NEW KING JAMES VERSION

The MACARTHUR DAILY BIBLE

READ *the* BIBLE *in* ONE YEAR *with* NOTES FROM

JOHN MACARTHUR

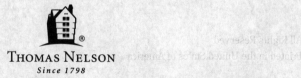

THOMAS NELSON
Since 1798

NASHVILLE DALLAS MEXICO CITY RIO DE JANEIRO

The MacArthur Daily Bible

Interior design, typesetting, and editorial development and research provided by
Koechel Peterson & Associates, Inc., Minneapolis, Minnesota.

Printed in the United States of America

11 12 13 14 15 - DP - 17 16 15 14

TABLE OF CONTENTS

MONTHS

THE OLD TESTAMENT

THE NEW TESTAMENT

TABLE OF ABBREVIATIONS

A.D.	in the year of our Lord
a.k.a.	also known as
a.m.	midnight to noon
B.C.	before Christ
ca.	about, approximately
cf.	compare
chap., chaps.	chapter, chapters
contra.	contrast
e.g.	for example
et al.	and others
etc.	and so forth
f., ff.	following verse, following verses
i.e.	that is
Mt.	Mount
p.m.	noon to midnight
v., vv.	verse, verses

WELCOME TO THE MACARTHUR DAILY BIBLE

No matter how much teaching and preaching you listen to, there can be no substitute for reading the Word of God daily yourself. The Bible is God's precious revelation of Himself to you. It's your point of contact with Him, where you learn the precious truth He has given to the Body of Christ. It's where you discover that history is His story, as you see the chain of events unfolding, always known to God, that led up to the birth, ministry, death, resurrection, and ascension of our Lord Jesus Christ. And it's where you learn what the future has in store in that wonderful day when the Lord returns.

This *MacArthur Daily Bible* provides a good way to develop a daily Bible reading habit. For each day of the year, it gives you a portion of the Old Testament, a bit from Psalms and Proverbs, and a portion of the New Testament, from the trusted New King James Version of the Bible.

It's all in Bible order: In each day's readings, you pick up where you left off the day before. If you stay in this *Daily Bible* every day for a year, you will have read through the entire Bible!

Along with each day's Scripture passages there are helpful comments and notes gleaned from the writings of John MacArthur.

WAYS TO WORK THE PLAN

There are several ways you might like to use the daily readings:

1) Bible in one year, once a day: Follow the plan. Read each day's readings during your daily Bible reading time, to finish the whole Bible in a year.

2) Bible in one year, twice a day: Like 1) above, but in two sittings. Read the Psalms, Proverbs, and New Testament readings in the morning and the Old Testament reading in the evening.

3) Bible in two years: Read the Psalms, Proverbs, and New Testament readings the first year, then the Old Testament readings the second year.

KEY MEMORY PASSAGES

If you like to focus on specific Bible passages, we have also included a section that spotlights 52 key scriptures, with additional comments from Dr. MacArthur. These passages are also good ones to memorize. Learn them by heart, and at year's end, you'll have 52 of the Bible's most important passages committed to memory.

OUR PRAYER FOR YOU

May the Lord use your reading of His Word to strengthen and guide you in your faith as you live for Him each day. As you read the Bible daily, may you be blessed with the peace and reassurance that only God can give.

FIFTY-TWO KEY PASSAGES OF THE BIBLE

Over the next year, you may wish to supplement your daily reading of Scripture with the following 52 weeks' worth of key passages of the Bible that have been selected and developed for you by Dr. John MacArthur. These passages provide a solid foundation upon which to build the Christian life, and gaining an understanding of these core biblical truths is the key to spiritual growth and development.

The intent is to provide you with the opportunity to focus on, and perhaps memorize, one important passage a week for a year. It is all a part of saturating and renewing your mind and thoughts with the Word of God. The page numbers where the passages are located among the daily readings are given so that you can study the context for the passages to ensure that you get the full meaning.

WEEK 1

Bless the LORD, O my soul; and all that is within me, bless His holy name! Bless the LORD, O my soul, and forget not all His benefits: who forgives all your iniquities, who heals all your diseases, who redeems your life from destruction, who crowns you with lovingkindness and tender mercies...—PSALM 103:1–4, page 865

King David learned the powerful habit of telling himself the truth. "Bless the LORD, O my soul." That's a good thing to tell yourself, isn't it? "And all that is within me, bless His holy name." That's a habit worth practicing. Train your soul to bless God. And how do you do that? By not forgetting His benefits. Whatever might be going wrong in your life, whatever might be a disappointment, even a serious illness or death, does not affect God's eternal blessing on you as His child. He has redeemed your life from destruction, and He crowns you with *lovingkindness*, which means grace and mercy. He pours out His tenderness. He heals all your diseases, not necessarily in time, but in eternity. And He forgives all your iniquities. Don't ever forget His benefits: forgiveness, absolute perfection in heaven, freedom from all sickness and death, abundant mercy, and everything you ever need. May everything that is in you bless His holy name!

WEEK 2

Thus says the LORD: "Let not the wise man glory in his wisdom, let not the mighty man glory in his might, nor let the rich man glory in his riches; but let him who glories glory in this, that he understands and knows Me, that I am the LORD, exercising lovingkindness, judgment, and righteousness in the earth. For in these I delight," says the LORD.—JEREMIAH 9:23,24, page 1028

What a wonderful promise, that God delights in those who understand and know Him. We live in a world full of people who glory in the big string of degrees after their names. They want people to be impressed by their achievements, insights, and wisdom. While some people glory in their physical strengths, others glory in the business they've built. We meet a lot of people who glory in their riches. "Glory" means "to boast." They proclaim it in the clothes they wear, the cars they drive, and the homes they own. That's just the way human, fallen, simple creatures are. But the Lord God says this: "If you're going to boast, boast in this, that you know and understand Me." Which is wonderful news! I know the God of the universe. Why would I glory in human wisdom and might and riches when I know the God of the universe? And, even more wonderfully, He knows me.

WEEK 3

And we know that all things work together for good to those who love God, to those who are the called according to His purpose.—ROMANS 8:28, page 797

The best manuscript evidence of the original Greek records this verse this way: "We know that God causes all things to work together for good." Now, we understand that there is evil, not only in the world, but in us. It isn't saying that all things are good. It says that God causes all things to work together for good. This leads us to the profound element of God's supreme authority and power over all the issues of life to produce out of them His own good purposes. God takes all the contingencies of life, all the choices, all the good, bad, and indifferent things, and weaves them together for ultimately a good purpose. That is the promise that God is giving to those who have been called to salvation. Every suffering, temptation, trial, even every sin, God works together into a tapestry that ultimately is for your good. You might not see it at the time. It's like looking at the back of a Persian rug. It's just a bunch of threads going into chaotic directions. But when you turn it over some day in eternity, you'll see how it all worked together for good.

WEEK 4

For the word of God is living and powerful, and sharper than any two-edged sword, piercing even to the division of soul and spirit, and of joints and marrow, and is a discerner of the thoughts and intents of the heart.—HEBREWS 4:12, page 1131

Many people think of the Bible as a comforting book, but the Scripture claims to be a sword—alive, powerful, sharp. It cuts and penetrates way down into the depth of soul and spirit. It becomes a discerner of the thoughts and intents of the heart. Nothing cuts and penetrates like the truth of God. You could take all the psychology and philosophy in the world, and it cannot dismantle a man at the level of his soul as the Word of God can. And the reason is because nobody knows a man like God knows a man. The heart of every one of us is exposed to God, and the Bible reveals that penetrating insight into our souls. Yes, the Bible knows how to build us up, but it also knows how to convict and unmask our hypocrisy, how to cut into our pride and self-will, how to uncover our secret sins. But wherever God cuts, He heals, and whatever He reveals, He cleanses. And it's that kind of cleansing that makes me able to bear more fruit to my own joy and to the glory of God.

WEEK 5

Or do you not know that your body is the temple of the Holy Spirit who is in you, whom you have from God, and you are not your own? For you were bought at a price; therefore glorify God in your body and in your spirit, which are God's.—1 CORINTHIANS 6:19,20, page 851

The Spirit of God lives in us. We literally are a temple in which God lives. We're not our own. We were bought, and the price was the precious blood of Jesus Christ as a Lamb without blemish and without spot. Therefore, we have the obligation to use this Holy Spirit temple in such a way that brings honor to God.

I had a friend who was visiting a great cathedral in New York City. When he came to a shrine to St. Joseph, there was a sign hanging around St. Joseph's neck that read: *Do not worship here. This shrine is out of order.* My friend said to himself, "I wonder if there aren't many days when that sign should be hanging around my neck. Don't expect to see Christ here. This shrine is out of order."

Your body is that shrine. It is that temple to the Holy Spirit because He lives there. Sometimes I'm afraid He is obscured. Make sure your shrine is in order. Glorify God in your body and in your spirit which are God's.

WEEK 6

Surely He has borne our griefs and carried our sorrows; yet we esteemed Him stricken, smitten by God, and afflicted. But He was wounded for our transgressions, He was bruised for our iniquities; the chastisement for our peace was upon Him, and by His stripes we are healed. All we like sheep have gone astray; we have turned, every one, to his own way; and the LORD has laid on Him the iniquity of us all.—ISAIAH 53:4–6, page 985

Isaiah speaks of God placing all our sins on His Son, the Lord Jesus Christ. He bore the grief for our sin, carried the sorrow for our lawlessness, was wounded for our transgressions and bruised for our iniquities. But by whom, and why? He was stricken, smitten, and afflicted by God, because God is the Judge. God alone can determine the appropriate punishment for sin; and God gave that punishment to His Son. He did that because there was no other one who could take our place, no other spotless Lamb, no other perfect sacrifice. So in order for us to have peace with God, Jesus paid the price for our sins. By His wounds we are healed spiritually. Every one of us has followed his own sinful path, and the Lord gathered all of our iniquity and laid it on Him. This is the amazing reality of Jesus Christ. He offered Himself, the sinless One, for the sinful ones. Every person has sinned, and for everyone who puts their trust in Jesus Christ that sin is paid for.

WEEK 7

Being confident of this very thing, that He who has begun a good work in you will complete it until the day of Jesus Christ...—PHILIPPIANS 1:6, page 1003

The Greek verb translated "has begun" is used only here and in Galatians 3:3, both times in reference to salvation. What it says is that when God begins a work of salvation in a person, He finishes it, He perfects it. You need to understand that salvation has three phases. There is justification, which occurs when you repent and put your faith in Jesus Christ. Then the second phase begins, which is sanctification. You are being continually separated from sin; that's an aspect of salvation. And the third phase is glorification. That occurs when we leave this world, enter into heaven, lose the residual fallen flesh, and the new creation is freed from any sinful impulses, from any reality of sin to enter into the full perfection and absolute holiness of eternal life. As a Christian, you have been justified. You are being sanctified, progressively set apart from sin by the work of the Holy Spirit through the Word. And you will one day be glorified, at which point you will be made like Jesus Christ. As much as glorified humanity can be like incarnate Deity, we will be like Jesus Christ!

WEEK 8

And without controversy great is the mystery of godliness: God was manifested in the flesh, justified in the Spirit, seen by angels, preached among the Gentiles, believed on in the world, received up in glory. —1 TIMOTHY 3:16, page 1073

This verse contains part of an early church hymn. It's uniformity, rhythm, and parallel as in the original language indicates this. Its six lines form a concise summary of the truth of the gospel. The "mystery of godliness" simply looks at Jesus Christ. The mystery is something that was hidden in the Old Testament age but is now revealed in the New Testament. And the greatest of mysteries was the mystery of God in human flesh, the mystery of Jesus Christ, the glorious reality of the Incarnation.

That becomes the theme for this early church hymn. God was manifested in human flesh through the virgin birth. He was righteous in His Spirit—perfectly righteous, perfectly holy. Angels holy and fallen acknowledged Him. He was preached among the nations. He was believed on by people in Galilee and Judea. After His resurrection, there were over 500 believers in Galilee. And when the church was founded on the Day of Pentecost, 3,000 believed on Him. At His ascension, He was received up into glory and seated at the right hand of the Father. So you have in that one verse a summation of the wonderful life of Jesus.

WEEK 9

All Scripture is given by inspiration of God, and is profitable for doctrine, for reproof, for correction, for instruction in righteousness, that the man of God may be complete, thoroughly equipped for every good work. —2 TIMOTHY 3:16,17, page 1094

If we ever hope to become spiritually strong and to do good works that glorify God, it all starts with teaching that confronts our sin and wrong thinking and then instructs us on how to walk in a righteous path. We find the truth that eliminates error, that brings truth and correct belief, and sets us in the path to righteousness in "all Scripture." All Scripture is given by inspiration of God and is profitable for that. Scripture brings us the sound teaching, the divine instruction that tears down what is wrong, builds up what is right, and puts us in the path of instruction to live a righteous life so that we can become mature and equipped to do the works that honor God. All Scripture is given by inspiration of God. It is, in the Greek, "God-breathed." Scripture is literally "out of the mouth of God." When you read the Bible, you are reading the very Word of God. God breathed it out; men wrote it down. And it is that powerful, living Word of God that brings to us the truth that equips us for every good work.

WEEK 10

The law of the LORD is perfect, converting the soul; the testimony of the LORD is sure, making wise the simple; the statutes of the LORD are right, rejoicing the heart; the commandment of the LORD is pure, enlightening the eyes; the fear of the LORD is clean, enduring forever; the judgments of the LORD are true and righteous altogether.—PSALM 19:7–9, page 127

These verses contain six titles about the Scripture. As the law of the Lord, it is God's standard for man's conduct. As the testimony of the Lord, Scripture is God's self-disclosure that describes who He is. As the statutes of the Lord, it is the doctrines and principles the Lord wants us to know. As the commandment of the Lord, it is the binding and authoritative mandate God gives to us. As the fear of the Lord, it is a manual on appropriately fearing and worshiping God. And as the judgments of the Lord, the Scripture provides for us the verdicts of God Himself.

These verses also tell us that Scripture is perfect and totally transforms the inner person. It is sure and reliable and makes the simple wise. It is right, meaning a right path as opposed to a wrong path, and brings joys to the heart. It is pure or translucent and makes things clear; even the dark things become understandable. It is clean—without flaw or blemish—and is not subject to cultural interpretation because it is everlasting. And it is true, absolutely righteous. What an amazing Book!

WEEK 11

For by grace you have been saved through faith, and that not of yourselves; it is the gift of God, not of works, lest anyone should boast.—EPHESIANS 2:8,9, page 983

These verses gather together all of the elements necessary to understand the work of salvation. It is by grace…through faith…the gift of God, not of works, so that we have no reason to be proud about some achievement. In fact, the only way to be saved is by grace, and grace means "unmerited favor." God graciously saves us. It isn't because we have earned, deserved, or achieved it. In fact, Paul tells us that our salvation is "that not of yourselves." "That" refers to the entire previous statement of salvation—not only the grace, but the faith. Although we are required to believe for salvation, we are also dead in trespasses and sins, so we can't believe. It's impossible for us to do that. Therefore, it isn't just the grace that comes from God; it is also the faith. The whole work of salvation is a miracle of God. We receive the Lord Jesus Christ, but it is God who awakens us and gives us the power and the understanding and the faith to do just that. None of us can boast about any of it. God's grace is preeminent in every aspect of salvation.

WEEK 12

And you, being dead in your trespasses and the uncircumcision of your flesh, He has made alive together with Him, having forgiven you all trespasses, having wiped out the handwriting of requirements that was against us, which was contrary to us. And He has taken it out of the way, having nailed it to the cross.—COLOSSIANS 2:13,14, page 1026

The language of these verses picks up on the legal concepts in the ancient world. When a person was crucified, the list of their crimes was nailed to the cross to demonstrate to everyone the reason they were there. With that imagery, the apostle Paul says the indictment against us as sinners, the handwriting of the laws we had broken, was taken and nailed to a cross. But we didn't have to die for them because Jesus was nailed there under our sins.

We were dead in sins. We were without cleansing. But we've been forgiven all our trespasses. We've been taken out of death and made alive because Jesus was nailed under our sins. He paid the penalty. Our crimes have been nailed to the Cross so that the whole world could see the violations are placed on Jesus Christ, the sinless One, who satisfies the just wrath of God for us. And this is why there are so many songs and hymns written about the Cross, because we can never stop singing its praises.

WEEK 13

"Go therefore and make disciples of all the nations, baptizing them in the name of the Father and of the Son and of the Holy Spirit, teaching them to observe all things that I have commanded you; and lo, I am with you always, even to the end of the age." Amen.—MATTHEW 28:19,20, page 163

If you ever wondered what our responsibility is in the world, here is the answer. Go and make disciples of all nations. Jesus said that to the apostles, but the Great Commission extends to all of us. We are to make disciples of Christ from all the nations. In fact, in the Greek the only verb here is "make disciples." The rest of the verb forms are participles that modify the main verb. Going, baptizing, and teaching are components of making disciples. And you're not alone in this enterprise. "Lo, I am with you always, even to the end of the age." Until the time is completely done for evangelism, Jesus is with you helping you to do so. This is our commission and the reason God leaves us here on earth—to bring people to Christ from all the nations by going, baptizing, and then teaching them so that they can observe everything the Lord commanded. Make sure you're involved in this joyous duty.

WEEK 14

"This Book of the Law shall not depart from your mouth, but you shall meditate in it day and night, that you may observe to do according to all that is written in it. For then you will make your way prosperous, and then you will have good success."—JOSHUA 1:8, page 333

In the case of Joshua, the "Book of the Law" specifically referred to Genesis through Deuteronomy as written by Moses. But it can be expanded, of course, to refer to all the Word of God. And it says that it should not depart from your mouth. You should be speaking the words of Scripture at all times. That will happen when you meditate in it day and night. It's a simple principle, isn't it? You saturate your mind and thoughts with the Word of God, and it comes out in your speech. When you're filled with the Word of God, that's what's going to come out of your mouth.

The verse also says that the purpose for this meditation is that you may observe to do according to all that is written in it. And that's what will happen. As you meditate or feed on the Word of God, it nourishes and shapes you as a person. It says that if you meditate, speak the Word, live the Word, you'll make your way prosperous and you'll have good success. The promise of God is a blessing on your spiritual effort and spiritual enterprise through the deep understanding and the application of Scripture.

WEEK 15

Therefore do not let sin reign in your mortal body, that you should obey it in its lusts. And do not present your members as instruments of unrighteousness to sin, but present yourselves to God as being alive from the dead, and your members as instruments of righteousness to God.—ROMANS 6:12,13, page 787

These verses speak about our physical body. Paul tells us that the only remaining repository where sin finds the believer vulnerable is in our humanness. It is physical, but it is also mental, because it mentions lusts. When you come to Christ, you are made a new creation. You are given a new nature with new desires, and you long to do what's right. The pattern of sin is broken, and you are no longer under the dominion of sin. But your new nature is still incarcerated in fallen humanness. That's going to be that way until we leave this world.

For all the wonders I'm looking forward to in heaven, what appeals most to me is the absence of sin. I hate the fact that there is residual sin in my life now. The appeal of heaven is to end the internal war with sin. But in the meantime, we're commanded to not let sin take over. Don't present your members as instruments of unrighteousness. Keep presenting yourself to God. Your members are instruments of righteousness to God. Fill your mind with biblical truth. And make sure that you stay in the presence of God so that His power and truth lead you to present yourself as an instrument of righteousness.

WEEK 16

Then He said to them all, "If anyone desires to come after Me, let him deny himself, and take up his cross daily, and follow Me. For whoever desires to save his life will lose it, but whoever loses his life for My sake will save it."—LUKE 9:23,24, page 342

With these words, Jesus clearly states the cost of following Him. This was Jesus' invitation to the crowd to follow Him; and the price, supreme. "If you want to come after Me, deny yourself." It's the end of you—your dreams, hopes, ambitions, goals. The gospel is not about self-fulfillment; it's about self-denial. In the Greek, the statement "deny himself" basically means "to refuse to associate with." That means that you're coming to Christ because you refuse to any longer associate with the person that you are. You're sick of yourself and your sin, and with desperation you willingly yield up that empty life you no longer want to associate with. You lose your life to gain it.

How extreme is this commitment? It involves taking up your cross daily. In the ancient world, the cross only meant one thing—a painful, horrible, shameful death. Jesus was saying, "If you want to follow Me, it's the end of you and not just your hopes and dreams. It may even cost you your physical life. But the infinite value of following Me is worth the high cost, because if you do lose your life for My sake, you'll save it forever." Ask yourself if you're truly following Jesus.

WEEK 17

For when we were still without strength, in due time Christ died for the ungodly. For scarcely for a righteous man will one die; yet perhaps for a good man someone would even dare to die. But God demonstrates His own love toward us, in that while we were still sinners, Christ died for us.—ROMANS 5:6–8, page 784

It's a powerful truth, isn't it? People rarely die for other people. Occasionally we read about someone giving his life for someone else. It's rare, even for the best of men, that someone would actually die on their behalf. It's notable when it happens. It is also true that sometimes for a good man someone will dare to die. But have you ever heard of anybody willing to die for a wicked, vile, evil man? That doesn't happen…unless you're Jesus Christ.

And what kind of love is it that causes Christ to die for the worst of us? That's the wonder of the love of God demonstrated toward us. Christ died for us. Christ died for the "ungodly." What a statement! It wasn't based on how worthy we were, how lovable we were, how godly we were. He died for the unworthy, the weak, the perverse. You can't say it any more directly than He died for the ungodly—not the righteous, not the good. He died for sinners, and He did it because of His love toward us. A love we didn't deserve produced a sacrifice we didn't deserve. But that's what grace does, and I hope you're overwhelmed with gratitude.

WEEK 18

Knowing that you were not redeemed with corruptible things, like silver or gold, from your aimless conduct received by tradition from your fathers, but with the precious blood of Christ, as of a lamb without blemish and without spot.—1 PETER 1:18,19, page 1193

Being redeemed is a tremendous concept. Redemption was a technical term for money paid to buy back a prisoner of war. It has the idea of paying a ransom to set someone free. We needed to be redeemed from the useless, aimless life passed down by tradition from our fathers. We needed to be rescued from that because the way of the world is the way of death and judgment.

We are redeemed by the precious blood of Christ. He alone was the acceptable sacrifice to God who paid the price for our sins. And He is pictured as a Lamb without blemish and without spot because throughout the Old Testament the whole sacrificial system of animals being offered as sin offerings to God all looked forward to the coming of the Lord Jesus Christ, who would be the final lamb. Which is why very soon after His death the city of Jerusalem was destroyed by the Romans in 70 A.D., and with that destruction, the entire sacrificial system came to an end. To this day there has never been a temple or a place for sacrifice, and none is needed because Jesus was the final sacrifice.

WEEK 19

For He made Him who knew no sin to be sin for us, that we might become the righteousness of God in Him.—2 CORINTHIANS 5:21, page 919

The fifteen words in the original Greek in this verse express the doctrine of substitution like no other single verse in the Bible. God made the only person who knew no sin, the Lord Jesus Christ, to be sin for us. Some people mistakenly think this means that Jesus became a sinner—that, on the cross, He actually was punished because He was a sinner. The truth is that, on the cross, Jesus was as holy as He ever was in the eternity before or the eternity after. On the cross, God treated Jesus as if He had personally committed every sin ever committed by every person who would ever believe, though, in fact, He committed none of them. God put the punishment for our sins on the sinless Son.

The rest of the verse says that "we might become the righteousness of God in Him." That's the other side of substitution. God treated Jesus as a sinner so that He could treat us as if we were righteous. He was not a sinner, and we're not righteous. That's substitution. He fulfilled all righteousness so that His sinless life could be credited to your account. Pretty amazing, isn't it? On the cross, God treats Jesus as if He lived your life so that He can treat you as if you lived His life. That is the heart of the gospel.

WEEK 20

Blessed be the God and Father of our Lord Jesus Christ, who according to His abundant mercy has begotten us again to a living hope through the resurrection of Jesus Christ from the dead, to an inheritance incorruptible and undefiled and that does not fade away, reserved in heaven for you.—1 PETER 1:3,4, page 1192

Throughout the Old Testament, God has a number of names. In the New Testament, He is most notably "the God and Father of our Lord Jesus Christ." He shares the same spiritual and eternal life, the same essential nature as Jesus Christ. He has begotten us again to a living hope as we put our trust in Jesus Christ. But everything that God has planned for those who belong to Him is not yet ours. And so we live in hope, a living hope of eternal life, because Christ rose from the dead. So we live by faith. We live today in the midst of God's blessings being poured out upon us, but there is a glorious reality yet ahead of us.

And then Peter adds that we have an inheritance that is incorruptible—not subject to termination, undefiled. It's not subject to any defect or tampering or fading away. But, rather, it is reserved intact in all its fullness, all its purity, all its glory in heaven for us. And so we not only enjoy what the Lord has done for us now, but we have our hope fixed on the day when the inheritance becomes a reality when we enter heaven.

WEEK 21

But the fruit of the Spirit is love, joy, peace, longsuffering, kindness, goodness, faithfulness, gentleness, self-control. Against such there is no law.—GALATIANS 5:22,23, page 972

This scripture tells us that when the Holy Spirit is in full control of your life, this is what you're going to be like. These nine characteristics are interlinked, and the fruit produced is this package. It's like a tree that bears nine different kinds of fruit. If we are walking in the Spirit, there will be *agape* love, which is the love of the will. It's not the love of emotion or physical attraction or a family bond. It's the love of willful self-sacrifice. And there will be a deep-down satisfaction of joy and an inner calm of peace that results from the Spirit of God superintending everything. There will be the longsuffering or the patience to endure irritation and difficulty, and a kindness or tender concern toward others. There will be goodness, moral and spiritual excellence. There will be faithfulness, loyalty, and trustworthiness. And there will be gentleness or humility and self-control, the restraining of passions.

Paul adds that "against such there is no law." Even if you had an external law, you couldn't force somebody to have this kind of character. You can't use the law to produce this. This fruit only flows up from within by the ministry of the Holy Spirit. And so how grateful should we be for that wonder-working Spirit, and how eager should we be to manifest that fruit as we walk in obedience to His revealed Word!

WEEK 22

Therefore, laying aside all malice, all deceit, hypocrisy, envy, and all evil speaking, as newborn babes, desire the pure milk of the word, that you may grow thereby...—1 PETER 2:1,2, page 1196

Spiritual growth happens when you desire the pure milk of the Word like a newborn baby desires milk. A baby basically desires milk, and that's it. Frankly, they don't care about much of anything except milk. It's that singularity of life that's so remarkable and so unique.

As a baby grows older, life gets more complicated. It's not just milk anymore; it's not just food anymore. But Peter is saying that if you want to grow, you need to set aside everything else. You need to set aside all malice or evil, and anything that's deceitful. Set aside any hypocrisy, envy, any evil speaking. Strip yourself of all those things that are wrong and focus on one thing—the pure milk of the Word.

That's the challenge. If you want to grow strong in the faith, you need to be singularly focused on desiring the pure milk of the Word. Every time you have an opportunity to drink that milk, you should rush to be satisfied. That's how you'll grow.

WEEK 23

Trust in the LORD with all your heart, and lean not on your own understanding; in all your ways acknowledge Him, and He shall direct your paths.—PROVERBS 3:5,6, page 32

These verses get to the core of Christian living. Can you trust the Lord fully? "With all your heart" means with everything. No matter what comes—good, bad, or indifferent; no matter what the pain or suffering; no matter what the trial or disappointment, can you trust the Lord wholeheartedly? The alternative is to lean on your own understanding, which is to interpret everything from your perspective.

You need to remember this: God loves you, and His promise is that in all things He is working together for your good. You have to trust Him for that. Don't lean on your own understanding and trust your own interpretation. Consider the life of Job. He lost all his children, possessions, health, and his wife and friends failed him. But after all Job's questions and suffering, when he finally encounters God, he can only say, "I have heard of You by the hearing of the ear, but now my eye sees You. Therefore I...repent." It all came down to simply trusting in God and His goodness.

Don't lean on your own interpretation of the things that go on in life. Always trust the Lord. In everything acknowledge Him. He'll open up a path you never even expected. This is His promise.

WEEK 24

Beloved, now we are children of God; and it has not yet been revealed what we shall be, but we know that when He is revealed, we shall be like Him, for we shall see Him as He is. And everyone who has this hope in Him purifies himself, just as He is pure.—1 JOHN 3:2,3, page 1232

Right now, if you believe in Jesus Christ, you are a child of God. But it hasn't been revealed what we shall be. We're sort of hidden at this time. But there's coming a day, the glorious manifestation of the children of God (Rom. 8:21), when the whole world is going to find out who we really are. And when that happens, we're going to be like Him, for we shall see Him as He is. This incredible promise is our hope. Someday we're going to be like Jesus Christ. We'll not only experience it, but everyone will see it and the truth will then be revealed that we are the children of God.

If you live in the anticipation of the coming of Christ, it changes the way you live. How should it alter the way we live when we anticipate the imminent return of Jesus Christ? He could come at any time. But the fact that we know He's coming, and He is perfectly pure, and that when He does come, He's going to make us like Himself, that should be a marvelous motivation for our own purity. Make sure that when He does come, He finds you living in a pure way.

WEEK 25

Now to Him who is able to keep you from stumbling, and to present you faultless before the presence of His glory with exceeding joy, to God our Savior, who alone is wise, be glory and majesty, dominion and power, both now and forever. Amen.—JUDE 24,25, page 1247

These verses are a doxology or benediction. There are many of them scattered throughout the Bible. A doxology is simply a praise to God. It is a pronunciation of blessing. And when we praise God and think about the immensity of blessing that comes from Him, nothing is more wonderful than this thought: God is able to keep you from stumbling and to present you faultless before the presence of His glory with exceeding joy. It means God is not going to lose you or let go of you. You're never going to stumble and fall to the temptation of abandoning the faith, to deny Christ. He will keep you from that.

How can He do that? Well, one day when He does present you to Himself in the presence of His glory, your fallen humanness will have disappeared, and you will be brought into His glorious presence absolutely faultless. You will literally be made a perfectly holy person, and no wonder there will be exceeding joy. The promise of God is that, if you are Christ's, He will keep you. Everyone the Father gives to Christ, Christ receives and keeps and raises to eternal glory. And so we praise our God for His keeping power.

WEEK 26

In this the love of God was manifested toward us, that God has sent His only begotten Son into the world, that we might live through Him. In this is love, not that we loved God, but that He loved us and sent His Son to be the propitiation for our sins.—1 JOHN 4:9,10, page 1235

The word "propitiation" means "satisfaction." That is essentially what Jesus came to do, to be a satisfaction for our sins. Who had to be satisfied? God had to be satisfied. After all, sin is a violation of the holy Law of God. Sin is a violation of God. It is an act of treachery against Him. God, then, if He is to forgive the sinner, must have that violation and that justice satisfied. Jesus comes to be that satisfaction. God was perfectly satisfied in His Son. Do you remember that the Father said at the baptism of Jesus, "This is My beloved Son, in whom I am well pleased"? He said the same thing again at the Transfiguration. The Father was perfectly satisfied with His Son so that His Son could be the perfect satisfaction for our sins.

How satisfied are you with Jesus? That's such an important question and such a basic spiritual reality. The Father is perfectly satisfied with the Son; the Son is perfectly satisfied with the Father. And how about you? Are you perfectly satisfied with Jesus Christ? Is He your purest and truest satisfaction? Do you find your highest joy in Him? If you do, it's going to have an impact on how you live your life. God is most pleased with us when we are most satisfied with His Son.

WEEK 27

"For God so loved the world that He gave His only begotten Son, that whoever believes in Him should not perish but have everlasting life. For God did not send His Son into the world to condemn the world, but that the world through Him might be saved."—JOHN 3:16,17, page 469

At the very heart of the message of God to us is a way to escape perishing. To "perish" connotes everlasting destruction, divine judgment and wrath, horrible punishment. Jesus said more about hell than He did about heaven. He talked about a fire never quenched, about a place where people experience permanent gnashing of teeth, loneliness, darkness, weeping, and wailing. That's perishing.

But God so loved the world that He sent His Son so that we don't have to perish, but we can have everlasting life. And that's not just a quantity of life; that's a quality of life. It isn't this temporal life; this kind of life forever. That would be a kind of hell in itself. It's another kind of life. God will give us eternal life, and that's why we have the word "saved" used here. It's the word "rescued." We are rescued from perishing and given not only a life different from this life, but a life also very different from the life of perishing. We are given everlasting life. It is God's kind of life. We literally participate in the bliss of divine immortality, the very life that belongs to God Himself. God gives us His own life, the very life that exists within His being and the being of the Son and the Holy Spirit. Rejoice always that you have been rescued by the love of God.

WEEK 28

Do not love the world or the things in the world. If anyone loves the world, the love of the Father is not in him. For all that is in the world—the lust of the flesh, the lust of the eyes, and the pride of life—is not of the Father but is of the world. And the world is passing away, and the lust of it; but he who does the will of God abides forever.—1 JOHN 2:15–17, page 1228

So what is the "world"? John is saying: "Don't love the invisible spiritual system of evil dominated by Satan, because if you love that, the love of the Father is not in you." The "world" is that evil system that appeals to our passions, our vision, and our pride. The world comes at our self-centeredness. I want what I want. I want to fulfill my lust, my passion. I want what I can see, what I covet, and I want what I want for my own personal benefit and self-aggrandizement. That's pride. That's what the world is all about.

But that's not of the Father, and so as believers we don't love that. We are tempted by it, and sometimes we fall into sin. But when we do, we hate that sin. And that's because it's part of the passing world. We are those, rather, who are motivated and characterized by doing the will of God, and, therefore, we abide forever. Not because we do the will of God, but because as we do the will of God, it is manifest that we are His and are the possessors of eternal life.

WEEK 29

Be diligent to present yourself approved to God, a worker who does not need to be ashamed, rightly dividing the word of truth.—2 TIMOTHY 2:15, page 1090

Christians desire to have God pleased with their lives. Certainly, you want to please the One who gave His Son for you. You want to please the One who loves you and promises to bless you and will someday give you an eternal reward and welcome you into His presence. Wanting to please God is just part of being a Christian.

But how do you present yourself to God for approval? Well, you have to be a worker who doesn't need to be ashamed. And the key to that is really important: Rightly dividing the word of truth. If I want God to approve my work, I need to rightly divide the word of truth or Scripture—all of it. To "rightly divide" means to "cut it straight." It refers to preciseness, exactness. For instance, if you were a leather worker such as Paul, cutting hides and making tents, you had to cut according to a pattern and sew the pattern together so that the tent was the way it should be. Precision and accuracy is the idea.

So if you want a life approved by God, and you want to be a worker who doesn't need to be ashamed, then heed these words: Handle accurately the Word of God in how you interpret and apply it.

WEEK 30

Teaching us that, denying ungodliness and worldly lusts, we should live soberly, righteously, and godly in the present age, looking for the blessed hope and glorious appearing of our great God and Savior Jesus Christ.—TITUS 2:12,13, page 1109

The Bible continually calls on us to live in the light of the return of Jesus Christ. He is coming, and we should love His appearing. No matter how much we may enjoy our lives, the fact is that the world at its best is far, far short of what heaven is going to be. Never become so involved in this world that heaven doesn't interest you anymore, because what God has prepared for us is infinitely beyond the best this life can offer.

But let's go beyond you. How long is Jesus Christ to endure the hostilities and hatred of this world, the demeaning, the denial of glory, the blasphemy of His name. How long must God the Father be blasphemed and maligned? How long does Satan run rampant over this planet doing everything he can to hinder God's work? How long should the Holy Spirit be grieved and quenched?

When you think about the Second Coming, the lofty thoughts are not just about you and me and heaven. It is longing for the final honoring of Jesus Christ and for the glorious appearing of our great God and Savior. Not just for my sake and what I'll receive, but for His.

WEEK 31

O God, You are my God; early will I seek You; my soul thirsts for You; my flesh longs for you in a dry and thirsty land where there is no water. So I have looked for You in the sanctuary, to see Your power and Your glory. Because Your lovingkindness is better than life, my lips shall praise You.—PSALM 63:1–3, page 483

This is the heart of a true believer. This is the panting heart, the thirsty heart that can only be satisfied by the presence and the power of God. This is all about a pure desire for God. The psalmist rises in the morning, and the first thing he wants is God. His soul is thirsty. He's like a wanderer in the desert who longs for water. In fact, David wrote this psalm while hiding in the wilderness, but longing to be back worshiping in Jerusalem. What did he want to see? God's power manifest in his life. He wanted to experience God's lovingkindness and mercy.

God had a relationship with David, but here we find that David had a relationship with God, and God was the priority of his life. That's the way it should be for every believer. Right now, is God your deepest desire? "Oh, God, it's You I want in my life. I feel dry and thirsty. I need Your power, Your glory, Your lovingkindness. It's better to me than to live, and I want to praise You." Cultivate that by being in the Word of God. Read through the Psalms and find out the greatness of your God.

WEEK 32

And He said to me, "My grace is sufficient for you, for My strength is made perfect in weakness." Therefore most gladly I will rather boast in my infirmities, that the power of Christ may rest upon me. Therefore I take pleasure in infirmities, in reproaches, in needs, in persecutions, in distresses, for Christ's sake. For when I am weak, then I am strong.—2 CORINTHIANS 12:9,10, page 948

Some people read the apostle Paul's testimony here and think it sounds like a death wish. Why in the world does he say this? He says it because, despite all these painful experiences in his life, God has a purpose in it. God spoke to Paul's heart and said, "My grace is sufficient for you." God was saying that every difficult time, every weakness, reproach, need, persecution, and distress is an opportunity for Him to manifest sufficient grace. But you won't get the grace until you get there. And when you do, His strength is perfected in your weakness. When you go through these kinds of trials, you become dependent on Him.

What do you believe in God for that only He can do, so that when He does it, He gets all the credit? There are issues in life, such as the suffering Paul was enduring, that only God can alter, and when He does, you know He did it. Suffering, then, is a way for God to display His grace and power. Embrace weakness. No one is too weak to be powerful. Embrace the suffering and see the grace and strength of God perfected in it.

WEEK 33

The LORD is my shepherd; I shall not want. He makes me to lie down in green pastures; He leads me beside the still waters. He restores my soul; He leads me in the paths of righteousness for His name's sake. Yea, though I walk through the valley of the shadow of death, I will fear no evil; for You are with me; Your rod and Your staff, they comfort me. You prepare a table before me in the presence of my enemies; You anoint my head with oil; my cup runs over. Surely goodness and mercy shall follow me all the days of my life; and I will dwell in the house of the LORD forever.—PSALM 23, page 158

"Yea, though I walk through the valley of the shadow of death, I will fear no evil." Sheep need to be fed. They need still water because they can't drink rushing water. They need to be led in safe places. And they need to be protected when they're in the shadow of death, which brings up a wonderful spiritual reality. We don't ever walk through the valley of death; we walk through the valley of the shadow of death. Think of it this way. As the sun is setting and a huge semi-truck sweeps past your car and casts its shadow over you, it is only the shadow running over you, not the truck itself. And so we fear no evil in the shadow of death. Death is but a harmless shadow for the sheep of the Good Shepherd. He takes care of us. He feeds us. He puts oil on our wounds. His goodness and mercy are available all the days of our life, and He will bring us into His eternal house forever.

WEEK 34

That if you confess with your mouth the Lord Jesus and believe in your heart that God has raised Him from the dead, you will be saved. For with the heart one believes unto righteousness, and with the mouth confession is made unto salvation.—ROMANS 10:9,10, page 806

It is not enough to simply acknowledge that Jesus is God. The demons acknowledge that and tremble (James 2:19), but that doesn't save them. To confess with your mouth the Lord Jesus means that you hold the deep personal conviction that Jesus is your master, without reservation. It's not about letting Jesus in your life to make you more successful or your marriage better. It's about you coming before Jesus and beating your breast and saying, "God, be merciful to me, a sinner." It's about you saying, "Jesus, I acknowledge You as my master and Lord, and I submit to whatever You desire."

The second aspect is to believe in your heart that Jesus died on the cross and rose from the dead and all that the Resurrection implies. You affirm both the deity and the sovereignty of Christ, His sinless life, substitutionary death, and literal bodily resurrection. You believe in your heart that God the Father put the stamp of divine approval on the perfect work of Jesus Christ. And you confess openly with your mouth unto salvation. And Jesus says, "Whoever confesses Me before men, him I will also confess before My Father" (Matt. 10:32).

WEEK 35

"Let your light so shine before men, that they may see your good works and glorify your Father in heaven."—MATTHEW 5:16, page 15

A German historian once said to a Christian, "Show me your redeemed life, and I might be inclined to be believe in your Redeemer." That's a pretty straightforward approach, isn't it? If I'm trying to tell you how great my doctor is, and I'm dying under his care, you might question his skill. This is something of the principle that's behind this verse. What good does it do to tell people how great our Savior is when they can't see the manifestation of His power in our lives? We must let the light shine.

What is "light" in the New Testament? Essentially, "light" means "eternal life." It's the life of God in us. It's the indwelling Christ, the indwelling Holy Spirit. In other words, "Let Christ shine through your life—the words you say, your attitudes, the things you do." And when people see that, they're going to say you do have a great Savior. You do have a great Father in heaven. A godly life lays the platform down on which individual testimony becomes convincing.

On the other hand, it's so sad for somebody to proclaim Jesus Christ as Savior and then live a sinful life. Not only does it dishonor Christ, but it's ineffective in terms of convincing anyone else of the power of Jesus Christ. As witnesses, our responsibility is to tell the world that Jesus Christ can transform lives. That's only believable if they see a transformed life.

WEEK 36

"I have been crucified with Christ; it is no longer I who live, but Christ lives in me; and the life which I now live in the flesh I live by faith in the Son of God, who loved me and gave Himself for me."—GALATIANS 2:20, page 959

To be "crucified with Christ" is a historical event that looks back at the Cross. Literally, you and I, who believe in Jesus, were there at the cross as He bore our sins. Which is why Paul says we were buried with Him into death and rose with Him in newness of life (Rom. 6). We were there. God literally placed us there even though we hadn't been born. Everybody who ever believed the truth of God, all the way back through the whole Old Testament, was there in Christ at His death. It's a glorious reality. You were there. Your sins were paid for. That's why you're not under condemnation.

Now we live this new life, and Paul says, "It's not really I who live it; it's Christ who lives in me." This is the glory of the mystery of Christ in us. Either you live this new life or you don't. Yet Paul says, "I live it, but Christ lives it." It takes all of us, but it's all of Him. Our old life is dead. We have a new life in Him. It takes all the discipline and obedience to live that life in the flesh by faith, and yet when it's all said and done, it's Christ Himself living in me.

WEEK 37

"A new commandment I give to you, that you love one another; as I have loved you, that you also love one another. By this all will know that you are My disciples, if you have love for one another."—JOHN 13:34,35, page 557

Clearly, the mark of true Christianity is love for one another. This is the command of Christ to love, but it was not new. In the Book of Deuteronomy, God commanded that we love Him and our neighbors. Yet Jesus' command regarding love presented a distinctly new standard. He said, "Love...as I have loved you." He gave a new model for this love, which He exemplified when He washed the disciples' feet. It was a common courtesy in the ancient world to provide a servant to wash feet. It was the lowest job on the servant ladder, yet Jesus stooped to do whatever they needed.

While that was a magnanimous gesture, it didn't come close to the lowliness of the One who went to the cross to bear the wrath of God for the sins of His own. He stooped all the way down, took upon Himself the form of a servant, was made in the likeness of man, went all the way down to a shameful death on the cross. So consider what Jesus meant when He told His disciples to love one another the way He loved them—sacrificially, selflessly, all the way down to most menial task and to giving your life for someone else. If you live like this, the world is going to know you're a disciple of Christ.

WEEK 38

"Come to Me, all you who labor and are heavy laden, and I will give you rest. Take My yoke upon you and learn from Me, for I am gentle and lowly in heart, and you will find rest for your souls. For My yoke is easy and My burden is light."—MATTHEW 11:28–30, page 52

These words of Jesus were wonderfully good news to the Jewish people. They were loaded down with a heavy burden of trying to earn their salvation by keeping the law and all the ordinances and traditions that had developed in Judaism. This was a weight no one could bear. And there are countless people who are still under that burden. While there may be many religions by name and description, there are only two religious systems. There is the truth of the gospel that salvation comes apart from works by faith alone through grace. And there is every other system, by whatever name, that says by religious ceremony, by moral deeds, and by good works you earn your way to heaven. It provides no peace and no rest because no one can be perfect.

Jesus came along and said, "Come to Me, and I'll give you rest. Instead of this horrendous yoke that has been imposed upon you, take My yoke. I'm gentle, I'm lowly in heart, and I'll give you rest because My yoke is easy and My burden is light." That is the wonderful promise of salvation by grace through faith.

WEEK 39

"In My Father's house are many mansions; if it were not so, I would have told you. I go to prepare a place for you. And if I go and prepare a place for you, I will come again and receive you to Myself; that where I am, there you may be also."—JOHN 14:2,3, page 560

Jesus, that last night before His death, gave His disciples many promises, and none more wonderful than that He was leaving for the purpose of preparing a place for them in heaven and that He would be back to take them there. When Jesus said, "In my Father's house are many mansions," the actual original language puts it this way: "In My Father's house are many rooms, many rooms." There's only one house—the Father's house—with many rooms. I'm not living 15 blocks from the Father's house; I'm in it. And so are you. I'm going to go there to be with the Lord. He will dwell forever with His people, and I shall dwell in His house.

What is the Lord Jesus doing right now? He's in heaven. One of the things He's doing is getting it ready for His children, and someday He's coming to take us all to be there. That looks at the Rapture when Jesus comes and snatches away His redeemed to heaven where we'll celebrate the marriage supper of the Lamb and receive our eternal rewards and find our room in the Father's house. And we'll dwell there throughout all of eternity, enjoying all the things that God has prepared for those who love Him.

WEEK 40

Finally, brethren, whatever things are true, whatever things are noble, whatever things are just, whatever things are pure, whatever things are lovely, whatever things are of good report, if there is any virtue and if there is anything praiseworthy—meditate on these things. —PHILIPPIANS 4:8, page 1017

We are the product of what we take in. If we take garbage in, garbage will come out. But Jesus said: "Not what goes into the mouth defiles a man; but what comes out of the mouth, this defiles a man" (Matt. 15:11). The real problem is what's in us. It's that fallen flesh. Sin doesn't come from the outside in; it comes from the inside out. This verse tells us there are all kinds of things outside that excite that sin inside.

Paul is saying, "Look, if you want to live a life that honors God, meditate on godliness." "Whatever is true" encompasses all the revelation of God. Truth is found in God, in Christ, in the Holy Spirit, in the Scripture. "Whatever is noble" means to meditate on what is worthy of respect, what is sacred as opposed to the profane. "Whatever is just" means to measure it by the divine standard of holiness. "Whatever is pure" means morally clean. "Whatever is lovely" means amiable or pleasing. "Whatever is of good report" is whatever is kind and gracious and edifying. So if there is any value in virtue, and if there is any value in a life that is worthy of praise, meditate on these things. Make sure the focus of your life is directed toward these things, and you will enjoy the wonderful fruit of this kind of godly thinking.

WEEK 41

"These things I have spoken to you, that in Me you may have peace. In the world you will have tribulation; but be of good cheer, I have overcome the world."—JOHN 16:33, page 570

Jesus said this to His beloved apostles in the Upper Room the night of His betrayal. He was going away, and they were going to be worried, fearful, anxious, troubled. Through that night He made promises to ease their troubled hearts. He even said, "Let not your heart be troubled." And He promised them love and the Holy Spirit and answered prayer and peace. He said to them, "There's no reason to be troubled. All that I've told you is so that you might have peace in your heart because you know the Holy Spirit is there. You have nothing to be anxious about. In the world, you will have tribulation." That word actually means "trouble." It comes from a word that means "pressure." "You will be squeezed tightly by the difficulties of this life, but in the midst of it, be of good cheer because in the end I've overcome the world." That is to say there's nothing the world can do to you that wins ultimately. Momentary pain, a momentary disappointment, but the world's opposition has been rendered null and void. And even though the world continues to attack the people of God, such attacks fall harmlessly, for Christ's victory has already accomplished a smashing defeat of the whole world system.

WEEK 42

I beseech you therefore, brethren, by the mercies of God, that you present your bodies a living sacrifice, holy, acceptable to God, which is your reasonable service. And do not be conformed to this world, but be transformed by the renewing of your mind, that you may prove what is that good and acceptable and perfect will of God. —ROMANS 12:1,2, page 815

The goal of these two verses is to live a life that pleases God, a life in the center of God's will. How do you do that? By being transformed through the renewing of your mind. This principle is all through Scripture. Transformation occurs as the Holy Spirit changes your thinking. As you meditate on the Word of God, it takes root in your heart and shapes your thinking. You have to have a mind transformed by the renewing of biblical truth.

Don't let yourself think and act according to the system of beliefs and values around you. You cannot allow yourself to be shaped by the spirit of the age. And the key to all of that is to present yourself as a living sacrifice to God. Paul is saying you need to get up on the altar and hold back nothing. And you're going to have to stay there, because we have a habit of crawling back off again. Get up on that altar, offer yourself to God as your act of reasonable or logical or spiritual worship. Paul says, "I beseech you to do that." And he bases it all on the mercies of God which are yours in Christ. He's been good to you. Do this in return.

WEEK 43

Therefore, my beloved brethren, be steadfast, immovable, always abounding in the work of the Lord, knowing that your labor is not in vain in the Lord. —1 CORINTHIANS 15:58, page 897

We live in a capitalistic system, and we understand the principle of rewarding people for their work. It's very different from the communist world, where there are no rewards to motivate people. Fortunately, our Lord isn't like that. Whatever you do in His name will receive an appropriate reward. You can count on that. God makes His promise that if you're abounding in the work of the Lord—in other words, if you're going over the top in serving the Lord—your labor is not in vain in the Lord. No work done in His name is wasted, no work done in His name is ever unaccounted for, and all work done in His name is appropriately rewarded. That's His promise.

And what is that reward? It might not be money or acknowledgment here, but there will be acknowledgment in the time of rewards when we stand before the Lord and He rewards every man according to his work. So serve the Lord with all your heart and know that He's keeping a record of your faithfulness, and you'll enjoy His loving reward when you see Him face-to-face.

WEEK 44

Blessed is the man who walks not in the counsel of the ungodly, nor stands in the path of sinners, nor sits in the seat of the scornful; but his delight is in the law of the LORD, and in His law he meditates day and night.—PSALM 1:1,2, page 2

This is a promise for spiritual well-being—for deep-seated heart-blessing contentment, peace, and joy that's below the surface of circumstances. If you want to be blessed like that, the psalmist says, don't walk in the counsel of the ungodly. Don't listen to their spin, their solution, their assessment, their evaluation. Don't even walk with them, and don't stop and stand in the path of sinners. Don't even engage yourself with them casually, and don't let that conversation become deeper and more penetrating. And don't sit in the seat of the scornful. Don't take your seat in their classroom while they scoff at divine truth.

You want to be blessed? Then find your delight in the law of the Lord. Walk in the counsel of the godly. Stand in the path of the righteous. Sit in the seat of the holy. You want to give your life to the law of the Lord so that rather than ungodly, sinful, scornful ideas permeating your thoughts day and night, you're literally filled with the law of God. Meditate on it. Let it grip your heart. Find your delight in the law of the Lord and let that be the content of your thought day and night. This is the path to blessing.

WEEK 45

For I am persuaded that neither death nor life, nor angels nor principalities nor powers, nor things present nor things to come, nor height nor depth, nor any other created thing, shall be able to separate us from the love of God which is in Christ Jesus our Lord.—ROMANS 8:38,39, page 797

This is one of those really monumental biblical passages. The apostle could have written that nothing can separate us from the love of God, but somebody would have said, "But what about this?" So Paul spoke in expansive terms of what could not separate us from God's love. "I am absolutely sure that neither the realm of death nor life, which covers all of existence, can do it. Nor angels, nor principalities, nor powers—all spirit beings, whether holy or unholy. Nor things present; nor things to come, which covers all of time, both now and in the future. And just in case that doesn't cover it, there's nothing all the way up into infinity, there's nothing all the way down into infinite depth, and there isn't any other created thing that can separate us from the love of God which is in Christ Jesus."

There is nothing in the created universe that can change your eternal relationship to God if you are in Christ Jesus our Lord. You can know this: the One who justified you, the One who sanctifies you, will one day glorify you. He will bring all His sons to glory. This is because God loves us with an everlasting love, and we are hidden with Christ in God's love.

WEEK 46

Who may ascend into the hill of the LORD? Or who may stand in His holy place? He who has clean hands and a pure heart, who has not lifted up his soul to an idol, nor sworn deceitfully. He shall receive blessing from the LORD, and righteousness from the God of his salvation.—PSALM 24:3–5, page 162

In the city of Jerusalem, the steps are still there that led up through the wall into the temple mount, the steps that even Jesus went up into the temple to worship. Here the people ascended "the holy hill." And as they went, it's likely the priests would ask the questions recorded in Psalm 24. "Who may ascend into the hill of the Lord? Who may stand in His holy place?" And the people antiphonally would give answers. "He who has clean hands and a pure heart, who has not lifted up his soul to an idol nor sworn deceitfully. He shall receive blessing from the Lord and righteousness from the God of his salvation."

Today we have worship bands and worship leaders, but do we ever ask ourselves: Do I have a right to come rushing into the holy presence of God? Because the Lord inhabits the praise of His people, He is there. Do I have a right to ascend into His presence? Not unless I come with clean hands and a pure heart; not if there is any sin in my life. If there is impurity, you will not receive blessing from the Lord and the mercies of His righteousness. To enjoy the blessing that God wants to give, make sure your heart is right as you enter His presence.

WEEK 47

No temptation has overtaken you except such as is common to man; but God is faithful, who will not allow you to be tempted beyond what you are able, but with the temptation will also make the way of escape, that you may be able to bear it.—1 CORINTHIANS 10:13, page 866

Despite what you may have heard, temptation is not about demons. It's just about being human. No temptation is ever going to come to you that is superhuman. You don't need to go through life in horror and dread of some demonic invasion. If you are a believer, you are Christ's. Greater is He that is in you than he that is in the world. God is faithful. He will not allow you to be tempted beyond what you are able.

And for a new Christian, it's different than for an older Christian. Some temptations that are very difficult for brand-new Christians who are just coming out of the world aren't a problem for an older believer who has walked with the Lord for years. But God is eminently, personally involved in our lives, sheltering us from the overwhelming temptation. And He says there will always be a way of escape, that we may be able to endure it. There's a path, and very often the path in the midst of the temptation is very clear to us. It's the path of resistance. It's the path of obedience. It's the path of prayer, of divine petition asking God to lead us out.

WEEK 48

I waited patiently for the LORD; and He inclined to me, and heard my cry. He also brought me up out of a horrible pit, out of the miry clay, and set my feet upon a rock, and established my steps. He has put a new song in my mouth—praise to our God; many will see it and fear, and will trust in the LORD.—PSALM 40:1–3, page 322

The psalmist actually says that praise is an evangelistic tool. He says when I have a new song in my mouth and I am praising God, many will see that and fear and trust in the Lord. There is a tremendous impact made upon the sinner by a believer filled with praise. We have a new song of redemption. The psalmist said, "I was in a horrible pit. I was in the miry clay." The picture is of hopelessness and helplessness, and the Lord "heard my cry...and set my feet upon a rock, and established my steps." That's a picture of salvation. And the response to that is a song of praise. And the more we sing it, and the louder we sing it, the more who hear it. Many will see our confidence and our joy and be drawn to Christ.

We don't often think about praise as an evangelistic tool, but it is. Those around us who are in the miry clay will see in our deliverance their own hope. Be filled with praise for what God has done for you, and that may draw someone to open their heart to see Him do it for them.

WEEK 49

Through the LORD's mercies we are not consumed, because His compassions fail not. They are new every morning; great is Your faithfulness.—LAMENTATIONS 3:22,23, page 1115

Jeremiah tells us that the Lord is merciful. Mercy means withholding what we deserve, not giving us the punishment we really have earned. And it is through the Lord's mercies that we are not consumed. We deserve judgment from God because we have broken His law, spurned His love, offended Him, and dishonored Him. Every time we sin we do that. We should be consumed by His justice, but His justice is tempered by mercy. And His mercy is based on His compassion.

Fortunately for us, His compassions fail not. They are new every morning. God never runs out of the supply, and every day is a new day. Isn't that wonderful? You get up and it's a new day, and you can expect all the compassions of God are available for that day. All the mercies of God are available for that day. Great is His faithfulness. The bedrock of God's mercy and compassion is His covenant. When He makes a promise, He keeps it, and He has promised us mercy and compassion if we believe in Him, and He will be faithful to His covenant.

WEEK 50

But we all, with unveiled face, beholding as in a mirror the glory of the Lord, are being transformed into the same image from glory to glory, just as by the Spirit of the Lord.—2 CORINTHIANS 3:18, page 913

Believers today, unlike the saints of the Old Testament, are able to behold the glory of the Lord in an unveiled way. Moses saw a portion of the glory of God when he was on the mountain, but the people never saw the unveiled face of the glory of God because that awaited the arrival of the Lord Jesus Christ. We have the unveiled glory of the Lord manifest in the face of Jesus Christ. And when I say "glory," I mean all the attributes of God. They're revealed to us in the Old Testament, but they are manifest alive to us in Jesus Christ, so that the glory of God shines more wonderfully in Christ than any other place.

And as we look at Him and see Him revealed in the New Testament, we are being transformed into the same image from one level of glory to the next by the Holy Spirit. This describes the dynamics of sanctification. As you see the wonder of Christ and are lost in the vision of Christ, you will be imperceptibly transformed into His image. This is spiritual growth and maturity. How do you move up to higher levels of manifesting holiness and righteousness? It's the work of the Spirit which He does as Jesus Christ becomes our consuming vision.

WEEK 51

That you may become blameless and harmless, children of God without fault in the midst of a crooked and perverse generation, among whom you shine as lights in the world, holding fast the word of life, so that I may rejoice in the day of Christ that I have not run in vain or labored in vain.—PHILIPPIANS 2:15,16, page 1008

The "day of Christ" is the day we get to heaven and meet the Lord. What would make that a day of rejoicing for Paul is seeing the believers who were gathered together in the presence of the Lord and being rewarded because they had lived godly lives in the midst of a crooked and perverse generation, where they had faithfully been shining as lights in the world.

Paul said on another occasion to a group of believers, "You are my joy and crown of rejoicing. When I get to heaven, my joy is going to be in seeing you there and seeing you rewarded for your faithful service" (a paraphrase of 1 Thess. 2:19). That's a wonderful eternal perspective. His only concern was to get into the presence of the Lord and know that his efforts had eternal consequences. That's why he wrote his letters, preached his gospel, and exhorted his churches. He wanted them to live blameless lives in the midst of what is a crooked, twisted, perverse world. And he wanted them to shine as lights in the world by holding forth the word of life, the word of Scripture. He wanted his people to live like that so that he could, with them, enjoy the eternal reward that the Lord would grant.

WEEK 52

My brethren, count it all joy when you fall into various trials, knowing that the testing of your faith produces patience. But let patience have its perfect work, that you may be perfect and complete, lacking nothing.—JAMES 1:2–4, page 1175

As a Christian, I would like to be in a position where I'm lacking nothing. But spiritual perfection and maturity comes with pain. If there's going to be completeness, the only way to get there is through trials. You are strengthened by the development of spiritual endurance, and endurance is developed as you persevere through trouble. People say, "Lord, I want to be strong in the faith and bold for You." Get ready, because when the Lord answers that prayer, it's going to be the testing of your faith, taking you to the edge, that produces the endurance so critical to increasing spiritual strength.

I want to be all that God wants me to be for His glory and for my usefulness. I don't just grit my teeth and endure the trial. James says, "Count it all joy." You can do that as you look past the trial to the goal, to the end, and that's where the joy comes from. The end of all our trials and all our suffering is our spiritual maturity. Here we are stronger than ever and less susceptible to besetting sins and debilitating temptations. I want that. I know you do, as well.

JANUARY 1

Genesis 1:1–2:25

1 In the beginning God created the heavens
and the earth. 2The earth was without form,
and void; and darkness *was* on the face of the
deep. And the Spirit of God was hovering over
the face of the waters.
3Then God said, "Let there be light"; and
there was light. 4And God saw the light, that *it
was* good; and God divided the light from the
darkness. 5God called the light Day, and the
darkness He called Night. So the evening and
the morning were the first day.

1:5 first day. God completed the creation in 7 days, which constituted a complete week. One "day" can refer to: 1) the light portion of a 24-hour period (1:5,14); an extended period of time (2:4); or 2) the whole 24-hour period while the earth completes a full rotation on its axis. Each "day" in Genesis refers to a 24-hour period. The cycle of light and dark means that the earth was rotating on its axis, receiving light from a source on one side of the earth, even though the sun was not yet created (v. 16).

6Then God said, "Let there be a firmament
in the midst of the waters, and let it divide the
waters from the waters." 7Thus God made the
firmament, and divided the waters which *were*
under the firmament from the waters which
were above the firmament; and it was so. 8And
God called the firmament Heaven. So the
evening and the morning were the second day.
9Then God said, "Let the waters under the
heavens be gathered together into one place,
and let the dry *land* appear"; and it was so.
10And God called the dry *land* Earth, and the
gathering together of the waters He called
Seas. And God saw that *it was* good.
11Then God said, "Let the earth bring forth
grass, the herb *that* yields seed, *and* the fruit
tree *that* yields fruit according to its kind,
whose seed *is* in itself, on the earth"; and it
was so. 12And the earth brought forth grass,
the herb *that* yields seed according to its kind,
and the tree *that* yields fruit, whose seed *is* in
itself according to its kind. And God saw that
it was good. 13So the evening and the morning
were the third day.
14Then God said, "Let there be lights in the
firmament of the heavens to divide the day
from the night; and let them be for signs and
seasons, and for days and years; 15and let them
be for lights in the firmament of the heavens
to give light on the earth"; and it was so.
16Then God made two great lights: the greater
light to rule the day, and the lesser light to
rule the night. *He made* the stars also. 17God
set them in the firmament of the heavens to
give light on the earth, 18and to rule over the
day and over the night, and to divide the light
from the darkness. And God saw that *it was*
good. 19So the evening and the morning were
the fourth day.
20Then God said, "Let the waters abound
with an abundance of living creatures, and let
birds fly above the earth across the face of the
firmament of the heavens." 21So God created
great sea creatures and every living thing that
moves, with which the waters abounded,
according to their kind, and every winged bird
according to its kind. And God saw that *it was*
good. 22And God blessed them, saying, "Be
fruitful and multiply, and fill the waters in the
seas, and let birds multiply on the earth." 23So
the evening and the morning were the fifth day.
24Then God said, "Let the earth bring forth
the living creature according to its kind: cattle
and creeping thing and beast of the earth,
each according to its kind"; and it was so.
25And God made the beast of the earth according to its kind, cattle according to its kind, and
everything that creeps on the earth according
to its kind. And God saw that *it was* good.
26Then God said, "Let Us make man in Our
image, according to Our likeness; let them have
dominion over the fish of the sea, over the birds
of the air, and over the cattle, over all the earth
and over every creeping thing that creeps on
the earth." 27So God created man in His *own*
image; in the image of God He created him;

1:26 Us...Our. The first clear reference to the three-person nature of God, as the Father, Son, and the Holy Spirit. This unique relationship is called the triunity of God. Even the very name of God, Elohim (1:1), is a plural form of El. **man.** The masterpiece of creation, a human being, was made in God's image to rule creation. **Our image.** This phrase defined man's unique relation to God and set him apart from the animals. He was like God in that he could reason and had intellect, will, and emotion. When he was first created, he was like God because he was good and sinless.

male and female He created them. 28 Then God
blessed them, and God said to them, "Be fruitful and multiply; fill the earth and subdue it;
have dominion over the fish of the sea, over
the birds of the air, and over every living thing
that moves on the earth."
29 And God said, "See, I have given you every
herb *that* yields seed which *is* on the face of all
the earth, and every tree whose fruit yields
seed; to you it shall be for food. 30 Also, to every
beast of the earth, to every bird of the air, and
to everything that creeps on the earth, in
which *there is* life, *I have given* every green
herb for food"; and it was so. 31 Then God saw
everything that He had made, and indeed *it*
was very good. So the evening and the morning were the sixth day.

2 Thus the heavens and the earth, and all
the host of them, were finished. 2 And on
the seventh day God ended His work which
He had done, and He rested on the seventh
day from all His work which He had done.
3 Then God blessed the seventh day and sanctified it, because in it He rested from all His
work which God had created and made.
4 This *is* the history of the heavens and the
earth when they were created, in the day that
the LORD God made the earth and the heavens, 5 before any plant of the field was in the
earth and before any herb of the field had
grown. For the LORD God had not caused it to
rain on the earth, and *there was* no man to till
the ground; 6 but a mist went up from the earth
and watered the whole face of the ground.
7 And the LORD God formed man *of* the dust of
the ground, and breathed into his nostrils the
breath of life; and man became a living being.
8 The LORD God planted a garden eastward
in Eden, and there He put the man whom He
had formed. 9 And out of the ground the LORD
God made every tree grow that is pleasant to
the sight and good for food. The tree of life
was also in the midst of the garden, and the
tree of the knowledge of good and evil.
10 Now a river went out of Eden to water the
garden, and from there it parted and became
four riverheads. 11 The name of the first *is*
Pishon; it *is* the one which skirts the whole
land of Havilah, where *there is* gold. 12 And the
gold of that land *is* good. Bdellium and the
onyx stone *are* there. 13 The name of the second river *is* Gihon; it *is* the one which goes
around the whole land of Cush. 14 The name of
the third river *is* Hiddekel; it *is* the one which
goes toward the east of Assyria. The fourth
river *is* the Euphrates.
15 Then the LORD God took the man and put
him in the garden of Eden to tend and keep it.
16 And the LORD God commanded the man, saying, "Of every tree of the garden you may
freely eat; 17 but of the tree of the knowledge of
good and evil you shall not eat, for in the day
that you eat of it you shall surely die."
18 And the LORD God said, "*It is* not good that
man should be alone; I will make him a helper
comparable to him." 19 Out of the ground the
LORD God formed every beast of the field and
every bird of the air, and brought *them* to
Adam to see what he would call them. And
whatever Adam called each living creature,
that *was* its name. 20 So Adam gave names to all
cattle, to the birds of the air, and to every
beast of the field. But for Adam there was not
found a helper comparable to him.
21 And the LORD God caused a deep sleep to
fall on Adam, and he slept; and He took one of
his ribs, and closed up the flesh in its place.
22 Then the rib which the LORD God had taken
from man He made into a woman, and He
brought her to the man.
23 And Adam said:

"This *is* now bone of my bones
And flesh of my flesh;
She shall be called Woman,
Because she was taken out of Man."

24 Therefore a man shall leave his father and
mother and be joined to his wife, and they
shall become one flesh.
25 And they were both naked, the man and
his wife, and were not ashamed.

Psalm 1:1–6

Blessed *is* the man
Who walks not in the counsel
of the ungodly,
Nor stands in the path of sinners,
Nor sits in the seat of the scornful;
2 But his delight *is* in the law
of the LORD,
And in His law he meditates day
and night.
3 He shall be like a tree
Planted by the rivers of water,
That brings forth its fruit
in its season,
Whose leaf also shall not wither;
And whatever he does shall prosper.
4 The ungodly *are* not so,
But *are* like the chaff which the wind
drives away.
5 Therefore the ungodly shall not stand
in the judgment,
Nor sinners in the congregation
of the righteous.

6 For the LORD knows the way of the
righteous,
But the way of the ungodly shall
perish.

Proverbs 1:1–7

1 The proverbs of Solomon the son of David,
king of Israel:

2 To know wisdom and instruction,
To perceive the words of
understanding,
3 To receive the instruction
of wisdom,
Justice, judgment, and equity;
4 To give prudence to the simple,
To the young man knowledge
and discretion—
5 A wise *man* will hear and increase
learning,
And a man of understanding will attain
wise counsel,
6 To understand a proverb and
an enigma,
The words of the wise and their
riddles.

7 The fear of the LORD *is* the beginning
of knowledge,
But fools despise wisdom
and instruction.

Matthew 1:1–25

1 The book of the genealogy of Jesus Christ,
the Son of David, the Son of Abraham:
[2]Abraham begot Isaac, Isaac begot Jacob,
and Jacob begot Judah and his brothers.
[3]Judah begot Perez and Zerah by Tamar,
Perez begot Hezron, and Hezron begot Ram.
[4]Ram begot Amminadab, Amminadab begot
Nahshon, and Nahshon begot Salmon.
[5]Salmon begot Boaz by Rahab, Boaz begot
Obed by Ruth, Obed begot Jesse, [6]and Jesse
begot David the king.
David the king begot Solomon by her *who
had been the wife* of Uriah. [7]Solomon begot
Rehoboam, Rehoboam begot Abijah, and
Abijah begot Asa. [8]Asa begot Jehoshaphat,
Jehoshaphat begot Joram, and Joram begot
Uzziah. [9]Uzziah begot Jotham, Jotham begot
Ahaz, and Ahaz begot Hezekiah. [10]Hezekiah
begot Manasseh, Manasseh begot Amon, and
Amon begot Josiah. [11]Josiah begot Jeconiah
and his brothers about the time they were carried away to Babylon.
[12]And after they were brought to Babylon,
Jeconiah begot Shealtiel, and Shealtiel begot
Zerubbabel. [13]Zerubbabel begot Abiud, Abiud
begot Eliakim, and Eliakim begot Azor. [14]Azor
begot Zadok, Zadok begot Achim, and Achim
begot Eliud. [15]Eliud begot Eleazar, Eleazar begot
Matthan, and Matthan begot Jacob. [16]And Jacob
begot Joseph the husband of Mary, of whom
was born Jesus who is called Christ.
[17]So all the generations from Abraham to
David *are* fourteen generations, from David
until the captivity in Babylon *are* fourteen generations, and from the captivity in Babylon
until the Christ *are* fourteen generations.

1:18 betrothed. Jewish betrothal was as binding as a modern marriage and could only be broken through divorce. The betrothal couple was legally considered husband and wife, even though physical union had not yet taken place.

[18]Now the birth of Jesus Christ was as follows: After His mother Mary was betrothed to
Joseph, before they came together, she was
found with child of the Holy Spirit. [19]Then Joseph her husband, being a just *man,* and not
wanting to make her a public example, was
minded to put her away secretly. [20]But while
he thought about these things, behold, an
angel of the Lord appeared to him in a dream,
saying, "Joseph, son of David, do not be afraid
to take to you Mary your wife, for that which
is conceived in her is of the Holy Spirit. [21]And
she will bring forth a Son, and you shall call
His name JESUS, for He will save His people
from their sins."
[22]So all this was done that it might be fulfilled which was spoken by the Lord through
the prophet, saying: [23]*"Behold, the virgin shall
be with child, and bear a Son, and they shall
call His name Immanuel,"* which is translated,
"God with us."
[24]Then Joseph, being aroused from sleep,
did as the angel of the Lord commanded him
and took to him his wife, [25]and did not know
her till she had brought forth her firstborn
Son. And he called His name JESUS.

1:22 that it might be fulfilled. Matthew often referred to places where Old Testament scriptures were fulfilled. He quoted from the Old Testament more than 60 times, more frequently than any other New Testament writer, except Paul in Romans.

DAY 1: How does the Bible challenge or agree with current scientific theories?

Scientific theories, by their very definition, are subject to change and adjustment. Scripture remains as God's revealed unchanging declaration of truth. The Bible was not written as a challenge to any particular scientific theory, but scientific theories have often been designed to challenge and undermine biblical statements. They either agree with scripture or are mistaken.

The description in Genesis 1:1 that "God created the heavens and the earth" yields three basic conclusions: 1) creation was a recent event measured in thousands not millions of years ago; 2) creation was ex nihilo, meaning that God created out of nothing; 3) creation was special, with light and time being the first of God's creative acts, since the day-count (Gen. 1:5) began before the creation of sun and moon (Gen. 1:16).

One key in evaluating scientific theories depends on our understanding of the biblical word "created." Although the Hebrew word used in Genesis 1:1 can be used to describe the act of shaping or altering existent matter (Is. 65:18), such is not the case with the Bible's first words. God spoke the heavens and earth into existence. Both context and the rest of Scripture bear witness to God's creativity without use of any preexisting material (Is. 40:28; 45:8,12,18; 48:13; Jer. 10:16; Acts 17:24).

JANUARY 2

Genesis 3:1–4:26

3 Now the serpent was more cunning than any beast of the field which the LORD God had made. And he said to the woman, "Has God indeed said, 'You shall not eat of every tree of the garden'?"
2 And the woman said to the serpent, "We may eat the fruit of the trees of the garden;
3 but of the fruit of the tree which *is* in the midst of the garden, God has said, 'You shall not eat it, nor shall you touch it, lest you die.' "
4 Then the serpent said to the woman, "You
will not surely die.
5 For God knows that in the day you eat of it your eyes will be opened, and you will be like God, knowing good and evil."
6 So when the woman saw that the tree *was* good for food, that it *was* pleasant to the eyes, and a tree desirable to make *one* wise, she took of its fruit and ate. She also gave to
her husband with her, and he ate.
7 Then the eyes of both of them were opened, and they knew that they *were* naked; and they sewed fig leaves together and made themselves coverings.
8 And they heard the sound of the LORD God walking in the garden in the cool of the day, and Adam and his wife hid themselves from the presence of the LORD God among the trees of the garden.
9 Then the LORD God called to Adam and said to him, "Where *are* you?"
10 So he said, "I heard Your voice in the garden, and I was afraid because I was naked; and I hid myself."
11 And He said, "Who told you that you *were* naked? Have you eaten from the tree of which I commanded you that you should not eat?"
12 Then the man said, "The woman whom You gave *to be* with me, she gave me of the tree, and I ate."
13 And the LORD God said to the woman, "What *is* this you have done?"

The woman said, "The serpent deceived me, and I ate."

14 So the LORD God said to the serpent:

"Because you have done this,
You *are* cursed more than all cattle,
And more than every beast
of the field;
On your belly you shall go,
And you shall eat dust
All the days of your life.
15 And I will put enmity
Between you and the woman,
And between your seed and her Seed;
He shall bruise your head,
And you shall bruise His heel."

16 To the woman He said:

"I will greatly multiply your sorrow and
your conception;
In pain you shall bring forth children;
Your desire *shall be* for your husband,
And he shall rule over you."

17 Then to Adam He said, "Because you have heeded the voice of your wife, and have eaten from the tree of which I commanded you, saying, 'You shall not eat of it':

"Cursed *is* the ground for your sake;
In toil you shall eat *of* it

3:15 bruise your head…bruise His heel. This is the first messianic prophecy, foretelling the coming of Jesus Christ. Ever since the Fall, Satan's "seed" (Satan and unbelievers, who are called the devil's children in John 8:44) has struggled against the woman's seed (Christ, a descendant of Eve, and His children). In the midst of this curse passage, God gives a message of hope—"He" is Christ, who will one day defeat Satan completely. Satan could only "bruise" Christ's heel (cause Him to suffer), while Christ will bruise Satan's head (destroy him with a fatal blow).

All the days of your life.
18 Both thorns and thistles it shall bring
forth for you,
And you shall eat the herb
of the field.
19 In the sweat of your face you shall eat
bread
Till you return to the ground,
For out of it you were taken;
For dust you *are,*
And to dust you shall return."

20And Adam called his wife's name Eve,
because she was the mother of all living.
21Also for Adam and his wife the LORD God
made tunics of skin, and clothed them.
22Then the LORD God said, "Behold, the man
has become like one of Us, to know good and
evil. And now, lest he put out his hand and
take also of the tree of life, and eat, and live
forever"— 23therefore the LORD God sent him
out of the garden of Eden to till the ground
from which he was taken. 24So He drove out
the man; and He placed cherubim at the east
of the garden of Eden, and a flaming sword
which turned every way, to guard the way to
the tree of life.

4 Now Adam knew Eve his wife, and she
conceived and bore Cain, and said, "I have
acquired a man from the LORD." 2Then she
bore again, this time his brother Abel. Now
Abel was a keeper of sheep, but Cain was a
tiller of the ground. 3And in the process of time
it came to pass that Cain brought an offering
of the fruit of the ground to the LORD. 4Abel
also brought of the firstborn of his flock and of
their fat. And the LORD respected Abel and his
offering, 5but He did not respect Cain and
his offering. And Cain was very angry, and
his countenance fell.
6So the LORD said to Cain, "Why are you

4:4,5 Abel's offering was acceptable (see Heb. 11:4), because it was in every way obediently given according to what God must have revealed, though the revelation is not recorded in Genesis. Abel's offering was an animal, it was the very best of what he had, and it was the culmination of a zealous heart for God. Cain, however, disdained the divine instruction and just brought what he wanted to bring: some of his crop.

angry? And why has your countenance fallen?
7If you do well, will you not be accepted? And if
you do not do well, sin lies at the door. And its
desire *is* for you, but you should rule over it."
8Now Cain talked with Abel his brother; and
it came to pass, when they were in the field,
that Cain rose up against Abel his brother and
killed him.
9Then the LORD said to Cain, "Where *is* Abel
your brother?"
He said, "I do not know. *Am* I my brother's
keeper?"
10And He said, "What have you done? The
voice of your brother's blood cries out to Me
from the ground. 11So now you *are* cursed
from the earth, which has opened its mouth to
receive your brother's blood from your hand.
12When you till the ground, it shall no longer
yield its strength to you. A fugitive and a
vagabond you shall be on the earth."
13And Cain said to the LORD, "My punishment *is* greater than I can bear! 14Surely You
have driven me out this day from the face of
the ground; I shall be hidden from Your face;
I shall be a fugitive and a vagabond on the
earth, and it will happen *that* anyone who finds
me will kill me."
15And the LORD said to him, "Therefore,
whoever kills Cain, vengeance shall be taken
on him sevenfold." And the LORD set a mark
on Cain, lest anyone finding him should kill
him.
16Then Cain went out from the presence of
the LORD and dwelt in the land of Nod on the
east of Eden. 17And Cain knew his wife, and she
conceived and bore Enoch. And he built a city,
and called the name of the city after the name
of his son—Enoch. 18To Enoch was born Irad;
and Irad begot Mehujael, and Mehujael begot
Methushael, and Methushael begot Lamech.
19Then Lamech took for himself two wives:
the name of one *was* Adah, and the name of
the second *was* Zillah. 20And Adah bore Jabal.

He was the father of those who dwell in tents
and have livestock. 21His brother's name *was*
Jubal. He was the father of all those who play
the harp and flute. 22And as for Zillah, she also
bore Tubal-Cain, an instructor of every craftsman in bronze and iron. And the sister of
Tubal-Cain *was* Naamah.

23Then Lamech said to his wives:

"Adah and Zillah, hear my voice;
Wives of Lamech, listen to my speech!
For I have killed a man for wounding
me,
Even a young man for hurting me.
24 If Cain shall be avenged sevenfold,
Then Lamech seventy-sevenfold."

25And Adam knew his wife again, and she
bore a son and named him Seth, "For God has
appointed another seed for me instead of Abel,
whom Cain killed." 26And as for Seth, to him
also a son was born; and he named him
Enosh. Then *men* began to call on the name of
the LORD.

Psalm 2:1–6

Why do the nations rage,
And the people plot a vain thing?
2 The kings of the earth set themselves,
And the rulers take counsel
together,
Against the LORD and against His
Anointed, *saying,*
3 "Let us break Their bonds in pieces
And cast away Their cords from us."

4 He who sits in the heavens shall
laugh;
The Lord shall hold them in derision.
5 Then He shall speak to them in His
wrath,
And distress them in His deep
displeasure:
6 "Yet I have set My King
On My holy hill of Zion."

Proverbs 1:8–9

8 My son, hear the instruction
of your father,
And do not forsake the law
of your mother;
9 For they *will be* a graceful ornament
on your head,
And chains about your neck.

Matthew 2:1–23

2 Now after Jesus was born in Bethlehem of
Judea in the days of Herod the king, behold,
wise men from the East came to Jerusalem,
2saying, "Where is He who has been born
King of the Jews? For we have seen His star in
the East and have come to worship Him."

3When Herod the king heard *this,* he was
troubled, and all Jerusalem with him. 4And
when he had gathered all the chief priests and
scribes of the people together, he inquired of
them where the Christ was to be born.

5So they said to him, "In Bethlehem of
Judea, for thus it is written by the prophet:

6 *'But you, Bethlehem,*
in the land of Judah,
Are not the least among the rulers
of Judah;
For out of you shall come
a Ruler
Who will shepherd My people Israel.' "

7Then Herod, when he had secretly called
the wise men, determined from them what
time the star appeared. 8And he sent them to
Bethlehem and said, "Go and search carefully
for the young Child, and when you have found
Him, bring back word to me, that I may come
and worship Him also."

9When they heard the king, they departed;
and behold, the star which they had seen in
the East went before them, till it came and
stood over where the young Child was.
10When they saw the star, they rejoiced with
exceedingly great joy. 11And when they had
come into the house, they saw the young
Child with Mary His mother, and fell down
and worshiped Him. And when they had
opened their treasures, they presented gifts to
Him: gold, frankincense, and myrrh.

12Then, being divinely warned in a dream
that they should not return to Herod, they
departed for their own country another way.

13Now when they had departed, behold, an
angel of the Lord appeared to Joseph in a
dream, saying, "Arise, take the young Child
and His mother, flee to Egypt, and stay there

2:1 in the days of Herod the king. Herod the Great was the first in a dynasty of rulers and is thought to be a descendant of Esau. A ruthless and cunning ruler, he saw the beginning of the rebuilding of the Jerusalem temple under his reign. **wise men from the East.** The number of men is not given, though the 3 gifts can be seen to represent one man each. These men were Magi—magicians and astrologers—not kings.

until I bring you word; for Herod will seek the
young Child to destroy Him."
[14]When he arose, he took the young Child
and His mother by night and departed for
Egypt, [15]and was there until the death of
Herod, that it might be fulfilled which was spoken by the Lord through the prophet, saying,
"Out of Egypt I called My Son."
[16]Then Herod, when he saw that he was
deceived by the wise men, was exceedingly
angry; and he sent forth and put to death all
the male children who were in Bethlehem and
in all its districts, from two years old and
under, according to the time which he had
determined from the wise men. [17]Then was fulfilled what was spoken by Jeremiah the
prophet, saying:

[18] *"A voice was heard in Ramah,*
Lamentation, weeping,
and great mourning,
Rachel weeping for her
children,
Refusing to be comforted,
Because they are no more."

[19]Now when Herod was dead, behold, an
angel of the Lord appeared in a dream to Joseph in Egypt, [20]saying, "Arise, take the young
Child and His mother, and go to the land of
Israel, for those who sought the young Child's
life are dead." [21]Then he arose, took the young
Child and His mother, and came into the land
of Israel.
[22]But when he heard that Archelaus was
reigning over Judea instead of his father
Herod, he was afraid to go there. And being
warned by God in a dream, he turned aside
into the region of Galilee. [23]And he came and
dwelt in a city called Nazareth, that it might be
fulfilled which was spoken by the prophets,
"He shall be called a Nazarene."

DAY 2: What do Christians mean when they talk about the Fall?

The Fall refers to that moment in time when human beings first disobeyed God. Genesis 3 tells the painful episode. What Eve set in motion, Adam confirmed and completed by joining her. They sinned together. The willful decision of Adam and Eve created a state of rebellion between the creation and her Creator.

The expression "the Fall" comes from the Bible itself. The apostle Paul uses the word in summarizing the human condition in Romans 3:23, "…for all have sinned and fall short of the glory of God." It carries with it the sense of defeat and destruction. Great cities fell. So did people. But another fall preceded all these—the fall of the angel Lucifer, who became known as Satan (Is. 14:12–15). In the Fall, our first ancestors declared us on Satan's side.

The Bible makes it clear that the Fall brought sin into every subsequent person's life: "Therefore, just as through one man sin entered the world, and death through sin, and thus death spread to all men, because all sinned" (Rom. 5:12). Our capacity for sin is inborn. We are sinners before we have the opportunity to sin. Not only are we sinners because we sin; we first sin because we are sinners. Why? Because we have all inherited the effects of Adam's fall.

JANUARY 3

Genesis 5:1–6:22

5 This is the book of the genealogy of Adam.
In the day that God created man, He made
him in the likeness of God. [2]He created them
male and female, and blessed them and called
them Mankind in the day they were created.
[3]And Adam lived one hundred and thirty
years, and begot *a son* in his own likeness,
after his image, and named him Seth. [4]After he
begot Seth, the days of Adam were eight hundred years; and he had sons and daughters.
[5]So all the days that Adam lived were nine hundred and thirty years; and he died.
[6]Seth lived one hundred and five years, and
begot Enosh. [7]After he begot Enosh, Seth lived
eight hundred and seven years, and had sons
and daughters. [8]So all the days of Seth were
nine hundred and twelve years; and he died.
[9]Enosh lived ninety years, and begot
Cainan. [10]After he begot Cainan, Enosh lived
eight hundred and fifteen years, and had sons
and daughters. [11]So all the days of Enosh were
nine hundred and five years; and he died.
[12]Cainan lived seventy years, and begot
Mahalalel. [13]After he begot Mahalalel, Cainan
lived eight hundred and forty years, and had
sons and daughters. [14]So all the days of Cainan
were nine hundred and ten years; and he died.
[15]Mahalalel lived sixty-five years, and begot
Jared. [16]After he begot Jared, Mahalalel lived
eight hundred and thirty years, and had sons
and daughters. [17]So all the days of Mahalalel

were eight hundred and ninety-five years; and
he died.
18Jared lived one hundred and sixty-two
years, and begot Enoch. 19After he begot Enoch,
Jared lived eight hundred years, and had sons
and daughters. 20So all the days of Jared were
nine hundred and sixty-two years; and he died.
21Enoch lived sixty-five years, and begot
Methuselah. 22After he begot Methuselah,
Enoch walked with God three hundred years,
and had sons and daughters. 23So all the days
of Enoch were three hundred and sixty-five
years. 24And Enoch walked with God; and he
was not, for God took him.
25Methuselah lived one hundred and eighty-
seven years, and begot Lamech. 26After he begot
Lamech, Methuselah lived seven hundred and
eighty-two years, and had sons and daughters.
27So all the days of Methuselah were nine
hundred and sixty-nine years; and he died.
28Lamech lived one hundred and eighty-two
years, and had a son. 29And he called his name
Noah, saying, "This *one* will comfort us concerning our work and the toil of our hands,
because of the ground which the LORD has
cursed." 30After he begot Noah, Lamech lived
five hundred and ninety-five years, and had
sons and daughters. 31So all the days of
Lamech were seven hundred and seventy-
seven years; and he died.
32And Noah was five hundred years old, and
Noah begot Shem, Ham, and Japheth.
6 Now it came to pass, when men began to
multiply on the face of the earth, and
daughters were born to them, 2that the sons of
God saw the daughters of men, that they *were*
beautiful; and they took wives for themselves
of all whom they chose.
3And the LORD said, "My Spirit shall not
strive with man forever, for he *is* indeed flesh;
yet his days shall be one hundred and twenty
years." 4There were giants on the earth in
those days, and also afterward, when the sons
of God came in to the daughters of men and
they bore *children* to them. Those *were* the
mighty men who *were* of old, men of renown.
5Then the LORD saw that the wickedness of
man *was* great in the earth, and *that* every intent of the thoughts of his heart *was* only evil
continually. 6And the LORD was sorry that He
had made man on the earth, and He was
grieved in His heart. 7So the LORD said, "I will
destroy man whom I have created from the
face of the earth, both man and beast, creeping thing and birds of the air, for I am sorry
that I have made them." 8But Noah found
grace in the eyes of the LORD.
9This is the genealogy of Noah. Noah was a
just man, perfect in his generations. Noah
walked with God. 10And Noah begot three
sons: Shem, Ham, and Japheth.
11The earth also was corrupt before God,
and the earth was filled with violence. 12So
God looked upon the earth, and indeed it was
corrupt; for all flesh had corrupted their way
on the earth.
13And God said to Noah, "The end of all
flesh has come before Me, for the earth is
filled with violence through them; and behold,
I will destroy them with the earth. 14Make
yourself an ark of gopherwood; make rooms
in the ark, and cover it inside and outside with
pitch. 15And this is how you shall make it: The
length of the ark *shall be* three hundred cubits, its width fifty cubits, and its height thirty
cubits. 16You shall make a window for the ark,
and you shall finish it to a cubit from above;
and set the door of the ark in its side. You shall
make it *with* lower, second, and third *decks.*
17And behold, I Myself am bringing floodwaters on the earth, to destroy from under heav-
en all flesh in which *is* the breath of life; everything that *is* on the earth shall die. 18But I will
establish My covenant with you; and you shall
go into the ark—you, your sons, your wife,
and your sons' wives with you. 19And of every
living thing of all flesh you shall bring two of
every *sort* into the ark, to keep *them* alive with
you; they shall be male and female. 20Of the
birds after their kind, of animals after their
kind, and of every creeping thing of the earth
after its kind, two of every *kind* will come to
you to keep *them* alive. 21And you shall take for
yourself of all food that is eaten, and you shall
gather *it* to yourself; and it shall be food for
you and for them."

6:15,16 The ark was not designed for beauty or speed, but these dimensions provided extraordinary stability in the tumultuous floodwaters. A cubit was about 18 inches long, which made the ark 450 feet long, 75 feet wide, and 45 feet high. A gigantic box of that size would be very stable in the water and impossible to capsize. The volume of space in the ark was 1.4 million cubic feet, equal to the capacity of 522 standard railroad box cars. It had 3 stories, each 15 feet high; each deck was equipped with rooms (literally, "nests"). "Pitch" was a resin substance to seal the seams and cracks in the wood. The "window" may have actually been a low wall around the flat roof to catch water for all on the ark.

22Thus Noah did; according to all that God commanded him, so he did.

Psalm 2:7–12

7 "I will declare the decree:
The LORD has said to Me,
'You *are* My Son,
Today I have begotten You.
8 Ask of Me, and I will give *You*
The nations *for* Your inheritance,

2:7 You *are* My Son. Second Samuel 7:8–16 is the only Old Testament reference to the Father/Son relationship in the Trinity, a relationship seen throughout the New Testament. **Today I have begotten You.** This expresses the privileges of relationship, with its prophetic application to the Son, the Messiah. This verse is quoted in the New Testament in reference to the birth of Jesus (Heb. 1:5,6) and to His resurrection (Acts 13:33,34) as the ultimate fulfillments of the verse.

2:12 Kiss the Son. This symbolic act indicates allegiance and submission (see 1 Sam. 10:1). This word for "Son" is not the Hebrew word for "son" that is used in v. 7. Rather, it is the Aramaic counterpart for the word (see Dan. 7:13), which addresses the command to "nations" (v. 1). **perish *in* the way.** These words pick up the major burden of Psalm 1.

And the ends of the earth *for*
Your possession.
9 You shall break them with a rod of iron;
You shall dash them to pieces like a
potter's vessel.' "

10 Now therefore, be wise, O kings;
Be instructed, you judges of the earth.
11 Serve the LORD with fear,
And rejoice with trembling.
12 Kiss the Son, lest He be angry,
And you perish *in* the way,
When His wrath is kindled but a little.
Blessed *are* all those who put their
trust in Him.

Proverbs 1:10–19

10 My son, if sinners entice you,
Do not consent.
11 If they say, "Come with us,
Let us lie in wait to *shed* blood;
Let us lurk secretly for the innocent
without cause;
12 Let us swallow them alive like Sheol,
And whole, like those who go down
to the Pit;
13 We shall find all *kinds* of
precious possessions,
We shall fill our houses with spoil;
14 Cast in your lot among us,
Let us all have one purse"—
15 My son, do not walk in the
way with them,
Keep your foot from their path;
16 For their feet run to evil,
And they make haste to shed blood.
17 Surely, in vain the net is spread
In the sight of any bird;
18 But they lie in wait for their *own* blood,
They lurk secretly for their *own* lives.
19 So *are* the ways of everyone who is
greedy for gain;
It takes away the life of its owners.

Matthew 3:1–17

3 In those days John the Baptist came
preaching in the wilderness of Judea, 2and
saying, "Repent, for the kingdom of heaven is
at hand!" 3For this is he who was spoken of by
the prophet Isaiah, saying:

"The voice of one crying in the
wilderness:
'Prepare the way of the LORD;
Make His paths straight.' "

4Now John himself was clothed in camel's
hair, with a leather belt around his waist; and
his food was locusts and wild honey. 5Then
Jerusalem, all Judea, and all the region around
the Jordan went out to him 6and were baptized
by him in the Jordan, confessing their sins.
7But when he saw many of the Pharisees
and Sadducees coming to his baptism, he said
to them, "Brood of vipers! Who warned you to
flee from the wrath to come? 8Therefore bear
fruits worthy of repentance, 9and do not think
to say to yourselves, 'We have Abraham as *our*
father.' For I say to you that God is able to
raise up children to Abraham from these
stones. 10And even now the ax is laid to the
root of the trees. Therefore every tree which
does not bear good fruit is cut down and
thrown into the fire. 11I indeed baptize you
with water unto repentance, but He who is
coming after me is mightier than I, whose sandals I am not worthy to carry. He will baptize
you with the Holy Spirit and fire. 12His winnowing fan *is* in His hand, and He will thoroughly
clean out His threshing floor, and gather His
wheat into the barn; but He will burn up the
chaff with unquenchable fire."
13Then Jesus came from Galilee to John at
the Jordan to be baptized by him. 14And John

tried to prevent Him, saying, "I need to be
baptized by You, and are You coming to me?"
15But Jesus answered and said to him, "Permit *it to be so* now, for thus it is fitting for us to
fulfill all righteousness." Then he allowed Him.
16When He had been baptized, Jesus came
up immediately from the water; and behold,
the heavens were opened to Him, and He saw
the Spirit of God descending like a dove and
alighting upon Him. 17And suddenly a voice
came from heaven, saying, "This is My
beloved Son, in whom I am well pleased."

DAY 3: What is the difference between the Pharisees and Sadducees?

The Pharisees were a small (about 6,000), legalistic sect of the Jews. Their name means "separated ones," not in the sense of isolationists but in the puritanical sense, i.e., they were highly zealous for ritual and religious purity according to the Mosaic Law as well as their own traditions that they added to the Old Testament legislation. They represented the orthodox core of Judaism and very strongly influenced the common people of Israel. Jesus' interaction with the Pharisees was usually adversarial. He rebuked them for using human tradition to nullify Scripture (15:3–9), and especially for rank hypocrisy (15:7,8; 22:18; 23:13,23,25,29; Luke 12:1).

The Sadducees were known for their denial of things supernatural. They denied the resurrection of the dead (22:23) and the existence of angels (Acts 23:8). Unlike the Pharisees, they rejected human tradition and scorned legalism. They accepted only the Pentateuch as authoritative. They tended to be wealthy, aristocratic, members of the priestly tribe, and in the days of Herod their sect controlled the temple, though they were fewer in number than the Pharisees.

Pharisees and Sadducees had little in common. Pharisees were ritualists; Sadducees were rationalists. Pharisees were legalists; Sadducees were liberals. Pharisees were separatists; Sadducees were compromisers and political opportunists. Yet they united together in their opposition of Christ (22:15,16,23,34,35). John publicly addressed them as deadly snakes.

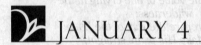

JANUARY 4

Genesis 7:1–8:22

7 Then the LORD said to Noah, "Come into
the ark, you and all your household,
because I have seen *that* you *are* righteous
before Me in this generation. 2You shall take
with you seven each of every clean animal, a
male and his female; two each of animals that
are unclean, a male and his female; 3also seven
each of birds of the air, male and female, to
keep the species alive on the face of all the
earth. 4For after seven more days I will cause
it to rain on the earth forty days and forty
nights, and I will destroy from the face of the
earth all living things that I have made." 5And
Noah did according to all that the LORD commanded him. 6Noah *was* six hundred years old
when the floodwaters were on the earth.
7So Noah, with his sons, his wife, and his
sons' wives, went into the ark because of the
waters of the flood. 8Of clean animals, of animals
that *are* unclean, of birds, and of everything
that creeps on the earth, 9two by two they
went into the ark to Noah, male and female, as
God had commanded Noah. 10And it came to
pass after seven days that the waters of the
flood were on the earth. 11In the six hundredth
year of Noah's life, in the second month, the
seventeenth day of the month, on that day all
the fountains of the great deep were broken
up, and the windows of heaven were opened.
12And the rain was on the earth forty days and
forty nights.
13On the very same day Noah and Noah's
sons, Shem, Ham, and Japheth, and Noah's
wife and the three wives of his sons with them,
entered the ark— 14they and every beast after
its kind, all cattle after their kind, every creeping thing that creeps on the earth after its

7:11 all the fountains of the great deep were broken up. The subterranean waters sprang up from deep fountains inside the earth to form the seas and rivers (1:10; 2:10–14), which were not produced by rainfall, since it never rained before the Flood. **the windows of heaven.** The celestial waters in the canopy encircling the globe were dumped on the earth and joined with the terrestrial and the subterranean waters (see 1:7). The Flood ended the water canopy surrounding the earth and unleashed the water in the earth. Thus began the earth's cycle of hydrology, with rain and evaporation (see Job 26:8; Eccl. 1:7; Is. 55:10; Amos 9:6).

kind, and every bird after its kind, every bird of every sort. [15]And they went into the ark to Noah, two by two, of all flesh in which *is* the breath of life. [16]So those that entered, male and female of all flesh, went in as God had commanded him; and the LORD shut him in.

[17]Now the flood was on the earth forty days. The waters increased and lifted up the ark, and it rose high above the earth. [18]The waters prevailed and greatly increased on the earth, and the ark moved about on the surface of the waters. [19]And the waters prevailed exceedingly on the earth, and all the high hills under the whole heaven were covered. [20]The waters prevailed fifteen cubits upward, and the mountains were covered. [21]And all flesh died that moved on the earth: birds and cattle and beasts and every creeping thing that creeps on the earth, and every man. [22]All in whose nostrils *was* the breath of the spirit of life, all that *was* on the dry *land,* died. [23]So He destroyed all living things which were on the face of the ground: both man and cattle, creeping thing and bird of the air. They were destroyed from the earth. Only Noah and those who *were* with him in the ark remained *alive.* [24]And the waters prevailed on the earth one hundred and fifty days.

8 Then God remembered Noah, and every living thing, and all the animals that *were* with him in the ark. And God made a wind to pass over the earth, and the waters subsided. [2]The fountains of the deep and the windows of heaven were also stopped, and the rain from heaven was restrained. [3]And the waters receded continually from the earth. At the end of the hundred and fifty days the waters decreased. [4]Then the ark rested in the seventh month, the seventeenth day of the month, on the mountains of Ararat. [5]And the waters decreased continually until the tenth month. In the tenth *month,* on the first *day* of the month, the tops of the mountains were seen.

[6]So it came to pass, at the end of forty days, that Noah opened the window of the ark which he had made. [7]Then he sent out a raven, which kept going to and fro until the waters had dried up from the earth. [8]He also sent out from himself a dove, to see if the waters had receded from the face of the ground. [9]But the dove found no resting place for the sole of her foot, and she returned into the ark to him, for the waters *were* on the face of the whole earth. So he put out his hand and took her, and drew her into the ark to himself. [10]And he waited yet another seven days, and again he sent the dove out from the ark. [11]Then the dove came to him in the evening, and behold, a freshly plucked olive leaf *was* in her mouth; and Noah knew that the waters had receded from the earth. [12]So he waited yet another seven days and sent out the dove, which did not return again to him anymore.

[13]And it came to pass in the six hundred and first year, in the first *month,* the first *day* of the month, that the waters were dried up from the earth; and Noah removed the covering of the ark and looked, and indeed the surface of the ground was dry. [14]And in the second month, on the twenty-seventh day of the month, the earth was dried.

[15]Then God spoke to Noah, saying, [16]"Go out of the ark, you and your wife, and your sons and your sons' wives with you. [17]Bring out with you every living thing of all flesh that *is* with you: birds and cattle and every creeping thing that creeps on the earth, so that they may abound on the earth, and be fruitful and multiply on the earth." [18]So Noah went out, and his sons and his wife and his sons' wives with him. [19]Every animal, every creeping thing, every bird, *and* whatever creeps on the earth, according to their families, went out of the ark.

[20]Then Noah built an altar to the LORD, and took of every clean animal and of every clean bird, and offered burnt offerings on the altar. [21]And the LORD smelled a soothing aroma. Then the LORD said in His heart, "I will never again curse the ground for man's sake, although the imagination of man's heart *is* evil from his youth; nor will I again destroy every living thing as I have done.

22 "While the earth remains,
Seedtime and harvest,
Cold and heat,
Winter and summer,
And day and night
Shall not cease."

Psalm 3:1–4

A Psalm of David when he fled from Absalom his son.

LORD, how they have increased
who trouble me!
Many *are* they who rise up against me.
2 Many *are* they who say of me,
"*There is* no help for him in God."
Selah
3 But You, O LORD, *are* a shield for me,
My glory and the One who lifts up my
head.
4 I cried to the LORD with my voice,
And He heard me from His
holy hill.
Selah

Proverbs 1:20–22

20 Wisdom calls aloud outside;
She raises her voice in the open
squares.
21 She cries out in the chief concourses,
At the openings of the gates in the city
She speaks her words:
22 "How long, you simple ones, will you
love simplicity?
For scorners delight in their scorning,
And fools hate knowledge.

1:22 How long. Three classes of people need wisdom: 1) the simple, who are ignorant; 2) scorners or mockers, who commit more serious, determined acts; and 3) fools or obstinate unbelievers, who will not listen to the truth. Proverbs directs its wisdom primarily at the first group.

Matthew 4:1–25

4 Then Jesus was led up by the Spirit into
the wilderness to be tempted by the devil.
2 And when He had fasted forty days and forty
nights, afterward He was hungry. 3 Now when
the tempter came to Him, he said, "If You are
the Son of God, command that these stones
become bread."
4 But He answered and said, "It is written,
'Man shall not live by bread alone, but by every
word that proceeds from the mouth of God.' "
5 Then the devil took Him up into the holy
city, set Him on the pinnacle of the temple,
6 and said to Him, "If You are the Son of God,
throw Yourself down. For it is written:

'He shall give His angels charge over you,'

and,

'In their hands they shall bear you up,
Lest you dash your foot against a stone.' "

7 Jesus said to him, "It is written again, *'You*
shall not tempt the LORD your God.' "
8 Again, the devil took Him up on an exceedingly high mountain, and showed Him all the
kingdoms of the world and their glory. 9 And
he said to Him, "All these things I will give
You if You will fall down and worship me."
10 Then Jesus said to him, "Away with you, Satan! For it is written, *'You shall worship the LORD*
your God, and Him only you shall serve.' "
11 Then the devil left Him, and behold, angels
came and ministered to Him.
12 Now when Jesus heard that John had been
put in prison, He departed to Galilee. 13 And leaving Nazareth, He came and dwelt in Capernaum,
which is by the sea, in the regions of Zebulun
and Naphtali, 14 that it might be fulfilled which
was spoken by Isaiah the prophet, saying:

15 *"The land of Zebulun and the land of*
Naphtali,
By the way of the sea, beyond the Jordan,
Galilee of the Gentiles:
16 *The people who sat in darkness have*
seen a great light,
And upon those who sat in the region
and shadow of death
Light has dawned."

17 From that time Jesus began to preach and
to say, "Repent, for the kingdom of heaven is
at hand."
18 And Jesus, walking by the Sea of Galilee, saw
two brothers, Simon called Peter, and Andrew
his brother, casting a net into the sea; for they
were fishermen. 19 Then He said to them, "Follow
Me, and I will make you fishers of men." 20 They
immediately left *their* nets and followed Him.
21 Going on from there, He saw two other
brothers, James *the son* of Zebedee, and John
his brother, in the boat with Zebedee their
father, mending their nets. He called them,
22 and immediately they left the boat and their
father, and followed Him.
23 And Jesus went about all Galilee, teaching
in their synagogues, preaching the gospel of
the kingdom, and healing all kinds of sickness
and all kinds of disease among the people.
24 Then His fame went throughout all Syria;
and they brought to Him all sick people who
were afflicted with various diseases and torments, and those who were demon-possessed,
epileptics, and paralytics; and He healed them.
25 Great multitudes followed Him—from Galilee, and *from* Decapolis, Jerusalem, Judea,
and beyond the Jordan.

4:4 It is written. All 3 of Jesus' replies to the devil were taken from Deuteronomy. This one, from Deuteronomy 8:3, states that God allowed Israel to hunger, so that He might feed them with manna and teach them to trust Him to provide for them. So the verse is directly applicable to Jesus' circumstances and a fitting reply to Satan's temptation. **every word that proceeds from the mouth of God.** A more important source of sustenance than food, it nurtures our spiritual needs in a way that benefits us eternally, rather than merely providing temporal relief from physical hunger.

DAY 4: How significant is the Flood in the overall biblical history?

The Bible treats the Flood as a worldwide event directly brought by God as a judgment on the sin of humanity. The flood hangs like a warning cloud over all subsequent history. Fortunately, that cloud also holds a rainbow of God's promised grace.

Conditions in Noah's day were ripe for judgment. "Then the LORD saw that the wickedness of man was great in the earth, and that every intent of the thoughts of his heart was only evil continually" (Gen. 6:5). This verse provides one of the strongest and clearest statements about man's sinful nature. Many other verses make it clear that God had every reason for radical action: Jeremiah 17:9,10; Matthew 12:34,35; 15:18,19; Mark 7:21; Luke 6:45. Other notable Scriptures on the worldwide flood brought by God include Job 12:15; 22:16; Psalms 29:10; 104:6–9; Isaiah 54:9; Matthew 24:37–39; Luke 17:26,27; Hebrews 11:7; 1 Peter 3:20; 2 Peter 2:5; 3:5,6.

The Flood illustrates several important aspects of God's character and God's relationship with His creation: 1) God retains ultimate control of world events; 2) God can and will judge sin; 3) God can and does exercise grace even in judgment; 4) An even more universal and final judgment will be carried out on the world based on God's timetable.

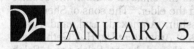

JANUARY 5

Genesis 9:1–10:32

9 So God blessed Noah and his sons, and said to them: "Be fruitful and multiply,
and fill the earth. 2And the fear of you and the
dread of you shall be on every beast of the
earth, on every bird of the air, on all that move
on the earth, and on all the fish of the sea.
They are given into your hand. 3Every moving
thing that lives shall be food for you. I have
given you all things, even as the green herbs.
4But you shall not eat flesh with its life, *that is,*
its blood. 5Surely for your lifeblood I will
demand *a reckoning;* from the hand of every
beast I will require it, and from the hand of
man. From the hand of every man's brother I
will require the life of man.

6 "Whoever sheds man's blood,
By man his blood shall be shed;
For in the image of God
He made man.
7 And as for you, be fruitful and multiply;
Bring forth abundantly in the earth
And multiply in it."

8Then God spoke to Noah and to his sons
with him, saying: 9"And as for Me, behold, I
establish My covenant with you and with your
descendants after you, 10and with every living
creature that *is* with you: the birds, the cattle,
and every beast of the earth with you, of all
that go out of the ark, every beast of the earth.
11Thus I establish My covenant with you:
Never again shall all flesh be cut off by the
waters of the flood; never again shall there be
a flood to destroy the earth."

12And God said: "This *is* the sign of the
covenant which I make between Me and you,
and every living creature that *is* with you, for
perpetual generations: 13I set My rainbow in
the cloud, and it shall be for the sign of the
covenant between Me and the earth. 14It shall
be, when I bring a cloud over the earth, that
the rainbow shall be seen in the cloud; 15and I
will remember My covenant which *is* between
Me and you and every living creature of all
flesh; the waters shall never again become a
flood to destroy all flesh. 16The rainbow shall
be in the cloud, and I will look on it to remember the everlasting covenant between God and
every living creature of all flesh that *is* on the
earth." 17And God said to Noah, "This *is* the
sign of the covenant which I have established
between Me and all flesh that *is* on the earth."

9:6 For in the image of God. The reason man could kill animals, but neither animals nor man could kill man, is because man alone was created in God's image.

9:16 the everlasting covenant. This covenant with Noah is the first of 5 divinely originated covenants that are described as "everlasting." The term "everlasting" can mean either 1) to the end of time and/or 2) through eternity future. It does not include eternity past. The other four such covenants include the following: 1) Abrahamic (Gen. 17:7); 2) Priestly (Num. 25:10–13); 3) Davidic (2 Sam. 23:5); and 4) New (Jer. 32:40).

[18]Now the sons of Noah who went out of the
ark were Shem, Ham, and Japheth. And Ham
was the father of Canaan. [19]These three *were*
the sons of Noah, and from these the whole
earth was populated.

[20]And Noah began *to be* a farmer, and he
planted a vineyard. [21]Then he drank of the wine
and was drunk, and became uncovered in his
tent. [22]And Ham, the father of Canaan, saw the
nakedness of his father, and told his two
brothers outside. [23]But Shem and Japheth took
a garment, laid *it* on both their shoulders, and
went backward and covered the nakedness of
their father. Their faces *were* turned away, and
they did not see their father's nakedness.

[24]So Noah awoke from his wine, and knew
what his younger son had done to him. [25]Then
he said:

"Cursed *be* Canaan;
A servant of servants
He shall be to his brethren."

[26]And he said:

"Blessed *be* the LORD,
The God of Shem,
And may Canaan be his servant.
27 May God enlarge Japheth,
And may he dwell in the tents of Shem;
And may Canaan be his servant."

[28]And Noah lived after the flood three hundred and fifty years. [29]So all the days of Noah
were nine hundred and fifty years; and he died.

10 Now this *is* the genealogy of the sons of
Noah: Shem, Ham, and Japheth. And
sons were born to them after the flood.

[2]The sons of Japheth *were* Gomer, Magog,
Madai, Javan, Tubal, Meshech, and Tiras.
[3]The sons of Gomer *were* Ashkenaz, Riphath,
and Togarmah. [4]The sons of Javan *were*
Elishah, Tarshish, Kittim, and Dodanim.
[5]From these the coastland *peoples* of the
Gentiles were separated into their lands,
everyone according to his language, according to their families, into their nations.

[6]The sons of Ham *were* Cush, Mizraim, Put,
and Canaan. [7]The sons of Cush *were* Seba,
Havilah, Sabtah, Raamah, and Sabtechah; and
the sons of Raamah *were* Sheba and Dedan.

[8]Cush begot Nimrod; he began to be a mighty
one on the earth. [9]He was a mighty hunter before the LORD; therefore it is said, "Like Nimrod
the mighty hunter before the LORD." [10]And the
beginning of his kingdom was Babel, Erech,
Accad, and Calneh, in the land of Shinar. [11]From
that land he went to Assyria and built Nineveh,
Rehoboth Ir, Calah, [12]and Resen between
Nineveh and Calah (that *is* the principal city).

[13]Mizraim begot Ludim, Anamim, Lehabim,
Naphtuhim, [14]Pathrusim, and Casluhim (from
whom came the Philistines and Caphtorim).

[15]Canaan begot Sidon his firstborn, and Heth;
[16]the Jebusite, the Amorite, and the Girgashite;
[17]the Hivite, the Arkite, and the Sinite; [18]the
Arvadite, the Zemarite, and the Hamathite.
Afterward the families of the Canaanites were
dispersed. [19]And the border of the Canaanites
was from Sidon as you go toward Gerar, as far
as Gaza; then as you go toward Sodom,
Gomorrah, Admah, and Zeboiim, as far as
Lasha. [20]These *were* the sons of Ham, according to their families, according to their languages, in their lands *and* in their nations.

[21]And *children* were born also to Shem, the
father of all the children of Eber, the brother
of Japheth the elder. [22]The sons of Shem *were*
Elam, Asshur, Arphaxad, Lud, and Aram.
[23]The sons of Aram *were* Uz, Hul, Gether, and
Mash. [24]Arphaxad begot Salah, and Salah
begot Eber. [25]To Eber were born two sons: the
name of one *was* Peleg, for in his days the
earth was divided; and his brother's name *was*
Joktan. [26]Joktan begot Almodad, Sheleph,
Hazarmaveth, Jerah, [27]Hadoram, Uzal, Diklah,
[28]Obal, Abimael, Sheba, [29]Ophir, Havilah, and
Jobab. All these *were* the sons of Joktan. [30]And
their dwelling place was from Mesha as you
go toward Sephar, the mountain of the east.
[31]These *were* the sons of Shem, according to
their families, according to their languages, in
their lands, according to their nations.

[32]These *were* the families of the sons of
Noah, according to their generations, in their
nations; and from these the nations were
divided on the earth after the flood.

Psalm 3:5–8

5 I lay down and slept;
I awoke, for the LORD sustained me.
6 I will not be afraid of ten thousands
of people
Who have set *themselves* against me
all around.

7 Arise, O LORD;
Save me, O my God!
For You have struck all my enemies
on the cheekbone;
You have broken the teeth of the
ungodly.
8 Salvation *belongs* to the LORD.
Your blessing *is* upon Your people.
Selah

Proverbs 1:23–27

23 Turn at my rebuke;
Surely I will pour out my spirit on you;

I will make my words known to you.
24 Because I have called and you refused,
I have stretched out my hand and no
one regarded,
25 Because you disdained all my counsel,
And would have none of my rebuke,
26 I also will laugh at your calamity;
I will mock when your terror comes,
27 When your terror comes like a storm,
And your destruction comes like
a whirlwind,
When distress and anguish come
upon you.

Matthew 5:1–26

5 And seeing the multitudes, He went up on
a mountain, and when He was seated His
disciples came to Him. 2Then He opened His
mouth and taught them, saying:

3 "Blessed *are* the poor in spirit,
For theirs is the kingdom
of heaven.
4 Blessed *are* those who mourn,
For they shall be comforted.
5 Blessed *are* the meek,
For they shall inherit
the earth.
6 Blessed *are* those who hunger and
thirst for righteousness,
For they shall be filled.
7 Blessed *are* the merciful,
For they shall obtain mercy.

5:3 Blessed. The word literally means "happy, fortunate, blissful." Here it speaks of more than a surface emotion. Jesus was describing the divinely bestowed well-being that belongs only to the faithful. The Beatitudes demonstrate that the way to heavenly blessedness is antithetical to the worldly path normally followed in pursuit of happiness. The worldly idea is that happiness is found in riches, merriment, abundance, leisure, and such things. The real truth is the very opposite. The Beatitudes give Jesus' description of the character of true faith. **poor in spirit.** The opposite of self-sufficiency. This speaks of deep humility of recognizing one's utter spiritual bankruptcy apart from God. It describes those who are acutely conscious of their own lostness and hopelessness apart from divine grace (9:12; Luke 18:13). **theirs is the kingdom of heaven.** Notice that the truth of salvation by grace is clearly presupposed in this opening verse of the Sermon on the Mount. Jesus was teaching that the kingdom is a gracious gift to those who sense their own poverty of spirit.

8 Blessed *are* the pure in heart,
For they shall see God.
9 Blessed *are* the peacemakers,
For they shall be called sons of God.
10 Blessed *are* those who are persecuted
for righteousness' sake,
For theirs is the kingdom of heaven.

11"Blessed are you when they revile and persecute you, and say all kinds of evil against you
falsely for My sake. 12Rejoice and be exceedingly glad, for great *is* your reward in heaven,
for so they persecuted the prophets who were
before you.

13"You are the salt of the earth; but if the salt
loses its flavor, how shall it be seasoned? It is
then good for nothing but to be thrown out
and trampled underfoot by men.

14"You are the light of the world. A city that
is set on a hill cannot be hidden. 15Nor do they
light a lamp and put it under a basket, but on
a lampstand, and it gives light to all *who are* in
the house. 16Let your light so shine before
men, that they may see your good works and
glorify your Father in heaven.

17"Do not think that I came to destroy the
Law or the Prophets. I did not come to destroy
but to fulfill. 18For assuredly, I say to you, till
heaven and earth pass away, one jot or one tittle will by no means pass from the law till all is
fulfilled. 19Whoever therefore breaks one of
the least of these commandments, and teaches men so, shall be called least in the kingdom
of heaven; but whoever does and teaches
them, he shall be called great in the kingdom
of heaven. 20For I say to you, that unless your
righteousness exceeds *the righteousness* of the
scribes and Pharisees, you will by no means
enter the kingdom of heaven.

21"You have heard that it was said to those of
old, '*You shall not murder,* and whoever murders will be in danger of the judgment.' 22But I
say to you that whoever is angry with his
brother without a cause shall be in danger of
the judgment. And whoever says to his brother, 'Raca!' shall be in danger of the council. But
whoever says, 'You fool!' shall be in danger of
hell fire. 23Therefore if you bring your gift to
the altar, and there remember that your brother has something against you, 24leave your gift
there before the altar, and go your way. First
be reconciled to your brother, and then come
and offer your gift. 25Agree with your adversary quickly, while you are on the way with
him, lest your adversary deliver you to the
judge, the judge hand you over to the officer,
and you be thrown into prison. 26Assuredly, I
say to you, you will by no means get out of
there till you have paid the last penny.

Day 5: Why did Jesus preach the Sermon on the Mount?

Matthew records five important discourses: the Sermon on the Mount (chaps. 5–7); the commissioning of the apostles (chap. 10); the parables about the kingdom of heaven (chap. 13); a discourse about the childlikeness of the believer (chap. 18); and the discourse on His second coming (chaps. 24;25). Each discourse ends with a variation of this phrase: "when Jesus had ended these sayings." That becomes a motif signaling a new narrative portion.

The Sermon on the Mount is a masterful exposition of the law and a potent assault on Pharisaic legalism, closing with a call to true faith and salvation (7:13–29). Matthew is keen to show the error of the Pharisees for the benefit of his Jewish audience—not for personal or self-aggrandizing reasons. Christ expounded the full meaning of the law, showing that its demands were humanly impossible (see 5:48). This is the proper use of the law with respect to salvation: It closes off every possible avenue of human merit and leaves sinners dependent on nothing but divine grace for salvation (see Rom. 3:19,20; Gal. 3:23,24). Christ plumbed the depth of the law, showing that its true demands went far beyond the surface meaning of the words (5:28,39,44) and set a standard that is higher than the most diligent students of the law had heretofore realized.

JANUARY 6

Genesis 11:1–12:20

11 Now the whole earth had one language and
one speech. 2And it came to pass, as they
journeyed from the east, that they found a
plain in the land of Shinar, and they dwelt
there. 3Then they said to one another, "Come,
let us make bricks and bake *them* thoroughly."
They had brick for stone, and they had asphalt
for mortar. 4And they said, "Come, let us build
ourselves a city, and a tower whose top *is* in
the heavens; let us make a name for ourselves,
lest we be scattered abroad over the face of
the whole earth."

11:3,4 build ourselves a city. After God commanded the people to scatter to fill the earth, the people, under the leadership of the powerful Nimrod, disobeyed God's command to disperse. They stopped to build a city and tower in their own honor. The tower itself was not the singular act of rebellion. Rather, human pride caused them to rebel against God.

5But the LORD came down to see the city and
the tower which the sons of men had built.
6And the LORD said, "Indeed the people *are*
one and they all have one language, and this is
what they begin to do; now nothing that they
propose to do will be withheld from them.
7Come, let Us go down and there confuse their
language, that they may not understand one
another's speech." 8So the LORD scattered
them abroad from there over the face of all the
earth, and they ceased building the city.
9Therefore its name is called Babel, because
there the LORD confused the language of all
the earth; and from there the LORD scattered
them abroad over the face of all the earth.

10This *is* the genealogy of Shem: Shem *was*
one hundred years old, and begot Arphaxad
two years after the flood. 11After he begot
Arphaxad, Shem lived five hundred years, and
begot sons and daughters.

12Arphaxad lived thirty-five years, and begot
Salah. 13After he begot Salah, Arphaxad lived
four hundred and three years, and begot sons
and daughters.

14Salah lived thirty years, and begot Eber.
15After he begot Eber, Salah lived four hundred and three years, and begot sons and
daughters.

16Eber lived thirty-four years, and begot
Peleg. 17After he begot Peleg, Eber lived four
hundred and thirty years, and begot sons and
daughters.

18Peleg lived thirty years, and begot Reu.
19After he begot Reu, Peleg lived two hundred
and nine years, and begot sons and daughters.

20Reu lived thirty-two years, and begot
Serug. 21After he begot Serug, Reu lived two
hundred and seven years, and begot sons and
daughters.

22Serug lived thirty years, and begot Nahor.
23After he begot Nahor, Serug lived two hundred years, and begot sons and daughters.

24Nahor lived twenty-nine years, and begot
Terah. 25After he begot Terah, Nahor lived one
hundred and nineteen years, and begot sons
and daughters.

26Now Terah lived seventy years, and begot
Abram, Nahor, and Haran.

27This *is* the genealogy of Terah: Terah
begot Abram, Nahor, and Haran. Haran begot

Lot. 28 And Haran died before his father Terah
in his native land, in Ur of the Chaldeans.
29 Then Abram and Nahor took wives: the
name of Abram's wife *was* Sarai, and the name
of Nahor's wife, Milcah, the daughter of Haran
the father of Milcah and the father of Iscah.
30 But Sarai was barren; she had no child.
31 And Terah took his son Abram and his
grandson Lot, the son of Haran, and his
daughter-in-law Sarai, his son Abram's wife,
and they went out with them from Ur of the
Chaldeans to go to the land of Canaan; and
they came to Haran and dwelt there. 32 So the
days of Terah were two hundred and five
years, and Terah died in Haran.

12 Now the LORD had said to Abram:

"Get out of your country,
From your family
And from your father's house,
To a land that I will show you.
2 I will make you a great nation;
I will bless you
And make your name great;
And you shall be a blessing.
3 I will bless those who bless you,
And I will curse him who curses you;
And in you all the families of the earth
shall be blessed."

4 So Abram departed as the LORD had spoken to him, and Lot went with him. And
Abram *was* seventy-five years old when he
departed from Haran. 5 Then Abram took Sarai
his wife and Lot his brother's son, and all their
possessions that they had gathered, and the
people whom they had acquired in Haran, and
they departed to go to the land of Canaan. So
they came to the land of Canaan. 6 Abram passed
through the land to the place of Shechem, as far
as the terebinth tree of Moreh. And the
Canaanites *were* then in the land.

12:1–3 the LORD...to Abram. This passage contains the promise whose fulfillment extends all through Scripture. It is an everlasting covenant which includes four components: 1) seed (see Gal. 3:8,16, referring to Christ); 2) land (15:18–21; 17:8); 3) a nation (12:2; 17:4); and 4) divine blessing and protection (12:3). The covenant is unconditional in the sense of its ultimate fulfillment of a kingdom and salvation. It has great national importance to Israel, as magnified by repeated references in the Old Testament, and great spiritual importance to all believers.

7 Then the LORD appeared to Abram and said,
"To your descendants I will give this land."
And there he built an altar to the LORD, who
had appeared to him. 8 And he moved from
there to the mountain east of Bethel, and he
pitched his tent *with* Bethel on the west and Ai
on the east; there he built an altar to the LORD
and called on the name of the LORD. 9 So Abram
journeyed, going on still toward the South.
10 Now there was a famine in the land, and
Abram went down to Egypt to dwell there, for
the famine *was* severe in the land. 11 And it
came to pass, when he was close to entering
Egypt, that he said to Sarai his wife, "Indeed I
know that you *are* a woman of beautiful countenance. 12 Therefore it will happen, when the
Egyptians see you, that they will say, 'This *is*
his wife'; and they will kill me, but they will let
you live. 13 Please say you *are* my sister, that it
may be well with me for your sake, and that I
may live because of you."
14 So it was, when Abram came into Egypt,
that the Egyptians saw the woman, that she
was very beautiful. 15 The princes of Pharaoh
also saw her and commended her to Pharaoh.
And the woman was taken to Pharaoh's house.
16 He treated Abram well for her sake. He had
sheep, oxen, male donkeys, male and female
servants, female donkeys, and camels.
17 But the LORD plagued Pharaoh and his
house with great plagues because of Sarai,
Abram's wife. 18 And Pharaoh called Abram
and said, "What *is* this you have done to me?
Why did you not tell me that she *was* your
wife? 19 Why did you say, 'She *is* my sister'? I
might have taken her as my wife. Now therefore, here is your wife; take *her* and go your
way." 20 So Pharaoh commanded *his* men concerning him; and they sent him away, with his
wife and all that he had.

Psalm 4:1–3

To the Chief Musician. With stringed instruments.
A Psalm of David.

Hear me when I call, O God of my
righteousness!

4:1 O God of my righteousness. The ultimate basis for divine intervention is God's righteousness, not the psalmist's (see Jer. 23:6). **distress.** This word describes the psalmist in painful situations. When he says "You have relieved me," he conveys the picture that God has provided space for him.

You have relieved me in *my* distress;
Have mercy on me, and hear my prayer.

2 How long, O you sons of men,
Will you turn my glory to shame?
How long will you love worthlessness
And seek falsehood? Selah
3 But know that the LORD has set apart
for Himself him who is godly;
The LORD will hear when I call to Him.

Proverbs 1:28–33

28 "Then they will call on me,
but I will not answer;
They will seek me diligently, but they
will not find me.
29 Because they hated knowledge
And did not choose the fear of the LORD,
30 They would have none of my counsel
And despised my every rebuke.
31 Therefore they shall eat the fruit of
their own way,
And be filled to the full with their own
fancies.
32 For the turning away of the simple will
slay them,
And the complacency of fools will
destroy them;
33 But whoever listens to me will dwell
safely,
And will be secure, without fear of evil."

Matthew 5:27–48

27"You have heard that it was said to those of old, *'You shall not commit adultery.'* 28But I say to you that whoever looks at a woman to lust for her has already committed adultery with her in his heart. 29If your right eye causes you to sin, pluck it out and cast *it* from you; for it is more profitable for you that one of your members perish, than for your whole body to be cast into hell. 30And if your right hand causes you to sin, cut it off and cast *it* from you; for it is more profitable for you that one of your members perish, than for your whole body to be cast into hell.

31"Furthermore it has been said, 'Whoever divorces his wife, let him give her a certificate of divorce.' 32But I say to you that whoever divorces his wife for any reason except sexual immorality causes her to commit adultery; and whoever marries a woman who is divorced commits adultery.

5:31 it has been said. The rabbis wrongly understood Deuteronomy 24:1–4 to mean that divorce only required regulated paperwork and could be granted for anything that displeased a man. Moses provided this as a concession to protect the woman who was divorced, not to justify or legalize divorce under all circumstances.

33"Again you have heard that it was said to those of old, 'You shall not swear falsely, but shall perform your oaths to the Lord.' 34But I say to you, do not swear at all: neither by heaven, for it is God's throne; 35nor by the earth, for it is His footstool; nor by Jerusalem, for it is the city of the great King. 36Nor shall you swear by your head, because you cannot make one hair white or black. 37But let your 'Yes' be 'Yes,' and your 'No,' 'No.' For whatever is more than these is from the evil one.

38"You have heard that it was said, *'An eye for an eye and a tooth for a tooth.'* 39But I tell you not to resist an evil person. But whoever slaps you on your right cheek, turn the other to him also. 40If anyone wants to sue you and take away your tunic, let him have *your* cloak also. 41And whoever compels you to go one mile, go with him two. 42Give to him who asks you, and from him who wants to borrow from you do not turn away.

43"You have heard that it was said, *'You shall love your neighbor* and hate your enemy.' 44But I say to you, love your enemies, bless those who curse you, do good to those who hate you, and pray for those who spitefully use you and persecute you, 45that you may be sons of your Father in heaven; for He makes His sun rise on the evil and on the good, and sends rain on the just and on the unjust. 46For if you love those who love you, what reward have you? Do not even the tax collectors do the same? 47And if you greet your brethren only, what do you do more *than others?* Do not even the tax collectors do so? 48Therefore you shall be perfect, just as your Father in heaven is perfect.

DAY 6: Why did God cause the multiplication of languages and the dispersion of peoples?

After the Flood, human civilization again began to spread across the earth. Those who traveled east under Nimrod (10:8–10) settled for a while in a place called Shinar. Later, they decided to establish a city as a tribute to themselves and as a way to keep from spreading across the earth (11:4). This was a double prideful rebellion against God. First, their city, with its proposed tower, was to be a monument to their self-reliance. Second, the permanence of their settlement represented an effort to disobey God's direct command to inhabit the whole earth.

Because it was God's purpose to fill the earth with custodians, He responded to the people's prideful rebellion. They had chosen to settle; He forced them to scatter. Their cooperation and self-reliance had been based on their shared language. Instead of using all their resources to obey God, they misused them for disobedience. God chose to complicate communication by multiplying the languages. The location where this confusion took place became known as Babel (related to a Hebrew word meaning "to confuse"). Later it became Babylon, the constant enemy of God's people, and throughout Scripture the capital of human rebellion against God (Rev. 16:19; 17:5).

JANUARY 7

Genesis 13:1–14:24

13 Then Abram went up from Egypt, he and
his wife and all that he had, and Lot with
him, to the South. 2Abram *was* very rich in
livestock, in silver, and in gold. 3And he went
on his journey from the South as far as Bethel,
to the place where his tent had been at the
beginning, between Bethel and Ai, 4to the
place of the altar which he had made there at
first. And there Abram called on the name of
the LORD.

5Lot also, who went with Abram, had flocks
and herds and tents. 6Now the land was not
able to support them, that they might dwell
together, for their possessions were so great
that they could not dwell together. 7And there
was strife between the herdsmen of Abram's
livestock and the herdsmen of Lot's livestock.
The Canaanites and the Perizzites then dwelt
in the land.

8So Abram said to Lot, "Please let there be
no strife between you and me, and between
my herdsmen and your herdsmen; for we *are*
brethren. 9*Is* not the whole land before you?
Please separate from me. If *you take* the left,
then I will go to the right; or, if *you go* to the
right, then I will go to the left."

10And Lot lifted his eyes and saw all the plain
of Jordan, that it *was* well watered everywhere
(before the LORD destroyed Sodom and
Gomorrah) like the garden of the LORD, like
the land of Egypt as you go toward Zoar. 11Then
Lot chose for himself all the plain of Jordan,
and Lot journeyed east. And they separated
from each other. 12Abram dwelt in the land of
Canaan, and Lot dwelt in the cities of the plain
and pitched *his* tent even as far as Sodom.
13But the men of Sodom *were* exceedingly
wicked and sinful against the LORD.

14And the LORD said to Abram, after Lot had
separated from him: "Lift your eyes now and
look from the place where you are—northward, southward, eastward, and westward; 15for
all the land which you see I give to you and
your descendants forever. 16And I will make
your descendants as the dust of the earth; so
that if a man could number the dust of the
earth, *then* your descendants also could be
numbered. 17Arise, walk in the land through
its length and its width, for I give it to you."

18Then Abram moved *his* tent, and went and
dwelt by the terebinth trees of Mamre, which
are in Hebron, and built an altar there to the
LORD.

14 And it came to pass in the days of
Amraphel king of Shinar, Arioch king of
Ellasar, Chedorlaomer king of Elam, and Tidal
king of nations, 2*that* they made war with Bera
king of Sodom, Birsha king of Gomorrah,
Shinab king of Admah, Shemeber king of
Zeboiim, and the king of Bela (that is, Zoar).
3All these joined together in the Valley of
Siddim (that is, the Salt Sea). 4Twelve years
they served Chedorlaomer, and in the thirteenth year they rebelled.

5In the fourteenth year Chedorlaomer and
the kings that *were* with him came and
attacked the Rephaim in Ashteroth Karnaim,
the Zuzim in Ham, the Emim in Shaveh
Kiriathaim, 6and the Horites in their mountain
of Seir, as far as El Paran, which *is* by the
wilderness. 7Then they turned back and came
to En Mishpat (that *is,* Kadesh), and attacked
all the country of the Amalekites, and also the
Amorites who dwelt in Hazezon Tamar.

8And the king of Sodom, the king of
Gomorrah, the king of Admah, the king of
Zeboiim, and the king of Bela (that *is,* Zoar)
went out and joined together in battle in the

13:8 we *are* brethren. Abram's whole reaction in resolving the strife between the two households and their personnel portrayed a different Abram than seen in Egypt—one whose attitude was not self-centered. Waving his rights to seniority, he gave the choice to his nephew, Lot.

Valley of Siddim 9against Chedorlaomer king
of Elam, Tidal king of nations, Amraphel king
of Shinar, and Arioch king of Ellasar—four
kings against five. 10Now the Valley of Siddim
was full of asphalt pits; and the kings of Sodom
and Gomorrah fled; *some* fell there, and the
remainder fled to the mountains. 11Then they
took all the goods of Sodom and Gomorrah, and
all their provisions, and went their way. 12They
also took Lot, Abram's brother's son who dwelt
in Sodom, and his goods, and departed.

13Then one who had escaped came and told
Abram the Hebrew, for he dwelt by the terebinth trees of Mamre the Amorite, brother of
Eshcol and brother of Aner; and they *were*
allies with Abram. 14Now when Abram heard
that his brother was taken captive, he armed
his three hundred and eighteen trained *servants* who were born in his own house, and
went in pursuit as far as Dan. 15He divided his
forces against them by night, and he and his
servants attacked them and pursued them as
far as Hobah, which *is* north of Damascus. 16So
he brought back all the goods, and also
brought back his brother Lot and his goods,
as well as the women and the people.

17And the king of Sodom went out to meet
him at the Valley of Shaveh (that *is*, the King's
Valley), after his return from the defeat of
Chedorlaomer and the kings who *were* with him.

18Then Melchizedek king of Salem brought
out bread and wine; he *was* the priest of God
Most High. 19And he blessed him and said:

"Blessed be Abram of God Most High,
Possessor of heaven and earth;
20 And blessed be God Most High,
Who has delivered your
enemies into your hand."

And he gave him a tithe of all.

21Now the king of Sodom said to Abram,
"Give me the persons, and take the goods for
yourself."

22But Abram said to the king of Sodom, "I
have raised my hand to the LORD, God Most
High, the Possessor of heaven and earth,
23that I *will take* nothing, from a thread to a
sandal strap, and that I will not take anything
that *is* yours, lest you should say, 'I have made
Abram rich'— 24except only what the young
men have eaten, and the portion of the men
who went with me: Aner, Eshcol, and Mamre;
let them take their portion."

14:18 Melchizedek king of Salem. The lack of biographical and genealogical particulars for this ruler, whose name meant "righteous king" and who was a king-priest over ancient Jerusalem, allowed for later revelation to use him as a type of Christ (see Ps. 110:4; Heb. 7:17,21). His superior status in Abram's day is witnessed 1) by the king of Sodom, the first to meet Abram returning in victory, deferring to Melchizedek before continuing with his request (vv. 17,21) and 2) by Abram, without demur, both accepting a blessing from him and also giving a tithe to him (vv. 19,20). **priest of God Most High.** The use of El Elyon (Sovereign Lord) for God's name indicated that Melchizedek, who used this title two times (vv. 18,19), worshiped, served, and represented no Canaanite deity, but the same one whom Abram also called Yahweh El Elyon (v. 22). That this was so is confirmed by the added description, "Possessor of heaven and earth," being used by both Abram and Melchizedek (vv. 19,22).

Psalm 4:4–8

4 Be angry, and do not sin.
Meditate within your heart on your
bed, and be still. Selah
5 Offer the sacrifices of righteousness,
And put your trust in the LORD.

6 *There are* many who say,
"Who will show us *any* good?"
LORD, lift up the light of Your
countenance upon us.
7 You have put gladness in my heart,
More than in the season that their
grain and wine increased.
8 I will both lie down in peace, and sleep;
For You alone, O LORD, make me dwell
in safety.

Proverbs 2:1–5

2 My son, if you receive my words,
And treasure my commands within you,
2 So that you incline your ear to wisdom,
And apply your heart to understanding;
3 Yes, if you cry out for discernment,
And lift up your voice for understanding,
4 If you seek her as silver,
And search for her as *for*
hidden treasures;

2:1 my words. Solomon made God's law his own by faith, obedience, and teaching. The wisdom of God's words is available to those who understand its value. Appropriating wisdom begins when one values it above all else.

5 Then you will understand the fear of
the LORD,
And find the knowledge of God.

Matthew 6:1–18

6 "Take heed that you do not do your
charitable deeds before men, to be seen
by them. Otherwise you have no reward
from your Father in heaven. 2 Therefore,
when you do a charitable deed, do not sound
a trumpet before you as the hypocrites do in
the synagogues and in the streets, that they
may have glory from men. Assuredly, I say to
you, they have their reward. 3 But when you
do a charitable deed, do not let your left hand
know what your right hand is doing, 4 that
your charitable deed may be in secret; and
your Father who sees in secret will Himself
reward you openly.
5 "And when you pray, you shall not be like
the hypocrites. For they love to pray standing
in the synagogues and on the corners of the
streets, that they may be seen by men.
Assuredly, I say to you, they have their
reward. 6 But you, when you pray, go into your
room, and when you have shut your door, pray
to your Father who *is* in the secret *place;* and
your Father who sees in secret will reward
you openly. 7 And when you pray, do not use
vain repetitions as the heathen *do.* For they
think that they will be heard for their many
words.
8 "Therefore do not be like them. For your
Father knows the things you have need of
before you ask Him. 9 In this manner, therefore, pray:

Our Father in heaven,
Hallowed be Your name.
10 Your kingdom come.
Your will be done
On earth as *it is* in heaven.
11 Give us this day our daily bread.
12 And forgive us our debts,
As we forgive our debtors.
13 And do not lead us into temptation,
But deliver us from the evil one.
For Yours is the kingdom
and the power and the glory
forever. Amen.

14 "For if you forgive men their trespasses,
your heavenly Father will also forgive you. 15 But
if you do not forgive men their trespasses, neither will your Father forgive your trespasses.
16 "Moreover, when you fast, do not be like
the hypocrites, with a sad countenance. For
they disfigure their faces that they may appear
to men to be fasting. Assuredly, I say to you,
they have their reward. 17 But you, when you
fast, anoint your head and wash your face, 18 so
that you do not appear to men to be fasting,
but to your Father who *is* in the secret *place;*
and your Father who sees in secret will
reward you openly.

DAY 7: What does the Lord's Prayer teach us about forgiveness?

The request, "Forgive us our debts" (6:12), is the heart of the prayer; it is what Jesus stressed in the words that followed the prayer (vv. 14,15; see Mark 11:25). The parallel passage in Luke 11:4 uses the word that means "sins," so that in context, spiritual debts are intended. Sinners are debtors to God in their violations of His laws.

When Jesus added that "if you do not forgive men their trespasses, neither will your Father forgive your trespasses" (v. 15), this is not to suggest that God will withdraw justification from those who have already received the free pardon He extends to all believers. Forgiveness in that sense—a permanent and complete acquittal from the guilt and ultimate penalty of sin—belongs to all who are in Christ (see John 5:24; Rom. 8:1; Eph. 1:7). Yet, Scripture also teaches that God chastens His children who disobey (Heb. 12:5–7). Believers are to confess their sins in order to obtain a day-to-day cleansing (1 John 1:9). This sort of forgiveness is a simple washing from the worldly defilements of sin; not a repeat of the wholesale cleansing from sin's corruption that comes with justification. It is like a washing of the feet rather than a bath (John 13:10). Forgiveness in this latter sense is what God threatens to withhold from Christians who refuse to forgive others.

JANUARY 8

Genesis 15:1–16:16

15 After these things the word of the LORD
came to Abram in a vision, saying, "Do
not be afraid, Abram. I *am* your shield, your
exceedingly great reward."
2 But Abram said, "Lord GOD, what will You
give me, seeing I go childless, and the heir of my
house *is* Eliezer of Damascus?" 3 Then Abram
said, "Look, You have given me no offspring;
indeed one born in my house is my heir!"

[4]And behold, the word of the LORD *came* to
him, saying, "This one shall not be your heir,
but one who will come from your own body
shall be your heir." [5]Then He brought him outside and said, "Look now toward heaven, and
count the stars if you are able to number
them." And He said to him, "So shall your
descendants be."

[6]And he believed in the LORD, and He accounted it to him for righteousness.

[7]Then He said to him, "I *am* the LORD, who
brought you out of Ur of the Chaldeans, to
give you this land to inherit it."

[8]And he said, "Lord GOD, how shall I know
that I will inherit it?"

[9]So He said to him, "Bring Me a three-year-
old heifer, a three-year-old female goat, a
three-year-old ram, a turtledove, and a young
pigeon." [10]Then he brought all these to Him
and cut them in two, down the middle, and
placed each piece opposite the other; but he
did not cut the birds in two. [11]And when the
vultures came down on the carcasses, Abram
drove them away.

[12]Now when the sun was going down, a deep
sleep fell upon Abram; and behold, horror *and*
great darkness fell upon him. [13]Then He said
to Abram: "Know certainly that your descendants will be strangers in a land *that is* not
theirs, and will serve them, and they will
afflict them four hundred years. [14]And also the
nation whom they serve I will judge; afterward they shall come out with great possessions. [15]Now as for you, you shall go to your
fathers in peace; you shall be buried at a good
old age. [16]But in the fourth generation they
shall return here, for the iniquity of the
Amorites *is* not yet complete."

[17]And it came to pass, when the sun went
down and it was dark, that behold, there
appeared a smoking oven and a burning torch
that passed between those pieces. [18]On the
same day the LORD made a covenant with
Abram, saying:

"To your descendants I have given this land,
from the river of Egypt to the great river, the
River Euphrates— [19]the Kenites, the Kenez-
zites, the Kadmonites, [20]the Hittites, the
Perizzites, the Rephaim, [21]the Amorites, the Canaanites, the Girgashites, and the Jebusites."

16 Now Sarai, Abram's wife, had borne him
no *children.* And she had an Egyptian
maidservant whose name was Hagar. [2]So Sarai
said to Abram, "See now, the LORD has
restrained me from bearing *children.* Please,
go in to my maid; perhaps I shall obtain children by her." And Abram heeded the voice of
Sarai. [3]Then Sarai, Abram's wife, took Hagar
her maid, the Egyptian, and gave her to her
husband Abram to be his wife, after Abram
had dwelt ten years in the land of Canaan. [4]So
he went in to Hagar, and she conceived. And
when she saw that she had conceived, her
mistress became despised in her eyes.

[5]Then Sarai said to Abram, "My wrong *be*
upon you! I gave my maid into your embrace;
and when she saw that she had conceived, I
became despised in her eyes. The LORD judge
between you and me."

[6]So Abram said to Sarai, "Indeed your maid
is in your hand; do to her as you please." And
when Sarai dealt harshly with her, she fled
from her presence.

[7]Now the Angel of the LORD found her by a
spring of water in the wilderness, by the
spring on the way to Shur. [8]And He said,
"Hagar, Sarai's maid, where have you come
from, and where are you going?"

She said, "I am fleeing from the presence of
my mistress Sarai."

[9]The Angel of the LORD said to her, "Return
to your mistress, and submit yourself under
her hand." [10]Then the Angel of the LORD said
to her, "I will multiply your descendants
exceedingly, so that they shall not be counted

16:3 gave her to her husband. After 10 childless years (see 12:4), Sarai resorted to the custom of the day by which a barren wife could get a child through one of her own maidservants (v. 2, "I shall obtain children by her"). Abram, ignoring divine reaction and assurance in response to his earlier attempt to appoint an heir (see 15:2–5), sinfully yielded to Sarai's insistence, and Ishmael was born.

16:7 the Angel of the LORD. This special individual spoke as though He were distinct from Yahweh, yet also spoke in the first person as though He were indeed to be identified as Yahweh Himself, with Hagar recognizing that in seeing this Angel, she had seen God (v. 13). Others had the same experience and came to the same conclusion (see Gen. 22:11–18; 31:11–13; Ex. 3:2–5; Num. 22:22–35; Judg. 6:11–23; 13:2–5; 1 Kin. 19:5–7). The Angel of the Lord, who does not appear after the birth of Christ, is often identified as the preincarnate Christ.

for multitude." 11And the Angel of the LORD
said to her:

"Behold, you *are* with child,
And you shall bear a son.
You shall call his name Ishmael,
Because the LORD has heard your
affliction.
12 He shall be a wild man;
His hand *shall be* against every man,
And every man's hand against him.
And he shall dwell in the presence of
all his brethren."

13Then she called the name of the LORD who
spoke to her, You-Are-the-God-Who-Sees; for
she said, "Have I also here seen Him who sees
me?" 14Therefore the well was called Beer Lahai
Roi; observe, *it is* between Kadesh and Bered.
15So Hagar bore Abram a son; and Abram
named his son, whom Hagar bore, Ishmael.
16Abram *was* eighty-six years old when Hagar
bore Ishmael to Abram.

Psalm 5:1–7

To the Chief Musician. With flutes.
A Psalm of David.

Give ear to my words, O LORD,
Consider my meditation.
2 Give heed to the voice of my cry,
My King and my God,
For to You I will pray.
3 My voice You shall hear in the
morning, O LORD;
In the morning I will direct *it* to You,
And I will look up.
4 For You *are* not a God
who takes pleasure in wickedness,
Nor shall evil dwell with You.
5 The boastful shall not stand in Your
sight;
You hate all workers of iniquity.
6 You shall destroy those who speak
falsehood;
The LORD abhors the bloodthirsty and
deceitful man.
7 But as for me, I will come into Your
house in the multitude of Your
mercy;
In fear of You I will worship toward
Your holy temple.

Proverbs 2:6–9

6 For the LORD gives wisdom;
From His mouth *come* knowledge and
understanding;
7 He stores up sound wisdom for the
upright;
He is a shield to those who walk
uprightly;
8 He guards the paths of justice,
And preserves the way of His saints.
9 Then you will understand
righteousness and justice,
Equity *and* every good path.

Matthew 6:19–34

19"Do not lay up for yourselves treasures on
earth, where moth and rust destroy and
where thieves break in and steal; 20but lay up
for yourselves treasures in heaven, where neither moth nor rust destroys and where
thieves do not break in and steal. 21For where
your treasure is, there your heart will be also.
22"The lamp of the body is the eye. If therefore your eye is good, your whole body will be
full of light. 23But if your eye is bad, your whole
body will be full of darkness. If therefore the
light that is in you is darkness, how great *is*
that darkness!

6:22,23 This is an argument from the lesser to the greater. The analogy is simple. If your eye is bad, no light can come in and you are left with darkness because of that malady. How much worse when the problem is not merely related to external perception, but an internal corruption of one's whole nature, so that the darkness actually emanates from within and affects one's whole being. He was indicting them for their superficial earthly religion that left their hearts dark.

24"No one can serve two masters; for either
he will hate the one and love the other, or else
he will be loyal to the one and despise the
other. You cannot serve God and mammon.
25"Therefore I say to you, do not worry
about your life, what you will eat or what you
will drink; nor about your body, what you will
put on. Is not life more than food and the body
more than clothing? 26Look at the birds of the
air, for they neither sow nor reap nor gather
into barns; yet your heavenly Father feeds
them. Are you not of more value than they?
27Which of you by worrying can add one cubit
to his stature?
28"So why do you worry about clothing?
Consider the lilies of the field, how they grow:
they neither toil nor spin; 29and yet I say to
you that even Solomon in all his glory was not
arrayed like one of these. 30Now if God so
clothes the grass of the field, which today is,

and tomorrow is thrown into the oven, *will He* not much more *clothe* you, O you of little faith?

31"Therefore do not worry, saying, 'What shall we eat?' or 'What shall we drink?' or 'What shall we wear?' 32For after all these things the Gentiles seek. For your heavenly Father knows that you need all these things. 33But seek first the kingdom of God and His righteousness, and all these things shall be added to you. 34Therefore do not worry about tomorrow, for tomorrow will worry about its own things. Sufficient for the day *is* its own trouble.

DAY 8: What does Abraham's faith teach us about justification?

In Genesis 15:6, we are told that when Abraham "believed" in the Lord, it was "accounted" to him for "righteousness." The apostle Paul quoted these words as an illustration of faith over and against works (Rom. 4:3,9,22; Gal. 3:6). Abraham was regenerated by faith, and so are we!

This quotation is one of the clearest statements in all Scripture about justification. Abraham's faith is not a meritorious work. It is never the ground of justification—it is simply the channel through which it is received and it, too, is a gift. His faith was "accounted" or "imputed" to him, which is a term used in both financial and legal settings. It means to take something that belongs to someone and credit to another's account. It is a one-sided transaction—Abraham did nothing to accumulate it: God simply credited it to him. In this case, God took His own righteousness and credited it to Abraham as if it were actually his. This God did because Abraham believed in Him.

The "righteousness" imputed to Abraham is unique: 1) God is its source (Is. 45:8); 2) it fulfills both the penalty and precept of God's law. Christ's death as a substitute pays the penalty exacted on those who failed to keep God's law, and His perfect obedience to every requirement of God's law fulfills God's demand for comprehensive righteousness (2 Cor. 5:21; 1 Pet. 2:24; see Heb. 9:28); and 3) because God's righteousness is eternal (Ps. 119:142; Is. 51:8; Dan. 9:24), the one who receives it from Him enjoys it forever.

JANUARY 9

Genesis 17:1–18:33

17 When Abram was ninety-nine years old, the LORD appeared to Abram and said to him, "I *am* Almighty God; walk before Me and be blameless. 2And I will make My covenant between Me and you, and will multiply you exceedingly." 3Then Abram fell on his face, and God talked with him, saying: 4"As for Me, behold, My covenant is with you, and you shall be a father of many nations. 5No longer shall your name be called Abram, but your name shall be Abraham; for I have made you a father of many nations. 6I will make you exceedingly fruitful; and I will make nations of you, and kings shall come from you. 7And I will establish My covenant between Me and you and your descendants after you in their generations, for an everlasting covenant, to be God to you and your descendants after you. 8Also I give to you and your descendants after you the land in which you are a stranger, all the land of Canaan, as an everlasting possession; and I will be their God."

17:5 your name shall be Abraham. The name meaning "father of many nations" reflected Abraham's new relationship to God as well as his new identity based on God's promise of seed.

9And God said to Abraham: "As for you, you shall keep My covenant, you and your descendants after you throughout their generations. 10This *is* My covenant which you shall keep, between Me and you and your descendants after you: Every male child among you shall be circumcised; 11and you shall be circumcised in the flesh of your foreskins, and it shall be a sign of the covenant between Me and you. 12He who is eight days old among you shall be circumcised, every male child in your generations, he who is born in your house or bought with money from any foreigner who is not your descendant. 13He who is born in your house and he who is bought with your money must be circumcised, and My covenant shall be in your flesh for an everlasting covenant. 14And the uncircumcised male child, who is not circumcised in the flesh of his foreskin, that person shall be cut off from his people; he has broken My covenant."

15Then God said to Abraham, "As for Sarai your wife, you shall not call her name Sarai, but Sarah *shall be* her name. 16And I will bless

17:15 Sarai...Sarah. Fittingly, since Sarai ("my princess") would be the ancestress of the promised nations and kings, God changed her name to Sarah, taking away the limiting personal pronoun "my," and calling her "princess" (v. 16).

her and also give you a son by her; then I will
bless her, and she shall be *a mother of* nations;
kings of peoples shall be from her."
[17]Then Abraham fell on his face and
laughed, and said in his heart, "Shall *a child*
be born to a man who is one hundred years
old? And shall Sarah, who is ninety years old,
bear *a child?*" [18]And Abraham said to God,
"Oh, that Ishmael might live before You!"
[19]Then God said: "No, Sarah your wife shall
bear you a son, and you shall call his name
Isaac; I will establish My covenant with him
for an everlasting covenant, *and* with his
descendants after him. [20]And as for Ishmael, I
have heard you. Behold, I have blessed him,
and will make him fruitful, and will multiply
him exceedingly. He shall beget twelve
princes, and I will make him a great nation.
[21]But My covenant I will establish with Isaac,
whom Sarah shall bear to you at this set time
next year." [22]Then He finished talking with
him, and God went up from Abraham.

17:19 call his name Isaac. The name of the promised son meant "he laughs," an appropriate reminder to Abraham of his initial, faithless reaction to God's promise.

[23]So Abraham took Ishmael his son, all who
were born in his house and all who were
bought with his money, every male among the
men of Abraham's house, and circumcised the
flesh of their foreskins that very same day, as
God had said to him. [24]Abraham *was* ninety-
nine years old when he was circumcised in the
flesh of his foreskin. [25]And Ishmael his son
was thirteen years old when he was circumcised in the flesh of his foreskin. [26]That very
same day Abraham was circumcised, and his
son Ishmael; [27]and all the men of his house,
born in the house or bought with money from
a foreigner, were circumcised with him.

18 Then the LORD appeared to him by the terebinth trees of Mamre, as he was sitting
in the tent door in the heat of the day. [2]So he
lifted his eyes and looked, and behold, three
men were standing by him; and when he saw
them, he ran from the tent door to meet them,
and bowed himself to the ground, [3]and said,
"My Lord, if I have now found favor in Your
sight, do not pass on by Your servant. [4]Please
let a little water be brought, and wash your feet,
and rest yourselves under the tree. [5]And I will
bring a morsel of bread, that you may refresh
your hearts. After that you may pass by, inasmuch as you have come to your servant."
They said, "Do as you have said."
[6]So Abraham hurried into the tent to Sarah
and said, "Quickly, make ready three measures of fine meal; knead *it* and make cakes."
[7]And Abraham ran to the herd, took a tender
and good calf, gave *it* to a young man, and he
hastened to prepare it. [8]So he took butter and
milk and the calf which he had prepared, and
set *it* before them; and he stood by them
under the tree as they ate.
[9]Then they said to him, "Where *is* Sarah
your wife?"
So he said, "Here, in the tent."
[10]And He said, "I will certainly return to you
according to the time of life, and behold,
Sarah your wife shall have a son."
(Sarah was listening in the tent door which
was behind him.) [11]Now Abraham and Sarah
were old, well advanced in age; *and* Sarah had
passed the age of childbearing. [12]Therefore Sarah laughed within herself, saying, "After I
have grown old, shall I have pleasure, my lord
being old also?"
[13]And the LORD said to Abraham, "Why did
Sarah laugh, saying, 'Shall I surely bear *a
child,* since I am old?' [14]Is anything too hard for
the LORD? At the appointed time I will return
to you, according to the time of life, and Sarah
shall have a son."
[15]But Sarah denied *it,* saying, "I did not
laugh," for she was afraid.
And He said, "No, but you did laugh!"
[16]Then the men rose from there and looked
toward Sodom, and Abraham went with them
to send them on the way. [17]And the LORD said,
"Shall I hide from Abraham what I am doing,
[18]since Abraham shall surely become a great
and mighty nation, and all the nations of the
earth shall be blessed in him? [19]For I have
known him, in order that he may command
his children and his household after him, that
they keep the way of the LORD, to do righteousness and justice, that the LORD may bring
to Abraham what He has spoken to him."
[20]And the LORD said, "Because the outcry
against Sodom and Gomorrah is great, and

because their sin is very grave, [21]I will go
down now and see whether they have done
altogether according to the outcry against it
that has come to Me; and if not, I will know."
[22]Then the men turned away from there and
went toward Sodom, but Abraham still stood
before the LORD. [23]And Abraham came near
and said, "Would You also destroy the righteous with the wicked? [24]Suppose there were
fifty righteous within the city; would You also
destroy the place and not spare *it* for the fifty
righteous that were in it? [25]Far be it from You
to do such a thing as this, to slay the righteous
with the wicked, so that the righteous should
be as the wicked; far be it from You! Shall not
the Judge of all the earth do right?"
[26]So the LORD said, "If I find in Sodom fifty
righteous within the city, then I will spare all
the place for their sakes."
[27]Then Abraham answered and said, "Indeed
now, I who *am but* dust and ashes have taken it
upon myself to speak to the Lord: [28]Suppose
there were five less than the fifty righteous;
would You destroy all of the city for *lack of* five?"
So He said, "If I find there forty-five, I will
not destroy *it*."
[29]And he spoke to Him yet again and said,
"Suppose there should be forty found there?"
So He said, "I will not do *it* for the sake of
forty."
[30]Then he said, "Let not the Lord be angry,
and I will speak: Suppose thirty should be
found there?"
So He said, "I will not do *it* if I find thirty
there."
[31]And he said, "Indeed now, I have taken it
upon myself to speak to the Lord: Suppose
twenty should be found there?"
So He said, "I will not destroy *it* for the sake
of twenty."
[32]Then he said, "Let not the Lord be angry,
and I will speak but once more: Suppose ten
should be found there?"
And He said, "I will not destroy *it* for the
sake of ten." [33]So the LORD went His way as
soon as He had finished speaking with Abraham; and Abraham returned to his place.

Psalm 5:8–12

8 Lead me, O LORD, in Your
righteousness because
of my enemies;
Make Your way straight before my face.
9 For *there is* no faithfulness in their
mouth;
Their inward part *is* destruction;
Their throat *is* an open tomb;
They flatter with their tongue.
10 Pronounce them guilty, O God!
Let them fall by their own counsels;
Cast them out in the multitude of their
transgressions,
For they have rebelled against You.
11 But let all those rejoice who put their
trust in You;
Let them ever shout for joy, because
You defend them;
Let those also who love Your name
Be joyful in You.
12 For You, O LORD, will bless the
righteous;
With favor You will surround him as
with a shield.

Proverbs 2:10–22

10 When wisdom enters your heart,
And knowledge is pleasant
to your soul,
11 Discretion will preserve you;
Understanding will keep you,
12 To deliver you from the way of evil,
From the man who speaks
perverse things,
13 From those who leave the paths of
uprightness
To walk in the ways of darkness;
14 Who rejoice in doing evil,
And delight in the perversity
of the wicked;
15 Whose ways *are* crooked,
And *who are* devious in their paths;
16 To deliver you from the immoral
woman,
From the seductress *who* flatters
with her words,
17 Who forsakes the companion of her
youth,
And forgets the covenant of her God.
18 For her house leads down to death,
And her paths to the dead;
19 None who go to her return,
Nor do they regain the paths of life—
20 So you may walk in the way
of goodness,
And keep *to* the paths of righteousness.
21 For the upright will dwell in the land,
And the blameless will remain in it;
22 But the wicked will be cut off from the
earth,
And the unfaithful will be uprooted
from it.

Matthew 7:1–29

7 "Judge not, that you be not judged. [2]For
with what judgment you judge, you will be
judged; and with the measure you use, it will

be measured back to you. 3And why do you look at the speck in your brother's eye, but do not consider the plank in your own eye? 4Or

7:1 Judge not. As the context reveals, this does not prohibit all types of judging (v. 16). There is a righteous kind of judgment we are supposed to exercise with careful discernment (John 7:24). Censorious, hypocritical, self-righteous, or other kinds of unfair judgments are forbidden; but in order to fulfill the commandments that follow, it is necessary to discern dogs and swine (v. 6) from one's own brethren (vv. 3–5).

how can you say to your brother, 'Let me remove the speck from your eye'; and look, a plank *is* in your own eye? 5Hypocrite! First remove the plank from your own eye, and then you will see clearly to remove the speck from your brother's eye.

6"Do not give what is holy to the dogs; nor cast your pearls before swine, lest they trample them under their feet, and turn and tear you in pieces.

7"Ask, and it will be given to you; seek, and you will find; knock, and it will be opened to you. 8For everyone who asks receives, and he who seeks finds, and to him who knocks it will be opened. 9Or what man is there among you who, if his son asks for bread, will give him a stone? 10Or if he asks for a fish, will he give him a serpent? 11If you then, being evil, know how to give good gifts to your children, how much more will your Father who is in heaven give good things to those who ask Him! 12Therefore, whatever you want men to do to you, do also to them, for this is the Law and the Prophets.

13"Enter by the narrow gate; for wide *is* the gate and broad *is* the way that leads to destruction, and there are many who go in by it. 14Because narrow *is* the gate and difficult *is* the way which leads to life, and there are few who find it.

15"Beware of false prophets, who come to you in sheep's clothing, but inwardly they are ravenous wolves. 16You will know them by their fruits. Do men gather grapes from thornbushes or figs from thistles? 17Even so, every good tree bears good fruit, but a bad tree bears bad fruit. 18A good tree cannot bear bad fruit, nor *can* a bad tree bear good fruit. 19Every tree that does not bear good fruit is cut down and thrown into the fire. 20Therefore by their fruits you will know them.

21"Not everyone who says to Me, 'Lord, Lord,' shall enter the kingdom of heaven, but he who does the will of My Father in heaven. 22Many will say to Me in that day, 'Lord, Lord, have we not prophesied in Your name, cast out demons in Your name, and done many wonders in Your name?' 23And then I will declare to them, 'I never knew you; depart from Me, you who practice lawlessness!'

24"Therefore whoever hears these sayings of Mine, and does them, I will liken him to a wise man who built his house on the rock: 25and the rain descended, the floods came, and the winds blew and beat on that house; and it did not fall, for it was founded on the rock.

26"But everyone who hears these sayings of Mine, and does not do them, will be like a foolish man who built his house on the sand: 27and the rain descended, the floods came, and the winds blew and beat on that house; and it fell. And great was its fall."

28And so it was, when Jesus had ended these sayings, that the people were astonished at His teaching, 29for He taught them as one having authority, and not as the scribes.

DAY 9: What did Jesus specify about the way to salvation?

In the closing section of the Sermon on the Mount (Matt. 7:13–29), Jesus gave a clear gospel application. Here are two gates, two ways, two destinations, and two groups of people (vv. 13,14); two kinds of trees and two kinds of fruit (vv. 17–20); two groups at the judgment (vv. 21–23); and two kinds of builders, building on two kinds of foundations (vv. 24–28). Christ is drawing the line as clearly as possible between the way that leads to destruction and the way which leads to life.

Both the narrow gate and the wide gate (vv. 13,14) are assumed to provide the entrance to God's kingdom. Two ways are offered to people. The narrow gate is by faith, only through Christ, constricted and precise. It represents true salvation in God's way that leads to life eternal. The wide gate includes all religions of works and self-righteousness, with no single way (see Acts 4:12), but leads to hell, not heaven.

Christ continually emphasized the difficulty of following Him (10:38; 16:24,25; John 15:18,19; 16:1–3; see Acts 14:22). Salvation is by grace alone, but is not easy. It calls for knowledge of the truth, repentance, submission to Christ as Lord, and a willingness to obey His will and Word.

JANUARY 10

Genesis 19:1–20:18

19 Now the two angels came to Sodom in the evening, and Lot was sitting in the gate of Sodom. When Lot saw *them,* he rose to meet them, and he bowed himself with his face toward the ground. [2]And he said, "Here now, my lords, please turn in to your servant's house and spend the night, and wash your feet; then you may rise early and go on your way."

And they said, "No, but we will spend the night in the open square."

[3]But he insisted strongly; so they turned in to him and entered his house. Then he made them a feast, and baked unleavened bread, and they ate.

[4]Now before they lay down, the men of the city, the men of Sodom, both old and young, all the people from every quarter, surrounded the house. [5]And they called to Lot and said to him, "Where are the men who came to you tonight? Bring them out to us that we may know them *carnally.*"

19:5 know them *carnally.* They sought homosexual relations with the visitors. God's attitude toward this vile behavior became clear when He destroyed the city (vv. 23–29). (See Lev. 18:22,29; 20:13; Rom. 1:26; 1 Cor. 6:9; 1 Tim. 1:10 where all homosexual behavior is prohibited and condemned by God.)

[6]So Lot went out to them through the doorway, shut the door behind him, [7]and said, "Please, my brethren, do not do so wickedly! [8]See now, I have two daughters who have not known a man; please, let me bring them out to you, and you may do to them as you wish; only do nothing to these men, since this is the reason they have come under the shadow of my roof."

[9]And they said, "Stand back!" Then they said, "This one came in to stay *here,* and he keeps acting as a judge; now we will deal worse with you than with them." So they pressed hard against the man Lot, and came near to break down the door. [10]But the men reached out their hands and pulled Lot into the house with them, and shut the door. [11]And they struck the men who *were* at the doorway of the house with blindness, both small and great, so that they became weary *trying* to find the door.

[12]Then the men said to Lot, "Have you anyone else here? Son-in-law, your sons, your daughters, and whomever you have in the city—take *them* out of this place! [13]For we will destroy this place, because the outcry against them has grown great before the face of the LORD, and the LORD has sent us to destroy it."

[14]So Lot went out and spoke to his sons-in-law, who had married his daughters, and said, "Get up, get out of this place; for the LORD will destroy this city!" But to his sons-in-law he seemed to be joking.

[15]When the morning dawned, the angels urged Lot to hurry, saying, "Arise, take your wife and your two daughters who are here, lest you be consumed in the punishment of the city." [16]And while he lingered, the men took hold of his hand, his wife's hand, and the hands of his two daughters, the LORD being merciful to him, and they brought him out and set him outside the city. [17]So it came to pass, when they had brought them outside, that he said, "Escape for your life! Do not look behind you nor stay anywhere in the plain. Escape to the mountains, lest you be destroyed."

[18]Then Lot said to them, "Please, no, my lords! [19]Indeed now, your servant has found favor in your sight, and you have increased your mercy which you have shown me by saving my life; but I cannot escape to the mountains, lest some evil overtake me and I die. [20]See now, this city *is* near *enough* to flee to, and it *is* a little one; please let me escape there (*is* it not a little one?) and my soul shall live."

[21]And he said to him, "See, I have favored you concerning this thing also, in that I will not overthrow this city for which you have spoken. [22]Hurry, escape there. For I cannot do anything until you arrive there."

Therefore the name of the city was called Zoar.

19:24 brimstone...from the LORD out of the heavens. When morning came (v. 23) judgment fell. Any natural explanation about how the Lord used combustible sulfur deposits to destroy that locale falters on this emphatic indication of miraculous judgment. "Brimstone" could refer to any inflammable substance; perhaps a volcanic eruption and an earthquake with a violent electrical storm "overthrew" (v. 25) the area. That area is now believed to be under the south end of the Dead Sea. Burning gases, sulfur, and magma blown into the air all fell to bury the region.

23 The sun had risen upon the earth when
Lot entered Zoar. 24 Then the LORD rained brimstone and fire on Sodom and Gomorrah, from
the LORD out of the heavens. 25 So He overthrew
those cities, all the plain, all the inhabitants of
the cities, and what grew on the ground.
26 But his wife looked back behind him, and
she became a pillar of salt.
27 And Abraham went early in the morning to
the place where he had stood before the LORD.
28 Then he looked toward Sodom and Gomorrah,
and toward all the land of the plain; and he saw,
and behold, the smoke of the land which went
up like the smoke of a furnace. 29 And it came to
pass, when God destroyed the cities of the
plain, that God remembered Abraham, and sent
Lot out of the midst of the overthrow, when He
overthrew the cities in which Lot had dwelt.
30 Then Lot went up out of Zoar and dwelt in
the mountains, and his two daughters were
with him; for he was afraid to dwell in Zoar. And
he and his two daughters dwelt in a cave. 31 Now
the firstborn said to the younger, "Our father *is*
old, and *there is* no man on the earth to come in
to us as is the custom of all the earth. 32 Come,
let us make our father drink wine, and we will
lie with him, that we may preserve the lineage
of our father." 33 So they made their father
drink wine that night. And the firstborn went
in and lay with her father, and he did not know
when she lay down or when she arose.
34 It happened on the next day that the firstborn said to the younger, "Indeed I lay with
my father last night; let us make him drink
wine tonight also, and you go in *and* lie with
him, that we may preserve the lineage of our
father." 35 Then they made their father drink
wine that night also. And the younger arose
and lay with him, and he did not know when
she lay down or when she arose.
36 Thus both the daughters of Lot were with
child by their father. 37 The firstborn bore a son
and called his name Moab; he *is* the father of the
Moabites to this day. 38 And the younger, she also
bore a son and called his name Ben-Ammi; he
is the father of the people of Ammon to this day.

20 And Abraham journeyed from there to
the South, and dwelt between Kadesh
and Shur, and stayed in Gerar. 2 Now Abraham
said of Sarah his wife, "She *is* my sister." And
Abimelech king of Gerar sent and took Sarah.
3 But God came to Abimelech in a dream by
night, and said to him, "Indeed you *are* a dead
man because of the woman whom you have
taken, for she *is* a man's wife."
4 But Abimelech had not come near her; and
he said, "Lord, will You slay a righteous nation
also? 5 Did he not say to me, 'She *is* my sister'?
And she, even she herself said, 'He *is* my
brother.' In the integrity of my heart and innocence of my hands I have done this."
6 And God said to him in a dream, "Yes, I know
that you did this in the integrity of your heart.
For I also withheld you from sinning against Me;
therefore I did not let you touch her. 7 Now
therefore, restore the man's wife; for he *is* a
prophet, and he will pray for you and you shall
live. But if you do not restore *her,* know that you
shall surely die, you and all who *are* yours."
8 So Abimelech rose early in the morning,
called all his servants, and told all these things
in their hearing; and the men were very much
afraid. 9 And Abimelech called Abraham and said
to him, "What have you done to us? How have I
offended you, that you have brought on me
and on my kingdom a great sin? You have done
deeds to me that ought not to be done." 10 Then
Abimelech said to Abraham, "What did you
have in view, that you have done this thing?"
11 And Abraham said, "Because I thought,
surely the fear of God *is* not in this place; and
they will kill me on account of my wife. 12 But
indeed *she is* truly my sister. She *is* the daughter of my father, but not the daughter of my
mother; and she became my wife. 13 And it
came to pass, when God caused me to wander
from my father's house, that I said to her,
'This *is* your kindness that you should do for
me: in every place, wherever we go, say of me,
"He *is* my brother." ' "
14 Then Abimelech took sheep, oxen, and male
and female servants, and gave *them* to Abraham;
and he restored Sarah his wife to him. 15 And
Abimelech said, "See, my land *is* before you;
dwell where it pleases you." 16 Then to Sarah
he said, "Behold, I have given your brother a
thousand *pieces* of silver; indeed this vindi-
cates you before all who *are* with you and
before everybody." Thus she was rebuked.
17 So Abraham prayed to God; and God healed
Abimelech, his wife, and his female servants.
Then they bore *children;* 18 for the LORD had
closed up all the wombs of the house of
Abimelech because of Sarah, Abraham's wife.

Psalm 6:1–5

To the Chief Musician. With stringed instruments.
On an eight-stringed harp.
A Psalm of David.

O LORD, do not rebuke me in
Your anger,
Nor chasten me in Your hot displeasure.
2 Have mercy on me, O LORD,
for I *am* weak;
O LORD, heal me, for my bones are
troubled.

3 My soul also is greatly troubled;
But You, O LORD—how long?

4 Return, O LORD, deliver me!
Oh, save me for Your mercies' sake!
5 For in death *there is* no remembrance
of You;
In the grave who will give You thanks?

Proverbs 3:1–4

3 My son, do not forget my law,
But let your heart keep my commands;
2 For length of days and long life
And peace they will add to you.
3 Let not mercy and truth forsake you;
Bind them around your neck,
Write them on the tablet of your heart,
4 *And* so find favor and high esteem
In the sight of God and man.

3:3 neck...heart. The virtues of mercy (the Hebrew word for lovingkindness and loyal love) and truth that come from God are to become part of us—outwardly in our behavior for all to see as an adornment of spiritual beauty and inwardly as the subject of our meditation (Deut. 6:4–9). Such inward and outward mercy and truth is evidence of New Covenant salvation (Jer. 31:33,34).

Matthew 8:1–17

8 When He had come down from the mountain, great multitudes followed Him. 2 And
behold, a leper came and worshiped Him, saying, "Lord, if You are willing, You can make
me clean."
3 Then Jesus put out *His* hand and touched
him, saying, "I am willing; be cleansed."
Immediately his leprosy was cleansed.
4 And Jesus said to him, "See that you tell no
one; but go your way, show yourself to the
priest, and offer the gift that Moses commanded, as a testimony to them."
5 Now when Jesus had entered Capernaum,
a centurion came to Him, pleading with Him,
6 saying, "Lord, my servant is lying at home
paralyzed, dreadfully tormented."
7 And Jesus said to him, "I will come and heal
him."
8 The centurion answered and said, "Lord, I
am not worthy that You should come under
my roof. But only speak a word, and my servant will be healed. 9 For I also am a man under
authority, having soldiers under me. And I say
to this *one*, 'Go,' and he goes; and to another,
'Come,' and he comes; and to my servant, 'Do
this,' and he does *it*."
10 When Jesus heard *it*, He marveled, and
said to those who followed, "Assuredly, I say
to you, I have not found such great faith, not
even in Israel! 11 And I say to you that many will
come from east and west, and sit down with
Abraham, Isaac, and Jacob in the kingdom of
heaven. 12 But the sons of the kingdom will be
cast out into outer darkness. There will be weeping and gnashing of teeth." 13 Then Jesus said
to the centurion, "Go your way; and as you
have believed, *so* let it be done for you." And
his servant was healed that same hour.
14 Now when Jesus had come into Peter's
house, He saw his wife's mother lying sick
with a fever. 15 So He touched her hand, and the
fever left her. And she arose and served them.
16 When evening had come, they brought to
Him many who were demon-possessed. And He
cast out the spirits with a word, and healed all
who were sick, 17 that it might be fulfilled which
was spoken by Isaiah the prophet, saying:

"He Himself took our infirmities
And bore our sicknesses."

DAY 10: How can we study and apply some of the Proverbs if we don't understand them?

More often than not, those Proverbs that at first seem unclear or contradictory turn out, instead, to be elusive and deep. Proverbs sometimes do state obvious truths. Their meaning is crystal clear: "A foolish son is a grief to his father, and bitterness to her who bore him" (17:25). But many proverbs require thoughtful meditation: "The lot is cast into the lap, but its every decision is from the LORD" (16:33) or "There is a way that seems right to a man, but its end is the way of death" (16:25). The fact that we may have to search the rest of the Scripture or work at thinking ought to make Proverbs dearer to us. If God has chosen this unusual approach to help us grow, why would we hesitate to give our full attention to Proverbs?

Given the context that surrounds Proverbs—the rest of God's Word—a student's failure to grasp a proverb ought not to lead to the conclusion that there's something wrong with this book. A better conclusion would be that the student doesn't know enough yet or hasn't paid enough attention. A wise person puts an elusive proverb on hold for further understanding rather than rejecting it as useless. God's further lessons in that person's life may well cast a new light on parts of the Bible that have been difficult to interpret.

JANUARY 11

Genesis 21:1–22:24

21 And the LORD visited Sarah as He had said, and the LORD did for Sarah as He had spoken. 2For Sarah conceived and bore Abraham a son in his old age, at the set time of which God had spoken to him. 3And Abraham called the name of his son who was born to him—whom Sarah bore to him—Isaac.

21:1 the LORD visited Sarah. To the aged couple (vv. 2,5,7), exactly as promised, a son was born and the 25-year suspense was finally over with the laughter of derision turning to rejoicing (v. 6). The barrenness of Sarah (11:26) had ended.

4Then Abraham circumcised his son Isaac when he was eight days old, as God had commanded him. 5Now Abraham was one hundred years old when his son Isaac was born to him. 6And Sarah said, "God has made me laugh, *and* all who hear will laugh with me." 7She also said, "Who would have said to Abraham that Sarah would nurse children? For I have borne *him* a son in his old age."

8So the child grew and was weaned. And Abraham made a great feast on the same day that Isaac was weaned.

9And Sarah saw the son of Hagar the Egyptian, whom she had borne to Abraham, scoffing. 10Therefore she said to Abraham, "Cast out this bondwoman and her son; for the son of this bondwoman shall not be heir with my son, *namely* with Isaac." 11And the matter was very displeasing in Abraham's sight because of his son.

21:10 Cast out...not be heir. Legal codes of Abraham's day—e.g., of Nuzi and of Hammurabi—forbade the putting out of a handmaiden's son if a rightful, natural heir was born. Sarah's request, thus, offended social law, Abraham's sensibilities, and his love for Ishmael (v. 11). Abraham, however, was given divine approval and assurances to overcome his scruples before sending Hagar and Ishmael out into the wilderness (vv. 12–15).

12But God said to Abraham, "Do not let it be displeasing in your sight because of the lad or because of your bondwoman. Whatever Sarah has said to you, listen to her voice; for in Isaac your seed shall be called. 13Yet I will also make a nation of the son of the bondwoman, because he *is* your seed."

14So Abraham rose early in the morning, and took bread and a skin of water; and putting *it* on her shoulder, he gave *it* and the boy to Hagar, and sent her away. Then she departed and wandered in the Wilderness of Beersheba. 15And the water in the skin was used up, and she placed the boy under one of the shrubs. 16Then she went and sat down across from *him* at a distance of about a bowshot; for she said to herself, "Let me not see the death of the boy." So she sat opposite *him,* and lifted her voice and wept.

17And God heard the voice of the lad. Then the angel of God called to Hagar out of heaven, and said to her, "What ails you, Hagar? Fear not, for God has heard the voice of the lad where he *is.* 18Arise, lift up the lad and hold him with your hand, for I will make him a great nation."

19Then God opened her eyes, and she saw a well of water. And she went and filled the skin with water, and gave the lad a drink. 20So God was with the lad; and he grew and dwelt in the wilderness, and became an archer. 21He dwelt in the Wilderness of Paran; and his mother took a wife for him from the land of Egypt.

22And it came to pass at that time that Abimelech and Phichol, the commander of his army, spoke to Abraham, saying, "God *is* with you in all that you do. 23Now therefore, swear to me by God that you will not deal falsely with me, with my offspring, or with my posterity; but that according to the kindness that I have done to you, you will do to me and to the land in which you have dwelt."

24And Abraham said, "I will swear."

25Then Abraham rebuked Abimelech because of a well of water which Abimelech's servants had seized. 26And Abimelech said, "I do not know who has done this thing; you did not tell me, nor had I heard *of it* until today." 27So Abraham took sheep and oxen and gave them to Abimelech, and the two of them made a covenant. 28And Abraham set seven ewe lambs of the flock by themselves.

29Then Abimelech asked Abraham, "What *is the meaning of* these seven ewe lambs which you have set by themselves?"

30And he said, "You will take *these* seven ewe lambs from my hand, that they may be my witness that I have dug this well." 31Therefore he

called that place Beersheba, because the two
of them swore an oath there.
32Thus they made a covenant at Beersheba.
So Abimelech rose with Phichol, the commander of his army, and they returned to the
land of the Philistines. 33Then *Abraham* planted a tamarisk tree in Beersheba, and there
called on the name of the LORD, the
Everlasting God. 34And Abraham stayed in the
land of the Philistines many days.

22 Now it came to pass after these things
that God tested Abraham, and said to
him, "Abraham!"

And he said, "Here I am."

2Then He said, "Take now your son, your
only *son* Isaac, whom you love, and go to the
land of Moriah, and offer him there as a burnt
offering on one of the mountains of which I
shall tell you."

3So Abraham rose early in the morning and
saddled his donkey, and took two of his young
men with him, and Isaac his son; and he split
the wood for the burnt offering, and arose and
went to the place of which God had told him.
4Then on the third day Abraham lifted his eyes
and saw the place afar off. 5And Abraham said
to his young men, "Stay here with the donkey;
the lad and I will go yonder and worship, and
we will come back to you."

6So Abraham took the wood of the burnt
offering and laid *it* on Isaac his son; and he
took the fire in his hand, and a knife, and the
two of them went together. 7But Isaac spoke to
Abraham his father and said, "My father!"

And he said, "Here I am, my son."

Then he said, "Look, the fire and the wood,
but where *is* the lamb for a burnt offering?"

8And Abraham said, "My son, God will provide for Himself the lamb for a burnt offering."
So the two of them went together.

9Then they came to the place of which God
had told him. And Abraham built an altar
there and placed the wood in order; and he
bound Isaac his son and laid him on the altar,
upon the wood. 10And Abraham stretched out
his hand and took the knife to slay his son.

11But the Angel of the LORD called to him
from heaven and said, "Abraham, Abraham!"

So he said, "Here I am."

12And He said, "Do not lay your hand on the
lad, or do anything to him; for now I know that
you fear God, since you have not withheld
your son, your only *son,* from Me."

13Then Abraham lifted his eyes and looked,
and there behind *him was* a ram caught in a
thicket by its horns. So Abraham went and
took the ram, and offered it up for a burnt
offering instead of his son. 14And Abraham
called the name of the place, The-LORD-Will-
Provide; as it is said *to* this day, "In the Mount
of the LORD it shall be provided."

15Then the Angel of the LORD called to Abraham a second time out of heaven, 16and said:
"By Myself I have sworn, says the LORD,
because you have done this thing, and have
not withheld your son, your only *son*— 17bless-
ing I will bless you, and multiplying I will multiply your descendants as the stars of the heav-
en and as the sand which *is* on the seashore;
and your descendants shall possess the gate
of their enemies. 18In your seed all the nations
of the earth shall be blessed, because you
have obeyed My voice." 19So Abraham
returned to his young men, and they rose and
went together to Beersheba; and Abraham
dwelt at Beersheba.

20Now it came to pass after these things that
it was told Abraham, saying, "Indeed Milcah
also has borne children to your brother
Nahor: 21Huz his firstborn, Buz his brother,
Kemuel the father of Aram, 22Chesed, Hazo,
Pildash, Jidlaph, and Bethuel." 23And Bethuel
begot Rebekah. These eight Milcah bore to
Nahor, Abraham's brother. 24His concubine,
whose name was Reumah, also bore Tebah,
Gaham, Thahash, and Maachah.

Psalm 6:6-10

6 I am weary with my groaning;
All night I make my bed swim;
I drench my couch with my tears.
7 My eye wastes away because
of grief;
It grows old because of all
my enemies.

8 Depart from me, all you
workers of iniquity;
For the LORD has heard the voice
of my weeping.
9 The LORD has heard my supplication;
The LORD will receive my prayer.
10 Let all my enemies be ashamed
and greatly troubled;
Let them turn back *and* be ashamed
suddenly.

Proverbs 3:5–6

5 Trust in the LORD with all your heart,
And lean not on your own
understanding;
6 In all your ways acknowledge Him,
And He shall direct your paths.

Matthew 8:18–34

18And when Jesus saw great multitudes
about Him, He gave a command to depart to

8:21 let me first go and bury my father. This does not mean that the man's father was already dead. The phrase "I must bury my father" was a common figure of speech, meaning "Let me wait until I receive my inheritance."

8:24 suddenly a great tempest arose. The Sea of Galilee is more than 690 feet below sea level. To the north, Mt. Hermon rises 9,200 feet, and from May to October strong winds often sweep through the narrow surrounding gorges into this valley, causing extremely sudden and violent storms. **He was asleep.** Just before the disciples saw one of the most awesome displays of His deity, they were given a touching picture of His humanity. He was so weary that not even the violent tossing of the boat awakened Him—even though the disciples feared they would drown (v. 25).

the other side. 19Then a certain scribe came and said to Him, "Teacher, I will follow You wherever You go."
20And Jesus said to him, "Foxes have holes and birds of the air *have* nests, but the Son of Man has nowhere to lay *His* head."
21Then another of His disciples said to Him, "Lord, let me first go and bury my father."
22But Jesus said to him, "Follow Me, and let the dead bury their own dead."
23Now when He got into a boat, His disciples
followed Him. 24And suddenly a great tempest
arose on the sea, so that the boat was covered
with the waves. But He was asleep. 25Then His
disciples came to *Him* and awoke Him, saying, "Lord, save us! We are perishing!"
26But He said to them, "Why are you fearful, O you of little faith?" Then He arose and rebuked the winds and the sea, and there was
a great calm. 27So the men marveled, saying, "Who can this be, that even the winds and the sea obey Him?"
28When He had come to the other side, to the country of the Gergesenes, there met Him two demon-possessed *men,* coming out of the tombs, exceedingly fierce, so that no one
could pass that way. 29And suddenly they cried
out, saying, "What have we to do with You, Jesus, You Son of God? Have You come here to torment us before the time?"
30Now a good way off from them there was a
herd of many swine feeding. 31So the demons
begged Him, saying, "If You cast us out, permit us to go away into the herd of swine."
32And He said to them, "Go." So when they had come out, they went into the herd of swine. And suddenly the whole herd of swine ran violently down the steep place into the sea, and perished in the water.
33Then those who kept *them* fled; and they went away into the city and told everything, including what *had happened* to the demon-possessed *men.*
34And behold, the whole city came out to meet Jesus. And when they saw Him, they begged *Him* to depart from their region.

DAY 11: What does it mean to be demon-possessed?

Matthew 8:16 and 8:28 refer to individuals who were demon-possessed. This means "demonized," or under the internal control of a demon. All of the cases of demonization dealt with by Christ involved the actual indwelling of demons who utterly controlled the bodies of their victims, even to the point of speaking through them (Mark 5:5–9), causing derangement (John 10:20), violence (Luke 8:29), or rendering them mute (Mark 9:17–22).

From Matthew 8:29, it is evident that even the demons not only recognized the deity of Jesus, but also knew there was a divinely appointed time for their judgment and He would be their judge. Their eschatology was factually correct, but it is one thing to know the truth and quite another thing to love it (see James 2:19). Luke 8:31 relates they pleaded not to be sent into the abyss, meaning the pit, the underworld, the prison of bound demons who disobeyed (2 Pet. 2:4; Jude 6). They knew Jesus had the power and authority to send them there if He desired.

Deliverance from demons and healing were a fulfillment of the words spoken by Isaiah the prophet concerning the atonement (Is. 53:4,5). Christ bore both the guilt and the curse of sin (see Gal. 3:13). Both physical healing and ultimate victory over death are guaranteed by Christ's atoning work, but these will not be fully realized until the very end (1 Cor. 15:26).

JANUARY 12

Genesis 23:1–24:67

23 Sarah lived one hundred and twenty-
seven years; *these were* the years of the
life of Sarah. 2So Sarah died in Kirjath Arba
(that *is,* Hebron) in the land of Canaan, and
Abraham came to mourn for Sarah and to
weep for her.
3Then Abraham stood up from before his
dead, and spoke to the sons of Heth, saying,
4"I *am* a foreigner and a visitor among you.
Give me property for a burial place among
you, that I may bury my dead out of my sight."

23:1,2 Although Sarah's age—the only woman's age at death recorded in Scripture—might suggest her importance in God's plan, it more importantly reminds of the birth of her only son well beyond childbearing age (at 90 years of age, see 17:17) and of God's intervention to bring about the fulfillment of His word to her and Abraham. Sarah's death occurred ca. 2028 B.C.

5And the sons of Heth answered Abraham,
saying to him, 6"Hear us, my lord: You *are* a
mighty prince among us; bury your dead in
the choicest of our burial places. None of us
will withhold from you his burial place, that
you may bury your dead."
7Then Abraham stood up and bowed himself to the people of the land, the sons of Heth.
8And he spoke with them, saying, "If it is your
wish that I bury my dead out of my sight, hear
me, and meet with Ephron the son of Zohar for
me, 9that he may give me the cave of Machpelah
which he has, which *is* at the end of his field.
Let him give it to me at the full price, as property for a burial place among you."
10Now Ephron dwelt among the sons of
Heth; and Ephron the Hittite answered Abraham in the presence of the sons of Heth, all
who entered at the gate of his city, saying,
11"No, my lord, hear me: I give you the field
and the cave that *is* in it; I give it to you in the
presence of the sons of my people. I give it to
you. Bury your dead!"
12Then Abraham bowed himself down
before the people of the land; 13and he spoke to
Ephron in the hearing of the people of the
land, saying, "If you *will give it,* please hear
me. I will give you money for the field; take *it*
from me and I will bury my dead there."
14And Ephron answered Abraham, saying to
him, 15"My lord, listen to me; the land *is worth*
four hundred shekels of silver. What *is* that
between you and me? So bury your dead."
16And Abraham listened to Ephron; and Abraham weighed out the silver for Ephron which
he had named in the hearing of the sons of
Heth, four hundred shekels of silver, currency
of the merchants.
17So the field of Ephron which *was* in
Machpelah, which *was* before Mamre, the
field and the cave which *was* in it, and all the
trees that *were* in the field, which *were* within
all the surrounding borders, were deeded 18to
Abraham as a possession in the presence of
the sons of Heth, before all who went in at the
gate of his city.
19And after this, Abraham buried Sarah his
wife in the cave of the field of Machpelah,
before Mamre (that *is,* Hebron) in the land of
Canaan. 20So the field and the cave that *is* in it
were deeded to Abraham by the sons of Heth
as property for a burial place.
24 Now Abraham was old, well advanced
in age; and the LORD had blessed Abraham in all things. 2So Abraham said to the oldest servant of his house, who ruled over all
that he had, "Please, put your hand under my
thigh, 3and I will make you swear by the LORD,
the God of heaven and the God of the earth,
that you will not take a wife for my son from
the daughters of the Canaanites, among
whom I dwell; 4but you shall go to my country
and to my family, and take a wife for my son
Isaac."
5And the servant said to him, "Perhaps the
woman will not be willing to follow me to this
land. Must I take your son back to the land
from which you came?"
6But Abraham said to him, "Beware that you
do not take my son back there. 7The LORD God

24:2–4 put your hand under my thigh... and...swear. A solemn pledge mentioning the Lord's name and formalized by an accepted customary gesture indicated just how serious an undertaking this was in Abraham's eyes. At his age (v. 1), Abraham was concerned to perpetuate his people and God's promise through the next generation, so he covenanted with his servant to return to Mesopotamia and bring back a wife for Isaac.

of heaven, who took me from my father's
house and from the land of my family, and who
spoke to me and swore to me, saying, 'To your
descendants I give this land,' He will send His
angel before you, and you shall take a wife for
my son from there. 8And if the woman is not
willing to follow you, then you will be released
from this oath; only do not take my son back
there." 9So the servant put his hand under the
thigh of Abraham his master, and swore to
him concerning this matter.

10Then the servant took ten of his master's
camels and departed, for all his master's
goods *were in* his hand. And he arose and
went to Mesopotamia, to the city of Nahor.
11And he made his camels kneel down outside
the city by a well of water at evening time, the
time when women go out to draw *water.*
12Then he said, "O LORD God of my master
Abraham, please give me success this day,
and show kindness to my master Abraham.
13Behold, *here* I stand by the well of water, and
the daughters of the men of the city are coming out to draw water. 14Now let it be that the
young woman to whom I say, 'Please let down
your pitcher that I may drink,' and she says,
'Drink, and I will also give your camels a
drink'—*let* her *be the one* You have appointed
for Your servant Isaac. And by this I will know
that You have shown kindness to my master."

15And it happened, before he had finished
speaking, that behold, Rebekah, who was
born to Bethuel, son of Milcah, the wife of
Nahor, Abraham's brother, came out with her
pitcher on her shoulder. 16Now the young
woman *was* very beautiful to behold, a virgin;
no man had known her. And she went down to
the well, filled her pitcher, and came up. 17And
the servant ran to meet her and said, "Please
let me drink a little water from your pitcher."

18So she said, "Drink, my lord." Then she
quickly let her pitcher down to her hand, and
gave him a drink. 19And when she had finished
giving him a drink, she said, "I will draw *water*
for your camels also, until they have finished
drinking." 20Then she quickly emptied her
pitcher into the trough, ran back to the well to
draw *water,* and drew for all his camels. 21And
the man, wondering at her, remained silent so
as to know whether the LORD had made his
journey prosperous or not.

22So it was, when the camels had finished
drinking, that the man took a golden nose ring
weighing half a shekel, and two bracelets for
her wrists weighing ten *shekels* of gold, 23and
said, "Whose daughter *are* you? Tell me,
please, is there room *in* your father's house
for us to lodge?"

24So she said to him, "I *am* the daughter of
Bethuel, Milcah's son, whom she bore to
Nahor." 25Moreover she said to him, "We have
both straw and feed enough, and room to
lodge."

26Then the man bowed down his head and
worshiped the LORD. 27And he said, "Blessed
be the LORD God of my master Abraham, who
has not forsaken His mercy and His truth
toward my master. As for me, being on the
way, the LORD led me to the house of my master's brethren." 28So the young woman ran and
told her mother's household these things.

29Now Rebekah had a brother whose name
was Laban, and Laban ran out to the man by
the well. 30So it came to pass, when he saw the
nose ring, and the bracelets on his sister's
wrists, and when he heard the words of his
sister Rebekah, saying, "Thus the man spoke
to me," that he went to the man. And there he
stood by the camels at the well. 31And he said,
"Come in, O blessed of the LORD! Why do you
stand outside? For I have prepared the house,
and a place for the camels."

32Then the man came to the house. And he
unloaded the camels, and provided straw and
feed for the camels, and water to wash his feet
and the feet of the men who *were* with him.
33*Food* was set before him to eat, but he said, "I
will not eat until I have told about my errand."

And he said, "Speak on."

34So he said, "I *am* Abraham's servant. 35The
LORD has blessed my master greatly, and he
has become great; and He has given him
flocks and herds, silver and gold, male and
female servants, and camels and donkeys.
36And Sarah my master's wife bore a son to my
master when she was old; and to him he has
given all that he has. 37Now my master made
me swear, saying, 'You shall not take a wife for
my son from the daughters of the Canaanites,
in whose land I dwell; 38but you shall go to my
father's house and to my family, and take a
wife for my son.' 39And I said to my master,
'Perhaps the woman will not follow me.' 40But
he said to me, 'The LORD, before whom I walk,
will send His angel with you and prosper your
way; and you shall take a wife for my son from
my family and from my father's house. 41You
will be clear from this oath when you arrive
among my family; for if they will not give *her*
to you, then you will be released from my
oath.'

42"And this day I came to the well and said,
'O LORD God of my master Abraham, if You
will now prosper the way in which I go, 43be-
hold, I stand by the well of water; and it shall
come to pass that when the virgin comes out

to draw *water,* and I say to her, "Please give me a little water from your pitcher to drink," 44 and she says to me, "Drink, and I will draw for your camels also,"—*let* her *be* the woman whom the LORD has appointed for my master's son.'

45 "But before I had finished speaking in my heart, there was Rebekah, coming out with her pitcher on her shoulder; and she went down to the well and drew *water.* And I said to her, 'Please let me drink.' 46 And she made haste and let her pitcher down from her *shoulder,* and said, 'Drink, and I will give your camels a drink also.' So I drank, and she gave the camels a drink also. 47 Then I asked her, and said, 'Whose daughter *are* you?' And she said, 'The daughter of Bethuel, Nahor's son, whom Milcah bore to him.' So I put the nose ring on her nose and the bracelets on her wrists. 48 And I bowed my head and worshiped the LORD, and blessed the LORD God of my master Abraham, who had led me in the way of truth to take the daughter of my master's brother for his son. 49 Now if you will deal kindly and truly with my master, tell me. And if not, tell me, that I may turn to the right hand or to the left."

50 Then Laban and Bethuel answered and said, "The thing comes from the LORD; we cannot speak to you either bad or good. 51 Here *is* Rebekah before you; take *her* and go, and let her be your master's son's wife, as the LORD has spoken."

52 And it came to pass, when Abraham's servant heard their words, that he worshiped the LORD, *bowing himself* to the earth. 53 Then the servant brought out jewelry of silver, jewelry of gold, and clothing, and gave *them* to Rebekah. He also gave precious things to her brother and to her mother.

54 And he and the men who *were* with him ate and drank and stayed all night. Then they arose in the morning, and he said, "Send me away to my master."

55 But her brother and her mother said, "Let the young woman stay with us *a few* days, at least ten; after that she may go."

56 And he said to them, "Do not hinder me, since the LORD has prospered my way; send me away so that I may go to my master."

57 So they said, "We will call the young woman and ask her personally." 58 Then they called Rebekah and said to her, "Will you go with this man?"

And she said, "I will go."

59 So they sent away Rebekah their sister and her nurse, and Abraham's servant and his men. 60 And they blessed Rebekah and said to her:

"Our sister, *may* you *become*
The mother of thousands of
ten thousands;
And may your descendants possess
The gates of those who hate them."

61 Then Rebekah and her maids arose, and they rode on the camels and followed the man. So the servant took Rebekah and departed.

62 Now Isaac came from the way of Beer Lahai Roi, for he dwelt in the South. 63 And Isaac went out to meditate in the field in the evening; and he lifted his eyes and looked, and there, the camels *were* coming. 64 Then Rebekah lifted her eyes, and when she saw Isaac she dismounted from her camel; 65 for she had said to the servant, "Who *is* this man walking in the field to meet us?"

The servant said, "It *is* my master." So she took a veil and covered herself.

66 And the servant told Isaac all the things that he had done. 67 Then Isaac brought her into his mother Sarah's tent; and he took Rebekah and she became his wife, and he loved her. So Isaac was comforted after his mother's *death.*

Psalm 7:1–5

A Meditation of David,
which he sang to the LORD concerning
the words of Cush, a Benjamite.

O LORD my God, in You I put
my trust;
Save me from all those who persecute
me;
And deliver me,
2 Lest they tear me like a lion,
Rending *me* in pieces, while *there is*
none to deliver.

3 O LORD my God, if I have done this:
If there is iniquity in my hands,
4 If I have repaid evil to him who was at
peace with me,
Or have plundered my enemy without
cause,
5 Let the enemy pursue me
and overtake *me;*
Yes, let him trample my life
to the earth,
And lay my honor in the dust.
Selah

Proverbs 3:7–8

7 Do not be wise in your own eyes;
Fear the LORD and depart from evil.
8 It will be health to your flesh,
And strength to your bones.

9:1 His own city. Capernaum is the city where Jesus settled. Jesus had left there to get away from the crowds for a time.

Matthew 9:1–17

9 So He got into a boat, crossed over, and came to His own city. [2]Then behold, they brought to Him a paralytic lying on a bed. When Jesus saw their faith, He said to the paralytic, "Son, be of good cheer; your sins are forgiven you."

[3]And at once some of the scribes said within themselves, "This Man blasphemes!"

[4]But Jesus, knowing their thoughts, said, "Why do you think evil in your hearts? [5]For which is easier, to say, *'Your* sins are forgiven you,' or to say, 'Arise and walk'? [6]But that you may know that the Son of Man has power on earth to forgive sins"—then He said to the paralytic, "Arise, take up your bed, and go to your house." [7]And he arose and departed to his house.

[8]Now when the multitudes saw *it,* they marveled and glorified God, who had given such power to men.

[9]As Jesus passed on from there, He saw a man named Matthew sitting at the tax office. And He said to him, "Follow Me." So he arose and followed Him.

[10]Now it happened, as Jesus sat at the table in the house, *that* behold, many tax collectors and sinners came and sat down with Him and His disciples. [11]And when the Pharisees saw *it,* they said to His disciples, "Why does your Teacher eat with tax collectors and sinners?"

[12]When Jesus heard *that,* He said to them, "Those who are well have no need of a physician, but those who are sick. [13]But go and learn what *this* means: *'I desire mercy and not sacrifice.'* For I did not come to call the righteous, but sinners, to repentance."

9:13 go and learn what *this* means. This phrase was commonly used as a rebuke for those who did not know something they should have known. The verse Jesus cites is Hosea 6:6, which emphasizes the absolute priority of the law's moral standards over the ceremonial requirements. The Pharisees tended to focus on the outward, ritual, and ceremonial aspects of God's law—to the neglect of its inward, eternal, and moral precepts. In doing so, they became harsh, judgmental, and self-righteously scornful of others. Jesus repeated this same criticism in 12:7.

[14]Then the disciples of John came to Him, saying, "Why do we and the Pharisees fast often, but Your disciples do not fast?"

[15]And Jesus said to them, "Can the friends of the bridegroom mourn as long as the bridegroom is with them? But the days will come when the bridegroom will be taken away from them, and then they will fast. [16]No one puts a piece of unshrunk cloth on an old garment; for the patch pulls away from the garment, and the tear is made worse. [17]Nor do they put new wine into old wineskins, or else the wineskins break, the wine is spilled, and the wineskins are ruined. But they put new wine into new wineskins, and both are preserved."

DAY 12: Why were the scribes upset that Christ forgave the paralytic?

In Matthew 9:1-8, the fact that the man was brought on a bed indicates that his paralysis was severe. Christ ignored the paralysis and addressed the man's greater needs. Christ's words of forgiveness may indicate that the paralysis was a direct consequence of the man's own sin (John 9:1–3).

The scribes outcry, "This Man blasphemes!" would be a true judgment about anyone but God incarnate, for only the One who has been sinned against has the prerogative to forgive. Jesus' words to the man were therefore an unequivocal claim of divine authority. That He asserted His prerogative that was God's alone was completely understood by the scribes.

Jesus then confronts the scribes directly. It is certainly easier to claim the power to pronounce absolution from sin than to demonstrate the power to heal. Christ actually proved His power to forgive by instantly healing the man of his paralysis. His ability to heal anyone and everyone at will—totally and immediately—was incontrovertible proof of His deity. If He could do the apparently harder, He could also do what seemed easier. The actual forgiving of the sins was in reality the more difficult task, however, because it ultimately required Him to sacrifice His life.

JANUARY 13

Genesis 25:1–26:35

25 Abraham again took a wife, and her
name *was* Keturah. 2And she bore him
Zimran, Jokshan, Medan, Midian, Ishbak, and
Shuah. 3Jokshan begot Sheba and Dedan. And
the sons of Dedan were Asshurim, Letushim,
and Leummim. 4And the sons of Midian *were*
Ephah, Epher, Hanoch, Abidah, and Eldaah.
All these *were* the children of Keturah.
5And Abraham gave all that he had to Isaac.
6But Abraham gave gifts to the sons of the concubines which Abraham had; and while he
was still living he sent them eastward, away
from Isaac his son, to the country of the east.
7This *is* the sum of the years of Abraham's
life which he lived: one hundred and seventy-
five years. 8Then Abraham breathed his last
and died in a good old age, an old man and full
of years, and was gathered to his people. 9And
his sons Isaac and Ishmael buried him in the
cave of Machpelah, which *is* before Mamre, in
the field of Ephron the son of Zohar the
Hittite, 10the field which Abraham purchased
from the sons of Heth. There Abraham was
buried, and Sarah his wife. 11And it came to
pass, after the death of Abraham, that God
blessed his son Isaac. And Isaac dwelt at Beer
Lahai Roi.

25:8 gathered to his people. A euphemism for death, but also an expression of personal continuance beyond death, which denoted a reunion with previously departed friends (ca. 1990 B.C.).

12Now this *is* the genealogy of Ishmael,
Abraham's son, whom Hagar the Egyptian, Sarah's maidservant, bore to Abraham. 13And
these *were* the names of the sons of Ishmael,
by their names, according to their generations: The firstborn of Ishmael, Nebajoth; then
Kedar, Adbeel, Mibsam, 14Mishma, Dumah,
Massa, 15Hadar, Tema, Jetur, Naphish, and
Kedemah. 16These *were* the sons of Ishmael
and these *were* their names, by their towns
and their settlements, twelve princes according to their nations. 17These *were* the years of
the life of Ishmael: one hundred and thirty-
seven years; and he breathed his last and died,
and was gathered to his people. 18(They dwelt
from Havilah as far as Shur, which *is* east of
Egypt as you go toward Assyria.) He died in
the presence of all his brethren.
19This *is* the genealogy of Isaac, Abraham's
son. Abraham begot Isaac. 20Isaac was forty
years old when he took Rebekah as wife, the
daughter of Bethuel the Syrian of Padan
Aram, the sister of Laban the Syrian. 21Now
Isaac pleaded with the LORD for his wife,
because she *was* barren; and the LORD granted his plea, and Rebekah his wife conceived.
22But the children struggled together within
her; and she said, "If *all is* well, why *am I like*
this?" So she went to inquire of the LORD.
23And the LORD said to her:

"Two nations *are* in your womb,
Two peoples shall be separated from
your body;
One people shall be stronger than the
other,
And the older shall serve the
younger."

25:23 the older shall serve the younger. This was contrary to the custom in patriarchal times when the elder son enjoyed the privileges of precedence in the household and at the father's death received a double share of the inheritance and became the recognized head of the family (see Ex. 22:29; Num 8:14–17; Deut. 21:17). Grave offenses could annul such primogeniture rights (see Gen. 35:22; 49:3,4; 1 Chr. 5:1); or the birthright could be sacrificed or legally transferred to another in the family, as in this case (vv. 29–34). In this case, God declared otherwise since His sovereign elective purposes did not necessarily have to follow custom (see Rom. 9:10–14, esp. v. 12).

24So when her days were fulfilled *for her* to
give birth, indeed *there were* twins in her
womb. 25And the first came out red. *He was*
like a hairy garment all over; so they called his
name Esau. 26Afterward his brother came out,
and his hand took hold of Esau's heel; so his
name was called Jacob. Isaac *was* sixty years
old when she bore them.
27So the boys grew. And Esau was a skillful
hunter, a man of the field; but Jacob was a mild
man, dwelling in tents. 28And Isaac loved Esau
because he ate *of his* game, but Rebekah loved
Jacob.

29Now Jacob cooked a stew; and Esau came
in from the field, and he *was* weary. 30And Esau
said to Jacob, "Please feed me with that same
red *stew,* for I *am* weary." Therefore his name
was called Edom.
31But Jacob said, "Sell me your birthright as
of this day."
32And Esau said, "Look, I *am* about to die; so
what *is* this birthright to me?"
33Then Jacob said, "Swear to me as of this day."
So he swore to him, and sold his birthright
to Jacob. 34And Jacob gave Esau bread and
stew of lentils; then he ate and drank, arose,
and went his way. Thus Esau despised *his*
birthright.

26 There was a famine in the land, besides
the first famine that was in the days of
Abraham. And Isaac went to Abimelech king
of the Philistines, in Gerar.
2Then the LORD appeared to him and said:
"Do not go down to Egypt; live in the land of
which I shall tell you. 3Dwell in this land, and I
will be with you and bless you; for to you and
your descendants I give all these lands, and I
will perform the oath which I swore to Abraham your father. 4And I will make your descendants multiply as the stars of heaven; I will
give to your descendants all these lands; and
in your seed all the nations of the earth shall
be blessed; 5because Abraham obeyed My
voice and kept My charge, My commandments, My statutes, and My laws."
6So Isaac dwelt in Gerar. 7And the men of
the place asked about his wife. And he said,
"She *is* my sister"; for he was afraid to say,
"*She is* my wife," *because he thought,* "lest the
men of the place kill me for Rebekah, because
she *is* beautiful to behold." 8Now it came to
pass, when he had been there a long time, that
Abimelech king of the Philistines looked
through a window, and saw, and there was
Isaac, showing endearment to Rebekah his
wife. 9Then Abimelech called Isaac and said,
"Quite obviously she *is* your wife; so how
could you say, 'She *is* my sister'?"
Isaac said to him, "Because I said, 'Lest I die
on account of her.' "
10And Abimelech said, "What *is* this you
have done to us? One of the people might soon
have lain with your wife, and you would have
brought guilt on us." 11So Abimelech charged
all *his* people, saying, "He who touches this
man or his wife shall surely be put to death."
12Then Isaac sowed in that land, and reaped
in the same year a hundredfold; and the LORD
blessed him. 13The man began to prosper, and
continued prospering until he became very
prosperous; 14for he had possessions of flocks
and possessions of herds and a great number
of servants. So the Philistines envied him.
15Now the Philistines had stopped up all the
wells which his father's servants had dug in
the days of Abraham his father, and they had
filled them with earth. 16And Abimelech said to
Isaac, "Go away from us, for you are much
mightier than we."
17Then Isaac departed from there and pitched
his tent in the Valley of Gerar, and dwelt there.
18And Isaac dug again the wells of water which
they had dug in the days of Abraham his
father, for the Philistines had stopped them up
after the death of Abraham. He called them by
the names which his father had called them.
19Also Isaac's servants dug in the valley, and
found a well of running water there. 20But the
herdsmen of Gerar quarreled with Isaac's
herdsmen, saying, "The water *is* ours." So he
called the name of the well Esek, because they
quarreled with him. 21Then they dug another
well, and they quarreled over that *one* also. So
he called its name Sitnah. 22And he moved
from there and dug another well, and they did
not quarrel over it. So he called its name
Rehoboth, because he said, "For now the
LORD has made room for us, and we shall be
fruitful in the land."
23Then he went up from there to Beersheba.
24And the LORD appeared to him the same
night and said, "I *am* the God of your father
Abraham; do not fear, for I *am* with you. I will
bless you and multiply your descendants for
My servant Abraham's sake." 25So he built an
altar there and called on the name of the LORD,
and he pitched his tent there; and there
Isaac's servants dug a well.
26Then Abimelech came to him from Gerar
with Ahuzzath, one of his friends, and Phichol
the commander of his army. 27And Isaac said to
them, "Why have you come to me, since you
hate me and have sent me away from you?"
28But they said, "We have certainly seen that
the LORD is with you. So we said, 'Let there
now be an oath between us, between you and
us; and let us make a covenant with you, 29that
you will do us no harm, since we have not
touched you, and since we have done nothing
to you but good and have sent you away in
peace. You *are* now the blessed of the LORD.' "
30So he made them a feast, and they ate and
drank. 31Then they arose early in the morning
and swore an oath with one another; and Isaac
sent them away, and they departed from him
in peace.
32It came to pass the same day that Isaac's
servants came and told him about the well
which they had dug, and said to him, "We

have found water." 33So he called it Shebah.
Therefore the name of the city *is* Beersheba to
this day.
34When Esau was forty years old, he took as
wives Judith the daughter of Beeri the Hittite,
and Basemath the daughter of Elon the
Hittite. 35And they were a grief of mind to Isaac
and Rebekah.

Psalm 7:6–8

6 Arise, O LORD, in Your anger;
Lift Yourself up because of the rage
of my enemies;
Rise up for me *to* the judgment
You have commanded!
7 So the congregation of the peoples
shall surround You;
For their sakes, therefore, return
on high.
8 The LORD shall judge the peoples;
Judge me, O LORD, according to my
righteousness,
And according to my integrity within me.

Proverbs 3:9–10

9 Honor the LORD with your possessions,
And with the firstfruits of all your
increase;
10 So your barns will be filled with plenty,
And your vats will overflow with new
wine.

3:9,10 Honor the LORD...possessions. A biblical view of possessions demands using them for honoring God. This is accomplished by trusting God (v. 5); by giving the first and best to God ("firstfruits"; see Ex. 22:29; 23:19; Deut. 18:4); by being fair (vv. 27,28); by giving generously (11:25); and by expressing gratitude for all He gives (Deut. 6:9–11). The result of such faithfulness to honor Him is prosperity and satisfaction.

Matthew 9:18–38

18While He spoke these things to them,
behold, a ruler came and worshiped Him, saying,
"My daughter has just died, but come and
lay Your hand on her and she will live." 19So
Jesus arose and followed him, and so *did* His
disciples.
20And suddenly, a woman who had a flow of
blood for twelve years came from behind and
touched the hem of His garment. 21For she said
to herself, "If only I may touch His garment, I
shall be made well." 22But Jesus turned around,
and when He saw her He said, "Be of good
cheer, daughter; your faith has made you well."
And the woman was made well from that hour.
23When Jesus came into the ruler's house,
and saw the flute players and the noisy crowd
wailing, 24He said to them, "Make room, for
the girl is not dead, but sleeping." And they
ridiculed Him. 25But when the crowd was put
outside, He went in and took her by the hand,
and the girl arose. 26And the report of this
went out into all that land.
27When Jesus departed from there, two
blind men followed Him, crying out and saying,
"Son of David, have mercy on us!"
28And when He had come into the house, the
blind men came to Him. And Jesus said to them,
"Do you believe that I am able to do this?"
They said to Him, "Yes, Lord."
29Then He touched their eyes, saying, "According
to your faith let it be to you." 30And
their eyes were opened. And Jesus sternly
warned them, saying, "See *that* no one knows
it." 31But when they had departed, they spread
the news about Him in all that country.
32As they went out, behold, they brought to
Him a man, mute and demon-possessed. 33And
when the demon was cast out, the mute
spoke. And the multitudes marveled, saying,
"It was never seen like this in Israel!"
34But the Pharisees said, "He casts out
demons by the ruler of the demons."
35Then Jesus went about all the cities and villages,
teaching in their synagogues, preaching
the gospel of the kingdom, and healing
every sickness and every disease among the
people. 36But when He saw the multitudes, He
was moved with compassion for them,
because they were weary and scattered, like
sheep having no shepherd. 37Then He said to
His disciples, "The harvest truly *is* plentiful,
but the laborers *are* few. 38Therefore pray the
Lord of the harvest to send out laborers into
His harvest."

DAY 13: Why is compassion the key to Christian service?

In Matthew 9:35, it describes Jesus' ministry of teaching and preaching the gospel of the kingdom and of healing every sickness and every disease among the people. Jesus banished illness in an unprecedented healing display, giving impressive evidence of His deity and making the Jews' rejection all the more heinous.

In v. 36 it adds that Jesus was "moved" with compassion when He saw the multitudes. Here the humanity of Christ allowed expression of His attitude toward sinners in terms of human passion. Whereas God, who is immutable, is not subject to the rise and fall and change of emotions (Num. 23:19), Christ, who was fully human with all the faculties of humanity, was on occasion moved to literal tears over the plight of sinners (Luke 19:41). God Himself expressed similar compassion through the prophets (Ex. 33:19; Ps. 86:15; Jer. 9:1; 13:17; 14:17). He saw these people as weary and scattered. Their spiritual needs were even more desperate than the need for physical healing.

Meeting those needs requires laborers (v. 37), which is where we come in. The Lord spoke of the spiritual harvest of souls for salvation; but apart from being "moved" with the same compassion, our service will be in vain.

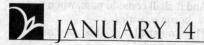

JANUARY 14

Genesis 27:1–28:22

27 Now it came to pass, when Isaac was
old and his eyes were so dim that he
could not see, that he called Esau his older
son and said to him, "My son."
And he answered him, "Here I am."
[2]Then he said, "Behold now, I am old. I do
not know the day of my death. [3]Now therefore,
please take your weapons, your quiver and
your bow, and go out to the field and hunt
game for me. [4]And make me savory food, such
as I love, and bring *it* to me that I may eat, that
my soul may bless you before I die."
[5]Now Rebekah was listening when Isaac
spoke to Esau his son. And Esau went to the
field to hunt game and to bring *it*. [6]So Rebekah
spoke to Jacob her son, saying, "Indeed I
heard your father speak to Esau your brother,
saying, [7]'Bring me game and make savory
food for me, that I may eat it and bless you in
the presence of the LORD before my death.'
[8]Now therefore, my son, obey my voice
according to what I command you. [9]Go now to
the flock and bring me from there two choice
kids of the goats, and I will make savory food
from them for your father, such as he loves.
[10]Then you shall take *it* to your father, that he
may eat *it*, and that he may bless you before
his death."
[11]And Jacob said to Rebekah his mother,
"Look, Esau my brother *is* a hairy man, and I
am a smooth-*skinned* man. [12]Perhaps my
father will feel me, and I shall seem to be a
deceiver to him; and I shall bring a curse on
myself and not a blessing."
[13]But his mother said to him, "*Let* your curse
be on me, my son; only obey my voice, and go,
get *them* for me." [14]And he went and got *them*
and brought *them* to his mother, and his mother
made savory food, such as his father loved.
[15]Then Rebekah took the choice clothes of her
elder son Esau, which *were* with her in the
house, and put them on Jacob her younger
son. [16]And she put the skins of the kids of the
goats on his hands and on the smooth part of
his neck. [17]Then she gave the savory food and
the bread, which she had prepared, into the
hand of her son Jacob.
[18]So he went to his father and said, "My
father."
And he said, "Here I am. Who *are* you, my
son?"
[19]Jacob said to his father, "I *am* Esau your
firstborn; I have done just as you told me;
please arise, sit and eat of my game, that your
soul may bless me."
[20]But Isaac said to his son, "How *is it* that
you have found *it* so quickly, my son?"
And he said, "Because the LORD your God
brought *it* to me."
[21]Isaac said to Jacob, "Please come near, that
I may feel you, my son, whether you *are* really
my son Esau or not." [22]So Jacob went near to
Isaac his father, and he felt him and said, "The
voice *is* Jacob's voice, but the hands *are* the
hands of Esau." [23]And he did not recognize
him, because his hands were hairy like his
brother Esau's hands; so he blessed him.
[24]Then he said, "*Are* you really my son Esau?"
He said, "I *am*."
[25]He said, "Bring *it* near to me, and I will eat
of my son's game, so that my soul may bless
you." So he brought *it* near to him, and he ate;
and he brought him wine, and he drank.
[26]Then his father Isaac said to him, "Come
near now and kiss me, my son." [27]And he came
near and kissed him; and he smelled the smell
of his clothing, and blessed him and said:

"Surely, the smell of my son
Is like the smell of a field
Which the LORD has blessed.
[28] Therefore may God give you
Of the dew of heaven,
Of the fatness of the earth,
And plenty of grain and wine.

29 Let peoples serve you,
And nations bow down to you.
Be master over your brethren,
And let your mother's sons bow down
to you.
Cursed *be* everyone who curses you,
And blessed *be* those who bless you!"

30 Now it happened, as soon as Isaac had finished blessing Jacob, and Jacob had scarcely
gone out from the presence of Isaac his father,
that Esau his brother came in from his hunting. 31 He also had made savory food, and
brought it to his father, and said to his father,
"Let my father arise and eat of his son's game,
that your soul may bless me."
32 And his father Isaac said to him, "Who *are*
you?"
So he said, "I *am* your son, your firstborn,
Esau."
33 Then Isaac trembled exceedingly, and
said, "Who? Where *is* the one who hunted
game and brought *it* to me? I ate all *of it* before
you came, and I have blessed him—*and*
indeed he shall be blessed."

27:33 Isaac trembled exceedingly. Visibly shocked when the scandal was uncovered by the entrance of Esau, the father, remembering the Lord's words to Rebekah (25:23), refused to withdraw the blessing and emphatically affirmed its validity—"Indeed he shall be blessed" and a little later "Indeed I have made him your master" and also "you shall serve your brother" (vv. 37,40). Sudden realization at having opposed God's will all those years likely made the shock more severe.

34 When Esau heard the words of his father,
he cried with an exceedingly great and bitter
cry, and said to his father, "Bless me—me
also, O my father!"
35 But he said, "Your brother came with
deceit and has taken away your blessing."
36 And *Esau* said, "Is he not rightly named
Jacob? For he has supplanted me these two
times. He took away my birthright, and now
look, he has taken away my blessing!" And he
said, "Have you not reserved a blessing for
me?"
37 Then Isaac answered and said to Esau, "Indeed I have made him your master, and all his
brethren I have given to him as servants; with
grain and wine I have sustained him. What
shall I do now for you, my son?"
38 And Esau said to his father, "Have you only
one blessing, my father? Bless me—me also,
O my father!" And Esau lifted up his voice and
wept.
39 Then Isaac his father answered and said to
him:

"Behold, your dwelling shall be of the
fatness of the earth,
And of the dew of heaven from above.
40 By your sword you shall live,
And you shall serve your brother;
And it shall come to pass, when you
become restless,
That you shall break his yoke from
your neck."

41 So Esau hated Jacob because of the blessing with which his father blessed him, and
Esau said in his heart, "The days of mourning
for my father are at hand; then I will kill my
brother Jacob."
42 And the words of Esau her older son were
told to Rebekah. So she sent and called Jacob
her younger son, and said to him, "Surely your
brother Esau comforts himself concerning you
by intending to kill you. 43 Now therefore, my
son, obey my voice: arise, flee to my brother
Laban in Haran. 44 And stay with him a few days,
until your brother's fury turns away, 45 until your
brother's anger turns away from you, and he
forgets what you have done to him; then I will
send and bring you from there. Why should I
be bereaved also of you both in one day?"
46 And Rebekah said to Isaac, "I am weary of
my life because of the daughters of Heth; if
Jacob takes a wife of the daughters of Heth,
like these *who are* the daughters of the land,
what good will my life be to me?"

28 Then Isaac called Jacob and blessed
him, and charged him, and said to him:
"You shall not take a wife from the daughters
of Canaan. 2 Arise, go to Padan Aram, to the
house of Bethuel your mother's father; and
take yourself a wife from there of the daughters of Laban your mother's brother.

3 "May God Almighty bless you,
And make you fruitful and
multiply you,
That you may be an assembly of
peoples;
4 And give you the blessing of Abraham,
To you and your descendants with
you,
That you may inherit the land
In which you are a stranger,
Which God gave to Abraham."

5 So Isaac sent Jacob away, and he went to

Padan Aram, to Laban the son of Bethuel the
Syrian, the brother of Rebekah, the mother of
Jacob and Esau.
6 Esau saw that Isaac had blessed Jacob and
sent him away to Padan Aram to take himself
a wife from there, *and that* as he blessed him
he gave him a charge, saying, "You shall not
take a wife from the daughters of Canaan,"
7 and that Jacob had obeyed his father and his
mother and had gone to Padan Aram. 8 Also
Esau saw that the daughters of Canaan did not
please his father Isaac. 9 So Esau went to
Ishmael and took Mahalath the daughter of
Ishmael, Abraham's son, the sister of
Nebajoth, to be his wife in addition to the
wives he had.
10 Now Jacob went out from Beersheba and
went toward Haran. 11 So he came to a certain
place and stayed there all night, because the
sun had set. And he took one of the stones of
that place and put it at his head, and he lay
down in that place to sleep. 12 Then he
dreamed, and behold, a ladder *was* set up on
the earth, and its top reached to heaven; and
there the angels of God were ascending and
descending on it.
13 And behold, the LORD stood above it and
said: "I *am* the LORD God of Abraham your
father and the God of Isaac; the land on which
you lie I will give to you and your descendants.
14 Also your descendants shall be as the dust of
the earth; you shall spread abroad to the west
and the east, to the north and the south; and in
you and in your seed all the families of the earth
shall be blessed. 15 Behold, I *am* with you and
will keep you wherever you go, and will bring
you back to this land; for I will not leave you
until I have done what I have spoken to you."
16 Then Jacob awoke from his sleep and
said, "Surely the LORD is in this place, and I
did not know *it*." 17 And he was afraid and said,
"How awesome *is* this place! This *is* none
other than the house of God, and this *is* the
gate of heaven!"
18 Then Jacob rose early in the morning, and
took the stone that he had put at his head, set
it up as a pillar, and poured oil on top of it.
19 And he called the name of that place Bethel;
but the name of that city had been Luz previously. 20 Then Jacob made a vow, saying, "If
God will be with me, and keep me in this way
that I am going, and give me bread to eat and
clothing to put on, 21 so that I come back to my
father's house in peace, then the LORD shall be
my God. 22 And this stone which I have set as a
pillar shall be God's house, and of all that You
give me I will surely give a tenth to You."

Psalm 7:9–17

9 Oh, let the wickedness of the wicked
come to an end,
But establish the just;
For the righteous God tests the hearts
and minds.
10 My defense *is* of God,
Who saves the upright
in heart.

11 God *is* a just judge,
And God is angry *with the wicked*
every day.
12 If he does not turn back,
He will sharpen His sword;
He bends His bow and makes
it ready.
13 He also prepares for Himself
instruments of death;
He makes His arrows into
fiery shafts.

14 Behold, *the wicked* brings forth
iniquity;
Yes, he conceives trouble and brings
forth falsehood.
15 He made a pit and dug it out,
And has fallen into the ditch *which* he
made.
16 His trouble shall return upon his own
head,
And his violent dealing
shall come down on
his own crown.

17 I will praise the LORD according
to His righteousness,
And will sing praise to the name
of the LORD Most High.

Proverbs 3:11–12

11 My son, do not despise the chastening
of the LORD,
Nor detest His correction;
12 For whom the LORD loves
He corrects,
Just as a father the son *in whom* he
delights.

3:11,12 not despise...chastening. Since even the wisest of God's children are subject to sin, there is necessity of God's fatherly discipline to increase wisdom and blessing. Such correction should not be resisted.

Matthew 10:1–20

10 And when He had called His twelve disciples to *Him,* He gave them power *over*
unclean spirits, to cast them out, and to heal
all kinds of sickness and all kinds of disease.
2Now the names of the twelve apostles are
these: first, Simon, who is called Peter, and
Andrew his brother; James the *son* of

10:1 He gave them power. Jesus delegated His power to the apostles to show clearly that He and His kingdom were sovereign over the physical and spiritual realms, the effects of sin, and the efforts of Satan. This was an unheard of display of power, never before seen in all redemptive history, to announce Messiah's arrival and authenticate Him plus His apostles who preached His gospel. This power was a preview of the power Christ will exhibit in His earthly kingdom, when Satan will be bound (Rev. 20) and the curse on physical life curtailed (Is. 65:20–25).

Zebedee, and John his brother; 3Philip and
Bartholomew; Thomas and Matthew the tax
collector; James the *son* of Alphaeus, and Leb-
baeus, whose surname was Thaddaeus;
4Simon the Cananite, and Judas Iscariot, who
also betrayed Him.
5These twelve Jesus sent out and commanded them, saying: "Do not go into the way of the
Gentiles, and do not enter a city of the Samaritans. 6But go rather to the lost sheep of the
house of Israel. 7And as you go, preach, saying, 'The kingdom of heaven is at hand.' 8Heal
the sick, cleanse the lepers, raise the dead,
cast out demons. Freely you have received,
freely give. 9Provide neither gold nor silver

10:8 Freely you have received, freely give. Jesus was giving them great power, to heal the sick and raise the dead. If they sold these gifts for money, they could have made quite a fortune. But that would have obscured the message of grace Christ sent them to preach. So He forbade them to charge money for their ministry. Yet they were permitted to accept support to meet their basic needs, for a workman is worthy of such support (v. 10).

nor copper in your money belts, 10nor bag for
your journey, nor two tunics, nor sandals, nor
staffs; for a worker is worthy of his food.
11"Now whatever city or town you enter,
inquire who in it is worthy, and stay there till
you go out. 12And when you go into a household, greet it. 13If the household is worthy, let
your peace come upon it. But if it is not worthy, let your peace return to you. 14And whoever will not receive you nor hear your words,
when you depart from that house or city,
shake off the dust from your feet. 15Assuredly,
I say to you, it will be more tolerable for the
land of Sodom and Gomorrah in the day of
judgment than for that city!
16"Behold, I send you out as sheep in the
midst of wolves. Therefore be wise as serpents
and harmless as doves. 17But beware of men, for
they will deliver you up to councils and scourge
you in their synagogues. 18You will be brought
before governors and kings for My sake, as a
testimony to them and to the Gentiles. 19But
when they deliver you up, do not worry about
how or what you should speak. For it will be
given to you in that hour what you should
speak; 20for it is not you who speak, but the
Spirit of your Father who speaks in you.

DAY 14: What does Jacob's deception teach us about lying?

When Jacob said, "I shall seem to be a deceiver to him" (Gen. 27:12), his objection to his mother's proposal that he lie to his father makes it clear he fully understood. The differences between him and Esau would surely not fool his father and might result in blessing being replaced with a curse as a fitting punishment for deception. But when Rebekah accepted full responsibility for the scheme and the curse it might incur, Jacob acquiesced and followed Rebekah's instructions.

Even Isaac's perfectly legitimate question in v. 20 afforded Jacob an escape route—confess and stop the deceit! Instead, Jacob, with consummate ease, knowing he needed Isaac's irrevocable confirmation even though he had bought the birthright, ascribed success in the hunt to God's providence. A lie had to sustain a lie, and a tangled web had begun to be woven (vv. 21–24). That principle always follows any lie we tell.

Although Jacob received Isaac's blessing that day, the deceit caused severe consequences: 1) he never saw his mother after that; 2) Esau wanted him dead; 3) Laban, his uncle, deceived him; 4) his family life was full of conflict; and 5) he was exiled for years from his family. By the promise of God he would have received the birthright (25:23). He didn't need to scheme this deception with his mother.

JANUARY 15

Genesis 29:1–30:43

29 So Jacob went on his journey and
came to the land of the people of the
East. 2And he looked, and saw a well in the
field; and behold, there *were* three flocks of
sheep lying by it; for out of that well they
watered the flocks. A large stone *was* on the
well's mouth. 3Now all the flocks would be
gathered there; and they would roll the stone
from the well's mouth, water the sheep, and put
the stone back in its place on the well's mouth.
4And Jacob said to them, "My brethren,
where *are* you from?"
And they said, "We *are* from Haran."
5Then he said to them, "Do you know Laban
the son of Nahor?"
And they said, "We know him."
6So he said to them, "Is he well?"
And they said, "*He is* well. And look, his
daughter Rachel is coming with the sheep."
7Then he said, "Look, *it is* still high day; *it is*
not time for the cattle to be gathered together.
Water the sheep, and go and feed *them.*"
8But they said, "We cannot until all the
flocks are gathered together, and they have
rolled the stone from the well's mouth; then
we water the sheep."
9Now while he was still speaking with them,
Rachel came with her father's sheep, for she
was a shepherdess. 10And it came to pass,
when Jacob saw Rachel the daughter of Laban
his mother's brother, and the sheep of Laban
his mother's brother, that Jacob went near and
rolled the stone from the well's mouth, and
watered the flock of Laban his mother's brother.
11Then Jacob kissed Rachel, and lifted up his
voice and wept. 12And Jacob told Rachel that he
was her father's relative and that he *was*
Rebekah's son. So she ran and told her father.
13Then it came to pass, when Laban heard
the report about Jacob his sister's son, that he
ran to meet him, and embraced him and
kissed him, and brought him to his house. So
he told Laban all these things. 14And Laban
said to him, "Surely you *are* my bone and my
flesh." And he stayed with him for a month.
15Then Laban said to Jacob, "Because you *are*
my relative, should you therefore serve me for
nothing? Tell me, what *should* your wages *be?*"
16Now Laban had two daughters: the name of the
elder *was* Leah, and the name of the younger
was Rachel. 17Leah's eyes *were* delicate, but
Rachel was beautiful of form and appearance.

29:17 eyes *were* delicate. Probably means that they were a pale color rather than the dark and sparkling eyes most common. Such paleness was viewed as a blemish.

18Now Jacob loved Rachel; so he said, "I will
serve you seven years for Rachel your
younger daughter."
19And Laban said, "*It is* better that I give her
to you than that I should give her to another
man. Stay with me." 20So Jacob served seven
years for Rachel, and they seemed *only* a few
days to him because of the love he had for her.
21Then Jacob said to Laban, "Give *me* my
wife, for my days are fulfilled, that I may go in
to her." 22And Laban gathered together all the
men of the place and made a feast. 23Now it
came to pass in the evening, that he took Leah
his daughter and brought her to Jacob; and he
went in to her. 24And Laban gave his maid
Zilpah to his daughter Leah *as* a maid. 25So it
came to pass in the morning, that behold, it
was Leah. And he said to Laban, "What is
this you have done to me? Was it not for
Rachel that I served you? Why then have you
deceived me?"
26And Laban said, "It must not be done so in
our country, to give the younger before the
firstborn. 27Fulfill her week, and we will give
you this one also for the service which you
will serve with me still another seven years."
28Then Jacob did so and fulfilled her week.
So he gave him his daughter Rachel as wife
also. 29And Laban gave his maid Bilhah to his
daughter Rachel as a maid. 30Then *Jacob* also
went in to Rachel, and he also loved Rachel
more than Leah. And he served with Laban
still another seven years.
31When the LORD saw that Leah *was* unloved, He opened her womb; but Rachel *was*
barren. 32So Leah conceived and bore a son,
and she called his name Reuben; for she said,
"The LORD has surely looked on my affliction.
Now therefore, my husband will love me."
33Then she conceived again and bore a son,
and said, "Because the LORD has heard that I
am unloved, He has therefore given me this
son also." And she called his name Simeon.
34She conceived again and bore a son, and
said, "Now this time my husband will become
attached to me, because I have borne him
three sons." Therefore his name was called
Levi. 35And she conceived again and bore a
son, and said, "Now I will praise the LORD."

Therefore she called his name Judah. Then she stopped bearing.

30 Now when Rachel saw that she bore Jacob no children, Rachel envied her sister, and said to Jacob, "Give me children, or else I die!"

2And Jacob's anger was aroused against Rachel, and he said, "*Am* I in the place of God, who has withheld from you the fruit of the womb?"

30:2 *Am* I in the place of God...? Although spoken in a moment of frustration with Rachel's pleading for children and the envy with which it was expressed, Jacob's words do indicate an understanding that ultimately God opened and closed the womb.

3So she said, "Here is my maid Bilhah; go in to her, and she will bear *a child* on my knees, that I also may have children by her." 4Then she gave him Bilhah her maid as wife, and Jacob went in to her. 5And Bilhah conceived and bore Jacob a son. 6Then Rachel said, "God has judged my case; and He has also heard my voice and given me a son." Therefore she called his name Dan. 7And Rachel's maid Bilhah conceived again and bore Jacob a second son. 8Then Rachel said, "With great wrestlings I have wrestled with my sister, *and* indeed I have prevailed." So she called his name Naphtali.

9When Leah saw that she had stopped bearing, she took Zilpah her maid and gave her to Jacob as wife. 10And Leah's maid Zilpah bore Jacob a son. 11Then Leah said, "A troop comes!" So she called his name Gad. 12And Leah's maid Zilpah bore Jacob a second son. 13Then Leah said, "I am happy, for the daughters will call me blessed." So she called his name Asher.

14Now Reuben went in the days of wheat harvest and found mandrakes in the field, and brought them to his mother Leah. Then Rachel said to Leah, "Please give me *some* of your son's mandrakes."

15But she said to her, "*Is it* a small matter that you have taken away my husband? Would you take away my son's mandrakes also?"

And Rachel said, "Therefore he will lie with you tonight for your son's mandrakes."

16When Jacob came out of the field in the evening, Leah went out to meet him and said, "You must come in to me, for I have surely hired you with my son's mandrakes." And he lay with her that night.

17And God listened to Leah, and she conceived and bore Jacob a fifth son. 18Leah said, "God has given me my wages, because I have given my maid to my husband." So she called his name Issachar. 19Then Leah conceived again and bore Jacob a sixth son. 20And Leah said, "God has endowed me *with* a good endowment; now my husband will dwell with me, because I have borne him six sons." So she called his name Zebulun. 21Afterward she bore a daughter, and called her name Dinah.

22Then God remembered Rachel, and God listened to her and opened her womb. 23And she conceived and bore a son, and said, "God has taken away my reproach." 24So she called his name Joseph, and said, "The LORD shall add to me another son."

25And it came to pass, when Rachel had borne Joseph, that Jacob said to Laban, "Send me away, that I may go to my own place and to my country. 26Give *me* my wives and my children for whom I have served you, and let me go; for you know my service which I have done for you."

27And Laban said to him, "Please *stay,* if I have found favor in your eyes, *for* I have learned by experience that the LORD has blessed me for your sake." 28Then he said, "Name me your wages, and I will give *it.*"

29So *Jacob* said to him, "You know how I have served you and how your livestock has been with me. 30For what you had before I *came was* little, and it has increased to a great amount; the LORD has blessed you since my coming. And now, when shall I also provide for my own house?"

31So he said, "What shall I give you?"

And Jacob said, "You shall not give me anything. If you will do this thing for me, I will again feed and keep your flocks: 32Let me pass through all your flock today, removing from there all the speckled and spotted sheep, and all the brown ones among the lambs, and the spotted and speckled among the goats; and *these* shall be my wages. 33So my righteousness will answer for me in time to come, when the subject of my wages comes before you: every one that *is* not speckled and spotted among the goats, and brown among the lambs, will be considered stolen, if *it is* with me."

34And Laban said, "Oh, that it were according to your word!" 35So he removed that day the male goats that were speckled and spotted, all the female goats that were speckled and spotted, every one that had *some* white in it, and all the brown ones among the lambs, and gave *them* into the hand of his sons.

36 Then he put three days' journey between
himself and Jacob, and Jacob fed the rest of
Laban's flocks.
37 Now Jacob took for himself rods of green
poplar and of the almond and chestnut trees,
peeled white strips in them, and exposed the
white which *was* in the rods. 38 And the rods
which he had peeled, he set before the flocks
in the gutters, in the watering troughs where
the flocks came to drink, so that they should
conceive when they came to drink. 39 So the
flocks conceived before the rods, and the
flocks brought forth streaked, speckled, and
spotted. 40 Then Jacob separated the lambs,
and made the flocks face toward the streaked
and all the brown in the flock of Laban; but he
put his own flocks by themselves and did not
put them with Laban's flock.
41 And it came to pass, whenever the stronger
livestock conceived, that Jacob placed the
rods before the eyes of the livestock in the
gutters, that they might conceive among the
rods. 42 But when the flocks were feeble, he did
not put *them* in; so the feebler were Laban's
and the stronger Jacob's. 43 Thus the man became exceedingly prosperous, and had large
flocks, female and male servants, and camels
and donkeys.

Psalm 8:1–5

To the Chief Musician.
On the instrument of Gath.
A Psalm of David.

O LORD, our Lord,
How excellent *is* Your name
in all the earth,
Who have set Your glory above the
heavens!

2 Out of the mouth of babes and nursing
infants
You have ordained strength,
Because of Your enemies,
That You may silence the enemy and
the avenger.

3 When I consider Your heavens, the
work of Your fingers,
The moon and the stars, which
You have ordained,
4 What is man that You are mindful of
him,
And the son of man that You
visit him?
5 For You have made him a little lower
than the angels,
And You have crowned him with glory
and honor.

8:3 Your heavens, the work of Your fingers. The heavens are created by God (Pss. 33:6,9; 102:25; 136:5). The anthropomorphism "Your fingers" miniaturizes the magnitude of the universe in the presence of the Creator.

8:4 What is man...? If the whole universe is diminutive in the sight of the Divine Creator, how much less is the significance of mankind! Even the word for "man" used in v. 4 alludes to his weakness (see Pss. 9:19,20; 90:3a; 103:15, etc.). **and the son of man.** This phrase also looks upon man as insignificant and transitory (e.g., Ps. 90:3b). Yet, the Aramaic counterpart of this phrase is found in Daniel 7:13, which has profound messianic overtones (see also Jesus' favorite self-designation in the New Testament, Son of Man).

Proverbs 3:13–18

13 Happy *is* the man *who* finds wisdom,
And the man *who* gains
understanding;
14 For her proceeds *are* better than the
profits of silver,
And her gain than fine gold.
15 She *is* more precious than rubies,
And all the things you may
desire cannot compare
with her.
16 Length of days *is* in her right hand,
In her left hand riches and honor.
17 Her ways *are* ways of
pleasantness,
And all her paths *are* peace.
18 She *is* a tree of life to those who take
hold of her,
And happy *are all* who
retain her.

Matthew 10:21–42

21 "Now brother will deliver up brother to
death, and a father *his* child; and children
will rise up against parents and cause them
to be put to death. 22 And you will be hated by
all for My name's sake. But he who endures
to the end will be saved. 23 When they persecute you in this city, flee to another. For
assuredly, I say to you, you will not have
gone through the cities of Israel before the
Son of Man comes.
24 "A disciple is not above *his* teacher, nor a
servant above his master. 25 It is enough for a
disciple that he be like his teacher, and a servant like his master. If they have called the

master of the house Beelzebub, how much
more *will they call* those of his household!
[26]Therefore do not fear them. For there is
nothing covered that will not be revealed, and
hidden that will not be known.

[27]"Whatever I tell you in the dark, speak in
the light; and what you hear in the ear, preach
on the housetops. [28]And do not fear those who
kill the body but cannot kill the soul. But
rather fear Him who is able to destroy both
soul and body in hell. [29]Are not two sparrows
sold for a copper coin? And not one of them
falls to the ground apart from your Father's
will. [30]But the very hairs of your head are all
numbered. [31]Do not fear therefore; you are of
more value than many sparrows.

[32]"Therefore whoever confesses Me before
men, him I will also confess before My Father
who is in heaven. [33]But whoever denies Me
before men, him I will also deny before My
Father who is in heaven.

[34]"Do not think that I came to bring peace on
earth. I did not come to bring peace but a
sword. [35]For I have come to '*set a man against
his father, a daughter against her mother, and
a daughter-in-law against her mother-in-law*';
[36]and '*a man's enemies will be those of his own
household.*' [37]He who loves father or mother
more than Me is not worthy of Me. And he
who loves son or daughter more than Me is
not worthy of Me. [38]And he who does not take
his cross and follow after Me is not worthy of
Me. [39]He who finds his life will lose it, and he
who loses his life for My sake will find it.

[40]"He who receives you receives Me, and he
who receives Me receives Him who sent Me.
[41]He who receives a prophet in the name of a
prophet shall receive a prophet's reward. And
he who receives a righteous man in the name
of a righteous man shall receive a righteous
man's reward. [42]And whoever gives one of
these little ones only a cup of cold *water* in the
name of a disciple, assuredly, I say to you, he
shall by no means lose his reward."

DAY 15: Should I expect to be persecuted for my faith?

In Matthew 10:32, Jesus makes the amazing promise that the person who acknowledges Him as Lord in life or in death, if necessary, is the one whom He will acknowledge personally before God as His own (Matt. 13:20; 2 Tim. 2:10–13). Conversely, He describes the soul-damning denial of Christ of those who through fear, shame, neglect, or love of the world reject all evidence and revelation and decline to confess Christ as Savior and King.

Though the ultimate end of the gospel is peace with God (John 14:27; Rom. 8:6), the immediate result of the gospel is frequently conflict (v. 34). Conversion to Christ can result in strained family relationships (vv. 35,36), persecution, and even martyrdom. Following Christ presupposes a willingness to endure such hardships (vv. 32,33,37–39). Though He is called "Prince of Peace" (Is. 9:6), Christ will have no one deluded into thinking that He calls believers to a life devoid of all conflict.

When Jesus adds that a disciple must "take his cross" (v. 38), it is His first mention of the word "cross" to His disciples. To them it would have evoked a picture of a violent, degrading death. He was demanding total commitment from them—even unto physical death—and making this call to full surrender a part of the message they were to proclaim to others. For those who come to Christ with self-renouncing faith, there will be true and eternal life (v. 39).

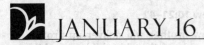

JANUARY 16

Genesis 31:1–32:32

31 Now *Jacob* heard the words of Laban's
sons, saying, "Jacob has taken away all
that was our father's, and from what was our
father's he has acquired all this wealth." [2]And
Jacob saw the countenance of Laban, and
indeed it *was* not *favorable* toward him as
before. [3]Then the LORD said to Jacob, "Return
to the land of your fathers and to your family,
and I will be with you."

[4]So Jacob sent and called Rachel and Leah
to the field, to his flock, [5]and said to them, "I
see your father's countenance, that it *is* not *favorable* toward me as before; but the God of my
father has been with me. [6]And you know that
with all my might I have served your father.
[7]Yet your father has deceived me and changed
my wages ten times, but God did not allow
him to hurt me. [8]If he said thus: 'The speckled
shall be your wages,' then all the flocks bore
speckled. And if he said thus: 'The streaked
shall be your wages,' then all the flocks bore
streaked. [9]So God has taken away the livestock of your father and given *them* to me.

[10]"And it happened, at the time when the
flocks conceived, that I lifted my eyes and saw

in a dream, and behold, the rams which
leaped upon the flocks *were* streaked, speckled, and gray-spotted. [11]Then the Angel of God
spoke to me in a dream, saying, 'Jacob.' And I
said, 'Here I am.' [12]And He said, 'Lift your eyes
now and see, all the rams which leap on the
flocks *are* streaked, speckled, and gray-spotted; for I have seen all that Laban is doing to
you. [13]I *am* the God of Bethel, where you
anointed the pillar *and* where you made a vow
to Me. Now arise, get out of this land, and
return to the land of your family.' "

31:19 household idols. Literally, teraphim (see 2 Kin. 23:24; Ezek. 21:21). These images or figurines of varying sizes, usually of nude goddesses with accentuated sexual features, either signaled special protection for, inheritance rights for, or guaranteed fertility for the bearer. Or, perhaps possession by Rachel would call for Jacob to be recognized as head of the household at Laban's death.

[14]Then Rachel and Leah answered and said
to him, "Is there still any portion or inheritance for us in our father's house? [15]Are we not
considered strangers by him? For he has sold
us, and also completely consumed our money.
[16]For all these riches which God has taken
from our father are *really* ours and our children's; now then, whatever God has said to
you, do it."

[17]Then Jacob rose and set his sons and his
wives on camels. [18]And he carried away all his
livestock and all his possessions which he had
gained, his acquired livestock which he had
gained in Padan Aram, to go to his father Isaac
in the land of Canaan. [19]Now Laban had gone
to shear his sheep, and Rachel had stolen the
household idols that were her father's. [20]And
Jacob stole away, unknown to Laban the Syrian, in that he did not tell him that he intended
to flee. [21]So he fled with all that he had. He
arose and crossed the river, and headed
toward the mountains of Gilead.

[22]And Laban was told on the third day that
Jacob had fled. [23]Then he took his brethren
with him and pursued him for seven days'
journey, and he overtook him in the mountains of Gilead. [24]But God had come to Laban
the Syrian in a dream by night, and said to
him, "Be careful that you speak to Jacob neither good nor bad."

[25]So Laban overtook Jacob. Now Jacob had
pitched his tent in the mountains, and Laban
with his brethren pitched in the mountains of
Gilead.

[26]And Laban said to Jacob: "What have you
done, that you have stolen away unknown to
me, and carried away my daughters like captives *taken* with the sword? [27]Why did you flee
away secretly, and steal away from me, and
not tell me; for I might have sent you away
with joy and songs, with timbrel and harp?
[28]And you did not allow me to kiss my sons and
my daughters. Now you have done foolishly in
so doing. [29]It is in my power to do you harm,
but the God of your father spoke to me last
night, saying, 'Be careful that you speak to
Jacob neither good nor bad.' [30]And now you
have surely gone because you greatly long for
your father's house, *but* why did you steal my
gods?"

[31]Then Jacob answered and said to Laban,
"Because I was afraid, for I said, 'Perhaps you
would take your daughters from me by force.'
[32]With whomever you find your gods, do not
let him live. In the presence of our brethren,
identify what I have of yours and take *it* with
you." For Jacob did not know that Rachel had
stolen them.

[33]And Laban went into Jacob's tent, into
Leah's tent, and into the two maids' tents, but
he did not find *them*. Then he went out of
Leah's tent and entered Rachel's tent. [34]Now
Rachel had taken the household idols, put
them in the camel's saddle, and sat on them.
And Laban searched all about the tent but did
not find *them*. [35]And she said to her father, "Let
it not displease my lord that I cannot rise
before you, for the manner of women *is* with
me." And he searched but did not find the
household idols.

[36]Then Jacob was angry and rebuked Laban,
and Jacob answered and said to Laban: "What
is my trespass? What *is* my sin, that you have
so hotly pursued me? [37]Although you have
searched all my things, what part of your
household things have you found? Set *it* here
before my brethren and your brethren, that
they may judge between us both! [38]These
twenty years I *have been* with you; your ewes
and your female goats have not miscarried
their young, and I have not eaten the rams of
your flock. [39]That which was torn *by beasts* I
did not bring to you; I bore the loss of it. You
required it from my hand, *whether* stolen by
day or stolen by night. [40]*There* I was! In the day
the drought consumed me, and the frost by
night, and my sleep departed from my eyes.
[41]Thus I have been in your house twenty years;
I served you fourteen years for your two

daughters, and six years for your flock, and
you have changed my wages ten times. 42Un-
less the God of my father, the God of Abraham
and the Fear of Isaac, had been with me, surely now you would have sent me away empty-
handed. God has seen my affliction and the
labor of my hands, and rebuked *you* last night."

43And Laban answered and said to Jacob,
"*These* daughters *are* my daughters, and *these*
children *are* my children, and *this* flock *is* my
flock; all that you see *is* mine. But what can I
do this day to these my daughters or to their
children whom they have borne? 44Now therefore, come, let us make a covenant, you and I,
and let it be a witness between you and me."

45So Jacob took a stone and set it up *as* a pillar. 46Then Jacob said to his brethren, "Gather
stones." And they took stones and made a
heap, and they ate there on the heap. 47Laban
called it Jegar Sahadutha, but Jacob called it
Galeed. 48And Laban said, "This heap *is* a witness between you and me this day." Therefore
its name was called Galeed, 49also Mizpah,
because he said, "May the LORD watch
between you and me when we are absent one
from another. 50If you afflict my daughters, or
if you take *other* wives besides my daughters,
although no man *is* with us—see, God *is* witness between you and me!"

51Then Laban said to Jacob, "Here is this
heap and here is *this* pillar, which I have
placed between you and me. 52This heap *is* a
witness, and *this* pillar *is* a witness, that I will
not pass beyond this heap to you, and you will
not pass beyond this heap and this pillar to
me, for harm. 53The God of Abraham, the God
of Nahor, and the God of their father judge
between us." And Jacob swore by the Fear of
his father Isaac. 54Then Jacob offered a sacrifice on the mountain, and called his brethren
to eat bread. And they ate bread and stayed all
night on the mountain. 55And early in the
morning Laban arose, and kissed his sons and
daughters and blessed them. Then Laban
departed and returned to his place.

32 So Jacob went on his way, and the
angels of God met him. 2When Jacob
saw them, he said, "This *is* God's camp." And
he called the name of that place Mahanaim.

3Then Jacob sent messengers before him to
Esau his brother in the land of Seir, the country of Edom. 4And he commanded them, saying, "Speak thus to my lord Esau, 'Thus your
servant Jacob says: "I have dwelt with Laban
and stayed there until now. 5I have oxen, donkeys, flocks, and male and female servants;
and I have sent to tell my lord, that I may find
favor in your sight." ' "

6Then the messengers returned to Jacob,
saying, "We came to your brother Esau, and
he also is coming to meet you, and four hundred men *are* with him." 7So Jacob was greatly
afraid and distressed; and he divided the people
that *were* with him, and the flocks and herds
and camels, into two companies. 8And he said,
"If Esau comes to the one company and attacks it, then the other company which is left
will escape."

9Then Jacob said, "O God of my father Abraham and God of my father Isaac, the LORD who
said to me, 'Return to your country and to
your family, and I will deal well with you': 10I
am not worthy of the least of all the mercies
and of all the truth which You have shown
Your servant; for I crossed over this Jordan
with my staff, and now I have become two
companies. 11Deliver me, I pray, from the hand
of my brother, from the hand of Esau; for I fear
him, lest he come and attack me *and* the
mother with the children. 12For You said, 'I will
surely treat you well, and make your descendants as the sand of the sea, which cannot be
numbered for multitude.' "

13So he lodged there that same night, and
took what came to his hand as a present for
Esau his brother: 14two hundred female goats
and twenty male goats, two hundred ewes and
twenty rams, 15thirty milk camels with their
colts, forty cows and ten bulls, twenty female
donkeys and ten foals. 16Then he delivered
them to the hand of his servants, every drove
by itself, and said to his servants, "Pass over
before me, and put some distance between
successive droves." 17And he commanded the
first one, saying, "When Esau my brother
meets you and asks you, saying, 'To whom do
you belong, and where are you going? Whose
are these in front of you?' 18then you shall say,
'They *are* your servant Jacob's. It *is* a present
sent to my lord Esau; and behold, he also *is*
behind us.' " 19So he commanded the second,
the third, and all who followed the droves, saying, "In this manner you shall speak to Esau
when you find him; 20and also say, 'Behold,
your servant Jacob *is* behind us.' " For he said,
"I will appease him with the present that goes
before me, and afterward I will see his face;
perhaps he will accept me." 21So the present
went on over before him, but he himself
lodged that night in the camp.

22And he arose that night and took his two
wives, his two female servants, and his eleven
sons, and crossed over the ford of Jabbok.
23He took them, sent them over the brook, and
sent over what he had. 24Then Jacob was left
alone; and a Man wrestled with him until the

breaking of day. 25 Now when He saw that He
did not prevail against him, He touched the
socket of his hip; and the socket of Jacob's hip
was out of joint as He wrestled with him. 26 And
He said, "Let Me go, for the day breaks."
But he said, "I will not let You go unless You
bless me!"
27 So He said to him, "What *is* your name?"
He said, "Jacob."
28 And He said, "Your name shall no longer be
called Jacob, but Israel; for you have struggled
with God and with men, and have prevailed."
29 Then Jacob asked, saying, "Tell *me* Your
name, I pray."
And He said, "Why *is* it *that* you ask about
My name?" And He blessed him there.
30 So Jacob called the name of the place
Peniel: "For I have seen God face to face, and
my life is preserved." 31 Just as he crossed over
Penuel the sun rose on him, and he limped on
his hip. 32 Therefore to this day the children of
Israel do not eat the muscle that shrank,
which *is* on the hip socket, because He
touched the socket of Jacob's hip in the muscle that shrank.

Psalm 8:6–9

6 You have made him to have dominion
over the works of Your hands;
You have put all *things* under his feet,
7 All sheep and oxen—
Even the beasts of the field,
8 The birds of the air,
And the fish of the sea
That pass through the paths
of the seas.
9 O LORD, our Lord,
How excellent *is* Your name in all the
earth!

Proverbs 3:19–20

19 The LORD by wisdom founded the
earth;
By understanding He established
the heavens;
20 By His knowledge the depths were
broken up,
And clouds drop down the dew.

Matthew 11:1–30

11 Now it came to pass, when Jesus finished
commanding His twelve disciples, that He
departed from there to teach and to preach in
their cities.
2 And when John had heard in prison about
the works of Christ, he sent two of his disciples
3 and said to Him, "Are You the Coming One,
or do we look for another?"

11:12 the kingdom of heaven suffers violence. From the time he began his preaching ministry, John the Baptist evoked a strong reaction. Having been imprisoned already, John ultimately fell victim to Herod's savagery. But the kingdom can never be subdued or opposed by human violence. Notice that where Matthew says, "the violent take it by force," Luke has, "everyone is pressing into it" (Luke 16:16). So the sense of this verse may be rendered this way: "The kingdom presses ahead relentlessly, and only the relentless press their way into it." Thus again Christ is magnifying the difficulty of entering the kingdom.

4 Jesus answered and said to them, "Go and
tell John the things which you hear and see:
5 *The* blind see and *the* lame walk; *the* lepers are
cleansed and *the* deaf hear; *the* dead are raised
up and *the* poor have the gospel preached to
them. 6 And blessed is he who is not offended
because of Me."
7 As they departed, Jesus began to say to the
multitudes concerning John: "What did you
go out into the wilderness to see? A reed shak-
en by the wind? 8 But what did you go out to
see? A man clothed in soft garments? Indeed,
those who wear soft *clothing* are in kings'
houses. 9 But what did you go out to see? A
prophet? Yes, I say to you, and more than a
prophet. 10 For this is *he* of whom it is written:

'Behold, I send My messenger before
Your face,
Who will prepare Your way
before You.'

11 "Assuredly, I say to you, among those born
of women there has not risen one greater than
John the Baptist; but he who is least in the
kingdom of heaven is greater than he. 12 And
from the days of John the Baptist until now the
kingdom of heaven suffers violence, and the
violent take it by force. 13 For all the prophets
and the law prophesied until John. 14 And if you
are willing to receive *it,* he is Elijah who is to
come. 15 He who has ears to hear, let him hear!
16 "But to what shall I liken this generation?
It is like children sitting in the marketplaces
and calling to their companions, 17 and saying:

'We played the flute for you,
And you did not dance;
We mourned to you,
And you did not lament.'

[18]For John came neither eating nor drinking,
and they say, 'He has a demon.' [19]The Son of
Man came eating and drinking, and they say,
'Look, a glutton and a winebibber, a friend of tax
collectors and sinners!' But wisdom is justified
by her children."
[20]Then He began to rebuke the cities in
which most of His mighty works had been
done, because they did not repent: [21]"Woe to
you, Chorazin! Woe to you, Bethsaida! For if
the mighty works which were done in you had
been done in Tyre and Sidon, they would have
repented long ago in sackcloth and ashes.
[22]But I say to you, it will be more tolerable for
Tyre and Sidon in the day of judgment than
for you. [23]And you, Capernaum, who are exalted to heaven, will be brought down to Hades;
for if the mighty works which were done in
you had been done in Sodom, it would have
remained until this day. [24]But I say to you that
it shall be more tolerable for the land of
Sodom in the day of judgment than for you."
[25]At that time Jesus answered and said, "I
thank You, Father, Lord of heaven and earth,
that You have hidden these things from *the*
wise and prudent and have revealed them to
babes. [26]Even so, Father, for so it seemed
good in Your sight. [27]All things have been
delivered to Me by My Father, and no one
knows the Son except the Father. Nor does
anyone know the Father except the Son, and
the one to whom the Son wills to reveal *Him.*
[28]Come to Me, all *you* who labor and are
heavy laden, and I will give you rest. [29]Take
My yoke upon you and learn from Me, for I
am gentle and lowly in heart, and you will
find rest for your souls. [30]For My yoke *is* easy
and My burden is light."

11:28–30 Come to Me, all *you* who labor and are heavy laden. There is an echo of the first beatitude (5:3) in this passage. Note that this is an open invitation to all who hear—but phrased in such a way that the only ones who will respond to the invitation are those who are burdened by their own spiritual bankruptcy and the weight of trying to save themselves by keeping the law. The stubbornness of humanity's sinful rebellion is such that without a sovereignly bestowed spiritual awakening, all sinners refuse to acknowledge the depth of their spiritual poverty. That is why, as Jesus says in v. 27, our salvation is the sovereign work of God. But the truth of divine election in v. 27 is not incompatible with the free offer to all in vv. 28–30.

DAY 16: List the false gods in the Old Testament.

1. Rachel's household gods (Gen. 31:19)
2. The golden calf at Sinai (Ex. 32)
3. Nanna, the moon god of Ur, worshiped by Abraham before his salvation (Josh. 24:2)
4. Asherah, or Ashtaroth, the chief goddess of Tyre, referred to as the lady of the sea (Judg. 6:24–32)
5. Dagon, the chief Philistine agriculture and sea god and father of Baal (Judg. 16:23–30)
6. Ashtoreth, a Canaanite goddess, another consort of Baal (1 Sam. 7:3,4)
7. Molech, the god of the Ammonites and the most horrible idol in the Scriptures (1 Kin. 11:7)
8. The two golden images made by King Jeroboam, set up at the shrines of Dan and Bethel (1 Kin. 12:28–31)
9. Baal, the chief deity of Canaan (1 Kin. 18:17–40; 2 Kin. 10:28; 11:18)
10. Rimmon, the Syrian god of Naaman the leper (2 Kin. 5:15–19)
11. Nishroch, the Assyrian god of Sennacherib (2 Kin. 19:37)
12. Nebo, the Babylonian god of wisdom and literature (Is. 46:1)
13. Merodach, also called Marduk, the chief god of the Babylonian pantheon (Jer. 50:2)
14. Tammuz, the husband and brother of Ishtar (Asherah), goddess of fertility (Ezek. 8:14)
15. The golden image in the plain of Dura (Dan. 2)

JANUARY 17

Genesis 33:1–34:31

33 Now Jacob lifted his eyes and looked,
and there, Esau was coming, and with
him were four hundred men. So he divided
the children among Leah, Rachel, and the two
maidservants. [2]And he put the maidservants
and their children in front, Leah and her children behind, and Rachel and Joseph last.
[3]Then he crossed over before them and bowed
himself to the ground seven times, until he
came near to his brother.
[4]But Esau ran to meet him, and embraced
him, and fell on his neck and kissed him, and
they wept. [5]And he lifted his eyes and saw the

33:3,4 Fearfully and deferentially, Jacob approached his brother as an inferior would a highly honored patron, while gladly and eagerly, Esau ran to greet his brother without restraint of emotion. "They wept" because, after 21 years of troubling separation, old memories were wiped away and murderous threats belonged to the distant past; hearts had been changed, brothers reconciled! See v. 10.

women and children, and said, "Who *are* these with you?"

So he said, "The children whom God has graciously given your servant." [6]Then the maidservants came near, they and their children, and bowed down. [7]And Leah also came near with her children, and they bowed down. Afterward Joseph and Rachel came near, and they bowed down.

[8]Then Esau said, "What *do* you *mean by* all this company which I met?"

And he said, "*These are* to find favor in the sight of my lord."

[9]But Esau said, "I have enough, my brother; keep what you have for yourself."

[10]And Jacob said, "No, please, if I have now found favor in your sight, then receive my present from my hand, inasmuch as I have seen your face as though I had seen the face of God, and you were pleased with me. [11]Please, take my blessing that is brought to you, because God has dealt graciously with me, and because I have enough." So he urged him, and he took *it.*

[12]Then Esau said, "Let us take our journey; let us go, and I will go before you."

[13]But Jacob said to him, "My lord knows that the children *are* weak, and the flocks and herds which are nursing *are* with me. And if the men should drive them hard one day, all the flock will die. [14]Please let my lord go on ahead before his servant. I will lead on slowly at a pace which the livestock that go before me, and the children, are able to endure, until I come to my lord in Seir."

[15]And Esau said, "Now let me leave with you *some* of the people who *are* with me."

But he said, "What need is there? Let me find favor in the sight of my lord." [16]So Esau returned that day on his way to Seir. [17]And Jacob journeyed to Succoth, built himself a house, and made booths for his livestock. Therefore the name of the place is called Succoth.

[18]Then Jacob came safely to the city of Shechem, which *is* in the land of Canaan, when he came from Padan Aram; and he pitched his tent before the city. [19]And he bought the parcel of land, where he had pitched his tent, from the children of Hamor, Shechem's father, for one hundred pieces of money. [20]Then he erected an altar there and called it El Elohe Israel.

34 Now Dinah the daughter of Leah, whom she had borne to Jacob, went out to see the daughters of the land. [2]And when Shechem the son of Hamor the Hivite, prince of the country, saw her, he took her and lay with her, and violated her. [3]His soul was strongly attracted to Dinah the daughter of Jacob, and he loved the young woman and spoke kindly to the young woman. [4]So Shechem spoke to his father Hamor, saying, "Get me this young woman as a wife."

[5]And Jacob heard that he had defiled Dinah his daughter. Now his sons were with his livestock in the field; so Jacob held his peace until they came. [6]Then Hamor the father of Shechem went out to Jacob to speak with him. [7]And the sons of Jacob came in from the field when they heard *it;* and the men were grieved and very angry, because he had done a disgraceful thing in Israel by lying with Jacob's daughter, a thing which ought not to be done. [8]But Hamor spoke with them, saying, "The soul of my son Shechem longs for your daughter. Please give her to him as a wife. [9]And make marriages with us; give your daughters to us, and take our daughters to yourselves. [10]So you shall dwell with us, and the land shall be before you. Dwell and trade in it, and acquire possessions for yourselves in it."

[11]Then Shechem said to her father and her brothers, "Let me find favor in your eyes, and whatever you say to me I will give. [12]Ask me ever so much dowry and gift, and I will give according to what you say to me; but give me the young woman as a wife."

[13]But the sons of Jacob answered Shechem and Hamor his father, and spoke deceitfully, because he had defiled Dinah their sister. [14]And they said to them, "We cannot do this thing, to give our sister to one who is uncircumcised, for that *would be* a reproach to us. [15]But on this *condition* we will consent to you: If you will become as we *are,* if every male of you is circumcised, [16]then we will give our daughters to you, and we will take your daughters to us; and we will dwell with you, and we will become one people. [17]But if you will not heed us and be circumcised, then we will take our daughter and be gone."

[18]And their words pleased Hamor and

Shechem, Hamor's son. [19]So the young man
did not delay to do the thing, because he
delighted in Jacob's daughter. He *was* more
honorable than all the household of his father.
[20]And Hamor and Shechem his son came to
the gate of their city, and spoke with the men
of their city, saying: [21]"These men *are* at peace
with us. Therefore let them dwell in the land
and trade in it. For indeed the land *is* large
enough for them. Let us take their daughters
to us as wives, and let us give them our daughters. [22]Only on this *condition* will the men consent to dwell with us, to be one people: if every
male among us is circumcised as they *are* circumcised. [23]*Will* not their livestock, their property, and every animal of theirs *be* ours? Only
let us consent to them, and they will dwell
with us." [24]And all who went out of the gate of
his city heeded Hamor and Shechem his son;
every male was circumcised, all who went out
of the gate of his city.
[25]Now it came to pass on the third day, when
they were in pain, that two of the sons of
Jacob, Simeon and Levi, Dinah's brothers,
each took his sword and came boldly upon the
city and killed all the males. [26]And they killed
Hamor and Shechem his son with the edge of
the sword, and took Dinah from Shechem's
house, and went out. [27]The sons of Jacob came
upon the slain, and plundered the city,
because their sister had been defiled. [28]They
took their sheep, their oxen, and their donkeys, what *was* in the city and what *was* in the
field, [29]and all their wealth. All their little ones
and their wives they took captive; and they
plundered even all that *was* in the houses.
[30]Then Jacob said to Simeon and Levi, "You
have troubled me by making me obnoxious
among the inhabitants of the land, among the
Canaanites and the Perizzites; and since I *am*
few in number, they will gather themselves
together against me and kill me. I shall be
destroyed, my household and I."
[31]But they said, "Should he treat our sister
like a harlot?"

Psalm 9:1–5

To the Chief Musician. To *the tune of* "Death of the Son." A Psalm of David.

I will praise *You,* O LORD, with
my whole heart;
I will tell of all Your marvelous works.
2 I will be glad and rejoice in You;
I will sing praise to Your name,
O Most High.

3 When my enemies turn back,
They shall fall and perish at
Your presence.
4 For You have maintained my right and
my cause;
You sat on the throne judging in
righteousness.
5 You have rebuked the nations,
You have destroyed the wicked;
You have blotted out their name
forever and ever.

Proverbs 3:21–26

21 My son, let them not depart from your
eyes—
Keep sound wisdom and
discretion;
22 So they will be life to your soul
And grace to your neck.

3:22 life to your soul. The association of wisdom with the inner spiritual life unfolds throughout the book (see 4:10,22; 7:2; 8:35; 9:11; 10:11,16,17; 11:19,30; 12:28; 13:14; 14:27; 15:4,24; 16:22; 19:23; 21:21; 22:4). **grace to your neck.** The wisdom of God will adorn one's life for all to see its beauty (see 1:9).

23 Then you will walk safely in your way,
And your foot will not stumble.
24 When you lie down, you will not be
afraid;
Yes, you will lie down and your sleep
will be sweet.
25 Do not be afraid of sudden
terror,
Nor of trouble from the
wicked when it comes;
26 For the LORD will be your confidence,
And will keep your foot from being
caught.

Matthew 12:1–21

12 At that time Jesus went through the
grainfields on the Sabbath. And His disciples were hungry, and began to pluck heads
of grain and to eat. [2]And when the Pharisees
saw *it,* they said to Him, "Look, Your disciples
are doing what is not lawful to do on the
Sabbath!"
[3]But He said to them, "Have you not read
what David did when he was hungry, he and
those who were with him: [4]how he entered the
house of God and ate the showbread which
was not lawful for him to eat, nor for those
who were with him, but only for the priests?

12:8 the Son of Man is Lord even of the Sabbath. Christ has the prerogative to rule over not only their man-made sabbatarian rules, but also over the Sabbath itself—which was designed for worshiping God. Again, this was an inescapable claim of Deity—and as such it prompted the Pharisees' violent outrage (v. 14).

[5]Or have you not read in the law that on the
Sabbath the priests in the temple profane the
Sabbath, and are blameless? [6]Yet I say to you
that in this place there is *One* greater than the
temple. [7]But if you had known what *this*
means, *'I desire mercy and not sacrifice,'* you
would not have condemned the guiltless. [8]For
the Son of Man is Lord even of the Sabbath."
[9]Now when He had departed from there, He
went into their synagogue. [10]And behold, there
was a man who had a withered hand. And they
asked Him, saying, "Is it lawful to heal on the
Sabbath?"—that they might accuse Him.
[11]Then He said to them, "What man is there
among you who has one sheep, and if it falls
into a pit on the Sabbath, will not lay hold of it
and lift *it* out? [12]Of how much more value then
is a man than a sheep? Therefore it is lawful to
do good on the Sabbath." [13]Then He said to the
man, "Stretch out your hand." And he stretched
it out, and it was restored as whole as the
other. [14]Then the Pharisees went out and plotted against Him, how they might destroy Him.

12:15 healed them all. In all of Old Testament history there was never a time or a person who exhibited such extensive healing power. Physical healings were very rare in the Old Testament. Christ chose to display His deity by healing, raising the dead, and liberating people from demons. That not only showed the Messiah's power over the physical and spiritual realms, but also demonstrated the compassion of God toward those affected by sin.

[15]But when Jesus knew *it,* He withdrew
from there. And great multitudes followed
Him, and He healed them all. [16]Yet He warned
them not to make Him known, [17]that it might
be fulfilled which was spoken by Isaiah the
prophet, saying:

18 *"Behold! My Servant whom*
I have chosen,
My Beloved in whom My soul is well
pleased!
I will put My Spirit upon Him,
And He will declare justice
to the Gentiles.
19 *He will not quarrel nor cry out,*
Nor will anyone hear His voice in the
streets.
20 *A bruised reed He will not break,*
And smoking flax He will not quench,
Till He sends forth justice to victory;
21 *And in His name Gentiles*
will trust."

DAY 17: How are we to interpret the Bible when the ancient customs were so different from our own?

Three tools help us in the task of interpreting events that happened so long ago and so far away: 1) The best interpretive tool in understanding a Bible passage is its immediate context. Surrounding verses will often yield clues to the observant about foreign or unusual details in a particular account. 2) One part of the Bible often explains, expands, and comments on another part. An ever-growing familiarity with all of Scripture will equip a student with significant insight into the culture of those who lived the history. 3) Some insight can be gained from ancient sources outside of Scripture, but these only supplement our primary sources in the Bible itself.

Once we are at home in the exotic and unfamiliar contexts of Scripture, we meet people in the Bible pages who are very much like us. These are not aliens, but our ancestors across the ages. Their struggles are ours. Their failures are all familiar to us. The God who spoke to them still speaks to us.

JANUARY 18

Genesis 35:1–36:43

35 Then God said to Jacob, "Arise, go up
to Bethel and dwell there; and make an
altar there to God, who appeared to you when
you fled from the face of Esau your brother."
[2]And Jacob said to his household and to all
who *were* with him, "Put away the foreign
gods that *are* among you, purify yourselves,
and change your garments. [3]Then let us arise

35:2–4 Put away the foreign gods. Moving to Bethel necessitated spiritual preparation beyond the level of an exercise in logistics. Possession of idolatrous symbols such as figurines, amulets, or cultic charms (v. 4, "earrings"), including Rachel's troubling teraphim (31:19), was no longer tolerable. Idols buried out of sight, plus bathing and changing to clean clothes, all served to portray both cleansing from defilement by idolatry and consecration of the heart to the Lord. It had been 8 or 10 years since Jacob's return to Canaan and, appropriately, time enough to clean up all traces of idolatry.

35:5 the terror of God. A supernaturally induced fear of Israel rendered the surrounding city-states unwilling and powerless to intervene and made Jacob's fear of their retaliation rather inconsequential (34:30).

---

and go up to Bethel; and I will make an altar there to God, who answered me in the day of my distress and has been with me in the way which I have gone." 4So they gave Jacob all the foreign gods which *were* in their hands, and the earrings which *were* in their ears; and Jacob hid them under the terebinth tree which *was* by Shechem.

5And they journeyed, and the terror of God was upon the cities that *were* all around them, and they did not pursue the sons of Jacob. 6So Jacob came to Luz (that *is,* Bethel), which *is* in the land of Canaan, he and all the people who *were* with him. 7And he built an altar there and called the place El Bethel, because there God appeared to him when he fled from the face of his brother.

8Now Deborah, Rebekah's nurse, died, and she was buried below Bethel under the terebinth tree. So the name of it was called Allon Bachuth.

9Then God appeared to Jacob again, when he came from Padan Aram, and blessed him. 10And God said to him, "Your name *is* Jacob; your name shall not be called Jacob anymore, but Israel shall be your name." So He called his name Israel. 11Also God said to him: "I *am* God Almighty. Be fruitful and multiply; a nation and a company of nations shall proceed from you, and kings shall come from your body. 12The land which I gave Abraham and Isaac I give to you; and to your descendants after you I give this land." 13Then God went up from him in the place where He talked with him. 14So Jacob set up a pillar in the place where He talked with him, a pillar of stone; and he poured a drink offering on it, and he poured oil on it. 15And Jacob called the name of the place where God spoke with him, Bethel.

16Then they journeyed from Bethel. And when there was but a little distance to go to Ephrath, Rachel labored *in childbirth,* and she had hard labor. 17Now it came to pass, when she was in hard labor, that the midwife said to her, "Do not fear; you will have this son also." 18And so it was, as her soul was departing (for she died), that she called his name Ben-Oni; but his father called him Benjamin. 19So Rachel died and was buried on the way to Ephrath (that *is,* Bethlehem). 20And Jacob set a pillar on her grave, which *is* the pillar of Rachel's grave to this day.

21Then Israel journeyed and pitched his tent beyond the tower of Eder. 22And it happened, when Israel dwelt in that land, that Reuben went and lay with Bilhah his father's concubine; and Israel heard *about it.*

Now the sons of Jacob were twelve: 23the sons of Leah *were* Reuben, Jacob's firstborn, and Simeon, Levi, Judah, Issachar, and Zebulun; 24the sons of Rachel *were* Joseph and Benjamin; 25the sons of Bilhah, Rachel's maidservant, *were* Dan and Naphtali; 26and the sons of Zilpah, Leah's maidservant, *were* Gad and Asher. These *were* the sons of Jacob who were born to him in Padan Aram.

27Then Jacob came to his father Isaac at Mamre, or Kirjath Arba (that *is,* Hebron), where Abraham and Isaac had dwelt. 28Now the days of Isaac were one hundred and eighty years. 29So Isaac breathed his last and died, and was gathered to his people, *being* old and full of days. And his sons Esau and Jacob buried him.

36 Now this *is* the genealogy of Esau, who is Edom. 2Esau took his wives from the daughters of Canaan: Adah the daughter of Elon the Hittite; Aholibamah the daughter of Anah, the daughter of Zibeon the Hivite; 3and Basemath, Ishmael's daughter, sister of Nebajoth. 4Now Adah bore Eliphaz to Esau, and Basemath bore Reuel. 5And Aholibamah bore Jeush, Jaalam, and Korah. These *were* the sons of Esau who were born to him in the land of Canaan.

6Then Esau took his wives, his sons, his daughters, and all the persons of his household, his cattle and all his animals, and all his goods which he had gained in the land of Canaan, and went to a country away from the presence of his brother Jacob. 7For their possessions were too great for them to dwell together, and the land where they were strangers could not

support them because of their livestock. 8So
Esau dwelt in Mount Seir. Esau *is* Edom.

9And this *is* the genealogy of Esau the father
of the Edomites in Mount Seir. 10These *were* the
names of Esau's sons: Eliphaz the son of Adah
the wife of Esau, and Reuel the son of Basemath
the wife of Esau. 11And the sons of Eliphaz were
Teman, Omar, Zepho, Gatam, and Kenaz.

12Now Timna was the concubine of Eliphaz,
Esau's son, and she bore Amalek to Eliphaz.
These *were* the sons of Adah, Esau's wife.

13These *were* the sons of Reuel: Nahath,
Zerah, Shammah, and Mizzah. These were
the sons of Basemath, Esau's wife.

14These were the sons of Aholibamah,
Esau's wife, the daughter of Anah, the daugh-
ter of Zibeon. And she bore to Esau: Jeush,
Jaalam, and Korah.

15These *were* the chiefs of the sons of Esau.
The sons of Eliphaz, the firstborn *son* of Esau,
were Chief Teman, Chief Omar, Chief Zepho,
Chief Kenaz, 16Chief Korah, Chief Gatam, *and*
Chief Amalek. These *were* the chiefs of
Eliphaz in the land of Edom. They *were* the
sons of Adah.

17These *were* the sons of Reuel, Esau's son:
Chief Nahath, Chief Zerah, Chief Shammah,
and Chief Mizzah. These *were* the chiefs of
Reuel in the land of Edom. These *were* the
sons of Basemath, Esau's wife.

18And these *were* the sons of Aholibamah,
Esau's wife: Chief Jeush, Chief Jaalam, and
Chief Korah. These *were* the chiefs *who
descended* from Aholibamah, Esau's wife, the
daughter of Anah. 19These *were* the sons of
Esau, who is Edom, and these *were* their chiefs.

20These *were* the sons of Seir the Horite who
inhabited the land: Lotan, Shobal, Zibeon,
Anah, 21Dishon, Ezer, and Dishan. These *were*
the chiefs of the Horites, the sons of Seir, in
the land of Edom.

22And the sons of Lotan were Hori and
Hemam. Lotan's sister *was* Timna.

23These *were* the sons of Shobal: Alvan,
Manahath, Ebal, Shepho, and Onam.

24These *were* the sons of Zibeon: both Ajah
and Anah. This *was the* Anah who found the
water in the wilderness as he pastured the
donkeys of his father Zibeon. 25These *were*
the children of Anah: Dishon and
Aholibamah the daughter of Anah.

26These *were* the sons of Dishon: Hemdan,
Eshban, Ithran, and Cheran. 27These *were* the
sons of Ezer: Bilhan, Zaavan, and Akan.
28These *were* the sons of Dishan: Uz and Aran.

29These *were* the chiefs of the Horites: Chief
Lotan, Chief Shobal, Chief Zibeon, Chief Anah,
30Chief Dishon, Chief Ezer, and Chief Dishan.
These *were* the chiefs of the Horites, according to their chiefs in the land of Seir.

31Now these *were* the kings who reigned in
the land of Edom before any king reigned over
the children of Israel: 32Bela the son of Beor
reigned in Edom, and the name of his city *was*
Dinhabah. 33And when Bela died, Jobab the
son of Zerah of Bozrah reigned in his place.
34When Jobab died, Husham of the land of the
Temanites reigned in his place. 35And when
Husham died, Hadad the son of Bedad, who
attacked Midian in the field of Moab, reigned
in his place. And the name of his city *was* Avith.
36When Hadad died, Samlah of Masrekah
reigned in his place. 37And when Samlah died,
Saul of Rehoboth-*by*-the-River reigned in his
place. 38When Saul died, Baal-Hanan the son of
Achbor reigned in his place. 39And when Baal-
Hanan the son of Achbor died, Hadar reigned
in his place; and the name of his city *was* Pau.
His wife's name *was* Mehetabel, the daughter
of Matred, the daughter of Mezahab.

40And these *were* the names of the chiefs of
Esau, according to their families and their
places, by their names: Chief Timnah, Chief
Alvah, Chief Jetheth, 41Chief Aholibamah,
Chief Elah, Chief Pinon, 42Chief Kenaz, Chief
Teman, Chief Mibzar, 43Chief Magdiel, and
Chief Iram. These *were* the chiefs of Edom,
according to their dwelling places in the land
of their possession. Esau *was* the father of the
Edomites.

Psalm 9:6–10

6 O enemy, destructions are
finished forever!
And you have destroyed cities;
Even their memory has perished.
7 But the LORD shall endure forever;
He has prepared His throne
for judgment.
8 He shall judge the world
in righteousness,
And He shall administer judgment for
the peoples in uprightness.

9 The LORD also will be a refuge for the
oppressed,
A refuge in times of trouble.
10 And those who know Your name
will put their trust in You;
For You, LORD, have not forsaken
those who seek You.

Proverbs 3:27–30

27 Do not withhold good from those to
whom it is due,
When it is in the power of your hand
to do *so*.

28 Do not say to your neighbor,
"Go, and come back,
And tomorrow I will give *it*,"
When you have it with you.
29 Do not devise evil against
your neighbor,
For he dwells by you for safety's sake.
30 Do not strive with a man
without cause,
If he has done you no harm.

Matthew 12:22–50

22Then one was brought to Him who was
demon-possessed, blind and mute; and He
healed him, so that the blind and mute man
both spoke and saw. 23And all the multitudes
were amazed and said, "Could this be the Son
of David?"
24Now when the Pharisees heard *it* they said,
"This *fellow* does not cast out demons except
by Beelzebub, the ruler of the demons."
25But Jesus knew their thoughts, and said to
them: "Every kingdom divided against itself is
brought to desolation, and every city or house
divided against itself will not stand. 26If Satan
casts out Satan, he is divided against himself.
How then will his kingdom stand? 27And if I
cast out demons by Beelzebub, by whom do
your sons cast *them* out? Therefore they shall
be your judges. 28But if I cast out demons by
the Spirit of God, surely the kingdom of God
has come upon you. 29Or how can one enter a
strong man's house and plunder his goods,
unless he first binds the strong man? And then
he will plunder his house. 30He who is not with
Me is against Me, and he who does not gather
with Me scatters abroad.
31"Therefore I say to you, every sin and blasphemy will be forgiven men, but the blasphemy *against* the Spirit will not be forgiven men.
32Anyone who speaks a word against the Son
of Man, it will be forgiven him; but whoever
speaks against the Holy Spirit, it will not be
forgiven him, either in this age or in the *age* to
come.
33"Either make the tree good and its fruit
good, or else make the tree bad and its fruit
bad; for a tree is known by *its* fruit. 34Brood of
vipers! How can you, being evil, speak good
things? For out of the abundance of the heart
the mouth speaks. 35A good man out of the
good treasure of his heart brings forth good
things, and an evil man out of the evil treasure
brings forth evil things. 36But I say to you that
for every idle word men may speak, they will
give account of it in the day of judgment. 37For
by your words you will be justified, and by
your words you will be condemned."
38Then some of the scribes and Pharisees
answered, saying, "Teacher, we want to see a
sign from You."
39But He answered and said to them, "An
evil and adulterous generation seeks after a
sign, and no sign will be given to it except the
sign of the prophet Jonah. 40For as Jonah was
three days and three nights in the belly of the
great fish, so will the Son of Man be three
days and three nights in the heart of the earth.
41The men of Nineveh will rise up in the judgment with this generation and condemn it, because they repented at the preaching of Jonah;
and indeed a greater than Jonah *is* here. 42The
queen of the South will rise up in the judgment with this generation and condemn it, for
she came from the ends of the earth to hear
the wisdom of Solomon; and indeed a greater
than Solomon *is* here.
43"When an unclean spirit goes out of a man,
he goes through dry places, seeking rest, and
finds none. 44Then he says, 'I will return to my
house from which I came.' And when he
comes, he finds *it* empty, swept, and put in
order. 45Then he goes and takes with him
seven other spirits more wicked than himself,
and they enter and dwell there; and the last
state of that man is worse than the first. So
shall it also be with this wicked generation."
46While He was still talking to the multitudes, behold, His mother and brothers stood
outside, seeking to speak with Him. 47Then
one said to Him, "Look, Your mother and Your
brothers are standing outside, seeking to
speak with You."
48But He answered and said to the one who
told Him, "Who is My mother and who are My
brothers?" 49And He stretched out His hand
toward His disciples and said, "Here are My
mother and My brothers! 50For whoever does
the will of My Father in heaven is My brother
and sister and mother."

12:46 brothers. These are actual siblings (half brothers) of Jesus. Matthew explicitly connects them with Mary, indicating that they were not cousins or Joseph's sons from a previous marriage, as some of the church fathers imagined. They are mentioned in all the Gospels (Mark 3:31; Luke 8:19–21; John 7:3–5). Matthew and Mark give the names of 4 of Jesus' brothers and mention that He had sisters, as well (13:55; Mark 6:3).

DAY 18: What is the unforgivable sin that Jesus spoke of?

According to Jesus' words in Matthew 12:31, the unforgivable sin is "the blasphemy against the Spirit." The sin He was confronting was the Pharisees' deliberate rejection of that which they knew to be of God (see John 11:48; Acts 4:16). They could not deny the reality of what the Holy Spirit had done through Him, so they attributed to Satan a work that they knew was of God (v. 24; Mark 3:22).

Someone never exposed to Christ's divine power and presence might reject Him in ignorance and "it will be forgiven him" (v. 32)—assuming the unbelief gives way to genuine repentance. Even a Pharisee such as Saul of Tarsus could be forgiven for speaking "against the Son of Man" or persecuting His followers—because his unbelief stemmed from ignorance (1 Tim. 1:13). But those who know His claims are true and reject Him anyway sin "against the Holy Spirit"—because it is the Holy Spirit who testifies of Christ and makes His truth known to us (John 15:26; 16:14,15). No forgiveness was possible for these Pharisees who witnessed His miracles firsthand, knew the truth of His claims, and still blasphemed the Holy Spirit—because they had already rejected the fullest possible revelation (Heb. 6:4–6; 10:29).

JANUARY 19

Genesis 37:1–38:30

37 Now Jacob dwelt in the land where his
father was a stranger, in the land of
Canaan. 2This *is* the history of Jacob.
Joseph, *being* seventeen years old, was feeding the flock with his brothers. And the lad
was with the sons of Bilhah and the sons of
Zilpah, his father's wives; and Joseph brought
a bad report of them to his father.
3Now Israel loved Joseph more than all his
children, because he *was* the son of his old age.
Also he made him a tunic of *many* colors. 4But
when his brothers saw that their father loved
him more than all his brothers, they hated him
and could not speak peaceably to him.

37:3,4 Overt favoritism of Joseph and tacit appointment of him as the primary son by the father conspired to estrange him from his brothers. They hated and envied him (vv. 4,5,11) and could not interact with him without conflict and hostility. Joseph must have noticed the situation.

5Now Joseph had a dream, and he told *it* to
his brothers; and they hated him even more.
6So he said to them, "Please hear this dream
which I have dreamed: 7There we were, binding sheaves in the field. Then behold, my
sheaf arose and also stood upright; and indeed
your sheaves stood all around and bowed
down to my sheaf."
8And his brothers said to him, "Shall you
indeed reign over us? Or shall you indeed
have dominion over us?" So they hated him
even more for his dreams and for his words.
9Then he dreamed still another dream and
told it to his brothers, and said, "Look, I have
dreamed another dream. And this time, the
sun, the moon, and the eleven stars bowed
down to me."
10So he told *it* to his father and his brothers;
and his father rebuked him and said to him,
"What *is* this dream that you have dreamed?
Shall your mother and I and your brothers
indeed come to bow down to the earth before
you?" 11And his brothers envied him, but his
father kept the matter *in mind.*
12Then his brothers went to feed their
father's flock in Shechem. 13And Israel said to
Joseph, "Are not your brothers feeding *the
flock* in Shechem? Come, I will send you to
them."
So he said to him, "Here I am."
14Then he said to him, "Please go and see if
it is well with your brothers and well with the
flocks, and bring back word to me." So he sent
him out of the Valley of Hebron, and he went
to Shechem.
15Now a certain man found him, and there
he was, wandering in the field. And the man
asked him, saying, "What are you seeking?"
16So he said, "I am seeking my brothers.
Please tell me where they are feeding *their
flocks.*"
17And the man said, "They have departed
from here, for I heard them say, 'Let us go to
Dothan.' " So Joseph went after his brothers
and found them in Dothan.
18Now when they saw him afar off, even
before he came near them, they conspired
against him to kill him. 19Then they said to one

another, "Look, this dreamer is coming!
[20]Come therefore, let us now kill him and cast
him into some pit; and we shall say, 'Some wild
beast has devoured him.' We shall see what
will become of his dreams!"
[21]But Reuben heard *it,* and he delivered him
out of their hands, and said, "Let us not kill
him." [22]And Reuben said to them, "Shed no
blood, *but* cast him into this pit which *is* in the
wilderness, and do not lay a hand on him"—
that he might deliver him out of their hands,
and bring him back to his father.
[23]So it came to pass, when Joseph had come
to his brothers, that they stripped Joseph *of*
his tunic, the tunic of *many* colors that *was* on
him. [24]Then they took him and cast him into a
pit. And the pit *was* empty; *there was* no water
in it.
[25]And they sat down to eat a meal. Then they
lifted their eyes and looked, and there was a
company of Ishmaelites, coming from Gilead
with their camels, bearing spices, balm, and
myrrh, on their way to carry *them* down to
Egypt. [26]So Judah said to his brothers, "What
profit *is there* if we kill our brother and conceal
his blood? [27]Come and let us sell him to the
Ishmaelites, and let not our hand be upon him,
for he *is* our brother *and* our flesh." And his
brothers listened. [28]Then Midianite traders
passed by; so *the brothers* pulled Joseph up
and lifted him out of the pit, and sold him to
the Ishmaelites for twenty *shekels* of silver.
And they took Joseph to Egypt.
[29]Then Reuben returned to the pit, and
indeed Joseph *was* not in the pit; and he tore
his clothes. [30]And he returned to his brothers
and said, "The lad *is* no *more;* and I, where
shall I go?"
[31]So they took Joseph's tunic, killed a kid of
the goats, and dipped the tunic in the blood.
[32]Then they sent the tunic of *many* colors, and
they brought *it* to their father and said, "We
have found this. Do you know whether it *is*
your son's tunic or not?"

37:36 Potiphar. He was a prominent court official and high-ranking officer in Egypt, perhaps captain of the royal bodyguard (see 40:3,4). His name, a most unusual grammatical form for that period, either meant "the one whom the god Ra has given" or "the one who is placed on earth by Ra," making it a descriptive epithet more than a personal name.

[33]And he recognized it and said, "*It is* my
son's tunic. A wild beast has devoured him.
Without doubt Joseph is torn to pieces."
[34]Then Jacob tore his clothes, put sackcloth on
his waist, and mourned for his son many days.
[35]And all his sons and all his daughters arose
to comfort him; but he refused to be comforted, and he said, "For I shall go down into the
grave to my son in mourning." Thus his father
wept for him.
[36]Now the Midianites had sold him in Egypt
to Potiphar, an officer of Pharaoh *and* captain
of the guard.

38

It came to pass at that time that Judah
departed from his brothers, and visited a certain Adullamite whose name *was*
Hirah. [2]And Judah saw there a daughter of a
certain Canaanite whose name *was* Shua, and
he married her and went in to her. [3]So she conceived and bore a son, and he called his name
Er. [4]She conceived again and bore a son, and
she called his name Onan. [5]And she conceived
yet again and bore a son, and called his name
Shelah. He was at Chezib when she bore him.
[6]Then Judah took a wife for Er his firstborn,
and her name *was* Tamar. [7]But Er, Judah's
firstborn, was wicked in the sight of the LORD,
and the LORD killed him. [8]And Judah said to
Onan, "Go in to your brother's wife and marry
her, and raise up an heir to your brother." [9]But
Onan knew that the heir would not be his; and
it came to pass, when he went in to his brother's wife, that he emitted on the ground, lest
he should give an heir to his brother. [10]And the
thing which he did displeased the LORD; therefore He killed him also.
[11]Then Judah said to Tamar his daughter-in-
law, "Remain a widow in your father's house
till my son Shelah is grown." For he said, "Lest
he also die like his brothers." And Tamar went
and dwelt in her father's house.
[12]Now in the process of time the daughter of
Shua, Judah's wife, died; and Judah was comforted, and went up to his sheepshearers at
Timnah, he and his friend Hirah the
Adullamite. [13]And it was told Tamar, saying,
"Look, your father-in-law is going up to
Timnah to shear his sheep." [14]So she took off
her widow's garments, covered *herself* with a
veil and wrapped herself, and sat in an open
place which *was* on the way to Timnah; for she
saw that Shelah was grown, and she was not
given to him as a wife. [15]When Judah saw her,
he thought she *was* a harlot, because she had
covered her face. [16]Then he turned to her by
the way, and said, "Please let me come in to
you"; for he did not know that she *was* his
daughter-in-law.

So she said, "What will you give me, that
you may come in to me?"
[17]And he said, "I will send a young goat from
the flock."
So she said, "Will you give *me* a pledge till
you send *it?*"
[18]Then he said, "What pledge shall I give you?"
So she said, "Your signet and cord, and your
staff that *is* in your hand." Then he gave *them*
to her, and went in to her, and she conceived
by him. [19]So she arose and went away, and laid
aside her veil and put on the garments of her
widowhood.
[20]And Judah sent the young goat by the
hand of his friend the Adullamite, to receive
his pledge from the woman's hand, but he did
not find her. [21]Then he asked the men of that
place, saying, "Where is the harlot who *was*
openly by the roadside?"
And they said, "There was no harlot in this
place."
[22]So he returned to Judah and said, "I cannot
find her. Also, the men of the place said there
was no harlot in this *place.*"
[23]Then Judah said, "Let her take *them* for
herself, lest we be shamed; for I sent this
young goat and you have not found her."
[24]And it came to pass, about three months
after, that Judah was told, saying, "Tamar your
daughter-in-law has played the harlot; furthermore she *is* with child by harlotry."
So Judah said, "Bring her out and let her be
burned!"
[25]When she *was* brought out, she sent to her
father-in-law, saying, "By the man to whom
these belong, I *am* with child." And she said,
"Please determine whose these *are*—the
signet and cord, and staff."
[26]So Judah acknowledged *them* and said,
"She has been more righteous than I, because
I did not give her to Shelah my son." And he
never knew her again.
[27]Now it came to pass, at the time for giving
birth, that behold, twins *were* in her womb.
[28]And so it was, when she was giving birth,
that *the one* put out *his* hand; and the midwife
took a scarlet *thread* and bound it on his hand,
saying, "This one came out first." [29]Then it
happened, as he drew back his hand, that his
brother came out unexpectedly; and she said,
"How did you break through? *This* breach *be*
upon you!" Therefore his name was called
Perez. [30]Afterward his brother came out who
had the scarlet *thread* on his hand. And his
name was called Zerah.

Psalm 9:11–20

11 Sing praises to the LORD,
who dwells in Zion!
Declare His deeds among the people.
12 When He avenges blood, He
remembers them;
He does not forget the cry
of the humble.

13 Have mercy on me, O LORD!
Consider my trouble from those who
hate me,
You who lift me up from the gates of
death,
14 That I may tell of all Your praise
In the gates of the daughter
of Zion.
I will rejoice in Your salvation.

15 The nations have sunk down in the pit
which they made;
In the net which they hid, their own
foot is caught.
16 The LORD is known *by* the judgment
He executes;
The wicked is snared in the work
of his own hands.
Meditation. Selah

17 The wicked shall be turned into hell,
And all the nations that forget God.
18 For the needy shall not always be
forgotten;
The expectation of the poor shall *not*
perish forever.

19 Arise, O LORD,
Do not let man prevail;
Let the nations be judged in Your
sight.
20 Put them in fear, O LORD,
That the nations may know
themselves *to be but* men. Selah

Proverbs 3:31–35

31 Do not envy the oppressor,
And choose none of his ways;
32 For the perverse *person is* an
abomination to the LORD,
But His secret counsel *is* with the
upright.
33 The curse of the LORD *is* on the house
of the wicked,
But He blesses the home of
the just.
34 Surely He scorns the scornful,
But gives grace to the humble.
35 The wise shall inherit glory,
But shame shall be the legacy of fools.

Matthew 13:1–30

13 On the same day Jesus went out of the
house and sat by the sea. [2]And great

13:3 parables. Parables were a common form of teaching in Judaism. The Greek term for "parable" appears 45 times in the LXX. A parable is a long analogy, often cast in the form of a story. Before this point in His ministry, Jesus had employed many graphic analogies (see 5:13–16), but their meaning was fairly clear in the context of His teaching. Parables required more explanation (see v. 36) and Jesus employed them to obscure the truth from unbelievers while making it clearer to His disciples (vv. 11,12). For the remainder of His Galilean ministry, He did not speak to the multitudes except in parables (v. 34). Jesus' veiling the truth from unbelievers this way was both an act of judgment and an act of mercy. It was "judgment" because it kept them in the darkness that they loved (see John 3:19), but it was "mercy" because they had already rejected the light, so any exposure to more truth would only increase their condemnation.

multitudes were gathered together to Him, so
that He got into a boat and sat; and the whole
multitude stood on the shore.
[3]Then He spoke many things to them in
parables, saying: "Behold, a sower went out to
sow. [4]And as he sowed, some *seed* fell by the
wayside; and the birds came and devoured
them. [5]Some fell on stony places, where they
did not have much earth; and they immediately sprang up because they had no depth of
earth. [6]But when the sun was up they were
scorched, and because they had no root they
withered away. [7]And some fell among thorns,
and the thorns sprang up and choked them.
[8]But others fell on good ground and yielded a
crop: some a hundredfold, some sixty, some
thirty. [9]He who has ears to hear, let him hear!"
[10]And the disciples came and said to Him,
"Why do You speak to them in parables?"
[11]He answered and said to them, "Because it
has been given to you to know the mysteries
of the kingdom of heaven, but to them it has
not been given. [12]For whoever has, to him
more will be given, and he will have abundance; but whoever does not have, even what
he has will be taken away from him. [13]There-
fore I speak to them in parables, because seeing they do not see, and hearing they do not
hear, nor do they understand. [14]And in them
the prophecy of Isaiah is fulfilled, which says:

'Hearing you will hear and shall not
understand,
And seeing you will see and
not perceive;
[15]*For the hearts of this people have*
grown dull.
Their ears are hard of hearing,
And their eyes they have closed,
Lest they should see with their eyes
and hear with their ears,
Lest they should understand
with their hearts and turn,
So that I should heal them.'

[16]But blessed *are* your eyes for they see, and
your ears for they hear; [17]for assuredly, I say
to you that many prophets and righteous *men*
desired to see what you see, and did not see
it, and to hear what you hear, and did not
hear *it.*
[18]"Therefore hear the parable of the sower:
[19]When anyone hears the word of the kingdom, and does not understand *it,* then the
wicked *one* comes and snatches away what
was sown in his heart. This is he who received
seed by the wayside. [20]But he who received
the seed on stony places, this is he who hears
the word and immediately receives it with joy;
[21]yet he has no root in himself, but endures
only for a while. For when tribulation or persecution arises because of the word, immediately he stumbles. [22]Now he who received
seed among the thorns is he who hears the
word, and the cares of this world and the
deceitfulness of riches choke the word, and he
becomes unfruitful. [23]But he who received
seed on the good ground is he who hears the
word and understands *it,* who indeed bears
fruit and produces: some a hundredfold, some
sixty, some thirty."
[24]Another parable He put forth to them,
saying: "The kingdom of heaven is like a
man who sowed good seed in his field; [25]but
while men slept, his enemy came and sowed
tares among the wheat and went his way.
[26]But when the grain had sprouted and produced a crop, then the tares also appeared.
[27]So the servants of the owner came and said
to him, 'Sir, did you not sow good seed in
your field? How then does it have tares?' [28]He
said to them, 'An enemy has done this.' The
servants said to him, 'Do you want us then to
go and gather them up?' [29]But he said, 'No,
lest while you gather up the tares you also
uproot the wheat with them. [30]Let both grow
together until the harvest, and at the time of
harvest I will say to the reapers, "First gather together the tares and bind them in bundles to burn them, but gather the wheat into
my barn." ' "

DAY 19: Why are some events in Matthew in a different order from the order in Mark or Luke?

In general, Matthew presents a topical or thematic approach to the life of Christ. He groups Jesus' teaching into five major discourses:

1. The Sermon on the Mount (chaps. 5–7)
2. The commissioning of the apostles (chap. 10)
3. The parables of the kingdom (chap. 13)
4. The childlikeness of the believer (chap. 18)
5. The discourse on His second coming (chaps. 24; 25)

Matthew makes no attempt to follow a strict chronology. A comparison of the synoptic Gospels reveals that he freely placed things out of order. He was dealing with themes and broad concepts, not laying out a timeline. Mark's and Luke's Gospels follow a chronological order more closely.

JANUARY 20

Genesis 39:1–40:23

39 Now Joseph had been taken down to
Egypt. And Potiphar, an officer of
Pharaoh, captain of the guard, an Egyptian,
bought him from the Ishmaelites who had
taken him down there. 2The LORD was with
Joseph, and he was a successful man; and he
was in the house of his master the Egyptian.
3And his master saw that the LORD *was* with
him and that the LORD made all he did to prosper in his hand. 4So Joseph found favor in his
sight, and served him. Then he made him
overseer of his house, and all *that* he had he
put under his authority. 5So it was, from the
time *that* he had made him overseer of his
house and all that he had, that the LORD
blessed the Egyptian's house for Joseph's
sake; and the blessing of the LORD was on all
that he had in the house and in the field. 6Thus
he left all that he had in Joseph's hand, and he
did not know what he had except for the bread
which he ate.
Now Joseph was handsome in form and
appearance.
7And it came to pass after these things that
his master's wife cast longing eyes on Joseph,
and she said, "Lie with me."
8But he refused and said to his master's
wife, "Look, my master does not know what *is*
with me in the house, and he has committed
all that he has to my hand. 9*There is* no one
greater in this house than I, nor has he kept
back anything from me but you, because you
are his wife. How then can I do this great
wickedness, and sin against God?"
10So it was, as she spoke to Joseph day by
day, that he did not heed her, to lie with her *or*
to be with her.
11But it happened about this time, when Joseph went into the house to do his work, and
none of the men of the house *was* inside, 12that
she caught him by his garment, saying, "Lie
with me." But he left his garment in her hand,
and fled and ran outside. 13And so it was, when
she saw that he had left his garment in her
hand and fled outside, 14that she called to the
men of her house and spoke to them, saying,
"See, he has brought in to us a Hebrew to
mock us. He came in to me to lie with me, and
I cried out with a loud voice. 15And it happened, when he heard that I lifted my voice
and cried out, that he left his garment with
me, and fled and went outside."
16So she kept his garment with her until his
master came home. 17Then she spoke to him
with words like these, saying, "The Hebrew
servant whom you brought to us came in to
me to mock me; 18so it happened, as I lifted my
voice and cried out, that he left his garment
with me and fled outside."

39:2 The LORD was with Joseph. Any and all ideas that Joseph, twice a victim of injustice, had been abandoned by the Lord are summarily banished by the employment of phrases highlighting God's oversight of his circumstances, e.g. "with him" (vv. 3,21), "made all he did to prosper" (vv. 3,23), "found/gave him favor" (vv. 4,21), "blessed/ blessing" (v. 5), and "showed him mercy" (v. 21). Neither being unjustly sold into slavery and forcibly removed from the Land (37:28), nor being unjustly accused of sexual harassment and imprisoned (vv. 13–18) were events signaling even a temporary loss of divine superintendence of Joseph's life and God's purpose for His people, Israel.

19So it was, when his master heard the words which his wife spoke to him, saying, "Your servant did to me after this manner," that his anger was aroused. 20Then Joseph's master took him and put him into the prison, a place where the king's prisoners *were* confined. And he was there in the prison. 21But the LORD was with Joseph and showed him mercy, and He gave him favor in the sight of the keeper of the prison. 22And the keeper of the prison committed to Joseph's hand all the prisoners who *were* in the prison; whatever they did there, it was his doing. 23The keeper of the prison did not look into anything *that was* under *Joseph's* authority, because the LORD was with him; and whatever he did, the LORD made *it* prosper.

40 It came to pass after these things *that* the butler and the baker of the king of Egypt offended their lord, the king of Egypt. 2And Pharaoh was angry with his two officers, the chief butler and the chief baker. 3So he put them in custody in the house of the captain of the guard, in the prison, the place where Joseph *was* confined. 4And the captain of the guard charged Joseph with them, and he served them; so they were in custody for a while.

5Then the butler and the baker of the king of Egypt, who *were* confined in the prison, had a dream, both of them, each man's dream in one night *and* each man's dream with its *own* interpretation. 6And Joseph came in to them in the morning and looked at them, and saw that they *were* sad. 7So he asked Pharaoh's officers who *were* with him in the custody of his lord's house, saying, "Why do you look *so* sad today?"

8And they said to him, "We each have had a dream, and *there is* no interpreter of it."

So Joseph said to them, "Do not interpretations belong to God? Tell *them* to me, please."

9Then the chief butler told his dream to Joseph, and said to him, "Behold, in my dream a vine *was* before me, 10and in the vine *were* three branches; it *was* as though it budded, its blossoms shot forth, and its clusters brought forth ripe grapes. 11Then Pharaoh's cup *was* in my hand; and I took the grapes and pressed them into Pharaoh's cup, and placed the cup in Pharaoh's hand."

12And Joseph said to him, "This *is* the interpretation of it: The three branches *are* three days. 13Now within three days Pharaoh will lift up your head and restore you to your place, and you will put Pharaoh's cup in his hand according to the former manner, when you were his butler. 14But remember me when it is well with you, and please show kindness to me; make mention of me to Pharaoh, and get me out of this house. 15For indeed I was stolen away from the land of the Hebrews; and also I have done nothing here that they should put me into the dungeon."

16When the chief baker saw that the interpretation was good, he said to Joseph, "I also *was* in my dream, and there *were* three white baskets on my head. 17In the uppermost basket *were* all kinds of baked goods for Pharaoh, and the birds ate them out of the basket on my head."

18So Joseph answered and said, "This *is* the interpretation of it: The three baskets *are* three days. 19Within three days Pharaoh will lift off your head from you and hang you on a tree; and the birds will eat your flesh from you."

20Now it came to pass on the third day, *which was* Pharaoh's birthday, that he made a feast for all his servants; and he lifted up the head of the chief butler and of the chief baker among his servants. 21Then he restored the chief butler to his butlership again, and he placed the cup in Pharaoh's hand. 22But he hanged the chief baker, as Joseph had interpreted to them. 23Yet the chief butler did not remember Joseph, but forgot him.

Psalm 10:1–11

Why do You stand afar off, O LORD?
Why do You hide in times of trouble?
2 The wicked in *his* pride
persecutes the poor;
Let them be caught in the plots which
they have devised.

3 For the wicked boasts of his heart's
desire;
He blesses the greedy *and* renounces
the LORD.
4 The wicked in his proud countenance
does not seek *God;*
God *is* in none of his thoughts.

5 His ways are always prospering;
Your judgments *are* far above, out of
his sight;
As for all his enemies, he sneers at
them.
6 He has said in his heart,
"I shall not be moved;
I shall never be in adversity."
7 His mouth is full of cursing and deceit
and oppression;
Under his tongue *is* trouble
and iniquity.

8 He sits in the lurking places
of the villages;

In the secret places he murders the innocent;
His eyes are secretly fixed on the helpless.
9 He lies in wait secretly, as a lion in his den;
He lies in wait to catch the poor;
He catches the poor when he draws him into his net.
10 So he crouches, he lies low,
That the helpless may fall by his strength.
11 He has said in his heart,
"God has forgotten;
He hides His face;
He will never see."

Proverbs 4:1–6

4 Hear, *my* children, the instruction of a father,
And give attention to know understanding;
2 For I give you good doctrine:
Do not forsake my law.

4:2 good doctrine...my law. There is no wisdom but that which is linked to good doctrine, which should be the focal point of all instruction (see 1 Tim. 1:10; 4:13,16; 5:17; 2 Tim. 3:10,16; 4:2; Titus 1:9; 2:1,10).

3 When I was my father's son,
Tender and the only one in the sight of my mother,
4 He also taught me,
and said to me:
"Let your heart retain my words;
Keep my commands, and live.
5 Get wisdom! Get understanding!
Do not forget, nor turn away from the words of my mouth.
6 Do not forsake her, and she will preserve you;
Love her, and she will keep you.

Matthew 13:31–58

31Another parable He put forth to them, saying: "The kingdom of heaven is like a mustard seed, which a man took and sowed in his field,
32which indeed is the least of all the seeds; but when it is grown it is greater than the herbs and becomes a tree, so that the birds of the air come and nest in its branches."

13:37 He who sows. The true sower of salvation seed is the Lord Himself. He alone can give the power in the heart to transform. He is the One who saves sinners, even through the preaching and witnessing of believers (Rom. 10:14).

33Another parable He spoke to them: "The kingdom of heaven is like leaven, which a woman took and hid in three measures of meal till it was all leavened."
34All these things Jesus spoke to the multitude in parables; and without a parable He did not speak to them,
35that it might be fulfilled which was spoken by the prophet, saying:

"I will open My mouth in parables;
I will utter things kept secret from the foundation of the world."

36Then Jesus sent the multitude away and went into the house. And His disciples came to Him, saying, "Explain to us the parable of the tares of the field."
37He answered and said to them: "He who sows the good seed is the Son of Man.
38The field is the world, the good seeds are the sons of the kingdom, but the tares are the sons of the wicked *one.*
39The enemy who sowed them is the devil, the harvest is the end of the age, and the reapers are the angels.
40Therefore as the tares are gathered and burned in the fire, so it will be at the end of this age.
41The Son of Man will send out His angels, and they will gather out of His kingdom all things that offend, and those who practice lawlessness,
42and will cast them into the furnace of fire. There will be wailing and gnashing of teeth.
43Then the righteous will shine forth as the sun in the kingdom of their Father. He who has ears to hear, let him hear!
44"Again, the kingdom of heaven is like treasure hidden in a field, which a man found and hid; and for joy over it he goes and sells all that he has and buys that field.
45"Again, the kingdom of heaven is like a merchant seeking beautiful pearls,
46who, when he had found one pearl of great price, went and sold all that he had and bought it.
47"Again, the kingdom of heaven is like a dragnet that was cast into the sea and gathered some of every kind,
48which, when it was full, they drew to shore; and they sat down and gathered the good into vessels, but threw the bad away.
49So it will be at the end of the age. The angels will come forth, separate the

13:57 A prophet…in his own country. This is an ancient proverb paralleling the modern saying "Familiarity breeds contempt." They knew Jesus too well as a boy and a young man from their own town—and they concluded that He was nothing special. Verse 58 gives the sad result (see Mark 6:4).

wicked from among the just, 50and cast them into the furnace of fire. There will be wailing and gnashing of teeth."

51Jesus said to them, "Have you understood all these things?"

They said to Him, "Yes, Lord."

52Then He said to them, "Therefore every scribe instructed concerning the kingdom of heaven is like a householder who brings out of his treasure *things* new and old."

53Now it came to pass, when Jesus had finished these parables, that He departed from there. 54When He had come to His own country, He taught them in their synagogue, so that they were astonished and said, "Where did this *Man* get this wisdom and *these* mighty works? 55Is this not the carpenter's son? Is not His mother called Mary? And His brothers James, Joses, Simon, and Judas? 56And His sisters, are they not all with us? Where then did this *Man* get all these things?" 57So they were offended at Him.

But Jesus said to them, "A prophet is not without honor except in his own country and in his own house." 58Now He did not do many mighty works there because of their unbelief.

DAY 20: What did Joseph understand about the interpretation of dreams?

Oneiromancy, the science or practice of interpreting dreams, flourished in ancient Egypt because dreams were thought to determine the future. Both Egypt and Babylon developed a professional class of dream interpreters. Deuteronomy 13:1–5 shows that such dream interpreters were part of ancient false religion and to be avoided by God's people. By some 500 years later, a detailed manual of dream interpretation had been compiled. Unlike Joseph, neither butler nor baker understood the significance of their dreams (see Gen. 37:5–11), and the sadness they project in Genesis 40:5 expresses their belief that the dreams required an interpretation.

Joseph believed that when it came to dreams that the "interpretations belong to God" (v. 8). He was careful to give credit to his Lord (see 41:16). Daniel, the only other Hebrew whom God allowed to accurately interpret revelatory dreams, was just as careful to do so (Dan. 2:28). Significantly, God chose both men to play an important role for Israel while serving pagan monarchs and stepping forward at the critical moment to interpret their dreams and reveal their futures.

JANUARY 21

Genesis 41:1–42:38

41 Then it came to pass, at the end of two
full years, that Pharaoh had a dream; and
behold, he stood by the river. 2Suddenly there
came up out of the river seven cows, fine looking and fat; and they fed in the meadow. 3Then
behold, seven other cows came up after them
out of the river, ugly and gaunt, and stood by
the *other* cows on the bank of the river. 4And
the ugly and gaunt cows ate up the seven fine
looking and fat cows. So Pharaoh awoke. 5He
slept and dreamed a second time; and suddenly seven heads of grain came up on one
stalk, plump and good. 6Then behold, seven
thin heads, blighted by the east wind, sprang
up after them. 7And the seven thin heads
devoured the seven plump and full heads. So
Pharaoh awoke, and indeed, *it was* a dream.
8Now it came to pass in the morning that his
spirit was troubled, and he sent and called for
all the magicians of Egypt and all its wise men.
And Pharaoh told them his dreams, but *there was* no one who could interpret them for
Pharaoh.

9Then the chief butler spoke to Pharaoh,
saying: "I remember my faults this day.
10When Pharaoh was angry with his servants,
and put me in custody in the house of the captain of the guard, *both* me and the chief baker,
11we each had a dream in one night, he and I.
Each of us dreamed according to the interpretation of his *own* dream. 12Now there *was* a
young Hebrew man with us there, a servant of
the captain of the guard. And we told him, and
he interpreted our dreams for us; to each man
he interpreted according to his *own* dream.
13And it came to pass, just as he interpreted for

us, so it happened. He restored me to my
office, and he hanged him."
14Then Pharaoh sent and called Joseph, and
they brought him quickly out of the dungeon;
and he shaved, changed his clothing, and
came to Pharaoh. 15And Pharaoh said to
Joseph, "I have had a dream, and *there is* no
one who can interpret it. But I have heard it
said of you *that* you can understand a dream,
to interpret it."
16So Joseph answered Pharaoh, saying, "*It is*
not in me; God will give Pharaoh an answer of
peace."
17Then Pharaoh said to Joseph: "Behold, in
my dream I stood on the bank of the river.
18Suddenly seven cows came up out of the
river, fine looking and fat; and they fed in the
meadow. 19Then behold, seven other cows
came up after them, poor and very ugly and
gaunt, such ugliness as I have never seen in all
the land of Egypt. 20And the gaunt and ugly
cows ate up the first seven, the fat cows.
21When they had eaten them up, no one would
have known that they had eaten them, for they
were just as ugly as at the beginning. So I
awoke. 22Also I saw in my dream, and suddenly seven heads came up on one stalk, full and
good. 23Then behold, seven heads, withered,
thin, *and* blighted by the east wind, sprang up
after them. 24And the thin heads devoured the
seven good heads. So I told *this* to the magicians, but *there was* no one who could explain
it to me."
25Then Joseph said to Pharaoh, "The dreams
of Pharaoh *are* one; God has shown Pharaoh
what He *is* about to do: 26The seven good cows
are seven years, and the seven good heads *are*
seven years; the dreams *are* one. 27And the
seven thin and ugly cows which came up after
them *are* seven years, and the seven empty
heads blighted by the east wind are seven
years of famine. 28This *is* the thing which I
have spoken to Pharaoh. God has shown
Pharaoh what He *is* about to do. 29Indeed
seven years of great plenty will come throughout all the land of Egypt; 30but after them seven
years of famine will arise, and all the plenty
will be forgotten in the land of Egypt; and the
famine will deplete the land. 31So the plenty
will not be known in the land because of the
famine following, for it *will be* very severe.
32And the dream was repeated to Pharaoh
twice because the thing *is* established by God,
and God will shortly bring it to pass.
33"Now therefore, let Pharaoh select a discerning and wise man, and set him over the
land of Egypt. 34Let Pharaoh do *this,* and let
him appoint officers over the land, to collect
one-fifth *of the produce* of the land of Egypt in
the seven plentiful years. 35And let them gather all the food of those good years that are
coming, and store up grain under the authority of Pharaoh, and let them keep food in the
cities. 36Then that food shall be as a reserve for
the land for the seven years of famine which
shall be in the land of Egypt, that the land may
not perish during the famine."
37So the advice was good in the eyes of
Pharaoh and in the eyes of all his servants.
38And Pharaoh said to his servants, "Can we
find *such a one* as this, a man in whom *is* the
Spirit of God?"
39Then Pharaoh said to Joseph, "Inasmuch
as God has shown you all this, *there is* no one
as discerning and wise as you. 40You shall be
over my house, and all my people shall be
ruled according to your word; only in regard
to the throne will I be greater than you." 41And
Pharaoh said to Joseph, "See, I have set you
over all the land of Egypt."
42Then Pharaoh took his signet ring off his
hand and put it on Joseph's hand; and he
clothed him in garments of fine linen and put
a gold chain around his neck. 43And he had
him ride in the second chariot which he had;
and they cried out before him, "Bow the
knee!" So he set him over all the land of Egypt.
44Pharaoh also said to Joseph, "I *am* Pharaoh,
and without your consent no man may lift his
hand or foot in all the land of Egypt." 45And
Pharaoh called Joseph's name Zaphnath-
Paaneah. And he gave him as a wife Asenath,
the daughter of Poti-Pherah priest of On. So
Joseph went out over *all* the land of Egypt.

41:42 signet ring...garments...gold chain. Emblems of office and a reward of clothing and jewelry suitable to the new rank accompanied Pharaoh's appointment of Joseph as vizier, or prime minister, the second-in-command (v. 40; 45:8,26). Joseph wore the royal seal on his finger, authorizing him to transact the affairs of state on behalf of Pharaoh himself.

46Joseph was thirty years old when he stood
before Pharaoh king of Egypt. And Joseph
went out from the presence of Pharaoh, and
went throughout all the land of Egypt. 47Now in
the seven plentiful years the ground brought
forth abundantly. 48So he gathered up all the
food of the seven years which were in the land
of Egypt, and laid up the food in the cities; he
laid up in every city the food of the fields

which surrounded them. 49Joseph gathered
very much grain, as the sand of the sea, until
he stopped counting, for *it was* immeasurable.
50And to Joseph were born two sons before
the years of famine came, whom Asenath, the
daughter of Poti-Pherah priest of On, bore to
him. 51Joseph called the name of the firstborn
Manasseh: "For God has made me forget all
my toil and all my father's house." 52And the
name of the second he called Ephraim: "For
God has caused me to be fruitful in the land of
my affliction."
53Then the seven years of plenty which were
in the land of Egypt ended, 54and the seven
years of famine began to come, as Joseph had
said. The famine was in all lands, but in all the
land of Egypt there was bread. 55So when all
the land of Egypt was famished, the people
cried to Pharaoh for bread. Then Pharaoh said
to all the Egyptians, "Go to Joseph; whatever
he says to you, do." 56The famine was over all
the face of the earth, and Joseph opened all
the storehouses and sold to the Egyptians.
And the famine became severe in the land of
Egypt. 57So all countries came to Joseph in
Egypt to buy *grain,* because the famine was
severe in all lands.

42 When Jacob saw that there was grain
in Egypt, Jacob said to his sons, "Why
do you look at one another?" 2And he said, "Indeed I have heard that there is grain in Egypt;
go down to that place and buy for us there,
that we may live and not die."
3So Joseph's ten brothers went down to buy
grain in Egypt. 4But Jacob did not send Joseph's brother Benjamin with his brothers, for
he said, "Lest some calamity befall him." 5And
the sons of Israel went to buy *grain* among
those who journeyed, for the famine was in
the land of Canaan.
6Now Joseph *was* governor over the land;
and it was he who sold to all the people of the
land. And Joseph's brothers came and bowed
down before him with *their* faces to the earth.

42:6 bowed down. Without his brothers' appreciating it at the time, Joseph's dream became reality (37:5–8). Recognition of Joseph was unlikely because: 1) over 15 years had elapsed and the teenager sold into slavery had become a mature adult; 2) he had become Egyptian in appearance and dress; 3) he treated them without a hint of familiarity (vv. 7,8); and 4) they thought he was dead (v. 13).

7Joseph saw his brothers and recognized
them, but he acted as a stranger to them and
spoke roughly to them. Then he said to them,
"Where do you come from?"
And they said, "From the land of Canaan to
buy food."
8So Joseph recognized his brothers, but
they did not recognize him. 9Then Joseph remembered the dreams which he had dreamed
about them, and said to them, "You *are* spies!
You have come to see the nakedness of the
land!"
10And they said to him, "No, my lord, but
your servants have come to buy food. 11We *are*
all one man's sons; we *are* honest *men;* your
servants are not spies."
12But he said to them, "No, but you have
come to see the nakedness of the land."
13And they said, "Your servants *are* twelve
brothers, the sons of one man in the land of
Canaan; and in fact, the youngest *is* with our
father today, and one *is* no more."
14But Joseph said to them, "It *is* as I spoke to
you, saying, 'You *are* spies!' 15In this *manner*
you shall be tested: By the life of Pharaoh, you
shall not leave this place unless your youngest
brother comes here. 16Send one of you, and let
him bring your brother; and you shall be kept
in prison, that your words may be tested to see
whether *there is* any truth in you; or else, by
the life of Pharaoh, surely you *are* spies!" 17So
he put them all together in prison three days.
18Then Joseph said to them the third day,
"Do this and live, *for* I fear God: 19If you *are* honest *men,* let one of your brothers be confined to
your prison house; but you, go and carry grain
for the famine of your houses. 20And bring your
youngest brother to me; so your words will be
verified, and you shall not die."
And they did so. 21Then they said to one
another, "We *are* truly guilty concerning our
brother, for we saw the anguish of his soul
when he pleaded with us, and we would not
hear; therefore this distress has come upon
us."
22And Reuben answered them, saying, "Did
I not speak to you, saying, 'Do not sin against
the boy'; and you would not listen? Therefore
behold, his blood is now required of us." 23But
they did not know that Joseph understood
them, for he spoke to them through an interpreter. 24And he turned himself away from
them and wept. Then he returned to them
again, and talked with them. And he took
Simeon from them and bound him before
their eyes.
25Then Joseph gave a command to fill their
sacks with grain, to restore every man's

money to his sack, and to give them provisions for the journey. Thus he did for them.
26So they loaded their donkeys with the grain
and departed from there. 27But as one *of them*
opened his sack to give his donkey feed at the
encampment, he saw his money; and there it
was, in the mouth of his sack. 28So he said to
his brothers, "My money has been restored,
and there it is, in my sack!" Then their hearts
failed *them* and they were afraid, saying to one
another, "What *is* this *that* God has done to us?"
29Then they went to Jacob their father in the
land of Canaan and told him all that had happened to them, saying: 30"The man *who is* lord
of the land spoke roughly to us, and took us
for spies of the country. 31But we said to him,
'We *are* honest *men;* we are not spies. 32We *are*
twelve brothers, sons of our father; one *is* no
more, and the youngest *is* with our father this
day in the land of Canaan.' 33Then the man, the
lord of the country, said to us, 'By this I will
know that you *are* honest *men:* Leave one of
your brothers *here* with me, take *food for* the
famine of your households, and be gone. 34And
bring your youngest brother to me; so I shall
know that you *are* not spies, but *that* you *are*
honest *men.* I will grant your brother to you,
and you may trade in the land.' "
35Then it happened as they emptied their
sacks, that surprisingly each man's bundle of
money *was* in his sack; and when they and
their father saw the bundles of money, they
were afraid. 36And Jacob their father said to
them, "You have bereaved me: Joseph is no
more, Simeon is no *more,* and you want to take
Benjamin. All these things are against me."
37Then Reuben spoke to his father, saying,
"Kill my two sons if I do not bring him *back* to
you; put him in my hands, and I will bring him
back to you."
38But he said, "My son shall not go down
with you, for his brother is dead, and he is left
alone. If any calamity should befall him along
the way in which you go, then you would bring
down my gray hair with sorrow to the grave."

Psalm 10:12–18

12 Arise, O LORD!
O God, lift up Your hand!
Do not forget the humble.
13 Why do the wicked renounce God?
He has said in his heart,
"You will not require *an account.*"
14 But You have seen, for You observe
trouble and grief,
To repay *it* by Your hand.
The helpless commits himself to You;

10:14 You are the helper of the fatherless. God is pictured as Helper or Advocate again, but this time in association with orphans. He is the Defender par excellence of the defenseless (on the imagery, see Ex. 22:21ff.; Deut. 10:18ff.; 1 Sam. 1:17; Jer. 7:6).

You are the helper of the fatherless.
15 Break the arm of the wicked and the
evil *man;*
Seek out his wickedness *until*
You find none.

16 The LORD *is* King forever
and ever;
The nations have perished out
of His land.
17 LORD, You have heard the desire
of the humble;
You will prepare their heart;
You will cause Your ear to hear,
18 To do justice to the fatherless
and the oppressed,
That the man of the earth may oppress
no more.

Proverbs 4:7–9

7 Wisdom *is* the principal thing;
Therefore get wisdom.
And in all your getting,
get understanding.
8 Exalt her, and she will promote you;
She will bring you honor, when you
embrace her.
9 She will place on your head
an ornament of grace;
A crown of glory she will deliver to you."

Matthew 14:1–21

14 At that time Herod the tetrarch heard
the report about Jesus 2and said to his
servants, "This is John the Baptist; he is risen
from the dead, and therefore these powers are
at work in him." 3For Herod had laid hold of
John and bound him, and put *him* in prison for
the sake of Herodias, his brother Philip's wife.
4Because John had said to him, "It is not lawful
for you to have her." 5And although he wanted
to put him to death, he feared the multitude,
because they counted him as a prophet.
6But when Herod's birthday was celebrated,
the daughter of Herodias danced before them
and pleased Herod. 7Therefore he promised
with an oath to give her whatever she might ask.

14:3 Herodias, his brother Philip's wife. Herodias was the daughter of Aristobulus, another son of Herod the Great; so when she married Philip, she was marrying her own father's brother. What precipitated the arrest of John the Baptist was that Herod Antipas (another of Herodias's uncles) talked Herodias into leaving her husband (his brother) in order to marry him (Mark 6:17)—thus compounding the incest, as well as violating Leviticus 18:16. John was outraged that a ruler in Israel would commit such a sin openly, so he rebuked Herod severely (v. 4). For this, he was imprisoned and later killed (Mark 6:14–29).

8So she, having been prompted by her
mother, said, "Give me John the Baptist's head
here on a platter."
9And the king was sorry; nevertheless,
because of the oaths and because of those
who sat with him, he commanded *it* to be
given to *her.* 10So he sent and had John beheaded in prison. 11And his head was brought on a
platter and given to the girl, and she brought
it to her mother. 12Then his disciples came and
took away the body and buried it, and went
and told Jesus.
13When Jesus heard *it,* He departed from
there by boat to a deserted place by Himself.
But when the multitudes heard it, they followed Him on foot from the cities. 14And when
Jesus went out He saw a great multitude; and
He was moved with compassion for them, and
healed their sick. 15When it was evening, His
disciples came to Him, saying, "This is a
deserted place, and the hour is already late.
Send the multitudes away, that they may go
into the villages and buy themselves food."
16But Jesus said to them, "They do not need
to go away. You give them something to eat."
17And they said to Him, "We have here only
five loaves and two fish."
18He said, "Bring them here to Me." 19Then He
commanded the multitudes to sit down on the
grass. And He took the five loaves and the two
fish, and looking up to heaven, He blessed and
broke and gave the loaves to the disciples; and
the disciples gave to the multitudes. 20So they
all ate and were filled, and they took up twelve
baskets full of the fragments that remained.
21Now those who had eaten were about five
thousand men, besides women and children.

DAY 21: How did Joseph's faithfulness lead to personal advancement?

Pharaoh's disturbing dreams in Genesis 41 were such that there was "no one who could interpret them" (v. 8). The combined expertise of a full council of Pharaoh's advisers and dream experts failed to provide an interpretation. Without knowing it, they had just set the stage for Joseph's entrance on the scene of Egyptian history. The chief butler spoke up and apprised Pharaoh of the Hebrew prisoner and his accurate interpretation of dreams two years earlier (vv. 10–13).

In the presence of Pharaoh, Joseph made his faith known: "It is not in me; God will give Pharaoh an answer of peace" (v. 16). Deprecating any innate ability, Joseph advised at the very outset that the answer Pharaoh desired could only come from God. And after hearing the dream described, Joseph's interpretation of what "God has shown Pharaoh" (v. 25) kept the focus fixed upon what God had determined for Egypt (vv. 28,32).

After interpreting the dream, Joseph told Pharaoh how to survive the next 14 years. Incongruously, Joseph, a slave and a prisoner, appended to the interpretation a long-term strategy for establishing reserves to meet the future need and included advice on the quality of the man to head up the project. Famines had ravaged Egypt before, but this time divine warning permitted serious and sustained advance planning. To Pharaoh and his royal retinue, no other candidate but Joseph qualified for the task of working out this good plan, because they recognized that he spoke God-given revelation and insight (v. 39).

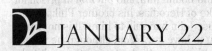

JANUARY 22

Genesis 43:1–44:34

43 Now the famine *was* severe in the
land. 2And it came to pass, when they
had eaten up the grain which they had
brought from Egypt, that their father said to
them, "Go back, buy us a little food."
3But Judah spoke to him, saying, "The man
solemnly warned us, saying, 'You shall not see
my face unless your brother *is* with you.' 4If
you send our brother with us, we will go down
and buy you food. 5But if you will not send

him, we will not go down; for the man said to
us, 'You shall not see my face unless your
brother *is* with you.' "
6And Israel said, "Why did you deal *so*
wrongfully with me *as* to tell the man whether
you had still *another* brother?"
7But they said, "The man asked us pointedly about ourselves and our family, saying, '*Is*
your father still alive? Have you *another* brother?' And we told him according to these
words. Could we possibly have known that he
would say, 'Bring your brother down'?"
8Then Judah said to Israel his father, "Send
the lad with me, and we will arise and go, that
we may live and not die, both we and you *and*
also our little ones. 9I myself will be surety for
him; from my hand you shall require him. If I
do not bring him *back* to you and set him
before you, then let me bear the blame forever. 10For if we had not lingered, surely by now
we would have returned this second time."
11And their father Israel said to them, "If *it*
must be so, then do this: Take some of the best
fruits of the land in your vessels and carry
down a present for the man—a little balm and
a little honey, spices and myrrh, pistachio nuts
and almonds. 12Take double money in your
hand, and take back in your hand the money
that was returned in the mouth of your sacks;
perhaps it was an oversight. 13Take your brother also, and arise, go back to the man. 14And
may God Almighty give you mercy before the
man, that he may release your other brother
and Benjamin. If I am bereaved, I am bereaved!"
15So the men took that present and Benjamin, and they took double money in their
hand, and arose and went down to Egypt; and
they stood before Joseph. 16When Joseph saw
Benjamin with them, he said to the steward of
his house, "Take *these* men to my home, and
slaughter an animal and make ready; for *these*
men will dine with me at noon." 17Then the
man did as Joseph ordered, and the man
brought the men into Joseph's house.
18Now the men were afraid because they
were brought into Joseph's house; and they
said, "*It is* because of the money, which was
returned in our sacks the first time, that we
are brought in, so that he may make a case
against us and seize us, to take us as slaves
with our donkeys."
19When they drew near to the steward of Joseph's house, they talked with him at the door
of the house, 20and said, "O sir, we indeed
came down the first time to buy food; 21but it
happened, when we came to the encampment,
that we opened our sacks, and there, *each*
man's money *was* in the mouth of his sack, our

43:33 the firstborn...the youngest. To be seated at the table in birth order in the house of an Egyptian official was startling—how did he know this of Jacob's sons? Enough clues had been given in Joseph's previous questions about the family and his use of God's name for them to wonder about him and his personal knowledge of them. Obviously, they simply did not believe Joseph was alive (44:20) and certainly not as a personage of such immense influence and authority. They had probably laughed through the years at the memory of Joseph's dreams of superiority.

money in full weight; so we have brought it
back in our hand. 22And we have brought down
other money in our hands to buy food. We do
not know who put our money in our sacks."
23But he said, "Peace *be* with you, do not be
afraid. Your God and the God of your father has
given you treasure in your sacks; I had your
money." Then he brought Simeon out to them.
24So the man brought the men into Joseph's
house and gave *them* water, and they washed
their feet; and he gave their donkeys feed.
25Then they made the present ready for Joseph's coming at noon, for they heard that
they would eat bread there.
26And when Joseph came home, they brought
him the present which *was* in their hand into
the house, and bowed down before him to the
earth. 27Then he asked them about *their* well-
being, and said, "*Is* your father well, the old
man of whom you spoke? *Is* he still alive?"
28And they answered, "Your servant our
father *is* in good health; he *is* still alive." And
they bowed their heads down and prostrated
themselves.
29Then he lifted his eyes and saw his brother Benjamin, his mother's son, and said, "*Is*
this your younger brother of whom you spoke
to me?" And he said, "God be gracious to you,
my son." 30Now his heart yearned for his
brother; so Joseph made haste and sought
somewhere to weep. And he went into *his*
chamber and wept there. 31Then he washed
his face and came out; and he restrained himself, and said, "Serve the bread."
32So they set him a place by himself, and them
by themselves, and the Egyptians who ate with
him by themselves; because the Egyptians
could not eat food with the Hebrews, for that *is*
an abomination to the Egyptians. 33And they sat
before him, the firstborn according to his birthright and the youngest according to his youth;

and the men looked in astonishment at one
another. [34]Then he took servings to them from
before him, but Benjamin's serving was five
times as much as any of theirs. So they drank
and were merry with him.

44 And he commanded the steward of his
house, saying, "Fill the men's sacks
with food, as much as they can carry, and put
each man's money in the mouth of his sack.
[2]Also put my cup, the silver cup, in the mouth
of the sack of the youngest, and his grain
money." So he did according to the word that
Joseph had spoken. [3]As soon as the morning
dawned, the men were sent away, they and
their donkeys. [4]When they had gone out of the
city, *and* were not *yet* far off, Joseph said to his
steward, "Get up, follow the men; and when
you overtake them, say to them, 'Why have
you repaid evil for good? [5]*Is* not this *the one*
from which my lord drinks, and with which he
indeed practices divination? You have done
evil in so doing.' "

[6]So he overtook them, and he spoke to them
these same words. [7]And they said to him,
"Why does my lord say these words? Far be it
from us that your servants should do such a
thing. [8]Look, we brought back to you from the
land of Canaan the money which we found in
the mouth of our sacks. How then could we
steal silver or gold from your lord's house?
[9]With whomever of your servants it is found, let
him die, and we also will be my lord's slaves."
[10]And he said, "Now also *let* it *be* according
to your words; he with whom it is found shall
be my slave, and you shall be blameless."
[11]Then each man speedily let down his sack to
the ground, and each opened his sack. [12]So he
searched. He began with the oldest and left off
with the youngest; and the cup was found in
Benjamin's sack. [13]Then they tore their
clothes, and each man loaded his donkey and
returned to the city.

[14]So Judah and his brothers came to Joseph's house, and he *was* still there; and they
fell before him on the ground. [15]And Joseph
said to them, "What deed *is* this you have
done? Did you not know that such a man as I
can certainly practice divination?"

[16]Then Judah said, "What shall we say to my
lord? What shall we speak? Or how shall we
clear ourselves? God has found out the iniquity of your servants; here we are, my lord's
slaves, both we and *he* also with whom the cup
was found."

[17]But he said, "Far be it from me that I
should do so; the man in whose hand the cup
was found, he shall be my slave. And as for
you, go up in peace to your father."

44:13 tore their clothes. A well-known ancient Near Eastern custom of visibly portraying the pain of heart being experienced. Benjamin's brothers were very upset that he might become a slave in Egypt (v. 10). Benjamin appears to have been speechless. They had passed a second test of devotion to Benjamin (the first in v. 34).

[18]Then Judah came near to him and said: "O
my lord, please let your servant speak a word
in my lord's hearing, and do not let your anger
burn against your servant; for you *are* even
like Pharaoh. [19]My lord asked his servants,
saying, 'Have you a father or a brother?' [20]And
we said to my lord, 'We have a father, an old
man, and a child of *his* old age, *who is* young;
his brother is dead, and he alone is left of his
mother's children, and his father loves him.'
[21]Then you said to your servants, 'Bring him
down to me, that I may set my eyes on him.'
[22]And we said to my lord, 'The lad cannot leave
his father, for *if* he should leave his father, *his
father* would die.' [23]But you said to your servants, 'Unless your youngest brother comes
down with you, you shall see my face no more.'
[24]"So it was, when we went up to your servant my father, that we told him the words of
my lord. [25]And our father said, 'Go back *and*
buy us a little food.' [26]But we said, 'We cannot
go down; if our youngest brother is with us,
then we will go down; for we may not see the
man's face unless our youngest brother *is* with
us.' [27]Then your servant my father said to us,
'You know that my wife bore me two sons; [28]and
the one went out from me, and I said, "Surely
he is torn to pieces"; and I have not seen him
since. [29]But if you take this one also from me,
and calamity befalls him, you shall bring down
my gray hair with sorrow to the grave.'

44:18–34 An eloquent and contrite plea for mercy, replete with reference to the aged father's delight in and doting upon the youngest son (vv. 20,30) and the fatal shock should he be lost (vv. 22,29,31,34). Judah's evident compassion for Jacob and readiness to substitute himself for Benjamin in slavery finally overwhelmed Joseph—these were not the same brothers of yesteryear (45:1).

30"Now therefore, when I come to your servant my father, and the lad *is* not with us, since
his life is bound up in the lad's life, 31it will happen, when he sees that the lad *is* not *with us,*
that he will die. So your servants will bring
down the gray hair of your servant our father
with sorrow to the grave. 32For your servant
became surety for the lad to my father, saying,
'If I do not bring him *back* to you, then I shall
bear the blame before my father forever.'
33Now therefore, please let your servant
remain instead of the lad as a slave to my lord,
and let the lad go up with his brothers. 34For
how shall I go up to my father if the lad *is* not
with me, lest perhaps I see the evil that would
come upon my father?"

Psalm 11:1–7

To the Chief Musician. *A Psalm* of David.

In the LORD I put my trust;
How can you say to my soul,
"Flee *as* a bird to your mountain"?
2 For look! The wicked bend *their* bow,
They make ready their arrow on the string,
That they may shoot secretly at the upright in heart.
3 If the foundations are destroyed,
What can the righteous do?

4 The LORD *is* in His holy temple,
The LORD's throne *is* in heaven;
His eyes behold,
His eyelids test the sons of men.
5 The LORD tests the righteous,
But the wicked and the one who loves violence His soul hates.
6 Upon the wicked He will rain coals;
Fire and brimstone and a burning wind
Shall be the portion of their cup.

7 For the LORD *is* righteous,
He loves righteousness;
His countenance beholds the upright.

Proverbs 4:10–13

10 Hear, my son, and receive my sayings,
And the years of your life will be many.
11 I have taught you in the way of wisdom;
I have led you in right paths.
12 When you walk, your steps will not be hindered,
And when you run, you will not stumble.
13 Take firm hold of instruction, do not let go;
Keep her, for she *is* your life.

Matthew 14:22–36

22Immediately Jesus made His disciples get
into the boat and go before Him to the other
side, while He sent the multitudes away. 23And
when He had sent the multitudes away, He
went up on the mountain by Himself to pray.
Now when evening came, He was alone there.
24But the boat was now in the middle of the
sea, tossed by the waves, for the wind was contrary.
25Now in the fourth watch of the night Jesus
went to them, walking on the sea. 26And when
the disciples saw Him walking on the sea, they
were troubled, saying, "It is a ghost!" And they
cried out for fear.
27But immediately Jesus spoke to them, saying, "Be of good cheer! It is I; do not be afraid."
28And Peter answered Him and said, "Lord,
if it is You, command me to come to You on
the water."
29So He said, "Come." And when Peter had
come down out of the boat, he walked on the
water to go to Jesus. 30But when he saw that
the wind *was* boisterous, he was afraid; and
beginning to sink he cried out, saying, "Lord,
save me!"
31And immediately Jesus stretched out *His*
hand and caught him, and said to him, "O you
of little faith, why did you doubt?" 32And when
they got into the boat, the wind ceased.
33Then those who were in the boat came and
worshiped Him, saying, "Truly You are the
Son of God."
34When they had crossed over, they came to
the land of Gennesaret. 35And when the men
of that place recognized Him, they sent out
into all that surrounding region, brought to
Him all who were sick, 36and begged Him that
they might only touch the hem of His garment. And as many as touched *it* were made
perfectly well.

DAY 22: When the world seems to be falling apart, who can I trust?

In Psalm 11, the panic that launched its writing was not David's but that of his apparently well-meaning counselors. Their mood in the face of wicked persecution is panic, the desire to flee, but David's is peace. Their words are the expressions of committed but confused saints. Their philosophical problem is,"In view of the crumbling of the theocratic society, what can one righteous person, out of a shrinking remnant, do?"

David's immediate response to panic is to say, "In the LORD I put my trust." Literally, he said, "I take refuge in the LORD." God is the exclusive refuge for His persecuted children (see Pss. 16:1; 36:7). After all, David adds, the Lord is "in His holy temple...in heaven." This emphasizes the transcendent throne room of God, yet God has sovereign sway over all the affairs of earth (see Hab. 2:20). "His eyes behold...His eyelids test"—His transcendence previously depicted does not negate His eminence here presented from the perspective of the divine scrutiny of all men, including the righteous (see Jer. 6:27–30; 17:10).

David had made up his mind to trust only in the Lord, and for good reason. In view of David's attitude, this psalm can be listed with the psalms of confidence (Pss. 4,16,23,27,62,125,131).

JANUARY 23

Genesis 45:1–46:34

45 Then Joseph could not restrain himself
before all those who stood by him, and
he cried out, "Make everyone go out from
me!" So no one stood with him while Joseph
made himself known to his brothers. 2And he
wept aloud, and the Egyptians and the house
of Pharaoh heard *it.*
3Then Joseph said to his brothers, "I *am* Joseph; does my father still live?" But his brothers could not answer him, for they were dismayed in his presence. 4And Joseph said to his
brothers, "Please come near to me." So they
came near. Then he said: "I *am* Joseph your
brother, whom you sold into Egypt. 5But now,
do not therefore be grieved or angry with
yourselves because you sold me here; for God
sent me before you to preserve life. 6For these
two years the famine *has been* in the land, and
there are still five years in which *there will be*
neither plowing nor harvesting. 7And God sent
me before you to preserve a posterity for you
in the earth, and to save your lives by a great
deliverance. 8So now *it was* not you *who* sent
me here, but God; and He has made me a
father to Pharaoh, and lord of all his house,
and a ruler throughout all the land of Egypt.
9"Hurry and go up to my father, and say to
him, 'Thus says your son Joseph: "God has
made me lord of all Egypt; come down to me,
do not tarry. 10You shall dwell in the land of
Goshen, and you shall be near to me, you and

45:1–8 Stunned by the revelation of who it really was with whom they dealt, the brothers then heard expressed a masterpiece of recognition of and submission to the sovereignty of God, i.e., His providential rule over the affairs of life, both good and bad.

your children, your children's children, your
flocks and your herds, and all that you have.
11There I will provide for you, lest you and
your household, and all that you have, come to
poverty; for *there are* still five years of famine." '
12"And behold, your eyes and the eyes of my
brother Benjamin see that *it is* my mouth that
speaks to you. 13So you shall tell my father of
all my glory in Egypt, and of all that you have
seen; and you shall hurry and bring my father
down here."
14Then he fell on his brother Benjamin's
neck and wept, and Benjamin wept on his
neck. 15Moreover he kissed all his brothers
and wept over them, and after that his brothers talked with him.
16Now the report of it was heard in Pharaoh's
house, saying, "Joseph's brothers have come."
So it pleased Pharaoh and his servants well.
17And Pharaoh said to Joseph, "Say to your
brothers, 'Do this: Load your animals and
depart; go to the land of Canaan. 18Bring your
father and your households and come to me; I
will give you the best of the land of Egypt, and
you will eat the fat of the land. 19Now you are
commanded—do this: Take carts out of the
land of Egypt for your little ones and your
wives; bring your father and come. 20Also do
not be concerned about your goods, for the
best of all the land of Egypt *is* yours.' "
21Then the sons of Israel did so; and Joseph
gave them carts, according to the command of
Pharaoh, and he gave them provisions for the
journey. 22He gave to all of them, to each man,
changes of garments; but to Benjamin he gave
three hundred *pieces* of silver and five changes
of garments. 23And he sent to his father these
things: ten donkeys loaded with the good things
of Egypt, and ten female donkeys loaded with
grain, bread, and food for his father for the
journey. 24So he sent his brothers away, and
they departed; and he said to them, "See that
you do not become troubled along the way."
25Then they went up out of Egypt, and came
to the land of Canaan to Jacob their father.

26And they told him, saying, "Joseph *is* still
alive, and he *is* governor over all the land of
Egypt." And Jacob's heart stood still, because
he did not believe them. 27But when they told
him all the words which Joseph had said to
them, and when he saw the carts which Joseph had sent to carry him, the spirit of Jacob
their father revived. 28Then Israel said, "*It is*
enough. Joseph my son *is* still alive. I will go
and see him before I die."

46 So Israel took his journey with all that
he had, and came to Beersheba, and
offered sacrifices to the God of his father
Isaac. 2Then God spoke to Israel in the visions
of the night, and said, "Jacob, Jacob!"

And he said, "Here I am."

3So He said, "I *am* God, the God of your
father; do not fear to go down to Egypt, for I
will make of you a great nation there. 4I will go
down with you to Egypt, and I will also surely
bring you up *again;* and Joseph will put his
hand on your eyes."

5Then Jacob arose from Beersheba; and the
sons of Israel carried their father Jacob, their
little ones, and their wives, in the carts which
Pharaoh had sent to carry him. 6So they took
their livestock and their goods, which they
had acquired in the land of Canaan, and went
to Egypt, Jacob and all his descendants with
him. 7His sons and his sons' sons, his daughters and his sons' daughters, and all his
descendants he brought with him to Egypt.

8Now these *were* the names of the children
of Israel, Jacob and his sons, who went to
Egypt: Reuben *was* Jacob's firstborn. 9The
sons of Reuben *were* Hanoch, Pallu, Hezron,
and Carmi. 10The sons of Simeon *were* Jemuel,
Jamin, Ohad, Jachin, Zohar, and Shaul, the son
of a Canaanite woman. 11The sons of Levi *were*
Gershon, Kohath, and Merari. 12The sons of
Judah *were* Er, Onan, Shelah, Perez, and
Zerah (but Er and Onan died in the land of
Canaan). The sons of Perez were Hezron and
Hamul. 13The sons of Issachar *were* Tola,
Puvah, Job, and Shimron. 14The sons of
Zebulun *were* Sered, Elon, and Jahleel. 15These
were the sons of Leah, whom she bore to
Jacob in Padan Aram, with his daughter
Dinah. All the persons, his sons and his
daughters, *were* thirty-three.

16The sons of Gad *were* Ziphion, Haggi,
Shuni, Ezbon, Eri, Arodi, and Areli. 17The sons
of Asher *were* Jimnah, Ishuah, Isui, Beriah,
and Serah, their sister. And the sons of Beriah
were Heber and Malchiel. 18These *were* the
sons of Zilpah, whom Laban gave to Leah his
daughter; and these she bore to Jacob: sixteen
persons.

19The sons of Rachel, Jacob's wife, *were* Jo-
seph and Benjamin. 20And to Joseph in the
land of Egypt were born Manasseh and
Ephraim, whom Asenath, the daughter of Poti-
Pherah priest of On, bore to him. 21The sons of
Benjamin *were* Belah, Becher, Ashbel, Gera,
Naaman, Ehi, Rosh, Muppim, Huppim, and
Ard. 22These *were* the sons of Rachel, who
were born to Jacob: fourteen persons in all.

23The son of Dan *was* Hushim. 24The sons of
Naphtali *were* Jahzeel, Guni, Jezer, and
Shillem. 25These *were* the sons of Bilhah,
whom Laban gave to Rachel his daughter, and
she bore these to Jacob: seven persons in all.

26All the persons who went with Jacob to
Egypt, who came from his body, besides
Jacob's sons' wives, *were* sixty-six persons in
all. 27And the sons of Joseph who were born to
him in Egypt *were* two persons. All the persons of the house of Jacob who went to Egypt
were seventy.

28Then he sent Judah before him to Joseph,
to point out before him *the way* to Goshen.
And they came to the land of Goshen. 29So Joseph made ready his chariot and went up to
Goshen to meet his father Israel; and he presented himself to him, and fell on his neck and
wept on his neck a good while.

30And Israel said to Joseph, "Now let me die,
since I have seen your face, because you *are*
still alive."

31Then Joseph said to his brothers and to his
father's household, "I will go up and tell
Pharaoh, and say to him, 'My brothers and
those of my father's house, who *were* in the
land of Canaan, have come to me. 32And the
men *are* shepherds, for their occupation has
been to feed livestock; and they have brought
their flocks, their herds, and all that they
have.' 33So it shall be, when Pharaoh calls you
and says, 'What is your occupation?' 34that you
shall say, 'Your servants' occupation has been
with livestock from our youth even till now,
both we *and* also our fathers,' that you may
dwell in the land of Goshen; for every shepherd *is* an abomination to the Egyptians."

46:31–34 Joseph's instructions about his preparatory interview with Pharaoh were designed to secure his relatives a place somewhat separate from the mainstream of Egyptian society. The social stigma regarding the Hebrews (43:32), who were shepherds, also (v. 34), played a crucial role in protecting Israel from intermingling and losing their identity in Egypt.

Psalm 12:1–8

To the Chief Musician. On an eight-stringed harp.
A Psalm of David.

Help, LORD, for the godly man ceases!
For the faithful disappear from among
the sons of men.
2 They speak idly everyone with his
neighbor;
With flattering lips *and* a double
heart they speak.

3 May the LORD cut off all flattering lips,
And the tongue that speaks proud
things,
4 Who have said,
"With our tongue we will prevail;
Our lips *are* our own;
Who *is* lord over us?"
5 "For the oppression of the poor, for the
sighing of the needy,
Now I will arise," says the LORD;
"I will set *him* in the safety for which
he yearns."

6 The words of the LORD *are* pure words,
Like silver tried in a furnace of earth,
Purified seven times.
7 You shall keep them, O LORD,
You shall preserve them from
this generation forever.

8 The wicked prowl on every side,
When vileness is exalted among the
sons of men.

Proverbs 4:14–17

14 Do not enter the path of the wicked,
And do not walk in the way of evil.
15 Avoid it, do not travel on it;
Turn away from it and pass on.
16 For they do not sleep unless they have
done evil;
And their sleep is taken away unless
they make *someone* fall.
17 For they eat the bread of
wickedness,
And drink the wine of violence.

Matthew 15:1–20

15 Then the scribes and Pharisees who were
from Jerusalem came to Jesus, saying,
2 "Why do Your disciples transgress the tradition of the elders? For they do not wash their
hands when they eat bread."
3 He answered and said to them, "Why do
you also transgress the commandment of God
because of your tradition? 4 For God commanded, saying, *'Honor your father and your
mother'*; and, *'He who curses father or mother, let him be put to death.'* 5 But you say, 'Whoever says to his father or mother, "Whatever
profit you might have received from me *is* a
gift *to God*"— 6 then he need not honor his
father or mother.' Thus you have made the
commandment of God of no effect by your tradition. 7 Hypocrites! Well did Isaiah prophesy
about you, saying:

8 *'These people draw near to Me
with their mouth,
And honor Me with their lips,
But their heart is far from Me.*
9 *And in vain they worship Me,
Teaching as doctrines the
commandments of men.'* "

10 When He had called the multitude to *Himself*, He said to them, "Hear and understand:
11 Not what goes into the mouth defiles a man;
but what comes out of the mouth, this defiles a
man."
12 Then His disciples came and said to Him,
"Do You know that the Pharisees were offended when they heard this saying?"
13 But He answered and said, "Every plant
which My heavenly Father has not planted
will be uprooted. 14 Let them alone. They are
blind leaders of the blind. And if the blind
leads the blind, both will fall into a ditch."
15 Then Peter answered and said to Him,
"Explain this parable to us."
16 So Jesus said, "Are you also still without
understanding? 17 Do you not yet understand
that whatever enters the mouth goes into the
stomach and is eliminated? 18 But those things
which proceed out of the mouth come from
the heart, and they defile a man. 19 For out of
the heart proceed evil thoughts, murders,
adulteries, fornications, thefts, false witness,
blasphemies. 20 These are *the things* which
defile a man, but to eat with unwashed hands
does not defile a man."

DAY 23: What were the "traditions of the elders"?

The "tradition of the elders" (Matt. 15:2) was a body of extrabiblical law that had existed only in oral form and only since the time of the Babylonian captivity. Later it was committed to writing in the *Mishna* near the end of the second century. The Law of Moses contained no commandment about washing one's hands before eating—except for priests who were required to wash before eating holy offerings (Lev. 22:6,7).

Jesus' problem with the Pharisees is that they used these traditions to dishonor their parents in a cleverly devised way (vv. 4–6). The commandments of God were clear (Ex. 20:12; 21:17; Deut. 5:16); but to circumvent them, some people claimed they could not financially assist their parents because they had dedicated a certain sum of money to God, who was greater than their parents. The rabbis had approved this exception to the commandments of Moses and thus in effect nullified God's law (v. 6).

Hypocritically, they made the commandment of God of no effect by their traditions (v. 6). "Making … of no effect" means, "to deprive of authority" or "to cancel." Jesus condemned this practice by showing that the Pharisees and scribes were guilty of canceling out God's Word through their tradition.

JANUARY 24

Genesis 47:1–48:22

47 Then Joseph went and told Pharaoh, and
said, "My father and my brothers, their
flocks and their herds and all that they possess,
have come from the land of Canaan; and indeed
they *are* in the land of Goshen." 2 And he took
five men from among his brothers and presented them to Pharaoh. 3 Then Pharaoh said to
his brothers, "What *is* your occupation?"
And they said to Pharaoh, "Your servants
are shepherds, both we *and* also our fathers."
4 And they said to Pharaoh, "We have come to
dwell in the land, because your servants have no
pasture for their flocks, for the famine *is* severe
in the land of Canaan. Now therefore, please let
your servants dwell in the land of Goshen."
5 Then Pharaoh spoke to Joseph, saying,
"Your father and your brothers have come to
you. 6 The land of Egypt *is* before you. Have your
father and brothers dwell in the best of the land;
let them dwell in the land of Goshen. And if you
know *any* competent men among them, then
make them chief herdsmen over my livestock."
7 Then Joseph brought in his father Jacob and
set him before Pharaoh; and Jacob blessed
Pharaoh. 8 Pharaoh said to Jacob, "How old *are*
you?"
9 And Jacob said to Pharaoh, "The days of the
years of my pilgrimage *are* one hundred and
thirty years; few and evil have been the days of
the years of my life, and they have not attained to
the days of the years of the life of my fathers in
the days of their pilgrimage." 10 So Jacob blessed
Pharaoh, and went out from before Pharaoh.
11 And Joseph situated his father and his
brothers, and gave them a possession in the
land of Egypt, in the best of the land, in the
land of Rameses, as Pharaoh had commanded.
12 Then Joseph provided his father, his brothers, and all his father's household with bread,
according to the number in *their* families.
13 Now *there was* no bread in all the land; for
the famine *was* very severe, so that the land of
Egypt and the land of Canaan languished
because of the famine. 14 And Joseph gathered
up all the money that was found in the land of
Egypt and in the land of Canaan, for the grain
which they bought; and Joseph brought the
money into Pharaoh's house.
15 So when the money failed in the land of
Egypt and in the land of Canaan, all the Egyptians came to Joseph and said, "Give us bread,
for why should we die in your presence? For
the money has failed."
16 Then Joseph said, "Give your livestock,
and I will give you *bread* for your livestock, if
the money is gone." 17 So they brought their
livestock to Joseph, and Joseph gave them
bread *in exchange* for the horses, the flocks,
the cattle of the herds, and for the donkeys.
Thus he fed them with bread *in exchange* for
all their livestock that year.
18 When that year had ended, they came to
him the next year and said to him, "We will not
hide from my lord that our money is gone; my
lord also has our herds of livestock. There is
nothing left in the sight of my lord but our
bodies and our lands. 19 Why should we die
before your eyes, both we and our land? Buy
us and our land for bread, and we and our land
will be servants of Pharaoh; give *us* seed, that
we may live and not die, that the land may not
be desolate."
20 Then Joseph bought all the land of Egypt
for Pharaoh; for every man of the Egyptians
sold his field, because the famine was severe
upon them. So the land became Pharaoh's.
21 And as for the people, he moved them into
the cities, from *one* end of the borders of
Egypt to the *other* end. 22 Only the land of the
priests he did not buy; for the priests had
rations *allotted to them* by Pharaoh, and they
ate their rations which Pharaoh gave them;
therefore they did not sell their lands.
23 Then Joseph said to the people, "Indeed I
have bought you and your land this day for
Pharaoh. Look, *here is* seed for you, and you

47:25,26 The extra measures imposed by Joseph to control the impact of the famine, i.e., moving parts of the population into cities (v. 21) and demanding a one-fifth tax on crop yields (v. 24), did not affect his approval ratings (v. 25). Whatever the gain to Pharaoh, the people obviously understood that Joseph had not enriched himself at their expense.

shall sow the land. [24]And it shall come to pass
in the harvest that you shall give one-fifth to
Pharaoh. Four-fifths shall be your own, as seed
for the field and for your food, for those of your
households and as food for your little ones."
[25]So they said, "You have saved our lives; let
us find favor in the sight of my lord, and we
will be Pharaoh's servants." [26]And Joseph
made it a law over the land of Egypt to this
day, *that* Pharaoh should have one-fifth, except for the land of the priests only, *which* did
not become Pharaoh's.
[27]So Israel dwelt in the land of Egypt, in the
country of Goshen; and they had possessions
there and grew and multiplied exceedingly.
[28]And Jacob lived in the land of Egypt seventeen years. So the length of Jacob's life was
one hundred and forty-seven years. [29]When
the time drew near that Israel must die, he
called his son Joseph and said to him, "Now if
I have found favor in your sight, please put
your hand under my thigh, and deal kindly
and truly with me. Please do not bury me in
Egypt, [30]but let me lie with my fathers; you
shall carry me out of Egypt and bury me in
their burial place."

And he said, "I will do as you have said."
[31]Then he said, "Swear to me." And he
swore to him. So Israel bowed himself on the
head of the bed.

48 Now it came to pass after these things
that Joseph was told, "Indeed your
father *is* sick"; and he took with him his two
sons, Manasseh and Ephraim. [2]And Jacob was
told, "Look, your son Joseph is coming to
you"; and Israel strengthened himself and sat
up on the bed. [3]Then Jacob said to Joseph:
"God Almighty appeared to me at Luz in the
land of Canaan and blessed me, [4]and said to
me, 'Behold, I will make you fruitful and multiply you, and I will make of you a multitude of
people, and give this land to your descendants
after you *as* an everlasting possession.' [5]And
now your two sons, Ephraim and Manasseh,
who were born to you in the land of Egypt
before I came to you in Egypt, *are* mine; as
Reuben and Simeon, they shall be mine. [6]Your
offspring whom you beget after them shall be
yours; they will be called by the name of their
brothers in their inheritance. [7]But as for me,
when I came from Padan, Rachel died beside
me in the land of Canaan on the way, when
there was but a little distance to go to Ephrath;
and I buried her there on the way to Ephrath
(that is, Bethlehem)."
[8]Then Israel saw Joseph's sons, and said,
"Who *are* these?"
[9]Joseph said to his father, "They *are* my
sons, whom God has given me in this *place*."

And he said, "Please bring them to me, and I
will bless them." [10]Now the eyes of Israel were
dim with age, *so that* he could not see. Then Joseph brought them near him, and he kissed
them and embraced them. [11]And Israel said to
Joseph, "I had not thought to see your face; but
in fact, God has also shown me your offspring!"
[12]So Joseph brought them from beside his
knees, and he bowed down with his face to the
earth. [13]And Joseph took them both, Ephraim
with his right hand toward Israel's left hand, and
Manasseh with his left hand toward Israel's
right hand, and brought *them* near him. [14]Then
Israel stretched out his right hand and laid *it*
on Ephraim's head, who *was* the younger, and
his left hand on Manasseh's head, guiding his
hands knowingly, for Manasseh *was* the firstborn. [15]And he blessed Joseph, and said:

"God, before whom my fathers
Abraham and Isaac walked,
The God who has fed me
all my life long to this day,
[16] The Angel who has redeemed me
from all evil,
Bless the lads;
Let my name be named upon them,
And the name of my fathers Abraham
and Isaac;
And let them grow into a multitude in
the midst of the earth."

[17]Now when Joseph saw that his father laid
his right hand on the head of Ephraim, it displeased him; so he took hold of his father's
hand to remove it from Ephraim's head to
Manasseh's head. [18]And Joseph said to his
father, "Not so, my father, for this *one is* the
firstborn; put your right hand on his head."
[19]But his father refused and said, "I know, my
son, I know. He also shall become a people, and
he also shall be great; but truly his younger
brother shall be greater than he, and his descendants shall become a multitude of nations."
[20]So he blessed them that day, saying, "By
you Israel will bless, saying, 'May God make
you as Ephraim and as Manasseh!' " And thus
he set Ephraim before Manasseh.

[21]Then Israel said to Joseph, "Behold, I am
dying, but God will be with you and bring you
back to the land of your fathers. [22]Moreover I
have given to you one portion above your
brothers, which I took from the hand of the
Amorite with my sword and my bow."

Psalm 13:1–6

To the Chief Musician. A Psalm of David.

1 How long, O LORD? Will You forget
me forever?
How long will You hide Your face from
me?
2 How long shall I take counsel in my soul,
Having sorrow in my heart daily?
How long will my enemy be exalted
over me?

3 Consider *and* hear me, O LORD my God;
Enlighten my eyes,
Lest I sleep the *sleep of* death;
4 Lest my enemy say,
"I have prevailed against him";
Lest those who trouble me rejoice
when I am moved.

5 But I have trusted in Your mercy;
My heart shall rejoice in Your
salvation.
6 I will sing to the LORD,
Because He has dealt bountifully
with me.

Proverbs 4:18–19

18 But the path of the just *is* like
the shining sun,
That shines ever brighter unto
the perfect day.
19 The way of the wicked *is* like darkness;
They do not know what makes them
stumble.

4:18 path of the…shining sun. The path of the believer is one of increasing light, just as a sunrise begins with the faint glow of dawn and proceeds to the splendor of noonday.

Matthew 15:21–39

[21]Then Jesus went out from there and
departed to the region of Tyre and Sidon.
[22]And behold, a woman of Canaan came from
that region and cried out to Him, saying,
"Have mercy on me, O Lord, Son of David! My
daughter is severely demon-possessed."
[23]But He answered her not a word.
And His disciples came and urged Him, saying, "Send her away, for she cries out after us."
[24]But He answered and said, "I was not sent
except to the lost sheep of the house of Israel."
[25]Then she came and worshiped Him, saying, "Lord, help me!"
[26]But He answered and said, "It is not good
to take the children's bread and throw *it* to the
little dogs."
[27]And she said, "Yes, Lord, yet even the little
dogs eat the crumbs which fall from their masters' table."
[28]Then Jesus answered and said to her, "O
woman, great *is* your faith! Let it be to you as
you desire." And her daughter was healed
from that very hour.
[29]Jesus departed from there, skirted the Sea
of Galilee, and went up on the mountain and
sat down there. [30]Then great multitudes came
to Him, having with them *the* lame, blind,
mute, maimed, and many others; and they laid
them down at Jesus' feet, and He healed them.
[31]So the multitude marveled when they saw
the mute speaking, *the* maimed made whole,
the lame walking, and *the* blind seeing; and
they glorified the God of Israel.
[32]Now Jesus called His disciples to *Himself*
and said, "I have compassion on the multitude,
because they have now continued with Me
three days and have nothing to eat. And I do
not want to send them away hungry, lest they
faint on the way."
[33]Then His disciples said to Him, "Where
could we get enough bread in the wilderness
to fill such a great multitude?"
[34]Jesus said to them, "How many loaves do
you have?"
And they said, "Seven, and a few little fish."
[35]So He commanded the multitude to sit
down on the ground. [36]And He took the seven
loaves and the fish and gave thanks, broke
them and gave *them* to His disciples; and the
disciples *gave* to the multitude. [37]So they all ate
and were filled, and they took up seven large
baskets full of the fragments that were left.
[38]Now those who ate were four thousand men,
besides women and children. [39]And He sent
away the multitude, got into the boat, and
came to the region of Magdala.

15:33 Where could we get enough bread…? No wonder our Lord called them men of little faith (8:26; 14:31; 16:8; 17:20), when they asked a question like that in the light of the recent feeding of the 5,000 (14:13–21).

DAY 24: How was Joseph a type of Christ?

Joseph	Parallels	Jesus
37:2	A shepherd of his father's family	John 10:11,27–29
37:3	His father loved him dearly	Matthew 3:17
37:4	Hated by his brothers	John 7:4,5
37:13,14	Sent by father to brothers	Hebrews 2:11
37:20	Others plotted to harm them	John 11:53
37:23	Robes taken from them	John 19:23,24
37:26	Taken to Egypt	Matthew 2:14,15
37:28	Sold for the price of a slave	Matthew 26:15
39:7	Tempted	Matthew 4:1
39:16–18	Falsely accused	Matthew 26:59,60
38:20	Bound in chains	Matthew 27:2
40:2,3	Placed with two other prisoners, one who was saved and the other lost	Luke 23:32
41:41	Exalted after suffering	Philippians 2:9–11
41:46	Both 30 years old at the beginning of public recognition	Luke 3:23
42:24; 45:2,14,15;46:29	Both wept	John 11:35
45:1–15	Forgave those who wronged them	Luke 23:34
45:7	Saved their nation	Matthew 1:21
50:20	What men did to hurt them, God turned to good	1 Corinthians 2:7,8

JANUARY 25

Genesis 49:1–50:26

49 And Jacob called his sons and said, "Gather together, that I may tell you what shall befall you in the last days:

2 "Gather together and hear, you sons of Jacob,
And listen to Israel your father.
3 "Reuben, you are my firstborn,
My might and the beginning of my strength,
The excellency of dignity and the excellency of power.
4 Unstable as water, you shall not excel,
Because you went up to your father's bed;
Then you defiled *it*—
He went up to my couch.

5 "Simeon and Levi *are* brothers;
Instruments of cruelty *are in* their dwelling place.
6 Let not my soul enter their council;
Let not my honor be united to their assembly;
For in their anger they slew a man,
And in their self-will they hamstrung an ox.
7 Cursed *be* their anger, for *it is* fierce;
And their wrath, for it is cruel!
I will divide them in Jacob
And scatter them in Israel.

8 "Judah, you *are he* whom your brothers shall praise;
Your hand *shall be* on the neck of your enemies;
Your father's children shall bow down before you.
9 Judah *is* a lion's whelp;
From the prey, my son, you have gone up.
He bows down, he lies down as a lion;
And as a lion, who shall rouse him?
10 The scepter shall not depart from Judah,
Nor a lawgiver from between his feet,
Until Shiloh comes;
And to Him *shall be* the obedience of the people.
11 Binding his donkey to the vine,
And his donkey's colt to the choice vine,

49:1–28 With Judah and Joseph receiving the most attention (vv. 8–12,22–26), the father's blessing portrayed the future history of each son, seemingly based upon their characters up to that time. The cryptic nature of the poetry demands rigorous analysis for correlating tribal history with Jacob's last word and testament. See Moses' blessing on the tribes in Deuteronomy 33, ca. 1405 B.C.

He washed his garments in wine,
And his clothes in the blood of grapes.
12 His eyes *are* darker than wine,
And his teeth whiter than milk.

13 "Zebulun shall dwell by the haven of the sea;
He *shall become* a haven for ships,
And his border shall adjoin Sidon.

14 "Issachar is a strong donkey,
Lying down between two burdens;
15 He saw that rest *was* good,
And that the land *was* pleasant;
He bowed his shoulder to bear *a burden,*
And became a band of slaves.

16 "Dan shall judge his people
As one of the tribes of Israel.
17 Dan shall be a serpent by the way,
A viper by the path,
That bites the horse's heels
So that its rider shall fall backward.
18 I have waited for Your salvation, O LORD!

19 "Gad, a troop shall tramp upon him,
But he shall triumph at last.

20 "Bread from Asher *shall be* rich,
And he shall yield royal dainties.

21 "Naphtali *is* a deer let loose;
He uses beautiful words.

22 "Joseph *is* a fruitful bough,
A fruitful bough by a well;
His branches run over the wall.
23 The archers have bitterly grieved him,
Shot *at him* and hated him.
24 But his bow remained in strength,
And the arms of his hands were made strong
By the hands of the Mighty *God* of Jacob
(From there *is* the Shepherd, the Stone of Israel),
25 By the God of your father who will help you,
And by the Almighty who will bless you
With blessings of heaven above,
Blessings of the deep that lies beneath,
Blessings of the breasts and of the womb.
26 The blessings of your father
Have excelled the blessings of my ancestors,
Up to the utmost bound of the everlasting hills.
They shall be on the head of Joseph,
And on the crown of the head of him who was separate from his brothers.

27 "Benjamin is a ravenous wolf;
In the morning he shall devour the prey,
And at night he shall divide the spoil."

28 All these *are* the twelve tribes of Israel, and
this *is* what their father spoke to them. And he
blessed them; he blessed each one according
to his own blessing.
29 Then he charged them and said to them:
"I am to be gathered to my people; bury me
with my fathers in the cave that *is* in the field
of Ephron the Hittite, 30 in the cave that *is* in
the field of Machpelah, which *is* before
Mamre in the land of Canaan, which Abraham
bought with the field of Ephron the Hittite as
a possession for a burial place. 31 There they
buried Abraham and Sarah his wife, there
they buried Isaac and Rebekah his wife, and
there I buried Leah. 32 The field and the cave
that *is* there *were* purchased from the sons of
Heth." 33 And when Jacob had finished commanding his sons, he drew his feet up into the
bed and breathed his last, and was gathered
to his people.

50 Then Joseph fell on his father's face
and wept over him, and kissed him.
2 And Joseph commanded his servants the
physicians to embalm his father. So the physicians embalmed Israel. 3 Forty days were
required for him, for such are the days
required for those who are embalmed; and the
Egyptians mourned for him seventy days.
4 Now when the days of his mourning were
past, Joseph spoke to the household of
Pharaoh, saying, "If now I have found favor in
your eyes, please speak in the hearing of
Pharaoh, saying, 5 'My father made me swear,
saying, "Behold, I am dying; in my grave
which I dug for myself in the land of Canaan,
there you shall bury me." Now therefore,
please let me go up and bury my father, and I
will come back.' "
6 And Pharaoh said, "Go up and bury your
father, as he made you swear."
7 So Joseph went up to bury his father; and
with him went up all the servants of Pharaoh,
the elders of his house, and all the elders of
the land of Egypt, 8 as well as all the house of
Joseph, his brothers, and his father's house.
Only their little ones, their flocks, and their
herds they left in the land of Goshen. 9 And
there went up with him both chariots and

horsemen, and it was a very great gathering.
10 Then they came to the threshing floor of
Atad, which *is* beyond the Jordan, and they
mourned there with a great and very solemn
lamentation. He observed seven days of
mourning for his father. 11 And when the inhabitants of the land, the Canaanites, saw the
mourning at the threshing floor of Atad, they
said, "This *is* a deep mourning of the Egyptians." Therefore its name was called Abel
Mizraim, which *is* beyond the Jordan.
12 So his sons did for him just as he had commanded them. 13 For his sons carried him to
the land of Canaan, and buried him in the cave
of the field of Machpelah, before Mamre,
which Abraham bought with the field from
Ephron the Hittite as property for a burial
place. 14 And after he had buried his father, Joseph returned to Egypt, he and his brothers
and all who went up with him to bury his
father.
15 When Joseph's brothers saw that their
father was dead, they said, "Perhaps Joseph
will hate us, and may actually repay us for all
the evil which we did to him." 16 So they sent
messengers to Joseph, saying, "Before your
father died he commanded, saying, 17 'Thus
you shall say to Joseph: "I beg you, please forgive the trespass of your brothers and their
sin; for they did evil to you." ' Now, please, forgive the trespass of the servants of the God of
your father." And Joseph wept when they
spoke to him.
18 Then his brothers also went and fell down
before his face, and they said, "Behold, we *are*
your servants."
19 Joseph said to them, "Do not be afraid, for
am I in the place of God? 20 But as for you, you
meant evil against me; *but* God meant it for
good, in order to bring it about as *it is* this day,
to save many people alive. 21 Now therefore, do
not be afraid; I will provide for you and your little ones." And he comforted them and spoke
kindly to them.
22 So Joseph dwelt in Egypt, he and his
father's household. And Joseph lived one hundred and ten years. 23 Joseph saw Ephraim's
children to the third *generation.* The children
of Machir, the son of Manasseh, were also
brought up on Joseph's knees.

50:20 *but* God meant it for good. Joseph's wise, theological answer has gone down in history as the classic statement of God's sovereignty over the affairs of men.

24 And Joseph said to his brethren, "I am
dying; but God will surely visit you, and bring
you out of this land to the land of which He
swore to Abraham, to Isaac, and to Jacob."
25 Then Joseph took an oath from the children
of Israel, saying, "God will surely visit you, and
you shall carry up my bones from here." 26 So
Joseph died, *being* one hundred and ten years
old; and they embalmed him, and he was put
in a coffin in Egypt.

Psalm 14:1–7

To the Chief Musician. *A Psalm* of David.

The fool has said in his heart,
"*There is* no God."
They are corrupt,
They have done abominable works,
There is none who does good.

2 The LORD looks down from heaven
upon the children of men,
To see if there are any who
understand, who seek God.
3 They have all turned aside,
They have together become corrupt;
There is none who does good,
No, not one.

4 Have all the workers of iniquity
no knowledge,
Who eat up my people *as* they eat
bread,
And do not call on the LORD?
5 There they are in great fear,
For God *is* with the generation of the
righteous.
6 You shame the counsel of the poor,
But the LORD *is* his refuge.

7 Oh, that the salvation of Israel *would
come* out of Zion!
When the LORD brings back the
captivity of His people,
Let Jacob rejoice *and* Israel be glad.

Proverbs 4:20–24

20 My son, give attention to my words;
Incline your ear to my sayings.
21 Do not let them depart from your
eyes;
Keep them in the midst of your heart;
22 For they *are* life to those
who find them,
And health to all their flesh.
23 Keep your heart with all diligence,
For out of it *spring* the issues of life.
24 Put away from you a deceitful mouth,
And put perverse lips far from you.

4:21–23 heart. The "heart" commonly refers to the mind as the center of thinking and reason (3:3; 6:21; 7:3), but also includes the emotions (15:15,30), the will (11:20; 14:14), and thus, the whole inner being (3:5). The heart is the depository of all wisdom and the source of whatever affects speech (v. 24), sight (v. 25), and conduct (vv. 26,27).

Matthew 16:1–28

16 Then the Pharisees and Sadducees
came, and testing Him asked that He
would show them a sign from heaven. 2He
answered and said to them, "When it is
evening you say, '*It will be* fair weather, for the
sky is red'; 3and in the morning, '*It will be* foul
weather today, for the sky is red and threatening.' Hypocrites! You know how to discern the
face of the sky, but you cannot *discern* the
signs of the times. 4A wicked and adulterous
generation seeks after a sign, and no sign shall
be given to it except the sign of the prophet
Jonah." And He left them and departed.
5Now when His disciples had come to the
other side, they had forgotten to take bread.
6Then Jesus said to them, "Take heed and
beware of the leaven of the Pharisees and the
Sadducees."
7And they reasoned among themselves, saying, "*It is* because we have taken no bread."
8But Jesus, being aware of *it,* said to them,
"O you of little faith, why do you reason
among yourselves because you have brought
no bread? 9Do you not yet understand, or
remember the five loaves of the five thousand
and how many baskets you took up? 10Nor the
seven loaves of the four thousand and how
many large baskets you took up? 11How is it
you do not understand that I did not speak to
you concerning bread?—*but* to beware of the
leaven of the Pharisees and Sadducees."
12Then they understood that He did not tell
them to beware of the leaven of bread, but of
the doctrine of the Pharisees and Sadducees.
13When Jesus came into the region of
Caesarea Philippi, He asked His disciples,
saying, "Who do men say that I, the Son of
Man, am?"
14So they said, "Some *say* John the Baptist,
some Elijah, and others Jeremiah or one of the
prophets."
15He said to them, "But who do you say that
I am?"
16Simon Peter answered and said, "You are
the Christ, the Son of the living God."
17Jesus answered and said to him, "Blessed
are you, Simon Bar-Jonah, for flesh and blood
has not revealed *this* to you, but My Father
who is in heaven. 18And I also say to you that
you are Peter, and on this rock I will build My
church, and the gates of Hades shall not prevail against it. 19And I will give you the keys of
the kingdom of heaven, and whatever you
bind on earth will be bound in heaven, and
whatever you loose on earth will be loosed in
heaven."
20Then He commanded His disciples that
they should tell no one that He was Jesus the
Christ.
21From that time Jesus began to show to His
disciples that He must go to Jerusalem, and
suffer many things from the elders and chief
priests and scribes, and be killed, and be
raised the third day.
22Then Peter took Him aside and began to
rebuke Him, saying, "Far be it from You, Lord;
this shall not happen to You!"
23But He turned and said to Peter, "Get
behind Me, Satan! You are an offense to Me,
for you are not mindful of the things of God,
but the things of men."

16:23 Get behind Me, Satan! The harshness of this rebuke contrasts sharply with Christ's words of commendation in vv. 17–19. Jesus suggested that Peter was being a mouthpiece for Satan. Jesus' death was part of God's sovereign plan (Acts 2:23; 4:27,28). "It pleased the LORD to bruise Him" (Is. 53:10). Christ had come with the express purpose of dying as an atonement for sin (John 12:27). And those who would thwart His mission were doing Satan's work.

24Then Jesus said to His disciples, "If anyone desires to come after Me, let him deny
himself, and take up his cross, and follow
Me. 25For whoever desires to save his life will
lose it, but whoever loses his life for My sake
will find it. 26For what profit is it to a man if
he gains the whole world, and loses his own
soul? Or what will a man give in exchange
for his soul? 27For the Son of Man will come
in the glory of His Father with His angels,
and then He will reward each according to
his works.
28Assuredly, I say to you, there are some
standing here who shall not taste death till they
see the Son of Man coming in His kingdom."

DAY 25: Why was Peter's confession of Christ so significant in Matthew 16:16?

To call Jesus the Son of "the living God" was an Old Testament name for God. Never before had He explicitly taught Peter and the apostles the fullness of His identity. God the Father had opened Peter's eyes to the full significance of those claims (v.17), and revealed to him who Jesus really was. Peter was not merely expressing an academic opinion about the identity of Christ; this was a confession of Peter's personal faith, made possible by a divinely regenerated heart.

Jesus said that "you are Peter, and on this rock I will build My church" (v. 18). The word for "Peter," *Petros*, means a small stone (John 1:42). Jesus used a play on words here with *petra*, which means a foundation boulder (see 7:24,25). Since the New Testament makes it abundantly clear that Christ is both the foundation (Acts 4:11,12; 1 Cor. 3:11) and the head (Eph. 5:23) of the church, it is a mistake to think that here He is giving either of those roles to Peter. There is a sense in which the apostles played a foundational role in the building of the church (Eph. 2:20), but the role of primacy is reserved for Christ alone, not assigned to Peter. So Jesus' words here are best interpreted as a simple play on words in that a boulderlike truth came from the mouth of one who was called a small stone. Peter himself explains the imagery in his first epistle: the church is built of "living stones" (1 Pet. 2:5) who, like Peter, confess that Jesus is the Christ, the Son of the living God. And Christ Himself is the "chief cornerstone" (1 Pet. 2:6,7).

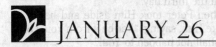

JANUARY 26

Exodus 1:1–2:25

1 Now these *are* the names of the children of
Israel who came to Egypt; each man and his
household came with Jacob: [2]Reuben, Simeon,
Levi, and Judah; [3]Issachar, Zebulun, and Benjamin; [4]Dan, Naphtali, Gad, and Asher. [5]All
those who were descendants of Jacob were
seventy persons (for Joseph was in Egypt
already). [6]And Joseph died, all his brothers,
and all that generation. [7]But the children of
Israel were fruitful and increased abundantly,
multiplied and grew exceedingly mighty; and
the land was filled with them.
[8]Now there arose a new king over Egypt,
who did not know Joseph. [9]And he said to his
people, "Look, the people of the children of
Israel *are* more and mightier than we; [10]come,
let us deal shrewdly with them, lest they multiply, and it happen, in the event of war, that
they also join our enemies and fight against
us, and *so* go up out of the land." [11]Therefore
they set taskmasters over them to afflict them
with their burdens. And they built for Pharaoh
supply cities, Pithom and Raamses. [12]But the
more they afflicted them, the more they multiplied and grew. And they were in dread of
the children of Israel. [13]So the Egyptians made
the children of Israel serve with rigor. [14]And
they made their lives bitter with hard
bondage—in mortar, in brick, and in all manner of service in the field. All their service in
which they made them serve *was* with rigor.
[15]Then the king of Egypt spoke to the Hebrew midwives, of whom the name of one *was*
Shiphrah and the name of the other Puah;
[16]and he said, "When you do the duties of a
midwife for the Hebrew women, and see *them*
on the birthstools, if it *is* a son, then you shall
kill him; but if it *is* a daughter, then she shall
live." [17]But the midwives feared God, and did
not do as the king of Egypt commanded them,
but saved the male children alive. [18]So the king
of Egypt called for the midwives and said to
them, "Why have you done this thing, and
saved the male children alive?"
[19]And the midwives said to Pharaoh, "Because the Hebrew women *are* not like the
Egyptian women; for they *are* lively and give
birth before the midwives come to them."
[20]Therefore God dealt well with the midwives, and the people multiplied and grew
very mighty. [21]And so it was, because the midwives feared God, that He provided households for them.
[22]So Pharaoh commanded all his people,
saying, "Every son who is born you shall cast
into the river, and every daughter you shall
save alive."

1:7 The growth of the nation (see 12:37) was phenomenal! It grew from 70 men to 603,000 males, 20 years of age and older, thus allowing for a total population of about 2 million (Num. 1:46) departing from Egypt. The seed of Abraham was no longer an extended family, but a nation. The promise that his descendants would be fruitful and multiply (Gen. 35:11,12) had indeed been fulfilled in Egypt.

2 And a man of the house of Levi went and
took *as wife* a daughter of Levi. 2So the
woman conceived and bore a son. And when
she saw that he *was* a beautiful *child,* she hid
him three months. 3But when she could no
longer hide him, she took an ark of bulrushes
for him, daubed it with asphalt and pitch, put
the child in it, and laid *it* in the reeds by the
river's bank. 4And his sister stood afar off, to
know what would be done to him.

5Then the daughter of Pharaoh came down
to bathe at the river. And her maidens walked
along the riverside; and when she saw the ark
among the reeds, she sent her maid to get it.
6And when she opened *it,* she saw the child,
and behold, the baby wept. So she had compassion on him, and said, "This is one of the
Hebrews' children."

7Then his sister said to Pharaoh's daughter,
"Shall I go and call a nurse for you from the
Hebrew women, that she may nurse the child
for you?"

8And Pharaoh's daughter said to her, "Go."
So the maiden went and called the child's
mother. 9Then Pharaoh's daughter said to her,
"Take this child away and nurse him for me,
and I will give *you* your wages." So the woman
took the child and nursed him. 10And the child
grew, and she brought him to Pharaoh's
daughter, and he became her son. So she
called his name Moses, saying, "Because I
drew him out of the water."

11Now it came to pass in those days, when
Moses was grown, that he went out to his
brethren and looked at their burdens. And he
saw an Egyptian beating a Hebrew, one of his
brethren. 12So he looked this way and that way,
and when he saw no one, he killed the Egyptian
and hid him in the sand. 13And when he went out
the second day, behold, two Hebrew men were
fighting, and he said to the one who did the
wrong, "Why are you striking your companion?"

14Then he said, "Who made you a prince and
a judge over us? Do you intend to kill me as
you killed the Egyptian?"

So Moses feared and said, "Surely this thing
is known!" 15When Pharaoh heard of this matter, he sought to kill Moses. But Moses fled
from the face of Pharaoh and dwelt in the land
of Midian; and he sat down by a well.

16Now the priest of Midian had seven daughters. And they came and drew water, and they
filled the troughs to water their father's flock.
17Then the shepherds came and drove them
away; but Moses stood up and helped them,
and watered their flock.

18When they came to Reuel their father, he
said, "How *is it that* you have come so soon
today?"

19And they said, "An Egyptian delivered us from
the hand of the shepherds, and he also drew
enough water for us and watered the flock."

20So he said to his daughters, "And where *is*
he? Why *is* it *that* you have left the man? Call
him, that he may eat bread."

21Then Moses was content to live with the
man, and he gave Zipporah his daughter to
Moses. 22And she bore *him* a son. He called
his name Gershom, for he said, "I have been a
stranger in a foreign land."

23Now it happened in the process of time
that the king of Egypt died. Then the children
of Israel groaned because of the bondage, and
they cried out; and their cry came up to God
because of the bondage. 24So God heard their
groaning, and God remembered His covenant
with Abraham, with Isaac, and with Jacob.
25And God looked upon the children of Israel,
and God acknowledged *them.*

2:10 became her son. The position of "son" undoubtedly granted Moses special privileges belonging to nobility, but none of these persuaded Moses to relinquish his native origin. Rather, as the New Testament advises, his spiritual maturity was such that when he came of age, he "refused to be called the son of Pharaoh's daughter" (Heb. 11:24). The formal education in the court of that time meant that Moses would have learned reading, writing, arithmetic, and perhaps one or more of the languages of Canaan. He would also have participated in various outdoor sports, e.g., archery and horseback riding, two favorites of the Eighteenth Dynasty court.

Psalm 15:1–5

A Psalm of David.

LORD, who may abide in Your tabernacle?
Who may dwell in Your holy hill?

2 He who walks uprightly,
And works righteousness,
And speaks the truth in his heart;
3 He *who* does not backbite with his tongue,
Nor does evil to his neighbor,
Nor does he take up a reproach against his friend;
4 In whose eyes a vile person is despised,
But he honors those who fear the LORD;
He *who* swears to his own hurt and does not change;

5 He *who* does not put out his money at
usury,
Nor does he take a bribe against
the innocent.

He who does these *things* shall never
be moved.

15:5 usury. Interest rates ran as high as 50 percent, but God's law put strict regulations on borrowing and lending. **He...shall never be moved.** This is an important promise in the light of its usage in Psalms and Proverbs (see Pss. 10:6; 13:4; 16:8; 46:5; 62:2,6; Prov. 10:30).

Proverbs 4:25–27

25 Let your eyes look straight ahead,
And your eyelids look right before you.
26 Ponder the path of your feet,
And let all your ways be established.
27 Do not turn to the right or the left;
Remove your foot from evil.

Matthew 17:1–27

17 Now after six days Jesus took Peter,
James, and John his brother, led them up
on a high mountain by themselves; [2]and He
was transfigured before them. His face shone
like the sun, and His clothes became as white
as the light. [3]And behold, Moses and Elijah
appeared to them, talking with Him. [4]Then Peter answered and said to Jesus, "Lord, it is
good for us to be here; if You wish, let us make
here three tabernacles: one for You, one for
Moses, and one for Elijah."
[5]While he was still speaking, behold, a
bright cloud overshadowed them; and suddenly a voice came out of the cloud, saying,
"This is My beloved Son, in whom I am well
pleased. Hear Him!" [6]And when the disciples
heard *it,* they fell on their faces and were
greatly afraid. [7]But Jesus came and touched
them and said, "Arise, and do not be afraid."
[8]When they had lifted up their eyes, they saw
no one but Jesus only.
[9]Now as they came down from the mountain, Jesus commanded them, saying, "Tell the
vision to no one until the Son of Man is risen
from the dead."
[10]And His disciples asked Him, saying,
"Why then do the scribes say that Elijah must
come first?"
[11]Jesus answered and said to them, "Indeed,
Elijah is coming first and will restore all
things. [12]But I say to you that Elijah has come
already, and they did not know him but did to
him whatever they wished. Likewise the Son
of Man is also about to suffer at their hands."
[13]Then the disciples understood that He spoke
to them of John the Baptist.
[14]And when they had come to the multitude,
a man came to Him, kneeling down to Him
and saying, [15]"Lord, have mercy on my son, for
he is an epileptic and suffers severely; for he
often falls into the fire and often into the water.
[16]So I brought him to Your disciples, but they
could not cure him."
[17]Then Jesus answered and said, "O faithless and perverse generation, how long shall I
be with you? How long shall I bear with you?
Bring him here to Me." [18]And Jesus rebuked
the demon, and it came out of him; and the
child was cured from that very hour.
[19]Then the disciples came to Jesus privately
and said, "Why could we not cast it out?"
[20]So Jesus said to them, "Because of your
unbelief; for assuredly, I say to you, if you have
faith as a mustard seed, you will say to this
mountain, 'Move from here to there,' and it
will move; and nothing will be impossible for
you. [21]However, this kind does not go out
except by prayer and fasting."
[22]Now while they were staying in Galilee,
Jesus said to them, "The Son of Man is about
to be betrayed into the hands of men, [23]and
they will kill Him, and the third day He will
be raised up." And they were exceedingly
sorrowful.
[24]When they had come to Capernaum, those
who received the *temple* tax came to Peter and
said, "Does your Teacher not pay the *temple*
tax?"
[25]He said, "Yes."
And when he had come into the house, Jesus anticipated him, saying, "What do you
think, Simon? From whom do the kings of the
earth take customs or taxes, from their sons
or from strangers?"
[26]Peter said to Him, "From strangers."
Jesus said to him, "Then the sons are free.
[27]Nevertheless, lest we offend them, go to the
sea, cast in a hook, and take the fish that
comes up first. And when you have opened its
mouth, you will find a piece of money; take
that and give it to them for Me and you."

17:3 Moses and Elijah. Representing the Law and the Prophets respectively, both of which had foretold Christ's death, and that is what Luke says the 3 of them were discussing (Luke 9:31).

DAY 26: How is genuine faith different from positive-thinking psychology?

Jesus' disappointment with His disciples' inability to cast the demon out of the epileptic boy is readily felt in the words, "O faithless and perverse generation, how long shall I be with you?" (Matt. 17:17).

Later, in privacy the disciples asked Jesus, "Why could we not cast it out?" (v. 19). When Christ sent the disciples out (Matt. 10:6–8), He explicitly commissioned them to do these kinds of miracles. Less than a year later, they failed where they had once succeeded. Christ's explanation for their failure was that their faith was deficient (v. 20). The deficiency did not consist in a lack of confidence; they were surprised that they could not cast out this demon. The problem probably lay in a failure to make God—rather than their own gifts—the object of their confidence.

True faith, even "faith as a mustard seed" (v. 20), by Christ's definition, always involves surrender to the will of God. What He was teaching here is nothing like positive-thinking psychology. He was saying that both the source and the object of all genuine faith—even the weak, mustard seed variety—is God. And "with God nothing will be impossible" (Luke 1:37). Here, Christ assumes the qualifying thought that is explicitly added by 1 John 5:14: what we ask for must be "according to His will."

JANUARY 27

Exodus 3:1–4:31

3 Now Moses was tending the flock of Jethro
his father-in-law, the priest of Midian. And
he led the flock to the back of the desert, and
came to Horeb, the mountain of God. 2And the
Angel of the LORD appeared to him in a flame
of fire from the midst of a bush. So he looked,
and behold, the bush was burning with fire,
but the bush *was* not consumed. 3Then Moses
said, "I will now turn aside and see this great
sight, why the bush does not burn."
4So when the LORD saw that he turned aside
to look, God called to him from the midst of
the bush and said, "Moses, Moses!"
And he said, "Here I am."
5Then He said, "Do not draw near this place.
Take your sandals off your feet, for the place
where you stand *is* holy ground." 6Moreover
He said, "I *am* the God of your father—the
God of Abraham, the God of Isaac, and the
God of Jacob." And Moses hid his face, for he
was afraid to look upon God.
7And the LORD said: "I have surely seen the
oppression of My people who *are* in Egypt,
and have heard their cry because of their
taskmasters, for I know their sorrows. 8So I
have come down to deliver them out of the
hand of the Egyptians, and to bring them up
from that land to a good and large land, to a
land flowing with milk and honey, to the place
of the Canaanites and the Hittites and the
Amorites and the Perizzites and the Hivites
and the Jebusites. 9Now therefore, behold, the
cry of the children of Israel has come to Me,
and I have also seen the oppression with
which the Egyptians oppress them. 10Come
now, therefore, and I will send you to Pharaoh
that you may bring My people, the children of
Israel, out of Egypt."
11But Moses said to God, "Who *am* I that I
should go to Pharaoh, and that I should bring
the children of Israel out of Egypt?"
12So He said, "I will certainly be with you.
And this *shall be* a sign to you that I have sent
you: When you have brought the people out of
Egypt, you shall serve God on this mountain."
13Then Moses said to God, "Indeed, *when* I
come to the children of Israel and say to them,
'The God of your fathers has sent me to you,'
and they say to me, 'What *is* His name?' what
shall I say to them?"
14And God said to Moses, "I AM WHO I
AM." And He said, "Thus you shall say to the
children of Israel, 'I AM has sent me to you.' "
15Moreover God said to Moses, "Thus you
shall say to the children of Israel: 'The LORD
God of your fathers, the God of Abraham, the
God of Isaac, and the God of Jacob, has sent
me to you. This *is* My name forever, and this
is My memorial to all generations.' 16Go and
gather the elders of Israel together, and say to
them, 'The LORD God of your fathers, the God
of Abraham, of Isaac, and of Jacob, appeared
to me, saying, "I have surely visited you and
seen what is done to you in Egypt; 17and I have
said I will bring you up out of the affliction of
Egypt to the land of the Canaanites and the
Hittites and the Amorites and the Perizzites
and the Hivites and the Jebusites, to a land
flowing with milk and honey." ' 18Then they
will heed your voice; and you shall come, you
and the elders of Israel, to the king of Egypt;
and you shall say to him, 'The LORD God of the

Hebrews has met with us; and now, please, let us go three days' journey into the wilderness, that we may sacrifice to the LORD our God.' 19 But I am sure that the king of Egypt will not let you go, no, not even by a mighty hand. 20 So I will stretch out My hand and strike Egypt with all My wonders which I will do in its midst; and after that he will let you go. 21 And I will give this people favor in the sight of the Egyptians; and it shall be, when you go, that you shall not go empty-handed. 22 But every woman shall ask of her neighbor, namely, of her who dwells near her house, articles of silver, articles of gold, and clothing; and you shall put *them* on your sons and on your daughters. So you shall plunder the Egyptians."

4 Then Moses answered and said, "But suppose they will not believe me or listen to my voice; suppose they say, 'The LORD has not appeared to you.' "

2 So the LORD said to him, "What *is* that in your hand?"

He said, "A rod."

3 And He said, "Cast it on the ground." So he cast it on the ground, and it became a serpent; and Moses fled from it. 4 Then the LORD said to Moses, "Reach out your hand and take *it* by the tail" (and he reached out his hand and caught it, and it became a rod in his hand), 5 "that they may believe that the LORD God of their fathers, the God of Abraham, the God of Isaac, and the God of Jacob, has appeared to you."

6 Furthermore the LORD said to him, "Now put your hand in your bosom." And he put his hand in his bosom, and when he took it out, behold, his hand *was* leprous, like snow. 7 And He said, "Put your hand in your bosom again." So he put his hand in his bosom again, and drew it out of his bosom, and behold, it was restored like his *other* flesh. 8 "Then it will be, if they do not believe you, nor heed the message of the first sign, that they may believe the message of the latter sign. 9 And it shall be, if they do not believe even these two signs, or listen to your voice, that you shall take water from the river and pour *it* on the dry *land*. The water which you take from the river will become blood on the dry *land*."

10 Then Moses said to the LORD, "O my Lord, I *am* not eloquent, neither before nor since You have spoken to Your servant; but I *am* slow of speech and slow of tongue."

11 So the LORD said to him, "Who has made man's mouth? Or who makes the mute, the deaf, the seeing, or the blind? *Have* not I, the LORD? 12 Now therefore, go, and I will be with your mouth and teach you what you shall say."

13 But he said, "O my Lord, please send by the hand of whomever *else* You may send."

14 So the anger of the LORD was kindled against Moses, and He said: "Is not Aaron the Levite your brother? I know that he can speak well. And look, he is also coming out to meet you. When he sees you, he will be glad in his heart. 15 Now you shall speak to him and put the words in his mouth. And I will be with your mouth and with his mouth, and I will teach you what you shall do. 16 So he shall be your spokesman to the people. And he himself shall be as a mouth for you, and you shall be to him as God. 17 And you shall take this rod in your hand, with which you shall do the signs."

18 So Moses went and returned to Jethro his father-in-law, and said to him, "Please let me go and return to my brethren who *are* in Egypt, and see whether they are still alive."

And Jethro said to Moses, "Go in peace."

19 Now the LORD said to Moses in Midian, "Go, return to Egypt; for all the men who sought your life are dead." 20 Then Moses took his wife and his sons and set them on a donkey, and he returned to the land of Egypt. And Moses took the rod of God in his hand.

21 And the LORD said to Moses, "When you go back to Egypt, see that you do all those

4:21 I will harden his heart. The Lord's personal and direct involvement in the affairs of men so that His purposes might be done is revealed as God informed Moses what would take place. Pharaoh was also warned that his own refusal would bring judgment on him (v. 23). Previously Moses had been told that God was certain of Pharaoh's refusal (3:19). This interplay between God's hardening and Pharaoh's hardening his heart must be kept in balance. Ten times (4:21; 7:3; 9:12; 10:1,20,27; 11:10; 14:4,8,17) the historical record notes specifically that God hardened the king's heart, and ten times (7:13,14,22; 8:15,19,32; 9:7,34,35; 13:15) the record indicates the king hardened his own heart. The apostle Paul used this hardening as an example of God's inscrutable will and absolute power to intervene as He chooses, yet obviously never without loss of personal responsibility for actions taken. The theological conundrum posed by such interplay of God's acting and Pharaoh's acting can only be resolved by accepting the record as it stands and by taking refuge in the omniscience and omnipotence of the God who planned and brought about His deliverance of Israel from Egypt and, in so doing, also judged Pharaoh's sinfulness.

wonders before Pharaoh which I have put in your hand. But I will harden his heart, so that he will not let the people go. 22Then you shall say to Pharaoh, 'Thus says the LORD: "Israel *is* My son, My firstborn. 23So I say to you, let My son go that he may serve Me. But if you refuse to let him go, indeed I will kill your son, your firstborn." ' "

24And it came to pass on the way, at the encampment, that the LORD met him and sought to kill him. 25Then Zipporah took a sharp stone and cut off the foreskin of her son and cast *it* at *Moses'* feet, and said, "Surely you *are* a husband of blood to me!" 26So He let him go. Then she said, "*You are* a husband of blood!"—because of the circumcision.

27And the LORD said to Aaron, "Go into the wilderness to meet Moses." So he went and met him on the mountain of God, and kissed him. 28So Moses told Aaron all the words of the LORD who had sent him, and all the signs which He had commanded him. 29Then Moses and Aaron went and gathered together all the elders of the children of Israel. 30And Aaron spoke all the words which the LORD had spoken to Moses. Then he did the signs in the sight of the people. 31So the people believed; and when they heard that the LORD had visited the children of Israel and that He had looked on their affliction, then they bowed their heads and worshiped.

Psalm 16:1–6

A Michtam of David.

Preserve me, O God, for in You
I put my trust.

2 *O my soul,* you have said to the LORD,
"You *are* my Lord,
My goodness is nothing apart from You."
3 As for the saints who *are* on the earth,
"They are the excellent ones, in whom
is all my delight."

4 Their sorrows shall be multiplied who
hasten *after* another *god;*
Their drink offerings of blood
I will not offer,
Nor take up their names on my lips.
5 O LORD, *You are* the portion of my
inheritance and my cup;
You maintain my lot.
6 The lines have fallen to me in pleasant
places;
Yes, I have a good inheritance.

Proverbs 5:1–6

5 My son, pay attention to
my wisdom;
Lend your ear to my understanding,
2 That you may preserve discretion,
And your lips may keep knowledge.
3 For the lips of an immoral woman drip
honey,
And her mouth *is* smoother than oil;
4 But in the end she is bitter
as wormwood,
Sharp as a two-edged sword.
5 Her feet go down to death,
Her steps lay hold of hell.
6 Lest you ponder *her* path of life—
Her ways are unstable;
You do not know *them.*

Matthew 18:1–20

18 At that time the disciples came to Jesus, saying, "Who then is greatest in the kingdom of heaven?"

2Then Jesus called a little child to Him, set him in the midst of them, 3and said, "Assuredly, I say to you, unless you are converted and become as little children, you will by no means enter the kingdom of heaven. 4Therefore whoever humbles himself as this little child is the greatest in the kingdom of heaven. 5Whoever receives one little child like this in My name receives Me.

18:3 become as little children. This is how Jesus characterized conversion. Like the Beatitudes, it pictures faith as the simple, helpless, trusting dependence of those who have no resources of their own. Like children, they have no achievements and no accomplishments to offer or commend themselves with.

6"Whoever causes one of these little ones who believe in Me to sin, it would be better for him if a millstone were hung around his neck, and he were drowned in the depth of the sea. 7Woe to the world because of offenses! For offenses must come, but woe to that man by whom the offense comes!

8"If your hand or foot causes you to sin, cut it off and cast *it* from you. It is better for you to enter into life lame or maimed, rather than having two hands or two feet, to be cast into the everlasting fire. 9And if your eye causes you to sin, pluck it out and cast *it* from you. It is better for you to enter into life with one eye, rather than having two eyes, to be cast into hell fire.

10"Take heed that you do not despise one of these little ones, for I say to you that in heaven their angels always see the face of My Father who is in heaven. [11]For the Son of Man has come to save that which was lost.

[12]"What do you think? If a man has a hundred sheep, and one of them goes astray, does he not leave the ninety-nine and go to the mountains to seek the one that is straying? [13]And if he should find it, assuredly, I say to you, he rejoices more over that *sheep* than over the ninety-nine that did not go astray. [14]Even so it is not the will of your Father who is in heaven that one of these little ones should perish.

[15]"Moreover if your brother sins against you, go and tell him his fault between you and him alone. If he hears you, you have gained your brother. [16]But if he will not hear, take with you one or two more, that *'by the mouth of two or three witnesses every word may be established.'* [17]And if he refuses to hear them, tell *it* to the church. But if he refuses even to hear the church, let him be to you like a heathen and a tax collector.

[18]"Assuredly, I say to you, whatever you bind on earth will be bound in heaven, and whatever you loose on earth will be loosed in heaven.

[19]"Again I say to you that if two of you agree on earth concerning anything that they ask, it will be done for them by My Father in heaven. [20]For where two or three are gathered together in My name, I am there in the midst of them."

18:20 two or three. Jewish tradition requires at least 10 men (a minyan) to constitute a synagogue or even hold public prayer. Here, Christ promised to be present in the midst of an even smaller flock—"two or three" witnesses gathered in His name for the purpose of discipline.

DAY 27: Is it okay to question God?

Upon hearing that God was sending Moses to be the leader/deliverer of Israel (Ex. 3:10), his response of "Who am I…?" is an expression of inadequacy for such a serious mission. It sounded reasonable, for after 40 years of absence from Egypt, what could he, a mere shepherd of Midian, do upon return?

But was Moses crossing the line from reasonable inquiry to unreasonable doubt in 3:13? God's patient replies instructing Moses on what He would do and what the results would be, including Israel's being viewed with favor by the Egyptians (3:21), ought to caution the reader from hastily classifying Moses' attitude as altogether wrong from the very beginning of the interaction between him and the Lord. Yes, Israel might ask for God's name in validation of Moses' declaration that he had been sent by the God of their fathers. Asking "What is His name?" meant they sought for the relevancy of the name to their circumstances—the character, quality, or essence of a person. God's answer was: "I AM WHO I AM" (v. 14). This name for God points to His self-existence and eternality; it denotes "I am the One who is/will be." The significance in relation to "God of your fathers" is immediately discernible: He's the same God throughout the ages!

A response of divine anger comes only in 4:14 at the very end of Moses' questions and objections, where he moved beyond inquiry into objection.

JANUARY 28

Exodus 5:1–6:30

5 Afterward Moses and Aaron went in and told Pharaoh, "Thus says the LORD God of Israel: 'Let My people go, that they may hold a feast to Me in the wilderness.' "

[2]And Pharaoh said, "Who *is* the LORD, that I should obey His voice to let Israel go? I do not know the LORD, nor will I let Israel go."

[3]So they said, "The God of the Hebrews has met with us. Please, let us go three days' journey into the desert and sacrifice to the LORD our God, lest He fall upon us with pestilence or with the sword."

[4]Then the king of Egypt said to them, "Moses and Aaron, why do you take the people

5:2 Who *is* the LORD…? In all likelihood Pharaoh knew of Israel's God, but his interrogative retort insolently and arrogantly rejected Him as having any power to make demands of Egypt's superior ruler.

from their work? Get *back* to your labor." 5And
Pharaoh said, "Look, the people of the land
are many now, and you make them rest from
their labor!"
6So the same day Pharaoh commanded the
taskmasters of the people and their officers,
saying, 7"You shall no longer give the people
straw to make brick as before. Let them go
and gather straw for themselves. 8And you
shall lay on them the quota of bricks which
they made before. You shall not reduce it. For
they are idle; therefore they cry out, saying,
'Let us go *and* sacrifice to our God.' 9Let more
work be laid on the men, that they may labor
in it, and let them not regard false words."
10And the taskmasters of the people and
their officers went out and spoke to the people,
saying, "Thus says Pharaoh: 'I will not give you
straw. 11Go, get yourselves straw where you
can find it; yet none of your work will be
reduced.'" 12So the people were scattered
abroad throughout all the land of Egypt to gather stubble instead of straw. 13And the taskmasters forced *them* to hurry, saying, "Fulfill your
work, *your* daily quota, as when there was
straw." 14Also the officers of the children of
Israel, whom Pharaoh's taskmasters had set
over them, were beaten *and* were asked, "Why
have you not fulfilled your task in making brick
both yesterday and today, as before?"
15Then the officers of the children of Israel
came and cried out to Pharaoh, saying, "Why
are you dealing thus with your servants?
16There is no straw given to your servants, and
they say to us, 'Make brick!' And indeed your
servants *are* beaten, but the fault *is* in your
own people."
17But he said, "You *are* idle! Idle! Therefore
you say, 'Let us go *and* sacrifice to the LORD.'
18Therefore go now *and* work; for no straw
shall be given you, yet you shall deliver the
quota of bricks." 19And the officers of the children of Israel saw *that* they *were* in trouble
after it was said, "You shall not reduce *any*
bricks from your daily quota."
20Then, as they came out from Pharaoh,
they met Moses and Aaron who stood there to
meet them. 21And they said to them, "Let the
LORD look on you and judge, because you have
made us abhorrent in the sight of Pharaoh
and in the sight of his servants, to put a sword
in their hand to kill us."
22So Moses returned to the LORD and said,
"Lord, why have You brought trouble on this
people? Why *is* it You have sent me? 23For
since I came to Pharaoh to speak in Your
name, he has done evil to this people; neither
have You delivered Your people at all."

5:22,23 Moses returned to the LORD. Whether Moses and his brother remonstrated with the foremen about their strong and wrong evaluation remains a moot point. Rather, the focus is upon Moses, who remonstrated with the Lord in prayer. Evidently, Moses did not anticipate what effect Pharaoh's refusal and reaction would have upon his own people. Confrontation with Pharaoh so far had provoked both angry resentment of Israel by the Egyptians and of Moses by Israel—this was not the expected scenario!

6 Then the LORD said to Moses, "Now you
shall see what I will do to Pharaoh. For
with a strong hand he will let them go, and
with a strong hand he will drive them out of
his land."
2And God spoke to Moses and said to him:
"I *am* the LORD. 3I appeared to Abraham, to
Isaac, and to Jacob, as God Almighty, but *by*
My name LORD I was not known to them. 4I
have also established My covenant with them,
to give them the land of Canaan, the land of
their pilgrimage, in which they were strangers. 5And I have also heard the groaning of
the children of Israel whom the Egyptians
keep in bondage, and I have remembered My
covenant. 6Therefore say to the children of
Israel: 'I *am* the LORD; I will bring you out from
under the burdens of the Egyptians, I will rescue you from their bondage, and I will redeem
you with an outstretched arm and with great
judgments. 7I will take you as My people, and
I will be your God. Then you shall know that I
am the LORD your God who brings you out
from under the burdens of the Egyptians.
8And I will bring you into the land which I
swore to give to Abraham, Isaac, and Jacob;
and I will give it to you *as* a heritage: I *am* the
LORD.'" 9So Moses spoke thus to the children
of Israel; but they did not heed Moses, because
of anguish of spirit and cruel bondage.
10And the LORD spoke to Moses, saying,
11"Go in, tell Pharaoh king of Egypt to let the
children of Israel go out of his land."
12And Moses spoke before the LORD, saying,
"The children of Israel have not heeded me.
How then shall Pharaoh heed me, for I *am* of
uncircumcised lips?"
13Then the LORD spoke to Moses and Aaron,
and gave them a command for the children of
Israel and for Pharaoh king of Egypt, to bring
the children of Israel out of the land of Egypt.

14 These *are* the heads of their fathers' houses: The sons of Reuben, the firstborn of Israel,
were Hanoch, Pallu, Hezron, and Carmi.
These are the families of Reuben. 15 And the
sons of Simeon *were* Jemuel, Jamin, Ohad,
Jachin, Zohar, and Shaul the son of a
Canaanite woman. These *are* the families of
Simeon. 16 These *are* the names of the sons of
Levi according to their generations: Gershon,
Kohath, and Merari. And the years of the life
of Levi *were* one hundred and thirty-seven.
17 The sons of Gershon *were* Libni and Shimi
according to their families. 18 And the sons of
Kohath *were* Amram, Izhar, Hebron, and
Uzziel. And the years of the life of Kohath *were*
one hundred and thirty-three. 19 The sons of
Merari *were* Mahli and Mushi. These *are* the
families of Levi according to their generations.
20 Now Amram took for himself Jochebed, his
father's sister, as wife; and she bore him Aaron
and Moses. And the years of the life of Amram
were one hundred and thirty-seven. 21 The sons
of Izhar *were* Korah, Nepheg, and Zichri. 22 And
the sons of Uzziel *were* Mishael, Elzaphan, and
Zithri. 23 Aaron took to himself Elisheba, daughter of Amminadab, sister of Nahshon, as wife;
and she bore him Nadab, Abihu, Eleazar, and
Ithamar. 24 And the sons of Korah *were* Assir,
Elkanah, and Abiasaph. These are the families
of the Korahites. 25 Eleazar, Aaron's son, took
for himself one of the daughters of Putiel as
wife; and she bore him Phinehas. These *are*
the heads of the fathers' houses of the Levites
according to their families.

26 These *are the same* Aaron and Moses to
whom the LORD said, "Bring out the children
of Israel from the land of Egypt according to
their armies." 27 These *are* the ones who spoke
to Pharaoh king of Egypt, to bring out the children of Israel from Egypt. These *are the same*
Moses and Aaron.

28 And it came to pass, on the day the LORD
spoke to Moses in the land of Egypt, 29 that the
LORD spoke to Moses, saying, "I *am* the LORD.
Speak to Pharaoh king of Egypt all that I say
to you."

30 But Moses said before the LORD, "Behold,
I *am* of uncircumcised lips, and how shall
Pharaoh heed me?"

Psalm 16:7–11

7 I will bless the LORD who has given me
counsel;
My heart also instructs me in the
night seasons.
8 I have set the LORD always before me;
Because *He is* at my right hand I shall
not be moved.
9 Therefore my heart is glad, and my
glory rejoices;
My flesh also will rest in hope.
10 For You will not leave my soul in
Sheol,
Nor will You allow Your Holy One to
see corruption.
11 You will show me the path of life;
In Your presence *is* fullness of joy;
At Your right hand *are* pleasures
forevermore.

Proverbs 5:7–14

7 Therefore hear me now, *my* children,
And do not depart from the words of
my mouth.
8 Remove your way far from her,
And do not go near the door of her
house,
9 Lest you give your honor to others,
And your years to the cruel *one;*
10 Lest aliens be filled with your wealth,
And your labors *go* to the house
of a foreigner;
11 And you mourn at last,
When your flesh and your body
are consumed,
12 And say:
"How I have hated instruction,
And my heart despised correction!
13 I have not obeyed the voice of my
teachers,
Nor inclined my ear to those who
instructed me!
14 I was on the verge of total ruin,
In the midst of the assembly
and congregation."

Matthew 18:21–35

21 Then Peter came to Him and said, "Lord,
how often shall my brother sin against me,
and I forgive him? Up to seven times?"
22 Jesus said to him, "I do not say to you, up
to seven times, but up to seventy times seven.
23 Therefore the kingdom of heaven is like a
certain king who wanted to settle accounts
with his servants. 24 And when he had begun to
settle accounts, one was brought to him who
owed him ten thousand talents. 25 But as he
was not able to pay, his master commanded
that he be sold, with his wife and children and
all that he had, and that payment be made.
26 The servant therefore fell down before him,
saying, 'Master, have patience with me, and I
will pay you all.' 27 Then the master of that servant was moved with compassion, released
him, and forgave him the debt.
28 "But that servant went out and found one

18:24 ten thousand talents. This represents an incomprehensible amount of money. The talent was the largest denomination of currency, and "ten thousand" in common parlance signified an infinite number.

of his fellow servants who owed him a hundred denarii; and he laid hands on him and
took *him* by the throat, saying, 'Pay me what
you owe!' [29]So his fellow servant fell down at
his feet and begged him, saying, 'Have
patience with me, and I will pay you all.' [30]And
he would not, but went and threw him into
prison till he should pay the debt. [31]So when
his fellow servants saw what had been done,
they were very grieved, and came and told
their master all that had been done. [32]Then his

18:28 a hundred denarii. About 3 months' wages. This was not a negligible amount by normal standards, but it was a pittance in comparison to what the servant had been forgiven.

master, after he had called him, said to him,
'You wicked servant! I forgave you all that
debt because you begged me. [33]Should you
not also have had compassion on your fellow
servant, just as I had pity on you?' [34]And his
master was angry, and delivered him to the
torturers until he should pay all that was due
to him.
[35]"So My heavenly Father also will do to you
if each of you, from his heart, does not forgive
his brother his trespasses."

DAY 28: Are there other messianic prophecies in the Psalms other than Psalm 16:10?

Prophecy	Psalm	Fulfillment
1. God will announce Christ to be His Son	2:7	Matthew 3:17; Acts 13:33; Hebrews 1:5
2. All things will be put under Christ's feet	8:6	1 Corinthians 15:27; Hebrews 2:8
3. Christ will be resurrected from the grave	16:10	Mark 16:6,7; Acts 13:35
4. God will forsake Christ in His moment of agony	22:1	Matthew 27:46; Mark 15:34
5. Christ will be scorned and ridiculed	22:7,8	Matthew 27:39–43; Luke 23:35
6. Christ's hands and feet will be pierced	22:16	John 20:25,27; Acts 2:23
7. Others will gamble for Christ's clothes	22:18	Matthew 27:35,36
8. Not one of Christ's bones will be broken	34:20	John 19:32,33,36
9. Christ will be hated unjustly	35:19	John 15:25
10. Christ will come to do God's will	40:7,8	Hebrews 10:7
11. Christ will be betrayed by a friend	41:9	John 13:18
12. Christ's throne will be eternal	45:6	Hebrews 1:8
13. Christ will ascend to heaven	68:18	Ephesians 4:8
14. Zeal for God's temple will consume Christ	69:9	John 2:17
15. Christ will be given vinegar and gall	69:21	Matthew 27:34; John 19:28–30
16. Christ's betrayer will be replaced	109:8	Acts 1:20
17. Christ's enemies will bow down to Him	110:1	Acts 2:34,35
18. Christ will be a priest like Melchizedek	110:4	Hebrews 5:6; 6:20; 7:17
19. Christ will be the chief cornerstone	118:22	Matthew 21:42; Acts 4:11
20. Christ will come in the name of the Lord	118:26	Matthew 21:9

JANUARY 29

Exodus 7:1–8:32

7 So the LORD said to Moses: "See, I have
made you *as* God to Pharaoh, and Aaron
your brother shall be your prophet. [2]You shall
speak all that I command you. And Aaron your
brother shall tell Pharaoh to send the children
of Israel out of his land. [3]And I will harden
Pharaoh's heart, and multiply My signs and
My wonders in the land of Egypt. [4]But
Pharaoh will not heed you, so that I may lay
My hand on Egypt and bring My armies *and*
My people, the children of Israel, out of the
land of Egypt by great judgments. [5]And the
Egyptians shall know that I *am* the LORD,
when I stretch out My hand on Egypt and
bring out the children of Israel from among
them."
[6]Then Moses and Aaron did *so;* just as the
LORD commanded them, so they did. [7]And

Moses *was* eighty years old and Aaron eighty-
three years old when they spoke to Pharaoh.
8Then the LORD spoke to Moses and Aaron,
saying, 9"When Pharaoh speaks to you, saying, 'Show a miracle for yourselves,' then you
shall say to Aaron, 'Take your rod and cast *it*
before Pharaoh, *and* let it become a serpent.' "
10So Moses and Aaron went in to Pharaoh, and
they did so, just as the LORD commanded. And
Aaron cast down his rod before Pharaoh and
before his servants, and it became a serpent.
11But Pharaoh also called the wise men and
the sorcerers; so the magicians of Egypt, they
also did in like manner with their enchantments. 12For every man threw down his rod,
and they became serpents. But Aaron's rod
swallowed up their rods. 13And Pharaoh's
heart grew hard, and he did not heed them, as
the LORD had said.

7:11 magicians. Magic and sorcery played a major role in the pantheistic religion of Egypt. Its ancient documents record the activities of the magicians, one of the most prominent being the charming of serpents. These men were also styled "wise men" and "sorcerers," i.e., the learned men of the day and the religious, as well (the word for sorcery being derived from a word meaning "to offer prayers"). Two of these men were named Jannes and Jambres (see 2 Tim. 3:8). Any supernatural power came from Satan (see 2 Cor. 11:13–15). **enchantments.** By means of their "secret arts" or "witchcraft," the wise men, sorcerers, and magicians demonstrated their abilities to perform a similar feat. Whether by optical illusion, sleight of hand, or learned physical manipulation of a snake, all sufficiently skillful enough to totally fool Pharaoh and his servants, or by evil supernaturalism, the evaluation given in the inspired record is simply "they also did in like manner." However, the turning of rods into snakes and later turning water into blood (7:22) and calling forth frogs (8:7) were not the same as trying to create lice from inanimate dust (8:18–19). At that point, the magicians had no option but to confess their failure.

14So the LORD said to Moses: "Pharaoh's
heart *is* hard; he refuses to let the people go.
15Go to Pharaoh in the morning, when he goes
out to the water, and you shall stand by the
river's bank to meet him; and the rod which
was turned to a serpent you shall take in your
hand. 16And you shall say to him, 'The LORD
God of the Hebrews has sent me to you, saying, "Let My people go, that they may serve
Me in the wilderness"; but indeed, until now
you would not hear! 17Thus says the LORD: "By
this you shall know that I *am* the LORD.
Behold, I will strike the waters which *are* in
the river with the rod that *is* in my hand, and
they shall be turned to blood. 18And the fish
that *are* in the river shall die, the river shall
stink, and the Egyptians will loathe to drink
the water of the river." ' "
19Then the LORD spoke to Moses, "Say to
Aaron, 'Take your rod and stretch out your
hand over the waters of Egypt, over their
streams, over their rivers, over their ponds,
and over all their pools of water, that they may
become blood. And there shall be blood
throughout all the land of Egypt, both in *buckets of* wood and *pitchers of* stone.' " 20And Moses and Aaron did so, just as the LORD commanded. So he lifted up the rod and struck the
waters that *were* in the river, in the sight of
Pharaoh and in the sight of his servants. And
all the waters that *were* in the river were
turned to blood. 21The fish that *were* in the
river died, the river stank, and the Egyptians
could not drink the water of the river. So there
was blood throughout all the land of Egypt.
22Then the magicians of Egypt did so with
their enchantments; and Pharaoh's heart grew
hard, and he did not heed them, as the LORD
had said. 23And Pharaoh turned and went into
his house. Neither was his heart moved by
this. 24So all the Egyptians dug all around the
river for water to drink, because they could not
drink the water of the river. 25And seven days
passed after the LORD had struck the river.
8 And the LORD spoke to Moses, "Go to
Pharaoh and say to him, 'Thus says the
LORD: "Let My people go, that they may serve
Me. 2But if you refuse to let *them* go, behold, I
will smite all your territory with frogs. 3So the
river shall bring forth frogs abundantly, which
shall go up and come into your house, into
your bedroom, on your bed, into the houses of
your servants, on your people, into your
ovens, and into your kneading bowls. 4And the
frogs shall come up on you, on your people,
and on all your servants." ' "
5Then the LORD spoke to Moses, "Say to
Aaron, 'Stretch out your hand with your rod
over the streams, over the rivers, and over the
ponds, and cause frogs to come up on the land
of Egypt.' " 6So Aaron stretched out his hand
over the waters of Egypt, and the frogs came
up and covered the land of Egypt. 7And the
magicians did so with their enchantments,
and brought up frogs on the land of Egypt.

[8]Then Pharaoh called for Moses and Aaron,
and said, "Entreat the LORD that He may take
away the frogs from me and from my people;
and I will let the people go, that they may sacrifice to the LORD."
[9]And Moses said to Pharaoh, "Accept the
honor of saying when I shall intercede for you,
for your servants, and for your people, to
destroy the frogs from you and your houses,
that they may remain in the river only."
[10]So he said, "Tomorrow." And he said, "*Let it
be* according to your word, that you may know
that *there is* no one like the LORD our God. [11]And
the frogs shall depart from you, from your
houses, from your servants, and from your
people. They shall remain in the river only."
[12]Then Moses and Aaron went out from
Pharaoh. And Moses cried out to the LORD
concerning the frogs which He had brought
against Pharaoh. [13]So the LORD did according
to the word of Moses. And the frogs died out of
the houses, out of the courtyards, and out of the
fields. [14]They gathered them together in heaps,
and the land stank. [15]But when Pharaoh saw
that there was relief, he hardened his heart
and did not heed them, as the LORD had said.
[16]So the LORD said to Moses, "Say to Aaron,
'Stretch out your rod, and strike the dust of
the land, so that it may become lice throughout all the land of Egypt.' " [17]And they did so.
For Aaron stretched out his hand with his rod
and struck the dust of the earth, and it became
lice on man and beast. All the dust of the land
became lice throughout all the land of Egypt.
[18]Now the magicians so worked with their
enchantments to bring forth lice, but they
could not. So there were lice on man and
beast. [19]Then the magicians said to Pharaoh,
"This *is* the finger of God." But Pharaoh's
heart grew hard, and he did not heed them,
just as the LORD had said.
[20]And the LORD said to Moses, "Rise early in
the morning and stand before Pharaoh as he
comes out to the water. Then say to him,
'Thus says the LORD: "Let My people go, that
they may serve Me. [21]Or else, if you will not let
My people go, behold, I will send swarms *of
flies* on you and your servants, on your people
and into your houses. The houses of the Egyptians shall be full of swarms *of flies,* and also
the ground on which they *stand.* [22]And in that
day I will set apart the land of Goshen, in
which My people dwell, that no swarms *of flies*
shall be there, in order that you may know
that I *am* the LORD in the midst of the land. [23]I
will make a difference between My people and
your people. Tomorrow this sign shall be." ' "
[24]And the LORD did so. Thick swarms *of flies*
came into the house of Pharaoh, *into* his servants' houses, and into all the land of Egypt.
The land was corrupted because of the
swarms *of flies.*
[25]Then Pharaoh called for Moses and Aaron,
and said, "Go, sacrifice to your God in the land."
[26]And Moses said, "It is not right to do so,
for we would be sacrificing the abomination of
the Egyptians to the LORD our God. If we sacrifice the abomination of the Egyptians before
their eyes, then will they not stone us? [27]We
will go three days' journey into the wilderness
and sacrifice to the LORD our God as He will
command us."
[28]So Pharaoh said, "I will let you go, that you
may sacrifice to the LORD your God in the
wilderness; only you shall not go very far
away. Intercede for me."
[29]Then Moses said, "Indeed I am going out
from you, and I will entreat the LORD, that the
swarms *of flies* may depart tomorrow from
Pharaoh, from his servants, and from his people. But let Pharaoh not deal deceitfully anymore in not letting the people go to sacrifice to
the LORD."
[30]So Moses went out from Pharaoh and entreated the LORD. [31]And the LORD did according to the word of Moses; He removed the
swarms *of flies* from Pharaoh, from his servants, and from his people. Not one remained.
[32]But Pharaoh hardened his heart at this time
also; neither would he let the people go.

Psalm 17:1–7

A Prayer of David.

Hear a just cause, O LORD,
Attend to my cry;
Give ear to my prayer *which is* not
from deceitful lips.
2 Let my vindication come from Your
presence;
Let Your eyes look on the things that
are upright.

3 You have tested my heart;
You have visited *me* in the night;
You have tried me and have found
nothing;
I have purposed that my mouth shall
not transgress.
4 Concerning the works of men,
By the word of Your lips,
I have kept away from the paths of the
destroyer.
5 Uphold my steps in Your paths,
That my footsteps may not slip.

6 I have called upon You, for You will
hear me, O God;

Incline Your ear to me, *and* hear my
speech.
7 Show Your marvelous lovingkindness
by Your right hand,
O You who save those who trust *in You*
From those who rise up *against them.*

Proverbs 5:15–20

15 Drink water from your own cistern,
And running water from your own
well.
16 Should your fountains be
dispersed abroad,
Streams of water in the streets?
17 Let them be only your own,
And not for strangers with you.
18 Let your fountain be blessed,
And rejoice with the wife of your
youth.
19 *As a* loving deer and a graceful doe,
Let her breasts satisfy you
at all times;
And always be enraptured with her love.
20 For why should you, my son, be
enraptured by an immoral woman,
And be embraced in the arms
of a seductress?

5:15–19 Using the imagery of water, the joy of a faithful marriage is contrasted with the disaster of infidelity (vv. 9–14). "Cistern" and "well" refer to the wife from whom the husband is to draw all his satisfying refreshment, sexually and affectionately (v. 19; see 9:17,18; Song 4:9–11).

Matthew 19:1–30

19 Now it came to pass, when Jesus had finished these sayings, *that* He departed
from Galilee and came to the region of Judea
beyond the Jordan. 2And great multitudes followed Him, and He healed them there.
3The Pharisees also came to Him, testing
Him, and saying to Him, "Is it lawful for a man
to divorce his wife for *just* any reason?"
4And He answered and said to them, "Have
you not read that He who made *them* at the
beginning *'made them male and female,'* 5and
said, *'For this reason a man shall leave his
father and mother and be joined to his wife, and
the two shall become one flesh'*? 6So then, they
are no longer two but one flesh. Therefore what
God has joined together, let not man separate."
7They said to Him, "Why then did Moses

19:7 Why then did Moses command to give a certificate of divorce...? The Pharisees misrepresented Deuteronomy 24:1–4. It was not a "command" for divorce, but a limitation on remarriage in the event of a divorce. While recognizing the legitimacy of divorce when a man "has found some uncleanness" (Deut. 24:1) in his wife (sexual sin, by Jesus' interpretation in v. 9), Moses did not "command" divorce.

command to give a certificate of divorce, and
to put her away?"
8He said to them, "Moses, because of the
hardness of your hearts, permitted you to
divorce your wives, but from the beginning it
was not so. 9And I say to you, whoever divorces
his wife, except for sexual immorality, and
marries another, commits adultery; and whoever marries her who is divorced commits
adultery."
10His disciples said to Him, "If such is the
case of the man with *his* wife, it is better not to
marry."
11But He said to them, "All cannot accept
this saying, but only *those* to whom it has been
given: 12For there are eunuchs who were born
thus from *their* mother's womb, and there are
eunuchs who were made eunuchs by men, and
there are eunuchs who have made themselves
eunuchs for the kingdom of heaven's sake. He
who is able to accept *it,* let him accept *it."*
13Then little children were brought to Him
that He might put *His* hands on them and
pray, but the disciples rebuked them. 14But Jesus said, "Let the little children come to Me,
and do not forbid them; for of such is the kingdom of heaven." 15And He laid *His* hands on
them and departed from there.
16Now behold, one came and said to Him,
"Good Teacher, what good thing shall I do that
I may have eternal life?"
17So He said to him, "Why do you call Me
good? No one *is* good but One, *that is,* God.
But if you want to enter into life, keep the commandments."
18He said to Him, "Which ones?"
Jesus said, "*'You shall not murder,' 'You
shall not commit adultery,' 'You shall not
steal,' 'You shall not bear false witness,'*
19*'Honor your father and your mother,'* and,
'You shall love your neighbor as yourself.'"
20The young man said to Him, "All these
things I have kept from my youth. What do I
still lack?"

19:21 go, sell what you have and give to the poor. Again, Jesus was not setting forth terms for salvation, but rather exposing the young man's true heart. His refusal to obey here revealed two things: 1) he was not blameless as far as the law was concerned, because he was guilty of loving himself and his possessions more than his neighbors (see v. 19); and 2) he lacked true faith, which involves a willingness to surrender all at Christ's bidding (16:24). Jesus was not teaching salvation by philanthropy; but He was demanding that this young man give Him first place. The young man failed the test (v. 22). **come, follow Me.** This was the answer to the young man's question in v. 16. It was a call to faith. It is likely that the young man never even heard or contemplated it, though, because his own love of his possessions was such a stumbling block that he had already rejected Jesus' claim to lordship over his life. Thus he walked away in unbelief.

21Jesus said to him, "If you want to be perfect, go, sell what you have and give to the poor, and you will have treasure in heaven; and come, follow Me."

22But when the young man heard that saying, he went away sorrowful, for he had great possessions.

23Then Jesus said to His disciples, "Assuredly, I say to you that it is hard for a rich
man to enter the kingdom of heaven. 24And
again I say to you, it is easier for a camel to go
through the eye of a needle than for a rich
man to enter the kingdom of God."

25When His disciples heard *it,* they were greatly astonished, saying, "Who then can be saved?"

26But Jesus looked at *them* and said to them, "With men this is impossible, but with God all things are possible."

27Then Peter answered and said to Him, "See, we have left all and followed You. Therefore what shall we have?"

28So Jesus said to them, "Assuredly I say to
you, that in the regeneration, when the Son of
Man sits on the throne of His glory, you who
have followed Me will also sit on twelve
thrones, judging the twelve tribes of Israel.
29And everyone who has left houses or brothers or sisters or father or mother or wife or
children or lands, for My name's sake, shall
receive a hundredfold, and inherit eternal life.
30But many *who are* first will be last, and the
last first.

DAY 29: Describe the ten plagues on Egypt.

The Plague	Egyptian Deity	The Effect
1. Blood (7:20)	Hapi	Pharaoh hardened (7:22)
2. Frogs (8:6)	Heqt	Pharaoh begs relief, promises freedom (8:8), but is hardened (8:15)
3. Lice (8:17)	Hathor, Nut	Pharaoh hardened (8:19)
4. Flies (8:24)	Shu, Isis	Pharaoh bargains (8:28), but is hardened (8:32)
5. Livestock diseased (9:6)	Apis	Pharaoh hardened (9:7)
6. Boils (9:10)	Sekhmet	Pharaoh hardened (9:12)
7. Hail (9:23)	Geb	Pharaoh begs relief (9:27), promises freedom (9:28), but is hardened (9:35)
8. Locusts (10:13)	Serapis	Pharaoh bargains (10:11), begs relief (10:17), but is hardened (10:20)
9. Darkness (10:22)	Ra	Pharaoh bargains (10:24), but is hardened (10:27)
10. Death of firstborn (12:29)		Pharaoh and Egyptians beg Israel to leave Egypt (12:31–33)

JANUARY 30

Exodus 9:1–10:29

9 Then the LORD said to Moses, "Go in to
Pharaoh and tell him, 'Thus says the LORD
God of the Hebrews: "Let My people go, that
they may serve Me. 2For if you refuse to let
them go, and still hold them, 3behold, the hand
of the LORD will be on your cattle in the field,
on the horses, on the donkeys, on the camels,
on the oxen, and on the sheep—a very severe
pestilence. 4And the LORD will make a difference between the livestock of Israel and the
livestock of Egypt. So nothing shall die of all
that belongs to the children of Israel." ' "

[5]Then the LORD appointed a set time, saying,
"Tomorrow the LORD will do this thing in the
land."
[6]So the LORD did this thing on the next day,
and all the livestock of Egypt died; but of the
livestock of the children of Israel, not one
died. [7]Then Pharaoh sent, and indeed, not
even one of the livestock of the Israelites was
dead. But the heart of Pharaoh became hard,
and he did not let the people go.
[8]So the LORD said to Moses and Aaron,
"Take for yourselves handfuls of ashes from a
furnace, and let Moses scatter it toward the
heavens in the sight of Pharaoh. [9]And it will
become fine dust in all the land of Egypt, and
it will cause boils that break out in sores on
man and beast throughout all the land of
Egypt." [10]Then they took ashes from the furnace and stood before Pharaoh, and Moses
scattered *them* toward heaven. And *they*
caused boils that break out in sores on man
and beast. [11]And the magicians could not stand
before Moses because of the boils, for the
boils were on the magicians and on all the
Egyptians. [12]But the LORD hardened the heart
of Pharaoh; and he did not heed them, just as
the LORD had spoken to Moses.

9:14 My plagues. God's use of the possessive pronoun specified what should have become abundantly clear to Pharaoh by then, namely, that these were God's own workings. **to your very heart.** "To send to the very heart" was apparently a colloquial expression denoting someone's being made to feel the full force of an act, to feel it strike home!

[13]Then the LORD said to Moses, "Rise early
in the morning and stand before Pharaoh, and
say to him, 'Thus says the LORD God of the Hebrews: "Let My people go, that they may serve
Me, [14]for at this time I will send all My plagues
to your very heart, and on your servants and
on your people, that you may know that *there*
is none like Me in all the earth. [15]Now if I had
stretched out My hand and struck you and
your people with pestilence, then you would
have been cut off from the earth. [16]But indeed
for this *purpose* I have raised you up, that I
may show My power *in* you, and that My
name may be declared in all the earth. [17]As yet
you exalt yourself against My people in that
you will not let them go. [18]Behold, tomorrow
about this time I will cause very heavy hail to
rain down, such as has not been in Egypt since
its founding until now. [19]Therefore send now
and gather your livestock and all that you have
in the field, for the hail shall come down on
every man and every animal which is found in
the field and is not brought home; and they
shall die."'"
[20]He who feared the word of the LORD
among the servants of Pharaoh made his servants and his livestock flee to the houses. [21]But
he who did not regard the word of the LORD
left his servants and his livestock in the field.
[22]Then the LORD said to Moses, "Stretch out
your hand toward heaven, that there may be
hail in all the land of Egypt—on man, on beast,
and on every herb of the field, throughout the
land of Egypt." [23]And Moses stretched out his
rod toward heaven; and the LORD sent thunder
and hail, and fire darted to the ground. And
the LORD rained hail on the land of Egypt. [24]So
there was hail, and fire mingled with the hail,
so very heavy that there was none like it in all
the land of Egypt since it became a nation.
[25]And the hail struck throughout the whole
land of Egypt, all that *was* in the field, both
man and beast; and the hail struck every herb
of the field and broke every tree of the field.
[26]Only in the land of Goshen, where the children of Israel *were,* there was no hail.
[27]And Pharaoh sent and called for Moses
and Aaron, and said to them, "I have sinned
this time. The LORD *is* righteous, and my people and I *are* wicked. [28]Entreat the LORD, that
there may be no *more* mighty thundering and
hail, for *it is* enough. I will let you go, and you
shall stay no longer."
[29]So Moses said to him, "As soon as I have
gone out of the city, I will spread out my hands
to the LORD; the thunder will cease, and there
will be no more hail, that you may know that
the earth *is* the LORD's. [30]But as for you and
your servants, I know that you will not yet fear
the LORD God."
[31]Now the flax and the barley were struck,
for the barley *was* in the head and the flax *was*
in bud. [32]But the wheat and the spelt were not
struck, for they *are* late crops.
[33]So Moses went out of the city from
Pharaoh and spread out his hands to the
LORD; then the thunder and the hail ceased,
and the rain was not poured on the earth.
[34]And when Pharaoh saw that the rain, the
hail, and the thunder had ceased, he sinned
yet more; and he hardened his heart, he and
his servants. [35]So the heart of Pharaoh was
hard; neither would he let the children of
Israel go, as the LORD had spoken by Moses.

10 Now the LORD said to Moses, "Go in to
Pharaoh; for I have hardened his heart
and the hearts of his servants, that I may
show these signs of Mine before him, 2and
that you may tell in the hearing of your son
and your son's son the mighty things I have
done in Egypt, and My signs which I have
done among them, that you may know that I
am the LORD."
3So Moses and Aaron came in to Pharaoh
and said to him, "Thus says the LORD God of
the Hebrews: 'How long will you refuse to
humble yourself before Me? Let My people
go, that they may serve Me. 4Or else, if you
refuse to let My people go, behold, tomorrow
I will bring locusts into your territory. 5And
they shall cover the face of the earth, so that
no one will be able to see the earth; and they
shall eat the residue of what is left, which
remains to you from the hail, and they shall
eat every tree which grows up for you out of
the field. 6They shall fill your houses, the
houses of all your servants, and the houses of
all the Egyptians—which neither your fathers
nor your fathers' fathers have seen, since the
day that they were on the earth to this day.' "
And he turned and went out from Pharaoh.
7Then Pharaoh's servants said to him, "How
long shall this man be a snare to us? Let the
men go, that they may serve the LORD their
God. Do you not yet know that Egypt is
destroyed?"
8So Moses and Aaron were brought again to
Pharaoh, and he said to them, "Go, serve the
LORD your God. Who *are* the ones that are
going?"
9And Moses said, "We will go with our
young and our old; with our sons and our
daughters, with our flocks and our herds we
will go, for we must hold a feast to the LORD."
10Then he said to them, "The LORD had better be with you when I let you and your little
ones go! Beware, for evil is ahead of you. 11Not
so! Go now, you *who are* men, and serve the
LORD, for that is what you desired." And they
were driven out from Pharaoh's presence.
12Then the LORD said to Moses, "Stretch out
your hand over the land of Egypt for the
locusts, that they may come upon the land of
Egypt, and eat every herb of the land—all that
the hail has left." 13So Moses stretched out his
rod over the land of Egypt, and the LORD
brought an east wind on the land all that day
and all *that* night. When it was morning, the
east wind brought the locusts. 14And the
locusts went up over all the land of Egypt and
rested on all the territory of Egypt. *They were*
very severe; previously there had been no
such locusts as they, nor shall there be such
after them. 15For they covered the face of the
whole earth, so that the land was darkened;
and they ate every herb of the land and all the
fruit of the trees which the hail had left. So
there remained nothing green on the trees or
on the plants of the field throughout all the
land of Egypt.
16Then Pharaoh called for Moses and Aaron
in haste, and said, "I have sinned against the
LORD your God and against you. 17Now therefore, please forgive my sin only this once, and
entreat the LORD your God, that He may take
away from me this death only." 18So he went
out from Pharaoh and entreated the LORD.
19And the LORD turned a very strong west
wind, which took the locusts away and blew
them into the Red Sea. There remained not
one locust in all the territory of Egypt. 20But
the LORD hardened Pharaoh's heart, and he
did not let the children of Israel go.
21Then the LORD said to Moses, "Stretch out
your hand toward heaven, that there may be
darkness over the land of Egypt, darkness
which may even be felt." 22So Moses stretched
out his hand toward heaven, and there was
thick darkness in all the land of Egypt three
days. 23They did not see one another; nor did
anyone rise from his place for three days. But
all the children of Israel had light in their
dwellings.
24Then Pharaoh called to Moses and said,
"Go, serve the LORD; only let your flocks and
your herds be kept back. Let your little ones
also go with you."
25But Moses said, "You must also give us
sacrifices and burnt offerings, that we may
sacrifice to the LORD our God. 26Our livestock
also shall go with us; not a hoof shall be left
behind. For we must take some of them to
serve the LORD our God, and even we do not
know with what we must serve the LORD until
we arrive there."
27But the LORD hardened Pharaoh's heart,
and he would not let them go. 28Then Pharaoh
said to him, "Get away from me! Take heed to
yourself and see my face no more! For in the
day you see my face you shall die!"
29So Moses said, "You have spoken well. I
will never see your face again."

10:13 an east wind. God used natural means, most probably the spring hot wind, or "sirocco," to bring the locusts into the country from the Arabian peninsula.

Psalm 17:8–15

8 Keep me as the apple of Your eye;
Hide me under the shadow of Your
wings,
9 From the wicked who oppress me,
From my deadly enemies who
surround me.
10 They have closed up their fat *hearts;*
With their mouths they speak
proudly.
11 They have now surrounded us
in our steps;
They have set their eyes, crouching
down to the earth,
12 As a lion is eager to tear his prey,
And like a young lion lurking
in secret places.

13 Arise, O LORD,
Confront him, cast him down;
Deliver my life from the wicked with
Your sword,
14 With Your hand from men,
O LORD,
From men of the world *who have*
their portion in *this* life,
And whose belly You fill with
Your hidden treasure.
They are satisfied with children,
And leave the rest of their *possession*
for their babes.

15 As for me, I will see Your face
in righteousness;
I shall be satisfied when I awake
in Your likeness.

Proverbs 5:21–23

21 For the ways of man *are* before the
eyes of the LORD,
And He ponders all his paths.
22 His own iniquities entrap the wicked
man,
And he is caught in the cords
of his sin.
23 He shall die for lack of instruction,
And in the greatness of his folly he
shall go astray.

Matthew 20:1–16

20 "For the kingdom of heaven is like a
landowner who went out early in the
morning to hire laborers for his vineyard.
2Now when he had agreed with the laborers
for a denarius a day, he sent them into his
vineyard. 3And he went out about the third
hour and saw others standing idle in the
marketplace, 4and said to them, 'You also go
into the vineyard, and whatever is right I will
give you.' So they went. 5Again he went out
about the sixth and the ninth hour, and did
likewise. 6And about the eleventh hour he
went out and found others standing idle, and
said to them, 'Why have you been standing
here idle all day?' 7They said to him, 'Because
no one hired us.' He said to them, 'You also
go into the vineyard, and whatever is right
you will receive.'
8"So when evening had come, the owner of
the vineyard said to his steward, 'Call the
laborers and give them *their* wages, beginning
with the last to the first.' 9And when those
came who *were hired* about the eleventh hour,
they each received a denarius. 10But when the
first came, they supposed that they would
receive more; and they likewise received each
a denarius. 11And when they had received *it,*
they complained against the landowner, 12say-
ing, 'These last *men* have worked *only* one
hour, and you made them equal to us who
have borne the burden and the heat of the
day.' 13But he answered one of them and said,
'Friend, I am doing you no wrong. Did you not
agree with me for a denarius? 14Take *what is*
yours and go your way. I wish to give to this
last man *the same* as to you. 15Is it not lawful for
me to do what I wish with my own things? Or
is your eye evil because I am good?' 16So the
last will be first, and the first last. For many
are called, but few chosen."

5:21,22 ponders...caught. The Lord sees all that man does and in mercy withholds immediate judgment, allowing the sinner time to repent or to be caught in his own sin (see Num. 32:23; Pss. 7:15,16; 57:6; Prov. 1:17; Gal. 6:7,8). Note the example of Haman (Esth. 5:9–14; 7:1–10).

20:16 the last will be first, and the first last. In other words, everyone finishes in a dead heat. No matter how long each of the workers worked, they each received a full day's wage. Similarly, the thief on the cross will enjoy the full blessings of heaven alongside those who have labored their whole lives for Christ. Such is the grace of God.

DAY 30: Why don't the Egyptian historical records acknowledge the events of the Exodus?

The absence of any Egyptian record of the devastation of Egypt by the 10 plagues and the major defeat of Pharaoh's elite army at the Red Sea should not give rise to speculation on whether the account is historically authentic. Egyptian historiography did not permit records of their pharaohs' embarrassments and ignominious defeats to be published. Interestingly, one of the subtle proofs of the truth of Scripture is the way in which it records both the triumphs and the tragedies of God's people. The Bible offers as many examples of failure as it does of faith.

Despite the absence of any extrabiblical, ancient Near Eastern records of the Hebrew bondage, the plagues, the Exodus, and the Conquest, archeological evidence corroborates Israel's dramatic exit from Egypt as occurring during the Eighteenth Dynasty (about 1445 B.C.), a setting of great political strength and economic strength in Egyptian history. Egypt was a world military, economic, and political superpower.

JANUARY 31

Exodus 11:1–12:51

11 And the LORD said to Moses, "I will bring
one more plague on Pharaoh and on
Egypt. Afterward he will let you go from here.
When he lets *you* go, he will surely drive you
out of here altogether. 2Speak now in the hearing of the people, and let every man ask from
his neighbor and every woman from her
neighbor, articles of silver and articles of
gold." 3And the LORD gave the people favor in
the sight of the Egyptians. Moreover the man
Moses *was* very great in the land of Egypt, in
the sight of Pharaoh's servants and in the
sight of the people.
4Then Moses said, "Thus says the LORD:
'About midnight I will go out into the midst of
Egypt; 5and all the firstborn in the land of
Egypt shall die, from the firstborn of Pharaoh
who sits on his throne, even to the firstborn of
the female servant who *is* behind the handmill,
and all the firstborn of the animals. 6Then there
shall be a great cry throughout all the land of
Egypt, such as was not like it *before,* nor shall
be like it again. 7But against none of the children of Israel shall a dog move its tongue,
against man or beast, that you may know that
the LORD does make a difference between the
Egyptians and Israel.' 8And all these your servants shall come down to me and bow down to
me, saying, 'Get out, and all the people who
follow you!' After that I will go out." Then he
went out from Pharaoh in great anger.
9But the LORD said to Moses, "Pharaoh will
not heed you, so that My wonders may be
multiplied in the land of Egypt." 10So Moses
and Aaron did all these wonders before
Pharaoh; and the LORD hardened Pharaoh's
heart, and he did not let the children of Israel
go out of his land.
12 Now the LORD spoke to Moses and Aaron
in the land of Egypt, saying, 2"This month
shall be your beginning of months; it *shall be*
the first month of the year to you. 3Speak to all
the congregation of Israel, saying: 'On the
tenth of this month every man shall take for
himself a lamb, according to the house of *his*
father, a lamb for a household. 4And if the
household is too small for the lamb, let him
and his neighbor next to his house take *it*
according to the number of the persons;
according to each man's need you shall make
your count for the lamb. 5Your lamb shall be
without blemish, a male of the first year. You
may take *it* from the sheep or from the goats.
6Now you shall keep it until the fourteenth day
of the same month. Then the whole assembly
of the congregation of Israel shall kill it at twilight. 7And they shall take *some* of the blood
and put *it* on the two doorposts and on the lintel of the houses where they eat it. 8Then they
shall eat the flesh on that night; roasted in fire,
with unleavened bread *and* with bitter *herbs*
they shall eat it. 9Do not eat it raw, nor boiled
at all with water, but roasted in fire—its head

11:5 the firstborn. The firstborn held a particularly important position in the family and society, not only inheriting a double portion of the father's estate, but also representing special qualities of life and strength (see Gen. 49:3). In Egypt, the firstborn would ascend to the throne and continue the dynasty. Whatever significance might have been attached religiously, politically, dynastically, and socially, it was all stripped away by the extent and intensity of the plague—namely, the execution of all the firstborn of all classes of the population including their animals.

with its legs and its entrails. 10You shall let
none of it remain until morning, and what
remains of it until morning you shall burn
with fire. 11And thus you shall eat it: *with* a belt
on your waist, your sandals on your feet, and
your staff in your hand. So you shall eat it in
haste. It *is* the LORD's Passover.

12"For I will pass through the land of Egypt
on that night, and will strike all the firstborn in
the land of Egypt, both man and beast; and
against all the gods of Egypt I will execute
judgment: I *am* the LORD. 13Now the blood
shall be a sign for you on the houses where
you *are.* And when I see the blood, I will pass
over you; and the plague shall not be on you to
destroy *you* when I strike the land of Egypt.

14"So this day shall be to you a memorial; and
you shall keep it as a feast to the LORD
throughout your generations. You shall keep it
as a feast by an everlasting ordinance. 15Seven
days you shall eat unleavened bread. On the
first day you shall remove leaven from your
houses. For whoever eats leavened bread
from the first day until the seventh day, that
person shall be cut off from Israel. 16On the
first day *there shall be* a holy convocation, and
on the seventh day there shall be a holy convocation for you. No manner of work shall be
done on them; but *that* which everyone must
eat—that only may be prepared by you. 17So
you shall observe *the Feast of* Unleavened
Bread, for on this same day I will have brought
your armies out of the land of Egypt. Therefore you shall observe this day throughout
your generations as an everlasting ordinance.
18In the first *month,* on the fourteenth day of
the month at evening, you shall eat unleavened bread, until the twenty-first day of the
month at evening. 19For seven days no leaven
shall be found in your houses, since whoever
eats what is leavened, that same person shall
be cut off from the congregation of Israel,
whether *he is* a stranger or a native of the land.
20You shall eat nothing leavened; in all your
dwellings you shall eat unleavened bread.' "

21Then Moses called for all the elders of
Israel and said to them, "Pick out and take
lambs for yourselves according to your families, and kill the Passover *lamb.* 22And you
shall take a bunch of hyssop, dip *it* in the
blood that *is* in the basin, and strike the lintel
and the two doorposts with the blood that *is* in
the basin. And none of you shall go out of the
door of his house until morning. 23For the
LORD will pass through to strike the Egyptians; and when He sees the blood on the lintel and on the two doorposts, the LORD will
pass over the door and not allow the destroyer
to come into your houses to strike *you.* 24And
you shall observe this thing as an ordinance
for you and your sons forever. 25It will come to
pass when you come to the land which the
LORD will give you, just as He promised, that
you shall keep this service. 26And it shall be,
when your children say to you, 'What do you
mean by this service?' 27that you shall say, 'It *is*
the Passover sacrifice of the LORD, who passed
over the houses of the children of Israel in
Egypt when He struck the Egyptians and
delivered our households.' " So the people
bowed their heads and worshiped. 28Then the
children of Israel went away and did *so;* just as
the LORD had commanded Moses and Aaron,
so they did.

29And it came to pass at midnight that the
LORD struck all the firstborn in the land of
Egypt, from the firstborn of Pharaoh who sat
on his throne to the firstborn of the captive
who *was* in the dungeon, and all the firstborn
of livestock. 30So Pharaoh rose in the night, he,
all his servants, and all the Egyptians; and
there was a great cry in Egypt, for *there was*
not a house where *there was* not one dead.

31Then he called for Moses and Aaron by
night, and said, "Rise, go out from among my
people, both you and the children of Israel.
And go, serve the LORD as you have said.
32Also take your flocks and your herds, as you
have said, and be gone; and bless me also."

33And the Egyptians urged the people, that
they might send them out of the land in haste.
For they said, "We *shall* all *be* dead." 34So the
people took their dough before it was leavened, having their kneading bowls bound up
in their clothes on their shoulders. 35Now
the children of Israel had done according to
the word of Moses, and they had asked from
the Egyptians articles of silver, articles of
gold, and clothing. 36And the LORD had given
the people favor in the sight of the Egyptians,
so that they granted them *what they requested.*
Thus they plundered the Egyptians.

37Then the children of Israel journeyed from
Rameses to Succoth, about six hundred thousand men on foot, besides children. 38A mixed
multitude went up with them also, and flocks
and herds—a great deal of livestock. 39And
they baked unleavened cakes of the dough
which they had brought out of Egypt; for it
was not leavened, because they were driven
out of Egypt and could not wait, nor had they
prepared provisions for themselves.

40Now the sojourn of the children of Israel
who lived in Egypt *was* four hundred and thirty years. 41And it came to pass at the end of the
four hundred and thirty years—on that very

same day—it came to pass that all the armies
of the LORD went out from the land of Egypt.
42 It *is* a night of solemn observance to the
LORD for bringing them out of the land of
Egypt. This *is* that night of the LORD, a solemn
observance for all the children of Israel
throughout their generations.
43 And the LORD said to Moses and Aaron,
"This *is* the ordinance of the Passover: No foreigner shall eat it. 44 But every man's servant
who is bought for money, when you have circumcised him, then he may eat it. 45 A sojourner and a hired servant shall not eat it. 46 In one
house it shall be eaten; you shall not carry any
of the flesh outside the house, nor shall you
break one of its bones. 47 All the congregation
of Israel shall keep it. 48 And when a stranger
dwells with you *and wants* to keep the
Passover to the LORD, let all his males be circumcised, and then let him come near and
keep it; and he shall be as a native of the land.
For no uncircumcised person shall eat it.
49 One law shall be for the native-born and for
the stranger who dwells among you."
50 Thus all the children of Israel did; as the
LORD commanded Moses and Aaron, so they
did. 51 And it came to pass, on that very same
day, that the LORD brought the children of
Israel out of the land of Egypt according to
their armies.

Psalm 18:1–12

To the Chief Musician. *A Psalm* of David the servant of the LORD, who spoke to the LORD the words of this song on the day that the LORD delivered him from the hand of all his enemies and from the hand of Saul. And he said:

I will love You, O LORD, my strength.
2 The LORD is my rock and my
fortress and my deliverer;
My God, my strength, in whom I will
trust;
My shield and the horn of my
salvation, my stronghold.
3 I will call upon the LORD, *who is worthy*
to be praised;
So shall I be saved from my enemies.

4 The pangs of death surrounded me,
And the floods of ungodliness made
me afraid.
5 The sorrows of Sheol surrounded me;
The snares of death confronted me.
6 In my distress I called upon the LORD,
And cried out to my God;
He heard my voice from His temple,
And my cry came before Him, *even* to
His ears.
7 Then the earth shook and trembled;
The foundations of the hills also
quaked and were shaken,
Because He was angry.
8 Smoke went up from His nostrils,
And devouring fire from
His mouth;
Coals were kindled by it.
9 He bowed the heavens also,
and came down
With darkness under His feet.
10 And He rode upon a cherub,
and flew;
He flew upon the wings of the wind.
11 He made darkness His secret place;
His canopy around Him *was* dark
waters
And thick clouds of the skies.
12 From the brightness before Him,
His thick clouds passed with hailstones
and coals of fire.

Proverbs 6:1–5

6 My son, if you become surety
for your friend,
If you have shaken hands in pledge
for a stranger,
2 You are snared by the words of your
mouth;
You are taken by the words
of your mouth.
3 So do this, my son, and deliver
yourself;
For you have come into the hand
of your friend:
Go and humble yourself;
Plead with your friend.
4 Give no sleep to your eyes,
Nor slumber to your eyelids.
5 Deliver yourself like a gazelle from
the hand *of the hunter,*
And like a bird from the hand
of the fowler.

6:2–4 snared...come into the hand. See 22:26, 27. Anyone who becomes responsible for another person's debt is trapped and controlled because he has yielded control of what God has given him as a stewardship. The situation is so serious that it is imperative to take control of one's own God-given resources and get out of such an intolerable arrangement immediately ("deliver yourself," vv. 3,4) before coming to poverty or slavery. See Genesis 43:9; 44:32,33.

Matthew 20:17–34

[17]Now Jesus, going up to Jerusalem, took
the twelve disciples aside on the road and said
to them, [18]"Behold, we are going up to Jerusalem, and the Son of Man will be betrayed to
the chief priests and to the scribes; and they
will condemn Him to death, [19]and deliver Him
to the Gentiles to mock and to scourge and to
crucify. And the third day He will rise again."
[20]Then the mother of Zebedee's sons came
to Him with her sons, kneeling down and asking something from Him.
[21]And He said to her, "What do you wish?"
She said to Him, "Grant that these two sons
of mine may sit, one on Your right hand and
the other on the left, in Your kingdom."
[22]But Jesus answered and said, "You do not
know what you ask. Are you able to drink the
cup that I am about to drink, and be baptized
with the baptism that I am baptized with?"
They said to Him, "We are able."
[23]So He said to them, "You will indeed drink
My cup, and be baptized with the baptism that
I am baptized with; but to sit on My right
hand and on My left is not Mine to give, but *it*
is for those for whom it is prepared by My
Father."
[24]And when the ten heard *it,* they were
greatly displeased with the two brothers. [25]But
Jesus called them to *Himself* and said, "You
know that the rulers of the Gentiles lord it
over them, and those who are great exercise
authority over them. [26]Yet it shall not be so
among you; but whoever desires to become
great among you, let him be your servant.
[27]And whoever desires to be first among you,
let him be your slave— [28]just as the Son of
Man did not come to be served, but to serve,
and to give His life a ransom for many."
[29]Now as they went out of Jericho, a great
multitude followed Him. [30]And behold, two
blind men sitting by the road, when they heard
that Jesus was passing by, cried out, saying,
"Have mercy on us, O Lord, Son of David!"
[31]Then the multitude warned them that they
should be quiet; but they cried out all the
more, saying, "Have mercy on us, O Lord, Son
of David!"
[32]So Jesus stood still and called them, and
said, "What do you want Me to do for you?"
[33]They said to Him, "Lord, that our eyes may
be opened." [34]So Jesus had compassion and
touched their eyes. And immediately their
eyes received sight, and they followed Him.

20:28 to give His life a ransom for many. The word translated "for" means "in the place of," underscoring the substitutionary nature of Christ's sacrifice. A "ransom" is a price paid to redeem a slave or a prisoner. Redemption does not involve a price paid to Satan. Rather, the ransom is offered to God—to satisfy His justice and wrath against sin. The price paid was Christ's own life—as a blood atonement (see Lev. 17:11; Heb. 9:22). This, then, is the meaning of the cross: Christ subjected Himself to the divine punishment against sin on our behalf (see Is. 53:4,5). Suffering the brunt of divine wrath in the place of sinners was the "cup" He spoke of having to drink, and the baptism He was preparing to undergo (v. 22).

DAY 31: Describe the chronology of the Exodus.

Date	Event	Reference
Fifteenth day, first month, first year	Exodus	Exodus 12
Fifteenth day, second month, first year	Arrival in Wilderness of Sin	Exodus 16:1
Third month, first year	Arrival in Wilderness of Sinai	Exodus 19:1
First day, first month, second year	Erection of Tabernacle	Exodus 40:1,17
	Dedication of Altar	Numbers 7:1
	Consecration of Levites	Numbers 8:1–26
Fourteenth day, first month, second year	Passover	Numbers 9:5
First day, second month, second year	Census	Numbers 1:1,18
Fourteenth day, second month, second year	Supplemental Passover	Numbers 9:11
Twentieth day, second month, second year	Departure from Sinai	Numbers 10:11
First month, fortieth year	In Wilderness of Zin	Numbers 20:1,22–29; 33:38
First day, fifth month, fortieth year	Death of Aaron	Numbers 20:22–29; 33:38
First day, eleventh month, fortieth year	Moses' Address	Deuteronomy 1:3

FEBRUARY 1

Exodus 13:1–14:31

13 Then the LORD spoke to Moses, saying,
2 "Consecrate to Me all the firstborn,
whatever opens the womb among the children
of Israel, *both* of man and beast; it is Mine."
3 And Moses said to the people: "Remember
this day in which you went out of Egypt, out of
the house of bondage; for by strength of hand
the LORD brought you out of this *place.* No
leavened bread shall be eaten. 4 On this day
you are going out, in the month Abib. 5 And it
shall be, when the LORD brings you into the
land of the Canaanites and the Hittites and the
Amorites and the Hivites and the Jebusites,
which He swore to your fathers to give you, a
land flowing with milk and honey, that you
shall keep this service in this month. 6 Seven
days you shall eat unleavened bread, and on
the seventh day *there shall be* a feast to the
LORD. 7 Unleavened bread shall be eaten seven
days. And no leavened bread shall be seen
among you, nor shall leaven be seen among
you in all your quarters. 8 And you shall tell your
son in that day, saying, '*This is done* because of
what the LORD did for me when I came up
from Egypt.' 9 It shall be as a sign to you on your
hand and as a memorial between your eyes,
that the LORD's law may be in your mouth; for
with a strong hand the LORD has brought you
out of Egypt. 10 You shall therefore keep this ordinance in its season from year to year.
11 "And it shall be, when the LORD brings you
into the land of the Canaanites, as He swore to
you and your fathers, and gives it to you, 12 that
you shall set apart to the LORD all that open the
womb, that is, every firstborn that comes from
an animal which you have; the males *shall be*
the LORD's. 13 But every firstborn of a donkey
you shall redeem with a lamb; and if you will
not redeem *it,* then you shall break its neck.
And all the firstborn of man among your sons
you shall redeem. 14 So it shall be, when your
son asks you in time to come, saying, 'What *is*
this?' that you shall say to him, 'By strength of
hand the LORD brought us out of Egypt, out of
the house of bondage. 15 And it came to pass,
when Pharaoh was stubborn about letting us
go, that the LORD killed all the firstborn in the
land of Egypt, both the firstborn of man and
the firstborn of beast. Therefore I sacrifice to
the LORD all males that open the womb, but
all the firstborn of my sons I redeem.' 16 It shall
be as a sign on your hand and as frontlets
between your eyes, for by strength of hand
the LORD brought us out of Egypt."
17 Then it came to pass, when Pharaoh had
let the people go, that God did not lead them
by way of the land of the Philistines, although
that *was* near; for God said, "Lest perhaps the
people change their minds when they see war,
and return to Egypt." 18 So God led the people
around *by* way of the wilderness of the Red
Sea. And the children of Israel went up in
orderly ranks out of the land of Egypt.
19 And Moses took the bones of Joseph with
him, for he had placed the children of Israel
under solemn oath, saying, "God will surely
visit you, and you shall carry up my bones
from here with you."
20 So they took their journey from Succoth
and camped in Etham at the edge of the
wilderness. 21 And the LORD went before them
by day in a pillar of cloud to lead the way, and
by night in a pillar of fire to give them light, so
as to go by day and night. 22 He did not take
away the pillar of cloud by day or the pillar of
fire by night *from* before the people.
14 Now the LORD spoke to Moses, saying:
2 "Speak to the children of Israel, that they
turn and camp before Pi Hahiroth, between
Migdol and the sea, opposite Baal Zephon;
you shall camp before it by the sea. 3 For
Pharaoh will say of the children of Israel,
'They *are* bewildered by the land; the wilderness has closed them in.' 4 Then I will harden
Pharaoh's heart, so that he will pursue them;
and I will gain honor over Pharaoh and over all
his army, that the Egyptians may know that I
am the LORD." And they did so.
5 Now it was told the king of Egypt that the
people had fled, and the heart of Pharaoh and
his servants was turned against the people;
and they said, "Why have we done this, that
we have let Israel go from serving us?" 6 So he
made ready his chariot and took his people
with him. 7 Also, he took six hundred choice
chariots, and all the chariots of Egypt with captains over every one of them. 8 And the LORD
hardened the heart of Pharaoh king of Egypt,
and he pursued the children of Israel; and the
children of Israel went out with boldness. 9 So
the Egyptians pursued them, all the horses
and chariots of Pharaoh, his horsemen and his
army, and overtook them camping by the sea
beside Pi Hahiroth, before Baal Zephon.
10 And when Pharaoh drew near, the children
of Israel lifted their eyes, and behold, the
Egyptians marched after them. So they were
very afraid, and the children of Israel cried out
to the LORD. 11 Then they said to Moses, "Because *there were* no graves in Egypt, have you

taken us away to die in the wilderness? Why
have you so dealt with us, to bring us up out of
Egypt? 12 *Is* this not the word that we told you
in Egypt, saying, 'Let us alone that we may
serve the Egyptians'? For *it would have been*
better for us to serve the Egyptians than that
we should die in the wilderness."
13 And Moses said to the people, "Do not be
afraid. Stand still, and see the salvation of the
LORD, which He will accomplish for you today.
For the Egyptians whom you see today, you
shall see again no more forever. 14 The LORD will
fight for you, and you shall hold your peace."
15 And the LORD said to Moses, "Why do you
cry to Me? Tell the children of Israel to go forward. 16 But lift up your rod, and stretch out
your hand over the sea and divide it. And the
children of Israel shall go on dry *ground*
through the midst of the sea. 17 And I indeed
will harden the hearts of the Egyptians, and
they shall follow them. So I will gain honor
over Pharaoh and over all his army, his chariots, and his horsemen. 18 Then the Egyptians
shall know that I *am* the LORD, when I have
gained honor for Myself over Pharaoh, his
chariots, and his horsemen."
19 And the Angel of God, who went before
the camp of Israel, moved and went behind
them; and the pillar of cloud went from before
them and stood behind them. 20 So it came
between the camp of the Egyptians and the
camp of Israel. Thus it was a cloud and darkness *to the one,* and it gave light by night *to the*
other, so that the one did not come near the
other all that night.
21 Then Moses stretched out his hand over
the sea; and the LORD caused the sea to go
back by a strong east wind all that night, and
made the sea into dry *land,* and the waters
were divided. 22 So the children of Israel went
into the midst of the sea on the dry *ground,*
and the waters *were* a wall to them on their
right hand and on their left. 23 And the Egyptians pursued and went after them into the
midst of the sea, all Pharaoh's horses, his
chariots, and his horsemen.

14:21 strong east wind. God's use of natural phenomena does not detract in any way from the miraculous nature of what took place that night. The psalmist recorded this event as the Lord dividing the sea by His strength (Ps. 74:13). The wind walled up the waters on either side of the pathway then opened (v. 22; 15:8; Ps. 78:13).

24 Now it came to pass, in the morning
watch, that the LORD looked down upon the
army of the Egyptians through the pillar of fire
and cloud, and He troubled the army of the
Egyptians. 25 And He took off their chariot
wheels, so that they drove them with difficulty; and the Egyptians said, "Let us flee from
the face of Israel, for the LORD fights for them
against the Egyptians."
26 Then the LORD said to Moses, "Stretch out
your hand over the sea, that the waters may
come back upon the Egyptians, on their chariots, and on their horsemen." 27 And Moses
stretched out his hand over the sea; and when
the morning appeared, the sea returned to its
full depth, while the Egyptians were fleeing
into it. So the LORD overthrew the Egyptians
in the midst of the sea. 28 Then the waters
returned and covered the chariots, the horsemen, *and* all the army of Pharaoh that came
into the sea after them. Not so much as one of
them remained. 29 But the children of Israel
had walked on dry *land* in the midst of the sea,
and the waters *were* a wall to them on their
right hand and on their left.
30 So the LORD saved Israel that day out of the
hand of the Egyptians, and Israel saw the
Egyptians dead on the seashore. 31 Thus Israel
saw the great work which the LORD had done
in Egypt; so the people feared the LORD, and
believed the LORD and His servant Moses.

Psalm 18:13–19

13 The LORD thundered from heaven,
And the Most High uttered His voice,
Hailstones and coals of fire.
14 He sent out His arrows and scattered
the foe,
Lightnings in abundance, and He
vanquished them.
15 Then the channels of the sea were
seen,
The foundations of the world were
uncovered
At Your rebuke, O LORD,
At the blast of the breath of Your nostrils.
16 He sent from above, He took me;
He drew me out of many waters.
17 He delivered me from my strong
enemy,
From those who hated me,
For they were too strong for me.
18 They confronted me in the day
of my calamity,
But the LORD was my support.
19 He also brought me out into a broad
place;

He delivered me because He delighted
in me.

Proverbs 6:6–11

6 Go to the ant, you sluggard!
Consider her ways and be wise,
7 Which, having no captain,
Overseer or ruler,
8 Provides her supplies in the summer,
And gathers her food in the harvest.
9 How long will you slumber, O sluggard?
When will you rise from your sleep?
10 A little sleep, a little slumber,
A little folding of the hands to sleep—
11 So shall your poverty come on you like
a prowler,
And your need like an armed man.

6:6 ant...sluggard. See 30:25. The ant is an example of industry, diligence, and planning (vv. 7, 8) and serves as a rebuke to a sluggard (a lazy one who lacks self-control). Folly sends a lazy man to learn from an ant (see 10:4,26; 12:24; 13:4; 15:19; 19:15; 20:4; 26:14–16).

Matthew 21:1–22

21 Now when they drew near Jerusalem,
and came to Bethphage, at the Mount of
Olives, then Jesus sent two disciples, 2saying
to them, "Go into the village opposite you, and
immediately you will find a donkey tied, and a
colt with her. Loose *them* and bring *them* to
Me. 3And if anyone says anything to you, you
shall say, 'The Lord has need of them,' and
immediately he will send them."
4All this was done that it might be fulfilled
which was spoken by the prophet, saying:

5 *"Tell the daughter of Zion,*
'Behold, your King is coming to you,
Lowly, and sitting on a donkey,
A colt, the foal of a donkey.' "

6So the disciples went and did as Jesus commanded them. 7They brought the donkey and
the colt, laid their clothes on them, and set *Him*
on them. 8And a very great multitude spread
their clothes on the road; others cut down
branches from the trees and spread *them* on
the road. 9Then the multitudes who went before
and those who followed cried out, saying:

"Hosanna to the Son of David!
'Blessed is He who comes in the name
of the L*ORD*!'
Hosanna in the highest!"

21:9 Hosanna. This transliterates the Hebrew expression which is translated "Save now" in Psalm 118:25. **Blessed is He.** This is an exact quotation from v. 26 of the same psalm. This, along with the messianic title "Son of David," make it clear that the crowd was acknowledging Christ's messianic claim. The date of this entry was Sunday, 9 Nisan, A.D. 30, exactly 483 years after the decree of Artaxerxes mentioned in Daniel 9:24–26.

10And when He had come into Jerusalem, all
the city was moved, saying, "Who is this?"
11So the multitudes said, "This is Jesus, the
prophet from Nazareth of Galilee."
12Then Jesus went into the temple of God
and drove out all those who bought and sold
in the temple, and overturned the tables of the
money changers and the seats of those who
sold doves. 13And He said to them, "It is written,
'My house shall be called a house of prayer,'
but you have made it a *'den of thieves.' "*
14Then *the* blind and *the* lame came to Him
in the temple, and He healed them. 15But when
the chief priests and scribes saw the wonderful things that He did, and the children crying
out in the temple and saying, "Hosanna to the
Son of David!" they were indignant 16and said
to Him, "Do You hear what these are saying?"
And Jesus said to them, "Yes. Have you
never read,

'Out of the mouth of babes
and nursing infants
You have perfected praise'? "

17Then He left them and went out of the city
to Bethany, and He lodged there.
18Now in the morning, as He returned to the
city, He was hungry. 19And seeing a fig tree by
the road, He came to it and found nothing on
it but leaves, and said to it, "Let no fruit grow

21:21 if you have faith and do not doubt. This presupposes that the thing requested is actually God's will—for only God-given faith is so doubt-free (see Mark 9:24). **it will be done.** A miracle on such a cosmic scale was precisely what the scribes and Pharisees wanted Christ to do, but He always declined. Here, He was speaking figuratively about the immeasurable power of God, unleashed in the lives of those with true faith.

on you ever again." Immediately the fig tree
withered away.
20And when the disciples saw *it,* they marveled, saying, "How did the fig tree wither
away so soon?"
21So Jesus answered and said to them,
"Assuredly, I say to you, if you have faith and
do not doubt, you will not only do what was
done to the fig tree, but also if you say to this
mountain, 'Be removed and be cast into the
sea,' it will be done. 22And whatever things you
ask in prayer, believing, you will receive."

DAY 1: Why did Jesus cleanse the temple in Matthew 21?

This was the second time Jesus cleansed the temple. John 2:14–16 describes a similar incident at the beginning of Christ's public ministry. He regarded both merchants and customers as guilty of desecrating the temple (Matt. 21:12). Items being bought and sold included "doves" and other animals for sacrifice. Currency-exchange agents, or "money changers," present in droves, were needed because Roman coins and other forms of currency were deemed unacceptable for temple offerings. Evidently, both merchants and money changers were charging such excessive rates that the temple marketplace took on the atmosphere of a thieves' den (v. 13). Religion had become crass and materialistic.

In verse 13, Jesus uses two Old Testament prophecies, Isaiah 56:7 ("My house shall be called a house of prayer for all nations") and Jeremiah 7:11 ("Has this house, which is called by My name, become a den of thieves in your eyes?") to justify His actions. When the holiness of God and His worship was at stake, Jesus took fast and furious action. The "all" (v. 12) indicates that He drove out not only men but also animals. Yet, although His physical action was forceful, it was not cruel. The moderation of His actions is seen in the fact that no riotous uproar occurred; otherwise the specially large contingent of Roman troops in Jerusalem at that time because of the Passover crowds, would have swiftly reacted. Although the primary reference is to the actions of the Messiah in the millennial kingdom, Jesus' actions in cleansing the temple was an initial fulfillment of Malachi 3:1–3 (and Zech. 14:20,21) that speak of the Messiah's purifying the religious worship of His people.

FEBRUARY 2

Exodus 15:1–16:36

15 Then Moses and the children of Israel sang this song to the LORD, and spoke, saying:

"I will sing to the LORD,
For He has triumphed gloriously!
The horse and its rider
He has thrown into the sea!
2 The LORD *is* my strength and song,
And He has become my salvation;
He *is* my God, and I will praise Him;
My father's God, and I will exalt Him.
3 The LORD *is* a man of war;
The LORD *is* His name.
4 Pharaoh's chariots and his army He has cast into the sea;
His chosen captains also are drowned in the Red Sea.
5 The depths have covered them;
They sank to the bottom like a stone.
6 "Your right hand, O LORD, has become glorious in power;
Your right hand, O LORD, has dashed the enemy in pieces.
7 And in the greatness of Your excellence
You have overthrown those who rose against You;
You sent forth Your wrath;
It consumed them like stubble.
8 And with the blast of Your nostrils
The waters were gathered together;
The floods stood upright like a heap;
The depths congealed in the heart of the sea.
9 The enemy said, 'I will pursue,
I will overtake,
I will divide the spoil;
My desire shall be satisfied on them.
I will draw my sword,
My hand shall destroy them.'
10 You blew with Your wind,
The sea covered them;
They sank like lead in the mighty waters.

11 "Who *is* like You, O LORD, among the gods?
Who *is* like You, glorious in holiness,
Fearful in praises, doing wonders?

12 You stretched out Your right hand;
The earth swallowed them.
13 You in Your mercy have led forth
The people whom You have redeemed;
You have guided *them* in Your strength
To Your holy habitation.

14 "The people will hear *and* be afraid;
Sorrow will take hold of the
inhabitants of Philistia.
15 Then the chiefs of Edom will be
dismayed;
The mighty men of Moab,
Trembling will take hold of them;
All the inhabitants of Canaan will melt
away.
16 Fear and dread will fall on them;
By the greatness of Your arm
They will be *as* still as a stone,
Till Your people pass over,
O LORD,
Till the people pass over
Whom You have purchased.
17 You will bring them in and plant them
In the mountain of Your
inheritance,
In the place, O LORD, *which* You have
made
For Your own dwelling,
The sanctuary, O Lord, *which* Your
hands have established.

18 "The LORD shall reign forever and
ever."

19 For the horses of Pharaoh went with his
chariots and his horsemen into the sea, and
the LORD brought back the waters of the sea
upon them. But the children of Israel went on
dry *land* in the midst of the sea.
20 Then Miriam the prophetess, the sister of
Aaron, took the timbrel in her hand; and all
the women went out after her with timbrels and
with dances. 21 And Miriam answered them:

15:20 the prophetess. Miriam was the first woman to be given this honor. She herself claimed the Lord had spoken through her (Num. 12:2). She apparently played an important role in these rescue events because the prophet Micah states that God delivered Israel by the hand of Moses, Aaron, and Miriam (Mic. 6:4). Other women to receive this rare honor were Deborah (Judg. 4:4); Huldah (2 Kin. 22:14); Isaiah's wife (Is. 8:3); Anna (Luke 2:36); and Philip's four daughters (Acts 21:9).

"Sing to the LORD,
For He has triumphed gloriously!
The horse and its rider
He has thrown into the sea!"

22 So Moses brought Israel from the Red Sea;
then they went out into the Wilderness of
Shur. And they went three days in the wilderness and found no water. 23 Now when they
came to Marah, they could not drink the
waters of Marah, for they *were* bitter.
Therefore the name of it was called Marah.
24 And the people complained against Moses,
saying, "What shall we drink?" 25 So he cried
out to the LORD, and the LORD showed him a
tree. When he cast *it* into the waters, the
waters were made sweet.
There He made a statute and an ordinance
for them, and there He tested them, 26 and said,
"If you diligently heed the voice of the LORD
your God and do what is right in His sight,
give ear to His commandments and keep all
His statutes, I will put none of the diseases on
you which I have brought on the Egyptians.
For I *am* the LORD who heals you."
27 Then they came to Elim, where there *were*
twelve wells of water and seventy palm trees;
so they camped there by the waters.

16 And they journeyed from Elim, and all
the congregation of the children of Israel
came to the Wilderness of Sin, which is
between Elim and Sinai, on the fifteenth day of
the second month after they departed from
the land of Egypt. 2 Then the whole congregation of the children of Israel complained
against Moses and Aaron in the wilderness.
3 And the children of Israel said to them, "Oh,
that we had died by the hand of the LORD in
the land of Egypt, when we sat by the pots of
meat *and* when we ate bread to the full! For
you have brought us out into this wilderness
to kill this whole assembly with hunger."
4 Then the LORD said to Moses, "Behold, I
will rain bread from heaven for you. And the
people shall go out and gather a certain quota
every day, that I may test them, whether they
will walk in My law or not. 5 And it shall be on
the sixth day that they shall prepare what they
bring in, and it shall be twice as much as they
gather daily."
6 Then Moses and Aaron said to all the children of Israel, "At evening you shall know that
the LORD has brought you out of the land of
Egypt. 7 And in the morning you shall see the
glory of the LORD; for He hears your complaints against the LORD. But what *are* we, that
you complain against us?" 8 Also Moses said,
"*This shall be seen* when the LORD gives you

meat to eat in the evening, and in the morning
bread to the full; for the LORD hears your complaints which you make against Him. And
what *are* we? Your complaints *are* not against
us but against the LORD."
9Then Moses spoke to Aaron, "Say to all the
congregation of the children of Israel, 'Come
near before the LORD, for He has heard your
complaints.' " 10Now it came to pass, as Aaron
spoke to the whole congregation of the children of Israel, that they looked toward the
wilderness, and behold, the glory of the LORD
appeared in the cloud.
11And the LORD spoke to Moses, saying, 12"I
have heard the complaints of the children of
Israel. Speak to them, saying, 'At twilight you
shall eat meat, and in the morning you shall be
filled with bread. And you shall know that I *am*
the LORD your God.' "
13So it was that quails came up at evening and
covered the camp, and in the morning the dew
lay all around the camp. 14And when the layer
of dew lifted, there, on the surface of the
wilderness, was a small round substance, *as*
fine as frost on the ground. 15So when the children of Israel saw *it,* they said to one another,
"What is it?" For they did not know what it
was.
And Moses said to them, "This *is* the bread
which the LORD has given you to eat. 16This is
the thing which the LORD has commanded:
'Let every man gather it according to each
one's need, one omer for each person, *according to the* number of persons; let every man
take for *those* who *are* in his tent.' "
17Then the children of Israel did so and gathered, some more, some less. 18So when they
measured *it* by omers, he who gathered much
had nothing left over, and he who gathered little had no lack. Every man had gathered
according to each one's need. 19And Moses
said, "Let no one leave any of it till morning."
20Notwithstanding they did not heed Moses.
But some of them left part of it until morning,
and it bred worms and stank. And Moses was
angry with them. 21So they gathered it every
morning, every man according to his need.
And when the sun became hot, it melted.
22And so it was, on the sixth day, *that* they
gathered twice as much bread, two omers for
each one. And all the rulers of the congregation came and told Moses. 23Then he said to
them, "This *is what* the LORD has said: 'Tomorrow *is* a Sabbath rest, a holy Sabbath to the
LORD. Bake what you will bake *today,* and boil
what you will boil; and lay up for yourselves all
that remains, to be kept until morning.' " 24So
they laid it up till morning, as Moses commanded; and it did not stink, nor were there
any worms in it. 25Then Moses said, "Eat that
today, for today *is* a Sabbath to the LORD; today
you will not find it in the field. 26Six days you
shall gather it, but on the seventh day, the
Sabbath, there will be none."
27Now it happened *that some* of the people
went out on the seventh day to gather, but
they found none. 28And the LORD said to Moses, "How long do you refuse to keep My commandments and My laws? 29See! For the LORD
has given you the Sabbath; therefore He gives
you on the sixth day bread for two days. Let
every man remain in his place; let no man go
out of his place on the seventh day." 30So the
people rested on the seventh day.
31And the house of Israel called its name
Manna. And it *was* like white coriander seed,
and the taste of it *was* like wafers *made* with
honey.

16:31 Manna. The arrival of the quails in much quantity (v. 13) was totally overshadowed by the arrival of manna the next morning. Despite the different descriptions given for its form and taste (vv. 14,31), the name chosen for it derived from the question they asked. "Manna" was an older form of their question, "What is it?" The psalmist referred to manna as the "bread of heaven" and "angels' food" which rained down after God had opened the windows of heaven (Ps. 78:23–25). Natural explanations for the manna, such as lichen growing on rocks or insect-excreted granules on tamarisk thickets, are totally inadequate to explain its presence in sufficient quantity on the ground under the dew every day except the Sabbath for the next 40 years (v. 35) to satisfy every family's hunger. It was supernaturally produced and supernaturally sustained to last for the Sabbath!

32Then Moses said, "This *is* the thing which
the LORD has commanded: 'Fill an omer with it,
to be kept for your generations, that they may
see the bread with which I fed you in the
wilderness, when I brought you out of the
land of Egypt.' " 33And Moses said to Aaron,
"Take a pot and put an omer of manna in it,
and lay it up before the LORD, to be kept for your
generations." 34As the LORD commanded Moses,
so Aaron laid it up before the Testimony, to be
kept. 35And the children of Israel ate manna
forty years, until they came to an inhabited
land; they ate manna until they came to the

border of the land of Canaan. 36Now an omer *is*
one-tenth of an ephah.

Psalm 18:20–27

20 The LORD rewarded me according to
my righteousness;
According to the cleanness of my hands
He has recompensed me.
21 For I have kept the ways of the LORD,
And have not wickedly departed from
my God.
22 For all His judgments *were* before me,
And I did not put away His statutes
from me.
23 I was also blameless before Him,
And I kept myself from my iniquity.
24 Therefore the LORD has recompensed
me according to my righteousness,
According to the cleanness of my
hands in His sight.

25 With the merciful You will show
Yourself merciful;
With a blameless man You will show
Yourself blameless;
26 With the pure You will show Yourself
pure;
And with the devious You will show
Yourself shrewd.
27 For You will save the humble people,
But will bring down haughty looks.

Proverbs 6:12–15

12 A worthless person, a wicked man,
Walks with a perverse mouth;
13 He winks with his eyes,
He shuffles his feet,
He points with his fingers;
14 Perversity *is* in his heart,
He devises evil continually,
He sows discord.
15 Therefore his calamity shall come
suddenly;
Suddenly he shall be broken without
remedy.

Matthew 21:23–46

23Now when He came into the temple, the
chief priests and the elders of the people confronted Him as He was teaching, and said, "By
what authority are You doing these things?
And who gave You this authority?"
24But Jesus answered and said to them, "I
also will ask you one thing, which if you tell
Me, I likewise will tell you by what authority I
do these things: 25The baptism of John—where
was it from? From heaven or from men?"
And they reasoned among themselves, say-

21:25 The baptism of John—where was it from? Jesus caught the Jewish leaders in their own trap. They had no doubt hoped that He would answer by asserting that His authority came directly from God (as He had many times before—see John 5:19–23; 10:18). They then accused Him of blasphemy and used the charge as an excuse to kill Him—as they had also attempted to do before (John 5:18; 10:31–33). Here, however, He asked a question that placed them in an impossible dilemma, because John was widely revered by the people. They could not affirm John's ministry without condemning themselves. And if they denied John's legitimacy, they feared the response of the people (v. 26). In effect, Jesus exposed their own lack of any authority to examine Him.

ing, "If we say, 'From heaven,' He will say to
us, 'Why then did you not believe him?' 26But if
we say, 'From men,' we fear the multitude, for
all count John as a prophet." 27So they
answered Jesus and said, "We do not know."
And He said to them, "Neither will I tell you
by what authority I do these things.
28"But what do you think? A man had two
sons, and he came to the first and said, 'Son,
go, work today in my vineyard.' 29He answered
and said, 'I will not,' but afterward he regretted it and went. 30Then he came to the second
and said likewise. And he answered and said,
'I *go,* sir,' but he did not go. 31Which of the two
did the will of *his* father?"
They said to Him, "The first."
Jesus said to them, "Assuredly, I say to you
that tax collectors and harlots enter the kingdom of God before you. 32For John came to
you in the way of righteousness, and you did
not believe him; but tax collectors and harlots
believed him; and when you saw *it,* you did
not afterward relent and believe him.
33"Hear another parable: There was a certain landowner who planted a vineyard and set
a hedge around it, dug a winepress in it and
built a tower. And he leased it to vinedressers
and went into a far country. 34Now when vintage-time drew near, he sent his servants to
the vinedressers, that they might receive its
fruit. 35And the vinedressers took his servants,
beat one, killed one, and stoned another.
36Again he sent other servants, more than the
first, and they did likewise to them. 37Then last
of all he sent his son to them, saying, 'They
will respect my son.' 38But when the vine-

dressers saw the son, they said among themselves, 'This is the heir. Come, let us kill him and seize his inheritance.' [39]So they took him and cast *him* out of the vineyard and killed *him*.

[40]"Therefore, when the owner of the vineyard comes, what will he do to those vinedressers?"

[41]They said to Him, "He will destroy those wicked men miserably, and lease *his* vineyard to other vinedressers who will render to him the fruits in their seasons."

[42]Jesus said to them, "Have you never read in the Scriptures:

'The stone which the builders rejected
Has become the chief cornerstone.
This was the LORD's doing,
And it is marvelous in our eyes'?

[43]"Therefore I say to you, the kingdom of God will be taken from you and given to a nation bearing the fruits of it. [44]And whoever falls on this stone will be broken; but on whomever it falls, it will grind him to powder."

[45]Now when the chief priests and Pharisees heard His parables, they perceived that He was speaking of them. [46]But when they sought to lay hands on Him, they feared the multitudes, because they took Him for a prophet.

21:42 The stone...rejected. This refers to His crucifixion; and the restoration of "the chief cornerstone" anticipates His resurrection. **the chief cornerstone.** To the superficial eye, this quotation from Psalm 118:22,23 is irrelevant to the parable that precedes it. But it is taken from a messianic psalm. Jesus cited it to suggest that the Son who was killed and thrown out of the vineyard was also "the chief cornerstone" in God's redemptive plan.

DAY 2: How are we to think about the astonishing miracles reported in Exodus?

The scientific materialism of many twenty-first-century people makes it difficult for them to consider any so-called miracles. If the laws of nature are considered supreme, the existence of a personal Supreme Being above the laws of nature and able to override them becomes inconceivable. Examples of miracles do little to convince someone who is already convinced that miracles are impossible.

Miracles can demonstrate God's existence; they don't prove it. Human beings display an amazing ability to come up with alternative explanations for God's activity in history. The situation is not that twenty-first-century people can't believe in miracles; rather, it is that twenty-first-century people often won't believe in miracles.

For Christians, the matter is settled by faith. In becoming Christians, we had to believe in the central miracle: God came in the flesh, Jesus Christ, who lived, died, and rose from the dead to reign eternally as Lord and Savior. In the light of that miracle, the miracles of Exodus become less a matter for speculation and more a matter of wonder and worship. They are examples of the lengths to which God went to communicate to people. Even twenty-first-century Christians are humbled and awestruck by God's amazing power!

FEBRUARY 3

Exodus 17:1–18:27

17 Then all the congregation of the children of Israel set out on their journey from the Wilderness of Sin, according to the commandment of the LORD, and camped in Rephidim; but *there was* no water for the people to drink. [2]Therefore the people contended with Moses, and said, "Give us water, that we may drink."

So Moses said to them, "Why do you contend with me? Why do you tempt the LORD?"

[3]And the people thirsted there for water, and the people complained against Moses, and said, "Why *is* it you have brought us up out of Egypt, to kill us and our children and our livestock with thirst?"

[4]So Moses cried out to the LORD, saying, "What shall I do with this people? They are almost ready to stone me!"

[5]And the LORD said to Moses, "Go on before the people, and take with you some of the elders of Israel. Also take in your hand your rod with which you struck the river, and go. [6]Behold, I will stand before you there on the rock in Horeb; and you shall strike the rock, and water will come out of it, that the people may drink."

GIFTS *of the* HOLY SPIRIT

The Bible clearly teaches that the Spirit distributes gifts to everyone who believes in Christ. The following is a list of gifts and the chapters where they are found.

	Rom 12	1 Cor 12	Eph 4
Apostleship		X	X
Prophecy	X	X	X
Evangelism			X
Pastoring			X
Teaching	X	X	X
Exhortation	X		
Knowledge		X	
Wisdom		X	
Discerning of Spirits		X	
Leadership	X		
Administration		X	
Service/Helps	X	X	
Acts of Mercy	X		
Giving	X		
Healing		X	
Faith		X	
Miracles		X	
Speaking & Interpreting Tongues		X	
Miscellaneous: Perhaps Celibacy (Matthew 19:12) Hospitality (Romans 12:13)			

Study Tip

In addition to Paul's list of gifts, the apostle Peter also mentions gifts, dividing them into speaking and serving categories (1 Peter 4:10–11). Compare Paul's list to see how it also divides roughly into half speaking and half serving gifts. The book of Acts is also another great place to see the gifts in action. As you read through the book make a note whenever you encounter the use of one of the gifts listed above.

The Holy Spirit gives gifts with particular spiritual functions for the benefit of the entire church. Paul's teaching in 1 Corinthians 12 speaks about the organic unity of Christ's body, the Church. The gifts complement each other and work together for the common good, much as the parts of the body are designed to do. Because this is true, the gifts are given to the church as a whole. It is only within the context of the believing community that the gifts are made to work and only within that community that they can be discovered in the first place.

Our understanding of gifts and gifting depends on how we view the Holy Spirit. He is God's gift to us as individuals and as a body (see Acts 2:38 and 10:45). Individuals who have come into this life, the life of Christ, are automatically part of a larger whole. These gifts operate as parts of a whole. Gifting, reception of the Spirit, and membership in the Body of Christ are all connected in the life of the believer and for the good of the whole church.

ROSE PUBLISHING

© 2008 Bristol Works, Inc.
Rose Publishing, Inc.
4733 Torrance Blvd., #259
Torrance, CA 90503 U.S.A.
email: info@rose-publishing.com
www.rose-publishing.com

Rose Publishing has more than 100 Bible reference pamphlets.

Editor: Benjamin Galan, MTS, ThM, Adjunct Professor of OT Hebrew and Literature at Fuller Seminary.

Author: William Brent Ashby

Other products available from Rose Publishing:
Names of God pamphlet, chart, and PowerPoint®
Names of Jesus pamphlet, chart, and PowerPoint®

Stock #665X *Names of the Holy Spirit* pamphlet
Retailers: Package of 10 pamphlets = Stock #667X (ISBN-13: 978-159636-208-6)

[illegible] Meanings

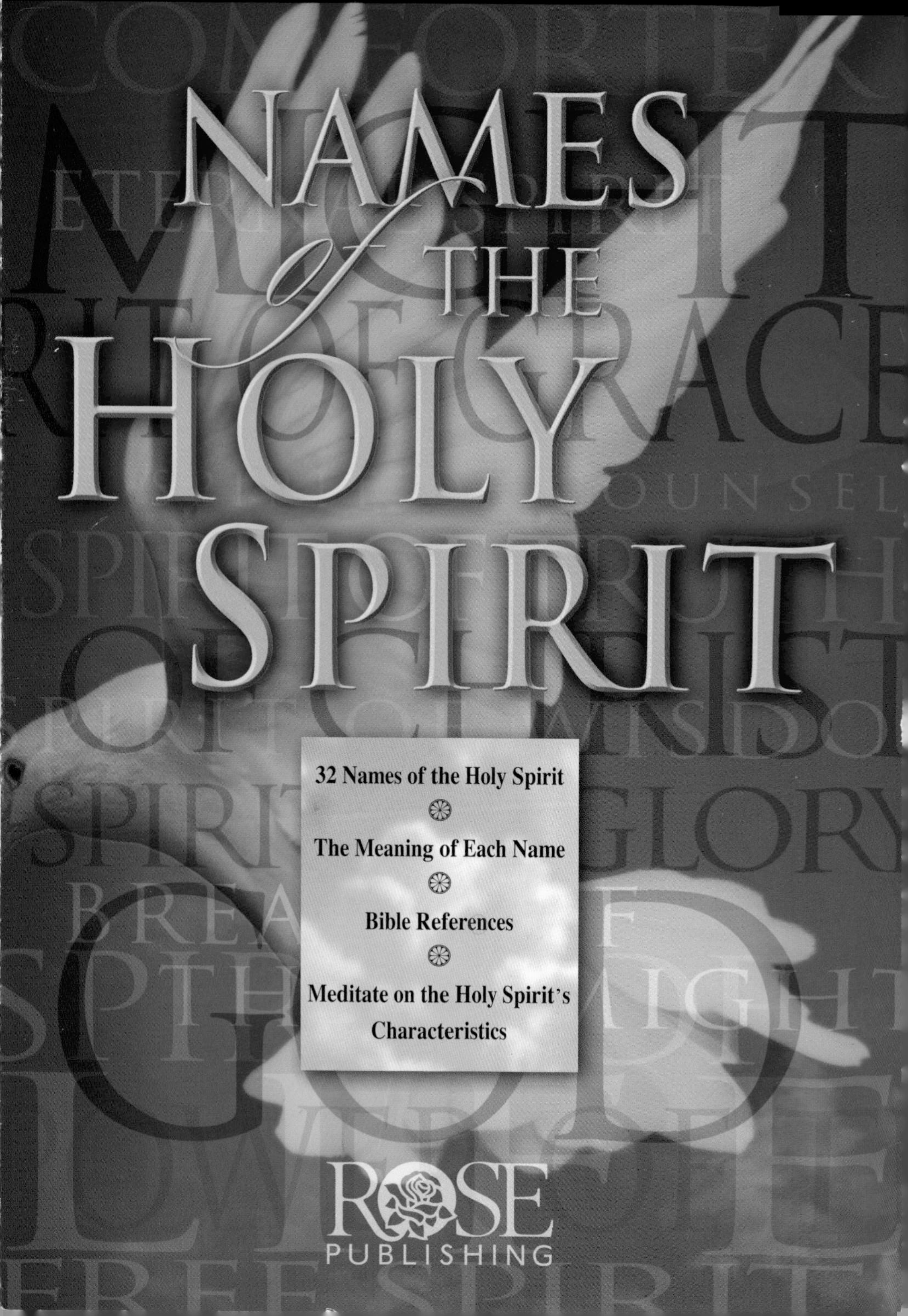

Names of the Holy Spirit

32 Names of the Holy Spirit

The Meaning of Each Name

Bible References

Meditate on the Holy Spirit's Characteristics

ROSE PUBLISHING

And Moses did so in the sight of the elders
of Israel. 7So he called the name of the place
Massah and Meribah, because of the contention of the children of Israel, and because
they tempted the LORD, saying, "Is the LORD
among us or not?"

8Now Amalek came and fought with Israel
in Rephidim. 9And Moses said to Joshua,
"Choose us some men and go out, fight with
Amalek. Tomorrow I will stand on the top of
the hill with the rod of God in my hand." 10So
Joshua did as Moses said to him, and fought
with Amalek. And Moses, Aaron, and Hur
went up to the top of the hill. 11And so it was,
when Moses held up his hand, that Israel prevailed; and when he let down his hand,
Amalek prevailed. 12But Moses' hands *became*
heavy; so they took a stone and put *it* under him,
and he sat on it. And Aaron and Hur supported his hands, one on one side, and the other
on the other side; and his hands were steady
until the going down of the sun. 13So Joshua
defeated Amalek and his people with the edge
of the sword.

14Then the LORD said to Moses, "Write this
for a memorial in the book and recount *it* in
the hearing of Joshua, that I will utterly blot
out the remembrance of Amalek from under
heaven." 15And Moses built an altar and called
its name, The-LORD-Is-My-Banner; 16for he
said, "Because the LORD has sworn: the LORD
will have war with Amalek from generation to
generation."

18 And Jethro, the priest of Midian, Moses'
father-in-law, heard of all that God had
done for Moses and for Israel His people—
that the LORD had brought Israel out of Egypt.
2Then Jethro, Moses' father-in-law, took
Zipporah, Moses' wife, after he had sent her
back, 3with her two sons, of whom the name of
one *was* Gershom (for he said, "I have been a
stranger in a foreign land") 4and the name of
the other *was* Eliezer (for *he said,* "The God of
my father *was* my help, and delivered me from
the sword of Pharaoh"); 5and Jethro, Moses'
father-in-law, came with his sons and his wife
to Moses in the wilderness, where he was
encamped at the mountain of God. 6Now he
had said to Moses, "I, your father-in-law
Jethro, am coming to you with your wife and
her two sons with her."

7So Moses went out to meet his father-in-
law, bowed down, and kissed him. And they
asked each other about *their* well-being, and
they went into the tent. 8And Moses told his
father-in-law all that the LORD had done to
Pharaoh and to the Egyptians for Israel's
sake, all the hardship that had come upon
them on the way, and *how* the LORD had delivered them. 9Then Jethro rejoiced for all the
good which the LORD had done for Israel,
whom He had delivered out of the hand of the
Egyptians. 10And Jethro said, "Blessed *be* the
LORD, who has delivered you out of the hand
of the Egyptians and out of the hand of
Pharaoh, *and* who has delivered the people
from under the hand of the Egyptians. 11Now I
know that the LORD *is* greater than all the
gods; for in the very thing in which they behaved proudly, *He was* above them." 12Then
Jethro, Moses' father-in-law, took a burnt offering and *other* sacrifices *to offer* to God. And
Aaron came with all the elders of Israel to eat
bread with Moses' father-in-law before God.

13And so it was, on the next day, that Moses
sat to judge the people; and the people stood
before Moses from morning until evening.
14So when Moses' father-in-law saw all that he
did for the people, he said, "What *is* this thing
that you are doing for the people? Why do you
alone sit, and all the people stand before you
from morning until evening?"

18:13–27 Jethro's practical wisdom was of immense benefit to Moses and Israel and has been lauded as an example of delegation and management organization by efficiency experts for centuries—and still is. Woven into Jethro's advice were statements about God and the virtues of godly men that cause one to respect this man as having his newfound faith well integrated into his thinking. Indeed, he fully recognized that Moses needed divine permission to enact his advice (v. 23). Moses apparently did not immediately implement Jethro's solution, but waited until the law had been given (see Deut. 1:9–15).

15And Moses said to his father-in-law, "Because the people come to me to inquire of
God. 16When they have a difficulty, they come
to me, and I judge between one and another;
and I make known the statutes of God and His
laws."

17So Moses' father-in-law said to him, "The
thing that you do *is* not good. 18Both you and
these people who *are* with you will surely wear
yourselves out. For this thing *is* too much for
you; you are not able to perform it by yourself.
19Listen now to my voice; I will give you counsel, and God will be with you: Stand before
God for the people, so that you may bring the
difficulties to God. 20And you shall teach them

the statutes and the laws, and show them the
way in which they must walk and the work
they must do. [21]Moreover you shall select from
all the people able men, such as fear God, men
of truth, hating covetousness; and place *such*
over them *to be* rulers of thousands, rulers of
hundreds, rulers of fifties, and rulers of tens.
[22]And let them judge the people at all times.
Then it will be *that* every great matter they
shall bring to you, but every small matter they
themselves shall judge. So it will be easier for
you, for they will bear *the burden* with you. [23]If
you do this thing, and God *so* commands you,
then you will be able to endure, and all this
people will also go to their place in peace."
[24]So Moses heeded the voice of his father-in-
law and did all that he had said. [25]And Moses
chose able men out of all Israel, and made
them heads over the people: rulers of thousands, rulers of hundreds, rulers of fifties, and
rulers of tens. [26]So they judged the people at
all times; the hard cases they brought to Moses, but they judged every small case themselves.
[27]Then Moses let his father-in-law depart,
and he went his way to his own land.

Psalm 18:28–36

28 For You will light my lamp;
The LORD my God will enlighten my
darkness.
29 For by You I can run against a troop,
By my God I can leap over a wall.
30 *As for* God, His way *is* perfect;
The word of the LORD is proven;
He *is* a shield to all who trust in Him.

31 For who *is* God, except the LORD?
And who *is* a rock, except our God?
32 *It is* God who arms me with strength,
And makes my way perfect.
33 He makes my feet like the *feet of* deer,
And sets me on my high places.
34 He teaches my hands to make war,
So that my arms can bend a bow of
bronze.
35 You have also given me the shield of
Your salvation;
Your right hand has held me up,
Your gentleness has made me great.
36 You enlarged my path under me,
So my feet did not slip.

Proverbs 6:16–19

16 These six *things* the LORD hates,
Yes, seven *are* an abomination to Him:
17 A proud look,
A lying tongue,
Hands that shed innocent blood,
18 A heart that devises wicked plans,
Feet that are swift in running to evil,
19 A false witness *who* speaks lies,
And one who sows discord among
brethren.

Matthew 22:1–22

22 And Jesus answered and spoke to them
again by parables and said: [2]"The kingdom of heaven is like a certain king who
arranged a marriage for his son, [3]and sent out
his servants to call those who were invited to
the wedding; and they were not willing to
come. [4]Again, he sent out other servants, saying, 'Tell those who are invited, "See, I have
prepared my dinner; my oxen and fatted cattle
are killed, and all things *are* ready. Come to
the wedding."' [5]But they made light of it and
went their ways, one to his own farm, another
to his business. [6]And the rest seized his servants, treated *them* spitefully, and killed *them.*
[7]But when the king heard *about it,* he was furious. And he sent out his armies, destroyed
those murderers, and burned up their city.
[8]Then he said to his servants, 'The wedding is
ready, but those who were invited were not
worthy. [9]Therefore go into the highways, and
as many as you find, invite to the wedding.'
[10]So those servants went out into the highways
and gathered together all whom they found,
both bad and good. And the wedding *hall* was
filled with guests.
[11]"But when the king came in to see the
guests, he saw a man there who did not have
on a wedding garment. [12]So he said to him,
'Friend, how did you come in here without a
wedding garment?' And he was speechless.
[13]Then the king said to the servants, 'Bind him
hand and foot, take him away, and cast *him*
into outer darkness; there will be weeping and
gnashing of teeth.'

22:13 outer darkness. This would describe the darkness farthest from the light, i.e., outer darkness. **weeping and gnashing of teeth.** This speaks of inconsolable grief and unremitting torment. Jesus commonly used the phrases in this verse to describe hell (see 13:42,50; 24:51).

[14]"For many are called, but few *are* chosen."
[15]Then the Pharisees went and plotted how
they might entangle Him in *His* talk. [16]And
they sent to Him their disciples with the

Herodians, saying, "Teacher, we know that You are true, and teach the way of God in truth; nor do You care about anyone, for You do not regard the person of men. 17Tell us, therefore, what do You think? Is it lawful to pay taxes to Caesar, or not?"

18But Jesus perceived their wickedness, and said, "Why do you test Me, *you* hypocrites? 19Show Me the tax money."

So they brought Him a denarius.

20And He said to them, "Whose image and inscription *is* this?"

21They said to Him, "Caesar's."

And He said to them, "Render therefore to Caesar the things that are Caesar's, and to God the things that are God's." 22When they had heard *these words,* they marveled, and left Him and went their way.

22:16 Herodians. A party of the Jews who supported the Roman-backed Herodian dynasty. The Herodians were not a religious party, like the Pharisees, but a political party, probably consisting largely of Sadducees (including the rulers of the temple). By contrast, the Pharisees hated Roman rule and the Herodian influence. The fact that these groups would conspire together to entrap Jesus reveals how seriously both groups viewed Him as a threat. Herod himself wanted Jesus dead (Luke 13:31), and the Pharisees were already plotting to kill Him, as well (John 11:53). So they joined efforts to seek their common goal.

DAY 3: Why was Moses' rod so important as Joshua went into battle? Did it have magic powers?

Joshua, the name of Moses' aide-de-camp, or personal minister (24:13; 33:11; Josh. 1:1), appears for the first time in Exodus 17:9. His assignment to muster a task force was part of his being groomed for military leadership in Israel. Actually, at this stage his name was still Hoshea, which later changed to Joshua at Kadesh just before the reconnaissance mission in Canaan (Num. 13:16). At this stage, Israel could not be described as a seasoned army and was not even militarily well prepared and trained.

The staff, or "the rod of God," that Moses held up in his hands was no magic wand. Rather, it had been previously used to initiate, via God's chosen leader, the miracles that God did and about which He had informed Moses in advance. It became, therefore, the symbol of God's personal and powerful involvement, with Moses' outstretched arms perhaps signifying an appeal to God.

The ebb and flow of battle in correlation with Moses' uplifted or drooping arms imparted more than psychological encouragement as the soldiers looked up to their leader on the hilltop, and more than Moses' interceding for them. It demonstrated and acknowledged their having to depend upon God for victory in battle and not upon their own strength and zeal. It also confirmed the position of Moses both in relation to God and the nation's well-being and safety. They had angrily chided him for their problems (Ex. 17:2), but God confirmed His appointment as leader.

FEBRUARY 4

Exodus 19:1–20:26

19 In the third month after the children of Israel had gone out of the land of Egypt, on the same day, they came *to* the Wilderness of Sinai. 2For they had departed from Rephidim, had come *to* the Wilderness of Sinai, and camped in the wilderness. So Israel camped there before the mountain.

3And Moses went up to God, and the LORD called to him from the mountain, saying, "Thus you shall say to the house of Jacob, and tell the children of Israel: 4'You have seen what I did to the Egyptians, and *how* I bore you on eagles' wings and brought you to Myself. 5Now therefore, if you will indeed obey My voice and keep My covenant, then you shall be a special treasure to Me above all people; for

19:4 bore you on eagles' wings. With a most appropriate metaphor, God described the Exodus and the journey to Sinai. Eagles were known to have carried their young out of the nests on their wings and taught them to fly, catching them when necessary on their outspread wings. Moses, in his final song, employed this metaphor of God's care for Israel and especially noted that there was only one Lord who did this (Deut. 32:11–12).

all the earth *is* Mine. 6And you shall be to Me
a kingdom of priests and a holy nation.' These
are the words which you shall speak to the
children of Israel."

7So Moses came and called for the elders of
the people, and laid before them all these
words which the LORD commanded him.
8Then all the people answered together and
said, "All that the LORD has spoken we will
do." So Moses brought back the words of the
people to the LORD. 9And the LORD said to Moses, "Behold, I come to you in the thick cloud,
that the people may hear when I speak with
you, and believe you forever."

So Moses told the words of the people to
the LORD.

10Then the LORD said to Moses, "Go to the
people and consecrate them today and tomorrow, and let them wash their clothes. 11And let
them be ready for the third day. For on the
third day the LORD will come down upon
Mount Sinai in the sight of all the people. 12You
shall set bounds for the people all around, saying, 'Take heed to yourselves *that* you do *not*
go up to the mountain or touch its base. Whoever touches the mountain shall surely be put
to death. 13Not a hand shall touch him, but he
shall surely be stoned or shot *with an arrow;*
whether man or beast, he shall not live.' When
the trumpet sounds long, they shall come near
the mountain."

14So Moses went down from the mountain to
the people and sanctified the people, and they
washed their clothes. 15And he said to the people, "Be ready for the third day; do not come
near *your* wives."

16Then it came to pass on the third day, in
the morning, that there were thunderings and
lightnings, and a thick cloud on the mountain;
and the sound of the trumpet was very loud,
so that all the people who *were* in the camp
trembled. 17And Moses brought the people out
of the camp to meet with God, and they stood
at the foot of the mountain. 18Now Mount Sinai
was completely in smoke, because the LORD
descended upon it in fire. Its smoke ascended
like the smoke of a furnace, and the whole
mountain quaked greatly. 19And when the blast
of the trumpet sounded long and became
louder and louder, Moses spoke, and God
answered him by voice. 20Then the LORD came
down upon Mount Sinai, on the top of the
mountain. And the LORD called Moses to the
top of the mountain, and Moses went up.

21And the LORD said to Moses, "Go down
and warn the people, lest they break through
to gaze at the LORD, and many of them perish.
22Also let the priests who come near the LORD
consecrate themselves, lest the LORD break
out against them."

23But Moses said to the LORD, "The people
cannot come up to Mount Sinai; for You
warned us, saying, 'Set bounds around the
mountain and consecrate it.' "

24Then the LORD said to him, "Away! Get
down and then come up, you and Aaron with
you. But do not let the priests and the people
break through to come up to the LORD, lest He
break out against them." 25So Moses went
down to the people and spoke to them.

20 And God spoke all these words, saying:

2 "I *am* the LORD your God, who brought
you out of the land of Egypt, out of the
house of bondage.

3 "You shall have no other gods before Me.

4 "You shall not make for yourself a carved
image—any likeness *of anything* that
is in heaven above, or that *is* in the
earth beneath, or that *is* in the water
under the earth; 5you shall not bow
down to them nor serve them. For I,
the LORD your God, *am* a jealous God,
visiting the iniquity of the fathers
upon the children to the third and
fourth *generations* of those who hate
Me, 6but showing mercy to thousands, to those who love Me and keep
My commandments.

7 "You shall not take the name of the LORD
your God in vain, for the LORD will not
hold *him* guiltless who takes His name
in vain.

8 "Remember the Sabbath day, to keep it
holy. 9Six days you shall labor and do
all your work, 10but the seventh day *is*
the Sabbath of the LORD your God. *In
it* you shall do no work: you, nor your
son, nor your daughter, nor your male
servant, nor your female servant, nor
your cattle, nor your stranger who *is*
within your gates. 11For *in* six days the
LORD made the heavens and the
earth, the sea, and all that *is* in them,
and rested the seventh day. Therefore
the LORD blessed the Sabbath day and
hallowed it.

12 "Honor your father and your mother, that
your days may be long upon the land
which the LORD your God is giving you.

13 "You shall not murder.

14 "You shall not commit adultery.

15 "You shall not steal.

16 "You shall not bear false witness against
your neighbor.

17 "You shall not covet your neighbor's
house; you shall not covet your neighbor's wife, nor his male servant, nor his female servant, nor his ox, nor his donkey, nor anything that *is* your neighbor's."

18Now all the people witnessed the thunderings, the lightning flashes, the sound of the trumpet, and the mountain smoking; and when the people saw *it,* they trembled and
stood afar off. 19Then they said to Moses, "You
speak with us, and we will hear; but let not God speak with us, lest we die."

20And Moses said to the people, "Do not fear;
for God has come to test you, and that His fear may be before you, so that you may not sin."
21So the people stood afar off, but Moses drew
near the thick darkness where God *was.*

22Then the LORD said to Moses, "Thus you
shall say to the children of Israel: 'You have seen that I have talked with you from heaven.
23You shall not make *anything to be* with Me—
gods of silver or gods of gold you shall not make
for yourselves. 24An altar of earth you shall
make for Me, and you shall sacrifice on it your burnt offerings and your peace offerings, your sheep and your oxen. In every place where I record My name I will come to you, and I will
bless you. 25And if you make Me an altar of
stone, you shall not build it of hewn stone; for if you use your tool on it, you have profaned it.
26Nor shall you go up by steps to My altar, that
your nakedness may not be exposed on it.'

Psalm 18:37–45

37 I have pursued my enemies and
overtaken them;
Neither did I turn back again till they
were destroyed.
38 I have wounded them,
So that they could not rise;
They have fallen under my feet.
39 For You have armed me with strength
for the battle;
You have subdued under me those
who rose up against me.
40 You have also given me the necks of
my enemies,
So that I destroyed those who hated
me.
41 They cried out, but *there was* none to
save;
Even to the LORD, but He did not
answer them.
42 Then I beat them as fine as the dust
before the wind;
I cast them out like dirt in the streets.
43 You have delivered me from the
strivings of the people;
You have made me the head
of the nations;
A people I have not known shall
serve me.
44 As soon as they hear of me they obey
me;
The foreigners submit to me.
45 The foreigners fade away,
And come frightened from their
hideouts.

Proverbs 6:20–25

20 My son, keep your father's command,
And do not forsake the law
of your mother.
21 Bind them continually upon your
heart;
Tie them around your neck.
22 When you roam, they will lead you;
When you sleep, they will keep you;
And *when* you awake, they will speak
with you.
23 For the commandment *is* a lamp,
And the law a light;
Reproofs of instruction *are* the way
of life,
24 To keep you from the evil woman,
From the flattering tongue
of a seductress.
25 Do not lust after her beauty
in your heart,
Nor let her allure you with her eyelids.

6:25 lust. Sexual sin is rooted in lust (imagination of the sinful act), as implied in Exodus 20:17 and addressed by Christ in Matthew 5:28. This initial attraction must be consistently rejected (James 1:14,15).

Matthew 22:23–46

23The same day the Sadducees, who say there
is no resurrection, came to Him and asked Him,
24saying: "Teacher, Moses said that if a man dies,
having no children, his brother shall marry his wife and raise up offspring for his brother.
25Now there were with us seven brothers. The
first died after he had married, and having no
offspring, left his wife to his brother. 26Like-
wise the second also, and the third, even to
the seventh. 27Last of all the woman died also.
28Therefore, in the resurrection, whose wife of
the seven will she be? For they all had her."

[29]Jesus answered and said to them, "You are mistaken, not knowing the Scriptures nor the power of God. [30]For in the resurrection they neither marry nor are given in marriage, but are like angels of God in heaven. [31]But concerning the resurrection of the dead, have you not read what was spoken to you by God, saying, [32]'*I am the God of Abraham, the God of Isaac, and the God of Jacob*'? God is not the God of the dead, but of the living." [33]And when the multitudes heard *this,* they were astonished at His teaching.

[34]But when the Pharisees heard that He had silenced the Sadducees, they gathered together. [35]Then one of them, a lawyer, asked *Him a question,* testing Him, and saying, [36]"Teacher, which *is* the great commandment in the law?"

[37]Jesus said to him, "'*You shall love the* LORD *your God with all your heart, with all your soul, and with all your mind.*' [38]This is *the* first and great commandment. [39]And *the* second *is* like it: '*You shall love your neighbor as yourself.*' [40]On these two commandments hang all the Law and the Prophets."

[41]While the Pharisees were gathered together, Jesus asked them, [42]saying, "What do you think about the Christ? Whose Son is He?"

They said to Him, "*The Son* of David."

22:45 David then calls Him 'Lord.' David would not have addressed a merely human descendant as "Lord." Here Jesus was not disputing whether "Son of David" was an appropriate title for the Messiah; after all, the title is based on what is revealed about the Messiah in the Old Testament (Is. 11:1; Jer. 23:5) and it is used as a messianic title in 1:1. But Jesus was pointing out that the title "son of David" did not begin to sum up all that is true about the Messiah who is also "Son of God" (Luke 22:70). The inescapable implication is that Jesus was declaring His deity.

[43]He said to them, "How then does David in the Spirit call Him '*Lord,*' saying:

[44] '*The* LORD *said to my Lord,*
"Sit at My right hand,
Till I make Your enemies
Your footstool" '?

[45]If David then calls Him '*Lord,*' how is He his Son?" [46]And no one was able to answer Him a word, nor from that day on did anyone dare question Him anymore.

DAY 4: Are the Ten Commandments outmoded expectations or divine demands?

People make a serious error when they speak about "breaking the Ten Commandments." History amply displays the fact that people persist in breaking themselves on the Ten Commandments. They represent God's absolute and unchanging standard despite any arguments over their interpretation and application.

The title "Ten Commandments" comes from Moses (Ex. 34:28). The emphasis on God Himself speaking and writing these words makes unacceptable any theories of Israel's borrowing legal patterns or concepts from surrounding nations.

The Ten Commandments may be grouped into two broad categories: the vertical—humanity's relationship to God (Ex. 20:2–11); and the horizontal—humanity's relationship to the community (Ex. 20:12–17). By these Ten Commandments, true theology and true worship, the name of God, family honor, life, marriage, property, truth, and virtue are well protected.

FEBRUARY 5

Exodus 21:1–22:31

21 "Now these *are* the judgments which you shall set before them: [2]If you buy a Hebrew servant, he shall serve six years; and in the seventh he shall go out free and pay nothing. [3]If he comes in by himself, he shall go out by himself; if he *comes in* married, then his wife shall go out with him. [4]If his master has given him a wife, and she has borne him sons or daughters, the wife and her children shall be her master's, and he shall go out by himself. [5]But if the servant plainly says, 'I love my master, my wife, and my children; I will not go out free,' [6]then his master shall bring him to the judges. He shall also bring him to the door, or to the doorpost, and his master shall pierce his ear with an awl; and he shall serve him forever.

[7]"And if a man sells his daughter to be a female slave, she shall not go out as the male slaves do. [8]If she does not please her master, who has betrothed her to himself, then he

shall let her be redeemed. He shall have no
right to sell her to a foreign people, since he
has dealt deceitfully with her. [9]And if he has
betrothed her to his son, he shall deal with her
according to the custom of daughters. [10]If he
takes another *wife,* he shall not diminish her
food, her clothing, and her marriage rights.
[11]And if he does not do these three for her, then
she shall go out free, without *paying* money.

[12]"He who strikes a man so that he dies shall
surely be put to death. [13]However, if he did not
lie in wait, but God delivered *him* into his
hand, then I will appoint for you a place where
he may flee.

[14]"But if a man acts with premeditation
against his neighbor, to kill him by treachery,
you shall take him from My altar, that he may
die.

[15]"And he who strikes his father or his mother shall surely be put to death.

[16]"He who kidnaps a man and sells him, or if
he is found in his hand, shall surely be put to
death.

[17]"And he who curses his father or his mother shall surely be put to death.

[18]"If men contend with each other, and one
strikes the other with a stone or with *his* fist,
and he does not die but is confined to *his* bed,
[19]if he rises again and walks about outside with
his staff, then he who struck *him* shall be acquitted. He shall only pay *for* the loss of his
time, and shall provide *for him* to be thoroughly healed.

[20]"And if a man beats his male or female servant with a rod, so that he dies under his hand,
he shall surely be punished. [21]Notwithstanding,
if he remains alive a day or two, he shall not be
punished; for he *is* his property.

[22]"If men fight, and hurt a woman with child,
so that she gives birth prematurely, yet no
harm follows, he shall surely be punished
accordingly as the woman's husband imposes
on him; and he shall pay as the judges *determine.* [23]But if *any* harm follows, then you shall
give life for life, [24]eye for eye, tooth for tooth,
hand for hand, foot for foot, [25]burn for burn,
wound for wound, stripe for stripe.

[26]"If a man strikes the eye of his male or
female servant, and destroys it, he shall let him
go free for the sake of his eye. [27]And if he knocks
out the tooth of his male or female servant, he
shall let him go free for the sake of his tooth.

[28]"If an ox gores a man or a woman to death,
then the ox shall surely be stoned, and its
flesh shall not be eaten; but the owner of the
ox *shall be* acquitted. [29]But if the ox tended to
thrust with its horn in times past, and it has
been made known to his owner, and he has
not kept it confined, so that it has killed a man
or a woman, the ox shall be stoned and its
owner also shall be put to death. [30]If there is
imposed on him a sum of money, then he shall
pay to redeem his life, whatever is imposed on
him. [31]Whether it has gored a son or gored a
daughter, according to this judgment it shall
be done to him. [32]If the ox gores a male or
female servant, he shall give to their master
thirty shekels of silver, and the ox shall be
stoned.

[33]"And if a man opens a pit, or if a man digs
a pit and does not cover it, and an ox or a donkey falls in it, [34]the owner of the pit shall make
it good; he shall give money to their owner,
but the dead *animal* shall be his.

[35]"If one man's ox hurts another's, so that it
dies, then they shall sell the live ox and divide
the money from it; and the dead *ox* they shall
also divide. [36]Or if it was known that the ox
tended to thrust in time past, and its owner
has not kept it confined, he shall surely pay ox
for ox, and the dead animal shall be his own.

22 "If a man steals an ox or a sheep, and
slaughters it or sells it, he shall restore
five oxen for an ox and four sheep for a sheep.
[2]If the thief is found breaking in, and he is
struck so that he dies, *there shall be* no guilt
for his bloodshed. [3]If the sun has risen on him,
there shall be guilt for his bloodshed. He
should make full restitution; if he has nothing,
then he shall be sold for his theft. [4]If the theft
is certainly found alive in his hand, whether it
is an ox or donkey or sheep, he shall restore
double.

[5]"If a man causes a field or vineyard to be
grazed, and lets loose his animal, and it feeds
in another man's field, he shall make restitution from the best of his own field and the best
of his own vineyard.

[6]"If fire breaks out and catches in thorns, so
that stacked grain, standing grain, or the field
is consumed, he who kindled the fire shall
surely make restitution.

[7]"If a man delivers to his neighbor money or
articles to keep, and it is stolen out of the
man's house, if the thief is found, he shall pay
double. [8]If the thief is not found, then the master of the house shall be brought to the judges
to see whether he has put his hand into his
neighbor's goods.

[9]"For any kind of trespass, *whether it concerns* an ox, a donkey, a sheep, or clothing, *or*
for any kind of lost thing which *another* claims
to be his, the cause of both parties shall come
before the judges; *and* whomever the judges
condemn shall pay double to his neighbor. [10]If
a man delivers to his neighbor a donkey, an

ox, a sheep, or any animal to keep, and it dies,
is hurt, or driven away, no one seeing *it,* 11 *then*
an oath of the LORD shall be between them
both, that he has not put his hand into his
neighbor's goods; and the owner of it shall
accept *that,* and he shall not make *it* good.
12 But if, in fact, it is stolen from him, he shall
make restitution to the owner of it. 13 If it is torn
to pieces *by a beast, then* he shall bring it as
evidence, *and* he shall not make good what
was torn.
14 "And if a man borrows *anything* from his
neighbor, and it becomes injured or dies, the
owner of it not *being* with it, he shall surely
make *it* good. 15 If its owner *was* with it, he shall
not make *it* good; if it *was* hired, it came for its
hire.
16 "If a man entices a virgin who is not
betrothed, and lies with her, he shall surely
pay the bride-price for her *to be* his wife. 17 If
her father utterly refuses to give her to him,
he shall pay money according to the bride-
price of virgins.
18 "You shall not permit a sorceress to live.
19 "Whoever lies with an animal shall surely
be put to death.
20 "He who sacrifices to *any* god, except to
the LORD only, he shall be utterly destroyed.
21 "You shall neither mistreat a stranger nor
oppress him, for you were strangers in the
land of Egypt.
22 "You shall not afflict any widow or fatherless child. 23 If you afflict them in any way, *and*
they cry at all to Me, I will surely hear their
cry; 24 and My wrath will become hot, and I will
kill you with the sword; your wives shall be
widows, and your children fatherless.

22:22 widow or fatherless child. God reserved His special attention for widows and orphans who often had no one to care for them. He also reserved a special reaction, His wrath, for those abusing and exploiting them. This wrath would work out in military invasions as the sword reduced the abusers' families to the same status of being without spouse or parents.

22:25 interest. One way in which the people showed their concern for the poor and needy was to take no business advantage of them. Charging interest was allowable (Lev. 25:35–37; Deut. 23:19,20), but not when it was exorbitant or worsened the plight of the borrower. The psalmist identified a righteous man as one who lends money without interest (Ps. 15:5).

25 "If you lend money to *any of* My people
who are poor among you, you shall not be like
a moneylender to him; you shall not charge
him interest. 26 If you ever take your neighbor's
garment as a pledge, you shall return it to him
before the sun goes down. 27 For that *is* his only
covering, it *is* his garment for his skin. What
will he sleep in? And it will be that when he
cries to Me, I will hear, for I *am* gracious.
28 "You shall not revile God, nor curse a ruler
of your people.
29 "You shall not delay *to offer* the first of your
ripe produce and your juices. The firstborn of
your sons you shall give to Me. 30 Likewise you
shall do with your oxen *and* your sheep. It
shall be with its mother seven days; on the
eighth day you shall give it to Me.
31 "And you shall be holy men to Me: you
shall not eat meat torn *by beasts* in the field;
you shall throw it to the dogs.

Psalm 18:46–50

46 The LORD lives!
Blessed *be* my Rock!
Let the God of my salvation be exalted.
47 *It is* God who avenges me,
And subdues the peoples under me;
48 He delivers me from my enemies.
You also lift me up above those who
rise against me;
You have delivered me from
the violent man.
49 Therefore I will give thanks to You,
O LORD, among the Gentiles,
And sing praises to Your name.
50 Great deliverance He gives to His king,
And shows mercy to His anointed,
To David and his descendants
forevermore.

Proverbs 6:26–29

26 For by means of a harlot
A man is reduced to a crust of bread;
And an adulteress will prey upon his
precious life.
27 Can a man take fire to his bosom,
And his clothes not be burned?
28 Can one walk on hot coals,
And his feet not be seared?

6:26 crust of bread. Here the smallest piece of bread demonstrates how the prostitute reduces the life of a man to insignificance, including the loss of his wealth, freedom, family, purity, dignity, and even his soul (v. 32).

29 So *is* he who goes in to his neighbor's wife;
Whoever touches her shall not be innocent.

Matthew 23:1–22

23 Then Jesus spoke to the multitudes and
to His disciples, [2]saying: "The scribes
and the Pharisees sit in Moses' seat. [3]Therefore
whatever they tell you to observe, *that* observe
and do, but do not do according to their works;
for they say, and do not do. [4]For they bind
heavy burdens, hard to bear, and lay *them* on
men's shoulders; but they *themselves* will not
move them with one of their fingers. [5]But all
their works they do to be seen by men. They
make their phylacteries broad and enlarge the
borders of their garments. [6]They love the best
places at feasts, the best seats in the synagogues, [7]greetings in the marketplaces, and to
be called by men, 'Rabbi, Rabbi.' [8]But you, do
not be called 'Rabbi'; for One is your Teacher,
the Christ, and you are all brethren. [9]Do not
call anyone on earth your father; for One is
your Father, He who is in heaven. [10]And do not
be called teachers; for One is your Teacher,
the Christ. [11]But he who is greatest among you
shall be your servant. [12]And whoever exalts
himself will be humbled, and he who humbles
himself will be exalted.
[13]"But woe to you, scribes and Pharisees,
hypocrites! For you shut up the kingdom of
heaven against men; for you neither go in
yourselves, nor do you allow those who are
entering to go in. [14]Woe to you, scribes and
Pharisees, hypocrites! For you devour widows' houses, and for a pretense make long
prayers. Therefore you will receive greater
condemnation.

23:5 phylacteries. Leather boxes containing a parchment on which is written in 4 columns (Ex. 13:1–10,11–16; Deut. 6:4–9; 11:13–21). These are worn by men during prayer—one on the middle of the forehead and one on the left arm just above the elbow. The use of phylacteries was based on an overly literal interpretation of passages like Exodus 13:9,10. Evidently the Pharisees would broaden the leather straps by which the phylacteries were bound to their arms and foreheads, in order to make the phylacteries more prominent. **the borders of their garments.** I.e., the tassels. Jesus Himself wore them, so it was not the tassels themselves that He condemned, only the mentality that would lengthen the tassels to make it appear that one was especially spiritual.

[15]"Woe to you, scribes and Pharisees, hypocrites! For you travel land and sea to win one
proselyte, and when he is won, you make him
twice as much a son of hell as yourselves.
[16]"Woe to you, blind guides, who say, 'Whoever swears by the temple, it is nothing; but
whoever swears by the gold of the temple, he
is obliged *to perform it.*' [17]Fools and blind! For
which is greater, the gold or the temple that
sanctifies the gold? [18]And, 'Whoever swears by
the altar, it is nothing; but whoever swears by
the gift that is on it, he is obliged *to perform it.*'
[19]Fools and blind! For which is greater, the gift
or the altar that sanctifies the gift? [20]Therefore
he who swears by the altar, swears by it and by
all things on it. [21]He who swears by the temple,
swears by it and by Him who dwells in it. [22]And
he who swears by heaven, swears by the
throne of God and by Him who sits on it.

DAY 5: Why did Jesus have such a hard time with the Pharisees?

Throughout Matthew 23, the words Jesus uses to characterize the Pharisees exposes their true nature. To say they "sit in Moses' seat" (v. 2) is an expression equivalent to a university's "chair of philosophy." It meant they had the highest authority to instruct people in the law. The expression here may be translated, "[they] have seated themselves in Moses' seat"—stressing the fact that this was an imaginary authority they claimed for themselves. There was a legitimate sense in which the priests and Levites had authority to decide matters of the law (Deut. 17:9), but the scribes and Pharisees had gone beyond any legitimate authority and were adding human tradition to the Word of God (Matt. 15:3–9). For that Jesus condemned them (vv. 8–36).

As regards the Pharisees, Jesus tells the multitude to "observe and do" (v. 3) only what accords with the Word of God. The Pharisees were prone to bind "heavy burdens" (v. 4) of extrabiblical traditions and put them on others' shoulders. Jesus explicitly condemned that sort of legalism. The Pharisees would even widen their "phylacteries" and lengthen their "tassels" to make it appear that they were especially spiritual.

Jesus warns against using the titles of "Rabbi…father…teachers" (vv. 8–10). Here Jesus condemns pride and pretense, not titles per se. Paul repeatedly speaks of "teachers" in the church, and even refers to himself as the Corinthians' "father" (1 Cor. 4:15). Obviously, this does not forbid the showing of respect either (see 1 Thess. 5:11,12; 1 Tim. 5:1). Christ is merely forbidding the use of such names as spiritual titles, or in an ostentatious sense that accords undue spiritual authority to a human being, as if he were the source of truth rather than God.

FEBRUARY 6

Exodus 23:1–24:18

23 "You shall not circulate a false report. Do not put your hand with the wicked to be an unrighteous witness. [2]You shall not follow a crowd to do evil; nor shall you testify in a dispute so as to turn aside after many to pervert *justice.* [3]You shall not show partiality to a poor man in his dispute.

[4]"If you meet your enemy's ox or his donkey going astray, you shall surely bring it back to him again. [5]If you see the donkey of one who hates you lying under its burden, and you would refrain from helping it, you shall surely help him with it.

[6]"You shall not pervert the judgment of your poor in his dispute. [7]Keep yourself far from a false matter; do not kill the innocent and righteous. For I will not justify the wicked. [8]And you shall take no bribe, for a bribe blinds the discerning and perverts the words of the righteous.

[9]"Also you shall not oppress a stranger, for you know the heart of a stranger, because you were strangers in the land of Egypt.

[10]"Six years you shall sow your land and gather in its produce, [11]but the seventh *year* you shall let it rest and lie fallow, that the poor of your people may eat; and what they leave, the beasts of the field may eat. In like manner you shall do with your vineyard *and* your olive grove. [12]Six days you shall do your work, and on the seventh day you shall rest, that your ox and your donkey may rest, and the son of your female servant and the stranger may be refreshed.

[13]"And in all that I have said to you, be circumspect and make no mention of the name of other gods, nor let it be heard from your mouth.

[14]"Three times you shall keep a feast to Me in the year: [15]You shall keep the Feast of Unleavened Bread (you shall eat unleavened bread seven days, as I commanded you, at the time appointed in the month of Abib, for in it you came out of Egypt; none shall appear before Me empty); [16]and the Feast of Harvest, the firstfruits of your labors which you have sown in the field; and the Feast of Ingathering at the end of the year, when you have gathered in *the fruit of* your labors from the field.

[17]"Three times in the year all your males shall appear before the Lord GOD.

[18]"You shall not offer the blood of My sacrifice with leavened bread; nor shall the fat of My sacrifice remain until morning. [19]The first of the firstfruits of your land you shall bring into the house of the LORD your God. You shall not boil a young goat in its mother's milk.

[20]"Behold, I send an Angel before you to keep you in the way and to bring you into the place which I have prepared. [21]Beware of Him and obey His voice; do not provoke Him, for He will not pardon your transgressions; for My name *is* in Him. [22]But if you indeed obey His voice and do all that I speak, then I will be an enemy to your enemies and an adversary to your adversaries. [23]For My Angel will go before you and bring you in to the Amorites and the Hittites and the Perizzites and the Canaanites and the Hivites and the Jebusites; and I will cut them off. [24]You shall not bow down to their gods, nor serve them, nor do according to their works; but you shall utterly overthrow them and completely break down their *sacred* pillars.

[25]"So you shall serve the LORD your God, and He will bless your bread and your water.

23:23 My Angel. Usually taken to be a reference to the Angel of Yahweh, who is distinguished from the Lord who talks about Him as another person. Yet, He is identified with Him by reason of His forgiving sin and the Lord's name being in Him (v. 21). Neither Moses nor some other messenger or guide qualify for such descriptions. The key to victory in the upcoming takeover of the Land would not be Israel's military skill but the presence of this Angel, who is the preincarnate Christ.

And I will take sickness away from the midst of you. 26No one shall suffer miscarriage or be barren in your land; I will fulfill the number of your days.

27"I will send My fear before you, I will cause confusion among all the people to whom you come, and will make all your enemies turn *their* backs to you. 28And I will send hornets before you, which shall drive out the Hivite, the Canaanite, and the Hittite from before you. 29I will not drive them out from before you in one year, lest the land become desolate and the beasts of the field become too numerous for you. 30Little by little I will drive them out from before you, until you have increased, and you inherit the land. 31And I will set your bounds from the Red Sea to the sea, Philistia, and from the desert to the River. For I will deliver the inhabitants of the land into your hand, and you shall drive them out before you. 32You shall make no covenant with them, nor with their gods. 33They shall not dwell in your land, lest they make you sin against Me. For *if* you serve their gods, it will surely be a snare to you."

24 Now He said to Moses, "Come up to the LORD, you and Aaron, Nadab and Abihu, and seventy of the elders of Israel, and worship from afar. 2And Moses alone shall come near the LORD, but they shall not come near; nor shall the people go up with him."

3So Moses came and told the people all the words of the LORD and all the judgments. And all the people answered with one voice and said, "All the words which the LORD has said we will do." 4And Moses wrote all the words of the LORD. And he rose early in the morning, and built an altar at the foot of the mountain, and twelve pillars according to the twelve tribes of Israel. 5Then he sent young men of the children of Israel, who offered burnt offerings and sacrificed peace offerings of oxen to the LORD. 6And Moses took half the blood and put *it* in basins, and half the blood he sprinkled on the altar. 7Then he took the Book of the Covenant and read in the hearing of the people. And they said, "All that the LORD has said we will do, and be obedient." 8And Moses took the blood, sprinkled *it* on the people, and said, "This is the blood of the covenant which the LORD has made with you according to all these words."

9Then Moses went up, also Aaron, Nadab, and Abihu, and seventy of the elders of Israel, 10and they saw the God of Israel. And *there was* under His feet as it were a paved work of sapphire stone, and it was like the very heavens in *its* clarity. 11But on the nobles of the children of Israel He did not lay His hand. So they saw God, and they ate and drank.

12Then the LORD said to Moses, "Come up to Me on the mountain and be there; and I will give you tablets of stone, and the law and commandments which I have written, that you may teach them."

13So Moses arose with his assistant Joshua, and Moses went up to the mountain of God. 14And he said to the elders, "Wait here for us until we come back to you. Indeed, Aaron and Hur *are* with you. If any man has a difficulty, let him go to them." 15Then Moses went up into the mountain, and a cloud covered the mountain.

16Now the glory of the LORD rested on Mount Sinai, and the cloud covered it six days. And on the seventh day He called to Moses out of the midst of the cloud. 17The sight of the glory of the LORD *was* like a consuming fire on the top of the mountain in the eyes of the children of Israel. 18So Moses went into the midst of the cloud and went up into the mountain. And Moses was on the mountain forty days and forty nights.

Psalm 19:1–6

To the Chief Musician. A Psalm of David.

The heavens declare the glory
of God;
And the firmament shows
His handiwork.
2 Day unto day utters speech,
And night unto night reveals knowledge.
3 *There is* no speech nor language
Where their voice is not heard.
4 Their line has gone out through all the
earth,
And their words to the end of the world.

In them He has set a tabernacle
for the sun,
5 Which *is* like a bridegroom coming out
of his chamber,
And rejoices like a strong man to run
its race.

19:1–6 The testimony of the universe comes forth consistently and clearly, but sinful mankind persistently resists it. For this reason, general revelation cannot convert sinners, but it does make them highly accountable (see Rom. 1:18ff.). Salvation comes ultimately only through special revelation, i.e., as the Word of God is effectually applied by the Spirit of God.

6 Its rising *is* from one end of heaven,
And its circuit to the other end;
And there is nothing hidden from its
heat.

Proverbs 6:30–31

30 *People* do not despise a thief
If he steals to satisfy himself when he
is starving.
31 Yet *when* he is found, he must restore
sevenfold;
He may have to give up all the
substance of his house.

Matthew 23:23–39

23“Woe to you, scribes and Pharisees, hypocrites! For you pay tithe of mint and anise
and cummin, and have neglected the weighti-
er *matters* of the law: justice and mercy and
faith. These you ought to have done, without
leaving the others undone. 24Blind guides, who
strain out a gnat and swallow a camel!
25“Woe to you, scribes and Pharisees, hypocrites! For you cleanse the outside of the cup
and dish, but inside they are full of extortion
and self-indulgence. 26Blind Pharisee, first
cleanse the inside of the cup and dish, that the
outside of them may be clean also.
27“Woe to you, scribes and Pharisees, hypocrites! For you are like whitewashed tombs
which indeed appear beautiful outwardly, but
inside are full of dead *men's* bones and all
uncleanness. 28Even so you also outwardly
appear righteous to men, but inside you are
full of hypocrisy and lawlessness.
29“Woe to you, scribes and Pharisees, hypocrites! Because you build the tombs of the
prophets and adorn the monuments of the
righteous, 30and say, ‘If we had lived in the days
of our fathers, we would not have been partakers with them in the blood of the prophets.’
31“Therefore you are witnesses against yourselves that you are sons of those who murdered the prophets. 32Fill up, then, the measure
of your fathers' *guilt.* 33Serpents, brood of
vipers! How can you escape the condemnation
of hell? 34Therefore, indeed, I send you
prophets, wise men, and scribes: *some* of them
you will kill and crucify, and *some* of them you
will scourge in your synagogues and persecute from city to city, 35that on you may come
all the righteous blood shed on the earth,
from the blood of righteous Abel to the blood
of Zechariah, son of Berechiah, whom you
murdered between the temple and the altar.
36Assuredly, I say to you, all these things will
come upon this generation.
37“O Jerusalem, Jerusalem, the one who kills
the prophets and stones those who are sent to
her! How often I wanted to gather your children
together, as a hen gathers her chicks under *her*
wings, but you were not willing! 38See! Your
house is left to you desolate; 39for I say to you,
you shall see Me no more till you say, *‘Blessed
is He who comes in the name of the LORD!’* ”

23:25 you cleanse the outside. The Pharisees' focus on external issues lay at the heart of their error. Who would want to drink from a cup that had been washed on the outside but was still filthy inside? Yet the Pharisees lived their lives as if external appearance were more important than internal reality. That was the very essence of their hypocrisy, and Jesus rebuked them for it repeatedly.

23:39 you shall see Me no more. Christ's public teaching ministry was over. He withdrew from national Israel until the time yet future when they will recognize Him as Messiah (Rom. 11:23–26). Then Christ quoted from Psalm 118:26.

DAY 6: What broke Jesus' heart about His people?

Read Jesus' lament over Jerusalem in Matthew 23:37: "I wanted to gather your children together, … but you were not willing!" God is utterly sovereign and therefore fully capable of bringing to pass whatever He desires (see Is. 46:10)—including the salvation of whomever He chooses (Eph. 1:4,5). Yet, He sometimes expresses a wish for that which He does not sovereignly bring to pass (see Gen. 6:6; Deut. 5:29; Ps. 81:13; Is. 48:18). Such expressions in no way suggest a limitation on the sovereignty of God or imply any actual change in Him (Num. 23:19). But these statements do reveal essential aspects of the divine character: He is full of compassion, sincerely good to all, desirous of good, not evil—and therefore not delighting in the destruction of the wicked (Ezek. 18:32; 33:11).

While affirming God's sovereignty, one must understand His pleas for the repentance of the reprobate as well-meant appeals—and His goodness toward the wicked as a genuine mercy designed to provoke them to repentance (Rom. 2:4). The emotion displayed by Christ here (and in all similar passages, such as Luke 19:41) is obviously a deep, sincere passion. All Christ's feelings must be in perfect harmony with the divine will (see John 8:29)—and therefore these lamentations should not be thought of as mere exhibitions of His humanity.

"Your house is left to you desolate" (v. 38). A few days earlier, Christ had referred to the temple as His Father's "house" (21:13). But the blessing and glory of God were being removed from Israel (see 1 Sam. 4:21). When Christ "departed from the temple" (24:1), the glory of God went with Him. Ezekiel 11:23 described Ezekiel's vision of the departure of the Shekinah glory in His day. The glory left the temple and stood on the Mount of Olives, exactly the same route Christ followed here (see 24:3).

FEBRUARY 7

Exodus 25:1–26:37

25 Then the LORD spoke to Moses, saying:
2"Speak to the children of Israel, that
they bring Me an offering. From everyone
who gives it willingly with his heart you shall
take My offering. 3And this *is* the offering
which you shall take from them: gold, silver,
and bronze; 4blue, purple, and scarlet *thread,*
fine linen, and goats' *hair;* 5ram skins dyed
red, badger skins, and acacia wood; 6oil for the
light, and spices for the anointing oil and for
the sweet incense; 7onyx stones, and stones to
be set in the ephod and in the breastplate.
8And let them make Me a sanctuary, that I
may dwell among them. 9According to all that
I show you, *that is,* the pattern of the tabernacle
and the pattern of all its furnishings, just
so you shall make *it.*
10"And they shall make an ark of acacia
wood; two and a half cubits *shall be* its length,
a cubit and a half its width, and a cubit and a
half its height. 11And you shall overlay it with
pure gold, inside and out you shall overlay it,
and shall make on it a molding of gold all
around. 12You shall cast four rings of gold for
it, and put *them* in its four corners; two rings
shall be on one side, and two rings on the
other side. 13And you shall make poles *of* acacia
wood, and overlay them with gold. 14You
shall put the poles into the rings on the sides
of the ark, that the ark may be carried by
them. 15The poles shall be in the rings of the
ark; they shall not be taken from it. 16And you
shall put into the ark the Testimony which I
will give you.
17"You shall make a mercy seat of pure gold;
two and a half cubits *shall be* its length and a
cubit and a half its width. 18And you shall make
two cherubim of gold; of hammered work you
shall make them at the two ends of the mercy
seat. 19Make one cherub at one end, and the
other cherub at the other end; you shall make
the cherubim at the two ends of it *of one piece*
with the mercy seat. 20And the cherubim shall
stretch out *their* wings above, covering the
mercy seat with their wings, and they shall
face one another; the faces of the cherubim
shall be toward the mercy seat. 21You shall put
the mercy seat on top of the ark, and in the ark
you shall put the Testimony that I will give
you. 22And there I will meet with you, and I will
speak with you from above the mercy seat,
from between the two cherubim which *are* on
the ark of the Testimony, about everything
which I will give you in commandment to the
children of Israel.
23"You shall also make a table of acacia wood;
two cubits *shall be* its length, a cubit its width,
and a cubit and a half its height. 24And you shall
overlay it with pure gold, and make a molding
of gold all around. 25You shall make for it a
frame of a handbreadth all around, and you
shall make a gold molding for the frame all
around. 26And you shall make for it four rings
of gold, and put the rings on the four corners
that *are* at its four legs. 27The rings shall be
close to the frame, as holders for the poles to
bear the table. 28And you shall make the poles
of acacia wood, and overlay them with gold,
that the table may be carried with them. 29You
shall make its dishes, its pans, its pitchers, and

25:17 mercy seat. The lid or cover of the ark was the "mercy seat" or the place at which atonement took place. Between the Shekinah glory cloud above the ark and the tablets of Law inside the ark was the blood-sprinkled cover. Blood from the sacrifices stood between God and the broken law of God!

its bowls for pouring. You shall make them of
pure gold. 30And you shall set the showbread
on the table before Me always.
31"You shall also make a lampstand of pure
gold; the lampstand shall be of hammered
work. Its shaft, its branches, its bowls, its *ornamental* knobs, and flowers shall be *of one*

25:31 lampstand. Situated opposite the table of showbread on the south side of the Holy Place stood an ornate lampstand, or menorah, patterned after a flowering almond tree. It provided light for the priests serving in the Holy Place. Care was taken, according to God's instructions (27:20,21; 30:7,8; Lev. 24:1–4), to keep it well supplied with pure olive oil so that it would not be extinguished. The lampstand is seen as typifying the Lord Jesus Christ, who was the true Light which came into the world (John 1:6–9; 8:12).

piece. 32And six branches shall come out of its
sides: three branches of the lampstand out of
one side, and three branches of the lampstand
out of the other side. 33Three bowls *shall be*
made like almond *blossoms* on one branch,
with an *ornamental* knob and a flower, and
three bowls made like almond *blossoms* on the
other branch, *with* an *ornamental* knob and a
flower—and so for the six branches that come
out of the lampstand. 34On the lampstand itself
four bowls *shall be* made like almond *blossoms,*
each with its *ornamental* knob and flower.
35And *there shall be* a knob under the *first* two
branches of the same, a knob under the *second*
two branches of the same, and a knob under
the *third* two branches of the same, according
to the six branches that extend from the lampstand. 36Their knobs and their branches *shall*
be of one piece; all of it *shall be* one hammered
piece of pure gold. 37You shall make seven
lamps for it, and they shall arrange its lamps
so that they give light in front of it. 38And its
wick-trimmers and their trays *shall be* of pure
gold. 39It shall be made of a talent of pure gold,
with all these utensils. 40And see to it that you
make *them* according to the pattern which was
shown you on the mountain.

26 "Moreover you shall make the tabernacle *with* ten curtains *of* fine woven linen
and blue, purple, and scarlet *thread;* with artistic designs of cherubim you shall weave them.
2The length of each curtain *shall be* twenty-
eight cubits, and the width of each curtain
four cubits. And every one of the curtains
shall have the same measurements. 3Five curtains shall be coupled to one another, and *the*
other five curtains *shall be* coupled to one
another. 4And you shall make loops of blue
yarn on the edge of the curtain on the
selvedge of *one* set, and likewise you shall do
on the outer edge of *the other* curtain of the
second set. 5Fifty loops you shall make in the
one curtain, and fifty loops you shall make on
the edge of the curtain that *is* on the end of the
second set, that the loops may be clasped to
one another. 6And you shall make fifty clasps
of gold, and couple the curtains together with
the clasps, so that it may be one tabernacle.
7"You shall also make curtains of goats' *hair,*
to be a tent over the tabernacle. You shall
make eleven curtains. 8The length of each curtain *shall be* thirty cubits, and the width of
each curtain four cubits; and the eleven curtains shall all have the same measurements.
9And you shall couple five curtains by themselves and six curtains by themselves, and
you shall double over the sixth curtain at the
forefront of the tent. 10You shall make fifty
loops on the edge of the curtain that is outermost in *one* set, and fifty loops on the edge of
the curtain of the second set. 11And you shall
make fifty bronze clasps, put the clasps into
the loops, and couple the tent together, that it
may be one. 12The remnant that remains of the
curtains of the tent, the half curtain that
remains, shall hang over the back of the tabernacle. 13And a cubit on one side and a cubit
on the other side, of what remains of the
length of the curtains of the tent, shall hang
over the sides of the tabernacle, on this side
and on that side, to cover it.
14"You shall also make a covering of ram
skins dyed red for the tent, and a covering of
badger skins above that.
15"And for the tabernacle you shall make the
boards of acacia wood, standing upright. 16Ten
cubits *shall be* the length of a board, and a
cubit and a half *shall be* the width of each
board. 17Two tenons *shall be* in each board for
binding one to another. Thus you shall make
for all the boards of the tabernacle. 18And you
shall make the boards for the tabernacle,
twenty boards for the south side. 19You shall
make forty sockets of silver under the twenty
boards: two sockets under each of the boards
for its two tenons. 20And for the second side of
the tabernacle, the north side, *there shall be*
twenty boards 21and their forty sockets of silver: two sockets under each of the boards.
22For the far side of the tabernacle, westward,
you shall make six boards. 23And you shall also
make two boards for the two back corners of

the tabernacle. [24]They shall be coupled together at the bottom and they shall be coupled together at the top by one ring. Thus it shall be for both of them. They shall be for the two corners. [25]So there shall be eight boards with their sockets of silver—sixteen sockets—two sockets under each of the boards.

[26]"And you shall make bars of acacia wood: five for the boards on one side of the tabernacle, [27]five bars for the boards on the other side of the tabernacle, and five bars for the boards of the side of the tabernacle, for the far side westward. [28]The middle bar shall pass through the midst of the boards from end to end. [29]You shall overlay the boards with gold, make their rings of gold *as* holders for the bars, and overlay the bars with gold. [30]And you shall raise up the tabernacle according to its pattern which you were shown on the mountain.

[31]"You shall make a veil woven of blue, purple, and scarlet *thread,* and fine woven linen. It shall be woven with an artistic design of cherubim. [32]You shall hang it upon the four pillars of acacia *wood* overlaid with gold. Their hooks *shall be* gold, upon four sockets of silver. [33]And you shall hang the veil from the clasps. Then you shall bring the ark of the Testimony in there, behind the veil. The veil shall be a divider for you between the holy *place* and the Most Holy. [34]You shall put the mercy seat upon the ark of the Testimony in the Most Holy. [35]You shall set the table outside the veil, and the lampstand across from the table on the side of the tabernacle toward the south; and you shall put the table on the north side.

[36]"You shall make a screen for the door of the tabernacle, *woven of* blue, purple, and scarlet *thread,* and fine woven linen, made by a weaver. [37]And you shall make for the screen five pillars of acacia *wood,* and overlay them with gold; their hooks *shall be* gold, and you shall cast five sockets of bronze for them.

Psalm 19:7–14

7 The law of the LORD *is* perfect,
converting the soul;
The testimony of the LORD *is* sure,
making wise the simple;
8 The statutes of the LORD *are* right,
rejoicing the heart;
The commandment of the LORD *is*
pure, enlightening the eyes;
9 The fear of the LORD *is* clean,
enduring forever;
The judgments of the LORD *are* true
and righteous altogether.
10 More to be desired *are they* than gold,
Yea, than much fine gold;
Sweeter also than honey and the
honeycomb.
11 Moreover by them Your servant is
warned,
And in keeping them *there is* great
reward.
12 Who can understand *his* errors?
Cleanse me from secret *faults.*
13 Keep back Your servant also
from presumptuous *sins;*
Let them not have dominion over me.
Then I shall be blameless,
And I shall be innocent of great
transgression.

14 Let the words of my mouth and the
meditation of my heart
Be acceptable in Your sight,
O LORD, my strength and my
Redeemer.

Proverbs 6:32–35

32 Whoever commits adultery with a
woman lacks understanding;
He *who* does so destroys his own soul.
33 Wounds and dishonor he will get,
And his reproach will not be
wiped away.
34 For jealousy *is* a husband's fury;
Therefore he will not spare in the day
of vengeance.
35 He will accept no recompense,
Nor will he be appeased though you
give many gifts.

Matthew 24:1–28

24 Then Jesus went out and departed from the temple, and His disciples came up to show Him the buildings of the temple. [2]And Jesus said to them, "Do you not see all these things? Assuredly, I say to you, not *one* stone shall be left here upon another, that shall not be thrown down."

[3]Now as He sat on the Mount of Olives, the disciples came to Him privately, saying, "Tell us, when will these things be? And what *will be* the sign of Your coming, and of the end of the age?"

[4]And Jesus answered and said to them: "Take heed that no one deceives you. [5]For many will come in My name, saying, 'I am the Christ,' and will deceive many. [6]And you will hear of wars and rumors of wars. See that you are not troubled; for all *these things* must come to pass, but the end is not yet. [7]For nation will rise against nation, and kingdom against kingdom. And there will be famines, pestilences, and earthquakes in various places. [8]All these *are* the beginning of sorrows.

24:2 not *one* stone shall be left here. These words were literally fulfilled in A.D. 70. Titus, the Roman general, built large wooden scaffolds around the walls of the temple buildings, piled them high with wood and other flammable items, and set them ablaze. The heat from the fires was so intense that the stones crumbled. The rubble was then sifted to retrieve the melted gold, and the remaining ruins were "thrown down" into the Kidron Valley.

24:14 preached in all the world. Despite all the tribulations that would come—the deception of false teachers, the wars, persecutions, natural disasters, defections from Christ, and all the obstacles to the spread of the gospel—the message ultimately penetrates every part of the globe. God is never without a witness, and He will proclaim the gospel from heaven itself if necessary (see Rev. 14:6). **and then the end will come.** "The end" refers to the final, excruciating birth pangs. This is how Christ characterizes the time of Great Tribulation described in the verses that follow.

9"Then they will deliver you up to tribulation
and kill you, and you will be hated by all nations
for My name's sake. 10And then many will be
offended, will betray one another, and will hate
one another. 11Then many false prophets will
rise up and deceive many. 12And because lawlessness will abound, the love of many will grow
cold. 13But he who endures to the end shall be
saved. 14And this gospel of the kingdom will be
preached in all the world as a witness to all the
nations, and then the end will come.
15"Therefore when you see the *'abomination
of desolation,'* spoken of by Daniel the
prophet, standing in the holy place" (whoever
reads, let him understand), 16"then let those
who are in Judea flee to the mountains. 17Let
him who is on the housetop not go down to
take anything out of his house. 18And let him
who is in the field not go back to get his
clothes. 19But woe to those who are pregnant
and to those who are nursing babies in those
days! 20And pray that your flight may not be in
winter or on the Sabbath. 21For then there will
be great tribulation, such as has not been
since the beginning of the world until this
time, no, nor ever shall be. 22And unless those
days were shortened, no flesh would be
saved; but for the elect's sake those days will
be shortened.
23"Then if anyone says to you, 'Look, here *is*
the Christ!' or 'There!' do not believe *it*. 24For
false christs and false prophets will rise and
show great signs and wonders to deceive, if
possible, even the elect. 25See, I have told you
beforehand.
26"Therefore if they say to you, 'Look, He is
in the desert!' do not go out; *or* 'Look, *He is* in
the inner rooms!' do not believe *it*. 27For as the
lightning comes from the east and flashes to
the west, so also will the coming of the Son of
Man be. 28For wherever the carcass is, there
the eagles will be gathered together.

DAY 7: Why all the specific details about the tabernacle, and what do they mean for us today?

Ever since God dictated the blueprints of the tabernacle to Moses, people have wondered about the significance of the exact details. Several terms are used to indicate times in the Bible when events, persons, or things represent larger ideas: typology and foreshadowing. For example, the sacrifice of the lambs in the Old Testament had not only a limited immediate significance in understanding the cost of forgiveness, but this practice also foreshadowed the eventual sacrifice of the Lamb of God, Jesus, on the cross.

Because at least some parts of the tabernacle hold special significance—the ark representing God's covenant with His people—students of Scripture have looked for other possible deeper meanings. Ingenuity in linking every item of furniture and every piece of building material to Christ may appear most intriguing; but if New Testament statements and allusions do not support such linkage and typology, students ought to proceed with caution. The beauty and efficiency of the tabernacle's design presents a tribute to God's creative character, but those who look for hidden meaning in every tent peg and covering stitch run the risk of missing the big picture in the details. The New Testament points repeatedly to the awesome fact of God's presence with people as represented in the Tabernacle. Other New Testament lessons (particularly the Book of Hebrews) help identify the intended symbols and deeper meanings.

FEBRUARY 8

Exodus 27:1–28:43

27 "You shall make an altar of acacia wood,
five cubits long and five cubits wide—
the altar shall be square—and its height *shall*
be three cubits. [2]You shall make its horns on
its four corners; its horns shall be of one
piece with it. And you shall overlay it with
bronze. [3]Also you shall make its pans to
receive its ashes, and its shovels and its basins
and its forks and its firepans; you shall make
all its utensils of bronze. [4]You shall make a
grate for it, a network of bronze; and on the
network you shall make four bronze rings at
its four corners. [5]You shall put it under the rim
of the altar beneath, that the network may be
midway up the altar. [6]And you shall make
poles for the altar, poles of acacia wood, and
overlay them with bronze. [7]The poles shall be
put in the rings, and the poles shall be on the
two sides of the altar to bear it. [8]You shall
make it hollow with boards; as it was shown
you on the mountain, so shall they make *it.*
[9]"You shall also make the court of the tabernacle. For the south side *there shall be* hangings for the court *made of* fine woven linen,
one hundred cubits long for one side. [10]And its
twenty pillars and their twenty sockets *shall be*
bronze. The hooks of the pillars and their
bands *shall be* silver. [11]Likewise along the
length of the north side *there shall be* hangings
one hundred *cubits* long, with its twenty pillars
and their twenty sockets of bronze, and the
hooks of the pillars and their bands of silver.

27:9 the court of the tabernacle. The dimensions of the rectangular courtyard space, bordered by curtains and poles around the tabernacle were also precisely given (vv. 9–19; 150 feet by 75 feet). The outer hangings were high enough, 5 cubits or 7.5 feet, to block all view of the interior of the courtyard (v. 18). Entry into the courtyard of God's dwelling place was not gained just generally and freely from all quarters.

[12]"And along the width of the court on the
west side *shall be* hangings of fifty cubits, with
their ten pillars and their ten sockets. [13]The
width of the court on the east side *shall be* fifty
cubits. [14]The hangings on *one* side *of the gate*
shall be fifteen cubits, *with* their three pillars
and their three sockets. [15]And on the other
side *shall be* hangings of fifteen *cubits, with*
their three pillars and their three sockets.
[16]"For the gate of the court *there shall be* a
screen twenty cubits long, *woven of* blue, purple, and scarlet *thread,* and fine woven linen,
made by a weaver. It *shall have* four pillars and
four sockets. [17]All the pillars around the court
shall have bands of silver; their hooks *shall be*
of silver and their sockets of bronze. [18]The
length of the court *shall be* one hundred cubits,
the width fifty throughout, and the height five
cubits, *made of* fine woven linen, and its sockets of bronze. [19]All the utensils of the tabernacle for all its service, all its pegs, and all the
pegs of the court, *shall be* of bronze.
[20]"And you shall command the children of
Israel that they bring you pure oil of pressed
olives for the light, to cause the lamp to burn
continually. [21]In the tabernacle of meeting, outside the veil which *is* before the Testimony,
Aaron and his sons shall tend it from evening
until morning before the LORD. *It shall be* a
statute forever to their generations on behalf
of the children of Israel.
28 "Now take Aaron your brother, and his
sons with him, from among the children of Israel, that he may minister to Me as
priest, Aaron *and* Aaron's sons: Nadab, Abihu,
Eleazar, and Ithamar. [2]And you shall make holy
garments for Aaron your brother, for glory and
for beauty. [3]So you shall speak to all *who are*
gifted artisans, whom I have filled with the
spirit of wisdom, that they may make Aaron's
garments, to consecrate him, that he may minister to Me as priest. [4]And these *are* the garments which they shall make: a breastplate,

28:1 minister to Me as priest. The 3-fold repetition of this phrase in the opening words about Aaron's priestly wardrobe would appear to stress the importance of his role in the religious life of the nation. Aaron's sons were part of the priesthood being set up. The Hebrew text groups the sons in two pairs, the first pair being Nadab and Abihu, both of whom died because of wanton disregard of God's instructions (Lev. 10:1,2). Aaron and his descendants, as well as the tribe of Levi, were selected by God to be Israel's priests—they did not appoint themselves to the position. The law clearly defined their duties for worship and the sacrifices in the tabernacle and for the individual worshiper and the nation's covenantal relationship to God.

an ephod, a robe, a skillfully woven tunic, a turban, and a sash. So they shall make holy garments for Aaron your brother and his sons, that he may minister to Me as priest.

5“They shall take the gold, blue, purple, and scarlet *thread,* and the fine linen, 6and they shall make the ephod of gold, blue, purple, *and* scarlet *thread,* and fine woven linen, artistically worked. 7It shall have two shoulder straps joined at its two edges, and *so* it shall be joined together. 8And the intricately woven band of the ephod, which *is* on it, shall be of the same workmanship, *made of* gold, blue, purple, and scarlet *thread,* and fine woven linen.

9“Then you shall take two onyx stones and engrave on them the names of the sons of Israel: 10six of their names on one stone and six names on the other stone, in order of their birth. 11With the work of an engraver in stone, *like* the engravings of a signet, you shall engrave the two stones with the names of the sons of Israel. You shall set them in settings of gold. 12And you shall put the two stones on the shoulders of the ephod *as* memorial stones for the sons of Israel. So Aaron shall bear their names before the LORD on his two shoulders as a memorial. 13You shall also make settings of gold, 14and you shall make two chains of pure gold like braided cords, and fasten the braided chains to the settings.

15“You shall make the breastplate of judgment. Artistically woven according to the workmanship of the ephod you shall make it: of gold, blue, purple, and scarlet *thread,* and fine woven linen, you shall make it. 16It shall be doubled into a square: a span *shall be* its length, and a span *shall be* its width. 17And you shall put settings of stones in it, four rows of stones: *The first* row *shall be* a sardius, a topaz, and an emerald; *this shall be* the first row; 18the second row *shall be* a turquoise, a sapphire, and a diamond; 19the third row, a jacinth, an agate, and an amethyst; 20and the fourth row, a beryl, an onyx, and a jasper. They shall be set in gold settings. 21And the stones shall have the names of the sons of Israel, twelve according to their names, *like* the engravings of a signet, each one with its own name; they shall be according to the twelve tribes.

22“You shall make chains for the breastplate at the end, like braided cords of pure gold. 23And you shall make two rings of gold for the breastplate, and put the two rings on the two ends of the breastplate. 24Then you shall put the two braided *chains* of gold in the two rings which are on the ends of the breastplate; 25and the *other* two ends of the two braided *chains* you shall fasten to the two settings, and put them on the shoulder straps of the ephod in the front.

26“You shall make two rings of gold, and put them on the two ends of the breastplate, on the edge of it, which is on the inner side of the ephod. 27And two *other* rings of gold you shall make, and put them on the two shoulder straps, underneath the ephod toward its front, right at the seam above the intricately woven band of the ephod. 28They shall bind the breastplate by means of its rings to the rings of the ephod, using a blue cord, so that it is above the intricately woven band of the ephod, and so that the breastplate does not come loose from the ephod.

29“So Aaron shall bear the names of the sons of Israel on the breastplate of judgment over his heart, when he goes into the holy *place,* as a memorial before the LORD continually. 30And you shall put in the breastplate of judgment the Urim and the Thummim, and they shall be over Aaron’s heart when he goes in before the LORD. So Aaron shall bear the judgment of the children of Israel over his heart before the LORD continually.

31“You shall make the robe of the ephod all of blue. 32There shall be an opening for his head in the middle of it; it shall have a woven binding all around its opening, like the opening in a coat of mail, so that it does not tear. 33And upon its hem you shall make pomegranates of blue, purple, and scarlet, all around its hem, and bells of gold between them all around: 34a golden bell and a pomegranate, a golden bell and a pomegranate, upon the hem of the robe all around. 35And it shall be upon Aaron when he ministers, and its sound will be heard when he goes into the holy *place* before the LORD and when he comes out, that he may not die.

36“You shall also make a plate of pure gold and engrave on it, *like* the engraving of a signet:

HOLINESS TO THE LORD.

37And you shall put it on a blue cord, that it may be on the turban; it shall be on the front of the turban. 38So it shall be on Aaron’s forehead, that Aaron may bear the iniquity of the holy things which the children of Israel hallow in all their holy gifts; and it shall always be on his forehead, that they may be accepted before the LORD.

39“You shall skillfully weave the tunic of fine linen *thread,* you shall make the turban of fine linen, and you shall make the sash of woven work.

40“For Aaron’s sons you shall make tunics, and you shall make sashes for them. And you

shall make hats for them, for glory and beauty.
[41]So you shall put them on Aaron your brother
and on his sons with him. You shall anoint
them, consecrate them, and sanctify them, that
they may minister to Me as priests. [42]And you
shall make for them linen trousers to cover
their nakedness; they shall reach from the waist
to the thighs. [43]They shall be on Aaron and on
his sons when they come into the tabernacle
of meeting, or when they come near the altar
to minister in the holy *place,* that they do not
incur iniquity and die. *It shall be* a statute forever to him and his descendants after him.

Psalm 20:1–5

To the Chief Musician. A Psalm of David.

May the LORD answer you in
the day of trouble;
May the name of the God of Jacob
defend you;
2 May He send you help from the
sanctuary,
And strengthen you out of Zion;
3 May He remember all your offerings,
And accept your burnt
sacrifice. Selah
4 May He grant you according to your
heart's *desire,*
And fulfill all your purpose.
5 We will rejoice in your salvation,
And in the name of our God we will set
up *our* banners!
May the LORD fulfill all your petitions.

Proverbs 7:1–5

7 My son, keep my words,
And treasure my commands
within you.
2 Keep my commands and live,
And my law as the apple of your eye.
3 Bind them on your fingers;
Write them on the tablet of your heart.
4 Say to wisdom, "You *are* my sister,"
And call understanding *your* nearest kin,
5 That they may keep you from the
immoral woman,
From the seductress *who* flatters
with her words.

Matthew 24:29–51

[29]"Immediately after the tribulation of those
days the sun will be darkened, and the moon
will not give its light; the stars will fall from
heaven, and the powers of the heavens will be
shaken. [30]Then the sign of the Son of Man will
appear in heaven, and then all the tribes of the
earth will mourn, and they will see the Son of
Man coming on the clouds of heaven with
power and great glory. [31]And He will send His
angels with a great sound of a trumpet, and they
will gather together His elect from the four
winds, from one end of heaven to the other.
[32]"Now learn this parable from the fig tree:
When its branch has already become tender
and puts forth leaves, you know that summer
is near. [33]So you also, when you see all these
things, know that it is near—at the doors! [34]As-
suredly, I say to you, this generation will by no
means pass away till all these things take
place. [35]Heaven and earth will pass away, but
My words will by no means pass away.
[36]"But of that day and hour no one knows,
not even the angels of heaven, but My Father
only. [37]But as the days of Noah *were,* so also
will the coming of the Son of Man be. [38]For as
in the days before the flood, they were eating
and drinking, marrying and giving in marriage, until the day that Noah entered the ark,
[39]and did not know until the flood came and
took them all away, so also will the coming of
the Son of Man be. [40]Then two *men* will be in
the field: one will be taken and the other left.
[41]Two *women will be* grinding at the mill: one
will be taken and the other left. [42]Watch therefore, for you do not know what hour your Lord
is coming. [43]But know this, that if the master of
the house had known what hour the thief
would come, he would have watched and not

7:2 apple of your eye. This expression refers to the pupil of the eye which, because it is the source of sight, is carefully protected (see Deut. 32:10; Ps. 17:8; Zech. 2:8). The son is to guard and protect his father's teachings because they give him spiritual and moral sight.

24:37 as the days of Noah *were.* Jesus' emphasis here is not so much on the extreme wickedness of Noah's day (Gen. 6:5), but on the people's preoccupation with mundane matters of everyday life ("eating and drinking, marrying and giving in marriage"—v. 38), when judgment fell suddenly. They had received warnings, in the form of Noah's preaching (2 Pet. 2:5)—and the ark itself, which was a testimony to the judgment that was to come. But they were unconcerned about such matters and therefore were swept away unexpectedly in the midst of their daily activities.

allowed his house to be broken into. 44There-
fore you also be ready, for the Son of Man is
coming at an hour you do not expect.
45"Who then is a faithful and wise servant,
whom his master made ruler over his household, to give them food in due season?
46Blessed *is* that servant whom his master,
when he comes, will find so doing. 47Assuredly,
I say to you that he will make him ruler over
all his goods. 48But if that evil servant says in
his heart, 'My master is delaying his coming,'
49and begins to beat *his* fellow servants, and to
eat and drink with the drunkards, 50the master
of that servant will come on a day when he is
not looking for *him* and at an hour that he is
not aware of, 51and will cut him in two and
appoint *him* his portion with the hypocrites.
There shall be weeping and gnashing of teeth.

DAY 8: How should Jesus' prophetic statements, many of which are found in Matthew 24 and 25, be interpreted?

The prophetic passages present a particular challenge for those seeking to understand a correct interpretation of Jesus' words. The Olivet discourse (Matthew 24; 25), for example, contains some details that evoke images of the violent destruction of Jerusalem in A.D. 70. Jesus' words in 24:34 have led some to conclude that all these things were fulfilled—albeit not literally—in the Roman conquest of that era. This view is known as "preterism." But this is a serious interpretive blunder, forcing the interpreter to read into these passages spiritualized, allegorical meanings unwarranted by normal exegetical study methods. The grammatical-historical hermeneutical approach to these passages is the approach to follow, and it yields a consistently futuristic interpretation of crucial prophecies.

FEBRUARY 9

Exodus 29:1–30:38

29 "And this is what you shall do to them
to hallow them for ministering to Me as
priests: Take one young bull and two rams
without blemish, 2and unleavened bread,
unleavened cakes mixed with oil, and unleavened wafers anointed with oil (you shall make
them of wheat flour). 3You shall put them in
one basket and bring them in the basket, with
the bull and the two rams.
4"And Aaron and his sons you shall bring to
the door of the tabernacle of meeting, and you
shall wash them with water. 5Then you shall
take the garments, put the tunic on Aaron, and
the robe of the ephod, the ephod, and the breastplate, and gird him with the intricately woven
band of the ephod. 6You shall put the turban
on his head, and put the holy crown on the turban. 7And you shall take the anointing oil, pour
it on his head, and anoint him. 8Then you shall
bring his sons and put tunics on them. 9And
you shall gird them with sashes, Aaron and
his sons, and put the hats on them. The priesthood shall be theirs for a perpetual statute. So
you shall consecrate Aaron and his sons.
10"You shall also have the bull brought
before the tabernacle of meeting, and Aaron
and his sons shall put their hands on the head
of the bull. 11Then you shall kill the bull before
the LORD, *by* the door of the tabernacle of
meeting. 12You shall take *some* of the blood of
the bull and put *it* on the horns of the altar
with your finger, and pour all the blood beside
the base of the altar. 13And you shall take all
the fat that covers the entrails, the fatty lobe
attached to the liver, and the two kidneys and
the fat that *is* on them, and burn *them* on the
altar. 14But the flesh of the bull, with its skin
and its offal, you shall burn with fire outside
the camp. It *is* a sin offering.
15"You shall also take one ram, and Aaron
and his sons shall put their hands on the head
of the ram; 16and you shall kill the ram, and you
shall take its blood and sprinkle *it* all around
on the altar. 17Then you shall cut the ram in
pieces, wash its entrails and its legs, and put
them with its pieces and with its head. 18And
you shall burn the whole ram on the altar. It *is*
a burnt offering to the LORD; it *is* a sweet
aroma, an offering made by fire to the LORD.
19"You shall also take the other ram, and
Aaron and his sons shall put their hands on
the head of the ram. 20Then you shall kill the
ram, and take some of its blood and put *it* on
the tip of the right ear of Aaron and on the tip
of the right ear of his sons, on the thumb of
their right hand and on the big toe of their
right foot, and sprinkle the blood all around on
the altar. 21And you shall take some of the
blood that is on the altar, and some of the
anointing oil, and sprinkle *it* on Aaron and on

his garments, on his sons and on the garments of his sons with him; and he and his garments shall be hallowed, and his sons and his sons' garments with him.

22"Also you shall take the fat of the ram, the fat tail, the fat that covers the entrails, the fatty lobe *attached to* the liver, the two kidneys and the fat on them, the right thigh (for it *is* a ram of consecration), 23one loaf of bread, one cake *made with* oil, and one wafer from the basket of the unleavened bread that *is* before the LORD; 24and you shall put all these in the hands of Aaron and in the hands of his sons, and you shall wave them *as* a wave offering before the LORD. 25You shall receive them back from their hands and burn *them* on the altar as a burnt offering, as a sweet aroma before the LORD. It *is* an offering made by fire to the LORD.

26"Then you shall take the breast of the ram of Aaron's consecration and wave it *as* a wave offering before the LORD; and it shall be your portion. 27And from the ram of the consecration you shall consecrate the breast of the wave offering which is waved, and the thigh of the heave offering which is raised, of *that* which *is* for Aaron and of *that* which is for his sons. 28It shall be from the children of Israel *for* Aaron and his sons by a statute forever. For it is a heave offering; it shall be a heave offering from the children of Israel from the sacrifices of their peace offerings, *that is,* their heave offering to the LORD.

29"And the holy garments of Aaron shall be his sons' after him, to be anointed in them and to be consecrated in them. 30That son who becomes priest in his place shall put them on for seven days, when he enters the tabernacle of meeting to minister in the holy *place.*

31"And you shall take the ram of the consecration and boil its flesh in the holy place. 32Then Aaron and his sons shall eat the flesh of the ram, and the bread that *is* in the basket, *by* the door of the tabernacle of meeting. 33They shall eat those things with which the atonement was made, to consecrate *and* to sanctify them; but an outsider shall not eat *them,* because they *are* holy. 34And if any of the flesh of the consecration offerings, or of the bread, remains until the morning, then you shall burn the remainder with fire. It shall not be eaten, because it *is* holy.

35"Thus you shall do to Aaron and his sons, according to all that I have commanded you. Seven days you shall consecrate them. 36And you shall offer a bull every day *as* a sin offering for atonement. You shall cleanse the altar when you make atonement for it, and you shall anoint it to sanctify it. 37Seven days you shall make atonement for the altar and sanctify it. And the altar shall be most holy. Whatever touches the altar must be holy.

38"Now this *is* what you shall offer on the altar: two lambs of the first year, day by day continually. 39One lamb you shall offer in the morning, and the other lamb you shall offer at twilight. 40With the one lamb shall be one-tenth *of an ephah* of flour mixed with one-fourth of a hin of pressed oil, and one-fourth of a hin of wine *as* a drink offering. 41And the other lamb you shall offer at twilight; and you shall offer with it the grain offering and the drink offering, as in the morning, for a sweet aroma, an offering made by fire to the LORD. 42*This shall be* a continual burnt offering throughout your generations *at* the door of the tabernacle of meeting before the LORD, where I will meet you to speak with you. 43And there I will meet with the children of Israel, and *the tabernacle* shall be sanctified by My glory. 44So I will consecrate the tabernacle of meeting and the altar. I will also consecrate both Aaron and his sons to minister to Me as priests. 45I will dwell among the children of Israel and will be their God. 46And they shall know that I *am* the LORD their God, who brought them up out of the land of Egypt, that I may dwell among them. I *am* the LORD their God.

29:45 I will dwell. That He would be God of the children of Israel and they would be His people was one thing, but that He would also dwell or tabernacle with them was a very important reality in the experience of the new nation. They were to understand not only the transcendence of their God, whose dwelling place was in the heaven of heavens, but also the immanence of their God, whose dwelling place was with them. Their redemption from Egypt was for this purpose (v. 46).

30 "You shall make an altar to burn incense on; you shall make it of acacia wood. 2A cubit *shall be* its length and a cubit its width—it shall be square—and two cubits *shall be* its height. Its horns *shall be* of one piece with it. 3And you shall overlay its top, its sides all around, and its horns with pure gold; and you shall make for it a molding of gold all around. 4Two gold rings you shall make for it, under the molding on both its sides. You shall place *them* on its two sides, and they will be holders for the poles with which to bear it.

5You shall make the poles of acacia wood, and
overlay them with gold. 6And you shall put it
before the veil that *is* before the ark of the
Testimony, before the mercy seat that *is* over
the Testimony, where I will meet with you.
7"Aaron shall burn on it sweet incense every
morning; when he tends the lamps, he shall
burn incense on it. 8And when Aaron lights the
lamps at twilight, he shall burn incense on it, a
perpetual incense before the LORD throughout
your generations. 9You shall not offer strange
incense on it, or a burnt offering, or a grain
offering; nor shall you pour a drink offering on
it. 10And Aaron shall make atonement upon its
horns once a year with the blood of the sin
offering of atonement; once a year he shall
make atonement upon it throughout your generations. It *is* most holy to the LORD."
11Then the LORD spoke to Moses, saying:
12"When you take the census of the children of
Israel for their number, then every man shall
give a ransom for himself to the LORD, when
you number them, that there may be no
plague among them when *you* number them.
13This is what everyone among those who are
numbered shall give: half a shekel according
to the shekel of the sanctuary (a shekel *is*
twenty gerahs). The half-shekel *shall be* an
offering to the LORD. 14Everyone included
among those who are numbered, from twenty
years old and above, shall give an offering to
the LORD. 15The rich shall not give more and
the poor shall not give less than half a shekel,
when *you* give an offering to the LORD, to
make atonement for yourselves. 16And you
shall take the atonement money of the children of Israel, and shall appoint it for the service of the tabernacle of meeting, that it may be
a memorial for the children of Israel before
the LORD, to make atonement for yourselves."
17Then the LORD spoke to Moses, saying:
18"You shall also make a laver of bronze, with
its base also of bronze, for washing. You shall
put it between the tabernacle of meeting and
the altar. And you shall put water in it, 19for
Aaron and his sons shall wash their hands and
their feet in water from it. 20When they go into
the tabernacle of meeting, or when they come
near the altar to minister, to burn an offering
made by fire to the LORD, they shall wash with
water, lest they die. 21So they shall wash their
hands and their feet, lest they die. And it shall
be a statute forever to them—to him and his
descendants throughout their generations."
22Moreover the LORD spoke to Moses, saying:
23"Also take for yourself quality spices—five
hundred *shekels* of liquid myrrh, half as much
sweet-smelling cinnamon (two hundred and
fifty *shekels*), two hundred and fifty *shekels* of
sweet-smelling cane, 24five hundred *shekels* of
cassia, according to the shekel of the sanctuary, and a hin of olive oil. 25And you shall make
from these a holy anointing oil, an ointment
compounded according to the art of the perfumer. It shall be a holy anointing oil. 26With it
you shall anoint the tabernacle of meeting and
the ark of the Testimony; 27the table and all its
utensils, the lampstand and its utensils, and
the altar of incense; 28the altar of burnt offering with all its utensils, and the laver and its
base. 29You shall consecrate them, that they
may be most holy; whatever touches them
must be holy. 30And you shall anoint Aaron and
his sons, and consecrate them, that *they* may
minister to Me as priests.
31"And you shall speak to the children of
Israel, saying: 'This shall be a holy anointing
oil to Me throughout your generations. 32It
shall not be poured on man's flesh; nor shall
you make *any other* like it, according to its
composition. It *is* holy, *and* it shall be holy to
you. 33Whoever compounds *any* like it, or whoever puts *any* of it on an outsider, shall be cut
off from his people.' "
34And the LORD said to Moses: "Take sweet
spices, stacte and onycha and galbanum, and
pure frankincense with *these* sweet spices;
there shall be equal amounts of each. 35You
shall make of these an incense, a compound
according to the art of the perfumer, salted,
pure, *and* holy. 36And you shall beat *some* of it
very fine, and put some of it before the
Testimony in the tabernacle of meeting where
I will meet with you. It shall be most holy to
you. 37But *as for* the incense which you shall
make, you shall not make any for yourselves,
according to its composition. It shall be to you
holy for the LORD. 38Whoever makes *any* like it,
to smell it, he shall be cut off from his people."

Psalm 20:6–9

6 Now I know that the LORD saves His
anointed;
He will answer him from His holy
heaven
With the saving strength of His right
hand.

7 Some *trust* in chariots, and some in
horses;
But we will remember the name of the
LORD our God.
8 They have bowed down and fallen;
But we have risen and stand upright.
9 Save, LORD!
May the King answer us when we call.

20:7 Some *trust* in... Trust, boast, and praise must not be directed to the wrong objects but only to God Himself (see, e.g., Deut. 17:16; 20:1–4; Lev. 26:7,8; Ps. 33:16,17; Is. 31:1–3; Jer. 9:23,24; Zech. 4:6).

Proverbs 7:6–23

6 For at the window of my house
I looked through my lattice,
7 And saw among the simple,
I perceived among the youths,
A young man devoid of
understanding,
8 Passing along the street near
her corner;
And he took the path to her house
9 In the twilight, in the evening,
In the black and dark night.

7:8 took the path. Against the advice of Proverbs 4:14,15, he put himself right in the harlot's place. "Fleeing immorality" (1 Cor. 6:18) starts by not being in the harlot's neighborhood at night.

10 And there a woman met him,
With the attire of a harlot, and a crafty
heart.
11 She *was* loud and rebellious,
Her feet would not stay at home.
12 At times *she was* outside, at times in
the open square,
Lurking at every corner.
13 So she caught him and kissed him;
With an impudent face she said to him:
14 "*I have* peace offerings with me;
Today I have paid my vows.
15 So I came out to meet you,
Diligently to seek your face,
And I have found you.
16 I have spread my bed with tapestry,
Colored coverings of Egyptian linen.
17 I have perfumed my bed
With myrrh, aloes, and cinnamon.
18 Come, let us take our fill of love until
morning;
Let us delight ourselves with love.
19 For my husband *is* not at home;
He has gone on a long journey;
20 He has taken a bag of money with him,
And will come home on the appointed
day."
21 With her enticing speech she caused
him to yield,
With her flattering lips she
seduced him.
22 Immediately he went after her,
as an ox goes to the slaughter,
Or as a fool to the correction of the
stocks,
23 Till an arrow struck his liver.
As a bird hastens to the snare,
He did not know it *would cost* his life.

Matthew 25:1–30

25 "Then the kingdom of heaven shall be
likened to ten virgins who took their
lamps and went out to meet the bridegroom.
2Now five of them were wise, and five *were*
foolish. 3Those who *were* foolish took their
lamps and took no oil with them, 4but the wise
took oil in their vessels with their lamps. 5But
while the bridegroom was delayed, they all
slumbered and slept.
6"And at midnight a cry was *heard:* 'Behold,
the bridegroom is coming; go out to meet
him!' 7Then all those virgins arose and
trimmed their lamps. 8And the foolish said to
the wise, 'Give us *some* of your oil, for our
lamps are going out.' 9But the wise answered,
saying, '*No,* lest there should not be enough
for us and you; but go rather to those who sell,
and buy for yourselves.' 10And while they went
to buy, the bridegroom came, and those who
were ready went in with him to the wedding;
and the door was shut.
11"Afterward the other virgins came also, saying, 'Lord, Lord, open to us!' 12But he answered
and said, 'Assuredly, I say to you, I do not
know you.'
13"Watch therefore, for you know neither the
day nor the hour in which the Son of Man is
coming.
14"For *the kingdom of heaven is* like a man
traveling to a far country, *who* called his own
servants and delivered his goods to them.
15And to one he gave five talents, to another
two, and to another one, to each according to
his own ability; and immediately he went on a
journey. 16Then he who had received the five
talents went and traded with them, and made
another five talents. 17And likewise he who *had*
received two gained two more also. 18But he
who had received one went and dug in the
ground, and hid his lord's money. 19After a
long time the lord of those servants came and
settled accounts with them.

25:15 talents. A talent was a measure of weight, not a specific coin, so that a talent of gold was more valuable than a talent of silver. A talent of silver (the word translated "money" in v. 18 is literally silver) was a considerable sum of money. The modern meaning of the word "talent," denoting a natural ability, stems from the fact that this parable is erroneously applied to the stewardship of one's natural gifts.

[20]"So he who had received five talents came and brought five other talents, saying, 'Lord, you delivered to me five talents; look, I have gained five more talents besides them.' [21]His lord said to him, 'Well *done,* good and faithful servant; you were faithful over a few things, I will make you ruler over many things. Enter into the joy of your lord.' [22]He also who had received two talents came and said, 'Lord, you delivered to me two talents; look, I have gained two more talents besides them.' [23]His lord said to him, 'Well *done,* good and faithful servant; you have been faithful over a few things, I will make you ruler over many things. Enter into the joy of your lord.'

[24]"Then he who had received the one talent came and said, 'Lord, I knew you to be a hard man, reaping where you have not sown, and gathering where you have not scattered seed. [25]And I was afraid, and went and hid your talent in the ground. Look, *there* you have *what is* yours.'

[26]"But his lord answered and said to him, 'You wicked and lazy servant, you knew that I reap where I have not sown, and gather where I have not scattered seed. [27]So you ought to have deposited my money with the bankers, and at my coming I would have received back my own with interest. [28]So take the talent from him, and give *it* to him who has ten talents.

[29]'For to everyone who has, more will be given, and he will have abundance; but from him who does not have, even what he has will be taken away. [30]And cast the unprofitable servant into the outer darkness. There will be weeping and gnashing of teeth.'

DAY 9: What do the parables of the 10 virgins and of the talents tell us about Christ's second coming?

The parable of the 10 virgins (Matt. 10:25:1–13) is given to underscore the importance of being ready for Christ's return in any event—even if He delays longer than expected. The wedding would begin at the bride's house when the bridegroom arrived to observe the wedding ritual. Then a procession would follow as the bridegroom took the bride to his house for the completion of festivities. For a night wedding, "lamps," which were actually torches, were needed for the procession. For those not prepared when He does return, there will be no second chances (vv. 11,12).

The parable of the talents (Matt. 25:14–30) illustrates the tragedy of wasted opportunity. The man who goes on the journey represents Christ, and the servants represent professing believers given different levels of responsibility. Faithfulness is what he demands of them (v. 23), but the parable suggests that all who are faithful will be fruitful to some degree. Both the man with five talents and the man with two received exactly the same reward, "the joy of your lord," indicating that the reward is based on faithfulness, not results. The slothful servant (v. 24) does not represent a genuine believer, for it is obvious that this man had no true knowledge of the master. This fruitless person is unmasked as a hypocrite and utterly destroyed (v. 30).

FEBRUARY 10

Exodus 31:1–32:35

31 Then the LORD spoke to Moses, saying:
[2]"See, I have called by name Bezalel the son of Uri, the son of Hur, of the tribe of Judah. [3]And I have filled him with the Spirit of God, in wisdom, in understanding, in knowledge, and in all *manner of* workmanship, [4]to design artistic works, to work in gold, in silver, in bronze, [5]in cutting jewels for setting, in carving wood, and to work in all *manner of* workmanship.

[6]"And I, indeed I, have appointed with him Aholiab the son of Ahisamach, of the tribe of Dan; and I have put wisdom in the hearts of all the gifted artisans, that they may make all that I have commanded you: [7]the tabernacle of meeting, the ark of the Testimony and the mercy seat that *is* on it, and all the furniture of the tabernacle—[8]the table and its utensils, the

pure *gold* lampstand with all its utensils, the
altar of incense, [9]the altar of burnt offering
with all its utensils, and the laver and its
base— [10]the garments of ministry, the holy
garments for Aaron the priest and the garments of his sons, to minister as priests, [11]and
the anointing oil and sweet incense for the
holy *place.* According to all that I have commanded you they shall do."

[12]And the LORD spoke to Moses, saying,
[13]"Speak also to the children of Israel, saying:
'Surely My Sabbaths you shall keep, for it *is* a
sign between Me and you throughout your
generations, that *you* may know that I *am* the
LORD who sanctifies you. [14]You shall keep the
Sabbath, therefore, for *it is* holy to you.
Everyone who profanes it shall surely be put
to death; for whoever does *any* work on it, that
person shall be cut off from among his people.
[15]Work shall be done for six days, but the seventh *is* the Sabbath of rest, holy to the LORD.
Whoever does *any* work on the Sabbath day,
he shall surely be put to death. [16]Therefore the
children of Israel shall keep the Sabbath, to
observe the Sabbath throughout their generations *as* a perpetual covenant. [17]It *is* a sign
between Me and the children of Israel forever;
for *in* six days the LORD made the heavens and
the earth, and on the seventh day He rested
and was refreshed.' "

[18]And when He had made an end of speaking with him on Mount Sinai, He gave Moses
two tablets of the Testimony, tablets of stone,
written with the finger of God.

32 Now when the people saw that Moses
delayed coming down from the moun-
tain, the people gathered together to Aaron, and
said to him, "Come, make us gods that shall go
before us; for *as for* this Moses, the man who
brought us up out of the land of Egypt, we do
not know what has become of him."

[2]And Aaron said to them, "Break off the
golden earrings which *are* in the ears of your
wives, your sons, and your daughters, and bring
them to me." [3]So all the people broke off the
golden earrings which *were* in their ears, and
brought *them* to Aaron. [4]And he received *the*
gold from their hand, and he fashioned it with
an engraving tool, and made a molded calf.

Then they said, "This *is* your god, O Israel,
that brought you out of the land of Egypt!"

[5]So when Aaron saw *it,* he built an altar
before it. And Aaron made a proclamation and
said, "Tomorrow *is* a feast to the LORD." [6]Then
they rose early on the next day, offered burnt
offerings, and brought peace offerings; and
the people sat down to eat and drink, and rose
up to play.

32:4 a molded calf. The young bull, which Aaron caused to be fashioned, was a pagan religious symbol of virile power. A miniature form of the golden calf, although made of bronze and silver, was found at the site of the ancient Philistine city of Ashkelon. Since it dates to about 1550 B.C. it indicates that calf worship was known not only in Egypt, but also in Canaan prior to the time of Moses. In worshiping the calf, the Israelites violated the first 3 commandments (20:3–7).

32:6 rose up to play. The Hebrew word allows for the inclusion of drunken and immoral activities so common to idolatrous fertility cults in their revelry. Syncretism had robbed the people of all ethical alertness and moral discernment (see 1 Cor. 10:7).

[7]And the LORD said to Moses, "Go, get down!
For your people whom you brought out of the
land of Egypt have corrupted *themselves.*
[8]They have turned aside quickly out of the way
which I commanded them. They have made
themselves a molded calf, and worshiped it
and sacrificed to it, and said, 'This *is* your god,
O Israel, that brought you out of the land of
Egypt!' " [9]And the LORD said to Moses, "I have
seen this people, and indeed it *is* a stiff-necked
people! [10]Now therefore, let Me alone, that My
wrath may burn hot against them and I may
consume them. And I will make of you a great
nation."

[11]Then Moses pleaded with the LORD his
God, and said: "LORD, why does Your wrath
burn hot against Your people whom You have
brought out of the land of Egypt with great
power and with a mighty hand? [12]Why should
the Egyptians speak, and say, 'He brought
them out to harm them, to kill them in the
mountains, and to consume them from the
face of the earth'? Turn from Your fierce
wrath, and relent from this harm to Your people. [13]Remember Abraham, Isaac, and Israel,
Your servants, to whom You swore by Your
own self, and said to them, 'I will multiply your
descendants as the stars of heaven; and all this
land that I have spoken of I give to your
descendants, and they shall inherit *it* forever.' "
[14]So the LORD relented from the harm which
He said He would do to His people.

[15]And Moses turned and went down from
the mountain, and the two tablets of the
Testimony *were* in his hand. The tablets *were*
written on both sides; on the one *side* and on

the other they were written. [16]Now the tablets *were* the work of God, and the writing *was* the writing of God engraved on the tablets.

[17]And when Joshua heard the noise of the people as they shouted, he said to Moses, "*There is* a noise of war in the camp."

[18]But he said:

"*It is* not the noise of the shout
of victory,
Nor the noise of the cry of defeat,
But the sound of singing I hear."

[19]So it was, as soon as he came near the camp, that he saw the calf *and* the dancing. So Moses' anger became hot, and he cast the tablets out of his hands and broke them at the foot of the mountain. [20]Then he took the calf which they had made, burned *it* in the fire, and ground *it* to powder; and he scattered *it* on the water and made the children of Israel drink *it*. [21]And Moses said to Aaron, "What did this people do to you that you have brought *so* great a sin upon them?"

[22]So Aaron said, "Do not let the anger of my lord become hot. You know the people, that they *are set* on evil. [23]For they said to me, 'Make us gods that shall go before us; *as for* this Moses, the man who brought us out of the land of Egypt, we do not know what has become of him.' [24]And I said to them, 'Whoever has any gold, let them break *it* off.' So they gave *it* to me, and I cast it into the fire, and this calf came out."

[25]Now when Moses saw that the people *were* unrestrained (for Aaron had not restrained them, to *their* shame among their enemies), [26]then Moses stood in the entrance of the camp, and said, "Whoever *is* on the LORD's side—*come* to me!" And all the sons of Levi gathered themselves together to him. [27]And he said to them, "Thus says the LORD God of Israel: 'Let every man put his sword on his side, and go in and out from entrance to entrance throughout the camp, and let every man kill his brother, every man his companion, and every man his neighbor.' " [28]So the sons of Levi did according to the word of Moses. And about three thousand men of the people fell that day. [29]Then Moses said, "Consecrate yourselves today to the LORD, that He may bestow on you a blessing this day, for every man has opposed his son and his brother."

[30]Now it came to pass on the next day that Moses said to the people, "You have committed a great sin. So now I will go up to the LORD; perhaps I can make atonement for your sin." [31]Then Moses returned to the LORD and said, "Oh, these people have committed a great sin,

32:32 blot me out of Your book. Nothing more strongly marked the love of Moses for his people than his sincere willingness to offer up his own life rather than see them disinherited and destroyed. The book to which Moses referred, the psalmist entitled "the book of the living" (Ps. 69:28). Untimely or premature death would constitute being blotted out of the book. The apostle Paul displayed a similar passionate devotion for his kinsmen (Rom. 9:1–3).

and have made for themselves a god of gold! [32]Yet now, if You will forgive their sin—but if not, I pray, blot me out of Your book which You have written."

[33]And the LORD said to Moses, "Whoever has sinned against Me, I will blot him out of My book. [34]Now therefore, go, lead the people to *the place* of which I have spoken to you. Behold, My Angel shall go before you. Nevertheless, in the day when I visit for punishment, I will visit punishment upon them for their sin."

[35]So the LORD plagued the people because of what they did with the calf which Aaron made.

Psalm 21:1–7

To the Chief Musician. A Psalm of David.

The king shall have joy in Your
strength, O LORD;
And in Your salvation how greatly shall
he rejoice!
2 You have given him his
heart's desire,
And have not withheld the request
of his lips. Selah

3 For You meet him with the blessings
of goodness;
You set a crown of pure gold upon his
head.
4 He asked life from You, *and* You gave
it to him—
Length of days forever and ever.
5 His glory *is* great in Your salvation;
Honor and majesty You have placed
upon him.

21:3 You set a crown of pure gold upon his head. This is symbolic of superlative blessing (note the reversal in Ezek. 21:25–27).

6 For You have made him most blessed
forever;
You have made him exceedingly glad
with Your presence.
7 For the king trusts in the LORD,
And through the mercy of the Most
High he shall not be moved.

Proverbs 7:24–27

24 Now therefore, listen to me, *my* children;
Pay attention to the words of my
mouth:
25 Do not let your heart turn aside
to her ways,
Do not stray into her paths;
26 For she has cast down many wounded,
And all who were slain by her were
strong *men.*
27 Her house *is* the way to hell,
Descending to the chambers of death.

Matthew 25:31–46

[31]"When the Son of Man comes in His glory,
and all the holy angels with Him, then He will
sit on the throne of His glory. [32]All the nations
will be gathered before Him, and He will separate them one from another, as a shepherd
divides *his* sheep from the goats. [33]And He will
set the sheep on His right hand, but the goats
on the left. [34]Then the King will say to those on
His right hand, 'Come, you blessed of My
Father, inherit the kingdom prepared for you
from the foundation of the world: [35]for I was
hungry and you gave Me food; I was thirsty
and you gave Me drink; I was a stranger and
you took Me in; [36]I *was* naked and you clothed
Me; I was sick and you visited Me; I was in
prison and you came to Me.'
[37]"Then the righteous will answer Him, saying, 'Lord, when did we see You hungry and feed
You, or thirsty and give *You* drink? [38]When did we
see You a stranger and take *You* in, or naked
and clothe *You?* [39]Or when did we see You sick,
or in prison, and come to You?' [40]And the King
will answer and say to them, 'Assuredly, I say
to you, inasmuch as you did *it* to one of the
least of these My brethren, you did *it* to Me.'
[41]"Then He will also say to those on the left
hand, 'Depart from Me, you cursed, into the
everlasting fire prepared for the devil and his
angels: [42]for I was hungry and you gave Me no
food; I was thirsty and you gave Me no drink;
[43]I was a stranger and you did not take Me in,
naked and you did not clothe Me, sick and in
prison and you did not visit Me.'
[44]"Then they also will answer Him, saying,
'Lord, when did we see You hungry or thirsty
or a stranger or naked or sick or in prison, and
did not minister to You?' [45]Then He will answer
them, saying, 'Assuredly, I say to you, inasmuch as you did not do *it* to one of the least of
these, you did not do *it* to Me.' [46]And these will
go away into everlasting punishment, but the
righteous into eternal life."

DAY 10: Did Jesus Christ believe in everlasting punishment for the wicked?

Look at His words in Matthew 25:46. "And these will go away into everlasting punishment, but the righteous into eternal life." The same Greek word is used in both instances. The punishment of the wicked is as never-ending as the bliss of the righteous. The wicked are not given a second chance, nor are they annihilated. The punishment of the wicked dead is described throughout Scripture as "everlasting fire" (v. 41); "unquenchable fire" (3:12); "shame and everlasting contempt" (Dan. 12:2); a place where "their worm does not die, and the fire is not quenched" (Mark 9:44–49); a place of "torments" and "flame" (Luke 16:23,24); "everlasting destruction" (2 Thess. 1:9); a place of torment with "fire and brimstone" where "the smoke of their torment ascends forever and ever" (Rev. 14:10,11); and a "lake of fire and brimstone" where the wicked are "tormented day and night forever and ever" (Rev. 20:10).

Here Jesus indicates that the punishment itself is everlasting—not merely the smoke and flames. The wicked are forever subject to the fury and the wrath of God. They consciously suffer shame and contempt and the assaults of an accusing conscience—along with the fiery wrath of an offended deity—for all of eternity. Even hell will acknowledge the perfect justice of God (Ps. 76:10); those who are there will know that their punishment is just and that they alone are to blame (see Deut. 32:3–5).

FEBRUARY 11

Exodus 33:1–34:35

33 Then the LORD said to Moses, "Depart
and go up from here, you and the people
whom you have brought out of the land of
Egypt, to the land of which I swore to Abraham, Isaac, and Jacob, saying, 'To your descendants I will give it.' [2]And I will send *My* Angel
before you, and I will drive out the Canaanite
and the Amorite and the Hittite and the
Perizzite and the Hivite and the Jebusite. [3]*Go*

up to a land flowing with milk and honey; for I
will not go up in your midst, lest I consume you
on the way, for you *are* a stiff-necked people."
4 And when the people heard this bad news,
they mourned, and no one put on his ornaments. 5 For the LORD had said to Moses, "Say
to the children of Israel, 'You *are* a stiff-necked
people. I could come up into your midst in one
moment and consume you. Now therefore,
take off your ornaments, that I may know
what to do to you.' " 6 So the children of Israel
stripped themselves of their ornaments by
Mount Horeb.
7 Moses took his tent and pitched it outside
the camp, far from the camp, and called it the
tabernacle of meeting. And it came to pass
that everyone who sought the LORD went out
to the tabernacle of meeting which *was* outside the camp. 8 So it was, whenever Moses
went out to the tabernacle, *that* all the people
rose, and each man stood *at* his tent door and
watched Moses until he had gone into the tabernacle. 9 And it came to pass, when Moses
entered the tabernacle, that the pillar of cloud
descended and stood *at* the door of the tabernacle, and *the LORD* talked with Moses. 10 All the
people saw the pillar of cloud standing *at* the
tabernacle door, and all the people rose and
worshiped, each man *in* his tent door. 11 So the
LORD spoke to Moses face to face, as a man
speaks to his friend. And he would return to the
camp, but his servant Joshua the son of Nun, a
young man, did not depart from the tabernacle.
12 Then Moses said to the LORD, "See, You
say to me, 'Bring up this people.' But You have
not let me know whom You will send with me.
Yet You have said, 'I know you by name, and
you have also found grace in My sight.' 13 Now
therefore, I pray, if I have found grace in Your
sight, show me now Your way, that I may know
You and that I may find grace in Your sight.
And consider that this nation *is* Your people."
14 And He said, "My Presence will go *with
you,* and I will give you rest."
15 Then he said to Him, "If Your Presence
does not go *with us,* do not bring us up from
here. 16 For how then will it be known that Your
people and I have found grace in Your sight,
except You go with us? So we shall be separate, Your people and I, from all the people
who *are* upon the face of the earth."
17 So the LORD said to Moses, "I will also do
this thing that you have spoken; for you have
found grace in My sight, and I know you by
name."
18 And he said, "Please, show me Your glory."
19 Then He said, "I will make all My goodness pass before you, and I will proclaim the
name of the LORD before you. I will be gracious to whom I will be gracious, and I will
have compassion on whom I will have compassion." 20 But He said, "You cannot see My
face; for no man shall see Me, and live." 21 And
the LORD said, "Here is a place by Me, and you
shall stand on the rock. 22 So it shall be, while
My glory passes by, that I will put you in the
cleft of the rock, and will cover you with My
hand while I pass by. 23 Then I will take away
My hand, and you shall see My back; but My
face shall not be seen."

34 And the LORD said to Moses, "Cut two
tablets of stone like the first *ones,* and I
will write on *these* tablets the words that were on
the first tablets which you broke. 2 So be ready
in the morning, and come up in the morning to
Mount Sinai, and present yourself to Me there
on the top of the mountain. 3 And no man shall
come up with you, and let no man be seen
throughout all the mountain; let neither flocks
nor herds feed before that mountain."
4 So he cut two tablets of stone like the first
ones. Then Moses rose early in the morning
and went up Mount Sinai, as the LORD had
commanded him; and he took in his hand the
two tablets of stone.
5 Now the LORD descended in the cloud and
stood with him there, and proclaimed the name
of the LORD. 6 And the LORD passed before him
and proclaimed, "The LORD, the LORD God,
merciful and gracious, longsuffering, and
abounding in goodness and truth, 7 keeping
mercy for thousands, forgiving iniquity and
transgression and sin, by no means clearing
the guilty, visiting the iniquity of the fathers
upon the children and the children's children
to the third and the fourth generation."
8 So Moses made haste and bowed his head
toward the earth, and worshiped. 9 Then he
said, "If now I have found grace in Your sight,
O Lord, let my Lord, I pray, go among us, even
though we *are* a stiff-necked people; and pardon our iniquity and our sin, and take us as
Your inheritance."

33:12–17 Again Moses entered earnestly and confidently into the role of intercessor before God for the nation whom he again referred to as "Your people" (vv. 13,16). Moses clearly understood that without God's presence they would not be a people set apart from other nations, so why travel any further? Moses' favored standing before the Lord comes out in the positive response to his intercession (v. 17).

10 And He said: "Behold, I make a covenant.
Before all your people I will do marvels such
as have not been done in all the earth, nor in
any nation; and all the people among whom
you *are* shall see the work of the LORD. For it
is an awesome thing that I will do with you.
11 Observe what I command you this day.
Behold, I am driving out from before you the
Amorite and the Canaanite and the Hittite and
the Perizzite and the Hivite and the Jebusite.
12 Take heed to yourself, lest you make a
covenant with the inhabitants of the land
where you are going, lest it be a snare in your
midst. 13 But you shall destroy their altars,
break their *sacred* pillars, and cut down their
wooden images 14 (for you shall worship no
other god, for the LORD, whose name *is*
Jealous, *is* a jealous God), 15 lest you make a
covenant with the inhabitants of the land, and
they play the harlot with their gods and make
sacrifice to their gods, and *one of them* invites
you and you eat of his sacrifice, 16 and you take
of his daughters for your sons, and his daughters play the harlot with their gods and make
your sons play the harlot with their gods.

17 "You shall make no molded gods for yourselves.

18 "The Feast of Unleavened Bread you shall
keep. Seven days you shall eat unleavened
bread, as I commanded you, in the appointed
time of the month of Abib; for in the month of
Abib you came out from Egypt.

19 "All that open the womb *are* Mine, and
every male firstborn among your livestock,
whether ox or sheep. 20 But the firstborn of a
donkey you shall redeem with a lamb. And if
you will not redeem *him,* then you shall break
his neck. All the firstborn of your sons you
shall redeem.

"And none shall appear before Me empty-
handed.

21 "Six days you shall work, but on the seventh day you shall rest; in plowing time and in
harvest you shall rest.

22 "And you shall observe the Feast of Weeks,
of the firstfruits of wheat harvest, and the
Feast of Ingathering at the year's end.

23 "Three times in the year all your men shall
appear before the Lord, the LORD God of Israel.
24 For I will cast out the nations before you and
enlarge your borders; neither will any man covet
your land when you go up to appear before the
LORD your God three times in the year.

25 "You shall not offer the blood of My sacrifice with leaven, nor shall the sacrifice of the
Feast of the Passover be left until morning.

26 "The first of the firstfruits of your land you
shall bring to the house of the LORD your God.
You shall not boil a young goat in its mother's
milk."

27 Then the LORD said to Moses, "Write these
words, for according to the tenor of these words
I have made a covenant with you and with Israel."
28 So he was there with the LORD forty days and
forty nights; he neither ate bread nor drank
water. And He wrote on the tablets the words
of the covenant, the Ten Commandments.

29 Now it was so, when Moses came down
from Mount Sinai (and the two tablets of the
Testimony *were* in Moses' hand when he came
down from the mountain), that Moses did not
know that the skin of his face shone while he
talked with Him. 30 So when Aaron and all the
children of Israel saw Moses, behold, the skin
of his face shone, and they were afraid to
come near him. 31 Then Moses called to them,
and Aaron and all the rulers of the congregation returned to him; and Moses talked with
them. 32 Afterward all the children of Israel
came near, and he gave them as commandments all that the LORD had spoken with him
on Mount Sinai. 33 And when Moses had finished speaking with them, he put a veil on his
face. 34 But whenever Moses went in before the
LORD to speak with Him, he would take the
veil off until he came out; and he would come
out and speak to the children of Israel whatever he had been commanded. 35 And whenever
the children of Israel saw the face of Moses,
that the skin of Moses' face shone, then Moses would put the veil on his face again, until
he went in to speak with Him.

Psalm 21:8–13

8 Your hand will find all Your enemies;
Your right hand will find those who
hate You.
9 You shall make them as a fiery oven in
the time of Your anger;
The LORD shall swallow them up in His
wrath,
And the fire shall devour them.
10 Their offspring You shall destroy from
the earth,
And their descendants from among the
sons of men.
11 For they intended evil against You;
They devised a plot *which* they are not
able *to perform.*
12 Therefore You will make them turn
their back;
You will make ready *Your arrows* on
Your string toward their faces.

13 Be exalted, O LORD, in Your own
strength!
We will sing and praise Your power.

Proverbs 8:1–5

8 Does not wisdom cry out,
And understanding lift up her voice?
2 She takes her stand on the top of the
high hill,
Beside the way, where the paths meet.
3 She cries out by the gates, at the entry
of the city,
At the entrance of the doors:
4 "To you, O men, I call,
And my voice *is* to the sons of men.
5 O you simple ones, understand
prudence,
And you fools, be of an
understanding heart.

Matthew 26:1–25

26 Now it came to pass, when Jesus had
finished all these sayings, *that* He said
to His disciples, 2 "You know that after two
days is the Passover, and the Son of Man will
be delivered up to be crucified."

26:2 Passover. This was God's chosen time for Christ to die. He was the antitype to which the Passover Lamb had always referred. Christ had always avoided His enemies' plots to kill Him (Luke 4:29,30; John 5:18; 10:39), but now it was His time. The true Lamb of God would take away the sin of the world (John 1:29).

3 Then the chief priests, the scribes, and the
elders of the people assembled at the palace of
the high priest, who was called Caiaphas, 4 and
plotted to take Jesus by trickery and kill *Him.*
5 But they said, "Not during the feast, lest there
be an uproar among the people."
6 And when Jesus was in Bethany at the house
of Simon the leper, 7 a woman came to Him
having an alabaster flask of very costly fragrant oil, and she poured *it* on His head as He
sat *at the table.* 8 But when His disciples saw *it,*
they were indignant, saying, "Why this waste?
9 For this fragrant oil might have been sold for
much and given to *the* poor."
10 But when Jesus was aware of *it,* He said to
them, "Why do you trouble the woman? For she
has done a good work for Me. 11 For you have

26:11 For you have the poor with you always. Jesus certainly was not disparaging ministry to the poor—especially so soon after the lesson of the sheep and goats judgment (see 25:35,36). However, He revealed here that there is a higher priority than any other earthly ministry, and that is worship rendered to Him. This would be an utter blasphemy for anyone less than God, so yet again He was implicitly affirming His deity.

the poor with you always, but Me you do not
have always. 12 For in pouring this fragrant oil on
My body, she did *it* for My burial. 13 Assuredly, I
say to you, wherever this gospel is preached
in the whole world, what this woman has done
will also be told as a memorial to her."
14 Then one of the twelve, called Judas Iscariot,
went to the chief priests 15 and said, "What are
you willing to give me if I deliver Him to you?"
And they counted out to him thirty pieces of
silver. 16 So from that time he sought opportunity to betray Him.
17 Now on the first *day of the Feast* of the
Unleavened Bread the disciples came to Jesus, saying to Him, "Where do You want us to
prepare for You to eat the Passover?"
18 And He said, "Go into the city to a certain
man, and say to him, 'The Teacher says, "My
time is at hand; I will keep the Passover at
your house with My disciples." ' "
19 So the disciples did as Jesus had directed
them; and they prepared the Passover.
20 When evening had come, He sat down
with the twelve. 21 Now as they were eating, He
said, "Assuredly, I say to you, one of you will
betray Me."
22 And they were exceedingly sorrowful, and
each of them began to say to Him, "Lord, is it I?"
23 He answered and said, "He who dipped *his*
hand with Me in the dish will betray Me. 24 The
Son of Man indeed goes just as it is written of
Him, but woe to that man by whom the Son of
Man is betrayed! It would have been good for
that man if he had not been born."
25 Then Judas, who was betraying Him,
answered and said, "Rabbi, is it I?"
He said to him, "You have said it."

DAY 11: How does Moses' veiled face represent the inadequacy of the Old Covenant?

The first time on Mount Sinai (Ex. 24:12–32:14), unlike the second time (34:29–35), had not left Moses with a face which was reflecting some radiance associated with being in the presence of the Lord for an extended period of time.

The second time, in comparison with the first, was not interrupted by the Lord's sending Moses away because of sin in the camp (32:7–10). A compliant and not defiant people feared the evidence of God's presence. When not speaking to the Lord or authoritatively on His behalf to the people, Moses veiled his face.

The apostle Paul advised that the veil prevented the people from seeing a fading glory and related it to the inadequacy of the Old Covenant and the blindness of the Jews in his day (2 Cor. 3:7–18). Paul says that "we all," not just Moses, or prophets, apostles, and preachers, but all believers are "with unveiled face." Believers in the New Covenant have nothing obstructing their vision of Christ and His glory as revealed in the Scripture. Though the vision is unobstructed and intimate ("beholding as in a mirror"), believers do not see a perfect representation of God's glory now, but will one day (see 1 Cor. 13:12). As they gaze at the glory of the Lord, believers are continually being transformed into Christlikeness. The ultimate goal of the believer is to be like Christ (see Rom. 8:29; Phil. 3:12–14; 1 John 3:2), and by continually focusing on Him the Spirit transforms the believer more and more into His image. "From glory to glory"—from one level of manifesting Christ to another. The more believers grow in their knowledge of Christ, the more He is revealed in their lives (see Phil. 3:12–14).

FEBRUARY 12

Exodus 35:1–36:38

35 Then Moses gathered all the congregation of the children of Israel together,
and said to them, "These *are* the words which
the LORD has commanded *you* to do: [2]Work
shall be done for six days, but the seventh day
shall be a holy day for you, a Sabbath of rest to
the LORD. Whoever does any work on it shall be
put to death. [3]You shall kindle no fire throughout your dwellings on the Sabbath day."
[4]And Moses spoke to all the congregation of
the children of Israel, saying, "This *is* the
thing which the LORD commanded, saying:
[5]'Take from among you an offering to the
LORD. Whoever *is* of a willing heart, let him
bring it as an offering to the LORD: gold, silver,
and bronze; [6]blue, purple, and scarlet *thread,*
fine linen, and goats' *hair;* [7]ram skins dyed
red, badger skins, and acacia wood; [8]oil for the
light, and spices for the anointing oil and for
the sweet incense; [9]onyx stones, and stones to
be set in the ephod and in the breastplate.
[10]'All *who are* gifted artisans among you shall
come and make all that the LORD has commanded: [11]the tabernacle, its tent, its covering,
its clasps, its boards, its bars, its pillars, and its
sockets; [12]the ark and its poles, *with* the mercy
seat, and the veil of the covering; [13]the table and
its poles, all its utensils, and the showbread;
[14]also the lampstand for the light, its utensils,
its lamps, and the oil for the light; [15]the incense
altar, its poles, the anointing oil, the sweet
incense, and the screen for the door at the
entrance of the tabernacle; [16]the altar of burnt
offering with its bronze grating, its poles, all
its utensils, *and* the laver and its base; [17]the
hangings of the court, its pillars, their sockets,
and the screen for the gate of the court; [18]the
pegs of the tabernacle, the pegs of the court,
and their cords; [19]the garments of ministry, for
ministering in the holy *place*—the holy garments for Aaron the priest and the garments
of his sons, to minister as priests.' "
[20]And all the congregation of the children of
Israel departed from the presence of Moses.
[21]Then everyone came whose heart was
stirred, and everyone whose spirit was willing, *and* they brought the LORD's offering for
the work of the tabernacle of meeting, for all
its service, and for the holy garments. [22]They
came, both men and women, as many as had a
willing heart, *and* brought earrings and nose
rings, rings and necklaces, all jewelry of gold,
that is, every man who *made* an offering of
gold to the LORD. [23]And every man, with whom
was found blue, purple, and scarlet *thread,* fine
linen, goats' *hair,* red skins of rams, and badger skins, brought *them.* [24]Everyone who
offered an offering of silver or bronze brought
the LORD's offering. And everyone with whom
was found acacia wood for any work of the
service, brought *it.* [25]All the women *who were*
gifted artisans spun yarn with their hands,
and brought what they had spun, of blue, purple, *and* scarlet, and fine linen. [26]And all the
women whose hearts stirred with wisdom
spun yarn of goats' *hair.* [27]The rulers brought
onyx stones, and the stones to be set in the
ephod and in the breastplate, [28]and spices and
oil for the light, for the anointing oil, and for
the sweet incense. [29]The children of Israel
brought a freewill offering to the LORD, all the

men and women whose hearts were willing to
bring *material* for all kinds of work which the
LORD, by the hand of Moses, had commanded
to be done.
30 And Moses said to the children of Israel,
“See, the LORD has called by name Bezalel the
son of Uri, the son of Hur, of the tribe of Judah; 31 and He has filled him with the Spirit of
God, in wisdom and understanding, in knowledge and all manner of workmanship, 32 to
design artistic works, to work in gold and silver and bronze, 33 in cutting jewels for setting,
in carving wood, and to work in all manner of
artistic workmanship.
34 “And He has put in his heart the ability to
teach, *in* him and Aholiab the son of Ahisamach,
of the tribe of Dan. 35 He has filled them with
skill to do all manner of work of the engraver
and the designer and the tapestry maker, in
blue, purple, and scarlet *thread,* and fine linen,
and of the weaver—those who do every work
and those who design artistic works.
36 “And Bezalel and Aholiab, and every
gifted artisan in whom the LORD has
put wisdom and understanding, to know how
to do all manner of work for the service of the
sanctuary, shall do according to all that the
LORD has commanded.”
2 Then Moses called Bezalel and Aholiab, and
every gifted artisan in whose heart the LORD
had put wisdom, everyone whose heart was
stirred, to come and do the work. 3 And they
received from Moses all the offering which the
children of Israel had brought for the work of
the service of making the sanctuary. So they
continued bringing to him freewill offerings
every morning. 4 Then all the craftsmen who
were doing all the work of the sanctuary came,
each from the work he was doing, 5 and they
spoke to Moses, saying, “The people bring
much more than enough for the service of the
work which the LORD commanded *us* to do.”
6 So Moses gave a commandment, and they
caused it to be proclaimed throughout the camp,
saying, “Let neither man nor woman do any
more work for the offering of the sanctuary.”
And the people were restrained from bringing, 7 for the material they had was sufficient
for all the work to be done—indeed too much.
8 Then all the gifted artisans among them
who worked on the tabernacle made ten curtains woven of fine linen, and of blue, purple,
and scarlet thread; *with* artistic designs of
cherubim they made them. 9 The length of
each curtain *was* twenty-eight cubits, and the
width of each curtain four cubits; the curtains
were all the same size. 10 And he coupled five
curtains to one another, and *the other* five curtains he coupled to one another. 11 He made
loops of blue *yarn* on the edge of the curtain
on the selvedge of one set; likewise he did on
the outer edge of *the other* curtain of the second set. 12 Fifty loops he made on one curtain,
and fifty loops he made on the edge of the curtain on the end of the second set; the loops
held one *curtain* to another. 13 And he made
fifty clasps of gold, and coupled the curtains to
one another with the clasps, that it might be
one tabernacle.
14 He made curtains of goats' *hair* for the tent
over the tabernacle; he made eleven curtains.
15 The length of each curtain *was* thirty cubits,
and the width of each curtain four cubits; the
eleven curtains *were* the same size. 16 He coupled five curtains by themselves and six curtains by themselves. 17 And he made fifty loops
on the edge of the curtain that is outermost in
one set, and fifty loops he made on the edge of
the curtain of the second set. 18 He also made
fifty bronze clasps to couple the tent together,
that it might be one. 19 Then he made a covering for the tent of ram skins dyed red, and a
covering of badger skins above *that.*
20 For the tabernacle he made boards of acacia wood, standing upright. 21 The length of
each board *was* ten cubits, and the width of
each board a cubit and a half. 22 Each board
had two tenons for binding one to another.
Thus he made for all the boards of the tabernacle. 23 And he made boards for the tabernacle, twenty boards for the south side. 24 Forty
sockets of silver he made to go under the
twenty boards: two sockets under each of the
boards for its two tenons. 25 And for the other
side of the tabernacle, the north side, he made
twenty boards 26 and their forty sockets of silver: two sockets under each of the boards.
27 For the west side of the tabernacle he made
six boards. 28 He also made two boards for the
two back corners of the tabernacle. 29 And they
were coupled at the bottom and coupled
together at the top by one ring. Thus he made
both of them for the two corners. 30 So there
were eight boards and their sockets—sixteen
sockets of silver—two sockets under each of
the boards.
31 And he made bars of acacia wood: five for
the boards on one side of the tabernacle, 32 five
bars for the boards on the other side of the
tabernacle, and five bars for the boards of the
tabernacle on the far side westward. 33 And he
made the middle bar to pass through the
boards from one end to the other. 34 He overlaid the boards with gold, made their rings of
gold *to be* holders for the bars, and overlaid
the bars with gold.

[35]And he made a veil of blue, purple, and
scarlet *thread,* and fine woven linen; it was
worked *with* an artistic design of cherubim.
[36]He made for it four pillars of acacia *wood,* and
overlaid them with gold, with their hooks of
gold; and he cast four sockets of silver for them.
[37]He also made a screen for the tabernacle
door, of blue, purple, and scarlet *thread,* and
fine woven linen, made by a weaver, [38]and its
five pillars with their hooks. And he overlaid
their capitals and their rings with gold, but
their five sockets *were* bronze.

Psalm 22:1–8

To the Chief Musician. Set to "The Deer of the Dawn." A Psalm of David.

My God, My God, why have
You forsaken Me?
Why are You so far from helping Me,
And from the words of My groaning?

22:1 This heavy lament rivals Job 3; Psalm 69; Jeremiah 20:14–18. **My God, My God, why have You forsaken Me?** The repeated noun of direct address to God reflects a personal molecule of hope in a seemingly hopeless situation. "Forsaken" is a strong expression for personal abandonment, intensely felt by David and supremely experienced by Christ on the cross (Matt. 27:46).

[2] O My God, I cry in the daytime, but
You do not hear;
And in the night season, and am not
silent.
[3] But You *are* holy,
Enthroned in the praises of Israel.
[4] Our fathers trusted in You;
They trusted, and You delivered them.
[5] They cried to You, and were
delivered;
They trusted in You, and were not
ashamed.
[6] But I *am* a worm, and no man;
A reproach of men, and despised by
the people.
[7] All those who see Me ridicule Me;
They shoot out the lip, they shake the
head, *saying,*
[8] "He trusted in the LORD, let Him rescue
Him;
Let Him deliver Him, since
He delights in Him!"

Proverbs 8:6–11

[6] Listen, for I will speak of excellent
things,
And from the opening of my lips
will come right things;
[7] For my mouth will speak truth;
Wickedness *is* an abomination
to my lips.
[8] All the words of my mouth *are* with
righteousness;
Nothing crooked or perverse *is* in
them.
[9] They *are* all plain to him who
understands,
And right to those who find knowledge.
[10] Receive my instruction, and not silver,
And knowledge rather than choice
gold;
[11] For wisdom *is* better than rubies,
And all the things one may desire
cannot be compared with her.

8:10,11 The most valuable reality a young person can attain is the insight to order his life by the standard of truth (see 3:14,15; 8:19–21; also Job 28:12–28; Ps. 19:10).

Matthew 26:26–50

[26]And as they were eating, Jesus took bread,
blessed and broke *it,* and gave *it* to the disciples and said, "Take, eat; this is My body."
[27]Then He took the cup, and gave thanks,
and gave *it* to them, saying, "Drink from it, all
of you. [28]For this is My blood of the new
covenant, which is shed for many for the remission of sins. [29]But I say to you, I will not
drink of this fruit of the vine from now on until that day when I drink it new with you in My
Father's kingdom."
[30]And when they had sung a hymn, they
went out to the Mount of Olives.
[31]Then Jesus said to them, "All of you will be
made to stumble because of Me this night, for
it is written:

'I will strike the Shepherd,
And the sheep of the flock
will be scattered.'

[32]But after I have been raised, I will go before
you to Galilee."
[33]Peter answered and said to Him, "Even if
all are made to stumble because of You, I will
never be made to stumble."
[34]Jesus said to him, "Assuredly, I say to you

26:39 this cup. See v. 42. A cup is often the symbol of divine wrath against sin in the Old Testament (Is. 51:17,22; Jer. 25:15–17,27–29; Lam. 4:21,22; Ezek. 23:31–34; Hab. 2:16). The next day Christ would "bear the sins of many" (Heb. 9:28)—and the fullness of divine wrath would fall on Him (Is. 53:10,11; 2 Cor. 5:21). This was the price of the sin He bore, and He paid it in full. His cry of anguish in 27:46 reflects the extreme bitterness of the cup of wrath He was given. **not as I will, but as You *will*.** This implies no conflict between the Persons of the Godhead. Rather, it graphically reveals how Christ in His humanity voluntarily surrendered His will to the will of the Father in all things—precisely so that there would be no conflict between the divine will and His desires. See John 4:34; 6:38; 8:29; Phil. 2:8.

that this night, before the rooster crows, you
will deny Me three times."
35 Peter said to Him, "Even if I have to die
with You, I will not deny You!"
And so said all the disciples.
36 Then Jesus came with them to a place
called Gethsemane, and said to the disciples,
"Sit here while I go and pray over there." 37 And
He took with Him Peter and the two sons of
Zebedee, and He began to be sorrowful and
deeply distressed. 38 Then He said to them,
"My soul is exceedingly sorrowful, even to
death. Stay here and watch with Me."
39 He went a little farther and fell on His face,
and prayed, saying, "O My Father, if it is possible, let this cup pass from Me; nevertheless,
not as I will, but as You *will*."
40 Then He came to the disciples and found
them sleeping, and said to Peter, "What! Could
you not watch with Me one hour? 41 Watch and
pray, lest you enter into temptation. The spirit
indeed *is* willing, but the flesh *is* weak."
42 Again, a second time, He went away and
prayed, saying, "O My Father, if this cup cannot pass away from Me unless I drink it, Your
will be done." 43 And He came and found them
asleep again, for their eyes were heavy.
44 So He left them, went away again, and
prayed the third time, saying the same words.
45 Then He came to His disciples and said to
them, "Are *you* still sleeping and resting?
Behold, the hour is at hand, and the Son of
Man is being betrayed into the hands of sinners. 46 Rise, let us be going. See, My betrayer
is at hand."
47 And while He was still speaking, behold,
Judas, one of the twelve, with a great multitude with swords and clubs, came from the
chief priests and elders of the people.
48 Now His betrayer had given them a sign,
saying, "Whomever I kiss, He is the One;
seize Him." 49 Immediately he went up to Jesus
and said, "Greetings, Rabbi!" and kissed Him.
50 But Jesus said to him, "Friend, why have
you come?"
Then they came and laid hands on Jesus
and took Him.

DAY 12: Why did Jesus institute the Lord's Supper?

In Matthew 26:26, "Jesus took bread, blessed and broke it, and gave it to the disciples and said, 'Take, eat; this is My body,'" thus transforming His last Passover into the first observance of the Lord's Supper. He is the central antitype in both ceremonies, being represented symbolically by both the paschal lamb of the Passover and the elements in the communion service. His statement, "this is My body," could not possibly have been taken in any literal sense by the disciples present that evening. Such metaphorical language was a typical Hebraism. No eucharistic miracle of transubstantiation was implied, nor could the disciples have missed the symbolic intent of His statement, for His actual body—yet unbroken—was before their very eyes.

When He took the cup of wine, He said that this is "My blood of the new covenant" (v. 28). Covenants were ratified with the blood of a sacrifice (Gen. 8:20; 15:9,10). Jesus' words here echo Moses' pronouncement in Exodus 24:8. The blood of the New Covenant is not an animal's blood, but Christ's own blood, shed for the remission of sins. See Jeremiah 31:31–34; Hebrews 8:1–10:18, especially 8:6. Thus He established the observance as an ordinance for worship (1 Cor. 11:23–26). Passover had looked forward to the sacrifice of Christ; He transformed it into an altogether different ceremony, which looks back in remembrance at His atoning death.

FEBRUARY 13

Exodus 37:1–38:31

37 Then Bezalel made the ark of acacia wood; two and a half cubits *was* its length, a cubit and a half its width, and a cubit and a half its height. 2He overlaid it with pure gold inside and outside, and made a molding of gold all around it. 3And he cast for it four rings of gold *to be set* in its four corners: two rings on one side, and two rings on the other side of it. 4He made poles of acacia wood, and overlaid them with gold. 5And he put the poles into the rings at the sides of the ark, to bear the ark. 6He also made the mercy seat of pure gold; two and a half cubits *was* its length and a cubit and a half its width. 7He made two cherubim of beaten gold; he made them of one piece at the two ends of the mercy seat: 8one cherub at one end on this side, and the other cherub at the *other* end on that side. He made the cherubim at the two ends *of one piece* with the mercy seat. 9The cherubim spread out *their* wings above, *and* covered the mercy seat with their wings. They faced one another; the faces of the cherubim were toward the mercy seat.

10He made the table of acacia wood; two cubits *was* its length, a cubit its width, and a cubit and a half its height. 11And he overlaid it with pure gold, and made a molding of gold all around it. 12Also he made a frame of a handbreadth all around it, and made a molding of gold for the frame all around it. 13And he cast for it four rings of gold, and put the rings on the four corners that *were* at its four legs. 14The rings were close to the frame, as holders for the poles to bear the table. 15And he made the poles of acacia wood to bear the table, and overlaid them with gold. 16He made of pure gold the utensils which were on the table: its dishes, its cups, its bowls, and its pitchers for pouring.

17He also made the lampstand of pure gold; of hammered work he made the lampstand. Its shaft, its branches, its bowls, its *ornamental* knobs, and its flowers were of the same piece. 18And six branches came out of its sides: three branches of the lampstand out of one side, and three branches of the lampstand out of the other side. 19There were three bowls made like almond *blossoms* on one branch, with an *ornamental* knob and a flower, and three bowls made like almond *blossoms* on the other branch, with an *ornamental* knob and a flower—and so for the six branches coming out of the lampstand. 20And on the lampstand itself *were* four bowls made like almond *blossoms, each with* its *ornamental* knob and flower. 21*There was* a knob under the *first* two branches of the same, a knob under the *second* two branches of the same, and a knob under the *third* two branches of the same, according to the six branches extending from it. 22Their knobs and their branches were of one piece; all of it *was* one hammered piece of pure gold. 23And he made its seven lamps, its wick-trimmers, and its trays of pure gold. 24Of a talent of pure gold he made it, with all its utensils.

25He made the incense altar of acacia wood. Its length *was* a cubit and its width a cubit—*it was* square—and two cubits *was* its height. Its horns were *of one piece* with it. 26And he overlaid it with pure gold: its top, its sides all around, and its horns. He also made for it a molding of gold all around it. 27He made two rings of gold for it under its molding, by its two corners on both sides, as holders for the poles with which to bear it. 28And he made the poles of acacia wood, and overlaid them with gold.

29He also made the holy anointing oil and the pure incense of sweet spices, according to the work of the perfumer.

38 He made the altar of burnt offering of acacia wood; five cubits *was* its length and five cubits its width—*it was* square—and its height *was* three cubits. 2He made its horns on its four corners; the horns were *of one piece* with it. And he overlaid it with bronze. 3He made all the utensils for the altar: the pans, the shovels, the basins, the forks, and the firepans; all its utensils he made of bronze. 4And he made a grate of bronze network for the altar, under its rim, midway from the bottom. 5He cast four rings for the four corners of the bronze grating, *as* holders for the poles. 6And he made the poles of acacia wood, and overlaid them with bronze. 7Then he put the poles into the rings on the sides of the altar, with which to bear it. He made the altar hollow with boards.

8He made the laver of bronze and its base of bronze, from the bronze mirrors of the serving women who assembled at the door of the tabernacle of meeting.

9Then he made the court on the south side; the hangings of the court *were of* fine woven linen, one hundred cubits long. 10There *were* twenty pillars for them, with twenty bronze sockets. The hooks of the pillars and their bands *were* silver. 11On the north side *the hangings were* one hundred cubits *long,* with twenty pillars and their twenty bronze sockets. The hooks of the pillars and their bands *were* silver. 12And on the west side *there were* hangings of fifty cubits, with ten pillars and

their ten sockets. The hooks of the pillars and
their bands *were* silver. 13 For the east side *the*
hangings were fifty cubits. 14 The hangings of
one side *of the gate were* fifteen cubits *long,*
with their three pillars and their three sockets,
15 and the same for the other side of the court
gate; on this side and that *were* hangings of fifteen cubits, *with* their three pillars and their
three sockets. 16 All the hangings of the court
all around *were of* fine woven linen. 17 The
sockets for the pillars *were* bronze, the hooks
of the pillars and their bands *were* silver, and
the overlay of their capitals *was* silver; and all
the pillars of the court had bands of silver.
18 The screen for the gate of the court *was*
woven of blue, purple, and scarlet *thread,* and
of fine woven linen. The length *was* twenty
cubits, and the height along its width *was* five
cubits, corresponding to the hangings of the
court. 19 And *there were* four pillars *with* their
four sockets of bronze; their hooks *were* silver, and the overlay of their capitals and their
bands *was* silver. 20 All the pegs of the tabernacle, and of the court all around, *were* bronze.

21 This is the inventory of the tabernacle, the
tabernacle of the Testimony, which was counted according to the commandment of Moses,
for the service of the Levites, by the hand of
Ithamar, son of Aaron the priest.

22 Bezalel the son of Uri, the son of Hur, of the
tribe of Judah, made all that the LORD had commanded Moses. 23 And with him *was* Aholiab
the son of Ahisamach, of the tribe of Dan, an
engraver and designer, a weaver of blue, purple, and scarlet *thread,* and of fine linen.

24 All the gold that was used in all the work of
the holy *place,* that is, the gold of the offering,
was twenty-nine talents and seven hundred
and thirty shekels, according to the shekel of
the sanctuary. 25 And the silver from those who
were numbered of the congregation *was* one
hundred talents and one thousand seven hundred and seventy-five shekels, according to
the shekel of the sanctuary: 26 a bekah for each
man (*that is,* half a shekel, according to the
shekel of the sanctuary), for everyone included in the numbering from twenty years old
and above, for six hundred and three thousand, five hundred and fifty *men.* 27 And from
the hundred talents of silver were cast the
sockets of the sanctuary and the bases of the
veil: one hundred sockets from the hundred
talents, one talent for each socket. 28 Then from
the one thousand seven hundred and seventy-
five *shekels* he made hooks for the pillars, overlaid their capitals, and made bands for them.

29 The offering of bronze *was* seventy talents
and two thousand four hundred shekels. 30 And
with it he made the sockets for the door of the
tabernacle of meeting, the bronze altar, the
bronze grating for it, and all the utensils for
the altar, 31 the sockets for the court all around,
the bases for the court gate, all the pegs for the
tabernacle, and all the pegs for the court all
around.

Psalm 22:9–15

9 But You *are* He who took Me out of
the womb;
You made Me trust *while* on
My mother's breasts.
10 I was cast upon You from birth.
From My mother's womb
You *have been* My God.
11 Be not far from Me,
For trouble *is* near;
For *there is* none to help.

12 Many bulls have surrounded Me;
Strong *bulls* of Bashan have encircled
Me.
13 They gape at Me *with* their mouths,
Like a raging and roaring lion.

14 I am poured out like water,
And all My bones are out of joint;
My heart is like wax;
It has melted within Me.
15 My strength is dried up like a potsherd,
And My tongue clings to My jaws;
You have brought Me to the dust of
death.

Proverbs 8:12–21

12 "I, wisdom, dwell with prudence,
And find out knowledge *and* discretion.
13 The fear of the LORD *is* to hate evil;
Pride and arrogance and the evil way
And the perverse mouth I hate.
14 Counsel *is* mine, and sound wisdom;
I *am* understanding, I have strength.
15 By me kings reign,
And rulers decree justice.
16 By me princes rule, and nobles,
All the judges of the earth.
17 I love those who love me,
And those who seek me diligently
will find me.
18 Riches and honor *are* with me,
Enduring riches and righteousness.
19 My fruit *is* better than gold, yes, than
fine gold,
And my revenue than choice silver.
20 I traverse the way of righteousness,
In the midst of the paths of justice,
21 That I may cause those who love me to
inherit wealth,
That I may fill their treasuries.

Matthew 26:51–75

51 And suddenly, one of those *who were* with Jesus stretched out *his* hand and drew his
sword, struck the servant of the high priest,
and cut off his ear.
52 But Jesus said to him, "Put your sword in
its place, for all who take the sword will perish
by the sword. 53 Or do you think that I cannot
now pray to My Father, and He will provide
Me with more than twelve legions of angels?
54 How then could the Scriptures be fulfilled,
that it must happen thus?"
55 In that hour Jesus said to the multitudes,
"Have you come out, as against a robber, with
swords and clubs to take Me? I sat daily with
you, teaching in the temple, and you did not
seize Me. 56 But all this was done that the Scriptures of the prophets might be fulfilled."
Then all the disciples forsook Him and fled.
57 And those who had laid hold of Jesus led
Him away to Caiaphas the high priest, where
the scribes and the elders were assembled.
58 But Peter followed Him at a distance to the
high priest's courtyard. And he went in and
sat with the servants to see the end.
59 Now the chief priests, the elders, and all
the council sought false testimony against Jesus to put Him to death, 60 but found none.
Even though many false witnesses came forward, they found none. But at last two false
witnesses came forward 61 and said, "This *fellow* said, 'I am able to destroy the temple of
God and to build it in three days.' "
62 And the high priest arose and said to Him,
"Do You answer nothing? What *is it* these men
testify against You?" 63 But Jesus kept silent.
And the high priest answered and said to Him,
"I put You under oath by the living God: Tell
us if You are the Christ, the Son of God!"

26:57 Caiaphas the high priest. From John 18:13, we learn that Christ was taken first to Annas (former high priest and father-in-law to Caiaphas). He then was sent bound to Caiaphas's house (John 18:24). The conspiracy was well planned, so that "the scribes and the elders" (the Sanhedrin) were already "assembled" at Caiaphas's house and ready to try Jesus. The time was sometime between midnight and the first rooster's crowing (v. 74). Such a hearing was illegal on several counts: criminal trials were not to be held at night; and trials in capital cases could only be held at the temple and only in public.

26:59 the council. The great Sanhedrin was the Supreme Court of Israel, consisting of 71 members, presided over by the high priest. They met daily in the temple to hold court, except on the Sabbath and other holy days. Technically, they did not have the power to administer capital punishment (John 18:31), but in the case of Stephen, for example, this was no deterrent to his stoning (see Acts 6:12–14; 7:58–60). Roman governors evidently sometimes ignored such incidents as a matter of political expediency. In Jesus' case, the men who were trying Him were the same ones who had conspired against Him (see John 11:47–50).

64 Jesus said to him, "*It is as* you said. Nevertheless, I say to you, hereafter you will see the
Son of Man sitting at the right hand of the
Power, and coming on the clouds of heaven."
65 Then the high priest tore his clothes, saying,
"He has spoken blasphemy! What further need
do we have of witnesses? Look, now you have
heard His blasphemy! 66 What do you think?"
They answered and said, "He is deserving
of death."
67 Then they spat in His face and beat Him;
and others struck *Him* with the palms of their
hands, 68 saying, "Prophesy to us, Christ! Who
is the one who struck You?"
69 Now Peter sat outside in the courtyard.
And a servant girl came to him, saying, "You
also were with Jesus of Galilee."
70 But he denied it before *them* all, saying, "I
do not know what you are saying."
71 And when he had gone out to the gateway,
another *girl* saw him and said to those *who
were* there, "This *fellow* also was with Jesus of
Nazareth."
72 But again he denied with an oath, "I do not
know the Man!"

26:75 And Peter remembered. Luke 22:61 records that Jesus made eye contact with Peter at this very moment, which must have magnified Peter's already unbearable sense of shame. "He went out"—evidently departing from Caiaphas's house—"and wept bitterly." The true Peter is seen not in his denial but in his repentance. This account reminds us of not only our own weakness, but also the richness of divine grace.

[73]And a little later those who stood by came
up and said to Peter, "Surely you also are *one*
of them, for your speech betrays you."
[74]Then he began to curse and swear, *saying,*
"I do not know the Man!"
Immediately a rooster crowed. [75]And Peter
remembered the word of Jesus who had said
to him, "Before the rooster crows, you will
deny Me three times." So he went out and
wept bitterly.

DAY 13: Why did Jesus refuse to take up arms and fight?

When the multitude comes to arrest Jesus in Matthew 26, one of His disciples strikes out with a sword. John identifies the swordsman as Peter (John 18:10). Clearly, Peter was not aiming for the ear, but for the head. Jesus' response was immediate. "Put your sword in its place, for all who take the sword will perish by the sword" (v. 52). Peter's action was vigilantism. No matter how unjust the arrest of Jesus, Peter had no right to take the law into his own hands in order to stop it. Jesus' reply was a restatement of the Genesis 9:6 principle: "Whoever sheds man's blood, by man his blood shall be shed," an affirmation that capital punishment is an appropriate penalty for murder.

Jesus said that if it were a matter of force, His Father would send "more than twelve legions" (v. 53). A Roman legion was composed of 6,000 soldiers, so this would represent more than 72,000 angels. In 2 Kings 19:35, a single angel killed more than 185,000 men in a single night, so this many angels would make a formidable army.

But it wasn't about force; it was that the "Scriptures…be fulfilled" (v. 54) God Himself had foreordained the very minutest details of how Jesus would die (Acts 2:23; 4:27,28). Dying was Christ's consummate act of submission to the Father's will. Jesus Himself was in absolute control (John 10:17,18). Yet it was not Jesus alone, but everyone around Him—His enemies included—who fulfilled precisely the details of the Old Testament prophecies. These events display His divine sovereignty.

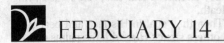

FEBRUARY 14

Exodus 39:1–40:38

39 Of the blue, purple, and scarlet *thread*
they made garments of ministry, for
ministering in the holy *place,* and made the
holy garments for Aaron, as the LORD had
commanded Moses.
[2]He made the ephod of gold, blue, purple,
and scarlet *thread,* and of fine woven linen.
[3]And they beat the gold into thin sheets and cut
it into threads, to work *it* in *with* the blue, purple, and scarlet *thread,* and the fine linen, *into*
artistic designs. [4]They made shoulder straps
for it to couple *it* together; it was coupled
together at its two edges. [5]And the intricately
woven band of his ephod that *was* on it *was* of
the same workmanship, *woven of* gold, blue,
purple, and scarlet *thread,* and of fine woven
linen, as the LORD had commanded Moses.
[6]And they set onyx stones, enclosed in settings of gold; they were engraved, as signets
are engraved, with the names of the sons of
Israel. [7]He put them on the shoulders of the
ephod *as* memorial stones for the sons of
Israel, as the LORD had commanded Moses.
[8]And he made the breastplate, artistically
woven like the workmanship of the ephod, of
gold, blue, purple, and scarlet *thread,* and of
fine woven linen. [9]They made the breastplate
square by doubling it; a span *was* its length
and a span its width when doubled. [10]And they
set in it four rows of stones: a row with a
sardius, a topaz, and an emerald was the first
row; [11]the second row, a turquoise, a sapphire,
and a diamond; [12]the third row, a jacinth, an
agate, and an amethyst; [13]the fourth row, a
beryl, an onyx, and a jasper. *They were*
enclosed in settings of gold in their mount-
ings. [14]*There were* twelve stones according to
the names of the sons of Israel: according to
their names, *engraved like* a signet, each one
with its own name according to the twelve
tribes. [15]And they made chains for the breastplate at the ends, like braided cords of pure
gold. [16]They also made two settings of gold
and two gold rings, and put the two rings on
the two ends of the breastplate. [17]And they put
the two braided *chains* of gold in the two rings
on the ends of the breastplate. [18]The two ends
of the two braided *chains* they fastened in the
two settings, and put them on the shoulder
straps of the ephod in the front. [19]And they
made two rings of gold and put *them* on the
two ends of the breastplate, on the edge of it,
which *was* on the inward side of the ephod.
[20]They made two *other* gold rings and put them
on the two shoulder straps, underneath the

ephod toward its front, right at the seam
above the intricately woven band of the ephod.
21And they bound the breastplate by means of
its rings to the rings of the ephod with a blue
cord, so that it would be above the intricately
woven band of the ephod, and that the breastplate would not come loose from the ephod, as
the LORD had commanded Moses.

22He made the robe of the ephod of woven
work, all of blue. 23And *there was* an opening in
the middle of the robe, like the opening in a
coat of mail, *with* a woven binding all around
the opening, so that it would not tear. 24They
made on the hem of the robe pomegranates of
blue, purple, and scarlet, and of fine woven
linen. 25And they made bells of pure gold, and
put the bells between the pomegranates on
the hem of the robe all around between the
pomegranates: 26a bell and a pomegranate, a
bell and a pomegranate, all around the hem of
the robe to minister in, as the LORD had commanded Moses.

27They made tunics, artistically woven of
fine linen, for Aaron and his sons, 28a turban of
fine linen, exquisite hats of fine linen, short
trousers of fine woven linen, 29and a sash of
fine woven linen with blue, purple, and scarlet
thread, made by a weaver, as the LORD had
commanded Moses.

30Then they made the plate of the holy
crown of pure gold, and wrote on it an inscription *like* the engraving of a signet:

HOLINESS TO THE LORD.

31And they tied to it a blue cord, to fasten *it*
above on the turban, as the LORD had commanded Moses.

32Thus all the work of the tabernacle of the
tent of meeting was finished. And the children
of Israel did according to all that the LORD had
commanded Moses; so they did. 33And they
brought the tabernacle to Moses, the tent and
all its furnishings: its clasps, its boards, its
bars, its pillars, and its sockets; 34the covering
of ram skins dyed red, the covering of badger
skins, and the veil of the covering; 35the ark of
the Testimony with its poles, and the mercy
seat; 36the table, all its utensils, and the showbread; 37the pure *gold* lampstand with its lamps
(the lamps set in order), all its utensils, and
the oil for light; 38the gold altar, the anointing
oil, and the sweet incense; the screen for the
tabernacle door; 39the bronze altar, its grate of
bronze, its poles, and all its utensils; the laver
with its base; 40the hangings of the court, its
pillars and its sockets, the screen for the court
gate, its cords, and its pegs; all the utensils for
the service of the tabernacle, for the tent of
meeting; 41and the garments of ministry, to
minister in the holy *place:* the holy garments
for Aaron the priest, and his sons' garments,
to minister as priests.

42According to all that the LORD had commanded Moses, so the children of Israel did
all the work. 43Then Moses looked over all the
work, and indeed they had done it; as the
LORD had commanded, just so they had done
it. And Moses blessed them.

40 Then the LORD spoke to Moses, saying: 2"On the first day of the first
month you shall set up the tabernacle of the
tent of meeting. 3You shall put in it the ark of
the Testimony, and partition off the ark with
the veil. 4You shall bring in the table and arrange the things that are to be set in order on
it; and you shall bring in the lampstand and
light its lamps. 5You shall also set the altar of
gold for the incense before the ark of the
Testimony, and put up the screen for the door
of the tabernacle. 6Then you shall set the altar
of the burnt offering before the door of the
tabernacle of the tent of meeting. 7And you
shall set the laver between the tabernacle of
meeting and the altar, and put water in it. 8You
shall set up the court all around, and hang up
the screen at the court gate.

9"And you shall take the anointing oil, and
anoint the tabernacle and all that *is* in it; and
you shall hallow it and all its utensils, and it
shall be holy. 10You shall anoint the altar of the
burnt offering and all its utensils, and consecrate the altar. The altar shall be most holy.
11And you shall anoint the laver and its base,
and consecrate it.

12"Then you shall bring Aaron and his sons
to the door of the tabernacle of meeting and
wash them with water. 13You shall put the holy
garments on Aaron, and anoint him and consecrate him, that he may minister to Me as
priest. 14And you shall bring his sons and
clothe them with tunics. 15You shall anoint
them, as you anointed their father, that they
may minister to Me as priests; for their anointing shall surely be an everlasting priesthood
throughout their generations."

16Thus Moses did; according to all that the
LORD had commanded him, so he did.

17And it came to pass in the first month of
the second year, on the first *day* of the month,
that the tabernacle was raised up. 18So Moses
raised up the tabernacle, fastened its sockets,
set up its boards, put in its bars, and raised up
its pillars. 19And he spread out the tent over
the tabernacle and put the covering of the tent
on top of it, as the LORD had commanded

Moses. 20 He took the Testimony and put *it* into
the ark, inserted the poles through the rings
of the ark, and put the mercy seat on top of the
ark. 21 And he brought the ark into the tabernacle, hung up the veil of the covering, and
partitioned off the ark of the Testimony, as the
LORD had commanded Moses.
22 He put the table in the tabernacle of meeting, on the north side of the tabernacle, outside the veil; 23 and he set the bread in order
upon it before the LORD, as the LORD had commanded Moses. 24 He put the lampstand in the
tabernacle of meeting, across from the table,
on the south side of the tabernacle; 25 and he lit
the lamps before the LORD, as the LORD had
commanded Moses. 26 He put the gold altar in
the tabernacle of meeting in front of the veil;
27 and he burned sweet incense on it, as the
LORD had commanded Moses. 28 He hung up
the screen *at* the door of the tabernacle. 29 And
he put the altar of burnt offering *before* the
door of the tabernacle of the tent of meeting,
and offered upon it the burnt offering and the
grain offering, as the LORD had commanded
Moses. 30 He set the laver between the tabernacle of meeting and the altar, and put water
there for washing; 31 and Moses, Aaron, and his
sons would wash their hands and their feet
with water from it. 32 Whenever they went into
the tabernacle of meeting, and when they
came near the altar, they washed, as the LORD
had commanded Moses. 33 And he raised up
the court all around the tabernacle and the
altar, and hung up the screen of the court
gate. So Moses finished the work.
34 Then the cloud covered the tabernacle of
meeting, and the glory of the LORD filled the
tabernacle. 35 And Moses was not able to enter
the tabernacle of meeting, because the cloud
rested above it, and the glory of the LORD
filled the tabernacle. 36 Whenever the cloud
was taken up from above the tabernacle, the
children of Israel would go onward in all their
journeys. 37 But if the cloud was not taken up,
then they did not journey till the day that it
was taken up. 38 For the cloud of the LORD *was*
above the tabernacle by day, and fire was over
it by night, in the sight of all the house of
Israel, throughout all their journeys.

Psalm 22:16–21

16 For dogs have surrounded Me;
The congregation of the wicked has
enclosed Me.
They pierced My hands and
My feet;
17 I can count all My bones.
They look *and* stare at Me.

22:16 They pierced My hands and My feet. The Hebrew text reads "like a lion," i.e., these vicious attacking enemies, like animals, have torn me. Likely, a messianic prediction with reference to crucifixion (see Is. 53:5; Zech. 12:10).

22:18 They divide...they cast. All 4 Gospel writers appeal to this imagery in describing Christ's crucifixion (Matt. 27:35; Mark 15:24; Luke 23:34; John 19:24).

18 They divide My garments among them,
And for My clothing they cast lots.
19 But You, O LORD, do not be far
from Me;
O My Strength, hasten to
help Me!
20 Deliver Me from the sword,
My precious *life* from the power
of the dog.
21 Save Me from the lion's mouth
And from the horns of the
wild oxen!

You have answered Me.

Proverbs 8:22–31

22 "The LORD possessed me at the
beginning of His way,
Before His works of old.
23 I have been established from
everlasting,
From the beginning, before there was
ever an earth.
24 When *there were* no depths
I was brought forth,
When *there were* no fountains
abounding with water.
25 Before the mountains were
settled,
Before the hills, I was brought forth;

8:27 circle on the face of the deep. The Hebrew word for circle indicates that the earth is a globe; therefore the horizon is circular (see Is. 40:22). This "deep" that surrounds the earth was the original world ocean that covered the surface of the earth before it was fully formed and given life (cf. Gen.1:2).

26 While as yet He had not made the
earth or the fields,
Or the primal dust of the world.
27 When He prepared the heavens,
I *was* there,
When He drew a circle on the face
of the deep,
28 When He established the clouds
above,
When He strengthened the fountains
of the deep,
29 When He assigned to the sea
its limit,
So that the waters would not
transgress His command,
When He marked out the foundations
of the earth,
30 Then I was beside Him *as* a master
craftsman;
And I was daily *His* delight,
Rejoicing always before Him,
31 Rejoicing in His inhabited world,
And my delight *was* with the
sons of men.

Matthew 27:1–26

27 When morning came, all the chief
priests and elders of the people plotted
against Jesus to put Him to death. [2]And when
they had bound Him, they led Him away and
delivered Him to Pontius Pilate the governor.
[3]Then Judas, His betrayer, seeing that He
had been condemned, was remorseful and
brought back the thirty pieces of silver to the
chief priests and elders, [4]saying, "I have
sinned by betraying innocent blood."
And they said, "What *is that* to us? You see
to it!"
[5]Then he threw down the pieces of silver in
the temple and departed, and went and
hanged himself.
[6]But the chief priests took the silver pieces
and said, "It is not lawful to put them into the
treasury, because they are the price of blood."
[7]And they consulted together and bought with
them the potter's field, to bury strangers in.
[8]Therefore that field has been called the Field
of Blood to this day.
[9]Then was fulfilled what was spoken by
Jeremiah the prophet, saying, *"And they took
the thirty pieces of silver, the value of Him
who was priced,* whom they of the children of
Israel priced, [10]*and gave them for the potter's
field, as the* L*ORD directed me."*
[11]Now Jesus stood before the governor. And
the governor asked Him, saying, "Are You the
King of the Jews?"
Jesus said to him, *"It is as* you say." [12]And
while He was being accused by the chief
priests and elders, He answered nothing.
[13]Then Pilate said to Him, "Do You not hear
how many things they testify against You?"
[14]But He answered him not one word, so that
the governor marveled greatly.
[15]Now at the feast the governor was accustomed to releasing to the multitude one prisoner whom they wished. [16]And at that time
they had a notorious prisoner called Barabbas.
[17]Therefore, when they had gathered together,
Pilate said to them, "Whom do you want me to
release to you? Barabbas, or Jesus who is
called Christ?" [18]For he knew that they had
handed Him over because of envy.
[19]While he was sitting on the judgment seat,
his wife sent to him, saying, "Have nothing to
do with that just Man, for I have suffered many
things today in a dream because of Him."
[20]But the chief priests and elders persuaded
the multitudes that they should ask for
Barabbas and destroy Jesus. [21]The governor
answered and said to them, "Which of the two
do you want me to release to you?"
They said, "Barabbas!"
[22]Pilate said to them, "What then shall I do
with Jesus who is called Christ?"
They all said to him, "Let Him be crucified!"
[23]Then the governor said, "Why, what evil
has He done?"
But they cried out all the more, saying, "Let
Him be crucified!"
[24]When Pilate saw that he could not prevail
at all, but rather *that* a tumult was rising, he
took water and washed *his* hands before the
multitude, saying, "I am innocent of the blood
of this just Person. You see *to it.*"
[25]And all the people answered and said, "His
blood *be* on us and on our children."
[26]Then he released Barabbas to them; and
when he had scourged Jesus, he delivered
Him to be crucified.

27:26 scourged. The whip used for scourging consisted of several strands of leather attached to a wooden handle. Each strand had a bit of metal or bone attached to the end. The victim was bound to a post by the wrists, high over his head, so that the flesh of the back would be taut. An expert at wielding the scourge could literally tear the flesh from the back, lacerating muscles, and sometimes even exposing the kidneys or other internal organs. Scourging alone was fatal in some cases.

DAY 14: Does Matthew include any material not found in the other Gospels?

Matthew includes nine events in Jesus' life that are unique to his Gospel:

1. Joseph's dream (1:20–24).
2. Visit of the wise men (2:1–12).
3. Flight into Egypt (2:13–15).
4. Herod kills the children (2:16–18).
5. Judas repents (27:3-10, but see Acts 1:18,19).
6. The dream of Pilate's wife (27:19).
7. Other resurrections (27:52).
8. The bribery of the soldiers (28:11–15).
9. The Great Commission (28:19,20).

FEBRUARY 15

Leviticus 1:1–2:16

1 Now the LORD called to Moses, and spoke to
him from the tabernacle of meeting, saying,
2“Speak to the children of Israel, and say to
them: ‘When any one of you brings an offering
to the LORD, you shall bring your offering of
the livestock—of the herd and of the flock.
3‘If his offering *is* a burnt sacrifice of the
herd, let him offer a male without blemish; he
shall offer it of his own free will at the door of
the tabernacle of meeting before the LORD.
4Then he shall put his hand on the head of the
burnt offering, and it will be accepted on his
behalf to make atonement for him. 5He shall
kill the bull before the LORD; and the priests,
Aaron's sons, shall bring the blood and sprinkle the blood all around on the altar that *is by*
the door of the tabernacle of meeting. 6And he
shall skin the burnt offering and cut it into its
pieces. 7The sons of Aaron the priest shall put
fire on the altar, and lay the wood in order on
the fire. 8Then the priests, Aaron's sons, shall
lay the parts, the head, and the fat in order on
the wood that *is* on the fire upon the altar; 9but
he shall wash its entrails and its legs with
water. And the priest shall burn all on the altar
as a burnt sacrifice, an offering made by fire,
a sweet aroma to the LORD.
10‘If his offering *is* of the flocks—of the sheep
or of the goats—as a burnt sacrifice, he shall
bring a male without blemish. 11He shall kill it
on the north side of the altar before the LORD;
and the priests, Aaron's sons, shall sprinkle its
blood all around on the altar. 12And he shall cut
it into its pieces, with its head and its fat; and
the priest shall lay them in order on the wood
that *is* on the fire upon the altar; 13but he shall
wash the entrails and the legs with water. Then
the priest shall bring *it* all and burn *it* on the
altar; it *is* a burnt sacrifice, an offering made
by fire, a sweet aroma to the LORD.
14‘And if the burnt sacrifice of his offering to
the LORD *is* of birds, then he shall bring his
offering of turtledoves or young pigeons. 15The
priest shall bring it to the altar, wring off its
head, and burn *it* on the altar; its blood shall be
drained out at the side of the altar. 16And he shall
remove its crop with its feathers and cast it beside the altar on the east side, into the place
for ashes. 17Then he shall split it at its wings,
but shall not divide *it* completely; and the priest
shall burn it on the altar, on the wood that *is* on
the fire. It *is* a burnt sacrifice, an offering made
by fire, a sweet aroma to the LORD.
2 ‘When anyone offers a grain offering to
the LORD, his offering shall be *of* fine flour.
And he shall pour oil on it, and put frankincense on it. 2He shall bring it to Aaron's sons,

1:4 put his hand on the head. This symbolic gesture pictured the transfer of the sacrificer's sin to the sacrificial animal and was likely done with a prayer of repentance and request for forgiveness (see Ps. 51:18,19). **on his behalf.** This was a substitutionary sacrifice that prefigured the ultimate substitute—Jesus Christ (see Is. 53; 2 Cor. 5:21). **make atonement.** The word means "cover." The psalmist defines it by saying, "Blessed is he whose transgression is forgiven, whose sin is covered" (Ps. 32:1). Theologically, the "atonement" of the Old Testament covered sin only temporarily, but it did not eliminate sin or later judgment (Heb. 10:4). The one-time sacrifice of Jesus Christ fully atoned for sin, thus satisfying God's wrath forever and insuring eternal salvation (see Heb. 9:12; 1 John 2:2), even to those who put saving faith in God for their redemption before Christ's death on the cross (see Rom. 3:25,26; Heb. 9:15).

the priests, one of whom shall take from it his
handful of fine flour and oil with all the frankincense. And the priest shall burn *it as* a
memorial on the altar, an offering made by
fire, a sweet aroma to the LORD. 3The rest of
the grain offering *shall be* Aaron's and his
sons'. *It is* most holy of the offerings to the
LORD made by fire.
4"And if you bring as an offering a grain
offering baked in the oven, *it shall be* unleavened cakes of fine flour mixed with oil, or
unleavened wafers anointed with oil. 5But if
your offering *is* a grain offering *baked* in a pan,
it shall be of fine flour, unleavened, mixed with
oil. 6You shall break it in pieces and pour oil on
it; it *is* a grain offering.
7"If your offering *is* a grain offering *baked* in
a covered pan, it shall be made *of* fine flour
with oil. 8You shall bring the grain offering
that is made of these things to the LORD. And
when it is presented to the priest, he shall
bring it to the altar. 9Then the priest shall take
from the grain offering a memorial portion,
and burn *it* on the altar. *It is* an offering made
by fire, a sweet aroma to the LORD. 10And what
is left of the grain offering *shall be* Aaron's and
his sons'. *It is* most holy of the offerings to the
LORD made by fire.
11"No grain offering which you bring to the
LORD shall be made with leaven, for you shall
burn no leaven nor any honey in any offering
to the LORD made by fire. 12As for the offering
of the firstfruits, you shall offer them to the
LORD, but they shall not be burned on the altar
for a sweet aroma. 13And every offering of your
grain offering you shall season with salt; you
shall not allow the salt of the covenant of your
God to be lacking from your grain offering.
With all your offerings you shall offer salt.
14"If you offer a grain offering of your firstfruits to the LORD, you shall offer for the grain
offering of your firstfruits green heads of
grain roasted on the fire, grain beaten from
full heads. 15And you shall put oil on it, and lay
frankincense on it. It *is* a grain offering. 16Then
the priest shall burn the memorial portion:
part of its beaten grain and *part* of its oil, with
all the frankincense, as an offering made by
fire to the LORD.

Psalm 22:22–31

22 I will declare Your name to
My brethren;
In the midst of the assembly
I will praise You.
23 You who fear the LORD, praise Him!
All you descendants of Jacob, glorify
Him,
And fear Him, all you offspring of Israel!
24 For He has not despised nor abhorred
the affliction of the afflicted;
Nor has He hidden His face from Him;
But when He cried to Him, He heard.

25 My praise *shall be* of You in the great
assembly;
I will pay My vows before those who
fear Him.
26 The poor shall eat and be satisfied;
Those who seek Him will praise the
LORD.
Let your heart live forever!

27 All the ends of the world
Shall remember and turn to the LORD,
And all the families of the nations
Shall worship before You.
28 For the kingdom *is* the LORD's,
And He rules over the nations.

29 All the prosperous of the earth
Shall eat and worship;
All those who go down to the dust
Shall bow before Him,
Even he who cannot keep himself
alive.
30 A posterity shall serve Him.
It will be recounted of the Lord to the
next generation,
31 They will come and declare His
righteousness to a people who
will be born,
That He has done *this*.

Proverbs 8:32–36

32 "Now therefore, listen to me,
my children,
For blessed *are those who* keep my
ways.
33 Hear instruction and be wise,
And do not disdain *it*.
34 Blessed is the man who listens to me,
Watching daily at my gates,
Waiting at the posts of my doors.
35 For whoever finds me finds life,
And obtains favor from the LORD;
36 But he who sins against me wrongs
his own soul;
All those who hate me love death."

Matthew 27:27–54

27Then the soldiers of the governor took Jesus into the Praetorium and gathered the
whole garrison around Him. 28And they
stripped Him and put a scarlet robe on Him.
29When they had twisted a crown of thorns,
they put *it* on His head, and a reed in His right

27:31 to be crucified. Crucifixion was a form of punishment that had been passed down to the Romans from the Persians, Phoenicians, and Carthaginians. Roman crucifixion was a lingering doom—by design. Roman executioners had perfected the art of slow torture while keeping the victim alive. Some victims even lingered until they were eaten alive by birds of prey or wild beasts. Most hung on the cross for days before dying of exhaustion, dehydration, traumatic fever, or—most likely—suffocation. When the legs would no longer support the weight of the body, the diaphragm was constricted in a way that made breathing impossible. That is why breaking the legs would hasten death (John 19:31–33), but this was unnecessary in Jesus' case. The hands were usually nailed through the wrists, and the feet through the instep or the Achilles tendon (sometimes using one nail for both feet). None of these wounds would be fatal, but their pain would become unbearable as the hours dragged on. The most notable feature of crucifixion was the stigma of disgrace that was attached to it (Gal. 3:13; 5:11; Heb. 12:2). One indignity was the humiliation of carrying one's own cross, which might weigh as much as 200 pounds. Normally a quaternion, 4 soldiers, would escort the prisoner through the crowds to the place of crucifixion. A placard bearing the indictment would be hung around the person's neck.

hand. And they bowed the knee before Him
and mocked Him, saying, "Hail, King of the
Jews!" 30 Then they spat on Him, and took the
reed and struck Him on the head. 31 And when
they had mocked Him, they took the robe off
Him, put His *own* clothes on Him, and led Him
away to be crucified.
32 Now as they came out, they found a man of
Cyrene, Simon by name. Him they compelled
to bear His cross. 33 And when they had come
to a place called Golgotha, that is to say, Place
of a Skull, 34 they gave Him sour wine mingled
with gall to drink. But when He had tasted *it,*
He would not drink.
35 Then they crucified Him, and divided His
garments, casting lots, that it might be fulfilled which was spoken by the prophet:

"They divided My garments among them,
And for My clothing they cast lots."

36 Sitting down, they kept watch over Him there.
37 And they put up over His head the accusation
written against Him:

THIS IS JESUS THE KING OF THE JEWS.

38 Then two robbers were crucified with Him,
one on the right and another on the left.
39 And those who passed by blasphemed
Him, wagging their heads 40 and saying, "You
who destroy the temple and build *it* in three
days, save Yourself! If You are the Son of God,
come down from the cross."
41 Likewise the chief priests also, mocking
with the scribes and elders, said, 42 "He saved
others; Himself He cannot save. If He is the
King of Israel, let Him now come down from
the cross, and we will believe Him. 43 He trusted in God; let Him deliver Him now if He will
have Him; for He said, 'I am the Son of God.' "
44 Even the robbers who were crucified with
Him reviled Him with the same thing.
45 Now from the sixth hour until the ninth
hour there was darkness over all the land. 46 And
about the ninth hour Jesus cried out with a loud
voice, saying, "Eli, Eli, lama sabachthani?" that is,
"My God, My God, why have You forsaken Me?"

27:46 Eli, Eli, lama sabachthani? "Eli" is Hebrew; the rest Aramaic. (Mark 15:34 gives the entire wail in Aramaic.) This cry is a fulfillment of Psalm 22:1, one of many striking parallels between that psalm and the specific events of the Crucifixion. Christ at that moment was experiencing the abandonment and despair that resulted from the outpouring of divine wrath on Him as sin-bearer.

47 Some of those who stood there, when they
heard *that,* said, "This Man is calling for Elijah!"
48 Immediately one of them ran and took a
sponge, filled *it* with sour wine and put *it* on a
reed, and offered it to Him to drink.
49 The rest said, "Let Him alone; let us see if
Elijah will come to save Him."
50 And Jesus cried out again with a loud
voice, and yielded up His spirit.
51 Then, behold, the veil of the temple was torn
in two from top to bottom; and the earth quaked,
and the rocks were split, 52 and the graves were
opened; and many bodies of the saints who
had fallen asleep were raised; 53 and coming
out of the graves after His resurrection, they
went into the holy city and appeared to many.
54 So when the centurion and those with him,
who were guarding Jesus, saw the earthquake
and the things that had happened, they feared
greatly, saying, "Truly this was the Son of God!"

DAY 15: How is Christ seen in the Levitical offerings?

Offering	Christ's Provision	Christ's Character
1. Burnt Offering (Leviticus 1:3–17; 6:8–13)	atonement	Christ's sinless nature
2. Grain Offering (Leviticus 2:1–16; 6:14–23)	dedication/consecration	Christ was wholly devoted to the Father's purposes
3. Peace Offering (Leviticus 3:1–17; 7:11–36)	reconciliation/fellowship	Christ was at peace with God
4. Sin Offering (Leviticus 4:1–5:13; 6:24–30)	propitiation	Christ's substitutionary death
5. Trespass Offering (Leviticus 5:14–6:7; 7:1–10)	repentance	Christ paid it all for redemption

FEBRUARY 16

Leviticus 3:1–4:35

3 'When his offering *is* a sacrifice of a peace
offering, if he offers *it* of the herd,
whether male or female, he shall offer it without blemish before the LORD. 2And he shall lay
his hand on the head of his offering, and kill it
at the door of the tabernacle of meeting; and
Aaron's sons, the priests, shall sprinkle the
blood all around on the altar. 3Then he shall
offer from the sacrifice of the peace offering
an offering made by fire to the LORD. The fat
that covers the entrails and all the fat that *is* on
the entrails, 4the two kidneys and the fat that *is*
on them by the flanks, and the fatty lobe
attached to the liver above the kidneys, he shall
remove; 5and Aaron's sons shall burn it on the
altar upon the burnt sacrifice, which *is* on the
wood that *is* on the fire, *as* an offering made by
fire, a sweet aroma to the LORD.

6'If his offering as a sacrifice of a peace offering to the LORD *is* of the flock, *whether* male or
female, he shall offer it without blemish. 7If he
offers a lamb as his offering, then he shall offer
it before the LORD. 8And he shall lay his hand on
the head of his offering, and kill it before the
tabernacle of meeting; and Aaron's sons shall
sprinkle its blood all around on the altar.

9'Then he shall offer from the sacrifice of
the peace offering, as an offering made by fire
to the LORD, its fat *and* the whole fat tail which
he shall remove close to the backbone. And
the fat that covers the entrails and all the fat
that *is* on the entrails, 10the two kidneys and
the fat that *is* on them by the flanks, and the
fatty lobe *attached* to the liver above the kidneys, he shall remove; 11and the priest shall
burn *them* on the altar *as* food, an offering
made by fire to the LORD.

12'And if his offering *is* a goat, then he shall
offer it before the LORD. 13He shall lay his hand
on its head and kill it before the tabernacle of
meeting; and the sons of Aaron shall sprinkle
its blood all around on the altar. 14Then he
shall offer from it his offering, as an offering
made by fire to the LORD. The fat that covers
the entrails and all the fat that *is* on the entrails,
15the two kidneys and the fat that *is* on them by
the flanks, and the fatty lobe *attached* to the
liver above the kidneys, he shall remove; 16and
the priest shall burn them on the altar *as* food,
an offering made by fire for a sweet aroma; all
the fat *is* the LORD's.

17'*This shall be* a perpetual statute throughout your generations in all your dwellings: you
shall eat neither fat nor blood.' "

4 Now the LORD spoke to Moses, saying,
2"Speak to the children of Israel, saying: 'If
a person sins unintentionally against any of
the commandments of the LORD *in anything*
which ought not to be done, and does any of
them, 3if the anointed priest sins, bringing
guilt on the people, then let him offer to the
LORD for his sin which he has sinned a young
bull without blemish as a sin offering. 4He shall
bring the bull to the door of the tabernacle of
meeting before the LORD, lay his hand on the
bull's head, and kill the bull before the LORD.
5Then the anointed priest shall take some of

3:1–17 See 7:11–36 for the priests' instructions. The peace offering symbolizes the peace and fellowship between the true worshiper and God (as a voluntary offering). It was the third freewill offering resulting in a sweet aroma to the Lord (3:5), which served as the appropriate corollary to the burnt offering of atonement and the grain offering of consecration and dedication. It symbolized the fruit of redemptive reconciliation between a sinner and God (see 2 Cor. 5:18).

the bull's blood and bring it to the tabernacle of meeting. 6The priest shall dip his finger in the blood and sprinkle some of the blood seven times before the LORD, in front of the veil of the sanctuary. 7And the priest shall put some of the blood on the horns of the altar of sweet incense before the LORD, which is in the tabernacle of meeting; and he shall pour the remaining blood of the bull at the base of the altar of the burnt offering, which is at the door of the tabernacle of meeting. 8He shall take from it all the fat of the bull as the sin offering. The fat that covers the entrails and all the fat which *is* on the entrails, 9the two kidneys and the fat that *is* on them by the flanks, and the fatty lobe *attached* to the liver above the kidneys, he shall remove, 10as it was taken from the bull of the sacrifice of the peace offering; and the priest shall burn them on the altar of the burnt offering. 11But the bull's hide and all its flesh, with its head and legs, its entrails and offal— 12the whole bull he shall carry outside the camp to a clean place, where the ashes are poured out, and burn it on wood with fire; where the ashes are poured out it shall be burned.

13"Now if the whole congregation of Israel sins unintentionally, and the thing is hidden from the eyes of the assembly, and they have done *something against* any of the commandments of the LORD *in anything* which should not be done, and are guilty; 14when the sin which they have committed becomes known, then the assembly shall offer a young bull for the sin, and bring it before the tabernacle of meeting. 15And the elders of the congregation shall lay their hands on the head of the bull before the LORD. Then the bull shall be killed before the LORD. 16The anointed priest shall bring some of the bull's blood to the tabernacle of meeting. 17Then the priest shall dip his finger in the blood and sprinkle *it* seven times before the LORD, in front of the veil. 18And he shall put *some* of the blood on the horns of the altar which *is* before the LORD, which *is* in the tabernacle of meeting; and he shall pour the remaining blood at the base of the altar of burnt offering, which is at the door of the tabernacle of meeting. 19He shall take all the fat from it and burn *it* on the altar. 20And he shall do with the bull as he did with the bull as a sin offering; thus he shall do with it. So the priest shall make atonement for them, and it shall be forgiven them. 21Then he shall carry the bull outside the camp, and burn it as he burned the first bull. It *is* a sin offering for the assembly.

22"When a ruler has sinned, and done *something* unintentionally *against* any of the commandments of the LORD his God *in anything* which should not be done, and is guilty, 23or if his sin which he has committed comes to his knowledge, he shall bring as his offering a kid of the goats, a male without blemish. 24And he shall lay his hand on the head of the goat, and kill it at the place where they kill the burnt offering before the LORD. It *is* a sin offering. 25The priest shall take some of the blood of the sin offering with his finger, put *it* on the horns of the altar of burnt offering, and pour its blood at the base of the altar of burnt offering. 26And he shall burn all its fat on the altar, like the fat of the sacrifice of the peace offering. So the priest shall make atonement for him concerning his sin, and it shall be forgiven him.

27"If anyone of the common people sins unintentionally by doing *something against* any of the commandments of the LORD *in anything* which ought not to be done, and is guilty, 28or if his sin which he has committed comes to his knowledge, then he shall bring as his offering a kid of the goats, a female without blemish, for his sin which he has committed. 29And he shall lay his hand on the head of the sin offering, and kill the sin offering at the place of the burnt offering. 30Then the priest shall take *some* of its blood with his finger, put *it* on the horns of the altar of burnt offering, and pour all *the remaining* blood at the base of the altar. 31He shall remove all its fat, as fat is removed from the sacrifice of the peace offering; and the priest shall burn it on the altar for a sweet aroma to the LORD. So the priest shall make atonement for him, and it shall be forgiven him.

32"If he brings a lamb as his sin offering, he shall bring a female without blemish. 33Then he shall lay his hand on the head of the sin offering, and kill it as a sin offering at the place where they kill the burnt offering. 34The priest shall take *some* of the blood of the sin offering with his finger, put *it* on the horns of the altar of burnt offering, and pour all *the remaining* blood at the base of the altar. 35He shall remove all its fat, as the fat of the lamb is removed from the sacrifice of the peace offering. Then the priest shall burn it on the altar, according to the offerings made by fire to the LORD. So the priest shall make atonement for his sin that he has committed, and it shall be forgiven him.

Psalm 23:1–6

A Psalm of David.

The LORD *is* my shepherd;
I shall not want.
2 He makes me to lie down in green
pastures;

He leads me beside the still waters.
3 He restores my soul;
He leads me in the paths
of righteousness
For His name's sake.

4 Yea, though I walk through the valley
of the shadow of death,
I will fear no evil;
For You *are* with me;
Your rod and Your staff,
they comfort me.

23:4 the valley of the shadow of death. Phraseology used to convey a perilously threatening environment (see Job 10:21,22; 38:17; Pss. 44:19; 107:10; Jer. 2:6; Luke. 1:79). **Your rod and Your staff.** The shepherd's club and crook are viewed as comforting instruments of protection and direction, respectively.

5 You prepare a table before me in the
presence of my enemies;
You anoint my head with oil;
My cup runs over.
6 Surely goodness and mercy
shall follow me
All the days of my life;
And I will dwell in the house
of the LORD
Forever.

Proverbs 9:1–6

9 Wisdom has built her house,
She has hewn out her seven pillars;
2 She has slaughtered her meat,
She has mixed her wine,
She has also furnished her table.
3 She has sent out her maidens,
She cries out from the highest places
of the city,
4 "Whoever *is* simple, let him turn in
here!"
As for him who lacks understanding,
she says to him,
5 "Come, eat of my bread
And drink of the wine I have
mixed.
6 Forsake foolishness and live,
And go in the way of understanding.

Matthew 27:55–66

55 And many women who followed Jesus
from Galilee, ministering to Him, were there
looking on from afar, 56 among whom were
Mary Magdalene, Mary the mother of James
and Joses, and the mother of Zebedee's sons.
57 Now when evening had come, there came
a rich man from Arimathea, named Joseph,
who himself had also become a disciple of Jesus.
58 This man went to Pilate and asked for
the body of Jesus. Then Pilate commanded
the body to be given to him. 59 When Joseph
had taken the body, he wrapped it in a clean
linen cloth, 60 and laid it in his new tomb which
he had hewn out of the rock; and he rolled a
large stone against the door of the tomb, and
departed. 61 And Mary Magdalene was there,
and the other Mary, sitting opposite the tomb.
62 On the next day, which followed the Day
of Preparation, the chief priests and
Pharisees gathered together to Pilate, 63 saying,
"Sir, we remember, while He was still
alive, how that deceiver said, 'After three days
I will rise.' 64 Therefore command that the
tomb be made secure until the third day, lest
His disciples come by night and steal Him
away, and say to the people, 'He has risen
from the dead.' So the last deception will be
worse than the first."
65 Pilate said to them, "You have a guard; go
your way, make *it* as secure as you know how."
66 So they went and made the tomb secure,
sealing the stone and setting the guard.

27:56 Mary Magdalene. She had been delivered from 7 demons (Luke 8:2); the other "Mary" ("wife of Clopas," John 19:25—a variant of Alphaeus) was the mother of the apostle known as "James the Less" (Mark 15:40). **the mother of Zebedee's sons.** Salome (Mark 15:40), mother of James and John. From John 19:26, we learn that Mary, the mother of Jesus, was also present at the Cross—possibly standing apart from these 3, who were "looking on from afar" (v. 55), as if they could not bear to watch His sufferings, but neither could they bear to leave Him.

27:57 Joseph. Mark 15:43 and Luke 23:50,51 identify him as a member of the Sanhedrin, though Luke says "he had not consented to their decision and deed" in condemning Christ. Joseph and Nicodemus (John 19:39), both being prominent Jewish leaders, buried Christ in Joseph's own "new tomb" (v. 60), thus fulfilling exactly the prophecy of Is. 53:9. **Arimathea.** A town about 15–20 miles northwest of Jerusalem.

DAY 16: Why are there so many uncomfortable expressions in the Psalms—for example in Psalms 23 and 139?

Because the Psalms genuinely reflect real life, we should expect that they will be uncomfortable in the same places that life is uncomfortable. According to the best-known Psalm 23, life isn't just about green pastures and still waters; it also includes death and enemies. The psalmists were convinced they knew the only true God. When someone was picking on them or their people, they would at times cry out for very specific judgment to be applied by God on their enemies. An amazing fact about the Psalms is their unblushing record of these cries to God that, if we are honest, echo some of our deepest hidden complaints before God.

In David's case, the role that he filled as the king and representative of God's people often blurs with his individual self-awareness. At times it is difficult to tell whether he is speaking for himself alone or for the people as a whole. This explains some of the vehemence behind the curse-pronouncing psalms. They unabashedly invoke God's righteous wrath and judgment against His enemies.

FEBRUARY 17

Leviticus 5:1–6:30

5 1'If a person sins in hearing the utterance
of an oath, and *is* a witness, whether he
has seen or known *of the matter*—if he does
not tell *it*, he bears guilt.
2'Or if a person touches any unclean thing,
whether *it is* the carcass of an unclean beast,
or the carcass of unclean livestock, or the carcass of unclean creeping things, and he is
unaware of it, he also shall be unclean and
guilty. 3Or if he touches human uncleanness—
whatever uncleanness with which a man may
be defiled, and he is unaware of it—when he
realizes *it*, then he shall be guilty.
4'Or if a person swears, speaking thoughtlessly with *his* lips to do evil or to do good,
whatever *it is* that a man may pronounce by an
oath, and he is unaware of it—when he realizes *it*, then he shall be guilty in any of these
matters.
5'And it shall be, when he is guilty in any of
these *matters*, that he shall confess that he has
sinned in that *thing*; 6and he shall bring his trespass offering to the LORD for his sin which he
has committed, a female from the flock, a lamb
or a kid of the goats as a sin offering. So the
priest shall make atonement for him concerning
his sin.
7'If he is not able to bring a lamb, then he
shall bring to the LORD, for his trespass which
he has committed, two turtledoves or two
young pigeons: one as a sin offering and the
other as a burnt offering. 8And he shall bring
them to the priest, who shall offer *that* which
is for the sin offering first, and wring off its
head from its neck, but shall not divide *it* completely. 9Then he shall sprinkle *some* of the
blood of the sin offering on the side of the
altar, and the rest of the blood shall be drained
out at the base of the altar. It *is* a sin offering.
10And he shall offer the second *as* a burnt
offering according to the prescribed manner.
So the priest shall make atonement on his
behalf for his sin which he has committed, and
it shall be forgiven him.
11'But if he is not able to bring two turtledoves or two young pigeons, then he who
sinned shall bring for his offering one-tenth of
an ephah of fine flour as a sin offering. He
shall put no oil on it, nor shall he put frankincense on it, for it *is* a sin offering. 12Then he
shall bring it to the priest, and the priest shall
take his handful of it as a memorial portion,
and burn *it* on the altar according to the offerings made by fire to the LORD. It *is* a sin offering. 13The priest shall make atonement for him,
for his sin that he has committed in any of
these matters; and it shall be forgiven him. *The
rest* shall be the priest's as a grain offering.' "
14Then the LORD spoke to Moses, saying:
15"If a person commits a trespass, and sins
unintentionally in regard to the holy things of
the LORD, then he shall bring to the LORD as
his trespass offering a ram without blemish
from the flocks, with your valuation in shekels
of silver according to the shekel of the sanctuary, as a trespass offering. 16And he shall make
restitution for the harm that he has done in

5:5 he shall confess. Confession must accompany the sacrifice as the outward expression of a repentant heart which openly acknowledged agreement with God concerning sin. Sacrifice minus true faith, repentance, and obedience was hypocrisy (see Ps. 26:4; Is. 9:17; Amos 5:21–26).

regard to the holy thing, and shall add one-fifth
to it and give it to the priest. So the priest shall
make atonement for him with the ram of the
trespass offering, and it shall be forgiven him.
[17]"If a person sins, and commits any of these
things which are forbidden to be done by the
commandments of the LORD, though he does
not know *it,* yet he is guilty and shall bear his
iniquity. [18]And he shall bring to the priest a
ram without blemish from the flock, with your
valuation, as a trespass offering. So the priest
shall make atonement for him regarding his
ignorance in which he erred and did not know
it, and it shall be forgiven him. [19]It is a trespass
offering; he has certainly trespassed against
the LORD."

6 And the LORD spoke to Moses, saying: [2]"If
a person sins and commits a trespass
against the LORD by lying to his neighbor
about what was delivered to him for safekeeping, or about a pledge, or about a robbery, or
if he has extorted from his neighbor, [3]or if he
has found what was lost and lies concerning it,
and swears falsely—in any one of these things
that a man may do in which he sins: [4]then it
shall be, because he has sinned and is guilty,
that he shall restore what he has stolen, or the
thing which he has extorted, or what was
delivered to him for safekeeping, or the lost
thing which he found, [5]or all that about which
he has sworn falsely. He shall restore its full
value, add one-fifth more to it, *and* give it to
whomever it belongs, on the day of his trespass offering. [6]And he shall bring his trespass
offering to the LORD, a ram without blemish
from the flock, with your valuation, as a trespass offering, to the priest. [7]So the priest shall
make atonement for him before the LORD, and
he shall be forgiven for any one of these
things that he may have done in which he
trespasses."

[8]Then the LORD spoke to Moses, saying,
[9]"Command Aaron and his sons, saying, 'This
is the law of the burnt offering: The burnt
offering *shall be* on the hearth upon the altar
all night until morning, and the fire of the altar
shall be kept burning on it. [10]And the priest
shall put on his linen garment, and his linen
trousers he shall put on his body, and take up
the ashes of the burnt offering which the fire
has consumed on the altar, and he shall put
them beside the altar. [11]Then he shall take off
his garments, put on other garments, and
carry the ashes outside the camp to a clean
place. [12]And the fire on the altar shall be kept
burning on it; it shall not be put out. And the
priest shall burn wood on it every morning,
and lay the burnt offering in order on it; and
he shall burn on it the fat of the peace offerings.
[13]A fire shall always be burning on the altar; it
shall never go out.

[14]"This *is* the law of the grain offering: The
sons of Aaron shall offer it on the altar before
the LORD. [15]He shall take from it his handful of
the fine flour of the grain offering, with its oil,
and all the frankincense which *is* on the grain
offering, and shall burn *it* on the altar *for* a
sweet aroma, as a memorial to the LORD. [16]And
the remainder of it Aaron and his sons shall
eat; with unleavened bread it shall be eaten in
a holy place; in the court of the tabernacle of
meeting they shall eat it. [17]It shall not be baked
with leaven. I have given it *as* their portion of
My offerings made by fire; it *is* most holy, like
the sin offering and the trespass offering. [18]All
the males among the children of Aaron may
eat it. *It shall be* a statute forever in your generations concerning the offerings made by
fire to the LORD. Everyone who touches them
must be holy.' "

[19]And the LORD spoke to Moses, saying,
[20]"This *is* the offering of Aaron and his sons,
which they shall offer to the LORD, *beginning*
on the day when he is anointed: one-tenth of
an ephah of fine flour as a daily grain offering,
half of it in the morning and half of it at night.
[21]It shall be made in a pan with oil. *When it is*
mixed, you shall bring it in. The baked pieces
of the grain offering you shall offer *for* a sweet
aroma to the LORD. [22]The priest from among
his sons, who is anointed in his place, shall
offer it. *It is* a statute forever to the LORD. It
shall be wholly burned. [23]For every grain
offering for the priest shall be wholly burned.
It shall not be eaten."

[24]Also the LORD spoke to Moses, saying,
[25]"Speak to Aaron and to his sons, saying,
'This *is* the law of the sin offering: In the place
where the burnt offering is killed, the sin
offering shall be killed before the LORD. It *is*
most holy. [26]The priest who offers it for sin
shall eat it. In a holy place it shall be eaten, in
the court of the tabernacle of meeting. [27]Eve-
ryone who touches its flesh must be holy. And
when its blood is sprinkled on any garment,
you shall wash that on which it was sprinkled,
in a holy place. [28]But the earthen vessel in
which it is boiled shall be broken. And if it is
boiled in a bronze pot, it shall be both scoured
and rinsed in water. [29]All the males among the
priests may eat it. It *is* most holy. [30]But no sin
offering from which *any* of the blood is
brought into the tabernacle of meeting, to
make atonement in the holy *place,* shall be
eaten. It shall be burned in the fire.

Psalm 24:1–6

A Psalm of David.

The earth *is* the LORD's,
And all its fullness,
The world and those who dwell therein.
2 For He has founded it upon the seas,
And established it upon the waters.

3 Who may ascend into the hill of the LORD?
Or who may stand in His holy place?
4 He who has clean hands and a pure heart,
Who has not lifted up his soul to an idol,
Nor sworn deceitfully.

24:4 These sample qualities do not signify sinless perfection, but rather basic integrity of inward motive and outward manner.

5 He shall receive blessing from the LORD,
And righteousness from the God of his salvation.
6 This *is* Jacob, the generation of those who seek Him,
Who seek Your face. Selah

Proverbs 9:7–9

7 "He who corrects a scoffer gets shame for himself,
And he who rebukes a wicked *man only* harms himself.
8 Do not correct a scoffer, lest he hate you;
Rebuke a wise *man,* and he will love you.
9 Give *instruction* to a wise *man,* and he will be still wiser;
Teach a just *man,* and he will increase in learning.

Matthew 28:1–20

28 Now after the Sabbath, as the first *day*
of the week began to dawn, Mary
Magdalene and the other Mary came to see
the tomb. 2And behold, there was a great
earthquake; for an angel of the Lord descended from heaven, and came and rolled back the
stone from the door, and sat on it. 3His countenance was like lightning, and his clothing as
white as snow. 4And the guards shook for fear
of him, and became like dead *men.*
5But the angel answered and said to the
women, "Do not be afraid, for I know that you
seek Jesus who was crucified. 6He is not here;
for He is risen, as He said. Come, see the place
where the Lord lay. 7And go quickly and tell

28:1 as the first *day* of the week began to dawn. Sabbath officially ended with sundown on Saturday. At that time the women could purchase and prepare spices (Luke 24:1). The event described here occurred the next morning, at dawn on Sunday, the first day of the week.

28:4 became like dead *men.* This suggests that they were not merely paralyzed with fear, but completely unconscious, totally traumatized by what they had seen. The word translated "shook" has the same root as the word for "earthquake" in v. 2. The sudden appearance of this angel, at the same time the women arrived, was their first clue that anything extraordinary was happening.

His disciples that He is risen from the dead, and
indeed He is going before you into Galilee;
there you will see Him. Behold, I have told you."
8So they went out quickly from the tomb
with fear and great joy, and ran to bring His
disciples word.
9And as they went to tell His disciples,
behold, Jesus met them, saying, "Rejoice!" So
they came and held Him by the feet and worshiped Him. 10Then Jesus said to them, "Do
not be afraid. Go *and* tell My brethren to go to
Galilee, and there they will see Me."
11Now while they were going, behold, some
of the guard came into the city and reported to
the chief priests all the things that had happened. 12When they had assembled with the
elders and consulted together, they gave a
large sum of money to the soldiers, 13saying,
"Tell them, 'His disciples came at night and
stole Him *away* while we slept.' 14And if this
comes to the governor's ears, we will appease
him and make you secure." 15So they took the
money and did as they were instructed; and
this saying is commonly reported among the
Jews until this day.
16Then the eleven disciples went away into

28:18 All authority. See 11:27; John 3:35. Absolute sovereign authority—lordship over all—is handed to Christ, "in heaven and on earth." This is clear proof of His deity. The time of His humiliation was at an end, and God had exalted Him above all (Phil. 2:9–11).

Galilee, to the mountain which Jesus had appointed for them. 17When they saw Him, they worshiped Him; but some doubted.

18And Jesus came and spoke to them, saying, "All authority has been given to Me in heaven and on earth. 19Go therefore and make disciples of all the nations, baptizing them in the name of the Father and of the Son and of the Holy Spirit, 20teaching them to observe all things that I have commanded you; and lo, I am with you always, *even* to the end of the age." Amen.

DAY 17: How are the Old Testament sacrifices compared to Christ's sacrifice?

Leviticus		Hebrews
1. Old Covenant (temporary)	Hebrews 7:22; 8:6,13; 10:20	1. New Covenant (permanent)
2. Obsolete promises	Hebrews 8:6–13	2. Better promises
3. A shadow	Hebrews 8:5; 9:23,24; 10:1	3. The reality
4. Aaronic priesthood (many)	Hebrews 6:19–7:25	4. Melchizedekian priesthood (one)
5. Sinful priesthood	Hebrews 7:26,27; 9:7	5. Sinless priest
6. Limited-by-death priesthood	Hebrews 7:16,17,23,24	6. Forever priesthood
7. Daily sacrifices	Hebrews 7:27; 9:12,25,26; 10:9,10,12	7. Once-for-all sacrifice
8. Animal sacrifices	Hebrews 9:11–15,26; 10:4–10,19	8. Sacrifice of God's Son
9. Ongoing sacrifices	Hebrews 10:11–14,18	9. Sacrifices no longer needed
10. One-year atonement	Hebrews 7:25; 9:12,15; 10:1–4,12	10. Eternal propitiation

FEBRUARY 18

Leviticus 7:1–8:36

7 'Likewise this *is* the law of the trespass offering (it *is* most holy): 2In the place where they kill the burnt offering they shall kill the trespass offering. And its blood he shall sprinkle all around on the altar. 3And he shall offer from it all its fat. The fat tail and the fat that covers the entrails, 4the two kidneys and the fat that *is* on them by the flanks, and the fatty lobe *attached* to the liver above the kidneys, he shall remove; 5and the priest shall burn them on the altar *as* an offering made by fire to the LORD. It *is* a trespass offering. 6Every male among the priests may eat it. It shall be eaten in a holy place. It *is* most holy. 7The trespass offering *is* like the sin offering; *there is* one law for them both: the priest who makes atonement with it shall have *it*. 8And the priest who offers anyone's burnt offering, that priest shall have for himself the skin of the burnt offering which he has offered. 9Also every grain offering that is baked in the oven and all that is prepared in the covered pan, or in a pan, shall be the priest's who offers it. 10Every grain offering, *whether* mixed with oil or dry, shall belong to all the sons of Aaron, to one *as much* as the other.

11'This *is* the law of the sacrifice of peace offerings which he shall offer to the LORD: 12If he offers it for a thanksgiving, then he shall offer, with the sacrifice of thanksgiving, unleavened cakes mixed with oil, unleavened wafers anointed with oil, or cakes of blended flour mixed with oil. 13Besides the cakes, *as* his offering he shall offer leavened bread with the sacrifice of thanksgiving of his peace offering. 14And from it he shall offer one cake from each offering *as* a heave offering to the LORD. It shall belong to the priest who sprinkles the blood of the peace offering.

15'The flesh of the sacrifice of his peace offering for thanksgiving shall be eaten the same day it is offered. He shall not leave any of it until morning. 16But if the sacrifice of his offering *is* a vow or a voluntary offering, it shall be eaten the same day that he offers his sacrifice; but on the next day the remainder of it also may be eaten; 17the remainder of the flesh of the sacrifice on the third day must be burned with fire. 18And if *any* of the flesh of the sacrifice of his peace offering is eaten at all on the third day, it shall not be accepted, nor shall it be imputed to him; it shall be an abomination *to* him who offers it, and the person who eats of it shall bear guilt.

19'The flesh that touches any unclean thing shall not be eaten. It shall be burned with fire. And as for the *clean* flesh, all who are clean may eat of it. 20But the person who eats the flesh of the sacrifice of the peace offering that *belongs* to the LORD, while he is unclean, that person shall be cut off from his people. 21Moreover the person who touches any unclean thing, *such as* human uncleanness, *an* unclean

animal, or any abominable unclean thing, and
who eats the flesh of the sacrifice of the peace
offering that *belongs* to the LORD, that person
shall be cut off from his people.' "
[22]And the LORD spoke to Moses, saying,
[23]"Speak to the children of Israel, saying: 'You
shall not eat any fat, of ox or sheep or goat.
[24]And the fat of an animal that dies *naturally,*
and the fat of what is torn by wild beasts, may
be used in any other way; but you shall by no
means eat it. [25]For whoever eats the fat of the
animal of which men offer an offering made
by fire to the LORD, the person who eats *it*
shall be cut off from his people. [26]Moreover
you shall not eat any blood in any of your
dwellings, *whether* of bird or beast. [27]Whoever
eats any blood, that person shall be cut off
from his people.' "
[28]Then the LORD spoke to Moses, saying,
[29]"Speak to the children of Israel, saying: 'He
who offers the sacrifice of his peace offering
to the LORD shall bring his offering to the
LORD from the sacrifice of his peace offering.
[30]His own hands shall bring the offerings made
by fire to the LORD. The fat with the breast he
shall bring, that the breast may be waved *as* a
wave offering before the LORD. [31]And the priest
shall burn the fat on the altar, but the breast
shall be Aaron's and his sons'. [32]Also the right
thigh you shall give to the priest *as* a heave
offering from the sacrifices of your peace
offerings. [33]He among the sons of Aaron, who
offers the blood of the peace offering and the
fat, shall have the right thigh for *his* part. [34]For
the breast of the wave offering and the thigh
of the heave offering I have taken from the
children of Israel, from the sacrifices of their
peace offerings, and I have given them to
Aaron the priest and to his sons from the children of Israel by a statute forever.' "
[35]This *is* the consecrated portion for Aaron
and his sons, from the offerings made by fire
to the LORD, on the day when *Moses* presented
them to minister to the LORD as priests. [36]The
LORD commanded this to be given to them by
the children of Israel, on the day that He
anointed them, *by* a statute forever throughout
their generations.
[37]This *is* the law of the burnt offering, the
grain offering, the sin offering, the trespass
offering, the consecrations, and the sacrifice
of the peace offering, [38]which the LORD commanded Moses on Mount Sinai, on the day
when He commanded the children of Israel to
offer their offerings to the LORD in the
Wilderness of Sinai.
8 And the LORD spoke to Moses, saying:
[2]"Take Aaron and his sons with him, and
the garments, the anointing oil, a bull as the sin
offering, two rams, and a basket of unleavened
bread; [3]and gather all the congregation together
at the door of the tabernacle of meeting."
[4]So Moses did as the LORD commanded him.
And the congregation was gathered together
at the door of the tabernacle of meeting. [5]And
Moses said to the congregation, "This *is* what
the LORD commanded to be done."
[6]Then Moses brought Aaron and his sons
and washed them with water. [7]And he put the
tunic on him, girded him with the sash,
clothed him with the robe, and put the ephod
on him; and he girded him with the intricately
woven band of the ephod, and with it tied *the
ephod* on him. [8]Then he put the breastplate on
him, and he put the Urim and the Thummim
in the breastplate. [9]And he put the turban on
his head. Also on the turban, on its front, he
put the golden plate, the holy crown, as the
LORD had commanded Moses.
[10]Also Moses took the anointing oil, and
anointed the tabernacle and all that *was* in it,
and consecrated them. [11]He sprinkled some of
it on the altar seven times, anointed the altar
and all its utensils, and the laver and its base,
to consecrate them. [12]And he poured some of
the anointing oil on Aaron's head and anointed
him, to consecrate him.
[13]Then Moses brought Aaron's sons and put
tunics on them, girded them with sashes, and
put hats on them, as the LORD had commanded
Moses.
[14]And he brought the bull for the sin offering. Then Aaron and his sons laid their hands
on the head of the bull for the sin offering,
[15]and Moses killed *it*. Then he took the blood,
and put *some* on the horns of the altar all
around with his finger, and purified the altar.
And he poured the blood at the base of the
altar, and consecrated it, to make atonement
for it. [16]Then he took all the fat that *was* on the
entrails, the fatty lobe *attached to* the liver, and
the two kidneys with their fat, and Moses
burned *them* on the altar. [17]But the bull, its hide,
its flesh, and its offal, he burned with fire outside the camp, as the LORD had commanded
Moses.
[18]Then he brought the ram as the burnt
offering. And Aaron and his sons laid their
hands on the head of the ram, [19]and Moses
killed *it*. Then he sprinkled the blood all
around on the altar. [20]And he cut the ram into
pieces; and Moses burned the head, the
pieces, and the fat. [21]Then he washed the
entrails and the legs in water. And Moses
burned the whole ram on the altar. It *was* a
burnt sacrifice for a sweet aroma, an offering

8:23,24 right ear…right hand…right foot. Using a part to represent the whole, Aaron and his sons were consecrated to listen to God's holy Word, to carry out His holy assignments, and to live holy lives.

made by fire to the LORD, as the LORD had
commanded Moses.
22And he brought the second ram, the ram
of consecration. Then Aaron and his sons laid
their hands on the head of the ram, 23and Moses killed *it.* Also he took *some* of its blood and
put it on the tip of Aaron's right ear, on the
thumb of his right hand, and on the big toe of
his right foot. 24Then he brought Aaron's sons.
And Moses put *some* of the blood on the tips of
their right ears, on the thumbs of their right
hands, and on the big toes of their right feet.
And Moses sprinkled the blood all around on
the altar. 25Then he took the fat and the fat tail,
all the fat that *was* on the entrails, the fatty
lobe *attached to* the liver, the two kidneys and
their fat, and the right thigh; 26and from the
basket of unleavened bread that was before
the LORD he took one unleavened cake, a cake
of bread *anointed with* oil, and one wafer, and
put *them* on the fat and on the right thigh;
27and he put all *these* in Aaron's hands and in
his sons' hands, and waved them *as* a wave
offering before the LORD. 28Then Moses took
them from their hands and burned *them* on
the altar, on the burnt offering. They *were* consecration offerings for a sweet aroma. That
was an offering made by fire to the LORD.
29And Moses took the breast and waved it *as* a
wave offering before the LORD. It was Moses'
part of the ram of consecration, as the LORD
had commanded Moses.
30Then Moses took some of the anointing oil
and some of the blood which *was* on the altar,
and sprinkled *it* on Aaron, on his garments, on
his sons, and on the garments of his sons with
him; and he consecrated Aaron, his garments,
his sons, and the garments of his sons with him.
31And Moses said to Aaron and his sons,
"Boil the flesh *at* the door of the tabernacle of
meeting, and eat it there with the bread that *is*
in the basket of consecration offerings, as I
commanded, saying, 'Aaron and his sons shall
eat it.' 32What remains of the flesh and of the
bread you shall burn with fire. 33And you shall
not go outside the door of the tabernacle of
meeting *for* seven days, until the days of your
consecration are ended. For seven days he
shall consecrate you. 34As he has done this
day, *so* the LORD has commanded to do, to
make atonement for you. 35Therefore you shall
stay *at* the door of the tabernacle of meeting
day and night for seven days, and keep the
charge of the LORD, so that you may not die;
for so I have been commanded." 36So Aaron
and his sons did all the things that the LORD
had commanded by the hand of Moses.

Psalm 24:7–10

7 Lift up your heads, O you gates!
And be lifted up, you
everlasting doors!
And the King of glory shall come in.
8 Who *is* this King of glory?
The LORD strong and mighty,
The LORD mighty in battle.
9 Lift up your heads, O you gates!
Lift up, you everlasting doors!
And the King of glory shall come in.
10 Who is this King of glory?
The LORD of hosts,
He is the King of glory. Selah

Proverbs 9:10–12

10 "The fear of the LORD *is* the beginning
of wisdom,
And the knowledge of the Holy One *is*
understanding.
11 For by me your days will be multiplied,
And years of life will be added to you.
12 If you are wise, you are wise
for yourself,
And *if* you scoff, you will bear
it alone."

Mark 1:1–22

1 The beginning of the gospel of Jesus Christ,
the Son of God. 2As it is written in the
Prophets:

"Behold, I send My messenger before
Your face,
Who will prepare Your way before
You."
3 *The voice of one crying in the*
wilderness:
'Prepare the way of the LORD;
Make His paths straight.'"

4John came baptizing in the wilderness and
preaching a baptism of repentance for the
remission of sins. 5Then all the land of Judea,
and those from Jerusalem, went out to him
and were all baptized by him in the Jordan
River, confessing their sins.
6Now John was clothed with camel's hair
and with a leather belt around his waist, and

he ate locusts and wild honey. [7]And he
preached, saying, "There comes One after me
who is mightier than I, whose sandal strap I
am not worthy to stoop down and loose. [8]I
indeed baptized you with water, but He will
baptize you with the Holy Spirit."
[9]It came to pass in those days *that* Jesus
came from Nazareth of Galilee, and was baptized by John in the Jordan. [10]And immediately,
coming up from the water, He saw the heavens
parting and the Spirit descending upon Him
like a dove. [11]Then a voice came from heaven,
"You are My beloved Son, in whom I am well
pleased."

1:15 The time is fulfilled. Not time in a chronological sense, but the time for decisive action on God's part. With the arrival of the King, a new era in God's dealings with men had come. **the kingdom of God.** God's sovereign rule over the sphere of salvation; at present in the hearts of His people (Luke 17:21), and in the future, in a literal, earthly kingdom (Rev. 20:4–6). **at hand.** Because the King was present. **Repent, and believe.** Repentance and faith are man's required response to God's gracious offer of salvation (see Acts 20:21).

1:17 Follow Me. Used frequently in the Gospels in reference to discipleship (2:14; 8:34; 10:21; Matt. 4:19; 8:22; 9:9; 10:38; 16:24; 19:21; Luke 9:23,59,61; 18:22; John 1:43; 10:27; 12:26). **fishers of men.** Evangelism was the primary purpose for which Jesus called the apostles, and it remains the central mission for His people (see Matt. 28:19,20; Acts 1:8).

[12]Immediately the Spirit drove Him into the
wilderness. [13]And He was there in the wilderness forty days, tempted by Satan, and was
with the wild beasts; and the angels ministered to Him.
[14]Now after John was put in prison, Jesus
came to Galilee, preaching the gospel of the
kingdom of God, [15]and saying, "The time is fulfilled, and the kingdom of God is at hand.
Repent, and believe in the gospel."
[16]And as He walked by the Sea of Galilee, He
saw Simon and Andrew his brother casting a
net into the sea; for they were fishermen.
[17]Then Jesus said to them, "Follow Me, and I
will make you become fishers of men." [18]They
immediately left their nets and followed Him.
[19]When He had gone a little farther from
there, He saw James the *son* of Zebedee, and
John his brother, who also *were* in the boat
mending their nets. [20]And immediately He called
them, and they left their father Zebedee in the
boat with the hired servants, and went after Him.
[21]Then they went into Capernaum, and
immediately on the Sabbath He entered the
synagogue and taught. [22]And they were astonished at His teaching, for He taught them as
one having authority, and not as the scribes.

1:22 authority. Jesus' authoritative teaching, as the spoken Word of God, was in sharp contrast to that of the scribes (experts in the Old Testament Scriptures), who based their authority largely on that of other rabbis. Jesus' direct, personal, and forceful teaching was so foreign to their experience that those who heard Him were "astonished" (see Titus 2:15).

DAY 18: What was the purpose of John's baptism?

The Gospels all introduce John the Baptist's ministry by quoting Isaiah 40:3 (see Matt. 3:3; Luke 3:4; John 1:23). John was called "My messenger" (Mark 1:2), the divinely promised messenger, sent to prepare the way for the Messiah. In ancient times, a king's envoys would travel ahead of him, making sure the roads were safe and fit for him to travel on, as well as announcing his arrival.

As the last Old Testament prophet and the divinely ordained forerunner of the Messiah, John was the culmination of Old Testament history and prophecy (Luke 16:16) as well as the beginning of the historical record of the gospel of Jesus Christ. Not surprisingly, Jesus designated John as the greatest man who had lived until his time (Matt. 11:11). John's baptism, being the distinctive mark of his ministry (Mark 1:4), differed from the ritual Jewish washings in that it was a one-time act. The Jews performed a similar one-time washing of Gentile proselytes, symbolizing their embracing of the true faith. That Jews would participate in such a rite was a startling admission that they needed to come to God through repentance and faith just like Gentiles.

John's baptism was for true repentance. His ministry was to call Israel to repentance in preparation for the coming of Messiah. Baptism did not produce repentance, but was its result (Matt. 3:7,8). Far more than a mere change of mind or remorse, repentance involves a turning from sin to God (1 Thess. 1:9), which results in righteous living. Genuine repentance is a work of God in the human heart (Acts 11:18). John's rite of baptism did not produce forgiveness of sin (Acts 2:38; 22:16); it was only the outward confession and illustration of the true repentance that results in forgiveness (Luke 24:47; Acts 3:19; 5:31; 2 Cor. 7:10).

FEBRUARY 19

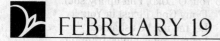

Leviticus 9:1–10:20

9 It came to pass on the eighth day that Moses called Aaron and his sons and the elders of Israel. 2And he said to Aaron, "Take for yourself a young bull as a sin offering and a ram as a burnt offering, without blemish, and offer *them* before the LORD. 3And to the children of Israel you shall speak, saying, 'Take a kid of the goats as a sin offering, and a calf and a lamb, *both* of the first year, without blemish, as a burnt offering, 4also a bull and a ram as peace offerings, to sacrifice before the LORD, and a grain offering mixed with oil; for today the LORD will appear to you.' "

5So they brought what Moses commanded before the tabernacle of meeting. And all the congregation drew near and stood before the LORD. 6Then Moses said, "This *is* the thing which the LORD commanded you to do, and the glory of the LORD will appear to you." 7And Moses said to Aaron, "Go to the altar, offer your sin offering and your burnt offering, and make atonement for yourself and for the people. Offer the offering of the people, and make atonement for them, as the LORD commanded."

8Aaron therefore went to the altar and killed the calf of the sin offering, which *was* for himself. 9Then the sons of Aaron brought the blood to him. And he dipped his finger in the blood, put *it* on the horns of the altar, and poured the blood at the base of the altar. 10But the fat, the kidneys, and the fatty lobe from the liver of the sin offering he burned on the altar, as the LORD had commanded Moses. 11The flesh and the hide he burned with fire outside the camp.

12And he killed the burnt offering; and Aaron's sons presented to him the blood, which he sprinkled all around on the altar. 13Then they presented the burnt offering to him, with its pieces and head, and he burned *them* on the altar. 14And he washed the entrails and the legs, and burned *them* with the burnt offering on the altar.

15Then he brought the people's offering, and took the goat, which *was* the sin offering for the people, and killed it and offered it for sin, like the first one. 16And he brought the burnt offering and offered it according to the prescribed manner. 17Then he brought the grain offering, took a handful of it, and burned *it* on the altar, besides the burnt sacrifice of the morning.

18He also killed the bull and the ram *as* sacrifices of peace offerings, which *were* for the people. And Aaron's sons presented to him the blood, which he sprinkled all around on the altar, 19and the fat from the bull and the ram—the fatty tail, what covers *the entrails* and the kidneys, and the fatty lobe *attached to* the liver; 20and they put the fat on the breasts. Then he burned the fat on the altar; 21but the breasts and the right thigh Aaron waved *as* a wave offering before the LORD, as Moses had commanded.

22Then Aaron lifted his hand toward the people, blessed them, and came down from offering the sin offering, the burnt offering, and peace offerings. 23And Moses and Aaron went into the tabernacle of meeting, and came out and blessed the people. Then the glory of the LORD appeared to all the people, 24and fire came out from before the LORD and consumed the burnt offering and the fat on the altar. When all the people saw *it,* they shouted and fell on their faces.

10 Then Nadab and Abihu, the sons of Aaron, each took his censer and put fire in it, put incense on it, and offered profane fire before the LORD, which He had not commanded them. 2So fire went out from the LORD and devoured them, and they died before the LORD. 3And Moses said to Aaron, "This is what the LORD spoke, saying:

'By those who come near Me
I must be regarded as holy;
And before all the people
I must be glorified.' "

So Aaron held his peace.

4Then Moses called Mishael and Elzaphan, the sons of Uzziel the uncle of Aaron, and said to them, "Come near, carry your brethren

from before the sanctuary out of the camp."
5 So they went near and carried them by their
tunics out of the camp, as Moses had said.
6 And Moses said to Aaron, and to Eleazar
and Ithamar, his sons, "Do not uncover your
heads nor tear your clothes, lest you die, and
wrath come upon all the people. But let your
brethren, the whole house of Israel, bewail the
burning which the LORD has kindled. 7 You
shall not go out from the door of the tabernacle of meeting, lest you die, for the anointing
oil of the LORD *is* upon you." And they did
according to the word of Moses.
8 Then the LORD spoke to Aaron, saying:
9 "Do not drink wine or intoxicating drink, you,
nor your sons with you, when you go into the
tabernacle of meeting, lest you die. *It shall be*
a statute forever throughout your generations,
10 that you may distinguish between holy and
unholy, and between unclean and clean, 11 and
that you may teach the children of Israel all
the statutes which the LORD has spoken to
them by the hand of Moses."
12 And Moses spoke to Aaron, and to
Eleazar and Ithamar, his sons who were left:
"Take the grain offering that remains of the
offerings made by fire to the LORD, and eat it
without leaven beside the altar; for it *is* most
holy. 13 You shall eat it in a holy place, because
it *is* your due and your sons' due, of the sacrifices made by fire to the LORD; for so I have
been commanded. 14 The breast of the wave
offering and the thigh of the heave offering
you shall eat in a clean place, you, your sons,
and your daughters with you; for *they are*
your due and your sons' due, *which* are given
from the sacrifices of peace offerings of the
children of Israel. 15 The thigh of the heave
offering and the breast of the wave offering
they shall bring with the offerings of fat
made by fire, to offer *as* a wave offering
before the LORD. And it shall be yours and
your sons' with you, by a statute forever, as
the LORD has commanded."
16 Then Moses made careful inquiry about
the goat of the sin offering, and there it was—
burned up. And he was angry with Eleazar
and Ithamar, the sons of Aaron *who were* left,
saying, 17 "Why have you not eaten the sin
offering in a holy place, since it *is* most holy,
and *God* has given it to you to bear the guilt of
the congregation, to make atonement for
them before the LORD? 18 See! Its blood was
not brought inside the holy *place;* indeed you
should have eaten it in a holy *place,* as I
commanded."
19 And Aaron said to Moses, "Look, this day
they have offered their sin offering and their
burnt offering before the LORD, and such
things have befallen me! *If* I had eaten the sin
offering today, would it have been accepted in
the sight of the LORD?" 20 So when Moses heard
that, he was content.

Psalm 25:1–7

A Psalm of David.

1 To You, O LORD, I lift up my soul.
2 O my God, I trust in You;
Let me not be ashamed;
Let not my enemies triumph
over me.
3 Indeed, let no one who waits on You
be ashamed;
Let those be ashamed who deal
treacherously without cause.

4 Show me Your ways, O LORD;
Teach me Your paths.
5 Lead me in Your truth and
teach me,
For You *are* the God of my
salvation;
On You I wait all the day.

6 Remember, O LORD, Your tender
mercies and Your lovingkindnesses,
For they *are* from of old.
7 Do not remember the sins
of my youth, nor my
transgressions;
According to Your mercy remember
me,
For Your goodness' sake,
O LORD.

25:6,7 Remember...Do not remember...remember. These are not concerns about God forgetting something, but the psalmist's prayer reminders about God's gracious covenant promises and provisions, all of which are grounded upon His "goodness' sake" (see v. 11, "Your name's sake").

Proverbs 9:13–18

13 A foolish woman is clamorous;
She is simple, and knows nothing.
14 For she sits at the door
of her house,
On a seat *by* the highest places
of the city,
15 To call to those who pass by,
Who go straight on their way:

[16] "Whoever *is* simple, let him turn in
here";
And *as for* him who lacks
understanding, she says to him,
[17] "Stolen water is sweet,
And bread *eaten* in secret
is pleasant."
[18] But he does not know that the dead
are there,
That her guests *are* in the depths
of hell.

Mark 1:23–45

[23]Now there was a man in their synagogue
with an unclean spirit. And he cried out, [24]say-
ing, "Let *us* alone! What have we to do with
You, Jesus of Nazareth? Did You come to
destroy us? I know who You are—the Holy
One of God!"

1:24 What have we to do with You...? Or, possibly, "Why do You interfere with us?" The demon was acutely aware that he and Jesus belonged to two radically different kingdoms, and thus had nothing in common. That the demon used the plural pronoun "we" indicates he spoke for all the demons. **the Holy One of God.** See Psalm 16:10; Daniel 9:24; Luke 4:34; Acts 2:27; 3:14; 4:27; Revelation 3:7. Amazingly, the demon affirmed Jesus' sinlessness and deity—truths which many in Israel denied and still deny.

[25]But Jesus rebuked him, saying, "Be quiet,
and come out of him!" [26]And when the
unclean spirit had convulsed him and cried
out with a loud voice, he came out of him.
[27]Then they were all amazed, so that they
questioned among themselves, saying, "What
is this? What new doctrine *is* this? For with
authority He commands even the unclean
spirits, and they obey Him." [28]And immediately His fame spread throughout all the region
around Galilee.
[29]Now as soon as they had come out of the
synagogue, they entered the house of Simon
and Andrew, with James and John. [30]But Simon's wife's mother lay sick with a fever, and
they told Him about her at once. [31]So He came
and took her by the hand and lifted her up,
and immediately the fever left her. And she
served them.
[32]At evening, when the sun had set, they
brought to Him all who were sick and those
who were demon-possessed. [33]And the whole
city was gathered together at the door. [34]Then
He healed many who were sick with various
diseases, and cast out many demons; and He
did not allow the demons to speak, because
they knew Him.
[35]Now in the morning, having risen a long
while before daylight, He went out and
departed to a solitary place; and there He
prayed. [36]And Simon and those *who were* with
Him searched for Him. [37]When they found
Him, they said to Him, "Everyone is looking
for You."
[38]But He said to them, "Let us go into the
next towns, that I may preach there also,
because for this purpose I have come forth."
[39]And He was preaching in their synagogues
throughout all Galilee, and casting out
demons.
[40]Now a leper came to Him, imploring Him,

1:40 leper. Lepers were considered ceremonially unclean and were outcasts from society (Lev. 13:11). While the Old Testament term for leprosy included other skin diseases, this man may have actually had true leprosy (Hansen's Disease), or else his cure would not have created such a sensation (v. 45).

1:41 compassion. Only Mark records Jesus' emotional reaction to the leper's desperate plight. The Greek word appears only in the synoptic Gospels and (apart from parables) is used only in reference to Jesus. **touched him.** Unlike rabbis, who avoided lepers lest they become ceremonially defiled, Jesus expressed His compassion with a physical gesture.

kneeling down to Him and saying to Him, "If
You are willing, You can make me clean."
[41]Then Jesus, moved with compassion,
stretched out *His* hand and touched him, and
said to him, "I am willing; be cleansed." [42]As
soon as He had spoken, immediately the leprosy left him, and he was cleansed. [43]And He
strictly warned him and sent him away at
once, [44]and said to him, "See that you say nothing to anyone; but go your way, show yourself
to the priest, and offer for your cleansing
those things which Moses commanded, as a
testimony to them."
[45]However, he went out and began to proclaim *it* freely, and to spread the matter, so
that Jesus could no longer openly enter the
city, but was outside in deserted places; and
they came to Him from every direction.

DAY 19: What was the incident with Nadab and Abihu about?

In Leviticus 9:23, it states that "the glory of the LORD appeared." The Bible speaks often of the glory of God—the visible appearance of His beauty and perfection reduced to blazing light. His glory appeared to Moses (Ex. 3:1–6; 24:15–17; 33:18–23). The glory of God also filled the tabernacle (Ex. 40:34), led the people as a pillar of fire and cloud (Ex. 40:35–38), and also filled the temple in Jerusalem (1 Kin. 8:10,11). When Aaron made the first sacrifice in the wilderness, as a priest, the "glory of the LORD appeared to all the people." In these manifestations, God was revealing His righteousness, holiness, truth, wisdom, and grace—the sum of all He is.

Nadab and Abihu were the two oldest sons of Aaron (10:1). The vessel in which the incense was burned in the Holy Place was to be used only for holy purposes. Though the exact infraction is not detailed, instead of taking the incense fire from the bronze altar, they had some other source and thus perpetrated a "profane" act, especially considering the descent of the miraculous fire they had just seen. The same divine fire that accepted the sacrifices (9:24) consumed the errant priests. The sons of Aaron were guilty of violating both requirements of God's absolute standard: "regarded as holy…be glorified" (10:3). That was not unlike the later deaths of Uzzah (2 Sam. 6:6,7) or Ananias and Sapphira (Acts 5:5,10).

FEBRUARY 20

Leviticus 11:1–12:8

11 Now the LORD spoke to Moses and Aaron,
saying to them, 2"Speak to the children of
Israel, saying, 'These *are* the animals which
you may eat among all the animals that *are* on
the earth: 3Among the animals, whatever
divides the hoof, having cloven hooves *and*
chewing the cud—that you may eat. 4Never-
theless these you shall not eat among those
that chew the cud or those that have cloven
hooves: the camel, because it chews the cud
but does not have cloven hooves, is unclean to
you; 5the rock hyrax, because it chews the cud
but does not have cloven hooves, *is* unclean to
you; 6the hare, because it chews the cud but
does not have cloven hooves, *is* unclean to
you; 7and the swine, though it divides the hoof,
having cloven hooves, yet does not chew the
cud, *is* unclean to you. 8Their flesh you shall
not eat, and their carcasses you shall not
touch. They *are* unclean to you.

9"These you may eat of all that *are* in the
water: whatever in the water has fins and
scales, whether in the seas or in the rivers—
that you may eat. 10But all in the seas or in the
rivers that do not have fins and scales, all that
move in the water or any living thing which *is*
in the water, they *are* an abomination to you.
11They shall be an abomination to you; you
shall not eat their flesh, but you shall regard
their carcasses as an abomination. 12Whatever
in the water does not have fins or scales—that
shall be an abomination to you.

13'And these you shall regard as an abomination among the birds; they shall not be eaten,
they *are* an abomination: the eagle, the vulture, the buzzard, 14the kite, and the falcon
after its kind; 15every raven after its kind, 16the
ostrich, the short-eared owl, the sea gull, and
the hawk after its kind; 17the little owl, the fisher owl, and the screech owl; 18the white owl,
the jackdaw, and the carrion vulture; 19the
stork, the heron after its kind, the hoopoe, and
the bat.

20'All flying insects that creep on *all* fours
shall be an abomination to you. 21Yet these you
may eat of every flying insect that creeps on
all fours: those which have jointed legs above
their feet with which to leap on the earth.
22These you may eat: the locust after its kind,
the destroying locust after its kind, the cricket
after its kind, and the grasshopper after its
kind. 23But all *other* flying insects which have
four feet *shall be* an abomination to you.

24'By these you shall become unclean; whoever touches the carcass of any of them shall
be unclean until evening; 25whoever carries
part of the carcass of any of them shall wash
his clothes and be unclean until evening: 26*The
carcass* of any animal which divides the foot,
but is not cloven-hoofed or does not chew the
cud, *is* unclean to you. Everyone who touches
it shall be unclean. 27And whatever goes on its
paws, among all kinds of animals that go on *all*
fours, those *are* unclean to you. Whoever
touches any such carcass shall be unclean
until evening. 28Whoever carries *any such* carcass shall wash his clothes and be unclean
until evening. It *is* unclean to you.

29'These also *shall be* unclean to you among
the creeping things that creep on the earth: the
mole, the mouse, and the large lizard after its
kind; 30the gecko, the monitor lizard, the sand
reptile, the sand lizard, and the chameleon.

31 These *are* unclean to you among all that creep. Whoever touches them when they are dead shall be unclean until evening. 32 Anything on which *any* of them falls, when they are dead shall be unclean, whether *it is* any item of wood or clothing or skin or sack, whatever item *it is,* in which *any* work is done, it must be put in water. And it shall be unclean until evening; then it shall be clean. 33 Any earthen vessel into which *any* of them falls you shall break; and whatever *is* in it shall be unclean: 34 in such a vessel, any edible food upon which water falls becomes unclean, and any drink that may be drunk from it becomes unclean. 35 And everything on which *a part* of *any such* carcass falls shall be unclean; *whether it is* an oven or cooking stove, it shall be broken down; *for* they *are* unclean, and shall be unclean to you. 36 Nevertheless a spring or a cistern, *in which there is* plenty of water, shall be clean, but whatever touches any such carcass becomes unclean. 37 And if a part of *any such* carcass falls on any planting seed which is to be sown, it *remains* clean. 38 But if water is put on the seed, and if *a part* of *any such* carcass falls on it, it *becomes* unclean to you.

39 'And if any animal which you may eat dies, he who touches its carcass shall be unclean until evening. 40 He who eats of its carcass shall wash his clothes and be unclean until evening. He also who carries its carcass shall wash his clothes and be unclean until evening.

41 'And every creeping thing that creeps on the earth *shall be* an abomination. It shall not be eaten. 42 Whatever crawls on its belly, whatever goes on *all* fours, or whatever has many feet among all creeping things that creep on the earth—these you shall not eat, for they *are* an abomination. 43 You shall not make yourselves abominable with any creeping thing that creeps; nor shall you make yourselves unclean with them, lest you be defiled by them. 44 For I *am* the LORD your God. You shall therefore consecrate yourselves, and you shall be holy; for I *am* holy. Neither shall you defile yourselves with any creeping thing that creeps on the earth. 45 For I *am* the LORD who brings you up out of the land of Egypt, to be your God. You shall therefore be holy, for I *am* holy.

46 'This *is* the law of the animals and the birds and every living creature that moves in the waters, and of every creature that creeps on the earth, 47 to distinguish between the unclean and the clean, and between the animal that may be eaten and the animal that may not be eaten.' "

12 Then the LORD spoke to Moses, saying, 2 "Speak to the children of Israel, saying: 'If a woman has conceived, and borne a male child, then she shall be unclean seven days; as in the days of her customary impurity she shall be unclean. 3 And on the eighth day the flesh of his foreskin shall be circumcised. 4 She shall then continue in the blood of *her* purification thirty-three days. She shall not touch any hallowed thing, nor come into the sanctuary until the days of her purification are fulfilled.

5 'But if she bears a female child, then she shall be unclean two weeks, as in her customary impurity, and she shall continue in the blood of *her* purification sixty-six days.

6 'When the days of her purification are fulfilled, whether for a son or a daughter, she shall bring to the priest a lamb of the first year as a burnt offering, and a young pigeon or a turtledove as a sin offering, to the door of the tabernacle of meeting. 7 Then he shall offer it before the LORD, and make atonement for her. And she shall be clean from the flow of her blood. This *is* the law for her who has borne a male or a female.

8 'And if she is not able to bring a lamb, then she may bring two turtledoves or two young pigeons—one as a burnt offering and the other as a sin offering. So the priest shall make atonement for her, and she will be clean.' "

Psalm 25:8–15

8 Good and upright *is* the LORD;
Therefore He teaches sinners in the way.
9 The humble He guides in justice,
And the humble He teaches His way.
10 All the paths of the LORD *are* mercy and truth,
To such as keep His covenant and His testimonies.
11 For Your name's sake, O LORD,
Pardon my iniquity, for it *is* great.

12 Who *is* the man that fears the LORD?
Him shall He teach in the way He chooses.
13 He himself shall dwell in prosperity,
And his descendants shall inherit the earth.
14 The secret of the LORD *is* with those who fear Him,
And He will show them His covenant.
15 My eyes *are* ever toward the LORD,
For He shall pluck my feet out of the net.

Proverbs 10:1–3

10 The proverbs of Solomon:

A wise son makes a glad father,
But a foolish son *is* the grief of his mother.

2 Treasures of wickedness
profit nothing,
But righteousness delivers from
death.
3 The LORD will not allow the righteous
soul to famish,
But He casts away the desire of the
wicked.

Mark 2:1–28

2 And again He entered Capernaum after
some days, and it was heard that He was in
the house. 2Immediately many gathered
together, so that there was no longer room to
receive *them,* not even near the door. And He
preached the word to them. 3Then they came
to Him, bringing a paralytic who was carried
by four *men.* 4And when they could not come
near Him because of the crowd, they uncovered the roof where He was. So when they had
broken through, they let down the bed on
which the paralytic was lying.
5When Jesus saw their faith, He said to the
paralytic, "Son, your sins are forgiven you."

2:5 When Jesus saw their faith. The aggressive, persistent effort of the paralytic's friends was visible evidence of their faith in Christ to heal. **"Son, your sins are forgiven you."** Many Jews in that day believed that all disease and affliction was a direct result of one's sins. This paralytic may have believed that as well; thus he would have welcomed forgiveness of his sins before healing. The Greek verb for "are forgiven" refers to sending or driving away (see Ps. 103:12; Jer. 31:34; Mic. 7:19). Thus Jesus dismissed the man's sin and freed him from the guilt of it.

6And some of the scribes were sitting there
and reasoning in their hearts, 7"Why does this
Man speak blasphemies like this? Who can
forgive sins but God alone?"
8But immediately, when Jesus perceived in
His spirit that they reasoned thus within themselves, He said to them, "Why do you reason
about these things in your hearts? 9Which is
easier, to say to the paralytic, '*Your* sins are
forgiven you,' or to say, 'Arise, take up your
bed and walk'? 10But that you may know that
the Son of Man has power on earth to forgive
sins"—He said to the paralytic, 11"I say to you,
arise, take up your bed, and go to your house."
12Immediately he arose, took up the bed, and
went out in the presence of them all, so that all
were amazed and glorified God, saying, "We
never saw *anything* like this!"
13Then He went out again by the sea; and
all the multitude came to Him, and He taught
them. 14As He passed by, He saw Levi the *son*
of Alphaeus sitting at the tax office. And He
said to him, "Follow Me." So he arose and
followed Him.
15Now it happened, as He was dining in
Levi's house, that many tax collectors and sinners also sat together with Jesus and His disciples; for there were many, and they followed
Him. 16And when the scribes and Pharisees
saw Him eating with the tax collectors and
sinners, they said to His disciples, "How *is it*
that He eats and drinks with tax collectors
and sinners?"
17When Jesus heard *it,* He said to them,
"Those who are well have no need of a
physician, but those who are sick. I did not
come to call *the* righteous, but sinners, to
repentance."
18The disciples of John and of the
Pharisees were fasting. Then they came and
said to Him, "Why do the disciples of John
and of the Pharisees fast, but Your disciples
do not fast?"
19And Jesus said to them, "Can the friends of
the bridegroom fast while the bridegroom is
with them? As long as they have the bridegroom with them they cannot fast. 20But the
days will come when the bridegroom will be
taken away from them, and then they will fast
in those days. 21No one sews a piece of
unshrunk cloth on an old garment; or else the
new piece pulls away from the old, and the
tear is made worse. 22And no one puts new
wine into old wineskins; or else the new wine
bursts the wineskins, the wine is spilled, and
the wineskins are ruined. But new wine must
be put into new wineskins."

2:24 what is not lawful on the Sabbath. Rabbinical tradition had interpreted the rubbing of grain in the hands (see Luke 6:1) as a form of threshing and forbidden it. Reaping for profit on the Sabbath was forbidden by Mosaic Law (Ex. 34:21), but that was obviously not the situation here. Actually the Pharisees' charge was itself sinful since they were holding their tradition on a par with God's Word.

2:27 The Sabbath was made for man. God instituted the Sabbath to benefit man by giving him a day to rest from his labors and to be a blessing to him. The Pharisees turned it into a burden and made man a slave to their myriad of man-made regulations.

2:28 also Lord of the Sabbath. Jesus claimed He was greater than the Sabbath, and thus was God. Based on that authority, Jesus could in fact reject the Pharisaic regulations concerning the Sabbath and restore God's original intention for Sabbath observance to be a blessing not a burden.

[23]Now it happened that He went through the
grainfields on the Sabbath; and as they went
His disciples began to pluck the heads of grain.
[24]And the Pharisees said to Him, "Look, why do
they do what is not lawful on the Sabbath?"
[25]But He said to them, "Have you never
read what David did when he was in need
and hungry, he and those with him: [26]how he
went into the house of God *in the days* of
Abiathar the high priest, and ate the showbread, which is not lawful to eat except for
the priests, and also gave some to those who
were with him?"
[27]And He said to them, "The Sabbath was
made for man, and not man for the Sabbath.
[28]Therefore the Son of Man is also Lord of the
Sabbath."

DAY 20: Does God expect us to be holy?

In Leviticus 11:44,45, God says "consecrate yourselves, and you shall be holy; for I am holy." In all of this, God is teaching His people to live antithetically. That is, He is using these clean and unclean distinctions to separate Israel from other idolatrous nations who have no such restrictions, and He is illustrating by these prescriptions that His people must learn to live His way. Through dietary laws and rituals, God is teaching them the reality of living His way in everything. They are being taught to obey God in every seemingly mundane area of life, so as to learn how crucial obedience is. Sacrifices, rituals, diet, and even clothing and cooking are all carefully ordered by God to teach them that they are to live differently from everyone else. This is to be an external illustration for the separation from sin in their hearts. Because the Lord is their God, they are to be utterly distinct.

In v. 44, for the first time the statement "I am the LORD your God" is made as a reason for the required separation and holiness. After this verse, that phrase is mentioned about 50 more times in this book alone, along with the equally instructive claim, "I am holy." Because God is holy and is their God, the people are to be holy in outward ceremonial behavior as an external expression of the greater necessity of heart holiness. The connection between ceremonial holiness carries over into personal holiness. The only motivation given for all these laws is to learn to be holy because God is holy. The holiness theme is central to Leviticus (see 10:3; 19:2; 20:7,26; 21:6–8).

FEBRUARY 21

Leviticus 13:1–59

13 And the LORD spoke to Moses and Aaron,
saying: [2]"When a man has on the skin of
his body a swelling, a scab, or a bright spot,
and it becomes on the skin of his body *like* a
leprous sore, then he shall be brought to Aaron
the priest or to one of his sons the priests. [3]The
priest shall examine the sore on the skin of
the body; and if the hair on the sore has turned
white, and the sore appears *to be* deeper than
the skin of his body, it *is* a leprous sore. Then
the priest shall examine him, and pronounce
him unclean. [4]But if the bright spot *is* white on
the skin of his body, and does not appear *to be*
deeper than the skin, and its hair has not
turned white, then the priest shall isolate *the*
one who has the sore seven days. [5]And the priest
shall examine him on the seventh day; and
indeed *if* the sore appears to be as it was, *and*
the sore has not spread on the skin, then the
priest shall isolate him another seven days.
[6]Then the priest shall examine him again on the
seventh day; and indeed *if* the sore has faded,
and the sore has not spread on the skin, then
the priest shall pronounce him clean; it *is only*
a scab, and he shall wash his clothes and be
clean. [7]But if the scab should at all spread over
the skin, after he has been seen by the priest
for his cleansing, he shall be seen by the priest
again. [8]And *if* the priest sees that the scab has
indeed spread on the skin, then the priest
shall pronounce him unclean. It *is* leprosy.
[9]"When the leprous sore is on a person,
then he shall be brought to the priest. [10]And
the priest shall examine *him;* and indeed *if* the

13:2 bright spot. This probably refers to inflammation. **a leprous sore.** This is a term referring to various ancient skin disorders that were sometimes superficial, sometimes serious. It may have included modern leprosy (Hansen's disease). The symptoms described in vv. 2, 6, 10, 18, 30, and 39 are not sufficient for a diagnosis of the clinical condition. For the protection of the people, observation and isolation were demanded for all suspected cases of what could be a contagious disease. This biblical leprosy involved some whiteness (v. 3; Ex. 4:6), which disfigured its victim but did not disable him. Naaman was able to exercise his functions as general of Syria's army, although a leper (2 Kin. 5:1,27). Both Old Testament and New Testament lepers went almost everywhere, indicating that this disease was not the leprosy of today that cripples. A victim of this scaly disease was unclean as long as the infection was partial. Once the body was covered with it, he was clean and could enter the place of worship (see vv. 12–17). Apparently the complete covering meant the contagious period was over. The allusion to a boil (vv. 18–28) with inflamed or raw areas and whitened hairs may refer to a related infection that was contagious. When lepers were cured by Christ, they were neither lame nor deformed. They were never brought on beds. Similar skin conditions are described in vv. 29–37 and vv. 38–44 (some inflammation from infection). The aim of these laws was to protect the people from disease, but more importantly, to inculcate into them by vivid object lessons how God desired purity, holiness, and cleanness among His people.

swelling on the skin *is* white, and it has turned
the hair white, and *there is* a spot of raw flesh
in the swelling, 11it *is* an old leprosy on the skin
of his body. The priest shall pronounce him
unclean, and shall not isolate him, for he *is*
unclean.
12"And if leprosy breaks out all over the skin,
and the leprosy covers all the skin of *the one*
who has the sore, from his head to his foot,
wherever the priest looks, 13then the priest
shall consider; and indeed *if* the leprosy has
covered all his body, he shall pronounce *him*
clean *who has* the sore. It has all turned white.
He *is* clean. 14But when raw flesh appears on
him, he shall be unclean. 15And the priest shall
examine the raw flesh and pronounce him to
be unclean; *for* the raw flesh *is* unclean. It *is*
leprosy. 16Or if the raw flesh changes and turns
white again, he shall come to the priest. 17And
the priest shall examine him; and indeed *if* the
sore has turned white, then the priest shall
pronounce *him* clean *who has* the sore. He *is*
clean.
18"If the body develops a boil in the skin, and
it is healed, 19and in the place of the boil there
comes a white swelling or a bright spot, reddish-white, then it shall be shown to the priest;
20and *if,* when the priest sees it, it indeed appears deeper than the skin, and its hair has
turned white, the priest shall pronounce him
unclean. It *is* a leprous sore which has broken
out of the boil. 21But if the priest examines it,
and indeed *there are* no white hairs in it, and it
is not deeper than the skin, but has faded,
then the priest shall isolate him seven days;
22and if it should at all spread over the skin,
then the priest shall pronounce him unclean.
It *is* a leprous sore. 23But if the bright spot
stays in one place, *and* has not spread, it *is* the
scar of the boil; and the priest shall pronounce
him clean.
24"Or if the body receives a burn on its skin
by fire, and the raw *flesh* of the burn becomes
a bright spot, reddish-white or white, 25then
the priest shall examine it; and indeed *if* the
hair of the bright spot has turned white, and it
appears deeper than the skin, it *is* leprosy broken out in the burn. Therefore the priest shall
pronounce him unclean. It *is* a leprous sore.
26But if the priest examines it, and indeed *there*
are no white hairs in the bright spot, and it *is*
not deeper than the skin, but has faded, then
the priest shall isolate him seven days. 27And
the priest shall examine him on the seventh
day. If it has at all spread over the skin, then
the priest shall pronounce him unclean. It *is* a
leprous sore. 28But if the bright spot stays in
one place, *and* has not spread on the skin, but
has faded, it *is* a swelling from the burn. The
priest shall pronounce him clean, for it *is* the
scar from the burn.
29"If a man or woman has a sore on the head
or the beard, 30then the priest shall examine
the sore; and indeed if it appears deeper than
the skin, *and there is* in it thin yellow hair, then
the priest shall pronounce him unclean. It *is* a
scaly leprosy of the head or beard. 31But if the
priest examines the scaly sore, and indeed it
does not appear deeper than the skin, and
there is no black hair in it, then the priest shall
isolate *the one who has* the scale seven days.
32And on the seventh day the priest shall
examine the sore; and indeed *if* the scale has
not spread, and there is no yellow hair in it,
and the scale does not appear deeper than the
skin, 33he shall shave himself, but the scale he

shall not shave. And the priest shall isolate *the*
one who has the scale another seven days. [34]On
the seventh day the priest shall examine the
scale; and indeed *if* the scale has not spread
over the skin, and does not appear deeper
than the skin, then the priest shall pronounce
him clean. He shall wash his clothes and be
clean. [35]But if the scale should at all spread over
the skin after his cleansing, [36]then the priest
shall examine him; and indeed *if* the scale has
spread over the skin, the priest need not seek
for yellow hair. He *is* unclean. [37]But if the scale
appears to be at a standstill, and there is black
hair grown up in it, the scale has healed. He *is*
clean, and the priest shall pronounce him clean.

[38]"If a man or a woman has bright spots on
the skin of the body, *specifically* white bright
spots, [39]then the priest shall look; and indeed *if*
the bright spots on the skin of the body *are*
dull white, it *is* a white spot *that* grows on the
skin. He *is* clean.

[40]"As for the man whose hair has fallen from
his head, he *is* bald, *but* he *is* clean. [41]He whose
hair has fallen from his forehead, he *is* bald on
the forehead, *but* he *is* clean. [42]And if there is
on the bald head or bald forehead a reddish-
white sore, it *is* leprosy breaking out on his
bald head or his bald forehead. [43]Then the
priest shall examine it; and indeed *if* the
swelling of the sore *is* reddish-white on his
bald head or on his bald forehead, as the
appearance of leprosy on the skin of the body,
[44]he is a leprous man. He *is* unclean. The priest
shall surely pronounce him unclean; his sore
is on his head.

[45]"Now the leper on whom the sore *is,* his
clothes shall be torn and his head bare; and he
shall cover his mustache, and cry, 'Unclean!
Unclean!' [46]He shall be unclean. All the days
he has the sore he shall be unclean. He *is*
unclean, and he shall dwell alone; his dwelling
shall be outside the camp.

[47]"Also, if a garment has a leprous plague in
it, *whether it is* a woolen garment or a linen
garment, [48]whether *it is* in the warp or woof of
linen or wool, whether in leather or in anything made of leather, [49]and if the plague is
greenish or reddish in the garment or in the
leather, whether in the warp or in the woof, or
in anything made of leather, it *is* a leprous
plague and shall be shown to the priest. [50]The
priest shall examine the plague and isolate
that which has the plague seven days. [51]And he
shall examine the plague on the seventh day.
If the plague has spread in the garment, either
in the warp or in the woof, in the leather *or* in
anything made of leather, the plague *is* an active
leprosy. It *is* unclean. [52]He shall therefore burn
that garment in which is the plague, whether
warp or woof, in wool or in linen, or anything
of leather, for it *is* an active leprosy; *the gar-*
ment shall be burned in the fire.

[53]"But if the priest examines *it,* and indeed
the plague has not spread in the garment,
either in the warp or in the woof, or in anything made of leather, [54]then the priest shall
command that they wash *the thing* in which *is*
the plague; and he shall isolate it another
seven days. [55]Then the priest shall examine
the plague after it has been washed; and
indeed *if* the plague has not changed its color,
though the plague has not spread, it *is*
unclean, and you shall burn it in the fire; it
continues eating away, *whether* the damage *is*
outside or inside. [56]If the priest examines *it,*
and indeed the plague has faded after washing
it, then he shall tear it out of the garment,
whether out of the warp or out of the woof, or
out of the leather. [57]But if it appears again in
the garment, either in the warp or in the woof,
or in anything made of leather, it *is* a spreading *plague;* you shall burn with fire that in
which is the plague. [58]And if you wash the garment, either warp or woof, or whatever is
made of leather, if the plague has disappeared
from it, then it shall be washed a second time,
and shall be clean.

[59]"This *is* the law of the leprous plague in a
garment of wool or linen, either in the warp or
woof, or in anything made of leather, to pronounce it clean or to pronounce it unclean."

Psalm 25:16–22

16 Turn Yourself to me, and have mercy
on me,
For I *am* desolate and afflicted.
17 The troubles of my heart have
enlarged;
Bring me out of my distresses!
18 Look on my affliction and my pain,
And forgive all my sins.
19 Consider my enemies, for they are
many;
And they hate me with cruel hatred.
20 Keep my soul, and deliver me;
Let me not be ashamed, for I put my
trust in You.
21 Let integrity and uprightness
preserve me,
For I wait for You.
22 Redeem Israel, O God,
Out of all their troubles!

Proverbs 10:4–5

4 He who has a slack hand becomes poor,
But the hand of the diligent makes rich.

[5] He who gathers in summer
is a wise son;
He who sleeps in harvest *is* a son who
causes shame.

Mark 3:1–19

3 And He entered the synagogue again, and
a man was there who had a withered hand.
[2]So they watched Him closely, whether He
would heal him on the Sabbath, so that they
might accuse Him. [3]And He said to the man
who had the withered hand, "Step forward."
[4]Then He said to them, "Is it lawful on the
Sabbath to do good or to do evil, to save life or
to kill?" But they kept silent. [5]And when He
had looked around at them with anger, being
grieved by the hardness of their hearts, He
said to the man, "Stretch out your hand." And
he stretched *it* out, and his hand was restored
as whole as the other. [6]Then the Pharisees
went out and immediately plotted with the
Herodians against Him, how they might
destroy Him.
[7]But Jesus withdrew with His disciples to
the sea. And a great multitude from Galilee followed Him, and from Judea [8]and Jerusalem
and Idumea and beyond the Jordan; and those
from Tyre and Sidon, a great multitude, when
they heard how many things He was doing,
came to Him. [9]So He told His disciples that a
small boat should be kept ready for Him
because of the multitude, lest they should
crush Him. [10]For He healed many, so that as
many as had afflictions pressed about Him to
touch Him. [11]And the unclean spirits, whenever they saw Him, fell down before Him and
cried out, saying, "You are the Son of God."

3:13 called…those He Himself wanted. The Greek verb "called" stresses that Jesus acted in His own sovereign interest when He chose the 12 disciples (see John 15:16).

3:14 appointed twelve. Christ, by an explicit act of His will, formed a distinct group of 12 men who were among His followers. This new group constituted the foundation of His church (see Eph. 2:20).

3:15 have power. This word is sometimes rendered "authority." Along with the main task of preaching, Jesus gave the 12 the right to expel demons (see Luke 9:1).

[12]But He sternly warned them that they should
not make Him known.
[13]And He went up on the mountain and
called to *Him* those He Himself wanted. And
they came to Him. [14]Then He appointed
twelve, that they might be with Him and that
He might send them out to preach, [15]and to
have power to heal sicknesses and to cast out
demons: [16]Simon, to whom He gave the name
Peter; [17]James the *son* of Zebedee and John the
brother of James, to whom He gave the name
Boanerges, that is, "Sons of Thunder"; [18]An-
drew, Philip, Bartholomew, Matthew,
Thomas, James the *son* of Alphaeus, Thaddaeus, Simon the Cananite; [19]and Judas
Iscariot, who also betrayed Him. And they
went into a house.

DAY 21: How does Jesus display the proper use of anger?

In Mark 3:1-6, Jesus was in a synagogue, where there was a man with a withered hand. This describes a condition of paralysis or deformity from an accident, a disease, or a congenital defect. It became another situation for the Pharisees to "accuse" Him (v. 2) of a violation of the Sabbath—an accusation they could bring before the Sanhedrin.

Jesus countered the Pharisees with a question that elevated the issue at hand from a legal to a moral problem. "Is it lawful on the Sabbath to do good…evil, to save…kill?" Jesus asks (v. 4). He was forcing the Pharisees to examine their tradition regarding the Sabbath to see if it was consistent with God's Old Testament law. Christ used a device common in the Middle East—He framed the issue in terms of clear-cut extremes. The obvious implication is that failure to do good or save a life was wrong and not in keeping with God's original intention for the Sabbath. But the Pharisees kept silent, and by so doing implied that their Sabbath views and practices were false.

Jesus' "anger" (v. 5) with human sin reveals a healthy, moral nature. His reaction was consistent with His divine nature and proved that He is the righteous Son of God. This kind of holy indignation with sinful attitudes and practices was to be more fully demonstrated when Jesus cleansed the temple (see 11:15–18; Matt. 21:12,13; Luke 19:45–48). The "hardness of their hearts" refers to an inability to understand because of a rebellious attitude (Ps. 95:8; Heb. 3:8,15). The Pharisees' hearts were becoming more and more obstinate and unresponsive to the truth (see 16:14; Rom. 9:18).

FEBRUARY 22

Leviticus 14:1–57

14 Then the LORD spoke to Moses, saying,
[2]"This shall be the law of the leper for the
day of his cleansing: He shall be brought to
the priest. [3]And the priest shall go out of the
camp, and the priest shall examine *him;* and
indeed, *if* the leprosy is healed in the leper,
[4]then the priest shall command to take for him
who is to be cleansed two living *and* clean
birds, cedar wood, scarlet, and hyssop. [5]And
the priest shall command that one of the birds
be killed in an earthen vessel over running
water. [6]As for the living bird, he shall take it,
the cedar wood and the scarlet and the hyssop, and dip them and the living bird in the
blood of the bird *that was* killed over the running water. [7]And he shall sprinkle it seven
times on him who is to be cleansed from the
leprosy, and shall pronounce him clean, and
shall let the living bird loose in the open field.
[8]He who is to be cleansed shall wash his
clothes, shave off all his hair, and wash himself
in water, that he may be clean. After that he
shall come into the camp, and shall stay outside his tent seven days. [9]But on the seventh
day he shall shave all the hair off his head and
his beard and his eyebrows—all his hair he
shall shave off. He shall wash his clothes and
wash his body in water, and he shall be clean.
[10]"And on the eighth day he shall take two
male lambs without blemish, one ewe lamb of
the first year without blemish, three-tenths *of
an ephah* of fine flour mixed with oil as a grain
offering, and one log of oil. [11]Then the priest
who makes *him* clean shall present the man
who is to be made clean, and those things,
before the LORD, *at* the door of the tabernacle
of meeting. [12]And the priest shall take one
male lamb and offer it as a trespass offering,
and the log of oil, and wave them *as* a wave
offering before the LORD. [13]Then he shall kill
the lamb in the place where he kills the sin
offering and the burnt offering, in a holy
place; for as the sin offering *is* the priest's, so
is the trespass offering. It *is* most holy. [14]The
priest shall take *some* of the blood of the trespass offering, and the priest shall put *it* on the
tip of the right ear of him who is to be
cleansed, on the thumb of his right hand, and
on the big toe of his right foot. [15]And the priest
shall take *some* of the log of oil, and pour *it* into
the palm of his own left hand. [16]Then the priest
shall dip his right finger in the oil that *is* in his
left hand, and shall sprinkle some of the oil
with his finger seven times before the LORD.
[17]And of the rest of the oil in his hand, the
priest shall put *some* on the tip of the right ear
of him who is to be cleansed, on the thumb of
his right hand, and on the big toe of his right
foot, on the blood of the trespass offering.
[18]The rest of the oil that *is* in the priest's hand
he shall put on the head of him who is to be
cleansed. So the priest shall make atonement
for him before the LORD.

14:18 put on the head. This would not have been understood as an anointing for entry into an office, but rather as a symbolic gesture of cleansing and healing. There could be a connection with the New Testament directive to anoint the sick for healing (Mark 6:13; 16:18; James 5:14).

[19]"Then the priest shall offer the sin offering, and make atonement for him who is to be
cleansed from his uncleanness. Afterward he
shall kill the burnt offering. [20]And the priest
shall offer the burnt offering and the grain
offering on the altar. So the priest shall make
atonement for him, and he shall be clean.
[21]"But if he *is* poor and cannot afford it, then
he shall take one male lamb *as* a trespass
offering to be waved, to make atonement for
him, one-tenth *of an ephah* of fine flour mixed
with oil as a grain offering, a log of oil, [22]and
two turtledoves or two young pigeons, such as
he is able to afford: one shall be a sin offering
and the other a burnt offering. [23]He shall bring
them to the priest on the eighth day for his
cleansing, to the door of the tabernacle of
meeting, before the LORD. [24]And the priest
shall take the lamb of the trespass offering
and the log of oil, and the priest shall wave
them *as* a wave offering before the LORD.
[25]Then he shall kill the lamb of the trespass
offering, and the priest shall take *some* of the
blood of the trespass offering and put *it* on the
tip of the right ear of him who is to be
cleansed, on the thumb of his right hand, and
on the big toe of his right foot. [26]And the priest
shall pour some of the oil into the palm of his
own left hand. [27]Then the priest shall sprinkle
with his right finger *some* of the oil that *is* in
his left hand seven times before the LORD.
[28]And the priest shall put *some* of the oil that *is*
in his hand on the tip of the right ear of him
who is to be cleansed, on the thumb of the

right hand, and on the big toe of his right foot,
on the place of the blood of the trespass offering. [29]The rest of the oil that *is* in the priest's
hand he shall put on the head of him who is to
be cleansed, to make atonement for him
before the LORD. [30]And he shall offer one of the
turtledoves or young pigeons, such as he can
afford— [31]such as he is able to afford, the one
as a sin offering and the other *as* a burnt offering, with the grain offering. So the priest shall
make atonement for him who is to be cleansed
before the LORD. [32]This *is* the law *for one* who
had a leprous sore, who cannot afford the
usual cleansing."

[33]And the LORD spoke to Moses and Aaron,
saying: [34]"When you have come into the land
of Canaan, which I give you as a possession,
and I put the leprous plague in a house in the
land of your possession, [35]and he who owns
the house comes and tells the priest, saying,
'It seems to me that *there is* some plague in the
house,' [36]then the priest shall command that
they empty the house, before the priest goes
into it to examine the plague, that all that *is* in
the house may not be made unclean; and afterward the priest shall go in to examine the
house. [37]And he shall examine the plague; and
indeed *if* the plague *is* on the walls of the
house with ingrained streaks, greenish or reddish, which appear to be deep in the wall,
[38]then the priest shall go out of the house, to
the door of the house, and shut up the house
seven days. [39]And the priest shall come again
on the seventh day and look; and indeed *if* the
plague has spread on the walls of the house,
[40]then the priest shall command that they take
away the stones in which *is* the plague, and
they shall cast them into an unclean place outside the city. [41]And he shall cause the house to
be scraped inside, all around, and the dust that
they scrape off they shall pour out in an
unclean place outside the city. [42]Then they
shall take other stones and put *them* in the
place of *those* stones, and he shall take other
mortar and plaster the house.

[43]"Now if the plague comes back and breaks
out in the house, after he has taken away the
stones, after he has scraped the house, and
after it is plastered, [44]then the priest shall
come and look; and indeed *if* the plague has
spread in the house, it *is* an active leprosy in
the house. It *is* unclean. [45]And he shall break
down the house, its stones, its timber, and all
the plaster of the house, and he shall carry
them outside the city to an unclean place.
[46]Moreover he who goes into the house at all
while it is shut up shall be unclean until
evening. [47]And he who lies down in the house
shall wash his clothes, and he who eats in the
house shall wash his clothes.

[48]"But if the priest comes in and examines *it,*
and indeed the plague has not spread in the
house after the house was plastered, then the
priest shall pronounce the house clean,
because the plague is healed. [49]And he shall
take, to cleanse the house, two birds, cedar
wood, scarlet, and hyssop. [50]Then he shall kill
one of the birds in an earthen vessel over running water; [51]and he shall take the cedar wood,
the hyssop, the scarlet, and the living bird,
and dip them in the blood of the slain bird and
in the running water, and sprinkle the house
seven times. [52]And he shall cleanse the house
with the blood of the bird and the running
water and the living bird, with the cedar wood,
the hyssop, and the scarlet. [53]Then he shall let
the living bird loose outside the city in the
open field, and make atonement for the house,
and it shall be clean.

[54]"This *is* the law for any leprous sore and
scale, [55]for the leprosy of a garment and of a
house, [56]for a swelling and a scab and a bright
spot, [57]to teach when *it is* unclean and when *it*
is clean. This *is* the law of leprosy."

Psalm 26:1–5

A Psalm of David.

Vindicate me, O LORD,
For I have walked in my integrity.
I have also trusted in the LORD;
I shall not slip.

26:1 Vindicate me. Literally, "Judge me!" This refers to exoneration of some false accusations and/or charges under the protection of the covenant stipulations of the theocratic law (see Pss. 7:8; 35:24; 43:1). **my integrity.** Again, this is not a claim to perfection, but of innocence, particularly as viewed within the context of ungrounded "legal" charges (see Ps. 7:8; Prov. 10:9; 19:1; 20:7; 28:6).

2 Examine me, O LORD, and prove me;
Try my mind and my heart.
3 For Your lovingkindness *is* before
my eyes,
And I have walked in Your truth.
4 I have not sat with idolatrous mortals,
Nor will I go in with hypocrites.
5 I have hated the assembly
of evildoers,
And will not sit with the wicked.

Proverbs 10:6–7

6 Blessings *are* on the head
of the righteous,
But violence covers the mouth of the
wicked.
7 The memory of the righteous *is*
blessed,
But the name of the wicked will rot.

Mark 3:20–35

[20]Then the multitude came together again,
so that they could not so much as eat bread.
[21]But when His own people heard *about this,*
they went out to lay hold of Him, for they said,
"He is out of His mind."
[22]And the scribes who came down from Jerusalem said, "He has Beelzebub," and, "By
the ruler of the demons He casts out demons."
[23]So He called them to *Himself* and said to
them in parables: "How can Satan cast out Satan? [24]If a kingdom is divided against itself,
that kingdom cannot stand. [25]And if a house is
divided against itself, that house cannot stand.
[26]And if Satan has risen up against himself, and
is divided, he cannot stand, but has an end.
[27]No one can enter a strong man's house and
plunder his goods, unless he first binds the
strong man. And then he will plunder his house.
[28]"Assuredly, I say to you, all sins will be forgiv-
en the sons of men, and whatever blasphemies
they may utter; [29]but he who blasphemes against
the Holy Spirit never has forgiveness, but is subject to eternal condemnation"— [30]because they
said, "He has an unclean spirit."
[31]Then His brothers and His mother came,
and standing outside they sent to Him, calling
Him. [32]And a multitude was sitting around
Him; and they said to Him, "Look, Your mother and Your brothers are outside seeking You."
[33]But He answered them, saying, "Who is
My mother, or My brothers?" [34]And He looked
around in a circle at those who sat about Him,
and said, "Here are My mother and My brothers! [35]For whoever does the will of God is My
brother and My sister and mother."

3:21 His own people. In Greek, this expression was used in various ways to describe someone's friends or close associates. In the strictest sense, it meant family, which is probably the best understanding here. **lay hold of Him.** Mark used this same term elsewhere to mean the arrest of a person (6:17; 12:12; 14:1,44,46,51). Jesus' relatives evidently heard the report of v. 20 and came to Capernaum to restrain Him from His many activities and bring Him under their care and control, all supposedly for His own good. **out of His mind.** Jesus' family could only explain His unconventional lifestyle, with its willingness for others always to impose on Him, by saying He was irrational or had lost His mind.

3:35 Jesus made a decisive and comprehensive statement on true Christian discipleship. Such discipleship involves a spiritual relationship that transcends the physical family and is open to all who are empowered by the Spirit of God to come to Christ in repentance and faith and enabled to live a life of obedience to God's Word.

DAY 22: How did Mark come to write one of the gospels if he wasn't one of the original disciples?

Although Mark was not one of the original apostles of Jesus, he was involved in many of the events recorded in the New Testament. He traveled as a close companion of the apostle Peter and appears repeatedly throughout the Book of Acts, where he is known as "John whose surname was Mark" (Acts 12:12,25; 15:37,39). When Peter was miraculously freed from prison, his first action was to go to Mark's mother's home in Jerusalem (Acts 12:12).

John Mark was also a cousin of Barnabas (Col. 4:10), and he joined Paul and Barnabas on their first missionary journey (Acts 12:25; 13:5). But Mark deserted the mission team while in Perga and returned to Jerusalem (Acts 13:13). Later, when Barnabas wanted to give Mark another opportunity to travel with Paul's second missionary team, Paul refused. The resulting friction between Paul and Barnabas led to their separation (Acts 15:38-40).

Eventually, Mark's youthful vacillation gave way to great strength and maturity. In time, he proved himself even to the apostle Paul. When Paul wrote to the Colossians, he told them that if John Mark came, they were to welcome him (Col. 4:10). Paul even listed Mark as a fellow worker (Philem. 24). Later, Paul told Timothy, "Get Mark and bring him with you, for he is useful to me for ministry" (2 Tim. 4:11).

John Mark's restoration to useful ministry and preparation for writing his Gospel was due, in part, to his extended close relationship with Peter (1 Pet. 5:13). The older apostle was no stranger to failure, and his influence on the younger man was no doubt instrumental. Mark grew out of the instability of his youth and into the strength and maturity he would need for the work to which God had called him. Mark's Gospel represents primarily Peter's version of the life of Jesus.

FEBRUARY 23

Leviticus 15:1–16:34

15 And the LORD spoke to Moses and
Aaron, saying, [2]"Speak to the children of
Israel, and say to them: 'When any man has a
discharge from his body, his discharge *is*
unclean. [3]And this shall be his uncleanness in
regard to his discharge—whether his body
runs with his discharge, or his body is
stopped up by his discharge, it *is* his uncleanness. [4]Every bed is unclean on which he who
has the discharge lies, and everything on
which he sits shall be unclean. [5]And whoever
touches his bed shall wash his clothes and
bathe in water, and be unclean until evening.
[6]He who sits on anything on which he who has
the discharge sat shall wash his clothes and
bathe in water, and be unclean until evening.
[7]And he who touches the body of him who has
the discharge shall wash his clothes and bathe
in water, and be unclean until evening. [8]If he
who has the discharge spits on him who is
clean, then he shall wash his clothes and
bathe in water, and be unclean until evening.
[9]Any saddle on which he who has the discharge rides shall be unclean. [10]Whoever
touches anything that was under him shall be
unclean until evening. He who carries *any of*
those things shall wash his clothes and bathe
in water, and be unclean until evening. [11]And
whomever the one who has the discharge
touches, and has not rinsed his hands in
water, he shall wash his clothes and bathe in
water, and be unclean until evening. [12]The vessel of earth that he who has the discharge
touches shall be broken, and every vessel of
wood shall be rinsed in water.

[13]'And when he who has a discharge is
cleansed of his discharge, then he shall count
for himself seven days for his cleansing, wash
his clothes, and bathe his body in running
water; then he shall be clean. [14]On the eighth
day he shall take for himself two turtledoves
or two young pigeons, and come before the
LORD, to the door of the tabernacle of meeting,
and give them to the priest. [15]Then the priest
shall offer them, the one *as* a sin offering and
the other *as* a burnt offering. So the priest
shall make atonement for him before the LORD
because of his discharge.

[16]'If any man has an emission of semen, then
he shall wash all his body in water, and be
unclean until evening. [17]And any garment and
any leather on which there is semen, it shall
be washed with water, and be unclean until
evening. [18]Also, when a woman lies with a
man, and *there is* an emission of semen, they
shall bathe in water, and be unclean until
evening.

[19]'If a woman has a discharge, *and* the discharge from her body is blood, she shall be
set apart seven days; and whoever touches
her shall be unclean until evening. [20]Every-
thing that she lies on during her impurity shall
be unclean; also everything that she sits on
shall be unclean. [21]Whoever touches her bed
shall wash his clothes and bathe in water, and
be unclean until evening. [22]And whoever
touches anything that she sat on shall wash
his clothes and bathe in water, and be unclean
until evening. [23]If *anything* is on *her* bed or on
anything on which she sits, when he touches it,
he shall be unclean until evening. [24]And if any
man lies with her at all, so that her impurity is
on him, he shall be unclean seven days; and
every bed on which he lies shall be unclean.

[25]'If a woman has a discharge of blood for
many days, other than at the time of her *customary* impurity, or if it runs beyond her *usual time
of* impurity, all the days of her unclean discharge shall be as the days of her *customary*
impurity. She *shall be* unclean. [26]Every bed on
which she lies all the days of her discharge
shall be to her as the bed of her impurity; and
whatever she sits on shall be unclean, as the
uncleanness of her impurity. [27]Whoever touches those things shall be unclean; he shall wash
his clothes and bathe in water, and be unclean
until evening.

[28]'But if she is cleansed of her discharge,

then she shall count for herself seven days,
and after that she shall be clean. [29]And on the
eighth day she shall take for herself two turtledoves or two young pigeons, and bring
them to the priest, to the door of the tabernacle of meeting. [30]Then the priest shall offer the
one *as* a sin offering and the other *as* a burnt
offering, and the priest shall make atonement
for her before the LORD for the discharge of
her uncleanness.

[31]"Thus you shall separate the children of
Israel from their uncleanness, lest they die in
their uncleanness when they defile My tabernacle that *is* among them. [32]This *is* the law for
one who has a discharge, and *for him* who
emits semen and is unclean thereby, [33]and for
her who is indisposed because of her *customary* impurity, and for one who has a discharge,
either man or woman, and for him who lies
with her who is unclean.' "

16 Now the LORD spoke to Moses after the
death of the two sons of Aaron, when
they offered *profane fire* before the LORD, and
died; [2]and the LORD said to Moses: "Tell Aaron
your brother not to come at *just* any time into
the Holy *Place* inside the veil, before the mercy
seat which *is* on the ark, lest he die; for I will
appear in the cloud above the mercy seat.

[3]"Thus Aaron shall come into the Holy *Place:*
with *the blood of* a young bull as a sin offering,
and *of* a ram as a burnt offering. [4]He shall put
the holy linen tunic and the linen trousers on
his body; he shall be girded with a linen sash,
and with the linen turban he shall be attired.
These *are* holy garments. Therefore he shall
wash his body in water, and put them on. [5]And
he shall take from the congregation of the
children of Israel two kids of the goats as a sin
offering, and one ram as a burnt offering.

[6]"Aaron shall offer the bull as a sin offering,
which *is* for himself, and make atonement for
himself and for his house. [7]He shall take the
two goats and present them before the LORD
at the door of the tabernacle of meeting. [8]Then
Aaron shall cast lots for the two goats: one lot
for the LORD and the other lot for the scapegoat. [9]And Aaron shall bring the goat on which
the LORD's lot fell, and offer it *as* a sin offering.
[10]But the goat on which the lot fell to be the
scapegoat shall be presented alive before the
LORD, to make atonement upon it, *and* to let it
go as the scapegoat into the wilderness.

[11]"And Aaron shall bring the bull of the sin
offering, which is for himself, and make atonement for himself and for his house, and shall
kill the bull as the sin offering which *is* for
himself. [12]Then he shall take a censer full of
burning coals of fire from the altar before the
LORD, with his hands full of sweet incense
beaten fine, and bring *it* inside the veil. [13]And
he shall put the incense on the fire before the
LORD, that the cloud of incense may cover the
mercy seat that *is* on the Testimony, lest he
die. [14]He shall take some of the blood of the
bull and sprinkle *it* with his finger on the
mercy seat on the east *side;* and before the
mercy seat he shall sprinkle some of the blood
with his finger seven times.

[15]"Then he shall kill the goat of the sin offering, which *is* for the people, bring its blood inside the veil, do with that blood as he did with
the blood of the bull, and sprinkle it on the
mercy seat and before the mercy seat. [16]So he
shall make atonement for the Holy *Place,*
because of the uncleanness of the children of
Israel, and because of their transgressions, for
all their sins; and so he shall do for the tabernacle of meeting which remains among them
in the midst of their uncleanness. [17]There shall
be no man in the tabernacle of meeting when
he goes in to make atonement in the Holy
Place, until he comes out, that he may make
atonement for himself, for his household, and
for all the assembly of Israel. [18]And he shall go
out to the altar that *is* before the LORD, and
make atonement for it, and shall take some of
the blood of the bull and some of the blood of
the goat, and put it on the horns of the altar all
around. [19]Then he shall sprinkle some of the
blood on it with his finger seven times, cleanse
it, and consecrate it from the uncleanness of
the children of Israel.

[20]"And when he has made an end of atoning
for the Holy *Place,* the tabernacle of meeting,
and the altar, he shall bring the live goat.
[21]Aaron shall lay both his hands on the head of
the live goat, confess over it all the iniquities
of the children of Israel, and all their transgressions, concerning all their sins, putting
them on the head of the goat, and shall send *it*
away into the wilderness by the hand of a suitable man. [22]The goat shall bear on itself all
their iniquities to an uninhabited land; and he
shall release the goat in the wilderness.

16:12 inside the veil. The veil separated all from the holy and consuming presence of God. It was this veil in Herod's temple that was torn open from top to bottom at the death of Christ, signifying access into God's presence through Jesus Christ (see Matt. 27:51; Mark 15:38; Luke 23:45).

16:20–22 This "sin offering of atonement" (Num. 29:11) portrayed Christ's substitutionary sacrifice (vv. 21, 22) with the result that the sinner's sins were removed (v. 22). Christ lived out this representation when He cried from the cross, "My God, My God, why have You forsaken Me?" (Matt. 27:46).

23 "Then Aaron shall come into the tabernacle of meeting, shall take off the linen garments which he put on when he went into the
Holy *Place,* and shall leave them there. 24 And
he shall wash his body with water in a holy
place, put on his garments, come out and offer
his burnt offering and the burnt offering of
the people, and make atonement for himself
and for the people. 25 The fat of the sin offering
he shall burn on the altar. 26 And he who
released the goat as the scapegoat shall wash
his clothes and bathe his body in water, and
afterward he may come into the camp. 27 The
bull *for* the sin offering and the goat *for* the sin
offering, whose blood was brought in to make
atonement in the Holy *Place,* shall be carried
outside the camp. And they shall burn in the
fire their skins, their flesh, and their offal.
28 Then he who burns them shall wash his
clothes and bathe his body in water, and afterward he may come into the camp.
29 "*This* shall be a statute forever for you: In
the seventh month, on the tenth *day* of the
month, you shall afflict your souls, and do no
work at all, *whether* a native of your own country or a stranger who dwells among you. 30 For
on that day *the priest* shall make atonement for
you, to cleanse you, *that* you may be clean from
all your sins before the LORD. 31 It *is* a sabbath of
solemn rest for you, and you shall afflict your
souls. *It is* a statute forever. 32 And the priest,
who is anointed and consecrated to minister as
priest in his father's place, shall make atonement, and put on the linen clothes, the holy
garments; 33 then he shall make atonement for

16:30 clean from all your sins. (See Ps. 103:12; Is. 38:17; Mic. 7:19.) This day provided ceremonial cleansing for one year, and pictured the forgiveness of God available to all who believed and repented. Actual atonement was based on cleansing through the sacrifice of Christ (see Rom. 3:25,26; Heb. 9:15).

the Holy Sanctuary, and he shall make atonement for the tabernacle of meeting and for the
altar, and he shall make atonement for the
priests and for all the people of the assembly.
34 This shall be an everlasting statute for you, to
make atonement for the children of Israel, for
all their sins, once a year." And he did as the
LORD commanded Moses.

Psalm 26:6–12

6 I will wash my hands in innocence;
So I will go about Your altar, O LORD,
7 That I may proclaim with the voice
of thanksgiving,
And tell of all Your wondrous works.
8 LORD, I have loved the habitation
of Your house,
And the place where Your glory dwells.

9 Do not gather my soul with sinners,
Nor my life with bloodthirsty men,
10 In whose hands *is* a sinister scheme,
And whose right hand is full of bribes.
11 But as for me, I will walk in
my integrity;
Redeem me and be merciful to me.
12 My foot stands in an even place;
In the congregations I will bless
the LORD.

Proverbs 10:8

8 The wise in heart will receive
commands,
But a prating fool will fall.

Mark 4:1–20

4 And again He began to teach by the sea.
And a great multitude was gathered to
Him, so that He got into a boat and sat *in it* on
the sea; and the whole multitude was on the
land facing the sea. 2 Then He taught them
many things by parables, and said to them in
His teaching:
3 "Listen! Behold, a sower went out to sow.
4 And it happened, as he sowed, *that* some *seed*
fell by the wayside; and the birds of the air
came and devoured it. 5 Some fell on stony
ground, where it did not have much earth; and
immediately it sprang up because it had no

4:2 parables. A common method of teaching in Judaism, which Jesus employed to conceal the truth from unbelievers while explaining it to His disciples.

depth of earth. 6But when the sun was up it
was scorched, and because it had no root it
withered away. 7And some *seed* fell among
thorns; and the thorns grew up and choked it,
and it yielded no crop. 8But other *seed* fell on
good ground and yielded a crop that sprang
up, increased and produced: some thirtyfold,
some sixty, and some a hundred."
9And He said to them, "He who has ears to
hear, let him hear!"
10But when He was alone, those around Him
with the twelve asked Him about the parable.
11And He said to them, "To you it has been
given to know the mystery of the kingdom of
God; but to those who are outside, all things
come in parables, 12so that

'Seeing they may see and not perceive,
And hearing they may hear and not
understand;
Lest they should turn,
And their sins be forgiven them.' "

13And He said to them, "Do you not understand this parable? How then will you understand all the parables? 14The sower sows the
word. 15And these are the ones by the wayside
where the word is sown. When they hear, Satan comes immediately and takes away the
word that was sown in their hearts. 16These
likewise are the ones sown on stony ground
who, when they hear the word, immediately
receive it with gladness; 17and they have no
root in themselves, and so endure only for a
time. Afterward, when tribulation or persecution arises for the word's sake, immediately
they stumble. 18Now these are the ones sown
among thorns; *they are* the ones who hear the
word, 19and the cares of this world, the deceitfulness of riches, and the desires for other
things entering in choke the word, and it
becomes unfruitful. 20But these are the ones
sown on good ground, those who hear the
word, accept *it,* and bear fruit: some thirtyfold, some sixty, and some a hundred."

DAY 23: What does the parable of the soils warn us about our heart?

Jesus made it clear that as the sower sows his seed, some of those seeds fall to the "wayside" (Mark 4:4)—either a road near a field's edge or a path that traversed a field, both of which were hard surfaces due to constant foot traffic. Other seed falls on "stony ground" (v. 5), where beds of solid rock lie under the surface of good soil. They are a little too deep for the plow to reach, and too shallow to allow a plant to reach water and develop a decent root system in the small amount of soil that covers them. Other seed falls among "thorns" (v. 7)—tough, thistle-bearing weeds that use up the available space, light, and water which good plants need.

Jesus warns in vv. 13-20 that our heart may be hard, like the stony ground, and the "word of God" never takes root in the soul and never transforms our life—there is only a temporary, surface change. Bring along the suffering, trials, and persecutions which result from one's association with God's Word and we fall away (John 8:31; 1 John 2:19). Then there are the "cares of this world," or "the distractions of the age." A preoccupation with the temporal issues of this present age blinds a person to any serious consideration of the gospel (James 4:4; 1 John 2:15,16). And "the deceitfulness of riches" come our way. Not only can money and material possessions not satisfy the desires of the heart or bring the lasting happiness they deceptively promise, but they also blind those who pursue them to eternal, spiritual concerns (1 Tim. 6:9,10).

FEBRUARY 24

Leviticus 17:1–18:30

17 And the LORD spoke to Moses, saying,
2"Speak to Aaron, to his sons, and to all
the children of Israel, and say to them, 'This *is*
the thing which the LORD has commanded,
saying: 3"Whatever man of the house of Israel
who kills an ox or lamb or goat in the camp, or
who kills *it* outside the camp, 4and does not
bring it to the door of the tabernacle of meeting to offer an offering to the LORD before the
tabernacle of the LORD, the guilt of bloodshed
shall be imputed to that man. He has shed
blood; and that man shall be cut off from
among his people, 5to the end that the children
of Israel may bring their sacrifices which they
offer in the open field, that they may bring
them to the LORD at the door of the tabernacle
of meeting, to the priest, and offer them *as*
peace offerings to the LORD. 6And the priest
shall sprinkle the blood on the altar of the
LORD *at* the door of the tabernacle of meeting,
and burn the fat for a sweet aroma to the
LORD. 7They shall no more offer their sacrifices to demons, after whom they have played
the harlot. This shall be a statute forever for
them throughout their generations." '

8“Also you shall say to them: ‘Whatever man
of the house of Israel, or of the strangers who
dwell among you, who offers a burnt offering
or sacrifice, 9and does not bring it to the door
of the tabernacle of meeting, to offer it to the
LORD, that man shall be cut off from among
his people.
10“And whatever man of the house of Israel,
or of the strangers who dwell among you, who
eats any blood, I will set My face against that
person who eats blood, and will cut him off
from among his people. 11For the life of the
flesh *is* in the blood, and I have given it to you
upon the altar to make atonement for your
souls; for it *is* the blood *that* makes atonement
for the soul.’ 12Therefore I said to the children
of Israel, ‘No one among you shall eat blood,
nor shall any stranger who dwells among you
eat blood.’

17:11 life of the flesh is in the blood. This phrase is amplified by "Its blood sustains its life" (17:14). Blood carries life-sustaining elements to all parts of the body; therefore it represents the essence of life. In contrast, the shedding of blood represents the shedding of life, i.e., death (see Gen. 9:4). New Testament references to the shedding of the blood of Jesus Christ are references to His death. **blood that makes atonement.** Since it contains the life, blood is sacred to God. Shed blood (death) from a substitute atones for, or covers, the sinner, who is then allowed to live.

13“Whatever man of the children of Israel, or
of the strangers who dwell among you, who
hunts and catches any animal or bird that may
be eaten, he shall pour out its blood and cover
it with dust; 14for *it is* the life of all flesh. Its
blood sustains its life. Therefore I said to the
children of Israel, ‘You shall not eat the blood
of any flesh, for the life of all flesh is its blood.
Whoever eats it shall be cut off.’
15“And every person who eats what died *nat-*
urally or what was torn *by beasts, whether he is*
a native of your own country or a stranger, he
shall both wash his clothes and bathe in water,
and be unclean until evening. Then he shall be
clean. 16But if he does not wash *them* or bathe
his body, then he shall bear his guilt.”
18 Then the LORD spoke to Moses, saying,
2“Speak to the children of Israel, and say
to them: ‘I am the LORD your God. 3According
to the doings of the land of Egypt, where you
dwelt, you shall not do; and according to the
doings of the land of Canaan, where I am
bringing you, you shall not do; nor shall you
walk in their ordinances. 4You shall observe
My judgments and keep My ordinances, to
walk in them: I *am* the LORD your God. 5You
shall therefore keep My statutes and My judgments, which if a man does, he shall live by
them: I *am* the LORD.
6‘None of you shall approach anyone who is
near of kin to him, to uncover his nakedness:
I *am* the LORD. 7The nakedness of your father
or the nakedness of your mother you shall not
uncover. She *is* your mother; you shall not
uncover her nakedness. 8The nakedness of
your father’s wife you shall not uncover; it *is*
your father’s nakedness. 9The nakedness of
your sister, the daughter of your father, or the
daughter of your mother, *whether* born at
home or elsewhere, their nakedness you shall
not uncover. 10The nakedness of your son’s
daughter or your daughter’s daughter, their
nakedness you shall not uncover; for theirs *is*
your own nakedness. 11The nakedness of your
father’s wife’s daughter, begotten by your
father—she *is* your sister—you shall not
uncover her nakedness. 12You shall not uncover the nakedness of your father’s sister; she *is*
near of kin to your father. 13You shall not
uncover the nakedness of your mother’s sister, for she *is* near of kin to your mother. 14You
shall not uncover the nakedness of your
father’s brother. You shall not approach his
wife; she *is* your aunt. 15You shall not uncover
the nakedness of your daughter-in-law—she *is*
your son’s wife—you shall not uncover her
nakedness. 16You shall not uncover the nakedness of your brother’s wife; it *is* your brother’s
nakedness. 17You shall not uncover the nakedness of a woman and her daughter, nor shall
you take her son’s daughter or her daughter’s
daughter, to uncover her nakedness. They *are*
near of kin to her. It *is* wickedness. 18Nor shall
you take a woman as a rival to her sister, to
uncover her nakedness while the other is
alive.
19‘Also you shall not approach a woman to
uncover her nakedness as long as she is in her
customary impurity. 20Moreover you shall not
lie carnally with your neighbor’s wife, to defile
yourself with her. 21And you shall not let any of
your descendants pass through *the fire* to
Molech, nor shall you profane the name of
your God: I *am* the LORD. 22You shall not lie
with a male as with a woman. It *is* an abomination. 23Nor shall you mate with any animal, to
defile yourself with it. Nor shall any woman
stand before an animal to mate with it. It *is* perversion.

18:21 Molech. This Semitic false deity (god of the Ammonites) was worshiped with child sacrifice (see Lev. 20:2–5; 1 Kin. 11:7; 2 Kin. 23:10; Jer. 32:35). Since this chapter deals otherwise with sexual deviation, there is likely an unmentioned sexual perversion connected with this pagan ritual. Jews giving false gods homage gave foreigners occasion to blaspheme the true God.

[24]'Do not defile yourselves with any of these
things; for by all these the nations are defiled,
which I am casting out before you. [25]For the
land is defiled; therefore I visit the punishment of its iniquity upon it, and the land vomits out its inhabitants. [26]You shall therefore
keep My statutes and My judgments, and
shall not commit *any* of these abominations,
either any of your own nation or any stranger
who dwells among you [27](for all these
abominations the men of the land have done,
who *were* before you, and thus the land is
defiled), [28]lest the land vomit you out also
when you defile it, as it vomited out the
nations that *were* before you. [29]For whoever
commits any of these abominations, the persons who commit *them* shall be cut off from
among their people.
[30]'Therefore you shall keep My ordinance,
so that *you* do not commit *any* of these abominable customs which were committed before
you, and that you do not defile yourselves by
them: I *am* the LORD your God.' "

Psalm 27:1–3

A Psalm of David.

The LORD *is* my light and
my salvation;
Whom shall I fear?
The LORD *is* the strength
of my life;
Of whom shall I be afraid?
2 When the wicked came against me
To eat up my flesh,
My enemies and foes,
They stumbled and fell.
3 Though an army may
encamp against me,
My heart shall not fear;
Though war may rise
against me,
In this I *will be* confident.

27:1 light. This important biblical word picture with exclusively positive connotations pictures the light of redemption in contrast to the darkness of condemnation (see Pss. 18:28; 36:9; 43:3; Is. 60:1,19,20; Mic. 7:8; John 8:12; 12:46; 1 John 1:5).

Proverbs 10:9

9 He who walks with integrity walks
securely,
But he who perverts his ways will
become known.

Mark 4:21–41

[21]Also He said to them, "Is a lamp brought to
be put under a basket or under a bed? Is it not
to be set on a lampstand? [22]For there is nothing hidden which will not be revealed, nor has
anything been kept secret but that it should
come to light. [23]If anyone has ears to hear, let
him hear."
[24]Then He said to them, "Take heed what
you hear. With the same measure you use, it
will be measured to you; and to you who hear,
more will be given. [25]For whoever has, to him
more will be given; but whoever does not
have, even what he has will be taken away
from him."
[26]And He said, "The kingdom of God is as if
a man should scatter seed on the ground,
[27]and should sleep by night and rise by day,
and the seed should sprout and grow, he himself does not know how. [28]For the earth yields
crops by itself: first the blade, then the head,
after that the full grain in the head. [29]But when
the grain ripens, immediately he puts in the
sickle, because the harvest has come."
[30]Then He said, "To what shall we liken the
kingdom of God? Or with what parable shall
we picture it? [31]*It is* like a mustard seed which,
when it is sown on the ground, is smaller than
all the seeds on earth; [32]but when it is sown, it

4:31 a mustard seed. A reference to the common black mustard plant. The leaves were used as a vegetable and the seed as a condiment. It also had medicinal benefits. **smaller than all.** The mustard seed is not the smallest of all seeds in existence, but it was in comparison to all the other seeds the Jews sowed in Palestine.

grows up and becomes greater than all herbs, and shoots out large branches, so that the birds of the air may nest under its shade."

33And with many such parables He spoke the word to them as they were able to hear *it.* 34But without a parable He did not speak to them. And when they were alone, He explained all things to His disciples.

35On the same day, when evening had come, He said to them, "Let us cross over to the other side." 36Now when they had left the multitude, they took Him along in the boat as He was. And other little boats were also with Him. 37And a great windstorm arose, and the waves beat into the boat, so that it was already filling. 38But He was in the stern, asleep on a pillow. And they awoke Him and said to Him, "Teacher, do You not care that we are perishing?"

39Then He arose and rebuked the wind, and said to the sea, "Peace, be still!" And the wind ceased and there was a great calm. 40But He said to them, "Why are you so fearful? How *is it* that you have no faith?" 41And they feared exceedingly, and said to one another, "Who can this be, that even the wind and the sea obey Him!"

DAY 24: Why would Jesus' own disciples fear Him?

In Mark 4:35, Jesus and His disciples were on the western shore of the Sea of Galilee. To escape the crowds for a brief respite, Jesus wanted to go to the eastern shore, which had no large cities and therefore fewer people. But as they crossed the lake, they were caught in a "great windstorm" (v. 37). Wind is a common occurrence on that lake, about 690 feet below sea level and surrounded by hills. The Greek word can also mean "whirlwind." In this case, it was a storm so severe that it took on the properties of a hurricane. The disciples, used to being on the lake in the wind, thought this storm would drown them (v. 38).

Meanwhile, Jesus was asleep (v. 38). He was so exhausted from a full day of healing and preaching, even that storm could not wake Him up. Thus they woke Him. He then rebuked the wind and said to the sea, "Peace, be still!" Literally, it means to "be silent, be muzzled." Storms normally subside gradually, but when the Creator gave the order, the natural elements of this storm ceased immediately (v. 39).

At that point, we are told "they feared exceedingly" (v. 41). This was not fear of being harmed by the storm, but a reverence for the supernatural power Jesus had just displayed. The only thing more terrifying than having a storm outside the boat was having God in the boat! "Who can this be..." This statement betrayed the disciples' wonderment.

FEBRUARY 25

Leviticus 19:1–20:27

19 And the LORD spoke to Moses, saying, 2"Speak to all the congregation of the children of Israel, and say to them: 'You shall be holy, for I the LORD your God *am* holy.

3'Every one of you shall revere his mother and his father, and keep My Sabbaths: I *am* the LORD your God.

19:2 I the LORD your God *am* holy. This basic statement, which gives the reason for holy living among God's people, is the central theme in Leviticus (see 20:26). See 1 Peter 1:16. Israel had been called to be a holy nation, and the perfectly holy character of God (see Is. 6:3) was the model after which the Israelites were to live (see 10:3; 20:26; 21:6–8).

4'Do not turn to idols, nor make for yourselves molded gods: I *am* the LORD your God.

5'And if you offer a sacrifice of a peace offering to the LORD, you shall offer it of your own free will. 6It shall be eaten the same day you offer *it,* and on the next day. And if any remains until the third day, it shall be burned in the fire. 7And if it is eaten at all on the third day, it *is* an abomination. It shall not be accepted. 8Therefore *everyone* who eats it shall bear his iniquity, because he has profaned the hallowed *offering* of the LORD; and that person shall be cut off from his people.

9'When you reap the harvest of your land, you shall not wholly reap the corners of your field, nor shall you gather the gleanings of your harvest. 10And you shall not glean your vineyard, nor shall you gather *every* grape of your vineyard; you shall leave them for the poor and the stranger: I *am* the LORD your God.

11'You shall not steal, nor deal falsely, nor lie to one another. 12And you shall not swear by

My name falsely, nor shall you profane the
name of your God: I *am* the LORD.
[13]'You shall not cheat your neighbor, nor rob
him. The wages of him who is hired shall not
remain with you all night until morning. [14]You
shall not curse the deaf, nor put a stumbling
block before the blind, but shall fear your
God: I *am* the LORD.
[15]'You shall do no injustice in judgment. You
shall not be partial to the poor, nor honor the
person of the mighty. In righteousness you
shall judge your neighbor. [16]You shall not go
about *as* a talebearer among your people; nor
shall you take a stand against the life of your
neighbor: I *am* the LORD.
[17]'You shall not hate your brother in your
heart. You shall surely rebuke your neighbor,
and not bear sin because of him. [18]You shall
not take vengeance, nor bear any grudge
against the children of your people, but you
shall love your neighbor as yourself: I *am* the
LORD.
[19]'You shall keep My statutes. You shall not
let your livestock breed with another kind.
You shall not sow your field with mixed seed.
Nor shall a garment of mixed linen and wool
come upon you.
[20]'Whoever lies carnally with a woman who
is betrothed to a man as a concubine, and who
has not at all been redeemed nor given her
freedom, for this there shall be scourging; *but*
they shall not be put to death, because she
was not free. [21]And he shall bring his trespass
offering to the LORD, to the door of the tabernacle of meeting, a ram as a trespass offering.
[22]The priest shall make atonement for him
with the ram of the trespass offering before
the LORD for his sin which he has committed.
And the sin which he has committed shall be
forgiven him.
[23]'When you come into the land, and have
planted all kinds of trees for food, then you
shall count their fruit as uncircumcised. Three
years it shall be as uncircumcised to you. *It*
shall not be eaten. [24]But in the fourth year all
its fruit shall be holy, a praise to the LORD.

19:26 divination...soothsaying. Attempting to tell the future with the help of snakes and clouds was a common ancient way of foretelling good or bad future. These were forbidden forms of witchcraft which involved demonic activity.

[25]And in the fifth year you may eat its fruit, that
it may yield to you its increase: I *am* the LORD
your God.
[26]'You shall not eat *anything* with the blood,
nor shall you practice divination or soothsaying. [27]You shall not shave around the sides of
your head, nor shall you disfigure the edges of
your beard. [28]You shall not make any cuttings
in your flesh for the dead, nor tattoo any
marks on you: I *am* the LORD.
[29]'Do not prostitute your daughter, to cause
her to be a harlot, lest the land fall into harlotry, and the land become full of wickedness.
[30]'You shall keep My Sabbaths and reverence My sanctuary: I *am* the LORD.
[31]'Give no regard to mediums and familiar
spirits; do not seek after them, to be defiled by
them: I *am* the LORD your God.
[32]'You shall rise before the gray headed and
honor the presence of an old man, and fear
your God: I *am* the LORD.
[33]'And if a stranger dwells with you in your
land, you shall not mistreat him. [34]The stranger who dwells among you shall be to you as
one born among you, and you shall love him
as yourself; for you were strangers in the land
of Egypt: I *am* the LORD your God.
[35]'You shall do no injustice in judgment, in
measurement of length, weight, or volume.
[36]You shall have honest scales, honest weights,
an honest ephah, and an honest hin: I *am* the
LORD your God, who brought you out of the
land of Egypt.
[37]'Therefore you shall observe all My
statutes and all My judgments, and perform
them: I *am* the LORD.' "

20 Then the LORD spoke to Moses, saying,
[2]"Again, you shall say to the children of
Israel: 'Whoever of the children of Israel, or of
the strangers who dwell in Israel, who gives
any of his descendants to Molech, he shall
surely be put to death. The people of the land
shall stone him with stones. [3]I will set My face
against that man, and will cut him off from his
people, because he has given *some* of his
descendants to Molech, to defile My sanctuary and profane My holy name. [4]And if the
people of the land should in any way hide their
eyes from the man, when he gives *some* of his
descendants to Molech, and they do not kill
him, [5]then I will set My face against that man
and against his family; and I will cut him off
from his people, and all who prostitute themselves with him to commit harlotry with
Molech.
[6]'And the person who turns to mediums and
familiar spirits, to prostitute himself with

them, I will set My face against that person
and cut him off from his people. 7Consecrate
yourselves therefore, and be holy, for I *am* the
LORD your God. 8And you shall keep My
statutes, and perform them: I *am* the LORD
who sanctifies you.
9"For everyone who curses his father or his
mother shall surely be put to death. He has
cursed his father or his mother. His blood
shall be upon him.
10"The man who commits adultery with *another* man's wife, *he* who commits adultery
with his neighbor's wife, the adulterer and the
adulteress, shall surely be put to death. 11The
man who lies with his father's wife has uncovered his father's nakedness; both of them
shall surely be put to death. Their blood *shall
be* upon them. 12If a man lies with his daughter-
in-law, both of them shall surely be put to
death. They have committed perversion.
Their blood *shall be* upon them. 13If a man lies
with a male as he lies with a woman, both of
them have committed an abomination. They
shall surely be put to death. Their blood *shall
be* upon them. 14If a man marries a woman and
her mother, it *is* wickedness. They shall be
burned with fire, both he and they, that there
may be no wickedness among you. 15If a man
mates with an animal, he shall surely be put to
death, and you shall kill the animal. 16If a
woman approaches any animal and mates with
it, you shall kill the woman and the animal.
They shall surely be put to death. Their blood
is upon them.
17"If a man takes his sister, his father's
daughter or his mother's daughter, and sees
her nakedness and she sees his nakedness, it
is a wicked thing. And they shall be cut off in
the sight of their people. He has uncovered
his sister's nakedness. He shall bear his guilt.
18If a man lies with a woman during her sickness and uncovers her nakedness, he has exposed her flow, and she has uncovered the
flow of her blood. Both of them shall be cut off
from their people.
19"You shall not uncover the nakedness of
your mother's sister nor of your father's sister,
for that would uncover his near of kin. They
shall bear their guilt. 20If a man lies with his uncle's wife, he has uncovered his uncle's
nakedness. They shall bear their sin; they
shall die childless. 21If a man takes his brother's wife, it *is* an unclean thing. He has uncovered his brother's nakedness. They shall be
childless.
22"You shall therefore keep all My statutes
and all My judgments, and perform them, that
the land where I am bringing you to dwell may
not vomit you out. 23And you shall not walk in
the statutes of the nation which I am casting
out before you; for they commit all these
things, and therefore I abhor them. 24But I
have said to you, "You shall inherit their land,
and I will give it to you to possess, a land flowing with milk and honey." I *am* the LORD your
God, who has separated you from the peoples.
25You shall therefore distinguish between
clean animals and unclean, between unclean
birds and clean, and you shall not make yourselves abominable by beast or by bird, or by
any kind of living thing that creeps on the
ground, which I have separated from you as
unclean. 26And you shall be holy to Me, for I
the LORD *am* holy, and have separated you
from the peoples, that you should be Mine.
27"A man or a woman who is a medium, or
who has familiar spirits, shall surely be put to
death; they shall stone them with stones.
Their blood *shall be* upon them.' "

Psalm 27:4–10

4 One *thing* I have desired
of the LORD,
That will I seek:
That I may dwell in the house
of the LORD
All the days of my life,
To behold the beauty of
the LORD,
And to inquire in His temple.
5 For in the time of trouble
He shall hide me in His pavilion;
In the secret place of
His tabernacle
He shall hide me;
He shall set me high upon
a rock.

6 And now my head shall be
lifted up above my enemies
all around me;
Therefore I will offer sacrifices of joy
in His tabernacle;

27:8,9 "Seek My face," ... "Your face," ... Your face. God's "face" indicates His personal presence or simply His being (Pss. 24:6; 105:4); and seeking His face is a primary characteristic of true believers who desire fellowship with God (see Deut. 4:29; 2 Chr. 11:16; 20:4; Ps. 40:16; Jer. 50:4; Hos. 3:5; Zech. 8:22).

I will sing, yes, I will sing praises to
the LORD.

7 Hear, O LORD, *when* I cry with my
voice!
Have mercy also upon me,
and answer me.
8 *When You said,* "Seek My face,"
My heart said to You, "Your face,
LORD, I will seek."
9 Do not hide Your face from me;
Do not turn Your servant away in
anger;
You have been my help;
Do not leave me nor
forsake me,
O God of my salvation.
10 When my father and my mother
forsake me,
Then the LORD will take care
of me.

Proverbs 10:10–12

10 He who winks with the eye causes
trouble,
But a prating fool will fall.
11 The mouth of the righteous
is a well of life,
But violence covers the mouth of the
wicked.

12 Hatred stirs up strife,
But love covers all sins.

Mark 5:1–20

5 Then they came to the other side of the
sea, to the country of the Gadarenes. 2And
when He had come out of the boat, immediately there met Him out of the tombs a man
with an unclean spirit, 3who had *his* dwelling
among the tombs; and no one could bind him,
not even with chains, 4because he had often
been bound with shackles and chains. And the
chains had been pulled apart by him, and the
shackles broken in pieces; neither could anyone tame him. 5And always, night and day, he
was in the mountains and in the tombs, crying
out and cutting himself with stones.
6When he saw Jesus from afar, he ran and
worshiped Him. 7And he cried out with a loud
voice and said, "What have I to do with You,
Jesus, Son of the Most High God? I implore
You by God that You do not torment me."
8For He said to him, "Come out of the man,
unclean spirit!" 9Then He asked him, "What *is*
your name?"
And he answered, saying, "My name *is*
Legion; for we are many." 10Also he begged
Him earnestly that He would not send them
out of the country.
11Now a large herd of swine was feeding
there near the mountains. 12So all the demons
begged Him, saying, "Send us to the swine,
that we may enter them." 13And at once Jesus
gave them permission. Then the unclean spirits went out and entered the swine (there were
about two thousand); and the herd ran violently down the steep place into the sea, and
drowned in the sea.
14So those who fed the swine fled, and they
told *it* in the city and in the country. And they
went out to see what it was that had happened.
15Then they came to Jesus, and saw the one
who had been demon-possessed and had the
legion, sitting and clothed and in his right
mind. And they were afraid. 16And those who
saw it told them how it happened to him *who
had been* demon-possessed, and about the
swine. 17Then they began to plead with Him to
depart from their region.
18And when He got into the boat, he who
had been demon-possessed begged Him that
he might be with Him. 19However, Jesus did
not permit him, but said to him, "Go home to
your friends, and tell them what great things
the Lord has done for you, and how He has
had compassion on you." 20And he departed
and began to proclaim in Decapolis all that Jesus had done for him; and all marveled.

5:5 crying out and cutting himself with stones. "Crying out" describes a continual unearthly scream uttered with intense emotion. The "stones" likely were rocks made of flint with sharp, jagged edges.

5:9 "What *is* your name?" Most likely, Jesus asked this in view of the demon's appeal not to be tormented. However, He did not need to know the demon's name in order to expel him. Rather, Jesus posed the question to bring the reality and complexity of this case into the open. **Legion.** A Latin term, by then common to Jews and Greeks, that defined a Roman military unit of 6,000 infantrymen. Such a name denotes that the man was controlled by an extremely large number of militant evil spirits, a truth reiterated by the expression "for we are many."

DAY 25: What does the term "type of Christ" mean when used to describe someone in the Old Testament?

Certain persons and practices recorded in the Old Testament serve as hints, clues, and preillustrations of what Jesus Christ would accomplish by His life, death, and resurrection. In most cases, the similarities or parallels are pointed out in the New Testament. The following people are some of those mentioned as representing, in a narrow way, what Christ accomplished perfectly: (1) Adam (Rom. 5:14; 1 Cor. 15:45); (2) Abel (Gen. 4:8,10; Heb. 12:24); (3) Aaron (Ex. 28:1; Heb. 5:4,5; 9:7,24); (4) David (2 Sam. 8:15; Phil. 2:9); (5) Jonah (Jon. 1:17; Matt. 12:40); (6) Melchizedek (Gen. 14:18–20; Heb. 7:1–17); (7) Moses (Num. 12:7; Heb. 3:2); (8) Noah (Gen. 5:29; 2 Cor. 1:5); (9) Samson (Judg. 16:30; Col. 2:14–15); (10) Solomon (2 Sam. 7:12,13; 1 Pet. 2:5).

The following events and practices also prefigure Christ: (1) Ark (Gen. 7:16; 1 Pet. 3:20,21); (2) Atonement sacrifices (Lev. 16:15,16; Heb. 9:12,24); (3) Bronze serpent (Num. 21:9; John 3:14,15); (4) Mercy seat (Ex. 25:17–22; Rom. 3:25; Heb. 4:16); (5) Passover lamb (Ex. 12:3–6,46; John 19:36; 1 Cor. 5:7); (6) Red heifer (Lev. 3:1; Eph. 2:14,16); (7) Rock of Horeb (Ex. 17:6; 1 Cor. 10:4); (8) Scapegoat (Lev. 16:20–22); (9) Tabernacle (Ex. 40:2; Heb. 9:11; Col. 2:9); (10) Veil of the tabernacle (Ex. 40:21; Heb. 10:20).

FEBRUARY 26

Leviticus 21:1–22:33

21 And the LORD said to Moses, "Speak to
the priests, the sons of Aaron, and say to
them: 'None shall defile himself for the dead
among his people, [2]except for his relatives who
are nearest to him: his mother, his father, his
son, his daughter, and his brother; [3]also his virgin sister who is near to him, who has had no
husband, for her he may defile himself. [4]*Otherwise* he shall not defile himself, *being* a chief
man among his people, to profane himself.

[5]'They shall not make any bald *place* on
their heads, nor shall they shave the edges of
their beards nor make any cuttings in their
flesh. [6]They shall be holy to their God and not
profane the name of their God, for they offer
the offerings of the LORD made by fire, *and* the
bread of their God; therefore they shall be
holy. [7]They shall not take a wife *who is* a harlot
or a defiled woman, nor shall they take a
woman divorced from her husband; for *the
priest* is holy to his God. [8]Therefore you shall
consecrate him, for he offers the bread of your
God. He shall be holy to you, for I the LORD,
who sanctify you, *am* holy. [9]The daughter of
any priest, if she profanes herself by playing
the harlot, she profanes her father. She shall
be burned with fire.

[10]'*He who is* the high priest among his
brethren, on whose head the anointing oil was
poured and who is consecrated to wear the
garments, shall not uncover his head nor tear
his clothes; [11]nor shall he go near any dead
body, nor defile himself for his father or his
mother; [12]nor shall he go out of the sanctuary,
nor profane the sanctuary of his God; for the
consecration of the anointing oil of his God *is*
upon him: I *am* the LORD. [13]And he shall take a
wife in her virginity. [14]A widow or a divorced
woman or a defiled woman *or* a harlot—these
he shall not marry; but he shall take a virgin
of his own people as wife. [15]Nor shall he profane his posterity among his people, for I the
LORD sanctify him.' "

[16]And the LORD spoke to Moses, saying,
[17]"Speak to Aaron, saying: 'No man of your
descendants in *succeeding* generations, who has
any defect, may approach to offer the bread of
his God. [18]For any man who has a defect shall
not approach: a man blind or lame, who has a
marred *face* or any *limb* too long, [19]a man who
has a broken foot or broken hand, [20]or is a
hunchback or a dwarf, or *a man* who has
a defect in his eye, or eczema or scab, or is a
eunuch. [21]No man of the descendants of Aaron
the priest, who has a defect, shall come near
to offer the offerings made by fire to the LORD.
He has a defect; he shall not come near to offer
the bread of his God. [22]He may eat the bread of

21:16–23 defect. Just as the sacrifice had to be without blemish, so did the one offering the sacrifice. As visible things exert strong impressions on the minds of people, any physical impurity or malformation tended to distract from the weight and authority of the sacred office, failed to externally exemplify the inward wholeness God sought, and failed to be a picture of Jesus Christ, the Perfect High Priest to come (see Heb. 7:26).

his God, *both* the most holy and the holy; 23only
he shall not go near the veil or approach the
altar, because he has a defect, lest he profane
My sanctuaries; for I the LORD sanctify them.' "
24And Moses told *it* to Aaron and his sons,
and to all the children of Israel.

22 Then the LORD spoke to Moses, saying,
2"Speak to Aaron and his sons, that
they separate themselves from the holy things
of the children of Israel, and that they do not
profane My holy name *by* what they dedicate to
Me: I *am* the LORD. 3Say to them: 'Whoever of all
your descendants throughout your generations,
who goes near the holy things which the children of Israel dedicate to the LORD, while he
has uncleanness upon him, that person shall
be cut off from My presence: I *am* the LORD.
4'Whatever man of the descendants of Aaron,
who *is* a leper or has a discharge, shall not eat
the holy offerings until he is clean. And whoever touches anything made unclean *by* a
corpse, or a man who has had an emission of
semen, 5or whoever touches any creeping thing
by which he would be made unclean, or any
person by whom he would become unclean,
whatever his uncleanness may be— 6the person who has touched any such thing shall be
unclean until evening, and shall not eat the
holy *offerings* unless he washes his body with
water. 7And when the sun goes down he shall
be clean; and afterward he may eat the holy *offerings,* because it *is* his food. 8Whatever dies
naturally or is torn *by beasts* he shall not eat, to
defile himself with it: I *am* the LORD.
9'They shall therefore keep My ordinance,
lest they bear sin for it and die thereby, if they
profane it: I the LORD sanctify them.
10'No outsider shall eat the holy *offering;* one
who dwells with the priest, or a hired servant,
shall not eat the holy thing. 11But if the priest
buys a person with his money, he may eat it;
and one who is born in his house may eat his
food. 12If the priest's daughter is married to an
outsider, she may not eat of the holy offerings.
13But if the priest's daughter is a widow or
divorced, and has no child, and has returned to
her father's house as in her youth, she may eat
her father's food; but no outsider shall eat it.
14'And if a man eats the holy *offering* unintentionally, then he shall restore a holy *offering* to the priest, and add one-fifth to it. 15They
shall not profane the holy *offerings* of the children of Israel, which they offer to the LORD,
16or allow them to bear the guilt of trespass
when they eat their holy *offerings;* for I the
LORD sanctify them.' "
17And the LORD spoke to Moses, saying,
18"Speak to Aaron and his sons, and to all the
children of Israel, and say to them: 'Whatever
man of the house of Israel, or of the strangers
in Israel, who offers his sacrifice for any of his
vows or for any of his freewill offerings, which
they offer to the LORD as a burnt offering—
19*you shall offer* of your own free will a male
without blemish from the cattle, from the
sheep, or from the goats. 20Whatever has a
defect, you shall not offer, for it shall not be
acceptable on your behalf. 21And whoever
offers a sacrifice of a peace offering to the
LORD, to fulfill *his* vow, or a freewill offering
from the cattle or the sheep, it must be perfect
to be accepted; there shall be no defect in it.
22Those *that are* blind or broken or maimed, or
have an ulcer or eczema or scabs, you shall
not offer to the LORD, nor make an offering by
fire of them on the altar to the LORD. 23Either a
bull or a lamb that has any limb too long or too
short you may offer *as* a freewill offering, but
for a vow it shall not be accepted.
24'You shall not offer to the LORD what is
bruised or crushed, or torn or cut; nor shall you
make *any offering of them* in your land. 25Nor
from a foreigner's hand shall you offer any of
these as the bread of your God, because their
corruption *is* in them, *and* defects *are* in them.
They shall not be accepted on your behalf.' "
26And the LORD spoke to Moses, saying:
27"When a bull or a sheep or a goat is born, it
shall be seven days with its mother; and from
the eighth day and thereafter it shall be
accepted as an offering made by fire to the
LORD. 28*Whether it is* a cow or ewe, do not kill
both her and her young on the same day. 29And
when you offer a sacrifice of thanksgiving to
the LORD, offer *it* of your own free will. 30On
the same day it shall be eaten; you shall leave
none of it until morning: I *am* the LORD.
31"Therefore you shall keep My commandments, and perform them: I *am* the LORD.
32You shall not profane My holy name, but I will
be hallowed among the children of Israel. I *am*
the LORD who sanctifies you, 33who brought you
out of the land of Egypt, to be your God: I *am*
the LORD."

Psalm 27:11–14

11 Teach me Your way, O LORD,
And lead me in a smooth path,
because of my enemies.
12 Do not deliver me to the will of my
adversaries;
For false witnesses have risen
against me,
And such as breathe out violence.
13 *I would have lost heart,* unless
I had believed

That I would see the goodness
of the LORD
In the land of the living.

14 Wait on the LORD;
Be of good courage,
And He shall strengthen your heart;
Wait, I say, on the LORD!

Proverbs 10:13–16

13 Wisdom is found on the lips of him
who has understanding,
But a rod *is* for the back of him
who is devoid of understanding.

14 Wise *people* store up knowledge,
But the mouth of the foolish *is* near
destruction.

15 The rich man's wealth *is* his strong city;
The destruction of the poor *is* their
poverty.

16 The labor of the righteous *leads* to life,
The wages of the wicked to sin.

10:13 rod. This first reference to corporal punishment applied to the backside (see 19:29; 26:3) recommends it as the most effective way of dealing with children and fools. See also 13:24; 18:6; 19:29; 22:15; 23:13,14; 26:3; 29:15.

Mark 5:21–43

21Now when Jesus had crossed over again
by boat to the other side, a great multitude
gathered to Him; and He was by the sea. 22And
behold, one of the rulers of the synagogue
came, Jairus by name. And when he saw Him,
he fell at His feet 23and begged Him earnestly,
saying, "My little daughter lies at the point of
death. Come and lay Your hands on her, that
she may be healed, and she will live." 24So *Jesus* went with him, and a great multitude followed Him and thronged Him.
25Now a certain woman had a flow of blood
for twelve years, 26and had suffered many things
from many physicians. She had spent all that
she had and was no better, but rather grew
worse. 27When she heard about Jesus, she came
behind *Him* in the crowd and touched His garment. 28For she said, "If only I may touch His
clothes, I shall be made well."
29Immediately the fountain of her blood was
dried up, and she felt in *her* body that she was
healed of the affliction. 30And Jesus, immediately knowing in Himself that power had gone
out of Him, turned around in the crowd and
said, "Who touched My clothes?"
31But His disciples said to Him, "You see the
multitude thronging You, and You say, 'Who
touched Me?' "
32And He looked around to see her who had
done this thing. 33But the woman, fearing and
trembling, knowing what had happened to
her, came and fell down before Him and told
Him the whole truth. 34And He said to her,

5:26 suffered many things from many physicians. In New Testament times, it was common practice in difficult medical cases for people to consult many different doctors and receive a variety of treatments. The supposed cures were often conflicting, abusive, and many times made the ailment worse, not better. (Luke, the physician, in Luke 8:43 suggested the woman was not helped because her condition was incurable.)

"Daughter, your faith has made you well. Go
in peace, and be healed of your affliction."
35While He was still speaking, *some* came
from the ruler of the synagogue's *house* who
said, "Your daughter is dead. Why trouble the
Teacher any further?"
36As soon as Jesus heard the word that was
spoken, He said to the ruler of the synagogue,
"Do not be afraid; only believe." 37And He permitted no one to follow Him except Peter,
James, and John the brother of James. 38Then
He came to the house of the ruler of the synagogue, and saw a tumult and those who wept
and wailed loudly. 39When He came in, He said
to them, "Why make this commotion and
weep? The child is not dead, but sleeping."
40And they ridiculed Him. But when He had
put them all outside, He took the father and the
mother of the child, and those *who were* with
Him, and entered where the child was lying.
41Then He took the child by the hand, and said
to her, "Talitha, cumi," which is translated,

5:38 wept and wailed. In that culture, a sure sign that a death had occurred. Because burial followed soon after death, it was the people's only opportunity to mourn publicly. The wailing was especially loud and mostly from paid mourners.

"Little girl, I say to you, arise." [42]Immediately
the girl arose and walked, for she was twelve
years *of age.* And they were overcome with
great amazement. [43]But He commanded them
strictly that no one should know it, and said
that *something* should be given her to eat.

DAY 26: What do the healings of Mark 5 teach us about faith?

Upon hearing about Jesus, the woman with the flow of blood said to herself, "If only I may touch His clothes, I shall be made well" (v. 28). Her faith in Jesus' healing powers was so great that she believed even indirect contact with Him through His garments would be enough to produce a cure. Jesus' response to her touch and healing was that "your faith has made you well" (v. 34). The form of the Greek verb translated "has made you well," which can also be rendered "has made you whole," indicates that her healing was complete. It is the same Greek word often translated "to save" and is the normal New Testament word for saving from sin, which strongly suggests that the woman's faith also led to spiritual salvation.

Jesus' response to the announced death of Jairus's daughter was simply, "Do not be afraid; only believe" (v. 36). The verb is a command for present, continuous action urging Jairus to maintain the faith he had initially demonstrated in coming to Jesus. Christ knew there was no other proper response to Jairus's helpless situation, and He was confident of faith's outcome (Luke 8:50). Even in the face of ridicule, Jesus said, "The child is not dead, but sleeping" (v. 39). With this figurative expression, Jesus meant that the girl was not dead in the normal sense, because her condition was temporary and would be reversed (see note on Matt. 9:24; see John 11:11–14; Acts 7:60; 13:36; 1 Cor. 11:30; 15:6,18,20,51; 1 Thess. 4:13,14).

FEBRUARY 27

Leviticus 23:1–24:23

23 And the LORD spoke to Moses, saying,
[2]"Speak to the children of Israel, and
say to them: 'The feasts of the LORD, which
you shall proclaim *to be* holy convocations,
these *are* My feasts.

23:2 proclaim *to be* holy convocations. These festivals did not involve gatherings of all Israel in every case. Only the feasts of 1) Unleavened Bread; 2) Weeks; and 3) Tabernacles required that all males gather in Jerusalem (see Ex. 23:14–17; Deut. 16:16,17).

[3]'Six days shall work be done, but the seventh day *is* a Sabbath of solemn rest, a holy
convocation. You shall do no work *on it;* it *is*
the Sabbath of the LORD in all your dwellings.
[4]'These *are* the feasts of the LORD, holy convocations which you shall proclaim at their
appointed times. [5]On the fourteenth *day* of the
first month at twilight *is* the LORD's Passover.
[6]And on the fifteenth day of the same month
is the Feast of Unleavened Bread to the
LORD; seven days you must eat unleavened
bread. [7]On the first day you shall have a holy
convocation; you shall do no customary work
on it. [8]But you shall offer an offering made by
fire to the LORD for seven days. The seventh
day *shall be* a holy convocation; you shall do
no customary work *on it.*' "
[9]And the LORD spoke to Moses, saying,
[10]"Speak to the children of Israel, and say to
them: 'When you come into the land which I
give to you, and reap its harvest, then you
shall bring a sheaf of the firstfruits of your harvest to the priest. [11]He shall wave the sheaf
before the LORD, to be accepted on your
behalf; on the day after the Sabbath the priest
shall wave it. [12]And you shall offer on that day,
when you wave the sheaf, a male lamb of the
first year, without blemish, as a burnt offering
to the LORD. [13]Its grain offering *shall be* two-
tenths *of an ephah* of fine flour mixed with oil,
an offering made by fire to the LORD, for a
sweet aroma; and its drink offering *shall be* of
wine, one-fourth of a hin. [14]You shall eat neither bread nor parched grain nor fresh grain
until the same day that you have brought an
offering to your God; *it shall be* a statute forever throughout your generations in all your
dwellings.
[15]'And you shall count for yourselves from
the day after the Sabbath, from the day that
you brought the sheaf of the wave offering:
seven Sabbaths shall be completed. [16]Count
fifty days to the day after the seventh Sabbath;
then you shall offer a new grain offering to the
LORD. [17]You shall bring from your dwellings

two wave *loaves* of two-tenths *of an ephah.*
They shall be of fine flour; they shall be baked
with leaven. *They are* the firstfruits to the
LORD. [18]And you shall offer with the bread
seven lambs of the first year, without blemish,
one young bull, and two rams. They shall be
as a burnt offering to the LORD, with their
grain offering and their drink offerings, an
offering made by fire for a sweet aroma to the
LORD. [19]Then you shall sacrifice one kid of the
goats as a sin offering, and two male lambs of
the first year as a sacrifice of a peace offering.
[20]The priest shall wave them with the bread of
the firstfruits *as* a wave offering before the
LORD, with the two lambs. They shall be holy
to the LORD for the priest. [21]And you shall proclaim on the same day *that* it is a holy convocation to you. You shall do no customary work
on it. It shall be a statute forever in all your
dwellings throughout your generations.
[22]'When you reap the harvest of your land,
you shall not wholly reap the corners of your
field when you reap, nor shall you gather any
gleaning from your harvest. You shall leave
them for the poor and for the stranger: I *am*
the LORD your God.' "
[23]Then the LORD spoke to Moses, saying,
[24]"Speak to the children of Israel, saying: 'In the
seventh month, on the first *day* of the month,
you shall have a sabbath-*rest,* a memorial of
blowing of trumpets, a holy convocation. [25]You
shall do no customary work *on it;* and you shall
offer an offering made by fire to the LORD.' "
[26]And the LORD spoke to Moses, saying:
[27]"Also the tenth *day* of this seventh month
shall be the Day of Atonement. It shall be a
holy convocation for you; you shall afflict your
souls, and offer an offering made by fire to the
LORD. [28]And you shall do no work on that same
day, for it *is* the Day of Atonement, to make
atonement for you before the LORD your God.
[29]For any person who is not afflicted *in soul* on
that same day shall be cut off from his people.
[30]And any person who does any work on that
same day, that person I will destroy from
among his people. [31]You shall do no manner of
work; *it shall be* a statute forever throughout
your generations in all your dwellings. [32]It
shall be to you a sabbath of *solemn* rest, and
you shall afflict your souls; on the ninth *day* of
the month at evening, from evening to
evening, you shall celebrate your sabbath."
[33]Then the LORD spoke to Moses, saying,
[34]"Speak to the children of Israel, saying: 'The
fifteenth day of this seventh month *shall be* the
Feast of Tabernacles *for* seven days to the
LORD. [35]On the first day *there shall be* a holy
convocation. You shall do no customary work
on it. [36]*For* seven days you shall offer an offering made by fire to the LORD. On the eighth
day you shall have a holy convocation, and you
shall offer an offering made by fire to the
LORD. It *is* a sacred assembly, *and* you shall do
no customary work *on it.*
[37]'These *are* the feasts of the LORD which you
shall proclaim *to be* holy convocations, to offer
an offering made by fire to the LORD, a burnt
offering and a grain offering, a sacrifice and
drink offerings, everything on its day— [38]be-
sides the Sabbaths of the LORD, besides your
gifts, besides all your vows, and besides all your
freewill offerings which you give to the LORD.
[39]'Also on the fifteenth day of the seventh
month, when you have gathered in the fruit of
the land, you shall keep the feast of the LORD
for seven days; on the first day *there shall be* a
sabbath-*rest,* and on the eighth day a sabbath-
rest. [40]And you shall take for yourselves on the
first day the fruit of beautiful trees, branches of
palm trees, the boughs of leafy trees, and willows of the brook; and you shall rejoice before
the LORD your God for seven days. [41]You shall
keep it as a feast to the LORD for seven days in
the year. *It shall be* a statute forever in your
generations. You shall celebrate it in the seventh month. [42]You shall dwell in booths for
seven days. All who are native Israelites shall
dwell in booths, [43]that your generations may
know that I made the children of Israel dwell
in booths when I brought them out of the land
of Egypt: I *am* the LORD your God.' "
[44]So Moses declared to the children of Israel
the feasts of the LORD.

24 Then the LORD spoke to Moses, saying:
[2]"Command the children of Israel that
they bring to you pure oil of pressed olives for
the light, to make the lamps burn continually.
[3]Outside the veil of the Testimony, in the tabernacle of meeting, Aaron shall be in charge
of it from evening until morning before the
LORD continually; *it shall be* a statute forever in
your generations. [4]He shall be in charge of the
lamps on the pure *gold* lampstand before the
LORD continually.
[5]"And you shall take fine flour and bake
twelve cakes with it. Two-tenths *of an ephah*
shall be in each cake. [6]You shall set them in
two rows, six in a row, on the pure *gold* table
before the LORD. [7]And you shall put pure
frankincense on *each* row, that it may be on
the bread for a memorial, an offering made by
fire to the LORD. [8]Every Sabbath he shall set it
in order before the LORD continually, *being*
taken from the children of Israel by an everlasting covenant. [9]And it shall be for Aaron and
his sons, and they shall eat it in a holy place;

for it *is* most holy to him from the offerings of
the LORD made by fire, by a perpetual statute."
[10]Now the son of an Israelite woman, whose
father *was* an Egyptian, went out among the
children of Israel; and this Israelite *woman's*
son and a man of Israel fought each other in
the camp. [11]And the Israelite woman's son
blasphemed the name *of the LORD* and cursed;
and so they brought him to Moses. (His mother's name *was* Shelomith the daughter of
Dibri, of the tribe of Dan.) [12]Then they put him
in custody, that the mind of the LORD might be
shown to them.
[13]And the LORD spoke to Moses, saying,
[14]"Take outside the camp him who has cursed;
then let all who heard *him* lay their hands on his
head, and let all the congregation stone him.
[15]"Then you shall speak to the children of
Israel, saying: 'Whoever curses his God shall
bear his sin. [16]And whoever blasphemes the
name of the LORD shall surely be put to death.
All the congregation shall certainly stone him,
the stranger as well as him who is born in the
land. When he blasphemes the name *of the
LORD,* he shall be put to death.
[17]'Whoever kills any man shall surely be put
to death. [18]Whoever kills an animal shall make
it good, animal for animal.
[19]'If a man causes disfigurement of his
neighbor, as he has done, so shall it be done to
him— [20]fracture for fracture, eye for eye, tooth
for tooth; as he has caused disfigurement of a
man, so shall it be done to him. [21]And whoever
kills an animal shall restore it; but whoever
kills a man shall be put to death. [22]You shall
have the same law for the stranger and for one
from your own country; for I *am* the LORD
your God.' "
[23]Then Moses spoke to the children of Israel;
and they took outside the camp him who had
cursed, and stoned him with stones. So the
children of Israel did as the LORD commanded
Moses.

Psalm 28:1–5

A Psalm of David.

To You I will cry, O LORD my Rock:
Do not be silent to me,
Lest, if You *are* silent to me,
I become like those who go down
to the pit.

2 Hear the voice of my supplications
When I cry to You,
When I lift up my hands toward Your
holy sanctuary.

3 Do not take me away with the wicked
And with the workers of iniquity,
Who speak peace to their neighbors,
But evil *is* in their hearts.

4 Give them according to their deeds,
And according to the wickedness of
their endeavors;
Give them according to the work of
their hands;
Render to them what they deserve.

5 Because they do not regard the works
of the LORD,
Nor the operation of His hands,
He shall destroy them
And not build them up.

Proverbs 10:17–18

17 He who keeps instruction *is in*
the way of life,
But he who refuses correction goes
astray.

18 Whoever hides hatred *has* lying lips,
And whoever spreads slander *is* a fool.

Mark 6:1–29

6 Then He went out from there and came to
His own country, and His disciples followed Him. [2]And when the Sabbath had come,
He began to teach in the synagogue. And
many hearing *Him* were astonished, saying,
"Where *did* this Man *get* these things? And
what wisdom *is* this which is given to Him,
that such mighty works are performed by His
hands! [3]Is this not the carpenter, the Son of
Mary, and brother of James, Joses, Judas, and
Simon? And are not His sisters here with us?"
So they were offended at Him.
[4]But Jesus said to them, "A prophet is not
without honor except in his own country,
among his own relatives, and in his own
house." [5]Now He could do no mighty work
there, except that He laid His hands on a few
sick people and healed *them.* [6]And He marveled because of their unbelief. Then He went
about the villages in a circuit, teaching.
[7]And He called the twelve to *Himself,* and
began to send them out two *by* two, and gave
them power over unclean spirits. [8]He commanded them to take nothing for the journey
except a staff—no bag, no bread, no copper in
their money belts— [9]but to wear sandals, and
not to put on two tunics.
[10]Also He said to them, "In whatever place
you enter a house, stay there till you depart
from that place. [11]And whoever will not receive
you nor hear you, when you depart from there,
shake off the dust under your feet as a testimony against them. Assuredly, I say to you, it
will be more tolerable for Sodom and Gomorrah

6:11 shake off the dust. A symbolic act that signified complete renunciation of further fellowship with those who rejected them. When the disciples made this gesture, it would show that the people had rejected Jesus and the gospel and were hence rejected by the disciples and by the Lord. **more tolerable for Sodom and Gomorrah.** People who reject Christ's gracious, saving gospel will face a fate worse than those pagans killed by divine judgment on the two Old Testament cities.

6:13 anointed with oil...sick. In Jesus' day olive oil was often used medicinally (see Luke 10:34). But here it represented the power and presence of the Holy Spirit and was used symbolically in relation to supernatural healing (see Is. 11:2; Zech. 4:1–6; Matt. 25:2–4; Rev. 1:4,12). As a well-known healing agent, the oil was an appropriate, tangible medium the people could identify with as the disciples ministered to the sick among them.

6:15 "It is Elijah." This identification of Jesus, which probably had been discussed repeatedly among the Jews, was based on the Jewish expectation that the prophet Elijah would return prior to Messiah's coming. **the Prophet...one of the prophets.** Some saw Jesus as the fulfillment of Deuteronomy 18:15, the messianic prophecy that looked to the One who, like Moses, would lead His people. Others were willing to identify Jesus only as a great prophet, or one who was resuming the suspended line of Old Testament prophets. These and the other opinions, although misplaced, show that the people still thought Jesus was special or somehow supernatural.

in the day of judgment than for that city!"
12So they went out and preached that *people*
should repent. 13And they cast out many
demons, and anointed with oil many who were
sick, and healed *them.*
14Now King Herod heard *of Him,* for His
name had become well known. And he said,
"John the Baptist is risen from the dead, and
therefore these powers are at work in him."
15Others said, "It is Elijah."
And others said, "It is the Prophet, or like
one of the prophets."
16But when Herod heard, he said, "This is
John, whom I beheaded; he has been raised
from the dead!" 17For Herod himself had sent
and laid hold of John, and bound him in prison
for the sake of Herodias, his brother Philip's
wife; for he had married her. 18Because John
had said to Herod, "It is not lawful for you to
have your brother's wife."
19Therefore Herodias held it against him
and wanted to kill him, but she could not; 20for
Herod feared John, knowing that he *was* a just
and holy man, and he protected him. And
when he heard him, he did many things, and
heard him gladly.
21Then an opportune day came when Herod
on his birthday gave a feast for his nobles, the
high officers, and the chief *men* of Galilee.
22And when Herodias' daughter herself came
in and danced, and pleased Herod and those
who sat with him, the king said to the girl, "Ask
me whatever you want, and I will give *it* to
you." 23He also swore to her, "Whatever you
ask me, I will give you, up to half my kingdom."
24So she went out and said to her mother,
"What shall I ask?"
And she said, "The head of John the
Baptist!"
25Immediately she came in with haste to the
king and asked, saying, "I want you to give
me at once the head of John the Baptist on a
platter."
26And the king was exceedingly sorry; *yet,*
because of the oaths and because of those
who sat with him, he did not want to refuse
her. 27Immediately the king sent an executioner and commanded his head to be brought.
And he went and beheaded him in prison,
28brought his head on a platter, and gave it to
the girl; and the girl gave it to her mother.
29When his disciples heard *of it,* they came and
took away his corpse and laid it in a tomb.

DAY 27: What is the relationship of unbelief and Jesus' working in people's lives?

Although the people in Jesus' hometown of Nazareth were "astonished" by Jesus' wisdom and mighty works (Mark 6:2), their initial reaction gave way to skepticism and a critical attitude toward Jesus. They still thought of Jesus as a carpenter and the son of Mary with brothers and sisters (v. 3). The residents of Nazareth were deeply offended at Jesus' posturing Himself as some great teacher because of His ordinary background, His limited formal education, and His lack of an officially sanctioned religious position.

In the face of this, Jesus "could do no mighty work there" (v. 5). This is not to suggest that His power was somehow diminished by their unbelief. It may suggest that because of their unbelief people were not coming to Him for healing or miracles the way they did in Capernaum and Jerusalem. Or, more importantly it may signify that Christ limited His ministry both as an act of mercy, so that the exposure to greater light would not result in a worse hardening that would only subject them to greater condemnation, and a judgment on their unbelief. He had the power to do more miracles, but not the will, because they rejected Him. Miracles belonged among those who were ready to believe.

"He marveled because of their unbelief" (v. 6). "Marveled" means Jesus was completely astonished and amazed at Nazareth's reaction to Him, His teaching, and His miracles. He was not surprised at the fact of the people's unbelief, but at how they could reject Him while claiming to know all about Him.

FEBRUARY 28

Leviticus 25:1–55

25 And the LORD spoke to Moses on
Mount Sinai, saying, 2"Speak to the
children of Israel, and say to them: 'When you
come into the land which I give you, then the
land shall keep a sabbath to the LORD. 3Six
years you shall sow your field, and six years
you shall prune your vineyard, and gather its
fruit; 4but in the seventh year there shall be a
sabbath of solemn rest for the land, a sabbath
to the LORD. You shall neither sow your field
nor prune your vineyard. 5What grows of its
own accord of your harvest you shall not reap,
nor gather the grapes of your untended vine,
for it is a year of rest for the land. 6And the sabbath *produce* of the land shall be food for you:
for you, your male and female servants, your
hired man, and the stranger who dwells with
you, 7for your livestock and the beasts that *are*
in your land—all its produce shall be for food.
8'And you shall count seven sabbaths of
years for yourself, seven times seven years;
and the time of the seven sabbaths of years
shall be to you forty-nine years. 9Then you
shall cause the trumpet of the Jubilee to sound
on the tenth *day* of the seventh month; on the
Day of Atonement you shall make the trumpet
to sound throughout all your land. 10And you
shall consecrate the fiftieth year, and proclaim
liberty throughout *all* the land to all its inhabitants. It shall be a Jubilee for you; and each of
you shall return to his possession, and each of
you shall return to his family. 11That fiftieth
year shall be a Jubilee to you; in it you shall
neither sow nor reap what grows of its own
accord, nor gather *the grapes* of your untended
vine. 12For it *is* the Jubilee; it shall be holy to
you; you shall eat its produce from the field.
13'In this Year of Jubilee, each of you shall
return to his possession. 14And if you sell anything to your neighbor or buy from your
neighbor's hand, you shall not oppress one
another. 15According to the number of years
after the Jubilee you shall buy from your
neighbor, and according to the number of
years of crops he shall sell to you. 16According
to the multitude of years you shall increase its
price, and according to the fewer number of
years you shall diminish its price; for he sells
to you *according* to the number *of the years* of
the crops. 17Therefore you shall not oppress
one another, but you shall fear your God; for I
am the LORD your God.
18'So you shall observe My statutes and
keep My judgments, and perform them; and
you will dwell in the land in safety. 19Then the
land will yield its fruit, and you will eat your
fill, and dwell there in safety.
20'And if you say, "What shall we eat in the
seventh year, since we shall not sow nor gather in our produce?" 21Then I will command My
blessing on you in the sixth year, and it will
bring forth produce enough for three years.
22And you shall sow in the eighth year, and eat
old produce until the ninth year; until its produce comes in, you shall eat *of* the old *harvest*.
23'The land shall not be sold permanently,
for the land *is* Mine; for you *are* strangers and

25:8–55 The Year of Jubilee involved a year of release from indebtedness (vv. 23–38) and bondage of all sorts (vv. 39–55). All prisoners and captives were set free, slaves released, and debtors absolved. All property reverted to original owners. This plan curbed inflation and moderated acquisitions. It also gave new opportunity to people who had fallen on hard times.

sojourners with Me. [24]And in all the land of
your possession you shall grant redemption of
the land.

[25]"If one of your brethren becomes poor, and
has sold *some* of his possession, and if his
redeeming relative comes to redeem it, then
he may redeem what his brother sold. [26]Or if
the man has no one to redeem it, but he himself becomes able to redeem it, [27]then let him
count the years since its sale, and restore the
remainder to the man to whom he sold it, that
he may return to his possession. [28]But if he is
not able to have *it* restored to himself, then
what was sold shall remain in the hand of him
who bought it until the Year of Jubilee; and in
the Jubilee it shall be released, and he shall
return to his possession.

[29]"If a man sells a house in a walled city, then
he may redeem it within a whole year after it
is sold; *within* a full year he may redeem it.
[30]But if it is not redeemed within the space of a
full year, then the house in the walled city
shall belong permanently to him who bought
it, throughout his generations. It shall not be
released in the Jubilee. [31]However the houses
of villages which have no wall around them
shall be counted as the fields of the country.
They may be redeemed, and they shall be
released in the Jubilee. [32]Nevertheless the
cities of the Levites, *and* the houses in the
cities of their possession, the Levites may
redeem at any time. [33]And if a man purchases
a house from the Levites, then the house that
was sold in the city of his possession shall be
released in the Jubilee; for the houses in the
cities of the Levites *are* their possession
among the children of Israel. [34]But the field of
the common-land of their cities may not be
sold, for it *is* their perpetual possession.

[35]"If one of your brethren becomes poor, and
falls into poverty among you, then you shall
help him, like a stranger or a sojourner, that
he may live with you. [36]Take no usury or interest from him; but fear your God, that your
brother may live with you. [37]You shall not lend
him your money for usury, nor lend him your
food at a profit. [38]I *am* the LORD your God, who
brought you out of the land of Egypt, to give
you the land of Canaan *and* to be your God.

[39]"And if *one of* your brethren *who dwells* by
you becomes poor, and sells himself to you,
you shall not compel him to serve as a slave.
[40]As a hired servant *and* a sojourner he shall
be with you, *and* shall serve you until the Year
of Jubilee. [41]And *then* he shall depart from
you—he and his children with him—and shall
return to his own family. He shall return to the
possession of his fathers. [42]For they *are* My
servants, whom I brought out of the land of
Egypt; they shall not be sold as slaves. [43]You
shall not rule over him with rigor, but you
shall fear your God. [44]And as for your male and
female slaves whom you may have—from the
nations that are around you, from them you
may buy male and female slaves. [45]Moreover
you may buy the children of the strangers who
dwell among you, and their families who are
with you, which they beget in your land; and
they shall become your property. [46]And you
may take them as an inheritance for your children after you, to inherit *them as* a possession;
they shall be your permanent slaves. But
regarding your brethren, the children of Israel,
you shall not rule over one another with rigor.

[47]"Now if a sojourner or stranger close to
you becomes rich, and *one of* your brethren
who dwells by him becomes poor, and sells
himself to the stranger *or* sojourner close to
you, or to a member of the stranger's family,
[48]after he is sold he may be redeemed again.
One of his brothers may redeem him; [49]or his
uncle or his uncle's son may redeem him; or
anyone who is near of kin to him in his family
may redeem him; or if he is able he may
redeem himself. [50]Thus he shall reckon with
him who bought him: The price of his release
shall be according to the number of years,
from the year that he was sold to him until the
Year of Jubilee; *it shall be* according to the
time of a hired servant for him. [51]If *there are*
still many years *remaining,* according to them
he shall repay the price of his redemption
from the money with which he was bought.
[52]And if there remain but a few years until the
Year of Jubilee, then he shall reckon with him,
and according to his years he shall repay him
the price of his redemption. [53]He shall be with
him as a yearly hired servant, and he shall not
rule with rigor over him in your sight. [54]And if
he is not redeemed in these *years,* then he
shall be released in the Year of Jubilee—he
and his children with him. [55]For the children
of Israel *are* servants to Me; they *are* My servants whom I brought out of the land of Egypt:
I *am* the LORD your God.

Psalm 28:6–9

6 Blessed *be* the LORD,
Because He has heard the voice of my
supplications!
7 The LORD *is* my strength and my
shield;
My heart trusted in Him,
and I am helped;
Therefore my heart greatly rejoices,
And with my song I will praise Him.

28:9 Your inheritance. God amazingly considers His people a most precious possession (see Deut. 7:6–16; 9:29; 1 Sam 10:1; Pss. 33:12; 94:5; Eph. 1:18).

8 The LORD *is* their strength,
And He *is* the saving refuge
of His anointed.
9 Save Your people,
And bless Your inheritance;
Shepherd them also,
And bear them up forever.

Proverbs 10:19–21

19 In the multitude of words sin
is not lacking,
But he who restrains his lips *is* wise.
20 The tongue of the righteous
is choice silver;
The heart of the wicked *is worth* little.
21 The lips of the righteous feed many,
But fools die for lack of wisdom.

Mark 6:30–56

30Then the apostles gathered to Jesus and
told Him all things, both what they had done
and what they had taught. 31And He said to
them, "Come aside by yourselves to a deserted place and rest a while." For there were
many coming and going, and they did not
even have time to eat. 32So they departed to a
deserted place in the boat by themselves.
33But the multitudes saw them departing,
and many knew Him and ran there on foot
from all the cities. They arrived before them
and came together to Him. 34And Jesus, when
He came out, saw a great multitude and was
moved with compassion for them, because
they were like sheep not having a shepherd.
So He began to teach them many things.
35When the day was now far spent, His disciples came to Him and said, "This is a deserted
place, and already the hour *is* late. 36Send them
away, that they may go into the surrounding
country and villages and buy themselves
bread; for they have nothing to eat."
37But He answered and said to them, "You
give them something to eat."

And they said to Him, "Shall we go and buy two hundred denarii worth of bread and give them *something* to eat?"

38But He said to them, "How many loaves do
you have? Go and see."

And when they found out they said, "Five, and two fish."

39Then He commanded them to make them
all sit down in groups on the green grass. 40So
they sat down in ranks, in hundreds and in
fifties. 41And when He had taken the five loaves
and the two fish, He looked up to heaven,
blessed and broke the loaves, and gave *them*
to His disciples to set before them; and the
two fish He divided among *them* all. 42So they
all ate and were filled. 43And they took up
twelve baskets full of fragments and of the
fish. 44Now those who had eaten the loaves
were about five thousand men.

6:44 five thousand men. The Greek word for "men" means strictly males, so the numerical estimate did not include women and children (see Matt. 14:21). The women and children were traditionally seated separately from the men for meals. When everyone was added, there could have been at least 20,000.

45Immediately He made His disciples get
into the boat and go before Him to the other
side, to Bethsaida, while He sent the multitude away. 46And when He had sent them
away, He departed to the mountain to pray.
47Now when evening came, the boat was in the
middle of the sea; and He *was* alone on the
land. 48Then He saw them straining at rowing,
for the wind was against them. Now about the
fourth watch of the night He came to them,
walking on the sea, and would have passed
them by. 49And when they saw Him walking on
the sea, they supposed it was a ghost, and cried
out; 50for they all saw Him and were troubled.
But immediately He talked with them and said
to them, "Be of good cheer! It is I; do not be
afraid." 51Then He went up into the boat to
them, and the wind ceased. And they were
greatly amazed in themselves beyond measure,
and marveled. 52For they had not understood

6:50 Be of good cheer! This command, always linked in the Gospels to a situation of fear and apprehension (see 10:49; Matt. 9:2,22; 14:27; Luke 8:48; John 16:33; Acts 23:11), urged the disciples to have a continuing attitude of courage. **It is I.** Literally, "I AM." This statement clearly identified the figure as the Lord Jesus, not some phantom. It echoed the Old Testament self-revelation of God (see Ex. 3:14).

about the loaves, because their heart was
hardened.
53When they had crossed over, they came to
the land of Gennesaret and anchored there.
54And when they came out of the boat, immediately the people recognized Him, 55ran
through that whole surrounding region, and
began to carry about on beds those who were
sick to wherever they heard He was. 56Wher-
ever He entered, into villages, cities, or the
country, they laid the sick in the marketplaces, and begged Him that they might just
touch the hem of His garment. And as many
as touched Him were made well.

DAY 28: List all the Jewish feasts and dates.

Feast of	Month on Jewish Calendar	Day	Corresponding Month	References
Passover	Nisan	14	Mar.–Apr.	Exodus 12:1–14; Matthew 26:17–20
*Unleavened Bread	Nisan	15-21	Mar.–Apr.	Exodus 12:15–20
Firstfruits	Nisan or Sivan	16 / 6	Mar.–Apr. / May–June	Leviticus 23:9–14; Numbers (28:26)
*Pentecost (Harvest or Weeks)	Sivan	6 (50 days after barley harvest)	May–June	Deuteronomy 16:9–12; Acts 2:1
Trumpets, Rosh Hashanah	Tishri	1, 2	Sept.–Oct.	Numbers 29:1–6
Day of Atonement, Yom Kippur	Tishri	10	Sept.–Oct.	Leviticus 23:26–32; Hebrews 9:7
*Tabernacles (Booths or Ingathering)	Tishri	15-22	Sept.–Oct.	Nehemiah 8:13–18; John 7:2
Dedication (Lights), Hanukkah	Chislev	25 (8 days)	Nov.–Dec.	John 10:22
Purim (Lots)	Adar	14,15	Feb.–Mar.	Esther 9:18–22

*The three major feasts for which all males of Israel were required to travel to the temple in Jerusalem (Ex. 23:14–19).

MARCH 1

Leviticus 26:1–27:34

26 'You shall not make idols for yourselves;
neither a carved image nor a *sacred* pillar shall you rear up for yourselves;
nor shall you set up an engraved stone in your land, to bow down to it;
for I *am* the LORD your God.
2 You shall keep My Sabbaths and reverence My sanctuary:
I *am* the LORD.
3 'If you walk in My statutes and keep My commandments, and perform them,
4 then I will give you rain in its season, the land shall yield its produce, and the trees of the field shall yield their fruit.
5 Your threshing shall last till the time of vintage, and the vintage shall last till the time of sowing;
you shall eat your bread to the full, and dwell in your land safely.
6 I will give peace in the land, and you shall lie down, and none will make *you* afraid;
I will rid the land of evil beasts,
and the sword will not go through your land.
7 You will chase your enemies, and they shall fall by the sword before you.
8 Five of you shall chase a hundred, and a hundred of you shall put ten thousand to flight;
your enemies shall fall by the sword before you.

26:9 make you fruitful, multiply you and confirm My covenant with you. What God commanded at creation and repeated after the Flood was contained in the covenant promise of seed (Gen. 12:1–3), which He will fulfill to the nation of Israel as promised to Abraham (Gen. 15:5,6).

26:12 your God...My people. The promise of an intimate covenant relationship with the God of the universe is given (see 2 Cor. 6:16).

9 'For I will look on you favorably and make you fruitful, multiply you and confirm My covenant with you.
10 You shall eat the old harvest, and clear out the old because of the new.
11 I will set My tabernacle among you, and My soul shall not abhor you.
12 I will walk among you and be your God, and you shall be My people.
13 I *am* the LORD your God, who brought you out of the land of Egypt, that *you* should not be their slaves;
I have broken the bands of your yoke and made you walk upright.
14 'But if you do not obey Me, and do not observe all these commandments,
15 and if you despise My statutes, or if your soul abhors My judgments, so that you do not perform all My commandments, *but* break My covenant,
16 I also will do this to you:
I will even appoint terror over you, wasting disease and fever which shall consume the eyes and cause sorrow of heart.
And you shall sow your seed in vain, for your enemies shall eat it.
17 I will set My face against you, and you shall be defeated by your enemies.
Those who hate you shall reign over you, and you shall flee when no one pursues you.
18 'And after all this, if you do not obey Me, then I will punish you seven times more for your sins.
19 I will break the pride of your power;
I will make your heavens like iron and your earth like bronze.
20 And your strength shall be spent in vain;
for your land shall not yield its produce, nor shall the trees of the land yield their fruit.
21 'Then, if you walk contrary to Me, and are not willing to obey Me, I will bring on you seven times more plagues, according to your sins.
22 I will also send wild beasts among you, which shall rob you of your children, destroy your livestock, and make you few in number;
and your highways shall be desolate.
23 'And if by these things you are not reformed by Me, but walk contrary to Me,

24 then I also will walk contrary to you, and
I will punish you yet seven times for
your sins.
25 And I will bring a sword against you
that will execute the vengeance of
the covenant;
when you are gathered together within
your cities I will send pestilence
among you;
and you shall be delivered into the hand
of the enemy.
26 When I have cut off your supply of
bread, ten women shall bake your
bread in one oven, and they shall
bring back your bread by weight, and
you shall eat and not be satisfied.

27 'And after all this, if you do not obey Me,
but walk contrary to Me,
28 then I also will walk contrary to you in
fury;
and I, even I, will chastise you seven
times for your sins.
29 You shall eat the flesh of your sons, and
you shall eat the flesh of your
daughters.
30 I will destroy your high places, cut
down your incense altars, and cast
your carcasses on the lifeless forms
of your idols;
and My soul shall abhor you.

26:30 high places. These were natural shrines for the worship of idols. Solomon disobeyed God by worshiping Him on the high places (1 Kin. 3:4); and not long afterward, he was serving the gods of his foreign wives (1 Kin. 11:1–9).

31 I will lay your cities waste and bring
your sanctuaries to desolation, and I
will not smell the fragrance of your
sweet aromas.
32 I will bring the land to desolation, and
your enemies who dwell in it shall
be astonished at it.
33 I will scatter you among the nations and
draw out a sword after you;
your land shall be desolate and your
cities waste.
34 Then the land shall enjoy its sabbaths
as long as it lies desolate and you
are in your enemies' land;
then the land shall rest and enjoy its
sabbaths.
35 As long as *it* lies desolate it shall rest—
for the time it did not rest on your sabbaths when you dwelt in it.

36 'And as for those of you who are left, I
will send faintness into their hearts
in the lands of their enemies;
the sound of a shaken leaf shall cause
them to flee;
they shall flee as though fleeing from a
sword, and they shall fall when no
one pursues.
37 They shall stumble over one another, as
it were before a sword, when no one
pursues;
and you shall have no *power* to stand
before your enemies.
38 You shall perish among the nations, and
the land of your enemies shall eat
you up.
39 And those of you who are left shall
waste away in their iniquity in your
enemies' lands;
also in their fathers' iniquities, which
are with them, they shall waste away.

40 '*But* if they confess their iniquity and the
iniquity of their fathers, with their
unfaithfulness in which they were
unfaithful to Me, and that they also
have walked contrary to Me,
41 and *that* I also have walked contrary to
them and have brought them into
the land of their enemies;
if their uncircumcised hearts are humbled, and they accept their guilt—
42 then I will remember My covenant with
Jacob, and My covenant with Isaac
and My covenant with Abraham I
will remember;
I will remember the land.
43 The land also shall be left empty by
them, and will enjoy its sabbaths
while it lies desolate without them;
they will accept their guilt, because
they despised My judgments and
because their soul abhorred My
statutes.
44 Yet for all that, when they are in the
land of their enemies, I will not cast
them away, nor shall I abhor them,
to utterly destroy them and break
My covenant with them;
for I *am* the LORD their God.
45 But for their sake I will remember the
covenant of their ancestors, whom I
brought out of the land of Egypt in
the sight of the nations, that I might
be their God:
I *am* the LORD.' "

[46]"These *are* the statutes and judgments and
laws which the LORD made between Himself
and the children of Israel on Mount Sinai by
the hand of Moses.

27 Now the LORD spoke to Moses, saying,
[2]"Speak to the children of Israel, and
say to them: 'When a man consecrates by a
vow certain persons to the LORD, according to
your valuation, [3]if your valuation is of a male
from twenty years old up to sixty years old,
then your valuation shall be fifty shekels of silver, according to the shekel of the sanctuary.
[4]If it *is* a female, then your valuation shall be
thirty shekels; [5]and if from five years old up to
twenty years old, then your valuation for a
male shall be twenty shekels, and for a female
ten shekels; [6]and if from a month old up to five
years old, then your valuation for a male shall
be five shekels of silver, and for a female your
valuation shall be three shekels of silver; [7]and
if from sixty years old and above, if *it is* a male,
then your valuation shall be fifteen shekels,
and for a female ten shekels.

[8]'But if he is too poor to pay your valuation,
then he shall present himself before the priest,
and the priest shall set a value for him; according to the ability of him who vowed, the priest
shall value him.

[9]'If *it is* an animal that men may bring as an
offering to the LORD, all that *anyone* gives to
the LORD shall be holy. [10]He shall not substitute
it or exchange it, good for bad or bad for good;
and if he at all exchanges animal for animal,
then both it and the one exchanged for it shall
be holy. [11]If *it is* an unclean animal which they
do not offer as a sacrifice to the LORD, then he
shall present the animal before the priest; [12]and
the priest shall set a value for it, whether it is
good or bad; as you, the priest, value it, so it
shall be. [13]But if he *wants* at all *to* redeem it,
then he must add one-fifth to your valuation.

[14]'And when a man dedicates his house *to be*
holy to the LORD, then the priest shall set a
value for it, whether it is good or bad; as the
priest values it, so it shall stand. [15]If he who
dedicated it *wants to* redeem his house, then
he must add one-fifth of the money of your valuation to it, and it shall be his.

[16]'If a man dedicates to the LORD *part* of a
field of his possession, then your valuation
shall be according to the seed for it. A homer
of barley seed *shall be valued* at fifty shekels of
silver. [17]If he dedicates his field from the Year
of Jubilee, according to your valuation it shall
stand. [18]But if he dedicates his field after the
Jubilee, then the priest shall reckon to him the
money due according to the years that remain
till the Year of Jubilee, and it shall be deducted
from your valuation. [19]And if he who dedicates
the field ever wishes to redeem it, then he
must add one-fifth of the money of your valuation to it, and it shall belong to him. [20]But if he
does not want to redeem the field, or if he has
sold the field to another man, it shall not be
redeemed anymore; [21]but the field, when it is
released in the Jubilee, shall be holy to the
LORD, as a devoted field; it shall be the possession of the priest.

[22]'And if a man dedicates to the LORD a field
which he has bought, which is not the field of
his possession, [23]then the priest shall reckon
to him the worth of your valuation, up to the
Year of Jubilee, and he shall give your valuation on that day *as* a holy *offering* to the LORD.
[24]In the Year of Jubilee the field shall return to
him from whom it was bought, to the one who
owned the land as a possession. [25]And all your
valuations shall be according to the shekel of
the sanctuary: twenty gerahs to the shekel.

[26]'But the firstborn of the animals, which
should be the LORD's firstborn, no man shall
dedicate; whether *it is* an ox or sheep, it *is* the
LORD's. [27]And if *it is* an unclean animal, then he
shall redeem *it* according to your valuation, and
shall add one-fifth to it; or if it is not redeemed,
then it shall be sold according to your valuation.

[28]'Nevertheless no devoted *offering* that a
man may devote to the LORD of all that he has,
both man and beast, or the field of his possession, shall be sold or redeemed; every devoted
offering is most holy to the LORD. [29]No person
under the ban, who may become doomed to
destruction among men, shall be redeemed,
but shall surely be put to death. [30]And all the
tithe of the land, *whether* of the seed of the
land *or* of the fruit of the tree, *is* the LORD's. It
is holy to the LORD. [31]If a man wants at all to
redeem *any* of his tithes, he shall add one-fifth
to it. [32]And concerning the tithe of the herd or
the flock, of whatever passes under the rod,
the tenth one shall be holy to the LORD. [33]He
shall not inquire whether it is good or bad, nor
shall he exchange it; and if he exchanges it at
all, then both it and the one exchanged for it
shall be holy; it shall not be redeemed.' "

[34]These *are* the commandments which the
LORD commanded Moses for the children of
Israel on Mount Sinai.

Psalm 29:1–6

A Psalm of David.

Give unto the LORD, O you mighty ones,
Give unto the LORD glory and strength.
2 Give unto the LORD the glory due to
His name;

29:1 mighty ones. Literally, "sons of God" (see Ps. 89:6 in its context of vv. 5–10; see the plural form of "gods" in Ex. 15:11). The reference here in Psalm 29 is most likely to Yahweh's mighty angels.

Worship the LORD in the beauty
of holiness.
3 The voice of the LORD *is* over
the waters;
The God of glory thunders;
The LORD *is* over many waters.
4 The voice of the LORD *is* powerful;
The voice of the LORD *is* full of majesty.
5 The voice of the LORD breaks
the cedars,
Yes, the LORD splinters the cedars
of Lebanon.
6 He makes them also skip like a calf,
Lebanon and Sirion like a young
wild ox.

Proverbs 10:22–25

22 The blessing of the LORD makes *one* rich,
And He adds no sorrow with it.

10:22 rich. While having more than one needs is not the object of wisdom, it is generally the result (see Deut. 6:11–15; 1 Kin. 3:10–14). **no sorrow.** None of the sorrow that is associated with ill-gotten wealth (see 13:11; 15:6; 16:19; 21:6; 28:6) is associated with wealth provided by the Lord.

23 To do evil *is* like sport to a fool,
But a man of understanding has
wisdom.
24 The fear of the wicked will come upon
him,
And the desire of the righteous will be
granted.
25 When the whirlwind passes by, the
wicked *is* no *more,*
But the righteous *has* an everlasting
foundation.

Mark 7:1–13

7 Then the Pharisees and some of the
scribes came together to Him, having
come from Jerusalem. 2Now when they saw
some of His disciples eat bread with defiled,
that is, with unwashed hands, they found fault.
3For the Pharisees and all the Jews do not eat
unless they wash *their* hands in a special way,
holding the tradition of the elders. 4*When they*
come from the marketplace, they do not eat
unless they wash. And there are many other
things which they have received and hold, *like*
the washing of cups, pitchers, copper vessels,
and couches.
5Then the Pharisees and scribes asked Him,
"Why do Your disciples not walk according to
the tradition of the elders, but eat bread with
unwashed hands?"
6He answered and said to them, "Well did
Isaiah prophesy of you hypocrites, as it is written:

'This people honors Me with their lips,
But their heart is far from Me.
7 *And in vain they worship Me,*
Teaching as doctrines the
commandments of men.'

8For laying aside the commandment of God,
you hold the tradition of men—the washing of
pitchers and cups, and many other such
things you do."
9He said to them, "*All too* well you reject the
commandment of God, that you may keep
your tradition. 10For Moses said, *'Honor your*
father and your mother'; and, *'He who curses*
father or mother, let him be put to death.' 11But
you say, 'If a man says to his father or mother,
"Whatever profit you might have received
from me *is* Corban"—' (that is, a gift *to God*),
12then you no longer let him do anything for
his father or his mother, 13making the word of
God of no effect through your tradition which
you have handed down. And many such
things you do."

DAY 1: What did the washing of hands have to do with spirituality?

In Mark 7:1, a delegation of leading representatives of Judaism came from Jerusalem perhaps at the request of the Galilean Pharisees. They immediately found fault with the disciples of Jesus, accusing them of eating with hands that had not been ceremonially cleansed and, thus, that had not been separated from the defilement associated with their having touched anything profane (v. 2). This washing had nothing to do with cleaning dirty hands but with a ceremonial rinsing. The ceremony involved someone pouring water out of a jar onto another's hands, whose fingers must be pointing up. As long as the water dripped off at the wrist, the person could proceed to the next step. He then had water poured over both hands with the fingers pointing down. Then each hand was to be rubbed with the fist of the other hand. This was according to the "tradition of the elders"—a body of extrabiblical laws and interpretations of Scripture that had in actuality supplanted Scripture as the highest religious authority in Judaism.

The Pharisees and scribes went to the disciples' Master for an explanation of the disciples' allegedly disgraceful conduct. In reality, they were accusing Jesus of teaching His disciples to disobey the tradition of the elders (v. 5). Jesus' reply was to quote Isaiah 29:13, whose prophecy perfectly fit the actions of the Pharisees. Not only were their hearts far from God but they were "hypocrites," or spiritual phonies (v. 6). They followed the traditions of men because such teaching required only mechanical and thoughtless conformity without a pure heart. And in doing so, they had abandoned all the commandments contained in God's Word and substituted a humanly designed standard for God's standard (v. 8).

MARCH 2

Numbers 1:1–2:34

1 Now the LORD spoke to Moses in the
Wilderness of Sinai, in the tabernacle of
meeting, on the first *day* of the second month,
in the second year after they had come out of
the land of Egypt, saying: 2"Take a census of
all the congregation of the children of Israel,
by their families, by their fathers' houses,
according to the number of names, every
male individually, 3from twenty years old and
above—all who *are able to* go to war in Israel.
You and Aaron shall number them by their
armies. 4And with you there shall be a man
from every tribe, each one the head of his
father's house.
5"These are the names of the men who shall
stand with you: from Reuben, Elizur the son
of Shedeur; 6from Simeon, Shelumiel the son of
Zurishaddai; 7from Judah, Nahshon the son
of Amminadab; 8from Issachar, Nethanel the
son of Zuar; 9from Zebulun, Eliab the son of
Helon; 10from the sons of Joseph: from
Ephraim, Elishama the son of Ammihud; from
Manasseh, Gamaliel the son of Pedahzur;
11from Benjamin, Abidan the son of Gideoni;
12from Dan, Ahiezer the son of Ammishaddai;
13from Asher, Pagiel the son of Ocran; 14from
Gad, Eliasaph the son of Deuel; 15from Naphtali, Ahira the son of Enan." 16These *were* chosen from the congregation, leaders of their
fathers' tribes, heads of the divisions in Israel.
17Then Moses and Aaron took these men
who had been mentioned by name, 18and they
assembled all the congregation together on the
first *day* of the second month; and they recited
their ancestry by families, by their fathers'
houses, according to the number of names,
from twenty years old and above, each one
individually. 19As the LORD commanded Moses,
so he numbered them in the Wilderness of
Sinai.
20Now the children of Reuben, Israel's oldest son, their genealogies by their families, by
their fathers' house, according to the number
of names, every male individually, from twenty years old and above, all who *were able to* go
to war: 21those who were numbered of the
tribe of Reuben *were* forty-six thousand five
hundred.
22From the children of Simeon, their
genealogies by their families, by their fathers'
house, of those who were numbered, according to the number of names, every male individually, from twenty years old and above, all
who *were able to* go to war: 23those who were
numbered of the tribe of Simeon *were* fifty-
nine thousand three hundred.
24From the children of Gad, their genealogies by their families, by their fathers' house,
according to the number of names, from twenty years old and above, all who *were able to* go
to war: 25those who were numbered of the
tribe of Gad *were* forty-five thousand six hundred and fifty.

1:2 a census. In Exodus 30:11–16, the Lord had commanded that a census of the males in Israel over 20 (excluding the Levites) be taken for the purpose of determining the ransom money for the service of the tabernacle. The result of that census is recorded in Exodus 38:25–28. The total number, 603,550 (Ex. 38:26), equals the number in 1:46.

1:3 go to war. The purpose of this census was to form a roster of fighting men. The Book of Numbers looks ahead to the invasion of the land promised to Abraham (see Gen. 12:1–3).

[26]From the children of Judah, their genealogies by their families, by their fathers' house,
according to the number of names, from twenty years old and above, all who *were able to* go
to war: [27]those who were numbered of the
tribe of Judah *were* seventy-four thousand six
hundred.

[28]From the children of Issachar, their
genealogies by their families, by their fathers'
house, according to the number of names,
from twenty years old and above, all who *were
able to* go to war: [29]those who were numbered
of the tribe of Issachar *were* fifty-four thousand
four hundred.

[30]From the children of Zebulun, their
genealogies by their families, by their fathers'
house, according to the number of names,
from twenty years old and above, all who *were
able to* go to war: [31]those who were numbered
of the tribe of Zebulun *were* fifty-seven thousand four hundred.

[32]From the sons of Joseph, the children of
Ephraim, their genealogies by their families,
by their fathers' house, according to the number of names, from twenty years old and above,
all who *were able to* go to war: [33]those who were
numbered of the tribe of Ephraim *were* forty
thousand five hundred.

[34]From the children of Manasseh, their
genealogies by their families, by their fathers'
house, according to the number of names,
from twenty years old and above, all who *were
able to* go to war: [35]those who were numbered
of the tribe of Manasseh *were* thirty-two thousand two hundred.

[36]From the children of Benjamin, their
genealogies by their families, by their fathers'
house, according to the number of names,
from twenty years old and above, all who *were
able to* go to war: [37]those who were numbered
of the tribe of Benjamin *were* thirty-five thousand four hundred.

[38]From the children of Dan, their genealogies
by their families, by their fathers' house,
according to the number of names, from twenty years old and above, all who *were able to* go
to war: [39]those who were numbered of the tribe
of Dan *were* sixty-two thousand seven hundred.

[40]From the children of Asher, their genealogies by their families, by their fathers' house,
according to the number of names, from twenty years old and above, all who *were able to* go
to war: [41]those who were numbered of the tribe
of Asher *were* forty-one thousand five hundred.

[42]From the children of Naphtali, their
genealogies by their families, by their fathers'
house, according to the number of names,
from twenty years old and above, all who *were
able to* go to war: [43]those who were numbered
of the tribe of Naphtali *were* fifty-three thousand four hundred.

[44]These are the ones who were numbered,
whom Moses and Aaron numbered, with the
leaders of Israel, twelve men, each one representing his father's house. [45]So all who
were numbered of the children of Israel, by
their fathers' houses, from twenty years old
and above, all who *were able to* go to war in
Israel— [46]all who were numbered were six
hundred and three thousand five hundred and
fifty.

[47]But the Levites were not numbered among
them by their fathers' tribe; [48]for the LORD had
spoken to Moses, saying: [49]"Only the tribe of
Levi you shall not number, nor take a census
of them among the children of Israel; [50]but you
shall appoint the Levites over the tabernacle of
the Testimony, over all its furnishings, and
over all things that belong to it; they shall
carry the tabernacle and all its furnishings;
they shall attend to it and camp around the
tabernacle. [51]And when the tabernacle is to go
forward, the Levites shall take it down; and
when the tabernacle is to be set up, the
Levites shall set it up. The outsider who comes
near shall be put to death. [52]The children of

1:51 The outsider. This word often refers to the "alien" or "stranger." The non-Levite Israelite was like a "foreigner" to the transporting of the tabernacle and had to keep his distance lest he die.

Israel shall pitch their tents, everyone by his
own camp, everyone by his own standard,
according to their armies; [53]but the Levites shall
camp around the tabernacle of the Testimony,
that there may be no wrath on the congregation of the children of Israel; and the Levites
shall keep charge of the tabernacle of the
Testimony."

[54]Thus the children of Israel did; according
to all that the LORD commanded Moses, so
they did.

2 And the LORD spoke to Moses and Aaron,
saying: [2]"Everyone of the children of Israel
shall camp by his own standard, beside the
emblems of his father's house; they shall
camp some distance from the tabernacle of
meeting. [3]On the east side, toward the rising
of the sun, those of the standard of the forces
with Judah shall camp according to their
armies; and Nahshon the son of Amminadab

shall be the leader of the children of Judah."
[4]And his army was numbered at seventy-four
thousand six hundred.
[5]"Those who camp next to him *shall be* the
tribe of Issachar, and Nethanel the son of Zuar
shall be the leader of the children of Issachar."
[6]And his army was numbered at fifty-four thousand four hundred.
[7]"Then *comes* the tribe of Zebulun, and Eliab
the son of Helon *shall be* the leader of the children of Zebulun." [8]And his army was numbered at fifty-seven thousand four hundred.
[9]"All who were numbered according to their
armies of the forces with Judah, one hundred
and eighty-six thousand four hundred—these
shall break camp first.
[10]"On the south side *shall be* the standard of
the forces with Reuben according to their
armies, and the leader of the children of Reuben *shall be* Elizur the son of Shedeur." [11]And
his army was numbered at forty-six thousand
five hundred.
[12]"Those who camp next to him *shall be* the
tribe of Simeon, and the leader of the children
of Simeon *shall be* Shelumiel the son of
Zurishaddai." [13]And his army was numbered at
fifty-nine thousand three hundred.
[14]"Then *comes* the tribe of Gad, and the
leader of the children of Gad *shall be* Eliasaph
the son of Reuel." [15]And his army was numbered at forty-five thousand six hundred and
fifty. [16]"All who were numbered according to
their armies of the forces with Reuben, one hundred and fifty-one thousand four hundred and
fifty—they shall be the second to break camp.
[17]"And the tabernacle of meeting shall move
out with the camp of the Levites in the middle
of the camps; as they camp, so they shall move
out, everyone in his place, by their standards.
[18]"On the west side *shall be* the standard of
the forces with Ephraim according to their
armies, and the leader of the children of
Ephraim *shall be* Elishama the son of Ammihud." [19]And his army was numbered at forty
thousand five hundred.
[20]"Next to him *comes* the tribe of Manasseh,
and the leader of the children of Manasseh
shall be Gamaliel the son of Pedahzur." [21]And
his army was numbered at thirty-two thousand two hundred.
[22]"Then *comes* the tribe of Benjamin, and the
leader of the children of Benjamin *shall be*
Abidan the son of Gideoni." [23]And his army
was numbered at thirty-five thousand four
hundred. [24]"All who were numbered according
to their armies of the forces with Ephraim, one
hundred and eight thousand one hundred—
they shall be the third to break camp.
[25]"The standard of the forces with Dan *shall*
be on the north side according to their armies,
and the leader of the children of Dan *shall be*
Ahiezer the son of Ammishaddai." [26]And his
army was numbered at sixty-two thousand
seven hundred.
[27]"Those who camp next to him *shall be* the
tribe of Asher, and the leader of the children of
Asher *shall be* Pagiel the son of Ocran." [28]And
his army was numbered at forty-one thousand
five hundred.
[29]"Then *comes* the tribe of Naphtali, and the
leader of the children of Naphtali *shall be* Ahira
the son of Enan." [30]And his army was numbered at fifty-three thousand four hundred.
[31]"All who were numbered of the forces with
Dan, one hundred and fifty-seven thousand six
hundred—they shall break camp last, with
their standards."
[32]These *are* the ones who were numbered of
the children of Israel by their fathers' houses.
All who were numbered according to their
armies of the forces *were* six hundred and
three thousand five hundred and fifty. [33]But the
Levites were not numbered among the children of Israel, just as the LORD commanded
Moses.
[34]Thus the children of Israel did according
to all that the LORD commanded Moses; so
they camped by their standards and so they
broke camp, each one by his family, according
to their fathers' houses.

Psalm 29:7–11

7 The voice of the LORD divides the
flames of fire.
8 The voice of the LORD shakes the
wilderness;
The LORD shakes the Wilderness of
Kadesh.
9 The voice of the LORD makes the deer
give birth,
And strips the forests bare;
And in His temple everyone says,
"Glory!"
10 The LORD sat *enthroned* at the Flood,
And the LORD sits as King forever.
11 The LORD will give strength to His
people;
The LORD will bless His people with
peace.

Proverbs 10:26–29

26 As vinegar to the teeth and smoke to
the eyes,
So *is* the lazy *man* to those who send
him.

27 The fear of the LORD prolongs days,
But the years of the wicked will be
shortened.
28 The hope of the righteous *will be*
gladness,
But the expectation of the wicked will
perish.
29 The way of the LORD *is* strength for the
upright,
But destruction *will come* to the
workers of iniquity.

Mark 7:14–37

14When He had called all the multitude to
Himself, He said to them, "Hear Me, everyone, and understand: 15There is nothing that
enters a man from outside which can defile
him; but the things which come out of him,
those are the things that defile a man. 16If anyone has ears to hear, let him hear!"
17When He had entered a house away from
the crowd, His disciples asked Him concerning the parable. 18So He said to them, "Are you
thus without understanding also? Do you not

7:19 Since food is merely physical, no one who eats it will defile his heart or inner person, which is spiritual. Physical pollution, no matter how corrupt, cannot cause spiritual or moral pollution. Neither can external ceremonies and rituals cleanse a person spiritually. ***thus* purifying all foods.** By overturning the tradition of hand washing, Jesus in effect removed the restrictions regarding dietary laws.

7:20 What comes out of a man. A person's defiled heart is expressed in both what he says and what he does.

perceive that whatever enters a man from outside cannot defile him, 19because it does not
enter his heart but his stomach, and is eliminated, *thus* purifying all foods?" 20And He said,
"What comes out of a man, that defiles a man.
21For from within, out of the heart of men, proceed evil thoughts, adulteries, fornications,
murders, 22thefts, covetousness, wickedness,
deceit, lewdness, an evil eye, blasphemy,
pride, foolishness. 23All these evil things come
from within and defile a man."
24From there He arose and went to the
region of Tyre and Sidon. And He entered a
house and wanted no one to know *it,* but He
could not be hidden. 25For a woman whose
young daughter had an unclean spirit heard
about Him, and she came and fell at His feet.
26The woman was a Greek, a Syro-Phoenician
by birth, and she kept asking Him to cast the
demon out of her daughter. 27But Jesus said to
her, "Let the children be filled first, for it is not
good to take the children's bread and throw *it*
to the little dogs."
28And she answered and said to Him, "Yes,
Lord, yet even the little dogs under the table
eat from the children's crumbs."
29Then He said to her, "For this saying go
your way; the demon has gone out of your
daughter."
30And when she had come to her house, she
found the demon gone out, and her daughter
lying on the bed.
31Again, departing from the region of Tyre
and Sidon, He came through the midst of the
region of Decapolis to the Sea of Galilee.
32Then they brought to Him one who was deaf
and had an impediment in his speech, and
they begged Him to put His hand on him.
33And He took him aside from the multitude,
and put His fingers in his ears, and He spat and
touched his tongue. 34Then, looking up to
heaven, He sighed, and said to him,
"Ephphatha," that is, "Be opened."
35Immediately his ears were opened, and the
impediment of his tongue was loosed, and he
spoke plainly. 36Then He commanded them
that they should tell no one; but the more He
commanded them, the more widely they proclaimed *it.* 37And they were astonished beyond
measure, saying, "He has done all things well.
He makes both the deaf to hear and the mute to
speak."

DAY 2: Did Moses perhaps inflate the numbers of Jews in the wilderness?

Twice during the wilderness wanderings a census of the people of Israel was taken (Numbers 1:46; 26:51). Each time the resulting total count of fighting men exceeded 600,000. These numbers indicate a population for Israel in the wilderness of around 2.5 million people at any time. Viewed naturally, this total appears too high to sustain in wilderness conditions.

Before concluding that Moses inflated the numbers, several factors must be considered. First, the Lord supernaturally took care of Israel for 40 years (Deut. 8:1–5). Miraculous provision of food was a daily event. Second, God also spelled out sanitary practices that prevented the kind of health crises that might have occurred under those conditions. Third, while Israel wandered in the wilderness for

40 years, they only moved camp about 40 times. Spending about a year in each campsite allowed for some normal life without creating a permanent settlement. This preserved some grazing for the herds while keeping the people's pollution to a manageable amount. Each census was meant to be an accurate accounting of God's people. They ought to be taken at face value.

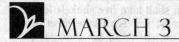

MARCH 3

Numbers 3:1–4:49

3 Now these *are* the records of Aaron and Moses when the LORD spoke with Moses on Mount Sinai. [2]And these *are* the names of the sons of Aaron: Nadab, the firstborn, and Abihu, Eleazar, and Ithamar. [3]These *are* the names of the sons of Aaron, the anointed priests, whom he consecrated to minister as priests. [4]Nadab and Abihu had died before the LORD when they offered profane fire before the LORD in the Wilderness of Sinai; and they had no children. So Eleazar and Ithamar ministered as priests in the presence of Aaron their father.

3:1 Aaron and Moses. Because Aaron and his sons are emphasized in this chapter, Aaron is named first. **Mount Sinai.** The Lord had first communicated to Moses His choice of Aaron and his sons as priests in Exodus 28:1–29:46, while he was in the midst of the cloud on Mt. Sinai (Ex. 24:18).

3:4 Eleazar and Ithamar. All of the future priests of Israel under the Mosaic Covenant were descendants of these two sons of Aaron. Eleazar and his descendants would later be singled out for great blessing (see Num. 25:10–13).

[5]And the LORD spoke to Moses, saying: [6]"Bring the tribe of Levi near, and present them before Aaron the priest, that they may serve him. [7]And they shall attend to his needs and the needs of the whole congregation before the tabernacle of meeting, to do the work of the tabernacle. [8]Also they shall attend to all the furnishings of the tabernacle of meeting, and to the needs of the children of Israel, to do the work of the tabernacle. [9]And you shall give the Levites to Aaron and his sons; they *are* given entirely to him from among the children of Israel. [10]So you shall appoint Aaron and his sons, and they shall attend to their priesthood; but the outsider who comes near shall be put to death."

[11]Then the LORD spoke to Moses, saying: [12]"Now behold, I Myself have taken the Levites from among the children of Israel instead of every firstborn who opens the womb among the children of Israel. Therefore the Levites shall be Mine, [13]because all the firstborn *are* Mine. On the day that I struck all the firstborn in the land of Egypt, I sanctified to Myself all the firstborn in Israel, both man and beast. They shall be Mine: I *am* the LORD."

[14]Then the LORD spoke to Moses in the Wilderness of Sinai, saying: [15]"Number the children of Levi by their fathers' houses, by their families; you shall number every male from a month old and above."

[16]So Moses numbered them according to the word of the LORD, as he was commanded. [17]These were the sons of Levi by their names: Gershon, Kohath, and Merari. [18]And these *are* the names of the sons of Gershon by their families: Libni and Shimei. [19]And the sons of Kohath by their families: Amram, Izehar, Hebron, and Uzziel. [20]And the sons of Merari by their families: Mahli and Mushi. These *are* the families of the Levites by their fathers' houses.

[21]From Gershon *came* the family of the Libnites and the family of the Shimites; these *were* the families of the Gershonites. [22]Those who were numbered, according to the number of all the males from a month old and above—of those who were numbered *there were* seven thousand five hundred. [23]The families of the Gershonites were to camp behind the tabernacle westward. [24]And the leader of the father's house of the Gershonites *was* Eliasaph the son of Lael. [25]The duties of the children of Gershon in the tabernacle of meeting *included* the tabernacle, the tent with its covering, the screen for the door of the tabernacle of meeting, [26]the screen for the door of the court, the hangings of the court which *are* around the tabernacle and the altar, and their cords, according to all the work relating to them.

[27]From Kohath *came* the family of the Amramites, the family of the Izharites, the family of the Hebronites, and the family of the Uzzielites; these *were* the families of the Kohathites. [28]According to the number of all the

males, from a month old and above, *there were*
eight thousand six hundred keeping charge of
the sanctuary. 29The families of the children of
Kohath were to camp on the south side of the
tabernacle. 30And the leader of the fathers'
house of the families of the Kohathites *was*
Elizaphan the son of Uzziel. 31Their duty *includ-*
ed the ark, the table, the lampstand, the altars,
the utensils of the sanctuary with which they
ministered, the screen, and all the work relating to them.

32And Eleazar the son of Aaron the priest
was to be chief over the leaders of the Levites,
with oversight of those who kept charge of the
sanctuary.

33From Merari *came* the family of the
Mahlites and the family of the Mushites; these
were the families of Merari. 34And those who
were numbered, according to the number of
all the males from a month old and above,
were six thousand two hundred. 35The leader
of the fathers' house of the families of Merari
was Zuriel the son of Abihail. These *were* to
camp on the north side of the tabernacle.
36And the appointed duty of the children of
Merari *included* the boards of the tabernacle,
its bars, its pillars, its sockets, its utensils, all
the work relating to them, 37and the pillars of
the court all around, with their sockets, their
pegs, and their cords.

38Moreover those who were to camp before
the tabernacle on the east, before the tabernacle of meeting, *were* Moses, Aaron, and his
sons, keeping charge of the sanctuary, to meet
the needs of the children of Israel; but the outsider who came near was to be put to death.
39All who were numbered of the Levites, whom
Moses and Aaron numbered at the commandment of the LORD, by their families, all the
males from a month old and above, *were*
twenty-two thousand.

40Then the LORD said to Moses: "Number all
the firstborn males of the children of Israel
from a month old and above, and take the
number of their names. 41And you shall take
the Levites for Me—I *am* the LORD—instead
of all the firstborn among the children of
Israel, and the livestock of the Levites instead
of all the firstborn among the livestock of the
children of Israel." 42So Moses numbered all
the firstborn among the children of Israel, as
the LORD commanded him. 43And all the firstborn males, according to the number of
names from a month old and above, of those
who were numbered of them, were twenty-two
thousand two hundred and seventy-three.

44Then the LORD spoke to Moses, saying:
45"Take the Levites instead of all the firstborn
among the children of Israel, and the livestock
of the Levites instead of their livestock. The
Levites shall be Mine: I *am* the LORD. 46And for
the redemption of the two hundred and
seventy-three of the firstborn of the children
of Israel, who are more than the number of the
Levites, 47you shall take five shekels for each
one individually; you shall take *them* in the
currency of the shekel of the sanctuary, the
shekel of twenty gerahs. 48And you shall give
the money, with which the excess number of
them is redeemed, to Aaron and his sons."

49So Moses took the redemption money
from those who were over and above those
who were redeemed by the Levites. 50From the
firstborn of the children of Israel he took the
money, one thousand three hundred and sixty-
five *shekels,* according to the shekel of the
sanctuary. 51And Moses gave their redemption
money to Aaron and his sons, according to the
word of the LORD, as the LORD commanded
Moses.

4 Then the LORD spoke to Moses and Aaron,
saying: 2"Take a census of the sons of
Kohath from among the children of Levi, by
their families, by their fathers' house, 3from
thirty years old and above, even to fifty years
old, all who enter the service to do the work in
the tabernacle of meeting.

4"This *is* the service of the sons of Kohath in
the tabernacle of meeting, *relating to* the most
holy things: 5When the camp prepares to journey, Aaron and his sons shall come, and they
shall take down the covering veil and cover
the ark of the Testimony with it. 6Then they
shall put on it a covering of badger skins, and
spread over *that* a cloth entirely of blue; and
they shall insert its poles.

7"On the table of showbread they shall
spread a blue cloth, and put on it the dishes, the
pans, the bowls, and the pitchers for pouring;
and the showbread shall be on it. 8They shall
spread over them a scarlet cloth, and cover
the same with a covering of badger skins; and
they shall insert its poles. 9And they shall take
a blue cloth and cover the lampstand of the
light, with its lamps, its wick-trimmers, its
trays, and all its oil vessels, with which they
service it. 10Then they shall put it with all its
utensils in a covering of badger skins, and put
it on a carrying beam.

11"Over the golden altar they shall spread a
blue cloth, and cover it with a covering of
badger skins; and they shall insert its poles.
12Then they shall take all the utensils of service with which they minister in the sanctuary,
put *them* in a blue cloth, cover them with a
covering of badger skins, and put *them* on a

carrying beam. [13]Also they shall take away the ashes from the altar, and spread a purple cloth over it. [14]They shall put on it all its implements with which they minister there—the firepans, the forks, the shovels, the basins, and all the utensils of the altar—and they shall spread on it a covering of badger skins, and insert its poles. [15]And when Aaron and his sons have finished covering the sanctuary and all the furnishings of the sanctuary, when the camp is set to go, then the sons of Kohath shall come to carry *them;* but they shall not touch any holy thing, lest they die.

"These *are* the things in the tabernacle of meeting which the sons of Kohath are to carry.

[16]"The appointed duty of Eleazar the son of Aaron the priest *is* the oil for the light, the sweet incense, the daily grain offering, the anointing oil, the oversight of all the tabernacle, of all that *is* in it, with the sanctuary and its furnishings."

[17]Then the LORD spoke to Moses and Aaron, saying: [18]"Do not cut off the tribe of the families of the Kohathites from among the Levites; [19]but do this in regard to them, that they may live and not die when they approach the most holy things: Aaron and his sons shall go in and appoint each of them to his service and his task. [20]But they shall not go in to watch while the holy things are being covered, lest they die."

[21]Then the LORD spoke to Moses, saying: [22]"Also take a census of the sons of Gershon, by their fathers' house, by their families. [23]From thirty years old and above, even to fifty years old, you shall number them, all who enter to perform the service, to do the work in the tabernacle of meeting. [24]This *is* the service of the families of the Gershonites, in serving and carrying: [25]They shall carry the curtains of the tabernacle and the tabernacle of meeting *with* its covering, the covering of badger skins that *is* on it, the screen for the door of the tabernacle of meeting, [26]the screen for the door of the gate of the court, the hangings of the court which *are* around the tabernacle and altar, and their cords, all the furnishings for their service and all that is made for these things: so shall they serve.

[27]"Aaron and his sons shall assign all the service of the sons of the Gershonites, all their tasks and all their service. And you shall appoint to them all their tasks as their duty. [28]This *is* the service of the families of the sons of Gershon in the tabernacle of meeting. And their duties *shall be* under the authority of Ithamar the son of Aaron the priest.

[29]"*As for* the sons of Merari, you shall number them by their families and by their fathers' house. [30]From thirty years old and above, even to fifty years old, you shall number them, everyone who enters the service to do the work of the tabernacle of meeting. [31]And this *is* what they must carry as all their service for the tabernacle of meeting: the boards of the tabernacle, its bars, its pillars, its sockets, [32]and the pillars around the court with their sockets, pegs, and cords, with all their furnishings and all their service; and you shall assign *to each man* by name the items he must carry. [33]This *is* the service of the families of the sons of Merari, as all their service for the tabernacle of meeting, under the authority of Ithamar the son of Aaron the priest."

[34]And Moses, Aaron, and the leaders of the congregation numbered the sons of the Kohathites by their families and by their fathers' house, [35]from thirty years old and above, even to fifty years old, everyone who entered the service for work in the tabernacle of meeting; [36]and those who were numbered by their families were two thousand seven hundred and fifty. [37]These *were* the ones who were numbered of the families of the Kohathites, all who might serve in the tabernacle of meeting, whom Moses and Aaron numbered according to the commandment of the LORD by the hand of Moses.

[38]And those who were numbered of the sons of Gershon, by their families and by their fathers' house, [39]from thirty years old and above, even to fifty years old, everyone who entered the service for work in the tabernacle of meeting— [40]those who were numbered by their families, by their fathers' house, were two thousand six hundred and thirty. [41]These *are* the ones who were numbered of the families of the sons of Gershon, of all who might serve in the tabernacle of meeting, whom Moses and Aaron numbered according to the commandment of the LORD.

[42]Those of the families of the sons of Merari who were numbered, by their families, by their fathers' house, [43]from thirty years old and above, even to fifty years old, everyone who entered the service for work in the tabernacle of meeting— [44]those who were numbered by their families were three thousand two hundred. [45]These *are* the ones who were numbered of the families of the sons of Merari, whom Moses and Aaron numbered according to the word of the LORD by the hand of Moses.

[46]All who were numbered of the Levites, whom Moses, Aaron, and the leaders of Israel numbered, by their families and by their

fathers' houses, [47]from thirty years old and above, even to fifty years old, everyone who came to do the work of service and the work of bearing burdens in the tabernacle of meeting— [48]those who were numbered were eight thousand five hundred and eighty.

[49]According to the commandment of the LORD they were numbered by the hand of Moses, each according to his service and according to his task; thus were they numbered by him, as the LORD commanded Moses.

Psalm 30:1–7

A Psalm. A Song at the dedication
of the house of David.

I will extol You, O LORD, for You have lifted
me up,
And have not let my foes rejoice over
me.
2 O LORD my God, I cried out to You,
And You healed me.
3 O LORD, You brought my soul up from
the grave;
You have kept me alive, that I should
not go down to the pit.
4 Sing praise to the LORD, you saints
of His,
And give thanks at the remembrance
of His holy name.
5 For His anger *is but for* a moment,
His favor *is for* life;
Weeping may endure for a night,
But joy *comes* in the morning.

30:2,3 You healed me. God alone is the unique healer (see Ex. 15:26; Deut. 32:39; Ps. 107:20). David is extolling God for bringing him back from a near-death experience.

30:5 This stark contrast constitutes one of the most worshipful testimonies from the Scriptures (see the principle in Is. 54:7,8; John 16:20–22; 2 Cor. 4:17).

6 Now in my prosperity I said,
"I shall never be moved."
7 LORD, by Your favor You have made my
mountain stand strong;
You hid Your face, *and* I was troubled.

Proverbs 10:30–32

30 The righteous will never be removed,
But the wicked will not inhabit the
earth.
31 The mouth of the righteous brings
forth wisdom,
But the perverse tongue will be cut
out.
32 The lips of the righteous know what is
acceptable,
But the mouth of the wicked *what is*
perverse.

Mark 8:1–21

8 In those days, the multitude being very great and having nothing to eat, Jesus called His disciples *to Him* and said to them,
[2]"I have compassion on the multitude, because they have now continued with Me three days and have nothing to eat. [3]And if I send them away hungry to their own houses, they will faint on the way; for some of them have come from afar."
[4]Then His disciples answered Him, "How can one satisfy these people with bread here in the wilderness?"
[5]He asked them, "How many loaves do you have?"
And they said, "Seven."
[6]So He commanded the multitude to sit down on the ground. And He took the seven loaves and gave thanks, broke *them* and gave *them* to His disciples to set before *them;* and they set *them* before the multitude. [7]They also had a few small fish; and having blessed them, He said to set them also before *them.* [8]So they ate and were filled, and they took up seven large baskets of leftover fragments. [9]Now those who had eaten were about four thousand. And He sent them away, [10]immediately got into the boat with His disciples, and came to the region of Dalmanutha.
[11]Then the Pharisees came out and began to dispute with Him, seeking from Him a sign from heaven, testing Him. [12]But He sighed deeply in His spirit, and said, "Why does this

8:2 I have compassion. Only here and in the parallel passage (Matt. 15:32) did Jesus use this word of Himself. When He fed the 5,000, Jesus expressed "compassion" for the people's lost spiritual condition (6:34). Here, He expressed "compassion" for people's physical needs. Jesus could empathize with their hunger, having experienced it Himself (Matt. 4:2).

generation seek a sign? Assuredly, I say to
you, no sign shall be given to this generation."
[13]And He left them, and getting into the boat
again, departed to the other side. [14]Now the
disciples had forgotten to take bread, and they
did not have more than one loaf with them in
the boat. [15]Then He charged them, saying,
"Take heed, beware of the leaven of the
Pharisees and the leaven of Herod."
[16]And they reasoned among themselves,
saying, "*It is* because we have no bread."
[17]But Jesus, being aware of *it,* said to them,
"Why do you reason because you have no
bread? Do you not yet perceive nor understand? Is your heart still hardened? [18]Having
eyes, do you not see? And having ears, do you
not hear? And do you not remember? [19]When I
broke the five loaves for the five thousand,
how many baskets full of fragments did you
take up?"
They said to Him, "Twelve."
[20]"Also, when I broke the seven for the four
thousand, how many large baskets full of fragments did you take up?"
And they said, "Seven."
[21]So He said to them, "How *is it* you do not
understand?"

DAY 3: What was the "leaven of the Pharisees and…of Herod" that Jesus warned about?

The skeptical Pharisees asked for a "sign from heaven" in Mark 8:11, demanding further miraculous proof of Jesus' messianic claims. Not content with the countless miracles He had performed on earth, they demanded some sort of astronomical miracle. Having already given them more than enough proof, Jesus refused to accommodate their spiritual blindness. The supreme sign verifying His claim to be the Son of God and Messiah was to be His resurrection (Matt. 16:39,40).

Jesus warned the disciples about "the leaven of the Pharisees and…of Herod." "Leaven" is a yeast that multiplies quietly and permeates all that it contacts. In the New Testament, "leaven" most often symbolizes the evil influence of sin. The "leaven" of the Pharisees included both their false teaching (Matt. 16:12) and their hypocritical behavior (Luke 12:1). The "leaven" of Herod Antipas was his immoral, corrupt conduct (see 6:17–29). The Pharisees and the Herodians were allied against Christ (3:6).

To Jesus' amazement, the disciples completely missed His point, thinking He was talking about physical bread. He was concerned with spiritual truth, not mundane physical matters. Jesus asks them, "Is your heart still hardened?" (v. 17), which implies that they were rebellious, spiritually insensitive, and unable to understand spiritual truth. And He also reminded them of His ability to provide anything they might lack.

MARCH 4

Numbers 5:1–6:27

5 And the LORD spoke to Moses, saying:
[2]"Command the children of Israel that
they put out of the camp every leper, everyone
who has a discharge, and whoever becomes
defiled by a corpse. [3]You shall put out both
male and female; you shall put them outside
the camp, that they may not defile their camps
in the midst of which I dwell." [4]And the children of Israel did so, and put them outside the
camp; as the LORD spoke to Moses, so the
children of Israel did.
[5]Then the LORD spoke to Moses, saying,
[6]"Speak to the children of Israel: 'When a man
or woman commits any sin that men commit
in unfaithfulness against the LORD, and that
person is guilty, [7]then he shall confess the sin
which he has committed. He shall make restitution for his trespass in full, plus one-fifth of
it, and give *it* to the one he has wronged. [8]But
if the man has no relative to whom restitution
may be made for the wrong, the restitution for
the wrong *must go* to the LORD for the priest,
in addition to the ram of the atonement with
which atonement is made for him. [9]Every offering of all the holy things of the children of
Israel, which they bring to the priest, shall be
his. [10]And every man's holy things shall be his;
whatever any man gives the priest shall be
his.' "
[11]And the LORD spoke to Moses, saying,
[12]"Speak to the children of Israel, and say to
them: 'If any man's wife goes astray and
behaves unfaithfully toward him, [13]and a man
lies with her carnally, and it is hidden from the
eyes of her husband, and it is concealed that
she has defiled herself, and *there was* no witness against her, nor was she caught— [14]if the
spirit of jealousy comes upon him and he
becomes jealous of his wife, who has defiled
herself; or if the spirit of jealousy comes upon
him and he becomes jealous of his wife,
although she has not defiled herself— [15]then

the man shall bring his wife to the priest. He
shall bring the offering required for her, one-
tenth of an ephah of barley meal; he shall pour
no oil on it and put no frankincense on it,
because it *is* a grain offering of jealousy, an
offering for remembering, for bringing iniquity
to remembrance.
[16]'And the priest shall bring her near, and set
her before the LORD. [17]The priest shall take
holy water in an earthen vessel, and take
some of the dust that is on the floor of the tabernacle and put *it* into the water. [18]Then the
priest shall stand the woman before the LORD,
uncover the woman's head, and put the offering for remembering in her hands, which *is* the
grain offering of jealousy. And the priest shall
have in his hand the bitter water that brings a
curse. [19]And the priest shall put her under oath,
and say to the woman, "If no man has lain with
you, and if you have not gone astray to
uncleanness *while* under your husband's *authority,* be free from this bitter water that
brings a curse. [20]But if you have gone astray
while under your husband's *authority,* and if
you have defiled yourself and some man other
than your husband has lain with you"— [21]then
the priest shall put the woman under the oath of
the curse, and he shall say to the woman—"the
LORD make you a curse and an oath among
your people, when the LORD makes your thigh
rot and your belly swell; [22]and may this water
that causes the curse go into your stomach,
and make *your* belly swell and *your* thigh rot."
Then the woman shall say, "Amen, so be it."
[23]'Then the priest shall write these curses in
a book, and he shall scrape *them* off into the
bitter water. [24]And he shall make the woman
drink the bitter water that brings a curse, and
the water that brings the curse shall enter her
to become bitter. [25]Then the priest shall take
the grain offering of jealousy from the
woman's hand, shall wave the offering before
the LORD, and bring it to the altar; [26]and the
priest shall take a handful of the offering, as
its memorial portion, burn *it* on the altar, and
afterward make the woman drink the water.
[27]When he has made her drink the water, then
it shall be, if she has defiled herself and
behaved unfaithfully toward her husband, that
the water that brings a curse will enter her
and become bitter, and her belly will swell, her
thigh will rot, and the woman will become a
curse among her people. [28]But if the woman
has not defiled herself, and is clean, then she
shall be free and may conceive children.
[29]'This *is* the law of jealousy, when a wife,
while under her husband's *authority,* goes
astray and defiles herself, [30]or when the spirit
of jealousy comes upon a man, and he becomes
jealous of his wife; then he shall stand the
woman before the LORD, and the priest shall
execute all this law upon her. [31]Then the man
shall be free from iniquity, but that woman
shall bear her guilt.'"

6 Then the LORD spoke to Moses, saying,
[2]"Speak to the children of Israel, and say to
them: 'When either a man or woman consecrates an offering to take the vow of a Nazirite,
to separate himself to the LORD, [3]he shall separate himself from wine and *similar* drink; he
shall drink neither vinegar made from wine
nor vinegar made from *similar* drink; neither
shall he drink any grape juice, nor eat fresh
grapes or raisins. [4]All the days of his separation he shall eat nothing that is produced by
the grapevine, from seed to skin.
[5]'All the days of the vow of his separation no
razor shall come upon his head; until the days
are fulfilled for which he separated himself to
the LORD, he shall be holy. *Then* he shall let
the locks of the hair of his head grow. [6]All the
days that he separates himself to the LORD he
shall not go near a dead body. [7]He shall not
make himself unclean even for his father or
his mother, for his brother or his sister, when
they die, because his separation to God *is* on
his head. [8]All the days of his separation he
shall be holy to the LORD.
[9]'And if anyone dies very suddenly beside
him, and he defiles his consecrated head, then
he shall shave his head on the day of his
cleansing; on the seventh day he shall shave it.
[10]Then on the eighth day he shall bring two turtledoves or two young pigeons to the priest, to

6:2 the vow of a Nazirite. The word "vow" here is related to the word "wonder," which signifies something out of the ordinary. "Nazirite" transliterates a Hebrew term meaning "dedication by separation." The Nazirite separated himself to the Lord by separating himself from 1) grape products (6:3,4), 2) the cutting of one's hair (6:5), and 3) contact with a dead body (6:6,7). The high priest was also forbidden 1) to drink wine while serving in the tabernacle (Lev. 10:9) and 2) to touch dead bodies (Lev. 21:11). Further, both the high priest's crown (Ex. 29:6; 39:30; Lev. 8:9) and the Nazirite's head (6:9,18) are referred to by the same Hebrew word. The Nazirite's hair was like the high priest's crown. Like the high priest, the Nazirite was holy to the Lord (6:8; Ex. 28:36) all the days (6:4,5,6,8) of his vow.

the door of the tabernacle of meeting; [11]and the priest shall offer one as a sin offering and *the* other as a burnt offering, and make atonement for him, because he sinned in regard to the corpse; and he shall sanctify his head that same day. [12]He shall consecrate to the LORD the days of his separation, and bring a male lamb in its first year as a trespass offering; but the former days shall be lost, because his separation was defiled.

[13]"Now this *is* the law of the Nazirite: When the days of his separation are fulfilled, he shall be brought to the door of the tabernacle of meeting. [14]And he shall present his offering to the LORD: one male lamb in its first year without blemish as a burnt offering, one ewe lamb in its first year without blemish as a sin offering, one ram without blemish as a peace offering, [15]a basket of unleavened bread, cakes of fine flour mixed with oil, unleavened wafers anointed with oil, and their grain offering with their drink offerings.

[16]"Then the priest shall bring *them* before the LORD and offer his sin offering and his burnt offering; [17]and he shall offer the ram as a sacrifice of a peace offering to the LORD, with the basket of unleavened bread; the priest shall also offer its grain offering and its drink offering. [18]Then the Nazirite shall shave his consecrated head *at* the door of the tabernacle of meeting, and shall take the hair from his consecrated head and put *it* on the fire which is under the sacrifice of the peace offering.

[19]"And the priest shall take the boiled shoulder of the ram, one unleavened cake from the basket, and one unleavened wafer, and put *them* upon the hands of the Nazirite after he has shaved his consecrated *hair,* [20]and the priest shall wave them as a wave offering before the LORD; they *are* holy for the priest, together with the breast of the wave offering and the thigh of the heave offering. After that the Nazirite may drink wine.'

[21]"This is the law of the Nazirite who vows to the LORD the offering for his separation, and besides that, whatever else his hand is able to provide; according to the vow which he takes, so he must do according to the law of his separation."

[22]And the LORD spoke to Moses, saying: [23]"Speak to Aaron and his sons, saying, 'This is the way you shall bless the children of Israel. Say to them:

24 "The LORD bless you and keep you;
25 The LORD make His face shine upon you,
And be gracious to you;
26 The LORD lift up His countenance upon you,
And give you peace." '

[27]"So they shall put My name on the children of Israel, and I will bless them."

Psalm 30:8–12

8 I cried out to You, O LORD;
And to the LORD I made supplication:
9 "What profit *is there* in my blood,
When I go down to the pit?
Will the dust praise You?
Will it declare Your truth?
10 Hear, O LORD, and have mercy on me;
LORD, be my helper!"

11 You have turned for me my mourning into dancing;
You have put off my sackcloth and clothed me with gladness,
12 To the end that *my* glory may sing praise to You and not be silent.
O LORD my God, I will give thanks to You forever.

Proverbs 11:1–3

11 Dishonest scales *are* an abomination to the LORD,
But a just weight *is* His delight.
2 When pride comes, then comes shame;
But with the humble *is* wisdom.

11:2 pride. From a root meaning "to boil," or "to run over," indicating an overwhelmingly arrogant attitude or behavior. It is used of ordinary men (Deut. 17:12,13); kings (Neh. 9:10); Israel (Neh. 9:16,29); false prophets (Deut. 18:20); and murderers (Ex. 21:14). **the humble.** A rare word, which appears in Micah 6:8: "walk humbly with your God." This humble and teachable spirit is first of all directed toward God (see 15:33; 16:18,19; 18:12; 22:4).

3 The integrity of the upright will guide them,
But the perversity of the unfaithful will destroy them.

Mark 8:22–38

[22]Then He came to Bethsaida; and they brought a blind man to Him, and begged Him to touch him. [23]So He took the blind man by the hand and led him out of the town. And when He had spit on his eyes and put His hands on him, He asked him if he saw anything.

8:23 spit on his eyes. This action and Jesus' touching his eyes with His hands (v. 25) were apparently meant to reassure the blind man (who would naturally depend on his other senses, such as touch) that Jesus would heal his eyes (see 7:33; John 9:6).

[24]And he looked up and said, "I see men like
trees, walking."
[25]Then He put *His* hands on his eyes again
and made him look up. And he was restored
and saw everyone clearly. [26]Then He sent him
away to his house, saying, "Neither go into the
town, nor tell anyone in the town."
[27]Now Jesus and His disciples went out to
the towns of Caesarea Philippi; and on the
road He asked His disciples, saying to them,
"Who do men say that I am?"
[28]So they answered, "John the Baptist; but
some *say,* Elijah; and others, one of the
prophets."
[29]He said to them, "But who do you say that
I am?"
Peter answered and said to Him, "You are
the Christ."
[30]Then He strictly warned them that they
should tell no one about Him.
[31]And He began to teach them that the Son
of Man must suffer many things, and be rejected by the elders and chief priests and
scribes, and be killed, and after three days rise

8:30 tell no one. Jesus' messianic mission cannot be understood apart from the Cross, which the disciples did not yet understand (see vv. 31–33; 9:30–32). For them to have proclaimed Jesus as Messiah at this point would have only furthered the misunderstanding that the Messiah was to be a political-military deliverer. The fallout was that the Jewish people, desperate to be rid of the yoke of Rome, would seek to make Jesus king by force (John 6:15; see 12:12–19).

again. [32]He spoke this word openly. Then Peter
took Him aside and began to rebuke Him.
[33]But when He had turned around and looked
at His disciples, He rebuked Peter, saying,
"Get behind Me, Satan! For you are not mindful of the things of God, but the things of men."
[34]When He had called the people to *Himself,*
with His disciples also, He said to them, "Whoever desires to come after Me, let him deny
himself, and take up his cross, and follow Me.
[35]For whoever desires to save his life will lose
it, but whoever loses his life for My sake and
the gospel's will save it. [36]For what will it profit a man if he gains the whole world, and loses
his own soul? [37]Or what will a man give in
exchange for his soul? [38]For whoever is
ashamed of Me and My words in this adulterous and sinful generation, of him the Son of
Man also will be ashamed when He comes in
the glory of His Father with the holy angels."

DAY 4: What does it mean to be a disciple of Jesus Christ?

In Mark 8:34, Jesus Christ makes it clear that no one who is unwilling to "deny himself" can legitimately claim to be a disciple. When He adds that one must "take up his cross," He reveals the extent of self-denial—to the point of death, if necessary. The extent of desperation on the part of the penitent sinner who is aware he can't save himself reaches the place where nothing is held back as He follows Jesus Christ (see Matt. 19:21,22).

Jesus says that whoever "loses his life for My sake and the gospel's will save it" (v. 35). This paradoxical saying reveals an important spiritual truth: those who pursue a life of ease, comfort, and acceptance by the world will not find eternal life. On the other hand, those who give up their lives for the sake of Christ and the gospel will find it.

To have all that the world has to offer yet not have Christ is to be eternally bankrupt. All the world's goods will not compensate for losing one's soul eternally (v. 36). It is the "soul," the real person, who will live forever in heaven or hell. Those who reject the demands of discipleship prove themselves to be ashamed of Jesus Christ and the truth He taught.

MARCH 5

Numbers 7:1–8:26

7 Now it came to pass, when Moses had finished setting up the tabernacle, that he
anointed it and consecrated it and all its furnishings, and the altar and all its utensils; so he
anointed them and consecrated them. [2]Then
the leaders of Israel, the heads of their fathers'
houses, who *were* the leaders of the tribes and
over those who were numbered, made an offering. [3]And they brought their offering before the

LORD, six covered carts and twelve oxen, a cart
for *every* two of the leaders, and for each one
an ox; and they presented them before the tabernacle.
[4]Then the LORD spoke to Moses, saying,
[5]"Accept *these* from them, that they may be
used in doing the work of the tabernacle of
meeting; and you shall give them to the Levites,
to every man according to his service." [6]So
Moses took the carts and the oxen, and gave
them to the Levites. [7]Two carts and four oxen
he gave to the sons of Gershon, according to
their service; [8]and four carts and eight oxen
he gave to the sons of Merari, according to
their service, under the authority of Ithamar
the son of Aaron the priest. [9]But to the sons of
Kohath he gave none, because theirs *was* the
service of the holy things, *which* they carried
on their shoulders.

[10]Now the leaders offered the dedication *offering* for the altar when it was anointed; so the
leaders offered their offering before the altar.
[11]For the LORD said to Moses, "They shall offer
their offering, one leader each day, for the
dedication of the altar."

[12]And the one who offered his offering on
the first day *was* Nahshon the son of
Amminadab, from the tribe of Judah. [13]His
offering *was* one silver platter, the weight of
which *was* one hundred and thirty *shekels,* and
one silver bowl of seventy shekels, according
to the shekel of the sanctuary, both of them
full of fine flour mixed with oil as a grain offering; [14]one gold pan of ten *shekels,* full of incense; [15]one young bull, one ram, and one
male lamb in its first year, as a burnt offering;
[16]one kid of the goats as a sin offering; [17]and for
the sacrifice of peace offerings: two oxen, five
rams, five male goats, and five male lambs in
their first year. This *was* the offering of
Nahshon the son of Amminadab.

[18]On the second day Nethanel the son of
Zuar, leader of Issachar, presented *an offering.*
[19]*For* his offering he offered one silver platter,
the weight of which *was* one hundred and thirty *shekels,* and one silver bowl of seventy
shekels, according to the shekel of the sanctuary, both of them full of fine flour mixed
with oil as a grain offering; [20]one gold pan of
ten *shekels,* full of incense; [21]one young bull,
one ram, and one male lamb in its first year, as
a burnt offering; [22]one kid of the goats as a sin
offering; [23]and as the sacrifice of peace offerings: two oxen, five rams, five male goats, and
five male lambs in their first year. This *was* the
offering of Nethanel the son of Zuar.

[24]On the third day Eliab the son of Helon,
leader of the children of Zebulun, *presented an
offering.* [25]His offering *was* one silver platter,
the weight of which *was* one hundred and thirty *shekels,* and one silver bowl of seventy
shekels, according to the shekel of the sanctuary, both of them full of fine flour mixed
with oil as a grain offering; [26]one gold pan of
ten *shekels,* full of incense; [27]one young bull,
one ram, and one male lamb in its first year, as
a burnt offering; [28]one kid of the goats as a sin
offering; [29]and for the sacrifice of peace offerings: two oxen, five rams, five male goats, and
five male lambs in their first year. This *was* the
offering of Eliab the son of Helon.

[30]On the fourth day Elizur the son of
Shedeur, leader of the children of Reuben, *presented an offering.* [31]His offering *was* one silver
platter, the weight of which *was* one hundred
and thirty *shekels,* and one silver bowl of seventy shekels, according to the shekel of the
sanctuary, both of them full of fine flour mixed
with oil as a grain offering; [32]one gold pan of
ten *shekels,* full of incense; [33]one young bull,
one ram, and one male lamb in its first year, as
a burnt offering; [34]one kid of the goats as a sin
offering; [35]and as the sacrifice of peace offerings: two oxen, five rams, five male goats, and
five male lambs in their first year. This *was* the
offering of Elizur the son of Shedeur.

[36]On the fifth day Shelumiel the son of
Zurishaddai, leader of the children of Simeon,
presented an offering. [37]His offering *was* one silver platter, the weight of which *was* one hundred and thirty *shekels,* and one silver bowl of
seventy shekels, according to the shekel of the
sanctuary, both of them full of fine flour mixed
with oil as a grain offering; [38]one gold pan of
ten *shekels,* full of incense; [39]one young bull,
one ram, and one male lamb in its first year, as
a burnt offering; [40]one kid of the goats as a sin
offering; [41]and as the sacrifice of peace offerings: two oxen, five rams, five male goats, and
five male lambs in their first year. This *was* the
offering of Shelumiel the son of Zurishaddai.

[42]On the sixth day Eliasaph the son of
Deuel, leader of the children of Gad, *presented
an offering.* [43]His offering *was* one silver platter, the weight of which *was* one hundred and
thirty *shekels,* and one silver bowl of seventy
shekels, according to the shekel of the sanctuary, both of them full of fine flour mixed
with oil as a grain offering; [44]one gold pan of
ten *shekels,* full of incense; [45]one young bull,
one ram, and one male lamb in its first year, as
a burnt offering; [46]one kid of the goats as a sin
offering; [47]and as the sacrifice of peace offerings: two oxen, five rams, five male goats, and
five male lambs in their first year. This *was* the
offering of Eliasaph the son of Deuel.

[48]On the seventh day Elishama the son of
Ammihud, leader of the children of Ephraim,
presented an offering. [49]His offering *was* one silver platter, the weight of which *was* one hundred and thirty *shekels,* and one silver bowl of
seventy shekels, according to the shekel of
the sanctuary, both of them full of fine flour
mixed with oil as a grain offering; [50]one gold
pan of ten *shekels,* full of incense; [51]one young
bull, one ram, and one male lamb in its first
year, as a burnt offering; [52]one kid of the goats
as a sin offering; [53]and as the sacrifice of peace
offerings: two oxen, five rams, five male goats,
and five male lambs in their first year. This
was the offering of Elishama the son of
Ammihud.

[54]On the eighth day Gamaliel the son of
Pedahzur, leader of the children of Manasseh,
presented an offering. [55]His offering *was* one silver platter, the weight of which *was* one hundred and thirty *shekels,* and one silver bowl of
seventy shekels, according to the shekel of
the sanctuary, both of them full of fine flour
mixed with oil as a grain offering; [56]one gold
pan of ten *shekels,* full of incense; [57]one young
bull, one ram, and one male lamb in its first
year, as a burnt offering; [58]one kid of the goats
as a sin offering; [59]and as the sacrifice of peace
offerings: two oxen, five rams, five male goats,
and five male lambs in their first year. This
was the offering of Gamaliel the son of
Pedahzur.

[60]On the ninth day Abidan the son of
Gideoni, leader of the children of Benjamin,
presented an offering. [61]His offering *was* one silver platter, the weight of which *was* one hundred and thirty *shekels,* and one silver bowl of
seventy shekels, according to the shekel of
the sanctuary, both of them full of fine flour
mixed with oil as a grain offering; [62]one gold
pan of ten *shekels,* full of incense; [63]one young
bull, one ram, and one male lamb in its first
year, as a burnt offering; [64]one kid of the goats
as a sin offering; [65]and as the sacrifice of peace
offerings: two oxen, five rams, five male goats,
and five male lambs in their first year. This
was the offering of Abidan the son of Gideoni.

[66]On the tenth day Ahiezer the son of Ammishaddai, leader of the children of Dan, *presented an offering.* [67]His offering *was* one silver
platter, the weight of which *was* one hundred
and thirty *shekels,* and one silver bowl of seventy shekels, according to the shekel of the
sanctuary, both of them full of fine flour mixed
with oil as a grain offering; [68]one gold pan of
ten *shekels,* full of incense; [69]one young bull,
one ram, and one male lamb in its first year, as
a burnt offering; [70]one kid of the goats as a sin
offering; [71]and as the sacrifice of peace offerings: two oxen, five rams, five male goats, and
five male lambs in their first year. This *was* the
offering of Ahiezer the son of Ammishaddai.

[72]On the eleventh day Pagiel the son of
Ocran, leader of the children of Asher, *presented an offering.* [73]His offering *was* one silver
platter, the weight of which *was* one hundred
and thirty *shekels,* and one silver bowl of seventy shekels, according to the shekel of the
sanctuary, both of them full of fine flour mixed
with oil as a grain offering; [74]one gold pan of
ten *shekels,* full of incense; [75]one young bull,
one ram, and one male lamb in its first year, as
a burnt offering; [76]one kid of the goats as a sin
offering; [77]and as the sacrifice of peace offerings: two oxen, five rams, five male goats, and
five male lambs in their first year. This *was* the
offering of Pagiel the son of Ocran.

[78]On the twelfth day Ahira the son of Enan,
leader of the children of Naphtali, *presented an
offering.* [79]His offering *was* one silver platter,
the weight of which *was* one hundred and thirty *shekels,* and one silver bowl of seventy
shekels, according to the shekel of the sanctuary, both of them full of fine flour mixed
with oil as a grain offering; [80]one gold pan of
ten *shekels,* full of incense; [81]one young bull,
one ram, and one male lamb in its first year, as
a burnt offering; [82]one kid of the goats as a sin
offering; [83]and as the sacrifice of peace offerings: two oxen, five rams, five male goats, and
five male lambs in their first year. This *was* the
offering of Ahira the son of Enan.

[84]This *was* the dedication *offering* for the
altar from the leaders of Israel, when it was
anointed: twelve silver platters, twelve silver
bowls, and twelve gold pans. [85]Each silver platter *weighed* one hundred and thirty *shekels* and
each bowl seventy *shekels.* All the silver of the
vessels *weighed* two thousand four hundred
shekels, according to the shekel of the sanctuary. [86]The twelve gold pans full of incense
weighed ten *shekels* apiece, according to the
shekel of the sanctuary; all the gold of the
pans *weighed* one hundred and twenty *shekels.*
[87]All the oxen for the burnt offering *were*
twelve young bulls, the rams twelve, the male
lambs in their first year twelve, with their grain
offering, and the kids of the goats as a sin
offering twelve. [88]And all the oxen for the sacrifice of peace offerings were twenty-four
bulls, the rams sixty, the male goats sixty, and
the lambs in their first year sixty. This *was* the
dedication *offering* for the altar after it was
anointed.

[89]Now when Moses went into the tabernacle
of meeting to speak with Him, he heard the

voice of One speaking to him from above the
mercy seat that *was* on the ark of the
Testimony, from between the two cherubim;
thus He spoke to him.

7:89 He spoke to him. With the completion of the tabernacle, the Lord communicated His word to Moses from the mercy seat in the Holy of Holies (see Lev. 1:1, Num. 1:1).

8 And the LORD spoke to Moses, saying:
[2]“Speak to Aaron, and say to him, ‘When
you arrange the lamps, the seven lamps shall
give light in front of the lampstand.’ ” [3]And
Aaron did so; he arranged the lamps to face
toward the front of the lampstand, as the LORD
commanded Moses. [4]Now this workmanship
of the lampstand *was* hammered gold; from its
shaft to its flowers it *was* hammered work. According to the pattern which the LORD had
shown Moses, so he made the lampstand.
[5]Then the LORD spoke to Moses, saying:
[6]“Take the Levites from among the children of
Israel and cleanse them *ceremonially.* [7]Thus
you shall do to them to cleanse them: Sprinkle
water of purification on them, and let them
shave all their body, and let them wash their
clothes, and *so* make themselves clean. [8]Then
let them take a young bull with its grain offering of fine flour mixed with oil, and you shall
take another young bull as a sin offering. [9]And
you shall bring the Levites before the tabernacle of meeting, and you shall gather together
the whole congregation of the children of
Israel. [10]So you shall bring the Levites before
the LORD, and the children of Israel shall lay
their hands on the Levites; [11]and Aaron shall offer the Levites before the LORD *like* a wave
offering from the children of Israel, that they
may perform the work of the LORD. [12]Then the
Levites shall lay their hands on the heads of
the young bulls, and you shall offer one as a
sin offering and the other as a burnt offering to
the LORD, to make atonement for the Levites.
[13]“And you shall stand the Levites before
Aaron and his sons, and then offer them *like* a
wave offering to the LORD. [14]Thus you shall separate the Levites from among the children of
Israel, and the Levites shall be Mine. [15]After that
the Levites shall go in to service the tabernacle
of meeting. So you shall cleanse them and offer
them *like* a wave offering. [16]For they *are* wholly
given to Me from among the children of Israel;
I have taken them for Myself instead of all
who open the womb, the firstborn of all the
children of Israel. [17]For all the firstborn among
the children of Israel *are* Mine, *both* man and
beast; on the day that I struck all the firstborn
in the land of Egypt I sanctified them to
Myself. [18]I have taken the Levites instead of all
the firstborn of the children of Israel. [19]And I
have given the Levites as a gift to Aaron and
his sons from among the children of Israel, to
do the work for the children of Israel in the tabernacle of meeting, and to make atonement for
the children of Israel, that there be no plague
among the children of Israel when the children
of Israel come near the sanctuary.”
[20]Thus Moses and Aaron and all the congregation of the children of Israel did to the
Levites; according to all that the LORD commanded Moses concerning the Levites, so the
children of Israel did to them. [21]And the Levites
purified themselves and washed their clothes;
then Aaron presented them *like* a wave offering before the LORD, and Aaron made atonement for them to cleanse them. [22]After that the
Levites went in to do their work in the tabernacle of meeting before Aaron and his sons; as
the LORD commanded Moses concerning the
Levites, so they did to them.
[23]Then the LORD spoke to Moses, saying,
[24]“This *is* what *pertains* to the Levites: From
twenty-five years old and above one may enter
to perform service in the work of the tabernacle of meeting; [25]and at the age of fifty years
they must cease performing this work, and
shall work no more. [26]They may minister with
their brethren in the tabernacle of meeting, to
attend to needs, but they *themselves* shall do
no work. Thus you shall do to the Levites
regarding their duties.”

Psalm 31:1–5

To the Chief Musician. A Psalm of David.

In You, O LORD, I put my trust;
Let me never be ashamed;
Deliver me in Your righteousness.
2 Bow down Your ear to me,
Deliver me speedily;
Be my rock of refuge,
A fortress of defense to save me.

3 For You *are* my rock and my fortress;
Therefore, for Your name’s sake,
Lead me and guide me.
4 Pull me out of the net which they have
secretly laid for me,
For You *are* my strength.
5 Into Your hand I commit my spirit;
You have redeemed me, O LORD God
of truth.

31:5 Into Your hand. This is applied to both the lesser David and the Greater David (Luke 23:46). Here it involves the common denominator of trust. This is a metaphor depicting God's power and control (see v. 15a; contra. vv. 8,15b).

Proverbs 11:4–6

4 Riches do not profit in the day of wrath,
But righteousness delivers from death.
5 The righteousness of the blameless
will direct his way aright,
But the wicked will fall by his own
wickedness.

11:4 day of wrath. Money buys no escape from death in the day of final accounting to God, the divine Judge (see Is. 10:3; Ezek. 7:19; Zeph. 1:18; Luke 12:16–21).

6 The righteousness of the upright will
deliver them,
But the unfaithful will be caught by
their lust.

Mark 9:1–29

9 And He said to them, "Assuredly, I say to
you that there are some standing here
who will not taste death till they see the kingdom of God present with power."
2 Now after six days Jesus took Peter, James,
and John, and led them up on a high mountain
apart by themselves; and He was transfigured
before them. 3 His clothes became shining,
exceedingly white, like snow, such as no laun-
derer on earth can whiten them. 4 And Elijah
appeared to them with Moses, and they were
talking with Jesus. 5 Then Peter answered and
said to Jesus, "Rabbi, it is good for us to be
here; and let us make three tabernacles: one
for You, one for Moses, and one for Elijah"—
6 because he did not know what to say, for they
were greatly afraid.
7 And a cloud came and overshadowed them;
and a voice came out of the cloud, saying, "This
is My beloved Son. Hear Him!" 8 Suddenly,
when they had looked around, they saw no
one anymore, but only Jesus with themselves.
9 Now as they came down from the mountain, He commanded them that they should
tell no one the things they had seen, till the
Son of Man had risen from the dead. 10 So they
kept this word to themselves, questioning
what the rising from the dead meant.
11 And they asked Him, saying, "Why do the
scribes say that Elijah must come first?"
12 Then He answered and told them, "Indeed,
Elijah is coming first and restores all things.
And how is it written concerning the Son of
Man, that He must suffer many things and be
treated with contempt? 13 But I say to you that
Elijah has also come, and they did to him whatever they wished, as it is written of him."
14 And when He came to the disciples, He
saw a great multitude around them, and
scribes disputing with them. 15 Immediately,
when they saw Him, all the people were greatly amazed, and running to *Him,* greeted Him.
16 And He asked the scribes, "What are you discussing with them?"
17 Then one of the crowd answered and said,
"Teacher, I brought You my son, who has a
mute spirit. 18 And wherever it seizes him, it
throws him down; he foams at the mouth,
gnashes his teeth, and becomes rigid. So I
spoke to Your disciples, that they should cast
it out, but they could not."
19 He answered him and said, "O faithless
generation, how long shall I be with you? How
long shall I bear with you? Bring him to Me."
20 Then they brought him to Him. And when he
saw Him, immediately the spirit convulsed
him, and he fell on the ground and wallowed,
foaming at the mouth.
21 So He asked his father, "How long has this
been happening to him?"
And he said, "From childhood. 22 And often
he has thrown him both into the fire and into
the water to destroy him. But if You can do anything, have compassion on us and help us."
23 Jesus said to him, "If you can believe, all

9:22 to destroy him. This demon was an especially violent and dangerous one. Open fires and unfenced bodies of water were common in first-century Palestine, providing ample opportunity for the demon's attempts to destroy the child. The father's statement added to the pathos of the situation. The boy himself was probably disfigured from burn scars, and possibly further ostracized because of them. His situation also created a hardship for his family, who would have had to watch the boy constantly to protect him from harm.

things *are* possible to him who believes."
24 Immediately the father of the child cried
out and said with tears, "Lord, I believe; help
my unbelief!"
25 When Jesus saw that the people came running together, He rebuked the unclean spirit,
saying to it, "Deaf and dumb spirit, I command
you, come out of him and enter him no more!"
26 Then *the spirit* cried out, convulsed him
greatly, and came out of him. And he became
as one dead, so that many said, "He is dead."
27 But Jesus took him by the hand and lifted
him up, and he arose.
28 And when He had come into the house,
His disciples asked Him privately, "Why could
we not cast it out?"
29 So He said to them, "This kind can come
out by nothing but prayer and fasting."

DAY 5: What was the purpose of Jesus' Transfiguration?

Matthew and Mark place the Transfiguration "six days" after Jesus' promise that some disciples would "see the kingdom of God present with power" (Mark 9:1). Peter, James, and John, as the inner circle of Jesus' disciples, were allowed to witness this great event on "a high mountain" (Mark 9:2), most likely Mt. Hermon, the highest mountain in the vicinity of Caesarea Philippi (see 8:27). Jesus was "transfigured," meaning "to change in form" or "to be transformed," in front of them. In some inexplicable way, Jesus manifested some of His divine glory to the 3 disciples (see 2 Pet. 1:16). The divine glory emanating from Jesus made even His clothing radiate brilliant white light (Mark 9:3). Light is often associated with God's visible presence (see Ps. 104:2; Dan. 7:9; 1 Tim. 6:16; Rev. 1:14; 21:23).

Also appearing with Jesus were "Elijah…with Moses" (Mark 9:4). They were symbolic of the Prophets and the Law, the two great divisions of the Old Testament. They "were talking with Jesus," and the subject was His coming death (Luke 9:31). Then "a cloud…overshadowed them" (v. 7). This is the glory cloud, Shekinah, which throughout the Old Testament was symbolic of God's presence (Ex. 13:21; 33:18–23; 40:34,35; Num. 9:15; 14:14; Deut. 9:33). And "a voice came out of the cloud," which was the Father's voice, saying, "This is My beloved Son"—repeating the affirmation of His love for the Son first given at Jesus' baptism (Mark 1:11). "Hear Him!" says the Father. Jesus, the One to whom the Law and Prophets pointed (see Deut. 18:15), is the One whom the disciples are to listen to and obey (see Heb. 1:1,2).

MARCH 6

Numbers 9:1–10:36

9 Now the LORD spoke to Moses in the
Wilderness of Sinai, in the first month of
the second year after they had come out of the
land of Egypt, saying: 2 "Let the children of
Israel keep the Passover at its appointed time.
3 On the fourteenth day of this month, at twilight, you shall keep it at its appointed time.
According to all its rites and ceremonies you
shall keep it." 4 So Moses told the children of
Israel that they should keep the Passover.
5 And they kept the Passover on the fourteenth
day of the first month, at twilight, in the
Wilderness of Sinai; according to all that the
LORD commanded Moses, so the children of
Israel did.
6 Now there were *certain* men who were defiled by a human corpse, so that they could not
keep the Passover on that day; and they came
before Moses and Aaron that day. 7 And those
men said to him, "We *became* defiled by a human
corpse. Why are we kept from presenting the
offering of the LORD at its appointed time
among the children of Israel?"
8 And Moses said to them, "Stand still, that I
may hear what the LORD will command concerning you."
9 Then the LORD spoke to Moses, saying,
10 "Speak to the children of Israel, saying: 'If
anyone of you or your posterity is unclean
because of a corpse, or *is* far away on a journey, he may still keep the LORD's Passover.
11 On the fourteenth day of the second month,
at twilight, they may keep it. They shall eat it
with unleavened bread and bitter herbs.
12 They shall leave none of it until morning, nor
break one of its bones. According to all the ordinances of the Passover they shall keep it.
13 But the man who *is* clean and is not on a journey, and ceases to keep the Passover, that
same person shall be cut off from among his
people, because he did not bring the offering
of the LORD at its appointed time; that man
shall bear his sin.
14 'And if a stranger dwells among you, and
would keep the LORD's Passover, he must do
so according to the rite of the Passover and
according to its ceremony; you shall have one

ordinance, both for the stranger and the native
of the land.' "
[15]Now on the day that the tabernacle was
raised up, the cloud covered the tabernacle,
the tent of the Testimony; from evening until
morning it was above the tabernacle like the
appearance of fire. [16]So it was always: the cloud
covered it *by day,* and the appearance of fire by
night. [17]Whenever the cloud was taken up
from above the tabernacle, after that the children of Israel would journey; and in the place
where the cloud settled, there the children of
Israel would pitch their tents. [18]At the command of the LORD the children of Israel would
journey, and at the command of the LORD they
would camp; as long as the cloud stayed above
the tabernacle they remained encamped.
[19]Even when the cloud continued long, many
days above the tabernacle, the children of
Israel kept the charge of the LORD and did not
journey. [20]So it was, when the cloud was above
the tabernacle a few days: according to the
command of the LORD they would remain
encamped, and according to the command of
the LORD they would journey. [21]So it was, when
the cloud remained only from evening until
morning: when the cloud was taken up in the
morning, then they would journey; whether
by day or by night, whenever the cloud was
taken up, they would journey. [22]*Whether it was*
two days, a month, or a year that the cloud
remained above the tabernacle, the children
of Israel would remain encamped and not journey; but when it was taken up, they would
journey. [23]At the command of the LORD they
remained encamped, and at the command of
the LORD they journeyed; they kept the charge
of the LORD, at the command of the LORD by
the hand of Moses.

10 And the LORD spoke to Moses, saying:
[2]"Make two silver trumpets for yourself;
you shall make them of hammered work; you
shall use them for calling the congregation
and for directing the movement of the camps.
[3]When they blow both of them, all the congregation shall gather before you at the door of
the tabernacle of meeting. [4]But if they blow
only one, then the leaders, the heads of the
divisions of Israel, shall gather to you. [5]When
you sound the advance, the camps that lie on
the east side shall then begin their journey.
[6]When you sound the advance the second
time, then the camps that lie on the south side
shall begin their journey; they shall sound the
call for them to begin their journeys. [7]And
when the assembly is to be gathered together,
you shall blow, but not sound the advance.
[8]The sons of Aaron, the priests, shall blow the
trumpets; and these shall be to you as an ordinance forever throughout your generations.
[9]"When you go to war in your land against
the enemy who oppresses you, then you shall
sound an alarm with the trumpets, and you will
be remembered before the LORD your God,
and you will be saved from your enemies.
[10]Also in the day of your gladness, in your
appointed feasts, and at the beginning of your
months, you shall blow the trumpets over
your burnt offerings and over the sacrifices of
your peace offerings; and they shall be a
memorial for you before your God: I *am* the
LORD your God."
[11]Now it came to pass on the twentieth *day* of
the second month, in the second year, that the
cloud was taken up from above the tabernacle
of the Testimony. [12]And the children of Israel
set out from the Wilderness of Sinai on their
journeys; then the cloud settled down in the
Wilderness of Paran. [13]So they started out for
the first time according to the command of the
LORD by the hand of Moses.
[14]The standard of the camp of the children of
Judah set out first according to their armies;
over their army was Nahshon the son of
Amminadab. [15]Over the army of the tribe of the
children of Issachar *was* Nethanel the son of
Zuar. [16]And over the army of the tribe of the
children of Zebulun *was* Eliab the son of Helon.
[17]Then the tabernacle was taken down; and
the sons of Gershon and the sons of Merari
set out, carrying the tabernacle.
[18]And the standard of the camp of Reuben
set out according to their armies; over their
army *was* Elizur the son of Shedeur. [19]Over the
army of the tribe of the children of Simeon
was Shelumiel the son of Zurishaddai. [20]And
over the army of the tribe of the children of
Gad *was* Eliasaph the son of Deuel.
[21]Then the Kohathites set out, carrying the
holy things. (The tabernacle would be prepared
for their arrival.)

9:15 tabernacle...raised up. The presence of the Lord arrived when the tabernacle was completed and erected on the first day of the first month of the second year after they had come out of Egypt.

9:16 cloud...fire. The presence of the Lord which was seen in the cloud by day became a fire that was seen at night (see Lev. 16:2).

[22]And the standard of the camp of the children of Ephraim set out according to their
armies; over their army *was* Elishama the son
of Ammihud. [23]Over the army of the tribe of
the children of Manasseh *was* Gamaliel the
son of Pedahzur. [24]And over the army of the
tribe of the children of Benjamin *was* Abidan
the son of Gideoni.
[25]Then the standard of the camp of the children of Dan (the rear guard of all the camps)
set out according to their armies; over their
army *was* Ahiezer the son of Ammishaddai.
[26]Over the army of the tribe of the children of
Asher *was* Pagiel the son of Ocran. [27]And over
the army of the tribe of the children of Naphtali
was Ahira the son of Enan.
[28]Thus *was* the order of march of the children of Israel, according to their armies, when
they began their journey.
[29]Now Moses said to Hobab the son of Reuel
the Midianite, Moses' father-in-law, "We are setting out for the place of which the LORD said, 'I
will give it to you.' Come with us, and we will
treat you well; for the LORD has promised good
things to Israel."
[30]And he said to him, "I will not go, but I will
depart to my *own* land and to my relatives."
[31]So *Moses* said, "Please do not leave, inasmuch as you know how we are to camp in the
wilderness, and you can be our eyes. [32]And it
shall be, if you go with us—indeed it shall
be—that whatever good the LORD will do to us,
the same we will do to you."
[33]So they departed from the mountain of the
LORD on a journey of three days; and the ark
of the covenant of the LORD went before them
for the three days' journey, to search out a
resting place for them. [34]And the cloud of the
LORD *was* above them by day when they went
out from the camp.
[35]So it was, whenever the ark set out, that
Moses said:

"Rise up, O LORD!
Let Your enemies be scattered,
And let those who hate You flee before
You."

[36]And when it rested, he said:

"Return, O LORD,
To the many thousands of Israel."

Psalm 31:6–14

6 I have hated those who regard useless
idols;
But I trust in the LORD.
7 I will be glad and rejoice in Your
mercy,
For You have considered my trouble;
You have known my soul in adversities,
8 And have not shut me up into the hand
of the enemy;
You have set my feet in a wide place.
9 Have mercy on me, O LORD, for I am in
trouble;
My eye wastes away with grief,
Yes, my soul and my body!
10 For my life is spent with grief,
And my years with sighing;
My strength fails because of my iniquity,
And my bones waste away.
11 I am a reproach among all my enemies,
But especially among my neighbors,
And *am* repulsive to my acquaintances;
Those who see me outside flee from me.
12 I am forgotten like a dead man, out of
mind;
I am like a broken vessel.
13 For I hear the slander of many;
Fear *is* on every side;
While they take counsel together
against me,
They scheme to take away my life.
14 But as for me, I trust in You, O LORD;
I say, "You *are* my God."

31:6 I have hated. See Psalm 26:5 on the proper basis for such hatred (see Ps. 139:21). **useless idols.** This is a common designation for false gods (see Deut. 32:21; 1 Kin. 16:13; Jer. 10:15; 14:22; 16:19; 18:15; Jon. 2:8). On the "idiocy" of idolatry, see Habakkuk 2:18–20.

Proverbs 11:7–11

7 When a wicked man dies, *his*
expectation will perish,
And the hope of the unjust perishes.
8 The righteous is delivered from
trouble,
And it comes to the wicked instead.
9 The hypocrite with *his* mouth destroys
his neighbor,
But through knowledge the righteous
will be delivered.
10 When it goes well with the righteous,
the city rejoices;
And when the wicked perish, *there is*
jubilation.
11 By the blessing of the upright the city
is exalted,
But it is overthrown by the mouth of
the wicked.

Mark 9:30–50

30Then they departed from there and passed
through Galilee, and He did not want anyone
to know *it.* 31For He taught His disciples and
said to them, "The Son of Man is being
betrayed into the hands of men, and they will
kill Him. And after He is killed, He will rise the
third day." 32But they did not understand this
saying, and were afraid to ask Him.

33Then He came to Capernaum. And when
He was in the house He asked them, "What
was it you disputed among yourselves on the
road?" 34But they kept silent, for on the road
they had disputed among themselves who
would be the greatest. 35And He sat down,
called the twelve, and said to them, "If anyone
desires to be first, he shall be last of all and
servant of all." 36Then He took a little child and
set him in the midst of them. And when He
had taken him in His arms, He said to them,
37"Whoever receives one of these little children in My name receives Me; and whoever
receives Me, receives not Me but Him who
sent Me."

38Now John answered Him, saying,
"Teacher, we saw someone who does not follow us casting out demons in Your name, and
we forbade him because he does not follow
us."

39But Jesus said, "Do not forbid him, for no
one who works a miracle in My name can
soon afterward speak evil of Me. 40For he who
is not against us is on our side. 41For whoever
gives you a cup of water to drink in My name,
because you belong to Christ, assuredly, I say
to you, he will by no means lose his reward.

42"But whoever causes one of these little
ones who believe in Me to stumble, it would
be better for him if a millstone were hung
around his neck, and he were thrown into the
sea. 43If your hand causes you to sin, cut it off.
It is better for you to enter into life maimed,
rather than having two hands, to go to hell,
into the fire that shall never be quenched—
44where

'Their worm does not die
And the fire is not quenched.'

45And if your foot causes you to sin, cut it off.
It is better for you to enter life lame, rather
than having two feet, to be cast into hell, into
the fire that shall never be quenched—
46where

'Their worm does not die
And the fire is not quenched.'

47And if your eye causes you to sin, pluck it
out. It is better for you to enter the kingdom of
God with one eye, rather than having two
eyes, to be cast into hell fire— 48where

'Their worm does not die
And the fire is not quenched.'

49"For everyone will be seasoned with fire,
and every sacrifice will be seasoned with salt.
50Salt *is* good, but if the salt loses its flavor, how
will you season it? Have salt in yourselves, and
have peace with one another."

9:43 cut it off. Jesus' words are to be taken figuratively. No amount of self-mutilation can deal with sin, which is an issue of the heart. The Lord is emphasizing the seriousness of sin and the need to do whatever is necessary to deal with it. **life.** The contrast of "life" with "hell" indicates that Jesus was referring to eternal life. **hell.** The Greek word refers to the Valley of Hinnom near Jerusalem, a garbage dump where fires constantly burned, furnishing a graphic symbol of eternal torment. **the fire that shall never be quenched.** That the punishment of hell lasts for eternity is the unmistakable teaching of Scripture (see Dan. 12:2; Matt. 25:41; 2 Thess. 1:9; Rev. 14:10,11; 20:10).

9:50 Salt *is* good. Salt was an essential item in first-century Palestine. In a hot climate, without refrigeration, salt was the practical means of preserving food. **Have salt in yourselves.** The work of the "word of Christ" (Col. 3:16) and the Spirit (Gal. 5:22,23) produce godly character, enabling a person to act as a preservative in society.

DAY 6: What essential element is Christ looking for in our character?

To be directly confronted by Christ with sin in your heart, as the disciples were in Mark 9:33, must have been powerfully convicting and embarrassing. We are told that "they kept silent"—they were speechless at His inquiry. They were caught in a dispute over "who would be the greatest" (v. 34), possibly triggered by the privilege granted Peter, James, and John to witness the

Transfiguration. The disciples' quarrel highlights their failure to apply Jesus' explicit teaching on humility (Matt. 5:3) and the example of His own suffering and death (vv. 31,32; 8:30–33). It also prompted them to ask Jesus to settle the issue, which He did—though not as they had expected.

Jesus "sat down" (v. 35)—rabbis usually sat down to teach—and said that "if anyone desires to be first," as the disciples undeniably did (v. 34; see 10:35–37), "he shall be last of all and servant of all." The disciples' concept of greatness and leadership, drawn from their culture, needed to be completely reversed. Not those who lord their position over others are great in God's kingdom, but those who humbly serve others (see 10:31,43–45; Matt. 19:30–20:16; 23:11,12; Luke 13:30; 14:8–11; 18:14; 22:24–27).

Then Jesus took "a little child"—the Greek word indicates an infant or toddler. If the house they were in was Peter's, this may have been one of his children. The child became in Jesus' masterful teaching an example of believers who have humbled themselves and become like trusting children.

MARCH 7

Numbers 11:1–12:16

11 Now *when* the people complained, it displeased the LORD; for the LORD heard *it,*
and His anger was aroused. So the fire of the
LORD burned among them, and consumed
some in the outskirts of the camp. [2]Then the
people cried out to Moses, and when Moses
prayed to the LORD, the fire was quenched. [3]So
he called the name of the place Taberah,
because the fire of the LORD had burned
among them.

[4]Now the mixed multitude who were among
them yielded to intense craving; so the children of Israel also wept again and said: "Who
will give us meat to eat? [5]We remember the
fish which we ate freely in Egypt, the cucumbers, the melons, the leeks, the onions, and
the garlic; [6]but now our whole being *is* dried
up; *there is* nothing at all except this manna *before* our eyes!"

[7]Now the manna *was* like coriander seed,
and its color like the color of bdellium. [8]The
people went about and gathered *it,* ground *it*
on millstones or beat *it* in the mortar, cooked
it in pans, and made cakes of it; and its taste
was like the taste of pastry prepared with oil.
[9]And when the dew fell on the camp in the
night, the manna fell on it.

[10]Then Moses heard the people weeping
throughout their families, everyone at the
door of his tent; and the anger of the LORD was
greatly aroused; Moses also was displeased.
[11]So Moses said to the LORD, "Why have You
afflicted Your servant? And why have I not
found favor in Your sight, that You have laid
the burden of all these people on me? [12]Did I
conceive all these people? Did I beget them,
that You should say to me, 'Carry them in your
bosom, as a guardian carries a nursing child,'
to the land which You swore to their fathers?
[13]Where am I to get meat to give to all these
people? For they weep all over me, saying,
'Give us meat, that we may eat.' [14]I am not able
to bear all these people alone, because the
burden *is* too heavy for me. [15]If You treat me
like this, please kill me here and now—if I
have found favor in Your sight—and do not let
me see my wretchedness!"

[16]So the LORD said to Moses: "Gather to Me
seventy men of the elders of Israel, whom you
know to be the elders of the people and officers over them; bring them to the tabernacle
of meeting, that they may stand there with
you. [17]Then I will come down and talk with you
there. I will take of the Spirit that *is* upon you
and will put *the same* upon them; and they
shall bear the burden of the people with you,
that you may not bear *it* yourself alone. [18]Then
you shall say to the people, 'Consecrate yourselves for tomorrow, and you shall eat meat;
for you have wept in the hearing of the LORD,
saying, "Who will give us meat to eat? For *it
was* well with us in Egypt." Therefore the
LORD will give you meat, and you shall eat.
[19]You shall eat, not one day, nor two days, nor
five days, nor ten days, nor twenty days, [20]but
for a whole month, until it comes out of your
nostrils and becomes loathsome to you,
because you have despised the LORD who is
among you, and have wept before Him, saying, "Why did we ever come up out of
Egypt?" ' "

[21]And Moses said, "The people whom I *am*

11:17 the Spirit. This refers to the Spirit of God. It was by means of the Holy Spirit that Moses was able to lead Israel. In v. 25, the Lord gave the Spirit to the 70 men in fulfillment of the word He gave to Moses.

among *are* six hundred thousand men on foot;
yet You have said, 'I will give them meat, that
they may eat *for* a whole month.' 22Shall flocks
and herds be slaughtered for them, to provide
enough for them? Or shall all the fish of the
sea be gathered together for them, to provide
enough for them?"

23And the LORD said to Moses, "Has the
LORD's arm been shortened? Now you shall
see whether what I say will happen to you or
not."

24So Moses went out and told the people the
words of the LORD, and he gathered the seventy men of the elders of the people and
placed them around the tabernacle. 25Then the
LORD came down in the cloud, and spoke to
him, and took of the Spirit that *was* upon him,
and placed *the same* upon the seventy elders;
and it happened, when the Spirit rested upon
them, that they prophesied, although they
never did *so* again.

26But two men had remained in the camp:
the name of one *was* Eldad, and the name of
the other Medad. And the Spirit rested upon
them. Now they *were* among those listed, but
who had not gone out to the tabernacle; yet
they prophesied in the camp. 27And a young
man ran and told Moses, and said, "Eldad and
Medad are prophesying in the camp."

28So Joshua the son of Nun, Moses' assistant, *one* of his choice men, answered and
said, "Moses my lord, forbid them!"

29Then Moses said to him, "Are you zealous
for my sake? Oh, that all the LORD's people
were prophets *and* that the LORD would put
His Spirit upon them!" 30And Moses returned
to the camp, he and the elders of Israel.

11:29 that the LORD would put His Spirit upon them! Moses desired and anticipated the day when all of God's people would have His Spirit within them. By this, he looked forward to the New Covenant. (See Ezek. 36:22–27; Jer. 31:31ff.; Joel 2:28.)

31Now a wind went out from the LORD, and it
brought quail from the sea and left *them* flut-
tering near the camp, about a day's journey on
this side and about a day's journey on the
other side, all around the camp, and about two
cubits above the surface of the ground. 32And
the people stayed up all that day, all night, and
all the next day, and gathered the quail (he
who gathered least gathered ten homers); and
they spread *them* out for themselves all
around the camp. 33But while the meat *was* still
between their teeth, before it was chewed, the
wrath of the LORD was aroused against the
people, and the LORD struck the people with a
very great plague. 34So he called the name of
that place Kibroth Hattaavah, because there
they buried the people who had yielded to
craving.

35From Kibroth Hattaavah the people moved
to Hazeroth, and camped at Hazeroth.

12 Then Miriam and Aaron spoke against
Moses because of the Ethiopian woman
whom he had married; for he had married an
Ethiopian woman. 2So they said, "Has the
LORD indeed spoken only through Moses?
Has He not spoken through us also?" And the
LORD heard *it*. 3(Now the man Moses *was* very
humble, more than all men who *were* on the
face of the earth.)

4Suddenly the LORD said to Moses, Aaron,
and Miriam, "Come out, you three, to the tabernacle of meeting!" So the three came out.
5Then the LORD came down in the pillar of
cloud and stood *in* the door of the tabernacle,
and called Aaron and Miriam. And they both
went forward. 6Then He said,

"Hear now My words:
If there is a prophet among you,
I, the LORD, make Myself known to him
in a vision;
I speak to him in a dream.
7 Not so with My servant Moses;
He *is* faithful in all My house.
8 I speak with him face to face,
Even plainly, and not in dark sayings;
And he sees the form of the LORD.
Why then were you not afraid
To speak against My servant Moses?"

9So the anger of the LORD was aroused
against them, and He departed. 10And when
the cloud departed from above the tabernacle,
suddenly Miriam *became* leprous, as *white as*
snow. Then Aaron turned toward Miriam, and
there she was, a leper. 11So Aaron said to
Moses, "Oh, my lord! Please do not lay *this* sin
on us, in which we have done foolishly and in
which we have sinned. 12Please do not let her
be as one dead, whose flesh is half consumed
when he comes out of his mother's womb!"

13So Moses cried out to the LORD, saying,
"Please heal her, O God, I pray!"

14Then the LORD said to Moses, "If her
father had but spit in her face, would she not
be shamed seven days? Let her be shut out of
the camp seven days, and afterward she may
be received *again*." 15So Miriam was shut out
of the camp seven days, and the people did not

journey till Miriam was brought in *again.* 16And
afterward the people moved from Hazeroth
and camped in the Wilderness of Paran.

Psalm 31:15–18

15 My times *are* in Your hand;
Deliver me from the hand of my
enemies,
And from those who persecute me.
16 Make Your face shine upon Your
servant;
Save me for Your mercies' sake.
17 Do not let me be ashamed, O LORD, for
I have called upon You;
Let the wicked be ashamed;
Let them be silent in the grave.
18 Let the lying lips be put to silence,
Which speak insolent things proudly
and contemptuously against the
righteous.

Proverbs 11:12–14

12 He who is devoid of wisdom despises
his neighbor,
But a man of understanding holds his
peace.
13 A talebearer reveals secrets,
But he who is of a faithful spirit
conceals a matter.
14 Where *there is* no counsel, the people
fall;
But in the multitude of counselors
there is safety.

Mark 10:1–31

10 Then He arose from there and came to
the region of Judea by the other side of
the Jordan. And multitudes gathered to Him
again, and as He was accustomed, He taught
them again.
2The Pharisees came and asked Him, "Is it
lawful for a man to divorce *his* wife?" testing
Him.
3And He answered and said to them, "What
did Moses command you?"
4They said, "Moses permitted *a man* to write
a certificate of divorce, and to dismiss *her.*"
5And Jesus answered and said to them, "Because of the hardness of your heart he wrote
you this precept. 6But from the beginning of
the creation, God *'made them male and
female.'* 7*'For this reason a man shall leave his
father and mother and be joined to his wife,*
8*and the two shall become one flesh'*; so then
they are no longer two, but one flesh. 9There-
fore what God has joined together, let not man
separate."
10In the house His disciples also asked Him
again about the same *matter.* 11So He said to
them, "Whoever divorces his wife and marries
another commits adultery against her. 12And if a
woman divorces her husband and marries
another, she commits adultery."
13Then they brought little children to Him,
that He might touch them; but the disciples
rebuked those who brought *them.* 14But when
Jesus saw *it,* He was greatly displeased and
said to them, "Let the little children come to
Me, and do not forbid them; for of such is the
kingdom of God. 15Assuredly, I say to you, whoever does not receive the kingdom of God as a
little child will by no means enter it." 16And He
took them up in His arms, laid *His* hands on
them, and blessed them.
17Now as He was going out on the road, one
came running, knelt before Him, and asked
Him, "Good Teacher, what shall I do that I
may inherit eternal life?"
18So Jesus said to him, "Why do you call Me
good? No one *is* good but One, *that is,* God.
19You know the commandments: *'Do not commit adultery,' 'Do not murder,' 'Do not steal,'
'Do not bear false witness,'* 'Do not defraud,'
'Honor your father and your mother.' "
20And he answered and said to Him,
"Teacher, all these things I have kept from my
youth."
21Then Jesus, looking at him, loved him, and
said to him, "One thing you lack: Go your way,

10:21 Jesus...loved him. Jesus felt great compassion for this sincere truth-seeker who was so hopelessly lost. And out of that great love He told the rich young man to **sell whatever you have.** Jesus was not making either philanthropy or poverty a requirement for salvation, but He was exposing the young man's heart. He was not blameless, as he maintained (v. 20), since he loved his possessions more than his neighbors (see Lev. 19:18). More importantly, he refused to obey Christ's direct command, choosing to serve riches instead of God (Matt. 6:24). The issue was to determine whether he would submit to the lordship of Christ no matter what He asked of him. So, as he would not acknowledge his sin and repent, neither would he submit to the Sovereign Savior. Such unwillingness on both counts kept him from the eternal life he sought. **treasure in heaven.** Salvation and all its benefits, given by the Father who dwells there, both in this life and the life to come (see Matt. 13:44–46).

sell whatever you have and give to the poor,
and you will have treasure in heaven; and
come, take up the cross, and follow Me."
22But he was sad at this word, and went
away sorrowful, for he had great possessions.
23Then Jesus looked around and said to His
disciples, "How hard it is for those who have
riches to enter the kingdom of God!" 24And the
disciples were astonished at His words. But
Jesus answered again and said to them, "Children, how hard it is for those who trust in riches to enter the kingdom of God! 25It is easier
for a camel to go through the eye of a needle
than for a rich man to enter the kingdom of
God."
26And they were greatly astonished, saying
among themselves, "Who then can be saved?"
27But Jesus looked at them and said, "With
men *it is* impossible, but not with God; for
with God all things are possible."
28Then Peter began to say to Him, "See, we
have left all and followed You."
29So Jesus answered and said, "Assuredly, I
say to you, there is no one who has left house
or brothers or sisters or father or mother or
wife or children or lands, for My sake and the
gospel's, 30who shall not receive a hundredfold
now in this time—houses and brothers and
sisters and mothers and children and lands,
with persecutions—and in the age to come,
eternal life. 31But many *who are* first will be
last, and the last first."

DAY 7: Is salvation harder for those who have riches?

Watching the rich young ruler walk away sorrowful in Mark 7:23, Jesus said, "How hard it is for those who have riches to enter the kingdom of God!" "Hard" in this context means impossible (see v. 25). "Riches" tend to breed self-sufficiency and a false sense of security, leading those who have them to imagine they do not need divine resources (see Luke 16:13; contra. Luke 19:2; see 1 Tim. 6:9,17,18).

Jesus adds that it is "easier for a camel to go through the eye of a needle" (v. 25). The Persians expressed impossibility by saying it would be easier to put an elephant through the eye of a needle. This was a Jewish colloquial adaptation of that expression denoting impossibility (the largest animal in Palestine was a camel). Many improbable interpretations have arisen that attempt to soften this phrase, but Jesus' use of this illustration was to explicitly say that salvation by human effort is impossible—it is wholly by God's grace.

The Jews believed that with alms a man purchased salvation (as recorded in the Talmud), so the more wealth one had, the more alms he could give, the more sacrifices and offerings he could offer, thus purchasing redemption. The disciples' question, "Who then can be saved?" (v. 26), makes it clear that they understood what Jesus meant—that not even the rich could buy salvation. Jesus' emphatic teaching that even the rich could not be saved by their own efforts left the bewildered disciples wondering what chance the poor stood. "With men it is impossible, but not with God," Jesus added (v. 27). It is impossible for anyone to be saved by his own efforts, since salvation is entirely a gracious, sovereign work of God.

MARCH 8

Numbers 13:1–14:45

13 And the LORD spoke to Moses, saying,
2"Send men to spy out the land of Canaan,
which I am giving to the children of Israel;
from each tribe of their fathers you shall send
a man, every one a leader among them."

13:1 the LORD spoke to Moses. According to Deuteronomy 1:22,23, the people had first requested the spies be sent out after Moses challenged them to take the land. Here, the Lord affirmed the peoples' desire and commanded Moses to send them.

3So Moses sent them from the Wilderness
of Paran according to the command of the
LORD, all of them men who *were* heads of the
children of Israel. 4Now these *were* their
names: from the tribe of Reuben, Shammua
the son of Zaccur; 5from the tribe of Simeon,
Shaphat the son of Hori; 6from the tribe of Judah, Caleb the son of Jephunneh; 7from the
tribe of Issachar, Igal the son of Joseph; 8from
the tribe of Ephraim, Hoshea the son of Nun;
9from the tribe of Benjamin, Palti the son of
Raphu; 10from the tribe of Zebulun, Gaddiel
the son of Sodi; 11from the tribe of Joseph, *that
is,* from the tribe of Manasseh, Gaddi the son
of Susi; 12from the tribe of Dan, Ammiel the
son of Gemalli; 13from the tribe of Asher,
Sethur the son of Michael; 14from the tribe of
Naphtali, Nahbi the son of Vophsi; 15from the
tribe of Gad, Geuel the son of Machi.
16These *are* the names of the men whom

Moses sent to spy out the land. And Moses
called Hoshea the son of Nun, Joshua.
17Then Moses sent them to spy out the land
of Canaan, and said to them, "Go up this *way*
into the South, and go up to the mountains,
18and see what the land is like: whether the
people who dwell in it *are* strong or weak, few
or many; 19whether the land they dwell in *is*
good or bad; whether the cities they inhabit
are like camps or strongholds; 20whether the
land *is* rich or poor; and whether there are
forests there or not. Be of good courage. And
bring some of the fruit of the land." Now the
time *was* the season of the first ripe grapes.
21So they went up and spied out the land
from the Wilderness of Zin as far as Rehob,
near the entrance of Hamath. 22And they went
up through the South and came to Hebron;
Ahiman, Sheshai, and Talmai, the descendants
of Anak, *were* there. (Now Hebron was built
seven years before Zoan in Egypt.) 23Then
they came to the Valley of Eshcol, and there
cut down a branch with one cluster of grapes;
they carried it between two of them on a pole.
They also *brought* some of the pomegranates
and figs. 24The place was called the Valley of
Eshcol, because of the cluster which the men
of Israel cut down there. 25And they returned
from spying out the land after forty days.
26Now they departed and came back to
Moses and Aaron and all the congregation of
the children of Israel in the Wilderness of Paran,
at Kadesh; they brought back word to them and
to all the congregation, and showed them the
fruit of the land. 27Then they told him, and said:
"We went to the land where you sent us. It truly
flows with milk and honey, and this *is* its fruit.
28Nevertheless the people who dwell in the land
are strong; the cities *are* fortified *and* very
large; moreover we saw the descendants of
Anak there. 29The Amalekites dwell in the land
of the South; the Hittites, the Jebusites, and the
Amorites dwell in the mountains; and the Canaanites dwell by the sea and along the banks
of the Jordan."
30Then Caleb quieted the people before
Moses, and said, "Let us go up at once and
take possession, for we are well able to overcome it."
31But the men who had gone up with him
said, "We are not able to go up against the people, for they *are* stronger than we." 32And they
gave the children of Israel a bad report of
the land which they had spied out, saying,
"The land through which we have gone as
spies *is* a land that devours its inhabitants, and
all the people whom we saw in it *are* men of
great stature. 33There we saw the giants (the
descendants of Anak came from the giants);
and we were like grasshoppers in our own
sight, and so we were in their sight."

14
So all the congregation lifted up their
voices and cried, and the people wept
that night. 2And all the children of Israel complained against Moses and Aaron, and the
whole congregation said to them, "If only we
had died in the land of Egypt! Or if only we
had died in this wilderness! 3Why has the
LORD brought us to this land to fall by the
sword, that our wives and children should
become victims? Would it not be better for us to
return to Egypt?" 4So they said to one another,
"Let us select a leader and return to Egypt."
5Then Moses and Aaron fell on their faces
before all the assembly of the congregation of
the children of Israel.
6But Joshua the son of Nun and Caleb the
son of Jephunneh, *who were* among those who
had spied out the land, tore their clothes; 7and
they spoke to all the congregation of the children of Israel, saying: "The land we passed
through to spy out *is* an exceedingly good
land. 8If the LORD delights in us, then He will
bring us into this land and give it to us, 'a land
which flows with milk and honey.' 9Only do not
rebel against the LORD, nor fear the people of
the land, for they *are* our bread; their protection has departed from them, and the LORD *is*
with us. Do not fear them."
10And all the congregation said to stone
them with stones. Now the glory of the LORD
appeared in the tabernacle of meeting before
all the children of Israel.
11Then the LORD said to Moses: "How long
will these people reject Me? And how long will
they not believe Me, with all the signs which I
have performed among them? 12I will strike
them with the pestilence and disinherit them,
and I will make of you a nation greater and
mightier than they."
13And Moses said to the LORD: "Then the
Egyptians will hear *it,* for by Your might You
brought these people up from among them,
14and they will tell *it* to the inhabitants of this
land. They have heard that You, LORD, *are*
among these people; that You, LORD, are seen
face to face and Your cloud stands above
them, and You go before them in a pillar of
cloud by day and in a pillar of fire by night.
15Now *if* You kill these people as one man, then
the nations which have heard of Your fame
will speak, saying, 16'Because the LORD was not
able to bring this people to the land which He
swore to give them, therefore He killed them
in the wilderness.' 17And now, I pray, let the
power of my Lord be great, just as You have

spoken, saying, 18 'The LORD is longsuffering
and abundant in mercy, forgiving iniquity and
transgression; but He by no means clears *the
guilty,* visiting the iniquity of the fathers on the
children to the third and fourth *generation.'*
19 Pardon the iniquity of this people, I pray, according to the greatness of Your mercy, just as
You have forgiven this people, from Egypt even
until now."

20 Then the LORD said: "I have pardoned, according to your word; 21 but truly, as I live, all
the earth shall be filled with the glory of the
LORD— 22 because all these men who have seen
My glory and the signs which I did in Egypt
and in the wilderness, and have put Me to the
test now these ten times, and have not heeded
My voice, 23 they certainly shall not see the
land of which I swore to their fathers, nor shall
any of those who rejected Me see it. 24 But My
servant Caleb, because he has a different spirit in him and has followed Me fully, I will bring
into the land where he went, and his descendants shall inherit it. 25 Now the Amalekites
and the Canaanites dwell in the valley; tomorrow turn and move out into the wilderness by
the Way of the Red Sea."

26 And the LORD spoke to Moses and Aaron,
saying, 27 "How long *shall I bear with* this evil
congregation who complain against Me? I
have heard the complaints which the children
of Israel make against Me. 28 Say to them, 'As I
live,' says the LORD, 'just as you have spoken
in My hearing, so I will do to you: 29 The carcasses of you who have complained against
Me shall fall in this wilderness, all of you who
were numbered, according to your entire number, from twenty years old and above. 30 Except
for Caleb the son of Jephunneh and Joshua the
son of Nun, you shall by no means enter the
land which I swore I would make you dwell in.
31 But your little ones, whom you said would be
victims, I will bring in, and they shall know the
land which you have despised. 32 But *as for* you,
your carcasses shall fall in this wilderness.
33 And your sons shall be shepherds in the
wilderness forty years, and bear the brunt of
your infidelity, until your carcasses are consumed in the wilderness. 34 According to the
number of the days in which you spied out the
land, forty days, for each day you shall bear
your guilt one year, *namely* forty years, and you
shall know My rejection. 35 I the LORD have spoken this. I will surely do so to all this evil congregation who are gathered together against
Me. In this wilderness they shall be consumed, and there they shall die.' "

36 Now the men whom Moses sent to spy
out the land, who returned and made all the
congregation complain against him by bringing a bad report of the land, 37 those very men
who brought the evil report about the land, died
by the plague before the LORD. 38 But Joshua the
son of Nun and Caleb the son of Jephunneh
remained alive, of the men who went to spy out
the land.

39 Then Moses told these words to all the
children of Israel, and the people mourned
greatly. 40 And they rose early in the morning
and went up to the top of the mountain, saying, "Here we are, and we will go up to the
place which the LORD has promised, for we
have sinned!"

41 And Moses said, "Now why do you transgress the command of the LORD? For this will
not succeed. 42 Do not go up, lest you be defeated by your enemies, for the LORD *is* not among
you. 43 For the Amalekites and the Canaanites
are there before you, and you shall fall by the
sword; because you have turned away from
the LORD, the LORD will not be with you."

44 But they presumed to go up to the mountaintop. Nevertheless, neither the ark of the
covenant of the LORD nor Moses departed from
the camp. 45 Then the Amalekites and the
Canaanites who dwelt in that mountain came
down and attacked them, and drove them back
as far as Hormah.

Psalm 31:19–24

19 Oh, how great *is* Your goodness,
Which You have laid up for those who
fear You,
Which You have prepared for those
who trust in You
In the presence of the sons of men!
20 You shall hide them in the secret place
of Your presence
From the plots of man;
You shall keep them secretly in a
pavilion
From the strife of tongues.

21 Blessed *be* the LORD,
For He has shown me His marvelous
kindness in a strong city!
22 For I said in my haste,
"I am cut off from before Your eyes";
Nevertheless You heard the voice of
my supplications
When I cried out to You.

23 Oh, love the LORD, all you
His saints!
For the LORD preserves
the faithful,
And fully repays the proud person.
24 Be of good courage,

31:23 love the Lord. Biblical love includes an attitudinal response and demonstrated obedience (see Deut. 6:4,5; 10:12; John 14:15,21; 15:10; 2 John 6). The assurance of both reward and retribution is a biblical maxim (e.g., Deut. 7:9,10).

And He shall strengthen your heart,
All you who hope in the Lord.

Proverbs 11:15

15 He who is surety for a stranger will suffer,
But one who hates being surety is secure.

Mark 10:32–52

32Now they were on the road, going up to Jerusalem, and Jesus was going before them;
and they were amazed. And as they followed
they were afraid. Then He took the twelve
aside again and began to tell them the things
that would happen to Him: 33"Behold, we are
going up to Jerusalem, and the Son of Man
will be betrayed to the chief priests and to the
scribes; and they will condemn Him to death
and deliver Him to the Gentiles; 34and they will
mock Him, and scourge Him, and spit on Him,
and kill Him. And the third day He will rise
again."
35Then James and John, the sons of
Zebedee, came to Him, saying, "Teacher, we
want You to do for us whatever we ask."
36And He said to them, "What do you want
Me to do for you?"
37They said to Him, "Grant us that we may
sit, one on Your right hand and the other on
Your left, in Your glory."
38But Jesus said to them, "You do not know
what you ask. Are you able to drink the cup
that I drink, and be baptized with the baptism
that I am baptized with?"
39They said to Him, "We are able."
So Jesus said to them, "You will indeed
drink the cup that I drink, and with the baptism I am baptized with you will be baptized;
40but to sit on My right hand and on My left is
not Mine to give, but *it is for those* for whom it
is prepared."
41And when the ten heard *it,* they began to
be greatly displeased with James and John.
42But Jesus called them to *Himself* and said to
them, "You know that those who are considered rulers over the Gentiles lord it over
them, and their great ones exercise authority
over them. 43Yet it shall not be so among you;
but whoever desires to become great among
you shall be your servant. 44And whoever of you
desires to be first shall be slave of all. 45For even
the Son of Man did not come to be served, but
to serve, and to give His life a ransom for
many."

10:45 Son of Man did not come to be served. Jesus was the supreme example of servant leadership (see John 13:13–15). The King of Kings and Lord of Lords (Rev. 19:16) relinquished His privileges (Phil. 2:5–8) and gave His life as a selfless sacrifice in serving others. **ransom for many.** "Ransom" refers to the price paid to free a slave or a prisoner; "for" means "in place of." Christ's substitutionary death on behalf of those who would put their faith in Him is the most glorious, blessed truth in all of Scripture (see Rom. 8:1–3; 1 Cor. 6:20; Gal. 3:13; 4:5; Eph. 1:7; Titus 2:14; 1 Pet. 1:18,19). The ransom was not paid to Satan, as some erroneous theories of the atonement teach. Satan is presented in Scripture as a foe to be defeated, not a ruler to be placated. The ransom price was paid to God to satisfy His justice and holy wrath against sin. In paying it, Christ "bore our sins in His own body on the [cross]" (1 Pet. 2:24).

46Now they came to Jericho. As He went out
of Jericho with His disciples and a great multitude, blind Bartimaeus, the son of Timaeus,
sat by the road begging. 47And when he heard
that it was Jesus of Nazareth, he began to cry
out and say, "Jesus, Son of David, have mercy
on me!"
48Then many warned him to be quiet; but he
cried out all the more, "Son of David, have
mercy on me!"
49So Jesus stood still and commanded him to
be called.
Then they called the blind man, saying to
him, "Be of good cheer. Rise, He is calling
you."
50And throwing aside his garment, he rose
and came to Jesus.
51So Jesus answered and said to him, "What
do you want Me to do for you?"
The blind man said to Him, "Rabboni, that I
may receive my sight."
52Then Jesus said to him, "Go your way;
your faith has made you well." And immediately he received his sight and followed Jesus
on the road.

DAY 8: If the report of the spies was true, why was it a "bad report"?

The spies were specifically called to explore the land that God had promised to Israel. This exploration gave valuable information to Moses for the conquest ahead. And while it was true that the land was flowing with milk and honey, it was also true that "the descendants of Anak" were in the fortified city of Hebron (Num. 13:22). Anak was probably the ancestor of Ahiman, Sheshai, and Talmai. They were noted for their height and strength (Deut. 2:21; 9:2). And "the people…are strong" (v. 28), as in too strong to be conquered (v. 31). "Giants" were in the land (v. 33). This term was used in Genesis 6:4 for a group of strong men who lived on the earth before the Flood. The descendants of Anak were, in exaggeration, compared to these giants, which led the spies to view themselves as grasshoppers before them.

In v. 30, Caleb concurred with the report of the other spies, but called the people to go up and take the land, knowing that with God's help they were able to overcome the strong people. The report of the 10 spies was evil because it exaggerated the dangers of the people in the land, sought to stir up and instill fear in the people of Israel, and, most importantly, it expressed their faithless attitude toward God and His promises (v. 32). The result was that "all the congregation…wept" over the circumstances (14:1) and "complained" to the point that they wished they had died in Egypt or the wilderness (v. 2). It was such a "bad report" that they were prepared to "select a leader and return to Egypt" (v. 4).

MARCH 9

Numbers 15:1–16:50

15 And the LORD spoke to Moses, saying, 2"Speak to the children of Israel, and say to them: 'When you have come into the land you are to inhabit, which I am giving to you, 3and you make an offering by fire to the LORD, a burnt offering or a sacrifice, to fulfill a vow or as a freewill offering or in your appointed feasts, to make a sweet aroma to the LORD, from the herd or the flock, 4then he who presents his offering to the LORD shall bring a grain offering of one-tenth *of an ephah* of fine flour mixed with one-fourth of a hin of oil; 5and one-fourth of a hin of wine as a drink offering you shall prepare with the burnt offering or the sacrifice, for each lamb. 6Or for a ram you shall prepare as a grain offering two-tenths *of an ephah* of fine flour mixed with one-third of a hin of oil; 7and as a drink offering you shall offer one-third of a hin of wine as a sweet aroma to the LORD. 8And when you prepare a young bull as a burnt offering, or as a sacrifice to fulfill a vow, or as a peace offering to the LORD, 9then shall be offered with the young bull a grain offering of three-tenths *of an ephah* of fine flour mixed with half a hin of oil; 10and you shall bring as the drink offering half a hin of wine as an offering made by fire, a sweet aroma to the LORD.

11'Thus it shall be done for each young bull, for each ram, or for each lamb or young goat. 12According to the number that you prepare, so you shall do with everyone according to their number. 13All who are native-born shall do these things in this manner, in presenting an offering made by fire, a sweet aroma to the LORD. 14And if a stranger dwells with you, or whoever *is* among you throughout your generations, and would present an offering made by fire, a sweet aroma to the LORD, just as you do, so shall he do. 15One ordinance *shall be* for you of the assembly and for the stranger who dwells *with you,* an ordinance forever throughout your generations; as you are, so shall the stranger be before the LORD. 16One law and one custom shall be for you and for the stranger who dwells with you.' "

17Again the LORD spoke to Moses, saying, 18"Speak to the children of Israel, and say to them: 'When you come into the land to which I bring you, 19then it will be, when you eat of the bread of the land, that you shall offer up a heave offering to the LORD. 20You shall offer up a cake of the first of your ground meal *as* a heave offering; as a heave offering of the threshing floor, so shall you offer it up. 21Of the first of your ground meal you shall give to the LORD a heave offering throughout your generations.

22'If you sin unintentionally, and do not observe all these commandments which the LORD has spoken to Moses— 23all that the LORD has commanded you by the hand of Moses, from the day the LORD gave commandment and onward throughout your generations— 24then it will be, if it is unintentionally committed, without the knowledge of the congregation, that the whole congregation shall offer one young bull as a burnt offering, as a sweet aroma to the LORD, with its grain offering and

its drink offering, according to the ordinance,
and one kid of the goats as a sin offering. 25So
the priest shall make atonement for the whole
congregation of the children of Israel, and it
shall be forgiven them, for it was unintentional;
they shall bring their offering, an offering
made by fire to the LORD, and their sin offering
before the LORD, for their unintended sin. 26It
shall be forgiven the whole congregation of the
children of Israel and the stranger who dwells
among them, because all the people *did it* unintentionally.

27'And if a person sins unintentionally, then
he shall bring a female goat in its first year as
a sin offering. 28So the priest shall make atonement for the person who sins unintentionally,
when he sins unintentionally before the LORD,
to make atonement for him; and it shall be forgiven him. 29You shall have one law for him
who sins unintentionally, *for* him who is native-
born among the children of Israel and for the
stranger who dwells among them.

30'But the person who does *anything* presumptuously, *whether he is* native-born or a
stranger, that one brings reproach on the
LORD, and he shall be cut off from among his
people. 31Because he has despised the word of
the LORD, and has broken His commandment,
that person shall be completely cut off; his
guilt *shall be* upon him.' "

32Now while the children of Israel were in
the wilderness, they found a man gathering
sticks on the Sabbath day. 33And those who
found him gathering sticks brought him to
Moses and Aaron, and to all the congregation.
34They put him under guard, because it had not
been explained what should be done to him.

35Then the LORD said to Moses, "The man
must surely be put to death; all the congregation shall stone him with stones outside the
camp." 36So, as the LORD commanded Moses,
all the congregation brought him outside the
camp and stoned him with stones, and he died.

37Again the LORD spoke to Moses, saying,
38"Speak to the children of Israel: Tell them to
make tassels on the corners of their garments
throughout their generations, and to put a
blue thread in the tassels of the corners. 39And
you shall have the tassel, that you may look
upon it and remember all the commandments
of the LORD and do them, and that you *may* not
follow the harlotry to which your own heart
and your own eyes are inclined, 40and that you
may remember and do all My commandments, and be holy for your God. 41I *am* the
LORD your God, who brought you out of the
land of Egypt, to be your God: I *am* the LORD
your God."

16 Now Korah the son of Izhar, the son of
Kohath, the son of Levi, with Dathan and
Abiram the sons of Eliab, and On the son of
Peleth, sons of Reuben, took *men;* 2and they
rose up before Moses with some of the children of Israel, two hundred and fifty leaders of
the congregation, representatives of the congregation, men of renown. 3They gathered
together against Moses and Aaron, and said to
them, "*You take* too much upon yourselves, for
all the congregation *is* holy, every one of
them, and the LORD *is* among them. Why then
do you exalt yourselves above the assembly of
the LORD?"

4So when Moses heard *it,* he fell on his face;
5and he spoke to Korah and all his company,
saying, "Tomorrow morning the LORD will
show who *is* His and *who is* holy, and will
cause *him* to come near to Him. That one
whom He chooses He will cause to come near
to Him. 6Do this: Take censers, Korah and all
your company; 7put fire in them and put
incense in them before the LORD tomorrow,
and it shall be *that* the man whom the LORD
chooses *is* the holy one. *You take* too much
upon yourselves, you sons of Levi!"

8Then Moses said to Korah, "Hear now, you
sons of Levi: 9*Is it* a small thing to you that the
God of Israel has separated you from the congregation of Israel, to bring you near to
Himself, to do the work of the tabernacle of
the LORD, and to stand before the congregation
to serve them; 10and that He has brought you
near *to Himself,* you and all your brethren, the
sons of Levi, with you? And are you seeking
the priesthood also? 11Therefore you and all
your company *are* gathered together against
the LORD. And what *is* Aaron that you complain
against him?"

12And Moses sent to call Dathan and Abiram
the sons of Eliab, but they said, "We will not
come up! 13*Is it* a small thing that you have
brought us up out of a land flowing with milk
and honey, to kill us in the wilderness, that
you should keep acting like a prince over us?
14Moreover you have not brought us into a
land flowing with milk and honey, nor given us
inheritance of fields and vineyards. Will you
put out the eyes of these men? We will not
come up!"

15Then Moses was very angry, and said to
the LORD, "Do not respect their offering. I
have not taken one donkey from them, nor
have I hurt one of them."

16And Moses said to Korah, "Tomorrow, you
and all your company be present before the
LORD—you and they, as well as Aaron. 17Let
each take his censer and put incense in it, and

each of you bring his censer before the LORD,
two hundred and fifty censers; both you and
Aaron, each *with* his censer." [18]So every man
took his censer, put fire in it, laid incense on it,
and stood at the door of the tabernacle of
meeting with Moses and Aaron. [19]And Korah
gathered all the congregation against them at
the door of the tabernacle of meeting. Then
the glory of the LORD appeared to all the congregation.
[20]And the LORD spoke to Moses and Aaron,
saying, [21]"Separate yourselves from among
this congregation, that I may consume them
in a moment."
[22]Then they fell on their faces, and said, "O
God, the God of the spirits of all flesh, shall
one man sin, and You be angry with all the
congregation?"

16:22 the God of the spirits of all flesh. This phrase appears only here and in 27:16. Moses called on omniscient God, who knows the heart of everyone, to judge those who had sinned, and those only.

[23]So the LORD spoke to Moses, saying,
[24]"Speak to the congregation, saying, 'Get
away from the tents of Korah, Dathan, and
Abiram.' "
[25]Then Moses rose and went to Dathan and
Abiram, and the elders of Israel followed him.
[26]And he spoke to the congregation, saying,
"Depart now from the tents of these wicked
men! Touch nothing of theirs, lest you be consumed in all their sins." [27]So they got away
from around the tents of Korah, Dathan, and
Abiram; and Dathan and Abiram came out and
stood at the door of their tents, with their
wives, their sons, and their little children.
[28]And Moses said: "By this you shall know
that the LORD has sent me to do all these
works, for *I have* not *done them* of my own will.
[29]If these men die naturally like all men, or if
they are visited by the common fate of all men,
then the LORD has not sent me. [30]But if the
LORD creates a new thing, and the earth opens
its mouth and swallows them up with all that
belongs to them, and they go down alive into
the pit, then you will understand that these
men have rejected the LORD."
[31]Now it came to pass, as he finished speaking all these words, that the ground split apart
under them, [32]and the earth opened its mouth
and swallowed them up, with their households

16:30 a new thing. This supernatural opening of the earth to swallow the rebels was a sign of God's wrath and the vindication of Moses and Aaron.

and all the men with Korah, with all *their*
goods. [33]So they and all those with them went
down alive into the pit; the earth closed over
them, and they perished from among the
assembly. [34]Then all Israel who *were* around
them fled at their cry, for they said, "Lest the
earth swallow us up *also!*"
[35]And a fire came out from the LORD and
consumed the two hundred and fifty men who
were offering incense.
[36]Then the LORD spoke to Moses, saying:
[37]"Tell Eleazar, the son of Aaron the priest, to
pick up the censers out of the blaze, for they
are holy, and scatter the fire some distance
away. [38]The censers of these men who sinned
against their own souls, let them be made into
hammered plates as a covering for the altar.
Because they presented them before the
LORD, therefore they are holy; and they shall
be a sign to the children of Israel." [39]So Eleazar
the priest took the bronze censers, which
those who were burned up had presented, and
they were hammered out as a covering on the
altar, [40]*to be* a memorial to the children of
Israel that no outsider, who *is* not a descendant of Aaron, should come near to offer
incense before the LORD, that he might not
become like Korah and his companions, just
as the LORD had said to him through Moses.
[41]On the next day all the congregation of the
children of Israel complained against Moses
and Aaron, saying, "You have killed the people
of the LORD." [42]Now it happened, when the
congregation had gathered against Moses and
Aaron, that they turned toward the tabernacle
of meeting; and suddenly the cloud covered it,
and the glory of the LORD appeared. [43]Then
Moses and Aaron came before the tabernacle
of meeting.
[44]And the LORD spoke to Moses, saying,
[45]"Get away from among this congregation,
that I may consume them in a moment."
And they fell on their faces.
[46]So Moses said to Aaron, "Take a censer
and put fire in it from the altar, put incense *on
it,* and take it quickly to the congregation and
make atonement for them; for wrath has gone
out from the LORD. The plague has begun."
[47]Then Aaron took *it* as Moses commanded,

and ran into the midst of the assembly; and
already the plague had begun among the people. So he put in the incense and made atonement for the people. 48And he stood between
the dead and the living; so the plague was
stopped. 49Now those who died in the plague
were fourteen thousand seven hundred,
besides those who died in the Korah incident.
50So Aaron returned to Moses at the door of
the tabernacle of meeting, for the plague had
stopped.

Psalm 32:1–5

A Psalm of David. A Contemplation.

Blessed *is he whose* transgression
is forgiven,
Whose sin *is* covered.
2 Blessed *is* the man to whom the LORD
does not impute iniquity,
And in whose spirit *there is* no deceit.

3 When I kept silent, my bones grew old
Through my groaning all the day long.
4 For day and night Your hand was
heavy upon me;
My vitality was turned into the drought
of summer. Selah
5 I acknowledged my sin to You,
And my iniquity I have not hidden.
I said, "I will confess my transgressions
to the LORD,"
And You forgave the iniquity of my sin.
Selah

Proverbs 11:16–18

16 A gracious woman retains honor,
But ruthless *men* retain riches.
17 The merciful man does good for his
own soul,
But *he who is* cruel troubles his own
flesh.
18 The wicked *man* does deceptive work,
But he who sows righteousness *will
have* a sure reward.

Mark 11:1–19

11 Now when they drew near Jerusalem, to
Bethphage and Bethany, at the Mount of
Olives, He sent two of His disciples; 2and He
said to them, "Go into the village opposite you;
and as soon as you have entered it you will find
a colt tied, on which no one has sat. Loose it
and bring *it*. 3And if anyone says to you, 'Why
are you doing this?' say, 'The Lord has need of
it,' and immediately he will send it here."
4So they went their way, and found the colt
tied by the door outside on the street, and they
loosed it. 5But some of those who stood there
said to them, "What are you doing, loosing the
colt?"
6And they spoke to them just as Jesus had
commanded. So they let them go. 7Then they
brought the colt to Jesus and threw their
clothes on it, and He sat on it. 8And many
spread their clothes on the road, and others cut
down leafy branches from the trees and spread
them on the road. 9Then those who went before
and those who followed cried out, saying:

"Hosanna!
*'Blessed is He who comes in the name
of the LORD!'*
10 Blessed *is* the kingdom of our father
David
That comes in the name of the Lord!
Hosanna in the highest!"

11:10 the kingdom of our father David. This tribute, recorded only by Mark, acknowledges Jesus as bringing in the messianic kingdom promised to David's Son. The crowd paraphrased the quote from Psalm 118:26 (v. 9) in anticipation that Jesus was fulfilling prophecy by bringing in the kingdom.

11And Jesus went into Jerusalem and into the
temple. So when He had looked around at all
things, as the hour was already late, He went
out to Bethany with the twelve.
12Now the next day, when they had come out
from Bethany, He was hungry. 13And seeing
from afar a fig tree having leaves, He went to
see if perhaps He would find something on it.
When He came to it, He found nothing but
leaves, for it was not the season for figs. 14In
response Jesus said to it, "Let no one eat fruit
from you ever again."
And His disciples heard *it*.
15So they came to Jerusalem. Then Jesus
went into the temple and began to drive out
those who bought and sold in the temple, and
overturned the tables of the money changers
and the seats of those who sold doves. 16And
He would not allow anyone to carry wares
through the temple. 17Then He taught, saying
to them, "Is it not written, *'My house shall be
called a house of prayer for all nations'*? But
you have made it a *'den of thieves.'*"
18And the scribes and chief priests heard it
and sought how they might destroy Him; for
they feared Him, because all the people were
astonished at His teaching. 19When evening
had come, He went out of the city.

DAY 9: Why did Jesus curse the fig tree in Mark 11:12–14?

Fig trees were common as a source of food. Three years were required from planting until fruit bearing. After that, a tree could be harvested twice a year, usually yielding much fruit. The figs normally grew with the leaves. This tree had leaves but, strangely, no fruit. That this tree was along the side of the road (see Matt. 21:19) implies it was public property. It was also apparently in good soil because its foliage was ahead of season and ahead of the surrounding fig trees. The abundance of leaves held out promise that the tree might also be ahead of schedule with its fruit. That it was "not the season for figs" (v. 13) recognizes that the next normal fig season was in June, more than a month away. This phrase, unique to Mark, emphasizes the unusual nature of this fig tree.

Jesus' direct address to the tree personified it and condemned it for not providing what its appearance promised. "Let no one eat fruit from you ever again" (v. 14). This incident was not the acting out of the parable of the fig tree (Luke 13:6–9), which was a warning against spiritual fruitlessness. Here, Jesus cursed the tree for its misleading appearance that suggested great productivity without providing it. It should have been full of fruit, but was barren. The fig tree was frequently an Old Testament type of the Jewish nation (Hos. 9:10; Nah. 3:12; Zech. 3:10)—and the barren fig tree often symbolizes divine judgment on Israel because of her spiritual fruitlessness despite an abundance of spiritual advantages (Jer. 8:13; Joel 1:12). In this instance Jesus used the tree by the road as a purposeful divine object lesson concerning Israel's spiritual hypocrisy and fruitlessness, exemplified in the rejection of their Messiah. It was not an impetuous act of frustration as some have stated.

MARCH 10

17:8 the rod of Aaron. God had stated that the stick of the man He had chosen would blossom (17:5). The stick of Aaron had not only blossomed, but had yielded ripe almonds. Thus God had exceeded the demands of the test, so there would be no uncertainty of the fact that Aaron had been chosen as high priest.

Numbers 17:1–18:32

17 And the LORD spoke to Moses, saying:
[2]"Speak to the children of Israel, and get from them a rod from each father's house, all their leaders according to their fathers' houses—twelve rods. Write each man's name on his rod.
[3]And you shall write Aaron's name on the rod of Levi. For there shall be one rod for the head of *each* father's house.
[4]Then you shall place them in the tabernacle of meeting before the Testimony, where I meet with you.
[5]And it shall be *that* the rod of the man whom I choose will blossom; thus I will rid Myself of the complaints of the children of Israel, which they make against you."
[6]So Moses spoke to the children of Israel, and each of their leaders gave him a rod apiece, for each leader according to their fathers' houses, twelve rods; and the rod of Aaron *was* among their rods.
[7]And Moses placed the rods before the LORD in the tabernacle of witness.
[8]Now it came to pass on the next day that Moses went into the tabernacle of witness, and behold, the rod of Aaron, of the house of Levi, had sprouted and put forth buds, had produced blossoms and yielded ripe almonds.
[9]Then Moses brought out all the rods from before the LORD to all the children of Israel; and they looked, and each man took his rod.
[10]And the LORD said to Moses, "Bring Aaron's rod back before the Testimony, to be kept as a sign against the rebels, that you may put their complaints away from Me, lest they die."
[11]Thus did Moses; just as the LORD had commanded him, so he did.
[12]So the children of Israel spoke to Moses, saying, "Surely we die, we perish, we all perish!
[13]Whoever even comes near the tabernacle of the LORD must die. Shall we all utterly die?"

18 Then the LORD said to Aaron: "You and your sons and your father's house with you shall bear the iniquity *related to* the sanctuary, and you and your sons with you shall bear the iniquity *associated with* your priesthood.
[2]Also bring with you your brethren of the tribe of Levi, the tribe of your father, that they may be joined with you and serve you while you and your sons *are* with you before the tabernacle of witness.
[3]They shall attend to your needs and all the needs of the tabernacle; but they shall not come near the articles of the sanctuary and the altar, lest they die—they and you also.
[4]They shall be joined with you and attend to the needs of the tabernacle of

meeting, for all the work of the tabernacle; but
an outsider shall not come near you. [5]And you
shall attend to the duties of the sanctuary and
the duties of the altar, that there *may* be no
more wrath on the children of Israel. [6]Behold, I
Myself have taken your brethren the Levites
from among the children of Israel; *they are* a
gift to you, given by the LORD, to do the work of
the tabernacle of meeting. [7]Therefore you and
your sons with you shall attend to your priesthood for everything at the altar and behind the
veil; and you shall serve. I give your priesthood
to you as a gift for service, but the outsider who
comes near shall be put to death."

[8]And the LORD spoke to Aaron: "Here, I
Myself have also given you charge of My heave
offerings, all the holy gifts of the children of
Israel; I have given them as a portion to you
and your sons, as an ordinance forever. [9]This
shall be yours of the most holy things *reserved*
from the fire: every offering of theirs, every
grain offering and every sin offering and
every trespass offering which they render to
Me, *shall be* most holy for you and your sons.
[10]In a most holy *place* you shall eat it; every
male shall eat it. It shall be holy to you.

[11]"This also *is* yours: the heave offering of
their gift, with all the wave offerings of the
children of Israel; I have given them to you,
and your sons and daughters with you, as an
ordinance forever. Everyone who is clean in
your house may eat it.

[12]"All the best of the oil, all the best of the
new wine and the grain, their firstfruits which
they offer to the LORD, I have given them to
you. [13]Whatever first ripe fruit is in their land,
which they bring to the LORD, shall be yours.
Everyone who is clean in your house may eat it.

[14]"Every devoted thing in Israel shall be
yours.

[15]"Everything that first opens the womb of
all flesh, which they bring to the LORD,
whether man or beast, shall be yours; nevertheless the firstborn of man you shall surely
redeem, and the firstborn of unclean animals
you shall redeem. [16]And those redeemed of the
devoted things you shall redeem when one
month old, according to your valuation, for five
shekels of silver, according to the shekel of the
sanctuary, which *is* twenty gerahs. [17]But the
firstborn of a cow, the firstborn of a sheep, or
the firstborn of a goat you shall not redeem;
they *are* holy. You shall sprinkle their blood on
the altar, and burn their fat *as* an offering made
by fire for a sweet aroma to the LORD. [18]And
their flesh shall be yours, just as the wave
breast and the right thigh are yours.

[19]"All the heave offerings of the holy things,
which the children of Israel offer to the LORD, I
have given to you and your sons and daughters
with you as an ordinance forever; it *is* a
covenant of salt forever before the LORD with
you and your descendants with you."

18:19 a covenant of salt forever. Salt, which does not burn, was a metaphor to speak of durability. As salt keeps its flavor, so the Lord's covenant with the priesthood was durable. The Lord would provide through the offerings of His people for His priests forever.

[20]Then the LORD said to Aaron: "You shall
have no inheritance in their land, nor shall you
have any portion among them; I *am* your portion and your inheritance among the children of
Israel.

[21]"Behold, I have given the children of Levi all
the tithes in Israel as an inheritance in return
for the work which they perform, the work of
the tabernacle of meeting. [22]Hereafter the children of Israel shall not come near the tabernacle of meeting, lest they bear sin and die. [23]But
the Levites shall perform the work of the tabernacle of meeting, and they shall bear their iniquity; *it shall be* a statute forever, throughout
your generations, that among the children of
Israel they shall have no inheritance. [24]For the
tithes of the children of Israel, which they offer
up *as* a heave offering to the LORD, I have given
to the Levites as an inheritance; therefore I have
said to them, 'Among the children of Israel they
shall have no inheritance.' "

[25]Then the LORD spoke to Moses, saying,
[26]"Speak thus to the Levites, and say to them:
'When you take from the children of Israel the
tithes which I have given you from them as your
inheritance, then you shall offer up a heave
offering of it to the LORD, a tenth of the tithe.
[27]And your heave offering shall be reckoned to
you as though *it were* the grain of the threshing
floor and as the fullness of the winepress. [28]Thus
you shall also offer a heave offering to the LORD
from all your tithes which you receive from the
children of Israel, and you shall give the LORD's
heave offering from it to Aaron the priest. [29]Of
all your gifts you shall offer up every heave
offering due to the LORD, from all the best of
them, the consecrated part of them.' [30]Therefore
you shall say to them: 'When you have lifted up
the best of it, then *the rest* shall be accounted to
the Levites as the produce of the threshing floor
and as the produce of the winepress. [31]You may

eat it in any place, you and your households, for it *is* your reward for your work in the tabernacle of meeting. [32]And you shall bear no sin because of it, when you have lifted up the best of it. But you shall not profane the holy gifts of the children of Israel, lest you die.' "

Psalm 32:6–11

6 For this cause everyone who is godly
shall pray to You
In a time when You may be found;
Surely in a flood of great waters
They shall not come near him.
7 You *are* my hiding place;
You shall preserve me from trouble;
You shall surround me with songs of
deliverance. Selah
8 I will instruct you and teach you in the
way you should go;
I will guide you with My eye.
9 Do not be like the horse *or* like the mule,
Which have no understanding,
Which must be harnessed with bit and
bridle,
Else they will not come near you.
10 Many sorrows *shall be* to the wicked;
But he who trusts in the LORD, mercy
shall surround him.
11 Be glad in the LORD and rejoice, you
righteous;
And shout for joy, all *you* upright in
heart!

Proverbs 11:19–21

19 As righteousness *leads* to life,
So he who pursues evil *pursues it* to his
own death.
20 Those who are of a perverse heart *are*
an abomination to the LORD,
But *the* blameless in their ways *are* His
delight.

11:20 abomination. Defined throughout Scripture as attitudes, this involves words and behaviors which God hates.

21 *Though they join* forces, the wicked will
not go unpunished;
But the posterity of the righteous will
be delivered.

Mark 11:20–33

[20]Now in the morning, as they passed by,
they saw the fig tree dried up from the roots.
[21]And Peter, remembering, said to Him,
"Rabbi, look! The fig tree which You cursed
has withered away."
[22]So Jesus answered and said to them,
"Have faith in God. [23]For assuredly, I say to
you, whoever says to this mountain, 'Be
removed and be cast into the sea,' and does
not doubt in his heart, but believes that those
things he says will be done, he will have whatever he says. [24]Therefore I say to you, whatever things you ask when you pray, believe
that you receive *them,* and you will have *them.*
[25]"And whenever you stand praying, if you
have anything against anyone, forgive him,
that your Father in heaven may also forgive
you your trespasses. [26]But if you do not forgive,

11:25 stand praying. The traditional Jewish prayer posture (see 1 Sam. 1:26; 1 Kin. 8:14,22; Neh. 9:4; Matt. 6:5; Luke 18:11,13). Kneeling or lying with one's face on the ground were used during extraordinary circumstances or for extremely urgent requests (see 1 Kin. 8:54; Ezra 9:5; Dan. 6:10; Matt. 26:39; Acts 7:60). **anything against anyone.** An all-inclusive statement that includes both sins and simple dislikes, which cause the believer to hold something against another person. "Anyone" incorporates believers and unbelievers. **forgive.** Jesus states the believer's ongoing duty to have a forgiving attitude. Successful prayer requires forgiveness as well as faith.

neither will your Father in heaven forgive your
trespasses."
[27]Then they came again to Jerusalem. And
as He was walking in the temple, the chief
priests, the scribes, and the elders came to
Him. [28]And they said to Him, "By what authority are You doing these things? And who gave
You this authority to do these things?"
[29]But Jesus answered and said to them, "I
also will ask you one question; then answer
Me, and I will tell you by what authority I do
these things: [30]The baptism of John—was it
from heaven or from men? Answer Me."
[31]And they reasoned among themselves,
saying, "If we say, 'From heaven,' He will say,
'Why then did you not believe him?' [32]But if we
say, 'From men' "—they feared the people, for
all counted John to have been a prophet
indeed. [33]So they answered and said to Jesus,
"We do not know."
And Jesus answered and said to them, "Neither will I tell you by what authority I do these
things."

DAY 10: How does one's faith move mountains?

When an amazed Peter noted to Jesus that the fig tree had withered, Jesus' response was simply that they should "have faith in God" (Mark 11:22). This was a gentle rebuke for the disciples' lack of faith in the power of His word. Such faith believes in God's revealed truth, His power, and seeks to do His will (see 1 John 5:14; Matt. 21:21).

The expression Jesus used, "this mountain…into the sea" (v. 23), was related to a common metaphor of that day, "rooter up of mountains," which was used in Jewish literature of great rabbis and spiritual leaders who could solve difficult problems and seemingly do the impossible. Obviously, Jesus did not literally uproot mountains. In fact, He refused to do such spectacular miracles for the unbelieving Jewish leaders (Matt. 12:38). Jesus' point is that, if believers sincerely trust in God and truly realize the unlimited power that is available through such faith in Him, they will see His mighty powers at work (see John 14:13,14).

"Whatever thing you ask when you pray, believe that you receive them, and you will have them" (v. 24). This places no limits on a believer's prayers, as long as they are according to God's will and purpose. This therefore means that man's faith and prayer are not inconsistent with God's sovereignty. And it is not the believer's responsibility to figure out how that can be true, but simply to be faithful and obedient to the clear teaching on prayer, as Jesus gives it in this passage. God's will is being unfolded through all of redemptive history by means of the prayers of His people—as His saving purpose is coming to pass through the faith of those who hear the gospel and repent. See James 5:16.

MARCH 11

Numbers 19:1–20:29

19 Now the LORD spoke to Moses and
Aaron, saying, 2"This *is* the ordinance of
the law which the LORD has commanded, saying: 'Speak to the children of Israel, that they
bring you a red heifer without blemish, in
which there *is* no defect *and* on which a yoke
has never come. 3You shall give it to Eleazar
the priest, that he may take it outside the
camp, and it shall be slaughtered before him;
4and Eleazar the priest shall take some of its
blood with his finger, and sprinkle some of its
blood seven times directly in front of the tabernacle of meeting. 5Then the heifer shall be
burned in his sight: its hide, its flesh, its
blood, and its offal shall be burned. 6And the
priest shall take cedar wood and hyssop and
scarlet, and cast *them* into the midst of the fire
burning the heifer. 7Then the priest shall wash
his clothes, he shall bathe in water, and afterward he shall come into the camp; the priest
shall be unclean until evening. 8And the one
who burns it shall wash his clothes in water,
bathe in water, and shall be unclean until
evening. 9Then a man *who is* clean shall gather up the ashes of the heifer, and store *them*
outside the camp in a clean place; and they
shall be kept for the congregation of the children of Israel for the water of purification; it *is*
for purifying from sin. 10And the one who gathers the ashes of the heifer shall wash his
clothes, and be unclean until evening. It shall
be a statute forever to the children of Israel
and to the stranger who dwells among them.
11'He who touches the dead body of anyone
shall be unclean seven days. 12He shall purify
himself with the water on the third day and on
the seventh day; *then* he will be clean. But if he
does not purify himself on the third day and
on the seventh day, he will not be clean. 13Who-
ever touches the body of anyone who has died,
and does not purify himself, defiles the tabernacle of the LORD. That person shall be cut off
from Israel. He shall be unclean, because the
water of purification was not sprinkled on him;
his uncleanness *is* still on him.
14'This *is* the law when a man dies in a tent:
All who come into the tent and all who *are* in
the tent shall be unclean seven days; 15and
every open vessel, which has no cover fastened on it, *is* unclean. 16Whoever in the open
field touches one who is slain by a sword or
who has died, or a bone of a man, or a grave,
shall be unclean seven days.
17'And for an unclean *person* they shall take
some of the ashes of the heifer burnt for purification from sin, and running water shall be
put on them in a vessel. 18A clean person shall
take hyssop and dip *it* in the water, sprinkle *it*
on the tent, on all the vessels, on the persons
who were there, or on the one who touched a
bone, the slain, the dead, or a grave. 19The clean
person shall sprinkle the unclean on the third
day and on the seventh day; and on the seventh day he shall purify himself, wash his
clothes, and bathe in water; and at evening he
shall be clean.

20“But the man who is unclean and does not
purify himself, that person shall be cut off
from among the assembly, because he has defiled the sanctuary of the LORD. The water of
purification has not been sprinkled on him; he
is unclean. 21It shall be a perpetual statute for
them. He who sprinkles the water of purification shall wash his clothes; and he who touches the water of purification shall be unclean
until evening. 22Whatever the unclean *person*
touches shall be unclean; and the person who
touches *it* shall be unclean until evening.’ ”

20 Then the children of Israel, the whole
congregation, came into the Wilderness of Zin in the first month, and the people
stayed in Kadesh; and Miriam died there and
was buried there.

2Now there was no water for the congregation; so they gathered together against Moses
and Aaron. 3And the people contended with
Moses and spoke, saying: “If only we had died
when our brethren died before the LORD!
4Why have you brought up the assembly of the
LORD into this wilderness, that we and our animals should die here? 5And why have you
made us come up out of Egypt, to bring us to
this evil place? It *is* not a place of grain or figs
or vines or pomegranates; nor *is* there any
water to drink.” 6So Moses and Aaron went
from the presence of the assembly to the door
of the tabernacle of meeting, and they fell on
their faces. And the glory of the LORD
appeared to them.

7Then the LORD spoke to Moses, saying,
8“Take the rod; you and your brother Aaron
gather the congregation together. Speak to
the rock before their eyes, and it will yield its
water; thus you shall bring water for them out
of the rock, and give drink to the congregation
and their animals.” 9So Moses took the rod
from before the LORD as He commanded him.

10And Moses and Aaron gathered the
assembly together before the rock; and he
said to them, “Hear now, you rebels! Must we
bring water for you out of this rock?” 11Then
Moses lifted his hand and struck the rock
twice with his rod; and water came out abundantly, and the congregation and their animals
drank.

12Then the LORD spoke to Moses and Aaron,
“Because you did not believe Me, to hallow
Me in the eyes of the children of Israel, therefore you shall not bring this assembly into the
land which I have given them.”

13This *was* the water of Meribah, because
the children of Israel contended with the
LORD, and He was hallowed among them.

14Now Moses sent messengers from Kadesh
to the king of Edom. “Thus says your brother
Israel: ‘You know all the hardship that has
befallen us, 15how our fathers went down to
Egypt, and we dwelt in Egypt a long time, and
the Egyptians afflicted us and our fathers.
16When we cried out to the LORD, He heard our
voice and sent the Angel and brought us up
out of Egypt; now here we are in Kadesh, a
city on the edge of your border. 17Please let us
pass through your country. We will not pass
through fields or vineyards, nor will we drink
water from wells; we will go along the King’s
Highway; we will not turn aside to the right
hand or to the left until we have passed
through your territory.’ ”

18Then Edom said to him, “You shall not
pass through my *land,* lest I come out against
you with the sword.”

19So the children of Israel said to him, “We
will go by the Highway, and if I or my livestock
drink any of your water, then I will pay for it;
let me only pass through on foot, nothing
more.”

20Then he said, “You shall not pass
through.” So Edom came out against them
with many men and with a strong hand. 21Thus
Edom refused to give Israel passage through
his territory; so Israel turned away from him.

22Now the children of Israel, the whole congregation, journeyed from Kadesh and came
to Mount Hor. 23And the LORD spoke to Moses
and Aaron in Mount Hor by the border of the
land of Edom, saying: 24“Aaron shall be gathered to his people, for he shall not enter the
land which I have given to the children of
Israel, because you rebelled against My word
at the water of Meribah. 25Take Aaron and
Eleazar his son, and bring them up to Mount
Hor; 26and strip Aaron of his garments and put
them on Eleazar his son; for Aaron shall be
gathered *to his people* and die there.” 27So
Moses did just as the LORD commanded, and

20:8 Speak to the rock. Though God told Moses to take his rod with which He had performed many wonders in the past (Ex. 4:1–5; 7:19–21; 14:16; 17:5,6), he was only to speak to the rock for it to yield water.

20:10 you rebels. Instead of speaking to the rock, Moses spoke to the people, accusing them of being rebels against God. By his actions, Moses joined the people in rebellion against God (see 27:14).

they went up to Mount Hor in the sight of all
the congregation. [28]Moses stripped Aaron of
his garments and put them on Eleazar his son;
and Aaron died there on the top of the mountain. Then Moses and Eleazar came down
from the mountain. [29]Now when all the congregation saw that Aaron was dead, all the
house of Israel mourned for Aaron thirty days.

Psalm 33:1–9

Rejoice in the LORD, O you righteous!
For praise from the upright is beautiful.
2 Praise the LORD with the harp;
Make melody to Him with an
instrument of ten strings.
3 Sing to Him a new song;
Play skillfully with a shout of joy.
4 For the word of the LORD *is* right,
And all His work *is done* in truth.
5 He loves righteousness and justice;
The earth is full of the goodness of
the LORD.
6 By the word of the LORD the heavens
were made,
And all the host of them by the breath
of His mouth.

33:3 a new song. I.e., a new occasion and impulse for expressing fresh praise to God (see Pss. 96:1; 98:1; 149:1).

33:6 host. This designation refers to stellar and planetary bodies (see Is. 40:26; 45:12) and/or heaven's complement of angels (see Ps. 103:20–22). The former emphasis is more prominent in the immediate context.

7 He gathers the waters of the sea
together as a heap;
He lays up the deep in storehouses.
8 Let all the earth fear the LORD;
Let all the inhabitants of the world
stand in awe of Him.
9 For He spoke, and it was *done;*
He commanded, and it stood fast.

Proverbs 11:22–24

22 *As* a ring of gold in a swine's snout,
So is a lovely woman who lacks
discretion.
23 The desire of the righteous *is* only good,
But the expectation of the wicked *is*
wrath.
24 There is *one* who scatters, yet
increases more;
And there is *one* who withholds more
than is right,
But it *leads* to poverty.

Mark 12:1–27

12 Then He began to speak to them in parables: "A man planted a vineyard and set a
hedge around *it,* dug *a place for* the wine vat
and built a tower. And he leased it to vinedressers and went into a far country. [2]Now at
vintage-time he sent a servant to the vinedressers, that he might receive some of the
fruit of the vineyard from the vinedressers.
[3]And they took *him* and beat him and sent *him*
away empty-handed. [4]Again he sent them
another servant, and at him they threw
stones, wounded *him* in the head, and sent
him away shamefully treated. [5]And again he
sent another, and him they killed; and many
others, beating some and killing some. [6]There-
fore still having one son, his beloved, he also
sent him to them last, saying, 'They will
respect my son.' [7]But those vinedressers said
among themselves, 'This is the heir. Come, let
us kill him, and the inheritance will be ours.'
[8]So they took him and killed *him* and cast *him*
out of the vineyard.

[9]"Therefore what will the owner of the vineyard do? He will come and destroy the vinedressers, and give the vineyard to others.
[10]Have you not even read this Scripture:

'The stone which the builders rejected
Has become the chief cornerstone.
11 *This was the LORD's doing,*
And it is marvelous in our eyes'?"

[12]And they sought to lay hands on Him, but
feared the multitude, for they knew He had
spoken the parable against them. So they left
Him and went away.

[13]Then they sent to Him some of the
Pharisees and the Herodians, to catch Him in
His words. [14]When they had come, they said to
Him, "Teacher, we know that You are true,
and care about no one; for You do not regard
the person of men, but teach the way of God in
truth. Is it lawful to pay taxes to Caesar, or
not? [15]Shall we pay, or shall we not pay?"

But He, knowing their hypocrisy, said to
them, "Why do you test Me? Bring Me a denarius that I may see *it.*" [16]So they brought *it.*

And He said to them, "Whose image and
inscription *is* this?" They said to Him, "Caesar's."

[17]And Jesus answered and said to them,
"Render to Caesar the things that are Caesar's,
and to God the things that are God's."

And they marveled at Him.
[18]Then *some* Sadducees, who say there is no
resurrection, came to Him; and they asked
Him, saying: [19]"Teacher, Moses wrote to us that
if a man's brother dies, and leaves *his* wife
behind, and leaves no children, his brother
should take his wife and raise up offspring for
his brother. [20]Now there were seven brothers.
The first took a wife; and dying, he left no offspring. [21]And the second took her, and he died;
nor did he leave any offspring. And the third
likewise. [22]So the seven had her and left no offspring. Last of all the woman died also.
[23]Therefore, in the resurrection, when they
rise, whose wife will she be? For all seven had
her as wife."
[24]Jesus answered and said to them, "Are you
not therefore mistaken, because you do not
know the Scriptures nor the power of God? [25]For
when they rise from the dead, they neither
marry nor are given in marriage, but are like
angels in heaven. [26]But concerning the dead,
that they rise, have you not read in the book
of Moses, in the *burning* bush *passage,* how
God spoke to him, saying, *'I am the God of
Abraham, the God of Isaac, and the God of Jacob'* ? [27]He is not the God of the dead, but the
God of the living. You are therefore greatly
mistaken."

12:24 the power of God. The Sadducees' ignorance of the Scriptures extended to their lack of understanding regarding the miracles God performed throughout the Old Testament. Such knowledge would have enabled them to believe in God's power to raise the dead.

DAY 11: What is the Christian response to taxes?

In Mark 12:13, the Pharisees and the Herodians came together to try to catch Jesus off guard by a seemingly sincere question: "Is it lawful to pay taxes to Caesar, or not? Shall we pay, or shall we not pay?" The Herodians were a political party of Jews who backed Herod Antipas, who in turn was but a puppet of Rome. The Greek word for "taxes" was borrowed from the Latin word that gives us the English word "census." The Romans counted all the citizens and made each one pay an annual poll tax of one denarius.

Jesus was fully aware of their hypocrisy, using a feigned interest in His teaching to hide their true intention to trap Him. "Why do you test Me?" (v. 15), He asked, and His response was to ask for a denarius. This small silver coin, minted by the Roman emperor, was the equivalent of a day's wage for a common laborer or soldier. On one side of the denarius was likely the image of the current emperor, Tiberius. If the coin was minted by Tiberius, it would have read, "Tiberius Caesar Augustus, the son of the Divine Augustus" on one side and "Chief Priest" on the other.

Based on the image on the denarius, Jesus answered, "Render to Caesar the things that are Caesar's." The Greek word for "render" means "to pay or give back," which implies a debt. All who lived within the realm of Caesar were obligated to return to him the tax that was owed him. It was not optional. Thus Jesus declared that all citizens are under divine obligation to pay taxes to whatever government is over them (see Rom. 13:1–7; 1 Pet. 2:13–17).

MARCH 12

Numbers 21:1–22:41

21 The king of Arad, the Canaanite, who
dwelt in the South, heard that Israel was
coming on the road to Atharim. Then he
fought against Israel and took *some* of them
prisoners. [2]So Israel made a vow to the LORD,
and said, "If You will indeed deliver this people
into my hand, then I will utterly destroy their
cities." [3]And the LORD listened to the voice of
Israel and delivered up the Canaanites, and
they utterly destroyed them and their cities.
So the name of that place was called Hormah.
[4]Then they journeyed from Mount Hor by
the Way of the Red Sea, to go around the land
of Edom; and the soul of the people became
very discouraged on the way. [5]And the people
spoke against God and against Moses: "Why
have you brought us up out of Egypt to die in
the wilderness? For *there is* no food and no
water, and our soul loathes this worthless
bread." [6]So the LORD sent fiery serpents
among the people, and they bit the people;
and many of the people of Israel died.
[7]Therefore the people came to Moses, and
said, "We have sinned, for we have spoken
against the LORD and against you; pray to the
LORD that He take away the serpents from us."
So Moses prayed for the people.
[8]Then the LORD said to Moses, "Make a fiery

serpent, and set it on a pole; and it shall be that
everyone who is bitten, when he looks at it,
shall live." [9]So Moses made a bronze serpent,
and put it on a pole; and so it was, if a serpent
had bitten anyone, when he looked at the
bronze serpent, he lived.

[10]Now the children of Israel moved on and
camped in Oboth. [11]And they journeyed from
Oboth and camped at Ije Abarim, in the
wilderness which *is* east of Moab, toward the
sunrise. [12]From there they moved and camped
in the Valley of Zered. [13]From there they
moved and camped on the other side of the
Arnon, which *is* in the wilderness that extends
from the border of the Amorites; for the
Arnon *is* the border of Moab, between Moab
and the Amorites. [14]Therefore it is said in the
Book of the Wars of the LORD:

"Waheb in Suphah,
The brooks of the Arnon,
15 And the slope of the brooks
That reaches to the dwelling of Ar,
And lies on the border of Moab."

[16]From there *they went* to Beer, which *is* the
well where the LORD said to Moses, "Gather the
people together, and I will give them water."
[17]Then Israel sang this song:

"Spring up, O well!
All of you sing to it—
18 The well the leaders sank,
Dug by the nation's nobles,
By the lawgiver, with their staves."

And from the wilderness *they went* to
Mattanah, [19]from Mattanah to Nahaliel, from
Nahaliel to Bamoth, [20]and from Bamoth, *in* the
valley that *is* in the country of Moab, to the top
of Pisgah which looks down on the wasteland.

[21]Then Israel sent messengers to Sihon king
of the Amorites, saying, [22]"Let me pass
through your land. We will not turn aside into
fields or vineyards; we will not drink water
from wells. We will go by the King's Highway
until we have passed through your territory."
[23]But Sihon would not allow Israel to pass
through his territory. So Sihon gathered all
his people together and went out against
Israel in the wilderness, and he came to Jahaz
and fought against Israel. [24]Then Israel defeated him with the edge of the sword, and took
possession of his land from the Arnon to the
Jabbok, as far as the people of Ammon; for the
border of the people of Ammon *was* fortified.
[25]So Israel took all these cities, and Israel
dwelt in all the cities of the Amorites, in
Heshbon and in all its villages. [26]For Heshbon
was the city of Sihon king of the Amorites,
who had fought against the former king of
Moab, and had taken all his land from his
hand as far as the Arnon. [27]Therefore those
who speak in proverbs say:

"Come to Heshbon, let it be built;
Let the city of Sihon be repaired.
28 "For fire went out from Heshbon,
A flame from the city of Sihon;
It consumed Ar of Moab,
The lords of the heights of the Arnon.
29 Woe to you, Moab!
You have perished, O people of
Chemosh!
He has given his sons as fugitives,
And his daughters into captivity,
To Sihon king of the Amorites.

30 "But we have shot at them;
Heshbon has perished as far as Dibon.
Then we laid waste as far as Nophah,
Which *reaches* to Medeba."

[31]Thus Israel dwelt in the land of the
Amorites. [32]Then Moses sent to spy out Jazer;
and they took its villages and drove out the
Amorites who *were* there.

[33]And they turned and went up by the way to
Bashan. So Og king of Bashan went out
against them, he and all his people, to battle at
Edrei. [34]Then the LORD said to Moses, "Do not
fear him, for I have delivered him into your
hand, with all his people and his land; and you
shall do to him as you did to Sihon king of the
Amorites, who dwelt at Heshbon." [35]So they
defeated him, his sons, and all his people, until
there was no survivor left him; and they took
possession of his land.

22 Then the children of Israel moved, and
camped in the plains of Moab on the
side of the Jordan *across from* Jericho.

[2]Now Balak the son of Zippor saw all that
Israel had done to the Amorites. [3]And Moab
was exceedingly afraid of the people because
they *were* many, and Moab was sick with
dread because of the children of Israel. [4]So
Moab said to the elders of Midian, "Now this
company will lick up everything around us, as
an ox licks up the grass of the field." And
Balak the son of Zippor *was* king of the
Moabites at that time. [5]Then he sent messengers to Balaam the son of Beor at Pethor,
which *is* near the River in the land of the sons
of his people, to call him, saying: "Look, a people has come from Egypt. See, they cover the
face of the earth, and are settling next to me!
[6]Therefore please come at once, curse this
people for me, for they *are* too mighty for me.
Perhaps I shall be able to defeat them and

22:5 Balaam. Balaam was from Pethor, a city on the Euphrates River, perhaps near Mari, where the existence of a cult of prophets whose activities resembled those of Balaam have been found. Balaam practiced magic and divination (24:1) and eventually led Israel into apostasy (31:16). Later Scripture identifies Balaam as a false prophet (Deut. 23:3–6; Josh. 13:22; 24:9,10; Neh. 13:1–3; Mic. 6:5; 2 Pet. 2:15,16; Jude 11; Rev. 2:14).

drive them out of the land, for I know that he whom you bless *is* blessed, and he whom you curse is cursed."

7So the elders of Moab and the elders of Midian departed with the diviner's fee in their hand, and they came to Balaam and spoke to him the words of Balak. 8And he said to them, "Lodge here tonight, and I will bring back word to you, as the LORD speaks to me." So the princes of Moab stayed with Balaam.

9Then God came to Balaam and said, "Who *are* these men with you?"

10So Balaam said to God, "Balak the son of Zippor, king of Moab, has sent to me, *saying,* 11'Look, a people has come out of Egypt, and they cover the face of the earth. Come now, curse them for me; perhaps I shall be able to overpower them and drive them out.' "

12And God said to Balaam, "You shall not go with them; you shall not curse the people, for they *are* blessed."

13So Balaam rose in the morning and said to the princes of Balak, "Go back to your land, for the LORD has refused to give me permission to go with you."

14And the princes of Moab rose and went to Balak, and said, "Balaam refuses to come with us."

15Then Balak again sent princes, more numerous and more honorable than they. 16And they came to Balaam and said to him, "Thus says Balak the son of Zippor: 'Please let nothing hinder you from coming to me; 17for I will certainly honor you greatly, and I will do whatever you say to me. Therefore please come, curse this people for me.' "

18Then Balaam answered and said to the servants of Balak, "Though Balak were to give me his house full of silver and gold, I could not go beyond the word of the LORD my God, to do less or more. 19Now therefore, please, you also stay here tonight, that I may know what more the LORD will say to me."

20And God came to Balaam at night and said to him, "If the men come to call you, rise *and* go with them; but only the word which I speak to you—that you shall do." 21So Balaam rose in the morning, saddled his donkey, and went with the princes of Moab.

22Then God's anger was aroused because he went, and the Angel of the LORD took His stand in the way as an adversary against him. And he was riding on his donkey, and his two servants *were* with him. 23Now the donkey saw the Angel of the LORD standing in the way with His drawn sword in His hand, and the donkey turned aside out of the way and went into the field. So Balaam struck the donkey to turn her back onto the road. 24Then the Angel of the LORD stood in a narrow path between the vineyards, *with* a wall on this side and a wall on that side. 25And when the donkey saw the Angel of the LORD, she pushed herself against the wall and crushed Balaam's foot against the wall; so he struck her again. 26Then the Angel of the LORD went further, and stood in a narrow place where there *was* no way to turn either to the right hand or to the left. 27And when the donkey saw the Angel of the LORD, she lay down under Balaam; so Balaam's anger was aroused, and he struck the donkey with his staff.

28Then the LORD opened the mouth of the donkey, and she said to Balaam, "What have I done to you, that you have struck me these three times?"

29And Balaam said to the donkey, "Because you have abused me. I wish there were a sword in my hand, for now I would kill you!"

30So the donkey said to Balaam, "*Am* I not your donkey on which you have ridden, ever since *I became* yours, to this day? Was I ever disposed to do this to you?"

And he said, "No."

31Then the LORD opened Balaam's eyes, and he saw the Angel of the LORD standing in the way with His drawn sword in His hand; and he bowed his head and fell flat on his face. 32And the Angel of the LORD said to him, "Why have you struck your donkey these three times? Behold, I have come out to stand against you, because *your* way is perverse before Me. 33The donkey saw Me and turned aside from Me these three times. If she had not turned aside from Me, surely I would also have killed you by now, and let her live."

34And Balaam said to the Angel of the LORD, "I have sinned, for I did not know You stood in the way against me. Now therefore, if it displeases You, I will turn back."

35Then the Angel of the LORD said to Balaam, "Go with the men, but only the word that I speak to you, that you shall speak." So Balaam went with the princes of Balak.

36Now when Balak heard that Balaam was coming, he went out to meet him at the city of Moab, which *is* on the border at the Arnon, the boundary of the territory. 37Then Balak said to Balaam, "Did I not earnestly send to you, calling for you? Why did you not come to me? Am I not able to honor you?"

38And Balaam said to Balak, "Look, I have come to you! Now, have I any power at all to say anything? The word that God puts in my mouth, that I must speak." 39So Balaam went with Balak, and they came to Kirjath Huzoth. 40Then Balak offered oxen and sheep, and he sent *some* to Balaam and to the princes who *were* with him.

41So it was, the next day, that Balak took Balaam and brought him up to the high places of Baal, that from there he might observe the extent of the people.

Psalm 33:10–17

10 The LORD brings the counsel of the
nations to nothing;
He makes the plans of the peoples of
no effect.
11 The counsel of the LORD stands
forever,
The plans of His heart to all
generations.
12 Blessed *is* the nation whose God *is* the
LORD,
The people He has chosen as His own
inheritance.

13 The LORD looks from heaven;
He sees all the sons of men.
14 From the place of His dwelling He looks
On all the inhabitants of the earth;
15 He fashions their hearts individually;
He considers all their works.
16 No king *is* saved by the multitude of an
army;
A mighty man is not delivered by great
strength.
17 A horse *is* a vain hope for safety;
Neither shall it deliver *any* by its great
strength.

Proverbs 11:25–26

25 The generous soul will be made rich,
And he who waters will also be
watered himself.
26 The people will curse him who
withholds grain,
But blessing *will be* on the head of him
who sells *it*.

Mark 12:28–44

28Then one of the scribes came, and having heard them reasoning together, perceiving that He had answered them well, asked Him, "Which is the first commandment of all?"

12:28 Which is the first commandment...? The rabbis had determined that there were 613 commandments contained in the Pentateuch, one for each letter of the Ten Commandments. Of the 613 commandments, 248 were seen as affirmative and 365 as negative. Those laws were also divided into heavy and light categories, with the heavy laws being more binding than the light ones. The scribes and rabbis, however, had been unable to agree on which were heavy and which were light. This orientation to the law led the Pharisees to think Jesus had devised His own theory. So the Pharisees asked this particular question to get Jesus to incriminate Himself by revealing His unorthodox and unilateral beliefs.

29Jesus answered him, "The first of all the commandments *is: 'Hear, O Israel, the LORD our God, the LORD is one.* 30*And you shall love the LORD your God with all your heart, with all your soul, with all your mind, and with all your strength.'* This *is* the first commandment. 31And the second, like *it, is* this: *'You shall love your neighbor as yourself.'* There is no other commandment greater than these."

32So the scribe said to Him, "Well *said*, Teacher. You have spoken the truth, for there is one God, and there is no other but He. 33And to love Him with all the heart, with all the understanding, with all the soul, and with all the strength, and to love one's neighbor as oneself, is more than all the whole burnt offerings and sacrifices."

34Now when Jesus saw that he answered wisely, He said to him, "You are not far from the kingdom of God."

But after that no one dared question Him.

35Then Jesus answered and said, while He taught in the temple, "How *is it* that the scribes say that the Christ is the Son of David? 36For David himself said by the Holy Spirit:

'The LORD said to my Lord,
"Sit at My right hand,
Till I make Your enemies Your
footstool."'

37Therefore David himself calls Him *'Lord'*; how is He *then* his Son?"

And the common people heard Him gladly.
[38]Then He said to them in His teaching, "Beware of the scribes, who desire to go around in long robes, *love* greetings in the marketplaces, [39]the best seats in the synagogues, and the best places at feasts, [40]who devour widows' houses, and for a pretense make long prayers. These will receive greater condemnation."
[41]Now Jesus sat opposite the treasury and saw how the people put money into the treasury. And many *who were* rich put in much. [42]Then one poor widow came and threw in two mites, which make a quadrans. [43]So He called His disciples to *Himself* and said to them, "Assuredly, I say to you that this poor widow has put in more than all those who have given to the treasury; [44]for they all put in out of their abundance, but she out of her poverty put in all that she had, her whole livelihood."

12:40 devour widows' houses. Jesus exposed the greedy, unscrupulous practice of the scribes. Scribes often served as estate planners for widows, which gave them the opportunity to convince distraught widows that they would be serving God by supporting the temple or the scribe's own holy work. In either case, the scribe benefited monetarily and effectively robbed the widow of her husband's legacy to her. **long prayers.** The Pharisees attempted to flaunt their piety by praying for long periods. Their motive was not devotion to God, but a desire to be revered by the people.

DAY 12: Wasn't it idol worship for the Israelites to look at the bronze serpent in Numbers 21:4–9?

The circumstances leading up to the casting of the bronze serpent were all too familiar. The people were tired and discouraged. They were angry with God and complained to Moses. They were convinced that things couldn't get any worse, but God showed them otherwise. He sent "fiery serpents" among the people and some of the Israelites died. Others suffered excruciating bites.

Realizing their mistake, the people came in repentance to Moses and begged for help. They were not worshiping the bronze serpent but were acting in faith, in obedience to God's and Moses' directions.

In John 3:14, Jesus said, "So must the Son of Man be lifted up." This is a veiled prediction of His death on the cross. It is in reference to the story of where the Israelite people who looked at the serpent lifted up by Moses were healed. The point of this illustration or analogy is in the "lifted up." Just as Moses lifted up the snake on the pole so that all who looked upon it might live physically, those who look to Christ, who was "lifted up" on the cross for the sins of the world, will live spiritually and eternally.

MARCH 13

Numbers 23:1–24:25

23 Then Balaam said to Balak, "Build seven altars for me here, and prepare for me here seven bulls and seven rams."
[2]And Balak did just as Balaam had spoken, and Balak and Balaam offered a bull and a ram on *each* altar. [3]Then Balaam said to Balak, "Stand by your burnt offering, and I will go; perhaps the LORD will come to meet me, and whatever He shows me I will tell you." So he went to a desolate height. [4]And God met Balaam, and he said to Him, "I have prepared the seven altars, and I have offered on *each* altar a bull and a ram."
[5]Then the LORD put a word in Balaam's mouth, and said, "Return to Balak, and thus you shall speak." [6]So he returned to him, and there he was, standing by his burnt offering, he and all the princes of Moab.
[7]And he took up his oracle and said:

> "Balak the king of Moab has brought
> me from Aram,
> From the mountains of the east.
> 'Come, curse Jacob for me,
> And come, denounce Israel!'

23:5 the LORD put a word in Balaam's mouth. Even though Balak and Balaam offered sacrifices on pagan altars, it was the Lord who gave Balaam his oracle.

8 "How shall I curse whom God has not
cursed?
And how shall I denounce *whom* the
LORD has not denounced?
9 For from the top of the rocks I see him,
And from the hills I behold him;
There! A people dwelling alone,
Not reckoning itself among the
nations.

10 "Who can count the dust of Jacob,
Or number one-fourth of Israel?
Let me die the death of the righteous,
And let my end be like his!"

11 Then Balak said to Balaam, "What have
you done to me? I took you to curse my enemies, and look, you have blessed *them* bountifully!"
12 So he answered and said, "Must I not take
heed to speak what the LORD has put in my
mouth?"
13 Then Balak said to him, "Please come with
me to another place from which you may see
them; you shall see only the outer part of
them, and shall not see them all; curse them
for me from there." 14 So he brought him to the
field of Zophim, to the top of Pisgah, and built
seven altars, and offered a bull and a ram on
each altar.
15 And he said to Balak, "Stand here by your
burnt offering while I meet *the LORD* over
there."
16 Then the LORD met Balaam, and put a
word in his mouth, and said, "Go back to
Balak, and thus you shall speak." 17 So he came
to him, and there he was, standing by his
burnt offering, and the princes of Moab were
with him. And Balak said to him, "What has
the LORD spoken?"
18 Then he took up his oracle and said:

"Rise up, Balak, and hear!
Listen to me, son of Zippor!

19 "God *is* not a man, that He should lie,
Nor a son of man, that He should
repent.
Has He said, and will He not do?
Or has He spoken, and will He not
make it good?
20 Behold, I have received *a command* to
bless;
He has blessed, and I cannot reverse
it.

21 "He has not observed iniquity in Jacob,
Nor has He seen wickedness in Israel.
The LORD his God *is* with him,
And the shout of a King *is* among
them.
22 God brings them out of Egypt;
He has strength like a wild ox.

23 "For *there is* no sorcery against Jacob,
Nor any divination against Israel.
It now must be said of Jacob
And of Israel, 'Oh, what God has done!'
24 Look, a people rises like a lioness,
And lifts itself up like a lion;
It shall not lie down until it devours
the prey,
And drinks the blood of the slain."

25 Then Balak said to Balaam, "Neither curse
them at all, nor bless them at all!"
26 So Balaam answered and said to Balak,
"Did I not tell you, saying, 'All that the LORD
speaks, that I must do'?"
27 Then Balak said to Balaam, "Please come, I
will take you to another place; perhaps it will
please God that you may curse them for me
from there." 28 So Balak took Balaam to the top
of Peor, that overlooks the wasteland. 29 Then
Balaam said to Balak, "Build for me here
seven altars, and prepare for me here seven
bulls and seven rams." 30 And Balak did as
Balaam had said, and offered a bull and a ram
on *every* altar.

24 Now when Balaam saw that it pleased
the LORD to bless Israel, he did not go as
at other times, to seek to use sorcery, but he set
his face toward the wilderness. 2 And Balaam
raised his eyes, and saw Israel encamped
according to their tribes; and the Spirit of God
came upon him.

24:2 the Spirit of God came upon him. This terminology was regularly used in the Old Testament for those whom God uniquely prepared to do His work (Judg. 3:10). Unlike the previous two oracles, Balaam does not involve himself in divination before giving this third oracle. He is empowered with the Holy Spirit to utter God's word accurately.

3 Then he took up his oracle and said:

"The utterance of Balaam the son of
Beor,
The utterance of the man whose eyes
are opened,
4 The utterance of him who hears the
words of God,
Who sees the vision of the Almighty,
Who falls down, with eyes wide open:

5 "How lovely are your tents, O Jacob!

Your dwellings, O Israel!
6 Like valleys that stretch out,
Like gardens by the riverside,
Like aloes planted by the LORD,
Like cedars beside the waters.
7 He shall pour water from his buckets,
And his seed *shall be* in many waters.

"His king shall be higher than Agag,
And his kingdom shall be exalted.

8 "God brings him out of Egypt;
He has strength like a wild ox;
He shall consume the nations, his
enemies;
He shall break their bones
And pierce *them* with his arrows.
9 'He bows down, he lies down as a lion;
And as a lion, who shall rouse him?'

"Blessed *is* he who blesses you,
And cursed *is* he who curses you."

10 Then Balak's anger was aroused against
Balaam, and he struck his hands together;
and Balak said to Balaam, "I called you to
curse my enemies, and look, you have bountifully blessed *them* these three times! 11 Now
therefore, flee to your place. I said I would
greatly honor you, but in fact, the LORD has
kept you back from honor."
12 So Balaam said to Balak, "Did I not also
speak to your messengers whom you sent to
me, saying, 13 'If Balak were to give me his
house full of silver and gold, I could not go
beyond the word of the LORD, to do good or bad
of my own will. What the LORD says, that I must
speak'? 14 And now, indeed, I am going to my
people. Come, I will advise you what this people
will do to your people in the latter days."
15 So he took up his oracle and said:

"The utterance of Balaam the son of
Beor,
And the utterance of the man whose
eyes are opened;
16 The utterance of him who hears the
words of God,
And has the knowledge of the Most
High,
Who sees the vision of the Almighty,
Who falls down, with eyes wide open:

17 "I see Him, but not now;
I behold Him, but not near;
A Star shall come out of Jacob;
A Scepter shall rise out of Israel,
And batter the brow of Moab,
And destroy all the sons of tumult.

18 "And Edom shall be a possession;
Seir also, his enemies, shall be a
possession,
While Israel does valiantly.
19 Out of Jacob One shall have dominion,
And destroy the remains of the city."

20 Then he looked on Amalek, and he took up
his oracle and said:

"Amalek *was* first among the nations,
But *shall be* last until he perishes."

21 Then he looked on the Kenites, and he
took up his oracle and said:

"Firm is your dwelling place,
And your nest is set in the rock;
22 Nevertheless Kain shall be burned.
How long until Asshur carries you
away captive?"

23 Then he took up his oracle and said:

"Alas! Who shall live when God does
this?
24 But ships *shall come* from the coasts of
Cyprus,
And they shall afflict Asshur and afflict
Eber,
And so shall *Amalek*, until he
perishes."

25 So Balaam rose and departed and returned to his place; Balak also went his way.

Psalm 33:18–22

18 Behold, the eye of the LORD *is* on those
who fear Him,
On those who hope in His mercy,
19 To deliver their soul from death,
And to keep them alive in famine.

20 Our soul waits for the LORD;
He *is* our help and our shield.
21 For our heart shall rejoice in Him,
Because we have trusted in His
holy name.
22 Let Your mercy, O LORD,
be upon us,
Just as we hope in You.

Proverbs 11:27

27 He who earnestly seeks good finds
favor,
But trouble will come to him who
seeks *evil*.

Mark 13:1–20

13 Then as He went out of the temple, one
of His disciples said to Him, "Teacher,
see what manner of stones and what buildings
are here!"

[2]And Jesus answered and said to him, "Do
you see these great buildings? Not *one* stone
shall be left upon another, that shall not be
thrown down."

13:2 Jesus answered. In response to the disciples' admiration, Jesus again predicted that the temple would be destroyed. About 40 years later, in A.D. 70, the Romans ransacked Jerusalem, killed a million Jews, and demolished the temple. **Not *one* stone.** The only stones left undisturbed were huge foundation stones that were not actually a part of the temple edifice but formed footings for the retaining wall under the entire temple mount. These can be viewed today in the "Rabbi's Tunnel" which runs north and south along the western wall. It is a portion of the western side of the retaining wall that today is called the Wailing Wall. More of that retaining wall, including the steps used to ascend and descend from the temple mount, has also been uncovered on the southern side.

[3]Now as He sat on the Mount of Olives
opposite the temple, Peter, James, John, and
Andrew asked Him privately, [4]"Tell us, when
will these things be? And what *will be* the sign
when all these things will be fulfilled?"
[5]And Jesus, answering them, began to say:
"Take heed that no one deceives you. [6]For
many will come in My name, saying, 'I am *He,*'
and will deceive many. [7]But when you hear of
wars and rumors of wars, do not be troubled;
for *such things* must happen, but the end *is* not
yet. [8]For nation will rise against nation, and
kingdom against kingdom. And there will be
earthquakes in various places, and there will
be famines and troubles. These *are* the beginnings of sorrows.
[9]"But watch out for yourselves, for they will
deliver you up to councils, and you will be
beaten in the synagogues. You will be brought
before rulers and kings for My sake, for a testimony to them. [10]And the gospel must first be
preached to all the nations. [11]But when they

13:8 the beginnings of sorrows. The Greek word for "sorrows" means "birth pangs." The Lord was referring to the pain a woman experiences in childbirth. Birth pains signal the end of pregnancy—they are infrequent at first and gradually increase just before the child is born. Likewise, the signs of vv. 6–8 will be infrequent, relatively speaking, in the beginning and will escalate to massive and tragic proportions just prior to Christ's Second Coming (see 1 Thess. 5:3; Matt. 24:8).

arrest *you* and deliver you up, do not worry
beforehand, or premeditate what you will
speak. But whatever is given you in that hour,
speak that; for it is not you who speak, but the
Holy Spirit. [12]Now brother will betray brother
to death, and a father *his* child; and children
will rise up against parents and cause them to
be put to death. [13]And you will be hated by all
for My name's sake. But he who endures to
the end shall be saved.
[14]"So when you see the *'abomination of desolation,'* spoken of by Daniel the prophet,
standing where it ought not" (let the reader
understand), "then let those who are in Judea
flee to the mountains. [15]Let him who is on the
housetop not go down into the house, nor
enter to take anything out of his house. [16]And
let him who is in the field not go back to get
his clothes. [17]But woe to those who are pregnant and to those who are nursing babies in
those days! [18]And pray that your flight may not
be in winter. [19]For *in* those days there will be
tribulation, such as has not been since the
beginning of the creation which God created
until this time, nor ever shall be. [20]And unless
the Lord had shortened those days, no flesh
would be saved; but for the elect's sake, whom
He chose, He shortened the days.

DAY 13: How does one makes sense of Balaam and his talking donkey?

Balaam, whose story is recorded in Numbers 22:2–24:25, does seem to receive special treatment in the biblical story. Even though Balaam claimed to know the Lord (Num. 22:18), Scripture consistently refers to him as a false prophet (2 Pet. 2:15,16; Jude 11). Apparently God placed such a priority on the message that the character of the messenger became a secondary consideration. The Lord used Balaam as His mouthpiece to speak the true words He put in his mouth. God had a purpose for Balaam despite the pagan prophet's own plans.

When it comes to the talking donkey, several observations come to mind. First, this incident was not recorded as a commonplace occurrence but as something unusual and noteworthy. Second, one can just as easily wonder why God didn't (or doesn't) use talking animals more often—

we'd all probably be better off. Third, why not recognize God's sense of humor in this account? Fourth, God's display of patience and persistence in these events ought to provoke in us a sense of humble worship. And, fifth, the incident, as unusual as it may be, should be accepted at face value.

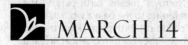

MARCH 14

Numbers 25:1–26:65

25 Now Israel remained in Acacia Grove,
and the people began to commit harlotry with the women of Moab. [2]They invited
the people to the sacrifices of their gods, and
the people ate and bowed down to their gods.
[3]So Israel was joined to Baal of Peor, and the
anger of the LORD was aroused against Israel.

25:3 joined to Baal of Peor. Israel engaged in acts of sexual immorality with the women of Moab. Since this was part of the pagan cult that was worshiped by the Moabites, the Israelites joined in these idolatrous practices. The Israelites yoked themselves to the false god of the Moabites and the Midianites, referred to as Baal of Peor. This was a violation of the first commandment.

[4]Then the LORD said to Moses, "Take all the
leaders of the people and hang the offenders
before the LORD, out in the sun, that the fierce
anger of the LORD may turn away from Israel."
[5]So Moses said to the judges of Israel,
"Every one of you kill his men who were
joined to Baal of Peor."
[6]And indeed, one of the children of Israel
came and presented to his brethren a
Midianite woman in the sight of Moses and in
the sight of all the congregation of the children of Israel, who *were* weeping at the door of
the tabernacle of meeting. [7]Now when
Phinehas the son of Eleazar, the son of Aaron
the priest, saw *it,* he rose from among the congregation and took a javelin in his hand; [8]and
he went after the man of Israel into the tent
and thrust both of them through, the man of
Israel, and the woman through her body. So
the plague was stopped among the children of
Israel. [9]And those who died in the plague were
twenty-four thousand.
[10]Then the LORD spoke to Moses, saying:
[11]"Phinehas the son of Eleazar, the son of
Aaron the priest, has turned back My wrath
from the children of Israel, because he was
zealous with My zeal among them, so that I
did not consume the children of Israel in My
zeal. [12]Therefore say, 'Behold, I give to him My
covenant of peace; [13]and it shall be to him and
his descendants after him a covenant of an
everlasting priesthood, because he was zealous for his God, and made atonement for the
children of Israel.' "

25:10–13 Because of Phinehas's zeal for God's holiness, the Lord made "a covenant of an everlasting priesthood" with him so that through his family line would come all future legitimate high priests (see Ps. 106:30,31). This promise will extend even into the millennial kingdom (see Ezek. 40:46; 44:10,15; 48:11).

[14]Now the name of the Israelite who was
killed, who was killed with the Midianite
woman, *was* Zimri the son of Salu, a leader of
a father's house among the Simeonites. [15]And
the name of the Midianite woman who was
killed *was* Cozbi the daughter of Zur; he *was*
head of the people of a father's house in
Midian.
[16]Then the LORD spoke to Moses, saying:
[17]"Harass the Midianites, and attack them; [18]for
they harassed you with their schemes by
which they seduced you in the matter of Peor
and in the matter of Cozbi, the daughter of a
leader of Midian, their sister, who was killed in
the day of the plague because of Peor."
26 And it came to pass, after the plague,
that the LORD spoke to Moses and
Eleazar the son of Aaron the priest, saying:
[2]"Take a census of all the congregation of the
children of Israel from twenty years old and
above, by their fathers' houses, all who are
able to go to war in Israel." [3]So Moses and
Eleazar the priest spoke with them in the
plains of Moab by the Jordan, *across from* Jericho, saying: [4]"*Take a census of the people* from
twenty years old and above, just as the LORD
commanded Moses and the children of Israel
who came out of the land of Egypt."
[5]Reuben *was* the firstborn of Israel. The

children of Reuben *were: of* Hanoch, the family
of the Hanochites; *of* Pallu, the family of the
Palluites; [6]*of* Hezron, the family of the Hezronites; *of* Carmi, the family of the Carmites.
[7]These *are* the families of the Reubenites:
those who were numbered of them were forty-
three thousand seven hundred and thirty. [8]And
the son of Pallu *was* Eliab. [9]The sons of Eliab
were Nemuel, Dathan, and Abiram. These *are*
the Dathan and Abiram, representatives of the
congregation, who contended against Moses
and Aaron in the company of Korah, when they
contended against the LORD; [10]and the earth
opened its mouth and swallowed them up
together with Korah when that company died,
when the fire devoured two hundred and fifty
men; and they became a sign. [11]Nevertheless
the children of Korah did not die.

[12]The sons of Simeon according to their families *were: of* Nemuel, the family of the Nem-
uelites; *of* Jamin, the family of the Jaminites;
of Jachin, the family of the Jachinites; [13]*of*
Zerah, the family of the Zarhites; *of* Shaul, the
family of the Shaulites. [14]These *are* the families
of the Simeonites: twenty-two thousand two
hundred.

[15]The sons of Gad according to their families
were: of Zephon, the family of the Zephonites;
of Haggi, the family of the Haggites; *of* Shuni,
the family of the Shunites; [16]*of* Ozni, the family
of the Oznites; *of* Eri, the family of the Erites;
[17]*of* Arod, the family of the Arodites; *of* Areli,
the family of the Arelites. [18]These *are* the families of the sons of Gad according to those who
were numbered of them: forty thousand five
hundred.

[19]The sons of Judah *were* Er and Onan; and
Er and Onan died in the land of Canaan. [20]And
the sons of Judah according to their families
were: *of* Shelah, the family of the Shelanites; *of*
Perez, the family of the Parzites; *of* Zerah, the
family of the Zarhites. [21]And the sons of Perez
were: *of* Hezron, the family of the Hezronites;
of Hamul, the family of the Hamulites. [22]These
are the families of Judah according to those
who were numbered of them: seventy-six
thousand five hundred.

[23]The sons of Issachar according to their
families *were: of* Tola, the family of the
Tolaites; of Puah, the family of the Punites; [24]of
Jashub, the family of the Jashubites; of
Shimron, the family of the Shimronites.
[25]These *are* the families of Issachar according
to those who were numbered of them: sixty-
four thousand three hundred.

[26]The sons of Zebulun according to their
families *were:* of Sered, the family of the
Sardites; of Elon, the family of the Elonites; of
Jahleel, the family of the Jahleelites. [27]These
are the families of the Zebulunites according
to those who were numbered of them: sixty
thousand five hundred.

[28]The sons of Joseph according to their families, by Manasseh and Ephraim, *were:* [29]The
sons of Manasseh: of Machir, the family of the
Machirites; and Machir begot Gilead; of Gilead,
the family of the Gileadites. [30]These *are* the
sons of Gilead: *of* Jeezer, the family of the Jee-
zerites; of Helek, the family of the Helekites; [31]*of*
Asriel, the family of the Asrielites; *of* Shechem,
the family of the Shechemites; [32]*of* Shemida, the
family of the Shemidaites; *of* Hepher, the family
of the Hepherites. [33]Now Zelophehad the son of
Hepher had no sons, but daughters; and the
names of the daughters of Zelophehad *were*
Mahlah, Noah, Hoglah, Milcah, and Tirzah.
[34]These *are* the families of Manasseh; and those
who were numbered of them *were* fifty-two
thousand seven hundred.

[35]These *are* the sons of Ephraim according
to their families: of Shuthelah, the family of
the Shuthalhites; of Becher, the family of the
Bachrites; of Tahan, the family of the
Tahanites. [36]And these *are* the sons of
Shuthelah: of Eran, the family of the Eranites.
[37]These *are* the families of the sons of Ephraim
according to those who were numbered of
them: thirty-two thousand five hundred.

These *are* the sons of Joseph according to
their families.

[38]The sons of Benjamin according to their
families were: of Bela, the family of the
Belaites; of Ashbel, the family of the Ash-
belites; of Ahiram, the family of the Ahiramites;
[39]of Shupham, the family of the Shuphamites;
of Hupham, the family of the Huphamites.
[40]And the sons of Bela were Ard and Naaman:
of Ard, the family of the Ardites; of Naaman,
the family of the Naamites. [41]These *are* the
sons of Benjamin according to their families;
and those who were numbered of them *were*
forty-five thousand six hundred.

[42]These *are* the sons of Dan according to
their families: of Shuham, the family of the
Shuhamites. These *are* the families of Dan
according to their families. [43]All the families of
the Shuhamites, according to those who were
numbered of them, *were* sixty-four thousand
four hundred.

[44]The sons of Asher according to their families *were:* of Jimna, the family of the Jimnites;
of Jesui, the family of the Jesuites; of Beriah,
the family of the Beriites. [45]Of the sons of
Beriah: of Heber, the family of the Heberites;
of Malchiel, the family of the Malchielites.
[46]And the name of the daughter of Asher *was*

Serah. 47These *are* the families of the sons of
Asher according to those who were numbered
of them: fifty-three thousand four hundred.
48The sons of Naphtali according to their
families *were:* of Jahzeel, the family of the
Jahzeelites; of Guni, the family of the Gunites;
49of Jezer, the family of the Jezerites; of Shillem,
the family of the Shillemites. 50These *are* the
families of Naphtali according to their families; and those who were numbered of them
were forty-five thousand four hundred.
51These *are* those who were numbered of
the children of Israel: six hundred and one
thousand seven hundred and thirty.
52Then the LORD spoke to Moses, saying:
53"To these the land shall be divided as an
inheritance, according to the number of
names. 54To a large *tribe* you shall give a larger inheritance, and to a small *tribe* you shall
give a smaller inheritance. Each shall be given
its inheritance according to those who were
numbered of them. 55But the land shall be divided by lot; they shall inherit according to the
names of the tribes of their fathers. 56Accord-
ing to the lot their inheritance shall be divided
between the larger and the smaller."
57And these *are* those who were numbered of
the Levites according to their families: of Gershon, the family of the Gershonites; of Kohath,
the family of the Kohathites; of Merari, the family of the Merarites. 58These *are* the families of
the Levites: the family of the Libnites, the family of the Hebronites, the family of the Mahlites, the family of the Mushites, and the family of the Korathites. And Kohath begot
Amram. 59The name of Amram's wife *was*
Jochebed the daughter of Levi, who was born
to Levi in Egypt; and to Amram she bore
Aaron and Moses and their sister Miriam. 60To
Aaron were born Nadab and Abihu, Eleazar
and Ithamar. 61And Nadab and Abihu died
when they offered profane fire before the
LORD.
62Now those who were numbered of them
were twenty-three thousand, every male from
a month old and above; for they were not
numbered among the other children of Israel,
because there was no inheritance given to
them among the children of Israel.
63These *are* those who were numbered by
Moses and Eleazar the priest, who numbered
the children of Israel in the plains of Moab by
the Jordan, *across from* Jericho. 64But among
these there was not a man of those who were
numbered by Moses and Aaron the priest
when they numbered the children of Israel in
the Wilderness of Sinai. 65For the LORD had
said of them, "They shall surely die in the
wilderness." So there was not left a man of
them, except Caleb the son of Jephunneh and
Joshua the son of Nun.

Psalm 34:1–7

A Psalm of David when he pretended madness before Abimelech, who drove him away, and he departed.

I will bless the LORD at all times;
His praise *shall* continually
be in my mouth.
2 My soul shall make its boast in the
LORD;
The humble shall hear *of it* and be
glad.
3 Oh, magnify the LORD with me,
And let us exalt His name together.

4 I sought the LORD, and He heard me,
And delivered me from all my fears.
5 They looked to Him and
were radiant,
And their faces were not ashamed.
6 This poor man cried out, and the LORD
heard *him,*
And saved him out of all his troubles.
7 The angel of the LORD encamps all
around those who fear Him,
And delivers them.

34:7 The angel of the LORD. A special manifestation of Yahweh Himself at strategic historical junctures (see Gen. 16:7ff,18,19; 31:11ff.; Josh. 5; Judg. 6; 13). A strong case can be made that these were preincarnate appearances of the Lord Jesus Christ.

Proverbs 11:28

28 He who trusts in his riches will fall,
But the righteous will flourish like
foliage.

Mark 13:21–37

21"Then if anyone says to you, 'Look, here *is*
the Christ!' or, 'Look, *He is* there!' do not believe
it. 22For false christs and false prophets will rise
and show signs and wonders to deceive, if possible, even the elect. 23But take heed; see, I have
told you all things beforehand.
24"But in those days, after that tribulation,
the sun will be darkened, and the moon will
not give its light; 25the stars of heaven will fall,
and the powers in the heavens will be shaken.
26Then they will see the Son of Man coming in

the clouds with great power and glory. [27]And
then He will send His angels, and gather
together His elect from the four winds, from the
farthest part of earth to the farthest part of
heaven.

13:26 Son of Man coming in the clouds with great power and glory. Jesus will return to earth in the same manner in which He left it (see Acts 1:9–11; Dan. 7:13,14; Rev. 1:7). The psalmist said that God uses "clouds" as His chariot (Ps. 104:3), and Isaiah 19:1 pictures the Lord riding on a cloud. Although these "clouds" could be natural, they more likely describe the supernatural "glory cloud" that represented God's presence in Old Testament Israel (Rev. 1:7). While Christ possesses "great power and glory," His return will be accompanied with visible manifestations of that power and glory (see Rev. 6:15–17; 11:15–19; 16:17–21; 19:11–16)—He will redeem the elect, restore the devastated earth, and establish His rule on earth.

[28]"Now learn this parable from the fig tree:
When its branch has already become tender,
and puts forth leaves, you know that summer
is near. [29]So you also, when you see these
things happening, know that it is near—at the
doors! [30]Assuredly, I say to you, this generation will by no means pass away till all these
things take place. [31]Heaven and earth will pass
away, but My words will by no means pass
away.
[32]"But of that day and hour no one knows,
not even the angels in heaven, nor the Son,
but only the Father. [33]Take heed, watch and
pray; for you do not know when the time is. [34]*It
is* like a man going to a far country, who left
his house and gave authority to his servants,
and to each his work, and commanded the
doorkeeper to watch. [35]Watch therefore, for
you do not know when the master of the
house is coming—in the evening, at midnight,
at the crowing of the rooster, or in the morning— [36]lest, coming suddenly, he find you
sleeping. [37]And what I say to you, I say to all:
Watch!"

DAY 14: Can anyone know the exact time and day of Christ's return?

Jesus' own words could not be clearer: "But of that day and hour no one knows, not even the angels in heaven, nor the Son, but only the Father" (Mark 13:32). The exact day and time of Christ's return will not be revealed in advance to any man. At this time, it was known only to God the Father. While all the angelic beings enjoy intimacy with God, hover around His throne to do His bidding (Is. 26:2–7), and continually behold Him (Matt. 18:10), they have no knowledge of the time of Christ's return.

When Jesus spoke these words to the disciples, even He had no knowledge of the date and time of His return. Although Jesus was fully God (John 1:1,14), when He became a man, He voluntarily restricted the use of certain divine attributes (Phil. 2:6–8). He did not manifest them unless directed by the Father (John 4:34; 5:30; 6:38). He demonstrated His omniscience on several occasions (see John 2:25; 3:13), but He voluntarily restricted that omniscience to only those things God wanted Him to know during the days of His humanity (John 15:15). Such was the case regarding the knowledge of the date and time of His return. After He was resurrected, Jesus resumed His full divine knowledge (see Matt. 28:18; Acts 1:7).

Based upon that, a Christian's role is to "watch and pray" (Mark 13:33). Christ sounded a warning for believers to be on guard in two practical ways: 1) "watch" is a call to stay awake and be alert, looking for approaching danger; and 2) "pray" emphasizes the believer's constant need for divine assistance in this endeavor. Even believers do not have in themselves sufficient resources to be alert to spiritual dangers that can so easily surprise them.

MARCH 15

Numbers 27:1–28:31

27 Then came the daughters of
Zelophehad the son of Hepher, the son
of Gilead, the son of Machir, the son of
Manasseh, from the families of Manasseh the
son of Joseph; and these *were* the names of his
daughters: Mahlah, Noah, Hoglah, Milcah,
and Tirzah. [2]And they stood before Moses,
before Eleazar the priest, and before the leaders and all the congregation, *by* the doorway of
the tabernacle of meeting, saying: [3]"Our father
died in the wilderness; but he was not in the
company of those who gathered together
against the LORD, in company with Korah, but
he died in his own sin; and he had no sons.
[4]Why should the name of our father be removed from among his family because he had
no son? Give us a possession among our
father's brothers."

5So Moses brought their case before the LORD.
6And the LORD spoke to Moses, saying:
7"The daughters of Zelophehad speak *what is*
right; you shall surely give them a possession
of inheritance among their father's brothers,
and cause the inheritance of their father to
pass to them. 8And you shall speak to the children of Israel, saying: 'If a man dies and has no
son, then you shall cause his inheritance to
pass to his daughter. 9If he has no daughter,
then you shall give his inheritance to his
brothers. 10If he has no brothers, then you
shall give his inheritance to his father's brothers. 11And if his father has no brothers, then
you shall give his inheritance to the relative
closest to him in his family, and he shall possess it.'" And it shall be to the children of
Israel a statute of judgment, just as the LORD
commanded Moses.
12Now the LORD said to Moses: "Go up into
this Mount Abarim, and see the land which I
have given to the children of Israel. 13And when
you have seen it, you also shall be gathered to
your people, as Aaron your brother was gathered. 14For in the Wilderness of Zin, during the
strife of the congregation, you rebelled against
My command to hallow Me at the waters
before their eyes." (These *are* the waters of
Meribah, at Kadesh in the Wilderness of Zin.)
15Then Moses spoke to the LORD, saying:
16"Let the LORD, the God of the spirits of all
flesh, set a man over the congregation, 17who
may go out before them and go in before
them, who may lead them out and bring them
in, that the congregation of the LORD may not
be like sheep which have no shepherd."
18And the LORD said to Moses: "Take Joshua
the son of Nun with you, a man in whom *is* the
Spirit, and lay your hand on him; 19set him
before Eleazar the priest and before all the
congregation, and inaugurate him in their
sight. 20And you shall give *some* of your authority to him, that all the congregation of the children of Israel may be obedient. 21He shall
stand before Eleazar the priest, who shall
inquire before the LORD for him by the judgment of the Urim. At his word they shall go
out, and at his word they shall come in, he and
all the children of Israel with him—all the congregation."
22So Moses did as the LORD commanded him.
He took Joshua and set him before Eleazar the
priest and before all the congregation. 23And he
laid his hands on him and inaugurated him, just
as the LORD commanded by the hand of Moses.
28 Now the LORD spoke to Moses, saying,
2"Command the children of Israel, and
say to them, 'My offering, My food for My

27:18 lay your hand on him. Joshua already had the inner endowment for leadership. He was empowered by the Holy Spirit. This inner endowment was to be recognized by an external ceremony. Moses publicly laid his hands upon Joshua. This act signified the transfer of Moses' leadership to Joshua. The laying on of hands can accompany a dedication to an office (see Num. 8:10).

27:21 Eleazar...shall inquire before the LORD for him. Moses had been able to communicate directly with God (12:8), but Joshua would receive the word from the Lord through the high priest. **Urim.** See Exodus 28:30 for this part of the high priest's breastplate (Ex. 39:8–21) as a means of determining God's will (see Deut. 33:8; 1 Sam. 28:6).

offerings made by fire as a sweet aroma to
Me, you shall be careful to offer to Me at their
appointed time.'
3"And you shall say to them, 'This *is* the
offering made by fire which you shall offer to
the LORD: two male lambs in their first year
without blemish, day by day, as a regular
burnt offering. 4The one lamb you shall offer
in the morning, the other lamb you shall offer
in the evening, 5and one-tenth of an ephah of
fine flour as a grain offering mixed with one-
fourth of a hin of pressed oil. 6*It is* a regular
burnt offering which was ordained at Mount
Sinai for a sweet aroma, an offering made by
fire to the LORD. 7And its drink offering *shall be*
one-fourth of a hin for each lamb; in a holy
place you shall pour out the drink to the LORD
as an offering. 8The other lamb you shall offer
in the evening; as the morning grain offering
and its drink offering, you shall offer *it* as an
offering made by fire, a sweet aroma to the
LORD.
9'And on the Sabbath day two lambs in their
first year, without blemish, and two-tenths *of*
an ephah of fine flour as a grain offering, mixed
with oil, with its drink offering— 10*this is* the
burnt offering for every Sabbath, besides the
regular burnt offering with its drink offering.
11'At the beginnings of your months you
shall present a burnt offering to the LORD: two
young bulls, one ram, and seven lambs in their
first year, without blemish; 12three-tenths *of an*
ephah of fine flour as a grain offering, mixed
with oil, for each bull; two-tenths *of an ephah*
of fine flour as a grain offering, mixed with oil,
for the one ram; 13and one-tenth *of an ephah* of

fine flour, mixed with oil, as a grain offering
for each lamb, as a burnt offering of sweet
aroma, an offering made by fire to the LORD.
14 Their drink offering shall be half a hin of
wine for a bull, one-third of a hin for a ram, and
one-fourth of a hin for a lamb; this *is* the burnt
offering for each month throughout the
months of the year. 15 Also one kid of the goats
as a sin offering to the LORD shall be offered,
besides the regular burnt offering and its
drink offering.

16 "On the fourteenth day of the first month *is*
the Passover of the LORD. 17 And on the fifteenth day of this month *is* the feast; unleavened bread shall be eaten for seven days. 18 On
the first day *you shall have* a holy convocation.
You shall do no customary work. 19 And you
shall present an offering made by fire as a
burnt offering to the LORD: two young bulls,
one ram, and seven lambs in their first year.
Be sure they are without blemish. 20 Their
grain offering shall be of fine flour mixed with
oil: three-tenths *of an ephah* you shall offer for
a bull, and two-tenths for a ram; 21 you shall
offer one-tenth *of an ephah* for each of the
seven lambs; 22 also one goat *as* a sin offering,
to make atonement for you. 23 You shall offer
these besides the burnt offering of the morning, which *is* for a regular burnt offering. 24 In
this manner you shall offer the food of the
offering made by fire daily for seven days, as a
sweet aroma to the LORD; it shall be offered
besides the regular burnt offering and its
drink offering. 25 And on the seventh day you
shall have a holy convocation. You shall do no
customary work.

26 'Also on the day of the firstfruits, when you
bring a new grain offering to the LORD at your
Feast of Weeks, you shall have a holy convocation. You shall do no customary work. 27 You
shall present a burnt offering as a sweet
aroma to the LORD: two young bulls, one ram,
and seven lambs in their first year, 28 with their
grain offering of fine flour mixed with oil:
three-tenths *of an ephah* for each bull, two-
tenths for the one ram, 29 and one-tenth for each
of the seven lambs; 30 *also* one kid of the goats,
to make atonement for you. 31 Be sure they are
without blemish. You shall present *them* with
their drink offerings, besides the regular burnt
offering with its grain offering.

Psalm 34:8–14

8 Oh, taste and see that the LORD *is* good;
Blessed *is* the man *who* trusts in Him!
9 Oh, fear the LORD, you His saints!
There is no want to those who fear
Him.
10 The young lions lack and suffer
hunger;
But those who seek the LORD shall not
lack any good *thing.*
11 Come, you children, listen to me;
I will teach you the fear of
the LORD.
12 Who *is* the man *who* desires life,
And loves *many* days, that he may
see good?
13 Keep your tongue from evil,
And your lips from speaking deceit.
14 Depart from evil and do good;
Seek peace and pursue it.

Proverbs 11:29

29 He who troubles his own house will
inherit the wind,
And the fool *will be* servant to the wise
of heart.

11:29 inherit the wind. The one who mismanages his house will see all he has blown away, and he will have nothing left in the end. He will serve the one who manages well (15:27).

Mark 14:1–26

14 After two days it was the Passover and *the*
Feast of Unleavened Bread. And the chief
priests and the scribes sought how they might
take Him by trickery and put *Him* to death.
2 But they said, "Not during the feast, lest there
be an uproar of the people."

3 And being in Bethany at the house of Simon
the leper, as He sat at the table, a woman came
having an alabaster flask of very costly oil of
spikenard. Then she broke the flask and poured
it on His head. 4 But there were some who were
indignant among themselves, and said, "Why
was this fragrant oil wasted? 5 For it might have
been sold for more than three hundred denarii
and given to the poor." And they criticized her
sharply.

6 But Jesus said, "Let her alone. Why do you
trouble her? She has done a good work for Me.
7 For you have the poor with you always, and
whenever you wish you may do them good;
but Me you do not have always. 8 She has done
what she could. She has come beforehand to
anoint My body for burial. 9 Assuredly, I say to
you, wherever this gospel is preached in the

whole world, what this woman has done will also be told as a memorial to her."

10 Then Judas Iscariot, one of the twelve, went to the chief priests to betray Him to them. 11 And when they heard *it,* they were glad, and promised to give him money. So he sought how he might conveniently betray Him.

12 Now on the first day of Unleavened Bread, when they killed the Passover *lamb,* His disciples said to Him, "Where do You want us to go and prepare, that You may eat the Passover?"

13 And He sent out two of His disciples and said to them, "Go into the city, and a man will meet you carrying a pitcher of water; follow him. 14 Wherever he goes in, say to the master of the house, 'The Teacher says, "Where is the guest room in which I may eat the Passover with My disciples?"' 15 Then he will show you a large upper room, furnished *and* prepared; there make ready for us."

16 So His disciples went out, and came into the city, and found it just as He had said to them; and they prepared the Passover.

17 In the evening He came with the twelve. 18 Now as they sat and ate, Jesus said, "Assuredly, I say to you, one of you who eats with Me will betray Me."

19 And they began to be sorrowful, and to say to Him one by one, "*Is* it I?" And another *said,* "*Is* it I?"

20 He answered and said to them, "*It is* one of the twelve, who dips with Me in the dish. 21 The Son of Man indeed goes just as it is written of Him, but woe to that man by whom the Son of Man is betrayed! It would have been good for that man if he had never been born."

22 And as they were eating, Jesus took bread, blessed and broke *it,* and gave *it* to them and said, "Take, eat; this is My body."

23 Then He took the cup, and when He had given thanks He gave *it* to them, and they all drank from it. 24 And He said to them, "This is My blood of the new covenant, which is shed for many. 25 Assuredly, I say to you, I will no longer drink of the fruit of the vine until that day when I drink it new in the kingdom of God."

26 And when they had sung a hymn, they went out to the Mount of Olives.

14:12 Unleavened Bread. Passover and the Feast of Unleavened Bread were so closely associated that both terms were used interchangeably to refer to the 8-day celebration that began with the Passover. Although Unleavened Bread is used here, Mark's clear intention is the preparation for Passover. **killed the Passover *lamb*.** The lambs were killed on 14 Nisan at twilight (Ex. 12:6), a Hebrew term meaning, "between the two evenings," or between 3:00 and 5:00 p.m. After the lamb was slaughtered and some of its blood sprinkled on the altar, the lamb was taken home, roasted whole, and eaten in the evening meal with unleavened bread, bitter herbs, *charoseth* (a paste made of crushed apples, dates, pomegranates, and nuts, into which they dipped bread), and wine.

DAY 15: Why did Mary's anointing of Jesus spark a controversy?

In Mark 14:3, Jesus was in the home of Simon the leper at Bethany. "A woman," who is identified in John 12:3 as Mary, the sister of Martha and Lazarus, brought an alabaster flask—a long-necked bottle made out of a special variety of marble, a material which proved to be the best container for preserving expensive perfumes and oils. The flask contained "spikenard," which represents two words in the Greek that could be translated "pure nard." The oil was derived from the nard plant, which was native to India. That it was pure meant it was genuine and unadulterated, which is what made it so costly. She may have simply broken the neck of the bottle so that she could pour out the contents more quickly, an expression of her sincere and total devotion to the Lord.

Some who were there became indignant (v. 4). John 12:4,5 says that Judas was the instigator, and Matthew 26:8 indicates that all the disciples, following Judas's lead, were angry with Mary's waste of a very valuable commodity. It was valued at three hundred denarii (v. 5). Since a denarius was a day's wage for a common laborer, it represented almost a year's work for such a person. This money could have been "given to the poor." While 11 of the disciples would have agreed to this use of the money, the fact is the poor may never have seen it. Since Judas was in reality a thief masquerading as the treasurer of the 12, he could have embezzled all of it (John 12:6).

In any case, Jesus' answer was that "you have the poor with you always" (v. 7). Opportunities to minister to the poor are "always" available, but Jesus would be in their presence for only a limited time. This was not a time for meeting the needs of the poor and the sick—it was a time for sacrificial worship of the One who would soon suffer and be crucified.

MARCH 16

Numbers 29:1–30:16

29 'And in the seventh month, on the first *day* of the month, you shall have a holy convocation. You shall do no customary work. For you it is a day of blowing the trumpets. [2]You shall offer a burnt offering as a sweet aroma to the LORD: one young bull, one ram, *and* seven lambs in their first year, without blemish. [3]Their grain offering *shall be* fine flour mixed with oil: three-tenths *of an ephah* for the bull, two-tenths for the ram, [4]and one-tenth for each of the seven lambs; [5]also one kid of the goats *as* a sin offering, to make atonement for you; [6]besides the burnt offering with its grain offering for the New Moon, the regular burnt offering with its grain offering, and their drink offerings, according to their ordinance, as a sweet aroma, an offering made by fire to the LORD.

[7]'On the tenth *day* of this seventh month you shall have a holy convocation. You shall afflict your souls; you shall not do any work. [8]You shall present a burnt offering to the LORD *as* a sweet aroma: one young bull, one ram, *and* seven lambs in their first year. Be sure they are without blemish. [9]Their grain offering *shall be of* fine flour mixed with oil: three-tenths *of an ephah* for the bull, two-tenths for the one ram, [10]and one-tenth for each of the seven lambs; [11]also one kid of the goats *as* a sin offering, besides the sin offering for atonement, the regular burnt offering with its grain offering, and their drink offerings.

[12]'On the fifteenth day of the seventh month you shall have a holy convocation. You shall do no customary work, and you shall keep a feast to the LORD seven days. [13]You shall present a burnt offering, an offering made by fire as a sweet aroma to the LORD: thirteen young bulls, two rams, *and* fourteen lambs in their first year. They shall be without blemish. [14]Their grain offering *shall be of* fine flour mixed with oil: three-tenths *of an ephah* for each of the thirteen bulls, two-tenths for each of the two rams, [15]and one-tenth for each of the fourteen lambs; [16]also one kid of the goats *as* a sin offering, besides the regular burnt offering, its grain offering, and its drink offering.

[17]'On the second day *present* twelve young bulls, two rams, fourteen lambs in their first year without blemish, [18]and their grain offering and their drink offerings for the bulls, for the rams, and for the lambs, by their number, according to the ordinance; [19]also one kid of the goats *as* a sin offering, besides the regular burnt offering with its grain offering, and their drink offerings.

[20]'On the third day *present* eleven bulls, two rams, fourteen lambs in their first year without blemish, [21]and their grain offering and their drink offerings for the bulls, for the rams, and for the lambs, by their number, according to the ordinance; [22]also one goat *as* a sin offering, besides the regular burnt offering, its grain offering, and its drink offering.

[23]'On the fourth day *present* ten bulls, two rams, *and* fourteen lambs in their first year, without blemish, [24]and their grain offering and their drink offerings for the bulls, for the rams, and for the lambs, by their number, according to the ordinance; [25]also one kid of the goats *as* a sin offering, besides the regular burnt offering, its grain offering, and its drink offering.

[26]'On the fifth day *present* nine bulls, two rams, *and* fourteen lambs in their first year without blemish, [27]and their grain offering and their drink offerings for the bulls, for the rams, and for the lambs, by their number, according to the ordinance; [28]also one goat *as* a sin offering, besides the regular burnt offering, its grain offering, and its drink offering.

[29]'On the sixth day *present* eight bulls, two rams, *and* fourteen lambs in their first year without blemish, [30]and their grain offering and their drink offerings for the bulls, for the rams, and for the lambs, by their number, according to the ordinance; [31]also one goat *as* a sin offering, besides the regular burnt offering, its grain offering, and its drink offering.

[32]'On the seventh day *present* seven bulls, two rams, *and* fourteen lambs in their first year without blemish, [33]and their grain offering and their drink offerings for the bulls, for the rams, and for the lambs, by their number, according to the ordinance; [34]also one goat *as* a sin offering, besides the regular burnt offering, its grain offering, and its drink offering.

[35]'On the eighth day you shall have a sacred assembly. You shall do no customary work. [36]You shall present a burnt offering, an offering made by fire as a sweet aroma to the LORD: one bull, one ram, seven lambs in their first year without blemish, [37]and their grain offering and their drink offerings for the bull, for the ram, and for the lambs, by their number, according to the ordinance; [38]also one goat *as* a sin offering, besides the regular burnt offering, its grain offering, and its drink offering.

[39]'These you shall present to the LORD at your appointed feasts (besides your vowed

offerings and your freewill offerings) as your
burnt offerings and your grain offerings, as
your drink offerings and your peace offerings.' "
40 So Moses told the children of Israel everything, just as the LORD commanded Moses.

30 Then Moses spoke to the heads of the
tribes concerning the children of
Israel, saying, "This *is* the thing which the
LORD has commanded: 2 If a man makes a vow
to the LORD, or swears an oath to bind himself
by some agreement, he shall not break his
word; he shall do according to all that proceeds out of his mouth.
3 "Or if a woman makes a vow to the LORD,
and binds *herself* by some agreement while in
her father's house in her youth, 4 and her
father hears her vow and the agreement by
which she has bound herself, and her father
holds his peace, then all her vows shall stand,
and every agreement with which she has
bound herself shall stand. 5 But if her father
overrules her on the day that he hears, then
none of her vows nor her agreements by
which she has bound herself shall stand; and
the LORD will release her, because her father
overruled her.
6 "If indeed she takes a husband, while
bound by her vows or by a rash utterance
from her lips by which she bound herself, 7 and
her husband hears *it,* and makes no response
to her on the day that he hears, then her vows
shall stand, and her agreements by which she
bound herself shall stand. 8 But if her husband
overrules her on the day that he hears *it,* he
shall make void her vow which she took and
what she uttered with her lips, by which she
bound herself, and the LORD will release her.
9 "Also any vow of a widow or a divorced
woman, by which she has bound herself, shall
stand against her.
10 "If she vowed in her husband's house, or
bound herself by an agreement with an oath,
11 and her husband heard *it,* and made no
response to her *and* did not overrule her, then
all her vows shall stand, and every agreement
by which she bound herself shall stand. 12 But
if her husband truly made them void on the
day he heard *them,* then whatever proceeded
from her lips concerning her vows or concerning the agreement binding her, it shall
not stand; her husband has made them void,
and the LORD will release her. 13 Every vow and
every binding oath to afflict her soul, her husband may confirm it, or her husband may
make it void. 14 Now if her husband makes no
response whatever to her from day to day,
then he confirms all her vows or all the agreements that bind her; he confirms them,
because he made no response to her on the
day that he heard *them.* 15 But if he does make
them void after he has heard *them,* then he
shall bear her guilt."
16 These *are* the statutes which the LORD
commanded Moses, between a man and his
wife, and between a father and his daughter in
her youth in her father's house.

Psalm 34:15–22

15 The eyes of the LORD *are* on the
righteous,
And His ears *are open* to their cry.
16 The face of the LORD *is* against those
who do evil,
To cut off the remembrance of them
from the earth.

17 *The righteous* cry out, and the LORD
hears,
And delivers them out of all their
troubles.
18 The LORD *is* near to those who have a
broken heart,
And saves such as have a contrite
spirit.

34:18 broken heart,...contrite spirit. These are graphic idioms that describe dependent disciples (see Pss. 51:17; 147:3; Is. 57:15; 61:1; 66:2; Matt. 5:3).

19 Many *are* the afflictions of the righteous,
But the LORD delivers him out of
them all.
20 He guards all his bones;
Not one of them is broken.
21 Evil shall slay the wicked,
And those who hate the righteous shall
be condemned.
22 The LORD redeems the soul of His
servants,
And none of those who trust in Him
shall be condemned.

Proverbs 11:30–31

30 The fruit of the righteous *is a* tree of
life,
And he who wins souls *is* wise.
31 If the righteous will be recompensed
on the earth,
How much more the ungodly and the
sinner.

11:30 wins souls. Literally, "to take lives," in the sense of doing them good or influencing them with wisdom's ways (see Luke 5:10). The word is also used for capturing people for evil purposes as in 6:25; Psalm 31:13; Ezekiel 13:18.

11:31 recompensed. God's final blessing and reward to the "righteous" and His judgment and punishment of the "ungodly and the sinner" come after life on this earth has ended. But there are foretastes of both during life on the earth, as the righteous experience God's personal care and goodness, while the wicked are void of it.

Mark 14:27–54

27Then Jesus said to them, "All of you will be
made to stumble because of Me this night, for
it is written:

'I will strike the Shepherd,
And the sheep will be scattered.'

28"But after I have been raised, I will go
before you to Galilee."

29Peter said to Him, "Even if all are made to
stumble, yet I *will* not *be*."

30Jesus said to him, "Assuredly, I say to you
that today, *even* this night, before the rooster
crows twice, you will deny Me three times."

31But he spoke more vehemently, "If I have
to die with You, I will not deny You!"
And they all said likewise.

32Then they came to a place which was named
Gethsemane; and He said to His disciples, "Sit
here while I pray." 33And He took Peter, James,
and John with Him, and He began to be troubled and deeply distressed. 34Then He said to
them, "My soul is exceedingly sorrowful, *even*
to death. Stay here and watch."

35He went a little farther, and fell on the
ground, and prayed that if it were possible, the
hour might pass from Him. 36And He said,
"Abba, Father, all things *are* possible for You.
Take this cup away from Me; nevertheless,
not what I will, but what You *will*."

14:32 Gethsemane. The name means "oil press" and referred to a garden filled with olive trees on a slope of the Mt. of Olives. Jesus frequented this spot with the disciples when He wanted to get away from the crowds to pray (John 18:12; Matt. 26:36).

14:36 Abba. An endearing, intimate Aramaic term that is essentially equivalent to the English word "Daddy" (see Rom. 8:15; Gal. 4:6). **all things *are* possible.** Jesus knew that it was in the scope of God's power and omniscience to provide an alternate plan of salvation, if He desired. **cup.** This was the cup of divine wrath referred to in the Old Testament (Ps. 75:8; Is. 51:17; Jer. 49:12). Christ was to endure the fury of God over sin, Satan, the power of death, and the guilt of iniquity. **not what I will, but what You *will*.** This reveals Jesus' total resolution and resignation to do the will of God. He came into the world to do God's will, and that remained His commitment while here (Matt. 26:39; John 6:38–40).

37Then He came and found them sleeping,
and said to Peter, "Simon, are you sleeping?
Could you not watch one hour? 38Watch and
pray, lest you enter into temptation. The spirit
indeed *is* willing, but the flesh *is* weak."

39Again He went away and prayed, and spoke
the same words. 40And when He returned, He
found them asleep again, for their eyes were
heavy; and they did not know what to answer
Him.

41Then He came the third time and said to
them, "Are you still sleeping and resting? It is
enough! The hour has come; behold, the Son
of Man is being betrayed into the hands of sinners. 42Rise, let us be going. See, My betrayer
is at hand."

43And immediately, while He was still speaking, Judas, one of the twelve, with a great multitude with swords and clubs, came from the
chief priests and the scribes and the elders.
44Now His betrayer had given them a signal,
saying, "Whomever I kiss, He is the One;
seize Him and lead *Him* away safely."

45As soon as he had come, immediately he
went up to Him and said to Him, "Rabbi,
Rabbi!" and kissed Him.

46Then they laid their hands on Him and
took Him. 47And one of those who stood by
drew his sword and struck the servant of the
high priest, and cut off his ear.

48Then Jesus answered and said to them,
"Have you come out, as against a robber, with
swords and clubs to take Me? 49I was daily with
you in the temple teaching, and you did not

seize Me. But the Scriptures must be fulfilled."
50"Then they all forsook Him and fled.
51Now a certain young man followed Him,
having a linen cloth thrown around *his* naked
body. And the young men laid hold of him, 52and
he left the linen cloth and fled from them naked.

53And they led Jesus away to the high priest;
and with him were assembled all the chief
priests, the elders, and the scribes. 54But Peter
followed Him at a distance, right into the
courtyard of the high priest. And he sat with
the servants and warmed himself at the fire.

DAY 16: Who was involved in the arrest of Jesus?

"Judas, one of the twelve," was the betrayer (Mark 14:43). All the Gospel writers refer to him this way (vv. 10,20; Matt. 26:14,47; Luke 22:47; John 6:71); and in so doing, they display remarkable restraint in describing and evaluating Judas. Especially in this context, such a simple description actually heightens the evil of his crime more than any series of derogatory epithets or negative criticisms could do. It also points out the precise fulfillment of Jesus' announcement in vv. 18–20.

"A great multitude with swords and clubs" also was there. This "multitude" was a carefully selected group whose sole purpose was arresting Jesus so He could be put to death. A cohort (600 men at full strength) of Roman soldiers (John 18:3,12) was in this crowd because the Jewish leaders (see Luke 22:52) who organized the throng needed permission from Rome to carry out the death penalty and feared the crowds. The "swords" were the regular small hand weapons of the Romans, and the wood "clubs" were ordinary weapons carried by the Jewish temple police.

Then there were the "chief priests…scribes…elders." Although 3 distinct sections of the Sanhedrin, they were acting in unity. These Jewish leaders had evidently for some time hoped to accuse Jesus of rebellion against Rome. Then, His execution could be blamed on the Romans and the leaders could escape potential reprisals from those Jews who admired Jesus. The Sanhedrin likely had hurried to Pontius Pilate, the Roman governor, to ask immediate use of his soldiers, or perhaps acted on a prearranged agreement for troop use on short notice. Whatever the case, the leaders procured the assistance of the Roman military from Fort Antonia in Jerusalem.

MARCH 17

Numbers 31:1–32:42

31 And the LORD spoke to Moses, saying:
2"Take vengeance on the Midianites for
the children of Israel. Afterward you shall be
gathered to your people."
3So Moses spoke to the people, saying,
"Arm some of yourselves for war, and let them
go against the Midianites to take vengeance
for the LORD on Midian. 4A thousand from
each tribe of all the tribes of Israel you shall
send to the war."
5So there were recruited from the divisions
of Israel one thousand from *each* tribe, twelve
thousand armed for war. 6Then Moses sent
them to the war, one thousand from *each* tribe;
he sent them to the war with Phinehas the son
of Eleazar the priest, with the holy articles and
the signal trumpets in his hand. 7And they
warred against the Midianites, just as the
LORD commanded Moses, and they killed all
the males. 8They killed the kings of Midian
with *the rest of* those who were killed—Evi,
Rekem, Zur, Hur, and Reba, the five kings of
Midian. Balaam the son of Beor they also
killed with the sword.
9And the children of Israel took the women
of Midian captive, with their little ones, and
took as spoil all their cattle, all their flocks, and
all their goods. 10They also burned with fire all
the cities where they dwelt, and all their forts.
11And they took all the spoil and all the booty—
of man and beast.
12Then they brought the captives, the booty,
and the spoil to Moses, to Eleazar the priest,
and to the congregation of the children of Israel,
to the camp in the plains of Moab by the Jordan,
across from Jericho. 13And Moses, Eleazar the
priest, and all the leaders of the congregation,
went to meet them outside the camp. 14But
Moses was angry with the officers of the army,
with the captains over thousands and captains
over hundreds, who had come from the battle.
15And Moses said to them: "Have you kept
all the women alive? 16Look, these *women*
caused the children of Israel, through the
counsel of Balaam, to trespass against the
LORD in the incident of Peor, and there was a
plague among the congregation of the LORD.
17Now therefore, kill every male among the little ones, and kill every woman who has known
a man intimately. 18But keep alive for yourselves all the young girls who have not known
a man intimately. 19And as for you, remain outside the camp seven days; whoever has killed
any person, and whoever has touched any

slain, purify yourselves and your captives on
the third day and on the seventh day. [20]Purify
every garment, everything made of leather,
everything woven of goats' *hair,* and everything made of wood."
[21]Then Eleazar the priest said to the men of
war who had gone to the battle, "This *is* the ordinance of the law which the LORD commanded Moses: [22]Only the gold, the silver, the
bronze, the iron, the tin, and the lead, [23]every-
thing that can endure fire, you shall put
through the fire, and it shall be clean; and it
shall be purified with the water of purification.
But all that cannot endure fire you shall put
through water. [24]And you shall wash your
clothes on the seventh day and be clean, and
afterward you may come into the camp."
[25]Now the LORD spoke to Moses, saying:
[26]"Count up the plunder that was taken—of
man and beast—you and Eleazar the priest
and the chief fathers of the congregation;
[27]and divide the plunder into two parts,
between those who took part in the war, who
went out to battle, and all the congregation.
[28]And levy a tribute for the LORD on the men of
war who went out to battle: one of every five
hundred of the persons, the cattle, the donkeys, and the sheep; [29]take *it* from their half,
and give *it* to Eleazar the priest as a heave
offering to the LORD. [30]And from the children
of Israel's half you shall take one of every fifty,
drawn from the persons, the cattle, the donkeys, and the sheep, from all the livestock,
and give them to the Levites who keep charge
of the tabernacle of the LORD." [31]So Moses and
Eleazar the priest did as the LORD commanded
Moses.
[32]The booty remaining from the plunder,
which the men of war had taken, was six
hundred and seventy-five thousand sheep,
[33]seventy-two thousand cattle, [34]sixty-one
thousand donkeys, [35]and thirty-two thousand
persons in all, of women who had not known a
man intimately. [36]And the half, the portion for
those who had gone out to war, was in number
three hundred and thirty-seven thousand five
hundred sheep; [37]and the LORD's tribute of the
sheep was six hundred and seventy-five. [38]The
cattle *were* thirty-six thousand, of which the
LORD's tribute *was* seventy-two. [39]The donkeys
were thirty thousand five hundred, of which
the LORD's tribute *was* sixty-one. [40]The persons
were sixteen thousand, of which the LORD's
tribute *was* thirty-two persons. [41]So Moses
gave the tribute *which was* the LORD's heave
offering to Eleazar the priest, as the LORD commanded Moses.
[42]And from the children of Israel's half,
which Moses separated from the men who
fought— [43]now the half belonging to the congregation was three hundred and thirty-seven
thousand five hundred sheep, [44]thirty-six thousand cattle, [45]thirty thousand five hundred donkeys, [46]and sixteen thousand persons— [47]and
from the children of Israel's half Moses took
one of every fifty, drawn from man and beast,
and gave them to the Levites, who kept charge
of the tabernacle of the LORD, as the LORD commanded Moses.
[48]Then the officers who *were* over thousands
of the army, the captains of thousands and
captains of hundreds, came near to Moses;
[49]and they said to Moses, "Your servants have
taken a count of the men of war who *are* under
our command, and not a man of us is missing.
[50]Therefore we have brought an offering for
the LORD, what every man found of ornaments
of gold: armlets and bracelets and signet rings
and earrings and necklaces, to make atonement for ourselves before the LORD." [51]So
Moses and Eleazar the priest received the
gold from them, all the fashioned ornaments.
[52]And all the gold of the offering that they
offered to the LORD, from the captains of thousands and captains of hundreds, was sixteen
thousand seven hundred and fifty shekels.
[53](The men of war had taken spoil, every man
for himself.) [54]And Moses and Eleazar the
priest received the gold from the captains of
thousands and of hundreds, and brought it
into the tabernacle of meeting as a memorial
for the children of Israel before the LORD.
32 Now the children of Reuben and the
children of Gad had a very great multitude of livestock; and when they saw the land
of Jazer and the land of Gilead, that indeed the
region *was* a place for livestock, [2]the children
of Gad and the children of Reuben came and
spoke to Moses, to Eleazar the priest, and to
the leaders of the congregation, saying,
[3]"Ataroth, Dibon, Jazer, Nimrah, Heshbon,
Elealeh, Shebam, Nebo, and Beon, [4]the country which the LORD defeated before the congregation of Israel, *is* a land for livestock, and
your servants have livestock." [5]Therefore they
said, "If we have found favor in your sight, let
this land be given to your servants as a possession. Do not take us over the Jordan."
[6]And Moses said to the children of Gad and
to the children of Reuben: "Shall your
brethren go to war while you sit here? [7]Now
why will you discourage the heart of the children of Israel from going over into the land
which the LORD has given them? [8]Thus your
fathers did when I sent them away from Kadesh
Barnea to see the land. [9]For when they went up

32:8 Thus your fathers did. Moses feared that if these two tribes were comfortably settled, they would not join with the other 10 tribes in conquering Canaan, and that could be the beginning of a general revolt against entering the land. As the 10 spies had dissuaded the people at Kadesh nearly 40 years earlier from conquering the land (vv. 9–13; 13:26–14:4), the refusal of these two tribes could cause the people to fail again (v. 15).

to the Valley of Eshcol and saw the land, they
discouraged the heart of the children of Israel,
so that they did not go into the land which the
LORD had given them. [10]So the LORD's anger
was aroused on that day, and He swore an
oath, saying, [11]'Surely none of the men who
came up from Egypt, from twenty years old
and above, shall see the land of which I swore
to Abraham, Isaac, and Jacob, because they
have not wholly followed Me, [12]except Caleb
the son of Jephunneh, the Kenizzite, and
Joshua the son of Nun, for they have wholly
followed the LORD.' [13]So the LORD's anger was
aroused against Israel, and He made them
wander in the wilderness forty years, until all
the generation that had done evil in the sight
of the LORD was gone. [14]And look! You have
risen in your fathers' place, a brood of sinful
men, to increase still more the fierce anger of
the LORD against Israel. [15]For if you turn away
from following Him, He will once again leave
them in the wilderness, and you will destroy
all these people."
[16]Then they came near to him and said: "We
will build sheepfolds here for our livestock,
and cities for our little ones, [17]but we ourselves
will be armed, ready *to go* before the children
of Israel until we have brought them to their
place; and our little ones will dwell in the fortified
cities because of the inhabitants of the
land. [18]We will not return to our homes until
every one of the children of Israel has received
his inheritance. [19]For we will not inherit
with them on the other side of the Jordan
and beyond, because our inheritance has fallen
to us on this eastern side of the Jordan."
[20]Then Moses said to them: "If you do this
thing, if you arm yourselves before the LORD
for the war, [21]and all your armed men cross
over the Jordan before the LORD until He has
driven out His enemies from before Him, [22]and
the land is subdued before the LORD, then
afterward you may return and be blameless
before the LORD and before Israel; and this land
shall be your possession before the LORD. [23]But
if you do not do so, then take note, you have
sinned against the LORD; and be sure your sin
will find you out. [24]Build cities for your little
ones and folds for your sheep, and do what has
proceeded out of your mouth."

32:23 your sin will find you out. The two tribes committed themselves to provide their warriors for the conquest of the land. This agreement satisfied Moses, although he added that nonparticipation would be sin and God would certainly find and judge the tribes for their sin.

[25]And the children of Gad and the children
of Reuben spoke to Moses, saying: "Your servants
will do as my lord commands. [26]Our little
ones, our wives, our flocks, and all our livestock
will be there in the cities of Gilead; [27]but
your servants will cross over, every man
armed for war, before the LORD to battle, just
as my lord says."
[28]So Moses gave command concerning
them to Eleazar the priest, to Joshua the son
of Nun, and to the chief fathers of the tribes of
the children of Israel. [29]And Moses said to
them: "If the children of Gad and the children
of Reuben cross over the Jordan with you,
every man armed for battle before the LORD,
and the land is subdued before you, then you
shall give them the land of Gilead as a possession.
[30]But if they do not cross over armed with
you, they shall have possessions among you in
the land of Canaan."
[31]Then the children of Gad and the children
of Reuben answered, saying: "As the LORD has
said to your servants, so we will do. [32]We will
cross over armed before the LORD into the
land of Canaan, but the possession of our
inheritance *shall remain* with us on this side of
the Jordan."
[33]So Moses gave to the children of Gad, to
the children of Reuben, and to half the tribe of
Manasseh the son of Joseph, the kingdom of
Sihon king of the Amorites and the kingdom
of Og king of Bashan, the land with its cities
within the borders, the cities of the surrounding
country. [34]And the children of Gad built
Dibon and Ataroth and Aroer, [35]Atroth and
Shophan and Jazer and Jogbehah, [36]Beth
Nimrah and Beth Haran, fortified cities, and
folds for sheep. [37]And the children of Reuben

built Heshbon and Elealeh and Kirjathaim,
38 Nebo and Baal Meon (*their* names being
changed) and Shibmah; and they gave *other*
names to the cities which they built.
39 And the children of Machir the son of
Manasseh went to Gilead and took it, and dispossessed the Amorites who *were* in it. 40 So
Moses gave Gilead to Machir the son of
Manasseh, and he dwelt in it. 41 Also Jair the
son of Manasseh went and took its small
towns, and called them Havoth Jair. 42 Then
Nobah went and took Kenath and its villages,
and he called it Nobah, after his own name.

Psalm 35:1–8

A Psalm of David.

Plead *my cause,* O LORD, with those
who strive with me;
Fight against those who fight against
me.
2 Take hold of shield and buckler,
And stand up for my help.
3 Also draw out the spear,
And stop those who pursue me.
Say to my soul,
"I *am* your salvation."

4 Let those be put to shame and brought
to dishonor
Who seek after my life;
Let those be turned back and brought
to confusion
Who plot my hurt.
5 Let them be like chaff before the wind,
And let the angel of the LORD chase
them.
6 Let their way be dark and slippery,
And let the angel of the LORD pursue
them.
7 For without cause they have hidden
their net for me *in* a pit,
Which they have dug without cause for
my life.
8 Let destruction come upon him
unexpectedly,
And let his net that he has hidden
catch himself;
Into that very destruction let him fall.

Proverbs 12:1

12 Whoever loves instruction loves
knowledge,
But he who hates correction
is stupid.

Mark 14:55–72

55 Now the chief priests and all the council
sought testimony against Jesus to put Him to
death, but found none. 56 For many bore false
witness against Him, but their testimonies did
not agree.
57 Then some rose up and bore false witness
against Him, saying, 58 "We heard Him say, 'I
will destroy this temple made with hands, and
within three days I will build another made
without hands.' " 59 But not even then did their
testimony agree.
60 And the high priest stood up in the midst
and asked Jesus, saying, "Do You answer nothing? What *is it* these men testify against You?"
61 But He kept silent and answered nothing.
Again the high priest asked Him, saying to
Him, "Are You the Christ, the Son of the
Blessed?"
62 Jesus said, "I am. And you will see the Son
of Man sitting at the right hand of the Power,
and coming with the clouds of heaven."
63 Then the high priest tore his clothes and
said, "What further need do we have of witnesses? 64 You have heard the blasphemy! What
do you think?"
And they all condemned Him to be deserving of death.
65 Then some began to spit on Him, and to

14:56 Because Jesus was innocent, the Jewish leaders could not convict Him except by relying on perjured testimony and perverted justice. The Jews were intent on doing whatever was necessary, even if they had to violate every biblical and rabbinical rule. **many bore false witness against Him.** There was no lack of people to come forward at the Sanhedrin's invitation to consciously present false, lying testimony. **did not agree.** The testimonies were grossly inconsistent. The law, however, required exact agreement between two witnesses (Deut. 17:6; 19:15).

14:65 spit on Him…beat Him. For the Jews, to "spit" in another's face was the grossest, most hateful form of personal insult (see Num. 12:14; Deut. 25:9). Their brutal cruelty reached a climax and revealed the great depravity of their hearts when they "beat Him," or hit Him with clenched fists. **"Prophesy!"** They jeeringly and disrespectfully ordered Jesus to use the prophetic powers He claimed to have—even in the frivolous manner of telling them who struck Him (Matt. 26:68).

blindfold Him, and to beat Him, and to say to
Him, "Prophesy!" And the officers struck Him
with the palms of their hands.
66 Now as Peter was below in the courtyard,
one of the servant girls of the high priest
came. 67 And when she saw Peter warming
himself, she looked at him and said, "You also
were with Jesus of Nazareth."
68 But he denied it, saying, "I neither know
nor understand what you are saying." And he
went out on the porch, and a rooster crowed.
69 And the servant girl saw him again, and
began to say to those who stood by, "This is
one of them." 70 But he denied it again.
And a little later those who stood by said to
Peter again, "Surely you are *one* of them; for
you are a Galilean, and your speech shows *it*."
71 Then he began to curse and swear, "I do
not know this Man of whom you speak!"
72 A second time *the* rooster crowed. Then
Peter called to mind the word that Jesus had
said to him, "Before the rooster crows twice,
you will deny Me three times." And when he
thought about it, he wept.

DAY 17: Did Jesus claim to be God during His trial?

In Mark 14:61, when Caiaphas, the high priest, asked Jesus if He was the "Christ," the term refers to Jesus' claim to be the promised Messiah. The "Son of the Blessed" clearly refers to Jesus' claim to Deity. This is the only New Testament use of the expression, and it is an example of Jewish wording that avoided using God's name. Jesus' acceptance of messiahship and Deity (see Luke 4:18–21; John 4:25,26; 5:17,18; 8:58) had always brought vigorous opposition from the Jewish leaders (John 5:19–47; 8:16–19; 10:29–39). Clearly, the high priest was asking this question in hopes that Jesus would affirm it and open Himself to the formal charge of blasphemy.

Jesus' response that "I am" (v. 62) was an explicit, unambiguous declaration that He was and is both the Messiah and "the Son of Man"—Jesus used this commonly acknowledged messianic title of Himself more than 80 times in the Gospels, here in a reference to Psalm 110:1 and Daniel 7:13 (see Rev. 1:13; 14:14). He added that His glorified position is next to the throne of God, "the right hand of the Power." Jesus' "Power" is another reference to God.

That Jesus' declaration was understood is seen when the high priest "tore his clothes" (v. 63), a ceremonial, and in this case contrived, display of grief and indignation over the presumed dishonoring of God's name by Jesus (see Gen. 37:29; Lev. 10:6; Job 1:20; Acts 14:13,19). Strictly speaking, Jesus' words were not "blasphemy" (v. 64) or defiant irreverence of God (Lev. 24:10–23), but Caiaphas regarded them as such because Jesus claimed for Himself equal power and prerogative with God.

MARCH 18

Numbers 33:1–34:29

33 These *are* the journeys of the children
of Israel, who went out of the land of
Egypt by their armies under the hand of
Moses and Aaron. 2 Now Moses wrote down
the starting points of their journeys at the
command of the LORD. And these *are* their
journeys according to their starting points:
3 They departed from Rameses in the first
month, on the fifteenth day of the first month;
on the day after the Passover the children of
Israel went out with boldness in the sight of all
the Egyptians. 4 For the Egyptians were burying all *their* firstborn, whom the LORD had
killed among them. Also on their gods the
LORD had executed judgments.
5 Then the children of Israel moved from
Rameses and camped at Succoth. 6 They
departed from Succoth and camped at Etham,
which *is* on the edge of the wilderness. 7 They
moved from Etham and turned back to Pi
Hahiroth, which *is* east of Baal Zephon; and
they camped near Migdol. 8 They departed
from before Hahiroth and passed through the
midst of the sea into the wilderness, went three
days' journey in the Wilderness of Etham, and
camped at Marah. 9 They moved from Marah
and came to Elim. At Elim *were* twelve springs
of water and seventy palm trees; so they
camped there.
10 They moved from Elim and camped by the
Red Sea. 11 They moved from the Red Sea and
camped in the Wilderness of Sin. 12 They journeyed from the Wilderness of Sin and camped
at Dophkah. 13 They departed from Dophkah
and camped at Alush. 14 They moved from
Alush and camped at Rephidim, where there
was no water for the people to drink.
15 They departed from Rephidim and
camped in the Wilderness of Sinai. 16 They
moved from the Wilderness of Sinai and
camped at Kibroth Hattaavah. 17 They departed
from Kibroth Hattaavah and camped at

Hazeroth. 18They departed from Hazeroth and
camped at Rithmah. 19They departed from
Rithmah and camped at Rimmon Perez. 20They
departed from Rimmon Perez and camped at
Libnah. 21They moved from Libnah and
camped at Rissah. 22They journeyed from
Rissah and camped at Kehelathah. 23They
went from Kehelathah and camped at Mount
Shepher. 24They moved from Mount Shepher
and camped at Haradah. 25They moved from
Haradah and camped at Makheloth. 26They
moved from Makheloth and camped at
Tahath. 27They departed from Tahath and
camped at Terah. 28They moved from Terah
and camped at Mithkah. 29They went from
Mithkah and camped at Hashmonah. 30They
departed from Hashmonah and camped at
Moseroth. 31They departed from Moseroth
and camped at Bene Jaakan. 32They moved
from Bene Jaakan and camped at Hor
Hagidgad. 33They went from Hor Hagidgad
and camped at Jotbathah. 34They moved from
Jotbathah and camped at Abronah. 35They
departed from Abronah and camped at Ezion
Geber. 36They moved from Ezion Geber and
camped in the Wilderness of Zin, which *is*
Kadesh. 37They moved from Kadesh and
camped at Mount Hor, on the boundary of the
land of Edom.

38Then Aaron the priest went up to Mount
Hor at the command of the LORD, and died
there in the fortieth year after the children of
Israel had come out of the land of Egypt, on the
first *day* of the fifth month. 39Aaron *was* one
hundred and twenty-three years old when he
died on Mount Hor.

40Now the king of Arad, the Canaanite, who
dwelt in the South in the land of Canaan,
heard of the coming of the children of Israel.

41So they departed from Mount Hor and
camped at Zalmonah. 42They departed from
Zalmonah and camped at Punon. 43They
departed from Punon and camped at Oboth.
44They departed from Oboth and camped at Ije
Abarim, at the border of Moab. 45They departed from Ijim and camped at Dibon Gad. 46They
moved from Dibon Gad and camped at Almon
Diblathaim. 47They moved from Almon
Diblathaim and camped in the mountains of
Abarim, before Nebo. 48They departed from
the mountains of Abarim and camped in the
plains of Moab by the Jordan, *across from* Jericho. 49They camped by the Jordan, from Beth
Jesimoth as far as the Abel Acacia Grove in
the plains of Moab.

50Now the LORD spoke to Moses in the
plains of Moab by the Jordan, *across from* Jericho, saying, 51"Speak to the children of Israel,
and say to them: 'When you have crossed the
Jordan into the land of Canaan, 52then you
shall drive out all the inhabitants of the land
from before you, destroy all their engraved
stones, destroy all their molded images, and
demolish all their high places; 53you shall
dispossess *the inhabitants of* the land and dwell
in it, for I have given you the land to possess.
54And you shall divide the land by lot as an
inheritance among your families; to the larger
you shall give a larger inheritance, and to the
smaller you shall give a smaller inheritance;
there everyone's *inheritance* shall be whatever falls to him by lot. You shall inherit according to the tribes of your fathers. 55But if you do
not drive out the inhabitants of the land from
before you, then it shall be that those whom
you let remain *shall be* irritants in your eyes
and thorns in your sides, and they shall harass
you in the land where you dwell. 56Moreover it
shall be *that* I will do to you as I thought to do
to them.' "

33:56 I will do to you as I thought to do to them. If Israel failed to obey God, she would be the object of God's punishment in exactly the same way as the Canaanites were.

34 Then the LORD spoke to Moses, saying,
2"Command the children of Israel, and
say to them: 'When you come into the land of
Canaan, this *is* the land that shall fall to you as
an inheritance—the land of Canaan to its boundaries. 3Your southern border shall be from the
Wilderness of Zin along the border of Edom;
then your southern border shall extend eastward to the end of the Salt Sea; 4your border
shall turn from the southern side of the Ascent
of Akrabbim, continue to Zin, and be on the
south of Kadesh Barnea; then it shall go on to
Hazar Addar, and continue to Azmon; 5the border shall turn from Azmon to the Brook of
Egypt, and it shall end at the Sea.

6'As for the western border, you shall have
the Great Sea for a border; this shall be your
western border.

7'And this shall be your northern border:
From the Great Sea you shall mark out your
border line to Mount Hor; 8from Mount Hor
you shall mark out *your border* to the entrance
of Hamath; then the direction of the border
shall be toward Zedad; 9the border shall proceed to Ziphron, and it shall end at Hazar
Enan. This shall be your northern border.

[10]"You shall mark out your eastern border
from Hazar Enan to Shepham; [11]the border
shall go down from Shepham to Riblah on the
east side of Ain; the border shall go down and
reach to the eastern side of the Sea of
Chinnereth; [12]the border shall go down along
the Jordan, and it shall end at the Salt Sea. This
shall be your land with its surrounding boundaries.' "
[13]Then Moses commanded the children of
Israel, saying: "This *is* the land which you
shall inherit by lot, which the LORD has commanded to give to the nine tribes and to the
half-tribe. [14]For the tribe of the children of Reuben according to the house of their fathers,
and the tribe of the children of Gad according
to the house of their fathers, have received
their inheritance; and the half-tribe of
Manasseh has received its inheritance. [15]The
two tribes and the half-tribe have received their
inheritance on this side of the Jordan, *across
from* Jericho eastward, toward the sunrise."
[16]And the LORD spoke to Moses, saying,
[17]"These *are* the names of the men who shall
divide the land among you as an inheritance:
Eleazar the priest and Joshua the son of Nun.
[18]And you shall take one leader of every tribe
to divide the land for the inheritance. [19]These
are the names of the men: from the tribe of Judah, Caleb the son of Jephunneh; [20]from the
tribe of the children of Simeon, Shemuel the
son of Ammihud; [21]from the tribe of Benjamin,
Elidad the son of Chislon; [22]a leader from the
tribe of the children of Dan, Bukki the son of
Jogli; [23]from the sons of Joseph: a leader from
the tribe of the children of Manasseh, Hanniel
the son of Ephod, [24]and a leader from the tribe
of the children of Ephraim, Kemuel the son of
Shiphtan; [25]a leader from the tribe of the children of Zebulun, Elizaphan the son of
Parnach; [26]a leader from the tribe of the children of Issachar, Paltiel the son of Azzan; [27]a
leader from the tribe of the children of Asher,
Ahihud the son of Shelomi; [28]and a leader from
the tribe of the children of Naphtali, Pedahel
the son of Ammihud."
[29]These *are* the ones the LORD commanded
to divide the inheritance among the children
of Israel in the land of Canaan.

Psalm 35:9–16

9 And my soul shall be joyful in the
LORD;
It shall rejoice in His salvation.
10 All my bones shall say,
"LORD, who *is* like You,
Delivering the poor from him who is
too strong for him,

35:10 LORD, who *is* like You...? This had become a canonized expression of awe at the uniqueness of Israel's great God (see Ex. 15:11; Mic. 7:18).

Yes, the poor and the needy from him
who plunders him?"
11 Fierce witnesses rise up;
They ask me *things* that I do not know.
12 They reward me evil for good,
To the sorrow of my soul.
13 But as for me, when they were sick,
My clothing *was* sackcloth;
I humbled myself with fasting;
And my prayer would return to my
own heart.
14 I paced about as though *he were* my
friend *or* brother;
I bowed down heavily, as one who
mourns *for his* mother.

15 But in my adversity they rejoiced
And gathered together;
Attackers gathered against me,
And I did not know *it;*
They tore *at me* and did not cease;
16 With ungodly mockers at feasts
They gnashed at me with their teeth.

Proverbs 12:2

2 A good *man* obtains favor from the
LORD,
But a man of wicked intentions He will
condemn.

Mark 15:1–24

15 Immediately, in the morning, the chief
priests held a consultation with the elders and scribes and the whole council; and
they bound Jesus, led *Him* away, and delivered *Him* to Pilate. [2]Then Pilate asked Him,
"Are You the King of the Jews?"
He answered and said to him, "*It is as* you
say."
[3]And the chief priests accused Him of many
things, but He answered nothing. [4]Then Pilate
asked Him again, saying, "Do You answer
nothing? See how many things they testify
against You!" [5]But Jesus still answered nothing, so that Pilate marveled.
[6]Now at the feast he was accustomed to
releasing one prisoner to them, whomever they
requested. [7]And there was one named
Barabbas, *who was* chained with his fellow

15:7 Barabbas. A robber (John 18:40) and murderer (Luke 23:18,19) in some way involved as an anti-Roman insurrectionist. Whether his involvement was motivated by political conviction or personal greed is not known. It is impossible to identify the specific insurrection in question, but such uprisings were common in Jesus' day and were precursors of the wholesale revolt of A.D. 66–70.

rebels; they had committed murder in the rebellion.
[8]Then the multitude, crying aloud, began to ask *him to do* just as he had always done for them.
[9]But Pilate answered them, saying, "Do you want me to release to you the King of the Jews?"
[10]For he knew that the chief priests had handed Him over because of envy.
[11]But the chief priests stirred up the crowd, so that he should rather release Barabbas to them.
[12]Pilate answered and said to them again, "What then do you want me to do *with Him* whom you call the King of the Jews?"
[13]So they cried out again, "Crucify Him!"
[14]Then Pilate said to them, "Why, what evil has He done?"

But they cried out all the more, "Crucify Him!"
[15]So Pilate, wanting to gratify the crowd, released Barabbas to them; and he delivered Jesus, after he had scourged *Him,* to be crucified.
[16]Then the soldiers led Him away into the hall called Praetorium, and they called together the whole garrison.
[17]And they clothed Him with purple; and they twisted a crown of thorns, put it on His *head,*
[18]and began to salute Him, "Hail, King of the Jews!"
[19]Then they struck Him on the head with a reed and spat on Him; and bowing the knee, they worshiped Him.
[20]And when they had mocked Him, they took the purple off Him, put His own clothes on Him, and led Him out to crucify Him.
[21]Then they compelled a certain man, Simon a Cyrenian, the father of Alexander and Rufus, as he was coming out of the country and passing by, to bear His cross.
[22]And they brought Him to the place Golgotha, which is translated, Place of a Skull.
[23]Then they gave Him wine mingled with myrrh to drink, but He did not take *it.*
[24]And when they crucified Him, they divided His garments, casting lots for them *to determine* what every man should take.

15:17 clothed Him with purple;...crown of thorns. "Purple" was the color traditionally worn by royalty. The "crown of thorns" was in mockery of a royal crown. The callous soldiers decided to hold a mock coronation of Jesus as king of the Jews.

15:21 Condemned prisoners were required to carry the heavy crossbeam of their cross to the execution site. Exhausted from a sleepless night and severely wounded and weakened by His scourging, Jesus was unable to continue. The Roman guards conscripted Simon, apparently at random, to carry Jesus' crossbeam the rest of the way. Simon, from the North African city of Cyrene, was on his way into Jerusalem. The identification of him as "the father of Alexander and Rufus" (Rom. 16:13) is evidence of Mark's connection with the church at Rome.

DAY 18: What are some general, time-tested principles that will help rightly interpret Proverbs?

One of the most common characteristics of Proverbs is the use of parallelism—placing truths side by side so that the second statement expands, completes, defines, and emphasizes the first. Sometimes a logical conclusion is reached; at other times, a logical contrast is demonstrated.

The following tools will assist a student in gaining greater confidence as he or she interprets these Proverbs: 1) determine what facts, principles, or circumstances make up the parallel ideas in that proverb—what two central concepts or persons are being compared or contrasted; 2) identify the figures of speech and rephrase the thought without those figures—for example, restate the idea behind "put a knife to your throat" (23:1–3); 3) summarize the lesson or principle of the proverb in a few words; 4) describe the behavior that is being taught or encouraged; and 5) think of examples from elsewhere in Scripture that illustrate the truth of that proverb.

MARCH 19

Numbers 35:1–36:13

35 And the LORD spoke to Moses in the plains of Moab by the Jordan *across from* Jericho, saying: 2"Command the children of Israel that they give the Levites cities to dwell in from the inheritance of their possession, and you shall *also* give the Levites common-land around the cities. 3They shall have the cities to dwell in; and their common-land shall be for their cattle, for their herds, and for all their animals. 4The common-land of the cities which you will give the Levites *shall extend* from the wall of the city outward a thousand cubits all around. 5And you shall measure outside the city on the east side two thousand cubits, on the south side two thousand cubits, on the west side two thousand cubits, and on the north side two thousand cubits. The city *shall be* in the middle. This shall belong to them as common-land for the cities.

6"Now among the cities which you will give to the Levites *you shall appoint* six cities of refuge, to which a manslayer may flee. And to these you shall add forty-two cities. 7So all the cities you will give to the Levites *shall be* forty-eight; these *you shall give* with their common-land. 8And the cities which you will give *shall be* from the possession of the children of Israel; from the larger *tribe* you shall give many, from the smaller you shall give few. Each shall give some of its cities to the Levites, in proportion to the inheritance that each receives."

9Then the LORD spoke to Moses, saying, 10"Speak to the children of Israel, and say to them: 'When you cross the Jordan into the land of Canaan, 11then you shall appoint cities to be cities of refuge for you, that the manslayer who kills any person accidentally may flee there. 12They shall be cities of refuge for you from the avenger, that the manslayer may not die until he stands before the congregation in judgment. 13And of the cities which you give, you shall have six cities of refuge. 14You shall appoint three cities on this side of the Jordan, and three cities you shall appoint in the land of Canaan, *which* will be cities of refuge. 15These six cities shall be for refuge for the children of Israel, for the stranger, and for the sojourner among them, that anyone who kills a person accidentally may flee there.

16'But if he strikes him with an iron implement, so that he dies, he *is* a murderer; the murderer shall surely be put to death. 17And if he strikes him with a stone in the hand, by which one could die, and he does die, he *is* a murderer; the murderer shall surely be put to death. 18Or *if* he strikes him with a wooden hand weapon, by which one could die, and he does die, he *is* a murderer; the murderer shall surely be put to death. 19The avenger of blood himself shall put the murderer to death; when he meets him, he shall put him to death. 20If he pushes him out of hatred or, while lying in wait, hurls something at him so that he dies, 21or in enmity he strikes him with his hand so that he dies, the one who struck *him* shall surely be put to death. He *is* a murderer. The avenger of blood shall put the murderer to death when he meets him.

22'However, if he pushes him suddenly without enmity, or throws anything at him without lying in wait, 23or uses a stone, by which a man could die, throwing *it* at him without seeing *him,* so that he dies, while he was not his enemy or seeking his harm, 24then the congregation shall judge between the manslayer and the avenger of blood according to these judgments. 25So the congregation shall deliver the manslayer from the hand of the avenger of blood, and the congregation shall return him to the city of refuge where he had fled, and he shall remain there until the death of the high priest who was anointed with the holy oil. 26But if the manslayer at any time goes outside the limits of the city of refuge where he fled, 27and the avenger of blood finds him outside the limits of his city of refuge, and the avenger of blood kills the manslayer, he shall not be guilty of blood, 28because he should have remained in his city of refuge until the death of the high priest. But after the death of the high priest the manslayer may return to the land of his possession.

29'And these *things* shall be a statute of judgment to you throughout your generations in all your dwellings. 30Whoever kills a person, the murderer shall be put to death on the testimony of witnesses; but one witness is not *sufficient* testimony against a person for the

35:12 the avenger. The meaning of this term is "near of kin." It refers to the person chosen by a family to deal with a loss suffered in that family. Here the close relative of a homicide victim would seek to avenge his death, but not until proper judgment was made.

death *penalty.* 31 Moreover you shall take no
ransom for the life of a murderer who *is* guilty
of death, but he shall surely be put to death.
32 And you shall take no ransom for him who
has fled to his city of refuge, that he may
return to dwell in the land before the death of
the priest. 33 So you shall not pollute the land
where you *are;* for blood defiles the land, and
no atonement can be made for the land, for the
blood that is shed on it, except by the blood of
him who shed it. 34 Therefore do not defile the

35:33 blood defiles the land. Though murder and inadvertent killing polluted the land, murder was atoned for by the death of the murderer. Failure to observe these principles would make the land unclean. If the whole land became unclean, then the Lord would no longer be able to dwell in their midst.

land which you inhabit, in the midst of which
I dwell; for I the LORD dwell among the children of Israel.' "

36 Now the chief fathers of the families of
the children of Gilead the son of
Machir, the son of Manasseh, of the families
of the sons of Joseph, came near and spoke
before Moses and before the leaders, the chief
fathers of the children of Israel. 2 And they
said: "The LORD commanded my lord *Moses* to
give the land as an inheritance by lot to the
children of Israel, and my lord was commanded by the LORD to give the inheritance of our
brother Zelophehad to his daughters. 3 Now if
they are married to any of the sons of the *other*
tribes of the children of Israel, then their
inheritance will be taken from the inheritance
of our fathers, and it will be added to the inheritance of the tribe into which they marry; so it
will be taken from the lot of our inheritance.
4 And when the Jubilee of the children of Israel
comes, then their inheritance will be added to
the inheritance of the tribe into which they
marry; so their inheritance will be taken away
from the inheritance of the tribe of our
fathers."

5 Then Moses commanded the children of
Israel according to the word of the LORD, saying: "What the tribe of the sons of Joseph
speaks is right. 6 This *is* what the LORD commands concerning the daughters of Zelophehad, saying, 'Let them marry whom they think
best, but they may marry only within the family of their father's tribe.' 7 So the inheritance of
the children of Israel shall not change hands
from tribe to tribe, for every one of the children of Israel shall keep the inheritance of the
tribe of his fathers. 8 And every daughter who
possesses an inheritance in any tribe of the
children of Israel shall be the wife of one of
the family of her father's tribe, so that the children of Israel each may possess the inheritance of his fathers. 9 Thus no inheritance shall
change hands from *one* tribe to another, but
every tribe of the children of Israel shall keep
its own inheritance."

10 Just as the LORD commanded Moses, so
did the daughters of Zelophehad; 11 for
Mahlah, Tirzah, Hoglah, Milcah, and Noah,
the daughters of Zelophehad, were married to
the sons of their father's brothers. 12 They were
married into the families of the children of
Manasseh the son of Joseph, and their inheritance remained in the tribe of their father's
family.

13 These *are* the commandments and the judgments which the LORD commanded the children of Israel by the hand of Moses in the plains
of Moab by the Jordan, *across from* Jericho.

Psalm 35:17–28

17 Lord, how long will You look on?
Rescue me from their destructions,
My precious *life* from the lions.
18 I will give You thanks in the great
assembly;
I will praise You among many people.

19 Let them not rejoice over me who are
wrongfully my enemies;
Nor let them wink with the eye who
hate me without a cause.
20 For they do not speak peace,
But they devise deceitful matters
Against *the* quiet ones in the land.
21 They also opened their mouth wide
against me,
And said, "Aha, aha!
Our eyes have seen *it.*"
22 *This* You have seen, O LORD;
Do not keep silence.
O Lord, do not be far from me.

35:21,22 Our eyes have seen *it.* *This* you have seen, O LORD. What David's enemy allegedly saw, the Lord has seen perfectly. David knew that his God would vindicate him based upon the true evidence, all in his favor.

23 Stir up Yourself, and awake to my
vindication,
To my cause, my God and my Lord.
24 Vindicate me, O LORD my God,
according to Your righteousness;
And let them not rejoice over me.
25 Let them not say in their hearts, "Ah,
so we would have it!"
Let them not say, "We have swallowed
him up."

26 Let them be ashamed and brought to
mutual confusion
Who rejoice at my hurt;
Let them be clothed with shame and
dishonor
Who exalt themselves against me.
27 Let them shout for joy and be glad,
Who favor my righteous cause;
And let them say continually,
"Let the LORD be magnified,
Who has pleasure in the prosperity of
His servant."
28 And my tongue shall speak of Your
righteousness
And of Your praise all the day long.

Proverbs 12:3

3 A man is not established by
wickedness,
But the root of the righteous cannot
be moved.

Mark 15:25–47

25 Now it was the third hour, and they crucified
Him. 26 And the inscription of His accusation was
written above:

THE KING OF THE JEWS.

27 With Him they also crucified two robbers,
one on His right and the other on His left. 28 So
the Scripture was fulfilled which says, *"And
He was numbered with the transgressors."*
29 And those who passed by blasphemed
Him, wagging their heads and saying, "Aha!
You who destroy the temple and build *it* in
three days, 30 save Yourself, and come down
from the cross!"
31 Likewise the chief priests also, mocking
among themselves with the scribes, said, "He
saved others; Himself He cannot save. 32 Let
the Christ, the King of Israel, descend now
from the cross, that we may see and believe."
Even those who were crucified with Him
reviled Him.
33 Now when the sixth hour had come, there
was darkness over the whole land until the
ninth hour. 34 And at the ninth hour Jesus cried
out with a loud voice, saying, "Eloi, Eloi, lama
sabachthani?" which is translated, *"My God,
My God, why have You forsaken Me?"*
35 Some of those who stood by, when they
heard *that,* said, "Look, He is calling for Elijah!"
36 Then someone ran and filled a sponge full of
sour wine, put *it* on a reed, and offered *it* to Him
to drink, saying, "Let Him alone; let us see if
Elijah will come to take Him down."
37 And Jesus cried out with a loud voice, and
breathed His last.
38 Then the veil of the temple was torn in two
from top to bottom. 39 So when the centurion,
who stood opposite Him, saw that He cried out
like this and breathed His last, he said, "Truly
this Man was the Son of God!"
40 There were also women looking on from
afar, among whom were Mary Magdalene,
Mary the mother of James the Less and of
Joses, and Salome, 41 who also followed Him
and ministered to Him when He was in Galilee, and many other women who came up with
Him to Jerusalem.

15:26 inscription of His accusation. The crime for which a condemned man was executed was written on a wooden board, which was fastened to the cross above his head. Jesus' inscription was written in Latin, Hebrew, and Greek (John 19:20). **THE KING OF THE JEWS.** Since Pilate had repeatedly declared Jesus to be innocent of any crime (Luke 23:4,14,15,22), he ordered this inscription written for Him. While Pilate's intent was probably neither to mock nor honor Jesus, he certainly intended it as an affront to the Jewish authorities, who had given him so much trouble. When the outraged Jewish leaders demanded the wording be changed, Pilate bluntly refused (John 19:22). A comparison of all 4 Gospel accounts reveals that the full inscription read: THIS IS JESUS OF NAZARETH, THE KING OF THE JEWS.

15:38 the veil of the temple was torn in two. The massive curtain separating the Holy of Holies from the rest of the sanctuary (Ex. 26:31–33; 40:20,21; Lev. 16:2; Heb. 9:3). Its rending signified that the way into God's presence was open by the death of His Son.

[42]Now when evening had come, because it
was the Preparation Day, that is, the day
before the Sabbath, [43]Joseph of Arimathea, a
prominent council member, who was himself
waiting for the kingdom of God, coming and
taking courage, went in to Pilate and asked
for the body of Jesus. [44]Pilate marveled that
He was already dead; and summoning the
centurion, he asked him if He had been dead
for some time. [45]So when he found out from
the centurion, he granted the body to Joseph.
[46]Then he bought fine linen, took Him down,
and wrapped Him in the linen. And he laid
Him in a tomb which had been hewn out of
the rock, and rolled a stone against the door
of the tomb. [47]And Mary Magdalene and
Mary *the mother* of Joses observed where He
was laid.

DAY 19: What happened to Jesus after His death?

Joseph of Arimathea, a prominent member of the "council" (or the Sanhedrin), who had opposed Jesus' condemnation (Luke 23:51), took courage and came forward (Mark 15:43). Pilate would not likely have been pleased to see a member of the Sanhedrin, after that group had forced him to crucify an innocent man. Further, Joseph's public identification with Jesus would enrage the other members of the Sanhedrin. Nevertheless, he "asked for the body of Jesus."

"Pilate marveled" that Jesus was already dead (v. 44). Victims of crucifixion often lingered for days, hence Pilate's surprise that Jesus was dead after only 6 hours. Before granting Jesus' body to Joseph, Pilate checked with the "centurion" in charge of the crucifixion to verify that Jesus was really dead. Having received confirmation from the centurion that Jesus was dead, Pilate granted Jesus' body to Joseph (v. 45). By that act, the Romans officially pronounced Jesus dead.

Then Jesus' body was wrapped in the linen (v. 46). The Jews did not embalm corpses, but wrapped them in perfumed burial cloths. Nicodemus, another prominent member of the Sanhedrin (see John 7:50), assisted Joseph in caring for the body of Jesus (John 19:39,40). These men, who had kept their allegiance to Jesus secret during His lifetime, then came forward publicly to bury Him, while the disciples, who had openly followed Jesus, hid (John 20:19). Then they laid Jesus in a "tomb…hewn out of the rock." This "tomb" was located near Golgotha (John 19:42). Matthew adds that it was Joseph's own tomb (Matt. 27:60), while Luke and John note that no one as yet had been buried in it (Luke 23:53; John 19:41).

MARCH 20

Deuteronomy 1:1–2:37

1 These *are* the words which Moses spoke to
all Israel on this side of the Jordan in the
wilderness, in the plain opposite Suph,
between Paran, Tophel, Laban, Hazeroth, and
Dizahab. [2]*It is* eleven days' *journey* from Horeb
by way of Mount Seir to Kadesh Barnea. [3]Now
it came to pass in the fortieth year, in the
eleventh month, on the first *day* of the month,
that Moses spoke to the children of Israel
according to all that the LORD had given him as
commandments to them, [4]after he had killed
Sihon king of the Amorites, who dwelt in
Heshbon, and Og king of Bashan, who dwelt at
Ashtaroth in Edrei.
[5]On this side of the Jordan in the land of
Moab, Moses began to explain this law, saying,
[6]"The LORD our God spoke to us in Horeb, saying: 'You have dwelt long enough at this mountain. [7]Turn and take your journey, and go to the
mountains of the Amorites, to all the neighboring *places* in the plain, in the mountains and in
the lowland, in the South and on the seacoast,
to the land of the Canaanites and to Lebanon,
as far as the great river, the River Euphrates.
[8]See, I have set the land before you; go in and
possess the land which the LORD swore to
your fathers—to Abraham, Isaac, and Jacob—
to give to them and their descendants after
them.'
[9]"And I spoke to you at that time, saying: 'I
alone am not able to bear you. [10]The LORD your
God has multiplied you, and here you *are* today,
as the stars of heaven in multitude. [11]May the
LORD God of your fathers make you a thousand
times more numerous than you are, and bless
you as He has promised you! [12]How can I alone
bear your problems and your burdens and your
complaints? [13]Choose wise, understanding, and
knowledgeable men from among your tribes,
and I will make them heads over you.' [14]And
you answered me and said, 'The thing which
you have told *us* to do *is* good.' [15]So I took the
heads of your tribes, wise and knowledgeable
men, and made them heads over you, leaders
of thousands, leaders of hundreds, leaders of
fifties, leaders of tens, and officers for your
tribes.
[16]"Then I commanded your judges at that

1:7,8 the land. The land which the Lord set before Israel to go in and possess was clearly described here. The mountains of the Amorites referred to the hill country to the west of the Dead Sea. The plain (Arabah) was the land in the rift valley from the Sea of Galilee in the north to the Dead Sea in the south. The mountains were the hills that run through the center of the land north and south. These hills are to the west of the Sea of Galilee and the Jordan River. The lowland referred to the low rolling hills that sloped toward the Mediterranean coast (Shephelah). The south (Negev) described the dry wasteland stretching southward from Beersheba to the wilderness. The seacoast referred to the land along the Mediterranean Sea. The boundaries of the land of the Canaanites were given in Numbers 34:1–15. Lebanon to the north marked the northwestern boundary on the coast. The northeast boundary of the land was the Euphrates River. See Numbers 34:1–12.

1:10 the stars of heaven. The Lord had promised Abraham that his descendants would be as numerous as the stars in the sky (Gen. 15:5; 22:17). The nation's growth proved both God's intention and ability to fulfill His original promises to Abraham.

time, saying, 'Hear *the cases* between your
brethren, and judge righteously between a
man and his brother or the stranger who is
with him. [17]You shall not show partiality in
judgment; you shall hear the small as well as
the great; you shall not be afraid in any man's
presence, for the judgment *is* God's. The case
that is too hard for you, bring to me, and I will
hear it.' [18]And I commanded you at that time all
the things which you should do.
[19]"So we departed from Horeb, and went
through all that great and terrible wilderness
which you saw on the way to the mountains of
the Amorites, as the LORD our God had commanded us. Then we came to Kadesh Barnea.
[20]And I said to you, 'You have come to the
mountains of the Amorites, which the LORD
our God is giving us. [21]Look, the LORD your
God has set the land before you; go up *and*
possess *it,* as the LORD God of your fathers has
spoken to you; do not fear or be discouraged.'
[22]"And every one of you came near to me
and said, 'Let us send men before us, and let
them search out the land for us, and bring
back word to us of the way by which we should
go up, and of the cities into which we shall
come.'
[23]"The plan pleased me well; so I took twelve
of your men, one man from *each* tribe. [24]And
they departed and went up into the mountains, and came to the Valley of Eshcol, and
spied it out. [25]They also took *some* of the fruit
of the land in their hands and brought *it* down
to us; and they brought back word to us, saying, '*It is* a good land which the LORD our God
is giving us.'
[26]"Nevertheless you would not go up, but
rebelled against the command of the LORD
your God; [27]and you complained in your tents,
and said, 'Because the LORD hates us, He has
brought us out of the land of Egypt to deliver
us into the hand of the Amorites, to destroy
us. [28]Where can we go up? Our brethren have
discouraged our hearts, saying, "The people
are greater and taller than we; the cities *are*
great and fortified up to heaven; moreover we
have seen the sons of the Anakim there." '
[29]"Then I said to you, 'Do not be terrified, or
afraid of them. [30]The LORD your God, who goes
before you, He will fight for you, according to
all He did for you in Egypt before your eyes,
[31]and in the wilderness where you saw how the
LORD your God carried you, as a man carries
his son, in all the way that you went until you
came to this place.' [32]Yet, for all that, you did
not believe the LORD your God, [33]who went in
the way before you to search out a place for you
to pitch your tents, to show you the way you
should go, in the fire by night and in the cloud
by day.
[34]"And the LORD heard the sound of your
words, and was angry, and took an oath, saying, [35]'Surely not one of these men of this evil
generation shall see that good land of which I
swore to give to your fathers, [36]except Caleb
the son of Jephunneh; he shall see it, and to
him and his children I am giving the land on
which he walked, because he wholly followed
the LORD.' [37]The LORD was also angry with me
for your sakes, saying, 'Even you shall not go
in there. [38]Joshua the son of Nun, who stands
before you, he shall go in there. Encourage
him, for he shall cause Israel to inherit it.
[39]"Moreover your little ones and your children, who you say will be victims, who today
have no knowledge of good and evil, they shall
go in there; to them I will give it, and they
shall possess it. [40]But *as for* you, turn and take
your journey into the wilderness by the Way
of the Red Sea.'
[41]"Then you answered and said to me, 'We
have sinned against the LORD; we will go up and

fight, just as the LORD our God commanded us.' And when everyone of you had girded on his weapons of war, you were ready to go up into the mountain.

42"And the LORD said to me, 'Tell them, "Do not go up nor fight, for I *am* not among you; lest you be defeated before your enemies." ' 43So I spoke to you; yet you would not listen, but rebelled against the command of the LORD, and presumptuously went up into the mountain. 44And the Amorites who dwelt in that mountain came out against you and chased you as bees do, and drove you back from Seir to Hormah. 45Then you returned and wept before the LORD, but the LORD would not listen to your voice nor give ear to you.

46"So you remained in Kadesh many days, according to the days that you spent *there.*

2 "Then we turned and journeyed into the wilderness of the Way of the Red Sea, as the LORD spoke to me, and we skirted Mount Seir for many days.

2"And the LORD spoke to me, saying: 3'You have skirted this mountain long enough; turn northward. 4And command the people, saying, "You *are about to* pass through the territory of your brethren, the descendants of Esau, who live in Seir; and they will be afraid of you. Therefore watch yourselves carefully. 5Do not meddle with them, for I will not give you *any* of their land, no, not so much as one footstep, because I have given Mount Seir to Esau *as* a possession. 6You shall buy food from them with money, that you may eat; and you shall also buy water from them with money, that you may drink.

7"For the LORD your God has blessed you in all the work of your hand. He knows your trudging through this great wilderness. These forty years the LORD your God *has been* with you; you have lacked nothing." '

8"And when we passed beyond our brethren, the descendants of Esau who dwell in Seir, away from the road of the plain, away from Elath and Ezion Geber, we turned and passed by way of the Wilderness of Moab. 9Then the LORD said to me, 'Do not harass Moab, nor contend with them in battle, for I will not give you *any* of their land *as* a possession, because I have given Ar to the descendants of Lot *as* a possession.' "

10(The Emim had dwelt there in times past, a people as great and numerous and tall as the Anakim. 11They were also regarded as giants, like the Anakim, but the Moabites call them Emim. 12The Horites formerly dwelt in Seir, but the descendants of Esau dispossessed them and destroyed them from before them, and dwelt in their place, just as Israel did to the land of their possession which the LORD gave them.)

13" 'Now rise and cross over the Valley of the Zered.' So we crossed over the Valley of the Zered. 14And the time we took to come from Kadesh Barnea until we crossed over the Valley of the Zered *was* thirty-eight years, until all the generation of the men of war was consumed from the midst of the camp, just as the LORD had sworn to them. 15For indeed the hand of the LORD was against them, to destroy them from the midst of the camp until they were consumed.

16"So it was, when all the men of war had finally perished from among the people, 17that the LORD spoke to me, saying: 18'This day you are to cross over at Ar, the boundary of Moab. 19And *when* you come near the people of Ammon, do not harass them or meddle with them, for I will not give you *any* of the land of the people of Ammon *as* a possession, because I have given it to the descendants of Lot *as* a possession.' "

20(That was also regarded as a land of giants; giants formerly dwelt there. But the Ammonites call them Zamzummim, 21a people as great and numerous and tall as the Anakim. But the LORD destroyed them before them, and they dispossessed them and dwelt in their place, 22just as He had done for the descendants of Esau, who dwelt in Seir, when He destroyed the Horites from before them. They dispossessed them and dwelt in their place, even to this day. 23And the Avim, who dwelt in villages as far as Gaza—the Caphtorim, who came from Caphtor, destroyed them and dwelt in their place.)

24" 'Rise, take your journey, and cross over the River Arnon. Look, I have given into your hand Sihon the Amorite, king of Heshbon, and his land. Begin to possess *it,* and engage him in battle. 25This day I will begin to put the dread and fear of you upon the nations under the whole heaven, who shall hear the report of you, and shall tremble and be in anguish because of you.'

26"And I sent messengers from the Wilderness of Kedemoth to Sihon king of Heshbon, with words of peace, saying, 27'Let me pass through your land; I will keep strictly to the road, and I will turn neither to the right nor to the left. 28You shall sell me food for money, that I may eat, and give me water for money, that I may drink; only let me pass through on foot, 29just as the descendants of Esau who dwell in Seir and the Moabites who dwell in Ar did for me, until I cross the Jordan

to the land which the LORD our God is giving
us.'
30"But Sihon king of Heshbon would not let
us pass through, for the LORD your God hardened his spirit and made his heart obstinate,
that He might deliver him into your hand, as *it*
is this day.
31"And the LORD said to me, 'See, I have
begun to give Sihon and his land over to you.
Begin to possess *it,* that you may inherit his
land.' 32Then Sihon and all his people came out
against us to fight at Jahaz. 33And the LORD our
God delivered him over to us; so we defeated
him, his sons, and all his people. 34We took all
his cities at that time, and we utterly
destroyed the men, women, and little ones of
every city; we left none remaining. 35We took
only the livestock as plunder for ourselves,
with the spoil of the cities which we took.
36From Aroer, which *is* on the bank of the River
Arnon, and *from* the city that *is* in the ravine, as
far as Gilead, there was not one city too strong
for us; the LORD our God delivered all to us.
37Only you did not go near the land of the people of Ammon—anywhere along the River
Jabbok, or to the cities of the mountains, or
wherever the LORD our God had forbidden us.

Psalm 36:1–6

To the Chief Musician.
A Psalm of David the servant of the LORD.

An oracle within my heart concerning the
transgression of the wicked:
There is no fear of God before his eyes.
2 For he flatters himself in his own eyes,
When he finds out his iniquity *and*
when he hates.
3 The words of his mouth *are*
wickedness and deceit;
He has ceased to be wise *and* to do
good.
4 He devises wickedness on his bed;
He sets himself in a way *that is* not
good;
He does not abhor evil.

5 Your mercy, O LORD, *is* in
the heavens;
Your faithfulness *reaches* to the clouds.
6 Your righteousness *is* like the great
mountains;
Your judgments *are* a great deep;
O LORD, You preserve man
and beast.

Proverbs 12:4–6

4 An excellent wife *is* the crown of her
husband,
But she who causes shame *is* like
rottenness in his bones.

5 The thoughts of the righteous *are*
right,
But the counsels of the wicked *are*
deceitful.
6 The words of the wicked *are,* "Lie in
wait for blood,"
But the mouth of the upright will
deliver them.

Mark 16:1–20

16 Now when the Sabbath was past, Mary
Magdalene, Mary *the mother* of James,
and Salome bought spices, that they might
come and anoint Him. 2Very early in the morning, on the first *day* of the week, they came to
the tomb when the sun had risen. 3And they
said among themselves, "Who will roll away
the stone from the door of the tomb for us?"

16:3 Who will roll away the stone...? Only Mark records this discussion on the way to the tomb. The women realized they had no men with them to move the heavy stone (v. 4) away from the entrance to the tomb. Since they had last visited the tomb on Friday evening, they did not know it had been sealed and a guard posted, which took place on Saturday (Matt. 27:62–66).

16:4 the stone had been rolled away. This was not to let Jesus out, but to let the witnesses in. When the angel rolled away the stone (Matt. 28:2), the earthquake may have affected only the area around the tomb, since the women apparently did not feel it.

4But when they looked up, they saw that the
stone had been rolled away—for it was very
large. 5And entering the tomb, they saw a
young man clothed in a long white robe sitting
on the right side; and they were alarmed.
6But he said to them, "Do not be alarmed.
You seek Jesus of Nazareth, who was crucified. He is risen! He is not here. See the place
where they laid Him. 7But go, tell His disciples—and Peter—that He is going before you
into Galilee; there you will see Him, as He said
to you."
8So they went out quickly and fled from the
tomb, for they trembled and were amazed.
And they said nothing to anyone, for they
were afraid.

[9]Now when *He* rose early on the first *day* of the week, He appeared first to Mary Magdalene, out of whom He had cast seven demons. [10]She went and told those who had been with Him, as they mourned and wept. [11]And when they heard that He was alive and had been seen by her, they did not believe.

[12]After that, He appeared in another form to two of them as they walked and went into the country. [13]And they went and told *it* to the rest, *but* they did not believe them either.

[14]Later He appeared to the eleven as they sat at the table; and He rebuked their unbelief and hardness of heart, because they did not believe those who had seen Him after He had risen. [15]And He said to them, "Go into all the world and preach the gospel to every creature. [16]He who believes and is baptized will be saved; but he who does not believe will be condemned. [17]And these signs will follow those who believe: In My name they will cast out demons; they will speak with new tongues; [18]they will take up serpents; and if they drink anything deadly, it will by no means hurt them; they will lay hands on the sick, and they will recover."

[19]So then, after the Lord had spoken to them, He was received up into heaven, and sat down at the right hand of God. [20]And they went out and preached everywhere, the Lord working with *them* and confirming the word through the accompanying signs. Amen.

DAY 20: Were the last 12 verses of Mark 16 originally in the Gospel?

The external evidence strongly suggests these verses were not originally part of Mark's Gospel. While the majority of Greek manuscripts contain these verses, the earliest and most reliable do not. A shorter ending also existed, but it is not included in the text. Further, some that include the passage note that it was missing from older Greek manuscripts, while others have scribal marks indicating the passage was considered spurious. The fourth-century church fathers Eusebius and Jerome noted that almost all of the Greek manuscripts available to them lacked vv. 9–20.

The internal evidence from this passage also weighs heavily against Mark's authorship. The grammatical transition between vv. 8 and 9 is abrupt and awkward. The vocabulary in these verses does not match the rest of Mark. Even the events and people mentioned in these verses appear in awkward fashion. For example, Mary Magdalene is introduced as if she were a new person on the scene rather than someone Mark had mentioned three times (v. 1; 15:40,47). Clearly, Mark16:9–20 represents an early attempt to complete Mark's Gospel.

While for the most part summarizing truths taught elsewhere in Scripture, these verses should always be compared with the rest of Scripture, and no doctrines should be formulated based solely on them. Further, in spite of all these considerations of the likely unreliability of this section, it is possible to be wrong on the issue. It is good to consider the meaning of this passage and leave it in the text, just as with John 7:53–8:11.

MARCH 21

Deuteronomy 3:1–4:49

3 "Then we turned and went up the road to Bashan; and Og king of Bashan came out against us, he and all his people, to battle at Edrei. [2]And the LORD said to me, 'Do not fear him, for I have delivered him and all his people and his land into your hand; you shall do to him as you did to Sihon king of the Amorites, who dwelt at Heshbon.'

[3]"So the LORD our God also delivered into our hands Og king of Bashan, with all his people, and we attacked him until he had no survivors remaining. [4]And we took all his cities at that time; there was not a city which we did not take from them: sixty cities, all the region of Argob, the kingdom of Og in Bashan. [5]All these cities *were* fortified with high walls, gates, and bars, besides a great many rural towns. [6]And we utterly destroyed them, as we did to Sihon king of Heshbon, utterly destroying the men, women, and children of every city. [7]But all the livestock and the spoil of the cities we took as booty for ourselves.

[8]"And at that time we took the land from the hand of the two kings of the Amorites who *were* on this side of the Jordan, from the River Arnon to Mount Hermon [9](the Sidonians call Hermon Sirion, and the Amorites call it Senir), [10]all the cities of the plain, all Gilead, and all Bashan, as far as Salcah and Edrei, cities of the kingdom of Og in Bashan.

[11]"For only Og king of Bashan remained of the remnant of the giants. Indeed his bedstead *was* an iron bedstead. (*Is* it not in Rabbah of the people of Ammon?) Nine cubits *is* its length and

3:11 an iron bedstead. The bedstead may actually have been a coffin, which would have been large enough to also hold tomb objects. The size of the "bedstead," 13.5 by 6 feet, emphasized the largeness of Og, who was a giant (the last of the Rephaim, a race of giants). As God had given Israel victory over the giant Og, so He would give them victory over the giants in the land.

four cubits its width, according to the standard
cubit.
12"And this land, *which* we possessed at that
time, from Aroer, which *is* by the River Arnon,
and half the mountains of Gilead and its cities, I
gave to the Reubenites and the Gadites. 13The
rest of Gilead, and all Bashan, the kingdom of
Og, I gave to half the tribe of Manasseh. (All
the region of Argob, with all Bashan, was
called the land of the giants. 14Jair the son of
Manasseh took all the region of Argob, as far
as the border of the Geshurites and the
Maachathites, and called Bashan after his own
name, Havoth Jair, to this day.)
15"Also I gave Gilead to Machir. 16And to the
Reubenites and the Gadites I gave from Gilead
as far as the River Arnon, the middle of the
river as *the* border, as far as the River Jabbok,
the border of the people of Ammon; 17the plain
also, with the Jordan as *the* border, from
Chinnereth as far as the east side of the Sea of
the Arabah (the Salt Sea), below the slopes of
Pisgah.
18"Then I commanded you at that time, saying: 'The LORD your God has given you this
land to possess. All you men of valor shall
cross over armed before your brethren, the
children of Israel. 19But your wives, your little
ones, and your livestock (I know that you have
much livestock) shall stay in your cities which
I have given you, 20until the LORD has given
rest to your brethren as to you, and they also
possess the land which the LORD your God is
giving them beyond the Jordan. Then each of
you may return to his possession which I have
given you.'
21"And I commanded Joshua at that time,
saying, 'Your eyes have seen all that the LORD
your God has done to these two kings; so will
the LORD do to all the kingdoms through
which you pass. 22You must not fear them, for
the LORD your God Himself fights for you.'
23"Then I pleaded with the LORD at that time,
saying: 24'O Lord GOD, You have begun to
show Your servant Your greatness and Your
mighty hand, for what god *is there* in heaven
or on earth who can do *anything* like Your
works and Your mighty *deeds?* 25I pray, let me
cross over and see the good land beyond the
Jordan, those pleasant mountains, and Lebanon.'
26"But the LORD was angry with me on your
account, and would not listen to me. So the
LORD said to me: 'Enough of that! Speak no
more to Me of this matter. 27Go up to the top of
Pisgah, and lift your eyes toward the west, the
north, the south, and the east; behold *it* with
your eyes, for you shall not cross over this Jordan. 28But command Joshua, and encourage
him and strengthen him; for he shall go over
before this people, and he shall cause them to
inherit the land which you will see.'
29"So we stayed in the valley opposite Beth
Peor.
4 "Now, O Israel, listen to the statutes and
the judgments which I teach you to
observe, that you may live, and go in and possess the land which the LORD God of your
fathers is giving you. 2You shall not add to the
word which I command you, nor take from it,
that you may keep the commandments of the
LORD your God which I command you. 3Your

4:2 You shall not add...nor take from. The word that God had given to Israel through Moses was complete and sufficient to direct the people. Thus, this Law, the gift of God at Horeb, could not be supplemented or reduced. Anything that adulterated or contradicted God's law would not be tolerated (see 12:32; Prov. 30:6; Rev. 22:18,19).

eyes have seen what the LORD did at Baal
Peor; for the LORD your God has destroyed
from among you all the men who followed
Baal of Peor. 4But you who held fast to the
LORD your God *are* alive today, every one of
you.
5"Surely I have taught you statutes and judgments, just as the LORD my God commanded
me, that you should act according *to them* in
the land which you go to possess. 6Therefore
be careful to observe *them;* for this *is* your wisdom and your understanding in the sight of
the peoples who will hear all these statutes,
and say, 'Surely this great nation *is* a wise and
understanding people.'
7"For what great nation *is there* that has God
so near to it, as the LORD our God *is* to us, for

whatever *reason* we may call upon Him? 8And
what great nation *is there* that has *such* statutes
and righteous judgments as are in all this law
which I set before you this day? 9Only take
heed to yourself, and diligently keep yourself,
lest you forget the things your eyes have seen,
and lest they depart from your heart all the
days of your life. And teach them to your children and your grandchildren, 10*especially concerning* the day you stood before the LORD
your God in Horeb, when the LORD said to me,
'Gather the people to Me, and I will let them
hear My words, that they may learn to fear Me
all the days they live on the earth, and *that*
they may teach their children.'

11"Then you came near and stood at the foot
of the mountain, and the mountain burned
with fire to the midst of heaven, with darkness,
cloud, and thick darkness. 12And the LORD
spoke to you out of the midst of the fire. You
heard the sound of the words, but saw no
form; *you* only *heard* a voice. 13So He declared
to you His covenant which He commanded you
to perform, the Ten Commandments; and He
wrote them on two tablets of stone. 14And the
LORD commanded me at that time to teach you
statutes and judgments, that you might observe them in the land which you cross over
to possess.

15"Take careful heed to yourselves, for you
saw no form when the LORD spoke to you at
Horeb out of the midst of the fire, 16lest you act
corruptly and make for yourselves a carved
image in the form of any figure: the likeness of
male or female, 17the likeness of any animal
that *is* on the earth or the likeness of any
winged bird that flies in the air, 18the likeness
of anything that creeps on the ground or the
likeness of any fish that *is* in the water beneath
the earth. 19And *take heed,* lest you lift your
eyes to heaven, and *when* you see the sun, the
moon, and the stars, all the host of heaven,
you feel driven to worship them and serve
them, which the LORD your God has given to
all the peoples under the whole heaven as a
heritage. 20But the LORD has taken you and
brought you out of the iron furnace, out of
Egypt, to be His people, an inheritance, as you
are this day. 21Furthermore the LORD was
angry with me for your sakes, and swore that
I would not cross over the Jordan, and that I
would not enter the good land which the LORD
your God is giving you as an inheritance. 22But
I must die in this land, I must not cross over
the Jordan; but you shall cross over and possess that good land. 23Take heed to yourselves,
lest you forget the covenant of the LORD your
God which He made with you, and make for
yourselves a carved image in the form of anything which the LORD your God has forbidden
you. 24For the LORD your God *is* a consuming
fire, a jealous God.

25"When you beget children and grandchildren and have grown old in the land, and act
corruptly and make a carved image in the
form of anything, and do evil in the sight of the
LORD your God to provoke Him to anger, 26I
call heaven and earth to witness against you
this day, that you will soon utterly perish from
the land which you cross over the Jordan to
possess; you will not prolong *your* days in it, but
will be utterly destroyed. 27And the LORD will
scatter you among the peoples, and you will be
left few in number among the nations where
the LORD will drive you. 28And there you will
serve gods, the work of men's hands, wood and
stone, which neither see nor hear nor eat nor
smell. 29But from there you will seek the LORD
your God, and you will find *Him* if you seek
Him with all your heart and with all your soul.
30When you are in distress, and all these
things come upon you in the latter days, when
you turn to the LORD your God and obey His
voice 31(for the LORD your God *is* a merciful
God), He will not forsake you nor destroy you,
nor forget the covenant of your fathers which
He swore to them.

32"For ask now concerning the days that are
past, which were before you, since the day
that God created man on the earth, and *ask*
from one end of heaven to the other, whether
any great *thing* like this has happened, or *anything* like it has been heard. 33Did *any* people
ever hear the voice of God speaking out of the
midst of the fire, as you have heard, and live?
34Or did God *ever* try to go *and* take for
Himself a nation from the midst of *another*
nation, by trials, by signs, by wonders, by war,
by a mighty hand and an outstretched arm,
and by great terrors, according to all that the
LORD your God did for you in Egypt before
your eyes? 35To you it was shown, that you
might know that the LORD Himself *is* God;
there is none other besides Him. 36Out of heav-
en He let you hear His voice, that He might
instruct you; on earth He showed you His
great fire, and you heard His words out of the
midst of the fire. 37And because He loved your
fathers, therefore He chose their descendants
after them; and He brought you out of Egypt
with His Presence, with His mighty power,
38driving out from before you nations greater
and mightier than you, to bring you in, to give
you their land *as* an inheritance, as *it is* this
day. 39Therefore know this day, and consider *it*
in your heart, that the LORD Himself *is* God in

heaven above and on the earth beneath; *there*
is no other. 40You shall therefore keep His
statutes and His commandments which I command you today, that it may go well with you
and with your children after you, and that you
may prolong *your* days in the land which the
LORD your God is giving you for all time."
41Then Moses set apart three cities on this
side of the Jordan, toward the rising of the
sun, 42that the manslayer might flee there, who
kills his neighbor unintentionally, without having hated him in time past, and that by fleeing
to one of these cities he might live: 43Bezer in
the wilderness on the plateau for the
Reubenites, Ramoth in Gilead for the Gadites,
and Golan in Bashan for the Manassites.
44Now this *is* the law which Moses set
before the children of Israel. 45These *are* the
testimonies, the statutes, and the judgments
which Moses spoke to the children of Israel
after they came out of Egypt, 46on this side of
the Jordan, in the valley opposite Beth Peor, in
the land of Sihon king of the Amorites, who
dwelt at Heshbon, whom Moses and the children of Israel defeated after they came out of
Egypt. 47And they took possession of his land
and the land of Og king of Bashan, two kings
of the Amorites, who *were* on this side of the
Jordan, toward the rising of the sun, 48from
Aroer, which *is* on the bank of the River
Arnon, even to Mount Sion (that is, Hermon),
49and all the plain on the east side of the Jordan
as far as the Sea of the Arabah, below the
slopes of Pisgah.

Psalm 36:7–12

7 How precious *is* Your lovingkindness,
O God!
Therefore the children of men put
their trust under the shadow of
Your wings.
8 They are abundantly satisfied with the
fullness of Your house,
And You give them drink from the
river of Your pleasures.
9 For with You *is* the fountain
of life;
In Your light we see light.
10 Oh, continue Your lovingkindness to
those who know You,
And Your righteousness to the upright
in heart.
11 Let not the foot of pride come against
me,
And let not the hand of the wicked
drive me away.
12 There the workers of iniquity have
fallen;
They have been cast down and are not
able to rise.

Proverbs 12:7

7 The wicked are overthrown and *are* no
more,
But the house of the righteous will stand.

Luke 1:1–20

1 Inasmuch as many have taken in hand to set
in order a narrative of those things which
have been fulfilled among us, 2just as those

1:1 many. Although Luke wrote direct divine revelation inspired by the Holy Spirit, he acknowledged the works of others who had set down in writing events from Christ's life. All those sources have been long lost, except for the inspired Gospels. Since Matthew and Mark were most likely written before Luke, it has been suggested that either one or both of those may have been among Luke's sources when he did his research. It is also known that he was personally acquainted with many first-hand witnesses to the events of Christ's life. And it is possible that some of his sources were word-of-mouth reports. About 60 percent of the material in Mark is repeated in Luke, and Luke seems to follow Mark's order of events closely. **to set in order.** Luke proposed to narrate the ministry of Christ in an authoritative, logical, and factual order. **those things which have been fulfilled.** I.e., the Old Testament messianic promises fulfilled in Christ. **among us.** I.e., in our generation. This phrase does not mean Luke was personally an eyewitness to the life of Christ.

who from the beginning were eyewitnesses
and ministers of the word delivered them to
us, 3it seemed good to me also, having had
perfect understanding of all things from the
very first, to write to you an orderly account,
most excellent Theophilus, 4that you may
know the certainty of those things in which
you were instructed.
5There was in the days of Herod, the king of
Judea, a certain priest named Zacharias, of the
division of Abijah. His wife *was* of the daughters of Aaron, and her name *was* Elizabeth.
6And they were both righteous before God,
walking in all the commandments and ordinances of the Lord blameless. 7But they had no
child, because Elizabeth was barren, and they
were both well advanced in years.

[8]So it was, that while he was serving as
priest before God in the order of his division,
[9]according to the custom of the priesthood, his
lot fell to burn incense when he went into the
temple of the Lord. [10]And the whole multitude
of the people was praying outside at the hour
of incense. [11]Then an angel of the Lord
appeared to him, standing on the right side of
the altar of incense. [12]And when Zacharias saw
him, he was troubled, and fear fell upon him.
[13]But the angel said to him, "Do not be
afraid, Zacharias, for your prayer is heard; and
your wife Elizabeth will bear you a son, and
you shall call his name John. [14]And you will
have joy and gladness, and many will rejoice at
his birth. [15]For he will be great in the sight of
the Lord, and shall drink neither wine nor
strong drink. He will also be filled with the
Holy Spirit, even from his mother's womb.
[16]And he will turn many of the children of Israel to the Lord their God. [17]He will also go
before Him in the spirit and power of Elijah, *'to
turn the hearts of the fathers to the children,'*
and the disobedient to the wisdom of the just,
to make ready a people prepared for the
Lord."
[18]And Zacharias said to the angel, "How
shall I know this? For I am an old man, and my
wife is well advanced in years."
[19]And the angel answered and said to him, "I
am Gabriel, who stands in the presence of
God, and was sent to speak to you and bring
you these glad tidings. [20]But behold, you will
be mute and not able to speak until the day
these things take place, because you did not
believe my words which will be fulfilled in
their own time."

1:19 Gabriel. Literally, "strong man of God." Gabriel also appears in Daniel 8:16; 9:21. He is one of only two holy angels whose names are given in Scripture, the other being Michael (Dan. 10:13,21; Jude 9; Rev. 12:7).

Day 21: Who was the writer Luke?

According to tradition, Luke was a Gentile. The apostle Paul seems to confirm this, distinguishing Luke from those who were "of the circumcision" (Col. 4:11,14). That would make Luke the only Gentile to pen any books of Scripture. He is responsible for a significant portion of the New Testament, having written both this Gospel and the Book of Acts.

Very little is known about Luke. He almost never included personal details about himself, and nothing definite is known about his background or his conversion. Both Eusebius and Jerome identified him as a native of Antioch (which may explain why so much of the Book of Acts centers on Antioch—see Acts 11:19–27; 13:1–3; 14:26; 15:22,23,30–35; 18:22,23). Luke was a frequent companion of the apostle Paul, at least from the time of Paul's Macedonian vision (Acts 16:9,10) right up to the time of Paul's martyrdom (2 Tim. 4:11).

The apostle Paul referred to Luke as a physician (Col. 4:14). Luke's interest in medical phenomena is evident in the high profile he gave to Jesus' healing ministry (e.g., 4:38–40; 5:15–25; 6:17–19; 7:11–15; 8:43–47, 49–56; 9:2,6,11; 13:11–13; 14:2–4; 17:12–14; 22:50,51). In Luke's day, physicians did not have a unique vocabulary of technical terminology; so when Luke discusses healings and other medical issues, his language is not markedly different from that of the other Gospel writers.

MARCH 22

Deuteronomy 5:1–6:25

5 And Moses called all Israel, and said to
them: "Hear, O Israel, the statutes and
judgments which I speak in your hearing
today, that you may learn them and be careful
to observe them. [2]The LORD our God made a
covenant with us in Horeb. [3]The LORD did not
make this covenant with our fathers, but with
us, those who *are* here today, all of us who *are*
alive. [4]The LORD talked with you face to face on
the mountain from the midst of the fire. [5]I
stood between the LORD and you at that time,
to declare to you the word of the LORD; for you
were afraid because of the fire, and you did
not go up the mountain. *He* said:

[6] 'I *am* the LORD your God who brought
you out of the land of Egypt, out of
the house of bondage.
[7] 'You shall have no other gods before Me.
[8] 'You shall not make for yourself a
carved image—any likeness *of
anything* that *is* in heaven above,
or that *is* in the earth beneath, or
that *is* in the water under the
earth; [9]you shall not bow down to
them nor serve them. For I, the

LORD your God, *am* a jealous God,
visiting the iniquity of the fathers
upon the children to the third and
fourth *generations* of those who
hate Me, [10]but showing mercy to
thousands, to those who love Me
and keep My commandments.

11 'You shall not take the name of the
LORD your God in vain, for the
LORD will not hold *him* guiltless
who takes His name in vain.

12 'Observe the Sabbath day, to keep it
holy, as the LORD your God
commanded you. [13]Six days you
shall labor and do all your work,
[14]but the seventh day *is* the Sabbath of the LORD your God. *In it*
you shall do no work: you, nor
your son, nor your daughter, nor
your male servant, nor your female
servant, nor your ox, nor your
donkey, nor any of your cattle, nor
your stranger who *is* within your
gates, that your male servant and
your female servant may rest as
well as you. [15]And remember that
you were a slave in the land of
Egypt, and the LORD your God
brought you out from there by a
mighty hand and by an outstretched arm; therefore the LORD
your God commanded you to keep
the Sabbath day.

16 'Honor your father and your mother, as
the LORD your God has com-
manded you, that your days may
be long, and that it may be well
with you in the land which the
LORD your God is giving you.

17 'You shall not murder.

18 'You shall not commit adultery.

19 'You shall not steal.

20 'You shall not bear false witness against
your neighbor.

21 'You shall not covet your neighbor's
wife; and you shall not desire your
neighbor's house, his field, his
male servant, his female servant,
his ox, his donkey, or anything
that *is* your neighbor's.'

[22]"These words the LORD spoke to all your
assembly, in the mountain from the midst of
the fire, the cloud, and the thick darkness,
with a loud voice; and He added no more. And
He wrote them on two tablets of stone and
gave them to me.

[23]"So it was, when you heard the voice from
the midst of the darkness, while the mountain
was burning with fire, that you came near to
me, all the heads of your tribes and your elders. [24]And you said: 'Surely the LORD our God
has shown us His glory and His greatness,
and we have heard His voice from the midst of
the fire. We have seen this day that God
speaks with man; yet he *still* lives. [25]Now therefore, why should we die? For this great fire
will consume us; if we hear the voice of the
LORD our God anymore, then we shall die.
[26]For who *is there* of all flesh who has heard
the voice of the living God speaking from the
midst of the fire, as we *have,* and lived? [27]You
go near and hear all that the LORD our God
may say, and tell us all that the LORD our God
says to you, and we will hear and do *it.*'

[28]"Then the LORD heard the voice of your
words when you spoke to me, and the LORD said
to me: 'I have heard the voice of the words of
this people which they have spoken to you.
They are right *in* all that they have spoken.
[29]Oh, that they had such a heart in them that
they would fear Me and always keep all My
commandments, that it might be well with them
and with their children forever! [30]Go and say to
them, "Return to your tents." [31]But as for you,
stand here by Me, and I will speak to you all the
commandments, the statutes, and the judgments which you shall teach them, that they
may observe *them* in the land which I am giving
them to possess.'

[32]"Therefore you shall be careful to do as the
LORD your God has commanded you; you shall
not turn aside to the right hand or to the left.
[33]You shall walk in all the ways which the LORD
your God has commanded you, that you may live
and *that it may be* well with you, and *that* you may
prolong *your* days in the land which you shall
possess.

6 "Now this *is* the commandment, *and these
are* the statutes and judgments which the
LORD your God has commanded to teach you,

5:22 and He added no more. These Ten Commandments alone were identified as direct quotations by God. The rest of the stipulations of the covenant were given to Moses, who in turn gave them to the Israelites. These basic rules, which reflect God's character, continue to be a means by which God reveals the sinful deeds of the flesh (see Rom. 7:7–14; Gal. 3:19–24; 5:13–26). They are also a holy standard for conduct that the saved live by through the Spirit's power, with the exception of keeping the Sabbath (see Col. 2:16,17).

that you may observe *them* in the land which you are crossing over to possess, 2that you may fear the LORD your God, to keep all His statutes and His commandments which I command you, you and your son and your grandson, all the days of your life, and that your days may be prolonged. 3Therefore hear, O Israel, and be careful to observe *it,* that it may be well with you, and that you may multiply greatly as the LORD God of your fathers has promised you—'a land flowing with milk and honey.'

4"Hear, O Israel: The LORD our God, the LORD *is* one! 5You shall love the LORD your God with all your heart, with all your soul, and with all your strength.

6"And these words which I command you today shall be in your heart. 7You shall teach them diligently to your children, and shall talk of them when you sit in your house, when you walk by the way, when you lie down, and when you rise up. 8You shall bind them as a sign on your hand, and they shall be as frontlets between your eyes. 9You shall write them on the doorposts of your house and on your gates.

10"So it shall be, when the LORD your God brings you into the land of which He swore to your fathers, to Abraham, Isaac, and Jacob, to give you large and beautiful cities which you did not build, 11houses full of all good things, which you did not fill, hewn-out wells which you did not dig, vineyards and olive trees which you did not plant—when you have eaten and are full— 12*then* beware, lest you forget the LORD who brought you out of the land of Egypt, from the house of bondage. 13You shall fear the LORD your God and serve Him, and shall take oaths in His name. 14You shall not go after other gods, the gods of the peoples who *are* all around you 15(for the LORD your God *is* a jealous God among you), lest the anger of the LORD your God be aroused against you and destroy you from the face of the earth.

16"You shall not tempt the LORD your God as you tempted *Him* in Massah. 17You shall diligently keep the commandments of the LORD your God, His testimonies, and His statutes which He has commanded you. 18And you shall do *what is* right and good in the sight of the LORD, that it may be well with you, and that you may go in and possess the good land of which the LORD swore to your fathers, 19to cast out all your enemies from before you, as the LORD has spoken.

20"When your son asks you in time to come, saying, 'What *is the meaning of* the testimonies, the statutes, and the judgments which the LORD our God has commanded you?' 21then you shall say to your son: 'We were slaves of Pharaoh in Egypt, and the LORD brought us out of Egypt with a mighty hand; 22and the LORD showed signs and wonders before our eyes, great and severe, against Egypt, Pharaoh, and all his household. 23Then He brought us out from there, that He might bring us in, to give us the land of which He swore to our fathers. 24And the LORD commanded us to observe all these statutes, to fear the LORD our God, for our good always, that He might preserve us alive, as *it is* this day. 25Then it will be righteousness for us, if we are careful to observe all these commandments before the LORD our God, as He has commanded us.'

Psalm 37:1–4

A Psalm of David.

Do not fret because of evildoers,
Nor be envious of the workers
of iniquity.
2 For they shall soon be cut down like
the grass,
And wither as the green herb.

3 Trust in the LORD, and do good;
Dwell in the land, and feed on His
faithfulness.
4 Delight yourself also in the LORD,
And He shall give you the desires of
your heart.

Proverbs 12:8

8 A man will be commended according
to his wisdom,
But he who is of a perverse heart will
be despised.

Luke 1:21–38

21And the people waited for Zacharias, and marveled that he lingered so long in the temple. 22But when he came out, he could not speak to them; and they perceived that he had seen a vision in the temple, for he beckoned to them and remained speechless.

23So it was, as soon as the days of his service were completed, that he departed to his own house. 24Now after those days his wife Elizabeth conceived; and she hid herself five months, saying, 25"Thus the Lord has dealt with me, in the days when He looked on *me,* to take away my reproach among people."

26Now in the sixth month the angel Gabriel was sent by God to a city of Galilee named Nazareth, 27to a virgin betrothed to a man whose name was Joseph, of the house of David. The virgin's name *was* Mary. 28And having come in, the angel said to her, "Rejoice, highly

1:27 a virgin. The importance of the virgin birth cannot be overstated. A right view of the incarnation hinges on the truth that Jesus was born of a virgin. Both Luke and Matthew expressly state that Mary was a virgin when Jesus was conceived (Matt. 1:23). The Holy Spirit wrought the conception through supernatural means (v. 35; Matt. 1:18). The nature of Christ's conception testifies of both His deity and His sinlessness.

1:34 I do not know a man. I.e., conjugally. Mary understood that the angel was speaking of an immediate conception, and she and Joseph were still in the midst of the long betrothal or engagement period (Matt. 1:18), before the actual marriage and consummation. Her question was born out of wonder, not doubt, nor disbelief, so the angel did not rebuke her as he had Zacharias (v. 20).

1:38 Let it be to me according to your word. Mary was in an extremely embarrassing and difficult position. Betrothed to Joseph, she faced the stigma of unwed motherhood. Joseph would obviously have known that the child was not his. She knew she would be accused of adultery—an offense punishable by stoning (Deut. 22:13–21; see John 8:3–5). Yet she willingly and graciously submitted to the will of God.

favored *one,* the Lord *is* with you; blessed *are*
you among women!"
29 But when she saw *him,* she was troubled at
his saying, and considered what manner of
greeting this was. 30 Then the angel said to her,
"Do not be afraid, Mary, for you have found favor with God.
31 And behold, you will conceive
in your womb and bring forth a Son, and shall
call His name JESUS. 32 He will be great, and will
be called the Son of the Highest; and the Lord
God will give Him the throne of His father David.
33 And He will reign over the house of Jacob forever, and of His kingdom there will be
no end."
34 Then Mary said to the angel, "How can
this be, since I do not know a man?"
35 And the angel answered and said to her,
"*The* Holy Spirit will come upon you, and the
power of the Highest will overshadow you;
therefore, also, that Holy One who is to be
born will be called the Son of God. 36 Now
indeed, Elizabeth your relative has also conceived a son in her old age; and this is now the
sixth month for her who was called barren.
37 For with God nothing will be impossible."
38 Then Mary said, "Behold the maidservant
of the Lord! Let it be to me according to your
word." And the angel departed from her.

DAY 22: What was the greatest of God's commandments?

Deuteronomy 6:4–9, known as the *Shema* (Hebrew for "hear"), has become the Jewish confession of faith, recited twice daily by the devout, along with 11:13–21 and Numbers 15:37–41. "Hear, O Israel: The LORD…LORD is one!" (v. 4). The intent of these words was to give a clear statement of the truth of monotheism, that there is only one God. Thus, it has also been translated "The LORD is our God, the LORD alone." The word used for "one" in this passage does not mean "singleness," but "unity." The same word is used in Genesis 2:24, where the husband and wife were said to be "one flesh." Thus, while this verse was intended as a clear and concise statement of monotheism, it does not exclude the concept of the Trinity.

"You shall love the LORD your God with all your heart, with all your soul, and with all your strength" (v. 5). First in the list of all that was essential for the Jew was an unreserved, wholehearted commitment expressed in love to God. Since this relationship of love for God could not be represented in any material way as with idols, it had to be demonstrated in obedience to God's law in daily life. See 11:16–21; Matthew 22:37; Luke 10:27.

"These words…in your heart" (v. 6). The people were to think about these commandments and meditate on them so that obedience would not be a matter of formal legalism, but a response based upon understanding. The law written upon the heart would be an essential characteristic of the later New Covenant (Jer. 31:33). And "teach them diligently to your children" (v. 7). The commandments were to be the subject of conversation, both inside and outside the home, from the beginning of the day to its end.

MARCH 23

Deuteronomy 7:1–8:20

7 "When the LORD your God brings you into
the land which you go to possess, and has
cast out many nations before you, the Hittites
and the Girgashites and the Amorites and
the Canaanites and the Perizzites and the
Hivites and the Jebusites, seven nations
greater and mightier than you, [2]and when the
LORD your God delivers them over to you, you
shall conquer them *and* utterly destroy them.

7:2 utterly destroy them. All the men, women, and children were to be put to death. Even though this action seems extreme, the following needs to be kept in mind: 1) the Canaanites deserved to die for their sin (9:4,5; see Gen. 15:16); 2) the Canaanites persisted in their hatred of God (7:10); and 3) the Canaanites constituted a moral cancer that had the potential of introducing idolatry and immorality which would spread rapidly among the Israelites (20:17,18).

You shall make no covenant with them nor
show mercy to them. [3]Nor shall you make marriages with them. You shall not give your
daughter to their son, nor take their daughter
for your son. [4]For they will turn your sons away
from following Me, to serve other gods; so the
anger of the LORD will be aroused against you
and destroy you suddenly. [5]But thus you shall
deal with them: you shall destroy their altars,
and break down their *sacred* pillars, and cut
down their wooden images, and burn their
carved images with fire.
[6]"For you *are* a holy people to the LORD your
God; the LORD your God has chosen you to be

7:6 a holy people to the LORD your God. The basis for the command to destroy the Canaanites is found in God's election of Israel. God had set apart Israel for His own special use, and they were His treasured possession. As God's people, Israel needed to be separated from the moral pollution of the Canaanites.

a people for Himself, a special treasure above
all the peoples on the face of the earth. [7]The
LORD did not set His love on you nor choose
you because you were more in number than
any other people, for you were the least of all
peoples; [8]but because the LORD loves you, and
because He would keep the oath which He
swore to your fathers, the LORD has brought
you out with a mighty hand, and redeemed
you from the house of bondage, from the hand
of Pharaoh king of Egypt.
[9]"Therefore know that the LORD your God,
He *is* God, the faithful God who keeps
covenant and mercy for a thousand generations with those who love Him and keep His
commandments; [10]and He repays those who
hate Him to their face, to destroy them. He will
not be slack with him who hates Him; He will
repay him to his face. [11]Therefore you shall
keep the commandment, the statutes, and the
judgments which I command you today, to
observe them.
[12]"Then it shall come to pass, because you
listen to these judgments, and keep and do
them, that the LORD your God will keep with
you the covenant and the mercy which He
swore to your fathers. [13]And He will love you
and bless you and multiply you; He will also
bless the fruit of your womb and the fruit of
your land, your grain and your new wine and
your oil, the increase of your cattle and the
offspring of your flock, in the land of which He
swore to your fathers to give you. [14]You shall
be blessed above all peoples; there shall not
be a male or female barren among you or
among your livestock. [15]And the LORD will take
away from you all sickness, and will afflict you
with none of the terrible diseases of Egypt
which you have known, but will lay *them* on all
those who hate you. [16]Also you shall destroy
all the peoples whom the LORD your God delivers over to you; your eye shall have no pity on
them; nor shall you serve their gods, for that
will be a snare to you.
[17]"If you should say in your heart, 'These
nations are greater than I; how can I dispossess them?'— [18]you shall not be afraid of them,
but you shall remember well what the LORD
your God did to Pharaoh and to all Egypt: [19]the
great trials which your eyes saw, the signs and
the wonders, the mighty hand and the outstretched arm, by which the LORD your God
brought you out. So shall the LORD your God
do to all the peoples of whom you are afraid.
[20]Moreover the LORD your God will send the
hornet among them until those who are left,
who hide themselves from you, are destroyed.
[21]You shall not be terrified of them; for the

LORD your God, the great and awesome God,
is among you. [22]And the LORD your God will
drive out those nations before you little by little; you will be unable to destroy them at once,
lest the beasts of the field become *too* numerous for you. [23]But the LORD your God will deliver them over to you, and will inflict defeat
upon them until they are destroyed. [24]And He
will deliver their kings into your hand, and you
will destroy their name from under heaven; no
one shall be able to stand against you until you
have destroyed them. [25]You shall burn the
carved images of their gods with fire; you shall
not covet the silver or gold *that is* on them, nor
take *it* for yourselves, lest you be snared by it;
for it *is* an abomination to the LORD your God.
[26]Nor shall you bring an abomination into your
house, lest you be doomed to destruction like
it. You shall utterly detest it and utterly abhor
it, for it *is* an accursed thing.

8 "Every commandment which I command
you today you must be careful to observe,
that you may live and multiply, and go in and
possess the land of which the LORD swore to
your fathers. [2]And you shall remember that
the LORD your God led you all the way these
forty years in the wilderness, to humble you
and test you, to know what *was* in your heart,
whether you would keep His commandments
or not. [3]So He humbled you, allowed you to
hunger, and fed you with manna which you
did not know nor did your fathers know, that
He might make you know that man shall not
live by bread alone; but man lives by every
word that proceeds from the mouth of the
LORD. [4]Your garments did not wear out on you,
nor did your foot swell these forty years. [5]You
should know in your heart that as a man chastens his son, *so* the LORD your God chastens
you.

[6]"Therefore you shall keep the commandments of the LORD your God, to walk in His
ways and to fear Him. [7]For the LORD your God
is bringing you into a good land, a land of
brooks of water, of fountains and springs, that
flow out of valleys and hills; [8]a land of wheat
and barley, of vines and fig trees and pomegranates, a land of olive oil and honey; [9]a land
in which you will eat bread without scarcity, in
which you will lack nothing; a land whose
stones *are* iron and out of whose hills you can
dig copper. [10]When you have eaten and are
full, then you shall bless the LORD your God
for the good land which He has given you.

[11]"Beware that you do not forget the LORD
your God by not keeping His commandments,
His judgments, and His statutes which I command you today, [12]lest—*when* you have eaten
and are full, and have built beautiful houses
and dwell *in them;* [13]and *when* your herds and
your flocks multiply, and your silver and your
gold are multiplied, and all that you have is
multiplied; [14]when your heart is lifted up, and
you forget the LORD your God who brought
you out of the land of Egypt, from the house of
bondage; [15]who led you through that great and
terrible wilderness, *in which were* fiery serpents and scorpions and thirsty land where
there was no water; who brought water for
you out of the flinty rock; [16]who fed you in the
wilderness with manna, which your fathers
did not know, that He might humble you and
that He might test you, to do you good in the
end— [17]then you say in your heart, 'My power
and the might of my hand have gained me this
wealth.'

[18]"And you shall remember the LORD your
God, for *it is* He who gives you power to get
wealth, that He may establish His covenant
which He swore to your fathers, as *it is* this
day. [19]Then it shall be, if you by any means forget the LORD your God, and follow other gods,
and serve them and worship them, I testify
against you this day that you shall surely perish. [20]As the nations which the LORD destroys
before you, so you shall perish, because you
would not be obedient to the voice of the LORD
your God.

8:11 do not forget the LORD your God. Sufficient food would lead to the satisfaction of Israel in the land (vv. 10,12). This satisfaction and security could lead to Israel forgetting God. Forgetting God means no longer having Him in the daily thoughts of one's life. This forgetfulness would lead to a disobedience of His commandments. Whereas, in the wilderness, Israel had to depend on God for the necessities of life, in the rich land there would be a tempting sense of self-sufficiency.

Psalm 37:5–11

5 Commit your way to the LORD,
Trust also in Him,
And He shall bring *it* to pass.
6 He shall bring forth your
righteousness as the light,
And your justice as the noonday.

7 Rest in the LORD, and wait patiently
for Him;

Do not fret because of him who
prospers in his way,
Because of the man who brings wicked
schemes to pass.
8 Cease from anger, and forsake
wrath;
Do not fret—*it* only *causes* harm.
9 For evildoers shall be cut off;
But those who wait on the LORD,
They shall inherit the earth.
10 For yet a little while and the wicked
shall be no *more;*
Indeed, you will look carefully for
his place,
But it *shall be* no *more.*
11 But the meek shall inherit
the earth,
And shall delight themselves in the
abundance of peace.

Proverbs 12:9–10

9 Better *is the one* who is slighted but
has a servant,
Than he who honors himself but
lacks bread.
10 A righteous *man* regards the life of
his animal,
But the tender mercies of the wicked
are cruel.

Luke 1:39–56

[39]Now Mary arose in those days and went
into the hill country with haste, to a city of Judah, [40]and entered the house of Zacharias and
greeted Elizabeth. [41]And it happened, when
Elizabeth heard the greeting of Mary, that the
babe leaped in her womb; and Elizabeth was
filled with the Holy Spirit. [42]Then she spoke
out with a loud voice and said, "Blessed *are*
you among women, and blessed *is* the fruit of
your womb! [43]But why *is* this *granted* to me,
that the mother of my Lord should come to
me? [44]For indeed, as soon as the voice of your
greeting sounded in my ears, the babe leaped
in my womb for joy. [45]Blessed *is* she who believed, for there will be a fulfillment of those
things which were told her from the Lord."
[46]And Mary said:

"My soul magnifies the Lord,
47 And my spirit has rejoiced in God my
Savior.

1:47 my Savior. Mary referred to God as "Savior," indicating both that she recognized her own need of a Savior, and that she knew the true God as her Savior. Nothing here or anywhere else in Scripture indicates Mary thought of herself as "immaculate" (free from the taint of original sin). Quite the opposite is true—she employed language typical of someone whose only hope for salvation is divine grace. Nothing in this passage lends support to the notion that Mary herself ought to be an object of adoration.

48 For He has regarded the lowly state
of His maidservant;
For behold, henceforth all generations
will call me blessed.
49 For He who is mighty has done great
things for me,
And holy *is* His name.
50 And His mercy *is* on those who fear
Him
From generation to generation.
51 He has shown strength with
His arm;
He has scattered *the* proud in the
imagination of their hearts.
52 He has put down the mighty from
their thrones,
And exalted *the* lowly.
53 He has filled *the* hungry with good
things,
And *the* rich He has sent away
empty.
54 He has helped His servant Israel,
In remembrance of *His* mercy,
55 As He spoke to our fathers,
To Abraham and to his seed forever."

[56]And Mary remained with her about three
months, and returned to her house.

DAY 23: Is Deuteronomy simply Moses' version of the secular covenants and treaties of his day, or does it represent a unique revelation from God?

The format that Moses used in recording not only the material in Deuteronomy but also the rest of the Pentateuch bears some resemblance to other official documents from a particular time in history. This fact can be used by historians in trying to establish a date for the book. This fact can also be used by those who question God's unique revelation when they claim that Moses must have merely been copying the style of other nations of his time.

The people whom God enlisted to record His revelation did not shed their personalities, education, or style as they wrote for God. Moses had the equivalent of advanced degrees in the best training Egypt had to offer young princes (Acts 7:22). If we think of the Pentateuch as Moses' God-guided journaling during the wilderness wanderings, it will not seem unusual that his writing style bears similarities to the official and political writings of his day. What sets Moses' writings, along with the rest of Scripture, apart is not so much the style but their authoritative and God-inspired content.

MARCH 24

Deuteronomy 9:1–10:22

9 "Hear, O Israel: You *are* to cross over the
Jordan today, and go in to dispossess
nations greater and mightier than yourself,
cities great and fortified up to heaven, 2 a people great and tall, the descendants of the
Anakim, whom you know, and *of whom* you
heard *it said,* 'Who can stand before the
descendants of Anak?' 3 Therefore understand
today that the LORD your God *is* He who goes
over before you *as* a consuming fire. He will
destroy them and bring them down before
you; so you shall drive them out and destroy
them quickly, as the LORD has said to you.
4 "Do not think in your heart, after the LORD
your God has cast them out before you, saying, 'Because of my righteousness the LORD
has brought me in to possess this land'; but *it*
is because of the wickedness of these nations
that the LORD is driving them out from before
you. 5 *It is* not because of your righteousness
or the uprightness of your heart *that* you go in
to possess their land, but because of the
wickedness of these nations *that* the LORD
your God drives them out from before you,
and that He may fulfill the word which the
LORD swore to your fathers, to Abraham,
Isaac, and Jacob. 6 Therefore understand that
the LORD your God is not giving you this good
land to possess because of your righteousness, for you *are* a stiff-necked people.
7 "Remember! Do not forget how you provoked the LORD your God to wrath in the
wilderness. From the day that you departed
from the land of Egypt until you came to this
place, you have been rebellious against the
LORD. 8 Also in Horeb you provoked the LORD
to wrath, so that the LORD was angry *enough*
with you to have destroyed you. 9 When I went
up into the mountain to receive the tablets of
stone, the tablets of the covenant which the
LORD made with you, then I stayed on the
mountain forty days and forty nights. I neither
ate bread nor drank water. 10 Then the LORD
delivered to me two tablets of stone written
with the finger of God, and on them *were* all
the words which the LORD had spoken to you
on the mountain from the midst of the fire in
the day of the assembly. 11 And it came to pass,
at the end of forty days and forty nights, *that*
the LORD gave me the two tablets of stone, the
tablets of the covenant.
12 "Then the LORD said to me, 'Arise, go
down quickly from here, for your people
whom you brought out of Egypt have acted
corruptly; they have quickly turned aside
from the way which I commanded them; they
have made themselves a molded image.'
13 "Furthermore the LORD spoke to me, saying, 'I have seen this people, and indeed they
are a stiff-necked people. 14 Let Me alone, that I
may destroy them and blot out their name
from under heaven; and I will make of you a
nation mightier and greater than they.'
15 "So I turned and came down from the
mountain, and the mountain burned with fire;
and the two tablets of the covenant *were* in my

9:3 a consuming fire. The Lord was pictured as a fire which burned everything in its path. So the Lord would go over into Canaan and exterminate Canaanites. **destroy them quickly.** Israel was to be the human agent of the Lord's destruction of the Canaanites. The military strength of the Canaanites would be destroyed quickly (Josh. 6:1–11:23), though the complete subjugation of the land would take time (7:22; Josh. 13:1).

9:4 Because of my righteousness. Three times in vv. 4–6, Moses emphasized that the victory was not because of Israel's goodness, but was entirely the work of God. It was the wickedness of the Canaanites that led to their expulsion from the land (see Rom. 10:6).

two hands. [16]And I looked, and behold, you
had sinned against the LORD your God—had
made for yourselves a molded calf! You had
turned aside quickly from the way which the
LORD had commanded you. [17]Then I took the
two tablets and threw them out of my two
hands and broke them before your eyes. [18]And
I fell down before the LORD, as at the first,
forty days and forty nights; I neither ate bread
nor drank water, because of all your sin which
you committed in doing wickedly in the sight
of the LORD, to provoke Him to anger. [19]For I
was afraid of the anger and hot displeasure
with which the LORD was angry with you, to
destroy you. But the LORD listened to me at
that time also. [20]And the LORD was very angry
with Aaron *and* would have destroyed him; so
I prayed for Aaron also at the same time.
[21]Then I took your sin, the calf which you had
made, and burned it with fire and crushed it
and ground *it* very small, until it was as fine as
dust; and I threw its dust into the brook that
descended from the mountain.

[22]"Also at Taberah and Massah and Kibroth
Hattaavah you provoked the LORD to wrath.
[23]Likewise, when the LORD sent you from
Kadesh Barnea, saying, 'Go up and possess
the land which I have given you,' then you
rebelled against the commandment of the
LORD your God, and you did not believe Him
nor obey His voice. [24]You have been rebellious
against the LORD from the day that I knew you.

[25]"Thus I prostrated myself before the LORD;
forty days and forty nights I kept prostrating
myself, because the LORD had said He would
destroy you. [26]Therefore I prayed to the LORD,
and said: 'O Lord GOD, do not destroy Your
people and Your inheritance whom You have
redeemed through Your greatness, whom You
have brought out of Egypt with a mighty hand.
[27]Remember Your servants, Abraham, Isaac,
and Jacob; do not look on the stubbornness of
this people, or on their wickedness or their
sin, [28]lest the land from which You brought us
should say, "Because the LORD was not able to
bring them to the land which He promised
them, and because He hated them, He has
brought them out to kill them in the wilderness." [29]Yet they *are* Your people and Your
inheritance, whom You brought out by Your
mighty power and by Your outstretched arm.'

10 "At that time the LORD said to me, 'Hew
for yourself two tablets of stone like the
first, and come up to Me on the mountain and
make yourself an ark of wood. [2]And I will write
on the tablets the words that were on the first
tablets, which you broke; and you shall put
them in the ark.'

[3]"So I made an ark of acacia wood, hewed
two tablets of stone like the first, and went up
the mountain, having the two tablets in my
hand. [4]And He wrote on the tablets according
to the first writing, the Ten Commandments,
which the LORD had spoken to you in the
mountain from the midst of the fire in the day
of the assembly; and the LORD gave them to
me. [5]Then I turned and came down from the
mountain, and put the tablets in the ark which
I had made; and there they are, just as the
LORD commanded me."

[6](Now the children of Israel journeyed from
the wells of Bene Jaakan to Moserah, where
Aaron died, and where he was buried; and
Eleazar his son ministered as priest in his
stead. [7]From there they journeyed to
Gudgodah, and from Gudgodah to Jotbathah,
a land of rivers of water. [8]At that time the LORD
separated the tribe of Levi to bear the ark of
the covenant of the LORD, to stand before the
LORD to minister to Him and to bless in His
name, to this day. [9]Therefore Levi has no portion nor inheritance with his brethren; the
LORD *is* his inheritance, just as the LORD your
God promised him.)

[10]"As at the first time, I stayed in the mountain forty days and forty nights; the LORD also
heard me at that time, *and* the LORD chose not
to destroy you. [11]Then the LORD said to me,
'Arise, begin *your* journey before the people,
that they may go in and possess the land
which I swore to their fathers to give them.'

[12]"And now, Israel, what does the LORD your
God require of you, but to fear the LORD your
God, to walk in all His ways and to love Him,
to serve the LORD your God with all your heart
and with all your soul, [13]*and* to keep the commandments of the LORD and His statutes
which I command you today for your good?
[14]Indeed heaven and the highest heavens
belong to the LORD your God, *also* the earth
with all that *is* in it. [15]The LORD delighted only
in your fathers, to love them; and He chose
their descendants after them, you above all
peoples, as *it is* this day. [16]Therefore circumcise
the foreskin of your heart, and be stiff-necked

10:16 Therefore circumcise...your heart. Moses called the Israelites to cut away all the sin in their hearts, as the circumcision surgery cut away the skin. This would leave them with a clean relationship to God (see 30:6; Lev. 26:40,41; Jer. 4:4; 9:25; Rom. 2:29).

no longer. 17 For the LORD your God *is* God of
gods and Lord of lords, the great God, mighty
and awesome, who shows no partiality nor
takes a bribe. 18 He administers justice for the
fatherless and the widow, and loves the stranger, giving him food and clothing. 19 Therefore
love the stranger, for you were strangers in
the land of Egypt. 20 You shall fear the LORD
your God; you shall serve Him, and to Him
you shall hold fast, and take oaths in His
name. 21 He *is* your praise, and He *is* your God,
who has done for you these great and awesome things which your eyes have seen.
22 Your fathers went down to Egypt with seventy
persons, and now the LORD your God has made
you as the stars of heaven in multitude.

Psalm 37:12–17

12 The wicked plots against the just,
And gnashes at him with his teeth.
13 The Lord laughs at him,
For He sees that his day is coming.
14 The wicked have drawn the sword
And have bent their bow,
To cast down the poor and needy,
To slay those who are of upright
conduct.
15 Their sword shall enter their own
heart,
And their bows shall be broken.
16 A little that a righteous man has
Is better than the riches of many
wicked.
17 For the arms of the wicked shall be
broken,
But the LORD upholds the
righteous.

Proverbs 12:11

11 He who tills his land will be satisfied
with bread,
But he who follows frivolity *is* devoid
of understanding.

Luke 1:57–80

57 Now Elizabeth's full time came for her to
be delivered, and she brought forth a son.
58 When her neighbors and relatives heard how
the Lord had shown great mercy to her, they
rejoiced with her.
59 So it was, on the eighth day, that they came
to circumcise the child; and they would have
called him by the name of his father,
Zacharias. 60 His mother answered and said,
"No; he shall be called John."
61 But they said to her, "There is no one
among your relatives who is called by this
name." 62 So they made signs to his father—
what he would have him called.
63 And he asked for a writing tablet, and
wrote, saying, "His name is John." So they all
marveled. 64 Immediately his mouth was
opened and his tongue *loosed,* and he spoke,
praising God. 65 Then fear came on all who
dwelt around them; and all these sayings were
discussed throughout all the hill country of
Judea. 66 And all those who heard *them* kept
them in their hearts, saying, "What kind of
child will this be?" And the hand of the Lord
was with him.
67 Now his father Zacharias was filled with
the Holy Spirit, and prophesied, saying:

68 "Blessed *is* the Lord God of Israel,
For He has visited and redeemed His
people,
69 And has raised up a horn of salvation
for us
In the house of His servant David,
70 As He spoke by the mouth of His holy
prophets,
Who *have been* since the world began,
71 That we should be saved from our
enemies
And from the hand of all who hate us,
72 To perform the mercy *promised* to our
fathers
And to remember His holy covenant,
73 The oath which He swore to our father
Abraham:
74 To grant us that we,
Being delivered from the hand of our
enemies,
Might serve Him without fear,
75 In holiness and righteousness before
Him all the days of our life.

76 "And you, child, will be called the
prophet of the Highest;

1:80 was in the deserts. Several groups of ascetics inhabited the wilderness regions east of Jerusalem. One was the famous Qumran community, source of the Dead Sea Scrolls. John's parents, already old when he was born, might have given him over to the care of someone with ties to such a community. In a similar way, Hannah consecrated Samuel to the Lord by entrusting him to Eli (1 Sam. 1:22–28). However, there is nothing concrete in Scripture to suggest that John was part of any such group. On the contrary, he is painted as a solitary figure, in the spirit of Elijah.

For you will go before the face of the
Lord to prepare His ways,
77 To give knowledge of salvation to His
people
By the remission of their sins,
78 Through the tender mercy of our God,
With which the Dayspring from on high
has visited us;
79 To give light to those who sit in
darkness and the shadow of death,
To guide our feet into the way of
peace."

80So the child grew and became strong in
spirit, and was in the deserts till the day of his
manifestation to Israel.

DAY 24: For whom did Luke write?

Luke, like Mark, and in contrast to Matthew, appears to target a Gentile readership. He identified locations that would have been familiar to all Jews (4:31; 23:51; 24:13), suggesting that his audience went beyond those who already had knowledge of Palestinian geography. He usually preferred Greek terminology over Hebraisms (e.g., "Calvary" instead of "Golgotha" in 23:33). The other Gospels all use occasional Semitic terms such as "Abba" (Mark 14:36), "rabbi" (Matt. 23:7,8; John 1:38,49), and "hosanna" (Matt. 21:9; Mark 11:9,10; John 12:13)—but Luke either omitted them or used Greek equivalents.

Luke quoted the Old Testament more sparingly than Matthew; and when citing Old Testament passages, he nearly always employed the Septuagint, a Greek translation of the Hebrew Scriptures. Furthermore, most of Luke's Old Testament citations are allusions rather than direct quotations, and many of them appear in Jesus' words rather than Luke's narration (2:23,24; 3:4–6; 4:4,8,10–12,18,19; 7:27; 10:27; 18:20; 19:46; 20:17,18,37,42,43; 22:37).

Luke, more than any of the other Gospel writers, highlighted the universal scope of the gospel invitation. He portrayed Jesus as the Son of Man, rejected by Israel, and then offered to the world. He repeatedly related accounts of Gentiles, Samaritans, and other outcasts who found grace in Jesus' eyes. This emphasis is precisely what we would expect from a close companion of the "apostle to the Gentiles" (Rom. 11:13).

MARCH 25

Deuteronomy 11:1–12:32

11 "Therefore you shall love the LORD your
God, and keep His charge, His statutes,
His judgments, and His commandments
always. 2Know today that *I do* not *speak* with
your children, who have not known and who
have not seen the chastening of the LORD your
God, His greatness and His mighty hand and
His outstretched arm— 3His signs and His
acts which He did in the midst of Egypt, to
Pharaoh king of Egypt, and to all his land;
4what He did to the army of Egypt, to their
horses and their chariots: how He made the
waters of the Red Sea overflow them as they
pursued you, and *how* the LORD has destroyed
them to this day; 5what He did for you in the
wilderness until you came to this place; 6and
what He did to Dathan and Abiram the sons of
Eliab, the son of Reuben: how the earth
opened its mouth and swallowed them up,
their households, their tents, and all the substance
that *was* in their possession, in the
midst of all Israel— 7but your eyes have seen
every great act of the LORD which He did.

8"Therefore you shall keep every commandment
which I command you today, that
you may be strong, and go in and possess the
land which you cross over to possess, 9and
that you may prolong *your* days in the land
which the LORD swore to give your fathers, to
them and their descendants, 'a land flowing
with milk and honey.' 10For the land which you
go to possess *is* not like the land of Egypt from
which you have come, where you sowed your
seed and watered *it* by foot, as a vegetable garden;
11but the land which you cross over to
possess *is* a land of hills and valleys, which
drinks water from the rain of heaven, 12a land
for which the LORD your God cares; the eyes
of the LORD your God *are* always on it, from
the beginning of the year to the very end of
the year.

13'And it shall be that if you earnestly obey
My commandments which I command you
today, to love the LORD your God and serve
Him with all your heart and with all your soul,
14then I will give *you* the rain for your land in its
season, the early rain and the latter rain, that
you may gather in your grain, your new wine,
and your oil. 15And I will send grass in your
fields for your livestock, that you may eat and
be filled.' 16Take heed to yourselves, lest your
heart be deceived, and you turn aside and

serve other gods and worship them, [17]lest the
LORD's anger be aroused against you, and He
shut up the heavens so that there be no rain,
and the land yield no produce, and you perish
quickly from the good land which the LORD is
giving you.
[18]"Therefore you shall lay up these words of
mine in your heart and in your soul, and bind
them as a sign on your hand, and they shall be
as frontlets between your eyes. [19]You shall
teach them to your children, speaking of them
when you sit in your house, when you walk by
the way, when you lie down, and when you
rise up. [20]And you shall write them on the
doorposts of your house and on your gates,
[21]that your days and the days of your children
may be multiplied in the land of which the
LORD swore to your fathers to give them, like
the days of the heavens above the earth.
[22]"For if you carefully keep all these commandments which I command you to do—to
love the LORD your God, to walk in all His
ways, and to hold fast to Him— [23]then the
LORD will drive out all these nations from
before you, and you will dispossess greater
and mightier nations than yourselves. [24]Every
place on which the sole of your foot treads
shall be yours: from the wilderness and Lebanon, from the river, the River Euphrates, even
to the Western Sea, shall be your territory.

11:24 Every place...your foot treads. In response to the obedience of Israel (vv. 22,23), the Lord promised to give to Israel all of the land they personally traversed to the extent of the boundaries that He had given. This same promise was repeated in Joshua 1:3–5. Had Israel obeyed God faithfully, her boundaries would have been enlarged to fulfill the promise made to Abraham (Gen. 15:18). But because of Israel's disobedience, the complete promise of the whole land still remains, to be fulfilled in the future kingdom of the Messiah (Ezek. 36:8–38).

[25]No man shall be able to stand against you;
the LORD your God will put the dread of you
and the fear of you upon all the land where
you tread, just as He has said to you.
[26]"Behold, I set before you today a blessing
and a curse: [27]the blessing, if you obey the
commandments of the LORD your God which I
command you today; [28]and the curse, if you do
not obey the commandments of the LORD your
God, but turn aside from the way which I
command you today, to go after other gods
which you have not known. [29]Now it shall be,
when the LORD your God has brought you into
the land which you go to possess, that you
shall put the blessing on Mount Gerizim and
the curse on Mount Ebal. [30]*Are* they not on the
other side of the Jordan, toward the setting
sun, in the land of the Canaanites who dwell in
the plain opposite Gilgal, beside the terebinth
trees of Moreh? [31]For you will cross over the
Jordan and go in to possess the land which the
LORD your God is giving you, and you will possess it and dwell in it. [32]And you shall be careful to observe all the statutes and judgments
which I set before you today.

12 "These *are* the statutes and judgments
which you shall be careful to observe in
the land which the LORD God of your fathers is
giving you to possess, all the days that you live
on the earth. [2]You shall utterly destroy all the
places where the nations which you shall
dispossess served their gods, on the high
mountains and on the hills and under every
green tree. [3]And you shall destroy their altars,
break their *sacred* pillars, and burn their
wooden images with fire; you shall cut down
the carved images of their gods and destroy
their names from that place. [4]You shall not
worship the LORD your God *with* such *things.*
[5]"But you shall seek the place where the
LORD your God chooses, out of all your tribes,
to put His name for His dwelling place; and
there you shall go. [6]There you shall take your
burnt offerings, your sacrifices, your tithes,
the heave offerings of your hand, your vowed
offerings, your freewill offerings, and the firstborn of your herds and flocks. [7]And there you
shall eat before the LORD your God, and you
shall rejoice in all to which you have put your
hand, you and your households, in which the
LORD your God has blessed you.
[8]"You shall not at all do as we are doing here
today—every man doing whatever *is* right in
his own eyes— [9]for as yet you have not come
to the rest and the inheritance which the LORD
your God is giving you. [10]But *when* you cross
over the Jordan and dwell in the land which
the LORD your God is giving you to inherit, and
He gives you rest from all your enemies round
about, so that you dwell in safety, [11]then there
will be the place where the LORD your God
chooses to make His name abide. There you
shall bring all that I command you: your burnt
offerings, your sacrifices, your tithes, the
heave offerings of your hand, and all your
choice offerings which you vow to the LORD.
[12]And you shall rejoice before the LORD your

God, you and your sons and your daughters,
your male and female servants, and the Levite
who *is* within your gates, since he has no portion nor inheritance with you. 13 Take heed to
yourself that you do not offer your burnt offerings in every place that you see; 14 but in the
place which the LORD chooses, in one of your
tribes, there you shall offer your burnt offerings, and there you shall do all that I command you.

15 "However, you may slaughter and eat meat
within all your gates, whatever your heart
desires, according to the blessing of the LORD
your God which He has given you; the unclean
and the clean may eat of it, of the gazelle and
the deer alike. 16 Only you shall not eat the
blood; you shall pour it on the earth like water.
17 You may not eat within your gates the tithe of
your grain or your new wine or your oil, of the
firstborn of your herd or your flock, of any of
your offerings which you vow, of your freewill
offerings, or of the heave offering of your
hand. 18 But you must eat them before the LORD
your God in the place which the LORD your
God chooses, you and your son and your
daughter, your male servant and your female
servant, and the Levite who *is* within your
gates; and you shall rejoice before the LORD
your God in all to which you put your hands.
19 Take heed to yourself that you do not forsake
the Levite as long as you live in your land.

20 "When the LORD your God enlarges your
border as He has promised you, and you say,
'Let me eat meat,' because you long to eat
meat, you may eat as much meat as your heart
desires. 21 If the place where the LORD your
God chooses to put His name is too far from
you, then you may slaughter from your herd
and from your flock which the LORD has given
you, just as I have commanded you, and you
may eat within your gates as much as your
heart desires. 22 Just as the gazelle and the
deer are eaten, so you may eat them; the
unclean and the clean alike may eat them.
23 Only be sure that you do not eat the blood,
for the blood *is* the life; you may not eat the life
with the meat. 24 You shall not eat it; you shall
pour it on the earth like water. 25 You shall not
eat it, that it may go well with you and your
children after you, when you do *what is* right
in the sight of the LORD. 26 Only the holy things
which you have, and your vowed offerings,
you shall take and go to the place which the
LORD chooses. 27 And you shall offer your burnt
offerings, the meat and the blood, on the altar
of the LORD your God; and the blood of your
sacrifices shall be poured out on the altar of
the LORD your God, and you shall eat the meat.
28 Observe and obey all these words which I
command you, that it may go well with you
and your children after you forever, when you
do *what is* good and right in the sight of the
LORD your God.

29 "When the LORD your God cuts off from
before you the nations which you go to dispossess, and you displace them and dwell in their
land, 30 take heed to yourself that you are not
ensnared to follow them, after they are
destroyed from before you, and that you do
not inquire after their gods, saying, 'How did
these nations serve their gods? I also will do
likewise.' 31 You shall not worship the LORD
your God in that way; for every abomination to
the LORD which He hates they have done to
their gods; for they burn even their sons and
daughters in the fire to their gods.

32 "Whatever I command you, be careful to
observe it; you shall not add to it nor take
away from it.

Psalm 37:18–22

18 The LORD knows the days of the
upright,
And their inheritance shall be forever.
19 They shall not be ashamed in the
evil time,
And in the days of famine they shall
be satisfied.
20 But the wicked shall perish;
And the enemies of the LORD,
Like the splendor of the meadows,
shall vanish.
Into smoke they shall vanish away.
21 The wicked borrows and does not
repay,
But the righteous shows mercy and
gives.
22 For *those* blessed by Him shall inherit
the earth,
But *those* cursed by Him shall be
cut off.

Proverbs 12:12–14

12 The wicked covet the catch of evil *men*,
But the root of the righteous yields
fruit.
13 The wicked is ensnared by the
transgression of *his* lips,
But the righteous will come through
trouble.
14 A man will be satisfied with good by the
fruit of *his* mouth,
And the recompense of a man's hands
will be rendered to him.

12:14 fruit of *his* mouth. This deals with the power of words; the reward of wise words is like the reward for physical labor (10:11; 15:4; 18:4).

Luke 2:1–24

2 And it came to pass in those days *that* a
decree went out from Caesar Augustus
that all the world should be registered. [2]This
census first took place while Quirinius was
governing Syria. [3]So all went to be registered,
everyone to his own city.
[4]Joseph also went up from Galilee, out of the
city of Nazareth, into Judea, to the city of David, which is called Bethlehem, because he
was of the house and lineage of David, [5]to be
registered with Mary, his betrothed wife, who
was with child. [6]So it was, that while they were
there, the days were completed for her to be
delivered. [7]And she brought forth her firstborn
Son, and wrapped Him in swaddling cloths,
and laid Him in a manger, because there was
no room for them in the inn.
[8]Now there were in the same country shepherds living out in the fields, keeping watch
over their flock by night. [9]And behold, an
angel of the Lord stood before them, and the
glory of the Lord shone around them, and
they were greatly afraid. [10]Then the angel said
to them, "Do not be afraid, for behold, I bring
you good tidings of great joy which will be to
all people. [11]For there is born to you this day in
the city of David a Savior, who is Christ the
Lord. [12]And this *will be* the sign to you: You will
find a Babe wrapped in swaddling cloths, lying
in a manger."
[13]And suddenly there was with the angel a
multitude of the heavenly host praising God
and saying:

[14] "Glory to God in the highest,
And on earth peace, goodwill toward
men!"

2:11 city of David. I.e., Bethlehem, the town where David was born—not the City of David, which was on the southern slope of Mt. Zion (2 Sam. 5:7–9). **a Savior.** This is one of only two places in the Gospels where Christ is referred to as "Savior"—the other being John 4:42, where the men of Sychar confessed Him as "Savior of the world." **Christ.** "Christ" is the Greek equivalent of "Messiah". **Lord.** The Greek word can mean "master"—but it is also the word used to translate the covenant name of God. Here (and in most of its New Testament occurrences), it is used in the latter sense, as a title of Deity.

[15]So it was, when the angels had gone away
from them into heaven, that the shepherds said
to one another, "Let us now go to Bethlehem
and see this thing that has come to pass, which
the Lord has made known to us." [16]And they
came with haste and found Mary and Joseph,
and the Babe lying in a manger. [17]Now when
they had seen *Him,* they made widely known
the saying which was told them concerning this
Child. [18]And all those who heard *it* marveled at
those things which were told them by the shepherds. [19]But Mary kept all these things and pondered *them* in her heart. [20]Then the shepherds
returned, glorifying and praising God for all the
things that they had heard and seen, as it was
told them.
[21]And when eight days were completed for
the circumcision of the Child, His name was
called JESUS, the name given by the angel before He was conceived in the womb.
[22]Now when the days of her purification
according to the law of Moses were completed,
they brought Him to Jerusalem to present *Him*
to the Lord [23](as it is written in the law of the
Lord, *"Every male who opens the womb shall
be called holy to the LORD"*), [24]and to offer a sacrifice according to what is said in the law of the
Lord, *"A pair of turtledoves or two young
pigeons."*

DAY 25: Why was there an emphasis on prescribed places of worship in the Old Testament?

In Deuteronomy 12:1–32, Moses begins by repeating his instructions concerning what to do with the false worship centers after Israel had taken possession of the land of the Canaanites (see 7:1–6). They were to destroy them completely. In v. 2, he speaks about "the high mountains… hills…every green tree." The Canaanite sanctuaries to be destroyed were located in places believed to have particular religious significance. The mountain or hill was thought to be the home of a god; and by ascending the mountain, the worshiper was in some symbolic sense closer to the deity. Certain trees were considered to be sacred and symbolized fertility, a dominant theme in Canaanite religion. And in v. 3, Moses addresses "their altars,…pillars,…wooden images…carved images."

These were elements of Canaanite worship, which included human sacrifice (v. 31). If they remained, the people might mix the worship of God with those places (v. 4).

In contrast to false worship centers, the Israelites are told "you shall seek the place where the LORD your God chooses, out of all your tribes, to put His name for His dwelling place" (v. 5). Various places of worship were chosen after the people settled in Canaan, such as Mt. Ebal (27:1–8; Josh. 8:30–35), Shechem (Josh. 24:1–28), and Shiloh (Josh. 18:1), which was the center of worship through the period of Judges (Judg. 21:19). The tabernacle, the Lord's dwelling place, was located in Canaan, where the Lord chose to dwell. The central importance of the tabernacle was in direct contrast to the multiple places (see v. 2) where the Canaanites practiced their worship of idols. Eventually, the tabernacle was brought to Jerusalem by David (2 Sam. 6:12–19).

MARCH 26

Deuteronomy 13:1–14:29

13 "If there arises among you a prophet or a
dreamer of dreams, and he gives you a
sign or a wonder, 2and the sign or the wonder
comes to pass, of which he spoke to you, saying, 'Let us go after other gods'—which you
have not known—'and let us serve them,' 3you

13:2 the sign or the wonder comes to pass. Miraculous signs alone were never meant to be a test of truth (see Pharaoh's magicians in Ex. 7–10). A prophet or a dreamer's prediction might come true; but if his message contradicted God's commands, the people were to trust God and His word rather than such experience. **Let us go after other gods.** The explicit temptation was to renounce allegiance to the Lord and go after other gods. The result of this apostasy would be the serving of these false gods by worshiping them, which would be in direct contradiction to the first commandment (5:7).

13:5 put away the evil from your midst. The object of the severe penalty was not only the punishment of the evildoer, but also the preservation of the community. Paul must have had this text in mind when he gave a similar command to the Corinthian church (1 Cor. 5:13; also Deut. 17:7; 19:19; 21:21; 22:21; 24:7).

shall not listen to the words of that prophet or
that dreamer of dreams, for the LORD your
God is testing you to know whether you love
the LORD your God with all your heart and
with all your soul. 4You shall walk after the
LORD your God and fear Him, and keep His
commandments and obey His voice; you shall
serve Him and hold fast to Him. 5But that
prophet or that dreamer of dreams shall be
put to death, because he has spoken in order
to turn *you* away from the LORD your God, who
brought you out of the land of Egypt and
redeemed you from the house of bondage, to
entice you from the way in which the LORD
your God commanded you to walk. So you
shall put away the evil from your midst.
6"If your brother, the son of your mother,
your son or your daughter, the wife of your
bosom, or your friend who is as your own soul,
secretly entices you, saying, 'Let us go and
serve other gods,' which you have not known,
neither you nor your fathers, 7of the gods of
the people which *are* all around you, near to
you or far off from you, from *one* end of the
earth to the *other* end of the earth, 8you shall
not consent to him or listen to him, nor shall
your eye pity him, nor shall you spare him or
conceal him; 9but you shall surely kill him;
your hand shall be first against him to put him
to death, and afterward the hand of all the
people. 10And you shall stone him with stones
until he dies, because he sought to entice you
away from the LORD your God, who brought
you out of the land of Egypt, from the house of
bondage. 11So all Israel shall hear and fear, and
not again do such wickedness as this among
you.
12"If you hear someone in one of your cities,
which the LORD your God gives you to dwell
in, saying, 13'Corrupt men have gone out from
among you and enticed the inhabitants of their
city, saying, "Let us go and serve other
gods" '—which you have not known— 14then
you shall inquire, search out, and ask diligently. And *if it is* indeed true *and* certain *that*
such an abomination was committed among
you, 15you shall surely strike the inhabitants of
that city with the edge of the sword, utterly
destroying it, all that is in it and its livestock—
with the edge of the sword. 16And you shall
gather all its plunder into the middle of the

street, and completely burn with fire the city
and all its plunder, for the LORD your God. It
shall be a heap forever; it shall not be built
again. 17 So none of the accursed things shall
remain in your hand, that the LORD may turn
from the fierceness of His anger and show you
mercy, have compassion on you and multiply
you, just as He swore to your fathers, 18 because you have listened to the voice of the
LORD your God, to keep all His commandments which I command you today, to do *what*
is right in the eyes of the LORD your God.

14 "You *are* the children of the LORD your
God; you shall not cut yourselves nor
shave the front of your head for the dead. 2 For
you *are* a holy people to the LORD your God,
and the LORD has chosen you to be a people
for Himself, a special treasure above all the
peoples who *are* on the face of the earth.
3 "You shall not eat any detestable thing.
4 These *are* the animals which you may eat: the
ox, the sheep, the goat, 5 the deer, the gazelle,
the roe deer, the wild goat, the mountain goat,
the antelope, and the mountain sheep. 6 And
you may eat every animal with cloven hooves,
having the hoof split into two parts, *and that*
chews the cud, among the animals. 7 Nevertheless, of those that chew the cud or have cloven
hooves, you shall not eat, *such as* these: the
camel, the hare, and the rock hyrax; for they
chew the cud but do not have cloven hooves;
they *are* unclean for you. 8 Also the swine is
unclean for you, because it has cloven hooves,
yet *does* not *chew* the cud; you shall not eat
their flesh or touch their dead carcasses.
9 "These you may eat of all that *are* in the
waters: you may eat all that have fins and
scales. 10 And whatever does not have fins and
scales you shall not eat; it *is* unclean for you.
11 "All clean birds you may eat. 12 But these you
shall not eat: the eagle, the vulture, the buzzard,
13 the red kite, the falcon, and the kite after their
kinds; 14 every raven after its kind; 15 the ostrich,
the short-eared owl, the sea gull, and the hawk
after their kinds; 16 the little owl, the screech owl,
the white owl, 17 the jackdaw, the carrion vulture,
the fisher owl, 18 the stork, the heron after its
kind, and the hoopoe and the bat.
19 "Also every creeping thing that flies is
unclean for you; they shall not be eaten.
20 "You may eat all clean birds.
21 "You shall not eat anything that dies *of*
itself; you may give it to the alien who *is* within your gates, that he may eat it, or you may
sell it to a foreigner; for you *are* a holy people
to the LORD your God.
"You shall not boil a young goat in its mother's milk.
22 "You shall truly tithe all the increase of
your grain that the field produces year by year.
23 And you shall eat before the LORD your God,
in the place where He chooses to make His
name abide, the tithe of your grain and your
new wine and your oil, of the firstborn of your
herds and your flocks, that you may learn to
fear the LORD your God always. 24 But if the
journey is too long for you, so that you are not
able to carry *the tithe, or* if the place where the
LORD your God chooses to put His name is too
far from you, when the LORD your God has
blessed you, 25 then you shall exchange *it* for
money, take the money in your hand, and go to
the place which the LORD your God chooses.
26 And you shall spend that money for whatever
your heart desires: for oxen or sheep, for wine
or similar drink, for whatever your heart
desires; you shall eat there before the LORD
your God, and you shall rejoice, you and your
household. 27 You shall not forsake the Levite
who *is* within your gates, for he has no part nor
inheritance with you.
28 "At the end of *every* third year you shall
bring out the tithe of your produce of that year
and store *it* up within your gates. 29 And the
Levite, because he has no portion nor inheritance with you, and the stranger and the
fatherless and the widow who *are* within your
gates, may come and eat and be satisfied, that
the LORD your God may bless you in all the
work of your hand which you do.

Psalm 37:23–29

23 The steps of a *good* man are ordered
by the LORD,
And He delights in his way.
24 Though he fall, he shall not be utterly
cast down;
For the LORD upholds *him with* His
hand.

25 I have been young, and *now* am old;
Yet I have not seen the righteous
forsaken,
Nor his descendants begging
bread.
26 *He is* ever merciful, and lends;
And his descendants *are* blessed.

27 Depart from evil, and do good;
And dwell forevermore.
28 For the LORD loves justice,
And does not forsake His saints;
They are preserved forever,
But the descendants of the wicked
shall be cut off.
29 The righteous shall inherit the land,
And dwell in it forever.

Proverbs 12:15–16

15 The way of a fool *is* right in his own
eyes,
But he who heeds counsel *is* wise.
16 A fool's wrath is known at once,
But a prudent *man* covers shame.

Luke 2:25–52

25And behold, there was a man in Jerusalem
whose name *was* Simeon, and this man *was*
just and devout, waiting for the Consolation of
Israel, and the Holy Spirit was upon him. 26And
it had been revealed to him by the Holy Spirit
that he would not see death before he had
seen the Lord's Christ. 27So he came by the
Spirit into the temple. And when the parents
brought in the Child Jesus, to do for Him
according to the custom of the law, 28he took
Him up in his arms and blessed God and said:

29 "Lord, now You are letting Your servant
depart in peace,
According to Your word;
30 For my eyes have seen Your salvation
31 Which You have prepared before the
face of all peoples,
32 A light to *bring* revelation to the
Gentiles,
And the glory of Your people Israel."

33And Joseph and His mother marveled at
those things which were spoken of Him.
34Then Simeon blessed them, and said to
Mary His mother, "Behold, this *Child* is destined for the fall and rising of many in Israel,
and for a sign which will be spoken against
35(yes, a sword will pierce through your own
soul also), that the thoughts of many hearts
may be revealed."
36Now there was one, Anna, a prophetess,
the daughter of Phanuel, of the tribe of Asher.
She was of a great age, and had lived with a
husband seven years from her virginity; 37and
this woman *was* a widow of about eighty-four
years, who did not depart from the temple, but
served *God* with fastings and prayers night
and day. 38And coming in that instant she gave
thanks to the Lord, and spoke of Him to all
those who looked for redemption in Jerusalem.
39So when they had performed all things
according to the law of the Lord, they
returned to Galilee, to their *own* city, Nazareth. 40And the Child grew and became strong
in spirit, filled with wisdom; and the grace of
God was upon Him.
41His parents went to Jerusalem every year
at the Feast of the Passover. 42And when He
was twelve years old, they went up to Jerusalem according to the custom of the feast.
43When they had finished the days, as they
returned, the Boy Jesus lingered behind in Jerusalem. And Joseph and His mother did not
know *it;* 44but supposing Him to have been in
the company, they went a day's journey, and
sought Him among *their* relatives and
acquaintances. 45So when they did not find
Him, they returned to Jerusalem, seeking
Him. 46Now so it was *that* after three days they
found Him in the temple, sitting in the midst
of the teachers, both listening to them and
asking them questions. 47And all who heard
Him were astonished at His understanding
and answers. 48So when they saw Him, they
were amazed; and His mother said to Him,
"Son, why have You done this to us? Look,

2:26 it had been revealed to him. It is significant that, with messianic expectations running so high (see 3:15) and with the many Old Testament prophecies that spoke of His coming, still only a handful of people realized the significance of Christ's birth. Most of them, including Simeon, received some angelic message or other special revelation to make the fulfillment of the Old Testament prophecies clear.

2:36 a prophetess. This refers to a woman who spoke God's word. She was a teacher of the Old Testament, not a source of revelation. The Old Testament mentions only 3 women who prophesied: Miriam (Ex. 15:20); Deborah (Judg. 4:4); Huldah (2 Kin. 22:14; 2 Chr. 34:22). One other, the "prophetess" Noadiah, was evidently a false prophet, grouped by Nehemiah with his enemies. Isaiah 8:3 refers to the prophet's wife as a "prophetess," but there is no evidence Isaiah's wife prophesied. Perhaps she is so-called because the child she bore was given a name that was prophetic (Is. 8:3,4). This use of the title for Isaiah's wife also shows that the title does not necessarily indicate an ongoing revelatory prophetic ministry. Rabbinical tradition also regarded Sarah, Hannah, Abigail, and Esther as prophetesses (apparently to make an even 7 with Miriam, Deborah, and Huldah). In the New Testament, the daughters of Philip prophesied (Acts 21:9).

Your father and I have sought You anxiously."
49And He said to them, "Why did you seek
Me? Did you not know that I must be about My
Father's business?" 50But they did not understand the statement which He spoke to them.
51Then He went down with them and came
to Nazareth, and was subject to them, but His
mother kept all these things in her heart.
52And Jesus increased in wisdom and stature,
and in favor with God and men.

DAY 26: What does Luke 2:41–52 tell us about the Boy Jesus?

When Jesus was 12 years old, He celebrated His first Feast of the Passover in preparation for that rite of passage into adulthood (*Bar mitzvah*). After the celebration, it says that "Jesus lingered" (v. 43). In stark contrast to the apocryphal gospels' spurious tales of youthful miracles and supernatural exploits, this lone biblical insight into the youth of Jesus portrays Him as a typical boy in a typical family. His lingering was neither mischievous nor disobedient—it was owing to a simple mistaken presumption on His parents' part (v. 44) that He was left behind.

Obviously Joseph and Mary were traveling with a large caravan of friends and relatives from Nazareth. Men and women in such a group might have been separated by some distance, and it appears each parent thought He was with the other. The reference to "three days" (v. 46) probably means they realized He was missing at the end of a full day's travel. That required another full day's journey back to Jerusalem, and the better part of another day was spent seeking Him. They found Jesus among the teachers in the temple, "listening to them and asking them questions." He was utterly respectful; but even at that young age, His questions showed a wisdom that put the teachers to shame (v. 47).

In the exchange of words that follow, Mary's words convey a tone of exasperation normal for any mother under such circumstances, but misplaced in this case. He was not hiding from them or defying their authority. In fact, He had done precisely what any child should do under such circumstances (being left by His parents)—He went to a safe, public place, in the presence of trusted adults, where His parents could be expected to come looking for Him (v. 49). Jesus' reference to "My Father's business" reveals a genuine amazement that they did not know where to look for Him. This also reveals that, even at so young an age, He had a clear consciousness of His identity and mission. However, He "was subject to them" (v. 51). His relationship with His heavenly Father did not override or nullify His duty to His earthly parents. His obedience to the fifth commandment was an essential part of the perfect legal obedience He rendered on our behalf (Heb. 4:4; 5:8,9).

MARCH 27

Deuteronomy 15:1–16:22

15 "At the end of *every* seven years you shall
grant a release *of debts.* 2And this *is* the
form of the release: Every creditor who has
lent *anything* to his neighbor shall release *it;*
he shall not require *it* of his neighbor or his
brother, because it is called the LORD's
release. 3Of a foreigner you may require *it;* but
you shall give up your claim to what is owed
by your brother, 4except when there may be
no poor among you; for the LORD will greatly
bless you in the land which the LORD your God
is giving you to possess *as* an inheritance—
5only if you carefully obey the voice of the
LORD your God, to observe with care all these
commandments which I command you today.
6For the LORD your God will bless you just as
He promised you; you shall lend to many
nations, but you shall not borrow; you shall
reign over many nations, but they shall not
reign over you.
7"If there is among you a poor man of your
brethren, within any of the gates in your land
which the LORD your God is giving you, you
shall not harden your heart nor shut your
hand from your poor brother, 8but you shall
open your hand wide to him and willingly lend
him sufficient for his need, whatever he
needs. 9Beware lest there be a wicked thought
in your heart, saying, 'The seventh year, the
year of release, is at hand,' and your eye be
evil against your poor brother and you give
him nothing, and he cry out to the LORD
against you, and it become sin among you.
10You shall surely give to him, and your heart
should not be grieved when you give to him,
because for this thing the LORD your God will
bless you in all your works and in all to which
you put your hand. 11For the poor will never
cease from the land; therefore I command
you, saying, 'You shall open your hand wide to
your brother, to your poor and your needy, in
your land.'
12"If your brother, a Hebrew man, or a Hebrew woman, is sold to you and serves you six
years, then in the seventh year you shall let him

go free from you. 13And when you send him
away free from you, you shall not let him go
away empty-handed; 14you shall supply him liberally from your flock, from your threshing
floor, and from your winepress. *From what* the
LORD your God has blessed you with, you shall
give to him. 15You shall remember that you were
a slave in the land of Egypt, and the LORD your
God redeemed you; therefore I command you
this thing today. 16And if it happens that he says
to you, 'I will not go away from you,' because he
loves you and your house, since he prospers
with you, 17then you shall take an awl and thrust
it through his ear to the door, and he shall be
your servant forever. Also to your female servant you shall do likewise. 18It shall not seem
hard to you when you send him away free from
you; for he has been worth a double hired servant in serving you six years. Then the LORD
your God will bless you in all that you do.

19"All the firstborn males that come from
your herd and your flock you shall sanctify to
the LORD your God; you shall do no work with
the firstborn of your herd, nor shear the firstborn of your flock. 20You and your household
shall eat *it* before the LORD your God year by
year in the place which the LORD chooses.
21But if there is a defect in it, *if it is* lame or
blind *or has* any serious defect, you shall not
sacrifice it to the LORD your God. 22You may eat
it within your gates; the unclean and the clean
person alike *may eat it,* as *if it were* a gazelle or
a deer. 23Only you shall not eat its blood; you
shall pour it on the ground like water.

16 "Observe the month of Abib, and keep
the Passover to the LORD your God, for in
the month of Abib the LORD your God brought
you out of Egypt by night. 2Therefore you
shall sacrifice the Passover to the LORD your
God, from the flock and the herd, in the place
where the LORD chooses to put His name. 3You
shall eat no leavened bread with it; seven days
you shall eat unleavened bread with it, *that is,*
the bread of affliction (for you came out of the
land of Egypt in haste), that you may remember the day in which you came out of the land
of Egypt all the days of your life. 4And no leav-
en shall be seen among you in all your territory for seven days, nor shall *any* of the meat
which you sacrifice the first day at twilight
remain overnight until morning.

5"You may not sacrifice the Passover within
any of your gates which the LORD your God
gives you; 6but at the place where the LORD
your God chooses to make His name abide,
there you shall sacrifice the Passover at twilight, at the going down of the sun, at the time
you came out of Egypt. 7And you shall roast
and eat *it* in the place which the LORD your
God chooses, and in the morning you shall
turn and go to your tents. 8Six days you shall
eat unleavened bread, and on the seventh day
there *shall be* a sacred assembly to the LORD
your God. You shall do no work *on it.*

9"You shall count seven weeks for yourself;
begin to count the seven weeks from *the time*
you begin *to put* the sickle to the grain. 10Then
you shall keep the Feast of Weeks to the LORD
your God with the tribute of a freewill offering
from your hand, which you shall give as the
LORD your God blesses you. 11You shall rejoice
before the LORD your God, you and your son
and your daughter, your male servant and
your female servant, the Levite who *is* within
your gates, the stranger and the fatherless and
the widow who *are* among you, at the place
where the LORD your God chooses to make His
name abide. 12And you shall remember that you
were a slave in Egypt, and you shall be careful to
observe these statutes.

13"You shall observe the Feast of Tabernacles seven days, when you have gathered
from your threshing floor and from your winepress. 14And you shall rejoice in your feast, you
and your son and your daughter, your male servant and your female servant and the Levite,
the stranger and the fatherless and the widow,
who *are* within your gates. 15Seven days you
shall keep a sacred feast to the LORD your God
in the place which the LORD chooses, because
the LORD your God will bless you in all your
produce and in all the work of your hands, so
that you surely rejoice.

16"Three times a year all your males shall
appear before the LORD your God in the place
which He chooses: at the Feast of Unleavened
Bread, at the Feast of Weeks, and at the Feast of
Tabernacles; and they shall not appear before
the LORD empty-handed. 17Every man *shall give*
as he is able, according to the blessing of the
LORD your God which He has given you.

18"You shall appoint judges and officers in all
your gates, which the LORD your God gives
you, according to your tribes, and they shall
judge the people with just judgment. 19You
shall not pervert justice; you shall not show
partiality, nor take a bribe, for a bribe blinds
the eyes of the wise and twists the words of
the righteous. 20You shall follow what is altogether just, that you may live and inherit the
land which the LORD your God is giving you.

21"You shall not plant for yourself any tree,
as a wooden image, near the altar which you
build for yourself to the LORD your God. 22You
shall not set up a *sacred* pillar, which the LORD
your God hates.

16:21,22 wooden image...*sacred* pillar. A reference to the wooden poles, images, or trees that represented the Canaanite goddess Asherah. A stone pillar symbolic of male fertility was also prevalent in the Canaanite religion. These were forbidden by the first two commandments (Ex. 20:3–6; Deut. 5:7–10).

Psalm 37:30–36

30 The mouth of the righteous speaks
wisdom,
And his tongue talks of justice.
31 The law of his God *is* in his heart;
None of his steps shall slide.

32 The wicked watches the righteous,
And seeks to slay him.
33 The LORD will not leave him in his
hand,
Nor condemn him when he is judged.
34 Wait on the LORD,
And keep His way,
And He shall exalt you to inherit the
land;
When the wicked are cut off, you shall
see *it.*
35 I have seen the wicked in great power,
And spreading himself like a native
green tree.
36 Yet he passed away, and behold, he *was*
no *more;*
Indeed I sought him, but he could not
be found.

Proverbs 12:17–19

17 He *who* speaks truth declares
righteousness,
But a false witness, deceit.
18 There is one who speaks like the
piercings of a sword,
But the tongue of the wise *promotes*
health.
19 The truthful lip shall be established
forever,
But a lying tongue *is* but for a moment.

12:18 speaks...piercings. The contrast here is between cutting words that are blurted out (Ps. 106:33) and thoughtful words that bring health (Eph. 4:29,30).

Luke 3:1–38

3 Now in the fifteenth year of the reign of
Tiberius Caesar, Pontius Pilate being governor of Judea, Herod being tetrarch of Galilee, his brother Philip tetrarch of Iturea and
the region of Trachonitis, and Lysanias tetrarch of Abilene,
2 while Annas and Caiaphas
were high priests, the word of God came to
John the son of Zacharias in the wilderness.
3 And he went into all the region around the Jordan, preaching a baptism of repentance for the
remission of sins,
4 as it is written in the book of
the words of Isaiah the prophet, saying:

3:2 Annas and Caiaphas were high priests. According to Josephus, Annas served as high priest A.D. 6–15, when he was deposed by Roman officials. He nonetheless retained *de facto* power, as seen in the fact that his successors included 5 of his sons and Caiaphas, a son-in-law (Matt. 26:3). Caiaphas was the actual high priest during the time Luke describes, but Annas still controlled the office. This is seen clearly in the fact that Christ was taken to Annas first after His arrest, then to Caiaphas (Matt. 26:57).

3:4 Make His paths straight. Quoted from Isaiah 40:3–5. A monarch traveling in wilderness regions would have a crew of workmen go ahead to make sure the road was clear of debris, obstructions, potholes, and other hazards that made the journey difficult. In a spiritual sense, John was calling the people of Israel to prepare their hearts for the coming of their Messiah.

*"The voice of one crying in the
wilderness:
'Prepare the way of the LORD;
Make His paths straight.*
5 *Every valley shall be filled
And every mountain and hill brought
low;
The crooked places shall be made
straight
And the rough ways smooth;*
6 *And all flesh shall see the salvation
of God.' "*

7 Then he said to the multitudes that came out
to be baptized by him, "Brood of vipers! Who
warned you to flee from the wrath to come?
8 Therefore bear fruits worthy of repentance,
and do not begin to say to yourselves, 'We have
Abraham as *our* father.' For I say to you that
God is able to raise up children to Abraham

from these stones. [9]And even now the ax is
laid to the root of the trees. Therefore every
tree which does not bear good fruit is cut
down and thrown into the fire."
[10]So the people asked him, saying, "What
shall we do then?"
[11]He answered and said to them, "He who has
two tunics, let him give to him who has none;
and he who has food, let him do likewise."
[12]Then tax collectors also came to be baptized,
and said to him, "Teacher, what shall we do?"
[13]And he said to them, "Collect no more
than what is appointed for you."
[14]Likewise the soldiers asked him, saying,
"And what shall we do?"
So he said to them, "Do not intimidate anyone or accuse falsely, and be content with your wages."
[15]Now as the people were in expectation, and
all reasoned in their hearts about John,
whether he was the Christ *or* not, [16]John
answered, saying to all, "I indeed baptize you
with water; but One mightier than I is coming,
whose sandal strap I am not worthy to loose.
He will baptize you with the Holy Spirit and
fire. [17]His winnowing fan *is* in His hand, and He
will thoroughly clean out His threshing floor,
and gather the wheat into His barn; but the
chaff He will burn with unquenchable fire."
[18]And with many other exhortations he
preached to the people. [19]But Herod the tetrarch, being rebuked by him concerning
Herodias, his brother Philip's wife, and for all
the evils which Herod had done, [20]also added
this, above all, that he shut John up in prison.
[21]When all the people were baptized, it came
to pass that Jesus also was baptized; and while
He prayed, the heaven was opened. [22]And the
Holy Spirit descended in bodily form like a
dove upon Him, and a voice came from heaven
which said, "You are My beloved Son; in You I
am well pleased."
[23]Now Jesus Himself began *His ministry at*
about thirty years of age, being (as was supposed) *the* son of Joseph, *the son* of Heli, [24]*the son*
of Matthat, *the son* of Levi, *the son* of Melchi, *the*
son of Janna, *the son* of Joseph, [25]*the son* of
Mattathiah, *the son* of Amos, *the son* of Nahum,
the son of Esli, *the son* of Naggai, [26]*the son* of
Maath, *the son* of Mattathiah, *the son* of Semei,
the son of Joseph, *the son* of Judah, [27]*the son* of
Joannas, *the son* of Rhesa, *the son* of
Zerubbabel, *the son* of Shealtiel, *the son* of Neri,
[28]*the son* of Melchi, *the son* of Addi, *the son* of
Cosam, *the son* of Elmodam, *the son* of Er, [29]*the*
son of Jose, *the son* of Eliezer, *the son* of Jorim,
the son of Matthat, *the son* of Levi, [30]*the son* of
Simeon, *the son* of Judah, *the son* of Joseph, *the*
son of Jonan, *the son* of Eliakim, [31]*the son* of
Melea, *the son* of Menan, *the son* of Mattathah,
the son of Nathan, *the son* of David, [32]*the son* of
Jesse, *the son* of Obed, *the son* of Boaz, *the son* of
Salmon, *the son* of Nahshon, [33]*the son* of Amminadab, *the son* of Ram, *the son* of Hezron, *the son*
of Perez, *the son* of Judah, [34]*the son* of Jacob, *the*
son of Isaac, *the son* of Abraham, *the son* of
Terah, *the son* of Nahor, [35]*the son* of Serug, *the*
son of Reu, *the son* of Peleg, *the son* of Eber, *the*
son of Shelah, [36]*the son* of Cainan, *the son* of
Arphaxad, *the son* of Shem, *the son* of Noah, *the*
son of Lamech, [37]*the son* of Methuselah, *the son*
of Enoch, *the son* of Jared, *the son* of Mahalalel,
the son of Cainan, [38]*the son* of Enosh, *the son* of
Seth, *the son* of Adam, *the son* of God.

DAY 27: How were God's people to treat the poor?

As the Israelites prepared to enter the Promised Land, Deuteronomy 15:4 has an interesting statement: "except when there may be no poor." Idealistically, there was the possibility that poverty would be eradicated in the land "for the LORD will greatly bless you in the land." The fullness of that blessing, however, would be contingent on the completeness of Israel's obedience. Thus, vv. 4–6 were an encouragement to strive for a reduction of poverty while at the same time they stressed the abundance of the provision God would make in the Promised Land.

God specifically warns them about hardening their hearts against the poor, but to "open your hand wide to him and willingly lend him sufficient for his need" (v. 8). The attitude of the Israelites toward the poor in their community was to be one of warmth and generosity. The poor were given whatever was necessary to meet their needs, even with the realization that such "loans" would never need to be paid back.

"For the poor will never cease from the land," Moses adds (v. 11). Realistically (in contrast to v. 4), the disobedience toward the Lord on Israel's part meant that there would always be poor people in the land of Israel. Jesus repeated this truism in Matthew 26:11. Even if a Hebrew was sold into a period of servitude for his debts, his master "shall not let him go away empty-handed" (Deut. 15:13). When a slave had completed his time of service, his former owner was to make ample provision for him so that he would not begin his state of new freedom in destitution.

MARCH 28

Deuteronomy 17:1–18:22

17 “You shall not sacrifice to the LORD your
God a bull or sheep which has any
blemish *or* defect, for that *is* an abomination to
the LORD your God.
2“If there is found among you, within any of
your gates which the LORD your God gives
you, a man or a woman who has been wicked
in the sight of the LORD your God, in transgressing His covenant, 3who has gone and
served other gods and worshiped them, either
the sun or moon or any of the host of heaven,
which I have not commanded, 4and it is told
you, and you hear *of it,* then you shall inquire
diligently. And if *it is* indeed true *and* certain
that such an abomination has been committed
in Israel, 5then you shall bring out to your
gates that man or woman who has committed
that wicked thing, and shall stone to death
that man or woman with stones. 6Whoever is
deserving of death shall be put to death on the
testimony of two or three witnesses; he shall
not be put to death on the testimony of one
witness. 7The hands of the witnesses shall be
the first against him to put him to death, and
afterward the hands of all the people. So you
shall put away the evil from among you.
8“If a matter arises which is too hard for you
to judge, between degrees of guilt for bloodshed, between one judgment or another, or
between one punishment or another, matters
of controversy within your gates, then you
shall arise and go up to the place which the
LORD your God chooses. 9And you shall come
to the priests, the Levites, and to the judge
there in those days, and inquire *of them;* they
shall pronounce upon you the sentence of
judgment. 10You shall do according to the sentence which they pronounce upon you in that
place which the LORD chooses. And you shall
be careful to do according to all that they
order you. 11According to the sentence of the
law in which they instruct you, according to
the judgment which they tell you, you shall
do; you shall not turn aside *to* the right hand
or *to* the left from the sentence which they
pronounce upon you. 12Now the man who acts
presumptuously and will not heed the priest
who stands to minister there before the LORD
your God, or the judge, that man shall die. So
you shall put away the evil from Israel. 13And
all the people shall hear and fear, and no
longer act presumptuously.
14“When you come to the land which the
LORD your God is giving you, and possess it
and dwell in it, and say, ‘I will set a king over
me like all the nations that *are* around me,’
15you shall surely set a king over you whom
the LORD your God chooses; *one* from among
your brethren you shall set as king over you;
you may not set a foreigner over you, who *is*
not your brother. 16But he shall not multiply
horses for himself, nor cause the people to
return to Egypt to multiply horses, for the
LORD has said to you, ‘You shall not return that
way again.’ 17Neither shall he multiply wives
for himself, lest his heart turn away; nor shall
he greatly multiply silver and gold for himself.

17:16,17 multiply...multiply...multiply. Restrictions were placed on the king: 1) he must not acquire many horses; 2) he must not take multiple wives; and 3) he must not accumulate much silver and gold. The king was not to rely on military strength, political alliances, or wealth for his position and authority, but he was to look to the Lord. Solomon violated all of those prohibitions, while his father, David, violated the last two. Solomon's wives brought idolatry into Jerusalem, which resulted in the kingdom being divided (1 Kin. 11:1–43).

18“Also it shall be, when he sits on the
throne of his kingdom, that he shall write for
himself a copy of this law in a book, from *the*
one before the priests, the Levites. 19And it
shall be with him, and he shall read it all the
days of his life, that he may learn to fear the
LORD his God and be careful to observe all
the words of this law and these statutes, 20that
his heart may not be lifted above his brethren,
that he may not turn aside from the commandment *to* the right hand or *to* the left, and
that he may prolong *his* days in his kingdom,
he and his children in the midst of Israel.

18 “The priests, the Levites—all the tribe of
Levi—shall have no part nor inheritance
with Israel; they shall eat the offerings of the
LORD made by fire, and His portion. 2There-
fore they shall have no inheritance among
their brethren; the LORD is their inheritance,
as He said to them.
3“And this shall be the priest's due from the
people, from those who offer a sacrifice,
whether *it is* bull or sheep: they shall give to
the priest the shoulder, the cheeks, and the
stomach. 4The firstfruits of your grain and
your new wine and your oil, and the first of the

fleece of your sheep, you shall give him. 5For
the LORD your God has chosen him out of all
your tribes to stand to minister in the name of
the LORD, him and his sons forever.
6"So if a Levite comes from any of your
gates, from where he dwells among all Israel,
and comes with all the desire of his mind to
the place which the LORD chooses, 7then he
may serve in the name of the LORD his God as
all his brethren the Levites *do,* who stand
there before the LORD. 8They shall have equal
portions to eat, besides what comes from the
sale of his inheritance.
9"When you come into the land which the
LORD your God is giving you, you shall not
learn to follow the abominations of those
nations. 10There shall not be found among you
anyone who makes his son or his daughter
pass through the fire, *or one* who practices
witchcraft, *or* a soothsayer, or one who interprets omens, or a sorcerer, 11or one who conjures spells, or a medium, or a spiritist, or one
who calls up the dead. 12For all who do these
things *are* an abomination to the LORD, and because of these abominations the LORD your
God drives them out from before you. 13You
shall be blameless before the LORD your God.
14For these nations which you will dispossess
listened to soothsayers and diviners; but as for
you, the LORD your God has not appointed
such for you.
15"The LORD your God will raise up for you a
Prophet like me from your midst, from your
brethren. Him you shall hear, 16according to all
you desired of the LORD your God in Horeb in
the day of the assembly, saying, 'Let me not
hear again the voice of the LORD my God, nor
let me see this great fire anymore, lest I die.'
17"And the LORD said to me: 'What they have
spoken is good. 18I will raise up for them a
Prophet like you from among their brethren,
and will put My words in His mouth, and He
shall speak to them all that I command Him.
19And it shall be *that* whoever will not hear My
words, which He speaks in My name, I will
require *it* of him. 20But the prophet who pre-
sumes to speak a word in My name, which I
have not commanded him to speak, or who
speaks in the name of other gods, that prophet
shall die.' 21And if you say in your heart, 'How
shall we know the word which the LORD has
not spoken?'— 22when a prophet speaks in the
name of the LORD, if the thing does not happen
or come to pass, that *is* the thing which the
LORD has not spoken; the prophet has spoken
it presumptuously; you shall not be afraid of
him.

Psalm 37:37–40

37 Mark the blameless *man,* and observe
the upright;
For the future of *that* man *is* peace.
38 But the transgressors shall be
destroyed together;
The future of the wicked shall be
cut off.
39 But the salvation of the righteous *is*
from the LORD;
He is their strength in the time of
trouble.
40 And the LORD shall help them and
deliver them;
He shall deliver them from the wicked,
And save them,
Because they trust in Him.

Proverbs 12:20–22

20 Deceit is in the heart of those who
devise evil,
But counselors of peace have joy.
21 No grave trouble will overtake the
righteous,
But the wicked shall be filled with evil.
22 Lying lips *are* an abomination to the
LORD,
But those who deal truthfully *are* His
delight.

Luke 4:1–30

4 Then Jesus, being filled with the Holy
Spirit, returned from the Jordan and was
led by the Spirit into the wilderness, 2being
tempted for forty days by the devil. And in
those days He ate nothing, and afterward,
when they had ended, He was hungry.
3And the devil said to Him, "If You are the Son
of God, command this stone to become bread."
4But Jesus answered him, saying, "It is written, *'Man shall not live by bread alone, but by
every word of God.'* "
5Then the devil, taking Him up on a high
mountain, showed Him all the kingdoms of the
world in a moment of time. 6And the devil said
to Him, "All this authority I will give You, and
their glory; for *this* has been delivered to me,
and I give it to whomever I wish. 7Therefore, if
You will worship before me, all will be Yours."
8And Jesus answered and said to him, "Get
behind Me, Satan! For it is written, *'You shall
worship the LORD your God, and Him only you
shall serve.'* "
9Then he brought Him to Jerusalem, set
Him on the pinnacle of the temple, and said to
Him, "If You are the Son of God, throw Yourself
down from here. 10For it is written:

'He shall give His angels charge over
you,
To keep you,'

11and,

'In their hands they shall bear you up,
Lest you dash your foot against a
stone.' "

12And Jesus answered and said to him, "It
has been said, *'You shall not tempt the LORD*
your God.' "
13Now when the devil had ended every temptation, he departed from Him until an opportune time.
14Then Jesus returned in the power of the
Spirit to Galilee, and news of Him went out
through all the surrounding region. 15And He
taught in their synagogues, being glorified by
all.
16So He came to Nazareth, where He had
been brought up. And as His custom was, He
went into the synagogue on the Sabbath day,
and stood up to read. 17And He was handed the
book of the prophet Isaiah. And when He had
opened the book, He found the place where it
was written:

18 *"The Spirit of the LORD is upon Me,*
Because He has anointed Me
To preach the gospel to the poor;
He has sent Me to heal the
brokenhearted,
To proclaim liberty to the captives
And recovery of sight to the blind,
To set at liberty those who are
oppressed;
19 *To proclaim the acceptable year*
of the LORD."

20Then He closed the book, and gave *it* back to
the attendant and sat down. And the eyes of all
who were in the synagogue were fixed on Him.
21And He began to say to them, "Today this
Scripture is fulfilled in your hearing." 22So all
bore witness to Him, and marveled at the gracious words which proceeded out of His mouth.
And they said, "Is this not Joseph's son?"
23He said to them, "You will surely say this
proverb to Me, 'Physician, heal yourself!

4:21 this Scripture is fulfilled. This was an unambiguous claim that Jesus was the Messiah who fulfilled the prophecy. His hearers correctly understood His meaning but could not accept such lofty claims from One whom they knew so well as the carpenter's son (v. 22; Matt. 13:55).

Whatever we have heard done in Capernaum,
do also here in Your country.' " 24Then He said,
"Assuredly, I say to you, no prophet is accepted in his own country. 25But I tell you truly,
many widows were in Israel in the days of
Elijah, when the heaven was shut up three
years and six months, and there was a great
famine throughout all the land; 26but to none of
them was Elijah sent except to Zarephath, *in*
the region of Sidon, to a woman *who was* a
widow. 27And many lepers were in Israel in the
time of Elisha the prophet, and none of them
was cleansed except Naaman the Syrian."
28So all those in the synagogue, when they
heard these things, were filled with wrath,
29and rose up and thrust Him out of the city;
and they led Him to the brow of the hill on
which their city was built, that they might
throw Him down over the cliff. 30Then passing
through the midst of them, He went His way.

4:28 filled with wrath. This is Luke's first mention of hostile opposition to Christ's ministry. What seems to have sparked the Nazarenes' fury was Christ's suggestion that divine grace might be withheld from them yet extended to Gentiles.

4:30 passing through the midst of them. The implication is that this was a miraculous escape—the first of several similar incidents in which Jesus escaped a premature death at the hands of a mob (John 7:30; 8:59; 10:39).

DAY 28: Who is the Prophet that Moses refers to in Deuteronomy 18:15–19?

Read through 18:15–19 again where Moses promises that "the LORD your God will raise up for you a Prophet like me from your midst." The singular pronoun emphasizes the ultimate Prophet who was to come. Both the Old Testament (34:10) and the New Testament (Acts 3:22,23; 7:37) interpret this passage as a reference to the coming Messiah, who, like Moses, would receive and preach divine revelation and lead His people (John 1:21,25,43–45; 6:14; 7:40). In fact, Jesus was like Moses in several other ways: 1) He was spared death as a baby (Ex. 2; Matt. 2:13–23); 2) He renounced a royal court (Phil. 2:5–8; Heb. 11:24–27); 3) He had compassion on His people (Num. 27:17; Matt. 9:36); 4) He made intercession for the people (Deut. 9:18; Heb. 7:25); 5) He spoke with God face-to-face (Ex. 34:29,30; 2 Cor. 3:7); and 6) He was the mediator of a covenant (Deut. 29:1; Heb. 8:6,7).

In contrast to the true Prophet, Moses predicted there would be false prophets who would come to Israel, speaking not in the name of the Lord, but in the name of false gods (vv. 20–22). How could the people tell if a prophet was authentically speaking for God? Moses said, "If the thing does not happen," it was not from God. The characteristic of false prophets is the failure of their predictions to always come true. Sometimes false prophets speak and it happens as they said, but they are representing false gods and trying to turn people from the true God—they must be rejected and executed (13:1–5). Other times, false prophets are more subtle and identify with the true God but speak lies. If ever a prophecy of such a prophet fails, he is shown to be false (Jer. 28:15–17; 29:30–32).

MARCH 29

Deuteronomy 19:1–20:20

19 "When the LORD your God has cut off the
nations whose land the LORD your God is
giving you, and you dispossess them and
dwell in their cities and in their houses, 2you
shall separate three cities for yourself in the
midst of your land which the LORD your God is
giving you to possess. 3You shall prepare
roads for yourself, and divide into three parts
the territory of your land which the LORD your
God is giving you to inherit, that any manslayer may flee there.
4"And this *is* the case of the manslayer who
flees there, that he may live: Whoever kills his
neighbor unintentionally, not having hated
him in time past— 5as when *a man* goes to the
woods with his neighbor to cut timber, and his
hand swings a stroke with the ax to cut down
the tree, and the head slips from the handle
and strikes his neighbor so that he dies—he
shall flee to one of these cities and live; 6lest
the avenger of blood, while his anger is hot,
pursue the manslayer and overtake him,
because the way is long, and kill him, though
he *was* not deserving of death, since he had
not hated the victim in time past. 7Therefore I
command you, saying, 'You shall separate
three cities for yourself.'
8"Now if the LORD your God enlarges your
territory, as He swore to your fathers, and
gives you the land which He promised to give
to your fathers, 9and if you keep all these commandments and do them, which I command
you today, to love the LORD your God and to
walk always in His ways, then you shall add
three more cities for yourself besides these
three, 10lest innocent blood be shed in the
midst of your land which the LORD your God is
giving you *as* an inheritance, and *thus* guilt of
bloodshed be upon you.
11"But if anyone hates his neighbor, lies in
wait for him, rises against him and strikes him
mortally, so that he dies, and he flees to one of
these cities, 12then the elders of his city shall
send and bring him from there, and deliver
him over to the hand of the avenger of blood,
that he may die. 13Your eye shall not pity him,
but you shall put away *the guilt of* innocent
blood from Israel, that it may go well with you.
14"You shall not remove your neighbor's landmark, which the men of old have set, in your
inheritance which you will inherit in the land
that the LORD your God is giving you to possess.
15"One witness shall not rise against a man
concerning any iniquity or any sin that he
commits; by the mouth of two or three witnesses the matter shall be established. 16If a
false witness rises against any man to testify
against him of wrongdoing, 17then both men in
the controversy shall stand before the LORD,
before the priests and the judges who serve in
those days. 18And the judges shall make careful inquiry, and indeed, *if* the witness *is* a false
witness, who has testified falsely against his
brother, 19then you shall do to him as he
thought to have done to his brother; so you
shall put away the evil from among you. 20And
those who remain shall hear and fear, and
hereafter they shall not again commit such
evil among you. 21Your eye shall not pity: life
shall be for life, eye for eye, tooth for tooth,
hand for hand, foot for foot.
20 "When you go out to battle against
your enemies, and see horses and
chariots *and* people more numerous than you,
do not be afraid of them; for the LORD your
God *is* with you, who brought you up from the
land of Egypt. 2So it shall be, when you are on
the verge of battle, that the priest shall
approach and speak to the people. 3And he
shall say to them, 'Hear, O Israel: Today you
are on the verge of battle with your enemies.
Do not let your heart faint, do not be afraid,
and do not tremble or be terrified because of
them; 4for the LORD your God *is* He who goes

with you, to fight for you against your enemies,
to save you.’
5“Then the officers shall speak to the people, saying: ‘What man *is there* who has built a
new house and has not dedicated it? Let him
go and return to his house, lest he die in the
battle and another man dedicate it. 6Also what
man *is there* who has planted a vineyard and
has not eaten of it? Let him go and return to
his house, lest he die in the battle and another
man eat of it. 7And what man *is there* who is betrothed to a woman and has not married her?
Let him go and return to his house, lest he die
in the battle and another man marry her.’

20:1 do not be afraid. When Israelites went into battle, they were never to fear an enemy’s horses or chariots because the outcome of a battle would never be determined by mere military strength. The command not to be afraid was based on God’s power and faithfulness, which had already been proved to Israel in their deliverance from Egypt.

20:5–8 Let him go and return to his house. Four exemptions from service in Israel’s volunteer army were cited to illustrate the principle that anyone whose heart was not in the fight should not be there. Those who had other matters on their minds or were afraid were allowed to leave the army and return to their homes, since they would be useless in battle and even influence others to lose courage (v. 8).

8“The officers shall speak further to the people, and say, ‘What man *is there who is* fearful
and fainthearted? Let him go and return to his
house, lest the heart of his brethren faint like
his heart.’ 9And so it shall be, when the officers have finished speaking to the people, that
they shall make captains of the armies to lead
the people.
10“When you go near a city to fight against it,
then proclaim an offer of peace to it. 11And it
shall be that if they accept your offer of peace,
and open to you, then all the people *who are*
found in it shall be placed under tribute to you,
and serve you. 12Now if *the city* will not make
peace with you, but war against you, then you
shall besiege it. 13And when the LORD your
God delivers it into your hands, you shall
strike every male in it with the edge of the
sword. 14But the women, the little ones, the
livestock, and all that is in the city, all its spoil,
you shall plunder for yourself; and you shall
eat the enemies’ plunder which the LORD your
God gives you. 15Thus you shall do to all the
cities *which are* very far from you, which *are*
not of the cities of these nations.
16“But of the cities of these peoples which
the LORD your God gives you *as* an inheritance, you shall let nothing that breathes
remain alive, 17but you shall utterly destroy
them: the Hittite and the Amorite and the
Canaanite and the Perizzite and the Hivite and
the Jebusite, just as the LORD your God has
commanded you, 18lest they teach you to do
according to all their abominations which they
have done for their gods, and you sin against
the LORD your God.
19“When you besiege a city for a long time,
while making war against it to take it, you
shall not destroy its trees by wielding an ax
against them; if you can eat of them, do not cut
them down to use in the siege, for the tree of
the field *is* man’s *food.* 20Only the trees which
you know *are* not trees for food you may
destroy and cut down, to build siegeworks
against the city that makes war with you, until
it is subdued.

Psalm 38:1–8

A Psalm of David. To bring to remembrance.

O LORD, do not rebuke me in Your wrath,
Nor chasten me in Your hot
displeasure!
2 For Your arrows pierce me deeply,
And Your hand presses me down.
3 *There is* no soundness in my flesh
Because of Your anger,
Nor *any* health in my bones
Because of my sin.
4 For my iniquities have gone over my
head;
Like a heavy burden they are too heavy
for me.
5 My wounds are foul *and* festering
Because of my foolishness.
6 I am troubled, I am bowed down greatly;
I go mourning all the day long.
7 For my loins are full of inflammation,
And *there is* no soundness in my flesh.
8 I am feeble and severely broken;
I groan because of the turmoil of my
heart.

Proverbs 12:23–25

23 A prudent man conceals knowledge,
But the heart of fools proclaims
foolishness.
24 The hand of the diligent will rule,

12:23 conceals. Unlike the fool who makes all hear his folly, the wise person is a model of restraint and humility, speaking what he knows at an appropriate time (see 29:11).

But the lazy *man* will be put to forced
labor.
25 Anxiety in the heart of man causes
depression,
But a good word makes it glad.

Luke 4:31–44

31Then He went down to Capernaum, a city
of Galilee, and was teaching them on the
Sabbaths. 32And they were astonished at His
teaching, for His word was with authority.
33Now in the synagogue there was a man who
had a spirit of an unclean demon. And he cried
out with a loud voice, 34saying, "Let *us* alone!
What have we to do with You, Jesus of Nazareth? Did You come to destroy us? I know who
You are—the Holy One of God!"
35But Jesus rebuked him, saying, "Be quiet,
and come out of him!" And when the demon
had thrown him in *their* midst, it came out of
him and did not hurt him. 36Then they were all
amazed and spoke among themselves, saying,
"What a word this *is!* For with authority and
power He commands the unclean spirits, and
they come out." 37And the report about Him
went out into every place in the surrounding
region.
38Now He arose from the synagogue and
entered Simon's house. But Simon's wife's
mother was sick with a high fever, and they
made request of Him concerning her. 39So He
stood over her and rebuked the fever, and it left
her. And immediately she arose and served
them.

4:38 Simon's wife's mother. Peter was married (1 Cor. 9:5), though no details about his wife are given anywhere in Scripture. **a high fever.** Matthew 8:14,15 and Mark 1:30,31 also report this miracle. But only Luke, the physician, remarks that the fever was "high" and makes note of the means Jesus used to heal her (v. 39).

40When the sun was setting, all those who
had any that were sick with various diseases
brought them to Him; and He laid His hands
on every one of them and healed them. 41And
demons also came out of many, crying out and
saying, "You are the Christ, the Son of God!"
And He, rebuking *them,* did not allow them
to speak, for they knew that He was the
Christ.
42Now when it was day, He departed and
went into a deserted place. And the crowd
sought Him and came to Him, and tried to keep
Him from leaving them; 43but He said to them,
"I must preach the kingdom of God to the
other cities also, because for this purpose I
have been sent." 44And He was preaching in
the synagogues of Galilee.

DAY 29: What did the law warn about bringing false witness against another person?

In Deuteronomy 19:15, the law required that "by the mouth of two or three witnesses the matter shall be established." More than one witness was necessary to convict a man of a crime. This principle was to act as a safeguard against the false witness who might bring an untruthful charge against a fellow Israelite. By requiring more than one witness, greater accuracy and objectivity was gained (Deut. 17:6; Matt. 18:15–17; 2 Cor. 13:1).

However, it was possible that "a false witness [might rise] against any man to testify against him of wrongdoing" (v. 16). In some cases, there would only be one witness who brought a charge against someone. When such a case was taken to the central tribunal of priests and judges for trial, and upon investigation the testimony of the witness was found to be false, the accuser received the punishment appropriate for the alleged crime (v. 19). Others looking on would be taught to "hear and fear, and hereafter they shall not again commit such evil among you" (v. 20). When the fate of the false witness became known in Israel, it would serve as a deterrent against giving false testimony in Israel's courts.

In Israel, the principle of legal justice (called *lex talionis,* "law of retaliation") or "eye for eye" (v. 21) was given to encourage appropriate punishment of a criminal in cases where there might be a tendency to be either too lenient or too strict (Ex. 21:23–25; Lev. 24:17–22). Jesus confronted the Jews of His day for taking this law out of the courts and using it for purposes of personal vengeance (Matt. 5:38–42).

MARCH 30

Deuteronomy 21:1–22:30

21 "If *anyone* is found slain, lying in the field in the land which the LORD your God is giving you to possess, *and* it is not known who killed him, 2then your elders and your judges shall go out and measure *the distance* from the slain man to the surrounding cities. 3And it shall be *that* the elders of the city nearest to the slain man will take a heifer which has not been worked *and* which has not pulled with a yoke. 4The elders of that city shall bring the heifer down to a valley with flowing water, which is neither plowed nor sown, and they shall break the heifer's neck there in the valley. 5Then the priests, the sons of Levi, shall come near, for the LORD your God has chosen them to minister to Him and to bless in the name of the LORD; by their word every controversy and every assault shall be *settled*. 6And all the elders of that city nearest to the slain *man* shall wash their hands over the heifer whose neck was broken in the valley. 7Then they shall answer and say, 'Our hands have not shed this blood, nor have our eyes seen *it*. 8Provide atonement, O LORD, for Your people Israel, whom You have redeemed, and do not lay innocent blood to the charge of Your people Israel.' And atonement shall be provided on their behalf for the blood. 9So you shall put away the *guilt of* innocent blood from among you when you do *what is* right in the sight of the LORD.

10"When you go out to war against your enemies, and the LORD your God delivers them into your hand, and you take them captive, 11and you see among the captives a beautiful woman, and desire her and would take her for your wife, 12then you shall bring her home to your house, and she shall shave her head and trim her nails. 13She shall put off the clothes of her captivity, remain in your house, and mourn her father and her mother a full month; after that you may go in to her and be her husband, and she shall be your wife. 14And it shall be, if you have no delight in her, then you shall set her free, but you certainly shall not sell her for money; you shall not treat her brutally, because you have humbled her.

15"If a man has two wives, one loved and the other unloved, and they have borne him children, *both* the loved and the unloved, and *if* the firstborn son is of her who is unloved, 16then it shall be, on the day he bequeaths his possessions to his sons, *that* he must not bestow firstborn status on the son of the loved wife in preference to the son of the unloved, the *true* firstborn. 17But he shall acknowledge the son of the unloved wife *as* the firstborn by giving him a double portion of all that he has, for he *is* the beginning of his strength; the right of the firstborn *is* his.

18"If a man has a stubborn and rebellious son who will not obey the voice of his father or the voice of his mother, and *who,* when they have chastened him, will not heed them, 19then his father and his mother shall take hold of him and bring him out to the elders of his city, to the gate of his city. 20And they shall say to the elders of his city, 'This son of ours is stubborn and rebellious; he will not obey our voice; he is a glutton and a drunkard.' 21Then all the men of his city shall stone him to death with stones; so you shall put away the evil from among you, and all Israel shall hear and fear.

22"If a man has committed a sin deserving of death, and he is put to death, and you hang him on a tree, 23his body shall not remain overnight on the tree, but you shall surely bury him that day, so that you do not defile the land which the LORD your God is giving you *as* an inheritance; for he who is hanged *is* accursed of God.

22 "You shall not see your brother's ox or his sheep going astray, and hide yourself from them; you shall certainly bring them back to your brother. 2And if your brother *is* not near you, or if you do not know him, then you shall bring it to your own house, and it shall remain with you until your brother seeks it; then you shall restore it to him. 3You shall do the same with his donkey, and so shall you do with his garment; with any lost thing of your brother's, which he has lost and you have found, you shall do likewise; you must not hide yourself.

4"You shall not see your brother's donkey or his ox fall down along the road, and hide yourself from them; you shall surely help him lift *them* up again.

5"A woman shall not wear anything that pertains to a man, nor shall a man put on a woman's garment, for all who do so *are* an abomination to the LORD your God.

6"If a bird's nest happens to be before you along the way, in any tree or on the ground, with young ones or eggs, with the mother sitting on the young or on the eggs, you shall not take the mother with the young; 7you shall surely let the mother go, and take the young for yourself, that it may be well with you and *that* you may prolong *your* days.

8"When you build a new house, then you shall make a parapet for your roof, that you may not

22:5 anything that pertains to a man... woman's garment. Found only here in the Pentateuch, this statute prohibited a man from wearing any item of feminine clothing or ornamentation or a woman from wearing any item of masculine clothing or ornamentation. The same word translated "abomination" was used to describe God's view of homosexuality (Lev. 18:22; 20:13). This instance specifically outlawed transvestism. The creation order distinctions between male and female were to be maintained without exception (Gen. 1:27).

bring guilt of bloodshed on your household if
anyone falls from it.
9"You shall not sow your vineyard with different kinds of seed, lest the yield of the seed which you have sown and the fruit of your vineyard be defiled.
10"You shall not plow with an ox and a donkey together.
11"You shall not wear a garment of different sorts, *such as* wool and linen mixed together.
12"You shall make tassels on the four corners of the clothing with which you cover *yourself.*
13"If any man takes a wife, and goes in to her,
and detests her, 14and charges her with shameful conduct, and brings a bad name on her, and says, 'I took this woman, and when I came
to her I found she *was* not a virgin,' 15then the
father and mother of the young woman shall take and bring out *the evidence of* the young woman's virginity to the elders of the city at
the gate. 16And the young woman's father shall
say to the elders, 'I gave my daughter to this man as wife, and he detests her. 17Now he has
charged her with shameful conduct, saying, "I found your daughter *was* not a virgin," and yet these *are the evidences of* my daughter's virginity.' And they shall spread the cloth before
the elders of the city. 18Then the elders of that
city shall take that man and punish him; 19and
they shall fine him one hundred *shekels* of silver and give *them* to the father of the young woman, because he has brought a bad name on a virgin of Israel. And she shall be his wife; he cannot divorce her all his days.
20"But if the thing is true, *and evidences of* vir-
ginity are not found for the young woman, 21then
they shall bring out the young woman to the door of her father's house, and the men of her city shall stone her to death with stones, because she has done a disgraceful thing in Israel, to play the harlot in her father's house. So you shall put away the evil from among you.
22"If a man is found lying with a woman married to a husband, then both of them shall die—the man that lay with the woman, and the woman; so you shall put away the evil from Israel.
23"If a young woman *who is* a virgin is be-
trothed to a husband, and a man finds her in
the city and lies with her, 24then you shall bring
them both out to the gate of that city, and you shall stone them to death with stones, the young woman because she did not cry out in the city, and the man because he humbled his neighbor's wife; so you shall put away the evil from among you.
25"But if a man finds a betrothed young woman in the countryside, and the man forces her and lies with her, then only the man who
lay with her shall die. 26But you shall do noth-
ing to the young woman; *there is* in the young woman no sin *deserving* of death, for just as when a man rises against his neighbor and
kills him, even so *is* this matter. 27For he found
her in the countryside, *and* the betrothed young woman cried out, but *there was* no one to save her.
28"If a man finds a young woman *who is* a vir-
gin, who is not betrothed, and he seizes her and lies with her, and they are found out,
29then the man who lay with her shall give to
the young woman's father fifty *shekels* of silver, and she shall be his wife because he has humbled her; he shall not be permitted to divorce her all his days.
30"A man shall not take his father's wife, nor
uncover his father's bed.

22:22–29 Adultery was punished by death for the two found in the act. If the adulterous persons were a man with a woman who was pledged to be married to someone else, this consentual act led to the death of both parties (vv. 23,24). However, if the man forced (i.e., raped) the woman, then only the man's life was required (vv. 25–27). If the woman was a virgin not pledged in marriage, then the man had to pay a fine, marry the girl, and keep her as his wife as long as he lived (vv. 28,29).

Psalm 38:9–22

9 Lord, all my desire *is* before You;
And my sighing is not hidden from You.
10 My heart pants, my strength fails me;
As for the light of my eyes, it also has
gone from me.

11 My loved ones and my friends stand
aloof from my plague,
And my relatives stand afar off.
12 Those also who seek my life lay snares
for me;
Those who seek my hurt speak of
destruction,
And plan deception all the day long.

13 But I, like a deaf *man,* do not hear;
And *I am* like a mute *who* does not
open his mouth.
14 Thus I am like a man who does not
hear,
And in whose mouth *is* no response.
15 For in You, O LORD, I hope;
You will hear, O Lord my God.
16 For I said, "*Hear me,* lest they rejoice
over me,
Lest, when my foot slips, they exalt
themselves against me."

17 For I *am* ready to fall,
And my sorrow *is* continually before
me.
18 For I will declare my iniquity;
I will be in anguish over my sin.
19 But my enemies *are* vigorous, *and* they
are strong;
And those who hate me wrongfully
have multiplied.
20 Those also who render evil for good,
They are my adversaries, because
I follow *what is* good.

21 Do not forsake me, O LORD;
O my God, be not far from me!
22 Make haste to help me,
O Lord, my salvation!

Proverbs 12:26–28

26 The righteous should choose his
friends carefully,
For the way of the wicked leads them
astray.
27 The lazy *man* does not roast what he
took in hunting,
But diligence *is* man's precious
possession.
28 In the way of righteousness *is* life,
And in *its* pathway *there is* no death.

Luke 5:1–16

5 So it was, as the multitude pressed about
Him to hear the word of God, that He
stood by the Lake of Gennesaret, 2and saw two
boats standing by the lake; but the fishermen
had gone from them and were washing *their*
nets. 3Then He got into one of the boats, which
was Simon's, and asked him to put out a little
from the land. And He sat down and taught
the multitudes from the boat.
4When He had stopped speaking, He said to
Simon, "Launch out into the deep and let
down your nets for a catch."

5:4 let down your nets. Normally, the fish that were netted in shallow water at night would migrate during the daylight hours to waters too deep to reach easily with nets, which is why Peter fished at night. Peter may have thought Jesus' directive made no sense, but he obeyed and was rewarded for his obedience (v. 6).

5But Simon answered and said to Him,
"Master, we have toiled all night and caught
nothing; nevertheless at Your word I will let
down the net." 6And when they had done this,
they caught a great number of fish, and their
net was breaking. 7So they signaled to *their*
partners in the other boat to come and help
them. And they came and filled both the boats,
so that they began to sink. 8When Simon Peter
saw *it,* he fell down at Jesus' knees, saying, "Depart from me, for I am a sinful man, O Lord!"
9For he and all who were with him were astonished at the catch of fish which they had
taken; 10and so also *were* James and John, the
sons of Zebedee, who were partners with
Simon. And Jesus said to Simon, "Do not be
afraid. From now on you will catch men." 11So
when they had brought their boats to land,
they forsook all and followed Him.
12And it happened when He was in a certain
city, that behold, a man who was full of leprosy
saw Jesus; and he fell on *his* face and implored
Him, saying, "Lord, if You are willing, You can
make me clean."
13Then He put out *His* hand and touched
him, saying, "I am willing; be cleansed." Immediately the leprosy left him. 14And He
charged him to tell no one, "But go and show
yourself to the priest, and make an offering for
your cleansing, as a testimony to them, just as
Moses commanded."
15However, the report went around concerning Him all the more; and great multitudes
came together to hear, and to be healed by
Him of their infirmities. 16So He Himself *often*
withdrew into the wilderness and prayed.

DAY 30: What specific crimes were listed in the Old Testament as deserving the death penalty?

CRIME	SCRIPTURE REFERENCE
1. Premeditated Murder	Genesis 9:6; Exodus 21:12–14,22,23
2. Kidnapping	Exodus 21:16; Deuteronomy 24:7
3. Striking or Cursing Parents	Exodus 21:15; Leviticus 20:9; Proverbs 20:20; Matthew 15:4; Mark 7:10
4. Magic and Divination	Exodus 22:18
5. Bestiality	Exodus 22:19; Leviticus 20:15,16
6. Sacrificing to False Gods	Exodus 22:20
7. Profaning the Sabbath	Exodus 35:2; Numbers 15:32–36
8. Offering Human Sacrifice	Leviticus 20:2
9. Adultery	Leviticus 20:10–21; Deuteronomy 22:22
10. Incest	Leviticus 20:11,12,14
11. Homosexuality	Leviticus 20:13
12. Blasphemy	Leviticus 24:11–14,16,23
13. False Prophecy	Deuteronomy 13:1–10
14. Incorrigible Rebelliousness	Deuteronomy 17:12;21:18–21
15. Fornication	Deuteronomy 22:20,21
16. Rape of Betrothed Virgin	Deuteronomy 22:23–27

MARCH 31

Deuteronomy 23:1–24:22

23 "He who is emasculated by crushing or
mutilation shall not enter the assembly
of the LORD.
2"One of illegitimate birth shall not enter
the assembly of the LORD; even to the tenth
generation none of his *descendants* shall enter
the assembly of the LORD.
3"An Ammonite or Moabite shall not enter
the assembly of the LORD; even to the tenth
generation none of his *descendants* shall enter
the assembly of the LORD forever, 4because
they did not meet you with bread and water on
the road when you came out of Egypt, and because they hired against you Balaam the son
of Beor from Pethor of Mesopotamia, to curse
you. 5Nevertheless the LORD your God would
not listen to Balaam, but the LORD your God
turned the curse into a blessing for you,
because the LORD your God loves you. 6You
shall not seek their peace nor their prosperity
all your days forever.
7"You shall not abhor an Edomite, for he *is*
your brother. You shall not abhor an Egyptian,
because you were an alien in his land. 8The
children of the third generation born to them
may enter the assembly of the LORD.
9"When the army goes out against your enemies, then keep yourself from every wicked
thing. 10If there is any man among you who
becomes unclean by some occurrence in the
night, then he shall go outside the camp; he
shall not come inside the camp. 11But it shall
be, when evening comes, that he shall wash
with water; and when the sun sets, he may
come into the camp.
12"Also you shall have a place outside the
camp, where you may go out; 13and you shall
have an implement among your equipment,
and when you sit down outside, you shall dig
with it and turn and cover your refuse. 14For
the LORD your God walks in the midst of your
camp, to deliver you and give your enemies
over to you; therefore your camp shall be holy,
that He may see no unclean thing among you,
and turn away from you.
15"You shall not give back to his master the
slave who has escaped from his master to you.
16He may dwell with you in your midst, in the
place which he chooses within one of your
gates, where it seems best to him; you shall
not oppress him.
17"There shall be no *ritual* harlot of the
daughters of Israel, or a perverted one of the
sons of Israel. 18You shall not bring the wages
of a harlot or the price of a dog to the house of
the LORD your God for any vowed offering, for
both of these *are* an abomination to the LORD
your God.
19"You shall not charge interest to your
brother—interest on money *or* food *or* anything that is lent out at interest. 20To a foreigner
you may charge interest, but to your brother
you shall not charge interest, that the LORD
your God may bless you in all to which you set
your hand in the land which you are entering
to possess.
21"When you make a vow to the LORD your

God, you shall not delay to pay it; for the LORD your God will surely require it of you, and it would be sin to you. 22But if you abstain from vowing, it shall not be sin to you. 23That which has gone from your lips you shall keep and perform, for you voluntarily vowed to the LORD your God what you have promised with your mouth.

24"When you come into your neighbor's vineyard, you may eat your fill of grapes at your pleasure, but you shall not put *any* in your container. 25When you come into your neighbor's standing grain, you may pluck the heads with your hand, but you shall not use a sickle on your neighbor's standing grain.

24 "When a man takes a wife and marries her, and it happens that she finds no favor in his eyes because he has found some uncleanness in her, and he writes her a certificate of divorce, puts *it* in her hand, and sends her out of his house, 2when she has departed from his house, and goes and becomes another man's *wife*, 3*if* the latter husband detests her and writes her a certificate of divorce, puts *it* in her hand, and sends her out of his house, or if the latter husband dies who took her as his wife, 4*then* her former husband who divorced her must not take her back to be his wife after she has been defiled; for that *is* an abomination before the LORD, and you shall not bring sin on the land which the LORD your God is giving you *as* an inheritance.

5"When a man has taken a new wife, he shall not go out to war or be charged with any business; he shall be free at home one year, and bring happiness to his wife whom he has taken.

6"No man shall take the lower or the upper millstone in pledge, for he takes *one's* living in pledge.

7"If a man is found kidnapping any of his brethren of the children of Israel, and mistreats him or sells him, then that kidnapper shall die; and you shall put away the evil from among you.

8"Take heed in an outbreak of leprosy, that you carefully observe and do according to all that the priests, the Levites, shall teach you; just as I commanded them, *so* you shall be careful to do. 9Remember what the LORD your God did to Miriam on the way when you came out of Egypt!

10"When you lend your brother anything, you shall not go into his house to get his pledge. 11You shall stand outside, and the man to whom you lend shall bring the pledge out to you. 12And if the man *is* poor, you shall not keep his pledge overnight. 13You shall in any case return the pledge to him again when the sun goes down, that he may sleep in his own garment and bless you; and it shall be righteousness to you before the LORD your God.

14"You shall not oppress a hired servant *who is* poor and needy, *whether* one of your brethren or one of the aliens who *is* in your land within your gates. 15Each day you shall give *him* his wages, and not let the sun go down on it, for he *is* poor and has set his heart on it; lest he cry out against you to the LORD, and it be sin to you.

16"Fathers shall not be put to death for *their* children, nor shall children be put to death for *their* fathers; a person shall be put to death for his own sin.

17"You shall not pervert justice due the stranger or the fatherless, nor take a widow's garment as a pledge. 18But you shall remember that you were a slave in Egypt, and the LORD your God redeemed you from there; therefore I command you to do this thing.

19"When you reap your harvest in your field, and forget a sheaf in the field, you shall not go back to get it; it shall be for the stranger, the fatherless, and the widow, that the LORD your God may bless you in all the work of your hands. 20When you beat your olive trees, you shall not go over the boughs again; it shall be for the stranger, the fatherless, and the widow. 21When you gather the grapes of your vineyard, you shall not glean *it* afterward; it shall be for the stranger, the fatherless, and the widow. 22And you shall remember that you were a slave in the land of Egypt; therefore I command you to do this thing.

Psalm 39:1–6

To the Chief Musician. To Jeduthun.
A Psalm of David.

I said, "I will guard my ways,
Lest I sin with my tongue;
I will restrain my mouth with a muzzle,
While the wicked are before me."
2 I was mute with silence,
I held my peace *even* from good;
And my sorrow was stirred up.
3 My heart was hot within me;
While I was musing, the fire burned.
Then I spoke with my tongue:

4 "LORD, make me to know my end,
And what *is* the measure of my days,
That I may know how frail I *am*.
5 Indeed, You have made my days *as* handbreadths,
And my age *is* as nothing before You;
Certainly every man at his best state is but vapor. Selah

39:5 handbreadths. He measures the length of his life with the smallest popular measuring unit of ancient times (1 Kin. 7:26); see "four fingers" (i.e., about 2.9 in.) in Jeremiah 52:21. **and my age *is* as nothing before You.** On "measuring" God's age, see Psalm 90:2. **vapor.** For the same Hebrew word, see Ecclesiastes 1:2ff., "vanity" (a total of 31 occurrences of this term are in Eccl.); Psalm 144:4. On the concept in the New Testament, see James 4:14.

6 Surely every man walks about like a
shadow;
Surely they busy themselves in vain;
He heaps up *riches*,
And does not know who will gather
them.

Proverbs 13:1–3

13 A wise son *heeds* his father's
instruction,
But a scoffer does not listen to rebuke.
2 A man shall eat well by the fruit of *his*
mouth,
But the soul of the unfaithful feeds on
violence.
3 He who guards his mouth preserves
his life,
But he who opens wide his lips shall
have destruction.

Luke 5:17–39

17Now it happened on a certain day, as He
was teaching, that there were Pharisees and
teachers of the law sitting by, who had come
out of every town of Galilee, Judea, and Jerusalem. And the power of the Lord was *present*
to heal them. 18Then behold, men brought on
a bed a man who was paralyzed, whom they
sought to bring in and lay before Him. 19And
when they could not find how they might
bring him in, because of the crowd, they went
up on the housetop and let him down with *his*
bed through the tiling into the midst before
Jesus.
20When He saw their faith, He said to him,
"Man, your sins are forgiven you."
21And the scribes and the Pharisees began
to reason, saying, "Who is this who speaks
blasphemies? Who can forgive sins but God
alone?"
22But when Jesus perceived their thoughts,
He answered and said to them, "Why are you
reasoning in your hearts? 23Which is easier, to
say, 'Your sins are forgiven you,' or to say,
'Rise up and walk'? 24But that you may know
that the Son of Man has power on earth to forgive sins"—He said to the man who was paralyzed, "I say to you, arise, take up your bed,
and go to your house."
25Immediately he rose up before them, took
up what he had been lying on, and departed to
his own house, glorifying God. 26And they
were all amazed, and they glorified God and
were filled with fear, saying, "We have seen
strange things today!"

5:26 strange things. The response is curiously noncommittal—not void of wonder and amazement, but utterly void of true faith.

27After these things He went out and saw a
tax collector named Levi, sitting at the tax
office. And He said to him, "Follow Me." 28So
he left all, rose up, and followed Him.
29Then Levi gave Him a great feast in his
own house. And there were a great number of
tax collectors and others who sat down with
them. 30And their scribes and the Pharisees
complained against His disciples, saying,
"Why do You eat and drink with tax collectors
and sinners?"
31Jesus answered and said to them, "Those
who are well have no need of a physician, but
those who are sick. 32I have not come to call
the righteous, but sinners, to repentance."

5:30 eat and drink. Consorting with outcasts on any level—even merely speaking to them—was bad enough. Eating and drinking with them implied a level of friendship that was abhorrent to the Pharisees (7:34; 15:2; 19:7).

5:33 fast often. Jesus did fast on at least one occasion (Matt. 4:2)—but privately, in accordance with His own teaching (Matt. 6:16–18). The law also prescribed a fast on the Day of Atonement (Lev. 16:29–31; 23:27)—but all other fasts were supposed to be voluntary, for specific reasons such as penitence and earnest prayer. The fact that these Pharisees raised this question shows that they thought of fasting as a public exercise to display one's own spirituality. Yet, the Old Testament also rebuked hypocritical fasting (Is. 58:3–6).

[33]Then they said to Him, "Why do the disciples of John fast often and make prayers, and likewise those of the Pharisees, but Yours eat and drink?"

[34]And He said to them, "Can you make the friends of the bridegroom fast while the bridegroom is with them? [35]But the days will come when the bridegroom will be taken away from them; then they will fast in those days."

[36]Then He spoke a parable to them: "No one puts a piece from a new garment on an old one; otherwise the new makes a tear, and also the piece that was *taken* out of the new does not match the old. [37]And no one puts new wine into old wineskins; or else the new wine will burst the wineskins and be spilled, and the wineskins will be ruined. [38]But new wine must be put into new wineskins, and both are preserved. [39]And no one, having drunk old *wine,* immediately desires new; for he says, 'The old is better.' "

DAY 31: What does Deuteronomy 24:1–4 say about divorce and remarriage?

This passage does not command, commend, condone, or even suggest divorce. Rather, it recognizes that divorce occurs and permits it only on restricted grounds. The case presented here is designed to convey the fact that divorcing produced defilement. Notice the following sequence:

1) if a man finds an uncleanness (some impurity or something vile, see 23:14) in his wife, other than adultery, which was punished by execution (see 22:22);

2) if he legally divorces her (although God hates divorce, as Mal. 2:16 says; He has designed marriage for life, as Gen. 2:24 declares; and He allowed divorce because of hard hearts, as Matt. 19:8 reveals);

3) if she then marries another man;

4) if the new husband then dies or divorces her, then that woman could not return to her first husband (v. 4). This is so because she was "defiled" with such a defilement that is an abomination to the Lord and a sinful pollution of the Promised Land.

What constitutes that defilement? Only one thing is possible—she was defiled in the remarriage because there was no ground for the divorce. So when she remarried, she became an adulteress (Matt. 5:31,32) and is thus defiled so that her former husband can't take her back. Illegitimate divorce proliferates adultery.

APRIL 1

Deuteronomy 25:1–26:19

25 "If there is a dispute between men, and
they come to court, that *the judges* may
judge them, and they justify the righteous and
condemn the wicked, 2then it shall be, if the
wicked man deserves to be beaten, that the
judge will cause him to lie down and be beaten
in his presence, according to his guilt, with a
certain number of blows. 3Forty blows he may
give him *and* no more, lest he should exceed
this and beat him with many blows above
these, and your brother be humiliated in your
sight.
4"You shall not muzzle an ox while it treads
out *the grain.*
5"If brothers dwell together, and one of them
dies and has no son, the widow of the dead
man shall not be *married* to a stranger outside
the family; her husband's brother shall go in to
her, take her as his wife, and perform the duty
of a husband's brother to her. 6And it shall be
that the firstborn son which she bears will succeed to the name of his dead brother, that his
name may not be blotted out of Israel. 7But if
the man does not want to take his brother's
wife, then let his brother's wife go up to the gate
to the elders, and say, 'My husband's brother
refuses to raise up a name to his brother in
Israel; he will not perform the duty of my husband's brother.' 8Then the elders of his city
shall call him and speak to him. But *if* he
stands firm and says, 'I do not want to take
her,' 9then his brother's wife shall come to him
in the presence of the elders, remove his sandal from his foot, spit in his face, and answer
and say, 'So shall it be done to the man who
will not build up his brother's house.' 10And his
name shall be called in Israel, 'The house of
him who had his sandal removed.'
11"If *two* men fight together, and the wife of
one draws near to rescue her husband from
the hand of the one attacking him, and puts
out her hand and seizes him by the genitals,
12then you shall cut off her hand; your eye
shall not pity *her.*
13"You shall not have in your bag differing
weights, a heavy and a light. 14You shall not
have in your house differing measures, a large
and a small. 15You shall have a perfect and just
weight, a perfect and just measure, that your
days may be lengthened in the land which the
LORD your God is giving you. 16For all who do
such things, all who behave unrighteously,
are an abomination to the LORD your God.
17"Remember what Amalek did to you on the
way as you were coming out of Egypt, 18how
he met you on the way and attacked your rear
ranks, all the stragglers at your rear, when you
were tired and weary; and he did not fear God.
19Therefore it shall be, when the LORD your
God has given you rest from your enemies all
around, in the land which the LORD your God
is giving you to possess *as* an inheritance, *that*
you will blot out the remembrance of Amalek
from under heaven. You shall not forget.

26 "And it shall be, when you come into
the land which the LORD your God is
giving you *as* an inheritance, and you possess
it and dwell in it, 2that you shall take some of
the first of all the produce of the ground, which
you shall bring from your land that the LORD
your God is giving you, and put *it* in a basket
and go to the place where the LORD your God
chooses to make His name abide. 3And you
shall go to the one who is priest in those days,
and say to him, 'I declare today to the LORD your
God that I have come to the country which the
LORD swore to our fathers to give us.'
4"Then the priest shall take the basket out
of your hand and set it down before the altar of
the LORD your God. 5And you shall answer and
say before the LORD your God: 'My father *was*
a Syrian, about to perish, and he went down to
Egypt and dwelt there, few in number; and
there he became a nation, great, mighty, and
populous. 6But the Egyptians mistreated us,
afflicted us, and laid hard bondage on us.
7Then we cried out to the LORD God of our
fathers, and the LORD heard our voice and
looked on our affliction and our labor and our
oppression. 8So the LORD brought us out of
Egypt with a mighty hand and with an outstretched arm, with great terror and with
signs and wonders. 9He has brought us to this
place and has given us this land, "a land flowing with milk and honey"; 10and now, behold, I
have brought the firstfruits of the land which
you, O LORD, have given me.'
"Then you shall set it before the LORD your
God, and worship before the LORD your God.
11So you shall rejoice in every good *thing*
which the LORD your God has given to you and
your house, you and the Levite and the stranger who *is* among you.
12"When you have finished laying aside all
the tithe of your increase in the third year—
the year of tithing—and have given *it* to the
Levite, the stranger, the fatherless, and the
widow, so that they may eat within your gates
and be filled, 13then you shall say before the
LORD your God: 'I have removed the holy *tithe*

26:13,14 you shall say before the LORD your God. The confession to be made in connection with the offering of this first tithe consisted of a statement of obedience (vv. 13,14) and a prayer for God's blessing (v. 15). In this manner, the Israelite confessed his continual dependence on God and lived in obedient expectance of God's continued gracious blessing.

26:15 Look down from...heaven. This was the first reference to God's dwelling place being in heaven. From His abode in heaven, God had given the Israelites the land flowing with milk and honey as He had promised to the patriarchs. His continued blessing on both the people and the land was requested.

from *my* house, and also have given them to the Levite, the stranger, the fatherless, and the widow, according to all Your commandments which You have commanded me; I have not transgressed Your commandments, nor have I forgotten *them*. 14I have not eaten any of it when in mourning, nor have I removed *any* of it for an unclean *use,* nor given *any* of it for the dead. I have obeyed the voice of the LORD my God, and have done according to all that You have commanded me. 15Look down from Your holy habitation, from heaven, and bless Your people Israel and the land which You have given us, just as You swore to our fathers, "a land flowing with milk and honey." '

16"This day the LORD your God commands you to observe these statutes and judgments; therefore you shall be careful to observe them with all your heart and with all your soul. 17Today you have proclaimed the LORD to be your God, and that you will walk in His ways and keep His statutes, His commandments, and His judgments, and that you will obey His voice. 18Also today the LORD has proclaimed you to be His special people, just as He promised you, that *you* should keep all His commandments, 19and that He will set you high above all nations which He has made, in praise, in name, and in honor, and that you may be a holy people to the LORD your God, just as He has spoken."

Psalm 39:7–11

7 "And now, Lord, what do I wait for?
My hope *is* in You.
8 Deliver me from all my transgressions;
Do not make me the reproach of the
foolish.
9 I was mute, I did not open my mouth,
Because it was You who did *it.*
10 Remove Your plague from me;
I am consumed by the blow
of Your hand.
11 When with rebukes You correct man
for iniquity,
You make his beauty melt away
like a moth;
Surely every man *is* vapor. Selah

39:11 like a moth. The moth normally represented one of the most destructive creatures, but here the delicacy of the moth is intended (see Job 13:28; Is. 50:9; 51:8; Matt. 6:19ff.).

Proverbs 13:4–6

4 The soul of a lazy *man* desires, and *has*
nothing;
But the soul of the diligent shall be
made rich.
5 A righteous *man* hates lying,
But a wicked *man* is loathsome and
comes to shame.
6 Righteousness guards *him whose* way
is blameless,
But wickedness overthrows the sinner.

Luke 6:1–26

6 Now it happened on the second Sabbath after the first that He went through the grainfields. And His disciples plucked the heads of grain and ate *them,* rubbing *them* in *their* hands. 2And some of the Pharisees said to them, "Why are you doing what is not lawful to do on the Sabbath?"

3But Jesus answering them said, "Have you not even read this, what David did when he was hungry, he and those who were with him: 4how he went into the house of God, took and ate the showbread, and also gave some to those with him, which is not lawful for any but the priests to eat?" 5And He said to them, "The Son of Man is also Lord of the Sabbath."

6Now it happened on another Sabbath, also, that He entered the synagogue and taught. And a man was there whose right hand was withered. 7So the scribes and Pharisees watched Him closely, whether He would heal on the Sabbath, that they might find an accusation against Him. 8But He knew their thoughts, and said to the man who had the withered hand, "Arise and stand here." And he arose and

stood. [9]Then Jesus said to them, "I will ask you
one thing: Is it lawful on the Sabbath to do
good or to do evil, to save life or to destroy?"
[10]And when He had looked around at them all,
He said to the man, "Stretch out your hand."
And he did so, and his hand was restored as
whole as the other. [11]But they were filled with
rage, and discussed with one another what
they might do to Jesus.

6:11 filled with rage. A curious response in the face of so glorious a miracle. Such irrational hatred was the scribes' and Pharisees' response to having been publicly humiliated—something they hated worse than anything (see Matt. 23:6,7). They were unable to answer His reasoning (vv. 9,10). And furthermore, by healing the man only with a command, He had performed no actual "work" that they could charge Him with. Desperately seeking a reason to accuse Him (v. 7), they could find none. Their response was blind fury.

6:12 continued all night in prayer. Luke frequently shows Jesus praying—and particularly before major events in His ministry. See 3:21; 5:16; 9:18,28,29; 11:1; 22:32,40–46.

[12]Now it came to pass in those days that He
went out to the mountain to pray, and continued all night in prayer to God. [13]And when it
was day, He called His disciples to *Himself;*
and from them He chose twelve whom He also
named apostles: [14]Simon, whom He also named
Peter, and Andrew his brother; James and
John; Philip and Bartholomew; [15]Matthew and
Thomas; James the *son* of Alphaeus, and Simon called the Zealot; [16]Judas *the son* of James,
and Judas Iscariot who also became a traitor.

[17]And He came down with them and stood
on a level place with a crowd of His disciples
and a great multitude of people from all Judea
and Jerusalem, and from the seacoast of Tyre
and Sidon, who came to hear Him and be
healed of their diseases, [18]as well as those who
were tormented with unclean spirits. And they
were healed. [19]And the whole multitude
sought to touch Him, for power went out from
Him and healed *them* all.

[20]Then He lifted up His eyes toward His disciples, and said:

"Blessed *are you* poor,
For yours is the kingdom of God.
[21] Blessed *are you* who hunger now,
For you shall be filled.
Blessed *are you* who weep now,
For you shall laugh.
[22] Blessed are you when men hate you,
And when they exclude you,
And revile *you,* and cast out your
name as evil,
For the Son of Man's sake.
[23] Rejoice in that day and leap for joy!
For indeed your reward *is* great in
heaven,
For in like manner their fathers did
to the prophets.

[24] "But woe to you who are rich,
For you have received your
consolation.
[25] Woe to you who are full,
For you shall hunger.
Woe to you who laugh now,
For you shall mourn and weep.
[26] Woe to you when all men speak well
of you,
For so did their fathers to the false
prophets.

DAY 1: How similar is the sermon in Luke 6:17–49 to the Sermon on the Mount?

The similarity of the Sermon on the Plateau in Luke to the Sermon on the Mount (Matt. 5:1–7:29) is remarkable. It is possible, of course, that Jesus simply preached the same sermon on more than one occasion. (It is evident that He often used the same material more than once—e.g., 12:58,59; see Matt. 5:25,26.) It appears more likely, however, that these are variant accounts of the same event. Luke's version is abbreviated somewhat, because he omitted sections from the sermon that are uniquely Jewish (particularly Christ's exposition of the law). Aside from that, the two sermons follow exactly the same flow of thought, beginning with the Beatitudes and ending with the parable about building on the rock. Differences in wording between the two accounts are undoubtedly owing to the fact that the sermon was originally delivered in Aramaic. Luke and Matthew translate into Greek with slight variances. Of course, both translations are equally inspired and authoritative.

Luke tells us the sermon was given on "a level place" (v. 17), after coming down from a mountain. In Matthew 5:1, it says "on a mountain." These harmonize easily if Luke is referring to either a plateau or a level place on the mountainside. Indeed, there is such a place at the site near Capernaum where tradition says this sermon was delivered.

Luke's account of the Beatitudes (vv. 20–23) is abbreviated (see Matt. 5:3–12). He lists only 4, and balances them with 4 parallel woes (vv. 24–26). One example of the difference in wording is in v. 20, "Blessed are you poor." Christ's concern for the poor and outcasts is one of Luke's favorite themes. Luke used a personal pronoun ("you") where Matthew 5:3 employed a definite article ("the"). Luke was underscoring the tender, personal sense of Christ's words. A comparison of the two passages reveals that Christ was dealing with something more significant than mere material poverty and wealth, however. The poverty spoken of here refers primarily to a sense of one's own spiritual impoverishment.

APRIL 2

Deuteronomy 27:1–28:68

27 Now Moses, with the elders of Israel,
commanded the people, saying: "Keep
all the commandments which I command you
today. 2And it shall be, on the day when you
cross over the Jordan to the land which the
LORD your God is giving you, that you shall set
up for yourselves large stones, and whitewash
them with lime. 3You shall write on them all
the words of this law, when you have crossed
over, that you may enter the land which the
LORD your God is giving you, 'a land flowing
with milk and honey,' just as the LORD God of
your fathers promised you. 4Therefore it shall
be, when you have crossed over the Jordan,
that on Mount Ebal you shall set up these
stones, which I command you today, and you
shall whitewash them with lime. 5And there
you shall build an altar to the LORD your God,
an altar of stones; you shall not use an iron *tool*
on them. 6You shall build with whole stones
the altar of the LORD your God, and offer burnt
offerings on it to the LORD your God. 7You
shall offer peace offerings, and shall eat there,
and rejoice before the LORD your God. 8And
you shall write very plainly on the stones all
the words of this law."

9Then Moses and the priests, the Levites,
spoke to all Israel, saying, "Take heed and listen, O Israel: This day you have become the
people of the LORD your God. 10Therefore you
shall obey the voice of the LORD your God, and
observe His commandments and His statutes
which I command you today."

11And Moses commanded the people on the
same day, saying, 12"These shall stand on
Mount Gerizim to bless the people, when you
have crossed over the Jordan: Simeon, Levi,
Judah, Issachar, Joseph, and Benjamin; 13and
these shall stand on Mount Ebal to curse: Reuben, Gad, Asher, Zebulun, Dan, and Naphtali.

14"And the Levites shall speak with a loud
voice and say to all the men of Israel: 15'Cursed
is the one who makes a carved or molded image,
an abomination to the LORD, the work of the
hands of the craftsman, and sets *it* up in secret.'

"And all the people shall answer and say,
'Amen!'

16'Cursed *is* the one who treats his father or
his mother with contempt.'

"And all the people shall say, 'Amen!'

17'Cursed *is* the one who moves his neighbor's landmark.'

"And all the people shall say, 'Amen!'

18'Cursed *is* the one who makes the blind to
wander off the road.'

"And all the people shall say, 'Amen!'

19'Cursed *is* the one who perverts the justice
due the stranger, the fatherless, and widow.'

"And all the people shall say, 'Amen!'

20'Cursed *is* the one who lies with his
father's wife, because he has uncovered his
father's bed.'

"And all the people shall say, 'Amen!'

21'Cursed *is* the one who lies with any kind
of animal.'

"And all the people shall say, 'Amen!'

22'Cursed *is* the one who lies with his sister,
the daughter of his father or the daughter of
his mother.'

"And all the people shall say, 'Amen!'

23'Cursed *is* the one who lies with his mother-
in-law.'

"And all the people shall say, 'Amen!'

24'Cursed *is* the one who attacks his neighbor secretly.'

"And all the people shall say, 'Amen!'

25'Cursed *is* the one who takes a bribe to slay
an innocent person.'

"And all the people shall say, 'Amen!'

26'Cursed *is* the one who does not confirm
all the words of this law by observing them.'

"And all the people shall say, 'Amen!' "

28 "Now it shall come to pass, if you diligently obey the voice of the LORD your
God, to observe carefully all His commandments which I command you today, that the
LORD your God will set you high above all
nations of the earth. 2And all these blessings
shall come upon you and overtake you, because
you obey the voice of the LORD your God:

28:1, 2 diligently obey the voice of the LORD your God. "Diligently obey" stressed the need for complete obedience on the part of Israel. The people could not legally or personally merit God's goodness and blessing; but their constant desire to obey, worship, and maintain a right relation to Him was evidence of their true faith in and love for Him (see 6:5). It was also evidence of God's gracious work in their hearts.

28:1 high above all nations. If Israel obeyed the Lord, ultimate blessing would be given in the form of preeminence above all the nations of the world (see 26:19). The indispensable condition for obtaining this blessing was salvation, resulting in obedience to the Lord in the form of keeping His commandments. This blessing will ultimately come to pass in the millennial kingdom, particularly designed to exalt Israel's King, the Messiah, and His nation (see Zech. 13:1–14:21; Rom. 11:25–27).

3"Blessed *shall* you *be* in the city, and blessed
shall you *be* in the country.
4"Blessed *shall be* the fruit of your body, the
produce of your ground and the increase of
your herds, the increase of your cattle and the
offspring of your flocks.
5"Blessed *shall be* your basket and your
kneading bowl.
6"Blessed *shall* you *be* when you come in,
and blessed *shall* you *be* when you go out.
7"The LORD will cause your enemies who
rise against you to be defeated before your
face; they shall come out against you one way
and flee before you seven ways.
8"The LORD will command the blessing on
you in your storehouses and in all to which
you set your hand, and He will bless you in the
land which the LORD your God is giving you.
9"The LORD will establish you as a holy people to Himself, just as He has sworn to you, if
you keep the commandments of the LORD
your God and walk in His ways. 10Then all peoples of the earth shall see that you are called
by the name of the LORD, and they shall be
afraid of you. 11And the LORD will grant you
plenty of goods, in the fruit of your body, in
the increase of your livestock, and in the produce of your ground, in the land of which the
LORD swore to your fathers to give you. 12The
LORD will open to you His good treasure, the
heavens, to give the rain to your land in its season, and to bless all the work of your hand.
You shall lend to many nations, but you shall
not borrow. 13And the LORD will make you the
head and not the tail; you shall be above only,
and not be beneath, if you heed the commandments of the LORD your God, which I
command you today, and are careful to
observe *them.* 14So you shall not turn aside
from any of the words which I command you
this day, *to* the right or the left, to go after
other gods to serve them.
15"But it shall come to pass, if you do not
obey the voice of the LORD your God, to
observe carefully all His commandments and
His statutes which I command you today, that
all these curses will come upon you and overtake you:
16"Cursed *shall* you *be* in the city, and cursed
shall you *be* in the country.
17"Cursed *shall be* your basket and your
kneading bowl.
18"Cursed *shall be* the fruit of your body and
the produce of your land, the increase of your
cattle and the offspring of your flocks.
19"Cursed *shall* you *be* when you come in,
and cursed *shall* you *be* when you go out.
20"The LORD will send on you cursing, confusion, and rebuke in all that you set your hand
to do, until you are destroyed and until you
perish quickly, because of the wickedness of
your doings in which you have forsaken Me.
21The LORD will make the plague cling to you
until He has consumed you from the land
which you are going to possess. 22The LORD
will strike you with consumption, with fever,
with inflammation, with severe burning fever,
with the sword, with scorching, and with
mildew; they shall pursue you until you perish. 23And your heavens which *are* over your
head shall be bronze, and the earth which is
under you *shall be* iron. 24The LORD will change
the rain of your land to powder and dust; from
the heaven it shall come down on you until
you are destroyed.
25"The LORD will cause you to be defeated
before your enemies; you shall go out one way
against them and flee seven ways before
them; and you shall become troublesome to
all the kingdoms of the earth. 26Your carcasses
shall be food for all the birds of the air and the
beasts of the earth, and no one shall frighten
them away. 27The LORD will strike you with the
boils of Egypt, with tumors, with the scab, and
with the itch, from which you cannot be healed.
28The LORD will strike you with madness and
blindness and confusion of heart. 29And you
shall grope at noonday, as a blind man gropes
in darkness; you shall not prosper in your ways;
you shall be only oppressed and plundered
continually, and no one shall save *you.*

30“You shall betroth a wife, but another man
shall lie with her; you shall build a house, but
you shall not dwell in it; you shall plant a vineyard, but shall not gather its grapes. 31Your ox
shall be slaughtered before your eyes, but
you shall not eat of it; your donkey *shall be*
violently taken away from before you, and
shall not be restored to you; your sheep *shall
be* given to your enemies, and you shall have
no one to rescue *them.* 32Your sons and your
daughters *shall be* given to another people,
and your eyes shall look and fail *with longing*
for them all day long; and *there shall be* no
strength in your hand. 33A nation whom you
have not known shall eat the fruit of your land
and the produce of your labor, and you shall
be only oppressed and crushed continually.
34So you shall be driven mad because of the
sight which your eyes see. 35The LORD will
strike you in the knees and on the legs with
severe boils which cannot be healed, and from
the sole of your foot to the top of your head.

36“The LORD will bring you and the king
whom you set over you to a nation which neither you nor your fathers have known, and
there you shall serve other gods—wood and
stone. 37And you shall become an astonishment, a proverb, and a byword among all
nations where the LORD will drive you.

38“You shall carry much seed out to the field
but gather little in, for the locust shall consume it. 39You shall plant vineyards and tend
them, but you shall neither drink *of* the wine
nor gather the *grapes;* for the worms shall eat
them. 40You shall have olive trees throughout
all your territory, but you shall not anoint *yourself* with the oil; for your olives shall drop off.
41You shall beget sons and daughters, but they
shall not be yours; for they shall go into captivity. 42Locusts shall consume all your trees
and the produce of your land.

43“The alien who *is* among you shall rise
higher and higher above you, and you shall
come down lower and lower. 44He shall lend to
you, but you shall not lend to him; he shall be
the head, and you shall be the tail.

45“Moreover all these curses shall come
upon you and pursue and overtake you, until
you are destroyed, because you did not obey
the voice of the LORD your God, to keep His
commandments and His statutes which He
commanded you. 46And they shall be upon you
for a sign and a wonder, and on your descendants forever.

47“Because you did not serve the LORD your
God with joy and gladness of heart, for the
abundance of everything, 48therefore you shall
serve your enemies, whom the LORD will send
against you, in hunger, in thirst, in nakedness,
and in need of everything; and He will put a
yoke of iron on your neck until He has
destroyed you. 49The LORD will bring a nation
against you from afar, from the end of the
earth, *as swift* as the eagle flies, a nation
whose language you will not understand, 50a
nation of fierce countenance, which does not
respect the elderly nor show favor to the
young. 51And they shall eat the increase of
your livestock and the produce of your land,
until you are destroyed; they shall not leave
you grain or new wine or oil, *or* the increase of
your cattle or the offspring of your flocks, until
they have destroyed you.

52“They shall besiege you at all your gates
until your high and fortified walls, in which
you trust, come down throughout all your
land; and they shall besiege you at all your
gates throughout all your land which the LORD
your God has given you. 53You shall eat the
fruit of your own body, the flesh of your sons
and your daughters whom the LORD your God
has given you, in the siege and desperate
straits in which your enemy shall distress you.
54The sensitive and very refined man among
you will be hostile toward his brother, toward
the wife of his bosom, and toward the rest of
his children whom he leaves behind, 55so that
he will not give any of them the flesh of his
children whom he will eat, because he has
nothing left in the siege and desperate straits
in which your enemy shall distress you at all
your gates. 56The tender and delicate woman
among you, who would not venture to set the
sole of her foot on the ground because of her
delicateness and sensitivity, will refuse to the
husband of her bosom, and to her son and her
daughter, 57her placenta which comes out from
between her feet and her children whom she
bears; for she will eat them secretly for lack of
everything in the siege and desperate straits
in which your enemy shall distress you at all
your gates.

58“If you do not carefully observe all the
words of this law that are written in this book,
that you may fear this glorious and awesome
name, THE LORD YOUR GOD, 59then the
LORD will bring upon you and your descendants extraordinary plagues—great and prolonged plagues—and serious and prolonged
sicknesses. 60Moreover He will bring back on
you all the diseases of Egypt, of which you
were afraid, and they shall cling to you. 61Also
every sickness and every plague, which *is* not
written in this Book of the Law, will the LORD
bring upon you until you are destroyed. 62You
shall be left few in number, whereas you were

as the stars of heaven in multitude, because
you would not obey the voice of the LORD your
God. [63]And it shall be, *that* just as the LORD rejoiced over you to do you good and multiply
you, so the LORD will rejoice over you to
destroy you and bring you to nothing; and you
shall be plucked from off the land which you
go to possess.

[64]"Then the LORD will scatter you among all
peoples, from one end of the earth to the
other, and there you shall serve other gods,
which neither you nor your fathers have
known—wood and stone. [65]And among those
nations you shall find no rest, nor shall the
sole of your foot have a resting place; but
there the LORD will give you a trembling heart,
failing eyes, and anguish of soul. [66]Your life
shall hang in doubt before you; you shall fear
day and night, and have no assurance of life.
[67]In the morning you shall say, 'Oh, that it
were evening!' And at evening you shall say,
'Oh, that it were morning!' because of the fear
which terrifies your heart, and because of the
sight which your eyes see.

[68]"And the LORD will take you back to Egypt
in ships, by the way of which I said to you, 'You
shall never see it again.' And there you shall be
offered for sale to your enemies as male and
female slaves, but no one will buy *you*."

Psalm 39:12–13

12 "Hear my prayer, O LORD,
And give ear to my cry;
Do not be silent at my tears;
For I *am* a stranger with You,
A sojourner, as all my fathers *were*.
13 Remove Your gaze from me, that
I may regain strength,
Before I go away and am no more."

Proverbs 13:7–8

7 There is one who makes himself rich,
yet *has* nothing;
And one who makes himself poor, yet
has great riches.

8 The ransom of a man's life
is his riches,
But the poor does not hear rebuke.

13:8 ransom...riches,...poor...rebuke. Riches deliver some from punishment, while others suffer, because they will not heed the rebuke of laziness, which keeps them poor.

Luke 6:27–49

[27]"But I say to you who hear: Love your enemies, do good to those who hate you, [28]bless
those who curse you, and pray for those who
spitefully use you. [29]To him who strikes you on
the *one* cheek, offer the other also. And from
him who takes away your cloak, do not withhold *your* tunic either. [30]Give to everyone who
asks of you. And from him who takes away
your goods do not ask *them* back. [31]And just as
you want men to do to you, you also do to
them likewise.

[32]"But if you love those who love you, what
credit is that to you? For even sinners love
those who love them. [33]And if you do good to
those who do good to you, what credit is that
to you? For even sinners do the same. [34]And if
you lend *to those* from whom you hope to
receive back, what credit is that to you? For
even sinners lend to sinners to receive as
much back. [35]But love your enemies, do good,
and lend, hoping for nothing in return; and
your reward will be great, and you will be sons
of the Most High. For He is kind to the
unthankful and evil. [36]Therefore be merciful,
just as your Father also is merciful.

[37]"Judge not, and you shall not be judged.
Condemn not, and you shall not be condemned. Forgive, and you will be forgiven.
[38]Give, and it will be given to you: good measure, pressed down, shaken together, and running over will be put into your bosom. For
with the same measure that you use, it will be
measured back to you."

[39]And He spoke a parable to them: "Can the
blind lead the blind? Will they not both fall
into the ditch? [40]A disciple is not above his
teacher, but everyone who is perfectly trained
will be like his teacher. [41]And why do you look
at the speck in your brother's eye, but do not
perceive the plank in your own eye? [42]Or how
can you say to your brother, 'Brother, let me
remove the speck that *is* in your eye,' when
you yourself do not see the plank that *is* in
your own eye? Hypocrite! First remove the
plank from your own eye, and then you will
see clearly to remove the speck that is in your
brother's eye.

6:41 speck...plank. The humor of the imagery was no doubt intentional. Christ often employed hyperbole to paint comical images (see 18:25; Matt. 23:24).

43"For a good tree does not bear bad fruit, nor does a bad tree bear good fruit. 44For every tree is known by its own fruit. For *men* do not gather figs from thorns, nor do they gather grapes from a bramble bush. 45A good man out of the good treasure of his heart brings forth good; and an evil man out of the evil treasure of his heart brings forth evil. For out of the abundance of the heart his mouth speaks.

46"But why do you call Me 'Lord, Lord,' and not do the things which I say? 47Whoever comes to Me, and hears My sayings and does them, I will show you whom he is like: 48He is like a man building a house, who dug deep and laid the foundation on the rock. And when the flood arose, the stream beat vehemently against that house, and could not shake it, for it was founded on the rock. 49But he who heard and did nothing is like a man who built a house on the earth without a foundation, against which the stream beat vehemently; and immediately it fell. And the ruin of that house was great."

6:46 you call Me 'Lord, Lord.' It is not sufficient to give lip service to Christ's lordship. Genuine faith produces obedience. A tree is known by its fruits (v. 44). See Matthew 7:21–23.

DAY 2: What did God promise would happen to Israel if they disobeyed the law?

Their obedience centers around "this glorious and awesome name, THE LORD YOUR GOD," as described in Deuteronomy 28:58 and would lead to fearing the Lord, whose "name" represents His presence and character. The title "LORD (Yahweh)" revealed the glory and greatness of God (see Ex. 3:15). Significantly, the phrase "the LORD your God" is used approximately 280 times in the Book of Deuteronomy. The full measure of the divine curse would come on Israel when its disobedience had been hardened into disregard for the glorious and awesome character of God. In vv. 15,45, Moses described curses for disobedience; hence, the worst of the curses come when disobedience is hardened into failure to fear God. Only God's grace would save a small remnant (v. 62), thus keeping Israel from being annihilated (see Mal. 2:2). In contrast to the promise made to Abraham in Genesis 15:5, the physical seed of Abraham under God's curse would be reduced. As God had multiplied the seed of the patriarchs in Egypt (see Ex. 1:7), He would decimate their numbers to make them as nothing until His restoration of the nation in a future day (see 30:5).

In v. 64, it warns that "the LORD will scatter you." The Jews remaining after the curses fall would be dispersed by the Lord ultimately to serve false gods, restlessly and fearfully throughout all the nations of the earth (see Neh. 1:8,9; Jer. 30:11; Ezek. 11:16). This dispersion began with the captivity of the northern kingdom, Israel (722 B.C.), then the southern kingdom, Judah (586 B.C.), and is still a reality today. In the future earthly kingdom of Messiah, Israel will experience its regathering in faith, salvation, and righteousness. (See Is. 59:19–21; Jer. 31:31–34; Ezek. 36:8–37:14; Zech. 12:10–14:21.)

In fact, Israel would be so abandoned by God that she would not even be able to sell herself into slavery (v. 68). The curse of God would bring Israel into a seemingly hopeless condition (see Hos. 8:13; 9:3). The specific mention of Egypt could be symbolic for any lands where the Jews have been taken into bondage or sold as slaves. But it is true that after the destruction of Jerusalem in A.D. 70, which was a judgment on the apostasy of Israel and their rejection and execution of the Messiah, this prophecy was actually fulfilled. The Roman general Titus, who conquered Jerusalem and Israel, sent 17,000 adult Jews to Egypt to perform hard labor there and had those who were under 17 years old publicly sold. Under the Roman emperor Hadrian, countless Jews were sold and suffered such bondage and cruelty.

APRIL 3

Deuteronomy 29:1–30:20

29 These *are* the words of the covenant which the LORD commanded Moses to make with the children of Israel in the land of Moab, besides the covenant which He made with them in Horeb.

2Now Moses called all Israel and said to them: "You have seen all that the LORD did before your eyes in the land of Egypt, to Pharaoh and to all his servants and to all his land— 3the great trials which your eyes have seen, the signs, and those great wonders. 4Yet the LORD has not given you a heart to perceive and eyes to see and ears to hear, to this *very* day. 5And I have led you forty years in the wilderness. Your clothes have not worn out on you, and your sandals have not worn out on

29:4 the LORD has not given you…eyes to see. In spite of all they had experienced (vv. 2,3), Israel was spiritually blind to the significance of what the Lord had done for them, lacking spiritual understanding, even as Moses was speaking. This spiritual blindness of Israel continues to the present day (Rom. 11:8), and it will not be reversed until Israel's future day of salvation (see Rom. 11:25–27). The Lord had not given them an understanding heart, simply because the people had not penitently sought it (see 2 Chr. 7:14).

your feet. [6]You have not eaten bread, nor have
you drunk wine or *similar* drink, that you may
know that I *am* the LORD your God. [7]And when
you came to this place, Sihon king of Heshbon
and Og king of Bashan came out against us to
battle, and we conquered them. [8]We took their
land and gave it as an inheritance to the
Reubenites, to the Gadites, and to half the
tribe of Manasseh. [9]Therefore keep the words
of this covenant, and do them, that you may
prosper in all that you do.
[10]"All of you stand today before the LORD
your God: your leaders and your tribes and
your elders and your officers, all the men of
Israel, [11]your little ones and your wives—also
the stranger who *is* in your camp, from the
one who cuts your wood to the one who draws
your water— [12]that you may enter into
covenant with the LORD your God, and into His
oath, which the LORD your God makes with
you today, [13]that He may establish you today as
a people for Himself, and *that* He may be God
to you, just as He has spoken to you, and just
as He has sworn to your fathers, to Abraham,
Isaac, and Jacob.
[14]"I make this covenant and this oath, not
with you alone, [15]but with *him* who stands here
with us today before the LORD our God, as well
as with *him* who *is* not here with us today [16](for
you know that we dwelt in the land of Egypt
and that we came through the nations which
you passed by, [17]and you saw their abominations and their idols which *were* among
them—wood and stone and silver and gold);
[18]so that there may not be among you man or
woman or family or tribe, whose heart turns
away today from the LORD our God, to go *and*
serve the gods of these nations, and that there
may not be among you a root bearing bitterness or wormwood; [19]and so it may not happen, when he hears the words of this curse,
that he blesses himself in his heart, saying, 'I
shall have peace, even though I follow the
dictates of my heart'—as though the drunkard could be included with the sober.
[20]"The LORD would not spare him; for then
the anger of the LORD and His jealousy would
burn against that man, and every curse that is
written in this book would settle on him, and
the LORD would blot out his name from under
heaven. [21]And the LORD would separate him
from all the tribes of Israel for adversity,
according to all the curses of the covenant that
are written in this Book of the Law, [22]so that
the coming generation of your children who
rise up after you, and the foreigner who comes
from a far land, would say, when they see the
plagues of that land and the sicknesses which
the LORD has laid on it:
[23]'The whole land *is* brimstone, salt, and
burning; it is not sown, nor does it bear, nor
does any grass grow there, like the overthrow
of Sodom and Gomorrah, Admah, and Zeboiim,
which the LORD overthrew in His anger and
His wrath.' [24]All nations would say, 'Why has
the LORD done so to this land? What does the
heat of this great anger mean?' [25]Then *people*
would say: 'Because they have forsaken the
covenant of the LORD God of their fathers,
which He made with them when He brought
them out of the land of Egypt; [26]for they went
and served other gods and worshiped them,
gods that they did not know and that He had
not given to them. [27]Then the anger of the LORD
was aroused against this land, to bring on it
every curse that is written in this book. [28]And
the LORD uprooted them from their land in
anger, in wrath, and in great indignation, and
cast them into another land, as *it is* this day.'
[29]"The secret *things belong* to the LORD our
God, but those *things which are* revealed
belong to us and to our children forever, that
we may do all the words of this law.

30 "Now it shall come to pass, when all
these things come upon you, the blessing and the curse which I have set before you,
and you call *them* to mind among all the

29:29 The secret *things*…those *things which are* revealed. That which is revealed included the law with its promises and threats. Consequently, that which is hidden only can refer to the specific way in which God will carry out His will in the future, which is revealed in His Word and completed in His great work of salvation, in spite of the apostasy of His people.

nations where the LORD your God drives you,
2and you return to the LORD your God and
obey His voice, according to all that I command you today, you and your children, with
all your heart and with all your soul, 3that the
LORD your God will bring you back from captivity, and have compassion on you, and gather you again from all the nations where the
LORD your God has scattered you. 4If *any* of
you are driven out to the farthest *parts* under
heaven, from there the LORD your God will
gather you, and from there He will bring you.
5Then the LORD your God will bring you to the
land which your fathers possessed, and you
shall possess it. He will prosper you and multiply you more than your fathers. 6And the
LORD your God will circumcise your heart and
the heart of your descendants, to love the
LORD your God with all your heart and with all
your soul, that you may live.

30:4,5 The gathering of Jews out of all the countries of the earth will follow Israel's final redemption. Restoration to the land will be in fulfillment of the promise of the covenant given to Abraham (see Gen. 12:7; 13:15; 15:18–21; 17:8) and so often reiterated by Moses and the prophets.

30:6 the LORD...will circumcise your heart. This work of God in the innermost being of the individual is the true salvation that grants a new will to obey Him in place of the former spiritual insensitivity and stubbornness (see Jer. 4:4; 9:25; Rom. 2:28,29). This new heart will allow the Israelite to love the Lord wholeheartedly and is the essential feature of the New Covenant (see 29:4,18; 30:10,17; Jer. 31:31–34; 32:37–42; Ezek. 11:19; 36:26).

7"Also the LORD your God will put all these
curses on your enemies and on those who hate
you, who persecuted you. 8And you will again
obey the voice of the LORD and do all His commandments which I command you today. 9The
LORD your God will make you abound in all the
work of your hand, in the fruit of your body, in
the increase of your livestock, and in the produce of your land for good. For the LORD will
again rejoice over you for good as He rejoiced
over your fathers, 10if you obey the voice of the
LORD your God, to keep His commandments
and His statutes which are written in this Book
of the Law, *and* if you turn to the LORD your
God with all your heart and with all your soul.

11"For this commandment which I command
you today *is* not *too* mysterious for you, nor *is*
it far off. 12It *is* not in heaven, that you should
say, 'Who will ascend into heaven for us and
bring it to us, that we may hear it and do it?'
13Nor *is* it beyond the sea, that you should say,
'Who will go over the sea for us and bring it to
us, that we may hear it and do it?' 14But the
word *is* very near you, in your mouth and in
your heart, that you may do it.

15"See, I have set before you today life and
good, death and evil, 16in that I command you
today to love the LORD your God, to walk in His
ways, and to keep His commandments, His
statutes, and His judgments, that you may live
and multiply; and the LORD your God will bless
you in the land which you go to possess. 17But
if your heart turns away so that you do not
hear, and are drawn away, and worship other
gods and serve them, 18I announce to you
today that you shall surely perish; you shall
not prolong *your* days in the land which you
cross over the Jordan to go in and possess. 19I
call heaven and earth as witnesses today
against you, *that* I have set before you life and
death, blessing and cursing; therefore choose
life, that both you and your descendants may
live; 20that you may love the LORD your God,
that you may obey His voice, and that you may
cling to Him, for He *is* your life and the length
of your days; and that you may dwell in the
land which the LORD swore to your fathers, to
Abraham, Isaac, and Jacob, to give them."

Psalm 40:1–5

To the Chief Musician. A Psalm of David.

I waited patiently for the LORD;
And He inclined to me,
And heard my cry.
2 He also brought me up out of a
horrible pit,
Out of the miry clay,
And set my feet upon a rock,
And established my steps.
3 He has put a new song in my mouth—
Praise to our God;
Many will see *it* and fear,
And will trust in the LORD.
4 Blessed *is* that man who makes the
LORD his trust,
And does not respect the proud, nor
such as turn aside to lies.
5 Many, O LORD my God, *are* Your
wonderful works
Which You have done;
And Your thoughts toward us
Cannot be recounted to You in order;

If I would declare and speak *of them,*
They are more than can be numbered.

Proverbs 13:9–10

9 The light of the righteous rejoices,
But the lamp of the wicked will be
put out.
10 By pride comes nothing but strife,
But with the well-advised *is* wisdom.

Luke 7:1–30

7 Now when He concluded all His sayings in
the hearing of the people, He entered
Capernaum. [2]And a certain centurion's servant, who was dear to him, was sick and ready
to die. [3]So when he heard about Jesus, he sent
elders of the Jews to Him, pleading with Him
to come and heal his servant. [4]And when they
came to Jesus, they begged Him earnestly,
saying that the one for whom He should do
this was deserving, [5]"for he loves our nation,
and has built us a synagogue."

[6]Then Jesus went with them. And when He
was already not far from the house, the centurion sent friends to Him, saying to Him, "Lord,
do not trouble Yourself, for I am not worthy
that You should enter under my roof. [7]There-
fore I did not even think myself worthy to
come to You. But say the word, and my servant will be healed. [8]For I also am a man placed
under authority, having soldiers under me.
And I say to one, 'Go,' and he goes; and to
another, 'Come,' and he comes; and to my servant, 'Do this,' and he does *it.*"

[9]When Jesus heard these things, He marveled at him, and turned around and said to the
crowd that followed Him, "I say to you, I have
not found such great faith, not even in Israel!"
[10]And those who were sent, returning to the
house, found the servant well who had been sick.

[11]Now it happened, the day after, *that* He
went into a city called Nain; and many of His
disciples went with Him, and a large crowd.
[12]And when He came near the gate of the city,
behold, a dead man was being carried out, the
only son of his mother; and she was a widow.
And a large crowd from the city was with her.
[13]When the Lord saw her, He had compassion
on her and said to her, "Do not weep." [14]Then
He came and touched the open coffin, and
those who carried *him* stood still. And He
said, "Young man, I say to you, arise." [15]So he
who was dead sat up and began to speak. And
He presented him to his mother.

[16]Then fear came upon all, and they glorified God, saying, "A great prophet has risen
up among us"; and, "God has visited His people." [17]And this report about Him went
throughout all Judea and all the surrounding
region.

[18]Then the disciples of John reported to him
concerning all these things. [19]And John, calling two of his disciples to *him,* sent *them* to Jesus, saying, "Are You the Coming One, or do
we look for another?"

[20]When the men had come to Him, they
said, "John the Baptist has sent us to You, saying, 'Are You the Coming One, or do we look
for another?' " [21]And that very hour He cured
many of infirmities, afflictions, and evil spirits;
and to many blind He gave sight.

[22]Jesus answered and said to them, "Go and
tell John the things you have seen and heard:
that *the* blind see, *the* lame walk, *the* lepers are
cleansed, *the* deaf hear, *the* dead are raised, *the*
poor have the gospel preached to them. [23]And
blessed is *he* who is not offended because of
Me."

[24]When the messengers of John had departed, He began to speak to the multitudes concerning John: "What did you go out into the
wilderness to see? A reed shaken by the wind?
[25]But what did you go out to see? A man clothed
in soft garments? Indeed those who are gorgeously appareled and live in luxury are in
kings' courts. [26]But what did you go out to see?
A prophet? Yes, I say to you, and more than a
prophet. [27]This is *he* of whom it is written:

'Behold, I send My messenger before
Your face,
Who will prepare Your way before You.'

[28]For I say to you, among those born of women
there is not a greater prophet than John the
Baptist; but he who is least in the kingdom of
God is greater than he."

[29]And when all the people heard *Him,* even
the tax collectors justified God, having been
baptized with the baptism of John. [30]But the
Pharisees and lawyers rejected the will of God
for themselves, not having been baptized by
him.

7:14 touched the open coffin. A ceremonially defiling act, normally. Jesus graphically illustrated how impervious He was to such defilements. When He touched the coffin, its defilement did not taint Him; rather, His power immediately dispelled the presence of all death and defilement. This was the first of 3 times Jesus raised people from the dead (see 8:49–56; John 11). Verse 22 implies that Christ also raised others who are not specifically mentioned.

DAY 3: Why are our choices in life so important?

In Deuteronomy 30:11–14, after remembering the failures of the past and the prospects for the future, Moses earnestly admonished the people to make the right choice. The issue facing them was to enjoy salvation and blessing by loving God so wholeheartedly that they would willingly live in obedience to His word. The choice was simple, yet profound. It was stated in simple terms so that they could understand and grasp what God expected of them (v. 11). Although God had spoken from heaven, He had spoken through Moses in words every person could understand (v. 12). Neither did they have to search at some point beyond the sea (v. 13). The truth was there, through Moses, now in their hearts and minds (v. 14). All the truth necessary for choosing to love and obey God and thus avoid disobedience and cursing, they had heard and known (v. 15).

In v. 15, Moses pinpoints the choice—to love and obey God is life and good; to reject God is death and evil. If they chose to love God and obey His word, they would enjoy all God's blessings (v. 16). If they refused to love and obey Him, they would be severely and immediately punished (vv. 17,18). Paul, in speaking about salvation in the New Testament, makes use of this appeal made by Moses (Rom. 10:1–13). Like Moses, Paul is saying that the message of salvation is plain and understandable.

So "choose life" (v. 19). Moses forces the decision, exhorting Israel on the plains of Moab before God (heaven) and man (earth) to choose, by believing in and loving God, the life available through the New Covenant (see v. 6). Sadly, Israel failed to respond to this call to the right choice (see 31:16–18,27–29). Choosing life or death was also emphasized by Jesus. The one who believed in Him had the promise of eternal life, while the one who refused to believe faced eternal death (see John 3:1–36). Every person faces this same choice.

APRIL 4

Deuteronomy 31:1–32:52

31 Then Moses went and spoke these words
to all Israel. 2And he said to them: "I *am*
one hundred and twenty years old today. I can
no longer go out and come in. Also the LORD
has said to me, 'You shall not cross over this
Jordan.' 3The LORD your God Himself crosses
over before you; He will destroy these nations
from before you, and you shall dispossess them.
Joshua himself crosses over before you, just as
the LORD has said. 4And the LORD will do to them
as He did to Sihon and Og, the kings of the
Amorites and their land, when He destroyed
them. 5The LORD will give them over to you,
that you may do to them according to every
commandment which I have commanded you.
6Be strong and of good courage, do not fear nor
be afraid of them; for the LORD your God, He *is*
the One who goes with you. He will not leave
you nor forsake you."
7Then Moses called Joshua and said to him
in the sight of all Israel, "Be strong and of
good courage, for you must go with this people to the land which the LORD has sworn to
their fathers to give them, and you shall cause
them to inherit it. 8And the LORD, He *is* the
One who goes before you. He will be with you,
He will not leave you nor forsake you; do not
fear nor be dismayed."
9So Moses wrote this law and delivered it
to the priests, the sons of Levi, who bore the
ark of the covenant of the LORD, and to all the
elders of Israel. 10And Moses commanded
them, saying: "At the end of *every* seven
years, at the appointed time in the year of
release, at the Feast of Tabernacles, 11when
all Israel comes to appear before the LORD
your God in the place which He chooses, you
shall read this law before all Israel in their
hearing. 12Gather the people together, men
and women and little ones, and the stranger
who *is* within your gates, that they may hear
and that they may learn to fear the LORD
your God and carefully observe all the words
of this law, 13and *that* their children, who
have not known it, may hear and learn to fear
the LORD your God as long as you live in the

31:6–8 Be strong and of good courage. The strength and courage of the warriors of Israel would come from their confidence that their God was with them and would not forsake them. In vv. 7,8, Moses repeated the substance of his exhortation, this time addressing it specifically to Joshua in the presence of the people to encourage him and to remind the people that Joshua's leadership was being assumed with the full approval of God. This principle for faith and confidence is repeated in 31:23; Josh. 1:5–7; 2 Sam. 10:12; 2 Kin. 2:2; 1 Chr. 22:11–13; 2 Chr. 32:1–8; Ps. 27:14. The writer of Hebrews quotes vv. 6,8 in 13:5.

land which you cross the Jordan to possess."
[14]Then the LORD said to Moses, "Behold, the
days approach when you must die; call
Joshua, and present yourselves in the tabernacle of meeting, that I may inaugurate him."
So Moses and Joshua went and presented
themselves in the tabernacle of meeting.
[15]Now the LORD appeared at the tabernacle in
a pillar of cloud, and the pillar of cloud stood
above the door of the tabernacle.
[16]And the LORD said to Moses: "Behold, you
will rest with your fathers; and this people will
rise and play the harlot with the gods of the
foreigners of the land, where they go *to be*
among them, and they will forsake Me and
break My covenant which I have made with
them. [17]Then My anger shall be aroused
against them in that day, and I will forsake
them, and I will hide My face from them, and
they shall be devoured. And many evils and
troubles shall befall them, so that they will say
in that day, 'Have not these evils come upon us
because our God *is* not among us?' [18]And I will
surely hide My face in that day because of all
the evil which they have done, in that they
have turned to other gods.
[19]"Now therefore, write down this song for
yourselves, and teach it to the children of
Israel; put it in their mouths, that this song may
be a witness for Me against the children of
Israel. [20]When I have brought them to the land
flowing with milk and honey, of which I swore
to their fathers, and they have eaten and filled
themselves and grown fat, then they will turn
to other gods and serve them; and they will
provoke Me and break My covenant. [21]Then it
shall be, when many evils and troubles have
come upon them, that this song will testify
against them as a witness; for it will not be forgotten in the mouths of their descendants, for
I know the inclination of their behavior today,
even before I have brought them to the land of
which I swore *to give them.*"
[22]Therefore Moses wrote this song the same
day, and taught it to the children of Israel.
[23]Then He inaugurated Joshua the son of Nun,
and said, "Be strong and of good courage; for
you shall bring the children of Israel into the
land of which I swore to them, and I will be
with you."
[24]So it was, when Moses had completed writing the words of this law in a book, when they
were finished, [25]that Moses commanded the
Levites, who bore the ark of the covenant of
the LORD, saying: [26]"Take this Book of the Law,
and put it beside the ark of the covenant of the
LORD your God, that it may be there as a witness against you; [27]for I know your rebellion
and your stiff neck. *If* today, while I am yet
alive with you, you have been rebellious
against the LORD, then how much more after
my death? [28]Gather to me all the elders of your
tribes, and your officers, that I may speak
these words in their hearing and call heaven
and earth to witness against them. [29]For I know
that after my death you will become utterly
corrupt, and turn aside from the way which I
have commanded you. And evil will befall you
in the latter days, because you will do evil in
the sight of the LORD, to provoke Him to anger
through the work of your hands."
[30]Then Moses spoke in the hearing of all the
assembly of Israel the words of this song until
they were ended:

32 "Give ear, O heavens, and I
will speak;
And hear, O earth, the words of my
mouth.
2 Let my teaching drop as the rain,
My speech distill as the dew,
As raindrops on the tender herb,
And as showers on the grass.
3 For I proclaim the name of the LORD:
Ascribe greatness to our God.
4 *He is* the Rock, His work *is* perfect;
For all His ways *are* justice,
A God of truth and without injustice;
Righteous and upright *is* He.

5 "They have corrupted themselves;
They are not His children,
Because of their blemish:
A perverse and crooked generation.
6 Do you thus deal with the LORD,
O foolish and unwise people?
Is He not your Father, *who* bought you?
Has He not made you and established
you?

7 "Remember the days of old,
Consider the years of many
generations.
Ask your father, and he will show you;
Your elders, and they will tell you:
8 When the Most High divided their
inheritance to the nations,
When He separated the sons of Adam,
He set the boundaries of the peoples
According to the number
of the children of Israel.
9 For the LORD'S portion *is* His people;
Jacob *is* the place of His inheritance.

10 "He found him in a desert land
And in the wasteland, a howling
wilderness;

He encircled him, He instructed him,
He kept him as the apple of His eye.
11 As an eagle stirs up its nest,
Hovers over its young,
Spreading out its wings, taking them up,
Carrying them on its wings,
12 *So* the LORD alone led him,
And *there was* no foreign god with him.

13 "He made him ride in the heights of the earth,
That he might eat the produce of the fields;
He made him draw honey from the rock,
And oil from the flinty rock;
14 Curds from the cattle, and milk of the flock,
With fat of lambs;
And rams of the breed of Bashan, and goats,
With the choicest wheat;
And you drank wine, the blood of the grapes.

15 "But Jeshurun grew fat and kicked;
You grew fat, you grew thick,
You are obese!
Then he forsook God *who* made him,
And scornfully esteemed the Rock of his salvation.
16 They provoked Him to jealousy with foreign *gods;*
With abominations they provoked Him to anger.
17 They sacrificed to demons, not to God,
To gods they did not know,
To new *gods,* new arrivals
That your fathers did not fear.
18 Of the Rock *who* begot you, you are unmindful,
And have forgotten the God who fathered you.

19 "And when the LORD saw *it,* He spurned *them,*
Because of the provocation of His sons and His daughters.
20 And He said: 'I will hide My face from them,
I will see what their end *will be,*
For they *are* a perverse generation,
Children in whom *is* no faith.
21 They have provoked Me to jealousy by *what* is not God;
They have moved Me to anger by their foolish idols.
But I will provoke them to jealousy by *those who are* not a nation;
I will move them to anger by a foolish nation.
22 For a fire is kindled in My anger,
And shall burn to the lowest hell;
It shall consume the earth with her increase,
And set on fire the foundations of the mountains.

23 'I will heap disasters on them;
I will spend My arrows on them.
24 *They shall be* wasted with hunger,
Devoured by pestilence and bitter destruction;
I will also send against them the teeth of beasts,
With the poison of serpents of the dust.
25 The sword shall destroy outside;
There shall be terror within
For the young man and virgin,
The nursing child with the man of gray hairs.
26 I would have said, "I will dash them in pieces,
I will make the memory of them to cease from among men,"
27 Had I not feared the wrath of the enemy,
Lest their adversaries should misunderstand,
Lest they should say, "Our hand *is* high;
And it is not the LORD who has done all this." '

28 "For they *are* a nation void of counsel,
Nor *is there any* understanding in them.
29 Oh, that they were wise, *that* they understood this,
That they would consider their latter end!
30 How could one chase a thousand,
And two put ten thousand to flight,
Unless their Rock had sold them,
And the LORD had surrendered them?
31 For their rock *is* not like our Rock,
Even our enemies themselves *being* judges.
32 For their vine *is* of the vine of Sodom
And of the fields of Gomorrah;
Their grapes *are* grapes of gall,
Their clusters *are* bitter.
33 Their wine *is* the poison of serpents,
And the cruel venom of cobras.
34 '*Is* this not laid up in store with Me,
Sealed up among My treasures?
35 Vengeance is Mine, and recompense;

Their foot shall slip in *due* time;
For the day of their calamity *is* at hand,
And the things to come hasten upon them.'

36 "For the LORD will judge His people
And have compassion on His servants,
When He sees that *their* power is gone,
And *there is* no one *remaining,* bond or free.
37 He will say: 'Where *are* their gods,
The rock in which they sought refuge?
38 Who ate the fat of their sacrifices,
And drank the wine of their drink offering?
Let them rise and help you,
And be your refuge.

39 'Now see that I, *even* I, *am* He,
And *there is* no God besides Me;
I kill and I make alive;
I wound and I heal;
Nor *is there any* who can deliver from My hand.
40 For I raise My hand to heaven,
And say, "*As* I live forever,
41 If I whet My glittering sword,
And My hand takes hold on judgment,
I will render vengeance to My enemies,
And repay those who hate Me.
42 I will make My arrows drunk with blood,
And My sword shall devour flesh,
With the blood of the slain and the captives,
From the heads of the leaders of the enemy." '

43 "Rejoice, O Gentiles, *with* His people;
For He will avenge the blood of His servants,
And render vengeance to His adversaries;
He will provide atonement for His land *and* His people."

44 So Moses came with Joshua the son of Nun and spoke all the words of this song in the
hearing of the people.
45 Moses finished speaking all these words to all Israel,
46 and he said to them: "Set your hearts on all the words which I testify among you today, which you shall command your children to be careful to
observe—all the words of this law.
47 For it *is* not a futile thing for you, because it *is* your life, and by this word you shall prolong *your* days in the land which you cross over the Jordan to possess."

48 Then the LORD spoke to Moses that very
same day, saying:
49 "Go up this mountain of the Abarim, Mount Nebo, which *is* in the land of Moab, across from Jericho; view the land of Canaan, which I give to the children of Israel
as a possession;
50 and die on the mountain which you ascend, and be gathered to your people, just as Aaron your brother died on Mount Hor and was gathered to his people;
51 because you trespassed against Me among the children of Israel at the waters of Meribah Kadesh, in the Wilderness of Zin, because you did not hallow Me in the midst of the children
of Israel.
52 Yet you shall see the land before *you,* though you shall not go there, into the land which I am giving to the children of Israel."

Psalm 40:6–12

6 Sacrifice and offering You did not desire;
My ears You have opened.
Burnt offering and sin offering You did not require.
7 Then I said, "Behold, I come;
In the scroll of the book *it is* written of me.

32:43 Rejoice, O Gentiles, *with* His people. As a result of the execution of God's vengeance, all nations will be called upon to praise with Israel the Lord who will have provided redemptively for them in Christ and also provided a new beginning in the land. This atonement for the land is the satisfaction of God's wrath by the sacrifice of His enemies in judgment. The atonement for the people is by the sacrifice of Jesus Christ on the cross (see Ps. 79:9). Paul quotes this passage in Romans 15:10, as does the writer of Hebrews (1:6).

40:6 Sacrifice and offering You did not desire. David is not negating the commandment to offer sacrifices, but is emphasizing their being offered with the right attitude of heart (contra. Saul, 1 Sam. 15:22,23; note the emphases on proper spiritual prerequisites for sacrifices in Pss. 19:14; 50:7–15; 51:15–17; 69:30–31; Is. 1:10–15; Jer. 7:21–26; Hos. 6:6; Amos 5:21–24; Mic. 6:6–8; Matt. 23:23). **My ears You have opened.** Literally, "ears" or "two ears You have dug for me." This pictures obedience and dedication.

8 I delight to do Your will, O my God,
And Your law *is* within my heart."

9 I have proclaimed the good news
of righteousness
In the great assembly;
Indeed, I do not restrain my lips,
O LORD, You Yourself know.
10 I have not hidden Your righteousness
within my heart;
I have declared Your faithfulness and
Your salvation;
I have not concealed Your
lovingkindness and Your truth
From the great assembly.

11 Do not withhold Your tender mercies
from me, O LORD;
Let Your lovingkindness and Your
truth continually preserve me.
12 For innumerable evils have
surrounded me;
My iniquities have overtaken me,
so that I am not able to look up;
They are more than the hairs of
my head;
Therefore my heart fails me.

Proverbs 13:11–12

11 Wealth *gained by* dishonesty will be
diminished,
But he who gathers by labor will
increase.

12 Hope deferred makes the
heart sick,
But *when* the desire comes, *it is*
a tree of life.

Luke 7:31–50

[31]And the Lord said, "To what then shall I
liken the men of this generation, and what are
they like? [32]They are like children sitting in the
marketplace and calling to one another, saying:

'We played the flute for you,
And you did not dance;
We mourned to you,
And you did not weep.'

[33]For John the Baptist came neither eating
bread nor drinking wine, and you say, 'He has
a demon.' [34]The Son of Man has come eating
and drinking, and you say, 'Look, a glutton and
a winebibber, a friend of tax collectors and sinners!' [35]But wisdom is justified by all her children."

[36]Then one of the Pharisees asked Him to eat
with him. And He went to the Pharisee's house,
and sat down to eat. [37]And behold, a woman in
the city who was a sinner, when she knew that
Jesus sat at the table in the Pharisee's house,
brought an alabaster flask of fragrant oil, [38]and
stood at His feet behind *Him* weeping; and she
began to wash His feet with her tears, and
wiped *them* with the hair of her head; and she
kissed His feet and anointed *them* with the fragrant oil. [39]Now when the Pharisee who had
invited Him saw *this,* he spoke to himself, saying, "This Man, if He were a prophet, would
know who and what manner of woman *this is*
who is touching Him, for she is a sinner."

[40]And Jesus answered and said to him,
"Simon, I have something to say to you."

So he said, "Teacher, say it."

[41]"There was a certain creditor who had two
debtors. One owed five hundred denarii, and
the other fifty. [42]And when they had nothing
with which to repay, he freely forgave them
both. Tell Me, therefore, which of them will
love him more?"

[43]Simon answered and said, "I suppose the
one whom he forgave more."

And He said to him, "You have rightly
judged." [44]Then He turned to the woman and
said to Simon, "Do you see this woman? I
entered your house; you gave Me no water for
My feet, but she has washed My feet with her
tears and wiped *them* with the hair of her
head. [45]You gave Me no kiss, but this woman
has not ceased to kiss My feet since the time I
came in. [46]You did not anoint My head with oil,
but this woman has anointed My feet with fragrant oil. [47]Therefore I say to you, her sins,
which *are* many, are forgiven, for she loved
much. But to whom little is forgiven, *the same*
loves little."

[48]Then He said to her, "Your sins are forgiven."

[49]And those who sat at the table with Him
began to say to themselves, "Who is this who
even forgives sins?"

[50]Then He said to the woman, "Your faith
has saved you. Go in peace."

7:32 like children. Christ used strong derision to rebuke the Pharisees. He suggested they were behaving childishly, determined not to be pleased, whether invited to "dance" (a reference to Christ's joyous style of ministry, "eating and drinking" with sinners—v. 34) or urged to "weep" (a reference to John the Baptist's call to repentance and John's more austere manner of ministry—v. 33).

DAY 4: How is God characterized in the Song of Moses in Deuteronomy 32?

The Song of Moses is a call to Israel to always "ascribe greatness to our God" (v. 3). This command refers to the greatness of God revealed in His acts of omnipotence. Read through the song and note the descriptions of God.

"The Rock" (v. 4). This word, representing the stability and permanence of God, was placed at the beginning of the verse for emphasis and was followed by a series of phrases which elaborated the attributes of God as the Rock of Israel. It is one of the principle themes in this song (see vv. 15,18,30,31), stressing the unchanging nature of God in contrast with the fickle nature of the people.

"Your Father" (v. 6). The foolishness and stupidity of Israel would be seen in the fact that they would rebel against God who as a Father had brought them forth and formed them into a nation. As Father, He was the progenitor and originator of the nation and the One who had matured and sustained it. This idea of God as Father of the nation is emphasized in the Old Testament (see 1 Chr. 29:10; Is. 63:16; 64:8; Mal. 2:10) while the idea of God as Father of individual believers is developed in the New Testament (see Rom. 8:15; Gal. 4:6).

"The Most High" (vv. 8,9). This title for God emphasized His sovereignty and authority over all the nations (see Gen. 11:9; 10:32; 14:18; Num. 24:16) with the amazing revelation that, in the whole plan for the world, God had as His goal the salvation of His chosen people. God ordained a plan where the number of nations (70, according to Gen. 10) corresponded to the number of the children of Israel (70, according to Gen. 46:27). Further, as God gave the nations their lands, He established their boundaries, leaving Israel enough land to sustain their expected population.

"Hovers over its young" (v. 11). The Lord exercised His loving care for Israel like an eagle caring for its young, especially as they were taught to fly. As they began to fly and had little strength, they would start to fall. At that point, an eagle would stop their fall by spreading its wings so they could land on them. So the Lord has carried Israel and not let the nation fall. He has been training Israel to fly on His wings of love and omnipotence.

APRIL 5

Deuteronomy 33:1–34:12

33 Now this *is* the blessing with which
Moses the man of God blessed the
children of Israel before his death. 2And he
said:

"The LORD came from Sinai,
And dawned on them from Seir;
He shone forth from Mount Paran,
And He came with ten thousands of saints;
From His right hand
Came a fiery law for them.
3 Yes, He loves the people;
All His saints *are* in Your hand;
They sit down at Your feet;
Everyone receives Your words.
4 Moses commanded a law for us,
A heritage of the congregation of Jacob.
5 And He was King in Jeshurun,
When the leaders of the people were gathered,
All the tribes of Israel together.
6 "Let Reuben live, and not die,
Nor let his men be few."

33:5 King in Jeshurun. Since Moses is nowhere else in Scripture referred to as king, most interpret this as a reference to the Lord as King over Israel. However, Moses is the closest antecedent of the pronoun "he" in this clause, and the most natural understanding is that Moses is being referred to as a king. Moses certainly exercised kingly authority over Israel and could be viewed as a prototype of the coming King. Thus, united in the figure of Moses, the coming Prophet like unto Moses (18:15) would be the Prophet-King.

7And this he said of Judah:

"Hear, LORD, the voice of Judah,
And bring him to his people;
Let his hands be sufficient for him,
And may You be a help against his enemies."

8And of Levi he said:

"*Let* Your Thummim and Your Urim *be* with Your holy one,
Whom You tested at Massah,
And with whom You contended at the waters of Meribah,
9 Who says of his father and mother,
'I have not seen them';

Nor did he acknowledge his brothers,
Or know his own children;
For they have observed Your word
And kept Your covenant.
10 They shall teach Jacob Your judgments,
And Israel Your law.
They shall put incense before You,
And a whole burnt sacrifice on Your altar.
11 Bless his substance, LORD,
And accept the work of his hands;
Strike the loins of those who rise against him,
And of those who hate him, that they rise not again."

12 Of Benjamin he said:

"The beloved of the LORD shall dwell in safety by Him,
Who shelters him all the day long;
And he shall dwell between His shoulders."

13 And of Joseph he said:

"Blessed of the LORD *is* his land,
With the precious things of heaven, with the dew,
And the deep lying beneath,
14 With the precious fruits of the sun,
With the precious produce of the months,
15 With the best things of the ancient mountains,
With the precious things of the everlasting hills,
16 With the precious things of the earth and its fullness,
And the favor of Him who dwelt in the bush.
Let *the blessing* come 'on the head of Joseph,
And on the crown of the head of him *who was* separate from his brothers.'
17 His glory *is like* a firstborn bull,
And his horns *like* the horns of the wild ox;
Together with them
He shall push the peoples
To the ends of the earth;
They *are* the ten thousands of Ephraim,
And they *are* the thousands of Manasseh."

18 And of Zebulun he said:

"Rejoice, Zebulun, in your going out,
And Issachar in your tents!
19 They shall call the peoples *to* the mountain;
There they shall offer sacrifices of righteousness;
For they shall partake *of* the abundance of the seas
And *of* treasures hidden in the sand."

20 And of Gad he said:

"Blessed *is* he who enlarges Gad;
He dwells as a lion,
And tears the arm and the crown of his head.
21 He provided the first *part* for himself,
Because a lawgiver's portion was reserved there.
He came *with* the heads of the people;
He administered the justice of the LORD,
And His judgments with Israel."

22 And of Dan he said:

"Dan *is* a lion's whelp;
He shall leap from Bashan."

23 And of Naphtali he said:

"O Naphtali, satisfied with favor,
And full of the blessing of the LORD,
Possess the west and the south."

24 And of Asher he said:

"Asher *is* most blessed of sons;
Let him be favored by his brothers,
And let him dip his foot in oil.
25 Your sandals *shall be* iron and bronze;
As your days, *so shall* your strength *be*.

26 "*There is* no one like the God of Jeshurun,
Who rides the heavens to help you,
And in His excellency on the clouds.
27 The eternal God *is your* refuge,
And underneath *are* the everlasting arms;
He will thrust out the enemy from before you,
And will say, 'Destroy!'
28 Then Israel shall dwell in safety,
The fountain of Jacob alone,
In a land of grain and new wine;
His heavens shall also drop dew.
29 Happy *are* you, O Israel!
Who *is* like you, a people saved by the LORD,
The shield of your help
And the sword of your majesty!
Your enemies shall submit to you,
And you shall tread down their high places."

34 Then Moses went up from the plains of Moab to Mount Nebo, to the top of Pisgah, which is across from Jericho. And the

LORD showed him all the land of Gilead as far
as Dan, [2]all Naphtali and the land of Ephraim
and Manasseh, all the land of Judah as far as
the Western Sea, [3]the South, and the plain of
the Valley of Jericho, the city of palm trees, as
far as Zoar. [4]Then the LORD said to him, "This
is the land of which I swore to give Abraham,
Isaac, and Jacob, saying, 'I will give it to your
descendants.' I have caused you to see *it* with
your eyes, but you shall not cross over there."
[5]So Moses the servant of the LORD died there
in the land of Moab, according to the word of
the LORD. [6]And He buried him in a valley in the
land of Moab, opposite Beth Peor; but no one
knows his grave to this day. [7]Moses *was* one hundred and twenty years old when he died. His
eyes were not dim nor his natural vigor diminished. [8]And the children of Israel wept for Moses
in the plains of Moab thirty days. So the days
of weeping *and* mourning for Moses ended.
[9]Now Joshua the son of Nun was full of the
spirit of wisdom, for Moses had laid his hands
on him; so the children of Israel heeded him,
and did as the LORD had commanded Moses.
[10]But since then there has not arisen in
Israel a prophet like Moses, whom the LORD
knew face to face, [11]in all the signs and wonders
which the LORD sent him to do in the land of
Egypt, before Pharaoh, before all his servants,
and in all his land, [12]and by all that mighty
power and all the great terror which Moses
performed in the sight of all Israel.

Psalm 40:13–17

13 Be pleased, O LORD, to deliver me;
O LORD, make haste to help me!
14 Let them be ashamed and brought to
mutual confusion
Who seek to destroy my life;
Let them be driven backward and
brought to dishonor
Who wish me evil.
15 Let them be confounded because of
their shame,
Who say to me, "Aha, aha!"
16 Let all those who seek You rejoice and
be glad in You;
Let such as love Your salvation say
continually,
"The LORD be magnified!"
17 But I *am* poor and needy;
Yet the LORD thinks upon me.
You *are* my help and my deliverer;
Do not delay, O my God.

Proverbs 13:13–14

13 He who despises the word will be
destroyed,
But he who fears the commandment
will be rewarded.
14 The law of the wise *is* a fountain of life,
To turn *one* away from the snares
of death.

Luke 8:1–25

8 Now it came to pass, afterward, that He
went through every city and village, preaching and bringing the glad tidings of the kingdom of God. And the twelve *were* with Him, [2]and
certain women who had been healed of evil spirits and infirmities—Mary called Magdalene,
out of whom had come seven demons, [3]and
Joanna the wife of Chuza, Herod's steward, and
Susanna, and many others who provided for
Him from their substance.
[4]And when a great multitude had gathered,
and they had come to Him from every city, He
spoke by a parable: [5]"A sower went out to sow
his seed. And as he sowed, some fell by the
wayside; and it was trampled down, and the
birds of the air devoured it. [6]Some fell on rock;
and as soon as it sprang up, it withered away
because it lacked moisture. [7]And some fell
among thorns, and the thorns sprang up with
it and choked it. [8]But others fell on good
ground, sprang up, and yielded a crop a hundredfold." When He had said these things He
cried, "He who has ears to hear, let him hear!"
[9]Then His disciples asked Him, saying,

8:2 certain women. Rabbis normally did not have women as disciples. **Mary called Magdalene.** Her name probably derives from the Galilean town of Magdala. Some believe she is the woman described in 7:37–50, but it seems highly unlikely that Luke would introduce her here by name for the first time if she were the main figure in the account he just completed. Also, while it is clear that she had suffered at the hands of "demons," there is no reason whatsoever to think that she had ever been a prostitute.

8:3 Joanna. This woman is also mentioned in 24:10, but nowhere else in Scripture. It is possible that she was a source for some of the details Luke recounts about Herod (see 23:8,12). **Susanna.** Aside from this reference, she is nowhere mentioned in Scripture. She is probably someone Luke knew personally. **from their substance.** It was a Jewish custom for disciples to support rabbis in this way. (See 10:7; 1 Cor. 9:4–11; Gal. 6:6; 1 Tim. 5:17,18.)

"What does this parable mean?"

[10]And He said, "To you it has been given to know the mysteries of the kingdom of God, but to the rest *it is given* in parables, that

> *'Seeing they may not see,*
> *And hearing they may not understand.'*

[11]"Now the parable is this: The seed is the word of God. [12]Those by the wayside are the ones who hear; then the devil comes and takes away the word out of their hearts, lest they should believe and be saved. [13]But the ones on the rock *are those* who, when they hear, receive the word with joy; and these have no root, who believe for a while and in time of temptation fall away. [14]Now the ones *that* fell among thorns are those who, when they have heard, go out and are choked with cares, riches, and pleasures of life, and bring no fruit to maturity. [15]But the ones *that* fell on the good ground are those who, having heard the word with a noble and good heart, keep *it* and bear fruit with patience.

8:18 take heed how you hear. One's response to the light in this life is crucial, because at the throne of judgment there will be no opportunity to embrace truth that was formerly spurned (Rev. 20:11–15). Those who scorn the light of the gospel now will have all light removed from them in eternity. See 19:26; Matthew 25:29.

[16]"No one, when he has lit a lamp, covers it with a vessel or puts *it* under a bed, but sets *it* on a lampstand, that those who enter may see the light. [17]For nothing is secret that will not be revealed, nor *anything* hidden that will not be known and come to light. [18]Therefore take heed how you hear. For whoever has, to him *more* will be given; and whoever does not have, even what he seems to have will be taken from him."

[19]Then His mother and brothers came to Him, and could not approach Him because of the crowd. [20]And it was told Him *by some,* who said, "Your mother and Your brothers are standing outside, desiring to see You."

[21]But He answered and said to them, "My mother and My brothers are these who hear the word of God and do it."

[22]Now it happened, on a certain day, that He got into a boat with His disciples. And He said to them, "Let us cross over to the other side of the lake." And they launched out. [23]But as they sailed He fell asleep. And a windstorm came down on the lake, and they were filling *with water,* and were in jeopardy. [24]And they came to Him and awoke Him, saying, "Master, Master, we are perishing!"

Then He arose and rebuked the wind and the raging of the water. And they ceased, and there was a calm. [25]But He said to them, "Where is your faith?"

And they were afraid, and marveled, saying to one another, "Who can this be? For He commands even the winds and water, and they obey Him!"

DAY 5: How is Moses described at the end of his life?

He is called "the man of God" in Deuteronomy 33:1. This is the first use of this phrase in Scripture. Subsequently, some 70 times in the Old Testament, messengers of God (especially prophets) are called "a man of God" (1 Sam. 2:27; 9:6; 1 Kin. 13:1; 17:18; 2 Kin. 4:7). The New Testament uses this title for Timothy (1 Tim. 6:11; 2 Tim. 3:17). Moses was viewed among such prophets in this conclusion to the book (see 34:10).

In Deuteronomy 34:1–4, he went to the top of Pisgah where "the LORD showed him" the panorama of the land the Lord had promised to give (the land of Canaan) to the patriarchs and their seed in Genesis 12:7; 13:15; 15:18–21; 26:4; 28:13,14. Remarkably, it adds that "He buried him" (v. 6). The context indicates that the Lord is the One who buried Moses, and man did not have a part in it. See Jude 9, which recounts Michael's and Satan's dispute over Moses' body.

At the end, Moses' physical vision and physical health were "not dim...diminished" (v. 7). It was not death by natural causes that kept Moses from leading Israel into the Promised Land. It was his unfaithfulness to the Lord at Meribah (see Num. 20:12). Before he passed on, Moses "laid his hands" on Joshua (v. 9), which was a confirmation of the military and administrative ability necessary to the task the Lord had given Joshua. It also confirmed that Joshua had the spiritual wisdom to rely on and to be committed to the Lord.

Moses was the greatest of all the Old Testament prophets (v. 10), one whom the Lord knew intimately. Not until John the Baptist was there another prophet greater than Moses (see Matt. 11:11). After John, the Prophet came of whom Moses wrote (see John 1:21,25; 6:14 with Deut. 18:15,18; Acts 3:22; 7:37). Moses next appeared on the Mt. of Transfiguration together with Elijah and Jesus Christ (Matt. 17:3; Mark 9:4; Luke 9:30,31).

APRIL 6

Joshua 1:1–2:24

1 After the death of Moses the servant of the
LORD, it came to pass that the LORD spoke to
Joshua the son of Nun, Moses' assistant, saying: 2"Moses My servant is dead. Now therefore, arise, go over this Jordan, you and all this
people, to the land which I am giving to
them—the children of Israel. 3Every place that
the sole of your foot will tread upon I have
given you, as I said to Moses. 4From the wilderness and this Lebanon as far as the great river,
the River Euphrates, all the land of the
Hittites, and to the Great Sea toward the going
down of the sun, shall be your territory. 5No
man shall *be able to* stand before you all the
days of your life; as I was with Moses, *so* I will
be with you. I will not leave you nor forsake
you. 6Be strong and of good courage, for to
this people you shall divide as an inheritance
the land which I swore to their fathers to give
them. 7Only be strong and very courageous,
that you may observe to do according to all the
law which Moses My servant commanded you;
do not turn from it to the right hand or to the
left, that you may prosper wherever you go.
8This Book of the Law shall not depart from
your mouth, but you shall meditate in it day and
night, that you may observe to do according to
all that is written in it. For then you will make
your way prosperous, and then you will have
good success. 9Have I not commanded you? Be
strong and of good courage; do not be afraid,
nor be dismayed, for the LORD your God *is*
with you wherever you go."
10Then Joshua commanded the officers of
the people, saying, 11"Pass through the camp
and command the people, saying, 'Prepare
provisions for yourselves, for within three
days you will cross over this Jordan, to go in to
possess the land which the LORD your God is
giving you to possess.'"
12And to the Reubenites, the Gadites, and half
the tribe of Manasseh Joshua spoke, saying,
13"Remember the word which Moses the servant of the LORD commanded you, saying, 'The
LORD your God is giving you rest and is giving
you this land.' 14Your wives, your little ones, and
your livestock shall remain in the land which
Moses gave you on this side of the Jordan. But
you shall pass before your brethren armed, all
your mighty men of valor, and help them, 15un-
til the LORD has given your brethren rest, as
He *gave* you, and they also have taken possession of the land which the LORD your God is
giving them. Then you shall return to the land
of your possession and enjoy it, which Moses
the LORD's servant gave you on this side of the
Jordan toward the sunrise."
16So they answered Joshua, saying, "All that
you command us we will do, and wherever
you send us we will go. 17Just as we heeded
Moses in all things, so we will heed you. Only
the LORD your God be with you, as He was
with Moses. 18Whoever rebels against your
command and does not heed your words, in
all that you command him, shall be put to
death. Only be strong and of good courage."
2 Now Joshua the son of Nun sent out two
men from Acacia Grove to spy secretly,
saying, "Go, view the land, especially Jericho."
So they went, and came to the house of a
harlot named Rahab, and lodged there. 2And it
was told the king of Jericho, saying, "Behold,
men have come here tonight from the children of Israel to search out the country."
3So the king of Jericho sent to Rahab, saying, "Bring out the men who have come to
you, who have entered your house, for they
have come to search out all the country."
4Then the woman took the two men and hid
them. So she said, "Yes, the men came to me,
but I did not know where they *were* from. 5And
it happened as the gate was being shut, when
it was dark, that the men went out. Where the
men went I do not know; pursue them quickly,

1:8 This Book of the Law. A reference to Scripture, specifically Genesis through Deuteronomy, written by Moses (see Ex. 17:14; Deut. 31:9–11, 24). **meditate in it.** To read with thoughtfulness, to linger over God's Word. The parts of Scripture they possessed have always been the main spiritual food of those who served Him, e.g., Job (Job 23:12); the psalmist (Ps. 1:1–3); Jeremiah (Jer. 15:16); and Jesus (John 4:34). **prosperous,...good success.** The promise of God's blessing on the great responsibility God has given Joshua. The principle here is central to all spiritual effort and enterprise, namely the deep understanding and application of Scripture at all times.

1:9 LORD...*is* with you. This assurance has always been the staying sufficiency for God's servants such as Abraham (Gen. 15:1), Moses and his people (Ex. 14:13), Isaiah (Is. 41:10), Jeremiah (Jer. 1:7, 8), and Christians through the centuries (Matt. 28:20; Heb. 13:5).

2:1 two men...to spy. These scouts would inform Joshua on various features of the topography, food, drinking water, and defenses to be overcome in the invasion. **house of a harlot.** Their purpose was not impure; rather, the spies sought a place where they would not be conspicuous. Resorting to such a house would be a good cover, from where they might learn something of Jericho. Also, a house on the city wall (v. 15) would allow a quick getaway. In spite of this precaution, their presence became known (vv. 2,3). God, in His sovereign providence, wanted them there for the salvation of the harlot. She would provide an example of His saving by faith a woman at the bottom of social strata, as He saved Abraham at the top (see James 2:18–25). Most importantly, by God's grace she was in the messianic line (Matt. 1:5).

for you may overtake them." [6](But she had brought them up to the roof and hidden them with the stalks of flax, which she had laid in order on the roof.) [7]Then the men pursued them by the road to the Jordan, to the fords. And as soon as those who pursued them had gone out, they shut the gate.

[8]Now before they lay down, she came up to them on the roof, [9]and said to the men: "I know that the LORD has given you the land, that the terror of you has fallen on us, and that all the inhabitants of the land are fainthearted because of you. [10]For we have heard how the LORD dried up the water of the Red Sea for you when you came out of Egypt, and what you did to the two kings of the Amorites who *were* on the other side of the Jordan, Sihon and Og, whom you utterly destroyed. [11]And as soon as we heard *these things,* our hearts melted; neither did there remain any more courage in anyone because of you, for the LORD your God, He *is* God in heaven above and on earth beneath. [12]Now therefore, I beg you, swear to me by the LORD, since I have shown you kindness, that you also will show kindness to my father's house, and give me a true token, [13]and spare my father, my mother, my brothers, my sisters, and all that they have, and deliver our lives from death."

[14]So the men answered her, "Our lives for yours, if none of you tell this business of ours. And it shall be, when the LORD has given us the land, that we will deal kindly and truly with you."

[15]Then she let them down by a rope through the window, for her house *was* on the city wall; she dwelt on the wall. [16]And she said to them, "Get to the mountain, lest the pursuers meet you. Hide there three days, until the pursuers have returned. Afterward you may go your way."

[17]So the men said to her: "We *will be* blameless of this oath of yours which you have made us swear, [18]unless, *when* we come into the land, you bind this line of scarlet cord in the window through which you let us down, and unless you bring your father, your mother, your brothers, and all your father's household to your own home. [19]So it shall be *that* whoever goes outside the doors of your house into the street, his blood *shall be* on his own head, and we *will be* guiltless. And whoever is with you in the house, his blood *shall be* on our head if a hand is laid on him. [20]And if you tell this business of ours, then we will be free from your oath which you made us swear."

[21]Then she said, "According to your words, so *be* it." And she sent them away, and they departed. And she bound the scarlet cord in the window.

[22]They departed and went to the mountain, and stayed there three days until the pursuers returned. The pursuers sought *them* all along the way, but did not find *them.* [23]So the two men returned, descended from the mountain, and crossed over; and they came to Joshua the son of Nun, and told him all that had befallen them. [24]And they said to Joshua, "Truly the LORD has delivered all the land into our hands, for indeed all the inhabitants of the country are fainthearted because of us."

Psalm 41:1–13

To the Chief Musician. A Psalm of David.

Blessed *is* he who considers
the poor;
The LORD will deliver him in time of
trouble.
2 The LORD will preserve him and keep
him alive,
And he will be blessed on the earth;
You will not deliver him to the will
of his enemies.
3 The LORD will strengthen him on his
bed of illness;
You will sustain him on his sickbed.

4 I said, "LORD, be merciful to me;
Heal my soul, for I have sinned
against You."
5 My enemies speak evil of me:
"When will he die, and his name perish?"
6 And if he comes to see *me,*
he speaks lies;
His heart gathers iniquity to itself;

When he goes out, he tells *it.*
7 All who hate me whisper together against me;
Against me they devise my hurt.
8 "An evil disease," *they say,* "clings to him.
And *now* that he lies down, he will rise up no more."
9 Even my own familiar friend in whom I trusted,
Who ate my bread,
Has lifted up *his* heel against me.
10 But You, O LORD, be merciful to me, and raise me up,
That I may repay them.
11 By this I know that You are well pleased with me,
Because my enemy does not triumph over me.
12 As for me, You uphold me in my integrity,
And set me before Your face forever.
13 Blessed *be* the LORD God of Israel
From everlasting to everlasting!
Amen and Amen.

41:13 Blessed *be.* The essence of the Hebrew root of "amen" is "it is true," i.e., reliable, confirmed, verified. Note that Book I of the Psalms (Pss. 1–41) closes with a doxology; see the endings of the other 4 books (Pss. 72:18,19; 89:52; 106:48; 150:6).

Proverbs 13:15–16

15 Good understanding gains favor,
But the way of the unfaithful *is* hard.
16 Every prudent *man* acts with knowledge,
But a fool lays open *his* folly.

Luke 8:26–56

26Then they sailed to the country of the
Gadarenes, which is opposite Galilee. 27And when
He stepped out on the land, there met Him a
certain man from the city who had demons for
a long time. And he wore no clothes, nor did he
live in a house but in the tombs. 28When he saw
Jesus, he cried out, fell down before Him, and
with a loud voice said, "What have I to do with
You, Jesus, Son of the Most High God? I beg
You, do not torment me!" 29For He had commanded the unclean spirit to come out of the man. For it had often seized him, and he was kept under guard, bound with chains and shackles; and he broke the bonds and was driven by the demon into the wilderness.
30Jesus asked him, saying, "What is your name?"

And he said, "Legion," because many demons
had entered him. 31And they begged Him that
He would not command them to go out into the abyss.
32Now a herd of many swine was feeding
there on the mountain. So they begged Him
that He would permit them to enter them. And
He permitted them. 33Then the demons went
out of the man and entered the swine, and the herd ran violently down the steep place into the lake and drowned.
34When those who fed *them* saw what had
happened, they fled and told *it* in the city and in
the country. 35Then they went out to see what
had happened, and came to Jesus, and found the man from whom the demons had departed, sitting at the feet of Jesus, clothed and in his
right mind. And they were afraid. 36They also
who had seen *it* told them by what means he who had been demon-possessed was healed.
37Then the whole multitude of the surrounding region of the Gadarenes asked Him to depart from them, for they were seized with great fear. And He got into the boat and returned.
38Now the man from whom the demons had departed begged Him that he might be with
Him. But Jesus sent him away, saying, 39"Return to your own house, and tell what great things God has done for you." And he went his way and proclaimed throughout the whole city what great things Jesus had done for him.
40So it was, when Jesus returned, that the multitude welcomed Him, for they were all
waiting for Him. 41And behold, there came a
man named Jairus, and he was a ruler of the synagogue. And he fell down at Jesus' feet and
begged Him to come to his house, 42for he had
an only daughter about twelve years of age, and she was dying.

But as He went, the multitudes thronged
Him. 43Now a woman, having a flow of blood
for twelve years, who had spent all her livelihood on physicians and could not be healed
by any, 44came from behind and touched the border of His garment. And immediately her flow of blood stopped.
45And Jesus said, "Who touched Me?"

When all denied it, Peter and those with him said, "Master, the multitudes throng and press You, and You say, 'Who touched Me?' "
46But Jesus said, "Somebody touched Me, for
I perceived power going out from Me." 47Now

when the woman saw that she was not hidden,
she came trembling; and falling down before
Him, she declared to Him in the presence of
all the people the reason she had touched Him
and how she was healed immediately.
[48]And He said to her, "Daughter, be of good
cheer; your faith has made you well. Go in
peace."
[49]While He was still speaking, someone
came from the ruler of the synagogue's *house*,
saying to him, "Your daughter is dead. Do not
trouble the Teacher."
[50]But when Jesus heard *it*, He answered
him, saying, "Do not be afraid; only believe,
and she will be made well." [51]When He came
into the house, He permitted no one to go in
except Peter, James, and John, and the father
and mother of the girl. [52]Now all wept and
mourned for her; but He said, "Do not weep;
she is not dead, but sleeping." [53]And they
ridiculed Him, knowing that she was dead.
[54]But He put them all outside, took her by
the hand and called, saying, "Little girl, arise."
[55]Then her spirit returned, and she arose
immediately. And He commanded that she be
given *something* to eat. [56]And her parents were
astonished, but He charged them to tell no one
what had happened.

DAY 6: What prepared Joshua for leading the nation of Israel?

1. Exodus 17:9,10,13,14—Joshua led the victorious battle against the Amalekites.
2. Exodus 24:13—Joshua, the servant of Moses, accompanied the Jewish leader to the mountain of God (see 32:17).
3. Numbers 11:28—Joshua was the attendant of Moses from his youth.
4. Numbers 13:16—Moses changed his name from Hosea ("salvation") to Joshua ("the Lord saves").
5. Numbers 14:6–10,30,38—Joshua, along with Caleb, spied out the land of Canaan with 10 others. Only Joshua and Caleb urged the nation to possess the land and, thus, only they of the 12 actually entered Canaan.
6. Numbers 27:18—Joshua was indwelt by the Holy Spirit.
7. Numbers 27:18–23—Joshua was commissioned for spiritual service the first time, to assist Moses.
8. Numbers 32:12—Joshua followed the Lord fully.
9. Deuteronomy 31:23—Joshua was commissioned a second time, to replace Moses.
10. Deuteronomy 34:9—Joshua was filled with the spirit of wisdom.

APRIL 7

Joshua 3:1–4:24

3 Then Joshua rose early in the morning;
and they set out from Acacia Grove and
came to the Jordan, he and all the children of
Israel, and lodged there before they crossed
over. [2]So it was, after three days, that the officers went through the camp; [3]and they commanded the people, saying, "When you see
the ark of the covenant of the LORD your God,
and the priests, the Levites, bearing it, then
you shall set out from your place and go after
it. [4]Yet there shall be a space between you and
it, about two thousand cubits by measure. Do
not come near it, that you may know the way
by which you must go, for you have not
passed *this* way before."
[5]And Joshua said to the people, "Sanctify
yourselves, for tomorrow the LORD will do
wonders among you." [6]Then Joshua spoke to
the priests, saying, "Take up the ark of the
covenant and cross over before the people."
So they took up the ark of the covenant and
went before the people.
[7]And the LORD said to Joshua, "This day I will
begin to exalt you in the sight of all Israel, that
they may know that, as I was with Moses, *so* I
will be with you. [8]You shall command the priests
who bear the ark of the covenant, saying, 'When
you have come to the edge of the water of the
Jordan, you shall stand in the Jordan.' "
[9]So Joshua said to the children of Israel,
"Come here, and hear the words of the LORD
your God." [10]And Joshua said, "By this you shall
know that the living God *is* among you, and
that He will without fail drive out from before
you the Canaanites and the Hittites and the
Hivites and the Perizzites and the Girgashites
and the Amorites and the Jebusites: [11]Behold,
the ark of the covenant of the Lord of all the
earth is crossing over before you into the
Jordan. [12]Now therefore, take for yourselves
twelve men from the tribes of Israel, one man
from every tribe. [13]And it shall come to pass,
as soon as the soles of the feet of the priests
who bear the ark of the LORD, the Lord of all
the earth, shall rest in the waters of the
Jordan, *that* the waters of the Jordan shall be

3:10 Canaanite people to be killed or defeated were sinful to the point of extreme (see Gen. 15:16; Lev. 18:24,25). God, as moral judge, has the right to deal with all people, as at the end (Rev. 20:11–15) or any other time when He deems it appropriate for His purposes. The question is not why God chose to destroy these sinners, but why He had let them live so long and why all sinners are not destroyed far sooner than they are. It is grace that allows any sinner to draw the breath of life (see Gen. 2:17; Ezek. 18:20; Rom. 6:23).

cut off, the waters that come down from
upstream, and they shall stand as a heap."
14So it was, when the people set out from
their camp to cross over the Jordan, with the
priests bearing the ark of the covenant before
the people, 15and as those who bore the ark
came to the Jordan, and the feet of the priests
who bore the ark dipped in the edge of the
water (for the Jordan overflows all its banks
during the whole time of harvest), 16that the
waters which came down from upstream
stood *still, and* rose in a heap very far away at
Adam, the city that *is* beside Zaretan. So the
waters that went down into the Sea of the
Arabah, the Salt Sea, failed, *and* were cut off;
and the people crossed over opposite Jericho.

3:16 rose in a heap. The God of all power, who created heaven, earth, and all else according to Genesis 1, worked miracles here. The waters were dammed up at Adam, a city 15 miles north of the crossing, and also in tributary creeks. Once the miracle was completed, God permitted the waters to flow again (4:18) after all the people had walked to the other side on dry ground (3:17). As the Exodus had begun (see Ex. 14), so it ended.

17Then the priests who bore the ark of the
covenant of the LORD stood firm on dry ground
in the midst of the Jordan; and all Israel crossed
over on dry ground, until all the people had
crossed completely over the Jordan.

4 And it came to pass, when all the people
had completely crossed over the Jordan,
that the LORD spoke to Joshua, saying: 2"Take
for yourselves twelve men from the people,
one man from every tribe, 3and command
them, saying, 'Take for yourselves twelve
stones from here, out of the midst of the Jordan,
from the place where the priests' feet stood
firm. You shall carry them over with you and
leave them in the lodging place where you
lodge tonight.' "
4Then Joshua called the twelve men whom
he had appointed from the children of Israel,
one man from every tribe; 5and Joshua said to
them: "Cross over before the ark of the LORD
your God into the midst of the Jordan, and
each one of you take up a stone on his shoulder, according to the number of the tribes of
the children of Israel, 6that this may be a sign
among you when your children ask in time to
come, saying, 'What do these stones *mean* to
you?' 7Then you shall answer them that the
waters of the Jordan were cut off before the ark
of the covenant of the LORD; when it crossed
over the Jordan, the waters of the Jordan were
cut off. And these stones shall be for a memorial to the children of Israel forever."
8And the children of Israel did so, just as
Joshua commanded, and took up twelve
stones from the midst of the Jordan, as the
LORD had spoken to Joshua, according to the
number of the tribes of the children of Israel,
and carried them over with them to the place
where they lodged, and laid them down there.
9Then Joshua set up twelve stones in the midst
of the Jordan, in the place where the feet of
the priests who bore the ark of the covenant
stood; and they are there to this day.
10So the priests who bore the ark stood in
the midst of the Jordan until everything was
finished that the LORD had commanded
Joshua to speak to the people, according to all
that Moses had commanded Joshua; and the
people hurried and crossed over. 11Then it
came to pass, when all the people had completely crossed over, that the ark of the LORD
and the priests crossed over in the presence of
the people. 12And the men of Reuben, the men
of Gad, and half the tribe of Manasseh crossed
over armed before the children of Israel, as
Moses had spoken to them. 13About forty
thousand prepared for war crossed over
before the LORD for battle, to the plains of Jericho. 14On that day the LORD exalted Joshua in
the sight of all Israel; and they feared him, as
they had feared Moses, all the days of his life.
15Then the LORD spoke to Joshua, saying,
16"Command the priests who bear the ark of
the Testimony to come up from the Jordan."
17Joshua therefore commanded the priests,
saying, "Come up from the Jordan." 18And it
came to pass, when the priests who bore the
ark of the covenant of the LORD had come

from the midst of the Jordan, *and* the soles of
the priests' feet touched the dry land, that the
waters of the Jordan returned to their place and
overflowed all its banks as before.
19Now the people came up from the Jordan
on the tenth *day* of the first month, and they
camped in Gilgal on the east border of Jericho.
20And those twelve stones which they took out
of the Jordan, Joshua set up in Gilgal. 21Then
he spoke to the children of Israel, saying:
"When your children ask their fathers in time
to come, saying, 'What *are* these stones?'
22then you shall let your children know, saying,
'Israel crossed over this Jordan on dry land';
23for the LORD your God dried up the waters of
the Jordan before you until you had crossed
over, as the LORD your God did to the Red Sea,
which He dried up before us until we had
crossed over, 24that all the peoples of the earth
may know the hand of the LORD, that it *is*
mighty, that you may fear the LORD your God
forever."

Psalm 42:1–5

To the Chief Musician.
A Contemplation of the sons of Korah.

As the deer pants for the
water brooks,
So pants my soul for You, O God.
2 My soul thirsts for God, for the living
God.
When shall I come and appear before
God?
3 My tears have been my food day and
night,
While they continually say to me,
"Where *is* your God?"

4 When I remember these *things,*
I pour out my soul within me.
For I used to go with the multitude;
I went with them to the house of God,
With the voice of joy and praise,
With a multitude that kept a pilgrim
feast.
5 Why are you cast down, O my soul?
And *why* are you disquieted within me?
Hope in God, for I shall yet praise Him
For the help of His countenance.

42:4 When I remember these *things,* I pour out my soul. Such language also characterizes Jeremiah's Lamentations, indicating a heavy dirge. On "pouring out one's soul" or "heart," see 1 Samuel 1:15; Psalm 62:8; Lamentations 2:19. These are attempts at trying to unburden oneself from intolerable pain, grief, and agony.

Proverbs 13:17–18

17 A wicked messenger falls into trouble,
But a faithful ambassador *brings*
health.
18 Poverty and shame *will come* to him
who disdains correction,
But he who regards a rebuke will be
honored.

Luke 9:1–17

9 Then He called His twelve disciples
together and gave them power and authority over all demons, and to cure diseases. 2He
sent them to preach the kingdom of God and
to heal the sick. 3And He said to them, "Take
nothing for the journey, neither staffs nor bag
nor bread nor money; and do not have two
tunics apiece.

9:3 Take nothing. Slight differences between Matthew, Mark, and Luke have troubled some. Matthew 10:9,10 and this text say the disciples were not to take staffs, but Mark 6:8 prohibited everything "except a staff." Mark 6:9 also instructed them to "wear sandals," but in Matthew 10:10 sandals were included in the things they were not to carry. Actually, however, what Matthew 10:10 and this verse prohibited was the packing of extra staffs and sandals. The disciples were not to be carrying baggage for the journey, but merely to go with the clothes on their backs.

4"Whatever house you enter, stay there, and
from there depart. 5And whoever will not receive
you, when you go out of that city, shake off the
very dust from your feet as a testimony
against them."
6So they departed and went through the
towns, preaching the gospel and healing
everywhere.
7Now Herod the tetrarch heard of all that was
done by Him; and he was perplexed, because it
was said by some that John had risen from the
dead, 8and by some that Elijah had appeared,
and by others that one of the old prophets had
risen again. 9Herod said, "John I have beheaded, but who is this of whom I hear such
things?" So he sought to see Him.
10And the apostles, when they had returned,
told Him all that they had done. Then He took

them and went aside privately into a deserted place belonging to the city called Bethsaida. [11]But when the multitudes knew *it,* they followed Him; and He received them and spoke to them about the kingdom of God, and healed those who had need of healing. [12]When the day began to wear away, the twelve came and said to Him, "Send the multitude away, that they may go into the surrounding towns and country, and lodge and get provisions; for we are in a deserted place here."

[13]But He said to them, "You give them something to eat."

And they said, "We have no more than five loaves and two fish, unless we go and buy food for all these people." [14]For there were about five thousand men.

Then He said to His disciples, "Make them sit down in groups of fifty." [15]And they did so, and made them all sit down.

[16]Then He took the five loaves and the two fish, and looking up to heaven, He blessed and broke them, and gave *them* to the disciples to set before the multitude. [17]So they all ate and were filled, and twelve baskets of the leftover fragments were taken up by them.

DAY 7: How do the Proverbs apply to specific life decisions and experiences?

Proverbs are divine guidelines and wise observations that teach underlying principles of life (24:3,4). They are not inflexible laws or absolute promises. This is because they are applied in life situations that are rately clear-cut or uncomplicated by other conditions. The consequences of a fool's behavior as described in Proverbs apply to the complete fool. Most people are only occasionally foolish and therefore experience the occasional consequences of foolish behavior. It becomes apparent that the proverbs usually do have exceptions due to the uncertainty of life and the unpredictable behavior of fallen people.

The marvelous challenge and principle expressed in 3:5,6 puts a heavy emphasis on trusting the Lord with "all your heart" and "in all your ways [acknowledging] Him." Even partly practicing the conditions of those phrases represents a major challenge. Because of God's grace, we don't have to perfectly carry out the conditions in order to experience the truth that "He shall direct your paths."

God does not guarantee uniform outcome or application for each proverb. By studying them and applying them, a believer is allowed to contemplate God's mind, character, attributes, works, and blessings. In Jesus Christ are hidden all the treasures of wisdom and knowledge which are only partly expressed in Proverbs (Col. 2:3).

APRIL 8

Joshua 5:1–6:27

5 So it was, when all the kings of the Amorites who *were* on the west side of the Jordan, and all the kings of the Canaanites who *were* by the sea, heard that the LORD had dried up the waters of the Jordan from before the children of Israel until we had crossed over, that their heart melted; and there was no spirit in them any longer because of the children of Israel.

[2]At that time the LORD said to Joshua, "Make flint knives for yourself, and circumcise the sons of Israel again the second time." [3]So Joshua made flint knives for himself, and circumcised the sons of Israel at the hill of the foreskins. [4]And this *is* the reason why Joshua circumcised them: All the people who came out of Egypt *who were* males, all the men of war, had died in the wilderness on the way, after they had come out of Egypt. [5]For all the people who came out had been circumcised, but all the people born in the wilderness, on the way as they came out of Egypt, had not been circumcised. [6]For the children of Israel walked forty years in the wilderness, till all the people *who were* men of war, who came out of Egypt, were consumed, because they did not obey the voice of the LORD—to whom the LORD swore that He would not show them the land which the LORD had sworn to their fathers that He would give us, "a land flowing

5:2 circumcise. God commanded Joshua to see that this was done to all males under 40. These were sons of the generation who died in the wilderness, survivors (see vv. 6,7) from the new generation God spared in Numbers 13 and 14. This surgical sign of a faith commitment to the Abrahamic Covenant (see Gen. 17:9–14) had been ignored during the wilderness trek. Now God wanted it reinstated, so the Israelites would start out right in the land they were possessing.

with milk and honey." 7Then Joshua circumcised their sons *whom* He raised up in their place; for they were uncircumcised, because they had not been circumcised on the way.

8So it was, when they had finished circumcising all the people, that they stayed in their places in the camp till they were healed. 9Then the LORD said to Joshua, "This day I have rolled away the reproach of Egypt from you." Therefore the name of the place is called Gilgal to this day.

10Now the children of Israel camped in Gilgal, and kept the Passover on the fourteenth day of the month at twilight on the plains of Jericho. 11And they ate of the produce of the land on the day after the Passover, unleavened bread and parched grain, on the very same day. 12Then the manna ceased on the day after they had eaten the produce of the land; and the children of Israel no longer had manna, but they ate the food of the land of Canaan that year.

13And it came to pass, when Joshua was by Jericho, that he lifted his eyes and looked, and behold, a Man stood opposite him with His sword drawn in His hand. And Joshua went to Him and said to Him, "*Are* You for us or for our adversaries?"

14So He said, "No, but *as* Commander of the army of the LORD I have now come."

And Joshua fell on his face to the earth and worshiped, and said to Him, "What does my Lord say to His servant?"

15Then the Commander of the LORD's army said to Joshua, "Take your sandal off your foot, for the place where you stand *is* holy." And Joshua did so.

6 Now Jericho was securely shut up because of the children of Israel; none went out, and none came in. 2And the LORD said to Joshua: "See! I have given Jericho into your hand, its king, *and* the mighty men of valor. 3You shall march around the city, all *you* men of war; you shall go all around the city once. This you shall do six days. 4And seven priests shall bear seven trumpets of rams' horns before the ark. But the seventh day you shall march around the city seven times, and the priests shall blow the trumpets. 5It shall come to pass, when they make a long *blast* with the ram's horn, *and* when you hear the sound of the trumpet, that all the people shall shout with a great shout; then the wall of the city will fall down flat. And the people shall go up every man straight before him."

6Then Joshua the son of Nun called the priests and said to them, "Take up the ark of the covenant, and let seven priests bear seven trumpets of rams' horns before the ark of the LORD." 7And he said to the people, "Proceed, and march around the city, and let him who is armed advance before the ark of the LORD."

8So it was, when Joshua had spoken to the people, that the seven priests bearing the seven trumpets of rams' horns before the LORD advanced and blew the trumpets, and the ark of the covenant of the LORD followed them. 9The armed men went before the priests who blew the trumpets, and the rear guard came after the ark, while *the priests* continued blowing the trumpets. 10Now Joshua had commanded the people, saying, "You shall not shout or make any noise with your voice, nor shall a word proceed out of your mouth, until the day I say to you, 'Shout!' Then you shall shout." 11So he had the ark of the LORD circle the city, going around *it* once. Then they came into the camp and lodged in the camp.

12And Joshua rose early in the morning, and the priests took up the ark of the LORD. 13Then seven priests bearing seven trumpets of rams' horns before the ark of the LORD went on continually and blew with the trumpets. And the armed men went before them. But the rear guard came after the ark of the LORD, while *the priests* continued blowing the trumpets. 14And the second day they marched around the city once and returned to the camp. So they did six days.

15But it came to pass on the seventh day that they rose early, about the dawning of the day, and marched around the city seven times in the same manner. On that day only they marched around the city seven times. 16And the seventh time it happened, when the priests blew the trumpets, that Joshua said to the people: "Shout, for the LORD has given you the city! 17Now the city shall be doomed by the LORD to destruction, it and all who *are* in it. Only Rahab the harlot shall live, she and all who *are* with her in the house, because she hid the messengers that we sent. 18And you, by all means abstain from the accursed things, lest you become accursed when you take of the accursed things, and make the camp of Israel a curse, and trouble it. 19But all the silver and gold, and vessels of bronze and iron, *are* consecrated to the LORD; they shall come into the treasury of the LORD."

20So the people shouted when *the priests* blew the trumpets. And it happened when the people heard the sound of the trumpet, and the people shouted with a great shout, that the wall fell down flat. Then the people went up into the city, every man straight before him, and they took the city. 21And they utterly destroyed all that *was* in the city, both man and woman, young and old, ox and sheep and donkey, with the edge of the sword.

[22]But Joshua had said to the two men who had spied out the country, "Go into the harlot's house, and from there bring out the woman and all that she has, as you swore to her." [23]And the young men who had been spies went in and brought out Rahab, her father, her mother, her brothers, and all that she had. So they brought out all her relatives and left them outside the camp of Israel. [24]But they burned the city and all that *was* in it with fire. Only the silver and gold, and the vessels of bronze and iron, they put into the treasury of the house of the LORD. [25]And Joshua spared Rahab the harlot, her father's household, and all that she had. So she dwells in Israel to this day, because she hid the messengers whom Joshua sent to spy out Jericho.

[26]Then Joshua charged *them* at that time, saying, "Cursed *be* the man before the LORD who rises up and builds this city Jericho; he shall lay its foundation with his firstborn, and with his youngest he shall set up its gates."

[27]So the LORD was with Joshua, and his fame spread throughout all the country.

Psalm 42:6–11

6 O my God, my soul is cast down within me;
Therefore I will remember You from the land of the Jordan,
And from the heights of Hermon,
From the Hill Mizar.
7 Deep calls unto deep at the noise of Your waterfalls;
All Your waves and billows have gone over me.
8 The LORD will command His lovingkindness in the daytime,
And in the night His song *shall be* with me—
A prayer to the God of my life.
9 I will say to God my Rock,
"Why have You forgotten me?
Why do I go mourning because of the oppression of the enemy?"
10 *As* with a breaking of my bones,
My enemies reproach me,
While they say to me all day long,
"Where *is* your God?"
11 Why are you cast down, O my soul?
And why are you disquieted within me?
Hope in God;
For I shall yet praise Him,
The help of my countenance and my God.

42:8 The LORD will command His lovingkindness. This statement of confidence interrupts the psalmist's laments (see their continuance in vv. 9,10), providing a few gracious gulps of divine "air" under the cascading inundations of his trials and tormentors.

Proverbs 13:19–21

19 A desire accomplished is sweet to the soul,
But *it is* an abomination to fools to depart from evil.
20 He who walks with wise *men* will be wise,
But the companion of fools will be destroyed.
21 Evil pursues sinners,
But to the righteous, good shall be repaid.

13:20 walks...companion. This speaks of the power of association to shape character. See 1:10,18; 2:12; 4:14; 16:29; 22:24,25; 23:20; 28:7, 19; Psalm 1.

Luke 9:18–36

[18]And it happened, as He was alone praying, *that* His disciples joined Him, and He asked them, saying, "Who do the crowds say that I am?"

[19]So they answered and said, "John the Baptist, but some *say* Elijah; and others *say* that one of the old prophets has risen again."

[20]He said to them, "But who do you say that I am?"

Peter answered and said, "The Christ of God."

9:23 cross. Self-denial was a common thread in Christ's teaching to His disciples (see 14:26,27; Matt. 10:38; 16:24; Mark 8:34; John 12:24–26). The kind of self-denial He sought was not a reclusive asceticism, but a willingness to obey His commandments, serve one another, and suffer—perhaps even die—for His sake.

[21]And He strictly warned and commanded
them to tell this to no one, [22]saying, "The Son of
Man must suffer many things, and be rejected
by the elders and chief priests and scribes,
and be killed, and be raised the third day."
[23]Then He said to *them* all, "If anyone desires
to come after Me, let him deny himself, and
take up his cross daily, and follow Me. [24]For
whoever desires to save his life will lose it, but
whoever loses his life for My sake will save it.
[25]For what profit is it to a man if he gains the
whole world, and is himself destroyed or lost?
[26]For whoever is ashamed of Me and My
words, of him the Son of Man will be ashamed
when He comes in His *own* glory, and *in His*
Father's, and of the holy angels.
[27]"But I tell you truly, there are some standing here who shall not taste death till they see
the kingdom of God."
[28]Now it came to pass, about eight days after
these sayings, that He took Peter, John, and
James and went up on the mountain to pray.
[29]As He prayed, the appearance of His face was
altered, and His robe *became* white *and* glistening. [30]And behold, two men talked with Him,
who were Moses and Elijah, [31]who appeared in
glory and spoke of His decease which He was
about to accomplish at Jerusalem. [32]But Peter
and those with him were heavy with sleep; and
when they were fully awake, they saw His
glory and the two men who stood with Him.
[33]Then it happened, as they were parting from
Him, *that* Peter said to Jesus, "Master, it is
good for us to be here; and let us make three
tabernacles: one for You, one for Moses, and
one for Elijah"—not knowing what he said.
[34]While he was saying this, a cloud came
and overshadowed them; and they were fearful as they entered the cloud. [35]And a voice
came out of the cloud, saying, "This is My
beloved Son. Hear Him!" [36]When the voice had
ceased, Jesus was found alone. But they kept
quiet, and told no one in those days any of the
things they had seen.

9:29 As He prayed. As at Jesus' baptism, while He was praying, the Father's voice came from heaven. **glistening.** Literally, "emitting light." This word is used only here in the New Testament. It suggests a brilliant flashing light, similar to lightning.

DAY 8: Why did God bless Rahab the prostitute?

Rahab's life was not spared because of her lie. It was spared because she put her faith in God. Rahab was given a gracious opportunity to side with God by protecting the two Israelite spies, and she acted within her circumstances. She lied daringly and elaborately. Perhaps her initial response was simply a habit of her profession. From the perspective of the king of Jericho, Rahab would have been guilty of treason, not just lying. She had a new allegiance, and she didn't yet know that the God she now wanted to trust had a rule about lying.

While those around her feared what the God of Israel might do, Rahab feared enough to boldly trust Him as the one true God, "for the LORD your God, He is God in heaven above and on earth beneath" (2:11b). She understood that God wasn't a local or a national god. She knew enough to act.

The spies were impressed and indebted. When Rahab asked them for protection, they recognized their obligation. They were exact in promising to preserve the lives of those in her house, indicated by the scarlet cord from the window.

The radical change that came into Rahab's life when those spies knocked on her door can be seen in several ways. She risked her life to trust God. The Book of Ruth, along with Matthew 1:5, also reveals that Rahab married and became the great-great-grandmother of King David and one of the ancestors of Jesus. Centuries later, Rahab was one of the women listed in Hebrews 11 because of her faith.

APRIL 9

Joshua 7:1–8:35

7 But the children of Israel committed a
trespass regarding the accursed things,
for Achan the son of Carmi, the son of Zabdi,
the son of Zerah, of the tribe of Judah, took of
the accursed things; so the anger of the
LORD burned against the children of Israel.
[2]Now Joshua sent men from Jericho to Ai,
which *is* beside Beth Aven, on the east side of
Bethel, and spoke to them, saying, "Go up
and spy out the country." So the men went up
and spied out Ai. [3]And they returned to
Joshua and said to him, "Do not let all the people go up, but let about two or three thousand
men go up and attack Ai. Do not weary all the
people there, for *the people of Ai are* few." [4]So

about three thousand men went up there from the people, but they fled before the men of Ai. 5And the men of Ai struck down about thirty-six men, for they chased them *from* before the gate as far as Shebarim, and struck them down on the descent; therefore the hearts of the people melted and became like water.

6Then Joshua tore his clothes, and fell to the earth on his face before the ark of the LORD until evening, he and the elders of Israel; and they put dust on their heads. 7And Joshua said, "Alas, Lord GOD, why have You brought this people over the Jordan at all—to deliver us into the hand of the Amorites, to destroy us? Oh, that we had been content, and dwelt on the other side of the Jordan! 8O Lord, what shall I say when Israel turns its back before its enemies? 9For the Canaanites and all the inhabitants of the land will hear *it,* and surround us, and cut off our name from the earth. Then what will You do for Your great name?"

7:9 what will You do for Your great name? The main issue is the glory and honor of God (see Daniel's prayer in Dan. 9:16–19).

10So the LORD said to Joshua: "Get up! Why do you lie thus on your face? 11Israel has sinned, and they have also transgressed My covenant which I commanded them. For they have even taken some of the accursed things, and have both stolen and deceived; and they have also put *it* among their own stuff. 12Therefore the children of Israel could not stand before their enemies, *but* turned *their* backs before their enemies, because they have become doomed to destruction. Neither will I be with you anymore, unless you destroy the accursed from among you. 13Get up, sanctify the people, and say, 'Sanctify yourselves for tomorrow, because thus says the LORD God of Israel: "*There is* an accursed thing in your midst, O Israel; you cannot stand before your enemies until you take away the accursed thing from among you." 14In the morning therefore you shall be brought according to your tribes. And it shall be *that* the tribe which the LORD takes shall come according to families; and the family which the LORD takes shall come by households; and the household which the LORD takes shall come man by man. 15Then it shall be *that* he who is taken with the accursed thing shall be burned with fire, he and all that he has, because he has transgressed the covenant of the LORD, and because he has done a disgraceful thing in Israel.' "

16So Joshua rose early in the morning and brought Israel by their tribes, and the tribe of Judah was taken. 17He brought the clan of Judah, and he took the family of the Zarhites; and he brought the family of the Zarhites man by man, and Zabdi was taken. 18Then he brought his household man by man, and Achan the son of Carmi, the son of Zabdi, the son of Zerah, of the tribe of Judah, was taken.

19Now Joshua said to Achan, "My son, I beg you, give glory to the LORD God of Israel, and make confession to Him, and tell me now what you have done; do not hide *it* from me."

20And Achan answered Joshua and said, "Indeed I have sinned against the LORD God of Israel, and this is what I have done: 21When I saw among the spoils a beautiful Babylonian garment, two hundred shekels of silver, and a wedge of gold weighing fifty shekels, I coveted them and took them. And there they are, hidden in the earth in the midst of my tent, with the silver under it."

22So Joshua sent messengers, and they ran to the tent; and there it was, hidden in his tent, with the silver under it. 23And they took them from the midst of the tent, brought them to Joshua and to all the children of Israel, and laid them out before the LORD. 24Then Joshua, and all Israel with him, took Achan the son of Zerah, the silver, the garment, the wedge of gold, his sons, his daughters, his oxen, his donkeys, his sheep, his tent, and all that he had, and they brought them to the Valley of Achor. 25And Joshua said, "Why have you troubled us? The LORD will trouble you this day." So all Israel stoned him with stones; and they burned them with fire after they had stoned them with stones.

26Then they raised over him a great heap of stones, still there to this day. So the LORD turned from the fierceness of His anger. Therefore the name of that place has been called the Valley of Achor to this day.

8 Now the LORD said to Joshua: "Do not be afraid, nor be dismayed; take all the people of war with you, and arise, go up to Ai. See, I have given into your hand the king of Ai, his people, his city, and his land. 2And you shall do to Ai and its king as you did to Jericho and its king. Only its spoil and its cattle you shall take as booty for yourselves. Lay an ambush for the city behind it."

3So Joshua arose, and all the people of war, to go up against Ai; and Joshua chose thirty thousand mighty men of valor and sent them away by night. 4And he commanded them, saying: "Behold, you shall lie in ambush against the city, behind the city. Do not go very far from the city, but all of you be ready. 5Then I and all the people who *are* with me will approach the city; and it will come about, when they come out against us as at the first, that we shall flee before them. 6For they will come out after us till we have drawn them from the city, for they will say, '*They are* fleeing before us as at the first.' Therefore we will flee before them. 7Then you shall rise from the ambush and seize the city, for the LORD your God will deliver it into your hand. 8And it will be, when you have taken the city, *that* you shall set the city on fire. According to the commandment of the LORD you shall do. See, I have commanded you."

9Joshua therefore sent them out; and they went to lie in ambush, and stayed between Bethel and Ai, on the west side of Ai; but Joshua lodged that night among the people. 10Then Joshua rose up early in the morning and mustered the people, and went up, he and the elders of Israel, before the people to Ai. 11And all the people of war who *were* with him went up and drew near; and they came before the city and camped on the north side of Ai. Now a valley *lay* between them and Ai. 12So he took about five thousand men and set them in ambush between Bethel and Ai, on the west side of the city. 13And when they had set the people, all the army that *was* on the north of the city, and its rear guard on the west of the city, Joshua went that night into the midst of the valley.

14Now it happened, when the king of Ai saw *it,* that the men of the city hurried and rose early and went out against Israel to battle, he and all his people, at an appointed place before the plain. But he did not know that *there was* an ambush against him behind the city. 15And Joshua and all Israel made as if they were beaten before them, and fled by the way of the wilderness. 16So all the people who *were* in Ai were called together to pursue them. And they pursued Joshua and were drawn away from the city. 17There was not a man left in Ai or Bethel who did not go out after Israel. So they left the city open and pursued Israel.

18Then the LORD said to Joshua, "Stretch out the spear that *is* in your hand toward Ai, for I will give it into your hand." And Joshua stretched out the spear that *was* in his hand toward the city. 19So *those in* ambush arose quickly out of their place; they ran as soon as he had stretched out his hand, and they entered the city and took it, and hurried to set the city on fire. 20And when the men of Ai looked behind them, they saw, and behold, the smoke of the city ascended to heaven. So they had no power to flee this way or that way, and the people who had fled to the wilderness turned back on the pursuers.

21Now when Joshua and all Israel saw that the ambush had taken the city and that the smoke of the city ascended, they turned back and struck down the men of Ai. 22Then the others came out of the city against them; so they were *caught* in the midst of Israel, some on this side and some on that side. And they struck them down, so that they let none of them remain or escape. 23But the king of Ai they took alive, and brought him to Joshua.

24And it came to pass when Israel had made an end of slaying all the inhabitants of Ai in the field, in the wilderness where they pursued them, and when they all had fallen by the edge of the sword until they were consumed, that all the Israelites returned to Ai and struck it with the edge of the sword. 25So it was *that* all who fell that day, both men and women, *were* twelve thousand—all the people of Ai. 26For Joshua did not draw back his hand, with which he stretched out the spear, until he had utterly destroyed all the inhabitants of Ai. 27Only the livestock and the spoil of that city Israel took as booty for themselves, according to the word of the LORD which He had commanded Joshua. 28So Joshua burned Ai and made it a heap forever, a desolation to this day. 29And the king of Ai he hanged on a tree until evening. And as soon as the sun was down, Joshua commanded that they should take his corpse down from the tree, cast it at the entrance of the gate of the city, and raise over it a great heap of stones *that remains* to this day.

30Now Joshua built an altar to the LORD God of Israel in Mount Ebal, 31as Moses the servant of the LORD had commanded the children of Israel, as it is written in the Book of the Law of Moses: "an altar of whole stones over which no man has wielded an iron *tool.*" And they offered on it burnt offerings to the LORD, and sacrificed peace offerings. 32And there, in the presence of the children of Israel, he wrote on the stones a copy of the law of Moses, which he had written. 33Then all Israel, with their elders and officers and judges, stood on either side of the ark before the priests, the Levites, who bore the ark of the covenant of the LORD, the stranger as well as he who was born among them. Half of them *were* in front of Mount Gerizim and half of them in front of Mount Ebal, as Moses the servant of the LORD had commanded before, that they should bless the

people of Israel. 34And afterward he read all
the words of the law, the blessings and the
cursings, according to all that is written in the
Book of the Law. 35There was not a word of all
that Moses had commanded which Joshua did
not read before all the assembly of Israel, with
the women, the little ones, and the strangers
who were living among them.

Psalm 43:1–5

Vindicate me, O God,
And plead my cause against
an ungodly nation;
Oh, deliver me from the deceitful and
unjust man!
2 For You *are* the God of my strength;
Why do You cast me off?
Why do I go mourning because of the
oppression of the enemy?
3 Oh, send out Your light and
Your truth!
Let them lead me;
Let them bring me to Your holy hill

43:3 Your light and Your truth! Let them lead me; let them bring me. These are bold personifications for divine guidance. The psalmist desired that these "messenger-attributes" divinely direct (see such "leading" and "guiding" in Gen. 24:48; Pss. 78:14,53,72; 107:30; Is. 57:18) so as to bring him successfully to his destination, i.e., Israel's designated place for worship.

And to Your tabernacle.
4 Then I will go to the altar of God,
To God my exceeding joy;
And on the harp I will praise You,
O God, my God.
5 Why are you cast down, O my soul?
And why are you disquieted
within me?
Hope in God;
For I shall yet praise Him,
The help of my countenance
and my God.

Proverbs 13:22–23

22 A good *man* leaves an inheritance to
his children's children,
But the wealth of the sinner is stored
up for the righteous.
23 Much food *is in* the fallow *ground* of
the poor,
And for lack of justice there is waste.

Luke 9:37–62

37Now it happened on the next day, when
they had come down from the mountain, that
a great multitude met Him. 38Suddenly a man
from the multitude cried out, saying, "Teacher,
I implore You, look on my son, for he is my
only child. 39And behold, a spirit seizes him,
and he suddenly cries out; it convulses him so
that he foams *at the mouth;* and it departs
from him with great difficulty, bruising him.
40So I implored Your disciples to cast it out, but
they could not."

41Then Jesus answered and said, "O faithless and perverse generation, how long shall I
be with you and bear with you? Bring your son
here." 42And as he was still coming, the demon
threw him down and convulsed *him.* Then Jesus rebuked the unclean spirit, healed the
child, and gave him back to his father.

43And they were all amazed at the majesty of
God.

But while everyone marveled at all the
things which Jesus did, He said to His disciples, 44"Let these words sink down into your
ears, for the Son of Man is about to be
betrayed into the hands of men." 45But they
did not understand this saying, and it was hidden from them so that they did not perceive it; and they were afraid to ask Him about this saying.

46Then a dispute arose among them as to
which of them would be greatest. 47And Jesus,
perceiving the thought of their heart, took a
little child and set him by Him, 48and said to
them, "Whoever receives this little child in My
name receives Me; and whoever receives Me
receives Him who sent Me. For he who is
least among you all will be great."

49Now John answered and said, "Master, we
saw someone casting out demons in Your name,
and we forbade him because he does not follow
with us."

50But Jesus said to him, "Do not forbid *him,*
for he who is not against us is on our side."

51Now it came to pass, when the time had
come for Him to be received up, that He steadfastly set His face to go to Jerusalem, 52and
sent messengers before His face. And as they
went, they entered a village of the Samaritans,
to prepare for Him. 53But they did not receive
Him, because His face was *set* for the journey
to Jerusalem. 54And when His disciples James
and John saw *this,* they said, "Lord, do You
want us to command fire to come down from
heaven and consume them, just as Elijah did?"
55But He turned and rebuked them, and

9:51 steadfastly set His face to go to Jerusalem. This begins a major section of Luke's Gospel. From here to 19:27, Christ's face was set toward Jerusalem, and Luke's narrative is a travelogue of that long journey to the Cross. This was a dramatic turning point in Christ's ministry. After this, Galilee was no longer His base of operation. Although 17:11–37 describes a return visit to Galilee, Luke included everything between this point and that short Galilean sojourn as part of the journey to Jerusalem. We know from a comparison of the Gospels that, during this period of Christ's ministry, He made short visits to Jerusalem to celebrate feasts. Nonetheless, those brief visits were only interludes in this period of ministry that would culminate in a final journey to Jerusalem for the purpose of dying there. Thus Luke underscored this turning point in Christ's ministry more dramatically than any of the other Gospels, by showing Christ's determination to complete His mission of going to the Cross.

said, "You do not know what manner of spirit
you are of. 56For the Son of Man did not come
to destroy men's lives but to save *them.*" And
they went to another village.
57Now it happened as they journeyed on the
road, *that* someone said to Him, "Lord, I will
follow You wherever You go."
58And Jesus said to him, "Foxes have holes
and birds of the air *have* nests, but the Son of
Man has nowhere to lay *His* head."
59Then He said to another, "Follow Me."
But he said, "Lord, let me first go and bury
my father."
60Jesus said to him, "Let the dead bury their
own dead, but you go and preach the kingdom
of God."
61And another also said, "Lord, I will follow
You, but let me first go *and* bid them farewell
who are at my house."
62But Jesus said to him, "No one, having put
his hand to the plow, and looking back, is fit for
the kingdom of God."

DAY 9: How should we respond to all forms of religious persecution?

Luke 9:51–56 show us Jesus' response to persecution. The Samaritans were descendants of Jewish mixed marriages from the days of captivity. They were rivals of the Jewish nation and had devised their own worship, a hybrid of Judaism and paganism, with a temple of their own on Mt. Gerizim. They were considered unclean by the Jews and were so hated that most Jewish travelers from Galilee to Judah took the longer route east of the Jordan to avoid traveling through Samaria.

The fact that Jesus was traveling to Jerusalem for worship implied rejection of the temple on Mt. Gerizim and a contempt for Samaritan worship. This was a strong point of contention between Jews and Samaritans (see John 4:20–22), and the Samaritan village would not take Him in (v. 53). James and John, whom Jesus nicknamed the "Sons of Thunder" (Mark 3:17), then suggested they call down fire from heaven as Elijah once did (v. 54). To which Christ "rebuked them" (v. 55).

Christ's response to the Samaritans exemplifies the attitude the church ought to have with regard to all forms of religious persecution. The Samaritans' worship was pagan at heart, plainly wrong. Compounding that was their intolerance. Yet, the Lord would not retaliate with force against them. Nor did He even revile them verbally. He had come to save, not to destroy, and so His response was grace rather than destructive fury (v. 56). Nonetheless, Christ's words of disapproval here must not be taken as condemnation of Elijah's actions in 1 Kings 18:38–40 or 2 Kings 1:10–12. Elijah was commissioned to a special ministry as prophet in a theocracy, and it was his God-ordained task to confront an evil monarch (Ahab) who was attempting to usurp God's authority. Elijah acted with an authority comparable to that of modern civil authorities (see Rom. 13:4)—not in a capacity that parallels that of ministers of the gospel.

APRIL 10

Joshua 9:1–10:43

9 And it came to pass when all the kings
who *were* on this side of the Jordan, in the
hills and in the lowland and in all the coasts of
the Great Sea toward Lebanon—the Hittite,
the Amorite, the Canaanite, the Perizzite, the
Hivite, and the Jebusite—heard *about it,* 2that
they gathered together to fight with Joshua
and Israel with one accord.
3But when the inhabitants of Gibeon heard
what Joshua had done to Jericho and Ai, 4they
worked craftily, and went and pretended to be
ambassadors. And they took old sacks on
their donkeys, old wineskins torn and mended,
5old and patched sandals on their feet, and
old garments on themselves; and all the bread
of their provision was dry *and* moldy. 6And

they went to Joshua, to the camp at Gilgal, and said to him and to the men of Israel, "We have come from a far country; now therefore, make a covenant with us."

7Then the men of Israel said to the Hivites, "Perhaps you dwell among us; so how can we make a covenant with you?"

8But they said to Joshua, "We *are* your servants."

And Joshua said to them, "Who *are* you, and where do you come from?"

9So they said to him: "From a very far country your servants have come, because of the name of the LORD your God; for we have heard of His fame, and all that He did in Egypt, 10and all that He did to the two kings of the Amorites who *were* beyond the Jordan—to Sihon king of Heshbon, and Og king of Bashan, who was at Ashtaroth. 11Therefore our elders and all the inhabitants of our country spoke to us, saying, 'Take provisions with you for the journey, and go to meet them, and say to them, "We *are* your servants; now therefore, make a covenant with us." ' 12This bread of ours we took hot *for* our provision from our houses on the day we departed to come to you. But now look, it is dry and moldy. 13And these wineskins which we filled *were* new, and see, they are torn; and these our garments and our sandals have become old because of the very long journey."

14Then the men of Israel took some of their provisions; but they did not ask counsel of the LORD. 15So Joshua made peace with them, and made a covenant with them to let them live; and the rulers of the congregation swore to them.

16And it happened at the end of three days, after they had made a covenant with them, that they heard that they *were* their neighbors who dwelt near them. 17Then the children of Israel journeyed and came to their cities on the third day. Now their cities *were* Gibeon, Chephirah, Beeroth, and Kirjath Jearim. 18But the children of Israel did not attack them, because the rulers of the congregation had sworn to them by the LORD God of Israel. And all the congregation complained against the rulers.

19Then all the rulers said to all the congregation, "We have sworn to them by the LORD God of Israel; now therefore, we may not touch them. 20This we will do to them: We will let them live, lest wrath be upon us because of the oath which we swore to them." 21And the rulers said to them, "Let them live, but let them be woodcutters and water carriers for all the congregation, as the rulers had promised them."

22Then Joshua called for them, and he spoke to them, saying, "Why have you deceived us, saying, 'We *are* very far from you,' when you dwell near us? 23Now therefore, you *are* cursed, and none of you shall be freed from being slaves—woodcutters and water carriers for the house of my God."

24So they answered Joshua and said, "Because your servants were clearly told that the LORD your God commanded His servant Moses to give you all the land, and to destroy all the inhabitants of the land from before you; therefore we were very much afraid for our lives because of you, and have done this thing. 25And now, here we are, in your hands; do with us as it seems good and right to do to us." 26So he did to them, and delivered them out of the hand of the children of Israel, so that they did not kill them. 27And that day Joshua made them woodcutters and water carriers for the congregation and for the altar of the LORD, in the place which He would choose, even to this day.

10 Now it came to pass when Adoni-Zedek king of Jerusalem heard how Joshua had taken Ai and had utterly destroyed it—as he had done to Jericho and its king, so he had done to Ai and its king—and how the inhabitants of Gibeon had made peace with Israel and were among them, 2that they feared greatly, because Gibeon *was* a great city, like one of the royal cities, and because it *was* greater than Ai, and all its men *were* mighty. 3Therefore Adoni-Zedek king of Jerusalem sent to Hoham king of Hebron, Piram king of Jarmuth, Japhia king of Lachish, and Debir king of Eglon, saying, 4"Come up to me and help me, that we may attack Gibeon, for it has made peace with Joshua and with the children of Israel." 5Therefore the five kings of the Amorites, the king of Jerusalem, the king of Hebron, the king of Jarmuth, the king of Lachish, *and* the king of Eglon, gathered together and went up, they and all their armies, and camped before Gibeon and made war against it.

6And the men of Gibeon sent to Joshua at the camp at Gilgal, saying, "Do not forsake your servants; come up to us quickly, save us and help us, for all the kings of the Amorites who dwell in the mountains have gathered together against us."

7So Joshua ascended from Gilgal, he and all the people of war with him, and all the mighty men of valor. 8And the LORD said to Joshua, "Do not fear them, for I have delivered them into your hand; not a man of them shall stand before you." 9Joshua therefore came upon them suddenly, having marched all night from Gilgal. 10So the LORD routed them before Israel, killed them with a great slaughter at

Gibeon, chased them along the road that goes
to Beth Horon, and struck them down as far
as Azekah and Makkedah. 11And it happened,
as they fled before Israel *and* were on the
descent of Beth Horon, that the LORD cast
down large hailstones from heaven on them as
far as Azekah, and they died. *There were* more
who died from the hailstones than the children of Israel killed with the sword.

10:11 The hailstones were miraculous. Note their: 1) source, God; 2) size, large; 3) slaughter, more by stones than by sword; 4) selectivity, only on the enemy; 5) swath, "as far as Azekah"; 6) situation, during a trek down a slope and while God caused the sun to stand still; and 7) similarity to miraculous stones God will fling down during the future wrath (Rev. 16:21).

12Then Joshua spoke to the LORD in the day
when the LORD delivered up the Amorites before
the children of Israel, and he said in the sight
of Israel:

"Sun, stand still over Gibeon;
And Moon, in the Valley of Aijalon."
13 So the sun stood still,

10:12–14 sun stood still, and the moon stopped. Some say an eclipse hid the sun, keeping its heat from Joshua's worn soldiers and allowing coolness for battle. Others suppose a local (not universal) refraction of the sun's rays such as the local darkness in Egypt (Ex. 10:21–23). Another view has it as only language of observation; i.e., it only seemed to Joshua's men that the sun and moon stopped as God helped them do in one literal 24-hour day what would normally take longer. Others view it as lavish poetic description, not literal fact. However, such ideas fail to do justice to 10:12–14 and needlessly question God's power as Creator. This is best accepted as an outright, monumental miracle. Joshua, moved by the Lord's will, commanded the sun to delay (Hebrew, "be still, silent, leave off"). The earth actually stopped revolving or, more likely, the sun moved in the same way to keep perfect pace with the battlefield. The moon also ceased its orbiting. This permitted Joshua's troops time to finish the battle with complete victory (v. 11).

And the moon stopped,
Till the people had revenge
Upon their enemies.

Is this not written in the Book of Jasher? So
the sun stood still in the midst of heaven, and
did not hasten to go *down* for about a whole
day. 14And there has been no day like that,
before it or after it, that the LORD heeded the
voice of a man; for the LORD fought for Israel.
15Then Joshua returned, and all Israel with
him, to the camp at Gilgal.
16But these five kings had fled and hidden
themselves in a cave at Makkedah. 17And it
was told Joshua, saying, "The five kings have
been found hidden in the cave at Makkedah."
18So Joshua said, "Roll large stones against
the mouth of the cave, and set men by it to
guard them. 19And do not stay *there* yourselves,
but pursue your enemies, and attack their rear
guard. Do not allow them to enter their cities,
for the LORD your God has delivered them into
your hand." 20Then it happened, while Joshua
and the children of Israel made an end of slaying them with a very great slaughter, till they
had finished, that those who escaped entered
fortified cities. 21And all the people returned to
the camp, to Joshua at Makkedah, in peace.
No one moved his tongue against any of the
children of Israel.
22Then Joshua said, "Open the mouth of the
cave, and bring out those five kings to me from
the cave." 23And they did so, and brought out
those five kings to him from the cave: the king
of Jerusalem, the king of Hebron, the king of
Jarmuth, the king of Lachish, *and* the king of
Eglon.
24So it was, when they brought out those
kings to Joshua, that Joshua called for all the
men of Israel, and said to the captains of the
men of war who went with him, "Come near,
put your feet on the necks of these kings."
And they drew near and put their feet on their
necks. 25Then Joshua said to them, "Do not be
afraid, nor be dismayed; be strong and of good
courage, for thus the LORD will do to all your
enemies against whom you fight." 26And afterward Joshua struck them and killed them, and
hanged them on five trees; and they were
hanging on the trees until evening. 27So it was
at the time of the going down of the sun *that*
Joshua commanded, and they took them down
from the trees, cast them into the cave where
they had been hidden, and laid large stones
against the cave's mouth, *which remain* until
this very day.
28On that day Joshua took Makkedah, and
struck it and its king with the edge of the
sword. He utterly destroyed them—all the

people who *were* in it. He let none remain. He
also did to the king of Makkedah as he had
done to the king of Jericho.
[29]Then Joshua passed from Makkedah, and
all Israel with him, to Libnah; and they fought
against Libnah. [30]And the LORD also delivered
it and its king into the hand of Israel; he struck
it and all the people who *were* in it with the
edge of the sword. He let none remain in it,
but did to its king as he had done to the king
of Jericho.
[31]Then Joshua passed from Libnah, and all
Israel with him, to Lachish; and they
encamped against it and fought against it.
[32]And the LORD delivered Lachish into the
hand of Israel, who took it on the second day,
and struck it and all the people who *were* in it
with the edge of the sword, according to all
that he had done to Libnah. [33]Then Horam
king of Gezer came up to help Lachish; and
Joshua struck him and his people, until he left
him none remaining.
[34]From Lachish Joshua passed to Eglon, and
all Israel with him; and they encamped against
it and fought against it. [35]They took it on that
day and struck it with the edge of the sword;
all the people who *were* in it he utterly
destroyed that day, according to all that he
had done to Lachish.
[36]So Joshua went up from Eglon, and all
Israel with him, to Hebron; and they fought
against it. [37]And they took it and struck it with
the edge of the sword—its king, all its cities,
and all the people who *were* in it; he left none
remaining, according to all that he had done to
Eglon, but utterly destroyed it and all the people who *were* in it.
[38]Then Joshua returned, and all Israel with
him, to Debir; and they fought against it. [39]And
he took it and its king and all its cities; they
struck them with the edge of the sword and
utterly destroyed all the people who *were* in it.
He left none remaining; as he had done to
Hebron, so he did to Debir and its king, as he
had done also to Libnah and its king.
[40]So Joshua conquered all the land: the
mountain country and the South and the lowland and the wilderness slopes, and all their
kings; he left none remaining, but utterly
destroyed all that breathed, as the LORD God
of Israel had commanded. [41]And Joshua conquered them from Kadesh Barnea as far as
Gaza, and all the country of Goshen, even as
far as Gibeon. [42]All these kings and their land
Joshua took at one time, because the LORD
God of Israel fought for Israel. [43]Then Joshua
returned, and all Israel with him, to the camp
at Gilgal.

Psalm 44:1–3

To the Chief Musician. A Contemplation of the sons of Korah.

We have heard with our ears,
O God,
Our fathers have told us,
The deeds You did in their days,
In days of old:
2 You drove out the nations with Your
hand,
But them You planted;
You afflicted the peoples, and cast
them out.
3 For they did not gain possession of the
land by their own sword,
Nor did their own arm save them;
But it was Your right hand, Your arm,
and the light of Your countenance,
Because You favored them.

Proverbs 13:24–25

24 He who spares his rod hates his son,
But he who loves him disciplines him
promptly.
25 The righteous eats to the satisfying of
his soul,
But the stomach of the wicked shall
be in want.

13:24 rod...disciplines...promptly. Early childhood teaching requires both parental discipline, including corporal punishment (see 10:13; 19:18; 22:15; 29:15,17) and balanced kindness and love. There is great hope that the use of the "divine ordinance" of the rod will produce godly virtue (see 23:13,14) and parental joy (see 10:1; 15:20; 17:21; 23:15,16,24,25; 28:7; 29:1,15,17). Such discipline must have the right motivation (Heb. 12:5–11) and appropriate severity (Eph. 6:4). One who has genuine affection for his child but withholds corporal punishment will produce the same kind of child as a parent who hates his offspring.

Luke 10:1–24

10 After these things the Lord appointed
seventy others also, and sent them two
by two before His face into every city and
place where He Himself was about to go.
[2]Then He said to them, "The harvest truly *is*
great, but the laborers *are* few; therefore pray
the Lord of the harvest to send out laborers
into His harvest. [3]Go your way; behold, I send

you out as lambs among wolves. 4Carry neither money bag, knapsack, nor sandals; and greet no one along the road. 5But whatever house you enter, first say, 'Peace to this house.' 6And if a son of peace is there, your peace will rest on it; if not, it will return to you. 7And remain in the same house, eating and drinking such things as they give, for the laborer is worthy of his wages. Do not go from house to house. 8Whatever city you enter, and they receive you, eat such things as are set before you. 9And heal the sick there, and say to them, 'The kingdom of God has come near to you.' 10But whatever city you enter, and they do not receive you, go out into its streets and say, 11'The very dust of your city which clings to us we wipe off against you. Nevertheless know this, that the kingdom of God has come near you.' 12But I say to you that it will be more tolerable in that Day for Sodom than for that city.

13"Woe to you, Chorazin! Woe to you, Bethsaida! For if the mighty works which were done in you had been done in Tyre and Sidon, they would have repented long ago, sitting in sackcloth and ashes. 14But it will be more tolerable for Tyre and Sidon at the judgment than for you. 15And you, Capernaum, who are exalted to heaven, will be brought down to Hades. 16He who hears you hears Me, he who rejects you rejects Me, and he who rejects Me rejects Him who sent Me."

17Then the seventy returned with joy, saying, "Lord, even the demons are subject to us in Your name."

18And He said to them, "I saw Satan fall like lightning from heaven. 19Behold, I give you the authority to trample on serpents and scorpions, and over all the power of the enemy, and nothing shall by any means hurt you. 20Nevertheless do not rejoice in this, that the spirits are subject to you, but rather rejoice because your names are written in heaven."

21In that hour Jesus rejoiced in the Spirit and said, "I thank You, Father, Lord of heaven and earth, that You have hidden these things from *the* wise and prudent and revealed them to babes. Even so, Father, for so it seemed good in Your sight. 22All things have been delivered to Me by My Father, and no one knows who the Son is except the Father, and who the Father is except the Son, and *the one* to whom the Son wills to reveal *Him.*"

23Then He turned to *His* disciples and said privately, "Blessed *are* the eyes which see the things you see; 24for I tell you that many prophets and kings have desired to see what you see, and have not seen *it,* and to hear what you hear, and have not heard *it.*"

DAY 10: What authority are Christians given over demonic power?

The commissioning of the 70 disciples is recorded only in Luke 10:1. Moses also appointed 70 elders as his representatives (Num. 11:16,24–26). The 12 disciples had been sent into Galilee (9:1–6); the 70 were sent into every city and place where Jesus was about to go—i.e., into Judea, and possibly Perea. They were to go out 2 by 2, as the 12 had been sent (Mark 6:7; see Eccl. 4:9,11; Acts 13:2; 15:27,39,40; 19:22; Rev. 11:3). Jesus warned them in Luke 10:3 that they would face hostility (see Ezek. 2:3–6; John 15:20) and spiritual danger (see Matt. 7:15; John 10:12). Yet we are told they "returned with joy" (v. 17). How long the mission lasted is not recorded. It may have been several weeks.

Regarding their experience, Jesus said, "I saw Satan fall like lightning from heaven" (v. 18). In this context, it appears Jesus' meaning was, "Don't be so surprised that the demons are subject to you. I saw their commander cast out of heaven, so it is no wonder if his minions are cast out on earth. After all, I am the source of the authority that makes them subject to you" (v. 19). He may also have intended a subtle reminder and warning against pride—the reason for Satan's fall (see 1 Tim. 3:6). Jesus gave them "authority to trample on serpents and scorpions." These appear to be figurative terms for demonic powers (see Rom. 16:20).

Nevertheless, Jesus says, "Do not rejoice in this" (v. 20). Rather than being so enthralled with extraordinary manifestations such as power over demons and the ability to work miracles, they should have realized that the greatest wonder of all is the reality of salvation—the whole point of the gospel message and the central issue to which all the miracles pointed—"because your names are written in heaven."

APRIL 11

Joshua 11:1–12:24

11 And it came to pass, when Jabin king of Hazor heard *these things,* that he sent to Jobab king of Madon, to the king of Shimron, to the king of Achshaph, 2and to the kings who *were* from the north, in the mountains, in the plain south of Chinneroth, in the lowland, and in the heights of Dor on the west, 3to the Canaanites in the east and in the west, the Amorite, the Hittite, the Perizzite, the Jebusite

in the mountains, and the Hivite below
Hermon in the land of Mizpah. 4So they went
out, they and all their armies with them, *as*
many people *as* the sand that *is* on the
seashore in multitude, with very many horses
and chariots. 5And when all these kings had
met together, they came and camped together
at the waters of Merom to fight against Israel.

6But the LORD said to Joshua, "Do not be
afraid because of them, for tomorrow about
this time I will deliver all of them slain before
Israel. You shall hamstring their horses and
burn their chariots with fire." 7So Joshua and
all the people of war with him came against
them suddenly by the waters of Merom, and
they attacked them. 8And the LORD delivered
them into the hand of Israel, who defeated
them and chased them to Greater Sidon, to
the Brook Misrephoth, and to the Valley of
Mizpah eastward; they attacked them until
they left none of them remaining. 9So Joshua
did to them as the LORD had told him: he hamstrung their horses and burned their chariots
with fire.

10Joshua turned back at that time and took
Hazor, and struck its king with the sword; for
Hazor was formerly the head of all those kingdoms. 11And they struck all the people who
were in it with the edge of the sword, utterly
destroying *them.* There was none left breathing. Then he burned Hazor with fire.

12So all the cities of those kings, and all their
kings, Joshua took and struck with the edge of
the sword. He utterly destroyed them, as
Moses the servant of the LORD had commanded. 13But *as for* the cities that stood on their
mounds, Israel burned none of them, except
Hazor only, *which* Joshua burned. 14And all the
spoil of these cities and the livestock, the children of Israel took as booty for themselves;
but they struck every man with the edge of
the sword until they had destroyed them, and
they left none breathing. 15As the LORD had
commanded Moses his servant, so Moses
commanded Joshua, and so Joshua did. He
left nothing undone of all that the LORD had
commanded Moses.

16Thus Joshua took all this land: the mountain country, all the South, all the land of
Goshen, the lowland, and the Jordan plain—
the mountains of Israel and its lowlands,
17from Mount Halak and the ascent to Seir,
even as far as Baal Gad in the Valley of Lebanon below Mount Hermon. He captured all
their kings, and struck them down and killed
them. 18Joshua made war a long time with all
those kings. 19There was not a city that made
peace with the children of Israel, except the

11:18 war a long time. The conquest took approximately 7 years. Only Gibeon submitted without a fight (v. 19).

Hivites, the inhabitants of Gibeon. All *the oth-*
ers they took in battle. 20For it was of the LORD
to harden their hearts, that they should come
against Israel in battle, that He might utterly
destroy them, *and* that they might receive no
mercy, but that He might destroy them, as the
LORD had commanded Moses.

21And at that time Joshua came and cut off
the Anakim from the mountains: from
Hebron, from Debir, from Anab, from all the
mountains of Judah, and from all the mountains of Israel; Joshua utterly destroyed them
with their cities. 22None of the Anakim were left
in the land of the children of Israel; they
remained only in Gaza, in Gath, and in Ashdod.

11:20 it was of the LORD to harden their hearts. God turned the Canaanites' hearts to fight in order that Israel might be His judging instrument to destroy them. They were willfully guilty of rejecting the true God with consequent great wickedness and were as unfit to remain in the land as vomit spewed out of the mouth (Lev. 18:24,25).

11:21 Anakim. Enemies who dwelt in the southern area which Joshua had defeated. They descended from Anak ("long-necked") and were related to the giants who made Israel's spies feel small as grasshoppers by comparison (Num. 13:28–33). Their territory was later given to Caleb as a reward for his loyalty (14:6–15).

23So Joshua took the whole land, according
to all that the LORD had said to Moses; and
Joshua gave it as an inheritance to Israel according to their divisions by their tribes. Then
the land rested from war.

12 These *are* the kings of the land whom
the children of Israel defeated, and
whose land they possessed on the other side
of the Jordan toward the rising of the sun,
from the River Arnon to Mount Hermon, and
all the eastern Jordan plain: 2*One king was*
Sihon king of the Amorites, who dwelt in
Heshbon *and* ruled half of Gilead, from Aroer,

which is on the bank of the River Arnon, from
the middle of that river, even as far as the
River Jabbok, *which is* the border of the
Ammonites, [3]and the eastern Jordan plain
from the Sea of Chinneroth as far as the Sea of
the Arabah (the Salt Sea), the road to Beth
Jeshimoth, and southward below the slopes of
Pisgah. [4]*The other king was* Og king of Bashan
and his territory, *who was* of the remnant of
the giants, who dwelt at Ashtaroth and at
Edrei, [5]and reigned over Mount Hermon, over
Salcah, over all Bashan, as far as the border of
the Geshurites and the Maachathites, and
over half of Gilead *to* the border of Sihon king
of Heshbon.

[6]These Moses the servant of the LORD and
the children of Israel had conquered; and
Moses the servant of the LORD had given it *as*
a possession to the Reubenites, the Gadites,
and half the tribe of Manasseh.

[7]And these *are* the kings of the country
which Joshua and the children of Israel conquered on this side of the Jordan, on the west,
from Baal Gad in the Valley of Lebanon as far
as Mount Halak and the ascent to Seir, which
Joshua gave to the tribes of Israel *as* a possession according to their divisions, [8]in the
mountain country, in the lowlands, in the
Jordan plain, in the slopes, in the wilderness,
and in the South—the Hittites, the Amorites,
the Canaanites, the Perizzites, the Hivites,
and the Jebusites: [9]the king of Jericho, one;
the king of Ai, which *is* beside Bethel, one;
[10]the king of Jerusalem, one; the king of
Hebron, one; [11]the king of Jarmuth, one; the
king of Lachish, one; [12]the king of Eglon, one;
the king of Gezer, one; [13]the king of Debir,
one; the king of Geder, one; [14]the king of
Hormah, one; the king of Arad, one; [15]the king
of Libnah, one; the king of Adullam, one; [16]the
king of Makkedah, one; the king of Bethel,
one; [17]the king of Tappuah, one; the king of
Hepher, one; [18]the king of Aphek, one; the
king of Lasharon, one; [19]the king of Madon,
one; the king of Hazor, one; [20]the king of Shimron Meron, one; the king of Achshaph, one;
[21]the king of Taanach, one; the king of
Megiddo, one; [22]the king of Kedesh, one; the
king of Jokneam in Carmel, one; [23]the king of
Dor in the heights of Dor, one; the king of the
people of Gilgal, one; [24]the king of Tirzah,
one—all the kings, thirty-one.

Psalm 44:4–19

4 You are my King, O God;
Command victories for Jacob.
5 Through You we will push down our
enemies;
Through Your name we will
trample those who rise up
against us.
6 For I will not trust in my bow,
Nor shall my sword save me.
7 But You have saved us from our
enemies,
And have put to shame those who
hated us.
8 In God we boast all day long,
And praise Your name forever.
Selah

9 But You have cast *us* off and put us to
shame,
And You do not go out with our armies.
10 You make us turn back from the
enemy,
And those who hate us have taken
spoil for themselves.
11 You have given us up like sheep
intended for food,
And have scattered us among the
nations.
12 You sell Your people for *next to*
nothing,
And are not enriched by selling them.
13 You make us a reproach to our
neighbors,
A scorn and a derision to those all
around us.
14 You make us a byword among the
nations,
A shaking of the head among the
peoples.
15 My dishonor *is* continually before me,
And the shame of my face has covered
me,
16 Because of the voice of him who
reproaches and reviles,
Because of the enemy and the avenger.
17 All this has come upon us;
But we have not forgotten You,
Nor have we dealt falsely with Your
covenant.
18 Our heart has not turned back,
Nor have our steps departed from
Your way;
19 But You have severely broken us in the
place of jackals,
And covered us with the shadow of
death.

Proverbs 14:1–2

14 The wise woman builds her
house,
But the foolish pulls it down with her
hands.

[2] He who walks in his uprightness fears
the LORD,
But *he who is* perverse in his ways
despises Him.

Luke 10:25–42

[25]And behold, a certain lawyer stood up and tested Him, saying, "Teacher, what shall I do to inherit eternal life?"
[26]He said to him, "What is written in the law? What is your reading *of it?*"
[27]So he answered and said, "*'You shall love the LORD your God with all your heart, with all your soul, with all your strength, and with all your mind,'* and *'your neighbor as yourself.'* "
[28]And He said to him, "You have answered rightly; do this and you will live."
[29]But he, wanting to justify himself, said to Jesus, "And who is my neighbor?"
[30]Then Jesus answered and said: "A certain *man* went down from Jerusalem to Jericho, and fell among thieves, who stripped him of his clothing, wounded *him,* and departed, leaving *him* half dead.
[31]Now by chance a certain priest came down that road. And when he saw him, he passed by on the other side.
[32]Likewise a Levite, when he arrived at the place, came and looked, and passed by on the other side.
[33]But a certain Samaritan, as he journeyed, came where he was. And when he saw him, he had compassion.
[34]So he went to *him* and bandaged his wounds, pouring on oil and wine; and he set him on his own animal, brought him to an inn, and took care of him.
[35]On the next day, when he departed, he took out two denarii, gave *them* to the innkeeper, and said to him, 'Take care of him; and whatever more you spend, when I come again, I will repay you.'
[36]So which of these three do you think was neighbor to him who fell among the thieves?"
[37]And he said, "He who showed mercy on him." Then Jesus said to him, "Go and do likewise."
[38]Now it happened as they went that He entered a certain village; and a certain woman named Martha welcomed Him into her house.
[39]And she had a sister called Mary, who also sat at Jesus' feet and heard His word.
[40]But Martha was distracted with much serving, and she approached Him and said, "Lord, do You not care that my sister has left me to serve alone? Therefore tell her to help me."
[41]And Jesus answered and said to her, "Martha, Martha, you are worried and troubled about many things.
[42]But one thing is needed, and Mary has chosen that good part, which will not be taken away from her."

10:42 one thing...good part. Jesus was not speaking of the number of dishes to be served. The one thing necessary was exemplified by Mary, i.e, an attitude of worship and meditation, listening with an open mind and heart to Jesus' words.

DAY 11: If we are to love our neighbor, who is our neighbor?

The lawyer who asked Jesus what he must do to inherit eternal life in Luke 10:25 knew the commandments well enough. But when he asked Jesus, "Who is my neighbor?" we are told that he was "wanting to justify himself" (v. 29). It revealed the man's self-righteous character, as well as his desire to test Christ.

The prevailing opinion among scribes and Pharisees was that one's neighbors were the righteous alone. According to them, the wicked—including rank sinners (such as tax collectors and prostitutes), Gentiles, and especially Samaritans—were to be hated because they were the enemies of God. They cited Psalm 139:21,22 to justify their position. As that passage suggests, hatred of evil is the natural corollary of loving righteousness. But the truly righteous person's "hatred" for sinners is not a malevolent enmity. It is a righteous abhorrence of all that is base and corrupt—not a spiteful, personal loathing of individuals. Godly hatred is marked by a brokenhearted grieving over the condition of the sinner. And as Jesus taught here and elsewhere (6:27–36; Matt. 5:44–48), it is also tempered by a genuine love. The Pharisees had elevated hostility toward the wicked to the status of a virtue, in effect nullifying the second Great Commandment. Jesus' answer to this lawyer demolished the Pharisaical excuse for hating one's enemies.

Contrasting the Levite, a religious person who assisted the priests in the work of the temple, with a despised Samaritan, who rescued the wounded person, Jesus reversed the lawyer's original question (v. 29). The lawyer assumed it was up to others to prove themselves neighbor to him. Jesus' reply makes it clear that each has a responsibility to be a neighbor—especially to those who are in need.

APRIL 12

Joshua 13:1–14:15

13 Now Joshua was old, advanced in years.
And the LORD said to him: "You are old,
advanced in years, and there remains very
much land yet to be possessed. 2This is the
land that yet remains: all the territory of the
Philistines and all *that of* the Geshurites, 3from
Sihor, which *is* east of Egypt, as far as the border of Ekron northward (*which* is counted as
Canaanite); the five lords of the Philistines—
the Gazites, the Ashdodites, the Ashkelonites,
the Gittites, and the Ekronites; also the Avites;
4from the south, all the land of the Canaanites,
and Mearah that belongs to the Sidonians as
far as Aphek, to the border of the Amorites;
5the land of the Gebalites, and all Lebanon,
toward the sunrise, from Baal Gad below
Mount Hermon as far as the entrance to
Hamath; 6all the inhabitants of the mountains
from Lebanon as far as the Brook Misrephoth,
and all the Sidonians—them I will drive out
from before the children of Israel; only divide
it by lot to Israel as an inheritance, as I have
commanded you. 7Now therefore, divide this
land as an inheritance to the nine tribes and
half the tribe of Manasseh."

8With the other half-tribe the Reubenites
and the Gadites received their inheritance,
which Moses had given them, beyond the
Jordan eastward, as Moses the servant of the
LORD had given them: 9from Aroer which *is* on
the bank of the River Arnon, and the town that
is in the midst of the ravine, and all the plain of
Medeba as far as Dibon; 10all the cities of Sihon
king of the Amorites, who reigned in Heshbon,
as far as the border of the children of Ammon;
11Gilead, and the border of the Geshurites and
Maachathites, all Mount Hermon, and all
Bashan as far as Salcah; 12all the kingdom of Og
in Bashan, who reigned in Ashtaroth and Edrei,
who remained of the remnant of the giants; for
Moses had defeated and cast out these.

13Nevertheless the children of Israel did not
drive out the Geshurites or the Maachathites,
but the Geshurites and the Maachathites
dwell among the Israelites until this day.

14Only to the tribe of Levi he had given no
inheritance; the sacrifices of the LORD God of
Israel made by fire *are* their inheritance, as He
said to them.

15And Moses had given to the tribe of the children of Reuben *an inheritance* according to
their families. 16Their territory was from Aroer,
which *is* on the bank of the River Arnon, and the
city that *is* in the midst of the ravine, and all the
plain by Medeba; 17Heshbon and all its cities
that *are* in the plain: Dibon, Bamoth Baal, Beth
Baal Meon, 18Jahaza, Kedemoth, Mephaath,
19Kirjathaim, Sibmah, Zereth Shahar on the
mountain of the valley, 20Beth Peor, the slopes of
Pisgah, and Beth Jeshimoth— 21all the cities of
the plain and all the kingdom of Sihon king of the
Amorites, who reigned in Heshbon, whom
Moses had struck with the princes of Midian:
Evi, Rekem, Zur, Hur, and Reba, who *were*
princes of Sihon dwelling in the country. 22The
children of Israel also killed with the sword
Balaam the son of Beor, the soothsayer, among
those who were killed by them. 23And the border of the children of Reuben was the bank of
the Jordan. This *was* the inheritance of the children of Reuben according to their families, the
cities and their villages.

13:22 Israel also killed...Balaam. This Israelite slaying of the infamous false prophet occurred at an unidentified point during the conquest (see Num. 31:16; Josh. 24:9,10; 2 Pet. 2:15,16; Jude 11; Rev. 2:14).

24Moses also had given *an inheritance* to the
tribe of Gad, to the children of Gad according
to their families. 25Their territory was Jazer,
and all the cities of Gilead, and half the land of
the Ammonites as far as Aroer, which *is* before
Rabbah, 26and from Heshbon to Ramath
Mizpah and Betonim, and from Mahanaim to
the border of Debir, 27and in the valley Beth
Haram, Beth Nimrah, Succoth, and Zaphon,
the rest of the kingdom of Sihon king of
Heshbon, with the Jordan as *its* border, as far
as the edge of the Sea of Chinnereth, on the
other side of the Jordan eastward. 28This *is* the
inheritance of the children of Gad according
to their families, the cities and their villages.

29Moses also had given *an inheritance* to
half the tribe of Manasseh; it was for half the
tribe of the children of Manasseh according to
their families: 30Their territory was from
Mahanaim, all Bashan, all the kingdom of Og
king of Bashan, and all the towns of Jair which
are in Bashan, sixty cities; 31half of Gilead, and
Ashtaroth and Edrei, cities of the kingdom of
Og in Bashan, *were* for the children of Machir
the son of Manasseh, for half of the children of
Machir according to their families.

32These *are the areas* which Moses had distributed as an inheritance in the plains of Moab

on the other side of the Jordan, by Jericho
eastward. [33]But to the tribe of Levi Moses had
given no inheritance; the LORD God of Israel
was their inheritance, as He had said to them.

14 These *are the areas* which the children of
Israel inherited in the land of Canaan,
which Eleazar the priest, Joshua the son of
Nun, and the heads of the fathers of the tribes
of the children of Israel distributed as an
inheritance to them. [2]Their inheritance *was* by
lot, as the LORD had commanded by the hand
of Moses, for the nine tribes and the half-tribe.
[3]For Moses had given the inheritance of the
two tribes and the half-tribe on the other side
of the Jordan; but to the Levites he had given
no inheritance among them. [4]For the children
of Joseph were two tribes: Manasseh and
Ephraim. And they gave no part to the Levites
in the land, except cities to dwell *in,* with their
common-lands for their livestock and their
property. [5]As the LORD had commanded
Moses, so the children of Israel did; and they
divided the land.

[6]Then the children of Judah came to Joshua
in Gilgal. And Caleb the son of Jephunneh the
Kenizzite said to him: "You know the word
which the LORD said to Moses the man of God
concerning you and me in Kadesh Barnea. [7]I
was forty years old when Moses the servant of
the LORD sent me from Kadesh Barnea to spy
out the land, and I brought back word to him
as *it was* in my heart. [8]Nevertheless my
brethren who went up with me made the heart
of the people melt, but I wholly followed the
LORD my God. [9]So Moses swore on that day,
saying, 'Surely the land where your foot has
trodden shall be your inheritance and your
children's forever, because you have wholly
followed the LORD my God.' [10]And now,
behold, the LORD has kept me alive, as He
said, these forty-five years, ever since the
LORD spoke this word to Moses while Israel
wandered in the wilderness; and now, here I
am this day, eighty-five years old. [11]As yet I *am*
as strong this day as on the day that Moses
sent me; just as my strength *was* then, so now
is my strength for war, both for going out and
for coming in. [12]Now therefore, give me this
mountain of which the LORD spoke in that day;
for you heard in that day how the Anakim *were*
there, and *that* the cities *were* great *and* fortified. It may be that the LORD *will be* with me,
and I shall be able to drive them out as the
LORD said."

[13]And Joshua blessed him, and gave Hebron
to Caleb the son of Jephunneh as an inheritance. [14]Hebron therefore became the inheritance of Caleb the son of Jephunneh the
Kenizzite to this day, because he wholly followed the LORD God of Israel. [15]And the name
of Hebron formerly was Kirjath Arba (*Arba*
was the greatest man among the Anakim).
Then the land had rest from war.

Psalm 44:20–26

20 If we had forgotten the name of our
God,
Or stretched out our hands to a foreign
god,

44:22 Yet for Your sake. They had no specific answers—only this inescapable conclusion that, by God's sovereign will, they were allowed to be destroyed by their enemies. See Paul's quote of this verse in Romans 8:36 and its general principle in Matthew 5:10–12; 1 Peter 3:13–17; 4:12–16.

21 Would not God search this out?
For He knows the secrets of the heart.
22 Yet for Your sake we are killed all day
long;
We are accounted as sheep for the
slaughter.
23 Awake! Why do You sleep, O Lord?
Arise! Do not cast *us* off forever.
24 Why do You hide Your face,
And forget our affliction and our
oppression?
25 For our soul is bowed down to the dust;
Our body clings to the ground.
26 Arise for our help,
And redeem us for Your mercies' sake.

Proverbs 14:3

3 In the mouth of a fool *is* a rod of pride,
But the lips of the wise will preserve
them.

Luke 11:1–28

11 Now it came to pass, as He was praying in
a certain place, when He ceased, *that* one

11:1 Lord, teach us to pray. Rabbis often composed prayers for their disciples to recite. Having seen Jesus pray many times, Jesus' disciples knew of His love for prayer, and they knew prayer was not just the reciting of words.

of His disciples said to Him, "Lord, teach us to pray, as John also taught his disciples."

[2]So He said to them, "When you pray, say:

Our Father in heaven,
Hallowed be Your name.
Your kingdom come.
Your will be done
On earth as *it is* in heaven.
3 Give us day by day our daily bread.
4 And forgive us our sins,
For we also forgive everyone who is
indebted to us.
And do not lead us into temptation,
But deliver us from the evil one."

[5]And He said to them, "Which of you shall have a friend, and go to him at midnight and say to him, 'Friend, lend me three loaves; [6]for a friend of mine has come to me on his journey, and I have nothing to set before him'; [7]and he will answer from within and say, 'Do not trouble me; the door is now shut, and my children are with me in bed; I cannot rise and give to you'? [8]I say to you, though he will not rise and give to him because he is his friend, yet because of his persistence he will rise and give him as many as he needs.

[9]"So I say to you, ask, and it will be given to you; seek, and you will find; knock, and it will be opened to you. [10]For everyone who asks receives, and he who seeks finds, and to him who knocks it will be opened. [11]If a son asks for bread from any father among you, will he give him a stone? Or if *he asks* for a fish, will he give him a serpent instead of a fish? [12]Or if he asks for an egg, will he offer him a scorpion? [13]If you then, being evil, know how to give good gifts to your children, how much more will *your* heavenly Father give the Holy Spirit to those who ask Him!"

[14]And He was casting out a demon, and it was mute. So it was, when the demon had gone out, that the mute spoke; and the multitudes marveled. [15]But some of them said, "He casts out demons by Beelzebub, the ruler of the demons."

[16]Others, testing *Him,* sought from Him a sign from heaven. [17]But He, knowing their thoughts, said to them: "Every kingdom divided against itself is brought to desolation, and a house *divided* against a house falls. [18]If Satan also is divided against himself, how will his kingdom stand? Because you say I cast out demons by Beelzebub. [19]And if I cast out demons by Beelzebub, by whom do your sons cast *them* out? Therefore they will be your judges. [20]But if I cast out demons with the finger of God, surely the kingdom of God has come upon you. [21]When a strong man, fully armed, guards his own palace, his goods are in peace. [22]But when a stronger than he comes upon him and overcomes him, he takes from him all his armor in which he trusted, and divides his spoils. [23]He who is not with Me is against Me, and he who does not gather with Me scatters.

[24]"When an unclean spirit goes out of a man, he goes through dry places, seeking rest; and finding none, he says, 'I will return to my house from which I came.' [25]And when he comes, he finds *it* swept and put in order. [26]Then he goes and takes with *him* seven other spirits more wicked than himself, and they enter and dwell there; and the last *state* of that man is worse than the first."

[27]And it happened, as He spoke these things, that a certain woman from the crowd raised her voice and said to Him, "Blessed *is* the womb that bore You, and *the* breasts which nursed You!"

[28]But He said, "More than that, blessed *are* those who hear the word of God and keep it!"

11:28 More than that. This has the sense of, "Yes, but rather...." While not denying the blessedness of Mary, Christ did not countenance any tendency to elevate Mary as an object of veneration. Mary's relationship to Him as His physical mother did not confer on her any greater honor than the blessedness of those who hear and obey the word of God.

DAY 12: How far would some go to explain away Jesus' power?

Having just watched Jesus cast a demon out of a person, some people said, "He casts out demons by Beelzebub, the ruler of demons" (Luke 11:15). Originally this referred to Baal-Zebul ("Baal, the prince"), chief god of the Philistine city of Ekron. The Israelites disdainfully referred to him as Baal-Zebub ("Lord of Flies").

Jesus reminded them that "every kingdom divided against itself is brought to desolation" (v. 17). This may have been a subtle jab at the Jewish nation, a kingdom divided in the time of Jeroboam, and still marked by various kinds of bitter internal strife and factionalism, right up to the destruction of Jerusalem in A.D. 70. He also questioned them: "By whom do your sons cast them out?" (v. 19). There were Jewish exorcists who claimed power to cast out demons (Acts 19:13–15). Jesus' point was that if such exorcisms could be done via satanic power, the Pharisaical exorcists must be suspect, as well. And in fact, the evidence in Acts 19 suggests that the sons of Sceva were charlatans who employed fraud and trickery to fabricate phony exorcisms. "They will be your judges" (v. 19), i.e., witnesses against you. This seems to suggest that the fraudulent exorcisms (which had their approval) stood as a testimony against the Pharisees themselves, who disapproved of Christ's genuine exorcisms.

"But if I cast out demons with the finger of God, surely the kingdom of God has come upon you" (v. 20). In Exodus 8:19, the phony magicians of Egypt were forced to confess that Moses' miracles were genuine works of God, not mere trickery such as they had performed. Here Jesus made a similar comparison between His exorcisms and the work of the Jewish exorcists.

APRIL 13

Joshua 15:1–16:10

15 So *this* was the lot of the tribe of the children of Judah according to their families:
The border of Edom at the Wilderness of Zin
southward *was* the extreme southern boundary. 2And their southern border began at the
shore of the Salt Sea, from the bay that faces
southward. 3Then it went out to the southern
side of the Ascent of Akrabbim, passed along
to Zin, ascended on the south side of Kadesh
Barnea, passed along to Hezron, went up to
Adar, and went around to Karkaa. 4*From there*
it passed toward Azmon and went out to the
Brook of Egypt; and the border ended at the
sea. This shall be your southern border.
5The east border *was* the Salt Sea as far as
the mouth of the Jordan.
And the border on the northern quarter *began* at the bay of the sea at the mouth of the
Jordan. 6The border went up to Beth Hoglah
and passed north of Beth Arabah; and the border went up to the stone of Bohan the son of
Reuben. 7Then the border went up toward
Debir from the Valley of Achor, and it turned
northward toward Gilgal, which *is* before the
Ascent of Adummim, which *is* on the south
side of the valley. The border continued
toward the waters of En Shemesh and ended
at En Rogel. 8And the border went up by the
Valley of the Son of Hinnom to the southern
slope of the Jebusite *city* (which *is* Jerusalem).
The border went up to the top of the mountain
that *lies* before the Valley of Hinnom westward,
which *is* at the end of the Valley of Rephaim
northward. 9Then the border went around
from the top of the hill to the fountain of the
water of Nephtoah, and extended to the cities
of Mount Ephron. And the border went
around to Baalah (which *is* Kirjath Jearim).
10Then the border turned westward from
Baalah to Mount Seir, passed along to the side
of Mount Jearim on the north (which *is*
Chesalon), went down to Beth Shemesh, and
passed on to Timnah. 11And the border went
out to the side of Ekron northward. Then the
border went around to Shicron, passed along
to Mount Baalah, and extended to Jabneel;
and the border ended at the sea.
12The west border *was* the coastline of the
Great Sea. This *is* the boundary of the children
of Judah all around according to their families.
13Now to Caleb the son of Jephunneh he
gave a share among the children of Judah,
according to the commandment of the LORD to
Joshua, *namely,* Kirjath Arba, which *is* Hebron
(*Arba was* the father of Anak). 14Caleb drove out
the three sons of Anak from there: Sheshai,
Ahiman, and Talmai, the children of Anak.
15Then he went up from there to the inhabitants of Debir (formerly the name of Debir
was Kirjath Sepher).
16And Caleb said, "He who attacks Kirjath
Sepher and takes it, to him I will give Achsah
my daughter as wife." 17So Othniel the son of
Kenaz, the brother of Caleb, took it; and he
gave him Achsah his daughter as wife. 18Now
it was so, when she came *to him,* that she persuaded him to ask her father for a field. So she
dismounted from *her* donkey, and Caleb said
to her, "What do you wish?" 19She answered,
"Give me a blessing; since you have given me
land in the South, give me also springs of
water." So he gave her the upper springs and
the lower springs.
20This *was* the inheritance of the tribe of the
children of Judah according to their families:
21The cities at the limits of the tribe of the
children of Judah, toward the border of Edom
in the South, were Kabzeel, Eder, Jagur, 22Kinah,
Dimonah, Adadah, 23Kedesh, Hazor, Ithnan,
24Ziph, Telem, Bealoth, 25Hazor, Hadattah,
Kerioth, Hezron (which *is* Hazor), 26Amam,
Shema, Moladah, 27Hazar Gaddah, Heshmon,
Beth Pelet, 28Hazar Shual, Beersheba,

Bizjothjah, 29Baalah, Ijim, Ezem, 30Eltolad,
Chesil, Hormah, 31Ziklag, Madmannah, Sansan-
nah, 32Lebaoth, Shilhim, Ain, and Rimmon: all
the cities *are* twenty-nine, with their villages.
33In the lowland: Eshtaol, Zorah, Ashnah,
34Zanoah, En Gannim, Tappuah, Enam,
35Jarmuth, Adullam, Socoh, Azekah, 36Sharaim,
Adithaim, Gederah, and Gederothaim: fourteen cities with their villages; 37Zenan,
Hadashah, Migdal Gad, 38Dilean, Mizpah,
Joktheel, 39Lachish, Bozkath, Eglon, 40Cabbon,
Lahmas, Kithlish, 41Gederoth, Beth Dagon,
Naamah, and Makkedah: sixteen cities with
their villages; 42Libnah, Ether, Ashan, 43Jiphtah,
Ashnah, Nezib, 44Keilah, Achzib, and
Mareshah: nine cities with their villages;
45Ekron, with its towns and villages; 46from
Ekron to the sea, all that *lay* near Ashdod, with
their villages; 47Ashdod with its towns and villages, Gaza with its towns and villages—as far
as the Brook of Egypt and the Great Sea with
its coastline.
48And in the mountain country: Shamir,
Jattir, Sochoh, 49Dannah, Kirjath Sannah
(which *is* Debir), 50Anab, Eshtemoh, Anim,
51Goshen, Holon, and Giloh: eleven cities with
their villages; 52Arab, Dumah, Eshean, 53Janum,
Beth Tappuah, Aphekah, 54Humtah, Kirjath
Arba (which *is* Hebron), and Zior: nine cities
with their villages; 55Maon, Carmel, Ziph,
Juttah, 56Jezreel, Jokdeam, Zanoah, 57Kain,
Gibeah, and Timnah: ten cities with their villages; 58Halhul, Beth Zur, Gedor, 59Maarath,
Beth Anoth, and Eltekon: six cities with their villages; 60Kirjath Baal (which *is* Kirjath Jearim)
and Rabbah: two cities with their villages.
61In the wilderness: Beth Arabah, Middin,
Secacah, 62Nibshan, the City of Salt, and En
Gedi: six cities with their villages.
63As for the Jebusites, the inhabitants of Jerusalem, the children of Judah could not drive
them out; but the Jebusites dwell with the children of Judah at Jerusalem to this day.

16 The lot fell to the children of Joseph
from the Jordan, by Jericho, to the
waters of Jericho on the east, to the wilderness that goes up from Jericho through the
mountains to Bethel, 2then went out from
Bethel to Luz, passed along to the border of
the Archites at Ataroth, 3and went down westward to the boundary of the Japhletites, as far
as the boundary of Lower Beth Horon to
Gezer; and it ended at the sea.
4So the children of Joseph, Manasseh and
Ephraim, took their inheritance.
5The border of the children of Ephraim,
according to their families, was *thus:* The border of their inheritance on the east side was
Ataroth Addar as far as Upper Beth Horon.
6And the border went out toward the sea on
the north side of Michmethath; then the border went around eastward to Taanath Shiloh,
and passed by it on the east of Janohah. 7Then
it went down from Janohah to Ataroth and
Naarah, reached to Jericho, and came out at
the Jordan.
8The border went out from Tappuah westward to the Brook Kanah, and it ended at the
sea. This *was* the inheritance of the tribe of the
children of Ephraim according to their families. 9The separate cities for the children of
Ephraim *were* among the inheritance of the
children of Manasseh, all the cities with their
villages.
10And they did not drive out the Canaanites
who dwelt in Gezer; but the Canaanites dwell
among the Ephraimites to this day and have
become forced laborers.

16:10 Ephraim did not drive the Canaanites from their area. This is the first mention of the fatal policy of neglecting to exterminate the idolaters (see Deut. 20:16).

Psalm 45:1–5

To the Chief Musician. Set to "The Lilies." A Contemplation of the sons of Korah. A Song of Love.

My heart is overflowing with
a good theme;
I recite my composition concerning
the King;
My tongue *is* the pen of a ready
writer.

2 You are fairer than the sons of men;
Grace is poured upon Your lips;
Therefore God has blessed You
forever.

3 Gird Your sword upon *Your* thigh,
O Mighty One,
With Your glory and Your majesty.

45:1 My heart is overflowing...my tongue. The psalmist is overwhelmed with emotion upon the occasion of the king's marriage. Consequently, he puts his stirred-up mind and feelings into words. In v. 2ff. his tongue is the brush that he uses to paint vivid word pictures.

4 And in Your majesty ride prosperously
because of truth, humility, *and* righteousness;
And Your right hand shall teach You
awesome things.
5 Your arrows *are* sharp in the heart
of the King's enemies;
The peoples fall under You.

Proverbs 14:4–5

4 Where no oxen *are,* the trough *is* clean;
But much increase *comes* by the
strength of an ox.
5 A faithful witness does not lie,
But a false witness will utter lies.

Luke 11:29–54

[29]And while the crowds were thickly gathered together, He began to say, "This is an evil generation. It seeks a sign, and no sign will be given to it except the sign of Jonah the prophet. [30]For as Jonah became a sign to the Ninevites, so also the Son of Man will be to this generation. [31]The queen of the South will rise up in the judgment with the men of this generation and condemn them, for she came from the ends of the earth to hear the wisdom of Solomon; and indeed a greater than Solomon *is* here. [32]The men of Nineveh will rise up in the judgment with this generation and condemn it, for they repented at the preaching of Jonah; and indeed a greater than Jonah *is* here.

[33]"No one, when he has lit a lamp, puts *it* in a secret place or under a basket, but on a lampstand, that those who come in may see the light. [34]The lamp of the body is the eye. Therefore, when your eye is good, your whole body also is full of light. But when *your eye* is bad, your body also *is* full of darkness. [35]Therefore take heed that the light which is in you is not darkness. [36]If then your whole body *is* full of light, having no part dark, *the* whole *body* will be full of light, as when the bright shining of a lamp gives you light."

[37]And as He spoke, a certain Pharisee asked Him to dine with him. So He went in and sat down to eat. [38]When the Pharisee saw *it,* he marveled that He had not first washed before dinner.

[39]Then the Lord said to him, "Now you Pharisees make the outside of the cup and dish clean, but your inward part is full of greed and wickedness. [40]Foolish ones! Did not He who made the outside make the inside also? [41]But rather give alms of such things as you have; then indeed all things are clean to you.

[42]"But woe to you Pharisees! For you tithe mint and rue and all manner of herbs, and pass by justice and the love of God. These you ought to have done, without leaving the others undone. [43]Woe to you Pharisees! For you love the best seats in the synagogues and greetings in the marketplaces. [44]Woe to you, scribes and Pharisees, hypocrites! For you are like graves which are not seen, and the men who walk over *them* are not aware *of them.*"

[45]Then one of the lawyers answered and said to Him, "Teacher, by saying these things You reproach us also."

[46]And He said, "Woe to you also, lawyers! For you load men with burdens hard to bear, and you yourselves do not touch the burdens with one of your fingers. [47]Woe to you! For you build the tombs of the prophets, and your fathers killed them. [48]In fact, you bear witness that you approve the deeds of your fathers; for they indeed killed them, and you build their tombs. [49]Therefore the wisdom of God also said, 'I will send them prophets and apostles, and *some* of them they will kill and persecute,' [50]that the blood of all the prophets which was shed from the foundation of the world may be required of this generation, [51]from the blood of Abel to the blood of Zechariah who perished between the altar and the temple. Yes, I say to you, it shall be required of this generation.

[52]"Woe to you lawyers! For you have taken away the key of knowledge. You did not enter in yourselves, and those who were entering in you hindered."

[53]And as He said these things to them, the scribes and the Pharisees began to assail *Him* vehemently, and to cross-examine Him about many things, [54]lying in wait for Him, and seeking to catch Him in something He might say, that they might accuse Him.

11:34 The lamp of the body. This is a different metaphor from the one in v. 33. There the lamp speaks of the word of God. Here the eye is the "lamp"—i.e., the source of light—for the body. **when *your eye* is bad.** The problem was their perception, not a lack of light. They did not need a sign. They needed hearts to believe the great display of divine power they had already seen.

11:38 He had not first washed. The Pharisee was concerned with ceremony, not hygiene. The Greek word for "washed" refers to a ceremonial ablution. Nothing in the law commanded such washings, but the Pharisees practiced them, believing the ritual cleansed them of any accidental ceremonial defilement.

DAY 13: How does God's guarantee of success to Joshua relate to us?

The Book of Joshua begins with God's commissioning of Israel's new leader. God described Joshua's mission—to go in and possess the Land (1:2–6). God hinged Joshua's success on three key factors: 1) God's own presence (v. 5); 2) Joshua's personal strength and courage (vv. 7,9); and 3) Joshua's attention to and application of God's word (vv. 7,8).

God spelled out this third factor with some detail for it was to be the basis for all of Joshua's actions. God's word was to be Joshua's constant conversation, continual meditation, and unswerving application. The phrase "This Book of the Law shall not depart from your mouth" (v. 8) deserves added attention. While a first impression might lead to the conclusion that Joshua was not supposed to talk about the Book of the Law, the direct opposite is the case: he was not supposed to stop talking about it.

Biblical meditation begins with the thoughtful, lingering reading of God's Word. It progresses to familiarity and memorization. In order to "meditate in it day and night" (v. 8), the Book of the Law would have been *in Joshua*. The purpose has been achieved when meditation leads us to "observe to do according to all that is written in it" (v. 8).

"Then," God told Joshua, "you will make your way prosperous, and then you will have good success" (v. 8). Joshua found the ultimate measure of prosperity and success—knowing how God wants His people to live and then living that way. God repeatedly assured Joshua of His own presence "wherever you go." What greater measurement of success could there be than to honor the ever-present God with our obedience?

APRIL 14

Joshua 17:1–18:28

17 There was also a lot for the tribe of
Manasseh, for he *was* the firstborn of Joseph: *namely* for Machir the firstborn of
Manasseh, the father of Gilead, because he
was a man of war; therefore he was given
Gilead and Bashan. [2]And there was *a lot* for
the rest of the children of Manasseh according to their families: for the children of
Abiezer, the children of Helek, the children of
Asriel, the children of Shechem, the children
of Hepher, and the children of Shemida; these
were the male children of Manasseh the son of
Joseph according to their families.
[3]But Zelophehad the son of Hepher, the son of
Gilead, the son of Machir, the son of Manasseh,
had no sons, but only daughters. And these *are*
the names of his daughters: Mahlah, Noah,
Hoglah, Milcah, and Tirzah. [4]And they came
near before Eleazar the priest, before Joshua
the son of Nun, and before the rulers, saying,
"The LORD commanded Moses to give us an
inheritance among our brothers." Therefore,
according to the commandment of the LORD,
he gave them an inheritance among their
father's brothers. [5]Ten shares fell to Manasseh, besides the land of Gilead and Bashan,
which *were* on the other side of the Jordan,
[6]because the daughters of Manasseh received
an inheritance among his sons; and the rest of
Manasseh's sons had the land of Gilead.
[7]And the territory of Manasseh was from
Asher to Michmethath, that *lies* east of
Shechem; and the border went along south to
the inhabitants of En Tappuah. [8]Manasseh had
the land of Tappuah, but Tappuah on the border of Manasseh *belonged* to the children of
Ephraim. [9]And the border descended to the
Brook Kanah, southward to the brook. These
cities of Ephraim *are* among the cities of
Manasseh. The border of Manasseh *was* on the
north side of the brook; and it ended at the sea.
[10]Southward *it was* Ephraim's, northward *it
was* Manasseh's, and the sea was its border.
Manasseh's territory was adjoining Asher on
the north and Issachar on the east. [11]And in
Issachar and in Asher, Manasseh had Beth
Shean and its towns, Ibleam and its towns, the
inhabitants of Dor and its towns, the inhabitants of En Dor and its towns, the inhabitants
of Taanach and its towns, and the inhabitants
of Megiddo and its towns—three hilly
regions. [12]Yet the children of Manasseh could
not drive out *the inhabitants of* those cities, but
the Canaanites were determined to dwell in
that land. [13]And it happened, when the children of Israel grew strong, that they put the
Canaanites to forced labor, but did not utterly
drive them out.
[14]Then the children of Joseph spoke to
Joshua, saying, "Why have you given us *only*
one lot and one share to inherit, since we *are*
a great people, inasmuch as the LORD has
blessed us until now?"
[15]So Joshua answered them, "If you *are* a
great people, *then* go up to the forest *country*
and clear a place for yourself there in the land

of the Perizzites and the giants, since the
mountains of Ephraim are too confined for
you."
[16]But the children of Joseph said, "The
mountain country is not enough for us; and all
the Canaanites who dwell in the land of the
valley have chariots of iron, *both those* who *are*
of Beth Shean and its towns and *those* who *are*
of the Valley of Jezreel."
[17]And Joshua spoke to the house of
Joseph—to Ephraim and Manasseh—saying,
"You *are* a great people and have great power;
you shall not have *only* one lot, [18]but the mountain country shall be yours. Although it *is*
wooded, you shall cut it down, and its farthest
extent shall be yours; for you shall drive out
the Canaanites, though they have iron chariots
and are strong."

17:12–18 children of Manasseh. Tribesmen of Manasseh complained that Joshua did not allot them land sufficient to their numbers and that the Canaanites were too tough for them to drive out altogether. He permitted them extra land in forested hills that they could clear. Joshua told them that they could drive out the Canaanites for God had promised to be with them in victory against chariots (Deut. 20:1).

18 Now the whole congregation of the children of Israel assembled together at
Shiloh, and set up the tabernacle of meeting
there. And the land was subdued before them.
[2]But there remained among the children of
Israel seven tribes which had not yet received
their inheritance.
[3]Then Joshua said to the children of Israel:
"How long will you neglect to go and possess
the land which the LORD God of your fathers
has given you? [4]Pick out from among you
three men for *each* tribe, and I will send them;
they shall rise and go through the land, survey it according to their inheritance, and come
back to me. [5]And they shall divide it into seven
parts. Judah shall remain in their territory on
the south, and the house of Joseph shall
remain in their territory on the north. [6]You
shall therefore survey the land in seven parts
and bring *the survey* here to me, that I may
cast lots for you here before the LORD our
God. [7]But the Levites have no part among you,
for the priesthood of the LORD *is* their inheritance. And Gad, Reuben, and half the tribe of
Manasseh have received their inheritance
beyond the Jordan on the east, which Moses
the servant of the LORD gave them."
[8]Then the men arose to go away; and Joshua
charged those who went to survey the land,
saying, "Go, walk through the land, survey it,
and come back to me, that I may cast lots for
you here before the LORD in Shiloh." [9]So the
men went, passed through the land, and wrote
the survey in a book in seven parts by cities;
and they came to Joshua at the camp in
Shiloh. [10]Then Joshua cast lots for them in
Shiloh before the LORD, and there Joshua
divided the land to the children of Israel
according to their divisions.
[11]Now the lot of the tribe of the children of
Benjamin came up according to their families,
and the territory of their lot came out
between the children of Judah and the children of Joseph. [12]Their border on the north
side began at the Jordan, and the border went
up to the side of Jericho on the north, and
went up through the mountains westward; it
ended at the Wilderness of Beth Aven. [13]The
border went over from there toward Luz, to
the side of Luz (which *is* Bethel) southward;
and the border descended to Ataroth Addar,
near the hill that *lies* on the south side of
Lower Beth Horon.
[14]Then the border extended around the
west side to the south, from the hill that *lies*
before Beth Horon southward; and it ended at
Kirjath Baal (which *is* Kirjath Jearim), a city of
the children of Judah. This *was* the west side.
[15]The south side *began* at the end of Kirjath
Jearim, and the border extended on the west
and went out to the spring of the waters of
Nephtoah. [16]Then the border came down to
the end of the mountain that *lies* before the
Valley of the Son of Hinnom, which *is* in the
Valley of the Rephaim on the north, descended to the Valley of Hinnom, to the side of the
Jebusite *city* on the south, and descended to
En Rogel. [17]And it went around from the north,
went out to En Shemesh, and extended
toward Geliloth, which is before the Ascent of
Adummim, and descended to the stone of
Bohan the son of Reuben. [18]Then it passed
along toward the north side of Arabah, and
went down to Arabah. [19]And the border passed
along to the north side of Beth Hoglah; then
the border ended at the north bay at the Salt
Sea, at the south end of the Jordan. This *was*
the southern boundary.
[20]The Jordan was its border on the east side.
This *was* the inheritance of the children of
Benjamin, according to its boundaries all
around, according to their families.

21 Now the cities of the tribe of the children
of Benjamin, according to their families, were
Jericho, Beth Hoglah, Emek Keziz, 22 Beth
Arabah, Zemaraim, Bethel, 23 Avim, Parah,
Ophrah, 24 Chephar Haammoni, Ophni, and
Gaba: twelve cities with their villages; 25 Gibeon,
Ramah, Beeroth, 26 Mizpah, Chephirah, Mozah,
27 Rekem, Irpeel, Taralah, 28 Zelah, Eleph, Jebus
(which *is* Jerusalem), Gibeath, *and* Kirjath:
fourteen cities with their villages. This was the
inheritance of the children of Benjamin
according to their families.

Psalm 45:6–17

6 Your throne, O God, *is* forever and ever;
A scepter of righteousness *is* the scepter
of Your kingdom.
7 You love righteousness and hate
wickedness;
Therefore God, Your God, has
anointed You
With the oil of gladness more than
Your companions.

45:6,7 Your throne, O God. Since this kinggroom was likely a member of the Davidic dynasty (e.g., 2 Sam. 7), there was a near and immediate application (see 1 Chr. 28:5; 29:23). Through progressive revelation (i.e., Heb. 1:8, 9), we learn of the ultimate application to "a greater than Solomon" who is God—the Lord Jesus Christ.

8 All Your garments *are scented* with
myrrh and aloes *and* cassia,
Out of the ivory palaces, by which they
have made You glad.
9 Kings' daughters *are* among Your
honorable women;
At Your right hand stands the queen
in gold from Ophir.

10 Listen, O daughter,
Consider and incline your ear;
Forget your own people also, and your
father's house;
11 So the King will greatly desire your
beauty;
Because He *is* your Lord, worship Him.
12 And the daughter of Tyre *will come*
with a gift;
The rich among the people will seek
your favor.
13 The royal daughter *is* all glorious
within *the palace;*
Her clothing *is* woven with gold.
14 She shall be brought to the King in robes
of many colors;
The virgins, her companions who
follow her, shall be brought to You.
15 With gladness and rejoicing they shall
be brought;
They shall enter the King's palace.

16 Instead of Your fathers shall be Your sons,
Whom You shall make princes in all
the earth.
17 I will make Your name to be
remembered in all generations;
Therefore the people shall praise You
forever and ever.

Proverbs 14:6

6 A scoffer seeks wisdom and does not
find it,
But knowledge *is* easy to him who
understands.

Luke 12:1–31

12 In the meantime, when an innumerable
multitude of people had gathered together, so that they trampled one another, He
began to say to His disciples first *of all,* "Beware of the leaven of the Pharisees, which is
hypocrisy. 2 For there is nothing covered that
will not be revealed, nor hidden that will not
be known. 3 Therefore whatever you have spoken in the dark will be heard in the light, and
what you have spoken in the ear in inner
rooms will be proclaimed on the housetops.
4 "And I say to you, My friends, do not be
afraid of those who kill the body, and after that
have no more that they can do. 5 But I will
show you whom you should fear: Fear Him
who, after He has killed, has power to cast into
hell; yes, I say to you, fear Him!
6 "Are not five sparrows sold for two copper
coins? And not one of them is forgotten before
God. 7 But the very hairs of your head are all
numbered. Do not fear therefore; you are of
more value than many sparrows.
8 "Also I say to you, whoever confesses Me
before men, him the Son of Man also will confess before the angels of God. 9 But he who denies Me before men will be denied before the
angels of God.
10 "And anyone who speaks a word against
the Son of Man, it will be forgiven him; but to
him who blasphemes against the Holy Spirit, it
will not be forgiven.
11 "Now when they bring you to the synagogues and magistrates and authorities, do
not worry about how or what you should
answer, or what you should say. 12 For the Holy

12:11 do not worry. I.e., do not be anxious. This does not suggest that ministers and teachers should forego preparation in their normal spiritual duties. To cite this passage and others like it (21:12–15; Matt. 10:19) to justify the neglect of study and meditation is to twist the meaning of Scripture. This verse is meant as a comfort for those under life-threatening persecution, not as an excuse for laziness in ministry. The exact same expression is used in v. 22, speaking of concern for one's material necessities. In neither context was Jesus condemning legitimate toil and preparation. He was promising the Holy Spirit's aid for times of persecution when there can be no preparation.

Spirit will teach you in that very hour what you
ought to say."
13 Then one from the crowd said to Him,
"Teacher, tell my brother to divide the inheritance with me."
14 But He said to him, "Man, who made Me a
judge or an arbitrator over you?" 15 And He said
to them, "Take heed and beware of covetousness, for one's life does not consist in the
abundance of the things he possesses."
16 Then He spoke a parable to them, saying:
"The ground of a certain rich man yielded
plentifully. 17 And he thought within himself,
saying, 'What shall I do, since I have no room
to store my crops?' 18 So he said, 'I will do this:
I will pull down my barns and build greater,
and there I will store all my crops and my
goods. 19 And I will say to my soul, "Soul, you
have many goods laid up for many years; take
your ease; eat, drink, *and* be merry." ' 20 But
God said to him, 'Fool! This night your soul
will be required of you; then whose will those
things be which you have provided?'
21 "So *is* he who lays up treasure for himself,
and is not rich toward God."
22 Then He said to His disciples, "Therefore
I say to you, do not worry about your life, what
you will eat; nor about the body, what you will
put on. 23 Life is more than food, and the body *is
more* than clothing. 24 Consider the ravens, for
they neither sow nor reap, which have neither
storehouse nor barn; and God feeds them. Of
how much more value are you than the birds?
25 And which of you by worrying can add one
cubit to his stature? 26 If you then are not able
to do *the* least, why are you anxious for the
rest? 27 Consider the lilies, how they grow: they
neither toil nor spin; and yet I say to you, even
Solomon in all his glory was not arrayed like
one of these. 28 If then God so clothes the
grass, which today is in the field and tomorrow is thrown into the oven, how much more
will He clothe you, O *you* of little faith?
29 "And do not seek what you should eat or
what you should drink, nor have an anxious
mind. 30 For all these things the nations of the
world seek after, and your Father knows that you
need these things. 31 But seek the kingdom of
God, and all these things shall be added to you.

DAY 14: What passages in Luke are unique to his Gospel?

Luke included 12 events or major passages not found in the other Gospels:

1. Events preceding the birth of John the Baptist and Jesus (1:5–80).
2. Scenes from Jesus' childhood (2:1–52).
3. Herod imprisons John the Baptist (3:19,20).
4. The people of Nazareth reject Jesus (4:16–30).
5. The first disciples are called (5:1–11).
6. A widow's son is raised (7:11–17).
7. A woman anoints Jesus' feet (7:36–50).
8. Certain women minister to Christ (8:1–3).
9. Events, teaching, and miracles during the months leading up to Christ's death (10:1–18:14).
10. Christ abides with Zacchaeus (19:1–27).
11. Herod tries Christ (23:6–12).
12. Some of Jesus' final words before His ascension (24:44–49).

APRIL 15

Joshua 19:1–20:9

19 The second lot came out for Simeon, for
the tribe of the children of Simeon
according to their families. And their inheritance was within the inheritance of the children of Judah. 2 They had in their inheritance
Beersheba (Sheba), Moladah, 3 Hazar Shual,
Balah, Ezem, 4 Eltolad, Bethul, Hormah,
5 Ziklag, Beth Marcaboth, Hazar Susah, 6 Beth
Lebaoth, and Sharuhen: thirteen cities and

their villages; 7Ain, Rimmon, Ether, and Ashan:
four cities and their villages; 8and all the villages that *were* all around these cities as far as
Baalath Beer, Ramah of the South. This *was*
the inheritance of the tribe of the children of
Simeon according to their families.

9The inheritance of the children of Simeon
was included in the share of the children of
Judah, for the share of the children of Judah
was too much for them. Therefore the children of Simeon had *their* inheritance within
the inheritance of that people.

10The third lot came out for the children of
Zebulun according to their families, and the
border of their inheritance was as far as
Sarid. 11Their border went toward the west
and to Maralah, went to Dabbasheth, and
extended along the brook that is east of
Jokneam. 12Then from Sarid it went eastward
toward the sunrise along the border of
Chisloth Tabor, and went out toward
Daberath, bypassing Japhia. 13And from there
it passed along on the east of Gath Hepher,
toward Eth Kazin, and extended to Rimmon,
which borders on Neah. 14Then the border
went around it on the north side of Han-
nathon, and it ended in the Valley of Jiphthah
El. 15Included were Kattath, Nahallal, Shimron, Idalah, and Bethlehem: twelve cities
with their villages. 16This *was* the inheritance
of the children of Zebulun according to their
families, these cities with their villages.

17The fourth lot came out to Issachar, for the
children of Issachar according to their families. 18And their territory went to Jezreel, and
included Chesulloth, Shunem, 19Haphraim,
Shion, Anaharath, 20Rabbith, Kishion, Abez,
21Remeth, En Gannim, En Haddah, and Beth
Pazzez. 22And the border reached to Tabor,
Shahazimah, and Beth Shemesh; their border
ended at the Jordan: sixteen cities with their
villages. 23This *was* the inheritance of the tribe
of the children of Issachar according to their
families, the cities and their villages.

24The fifth lot came out for the tribe of the
children of Asher according to their families.
25And their territory included Helkath, Hali,
Beten, Achshaph, 26Alammelech, Amad, and
Mishal; it reached to Mount Carmel westward, along *the Brook* Shihor Libnath. 27It
turned toward the sunrise to Beth Dagon; and
it reached to Zebulun and to the Valley of
Jiphthah El, then northward beyond Beth
Emek and Neiel, bypassing Cabul *which was*
on the left, 28including Ebron, Rehob,
Hammon, and Kanah, as far as Greater Sidon.
29And the border turned to Ramah and to the
fortified city of Tyre; then the border turned
to Hosah, and ended at the sea by the region
of Achzib. 30Also Ummah, Aphek, and Rehob
were included: twenty-two cities with their villages. 31This *was* the inheritance of the tribe of
the children of Asher according to their families, these cities with their villages.

32The sixth lot came out to the children of
Naphtali, for the children of Naphtali according to their families. 33And their border began
at Heleph, enclosing the territory from the
terebinth tree in Zaanannim, Adami Nekeb,
and Jabneel, as far as Lakkum; it ended at the
Jordan. 34From Heleph the border extended
westward to Aznoth Tabor, and went out from
there toward Hukkok; it adjoined Zebulun on
the south side and Asher on the west side, and
ended at Judah by the Jordan toward the sunrise. 35And the fortified cities *are* Ziddim, Zer,
Hammath, Rakkath, Chinnereth, 36Adamah,
Ramah, Hazor, 37Kedesh, Edrei, En Hazor,
38Iron, Migdal El, Horem, Beth Anath, and
Beth Shemesh: nineteen cities with their villages. 39This *was* the inheritance of the tribe of
the children of Naphtali according to their
families, the cities and their villages.

40The seventh lot came out for the tribe of
the children of Dan according to their families. 41And the territory of their inheritance
was Zorah, Eshtaol, Ir Shemesh, 42Shaalabbin,
Aijalon, Jethlah, 43Elon, Timnah, Ekron, 44Elte-
keh, Gibbethon, Baalath, 45Jehud, Bene Berak,
Gath Rimmon, 46Me Jarkon, and Rakkon, with
the region near Joppa. 47And the border of the
children of Dan went beyond these, because
the children of Dan went up to fight against
Leshem and took it; and they struck it with the
edge of the sword, took possession of it, and
dwelt in it. They called Leshem, Dan, after the
name of Dan their father. 48This *is* the inheritance of the tribe of the children of Dan
according to their families, these cities with
their villages.

49When they had made an end of dividing
the land as an inheritance according to their
borders, the children of Israel gave an inheritance among them to Joshua the son of Nun.
50According to the word of the LORD they gave
him the city which he asked for, Timnath
Serah in the mountains of Ephraim; and he
built the city and dwelt in it.

51These *were* the inheritances which Eleazar
the priest, Joshua the son of Nun, and the
heads of the fathers of the tribes of the children of Israel divided as an inheritance by lot
in Shiloh before the LORD, at the door of the
tabernacle of meeting. So they made an end of
dividing the country.

20 The LORD also spoke to Joshua, saying,
[2]"Speak to the children of Israel, saying: 'Appoint for yourselves cities of refuge, of
which I spoke to you through Moses, [3]that the
slayer who kills a person accidentally *or* unintentionally may flee there; and they shall be
your refuge from the avenger of blood. [4]And
when he flees to one of those cities, and stands
at the entrance of the gate of the city, and declares his case in the hearing of the elders of
that city, they shall take him into the city as
one of them, and give him a place, that he may
dwell among them. [5]Then if the avenger of
blood pursues him, they shall not deliver the
slayer into his hand, because he struck his
neighbor unintentionally, but did not hate him
beforehand. [6]And he shall dwell in that city until he stands before the congregation for judgment, *and* until the death of the one who is
high priest in those days. Then the slayer may
return and come to his own city and his own
house, to the city from which he fled.' "
[7]So they appointed Kedesh in Galilee, in the
mountains of Naphtali, Shechem in the mountains of Ephraim, and Kirjath Arba (which *is*
Hebron) in the mountains of Judah. [8]And on
the other side of the Jordan, by Jericho eastward, they assigned Bezer in the wilderness
on the plain, from the tribe of Reuben, Ramoth
in Gilead, from the tribe of Gad, and Golan in
Bashan, from the tribe of Manasseh. [9]These
were the cities appointed for all the children of
Israel and for the stranger who dwelt among
them, that whoever killed a person accidentally
might flee there, and not die by the hand of
the avenger of blood until he stood before the
congregation.

20:1–9 cities of refuge. Moses had spoken God's word to name 6 cities in Israel as refuge centers. A person who inadvertently killed another could flee to the nearest of these for protection (see Num. 35:9–34). Three lay west of the Jordan, and 3 lay to the east, each reachable in a day for those in its area. The slayer could flee there to escape pursuit by a family member seeking to exact private justice. Authorities at the refuge protected him and escorted him to a trial. If found innocent, he was guarded at the refuge until the death of the current high priest, a kind of statute of limitations (Josh. 20:6). He could then return home. If found guilty of murder, he suffered due punishment.

Psalm 46:1–6

To the Chief Musician. *A Psalm* of the sons of Korah. A Song for Alamoth.

God *is* our refuge and strength,
A very present help in trouble.
2 Therefore we will not fear,
Even though the earth be removed,
And though the mountains be carried
into the midst of the sea;
3 *Though* its waters roar *and* be troubled,
Though the mountains shake with its
swelling. Selah

4 *There is* a river whose streams shall
make glad the city of God,
The holy *place* of the tabernacle of the
Most High.
5 God *is* in the midst of her, she shall not
be moved;
God shall help her, just at the break of
dawn.
6 The nations raged, the kingdoms were
moved;
He uttered His voice, the earth melted.

Proverbs 14:7–11

7 Go from the presence of a foolish man,
When you do not perceive *in him* the
lips of knowledge.
8 The wisdom of the prudent *is* to
understand his way,
But the folly of fools *is* deceit.

9 Fools mock at sin,
But among the upright *there is* favor.
10 The heart knows its own bitterness,
And a stranger does not share its joy.
11 The house of the wicked will be
overthrown,
But the tent of the upright will flourish.

14:10 At its depth, suffering and rejoicing are personal and private. No one is able to communicate them fully (1 Sam 1:10; 1 Kin. 8:38; Matt 2:18; 26:39–42,75).

Luke 12:32–59

[32]"Do not fear, little flock, for it is your
Father's good pleasure to give you the kingdom. [33]Sell what you have and give alms; provide yourselves money bags which do not
grow old, a treasure in the heavens that does
not fail, where no thief approaches nor moth

destroys. 34For where your treasure is, there
your heart will be also.
35"Let your waist be girded and *your* lamps
burning; 36and you yourselves be like men
who wait for their master, when he will return
from the wedding, that when he comes and
knocks they may open to him immediately.
37Blessed *are* those servants whom the master, when he comes, will find watching.
Assuredly, I say to you that he will gird himself and have them sit down *to eat,* and will
come and serve them. 38And if he should come
in the second watch, or come in the third
watch, and find *them* so, blessed are those servants. 39But know this, that if the master of the
house had known what hour the thief would
come, he would have watched and not allowed
his house to be broken into. 40Therefore you
also be ready, for the Son of Man is coming at
an hour you do not expect."
41Then Peter said to Him, "Lord, do You
speak this parable *only* to us, or to all *people?*"
42And the Lord said, "Who then is that faithful and wise steward, whom *his* master will
make ruler over his household, to give *them*
their portion of food in due season? 43Blessed
is that servant whom his master will find so
doing when he comes. 44Truly, I say to you
that he will make him ruler over all that he
has. 45But if that servant says in his heart, 'My
master is delaying his coming,' and begins to
beat the male and female servants, and to eat
and drink and be drunk, 46the master of that
servant will come on a day when he is not
looking for *him,* and at an hour when he is not
aware, and will cut him in two and appoint *him*
his portion with the unbelievers. 47And that
servant who knew his master's will, and did
not prepare *himself* or do according to his will,
shall be beaten with many *stripes.* 48But he who
did not know, yet committed things deserving
of stripes, shall be beaten with few. For everyone to whom much is given, from him much
will be required; and to whom much has been
committed, of him they will ask the more.
49"I came to send fire on the earth, and how
I wish it were already kindled! 50But I have a
baptism to be baptized with, and how distressed I am till it is accomplished! 51Do *you*
suppose that I came to give peace on earth? I

12:33 Sell what you have and give alms. Those who amassed earthly possessions, falsely thinking their security lay in material resources (vv. 16–20), needed to lay up treasure in heaven instead. Believers in the early church did sell their goods to meet the basic needs of poorer brethren (Acts 2:44,45; 4:32–37). But this commandment is not to be twisted into an absolute prohibition of all earthly possessions. In fact, Peter's words to Ananias in Acts 5:4 make it clear that the selling of one's possessions was optional. **money bags which do not grow old.** These purses that do not wear out (so as to lose the money) are defined as "treasure in the heavens that does not fail." The surest place to put one's money is in such a purse—in heaven, where it is safe from thieves and decay, as well.

12:34 your heart will be also. Where one puts his money reveals the priorities of his heart. See 16:1–13; Matthew 6:21.

tell you, not at all, but rather division. 52For from
now on five in one house will be divided: three
against two, and two against three. 53Father
will be divided against son and son against
father, mother against daughter and daughter
against mother, mother-in-law against her
daughter-in-law and daughter-in-law against
her mother-in-law."
54Then He also said to the multitudes,
"Whenever you see a cloud rising out of the
west, immediately you say, 'A shower is coming'; and so it is. 55And when *you see* the south
wind blow, you say, 'There will be hot weather'; and there is. 56Hypocrites! You can discern
the face of the sky and of the earth, but how *is*
it you do not discern this time?
57"Yes, and why, even of yourselves, do you
not judge what is right? 58When you go with
your adversary to the magistrate, make every
effort along the way to settle with him, lest he
drag you to the judge, the judge deliver you to
the officer, and the officer throw you into
prison. 59I tell you, you shall not depart from
there till you have paid the very last mite."

DAY 15: Where can we find stability in troubled times?

Psalm 46 was the scriptural catalyst for Martin Luther's great hymn "A Mighty Fortress Is Our God." This psalm extols the adequacy of God in facing threats from nature and the nations. God indeed protects (see vv. 1,7,11) His people upon the earth (see vv. 2,6,8,9,10). The major burden of Psalm 46 is that God provides stability for His people who live in two exceedingly unstable environments.

Specifically, "Even though the earth be removed" (v. 2). I.e., "When earth changes and when mountains move or shake or totter or slip" (see the language of Is. 24:19,20; 54:10; Hag. 2:6). These are poetic allusions to earthquakes. Since "the earth" and "mountains" are regarded by men as symbols of stability, when they "dance," great terror normally ensues. But when the most stable becomes unstable, there should be "no fear" because of the transcendent stability of God. And "though its waters roar" (v. 3). This is an illustration of powerfully surging and potentially destructive floods of waters. These will not erode God's protective fortifications.

"There is a river whose streams shall make glad the city of God" (v. 4). Refreshing waters contrast with those threatening torrents of v. 3. See the garden of paradise concept often mentioned in ancient Near Eastern literature, but most importantly, see the biblical revelation, noting especially the "bookends" of Genesis 2:10 and Revelation 22:1, 2. "She shall not be moved" (vv. 5,6). These verses pick up some of the key terms about moving, slipping, tottering, sliding, and roaring from vv. 1–3. However, here, because of the presence of God, the forces of nature and the nations are no longer a threat to the people of God who dwell with Him.

APRIL 16

Joshua 21:1–22:34

21 Then the heads of the fathers' *houses* of
the Levites came near to Eleazar the
priest, to Joshua the son of Nun, and to the
heads of the fathers' *houses* of the tribes of the
children of Israel. [2]And they spoke to them at
Shiloh in the land of Canaan, saying, "The LORD
commanded through Moses to give us cities to
dwell in, with their common-lands for our livestock." [3]So the children of Israel gave to the
Levites from their inheritance, at the commandment of the LORD, these cities and their
common-lands:

[4]Now the lot came out for the families of the
Kohathites. And the children of Aaron the
priest, *who were* of the Levites, had thirteen
cities by lot from the tribe of Judah, from the
tribe of Simeon, and from the tribe of Benjamin. [5]The rest of the children of Kohath had
ten cities by lot from the families of the tribe
of Ephraim, from the tribe of Dan, and from
the half-tribe of Manasseh.

[6]And the children of Gershon had thirteen
cities by lot from the families of the tribe of
Issachar, from the tribe of Asher, from the
tribe of Naphtali, and from the half-tribe of
Manasseh in Bashan.

[7]The children of Merari according to their
families had twelve cities from the tribe of
Reuben, from the tribe of Gad, and from the
tribe of Zebulun.

[8]And the children of Israel gave these cities
with their common-lands by lot to the Levites, as
the LORD had commanded by the hand of Moses.

[9]So they gave from the tribe of the children
of Judah and from the tribe of the children of
Simeon these cities which are designated by
name, [10]which were for the children of Aaron,
one of the families of the Kohathites, *who were*
of the children of Levi; for the lot was theirs
first. [11]And they gave them Kirjath Arba (*Arba*
was the father of Anak), which *is* Hebron, in
the mountains of Judah, with the common-
land surrounding it. [12]But the fields of the city
and its villages they gave to Caleb the son of
Jephunneh as his possession.

[13]Thus to the children of Aaron the priest
they gave Hebron with its common-land (a
city of refuge for the slayer), Libnah with its
common-land, [14]Jattir with its common-land,
Eshtemoa with its common-land, [15]Holon with its
common-land, Debir with its common-land, [16]Ain
with its common-land, Juttah with its common-
land, and Beth Shemesh with its common-land:
nine cities from those two tribes; [17]and from the
tribe of Benjamin, Gibeon with its common-
land, Geba with its common-land, [18]Anathoth
with its common-land, and Almon with its
common-land: four cities. [19]All the cities of the
children of Aaron, the priests, *were* thirteen
cities with their common-lands.

[20]And the families of the children of Kohath,
the Levites, the rest of the children of Kohath,
even they had the cities of their lot from the
tribe of Ephraim. [21]For they gave them
Shechem with its common-land in the mountains of Ephraim (a city of refuge for the slayer),
Gezer with its common-land, [22]Kibzaim with its
common-land, and Beth Horon with its common-land: four cities; [23]and from the tribe of
Dan, Eltekeh with its common-land, Gibbethon
with its common-land, [24]Aijalon with its common-
land, *and* Gath Rimmon with its common-land:
four cities; [25]and from the half-tribe of
Manasseh, Tanach with its common-land and
Gath Rimmon with its common-land: two
cities. [26]All the ten cities with their common-
lands were for the rest of the families of the
children of Kohath.

[27]Also to the children of Gershon, of the families of the Levites, from the *other* half-tribe of Manasseh, *they gave* Golan in Bashan with its common-land (a city of refuge for the slayer), and Be Eshterah with its common-land: two cities; [28]and from the tribe of Issachar, Kishion with its common-land, Daberath with its common-land, [29]Jarmuth with its common-land, *and* En Gannim with its common-land: four cities; [30]and from the tribe of Asher, Mishal with its common-land, Abdon with its common-land, [31]Helkath with its common-land, and Rehob with its common-land: four cities; [32]and from the tribe of Naphtali, Kedesh in Galilee with its common-land (a city of refuge for the slayer), Hammoth Dor with its common-land, and Kartan with its common-land: three cities. [33]All the cities of the Gershonites according to their families *were* thirteen cities with their common-lands.

[34]And to the families of the children of Merari, the rest of the Levites, from the tribe of Zebulun, Jokneam with its common-land, Kartah with its common-land, [35]Dimnah with its common-land, *and* Nahalal with its common-land: four cities; [36]and from the tribe of Reuben, Bezer with its common-land, Jahaz with its common-land, [37]Kedemoth with its common-land, and Mephaath with its common-land: four cities; [38]and from the tribe of Gad, Ramoth in Gilead with its common-land (a city of refuge for the slayer), Mahanaim with its common-land, [39]Heshbon with its common-land, *and* Jazer with its common-land: four cities in all. [40]So all the cities for the children of Merari according to their families, the rest of the families of the Levites, were *by* their lot twelve cities.

[41]All the cities of the Levites within the possession of the children of Israel *were* forty-eight cities with their common-lands. [42]Every one of these cities had its common-land surrounding it; thus *were* all these cities.

[43]So the LORD gave to Israel all the land of which He had sworn to give to their fathers, and they took possession of it and dwelt in it. [44]The LORD gave them rest all around, according to all that He had sworn to their fathers. And not a man of all their enemies stood against them; the LORD delivered all their enemies into their hand. [45]Not a word failed of any good thing which the LORD had spoken to the house of Israel. All came to pass.

22 Then Joshua called the Reubenites, the Gadites, and half the tribe of Manasseh, [2]and said to them: "You have kept all that Moses the servant of the LORD commanded you, and have obeyed my voice in all that I commanded you. [3]You have not left your brethren these many days, up to this day, but have kept the charge of the commandment of the LORD your God. [4]And now the LORD your God has given rest to your brethren, as He promised them; now therefore, return and go to your tents *and* to the land of your possession, which Moses the servant of the LORD gave you on the other side of the Jordan. [5]But take careful heed to do the commandment and the law which Moses the servant of the LORD commanded you, to love the LORD your God, to walk in all His ways, to keep His commandments, to hold fast to Him, and to serve Him with all your heart and with all your soul." [6]So Joshua blessed them and sent them away, and they went to their tents.

[7]Now to half the tribe of Manasseh Moses had given a possession in Bashan, but to the *other* half of it Joshua gave *a possession* among their brethren on this side of the Jordan, westward. And indeed, when Joshua sent them away to their tents, he blessed them, [8]and spoke to them, saying, "Return with much riches to your tents, with very much livestock, with silver, with gold, with bronze, with iron, and with very much clothing. Divide the spoil of your enemies with your brethren."

[9]So the children of Reuben, the children of Gad, and half the tribe of Manasseh returned, and departed from the children of Israel at Shiloh, which *is* in the land of Canaan, to go to the country of Gilead, to the land of their possession, which they had obtained according to the word of the LORD by the hand of Moses.

[10]And when they came to the region of the Jordan which *is* in the land of Canaan, the children of Reuben, the children of Gad, and half the tribe of Manasseh built an altar there by the Jordan—a great, impressive altar. [11]Now the children of Israel heard *someone* say, "Behold, the children of Reuben, the children of Gad, and half the tribe of Manasseh have built an altar on the frontier of the land of Canaan, in

21:43–45 So the LORD gave to Israel all the land. This sums up God's fulfillment of His covenant promise to give Abraham's people the land (Gen. 12:7; Josh. 1:2,5–9). God also kept His Word in giving the people rest (Deut. 12:9,10). In a valid sense, the Canaanites were in check, under military conquest as God had pledged (Josh. 1:5), not posing an immediate threat. Not every enemy had been driven out, however, leaving some to stir up trouble later. But God's people failed to exercise their responsibility and possess their land to the full degree in various areas.

the region of the Jordan—on the children of
Israel's side." 12And when the children of Israel
heard *of it,* the whole congregation of the children of Israel gathered together at Shiloh to
go to war against them.

13Then the children of Israel sent Phinehas
the son of Eleazar the priest to the children of
Reuben, to the children of Gad, and to half the
tribe of Manasseh, into the land of Gilead,
14and with him ten rulers, one ruler each from
the chief house of every tribe of Israel; and
each one *was* the head of the house of his
father among the divisions of Israel. 15Then
they came to the children of Reuben, to the
children of Gad, and to half the tribe of
Manasseh, to the land of Gilead, and they
spoke with them, saying, 16"Thus says the
whole congregation of the LORD: 'What treachery *is* this that you have committed against
the God of Israel, to turn away this day from
following the LORD, in that you have built for
yourselves an altar, that you might rebel this
day against the LORD? 17*Is* the iniquity of Peor
not enough for us, from which we are not
cleansed till this day, although there was a
plague in the congregation of the LORD, 18but
that you must turn away this day from following the LORD? And it shall be, if you rebel
today against the LORD, that tomorrow He will
be angry with the whole congregation of
Israel. 19Nevertheless, if the land of your possession *is* unclean, *then* cross over to the land
of the possession of the LORD, where the
LORD's tabernacle stands, and take possession
among us; but do not rebel against the LORD,
nor rebel against us, by building yourselves an
altar besides the altar of the LORD our God.
20Did not Achan the son of Zerah commit a
trespass in the accursed thing, and wrath fell
on all the congregation of Israel? And that
man did not perish alone in his iniquity.' "

21Then the children of Reuben, the children
of Gad, and half the tribe of Manasseh
answered and said to the heads of the divisions of Israel: 22"The LORD God of gods, the
LORD God of gods, He knows, and let Israel
itself know—if *it is* in rebellion, or if in treachery against the LORD, do not save us this day.
23If we have built ourselves an altar to turn from
following the LORD, or if to offer on it burnt offerings or grain offerings, or if to offer peace offerings on it, let the LORD Himself require *an
account.* 24But in fact we have done it for fear, for
a reason, saying, 'In time to come your descendants may speak to our descendants, saying,
"What have you to do with the LORD God of
Israel? 25For the LORD has made the Jordan a
border between you and us, *you* children of
Reuben and children of Gad. You have no part
in the LORD." So your descendants would
make our descendants cease fearing the
LORD.' 26Therefore we said, 'Let us now prepare to build ourselves an altar, not for burnt
offering nor for sacrifice, 27but *that* it *may be* a
witness between you and us and our generations after us, that we may perform the service of the LORD before Him with our burnt
offerings, with our sacrifices, and with our
peace offerings; that your descendants may
not say to our descendants in time to come,
"You have no part in the LORD." ' 28Therefore
we said that it will be, when they say *this* to us
or to our generations in time to come, that we
may say, 'Here is the replica of the altar of the
LORD which our fathers made, though not for
burnt offerings nor for sacrifices; but it *is* a
witness between you and us.' 29Far be it from
us that we should rebel against the LORD, and
turn from following the LORD this day, to build
an altar for burnt offerings, for grain offerings,
or for sacrifices, besides the altar of the LORD
our God which *is* before His tabernacle."

30Now when Phinehas the priest and the rulers
of the congregation, the heads of the divisions of
Israel who *were* with him, heard the words that
the children of Reuben, the children of Gad, and
the children of Manasseh spoke, it pleased them.
31Then Phinehas the son of Eleazar the priest
said to the children of Reuben, the children of
Gad, and the children of Manasseh, "This day
we perceive that the LORD *is* among us, because
you have not committed this treachery against
the LORD. Now you have delivered the children
of Israel out of the hand of the LORD."

32And Phinehas the son of Eleazar the priest,
and the rulers, returned from the children of
Reuben and the children of Gad, from the land
of Gilead to the land of Canaan, to the children
of Israel, and brought back word to them. 33So
the thing pleased the children of Israel, and
the children of Israel blessed God; they spoke
no more of going against them in battle, to
destroy the land where the children of Reuben
and Gad dwelt.

34The children of Reuben and the children of
Gad called the altar, *Witness,* "For *it is* a witness between us that the LORD *is* God."

Psalm 46:7–11

7 The LORD of hosts *is* with us;
The God of Jacob is our refuge.
Selah

8 Come, behold the works of the LORD,
Who has made desolations in the earth.
9 He makes wars cease to the end of the
earth;

46:7 The LORD of hosts *is* with us. The precious personal presence (see "God with us" in Is. 7:14; 8:8,10) of the Divine Warrior (see "LORD of hosts" or "armies," e.g., Pss. 24:10; 48:8; 59:5) secures the safety of His people.

He breaks the bow and cuts the spear
in two;
He burns the chariot in the fire.

10 Be still, and know that I *am* God;
I will be exalted among the nations,
I will be exalted in the earth!

11 The LORD of hosts *is* with us;
The God of Jacob is our refuge.
Selah

46:10 Be still, and know that I *am* God. This twin command to not panic and to recognize His sovereignty is probably directed to both His nation for comfort and all other nations for warning.

Proverbs 14:12–13

12 There is a way *that seems* right to a man,
But its end *is* the way of death.

13 Even in laughter the heart may sorrow,
And the end of mirth *may be* grief.

Luke 13:1–22

13 There were present at that season some
who told Him about the Galileans whose
blood Pilate had mingled with their sacrifices.
2And Jesus answered and said to them, "Do
you suppose that these Galileans were worse
sinners than all *other* Galileans, because they
suffered such things? 3I tell you, no; but unless
you repent you will all likewise perish. 4Or
those eighteen on whom the tower in Siloam
fell and killed them, do you think that they
were worse sinners than all *other* men who
dwelt in Jerusalem? 5I tell you, no; but unless
you repent you will all likewise perish."

6He also spoke this parable: "A certain *man*
had a fig tree planted in his vineyard, and he
came seeking fruit on it and found none.
7Then he said to the keeper of his vineyard,
'Look, for three years I have come seeking
fruit on this fig tree and find none. Cut it
down; why does it use up the ground?' 8But he
answered and said to him, 'Sir, let it alone this

13:11 had a spirit of infirmity. This suggests that her physical ailment, which left her unable to stand erect, was caused by an evil spirit. However, Christ did not have to confront and drive out a demon, but simply declared her loosed (v. 12), so her case appears somewhat different from other cases of demonic possession He often encountered.

13:12 He called *her* to *Him*. The healing was unsolicited; He took the initiative (see 7:12–14). Furthermore, no special faith was required on her part or anyone else's. Jesus sometimes called for faith, but not always (see 8:48; Mark 5:34).

year also, until I dig around it and fertilize *it*.
9And if it bears fruit, *well*. But if not, after that
you can cut it down.' "

10Now He was teaching in one of the synagogues on the Sabbath. 11And behold, there
was a woman who had a spirit of infirmity
eighteen years, and was bent over and could in
no way raise *herself* up. 12But when Jesus saw
her, He called *her* to *Him* and said to her,
"Woman, you are loosed from your infirmity."
13And He laid *His* hands on her, and immediately she was made straight, and glorified God.
14But the ruler of the synagogue answered
with indignation, because Jesus had healed on
the Sabbath; and he said to the crowd, "There
are six days on which men ought to work;
therefore come and be healed on them, and
not on the Sabbath day."

15The Lord then answered him and said, "Hypocrite! Does not each one of you on the Sabbath
loose his ox or donkey from the stall, and lead *it*
away to water it? 16So ought not this woman, being a daughter of Abraham, whom Satan has
bound—think of it—for eighteen years, be
loosed from this bond on the Sabbath?" 17And
when He said these things, all His adversaries
were put to shame; and all the multitude rejoiced
for all the glorious things that were done by Him.

18Then He said, "What is the kingdom of God
like? And to what shall I compare it? 19It is like a
mustard seed, which a man took and put in his
garden; and it grew and became a large tree,
and the birds of the air nested in its branches."

20And again He said, "To what shall I liken
the kingdom of God? 21It is like leaven, which
a woman took and hid in three measures of
meal till it was all leavened."

22And He went through the cities and villages,
teaching, and journeying toward Jerusalem.

DAY 16: Are catastrophes a sign of God's judgment?

Upon hearing about an incident where Galileans were sought out and killed in the temple by Roman authorities while in the process of offering a sacrifice, perhaps because they were seditious zealots, Jesus asked His listeners, "Do you suppose that these Galileans were worse sinners…because they suffered such things?" (Luke 13:2). It was the belief of many that disaster and sudden death always signified divine displeasure over particular sins (see Job 4:7). Those who suffered in uncommon ways were therefore assumed to be guilty of some more severe immorality (see John 9:2).

Jesus did not deny the connection between catastrophe and human evil, for all such afflictions ultimately stem from the curse of humanity's fallenness (Gen. 3:17–19). Furthermore, specific calamities may indeed be the fruit of certain iniquities (Prov. 24:16). But Christ challenged the people's notion that they were morally superior to those who suffered in such catastrophes. He called all to repent (v. 3), for all were in danger of sudden destruction. No one is guaranteed time to prepare for death, so now is the time for repentance for all (see 2 Cor. 6:2).

Jesus also mentions another disaster in Siloam, where evidently one of the towers guarding an aqueduct collapsed, perhaps while under construction, killing some people (v. 4). Again, the question in the minds of people was regarding the connection between calamity and iniquity ("worse sinners"). Jesus responded by saying that such a calamity was not God's way to single out an especially evil group for death, but a means of warning to all sinners.

APRIL 17

Joshua 23:1–24:33

23 Now it came to pass, a long time after
the LORD had given rest to Israel from
all their enemies round about, that Joshua was
old, advanced in age. 2And Joshua called for all
Israel, for their elders, for their heads, for their
judges, and for their officers, and said to them:
"I am old, advanced in age. 3You have seen
all that the LORD your God has done to all
these nations because of you, for the LORD
your God *is* He who has fought for you. 4See, I
have divided to you by lot these nations that
remain, to be an inheritance for your tribes,
from the Jordan, with all the nations that I
have cut off, as far as the Great Sea westward.
5And the LORD your God will expel them from
before you and drive them out of your sight.
So you shall possess their land, as the LORD
your God promised you. 6Therefore be very
courageous to keep and to do all that is written
in the Book of the Law of Moses, lest you turn
aside from it to the right hand or to the left,
7*and* lest you go among these nations, these
who remain among you. You shall not make
mention of the name of their gods, nor cause
anyone to swear *by them;* you shall not serve
them nor bow down to them, 8but you shall
hold fast to the LORD your God, as you have
done to this day. 9For the LORD has driven out
from before you great and strong nations; but
as for you, no one has been able to stand
against you to this day. 10One man of you shall
chase a thousand, for the LORD your God *is* He
who fights for you, as He promised you.
11Therefore take careful heed to yourselves,
that you love the LORD your God. 12Or else, if
indeed you do go back, and cling to the remnant of these nations—these that remain
among you—and make marriages with them,
and go in to them and they to you, 13know for
certain that the LORD your God will no longer
drive out these nations from before you. But
they shall be snares and traps to you, and
scourges on your sides and thorns in your
eyes, until you perish from this good land
which the LORD your God has given you.
14"Behold, this day I *am* going the way of all
the earth. And you know in all your hearts and
in all your souls that not one thing has failed of
all the good things which the LORD your God
spoke concerning you. All have come to pass
for you; not one word of them has failed.
15Therefore it shall come to pass, that as all the
good things have come upon you which the
LORD your God promised you, so the LORD will
bring upon you all harmful things, until He
has destroyed you from this good land which
the LORD your God has given you. 16When you
have transgressed the covenant of the LORD
your God, which He commanded you, and
have gone and served other gods, and bowed
down to them, then the anger of the LORD will
burn against you, and you shall perish quickly
from the good land which He has given you."

24 Then Joshua gathered all the tribes of
Israel to Shechem and called for the
elders of Israel, for their heads, for their
judges, and for their officers; and they presented themselves before God. 2And Joshua
said to all the people, "Thus says the LORD
God of Israel: 'Your fathers, *including* Terah,

the father of Abraham and the father of Nahor,
dwelt on the other side of the River in old
times; and they served other gods. [3]Then I
took your father Abraham from the other side
of the River, led him throughout all the land of
Canaan, and multiplied his descendants and
gave him Isaac. [4]To Isaac I gave Jacob and
Esau. To Esau I gave the mountains of Seir to
possess, but Jacob and his children went down
to Egypt. [5]Also I sent Moses and Aaron, and I
plagued Egypt, according to what I did among
them. Afterward I brought you out.

[6]"Then I brought your fathers out of Egypt,
and you came to the sea; and the Egyptians
pursued your fathers with chariots and horsemen to the Red Sea. [7]So they cried out to the
LORD; and He put darkness between you and
the Egyptians, brought the sea upon them,
and covered them. And your eyes saw what I
did in Egypt. Then you dwelt in the wilderness
a long time. [8]And I brought you into the land
of the Amorites, who dwelt on the other side
of the Jordan, and they fought with you. But I
gave them into your hand, that you might possess their land, and I destroyed them from
before you. [9]Then Balak the son of Zippor, king
of Moab, arose to make war against Israel, and
sent and called Balaam the son of Beor to
curse you. [10]But I would not listen to Balaam;
therefore he continued to bless you. So I delivered you out of his hand. [11]Then you went over
the Jordan and came to Jericho. And the men
of Jericho fought against you—*also* the
Amorites, the Perizzites, the Canaanites, the
Hittites, the Girgashites, the Hivites, and the
Jebusites. But I delivered them into your
hand. [12]I sent the hornet before you which
drove them out from before you, *also* the two
kings of the Amorites, *but* not with your sword
or with your bow. [13]I have given you a land for
which you did not labor, and cities which you
did not build, and you dwell in them; you eat
of the vineyards and olive groves which you
did not plant.'

[14]"Now therefore, fear the LORD, serve Him
in sincerity and in truth, and put away the
gods which your fathers served on the other
side of the River and in Egypt. Serve the LORD!
[15]And if it seems evil to you to serve the LORD,
choose for yourselves this day whom you will
serve, whether the gods which your fathers
served that *were* on the other side of the River,
or the gods of the Amorites, in whose land you
dwell. But as for me and my house, we will
serve the LORD."

[16]So the people answered and said: "Far be it
from us that we should forsake the LORD to
serve other gods; [17]for the LORD our God *is* He

24:15 choose...this day whom you will serve. Joshua's fatherly model (reminiscent of Abraham's, Gen. 18:19) was for himself and his family to serve the Lord, not false gods. He called others in Israel to this, and they committed themselves to serve the Lord also (vv. 21,24).

who brought us and our fathers up out of the
land of Egypt, from the house of bondage,
who did those great signs in our sight, and
preserved us in all the way that we went and
among all the people through whom we
passed. [18]And the LORD drove out from before
us all the people, including the Amorites who
dwelt in the land. We also will serve the LORD,
for He *is* our God."

[19]But Joshua said to the people, "You cannot
serve the LORD, for He *is* a holy God. He *is* a
jealous God; He will not forgive your transgressions nor your sins. [20]If you forsake the
LORD and serve foreign gods, then He will
turn and do you harm and consume you, after
He has done you good."

[21]And the people said to Joshua, "No, but we
will serve the LORD!"

[22]So Joshua said to the people, "You *are* witnesses against yourselves that you have chosen the LORD for yourselves, to serve Him."

And they said, "*We are* witnesses!"

[23]"Now therefore," *he said,* "put away the foreign gods which *are* among you, and incline
your heart to the LORD God of Israel."

[24]And the people said to Joshua, "The LORD
our God we will serve, and His voice we will
obey!"

[25]So Joshua made a covenant with the people that day, and made for them a statute and
an ordinance in Shechem.

[26]Then Joshua wrote these words in the
Book of the Law of God. And he took a large
stone, and set it up there under the oak that
was by the sanctuary of the LORD. [27]And Joshua
said to all the people, "Behold, this stone shall
be a witness to us, for it has heard all the
words of the LORD which He spoke to us. It
shall therefore be a witness to you, lest you
deny your God." [28]So Joshua let the people
depart, each to his own inheritance.

[29]Now it came to pass after these things that
Joshua the son of Nun, the servant of the
LORD, died, *being* one hundred and ten years
old. [30]And they buried him within the border of
his inheritance at Timnath Serah, which *is* in
the mountains of Ephraim, on the north side
of Mount Gaash.

31 Israel served the LORD all the days of
Joshua, and all the days of the elders who outlived Joshua, who had known all the works of
the LORD which He had done for Israel.
32 The bones of Joseph, which the children of
Israel had brought up out of Egypt, they buried
at Shechem, in the plot of ground which Jacob
had bought from the sons of Hamor the father
of Shechem for one hundred pieces of silver,
and which had become an inheritance of the
children of Joseph.
33 And Eleazar the son of Aaron died. They
buried him in a hill *belonging to* Phinehas his
son, which was given to him in the mountains
of Ephraim.

Psalm 47:1–9

To the Chief Musician. A Psalm of the sons of Korah.

Oh, clap your hands, all you peoples!
Shout to God with the voice
of triumph!
2 For the LORD Most High *is* awesome;
He is a great King over all the earth.
3 He will subdue the peoples under us,
And the nations under our feet.
4 He will choose our inheritance for us,
The excellence of Jacob whom
He loves. Selah

5 God has gone up with a shout,
The LORD with the sound of a trumpet.
6 Sing praises to God, sing praises!
Sing praises to our King, sing praises!
7 For God *is* the King of all the earth;
Sing praises with understanding.

8 God reigns over the nations;
God sits on His holy throne.
9 The princes of the people have
gathered together,
The people of the God of Abraham.
For the shields of the earth *belong* to God;
He is greatly exalted.

Proverbs 14:14

14 The backslider in heart will be filled
with his own ways,
But a good man *will be satisfied* from
above.

14:14 backslider in heart. This term, so often used by the prophets (Is. 57:17; Jer. 3:6,8, 11,12,14,22; 8:5; 31:22; 49:4; Hos. 11:7; 14:4), is here used in such a way as to clarify who is a backslider. He belongs in the category of the fool, the wicked, and the disobedient, and he is contrasted with the godly wise. It is a word that the prophets used of apostate unbelievers.

Luke 13:23–35

23 Then one said to Him, "Lord, are there few
who are saved?"
And He said to them, 24 "Strive to enter
through the narrow gate, for many, I say to
you, will seek to enter and will not be able.
25 When once the Master of the house has risen
up and shut the door, and you begin to stand
outside and knock at the door, saying, 'Lord,
Lord, open for us,' and He will answer and say
to you, 'I do not know you, where you are
from,' 26 then you will begin to say, 'We ate and
drank in Your presence, and You taught in our
streets.' 27 But He will say, 'I tell you I do not
know you, where you are from. Depart from
Me, all you workers of iniquity.' 28 There will be
weeping and gnashing of teeth, when you see
Abraham and Isaac and Jacob and all the
prophets in the kingdom of God, and yourselves thrust out. 29 They will come from the
east and the west, from the north and the

13:23 are there few who are saved? That question may have been prompted by a number of factors. The great multitudes that had once followed Christ were subsiding to a faithful few (see John 6:66). Great crowds still came to hear (14:25), but committed followers were increasingly scarce. Moreover, Christ's messages often seemed designed to discourage the halfhearted. And He Himself had stated that the way is so narrow that few find it (Matt. 7:14). This contradicted the Jewish belief that all Jews, except for tax collectors and other notorious sinners, would be saved. Christ's reply once again underscored the difficulty of entering at the narrow gate. After the resurrection, only 120 disciples gathered in the upper room in Jerusalem (Acts 1:15) and only about 500 in Galilee (1 Cor. 15:6).

13:29 They will come. By including people from the 4 corners of the earth, Jesus made it clear that even Gentiles would be invited to the heavenly banquet table. This was contrary to prevailing rabbinical thought, but perfectly consistent with the Old Testament Scriptures (Ps. 107:3; Is. 66:18,19; Mal. 1:11).

south, and sit down in the kingdom of God.
30And indeed there are last who will be first,
and there are first who will be last."
31On that very day some Pharisees came,
saying to Him, "Get out and depart from here,
for Herod wants to kill You."
32And He said to them, "Go, tell that fox, 'Behold, I cast out demons and perform cures
today and tomorrow, and the third *day* I shall
be perfected.' 33Nevertheless I must journey
today, tomorrow, and the *day* following; for it
cannot be that a prophet should perish outside
of Jerusalem.
34"O Jerusalem, Jerusalem, the one who
kills the prophets and stones those who are
sent to her! How often I wanted to gather your
children together, as a hen *gathers* her brood
under *her* wings, but you were not willing!
35See! Your house is left to you desolate; and assuredly, I say to you, you shall not see Me until
the time comes when you say, *'Blessed is He
who comes in the name of the LORD!'* "

DAY 17: Why would Jesus call Herod a "fox" in Luke 13:32?

Some have suggested that Jesus' use of this expression is hard to reconcile with Exodus 22:28; Ecclesiastes 10:20; and Acts 23:5. However, those verses apply to everyday discourse. Prophets, speaking as mouthpieces of God and with divine authority, were often commissioned to rebuke leaders publicly (see Is. 1:23; Ezek. 22:27; Hos. 7:3–7; Zeph. 3:3). Since Jesus spoke with perfect divine authority, He had every right to speak of Herod in such terms. Rabbinical writings often used "the fox" to signify someone who was both crafty and worthless. The Pharisees, who trembled at Herod's power, must have been astonished at Christ's boldness.

Jesus' message to Herod was: "Behold, I cast out demons and perform cures today and tomorrow, and the third day I shall be perfected" (v. 32). This expression signified only that Christ was on His own divine timetable; it was not meant to lay out a literal 3-day schedule. Expressions like this were common in Semitic usage and seldom were employed in a literal sense to specify precise intervals of time. To "be perfected," i.e., by death, in the finishing of His work. (See Heb. 2:10; John 17:4,5; 19:30.) Herod was threatening to kill Him, but no one could kill Christ before His time (John 10:17,18).

Jesus adds that "it cannot be that a prophet should perish outside of Jerusalem" (v. 33). Not all prophets who were martyred died in Jerusalem, of course. This saying was probably a familiar proverb. The statement is full of irony, noting that most of the Old Testament prophets were martyred at the hands of the Jewish people, not by foreign enemies. Luke's inclusion of this saying underscores his theme in this section of his Gospel—Jesus' relentless journey to Jerusalem for the purpose of dying.

APRIL 18

Judges 1:1–2:23

1 Now after the death of Joshua it came to
pass that the children of Israel asked the
LORD, saying, "Who shall be first to go up for
us against the Canaanites to fight against
them?"
2And the LORD said, "Judah shall go up.
Indeed I have delivered the land into his hand."
3So Judah said to Simeon his brother,
"Come up with me to my allotted territory,
that we may fight against the Canaanites; and
I will likewise go with you to your allotted territory." And Simeon went with him. 4Then Judah went up, and the LORD delivered the
Canaanites and the Perizzites into their hand;
and they killed ten thousand men at Bezek.
5And they found Adoni-Bezek in Bezek, and
fought against him; and they defeated the
Canaanites and the Perizzites. 6Then Adoni-
Bezek fled, and they pursued him and caught
him and cut off his thumbs and big toes. 7And
Adoni-Bezek said, "Seventy kings with their
thumbs and big toes cut off used to gather
scraps under my table; as I have done, so God
has repaid me." Then they brought him to Jerusalem, and there he died.
8Now the children of Judah fought against
Jerusalem and took it; they struck it with the
edge of the sword and set the city on fire. 9And
afterward the children of Judah went down to
fight against the Canaanites who dwelt in the
mountains, in the South, and in the lowland.
10Then Judah went against the Canaanites who
dwelt in Hebron. (Now the name of Hebron
was formerly Kirjath Arba.) And they killed
Sheshai, Ahiman, and Talmai.
11From there they went against the inhabitants of Debir. (The name of Debir *was* formerly Kirjath Sepher.)
12Then Caleb said, "Whoever attacks Kirjath
Sepher and takes it, to him I will give my
daughter Achsah as wife." 13And Othniel the
son of Kenaz, Caleb's younger brother, took it;

so he gave him his daughter Achsah as wife.
[14]Now it happened, when she came *to him,* that
she urged him to ask her father for a field.
And she dismounted from *her* donkey, and Caleb said to her, "What do you wish?" [15]So she
said to him, "Give me a blessing; since you
have given me land in the South, give me also
springs of water."

And Caleb gave her the upper springs and
the lower springs.

[16]Now the children of the Kenite, Moses'
father-in-law, went up from the City of Palms
with the children of Judah into the Wilderness
of Judah, which *lies* in the South *near* Arad;
and they went and dwelt among the people.
[17]And Judah went with his brother Simeon,
and they attacked the Canaanites who inhabited Zephath, and utterly destroyed it. So the
name of the city was called Hormah. [18]Also Judah took Gaza with its territory, Ashkelon
with its territory, and Ekron with its territory.
[19]So the LORD was with Judah. And they drove
out the mountaineers, but they could not drive
out the inhabitants of the lowland, because
they had chariots of iron. [20]And they gave
Hebron to Caleb, as Moses had said. Then he
expelled from there the three sons of Anak.

1:19 they could not drive out. "They" of Judah could not. They had been promised by Joshua that they could conquer the lowland (Josh. 17:16,18) and should have remembered Joshua 11:4–9. This is a recurring failure among the tribes to rise to full trust and obedience for victory by God's power. Compromising for less than what God was able to give (Josh. 1:6–9) began even in Joshua's day (Judg. 2:2–6) and earlier (Num. 13; 14). In another sense, God permitted enemies to hold out as a test to display whether His people would obey Him (2:20–23; 3:1,4). Another factor involved keeping the wild animal count from rising too fast (Deut. 7:22).

[21]But the children of Benjamin did not drive
out the Jebusites who inhabited Jerusalem; so
the Jebusites dwell with the children of Benjamin in Jerusalem to this day.

[22]And the house of Joseph also went up
against Bethel, and the LORD *was* with them.
[23]So the house of Joseph sent men to spy out
Bethel. (The name of the city *was* formerly
Luz.) [24]And when the spies saw a man coming
out of the city, they said to him, "Please show
us the entrance to the city, and we will show
you mercy." [25]So he showed them the entrance
to the city, and they struck the city with the
edge of the sword; but they let the man and all
his family go. [26]And the man went to the land
of the Hittites, built a city, and called its name
Luz, which *is* its name to this day.

[27]However, Manasseh did not drive out *the
inhabitants of* Beth Shean and its villages, or
Taanach and its villages, or the inhabitants of
Dor and its villages, or the inhabitants of Ibleam
and its villages, or the inhabitants of Megiddo
and its villages; for the Canaanites were determined to dwell in that land. [28]And it came to
pass, when Israel was strong, that they put the
Canaanites under tribute, but did not completely drive them out.

[29]Nor did Ephraim drive out the Canaanites
who dwelt in Gezer; so the Canaanites dwelt in
Gezer among them.

[30]Nor did Zebulun drive out the inhabitants
of Kitron or the inhabitants of Nahalol; so the
Canaanites dwelt among them, and were put
under tribute.

[31]Nor did Asher drive out the inhabitants of
Acco or the inhabitants of Sidon, or of Ahlab,
Achzib, Helbah, Aphik, or Rehob. [32]So the
Asherites dwelt among the Canaanites, the
inhabitants of the land; for they did not drive
them out.

[33]Nor did Naphtali drive out the inhabitants
of Beth Shemesh or the inhabitants of Beth
Anath; but they dwelt among the Canaanites,
the inhabitants of the land. Nevertheless the
inhabitants of Beth Shemesh and Beth Anath
were put under tribute to them.

[34]And the Amorites forced the children of
Dan into the mountains, for they would not
allow them to come down to the valley;
[35]and the Amorites were determined to
dwell in Mount Heres, in Aijalon, and in
Shaalbim; yet when the strength of the
house of Joseph became greater, they were
put under tribute.

[36]Now the boundary of the Amorites *was*
from the Ascent of Akrabbim, from Sela, and
upward.

2 Then the Angel of the LORD came up from
Gilgal to Bochim, and said: "I led you up
from Egypt and brought you to the land of
which I swore to your fathers; and I said, 'I will
never break My covenant with you. [2]And you
shall make no covenant with the inhabitants of
this land; you shall tear down their altars.' But
you have not obeyed My voice. Why have you
done this? [3]Therefore I also said, 'I will not
drive them out before you; but they shall be
thorns in your side, and their gods shall be a
snare to you.' " [4]So it was, when the Angel of
the LORD spoke these words to all the children

2:1 the Angel of the LORD. One of 3 preincarnate theophanies by the Lord Jesus Christ in Judges (see 6:11–18; 13:3–23). This same Divine Messenger had earlier led Israel out of Egypt (see Ex. 14:19). **I will never break My covenant with you.** God would be faithful until the end, but the people would forfeit blessing for trouble, due to their disobedience (see v. 3).

of Israel, that the people lifted up their voices
and wept.
[5]Then they called the name of that place
Bochim; and they sacrificed there to the LORD.
[6]And when Joshua had dismissed the people,
the children of Israel went each to his own
inheritance to possess the land.
[7]So the people served the LORD all the days
of Joshua, and all the days of the elders who
outlived Joshua, who had seen all the great
works of the LORD which He had done for Israel. [8]Now Joshua the son of Nun, the servant
of the LORD, died *when he was* one hundred
and ten years old. [9]And they buried him within the border of his inheritance at Timnath
Heres, in the mountains of Ephraim, on the
north side of Mount Gaash. [10]When all that
generation had been gathered to their fathers,
another generation arose after them who did
not know the LORD nor the work which He had
done for Israel.
[11]Then the children of Israel did evil in the
sight of the LORD, and served the Baals; [12]and
they forsook the LORD God of their fathers,
who had brought them out of the land of
Egypt; and they followed other gods from
among the gods of the people who *were* all
around them, and they bowed down to them;
and they provoked the LORD to anger. [13]They
forsook the LORD and served Baal and the
Ashtoreths. [14]And the anger of the LORD was
hot against Israel. So He delivered them into
the hands of plunderers who despoiled them;
and He sold them into the hands of their enemies all around, so that they could no longer
stand before their enemies. [15]Wherever they
went out, the hand of the LORD was against
them for calamity, as the LORD had said, and as
the LORD had sworn to them. And they were
greatly distressed.
[16]Nevertheless, the LORD raised up judges
who delivered them out of the hand of those
who plundered them. [17]Yet they would not listen to their judges, but they played the harlot
with other gods, and bowed down to them.
They turned quickly from the way in which
their fathers walked, in obeying the commandments of the LORD; they did not do so. [18]And
when the LORD raised up judges for them, the
LORD was with the judge and delivered them
out of the hand of their enemies all the days of
the judge; for the LORD was moved to pity by
their groaning because of those who oppressed
them and harassed them. [19]And it came to
pass, when the judge was dead, that they
reverted and behaved more corruptly than
their fathers, by following other gods, to serve
them and bow down to them. They did not
cease from their own doings nor from their
stubborn way.
[20]Then the anger of the LORD was hot against
Israel; and He said, "Because this nation has
transgressed My covenant which I commanded their fathers, and has not heeded My voice,
[21]I also will no longer drive out before them
any of the nations which Joshua left when he
died, [22]so that through them I may test Israel,
whether they will keep the ways of the LORD,
to walk in them as their fathers kept *them,* or
not." [23]Therefore the LORD left those nations,
without driving them out immediately; nor did
He deliver them into the hand of Joshua.

Psalm 48:1–8

A Song. A Psalm of the sons of Korah.

Great *is* the LORD, and greatly
to be praised
In the city of our God,
In His holy mountain.
2 Beautiful in elevation,
The joy of the whole earth,
Is Mount Zion *on* the sides of the north,
The city of the great King.

48:2 The joy of the whole earth. See the judgment context of Lamentations 2:15. **the sides of the north.** "North" is an interpretive translation of a word that occurs as a Semitic place name, i.e., "Zaphon." In Canaanite mythology Zaphon was an ancient Near Eastern equivalent to Mt. Olympus, the dwelling place of pagan gods. If this was the psalmist's intention in Psalm 48:2, the reference becomes a polemical description of the Lord. He is not only King of Kings but also is God of all so-called gods. **The city of the great King.** See Psalm 47:2 and Matthew 5:34,35. God Himself has always been the King of Kings.

3 God *is* in her palaces;
He is known as her refuge.

4 For behold, the kings assembled,
They passed by together.
5 They saw *it, and* so they marveled;
They were troubled, they hastened
away.
6 Fear took hold of them there,
And pain, as of a woman in birth pangs,
7 *As when* You break the ships of
Tarshish
With an east wind.

8 As we have heard,
So we have seen
In the city of the LORD of hosts,
In the city of our God:
God will establish it forever. Selah

Proverbs 14:15–17

15 The simple believes every word,
But the prudent considers well his
steps.
16 A wise *man* fears and departs from
evil,
But a fool rages and is self-confident.
17 A quick-tempered *man* acts foolishly,
And a man of wicked intentions
is hated.

Luke 14:1–24

14 Now it happened, as He went into the
house of one of the rulers of the
Pharisees to eat bread on the Sabbath, that
they watched Him closely. [2]And behold,
there was a certain man before Him who had
dropsy. [3]And Jesus, answering, spoke to the
lawyers and Pharisees, saying, "Is it lawful to
heal on the Sabbath?"
[4]But they kept silent. And He took *him* and
healed him, and let him go. [5]Then He
answered them, saying, "Which of you, having
a donkey or an ox that has fallen into a pit, will
not immediately pull him out on the Sabbath
day?" [6]And they could not answer Him regarding these things.
[7]So He told a parable to those who were
invited, when He noted how they chose the
best places, saying to them: [8]"When you are
invited by anyone to a wedding feast, do not sit
down in the best place, lest one more honorable than you be invited by him; [9]and he who
invited you and him come and say to you,
'Give place to this man,' and then you begin
with shame to take the lowest place. [10]But
when you are invited, go and sit down in the
lowest place, so that when he who invited you
comes he may say to you, 'Friend, go up higher.' Then you will have glory in the presence
of those who sit at the table with you. [11]For
whoever exalts himself will be humbled, and
he who humbles himself will be exalted."
[12]Then He also said to him who invited Him,
"When you give a dinner or a supper, do not
ask your friends, your brothers, your relatives,
nor rich neighbors, lest they also invite you
back, and you be repaid. [13]But when you give
a feast, invite *the* poor, *the* maimed, *the* lame,
the blind. [14]And you will be blessed, because
they cannot repay you; for you shall be repaid
at the resurrection of the just."
[15]Now when one of those who sat at the
table with Him heard these things, he said to
Him, "Blessed *is* he who shall eat bread in the
kingdom of God!"
[16]Then He said to him, "A certain man gave
a great supper and invited many, [17]and sent his
servant at supper time to say to those who
were invited, 'Come, for all things are now
ready.' [18]But they all with one *accord* began to
make excuses. The first said to him, 'I have
bought a piece of ground, and I must go and
see it. I ask you to have me excused.' [19]And
another said, 'I have bought five yoke of oxen,
and I am going to test them. I ask you to have
me excused.' [20]Still another said, 'I have married a wife, and therefore I cannot come.' [21]So
that servant came and reported these things
to his master. Then the master of the house,
being angry, said to his servant, 'Go out quickly into the streets and lanes of the city, and
bring in here *the* poor and *the* maimed and *the*
lame and *the* blind.' [22]And the servant said,
'Master, it is done as you commanded, and
still there is room.' [23]Then the master said to
the servant, 'Go out into the highways and
hedges, and compel *them* to come in, that my
house may be filled. [24]For I say to you that
none of those men who were invited shall
taste my supper.' "

14:21 *the* poor and *the* maimed and *the* lame and *the* blind. I.e., people the Pharisees tended to regard as unclean or unworthy. The religious leaders condemned Jesus for His associations with prostitutes and tax collectors (see 5:29,30; 15:1; Matt. 9:10,11; 11:19; 21:31,32; Mark 2:15,16).

14:23 into the highways and hedges. This evidently represents the Gentile regions. **compel *them* to come in.** I.e., not by force or violence, but by earnest persuasion.

DAY 18: Why was there a need for the judges?

"Another generation arose after them who did not know the LORD nor the work which He had done" (Judg. 2:10). The first people in the land had vivid recollections of all the miracles and judgments and were devoted to faith, duty, and purity. The new generation were ignorant of the experiences of their parents and yielded more easily to corruption. To a marked degree the people of this new generation were not true believers.

The new generation "followed other gods" (v. 12). Idol worship, such as the golden calf in the wilderness (Ex. 32), flared up again. Spurious gods of Canaan were plentiful. El was the supreme Canaanite deity, a god of uncontrolled lust and a bloody tyrant, as shown in writings found at Ras Shamra in northern Syria. His name means "strong, powerful." Baal, son and successor of El, was "lord of heaven," a farm god of rain and storm, his name meaning "lord, possessor." His cult at Phoenicia included animal sacrifices, ritual meals, and licentious dances. Chambers catered to sacred prostitution by men and women (see 1 Kin. 14:23,24; 2 Kin. 23:7). Anath, sister-wife of Baal, also called Ashtoreth (Astarte), patroness of sex and war, was called "virgin" and "holy," but was actually a "sacred prostitute." Many other gods besides these also attracted worship.

"The anger of the LORD was hot" against them (v. 14), which was followed by plunderers and calamities designed as chastisement to lead the people to repentance. During these times, "the LORD raised up judges" (v. 16). A "judge" or deliverer guided military expeditions against foes and arbitrated judicial matters (see 4:5). There was no succession or national rule. They were local deliverers, lifted up to leadership by God when the deplorable condition of Israel in the region around them prompted God to rescue the people.

APRIL 19

Judges 3:1–4:24

3 Now these *are* the nations which the LORD left, that He might test Israel by them, *that is,* all who had not known any of the wars in Canaan 2(*this was* only so that the generations of the children of Israel might be taught to know war, at least those who had not formerly known it), 3*namely,* five lords of the Philistines, all the Canaanites, the Sidonians, and the Hivites who dwelt in Mount Lebanon, from Mount Baal Hermon to the entrance of Hamath. 4And they were *left, that He might* test Israel by them, to know whether they would obey the commandments of the LORD, which He had commanded their fathers by the hand of Moses.

5Thus the children of Israel dwelt among the Canaanites, the Hittites, the Amorites, the Perizzites, the Hivites, and the Jebusites. 6And they took their daughters to be their wives, and gave their daughters to their sons; and they served their gods.

7So the children of Israel did evil in the sight of the LORD. They forgot the LORD their God, and served the Baals and Asherahs. 8Therefore the anger of the LORD was hot against Israel, and He sold them into the hand of Cushan-Rishathaim king of Mesopotamia; and the children of Israel served Cushan-Rishathaim eight years. 9When the children of Israel cried out to the LORD, the LORD raised up a deliverer for the children of Israel, who delivered them: Othniel the son of Kenaz, Caleb's younger brother. 10The Spirit of the LORD came upon him, and he judged Israel. He went out to war, and the LORD delivered Cushan-Rishathaim king of Mesopotamia into his hand; and his hand prevailed over Cushan-Rishathaim. 11So the land had rest for forty years. Then Othniel the son of Kenaz died.

12And the children of Israel again did evil in the sight of the LORD. So the LORD strengthened Eglon king of Moab against Israel, because they had done evil in the sight of the LORD. 13Then he gathered to himself the people of Ammon and Amalek, went and defeated Israel, and took possession of the City of Palms. 14So the children of Israel served Eglon king of Moab eighteen years.

15But when the children of Israel cried out to the LORD, the LORD raised up a deliverer for

3:10 The Spirit of the LORD came. Certain judges were expressly said to have the Spirit of the Lord come upon them (6:34; 11:29; 13:25; 14:6,19; 15:14); others apparently also had this experience. This is a common Old Testament expression signifying a unique act of God which conferred power and wisdom for victory. But this did not guarantee that the will of God would be done in absolutely all details, as is apparent in Gideon (8:24–27,30), Jephthah (11:34–40), and Samson (16:1).

them: Ehud the son of Gera, the Benjamite, a left-handed man. By him the children of Israel sent tribute to Eglon king of Moab. 16Now Ehud made himself a dagger (it was double-edged and a cubit in length) and fastened it under his clothes on his right thigh. 17So he brought the tribute to Eglon king of Moab. (Now Eglon *was* a very fat man.) 18And when he had finished presenting the tribute, he sent away the people who had carried the tribute. 19But he himself turned back from the stone images that *were* at Gilgal, and said, "I have a secret message for you, O king."

He said, "Keep silence!" And all who attended him went out from him.

20So Ehud came to him (now he was sitting upstairs in his cool private chamber). Then Ehud said, "I have a message from God for you." So he arose from *his* seat. 21Then Ehud reached with his left hand, took the dagger from his right thigh, and thrust it into his belly. 22Even the hilt went in after the blade, and the fat closed over the blade, for he did not draw the dagger out of his belly; and his entrails came out. 23Then Ehud went out through the porch and shut the doors of the upper room behind him and locked them.

3:20 "I have a message from God for you." Ehud claimed he came to do God's will in answer to prayer (v. 15). Calmly and confidently, Ehud acted and later credited the defeat of the wicked king to God (v. 28; see Ps. 75:6,7,10; Dan. 4:25), though it was by means of Ehud, as Jael used her way (4:21) and Israel's armies used the sword (4:16). By God's power, Ehud's army would slay a greater number (v. 29). Men's evil provokes God's judgment (Lev. 18:25).

24When he had gone out, *Eglon's* servants came to look, and *to their* surprise, the doors of the upper room were locked. So they said, "He is probably attending to his needs in the cool chamber." 25So they waited till they were embarrassed, and still he had not opened the doors of the upper room. Therefore they took the key and opened *them*. And there was their master, fallen dead on the floor.

26But Ehud had escaped while they delayed, and passed beyond the stone images and escaped to Seirah. 27And it happened, when he arrived, that he blew the trumpet in the mountains of Ephraim, and the children of Israel went down with him from the mountains; and he led them. 28Then he said to them, "Follow *me*, for the LORD has delivered your enemies the Moabites into your hand." So they went down after him, seized the fords of the Jordan leading to Moab, and did not allow anyone to cross over. 29And at that time they killed about ten thousand men of Moab, all stout men of valor; not a man escaped. 30So Moab was subdued that day under the hand of Israel. And the land had rest for eighty years.

31After him was Shamgar the son of Anath, who killed six hundred men of the Philistines with an ox goad; and he also delivered Israel.

3:31 Shamgar. His extraordinary exploit causes one to think of Samson (15:16). **an ox goad.** This was a stout stick about 8 to 10 feet long and 6 inches around, with a sharp metal tip to prod or turn oxen. The other end was a flat, curved blade for cleaning a plow.

4 When Ehud was dead, the children of Israel again did evil in the sight of the LORD. 2So the LORD sold them into the hand of Jabin king of Canaan, who reigned in Hazor. The commander of his army *was* Sisera, who dwelt in Harosheth Hagoyim. 3And the children of Israel cried out to the LORD; for Jabin had nine hundred chariots of iron, and for twenty years he had harshly oppressed the children of Israel.

4Now Deborah, a prophetess, the wife of Lapidoth, was judging Israel at that time. 5And she would sit under the palm tree of Deborah between Ramah and Bethel in the mountains of Ephraim. And the children of Israel came up to her for judgment. 6Then she sent and called for Barak the son of Abinoam from Kedesh in Naphtali, and said to him, "Has not

4:4 Deborah, a prophetess. She was an unusual woman of wisdom and influence who did the tasks of a judge, except for military leadership. God can use women mightily for civil, religious, or other tasks, e.g., Huldah the prophetess (2 Kin. 22:14), Philip's daughters in prophesying (Acts 21:8,9), and Phoebe a deaconess (Rom. 16:1). Deborah's rise to such a role is the exception in the book because of Barak's failure to show the courage to lead courageously (vv. 8,14). God rebuked his cowardice by the pledge that a woman would slay Sisera (v. 9).

the LORD God of Israel commanded, 'Go and
deploy *troops* at Mount Tabor; take with you
ten thousand men of the sons of Naphtali and
of the sons of Zebulun; 7and against you I will
deploy Sisera, the commander of Jabin's army,
with his chariots and his multitude at the River
Kishon; and I will deliver him into your
hand'?"
8And Barak said to her, "If you will go with
me, then I will go; but if you will not go with
me, I will not go!"
9So she said, "I will surely go with you; nevertheless there will be no glory for you in the
journey you are taking, for the LORD will sell
Sisera into the hand of a woman." Then
Deborah arose and went with Barak to
Kedesh. 10And Barak called Zebulun and
Naphtali to Kedesh; he went up with ten thousand men under his command, and Deborah
went up with him.
11Now Heber the Kenite, of the children of
Hobab the father-in-law of Moses, had separated himself from the Kenites and pitched his
tent near the terebinth tree at Zaanaim, which
is beside Kedesh.
12And they reported to Sisera that Barak the
son of Abinoam had gone up to Mount Tabor.
13So Sisera gathered together all his chariots,
nine hundred chariots of iron, and all the people who *were* with him, from Harosheth
Hagoyim to the River Kishon.
14Then Deborah said to Barak, "Up! For this
is the day in which the LORD has delivered
Sisera into your hand. Has not the LORD gone
out before you?" So Barak went down from
Mount Tabor with ten thousand men following him. 15And the LORD routed Sisera and all
his chariots and all *his* army with the edge of
the sword before Barak; and Sisera alighted
from *his* chariot and fled away on foot. 16But
Barak pursued the chariots and the army as far
as Harosheth Hagoyim, and all the army of
Sisera fell by the edge of the sword; not a man
was left.
17However, Sisera had fled away on foot to
the tent of Jael, the wife of Heber the Kenite;
for *there was* peace between Jabin king of
Hazor and the house of Heber the Kenite.
18And Jael went out to meet Sisera, and said to
him, "Turn aside, my lord, turn aside to me;
do not fear." And when he had turned aside
with her into the tent, she covered him with a
blanket.
19Then he said to her, "Please give me a little water to drink, for I am thirsty." So she
opened a jug of milk, gave him a drink, and
covered him. 20And he said to her, "Stand at
the door of the tent, and if any man comes and
inquires of you, and says, 'Is there any man
here?' you shall say, 'No.' "
21Then Jael, Heber's wife, took a tent peg
and took a hammer in her hand, and went softly to him and drove the peg into his temple,
and it went down into the ground; for he was
fast asleep and weary. So he died. 22And then,
as Barak pursued Sisera, Jael came out to
meet him, and said to him, "Come, I will show
you the man whom you seek." And when he
went into her *tent,* there lay Sisera, dead with
the peg in his temple.
23So on that day God subdued Jabin king of
Canaan in the presence of the children of Israel. 24And the hand of the children of Israel
grew stronger and stronger against Jabin king
of Canaan, until they had destroyed Jabin king
of Canaan.

Psalm 48:9–14

9 We have thought, O God, on Your
lovingkindness,
In the midst of Your temple.
10 According to Your name, O God,
So *is* Your praise to the ends of the
earth;
Your right hand is full of righteousness.
11 Let Mount Zion rejoice,
Let the daughters of Judah be glad,
Because of Your judgments.

12 Walk about Zion,
And go all around her.
Count her towers;
13 Mark well her bulwarks;
Consider her palaces;
That you may tell *it* to the generation
following.
14 For this *is* God,
Our God forever and ever;
He will be our guide
Even to death.

Proverbs 14:18–19

18 The simple inherit folly,
But the prudent are crowned with
knowledge.
19 The evil will bow before the good,
And the wicked at the gates of the
righteous.

14:19 evil will bow. The ancient custom was for the inferior to prostrate himself before the superior or wait humbly before the great one's gate seeking favor. Good will humble evil.

Luke 14:25–35

[25]Now great multitudes went with Him. And
He turned and said to them, [26]"If anyone
comes to Me and does not hate his father and
mother, wife and children, brothers and sisters, yes, and his own life also, he cannot be
My disciple. [27]And whoever does not bear his
cross and come after Me cannot be My disciple. [28]For which of you, intending to build a
tower, does not sit down first and count the
cost, whether he has *enough* to finish *it*—
[29]lest, after he has laid the foundation, and is
not able to finish, all who see *it* begin to mock
him, [30]saying, 'This man began to build and
was not able to finish.' [31]Or what king, going to
make war against another king, does not sit
down first and consider whether he is able
with ten thousand to meet him who comes
against him with twenty thousand? [32]Or else,
while the other is still a great way off, he
sends a delegation and asks conditions of
peace. [33]So likewise, whoever of you does not
forsake all that he has cannot be My disciple.
[34]"Salt *is* good; but if the salt has lost its flavor, how shall it be seasoned? [35]It is neither fit
for the land nor for the dunghill, *but* men throw
it out. He who has ears to hear, let him hear!"

DAY 19: How deep of a commitment does Christ ask of His followers?

From the teaching in Luke 14:25–35, it is clear that Christ's aim was not to gather appreciative crowds, but to make true disciples. He never adapted His message to majority preferences, but always plainly declared the high cost of discipleship. Here He made several bold demands that would discourage the halfhearted.

"Hate" (v. 26). A similar statement in Matthew 10:37 is the key to understanding this difficult command. The "hatred" called for here is actually a lesser love. Jesus was calling His disciples to cultivate such a devotion to Him that their attachment to everything else—including their own lives—would seem like hatred by comparison. See 16:13; Genesis 29:30,31 for similar usages of the word "hate."

"Bear his cross" (v. 27). I.e., willingly. This parallels the idea of hating one's own life in v. 26. "Count the cost" (v. 28). The multitudes were positive but uncommitted. Far from making it easy for them to respond positively, He set the cost of discipleship as high as possible and encouraged them to do a careful inventory before declaring their willingness to follow.

"Forsake all" (v. 33). Only those willing to carefully assess the cost and invest all they had in His kingdom were worthy to enter. This speaks of something far more than mere abandonment of one's material possessions. It is an absolute, unconditional surrender. His disciples were permitted to retain no privileges and make no demands. They were to safeguard no cherished sins, treasure no earthly possessions, and cling to no secret self-indulgences. Their commitment to Him must be without reservation.

APRIL 20

Judges 5:1–6:40

5 Then Deborah and Barak the son of Abinoam sang on that day, saying:

2 "When leaders lead in Israel,
When the people willingly offer
themselves,
Bless the LORD!
3 "Hear, O kings! Give ear, O princes!
I, *even* I, will sing to the LORD;
I will sing praise to the LORD God
of Israel.
4 "LORD, when You went out from Seir,
When You marched from the field
of Edom,
The earth trembled and the heavens
poured,
The clouds also poured water;
5 The mountains gushed before the LORD,
This Sinai, before the LORD God
of Israel.
6 "In the days of Shamgar, son of Anath,
In the days of Jael,
The highways were deserted,
And the travelers walked along the
byways.
7 Village life ceased, it ceased in Israel,
Until I, Deborah, arose,
Arose a mother in Israel.
8 They chose new gods;
Then *there was* war in the gates;
Not a shield or spear was seen among
forty thousand in Israel.
9 My heart *is* with the rulers of Israel
Who offered themselves willingly with
the people.
Bless the LORD!
10 "Speak, you who ride on white
donkeys,

Who sit in judges' attire,
And who walk along the road.
11 Far from the noise of the archers,
among the watering places,
There they shall recount the righteous
acts of the LORD,
The righteous acts *for* His villagers in
Israel;
Then the people of the LORD shall go
down to the gates.

12 "Awake, awake, Deborah!
Awake, awake, sing a song!
Arise, Barak, and lead your captives
away,
O son of Abinoam!

13 "Then the survivors came down, the
people against the nobles;
The LORD came down for me against
the mighty.
14 From Ephraim *were* those whose roots
were in Amalek.
After you, Benjamin, with your
peoples,
From Machir rulers came down,
And from Zebulun those who bear the
recruiter's staff.
15 And the princes of Issachar *were* with
Deborah;
As Issachar, so *was* Barak
Sent into the valley under his
command;
Among the divisions of Reuben
There were great resolves of heart.
16 Why did you sit among the
sheepfolds,
To hear the pipings for the flocks?
The divisions of Reuben have great
searchings of heart.
17 Gilead stayed beyond the Jordan,
And why did Dan remain on ships?
Asher continued at the seashore,
And stayed by his inlets.
18 Zebulun *is* a people *who* jeopardized
their lives to the point of death,
Naphtali also, on the heights of the
battlefield.

19 "The kings came *and* fought,
Then the kings of Canaan fought
In Taanach, by the waters of Megiddo;
They took no spoils of silver.
20 They fought from the heavens;
The stars from their courses fought
against Sisera.
21 The torrent of Kishon swept them away,
That ancient torrent, the torrent of
Kishon.
O my soul, march on in strength!

22 Then the horses' hooves pounded,
The galloping, galloping of his steeds.
23 'Curse Meroz,' said the angel of the
LORD,
'Curse its inhabitants bitterly,
Because they did not come to the help
of the LORD,
To the help of the LORD against the
mighty.'

24 "Most blessed among women is Jael,
The wife of Heber the Kenite;
Blessed is she among women in tents.
25 He asked for water, she gave milk;
She brought out cream in a lordly
bowl.
26 She stretched her hand to the
tent peg,
Her right hand to the workmen's
hammer;
She pounded Sisera, she pierced his
head,
She split and struck through his
temple.
27 At her feet he sank, he fell, he lay still;
At her feet he sank, he fell;
Where he sank, there he fell dead.

28 "The mother of Sisera looked through
the window,
And cried out through the lattice,
'Why is his chariot *so* long in coming?
Why tarries the clatter of his
chariots?'
29 Her wisest ladies answered her,
Yes, she answered herself,
30 'Are they not finding and dividing the
spoil:
To every man a girl *or* two;
For Sisera, plunder of dyed garments,
Plunder of garments embroidered
and dyed,
Two pieces of dyed embroidery
for the neck of the looter?'

31 "Thus let all Your enemies perish,
O LORD!
But *let* those who love Him *be* like the
sun
When it comes out in full strength."

So the land had rest for forty years.

6 Then the children of Israel did evil in the
sight of the LORD. So the LORD delivered
them into the hand of Midian for seven years,
2and the hand of Midian prevailed against Israel.
Because of the Midianites, the children of Israel made for themselves the dens, the caves,
and the strongholds which *are* in the mountains. 3So it was, whenever Israel had sown,

Midianites would come up; also Amalekites
and the people of the East would come up
against them. [4]Then they would encamp
against them and destroy the produce of the
earth as far as Gaza, and leave no sustenance
for Israel, neither sheep nor ox nor donkey.
[5]For they would come up with their livestock
and their tents, coming in as numerous as
locusts; both they and their camels were without number; and they would enter the land to
destroy it. [6]So Israel was greatly impoverished
because of the Midianites, and the children of
Israel cried out to the LORD.

[7]And it came to pass, when the children of
Israel cried out to the LORD because of the
Midianites, [8]that the LORD sent a prophet to
the children of Israel, who said to them, "Thus
says the LORD God of Israel: 'I brought you up
from Egypt and brought you out of the house of
bondage; [9]and I delivered you out of the hand of
the Egyptians and out of the hand of all who
oppressed you, and drove them out before you

6:8 the LORD sent a prophet. He used prophets in isolated cases before Samuel, the band of prophets Samuel probably founded (1 Sam. 10:5), and later such prophets as Elijah, Elisha, and the writing prophets—major and minor. Here the prophet is sent to bring the divine curse because of their infidelity (v. 10).

and gave you their land. [10]Also I said to you, "I
am the LORD your God; do not fear the gods of
the Amorites, in whose land you dwell." But
you have not obeyed My voice.' "

[11]Now the Angel of the LORD came and sat
under the terebinth tree which *was* in Ophrah,
which *belonged* to Joash the Abiezrite, while
his son Gideon threshed wheat in the winepress, in order to hide *it* from the Midianites.
[12]And the Angel of the LORD appeared to him,
and said to him, "The LORD *is* with you, you
mighty man of valor!"

[13]Gideon said to Him, "O my lord, if the
LORD is with us, why then has all this happened to us? And where *are* all His miracles
which our fathers told us about, saying, 'Did
not the LORD bring us up from Egypt?' But
now the LORD has forsaken us and delivered
us into the hands of the Midianites."

[14]Then the LORD turned to him and said, "Go
in this might of yours, and you shall save Israel from the hand of the Midianites. Have I
not sent you?"

[15]So he said to Him, "O my Lord, how can I
save Israel? Indeed my clan *is* the weakest in
Manasseh, and I *am* the least in my father's
house."

[16]And the LORD said to him, "Surely I will be
with you, and you shall defeat the Midianites
as one man."

[17]Then he said to Him, "If now I have found
favor in Your sight, then show me a sign that
it is You who talk with me. [18]Do not depart
from here, I pray, until I come to You and
bring out my offering and set *it* before You."

And He said, "I will wait until you come back."
[19]So Gideon went in and prepared a young
goat, and unleavened bread from an ephah of
flour. The meat he put in a basket, and he put
the broth in a pot; and he brought *them* out to
Him under the terebinth tree and presented
them. [20]The Angel of God said to him, "Take
the meat and the unleavened bread and lay
them on this rock, and pour out the broth." And
he did so.

[21]Then the Angel of the LORD put out the end
of the staff that *was* in His hand, and touched
the meat and the unleavened bread; and fire
rose out of the rock and consumed the meat
and the unleavened bread. And the Angel of
the LORD departed out of his sight.

[22]Now Gideon perceived that He *was* the
Angel of the LORD. So Gideon said, "Alas, O Lord
GOD! For I have seen the Angel of the LORD face
to face."

[23]Then the LORD said to him, "Peace *be* with
you; do not fear, you shall not die." [24]So Gideon
built an altar there to the LORD, and called it
The-LORD-*Is*-Peace. To this day it *is* still in
Ophrah of the Abiezrites.

[25]Now it came to pass the same night that
the LORD said to him, "Take your father's
young bull, the second bull of seven years old,
and tear down the altar of Baal that your father
has, and cut down the wooden image that *is*
beside it; [26]and build an altar to the LORD your
God on top of this rock in the proper arrangement, and take the second bull and offer a burnt
sacrifice with the wood of the image which you
shall cut down." [27]So Gideon took ten men
from among his servants and did as the LORD
had said to him. But because he feared his
father's household and the men of the city too
much to do *it* by day, he did *it* by night.

[28]And when the men of the city arose early
in the morning, there was the altar of Baal,
torn down; and the wooden image that *was*
beside it was cut down, and the second bull
was being offered on the altar *which had been*
built. [29]So they said to one another, "Who has
done this thing?" And when they had inquired
and asked, they said, "Gideon the son of Joash

has done this thing." [30]Then the men of the
city said to Joash, "Bring out your son, that he
may die, because he has torn down the altar of
Baal, and because he has cut down the wooden
image that *was* beside it."
[31]But Joash said to all who stood against
him, "Would you plead for Baal? Would you
save him? Let the one who would plead for
him be put to death by morning! If he *is* a god,
let him plead for himself, because his altar has
been torn down!" [32]Therefore on that day he
called him Jerubbaal, saying, "Let Baal plead
against him, because he has torn down his
altar."
[33]Then all the Midianites and Amalekites,
the people of the East, gathered together; and
they crossed over and encamped in the Valley
of Jezreel. [34]But the Spirit of the LORD came
upon Gideon; then he blew the trumpet, and
the Abiezrites gathered behind him. [35]And he
sent messengers throughout all Manasseh,
who also gathered behind him. He also sent
messengers to Asher, Zebulun, and Naphtali;
and they came up to meet them.
[36]So Gideon said to God, "If You will save Israel by my hand as You have said— [37]look, I
shall put a fleece of wool on the threshing
floor; if there is dew on the fleece only, and *it
is* dry on all the ground, then I shall know that
You will save Israel by my hand, as You have
said." [38]And it was so. When he rose early the
next morning and squeezed the fleece together, he wrung the dew out of the fleece, a bowl-
ful of water. [39]Then Gideon said to God, "Do
not be angry with me, but let me speak just
once more: Let me test, I pray, just once more
with the fleece; let it now be dry only on the
fleece, but on all the ground let there be dew."
[40]And God did so that night. It was dry on the
fleece only, but there was dew on all the
ground.

Psalm 49:1–9

To the Chief Musician.
A Psalm of the sons of Korah.

Hear this, all peoples;
Give ear, all inhabitants of the world,
2 Both low and high,
Rich and poor together.
3 My mouth shall speak wisdom,
And the meditation of my heart *shall
give* understanding.
4 I will incline my ear to a proverb;
I will disclose my dark saying
on the harp.
5 Why should I fear in the days
of evil,

49:6 Those who trust in their wealth. Mankind's propensity to trust in his own material goods is well attested in Scripture (e.g., Ps. 52:7; Jer. 17:5). Biblically this is exposed as the epitome of stupidity (see Prov. 23:4,5; Luke 12:16ff.).

When the iniquity at my heels
surrounds me?
6 Those who trust in their wealth
And boast in the multitude of their
riches,
7 None *of them* can by any means
redeem *his* brother,
Nor give to God a ransom for him—
8 For the redemption of their souls *is*
costly,
And it shall cease forever—
9 That he should continue to live
eternally,
And not see the Pit.

Proverbs 14:20–21

20 The poor *man* is hated even by his own
neighbor,
But the rich *has* many friends.
21 He who despises his neighbor sins;

14:20 This sad-but-true picture of human nature is not given approvingly, but only as a fact.

But he who has mercy on the poor,
happy *is* he.

Luke 15:1–10

15 Then all the tax collectors and the sinners drew near to Him to hear Him. [2]And
the Pharisees and scribes complained, saying,
"This Man receives sinners and eats with them."
[3]So He spoke this parable to them, saying:
[4]"What man of you, having a hundred
sheep, if he loses one of them, does not leave
the ninety-nine in the wilderness, and go after
the one which is lost until he finds it? [5]And
when he has found *it,* he lays *it* on his shoulders, rejoicing. [6]And when he comes home, he
calls together *his* friends and neighbors, saying to them, 'Rejoice with me, for I have found
my sheep which was lost!' [7]I say to you that
likewise there will be more joy in heaven over

one sinner who repents than over ninety-nine just persons who need no repentance.

[8]"Or what woman, having ten silver coins, if she loses one coin, does not light a lamp, sweep the house, and search carefully until she finds *it?* [9]And when she has found *it*, she calls *her* friends and neighbors together, saying, 'Rejoice with me, for I have found the piece which I lost!' [10]Likewise, I say to you, there is joy in the presence of the angels of God over one sinner who repents."

15:7 joy in heaven. A reference to the joy of God Himself. There was complaining on earth, among the Pharisees (v. 2); but there was great joy with God and among the angels (v. 10). **persons who need no repentance.** I.e., those who think themselves righteous (see 5:32; 16:15; 18:9).

DAY 20: Was it right for Gideon to ask God for signs?

In Judges 6:11, Gideon received a visitation from the "Angel of the LORD." This is identified as "the LORD" Himself (vv. 14,16,23,25,27). See Genesis 16:7–14; 18:1; 32:24–30 for other appearances. Conditions in the land were grim due to the Midianites, which led Gideon to express his frustration that the Lord had forsaken them utterly.

Like Moses (Ex. 33), Gideon desired a sign when the Lord directed him to rise up and lead a deliverance (v. 17). In both incidents, revelation was so rare and wickedness so prevalent that they desired full assurance. God graciously gave it. In vv. 18–23, the fire from God brought the realization of the presence of God to Gideon, filling him with awe and even the fear of death. When he saw the Lord, he knew the Lord had also seen him in his fallenness. Thus he feared the death that sinners should die before Holy God. But God graciously promised life (v. 23).

In vv. 36–40, Gideon's two requests for signs in the fleece should be viewed as weak faith. Even Gideon recognized this when he said, "Do not be angry with me" (v. 39), since God had already specifically promised His presence and victory (vv. 12,14,16). But they were also legitimate requests for confirmation of victory against seemingly impossible odds (6:5; 7:2,12). God nowhere reprimanded Gideon, but was very compassionate in giving what his inadequacy requested. In 7:10–15, God volunteered a sign to boost Gideon's faith.

APRIL 21

Judges 7:1–8:35

7 Then Jerubbaal (that *is,* Gideon) and all the people who *were* with him rose early and encamped beside the well of Harod, so that the camp of the Midianites was on the north side of them by the hill of Moreh in the valley.

[2]And the LORD said to Gideon, "The people who *are* with you *are* too many for Me to give the Midianites into their hands, lest Israel claim glory for itself against Me, saying, 'My own hand has saved me.' [3]Now therefore, proclaim in the hearing of the people, saying, 'Whoever *is* fearful and afraid, let him turn and depart at once from Mount Gilead.'" And twenty-two thousand of the people returned, and ten thousand remained.

[4]But the LORD said to Gideon, "The people *are* still *too* many; bring them down to the water, and I will test them for you there. Then it will be, *that* of whom I say to you, 'This one shall go with you,' the same shall go with you; and of whomever I say to you, 'This one shall not go with you,' the same shall not go." [5]So he brought the people down to the water. And the LORD said to Gideon, "Everyone who laps from the water with his tongue, as a dog laps, you shall set apart by himself; likewise everyone who gets down on his knees to drink." [6]And the number of those who lapped, *putting* their hand to their mouth, was three hundred men; but all the rest of the people got down on their knees to drink water. [7]Then the LORD said to Gideon, "By the three hundred men who lapped I will save you, and deliver the Midianites into your hand. Let all the *other* people go, every man to his place." [8]So the people took provisions and their trumpets in their hands. And he sent away all *the rest of* Israel, every man to his tent, and retained those three hundred men. Now the camp of Midian was below him in the valley.

[9]It happened on the same night that the LORD said to him, "Arise, go down against the camp, for I have delivered it into your hand. [10]But if you are afraid to go down, go down to the camp with Purah your servant, [11]and you shall hear what they say; and afterward your hands shall be strengthened to go down against the camp." Then he went down with

Purah his servant to the outpost of the armed
men who *were* in the camp. [12]Now the
Midianites and Amalekites, all the people of
the East, were lying in the valley as numerous
as locusts; and their camels *were* without number, as the sand by the seashore in multitude.
[13]And when Gideon had come, there was a
man telling a dream to his companion. He
said, "I have had a dream: *To my* surprise, a
loaf of barley bread tumbled into the camp of
Midian; it came to a tent and struck it so that
it fell and overturned, and the tent collapsed."
[14]Then his companion answered and said,
"This *is* nothing else but the sword of Gideon
the son of Joash, a man of Israel! Into his hand
God has delivered Midian and the whole
camp."
[15]And so it was, when Gideon heard the
telling of the dream and its interpretation, that
he worshiped. He returned to the camp of Israel, and said, "Arise, for the LORD has delivered the camp of Midian into your hand."
[16]Then he divided the three hundred men *into*
three companies, and he put a trumpet into
every man's hand, with empty pitchers, and
torches inside the pitchers. [17]And he said to
them, "Look at me and do likewise; watch, and
when I come to the edge of the camp you shall
do as I do: [18]When I blow the trumpet, I and all
who *are* with me, then you also blow the trumpets on every side of the whole camp, and say,
'*The sword of* the LORD and of Gideon!' "

7:18 *The sword of* the LORD and of Gideon!
Here was the power of God in harmony with the obedience of man. Such shouts reminded the enemies that the threat of the sword of Gideon and of God was for real. The impression was one of doom and terror.

[19]So Gideon and the hundred men who *were*
with him came to the outpost of the camp at
the beginning of the middle watch, just as they
had posted the watch; and they blew the trumpets and broke the pitchers that *were* in their
hands. [20]Then the three companies blew the
trumpets and broke the pitchers—they held
the torches in their left hands and the trumpets in their right hands for blowing—and they
cried, "The sword of the LORD and of Gideon!"
[21]And every man stood in his place all around
the camp; and the whole army ran and cried
out and fled. [22]When the three hundred blew
the trumpets, the LORD set every man's sword
against his companion throughout the whole
camp; and the army fled to Beth Acacia,
toward Zererah, as far as the border of Abel
Meholah, by Tabbath.
[23]And the men of Israel gathered together
from Naphtali, Asher, and all Manasseh, and
pursued the Midianites.
[24]Then Gideon sent messengers throughout
all the mountains of Ephraim, saying, "Come
down against the Midianites, and seize from
them the watering places as far as Beth Barah
and the Jordan." Then all the men of Ephraim
gathered together and seized the watering
places as far as Beth Barah and the Jordan.
[25]And they captured two princes of the Midianites, Oreb and Zeeb. They killed Oreb at the
rock of Oreb, and Zeeb they killed at the winepress of Zeeb. They pursued Midian and
brought the heads of Oreb and Zeeb to Gideon
on the other side of the Jordan.

8 Now the men of Ephraim said to him,
"Why have you done this to us by not calling us when you went to fight with the
Midianites?" And they reprimanded him
sharply.
[2]So he said to them, "What have I done now
in comparison with you? *Is* not the gleaning *of
the grapes* of Ephraim better than the vintage
of Abiezer? [3]God has delivered into your
hands the princes of Midian, Oreb and Zeeb.
And what was I able to do in comparison with
you?" Then their anger toward him subsided
when he said that.
[4]When Gideon came to the Jordan, he and
the three hundred men who *were* with him
crossed over, exhausted but still in pursuit.
[5]Then he said to the men of Succoth, "Please
give loaves of bread to the people who follow
me, for they are exhausted, and I am pursuing
Zebah and Zalmunna, kings of Midian."
[6]And the leaders of Succoth said, "*Are* the
hands of Zebah and Zalmunna now in your
hand, that we should give bread to your army?"
[7]So Gideon said, "For this cause, when the
LORD has delivered Zebah and Zalmunna into
my hand, then I will tear your flesh with the
thorns of the wilderness and with briers!"
[8]Then he went up from there to Penuel and
spoke to them in the same way. And the men
of Penuel answered him as the men of
Succoth had answered. [9]So he also spoke to
the men of Penuel, saying, "When I come
back in peace, I will tear down this tower!"
[10]Now Zebah and Zalmunna *were* at Karkor,
and their armies with them, about fifteen thousand, all who were left of all the army of the
people of the East; for one hundred and twenty
thousand men who drew the sword had fallen.

11 Then Gideon went up by the road of those
who dwell in tents on the east of Nobah and
Jogbehah; and he attacked the army while the
camp felt secure. 12 When Zebah and Zalmunna
fled, he pursued them; and he took the two
kings of Midian, Zebah and Zalmunna, and
routed the whole army.

13 Then Gideon the son of Joash returned
from battle, from the Ascent of Heres. 14 And
he caught a young man of the men of Succoth
and interrogated him; and he wrote down for
him the leaders of Succoth and its elders,
seventy-seven men. 15 Then he came to the
men of Succoth and said, "Here are Zebah and
Zalmunna, about whom you ridiculed me, saying, '*Are* the hands of Zebah and Zalmunna
now in your hand, that we should give bread
to your weary men?' " 16 And he took the elders
of the city, and thorns of the wilderness and
briers, and with them he taught the men of
Succoth. 17 Then he tore down the tower of
Penuel and killed the men of the city.

18 And he said to Zebah and Zalmunna,
"What kind of men *were they* whom you killed
at Tabor?"

So they answered, "As you *are,* so *were*
they; each one resembled the son of a king."

19 Then he said, "They *were* my brothers, the
sons of my mother. *As* the LORD lives, if you had
let them live, I would not kill you." 20 And he said
to Jether his firstborn, "Rise, kill them!" But the
youth would not draw his sword; for he was
afraid, because he *was* still a youth.

21 So Zebah and Zalmunna said, "Rise yourself, and kill us; for as a man *is, so is* his
strength." So Gideon arose and killed Zebah
and Zalmunna, and took the crescent ornaments that *were* on their camels' necks.

22 Then the men of Israel said to Gideon,
"Rule over us, both you and your son, and
your grandson also; for you have delivered us
from the hand of Midian."

23 But Gideon said to them, "I will not rule
over you, nor shall my son rule over you; the
LORD shall rule over you." 24 Then Gideon said
to them, "I would like to make a request of
you, that each of you would give me the earrings from his plunder." For they had golden
earrings, because they *were* Ishmaelites.

25 So they answered, "We will gladly give
them." And they spread out a garment, and
each man threw into it the earrings from his
plunder. 26 Now the weight of the gold earrings
that he requested was one thousand seven
hundred *shekels* of gold, besides the crescent
ornaments, pendants, and purple robes which
were on the kings of Midian, and besides the
chains that *were* around their camels' necks.

8:24–27 Gideon made…an ephod. This was certainly a sad end to Gideon's influence as he, perhaps in an expression of pride, sought to lift himself up in the eyes of the people. Gideon intended nothing more than to make a breastplate as David did (1 Chr. 15:27) to indicate civil, not priestly, rule. It was never intended to set up idolatrous worship, but to be a symbol of civil power. That no evil was intended can be noted from the subduing of Midian (v. 28), quietness from wars (v. 28), and the fact that idolatry came after Gideon's death (v. 33), as well as the commendation of Gideon (v. 35).

27 Then Gideon made it into an ephod and set it
up in his city, Ophrah. And all Israel played
the harlot with it there. It became a snare to
Gideon and to his house.

28 Thus Midian was subdued before the children of Israel, so that they lifted their heads
no more. And the country was quiet for forty
years in the days of Gideon.

29 Then Jerubbaal the son of Joash went and
dwelt in his own house. 30 Gideon had seventy
sons who were his own offspring, for he had
many wives. 31 And his concubine who *was* in
Shechem also bore him a son, whose name he
called Abimelech. 32 Now Gideon the son of
Joash died at a good old age, and was buried in
the tomb of Joash his father, in Ophrah of the
Abiezrites.

33 So it was, as soon as Gideon was dead, that
the children of Israel again played the harlot
with the Baals, and made Baal-Berith their
god. 34 Thus the children of Israel did not
remember the LORD their God, who had delivered them from the hands of all their enemies
on every side; 35 nor did they show kindness to
the house of Jerubbaal (Gideon) in accordance with the good he had done for Israel.

Psalm 49:10–20

10 For he sees wise men die;
Likewise the fool and the senseless
person perish,
And leave their wealth to others.
11 Their inner thought *is that* their houses
will last forever,
Their dwelling places to all
generations;
They call *their* lands after their own
names.
12 Nevertheless man, *though* in honor,
does not remain;

He is like the beasts *that* perish.

13 This is the way of those who *are* foolish,
And of their posterity who approve
their sayings. Selah
14 Like sheep they are laid in the grave;
Death shall feed on them;
The upright shall have dominion over
them in the morning;
And their beauty shall be consumed in
the grave, far from their dwelling.
15 But God will redeem my soul from the
power of the grave,
For He shall receive me. Selah

49:15 But God will redeem my soul...He shall receive me. This is one of the greatest affirmations of confidence in God in the Psalms. Although the faithless person cannot buy his way out of death (v. 7ff.), the faithful one is redeemed by the only Redeemer, God Himself. (On the significance of the word "receive," see Gen. 5:24; 2 Kin. 2:10; Ps. 73:24; Heb. 11:5.) So in v. 15 the psalmist expresses his confidence in God, that He would raise him to eternal life.

16 Do not be afraid when one becomes rich,
When the glory of his house is
increased;
17 For when he dies he shall carry
nothing away;
His glory shall not descend after him.
18 Though while he lives he blesses
himself
(For *men* will praise you when you do
well for yourself),
19 He shall go to the generation of his
fathers;
They shall never see light.
20 A man *who is* in honor, yet does not
understand,
Is like the beasts *that* perish.

Proverbs 14:22–24

22 Do they not go astray who devise evil?
But mercy and truth *belong* to those
who devise good.

23 In all labor there is profit,
But idle chatter *leads* only to poverty.

24 The crown of the wise is their riches,
But the foolishness of fools *is* folly.

Luke 15:11–32

11Then He said: "A certain man had two
sons. 12And the younger of them said to *his*
father, 'Father, give me the portion of goods
that falls *to me.*' So he divided to them *his*
livelihood. 13And not many days after, the
younger son gathered all together, journeyed
to a far country, and there wasted his possessions with prodigal living. 14But when he had
spent all, there arose a severe famine in that
land, and he began to be in want. 15Then he
went and joined himself to a citizen of that
country, and he sent him into his fields to feed
swine. 16And he would gladly have filled his
stomach with the pods that the swine ate, and
no one gave him *anything.*
17"But when he came to himself, he said,
'How many of my father's hired servants have
bread enough and to spare, and I perish with
hunger! 18I will arise and go to my father, and
will say to him, "Father, I have sinned against
heaven and before you, 19and I am no longer
worthy to be called your son. Make me like
one of your hired servants." '
20"And he arose and came to his father. But
when he was still a great way off, his father
saw him and had compassion, and ran and fell
on his neck and kissed him. 21And the son said
to him, 'Father, I have sinned against heaven
and in your sight, and am no longer worthy to
be called your son.'
22"But the father said to his servants, 'Bring
out the best robe and put *it* on him, and put a
ring on his hand and sandals on *his* feet. 23And
bring the fatted calf here and kill *it,* and let us
eat and be merry; 24for this my son was dead
and is alive again; he was lost and is found.'
And they began to be merry.
25"Now his older son was in the field. And as
he came and drew near to the house, he heard
music and dancing. 26So he called one of the
servants and asked what these things meant.

15:29 I never transgressed your commandment at any time. Unlikely, given the boy's obvious contempt for his father, shown by his refusal to participate in the father's great joy. This statement reveals the telltale problem with all religious hypocrites. They will not recognize their sin and repent. The elder son's comment reeks of the same spirit as the words of the Pharisee in 18:11. **you never gave me a young goat.** All those years of service to the father appear to have been motivated too much by concern for what he could get for himself. This son's self-righteous behavior was more socially acceptable than the younger brother's debauchery, but it was equally dishonoring to the father—and called for repentance.

27And he said to him, 'Your brother has come,
and because he has received him safe and
sound, your father has killed the fatted calf.'
28"But he was angry and would not go in.
Therefore his father came out and pleaded with
him. 29So he answered and said to *his* father,
'Lo, these many years I have been serving you;
I never transgressed your commandment at
any time; and yet you never gave me a young
goat, that I might make merry with my
friends. 30But as soon as this son of yours
came, who has devoured your livelihood with
harlots, you killed the fatted calf for him.'
31"And he said to him, 'Son, you are always
with me, and all that I have is yours. 32It was
right that we should make merry and be glad,
for your brother was dead and is alive again,
and was lost and is found.' "

DAY 21: What is the main feature of the parable of the prodigal son?

The parable in Luke 15:11–32, unlike most parables, has more than one lesson. The prodigal is an example of sound repentance. The elder brother illustrates the wickedness of the Pharisees' self-righteousness, prejudice, and indifference toward repenting sinners. And the father pictures God, eager to forgive and longing for the return of the sinner. The main feature, however, is the joy of God, the celebrations that fill heaven when a sinner repents.

For the son to demand "the portion of goods that falls to me" (v. 12) is tantamount to saying he wished his father were dead. He was not entitled to any inheritance while his father still lived. Yet the father graciously fulfilled the request, giving him his full portion, which would have been one-third of the entire estate—because the right of the firstborn (Deut. 21:17) gave the elder brother a double portion. This act pictures all sinners (related to God the Father by creation), who waste their potential privileges and refuse any relationship with Him, choosing instead a life of sinful self-indulgence. The Greek word for "prodigal" means "dissolute" and conveys the idea of an utterly debauched lifestyle. "To feed swine" (v. 15) was the worst sort of degradation imaginable for Jesus' Jewish audience; swine were the worst sort of unclean animals. His situation could hardly have been more desperate.

Nevertheless, when "his father saw him [he] had compassion, and ran and fell on his neck and kissed him" (v. 20). Clearly, the father had been waiting and looking for his son's return. The father's eagerness and joy at his son's return is unmistakable. This is the magnificent attribute of God that sets Him apart from all the false gods invented by men and demons. He is not indifferent or hostile, but a Savior by nature, longing to see sinners repent and rejoicing when they do. From Genesis 3:8 to Revelation 22:17, from the Fall to the Consummation, God has been and will be seeking to save sinners, and rejoices each time one repents and is converted.

APRIL 22

Judges 9:1–10:18

9 Then Abimelech the son of Jerubbaal
went to Shechem, to his mother's brothers, and spoke with them and with all the family of the house of his mother's father, saying,
2"Please speak in the hearing of all the men of
Shechem: 'Which is better for you, that all seventy of the sons of Jerubbaal reign over you,
or that one reign over you?' Remember that I
am your own flesh and bone."
3And his mother's brothers spoke all these
words concerning him in the hearing of all the
men of Shechem; and their heart was inclined
to follow Abimelech, for they said, "He is our
brother." 4So they gave him seventy *shekels* of
silver from the temple of Baal-Berith, with
which Abimelech hired worthless and reckless men; and they followed him. 5Then he
went to his father's house at Ophrah and killed
his brothers, the seventy sons of Jerubbaal, on
one stone. But Jotham the youngest son of
Jerubbaal was left, because he hid himself.
6And all the men of Shechem gathered together, all of Beth Millo, and they went and made
Abimelech king beside the terebinth tree at
the pillar that *was* in Shechem.
7Now when they told Jotham, he went and
stood on top of Mount Gerizim, and lifted his
voice and cried out. And he said to them:

"Listen to me, you men of Shechem,
That God may listen to you!

8 "The trees once went forth to anoint a
king over them.
And they said to the olive tree,
'Reign over us!'
9 But the olive tree said to them,
'Should I cease giving my oil,
With which they honor God and men,
And go to sway over trees?'

10 "Then the trees said to the fig tree,
'You come *and* reign over us!'
11 But the fig tree said to them,
'Should I cease my sweetness and my good fruit,
And go to sway over trees?'

12 "Then the trees said to the vine,
'You come *and* reign over us!'
13 But the vine said to them,
'Should I cease my new wine,
Which cheers *both* God and men,
And go to sway over trees?'

14 "Then all the trees said to the bramble,
'You come *and* reign over us!'
15 And the bramble said to the trees,
'If in truth you anoint me as king over you,
Then come *and* take shelter in my shade;
But if not, let fire come out of the bramble
And devour the cedars of Lebanon!'

16 "Now therefore, if you have acted in truth
and sincerity in making Abimelech king, and if
you have dealt well with Jerubbaal and his
house, and have done to him as he deserves—
17 for my father fought for you, risked his life,
and delivered you out of the hand of Midian;
18 but you have risen up against my father's
house this day, and killed his seventy sons on
one stone, and made Abimelech, the son of his
female servant, king over the men of Shechem,
because he is your brother— 19 if then you have
acted in truth and sincerity with Jerubbaal and
with his house this day, *then* rejoice in
Abimelech, and let him also rejoice in you.
20 But if not, let fire come from Abimelech and
devour the men of Shechem and Beth Millo;
and let fire come from the men of Shechem
and from Beth Millo and devour Abimelech!"
21 And Jotham ran away and fled; and he went
to Beer and dwelt there, for fear of Abimelech
his brother.

22 After Abimelech had reigned over Israel
three years, 23 God sent a spirit of ill will
between Abimelech and the men of Shechem;
and the men of Shechem dealt treacherously
with Abimelech, 24 that the crime *done* to the
seventy sons of Jerubbaal might be settled
and their blood be laid on Abimelech their
brother, who killed them, and on the men of
Shechem, who aided him in the killing of his
brothers. 25 And the men of Shechem set men in
ambush against him on the tops of the mountains, and they robbed all who passed by them
along that way; and it was told Abimelech.

26 Now Gaal the son of Ebed came with his
brothers and went over to Shechem; and the
men of Shechem put their confidence in him.
27 So they went out into the fields, and gathered
grapes from their vineyards and trod *them,* and
made merry. And they went into the house of
their god, and ate and drank, and cursed
Abimelech. 28 Then Gaal the son of Ebed said,
"Who *is* Abimelech, and who *is* Shechem, that
we should serve him? *Is he* not the son of
Jerubbaal, and *is not* Zebul his officer? Serve
the men of Hamor the father of Shechem; but
why should we serve him? 29 If only this people
were under my authority! Then I would
remove Abimelech." So he said to Abimelech,
"Increase your army and come out!"

30 When Zebul, the ruler of the city, heard
the words of Gaal the son of Ebed, his anger
was aroused. 31 And he sent messengers to
Abimelech secretly, saying, "Take note! Gaal
the son of Ebed and his brothers have come to
Shechem; and here they are, fortifying the
city against you. 32 Now therefore, get up by
night, you and the people who *are* with you,
and lie in wait in the field. 33 And it shall be, as
soon as the sun is up in the morning, *that* you
shall rise early and rush upon the city; and
when he and the people who are with him
come out against you, you may then do to
them as you find opportunity."

34 So Abimelech and all the people who *were*
with him rose by night, and lay in wait against
Shechem in four companies. 35 When Gaal the
son of Ebed went out and stood in the entrance
to the city gate, Abimelech and the people who
were with him rose from lying in wait. 36 And
when Gaal saw the people, he said to Zebul,
"Look, people are coming down from the tops
of the mountains!"

But Zebul said to him, "You see the shadows of the mountains as *if they were* men."

37 So Gaal spoke again and said, "See, people
are coming down from the center of the land,
and another company is coming from the Diviners' Terebinth Tree."

38 Then Zebul said to him, "Where indeed *is*
your mouth now, with which you said, 'Who is
Abimelech, that we should serve him?' *Are* not
these the people whom you despised? Go out,
if you will, and fight with them now."

39 So Gaal went out, leading the men of
Shechem, and fought with Abimelech. 40 And
Abimelech chased him, and he fled from him;
and many fell wounded, to the *very* entrance of
the gate. 41 Then Abimelech dwelt at Arumah,
and Zebul drove out Gaal and his brothers, so
that they would not dwell in Shechem.

42 And it came about on the next day that the

people went out into the field, and they told
Abimelech. 43So he took his people, divided
them into three companies, and lay in wait in
the field. And he looked, and there were the
people, coming out of the city; and he rose
against them and attacked them. 44Then
Abimelech and the company that *was* with
him rushed forward and stood at the entrance
of the gate of the city; and the *other* two companies rushed upon all who *were* in the fields
and killed them. 45So Abimelech fought against
the city all that day; he took the city and killed
the people who *were* in it; and he demolished
the city and sowed it with salt.

46Now when all the men of the tower of
Shechem had heard *that,* they entered the
stronghold of the temple of the god Berith.
47And it was told Abimelech that all the men of
the tower of Shechem were gathered together.
48Then Abimelech went up to Mount Zalmon,
he and all the people who *were* with him. And
Abimelech took an ax in his hand and cut down
a bough from the trees, and took it and laid *it*
on his shoulder; then he said to the people
who were with him, "What you have seen me
do, make haste *and* do as I *have done.*" 49So
each of the people likewise cut down his own
bough and followed Abimelech, put *them*
against the stronghold, and set the stronghold
on fire above them, so that all the people of the
tower of Shechem died, about a thousand men
and women.

50Then Abimelech went to Thebez, and he
encamped against Thebez and took it. 51But
there was a strong tower in the city, and all the
men and women—all the people of the city—
fled there and shut themselves in; then they
went up to the top of the tower. 52So Abimelech
came as far as the tower and fought against it;
and he drew near the door of the tower to burn
it with fire. 53But a certain woman dropped an
upper millstone on Abimelech's head and
crushed his skull. 54Then he called quickly to
the young man, his armorbearer, and said to
him, "Draw your sword and kill me, lest men
say of me, 'A woman killed him.'" So his
young man thrust him through, and he died.
55And when the men of Israel saw that
Abimelech was dead, they departed, every
man to his place.

56Thus God repaid the wickedness of
Abimelech, which he had done to his father by
killing his seventy brothers. 57And all the evil
of the men of Shechem God returned on their
own heads, and on them came the curse of
Jotham the son of Jerubbaal.

10 After Abimelech there arose to save Israel Tola the son of Puah, the son of
Dodo, a man of Issachar; and he dwelt in
Shamir in the mountains of Ephraim. 2He
judged Israel twenty-three years; and he died
and was buried in Shamir.

3After him arose Jair, a Gileadite; and he
judged Israel twenty-two years. 4Now he had
thirty sons who rode on thirty donkeys; they
also had thirty towns, which are called
"Havoth Jair" to this day, which *are* in the land
of Gilead. 5And Jair died and was buried in
Camon.

6Then the children of Israel again did evil in
the sight of the LORD, and served the Baals
and the Ashtoreths, the gods of Syria, the
gods of Sidon, the gods of Moab, the gods of
the people of Ammon, and the gods of the
Philistines; and they forsook the LORD and did
not serve Him. 7So the anger of the LORD was
hot against Israel; and He sold them into the
hands of the Philistines and into the hands of
the people of Ammon. 8From that year they harassed and oppressed the children of Israel for
eighteen years—all the children of Israel who
were on the other side of the Jordan in the land
of the Amorites, in Gilead. 9Moreover the people of Ammon crossed over the Jordan to fight
against Judah also, against Benjamin, and
against the house of Ephraim, so that Israel
was severely distressed.

10And the children of Israel cried out to the
LORD, saying, "We have sinned against You,
because we have both forsaken our God and
served the Baals!"

11So the LORD said to the children of Israel,
"*Did I* not *deliver you* from the Egyptians and
from the Amorites and from the people of
Ammon and from the Philistines? 12Also the
Sidonians and Amalekites and Maonites oppressed you; and you cried out to Me, and I
delivered you from their hand. 13Yet you have
forsaken Me and served other gods. Therefore
I will deliver you no more. 14Go and cry out to
the gods which you have chosen; let them
deliver you in your time of distress."

15And the children of Israel said to the LORD,
"We have sinned! Do to us whatever seems best
to You; only deliver us this day, we pray." 16So
they put away the foreign gods from among
them and served the LORD. And His soul could
no longer endure the misery of Israel.

17Then the people of Ammon gathered
together and encamped in Gilead. And the children of Israel assembled together and
encamped in Mizpah. 18And the people, the
leaders of Gilead, said to one another, "Who *is*
the man who will begin the fight against the
people of Ammon? He shall be head over all
the inhabitants of Gilead."

Psalm 50:1–6

A Psalm of Asaph.

The Mighty One, God the LORD,
Has spoken and called the earth
From the rising of the sun to its going
down.

50:1 The Mighty One, God the LORD. The Divine Judge is introduced with three significant Old Testament names. The first two are the short and longer forms of the most common word for "God" in the Old Testament, and the third is the name for Israel's God par excellence, i.e., Yahweh. **From the rising of the sun to its going down.** A common Old Testament idiom conveying from east to west, i.e., all over the planet.

2 Out of Zion, the perfection of beauty,
God will shine forth.
3 Our God shall come, and shall not
keep silent;
A fire shall devour before Him,
And it shall be very tempestuous all
around Him.
4 He shall call to the heavens from
above,
And to the earth, that He may judge
His people:
5 "Gather My saints together to Me,
Those who have made a covenant with
Me by sacrifice."
6 Let the heavens declare His
righteousness,
For God Himself *is* Judge. Selah

Proverbs 14:25–27

25 A true witness delivers souls,
But a deceitful *witness* speaks lies.
26 In the fear of the LORD *there is* strong
confidence,
And His children will have a place of
refuge.
27 The fear of the LORD *is* a fountain of
life,
To turn *one* away from the snares of
death.

Luke 16:1–31

16 He also said to His disciples: "There was
a certain rich man who had a steward,
and an accusation was brought to him that this
man was wasting his goods. 2 So he called him
and said to him, 'What is this I hear about you?

16:13 You cannot serve God and mammon. Many of the Pharisees taught that devotion to money and devotion to God were perfectly compatible (v. 14). This went hand-in-hand with the commonly held notion that earthly riches signified divine blessing. Rich people were therefore regarded as God's favorites. While not condemning wealth per se, Christ denounced both love of wealth and devotion to mammon.

16:15 justify yourselves. The Pharisees' belief was that their own goodness was what justified them (see Rom. 10:3). This is the very definition of "self-righteousness." But, as Jesus suggested, their righteousness was flawed, being an external veneer only. That might be enough to justify them before men, but not before God, because He knew their hearts. He repeatedly exposed their habit of seeking the approval of people (see Matt. 6:2,5,16; 23:28).

Give an account of your stewardship, for you
can no longer be steward.'
3 "Then the steward said within himself,
'What shall I do? For my master is taking the
stewardship away from me. I cannot dig; I am
ashamed to beg. 4 I have resolved what to do,
that when I am put out of the stewardship, they
may receive me into their houses.'
5 "So he called every one of his master's
debtors to *him,* and said to the first, 'How much
do you owe my master?' 6 And he said, 'A hundred measures of oil.' So he said to him, 'Take
your bill, and sit down quickly and write fifty.'
7 Then he said to another, 'And how much do
you owe?' So he said, 'A hundred measures of
wheat.' And he said to him, 'Take your bill, and
write eighty.' 8 So the master commended the
unjust steward because he had dealt shrewdly.
For the sons of this world are more shrewd in
their generation than the sons of light.
9 "And I say to you, make friends for yourselves by unrighteous mammon, that when
you fail, they may receive you into an everlasting home. 10 He who *is* faithful in *what is* least
is faithful also in much; and he who is unjust
in *what is* least is unjust also in much. 11 Therefore if you have not been faithful in the
unrighteous mammon, who will commit to
your trust the true *riches?* 12 And if you have
not been faithful in what is another man's, who
will give you what is your own?
13 "No servant can serve two masters; for
either he will hate the one and love the other,

or else he will be loyal to the one and despise the
other. You cannot serve God and mammon."
14 Now the Pharisees, who were lovers of
money, also heard all these things, and they
derided Him. 15 And He said to them, "You are
those who justify yourselves before men, but
God knows your hearts. For what is highly
esteemed among men is an abomination in the
sight of God.
16 "The law and the prophets *were* until John.
Since that time the kingdom of God has been
preached, and everyone is pressing into it.
17 And it is easier for heaven and earth to pass
away than for one tittle of the law to fail.
18 "Whoever divorces his wife and marries
another commits adultery; and whoever marries her who is divorced from *her* husband
commits adultery.
19 "There was a certain rich man who was
clothed in purple and fine linen and fared sumptuously every day. 20 But there was a certain beggar named Lazarus, full of sores, who was laid at
his gate, 21 desiring to be fed with the crumbs
which fell from the rich man's table. Moreover
the dogs came and licked his sores. 22 So it was
that the beggar died, and was carried by the
angels to Abraham's bosom. The rich man also
died and was buried. 23 And being in torments in
Hades, he lifted up his eyes and saw Abraham
afar off, and Lazarus in his bosom.
24 "Then he cried and said, 'Father Abraham,
have mercy on me, and send Lazarus that he
may dip the tip of his finger in water and cool
my tongue; for I am tormented in this flame.'

16:31 neither will they be persuaded. This speaks powerfully of the singular sufficiency of Scripture to overcome unbelief. The gospel itself is the power of God unto salvation (Rom. 1:16). Since unbelief is at heart a moral rather than an intellectual problem, no amount of evidences will ever turn unbelief to faith. But the revealed Word of God has inherent power to do so (see John 6:63; Heb. 4:12; James 1:18; 1 Pet. 1:23).

25 But Abraham said, 'Son, remember that in
your lifetime you received your good things,
and likewise Lazarus evil things; but now he is
comforted and you are tormented. 26 And
besides all this, between us and you there is a
great gulf fixed, so that those who want to
pass from here to you cannot, nor can those
from there pass to us.'
27 "Then he said, 'I beg you therefore, father,
that you would send him to my father's house,
28 for I have five brothers, that he may testify to
them, lest they also come to this place of torment.' 29 Abraham said to him, 'They have Moses and the prophets; let them hear them.'
30 And he said, 'No, father Abraham; but if one
goes to them from the dead, they will repent.'
31 But he said to him, 'If they do not hear Moses and the prophets, neither will they be persuaded though one rise from the dead.' "

DAY 22: Why would the parable of the rich man scandalize the Pharisees?

The parable of the rich man and Lazarus (Luke 16:19–31) was employed in the same fashion as all Christ's parables, to teach a lesson, in this case for the benefit of the Pharisees. The mention of table scraps, sores, and dogs all made this poor man appear odious in the eyes of the Pharisees (v. 21). They were inclined to see all such things as proof of divine disfavor.

The idea was that Lazarus was given a place of high honor, reclining next to Abraham at the heavenly banquet, "Abraham's bosom" (v. 22). This same expression (found only here in Scripture) was used in the Talmud as a figure for heaven. Yet the rich man was "in Hades" (v. 23). The suggestion that a rich man would be excluded from heaven would have scandalized the Pharisees. Especially galling was the idea that a beggar who ate scraps from his table was granted the place of honor next to Abraham.

"Hades" was the Greek term for the abode of the dead. In the Greek Old Testament, it was used to translate the Hebrew *Sheol,* which referred to the realm of the dead in general, without necessarily distinguishing between righteous or unrighteous souls. However, in New Testament usage, "Hades" always refers to the place of the wicked prior to final judgment in hell. The imagery Jesus used fit the erroneous common rabbinical idea that Sheol had two parts, one for the souls of the righteous and the other for the souls of the wicked—separated by an impassable gulf. But there is no reason to suppose, as some do, that "Abraham's bosom" spoke of a temporary prison for the souls of Old Testament saints, who were brought to heaven only after He had actually atoned for their sins. Scripture consistently teaches that the spirits of the righteous dead go immediately into the presence of God (see 23:43; 2 Cor. 5:8; Phil. 1:23). And the presence of Moses and Elijah on the Mount of Transfiguration (9:30) belies the notion that they were confined in a compartment of Sheol until Christ finished His work.

APRIL 23

Judges 11:1–12:15

11 Now Jephthah the Gileadite was a mighty
man of valor, but he *was* the son of a harlot; and Gilead begot Jephthah. 2Gilead's wife
bore sons; and when his wife's sons grew up,
they drove Jephthah out, and said to him,
"You shall have no inheritance in our father's
house, for you *are* the son of another woman."
3Then Jephthah fled from his brothers and
dwelt in the land of Tob; and worthless men
banded together with Jephthah and went out
raiding with him.

4It came to pass after a time that the people
of Ammon made war against Israel. 5And so it
was, when the people of Ammon made war
against Israel, that the elders of Gilead went to
get Jephthah from the land of Tob. 6Then they
said to Jephthah, "Come and be our commander, that we may fight against the people
of Ammon."

7So Jephthah said to the elders of Gilead,
"Did you not hate me, and expel me from my
father's house? Why have you come to me
now when you are in distress?"

8And the elders of Gilead said to Jephthah,
"That is why we have turned again to you now,
that you may go with us and fight against the
people of Ammon, and be our head over all the
inhabitants of Gilead."

9So Jephthah said to the elders of Gilead, "If
you take me back home to fight against the
people of Ammon, and the LORD delivers them
to me, shall I be your head?"

10And the elders of Gilead said to Jephthah,
"The LORD will be a witness between us, if we
do not do according to your words." 11Then
Jephthah went with the elders of Gilead, and
the people made him head and commander
over them; and Jephthah spoke all his words
before the LORD in Mizpah.

12Now Jephthah sent messengers to the
king of the people of Ammon, saying, "What
do you have against me, that you have come to
fight against me in my land?"

13And the king of the people of Ammon
answered the messengers of Jephthah, "Because Israel took away my land when they
came up out of Egypt, from the Arnon as far as
the Jabbok, and to the Jordan. Now therefore,
restore those *lands* peaceably."

14So Jephthah again sent messengers to the
king of the people of Ammon, 15and said to
him, "Thus says Jephthah: 'Israel did not take
away the land of Moab, nor the land of the
people of Ammon; 16for when Israel came up
from Egypt, they walked through the wilderness as far as the Red Sea and came to Kadesh.
17Then Israel sent messengers to the king of
Edom, saying, "Please let me pass through
your land." But the king of Edom would not
heed. And in like manner they sent to the king
of Moab, but he would not *consent.* So Israel
remained in Kadesh. 18And they went along
through the wilderness and bypassed the land
of Edom and the land of Moab, came to the
east side of the land of Moab, and encamped
on the other side of the Arnon. But they did
not enter the border of Moab, for the Arnon
was the border of Moab. 19Then Israel sent
messengers to Sihon king of the Amorites,
king of Heshbon; and Israel said to him, "Please
let us pass through your land into our place."
20But Sihon did not trust Israel to pass through
his territory. So Sihon gathered all his people
together, encamped in Jahaz, and fought
against Israel. 21And the LORD God of Israel delivered Sihon and all his people into the hand
of Israel, and they defeated them. Thus Israel
gained possession of all the land of the
Amorites, who inhabited that country. 22They
took possession of all the territory of the
Amorites, from the Arnon to the Jabbok and
from the wilderness to the Jordan.

23'And now the LORD God of Israel has dispossessed the Amorites from before His people
Israel; should you then possess it? 24Will you
not possess whatever Chemosh your god gives
you to possess? So whatever the LORD our God
takes possession of before us, we will possess.
25And now, *are* you any better than Balak the
son of Zippor, king of Moab? Did he ever
strive against Israel? Did he ever fight against
them? 26While Israel dwelt in Heshbon and its
villages, in Aroer and its villages, and in all the
cities along the banks of the Arnon, for three
hundred years, why did you not recover *them*
within that time? 27Therefore I have not sinned
against you, but you wronged me by fighting
against me. May the LORD, the Judge, render
judgment this day between the children of Israel and the people of Ammon.' " 28However,
the king of the people of Ammon did not heed
the words which Jephthah sent him.

29Then the Spirit of the LORD came upon
Jephthah, and he passed through Gilead and
Manasseh, and passed through Mizpah of
Gilead; and from Mizpah of Gilead he
advanced *toward* the people of Ammon. 30And
Jephthah made a vow to the LORD, and said, "If
You will indeed deliver the people of Ammon
into my hands, 31then it will be that whatever

11:31 I will offer it. Some interpreters reason that Jephthah offered his daughter as a living sacrifice in perpetual virginity. With this idea, v. 31 is made to mean "shall surely be the LORD's" or "I will offer it up as a burnt offering." The view sees only perpetual virginity in vv. 37–40 and rejects his offering a human sacrifice as being against God's revealed will (Deut. 12:31). On the other hand, since he was 1) beyond the Jordan, 2) far from the tabernacle, 3) a hypocrite in religious devotion, 4) familiar with human sacrifice among other nations, 5) influenced by such superstition, and 6) wanting victory badly, he likely meant a burnt offering. The translation in v. 31 is "and," not "or." His act came in an era of bizarre things, even inconsistency by leaders whom God otherwise empowered (see Gideon in 8:27).

comes out of the doors of my house to meet
me, when I return in peace from the people of
Ammon, shall surely be the LORD's, and I will
offer it up as a burnt offering."
32 So Jephthah advanced toward the people
of Ammon to fight against them, and the LORD
delivered them into his hands. 33 And he defeated them from Aroer as far as Minnith—
twenty cities—and to Abel Keramim, with a very
great slaughter. Thus the people of Ammon
were subdued before the children of Israel.
34 When Jephthah came to his house at
Mizpah, there was his daughter, coming out to
meet him with timbrels and dancing; and she
was his only child. Besides her he had neither
son nor daughter. 35 And it came to pass, when
he saw her, that he tore his clothes, and said,
"Alas, my daughter! You have brought me
very low! You are among those who trouble
me! For I have given my word to the LORD, and
I cannot go back on it."
36 So she said to him, "My father, *if* you have
given your word to the LORD, do to me according to what has gone out of your mouth,
because the LORD has avenged you of your
enemies, the people of Ammon." 37 Then she
said to her father, "Let this thing be done for
me: let me alone for two months, that I may go
and wander on the mountains and bewail my
virginity, my friends and I."
38 So he said, "Go." And he sent her away *for*
two months; and she went with her friends,
and bewailed her virginity on the mountains.
39 And it was so at the end of two months that
she returned to her father, and he carried out
his vow with her which he had vowed. She
knew no man.
And it became a custom in Israel 40 *that* the
daughters of Israel went four days each year to
lament the daughter of Jephthah the Gileadite.

12 Then the men of Ephraim gathered
together, crossed over toward Zaphon,
and said to Jephthah, "Why did you cross over
to fight against the people of Ammon, and did
not call us to go with you? We will burn your
house down on you with fire!"
2 And Jephthah said to them, "My people and
I were in a great struggle with the people of
Ammon; and when I called you, you did not
deliver me out of their hands. 3 So when I saw
that you would not deliver *me,* I took my life in
my hands and crossed over against the people
of Ammon; and the LORD delivered them into
my hand. Why then have you come up to me
this day to fight against me?" 4 Now Jephthah
gathered together all the men of Gilead and
fought against Ephraim. And the men of
Gilead defeated Ephraim, because they said,
"You Gileadites *are* fugitives of Ephraim
among the Ephraimites *and* among the
Manassites." 5 The Gileadites seized the fords
of the Jordan before the Ephraimites *arrived.*
And when *any* Ephraimite who escaped said,
"Let me cross over," the men of Gilead would
say to him, "*Are* you an Ephraimite?" If he
said, "No," 6 then they would say to him, "Then
say, 'Shibboleth'!" And he would say,
"Sibboleth," for he could not pronounce *it*
right. Then they would take him and kill him
at the fords of the Jordan. There fell at that
time forty-two thousand Ephraimites.
7 And Jephthah judged Israel six years. Then
Jephthah the Gileadite died and was buried
among the cities of Gilead.
8 After him, Ibzan of Bethlehem judged Israel. 9 He had thirty sons. And he gave away
thirty daughters in marriage, and brought in
thirty daughters from elsewhere for his sons.
He judged Israel seven years. 10 Then Ibzan
died and was buried at Bethlehem.
11 After him, Elon the Zebulunite judged Israel. He judged Israel ten years. 12 And Elon
the Zebulunite died and was buried at Aijalon
in the country of Zebulun.
13 After him, Abdon the son of Hillel the
Pirathonite judged Israel. 14 He had forty sons
and thirty grandsons, who rode on seventy
young donkeys. He judged Israel eight years.
15 Then Abdon the son of Hillel the Pirathonite
died and was buried in Pirathon in the land of
Ephraim, in the mountains of the Amalekites.

Psalm 50:7–15

7 "Hear, O My people, and I will speak,
O Israel, and I will testify against you;

I *am* God, your God!
8 I will not rebuke you for your sacrifices
Or your burnt offerings,
Which are continually before Me.
9 I will not take a bull from your house,
Nor goats out of your folds.
10 For every beast of the forest *is* Mine,
And the cattle on a thousand hills.
11 I know all the birds of the mountains,
And the wild beasts of the field *are* Mine.
12 "If I were hungry, I would not tell you;
For the world *is* Mine, and all its fullness.
13 Will I eat the flesh of bulls,
Or drink the blood of goats?

50:8 I will not rebuke you for your sacrifices. The divine Judge's condemnations are directed not at the act of sacrifice but at the people's attitude in sacrificing (see 1 Sam. 15:22; Pss. 40:6–8; 51:17; 69:30; Is. 1:12; Jer. 7:21–26; Hos. 6:6; Mic. 6:6–8).

50:9–13 will not take a bull from your house. God refuses mere ritual; it is an abomination to Him. He, unlike the pagan deities, needs nothing. He created everything and owns everything.

14 Offer to God thanksgiving,
And pay your vows to the Most High.
15 Call upon Me in the day of trouble;
I will deliver you, and you shall glorify Me."

Proverbs 14:28

28 In a multitude of people *is* a king's honor,
But in the lack of people *is* the downfall of a prince.

Luke 17:1–19

17 Then He said to the disciples, "It is impossible that no offenses should come, but woe *to him* through whom they do come! 2It would be better for him if a millstone were hung around his neck, and he were thrown into the sea, than that he should offend one of these little ones. 3Take heed to yourselves. If your brother sins against you, rebuke him; and if he repents, forgive him. 4And if he sins against you seven times in a day, and seven times in a day returns to you, saying, 'I repent,' you shall forgive him."

5And the apostles said to the Lord, "Increase our faith."

6So the Lord said, "If you have faith as a mustard seed, you can say to this mulberry tree, 'Be pulled up by the roots and be planted in the sea,' and it would obey you. 7And which of you, having a servant plowing or tending sheep, will say to him when he has come in from the field, 'Come at once and sit down to eat'? 8But will he not rather say to him, 'Prepare something for my supper, and gird yourself and serve me till I have eaten and drunk, and afterward you will eat and drink'? 9Does he thank that servant because he did the things that were commanded him? I think not. 10So likewise you, when you have done all those things which you are commanded, say, 'We are unprofitable servants. We have done what was our duty to do.' "

11Now it happened as He went to Jerusalem that He passed through the midst of Samaria and Galilee. 12Then as He entered a certain village, there met Him ten men who were lepers, who stood afar off. 13And they lifted up *their* voices and said, "Jesus, Master, have mercy on us!"

14So when He saw *them,* He said to them, "Go, show yourselves to the priests." And so it was that as they went, they were cleansed.

15And one of them, when he saw that he was healed, returned, and with a loud voice glorified God, 16and fell down on *his* face at His feet, giving Him thanks. And he was a Samaritan.

17So Jesus answered and said, "Were there not ten cleansed? But where *are* the nine? 18Were there not any found who returned to give glory to God except this foreigner?" 19And He said to him, "Arise, go your way. Your faith has made you well."

17:16 he was a Samaritan. Jesus' sending the lepers to show themselves to the priest suggests that they were Jewish. This Samaritan had been permitted to associate with them when all were ceremonially unclean, but in their healing they did not share his deep gratitude.

DAY 23: Why does God make use of leaders who display such obvious weaknesses?

It is true that judges such as Gideon, Jephthah, and Samson exhibited gross failures, as well as successes. But as long as God chooses to use people at all, He will end up using people with obvious weaknesses. No one escapes that category. The point is that God uses people in His plans in spite of it.

This does not excuse the sins of a leader. Note for example that Moses forfeited his opportunity to enter the Promised Land because of an angry outburst (Num. 20:10; Deut. 3:24–27). Jephthah made a rash vow for which his daughter had to bear the primary consequence (Judg. 11:29–40). What probably ought to attract our attention to these servants of God is not so much their weaknesses, or even the great accomplishments, but the fact that they remained faithful to God despite their failures.

When we study the lives of the judges, we discover ourselves. The shared victories, defeats, mistakes, and right choices form a common link across the centuries and turn our attention to the God who worked in their lives. The invitation from the ancients remains silently compelling: If we are to live as boldly for God, surely we would discover each day that same kind of God's immediate presence that was such a part of their experience.

APRIL 24

Judges 13:1–14:20

13 Again the children of Israel did evil in the
sight of the LORD, and the LORD delivered
them into the hand of the Philistines for forty
years.
2 Now there was a certain man from Zorah,
of the family of the Danites, whose name *was*
Manoah; and his wife *was* barren and had no
children. 3 And the Angel of the LORD appeared
to the woman and said to her, "Indeed now,
you are barren and have borne no children,
but you shall conceive and bear a son. 4 Now
therefore, please be careful not to drink wine
or *similar* drink, and not to eat anything
unclean. 5 For behold, you shall conceive and
bear a son. And no razor shall come upon his
head, for the child shall be a Nazirite to God
from the womb; and he shall begin to deliver
Israel out of the hand of the Philistines."
6 So the woman came and told her husband,
saying, "A Man of God came to me, and His
countenance *was* like the countenance of the
Angel of God, very awesome; but I did not ask
Him where He *was* from, and He did not tell
me His name. 7 And He said to me, 'Behold,
you shall conceive and bear a son. Now drink
no wine or *similar* drink, nor eat anything
unclean, for the child shall be a Nazirite to God
from the womb to the day of his death.'"
8 Then Manoah prayed to the LORD, and said,
"O my Lord, please let the Man of God whom
You sent come to us again and teach us what
we shall do for the child who will be born."
9 And God listened to the voice of Manoah,
and the Angel of God came to the woman again
as she was sitting in the field; but Manoah her
husband *was* not with her. 10 Then the woman
ran in haste and told her husband, and said to
him, "Look, the Man who came to me the
other day has just now appeared to me!"
11 So Manoah arose and followed his wife.
When he came to the Man, he said to Him,
"Are You the Man who spoke to this woman?"
And He said, "I *am.*"
12 Manoah said, "Now let Your words come
to pass! What will be the boy's rule of life, and
his work?"
13 So the Angel of the LORD said to Manoah,
"Of all that I said to the woman let her be careful.
14 She may not eat anything that comes
from the vine, nor may she drink wine or similar
drink, nor eat anything unclean. All that I
commanded her let her observe."
15 Then Manoah said to the Angel of the
LORD, "Please let us detain You, and we will prepare
a young goat for You."
16 And the Angel of the LORD said to Manoah,
"Though you detain Me, I will not eat your
food. But if you offer a burnt offering, you
must offer it to the LORD." (For Manoah did
not know He *was* the Angel of the LORD.)
17 Then Manoah said to the Angel of the
LORD, "What *is* Your name, that when Your
words come *to pass* we may honor You?"

13:5 Nazirite. The word is from the Hebrew "to separate." For rigid Nazirite restrictions, such as here in Samson's case, see Numbers 6:1–8. God gave 3 restrictions: no wine (vv. 3,4), no razor cutting the hair (v. 5), no touching a dead body and being defiled (v. 6). Such outward actions indicated an inner dedication to God.

18 And the Angel of the LORD said to him,
"Why do you ask My name, seeing it *is* wonderful?"

19 So Manoah took the young goat with the
grain offering, and offered it upon the rock to
the LORD. And He did a wondrous thing while
Manoah and his wife looked on— 20 it happened as the flame went up toward heaven
from the altar—the Angel of the LORD ascended in the flame of the altar! When Manoah and
his wife saw *this,* they fell on their faces to the
ground. 21 When the Angel of the LORD
appeared no more to Manoah and his wife,
then Manoah knew that He *was* the Angel of
the LORD.

22 And Manoah said to his wife, "We shall
surely die, because we have seen God!"

23 But his wife said to him, "If the LORD had
desired to kill us, He would not have accepted
a burnt offering and a grain offering from our
hands, nor would He have shown us all these
things, nor would He have told us *such things*
as these at this time."

24 So the woman bore a son and called his
name Samson; and the child grew, and the
LORD blessed him. 25 And the Spirit of the LORD
began to move upon him at Mahaneh Dan between Zorah and Eshtaol.

14 Now Samson went down to Timnah, and
saw a woman in Timnah of the daughters
of the Philistines. 2 So he went up and told his
father and mother, saying, "I have seen a
woman in Timnah of the daughters of the
Philistines; now therefore, get her for me as a
wife."

3 Then his father and mother said to him, "*Is*
there no woman among the daughters of your
brethren, or among all my people, that you
must go and get a wife from the uncircumcised Philistines?"

And Samson said to his father, "Get her for
me, for she pleases me well."

14:1–4 she pleases me well. The Philistines were not among the 7 nations of Canaan which Israel was specifically forbidden to marry. Nonetheless Samson's choice was seriously weak. Samson sins here, but God is sovereign and was able to turn the situation to please Him (14:4). He was not at a loss, but used the opportunity to work against the wicked Philistines and provided gracious help to His people. He achieved destruction of these people, not by an army, but by the miraculous power of one man.

4 But his father and mother did not know
that it was of the LORD—that He was seeking
an occasion to move against the Philistines.
For at that time the Philistines had dominion
over Israel.

5 So Samson went down to Timnah with his
father and mother, and came to the vineyards
of Timnah.

Now *to his* surprise, a young lion *came* roaring against him. 6 And the Spirit of the LORD
came mightily upon him, and he tore the lion
apart as one would have torn apart a young
goat, though *he had* nothing in his hand. But
he did not tell his father or his mother what he
had done.

7 Then he went down and talked with the
woman; and she pleased Samson well. 8 After
some time, when he returned to get her, he
turned aside to see the carcass of the lion. And
behold, a swarm of bees and honey *were* in the
carcass of the lion. 9 He took some of it in his
hands and went along, eating. When he came
to his father and mother, he gave *some* to
them, and they also ate. But he did not tell
them that he had taken the honey out of the
carcass of the lion.

10 So his father went down to the woman.
And Samson gave a feast there, for young men
used to do so. 11 And it happened, when they
saw him, that they brought thirty companions
to be with him.

12 Then Samson said to them, "Let me pose a
riddle to you. If you can correctly solve and
explain it to me within the seven days of the
feast, then I will give you thirty linen garments
and thirty changes of clothing. 13 But if you
cannot explain *it* to me, then you shall give me
thirty linen garments and thirty changes of
clothing."

And they said to him, "Pose your riddle, that
we may hear it."

14 So he said to them:

"Out of the eater came something to eat,
And out of the strong came something
sweet."

Now for three days they could not explain the
riddle.

15 But it came to pass on the seventh day that
they said to Samson's wife, "Entice your husband, that he may explain the riddle to us, or
else we will burn you and your father's house
with fire. Have you invited us in order to take
what is ours? *Is that* not *so?*"

16 Then Samson's wife wept on him, and said,
"You only hate me! You do not love me! You
have posed a riddle to the sons of my people,
but you have not explained *it* to me."

And he said to her, "Look, I have not
explained *it* to my father or my mother; so
should I explain *it* to you?" [17]Now she had wept
on him the seven days while their feast lasted.
And it happened on the seventh day that he
told her, because she pressed him so much.
Then she explained the riddle to the sons of
her people. [18]So the men of the city said to him
on the seventh day before the sun went down:

"What *is* sweeter than honey?
And what *is* stronger than a lion?"

And he said to them:

"If you had not plowed with my heifer,
You would not have solved my riddle!"

[19]Then the Spirit of the LORD came upon him
mightily, and he went down to Ashkelon and
killed thirty of their men, took their apparel,
and gave the changes *of clothing* to those who
had explained the riddle. So his anger was
aroused, and he went back up to his father's
house. [20]And Samson's wife was *given* to his
companion, who had been his best man.

Psalm 50:16–23

16 But to the wicked God says:
"What *right* have you to declare My statutes,
Or take My covenant in your mouth,
17 Seeing you hate instruction
And cast My words behind you?
18 When you saw a thief, you consented with him,
And have been a partaker with adulterers.
19 You give your mouth to evil,
And your tongue frames deceit.
20 You sit *and* speak against your brother;
You slander your own mother's son.
21 These *things* you have done, and I kept silent;
You thought that I was altogether like you;
But I will rebuke you,
And set *them* in order before your eyes.
22 "Now consider this, you who forget God,
Lest I tear *you* in pieces,
And *there be* none to deliver:
23 Whoever offers praise glorifies Me;
And to him who orders *his* conduct *aright*
I will show the salvation of God."

Proverbs 14:29–30

29 *He who is* slow to wrath has great understanding,
But *he who is* impulsive exalts folly.
30 A sound heart *is* life to the body,
But envy *is* rottenness to the bones.

Luke 17:20–37

[20]Now when He was asked by the Pharisees
when the kingdom of God would come, He
answered them and said, "The kingdom of
God does not come with observation; [21]nor will
they say, 'See here!' or 'See there!' For indeed,
the kingdom of God is within you."

[22]Then He said to the disciples, "The days
will come when you will desire to see one of
the days of the Son of Man, and you will not see
it. [23]And they will say to you, 'Look here!' or
'Look there!' Do not go after *them* or follow
them. [24]For as the lightning that flashes out of
one *part* under heaven shines to the other *part*
under heaven, so also the Son of Man will be in
His day. [25]But first He must suffer many things
and be rejected by this generation. [26]And as it
was in the days of Noah, so it will be also in
the days of the Son of Man: [27]They ate, they
drank, they married wives, they were given in

17:20 when the kingdom of God would come. They may have asked the question mockingly, having already concluded that He was not the Messiah. **does not come with observation.** The Pharisees believed that the Messiah's triumph would be immediate. They were looking for Him to come, overthrow Rome, and set up the millennial kingdom. Christ's program was altogether different. He was inaugurating an era in which the kingdom would be manifest in the rule of God in men's hearts through faith in the Savior (v. 21; see Rom. 14:17). That kingdom was neither confined to a particular geographical location nor visible to human eyes. It would come quietly, invisibly, and without the normal pomp and splendor associated with the arrival of a king. Jesus did not suggest that the Old Testament promises of an earthly kingdom were hereby nullified. Rather, that earthly, visible manifestation of the kingdom is yet to come (Rev. 20:1–6).

17:22 The days will come. This introduces a brief discourse that has some similarities to the Olivet Discourse of Matthew 24 and 25. **you will desire to see one of the days of the Son of Man.** I.e., desire to have Him physically present. This suggests a longing for His return to set things right (see Rev. 6:9–11; 22:20).

marriage, until the day that Noah entered the
ark, and the flood came and destroyed them
all. 28Likewise as it was also in the days of Lot:
They ate, they drank, they bought, they sold,
they planted, they built; 29but on the day that
Lot went out of Sodom it rained fire and brimstone from heaven and destroyed *them* all.
30Even so will it be in the day when the Son of
Man is revealed.

31"In that day, he who is on the housetop,
and his goods *are* in the house, let him not
come down to take them away. And likewise
the one who is in the field, let him not turn
back. 32Remember Lot's wife. 33Whoever
seeks to save his life will lose it, and whoever
loses his life will preserve it. 34I tell you, in that
night there will be two *men* in one bed: the
one will be taken and the other will be left.
35Two *women* will be grinding together: the
one will be taken and the other left. 36Two *men*
will be in the field: the one will be taken and
the other left."

37And they answered and said to Him,
"Where, Lord?"

So He said to them, "Wherever the body is, there the eagles will be gathered together."

DAY 24: What about those who claim to see a wide gap between Luke's theology and Paul's theology?

Although Luke, more than any of the other Gospel writers, highlighted the univeral scope of the gospel invitation, some have questioned why a companion of Paul's would use so little of Paul's language in explaining the process of salvation. But a difference in vocabulary does not necessarily imply a difference in thought or underlying theology.

Luke certainly wrote in his own style. He was an astute observer and careful thinker. In writing the Gospel, he was careful not to insert Pauline language back into the Gospel account. The theology of Luke's record parallels Paul's exactly. Luke repeatedly related accounts of Gentiles, Samaritans, and other outcasts who found grace in Jesus' eyes. This emphasis not only records Jesus' appeal, but also proves to be precisely what we would expect from the close companion of the "apostle to the Gentiles" (Rom. 11:13).

A compelling illustration of this parallel involves Luke's treatment of the centerpiece of Paul's doctrine—justification by faith. Luke highlighted and illustrated justification by faith in many of the incidents and parables he related in his Gospel. For example, the account of the Pharisee and the publican (18:9–14), the familiar story of the prodigal son (15:11–32), the incident at Simon's house (7:36–50), and the salvation of Zacchaeus (19:1–10) all serve to demonstrate that Jesus taught justification by faith long before Paul wrote about it.

APRIL 25

Judges 15:1–16:31

15 After a while, in the time of wheat harvest, it happened that Samson visited his
wife with a young goat. And he said, "Let me
go in to my wife, into *her* room." But her father
would not permit him to go in.

2Her father said, "I really thought that you
thoroughly hated her; therefore I gave her to
your companion. *Is* not her younger sister better than she? Please, take her instead."

3And Samson said to them, "This time I shall
be blameless regarding the Philistines if I
harm them!" 4Then Samson went and caught
three hundred foxes; and he took torches,
turned *the foxes* tail to tail, and put a torch
between each pair of tails. 5When he had set
the torches on fire, he let *the foxes* go into the
standing grain of the Philistines, and burned
up both the shocks and the standing grain, as
well as the vineyards *and* olive groves.

6Then the Philistines said, "Who has done
this?"

And they answered, "Samson, the son-in-law of the Timnite, because he has taken his wife and given her to his companion." So the Philistines came up and burned her and her father with fire.

7Samson said to them, "Since you would do
a thing like this, I will surely take revenge on
you, and after that I will cease." 8So he attacked
them hip and thigh with a great slaughter;
then he went down and dwelt in the cleft of the
rock of Etam.

9Now the Philistines went up, encamped in
Judah, and deployed themselves against Lehi.
10And the men of Judah said, "Why have you
come up against us?"

So they answered, "We have come up to arrest Samson, to do to him as he has done to us."

11Then three thousand men of Judah went
down to the cleft of the rock of Etam, and said

to Samson, "Do you not know that the
Philistines rule over us? What *is* this you have
done to us?"
And he said to them, "As they did to me, so
I have done to them."
12But they said to him, "We have come down
to arrest you, that we may deliver you into the
hand of the Philistines."
Then Samson said to them, "Swear to me
that you will not kill me yourselves."
13So they spoke to him, saying, "No, but we
will tie you securely and deliver you into their
hand; but we will surely not kill you." And they
bound him with two new ropes and brought
him up from the rock.
14When he came to Lehi, the Philistines
came shouting against him. Then the Spirit of
the LORD came mightily upon him; and the
ropes that *were* on his arms became like flax
that is burned with fire, and his bonds broke
loose from his hands. 15He found a fresh jawbone of a donkey, reached out his hand and
took it, and killed a thousand men with it.
16Then Samson said:

"With the jawbone of a donkey,
Heaps upon heaps,
With the jawbone of a donkey
I have slain a thousand men!"

17And so it was, when he had finished speaking, that he threw the jawbone from his hand,
and called that place Ramath Lehi.
18Then he became very thirsty; so he cried
out to the LORD and said, "You have given this
great deliverance by the hand of Your servant;
and now shall I die of thirst and fall into the
hand of the uncircumcised?" 19So God split the
hollow place that *is* in Lehi, and water came
out, and he drank; and his spirit returned, and
he revived. Therefore he called its name En
Hakkore, which is in Lehi to this day. 20And he
judged Israel twenty years in the days of the
Philistines.

16 Now Samson went to Gaza and saw a
harlot there, and went in to her. 2*When*
the Gazites *were told,* "Samson has come
here!" they surrounded *the place* and lay in
wait for him all night at the gate of the city.
They were quiet all night, saying, "In the
morning, when it is daylight, we will kill him."
3And Samson lay *low* till midnight; then he
arose at midnight, took hold of the doors of
the gate of the city and the two gateposts,
pulled them up, bar and all, put *them* on his
shoulders, and carried them to the top of the
hill that faces Hebron.
4Afterward it happened that he loved a
woman in the Valley of Sorek, whose name
was Delilah. 5And the lords of the Philistines
came up to her and said to her, "Entice him,
and find out where his great strength *lies,* and
by what *means* we may overpower him, that
we may bind him to afflict him; and every one
of us will give you eleven hundred *pieces* of
silver."
6So Delilah said to Samson, "Please tell me
where your great strength *lies,* and with what
you may be bound to afflict you."
7And Samson said to her, "If they bind me
with seven fresh bowstrings, not yet dried,
then I shall become weak, and be like any
other man."
8So the lords of the Philistines brought up to
her seven fresh bowstrings, not yet dried, and
she bound him with them. 9Now *men were*
lying in wait, staying with her in the room.
And she said to him, "The Philistines *are* upon
you, Samson!" But he broke the bowstrings as
a strand of yarn breaks when it touches fire.
So the secret of his strength was not known.
10Then Delilah said to Samson, "Look, you
have mocked me and told me lies. Now, please
tell me what you may be bound with."
11So he said to her, "If they bind me securely with new ropes that have never been used,
then I shall become weak, and be like any
other man."
12Therefore Delilah took new ropes and
bound him with them, and said to him, "The
Philistines *are* upon you, Samson!" And *men*
were lying in wait, staying in the room. But he
broke them off his arms like a thread.
13Delilah said to Samson, "Until now you
have mocked me and told me lies. Tell me
what you may be bound with."
And he said to her, "If you weave the seven
locks of my head into the web of the loom"—
14So she wove *it* tightly with the batten of the
loom, and said to him, "The Philistines *are*
upon you, Samson!" But he awoke from his
sleep, and pulled out the batten and the web
from the loom.
15Then she said to him, "How can you say, 'I
love you,' when your heart *is* not with me? You
have mocked me these three times, and have
not told me where your great strength *lies.*"
16And it came to pass, when she pestered him
daily with her words and pressed him, *so* that
his soul was vexed to death, 17that he told her
all his heart, and said to her, "No razor has ever
come upon my head, for I *have been* a Nazirite
to God from my mother's womb. If I am
shaven, then my strength will leave me, and I
shall become weak, and be like any *other* man."
18When Delilah saw that he had told her all
his heart, she sent and called for the lords of

the Philistines, saying, "Come up once more, for he has told me all his heart." So the lords of the Philistines came up to her and brought the money in their hand. [19]Then she lulled him to sleep on her knees, and called for a man and had him shave off the seven locks of his head. Then she began to torment him, and his strength left him. [20]And she said, "The Philistines *are* upon you, Samson!" So he awoke from his sleep, and said, "I will go out as before, at other times, and shake myself free!" But he did not know that the LORD had depared from him.

16:20 he did not know that the LORD had departed from him. Here was the tragedy of the wrath of abandonment. His sin had caused him to forfeit the power of God's presence. This principle is seen throughout Scripture (Gen. 6:3; Prov. 1:24–31; Matt. 15:14; Rom. 1:24–32).

[21]Then the Philistines took him and put out his eyes, and brought him down to Gaza. They bound him with bronze fetters, and he became a grinder in the prison. [22]However, the hair of his head began to grow again after it had been shaven.

[23]Now the lords of the Philistines gathered together to offer a great sacrifice to Dagon their god, and to rejoice. And they said:

"Our god has delivered into our hands
Samson our enemy!"

[24]When the people saw him, they praised their god; for they said:

"Our god has delivered into our hands
our enemy,
The destroyer of our land,
And the one who multiplied our dead."

[25]So it happened, when their hearts were merry, that they said, "Call for Samson, that he may perform for us." So they called for Samson from the prison, and he performed for them. And they stationed him between the pillars. [26]Then

16:24 they praised their god. It is tragic when a person's sin contributes to the unsaved community's giving praise to a false god, for God alone is worthy of praise.

Samson said to the lad who held him by the hand, "Let me feel the pillars which support the temple, so that I can lean on them." [27]Now the temple was full of men and women. All the lords of the Philistines *were* there—about three thousand men and women on the roof watching while Samson performed.

[28]Then Samson called to the LORD, saying, "O Lord GOD, remember me, I pray! Strengthen me, I pray, just this once, O God, that I may with one *blow* take vengeance on the Philistines for my two eyes!" [29]And Samson took hold of the two middle pillars which supported the temple, and he braced himself against them, one on his right and the other on his left. [30]Then Samson said, "Let me die with the Philistines!" And he pushed with *all his* might, and the temple fell on the lords and all the people who *were* in it. So the dead that he killed at his death were more than he had killed in his life.

[31]And his brothers and all his father's household came down and took him, and brought *him* up and buried him between Zorah and Eshtaol in the tomb of his father Manoah. He had judged Israel twenty years.

Psalm 51:1–6

To the Chief Musician. A Psalm of David when Nathan the prophet went to him, after he had gone in to Bathsheba.

Have mercy upon me, O God,
According to Your lovingkindness;
According to the multitude of Your
tender mercies,
Blot out my transgressions.

51:1 lovingkindness. Even though he had sinned horribly, David knew that forgiveness was available, based on God's covenant love.

2 Wash me thoroughly from my iniquity,
And cleanse me from my sin.
3 For I acknowledge my transgressions,
And my sin *is* always before me.
4 Against You, You only, have I sinned,
And done *this* evil in Your sight—
That You may be found just when You
speak,
And blameless when You judge.

5 Behold, I was brought forth in iniquity,
And in sin my mother conceived me.
6 Behold, You desire truth in the inward
parts,

51:4 Against You, You only. David realized what every believer seeking forgiveness must, that even though he had tragically wronged Bathsheba and Uriah, his ultimate crime was against God and His holy law (see 2 Sam. 11:27).

51:5 brought forth in iniquity. David also acknowledged that his sin was not God's fault in any way (vv. 4b,6) nor was it some aberration. Rather, the source of David's sin was a fallen, sinful disposition, his since conception.

And in the hidden *part* You will make
me to know wisdom.

Proverbs 14:31–32

31 He who oppresses the poor reproaches
his Maker,
But he who honors Him has mercy on
the needy.
32 The wicked is banished in his
wickedness,
But the righteous has a refuge in his
death.

Luke 18:1–23

18 Then He spoke a parable to them, that
men always ought to pray and not lose
heart, 2saying: "There was in a certain city a
judge who did not fear God nor regard man.
3Now there was a widow in that city; and she
came to him, saying, 'Get justice for me from
my adversary.' 4And he would not for a while;
but afterward he said within himself, 'Though
I do not fear God nor regard man, 5yet because
this widow troubles me I will avenge her, lest
by her continual coming she weary me.' "
6Then the Lord said, "Hear what the unjust
judge said. 7And shall God not avenge His own
elect who cry out day and night to Him, though
He bears long with them? 8I tell you that He will
avenge them speedily. Nevertheless, when
the Son of Man comes, will He really find faith
on the earth?"
9Also He spoke this parable to some who
trusted in themselves that they were righteous, and despised others: 10"Two men went
up to the temple to pray, one a Pharisee and
the other a tax collector. 11The Pharisee stood
and prayed thus with himself, 'God, I thank
You that I am not like other men—extortioners, unjust, adulterers, or even as this
tax collector. 12I fast twice a week; I give tithes
of all that I possess.' 13And the tax collector,
standing afar off, would not so much as raise
his eyes to heaven, but beat his breast, saying,
'God, be merciful to me a sinner!' 14I tell you,
this man went down to his house justified
rather than the other; for everyone who exalts
himself will be humbled, and he who humbles
himself will be exalted."
15Then they also brought infants to Him that
He might touch them; but when the disciples
saw *it,* they rebuked them. 16But Jesus called
them to *Him* and said, "Let the little children
come to Me, and do not forbid them; for of such
is the kingdom of God. 17Assuredly, I say to
you, whoever does not receive the kingdom of
God as a little child will by no means enter it."
18Now a certain ruler asked Him, saying,
"Good Teacher, what shall I do to inherit eternal
life?"
19So Jesus said to him, "Why do you call Me
good? No one *is* good but One, *that is,* God.
20You know the commandments: *'Do not commit adultery,' 'Do not murder,' 'Do not steal,'
'Do not bear false witness,' 'Honor your father
and your mother.'* "
21And he said, "All these things I have kept
from my youth."
22So when Jesus heard these things, He said
to him, "You still lack one thing. Sell all that you
have and distribute to the poor, and you will
have treasure in heaven; and come, follow Me."
23But when he heard this, he became very
sorrowful, for he was very rich.

DAY 25: Why is human righteousness so insufficient for salvation?

The parable of the Pharisee and the tax collector in Luke 18:9–14 is rich with truth about the doctrine of justification by faith. It illustrates perfectly how a sinner who is utterly devoid of personal righteousness may be declared righteous before God instantaneously through an act of repentant faith. The parable is addressed to Pharisees who trusted their own righteousness (vv. 10,11). Such confidence in one's inherent righteousness is a damning hope (see Rom. 10:3; Phil. 3:9), because human righteousness—even the righteousness of the most fastidious Pharisee—falls short of the divine standard (Matt. 5:48). Scripture consistently teaches that sinners are justified when God's perfect righteousness is imputed to their account (see Gen. 15:6; Rom. 4:4,5; 2 Cor. 5:21; Phil. 3:4–9)—and it was only on that basis that this tax collector (or anyone else) could be saved.

For the Pharisee to fast twice a week (v. 12) was more than is required by any biblical standard. By exalting his own works, the Pharisee revealed that his entire hope lay in his not being as bad as someone else. He utterly lacked any sense of his own unworthiness and sin.

The tax collector's humility is notable in everything about his posture and behavior (v. 13). Here was a man who had been made to face the reality of his own sin, and his only response was abject humility and repentance. He contrasts with the Pharisee in virtually every detail. "God, be merciful to me a sinner!" He had no hope but the mercy of God. This is the point to which the law aims to bring every sinner (see Rom. 3:19,20; 7:13; Gal 3:22–24). He was "justified" (v. 14), i.e., reckoned righteous before God by means of an imputed righteousness.

APRIL 26

Judges 17:1–19:30

17 Now there was a man from the mountains of Ephraim, whose name *was*
Micah. 2And he said to his mother, "The
eleven hundred *shekels* of silver that were
taken from you, and on which you put a curse,
even saying it in my ears—here *is* the silver
with me; I took it."

And his mother said, "*May you be* blessed
by the LORD, my son!" 3So when he had
returned the eleven hundred *shekels* of silver
to his mother, his mother said, "I had wholly
dedicated the silver from my hand to the LORD
for my son, to make a carved image and a molded image; now therefore, I will return it to you."
4Thus he returned the silver to his mother.
Then his mother took two hundred *shekels* of
silver and gave them to the silversmith, and he
made it into a carved image and a molded
image; and they were in the house of Micah.
5The man Micah had a shrine, and made an
ephod and household idols; and he consecrated one of his sons, who became his priest. 6In
those days *there was* no king in Israel; everyone did *what was* right in his own eyes.
7Now there was a young man from Bethlehem in Judah, of the family of Judah; he *was* a
Levite, and was staying there. 8The man
departed from the city of Bethlehem in Judah
to stay wherever he could find *a place*. Then he
came to the mountains of Ephraim, to the
house of Micah, as he journeyed. 9And Micah
said to him, "Where do you come from?"

So he said to him, "I *am* a Levite from Bethlehem in Judah, and I am on my way to find *a
place* to stay."
10Micah said to him, "Dwell with me, and be
a father and a priest to me, and I will give you
ten *shekels* of silver per year, a suit of clothes,
and your sustenance." So the Levite went in.
11Then the Levite was content to dwell with the
man; and the young man became like one of
his sons to him. 12So Micah consecrated the
Levite, and the young man became his priest,
and lived in the house of Micah. 13Then Micah
said, "Now I know that the LORD will be good
to me, since I have a Levite as priest!"

18 In those days *there was* no king in Israel.
And in those days the tribe of the
Danites was seeking an inheritance for itself
to dwell in; for until that day *their* inheritance
among the tribes of Israel had not fallen to
them. 2So the children of Dan sent five men of
their family from their territory, men of valor
from Zorah and Eshtaol, to spy out the land
and search it. They said to them, "Go, search
the land." So they went to the mountains of
Ephraim, to the house of Micah, and lodged
there. 3While they *were* at the house of Micah,
they recognized the voice of the young Levite.
They turned aside and said to him, "Who
brought you here? What are you doing in this
place? What do you have here?"
4He said to them, "Thus and so Micah did
for me. He has hired me, and I have become
his priest."
5So they said to him, "Please inquire of God,
that we may know whether the journey on
which we go will be prosperous."
6And the priest said to them, "Go in peace.
The presence of the LORD *be* with you on your
way."
7So the five men departed and went to
Laish. They saw the people who *were* there,
how they dwelt safely, in the manner of the
Sidonians, quiet and secure. *There were* no
rulers in the land who might put *them* to
shame for anything. They *were* far from the
Sidonians, and they had no ties with anyone.
8Then *the spies* came back to their brethren
at Zorah and Eshtaol, and their brethren said
to them, "What *is* your *report?*"
9So they said, "Arise, let us go up against
them. For we have seen the land, and indeed it
is very good. *Would* you *do* nothing? Do not hesitate to go, *and* enter to possess the land.
10When you go, you will come to a secure people

and a large land. For God has given it into your
hands, a place where *there is* no lack of anything
that *is* on the earth."
11And six hundred men of the family of the
Danites went from there, from Zorah and
Eshtaol, armed with weapons of war. 12Then
they went up and encamped in Kirjath Jearim
in Judah. (Therefore they call that place
Mahaneh Dan to this day. There *it is,* west of
Kirjath Jearim.) 13And they passed from there
to the mountains of Ephraim, and came to the
house of Micah.
14Then the five men who had gone to spy out
the country of Laish answered and said to
their brethren, "Do you know that there are in
these houses an ephod, household idols, a
carved image, and a molded image? Now
therefore, consider what you should do." 15So
they turned aside there, and came to the
house of the young Levite man—to the house
of Micah—and greeted him. 16The six hundred men armed with their weapons of war,
who *were* of the children of Dan, stood by the
entrance of the gate. 17Then the five men who
had gone to spy out the land went up. Entering
there, they took the carved image, the ephod,
the household idols, and the molded image.
The priest stood at the entrance of the gate
with the six hundred men *who were* armed
with weapons of war.
18When these went into Micah's house and
took the carved image, the ephod, the household idols, and the molded image, the priest
said to them, "What are you doing?"
19And they said to him, "Be quiet, put your
hand over your mouth, and come with us; be a
father and a priest to us. *Is it* better for you to
be a priest to the household of one man, or that
you be a priest to a tribe and a family in Israel?"
20So the priest's heart was glad; and he took
the ephod, the household idols, and the
carved image, and took his place among the
people.
21Then they turned and departed, and put
the little ones, the livestock, and the goods in
front of them. 22When they were a good way
from the house of Micah, the men who *were*
in the houses near Micah's house gathered
together and overtook the children of Dan.
23And they called out to the children of Dan.
So they turned around and said to Micah,
"What ails you, that you have gathered such a
company?"
24So he said, "You have taken away my gods
which I made, and the priest, and you have
gone away. Now what more do I have? How
can you say to me, 'What ails you?' "
25And the children of Dan said to him, "Do
not let your voice be heard among us, lest angry men fall upon you, and you lose your life,
with the lives of your household!" 26Then the
children of Dan went their way. And when
Micah saw that they *were* too strong for him,
he turned and went back to his house.
27So they took *the things* Micah had made,
and the priest who had belonged to him, and
went to Laish, to a people quiet and secure;
and they struck them with the edge of the
sword and burned the city with fire. 28*There
was* no deliverer, because it *was* far from
Sidon, and they had no ties with anyone. It
was in the valley that belongs to Beth Rehob.
So they rebuilt the city and dwelt there. 29And
they called the name of the city Dan, after the
name of Dan their father, who was born to Israel. However, the name of the city formerly
was Laish.
30Then the children of Dan set up for themselves the carved image; and Jonathan the son
of Gershom, the son of Manasseh, and his
sons were priests to the tribe of Dan until the
day of the captivity of the land. 31So they set up
for themselves Micah's carved image which
he made, all the time that the house of God
was in Shiloh.

19 And it came to pass in those days, when
there was no king in Israel, that there was
a certain Levite staying in the remote mountains of Ephraim. He took for himself a concubine from Bethlehem in Judah. 2But his concubine played the harlot against him, and
went away from him to her father's house at
Bethlehem in Judah, and was there four whole
months. 3Then her husband arose and went
after her, to speak kindly to her *and* bring her
back, having his servant and a couple of donkeys with him. So she brought him into her
father's house; and when the father of the
young woman saw him, he was glad to meet
him. 4Now his father-in-law, the young
woman's father, detained him; and he stayed
with him three days. So they ate and drank
and lodged there.
5Then it came to pass on the fourth day that
they arose early in the morning, and he stood
to depart; but the young woman's father said
to his son-in-law, "Refresh your heart with a
morsel of bread, and afterward go your way."
6So they sat down, and the two of them ate
and drank together. Then the young woman's
father said to the man, "Please be content to
stay all night, and let your heart be merry."
7And when the man stood to depart, his father-
in-law urged him; so he lodged there again.
8Then he arose early in the morning on the fifth
day to depart, but the young woman's father

said, "Please refresh your heart." So they
delayed until afternoon; and both of them ate.
9And when the man stood to depart—he
and his concubine and his servant—his father-
in-law, the young woman's father, said to him,
"Look, the day is now drawing toward
evening; please spend the night. See, the day
is coming to an end; lodge here, that your
heart may be merry. Tomorrow go your way
early, so that you may get home."
10However, the man was not willing to spend
that night; so he rose and departed, and came
opposite Jebus (that *is,* Jerusalem). With him
were the two saddled donkeys; his concubine
was also with him. 11They *were* near Jebus, and
the day was far spent; and the servant said to
his master, "Come, please, and let us turn
aside into this city of the Jebusites and lodge
in it."
12But his master said to him, "We will not
turn aside here into a city of foreigners, who
are not of the children of Israel; we will go on
to Gibeah." 13So he said to his servant, "Come,
let us draw near to one of these places, and
spend the night in Gibeah or in Ramah." 14And
they passed by and went their way; and the
sun went down on them near Gibeah, which
belongs to Benjamin. 15They turned aside
there to go in to lodge in Gibeah. And when he
went in, he sat down in the open square of the
city, for no one would take them into *his* house
to spend the night.
16Just then an old man came in from his
work in the field at evening, who also *was* from
the mountains of Ephraim; he was staying in
Gibeah, whereas the men of the place *were*
Benjamites. 17And when he raised his eyes, he
saw the traveler in the open square of the city;
and the old man said, "Where are you going,
and where do you come from?"
18So he said to him, "We *are* passing from
Bethlehem in Judah toward the remote mountains of Ephraim; I *am* from there. I went to
Bethlehem in Judah; *now* I am going to the
house of the LORD. But there *is* no one who
will take me into his house, 19although we have
both straw and fodder for our donkeys, and
bread and wine for myself, for your female servant, and for the young man *who is* with your
servant; *there is* no lack of anything."
20And the old man said, "Peace *be* with you!
However, *let* all your needs *be* my responsibility; only do not spend the night in the open
square." 21So he brought him into his house,
and gave fodder to the donkeys. And they
washed their feet, and ate and drank.
22As they were enjoying themselves, suddenly certain men of the city, perverted men,
surrounded the house *and* beat on the door.
They spoke to the master of the house, the old
man, saying, "Bring out the man who came to
your house, that we may know him *carnally!*"

19:22 perverted men. Literally, "sons of Belial," i.e., worthless men, who desired to commit sodomy against the Levite. The phrase elsewhere is used for idolaters (Deut. 13:13), neglecters of the poor (Deut. 15:9), drunks (1 Sam. 1:16), immoral people (1 Sam. 2:12), and rebels against the civil authority (2 Sam. 20:1; Prov. 19:28). "Belial" can be traced to the false god Baal and is also a term for yoke (they cast off the yoke of decency) and a term for entangling or injuring. It is used in the New Testament of Satan (2 Cor. 6:15).

23But the man, the master of the house,
went out to them and said to them, "No, my
brethren! I beg you, do not act *so* wickedly!
Seeing this man has come into my house, do
not commit this outrage. 24Look, *here is* my
virgin daughter and *the man's* concubine; let
me bring them out now. Humble them, and
do with them as you please; but to this man
do not do such a vile thing!" 25But the men
would not heed him. So the man took his concubine and brought *her* out to them. And
they knew her and abused her all night until
morning; and when the day began to break,
they let her go.

19:25 the man took his concubine...to them. This is unthinkable weakness and cowardice for any man, especially a priest of God. Apparently he even slept through the night or stayed in bed out of fear, since he didn't see her again until he awakened and prepared to leave (see vv. 27,28).

26Then the woman came as the day was
dawning, and fell down at the door of the
man's house where her master *was,* till it was
light.
27When her master arose in the morning,
and opened the doors of the house and went
out to go his way, there was his concubine,
fallen *at* the door of the house with her hands
on the threshold. 28And he said to her, "Get up
and let us be going." But there was no answer.

So the man lifted her onto the donkey; and the
man got up and went to his place.
[29]When he entered his house he took a
knife, laid hold of his concubine, and divided
her into twelve pieces, limb by limb, and sent
her throughout all the territory of Israel. [30]And
so it was that all who saw it said, "No such
deed has been done or seen from the day that
the children of Israel came up from the land of
Egypt until this day. Consider it, confer, and
speak up!"

Psalm 51:7–11

7 Purge me with hyssop, and I shall be
clean;
Wash me, and I shall be whiter than
snow.

51:7 hyssop. Old Testament priests used hyssop, a leafy plant, to sprinkle blood or water on a person being ceremonially cleansed from defilements such as leprosy or touching a dead body (see Lev. 14:6ff.; Num. 19:16–19). Here hyssop is a figure for David's longing to be spiritually cleansed from his moral defilement. In forgiveness, God washes away sin (see Ps. 103:12; Is. 1:16; Mic. 7:19).

8 Make me hear joy and gladness,
That the bones You have broken may
rejoice.
9 Hide Your face from my sins,
And blot out all my iniquities.
10 Create in me a clean heart, O God,
And renew a steadfast spirit
within me.
11 Do not cast me away from Your
presence,
And do not take Your Holy Spirit
from me.

Proverbs 14:33–35

33 Wisdom rests in the heart of him who
has understanding,
But *what is* in the heart of fools is
made known.

14:33 is made known. Wisdom is quietly preserved in the heart of the wise for the time of proper use, while fools are eager to blurt out their folly (see 12:23; 13:16; 15:2,14).

34 Righteousness exalts a nation,
But sin *is* a reproach to *any* people.
35 The king's favor *is* toward a wise
servant,
But his wrath *is against* him who
causes shame.

Luke 18:24–43

[24]And when Jesus saw that he became very
sorrowful, He said, "How hard it is for those
who have riches to enter the kingdom of God!
[25]For it is easier for a camel to go through the
eye of a needle than for a rich man to enter the
kingdom of God."
[26]And those who heard it said, "Who then
can be saved?"
[27]But He said, "The things which are impossible with men are possible with God."
[28]Then Peter said, "See, we have left all and
followed You."
[29]So He said to them, "Assuredly, I say to
you, there is no one who has left house or parents or brothers or wife or children, for the
sake of the kingdom of God, [30]who shall not
receive many times more in this present time,
and in the age to come eternal life."
[31]Then He took the twelve aside and said to
them, "Behold, we are going up to Jerusalem,
and all things that are written by the prophets
concerning the Son of Man will be accomplished. [32]For He will be delivered to the
Gentiles and will be mocked and insulted and
spit upon. [33]They will scourge *Him* and kill
Him. And the third day He will rise again."
[34]But they understood none of these things;
this saying was hidden from them, and they
did not know the things which were spoken.
[35]Then it happened, as He was coming near
Jericho, that a certain blind man sat by the
road begging. [36]And hearing a multitude passing by, he asked what it meant. [37]So they told
him that Jesus of Nazareth was passing by.
[38]And he cried out, saying, "Jesus, Son of David,
have mercy on me!"
[39]Then those who went before warned him
that he should be quiet; but he cried out all the
more, "Son of David, have mercy on me!"
[40]So Jesus stood still and commanded him to
be brought to Him. And when he had come
near, He asked him, [41]saying, "What do you
want Me to do for you?"
He said, "Lord, that I may receive my sight."
[42]Then Jesus said to him, "Receive your
sight; your faith has made you well." [43]And
immediately he received his sight, and followed Him, glorifying God. And all the people,
when they saw *it*, gave praise to God.

DAY 26: What did the anointing of the Holy Spirit mean in the Old Testament?

Old Testament Israel had mediators who stood between God and His people. To empower the Old Testament mediators, the Holy Spirit gave special administrative ability to carry out the management of the nation and military skills which enabled them to defeat the theocracy's enemies. The Lord first anointed Moses with this ministry of the Spirit, and then in a truly dramatic scene, took some of this ministry of the Spirit and shared it with the 70 elders. Thus they were enabled to help Moses administer Israel (Num. 11:17–25).

Also Joshua (Deut. 34:9), the judges (Judg. 3:10; 6:34), and the kings of united Israel and the southern kingdom were anointed with this special ministry of the Spirit. When the Spirit of the Lord came upon King Saul, for example, he was in effect given "another heart" (1 Sam. 10:6–10). This does not mean that he was regenerated at this point in his life, but that he was given skills to be a king. Later the theocratic anointing was taken from Saul and given to David (1 Sam. 16:1–14). Saul, from that time on, became a totally incapable leader.

King David no doubt had this special ministry of the Spirit in mind in his prayer of repentance in Psalm 51. He was not afraid of losing his salvation when he prayed, "Do not take Your Holy Spirit from me" (Ps. 51:11), but rather was concerned that God would remove this spiritual wisdom and administrative skill from him. David had earlier seen such the tragedy in the life of Saul when that king of Israel lost the anointing of the Holy Spirit. David was thus pleading with God not to remove His hand of guidance.

King Solomon also perceived his youthful inabilities at the beginning of his reign and requested God to give him special wisdom in administering Israel. God was greatly pleased with this request and granted an extra measure to the young man (1 Kin. 3:7–12,28; 4:29–34). Although the Old Testament is silent in this regard about the kings who succeeded Solomon, the theocratic anointing of the Spirit likely came on all the descendants of David in connection with the Davidic Covenant.

When the theocracy went out of existence as Judah was carried away into captivity and the last Davidic king was disempowered, the theocratic anointing was no longer given (Ezek. 8–11). The kings of the northern tribes, on the other hand, being essentially apostate and not in the Davidic line, never had the benefit of this special ministry of the Spirit.

APRIL 27

Judges 20:1–21:25

20 So all the children of Israel came out,
from Dan to Beersheba, as well as from
the land of Gilead, and the congregation gathered
together as one man before the LORD at
Mizpah. 2And the leaders of all the people, all
the tribes of Israel, presented themselves in the
assembly of the people of God, four hundred
thousand foot soldiers who drew the sword.
3(Now the children of Benjamin heard that the
children of Israel had gone up to Mizpah.)
Then the children of Israel said, "Tell *us,* how
did this wicked deed happen?"
4So the Levite, the husband of the woman
who was murdered, answered and said, "My
concubine and I went into Gibeah, which
belongs to Benjamin, to spend the night. 5And
the men of Gibeah rose against me, and surrounded
the house at night because of me.
They intended to kill me, but instead they ravished
my concubine so that she died. 6So I
took hold of my concubine, cut her in pieces,
and sent her throughout all the territory of the
inheritance of Israel, because they committed
lewdness and outrage in Israel. 7Look! All of
you *are* children of Israel; give your advice
and counsel here and now!"
8So all the people arose as one man, saying,
"None *of us* will go to his tent, nor will any turn
back to his house; 9but now this *is* the thing
which we will do to Gibeah: *We will go up*
against it by lot. 10We will take ten men out of
every hundred throughout all the tribes of Israel,
a hundred out of *every* thousand, and a
thousand out of *every* ten thousand, to make
provisions for the people, that when they come
to Gibeah in Benjamin, they may repay all the
vileness that they have done in Israel." 11So all
the men of Israel were gathered against the
city, united together as one man.
12Then the tribes of Israel sent men through
all the tribe of Benjamin, saying, "What *is* this
wickedness that has occurred among you?
13Now therefore, deliver up the men, the perverted
men who *are* in Gibeah, that we may
put them to death and remove the evil from Israel!"
But the children of Benjamin would not
listen to the voice of their brethren, the children
of Israel. 14Instead, the children of Benjamin
gathered together from their cities to

Gibeah, to go to battle against the children of
Israel. [15]And from their cities at that time the
children of Benjamin numbered twenty-six
thousand men who drew the sword, besides
the inhabitants of Gibeah, who numbered
seven hundred select men. [16]Among all this
people *were* seven hundred select men *who*
were left-handed; every one could sling a stone
at a hair's *breadth* and not miss. [17]Now besides
Benjamin, the men of Israel numbered four
hundred thousand men who drew the sword;
all of these *were* men of war.

[18]Then the children of Israel arose and went
up to the house of God to inquire of God. They
said, "Which of us shall go up first to battle
against the children of Benjamin?"

The LORD said, "Judah first!"

20:18 to inquire of God. The Lord gave His counsel from the location of the ark at Shiloh, probably through the Urim and Thummim (vv. 27,28). The tribe of Judah was responsible to lead in battle since God had chosen a leadership role for that tribe (Gen. 49:8–12; 1 Chr. 5:1,2).

---

[19]So the children of Israel rose in the morning and encamped against Gibeah. [20]And the
men of Israel went out to battle against Benjamin, and the men of Israel put themselves in
battle array to fight against them at Gibeah.
[21]Then the children of Benjamin came out of
Gibeah, and on that day cut down to the
ground twenty-two thousand men of the Israelites. [22]And the people, that is, the men of Israel, encouraged themselves and again
formed the battle line at the place where they
had put themselves in array on the first day.
[23]Then the children of Israel went up and wept
before the LORD until evening, and asked
counsel of the LORD, saying, "Shall I again
draw near for battle against the children of my
brother Benjamin?"

And the LORD said, "Go up against him."

[24]So the children of Israel approached the
children of Benjamin on the second day. [25]And
Benjamin went out against them from Gibeah
on the second day, and cut down to the ground
eighteen thousand more of the children of Israel; all these drew the sword.

[26]Then all the children of Israel, that is, all
the people, went up and came to the house of
God and wept. They sat there before the LORD
and fasted that day until evening; and they
offered burnt offerings and peace offerings
before the LORD. [27]So the children of Israel

20:22–25 The Lord twice allowed great defeat and death to Israel to bring them to their spiritual senses regarding the cost of tolerating apostasy. Also, while they sought counsel, they placed too much reliance on their own prowess and on satisfying their own outrage. Finally, when desperate enough, they fasted and offered sacrifices (v. 26). The Lord then gave victory with strategy similar to that at Ai (Josh. 8).

---

inquired of the LORD (the ark of the covenant
of God *was* there in those days, [28]and Phinehas
the son of Eleazar, the son of Aaron, stood
before it in those days), saying, "Shall I yet
again go out to battle against the children of
my brother Benjamin, or shall I cease?"

And the LORD said, "Go up, for tomorrow I will
deliver them into your hand."

[29]Then Israel set men in ambush all around
Gibeah. [30]And the children of Israel went up
against the children of Benjamin on the third
day, and put themselves in battle array against
Gibeah as at the other times. [31]So the children
of Benjamin went out against the people, *and*
were drawn away from the city. They began to
strike down *and* kill some of the people, as at
the other times, in the highways (one of which
goes up to Bethel and the other to Gibeah)
and in the field, about thirty men of Israel.
[32]And the children of Benjamin said, "They *are*
defeated before us, as at first."

But the children of Israel said, "Let us flee
and draw them away from the city to the highways." [33]So all the men of Israel rose from their
place and put themselves in battle array at Baal
Tamar. Then Israel's men in ambush burst
forth from their position in the plain of Geba.
[34]And ten thousand select men from all Israel
came against Gibeah, and the battle was fierce.
But *the Benjamites* did not know that disaster
was upon them. [35]The LORD defeated Benjamin
before Israel. And the children of Israel
destroyed that day twenty-five thousand one
hundred Benjamites; all these drew the sword.

[36]So the children of Benjamin saw that they
were defeated. The men of Israel had given
ground to the Benjamites, because they relied
on the men in ambush whom they had set
against Gibeah. [37]And the men in ambush
quickly rushed upon Gibeah; the men in
ambush spread out and struck the whole city
with the edge of the sword. [38]Now the appointed signal between the men of Israel and the

men in ambush was that they would make a
great cloud of smoke rise up from the city,
39whereupon the men of Israel would turn in
battle. Now Benjamin had begun to strike *and*
kill about thirty of the men of Israel. For they
said, "Surely they are defeated before us, as *in*
the first battle." 40But when the cloud began to
rise from the city in a column of smoke, the
Benjamites looked behind them, and there
was the whole city going up *in smoke* to heav-
en. 41And when the men of Israel turned back,
the men of Benjamin panicked, for they saw
that disaster had come upon them. 42Therefore
they turned *their backs* before the men of Israel in the direction of the wilderness; but the
battle overtook them, and whoever *came* out
of the cities they destroyed in their midst.
43They surrounded the Benjamites, chased
them, *and* easily trampled them down as far as
the front of Gibeah toward the east. 44And
eighteen thousand men of Benjamin fell; all
these *were* men of valor. 45Then they turned
and fled toward the wilderness to the rock of
Rimmon; and they cut down five thousand of
them on the highways. Then they pursued
them relentlessly up to Gidom, and killed two
thousand of them. 46So all who fell of Benjamin
that day were twenty-five thousand men who
drew the sword; all these *were* men of valor.

47But six hundred men turned and fled
toward the wilderness to the rock of Rimmon,
and they stayed at the rock of Rimmon for four
months. 48And the men of Israel turned back
against the children of Benjamin, and struck
them down with the edge of the sword—from
every city, men and beasts, all who were found.
They also set fire to all the cities they came to.

21 Now the men of Israel had sworn an oath
at Mizpah, saying, "None of us shall give
his daughter to Benjamin as a wife." 2Then the
people came to the house of God, and
remained there before God till evening. They
lifted up their voices and wept bitterly, 3and
said, "O LORD God of Israel, why has this
come to pass in Israel, that today there should
be one tribe *missing* in Israel?"

4So it was, on the next morning, that the people rose early and built an altar there, and
offered burnt offerings and peace offerings.
5The children of Israel said, "Who *is there*
among all the tribes of Israel who did not come
up with the assembly to the LORD?" For they
had made a great oath concerning anyone who
had not come up to the LORD at Mizpah, saying,
"He shall surely be put to death." 6And the children of Israel grieved for Benjamin their brother, and said, "One tribe is cut off from Israel
today. 7What shall we do for wives for those
who remain, seeing we have sworn by the LORD
that we will not give them our daughters as
wives?"

8And they said, "What one *is there* from the
tribes of Israel who did not come up to Mizpah
to the LORD?" And, in fact, no one had come to
the camp from Jabesh Gilead to the assembly.
9For when the people were counted, indeed,
not one of the inhabitants of Jabesh Gilead
was there. 10So the congregation sent out there
twelve thousand of their most valiant men, and
commanded them, saying, "Go and strike the
inhabitants of Jabesh Gilead with the edge of
the sword, including the women and children.
11And this *is* the thing that you shall do: You
shall utterly destroy every male, and every
woman who has known a man intimately." 12So
they found among the inhabitants of Jabesh
Gilead four hundred young virgins who had
not known a man intimately; and they brought
them to the camp at Shiloh, which is in the
land of Canaan.

13Then the whole congregation sent *word* to
the children of Benjamin who *were* at the rock
of Rimmon, and announced peace to them.
14So Benjamin came back at that time, and
they gave them the women whom they had
saved alive of the women of Jabesh Gilead;
and yet they had not found enough for them.

15And the people grieved for Benjamin,
because the LORD had made a void in the
tribes of Israel.

16Then the elders of the congregation said,
"What shall we do for wives for those who
remain, since the women of Benjamin have
been destroyed?" 17And they said, "*There must
be* an inheritance for the survivors of Benjamin, that a tribe may not be destroyed from Israel. 18However, we cannot give them wives
from our daughters, for the children of Israel
have sworn an oath, saying, 'Cursed *be* the one
who gives a wife to Benjamin.'" 19Then they
said, "In fact, *there is* a yearly feast of the LORD
in Shiloh, which *is* north of Bethel, on the east
side of the highway that goes up from Bethel
to Shechem, and south of Lebonah."

20Therefore they instructed the children of
Benjamin, saying, "Go, lie in wait in the vineyards, 21and watch; and just when the daughters of Shiloh come out to perform their
dances, then come out from the vineyards,
and every man catch a wife for himself from
the daughters of Shiloh; then go to the land of
Benjamin. 22Then it shall be, when their
fathers or their brothers come to us to complain, that we will say to them, 'Be kind to
them for our sakes, because we did not take a
wife for any of them in the war; for *it is* not *as*

though you have given the *women* to them at
this time, making yourselves guilty of your
oath.' "
23And the children of Benjamin did so; they
took enough wives for their number from
those who danced, whom they caught. Then
they went and returned to their inheritance,
and they rebuilt the cities and dwelt in them.
24So the children of Israel departed from there
at that time, every man to his tribe and family;
they went out from there, every man to his
inheritance.
25In those days *there was* no king in Israel;
everyone did *what was* right in his own eyes.

21:25 Judges 17–21 vividly demonstrates how bizarre and deep sin can become when people throw off the authority of God as mediated through the king (see 17:6). This was the appropriate but tragic conclusion to a bleak period of Israelite history (see Deut. 12:8).

Psalm 51:12–19

12 Restore to me the joy of Your salvation,
And uphold me *by Your* generous
Spirit.
13 *Then* I will teach transgressors Your
ways,
And sinners shall be converted
to You.

14 Deliver me from the guilt of
bloodshed, O God,
The God of my salvation,
And my tongue shall sing aloud of Your
righteousness.
15 O Lord, open my lips,
And my mouth shall show forth Your
praise.
16 For You do not desire sacrifice, or else I
would give *it;*
You do not delight in burnt offering.
17 The sacrifices of God *are* a broken
spirit,
A broken and a contrite heart—
These, O God, You will not despise.
18 Do good in Your good pleasure to Zion;
Build the walls of Jerusalem.
19 Then You shall be pleased with the
sacrifices of righteousness,
With burnt offering and whole burnt
offering;
Then they shall offer bulls on
Your altar.

Proverbs 15:1–3

15 A soft answer turns away wrath,
But a harsh word stirs up anger.
2 The tongue of the wise uses
knowledge rightly,
But the mouth of fools pours forth
foolishness.
3 The eyes of the LORD *are* in every
place,
Keeping watch on the evil and the
good.

Luke 19:1–27

19 Then *Jesus* entered and passed through
Jericho. 2Now behold, *there was* a man
named Zacchaeus who was a chief tax collector, and he was rich. 3And he sought to see
who Jesus was, but could not because of the
crowd, for he was of short stature. 4So he ran
ahead and climbed up into a sycamore tree to
see Him, for He was going to pass that *way.*
5And when Jesus came to the place, He looked
up and saw him, and said to him, "Zacchaeus,
make haste and come down, for today I must
stay at your house." 6So he made haste and
came down, and received Him joyfully. 7But
when they saw *it,* they all complained, saying,
"He has gone to be a guest with a man who is
a sinner."
8Then Zacchaeus stood and said to the
Lord, "Look, Lord, I give half of my goods to
the poor; and if I have taken anything from
anyone by false accusation, I restore fourfold."
9And Jesus said to him, "Today salvation has
come to this house, because he also is a son of
Abraham; 10for the Son of Man has come to
seek and to save that which was lost."
11Now as they heard these things, He spoke
another parable, because He was near Jerusalem and because they thought the kingdom of
God would appear immediately. 12Therefore
He said: "A certain nobleman went into a far
country to receive for himself a kingdom and to
return. 13So he called ten of his servants, delivered to them ten minas, and said to them, 'Do
business till I come.' 14But his citizens hated
him, and sent a delegation after him, saying,
'We will not have this *man* to reign over us.'
15"And so it was that when he returned, having received the kingdom, he then commanded these servants, to whom he had given the
money, to be called to him, that he might
know how much every man had gained by
trading. 16Then came the first, saying, 'Master,
your mina has earned ten minas.' 17And he
said to him, 'Well *done,* good servant; because
you were faithful in a very little, have authority

19:17 faithful in a very little. Those with relatively small gifts and opportunities are just as responsible to use them faithfully as those who are given much more. **over ten cities.** The reward is incomparably greater than the 10 minas warranted. Note also that the rewards were apportioned according to the servants' diligence: the one who gained 10 minas was given 10 cities, the one who gained 5 minas, 5 cities (v. 19), and so on.

over ten cities.' [18]And the second came, saying,
'Master, your mina has earned five minas.'
[19]Likewise he said to him, 'You also be over
five cities.'
[20]"Then another came, saying, 'Master,
here is your mina, which I have kept put
away in a handkerchief. [21]For I feared you,
because you are an austere man. You collect
what you did not deposit, and reap what you
did not sow.' [22]And he said to him, 'Out of
your own mouth I will judge you, *you* wicked
servant. You knew that I was an austere man,
collecting what I did not deposit and reaping
what I did not sow. [23]Why then did you not
put my money in the bank, that at my coming
I might have collected it with interest?'
[24]"And he said to those who stood by, 'Take
the mina from him, and give *it* to him who has
ten minas.' [25](But they said to him, 'Master, he
has ten minas.') [26]'For I say to you, that to
everyone who has will be given; and from him
who does not have, even what he has will be
taken away from him. [27]But bring here those
enemies of mine, who did not want me to
reign over them, and slay *them* before me.'"

DAY 27: How did Zacchaeus personify why Jesus came to this world?

Zacchaeus was a chief tax collector, who probably oversaw a large tax district and had other tax collectors working for him (Luke 19:2). Jericho alone was a prosperous trading center, so it is certain that Zacchaeus was a wealthy man. Zacchaeus was among "the crowd" in Jericho who lined the street to see Jesus pass through. They had undoubtedly heard about the recent raising of Lazarus in Bethany, less than 15 miles away (John 11). That, combined with His fame as a healer and teacher, stirred the entire city when word arrived that He was coming. Zacchaeus was so desperate to see Christ that he took an undignified position for someone of his rank (v. 4).

Both the religious elite and the common people hated Zacchaeus. They did not understand, and in their blind pride refused to see, what possible righteous purpose Jesus had in visiting such a notorious sinner (v. 7). But He had come to seek and to save the lost, which is exactly what happened here (v. 10).

Not only did Zacchaeus receive Jesus joyfully (v. 6), but his willingness to make restitution was proof that his conversion was genuine (v. 8). It was the fruit, not the condition, of his salvation. The law required a penalty of one-fifth as restitution for money acquired by fraud (Lev. 6:5; Num. 5:6,7), so Zacchaeus was doing more than was required. Zacchaeus judged his own crime severely, acknowledging that he was as guilty as the lowest common robber. Since much of his wealth had probably been acquired fraudulently, this was a costly commitment. On top of that, he gave half his goods to the poor. But Zacchaeus had just found incomprehensible spiritual riches and did not mind the loss of material wealth.

APRIL 28

Ruth 1:1–2:23

1 Now it came to pass, in the days when the
judges ruled, that there was a famine in the
land. And a certain man of Bethehem, Judah,
went to dwell in the country of Moab, he and
his wife and his two sons. [2]The name of the man
was Elimelech, the name of his wife *was* Naomi,
and the names of his two sons *were* Mahlon
and Chilion—Ephrathites of Bethlehem,
Judah. And they went to the country of Moab
and remained there. [3]Then Elimelech,
Naomi's husband, died; and she was left, and
her two sons. [4]Now they took wives of the
women of Moab: the name of the one *was*
Orpah, and the name of the other Ruth. And
they dwelt there about ten years. [5]Then both
Mahlon and Chilion also died; so the woman
survived her two sons and her husband.
[6]Then she arose with her daughters-in-law
that she might return from the country of
Moab, for she had heard in the country of
Moab that the LORD had visited His people by
giving them bread. [7]Therefore she went out

from the place where she was, and her two
daughters-in-law with her; and they went on
the way to return to the land of Judah. [8]And
Naomi said to her two daughters-in-law, "Go,
return each to her mother's house. The LORD
deal kindly with you, as you have dealt with
the dead and with me. [9]The LORD grant that
you may find rest, each in the house of her
husband."

So she kissed them, and they lifted up their
voices and wept. [10]And they said to her, "Surely
we will return with you to your people."

[11]But Naomi said, "Turn back, my daughters; why will you go with me? *Are* there still
sons in my womb, that they may be your husbands? [12]Turn back, my daughters, go—for I
am too old to have a husband. If I should say I
have hope, *if* I should have a husband tonight
and should also bear sons, [13]would you wait for
them till they were grown? Would you restrain
yourselves from having husbands? No, my
daughters; for it grieves me very much for
your sakes that the hand of the LORD has gone
out against me!"

[14]Then they lifted up their voices and wept
again; and Orpah kissed her mother-in-law,
but Ruth clung to her.

[15]And she said, "Look, your sister-in-law has
gone back to her people and to her gods;
return after your sister-in-law."

[16]But Ruth said:

"Entreat me not to leave you,
Or to turn back from following
after you;
For wherever you go, I will go;
And wherever you lodge,
I will lodge;
Your people *shall be* my people,
And your God, my God.
17 Where you die, I will die,
And there will I be buried.
The LORD do so to me, and
more also,
If *anything but* death parts you
and me."

[18]When she saw that she was determined to go
with her, she stopped speaking to her.

1:16 And your God, my God. This testimony evidenced Ruth's conversion from worshiping Chemosh to Yahweh of Israel (see 1 Thess. 1:9,10).

[19]Now the two of them went until they came
to Bethlehem. And it happened, when they
had come to Bethlehem, that all the city was
excited because of them; and the women said,
"*Is* this Naomi?"

[20]But she said to them, "Do not call me
Naomi; call me Mara, for the Almighty has
dealt very bitterly with me. [21]I went out full,
and the LORD has brought me home again
empty. Why do you call me Naomi, since the
LORD has testified against me, and the
Almighty has afflicted me?"

[22]So Naomi returned, and Ruth the
Moabitess her daughter-in-law with her, who
returned from the country of Moab. Now they
came to Bethlehem at the beginning of barley
harvest.

2 There was a relative of Naomi's husband,
a man of great wealth, of the family of
Elimelech. His name *was* Boaz. [2]So Ruth the
Moabitess said to Naomi, "Please let me go to
the field, and glean heads of grain after *him* in
whose sight I may find favor."

And she said to her, "Go, my daughter."
[3]Then she left, and went and gleaned in the
field after the reapers. And she happened to
come to the part of the field *belonging* to Boaz,
who *was* of the family of Elimelech.

[4]Now behold, Boaz came from Bethlehem,
and said to the reapers, "The LORD *be* with you!"

And they answered him, "The LORD bless
you!"

[5]Then Boaz said to his servant who was in
charge of the reapers, "Whose young woman
is this?"

[6]So the servant who was in charge of the
reapers answered and said, "It *is* the young
Moabite woman who came back with Naomi
from the country of Moab. [7]And she said, 'Please
let me glean and gather after the reapers among
the sheaves.' So she came and has continued
from morning until now, though she rested a
little in the house."

[8]Then Boaz said to Ruth, "You will listen, my
daughter, will you not? Do not go to glean in
another field, nor go from here, but stay close
by my young women. [9]*Let* your eyes *be* on the
field which they reap, and go after them. Have
I not commanded the young men not to touch
you? And when you are thirsty, go to the vessels and drink from what the young men have
drawn."

[10]So she fell on her face, bowed down to the
ground, and said to him, "Why have I found favor in your eyes, that you should take notice of
me, since I *am* a foreigner?"

[11]And Boaz answered and said to her, "It has
been fully reported to me, all that you have

done for your mother-in-law since the death of
your husband, and *how* you have left your
father and your mother and the land of your
birth, and have come to a people whom you
did not know before. 12The LORD repay your
work, and a full reward be given you by the
LORD God of Israel, under whose wings you
have come for refuge."

2:12 wings...refuge. Scripture pictures God as catching Israel up on His wings in the Exodus (Ex. 19:4; Deut. 32:11). God is here portrayed as a mother bird sheltering the young and fragile with her wings (see Pss. 17:8; 36:7; 57:1; 61:4; 63:7; 91:1,4). Boaz blessed Ruth in light of her newfound commitment to and dependence on the Lord. Later, he would become God's answer to this prayer (see 3:9).

13Then she said, "Let me find favor in your
sight, my lord; for you have comforted me, and
have spoken kindly to your maidservant,
though I am not like one of your maidservants."
14Now Boaz said to her at mealtime, "Come
here, and eat of the bread, and dip your piece
of bread in the vinegar." So she sat beside the
reapers, and he passed parched *grain* to her;
and she ate and was satisfied, and kept some
back. 15And when she rose up to glean, Boaz
commanded his young men, saying, "Let her
glean even among the sheaves, and do not reproach her. 16Also let *grain* from the bundles
fall purposely for her; leave *it* that she may
glean, and do not rebuke her."
17So she gleaned in the field until evening,
and beat out what she had gleaned, and it was
about an ephah of barley. 18Then she took *it* up
and went into the city, and her mother-in-law
saw what she had gleaned. So she brought out
and gave to her what she had kept back after
she had been satisfied.
19And her mother-in-law said to her, "Where
have you gleaned today? And where did you
work? Blessed be the one who took notice of
you."
So she told her mother-in-law with whom
she had worked, and said, "The man's name
with whom I worked today *is* Boaz."
20Then Naomi said to her daughter-in-law,
"Blessed *be* he of the LORD, who has not forsaken His kindness to the living and the
dead!" And Naomi said to her, "This man *is* a
relation of ours, one of our close relatives."
21Ruth the Moabitess said, "He also said to
me, 'You shall stay close by my young men
until they have finished all my harvest.'"
22And Naomi said to Ruth her daughter-in-
law, "*It is* good, my daughter, that you go out
with his young women, and that people do not
meet you in any other field." 23So she stayed
close by the young women of Boaz, to glean
until the end of barley harvest and wheat harvest; and she dwelt with her mother-in-law.

Psalm 52:1–5

To the Chief Musician. A Contemplation of David when Doeg the Edomite went and told Saul, and said to him, "David has gone to the house of Ahimelech."

Why do you boast in evil,
O mighty man?
The goodness of God *endures*
continually.

52:1 mighty man. A reference to Doeg, the chief of Saul's shepherds, who reported to Saul that the priests of Nob had aided David when he was a fugitive (see 1 Sam. 22:9,18,19).

2 Your tongue devises destruction,
Like a sharp razor, working
deceitfully.
3 You love evil more than good,
Lying rather than speaking
righteousness. Selah
4 You love all devouring words,
You deceitful tongue.
5 God shall likewise destroy
you forever;
He shall take you away, and pluck you
out of *your* dwelling place,
And uproot you from the land
of the living. Selah

Proverbs 15:4–5

4 A wholesome tongue *is* a tree of life,
But perverseness in it breaks the
spirit.
5 A fool despises his father's instruction,
But he who receives correction
is prudent.

Luke 19:28–48

28When He had said this, He went on ahead,
going up to Jerusalem. 29And it came to pass,
when He drew near to Bethphage and
Bethany, at the mountain called Olivet, *that* He

sent two of His disciples, [30]saying, "Go into the
village opposite *you,* where as you enter you
will find a colt tied, on which no one has ever
sat. Loose it and bring *it here.* [31]And if anyone
asks you, 'Why are you loosing *it?*' thus you
shall say to him, 'Because the Lord has need
of it.' "

[32]So those who were sent went their way and
found *it* just as He had said to them. [33]But as
they were loosing the colt, the owners of it
said to them, "Why are you loosing the colt?"
[34]And they said, "The Lord has need of
him." [35]Then they brought him to Jesus. And
they threw their own clothes on the colt, and
they set Jesus on him. [36]And as He went, *many*
spread their clothes on the road.

[37]Then, as He was now drawing near the
descent of the Mount of Olives, the whole multitude of the disciples began to rejoice and
praise God with a loud voice for all the mighty
works they had seen, [38]saying:

"'*Blessed is the King who comes in the*
name of the LORD!'
Peace in heaven and glory in the
highest!"

[39]And some of the Pharisees called to Him
from the crowd, "Teacher, rebuke Your disciples."

[40]But He answered and said to them, "I tell
you that if these should keep silent, the stones
would immediately cry out."

[41]Now as He drew near, He saw the city and
wept over it, [42]saying, "If you had known, even
you, especially in this your day, the things *that*
make for your peace! But now they are hidden
from your eyes. [43]For days will come upon you
when your enemies will build an embankment
around you, surround you and close you in on
every side, [44]and level you, and your children
within you, to the ground; and they will not
leave in you one stone upon another, because
you did not know the time of your visitation."

[45]Then He went into the temple and began
to drive out those who bought and sold in it,
[46]saying to them, "It is written, '*My house is a*
house of prayer,' but you have made it a '*den*
of thieves.' "

[47]And He was teaching daily in the temple.
But the chief priests, the scribes, and the
leaders of the people sought to destroy Him,
[48]and were unable to do anything; for all the
people were very attentive to hear Him.

19:40 the stones would immediately cry out. This was a strong claim of Deity and perhaps a reference to the words of Habakkuk 2:11. Scripture often speaks of inanimate nature praising God. (See Pss. 96:11; 98:7–9; 114:7; Is. 55:12.) See also the words of John the Baptist in Matthew 3:9; note the fulfillment of Jesus' words in Matthew 27:51.

19:41,42 Only Luke recorded the weeping of Jesus over the city of Jerusalem. Christ grieved over Jerusalem on at least two other occasions (13:34; Matt. 23:37). The timing of this lament may seem incongruous with the Triumphal Entry, but it reveals that Jesus knew the true superficiality of the peoples' hearts, and His mood was anything but giddy as He rode into the city. The same crowd would soon cry for His death (23:21).

DAY 28: Why is the "kinsman-redeemer" a prominent part in the story of Ruth?

In Ruth 2:20, the great kinsman-redeemer theme of Ruth begins (cf. 3:9,12; 4:1,3,6,8,14). A close relative could redeem 1) a family member sold into slavery (Lev. 25:47–49), 2) land which needed to be sold under economic hardship (Lev. 25:23–28), and/or 3) the family name by virtue of a levirate marriage (Deut. 25:5–10). This earthly custom pictures the reality of God the Redeemer doing a greater work (Pss. 19:14; 78:35; Is. 41:14; 43:14) by reclaiming those who needed to be spiritually redeemed out of slavery to sin (Ps. 107:2; Is. 62:12). Thus, Boaz pictures Christ, who as a Brother (Heb. 2:17) redeemed those who 1) were slaves to sin (Rom. 6:15–18), 2) had lost all earthly possessions/privilege in the Fall (Gen. 3:17–19), and 3) had been alienated by sin from God (2 Cor. 5:18–21). Boaz stands in the direct line of Christ (Matt. 1:5; Luke 3:32). This turn of events marks the point where Naomi's human emptiness (1:21) begins to be refilled by the Lord. Her night of earthly doubt has been broken by the dawning of new hope (cf. Rom. 8:28–39).

When Boaz negotiated with another relative about the settlement of Elimelech and Naomi's estate in Ruth 4:1–12, he referred to a law established by Moses in Deuteronomy 25:5–10. That law set out specific actions to be taken by the surviving family if a married son were to die without a son to inherit or carry on his name. Another (presumably unmarried) man in the family was to marry the widow. The first resulting child would inherit the estate of the man who had died.

APRIL 29

Ruth 3:1–4:22

3 Then Naomi her mother-in-law said to her, "My daughter, shall I not seek security for you, that it may be well with you? [2]Now Boaz, whose young women you were with, *is he* not our relative? In fact, he is winnowing barley tonight at the threshing floor. [3]Therefore wash yourself and anoint yourself, put on your *best* garment and go down to the threshing floor; *but* do not make yourself known to the man until he has finished eating and drinking. [4]Then it shall be, when he lies down, that you shall notice the place where he lies; and you shall go in, uncover his feet, and lie down; and he will tell you what you should do."

[5]And she said to her, "All that you say to me I will do."

[6]So she went down to the threshing floor and did according to all that her mother-in-law instructed her. [7]And after Boaz had eaten and drunk, and his heart was cheerful, he went to lie down at the end of the heap of grain; and she came softly, uncovered his feet, and lay down.

[8]Now it happened at midnight that the man was startled, and turned himself; and there, a woman was lying at his feet. [9]And he said, "Who *are* you?"

So she answered, "I *am* Ruth, your maidservant. Take your maidservant under your wing, for you are a close relative."

[10]Then he said, "Blessed *are* you of the LORD, my daughter! For you have shown more kindness at the end than at the beginning, in that you did not go after young men, whether poor or rich. [11]And now, my daughter, do not fear. I will do for you all that you request, for all the people of my town know that you *are* a virtuous woman. [12]Now it is true that I *am* a close relative; however, there is a relative closer than I. [13]Stay this night, and in the morning it shall be *that* if he will perform the duty of a close relative for you—good; let him do it. But if he does not want to perform the duty for you, then I will perform the duty for you, *as* the LORD lives! Lie down until morning."

[14]So she lay at his feet until morning, and she arose before one could recognize another. Then he said, "Do not let it be known that the woman came to the threshing floor." [15]Also he said, "Bring the shawl that *is* on you and hold it." And when she held it, he measured six *ephahs* of barley, and laid *it* on her. Then she went into the city.

[16]When she came to her mother-in-law, she said, "*Is* that you, my daughter?"

Then she told her all that the man had done for her. [17]And she said, "These six *ephahs* of barley he gave me; for he said to me, 'Do not go empty-handed to your mother-in-law.' "

[18]Then she said, "Sit still, my daughter, until you know how the matter will turn out; for the man will not rest until he has concluded the matter this day."

4 Now Boaz went up to the gate and sat down there; and behold, the close relative of whom Boaz had spoken came by. So Boaz said, "Come aside, friend, sit down here." So he came aside and sat down. [2]And he took ten men of the elders of the city, and said, "Sit down here." So they sat down. [3]Then he said to the close relative, "Naomi, who has come back from the country of Moab, sold the piece of land which *belonged* to our brother Elimelech. [4]And I thought to inform you, saying, 'Buy *it* back in the presence of the inhabitants and the elders of my people. If you will redeem *it,* redeem *it;* but if you will not redeem *it, then* tell me, that I may know; for *there is* no one but you to redeem *it,* and I *am* next after you.' "

And he said, "I will redeem *it.*"

[5]Then Boaz said, "On the day you buy the field from the hand of Naomi, you must also buy *it* from Ruth the Moabitess, the wife of the dead, to perpetuate the name of the dead through his inheritance."

[6]And the close relative said, "I cannot redeem *it* for myself, lest I ruin my own inheritance. You redeem my right of redemption for yourself, for I cannot redeem *it.*"

[7]Now this *was the custom* in former times in Israel concerning redeeming and exchanging, to confirm anything: one man took off his sandal and gave *it* to the other, and this *was* a confirmation in Israel.

[8]Therefore the close relative said to Boaz, "Buy *it* for yourself." So he took off his sandal. [9]And Boaz said to the elders and all the people,

4:7 took off his sandal. The scripture writer explained to his own generation what had been a custom in former generations. This kind of tradition appears in Deuteronomy 25:5–10 and apparently continued at least to the time of Amos (see 2:6; 8:6). The closer relative legally transferred his right to the property as symbolized by the sandal, most likely that of the nearer relative.

"You *are* witnesses this day that I have bought
all that was Elimelech's, and all that *was*
Chilion's and Mahlon's, from the hand of
Naomi. 10Moreover, Ruth the Moabitess, the
widow of Mahlon, I have acquired as my wife,
to perpetuate the name of the dead through
his inheritance, that the name of the dead may
not be cut off from among his brethren and
from his position at the gate. You *are* witnesses this day."
11And all the people who *were* at the gate,
and the elders, said, "*We are* witnesses. The
LORD make the woman who is coming to your
house like Rachel and Leah, the two who built
the house of Israel; and may you prosper in
Ephrathah and be famous in Bethlehem. 12May
your house be like the house of Perez, whom
Tamar bore to Judah, because of the offspring
which the LORD will give you from this young
woman."
13So Boaz took Ruth and she became his
wife; and when he went in to her, the LORD
gave her conception, and she bore a son.
14Then the women said to Naomi, "Blessed *be*
the LORD, who has not left you this day without
a close relative; and may his name be famous
in Israel! 15And may he be to you a restorer of
life and a nourisher of your old age; for your
daughter-in-law, who loves you, who is better
to you than seven sons, has borne him."
16Then Naomi took the child and laid him on
her bosom, and became a nurse to him. 17Also
the neighbor women gave him a name, saying,
"There is a son born to Naomi." And they
called his name Obed. He *is* the father of
Jesse, the father of David.
18Now this *is* the genealogy of Perez: Perez
begot Hezron; 19Hezron begot Ram, and Ram
begot Amminadab; 20Amminadab begot
Nahshon, and Nahshon begot Salmon;
21Salmon begot Boaz, and Boaz begot Obed;
22Obed begot Jesse, and Jesse begot David.

4:22 David. Looking back at Ruth from a New Testament perspective, latent messianic implications become more apparent (see Matt. 1:1). The fruit which is promised later on in the Davidic Covenant (2 Sam. 7:1–17) finds its seedbed here. The hope of a messianic king and kingdom (2 Sam. 7:12–14) will be fulfilled in the Lord Jesus Christ (Rev. 19–20) through the lineage of David's grandfather Obed who was born to Boaz and Ruth the Moabitess.

Psalm 52:6–9

6 The righteous also shall see and fear,
And shall laugh at him, *saying*,
7 "Here is the man *who* did not make God
his strength,
But trusted in the abundance of his
riches,
And strengthened himself in his
wickedness."

8 But I *am* like a green olive tree in the
house of God;
I trust in the mercy of God forever
and ever.

52:8 green olive tree. The psalmist exults (through this simile) that the one who trusts in the mercy of God is productive and secure.

9 I will praise You forever,
Because You have done *it;*
And in the presence of Your saints
I will wait on Your name,
for *it is* good.

Proverbs 15:6–7

6 *In* the house of the righteous
there is much treasure,
But in the revenue of the wicked
is trouble.
7 The lips of the wise disperse
knowledge,
But the heart of the fool *does* not
do so.

Luke 20:1–26

20 Now it happened on one of those days,
as He taught the people in the temple
and preached the gospel, *that* the chief
priests and the scribes, together with the elders, confronted *Him* 2and spoke to Him, saying, "Tell us, by what authority are You doing
these things? Or who is he who gave You this
authority?"
3But He answered and said to them, "I also
will ask you one thing, and answer Me: 4The
baptism of John—was it from heaven or from
men?"
5And they reasoned among themselves, saying, "If we say, 'From heaven,' He will say,
'Why then did you not believe him?' 6But if we
say, 'From men,' all the people will stone us, for
they are persuaded that John was a prophet."

20:5 Why then did you not believe him? John had clearly testified that Jesus was the Messiah. If John was a prophet whose words were true, they ought to believe his testimony about Christ. On the other hand, it would have been political folly for the Pharisees to attack the legitimacy of John the Baptist or deny his authority as a prophet of God. John was enormously popular with the people and a martyr at the hands of the despised Herod. For the Pharisees to question John's authority was to attack a national hero, and they knew better than that. So they pleaded ignorance (v. 7).

7So they answered that they did not know where *it was* from.

8And Jesus said to them, "Neither will I tell you by what authority I do these things."

9Then He began to tell the people this parable: "A certain man planted a vineyard, leased it to vinedressers, and went into a far country for a long time. 10Now at vintage-time he sent a servant to the vinedressers, that they might give him some of the fruit of the vineyard. But the vinedressers beat him and sent *him* away empty-handed. 11Again he sent another servant; and they beat him also, treated *him* shamefully, and sent *him* away empty-handed. 12And again he sent a third; and they wounded him also and cast *him* out.

13"Then the owner of the vineyard said, 'What shall I do? I will send my beloved son. Probably they will respect *him* when they see him.' 14But when the vinedressers saw him, they reasoned among themselves, saying, 'This is the heir. Come, let us kill him, that the inheritance may be ours.' 15So they cast him out of the vineyard and killed *him*. Therefore what will the owner of the vineyard do to them? 16He will come and destroy those vinedressers and give the vineyard to others."

And when they heard *it* they said, "Certainly not!"

17Then He looked at them and said, "What then is this that is written:

'The stone which the builders rejected
Has become the chief cornerstone'?

18Whoever falls on that stone will be broken; but on whomever it falls, it will grind him to powder."

19And the chief priests and the scribes that very hour sought to lay hands on Him, but they feared the people—for they knew He had spoken this parable against them.

20So they watched *Him*, and sent spies who pretended to be righteous, that they might seize on His words, in order to deliver Him to the power and the authority of the governor.

21Then they asked Him, saying, "Teacher, we know that You say and teach rightly, and You do not show personal favoritism, but teach the way of God in truth: 22Is it lawful for us to pay taxes to Caesar or not?"

23But He perceived their craftiness, and said to them, "Why do you test Me? 24Show Me a denarius. Whose image and inscription does it have?"

They answered and said, "Caesar's."

25And He said to them, "Render therefore to Caesar the things that are Caesar's, and to God the things that are God's."

26But they could not catch Him in His words in the presence of the people. And they marveled at His answer and kept silent.

DAY 29: How does Ruth exemplify the Proverbs 31 wife?

The "virtuous" wife of Proverbs 31:10 is personified by "virtuous" Ruth of whom the same Hebrew word is used (Ruth 3:11). With amazing parallel, they share at least 8 character traits (see below). One wonders (in concert with Jewish tradition) if King Lemuel's mother might not have been Bathsheba, who orally passed the family heritage of Ruth's spotless reputation along to David's son Solomon. Lemuel, which means "devoted to God," could have been a family name for Solomon (see Jedidiah, 2 Sam. 12:25), who then could have penned Proverbs 31:10–31 with Ruth in mind:

1. Devoted to her family (Ruth 1:15–18 // Prov. 31:10–12,23).
2. Delighted in her work (Ruth 2:2 // Prov. 31:13).
3. Diligent in her labor (Ruth 2:7,17,23 // Prov. 31:14–18,19–21,24,27).
4. Dedicated to godly speech (Ruth 2:10,13 // Prov. 13:26).
5. Dependent on God (Ruth 2:12 // Prov. 31:25b,30).
6. Dressed with care (Ruth 3:3 // Prov. 31:22,25a).
7. Discreet with men (Ruth 3:6–13 // Prov. 31:11,12,23).
8. Delivered blessings (Ruth 4:14,15 // Prov. 31:28,29,31)

APRIL 30

1 Samuel 1:1–3:21

1 Now there was a certain man of Ramathaim Zophim, of the mountains of Ephraim, and his name *was* Elkanah the son of Jeroham, the son of Elihu, the son of Tohu, the son of Zuph, an Ephraimite. 2And he had two wives: the name of one *was* Hannah, and the name of the other Peninnah. Peninnah had children, but Hannah had no children. 3This man went up from his city yearly to worship and sacrifice to the LORD of hosts in Shiloh. Also the two sons of Eli, Hophni and Phinehas, the priests of the LORD, *were* there. 4And whenever the time came for Elkanah to make an offering, he would give portions to Peninnah his wife and to all her sons and daughters. 5But to Hannah he would give a double portion, for he loved Hannah, although the LORD had closed her womb. 6And her rival also provoked her severely, to make her miserable, because the LORD had closed her womb. 7So it was, year by year, when she went up to the house of the LORD, that she provoked her; therefore she wept and did not eat.

8Then Elkanah her husband said to her, "Hannah, why do you weep? Why do you not eat? And why is your heart grieved? *Am* I not better to you than ten sons?"

9So Hannah arose after they had finished eating and drinking in Shiloh. Now Eli the priest was sitting on the seat by the doorpost of the tabernacle of the LORD. 10And she *was* in bitterness of soul, and prayed to the LORD and wept in anguish. 11Then she made a vow and said, "O LORD of hosts, if You will indeed look on the affliction of Your maidservant and remember me, and not forget Your maidservant, but will give Your maidservant a male child, then I will give him to the LORD all the days of his life, and no razor shall come upon his head."

12And it happened, as she continued praying before the LORD, that Eli watched her mouth. 13Now Hannah spoke in her heart; only her lips moved, but her voice was not heard. Therefore Eli thought she was drunk. 14So Eli said to her, "How long will you be drunk? Put your wine away from you!"

15But Hannah answered and said, "No, my lord, I *am* a woman of sorrowful spirit. I have drunk neither wine nor intoxicating drink, but have poured out my soul before the LORD. 16Do not consider your maidservant a wicked woman, for out of the abundance of my complaint and grief I have spoken until now."

17Then Eli answered and said, "Go in peace, and the God of Israel grant your petition which you have asked of Him."

18And she said, "Let your maidservant find favor in your sight." So the woman went her way and ate, and her face was no longer *sad.*

19Then they rose early in the morning and worshiped before the LORD, and returned and came to their house at Ramah. And Elkanah knew Hannah his wife, and the LORD remembered her. 20So it came to pass in the process of time that Hannah conceived and bore a son, and called his name Samuel, *saying,* "Because I have asked for him from the LORD."

21Now the man Elkanah and all his house went up to offer to the LORD the yearly sacrifice and his vow. 22But Hannah did not go up, for she said to her husband, "*Not* until the child is weaned; then I will take him, that he may appear before the LORD and remain there forever."

23So Elkanah her husband said to her, "Do what seems best to you; wait until you have weaned him. Only let the LORD establish His word." Then the woman stayed and nursed her son until she had weaned him.

24Now when she had weaned him, she took him up with her, with three bulls, one ephah of flour, and a skin of wine, and brought him to the house of the LORD in Shiloh. And the child *was* young. 25Then they slaughtered a bull, and brought the child to Eli. 26And she said, "O my lord! As your soul lives, my lord, I *am* the woman who stood by you here, praying to the LORD. 27For this child I prayed, and the LORD has granted me my petition which I asked of Him. 28Therefore I also have lent him to the LORD; as long as he lives he shall be lent to the LORD." So they worshiped the LORD there.

2 And Hannah prayed and said:

"My heart rejoices in the LORD;
My horn is exalted in the LORD.
I smile at my enemies,
Because I rejoice in Your salvation.

2 "No one is holy like the LORD,
For *there is* none besides You,
Nor *is there* any rock like our God.

3 "Talk no more so very proudly;
Let no arrogance come from your mouth,
For the LORD *is* the God of knowledge;
And by Him actions are weighed.

4 "The bows of the mighty men *are* broken,
And those who stumbled are girded with strength.

5 *Those who were* full have hired
themselves out for bread,
And the hungry have ceased
to hunger.
Even the barren has borne seven,
And she who has many children has
become feeble.

6 "The LORD kills and makes alive;
He brings down to the grave and
brings up.
7 The LORD makes poor and makes rich;
He brings low and lifts up.
8 He raises the poor from the dust
And lifts the beggar from the ash heap,
To set *them* among princes
And make them inherit the throne of
glory.
"For the pillars of the earth *are* the
LORD's,
And He has set the world upon them.
9 He will guard the feet of His saints,
But the wicked shall be silent in
darkness.
"For by strength no man shall prevail.
10 The adversaries of the LORD shall be
broken in pieces;
From heaven He will thunder against
them.
The LORD will judge the ends of the
earth.
"He will give strength to His king,
And exalt the horn of His anointed."

11 Then Elkanah went to his house at Ramah.
But the child ministered to the LORD before
Eli the priest.
12 Now the sons of Eli *were* corrupt; they did
not know the LORD. 13 And the priests' custom
with the people *was that* when any man
offered a sacrifice, the priest's servant would
come with a three-pronged fleshhook in his
hand while the meat was boiling. 14 Then he
would thrust *it* into the pan, or kettle, or caldron, or pot; and the priest would take for himself all that the fleshhook brought up. So they
did in Shiloh to all the Israelites who came
there. 15 Also, before they burned the fat, the
priest's servant would come and say to the
man who sacrificed, "Give meat for roasting to
the priest, for he will not take boiled meat
from you, but raw."
16 And *if* the man said to him, "They should
really burn the fat first; *then* you may take *as
much* as your heart desires," he would then
answer him, "*No,* but you must give *it* now;
and if not, I will take *it* by force."
17 Therefore the sin of the young men was
very great before the LORD, for men abhorred
the offering of the LORD.
18 But Samuel ministered before the LORD,
even as a child, wearing a linen ephod. 19 Moreover his mother used to make him a little
robe, and bring *it* to him year by year when
she came up with her husband to offer the
yearly sacrifice. 20 And Eli would bless Elkanah
and his wife, and say, "The LORD give you
descendants from this woman for the loan that
was given to the LORD." Then they would go to
their own home.
21 And the LORD visited Hannah, so that she
conceived and bore three sons and two daughters. Meanwhile the child Samuel grew before
the LORD.
22 Now Eli was very old; and he heard
everything his sons did to all Israel, and how
they lay with the women who assembled at
the door of the tabernacle of meeting. 23 So he
said to them, "Why do you do such things?
For I hear of your evil dealings from all the
people. 24 No, my sons! For *it is* not a good
report that I hear. You make the LORD's people transgress. 25 If one man sins against
another, God will judge him. But if a man sins
against the LORD, who will intercede for
him?" Nevertheless they did not heed the
voice of their father, because the LORD
desired to kill them.
26 And the child Samuel grew in stature, and
in favor both with the LORD and men.
27 Then a man of God came to Eli and said to
him, "Thus says the LORD: 'Did I not clearly
reveal Myself to the house of your father when
they were in Egypt in Pharaoh's house? 28 Did I
not choose him out of all the tribes of Israel *to
be* My priest, to offer upon My altar, to burn
incense, and to wear an ephod before Me?
And did I not give to the house of your father
all the offerings of the children of Israel made
by fire? 29 Why do you kick at My sacrifice and
My offering which I have commanded *in My*
dwelling place, and honor your sons more
than Me, to make yourselves fat with the best
of all the offerings of Israel My people?'
30 Therefore the LORD God of Israel says: 'I said
indeed *that* your house and the house of your
father would walk before Me forever.' But now
the LORD says: 'Far be it from Me; for those
who honor Me I will honor, and those who
despise Me shall be lightly esteemed. 31 Behold, the days are coming that I will cut off
your arm and the arm of your father's house,
so that there will not be an old man in your
house. 32 And you will see an enemy *in My*
dwelling place, *despite* all the good which God

does for Israel. And there shall not be an old man in your house forever. 33 But any of your men *whom* I do not cut off from My altar shall consume your eyes and grieve your heart. And all the descendants of your house shall die in the flower of their age. 34 Now this *shall be* a sign to you that will come upon your two sons, on Hophni and Phinehas: in one day they shall die, both of them. 35 Then I will raise up for Myself a faithful priest *who* shall do according to what *is* in My heart and in My mind. I will build him a sure house, and he shall walk before My anointed forever. 36 And it shall come to pass that everyone who is left in your house will come *and* bow down to him for a piece of silver and a morsel of bread, and say, "Please, put me in one of the priestly positions, that I may eat a piece of bread." ' "

3 Now the boy Samuel ministered to the LORD before Eli. And the word of the LORD was rare in those days; *there was* no widespread revelation. 2 And it came to pass at that time, while Eli *was* lying down in his place, and when his eyes had begun to grow so dim that he could not see, 3 and before the lamp of God went out in the tabernacle of the LORD where the ark of God *was,* and while Samuel was lying down, 4 that the LORD called Samuel. And he answered, "Here I am!" 5 So he ran to

3:1 the boy Samuel. Samuel was no longer a child (2:21,26). While Jewish historian Josephus suggested he was 12 years of age, he was probably a teenager at this time. The same Hebrew term translated here "boy" was used of David when he slew Goliath (17:33). **the word of the LORD was rare.** The time of the judges was a period of extremely limited prophetic activity. The few visions that God did give were not widely known. **revelation.** Literally, "vision." A divine revelation mediated through an auditory or visual encounter.

Eli and said, "Here I am, for you called me."

And he said, "I did not call; lie down again." And he went and lay down.

6 Then the LORD called yet again, "Samuel!"

So Samuel arose and went to Eli, and said, "Here I am, for you called me." He answered, "I did not call, my son; lie down again." 7 (Now Samuel did not yet know the LORD, nor was the word of the LORD yet revealed to him.)

8 And the LORD called Samuel again the third time. So he arose and went to Eli, and said, "Here I am, for you did call me."

Then Eli perceived that the LORD had called the boy. 9 Therefore Eli said to Samuel, "Go, lie down; and it shall be, if He calls you, that you must say, 'Speak, LORD, for Your servant hears.' " So Samuel went and lay down in his place.

10 Now the LORD came and stood and called as at other times, "Samuel! Samuel!"

And Samuel answered, "Speak, for Your servant hears."

11 Then the LORD said to Samuel: "Behold, I will do something in Israel at which both ears of everyone who hears it will tingle. 12 In that day I will perform against Eli all that I have spoken concerning his house, from beginning to end. 13 For I have told him that I will judge his house forever for the iniquity which he knows, because his sons made themselves vile, and he did not restrain them. 14 And therefore I have sworn to the house of Eli that the iniquity of Eli's house shall not be atoned for by sacrifice or offering forever."

15 So Samuel lay down until morning, and opened the doors of the house of the LORD. And Samuel was afraid to tell Eli the vision. 16 Then Eli called Samuel and said, "Samuel, my son!"

He answered, "Here I am."

17 And he said, "What *is* the word that *the LORD* spoke to you? Please do not hide *it* from me. God do so to you, and more also, if you hide anything from me of all the things that He said to you." 18 Then Samuel told him everything, and hid nothing from him. And he said, "It *is* the LORD. Let Him do what seems good to Him."

19 So Samuel grew, and the LORD was with him and let none of his words fall to the ground. 20 And all Israel from Dan to Beersheba knew that Samuel *had been* established as a prophet of the LORD. 21 Then the LORD appeared again in Shiloh. For the LORD revealed Himself to Samuel in Shiloh by the word of the LORD.

3:19 the LORD was with him. The Lord's presence was with Samuel, as it would be later with David (16:18; 18:12). The Lord's presence validated His choice of a man for His service. **let none of his words fall to the ground.** Everything Samuel said with divine authorization came true. This fulfillment of Samuel's word proved that he was a true prophet of God (see Deut. 18:21,22).

Psalm 53:1–6

To the Chief Musician. Set to "Mahalath."
A Contemplation of David.

The fool has said in his heart,
"*There is* no God."
They are corrupt, and have done
abominable iniquity;
There is none who does good.

2 God looks down from heaven upon
the children of men,
To see if there are *any* who
understand, who seek God.
3 Every one of them has turned aside;
They have together become corrupt;
There is none who does good,
No, not one.

4 Have the workers of iniquity no
knowledge,
Who eat up my people *as* they eat
bread,
And do not call upon God?
5 There they are in great fear
Where no fear was,
For God has scattered the bones of
him who encamps against you;
You have put *them* to shame,
Because God has despised them.

6 Oh, that the salvation of Israel would
come out of Zion!
When God brings back the captivity
of His people,
Let Jacob rejoice *and* Israel be glad.

Proverbs 15:8–11

8 The sacrifice of the wicked *is* an
abomination to the LORD,
But the prayer of the upright *is* His
delight.
9 The way of the wicked *is* an
abomination to the LORD,
But He loves him who follows
righteousness.

10 Harsh discipline *is* for him who
forsakes the way,
And he who hates correction
will die.

15:11 Hell and Destruction. See 27:20. Hell or Sheol is the place of the dead. "Destruction" refers to the experience of external punishment. See Job 26:6.

11 Hell and Destruction *are* before the
LORD;
So how much more the hearts of the
sons of men.

Luke 20:27–47

27 Then some of the Sadducees, who deny
that there is a resurrection, came to *Him* and
asked Him, 28 saying: "Teacher, Moses wrote
to us *that* if a man's brother dies, having a
wife, and he dies without children, his brother should take his wife and raise up offspring
for his brother. 29 Now there were seven
brothers. And the first took a wife, and died
without children. 30 And the second took her
as wife, and he died childless. 31 Then the
third took her, and in like manner the seven
also; and they left no children, and died.
32 Last of all the woman died also. 33 Therefore,
in the resurrection, whose wife does she
become? For all seven had her as wife."

34 Jesus answered and said to them, "The
sons of this age marry and are given in marriage. 35 But those who are counted worthy to
attain that age, and the resurrection from the
dead, neither marry nor are given in marriage;
36 nor can they die anymore, for they are equal to
the angels and are sons of God, being sons of the
resurrection. 37 But even Moses showed in the
burning bush *passage* that the dead are raised,
when he called the Lord *'the God of Abraham,
the God of Isaac, and the God of Jacob.'* 38 For He
is not the God of the dead but of the living, for
all live to Him."

20:37 the *burning* bush *passage*. Exodus 3:1–4:17. In that passage God identified Himself to Moses as the God of Abraham, Isaac, and Jacob—using the present tense. He didn't say He *was* their God, but "I AM" their God, indicating that their existence had not ended with their deaths.

39 Then some of the scribes answered and
said, "Teacher, You have spoken well." 40 But
after that they dared not question Him anymore.

41 And He said to them, "How can they say
that the Christ is the Son of David? 42 Now David himself said in the Book of Psalms:

*'The LORD said to my Lord,
"Sit at My right hand,*
43 *Till I make Your enemies Your
footstool."'*

44"Therefore David calls Him *'Lord'*; how is He then his Son?"

45Then, in the hearing of all the people, He said to His disciples, 46"Beware of the scribes, who desire to go around in long robes, love greetings in the marketplaces, the best seats in the synagogues, and the best places at feasts, 47who devour widows' houses, and for a pretense make long prayers. These will receive greater condemnation."

20:40 they dared not question Him. The more questions Jesus answered the clearer it became that His understanding and authority were vastly superior to that of the scribes and Pharisees.

DAY 30: What do the two prayers of Hannah teach us about prayer?

In 1 Samuel 1:10,11, Hannah vowed in "bitterness of soul" to give the Lord her son in return for God's favor in giving her that son. She prayed as a "maidservant"—a humble, submissive way of referring to herself in the presence of her superior, sovereign God. "Remember me," she requested, asking for special attention and care from the Lord. She would give the child to the Lord "all the days of his life," which was in contrast to the normal Nazirite vow, which was only for a specified period of time (see Num. 6:4,5,8).

In contrast to the prayer that came from her bitterness, Hannah prayed from joy in 2:1–10. The prominent idea in Hannah's prayer is that the Lord is a righteous Judge. He had brought down the proud (Peninnah) and exalted the humble (Hannah). The prayer has four sections: 1) Hannah prayed to the Lord for His salvation (vv. 1, 2); 2) Hannah warned the proud of the Lord's humbling (vv. 3–8d); 3) Hannah affirmed the Lord's faithful care for His saints (vv. 8e–9b); 4) Hannah petitioned the Lord to judge the world and to prosper His anointed king (vv. 10d-e). This prayer has a number of striking verbal similarities with David's song of 2 Samuel 22:2–51: "horn" (2:1; 22:3), "rock" (2:2; 22:2,3), salvation/deliverance (2:1,2; 22:2,3), grave/Sheol (2:6; 22:6), "thunder" (2:10; 22:14), "king" (2:10; 22:51), and "anointed" (2:10; 22:51).

MAY 1

1 Samuel 4:1–5:12

4 And the word of Samuel came to all
Israel.
Now Israel went out to battle against the
Philistines, and encamped beside Ebenezer;
and the Philistines encamped in Aphek. 2Then
the Philistines put themselves in battle array
against Israel. And when they joined battle,
Israel was defeated by the Philistines, who
killed about four thousand men of the army in
the field. 3And when the people had come into
the camp, the elders of Israel said, "Why has the
LORD defeated us today before the Philistines?
Let us bring the ark of the covenant of the
LORD from Shiloh to us, that when it comes
among us it may save us from the hand of our
enemies." 4So the people sent to Shiloh, that
they might bring from there the ark of the
covenant of the LORD of hosts, who dwells *between* the cherubim. And the two sons of Eli,
Hophni and Phinehas, *were* there with the ark
of the covenant of God.

4:4 dwells *between* the cherubim. A repeated phrase used to describe the Lord (see 2 Sam. 6:2; 2 Kin. 19:15; 1 Chr. 13:6; Ps. 80:1; 99:1; Is. 37:16). It spoke of His sovereign majesty. **Hophni and Phinehas.** These were the two wicked sons of Eli (2:12–17,27–37), of whom it was said that they "did not know the LORD" (2:12). The fact that they were mentioned together recalls the prophecy that they would die together (2:34).

5And when the ark of the covenant of the
LORD came into the camp, all Israel shouted so
loudly that the earth shook. 6Now when the
Philistines heard the noise of the shout, they
said, "What *does* the sound of this great shout in
the camp of the Hebrews *mean?*" Then they
understood that the ark of the LORD had come
into the camp. 7So the Philistines were afraid,
for they said, "God has come into the camp!"
And they said, "Woe to us! For such a thing
has never happened before. 8Woe to us! Who
will deliver us from the hand of these mighty
gods? These *are* the gods who struck the Egyptians with all the plagues in the wilderness. 9Be
strong and conduct yourselves like men, you
Philistines, that you do not become servants of
the Hebrews, as they have been to you. Conduct yourselves like men, and fight!"
10So the Philistines fought, and Israel was defeated, and every man fled to his tent. There
was a very great slaughter, and there fell of
Israel thirty thousand foot soldiers. 11Also the
ark of God was captured; and the two sons of
Eli, Hophni and Phinehas, died.

4:11 the ark of God was captured. In spite of their hopes to manipulate God into giving them the victory, Israel was defeated and the ark fell into the hands of the Philistines. The view of having the ark of God being equivalent to having control of God, possessed both by Israel and then the Philistines, is to be contrasted with the power and providence of God in the remaining narrative.

12Then a man of Benjamin ran from the battle line the same day, and came to Shiloh with
his clothes torn and dirt on his head. 13Now
when he came, there was Eli, sitting on a seat
by the wayside watching, for his heart trembled for the ark of God. And when the man
came into the city and told *it,* all the city cried
out. 14When Eli heard the noise of the outcry,
he said, "What *does* the sound of this tumult
mean?" And the man came quickly and told Eli.
15Eli was ninety-eight years old, and his eyes
were so dim that he could not see.
16Then the man said to Eli, "I *am* he who
came from the battle. And I fled today from
the battle line."
And he said, "What happened, my son?"
17So the messenger answered and said,
"Israel has fled before the Philistines, and there
has been a great slaughter among the people.
Also your two sons, Hophni and Phinehas, are
dead; and the ark of God has been captured."
18Then it happened, when he made mention
of the ark of God, that Eli fell off the seat backward by the side of the gate; and his neck was
broken and he died, for the man was old and
heavy. And he had judged Israel forty years.
19Now his daughter-in-law, Phinehas' wife,
was with child, *due* to be delivered; and when
she heard the news that the ark of God was
captured, and that her father-in-law and her
husband were dead, she bowed herself and
gave birth, for her labor pains came upon her.
20And about the time of her death the women
who stood by her said to her, "Do not fear, for
you have borne a son." But she did not answer,
nor did she regard *it.* 21Then she named the
child Ichabod, saying, "The glory has departed

from Israel!" because the ark of God had been
captured and because of her father-in-law and
her husband. 22And she said, "The glory has
departed from Israel, for the ark of God has
been captured."

4:21 Ichabod…The glory has departed. Due primarily to the loss of the ark, the symbol of God's presence, Phinehas's wife names her child Ichabod, meaning either "Where is the glory?" or "no glory." To the Hebrew, "glory" was often used to refer to God's presence; hence, the text means "Where is God?" The word "departed" carries the idea of having gone into exile. Thus, to the people of Israel, the capturing of the ark was a symbol that God had gone into exile. Although this was the mind-set of Israel, the text narrative will reveal that God was present, even when He disciplined His people.

5 Then the Philistines took the ark of God
and brought it from Ebenezer to Ashdod.
2When the Philistines took the ark of God, they
brought it into the house of Dagon and set it by
Dagon. 3And when the people of Ashdod arose
early in the morning, there was Dagon, fallen
on its face to the earth before the ark of the
LORD. So they took Dagon and set it in its
place again. 4And when they arose early the
next morning, there was Dagon, fallen on its
face to the ground before the ark of the LORD.
The head of Dagon and both the palms of its
hands *were* broken off on the threshold; only
Dagon's *torso* was left of it. 5Therefore neither
the priests of Dagon nor any who come into
Dagon's house tread on the threshold of
Dagon in Ashdod to this day.

6But the hand of the LORD was heavy on the
people of Ashdod, and He ravaged them and
struck them with tumors, *both* Ashdod and its
territory. 7And when the men of Ashdod saw
how *it was,* they said, "The ark of the God of
Israel must not remain with us, for His hand is
harsh toward us and Dagon our god." 8There-
fore they sent and gathered to themselves all
the lords of the Philistines, and said, "What
shall we do with the ark of the God of Israel?"

And they answered, "Let the ark of the God
of Israel be carried away to Gath." So they carried the ark of the God of Israel away. 9So it
was, after they had carried it away, that the
hand of the LORD was against the city with a
very great destruction; and He struck the
men of the city, both small and great, and
tumors broke out on them.

10Therefore they sent the ark of God to
Ekron. So it was, as the ark of God came to
Ekron, that the Ekronites cried out, saying,
"They have brought the ark of the God of
Israel to us, to kill us and our people!" 11So they
sent and gathered together all the lords of the
Philistines, and said, "Send away the ark of the
God of Israel, and let it go back to its own
place, so that it does not kill us and our people." For there was a deadly destruction
throughout all the city; the hand of God was
very heavy there. 12And the men who did not
die were stricken with the tumors, and the cry
of the city went up to heaven.

Psalm 54:1–7

To the Chief Musician. With stringed instruments.
A Contemplation of David when the Ziphites went
and said to Saul, "Is David not hiding with us?"

Save me, O God, by Your name,
And vindicate me by Your strength.
2 Hear my prayer, O God;
Give ear to the words of my mouth.

54:1 by Your name. In the ancient world, a person's name was essentially the person himself. Here, God's name includes His covenant protection. **vindicate.** David requests that God will execute justice for him, as in a court trial when a defendant is declared not guilty.

3 For strangers have risen up against me,
And oppressors have sought after my life;
They have not set God before them. Selah
4 Behold, God *is* my helper;
The Lord *is* with those who uphold my life.
5 He will repay my enemies for their evil.
Cut them off in Your truth.
6 I will freely sacrifice to You;
I will praise Your name, O LORD, for *it is* good.
7 For He has delivered me out of all trouble;
And my eye has seen *its desire* upon my enemies.

Proverbs 15:12–13

12 A scoffer does not love one who corrects him,
Nor will he go to the wise.

13 A merry heart makes a cheerful
countenance,
But by sorrow of the heart the spirit
is broken.

Luke 21:1–19

21 And He looked up and saw the rich putting their gifts into the treasury, 2and He
saw also a certain poor widow putting in two
mites. 3So He said, "Truly I say to you that this
poor widow has put in more than all; 4for all
these out of their abundance have put in offerings for God, but she out of her poverty put in
all the livelihood that she had."

5Then, as some spoke of the temple, how it
was adorned with beautiful stones and donations, He said, 6"These things which you
see—the days will come in which not *one*
stone shall be left upon another that shall not
be thrown down."

7So they asked Him, saying, "Teacher, but
when will these things be? And what sign *will
there be* when these things are about to take
place?"

8And He said: "Take heed that you not be
deceived. For many will come in My name, saying, 'I am *He*,' and, 'The time has drawn near.'
Therefore do not go after them. 9But when you
hear of wars and commotions, do not be terrified; for these things must come to pass first,
but the end *will* not *come* immediately."

10Then He said to them, "Nation will rise
against nation, and kingdom against kingdom.
11And there will be great earthquakes in various places, and famines and pestilences; and
there will be fearful sights and great signs
from heaven. 12But before all these things,
they will lay their hands on you and persecute
you, delivering *you* up to the synagogues and
prisons. You will be brought before kings and
rulers for My name's sake. 13But it will turn
out for you as an occasion for testimony.
14Therefore settle *it* in your hearts not to meditate beforehand on what you will answer; 15for
I will give you a mouth and wisdom which all
your adversaries will not be able to contradict
or resist. 16You will be betrayed even by parents and brothers, relatives and friends; and
they will put *some* of you to death. 17And you
will be hated by all for My name's sake. 18But
not a hair of your head shall be lost. 19By your
patience possess your souls.

21:1 the treasury. Thirteen chests with funnel-shaped openings stood in the court of the women. Each was labeled for a specific use, and donations were given accordingly.

21:5 donations. Wealthy people gave gifts of gold sculpture, golden plaques, and other treasures to the temple. Herod had donated a golden vine with clusters of golden grapes nearly 6 feet tall. The gifts were displayed on the walls and suspended in the portico. They constituted an unimaginable collection of wealth. All of these riches were looted by the Romans when the temple was destroyed (v. 6).

DAY 1: Contrast the pagan god of the Philistines and the living God.

In Judges 5:2, Dagon is mentioned. Ugaritic literature identifies this deity as a god of grain or vegetation, whose image had the lower body of a fish and upper body of a man. Dagon seems to have been the leader of the Philistine pantheon (Judg. 16:23) and is noted to be the father of Baal. The placing of the ark of God in the temple of Dagon was supposed to be a sign of Dagon's power and Yahweh's inferiority, a visual representation that the god of the Philistines was victorious over the God of the Hebrews.

The next morning the Philistines found Dagon had "fallen on its face" (1 Sam. 5:3). Ironically, God Himself overturned the supposed supremacy of Dagon by having Dagon fallen over, as if paying homage to the Lord. The same thing happened the next morning, but this time the "head… hands were broken off" (v. 4). The first display of God's authority over Dagon was not perceived. God's second display of authority, the cutting off of Dagon's head and hands, was a common sign that the enemy was dead (Judg. 7:25; 8:6; 1 Sam. 17:54; 31:9; 2 Sam. 4:12), and was to be understood as God's divine judgment on the false idol. Because the head and hands of Dagon fell on the threshold, superstition developed that it was cursed; therefore, the Philistines would not tread on it (v. 5).

In contrast to the hands of Dagon being cut off, symbolizing his helplessness against the power of Yahweh, the Lord was pictured to be actively involved in judging the Philistines. "The hand of the LORD was heavy" on the people (v. 6). The imagery of God's hand is found throughout the ark narrative (4:8; 5:6,7,9,11; 6:3,5,9). It has been suggested that "tumors" refers to the sores or boils caused by an epidemic of the bubonic plague carried by rats (6:4,5). The spread of the disease and its deadly effect (5:6,9,12; 6:11,17) make this a likely view.

MAY 2

1 Samuel 6:1–7:17

6 Now the ark of the LORD was in the country of the Philistines seven months. [2]And
the Philistines called for the priests and the
diviners, saying, "What shall we do with the
ark of the LORD? Tell us how we should send it
to its place."

[3]So they said, "If you send away the ark of the
God of Israel, do not send it empty; but by all
means return *it* to Him *with* a trespass offering.
Then you will be healed, and it will be known to
you why His hand is not removed from you."

[4]Then they said, "What *is* the trespass offering which we shall return to Him?"

They answered, "Five golden tumors and five
golden rats, *according to* the number of the lords
of the Philistines. For the same plague *was* on
all of you and on your lords. [5]Therefore you
shall make images of your tumors and images
of your rats that ravage the land, and you shall
give glory to the God of Israel; perhaps He will
lighten His hand from you, from your gods,
and from your land. [6]Why then do you harden
your hearts as the Egyptians and Pharaoh
hardened their hearts? When He did mighty
things among them, did they not let the people
go, that they might depart? [7]Now therefore,
make a new cart, take two milk cows which
have never been yoked, and hitch the cows to
the cart; and take their calves home, away from
them. [8]Then take the ark of the LORD and set it
on the cart; and put the articles of gold which
you are returning to Him *as* a trespass offering
in a chest by its side. Then send it away, and let
it go. [9]And watch: if it goes up the road to its
own territory, to Beth Shemesh, *then* He has
done us this great evil. But if not, then we shall
know that *it is* not His hand *that* struck us—it
happened to us by chance."

[10]Then the men did so; they took two milk
cows and hitched them to the cart, and shut
up their calves at home. [11]And they set the ark
of the LORD on the cart, and the chest with the
gold rats and the images of their tumors.
[12]Then the cows headed straight for the road
to Beth Shemesh, *and* went along the highway, lowing as they went, and did not turn
aside to the right hand or the left. And the
lords of the Philistines went after them to the
border of Beth Shemesh.

[13]Now *the people of* Beth Shemesh *were* reaping their wheat harvest in the valley; and they
lifted their eyes and saw the ark, and rejoiced
to see *it*. [14]Then the cart came into the field of
Joshua of Beth Shemesh, and stood there; a
large stone *was* there. So they split the wood
of the cart and offered the cows as a burnt
offering to the LORD. [15]The Levites took down
the ark of the LORD and the chest that *was* with
it, in which *were* the articles of gold, and put
them on the large stone. Then the men of Beth
Shemesh offered burnt offerings and made
sacrifices the same day to the LORD. [16]So when
the five lords of the Philistines had seen *it*,
they returned to Ekron the same day.

[17]These *are* the golden tumors which the
Philistines returned *as* a trespass offering to
the LORD: one for Ashdod, one for Gaza, one
for Ashkelon, one for Gath, one for Ekron;
[18]and the golden rats, *according to* the number
of all the cities of the Philistines *belonging* to
the five lords, *both* fortified cities and country
villages, even as far as the large *stone of* Abel
on which they set the ark of the LORD, *which
stone remains* to this day in the field of Joshua
of Beth Shemesh.

[19]Then He struck the men of Beth Shemesh,
because they had looked into the ark of the
LORD. He struck fifty thousand and seventy
men of the people, and the people lamented
because the LORD had struck the people with
a great slaughter.

[20]And the men of Beth Shemesh said, "Who
is able to stand before this holy LORD God?
And to whom shall it go up from us?" [21]So they
sent messengers to the inhabitants of Kirjath
Jearim, saying, "The Philistines have brought
back the ark of the LORD; come down *and* take
it up with you."

7 Then the men of Kirjath Jearim came and
took the ark of the LORD, and brought it
into the house of Abinadab on the hill, and
consecrated Eleazar his son to keep the ark of
the LORD.

6:19 looked into the ark. This action on the part of the men of Beth Shemesh constituted the sin of presumption. This is first addressed in Numbers 4:20 and is mentioned again in 2 Samuel 6:6,7. **fifty thousand and seventy men.** Some debate whether this figure is too large. However, retaining the larger number is more consistent with the context of "a great slaughter" and the reference to 30,000 in 4:10 (see 11:8). However, a scribal error could have occurred, in which case the number would omit the 50,000 and likely be "seventy," as in the LXX, the Greek translation of the Old Testament.

2 So it was that the ark remained in Kirjath
Jearim a long time; it was there twenty years.
And all the house of Israel lamented after the
LORD.

3 Then Samuel spoke to all the house of
Israel, saying, "If you return to the LORD with
all your hearts, *then* put away the foreign gods
and the Ashtoreths from among you, and prepare your hearts for the LORD, and serve Him
only; and He will deliver you from the hand of
the Philistines." 4 So the children of Israel put
away the Baals and the Ashtoreths, and
served the LORD only.

5 And Samuel said, "Gather all Israel to
Mizpah, and I will pray to the LORD for you."
6 So they gathered together at Mizpah, drew
water, and poured *it* out before the LORD. And
they fasted that day, and said there, "We have
sinned against the LORD." And Samuel judged
the children of Israel at Mizpah.

7:6 drew water, and poured *it* out before the LORD. The pouring out of water before the Lord was a sign of repentance. This act is repeated in 2 Samuel 23:16. **We have sinned against the LORD.** The symbol of Samuel pouring out the water and the acknowledgment of the people reveal a situation where true repentance had taken place. The condition of the heart superseded the importance or righteousness of the ritual. **Samuel judged.** At this point Samuel is introduced as the judge of Israel. His judgeship encompassed both domestic leadership and the conduct of war. The word links the text back to the last comment about Eli who judged 40 years (4:18). Samuel is shown to be the one taking over Eli's judgeship. He served as the last judge before the first king (see 1 Sam. 8:50).

7 Now when the Philistines heard that the
children of Israel had gathered together at
Mizpah, the lords of the Philistines went up
against Israel. And when the children of Israel
heard *of it,* they were afraid of the Philistines.
8 So the children of Israel said to Samuel, "Do
not cease to cry out to the LORD our God for
us, that He may save us from the hand of the
Philistines."

9 And Samuel took a suckling lamb and
offered *it as* a whole burnt offering to the
LORD. Then Samuel cried out to the LORD for
Israel, and the LORD answered him. 10 Now as
Samuel was offering up the burnt offering, the
Philistines drew near to battle against Israel.
But the LORD thundered with a loud thunder
upon the Philistines that day, and so confused
them that they were overcome before Israel.
11 And the men of Israel went out of Mizpah
and pursued the Philistines, and drove them
back as far as below Beth Car. 12 Then Samuel
took a stone and set *it* up between Mizpah and
Shen, and called its name Ebenezer, saying,
"Thus far the LORD has helped us."

13 So the Philistines were subdued, and they
did not come anymore into the territory of
Israel. And the hand of the LORD was against
the Philistines all the days of Samuel. 14 Then
the cities which the Philistines had taken from
Israel were restored to Israel, from Ekron to
Gath; and Israel recovered its territory from
the hands of the Philistines. Also there was
peace between Israel and the Amorites.

15 And Samuel judged Israel all the days of
his life. 16 He went from year to year on a circuit
to Bethel, Gilgal, and Mizpah, and judged
Israel in all those places. 17 But he always
returned to Ramah, for his home *was* there.
There he judged Israel, and there he built an
altar to the LORD.

7:16 a circuit. The circuit was an annual trip made by Samuel; he would travel to Bethel, Gilgal, Mizpah, and return once again to Ramah, which allowed him to manage the affairs of the people.

Psalm 55:1–8

To the Chief Musician. With stringed instruments.
A Contemplation of David.

Give ear to my prayer, O God,
And do not hide Yourself
from my supplication.
2 Attend to me, and hear me;
I am restless in my complaint, and
moan noisily,
3 Because of the voice of the enemy,
Because of the oppression of the
wicked;
For they bring down trouble upon me,
And in wrath they hate me.

4 My heart is severely pained within me,
And the terrors of death have fallen
upon me.
5 Fearfulness and trembling have come
upon me,
And horror has overwhelmed me.
6 So I said, "Oh, that I had wings like a
dove!

I would fly away and be at rest.
7 Indeed, I would wander far off,
And remain in the wilderness. Selah
8 I would hasten my escape
From the windy storm *and* tempest."

Proverbs 15:14

14 The heart of him who has understanding seeks knowledge,
But the mouth of fools feeds on foolishness.

Luke 21:20–38

20"But when you see Jerusalem surrounded
by armies, then know that its desolation is
near. 21Then let those who are in Judea flee to
the mountains, let those who are in the midst
of her depart, and let not those who are in the

21:20 Jerusalem surrounded by armies. A comparison with Matthew 24:15,16 and Mark 13:14 suggests that this sign is closely associated with "the abomination of desolation" (see Matt. 24:15; Dan. 9:27; 11:31). This sign of Jerusalem under siege was previewed in A.D. 70, but awaits its fulfillment in the future.

country enter her. 22For these are the days of
vengeance, that all things which are written
may be fulfilled. 23But woe to those who are
pregnant and to those who are nursing babies
in those days! For there will be great distress
in the land and wrath upon this people. 24And
they will fall by the edge of the sword, and be
led away captive into all nations. And Jerusalem will be trampled by Gentiles until the
times of the Gentiles are fulfilled.
25"And there will be signs in the sun, in the
moon, and in the stars; and on the earth distress of nations, with perplexity, the sea and the
waves roaring; 26men's hearts failing them from

21:24 the times of the Gentiles. This expression is unique to Luke. It identifies the era from Israel's captivity (ca. 586 B.C. to Babylon; see 2 Kin. 25) to her restoration in the kingdom (Rev. 20:1–6). It has been a time during which, in accord with God's purpose, Gentiles have dominated or threatened Jerusalem. The era has also been marked by vast spiritual privileges for the Gentile nations (see Is. 66:12; Mal. 1:11; Matt. 24:14; Mark 13:10).

fear and the expectation of those things which
are coming on the earth, for the powers of the
heavens will be shaken. 27Then they will see
the Son of Man coming in a cloud with power
and great glory. 28Now when these things
begin to happen, look up and lift up your
heads, because your redemption draws near."
29Then He spoke to them a parable: "Look at
the fig tree, and all the trees. 30When they are
already budding, you see and know for yourselves that summer is now near. 31So you also,
when you see these things happening, know
that the kingdom of God is near. 32Assuredly, I
say to you, this generation will by no means
pass away till all things take place. 33Heaven
and earth will pass away, but My words will by
no means pass away.
34"But take heed to yourselves, lest your
hearts be weighed down with carousing,
drunkenness, and cares of this life, and that
Day come on you unexpectedly. 35For it will
come as a snare on all those who dwell on the
face of the whole earth. 36Watch therefore, and
pray always that you may be counted worthy
to escape all these things that will come to
pass, and to stand before the Son of Man."
37And in the daytime He was teaching in the
temple, but at night He went out and stayed on
the mountain called Olivet. 38Then early in the
morning all the people came to Him in the
temple to hear Him.

DAY 2: How did the Philistines attempt to stop the plague?

"The priests and the diviners" (1 Sam. 6:2) of the Philistines were summoned to figure out how to appease God so that He would stop the plague. They understood that they had offended God. Their diviners decided to rightfully appease His wrath by sending the ark back to Israel. These pagans recognized their sin and the need for manifest repentance, which they did according to their religious tradition by means of a "trespass offering" (v. 3) to compensate for their trespass of dishonoring the God of Israel. It was their custom to make models of their sores (and the rats which brought the plague), in hopes that the deity would recognize that they knew why he was angry and remove the evil which had fallen upon them (v. 4).

"Give glory to the God of Israel...He will lighten His hand" (v. 5). While sympathetic magic was the Philistine custom, this statement expressly affirms the intention behind the offerings: They were to halt the dishonor, confess their sin, and give glory to the God of Israel by acknowledging who it was that they had offended and who was the supreme Deity. The diviners correlate the Philistines' actions of not recognizing God with those of Pharaoh and the Egyptians. "Why then do you harden your hearts...?" (v. 6). This is the same word "harden" that was used in Exodus 7:14; 8:15,32. It is an interesting correlation, because the dominant purpose in Exodus 5–14 is that the Egyptians might "know that I am the LORD" (Ex. 7:5).

To know without a doubt that the God of Israel was behind all of their troubles, the diviners devised a plan that would reveal whether God was the One responsible. Using cows that had "never been yoked" (v. 7) meant using animals that were untrained to pull a cart and probably would not go anywhere. The second element in their plan was to use nursing cows taken away from their calves. For the cows unnaturally to head off in the opposite direction from their calves would be a clear sign that the cause of their judgment was supernatural, which is precisely what happened (v. 12).

MAY 3

1 Samuel 8:1–9:27

8 Now it came to pass when Samuel was old
that he made his sons judges over Israel.
2The name of his firstborn was Joel, and the
name of his second, Abijah; *they were* judges in
Beersheba. 3But his sons did not walk in his
ways; they turned aside after dishonest gain,
took bribes, and perverted justice.
4Then all the elders of Israel gathered
together and came to Samuel at Ramah, 5and
said to him, "Look, you are old, and your sons
do not walk in your ways. Now make us a king
to judge us like all the nations."
6But the thing displeased Samuel when they
said, "Give us a king to judge us." So Samuel
prayed to the LORD. 7And the LORD said to
Samuel, "Heed the voice of the people in all
that they say to you; for they have not rejected
you, but they have rejected Me, that I should
not reign over them. 8According to all the
works which they have done since the day
that I brought them up out of Egypt, even to
this day—with which they have forsaken Me
and served other gods—so they are doing to
you also. 9Now therefore, heed their voice.
However, you shall solemnly forewarn them,
and show them the behavior of the king who
will reign over them."
10So Samuel told all the words of the LORD to
the people who asked him for a king. 11And he
said, "This will be the behavior of the king
who will reign over you: He will take your
sons and appoint *them* for his own chariots
and *to be* his horsemen, and *some* will run
before his chariots. 12He will appoint captains
over his thousands and captains over his
fifties, *will set some* to plow his ground and
reap his harvest, and *some* to make his
weapons of war and equipment for his chariots. 13He will take your daughters *to be* perfumers, cooks, and bakers. 14And he will take
the best of your fields, your vineyards, and
your olive groves, and give *them* to his servants. 15He will take a tenth of your grain and
your vintage, and give it to his officers and servants. 16And he will take your male servants,
your female servants, your finest young men,
and your donkeys, and put *them* to his work.
17He will take a tenth of your sheep. And you
will be his servants. 18And you will cry out in
that day because of your king whom you have
chosen for yourselves, and the LORD will not
hear you in that day."
19Nevertheless the people refused to obey
the voice of Samuel; and they said, "No, but
we will have a king over us, 20that we also may
be like all the nations, and that our king may
judge us and go out before us and fight our
battles."
21And Samuel heard all the words of the people, and he repeated them in the hearing of
the LORD. 22So the LORD said to Samuel, "Heed
their voice, and make them a king."
And Samuel said to the men of Israel,
"Every man go to his city."

9 There was a man of Benjamin whose
name *was* Kish the son of Abiel, the son of
Zeror, the son of Bechorath, the son of
Aphiah, a Benjamite, a mighty man of power.
2And he had a choice and handsome son
whose name *was* Saul. *There was* not a more
handsome person than he among the children
of Israel. From his shoulders upward *he was*
taller than any of the people.
3Now the donkeys of Kish, Saul's father,
were lost. And Kish said to his son Saul,
"Please take one of the servants with you, and
arise, go and look for the donkeys." 4So he
passed through the mountains of Ephraim and

through the land of Shalisha, but they did not
find *them.* Then they passed through the land
of Shaalim, and *they were* not *there.* Then he
passed through the land of the Benjamites, but
they did not find *them.*
5When they had come to the land of Zuph,
Saul said to his servant who *was* with him,
“Come, let us return, lest my father cease *car-*
ing about the donkeys and become worried
about us.”
6And he said to him, “Look now, *there is* in
this city a man of God, and *he is* an honorable
man; all that he says surely comes to pass. So
let us go there; perhaps he can show us the
way that we should go.”
7Then Saul said to his servant, “But look, *if*
we go, what shall we bring the man? For the
bread in our vessels is all gone, and *there is* no
present to bring to the man of God. What do
we have?”
8And the servant answered Saul again and
said, “Look, I have here at hand one-fourth of
a shekel of silver. I will give *that* to the man of
God, to tell us our way.” 9(Formerly in Israel,
when a man went to inquire of God, he spoke
thus: “Come, let us go to the seer”; for *he who*
is now *called* a prophet was formerly called a
seer.)
10Then Saul said to his servant, “Well said;
come, let us go.” So they went to the city
where the man of God *was.*
11As they went up the hill to the city, they
met some young women going out to draw
water, and said to them, “Is the seer here?”
12And they answered them and said, “Yes,
there he is, just ahead of you. Hurry now; for
today he came to this city, because there is a
sacrifice of the people today on the high place.
13As soon as you come into the city, you will
surely find him before he goes up to the high
place to eat. For the people will not eat until he
comes, because he must bless the sacrifice;
afterward those who are invited will eat. Now
therefore, go up, for about this time you will
find him.” 14So they went up to the city. As they
were coming into the city, there was Samuel,
coming out toward them on his way up to the
high place.
15Now the LORD had told Samuel in his ear
the day before Saul came, saying, 16“Tomorrow about this time I will send you a man from
the land of Benjamin, and you shall anoint him
commander over My people Israel, that he
may save My people from the hand of the
Philistines; for I have looked upon My people,
because their cry has come to Me.”
17So when Samuel saw Saul, the LORD said to
him, “There he is, the man of whom I spoke to

9:16 anoint him. This represents a setting apart for service to the Lord, which occurs in 10:1. **commander.** Literally, “one given prominence, one placed in front.” The title referred to “one designated to rule” (see 1 Kin. 1:35; 2 Chr. 11:22). **their cry has come to Me.** The people had been crying out for deliverance from the Philistines, their longstanding rivals, just as they did for liberation from Egypt (see Ex. 2:25; 3:9).

9:17 This one shall reign over My people. God identified Saul to Samuel, assuring there was no mistaking whom God was choosing to be king.

you. This one shall reign over My people.”
18Then Saul drew near to Samuel in the gate,
and said, “Please tell me, where *is* the seer’s
house?”
19Samuel answered Saul and said, “I *am* the
seer. Go up before me to the high place, for
you shall eat with me today; and tomorrow I
will let you go and will tell you all that *is* in
your heart. 20But as for your donkeys that
were lost three days ago, do not be anxious
about them, for they have been found. And on
whom *is* all the desire of Israel? *Is it* not on you
and on all your father’s house?”
21And Saul answered and said, “*Am* I not a
Benjamite, of the smallest of the tribes of
Israel, and my family the least of all the families of the tribe of Benjamin? Why then do you
speak like this to me?”
22Now Samuel took Saul and his servant and
brought them into the hall, and had them sit in
the place of honor among those who were
invited; there *were* about thirty persons. 23And
Samuel said to the cook, “Bring the portion
which I gave you, of which I said to you, ‘Set it
apart.’ ” 24So the cook took up the thigh with
its upper part and set *it* before Saul. And *Sam-*
uel said, “Here it is, what was kept back. *It* was
set apart for you. Eat; for until this time it has
been kept for you, since I said I invited the
people.” So Saul ate with Samuel that day.
25When they had come down from the high
place into the city, *Samuel* spoke with Saul on
the top of the house. 26They arose early; and it
was about the dawning of the day that Samuel
called to Saul on the top of the house, saying,
“Get up, that I may send you on your way.”
And Saul arose, and both of them went outside, he and Samuel.
27As they were going down to the outskirts of

the city, Samuel said to Saul, "Tell the servant to go on ahead of us." And he went on. "But you stand here awhile, that I may announce to you the word of God."

Psalm 55:9–15

9 Destroy, O Lord, *and* divide their
tongues,
For I have seen violence and strife in
the city.
10 Day and night they go around it on its
walls;
Iniquity and trouble *are* also in the
midst of it.
11 Destruction *is* in its midst;
Oppression and deceit do not depart
from its streets.

12 For *it is* not an enemy *who* reproaches
me;
Then I could bear *it*.
Nor *is it* one *who* hates me who has
exalted *himself* against me;
Then I could hide from him.
13 But *it was* you, a man my equal,
My companion and my acquaintance.
14 We took sweet counsel together,
And walked to the house of God
in the throng.

15 Let death seize them;
Let them go down alive into hell,
For wickedness *is* in their dwellings
and among them.

Proverbs 15:15–17

15 All the days of the afflicted *are* evil,
But he who is of a merry heart *has* a
continual feast.
16 Better *is* a little with the fear of the
LORD,
Than great treasure with trouble.
17 Better *is* a dinner of herbs where
love is,
Than a fatted calf with hatred.

Luke 22:1–23

22 Now the Feast of Unleavened Bread
drew near, which is called Passover.
2And the chief priests and the scribes sought
how they might kill Him, for they feared the
people.
3Then Satan entered Judas, surnamed
Iscariot, who was numbered among the
twelve. 4So he went his way and conferred
with the chief priests and captains, how he
might betray Him to them. 5And they were
glad, and agreed to give him money. 6So he

22:3 Satan entered. I.e., Judas was possessed by Satan himself. Satan evidently gained direct control over Judas on two occasions—once just before Judas arranged his betrayal with the chief priests and again during the Last Supper (John 13:27), immediately before the betrayal was actually carried out.

promised and sought opportunity to betray
Him to them in the absence of the multitude.
7Then came the Day of Unleavened Bread,
when the Passover must be killed. 8And He
sent Peter and John, saying, "Go and prepare
the Passover for us, that we may eat."
9So they said to Him, "Where do You want
us to prepare?"
10And He said to them, "Behold, when you
have entered the city, a man will meet you carrying a pitcher of water; follow him into the
house which he enters. 11Then you shall say to
the master of the house, 'The Teacher says to
you, "Where is the guest room where I may eat
the Passover with My disciples?"' 12Then he
will show you a large, furnished upper room;
there make ready."

22:12 a large, furnished upper room. One of many such rooms for rent in Jerusalem that were maintained for the express purpose of providing pilgrims a place to celebrate feasts. The furnishings undoubtedly included a large banquet table and everything necessary to prepare and serve a meal.

13So they went and found it just as He had
said to them, and they prepared the
Passover.
14When the hour had come, He sat down,
and the twelve apostles with Him. 15Then He
said to them, "With *fervent* desire I have
desired to eat this Passover with you before
I suffer; 16for I say to you, I will no longer eat
of it until it is fulfilled in the kingdom of
God."
17Then He took the cup, and gave thanks,
and said, "Take this and divide *it* among yourselves; 18for I say to you, I will not drink of the
fruit of the vine until the kingdom of God
comes."
19And He took bread, gave thanks and broke

it, and gave *it* to them, saying, "This is My
body which is given for you; do this in
remembrance of Me."
[20]Likewise He also *took* the cup after supper,
saying, "This cup *is* the new covenant in My
blood, which is shed for you. [21]But behold, the
hand of My betrayer *is* with Me on the table.
[22]And truly the Son of Man goes as it has been
determined, but woe to that man by whom He
is betrayed!"
[23]Then they began to question among themselves, which of them it was who would do this
thing.

22:22 as it has been determined. Every detail of the crucifixion of Christ was under the sovereign control of God and in accord with His eternal purposes. See Acts 2:23; 4:26–28. **but woe.** The fact that Judas's betrayal was part of God's plan does not free him from the guilt of a crime he entered into willfully. God's sovereignty is never a legitimate excuse for human guilt.

DAY 3: What was wrong with Israel wanting a king?

"Now make us a king…like all the nations" (1 Samuel 8:5). When Israel entered the land, they encountered Canaanite city-states that were led by kings (Josh. 12:7–24) and were later enslaved by nations that were led by kings (Judg. 3:8,12; 4:2; 8:5; 11:12). However, at the time of the judges, there was no king in Israel (Judg. 17:6; 18:1; 19:1; 21:25).

According to Deuteronomy 17:14, God knew this would be their desire and He would allow it to occur. "Heed the voice of the people," the Lord told Samuel (v. 7) and give them a king. "They have not rejected you, but…Me." The nature of this rejection of the Lord by Israel is explained in vv. 19, 20.

Samuel obeyed the Lord by warning them of the behavior of a human king in vv. 10–18. A king would: 1) draft young men and women for his service (vv. 11–13); 2) tax the people's crops and flocks (vv. 14,15,17a); 3) appropriate the best of their animals and servants (v. 16); and 4) place limitations on their personal freedom (v. 17b). Additionally, Samuel told them "you will cry out…because of your king" (v. 18). They would later cry out for freedom from his rule (1 Kin. 12:4), but "the LORD will not hear you." In contrast to the Lord's response to Israel during the period of the judges (Judg. 2:18), the Lord would refuse to deliver the people out of the hand of their king who oppressed them.

In spite of Samuel's warnings, the people demanded a king who will "fight our battles" (v. 20). Up until this point, the Lord Himself had fought the battles for Israel and given continual victory (Josh. 10:14; 1 Sam. 7:10). Israel no longer wanted the Lord to be their warrior—replacing Him with a human king was their desire. It was in this way that Israel rejected the Lord. The problem was not in having a king; but, rather the reason the people wanted a king, i.e., to be like other nations. They also foolishly assumed there would be some greater power in a king leading them in battle.

MAY 4

1 Samuel 10:1–11:15

10 Then Samuel took a flask of oil and
poured *it* on his head, and kissed him
and said: "*Is it* not because the LORD has
anointed you commander over His inheritance? [2]When you have departed from me
today, you will find two men by Rachel's tomb
in the territory of Benjamin at Zelzah; and they
will say to you, 'The donkeys which you went to
look for have been found. And now your father
has ceased caring about the donkeys and is
worrying about you, saying, "What shall I do
about my son?" ' [3]Then you shall go on forward from there and come to the terebinth
tree of Tabor. There three men going up to
God at Bethel will meet you, one carrying
three young goats, another carrying three
loaves of bread, and another carrying a skin of
wine. [4]And they will greet you and give you
two *loaves* of bread, which you shall receive
from their hands. [5]After that you shall come to
the hill of God where the Philistine garrison *is.*
And it will happen, when you have come there

10:1 the LORD has anointed you commander. The Lord chose Saul to be the leader of Israel and communicated His choice through the private anointing by Samuel, signifying a setting aside for God's service. **His inheritance.** The inheritance was God's nation, Israel, in the sense that she uniquely belonged to Him (Deut. 4:20; 9:26).

to the city, that you will meet a group of
prophets coming down from the high place
with a stringed instrument, a tambourine, a
flute, and a harp before them; and they will be
prophesying. 6Then the Spirit of the LORD will
come upon you, and you will prophesy with
them and be turned into another man. 7And let
it be, when these signs come to you, *that* you
do as the occasion demands; for God *is* with
you. 8You shall go down before me to Gilgal;
and surely I will come down to you to offer
burnt offerings *and* make sacrifices of peace
offerings. Seven days you shall wait, till I come
to you and show you what you should do."

10:6 the Spirit of the LORD will come upon you. The Holy Spirit would enable Saul to declare the word of the Lord with the prophets. **turned into another man.** With this empowerment by the Holy Spirit, Saul would emerge another man (see 10:9), equipped in the manner of Gideon and Jephthah for deeds of valor (see v. 9; Judg. 6:34; 11:29).

9So it was, when he had turned his back to
go from Samuel, that God gave him another
heart; and all those signs came to pass that
day. 10When they came there to the hill, there
was a group of prophets to meet him; then the
Spirit of God came upon him, and he prophesied among them. 11And it happened, when all
who knew him formerly saw that he indeed
prophesied among the prophets, that the people said to one another, "What *is* this *that* has
come upon the son of Kish? *Is* Saul also among
the prophets?" 12Then a man from there
answered and said, "But who *is* their father?"
Therefore it became a proverb: "*Is* Saul also
among the prophets?" 13And when he had finished prophesying, he went to the high place.
14Then Saul's uncle said to him and his servant, "Where did you go?"

So he said, "To look for the donkeys. When
we saw that *they were* nowhere *to be found,* we
went to Samuel."

15And Saul's uncle said, "Tell me, please,
what Samuel said to you."

16So Saul said to his uncle, "He told us plainly
that the donkeys had been found." But about
the matter of the kingdom, he did not tell him
what Samuel had said.

17Then Samuel called the people together to
the LORD at Mizpah, 18and said to the children
of Israel, "Thus says the LORD God of Israel: 'I
brought up Israel out of Egypt, and delivered
you from the hand of the Egyptians *and* from
the hand of all kingdoms and from those who
oppressed you.' 19But you have today rejected
your God, who Himself saved you from all
your adversities and your tribulations; and you
have said to Him, 'No, set a king over us!' Now
therefore, present yourselves before the LORD
by your tribes and by your clans."

20And when Samuel had caused all the tribes
of Israel to come near, the tribe of Benjamin
was chosen. 21When he had caused the tribe of
Benjamin to come near by their families, the
family of Matri was chosen. And Saul the son
of Kish was chosen. But when they sought
him, he could not be found. 22Therefore they
inquired of the LORD further, "Has the man
come here yet?"

And the LORD answered, "There he is, hidden among the equipment."

23So they ran and brought him from there;
and when he stood among the people, he was
taller than any of the people from his shoulders upward. 24And Samuel said to all the people, "Do you see him whom the LORD has
chosen, that *there is* no one like him among all
the people?"

So all the people shouted and said, "Long
live the king!"

25Then Samuel explained to the people the
behavior of royalty, and wrote *it* in a book and
laid *it* up before the LORD. And Samuel sent all
the people away, every man to his house.
26And Saul also went home to Gibeah; and
valiant *men* went with him, whose hearts God
had touched. 27But some rebels said, "How can
this man save us?" So they despised him, and
brought him no presents. But he held his
peace.

11 Then Nahash the Ammonite came up and
encamped against Jabesh Gilead; and all
the men of Jabesh said to Nahash, "Make a
covenant with us, and we will serve you."

2And Nahash the Ammonite answered
them, "On this *condition* I will make *a
covenant* with you, that I may put out all your
right eyes, and bring reproach on all Israel."

3Then the elders of Jabesh said to him,
"Hold off for seven days, that we may send
messengers to all the territory of Israel. And
then, if *there is* no one to save us, we will come
out to you."

4So the messengers came to Gibeah of Saul
and told the news in the hearing of the people.
And all the people lifted up their voices and
wept. 5Now there was Saul, coming behind the
herd from the field; and Saul said, "What *troubles* the people, that they weep?" And they told
him the words of the men of Jabesh. 6Then the

Spirit of God came upon Saul when he heard
this news, and his anger was greatly aroused.
7So he took a yoke of oxen and cut them in
pieces, and sent *them* throughout all the territory of Israel by the hands of messengers, saying, "Whoever does not go out with Saul and
Samuel to battle, so it shall be done to his
oxen."

And the fear of the LORD fell on the people,
and they came out with one consent. 8When
he numbered them in Bezek, the children of
Israel were three hundred thousand, and the
men of Judah thirty thousand. 9And they said
to the messengers who came, "Thus you shall
say to the men of Jabesh Gilead: 'Tomorrow,
by *the time* the sun is hot, you shall have
help.'" Then the messengers came and
reported *it* to the men of Jabesh, and they
were glad. 10Therefore the men of Jabesh said,
"Tomorrow we will come out to you, and you
may do with us whatever seems good to you."

11So it was, on the next day, that Saul put the
people in three companies; and they came into
the midst of the camp in the morning watch,
and killed Ammonites until the heat of the day.
And it happened that those who survived were
scattered, so that no two of them were left
together.

12Then the people said to Samuel, "Who *is*
he who said, 'Shall Saul reign over us?' Bring
the men, that we may put them to death."

13But Saul said, "Not a man shall be put to
death this day, for today the LORD has accomplished salvation in Israel."

14Then Samuel said to the people, "Come, let
us go to Gilgal and renew the kingdom there."
15So all the people went to Gilgal, and there
they made Saul king before the LORD in Gilgal.
There they made sacrifices of peace offerings
before the LORD, and there Saul and all the
men of Israel rejoiced greatly.

11:15 they made Saul king before the LORD. All the people came to crown Saul king that day. The process of entering the kingship was the same for both Saul and David: 1) commissioned by the Lord (9:1–10:16; 16:1–13); 2) confirmed by military victory (10:17–11:11; 16:14; 2 Sam. 1:27); and 3) crowned (11:12–15; 2 Sam. 2:4; 5:3). **peace offerings.** Sacrifices of thanksgiving (see Lev. 7:13). **rejoiced greatly.** Along with the victory over the Ammonites, there was a great celebration over the nation being united.

Psalm 55:16–23

16 As for me, I will call upon God,
And the LORD shall save me.
17 Evening and morning and at noon
I will pray, and cry aloud,
And He shall hear my voice.
18 He has redeemed my soul in peace
from the battle *that was*
against me,
For there were many against me.
19 God will hear, and afflict them,
Even He who abides from of old.
Selah
Because they do not change,
Therefore they do not fear God.

20 He has put forth his hands against
those who were at peace
with him;
He has broken his covenant.
21 *The words* of his mouth were smoother
than butter,
But war *was* in his heart;
His words were softer than oil,
Yet they *were* drawn swords.
22 Cast your burden on the LORD,
And He shall sustain you;
He shall never permit the righteous to
be moved.

23 But You, O God, shall bring
them down to the pit of destruction;
Bloodthirsty and deceitful men shall
not live out half their days;
But I will trust in You.

55:22 Cast your burden on the LORD. The word for "burden" implies one's circumstances, one's lot. The psalmist promises that the Lord will uphold the believer in the struggles of life.

Proverbs 15:18–20

18 A wrathful man stirs up strife,
But *he who is* slow to anger allays
contention.

19 The way of the lazy *man is* like
a hedge of thorns,
But the way of the upright
is a highway.

20 A wise son makes a father glad,
But a foolish man despises
his mother.

Luke 22:24–46

24 Now there was also a dispute among them,
as to which of them should be considered the
greatest. 25 And He said to them, "The kings of
the Gentiles exercise lordship over them, and
those who exercise authority over them are
called 'benefactors.' 26 But not so *among* you;
on the contrary, he who is greatest among
you, let him be as the younger, and he who
governs as he who serves. 27 For who *is*
greater, he who sits at the table, or he who
serves? *Is* it not he who sits at the table? Yet I
am among you as the One who serves.

28 "But you are those who have continued
with Me in My trials. 29 And I bestow upon you a
kingdom, just as My Father bestowed *one*
upon Me, 30 that you may eat and drink at My
table in My kingdom, and sit on thrones judging the twelve tribes of Israel."

31 And the Lord said, "Simon, Simon! Indeed,
Satan has asked for you, that he may sift *you* as
wheat. 32 But I have prayed for you, that your
faith should not fail; and when you have
returned to *Me,* strengthen your brethren."

33 But he said to Him, "Lord, I am ready to go
with You, both to prison and to death."

34 Then He said, "I tell you, Peter, the rooster
shall not crow this day before you will deny
three times that you know Me."

35 And He said to them, "When I sent you
without money bag, knapsack, and sandals, did
you lack anything?"

So they said, "Nothing."

36 Then He said to them, "But now, he who
has a money bag, let him take *it,* and likewise a
knapsack; and he who has no sword, let him sell
his garment and buy one. 37 For I say to you that
this which is written must still be accomplished
in Me: *'And He was numbered with the transgressors.'* For the things concerning Me have
an end."

38 So they said, "Lord, look, here *are* two
swords."

And He said to them, "It is enough."

39 Coming out, He went to the Mount of
Olives, as He was accustomed, and His disciples also followed Him. 40 When He came to the
place, He said to them, "Pray that you may not
enter into temptation."

41 And He was withdrawn from them about a
stone's throw, and He knelt down and prayed,
42 saying, "Father, if it is Your will, take this cup
away from Me; nevertheless not My will, but
Yours, be done." 43 Then an angel appeared to
Him from heaven, strengthening Him. 44 And
being in agony, He prayed more earnestly.
Then His sweat became like great drops of
blood falling down to the ground.

45 When He rose up from prayer, and had
come to His disciples, He found them sleeping
from sorrow. 46 Then He said to them, "Why do
you sleep? Rise and pray, lest you enter into
temptation."

22:44 like great drops of blood. This suggests a dangerous condition known as *hematidrosis,* the effusion of blood in one's perspiration. It can be caused by extreme anguish or physical strain. Subcutaneous capillaries dilate and burst, mingling blood with sweat. Christ Himself stated that His distress had brought Him to the threshold of death (see Matt. 26:38; Mark 14:34; Heb. 12:3,4).

DAY 4: How can we face temptation with confidence?

Shortly after a dispute among the disciples as to which one should be considered the greatest (Luke 22:24), Jesus specifically addresses Peter as "Simon, Simon" (v. 31). The repetition of the name (see 10:41; Acts 9:4) implied an earnest and somber tone of warning. Christ Himself had given Simon the name Peter (6:14), but here He reverted to his old name, perhaps to intensify His rebuke about Peter's fleshly overconfidence. The context also suggests that Peter may have been one of the more vocal participants in the dispute of v. 24.

"Satan," Jesus told him, "has asked for you." Though addressed specifically to Peter, this warning embraced the other disciples as well. The pronoun "you" is plural in the Greek text. "That he may sift you as wheat." The imagery is apt. It suggests that such trials, though unsettling and undesirable, have a necessary refining effect.

Nevertheless, Jesus said, "I have prayed for you" (v. 32). The pronoun "you" is singular. Although it is clear that He prayed for all of them (John 17:6–19), He personally assured Peter of His prayers and of Peter's ultimate victory, even encouraging Peter to be an encourager to the others. "That your faith should not fail." Peter himself failed miserably, but his faith was never overthrown (see John 21:18,19).

MAY 5

1 Samuel 12:1–13:23

12 Now Samuel said to all Israel: "Indeed I
have heeded your voice in all that you
said to me, and have made a king over you.
2And now here is the king, walking before you;
and I am old and gray headed, and look, my
sons *are* with you. I have walked before you
from my childhood to this day. 3Here I am.
Witness against me before the LORD and before
His anointed: Whose ox have I taken, or whose
donkey have I taken, or whom have I cheated?
Whom have I oppressed, or from whose hand
have I received *any* bribe with which to blind
my eyes? I will restore *it* to you."
4And they said, "You have not cheated us or
oppressed us, nor have you taken anything
from any man's hand."
5Then he said to them, "The LORD *is* witness
against you, and His anointed *is* witness this day,
that you have not found anything in my hand."
And they answered, "*He is* witness."
6Then Samuel said to the people, "*It is* the
LORD who raised up Moses and Aaron, and
who brought your fathers up from the land of
Egypt. 7Now therefore, stand still, that I may
reason with you before the LORD concerning
all the righteous acts of the LORD which He did
to you and your fathers: 8When Jacob had
gone into Egypt, and your fathers cried out to
the LORD, then the LORD sent Moses and
Aaron, who brought your fathers out of Egypt
and made them dwell in this place. 9And when
they forgot the LORD their God, He sold them
into the hand of Sisera, commander of the
army of Hazor, into the hand of the Philistines,
and into the hand of the king of Moab; and
they fought against them. 10Then they cried
out to the LORD, and said, 'We have sinned,
because we have forsaken the LORD and
served the Baals and Ashtoreths; but now
deliver us from the hand of our enemies, and
we will serve You.' 11And the LORD sent
Jerubbaal, Bedan, Jephthah, and Samuel, and
delivered you out of the hand of your enemies
on every side; and you dwelt in safety. 12And
when you saw that Nahash king of the
Ammonites came against you, you said to me,
'No, but a king shall reign over us,' when the
LORD your God *was* your king.
13"Now therefore, here is the king whom
you have chosen *and* whom you have desired.
And take note, the LORD has set a king over
you. 14If you fear the LORD and serve Him and

12:12 when you saw that Nahash king of the Ammonites came against you. According to the Dead Sea Scrolls and Josephus, Nahash was campaigning over a large area. It was that Ammonite threat that seemingly provoked Israel to demand a human king (8:1–20). **the LORD your God *was* your king.** The clearest indictment of Israel for choosing a mere man to fight for her instead of the Lord God (see 8:20).

obey His voice, and do not rebel against the
commandment of the LORD, then both you and
the king who reigns over you will continue following the LORD your God. 15However, if you do
not obey the voice of the LORD, but rebel
against the commandment of the LORD, then
the hand of the LORD will be against you, as *it*
was against your fathers.
16"Now therefore, stand and see this great
thing which the LORD will do before your eyes:
17*Is* today not the wheat harvest? I will call to the
LORD, and He will send thunder and rain, that
you may perceive and see that your wickedness
is great, which you have done in the sight of
the LORD, in asking a king for yourselves."
18So Samuel called to the LORD, and the LORD
sent thunder and rain that day; and all the people greatly feared the LORD and Samuel.
19And all the people said to Samuel, "Pray
for your servants to the LORD your God, that
we may not die; for we have added to all our
sins the evil of asking a king for ourselves."
20Then Samuel said to the people, "Do not
fear. You have done all this wickedness; yet do
not turn aside from following the LORD, but
serve the LORD with all your heart. 21And do
not turn aside; for *then you would go* after
empty things which cannot profit or deliver,
for they *are* nothing. 22For the LORD will not
forsake His people, for His great name's sake,
because it has pleased the LORD to make you
His people. 23Moreover, as for me, far be it
from me that I should sin against the LORD in
ceasing to pray for you; but I will teach you the
good and the right way. 24Only fear the LORD,
and serve Him in truth with all your heart; for
consider what great things He has done for
you. 25But if you still do wickedly, you shall be
swept away, both you and your king."
13 Saul reigned one year; and when he had
reigned two years over Israel, 2Saul chose
for himself three thousand *men* of Israel. Two
thousand were with Saul in Michmash and in
the mountains of Bethel, and a thousand were

with Jonathan in Gibeah of Benjamin. The rest
of the people he sent away, every man to his
tent.
[3]And Jonathan attacked the garrison of the
Philistines that *was* in Geba, and the Philistines
heard *of it.* Then Saul blew the trumpet
throughout all the land, saying, "Let the Hebrews hear!" [4]Now all Israel heard it said *that*
Saul had attacked a garrison of the Philistines,
and *that* Israel had also become an abomination to the Philistines. And the people were
called together to Saul at Gilgal.
[5]Then the Philistines gathered together to
fight with Israel, thirty thousand chariots and
six thousand horsemen, and people as the
sand which *is* on the seashore in multitude.
And they came up and encamped in
Michmash, to the east of Beth Aven. [6]When
the men of Israel saw that they were in danger
(for the people were distressed), then the people hid in caves, in thickets, in rocks, in holes,
and in pits. [7]And *some of* the Hebrews crossed
over the Jordan to the land of Gad and Gilead.
As for Saul, he *was* still in Gilgal, and all the
people followed him trembling. [8]Then he waited seven days, according to the time set by
Samuel. But Samuel did not come to Gilgal;
and the people were scattered from him. [9]So
Saul said, "Bring a burnt offering and peace
offerings here to me." And he offered the
burnt offering. [10]Now it happened, as soon as
he had finished presenting the burnt offering,
that Samuel came; and Saul went out to meet
him, that he might greet him.
[11]And Samuel said, "What have you done?"
Saul said, "When I saw that the people were
scattered from me, and *that* you did not come
within the days appointed, and *that* the
Philistines gathered together at Michmash,
[12]then I said, 'The Philistines will now come
down on me at Gilgal, and I have not made supplication to the LORD.' Therefore I felt compelled, and offered a burnt offering."
[13]And Samuel said to Saul, "You have done
foolishly. You have not kept the commandment of the LORD your God, which He commanded you. For now the LORD would have
established your kingdom over Israel forever.
[14]But now your kingdom shall not continue.
The LORD has sought for Himself a man after
His own heart, and the LORD has commanded
him *to be* commander over His people,
because you have not kept what the LORD
commanded you."
[15]Then Samuel arose and went up from
Gilgal to Gibeah of Benjamin. And Saul numbered the people present with him, about six
hundred men.
[16]Saul, Jonathan his son, and the people present with them remained in Gibeah of Benjamin.
But the Philistines encamped in Michmash.
[17]Then raiders came out of the camp of the
Philistines in three companies. One company
turned onto the road to Ophrah, to the land of
Shual, [18]another company turned to the road *to*
Beth Horon, and another company turned *to*
the road of the border that overlooks the
Valley of Zeboim toward the wilderness.
[19]Now there was no blacksmith to be found
throughout all the land of Israel, for the
Philistines said, "Lest the Hebrews make
swords or spears." [20]But all the Israelites would
go down to the Philistines to sharpen each
man's plowshare, his mattock, his ax, and his
sickle; [21]and the charge for a sharpening was a
pim for the plowshares, the mattocks, the
forks, and the axes, and to set the points of the
goads. [22]So it came about, on the day of battle,
that there was neither sword nor spear found
in the hand of any of the people who *were* with
Saul and Jonathan. But they were found with
Saul and Jonathan his son.
[23]And the garrison of the Philistines went
out to the pass of Michmash.

13:19 no blacksmith. The Philistines had superior iron- and metal-working craftsmen until David's time (see 1 Chr. 22:3), accounting for their formidable military force.

Psalm 56:1–13

To the Chief Musician. Set to "The Silent Dove in Distant Lands." A Michtam of David when the Philistines captured him in Gath.

Be merciful to me, O God, for
man would swallow me up;
Fighting all day he oppresses me.
2 My enemies would hound *me* all day,
For *there are* many who fight against
me, O Most High.

3 Whenever I am afraid,
I will trust in You.
4 In God (I will praise His word),
In God I have put my trust;
I will not fear.
What can flesh do to me?

5 All day they twist my words;
All their thoughts *are* against me for
evil.
6 They gather together,

They hide, they mark my steps,
When they lie in wait for my life.
7 Shall they escape by iniquity?
In anger cast down the peoples, O God!

8 You number my wanderings;
Put my tears into Your bottle;
Are they not in Your book?

56:8 my tears...Your bottle. David asked God to keep a remembrance of all of his sufferings, so that God would eventually vindicate him.

9 When I cry out *to You,*
Then my enemies will turn back;
This I know, because God *is* for me.
10 In God (I will praise *His* word),
In the LORD (I will praise *His* word),
11 In God I have put my trust;
I will not be afraid.
What can man do to me?

12 Vows *made* to You *are binding* upon me, O God;
I will render praises to You,
13 For You have delivered my soul from death.
Have You not *kept* my feet from falling,
That I may walk before God
In the light of the living?

Proverbs 15:21–23

21 Folly *is* joy *to him who is* destitute of discernment,
But a man of understanding walks uprightly.

22 Without counsel, plans go awry,
But in the multitude of counselors they are established.

23 A man has joy by the answer of his mouth,
And a word *spoken* in due season, how good *it is!*

Luke 22:47–71

47And while He was still speaking, behold, a
multitude; and he who was called Judas, one of
the twelve, went before them and drew near to
Jesus to kiss Him. 48But Jesus said to him, "Judas,
are you betraying the Son of Man with a kiss?"
49When those around Him saw what was
going to happen, they said to Him, "Lord, shall
we strike with the sword?" 50And one of them
struck the servant of the high priest and cut off
his right ear.
51But Jesus answered and said, "Permit even
this." And He touched his ear and healed him.
52Then Jesus said to the chief priests, captains
of the temple, and the elders who had come to
Him, "Have you come out, as against a robber,
with swords and clubs? 53When I was with you
daily in the temple, you did not try to seize
Me. But this is your hour, and the power of
darkness."

22:51 Permit even this. I.e., the betrayal and arrest (see John 18:11). All was proceeding according to the divine timetable. **touched his ear and healed him.** This is the only instance in all of Scripture where Christ healed a fresh wound. The miracle is also unique in that Christ healed an enemy, unasked, and without any evidence of faith in the recipient. It is also remarkable that such a dramatic miracle had no effect whatsoever on the hearts of those men. Neither had the explosive power of Jesus' words, which knocked them to the ground (John 18:6). They carried on with the arrest as if nothing peculiar had happened (v. 54).

22:53 this is your hour. I.e., nighttime, the hour of darkness. The arresting group had not the courage to confront Jesus in the presence of the crowds at the temple, where He had openly taught each day. Their skulking tactics betrayed the truth about their hearts. Nighttime was a fitting hour for the servants of the power of darkness (Satan) to be afoot (see John 3:20,21; Eph. 5:8,12–15; 1 Thess. 5:5–7).

54Having arrested Him, they led *Him* and
brought Him into the high priest's house. But
Peter followed at a distance. 55Now when they
had kindled a fire in the midst of the courtyard
and sat down together, Peter sat among them.
56And a certain servant girl, seeing him as he
sat by the fire, looked intently at him and said,
"This man was also with Him."
57But he denied Him, saying, "Woman, I do
not know Him."
58And after a little while another saw him
and said, "You also are of them."
But Peter said, "Man, I am not!"
59Then after about an hour had passed, another
confidently affirmed, saying, "Surely this *fellow*
also was with Him, for he is a Galilean."
60But Peter said, "Man, I do not know what
you are saying!"
Immediately, while he was still speaking,
the rooster crowed. 61And the Lord turned

and looked at Peter. Then Peter remembered the word of the Lord, how He had said to him, "Before the rooster crows, you will deny Me three times." 62So Peter went out and wept bitterly.

63Now the men who held Jesus mocked Him and beat Him. 64And having blindfolded Him, they struck Him on the face and asked Him, saying, "Prophesy! Who is the one who struck You?" 65And many other things they blasphemously spoke against Him.

66As soon as it was day, the elders of the people, both chief priests and scribes, came together and led Him into their council, saying, 67"If You are the Christ, tell us."

But He said to them, "If I tell you, you will by no means believe. 68And if I also ask *you,* you will by no means answer Me or let *Me* go. 69Hereafter the Son of Man will sit on the right hand of the power of God."

70Then they all said, "Are You then the Son of God?"

So He said to them, "You *rightly* say that I am."

71And they said, "What further testimony do we need? For we have heard it ourselves from His own mouth."

DAY 5: Why was Saul judged so severely?

When Saul was anointed king by Samuel, Saul was commanded to wait 7 days to meet Samuel in Gilgal. Samuel would offer burnt offerings and peace offerings, and he would show Saul what he should do (1 Sam. 10:8). After 7 days of waiting and Samuel had not come, the people were scattered (1 Sam. 13:8). Saul's men were deserting him because of anxiety and fear over the coming battle.

Rather than continue to wait, Saul "offered the burnt offering" (v. 9). Saul's sin was not specifically that he made a sacrifice (see 2 Sam. 24:25; 1 Kin. 8:62–64), but that he did not wait for priestly assistance from Samuel. He wished to rule as an autocrat, who possessed absolute power in civil and sacred matters. Samuel had waited the 7 days as a test of Saul's character and obedience to God, but Saul failed it by invading the priestly office himself.

Confronted by Samuel, Saul's response was "When I saw…" (v. 11). Saul reacted disobediently based upon what he saw and not by faith. He feared losing his men and did not properly consider what God would have him do. Consequently, Samuel places the responsibility fully on Saul's shoulders: "You have not kept the commandment" (v. 13). "Now your kingdom shall not continue" (v. 14). Instead of Saul, God was going to choose one whose heart was like His own, i.e., one who had a will to obey God. Paul quotes this passage in Acts 13:22 of David. Someone else, namely David, had already been chosen to be God's leader over His people.

MAY 6

1 Samuel 14:1–15:35

14 Now it happened one day that Jonathan the son of Saul said to the young man who bore his armor, "Come, let us go over to the Philistines' garrison that *is* on the other side." But he did not tell his father. 2And Saul was sitting in the outskirts of Gibeah under a pomegranate tree which *is* in Migron. The people who *were* with him *were* about six hundred men. 3Ahijah the son of Ahitub, Ichabod's brother, the son of Phinehas, the son of Eli, the LORD's priest in Shiloh, was wearing an ephod. But the people did not know that Jonathan had gone.

4Between the passes, by which Jonathan sought to go over to the Philistines' garrison, *there was* a sharp rock on one side and a sharp rock on the other side. And the name of one *was* Bozez, and the name of the other Seneh. 5The front of one faced northward opposite Michmash, and the other southward opposite Gibeah.

6Then Jonathan said to the young man who bore his armor, "Come, let us go over to the garrison of these uncircumcised; it may be that the LORD will work for us. For nothing restrains the LORD from saving by many or by few."

7So his armorbearer said to him, "Do all that is in your heart. Go then; here I am with you, according to your heart."

8Then Jonathan said, "Very well, let us cross over to *these* men, and we will show ourselves to them. 9If they say thus to us, 'Wait until we come to you,' then we will stand still in our place and not go up to them. 10But if they say thus, 'Come up to us,' then we will go up. For the LORD has delivered them into our hand, and this *will be* a sign to us."

11So both of them showed themselves to the garrison of the Philistines. And the Philistines said, "Look, the Hebrews are coming out of the holes where they have hidden." 12Then the men of the garrison called to Jonathan and his armorbearer, and said, "Come up to us, and we will show you something."

Jonathan said to his armorbearer, "Come up after me, for the LORD has delivered them into

the hand of Israel." 13And Jonathan climbed up
on his hands and knees with his armorbearer
after him; and they fell before Jonathan. And
as he came after him, his armorbearer killed
them. 14That first slaughter which Jonathan
and his armorbearer made was about twenty
men within about half an acre of land.
15And there was trembling in the camp, in
the field, and among all the people. The garrison and the raiders also trembled; and the
earth quaked, so that it was a very great trembling. 16Now the watchmen of Saul in Gibeah
of Benjamin looked, and *there* was the multitude, melting away; and they went here and

14:15 the earth quaked. The earthquake affirms the fact that divine intervention aided Jonathan and his armorbearer in their raid. The earthquake caused a panic among the Philistines. God would have intervened on Saul's behalf in such a manner had he chosen to be faithfully patient (see 13:9).

there. 17Then Saul said to the people who *were*
with him, "Now call the roll and see who has
gone from us." And when they had called the
roll, surprisingly, Jonathan and his armorbearer *were* not *there.* 18And Saul said to Ahijah,
"Bring the ark of God here" (for at that time
the ark of God was with the children of Israel).
19Now it happened, while Saul talked to the
priest, that the noise which *was* in the camp of
the Philistines continued to increase; so Saul
said to the priest, "Withdraw your hand."
20Then Saul and all the people who *were* with
him assembled, and they went to the battle;
and indeed every man's sword was against his
neighbor, *and there was* very great confusion.
21Moreover the Hebrews *who* were with the
Philistines before that time, who went up with
them into the camp *from the* surrounding
country, they also joined the Israelites who
were with Saul and Jonathan. 22Likewise all the
men of Israel who had hidden in the mountains of Ephraim, *when* they heard that the
Philistines fled, they also followed hard after
them in the battle. 23So the LORD saved Israel
that day, and the battle shifted to Beth Aven.
24And the men of Israel were distressed that
day, for Saul had placed the people under oath,
saying, "Cursed *is* the man who eats *any* food
until evening, before I have taken vengeance on
my enemies." So none of the people tasted
food. 25Now all *the people* of the land came to a
forest; and there was honey on the ground.
26And when the people had come into the
woods, there was the honey, dripping; but no
one put his hand to his mouth, for the people
feared the oath. 27But Jonathan had not heard
his father charge the people with the oath;
therefore he stretched out the end of the rod
that *was* in his hand and dipped it in a honeycomb, and put his hand to his mouth; and his
countenance brightened. 28Then one of the people said, "Your father strictly charged the people
with an oath, saying, 'Cursed *is* the man who
eats food this day.'" And the people were faint.
29But Jonathan said, "My father has troubled
the land. Look now, how my countenance has
brightened because I tasted a little of this
honey. 30How much better if the people had
eaten freely today of the spoil of their enemies
which they found! For now would there not
have been a much greater slaughter among
the Philistines?"
31Now they had driven back the Philistines
that day from Michmash to Aijalon. So the people were very faint. 32And the people rushed on
the spoil, and took sheep, oxen, and calves,
and slaughtered *them* on the ground; and the
people ate *them* with the blood. 33Then they
told Saul, saying, "Look, the people are sinning
against the LORD by eating with the blood!"
So he said, "You have dealt treacherously;
roll a large stone to me this day." 34Then Saul
said, "Disperse yourselves among the people,
and say to them, 'Bring me here every man's
ox and every man's sheep, slaughter *them*
here, and eat; and do not sin against the LORD
by eating with the blood.'" So every one of the
people brought his ox with him that night, and
slaughtered *it* there. 35Then Saul built an altar
to the LORD. This was the first altar that he
built to the LORD.
36Now Saul said, "Let us go down after the
Philistines by night, and plunder them until
the morning light; and let us not leave a man
of them."
And they said, "Do whatever seems good to
you."
Then the priest said, "Let us draw near to
God here."
37So Saul asked counsel of God, "Shall I go
down after the Philistines? Will You deliver
them into the hand of Israel?" But He did not
answer him that day. 38And Saul said, "Come
over here, all you chiefs of the people, and know
and see what this sin was today. 39For *as* the
LORD lives, who saves Israel, though it be in Jonathan my son, he shall surely die." But not a
man among all the people answered him. 40Then
he said to all Israel, "You be on one side, and my
son Jonathan and I will be on the other side."

14:37 Saul asked counsel of God. At the request of Ahijah, Saul inquired of the Lord regarding his battle plan. **He did not answer him.** Because of the sin that Saul had caused in his army, God did not answer his inquiry. This would not be the last time that the Lord would refuse to respond to sinful Saul (see 28:6).

And the people said to Saul, "Do what seems
good to you."
[41]Therefore Saul said to the LORD God of
Israel, "Give a perfect *lot*." So Saul and Jonathan were taken, but the people escaped. [42]And
Saul said, "Cast *lots* between my son Jonathan
and me." So Jonathan was taken. [43]Then Saul
said to Jonathan, "Tell me what you have done."
And Jonathan told him, and said, "I only
tasted a little honey with the end of the rod
that *was* in my hand. So now I must die!"
[44]Saul answered, "God do so and more also;
for you shall surely die, Jonathan."
[45]But the people said to Saul, "Shall Jonathan die, who has accomplished this great
deliverance in Israel? Certainly not! *As* the
LORD lives, not one hair of his head shall fall to
the ground, for he has worked with God this
day." So the people rescued Jonathan, and he
did not die.
[46]Then Saul returned from pursuing the Philistines, and the Philistines went to their own
place.
[47]So Saul established his sovereignty over
Israel, and fought against all his enemies on
every side, against Moab, against the people
of Ammon, against Edom, against the kings of
Zobah, and against the Philistines. Wherever
he turned, he harassed *them*. [48]And he gathered an army and attacked the Amalekites,
and delivered Israel from the hands of those
who plundered them.
[49]The sons of Saul were Jonathan, Jishui, and
Malchishua. And the names of his two daughters *were these:* the name of the firstborn Merab,
and the name of the younger Michal. [50]The
name of Saul's wife *was* Ahinoam the daughter
of Ahimaaz. And the name of the commander
of his army *was* Abner the son of Ner, Saul's
uncle. [51]Kish *was* the father of Saul, and Ner
the father of Abner *was* the son of Abiel.
[52]Now there was fierce war with the
Philistines all the days of Saul. And when Saul
saw any strong man or any valiant man, he
took him for himself.

15 Samuel also said to Saul, "The LORD sent
me to anoint you king over His people,
over Israel. Now therefore, heed the voice of
the words of the LORD. [2]Thus says the LORD of
hosts: 'I will punish Amalek *for* what he did to
Israel, how he ambushed him on the way
when he came up from Egypt. [3]Now go and attack Amalek, and utterly destroy all that they
have, and do not spare them. But kill both
man and woman, infant and nursing child, ox
and sheep, camel and donkey.' "
[4]So Saul gathered the people together and
numbered them in Telaim, two hundred thousand foot soldiers and ten thousand men of Judah. [5]And Saul came to a city of Amalek, and
lay in wait in the valley.
[6]Then Saul said to the Kenites, "Go, depart,
get down from among the Amalekites, lest I
destroy you with them. For you showed kindness to all the children of Israel when they
came up out of Egypt." So the Kenites departed from among the Amalekites. [7]And Saul
attacked the Amalekites, from Havilah all the
way to Shur, which is east of Egypt. [8]He also
took Agag king of the Amalekites alive, and utterly destroyed all the people with the edge of
the sword. [9]But Saul and the people spared
Agag and the best of the sheep, the oxen, the
fatlings, the lambs, and all *that was* good, and
were unwilling to utterly destroy them. But
everything despised and worthless, that they
utterly destroyed.
[10]Now the word of the LORD came to Samuel,
saying, [11]"I greatly regret that I have set up
Saul *as* king, for he has turned back from following Me, and has not performed My commandments." And it grieved Samuel, and he
cried out to the LORD all night. [12]So when Samuel rose early in the morning to meet Saul, it
was told Samuel, saying, "Saul went to
Carmel, and indeed, he set up a monument for
himself; and he has gone on around, passed
by, and gone down to Gilgal." [13]Then Samuel
went to Saul, and Saul said to him, "Blessed
are you of the LORD! I have performed the
commandment of the LORD."
[14]But Samuel said, "What then *is* this bleat-
ing of the sheep in my ears, and the lowing of
the oxen which I hear?"
[15]And Saul said, "They have brought them
from the Amalekites; for the people spared the
best of the sheep and the oxen, to sacrifice to the
LORD your God; and the rest we have utterly
destroyed."
[16]Then Samuel said to Saul, "Be quiet! And I
will tell you what the LORD said to me last night."
And he said to him, "Speak on."
[17]So Samuel said, "When you *were* little in
your own eyes, *were* you not head of the tribes
of Israel? And did not the LORD anoint you

king over Israel? 18Now the LORD sent you on a
mission, and said, 'Go, and utterly destroy the
sinners, the Amalekites, and fight against
them until they are consumed.' 19Why then did
you not obey the voice of the LORD? Why did
you swoop down on the spoil, and do evil in
the sight of the LORD?"

20And Saul said to Samuel, "But I have obeyed
the voice of the LORD, and gone on the mission
on which the LORD sent me, and brought back
Agag king of Amalek; I have utterly destroyed
the Amalekites. 21But the people took of the
plunder, sheep and oxen, the best of the
things which should have been utterly
destroyed, to sacrifice to the LORD your God in
Gilgal."

22So Samuel said:

"Has the LORD *as great* delight in burnt
offerings and sacrifices,
As in obeying the voice of the LORD?
Behold, to obey is better than sacrifice,
And to heed than the fat of rams.
23 For rebellion *is as* the sin of witchcraft,
And stubbornness *is as* iniquity and
idolatry.
Because you have rejected the word of
the LORD,
He also has rejected you from *being*
king."

24Then Saul said to Samuel, "I have sinned,
for I have transgressed the commandment of
the LORD and your words, because I feared the
people and obeyed their voice. 25Now therefore, please pardon my sin, and return with
me, that I may worship the LORD."

26But Samuel said to Saul, "I will not return
with you, for you have rejected the word of the
LORD, and the LORD has rejected you from
being king over Israel."

27And as Samuel turned around to go away,
Saul seized the edge of his robe, and it tore.
28So Samuel said to him, "The LORD has torn
the kingdom of Israel from you today, and has
given it to a neighbor of yours, *who is* better
than you. 29And also the Strength of Israel will
not lie nor relent. For He *is* not a man, that He
should relent."

30Then he said, "I have sinned; *yet* honor me
now, please, before the elders of my people and
before Israel, and return with me, that I may
worship the LORD your God." 31So Samuel turned
back after Saul, and Saul worshiped the LORD.

32Then Samuel said, "Bring Agag king of the
Amalekites here to me." So Agag came to him
cautiously.

And Agag said, "Surely the bitterness of
death is past."

33But Samuel said, "As your sword has made
women childless, so shall your mother be
childless among women." And Samuel hacked
Agag in pieces before the LORD in Gilgal.

34Then Samuel went to Ramah, and Saul
went up to his house at Gibeah of Saul. 35And
Samuel went no more to see Saul until the day
of his death. Nevertheless Samuel mourned
for Saul, and the LORD regretted that He had
made Saul king over Israel.

Psalm 57:1–3

To the Chief Musician. Set to "Do Not Destroy."
A Michtam of David when he fled from Saul
into the cave.

Be merciful to me, O God,
be merciful to me!
For my soul trusts in You;
And in the shadow of Your wings I will
make my refuge,
Until *these* calamities have passed by.

57:1 the shadow of Your wings. Metaphorically, God cares for His own as a mother bird protects its young. Symbolically, there may be a reference here to the cherubim wings on the ark of the covenant where God was specifically present (see Ex. 37:1–16; Pss. 17:8; 36:7; 61:4; 63:7; 91:1,4). **I will make my refuge.** When life becomes bizarre, only one's relationship with his God calms the soul.

2 I will cry out to God Most High,
To God who performs *all things* for me.
3 He shall send from heaven and save me;
He reproaches the one who would
swallow me up. Selah
God shall send forth His mercy and
His truth.

Proverbs 15:24–25

24 The way of life *winds* upward for the
wise,
That he may turn away from hell below.
25 The LORD will destroy the house of the
proud,
But He will establish the boundary of
the widow.

Luke 23:1–25

23 Then the whole multitude of them
arose and led Him to Pilate. 2And they
began to accuse Him, saying, "We found this
fellow perverting the nation, and forbidding to

pay taxes to Caesar, saying that He Himself is
Christ, a King."
3 Then Pilate asked Him, saying, "Are You
the King of the Jews?"
He answered him and said, "*It is as* you say."
4 So Pilate said to the chief priests and the
crowd, "I find no fault in this Man."
5 But they were the more fierce, saying, "He
stirs up the people, teaching throughout all
Judea, beginning from Galilee to this place."
6 When Pilate heard of Galilee, he asked if
the Man were a Galilean. 7 And as soon as he
knew that He belonged to Herod's jurisdiction, he sent Him to Herod, who was also in Jerusalem at that time. 8 Now when Herod saw
Jesus, he was exceedingly glad; for he had
desired for a long *time* to see Him, because he
had heard many things about Him, and he
hoped to see some miracle done by Him.
9 Then he questioned Him with many words,
but He answered him nothing. 10 And the chief
priests and scribes stood and vehemently
accused Him. 11 Then Herod, with his men of
war, treated Him with contempt and mocked
Him, arrayed Him in a gorgeous robe, and
sent Him back to Pilate. 12 That very day Pilate
and Herod became friends with each other, for
previously they had been at enmity with each
other.
13 Then Pilate, when he had called together
the chief priests, the rulers, and the people,
14 said to them, "You have brought this Man to
me, as one who misleads the people. And
indeed, having examined *Him* in your presence,
I have found no fault in this Man concerning
those things of which you accuse Him; 15 no, neither did Herod, for I sent you back to him; and
indeed nothing deserving of death has been
done by Him. 16 I will therefore chastise Him and
release *Him*" 17 (for it was necessary for him to
release one to them at the feast).

23:8 desired...to see Him. Herod's interest in Christ was fueled by the fact that Christ reminded him of his late nemesis, John the Baptist. At one time Herod had apparently threatened to kill Jesus (13:31–33), but with Christ in Judea rather than Galilee and Perea (where Herod ruled), the king's concern seems to have been nothing more than an eager curiosity.

23:9 answered him nothing. It is significant that in all Jesus' various interrogations, Herod was the only one to whom He refused to speak. See Matthew 7:6. Herod had summarily rejected the truth when he heard it from John the Baptist, so it would have been pointless for Jesus to answer him.

18 And they all cried out at once, saying,
"Away with this *Man,* and release to us
Barabbas"— 19 who had been thrown into
prison for a certain rebellion made in the city,
and for murder.
20 Pilate, therefore, wishing to release Jesus,
again called out to them. 21 But they shouted,
saying, "Crucify *Him,* crucify Him!"
22 Then he said to them the third time, "Why,
what evil has He done? I have found no reason
for death in Him. I will therefore chastise Him
and let *Him* go."
23 But they were insistent, demanding with
loud voices that He be crucified. And the voices of these men and of the chief priests prevailed. 24 So Pilate gave sentence that it should
be as they requested. 25 And he released to
them the one they requested, who for rebellion and murder had been thrown into prison;
but he delivered Jesus to their will.

DAY 6: Why is obedience so important?

Samuel's specific command to Saul was to destroy all the Amalekites and their animals, but instead he spared their king and the best of the animals (1 Sam. 15:3,9). But when confronted by Samuel, Saul's response was: "I have performed the commandment of the Lord" (v. 13). Saul, either ignorantly or deceitfully, maintained that he did what was commanded (15:20). Saul also began to place blame on others (vv. 11,12), making room for his own excuses just as he had done earlier. Then he tried to justify his sin by saying that the animals would be used to sacrifice to the God of Samuel. Saul's blatant disobedience at least pained his conscience so that he could not claim God as his God. Instead of confessing his sin and repenting, Saul continued to justify himself.

"Behold," Samuel told Saul, "to obey is better than sacrifice" (v. 22). This is an essential Old Testament truth. Samuel stated that God desires heart obedience over the ritual sacrifice of animals (Ps. 51:16,17; Is. 1:10–17). The sacrificial system was never intended to function in place of living an obedient life, but was rather to be an expression of it (Hos. 6:6; Amos 5:21–27; Mic. 6:6–8).

Saul needed to see that his real worship was indicated by his behavior and not by his sacrifices. He demonstrated himself to be an idolater whose idol was himself. He had failed the conditions (12:13–15) which would have brought blessing on the nation. His disobedience here was on the same level as witchcraft and idolatry, sins worthy of death (v. 23)."Because you have rejected the word of the LORD, He also has rejected you." A universal principle is given here that those who continually reject God will one day be rejected by Him. The sins of Saul caused God to immediately depose Saul and his descendants forever from the throne of Israel.

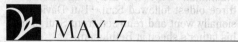

MAY 7

1 Samuel 16:1–17:58

16 Now the LORD said to Samuel, "How long
will you mourn for Saul, seeing I have
rejected him from reigning over Israel? Fill
your horn with oil, and go; I am sending you to
Jesse the Bethlehemite. For I have provided
Myself a king among his sons."
[2]And Samuel said, "How can I go? If Saul
hears *it,* he will kill me."
But the LORD said, "Take a heifer with you,
and say, 'I have come to sacrifice to the LORD.'
[3]Then invite Jesse to the sacrifice, and I will
show you what you shall do; you shall anoint
for Me the one I name to you."
[4]So Samuel did what the LORD said, and went
to Bethlehem. And the elders of the town trembled at his coming, and said, "Do you come
peaceably?"
[5]And he said, "Peaceably; I have come to
sacrifice to the LORD. Sanctify yourselves, and
come with me to the sacrifice." Then he consecrated Jesse and his sons, and invited them
to the sacrifice.
[6]So it was, when they came, that he looked
at Eliab and said, "Surely the LORD's anointed
is before Him!"
[7]But the LORD said to Samuel, "Do not look
at his appearance or at his physical stature,
because I have refused him. For *the LORD does*
not *see* as man sees; for man looks at the outward appearance, but the LORD looks at the
heart."
[8]So Jesse called Abinadab, and made him
pass before Samuel. And he said, "Neither has
the LORD chosen this one." [9]Then Jesse made
Shammah pass by. And he said, "Neither has
the LORD chosen this one." [10]Thus Jesse made
seven of his sons pass before Samuel. And
Samuel said to Jesse, "The LORD has not chosen these." [11]And Samuel said to Jesse, "Are all
the young men here?" Then he said, "There
remains yet the youngest, and there he is,
keeping the sheep."
And Samuel said to Jesse, "Send and bring
him. For we will not sit down till he comes
here." [12]So he sent and brought him in. Now
he *was* ruddy, with bright eyes, and good-looking. And the LORD said, "Arise, anoint him; for
this *is* the one!" [13]Then Samuel took the horn
of oil and anointed him in the midst of his
brothers; and the Spirit of the LORD came
upon David from that day forward. So Samuel
arose and went to Ramah.
[14]But the Spirit of the LORD departed from
Saul, and a distressing spirit from the LORD
troubled him. [15]And Saul's servants said to
him, "Surely, a distressing spirit from God is
troubling you. [16]Let our master now command
your servants, *who are* before you, to seek out
a man *who is* a skillful player on the harp. And
it shall be that he will play it with his hand
when the distressing spirit from God is upon
you, and you shall be well."
[17]So Saul said to his servants, "Provide me
now a man who can play well, and bring *him* to
me."
[18]Then one of the servants answered and
said, "Look, I have seen a son of Jesse the
Bethlehemite, *who is* skillful in playing, a
mighty man of valor, a man of war, prudent in
speech, and a handsome person; and the LORD
is with him."
[19]Therefore Saul sent messengers to Jesse,
and said, "Send me your son David, who *is* with
the sheep." [20]And Jesse took a donkey *loaded
with* bread, a skin of wine, and a young goat, and
sent *them* by his son David to Saul. [21]So David
came to Saul and stood before him. And he

16:7 his appearance...physical stature. Samuel needed to be reminded that God's anointed was not chosen because of physical attributes. This was initially a difficult concept for Samuel as he was accustomed to a king whose only positive attributes were physical. **the LORD looks at the heart.** The Hebrew concept of "heart" embodies emotions, will, intellect, and desires. The life of the man will reflect his heart (see Matt. 12:34,35).

loved him greatly, and he became his armorbearer. 22Then Saul sent to Jesse, saying, "Please
let David stand before me, for he has found
favor in my sight." 23And so it was, whenever the
spirit from God was upon Saul, that David would
take a harp and play *it* with his hand. Then Saul
would become refreshed and well, and the distressing spirit would depart from him.

17 Now the Philistines gathered their
armies together to battle, and were gathered at Sochoh, which *belongs* to Judah; they
encamped between Sochoh and Azekah, in
Ephes Dammim. 2And Saul and the men of Israel
were gathered together, and they encamped in
the Valley of Elah, and drew up in battle array
against the Philistines. 3The Philistines stood on
a mountain on one side, and Israel stood on a
mountain on the other side, with a valley
between them.

17:4 champion. Literally, "the man between two." An appropriate appellation as Goliath stood between the two armies and offered his challenge to a "duel" of hand-to-hand combat, the outcome of which would settle the battle for both sides. **six cubits and a span.** One cubit measures approximately 18 inches and one span about 9 inches, making Goliath about 9 feet 9 inches in height.

4And a champion went out from the camp of
the Philistines, named Goliath, from Gath,
whose height *was* six cubits and a span. 5*He*
had a bronze helmet on his head, and he *was*
armed with a coat of mail, and the weight of
the coat *was* five thousand shekels of bronze.
6And *he had* bronze armor on his legs and a
bronze javelin between his shoulders. 7Now
the staff of his spear *was* like a weaver's beam,
and his iron spearhead *weighed* six hundred
shekels; and a shield-bearer went before him.
8Then he stood and cried out to the armies of
Israel, and said to them, "Why have you come
out to line up for battle? *Am* I not a Philistine,
and you the servants of Saul? Choose a man
for yourselves, and let him come down to me.
9If he is able to fight with me and kill me, then
we will be your servants. But if I prevail against
him and kill him, then you shall be our servants and serve us." 10And the Philistine said,
"I defy the armies of Israel this day; give me a
man, that we may fight together." 11When Saul
and all Israel heard these words of the Philistine,
they were dismayed and greatly afraid.

12Now David *was* the son of that Ephrathite of
Bethlehem Judah, whose name *was* Jesse, and
who had eight sons. And the man was old,
advanced *in years,* in the days of Saul. 13The
three oldest sons of Jesse had gone to follow
Saul to the battle. The names of his three sons
who went to the battle *were* Eliab the firstborn, next to him Abinadab, and the third
Shammah. 14David *was* the youngest. And the
three oldest followed Saul. 15But David occasionally went and returned from Saul to feed
his father's sheep at Bethlehem.

16And the Philistine drew near and presented himself forty days, morning and evening.

17Then Jesse said to his son David, "Take
now for your brothers an ephah of this dried
grain and these ten loaves, and run to your
brothers at the camp. 18And carry these ten
cheeses to the captain of *their* thousand, and
see how your brothers fare, and bring back
news of them." 19Now Saul and they and all the
men of Israel *were* in the Valley of Elah, fighting with the Philistines.

20So David rose early in the morning, left the
sheep with a keeper, and took *the things* and
went as Jesse had commanded him. And he
came to the camp as the army was going out
to the fight and shouting for the battle. 21For
Israel and the Philistines had drawn up in battle array, army against army. 22And David left
his supplies in the hand of the supply keeper,
ran to the army, and came and greeted his
brothers. 23Then as he talked with them, there
was the champion, the Philistine of Gath, Goliath by name, coming up from the armies of
the Philistines; and he spoke according to the
same words. So David heard *them.* 24And all
the men of Israel, when they saw the man, fled
from him and were dreadfully afraid. 25So the
men of Israel said, "Have you seen this man
who has come up? Surely he has come up to
defy Israel; and it shall be *that* the man who
kills him the king will enrich with great riches, will give him his daughter, and give his
father's house exemption *from taxes* in Israel."

26Then David spoke to the men who stood
by him, saying, "What shall be done for the
man who kills this Philistine and takes away
the reproach from Israel? For who *is* this uncircumcised Philistine, that he should defy the
armies of the living God?"

27And the people answered him in this manner, saying, "So shall it be done for the man
who kills him."

28Now Eliab his oldest brother heard when
he spoke to the men; and Eliab's anger was
aroused against David, and he said, "Why did
you come down here? And with whom have you

left those few sheep in the wilderness? I know
your pride and the insolence of your heart, for
you have come down to see the battle."
29And David said, "What have I done now? *Is
there* not a cause?" 30Then he turned from him
toward another and said the same thing; and
these people answered him as the first ones *did.*
31Now when the words which David spoke
were heard, they reported *them* to Saul; and
he sent for him. 32Then David said to Saul, "Let
no man's heart fail because of him; your servant will go and fight with this Philistine."

17:32 Let no man's heart fail. Joshua and Caleb exhorted Israel in the same fashion regarding the giant Anakim 400 years prior (Num. 13:30; 14:8,9). The heathens' hearts fail at the name of the Lord God of Israel (Josh. 2:11).

33And Saul said to David, "You are not able
to go against this Philistine to fight with him;
for you *are* a youth, and he a man of war from
his youth."
34But David said to Saul, "Your servant used
to keep his father's sheep, and when a lion or
a bear came and took a lamb out of the flock, 35I
went out after it and struck it, and delivered
the lamb from its mouth; and when it arose
against me, I caught *it* by its beard, and struck
and killed it. 36Your servant has killed both lion
and bear; and this uncircumcised Philistine
will be like one of them, seeing he has defied
the armies of the living God." 37Moreover
David said, "The LORD, who delivered me
from the paw of the lion and from the paw of
the bear, He will deliver me from the hand of
this Philistine."
And Saul said to David, "Go, and the LORD
be with you!"
38So Saul clothed David with his armor, and
he put a bronze helmet on his head; he also
clothed him with a coat of mail. 39David fastened his sword to his armor and tried to walk,
for he had not tested *them.* And David said to
Saul, "I cannot walk with these, for I have not
tested *them.*" So David took them off.
40Then he took his staff in his hand; and he
chose for himself five smooth stones from the
brook, and put them in a shepherd's bag, in a
pouch which he had, and his sling was in his
hand. And he drew near to the Philistine. 41So
the Philistine came, and began drawing near
to David, and the man who bore the shield
went before him. 42And when the Philistine
looked about and saw David, he disdained
him; for he was *only* a youth, ruddy and good-
looking. 43So the Philistine said to David, "*Am* I
a dog, that you come to me with sticks?" And
the Philistine cursed David by his gods. 44And
the Philistine said to David, "Come to me,
and I will give your flesh to the birds of the
air and the beasts of the field!"
45Then David said to the Philistine, "You
come to me with a sword, with a spear, and
with a javelin. But I come to you in the name
of the LORD of hosts, the God of the armies of
Israel, whom you have defied. 46This day the
LORD will deliver you into my hand, and I will
strike you and take your head from you. And
this day I will give the carcasses of the camp
of the Philistines to the birds of the air and the
wild beasts of the earth, that all the earth may
know that there is a God in Israel. 47Then all
this assembly shall know that the LORD does not
save with sword and spear; for the battle *is* the
LORD's, and He will give you into our hands."
48So it was, when the Philistine arose and
came and drew near to meet David, that David
hurried and ran toward the army to meet the
Philistine. 49Then David put his hand in his bag
and took out a stone; and he slung *it* and
struck the Philistine in his forehead, so that
the stone sank into his forehead, and he fell on
his face to the earth. 50So David prevailed over
the Philistine with a sling and a stone, and
struck the Philistine and killed him. But *there
was* no sword in the hand of David. 51Therefore
David ran and stood over the Philistine, took
his sword and drew it out of its sheath and
killed him, and cut off his head with it.
And when the Philistines saw that their
champion was dead, they fled. 52Now the men
of Israel and Judah arose and shouted, and
pursued the Philistines as far as the entrance
of the valley and to the gates of Ekron. And
the wounded of the Philistines fell along the
road to Shaaraim, even as far as Gath and
Ekron. 53Then the children of Israel returned
from chasing the Philistines, and they plundered their tents. 54And David took the head of
the Philistine and brought it to Jerusalem, but
he put his armor in his tent.

17:37 The LORD...He will deliver me. Just as Jonathan believed earlier (14:6). David had a wholehearted faith in the God of Israel. **the LORD be with you.** One of the first explicit indications in the text that Saul knew that the Lord was with David (see 15:28).

[55]When Saul saw David going out against the
Philistine, he said to Abner, the commander of
the army, "Abner, whose son *is* this youth?"
And Abner said, "As your soul lives, O king,
I do not know."
[56]So the king said, "Inquire whose son this
young man *is*."
[57]Then, as David returned from the slaughter of the Philistine, Abner took him and
brought him before Saul with the head of the
Philistine in his hand. [58]And Saul said to him,
"Whose son *are* you, young man?"
So David answered, "*I am* the son of your
servant Jesse the Bethlehemite."

Psalm 57:4–11

4 My soul *is* among lions;
I lie *among* the sons of men
Who are set on fire,
Whose teeth *are* spears and arrows,
And their tongue a sharp sword.
5 Be exalted, O God, above the heavens;
Let Your glory *be* above all the earth.

6 They have prepared a net for
my steps;
My soul is bowed down;
They have dug a pit before me;
Into the midst of it they *themselves*
have fallen. Selah
7 My heart is steadfast, O God, my heart
is steadfast;
I will sing and give praise.
8 Awake, my glory!
Awake, lute and harp!
I will awaken the dawn.

9 I will praise You, O Lord, among the
peoples;
I will sing to You among the nations.
10 For Your mercy reaches unto the
heavens,
And Your truth unto the clouds.
11 Be exalted, O God, above the heavens;
Let Your glory *be* above all the earth.

Proverbs 15:26

26 The thoughts of the wicked *are* an
abomination to the LORD,
But the words of the pure *are* pleasant.

Luke 23:26–56

[26]Now as they led Him away, they laid hold
of a certain man, Simon a Cyrenian, who was
coming from the country, and on him they laid
the cross that he might bear *it* after Jesus.
[27]And a great multitude of the people followed Him, and women who also mourned
and lamented Him. [28]But Jesus, turning to
them, said, "Daughters of Jerusalem, do not
weep for Me, but weep for yourselves and for
your children. [29]For indeed the days are coming in which they will say, 'Blessed *are* the barren, wombs that never bore, and breasts which
never nursed!' [30]Then they will begin *'to say to
the mountains, "Fall on us!" and to the hills,
"Cover us!"'* [31]For if they do these things in
the green wood, what will be done in the dry?"
[32]There were also two others, criminals, led
with Him to be put to death. [33]And when they
had come to the place called Calvary, there
they crucified Him, and the criminals, one on
the right hand and the other on the left. [34]Then
Jesus said, "Father, forgive them, for they do
not know what they do."
And they divided His garments and cast
lots. [35]And the people stood looking on. But
even the rulers with them sneered, saying,
"He saved others; let Him save Himself if He
is the Christ, the chosen of God."
[36]The soldiers also mocked Him, coming
and offering Him sour wine, [37]and saying, "If
You are the King of the Jews, save Yourself."
[38]And an inscription also was written over
Him in letters of Greek, Latin, and Hebrew:

THIS IS THE KING OF THE JEWS.

[39]Then one of the criminals who were
hanged blasphemed Him, saying, "If You are
the Christ, save Yourself and us."
[40]But the other, answering, rebuked him, saying, "Do you not even fear God, seeing you are
under the same condemnation? [41]And we indeed
justly, for we receive the due reward of our
deeds; but this Man has done nothing wrong."
[42]Then he said to Jesus, "Lord, remember me
when You come into Your kingdom."

23:42 Lord, remember me. The penitent thief's prayer reflected his belief that the soul lives on after death; that Christ had a right to rule over a kingdom of the souls of men; and that He would soon enter that kingdom despite His impending death. His request to be remembered was a plea for mercy, which also reveals that the thief understood he had no hope but divine grace and that the dispensing of that grace lay in Jesus' power. All of this demonstrates true faith on the part of the dying thief, and Christ graciously affirmed the man's salvation (v. 43).

43And Jesus said to him, "Assuredly, I say to
you, today you will be with Me in Paradise."
44Now it was about the sixth hour, and there
was darkness over all the earth until the ninth
hour. 45Then the sun was darkened, and the
veil of the temple was torn in two. 46And when
Jesus had cried out with a loud voice, He said,
"Father, *'into Your hands I commit My spirit.'* "
Having said this, He breathed His last.
47So when the centurion saw what had happened, he glorified God, saying, "Certainly this
was a righteous Man!"
48And the whole crowd who came together to
that sight, seeing what had been done, beat their
breasts and returned. 49But all His acquaintances, and the women who followed Him from Galilee, stood at a distance, watching these things.
50Now behold, *there was* a man named Joseph,
a council member, a good and just man. 51He
had not consented to their decision and deed.
He was from Arimathea, a city of the Jews, who
himself was also waiting for the kingdom of
God. 52This man went to Pilate and asked for the
body of Jesus. 53Then he took it down, wrapped
it in linen, and laid it in a tomb *that was* hewn
out of the rock, where no one had ever lain
before. 54That day was the Preparation, and the
Sabbath drew near.
55And the women who had come with Him
from Galilee followed after, and they observed
the tomb and how His body was laid. 56Then they
returned and prepared spices and fragrant oils.
And they rested on the Sabbath according to
the commandment.

DAY 7: Contrast the spiritual anointings of David and Saul.

David was first anointed by Samuel "in the midst of his brothers" (1 Sam. 16:13). David's first anointing was before his family/house. His second anointing would be before the assembly of his tribe, Judah; and his third anointing would be before the nation Israel. At this time, "the Spirit of the LORD came upon David." This familiar Old Testament expression relates to empowerment for some God-given task (see 10:6,11; 11:6; 19:20,23; 2 Sam. 23:2; 2 Chr. 20:14; Is. 11:2; 61:1; Ezek. 11:5; 37:1). David's anointing was an external symbol of an inward work of God. The operation of the Holy Spirit in this case was not for regeneration, but for empowerment to perform his (David's) role in God's program for Israel. After David sinned with Bathsheba (2 Sam. 11; 12), he prayed, "Do not take Your Holy Spirit from me" (Ps. 51:11).

When David's ascent to the throne began, Saul's slow and painful descent began also. "The Spirit of the LORD departed from Saul" (1 Sam. 16:14). Without God's empowering Holy Spirit, Saul was effectively no longer king over Israel (15:28), although his physical removal from the throne, and his death, happened many years later. "And a distressing spirit from the LORD troubled him." God, in His sovereignty, allowed an evil spirit to torment Saul (see Judg. 9:23; 1 Kin. 22:19–23; Job 1:6–12) for His purpose of establishing the throne of David. This spirit, a messenger from Satan, is to be distinguished from a troubled emotional state brought on by indwelling sin or the harmful consequences of the sinful acts of others (e.g., spirit of jealousy, Num. 5:14). This demon spirit attacked Saul from without, for there is no evidence that the demon indwelt Saul. Saul, whose inward constitution was already prone to questionable judgment and the fear of men, began to experience God's judgment in the form of severe bouts of depression, anger, and delusion, initiated and aggravated by the evil spirit assigned to him. There are several New Testament occasions where God turned people over to demons or Satan for judgment (see Acts 5:1–3; 1 Cor. 5:1–7; 1 Tim. 1:18–20).

MAY 8

1 Samuel 18:1–19:24

18 Now when he had finished speaking to
Saul, the soul of Jonathan was knit to the
soul of David, and Jonathan loved him as his
own soul. 2Saul took him that day, and would
not let him go home to his father's house anymore. 3Then Jonathan and David made a
covenant, because he loved him as his own
soul. 4And Jonathan took off the robe that *was*
on him and gave it to David, with his armor,
even to his sword and his bow and his belt.
5So David went out wherever Saul sent him,
and behaved wisely. And Saul set him over the
men of war, and he was accepted in the sight
of all the people and also in the sight of Saul's

18:1 Jonathan loved him. Jonathan loved David with a loyalty and devotion indicative of covenantal love (18:3). Hiram of Tyre had much the same covenantal love for David (see 2 Sam. 5:11; 1 Kin. 5:1; 9:11). David's later reign from Jerusalem is marked by loyalty to his covenant with Jonathan (2 Sam. 9:1).

servants. 6Now it had happened as they were
coming *home,* when David was returning from
the slaughter of the Philistine, that the women
had come out of all the cities of Israel, singing
and dancing, to meet King Saul, with tambourines, with joy, and with musical instruments. 7So the women sang as they danced,
and said:

"Saul has slain his thousands,
And David his ten thousands."

8Then Saul was very angry, and the saying displeased him; and he said, "They have ascribed
to David ten thousands, and to me they have
ascribed *only* thousands. Now *what* more can
he have but the kingdom?" 9So Saul eyed David
from that day forward.

10And it happened on the next day that the
distressing spirit from God came upon Saul,
and he prophesied inside the house. So David
played *music* with his hand, as at other times;
but *there was* a spear in Saul's hand. 11And Saul
cast the spear, for he said, "I will pin David to
the wall!" But David escaped his presence
twice.

12Now Saul was afraid of David, because the
LORD was with him, but had departed from
Saul. 13Therefore Saul removed him from his
presence, and made him his captain over a
thousand; and he went out and came in before
the people. 14And David behaved wisely in all
his ways, and the LORD *was* with him. 15There-
fore, when Saul saw that he behaved very
wisely, he was afraid of him. 16But all Israel and
Judah loved David, because he went out and
came in before them.

17Then Saul said to David, "Here is my older
daughter Merab; I will give her to you as a
wife. Only be valiant for me, and fight the
LORD's battles." For Saul thought, "Let my
hand not be against him, but let the hand of
the Philistines be against him."

18So David said to Saul, "Who *am* I, and what
is my life *or* my father's family in Israel, that I
should be son-in-law to the king?" 19But it happened at the time when Merab, Saul's daughter, should have been given to David, that she
was given to Adriel the Meholathite as a wife.

20Now Michal, Saul's daughter, loved David.
And they told Saul, and the thing pleased him.
21So Saul said, "I will give her to him, that she
may be a snare to him, and that the hand of the
Philistines may be against him." Therefore Saul
said to David a second time, "You shall be my
son-in-law today."

22And Saul commanded his servants, "Communicate with David secretly, and say, 'Look,
the king has delight in you, and all his servants
love you. Now therefore, become the king's
son-in-law.' "

23So Saul's servants spoke those words in
the hearing of David. And David said, "Does it
seem to you *a* light *thing* to be a king's son-in-
law, seeing I *am* a poor and lightly esteemed
man?" 24And the servants of Saul told him, saying, "In this manner David spoke."

25Then Saul said, "Thus you shall say to
David: 'The king does not desire any dowry but
one hundred foreskins of the Philistines, to
take vengeance on the king's enemies.' " But
Saul thought to make David fall by the hand of
the Philistines. 26So when his servants told
David these words, it pleased David well to
become the king's son-in-law. Now the days
had not expired; 27therefore David arose and
went, he and his men, and killed two hundred
men of the Philistines. And David brought
their foreskins, and they gave them in full
count to the king, that he might become the
king's son-in-law. Then Saul gave him Michal
his daughter as a wife.

28Thus Saul saw and knew that the LORD *was*
with David, and *that* Michal, Saul's daughter,
loved him; 29and Saul was still more afraid of
David. So Saul became David's enemy continually. 30Then the princes of the Philistines went
out *to war.* And so it was, whenever they went
out, *that* David behaved more wisely than all
the servants of Saul, so that his name became
highly esteemed.

19 Now Saul spoke to Jonathan his son and
to all his servants, that they should kill
David; but Jonathan, Saul's son, delighted
greatly in David. 2So Jonathan told David, saying, "My father Saul seeks to kill you. Therefore please be on your guard until morning,
and stay in a secret *place* and hide. 3And I will
go out and stand beside my father in the field
where you *are,* and I will speak with my father
about you. Then what I observe, I will tell you."

4Thus Jonathan spoke well of David to Saul
his father, and said to him, "Let not the king
sin against his servant, against David, because
he has not sinned against you, and because
his works *have been* very good toward you.
5For he took his life in his hands and killed the
Philistine, and the LORD brought about a great
deliverance for all Israel. You saw *it* and
rejoiced. Why then will you sin against innocent blood, to kill David without a cause?"

6So Saul heeded the voice of Jonathan, and
Saul swore, "*As* the LORD lives, he shall not
be killed." 7Then Jonathan called David, and
Jonathan told him all these things. So Jonathan brought David to Saul, and he was in his
presence as in times past.

8And there was war again; and David went out
and fought with the Philistines, and struck them
with a mighty blow, and they fled from him.
9Now the distressing spirit from the LORD
came upon Saul as he sat in his house with his
spear in his hand. And David was playing *music* with *his* hand. 10Then Saul sought to pin
David to the wall with the spear, but he slipped
away from Saul's presence; and he drove the
spear into the wall. So David fled and escaped
that night.
11Saul also sent messengers to David's
house to watch him and to kill him in the
morning. And Michal, David's wife, told him,
saying, "If you do not save your life tonight,
tomorrow you will be killed." 12So Michal let
David down through a window. And he went
and fled and escaped. 13And Michal took an
image and laid *it* in the bed, put a cover of
goats' *hair* for his head, and covered *it* with
clothes. 14So when Saul sent messengers to
take David, she said, "He *is* sick."
15Then Saul sent the messengers *back* to see
David, saying, "Bring him up to me in the bed,
that I may kill him." 16And when the messengers
had come in, there was the image in the bed,
with a cover of goats' *hair* for his head. 17Then
Saul said to Michal, "Why have you deceived
me like this, and sent my enemy away, so that
he has escaped?"

And Michal answered Saul, "He said to me,
'Let me go! Why should I kill you?' "
18So David fled and escaped, and went to
Samuel at Ramah, and told him all that Saul
had done to him. And he and Samuel went and
stayed in Naioth. 19Now it was told Saul, saying, "Take note, David *is* at Naioth in Ramah!"
20Then Saul sent messengers to take David.
And when they saw the group of prophets
prophesying, and Samuel standing *as* leader
over them, the Spirit of God came upon the
messengers of Saul, and they also prophesied.
21And when Saul was told, he sent other messengers, and they prophesied likewise. Then
Saul sent messengers again the third time,
and they prophesied also. 22Then he also went
to Ramah, and came to the great well that *is* at
Sechu. So he asked, and said, "Where *are*
Samuel and David?"

And *someone* said, "Indeed *they are* at
Naioth in Ramah." 23So he went there to
Naioth in Ramah. Then the Spirit of God was
upon him also, and he went on and prophesied
until he came to Naioth in Ramah. 24And he
also stripped off his clothes and prophesied
before Samuel in like manner, and lay down
naked all that day and all that night. Therefore
they say, "*Is* Saul also among the prophets?"

19:23 the Spirit of God was upon him. This was the last time the Spirit of the Lord would rest on Saul. God turned Saul's heart to prophesy and not to harm David.

19:24 stripped off his clothes. Saul removed his armor and royal garments, prompted by the Spirit of God, thus signifying God's rejection of Saul as king over Israel. **lay down naked.** Without the royal garments, Saul was figuratively "naked," perhaps so overwhelmed by the Spirit of God as to be in a deep sleep. Other than Saul's utter despair and pitiful state at the home of the medium at En Dor (28:20) and his end at Mt. Gilboa (31:4–6), this episode represents one of the severest humblings in Saul's life. ***Is* Saul also among the prophets?** This is a final editorial comment tying together the Spirit of God's presence at Saul's inauguration (10:10,11), and the final departure of the same at his rejection (19:24).

Psalm 58:1–11

To the Chief Musician. Set to "Do Not Destroy."
A Michtam of David.

Do you indeed speak righteousness,
you silent ones?
Do you judge uprightly, you sons of
men?
2 No, in heart you work wickedness;
You weigh out the violence of your
hands in the earth.

3 The wicked are estranged from the
womb;
They go astray as soon as they are
born, speaking lies.
4 Their poison *is* like the poison of a
serpent;
They are like the deaf cobra *that* stops
its ear,
5 Which will not heed the voice of
charmers,
Charming ever so skillfully.

58:4 Their poison. The words and actions of these tyrants are like poisonous venom in a serpent's fangs. **deaf cobra.** Like a cobra which cannot hear its charmer are these stubborn rulers, who ignore all encouragements to righteousness.

6 Break their teeth in their mouth,
O God!
Break out the fangs of the young lions,
O LORD!
7 Let them flow away as waters *which*
run continually;
When he bends *his bow,*
Let his arrows be as if cut in pieces.
8 *Let them be* like a snail which melts
away as it goes,
Like a stillborn child of a woman, that
they may not see the sun.

9 Before your pots can feel *the burning*
thorns,
He shall take them away as with a
whirlwind,
As in His living and burning wrath.
10 The righteous shall rejoice when he
sees the vengeance;
He shall wash his feet in the blood
of the wicked,
11 So that men will say,
"Surely *there is* a reward for the
righteous;
Surely He is God who judges in the
earth."

Proverbs 15:27–30

27 He who is greedy for gain troubles his
own house,
But he who hates bribes will live.

28 The heart of the righteous studies how
to answer,
But the mouth of the wicked pours
forth evil.

29 The LORD *is* far from the wicked,
But He hears the prayer of the
righteous.

30 The light of the eyes rejoices the heart,
And a good report makes the bones
healthy.

Luke 24:1–35

24 Now on the first *day* of the week, very
early in the morning, they, and certain
other women with them, came to the tomb
bringing the spices which they had prepared.
2But they found the stone rolled away from the
tomb. 3Then they went in and did not find the
body of the Lord Jesus. 4And it happened, as
they were greatly perplexed about this, that
behold, two men stood by them in shining garments. 5Then, as they were afraid and bowed
their faces to the earth, they said to them,
"Why do you seek the living among the dead?
6He is not here, but is risen! Remember how
He spoke to you when He was still in Galilee,
7saying, 'The Son of Man must be delivered
into the hands of sinful men, and be crucified,
and the third day rise again.'"
8And they remembered His words. 9Then
they returned from the tomb and told all these
things to the eleven and to all the rest. 10It was
Mary Magdalene, Joanna, Mary *the mother* of
James, and the other *women* with them, who
told these things to the apostles. 11And their
words seemed to them like idle tales, and they
did not believe them. 12But Peter arose and ran
to the tomb; and stooping down, he saw the
linen cloths lying by themselves; and he departed, marveling to himself at what had happened.
13Now behold, two of them were traveling
that same day to a village called Emmaus,
which was seven miles from Jerusalem. 14And
they talked together of all these things which
had happened. 15So it was, while they conversed and reasoned, that Jesus Himself drew
near and went with them. 16But their eyes were
restrained, so that they did not know Him.
17And He said to them, "What kind of conversation *is* this that you have with one another as you walk and are sad?"
18Then the one whose name was Cleopas
answered and said to Him, "Are You the only
stranger in Jerusalem, and have You not known
the things which happened there in these days?"
19And He said to them, "What things?"
So they said to Him, "The things concerning Jesus of Nazareth, who was a Prophet
mighty in deed and word before God and all
the people, 20and how the chief priests and our
rulers delivered Him to be condemned to
death, and crucified Him. 21But we were hoping that it was He who was going to redeem Israel. Indeed, besides all this, today is the third
day since these things happened. 22Yes, and
certain women of our company, who arrived at
the tomb early, astonished us. 23When they did
not find His body, they came saying that they
had also seen a vision of angels who said He
was alive. 24And certain of those *who were* with
us went to the tomb and found *it* just as the
women had said; but Him they did not see."
25Then He said to them, "O foolish ones, and
slow of heart to believe in all that the prophets
have spoken! 26Ought not the Christ to have
suffered these things and to enter into His
glory?" 27And beginning at Moses and all the
Prophets, He expounded to them in all the
Scriptures the things concerning Himself.
28Then they drew near to the village where
they were going, and He indicated that He
would have gone farther. 29But they con-
strained Him, saying, "Abide with us, for it is
toward evening, and the day is far spent." And
He went in to stay with them.

[30]Now it came to pass, as He sat at the table
with them, that He took bread, blessed and
broke *it,* and gave it to them. [31]Then their eyes
were opened and they knew Him; and He vanished from their sight.

[32]And they said to one another, "Did not our
heart burn within us while He talked with us on
the road, and while He opened the Scriptures
to us?" [33]So they rose up that very hour and
returned to Jerusalem, and found the eleven
and those *who were* with them gathered together, [34]saying, "The Lord is risen indeed, and has
appeared to Simon!" [35]And they told about the
things *that had happened* on the road, and how
He was known to them in the breaking of
bread.

DAY 8: What happened on the day that Christ was resurrected from the dead?

Early in the morning, certain women came to the tomb "bringing the spices which they had prepared" (Luke 24:1). But they found "the stone rolled away" (v. 2). Matthew 28:2–4 records that an earthquake occurred and an angel rolled the stone away. The Roman guards fainted with fear. Mark, Luke, and John make no mention of the guards, so it appears they fled when they awoke to find the empty tomb. The women must have arrived shortly after.

Finding the stone rolled away, the women entered the tomb, but found it empty (v. 3). While they were still in the tomb, the angels suddenly appeared (v. 4; Mark 16:5). Only Luke mentioned both angels. Mark was concerned only with the one who spoke for the duo. Such minor differences in the Gospel accounts are all reconcilable.

The angel who spoke reminded them of Jesus' promises (vv. 6–8), then sent them to find Peter and the disciples to report that Jesus was risen (Matt. 28:7,8; Mark 16:7,8). The women did as they were told (vv. 9–11). The disciples were skeptical at first (v. 11), but ran to where the tomb was, John arriving first (John 20:4), but Peter actually entering the tomb first (John 20:6). They saw the linen wrappings intact but empty, proof that Jesus was risen (v. 12; John 20:6–8). They left immediately (v. 12; John 20:10).

Meanwhile, Mary Magdalene returned to the tomb and was standing outside weeping when Christ suddenly appeared to her (John 20:11–18). That was His first appearance (Mark 16:9). Sometime soon after that, He met the other women on the road and appeared to them, as well (Matt. 28:9,10). Later that day He appeared to two of the disciples on the road to Emmaus (vv. 13–32) and to Peter (v. 34).

MAY 9

1 Samuel 20:1–21:15

20 Then David fled from Naioth in
Ramah, and went and said to Jonathan,
"What have I done? What *is* my iniquity, and
what *is* my sin before your father, that he
seeks my life?"

[2]So Jonathan said to him, "By no means!
You shall not die! Indeed, my father will do
nothing either great or small without first
telling me. And why should my father hide
this thing from me? It *is* not *so!*"

[3]Then David took an oath again, and said,
"Your father certainly knows that I have found
favor in your eyes, and he has said, 'Do not let
Jonathan know this, lest he be grieved.' But
truly, *as* the LORD lives and *as* your soul lives,
there is but a step between me and death."

[4]So Jonathan said to David, "Whatever you
yourself desire, I will do *it* for you."

[5]And David said to Jonathan, "Indeed tomorrow *is* the New Moon, and I should not fail to sit
with the king to eat. But let me go, that I may
hide in the field until the third *day* at evening. [6]If
your father misses me at all, then say, 'David
earnestly asked *permission* of me that he might
run over to Bethlehem, his city, for *there is* a yearly sacrifice there for all the family.' [7]If he says
thus: '*It is* well,' your servant will be safe. But if he
is very angry, be sure that evil is determined by
him. [8]Therefore you shall deal kindly with your
servant, for you have brought your servant into
a covenant of the LORD with you. Nevertheless,
if there is iniquity in me, kill me yourself, for why
should you bring me to your father?"

[9]But Jonathan said, "Far be it from you! For
if I knew certainly that evil was determined by
my father to come upon you, then would I not
tell you?"

[10]Then David said to Jonathan, "Who will tell
me, or what *if* your father answers you roughly?"

[11]And Jonathan said to David, "Come, let us
go out into the field." So both of them went out
into the field. [12]Then Jonathan said to David:
"The LORD God of Israel *is witness!* When I
have sounded out my father sometime tomorrow, *or* the third *day,* and indeed *there is* good
toward David, and I do not send to you and tell

you, 13may the LORD do so and much more to
Jonathan. But if it pleases my father *to do* you
evil, then I will report it to you and send you
away, that you may go in safety. And the LORD
be with you as He has been with my father.
14And you shall not only show me the kindness
of the LORD while I still live, that I may not die;
15but you shall not cut off your kindness from my
house forever, no, not when the LORD has cut off
every one of the enemies of David from the face
of the earth." 16So Jonathan made *a covenant*
with the house of David, *saying,* "Let the LORD
require *it* at the hand of David's enemies."

17Now Jonathan again caused David to vow,
because he loved him; for he loved him as he
loved his own soul. 18Then Jonathan said to
David, "Tomorrow *is* the New Moon; and you
will be missed, because your seat will be
empty. 19And *when* you have stayed three days,
go down quickly and come to the place where
you hid on the day of the deed; and remain by
the stone Ezel. 20Then I will shoot three
arrows to the side, as though I shot at a target;
21and there I will send a lad, *saying,* 'Go, find
the arrows.' If I expressly say to the lad, 'Look,
the arrows *are* on this side of you; get them
and come'—then, as the LORD lives, *there is*
safety for you and no harm. 22But if I say thus
to the young man, 'Look, the arrows *are*
beyond you'—go your way, for the LORD has
sent you away. 23And as for the matter which
you and I have spoken of, indeed the LORD *be*
between you and me forever."

24Then David hid in the field. And when the
New Moon had come, the king sat down to eat
the feast. 25Now the king sat on his seat, as at
other times, on a seat by the wall. And Jonathan arose, and Abner sat by Saul's side, but
David's place was empty. 26Nevertheless Saul
did not say anything that day, for he thought,
"Something has happened to him; he *is* unclean,
surely he *is* unclean." 27And it happened the next
day, the second *day* of the month, that David's
place was empty. And Saul said to Jonathan his
son, "Why has the son of Jesse not come to eat,
either yesterday or today?"

28So Jonathan answered Saul, "David
earnestly asked *permission* of me *to go* to Bethlehem. 29And he said, 'Please let me go, for our
family has a sacrifice in the city, and my brother has commanded me *to be there.* And now, if
I have found favor in your eyes, please let me
get away and see my brothers.' Therefore he
has not come to the king's table."

30Then Saul's anger was aroused against
Jonathan, and he said to him, "You son of a
perverse, rebellious *woman!* Do I not know
that you have chosen the son of Jesse to your
own shame and to the shame of your mother's
nakedness? 31For as long as the son of Jesse
lives on the earth, you shall not be established,
nor your kingdom. Now therefore, send and
bring him to me, for he shall surely die."

32And Jonathan answered Saul his father,
and said to him, "Why should he be killed?
What has he done?" 33Then Saul cast a spear at
him to kill him, by which Jonathan knew that
it was determined by his father to kill David.

34So Jonathan arose from the table in fierce
anger, and ate no food the second day of the
month, for he was grieved for David, because
his father had treated him shamefully.

35And so it was, in the morning, that Jonathan went out into the field at the time appointed with David, and a little lad *was* with him.
36Then he said to his lad, "Now run, find the
arrows which I shoot." As the lad ran, he shot
an arrow beyond him. 37When the lad had
come to the place where the arrow was which
Jonathan had shot, Jonathan cried out after the
lad and said, "*Is* not the arrow beyond you?"
38And Jonathan cried out after the lad, "Make
haste, hurry, do not delay!" So Jonathan's lad
gathered up the arrows and came back to his
master. 39But the lad did not know anything.
Only Jonathan and David knew of the matter.
40Then Jonathan gave his weapons to his lad,
and said to him, "Go, carry *them* to the city."

41As soon as the lad had gone, David arose
from *a place* toward the south, fell on his face
to the ground, and bowed down three times.
And they kissed one another; and they wept
together, but David more so. 42Then Jonathan
said to David, "Go in peace, since we have
both sworn in the name of the LORD, saying,
'May the LORD be between you and me, and
between your descendants and my descendants, forever.'" So he arose and departed,
and Jonathan went into the city.

21 Now David came to Nob, to Ahimelech
the priest. And Ahimelech was afraid
when he met David, and said to him, "Why *are*
you alone, and no one is with you?"

2So David said to Ahimelech the priest,
"The king has ordered me on some business,
and said to me, 'Do not let anyone know anything about the business on which I send you,
or what I have commanded you.' And I have
directed *my* young men to such and such a
place. 3Now therefore, what have you on
hand? Give *me* five *loaves of* bread in my hand,
or whatever can be found."

4And the priest answered David and said,
"*There is* no common bread on hand; but there
is holy bread, if the young men have at least
kept themselves from women."

21:2 The king has ordered me. David, fearing someone might tell Saul where he was, deceived Ahimelech the priest into thinking that he was on official business for the king. He supposed, as many do, that it is excusable to lie for the purpose of saving one's life. But what is essentially sinful can never, because of circumstances, change its immoral character (see Ps. 119:29). David's lying led tragically to the deaths of the priests (22:9–18).

5Then David answered the priest, and said
to him, "Truly, women *have been* kept from us
about three days since I came out. And the
vessels of the young men are holy, and *the*
bread is in effect common, even though it was
consecrated in the vessel this day."
6So the priest gave him holy *bread;* for there
was no bread there but the showbread which
had been taken from before the LORD, in order
to put hot bread *in its place* on the day when it
was taken away.

21:5,6 *bread*...common. Since that bread was no longer on the Lord's table, having been replaced by hot bread, it was to be eaten by the priests and in these exigencies, by David under the law of necessity and mercy. The removal of the old bread and the replacing with new was done on the Sabbath (Lev. 24:8).

7Now a certain man of the servants of Saul
was there that day, detained before the LORD.
And his name *was* Doeg, an Edomite, the chief
of the herdsmen who *belonged* to Saul.
8And David said to Ahimelech, "Is there not
here on hand a spear or a sword? For I have
brought neither my sword nor my weapons
with me, because the king's business required
haste."
9So the priest said, "The sword of Goliath
the Philistine, whom you killed in the Valley of
Elah, there it is, wrapped in a cloth behind the
ephod. If you will take that, take *it.* For *there is*
no other except that one here."
And David said, "*There is* none like it; give it
to me."
10Then David arose and fled that day from
before Saul, and went to Achish the king of
Gath. 11And the servants of Achish said to him,
"*Is* this not David the king of the land? Did
they not sing of him to one another in dances,
saying:

'Saul has slain his thousands,
And David his ten thousands'?"

12Now David took these words to heart, and
was very much afraid of Achish the king of
Gath. 13So he changed his behavior before
them, pretended madness in their hands,
scratched on the doors of the gate, and let his
saliva fall down on his beard. 14Then Achish
said to his servants, "Look, you see the man is
insane. Why have you brought him to me?
15Have I need of madmen, that you have brought
this *fellow* to play the madman in my presence?
Shall this *fellow* come into my house?"

21:13 changed his behavior. David feared for his life, lacked trust in God to deliver him, and feigned insanity to persuade Achish to send him away. See the titles of Psalms 34 and 56. Drooling in one's beard was considered in the East an intolerable indignity, as was spitting in another's beard.

Psalm 59:1–5

To the Chief Musician. Set to "Do Not Destroy."
A Michtam of David when Saul sent men,
and they watched the house in order to kill him.

Deliver me from my enemies,
O my God;
Defend me from those who rise up
against me.
2 Deliver me from the workers of
iniquity,
And save me from bloodthirsty men.

3 For look, they lie in wait for my life;
The mighty gather against me,
Not *for* my transgression nor *for* my
sin, O LORD.
4 They run and prepare themselves
through no fault *of mine.*

Awake to help me, and behold!
5 You therefore, O LORD God of hosts,
the God of Israel,
Awake to punish all the nations;
Do not be merciful to any wicked
transgressors. Selah

Proverbs 15:31–33

31 The ear that hears the rebukes of life
Will abide among the wise.

32 He who disdains instruction despises
his own soul,
But he who heeds rebuke gets
understanding.
33 The fear of the LORD *is* the instruction
of wisdom,
And before honor *is* humility.

Luke 24:36–53

36Now as they said these things, Jesus
Himself stood in the midst of them, and said to
them, "Peace to you." 37But they were terrified
and frightened, and supposed they had seen a
spirit. 38And He said to them, "Why are you
troubled? And why do doubts arise in your
hearts? 39Behold My hands and My feet, that it
is I Myself. Handle Me and see, for a spirit does
not have flesh and bones as you see I have."
40When He had said this, He showed them His
hands and His feet. 41But while they still did not
believe for joy, and marveled, He said to them,
"Have you any food here?" 42So they gave Him a
piece of a broiled fish and some honeycomb.
43And He took *it* and ate in their presence.
44Then He said to them, "These *are* the
words which I spoke to you while I was still
with you, that all things must be fulfilled which
were written in the Law of Moses and *the*
Prophets and *the* Psalms concerning Me."
45And He opened their understanding, that
they might comprehend the Scriptures.

24:45 opened their understanding. He undoubtedly taught them from the Old Testament, as He had on the road to Emmaus. But the gist of the expression also seems to convey a supernatural opening of their minds to receive the truths He unfolded. Whereas their understanding was once dull (9:45), they finally saw clearly (see Ps. 119:18; Is. 29:18,19; 2 Cor. 3:14–16).

46Then He said to them, "Thus it is written,
and thus it was necessary for the Christ to suffer and to rise from the dead the third day,
47and that repentance and remission of sins
should be preached in His name to all nations,
beginning at Jerusalem. 48And you are witnesses of these things. 49Behold, I send the
Promise of My Father upon you; but tarry in
the city of Jerusalem until you are endued
with power from on high."
50And He led them out as far as Bethany, and
He lifted up His hands and blessed them. 51Now
it came to pass, while He blessed them, that He
was parted from them and carried up into heav-
en. 52And they worshiped Him, and returned to
Jerusalem with great joy, 53and were continually
in the temple praising and blessing God. Amen.

DAY 9: What was the resurrected body of Christ like?

In Luke 24:31, it tells us that after the two men had traveled with Jesus on the road to Emmaus, "their eyes were opened," i.e., by God. They had been sovereignly kept from recognizing Him until this point (v. 16). His resurrection body was glorified and altered from its previous appearance (see John's description in Rev. 1:13–16), and this surely explains why even Mary did not recognize Him at first (John 20:14–16). But in this case, God actively intervened to keep them from recognizing Him until it was time for Him to depart.

"He vanished from their sight." His resurrection body, though real and tangible (John 20:27)—and even capable of ingesting earthly food (vv. 42,43)—nonetheless possessed certain properties that indicate it was glorified, altered in a mysterious way (1 Cor. 15:35–54; Phil. 3:21). Christ could appear and disappear bodily, as seen in this text. His body could pass through solid objects—such as the graveclothes (v. 12) or the walls and doors of a closed room (John 20:19,26). He could apparently travel great distances in a moment, for by the time these disciples returned to Jerusalem, Christ had already appeared to Peter (v. 34). The fact that He ascended into heaven bodily demonstrated that His resurrection body was already fit for heaven. Yet it was His body, the same one that was missing from the tomb, even retaining identifying features such as the nail wounds (John 20:25–27). He was no ghost or phantom.

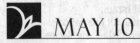

MAY 10

1 Samuel 22:1–23:29

22 David therefore departed from there
and escaped to the cave of Adullam. So
when his brothers and all his father's house
heard *it,* they went down there to him. 2And
everyone *who was* in distress, everyone who
was in debt, and everyone *who was* discon-
tented gathered to him. So he became captain
over them. And there were about four hundred
men with him.

22:1 cave of Adullam. A cave near Adullam was David's refuge. Adullam, which may mean "refuge," was located in the western foothills of Judah (Josh. 15:33), about 17 miles southwest of Jerusalem and 10 miles southeast of Gath. See titles of Psalms 57 and 142, which could possibly refer to 1 Samuel 24:3. **brothers and all his father's house.** David's family members went down from Bethlehem to join David in Adullam, a journey of about 12 miles.

3 Then David went from there to Mizpah of
Moab; and he said to the king of Moab,
"Please let my father and mother come here
with you, till I know what God will do for me."
4 So he brought them before the king of Moab,
and they dwelt with him all the time that David
was in the stronghold.
5 Now the prophet Gad said to David, "Do
not stay in the stronghold; depart, and go to
the land of Judah." So David departed and
went into the forest of Hereth.
6 When Saul heard that David and the men
who *were* with him had been discovered—now
Saul was staying in Gibeah under a tamarisk
tree in Ramah, with his spear in his hand, and
all his servants standing about him— 7 then
Saul said to his servants who stood about him,
"Hear now, you Benjamites! Will the son of
Jesse give every one of you fields and vineyards,
and make you all captains of thousands
and captains of hundreds? 8 All of you have
conspired against me, and *there is* no one who
reveals to me that my son has made a
covenant with the son of Jesse; and *there is* not
one of you who is sorry for me or reveals to
me that my son has stirred up my servant
against me, to lie in wait, as *it is* this day."
9 Then answered Doeg the Edomite, who
was set over the servants of Saul, and said, "I
saw the son of Jesse going to Nob, to
Ahimelech the son of Ahitub. 10 And he
inquired of the LORD for him, gave him provisions,
and gave him the sword of Goliath the
Philistine."
11 So the king sent to call Ahimelech the
priest, the son of Ahitub, and all his father's
house, the priests who *were* in Nob. And they
all came to the king. 12 And Saul said, "Hear
now, son of Ahitub!"

He answered, "Here I am, my lord."
13 Then Saul said to him, "Why have you conspired
against me, you and the son of Jesse, in
that you have given him bread and a sword,
and have inquired of God for him, that he
should rise against me, to lie in wait, as it is
this day?"
14 So Ahimelech answered the king and said,
"And who among all your servants *is as* faithful
as David, who is the king's son-in-law, who
goes at your bidding, and is honorable in your
house? 15 Did I then begin to inquire of God for
him? Far be it from me! Let not the king
impute anything to his servant, *or* to any in the
house of my father. For your servant knew
nothing of all this, little or much."
16 And the king said, "You shall surely die,
Ahimelech, you and all your father's house!"
17 Then the king said to the guards who stood
about him, "Turn and kill the priests of the
LORD, because their hand also *is* with David,
and because they knew when he fled and did
not tell it to me." But the servants of the king
would not lift their hands to strike the priests
of the LORD. 18 And the king said to Doeg, "You
turn and kill the priests!" So Doeg the
Edomite turned and struck the priests, and
killed on that day eighty-five men who wore a
linen ephod. 19 Also Nob, the city of the priests,
he struck with the edge of the sword, both
men and women, children and nursing infants,
oxen and donkeys and sheep—with the edge
of the sword.
20 Now one of the sons of Ahimelech the son
of Ahitub, named Abiathar, escaped and fled
after David. 21 And Abiathar told David that
Saul had killed the LORD's priests. 22 So David
said to Abiathar, "I knew that day, when Doeg
the Edomite *was* there, that he would surely
tell Saul. I have caused *the death* of all the persons
of your father's house. 23 Stay with me; do
not fear. For he who seeks my life seeks your
life, but with me you *shall be* safe."

23 Then they told David, saying, "Look,
the Philistines are fighting against
Keilah, and they are robbing the threshing
floors."
2 Therefore David inquired of the LORD, saying,
"Shall I go and attack these Philistines?"

And the LORD said to David, "Go and attack
the Philistines, and save Keilah."
3 But David's men said to him, "Look, we are
afraid here in Judah. How much more then if
we go to Keilah against the armies of the
Philistines?" 4 Then David inquired of the LORD
once again.

And the LORD answered him and said,
"Arise, go down to Keilah. For I will deliver
the Philistines into your hand." 5 And David
and his men went to Keilah and fought with
the Philistines, struck them with a mighty
blow, and took away their livestock. So David
saved the inhabitants of Keilah.

6 Now it happened, when Abiathar the son of
Ahimelech fled to David at Keilah, *that* he
went down *with* an ephod in his hand.
7 And Saul was told that David had gone to
Keilah. So Saul said, "God has delivered him
into my hand, for he has shut himself in by
entering a town that has gates and bars." 8 Then
Saul called all the people together for war, to go
down to Keilah to besiege David and his men.
9 When David knew that Saul plotted evil
against him, he said to Abiathar the priest,
"Bring the ephod here." 10 Then David said, "O
LORD God of Israel, Your servant has certainly
heard that Saul seeks to come to Keilah to
destroy the city for my sake. 11 Will the men of
Keilah deliver me into his hand? Will Saul
come down, as Your servant has heard? O
LORD God of Israel, I pray, tell Your servant."
And the LORD said, "He will come down."
12 Then David said, "Will the men of Keilah
deliver me and my men into the hand of Saul?"
And the LORD said, "They will deliver *you*."
13 So David and his men, about six hundred,
arose and departed from Keilah and went
wherever they could go. Then it was told Saul
that David had escaped from Keilah; so he
halted the expedition.
14 And David stayed in strongholds in the
wilderness, and remained in the mountains in
the Wilderness of Ziph. Saul sought him
every day, but God did not deliver him into his
hand. 15 So David saw that Saul had come out to
seek his life. And David *was* in the Wilderness
of Ziph in a forest. 16 Then Jonathan, Saul's son,
arose and went to David in the woods and
strengthened his hand in God. 17 And he said to
him, "Do not fear, for the hand of Saul my
father shall not find you. You shall be king
over Israel, and I shall be next to you. Even my
father Saul knows that." 18 So the two of them
made a covenant before the LORD. And David
stayed in the woods, and Jonathan went to his
own house.
19 Then the Ziphites came up to Saul at Gibeah,
saying, "Is David not hiding with us in strongholds in the woods, in the hill of Hachilah,
which *is* on the south of Jeshimon? 20 Now therefore, O king, come down according to all the
desire of your soul to come down; and our part
shall be to deliver him into the king's hand."
21 And Saul said, "Blessed *are* you of the LORD,
for you have compassion on me. 22 Please go
and find out for sure, and see the place where
his hideout is, *and* who has seen him there.
For I am told he is very crafty. 23 See therefore,
and take knowledge of all the lurking places
where he hides; and come back to me with
certainty, and I will go with you. And it shall
be, if he is in the land, that I will search for
him throughout all the clans of Judah."
24 So they arose and went to Ziph before
Saul. But David and his men *were* in the
Wilderness of Maon, in the plain on the south
of Jeshimon. 25 When Saul and his men went to
seek *him,* they told David. Therefore he went
down to the rock, and stayed in the Wilderness
of Maon. And when Saul heard *that,* he pursued David in the Wilderness of Maon. 26 Then
Saul went on one side of the mountain, and
David and his men on the other side of the
mountain. So David made haste to get away
from Saul, for Saul and his men were encircling David and his men to take them.
27 But a messenger came to Saul, saying,
"Hurry and come, for the Philistines have
invaded the land!" 28 Therefore Saul returned
from pursuing David, and went against the
Philistines; so they called that place the Rock
of Escape. 29 Then David went up from there
and dwelt in strongholds at En Gedi.

Psalm 59:6–17

6 At evening they return,
They growl like a dog,
And go all around the city.
7 Indeed, they belch with their mouth;
Swords *are* in their lips;
For *they say,* "Who hears?"

8 But You, O LORD, shall laugh at them;
You shall have all the nations in
derision.
9 I will wait for You, O You his Strength;
For God *is* my defense.
10 My God of mercy shall come to meet
me;
God shall let me see *my desire* on my
enemies.

11 Do not slay them, lest my people forget;
Scatter them by Your power,
And bring them down,
O Lord our shield.
12 *For* the sin of their mouth *and* the
words of their lips,
Let them even be taken in their pride,
And for the cursing and lying *which*
they speak.
13 Consume *them* in wrath, consume
them,
That they *may* not *be;*
And let them know that God rules in
Jacob
To the ends of the earth. Selah

14 And at evening they return,
They growl like a dog,
And go all around the city.

15 They wander up and down for food,
And howl if they are not satisfied.

16 But I will sing of Your power;
Yes, I will sing aloud of Your mercy in
the morning;
For You have been my defense
And refuge in the day of my trouble.
17 To You, O my Strength, I will sing
praises;
For God *is* my defense,
My God of mercy.

Proverbs 16:1–2

16 The preparations of the heart
belong to man,
But the answer of the tongue *is* from
the LORD.
2 All the ways of a man *are* pure in his
own eyes,
But the LORD weighs the spirits.

John 1:1–28

1 In the beginning was the Word, and the
Word was with God, and the Word was God.
2He was in the beginning with God. 3All things
were made through Him, and without Him
nothing was made that was made. 4In Him was
life, and the life was the light of men. 5And the
light shines in the darkness, and the darkness
did not comprehend it.
6There was a man sent from God, whose
name *was* John. 7This man came for a witness,
to bear witness of the Light, that all through
him might believe. 8He was not that Light, but
was sent to bear witness of that Light. 9That
was the true Light which gives light to every
man coming into the world.
10He was in the world, and the world was
made through Him, and the world did not
know Him. 11He came to His own, and His own
did not receive Him. 12But as many as received
Him, to them He gave the right to become
children of God, to those who believe in His
name: 13who were born, not of blood, nor of
the will of the flesh, nor of the will of man, but
of God.
14And the Word became flesh and dwelt
among us, and we beheld His glory, the glory
as of the only begotten of the Father, full of
grace and truth.
15John bore witness of Him and cried out,
saying, "This was He of whom I said, 'He who
comes after me is preferred before me, for He
was before me.' "
16And of His fullness we have all received,
and grace for grace. 17For the law was given
through Moses, *but* grace and truth came
through Jesus Christ. 18No one has seen God
at any time. The only begotten Son, who is in
the bosom of the Father, He has declared
Him.
19Now this is the testimony of John, when
the Jews sent priests and Levites from Jerusalem to ask him, "Who are you?"
20He confessed, and did not deny, but confessed, "I am not the Christ."
21And they asked him, "What then? Are you
Elijah?"
He said, "I am not."
"Are you the Prophet?"
And he answered, "No."
22Then they said to him, "Who are you, that

1:12 as many as received Him…to those who believe in His name. The second phrase describes the first. To receive Him who is the Word of God means to acknowledge His claims, place one's faith in Him, and thereby yield allegiance to Him. **gave.** The term emphasizes the grace of God involved in the gift of salvation (Eph. 2:8–10). **the right.** Those who receive Jesus, the Word, receive full authority to claim the exalted title of "God's children." **His name.** Denotes the character of the person himself.

1:14 the Word became flesh. While Christ as God was uncreated and eternal, the word "became" emphasizes Christ's taking on humanity (see Heb. 1:1–3; 2:14–18). This reality is surely the most profound ever because it indicates that the Infinite became finite; the Eternal was conformed to time; the Invisible became visible; the supernatural One reduced Himself to the natural. In the Incarnation, however, the Word did not cease to be God but became God in human flesh, i.e., undiminished Deity in human form as a man (1 Tim. 3:16). **dwelt.** Meaning "to pitch a tabernacle," or "live in a tent." The term recalls the Old Testament tabernacle where God met with Israel before the temple was constructed (Ex. 25:8). It was called the "tabernacle of meeting" (Ex. 33:7) where "the LORD spoke to Moses face to face, as a man speaks to his friend" (Ex. 33:11). In the New Testament, God chose to dwell among His people in a far more personal way through becoming a man. In the Old Testament, when the tabernacle was completed, God's Shekinah presence filled the entire structure (Ex. 40:34; 1 Kin. 8:10). When the Word became flesh, the glorious presence of Deity was embodied in Him (Col. 2:9).

we may give an answer to those who sent us?
What do you say about yourself?"
23He said: "I *am*

'The voice of one crying in the wilderness:
"Make straight the way of the LORD,"'

as the prophet Isaiah said."
24Now those who were sent were from the
Pharisees. 25And they asked him, saying,
"Why then do you baptize if you are not the
Christ, nor Elijah, nor the Prophet?"
26John answered them, saying, "I baptize
with water, but there stands One among you
whom you do not know. 27It is He who, coming
after me, is preferred before me, whose sandal strap I am not worthy to loose."
28These things were done in Bethabara
beyond the Jordan, where John was baptizing.

DAY 10: Note the powerful words loaded into John 1:1.

"In the beginning." In contrast to 1 John 1:1 where John used a similar phrase ("from the beginning") to refer to the starting point of Jesus' ministry and gospel preaching, this phrase parallels Genesis 1:1 where the same phrase is used. John used the phrase in an absolute sense to refer to the beginning of the time-space-material universe. "Was." The verb highlights the eternal preexistence of the Word, i.e., Jesus Christ. Before the universe began, the Second Person of the Trinity always existed; i.e., He always was (see 8:58). This word is used in contrast with the verb "was made" (or "were made") in v. 3, which indicate a beginning in time. Because of John's theme that Jesus Christ is the eternal God, the Second Person of the Trinity, he did not include a genealogy as Matthew and Luke did. In terms of Jesus' humanity, He had a human genealogy; but in terms of His deity, He has no genealogy.

"The Word." John borrowed the use of the term "Word" not only from the vocabulary of the Old Testament but also from Greek philosophy, in which the term was essentially impersonal, signifying the rational principle of "divine reason," "mind," or even "wisdom." John, however, imbued the term entirely with Old Testament and Christian meaning (e.g., Gen. 1:3 where God's Word brought the world into being; Pss. 33:6; 107:20; Prov. 8:27 where God's Word is His powerful self-expression in creation, wisdom, revelation, and salvation) and made it refer to a person, i.e., Jesus Christ. Greek philosophical usage, therefore, is not the exclusive background of John's thought. Strategically, the term "Word" serves as a bridge-word to reach not only Jews but also the unsaved Greeks. John chose this concept because both Jews and Greeks were familiar with it.

"The Word was with God." The Word, as the Second Person of the Trinity, was in intimate fellowship with God the Father throughout all eternity. Yet, although the Word enjoyed the splendors of heaven and eternity with the Father (Is. 6:1–13; see 12:41; 17:5), He willingly gave up His heavenly status, taking the form of a man, and became subject to the death of the cross (Phil. 2:6–8). "Was God." The Greek construction emphasizes that the Word had all the essence or attributes of Deity, i.e., Jesus the Messiah was fully God (Col. 2:9). Even in His incarnation when He emptied Himself, He did not cease to be God but took on a genuine human nature/body and voluntarily refrained from the independent exercise of the attributes of Deity.

MAY 11

1 Samuel 24:1–25:44

24 Now it happened, when Saul had
returned from following the Philistines,
that it was told him, saying, "Take note! David
is in the Wilderness of En Gedi." 2Then Saul
took three thousand chosen men from all
Israel, and went to seek David and his men on
the Rocks of the Wild Goats. 3So he came to
the sheepfolds by the road, where there *was* a
cave; and Saul went in to attend to his needs.
(David and his men were staying in the
recesses of the cave.) 4Then the men of David
said to him, "This is the day of which the LORD
said to you, 'Behold, I will deliver your enemy
into your hand, that you may do to him as it
seems good to you.'" And David arose and
secretly cut off a corner of Saul's robe. 5Now it
happened afterward that David's heart troubled
him because he had cut Saul's robe. 6And he

24:4 the day of which the LORD said to you. David's men perhaps believed that God had providentially placed Saul in the same cave where they were hiding so David could kill the king. However, nothing revelatory had previously been said by the Lord that indicated He wanted David to lift a hand against Saul.

24:5 David's heart troubled him. David was able to cut off a piece of Saul's robe undetected. However, touching Saul's clothing was tantamount to touching his person, and David's conscience troubled him on this account.

24:6 LORD's anointed. David recognized that the Lord Himself had placed Saul into the kingship. Thus the judgment and removal of Saul had to be left to the Lord.

said to his men, "The LORD forbid that I should
do this thing to my master, the LORD's anointed, to stretch out my hand against him, seeing
he *is* the anointed of the LORD." 7So David restrained his servants with *these* words, and did
not allow them to rise against Saul. And Saul
got up from the cave and went on *his* way.
8David also arose afterward, went out of the
cave, and called out to Saul, saying, "My lord
the king!" And when Saul looked behind him,
David stooped with his face to the earth, and
bowed down. 9And David said to Saul: "Why do
you listen to the words of men who say, 'Indeed
David seeks your harm'? 10Look, this day your
eyes have seen that the LORD delivered you
today into my hand in the cave, and *someone*
urged *me* to kill you. But *my eye* spared you, and
I said, 'I will not stretch out my hand against my
lord, for he *is* the LORD's anointed.' 11Moreover,
my father, see! Yes, see the corner of your robe
in my hand! For in that I cut off the corner of
your robe, and did not kill you, know and see
that *there is* neither evil nor rebellion in my hand,
and I have not sinned against you. Yet you hunt
my life to take it. 12Let the LORD judge between
you and me, and let the LORD avenge me on you.
But my hand shall not be against you. 13As the
proverb of the ancients says, 'Wickedness proceeds from the wicked.' But my hand shall not
be against you. 14After whom has the king of
Israel come out? Whom do you pursue? A dead
dog? A flea? 15Therefore let the LORD be judge,
and judge between you and me, and see and
plead my case, and deliver me out of your hand."
16So it was, when David had finished speaking these words to Saul, that Saul said, "*Is* this
your voice, my son David?" And Saul lifted up
his voice and wept. 17Then he said to David:
"You *are* more righteous than I; for you have
rewarded me with good, whereas I have
rewarded you with evil. 18And you have shown
this day how you have dealt well with me; for
when the LORD delivered me into your hand,
you did not kill me. 19For if a man finds his
enemy, will he let him get away safely? Therefore may the LORD reward you with good for
what you have done to me this day. 20And now
I know indeed that you shall surely be king,
and that the kingdom of Israel shall be established in your hand. 21Therefore swear now to
me by the LORD that you will not cut off my
descendants after me, and that you will not
destroy my name from my father's house."
22So David swore to Saul. And Saul went
home, but David and his men went up to the
stronghold.

25 Then Samuel died; and the Israelites
gathered together and lamented for
him, and buried him at his home in Ramah.
And David arose and went down to the Wilderness of Paran.
2Now *there was* a man in Maon whose business *was* in Carmel, and the man *was* very rich.
He had three thousand sheep and a thousand
goats. And he was shearing his sheep in
Carmel. 3The name of the man *was* Nabal, and
the name of his wife Abigail. And *she was* a
woman of good understanding and beautiful
appearance; but the man *was* harsh and evil in
his doings. He *was of the house of* Caleb.
4When David heard in the wilderness that
Nabal was shearing his sheep, 5David sent ten
young men; and David said to the young men,
"Go up to Carmel, go to Nabal, and greet him
in my name. 6And thus you shall say to him
who lives *in prosperity:* 'Peace *be* to you, peace
to your house, and peace to all that you have!
7Now I have heard that you have shearers.
Your shepherds were with us, and we did not
hurt them, nor was there anything missing
from them all the while they were in Carmel.
8Ask your young men, and they will tell you.
Therefore let *my* young men find favor in your
eyes, for we come on a feast day. Please give
whatever comes to your hand to your servants
and to your son David.' "
9So when David's young men came, they
spoke to Nabal according to all these words in
the name of David, and waited.
10Then Nabal answered David's servants,
and said, "Who *is* David, and who *is* the son of
Jesse? There are many servants nowadays
who break away each one from his master.
11Shall I then take my bread and my water and
my meat that I have killed for my shearers,
and give *it* to men when I do not know where
they *are* from?"
12So David's young men turned on their
heels and went back; and they came and told
him all these words. 13Then David said to his
men, "Every man gird on his sword." So every

man girded on his sword, and David also girded on his sword. And about four hundred men
went with David, and two hundred stayed with
the supplies.
14Now one of the young men told Abigail,
Nabal's wife, saying, "Look, David sent messengers from the wilderness to greet our master; and he reviled them. 15But the men *were*
very good to us, and we were not hurt, nor did
we miss anything as long as we accompanied
them, when we were in the fields. 16They were
a wall to us both by night and day, all the time
we were with them keeping the sheep. 17Now
therefore, know and consider what you will
do, for harm is determined against our master
and against all his household. For he *is such* a
scoundrel that *one* cannot speak to him."
18Then Abigail made haste and took two
hundred *loaves* of bread, two skins of wine, five
sheep already dressed, five seahs of roasted
grain, one hundred clusters of raisins, and two
hundred cakes of figs, and loaded *them* on
donkeys. 19And she said to her servants, "Go
on before me; see, I am coming after you." But
she did not tell her husband Nabal.
20So it was, *as* she rode on the donkey, that
she went down under cover of the hill; and
there were David and his men, coming down
toward her, and she met them. 21Now David
had said, "Surely in vain I have protected all
that this *fellow* has in the wilderness, so that
nothing was missed of all that *belongs* to him.
And he has repaid me evil for good. 22May God
do so, and more also, to the enemies of David,
if I leave one male of all who *belong* to him by
morning light."
23Now when Abigail saw David, she dismounted quickly from the donkey, fell on her
face before David, and bowed down to the
ground. 24So she fell at his feet and said: "On
me, my lord, *on* me *let* this iniquity *be!* And
please let your maidservant speak in your
ears, and hear the words of your maidservant.
25Please, let not my lord regard this scoundrel
Nabal. For as his name *is,* so *is* he: Nabal *is* his
name, and folly *is* with him! But I, your
maidservant, did not see the young men of my
lord whom you sent. 26Now therefore, my lord,
as the LORD lives and *as* your soul lives, since
the LORD has held you back from coming to
bloodshed and from avenging yourself with
your own hand, now then, let your enemies
and those who seek harm for my lord be as
Nabal. 27And now this present which your
maidservant has brought to my lord, let it be
given to the young men who follow my lord.
28Please forgive the trespass of your maidservant. For the LORD will certainly make for my
lord an enduring house, because my lord
fights the battles of the LORD, and evil is not
found in you throughout your days. 29Yet a
man has risen to pursue you and seek your
life, but the life of my lord shall be bound in
the bundle of the living with the LORD your
God; and the lives of your enemies He shall
sling out, *as from* the pocket of a sling. 30And it
shall come to pass, when the LORD has done
for my lord according to all the good that He
has spoken concerning you, and has appointed you ruler over Israel, 31that this will be no
grief to you, nor offense of heart to my lord,
either that you have shed blood without cause,
or that my lord has avenged himself. But
when the LORD has dealt well with my lord,
then remember your maidservant."
32Then David said to Abigail: "Blessed *is* the
LORD God of Israel, who sent you this day to
meet me! 33And blessed *is* your advice and
blessed *are* you, because you have kept me this
day from coming to bloodshed and from avenging myself with my own hand. 34For indeed, *as*
the LORD God of Israel lives, who has kept me
back from hurting you, unless you had hurried and come to meet me, surely by morning
light no males would have been left to Nabal!"
35So David received from her hand what she
had brought him, and said to her, "Go up in
peace to your house. See, I have heeded your
voice and respected your person."
36Now Abigail went to Nabal, and there he
was, holding a feast in his house, like the feast
of a king. And Nabal's heart *was* merry within
him, for he *was* very drunk; therefore she told
him nothing, little or much, until morning
light. 37So it was, in the morning, when the
wine had gone from Nabal, and his wife had
told him these things, that his heart died within him, and he became *like* a stone. 38Then it
happened, *after* about ten days, that the LORD
struck Nabal, and he died.
39So when David heard that Nabal was dead,
he said, "Blessed *be* the LORD, who has pleaded the cause of my reproach from the hand of
Nabal, and has kept His servant from evil! For
the LORD has returned the wickedness of
Nabal on his own head."
And David sent and proposed to Abigail, to
take her as his wife. 40When the servants of
David had come to Abigail at Carmel, they
spoke to her saying, "David sent us to you, to
ask you to become his wife."
41Then she arose, bowed her face to the
earth, and said, "Here is your maidservant, a
servant to wash the feet of the servants of my
lord." 42So Abigail rose in haste and rode on a
donkey, attended by five of her maidens; and

she followed the messengers of David, and became his wife. [43]David also took Ahinoam of Jezreel, and so both of them were his wives.

[44]But Saul had given Michal his daughter, David's wife, to Palti the son of Laish, who *was* from Gallim.

Psalm 60:1–5

To the Chief Musician. Set to "Lily of the Testimony." A Michtam of David. For teaching. When he fought against Mesopotamia and Syria of Zobah, and Joab returned and killed twelve thousand Edomites in the Valley of Salt.

O God, You have cast us off;
You have broken us down;
You have been displeased;
Oh, restore us again!
2 You have made the earth tremble;
You have broken it;
Heal its breaches, for it is shaking.
3 You have shown Your people hard things;
You have made us drink the wine of confusion.
4 You have given a banner to those who fear You,
That it may be displayed because of the truth. Selah
5 That Your beloved may be delivered,
Save *with* Your right hand, and hear me.

Proverbs 16:3

3 Commit your works to the LORD,
And your thoughts will be established.

16:3 Commit. Literally, "roll upon" in the sense of both total trust (3:5,6) and submission to the will of God (Pss. 22:8; 37:5; 119:133). He will fulfill your righteous plans.

John 1:29–51

[29]The next day John saw Jesus coming toward him, and said, "Behold! The Lamb of God who takes away the sin of the world! [30]This is He of whom I said, 'After me comes a Man who is preferred before me, for He was before me.' [31]I did not know Him; but that He should be revealed to Israel, therefore I came baptizing with water."

[32]And John bore witness, saying, "I saw the Spirit descending from heaven like a dove, and He remained upon Him. [33]I did not know Him, but He who sent me to baptize with water said to me, 'Upon whom you see the Spirit descending, and remaining on Him, this is He who baptizes with the Holy Spirit.' [34]And I have seen and testified that this is the Son of God."

[35]Again, the next day, John stood with two of his disciples. [36]And looking at Jesus as He walked, he said, "Behold the Lamb of God!"

[37]The two disciples heard him speak, and they followed Jesus. [38]Then Jesus turned, and seeing them following, said to them, "What do you seek?"

They said to Him, "Rabbi" (which is to say, when translated, Teacher), "where are You staying?"

[39]He said to them, "Come and see." They came and saw where He was staying, and remained with Him that day (now it was about the tenth hour).

[40]One of the two who heard John *speak,* and followed Him, was Andrew, Simon Peter's brother. [41]He first found his own brother Simon, and said to him, "We have found the Messiah" (which is translated, the Christ). [42]And he brought him to Jesus.

1:41 Messiah. The term "Messiah" is a transliteration of a Hebrew or Aramaic verbal adjective that means "Anointed One." It comes from a verb that means "to anoint" someone as an action involved in consecrating that person to a particular office or function. While the term at first applied to the king of Israel ("the LORD's anointed," 1 Sam. 16:6), the high priest ("the anointed priest," Lev. 4:3) and, in one passage, the patriarchs ("My anointed ones," Ps. 105:15), the term eventually came to point above all to the prophesied "Coming One" or "Messiah" in His role as prophet, priest, and king. The term "Christ," a Greek word (verbal adjective) that comes from a verb meaning "to anoint," is used in translating the Hebrew term, so that the terms "Messiah" or "Christ" are titles and not personal names of Jesus.

Now when Jesus looked at him, He said, "You are Simon the son of Jonah. You shall be called Cephas" (which is translated, A Stone).

[43]The following day Jesus wanted to go to Galilee, and He found Philip and said to him, "Follow Me." [44]Now Philip was from Bethsaida, the city of Andrew and Peter. [45]Philip found Nathanael and said to him, "We have found Him of whom Moses in the law, and also the prophets, wrote—Jesus of Nazareth, the son of Joseph."

[46]And Nathanael said to him, "Can anything good come out of Nazareth?"

Philip said to him, "Come and see."
47Jesus saw Nathanael coming toward Him,
and said of him, "Behold, an Israelite indeed,
in whom is no deceit!"
48Nathanael said to Him, "How do You know
me?"
Jesus answered and said to him, "Before
Philip called you, when you were under the fig
tree, I saw you."
49Nathanael answered and said to Him,
"Rabbi, You are the Son of God! You are the
King of Israel!"
50Jesus answered and said to him, "Because I said to you, 'I saw you under the fig
tree,' do you believe? You will see greater
things than these." 51And He said to him,
"Most assuredly, I say to you, hereafter you
shall see heaven open, and the angels of God
ascending and descending upon the Son of
Man."

DAY 11: How did John the Baptist characterize Jesus Christ?

John the Baptist's witness to Jesus in John 1 introduces a lengthy list of titles applied to Jesus: Lamb of God (vv. 29,36), Rabbi (vv. 38,49), Messiah/Christ (v. 41), Son of God (vv. 34,49), King of Israel (v. 49), Son of Man (v. 51), and "Him of whom Moses in the law, and also the prophets, wrote" (v. 45).

In John 1:29, John the Baptist refers to Jesus as "The Lamb of God." The use of a lamb for sacrifice was very familiar to Jews. A lamb was used as a sacrifice during Passover (Ex. 12:1–36); a lamb was led to the slaughter in the prophecies of Isaiah (Is. 53:7); a lamb was offered in the daily sacrifices of Israel (Lev. 14:12–21; Heb. 10:5–7). John the Baptist used this expression as a reference to the ultimate sacrifice of Jesus on the cross to atone for the sins of the world, a theme which John the apostle carries throughout his writings (19:36; see Rev. 5:1–6; 7:17; 17:14) and that appears in other New Testament writings (e.g., 1 Pet. 1:19).

"Who takes away the sin of the world." In this context "world" has the connotation of humanity in general, not specifically every person. The use of the singular "sin" in conjunction with "of the world" indicates that Jesus' sacrifice for sin potentially reaches all human beings without distinction (1 John 2:2). John makes clear, however, that its efficacious effect is only for those who receive Christ (vv. 11,12).

John adds that "I saw the Spirit descending...upon Him" (v. 32). God had previously communicated to John that this sign was to indicate the promised Messiah (v. 33), so when John witnessed this act, he was able to identify the Messiah as Jesus (Matt. 3:16; Mark 1:10; Luke 3:22). "I have seen and testified that this is the Son of God" (v. 34). Although, in a limited sense, believers can be called "sons of God" (v. 12; Matt. 5:9; Rom. 8:14), John uses this phrase with the full force as a title that points to the unique oneness and intimacy that Jesus sustains to the Father as "Son." The term carries the idea of the deity of Jesus as Messiah (v. 49; 5:16–30; 2 Sam. 7:14; Ps. 2:7; Heb. 1:1–9).

MAY 12

1 Samuel 26:1–27:12

26 Now the Ziphites came to Saul at
Gibeah, saying, "Is David not hiding in
the hill of Hachilah, opposite Jeshimon?" 2Then
Saul arose and went down to the Wilderness of
Ziph, having three thousand chosen men of
Israel with him, to seek David in the Wilderness of Ziph. 3And Saul encamped in the hill of
Hachilah, which *is* opposite Jeshimon, by the
road. But David stayed in the wilderness, and
he saw that Saul came after him into the
wilderness. 4David therefore sent out spies,
and understood that Saul had indeed come.
5So David arose and came to the place
where Saul had encamped. And David saw the
place where Saul lay, and Abner the son of
Ner, the commander of his army. Now Saul lay
within the camp, with the people encamped all
around him. 6Then David answered, and said to
Ahimelech the Hittite and to Abishai the son of
Zeruiah, brother of Joab, saying, "Who will go
down with me to Saul in the camp?"
And Abishai said, "I will go down with you."
7So David and Abishai came to the people
by night; and there Saul lay sleeping within
the camp, with his spear stuck in the ground
by his head. And Abner and the people lay all
around him. 8Then Abishai said to David, "God
has delivered your enemy into your hand this
day. Now therefore, please, let me strike him at
once with the spear, right to the earth; and I will
not *have to strike* him a second time!"
9But David said to Abishai, "Do not destroy
him; for who can stretch out his hand against
the LORD's anointed, and be guiltless?" 10David
said furthermore, "*As* the LORD lives, the LORD
shall strike him, or his day shall come to die,
or he shall go out to battle and perish. 11The
LORD forbid that I should stretch out my hand
against the LORD's anointed. But please, take

now the spear and the jug of water that *are* by his head, and let us go." 12 So David took the spear and the jug of water *by* Saul's head, and they got away; and no man saw or knew *it* or awoke. For they *were* all asleep, because a deep sleep from the LORD had fallen on them.

13 Now David went over to the other side, and stood on the top of a hill afar off, a great distance *being* between them. 14 And David called out to the people and to Abner the son of Ner, saying, "Do you not answer, Abner?"

Then Abner answered and said, "Who *are* you, calling out to the king?"

15 So David said to Abner, "*Are* you not a man? And who *is* like you in Israel? Why then have you not guarded your lord the king? For one of the people came in to destroy your lord the king. 16 This thing that you have done *is* not good. *As* the LORD lives, you deserve to die, because you have not guarded your master, the LORD's anointed. And now see where the king's spear *is,* and the jug of water that *was* by his head."

17 Then Saul knew David's voice, and said, "*Is* that your voice, my son David?"

David said, "*It is* my voice, my lord, O king." 18 And he said, "Why does my lord thus pursue his servant? For what have I done, or what evil *is* in my hand? 19 Now therefore, please, let my lord the king hear the words of his servant: If the LORD has stirred you up against me, let Him accept an offering. But if *it is* the children of men, *may* they *be* cursed before the LORD, for they have driven me out this day from sharing in the inheritance of the LORD, saying, 'Go, serve other gods.' 20 So now, do not let my blood fall to the earth before the face of the LORD. For the king of Israel has come out to seek a flea, as when one hunts a partridge in the mountains."

21 Then Saul said, "I have sinned. Return, my son David. For I will harm you no more, because my life was precious in your eyes this day. Indeed I have played the fool and erred exceedingly."

26:21 I have sinned. As in 24:17, Saul confessed his sin and wrongdoing. Although Saul may have been sincere, he could not be trusted and David wisely did not accept his invitation to return with him. **I have played the fool.** Saul had been foolish in his actions toward David, as had Nabal.

22 And David answered and said, "Here is the king's spear. Let one of the young men come over and get it. 23 May the LORD repay every man *for* his righteousness and his faithfulness; for the LORD delivered you into *my* hand today, but I would not stretch out my hand against the LORD's anointed. 24 And indeed, as your life was valued much this day in my eyes, so let my life be valued much in the eyes of the LORD, and let Him deliver me out of all tribulation."

25 Then Saul said to David, "*May* you *be* blessed, my son David! You shall both do great things and also still prevail."

So David went on his way, and Saul returned to his place.

27 And David said in his heart, "Now I shall perish someday by the hand of Saul. *There is* nothing better for me than that I should speedily escape to the land of the Philistines; and Saul will despair of me, to seek me anymore in any part of Israel. So I shall escape out of his hand." 2 Then David arose and went over with the six hundred men who *were* with him to Achish the son of Maoch, king of Gath. 3 So David dwelt with Achish at Gath, he and his men, each man with his household, *and* David with his two wives, Ahinoam the Jezreelitess, and Abigail the Carmelitess, Nabal's widow. 4 And it was told Saul that David had fled to Gath; so he sought him no more.

27:1 by the hand of Saul. In direct contrast to Saul's word that David would prevail (26:25), David thought that Saul would ultimately kill him. This anxious thinking and the fear that fell upon him explain David's actions in this chapter. God had told him to stay in Judah (22:5), but he was afraid and sought protection again among the Philistine enemies of Israel (21:10–15).

5 Then David said to Achish, "If I have now found favor in your eyes, let them give me a place in some town in the country, that I may dwell there. For why should your servant dwell in the royal city with you?" 6 So Achish gave him Ziklag that day. Therefore Ziklag has belonged to the kings of Judah to this day. 7 Now the time that David dwelt in the country of the Philistines was one full year and four months. 8 And David and his men went up and raided the Geshurites, the Girzites, and the Amalekites. For those *nations* were the inhabitants of the land from of old, as you go to Shur, even as far as the land of Egypt. 9 Whenever David attacked

the land, he left neither man nor woman alive,
but took away the sheep, the oxen, the donkeys, the camels, and the apparel, and returned
and came to Achish. 10 Then Achish would say,
"Where have you made a raid today?" And David would say, "Against the southern *area* of
Judah, or against the southern *area* of the
Jerahmeelites, or against the southern *area* of
the Kenites." 11 David would save neither man
nor woman alive, to bring *news* to Gath, saying, "Lest they should inform on us, saying,
'Thus David did.' " And thus *was* his behavior
all the time he dwelt in the country of the
Philistines. 12 So Achish believed David, saying,
"He has made his people Israel utterly abhor
him; therefore he will be my servant forever."

Psalm 60:6–12

6 God has spoken in His holiness:
"I will rejoice;
I will divide Shechem
And measure out the Valley of Succoth.
7 Gilead *is* Mine, and Manasseh *is* Mine;
Ephraim also *is* the helmet for My head;
Judah *is* My lawgiver.
8 Moab *is* My washpot;
Over Edom I will cast My shoe;
Philistia, shout in triumph because
of Me."
9 Who will bring me *to* the strong city?
Who will lead me to Edom?
10 *Is it* not You, O God, *who* cast us off?
And You, O God, *who* did not go out
with our armies?
11 Give us help from trouble,
For the help of man *is* useless.
12 Through God we will do valiantly,
For *it is* He *who* shall tread down our
enemies.

Proverbs 16:4–5

4 The LORD has made all for Himself,
Yes, even the wicked for the day of doom.

5 Everyone proud in heart *is* an
abomination to the LORD;
Though they join forces, none will
go unpunished.

John 2:1–25

2 On the third day there was a wedding in
Cana of Galilee, and the mother of Jesus
was there. 2 Now both Jesus and His disciples
were invited to the wedding. 3 And when they
ran out of wine, the mother of Jesus said to
Him, "They have no wine."
4 Jesus said to her, "Woman, what does your
concern have to do with Me? My hour has not
yet come."

2:2,3 both Jesus and His disciples were invited. The fact that Jesus, His mother, and His disciples all attended the wedding suggests that the wedding may have been for a relative or close family friend. Andrew, Simon Peter, Philip, Nathanael, and the unnamed disciple (1:35), who was surely John, witnessed this miracle. **wine.** The wine served was subject to fermentation. In the ancient world, however, to quench thirst without inducing drunkenness, wine was diluted with water to between one-third and one-tenth of its strength. Due to the climate and circumstances, even "new wine" fermented quickly and had an inebriating effect if not mixed (Acts 2:13). Because of a lack of water purification process, wine mixed with water was also safer to drink than water alone. While the Bible condemns drunkenness, it does not necessarily condemn the consumption of wine (Ps. 104:15; Prov. 20:1; Eph. 5:18).

5 His mother said to the servants, "Whatever
He says to you, do *it*."
6 Now there were set there six waterpots of
stone, according to the manner of purification
of the Jews, containing twenty or thirty gal-
lons apiece. 7 Jesus said to them, "Fill the
waterpots with water." And they filled them up
to the brim. 8 And He said to them, "Draw *some*
out now, and take *it* to the master of the feast."
And they took *it*. 9 When the master of the feast
had tasted the water that was made wine, and
did not know where it came from (but the servants who had drawn the water knew), the
master of the feast called the bridegroom.
10 And he said to him, "Every man at the beginning sets out the good wine, and when the
guests have well drunk, then the inferior. You
have kept the good wine until now!"
11 This beginning of signs Jesus did in Cana
of Galilee, and manifested His glory; and His
disciples believed in Him.
12 After this He went down to Capernaum,
He, His mother, His brothers, and His disciples; and they did not stay there many days.
13 Now the Passover of the Jews was at hand,
and Jesus went up to Jerusalem. 14 And He
found in the temple those who sold oxen and
sheep and doves, and the money changers doing business. 15 When He had made a whip of
cords, He drove them all out of the temple, with
the sheep and the oxen, and poured out the
changers' money and overturned the tables.
16 And He said to those who sold doves, "Take
these things away! Do not make My Father's

house a house of merchandise!" 17Then His disciples remembered that it was written, *"Zeal
for Your house has eaten Me up."*
18So the Jews answered and said to Him,
"What sign do You show to us, since You do
these things?"
19Jesus answered and said to them, "Destroy
this temple, and in three days I will raise it up."
20Then the Jews said, "It has taken forty-six
years to build this temple, and will You raise it
up in three days?"
21But He was speaking of the temple of His
body. 22Therefore, when He had risen from the
dead, His disciples remembered that He had
said this to them; and they believed the Scripture and the word which Jesus had said.
23Now when He was in Jerusalem at the
Passover, during the feast, many believed in
His name when they saw the signs which He
did. 24But Jesus did not commit Himself to
them, because He knew all *men,* 25and had no
need that anyone should testify of man, for He
knew what was in man.

2:23,24 many believed in His name.... But Jesus did not commit Himself. John based these two phrases on the same Greek verb for "believe." This verse subtly reveals the true nature of belief from a biblical standpoint. Because of what they knew of Jesus from His miraculous signs, many came to believe in Him. However, Jesus made it His habit not to wholeheartedly "entrust" or "commit" Himself to them because He knew their hearts. Verse 24 indicates that Jesus looked for genuine conversion rather than enthusiasm for the spectacular. The latter verse also leaves a subtle doubt as to the genuineness of the conversion of some (8:31,32). This emphatic contrast between vv. 23,24 in terms of type of trust, therefore, reveals that, literally, "belief into His name" involved much more than intellectual assent. It called for wholehearted commitment of one's life as Jesus' disciple (Matt. 10:37; 16:24–26).

DAY 12: What did Jesus mean by His comments about the temple in John 2?

In John 2:18, the Jews demanded that Jesus show some type of miraculous sign that would indicate His authority for the actions that He had just taken in regulating the activities of the temple. Their demand of a sign reveals that they had not grasped the significance of Jesus' rebuke that centered in their need for proper attitudes and holiness in worship. Such an action itself constituted a "sign" of Jesus' person and authority. Moreover, they were requesting from Jesus a crass display of miracles on demand, further displaying their unbelief.

"Destroy this temple, and in three days I will raise it up" (v. 19). At His trial, the authorities charged Jesus (Mark 14:29,58) with making a threatening statement against the temple, revealing that they did not understand Jesus' response here. Once again John's Gospel supplements the other Gospels at this point by indicating that Jesus enigmatically referred to His resurrection. As with His usage of parables, Jesus' cryptic statement most likely was designed to reveal the truth to His disciples but conceal its meaning from unbelievers who questioned Him (Matt. 13:10,11). Only after His resurrection, however, did the disciples understand the real significance of this statement (v. 22; Matt. 12:40). Importantly, through the death and resurrection of Christ, temple worship in Jerusalem was destroyed (see 4:21) and reinstituted in the hearts of those who were built into a spiritual temple called the church (Eph. 2:19–22).

"It has taken forty-six years to build this temple" (v. 20). This was not a reference to the Solomonic temple, since it had been destroyed during the Babylonian conquest in 586 B.C. When the captives returned from Babylon, Zerubbabel and Joshua began rebuilding the temple (Ezra 1–4). Encouraged by the prophets Haggai and Zechariah (Ezra 5:1–6:18), the Jews completed the work in 516 B.C. In 20/19 B.C., Herod the Great began a reconstruction and expansion. Workers completed the main part of the project in 10 years, but other parts were still being constructed even at the time Jesus cleansed the temple. The famous "Wailing Wall" is built on part of the Herodian temple foundation.

MAY 13

1 Samuel 28:1–25

28 Now it happened in those days that
the Philistines gathered their armies
together for war, to fight with Israel. And
Achish said to David, "You assuredly know that
you will go out with me to battle, you and your
men."
2So David said to Achish, "Surely you know
what your servant can do."
And Achish said to David, "Therefore I will
make you one of my chief guardians forever."
3Now Samuel had died, and all Israel had

28:3 mediums and the spiritists. By divine law, they were banned from Israel (Deut. 18:11), and Israel was not to be defiled by them (Lev. 19:31). Turning to them was tantamount to playing the harlot and would result in God setting His face against the person and cutting him off from among His people (Lev. 20:6). Mediums and spiritists were to be put to death by stoning (Lev. 20:27). Even Saul understood this and had previously dealt with the issue (v. 9).

28:12 the woman saw Samuel. Though questions have arisen as to the nature of Samuel's appearance, the text clearly indicates that Samuel, not an apparition, was evident to the eyes of the medium. God miraculously permitted the actual spirit of Samuel to speak (vv. 16–19). Because she understood her inability to raise the dead in this manner, she immediately knew 1) that it must have been by the power of God and 2) that her disguised inquirer must be Saul.

lamented for him and buried him in Ramah, in
his own city. And Saul had put the mediums
and the spiritists out of the land.
4 Then the Philistines gathered together, and
came and encamped at Shunem. So Saul gathered all Israel together, and they encamped at
Gilboa. 5 When Saul saw the army of the
Philistines, he was afraid, and his heart trembled greatly. 6 And when Saul inquired of the
LORD, the LORD did not answer him, either by
dreams or by Urim or by the prophets.
7 Then Saul said to his servants, "Find me a
woman who is a medium, that I may go to her
and inquire of her."
And his servants said to him, "In fact, *there
is* a woman who is a medium at En Dor."
8 So Saul disguised himself and put on other
clothes, and he went, and two men with him;
and they came to the woman by night. And he
said, "Please conduct a séance for me, and
bring up for me the one I shall name to you."
9 Then the woman said to him, "Look, you
know what Saul has done, how he has cut off
the mediums and the spiritists from the land.
Why then do you lay a snare for my life, to
cause me to die?"
10 And Saul swore to her by the LORD, saying,
"*As* the LORD lives, no punishment shall come
upon you for this thing."
11 Then the woman said, "Whom shall I bring
up for you?"
And he said, "Bring up Samuel for me."
12 When the woman saw Samuel, she cried
out with a loud voice. And the woman spoke to
Saul, saying, "Why have you deceived me? For
you *are* Saul!"
13 And the king said to her, "Do not be afraid.
What did you see?"
And the woman said to Saul, "I saw a spirit
ascending out of the earth."
14 So he said to her, "What *is* his form?"
And she said, "An old man is coming up,
and he *is* covered with a mantle." And Saul
perceived that it *was* Samuel, and he stooped
with *his* face to the ground and bowed down.
15 Now Samuel said to Saul, "Why have you
disturbed me by bringing me up?"
And Saul answered, "I am deeply distressed; for the Philistines make war against
me, and God has departed from me and does
not answer me anymore, neither by prophets
nor by dreams. Therefore I have called you,
that you may reveal to me what I should do."
16 Then Samuel said: "So why do you ask me,
seeing the LORD has departed from you and
has become your enemy? 17 And the LORD has
done for Himself as He spoke by me. For the
LORD has torn the kingdom out of your hand
and given it to your neighbor, David. 18 Because you did not obey the voice of the LORD
nor execute His fierce wrath upon Amalek,
therefore the LORD has done this thing to you
this day. 19 Moreover the LORD will also deliver
Israel with you into the hand of the Philistines.
And tomorrow you and your sons *will be* with
me. The LORD will also deliver the army of
Israel into the hand of the Philistines."
20 Immediately Saul fell full length on the
ground, and was dreadfully afraid because of
the words of Samuel. And there was no
strength in him, for he had eaten no food all
day or all night.
21 And the woman came to Saul and saw that
he was severely troubled, and said to him,
"Look, your maidservant has obeyed your
voice, and I have put my life in my hands and
heeded the words which you spoke to me.
22 Now therefore, please, heed also the voice of
your maidservant, and let me set a piece of
bread before you; and eat, that you may have
strength when you go on *your* way."
23 But he refused and said, "I will not eat."
So his servants, together with the woman,
urged him; and he heeded their voice. Then

he arose from the ground and sat on the bed.
[24]Now the woman had a fatted calf in the
house, and she hastened to kill it. And she
took flour and kneaded *it,* and baked unleavened bread from it. [25]So she brought *it* before
Saul and his servants, and they ate. Then they
rose and went away that night.

Psalm 61:1–4

To the Chief Musician.
On a stringed instrument.
A Psalm of David.

Hear my cry, O God;
Attend to my prayer.
2 From the end of the earth I will cry
to You,
When my heart is overwhelmed;
Lead me to the rock that is higher
than I.
3 For You have been a shelter for me,
A strong tower from the enemy.
4 I will abide in Your tabernacle forever;
I will trust in the shelter of Your
wings. Selah

Proverbs 16:6

6 In mercy and truth
Atonement is provided for iniquity;
And by the fear of the LORD *one*
departs from evil.

John 3:1–18

3 There was a man of the Pharisees named
Nicodemus, a ruler of the Jews. [2]This man
came to Jesus by night and said to Him,
"Rabbi, we know that You are a teacher come
from God; for no one can do these signs that
You do unless God is with him."
[3]Jesus answered and said to him, "Most
assuredly, I say to you, unless one is born
again, he cannot see the kingdom of God."
[4]Nicodemus said to Him, "How can a man
be born when he is old? Can he enter a second
time into his mother's womb and be born?"
[5]Jesus answered, "Most assuredly, I say to
you, unless one is born of water and the Spirit,
he cannot enter the kingdom of God. [6]That
which is born of the flesh is flesh, and that which
is born of the Spirit is spirit. [7]Do not marvel
that I said to you, 'You must be born again.'
[8]The wind blows where it wishes, and you
hear the sound of it, but cannot tell where it
comes from and where it goes. So is everyone
who is born of the Spirit."
[9]Nicodemus answered and said to Him,
"How can these things be?"
[10]Jesus answered and said to him, "Are you
the teacher of Israel, and do not know these
things? [11]Most assuredly, I say to you, We
speak what We know and testify what We have
seen, and you do not receive Our witness. [12]If
I have told you earthly things and you do not
believe, how will you believe if I tell you heavenly things? [13]No one has ascended to heaven
but He who came down from heaven, *that is,*
the Son of Man who is in heaven. [14]And as Moses lifted up the serpent in the wilderness,
even so must the Son of Man be lifted up,
[15]that whoever believes in Him should not perish but have eternal life. [16]For God so loved the

3:15 eternal life. This is the first of 10 references to "eternal life" in John's Gospel. The same Greek word is translated 8 times as "everlasting life." The two expressions appear in the New Testament nearly 50 times. Eternal life refers not only to eternal quantity but divine quality of life. It means literally "life of the age to come" and refers therefore to resurrection and heavenly existence in perfect glory and holiness. This life for believers in the Lord Jesus is experienced before heaven is reached. This "eternal life" is in essence nothing less than participation in the eternal life of the Living Word, Jesus Christ. It is the life of God in every believer, yet not fully manifest until the resurrection (Rom. 8:19–23; Phil. 3:20,21).

world that He gave His only begotten Son, that
whoever believes in Him should not perish
but have everlasting life. [17]For God did not
send His Son into the world to condemn the
world, but that the world through Him might
be saved.
[18]"He who believes in Him is not condemned;
but he who does not believe is condemned
already, because he has not believed in the
name of the only begotten Son of God.

3:16 For God so loved the world. The Son's mission is bound up in the supreme love of God for the evil, sinful "world" of humanity (see 6:32,51;12:47) that is in rebellion against Him. The word "so" emphasizes the intensity or greatness of His love. The Father gave His unique and beloved Son to die on behalf of sinful men (2 Cor. 5:21).

DAY 13: What does it mean to be "born again"?

In John 3:3, Jesus answered a question that Nicodemus does not even ask. He read Nicodemus's heart and came to the very core of his problem, i.e., the need for spiritual transformation or regeneration produced by the Holy Spirit. He tells Nicodemus that he must be "born again." The phrase literally means "born from above." New birth is an act of God whereby eternal life is imparted to the believer (2 Cor. 5:17; Titus 3:5; 1 Pet. 1:3; 1 John 2:29; 3:9; 4:7; 5:1,4,18). Chapter 1:12,13 indicates that "born again" also carries the idea "to become children of God" through trust in the name of the incarnate Word.

Unless one is born again, he "cannot see the kingdom of God." In context, this is primarily a reference to participation in the millennial kingdom at the end of the age, fervently anticipated by the Pharisees and other Jews. Since the Pharisees were supernaturalists, they naturally and eagerly expected the coming of the prophesied resurrection of the saints and institution of the messianic kingdom (Is. 11:1–16; Dan. 12:2). Their problem was that they thought that mere physical lineage and keeping of religious externals qualified them for entrance into the kingdom rather than the needed spiritual transformation which Jesus emphasized (see 8:33–39; Gal. 6:15). The coming of the kingdom at the end of the age can be described as the "regeneration" of the world (Matt. 19:28), but regeneration of the individual is required before the end of the world in order to enter the kingdom.

Restating it, Jesus said that one must be "born of water and the Spirit" (v. 5). Jesus referred not to literal water here but to the need for "cleansing" (Ezek. 36:24–27). When water is used figuratively in the Old Testament, it consistently refers to renewal or spiritual cleansing, especially when used in conjunction with "spirit" (Num. 19:17–19; Ps. 51:9,10; Is. 32:15; 44:3–5; 55:1–3; Jer. 2:13; Joel 2:28,29). Thus, Jesus made reference to the spiritual washing or purification of the soul, accomplished by the Holy Spirit through the Word of God at the moment of salvation (Eph. 5:26; Titus 3:5), required for belonging to His kingdom.

MAY 14

1 Samuel 29:1–31:13

29 Then the Philistines gathered together
all their armies at Aphek, and the
Israelites encamped by a fountain which *is* in
Jezreel. [2]And the lords of the Philistines passed
in review by hundreds and by thousands, but
David and his men passed in review at the rear
with Achish. [3]Then the princes of the Philistines
said, "What *are* these Hebrews *doing here?*"
And Achish said to the princes of the
Philistines, "*Is* this not David, the servant of
Saul king of Israel, who has been with me these
days, or these years? And to this day I have
found no fault in him since he defected *to me.*"
[4]But the princes of the Philistines were angry
with him; so the princes of the Philistines said
to him, "Make this fellow return, that he may
go back to the place which you have appointed for him, and do not let him go down with us
to battle, lest in the battle he become our
adversary. For with what could he reconcile
himself to his master, if not with the heads of
these men? [5]*Is* this not David, of whom they
sang to one another in dances, saying:

'Saul has slain his thousands,
And David his ten thousands'?"

[6]Then Achish called David and said to him,
"Surely, *as* the LORD lives, you have been
upright, and your going out and your coming
in with me in the army *is* good in my sight. For
to this day I have not found evil in you since
the day of your coming to me. Nevertheless
the lords do not favor you. [7]Therefore return
now, and go in peace, that you may not displease the lords of the Philistines."
[8]So David said to Achish, "But what have I
done? And to this day what have you found in
your servant as long as I have been with you,
that I may not go and fight against the enemies of my lord the king?"
[9]Then Achish answered and said to David,
"I know that you *are* as good in my sight as an
angel of God; nevertheless the princes of the
Philistines have said, 'He shall not go up with
us to the battle.' [10]Now therefore, rise early in
the morning with your master's servants who
have come with you. And as soon as you are up
early in the morning and have light, depart."
[11]So David and his men rose early to depart
in the morning, to return to the land of the
Philistines. And the Philistines went up to
Jezreel.

30 Now it happened, when David and his
men came to Ziklag, on the third day,
that the Amalekites had invaded the South and
Ziklag, attacked Ziklag and burned it with fire,
[2]and had taken captive the women and those
who *were* there, from small to great; they did
not kill anyone, but carried *them* away and
went their way. [3]So David and his men came to

the city, and there it was, burned with fire; and
their wives, their sons, and their daughters had
been taken captive. 4Then David and the people who *were* with him lifted up their voices and
wept, until they had no more power to weep.
5And David's two wives, Ahinoam the Jezreelitess, and Abigail the widow of Nabal the
Carmelite, had been taken captive. 6Now David
was greatly distressed, for the people spoke of
stoning him, because the soul of all the people
was grieved, every man for his sons and his
daughters. But David strengthened himself in
the LORD his God.

30:6 distressed...grieved. Arriving home to the reality of their great tragedy caused David immense distress and provoked the wickedness of his men to entertain the treasonous idea of stoning him. Having not inquired of the Lord before his departure to support Achish in battle, David was in need of God's getting his attention. **strengthened himself in the LORD his God.** This was the key to David's being a man after God's heart (1 Sam. 13:14; Acts 13:22).

7Then David said to Abiathar the priest,
Ahimelech's son, "Please bring the ephod
here to me." And Abiathar brought the ephod
to David. 8So David inquired of the LORD, saying, "Shall I pursue this troop? Shall I overtake
them?"

And He answered him, "Pursue, for you
shall surely overtake *them* and without fail
recover *all*."

9So David went, he and the six hundred
men who *were* with him, and came to the
Brook Besor, where those stayed who were
left behind. 10But David pursued, he and four
hundred men; for two hundred stayed *behind*,
who were so weary that they could not cross
the Brook Besor.

11Then they found an Egyptian in the field,
and brought him to David; and they gave him
bread and he ate, and they let him drink water.
12And they gave him a piece of a cake of figs
and two clusters of raisins. So when he had
eaten, his strength came back to him; for he
had eaten no bread nor drunk water for three
days and three nights. 13Then David said to
him, "To whom do you *belong*, and where *are*
you from?"

And he said, "I *am* a young man from Egypt,
servant of an Amalekite; and my master left
me behind, because three days ago I fell sick.
14We made an invasion of the southern *area* of
the Cherethites, in the *territory* which *belongs*
to Judah, and of the southern *area* of Caleb;
and we burned Ziklag with fire."

15And David said to him, "Can you take me
down to this troop?"

So he said, "Swear to me by God that you
will neither kill me nor deliver me into the
hands of my master, and I will take you down
to this troop."

16And when he had brought him down, there
they were, spread out over all the land, eating
and drinking and dancing, because of all the
great spoil which they had taken from the land
of the Philistines and from the land of Judah.
17Then David attacked them from twilight until
the evening of the next day. Not a man of them
escaped, except four hundred young men who
rode on camels and fled. 18So David recovered
all that the Amalekites had carried away, and
David rescued his two wives. 19And nothing of
theirs was lacking, either small or great, sons
or daughters, spoil or anything which they
had taken from them; David recovered all.
20Then David took all the flocks and herds
they had driven before those *other* livestock,
and said, "This *is* David's spoil."

30:19 nothing...was lacking. In spite of David's previous failures, God showed Himself to be more than gracious and abundant in His stewardship of the wives, children, livestock, and possessions of David and his men.

21Now David came to the two hundred men
who had been so weary that they could not follow David, whom they also had made to stay at
the Brook Besor. So they went out to meet David and to meet the people who *were* with him.
And when David came near the people, he
greeted them. 22Then all the wicked and
worthless men of those who went with David
answered and said, "Because they did not go
with us, we will not give them *any* of the spoil
that we have recovered, except for every
man's wife and children, that they may lead
them away and depart."

23But David said, "My brethren, you shall
not do so with what the LORD has given us,
who has preserved us and delivered into our
hand the troop that came against us. 24For who
will heed you in this matter? But as his part *is*
who goes down to the battle, so *shall* his part
be who stays by the supplies; they shall share

alike." [25]So it was, from that day forward; he
made it a statute and an ordinance for Israel to
this day.

[26]Now when David came to Ziklag, he sent
some of the spoil to the elders of Judah, to his
friends, saying, "Here is a present for you
from the spoil of the enemies of the LORD"—
[27]to *those* who *were* in Bethel, *those* who *were* in
Ramoth of the South, *those* who *were* in Jattir,
[28]*those* who *were* in Aroer, *those* who *were* in
Siphmoth, *those* who *were* in Eshtemoa, [29]*those*
who *were* in Rachal, *those* who *were* in the
cities of the Jerahmeelites, *those* who *were* in the
cities of the Kenites, [30]*those* who *were* in
Hormah, *those* who *were* in Chorashan, *those*
who *were* in Athach, [31]*those* who *were* in Hebron,
and to all the places where David himself and
his men were accustomed to rove.

31 Now the Philistines fought against
Israel; and the men of Israel fled from
before the Philistines, and fell slain on Mount
Gilboa. [2]Then the Philistines followed hard
after Saul and his sons. And the Philistines
killed Jonathan, Abinadab, and Malchishua,
Saul's sons. [3]The battle became fierce against
Saul. The archers hit him, and he was severely wounded by the archers.

[4]Then Saul said to his armorbearer, "Draw
your sword, and thrust me through with it,
lest these uncircumcised men come and
thrust me through and abuse me."

But his armorbearer would not, for he was
greatly afraid. Therefore Saul took a sword
and fell on it. [5]And when his armorbearer saw
that Saul was dead, he also fell on his sword,
and died with him. [6]So Saul, his three sons, his
armorbearer, and all his men died together
that same day.

[7]And when the men of Israel who *were* on
the other side of the valley, and *those* who *were*
on the other side of the Jordan, saw that the
men of Israel had fled and that Saul and his
sons were dead, they forsook the cities and
fled; and the Philistines came and dwelt in
them. [8]So it happened the next day, when the
Philistines came to strip the slain, that they
found Saul and his three sons fallen on Mount
Gilboa. [9]And they cut off his head and stripped
off his armor, and sent *word* throughout the
land of the Philistines, to proclaim *it in* the
temple of their idols and among the people.
[10]Then they put his armor in the temple of the
Ashtoreths, and they fastened his body to the
wall of Beth Shan.

[11]Now when the inhabitants of Jabesh
Gilead heard what the Philistines had done to
Saul, [12]all the valiant men arose and traveled
all night, and took the body of Saul and the
bodies of his sons from the wall of Beth Shan;
and they came to Jabesh and burned them
there. [13]Then they took their bones and buried
them under the tamarisk tree at Jabesh, and
fasted seven days.

31:4 uncircumcised men. A common term of derision used among Israelites to designate non-Israelites. Circumcision was given as the sign of the Abrahamic Covenant in Genesis 17:10–14. **abuse.** Having engaged in several battles against the Philistines, Saul had succeeded in provoking their hatred and resentment. As the king, Saul would certainly have received especially cruel treatment from the hands of his enemies, who would have likely made sport of him and tortured him before his death. **Saul took a sword and fell on it.** Though Saul's suicide is considered by some to be an act of heroism, Saul should have found his strength and courage in God as David did in 23:16 and 30:6 to fight to the end or to surrender. Saul's suicide is the ultimate expression of his faithlessness toward God at this moment in his life.

Psalm 61:5–8

5 For You, O God, have heard
my vows;
You have given *me* the heritage of
those who fear Your name.
6 You will prolong the king's life,
His years as many generations.
7 He shall abide before God forever.
Oh, prepare mercy and truth, *which*
may preserve him!

8 So I will sing praise to Your name
forever,
That I may daily perform my vows.

61:7 forever. The Davidic Covenant guaranteed that on the basis of God's merciful and faithful dealings with David and the nation, David's descendants would rule on the throne of Israel forever (2 Sam. 7; Pss. 40:11; 89:4,33–37).

Proverbs 16:7–9

7 When a man's ways please
the LORD,
He makes even his enemies
to be at peace with him.

16:9 Sovereign God overrules the plans of men to fulfill His purposes. (See Gen. 50:20; 1 Kin. 12:15; Ps. 119:133; Jer. 10:23; Dan. 5:23–30; 1 Cor. 3:19,20.)

8 Better *is* a little with righteousness,
Than vast revenues without justice.

9 A man's heart plans his way,
But the LORD directs his steps.

John 3:19–36

19 And this is the condemnation, that the light
has come into the world, and men loved darkness rather than light, because their deeds
were evil. 20 For everyone practicing evil hates
the light and does not come to the light, lest
his deeds should be exposed. 21 But he who
does the truth comes to the light, that his
deeds may be clearly seen, that they have
been done in God."
22 After these things Jesus and His disciples came into the land of Judea, and there
He remained with them and baptized. 23 Now
John also was baptizing in Aenon near
Salim, because there was much water there.
And they came and were baptized. 24 For
John had not yet been thrown into prison.
25 Then there arose a dispute between *some*
of John's disciples and the Jews about purification. 26 And they came to John and said to
him, "Rabbi, He who was with you beyond the
Jordan, to whom you have testified—behold,
He is baptizing, and all are coming to Him!"
27 John answered and said, "A man can
receive nothing unless it has been given to him
from heaven. 28 You yourselves bear me witness, that I said, 'I am not the Christ,' but, 'I
have been sent before Him.' 29 He who has the
bride is the bridegroom; but the friend of the
bridegroom, who stands and hears him, rejoices greatly because of the bridegroom's voice.
Therefore this joy of mine is fulfilled. 30 He must
increase, but I *must* decrease. 31 He who comes
from above is above all; he who is of the earth
is earthly and speaks of the earth. He who
comes from heaven is above all. 32 And what He
has seen and heard, that He testifies; and no
one receives His testimony. 33 He who has
received His testimony has certified that God
is true. 34 For He whom God has sent speaks
the words of God, for God does not give the
Spirit by measure. 35 The Father loves the Son,
and has given all things into His hand. 36 He
who believes in the Son has everlasting life;
and he who does not believe the Son shall not
see life, but the wrath of God abides on him."

DAY 14: How did John the Baptist respond to the growing ministry of Christ?

The potential conflict between John and Jesus as depicted in John 3:26 was heightened by the fact that both were engaged in ministry in close proximity to each other. Because baptism is mentioned in v. 22, Jesus may have been close to Jericho near the fords of the Jordan, while John was a short distance north baptizing at Aenon. John's followers were especially disturbed by the fact that so many were flocking to Jesus whereas formerly they had come to John.

John's response was to emphasize God's sovereign authority in granting any ministry opportunity (v. 27). It must be "given to him from heaven." And he conveyed his understanding of his own role through the use of a parable (v. 29). The "friend of the bridegroom" was the ancient equivalent of the best man who organized the details and presided over the Judean wedding. This friend found his greatest joy in watching the ceremony proceed without problems. Most likely, John was also alluding to Old Testament passages where faithful Israel is depicted as the bride of the Lord (Is. 62:4,5; Jer. 2:2; Hos. 2:16–20).

In vv. 31–36, John the Baptist gave 5 reasons for Christ's superiority to him: 1) Christ had a heavenly origin (v. 31); 2) Christ knew what was true by firsthand experience (v. 32); 3) Christ's testimony always agreed with God (v. 33); 4) Christ experienced the Holy Spirit in an unlimited manner (v. 34); and 5) Christ was supreme because the Father sovereignly had granted that status to Him (v. 35).

In a fitting climax to the chapter (v. 36), John the Baptist laid out two alternatives, genuine faith and defiant disobedience, thereby bringing to the forefront the threat of looming judgment. As John faded from the forefront, he offered an invitation to faith in the Son and clearly expressed the ultimate consequence of failure to believe, i.e., "the wrath of God."

MAY 15

2 Samuel 1:1–2:32

1 Now it came to pass after the death of Saul, when David had returned from the slaughter of the Amalekites, and David had stayed two days in Ziklag, 2on the third day, behold, it happened that a man came from Saul's camp with his clothes torn and dust on his head. So it was, when he came to David, that he fell to the ground and prostrated himself.

3And David said to him, "Where have you come from?"

So he said to him, "I have escaped from the camp of Israel."

4Then David said to him, "How did the matter go? Please tell me."

And he answered, "The people have fled from the battle, many of the people are fallen and dead, and Saul and Jonathan his son are dead also."

5So David said to the young man who told him, "How do you know that Saul and Jonathan his son are dead?"

6Then the young man who told him said, "As I happened by chance *to be* on Mount Gilboa, there was Saul, leaning on his spear; and indeed the chariots and horsemen followed hard after him. 7Now when he looked behind him, he saw me and called to me. And I answered, 'Here I am.' 8And he said to me, 'Who *are* you?' So I answered him, 'I *am* an Amalekite.' 9He said to me again, 'Please stand over me and kill me, for anguish has come upon me, but my life still *remains* in me.' 10So I stood over him and killed him, because I was sure that he could not live after he had fallen. And I took the crown that *was* on his head and the bracelet that *was* on his arm, and have brought them here to my lord."

11Therefore David took hold of his own clothes and tore them, and *so did* all the men who *were* with him. 12And they mourned and wept and fasted until evening for Saul and for Jonathan his son, for the people of the LORD and for the house of Israel, because they had fallen by the sword.

13Then David said to the young man who told him, "Where *are* you from?"

And he answered, "I *am* the son of an alien, an Amalekite."

14So David said to him, "How was it you were not afraid to put forth your hand to destroy the LORD's anointed?" 15Then David called one of the young men and said, "Go near, *and* execute him!" And he struck him so that he died. 16So David said to him, "Your blood *is* on your own head, for your own mouth has testified against you, saying, 'I have killed the LORD's anointed.' "

17Then David lamented with this lamentation over Saul and over Jonathan his son, 18and he told *them* to teach the children of Judah *the Song of* the Bow; indeed *it is* written in the Book of Jasher:

19 "The beauty of Israel is slain on your
high places!
How the mighty have fallen!
20 Tell *it* not in Gath,
Proclaim *it* not in the streets of
Ashkelon—
Lest the daughters of the Philistines
rejoice,
Lest the daughters of the uncircumcised
triumph.

21 "O mountains of Gilboa,
Let there be no dew nor rain upon you,
Nor fields of offerings.
For the shield of the mighty is cast
away there!
The shield of Saul, not anointed with oil.
22 From the blood of the slain,
From the fat of the mighty,
The bow of Jonathan did not turn
back,
And the sword of Saul did not return
empty.

23 "Saul and Jonathan *were* beloved and
pleasant in their lives,
And in their death they were not
divided;
They were swifter than eagles,
They were stronger than lions.

24 "O daughters of Israel, weep over Saul,
Who clothed you in scarlet, with luxury;

1:19 The beauty of Israel. Literally, the gazelle or antelope of Israel, the chosen symbol of youthful elegance and symmetry, most likely referring to Jonathan. Thus, the song began and ended with Saul's noble son (vv. 25,26). **high places.** These were open-air worship sites generally established at high elevations. In this case, the high place was Mt. Gilboa, where Saul had died. **How the mighty have fallen!** They were not only Israel's slain "beauty," but Saul and Jonathan were mighty men who had fallen in battle. This phrase is repeated as a refrain in vv. 25 and 27.

Who put ornaments of gold on your
apparel.

25 "How the mighty have fallen in the
midst of the battle!
Jonathan *was* slain in your high places.
26 I am distressed for you, my brother
Jonathan;
You have been very pleasant to me;
Your love to me was wonderful,
Surpassing the love of women.

27 "How the mighty have fallen,
And the weapons of war perished!"

2 It happened after this that David inquired
of the LORD, saying, "Shall I go up to any
of the cities of Judah?"
And the LORD said to him, "Go up."
David said, "Where shall I go up?"
And He said, "To Hebron."
2 So David went up there, and his two wives
also, Ahinoam the Jezreelitess, and Abigail the
widow of Nabal the Carmelite. 3 And David
brought up the men who *were* with him, every
man with his household. So they dwelt in the
cities of Hebron.
4 Then the men of Judah came, and there
they anointed David king over the house of Judah. And they told David, saying, "The men of
Jabesh Gilead *were the ones* who buried Saul."
5 So David sent messengers to the men of
Jabesh Gilead, and said to them, "You *are*
blessed of the LORD, for you have shown this
kindness to your lord, to Saul, and have buried
him. 6 And now may the LORD show kindness
and truth to you. I also will repay you this
kindness, because you have done this thing.
7 Now therefore, let your hands be strengthened, and be valiant; for your master Saul is
dead, and also the house of Judah has anointed me king over them."
8 But Abner the son of Ner, commander of
Saul's army, took Ishbosheth the son of Saul
and brought him over to Mahanaim; 9 and he
made him king over Gilead, over the Ashurites,

2:4 anointed David king. David had already been privately anointed king by Samuel (1 Sam. 16:3). This anointing recognized his rule in the southern area of Judah. Later he would be anointed as king over all Israel (2 Sam. 5:3). **men of Jabesh Gilead.** Jabesh, a city of Israel east of the Jordan, demonstrated its loyalty to Saul by giving him a proper burial (1 Sam. 31:11–13).

over Jezreel, over Ephraim, over Benjamin,
and over all Israel. 10 Ishbosheth, Saul's son,
was forty years old when he began to reign
over Israel, and he reigned two years. Only
the house of Judah followed David. 11 And the
time that David was king in Hebron over the
house of Judah was seven years and six
months.
12 Now Abner the son of Ner, and the servants of Ishbosheth the son of Saul, went out
from Mahanaim to Gibeon. 13 And Joab the son
of Zeruiah, and the servants of David, went
out and met them by the pool of Gibeon. So
they sat down, one on one side of the pool and
the other on the other side of the pool. 14 Then
Abner said to Joab, "Let the young men now
arise and compete before us."
And Joab said, "Let them arise."
15 So they arose and went over by number,
twelve from Benjamin, *followers* of Ishbosheth
the son of Saul, and twelve from the servants
of David. 16 And each one grasped his opponent
by the head and *thrust* his sword in his opponent's side; so they fell down together.
Therefore that place was called the Field of
Sharp Swords, which *is* in Gibeon. 17 So there
was a very fierce battle that day, and Abner
and the men of Israel were beaten before the
servants of David.
18 Now the three sons of Zeruiah were there:
Joab and Abishai and Asahel. And Asahel *was as*
fleet of foot as a wild gazelle. 19 So Asahel pursued Abner, and in going he did not turn to the
right hand or to the left from following Abner.
20 Then Abner looked behind him and said,
"*Are* you Asahel?"
He answered, "I *am*."
21 And Abner said to him, "Turn aside to your
right hand or to your left, and lay hold on one
of the young men and take his armor for yourself." But Asahel would not turn aside from
following him. 22 So Abner said again to Asahel,
"Turn aside from following me. Why should I
strike you to the ground? How then could I
face your brother Joab?" 23 However, he
refused to turn aside. Therefore Abner struck
him in the stomach with the blunt end of the
spear, so that the spear came out of his back;
and he fell down there and died on the spot.
So it was *that* as many as came to the place
where Asahel fell down and died, stood still.
24 Joab and Abishai also pursued Abner. And
the sun was going down when they came to
the hill of Ammah, which *is* before Giah by the
road to the Wilderness of Gibeon. 25 Now the
children of Benjamin gathered together
behind Abner and became a unit, and took
their stand on top of a hill. 26 Then Abner called

to Joab and said, "Shall the sword devour forever? Do you not know that it will be bitter in
the latter end? How long will it be then until
you tell the people to return from pursuing
their brethren?"
27And Joab said, "*As* God lives, unless you had
spoken, surely then by morning all the people
would have given up pursuing their brethren."
28So Joab blew a trumpet; and all the people
stood still and did not pursue Israel anymore,
nor did they fight anymore. 29Then Abner and
his men went on all that night through the plain,
crossed over the Jordan, and went through all
Bithron; and they came to Mahanaim.
30So Joab returned from pursuing Abner.
And when he had gathered all the people
together, there were missing of David's servants nineteen men and Asahel. 31But the servants of David had struck down, of Benjamin
and Abner's men, three hundred and sixty
men who died. 32Then they took up Asahel and
buried him in his father's tomb, which *was in*
Bethlehem. And Joab and his men went all
night, and they came to Hebron at daybreak.

Psalm 62:1–4

To the Chief Musician. To Jeduthun.
A Psalm of David.

Truly my soul silently *waits*
for God;
From Him *comes* my salvation.
2 He only *is* my rock and my salvation;
He is my defense;
I shall not be greatly moved.
3 How long will you attack a man?
You shall be slain, all of you,
Like a leaning wall and a tottering
fence.
4 They only consult to cast *him* down
from his high position;
They delight in lies;
They bless with their mouth,
But they curse inwardly. Selah

Proverbs 16:10–12

10 Divination *is* on the lips
of the king;
His mouth must not transgress in
judgment.
11 Honest weights and scales *are* the
LORD's;
All the weights in the bag *are* His
work.
12 *It is* an abomination for kings to
commit wickedness,
For a throne is established by
righteousness.

4:4 Samaria. When the nation of Israel split politically after Solomon's rule, King Omri named the capital of the northern kingdom of Israel "Samaria" (1 Kin. 16:24). The name eventually referred to the entire district and sometimes to the entire northern kingdom, which had been taken captive (capital, Samaria) by Assyria in 722 B.C. (2 Kin. 17:1–6). While Assyria led most of the populace of the 10 northern tribes away (into the region which today is northern Iraq), it left a sizable population of Jews in the northern Samaritan region and transported many non-Jews into Samaria. These groups intermingled to form a mixed race through intermarriage. Eventually tension developed between the Jews who returned from captivity and the Samaritans. The Samaritans withdrew from the worship of Yahweh at Jerusalem and established their worship at Mt. Gerizim in Samaria (vv. 20–22). Samaritans regarded only the Pentateuch as authoritative. As a result of this history, Jews repudiated Samaritans and considered them heretical. Intense ethnic and cultural tensions raged historically between the two groups so that both avoided contact as much as possible (v. 9; Ezra 4:1–24; Neh. 4:1–6; Luke 10:25–37).

John 4:1–30

4 Therefore, when the Lord knew that the
Pharisees had heard that Jesus made and
baptized more disciples than John 2(though Jesus Himself did not baptize, but His disciples),
3He left Judea and departed again to Galilee.
4But He needed to go through Samaria.
5So He came to a city of Samaria which is
called Sychar, near the plot of ground that Jacob gave to his son Joseph. 6Now Jacob's well
was there. Jesus therefore, being wearied
from *His* journey, sat thus by the well. It was
about the sixth hour.
7A woman of Samaria came to draw water.
Jesus said to her, "Give Me a drink." 8For His
disciples had gone away into the city to buy
food.
9Then the woman of Samaria said to Him,
"How is it that You, being a Jew, ask a drink
from me, a Samaritan woman?" For Jews have
no dealings with Samaritans.
10Jesus answered and said to her, "If you
knew the gift of God, and who it is who says to
you, 'Give Me a drink,' you would have asked
Him, and He would have given you living water."
11The woman said to Him, "Sir, You have
nothing to draw with, and the well is deep.

4:10 living water. The Old Testament is the background for this term, which has important metaphorical significance. In Jeremiah 2:13, Yahweh decries the disobedient Jews for rejecting Him, the "fountain of living waters." The Old Testament prophets looked forward to a time when "living waters shall flow from Jerusalem" (Zech. 14:8; Ezek. 47:9). The Old Testament metaphor spoke of the knowledge of God and His grace which provides cleansing, spiritual life, and the transforming power of the Holy Spirit (Is. 1:16–18; 12:3; 44:3; Ezek. 36:25–27). John applies these themes to Jesus Christ as the living water which is symbolic of eternal life mediated by the Holy Spirit from Him (v. 14; 6:35; 7:37–39). Jesus used the woman's need for physical water to sustain life in this arid region in order to serve as an object lesson for her need for spiritual transformation.

Where then do You get that living water? 12Are
You greater than our father Jacob, who gave
us the well, and drank from it himself, as well
as his sons and his livestock?"
13Jesus answered and said to her, "Whoever
drinks of this water will thirst again, 14but whoever drinks of the water that I shall give him will
never thirst. But the water that I shall give him
will become in him a fountain of water springing
up into everlasting life."
15The woman said to Him, "Sir, give me this
water, that I may not thirst, nor come here to
draw."
16Jesus said to her, "Go, call your husband,
and come here."
17The woman answered and said, "I have no
husband."
Jesus said to her, "You have well said, 'I
have no husband,' 18for you have had five husbands, and the one whom you now have is not
your husband; in that you spoke truly."
19The woman said to Him, "Sir, I perceive that
You are a prophet. 20Our fathers worshiped on
this mountain, and you *Jews* say that in Jerusalem is the place where one ought to worship."
21Jesus said to her, "Woman, believe Me, the
hour is coming when you will neither on this
mountain, nor in Jerusalem, worship the
Father. 22You worship what you do not know;
we know what we worship, for salvation is of
the Jews. 23But the hour is coming, and now is,
when the true worshipers will worship the
Father in spirit and truth; for the Father is
seeking such to worship Him. 24God *is* Spirit,
and those who worship Him must worship in
spirit and truth."
25The woman said to Him, "I know that Messiah is coming" (who is called Christ). "When
He comes, He will tell us all things."
26Jesus said to her, "I who speak to you am
He."
27And at this *point* His disciples came, and
they marveled that He talked with a woman;
yet no one said, "What do You seek?" or, "Why
are You talking with her?"
28The woman then left her waterpot, went
her way into the city, and said to the men,
29"Come, see a Man who told me all things that
I ever did. Could this be the Christ?" 30Then
they went out of the city and came to Him.

DAY 15: What aspect of worship toward God is absolutely essential?

In His conversation with the Samaritan woman in John 4:24, Jesus reminded her that "God is Spirit." This verse represents the classical statement on the nature of God as Spirit. The phrase means that God is invisible (Col. 1:15; 1 Tim. 1:17; Heb. 11:27) as opposed to the physical or material nature of man (1:18; 3:6). The word order of this phrase puts an emphasis on "Spirit," and the statement is essentially emphatic. Man could never comprehend the invisible God unless He revealed Himself, as He did in Scripture and the Incarnation.

"Must worship." Jesus is not speaking of a desirable element in worship but that which is absolutely necessary. "In spirit and truth." The word "spirit" does not refer to the Holy Spirit but to the human spirit. Jesus' point here is that a person must worship not simply by external conformity to religious rituals and places (outwardly) but inwardly ("in spirit") with the proper heart attitude. The reference to "truth" refers to worship of God consistent with the revealed Scripture and centered on the "Word made flesh" who ultimately revealed His Father (14:6).

The Samaritans also anticipated Messiah's coming. The Samaritan woman responded, pushing toward the future. "I who speak to you am He"—Jesus forthrightly declared Himself to be Messiah, though His habit was to avoid such declarations to His own Jewish people, who had such crassly political and militaristic views regarding Messiah (10:24; Mark 9:41). The "He" in this translation is not in the original Greek for Jesus literally said "I who speak to you am." The usage of "I am" is reminiscent of 8:58. This claim constitutes the main point of the story regarding the Samaritan woman, upon which all worship is centered.

MAY 16

2 Samuel 3:1–4:12

3 Now there was a long war between the
house of Saul and the house of David. But
David grew stronger and stronger, and the
house of Saul grew weaker and weaker.
2 Sons were born to David in Hebron: His firstborn was Amnon by Ahinoam the Jezreelitess;
3 his second, Chileab, by Abigail the widow of
Nabal the Carmelite; the third, Absalom the
son of Maacah, the daughter of Talmai, king of
Geshur; 4 the fourth, Adonijah the son of
Haggith; the fifth, Shephatiah the son of Abital;
5 and the sixth, Ithream, by David's wife Eglah.
These were born to David in Hebron.
6 Now it was so, while there was war
between the house of Saul and the house of
David, that Abner was strengthening *his hold*
on the house of Saul.
7 And Saul had a concubine, whose name *was*
Rizpah, the daughter of Aiah. So *Ishbosheth*
said to Abner, "Why have you gone in to my
father's concubine?"
8 Then Abner became very angry at the
words of Ishbosheth, and said, "*Am* I a dog's
head that belongs to Judah? Today I show loyalty to the house of Saul your father, to his
brothers, and to his friends, and have not
delivered you into the hand of David; and you
charge me today with a fault concerning this
woman? 9 May God do so to Abner, and more
also, if I do not do for David as the LORD has
sworn to him— 10 to transfer the kingdom from
the house of Saul, and set up the throne of David over Israel and over Judah, from Dan to
Beersheba." 11 And he could not answer Abner
another word, because he feared him.
12 Then Abner sent messengers on his behalf
to David, saying, "Whose *is* the land?" saying
also, "Make your covenant with me, and
indeed my hand *shall be* with you to bring all
Israel to you."
13 And *David* said, "Good, I will make a
covenant with you. But one thing I require of
you: you shall not see my face unless you first
bring Michal, Saul's daughter, when you
come to see my face." 14 So David sent messengers to Ishbosheth, Saul's son, saying,
"Give *me* my wife Michal, whom I betrothed
to myself for a hundred foreskins of the
Philistines." 15 And Ishbosheth sent and took
her from *her* husband, from Paltiel the son of
Laish. 16 Then her husband went along with her
to Bahurim, weeping behind her. So Abner
said to him, "Go, return!" And he returned.
17 Now Abner had communicated with the
elders of Israel, saying, "In time past you were
seeking for David *to be* king over you. 18 Now
then, do *it!* For the LORD has spoken of David,
saying, 'By the hand of My servant David, I
will save My people Israel from the hand of
the Philistines and the hand of all their enemies.' " 19 And Abner also spoke in the hearing
of Benjamin. Then Abner also went to speak in
the hearing of David in Hebron all that
seemed good to Israel and the whole house of
Benjamin.
20 So Abner and twenty men with him came
to David at Hebron. And David made a feast
for Abner and the men who *were* with him.
21 Then Abner said to David, "I will arise and
go, and gather all Israel to my lord the king,
that they may make a covenant with you, and
that you may reign over all that your heart
desires." So David sent Abner away, and he
went in peace.
22 At that moment the servants of David and
Joab came from a raid and brought much spoil
with them. But Abner *was* not with David in
Hebron, for he had sent him away, and he had
gone in peace. 23 When Joab and all the troops
that *were* with him had come, they told Joab,
saying, "Abner the son of Ner came to the
king, and he sent him away, and he has gone
in peace." 24 Then Joab came to the king and
said, "What have you done? Look, Abner came
to you; why *is* it *that* you sent him away, and he
has already gone? 25 Surely you realize that
Abner the son of Ner came to deceive you, to
know your going out and your coming in, and
to know all that you are doing."
26 And when Joab had gone from David's
presence, he sent messengers after Abner,
who brought him back from the well of Sirah.
But David did not know *it.* 27 Now when Abner
had returned to Hebron, Joab took him aside
in the gate to speak with him privately, and
there stabbed him in the stomach, so that he
died for the blood of Asahel his brother.

3:25 Abner...came to deceive you. It is ironic that Joab accused Abner of deception in spying on David in v. 25 when in v. 26 he deceived David by not telling him of his request to have Abner returned to Hebron. Joab used this deception to slay Abner out of personal vengeance for the death of his brother Asahel (v. 27; 2:19–23).

28 Afterward, when David heard *it,* he said, "My kingdom and I *are* guiltless before the LORD forever of the blood of Abner the son of Ner. 29 Let it rest on the head of Joab and on all his father's house; and let there never fail to be in the house of Joab one who has a discharge or is a leper, who leans on a staff or falls by the sword, or who lacks bread." 30 So Joab and Abishai his brother killed Abner, because he had killed their brother Asahel at Gibeon in the battle.

31 Then David said to Joab and to all the people who were with him, "Tear your clothes, gird yourselves with sackcloth, and mourn for Abner." And King David followed the coffin. 32 So they buried Abner in Hebron; and the king lifted up his voice and wept at the grave of Abner, and all the people wept. 33 And the king sang *a lament* over Abner and said:

"Should Abner die as a fool dies?
34 Your hands were not bound
Nor your feet put into fetters;
As a man falls before wicked men,
so you fell."

Then all the people wept over him again.

35 And when all the people came to persuade David to eat food while it was still day, David took an oath, saying, "God do so to me, and more also, if I taste bread or anything else till the sun goes down!" 36 Now all the people took note *of it,* and it pleased them, since whatever the king did pleased all the people. 37 For all the people and all Israel understood that day that it had not been the king's *intent* to kill Abner the son of Ner. 38 Then the king said to his servants, "Do you not know that a prince and a great man has fallen this day in Israel? 39 And I *am* weak today, though anointed king; and these men, the sons of Zeruiah, *are* too harsh for me. The LORD shall repay the evildoer according to his wickedness."

4 When Saul's son heard that Abner had died in Hebron, he lost heart, and all Israel was troubled. 2 Now Saul's son *had* two men *who were* captains of troops. The name of one *was* Baanah and the name of the other Rechab, the sons of Rimmon the Beerothite, of the children of Benjamin. (For Beeroth also was *part* of Benjamin, 3 because the Beerothites fled to Gittaim and have been sojourners there until this day.)

4 Jonathan, Saul's son, had a son *who was* lame in *his* feet. He was five years old when the news about Saul and Jonathan came from Jezreel; and his nurse took him up and fled. And it happened, as she made haste to flee, that he fell and became lame. His name *was* Mephibosheth.

4:4 Mephibosheth. He may be introduced here to demonstrate that his youth and physical handicap disqualified him from being considered for ruling Israel. He would have been only 12 years old at the time of Ishbosheth's death. For the history of this man, see 9:6–13; 16:1–4; 19:24–30; 21:7.

5 Then the sons of Rimmon the Beerothite, Rechab and Baanah, set out and came at about the heat of the day to the house of Ishbosheth, who was lying on his bed at noon. 6 And they came there, all the way into the house, *as though* to get wheat, and they stabbed him in the stomach. Then Rechab and Baanah his brother escaped. 7 For when they came into the house, he was lying on his bed in his bedroom; then they struck him and killed him, beheaded him and took his head, and were all night escaping through the plain. 8 And they brought the head of Ishbosheth to David at Hebron, and said to the king, "Here is the head of Ishbosheth, the son of Saul your enemy, who sought your life; and the LORD has avenged my lord the king this day of Saul and his descendants."

9 But David answered Rechab and Baanah his brother, the sons of Rimmon the Beerothite, and said to them, "*As* the LORD lives, who has redeemed my life from all adversity, 10 when someone told me, saying, 'Look, Saul is dead,' thinking to have brought good news, I arrested him and had him executed in Ziklag—the one who *thought* I would give him a reward for *his* news. 11 How much more, when wicked men have killed a righteous person in his own house on his bed? Therefore, shall I not now require his blood at your hand and remove you from the earth?" 12 So David commanded his young men, and they executed them, cut off their hands and feet, and hanged *them* by the pool in Hebron. But they took the head of Ishbosheth and buried *it* in the tomb of Abner in Hebron.

Psalm 62:5–12

5 My soul, wait silently for God alone,
For my expectation *is* from Him.
6 He only *is* my rock and my salvation;
He is my defense;
I shall not be moved.
7 In God *is* my salvation and my glory;
The rock of my strength,
And my refuge, *is* in God.

8 Trust in Him at all times, you people;
Pour out your heart before Him;
God is a refuge for us. Selah

9 Surely men of low degree *are* a vapor,
Men of high degree *are* a lie;
If they are weighed on the scales,
They *are* altogether *lighter* than vapor.
10 Do not trust in oppression,
Nor vainly hope in robbery;
If riches increase,
Do not set *your* heart *on them.*

11 God has spoken once,
Twice I have heard this:
That power *belongs* to God.
12 Also to You, O Lord, *belongs* mercy;
For You render to each one according
to his work.

Proverbs 16:13–15

13 Righteous lips *are* the delight of kings,
And they love him who speaks *what is*
right.
14 As messengers of death *is* the king's
wrath,
But a wise man will appease it.
15 In the light of the king's face *is* life,
And his favor *is* like a cloud of the
latter rain.

16:15 cloud of the latter rain. The late spring rain, which matured the crop, fell before the harvest (2 Sam. 23:3,4; Ps. 72:6) and is here compared to the king's power to grace his subjects with encouragement.

John 4:31–54

31In the meantime His disciples urged Him,
saying, "Rabbi, eat."
32But He said to them, "I have food to eat of
which you do not know."
33Therefore the disciples said to one another,
"Has anyone brought Him *anything* to eat?"
34Jesus said to them, "My food is to do the
will of Him who sent Me, and to finish His
work. 35Do you not say, 'There are still four
months and *then* comes the harvest'? Behold,
I say to you, lift up your eyes and look at the
fields, for they are already white for harvest!
36And he who reaps receives wages, and gathers fruit for eternal life, that both he who sows
and he who reaps may rejoice together. 37For in
this the saying is true: 'One sows and another
reaps.' 38I sent you to reap that for which you
have not labored; others have labored, and you
have entered into their labors."
39And many of the Samaritans of that city
believed in Him because of the word of the
woman who testified, "He told me all that I *ever*
did." 40So when the Samaritans had come to
Him, they urged Him to stay with them; and
He stayed there two days. 41And many more
believed because of His own word.
42Then they said to the woman, "Now we believe, not because of what you said, for we ourselves have heard *Him* and we know that this
is indeed the Christ, the Savior of the world."
43Now after the two days He departed from
there and went to Galilee. 44For Jesus Himself
testified that a prophet has no honor in his
own country. 45So when He came to Galilee,
the Galileans received Him, having seen all
the things He did in Jerusalem at the feast; for
they also had gone to the feast.

4:44 prophet has no honor in his own country. This proverb (also in Matt. 13:57; Mark 6:4) contrasts the believing response of the Samaritans (v. 39) with the characteristic unbelief of Jesus' own people in Galilee (and Judea) whose reticent faith depended so much on Jesus' performance of miracles (v. 48). While in Samaria, Jesus had enjoyed His first unqualified and unopposed success. His own people's hearts were not open to Him, but exhibited reluctance and hardness.

46So Jesus came again to Cana of Galilee
where He had made the water wine. And there
was a certain nobleman whose son was sick at
Capernaum. 47When he heard that Jesus had
come out of Judea into Galilee, he went to Him
and implored Him to come down and heal His
son, for he was at the point of death. 48Then Jesus said to him, "Unless you *people* see signs
and wonders, you will by no means believe."

4:48 Unless you *people* see signs and wonders. The "you" is plural. Jesus addresses these words to the Galileans as a whole and not just to the nobleman (vv. 45,46). The response of the Galileans was fundamentally flawed because it disregarded the person of Christ and centered in the need for a constant display of miraculous signs. Such an attitude represents the deepest state of unbelief.

[49]The nobleman said to Him, "Sir, come
down before my child dies!"
[50]Jesus said to him, "Go your way; your son
lives." So the man believed the word that Jesus spoke to him, and he went his way. [51]And
as he was now going down, his servants met
him and told *him,* saying, "Your son lives!"
[52]Then he inquired of them the hour when
he got better. And they said to him,
"Yesterday at the seventh hour the fever left
him." [53]So the father knew that *it was* at the
same hour in which Jesus said to him, "Your
son lives." And he himself believed, and his
whole household.
[54]This again *is* the second sign Jesus did
when He had come out of Judea into Galilee.

DAY 16: What is a believer's role in the evangelism of the world?

In the context of the Samaritan woman and village coming to faith in Christ, Jesus spoke of the harvest and the need for workers in John 4:35. Jesus used the fact that they were surrounded by crops growing in the field and waiting to be harvested as an object lesson to illustrate His urgency about reaching the lost, which the "harvest" symbolized. The event probably happened in December or January, which was 4 months before the normal spring harvest (mid-April). Crops were planted in November, and by December or January the grain would be sprouting up in vibrant green color. Jesus points out the Samaritan woman and people of Sychar ("lift up your eyes") who were at that moment coming upon the scene (v. 30) looking like a ripened "harvest" that urgently need to be "gathered," i.e., evangelized. "Already white for harvest." Their white clothing seen above the growing grain may have looked like white heads on the stalks, an indication of readiness for harvest. Jesus knew the hearts of all (2:24), so was able to state their readiness for salvation (vv. 39–41).

This episode represents the first instance of cross-cultural evangelism (Acts 1:8). In vv. 36–38, the Lord's call to His disciples to do the work of evangelism both then and now contains promises of reward ("wages"), fruit that brings eternal joy (v. 36), and the mutual partnership of shared privilege (vv. 37,38).

When He talked with the Samaritan woman, Jesus was performing the will of the Father and thereby received greater sustenance and satisfaction than any mere physical food could offer Him (v. 34). Obedience to and dependence upon God's will summed up Jesus' whole life (Eph. 5:17). Certainly, the same is true for any follower of Christ.

MAY 17

2 Samuel 5:1–6:23

5 Then all the tribes of Israel came to David
at Hebron and spoke, saying, "Indeed we
are your bone and your flesh. [2]Also, in time
past, when Saul was king over us, you were the
one who led Israel out and brought them in;
and the LORD said to you, 'You shall shepherd
My people Israel, and be ruler over Israel.' "
[3]Therefore all the elders of Israel came to the
king at Hebron, and King David made a
covenant with them at Hebron before the
LORD. And they anointed David king over Israel. [4]David *was* thirty years old when he
began to reign, *and* he reigned forty years. [5]In
Hebron he reigned over Judah seven years
and six months, and in Jerusalem he reigned
thirty-three years over all Israel and Judah.
[6]And the king and his men went to Jerusalem
against the Jebusites, the inhabitants of the
land, who spoke to David, saying, "You shall
not come in here; but the blind and the lame
will repel you," thinking, "David cannot come
in here." [7]Nevertheless David took the stronghold of Zion (that *is,* the City of David).
[8]Now David said on that day, "Whoever
climbs up by way of the water shaft and defeats
the Jebusites (the lame and the blind, *who are*
hated by David's soul), *he shall be chief and
captain."* Therefore they say, "The blind and
the lame shall not come into the house."
[9]Then David dwelt in the stronghold, and
called it the City of David. And David built all

5:1,2 all the tribes of Israel. The term "all" is used 3 times (vv. 1,3,5) to emphasize that the kingdom established under King David was truly a united monarchy. The "elders" of Israel (v. 3), representing the "tribes" (v. 1), came to David at Hebron with the express purpose of submitting to his rule. Three reasons were given by the Israelites for wanting to make David king: 1) he was an Israelite brother (Deut. 17:15); 2) he was Israel's best warrior and commander; and 3) he had been chosen by the Lord to be the king of Israel.

around from the Millo and inward. [10]So David went on and became great, and the LORD God of hosts *was* with him.

[11]Then Hiram king of Tyre sent messengers to David, and cedar trees, and carpenters and masons. And they built David a house. [12]So David knew that the LORD had established him as king over Israel, and that He had exalted His kingdom for the sake of His people Israel.

[13]And David took more concubines and wives from Jerusalem, after he had come from Hebron. Also more sons and daughters were born to David. [14]Now these *are* the names of those who were born to him in Jerusalem: Shammua, Shobab, Nathan, Solomon, [15]Ibhar, Elishua, Nepheg, Japhia, [16]Elishama, Eliada, and Eliphelet.

[17]Now when the Philistines heard that they had anointed David king over Israel, all the Philistines went up to search for David. And David heard *of it* and went down to the stronghold. [18]The Philistines also went and deployed themselves in the Valley of Rephaim. [19]So David inquired of the LORD, saying, "Shall I go up against the Philistines? Will You deliver them into my hand?"

And the LORD said to David, "Go up, for I will doubtless deliver the Philistines into your hand."

[20]So David went to Baal Perazim, and David defeated them there; and he said, "The LORD has broken through my enemies before me, like a breakthrough of water." Therefore he called the name of that place Baal Perazim. [21]And they left their images there, and David and his men carried them away.

[22]Then the Philistines went up once again and deployed themselves in the Valley of Rephaim. [23]Therefore David inquired of the LORD, and He said, "You shall not go up; circle around behind them, and come upon them in front of the mulberry trees. [24]And it shall be, when you hear the sound of marching in the tops of the mulberry trees, then you shall advance quickly. For then the LORD will go out before you to strike the camp of the Philistines." [25]And David did so, as the LORD commanded him; and he drove back the Philistines from Geba as far as Gezer.

6 Again David gathered all *the* choice *men* of Israel, thirty thousand. [2]And David arose and went with all the people who *were* with him from Baale Judah to bring up from there the ark of God, whose name is called by the Name, the LORD of Hosts, who dwells *between* the cherubim. [3]So they set the ark of God on a new cart, and brought it out of the house of Abinadab, which *was* on the hill; and Uzzah and Ahio, the sons of Abinadab, drove the new cart. [4]And they brought it out of the house of Abinadab, which *was* on the hill, accompanying the ark of God; and Ahio went before the ark. [5]Then David and all the house of Israel played *music* before the LORD on all kinds of *instruments of* fir wood, on harps, on stringed instruments, on tambourines, on sistrums, and on cymbals.

[6]And when they came to Nachon's threshing floor, Uzzah put out *his hand* to the ark of God and took hold of it, for the oxen stumbled. [7]Then the anger of the LORD was aroused against Uzzah, and God struck him there for *his* error; and he died there by the ark of God. [8]And David became angry because of the LORD's outbreak against Uzzah; and he called the name of the place Perez Uzzah to this day. [9]David was afraid of the LORD that day; and he said, "How can the ark of the LORD come to me?" [10]So David would not move the ark of the LORD with him into the City of David; but David took it aside into the house of Obed-Edom the Gittite. [11]The ark of the LORD remained in the house of Obed-Edom the Gittite three months. And the LORD blessed Obed-Edom and all his household.

[12]Now it was told King David, saying, "The LORD has blessed the house of Obed-Edom and all that *belongs* to him, because of the ark of God." So David went and brought up the ark of God from the house of Obed-Edom to the City of David with gladness. [13]And so it was, when those bearing the ark of the LORD had gone six paces, that he sacrificed oxen and fatted sheep. [14]Then David danced before the LORD with all *his* might; and David *was* wearing a linen ephod. [15]So David and all the house of Israel brought up the ark of the LORD with shouting and with the sound of the trumpet.

[16]Now as the ark of the LORD came into the City of David, Michal, Saul's daughter, looked through a window and saw King David leaping and whirling before the LORD; and she despised him in her heart. [17]So they brought the ark of the LORD, and set it in its place in the midst of the tabernacle that David had erected for it. Then David offered burnt offerings and peace offerings before the LORD. [18]And when David had finished offering burnt offerings and peace offerings, he blessed the people in the name of the LORD of hosts. [19]Then he distributed among all the people, among the whole multitude of Israel, both the women and the men, to everyone a loaf of bread, a piece *of meat,* and a cake of raisins. So all the people departed, everyone to his house.

[20]Then David returned to bless his household. And Michal the daughter of Saul came out

to meet David, and said, "How glorious was the king of Israel today, uncovering himself today in the eyes of the maids of his servants, as one of the base fellows shamelessly uncovers himself!"
[21]So David said to Michal, "*It was* before the LORD, who chose me instead of your father and all his house, to appoint me ruler over the people of the LORD, over Israel. Therefore I will play *music* before the LORD. [22]And I will be even more undignified than this, and will be humble in my own sight. But as for the maidservants of whom you have spoken, by them I will be held in honor."
[23]Therefore Michal the daughter of Saul had no children to the day of her death.

Psalm 63:1–11

A Psalm of David when he was in the wilderness of Judah.

O God, You *are* my God;
Early will I seek You;
My soul thirsts for You;
My flesh longs for You
In a dry and thirsty land
Where there is no water.
2 So I have looked for You in the sanctuary,
To see Your power and Your glory.

63:1 Early will I seek You. Eagerness to be with the Lord in every situation is more in view than the time of day. **My soul thirsts.** David longs for God's presence like a wanderer in a desert longs for water. **In a dry and thirsty land.** David writes this psalm while hiding in the wilderness of Judea, but longing to be back worshiping in Jerusalem.

3 Because Your lovingkindness *is* better than life,
My lips shall praise You.
4 Thus I will bless You while I live;
I will lift up my hands in Your name.
5 My soul shall be satisfied as with marrow and fatness,
And my mouth shall praise *You* with joyful lips.
6 When I remember You on my bed,
I meditate on You in the *night* watches.
7 Because You have been my help,
Therefore in the shadow of Your wings I will rejoice.
8 My soul follows close behind You;
Your right hand upholds me.
9 But those *who* seek my life, to destroy *it*,
Shall go into the lower parts of the earth.
10 They shall fall by the sword;
They shall be a portion for jackals.
11 But the king shall rejoice in God;
Everyone who swears by Him shall glory;
But the mouth of those who speak lies shall be stopped.

Proverbs 16:16–17

16 How much better to get wisdom than gold!
And to get understanding is to be chosen rather than silver.
17 The highway of the upright *is* to depart from evil;
He who keeps his way preserves his soul.

John 5:1–23

5 After this there was a feast of the Jews,
and Jesus went up to Jerusalem. [2]Now
there is in Jerusalem by the Sheep *Gate* a
pool, which is called in Hebrew, Bethesda,
having five porches. [3]In these lay a great multitude of sick people, blind, lame, paralyzed,
waiting for the moving of the water. [4]For an
angel went down at a certain time into the
pool and stirred up the water; then whoever
stepped in first, after the stirring of the water,
was made well of whatever disease he had.
[5]Now a certain man was there who had an
infirmity thirty-eight years. [6]When Jesus saw
him lying there, and knew that he already had

5:10,11 The Old Testament had forbidden work on the Sabbath but did not stipulate what "work" was specifically indicated (Ex. 20:8–11). The assumption in Scripture seems to be that "work" was one's customary employment, but rabbinical opinion had developed oral tradition beyond the Old Testament which stipulated 39 activities forbidden (Mishnah *Shabbath* 7:2; 10:5), including carrying anything from one domain to another. Thus, the man had broken oral tradition, not Old Testament law.

5:14 Sin no more, lest a worse thing come upon you. The basic thrust of Jesus' comments here indicates that sin has its inevitable consequences (Gal. 6:7,8). Although Scripture makes clear that not all disease is a consequence of sin (9:1–3; Luke 13:1–5), illness at times may be directly tied into one's moral turpitude (1 Cor. 11:29,30; James 5:15). Jesus may specifically have chosen this man in order to highlight this point.

been *in that condition* a long time, He said to
him, "Do you want to be made well?"
7The sick man answered Him, "Sir, I have no
man to put me into the pool when the water is
stirred up; but while I am coming, another
steps down before me."
8Jesus said to him, "Rise, take up your bed
and walk." 9And immediately the man was
made well, took up his bed, and walked.
And that day was the Sabbath. 10The Jews
therefore said to him who was cured, "It is the
Sabbath; it is not lawful for you to carry your
bed."
11He answered them, "He who made me
well said to me, 'Take up your bed and walk.'"
12Then they asked him, "Who is the Man
who said to you, 'Take up your bed and walk'?"
13But the one who was healed did not know
who it was, for Jesus had withdrawn, a multitude being in *that* place. 14Afterward Jesus
found him in the temple, and said to him, "See,
you have been made well. Sin no more, lest a
worse thing come upon you."
15The man departed and told the Jews that it
was Jesus who had made him well.
16For this reason the Jews persecuted Jesus,
and sought to kill Him, because He had done
these things on the Sabbath. 17But Jesus
answered them, "My Father has been working
until now, and I have been working."
18Therefore the Jews sought all the more to
kill Him, because He not only broke the
Sabbath, but also said that God was His
Father, making Himself equal with God.
19Then Jesus answered and said to them,
"Most assuredly, I say to you, the Son can do
nothing of Himself, but what He sees the
Father do; for whatever He does, the Son also
does in like manner. 20For the Father loves the
Son, and shows Him all things that He Himself
does; and He will show Him greater works
than these, that you may marvel. 21For as the
Father raises the dead and gives life to *them,*
even so the Son gives life to whom He will.
22For the Father judges no one, but has committed all judgment to the Son, 23that all should
honor the Son just as they honor the Father.
He who does not honor the Son does not
honor the Father who sent Him.

DAY 17: Why did Jesus not back down to religious hypocrisy?

A careful reading of John 5:17–47 reveals the ultimate reason Jesus confronted the Jews' religious hypocrisy, i.e., the opportunity to declare who He was. This section is Christ's own personal statement of His deity. As such, it is one of the greatest Christological discourses in Scripture. Herein Jesus makes 5 claims to equality with God: 1) He is equal with God in His person (vv. 17,18); 2) He is equal with God in His works (vv. 19,20); 3) He is equal with God in His power and sovereignty (v. 21); 4) He is equal with God in His judgment (v. 22); and 5) He is equal with God in His honor (v. 23).

In v. 17, Jesus' point is that whether He broke the Sabbath or not, God was working continuously and, since Jesus Himself worked continuously, He also must be God. Furthermore, God does not need a day of rest for He never wearies (Is. 40:28). For Jesus' self-defense to be valid, the same factors that apply to God must also apply to Him. Jesus is Lord of the Sabbath! (Matt. 12:8). Interestingly, even the rabbis admitted that God's work had not ceased after the Sabbath because He sustains the universe.

In response to Jewish hostility at the implications of His assertions of equality with God (v. 18), Jesus became even more fearless, forceful, and emphatic. "Most assuredly" (v. 19) is an emphatic way of saying "I'm telling you the truth." Jesus essentially tied His activities of healing on the Sabbath directly to the Father. The Son never took independent action that set Him against the Father because the Son only did those things that were coincident with and coextensive with all that the Father does. Jesus thus implied that the only One who could do what the Father does must be as great as the Father.

MAY 18

2 Samuel 7:1–8:18

7 Now it came to pass when the king was
dwelling in his house, and the LORD had
given him rest from all his enemies all around,
2 that the king said to Nathan the prophet, "See
now, I dwell in a house of cedar, but the ark of
God dwells inside tent curtains."
3 Then Nathan said to the king, "Go, do all
that *is* in your heart, for the LORD *is* with you."
4 But it happened that night that the word of
the LORD came to Nathan, saying, 5 "Go and tell
My servant David, 'Thus says the LORD:
"Would you build a house for Me to dwell in?
6 For I have not dwelt in a house since the time
that I brought the children of Israel up from
Egypt, even to this day, but have moved about
in a tent and in a tabernacle. 7 Wherever I have
moved about with all the children of Israel,
have I ever spoken a word to anyone from the
tribes of Israel, whom I commanded to shepherd My people Israel, saying, 'Why have you
not built Me a house of cedar?' " ' 8 Now there-
fore, thus shall you say to My servant David,
'Thus says the LORD of hosts: "I took you from
the sheepfold, from following the sheep, to be
ruler over My people, over Israel. 9 And I have
been with you wherever you have gone, and
have cut off all your enemies from before you,
and have made you a great name, like the
name of the great men who *are* on the earth.
10 Moreover I will appoint a place for My people
Israel, and will plant them, that they may dwell
in a place of their own and move no more; nor
shall the sons of wickedness oppress them
anymore, as previously, 11 since the time that I
commanded judges *to be* over My people Israel, and have caused you to rest from all your
enemies. Also the LORD tells you that He will
make you a house.
12 "When your days are fulfilled and you rest
with your fathers, I will set up your seed after
you, who will come from your body, and I will
establish his kingdom. 13 He shall build a house
for My name, and I will establish the throne of
his kingdom forever. 14 I will be his Father, and
he shall be My son. If he commits iniquity, I
will chasten him with the rod of men and with
the blows of the sons of men. 15 But My mercy
shall not depart from him, as I took *it* from
Saul, whom I removed from before you. 16 And
your house and your kingdom shall be established forever before you. Your throne shall be
established forever." ' "

7:14 his Father...My son. These words are directly related to Jesus the Messiah in Hebrews 1:5. In Semitic thought, since the son had the full character of the father, the future seed of David would have the same essence of God. That Jesus Christ was God incarnate is the central theme of John's Gospel. **If he commits iniquity.** As a human father disciplines his sons, so the Lord would discipline the seed, if he committed iniquity. This has reference to the intermediary seed until Messiah's arrival (any king of David's line from Solomon on). However, the ultimate Seed of David will not be a sinner like David and his descendants were, as recorded in Samuel and Kings (see 2 Cor. 5:21). Significantly, Chronicles, focusing more directly on the Messiah, does not include this statement in its record of Nathan's words (1 Chr. 17:13).

7:16 your house...your kingdom...Your throne. Luke 1:32b,33 indicates that these 3 terms are fulfilled in Jesus, "...and the Lord God will give Him the *throne* of His father David. And He will reign over the *house* of Jacob forever, and of His *kingdom* there will be no end." **forever.** This word conveys the idea of 1) an indeterminately long time or 2) into eternity future. It does not mean that there cannot be interruptions, but rather that the outcome is guaranteed. Christ's Davidic reign will conclude human history.

17 According to all these words and according
to all this vision, so Nathan spoke to David.
18 Then King David went in and sat before
the LORD; and he said: "Who *am* I, O Lord
GOD? And what is my house, that You have
brought me this far? 19 And yet this was a
small thing in Your sight, O Lord GOD; and
You have also spoken of Your servant's house
for a great while to come. *Is* this the manner
of man, O Lord GOD? 20 Now what more can
David say to You? For You, Lord GOD, know
Your servant. 21 For Your word's sake, and
according to Your own heart, You have done
all these great things, to make Your servant
know *them*. 22 Therefore You are great, O Lord
GOD. For *there is* none like You, nor *is there*
any God besides You, according to all that we
have heard with our ears. 23 And who *is* like
Your people, like Israel, the one nation on the
earth whom God went to redeem for Himself
as a people, to make for Himself a name—

and to do for Yourself great and awesome deeds for Your land—before Your people whom You redeemed for Yourself from Egypt, the nations, and their gods? [24]For You have made Your people Israel Your very own people forever; and You, LORD, have become their God.

[25]"Now, O LORD God, the word which You have spoken concerning Your servant and concerning his house, establish *it* forever and do as You have said. [26]So let Your name be magnified forever, saying, 'The LORD of hosts *is* the God over Israel.' And let the house of Your servant David be established before You. [27]For You, O LORD of hosts, God of Israel, have revealed *this* to Your servant, saying, 'I will build you a house.' Therefore Your servant has found it in his heart to pray this prayer to You.

[28]"And now, O Lord GOD, You are God, and Your words are true, and You have promised this goodness to Your servant. [29]Now therefore, let it please You to bless the house of Your servant, that it may continue before You forever; for You, O Lord GOD, have spoken *it,* and with Your blessing let the house of Your servant be blessed forever."

8 After this it came to pass that David attacked the Philistines and subdued them. And David took Metheg Ammah from the hand of the Philistines.

[2]Then he defeated Moab. Forcing them down to the ground, he measured them off with a line. With two lines he measured off those to be put to death, and with one full line those to be kept alive. So the Moabites became David's servants, *and* brought tribute.

[3]David also defeated Hadadezer the son of Rehob, king of Zobah, as he went to recover his territory at the River Euphrates. [4]David took from him one thousand *chariots,* seven hundred horsemen, and twenty thousand foot soldiers. Also David hamstrung all the chariot *horses,* except that he spared *enough* of them for one hundred chariots.

[5]When the Syrians of Damascus came to help Hadadezer king of Zobah, David killed twenty-two thousand of the Syrians. [6]Then David put garrisons in Syria of Damascus; and the Syrians became David's servants, *and* brought tribute. So the LORD preserved David wherever he went. [7]And David took the shields of gold that had belonged to the servants of Hadadezer, and brought them to Jerusalem. [8]Also from Betah and from Berothai, cities of Hadadezer, King David took a large amount of bronze.

[9]When Toi king of Hamath heard that David had defeated all the army of Hadadezer, [10]then Toi sent Joram his son to King David, to greet him and bless him, because he had fought against Hadadezer and defeated him (for Hadadezer had been at war with Toi); and *Joram* brought with him articles of silver, articles of gold, and articles of bronze. [11]King David also dedicated these to the LORD, along with the silver and gold that he had dedicated from all the nations which he had subdued—[12]from Syria, from Moab, from the people of Ammon, from the Philistines, from Amalek, and from the spoil of Hadadezer the son of Rehob, king of Zobah.

[13]And David made *himself* a name when he returned from killing eighteen thousand Syrians in the Valley of Salt. [14]He also put garrisons in Edom; throughout all Edom he put garrisons, and all the Edomites became David's servants. And the LORD preserved David wherever he went.

[15]So David reigned over all Israel; and David administered judgment and justice to all his people. [16]Joab the son of Zeruiah *was* over the army; Jehoshaphat the son of Ahilud *was* recorder; [17]Zadok the son of Ahitub and Ahimelech the son of Abiathar *were* the priests; Seraiah *was* the scribe; [18]Benaiah the son of Jehoiada *was over* both the Cherethites and the Pelethites; and David's sons were chief ministers.

64:1 Preserve...from fear. This word for "fear" means "dread" and is a different Hebrew word than the "fear" in verses 4 and 9. The psalmist recognized that the fear of an enemy can be as destructive as an actual assault.

Psalm 64:1–10

To the Chief Musician. A Psalm of David.

Hear my voice, O God, in
my meditation;
Preserve my life from fear of the
enemy.
2 Hide me from the secret plots
of the wicked,
From the rebellion of the workers
of iniquity,
3 Who sharpen their tongue
like a sword,
And bend *their bows to shoot* their
arrows—bitter words,

5:36 the very works that I do. See 10:25. The miracles of Jesus were witness to His deity and messiahship. Such miracles are the major signs recorded by John in this Gospel, so as to fulfill His purpose in 20:30,31.

5:39 You search. Although the verb "search" could also be understood as a command (i.e., "Search the Scriptures!"), most prefer this translation as an indicative. The verb implies diligent scrutiny in investigating the Scriptures to find "eternal life." However, Jesus points out that with all their fastidious effort, they miserably failed in their understanding of the true way to eternal life through the Son of God. **testify of Me.** See v. 45. Christ is the main theme of Scripture.

4 That they may shoot in secret at the
blameless;
Suddenly they shoot at him and
do not fear.

5 They encourage themselves
in an evil matter;
They talk of laying snares secretly;
They say, "Who will see them?"
6 They devise iniquities:
"We have perfected a shrewd
scheme."
Both the inward thought and
the heart of man are deep.

7 But God shall shoot at them *with* an
arrow;
Suddenly they shall be wounded.
8 So He will make them stumble over
their own tongue;
All who see them shall flee away.
9 All men shall fear,
And shall declare the work of God;
For they shall wisely consider His
doing.
10 The righteous shall be glad in the
LORD, and trust in Him.
And all the upright in heart
shall glory.

Proverbs 16:18–19

18 Pride *goes* before destruction,
And a haughty spirit before a fall.
19 Better *to be* of a humble spirit with
the lowly,
Than to divide the spoil with
the proud.

John 5:24–47

24 "Most assuredly, I say to you, he who
hears My word and believes in Him who sent
Me has everlasting life, and shall not come
into judgment, but has passed from death into
life. 25 Most assuredly, I say to you, the hour is
coming, and now is, when the dead will hear
the voice of the Son of God; and those who
hear will live. 26 For as the Father has life in
Himself, so He has granted the Son to have
life in Himself, 27 and has given Him authority to
execute judgment also, because He is the Son
of Man. 28 Do not marvel at this; for the hour is
coming in which all who are in the graves will
hear His voice 29 and come forth—those who
have done good, to the resurrection of life,
and those who have done evil, to the resurrection of condemnation. 30 I can of Myself do
nothing. As I hear, I judge; and My judgment
is righteous, because I do not seek My own
will but the will of the Father who sent Me.

31 "If I bear witness of Myself, My witness is
not true. 32 There is another who bears witness
of Me, and I know that the witness which He
witnesses of Me is true. 33 You have sent to
John, and he has borne witness to the truth.
34 Yet I do not receive testimony from man, but
I say these things that you may be saved. 35 He
was the burning and shining lamp, and you
were willing for a time to rejoice in his light.
36 But I have a greater witness than John's; for
the works which the Father has given Me to
finish—the very works that I do—bear witness of Me, that the Father has sent Me. 37 And
the Father Himself, who sent Me, has testified
of Me. You have neither heard His voice at any
time, nor seen His form. 38 But you do not have
His word abiding in you, because whom He
sent, Him you do not believe. 39 You search the
Scriptures, for in them you think you have
eternal life; and these are they which testify of
Me. 40 But you are not willing to come to Me
that you may have life.

41 "I do not receive honor from men. 42 But I
know you, that you do not have the love of
God in you. 43 I have come in My Father's
name, and you do not receive Me; if another
comes in his own name, him you will receive.
44 How can you believe, who receive honor
from one another, and do not seek the honor
that *comes* from the only God? 45 Do not think
that I shall accuse you to the Father; there is
one who accuses you—Moses, in whom you
trust. 46 For if you believed Moses, you would
believe Me; for he wrote about Me. 47 But if you
do not believe his writings, how will you
believe My words?"

DAY 18: What was the Davidic Covenant?

Second Samuel 7:1–17 record the establishment of the Davidic Covenant, God's unconditional promise to David and his posterity. While not called a covenant here, it is later (23:5). This promise is an important key to understanding God's irrevocable pledge of a king from the line of David to rule forever (v. 16). It has been estimated that over 40 individual biblical passages are directly related to these verses (see Pss. 89; 110; 132); thus, this text is a major highlight in the Old Testament. The ultimate fulfillment comes at Christ's Second Advent when He sets up His millennial kingdom on earth (see Ezek. 37; Zech. 14; Rev. 19). This is the fourth of 5 irrevocable, unconditional covenants made by God. The first 3 include: 1) the Noahic Covenant (Gen. 9:8–17); 2) the Abrahamic Covenant (Gen. 15:12–21); and 3) the Levitic or Priestly Covenant (Num. 3:1–18; 18:1–20; 25:10–13). The New Covenant, which actually provided redemption, was revealed later through Jeremiah (Jer. 31:31–34) and accomplished by the death and resurrection of Jesus Christ.

Specifically, 2 Samuel 7:8–16 state the promises the Lord gave to David. Verses 8–11a give the promises to be realized during David's lifetime. Verses 11b–16 state the promises that would be fulfilled after David's death. During David's lifetime, the Lord: 1) gave David "a great name"; 2) appointed a place for Israel; and 3) gave David "rest" from all his enemies. After David's death, the Lord gave David: 1) a son to sit on his national throne, whom the Lord would oversee as a father with necessary chastening, discipline, and mercy (Solomon); and 2) a Son who would rule a kingdom that will be established forever (Messiah). This prophecy referred in its immediacy to Solomon and to the temporal kingdom of David's family in the land. But in a larger and more sublime sense, it refers to David's greater Son of another nature, Jesus Christ (Heb. 1:8).

MAY 19

2 Samuel 9:1–10:19

9 Now David said, "Is there still anyone who
is left of the house of Saul, that I may show
him kindness for Jonathan's sake?"
2And *there was* a servant of the house of Saul
whose name *was* Ziba. So when they had
called him to David, the king said to him, "*Are*
you Ziba?"
He said, "At your service!"
3Then the king said, "*Is* there not still someone
of the house of Saul, to whom I may show
the kindness of God?"
And Ziba said to the king, "There is still a
son of Jonathan *who is* lame in *his* feet."
4So the king said to him, "Where *is* he?"
And Ziba said to the king, "Indeed he *is* in
the house of Machir the son of Ammiel, in Lo
Debar."
5Then King David sent and brought him out
of the house of Machir the son of Ammiel,
from Lo Debar.
6Now when Mephibosheth the son of Jonathan,
the son of Saul, had come to David, he
fell on his face and prostrated himself. Then
David said, "Mephibosheth?"
And he answered, "Here is your servant!"
7So David said to him, "Do not fear, for I will
surely show you kindness for Jonathan your
father's sake, and will restore to you all the
land of Saul your grandfather; and you shall
eat bread at my table continually."
8Then he bowed himself, and said, "What *is*
your servant, that you should look upon such
a dead dog as I?"

9:8 dead dog. A "dead dog" was considered contemptible and useless. Mephibosheth saw himself as such in that he knew that he had not merited David's kindness and that there was no way for him to repay it. David's offer was an extraordinary expression of grace and beauty to his covenant with Jonathan (1 Sam. 18:3; 20:15,42).

9And the king called to Ziba, Saul's servant,
and said to him, "I have given to your master's
son all that belonged to Saul and to all his
house. 10You therefore, and your sons and your
servants, shall work the land for him, and you
shall bring in *the harvest,* that your master's
son may have food to eat. But Mephibosheth
your master's son shall eat bread at my table
always." Now Ziba had fifteen sons and twenty
servants.
11Then Ziba said to the king, "According to
all that my lord the king has commanded his
servant, so will your servant do."
"As for Mephibosheth," *said the king,* "he
shall eat at my table like one of the king's
sons." 12Mephibosheth had a young son whose
name *was* Micha. And all who dwelt in the
house of Ziba *were* servants of Mephibosheth.
13So Mephibosheth dwelt in Jerusalem, for he

ate continually at the king's table. And he was lame in both his feet.

10 It happened after this that the king of the people of Ammon died, and Hanun his son reigned in his place. 2Then David said, "I will show kindness to Hanun the son of Nahash, as his father showed kindness to me."

So David sent by the hand of his servants to comfort him concerning his father. And David's servants came into the land of the people of Ammon. 3And the princes of the people of Ammon said to Hanun their lord, "Do you think that David really honors your father because he has sent comforters to you? Has David not *rather* sent his servants to you to search the city, to spy it out, and to overthrow it?"

4Therefore Hanun took David's servants, shaved off half of their beards, cut off their garments in the middle, at their buttocks, and sent them away. 5When they told David, he sent to meet them, because the men were greatly ashamed. And the king said, "Wait at Jericho until your beards have grown, and *then* return."

10:4 shaved off half of their beards. Forced shaving was considered an insult and a sign of submission (Is. 7:20). **cut off their garments...at their buttocks.** To those who wore long garments in that time, exposure of the buttocks was a shameful practice inflicted on prisoners of war (Is. 20:4).

6When the people of Ammon saw that they had made themselves repulsive to David, the people of Ammon sent and hired the Syrians of Beth Rehob and the Syrians of Zoba, twenty thousand foot soldiers; and from the king of Maacah one thousand men, and from Ish-Tob twelve thousand men. 7Now when David heard *of it,* he sent Joab and all the army of the mighty men. 8Then the people of Ammon came out and put themselves in battle array at the entrance of the gate. And the Syrians of Zoba, Beth Rehob, Ish-Tob, and Maacah *were* by themselves in the field.

9When Joab saw that the battle line was against him before and behind, he chose some of Israel's best and put *them* in battle array against the Syrians. 10And the rest of the people he put under the command of Abishai his brother, that he might set *them* in battle array against the people of Ammon. 11Then he said, "If the Syrians are too strong for me, then you shall help me; but if the people of Ammon are too strong for you, then I will come and help you. 12Be of good courage, and let us be strong for our people and for the cities of our God. And may the LORD do *what is* good in His sight."

13So Joab and the people who *were* with him drew near for the battle against the Syrians, and they fled before him. 14When the people of Ammon saw that the Syrians were fleeing, they also fled before Abishai, and entered the city. So Joab returned from the people of Ammon and went to Jerusalem.

15When the Syrians saw that they had been defeated by Israel, they gathered together. 16Then Hadadezer sent and brought out the Syrians who *were* beyond the River, and they came to Helam. And Shobach the commander of Hadadezer's army *went* before them. 17When it was told David, he gathered all Israel, crossed over the Jordan, and came to Helam. And the Syrians set themselves in battle array against David and fought with him. 18Then the Syrians fled before Israel; and David killed seven hundred charioteers and forty thousand horsemen of the Syrians, and struck Shobach the commander of their army, who died there. 19And when all the kings *who were* servants to Hadadezer saw that they were defeated by Israel, they made peace with Israel and served them. So the Syrians were afraid to help the people of Ammon anymore.

Psalm 65:1–8

To the Chief Musician. A Psalm of David. A Song.

Praise is awaiting You,
O God, in Zion;
And to You the vow shall be performed.
2 O You who hear prayer,
To You all flesh will come.
3 Iniquities prevail against me;
As for our transgressions,
You will provide atonement for them.
4 Blessed *is the man* You choose,
And cause to approach *You,*
That he may dwell in Your courts.
We shall be satisfied with the goodness
of Your house,
Of Your holy temple.
5 *By* awesome deeds in righteousness You
will answer us,
O God of our salvation,
You who are the confidence of all the
ends of the earth,
And of the far-off seas;
6 Who established the mountains by His
strength,
Being clothed with power;
7 You who still the noise of the seas,

The noise of their waves,
And the tumult of the peoples.
8 They also who dwell in the farthest parts are afraid of Your signs;
You make the outgoings of the morning and evening rejoice.

Proverbs 16:20–21

20 He who heeds the word wisely will find good,
And whoever trusts in the LORD, happy *is* he.

21 The wise in heart will be called prudent,
And sweetness of the lips increases learning.

16:21 sweetness of the lips. "Honeyed words," which reflect intelligence, judiciousness, and discernment in speech. This refers to eloquent discourse from the wise (v. 24).

John 6:1–21

6 After these things Jesus went over the Sea
of Galilee, which is *the Sea* of Tiberias. [2]Then
a great multitude followed Him, because they
saw His signs which He performed on those
who were diseased. [3]And Jesus went up on the
mountain, and there He sat with His disciples.
[4]Now the Passover, a feast of the Jews, was
near. [5]Then Jesus lifted up *His* eyes, and seeing a great multitude coming toward Him, He
said to Philip, "Where shall we buy bread, that
these may eat?" [6]But this He said to test him, for
He Himself knew what He would do.
[7]Philip answered Him, "Two hundred denarii
worth of bread is not sufficient for them, that
every one of them may have a little."
[8]One of His disciples, Andrew, Simon Peter's brother, said to Him, [9]"There is a lad
here who has five barley loaves and two small
fish, but what are they among so many?"

6:19,20 Jesus walking on the sea. The Synoptics reveal that in fear and the darkness, the disciples thought Jesus was a ghost (Matt. 14:26; Mark 6:49). The Son of God, who made the world, was in control of its forces; and, in this case, He suspended the law of gravity. The act was not frivolous on Jesus' part, for it constituted a dramatic object lesson to the disciples of Jesus' true identity as the sovereign Lord of all creation (1:3).

[10]Then Jesus said, "Make the people sit down."
Now there was much grass in the place. So the
men sat down, in number about five thousand.
[11]And Jesus took the loaves, and when He had
given thanks He distributed *them* to the disciples,
and the disciples to those sitting down; and likewise of the fish, as much as they wanted. [12]So when
they were filled, He said to His disciples, "Gather
up the fragments that remain, so that nothing is
lost." [13]Therefore they gathered *them* up, and filled
twelve baskets with the fragments of the five barley loaves which were left over by those who had
eaten. [14]Then those men, when they had seen the
sign that Jesus did, said, "This is truly the Prophet
who is to come into the world."
[15]Therefore when Jesus perceived that they
were about to come and take Him by force to
make Him king, He departed again to the
mountain by Himself alone.
[16]Now when evening came, His disciples went
down to the sea, [17]got into the boat, and went
over the sea toward Capernaum. And it was
already dark, and Jesus had not come to them.
[18]Then the sea arose because a great wind was
blowing. [19]So when they had rowed about
three or four miles, they saw Jesus walking on
the sea and drawing near the boat; and they
were afraid. [20]But He said to them, "It is I; do
not be afraid." [21]Then they willingly received
Him into the boat, and immediately the boat
was at the land where they were going.

DAY 19: Why were the crowds who followed Jesus a potential liability?

In John 6:2, it says that the multitudes followed Jesus "because they saw His signs." The crowds followed not out of belief but out of curiosity concerning the miracles that He performed (v. 26). However, in spite of the crowd's crass motivations, Jesus, having compassion on them, healed their sick and fed them (Matt. 13:14; Mark 6:34).

The crowd's declaration of Jesus as "the Prophet" (v. 14) is a reference to Deuteronomy 18:15. Sadly, these comments, coming right after Jesus healed and fed them, indicate that the people desired a Messiah who met their physical, rather than spiritual, needs. Apparently, no recognition existed for the need of spiritual repentance and preparation for the kingdom (Matt. 4:17). They wanted an earthly, political Messiah to meet all their needs and to deliver them from Roman oppression. Their reaction typifies many who want a "Christ" that makes no demands of them (Matt. 10:34–39; 16:24–26), but of whom they can make their selfish personal requests.

Jesus "perceived that they were about to come and take Him by force to make Him king" (v. 15). John supplemented the information in Matthew and Mark by indicating that the reason Jesus dismissed the disciples and withdrew from the crowd into a mountain alone was because of His supernatural knowledge of their intention to make Him king in light of His healing and feeding of them. The crowd, incited by mob enthusiasm, was ready to proceed with crassly political intentions that would have jeopardized God's will.

MAY 20

2 Samuel 11:1–12:31

11 It happened in the spring of the year, at
the time when kings go out *to battle,* that
David sent Joab and his servants with him,
and all Israel; and they destroyed the people of
Ammon and besieged Rabbah. But David
remained at Jerusalem.
2Then it happened one evening that David
arose from his bed and walked on the roof of
the king's house. And from the roof he saw a
woman bathing, and the woman *was* very beautiful to behold. 3So David sent and inquired
about the woman. And *someone* said, "*Is* this
not Bathsheba, the daughter of Eliam, the wife
of Uriah the Hittite?" 4Then David sent messengers, and took her; and she came to him,
and he lay with her, for she was cleansed from
her impurity; and she returned to her house.
5And the woman conceived; so she sent and
told David, and said, "I *am* with child."
6Then David sent to Joab, *saying,* "Send me
Uriah the Hittite." And Joab sent Uriah to David. 7When Uriah had come to him, David
asked how Joab was doing, and how the people
were doing, and how the war prospered. 8And
David said to Uriah, "Go down to your house
and wash your feet." So Uriah departed from
the king's house, and a gift *of food* from the
king followed him. 9But Uriah slept at the door
of the king's house with all the servants of his
lord, and did not go down to his house. 10So
when they told David, saying, "Uriah did not
go down to his house," David said to Uriah,
"Did you not come from a journey? Why did
you not go down to your house?"
11And Uriah said to David, "The ark and Israel and Judah are dwelling in tents, and my
lord Joab and the servants of my lord are
encamped in the open fields. Shall I then go to
my house to eat and drink, and to lie with my
wife? *As* you live, and *as* your soul lives, I will
not do this thing."
12Then David said to Uriah, "Wait here today
also, and tomorrow I will let you depart." So
Uriah remained in Jerusalem that day and the
next. 13Now when David called him, he ate and
drank before him; and he made him drunk.
And at evening he went out to lie on his bed
with the servants of his lord, but he did not go
down to his house.
14In the morning it happened that David
wrote a letter to Joab and sent *it* by the hand
of Uriah. 15And he wrote in the letter, saying,
"Set Uriah in the forefront of the hottest battle,
and retreat from him, that he may be struck
down and die." 16So it was, while Joab besieged
the city, that he assigned Uriah to a place
where he knew there *were* valiant men. 17Then
the men of the city came out and fought with
Joab. And *some* of the people of the servants of
David fell; and Uriah the Hittite died also.

11:3 Bathsheba. Not until 12:24 is her name used again. Rather, to intensify the sin of adultery, it is emphasized that she was the wife of Uriah (vv. 3,26; 12:10,15). Even the New Testament says "her of Uriah" (Matt. 1:6). **Eliam.** The father of Bathsheba was one of David's mighty men (23:34). Since Eliam was the son of Ahithophel, Bathsheba was Ahithophel's granddaughter (15:12; 16:15). This could explain why Ahithophel, one of David's counselors (15:12), later gave his allegiance to Absalom in his revolt against David. **Uriah.** Also one of David's mighty men (23:39). Although a Hittite (see Gen. 15:20; Ex. 3:8,17,23), Uriah bore a Hebrew name meaning "the LORD is my light," indicating he was a worshiper of the one true God.

11:15 he may…die. Failing twice to cover up his sin with Bathsheba, the frustrated and panicked David plotted the murder of Uriah by taking advantage of Uriah's unswerving loyalty to him as king, even having Uriah deliver his own death warrant. Thus David engaged in another crime deserving of capital punishment (Lev. 24:17). This is graphic proof of the extremes people go to in pursuit of sin and in the absence of restraining grace.

18Then Joab sent and told David all the things concerning the war, 19and charged the messenger, saying, "When you have finished telling the matters of the war to the king, 20if it happens that the king's wrath rises, and he says to you: 'Why did you approach so near to the city when you fought? Did you not know that they would shoot from the wall? 21Who struck Abimelech the son of Jerubbesheth? Was it not a woman who cast a piece of a millstone on him from the wall, so that he died in Thebez? Why did you go near the wall?'—then you shall say, 'Your servant Uriah the Hittite is dead also.' "

22So the messenger went, and came and told David all that Joab had sent by him. 23And the messenger said to David, "Surely the men prevailed against us and came out to us in the field; then we drove them back as far as the entrance of the gate. 24The archers shot from the wall at your servants; and *some* of the king's servants are dead, and your servant Uriah the Hittite is dead also."

25Then David said to the messenger, "Thus you shall say to Joab: 'Do not let this thing displease you, for the sword devours one as well as another. Strengthen your attack against the city, and overthrow it.' So encourage him."

26When the wife of Uriah heard that Uriah her husband was dead, she mourned for her husband. 27And when her mourning was over, David sent and brought her to his house, and she became his wife and bore him a son. But the thing that David had done displeased the LORD.

12 Then the LORD sent Nathan to David. And he came to him, and said to him: "There were two men in one city, one rich and the other poor. 2The rich *man* had exceedingly many flocks and herds. 3But the poor *man* had nothing, except one little ewe lamb which he had bought and nourished; and it grew up together with him and with his children. It ate of his own food and drank from his own cup and lay in his bosom; and it was like a daughter to him. 4And a traveler came to the rich man, who refused to take from his own flock and from his own herd to prepare one for the wayfaring man who had come to him; but he took the poor man's lamb and prepared it for the man who had come to him."

5So David's anger was greatly aroused against the man, and he said to Nathan, "*As* the LORD lives, the man who has done this shall surely die! 6And he shall restore fourfold for the lamb, because he did this thing and because he had no pity."

7Then Nathan said to David, "You *are* the man! Thus says the LORD God of Israel: 'I anointed you king over Israel, and I delivered you from the hand of Saul. 8I gave you your master's house and your master's wives into your keeping, and gave you the house of Israel and Judah. And if *that had been* too little, I also would have given you much more! 9Why have you despised the commandment of the LORD, to do evil in His sight? You have killed Uriah the Hittite with the sword; you have taken his wife *to be* your wife, and have killed him with the sword of the people of Ammon. 10Now therefore, the sword shall never depart from your house, because you have despised Me, and have taken the wife of Uriah the Hittite to be your wife.' 11Thus says the LORD: 'Behold, I will raise up adversity against you from your own house; and I will take your wives before your eyes and give *them* to your neighbor, and he shall lie with your wives in the sight of this sun. 12For you did *it* secretly, but I will do this thing before all Israel, before the sun.' "

13So David said to Nathan, "I have sinned against the LORD."

And Nathan said to David, "The LORD also has put away your sin; you shall not die. 14However, because by this deed you have given great occasion to the enemies of the LORD to blaspheme, the child also *who is* born to you shall surely die." 15Then Nathan departed to his house.

And the LORD struck the child that Uriah's wife bore to David, and it became ill. 16David therefore pleaded with God for the child, and David fasted and went in and lay all night on the ground. 17So the elders of his house arose *and went* to him, to raise him up from the ground. But he would not, nor did he eat food with them. 18Then on the seventh day it came to pass that the child died. And the servants of David were afraid to tell him that the child was dead. For they said, "Indeed, while the child was alive, we spoke to him, and he would not heed our voice. How can we tell him that the child is dead? He may do some harm!"

19When David saw that his servants were whispering, David perceived that the child was dead. Therefore David said to his servants, "Is the child dead?"

And they said, "He is dead."

20So David arose from the ground, washed and anointed himself, and changed his clothes; and he went into the house of the LORD and worshiped. Then he went to his own house; and when he requested, they set food before him, and he ate. 21Then his servants said to him, "What *is* this that you have done? You fasted and wept for the child *while he was* alive, but when the child died, you arose and ate food."

22And he said, "While the child was alive, I fasted and wept; for I said, 'Who can tell

whether the LORD will be gracious to me, that
the child may live?' [23]But now he is dead; why
should I fast? Can I bring him back again? I
shall go to him, but he shall not return to me."
[24]Then David comforted Bathsheba his wife,
and went in to her and lay with her. So she
bore a son, and he called his name Solomon.
Now the LORD loved him, [25]and He sent *word*
by the hand of Nathan the prophet: So he
called his name Jedidiah, because of the LORD.
[26]Now Joab fought against Rabbah of the
people of Ammon, and took the royal city.
[27]And Joab sent messengers to David, and
said, "I have fought against Rabbah, and I
have taken the city's water *supply.* [28]Now
therefore, gather the rest of the people
together and encamp against the city and take
it, lest I take the city and it be called after my
name." [29]So David gathered all the people
together and went to Rabbah, fought against
it, and took it. [30]Then he took their king's
crown from his head. Its weight *was* a talent
of gold, with precious stones. And it was *set*
on David's head. Also he brought out the
spoil of the city in great abundance. [31]And he
brought out the people who *were* in it, and put
them to work with saws and iron picks and iron
axes, and made them cross over to the brick
works. So he did to all the cities of the people
of Ammon. Then David and all the people
returned to Jerusalem.

Psalm 65:9–13

9 You visit the earth and water it,
You greatly enrich it;
The river of God is full of water;
You provide their grain,
For so You have prepared it.
10 You water its ridges abundantly,
You settle its furrows;
You make it soft with showers,
You bless its growth.

11 You crown the year with Your
goodness,
And Your paths drip *with* abundance.
12 They drop *on* the pastures of the
wilderness,
And the little hills rejoice on every
side.
13 The pastures are clothed with flocks;
The valleys also are covered with
grain;
They shout for joy, they also sing.

Proverbs 16:22–24

22 Understanding *is* a wellspring of life to
him who has it.
But the correction of fools *is* folly.
23 The heart of the wise teaches
his mouth,
And adds learning to his lips.
24 Pleasant words *are like* a honeycomb,
Sweetness to the soul and health
to the bones.

John 6:22–51

[22]On the following day, when the people who
were standing on the other side of the sea saw
that there was no other boat there, except that
one which His disciples had entered, and that
Jesus had not entered the boat with His disciples, but His disciples had gone away alone—
[23]however, other boats came from Tiberias,
near the place where they ate bread after the
Lord had given thanks— [24]when the people
therefore saw that Jesus was not there, nor
His disciples, they also got into boats and
came to Capernaum, seeking Jesus. [25]And
when they found Him on the other side of the
sea, they said to Him, "Rabbi, when did You
come here?"
[26]Jesus answered them and said, "Most
assuredly, I say to you, you seek Me, not
because you saw the signs, but because you
ate of the loaves and were filled. [27]Do not labor
for the food which perishes, but for the food
which endures to everlasting life, which the
Son of Man will give you, because God the
Father has set His seal on Him."
[28]Then they said to Him, "What shall we do,
that we may work the works of God?"
[29]Jesus answered and said to them, "This is
the work of God, that you believe in Him
whom He sent."
[30]Therefore they said to Him, "What sign
will You perform then, that we may see it and
believe You? What work will You do? [31]Our
fathers ate the manna in the desert; as it is
written, *'He gave them bread from heaven to
eat.' "*
[32]Then Jesus said to them, "Most assuredly,
I say to you, Moses did not give you the bread
from heaven, but My Father gives you the
true bread from heaven. [33]For the bread of
God is He who comes down from heaven and
gives life to the world."
[34]Then they said to Him, "Lord, give us this
bread always."
[35]And Jesus said to them, "I am the bread of
life. He who comes to Me shall never hunger,
and he who believes in Me shall never thirst.
[36]But I said to you that you have seen Me and
yet do not believe. [37]All that the Father gives
Me will come to Me, and the one who comes

to Me I will by no means cast out. [38]For I have
come down from heaven, not to do My own
will, but the will of Him who sent Me. [39]This is
the will of the Father who sent Me, that of all
He has given Me I should lose nothing, but
should raise it up at the last day. [40]And this is

6:40 everyone who sees the Son and believes in Him. This verse emphasizes human responsibility in salvation. Although God is sovereign, He works through faith, so that a man must believe in Jesus as the Messiah and Son of God who alone offers the only way of salvation (14:6). However, even faith is a gift of God (Rom. 12:3; Eph. 2:8,9). Intellectually harmonizing the sovereignty of God and the responsibility of man is impossible humanly, but perfectly resolved in the infinite mind of God.

the will of Him who sent Me, that everyone
who sees the Son and believes in Him may
have everlasting life; and I will raise him up at
the last day."
[41]The Jews then complained about Him,
because He said, "I am the bread which came
down from heaven." [42]And they said, "Is not
this Jesus, the son of Joseph, whose father and
mother we know? How is it then that He says,
'I have come down from heaven'?"
[43]Jesus therefore answered and said to
them, "Do not murmur among yourselves.
[44]No one can come to Me unless the Father
who sent Me draws him; and I will raise him
up at the last day. [45]It is written in the prophets,
'And they shall all be taught by God.' Therefore everyone who has heard and learned
from the Father comes to Me. [46]Not that anyone has seen the Father, except He who is
from God; He has seen the Father. [47]Most
assuredly, I say to you, he who believes in Me
has everlasting life. [48]I am the bread of life.
[49]Your fathers ate the manna in the wilderness,
and are dead. [50]This is the bread which comes
down from heaven, that one may eat of it and
not die. [51]I am the living bread which came
down from heaven. If anyone eats of this
bread, he will live forever; and the bread that I
shall give is My flesh, which I shall give for
the life of the world."

6:51 This pronouncement exactly reiterates vv. 33,35,47,48. **My flesh, which I shall give for the life of the world.** Jesus refers here prophetically to His impending sacrifice upon the cross (2 Cor. 5:21; 1 Pet. 2:24). Jesus voluntarily laid down His life for evil, sinful mankind (10:18; 1 John 2:2).

DAY 20: How do Jesus' "I am" statements in the Book of John express His saving relationship toward the world?

After the miraculous feeding of the 5,000, Jesus was challenged by the crowd to perform an even greater miracle in John 6:30. "Our fathers ate the manna," they said (v. 31), implying that Jesus' miraculous feeding was a small miracle compared to what Moses did. In order for them to believe in Him, they would need to see Him feed the nation of Israel on the same scale that God did when He sent manna and fed the entire nation of Israel during their wilderness wanderings for 40 years (Ex. 16:11–36). They were demanding that Jesus outdo Moses if they were to believe in Him.

Jesus responded that the manna God gave was temporary and perished and was only a meager shadow of what God offered them in the true bread, Himself, who gives spiritual and eternal life to mankind ("world"). He is the "true bread from heaven," and in case that wasn't understood, He added, "I am the bread of life" (v. 35).

Twenty-three times in all we find our Lord's meaningful "I AM" in the Greek text of this Gospel (4:26; 6:20,35,41,48,51; 8:12,18,24,28,58; 10:7,9,11,14; 11:25; 13:19; 14:6; 15:1,5; 18:5,6,8). In several of these, He joins His "I AM" with seven tremendous metaphors which are expressive of His saving relationship toward the world.

"I AM the Bread of life" (6:35,41,48,51).
"I AM the Light of the world" (8:12).
"I AM the Door of the sheep" (10:7,9).
"I AM the Good Shepherd" (10:11,14).
"I AM the Resurrection and the Life" (11:25).
"I AM the Way, the Truth, and the Life" (14:6).
"I AM the true Vine" (15:1,5).

MAY 21

2 Samuel 13:1–14:33

13 After this Absalom the son of David had
a lovely sister, whose name *was* Tamar;
and Amnon the son of David loved her.
[2]Amnon was so distressed over his sister
Tamar that he became sick; for she *was* a virgin. And it was improper for Amnon to do anything to her. [3]But Amnon had a friend whose
name *was* Jonadab the son of Shimeah, David's brother. Now Jonadab *was* a very crafty
man. [4]And he said to him, "Why *are* you, the
king's son, becoming thinner day after day?
Will you not tell me?"

Amnon said to him, "I love Tamar, my
brother Absalom's sister."

[5]So Jonadab said to him, "Lie down on your
bed and pretend to be ill. And when your
father comes to see you, say to him, 'Please let
my sister Tamar come and give me food, and
prepare the food in my sight, that I may see *it*
and eat it from her hand.' " [6]Then Amnon lay
down and pretended to be ill; and when the
king came to see him, Amnon said to the king,
"Please let Tamar my sister come and make a
couple of cakes for me in my sight, that I may
eat from her hand."

[7]And David sent home to Tamar, saying,
"Now go to your brother Amnon's house, and
prepare food for him." [8]So Tamar went to her
brother Amnon's house; and he was lying
down. Then she took flour and kneaded *it,*
made cakes in his sight, and baked the cakes.
[9]And she took the pan and placed *them* out
before him, but he refused to eat. Then
Amnon said, "Have everyone go out from me."
And they all went out from him. [10]Then Amnon
said to Tamar, "Bring the food into the bedroom, that I may eat from your hand." And
Tamar took the cakes which she had made,
and brought *them* to Amnon her brother in the
bedroom. [11]Now when she had brought *them*
to him to eat, he took hold of her and said to
her, "Come, lie with me, my sister."

[12]But she answered him, "No, my brother,
do not force me, for no such thing should be
done in Israel. Do not do this disgraceful
thing! [13]And I, where could I take my shame?
And as for you, you would be like one of the
fools in Israel. Now therefore, please speak to
the king; for he will not withhold me from
you." [14]However, he would not heed her voice;
and being stronger than she, he forced her
and lay with her.

[15]Then Amnon hated her exceedingly, so
that the hatred with which he hated her *was*
greater than the love with which he had loved
her. And Amnon said to her, "Arise, be gone!"

[16]So she said to him, "No, indeed! This evil
of sending me away *is* worse than the other
that you did to me."

13:15 hated her. Amnon's "love" (v. 1) was nothing but sensual desire that, once gratified, turned to hatred. His sudden revulsion was the result of Tamar's unwilling resistance, the atrocity of what he had done, feelings of remorse, and dread of exposure and punishment. All of these rendered her intolerably undesirable to him.

But he would not listen to her. [17]Then he
called his servant who attended him, and said,
"Here! Put this *woman* out, away from me, and
bolt the door behind her." [18]Now she had on a
robe of many colors, for the king's virgin
daughters wore such apparel. And his servant
put her out and bolted the door behind her.

[19]Then Tamar put ashes on her head, and
tore her robe of many colors that *was* on her,
and laid her hand on her head and went away
crying bitterly. [20]And Absalom her brother
said to her, "Has Amnon your brother been
with you? But now hold your peace, my sister.
He *is* your brother; do not take this thing to
heart." So Tamar remained desolate in her
brother Absalom's house.

[21]But when King David heard of all these
things, he was very angry. [22]And Absalom
spoke to his brother Amnon neither good nor
bad. For Absalom hated Amnon, because he
had forced his sister Tamar.

[23]And it came to pass, after two full years,
that Absalom had sheepshearers in Baal
Hazor, which *is* near Ephraim; so Absalom
invited all the king's sons. [24]Then Absalom
came to the king and said, "Kindly note, your
servant has sheepshearers; please, let the
king and his servants go with your servant."

[25]But the king said to Absalom, "No, my son,
let us not all go now, lest we be a burden to
you." Then he urged him, but he would not
go; and he blessed him.

[26]Then Absalom said, "If not, please let my
brother Amnon go with us."

And the king said to him, "Why should he
go with you?" [27]But Absalom urged him; so he
let Amnon and all the king's sons go with him.

[28]Now Absalom had commanded his servants,

saying, "Watch now, when Amnon's heart is
merry with wine, and when I say to you,
'Strike Amnon!' then kill him. Do not be afraid.
Have I not commanded you? Be courageous
and valiant." 29So the servants of Absalom did
to Amnon as Absalom had commanded. Then
all the king's sons arose, and each one got on
his mule and fled.

30And it came to pass, while they were on the
way, that news came to David, saying, "Absalom has killed all the king's sons, and not one
of them is left!" 31So the king arose and tore his
garments and lay on the ground, and all his servants stood by with their clothes torn. 32Then
Jonadab the son of Shimeah, David's brother,
answered and said, "Let not my lord suppose
they have killed all the young men, the king's
sons, for only Amnon is dead. For by the command of Absalom this has been determined
from the day that he forced his sister Tamar.
33Now therefore, let not my lord the king take
the thing to his heart, to think that all the
king's sons are dead. For only Amnon is dead."

34Then Absalom fled. And the young man
who was keeping watch lifted his eyes and
looked, and there, many people were coming
from the road on the hillside behind him. 35And
Jonadab said to the king, "Look, the king's
sons are coming; as your servant said, so it is."
36So it was, as soon as he had finished speaking, that the king's sons indeed came, and they
lifted up their voice and wept. Also the king
and all his servants wept very bitterly.

37But Absalom fled and went to Talmai the
son of Ammihud, king of Geshur. And *David*
mourned for his son every day. 38So Absalom
fled and went to Geshur, and was there three
years. 39And King David longed to go to
Absalom. For he had been comforted concerning Amnon, because he was dead.

14 So Joab the son of Zeruiah perceived that
the king's heart *was* concerned about
Absalom. 2And Joab sent to Tekoa and
brought from there a wise woman, and said to
her, "Please pretend to be a mourner, and put
on mourning apparel; do not anoint yourself
with oil, but act like a woman who has been
mourning a long time for the dead. 3Go to the
king and speak to him in this manner." So Joab
put the words in her mouth.

4And when the woman of Tekoa spoke to
the king, she fell on her face to the ground and
prostrated herself, and said, "Help, O king!"

5Then the king said to her, "What troubles
you?"

And she answered, "Indeed I *am* a widow,
my husband is dead. 6Now your maidservant
had two sons; and the two fought with each
other in the field, and *there was* no one to part
them, but the one struck the other and killed
him. 7And now the whole family has risen up
against your maidservant, and they said, 'Deliver him who struck his brother, that we may
execute him for the life of his brother whom he
killed; and we will destroy the heir also.' So
they would extinguish my ember that is left,
and leave to my husband *neither* name nor
remnant on the earth."

8Then the king said to the woman, "Go to your
house, and I will give orders concerning you."

9And the woman of Tekoa said to the king,
"My lord, O king, *let* the iniquity *be* on me and
on my father's house, and the king and his
throne *be* guiltless."

10So the king said, "Whoever says *anything*
to you, bring him to me, and he shall not touch
you anymore."

11Then she said, "Please let the king remember the LORD your God, and do not permit the
avenger of blood to destroy anymore, lest they
destroy my son."

And he said, "*As* the LORD lives, not one hair
of your son shall fall to the ground."

12Therefore the woman said, "Please, let your
maidservant speak *another* word to my lord
the king."

And he said, "Say on."

13So the woman said: "Why then have you
schemed such a thing against the people of
God? For the king speaks this thing as one
who is guilty, *in that* the king does not bring
his banished one home again. 14For we will
surely die and *become* like water spilled on the
ground, which cannot be gathered up again.
Yet God does not take away a life; but He devises means, so that His banished ones are not
expelled from Him. 15Now therefore, I have
come to speak of this thing to my lord the king
because the people have made me afraid. And
your maidservant said, 'I will now speak to the
king; it may be that the king will perform the
request of his maidservant. 16For the king will
hear and deliver his maidservant from the
hand of the man *who would* destroy me and
my son together from the inheritance of God.'

14:13 against the people of God. The woman asserted that by allowing Absalom to remain in exile, David had jeopardized the future welfare of Israel. If he would be so generous to a son he did not know in a family he did not know, would he not forgive his own son?

17 Your maidservant said, 'The word of my lord
the king will now be comforting; for as the
angel of God, so *is* my lord the king in discerning good and evil. And may the LORD your God
be with you.' "
18 Then the king answered and said to the
woman, "Please do not hide from me anything
that I ask you."
And the woman said, "Please, let my lord
the king speak."
19 So the king said, "*Is* the hand of Joab with
you in all this?" And the woman answered and
said, "*As* you live, my lord the king, no one can
turn to the right hand or to the left from anything that my lord the king has spoken. For your
servant Joab commanded me, and he put all
these words in the mouth of your maidservant.
20 To bring about this change of affairs your servant Joab has done this thing; but my lord *is*
wise, according to the wisdom of the angel of
God, to know everything that *is* in the earth."
21 And the king said to Joab, "All right, I have
granted this thing. Go therefore, bring back
the young man Absalom."
22 Then Joab fell to the ground on his face
and bowed himself, and thanked the king. And
Joab said, "Today your servant knows that I
have found favor in your sight, my lord, O
king, in that the king has fulfilled the request
of his servant." 23 So Joab arose and went to
Geshur, and brought Absalom to Jerusalem.
24 And the king said, "Let him return to his own
house, but do not let him see my face." So
Absalom returned to his own house, but did
not see the king's face.
25 Now in all Israel there was no one who was
praised as much as Absalom for his good
looks. From the sole of his foot to the crown of
his head there was no blemish in him. 26 And
when he cut the hair of his head—at the end
of every year he cut *it* because it was heavy on
him—when he cut it, he weighed the hair of his
head at two hundred shekels according to the
king's standard. 27 To Absalom were born three
sons, and one daughter whose name *was* Tamar.
She was a woman of beautiful appearance.
28 And Absalom dwelt two full years in Jerusalem, but did not see the king's face. 29 Therefore Absalom sent for Joab, to send him to the
king, but he would not come to him. And
when he sent again the second time, he would
not come. 30 So he said to his servants, "See,
Joab's field is near mine, and he has barley
there; go and set it on fire." And Absalom's
servants set the field on fire.
31 Then Joab arose and came to Absalom's
house, and said to him, "Why have your servants set my field on fire?"
32 And Absalom answered Joab, "Look, I sent
to you, saying, 'Come here, so that I may send
you to the king, to say, "Why have I come from
Geshur? *It would be* better for me *to be* there
still." ' Now therefore, let me see the king's
face; but if there is iniquity in me, let him execute me."
33 So Joab went to the king and told him. And
when he had called for Absalom, he came to
the king and bowed himself on his face to the
ground before the king. Then the king kissed
Absalom.

Psalm 66:1–7

To the Chief Musician. A Song. A Psalm.

Make a joyful shout to God,
all the earth!
2 Sing out the honor of His name;
Make His praise glorious.
3 Say to God,
"How awesome are Your works!
Through the greatness of Your power
Your enemies shall submit themselves
to You.
4 All the earth shall worship You
And sing praises to You;
They shall sing praises *to* Your name."
Selah

66:4 All the earth shall worship You. This praise is not only an acknowledgment of God's universal Lordship, but also an intimation of the people's belief in a future worldwide kingdom where God will be worshiped (Is. 66:23; Zech. 14:16; Phil. 2:10,11).

5 Come and see the works of God;
He is awesome *in His* doing toward the
sons of men.
6 He turned the sea into dry *land;*
They went through the river on foot.
There we will rejoice in Him.
7 He rules by His power forever;
His eyes observe the nations;
Do not let the rebellious exalt
themselves. Selah

Proverbs 16:25–26

25 There is a way *that seems* right to a
man,
But its end *is* the way of death.

26 The person who labors, labors for
himself,
For his *hungry* mouth drives him *on.*

John 6:52–71

52The Jews therefore quarreled among
themselves, saying, "How can this Man give
us *His* flesh to eat?"
53Then Jesus said to them, "Most assuredly,
I say to you, unless you eat the flesh of the Son
of Man and drink His blood, you have no life
in you. 54Whoever eats My flesh and drinks
My blood has eternal life, and I will raise him
up at the last day. 55For My flesh is food indeed,
and My blood is drink indeed. 56He who eats
My flesh and drinks My blood abides in Me,
and I in him. 57As the living Father sent Me,
and I live because of the Father, so he who
feeds on Me will live because of Me. 58This is
the bread which came down from heaven—
not as your fathers ate the manna, and are
dead. He who eats this bread will live forever."
59These things He said in the synagogue as
He taught in Capernaum.
60Therefore many of His disciples, when
they heard *this,* said, "This is a hard saying;
who can understand it?"
61When Jesus knew in Himself that His disciples complained about this, He said to them,
"Does this offend you? 62*What* then if you
should see the Son of Man ascend where He
was before? 63It is the Spirit who gives life; the
flesh profits nothing. The words that I speak to
you are spirit, and *they* are life. 64But there are
some of you who do not believe." For Jesus
knew from the beginning who they were who
did not believe, and who would betray Him.
65And He said, "Therefore I have said to you
that no one can come to Me unless it has been
granted to him by My Father."
66From that *time* many of His disciples went
back and walked with Him no more. 67Then
Jesus said to the twelve, "Do you also want to
go away?"
68But Simon Peter answered Him, "Lord, to
whom shall we go? You have the words of eternal life. 69Also we have come to believe and
know that You are the Christ, the Son of the
living God."
70Jesus answered them, "Did I not choose
you, the twelve, and one of you is a devil?" 71He
spoke of Judas Iscariot, *the son* of Simon, for it
was he who would betray Him, being one of
the twelve.

6:64 Jesus knew. Reminiscent of Jesus' words in 2:23–25, Jesus knew the hearts of men, including those disciples who followed Him. He supernaturally knew that many did not believe in Him as Messiah and Son of God so He did not entrust Himself to them. These false disciples were simply attracted to the physical phenomena (miracles and food) and failed to understand the true significance of Jesus' teaching (v. 61).

DAY 21: If we accept the scholarly view that the surviving ancient manuscripts of 1 and 2 Samuel were poorly preserved, what should be our attitude toward these books?

Given the challenges involved in hand-copying and preserving scrolls, it is a wonder that we have the ancient documents that we do have. Our attitude ought to lean more toward amazement that we have such few discrepancies rather than toward concern over the ones that puzzle and challenge us.

Many of the discoveries in the science of analyzing ancient manuscripts involve the typical errors that commonly appear when handwritten documents are copied. For example, when two lines of text end with the same word or words, the eye of the copyist tends to skip the second line, deleting it completely. Careful comparisons between manuscripts and reconstruction of the text often reveal these simple errors.

In the case of 1 and 2 Samuel we have two ancient text families: 1) the Masoretic text in the Hebrew language and 2) the LXX (Septuagint) text in Greek that was translated by Jewish scholars in about 100 B.C. Comparing the two, it is clear that the two differ in more places with the Samuel books than with other Old Testament books. There are frequent disagreements between the texts when it comes to numbers. In settling these discrepancies, the age and language of the Masoretic text is generally considered a closer version of the original manuscript unless grammar and context indicate a copying error.

When thinking about the possibility of textual errors in the Scriptures, it is crucial to remember this: The central doctrines of the Christian faith are never based on a single verse of Scripture, nor do they rely on a disputed section of Scripture. God's plan of salvation and the main outline of Christian teaching can be found throughout Scripture.

MAY 22

2 Samuel 15:1–16:23

15 After this it happened that Absalom provided himself with chariots and horses, and fifty men to run before him. [2]Now Absalom would rise early and stand beside the way to the gate. *So* it was, whenever anyone who had a lawsuit came to the king for a decision, that Absalom would call to him and say, "What city *are* you from?" And he would say, "Your servant *is* from such and such a tribe of Israel." [3]Then Absalom would say to him, "Look, your case *is* good and right; but *there is* no deputy of the king to hear you." [4]Moreover Absalom would say, "Oh, that I were made judge in the land, and everyone who has any suit or cause would come to me; then I would give him justice." [5]And *so* it was, whenever anyone came near to bow down to him, that he would put out his hand and take him and kiss him. [6]In this manner Absalom acted toward all Israel who came to the king for judgment. So Absalom stole the hearts of the men of Israel.

15:1–6 stole the hearts. Public hearings were always conducted early in the morning in a court held outside by the city gates. Absalom positioned himself there to win favor. Because King David was busy with other matters or with wars, and was also aging, many matters were left unresolved, building a deep feeling of resentment among the people. Absalom used that situation to undermine his father, by gratifying all he could with a favorable settlement and showing them all warm cordiality. Thus, he won the people to himself, without them knowing his wicked ambition.

[7]Now it came to pass after forty years that Absalom said to the king, "Please, let me go to Hebron and pay the vow which I made to the LORD. [8]For your servant took a vow while I dwelt at Geshur in Syria, saying, 'If the LORD indeed brings me back to Jerusalem, then I will serve the LORD.' "

[9]And the king said to him, "Go in peace." So he arose and went to Hebron.

[10]Then Absalom sent spies throughout all the tribes of Israel, saying, "As soon as you hear the sound of the trumpet, then you shall say, 'Absalom reigns in Hebron!' " [11]And with

15:10–12 Absalom formed a conspiracy, which included taking some of the leading men to create the impression that the king supported this action and was in his old age sharing the kingdom. All of this was a subtle disguise so Absalom could have freedom to plan his revolution. Absalom was able to do this against his father not merely because of his cleverness, but also because of the laxness of his father (1 Kin. 1:6).

Absalom went two hundred men invited from Jerusalem, and they went along innocently and did not know anything. [12]Then Absalom sent for Ahithophel the Gilonite, David's counselor, from his city—from Giloh—while he offered sacrifices. And the conspiracy grew strong, for the people with Absalom continually increased in number.

[13]Now a messenger came to David, saying, "The hearts of the men of Israel are with Absalom."

[14]So David said to all his servants who *were* with him at Jerusalem, "Arise, and let us flee, or we shall not escape from Absalom. Make haste to depart, lest he overtake us suddenly and bring disaster upon us, and strike the city with the edge of the sword."

[15]And the king's servants said to the king, "We *are* your servants, *ready to do* whatever my lord the king commands." [16]Then the king went out with all his household after him. But the king left ten women, concubines, to keep the house. [17]And the king went out with all the people after him, and stopped at the outskirts. [18]Then all his servants passed before him; and all the Cherethites, all the Pelethites, and all the Gittites, six hundred men who had followed him from Gath, passed before the king.

[19]Then the king said to Ittai the Gittite, "Why are you also going with us? Return and remain with the king. For you *are* a foreigner and also an exile from your own place. [20]In fact, you came *only* yesterday. Should I make you wander up and down with us today, since I go I know not where? Return, and take your brethren back. Mercy and truth *be* with you."

[21]But Ittai answered the king and said, "*As* the LORD lives, and *as* my lord the king lives, surely in whatever place my lord the king shall be, whether in death or life, even there also your servant will be."

[22]So David said to Ittai, "Go, and cross over." Then Ittai the Gittite and all his men and all the little ones who *were* with him crossed over. [23]And all the country wept with a loud voice,

and all the people crossed over. The king himself also crossed over the Brook Kidron, and
all the people crossed over toward the way of
the wilderness.

24There was Zadok also, and all the Levites
with him, bearing the ark of the covenant of
God. And they set down the ark of God, and
Abiathar went up until all the people had finished crossing over from the city. 25Then the
king said to Zadok, "Carry the ark of God back
into the city. If I find favor in the eyes of the
LORD, He will bring me back and show me *both*
it and His dwelling place. 26But if He says thus:
'I have no delight in you,' here I am, let Him do
to me as seems good to Him." 27The king also
said to Zadok the priest, "*Are* you *not* a seer?
Return to the city in peace, and your two sons
with you, Ahimaaz your son, and Jonathan the
son of Abiathar. 28See, I will wait in the plains of
the wilderness until word comes from you to
inform me." 29Therefore Zadok and Abiathar
carried the ark of God back to Jerusalem. And
they remained there.

30So David went up by the Ascent of the
Mount of Olives, and wept as he went up; and he
had his head covered and went barefoot. And all
the people who *were* with him covered their
heads and went up, weeping as they went up.
31Then *someone* told David, saying, "Ahithophel
is among the conspirators with Absalom." And
David said, "O LORD, I pray, turn the counsel
of Ahithophel into foolishness!"

32Now it happened when David had come to
the top *of the mountain,* where he worshiped
God—there was Hushai the Archite coming to
meet him with his robe torn and dust on his
head. 33David said to him, "If you go on with me,
then you will become a burden to me. 34But if
you return to the city, and say to Absalom, 'I
will be your servant, O king; *as* I *was* your
father's servant previously, so I *will* now also *be*
your servant,' then you may defeat the counsel
of Ahithophel for me. 35And *do* you not *have*
Zadok and Abiathar the priests with you there?
Therefore it will be *that* whatever you hear from
the king's house, you shall tell to Zadok and
Abiathar the priests. 36Indeed *they have* there
with them their two sons, Ahimaaz, Zadok's *son,*
and Jonathan, Abiathar's *son;* and by them you
shall send me everything you hear."

37So Hushai, David's friend, went into the
city. And Absalom came into Jerusalem.

16 When David was a little past the top *of
the mountain,* there was Ziba the servant
of Mephibosheth, who met him with a couple
of saddled donkeys, and on them two hundred
loaves of bread, one hundred clusters of
raisins, one hundred summer fruits, and a
skin of wine. 2And the king said to Ziba, "What
do you mean to do with these?"

So Ziba said, "The donkeys *are* for the king's
household to ride on, the bread and summer
fruit for the young men to eat, and the wine for
those who are faint in the wilderness to drink."

3Then the king said, "And where *is* your
master's son?"

And Ziba said to the king, "Indeed he is
staying in Jerusalem, for he said, 'Today the
house of Israel will restore the kingdom of my
father to me.' "

4So the king said to Ziba, "Here, all that
belongs to Mephibosheth *is* yours."

And Ziba said, "I humbly bow before you, *that*
I may find favor in your sight, my lord, O king!"

5Now when King David came to Bahurim,
there was a man from the family of the house of
Saul, whose name *was* Shimei the son of Gera,
coming from there. He came out, cursing continuously as he came. 6And he threw stones at David
and at all the servants of King David. And all the
people and all the mighty men *were* on his right
hand and on his left. 7Also Shimei said thus when
he cursed: "Come out! Come out! You bloodthirsty man, you rogue! 8The LORD has brought
upon you all the blood of the house of Saul, in
whose place you have reigned; and the LORD has
delivered the kingdom into the hand of Absalom
your son. So now you *are caught* in your own
evil, because you are a bloodthirsty man!"

9Then Abishai the son of Zeruiah said to the
king, "Why should this dead dog curse my lord
the king? Please, let me go over and take off his
head!"

10But the king said, "What have I to do with
you, you sons of Zeruiah? So let him curse,
because the LORD has said to him, 'Curse David.'
Who then shall say, 'Why have you done so?' "

11And David said to Abishai and all his servants, "See how my son who came from my own
body seeks my life. How much more now *may
this* Benjamite? Let him alone, and let him
curse; for so the LORD has ordered him. 12It may
be that the LORD will look on my affliction, and
that the LORD will repay me with good for his
cursing this day." 13And as David and his men
went along the road, Shimei went along the hillside opposite him and cursed as he went, threw
stones at him and kicked up dust. 14Now the king
and all the people who *were* with him became
weary; so they refreshed themselves there.

15Meanwhile Absalom and all the people, the
men of Israel, came to Jerusalem; and
Ahithophel *was* with him. 16And so it was, when
Hushai the Archite, David's friend, came to Absalom, that Hushai said to Absalom, "*Long* live
the king! *Long* live the king!"

17 So Absalom said to Hushai, "*Is* this your
loyalty to your friend? Why did you not go
with your friend?"
18 And Hushai said to Absalom, "No, but
whom the LORD and this people and all the men
of Israel choose, his I will be, and with him I
will remain. 19 Furthermore, whom should I
serve? *Should I* not *serve* in the presence of his
son? As I have served in your father's presence,
so will I be in your presence."
20 Then Absalom said to Ahithophel, "Give
advice as to what we should do."
21 And Ahithophel said to Absalom, "Go in to
your father's concubines, whom he has left to
keep the house; and all Israel will hear that
you are abhorred by your father. Then the
hands of all who are with you will be strong."
22 So they pitched a tent for Absalom on the top
of the house, and Absalom went in to his
father's concubines in the sight of all Israel.
23 Now the advice of Ahithophel, which he
gave in those days, *was* as if one had inquired
at the oracle of God. So *was* all the advice of
Ahithophel both with David and with Absalom.

Psalm 66:8–15

8 Oh, bless our God, you peoples!
And make the voice of His praise
to be heard,
9 Who keeps our soul among the living,
And does not allow our feet to be
moved.
10 For You, O God, have tested us;
You have refined us as silver is refined.
11 You brought us into the net;
You laid affliction on our backs.
12 You have caused men to ride over our
heads;
We went through fire and through water;
But You brought us out to rich *fulfillment.*
13 I will go into Your house with burnt
offerings;
I will pay You my vows,
14 Which my lips have uttered
And my mouth has spoken when I was
in trouble.
15 I will offer You burnt sacrifices of fat
animals,
With the sweet aroma of rams;
I will offer bulls with goats. Selah

Proverbs 16:27–30

27 An ungodly man digs up evil,
And *it is* on his lips like a burning fire.
28 A perverse man sows strife,
And a whisperer separates the best
of friends.
29 A violent man entices his neighbor,
And leads him in a way *that is* not good.
30 He winks his eye to devise perverse
things;
He purses his lips *and* brings about evil.

John 7:1–27

7 After these things Jesus walked in Galilee;
for He did not want to walk in Judea, because the Jews sought to kill Him. 2 Now the
Jews' Feast of Tabernacles was at hand. 3 His
brothers therefore said to Him, "Depart from
here and go into Judea, that Your disciples also
may see the works that You are doing. 4 For no
one does anything in secret while he himself
seeks to be known openly. If You do these
things, show Yourself to the world." 5 For even
His brothers did not believe in Him.

7:4 to be known openly….show Yourself to the world. Jesus' brothers wanted Him to put on a display of His miracles. Although the text does not clearly state their motivation, perhaps they made the request for two reasons: 1) they wanted to see the miracles for themselves to determine their genuineness, and 2) they may have had similar crass political motives as did the people, namely that He would become their social and political Messiah. Jerusalem's acceptance of Him was to be the acid test for them as to whether His own family would believe in Him as Messiah.

6 Then Jesus said to them, "My time has not
yet come, but your time is always ready. 7 The
world cannot hate you, but it hates Me because I testify of it that its works are evil. 8 You
go up to this feast. I am not yet going up to this
feast, for My time has not yet fully come."
9 When He had said these things to them, He
remained in Galilee.
10 But when His brothers had gone up, then
He also went up to the feast, not openly, but as
it were in secret. 11 Then the Jews sought Him
at the feast, and said, "Where is He?" 12 And
there was much complaining among the people concerning Him. Some said, "He is good";
others said, "No, on the contrary, He deceives
the people." 13 However, no one spoke openly
of Him for fear of the Jews.
14 Now about the middle of the feast Jesus
went up into the temple and taught. 15 And the
Jews marveled, saying, "How does this Man
know letters, having never studied?"
16 Jesus answered them and said, "My doctrine

is not Mine, but His who sent Me. [17]If anyone wills to do His will, he shall know concerning the doctrine, whether it is from God or *whether* I speak on My own *authority.* [18]He who speaks from himself seeks his own glory; but He who seeks the glory of the One who sent Him is true, and no unrighteousness is in Him. [19]Did not Moses give you the law, yet none of you keeps the law? Why do you seek to kill Me?"

[20]The people answered and said, "You have a demon. Who is seeking to kill You?"

[21]Jesus answered and said to them, "I did one work, and you all marvel. [22]Moses therefore gave you circumcision (not that it is from Moses, but from the fathers), and you circumcise a man on the Sabbath. [23]If a man receives circumcision on the Sabbath, so that the law of Moses should not be broken, are you angry with Me because I made a man completely well on the Sabbath? [24]Do not judge according to appearance, but judge with righteous judgment."

[25]Now some of them from Jerusalem said, "Is this not He whom they seek to kill? [26]But look! He speaks boldly, and they say nothing to Him. Do the rulers know indeed that this is truly the Christ? [27]However, we know where this Man is from; but when the Christ comes, no one knows where He is from."

7:17 If anyone wills to do His will, he shall know. Those who are fundamentally committed to doing God's will will be guided by Him in the affirmation of His truth. God's truth is self-authenticating through the teaching ministry of the Holy Spirit (16:13; 1 John 2:20,27).

DAY 22: How confused were the Jewish people about who Jesus was?

John 7:12–27 reflects the confusion among the people. In vv. 12,13 the crowds, made up of Judeans, Galileans, and Diaspora (scattered) Jews, expressed various opinions regarding Christ. The spectrum ranged from superficial acceptance ("He is good") to cynical rejection ("He deceives the people"). The Jewish Talmud reveals that the latter view of deception became the predominant opinion of many Jews.

Jesus' knowledge of Scripture was supernatural. The people "marveled" (v. 15) that someone who had never studied at any great rabbinical centers or under any great rabbis could display such profound mastery of Scripture. Both the content and manner of Jesus' teachings were qualitatively different from those of any other teacher. And the people were surprised that, in spite of the ominous threat from the religious authorities (vv. 20,32), Jesus boldly proclaimed His identity (v. 26).

"Do the rulers know indeed that this is truly the Christ?" they asked. The question indicates the level of confusion and uncertainty as to who Jesus was and what to do about Him. They did not really have any firm convictions regarding Jesus' identity. They were also perplexed at the religious leaders' failure to arrest and silence Him if He really were a fraud. Such dense confusion caused the crowd to wonder if the religious authorities in private concluded that He was indeed the Christ. Mass confusion among all groups reigned regarding Jesus.

"No one knows where He is from" (v. 27). Only information regarding the Messiah's birthplace was revealed in Scripture (Mic. 5:2; Matt. 2:5,6). Beyond that, a tradition had developed in Jewish circles that the Messiah would appear suddenly to the people, based on a misinterpretation of Isaiah 53:8 and Malachi 3:1. In light of this, the meaning of this phrase most likely is that the identity of the Messiah would be wholly unknown until He suddenly appeared in Israel and accomplished Israel's redemption. In contrast, Jesus had lived His life in Nazareth and was known (at least superficially) to the people (v. 28).

MAY 23

2 Samuel 17:1–18:33

17 Moreover Ahithophel said to Absalom, "Now let me choose twelve thousand men, and I will arise and pursue David tonight. [2]I will come upon him while he *is* weary and weak, and make him afraid. And all the people who *are* with him will flee, and I will strike only the king. [3]Then I will bring back all the people to you. When all return except the man whom you seek, all the people will be at peace." [4]And the saying pleased Absalom and all the elders of Israel.

[5]Then Absalom said, "Now call Hushai the Archite also, and let us hear what he says too." [6]And when Hushai came to Absalom, Absalom spoke to him, saying, "Ahithophel has spoken

in this manner. Shall we do as he says? If not,
speak up."
7 So Hushai said to Absalom: "The advice that
Ahithophel has given *is* not good at this time.
8 "For," said Hushai, "you know your father and
his men, that they *are* mighty men, and they
are enraged in their minds, like a bear robbed
of her cubs in the field; and your father *is* a
man of war, and will not camp with the people.
9 Surely by now he is hidden in some pit, or in
some *other* place. And it will be, when some of
them are overthrown at the first, that whoever
hears *it* will say, 'There is a slaughter among
the people who follow Absalom.' 10 And even he
who is valiant, whose heart *is* like the heart of
a lion, will melt completely. For all Israel
knows that your father *is* a mighty man, and
those who *are* with him *are* valiant men.
11 Therefore I advise that all Israel be fully gathered to you, from Dan to Beersheba, like the
sand that *is* by the sea for multitude, and that
you go to battle in person. 12 So we will come
upon him in some place where he may be
found, and we will fall on him as the dew falls
on the ground. And of him and all the men
who *are* with him there shall not be left so
much as one. 13 Moreover, if he has withdrawn
into a city, then all Israel shall bring ropes to
that city; and we will pull it into the river, until
there is not one small stone found there."

14 So Absalom and all the men of Israel said,
"The advice of Hushai the Archite *is* better
than the advice of Ahithophel." For the LORD
had purposed to defeat the good advice of
Ahithophel, to the intent that the LORD might
bring disaster on Absalom.

15 Then Hushai said to Zadok and Abiathar
the priests, "Thus and so Ahithophel advised
Absalom and the elders of Israel, and thus and
so I have advised. 16 Now therefore, send quickly and tell David, saying, 'Do not spend this
night in the plains of the wilderness, but speedily cross over, lest the king and all the people
who *are* with him be swallowed up.' " 17 Now
Jonathan and Ahimaaz stayed at En Rogel, for
they dared not be seen coming into the city; so a
female servant would come and tell them, and
they would go and tell King David. 18 Nevertheless a lad saw them, and told Absalom. But both
of them went away quickly and came to a man's
house in Bahurim, who had a well in his court;
and they went down into it. 19 Then the woman
took and spread a covering over the well's
mouth, and spread ground grain on it; and the
thing was not known. 20 And when Absalom's
servants came to the woman at the house, they
said, "Where *are* Ahimaaz and Jonathan?"

So the woman said to them, "They have
gone over the water brook."

And when they had searched and could not
find *them,* they returned to Jerusalem. 21 Now it
came to pass, after they had departed, that they
came up out of the well and went and told King
David, and said to David, "Arise and cross over
the water quickly. For thus has Ahithophel
advised against you." 22 So David and all the people who *were* with him arose and crossed over
the Jordan. By morning light not one of them
was left who had not gone over the Jordan.

23 Now when Ahithophel saw that his advice
was not followed, he saddled a donkey, and
arose and went home to his house, to his city.
Then he put his household in order, and
hanged himself, and died; and he was buried
in his father's tomb.

24 Then David went to Mahanaim. And
Absalom crossed over the Jordan, he and all
the men of Israel with him. 25 And Absalom
made Amasa captain of the army instead of
Joab. This Amasa *was* the son of a man whose
name *was* Jithra, an Israelite, who had gone in
to Abigail the daughter of Nahash, sister of
Zeruiah, Joab's mother. 26 So Israel and
Absalom encamped in the land of Gilead.

27 Now it happened, when David had come to
Mahanaim, that Shobi the son of Nahash from
Rabbah of the people of Ammon, Machir the
son of Ammiel from Lo Debar, and Barzillai
the Gileadite from Rogelim, 28 brought beds
and basins, earthen vessels and wheat, barley
and flour, parched *grain* and beans, lentils and
parched *seeds,* 29 honey and curds, sheep and
cheese of the herd, for David and the people
who *were* with him to eat. For they said, "The

17:7–13 Providentially, the Lord took control of the situation through the counsel of Hushai (15:32) who advised Absalom in such a way as to give David time to prepare for war with Absalom. Hushai's plan seemed best to the elders. It had two features: 1) the need for an army larger than 12,000 (v. 1), so that Absalom would not lose, and 2) the king leading the army into battle (an appeal to Absalom's arrogance).

17:14 the LORD had purposed. The text notes that Ahithophel's advice was rejected by Absalom because the Lord had determined to defeat the rebellion of Absalom, as prayed for by David (15:31). God's providence was controlling all the intrigues among the usurper's counselors.

people are hungry and weary and thirsty in
the wilderness."
18 And David numbered the people who
were with him, and set captains of thousands and captains of hundreds over them.
2Then David sent out one third of the people
under the hand of Joab, one third under the
hand of Abishai the son of Zeruiah, Joab's
brother, and one third under the hand of Ittai
the Gittite. And the king said to the people, "I
also will surely go out with you myself."
3But the people answered, "You shall not go
out! For if we flee away, they will not care about
us; nor if half of us die, will they care about us.
But *you are* worth ten thousand of us now. For
you are now more help to us in the city."
4Then the king said to them, "Whatever
seems best to you I will do." So the king stood
beside the gate, and all the people went out by
hundreds and by thousands. 5Now the king had
commanded Joab, Abishai, and Ittai, saying,
"*Deal* gently for my sake with the young man
Absalom." And all the people heard when the
king gave all the captains orders concerning
Absalom.
6So the people went out into the field of battle against Israel. And the battle was in the
woods of Ephraim. 7The people of Israel were
overthrown there before the servants of David, and a great slaughter of twenty thousand
took place there that day. 8For the battle there
was scattered over the face of the whole countryside, and the woods devoured more people
that day than the sword devoured.
9Then Absalom met the servants of David.
Absalom rode on a mule. The mule went under
the thick boughs of a great terebinth tree, and
his head caught in the terebinth; so he was left
hanging between heaven and earth. And the
mule which *was* under him went on. 10Now a
certain man saw *it* and told Joab, and said, "I
just saw Absalom hanging in a terebinth tree!"
11So Joab said to the man who told him, "You
just saw *him!* And why did you not strike him
there to the ground? I would have given you
ten *shekels* of silver and a belt."
12But the man said to Joab, "Though I were
to receive a thousand *shekels* of silver in my
hand, I would not raise my hand against the
king's son. For in our hearing the king commanded you and Abishai and Ittai, saying, 'Beware lest anyone *touch* the young man
Absalom!' 13Otherwise I would have dealt
falsely against my own life. For there is nothing hidden from the king, and you yourself
would have set yourself against *me*."
14Then Joab said, "I cannot linger with you."
And he took three spears in his hand and thrust
them through Absalom's heart, while he was
still alive in the midst of the terebinth tree. 15And
ten young men who bore Joab's armor surrounded Absalom, and struck and killed him.
16So Joab blew the trumpet, and the people
returned from pursuing Israel. For Joab held
back the people. 17And they took Absalom and
cast him into a large pit in the woods, and laid
a very large heap of stones over him. Then all
Israel fled, everyone to his tent.
18Now Absalom in his lifetime had taken and
set up a pillar for himself, which *is* in the
King's Valley. For he said, "I have no son to
keep my name in remembrance." He called
the pillar after his own name. And to this day
it is called Absalom's Monument.
19Then Ahimaaz the son of Zadok said, "Let
me run now and take the news to the king, how
the LORD has avenged him of his enemies."
20And Joab said to him, "You shall not take
the news this day, for you shall take the news
another day. But today you shall take no news,
because the king's son is dead." 21Then Joab
said to the Cushite, "Go, tell the king what you
have seen." So the Cushite bowed himself to
Joab and ran.
22And Ahimaaz the son of Zadok said again
to Joab, "But whatever happens, please let me
also run after the Cushite."
So Joab said, "Why will you run, my son,
since you have no news ready?"
23"But whatever happens," *he said,* "let me
run."
So he said to him, "Run." Then Ahimaaz ran
by way of the plain, and outran the Cushite.
24Now David was sitting between the two
gates. And the watchman went up to the roof
over the gate, to the wall, lifted his eyes and
looked, and there was a man, running alone.
25Then the watchman cried out and told the
king. And the king said, "If he *is* alone, *there is*
news in his mouth." And he came rapidly and
drew near.
26Then the watchman saw *another* man running, and the watchman called to the gatekeeper
and said, "There is *another* man, running alone!"
And the king said, "He also brings news."
27So the watchman said, "I think the running
of the first is like the running of Ahimaaz the
son of Zadok."
And the king said, "He *is* a good man, and
comes with good news."
28So Ahimaaz called out and said to the king,
"All is well!" Then he bowed down with his
face to the earth before the king, and said,
"Blessed *be* the LORD your God, who has delivered up the men who raised their hand against
my lord the king!"

29 The king said, "Is the young man Absalom
safe?"
Ahimaaz answered, "When Joab sent the
king's servant and *me* your servant, I saw a
great tumult, but I did not know what *it was*
about."
30 And the king said, "Turn aside *and* stand
here." So he turned aside and stood still.
31 Just then the Cushite came, and the
Cushite said, "There is good news, my lord
the king! For the LORD has avenged you this
day of all those who rose against you."
32 And the king said to the Cushite, "Is the
young man Absalom safe?"
So the Cushite answered, "May the enemies
of my lord the king, and all who rise against
you to do harm, be like *that* young man!"
33 Then the king was deeply moved, and went
up to the chamber over the gate, and wept. And
as he went, he said thus: "O my son Absalom—
my son, my son Absalom—if only I had died in
your place! O Absalom my son, my son!"

18:33 my son. Repeated 5 times in this verse, David lamented the death of Absalom, his son (19:5). In spite of all the harm that Absalom had caused, David was preoccupied with his personal loss in a melancholy way that seems to be consistent with his weakness as a father. It was an unwarranted zeal for such a worthless son and a warning about the pitiful results of sin.

Psalm 66:16–20

16 Come *and* hear, all you who fear God,
And I will declare what He has done
for my soul.
17 I cried to Him with my mouth,
And He was extolled with my tongue.
18 If I regard iniquity in my heart,
The Lord will not hear.
19 *But* certainly God has heard *me;*
He has attended to the voice of my prayer.
20 Blessed *be* God,
Who has not turned away my prayer,
Nor His mercy from me!

Proverbs 16:31–32

31 The silver-haired head *is* a crown of glory,
If it is found in the way of righteousness.
32 *He who is* slow to anger *is* better than
the mighty,
And he who rules his spirit than he
who takes a city.

7:31 many…believed. Divided conviction existed among the people regarding Jesus. While some wanted to seize Him, a small remnant of genuine believers existed among the crowds. The question here anticipates a negative answer, i.e., the Messiah could do no greater kinds of miracles than those Jesus had done.

John 7:28–53

28 Then Jesus cried out, as He taught in the
temple, saying, "You both know Me, and you
know where I am from; and I have not come of
Myself, but He who sent Me is true, whom
you do not know. 29 But I know Him, for I am
from Him, and He sent Me."
30 Therefore they sought to take Him; but no
one laid a hand on Him, because His hour had
not yet come. 31 And many of the people
believed in Him, and said, "When the Christ
comes, will He do more signs than these
which this *Man* has done?"
32 The Pharisees heard the crowd murmur-
ing these things concerning Him, and the
Pharisees and the chief priests sent officers to
take Him. 33 Then Jesus said to them, "I shall be
with you a little while longer, and *then* I go to
Him who sent Me. 34 You will seek Me and not
find *Me,* and where I am you cannot come."
35 Then the Jews said among themselves,
"Where does He intend to go that we shall not
find Him? Does He intend to go to the
Dispersion among the Greeks and teach the
Greeks? 36 What is this thing that He said, 'You
will seek Me and not find Me, and where I am
you cannot come'?"
37 On the last day, that great *day* of the feast,
Jesus stood and cried out, saying, "If anyone
thirsts, let him come to Me and drink. 38 He
who believes in Me, as the Scripture has said,
out of his heart will flow rivers of living
water." 39 But this He spoke concerning the
Spirit, whom those believing in Him would
receive; for the Holy Spirit was not yet *given,*
because Jesus was not yet glorified.
40 Therefore many from the crowd, when
they heard this saying, said, "Truly this is the
Prophet." 41 Others said, "This is the Christ."
But some said, "Will the Christ come out of
Galilee? 42 Has not the Scripture said that the
Christ comes from the seed of David and from
the town of Bethlehem, where David was?"
43 So there was a division among the people
because of Him. 44 Now some of them wanted
to take Him, but no one laid hands on Him.

[45]Then the officers came to the chief priests and Pharisees, who said to them, "Why have you not brought Him?"

[46]The officers answered, "No man ever spoke like this Man!"

[47]Then the Pharisees answered them, "Are
you also deceived? [48]Have any of the rulers or
the Pharisees believed in Him? [49]But this
crowd that does not know the law is accursed."

[50]Nicodemus (he who came to Jesus by
night, being one of them) said to them,
[51]"Does our law judge a man before it hears
him and knows what he is doing?"

[52]They answered and said to him, "Are you also from Galilee? Search and look, for no prophet has arisen out of Galilee."

[53]And everyone went to his *own* house.

7:37–52 This section catalogues the different reactions of people to Jesus' claims. These reactions have become universal patterns for reactions to Him through the ages. This section may be divided into the claim of Christ (vv. 37–39) and the reactions to Christ (vv. 40–52). The reactions may be subdivided into 5 sections: 1) the reaction of the convinced (vv. 40,41a); 2) the reaction of the contrary (vv. 41b,42); 3) the reaction of the hostile (vv. 43, 44); 4) the rejection of the confused (vv. 45, 46); and 5) the reaction of the religious authorities (vv. 47–52).

DAY 23: What does the "living water" have to do with Jesus?

A tradition grew up in the few centuries before Jesus that on the 7 days of the Feast of Tabernacles, a golden container filled with water from the pool of Siloam was carried in procession by the high priest back to the temple. As the procession came to the Watergate on the south side of the inner temple court, 3 trumpet blasts were made to mark the joy of the occasion and the people recited Isaiah 12:3, "With joy you will draw water from the wells of salvation." At the temple, while onlookers watched, the priests would march around the altar with the water container while the temple choir sang the Hallel (Pss. 113–118). The water was offered in sacrifice to God at the time of the morning sacrifice. The use of the water symbolized the blessing of adequate rainfall for crops.

In John 7:37, Jesus used this event as an object lesson and opportunity to make a very public invitation on the last day of the feast for His people to accept Him as the living water. His words recall Isaiah 55:1. "If anyone *thirsts*, let him *come* to Me and *drink*." These 3 words summarize the gospel invitation. A recognition of need leads to an approach to the source of provision, followed by receiving what is needed. The thirsty, needy soul feels the craving to come to the Savior and drink, i.e., receive the salvation that He offers.

"Out of his heart will flow rivers of living water" (v. 38). The water-pouring rite was also associated within Jewish tradition as a foreshadowing of the eschatological rivers of living water foreseen in Ezekiel 47:1–9 and Zechariah 13:1. The significance of Jesus' invitation centers in the fact that He was the fulfillment of all the Feast of Tabernacles anticipated, i.e., He was the One who provided the living water that gives eternal life to man (4:10,11). By this "He spoke concerning the Spirit" (v. 39). The impartation of the Holy Spirit is the source of spiritual and eternal life.

MAY 24

2 Samuel 19:1–20:26

19 And Joab was told, "Behold, the king is
weeping and mourning for Absalom."
[2]So the victory that day was *turned* into
mourning for all the people. For the people
heard it said that day, "The king is grieved for
his son." [3]And the people stole back into the
city that day, as people who are ashamed steal
away when they flee in battle. [4]But the king
covered his face, and the king cried out with a
loud voice, "O my son Absalom! O Absalom,
my son, my son!"
[5]Then Joab came into the house to the king,
and said, "Today you have disgraced all your
servants who today have saved your life, the
lives of your sons and daughters, the lives of
your wives and the lives of your concubines,
[6]in that you love your enemies and hate your
friends. For you have declared today that you
regard neither princes nor servants; for today
I perceive that if Absalom had lived and all of
us had died today, then it would have pleased
you well. [7]Now therefore, arise, go out and
speak comfort to your servants. For I swear
by the LORD, if you do not go out, not one will
stay with you this night. And that will be worse
for you than all the evil that has befallen you
from your youth until now." [8]Then the king
arose and sat in the gate. And they told all the
people, saying, "There is the king, sitting in

19:7 not one will stay with you. Joab, who was the esteemed general of the army, was a dangerous person because of that power. He was also dangerous to David because he had disobeyed his command to spare Absalom and killed him with no remorse. When he warned David that he would be in deep trouble if he did not immediately express appreciation to his men for their victory, David knew he could be in serious danger.

the gate." So all the people came before the
king.
For everyone of Israel had fled to his tent.
9Now all the people were in a dispute
throughout all the tribes of Israel, saying, "The
king saved us from the hand of our enemies,
he delivered us from the hand of the
Philistines, and now he has fled from the land
because of Absalom. 10But Absalom, whom we
anointed over us, has died in battle. Now therefore, why do you say nothing about bringing
back the king?"
11So King David sent to Zadok and Abiathar
the priests, saying, "Speak to the elders of Judah, saying, 'Why are you the last to bring the
king back to his house, since the words of all
Israel have come to the king, to his *very*
house? 12You *are* my brethren, you *are* my
bone and my flesh. Why then are you the last
to bring back the king?' 13And say to Amasa,
'*Are* you not my bone and my flesh? God do so
to me, and more also, if you are not commander of the army before me continually in place
of Joab.' " 14So he swayed the hearts of all the
men of Judah, just as *the heart of* one man, so
that they sent *this word* to the king: "Return,
you and all your servants!"
15Then the king returned and came to the
Jordan. And Judah came to Gilgal, to go to
meet the king, to escort the king across the

19:13 Amasa...commander of the army...in place of Joab. David appointed Amasa commander of his army, hoping to secure the allegiance of those who had followed Amasa when he led Absalom's forces, especially those of Judah. This appointment did persuade the tribe of Judah to support David's return to the kingship (v. 14) and secured the animosity of Joab against Amasa for taking his position (20:8–10).

Jordan. 16And Shimei the son of Gera, a
Benjamite, who *was* from Bahurim, hurried
and came down with the men of Judah to meet
King David. 17*There were* a thousand men of
Benjamin with him, and Ziba the servant of
the house of Saul, and his fifteen sons and his
twenty servants with him; and they went over
the Jordan before the king. 18Then a ferryboat
went across to carry over the king's household, and to do what he thought good.
Now Shimei the son of Gera fell down before
the king when he had crossed the Jordan.
19Then he said to the king, "Do not let my lord
impute iniquity to me, or remember what
wrong your servant did on the day that my
lord the king left Jerusalem, that the king
should take *it* to heart. 20For I, your servant,
know that I have sinned. Therefore here I am,
the first to come today of all the house of Joseph to go down to meet my lord the king."
21But Abishai the son of Zeruiah answered
and said, "Shall not Shimei be put to death for
this, because he cursed the LORD's anointed?"
22And David said, "What have I to do with
you, you sons of Zeruiah, that you should be
adversaries to me today? Shall any man be put
to death today in Israel? For do I not know that
today I *am* king over Israel?" 23Therefore the
king said to Shimei, "You shall not die." And
the king swore to him.
24Now Mephibosheth the son of Saul came
down to meet the king. And he had not cared
for his feet, nor trimmed his mustache, nor
washed his clothes, from the day the king
departed until the day he returned in peace.
25So it was, when he had come to Jerusalem to
meet the king, that the king said to him, "Why
did you not go with me, Mephibosheth?"
26And he answered, "My lord, O king, my servant deceived me. For your servant said, 'I will
saddle a donkey for myself, that I may ride on
it and go to the king,' because your servant *is*
lame. 27And he has slandered your servant to
my lord the king, but my lord the king *is* like
the angel of God. Therefore do *what is* good in
your eyes. 28For all my father's house were but
dead men before my lord the king. Yet you set
your servant among those who eat at your
own table. Therefore what right have I still to
cry out anymore to the king?"
29So the king said to him, "Why do you
speak anymore of your matters? I have said,
'You and Ziba divide the land.' "
30Then Mephibosheth said to the king, "Rather,
let him take it all, inasmuch as my lord the king
has come back in peace to his own house."
31And Barzillai the Gileadite came down
from Rogelim and went across the Jordan

with the king, to escort him across the Jordan. 32Now Barzillai was a very aged man,
eighty years old. And he had provided the
king with supplies while he stayed at Mahanaim, for he *was* a very rich man. 33And the
king said to Barzillai, "Come across with me,
and I will provide for you while you are with
me in Jerusalem."

34But Barzillai said to the king, "How long
have I to live, that I should go up with the king
to Jerusalem? 35I *am* today eighty years old.
Can I discern between the good and bad? Can
your servant taste what I eat or what I drink?
Can I hear any longer the voice of singing men
and singing women? Why then should your
servant be a further burden to my lord the
king? 36Your servant will go a little way across
the Jordan with the king. And why should the
king repay me *with* such a reward? 37Please let
your servant turn back again, that I may die in
my own city, near the grave of my father and
mother. But here is your servant Chimham;
let him cross over with my lord the king, and
do for him what seems good to you."

38And the king answered, "Chimham shall
cross over with me, and I will do for him what
seems good to you. Now whatever you
request of me, I will do for you." 39Then all the
people went over the Jordan. And when the
king had crossed over, the king kissed
Barzillai and blessed him, and he returned to
his own place.

40Now the king went on to Gilgal, and
Chimham went on with him. And all the people of Judah escorted the king, and also half
the people of Israel. 41Just then all the men of
Israel came to the king, and said to the king,
"Why have our brethren, the men of Judah,
stolen you away and brought the king, his
household, and all David's men with him
across the Jordan?"

42So all the men of Judah answered the men
of Israel, "Because the king *is* a close relative
of ours. Why then are you angry over this matter? Have we ever eaten at the king's *expense*?
Or has he given us any gift?"

43And the men of Israel answered the men of
Judah, and said, "We have ten shares in the king;
therefore we also have more *right* to David than
you. Why then do you despise us—were we not
the first to advise bringing back our king?"

Yet the words of the men of Judah were
fiercer than the words of the men of Israel.

20 And there happened to be there a
rebel, whose name *was* Sheba the son
of Bichri, a Benjamite. And he blew a trumpet,
and said:

"We have no share in David,
Nor do we have inheritance in the son
of Jesse;
Every man to his tents, O Israel!"

2So every man of Israel deserted David, *and*
followed Sheba the son of Bichri. But the men
of Judah, from the Jordan as far as Jerusalem,
remained loyal to their king.

3Now David came to his house at Jerusalem.
And the king took the ten women, his concubines whom he had left to keep the house, and
put them in seclusion and supported them,
but did not go in to them. So they were shut up
to the day of their death, living in widowhood.

4And the king said to Amasa, "Assemble the
men of Judah for me within three days, and be
present here yourself." 5So Amasa went to
assemble *the men of* Judah. But he delayed
longer than the set time which David had
appointed him. 6And David said to Abishai,
"Now Sheba the son of Bichri will do us more
harm than Absalom. Take your lord's servants
and pursue him, lest he find for himself fortified cities, and escape us." 7So Joab's men,
with the Cherethites, the Pelethites, and all
the mighty men, went out after him. And they
went out of Jerusalem to pursue Sheba the
son of Bichri. 8When they *were* at the large
stone which *is* in Gibeon, Amasa came before
them. Now Joab was dressed in battle armor;
on it was a belt *with* a sword fastened in its
sheath at his hips; and as he was going forward, it fell out. 9Then Joab said to Amasa,
"*Are* you in health, my brother?" And Joab
took Amasa by the beard with his right hand
to kiss him. 10But Amasa did not notice the
sword that *was* in Joab's hand. And he struck
him with it in the stomach, and his entrails
poured out on the ground; and he did not
strike him again. Thus he died.

Then Joab and Abishai his brother pursued
Sheba the son of Bichri. 11Meanwhile one of
Joab's men stood near Amasa, and said, "Whoever favors Joab and whoever *is* for David—
follow Joab!" 12But Amasa wallowed in *his* blood
in the middle of the highway. And when the man

20:11 one of Joab's men. Joab was reinstated as commander of David's army by his troops. It is a striking illustration of Joab's influence over the army that he could murder the commander whom David had chosen, a killing right before their eyes, and they would follow him unanimously as their leader in pursuit of Sheba.

saw that all the people stood still, he moved
Amasa from the highway to the field and threw
a garment over him, when he saw that everyone who came upon him halted. 13When he was
removed from the highway, all the people went
on after Joab to pursue Sheba the son of Bichri.
14And he went through all the tribes of Israel
to Abel and Beth Maachah and all the Berites.
So they were gathered together and also went
after *Sheba.* 15Then they came and besieged
him in Abel of Beth Maachah; and they cast up
a siege mound against the city, and it stood by
the rampart. And all the people who *were* with
Joab battered the wall to throw it down.
16Then a wise woman cried out from the city,
"Hear, hear! Please say to Joab, 'Come nearby,
that I may speak with you.' " 17When he had come
near to her, the woman said, "*Are* you Joab?"

He answered, "I *am.*"

Then she said to him, "Hear the words of your maidservant."

And he answered, "I am listening."

18So she spoke, saying, "They used to talk in
former times, saying, 'They shall surely seek
guidance at Abel,' and so they would end *dis-*
putes. 19I *am among the* peaceable *and* faithful
in Israel. You seek to destroy a city and a
mother in Israel. Why would you swallow up
the inheritance of the LORD?"
20And Joab answered and said, "Far be it, far
be it from me, that I should swallow up or
destroy! 21That *is* not so. But a man from the
mountains of Ephraim, Sheba the son of
Bichri by name, has raised his hand against
the king, against David. Deliver him only, and
I will depart from the city."

So the woman said to Joab, "Watch, his head
will be thrown to you over the wall." 22Then the
woman in her wisdom went to all the people.
And they cut off the head of Sheba the son of
Bichri, and threw *it* out to Joab. Then he blew
a trumpet, and they withdrew from the city,
every man to his tent. So Joab returned to the
king at Jerusalem.
23And Joab *was* over all the army of Israel;
Benaiah the son of Jehoiada *was* over the
Cherethites and the Pelethites; 24Adoram *was*
in charge of revenue; Jehoshaphat the son of
Ahilud *was* recorder; 25Sheva *was* scribe;
Zadok and Abiathar *were* the priests; 26and Ira
the Jairite was a chief minister under David.

Psalm 67:1–7

To the Chief Musician. On stringed instruments.
A Psalm. A Song.

God be merciful to us and bless us,
And cause His face to
shine upon us, Selah
2 That Your way may be known on earth,
Your salvation among all nations.

3 Let the peoples praise You, O God;
Let all the peoples praise You.
4 Oh, let the nations be glad and sing for
joy!
For You shall judge the people
righteously,
And govern the nations on earth.
Selah

5 Let the peoples praise You, O God;
Let all the peoples praise You.
6 *Then* the earth shall yield her increase;
God, our own God, shall bless us.
7 God shall bless us,
And all the ends of the earth shall fear
Him.

Proverbs 16:33–17:1

33 The lot is cast into the lap,
But its every decision *is* from the LORD.

17 Better *is* a dry morsel with
quietness,
Than a house full of feasting *with* strife.

16:33 lot. Casting lots was a method often used to reveal God's purposes in a matter (Josh. 14:1,2; 1 Sam. 14:38–43; 1 Chr. 25:8–31; Jon. 1:7; Acts 1:26). The high priest may have carried lots in his sacred vest, along with the Urim and Thummim (Ex. 28:30).

John 8:1–27

8 But Jesus went to the Mount of Olives.
2Now early in the morning He came
again into the temple, and all the people came
to Him; and He sat down and taught them.
3Then the scribes and Pharisees brought to
Him a woman caught in adultery. And when
they had set her in the midst, 4they said to
Him, "Teacher, this woman was caught in
adultery, in the very act. 5Now Moses, in the
law, commanded us that such should be
stoned. But what do You say?" 6This they said,
testing Him, that they might have *something* of
which to accuse Him. But Jesus stooped down
and wrote on the ground with *His* finger, as
though He did not hear.
7So when they continued asking Him, He
raised Himself up and said to them, "He who is
without sin among you, let him throw a stone
at her first." 8And again He stooped down and
wrote on the ground. 9Then those who heard *it,*

being convicted by *their* conscience, went out
one by one, beginning with the oldest *even* to the
last. And Jesus was left alone, and the woman
standing in the midst. 10When Jesus had raised
Himself up and saw no one but the woman, He
said to her, "Woman, where are those accusers
of yours? Has no one condemned you?"
11She said, "No one, Lord."
And Jesus said to her, "Neither do I condemn you; go and sin no more."
12Then Jesus spoke to them again, saying, "I
am the light of the world. He who follows Me
shall not walk in darkness, but have the light
of life."
13The Pharisees therefore said to Him, "You
bear witness of Yourself; Your witness is not
true."
14Jesus answered and said to them, "Even if
I bear witness of Myself, My witness is true,
for I know where I came from and where I am
going; but you do not know where I come
from and where I am going. 15You judge
according to the flesh; I judge no one. 16And
yet if I do judge, My judgment is true; for I am
not alone, but I *am* with the Father who sent
Me. 17It is also written in your law that the testimony of two men is true. 18I am One who
bears witness of Myself, and the Father who
sent Me bears witness of Me."
19Then they said to Him, "Where is Your
Father?"
Jesus answered, "You know neither Me nor
My Father. If you had known Me, you would
have known My Father also."
20These words Jesus spoke in the treasury,
as He taught in the temple; and no one laid
hands on Him, for His hour had not yet come.
21Then Jesus said to them again, "I am going
away, and you will seek Me, and will die in
your sin. Where I go you cannot come."
22So the Jews said, "Will He kill Himself,
because He says, 'Where I go you cannot come'?"
23And He said to them, "You are from beneath;
I am from above. You are of this world; I am not
of this world. 24Therefore I said to you that you
will die in your sins; for if you do not believe that
I am *He,* you will die in your sins."
25Then they said to Him, "Who are You?"
And Jesus said to them, "Just what I have
been saying to you from the beginning. 26I
have many things to say and to judge concerning you, but He who sent Me is true; and
I speak to the world those things which I
heard from Him."
27They did not understand that He spoke to
them of the Father.

8:24 if you do not believe. Jesus emphasized that the fatal, unforgivable, and eternal sin is failure to believe in Him as Messiah and Son of God. In truth, all other sins can be forgiven if this one is repented of. **I am *He*.** "*He*" is not part of the original statement. Jesus' words were not constructed normally but were influenced by Old Testament Hebrew usage. It is an absolute usage meaning "I AM" and has immense theological significance. The reference may be to both Exodus 3:14 where the Lord declared His name as "I AM" and to Isaiah 40–55 where the phrase "I am" occurs repeatedly (especially 43:10,13,25; 46:4; 48:12). In this, Jesus referred to Himself as the God (Yahweh—the LORD) of the Old Testament and directly claimed full Deity for Himself, prompting the Jews' question of v. 25.

DAY 24: How is Jesus the light of the world?

In John 8:12–21, the word "again" indicates that Jesus spoke once more to the people at this same Feast of Tabernacles (7:2,10). While Jesus first used the water-drawing rite (7:37–39) as a metaphor to portray the ultimate spiritual truth of Himself as Messiah who fulfills all that the feast anticipated, He then turned to another rite that traditionally occurred at the feast: the lighting ceremony. During Tabernacles, 4 large lamps in the temple's court of women were lit and an exuberant nightly celebration took place under their light with people dancing through the night and holding burning torches in their hands while singing songs and praises. The Levitical orchestras also played.

Jesus took this opportunity of the lighting celebration to portray another spiritual analogy for the people: "I am the light of the world" (v. 12). This is the second "I AM" statement (6:35). John has already used the "light" metaphor for Jesus (1:4). Jesus' metaphor here is steeped in Old Testament allusions (Ex. 13:21,22; 14:19–25; Pss. 27:1; 119:105; Prov. 6:23; Ezek. 1:4,13,26–28; Hab. 3:3,4). The phrase highlights Jesus' role as Messiah and Son of God (Ps. 27:1; Mal. 4:2). The Old Testament indicates that the coming age of Messiah would be a time when the Lord would be a light for His people (Is. 60:19–22; see Rev. 21:23,24), as well as for the whole earth (Is. 42:6; 49:6). Zechariah 14:5b–8 has an emphasis on God as the light of the world who gives living waters to His people. This latter passage probably formed the liturgical readings for the Feast of Tabernacles.

"He who follows Me shall not walk in darkness, but have the light of life." The word "follows" conveys the idea of someone who gives himself completely to the person followed. No half-hearted followers exist in Jesus' mind (Matt. 8:18–22; 10:38,39). A veiled reference exists here to the Jews, following the pillar of cloud and fire that led them during the Exodus (Ex. 13:21).

MAY 25

2 Samuel 21:1–22:51

21 Now there was a famine in the days of
David for three years, year after year;
and David inquired of the LORD. And the LORD
answered, "*It is* because of Saul and *his* bloodthirsty house, because he killed the Gibeonites." [2]So the king called the Gibeonites and
spoke to them. Now the Gibeonites *were* not of
the children of Israel, but of the remnant of the
Amorites; the children of Israel had sworn protection to them, but Saul had sought to kill them
in his zeal for the children of Israel and Judah.

21:1,2 Saul and *his* bloodthirsty house. By divine revelation David learned that the famine was a result of sin committed by Saul; namely, that he had slain the Gibeonites. There is no further reference to this event. Saul was probably trying to do as God commanded and rid the land of the remnant of heathen in order that Israel might prosper (v. 2). But in his zeal he had committed a serious sin. He had broken a covenant that had been made 400 years before between Joshua and the Gibeonites, who were in the land when Israel took possession of it. They deceived Joshua into making the covenant, but it was, nevertheless, a covenant (Josh. 9:3–27). Covenant keeping was no small matter to God (Josh. 9:20).

[3]Therefore David said to the Gibeonites,
"What shall I do for you? And with what shall
I make atonement, that you may bless the
inheritance of the LORD?"
[4]And the Gibeonites said to him, "We will have
no silver or gold from Saul or from his house,
nor shall you kill any man in Israel for us."
So he said, "Whatever you say, I will do for
you."
[5]Then they answered the king, "As for the
man who consumed us and plotted against us,
that we should be destroyed from remaining in
any of the territories of Israel, [6]let seven men of
his descendants be delivered to us, and we will
hang them before the LORD in Gibeah of Saul,
whom the LORD chose."
And the king said, "I will give *them.*"
[7]But the king spared Mephibosheth the son
of Jonathan, the son of Saul, because of the
LORD's oath that *was* between them, between
David and Jonathan the son of Saul. [8]So the king
took Armoni and Mephibosheth, the two sons
of Rizpah the daughter of Aiah, whom she bore
to Saul, and the five sons of Michal the daughter of Saul, whom she brought up for Adriel the
son of Barzillai the Meholathite; [9]and he delivered them into the hands of the Gibeonites, and
they hanged them on the hill before the LORD.
So they fell, *all* seven together, and were put to
death in the days of harvest, in the first *days,* in
the beginning of barley harvest.
[10]Now Rizpah the daughter of Aiah took
sackcloth and spread it for herself on the rock,
from the beginning of harvest until the late
rains poured on them from heaven. And she
did not allow the birds of the air to rest on them
by day nor the beasts of the field by night.
[11]And David was told what Rizpah the daughter of Aiah, the concubine of Saul, had done.
[12]Then David went and took the bones of Saul,
and the bones of Jonathan his son, from the
men of Jabesh Gilead who had stolen them
from the street of Beth Shan, where the
Philistines had hung them up, after the
Philistines had struck down Saul in Gilboa.
[13]So he brought up the bones of Saul and the
bones of Jonathan his son from there; and they
gathered the bones of those who had been
hanged. [14]They buried the bones of Saul and
Jonathan his son in the country of Benjamin in
Zelah, in the tomb of Kish his father. So they
performed all that the king commanded. And
after that God heeded the prayer for the land.
[15]When the Philistines were at war again with
Israel, David and his servants with him went
down and fought against the Philistines; and David grew faint. [16]Then Ishbi-Benob, who *was* one
of the sons of the giant, the weight of whose
bronze spear *was* three hundred *shekels,* who
was bearing a new *sword,* thought he could kill
David. [17]But Abishai the son of Zeruiah came to
his aid, and struck the Philistine and killed him.
Then the men of David swore to him, saying,
"You shall go out no more with us to battle, lest
you quench the lamp of Israel."

[18]Now it happened afterward that there was
again a battle with the Philistines at Gob. Then
Sibbechai the Hushathite killed Saph, who *was*
one of the sons of the giant. [19]Again there was
war at Gob with the Philistines, where Elhanan
the son of Jaare-Oregim the Bethlehemite
killed *the brother of* Goliath the Gittite, the shaft
of whose spear *was* like a weaver's beam.

[20]Yet again there was war at Gath, where
there was a man of *great* stature, who had six
fingers on each hand and six toes on each
foot, twenty-four in number; and he also was
born to the giant. [21]So when he defied Israel,
Jonathan the son of Shimea, David's brother,
killed him.

[22]These four were born to the giant in Gath,
and fell by the hand of David and by the hand
of his servants.

22 Then David spoke to the LORD the words of this song, on the day when the LORD had delivered him from the hand of all his enemies, and from the hand of Saul. [2]And he said:

"The LORD *is* my rock and my fortress
and my deliverer;
[3] The God of my strength, in whom I will
trust;
My shield and the horn of my
salvation,
My stronghold and my refuge;
My Savior, You save me from violence.
[4] I will call upon the LORD, *who is worthy*
to be praised;
So shall I be saved from my enemies.

[5] "When the waves of death surrounded
me,
The floods of ungodliness made me
afraid.
[6] The sorrows of Sheol surrounded me;
The snares of death confronted me.
[7] In my distress I called upon the LORD,
And cried out to my God;
He heard my voice from His temple,
And my cry *entered* His ears.

[8] "Then the earth shook and trembled;
The foundations of heaven quaked and
were shaken,
Because He was angry.
[9] Smoke went up from His nostrils,
And devouring fire from His mouth;
Coals were kindled by it.
[10] He bowed the heavens also,
and came down
With darkness under His feet.
[11] He rode upon a cherub, and flew;
And He was seen upon the wings of
the wind.
[12] He made darkness canopies around Him,
Dark waters *and* thick clouds of the
skies.
[13] From the brightness before Him
Coals of fire were kindled.

[14] "The LORD thundered from heaven,
And the Most High uttered His voice.
[15] He sent out arrows and scattered them;
Lightning bolts, and He vanquished
them.
[16] Then the channels of the sea were seen,
The foundations of the world were
uncovered,
At the rebuke of the LORD,
At the blast of the breath of His
nostrils.

[17] "He sent from above, He took me,
He drew me out of many waters.
[18] He delivered me from my strong
enemy,
From those who hated me;
For they were too strong for me.
[19] They confronted me in the day of my
calamity,
But the LORD was my support.
[20] He also brought me out into a broad
place;
He delivered me because He delighted
in me.

[21] "The LORD rewarded me according to
my righteousness;
According to the cleanness of my
hands
He has recompensed me.
[22] For I have kept the ways of the LORD,
And have not wickedly departed from
my God.
[23] For all His judgments *were* before me;
And *as for* His statutes, I did not depart
from them.
[24] I was also blameless before Him,
And I kept myself from my iniquity.
[25] Therefore the LORD has recompensed
me according to my righteousness,
According to my cleanness in His eyes.

[26] "With the merciful You will show
Yourself merciful;
With a blameless man You will show
Yourself blameless;
[27] With the pure You will show Yourself
pure;
And with the devious You will show
Yourself shrewd.
[28] You will save the humble people;
But Your eyes *are* on the haughty, *that*
You may bring *them* down.

29 "For You *are* my lamp, O LORD;
The LORD shall enlighten my darkness.
30 For by You I can run against a troop;
By my God I can leap over a wall.
31 *As for* God, His way *is* perfect;
The word of the LORD *is* proven;
He *is* a shield to all who trust in Him.
32 "For who *is* God, except the LORD?
And who *is* a rock, except our God?
33 God *is* my strength *and* power,
And He makes my way perfect.
34 He makes my feet like the *feet* of deer,
And sets me on my high places.
35 He teaches my hands to make war,
So that my arms can bend a bow of bronze.

36 "You have also given me the shield of Your salvation;
Your gentleness has made me great.
37 You enlarged my path under me;
So my feet did not slip.

38 "I have pursued my enemies and destroyed them;
Neither did I turn back again till they were destroyed.
39 And I have destroyed them and wounded them,
So that they could not rise;
They have fallen under my feet.
40 For You have armed me with strength for the battle;
You have subdued under me those who rose against me.
41 You have also given me the necks of my enemies,
So that I destroyed those who hated me.
42 They looked, but *there was* none to save;
Even to the LORD, but He did not answer them.
43 Then I beat them as fine as the dust of the earth;
I trod them like dirt in the streets,
And I spread them out.

44 "You have also delivered me from the strivings of my people;
You have kept me as the head of the nations.
A people I have not known shall serve me.
45 The foreigners submit to me;
As soon as they hear, they obey me.
46 The foreigners fade away,
And come frightened from their hideouts.

47 "The LORD lives!
Blessed *be* my Rock!
Let God be exalted,
The Rock of my salvation!
48 *It is* God who avenges me,
And subdues the peoples under me;
49 He delivers me from my enemies.
You also lift me up above those who rise against me;
You have delivered me from the violent man.
50 Therefore I will give thanks to You, O LORD, among the Gentiles,
And sing praises to Your name.

51 *He* is the tower of salvation to His king,
And shows mercy to His anointed,
To David and his descendants forevermore."

22:1–51 David's song of praise here is almost identical to Psalm 18. This song also has many verbal links to Hannah's prayer (1 Sam. 2:1–10) and together with it forms the framework for the books of Samuel. This song focuses on the Lord's deliverance of David from all his enemies, in response to which David praised the Lord, his deliverer (vv. 2–4). The major part of the song (vv. 5–46) states the reason for this praise of the Lord. David first describes how the Lord had delivered him from his enemies (vv. 5–20), then declares why the Lord had delivered him from his enemies (vv. 21–28), then states the extent of the Lord's deliverance from his enemies (vv. 29–46). The song concludes with David's resolve to praise his delivering Lord, even among the Gentiles (vv. 47–51).

Psalm 68:1–6

To the Chief Musician. A Psalm of David. A Song.

Let God arise,
Let His enemies be scattered;
Let those also who hate Him flee before Him.
2 As smoke is driven away,
So drive *them* away;
As wax melts before the fire,
So let the wicked perish at the presence of God.
3 But let the righteous be glad;
Let them rejoice before God;
Yes, let them rejoice exceedingly.

4 Sing to God, sing praises to His name;
Extol Him who rides on the clouds,
By His name YAH,
And rejoice before Him.

5 A father of the fatherless, a defender of widows,
Is God in His holy habitation.
6 God sets the solitary in families;
He brings out those who are bound into prosperity;
But the rebellious dwell in a dry *land.*

Proverbs 17:2–4

2 A wise servant will rule over a son who causes shame,
And will share an inheritance among the brothers.

3 The refining pot *is* for silver and the furnace for gold,
But the LORD tests the hearts.

4 An evildoer gives heed to false lips;
A liar listens eagerly to a spiteful tongue.

John 8:28–59

28Then Jesus said to them, "When you lift up the Son of Man, then you will know that I am *He,* and *that* I do nothing of Myself; but as My Father taught Me, I speak these things. 29And He who sent Me is with Me. The Father has not left Me alone, for I always do those things that please Him." 30As He spoke these words, many believed in Him.

31Then Jesus said to those Jews who believed Him, "If you abide in My word, you are My disciples indeed. 32And you shall know the truth, and the truth shall make you free."

33They answered Him, "We are Abraham's descendants, and have never been in bondage to anyone. How *can* You say, 'You will be made free'?"

34Jesus answered them, "Most assuredly, I say to you, whoever commits sin is a slave of sin. 35And a slave does not abide in the house forever, *but* a son abides forever. 36Therefore if the Son makes you free, you shall be free indeed.

37"I know that you are Abraham's descendants, but you seek to kill Me, because My word has no place in you. 38I speak what I have seen with My Father, and you do what you have seen with your father."

39They answered and said to Him, "Abraham is our father."

Jesus said to them, "If you were Abraham's children, you would do the works of Abraham. 40But now you seek to kill Me, a Man who has told you the truth which I heard from God. Abraham did not do this. 41You do the deeds of your father."

Then they said to Him, "We were not born of fornication; we have one Father—God."

8:39 If you were Abraham's children. The construction of this phrase indicates that Jesus was denying that mere physical lineage was sufficient for salvation (Phil. 3:4–9). The sense would be "if you were Abraham's children, but you are not, then you would act like Abraham did." Just as children inherit genetic characteristics from their parents, so also those who are truly Abraham's offspring will act like Abraham, i.e., imitate Abraham's faith and obedience (Rom. 4:16; Gal. 3:6–9; Heb. 11:8–19; James 2:21–24). **works of Abraham.** Abraham's faith was demonstrated through his obedience to God (James 2:21–24). Jesus' point was that the conduct of the unbelieving Jews was diametrically opposed by the conduct of Abraham, who lived a life of obedience to all that God had commanded. Their conduct toward Jesus demonstrated that their real father was Satan (vv. 41,44).

42Jesus said to them, "If God were your Father, you would love Me, for I proceeded forth and came from God; nor have I come of Myself, but He sent Me. 43Why do you not understand My speech? Because you are not able to listen to My word. 44You are of *your* father the devil, and the desires of your father you want to do. He was a murderer from the beginning, and does not stand in the truth, because there is no truth in him. When he speaks a lie, he speaks from his own *resources,* for he is a liar and the father of it. 45But because I tell the truth, you do not believe Me. 46Which of you convicts Me of sin? And if I tell the truth, why do you not believe Me? 47He who is of God hears God's words; therefore you do not hear, because you are not of God."

48Then the Jews answered and said to Him, "Do we not say rightly that You are a Samaritan and have a demon?"

49Jesus answered, "I do not have a demon; but I honor My Father, and you dishonor Me. 50And I do not seek My *own* glory; there is One who seeks and judges. 51Most assuredly, I say to you, if anyone keeps My word he shall never see death."

52Then the Jews said to Him, "Now we know that You have a demon! Abraham is dead, and the prophets; and You say, 'If anyone keeps My word he shall never taste death.' 53Are You greater than our father Abraham, who is dead? And the prophets are dead. Who do You make Yourself out to be?"

54Jesus answered, "If I honor Myself, My honor is nothing. It is My Father who honors Me, of whom you say that He is your God.

[55]Yet you have not known Him, but I know Him. And if I say, 'I do not know Him,' I shall be a liar like you; but I do know Him and keep His word. [56]Your father Abraham rejoiced to see My day, and he saw *it* and was glad."

[57]Then the Jews said to Him, "You are not yet fifty years old, and have You seen Abraham?"

[58]Jesus said to them, "Most assuredly, I say to you, before Abraham was, I AM."

[59]Then they took up stones to throw at Him; but Jesus hid Himself and went out of the temple, going through the midst of them, and so passed by.

8:58 Most assuredly...I AM. Here Jesus declared Himself to be Yahweh, i.e., the Lord of the Old Testament. Basic to the expression are such passages as Exodus 3:14; Deuteronomy 32:39; Isaiah 41:4; 43:10, where God declared Himself to be the eternally preexistent God who revealed Himself in the Old Testament to the Jews.

DAY 25: What are the steps toward true Christian discipleship?

John 8:31–36 is a pivotal section of Scripture in understanding genuine salvation and true discipleship. John emphasized these realities by stressing truth and freedom. The focus in the passage is upon those who were exercising the beginnings of faith in Jesus as Messiah and Son of God. Jesus desired them to move on in their faith. Saving faith is not fickle but firm and settled. Such maturity expresses itself in full commitment to the truth in Jesus Christ resulting in genuine freedom.

The first step in the progress toward true discipleship is belief in Jesus Christ as Messiah and Son of God (v. 31). "If you abide in My word, you are My disciples indeed" reveals the second step in the progress toward true discipleship. Perseverance in obedience to Scripture (Matt. 28:19,20) is the fruit or evidence of genuine faith (Eph. 2:10). The word "abide" means to habitually abide in Jesus' words. A genuine believer holds fast, obeys, and practices Jesus' teaching. The one who continues in His teaching has both the Father and the Son (2 John 9; Heb. 3:14; Rev. 2:26). Real disciples are both learners (the basic meaning of the word) and faithful followers.

"The truth" (v. 32) has reference not only to the facts surrounding Jesus as the Messiah and Son of God but also to the teaching that He brought. A genuinely saved and obedient follower of the Lord Jesus will know divine truth and both freedom from sin (v. 34) and the search for reality. This divine truth comes not merely by intellectual assent (1 Cor. 2:14) but by saving commitment to Christ (Titus 1:1,2).

"Whoever commits sin" (v. 34). The kind of slavery that Jesus had in mind was not physical slavery but slavery to sin (Rom. 6:17,18). The idea of "commits sin" means to practice sin habitually (1 John 3:4,8,9). The ultimate bondage is not political or economic enslavement but spiritual bondage to sin and rebellion against God. Thus, this also explains why Jesus would not let Himself be reduced to merely a political Messiah (6:14,15).

MAY 26

2 Samuel 23:1–24:25

23 Now these *are* the last words of David.

Thus says David the son of Jesse;
Thus says the man raised up on high,
The anointed of the God of Jacob,
And the sweet psalmist of Israel:

2 "The Spirit of the LORD spoke by me,
And His word *was* on my tongue.
3 The God of Israel said,
The Rock of Israel spoke to me:
'He who rules over men *must be* just,
Ruling in the fear of God.
4 And *he shall be* like the light of the morning *when* the sun rises,
A morning without clouds,
Like the tender grass *springing* out of the earth,
By clear shining after rain.'

5 "Although my house *is* not so with God,
Yet He has made with me an everlasting covenant,
Ordered in all *things* and secure.
For *this is* all my salvation and all *my* desire;
Will He not make *it* increase?
6 But *the sons* of rebellion *shall* all *be* as thorns thrust away,
Because they cannot be taken with hands.
7 But the man *who* touches them

Must be armed with iron and the shaft
of a spear,
And they shall be utterly burned with
fire in *their* place."

[8]These *are* the names of the mighty men
whom David had: Josheb-Basshebeth the
Tachmonite, chief among the captains. He
was called Adino the Eznite, because he had
killed eight hundred men at one time. [9]And
after him *was* Eleazar the son of Dodo, the
Ahohite, *one* of the three mighty men with David when they defied the Philistines *who* were
gathered there for battle, and the men of Israel had retreated. [10]He arose and attacked the
Philistines until his hand was weary, and his
hand stuck to the sword. The LORD brought
about a great victory that day; and the people
returned after him only to plunder. [11]And after
him *was* Shammah the son of Agee the
Hararite. The Philistines had gathered together into a troop where there was a piece of
ground full of lentils. So the people fled from
the Philistines. [12]But he stationed himself in the
middle of the field, defended it, and killed the
Philistines. So the LORD brought about a great
victory.

[13]Then three of the thirty chief men went
down at harvest time and came to David at the
cave of Adullam. And the troop of Philistines
encamped in the Valley of Rephaim. [14]David
was then in the stronghold, and the garrison of
the Philistines *was* then *in* Bethlehem. [15]And
David said with longing, "Oh, that someone
would give me a drink of the water from the
well of Bethlehem, which *is* by the gate!" [16]So
the three mighty men broke through the
camp of the Philistines, drew water from the
well of Bethlehem that *was* by the gate, and
took it and brought *it* to David. Nevertheless
he would not drink it, but poured it out to the
LORD. [17]And he said, "Far be it from me, O
LORD, that I should do this! Is *this not* the
blood of the men who went in *jeopardy of* their
lives?" Therefore he would not drink it.

These things were done by the three
mighty men.

[18]Now Abishai the brother of Joab, the son of
Zeruiah, was chief of *another* three. He lifted
his spear against three hundred *men,* killed
them, and won a name among *these* three.
[19]Was he not the most honored of three?
Therefore he became their captain. However,
he did not attain to the *first* three.

[20]Benaiah *was* the son of Jehoiada, the son
of a valiant man from Kabzeel, who had done
many deeds. He had killed two lion-like
heroes of Moab. He also had gone down and
killed a lion in the midst of a pit on a snowy
day. [21]And he killed an Egyptian, a spectacular
man. The Egyptian *had* a spear in his hand; so
he went down to him with a staff, wrested the
spear out of the Egyptian's hand, and killed
him with his own spear. [22]These *things*
Benaiah the son of Jehoiada did, and won a
name among three mighty men. [23]He was
more honored than the thirty, but he did not
attain to the *first* three. And David appointed
him over his guard.

[24]Asahel the brother of Joab *was* one of the
thirty; Elhanan the son of Dodo of Bethlehem,
[25]Shammah the Harodite, Elika the Harodite,
[26]Helez the Paltite, Ira the son of Ikkesh the
Tekoite, [27]Abiezer the Anathothite, Mebunnai
the Hushathite, [28]Zalmon the Ahohite,
Maharai the Netophathite, [29]Heleb the son of
Baanah (the Netophathite), Ittai the son of
Ribai from Gibeah of the children of Benjamin, [30]Benaiah a Pirathonite, Hiddai from the
brooks of Gaash, [31]Abi-Albon the Arbathite,
Azmaveth the Barhumite, [32]Eliahba the Shaalbonite (of the sons of Jashen), Jonathan,
[33]Shammah the Hararite, Ahiam the son of
Sharar the Hararite, [34]Eliphelet the son of
Ahasbai, the son of the Maachathite, Eliam
the son of Ahithophel the Gilonite, [35]Hezrai
the Carmelite, Paarai the Arbite, [36]Igal the son
of Nathan of Zobah, Bani the Gadite, [37]Zelek
the Ammonite, Naharai the Beerothite (armorbearer of Joab the son of Zeruiah), [38]Ira the
Ithrite, Gareb the Ithrite, [39]*and* Uriah the Hittite: thirty-seven in all.

24 Again the anger of the LORD was
aroused against Israel, and He moved
David against them to say, "Go, number Israel
and Judah."

[2]So the king said to Joab the commander of
the army who *was* with him, "Now go throughout all the tribes of Israel, from Dan to
Beersheba, and count the people, that I may
know the number of the people."

[3]And Joab said to the king, "Now may the
LORD your God add to the people a hundred
times more than there are, and may the eyes
of my lord the king see *it.* But why does my
lord the king desire this thing?" [4]Nevertheless
the king's word prevailed against Joab and
against the captains of the army. Therefore
Joab and the captains of the army went out
from the presence of the king to count the
people of Israel.

[5]And they crossed over the Jordan and
camped in Aroer, on the right side of the town
which *is* in the midst of the ravine of Gad, and
toward Jazer. [6]Then they came to Gilead and
to the land of Tahtim Hodshi; they came to
Dan Jaan and around to Sidon; [7]and they came

24:1 Again. A second outbreak of the divine wrath occurred after the 3-year famine recorded in 21:1. **against Israel.** The inciting of David to conduct a census was a punishment on Israel from the Lord for some unspecified sins. Perhaps sins of pride and ambition had led him to increase the size of his army unnecessarily and place heavy burdens of support on the people. Whatever the sin, it is clear God was dissatisfied with David's motives, goals, and actions and brought judgment. **He moved David.** Satan incited David to take this census, and the Lord sovereignly and permissively used Satan to accomplish His will (1 Chr. 21:1). **number Israel and Judah.** A census was usually for military purposes, which seems to be the case here (v. 9). Numbering the potential army of Israel had been done in the past (Num. 1:1,2; 26:1–4). However, this census of Israel's potential army did not have the sanction of the Lord and proceeded from wrong motives. David either wanted to glory in the size of his fighting force or take more territory than what the Lord had granted him. He shifted his trust from God to military power (this is a constant theme in the Psalms; see 20:7; 25:2; 44:6).

to the stronghold of Tyre and to all the cities of
the Hivites and the Canaanites. Then they went
out to South Judah *as far as* Beersheba. [8]So
when they had gone through all the land, they
came to Jerusalem at the end of nine months
and twenty days. [9]Then Joab gave the sum of
the number of the people to the king. And
there were in Israel eight hundred thousand
valiant men who drew the sword, and the men
of Judah were five hundred thousand men.
[10]And David's heart condemned him after he
had numbered the people. So David said to the
LORD, "I have sinned greatly in what I have done;
but now, I pray, O LORD, take away the iniquity of
Your servant, for I have done very foolishly."
[11]Now when David arose in the morning, the
word of the LORD came to the prophet Gad, David's seer, saying, [12]"Go and tell David, 'Thus
says the LORD: "I offer you three *things;* choose
one of them for yourself, that I may do *it* to
you." ' " [13]So Gad came to David and told him;
and he said to him, "Shall seven years of famine
come to you in your land? Or shall you flee
three months before your enemies, while they
pursue you? Or shall there be three days'
plague in your land? Now consider and see what
answer I should take back to Him who sent me."
[14]And David said to Gad, "I am in great distress. Please let us fall into the hand of the
LORD, for His mercies *are* great; but do not let
me fall into the hand of man."
[15]So the LORD sent a plague upon Israel from
the morning till the appointed time. From Dan
to Beersheba seventy thousand men of the
people died. [16]And when the angel stretched
out His hand over Jerusalem to destroy it, the
LORD relented from the destruction, and said
to the angel who was destroying the people,
"It is enough; now restrain your hand." And
the angel of the LORD was by the threshing
floor of Araunah the Jebusite.
[17]Then David spoke to the LORD when he
saw the angel who was striking the people, and
said, "Surely I have sinned, and I have done
wickedly; but these sheep, what have they
done? Let Your hand, I pray, be against me and
against my father's house."
[18]And Gad came that day to David and said to
him, "Go up, erect an altar to the LORD on the
threshing floor of Araunah the Jebusite." [19]So
David, according to the word of Gad, went up as
the LORD commanded. [20]Now Araunah looked,
and saw the king and his servants coming
toward him. So Araunah went out and bowed
before the king with his face to the ground.
[21]Then Araunah said, "Why has my lord the
king come to his servant?"

And David said, "To buy the threshing floor
from you, to build an altar to the LORD, that the
plague may be withdrawn from the people."
[22]Now Araunah said to David, "Let my lord
the king take and offer up whatever *seems*
good to him. Look, *here are* oxen for burnt
sacrifice, and threshing implements and the
yokes of the oxen for wood. [23]All these, O king,
Araunah has given to the king."

And Araunah said to the king, "May the
LORD your God accept you."
[24]Then the king said to Araunah, "No, but I
will surely buy *it* from you for a price; nor will
I offer burnt offerings to the LORD my God
with that which costs me nothing." So David
bought the threshing floor and the oxen for
fifty shekels of silver. [25]And David built there
an altar to the LORD, and offered burnt offerings and peace offerings. So the LORD heeded
the prayers for the land, and the plague was
withdrawn from Israel.

Psalm 68:7–10

7 O God, when You went out before
Your people,
When You marched through the
wilderness, Selah
8 The earth shook;
The heavens also dropped *rain* at the
presence of God;

Sinai itself *was moved* at the presence
of God, the God of Israel.
9 You, O God, sent a plentiful rain,
Whereby You confirmed Your
inheritance,
When it was weary.
10 Your congregation dwelt in it;
You, O God, provided from Your
goodness for the poor.

Proverbs 17:5–6

5 He who mocks the poor reproaches his
Maker;
He who is glad at calamity will not go
unpunished.

6 Children's children *are* the crown of
old men,
And the glory of children *is* their father.

John 9:1–23

9 Now as *Jesus* passed by, He saw a man who
was blind from birth. 2And His disciples
asked Him, saying, "Rabbi, who sinned, this
man or his parents, that he was born blind?"
3Jesus answered, "Neither this man nor his
parents sinned, but that the works of God
should be revealed in him. 4I must work the
works of Him who sent Me while it is day; *the*
night is coming when no one can work. 5As
long as I am in the world, I am the light of the
world."
6When He had said these things, He spat on
the ground and made clay with the saliva; and
He anointed the eyes of the blind man with the
clay. 7And He said to him, "Go, wash in the
pool of Siloam" (which is translated, Sent). So
he went and washed, and came back seeing.
8Therefore the neighbors and those who
previously had seen that he was blind said, "Is
not this he who sat and begged?"
9Some said, "This is he." Others *said,* "He is
like him."
He said, "I am *he.*"
10Therefore they said to him, "How were
your eyes opened?"
11He answered and said, "A Man called Jesus made clay and anointed my eyes and said
to me, 'Go to the pool of Siloam and wash.' So
I went and washed, and I received sight."
12Then they said to him, "Where is He?"
He said, "I do not know."
13They brought him who formerly was blind
to the Pharisees. 14Now it was a Sabbath when
Jesus made the clay and opened his eyes.
15Then the Pharisees also asked him again how
he had received his sight. He said to them, "He
put clay on my eyes, and I washed, and I see."
16Therefore some of the Pharisees said,
"This Man is not from God, because He does
not keep the Sabbath."
Others said, "How can a man who is a sinner do such signs?" And there was a division
among them.
17They said to the blind man again, "What do
you say about Him because He opened your
eyes?"
He said, "He is a prophet."
18But the Jews did not believe concerning
him, that he had been blind and received his

9:17 He is a prophet. While the blind man saw clearly that Jesus was more than a mere man, the sighted but obstinate Pharisees were spiritually blind to that truth (v. 39). Blindness in the Bible is a metaphor for spiritual darkness, i.e., inability to discern God or His truth (2 Cor. 4:3–6; Col. 1:12–14).

sight, until they called the parents of him who
had received his sight. 19And they asked them,
saying, "Is this your son, who you say was
born blind? How then does he now see?"
20His parents answered them and said, "We
know that this is our son, and that he was born
blind; 21but by what means he now sees we do not
know, or who opened his eyes we do not know.
He is of age; ask him. He will speak for himself."
22His parents said these *things* because they
feared the Jews, for the Jews had agreed already
that if anyone confessed *that* He *was* Christ, he
would be put out of the synagogue. 23Therefore
his parents said, "He is of age; ask him."

9:2 who sinned. While sin may be a cause of suffering, as clearly indicated in Scripture (5:14; Num. 12; 1 Cor. 11:30; James 5:15), it is not always the case necessarily (see Job; 2 Cor. 12:7; Gal. 4:13). The disciples assumed, like most Palestinians of their day, that sin was the primary, if not exclusive, cause of all suffering. In this instance, however, Jesus made it clear that personal sin was not the reason for the blindness (v. 3).

9:3 Jesus did not deny the general connection between sin and suffering, but refuted the idea that personal acts of sin were the direct cause. God's sovereignty and purposes play a part in such matters, as is clear from Job 1 and 2.

DAY 26: What does the healing of the blind man in John 9 teach us about unbelief?

In ancient times, severe physical deformities, such as congenital blindness (vv. 8,9), sentenced a person to begging as the only means of support (Acts 3:1–7). The drastic change in the healed man caused many to faithlessly believe that he was not the person born blind.

If you read through vv. 13–34, this section in the story of the healing of the blind man reveals some key characteristics of willful unbelief: 1) unbelief sets false standards; 2) unbelief always wants more evidence but never has enough; 3) unbelief does biased research on a purely subjective basis; 4) unbelief rejects the facts; and 5) unbelief is self-centered. John included this section on the dialogue of the Pharisees with the blind man most likely for two reasons: 1) the dialogue carefully demonstrates the character of willful and fixed unbelief, and 2) the story confirms the first great schism between the synagogue and Christ's new followers. The blind man was the first known person thrown out of the synagogue because he chose to follow Christ (see 16:1–3).

Even though the neighbors had confirmed that the man had in fact been blind (v. 9), that was not evidence enough. So the authorities called the parents (v. 18). While neighbors may have been mistaken as to the man's identity, the parents would know if this was their own son. And the authorities considered the witness of the healed man worthless.

MAY 27

1 Kings 1:1–2:46

1 Now King David was old, advanced in years;
and they put covers on him, but he could not
get warm. 2Therefore his servants said to him,
"Let a young woman, a virgin, be sought for
our lord the king, and let her stand before the
king, and let her care for him; and let her lie in
your bosom, that our lord the king may be
warm." 3So they sought for a lovely young
woman throughout all the territory of Israel, and
found Abishag the Shunammite, and brought
her to the king. 4The young woman *was* very
lovely; and she cared for the king, and served
him; but the king did not know her.
5Then Adonijah the son of Haggith exalted
himself, saying, "I will be king"; and he prepared for himself chariots and horsemen, and
fifty men to run before him. 6(And his father
had not rebuked him at any time by saying,
"Why have you done so?" He *was* also very
good-looking. *His mother* had borne him after
Absalom.) 7Then he conferred with Joab the
son of Zeruiah and with Abiathar the priest,
and they followed and helped Adonijah. 8But
Zadok the priest, Benaiah the son of Jehoiada,
Nathan the prophet, Shimei, Rei, and the
mighty men who *belonged* to David were not
with Adonijah.
9And Adonijah sacrificed sheep and oxen
and fattened cattle by the stone of Zoheleth,
which *is* by En Rogel; he also invited all his
brothers, the king's sons, and all the men of
Judah, the king's servants. 10But he did not
invite Nathan the prophet, Benaiah, the
mighty men, or Solomon his brother.
11So Nathan spoke to Bathsheba the mother
of Solomon, saying, "Have you not heard that
Adonijah the son of Haggith has become king,
and David our lord does not know *it?* 12Come,
please, let me now give you advice, that you
may save your own life and the life of your son
Solomon. 13Go immediately to King David and
say to him, 'Did you not, my lord, O king,
swear to your maidservant, saying, "Assuredly your son Solomon shall reign after
me, and he shall sit on my throne"? Why then
has Adonijah become king?' 14Then, while you

1:5 Adonijah. Adonijah was the fourth son of David (2 Sam. 3:4) and probably the oldest living son, since Amnon (2 Sam. 13:28,29) and Absalom (2 Sam. 18:14,15) had been killed, and Chileab apparently died in his youth, since there is no mention of him beyond his birth. As David's oldest surviving heir, Adonijah attempted to claim the kingship. **chariots and horsemen.** Like Absalom (2 Sam. 15:1), Adonijah sought to confirm and support his claim to kingship by raising a small army.

1:13 Did you not...swear...? This oath was given privately (unrecorded in Scripture) by David, perhaps to both Nathan and Bathsheba. Solomon's choice by the Lord was implicit in his name Jedidiah, meaning "loved by the Lord" (2 Sam. 12:24,25) and explicit in David's declaration to Solomon (1 Chr. 22:6–13).

are still talking there with the king, I also will
come in after you and confirm your words."
15So Bathsheba went into the chamber to
the king. (Now the king was very old, and
Abishag the Shunammite was serving the
king.) 16And Bathsheba bowed and did homage to the king. Then the king said, "What is
your wish?"
17Then she said to him, "My lord, you swore
by the LORD your God to your maidservant,
saying, 'Assuredly Solomon your son shall
reign after me, and he shall sit on my throne.'
18So now, look! Adonijah has become king; and
now, my lord the king, you do not know about
it. 19He has sacrificed oxen and fattened cattle
and sheep in abundance, and has invited all
the sons of the king, Abiathar the priest, and
Joab the commander of the army; but Solomon your servant he has not invited. 20And as
for you, my lord, O king, the eyes of all Israel
are on you, that you should tell them who will
sit on the throne of my lord the king after him.
21Otherwise it will happen, when my lord the
king rests with his fathers, that I and my son
Solomon will be counted as offenders."
22And just then, while she was still talking
with the king, Nathan the prophet also came
in. 23So they told the king, saying, "Here is Nathan the prophet." And when he came in
before the king, he bowed down before the
king with his face to the ground. 24And Nathan
said, "My lord, O king, have you said,
'Adonijah shall reign after me, and he shall sit
on my throne'? 25For he has gone down today,
and has sacrificed oxen and fattened cattle
and sheep in abundance, and has invited all
the king's sons, and the commanders of the
army, and Abiathar the priest; and look! They
are eating and drinking before him; and they
say, '*Long* live King Adonijah!' 26But he has not
invited me—me your servant—nor Zadok the
priest, nor Benaiah the son of Jehoiada, nor
your servant Solomon. 27Has this thing been
done by my lord the king, and you have not
told your servant who should sit on the throne
of my lord the king after him?"
28Then King David answered and said, "Call
Bathsheba to me." So she came into the king's
presence and stood before the king. 29And the
king took an oath and said, "*As* the LORD lives,
who has redeemed my life from every distress,
30just as I swore to you by the LORD God of Israel, saying, 'Assuredly Solomon your son shall
be king after me, and he shall sit on my throne
in my place,' so I certainly will do this day."
31Then Bathsheba bowed with *her* face to
the earth, and paid homage to the king, and
said, "Let my lord King David live forever!"
32And King David said, "Call to me Zadok
the priest, Nathan the prophet, and Benaiah
the son of Jehoiada." So they came before the
king. 33The king also said to them, "Take with
you the servants of your lord, and have Solomon my son ride on my own mule, and take
him down to Gihon. 34There let Zadok the priest
and Nathan the prophet anoint him king over
Israel; and blow the horn, and say, '*Long* live
King Solomon!' 35Then you shall come up after
him, and he shall come and sit on my throne, and
he shall be king in my place. For I have appointed him to be ruler over Israel and Judah."
36Benaiah the son of Jehoiada answered the
king and said, "Amen! May the LORD God of
my lord the king say so *too.* 37As the LORD has
been with my lord the king, even so may He
be with Solomon, and make his throne greater
than the throne of my lord King David."
38So Zadok the priest, Nathan the prophet,
Benaiah the son of Jehoiada, the Cherethites,
and the Pelethites went down and had Solomon ride on King David's mule, and took
him to Gihon. 39Then Zadok the priest took a
horn of oil from the tabernacle and anointed
Solomon. And they blew the horn, and all the
people said, "*Long* live King Solomon!" 40And
all the people went up after him; and the people played the flutes and rejoiced with great
joy, so that the earth *seemed to* split with their
sound.
41Now Adonijah and all the guests who *were*
with him heard *it* as they finished eating. And
when Joab heard the sound of the horn, he
said, "Why *is* the city in such a noisy uproar?"
42While he was still speaking, there came Jonathan, the son of Abiathar the priest. And
Adonijah said to him, "Come in, for you *are* a
prominent man, and bring good news."
43Then Jonathan answered and said to
Adonijah, "No! Our lord King David has made
Solomon king. 44The king has sent with him
Zadok the priest, Nathan the prophet, Benaiah
the son of Jehoiada, the Cherethites, and the
Pelethites; and they have made him ride on
the king's mule. 45So Zadok the priest and Nathan the prophet have anointed him king at
Gihon; and they have gone up from there
rejoicing, so that the city is in an uproar. This
is the noise that you have heard. 46Also Solomon sits on the throne of the kingdom. 47And
moreover the king's servants have gone to
bless our lord King David, saying, 'May God
make the name of Solomon better than your
name, and may He make his throne greater
than your throne.' Then the king bowed himself on the bed. 48Also the king said thus,
'Blessed *be* the LORD God of Israel, who has

given *one* to sit on my throne this day, while
my eyes see *it!'* "
[49]So all the guests who were with Adonijah
were afraid, and arose, and each one went his
way.
[50]Now Adonijah was afraid of Solomon; so
he arose, and went and took hold of the horns
of the altar. [51]And it was told Solomon, saying,
"Indeed Adonijah is afraid of King Solomon;
for look, he has taken hold of the horns of the
altar, saying, 'Let King Solomon swear to me
today that he will not put his servant to death
with the sword.' "
[52]Then Solomon said, "If he proves himself a
worthy man, not one hair of him shall fall to
the earth; but if wickedness is found in him,
he shall die." [53]So King Solomon sent them to
bring him down from the altar. And he came
and fell down before King Solomon; and Solomon said to him, "Go to your house."
2 Now the days of David drew near that he
should die, and he charged Solomon his
son, saying: [2]"I go the way of all the earth; be
strong, therefore, and prove yourself a man.
[3]And keep the charge of the LORD your God: to
walk in His ways, to keep His statutes, His
commandments, His judgments, and His testimonies, as it is written in the Law of Moses,
that you may prosper in all that you do and
wherever you turn; [4]that the LORD may fulfill
His word which He spoke concerning me, saying, 'If your sons take heed to their way, to
walk before Me in truth with all their heart
and with all their soul,' He said, 'you shall not
lack a man on the throne of Israel.'
[5]"Moreover you know also what Joab the
son of Zeruiah did to me, *and* what he did to
the two commanders of the armies of Israel, to
Abner the son of Ner and Amasa the son of
Jether, whom he killed. And he shed the blood
of war in peacetime, and put the blood of war
on his belt that *was* around his waist, and on
his sandals that *were* on his feet. [6]Therefore do
according to your wisdom, and do not let his
gray hair go down to the grave in peace.
[7]"But show kindness to the sons of Barzillai
the Gileadite, and let them be among those
who eat at your table, for so they came to me
when I fled from Absalom your brother.
[8]"And see, *you have* with you Shimei the son
of Gera, a Benjamite from Bahurim, who
cursed me with a malicious curse in the day
when I went to Mahanaim. But he came down
to meet me at the Jordan, and I swore to him
by the LORD, saying, 'I will not put you to death
with the sword.' [9]Now therefore, do not hold
him guiltless, for you *are* a wise man and
know what you ought to do to him; but bring
his gray hair down to the grave with blood."
[10]So David rested with his fathers, and was
buried in the City of David. [11]The period that
David reigned over Israel *was* forty years;
seven years he reigned in Hebron, and in Jerusalem he reigned thirty-three years. [12]Then
Solomon sat on the throne of his father David;
and his kingdom was firmly established.
[13]Now Adonijah the son of Haggith came to
Bathsheba the mother of Solomon. So she
said, "Do you come peaceably?"
And he said, "Peaceably." [14]Moreover he
said, "I have something *to say* to you."
And she said, "Say it."
[15]Then he said, "You know that the kingdom
was mine, and all Israel had set their expectations on me, that I should reign. However, the
kingdom has been turned over, and has
become my brother's; for it was his from the
LORD. [16]Now I ask one petition of you; do not
deny me."
And she said to him, "Say it."
[17]Then he said, "Please speak to King Solomon, for he will not refuse you, that he may
give me Abishag the Shunammite as wife."
[18]So Bathsheba said, "Very well, I will speak
for you to the king."
[19]Bathsheba therefore went to King Solomon, to speak to him for Adonijah. And the
king rose up to meet her and bowed down to
her, and sat down on his throne and had a
throne set for the king's mother; so she sat at
his right hand. [20]Then she said, "I desire one
small petition of you; do not refuse me."
And the king said to her, "Ask it, my mother,
for I will not refuse you."
[21]So she said, "Let Abishag the Shunammite
be given to Adonijah your brother as wife."

2:4 His word. The unconditional Davidic covenant was made by God with David in 2 Samuel 7:4–17 and confirmed to Solomon in 1 Kings 9:5, promising the perpetuation of the Davidic dynasty over Israel. **If your sons take heed to their way.** David declared that the king's obedience to the Law of Moses was a necessary condition for the fulfillment of divine promise. The Book of Kings demonstrates that none of the descendants of David remained faithful to God's law; none of them met the conditions for the fulfillment of the divine promise. Rather, David's words provided a basis for explaining the Exile. Thus, the ultimate and final King of Israel would appear at a later, undesignated time.

22 And King Solomon answered and said to
his mother, "Now why do you ask Abishag the
Shunammite for Adonijah? Ask for him the
kingdom also—for he *is* my older brother—
for him, and for Abiathar the priest, and for
Joab the son of Zeruiah." 23 Then King Solomon swore by the LORD, saying, "May God
do so to me, and more also, if Adonijah has not
spoken this word against his own life! 24 Now
therefore, *as* the LORD lives, who has confirmed me and set me on the throne of David
my father, and who has established a house
for me, as He promised, Adonijah shall be put
to death today!"

25 So King Solomon sent by the hand of
Benaiah the son of Jehoiada; and he struck
him down, and he died.

26 And to Abiathar the priest the king said,
"Go to Anathoth, to your own fields, for you
are deserving of death; but I will not put you
to death at this time, because you carried the
ark of the Lord GOD before my father David,
and because you were afflicted every time my
father was afflicted." 27 So Solomon removed
Abiathar from being priest to the LORD, that he
might fulfill the word of the LORD which He
spoke concerning the house of Eli at Shiloh.

28 Then news came to Joab, for Joab had
defected to Adonijah, though he had not
defected to Absalom. So Joab fled to the tabernacle of the LORD, and took hold of the
horns of the altar. 29 And King Solomon was
told, "Joab has fled to the tabernacle of the
LORD; there *he is,* by the altar." Then Solomon
sent Benaiah the son of Jehoiada, saying, "Go,
strike him down." 30 So Benaiah went to the
tabernacle of the LORD, and said to him, "Thus
says the king, 'Come out!' "

And he said, "No, but I will die here." And
Benaiah brought back word to the king, saying,
"Thus said Joab, and thus he answered me."

31 Then the king said to him, "Do as he has
said, and strike him down and bury him, that
you may take away from me and from the
house of my father the innocent blood which
Joab shed. 32 So the LORD will return his blood
on his head, because he struck down two men
more righteous and better than he, and killed
them with the sword—Abner the son of Ner,
the commander of the army of Israel, and
Amasa the son of Jether, the commander of
the army of Judah—though my father David
did not know *it.* 33 Their blood shall therefore
return upon the head of Joab and upon the
head of his descendants forever. But upon David and his descendants, upon his house and
his throne, there shall be peace forever from
the LORD."

34 So Benaiah the son of Jehoiada went up
and struck and killed him; and he was buried
in his own house in the wilderness. 35 The king
put Benaiah the son of Jehoiada in his place
over the army, and the king put Zadok the
priest in the place of Abiathar.

36 Then the king sent and called for Shimei,
and said to him, "Build yourself a house in Jerusalem and dwell there, and do not go out
from there anywhere. 37 For it shall be, on the
day you go out and cross the Brook Kidron,
know for certain you shall surely die; your
blood shall be on your own head."

38 And Shimei said to the king, "The saying *is*
good. As my lord the king has said, so your
servant will do." So Shimei dwelt in Jerusalem
many days.

39 Now it happened at the end of three years,
that two slaves of Shimei ran away to Achish the
son of Maachah, king of Gath. And they told
Shimei, saying, "Look, your slaves *are* in
Gath!" 40 So Shimei arose, saddled his donkey,
and went to Achish at Gath to seek his slaves.
And Shimei went and brought his slaves from
Gath. 41 And Solomon was told that Shimei had
gone from Jerusalem to Gath and had come
back. 42 Then the king sent and called for
Shimei, and said to him, "Did I not make you
swear by the LORD, and warn you, saying,
'Know for certain that on the day you go out
and travel anywhere, you shall surely die'? And
you said to me, 'The word I have heard *is* good.'
43 Why then have you not kept the oath of the
LORD and the commandment that I gave you?"
44 The king said moreover to Shimei, "You know,
as your heart acknowledges, all the wickedness that you did to my father David; therefore
the LORD will return your wickedness on your
own head. 45 But King Solomon *shall be* blessed,
and the throne of David shall be established
before the LORD forever."

46 So the king commanded Benaiah the son
of Jehoiada; and he went out and struck him
down, and he died. Thus the kingdom was
established in the hand of Solomon.

Psalm 68:11–14

11 The Lord gave the word;
Great *was* the company of those who
proclaimed *it:*
12 "Kings of armies flee, they flee,
And she who remains at home divides
the spoil.
13 Though you lie down among the
sheepfolds,
You will be like the wings of a dove
covered with silver,
And her feathers with yellow gold."

14 When the Almighty scattered kings in it,
It was *white* as snow in Zalmon.

Proverbs 17:7–9

7 Excellent speech is not becoming to a fool,
Much less lying lips to a prince.

8 A present *is* a precious stone in the eyes of its possessor;
Wherever he turns, he prospers.

9 He who covers a transgression seeks love,
But he who repeats a matter separates friends.

John 9:24–41

24So they again called the man who was
blind, and said to him, "Give God the glory!
We know that this Man is a sinner."
25He answered and said, "Whether He is a
sinner *or not* I do not know. One thing I know:
that though I was blind, now I see."
26Then they said to him again, "What did He
do to you? How did He open your eyes?"
27He answered them, "I told you already, and
you did not listen. Why do you want to hear *it*
again? Do you also want to become His disciples?"
28Then they reviled him and said, "You are
His disciple, but we are Moses' disciples. 29We
know that God spoke to Moses; *as for* this *fel-*
low, we do not know where He is from."
30The man answered and said to them,
"Why, this is a marvelous thing, that you do
not know where He is from; yet He has
opened my eyes! 31Now we know that God
does not hear sinners; but if anyone is a worshiper of God and does His will, He hears him.
32Since the world began it has been unheard of
that anyone opened the eyes of one who was
born blind. 33If this Man were not from God,
He could do nothing."
34They answered and said to him, "You were
completely born in sins, and are you teaching
us?" And they cast him out.
35Jesus heard that they had cast him out;
and when He had found him, He said to him,
"Do you believe in the Son of God?"

9:35 Do you believe…? Jesus invited the man to put his trust in Him as the One who revealed God to man. Jesus placed great emphasis on public acknowledgment of who He was and confession of faith in Him (Matt. 10:32; Luke 12:8). **Son of God.** This should be Son of Man (see 1:51; 3:13,14; 5:27; 6:27,53,62; 8:28).

36He answered and said, "Who is He, Lord,
that I may believe in Him?"
37And Jesus said to him, "You have both
seen Him and it is He who is talking with you."
38Then he said, "Lord, I believe!" And he
worshiped Him.
39And Jesus said, "For judgment I have
come into this world, that those who do not
see may see, and that those who see may be
made blind."
40Then *some* of the Pharisees who were with
Him heard these words, and said to Him, "Are
we blind also?"
41Jesus said to them, "If you were blind, you
would have no sin; but now you say, 'We see.'
Therefore your sin remains.

9:41 your sin remains. Jesus had particular reference to the sin of unbelief and rejection of Him as Messiah and Son of God. If they knew their lostness and darkness and cried out for spiritual light, they would no longer be guilty of the sin of unbelief in Christ. But satisfied that their darkness was light and continuing in rejection of Christ, their sin remained.

DAY 27: How did the simple logic of the healed man outwit the religious authorities?

In John 9, the religious authorites wanted the man to own up and admit the truth that Jesus was a sinner because He violated their traditions and threatened their influence (see Josh. 7:19). "Give God the glory! We know that this Man is a sinner" (v. 24). Enough unanimity existed among the religious authorities to conclude that Jesus was a sinner (8:46). Because of this already predetermined opinion, they refused to accept any of the testimony that a miracle had actually taken place.

In order to forcefully emphasize their hypocrisy, the healed man resorted to biting sarcasm when he suggested they desired to be Jesus' disciples (v. 27).

"You are His disciple, but we are Moses' disciples" (v. 28). At this point, the meeting degenerated into a shouting match of insults. The healed man's wit had exposed the bias of his inquisitors. As far as the authorities were concerned, the conflict between Jesus and Moses was irreconcilable. If the healed man defended Jesus, then such defense could only mean that he was Jesus' disciple.

In vv. 30–33, the healed man demonstrated more spiritual insight and common sense than all of the religious authorities combined who sat in judgment of Jesus and him. His penetrating wit focused in on their intractable unbelief. His logic was that such an extraordinary miracle could only indicate that Jesus was from God, for the Jews believed that God responds in proportion to the righteousness of the one praying (Job 27:9; 35:13; Pss. 66:18; 109:7; Prov. 15:29; Is. 1:15; see 14:13,14; 16:23–27; 1 John 3:21,22). The greatness of the miracle could only indicate that Jesus was actually from God.

"You were completely born in sins, and are you teaching us?" (v. 34). The Pharisees were incensed with the man, and their anger prevented them from seeing the penetrating insight that the uneducated healed man had demonstrated. The phrase also revealed their ignorance of Scripture, for the Old Testament indicated that the coming messianic age would be evidenced by restoration of sight to the blind (Is. 29:18; 35:5; 42:7; Matt. 11:4,5; Luke 4:18,19).

MAY 28

1 Kings 3:1–4:34

3 Now Solomon made a treaty with Pharaoh
king of Egypt, and married Pharaoh's
daughter; then he brought her to the City of
David until he had finished building his own
house, and the house of the LORD, and the wall
all around Jerusalem. 2Meanwhile the people
sacrificed at the high places, because there
was no house built for the name of the LORD
until those days. 3And Solomon loved the
LORD, walking in the statutes of his father David, except that he sacrificed and burned
incense at the high places.

4Now the king went to Gibeon to sacrifice
there, for that *was* the great high place: Solomon offered a thousand burnt offerings on
that altar. 5At Gibeon the LORD appeared to
Solomon in a dream by night; and God said,
"Ask! What shall I give you?"

6And Solomon said: "You have shown great
mercy to Your servant David my father,
because he walked before You in truth, in
righteousness, and in uprightness of heart
with You; You have continued this great kindness for him, and You have given him a son to
sit on his throne, as *it is* this day. 7Now, O LORD
my God, You have made Your servant king
instead of my father David, but I *am* a little
child; I do not know *how* to go out or come in.
8And Your servant *is* in the midst of Your people whom You have chosen, a great people,
too numerous to be numbered or counted.
9Therefore give to Your servant an understanding heart to judge Your people, that I
may discern between good and evil. For who
is able to judge this great people of Yours?"

10The speech pleased the Lord, that Solomon had asked this thing. 11Then God said to
him: "Because you have asked this thing, and
have not asked long life for yourself, nor have

3:7 little child. Since Solomon was probably only about 20 years of age, he readily admitted his lack of qualification and experience to be king (1 Chr. 22:5; 29:1).

3:8 a great people. Based on the census, which recorded 800,000 men of fighting age in Israel and 500,000 in Judah (2 Sam. 24:9), the total population was over 4 million, approximately double what it had been at the time of the conquest (Num. 26:1–65).

3:9 an understanding heart. Humbly admitting his need, Solomon sought "a listening heart" to govern God's people with wisdom.

3:10 pleased the Lord. The Lord was delighted that Solomon had not asked for personal benefits—long life, wealth, or the death of his enemies.

asked riches for yourself, nor have asked the
life of your enemies, but have asked for yourself understanding to discern justice, 12behold,
I have done according to your words; see, I
have given you a wise and understanding
heart, so that there has not been anyone like
you before you, nor shall any like you arise
after you. 13And I have also given you what you
have not asked: both riches and honor, so that
there shall not be anyone like you among the
kings all your days. 14So if you walk in My ways,
to keep My statutes and My commandments, as
your father David walked, then I will lengthen
your days."

15Then Solomon awoke; and indeed it had
been a dream. And he came to Jerusalem and
stood before the ark of the covenant of the
LORD, offered up burnt offerings, offered peace
offerings, and made a feast for all his servants.
16Now two women *who were* harlots came to

the king, and stood before him. 17And one
woman said, "O my lord, this woman and I dwell
in the same house; and I gave birth while she
was in the house. 18Then it happened, the third
day after I had given birth, that this woman
also gave birth. And we *were* together; no one
was with us in the house, except the two of us
in the house. 19And this woman's son died in the
night, because she lay on him. 20So she arose in
the middle of the night and took my son from
my side, while your maidservant slept, and laid
him in her bosom, and laid her dead child in my
bosom. 21And when I rose in the morning to
nurse my son, there he was, dead. But when I
had examined him in the morning, indeed, he
was not my son whom I had borne."

22Then the other woman said, "No! But the
living one *is* my son, and the dead one *is* your
son."

And the first woman said, "No! But the dead
one *is* your son, and the living one *is* my son."

Thus they spoke before the king.

23And the king said, "The one says, 'This *is*
my son, who lives, and your son *is* the dead
one'; and the other says, 'No! But your son *is*
the dead one, and my son *is* the living one.' "
24Then the king said, "Bring me a sword." So
they brought a sword before the king. 25And the
king said, "Divide the living child in two, and
give half to one, and half to the other."

26Then the woman whose son *was* living spoke
to the king, for she yearned with compassion for
her son; and she said, "O my lord, give her the
living child, and by no means kill him!"

But the other said, "Let him be neither mine
nor yours, *but* divide *him.*"

27So the king answered and said, "Give the
first woman the living child, and by no means
kill him; she *is* his mother."

28And all Israel heard of the judgment which
the king had rendered; and they feared the
king, for they saw that the wisdom of God *was*
in him to administer justice.

4 So King Solomon was king over all Israel.
2And these *were* his officials: Azariah the
son of Zadok, the priest; 3Elihoreph and
Ahijah, the sons of Shisha, scribes;
Jehoshaphat the son of Ahilud, the recorder;
4Benaiah the son of Jehoiada, over the army;
Zadok and Abiathar, the priests; 5Azariah the
son of Nathan, over the officers; Zabud the
son of Nathan, a priest *and* the king's friend;
6Ahishar, over the household; and Adoniram
the son of Abda, over the labor force.

7And Solomon had twelve governors over all
Israel, who provided food for the king and his
household; each one made provision for one
month of the year. 8These *are* their names:
Ben-Hur, in the mountains of Ephraim; 9Ben-
Deker, in Makaz, Shaalbim, Beth Shemesh,
and Elon Beth Hanan; 10Ben-Hesed, in
Arubboth; to him *belonged* Sochoh and all the
land of Hepher; 11Ben-Abinadab, *in* all the
regions of Dor; he had Taphath the daughter
of Solomon as wife; 12Baana the son of Ahilud,
in Taanach, Megiddo, and all Beth Shean,
which *is* beside Zaretan below Jezreel, from
Beth Shean to Abel Meholah, as far as the
other side of Jokneam; 13Ben-Geber, in
Ramoth Gilead; to him *belonged* the towns of
Jair the son of Manasseh, in Gilead; to him
also belonged the region of Argob in Bashan—
sixty large cities with walls and bronze gate-
bars; 14Ahinadab the son of Iddo, *in* Mahanaim;
15Ahimaaz, in Naphtali; he also took Basemath
the daughter of Solomon as wife; 16Baanah the
son of Hushai, in Asher and Aloth; 17Jehosh-
aphat the son of Paruah, in Issachar; 18Shimei
the son of Elah, in Benjamin; 19Geber the son
of Uri, in the land of Gilead, *in* the country of
Sihon king of the Amorites, and of Og king of
Bashan. *He was* the only governor who *was* in
the land.

20Judah and Israel *were* as numerous as the
sand by the sea in multitude, eating and drinking and rejoicing. 21So Solomon reigned over
all kingdoms from the River *to* the land of the
Philistines, as far as the border of Egypt. *They*
brought tribute and served Solomon all the
days of his life.

22Now Solomon's provision for one day was
thirty kors of fine flour, sixty kors of meal,
23ten fatted oxen, twenty oxen from the pastures, and one hundred sheep, besides deer,
gazelles, roebucks, and fatted fowl.

24For he had dominion over all *the region* on
this side of the River from Tiphsah even to
Gaza, namely over all the kings on this side of
the River; and he had peace on every side all
around him. 25And Judah and Israel dwelt safely, each man under his vine and his fig tree,
from Dan as far as Beersheba, all the days of
Solomon.

26Solomon had forty thousand stalls of horses for his chariots, and twelve thousand horsemen. 27And these governors, each man in his
month, provided food for King Solomon and
for all who came to King Solomon's table.
There was no lack in their supply. 28They also
brought barley and straw to the proper place,
for the horses and steeds, each man according
to his charge.

29And God gave Solomon wisdom and exceedingly great understanding, and largeness of
heart like the sand on the seashore. 30Thus
Solomon's wisdom excelled the wisdom of all

the men of the East and all the wisdom of
Egypt. [31]For he was wiser than all men—than
Ethan the Ezrahite, and Heman, Chalcol, and
Darda, the sons of Mahol; and his fame was in
all the surrounding nations. [32]He spoke three
thousand proverbs, and his songs were one
thousand and five. [33]Also he spoke of trees,
from the cedar tree of Lebanon even to the
hyssop that springs out of the wall; he spoke
also of animals, of birds, of creeping things,
and of fish. [34]And men of all nations, from all
the kings of the earth who had heard of his
wisdom, came to hear the wisdom of Solomon.

Psalm 68:15–20

15 A mountain of God *is* the mountain of
Bashan;
A mountain *of many* peaks *is* the
mountain of Bashan.
16 Why do you fume with envy, you
mountains of *many* peaks?
This is the mountain *which* God desires
to dwell in;
Yes, the LORD will dwell *in it* forever.

17 The chariots of God *are* twenty
thousand,
Even thousands of thousands;
The Lord is among them *as in* Sinai, in
the Holy *Place.*
18 You have ascended on high,
You have led captivity captive;
You have received gifts among men,
Even *from* the rebellious,
That the LORD God might dwell *there.*
19 Blessed *be* the Lord,
Who daily loads us *with benefits,*
The God of our salvation! Selah
20 Our God *is* the God of salvation;
And to GOD the Lord *belong* escapes
from death.

Proverbs 17:10–12

10 Rebuke is more effective for a wise
man
Than a hundred blows on a fool.

11 An evil *man* seeks only rebellion;
Therefore a cruel messenger will be
sent against him.
12 Let a man meet a bear robbed of her
cubs,
Rather than a fool in his folly.

John 10:1–23

10 "Most assuredly, I say to you, he who
does not enter the sheepfold by the door,
but climbs up some other way, the same is a
thief and a robber. [2]But he who enters by the
door is the shepherd of the sheep. [3]To him the
doorkeeper opens, and the sheep hear his
voice; and he calls his own sheep by name and
leads them out. [4]And when he brings out his
own sheep, he goes before them; and the
sheep follow him, for they know his voice. [5]Yet
they will by no means follow a stranger, but
will flee from him, for they do not know the
voice of strangers." [6]Jesus used this illustration, but they did not understand the things
which He spoke to them.

[7]Then Jesus said to them again, "Most
assuredly, I say to you, I am the door of the
sheep. [8]All who *ever* came before Me are
thieves and robbers, but the sheep did not
hear them. [9]I am the door. If anyone enters by
Me, he will be saved, and will go in and out
and find pasture. [10]The thief does not come
except to steal, and to kill, and to destroy. I
have come that they may have life, and that
they may have *it* more abundantly.

10:7–10 I am the door. This is the third of 7 "I AM" statements of Jesus (6:35; 8:12). Here, He changes the metaphor slightly. While in vv. 1–5 He was the shepherd, here He is the gate. While in vv. 1–5, the shepherd led the sheep out of the pen, here He is the entrance to the pen (v. 9) that leads to proper pasture. This section echoes Jesus' words in 14:6 that He is the only way to the Father. His point is that He serves as the sole means to approach the Father and partake of God's promised salvation. As some Near Eastern shepherds slept in the gateway to guard the sheep, Jesus here pictures Himself as the gate.

[11]"I am the good shepherd. The good shepherd gives His life for the sheep. [12]But a hireling, *he who is* not the shepherd, one who does
not own the sheep, sees the wolf coming and
leaves the sheep and flees; and the wolf catches the sheep and scatters them. [13]The hireling
flees because he is a hireling and does not
care about the sheep. [14]I am the good shepherd; and I know My *sheep,* and am known by
My own. [15]As the Father knows Me, even so I
know the Father; and I lay down My life for
the sheep. [16]And other sheep I have which are
not of this fold; them also I must bring, and
they will hear My voice; and there will be one
flock *and* one shepherd.

[17]"Therefore My Father loves Me, because I
lay down My life that I may take it again. [18]No

one takes it from Me, but I lay it down of Myself. I have power to lay it down, and I have power to take it again. This command I have received from My Father."

19Therefore there was a division again among the Jews because of these sayings. 20And many of them said, "He has a demon and is mad. Why do you listen to Him?"

21Others said, "These are not the words of one who has a demon. Can a demon open the eyes of the blind?"

22Now it was the Feast of Dedication in Jerusalem, and it was winter. 23And Jesus walked in the temple, in Solomon's porch.

10:17,18 take it again. Jesus repeated this phrase twice in these two verses indicating that His sacrificial death was not the end. His resurrection followed in demonstration of His messiahship and deity (Rom. 1:4). His death and resurrection resulted in His ultimate glorification (12:23; 17:5) and the outpouring of the Holy Spirit (7:37–39; Acts 2:16–39).

DAY 28: What does it mean to have Jesus as the "Good Shepherd"?

In John 10:1–39, Jesus' discourse on Himself as the "Good Shepherd" flowed directly from chapter 9, as Jesus continued to talk to the very same people. The problem of chapter 9 was that Israel was led by false shepherds who drew them astray from the true knowledge and kingdom of Messiah (9:39–41). In chapter 10, Jesus declared Himself to be the "Good Shepherd" who was appointed by His Father as Savior and King, in contrast to the false shepherds of Israel who were self-appointed and self-righteous (Ps. 23:1; Is. 40:11; Jer. 3:15; see Is. 56:9–12; Jer. 23:1–4; 25:32–38; Ezek. 34:1–31; Zech. 11:16).

Jesus spoke in vv. 1–30 using a sustained metaphor based on first-century sheep ranching. The sheep were kept in a pen, which had a gate through which the sheep entered and left. The shepherd engaged a "doorkeeper" (v. 3) or "hireling" (v. 12) as an undershepherd to guard the gate. The shepherd entered through that gate. He whose interest was stealing or wounding the sheep would chose another way to attempt entrance. The words of Ezekiel 34 most likely form the background to Jesus' teaching since God decried the false shepherds of Israel (i.e., the spiritual leaders of the nation) for not caring properly for the flock of Israel (i.e., the nation). The Gospels themselves contain extensive sheep/shepherd imagery (Matt. 9:36; Mark 6:34; 14:27; Luke 15:1–7).

The doorkeeper was a hired undershepherd who recognized the true shepherd of the flock, opened the gate for Him, assisted the shepherd in caring for the flock, and especially guarded them at night (v. 3). "The sheep hear his voice." Near Eastern shepherds stand at different locations outside the sheep pen, sounding out their own unique calls which their sheep recognize. As a result, the sheep gather around the shepherd. "He calls his own sheep by name." This shepherd goes even further by calling each sheep by its own special name (see 3 John 15). Jesus' point is that He comes to the fold of Israel and calls out His own sheep individually to come into His own messianic fold. The assumption is that they are already in some way His sheep even before He calls them by name (vv. 25–27; 6:37,39,44,64,65; 17:6,9,24; 18:9).

Unlike Western shepherds who drive the sheep from the side or behind, often using sheep dogs, Near Eastern shepherds lead their flocks, their voice calling them to move on (vv. 4,5). This draws a remarkable picture of the master/disciple relationship. New Testament spiritual leadership is always by example, i.e., a call to imitate conduct (1 Tim. 4:12; 1 Pet. 5:1–3).

MAY 29

1 Kings 5:1–6:38

5 Now Hiram king of Tyre sent his servants to Solomon, because he heard that they had anointed him king in place of his father, for Hiram had always loved David. 2Then Solomon sent to Hiram, saying:

3 You know how my father David could
not build a house for the name of the
LORD his God because of the wars
which were fought against him on
every side, until the LORD put *his foes*
under the soles of his feet.
4 But now the LORD my God has given
me rest on every side; *there is* neither
adversary nor evil occurrence.
5 And behold, I propose to build a house
for the name of the LORD my God, as
the LORD spoke to my father David,
saying, "Your son, whom I will set on
your throne in your place, he shall
build the house for My name."

6 Now therefore, command that they cut
down cedars for me from Lebanon; and
my servants will be with your servants,
and I will pay you wages for your servants
according to whatever you say. For you
know *there is* none among us who has
skill to cut timber like the Sidonians.

5:6 cedars…from Lebanon. The cedars of Lebanon symbolized majesty and might (Ps. 92:12; Ezek. 31:3). Because cedar was durable, resistant to rot and worms, closely grained, and could be polished to a fine shine, its wood was regarded as the best timber for building. The logs were tied together and floated down the Mediterranean to Joppa (v. 9; 2 Chr. 2:16), from where they could be transported to Jerusalem, 35 miles inland.

7 So it was, when Hiram heard the words of
Solomon, that he rejoiced greatly and said,

Blessed *be* the LORD this day, for He
has given David a wise son over this
great people!

8 Then Hiram sent to Solomon, saying:

I have considered *the message* which
you sent me, *and* I will do all you
desire concerning the cedar and
cypress logs.
9 My servants shall bring *them* down
from Lebanon to the sea; I will float
them in rafts by sea to the place you
indicate to me, and will have them
broken apart there; then you can take
them away. And you shall fulfill my
desire by giving food for my household.

10 Then Hiram gave Solomon cedar and
cypress logs *according to* all his desire. 11 And
Solomon gave Hiram twenty thousand kors of
wheat *as* food for his household, and twenty
kors of pressed oil. Thus Solomon gave to
Hiram year by year.

12 So the LORD gave Solomon wisdom, as He
had promised him; and there was peace
between Hiram and Solomon, and the two of
them made a treaty together.

13 Then King Solomon raised up a labor force
out of all Israel; and the labor force was thirty
thousand men. 14 And he sent them to Lebanon,
ten thousand a month in shifts: they were one
month in Lebanon *and* two months at home;
Adoniram *was* in charge of the labor force.
15 Solomon had seventy thousand who carried
burdens, and eighty thousand who quarried
stone in the mountains, 16 besides three thousand
three hundred from the chiefs of Solomon's
deputies, who supervised the people who
labored in the work. 17 And the king commanded
them to quarry large stones, costly stones, *and*
hewn stones, to lay the foundation of the temple. 18 So Solomon's builders, Hiram's builders,
and the Gebalites quarried *them;* and they prepared timber and stones to build the temple.

6 And it came to pass in the four hundred and
eightieth year after the children of Israel
had come out of the land of Egypt, in the fourth
year of Solomon's reign over Israel, in the
month of Ziv, which *is* the second month, that he
began to build the house of the LORD. 2 Now the
house which King Solomon built for the LORD,
its length *was* sixty cubits, its width twenty, and
its height thirty cubits. 3 The vestibule in front
of the sanctuary of the house *was* twenty
cubits long across the width of the house, *and*
the width of *the vestibule extended* ten cubits
from the front of the house. 4 And he made for
the house windows with beveled frames.

5 Against the wall of the temple he built
chambers all around, *against* the walls of the
temple, all around the sanctuary and the inner
sanctuary. Thus he made side chambers all
around it. 6 The lowest chamber *was* five cubits
wide, the middle *was* six cubits wide, and the
third *was* seven cubits wide; for he made narrow ledges around the outside of the temple,
so that *the support beams* would not be fastened into the walls of the temple. 7 And the
temple, when it was being built, was built with
stone finished at the quarry, so that no hammer or chisel *or* any iron tool was heard in the
temple while it was being built. 8 The doorway
for the middle story *was* on the right side of
the temple. They went up by stairs to the middle *story,* and from the middle to the third.

9 So he built the temple and finished it, and
he paneled the temple with beams and boards
of cedar. 10 And he built side chambers against
the entire temple, each five cubits high; they
were attached to the temple with cedar beams.

11 Then the word of the LORD came to Solomon, saying: 12 "*Concerning* this temple which
you are building, if you walk in My statutes,
execute My judgments, keep all My commandments, and walk in them, then I will perform My word with you, which I spoke to your
father David. 13 And I will dwell among the children of Israel, and will not forsake My people
Israel."

14 So Solomon built the temple and finished it.
15 And he built the inside walls of the temple with
cedar boards; from the floor of the temple to the

ceiling he paneled the inside with wood; and he
covered the floor of the temple with planks of
cypress. 16Then he built the twenty-cubit room
at the rear of the temple, from floor to ceiling,
with cedar boards; he built *it* inside as the inner
sanctuary, as the Most Holy *Place*. 17And in front
of it the temple sanctuary was forty cubits *long*.
18The inside of the temple was cedar, carved
with ornamental buds and open flowers. All *was*
cedar; there was no stone *to be* seen.

6:16 the Most Holy *Place*. This inner sanctuary, partitioned off from the main hall by cedar planks, was a perfect cube about 30 feet on a side (v. 20) and was the most sacred area of the temple. The Most Holy Place is further described in vv. 19–28. The tabernacle also had a Most Holy Place (Ex. 26:33,34).

19And he prepared the inner sanctuary
inside the temple, to set the ark of the
covenant of the LORD there. 20The inner sanctuary *was* twenty cubits long, twenty cubits
wide, and twenty cubits high. He overlaid it
with pure gold, and overlaid the altar of cedar.
21So Solomon overlaid the inside of the temple
with pure gold. He stretched gold chains
across the front of the inner sanctuary, and
overlaid it with gold. 22The whole temple he
overlaid with gold, until he had finished all the
temple; also he overlaid with gold the entire
altar that *was* by the inner sanctuary.
23Inside the inner sanctuary he made two
cherubim *of* olive wood, *each* ten cubits high.
24One wing of the cherub *was* five cubits, and
the other wing of the cherub five cubits: ten
cubits from the tip of one wing to the tip of the
other. 25And the other cherub *was* ten cubits;
both cherubim *were* of the same size and
shape. 26The height of one cherub *was* ten
cubits, and so *was* the other cherub. 27Then he
set the cherubim inside the inner room; and
they stretched out the wings of the cherubim
so that the wing of the one touched *one* wall,
and the wing of the other cherub touched the
other wall. And their wings touched each
other in the middle of the room. 28Also he overlaid the cherubim with gold.
29Then he carved all the walls of the temple
all around, both the inner and outer *sanctuaries,* with carved figures of cherubim, palm
trees, and open flowers. 30And the floor of the
temple he overlaid with gold, both the inner
and outer *sanctuaries*.
31For the entrance of the inner sanctuary he
made doors *of* olive wood; the lintel *and* doorposts *were* one-fifth *of the wall*. 32The two doors
were of olive wood; and he carved on them figures of cherubim, palm trees, and open flowers, and overlaid *them* with gold; and he
spread gold on the cherubim and on the palm
trees. 33So for the door of the sanctuary he also
made doorposts *of* olive wood, one-fourth *of
the wall*. 34And the two doors *were of* cypress
wood; two panels *comprised* one folding door,
and two panels *comprised* the other folding
door. 35Then he carved cherubim, palm trees,
and open flowers *on them,* and overlaid *them*
with gold applied evenly on the carved work.
36And he built the inner court with three
rows of hewn stone and a row of cedar beams.
37In the fourth year the foundation of the
house of the LORD was laid, in the month of
Ziv. 38And in the eleventh year, in the month
of Bul, which is the eighth month, the house
was finished in all its details and according
to all its plans. So he was seven years in
building it.

Psalm 68:21–27

21 But God will wound the head of His
enemies,
The hairy scalp of the one who still
goes on in his trespasses.
22 The Lord said, "I will bring back from
Bashan,
I will bring *them* back from the depths
of the sea,
23 That your foot may crush *them* in
blood,
And the tongues of your dogs *may have*
their portion from *your* enemies."

24 They have seen Your procession,
O God,
The procession of my God, my King,
into the sanctuary.
25 The singers went before, the players
on instruments *followed* after;
Among *them were* the maidens playing
timbrels.
26 Bless God in the congregations,
The Lord, from the fountain of Israel.
27 There *is* little Benjamin, their leader,
The princes of Judah *and* their
company,
The princes of Zebulun *and* the princes
of Naphtali.

Proverbs 17:13–15

13 Whoever rewards evil for good,
Evil will not depart from his house.

17:13 evil for good. Solomon knew this proverb well since his father mistreated Uriah (2 Sam. 12:10–31). Contrast this with the man who repays evil with good (20:22; Matt. 5:43–48; 1 Pet. 3:9).

14 The beginning of strife *is like* releasing
water;
Therefore stop contention before a
quarrel starts.

15 He who justifies the wicked, and he who
condemns the just,
Both of them alike *are* an abomination
to the LORD.

John 10:24–42

24Then the Jews surrounded Him and said to
Him, "How long do You keep us in doubt? If
You are the Christ, tell us plainly."
25Jesus answered them, "I told you, and you
do not believe. The works that I do in My
Father's name, they bear witness of Me. 26But
you do not believe, because you are not of My
sheep, as I said to you. 27My sheep hear My
voice, and I know them, and they follow Me.
28And I give them eternal life, and they shall
never perish; neither shall anyone snatch
them out of My hand. 29My Father, who has
given *them* to Me, is greater than all; and no
one is able to snatch *them* out of My Father's
hand. 30I and *My* Father are one."
31Then the Jews took up stones again to
stone Him. 32Jesus answered them, "Many
good works I have shown you from My Father.
For which of those works do you stone Me?"
33The Jews answered Him, saying, "For a
good work we do not stone You, but for blasphemy, and because You, being a Man, make
Yourself God."
34Jesus answered them, "Is it not written in
your law, *'I said, "You are gods"'*? 35If He
called them gods, to whom the word of God
came (and the Scripture cannot be broken),
36do you say of Him whom the Father sanctified and sent into the world, 'You are blaspheming,' because I said, 'I am the Son of
God'? 37If I do not do the works of My Father,
do not believe Me; 38but if I do, though you do
not believe Me, believe the works, that you
may know and believe that the Father *is* in
Me, and I in Him." 39Therefore they sought
again to seize Him, but He escaped out of
their hand.
40And He went away again beyond the Jordan to the place where John was baptizing at
first, and there He stayed. 41Then many came
to Him and said, "John performed no sign,
but all the things that John spoke about this
Man were true." 42And many believed in Him
there.

10:38 believe the works. Jesus did not expect to be believed merely on His own assertions. Since He did the same things that the Father does (5:19), His enemies should consider this in their evaluation of Him. The implication is, however, that they were so ignorant of God that they could not recognize the works of the Father or the One whom the Father sent (see also 14:10,11).

DAY 29: How secure is the believer in Christ?

In John 10:24, the Jews surrounded Him and said, "If you are the Christ, tell us plainly." In light of the context of vv. 31–39, the Jews were not seeking merely for clarity and understanding regarding who Jesus was, but rather wanted Him to declare openly that He was Messiah in order to justify attacking Him.

Jesus' response is that He has told them and that His works confirm the truth of who He is. The problem is that they do not believe because they "are not of My sheep" (v. 26). This clearly indicates that God has chosen His sheep and it is they who believe and follow.

But for those who do believe and follow Christ, "I give them eternal life, and they shall never perish" (v. 28). The security of Jesus' sheep rests with Him as the Good Shepherd, who has the power to keep them safe. Neither thieves and robbers (vv. 1,8) nor the wolf (v. 12) can harm them. Verse 29 makes clear that the Father ultimately stands behind the sheep's security, for no one is able to steal from God, who is in sovereign control of all things (Col. 3:3; Rom. 8:31–39). No stronger passage in the Old Testament or New Testament exists for the absolute, eternal security of every true Christian.

"I and My Father are one" (v. 30). Both Father and Son are committed to the perfect protection and preservation of Jesus' sheep. The sentence, stressing the united purpose and action of both in the security and safety of the flock, presupposes unity of nature and essence (see 5:17–23; 17:22).

MAY 30

1 Kings 7:1–8:66

7 But Solomon took thirteen years to build
his own house; so he finished all his
house.
2He also built the House of the Forest of
Lebanon; its length *was* one hundred cubits,
its width fifty cubits, and its height thirty
cubits, with four rows of cedar pillars, and
cedar beams on the pillars. 3And *it was* paneled with cedar above the beams that *were* on
forty-five pillars, fifteen *to* a row. 4*There were*
windows *with beveled frames in* three rows,
and window *was* opposite window *in* three
tiers. 5And all the doorways and doorposts *had*
rectangular frames; and window *was* opposite
window *in* three tiers.
6He also made the Hall of Pillars: its length
was fifty cubits, and its width thirty cubits; and
in front of them *was* a portico with pillars, and
a canopy *was* in front of them.
7Then he made a hall for the throne, the
Hall of Judgment, where he might judge; and
it was paneled with cedar from floor to ceiling.
8And the house where he dwelt *had* another
court inside the hall, of like workmanship. Solomon also made a house like this hall for
Pharaoh's daughter, whom he had taken *as wife.*
9All these *were of* costly stones cut to size,
trimmed with saws, inside and out, from the
foundation to the eaves, and also on the outside to the great court. 10The foundation *was of*
costly stones, large stones, some ten cubits
and some eight cubits. 11And above *were* costly stones, hewn to size, and cedar wood. 12The
great court *was* enclosed with three rows of
hewn stones and a row of cedar beams. So
were the inner court of the house of the LORD
and the vestibule of the temple.
13Now King Solomon sent and brought
Huram from Tyre. 14He *was* the son of a widow
from the tribe of Naphtali, and his father *was* a
man of Tyre, a bronze worker; he was filled
with wisdom and understanding and skill in
working with all kinds of bronze work. So he
came to King Solomon and did all his work.
15And he cast two pillars of bronze, each one
eighteen cubits high, and a line of twelve
cubits measured the circumference of each.
16Then he made two capitals *of* cast bronze, to
set on the tops of the pillars. The height of one
capital *was* five cubits, and the height of the
other capital *was* five cubits. 17*He made* a lattice network, with wreaths of chainwork, for
the capitals which *were* on top of the pillars:
seven chains for one capital and seven for the
other capital. 18So he made the pillars, and two
rows of pomegranates above the network all
around to cover the capitals that *were* on top;
and thus he did for the other capital.
19The capitals which *were* on top of the pillars in the hall *were* in the shape of lilies, four
cubits. 20The capitals on the two pillars also
had pomegranates above, by the convex surface which *was* next to the network; and there
were two hundred such pomegranates in rows
on each of the capitals all around.
21Then he set up the pillars by the vestibule
of the temple; he set up the pillar on the right
and called its name Jachin, and he set up the
pillar on the left and called its name Boaz.
22The tops of the pillars were in the shape of
lilies. So the work of the pillars was finished.
23And he made the Sea of cast bronze, ten
cubits from one brim to the other; *it was* completely round. Its height *was* five cubits, and a
line of thirty cubits measured its circumference.
24Below its brim *were* ornamental buds encircling it all around, ten to a cubit, all the way
around the Sea. The ornamental buds *were*
cast in two rows when it was cast. 25It stood on
twelve oxen: three looking toward the north,
three looking toward the west, three looking
toward the south, and three looking toward
the east; the Sea *was set* upon them, and all
their back parts *pointed* inward. 26It *was* a handbreadth thick; and its brim was shaped like the
brim of a cup, *like* a lily blossom. It contained
two thousand baths.
27He also made ten carts of bronze; four
cubits *was* the length of each cart, four cubits
its width, and three cubits its height. 28And this
was the design of the carts: They had panels,
and the panels *were* between frames; 29on the
panels that *were* between the frames *were*
lions, oxen, and cherubim. And on the frames
was a pedestal on top. Below the lions and
oxen *were* wreaths of plaited work. 30Every
cart had four bronze wheels and axles of
bronze, and its four feet had supports. Under
the laver *were* supports of cast *bronze* beside
each wreath. 31Its opening inside the crown at
the top *was* one cubit in diameter; and the
opening *was* round, shaped *like* a pedestal, one
and a half cubits in outside diameter; and also
on the opening *were* engravings, but the panels
were square, not round. 32Under the panels
were the four wheels, and the axles of the
wheels *were joined* to the cart. The height of a
wheel *was* one and a half cubits. 33The workmanship of the wheels *was* like the workmanship of a chariot wheel; their axle pins, their

rims, their spokes, and their hubs *were* all of
cast *bronze.* [34]And *there were* four supports at
the four corners of each cart; its supports *were*
part of the cart itself. [35]On the top of the cart,
at the height of half a cubit, *it was* perfectly
round. And on the top of the cart, its flanges
and its panels *were* of the same casting. [36]On the
plates of its flanges and on its panels he
engraved cherubim, lions, and palm trees,
wherever there was a clear space on each, with
wreaths all around. [37]Thus he made the ten
carts. All of them were of the same mold, one
measure, *and* one shape.

[38]Then he made ten lavers of bronze; each
laver contained forty baths, *and* each laver *was*
four cubits. On each of the ten carts *was* a laver.
[39]And he put five carts on the right side of the
house, and five on the left side of the house. He
set the Sea on the right side of the house,
toward the southeast.

[40]Huram made the lavers and the shovels
and the bowls. So Huram finished doing all
the work that he was to do for King Solomon
for the house of the LORD: [41]the two pillars, the
two bowl-shaped capitals that *were* on top of
the two pillars; the two networks covering the
two bowl-shaped capitals which *were* on top of
the pillars; [42]four hundred pomegranates for
the two networks (two rows of pomegranates
for each network, to cover the two bowl-
shaped capitals that *were* on top of the pillars);
[43]the ten carts, and ten lavers on the carts;
[44]one Sea, and twelve oxen under the Sea; [45]the
pots, the shovels, and the bowls.

All these articles which Huram made for
King Solomon *for* the house of the LORD *were*
of burnished bronze. [46]In the plain of Jordan
the king had them cast in clay molds,
between Succoth and Zaretan. [47]And Solomon
did not weigh all the articles, because *there*
were so many; the weight of the bronze was
not determined.

[48]Thus Solomon had all the furnishings
made for the house of the LORD: the altar of
gold, and the table of gold on which *was* the
showbread; [49]the lampstands of pure gold, five
on the right *side* and five on the left in front of
the inner sanctuary, with the flowers and the
lamps and the wick-trimmers of gold; [50]the
basins, the trimmers, the bowls, the ladles,
and the censers of pure gold; and the hinges
of gold, *both* for the doors of the inner room
(the Most Holy *Place*) *and* for the doors of the
main hall of the temple.

[51]So all the work that King Solomon had
done for the house of the LORD was finished;
and Solomon brought in the things which his
father David had dedicated: the silver and the
gold and the furnishings. He put them in the
treasuries of the house of the LORD.

8 Now Solomon assembled the elders of Israel and all the heads of the tribes, the
chief fathers of the children of Israel, to King
Solomon in Jerusalem, that they might bring
up the ark of the covenant of the LORD from the
City of David, which *is* Zion. [2]Therefore all the
men of Israel assembled with King Solomon at
the feast in the month of Ethanim, which *is* the
seventh month. [3]So all the elders of Israel
came, and the priests took up the ark. [4]Then
they brought up the ark of the LORD, the tabernacle of meeting, and all the holy furnishings that *were* in the tabernacle. The priests
and the Levites brought them up. [5]Also King
Solomon, and all the congregation of Israel
who were assembled with him, *were* with him
before the ark, sacrificing sheep and oxen that
could not be counted or numbered for multitude. [6]Then the priests brought in the ark of
the covenant of the LORD to its place, into the
inner sanctuary of the temple, to the Most
Holy *Place,* under the wings of the cherubim.
[7]For the cherubim spread *their* two wings over
the place of the ark, and the cherubim overshadowed the ark and its poles. [8]The poles extended so that the ends of the poles could be
seen from the holy *place,* in front of the inner
sanctuary; but they could not be seen from
outside. And they are there to this day. [9]Noth-
ing *was* in the ark except the two tablets of
stone which Moses put there at Horeb, when
the LORD made *a covenant* with the children of
Israel, when they came out of the land of Egypt.

[10]And it came to pass, when the priests came
out of the holy *place,* that the cloud filled the
house of the LORD, [11]so that the priests could
not continue ministering because of the cloud;
for the glory of the LORD filled the house of the
LORD.

[12]Then Solomon spoke:

"The LORD said He would dwell in the
dark cloud.
[13] I have surely built You an exalted
house,
And a place for You to dwell in forever."

8:10 the cloud. The cloud was "the glory of the LORD," the visible symbol of God's presence. It signaled the Lord's approval of this new temple. A similar manifestation took place when the tabernacle was dedicated (Ex. 40:34,35).

[14]Then the king turned around and blessed the whole assembly of Israel, while all the assembly of Israel was standing. [15]And he said: "Blessed *be* the LORD God of Israel, who spoke with His mouth to my father David, and with His hand has fulfilled *it,* saying, [16]'Since the day that I brought My people Israel out of Egypt, I have chosen no city from any tribe of Israel *in which* to build a house, that My name might be there; but I chose David to be over My people Israel.' [17]Now it was in the heart of my father David to build a temple for the name of the LORD God of Israel. [18]But the LORD said to my father David, 'Whereas it was in your heart to build a temple for My name, you did well that it was in your heart. [19]Nevertheless you shall not build the temple, but your son who will come from your body, he shall build the temple for My name.' [20]So the LORD has fulfilled His word which He spoke; and I have filled the position of my father David, and sit on the throne of Israel, as the LORD promised; and I have built a temple for the name of the LORD God of Israel. [21]And there I have made a place for the ark, in which *is* the covenant of the LORD which He made with our fathers, when He brought them out of the land of Egypt."

[22]Then Solomon stood before the altar of the LORD in the presence of all the assembly of Israel, and spread out his hands toward heaven; [23]and he said: "LORD God of Israel, *there is* no God in heaven above or on earth below like You, who keep *Your* covenant and mercy with Your servants who walk before You with all their hearts. [24]You have kept what You promised Your servant David my father; You have both spoken with Your mouth and fulfilled *it* with Your hand, as *it is* this day. [25]Therefore, LORD God of Israel, now keep what You promised Your servant David my father, saying, 'You shall not fail to have a man sit before Me on the throne of Israel, only if your sons take heed to their way, that they walk before Me as you have walked before Me.' [26]And now I pray, O God of Israel, let Your word come true, which You have spoken to Your servant David my father.

[27]"But will God indeed dwell on the earth? Behold, heaven and the heaven of heavens cannot contain You. How much less this temple which I have built! [28]Yet regard the prayer of Your servant and his supplication, O LORD my God, and listen to the cry and the prayer which Your servant is praying before You today: [29]that Your eyes may be open toward this temple night and day, toward the place of which You said, 'My name shall be there,' that You may hear the prayer which Your servant makes toward this place. [30]And may You hear the supplication of Your servant and of Your people Israel, when they pray toward this place. Hear in heaven Your dwelling place; and when You hear, forgive.

[31]"When anyone sins against his neighbor, and is forced to take an oath, and comes *and* takes an oath before Your altar in this temple, [32]then hear in heaven, and act, and judge Your servants, condemning the wicked, bringing his way on his head, and justifying the righteous by giving him according to his righteousness.

[33]"When Your people Israel are defeated before an enemy because they have sinned against You, and when they turn back to You and confess Your name, and pray and make supplication to You in this temple, [34]then hear in heaven, and forgive the sin of Your people Israel, and bring them back to the land which You gave to their fathers.

[35]"When the heavens are shut up and there is no rain because they have sinned against You, when they pray toward this place and confess Your name, and turn from their sin because You afflict them, [36]then hear in heaven, and forgive the sin of Your servants, Your people Israel, that You may teach them the good way in which they should walk; and send rain on Your land which You have given to Your people as an inheritance.

[37]"When there is famine in the land, pestilence *or* blight *or* mildew, locusts *or* grasshoppers; when their enemy besieges them in the land of their cities; whatever plague or whatever sickness *there is;* [38]whatever prayer, whatever supplication is made by anyone, *or* by all Your people Israel, when each one knows the plague of his own heart, and spreads out his hands toward this temple: [39]then hear in heaven Your dwelling place, and forgive, and act, and give to everyone according to all his ways, whose heart You know (for You alone know the hearts of all the sons of men), [40]that they may fear You all the days that they live in the land which You gave to our fathers.

[41]"Moreover, concerning a foreigner, who *is* not of Your people Israel, but has come from a far country for Your name's sake [42](for they will hear of Your great name and Your strong hand and Your outstretched arm), when he comes and prays toward this temple, [43]hear in heaven Your dwelling place, and do according to all for which the foreigner calls to You, that all peoples of the earth may know Your name and fear You, as *do* Your people Israel, and that they may know that this temple which I have built is called by Your name.

[44]"When Your people go out to battle against their enemy, wherever You send them, and

when they pray to the LORD toward the city
which You have chosen and the temple which
I have built for Your name, [45]then hear in heav-
en their prayer and their supplication, and
maintain their cause.
[46]"When they sin against You (for *there is* no
one who does not sin), and You become angry
with them and deliver them to the enemy, and
they take them captive to the land of the
enemy, far or near; [47]*yet* when they come to
themselves in the land where they were carried captive, and repent, and make supplication to You in the land of those who took them
captive, saying, 'We have sinned and done
wrong, we have committed wickedness'; [48]and
when they return to You with all their heart
and with all their soul in the land of their enemies who led them away captive, and pray to
You toward their land which You gave to their
fathers, the city which You have chosen and
the temple which I have built for Your name:
[49]then hear in heaven Your dwelling place their
prayer and their supplication, and maintain
their cause, [50]and forgive Your people who have
sinned against You, and all their transgressions
which they have transgressed against You; and
grant them compassion before those who took
them captive, that they may have compassion
on them [51](for they *are* Your people and Your
inheritance, whom You brought out of Egypt,
out of the iron furnace), [52]that Your eyes may be
open to the supplication of Your servant and
the supplication of Your people Israel, to listen
to them whenever they call to You. [53]For You
separated them from among all the peoples of
the earth *to be* Your inheritance, as You spoke
by Your servant Moses, when You brought
our fathers out of Egypt, O Lord GOD."
[54]And so it was, when Solomon had finished
praying all this prayer and supplication to the
LORD, that he arose from before the altar of
the LORD, from kneeling on his knees with his
hands spread up to heaven. [55]Then he stood
and blessed all the assembly of Israel with a
loud voice, saying: [56]"Blessed *be* the LORD, who
has given rest to His people Israel, according
to all that He promised. There has not failed
one word of all His good promise, which He
promised through His servant Moses. [57]May
the LORD our God be with us, as He was with
our fathers. May He not leave us nor forsake
us, [58]that He may incline our hearts to Himself,
to walk in all His ways, and to keep His commandments and His statutes and His judgments, which He commanded our fathers.
[59]And may these words of mine, with which I
have made supplication before the LORD, be
near the LORD our God day and night, that He
may maintain the cause of His servant and the
cause of His people Israel, as each day may
require, [60]that all the peoples of the earth may
know that the LORD *is* God; *there is* no other.
[61]Let your heart therefore be loyal to the LORD
our God, to walk in His statutes and keep His
commandments, as at this day."
[62]Then the king and all Israel with him
offered sacrifices before the LORD. [63]And Solomon offered a sacrifice of peace offerings,
which he offered to the LORD, twenty-two
thousand bulls and one hundred and twenty
thousand sheep. So the king and all the children of Israel dedicated the house of the LORD.
[64]On the same day the king consecrated the
middle of the court that *was* in front of the
house of the LORD; for there he offered burnt
offerings, grain offerings, and the fat of the
peace offerings, because the bronze altar that
was before the LORD *was* too small to receive
the burnt offerings, the grain offerings, and
the fat of the peace offerings.
[65]At that time Solomon held a feast, and all
Israel with him, a great assembly from the
entrance of Hamath to the Brook of Egypt,
before the LORD our God, seven days and
seven *more* days—fourteen days. [66]On the
eighth day he sent the people away; and they
blessed the king, and went to their tents joyful
and glad of heart for all the good that the LORD
had done for His servant David, and for Israel
His people.

8:22–53 Solomon moved to the altar of burnt offering to offer a lengthy prayer of consecration to the Lord. First, he affirmed that no god could compare to Israel's God, the Lord (vv. 23,24). Second, he asked the Lord for His continued presence and protection (vv. 25–30). Third, he listed 7 typical Israelite prayers that would require the Lord's response (vv. 31–54). These supplications recalled the detailed list of curses that Deuteronomy 28:15–68 ascribed for the breaking of the law. Specifically, Solomon prayed that the Lord would judge between the wicked and the righteous (vv. 31,32); the Lord would forgive the sins that had caused defeat in battle (vv. 33,34); the Lord would forgive the sins that had brought on drought (vv. 35,36); the Lord would forgive the sins that had resulted in national calamities (vv. 37–40); the Lord would show mercy to God-fearing foreigners (vv. 41–43); the Lord would give victory in battle (vv. 44,45); and the Lord would bring restoration after captivity (vv. 46–54).

Psalm 68:28–35

28 Your God has commanded your
strength;
Strengthen, O God, what You have
done for us.
29 Because of Your temple at Jerusalem,
Kings will bring presents to You.
30 Rebuke the beasts of the reeds,
The herd of bulls with the calves of the
peoples,
Till everyone submits himself with
pieces of silver.
Scatter the peoples *who* delight in war.
31 Envoys will come out of Egypt;
Ethiopia will quickly stretch out her
hands to God.
32 Sing to God, you kingdoms of the earth;
Oh, sing praises to the Lord,
Selah
33 To Him who rides on the heaven of
heavens, *which were* of old!
Indeed, He sends out His voice, a
mighty voice.
34 Ascribe strength to God;
His excellence *is* over Israel,
And His strength *is* in the clouds.
35 O God, *You are* more awesome than
Your holy places.
The God of Israel *is* He who gives
strength and power to *His* people.

Blessed *be* God!

Proverbs 17:16–17

16 Why *is there* in the hand of a fool the
purchase price of wisdom,
Since *he has* no heart *for it?*

17 A friend loves at all times,
And a brother is born for adversity.

17:17 The difference between a friend and a brother is noted here. A true friend is a constant source of love, while a brother in one's family may not be close, but is drawn near to help in trouble. Friends are closer than brothers because they are available all the time, not just in the crisis.

John 11:1–29

11 Now a certain *man* was sick, Lazarus of
Bethany, the town of Mary and her sister
Martha. 2 It was *that* Mary who anointed the
Lord with fragrant oil and wiped His feet with
her hair, whose brother Lazarus was sick.
3 Therefore the sisters sent to Him, saying,
"Lord, behold, he whom You love is sick."
4 When Jesus heard *that,* He said, "This sickness is not unto death, but for the glory of
God, that the Son of God may be glorified
through it."
5 Now Jesus loved Martha and her sister and
Lazarus. 6 So, when He heard that he was sick,
He stayed two more days in the place where
He was. 7 Then after this He said to *the* disciples, "Let us go to Judea again."
8 *The* disciples said to Him, "Rabbi, lately the
Jews sought to stone You, and are You going
there again?"
9 Jesus answered, "Are there not twelve
hours in the day? If anyone walks in the day, he
does not stumble, because he sees the light of
this world. 10 But if one walks in the night, he
stumbles, because the light is not in him."
11 These things He said, and after that He said
to them, "Our friend Lazarus sleeps, but I go
that I may wake him up."
12 Then His disciples said, "Lord, if he sleeps
he will get well." 13 However, Jesus spoke of his
death, but they thought that He was speaking
about taking rest in sleep.
14 Then Jesus said to them plainly, "Lazarus
is dead. 15 And I am glad for your sakes that I
was not there, that you may believe.
Nevertheless let us go to him."
16 Then Thomas, who is called the Twin, said
to his fellow disciples, "Let us also go, that we
may die with Him."
17 So when Jesus came, He found that he had
already been in the tomb four days. 18 Now
Bethany was near Jerusalem, about two miles
away. 19 And many of the Jews had joined the
women around Martha and Mary, to comfort
them concerning their brother.
20 Now Martha, as soon as she heard that
Jesus was coming, went and met Him, but

11:17 in the tomb. The term "tomb" means a stone sepulcher. In Palestine such a grave was common. Either a cave or rock area would be hewn out, the floor inside leveled and graded to make a shallow descent. Shelves were cut out or constructed inside the area in order to bury additional family members. A rock was rolled in front to prevent wild animals or grave robbers from entering. The evangelist made special mention of the fourth day in order to stress the magnitude of the miracle, for the Jews did not embalm and by then the body would have been in a state of rapid decomposition.

Mary was sitting in the house. [21]Now Martha
said to Jesus, "Lord, if You had been here, my
brother would not have died. [22]But even now I
know that whatever You ask of God, God will
give You."
[23]Jesus said to her, "Your brother will rise
again."
[24]Martha said to Him, "I know that he will
rise again in the resurrection at the last day."
[25]Jesus said to her, "I am the resurrection
and the life. He who believes in Me, though he
may die, he shall live. [26]And whoever lives and
believes in Me shall never die. Do you believe
this?"
[27]She said to Him, "Yes, Lord, I believe that
You are the Christ, the Son of God, who is to
come into the world."
[28]And when she had said these things, she
went her way and secretly called Mary her sister, saying, "The Teacher has come and is calling for you." [29]As soon as she heard *that,* she
arose quickly and came to Him.

DAY 30: Why did Jesus delay when He heard that Lazarus was sick?

The resurrection of Lazarus in John 11 is the climactic and most dramatic sign in this Gospel and the capstone of Christ's public ministry. Six miracles have already been presented (water into wine [2:1–11], healing of the nobleman's son [4:46–54], restoring the impotent man [5:1–15], multiplying the loaves and fishes [6:1–14], walking on the water [6:15–21], and curing the man born blind [9:1–12]). Lazarus's resurrection is more potent than all those and even more monumental than the raising of the widow's son in Nain (Luke 7:11–16) or Jairus's daughter (Luke 8:40–56) because those two resurrections occurred immediately after death. Lazarus was raised after 4 days of being in the grave with the process of decomposition already having started (v. 39).

Upon hearing that Lazarus is sick, Jesus' immediate response is that it is "for the glory of God, that the Son of God may be glorified through it" (v. 4). This phrase reveals the real purpose behind Lazarus's sickness, i.e., not death, but that the Son of God might be glorified through his resurrection. So He stayed two more days. The decision to delay coming did not bring about Lazarus's death, since Jesus already supernaturally knew his plight. Most likely by the time the messenger arrived to inform Jesus, Lazarus was already dead. The delay was because He loved the family (v. 5) and that love would be clear as He greatly strengthened their faith by raising Lazarus from the dead. The delay also ensured that Lazarus had been dead long enough that no one could misinterpret the miracle as a fraud or mere resuscitation.

Coming to Martha, Jesus said, "I am the resurrection and the life" (v. 25). This is the fifth in a series of 7 great "I AM" statements of Jesus (6:35; 8:12; 10:7,9; 10:11,14). With this statement, Jesus moved Mary from an abstract belief in the resurrection that will take place "at the last day" (see 5:28, 29) to a personalized trust in Him who alone can raise the dead. No resurrection or eternal life exists outside of the Son of God. Time ("at the last day") is no barrier to the One who has the power of resurrection and life (1:4) for He can give life at any time.

MAY 31

1 Kings 9:1–10:29

9 And it came to pass, when Solomon had
finished building the house of the LORD
and the king's house, and all Solomon's desire
which he wanted to do, [2]that the LORD
appeared to Solomon the second time, as He
had appeared to him at Gibeon. [3]And the LORD
said to him: "I have heard your prayer and
your supplication that you have made before
Me; I have consecrated this house which you
have built to put My name there forever, and
My eyes and My heart will be there perpetually. [4]Now if you walk before Me as your father
David walked, in integrity of heart and in
uprightness, to do according to all that I have
commanded you, *and* if you keep My statutes
and My judgments, [5]then I will establish the
throne of your kingdom over Israel forever, as
I promised David your father, saying, 'You
shall not fail to have a man on the throne of Israel.' [6]*But* if you or your sons at all turn from
following Me, and do not keep My commandments *and* My statutes which I have set before
you, but go and serve other gods and worship
them, [7]then I will cut off Israel from the land
which I have given them; and this house which
I have consecrated for My name I will cast out
of My sight. Israel will be a proverb and a
byword among all peoples. [8]And *as for* this
house, *which* is exalted, everyone who passes
by it will be astonished and will hiss, and say,
'Why has the LORD done thus to this land and
to this house?' [9]Then they will answer, 'Because they forsook the LORD their God, who
brought their fathers out of the land of Egypt,

9:3 consecrated. The Lord made the temple holy by being present in the cloud (8:10). As proof of the temple's consecration, the Lord told Solomon that He had put His name there (3:2). **forever.** God was not saying He will dwell in that building forever, since in less than 400 years it was destroyed by the Babylonians (vv. 7–9). He was saying that Jerusalem and the temple mount are to be His earthly throne as long as the earth remains, through the millennial kingdom (Is. 2:1–4; Zech. 14:16). Even during the new heaven and new earth, the eternal state, there will be the heavenly Jerusalem, where God will eternally dwell (Rev. 21:1,2). **eyes...heart.** These symbolized, respectively, the Lord's constant attention toward and deep affection for Israel. By implication, He promised them access to His presence and answers to their prayers.

and have embraced other gods, and worshiped
them and served them; therefore the LORD
has brought all this calamity on them.' "
[10]Now it happened at the end of twenty
years, when Solomon had built the two houses, the house of the LORD and the king's house
[11](Hiram the king of Tyre had supplied Solomon with cedar and cypress and gold, as
much as he desired), *that* King Solomon then
gave Hiram twenty cities in the land of Galilee.
[12]Then Hiram went from Tyre to see the cities
which Solomon had given him, but they did not
please him. [13]So he said, "What *kind of* cities *are*
these which you have given me, my brother?"
And he called them the land of Cabul, as they
are to this day. [14]Then Hiram sent the king one
hundred and twenty talents of gold.
[15]And this *is* the reason for the labor force
which King Solomon raised: to build the
house of the LORD, his own house, the Millo,
the wall of Jerusalem, Hazor, Megiddo, and
Gezer. [16](Pharaoh king of Egypt had gone up
and taken Gezer and burned it with fire, had
killed the Canaanites who dwelt in the city,
and had given it *as* a dowry to his daughter,
Solomon's wife.) [17]And Solomon built Gezer,
Lower Beth Horon, [18]Baalath, and Tadmor in
the wilderness, in the land *of Judah,* [19]all the
storage cities that Solomon had, cities for his
chariots and cities for his cavalry, and whatever Solomon desired to build in Jerusalem, in
Lebanon, and in all the land of his dominion.
[20]All the people *who were* left of the Amorites,
Hittites, Perizzites, Hivites, and Jebusites, who
were not of the children of Israel— [21]that is,
their descendants who were left in the land
after them, whom the children of Israel had
not been able to destroy completely—from
these Solomon raised forced labor, as it is to
this day. [22]But of the children of Israel Solomon made no forced laborers, because they
were men of war and his servants: his officers,
his captains, commanders of his chariots, and
his cavalry.
[23]Others *were* chiefs of the officials who *were*
over Solomon's work: five hundred and fifty,
who ruled over the people who did the work.
[24]But Pharaoh's daughter came up from the
City of David to her house which *Solomon* had
built for her. Then he built the Millo.
[25]Now three times a year Solomon offered
burnt offerings and peace offerings on the altar
which he had built for the LORD, and he burned
incense with them *on the altar* that *was* before
the LORD. So he finished the temple.
[26]King Solomon also built a fleet of ships at
Ezion Geber, which *is* near Elath on the shore
of the Red Sea, in the land of Edom. [27]Then
Hiram sent his servants with the fleet, seamen
who knew the sea, to work with the servants of
Solomon. [28]And they went to Ophir, and acquired
four hundred and twenty talents of gold from
there, and brought *it* to King Solomon.
10 Now when the queen of Sheba heard of
the fame of Solomon concerning the
name of the LORD, she came to test him with
hard questions. [2]She came to Jerusalem with a
very great retinue, with camels that bore
spices, very much gold, and precious stones;
and when she came to Solomon, she spoke
with him about all that was in her heart. [3]So
Solomon answered all her questions; there
was nothing so difficult for the king that he
could not explain *it* to her. [4]And when the
queen of Sheba had seen all the wisdom of
Solomon, the house that he had built, [5]the
food on his table, the seating of his servants,
the service of his waiters and their apparel, his
cupbearers, and his entryway by which he
went up to the house of the LORD, there was no
more spirit in her. [6]Then she said to the king:
"It was a true report which I heard in my own

10:1 Sheba. Sheba was located in southwestern Arabia, about 1,200 miles from Jerusalem. **concerning the name of the LORD.** The primary motive for the queen's visit was to verify Solomon's reputation for wisdom and devotion to the Lord. **hard questions.** Riddles designed to stump the hearer (Judg. 14:12).

land about your words and your wisdom. 7However I did not believe the words until I came and saw with my own eyes; and indeed the half was not told me. Your wisdom and prosperity exceed the fame of which I heard. 8Happy *are* your men and happy *are* these your servants, who stand continually before you *and* hear your wisdom! 9Blessed be the LORD your God, who delighted in you, setting you on the throne of Israel! Because the LORD has loved Israel forever, therefore He made you king, to do justice and righteousness."

10Then she gave the king one hundred and twenty talents of gold, spices in great quantity, and precious stones. There never again came such abundance of spices as the queen of Sheba gave to King Solomon. 11Also, the ships of Hiram, which brought gold from Ophir, brought great quantities of almug wood and precious stones from Ophir. 12And the king made steps of the almug wood for the house of the LORD and for the king's house, also harps and stringed instruments for singers. There never again came such almug wood, nor has the like been seen to this day.

13Now King Solomon gave the queen of Sheba all she desired, whatever she asked, besides what Solomon had given her according to the royal generosity. So she turned and went to her own country, she and her servants.

14The weight of gold that came to Solomon yearly was six hundred and sixty-six talents of gold, 15besides *that* from the traveling merchants, from the income of traders, from all the kings of Arabia, and from the governors of the country.

16And King Solomon made two hundred large shields *of* hammered gold; six hundred *shekels* of gold went into each shield. 17He also *made* three hundred shields *of* hammered gold; three minas of gold went into each shield. The king put them in the House of the Forest of Lebanon.

18Moreover the king made a great throne of ivory, and overlaid it with pure gold. 19The throne had six steps, and the top of the throne *was* round at the back; *there were* armrests on either side of the place of the seat, and two lions stood beside the armrests. 20Twelve lions stood there, one on each side of the six steps; nothing like *this* had been made for any *other* kingdom.

21All King Solomon's drinking vessels *were* gold, and all the vessels of the House of the Forest of Lebanon *were* pure gold. Not *one was* silver, for this was accounted as nothing in the days of Solomon. 22For the king had merchant ships at sea with the fleet of Hiram. Once every three years the merchant ships came bringing gold, silver, ivory, apes, and monkeys. 23So King Solomon surpassed all the kings of the earth in riches and wisdom.

24Now all the earth sought the presence of Solomon to hear his wisdom, which God had put in his heart. 25Each man brought his present: articles of silver and gold, garments, armor, spices, horses, and mules, at a set rate year by year.

10:25 silver and gold...horses. The wisdom God had given to Solomon (v. 24) caused many rulers, like the queen of Sheba (vv. 1–13), to bring presents to Solomon as they sought to buy his wisdom to be applied in their own nations. These gifts led Solomon to multiply for himself horses, as well as silver and gold, precisely that which God's king was warned against in Deuteronomy 17:16,17. Solomon became ensnared by the blessings of his own wisdom and disobeyed God's commands.

26And Solomon gathered chariots and horsemen; he had one thousand four hundred chariots and twelve thousand horsemen, whom he stationed in the chariot cities and with the king at Jerusalem. 27The king made silver *as common* in Jerusalem as stones, and he made cedar trees as abundant as the sycamores which *are* in the lowland.

28Also Solomon had horses imported from Egypt and Keveh; the king's merchants bought them in Keveh at the *current* price. 29Now a chariot that was imported from Egypt cost six hundred *shekels* of silver, and a horse one hundred and fifty; and thus, through their agents, they exported *them* to all the kings of the Hittites and the kings of Syria.

Psalm 69:1–4

To the Chief Musician. Set to "The Lilies."
A Psalm of David.

Save me, O God!
For the waters have come up to *my* neck.
2 I sink in deep mire,
Where *there is* no standing;
I have come into deep waters,
Where the floods overflow me.
3 I am weary with my crying;
My throat is dry;
My eyes fail while I wait for my God.
4 Those who hate me without a cause
Are more than the hairs of my head;

They are mighty who would
destroy me,
Being my enemies wrongfully;
Though I have stolen nothing,
I *still* must restore *it.*

Proverbs 17:18–19

18 A man devoid of understanding shakes
hands in a pledge,
And becomes surety for his friend.

19 He who loves transgression loves strife,
And he who exalts his gate seeks
destruction.

John 11:30–57

30 Now Jesus had not yet come into the town,
but was in the place where Martha met Him.
31 Then the Jews who were with her in the
house, and comforting her, when they saw
that Mary rose up quickly and went out, followed her, saying, "She is going to the tomb to
weep there."

32 Then, when Mary came where Jesus was,
and saw Him, she fell down at His feet, saying
to Him, "Lord, if You had been here, my brother would not have died."

33 Therefore, when Jesus saw her weeping,
and the Jews who came with her weeping, He
groaned in the spirit and was troubled. 34 And
He said, "Where have you laid him?"

They said to Him, "Lord, come and see."

35 Jesus wept. 36 Then the Jews said, "See how
He loved him!"

37 And some of them said, "Could not this
Man, who opened the eyes of the blind, also
have kept this man from dying?"

38 Then Jesus, again groaning in Himself,
came to the tomb. It was a cave, and a stone
lay against it. 39 Jesus said, "Take away the
stone."

Martha, the sister of him who was dead,
said to Him, "Lord, by this time there is a
stench, for he has been *dead* four days."

40 Jesus said to her, "Did I not say to you that if
you would believe you would see the glory of
God?" 41 Then they took away the stone *from the
place* where the dead man was lying. And Jesus
lifted up *His* eyes and said, "Father, I thank You
that You have heard Me. 42 And I know that You
always hear Me, but because of the people who
are standing by I said *this,* that they may believe
that You sent Me." 43 Now when He had said
these things, He cried with a loud voice,
"Lazarus, come forth!" 44 And he who had died
came out bound hand and foot with graveclothes, and his face was wrapped with a cloth.
Jesus said to them, "Loose him, and let him go."

45 Then many of the Jews who had come to
Mary, and had seen the things Jesus did,
believed in Him. 46 But some of them went
away to the Pharisees and told them the
things Jesus did. 47 Then the chief priests and
the Pharisees gathered a council and said,
"What shall we do? For this Man works many
signs. 48 If we let Him alone like this, everyone
will believe in Him, and the Romans will come
and take away both our place and nation."

49 And one of them, Caiaphas, being high
priest that year, said to them, "You know nothing at all, 50 nor do you consider that it is expedient for us that one man should die for the
people, and not that the whole nation should
perish." 51 Now this he did not say on his own
authority; but being high priest that year he
prophesied that Jesus would die for the
nation, 52 and not for that nation only, but also
that He would gather together in one the children of God who were scattered abroad.

11:50 one man should die for the people. He only meant that Jesus should be executed in order to spare their own positions and nation from Roman reprisals, but Caiaphas unwittingly used sacrificial, substitutionary language and prophesied the death of Christ for sinners.

11:51 he prophesied. Caiaphas did not realize the implications of what he spoke. While he uttered blasphemy against Christ, God parodied his statement into truth (Ps. 76:10). The responsibility for the wicked meaning of his words belonged to Caiaphas, but God's providence directed the choice of words so as to express the heart of God's glorious plan of salvation (Acts 4:27,28). He actually was used by God as a prophet because he was the high priest and originally the high priest was the means of God's will being revealed (2 Sam. 15:27).

53 Then, from that day on, they plotted to put
Him to death. 54 Therefore Jesus no longer
walked openly among the Jews, but went from
there into the country near the wilderness, to
a city called Ephraim, and there remained
with His disciples.

55 And the Passover of the Jews was near,
and many went from the country up to Jerusalem before the Passover, to purify themselves.
56 Then they sought Jesus, and spoke among
themselves as they stood in the temple, "What
do you think—that He will not come to the

feast?" [57]Now both the chief priests and the Pharisees had given a command, that if anyone knew where He was, he should report *it,* that they might seize Him.

DAY 31: What so troubled Christ at the death of His friend Lazarus?

Jesus was met by Mary, who fell brokenhearted at His feet and "the Jews who came with her weeping" (John 11:33). According to Jewish oral tradition, the funeral custom indicated that even a poor family must hire at least two flute players and a professional wailing woman to mourn the dead. Because the family may have been well-to-do, a rather large group appears present.

"He groaned in the spirit and was troubled." The phrase here does not mean merely that Jesus was deeply touched or moved with sympathy at the sight. The Greek term "groaned" always suggests anger, outrage, or emotional indignation (v. 38; Matt. 9:30; Mark 1:43; 14:5). Most likely Jesus was angered at the emotional grief of the people because it implicitly revealed unbelief in the resurrection and the temporary nature of death. The group was acting like pagans who had no hope (1 Thess. 4:13). While grief is understandable, the group was acting in despair, thus indicating a tacit denial of the resurrection and the Scripture that promised it. Jesus may also have been angered because He was indignant at the pain and sorrow in death that sin brought into the human condition.

"Jesus wept" (v. 35). The Greek word here has the connotation of silently bursting into tears in contrast to the loud lament of the group. His tears here were not generated out of mourning, since He was to raise Lazarus, but out of grief for a fallen world entangled in sin-caused sorrow and death. He was "a Man of sorrows and acquainted with grief" (3:16; Is. 53:3).

Jesus' prayer in vv. 41,42 was not really a petition, but thanksgiving to the Father. The reason for the miracle was to authenticate His claims to be the Messiah and Son of God.

JUNE 1

1 Kings 11:1–12:33

11 But King Solomon loved many foreign
women, as well as the daughter of
Pharaoh: women of the Moabites, Ammonites,
Edomites, Sidonians, *and* Hittites— 2from the
nations of whom the LORD had said to the children of Israel, "You shall not intermarry with
them, nor they with you. Surely they will turn
away your hearts after their gods." Solomon
clung to these in love. 3And he had seven hundred wives, princesses, and three hundred
concubines; and his wives turned away his
heart. 4For it was so, when Solomon was old,
that his wives turned his heart after other
gods; and his heart was not loyal to the LORD
his God, as *was* the heart of his father David.
5For Solomon went after Ashtoreth the goddess of the Sidonians, and after Milcom the
abomination of the Ammonites. 6Solomon did
evil in the sight of the LORD, and did not fully
follow the LORD, as *did* his father David. 7Then
Solomon built a high place for Chemosh the
abomination of Moab, on the hill that *is* east of
Jerusalem, and for Molech the abomination of
the people of Ammon. 8And he did likewise for
all his foreign wives, who burned incense and
sacrificed to their gods.

9So the LORD became angry with Solomon,
because his heart had turned from the LORD
God of Israel, who had appeared to him twice,
10and had commanded him concerning this
thing, that he should not go after other gods;
but he did not keep what the LORD had commanded. 11Therefore the LORD said to Solomon, "Because you have done this, and have
not kept My covenant and My statutes, which
I have commanded you, I will surely tear the
kingdom away from you and give it to your
servant. 12Nevertheless I will not do it in your
days, for the sake of your father David; I will
tear it out of the hand of your son. 13However I
will not tear away the whole kingdom; I will
give one tribe to your son for the sake of My
servant David, and for the sake of Jerusalem
which I have chosen."

14Now the LORD raised up an adversary
against Solomon, Hadad the Edomite; he *was*
a descendant of the king in Edom. 15For it happened, when David was in Edom, and Joab the
commander of the army had gone up to bury
the slain, after he had killed every male in
Edom 16(because for six months Joab
remained there with all Israel, until he had cut
down every male in Edom), 17that Hadad fled
to go to Egypt, he and certain Edomites of his
father's servants with him. Hadad *was* still a
little child. 18Then they arose from Midian and
came to Paran; and they took men with them
from Paran and came to Egypt, to Pharaoh
king of Egypt, who gave him a house, apportioned food for him, and gave him land. 19And
Hadad found great favor in the sight of
Pharaoh, so that he gave him as wife the sister
of his own wife, that is, the sister of Queen
Tahpenes. 20Then the sister of Tahpenes bore
him Genubath his son, whom Tahpenes
weaned in Pharaoh's house. And Genubath
was in Pharaoh's household among the sons of
Pharaoh.

21So when Hadad heard in Egypt that David
rested with his fathers, and that Joab the commander of the army was dead, Hadad said to
Pharaoh, "Let me depart, that I may go to my
own country."

22Then Pharaoh said to him, "But what have
you lacked with me, that suddenly you seek to
go to your own country?"

So he answered, "Nothing, but do let me go
anyway."

23And God raised up *another* adversary
against him, Rezon the son of Eliadah, who
had fled from his lord, Hadadezer king of
Zobah. 24So he gathered men to him and
became captain over a band *of raiders,* when
David killed those *of Zobah.* And they went to
Damascus and dwelt there, and reigned in Damascus. 25He was an adversary of Israel all the
days of Solomon (besides the trouble that
Hadad *caused*); and he abhorred Israel, and
reigned over Syria.

26Then Solomon's servant, Jeroboam the son
of Nebat, an Ephraimite from Zereda, whose
mother's name *was* Zeruah, a widow, also rebelled against the king.

27And this *is* what caused him to rebel
against the king: Solomon had built the Millo

11:26 Jeroboam the son of Nebat. In contrast to Hadad and Rezon, who were external adversaries of Solomon, God raised up Jeroboam from a town in Ephraim as an internal adversary. Jeroboam was from Ephraim, the leading tribe of Israel's northern 10 tribes. He was a young man of talent and energy who, having been appointed by Solomon as leader over the building works around Jerusalem, rose to public notice.

and repaired the damages to the City of David
his father. 28The man Jeroboam *was* a mighty
man of valor; and Solomon, seeing that the
young man was industrious, made him the
officer over all the labor force of the house of
Joseph.
29Now it happened at that time, when
Jeroboam went out of Jerusalem, that the
prophet Ahijah the Shilonite met him on the
way; and he had clothed himself with a new
garment, and the two *were* alone in the field.
30Then Ahijah took hold of the new garment
that *was* on him, and tore it *into* twelve pieces.
31And he said to Jeroboam, "Take for yourself
ten pieces, for thus says the LORD, the God of
Israel: 'Behold, I will tear the kingdom out of
the hand of Solomon and will give ten tribes to
you 32(but he shall have one tribe for the sake
of My servant David, and for the sake of Jerusalem, the city which I have chosen out of all
the tribes of Israel), 33because they have forsak-
en Me, and worshiped Ashtoreth the goddess of
the Sidonians, Chemosh the god of the
Moabites, and Milcom the god of the people of
Ammon, and have not walked in My ways to
do *what is* right in My eyes and *keep* My
statutes and My judgments, as *did* his father
David. 34However I will not take the whole
kingdom out of his hand, because I have made
him ruler all the days of his life for the sake of
My servant David, whom I chose because he
kept My commandments and My statutes.
35But I will take the kingdom out of his son's
hand and give it to you—ten tribes. 36And to
his son I will give one tribe, that My servant
David may always have a lamp before Me in
Jerusalem, the city which I have chosen for
Myself, to put My name there. 37So I will take
you, and you shall reign over all your heart
desires, and you shall be king over Israel.
38Then it shall be, if you heed all that I command you, walk in My ways, and do *what is*
right in My sight, to keep My statutes and My
commandments, as My servant David did, then
I will be with you and build for you an enduring
house, as I built for David, and will give Israel
to you. 39And I will afflict the descendants of David because of this, but not forever.' "
40Solomon therefore sought to kill Jeroboam.
But Jeroboam arose and fled to Egypt, to
Shishak king of Egypt, and was in Egypt until
the death of Solomon.
41Now the rest of the acts of Solomon, all
that he did, and his wisdom, *are* they not written in the book of the acts of Solomon? 42And
the period that Solomon reigned in Jerusalem
over all Israel *was* forty years. 43Then Solomon
rested with his fathers, and was buried in the
City of David his father. And Rehoboam his
son reigned in his place.

11:38 if you heed all that I command you. The Lord gave to Jeroboam the same promise that He had made to David—an enduring royal dynasty over Israel, the 10 northern tribes, if he obeyed God's law. The Lord imposed on Jeroboam the same conditions for his kingship that He had imposed on David (2:3,4; 3:14).

11:39 but not forever. This statement implied that the kingdom's division was not to be permanent and that David's house would ultimately rule all the tribes of Israel again (Ezek. 37:15–28).

12 And Rehoboam went to Shechem, for all
Israel had gone to Shechem to make him
king. 2So it happened, when Jeroboam the son
of Nebat heard *it* (he was still in Egypt, for he
had fled from the presence of King Solomon
and had been dwelling in Egypt), 3that they
sent and called him. Then Jeroboam and the
whole assembly of Israel came and spoke to
Rehoboam, saying, 4"Your father made our
yoke heavy; now therefore, lighten the burdensome service of your father, and his heavy
yoke which he put on us, and we will serve
you."
5So he said to them, "Depart *for* three days,
then come back to me." And the people
departed.
6Then King Rehoboam consulted the elders
who stood before his father Solomon while he
still lived, and he said, "How do you advise *me*
to answer these people?"
7And they spoke to him, saying, "If you will
be a servant to these people today, and serve
them, and answer them, and speak good
words to them, then they will be your servants forever."
8But he rejected the advice which the elders
had given him, and consulted the young men
who had grown up with him, who stood before
him. 9And he said to them, "What advice do
you give? How should we answer this people
who have spoken to me, saying, 'Lighten the
yoke which your father put on us'?"
10Then the young men who had grown up
with him spoke to him, saying, "Thus you
should speak to this people who have spoken
to you, saying, 'Your father made our yoke
heavy, but you make *it* lighter on us'—thus
you shall say to them: 'My little *finger* shall be

thicker than my father's waist! 11And now, whereas my father put a heavy yoke on you, I will add to your yoke; my father chastised you with whips, but I will chastise you with scourges!' "

12So Jeroboam and all the people came to Rehoboam the third day, as the king had directed, saying, "Come back to me the third day." 13Then the king answered the people roughly, and rejected the advice which the elders had given him; 14and he spoke to them according to the advice of the young men, saying, "My father made your yoke heavy, but I will add to your yoke; my father chastised you with whips, but I will chastise you with scourges!" 15So the king did not listen to the people; for the turn *of events* was from the LORD, that He might fulfill His word, which the LORD had spoken by Ahijah the Shilonite to Jeroboam the son of Nebat.

16Now when all Israel saw that the king did not listen to them, the people answered the king, saying:

"What share have we in David?
We have no inheritance in the son of Jesse.
To your tents, O Israel!
Now, see to your own house, O David!"

So Israel departed to their tents. 17But Rehoboam reigned over the children of Israel who dwelt in the cities of Judah.

18Then King Rehoboam sent Adoram, who *was* in charge of the revenue; but all Israel stoned him with stones, and he died. Therefore King Rehoboam mounted his chariot in haste to flee to Jerusalem. 19So Israel has been in rebellion against the house of David to this day.

20Now it came to pass when all Israel heard that Jeroboam had come back, they sent for him and called him to the congregation, and made him king over all Israel. There was none who followed the house of David, but the tribe of Judah only.

21And when Rehoboam came to Jerusalem, he assembled all the house of Judah with the tribe of Benjamin, one hundred and eighty thousand chosen *men* who were warriors, to fight against the house of Israel, that he might restore the kingdom to Rehoboam the son of Solomon. 22But the word of God came to Shemaiah the man of God, saying, 23"Speak to Rehoboam the son of Solomon, king of Judah, to all the house of Judah and Benjamin, and to the rest of the people, saying, 24'Thus says the LORD: "You shall not go up nor fight against your brethren the children of Israel. Let every man return to his house, for this thing is from Me." ' " Therefore they obeyed the word of the LORD, and turned back, according to the word of the LORD.

25Then Jeroboam built Shechem in the mountains of Ephraim, and dwelt there. Also he went out from there and built Penuel. 26And Jeroboam said in his heart, "Now the kingdom may return to the house of David: 27If these people go up to offer sacrifices in the house of

12:26 return to the house of David. The Lord had ordained a political, not a religious, division of Solomon's kingdom. The Lord had promised Jeroboam political control of the 10 northern tribes (11:31,35,37). However, Jeroboam was to religiously follow the Mosaic Law, which demanded that he follow the Lord's sacrificial system at the temple in Jerusalem (11:38). Having received the kingdom from God, he should have relied on divine protection, but he did not. Seeking to keep his subjects from being influenced by Rehoboam when they went to Jerusalem to worship, he set up worship in the north (vv. 27,28).

the LORD at Jerusalem, then the heart of this people will turn back to their lord, Rehoboam king of Judah, and they will kill me and go back to Rehoboam king of Judah."

28Therefore the king asked advice, made two calves of gold, and said to the people, "It is too much for you to go up to Jerusalem. Here are your gods, O Israel, which brought you up from the land of Egypt!" 29And he set up one in Bethel, and the other he put in Dan. 30Now this thing became a sin, for the people went *to worship* before the one as far as Dan. 31He made shrines on the high places, and made priests from every class of people, who were not of the sons of Levi.

32Jeroboam ordained a feast on the fifteenth day of the eighth month, like the feast that *was* in Judah, and offered sacrifices on the altar. So he did at Bethel, sacrificing to the calves that he had made. And at Bethel he installed the priests of the high places which he had made. 33So he made offerings on the altar which he had made at Bethel on the fifteenth day of the eighth month, in the month which he had devised in his own heart. And he ordained a feast for the children of Israel, and offered sacrifices on the altar and burned incense.

Psalm 69:5–15

5 O God, You know my foolishness;
And my sins are not hidden from You.

6 Let not those who wait for You, O Lord
GOD of hosts, be ashamed because
of me;
Let not those who seek You be
confounded because of me, O God
of Israel.
7 Because for Your sake I have borne
reproach;
Shame has covered my face.
8 I have become a stranger to my
brothers,
And an alien to my mother's children;
9 Because zeal for Your house has eaten
me up,
And the reproaches of those who
reproach You have fallen on me.

69:9 has eaten me up. The psalmist has brought hatred and hostility on himself by his unyielding insistence that the behavior of the people measure up to their outward claim of devotion to God. Whenever God was dishonored, he felt the pain, because he loved God so greatly. Jesus claimed for Himself this attitude, as indicated in John 2:17; Romans 15:3.

---

10 When I wept *and chastened* my soul
with fasting,
That became my reproach.
11 I also made sackcloth my garment;
I became a byword to them.
12 Those who sit in the gate speak
against me,
And I *am* the song of the drunkards.

13 But as for me, my prayer *is* to You,
O LORD, *in* the acceptable time;
O God, in the multitude of Your mercy,
Hear me in the truth of Your salvation.
14 Deliver me out of the mire,
And let me not sink;
Let me be delivered from those who
hate me,
And out of the deep waters.
15 Let not the floodwater overflow me,
Nor let the deep swallow me up;
And let not the pit shut its mouth on me.

Proverbs 17:20–22

20 He who has a deceitful heart finds no
good,
And he who has a perverse tongue falls
into evil.

21 He who begets a scoffer *does so* to his
sorrow,
And the father of a fool has no joy.
22 A merry heart does good, *like*
medicine,
But a broken spirit dries the bones.

John 12:1–26

12 Then, six days before the Passover, Jesus
came to Bethany, where Lazarus was
who had been dead, whom He had raised
from the dead. 2There they made Him a supper; and Martha served, but Lazarus was one
of those who sat at the table with Him. 3Then
Mary took a pound of very costly oil of spikenard, anointed the feet of Jesus, and wiped His
feet with her hair. And the house was filled
with the fragrance of the oil.
4But one of His disciples, Judas Iscariot, Simon's *son,* who would betray Him, said, 5"Why
was this fragrant oil not sold for three hundred denarii and given to the poor?" 6This he
said, not that he cared for the poor, but
because he was a thief, and had the money
box; and he used to take what was put in it.
7But Jesus said, "Let her alone; she has kept
this for the day of My burial. 8For the poor you
have with you always, but Me you do not have
always."
9Now a great many of the Jews knew that He
was there; and they came, not for Jesus' sake
only, but that they might also see Lazarus,
whom He had raised from the dead. 10But the
chief priests plotted to put Lazarus to death
also, 11because on account of him many of the
Jews went away and believed in Jesus.
12The next day a great multitude that had
come to the feast, when they heard that Jesus
was coming to Jerusalem, 13took branches of
palm trees and went out to meet Him, and
cried out:

"Hosanna!
*'Blessed is He who comes in the name
of the LORD!'*
The King of Israel!"

14Then Jesus, when He had found a young
donkey, sat on it; as it is written:

15 *"Fear not, daughter of Zion;
Behold, your King is coming,
Sitting on a donkey's colt."*

16His disciples did not understand these
things at first; but when Jesus was glorified,
then they remembered that these things were
written about Him and *that* they had done
these things to Him.
17Therefore the people, who were with Him
when He called Lazarus out of his tomb and

raised him from the dead, bore witness. [18]For
this reason the people also met Him, because
they heard that He had done this sign. [19]The
Pharisees therefore said among themselves,
"You see that you are accomplishing nothing.
Look, the world has gone after Him!"
[20]Now there were certain Greeks among
those who came up to worship at the feast.
[21]Then they came to Philip, who was from
Bethsaida of Galilee, and asked him, saying,
"Sir, we wish to see Jesus."
[22]Philip came and told Andrew, and in turn
Andrew and Philip told Jesus.
[23]But Jesus answered them, saying, "The
hour has come that the Son of Man should be
glorified. [24]Most assuredly, I say to you, unless
a grain of wheat falls into the ground and dies,
it remains alone; but if it dies, it produces
much grain. [25]He who loves his life will lose it,
and he who hates his life in this world will
keep it for eternal life. [26]If anyone serves Me,
let him follow Me; and where I am, there My
servant will be also. If anyone serves Me, him
My Father will honor.

12:19 the world has gone after Him. The world means the people in general, as opposed to everyone in particular. Clearly, most people in the world did not even know of Him at that time, and many in Israel did not believe in Him. Often, world is used in this general sense (v. 47; 1:29; 3:17; 4:42; 14:22; 17:9,21).

Day 1: What was Solomon's main downfall?

"But King Solomon loved many foreign women" (1 Kin. 11:1). Many of Solomon's marriages were for the purpose of ratifying treaties with other nations, a common practice in the ancient Near East. The practice of multiplying royal wives, prohibited in Deuteronomy 17:17 because the practice would turn the king's heart away from the Lord, proved to be accurate in the experience of Solomon. His love for his wives (vv. 1,2) led him to abandon his loyalty to the Lord and worship other gods (vv. 3–6). No sadder picture can be imagined than the ugly apostasy of his later years (over 50), which can be traced back to his sins with foreign wives. Polygamy was tolerated among the ancient Hebrews, though most in the East had only one wife. A number of wives was seen as a sign of wealth and importance. The king desired to have a larger harem than any of his subjects, and Solomon resorted to this form of state magnificence. But it was a sin directly violating God's law, and the very result which that law was designed to prevent happened.

"Solomon did evil in the sight of the LORD" (v. 6). The particular evil of Solomon was his tolerance of and personal practice of idolatry. These same words were used throughout the Book of Kings to describe the rulers who promoted and practiced idolatry (15:26,34; 16:19,25,30; 22:52; 2 Kin. 3:2; 8:18,27; 13:2,11; 14:24; 15:9,18,24,28; 17:2; 21:2,20; 23:32; 24:9,19). Solomon became an open idolater, worshiping images of wood and stone in the sight of the temple which, in his early years, he had erected to the one true God.

The Lord appeared to him twice (vv. 9,10). Once was at Gibeon (3:5), the next at Jerusalem (9:2). On both occasions, God had warned Solomon, so he had no excuses. "Because you have done this,…I will surely tear the kingdom away from you" (v. 11). Solomon failed to obey the commandments to honor God (Ex. 20:3–6), which were part of the Mosaic Covenant. Obedience to that Covenant was necessary for receiving the blessings of the Davidic Covenant (2:3, 4). The Lord's tearing of the kingdom from Solomon was announced in Ahijah's symbolic action of tearing his garment in vv. 29–39.

JUNE 2

1 Kings 13:1–14:31

13 And behold, a man of God went from Judah to Bethel by the word of the LORD,
and Jeroboam stood by the altar to burn
incense. [2]Then he cried out against the altar
by the word of the LORD, and said, "O altar,
altar! Thus says the LORD: 'Behold, a child,
Josiah by name, shall be born to the house of
David; and on you he shall sacrifice the priests
of the high places who burn incense on you,
and men's bones shall be burned on you.' "
[3]And he gave a sign the same day, saying,
"This *is* the sign which the LORD has spoken:
Surely the altar shall split apart, and the ashes
on it shall be poured out."
[4]So it came to pass when King Jeroboam
heard the saying of the man of God, who cried
out against the altar in Bethel, that he
stretched out his hand from the altar, saying,

"Arrest him!" Then his hand, which he
stretched out toward him, withered, so that he
could not pull it back to himself. 5The altar also
was split apart, and the ashes poured out from
the altar, according to the sign which the man
of God had given by the word of the LORD.
6Then the king answered and said to the man
of God, "Please entreat the favor of the LORD
your God, and pray for me, that my hand may
be restored to me."

So the man of God entreated the LORD, and
the king's hand was restored to him, and
became as before. 7Then the king said to the
man of God, "Come home with me and refresh
yourself, and I will give you a reward."

8But the man of God said to the king, "If you
were to give me half your house, I would not
go in with you; nor would I eat bread nor drink
water in this place. 9For so it was commanded
me by the word of the LORD, saying, 'You shall
not eat bread, nor drink water, nor return by
the same way you came.' " 10So he went another way and did not return by the way he came
to Bethel.

11Now an old prophet dwelt in Bethel, and
his sons came and told him all the works that
the man of God had done that day in Bethel;
they also told their father the words which he
had spoken to the king. 12And their father said
to them, "Which way did he go?" For his sons
had seen which way the man of God went who
came from Judah. 13Then he said to his sons,
"Saddle the donkey for me." So they saddled
the donkey for him; and he rode on it, 14and
went after the man of God, and found him sitting under an oak. Then he said to him, "*Are*
you the man of God who came from Judah?"

And he said, "I *am.*"

15Then he said to him, "Come home with me
and eat bread."

16And he said, "I cannot return with you nor
go in with you; neither can I eat bread nor
drink water with you in this place. 17For I have
been told by the word of the LORD, 'You shall
not eat bread nor drink water there, nor
return by going the way you came.' "

18He said to him, "I too *am* a prophet as you
are, and an angel spoke to me by the word of
the LORD, saying, 'Bring him back with you to
your house, that he may eat bread and drink
water.' " (He was lying to him.)

19So he went back with him, and ate bread in
his house, and drank water.

20Now it happened, as they sat at the table,
that the word of the LORD came to the prophet
who had brought him back; 21and he cried out
to the man of God who came from Judah, saying, "Thus says the LORD: 'Because you have
disobeyed the word of the LORD, and have not
kept the commandment which the LORD your
God commanded you, 22but you came back,
ate bread, and drank water in the place of
which *the LORD* said to you, "Eat no bread and
drink no water," your corpse shall not come to
the tomb of your fathers.' "

23So it was, after he had eaten bread and
after he had drunk, that he saddled the donkey for him, the prophet whom he had
brought back. 24When he was gone, a lion met
him on the road and killed him. And his
corpse was thrown on the road, and the donkey stood by it. The lion also stood by the
corpse. 25And there, men passed by and saw
the corpse thrown on the road, and the lion
standing by the corpse. Then they went and
told *it* in the city where the old prophet dwelt.

26Now when the prophet who had brought
him back from the way heard *it,* he said, "It *is*
the man of God who was disobedient to the
word of the LORD. Therefore the LORD has
delivered him to the lion, which has torn him
and killed him, according to the word of the
LORD which He spoke to him." 27And he spoke
to his sons, saying, "Saddle the donkey for
me." So they saddled *it.* 28Then he went and
found his corpse thrown on the road, and the
donkey and the lion standing by the corpse.
The lion had not eaten the corpse nor torn the
donkey. 29And the prophet took up the corpse
of the man of God, laid it on the donkey, and
brought it back. So the old prophet came to
the city to mourn, and to bury him. 30Then he
laid the corpse in his own tomb; and they
mourned over him, *saying,* "Alas, my brother!"
31So it was, after he had buried him, that he
spoke to his sons, saying, "When I am dead,
then bury me in the tomb where the man of
God *is* buried; lay my bones beside his bones.
32For the saying which he cried out by the
word of the LORD against the altar in Bethel,

13:18 He was lying to him. Why the old prophet deceived the man of God the text does not state. It may be that his own sons were worshipers at Bethel or perhaps priests, and this man wanted to gain favor with the king by showing up the man of God as an imposter who acted contrary to his own claim to have heard from God. Accustomed to receiving direct revelations, the Judean prophet should have regarded the supposed angelic message with suspicion and sought divine verification of this revised order.

and against all the shrines on the high places
which *are* in the cities of Samaria, will surely
come to pass."
33After this event Jeroboam did not turn
from his evil way, but again he made priests
from every class of people for the high places;
whoever wished, he consecrated him, and he
became *one* of the priests of the high places.
34And this thing was the sin of the house of
Jeroboam, so as to exterminate and destroy *it*
from the face of the earth.
14 At that time Abijah the son of Jeroboam
became sick. 2And Jeroboam said to his
wife, "Please arise, and disguise yourself, that
they may not recognize you as the wife of Jeroboam, and go to Shiloh. Indeed, Ahijah the
prophet *is* there, who told me that *I would be*
king over this people. 3Also take with you ten
loaves, *some* cakes, and a jar of honey, and go
to him; he will tell you what will become of the
child." 4And Jeroboam's wife did so; she arose
and went to Shiloh, and came to the house of
Ahijah. But Ahijah could not see, for his eyes
were glazed by reason of his age.
5Now the LORD had said to Ahijah, "Here is
the wife of Jeroboam, coming to ask you
something about her son, for he *is* sick. Thus
and thus you shall say to her; for it will be,
when she comes in, that she will pretend *to be*
another *woman*."
6And so it was, when Ahijah heard the sound
of her footsteps as she came through the door,
he said, "Come in, wife of Jeroboam. Why do
you pretend *to be* another *person?* For I *have*
been sent to you *with* bad *news*. 7Go, tell
Jeroboam, 'Thus says the LORD God of Israel:
"Because I exalted you from among the people, and made you ruler over My people Israel, 8and tore the kingdom away from the
house of David, and gave it to you; and *yet* you
have not been as My servant David, who kept
My commandments and who followed Me
with all his heart, to do only *what was* right in
My eyes; 9but you have done more evil than all
who were before you, for you have gone and
made for yourself other gods and molded
images to provoke Me to anger, and have cast
Me behind your back— 10therefore behold! I
will bring disaster on the house of Jeroboam,
and will cut off from Jeroboam every male in
Israel, bond and free; I will take away the remnant of the house of Jeroboam, as one takes
away refuse until it is all gone. 11The dogs shall
eat whoever belongs to Jeroboam and dies in
the city, and the birds of the air shall eat whoever dies in the field; for the LORD has spoken!"' 12Arise therefore, go to your own
house. When your feet enter the city, the child
shall die. 13And all Israel shall mourn for him
and bury him, for he is the only one of
Jeroboam who shall come to the grave,
because in him there is found something good
toward the LORD God of Israel in the house of
Jeroboam.
14"Moreover the LORD will raise up for
Himself a king over Israel who shall cut off the
house of Jeroboam; this is the day. What?
Even now! 15For the LORD will strike Israel, as
a reed is shaken in the water. He will uproot
Israel from this good land which He gave to
their fathers, and will scatter them beyond the
River, because they have made their wooden
images, provoking the LORD to anger. 16And

14:15 Ahijah announced God's stern judgment on Israel for joining Jeroboam's apostasy. Struck by the Lord, Israel would sway like a reed in a rushing river, a biblical metaphor for political instability (Matt. 11:7; Luke 7:24). One day, the Lord would uproot Israel from Palestinian soil and scatter it in exile east of the Euphrates. The fulfillment of this prophecy is recorded in 2 Kings 17:23.

He will give Israel up because of the sins of
Jeroboam, who sinned and who made Israel
sin."
17Then Jeroboam's wife arose and departed,
and came to Tirzah. When she came to the
threshold of the house, the child died. 18And
they buried him; and all Israel mourned for
him, according to the word of the LORD which
He spoke through His servant Ahijah the
prophet.
19Now the rest of the acts of Jeroboam, how
he made war and how he reigned, indeed they
are written in the book of the chronicles of the
kings of Israel. 20The period that Jeroboam
reigned *was* twenty-two years. So he rested
with his fathers. Then Nadab his son reigned
in his place.
21And Rehoboam the son of Solomon
reigned in Judah. Rehoboam *was* forty-one
years old when he became king. He reigned
seventeen years in Jerusalem, the city which
the LORD had chosen out of all the tribes of Israel, to put His name there. His mother's
name *was* Naamah, an Ammonitess. 22Now Judah did evil in the sight of the LORD, and they
provoked Him to jealousy with their sins
which they committed, more than all that their
fathers had done. 23For they also built for themselves high places, *sacred* pillars, and wooden

images on every high hill and under every
green tree. [24]And there were also perverted
persons in the land. They did according to all
the abominations of the nations which the
LORD had cast out before the children of Israel.

[25]It happened in the fifth year of King
Rehoboam *that* Shishak king of Egypt came
up against Jerusalem. [26]And he took away the
treasures of the house of the LORD and the
treasures of the king's house; he took away
everything. He also took away all the gold
shields which Solomon had made. [27]Then
King Rehoboam made bronze shields in their
place, and committed *them* to the hands of the
captains of the guard, who guarded the doorway of the king's house. [28]And whenever the
king entered the house of the LORD, the
guards carried them, then brought them back
into the guardroom.

[29]Now the rest of the acts of Rehoboam, and
all that he did, *are* they not written in the book
of the chronicles of the kings of Judah? [30]And
there was war between Rehoboam and Jeroboam all *their* days. [31]So Rehoboam rested with
his fathers, and was buried with his fathers in
the City of David. His mother's name *was*
Naamah, an Ammonitess. Then Abijam his
son reigned in his place.

69:21 gall...vinegar. Gall was a poisonous herb. Here it serves as a metaphor for betrayal. Friends who should provide sustenance to the psalmist had turned against him. Gall in vinegar was actually offered to Christ while He was on the cross (Matt. 27:34).

Psalm 69:16–21

16 Hear me, O LORD, for Your
lovingkindness *is* good;
Turn to me according to the multitude
of Your tender mercies.
17 And do not hide Your face from Your
servant,
For I am in trouble;
Hear me speedily.
18 Draw near to my soul, *and* redeem it;
Deliver me because of my enemies.

19 You know my reproach, my shame,
and my dishonor;
My adversaries *are* all before You.
20 Reproach has broken my heart,
And I am full of heaviness;
I looked *for someone* to take pity, but
there was none;
And for comforters, but I found none.
21 They also gave me gall for my food,
And for my thirst they gave me vinegar
to drink.

Proverbs 17:23–24

23 A wicked *man* accepts a bribe behind
the back
To pervert the ways of justice.

24 Wisdom *is* in the sight of him who has
understanding,
But the eyes of a fool *are* on the ends
of the earth.

John 12:27–50

[27]"Now My soul is troubled, and what shall I
say? 'Father, save Me from this hour'? But for
this purpose I came to this hour. [28]Father, glorify Your name."

Then a voice came from heaven, *saying,* "I
have both glorified *it* and will glorify *it* again."

[29]Therefore the people who stood by and
heard *it* said that it had thundered. Others said,
"An angel has spoken to Him."

[30]Jesus answered and said, "This voice did
not come because of Me, but for your sake.
[31]Now is the judgment of this world; now the
ruler of this world will be cast out. [32]And I, if I
am lifted up from the earth, will draw all *peoples* to Myself." [33]This He said, signifying by
what death He would die.

[34]The people answered Him, "We have heard
from the law that the Christ remains forever;
and how *can* You say, 'The Son of Man must be
lifted up'? Who is this Son of Man?"

[35]Then Jesus said to them, "A little while
longer the light is with you. Walk while you
have the light, lest darkness overtake you; he
who walks in darkness does not know where
he is going. [36]While you have the light, believe
in the light, that you may become sons of
light." These things Jesus spoke, and departed, and was hidden from them.

[37]But although He had done so many signs
before them, they did not believe in Him, [38]that
the word of Isaiah the prophet might be fulfilled, which he spoke:

*"Lord, who has believed our report?
And to whom has the arm of the* LORD
been revealed?"

[39]Therefore they could not believe, because
Isaiah said again:

40 *"He has blinded their eyes and
hardened their hearts,*

Lest they should see with their eyes,
Lest they should understand with their
hearts and turn,
So that I should heal them."

[41]These things Isaiah said when he saw His
glory and spoke of Him.

[42]Nevertheless even among the rulers many
believed in Him, but because of the Pharisees
they did not confess *Him,* lest they should be
put out of the synagogue; [43]for they loved the
praise of men more than the praise of God.

[44]Then Jesus cried out and said, "He who
believes in Me, believes not in Me but in Him
who sent Me. [45]And he who sees Me sees Him
who sent Me. [46]I have come *as* a light into the
world, that whoever believes in Me should not
abide in darkness. [47]And if anyone hears My
words and does not believe, I do not judge him;
for I did not come to judge the world but to save
the world. [48]He who rejects Me, and does not
receive My words, has that which judges him—
the word that I have spoken will judge him in
the last day. [49]For I have not spoken on My own
authority; but the Father who sent Me gave Me
a command, what I should say and what I
should speak. [50]And I know that His command
is everlasting life. Therefore, whatever I speak,
just as the Father has told Me, so I speak."

12:42,43 The indictment of vv. 37–41 is followed by the exceptions of vv. 42,43. While the people seemed to trust Jesus with much more candor and fervency, the leaders of Israel who believed in Him demonstrated inadequate, irresolute, even spurious faith. The faith of the latter was so weak that they refused to take any position that would threaten their position in the synagogue. This is one of the saddest statements about spiritual leadership, for they preferred the praises of men above the praises of God in their refusal to publicly acknowledge Jesus as Messiah and Son of God.

DAY 2: As Jesus approached His death, what kept Him going?

In John 12:23, Jesus knew that "the hour" had come for His death. Considering what was ahead, He confessed, "Now My soul is troubled" (v. 27). The term used here is strong and signifies horror, anxiety, and agitation. Jesus' contemplation of taking on the wrath of God for the sins of the world caused revulsion in the sinless Savior (2 Cor. 5:21).

What kept Him going was the principle that Jesus lived by and would die by: "Father, glorify Your name" (v. 28). See 7:18; 8:29,50. The fact that the Father answered the Son in an audible voice signifies its importance: "I have both glorified it and will glorify." This is only one of three instances during Jesus' ministry when this took place (Matt. 3:17—His baptism; 17:5—His transfiguration).

Jesus acknowledged that "the ruler of this world" was involved (v. 31). This is a reference to Satan (see 14:30; 16:11; Matt. 4:8,9; Luke 4:6,7; 2 Cor. 4:4; Eph. 2:2; 6:12). Although the Cross might have appeared to signal Satan's victory over God, in reality it marked Satan's defeat (Rom. 16:20; Heb. 2:14). This would occur as Jesus was "lifted up from the earth" (v. 32), referring to His crucifixion (v. 33; 18:32). This is a veiled prediction of Jesus' death on the cross. Jesus referred to the story of Numbers 21:5–9 where the Israelite people who looked at the serpent lifted up by Moses were healed. The point of this illustration or analogy is in the "lifted up." Just as Moses lifted up the snake on the pole so that all who looked upon it might live physically, those who look to Christ, who was lifted up on the cross for the sins of the world, will live spiritually and eternally.

The people's response was to ask Him, "We have heard from the law that the Christ remains forever; and how can You say, 'The Son of Man must be lifted up'?" (v. 34). The term "law" was used broadly enough to include not only the 5 books of Moses but also the whole of the Old Testament (Rom. 10:4). Perhaps they had in mind Isaiah 9:7 which promised that Messiah's kingdom would last forever or Ezekiel 37:25 where God promised that the final David would be Israel's prince forever (Ps. 89:35–37). To their question, Jesus offered them a final invitation to focus on His theme of believing in the Messiah and Son of God (vv. 35,36).

JUNE 3

1 Kings 15:1–16:34

15 In the eighteenth year of King Jeroboam
the son of Nebat, Abijam became king over
Judah. [2]He reigned three years in Jerusalem.
His mother's name *was* Maachah the granddaughter of Abishalom. [3]And he walked in all
the sins of his father, which he had done before
him; his heart was not loyal to the LORD his
God, as was the heart of his father David. [4]Nev-
ertheless for David's sake the LORD his God
gave him a lamp in Jerusalem, by setting up his
son after him and by establishing Jerusalem;

[5]because David did *what was* right in the eyes
of the LORD, and had not turned aside from
anything that He commanded him all the days
of his life, except in the matter of Uriah the Hittite. [6]And there was war between Rehoboam
and Jeroboam all the days of his life. [7]Now the
rest of the acts of Abijam, and all that he did,
are they not written in the book of the chronicles of the kings of Judah? And there was war
between Abijam and Jeroboam.
[8]So Abijam rested with his fathers, and they
buried him in the City of David. Then Asa his
son reigned in his place.
[9]In the twentieth year of Jeroboam king of
Israel, Asa became king over Judah. [10]And he
reigned forty-one years in Jerusalem. His
grandmother's name *was* Maachah the granddaughter of Abishalom. [11]Asa did *what was* right
in the eyes of the LORD, as *did* his father David.
[12]And he banished the perverted persons from
the land, and removed all the idols that his
fathers had made. [13]Also he removed Maachah
his grandmother from *being* queen mother,
because she had made an obscene image of
Asherah. And Asa cut down her obscene image
and burned *it* by the Brook Kidron. [14]But the
high places were not removed. Nevertheless
Asa's heart was loyal to the LORD all his days.
[15]He also brought into the house of the LORD
the things which his father had dedicated, and
the things which he himself had dedicated: silver and gold and utensils.
[16]Now there was war between Asa and
Baasha king of Israel all their days. [17]And
Baasha king of Israel came up against Judah,
and built Ramah, that he might let none go out
or come in to Asa king of Judah. [18]Then Asa
took all the silver and gold *that was* left in the
treasuries of the house of the LORD and the
treasuries of the king's house, and delivered
them into the hand of his servants. And King
Asa sent them to Ben-Hadad the son of
Tabrimmon, the son of Hezion, king of Syria,
who dwelt in Damascus, saying, [19]"*Let there be*
a treaty between you and me, as there was
between my father and your father. See, I have
sent you a present of silver and gold. Come
and break your treaty with Baasha king of Israel, so that he will withdraw from me."
[20]So Ben-Hadad heeded King Asa, and sent
the captains of his armies against the cities of
Israel. He attacked Ijon, Dan, Abel Beth
Maachah, and all Chinneroth, with all the land
of Naphtali. [21]Now it happened, when Baasha
heard *it,* that he stopped building Ramah, and
remained in Tirzah.
[22]Then King Asa made a proclamation
throughout all Judah; none *was* exempted.
And they took away the stones and timber of
Ramah, which Baasha had used for building;
and with them King Asa built Geba of Benjamin, and Mizpah.
[23]The rest of all the acts of Asa, all his might,
all that he did, and the cities which he built,
are they not written in the book of the chronicles of the kings of Judah? But in the time of
his old age he was diseased in his feet. [24]So
Asa rested with his fathers, and was buried
with his fathers in the City of David his father.
Then Jehoshaphat his son reigned in his
place.
[25]Now Nadab the son of Jeroboam became
king over Israel in the second year of Asa king
of Judah, and he reigned over Israel two years.
[26]And he did evil in the sight of the LORD, and
walked in the way of his father, and in his sin
by which he had made Israel sin.
[27]Then Baasha the son of Ahijah, of the house
of Issachar, conspired against him. And Baasha
killed him at Gibbethon, which *belonged* to the
Philistines, while Nadab and all Israel laid siege
to Gibbethon. [28]Baasha killed him in the third
year of Asa king of Judah, and reigned in his
place. [29]And it was so, when he became king,
that he killed all the house of Jeroboam. He did
not leave to Jeroboam anyone that breathed,
until he had destroyed him, according to the
word of the LORD which He had spoken by His
servant Ahijah the Shilonite, [30]because of the
sins of Jeroboam, which he had sinned and by
which he had made Israel sin, because of his
provocation with which he had provoked the
LORD God of Israel to anger.
[31]Now the rest of the acts of Nadab, and all

15:11–15 Asa did 4 good things: 1) he removed the sacred prostitutes (v. 12); 2) he rid the land of all the idols made by his predecessors (v. 12); 3) he removed the corrupt queen mother and burned the idol she had made; and 4) he placed holy things, items that he and his father had dedicated to the Lord, back in the temple (v. 15). Though he never engaged in idolatry, Asa's failure was his toleration of the high places (v. 14).

15:13 obscene image. This term is derived from the verb "to shudder" (Job 9:6). It suggests a shocking, perhaps even a sexually explicit, idol. Asa removed his grandmother, Maacah, the official queen mother, because of her association with this idol.

15:29 he killed all the house of Jeroboam. Baasha, the northern king, in a vicious practice too common in the ancient Near East, annihilated all of Jeroboam's family. This act fulfilled Ahijah's prophecy against Jeroboam (14:9–11). However, Baasha went beyond the words of the prophecy, since 14:10 specified judgment only on every male, while Baasha killed all men, women, and children.

that he did, *are* they not written in the book of
the chronicles of the kings of Israel? 32And
there was war between Asa and Baasha king
of Israel all their days.
33In the third year of Asa king of Judah,
Baasha the son of Ahijah became king over all
Israel in Tirzah, and *reigned* twenty-four years.
34He did evil in the sight of the LORD, and walked
in the way of Jeroboam, and in his sin by which
he had made Israel sin.
16 Then the word of the LORD came to Jehu
the son of Hanani, against Baasha, saying: 2"Inasmuch as I lifted you out of the dust
and made you ruler over My people Israel, and
you have walked in the way of Jeroboam, and
have made My people Israel sin, to provoke
Me to anger with their sins, 3surely I will take
away the posterity of Baasha and the posterity
of his house, and I will make your house like
the house of Jeroboam the son of Nebat. 4The
dogs shall eat whoever belongs to Baasha and
dies in the city, and the birds of the air shall eat
whoever dies in the fields."
5Now the rest of the acts of Baasha, what he
did, and his might, *are* they not written in the
book of the chronicles of the kings of Israel?
6So Baasha rested with his fathers and was
buried in Tirzah. Then Elah his son reigned in
his place.
7And also the word of the LORD came by the
prophet Jehu the son of Hanani against
Baasha and his house, because of all the evil
that he did in the sight of the LORD in provoking Him to anger with the work of his hands,
in being like the house of Jeroboam, and
because he killed them.
8In the twenty-sixth year of Asa king of Judah, Elah the son of Baasha became king over
Israel, *and reigned* two years in Tirzah. 9Now
his servant Zimri, commander of half *his* chariots, conspired against him as he was in
Tirzah drinking himself drunk in the house of
Arza, steward of *his* house in Tirzah. 10And
Zimri went in and struck him and killed him
in the twenty-seventh year of Asa king of
Judah, and reigned in his place.
11Then it came to pass, when he began to
reign, as soon as he was seated on his throne,
that he killed all the household of Baasha; he
did not leave him one male, neither of his relatives nor of his friends. 12Thus Zimri
destroyed all the household of Baasha, according to the word of the LORD, which He spoke
against Baasha by Jehu the prophet, 13for all
the sins of Baasha and the sins of Elah his son,
by which they had sinned and by which they
had made Israel sin, in provoking the LORD
God of Israel to anger with their idols.
14Now the rest of the acts of Elah, and all
that he did, *are* they not written in the book of
the chronicles of the kings of Israel?
15In the twenty-seventh year of Asa king of
Judah, Zimri had reigned in Tirzah seven days.
And the people *were* encamped against
Gibbethon, which *belonged* to the Philistines.
16Now the people *who were* encamped heard it
said, "Zimri has conspired and also has killed
the king." So all Israel made Omri, the commander of the army, king over Israel that day in
the camp. 17Then Omri and all Israel with him
went up from Gibbethon, and they besieged
Tirzah. 18And it happened, when Zimri saw that
the city was taken, that he went into the citadel
of the king's house and burned the king's
house down upon himself with fire, and died,
19because of the sins which he had committed
in doing evil in the sight of the LORD, in walking
in the way of Jeroboam, and in his sin which he
had committed to make Israel sin.
20Now the rest of the acts of Zimri, and the
treason he committed, *are* they not written in
the book of the chronicles of the kings of Israel?
21Then the people of Israel were divided into
two parts: half of the people followed Tibni the
son of Ginath, to make him king, and half followed Omri. 22But the people who followed
Omri prevailed over the people who followed
Tibni the son of Ginath. So Tibni died and
Omri reigned. 23In the thirty-first year of Asa
king of Judah, Omri became king over Israel,
and reigned twelve years. Six years he reigned
in Tirzah. 24And he bought the hill of Samaria
from Shemer for two talents of silver; then he
built on the hill, and called the name of the city
which he built, Samaria, after the name of
Shemer, owner of the hill. 25Omri did evil in
the eyes of the LORD, and did worse than all
who *were* before him. 26For he walked in all the
ways of Jeroboam the son of Nebat, and in his
sin by which he had made Israel sin, provoking the LORD God of Israel to anger with their
idols.

27 Now the rest of the acts of Omri which he
did, and the might that he showed, *are* they
not written in the book of the chronicles of the
kings of Israel?
28 So Omri rested with his fathers and was
buried in Samaria. Then Ahab his son reigned
in his place.
29 In the thirty-eighth year of Asa king of Judah, Ahab the son of Omri became king over
Israel; and Ahab the son of Omri reigned over
Israel in Samaria twenty-two years. 30 Now
Ahab the son of Omri did evil in the sight of
the LORD, more than all who *were* before him.

16:30 evil...more than all who *were* before him. With Ahab, Israel's spiritual decay reached its lowest point. He was even worse than his father, Omri, who was more wicked than all before him (v. 25). Ahab's evil consisted of perpetuating all the sins of Jeroboam and promoting the worship of Baal in Israel (vv. 31,32). Of all Israel's kings, Ahab outraged the Lord most (v. 33).

31 And it came to pass, as though it had been a
trivial thing for him to walk in the sins of
Jeroboam the son of Nebat, that he took as
wife Jezebel the daughter of Ethbaal, king of
the Sidonians; and he went and served Baal
and worshiped him. 32 Then he set up an altar
for Baal in the temple of Baal, which he had
built in Samaria. 33 And Ahab made a wooden
image. Ahab did more to provoke the LORD
God of Israel to anger than all the kings of Israel who were before him. 34 In his days Hiel of
Bethel built Jericho. He laid its foundation
with Abiram his firstborn, and with his
youngest *son* Segub he set up its gates, according to the word of the LORD, which He
had spoken through Joshua the son of Nun.

Psalm 69:22–28

22 Let their table become a snare before
them,
And their well-being a trap.
23 Let their eyes be darkened, so that
they do not see;
And make their loins shake continually.
24 Pour out Your indignation upon them,
And let Your wrathful anger take hold
of them.
25 Let their dwelling place be desolate;
Let no one live in their tents.
26 For they persecute the *ones* You have
struck,

69:26 the *ones* You have struck. Those hostile to the psalmist were ridiculing him as one suffering from God's chastisement. In its messianic application, the suffering of the Messiah was a part of God's plan from eternity past (Is. 53:10).

And talk of the grief of those You have
wounded.
27 Add iniquity to their iniquity,
And let them not come into Your
righteousness.
28 Let them be blotted out of the book of
the living,
And not be written with the righteous.

Proverbs 17:25–26

25 A foolish son *is* a grief to his father,
And bitterness to her who bore him.
26 Also, to punish the righteous *is* not
good,
Nor to strike princes for *their*
uprightness.

17:26 punish...strike. Here is a clear statement on political and religious injustice, focusing on the equally bad mistreatment of the innocent and the noble.

John 13:1–20

13 Now before the Feast of the Passover,
when Jesus knew that His hour had come
that He should depart from this world to the
Father, having loved His own who were in the
world, He loved them to the end.
2 And supper being ended, the devil having
already put it into the heart of Judas Iscariot,
Simon's *son,* to betray Him, 3 Jesus, knowing
that the Father had given all things into His
hands, and that He had come from God and
was going to God, 4 rose from supper and laid
aside His garments, took a towel and girded
Himself. 5 After that, He poured water into a
basin and began to wash the disciples' feet,
and to wipe *them* with the towel with which He
was girded. 6 Then He came to Simon Peter.
And *Peter* said to Him, "Lord, are You washing
my feet?"
7 Jesus answered and said to him, "What I am
doing you do not understand now, but you will
know after this."

8Peter said to Him, "You shall never wash
my feet!"
Jesus answered him, "If I do not wash you,
you have no part with Me."
9Simon Peter said to Him, "Lord, not my feet
only, but also *my* hands and *my* head!"
10Jesus said to him, "He who is bathed needs
only to wash *his* feet, but is completely clean;
and you are clean, but not all of you." 11For He
knew who would betray Him; therefore He
said, "You are not all clean."
12So when He had washed their feet, taken His
garments, and sat down again, He said to them,
"Do you know what I have done to you? 13You
call Me Teacher and Lord, and you say well, for
so I am. 14If I then, *your* Lord and Teacher, have
washed your feet, you also ought to wash one
another's feet. 15For I have given you an example, that you should do as I have done to you.
16Most assuredly, I say to you, a servant is not
greater than his master; nor is he who is sent
greater than he who sent him. 17If you know
these things, blessed are you if you do them.
18"I do not speak concerning all of you. I
know whom I have chosen; but that the Scripture may be fulfilled, *'He who eats bread with
Me has lifted up his heel against Me.'* 19Now I
tell you before it comes, that when it does
come to pass, you may believe that I am *He.*
20Most assuredly, I say to you, he who receives
whomever I send receives Me; and he who
receives Me receives Him who sent Me."

DAY 3: Why was Jesus' washing of the disciples' feet so powerful a lesson?

The dusty and dirty conditions of the region necessitated the need for footwashing. Although the disciples most likely would have been happy to wash Jesus' feet, they could not conceive of washing one another's feet (John 13:4–17). This was because in the society of the time footwashing was reserved for the lowliest of menial servants. Peers did not wash one another's feet, except very rarely and as a mark of great love. Luke points out (22:24) that they were arguing about who was the greatest of them, so that none was willing to stoop to wash feet. When Jesus moved to wash their feet, they were shocked. His actions serve also as symbolic of spiritual cleansing (vv. 6–9) and a model of Christian humility (vv. 12–17). Through this action Jesus taught the lesson of selfless service that was supremely exemplified by His death on the cross.

These proceedings embarrassed all of the disciples (vv. 6–10). While others remained silent, Peter spoke up in indignation that Jesus would stoop so low as to wash his feet. He failed to see beyond the humble service itself to the symbolism of spiritual cleansing involved (v. 7; 1 John 1:7–9). Jesus' response made the real point of His actions clear: Unless the Lamb of God cleanses a person's sin (i.e., as portrayed in the symbolism of washing), one can have no part with Him. The cleansing that Christ does at salvation never needs to be repeated—atonement is complete at that point. But all who have been cleansed by God's gracious justification need constant washing in the experiential sense as they battle sin in the flesh. Believers are justified and granted imputed righteousness (Phil. 3:8,9), but still need sanctification and personal righteousness (Phil. 3:12–14).

Jesus said, "I have given you an example" (v. 15). The word used here suggests both example and pattern. Jesus' purpose in this action was to establish the model of loving humility. "If you know these things, blessed are you if you do them" (v. 17). Joy is always tied to obedience to God's revealed Word.

JUNE 4

1 Kings 17:1–18:46

17 And Elijah the Tishbite, of the inhabitants
of Gilead, said to Ahab, "*As* the LORD God
of Israel lives, before whom I stand, there shall
not be dew nor rain these years, except at my
word."
2Then the word of the LORD came to him,
saying, 3"Get away from here and turn eastward, and hide by the Brook Cherith, which
flows into the Jordan. 4And it will be *that* you
shall drink from the brook, and I have commanded the ravens to feed you there."
5So he went and did according to the word
of the LORD, for he went and stayed by the
Brook Cherith, which flows into the Jordan.
6The ravens brought him bread and meat in
the morning, and bread and meat in the
evening; and he drank from the brook. 7And it
happened after a while that the brook dried
up, because there had been no rain in the
land.
8Then the word of the LORD came to him,
saying, 9"Arise, go to Zarephath, which *belongs*
to Sidon, and dwell there. See, I have commanded a widow there to provide for you."
10So he arose and went to Zarephath. And
when he came to the gate of the city, indeed a
widow *was* there gathering sticks. And he
called to her and said, "Please bring me a little

17:1 Elijah. His name means "the LORD is God." The prophet Elijah's ministry corresponded to his name: He was sent by God to confront Baalism and to declare to Israel that the Lord was God and there was no other. **Tishbite.** Elijah lived in a town called Tishbe, east of the Jordan River in the vicinity of the Jabbok River. **not be dew nor rain.** The autumn and spring rains and summer dew were necessities for the crops of Israel. The Lord had threatened to withhold these from the Land if His people turned from Him to serve other gods (Lev. 26:18,19; Deut. 11:16,17; 28:23,24). Elijah had prayed for the drought (James 5:17) and God answered. It lasted 3 years and 6 months. The drought proved that Baal, the god of the rains and fertility, was impotent before the Lord.

water in a cup, that I may drink." 11And as she
was going to get *it,* he called to her and said,
"Please bring me a morsel of bread in your
hand."
12So she said, "As the LORD your God lives, I
do not have bread, only a handful of flour in a
bin, and a little oil in a jar; and see, I *am* gathering a couple of sticks that I may go in and
prepare it for myself and my son, that we may
eat it, and die."
13And Elijah said to her, "Do not fear; go *and*
do as you have said, but make me a small cake
from it first, and bring *it* to me; and afterward
make *some* for yourself and your son. 14For
thus says the LORD God of Israel: 'The bin of
flour shall not be used up, nor shall the jar of
oil run dry, until the day the LORD sends rain
on the earth.' "
15So she went away and did according to the
word of Elijah; and she and he and her household ate for *many* days. 16The bin of flour was
not used up, nor did the jar of oil run dry,
according to the word of the LORD which He
spoke by Elijah.
17Now it happened after these things *that*
the son of the woman who owned the house
became sick. And his sickness was so serious
that there was no breath left in him. 18So she
said to Elijah, "What have I to do with you, O
man of God? Have you come to me to bring
my sin to remembrance, and to kill my son?"
19And he said to her, "Give me your son." So
he took him out of her arms and carried him
to the upper room where he was staying, and
laid him on his own bed. 20Then he cried out to
the LORD and said, "O LORD my God, have You
also brought tragedy on the widow with whom
I lodge, by killing her son?" 21And he stretched
himself out on the child three times, and cried
out to the LORD and said, "O LORD my God, I
pray, let this child's soul come back to him."
22Then the LORD heard the voice of Elijah; and
the soul of the child came back to him, and he
revived.
23And Elijah took the child and brought him
down from the upper room into the house, and
gave him to his mother. And Elijah said, "See,
your son lives!"
24Then the woman said to Elijah, "Now by
this I know that you *are* a man of God, *and* that
the word of the LORD in your mouth *is* the
truth."

18 And it came to pass *after* many days that
the word of the LORD came to Elijah, in
the third year, saying, "Go, present yourself to
Ahab, and I will send rain on the earth."
2So Elijah went to present himself to Ahab;
and *there was* a severe famine in Samaria. 3And
Ahab had called Obadiah, who *was* in charge
of *his* house. (Now Obadiah feared the LORD
greatly. 4For so it was, while Jezebel massacred

18:3 Obadiah. His name means "servant of the LORD." He was the manager of Ahab's royal palace and a devout worshiper of the Lord, who had demonstrated his devotion to the Lord by protecting 100 of the Lord's prophets from death by Jezebel (vv. 4,13), which had put him on tenuous ground with Ahab.

the prophets of the LORD, that Obadiah had
taken one hundred prophets and hidden them,
fifty to a cave, and had fed them with bread and
water.) 5And Ahab had said to Obadiah, "Go
into the land to all the springs of water and to
all the brooks; perhaps we may find grass to
keep the horses and mules alive, so that we
will not have to kill any livestock." 6So they
divided the land between them to explore it;
Ahab went one way by himself, and Obadiah
went another way by himself.
7Now as Obadiah was on his way, suddenly
Elijah met him; and he recognized him, and
fell on his face, and said, "*Is* that you, my lord
Elijah?"
8And he answered him, "*It is* I. Go, tell your
master, 'Elijah *is here.*' "
9So he said, "How have I sinned, that you
are delivering your servant into the hand of
Ahab, to kill me? 10*As* the LORD your God lives,
there is no nation or kingdom where my master has not sent someone to hunt for you; and

when they said, '*He is* not *here,*' he took an
oath from the kingdom or nation that they
could not find you. 11And now you say, 'Go, tell
your master, "Elijah *is here*" '! 12And it shall
come to pass, *as soon as* I am gone from you,
that the Spirit of the LORD will carry you to a
place I do not know; so when I go and tell Ahab,
and he cannot find you, he will kill me. But I
your servant have feared the LORD from my
youth. 13Was it not reported to my lord what I

18:12 the Spirit of the LORD will carry you. The servant had been asked to tell Ahab Elijah was present to speak with him (vv. 7,18), but he was afraid because Ahab was seeking Elijah so intensely. Since Elijah had disappeared from sight earlier (17:5), Obadiah was afraid that the Holy Spirit would carry Elijah away again (2 Kin. 2:16) and the irrational Ahab would kill him for the false report of Elijah's presence.

did when Jezebel killed the prophets of the
LORD, how I hid one hundred men of the LORD's
prophets, fifty to a cave, and fed them with
bread and water? 14And now you say, 'Go, tell
your master, "Elijah *is here.*" ' He will kill me!"
15Then Elijah said, "*As* the LORD of hosts
lives, before whom I stand, I will surely present myself to him today."
16So Obadiah went to meet Ahab, and told
him; and Ahab went to meet Elijah.
17Then it happened, when Ahab saw Elijah,
that Ahab said to him, "*Is that* you, O troubler
of Israel?"
18And he answered, "I have not troubled Israel, but you and your father's house *have,* in
that you have forsaken the commandments of
the LORD and have followed the Baals. 19Now
therefore, send *and* gather all Israel to me on
Mount Carmel, the four hundred and fifty
prophets of Baal, and the four hundred
prophets of Asherah, who eat at Jezebel's table."
20So Ahab sent for all the children of Israel,
and gathered the prophets together on Mount
Carmel. 21And Elijah came to all the people,
and said, "How long will you falter between
two opinions? If the LORD *is* God, follow Him;
but if Baal, follow him." But the people
answered him not a word. 22Then Elijah said to
the people, "I alone am left a prophet of the
LORD; but Baal's prophets *are* four hundred
and fifty men. 23Therefore let them give us two
bulls; and let them choose one bull for themselves, cut it in pieces, and lay *it* on the wood,
but put no fire *under it;* and I will prepare the

18:21 falter between two opinions. Literally, limp along on or between two twigs. Israel had not totally rejected the Lord, but was seeking to combine worship of Him with the worship of Baal. The issue posed by Elijah was that Israel had to choose who was God, the Lord or Baal, and then serve God wholeheartedly. Rather than decide by his message, Elijah sought a visible sign from heaven.

18:24 the God who answers by fire. Since Baal's followers believed that he controlled the thunder, lightning, and storms, and the Lord's followers declared the same (Ps. 18:14; 29:3–9; 104:3), this would prove to be a fair test to show who was God.

other bull, and lay *it* on the wood, but put no
fire *under it.* 24Then you call on the name of
your gods, and I will call on the name of the
LORD; and the God who answers by fire, He is
God."
So all the people answered and said, "It is
well spoken."
25Now Elijah said to the prophets of Baal,
"Choose one bull for yourselves and prepare *it*
first, for you *are* many; and call on the name of
your god, but put no fire *under it.*"
26So they took the bull which was given
them, and they prepared *it,* and called on the
name of Baal from morning even till noon, saying, "O Baal, hear us!" But *there was* no voice;
no one answered. Then they leaped about the
altar which they had made.
27And so it was, at noon, that Elijah mocked
them and said, "Cry aloud, for he *is* a god;
either he is meditating, or he is busy, or he is
on a journey, *or* perhaps he is sleeping and
must be awakened." 28So they cried aloud, and
cut themselves, as was their custom, with
knives and lances, until the blood gushed out
on them. 29And when midday was past, they
prophesied until the *time* of the offering of the
evening sacrifice. But *there was* no voice; no
one answered, no one paid attention.
30Then Elijah said to all the people, "Come
near to me." So all the people came near to
him. And he repaired the altar of the LORD *that
was* broken down. 31And Elijah took twelve
stones, according to the number of the tribes
of the sons of Jacob, to whom the word of the
LORD had come, saying, "Israel shall be your
name." 32Then with the stones he built an altar
in the name of the LORD; and he made a trench

around the altar large enough to hold two
seahs of seed. 33And he put the wood in order,
cut the bull in pieces, and laid *it* on the wood,
and said, "Fill four waterpots with water, and
pour *it* on the burnt sacrifice and on the
wood." 34Then he said, "Do *it* a second time,"
and they did *it* a second time; and he said, "Do
it a third time," and they did *it* a third time. 35So
the water ran all around the altar; and he also
filled the trench with water.

36And it came to pass, at *the time of* the offering of the *evening* sacrifice, that Elijah the prophet came near and said, "LORD God of Abraham, Isaac, and Israel, let it be known this day that You *are* God in Israel and I *am* Your servant, and *that* I have done all these things at Your word.
37Hear me, O LORD, hear
me, that this people may know that You *are* the LORD God, and *that* You have turned their hearts back *to You* again."

38Then the fire of the LORD fell and consumed the burnt sacrifice, and the wood and the stones and the dust, and it licked up the water that *was* in the trench.
39Now when all
the people saw *it,* they fell on their faces; and they said, "The LORD, He *is* God! The LORD, He *is* God!"

40And Elijah said to them, "Seize the prophets of Baal! Do not let one of them escape!" So they seized them; and Elijah brought them down to the Brook Kishon and executed them there.

41Then Elijah said to Ahab, "Go up, eat and drink; for *there is* the sound of abundance of
rain." 42So Ahab went up to eat and drink. And
Elijah went up to the top of Carmel; then he bowed down on the ground, and put his face
between his knees, 43and said to his servant,
"Go up now, look toward the sea."

So he went up and looked, and said, "*There is* nothing." And seven times he said, "Go again."

44Then it came to pass the seventh *time,* that he said, "There is a cloud, as small as a man's hand, rising out of the sea!" So he said, "Go up, say to Ahab, 'Prepare *your chariot,* and go down before the rain stops you.' "

45Now it happened in the meantime that the sky became black with clouds and wind, and there was a heavy rain. So Ahab rode away
and went to Jezreel. 46Then the hand of the
LORD came upon Elijah; and he girded up his loins and ran ahead of Ahab to the entrance of Jezreel.

Psalm 69:29–36

29 But I *am* poor and sorrowful;
Let Your salvation, O God, set me up on high.

30 I will praise the name of God with a song,
And will magnify Him with thanksgiving.

31 *This* also shall please the LORD better than an ox *or* bull,
Which has horns and hooves.

32 The humble shall see *this and* be glad;
And you who seek God, your hearts shall live.

33 For the LORD hears the poor,
And does not despise His prisoners.

34 Let heaven and earth praise Him,
The seas and everything that moves in them.

35 For God will save Zion
And build the cities of Judah,
That they may dwell there and possess it.

36 Also, the descendants of His servants shall inherit it,
And those who love His name shall dwell in it.

Proverbs 17:27–28

27 He who has knowledge spares his words,
And a man of understanding is of a calm spirit.

28 Even a fool is counted wise when he holds his peace;
When he shuts his lips, *he is considered* perceptive.

John 13:21–38

21When Jesus had said these things, He was troubled in spirit, and testified and said, "Most assuredly, I say to you, one of you will betray
Me." 22Then the disciples looked at one another, perplexed about whom He spoke.

23Now there was leaning on Jesus' bosom
one of His disciples, whom Jesus loved. 24Si-
mon Peter therefore motioned to him to ask who it was of whom He spoke.

25Then, leaning back on Jesus' breast, he said to Him, "Lord, who is it?"

26Jesus answered, "It is he to whom I shall give a piece of bread when I have dipped *it.*" And having dipped the bread, He gave *it* to Judas Iscariot, *the son* of Simon. 27Now after the
piece of bread, Satan entered him. Then Jesus
said to him, "What you do, do quickly." 28But
no one at the table knew for what reason He
said this to him. 29For some thought, because
Judas had the money box, that Jesus had said to him, "Buy *those things* we need for the feast," or that he should give something to the poor.

13:26 He gave *it* to Judas Iscariot. The host at a feast (whose role was filled by Jesus) would dip into a common bowl and pull out a particularly tasty bit and pass it to a guest as a special mark of honor or friendship. Because Jesus passed it so easily to Judas, it has been suggested that he was seated near the Lord in a place of honor. Jesus was demonstrating a final gesture of His love for Judas even though he would betray Him.

30 Having received the piece of bread, he then went out immediately. And it was night.
31 So, when he had gone out, Jesus said, "Now the Son of Man is glorified, and God is glorified in Him. 32 If God is glorified in Him, God will also glorify Him in Himself, and glorify Him immediately. 33 Little children, I shall be with you a little while longer. You will seek Me; and as I said to the Jews, 'Where I am going, you cannot come,' so now I say to you.
34 A new commandment I give to you, that you love one another; as I have loved you, that you also love one another. 35 By this all will know that you are My disciples, if you have love for one another."

13:34 A new commandment...as I have loved you. The commandment to love was not new. Deuteronomy 6:5 commanded love for God and Leviticus 19:18 commanded loving one's neighbor as oneself (Matt. 22:34–40; Rom. 13:8–10; Gal. 5:14; James 2:8). However, Jesus' command regarding love presented a distinctly new standard for two reasons: 1) it was sacrificial love modeled after His love (as I loved you; 15:13), and 2) it is produced through the New Covenant by the transforming power of the Holy Spirit (Jer. 31:29–34; Ezek. 36:24–26; Gal. 5:22).

36 Simon Peter said to Him, "Lord, where are You going?"
Jesus answered him, "Where I am going you cannot follow Me now, but you shall follow Me afterward."
37 Peter said to Him, "Lord, why can I not follow You now? I will lay down my life for Your sake."
38 Jesus answered him, "Will you lay down your life for My sake? Most assuredly, I say to you, the rooster shall not crow till you have denied Me three times.

DAY 4: How do scholars conclude that the expression "whom Jesus loved" was John's way of referring to himself?

Three obvious clues about John's Gospel help identify the unnamed disciple who called himself the disciple "whom Jesus loved" (13:23; 19:26; 20:2; 21:7,20).

Early church fathers invariably identify the apostle John as the author of this Gospel. John is frequently mentioned by the other Gospel writers as an active participant among the disciples of Jesus, yet John's name is absent from the fourth Gospel.

If four people take a trip together and each carries a camera, the group-shots each person takes will naturally not include them. In fact, someone else could probably guess who took which pictures by which member of the group was absent. The Gospel of John functions this way—John's absence by name shouts his presence.

As for his signature phrase, the words "whom Jesus loved" convey both a sense of the apostle's humility and the depth of his relationship to Jesus. The phrase doesn't mean that John thought of himself as the only disciple Jesus loved. It simply expresses with disarming honesty the wonder of this disciple over the fact that the Lord loved him!

JUNE 5

1 Kings 19:1–20:43

19 And Ahab told Jezebel all that Elijah had
done, also how he had executed all the
prophets with the sword. 2 Then Jezebel sent a
messenger to Elijah, saying, "So let the gods
do *to me,* and more also, if I do not make your
life as the life of one of them by tomorrow
about this time." 3 And when he saw *that,* he
arose and ran for his life, and went to
Beersheba, which *belongs* to Judah, and left
his servant there.
4 But he himself went a day's journey into
the wilderness, and came and sat down under
a broom tree. And he prayed that he might
die, and said, "It is enough! Now, LORD, take
my life, for I *am* no better than my fathers!"

19:3 he saw. His hope shattered, Elijah fled as a prophet, broken by Jezebel's threats (v. 2), her unrepentant Baalism, and her continuing power over Israel. Elijah expected Jezebel to surrender. When she did not capitulate, he became a discouraged man (vv. 4,10,14).

19:4 broom tree. A desert bush that grew to a height of 10 feet. It had slender branches featuring small leaves and fragrant blossoms. **take my life.** Since Israelites believed that suicide was an affront to the Lord, it was not an option, whatever the distress. So Elijah asked the Lord for death (Jon. 4:3,8) because he viewed the situation as hopeless. Job (Job 6:8,9), Moses (Num. 11:10–15), and Jeremiah (Jer. 20:14–18) had also reacted in similar fashion during their ministries.

5Then as he lay and slept under a broom
tree, suddenly an angel touched him, and said
to him, "Arise *and* eat." 6Then he looked, and
there by his head *was* a cake baked on coals,
and a jar of water. So he ate and drank, and lay
down again. 7And the angel of the LORD came
back the second time, and touched him, and
said, "Arise *and* eat, because the journey *is* too
great for you." 8So he arose, and ate and
drank; and he went in the strength of that food
forty days and forty nights as far as Horeb, the
mountain of God.
9And there he went into a cave, and spent
the night in that place; and behold, the word of
the LORD *came* to him, and He said to him,
"What are you doing here, Elijah?"
10So he said, "I have been very zealous for the
LORD God of hosts; for the children of Israel
have forsaken Your covenant, torn down Your
altars, and killed Your prophets with the sword.
I alone am left; and they seek to take my life."
11Then He said, "Go out, and stand on the
mountain before the LORD." And behold, the
LORD passed by, and a great and strong wind
tore into the mountains and broke the rocks in
pieces before the LORD, *but* the LORD *was* not in
the wind; and after the wind an earthquake,
but the LORD *was* not in the earthquake; 12and
after the earthquake a fire, *but* the LORD *was*
not in the fire; and after the fire a still small
voice.
13So it was, when Elijah heard *it,* that he
wrapped his face in his mantle and went out
and stood in the entrance of the cave. Suddenly a voice *came* to him, and said, "What are
you doing here, Elijah?"

19:11 the LORD passed by. The 3 phenomena, wind, earthquake, and fire, announced the imminent arrival of the Lord (Ex. 19:16–19; Ps. 18:7–15; Hab. 3:3–6). The Lord's self-revelation to Elijah came in a faint, whispering voice (v. 12). The lesson for Elijah was that Almighty God was quietly, sometimes imperceptibly, doing His work in Israel (v. 18).

14And he said, "I have been very zealous for
the LORD God of hosts; because the children of
Israel have forsaken Your covenant, torn
down Your altars, and killed Your prophets
with the sword. I alone am left; and they seek
to take my life."
15Then the LORD said to him: "Go, return on
your way to the Wilderness of Damascus; and
when you arrive, anoint Hazael *as* king over
Syria. 16Also you shall anoint Jehu the son of
Nimshi *as* king over Israel. And Elisha the son
of Shaphat of Abel Meholah you shall anoint *as*
prophet in your place. 17It shall be *that* whoever
escapes the sword of Hazael, Jehu will kill; and
whoever escapes the sword of Jehu, Elisha will
kill. 18Yet I have reserved seven thousand in Israel, all whose knees have not bowed to Baal,
and every mouth that has not kissed him."
19So he departed from there, and found
Elisha the son of Shaphat, who *was* plowing
with twelve yoke *of oxen* before him, and he
was with the twelfth. Then Elijah passed by
him and threw his mantle on him. 20And he left

19:19 Elisha. This name means "my God is salvation" and belonged to Elisha, the successor to Elijah (2 Kin. 2:9–15). It was a common practice for several teams of oxen, each with his own plow and driver, to work together in a row. After letting the others pass, Elijah threw his mantle around the last man, Elisha, thus designating him as his successor.

the oxen and ran after Elijah, and said, "Please
let me kiss my father and my mother, and *then*
I will follow you."
And he said to him, "Go back again, for
what have I done to you?"
21So *Elisha* turned back from him, and took
a yoke of oxen and slaughtered them and
boiled their flesh, using the oxen's equipment,
and gave it to the people, and they ate. Then

he arose and followed Elijah, and became his
servant.

20 Now Ben-Hadad the king of Syria gathered all his forces together; thirty-two
kings *were* with him, with horses and chariots.
And he went up and besieged Samaria, and
made war against it. [2]Then he sent messengers into the city to Ahab king of Israel, and
said to him, "Thus says Ben-Hadad: [3]'Your silver and your gold *are* mine; your loveliest
wives and children are mine.' "

[4]And the king of Israel answered and said,
"My lord, O king, just as you say, I and all that
I have *are* yours."

[5]Then the messengers came back and said,
"Thus speaks Ben-Hadad, saying, 'Indeed I have
sent to you, saying, "You shall deliver to me your
silver and your gold, your wives and your children"; [6]but I will send my servants to you tomorrow about this time, and they shall search your
house and the houses of your servants. And it
shall be, *that* whatever is pleasant in your eyes,
they will put *it* in their hands and take *it*.' "

[7]So the king of Israel called all the elders of
the land, and said, "Notice, please, and see
how this *man* seeks trouble, for he sent to me
for my wives, my children, my silver, and my
gold; and I did not deny him."

[8]And all the elders and all the people said to
him, "Do not listen or consent."

[9]Therefore he said to the messengers of
Ben-Hadad, "Tell my lord the king, 'All that
you sent for to your servant the first time I will
do, but this thing I cannot do.' "

And the messengers departed and brought
back word to him.

[10]Then Ben-Hadad sent to him and said,
"The gods do so to me, and more also, if
enough dust is left of Samaria for a handful for
each of the people who follow me."

[11]So the king of Israel answered and said,
"Tell *him*, 'Let not the one who puts on *his
armor* boast like the one who takes *it off*.' "

[12]And it happened when *Ben-Hadad* heard
this message, as he and the kings *were* drinking at the command post, that he said to his
servants, "Get ready." And they got ready to
attack the city.

[13]Suddenly a prophet approached Ahab king
of Israel, saying, "Thus says the LORD: 'Have
you seen all this great multitude? Behold, I
will deliver it into your hand today, and you
shall know that I *am* the LORD.' "

[14]So Ahab said, "By whom?"

And he said, "Thus says the LORD: 'By the
young leaders of the provinces.' "

Then he said, "Who will set the battle in
order?"

And he answered, "You."

[15]Then he mustered the young leaders of
the provinces, and there were two hundred
and thirty-two; and after them he mustered all
the people, all the children of Israel—seven
thousand.

[16]So they went out at noon. Meanwhile Ben-
Hadad and the thirty-two kings helping him
were getting drunk at the command post.
[17]The young leaders of the provinces went out
first. And Ben-Hadad sent out *a patrol*, and
they told him, saying, "Men are coming out of
Samaria!" [18]So he said, "If they have come out
for peace, take them alive; and if they have
come out for war, take them alive."

[19]Then these young leaders of the provinces
went out of the city with the army which followed them. [20]And each one killed his man; so
the Syrians fled, and Israel pursued them; and
Ben-Hadad the king of Syria escaped on a
horse with the cavalry. [21]Then the king of Israel went out and attacked the horses and
chariots, and killed the Syrians with a great
slaughter.

[22]And the prophet came to the king of Israel
and said to him, "Go, strengthen yourself; take
note, and see what you should do, for in the
spring of the year the king of Syria will come
up against you."

[23]Then the servants of the king of Syria said
to him, "Their gods *are* gods of the hills.
Therefore they were stronger than we; but if
we fight against them in the plain, surely we
will be stronger than they. [24]So do this thing:
Dismiss the kings, each from his position, and
put captains in their places; [25]and you shall
muster an army like the army that you have
lost, horse for horse and chariot for chariot.
Then we will fight against them in the plain;
surely we will be stronger than they."

And he listened to their voice and did so.

[26]So it was, in the spring of the year, that
Ben-Hadad mustered the Syrians and went up
to Aphek to fight against Israel. [27]And the children of Israel were mustered and given provisions, and they went against them. Now the
children of Israel encamped before them like
two little flocks of goats, while the Syrians
filled the countryside.

[28]Then a man of God came and spoke to the
king of Israel, and said, "Thus says the LORD:
'Because the Syrians have said, "The LORD *is*
God of the hills, but He *is* not God of the valleys," therefore I will deliver all this great multitude into your hand, and you shall know that I
am the LORD.' " [29]And they encamped opposite
each other for seven days. So it was that on
the seventh day the battle was joined; and the

children of Israel killed one hundred thousand
foot soldiers *of* the Syrians in one day. 30But the
rest fled to Aphek, into the city; then a wall fell
on twenty-seven thousand of the men *who
were* left.

And Ben-Hadad fled and went into the city,
into an inner chamber.

31Then his servants said to him, "Look now,
we have heard that the kings of the house of
Israel *are* merciful kings. Please, let us put
sackcloth around our waists and ropes around
our heads, and go out to the king of Israel; perhaps he will spare your life." 32So they wore
sackcloth around their waists and *put* ropes
around their heads, and came to the king of Israel and said, "Your servant Ben-Hadad says,
'Please let me live.' "

And he said, "*Is* he still alive? He *is* my
brother."

33Now the men were watching closely to see
whether *any sign of mercy would come* from
him; and they quickly grasped *at this word* and
said, "Your brother Ben-Hadad."

So he said, "Go, bring him." Then Ben-
Hadad came out to him; and he had him come
up into the chariot.

34So *Ben-Hadad* said to him, "The cities
which my father took from your father I will
restore; and you may set up marketplaces for
yourself in Damascus, as my father did in Samaria."

Then *Ahab said,* "I will send you away with
this treaty." So he made a treaty with him and
sent him away.

35Now a certain man of the sons of the
prophets said to his neighbor by the word of
the LORD, "Strike me, please." And the man
refused to strike him. 36Then he said to him,
"Because you have not obeyed the voice of the
LORD, surely, as soon as you depart from me,
a lion shall kill you." And as soon as he left
him, a lion found him and killed him.

37And he found another man, and said,
"Strike me, please." So the man struck him,
inflicting a wound. 38Then the prophet departed and waited for the king by the road, and
disguised himself with a bandage over his
eyes. 39Now as the king passed by, he cried out
to the king and said, "Your servant went out
into the midst of the battle; and there, a man
came over and brought a man to me, and said,
'Guard this man; if by any means he is missing, your life shall be for his life, or else you
shall pay a talent of silver.' 40While your servant was busy here and there, he was gone."

Then the king of Israel said to him, "So *shall*
your judgment *be;* you yourself have decided *it.*"
41And he hastened to take the bandage away
from his eyes; and the king of Israel recognized him as one of the prophets. 42Then he
said to him, "Thus says the LORD: 'Because
you have let slip out of *your* hand a man whom
I appointed to utter destruction, therefore
your life shall go for his life, and your people
for his people.' "

43So the king of Israel went to his house
sullen and displeased, and came to Samaria.

Psalm 70:1–5

To the Chief Musician. *A Psalm* of David. To bring to remembrance.

Make haste, O God, to deliver me!
Make haste to help me, O LORD!

2 Let them be ashamed and confounded
Who seek my life;
Let them be turned back and confused
Who desire my hurt.

3 Let them be turned back because of
their shame,
Who say, "Aha, aha!"

4 Let all those who seek You rejoice and
be glad in You;
And let those who love Your salvation
say continually,
"Let God be magnified!"

5 But I *am* poor and needy;
Make haste to me, O God!
You *are* my help and my deliverer;
O LORD, do not delay.

Proverbs 18:1–2

18 A man who isolates himself
seeks his own desire;
He rages against all wise judgment.

2 A fool has no delight in understanding,
But in expressing his own heart.

John 14:1–31

14 "Let not your heart be troubled; you
believe in God, believe also in Me. 2In My
Father's house are many mansions; if *it were*
not *so,* I would have told you. I go to prepare a
place for you. 3And if I go and prepare a place
for you, I will come again and receive you to
Myself; that where I am, *there* you may be
also. 4And where I go you know, and the way
you know."

5Thomas said to Him, "Lord, we do not
know where You are going, and how can we
know the way?"

6Jesus said to him, "I am the way, the truth,
and the life. No one comes to the Father except through Me.

7"If you had known Me, you would have

14:6 This is the sixth I AM statement of Jesus in John (6:35; 8:12; 10:7,9; 10:11,14; 11:25; 15:1,5). In response to Thomas's query (v. 4), Jesus declared that He is the way to God because He is the truth of God (1:14) and the life of God (1:4; 3:15; 11:25). In this verse, the exclusiveness of Jesus as the only approach to the Father is emphatic. Only one way, not many ways, exist to God, i.e., Jesus Christ (10:7–9; Matt. 7:13,14; Luke 13:24; Acts 4:12).

known My Father also; and from now on you
know Him and have seen Him."
8Philip said to Him, "Lord, show us the
Father, and it is sufficient for us."
9Jesus said to him, "Have I been with you so
long, and yet you have not known Me, Philip?
He who has seen Me has seen the Father; so
how can you say, 'Show us the Father'? 10Do
you not believe that I am in the Father, and the
Father in Me? The words that I speak to you I
do not speak on My own *authority;* but the
Father who dwells in Me does the works. 11Be-
lieve Me that I *am* in the Father and the
Father in Me, or else believe Me for the sake
of the works themselves.
12"Most assuredly, I say to you, he who
believes in Me, the works that I do he will do
also; and greater *works* than these he will do,
because I go to My Father. 13And whatever you

14:12 greater *works* than these he will do. Jesus did not mean greater works in power, but in extent. They would become witnesses to all the world through the power of the indwelling and infilling of the Holy Spirit (Acts 1:8) and would bring many to salvation because of the Comforter dwelling in them. The focus is on spiritual rather than physical miracles. The Book of Acts constitutes the beginning historical record of the impact that the Spirit-empowered disciples had on the world (Acts 17:6).

ask in My name, that I will do, that the Father
may be glorified in the Son. 14If you ask anything in My name, I will do *it.*
15"If you love Me, keep My commandments.
16And I will pray the Father, and He will give
you another Helper, that He may abide with
you forever—17the Spirit of truth, whom the
world cannot receive, because it neither sees
Him nor knows Him; but you know Him, for
He dwells with you and will be in you. 18I will
not leave you orphans; I will come to you.
19"A little while longer and the world will see
Me no more, but you will see Me. Because I
live, you will live also. 20At that day you will
know that I *am* in My Father, and you in Me,
and I in you. 21He who has My commandments
and keeps them, it is he who loves Me. And he
who loves Me will be loved by My Father, and
I will love him and manifest Myself to him."
22Judas (not Iscariot) said to Him, "Lord,
how is it that You will manifest Yourself to us,
and not to the world?"
23Jesus answered and said to him, "If anyone
loves Me, he will keep My word; and My
Father will love him, and We will come to him
and make Our home with him. 24He who does
not love Me does not keep My words; and the
word which you hear is not Mine but the
Father's who sent Me.
25"These things I have spoken to you while
being present with you. 26But the Helper, the
Holy Spirit, whom the Father will send in My
name, He will teach you all things, and bring to
your remembrance all things that I said to you.
27Peace I leave with you, My peace I give to you;
not as the world gives do I give to you. Let not
your heart be troubled, neither let it be afraid.
28You have heard Me say to you, 'I am going
away and coming *back* to you.' If you loved Me,
you would rejoice because I said, 'I am going to
the Father,' for My Father is greater than I.
29"And now I have told you before it comes,
that when it does come to pass, you may
believe. 30I will no longer talk much with you,
for the ruler of this world is coming, and he
has nothing in Me. 31But that the world may
know that I love the Father, and as the Father
gave Me commandment, so I do. Arise, let us
go from here.

DAY 5: How is the role of the Holy Spirit explained in John 14?

Jesus said, "I will pray the Father, and He will give you another Helper, that He may abide with you forever" (v. 16). The priestly and intercessory work of Christ began with the request that the Father send the Holy Spirit to indwell in the people of faith (7:39; 15:26; 16:7; 20:22; Acts 1:8; 2:4,33). The Greek word specifically means "another of the same kind," i.e., someone like Jesus Himself who will take His place and do His work. The Spirit of Christ is the Third Person of the Trinity, having the same essence of Deity as Jesus and as perfectly one with Him as He is with the Father. A "Helper" literally means one called alongside to help and has the idea of someone who encourages and exhorts. Abiding has to do with His permanent residence in believers (Rom. 8:9; 1 Cor. 6:19,20; 12:13).

He is the "Spirit of truth" (v. 17) in that He is the source of truth and communicates the truth to His own (v. 26; 16:12–15). Apart from Him, men cannot know God's truth (1 Cor. 2:12–16; 1 John 2:20,27). He "dwells with you and will be in you." This indicates some distinction between the ministry of the Holy Spirit to believers before and after Pentecost. While clearly the Holy Spirit has been with all who have ever believed throughout redemptive history as the source of truth, faith, and life, Jesus is saying something new is coming in His ministry. John 7:37–39 indicates this unique ministry would be like rivers of living water. Acts 19:1–7 introduces some Old Covenant believers who had not received the Holy Spirit in this unique fullness and intimacy.

He "will teach you all things" (v. 26). The Holy Spirit energized the hearts and minds of the apostles in their ministry, helping them to produce the New Testament scriptures. The disciples had failed to understand many things about Jesus and what He taught; but because of this supernatural work, they came to an inerrant and accurate understanding of the Lord and His work and recorded it in the Gospels and the rest of the New Testament scriptures (2 Tim. 3:16; 2 Pet. 1:20,21).

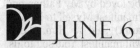

JUNE 6

1 Kings 21:1–22:53

21 And it came to pass after these things *that*
Naboth the Jezreelite had a vineyard
which *was* in Jezreel, next to the palace of Ahab
king of Samaria. 2So Ahab spoke to Naboth,
saying, "Give me your vineyard, that I may
have it for a vegetable garden, because it *is*
near, next to my house; and for it I will give you
a vineyard better than it. *Or,* if it seems good to
you, I will give you its worth in money."
3But Naboth said to Ahab, "The LORD forbid
that I should give the inheritance of my
fathers to you!"

21:3 The LORD forbid. Naboth's words implied that trading or selling his property would be a disregard of the law and thus displeasing in God's eyes (1 Sam. 24:6; 26:11; 2 Sam. 23:17). The reason was that the vineyard was his ancestral property. The Lord, the owner of all of the land of Israel, had forbidden Israelite families to surrender ownership of family lands permanently (Lev. 25:23–28; Num. 36:7–9). Out of loyalty to God, Naboth declined Ahab's offer.

4So Ahab went into his house sullen and displeased because of the word which Naboth the
Jezreelite had spoken to him; for he had said, "I
will not give you the inheritance of my fathers."
And he lay down on his bed, and turned away
his face, and would eat no food. 5But Jezebel his
wife came to him, and said to him, "Why is your
spirit so sullen that you eat no food?"
6He said to her, "Because I spoke to Naboth
the Jezreelite, and said to him, 'Give me your
vineyard for money; or else, if it pleases you, I
will give you *another* vineyard for it.' And he
answered, 'I will not give you my vineyard.' "
7Then Jezebel his wife said to him, "You now
exercise authority over Israel! Arise, eat food,
and let your heart be cheerful; I will give you
the vineyard of Naboth the Jezreelite."
8And she wrote letters in Ahab's name,
sealed *them* with his seal, and sent the letters
to the elders and the nobles who *were*
dwelling in the city with Naboth. 9She wrote in
the letters, saying,

> Proclaim a fast, and seat Naboth with
> high honor among the people; 10and
> seat two men, scoundrels, before him
> to bear witness against him, saying,
> "You have blasphemed God and the
> king." *Then* take him out, and stone
> him, that he may die.

11So the men of his city, the elders and
nobles who were inhabitants of his city, did as
Jezebel had sent to them, as it *was* written in
the letters which she had sent to them. 12They
proclaimed a fast, and seated Naboth with high
honor among the people. 13And two men,
scoundrels, came in and sat before him; and
the scoundrels witnessed against him, against
Naboth, in the presence of the people, saying,
"Naboth has blasphemed God and the king!"
Then they took him outside the city and
stoned him with stones, so that he died. 14Then
they sent to Jezebel, saying, "Naboth has been
stoned and is dead."
15And it came to pass, when Jezebel heard
that Naboth had been stoned and was dead, that

Jezebel said to Ahab, "Arise, take possession of
the vineyard of Naboth the Jezreelite, which
he refused to give you for money; for Naboth
is not alive, but dead." 16So it was, when Ahab
heard that Naboth was dead, that Ahab got up
and went down to take possession of the vineyard of Naboth the Jezreelite.
17Then the word of the LORD came to Elijah
the Tishbite, saying, 18"Arise, go down to meet
Ahab king of Israel, who *lives* in Samaria. There
he is, in the vineyard of Naboth, where he has
gone down to take possession of it. 19You shall
speak to him, saying, 'Thus says the LORD:
"Have you murdered and also taken possession?"' And you shall speak to him, saying,
'Thus says the LORD: "In the place where dogs
licked the blood of Naboth, dogs shall lick your
blood, even yours."'"
20So Ahab said to Elijah, "Have you found
me, O my enemy?"
And he answered, "I have found *you,* because
you have sold yourself to do evil in the sight of
the LORD: 21'Behold, I will bring calamity on
you. I will take away your posterity, and will cut
off from Ahab every male in Israel, both bond
and free. 22I will make your house like the
house of Jeroboam the son of Nebat, and like
the house of Baasha the son of Ahijah, because
of the provocation with which you have provoked *Me* to anger, and made Israel sin.' 23And
concerning Jezebel the LORD also spoke, saying, 'The dogs shall eat Jezebel by the wall of
Jezreel.' 24The dogs shall eat whoever belongs
to Ahab and dies in the city, and the birds of the
air shall eat whoever dies in the field."
25But there was no one like Ahab who sold
himself to do wickedness in the sight of the
LORD, because Jezebel his wife stirred him up.
26And he behaved very abominably in following
idols, according to all *that* the Amorites had
done, whom the LORD had cast out before the
children of Israel.
27So it was, when Ahab heard those words,
that he tore his clothes and put sackcloth on
his body, and fasted and lay in sackcloth, and
went about mourning.
28And the word of the LORD came to Elijah
the Tishbite, saying, 29"See how Ahab has
humbled himself before Me? Because he has
humbled himself before Me, I will not bring
the calamity in his days. In the days of his son
I will bring the calamity on his house."
22 Now three years passed without war
between Syria and Israel. 2Then it came
to pass, in the third year, that Jehoshaphat the
king of Judah went down to *visit* the king of
Israel.
3And the king of Israel said to his servants,
"Do you know that Ramoth in Gilead *is* ours,
but we hesitate to take it out of the hand of the
king of Syria?" 4So he said to Jehoshaphat, "Will
you go with me to fight at Ramoth Gilead?"
Jehoshaphat said to the king of Israel, "I *am*
as you *are,* my people as your people, my horses as your horses." 5Also Jehoshaphat said to
the king of Israel, "Please inquire for the word
of the LORD today."
6Then the king of Israel gathered the
prophets together, about four hundred men,
and said to them, "Shall I go against Ramoth
Gilead to fight, or shall I refrain?"
So they said, "Go up, for the Lord will deliver
it into the hand of the king."

22:6 prophets. These 400 prophets of Ahab were not true prophets of the Lord. They worshiped at Bethel in the golden-calf center set up by Jeroboam (12:28,29) and were supported by Ahab, whose religious policy also permitted Baal worship. Their words were designed to please Ahab (v. 8), so they refused to begin with the authoritative "thus says the LORD" and did not use the covenant name for Israel's God, "LORD."

7And Jehoshaphat said, "*Is there* not still a
prophet of the LORD here, that we may inquire
of Him?"
8So the king of Israel said to Jehoshaphat,
"*There is* still one man, Micaiah the son of
Imlah, by whom we may inquire of the LORD;
but I hate him, because he does not prophesy
good concerning me, but evil."
And Jehoshaphat said, "Let not the king say
such things!"
9Then the king of Israel called an officer and
said, "Bring Micaiah the son of Imlah quickly!"
10The king of Israel and Jehoshaphat the
king of Judah, having put on *their* robes, sat
each on his throne, at a threshing floor at the
entrance of the gate of Samaria; and all the
prophets prophesied before them. 11Now
Zedekiah the son of Chenaanah had made
horns of iron for himself; and he said, "Thus
says the LORD: 'With these you shall gore the
Syrians until they are destroyed.'" 12And all
the prophets prophesied so, saying, "Go up to
Ramoth Gilead and prosper, for the LORD will
deliver *it* into the king's hand."
13Then the messenger who had gone to call
Micaiah spoke to him, saying, "Now listen, the
words of the prophets with one accord encourage the king. Please, let your word be like the

word of one of them, and speak encouragement."
14And Micaiah said, "*As* the LORD lives, whatever the LORD says to me, that I will speak."
15Then he came to the king; and the king
said to him, "Micaiah, shall we go to war
against Ramoth Gilead, or shall we refrain?"

And he answered him, "Go and prosper, for
the LORD will deliver *it* into the hand of the king!"
16So the king said to him, "How many times
shall I make you swear that you tell me nothing but the truth in the name of the LORD?"
17Then he said, "I saw all Israel scattered on
the mountains, as sheep that have no shepherd. And the LORD said, 'These have no master. Let each return to his house in peace.' "
18And the king of Israel said to Jehoshaphat,
"Did I not tell you he would not prophesy
good concerning me, but evil?"
19Then *Micaiah* said, "Therefore hear the
word of the LORD: I saw the LORD sitting on
His throne, and all the host of heaven standing
by, on His right hand and on His left. 20And the
LORD said, 'Who will persuade Ahab to go up,
that he may fall at Ramoth Gilead?' So one
spoke in this manner, and another spoke in
that manner. 21Then a spirit came forward and
stood before the LORD, and said, 'I will persuade him.' 22The LORD said to him, 'In what
way?' So he said, 'I will go out and be a lying
spirit in the mouth of all his prophets.' And the
LORD said, 'You shall persuade *him*, and also
prevail. Go out and do so.' 23Therefore look!
The LORD has put a lying spirit in the mouth of
all these prophets of yours, and the LORD has
declared disaster against you."
24Now Zedekiah the son of Chenaanah went
near and struck Micaiah on the cheek, and
said, "Which way did the spirit from the LORD
go from me to speak to you?"
25And Micaiah said, "Indeed, you shall see
on that day when you go into an inner chamber to hide!"
26So the king of Israel said, "Take Micaiah,
and return him to Amon the governor of the
city and to Joash the king's son; 27and say,
'Thus says the king: "Put this *fellow* in prison,
and feed him with bread of affliction and water
of affliction, until I come in peace." ' "
28But Micaiah said, "If you ever return in
peace, the LORD has not spoken by me." And
he said, "Take heed, all you people!"
29So the king of Israel and Jehoshaphat the
king of Judah went up to Ramoth Gilead. 30And
the king of Israel said to Jehoshaphat, "I will
disguise myself and go into battle; but you put
on your robes." So the king of Israel disguised
himself and went into battle.
31Now the king of Syria had commanded the
thirty-two captains of his chariots, saying,
"Fight with no one small or great, but only with
the king of Israel." 32So it was, when the captains
of the chariots saw Jehoshaphat, that they said,
"Surely it *is* the king of Israel!" Therefore they
turned aside to fight against him, and
Jehoshaphat cried out. 33And it happened, when
the captains of the chariots saw that it *was* not
the king of Israel, that they turned back from
pursuing him. 34Now a *certain* man drew a bow
at random, and struck the king of Israel
between the joints of his armor. So he said to
the driver of his chariot, "Turn around and
take me out of the battle, for I am wounded."
35The battle increased that day; and the king
was propped up in his chariot, facing the Syrians, and died at evening. The blood ran out
from the wound onto the floor of the chariot.
36Then, as the sun was going down, a shout
went throughout the army, saying, "Every man
to his city, and every man to his own country!"
37So the king died, and was brought to Samaria. And they buried the king in Samaria.
38Then *someone* washed the chariot at a pool in
Samaria, and the dogs licked up his blood
while the harlots bathed, according to the
word of the LORD which He had spoken.
39Now the rest of the acts of Ahab, and all
that he did, the ivory house which he built and
all the cities that he built, *are* they not written
in the book of the chronicles of the kings of Israel? 40So Ahab rested with his fathers. Then
Ahaziah his son reigned in his place.
41Jehoshaphat the son of Asa had become
king over Judah in the fourth year of Ahab
king of Israel. 42Jehoshaphat *was* thirty-five
years old when he became king, and he
reigned twenty-five years in Jerusalem. His
mother's name *was* Azubah the daughter of
Shilhi. 43And he walked in all the ways of his
father Asa. He did not turn aside from them,
doing *what was* right in the eyes of the LORD.
Nevertheless the high places were not taken
away, *for* the people offered sacrifices and
burned incense on the high places. 44Also
Jehoshaphat made peace with the king of Israel.
45Now the rest of the acts of Jehoshaphat, the
might that he showed, and how he made war,
are they not written in the book of the chronicles of the kings of Judah? 46And the rest of the
perverted persons, who remained in the days
of his father Asa, he banished from the land.
47*There was* then no king in Edom, only a
deputy of the king.
48Jehoshaphat made merchant ships to go to
Ophir for gold; but they never sailed, for the

ships were wrecked at Ezion Geber. 49Then
Ahaziah the son of Ahab said to Jehoshaphat,
"Let my servants go with your servants in the
ships." But Jehoshaphat would not.
50And Jehoshaphat rested with his fathers,
and was buried with his fathers in the City of
David his father. Then Jehoram his son reigned
in his place.
51Ahaziah the son of Ahab became king over
Israel in Samaria in the seventeenth year of
Jehoshaphat king of Judah, and reigned two
years over Israel. 52He did evil in the sight of
the LORD, and walked in the way of his father
and in the way of his mother and in the way of
Jeroboam the son of Nebat, who had made Israel sin; 53for he served Baal and worshiped
him, and provoked the LORD God of Israel to
anger, according to all that his father had done.

Psalm 71:1–8

In You, O LORD, I put my trust;
Let me never be put to shame.
2 Deliver me in Your righteousness, and
cause me to escape;
Incline Your ear to me, and save me.
3 Be my strong refuge,
To which I may resort continually;
You have given the commandment to
save me,
For You *are* my rock and
my fortress.

4 Deliver me, O my God, out of the
hand of the wicked,
Out of the hand of the unrighteous
and cruel man.
5 For You are my hope, O Lord GOD;
You are my trust from my youth.
6 By You I have been upheld from birth;
You are He who took me out of my
mother's womb.
My praise *shall be* continually of You.
7 I have become as a wonder to many,
But You *are* my strong refuge.
8 Let my mouth be filled *with* Your praise
And with Your glory all the day.

Proverbs 18:3–5

3 When the wicked comes, contempt
comes also;
And with dishonor *comes* reproach.

4 The words of a man's mouth *are* deep
waters;
The wellspring of wisdom *is* a flowing
brook.

5 *It is* not good to show partiality to the
wicked,
Or to overthrow the righteous in
judgment.

John 15:1–27

15 "I am the true vine, and My Father is the
vinedresser. 2Every branch in Me that
does not bear fruit He takes away; and every
branch that bears fruit He prunes, that it may
bear more fruit. 3You are already clean because
of the word which I have spoken to you. 4Abide
in Me, and I in you. As the branch cannot bear
fruit of itself, unless it abides in the vine, neither can you, unless you abide in Me.
5"I am the vine, you *are* the branches. He who
abides in Me, and I in him, bears much fruit;
for without Me you can do nothing. 6If anyone
does not abide in Me, he is cast out as a
branch and is withered; and they gather them
and throw *them* into the fire, and they are
burned. 7If you abide in Me, and My words
abide in you, you will ask what you desire, and
it shall be done for you. 8By this My Father is
glorified, that you bear much fruit; so you will
be My disciples.
9"As the Father loved Me, I also have loved
you; abide in My love. 10If you keep My commandments, you will abide in My love, just as
I have kept My Father's commandments and
abide in His love.
11"These things I have spoken to you, that
My joy may remain in you, and *that* your joy
may be full. 12This is My commandment, that
you love one another as I have loved you.
13Greater love has no one than this, than to lay
down one's life for his friends. 14You are My
friends if you do whatever I command you.
15No longer do I call you servants, for a servant does not know what his master is doing;
but I have called you friends, for all things that
I heard from My Father I have made known to
you. 16You did not choose Me, but I chose you
and appointed you that you should go and
bear fruit, and *that* your fruit should remain,
that whatever you ask the Father in My name
He may give you. 17These things I command
you, that you love one another.
18"If the world hates you, you know that it
hated Me before *it hated* you. 19If you were of
the world, the world would love its own. Yet
because you are not of the world, but I chose
you out of the world, therefore the world hates
you. 20Remember the word that I said to you,
'A servant is not greater than his master.' If
they persecuted Me, they will also persecute
you. If they kept My word, they will keep
yours also. 21But all these things they will do to
you for My name's sake, because they do not
know Him who sent Me. 22If I had not come

15:14,15 friends. Just as Abraham was called the friend of God (2 Chr. 20:7; James 2:23) because he enjoyed extraordinary access to the mind of God through God's revelation to him which he believed, so also those who follow Christ are privileged with extraordinary revelation through the Messiah and Son of God and, believing, become friends of God also. It was for His friends that the Lord laid down His life (v. 13; 10:11,15,17).

and spoken to them, they would have no sin, but now they have no excuse for their sin. [23]He who hates Me hates My Father also. [24]If I had not done among them the works which no one else did, they would have no sin; but now they have seen and also hated both Me and My Father. [25]But *this happened* that the word might be fulfilled which is written in their law, '*They hated Me without a cause.*'

[26]"But when the Helper comes, whom I shall send to you from the Father, the Spirit of truth who proceeds from the Father, He will testify of Me. [27]And you also will bear witness, because you have been with Me from the beginning.

DAY 6: What serious warning is sounded in the lesson of the vine and branches?

In John 15:1–17, Jesus used the extended metaphor of the vine and branches to set forth the basis of Christian living. Jesus used the imagery of agricultural life at the time, i.e., vines and vine crops (see also Matt. 20:1–16; 21:23–41; Mark 12:1–9; Luke 13:6–9; 20:9–16). In the Old Testament, the vine is used commonly as a symbol for Israel (Ps. 80:9–16; Is. 5:1–7; 27:2–6; Jer. 2:21; 12:10; Ezek. 15:1–8; 17:1–21; 19:10–14; Hos. 10:1,2). He specifically identified Himself as the true vine and the Father as the vinedresser or caretaker of the vine.

The vine has two types of branches: 1) branches that bear fruit (vv. 2,8), and 2) branches that do not (vv. 2,6). The branches that bear fruit are genuine believers. Though in immediate context the focus is upon the 11 faithful disciples, the imagery also encompasses all believers down through the ages. The branches that do not bear fruit are those who profess to believe, but their lack of fruit indicates genuine salvation has never taken place and they have no life from the vine. Especially in the immediate context, Judas was in view, but the imagery extends from him to all those who make a profession of faith in Christ but do not actually possess salvation. The image of non-fruit-bearing branches being burned pictures eschatological judgment and eternal rejection (Ezek. 15:6–8).

"Abide in Me," Jesus said (vv. 4–6). The word "abide" means to remain or stay around. The remaining is evidence that salvation has already taken place (1 John 2:19) and not vice versa. The fruit or evidence of salvation is continuance in service to Him and in His teaching (8:31; 1 John 2:24; Col. 1:23). The abiding believer is the only legitimate believer. Abiding and believing actually are addressing the same issue of genuine salvation (Heb. 3:6–19). "Abide in My love" (vv. 9,10; Jude 21). This is not emotional or mystical, but defined in v. 10 as obedience. Jesus set the model by His perfect obedience to the Father, which we are to use as the pattern for our obedience to Him.

JUNE 7

2 Kings 1:1–2:25

1 Moab rebelled against Israel after the death of Ahab. [2]Now Ahaziah fell through the lattice of his upper room in Samaria, and was injured; so he sent messengers and said to them, "Go, inquire of Baal-Zebub, the god of Ekron, whether I shall recover from this injury." [3]But the angel of the LORD said to Elijah the Tishbite, "Arise, go up to meet the messengers of the king of Samaria, and say to them, '*Is it* because *there is* no God in Israel *that* you are going to inquire of Baal-Zebub, the god of Ekron?' [4]Now therefore, thus says the LORD: 'You shall not come down from the bed to which you have gone up, but you shall surely die.' " So Elijah departed.

[5]And when the messengers returned to him, he said to them, "Why have you come back?"

[6]So they said to him, "A man came up to meet us, and said to us, 'Go, return to the king who sent you, and say to him, "Thus says the LORD: '*Is it* because *there is* no God in Israel *that* you are sending to inquire of Baal-Zebub, the god of Ekron? Therefore you shall not come down from the bed to which you have gone up, but you shall surely die.' " ' "

[7]Then he said to them, "What kind of man *was it* who came up to meet you and told you these words?"

[8]So they answered him, "A hairy man wearing a leather belt around his waist."

And he said, "It *is* Elijah the Tishbite."

[9]Then the king sent to him a captain of fifty

with his fifty men. So he went up to him; and there he was, sitting on the top of a hill. And he spoke to him: "Man of God, the king has said, 'Come down!' "

10 So Elijah answered and said to the captain of fifty, "If I *am* a man of God, then let fire come down from heaven and consume you and your fifty men." And fire came down from heaven and consumed him and his fifty. 11 Then he sent to him another captain of fifty with his fifty men.

And he answered and said to him: "Man of God, thus has the king said, 'Come down quickly!' "

12 So Elijah answered and said to them, "If I *am* a man of God, let fire come down from heaven and consume you and your fifty men." And the fire of God came down from heaven and consumed him and his fifty.

13 Again, he sent a third captain of fifty with his fifty men. And the third captain of fifty went up, and came and fell on his knees before Elijah, and pleaded with him, and said to him: "Man of God, please let my life and the life of these fifty servants of yours be precious in your sight. 14 Look, fire has come down from heaven and burned up the first two captains of fifties with their fifties. But let my life now be precious in your sight."

15 And the angel of the LORD said to Elijah, "Go down with him; do not be afraid of him." So he arose and went down with him to the king. 16 Then he said to him, "Thus says the LORD: 'Because you have sent messengers to inquire of Baal-Zebub, the god of Ekron, *is it* because *there is* no God in Israel to inquire of His word? Therefore you shall not come down from the bed to which you have gone up, but you shall surely die.' "

17 So *Ahaziah* died according to the word of the LORD which Elijah had spoken. Because he had no son, Jehoram became king in his place, in the second year of Jehoram the son of Jehoshaphat, king of Judah.

18 Now the rest of the acts of Ahaziah which he did, *are* they not written in the book of the chronicles of the kings of Israel?

2 And it came to pass, when the LORD was about to take up Elijah into heaven by a whirlwind, that Elijah went with Elisha from Gilgal. 2 Then Elijah said to Elisha, "Stay here, please, for the LORD has sent me on to Bethel."

But Elisha said, "*As* the LORD lives, and *as* your soul lives, I will not leave you!" So they went down to Bethel.

3 Now the sons of the prophets who *were* at Bethel came out to Elisha, and said to him, "Do you know that the LORD will take away your master from over you today?"

2:1 by a whirlwind. Literally, "in the whirlwind." This was a reference to the specific storm with lightning and thunder in which Elijah was taken to heaven (v. 11). The Lord's presence was connected with a whirlwind in Job 38:1; 40:6; Jer. 23:19; 25:32; 30:23; Zech. 9:14. **Elisha.** The record of this prophet, who was the successor to Elijah, begins in 1 Kings 19:16 and extends to his death in 2 Kings 13:20.

2:3 the sons of the prophets. See 1 Kings 20:35. **take away**. The same term was used of Enoch's translation to heaven in Genesis 5:24. The question from the sons of the prophets implied that the Lord had revealed Elijah's imminent departure to them. Elisha's response that he didn't need to hear about it (keep silent) explicitly stated that Elijah's departure had been revealed by the Lord to him also (v. 5). **from over you**. I.e., from supervising you, an allusion to the habit of students sitting beneath the feet of their master, elevated on a platform. Elisha would soon change from being Elijah's assistant to serving as the leader among the prophets.

And he said, "Yes, I know; keep silent!"

4 Then Elijah said to him, "Elisha, stay here, please, for the LORD has sent me on to Jericho."

But he said, "*As* the LORD lives, and *as* your soul lives, I will not leave you!" So they came to Jericho.

5 Now the sons of the prophets who *were* at Jericho came to Elisha and said to him, "Do you know that the LORD will take away your master from over you today?"

So he answered, "Yes, I know; keep silent!"

6 Then Elijah said to him, "Stay here, please, for the LORD has sent me on to the Jordan."

But he said, "*As* the LORD lives, and *as* your soul lives, I will not leave you!" So the two of them went on. 7 And fifty men of the sons of the prophets went and stood facing *them* at a distance, while the two of them stood by the Jordan. 8 Now Elijah took his mantle, rolled *it* up, and struck the water; and it was divided this way and that, so that the two of them crossed over on dry ground.

9 And so it was, when they had crossed over, that Elijah said to Elisha, "Ask! What may I do for you, before I am taken away from you?"

Elisha said, "Please let a double portion of your spirit be upon me."

10 So he said, "You have asked a hard thing. *Nevertheless,* if you see me *when I am* taken

from you, it shall be so for you; but if not, it
shall not be *so*.” 11Then it happened, as they
continued on and talked, that suddenly a chariot of fire *appeared* with horses of fire, and separated the two of them; and Elijah went up by
a whirlwind into heaven.

2:11 chariot of fire...with horses of fire. The horse-drawn chariot was the fastest means of transport and the mightiest means of warfare in that day. Thus, the chariot and horses symbolized God's powerful protection, which was the true safety of Israel (v. 12). As earthly kingdoms are dependent for their defense on such military force as represented by horses and chariots, one single prophet had done more by God's power to preserve his nation than all their military preparations.

12And Elisha saw *it*, and he cried out, “My
father, my father, the chariot of Israel and its
horsemen!” So he saw him no more. And he
took hold of his own clothes and tore them
into two pieces. 13He also took up the mantle of
Elijah that had fallen from him, and went back
and stood by the bank of the Jordan. 14Then he
took the mantle of Elijah that had fallen from
him, and struck the water, and said, “Where *is*
the LORD God of Elijah?” And when he also
had struck the water, it was divided this way
and that; and Elisha crossed over.

15Now when the sons of the prophets who
were from Jericho saw him, they said, “The
spirit of Elijah rests on Elisha.” And they came
to meet him, and bowed to the ground before
him. 16Then they said to him, “Look now, there
are fifty strong men with your servants. Please
let them go and search for your master, lest
perhaps the Spirit of the LORD has taken him
up and cast him upon some mountain or into
some valley.”

And he said, “You shall not send anyone.”

17But when they urged him till he was
ashamed, he said, “Send *them!*” Therefore
they sent fifty men, and they searched for
three days but did not find him. 18And when
they came back to him, for he had stayed in
Jericho, he said to them, “Did I not say to you,
‘Do not go’?”

19Then the men of the city said to Elisha,
“Please notice, the situation of this city *is*
pleasant, as my lord sees; but the water *is* bad,
and the ground barren.”

20And he said, “Bring me a new bowl, and
put salt in it.” So they brought *it* to him. 21Then
he went out to the source of the water, and
cast in the salt there, and said, “Thus says the
LORD: ‘I have healed this water; from it there
shall be no more death or barrenness.’ ” 22So
the water remains healed to this day, according to the word of Elisha which he spoke.

23Then he went up from there to Bethel; and
as he was going up the road, some youths
came from the city and mocked him, and said
to him, “Go up, you baldhead! Go up, you baldhead!”

24So he turned around and looked at them,
and pronounced a curse on them in the name
of the LORD. And two female bears came out of
the woods and mauled forty-two of the youths.

25Then he went from there to Mount Carmel,
and from there he returned to Samaria.

2:24 pronounced a curse. Because these young people of about 20 years of age or older (the same term is used of Solomon in 1 Kin. 3:7) so despised the prophet of the Lord, Elisha called upon the Lord to deal with the rebels as He saw fit. The Lord's punishment was the mauling of 42 youths by two female bears. The penalty was clearly justified, for to ridicule Elisha was to ridicule the Lord Himself. The gravity of the penalty mirrored the gravity of the crime. The appalling judgment was God's warning to any and all who attempted to interfere with the newly invested prophet's ministry.

Psalm 71:9–16

9 Do not cast me off in the time of old age;
Do not forsake me when my strength
fails.
10 For my enemies speak against me;
And those who lie in wait for my life
take counsel together,
11 Saying, “God has forsaken him;
Pursue and take him, for *there is* none
to deliver *him*.”

12 O God, do not be far from me;
O my God, make haste to help me!
13 Let them be confounded *and*
consumed
Who are adversaries of my life;
Let them be covered *with* reproach
and dishonor
Who seek my hurt.

14 But I will hope continually,
And will praise You yet more and more.
15 My mouth shall tell of Your
righteousness

And Your salvation all the day,
For I do not know *their* limits.
16 I will go in the strength of the Lord GOD;
I will make mention of Your righteousness, of Yours only.

Proverbs 18:6–8

6 A fool's lips enter into contention,
And his mouth calls for blows.
7 A fool's mouth *is* his destruction,
And his lips *are* the snare of his soul.
8 The words of a talebearer *are* like tasty trifles,
And they go down into the inmost body.

John 16:1–33

16 "These things I have spoken to you, that
you should not be made to stumble. 2They
will put you out of the synagogues; yes, the
time is coming that whoever kills you will
think that he offers God service. 3And these
things they will do to you because they have
not known the Father nor Me. 4But these
things I have told you, that when the time
comes, you may remember that I told you of
them.
"And these things I did not say to you at the
beginning, because I was with you.
5"But now I go away to Him who sent Me,
and none of you asks Me, 'Where are You
going?' 6But because I have said these things
to you, sorrow has filled your heart. 7Never-
theless I tell you the truth. It is to your advantage that I go away; for if I do not go away, the
Helper will not come to you; but if I depart, I
will send Him to you. 8And when He has come,
He will convict the world of sin, and of righteousness, and of judgment: 9of sin, because
they do not believe in Me; 10of righteousness,
because I go to My Father and you see Me no
more; 11of judgment, because the ruler of this
world is judged.
12"I still have many things to say to you, but
you cannot bear *them* now. 13However, when
He, the Spirit of truth, has come, He will guide
you into all truth; for He will not speak on His
own *authority,* but whatever He hears He will
speak; and He will tell you things to come.
14He will glorify Me, for He will take of what is
Mine and declare *it* to you. 15All things that the
Father has are Mine. Therefore I said that He
will take of Mine and declare *it* to you.
16"A little while, and you will not see Me; and
again a little while, and you will see Me, because
I go to the Father."
17Then *some* of His disciples said among
themselves, "What is this that He says to us,
'A little while, and you will not see Me; and
again a little while, and you will see Me'; and,
'because I go to the Father'?" 18They said
therefore, "What is this that He says, 'A little
while'? We do not know what He is saying."
19Now Jesus knew that they desired to ask
Him, and He said to them, "Are you inquiring
among yourselves about what I said, 'A little
while, and you will not see Me; and again a little while, and you will see Me'? 20Most assuredly, I say to you that you will weep and lament,
but the world will rejoice; and you will be sorrowful, but your sorrow will be turned into joy.
21A woman, when she is in labor, has sorrow
because her hour has come; but as soon as
she has given birth to the child, she no longer
remembers the anguish, for joy that a human
being has been born into the world. 22There-
fore you now have sorrow; but I will see you
again and your heart will rejoice, and your joy
no one will take from you.
23"And in that day you will ask Me nothing.
Most assuredly, I say to you, whatever you ask
the Father in My name He will give you. 24Un-
til now you have asked nothing in My name.
Ask, and you will receive, that your joy may be
full.
25"These things I have spoken to you in figurative language; but the time is coming when
I will no longer speak to you in figurative language, but I will tell you plainly about the
Father. 26In that day you will ask in My name,

16:25 in figurative language. The word means a veiled, pointed statement that is pregnant with meaning, i.e., something that is obscure. What seemed hard to understand for the disciples during the life of Jesus would become clear after His death, resurrection, and the coming of the Holy Spirit (vv. 13,14; 14:26; 15:26,27). They would actually understand the ministry of Christ better than they had while they were with Him, as the Spirit inspired them to write the Gospels and Epistles and ministered in and through them.

and I do not say to you that I shall pray the
Father for you; 27for the Father Himself loves
you, because you have loved Me, and have
believed that I came forth from God. 28I came
forth from the Father and have come into the
world. Again, I leave the world and go to the
Father."
29His disciples said to Him, "See, now You are

speaking plainly, and using no figure of speech!
30Now we are sure that You know all things,
and have no need that anyone should question
You. By this we believe that You came forth
from God."
31Jesus answered them, "Do you now
believe? 32Indeed the hour is coming, yes, has
now come, that you will be scattered, each to
his own, and will leave Me alone. And yet I am
not alone, because the Father is with Me.
33These things I have spoken to you, that in
Me you may have peace. In the world you will
have tribulation; but be of good cheer, I have
overcome the world."

DAY 7: What very specific ministry does the Holy Spirit have on people's lives?

In John 16:8, the coming of the Holy Spirit at Pentecost was approximately 40 or more days away at this point (Acts 2:1–13). Jesus says that the Holy Spirit's ministry is to "convict" people. This word has two meanings: 1) the judicial act of conviction with a view toward sentencing (i.e., a courtroom term—conviction of sin) or 2) the act of convincing. Here the second idea is best, since the purpose of the Holy Spirit is not condemnation but conviction of the need for the Savior. The Son does the judgment, with the Father (5:22,27,30). In v. 14, it is said that He will reveal the glories of Christ to His people. He will also inspire the writing of the New Testament, guiding the apostles to write it (v. 13), and He will reveal things to come, through the New Testament prophecies (v. 13).

The Holy Spirit convicts of "sin" (v. 9). The singular indicates that a specific sin is in view; i.e., that of not believing in Jesus as Messiah and Son of God. This is the only sin, ultimately, that damns people to hell. Though all men are depraved, cursed by their violation of God's law, and sinful by nature, what ultimately damns them to hell is their unwillingness to believe in the Lord Jesus Christ as Savior (8:24).

He convicts of "righteousness" (v. 10). The Holy Spirit's purpose here is to shatter the pretensions of self-righteousness (hypocrisy), exposing the darkness of the heart. While Jesus was on the earth, He performed this task especially toward the shallowness and emptiness of Judaism that had degenerated into legalistic modes without life-giving reality. With Jesus gone to the Father, the Holy Spirit continues His convicting role.

And of "judgment" (v. 11). The judgment here in context is that of the world under Satan's control. Its judgments are blind, faulty, and evil as evidenced in their verdict on Christ. The world can't make righteous judgments (7:24), but the Spirit of Christ does (8:16). All Satan's adjudications are lies (8:44–47), so the Spirit convicts men of their false judgment of Christ. Satan, the ruler of the world (14:30; Eph. 2:1–3) who, as the god of this world, has perverted the world's judgment and turned people from believing in Jesus as the Messiah and Son of God (2 Cor. 4:4), was defeated at the Cross. While Christ's death looked like Satan's greatest victory, it actually was Satan's destruction (Col. 2:15; Heb. 2:14,15; Rev. 20:10). The Spirit will lead sinners to true judgment.

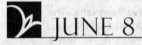

JUNE 8

2 Kings 3:1–4:44

3 Now Jehoram the son of Ahab became
king over Israel at Samaria in the eighteenth year of Jehoshaphat king of Judah, and
reigned twelve years. 2And he did evil in the
sight of the LORD, but not like his father and
mother; for he put away the *sacred* pillar of
Baal that his father had made. 3Nevertheless
he persisted in the sins of Jeroboam the son of
Nebat, who had made Israel sin; he did not
depart from them.
4Now Mesha king of Moab was a sheepbreeder, and he regularly paid the king of Israel one hundred thousand lambs and the
wool of one hundred thousand rams. 5But it
happened, when Ahab died, that the king of
Moab rebelled against the king of Israel.
6So King Jehoram went out of Samaria at that
time and mustered all Israel. 7Then he went and
sent to Jehoshaphat king of Judah, saying, "The
king of Moab has rebelled against me. Will you
go with me to fight against Moab?"
And he said, "I will go up; I *am* as you *are,*
my people as your people, my horses as your
horses." 8Then he said, "Which way shall we
go up?"
And he answered, "By way of the Wilderness of Edom."
9So the king of Israel went with the king of
Judah and the king of Edom, and they
marched on that roundabout route seven
days; and there was no water for the army, nor
for the animals that followed them. 10And the
king of Israel said, "Alas! For the LORD has
called these three kings together to deliver
them into the hand of Moab."
11But Jehoshaphat said, "*Is there* no prophet
of the LORD here, that we may inquire of the
LORD by him?"

So one of the servants of the king of Israel
answered and said, "Elisha the son of Shaphat
is here, who poured water on the hands of
Elijah."
12And Jehoshaphat said, "The word of the
LORD is with him." So the king of Israel and
Jehoshaphat and the king of Edom went down
to him.
13Then Elisha said to the king of Israel, "What
have I to do with you? Go to the prophets of
your father and the prophets of your mother."
But the king of Israel said to him, "No, for
the LORD has called these three kings *together*
to deliver them into the hand of Moab."
14And Elisha said, "*As* the LORD of hosts
lives, before whom I stand, surely were it not
that I regard the presence of Jehoshaphat king
of Judah, I would not look at you, nor see you.
15But now bring me a musician."

3:15 a musician. The music was used to accompany praise and prayer, which calmed the mind of the prophet that he might clearly hear the word of the Lord. Music often accompanied prophecies in the Old Testament (1 Chr. 25:1).

Then it happened, when the musician
played, that the hand of the LORD came upon
him. 16And he said, "Thus says the LORD:
'Make this valley full of ditches.' 17For thus
says the LORD: 'You shall not see wind, nor
shall you see rain; yet that valley shall be filled
with water, so that you, your cattle, and your
animals may drink.' 18And this is a simple matter in the sight of the LORD; He will also deliver the Moabites into your hand. 19Also you
shall attack every fortified city and every
choice city, and shall cut down every good
tree, and stop up every spring of water, and
ruin every good piece of land with stones."
20Now it happened in the morning, when the
grain offering was offered, that suddenly
water came by way of Edom, and the land was
filled with water.
21And when all the Moabites heard that the
kings had come up to fight against them, all
who were able to bear arms and older were
gathered; and they stood at the border. 22Then
they rose up early in the morning, and the sun
was shining on the water; and the Moabites
saw the water on the other side *as* red as
blood. 23And they said, "This is blood; the
kings have surely struck swords and have
killed one another; now therefore, Moab, to
the spoil!"
24So when they came to the camp of Israel,
Israel rose up and attacked the Moabites, so
that they fled before them; and they entered
their land, killing the Moabites. 25Then they
destroyed the cities, and each man threw a
stone on every good piece of land and filled it;
and they stopped up all the springs of water
and cut down all the good trees. But they left
the stones of Kir Haraseth *intact*. However the
slingers surrounded and attacked it.
26And when the king of Moab saw that the
battle was too fierce for him, he took with him
seven hundred men who drew swords, to
break through to the king of Edom, but they
could not. 27Then he took his eldest son who
would have reigned in his place, and offered
him *as* a burnt offering upon the wall; and
there was great indignation against Israel. So
they departed from him and returned to *their*
own land.

4 A certain woman of the wives of the sons
of the prophets cried out to Elisha, saying,
"Your servant my husband is dead, and you
know that your servant feared the LORD. And
the creditor is coming to take my two sons to
be his slaves."
2So Elisha said to her, "What shall I do for
you? Tell me, what do you have in the house?"
And she said, "Your maidservant has nothing
in the house but a jar of oil."
3Then he said, "Go, borrow vessels from
everywhere, from all your neighbors—empty
vessels; do not gather just a few. 4And when
you have come in, you shall shut the door
behind you and your sons; then pour it into all
those vessels, and set aside the full ones."

4:4 shut the door behind you. Since the widow's need was private, the provision was to be private also. Further, the absence of Elisha demonstrated that the miracle happened only by God's power. God's power multiplied little into much, filling all the vessels to meet the widow's need (1 Kin. 17:7–16).

5So she went from him and shut the door
behind her and her sons, who brought *the ves-*
sels to her; and she poured *it* out. 6Now it came
to pass, when the vessels were full, that she
said to her son, "Bring me another vessel."
And he said to her, "*There is* not another
vessel." So the oil ceased. 7Then she came and
told the man of God. And he said, "Go, sell the
oil and pay your debt; and you *and* your sons
live on the rest."

8Now it happened one day that Elisha went to Shunem, where there *was* a notable woman, and she persuaded him to eat some food. So it was, as often as he passed by, he would turn in there to eat some food. 9And she said to her husband, "Look now, I know that this *is* a holy man of God, who passes by us regularly. 10Please, let us make a small upper room on the wall; and let us put a bed for him there, and a table and a chair and a lampstand; so it will be, whenever he comes to us, he can turn in there."

11And it happened one day that he came there, and he turned in to the upper room and lay down there. 12Then he said to Gehazi his servant, "Call this Shunammite woman." When he had called her, she stood before him. 13And he said to him, "Say now to her, 'Look, you have been concerned for us with all this care. What *can I* do for you? Do you want me to speak on your behalf to the king or to the commander of the army?' "

She answered, "I dwell among my own people."

14So he said, "What then *is* to be done for her?"

And Gehazi answered, "Actually, she has no son, and her husband is old."

15So he said, "Call her." When he had called her, she stood in the doorway. 16Then he said, "About this time next year you shall embrace a son."

And she said, "No, my lord. Man of God, do not lie to your maidservant!"

17But the woman conceived, and bore a son when the appointed time had come, of which Elisha had told her.

18And the child grew. Now it happened one day that he went out to his father, to the reapers. 19And he said to his father, "My head, my head!"

So he said to a servant, "Carry him to his mother." 20When he had taken him and brought him to his mother, he sat on her knees till noon, and *then* died. 21And she went up and laid him on the bed of the man of God, shut *the door* upon him, and went out. 22Then she called to her husband, and said, "Please send me one of the young men and one of the donkeys, that I may run to the man of God and come back."

23So he said, "Why are you going to him today? *It is* neither the New Moon nor the Sabbath."

And she said, "*It is* well." 24Then she saddled a donkey, and said to her servant, "Drive, and go forward; do not slacken the pace for me unless I tell you." 25And so she departed, and went to the man of God at Mount Carmel.

So it was, when the man of God saw her afar off, that he said to his servant Gehazi, "Look, the Shunammite woman! 26Please run now to meet her, and say to her, '*Is it* well with you? *Is it* well with your husband? *Is it* well with the child?' "

And she answered, "*It is* well." 27Now when she came to the man of God at the hill, she caught him by the feet, but Gehazi came near to push her away. But the man of God said, "Let her alone; for her soul *is* in deep distress, and the LORD has hidden *it* from me, and has not told me."

28So she said, "Did I ask a son of my lord? Did I not say, 'Do not deceive me'?"

29Then he said to Gehazi, "Get yourself ready, and take my staff in your hand, and be on your way. If you meet anyone, do not greet him; and if anyone greets you, do not answer him; but lay my staff on the face of the child."

30And the mother of the child said, "*As* the LORD lives, and *as* your soul lives, I will not leave you." So he arose and followed her. 31Now Gehazi went on ahead of them, and laid the staff on the face of the child; but *there was* neither voice nor hearing. Therefore he went back to meet him, and told him, saying, "The child has not awakened."

32When Elisha came into the house, there was the child, lying dead on his bed. 33He went in therefore, shut the door behind the two of them, and prayed to the LORD. 34And he went up and lay on the child, and put his mouth on his mouth, his eyes on his eyes, and his hands on his hands; and he stretched himself out on the child, and the flesh of the child became warm. 35He returned and walked back and forth in the house, and again went up and stretched himself out on him; then the child sneezed seven times, and the child opened his eyes. 36And he called Gehazi and said, "Call this Shunammite woman." So he called her. And when she came in to him, he said, "Pick up your son." 37So she went in, fell at his feet, and bowed to the ground; then she picked up her son and went out.

38And Elisha returned to Gilgal, and *there was* a famine in the land. Now the sons of the prophets *were* sitting before him; and he said to his servant, "Put on the large pot, and boil stew for the sons of the prophets." 39So one went out into the field to gather herbs, and found a wild vine, and gathered from it a lapful of wild gourds, and came and sliced *them* into the pot of stew, though they did not know *what they were.* 40Then they served it to the men to eat. Now it happened, as they were eating the stew, that they cried out and said, "Man of God, *there is* death in the pot!" And they could not eat *it.*

[41]So he said, "Then bring some flour." And
he put *it* into the pot, and said, "Serve *it* to the
people, that they may eat." And there was
nothing harmful in the pot.
[42]Then a man came from Baal Shalisha, and
brought the man of God bread of the firstfruits, twenty loaves of barley bread, and newly
ripened grain in his knapsack. And he said,
"Give *it* to the people, that they may eat."
[43]But his servant said, "What? Shall I set this
before one hundred men?"

He said again, "Give it to the people, that
they may eat; for thus says the LORD: 'They
shall eat and have *some* left over.' " [44]So he set
it before them; and they ate and had *some* left
over, according to the word of the LORD.

Psalm 71:17–24

17 O God, You have taught me from my
youth;
And to this *day* I declare Your
wondrous works.
18 Now also when *I am* old and
grayheaded,
O God, do not forsake me,
Until I declare Your strength to *this*
generation,
Your power to everyone *who* is to come.
19 Also Your righteousness, O God, *is*
very high,
You who have done great things;
O God, who *is* like You?
20 *You,* who have shown me great and
severe troubles,
Shall revive me again,
And bring me up again from the depths
of the earth.
21 You shall increase my greatness,
And comfort me on every side.
22 Also with the lute I will praise You—
And Your faithfulness, O my God!
To You I will sing with the harp,
O Holy One of Israel.
23 My lips shall greatly rejoice when I
sing to You,
And my soul, which You have
redeemed.
24 My tongue also shall talk of Your
righteousness all the day long;
For they are confounded,
For they are brought to shame
Who seek my hurt.

Proverbs 18:9

9 He who is slothful in his work
Is a brother to him who is a great
destroyer.

John 17:1–26

17 Jesus spoke these words, lifted up His
eyes to heaven, and said: "Father, the
hour has come. Glorify Your Son, that Your
Son also may glorify You, [2]as You have given
Him authority over all flesh, that He should
give eternal life to as many as You have given
Him. [3]And this is eternal life, that they may
know You, the only true God, and Jesus Christ
whom You have sent. [4]I have glorified You on
the earth. I have finished the work which You
have given Me to do. [5]And now, O Father, glorify Me together with Yourself, with the glory
which I had with You before the world was.
[6]"I have manifested Your name to the men
whom You have given Me out of the world.
They were Yours, You gave them to Me, and
they have kept Your word. [7]Now they have
known that all things which You have given Me
are from You. [8]For I have given to them the
words which You have given Me; and they
have received *them,* and have known surely
that I came forth from You; and they have
believed that You sent Me.
[9]"I pray for them. I do not pray for the world
but for those whom You have given Me, for
they are Yours. [10]And all Mine are Yours, and
Yours are Mine, and I am glorified in them.
[11]Now I am no longer in the world, but these
are in the world, and I come to You. Holy
Father, keep through Your name those whom
You have given Me, that they may be one as
We *are.* [12]While I was with them in the world,
I kept them in Your name. Those whom You
gave Me I have kept; and none of them is lost
except the son of perdition, that the Scripture
might be fulfilled. [13]But now I come to You,
and these things I speak in the world, that
they may have My joy fulfilled in themselves.
[14]I have given them Your word; and the world
has hated them because they are not of the
world, just as I am not of the world. [15]I do not
pray that You should take them out of the
world, but that You should keep them from
the evil one. [16]They are not of the world, just as
I am not of the world. [17]Sanctify them by Your
truth. Your word is truth. [18]As You sent Me
into the world, I also have sent them into the
world. [19]And for their sakes I sanctify Myself,
that they also may be sanctified by the truth.
[20]"I do not pray for these alone, but also for
those who will believe in Me through their
word; [21]that they all may be one, as You, Father,
are in Me, and I in You; that they also may be
one in Us, that the world may believe that You
sent Me. [22]And the glory which You gave Me I
have given them, that they may be one just as

We are one: [23]I in them, and You in Me; that they
may be made perfect in one, and that the world
may know that You have sent Me, and have
loved them as You have loved Me.
[24]"Father, I desire that they also whom You
gave Me may be with Me where I am, that
they may behold My glory which You have
given Me; for You loved Me before the foundation of the world. [25]O righteous Father! The
world has not known You, but I have known
You; and these have known that You sent Me.
[26]And I have declared to them Your name, and
will declare *it*, that the love with which You
loved Me may be in them, and I in them."

17:17 Sanctify. This verb also occurs in John's Gospel at v. 19; 10:36. The idea of sanctification is the setting apart of something for a particular use. Accordingly, believers are set apart for God and His purposes alone so that the believer does only what God wants and hates all that God hates (Lev. 11:44,45; 1 Pet. 1:16). Sanctification is accomplished by means of the truth, which is the revelation that the Son gave regarding all that the Father commanded Him to communicate and is now contained in the scriptures left by the apostles.

17:21 they all may be one. The basis of this unity centers in adherence to the revelation the Father mediated to His first disciples through His Son. Believers are also to be united in the common belief of the truth that was received in the Word of God (Phil. 2:2). This is not still a wish, but it became a reality when the Spirit came (Acts 2:4; 1 Cor. 12:13). It is not experiential unity, but the unity of common eternal life shared by all who believe the truth, and it results in the one body of Christ all sharing His life.

DAY 8: What was Jesus' prayer in John 17 about?

Although Matthew 6:9–13 and Luke 11:2–4 have become known popularly as the Lord's Prayer, that prayer was actually a prayer taught to the disciples by Jesus as a pattern for their prayers. The prayer recorded in John 17:1–26 is truly the Lord's Prayer, exhibiting the face-to-face communion the Son had with the Father. Very little is recorded of the content of Jesus' frequent prayers to the Father (Matt. 14:23; Luke 5:16), so this prayer reveals some of the precious content of the Son's communion and intercession with Him.

This chapter is a transitional chapter, marking the end of Jesus' earthly ministry and the beginning of His intercessory ministry for believers (Heb. 7:25). In many respects, the prayer is a summary of John's entire Gospel. Its principle themes include: 1) Jesus' obedience to His Father; 2) the glorification of His Father through His death and exaltation; 3) the revelation of God in Jesus Christ; 4) the choosing of the disciples out of the world; 5) their mission to the world; 6) their unity modeled on the unity of the Father and Son; and 7) the believer's final destiny in the presence of the Father and Son. The chapter divides into three parts: 1) Jesus' prayer for Himself (vv. 1–5); 2) Jesus' prayer for the apostles (vv. 6–19); and 3) Jesus' prayer for all New Testament believers who will form the church (vv. 20–26).

Jesus speaks to His Father that the hour of His death has come (v. 1). "Glorify Your Son." The very event that would glorify the Son was His death. By it, He has received the adoration, worship, and love of millions whose sins He bore. He accepted this path to glory, knowing that by it He would be exalted to the Father. The goal is that the Father may be glorified for His redemptive plan in the Son.

Note Jesus' concern that the Father keep His disciples "from the evil one" (v. 15). The reference here refers to protection from Satan and all the wicked forces following him (Matt. 6:13; 1 John 2:13,14; 3:12; 5:18,19). Though Jesus' sacrifice on the cross was the defeat of Satan, he is still loose and orchestrating his evil system against believers. He seeks to destroy believers (1 Pet. 5:8; Eph. 6:12), but God is their strong protector (12:31; 16:11; Ps. 27:1–3; 2 Cor. 4:4; Jude 24,25).

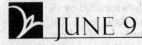

JUNE 9

2 Kings 5:1–6:33

5 Now Naaman, commander of the army of
the king of Syria, was a great and honorable
man in the eyes of his master, because by him
the LORD had given victory to Syria. He was
also a mighty man of valor, *but* a leper. [2]And the
Syrians had gone out on raids, and had brought
back captive a young girl from the land of Israel. She waited on Naaman's wife. [3]Then she
said to her mistress, "If only my master *were*
with the prophet who *is* in Samaria! For he

would heal him of his leprosy." [4]And *Naaman*
went in and told his master, saying, "Thus and
thus said the girl who *is* from the land of Israel."
[5]Then the king of Syria said, "Go now, and I
will send a letter to the king of Israel."

So he departed and took with him ten talents of silver, six thousand *shekels* of gold, and
ten changes of clothing. [6]Then he brought the
letter to the king of Israel, which said,

> Now be advised, when this letter comes to you, that I have sent Naaman my servant to you, that you may heal him of his leprosy.

[7]And it happened, when the king of Israel read
the letter, that he tore his clothes and said,
"*Am* I God, to kill and make alive, that this man
sends a man to me to heal him of his leprosy?
Therefore please consider, and see how he
seeks a quarrel with me."
[8]So it was, when Elisha the man of God
heard that the king of Israel had torn his
clothes, that he sent to the king, saying, "Why
have you torn your clothes? Please let him
come to me, and he shall know that there is a
prophet in Israel."
[9]Then Naaman went with his horses and
chariot, and he stood at the door of Elisha's
house. [10]And Elisha sent a messenger to him,
saying, "Go and wash in the Jordan seven
times, and your flesh shall be restored to you,
and *you shall* be clean." [11]But Naaman became
furious, and went away and said, "Indeed, I
said to myself, 'He will surely come out *to me,*
and stand and call on the name of the LORD his
God, and wave his hand over the place, and
heal the leprosy.' [12]*Are* not the Abanah and the
Pharpar, the rivers of Damascus, better than
all the waters of Israel? Could I not wash in
them and be clean?" So he turned and went
away in a rage. [13]And his servants came near
and spoke to him, and said, "My father, *if* the
prophet had told you *to do* something great,
would you not have done *it?* How much more
then, when he says to you, 'Wash, and be
clean'?" [14]So he went down and dipped seven
times in the Jordan, according to the saying of
the man of God; and his flesh was restored
like the flesh of a little child, and he was clean.
[15]And he returned to the man of God, he and
all his aides, and came and stood before him;
and he said, "Indeed, now I know that *there is*
no God in all the earth, except in Israel; now
therefore, please take a gift from your servant."
[16]But he said, "*As* the LORD lives, before
whom I stand, I will receive nothing." And he
urged him to take *it,* but he refused.
[17]So Naaman said, "Then, if not, please let
your servant be given two mule-loads of earth;
for your servant will no longer offer either
burnt offering or sacrifice to other gods, but to
the LORD. [18]Yet in this thing may the LORD pardon your servant: when my master goes into
the temple of Rimmon to worship there, and he
leans on my hand, and I bow down in the temple of Rimmon—when I bow down in the
temple of Rimmon, may the LORD please pardon your servant in this thing."
[19]Then he said to him, "Go in peace." So he
departed from him a short distance.
[20]But Gehazi, the servant of Elisha the man
of God, said, "Look, my master has spared
Naaman this Syrian, while not receiving from
his hands what he brought; but *as* the LORD
lives, I will run after him and take something
from him." [21]So Gehazi pursued Naaman.
When Naaman saw *him* running after him, he
got down from the chariot to meet him, and
said, "*Is* all well?"
[22]And he said, "All *is* well. My master has
sent me, saying, 'Indeed, just now two young
men of the sons of the prophets have come to
me from the mountains of Ephraim. Please
give them a talent of silver and two changes of
garments.' "
[23]So Naaman said, "Please, take two talents."
And he urged him, and bound two talents of
silver in two bags, with two changes of garments, and handed *them* to two of his servants; and they carried *them* on ahead of him.
[24]When he came to the citadel, he took *them*
from their hand, and stored *them* away in the
house; then he let the men go, and they
departed. [25]Now he went in and stood before
his master. Elisha said to him, "Where *did you*
go, Gehazi?"
And he said, "Your servant did not go anywhere."
[26]Then he said to him, "Did not my heart go

5:17 two mule-loads of earth. In the ancient Near East, it was thought that a god could be worshiped only on the soil of the nation to which he was bound. Therefore, Naaman wanted a load of Israelite soil on which to make burnt offerings and sacrifices to the Lord when he returned to Damascus. This request confirmed how Naaman had changed—whereas he had previously disparaged Israel's river, now he wanted to take a pile of Israel's soil to Damascus.

with you when the man turned back from his
chariot to meet you? *Is it* time to receive
money and to receive clothing, olive groves
and vineyards, sheep and oxen, male and
female servants? 27Therefore the leprosy of
Naaman shall cling to you and your descendants forever." And he went out from his presence leprous, *as white* as snow.

5:27 leprosy...shall cling to you. Gehazi's greed had cast a shadow over the integrity of Elisha's prophetic office. This made him no better in the people's thinking than Israel's false prophets, who prophesied for material gain, the very thing he wanted to avoid (vv. 15,16). Gehazi's act betrayed a lack of faith in the Lord's ability to provide. As a result, Elisha condemned Gehazi and his descendants to suffer Naaman's skin disease forever. The punishment was a twist for Gehazi, who had gone to take something from Naaman (v. 20), but what he received was Naaman's disease.

6 And the sons of the prophets said to
Elisha, "See now, the place where we
dwell with you is too small for us. 2Please, let
us go to the Jordan, and let every man take a
beam from there, and let us make there a
place where we may dwell."

So he answered, "Go."

3Then one said, "Please consent to go with
your servants."

And he answered, "I will go." 4So he went
with them. And when they came to the Jordan,
they cut down trees. 5But as one was cutting
down a tree, the iron *ax head* fell into the
water; and he cried out and said, "Alas, master! For it was borrowed."

6:5 iron...borrowed. Iron was expensive and relatively rare in Israel at that time, and the student-prophet was very poor. The ax head was loaned to the prophet since he could not have afforded it on his own and would have had no means to reimburse the owner for it.

6So the man of God said, "Where did it fall?"
And he showed him the place. So he cut off a
stick, and threw *it* in there; and he made the
iron float. 7Therefore he said, "Pick *it* up for
yourself." So he reached out his hand and
took it.

8Now the king of Syria was making war
against Israel; and he consulted with his servants, saying, "My camp *will be* in such and
such a place." 9And the man of God sent to the
king of Israel, saying, "Beware that you do not
pass this place, for the Syrians are coming
down there." 10Then the king of Israel sent
someone to the place of which the man of God
had told him. Thus he warned him, and he
was watchful there, not just once or twice.

11Therefore the heart of the king of Syria
was greatly troubled by this thing; and he called
his servants and said to them, "Will you not
show me which of us *is* for the king of Israel?"

12And one of his servants said, "None, my
lord, O king; but Elisha, the prophet who *is* in
Israel, tells the king of Israel the words that
you speak in your bedroom."

13So he said, "Go and see where he *is,* that I
may send and get him."

And it was told him, saying, "Surely *he is* in
Dothan."

14Therefore he sent horses and chariots and
a great army there, and they came by night
and surrounded the city. 15And when the servant of the man of God arose early and went
out, there was an army, surrounding the city
with horses and chariots. And his servant said
to him, "Alas, my master! What shall we do?"

16So he answered, "Do not fear, for those
who *are* with us *are* more than those who *are*
with them." 17And Elisha prayed, and said,
"LORD, I pray, open his eyes that he may see."
Then the LORD opened the eyes of the young
man, and he saw. And behold, the mountain
was full of horses and chariots of fire all
around Elisha. 18So when *the Syrians* came
down to him, Elisha prayed to the LORD, and
said, "Strike this people, I pray, with blindness." And He struck them with blindness
according to the word of Elisha.

19Now Elisha said to them, "This *is* not the
way, nor *is* this the city. Follow me, and I will
bring you to the man whom you seek." But he
led them to Samaria.

20So it was, when they had come to Samaria,
that Elisha said, "LORD, open the eyes of these
men, that they may see." And the LORD opened
their eyes, and they saw; and there *they were,*
inside Samaria!

21Now when the king of Israel saw them, he
said to Elisha, "My father, shall I kill *them?*
Shall I kill *them?*"

22But he answered, "You shall not kill *them.*
Would you kill those whom you have taken
captive with your sword and your bow? Set
food and water before them, that they may eat
and drink and go to their master." 23Then he

prepared a great feast for them; and after they
ate and drank, he sent them away and they
went to their master. So the bands of Syrian
raiders came no more into the land of Israel.
[24]And it happened after this that Ben-Hadad
king of Syria gathered all his army, and went
up and besieged Samaria. [25]And there was a
great famine in Samaria; and indeed they
besieged it until a donkey's head was *sold* for
eighty *shekels* of silver, and one-fourth of a kab
of dove droppings for five *shekels* of silver.
[26]Then, as the king of Israel was passing by
on the wall, a woman cried out to him, saying,
"Help, my lord, O king!"
[27]And he said, "If the LORD does not help
you, where can I find help for you? From the
threshing floor or from the winepress?" [28]Then
the king said to her, "What is troubling you?"
And she answered, "This woman said to me,
'Give your son, that we may eat him today, and
we will eat my son tomorrow.' [29]So we boiled
my son, and ate him. And I said to her on the
next day, 'Give your son, that we may eat him';
but she has hidden her son."
[30]Now it happened, when the king heard the
words of the woman, that he tore his clothes;
and as he passed by on the wall, the people
looked, and there underneath *he had* sackcloth
on his body. [31]Then he said, "God do so to me
and more also, if the head of Elisha the son of
Shaphat remains on him today!"
[32]But Elisha was sitting in his house, and the
elders were sitting with him. And *the king* sent
a man ahead of him, but before the messenger
came to him, he said to the elders, "Do you see
how this son of a murderer has sent someone
to take away my head? Look, when the messenger
comes, shut the door, and hold him fast
at the door. *Is* not the sound of his master's feet
behind him?" [33]And while he was still talking
with them, there was the messenger, coming
down to him; and then *the king* said, "Surely
this calamity *is* from the LORD; why should I
wait for the LORD any longer?"

Psalm 72:1–7

A Psalm of Solomon.

Give the king Your judgments, O God,
And Your righteousness to the king's Son.
2 He will judge Your people with righteousness,
And Your poor with justice.
3 The mountains will bring peace to the people,
And the little hills, by righteousness.
4 He will bring justice to the poor of the people;
He will save the children of the needy,
And will break in pieces the oppressor.

5 They shall fear You
As long as the sun and moon endure,
Throughout all generations.
6 He shall come down like rain upon the grass before mowing,
Like showers *that* water the earth.
7 In His days the righteous shall flourish,
And abundance of peace,
Until the moon is no more.

Proverbs 18:10–11

10 The name of the LORD *is* a strong tower;
The righteous run to it and are safe.
11 The rich man's wealth *is* his strong city,
And like a high wall in his own esteem.

John 18:1–18

18 When Jesus had spoken these words, He
went out with His disciples over the
Brook Kidron, where there was a garden,
which He and His disciples entered. [2]And Judas,
who betrayed Him, also knew the place;
for Jesus often met there with His disciples.
[3]Then Judas, having received a detachment *of
troops,* and officers from the chief priests and
Pharisees, came there with lanterns, torches,
and weapons. [4]Jesus therefore, knowing all
things that would come upon Him, went forward
and said to them, "Whom are you seeking?"
[5]They answered Him, "Jesus of Nazareth."
Jesus said to them, "I am *He.*" And Judas,

18:4–8 Whom are you seeking? By twice asking that question (vv. 4,7), to which they replied, "Jesus of Nazareth" (vv. 5,7), Jesus was forcing them to acknowledge that they had no authority to take His disciples. In fact, He demanded that they let the disciples go (v. 8). The force of His demand was established by the power of His words. When He spoke, "I am He" (v. 6), a designation He had used before to declare Himself God (8:28,58; 6:35; 8:12; 10:7,9,11,14; 11:25; 14:6; 15:1,5), they were jolted backward and to the ground (v. 6). This power display and the authoritative demand not to take the disciples was of immense significance, as the next verse indicates.

who betrayed Him, also stood with them.
6Now when He said to them, "I am *He,*" they
drew back and fell to the ground.
7Then He asked them again, "Whom are you
seeking?"

And they said, "Jesus of Nazareth."

8Jesus answered, "I have told you that I am
He. Therefore, if you seek Me, let these go
their way," 9that the saying might be fulfilled
which He spoke, "Of those whom You gave
Me I have lost none."
10Then Simon Peter, having a sword, drew it
and struck the high priest's servant, and cut off
his right ear. The servant's name was Malchus.
11So Jesus said to Peter, "Put your sword
into the sheath. Shall I not drink the cup
which My Father has given Me?"
12Then the detachment *of troops* and the captain and the officers of the Jews arrested Jesus
and bound Him. 13And they led Him away to
Annas first, for he was the father-in-law of
Caiaphas who was high priest that year. 14Now
it was Caiaphas who advised the Jews that it
was expedient that one man should die for the
people.
15And Simon Peter followed Jesus, and so
did another disciple. Now that disciple was
known to the high priest, and went with Jesus
into the courtyard of the high priest. 16But Peter stood at the door outside. Then the other
disciple, who was known to the high priest,
went out and spoke to her who kept the door,
and brought Peter in. 17Then the servant girl
who kept the door said to Peter, "You are not
also *one* of this Man's disciples, are you?"

He said, "I am not."

18Now the servants and officers who had
made a fire of coals stood there, for it was
cold, and they warmed themselves. And Peter
stood with them and warmed himself.

18:13 Annas first. Annas held the high priesthood office from A.D. 6–15 when Valerius Gratus, Pilate's predecessor, removed him from office. In spite of this, Annas continued to wield influence over the office, most likely because he was still regarded as the true high priest and also because no fewer than 5 of his sons, and his son-in-law Caiaphas, held the office at one time or another. Two trials occurred: one Jewish and one Roman. The Jewish phase began with the informal examination by Annas (vv. 12–14, 19–23), probably giving time for the members of the Sanhedrin to hurriedly gather together. A session before the Sanhedrin was next (Matt. 26:57–68) at which consensus was reached to send Jesus to Pilate (Matt. 27:1,2). The Roman phase began with a first examination before Pilate (vv. 28–38a; Matt. 27:11–14) and then Herod Antipas ("that fox"—Luke 13:32) interrogated Him (Luke 23:6–12). Lastly, Jesus appeared again before Pilate (vv. 38b–19:16; Matt. 27:15–31).

DAY 9: Who was Naaman, and what does he teach us about obedience to God?

In 2 Kings 5:1, four phrases describe the importance of Naaman: 1) he was the supreme commander of the army of Syria as indicated by the term "commander," used of an army's highest ranking officer (Gen. 21:22; 1 Sam. 12:9; 1 Chr. 27:34); 2) he was a great man, a man of high social standing and prominence; 3) he was an honorable man in the eyes of his master, a man highly regarded by the king of Syria because of the military victories he had won; and 4) he was a mighty man of valor, a term used in the Old Testament for both a man of great wealth (Ruth 2:1) and a courageous warrior (Judg. 6:12; 11:1). Severely mitigating against all of this was the fact that he suffered from leprosy, a serious skin disease (v. 27). Naaman's military success was attributable to the God of Israel, who is sovereign over all the nations (Is. 10:13; Amos 9:7).

Because of his personal greatness (v. 1), his huge gift of ten talents of silver, six thousand *shekels* of gold (about 750 pounds of silver and 150 pounds of gold in v. 5), and diplomatic letter (v. 6), Naaman expected that Elisha would "surely come out to me" (v.11). He expected personal attention to his need. However, Elisha did not even go out to meet him. Instead, he sent his instructions for healing through a messenger (v. 10). Naaman was angry because he anticipated a personal cleansing ceremony from the prophet himself. Besides, if Naaman needed to wash in a river, two Syrian rivers were superior to the muddy Jordan. However, it was obedience to God's word that was the issue, not the quality of the water.

Fortunately, Naaman had a servant who pointed out to him that he had been willing to do anything, no matter how hard, to be cured. He should be even more willing, therefore, to do something as easy as washing in a muddy river. Naaman's healing restored his flesh to that "of a little child" (v. 14). Upon his healing, Naaman returned from the Jordan River to Elisha's house in Samaria to give confession of his new belief: "there is no God...except in Israel" (v. 15).

JUNE 10

2 Kings 7:1–8:29

7 Then Elisha said, "Hear the word of the LORD. Thus says the LORD: 'Tomorrow about this time a seah of fine flour *shall be sold* for a shekel, and two seahs of barley for a shekel, at the gate of Samaria.' "

[2]So an officer on whose hand the king leaned answered the man of God and said, "Look, *if* the LORD would make windows in heaven, could this thing be?"

And he said, "In fact, you shall see *it* with your eyes, but you shall not eat of it."

[3]Now there were four leprous men at the entrance of the gate; and they said to one another, "Why are we sitting here until we die? [4]If we say, 'We will enter the city,' the famine *is* in the city, and we shall die there. And if we sit here, we die also. Now therefore, come, let us surrender to the army of the Syrians. If they keep us alive, we shall live; and if they kill us, we shall only die." [5]And they rose at twilight to go to the camp of the Syrians; and when they had come to the outskirts of the Syrian camp, to their surprise no one *was* there. [6]For the Lord had caused the army of the Syrians to hear the noise of chariots and the noise of horses—the noise of a great army; so they said to one another, "Look, the king of Israel has hired against us the kings of the Hittites and the kings of the Egyptians to attack us!" [7]Therefore they arose and fled at twilight, and left the camp intact—their tents, their horses, and their donkeys—and they fled for their lives. [8]And when these lepers came to the outskirts of the camp, they went into one tent and ate and drank, and carried from it silver and gold and clothing, and went and hid *them;* then they came back and entered another tent, and carried *some* from there *also,* and went and hid *it.*

[9]Then they said to one another, "We are not doing right. This day *is* a day of good news, and we remain silent. If we wait until morning light, some punishment will come upon us. Now therefore, come, let us go and tell the king's household." [10]So they went and called to the gatekeepers of the city, and told them, saying, "We went to the Syrian camp, and surprisingly no one *was* there, not a human sound—only horses and donkeys tied, and the tents intact." [11]And the gatekeepers called out, and they told *it* to the king's household inside.

[12]So the king arose in the night and said to his servants, "Let me now tell you what the Syrians have done to us. They know that we *are* hungry; therefore they have gone out of the camp to hide themselves in the field, saying, 'When they come out of the city, we shall catch them alive, and get into the city.' "

[13]And one of his servants answered and said, "Please, let several *men* take five of the remaining horses which are left in the city. Look, they *may either become* like all the multitude of Israel that are left in it; or indeed, *I say,* they *may become* like all the multitude of Israel left from those who are consumed; so let us send them and see." [14]Therefore they took two chariots with horses; and the king sent them in the direction of the Syrian army, saying, "Go and see." [15]And they went after them to the Jordan; and indeed all the road *was* full of garments and weapons which the Syrians had thrown away in their haste. So the messengers returned and told the king. [16]Then the people went out and plundered the tents of the Syrians. So a seah of fine flour was *sold* for a shekel, and two seahs of barley for a shekel, according to the word of the LORD.

[17]Now the king had appointed the officer on whose hand he leaned to have charge of the gate. But the people trampled him in the gate, and he died, just as the man of God had said, who spoke when the king came down to him. [18]So it happened just as the man of God had spoken to the king, saying, "Two seahs of barley for a shekel, and a seah of fine flour for a shekel, shall be *sold* tomorrow about this time in the gate of Samaria."

[19]Then that officer had answered the man of God, and said, "Now look, *if* the LORD would make windows in heaven, could such a thing be?"

And he had said, "In fact, you shall see *it* with your eyes, but you shall not eat of it." [20]And so it happened to him, for the people trampled him in the gate, and he died.

7:6 the Hittites and...Egyptians. Sometime before the arrival of the lepers, the Lord had made the Syrians hear the terrifying sound of a huge army approaching. They thought the Israelite king had hired two massive foreign armies to attack them. The Hittites were descendants of the once-great Hittite Empire who lived in small groups across northern Syria (1 Kin. 10:29). Egypt was in decline at this time, but its army would still have represented a great danger to the Syrians.

8 Then Elisha spoke to the woman whose
son he had restored to life, saying, "Arise
and go, you and your household, and stay
wherever you can; for the LORD has called for
a famine, and furthermore, it will come upon
the land for seven years." 2So the woman arose
and did according to the saying of the man of
God, and she went with her household and
dwelt in the land of the Philistines seven years.
3It came to pass, at the end of seven years,
that the woman returned from the land of the
Philistines; and she went to make an appeal to
the king for her house and for her land. 4Then
the king talked with Gehazi, the servant of the
man of God, saying, "Tell me, please, all the
great things Elisha has done." 5Now it happened, as he was telling the king how he had
restored the dead to life, that there was the
woman whose son he had restored to life,
appealing to the king for her house and for her
land. And Gehazi said, "My lord, O king, this
is the woman, and this *is* her son whom Elisha
restored to life." 6And when the king asked the
woman, she told him.
So the king appointed a certain officer for
her, saying, "Restore all that *was* hers, and all
the proceeds of the field from the day that she
left the land until now."
7Then Elisha went to Damascus, and Ben-
Hadad king of Syria was sick; and it was told
him, saying, "The man of God has come here."
8And the king said to Hazael, "Take a present
in your hand, and go to meet the man of God,
and inquire of the LORD by him, saying, 'Shall
I recover from this disease?' " 9So Hazael went
to meet him and took a present with him, of
every good thing of Damascus, forty camel-
loads; and he came and stood before him, and
said, "Your son Ben-Hadad king of Syria has
sent me to you, saying, 'Shall I recover from
this disease?' "
10And Elisha said to him, "Go, say to him,
'You shall certainly recover.' However the
LORD has shown me that he will really die."
11Then he set his countenance in a stare until
he was ashamed; and the man of God wept.
12And Hazael said, "Why is my lord weeping?"
He answered, "Because I know the evil that
you will do to the children of Israel: Their
strongholds you will set on fire, and their
young men you will kill with the sword; and
you will dash their children, and rip open their
women with child."
13So Hazael said, "But what *is* your servant—a dog, that he should do this gross
thing?"
And Elisha answered, "The LORD has shown
me that you *will become* king over Syria."

8:10 recover...die. Ben-Hadad wanted to know whether or not he would recover from his present illness. In response, Elisha affirmed two interrelated things: 1) Ben-Hadad would be restored to health; his present sickness would not be the means of his death. 2) Ben-Hadad would surely die by some other means.

8:11 he was ashamed. With a fixed gaze, Elisha stared at Hazael because it had been revealed to him what Hazael would do, including the murder of Ben-Hadad (v. 15). Hazael was embarrassed, knowing that Elisha knew of his plan to assassinate the Syrian king.

14Then he departed from Elisha, and came to
his master, who said to him, "What did Elisha
say to you?" And he answered, "He told me
you would surely recover." 15But it happened
on the next day that he took a thick cloth and
dipped *it* in water, and spread *it* over his face
so that he died; and Hazael reigned in his
place.
16Now in the fifth year of Joram the son of
Ahab, king of Israel, Jehoshaphat *having been*
king of Judah, Jehoram the son of Jehoshaphat began to reign as king of Judah. 17He was
thirty-two years old when he became king,
and he reigned eight years in Jerusalem. 18And
he walked in the way of the kings of Israel, just
as the house of Ahab had done, for the daughter of Ahab was his wife; and he did evil in the
sight of the LORD. 19Yet the LORD would not
destroy Judah, for the sake of His servant David, as He promised him to give a lamp to him
and his sons forever.
20In his days Edom revolted against Judah's
authority, and made a king over themselves.
21So Joram went to Zair, and all his chariots
with him. Then he rose by night and attacked
the Edomites who had surrounded him and
the captains of the chariots; and the troops
fled to their tents. 22Thus Edom has been in
revolt against Judah's authority to this day.
And Libnah revolted at that time.
23Now the rest of the acts of Joram, and all
that he did, *are* they not written in the book of
the chronicles of the kings of Judah? 24So
Joram rested with his fathers, and was buried
with his fathers in the City of David. Then
Ahaziah his son reigned in his place.
25In the twelfth year of Joram the son of Ahab,
king of Israel, Ahaziah the son of Jehoram, king
of Judah, began to reign. 26Ahaziah *was* twenty-
two years old when he became king, and he

reigned one year in Jerusalem. His mother's
name *was* Athaliah the granddaughter of Omri,
king of Israel. [27]And he walked in the way of
the house of Ahab, and did evil in the sight of
the LORD, like the house of Ahab, for he *was* the
son-in-law of the house of Ahab.

[28]Now he went with Joram the son of Ahab
to war against Hazael king of Syria at Ramoth
Gilead; and the Syrians wounded Joram.
[29]Then King Joram went back to Jezreel to
recover from the wounds which the Syrians
had inflicted on him at Ramah, when he
fought against Hazael king of Syria. And
Ahaziah the son of Jehoram, king of Judah,
went down to see Joram the son of Ahab in
Jezreel, because he was sick.

Psalm 72:8–16

8 He shall have dominion also from sea
to sea,
And from the River to the ends of the
earth.
9 Those who dwell in the wilderness will
bow before Him,
And His enemies will lick the dust.
10 The kings of Tarshish and of the isles
Will bring presents;
The kings of Sheba and Seba
Will offer gifts.

72:10 Tarshish...Seba. Countries near and far which brought tribute to Solomon (1 Kin. 4:21; 10:1,23,24; Is. 60:4–7; Jer. 6:20). Tarshish is probably in Spain; Sheba, a kingdom in southern Arabia (modern Yemen); and Seba, a North African nation.

11 Yes, all kings shall fall down before Him;
All nations shall serve Him.
12 For He will deliver the needy when he
cries,
The poor also, and *him* who has no
helper.
13 He will spare the poor and needy,
And will save the souls of the needy.
14 He will redeem their life from
oppression and violence;
And precious shall be their blood in
His sight.
15 And He shall live;
And the gold of Sheba will be given to
Him;
Prayer also will be made for Him
continually,
And daily He shall be praised.
16 There will be an abundance of grain in
the earth,
On the top of the mountains;
Its fruit shall wave like Lebanon;
And *those* of the city shall flourish like
grass of the earth.

Proverbs 18:12–13

12 Before destruction the heart of a man
is haughty,
And before honor *is* humility.
13 He who answers a matter before he
hears *it,*
It *is* folly and shame to him.

John 18:19–40

[19]The high priest then asked Jesus about
His disciples and His doctrine.
[20]Jesus answered him, "I spoke openly to the
world. I always taught in synagogues and in
the temple, where the Jews always meet, and
in secret I have said nothing. [21]Why do you ask
Me? Ask those who have heard Me what I said
to them. Indeed they know what I said."
[22]And when He had said these things, one of
the officers who stood by struck Jesus with the
palm of his hand, saying, "Do You answer the
high priest like that?"
[23]Jesus answered him, "If I have spoken evil,
bear witness of the evil; but if well, why do you
strike Me?"
[24]Then Annas sent Him bound to Caiaphas
the high priest.
[25]Now Simon Peter stood and warmed himself. Therefore they said to him, "You are not
also *one* of His disciples, are you?"
He denied *it* and said, "I am not!"
[26]One of the servants of the high priest, a
relative *of him* whose ear Peter cut off, said,
"Did I not see you in the garden with Him?"
[27]Peter then denied again; and immediately a
rooster crowed.
[28]Then they led Jesus from Caiaphas to the
Praetorium, and it was early morning. But
they themselves did not go into the Praetorium, lest they should be defiled, but that they
might eat the Passover. [29]Pilate then went out
to them and said, "What accusation do you
bring against this Man?"
[30]They answered and said to him, "If He
were not an evildoer, we would not have delivered Him up to you."
[31]Then Pilate said to them, "You take Him
and judge Him according to your law."
Therefore the Jews said to him, "It is not
lawful for us to put anyone to death," [32]that the

saying of Jesus might be fulfilled which He
spoke, signifying by what death He would die.
33Then Pilate entered the Praetorium again,
called Jesus, and said to Him, "Are You the King
of the Jews?"
34Jesus answered him, "Are you speaking for
yourself about this, or did others tell you this
concerning Me?"
35Pilate answered, "Am I a Jew? Your own
nation and the chief priests have delivered
You to me. What have You done?"
36Jesus answered, "My kingdom is not of
this world. If My kingdom were of this world,
My servants would fight, so that I should not
be delivered to the Jews; but now My kingdom is not from here."
37Pilate therefore said to Him, "Are You a
king then?"
Jesus answered, "You say *rightly* that I am a
king. For this cause I was born, and for this
cause I have come into the world, that I should
bear witness to the truth. Everyone who is of
the truth hears My voice."
38Pilate said to Him, "What is truth?" And
when he had said this, he went out again to
the Jews, and said to them, "I find no fault in
Him at all.
39"But you have a custom that I should
release someone to you at the Passover. Do
you therefore want me to release to you the
King of the Jews?"
40Then they all cried again, saying, "Not this
Man, but Barabbas!" Now Barabbas was a robber.

18:36 My kingdom is not of this world. By this phrase, Jesus meant that His kingdom is not connected to earthly political and national entities, nor does it have its origin in the evil world system that is in rebellion against God. If His kingdom was of this world, He would have fought. The kingships of this world preserve themselves by fighting with force. Messiah's kingdom does not originate in the efforts of man but with the Son of Man forcefully and decisively conquering sin in the lives of His people and someday conquering the evil world system at His Second Coming when He establishes the earthly form of His kingdom. His kingdom was no threat to the national identity of Israel or the political and military identity of Rome. It exists in the spiritual dimension until the end of the age (Rev. 11:15).

DAY 10: Why was the trial of Jesus conducted by the Romans rather than the Sanhedrin?

Jesus was led from the trial before Caiaphas to the Praetorium in John 18:28. This was the headquarters of the commanding officer of the Roman military camp or the headquarters of the Roman military governor (i.e., Pilate). Pilate's normal headquarters was in Caesarea, in the palace that Herod the Great had built for himself. However, Pilate and his predecessors made it a point to be in Jerusalem during the feasts in order to quell any riots. Jerusalem became his *praetorium* or headquarters. It was "early morning." The word is ambiguous. Most likely, it refers to around 6:00 a.m. since many Roman officials began their day very early and finished by 10:00 or 11:00 a.m. Those who brought Jesus did not go into the Praetorium "lest they should be defiled." Jewish oral law gives evidence that a Jew who entered the dwelling places of Gentiles became ceremonially unclean. Their remaining outside in the colonnade avoided that pollution. John loads this statement with great irony by noting the chief priests' scrupulousness in the matter of ceremonial cleansing, when all the time they were incurring incomparably greater moral defilement by their proceedings against Jesus.

"What accusation…?" (v. 29). This question formally opened the Roman civil phase of proceedings against Jesus. The fact that Roman troops were used at the arrest proves that the Jewish authorities communicated something about this case to Pilate in advance. Although they most likely had expected Pilate to confirm their judgment against Jesus and order His death sentence, Pilate ordered instead a fresh hearing in his presence.

When Pilate told them to take Jesus back and try Him themselves, the Jews objected on the basis that "It is not lawful for us to put anyone to death" (v. 31). When Rome took over Judea and began direct rule through a prefect in A.D. 6, capital jurisdiction (i.e., the right to execute) was taken away from the Jews and given to the Roman governor. Capital punishment was the most jealously guarded of all the attributes in Roman provincial administration.

By a Roman crucifixion, it also fulfilled "the saying of Jesus" (v. 32) that He would die by being lifted up (3:14; 8:28; 12:32,33). If the Jews had executed Him, it would have been by throwing Him down and stoning Him. But God providentially controlled all the political procedures to assure that, when sentence was finally passed, He would be crucified by the Romans and not stoned by the Jews, as was Stephen (Acts 7:59).

JUNE 11

2 Kings 9:1–10:36

9 And Elisha the prophet called one of the
sons of the prophets, and said to him, "Get
yourself ready, take this flask of oil in your
hand, and go to Ramoth Gilead. [2]Now when
you arrive at that place, look there for Jehu the
son of Jehoshaphat, the son of Nimshi, and go
in and make him rise up from among his associates, and take him to an inner room. [3]Then
take the flask of oil, and pour *it* on his head,
and say, 'Thus says the LORD: "I have anointed
you king over Israel." ' Then open the door and
flee, and do not delay."

9:2 Jehu. The Lord had previously told Elijah that Jehu would become king over Israel and kill those involved in the worship of Baal (1 Kin. 19:16,17). The fulfillment of the prophecy is recorded from 9:1–10:31. **inner room.** A private room that could be closed off to the public. Elisha commissioned one of the younger prophets to anoint Jehu alone behind closed doors. The rite was to be a secret affair without Elisha present so that Jehoram would not suspect that a coup was coming.

9:3 anointed you king over Israel. The anointing with olive oil by a prophet of the Lord confirmed that God Himself had earlier chosen that man to be king (1 Sam. 10:1; 16:13). This action of anointing by a commissioned prophet indicated divine investiture with God's sovereign power to Jehu. **flee, and do not delay.** The need for haste by the young prophet underscored the danger of the assignment. A prophet in the midst of Israel's army camp would alert the pro-Jehoram elements to the possibility of the coup.

[4]So the young man, the servant of the
prophet, went to Ramoth Gilead. [5]And when he
arrived, there *were* the captains of the army sitting; and he said, "I have a message for you,
Commander."

Jehu said, "For which *one* of us?"

And he said, "For you, Commander." [6]Then
he arose and went into the house. And he
poured the oil on his head, and said to him,
"Thus says the LORD God of Israel: 'I have
anointed you king over the people of the LORD,
over Israel. [7]You shall strike down the house of
Ahab your master, that I may avenge the blood
of My servants the prophets, and the blood of all
the servants of the LORD, at the hand of Jezebel.
[8]For the whole house of Ahab shall perish; and
I will cut off from Ahab all the males in Israel,
both bond and free. [9]So I will make the house
of Ahab like the house of Jeroboam the son
of Nebat, and like the house of Baasha the
son of Ahijah. [10]The dogs shall eat Jezebel on
the plot *of ground* at Jezreel, and *there shall be*
none to bury *her.*' " And he opened the door and
fled.

[11]Then Jehu came out to the servants of his
master, and *one* said to him, "*Is* all well? Why
did this madman come to you?"

And he said to them, "You know the man
and his babble."

[12]And they said, "A lie! Tell us now."

So he said, "Thus and thus he spoke to me,
saying, 'Thus says the LORD: "I have anointed
you king over Israel." ' "

[13]Then each man hastened to take his garment and put *it* under him on the top of the
steps; and they blew trumpets, saying, "Jehu
is king!"

[14]So Jehu the son of Jehoshaphat, the son of
Nimshi, conspired against Joram. (Now Joram
had been defending Ramoth Gilead, he and all
Israel, against Hazael king of Syria. [15]But King
Joram had returned to Jezreel to recover from
the wounds which the Syrians had inflicted on
him when he fought with Hazael king of Syria.)
And Jehu said, "If you are so minded, let no
one leave *or* escape from the city to go and tell
it in Jezreel." [16]So Jehu rode in a chariot and
went to Jezreel, for Joram was laid up there;
and Ahaziah king of Judah had come down to
see Joram.

[17]Now a watchman stood on the tower in
Jezreel, and he saw the company of Jehu as he
came, and said, "I see a company of men."

And Joram said, "Get a horseman and send
him to meet them, and let him say, '*Is it*
peace?' "

[18]So the horseman went to meet him, and
said, "Thus says the king: '*Is it* peace?' "

And Jehu said, "What have you to do with
peace? Turn around and follow me."

So the watchman reported, saying, "The
messenger went to them, but is not coming
back."

[19]Then he sent out a second horseman who
came to them, and said, "Thus says the king:
'*Is it* peace?' "

And Jehu answered, "What have you to do
with peace? Turn around and follow me."

[20]So the watchman reported, saying, "He
went up to them and is not coming back; and

the driving *is* like the driving of Jehu the son
of Nimshi, for he drives furiously!"
[21]Then Joram said, "Make ready." And his
chariot was made ready. Then Joram king of
Israel and Ahaziah king of Judah went out,
each in his chariot; and they went out to meet
Jehu, and met him on the property of Naboth
the Jezreelite. [22]Now it happened, when Joram
saw Jehu, that he said, "*Is it* peace, Jehu?"
So he answered, "What peace, as long as
the harlotries of your mother Jezebel and her
witchcraft *are so* many?"
[23]Then Joram turned around and fled, and
said to Ahaziah, "Treachery, Ahaziah!" [24]Now
Jehu drew his bow with full strength and shot
Jehoram between his arms; and the arrow
came out at his heart, and he sank down in his
chariot. [25]Then *Jehu* said to Bidkar his captain,
"Pick *him* up, *and* throw him into the tract of
the field of Naboth the Jezreelite; for remember, when you and I were riding together
behind Ahab his father, that the LORD laid this
burden upon him: [26]'Surely I saw yesterday the
blood of Naboth and the blood of his sons,'
says the LORD, 'and I will repay you in this
plot,' says the LORD. Now therefore, take *and*
throw him on the plot *of ground,* according to
the word of the LORD."
[27]But when Ahaziah king of Judah saw *this,*
he fled by the road to Beth Haggan. So Jehu
pursued him, and said, "Shoot him also in the
chariot." *And they shot him* at the Ascent of
Gur, which is by Ibleam. Then he fled to
Megiddo, and died there. [28]And his servants carried him in the chariot to Jerusalem, and buried
him in his tomb with his fathers in the City of
David. [29]In the eleventh year of Joram the son of
Ahab, Ahaziah had become king over Judah.
[30]Now when Jehu had come to Jezreel,
Jezebel heard *of it;* and she put paint on her
eyes and adorned her head, and looked

9:30 paint on her eyes. The painting of the eyelids with a black powder mixed with oil and applied with a brush, darkened them to give an enlarged effect. Jezebel's appearance at the window gave the air of a royal audience to awe Jehu.

through a window. [31]Then, as Jehu entered at
the gate, she said, "*Is it* peace, Zimri, murderer of your master?"
[32]And he looked up at the window, and said,
"Who *is* on my side? Who?" So two *or* three
eunuchs looked out at him. [33]Then he said,
"Throw her down." So they threw her down,
and *some* of her blood spattered on the wall
and on the horses; and he trampled her underfoot. [34]And when he had gone in, he ate and
drank. Then he said, "Go now, see to this
accursed *woman,* and bury her, for she was a
king's daughter." [35]So they went to bury her,
but they found no more of her than the skull
and the feet and the palms of *her* hands.
[36]Therefore they came back and told him. And
he said, "This *is* the word of the LORD, which
He spoke by His servant Elijah the Tishbite,
saying, 'On the plot *of ground* at Jezreel dogs
shall eat the flesh of Jezebel; [37]and the corpse
of Jezebel shall be as refuse on the surface of
the field, in the plot at Jezreel, so that they
shall not say, "Here *lies* Jezebel." ' "

10 Now Ahab had seventy sons in Samaria.
And Jehu wrote and sent letters to Samaria, to the rulers of Jezreel, to the elders,
and to those who reared Ahab's *sons,* saying:

> [2] Now as soon as this letter comes to
> you, since your master's sons *are* with
> you, and you have chariots and horses,
> a fortified city also, and weapons,
> [3]choose the best qualified of your
> master's sons, set *him* on his father's
> throne, and fight for your master's
> house.

[4]But they were exceedingly afraid, and said,
"Look, two kings could not stand up to him;
how then can we stand?" [5]And he who *was* in
charge of the house, and he who *was* in
charge of the city, the elders also, and those
who reared *the sons,* sent to Jehu, saying, "We
are your servants, we will do all you tell us; but
we will not make anyone king. Do *what is*
good in your sight." [6]Then he wrote a second
letter to them, saying:

> If you *are* for me and will obey my
> voice, take the heads of the men, your
> master's sons, and come to me at
> Jezreel by this time tomorrow.

Now the king's sons, seventy persons, *were*
with the great men of the city, *who* were rear-
ing them. [7]So it was, when the letter came to
them, that they took the king's sons and
slaughtered seventy persons, put their heads
in baskets and sent *them* to him at Jezreel.
[8]Then a messenger came and told him, saying, "They have brought the heads of the
king's sons."
And he said, "Lay them in two heaps at the
entrance of the gate until morning."
[9]So it was, in the morning, that he went out
and stood, and said to all the people, "You *are*

righteous. Indeed I conspired against my master and killed him; but who killed all these?
10 Know now that nothing shall fall to the earth
of the word of the Lord which the Lord spoke
concerning the house of Ahab; for the Lord
has done what He spoke by His servant
Elijah." 11 So Jehu killed all who remained of
the house of Ahab in Jezreel, and all his great
men and his close acquaintances and his
priests, until he left him none remaining.

12 And he arose and departed and went to Sa-
maria. On the way, at Beth Eked of the
Shepherds, 13 Jehu met with the brothers of
Ahaziah king of Judah, and said, "Who *are* you?"

So they answered, "We *are* the brothers of
Ahaziah; we have come down to greet the
sons of the king and the sons of the queen
mother."

14 And he said, "Take them alive!" So they
took them alive, and killed them at the well of
Beth Eked, forty-two men; and he left none of
them.

15 Now when he departed from there, he met
Jehonadab the son of Rechab, *coming* to meet
him; and he greeted him and said to him, "Is
your heart right, as my heart *is* toward your
heart?"

And Jehonadab answered, "It is."

Jehu said, "If it is, give *me* your hand." So he
gave *him* his hand, and he took him up to him
into the chariot. 16 Then he said, "Come with
me, and see my zeal for the Lord." So they
had him ride in his chariot. 17 And when he
came to Samaria, he killed all who remained to
Ahab in Samaria, till he had destroyed them,
according to the word of the Lord which He
spoke to Elijah.

18 Then Jehu gathered all the people together, and said to them, "Ahab served Baal a little,
Jehu will serve him much. 19 Now therefore,
call to me all the prophets of Baal, all his servants, and all his priests. Let no one be missing,
for I have a great sacrifice for Baal. Whoever is
missing shall not live." But Jehu acted deceptively, with the intent of destroying the worshipers of Baal. 20 And Jehu said, "Proclaim a
solemn assembly for Baal." So they proclaimed
it. 21 Then Jehu sent throughout all Israel; and
all the worshipers of Baal came, so that there
was not a man left who did not come. So they
came into the temple of Baal, and the temple of
Baal was full from one end to the other. 22 And
he said to the one in charge of the wardrobe,
"Bring out vestments for all the worshipers of
Baal." So he brought out vestments for them.
23 Then Jehu and Jehonadab the son of Rechab
went into the temple of Baal, and said to the
worshipers of Baal, "Search and see that no
servants of the Lord are here with you, but
only the worshipers of Baal." 24 So they went in
to offer sacrifices and burnt offerings. Now
Jehu had appointed for himself eighty men on
the outside, and had said, "*If* any of the men
whom I have brought into your hands escapes,
whoever lets him escape, it shall be his life for
the life of the other."

25 Now it happened, as soon as he had made
an end of offering the burnt offering, that Jehu
said to the guard and to the captains, "Go in
and kill them; let no one come out!" And they
killed them with the edge of the sword; then
the guards and the officers threw *them* out,
and went into the inner room of the temple of
Baal. 26 And they brought the *sacred* pillars out
of the temple of Baal and burned them. 27 Then
they broke down the *sacred* pillar of Baal, and
tore down the temple of Baal and made it a
refuse dump to this day. 28 Thus Jehu destroyed Baal from Israel.

29 However Jehu did not turn away from the
sins of Jeroboam the son of Nebat, who had
made Israel sin, *that is,* from the golden calves
that *were* at Bethel and Dan. 30 And the Lord
said to Jehu, "Because you have done well in
doing *what is* right in My sight, *and* have done
to the house of Ahab all that *was* in My heart,
your sons shall sit on the throne of Israel to
the fourth *generation.*" 31 But Jehu took no
heed to walk in the law of the Lord God of Israel with all his heart; for he did not depart
from the sins of Jeroboam, who had made Israel sin.

32 In those days the Lord began to cut off *parts*
of Israel; and Hazael conquered them in all the
territory of Israel 33 from the Jordan eastward: all
the land of Gilead—Gad, Reuben, and Manasseh—from Aroer, which *is* by the River Arnon,
including Gilead and Bashan.

34 Now the rest of the acts of Jehu, all that he
did, and all his might, *are* they not written in
the book of the chronicles of the kings of Israel? 35 So Jehu rested with his fathers, and they
buried him in Samaria. Then Jehoahaz his son
reigned in his place. 36 And the period that Jehu
reigned over Israel in Samaria *was* twenty-
eight years.

Psalm 72:17–20

17 His name shall endure forever;
His name shall continue as long as
the sun.
And *men* shall be blessed in Him;
All nations shall call Him blessed.

18 Blessed *be* the Lord God, the God
of Israel,

Who only does wondrous things!
19 And blessed *be* His glorious name
forever!
And let the whole earth be filled *with*
His glory.
Amen and Amen.
20 The prayers of David the son of Jesse
are ended.

Proverbs 18:14–15

14 The spirit of a man will sustain him in
sickness,
But who can bear a broken spirit?
15 The heart of the prudent acquires
knowledge,
And the ear of the wise seeks
knowledge.

John 19:1–22

19 So then Pilate took Jesus and scourged
Him. [2]And the soldiers twisted a crown of
thorns and put *it* on His head, and they put on
Him a purple robe. [3]Then they said, "Hail,
King of the Jews!" And they struck Him with
their hands.
[4]Pilate then went out again, and said to
them, "Behold, I am bringing Him out to you,
that you may know that I find no fault in Him."
[5]Then Jesus came out, wearing the crown of
thorns and the purple robe. And *Pilate* said to
them, "Behold the Man!"
[6]Therefore, when the chief priests and officers saw Him, they cried out, saying, "Crucify
Him, crucify *Him!*"
Pilate said to them, "You take Him and crucify *Him,* for I find no fault in Him."
[7]The Jews answered him, "We have a law,
and according to our law He ought to die,
because He made Himself the Son of God."
[8]Therefore, when Pilate heard that saying,
he was the more afraid, [9]and went again into
the Praetorium, and said to Jesus, "Where are
You from?" But Jesus gave him no answer.
[10]Then Pilate said to Him, "Are You not
speaking to me? Do You not know that I have
power to crucify You, and power to release
You?"
[11]Jesus answered, "You could have no power
at all against Me unless it had been given you
from above. Therefore the one who delivered
Me to you has the greater sin."
[12]From then on Pilate sought to release
Him, but the Jews cried out, saying, "If you let
this Man go, you are not Caesar's friend.
Whoever makes himself a king speaks against
Caesar."

19:12 not Caesar's friend. This statement by the Jews was loaded with irony, for the Jews' hatred of Rome certainly indicated they too were no friends of Caesar. But they knew Pilate feared Tiberius Caesar (the Roman emperor at the time of Jesus' crucifixion) since he had a highly suspicious personality and exacted ruthless punishment. Pilate had already created upheaval in Palestine by several foolish acts that had infuriated the Jews, and so was under the scrutiny of Rome to see if his ineptness continued. The Jews were intimidating him by threatening another upheaval that could spell the end of his power in Palestine, if he did not execute Jesus.

[13]When Pilate therefore heard that saying,
he brought Jesus out and sat down in the judgment seat in a place that is called *The*
Pavement, but in Hebrew, Gabbatha. [14]Now it
was the Preparation Day of the Passover, and
about the sixth hour. And he said to the Jews,
"Behold your King!"
[15]But they cried out, "Away with *Him,* away
with *Him!* Crucify Him!"
Pilate said to them, "Shall I crucify your
King?"

19:18 crucified Him. Jesus was made to lie on the ground while His arms were stretched out and nailed to the horizontal beam that He carried. The beam was then hoisted up, along with the victim, and fastened to the vertical beam. His feet were nailed to the vertical beam to which sometimes was attached a piece of wood that served as a kind of seat that partially supported the weight of the body. The latter, however, was designed to prolong and increase the agony, not relieve it. Having been stripped naked and beaten, Jesus could hang in the hot sun for hours if not days. To breathe, it was necessary to push with the legs and pull with the arms, creating excruciating pain. Terrible muscle spasms wracked the entire body; but since collapse meant asphyxiation, the struggle for life continued. **two others.** Matthew (27:38) and Luke (23:33) use the same word for these two as John used for Barabbas, i.e., guerrilla fighters.

The chief priests answered, "We have no
king but Caesar!"
16Then he delivered Him to them to be crucified. Then they took Jesus and led *Him*
away.
17And He, bearing His cross, went out to a
place called *the Place* of a Skull, which is called
in Hebrew, Golgotha, 18where they crucified
Him, and two others with Him, one on either
side, and Jesus in the center. 19Now Pilate
wrote a title and put *it* on the cross. And the
writing was:

JESUS OF NAZARETH,
THE KING OF THE JEWS.

20Then many of the Jews read this title, for the
place where Jesus was crucified was near the
city; and it was written in Hebrew, Greek, *and*
Latin.
21Therefore the chief priests of the Jews said
to Pilate, "Do not write, 'The King of the Jews,'
but, 'He said, "I am the King of the Jews." ' "
22Pilate answered, "What I have written, I
have written."

DAY 11: Describe the abuse that Christ endured during the trial?

In John 19:1, it says that "Pilate took Jesus and scourged Him." Pilate appears to have flogged Jesus as a strategy to set Him free (vv. 4–6). He was hoping that the Jews would be appeased by this action and that sympathy for Jesus' suffering would result in their desire that He be released (Luke 23:13–16). Scourging was a horribly cruel act in which the victim was stripped, tied to a post and beaten by several torturers, i.e., soldiers who alternated when exhausted. For victims who were not Roman citizens, the preferred instrument was a short wooden handle to which several leather thongs were attached. Each leather thong had pieces of bones or metal on the end. The beatings were so savage that sometimes victims died. The body could be torn or lacerated to such an extent that muscles, veins, or bones were exposed. Such flogging often preceded execution in order to weaken and dehumanize the victim (Is. 53:5). Apparently, however, Pilate intended this to create sympathy for Jesus.

Then there was the "crown of thorns" (v. 2). This crown was made from the long spikes (up to 12 inches) of a date palm formed into an imitation of the radiating crowns which oriental kings wore. The long thorns would have cut deeply into Jesus' head, adding to the pain and bleeding. The use of the "purple robe" represented royalty. The robe probably was a military cloak flung around Jesus' shoulders, intended to mock His claim to be King of the Jews.

Pilate declared to the people, "I find no fault in Him" (v. 4), and when he brought Jesus out, he cried, "Behold the Man!" (v. 5). Pilate dramatically presented Jesus after His torturous treatment by the soldiers. Jesus would have been swollen, bruised, and bleeding. Pilate displayed Jesus as a beaten and pathetic figure, hoping to gain the people's choice of Jesus for release. Pilate's phrase is filled with sarcasm since he was attempting to impress upon the Jewish authorities that Jesus was not the dangerous man that they had made Him out to be.

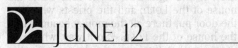

JUNE 12

2 Kings 11:1–13:25

11 When Athaliah the mother of Ahaziah saw
that her son was dead, she arose and
destroyed all the royal heirs. 2But Jehosheba,
the daughter of King Joram, sister of Ahaziah,
took Joash the son of Ahaziah, and stole him
away from among the king's sons *who were*
being murdered; and they hid him and his
nurse in the bedroom, from Athaliah, so that he
was not killed. 3So he was hidden with her in
the house of the LORD for six years, while
Athaliah reigned over the land.
4In the seventh year Jehoiada sent and
brought the captains of hundreds—of the
bodyguards and the escorts—and brought
them into the house of the LORD to him. And he
made a covenant with them and took an oath
from them in the house of the LORD, and
showed them the king's son. 5Then he commanded them, saying, "This *is* what you shall
do: One-third of you who come on duty on the
Sabbath shall be keeping watch over the
king's house, 6one-third *shall be* at the gate of
Sur, and one-third at the gate behind the
escorts. You shall keep the watch of the
house, lest it be broken down. 7The two con-
tingents of you who go off duty on the Sabbath
shall keep the watch of the house of the LORD
for the king. 8But you shall surround the king
on all sides, every man with his weapons in his
hand; and whoever comes within range, let
him be put to death. You are to be with the
king as he goes out and as he comes in."
9So the captains of the hundreds did according to all that Jehoiada the priest commanded.
Each of them took his men who were to be on
duty on the Sabbath, with those who were

going off duty on the Sabbath, and came to
Jehoiada the priest. 10And the priest gave the
captains of hundreds the spears and shields
which *had belonged* to King David, that were in
the temple of the LORD. 11Then the escorts
stood, every man with his weapons in his
hand, all around the king, from the right side
of the temple to the left side of the temple, by
the altar and the house. 12And he brought out
the king's son, put the crown on him, and *gave*
him the Testimony; they made him king and
anointed him, and they clapped their hands
and said, "Long live the king!"

13Now when Athaliah heard the noise of the
escorts *and* the people, she came to the people *in* the temple of the LORD. 14When she
looked, there was the king standing by a pillar
according to custom; and the leaders and the
trumpeters were by the king. All the people of
the land were rejoicing and blowing trumpets.
So Athaliah tore her clothes and cried out,
"Treason! Treason!"

15And Jehoiada the priest commanded the
captains of the hundreds, the officers of the
army, and said to them, "Take her outside under guard, and slay with the sword whoever
follows her." For the priest had said, "Do not
let her be killed in the house of the LORD." 16So
they seized her; and she went by way of the
horses' entrance *into* the king's house, and
there she was killed.

17Then Jehoiada made a covenant between
the LORD, the king, and the people, that they
should be the LORD's people, and *also* between
the king and the people. 18And all the people of

11:17 a covenant. The renewal of the agreement between the people and the Lord and between the house of David and the people was appropriate because of the disruption under Athaliah. A similar ceremony was held later, during the reign of Josiah (23:1–3).

the land went to the temple of Baal, and tore it
down. They thoroughly broke in pieces its
altars and images, and killed Mattan the priest
of Baal before the altars. And the priest
appointed officers over the house of the LORD.
19Then he took the captains of hundreds, the
bodyguards, the escorts, and all the people of
the land; and they brought the king down
from the house of the LORD, and went by way
of the gate of the escorts to the king's house.
Then he sat on the throne of the kings. 20So all
the people of the land rejoiced; and the city
was quiet, for they had slain Athaliah with the
sword *in* the king's house. 21Jehoash *was*
seven years old when he became king.

12 In the seventh year of Jehu, Jehoash
became king, and he reigned forty years
in Jerusalem. His mother's name *was* Zibiah of
Beersheba. 2Jehoash did *what was* right in the
sight of the LORD all the days in which
Jehoiada the priest instructed him. 3But the
high places were not taken away; the people
still sacrificed and burned incense on the high
places.

4And Jehoash said to the priests, "All the
money of the dedicated gifts that are brought
into the house of the LORD—each man's census
money, each man's assessment money—*and* all
the money that a man purposes in his heart to
bring into the house of the LORD, 5let the priests
take *it* themselves, each from his constituency;
and let them repair the damages of the temple,
wherever any dilapidation is found."

6Now it was so, by the twenty-third year of
King Jehoash, *that* the priests had not
repaired the damages of the temple. 7So King
Jehoash called Jehoiada the priest and the
other priests, and said to them, "Why have you
not repaired the damages of the temple? Now
therefore, do not take *more* money from your
constituency, but deliver it for repairing the
damages of the temple." 8And the priests
agreed that they would neither receive *more*
money from the people, nor repair the damages of the temple.

9Then Jehoiada the priest took a chest,
bored a hole in its lid, and set it beside the
altar, on the right side as one comes into the
house of the LORD; and the priests who kept
the door put there all the money brought into
the house of the LORD. 10So it was, whenever
they saw that *there was* much money in the
chest, that the king's scribe and the high
priest came up and put it in bags, and counted
the money that was found in the house of the
LORD. 11Then they gave the money, which had
been apportioned, into the hands of those who
did the work, who had the oversight of the
house of the LORD; and they paid it out to the carpenters and builders who worked on the
house of the LORD, 12and to masons and
stonecutters, and for buying timber and hewn
stone, to repair the damage of the house of the
LORD, and for all that was paid out to repair the
temple. 13However there were not made for
the house of the LORD basins of silver, trimmers, sprinkling-bowls, trumpets, any articles
of gold or articles of silver, from the money
brought into the house of the LORD. 14But they

gave that to the workmen, and they repaired
the house of the LORD with it. 15 Moreover they
did not require an account from the men into
whose hand they delivered the money to be
paid to workmen, for they dealt faithfully. 16 The
money from the trespass offerings and the
money from the sin offerings was not brought
into the house of the LORD. It belonged to the
priests.

17 Hazael king of Syria went up and fought
against Gath, and took it; then Hazael set his
face to go up to Jerusalem. 18 And Jehoash king
of Judah took all the sacred things that his
fathers, Jehoshaphat and Jehoram and Ahaziah,
kings of Judah, had dedicated, and his own
sacred things, and all the gold found in the
treasuries of the house of the LORD and in the
king's house, and sent *them* to Hazael king of
Syria. Then he went away from Jerusalem.

19 Now the rest of the acts of Joash, and all
that he did, *are* they not written in the book of
the chronicles of the kings of Judah?

20 And his servants arose and formed a conspiracy, and killed Joash in the house of the
Millo, which goes down to Silla. 21 For Jozachar
the son of Shimeath and Jehozabad the son of
Shomer, his servants, struck him. So he died,
and they buried him with his fathers in the
City of David. Then Amaziah his son reigned
in his place.

13 In the twenty-third year of Joash the son
of Ahaziah, king of Judah, Jehoahaz the
son of Jehu became king over Israel in Samaria,
and reigned seventeen years. 2 And he did evil in
the sight of the LORD, and followed the sins of
Jeroboam the son of Nebat, who had made Israel sin. He did not depart from them.

3 Then the anger of the LORD was aroused
against Israel, and He delivered them into the
hand of Hazael king of Syria, and into the hand
of Ben-Hadad the son of Hazael, all *their* days.
4 So Jehoahaz pleaded with the LORD, and the
LORD listened to him; for He saw the oppression of Israel, because the king of Syria
oppressed them. 5 Then the LORD gave Israel a
deliverer, so that they escaped from under the
hand of the Syrians; and the children of Israel
dwelt in their tents as before. 6 Nevertheless
they did not depart from the sins of the house
of Jeroboam, who had made Israel sin, *but*
walked in them; and the wooden image also
remained in Samaria. 7 For He left of the army
of Jehoahaz only fifty horsemen, ten chariots,
and ten thousand foot soldiers; for the king of
Syria had destroyed them and made them like
the dust at threshing.

8 Now the rest of the acts of Jehoahaz, all
that he did, and his might, *are* they not written
in the book of the chronicles of the kings of Israel? 9 So Jehoahaz rested with his fathers, and
they buried him in Samaria. Then Joash his
son reigned in his place.

10 In the thirty-seventh year of Joash king of
Judah, Jehoash the son of Jehoahaz became
king over Israel in Samaria, *and reigned* sixteen years. 11 And he did evil in the sight of the
LORD. He did not depart from all the sins of
Jeroboam the son of Nebat, who made Israel
sin, *but* walked in them.

12 Now the rest of the acts of Joash, all that
he did, and his might with which he fought
against Amaziah king of Judah, *are* they not
written in the book of the chronicles of the
kings of Israel? 13 So Joash rested with his
fathers. Then Jeroboam sat on his throne. And
Joash was buried in Samaria with the kings of
Israel.

14 Elisha had become sick with the illness of
which he would die. Then Joash the king of Israel came down to him, and wept over his face,
and said, "O my father, my father, the chariots
of Israel and their horsemen!"

15 And Elisha said to him, "Take a bow and
some arrows." So he took himself a bow and
some arrows. 16 Then he said to the king of Israel, "Put your hand on the bow." So he put his
hand *on it,* and Elisha put his hands on the
king's hands. 17 And he said, "Open the east
window"; and he opened *it.* Then Elisha said,
"Shoot"; and he shot. And he said, "The arrow
of the LORD's deliverance and the arrow of
deliverance from Syria; for you must strike the
Syrians at Aphek till you have destroyed
them." 18 Then he said, "Take the arrows"; so
he took *them.* And he said to the king of Israel,
"Strike the ground"; so he struck three times,
and stopped. 19 And the man of God was angry
with him, and said, "You should have struck
five or six times; then you would have struck
Syria till you had destroyed *it!* But now you will
strike Syria *only* three times."

20 Then Elisha died, and they buried him.
And the *raiding* bands from Moab invaded the
land in the spring of the year. 21 So it was, as
they were burying a man, that suddenly they
spied a band *of raiders;* and they put the man
in the tomb of Elisha; and when the man was
let down and touched the bones of Elisha, he
revived and stood on his feet.

22 And Hazael king of Syria oppressed Israel
all the days of Jehoahaz. 23 But the LORD was
gracious to them, had compassion on them,
and regarded them, because of His covenant
with Abraham, Isaac, and Jacob, and would
not yet destroy them or cast them from His
presence.

13:21 he revived. A dead man returned to life after touching Elisha's bones. This miracle was a sign that God's power continued to work in relationship to Elisha even after his death. What God had promised to Jehoash through Elisha when he was alive would surely come to pass after the prophet's death (vv. 19,25) in the defeat of the enemy, the recovery of the cities that had been taken, and their restoration to the kingdom of Israel (vv. 22–25).

[24]Now Hazael king of Syria died. Then Ben-Hadad his son reigned in his place. [25]And Jehoash the son of Jehoahaz recaptured from the hand of Ben-Hadad, the son of Hazael, the cities which he had taken out of the hand of Jehoahaz his father by war. Three times Joash defeated him and recaptured the cities of Israel.

Psalm 73:1–9

A Psalm of Asaph.

Truly God *is* good to Israel,
To such as are pure in heart.
2 But as for me, my feet had almost stumbled;
My steps had nearly slipped.
3 For I *was* envious of the boastful,
When I saw the prosperity of the wicked.

4 For *there are* no pangs in their death,
But their strength *is* firm.
5 They *are* not in trouble *as other* men,
Nor are they plagued like *other* men.
6 Therefore pride serves as their necklace;
Violence covers them *like* a garment.
7 Their eyes bulge with abundance;
They have more than heart could wish.
8 They scoff and speak wickedly *concerning* oppression;
They speak loftily.
9 They set their mouth against the heavens,
And their tongue walks through the earth.

Proverbs 18:16–17

16 A man's gift makes room for him,
And brings him before great men.
17 The first *one* to plead his cause *seems* right,
Until his neighbor comes and examines him.

18:16 man's gift. This is not the word for a bribe (17:23), but rather the word for a present given to someone (Jacob's gift, Gen. 32:20,21; Joseph's gift, Gen. 43:11; David's gift, 1 Sam. 17:17,18; and Abigail's gift, 1 Sam. 25:27).

John 19:23–42

[23]Then the soldiers, when they had crucified Jesus, took His garments and made four parts, to each soldier a part, and also the tunic. Now the tunic was without seam, woven from the top in one piece. [24]They said therefore among themselves, "Let us not tear it, but cast lots for it, whose it shall be," that the Scripture might be fulfilled which says:

"They divided My garments among them,
And for My clothing they cast lots."

Therefore the soldiers did these things.

19:23 His garments...and also the tunic. By custom, the clothes of the condemned person were the property of the executioners. The division of the garments suggests that the execution squad was made up of 4 soldiers (Acts 12:4). The tunic was worn next to the skin. The plural garments probably refers to other clothes, including an outer garment, belt, sandals, and head covering.

19:24 John cites Psalm 22:18. In the psalm, David, beset by physical distress and mockery by his opponents, used the symbolism of the common practice in an execution scene in which the executioner divided the victim's clothes to portray the depth of his trouble. It is notable that David precisely described a form of execution that he had never seen. The passage was typologically prophetic of Jesus, David's heir to the messianic throne (Matt. 27:46; Mark 15:34).

[25]Now there stood by the cross of Jesus His mother, and His mother's sister, Mary the *wife* of Clopas, and Mary Magdalene. [26]When Jesus therefore saw His mother, and the disciple whom He loved standing by, He said to His mother, "Woman, behold your son!" [27]Then He said to the disciple, "Behold your mother!" And from that hour that disciple took her to his own *home*.

28After this, Jesus, knowing that all things were now accomplished, that the Scripture might be fulfilled, said, "I thirst!" 29Now a vessel full of sour wine was sitting there; and they filled a sponge with sour wine, put *it* on hyssop, and put *it* to His mouth. 30So when Jesus had received the sour wine, He said, "It is finished!" And bowing His head, He gave up His spirit.

31Therefore, because it was the Preparation *Day,* that the bodies should not remain on the cross on the Sabbath (for that Sabbath was a high day), the Jews asked Pilate that their legs might be broken, and *that* they might be taken away. 32Then the soldiers came and broke the legs of the first and of the other who was crucified with Him. 33But when they came to Jesus and saw that He was already dead, they did not break His legs. 34But one of the soldiers pierced His side with a spear, and immediately blood and water came out. 35And he who has seen has testified, and his testimony is true; and he knows that he is telling the truth, so that you may believe. 36For these things were done that the Scripture should be fulfilled, *"Not one of His bones shall be broken."* 37And again another Scripture says, *"They shall look on Him whom they pierced."*

38After this, Joseph of Arimathea, being a disciple of Jesus, but secretly, for fear of the Jews, asked Pilate that he might take away the body of Jesus; and Pilate gave *him* permission. So he came and took the body of Jesus. 39And Nicodemus, who at first came to Jesus by night, also came, bringing a mixture of myrrh and aloes, about a hundred pounds. 40Then they took the body of Jesus, and bound it in strips of linen with the spices, as the custom of the Jews is to bury. 41Now in the place where He was crucified there was a garden, and in the garden a new tomb in which no one had yet been laid. 42So there they laid Jesus, because of the Jews' Preparation *Day,* for the tomb was nearby.

DAY 12: Was there any question as to whether Jesus died or not?

In His death on the cross, Jesus finally cried out, "It is finished!" (John 19:30). The verb here carries the idea of fulfilling one's task and, in religious contexts, has the idea of fulfilling one's religious obligations. The entire work of redemption had been brought to completion. The single Greek word here (translated "it is finished") has been found in the papyri being placed on receipts for taxes meaning paid in full (Col. 3:13,14). "He gave up His spirit." The sentence signaled that Jesus handed over His spirit as an act of His will. No one took His life from Him, for He voluntarily and willingly gave it up (10:17,18).

It was "Preparation Day" (v. 31). This refers to Friday, the day before or the preparation day for the Sabbath. "Bodies should not remain on the cross on the Sabbath." The normal Roman practice was to leave crucified men and women on the cross until they died (and this could take days) and then leave their rotting bodies hanging there to be devoured by vultures. The Mosaic Law insisted that anyone being impaled (usually after execution) should not remain there overnight (Deut. 21:22,23). Such a person was under God's curse, and to leave him exposed would be to desecrate the land in their minds. So "the Jews asked Pilate that their legs might be broken." In order to hasten death for certain reasons, soldiers would smash the legs of the victim with an iron mallet. Not only did this action induce shock and additional loss of blood, but it prevented the victim from pushing with his legs to keep breathing, and thus the victim died due to asphyxiation.

However, the soldier's stabbing of Jesus' side caused significant penetration because of the sudden flow of blood and water (v. 34). Either the spear pierced Jesus' heart or the chest cavity was pierced at the bottom. In either event, John mentioned the outflow of blood and water to emphasize that Jesus was unquestionably dead.

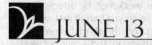

JUNE 13

2 Kings 14:1–29

14 In the second year of Joash the son of Jehoahaz, king of Israel, Amaziah the son of Joash, king of Judah, became king. 2He was twenty-five years old when he became king, and he reigned twenty-nine years in Jerusalem. His mother's name was Jehoaddan of Jerusalem. 3And he did *what was* right in the sight of the LORD, yet not like his father David; he did everything as his father Joash had done. 4However the high places were not taken away, and the people still sacrificed and burned incense on the high places.

5Now it happened, as soon as the kingdom was established in his hand, that he executed his servants who had murdered his father the king. 6But the children of the murderers he

14:1–15:38 This section quickly surveys the kings and selected events of the northern and southern kingdoms from 796 to 735 B.C. In contrast to the previous 19 chapters (1 Kin. 17:1–2 Kin. 13:25), which narrated 90 years of history (885–796 B.C.) with a concentration on the ministries of Elijah and Elisha during the final 65 years of that period (860–796 B.C.), 62 years are covered in these two chapters. The previous section concluded with a shadow of hope: officially sanctioned Baal worship had been eradicated in both Israel (10:18–28) and Judah (11:17,18); the temple of the Lord in Jerusalem had been repaired (12:9–15); and the Syrian threat to Israel had been overcome (13:25). However, this section emphasizes that the fundamental problems still remained: the false religion established by Jeroboam I continued in Israel even with the change of royal families (14:24–15:9,18,24,28), and the high places were not removed in Judah even though there were only good kings there during those years (14:4; 15:4,35).

did not execute, according to what is written in
the Book of the Law of Moses, in which the
LORD commanded, saying, "Fathers shall not
be put to death for their children, nor shall
children be put to death for their fathers; but a
person shall be put to death for his own sin."
[7]He killed ten thousand Edomites in the
Valley of Salt, and took Sela by war, and called
its name Joktheel to this day.
[8]Then Amaziah sent messengers to Jehoash
the son of Jehoahaz, the son of Jehu, king of
Israel, saying, "Come, let us face one another
in battle." [9]And Jehoash king of Israel sent to
Amaziah king of Judah, saying, "The thistle
that *was* in Lebanon sent to the cedar that *was*
in Lebanon, saying, 'Give your daughter to my
son as wife'; and a wild beast that *was* in Lebanon passed by and trampled the thistle. [10]You
have indeed defeated Edom, and your heart
has lifted you up. Glory *in that,* and stay at
home; for why should you meddle with trouble so that you fall—you and Judah with you?"
[11]But Amaziah would not heed. Therefore
Jehoash king of Israel went out; so he and
Amaziah king of Judah faced one another at
Beth Shemesh, which *belongs* to Judah. [12]And
Judah was defeated by Israel, and every man
fled to his tent. [13]Then Jehoash king of Israel
captured Amaziah king of Judah, the son of
Jehoash, the son of Ahaziah, at Beth Shemesh;
and he went to Jerusalem, and broke down the
wall of Jerusalem from the Gate of Ephraim to
the Corner Gate—four hundred cubits. [14]And
he took all the gold and silver, all the articles
that were found in the house of the LORD and
in the treasuries of the king's house, and
hostages, and returned to Samaria.
[15]Now the rest of the acts of Jehoash which
he did—his might, and how he fought with
Amaziah king of Judah—*are* they not written
in the book of the chronicles of the kings of Israel? [16]So Jehoash rested with his fathers, and
was buried in Samaria with the kings of Israel.
Then Jeroboam his son reigned in his place.
[17]Amaziah the son of Joash, king of Judah,
lived fifteen years after the death of Jehoash
the son of Jehoahaz, king of Israel. [18]Now the
rest of the acts of Amaziah, *are* they not written in the book of the chronicles of the kings of
Judah? [19]And they formed a conspiracy against
him in Jerusalem, and he fled to Lachish; but
they sent after him to Lachish and killed him
there. [20]Then they brought him on horses, and
he was buried at Jerusalem with his fathers in
the City of David.
[21]And all the people of Judah took Azariah,
who *was* sixteen years old, and made him king
instead of his father Amaziah. [22]He built Elath
and restored it to Judah, after the king rested
with his fathers.

14:25 restored the territory of Israel. Jeroboam II's greatest accomplishment was the restoration of Israel's boundaries to approximately their extent in Solomon's time, excluding the territory belonging to Judah. The northern boundary was the entrance of Hamath, the same as Solomon's (1 Kin. 8:65) and the southern boundary was the Sea of the Arabah, the Dead Sea (Josh. 3:16; 12:3). Jeroboam II took Hamath, a major city located on the Orontes River, about 160 miles north of the Sea of Galilee. He also controlled Damascus, indicating that the Transjordan territory south to Moab was also under his authority. These victories of Jeroboam II were accomplished because the Syrians had been weakened by attacks from the Assyrians, while Assyria herself was weak at this time, suffering from threats on her northern border, internal dissension, and a series of weak kings. **Jonah.** The territorial extension of Jeroboam II was in accordance with the will of the Lord as revealed through the prophet Jonah. This was the same Jonah who traveled to Nineveh with God's message of repentance for the Assyrians.

23 In the fifteenth year of Amaziah the son of
Joash, king of Judah, Jeroboam the son of
Joash, king of Israel, became king in Samaria,
and reigned forty-one years. 24 And he did evil in
the sight of the LORD; he did not depart from
all the sins of Jeroboam the son of Nebat, who
had made Israel sin. 25 He restored the territory
of Israel from the entrance of Hamath to the
Sea of the Arabah, according to the word of the
LORD God of Israel, which He had spoken
through His servant Jonah the son of Amittai,
the prophet who *was* from Gath Hepher. 26 For
the LORD saw *that* the affliction of Israel *was*
very bitter; and whether bond or free, there
was no helper for Israel. 27 And the LORD did not
say that He would blot out the name of Israel
from under heaven; but He saved them by the
hand of Jeroboam the son of Joash.
28 Now the rest of the acts of Jeroboam, and
all that he did—his might, how he made war,
and how he recaptured for Israel, from Damascus and Hamath, *what had belonged* to Judah—*are* they not written in the book of the chronicles of the kings of Israel? 29 So Jeroboam rested with his fathers, the kings of Israel. Then
Zechariah his son reigned in his place.

Psalm 73:10–20

10 Therefore his people return here,
And waters of a full *cup* are drained by them.
11 And they say, "How does God know?
And is there knowledge in the Most High?"
12 Behold, these *are* the ungodly,
Who are always at ease;
They increase *in* riches.
13 Surely I have cleansed my heart *in* vain,
And washed my hands in innocence.
14 For all day long I have been plagued,
And chastened every morning.

15 If I had said, "I will speak thus,"
Behold, I would have been untrue to the generation of Your children.
16 When I thought *how* to understand this,
It *was* too painful for me—
17 Until I went into the sanctuary of God;
Then I understood their end.

18 Surely You set them in slippery places;
You cast them down to destruction.
19 Oh, how they are *brought* to desolation, as in a moment!
They are utterly consumed with terrors.
20 As a dream when *one* awakes,
So, Lord, when You awake,
You shall despise their image.

Proverbs 18:18–19

18 Casting lots causes contentions to cease,
And keeps the mighty apart.

19 A brother offended *is harder to win* than a strong city,
And contentions *are* like the bars of a castle.

18:19 There are no feuds as difficult to resolve as those with relatives; no barriers are so hard to bring down. Hence, great care should be taken to avoid such conflicts.

John 20:1–31

20 Now the first *day* of the week Mary
Magdalene went to the tomb early,
while it was still dark, and saw *that* the stone
had been taken away from the tomb. 2 Then
she ran and came to Simon Peter, and to the
other disciple, whom Jesus loved, and said to
them, "They have taken away the Lord out of
the tomb, and we do not know where they
have laid Him."
3 Peter therefore went out, and the other disciple, and were going to the tomb. 4 So they both
ran together, and the other disciple outran Peter and came to the tomb first. 5 And he, stooping down and looking in, saw the linen cloths
lying *there;* yet he did not go in. 6 Then Simon
Peter came, following him, and went into the
tomb; and he saw the linen cloths lying *there,*
7 and the handkerchief that had been around
His head, not lying with the linen cloths, but
folded together in a place by itself. 8 Then the
other disciple, who came to the tomb first, went
in also; and he saw and believed. 9 For as yet
they did not know the Scripture, that He must
rise again from the dead. 10 Then the disciples
went away again to their own homes.
11 But Mary stood outside by the tomb weeping, and as she wept she stooped down *and*
looked into the tomb. 12 And she saw two angels
in white sitting, one at the head and the other
at the feet, where the body of Jesus had lain.
13 Then they said to her, "Woman, why are you
weeping?"
She said to them, "Because they have taken away my Lord, and I do not know where they have laid Him."

20:9 did not know the Scripture. Neither Peter nor John understood that Scripture said Jesus would rise (Ps. 16:10). This is evident by the reports of Luke (24:25–27,32,44–47). Jesus had foretold His resurrection (2:19; Matt. 16:21; Mark 8:31; 9:31; Luke 9:22), but they would not accept it (Matt. 16:22; Luke 9:44,45). By the time John wrote this Gospel, the church had developed an understanding of the Old Testament prediction of Messiah's resurrection.

[14]Now when she had said this, she turned
around and saw Jesus standing *there,* and did
not know that it was Jesus. [15]Jesus said to her,
"Woman, why are you weeping? Whom are
you seeking?"

She, supposing Him to be the gardener, said to Him, "Sir, if You have carried Him away, tell me where You have laid Him, and I will take Him away."

[16]Jesus said to her, "Mary!"

She turned and said to Him, "Rabboni!" (which is to say, Teacher).

[17]Jesus said to her, "Do not cling to Me, for I have not yet ascended to My Father; but go to My brethren and say to them, 'I am ascending to My Father and your Father, and *to* My God and your God.' "

[18]Mary Magdalene came and told the disciples that she had seen the Lord, and *that* He had spoken these things to her.

[19]Then, the same day at evening, being the first *day* of the week, when the doors were shut where the disciples were assembled, for fear of the Jews, Jesus came and stood in the midst, and said to them, "Peace *be* with you."
[20]When He had said this, He showed them *His*
hands and His side. Then the disciples were glad when they saw the Lord.

[21]So Jesus said to them again, "Peace to you! As the Father has sent Me, I also send you."
[22]And when He had said this, He breathed on
them, and said to them, "Receive the Holy
Spirit. [23]If you forgive the sins of any, they are
forgiven them; if you retain the *sins* of any, they are retained."

[24]Now Thomas, called the Twin, one of the twelve, was not with them when Jesus came.
[25]The other disciples therefore said to him,
"We have seen the Lord."

So he said to them, "Unless I see in His hands the print of the nails, and put my finger into the print of the nails, and put my hand into His side, I will not believe."

[26]And after eight days His disciples were
again inside, and Thomas with them. Jesus
came, the doors being shut, and stood in the
midst, and said, "Peace to you!" [27]Then He said
to Thomas, "Reach your finger here, and look at My hands; and reach your hand *here,* and put *it* into My side. Do not be unbelieving, but believing."

[28]And Thomas answered and said to Him, "My Lord and my God!"

[29]Jesus said to him, "Thomas, because you have seen Me, you have believed. Blessed *are* those who have not seen and *yet* have believed."

[30]And truly Jesus did many other signs in
the presence of His disciples, which are not
written in this book; [31]but these are written
that you may believe that Jesus is the Christ, the Son of God, and that believing you may have life in His name.

DAY 13: Describe the resurrection appearances of Jesus to His followers.

John 20 records the appearances of Jesus to His own followers: 1) the appearance to Mary Magdalene (vv. 1–18); 2) the appearance to the 10 disciples (vv. 19–23); and 3) the appearance to Thomas (vv. 24–29). Jesus did not appear to unbelievers (see 14:19; 16:16,22) because the evidence of His resurrection would not have convinced them as the miracles had not (Luke 16:31). The god of this world had blinded them and prevented their belief (2 Cor. 4:4). Jesus, therefore, appears exclusively to His own in order to confirm their faith in the living Christ. Such appearances were so profound that they transformed the disciples from cowardly men hiding in fear to bold witnesses for Jesus (e.g., Peter; see 18:27; Acts 2:14–39). Once again John's purpose in recording these resurrection appearances was to demonstrate that Jesus' physical and bodily resurrection was the crowning proof that He truly is the Messiah and Son of God who laid down His life for His own (10:17,18; 15:13; Rom. 1:4).

In particular, His appearance to Thomas, who has already been portrayed as loyal but pessimistic, is insightful (vv. 24–26). Jesus did not rebuke Thomas for his failure, but instead compassionately offered him proof of His resurrection. Jesus lovingly met him at the point of his weakness (2 Tim. 2:13). Thomas's actions indicated that Jesus had to convince the disciples rather forcefully of His resurrection, i.e., they were not gullible people predisposed to believing in resurrection. The point is they would not have fabricated it or hallucinated it, since they were so reluctant to believe even with the evidence they could see.

With the words "My Lord and my God!" (v. 28), Thomas declared his firm belief in the resurrection and, therefore, the deity of Jesus the Messiah and Son of God (Titus 2:13). This is the greatest confession a person can make. Thomas's confession functions as the fitting capstone of John's purpose in writing (vv. 30,31).

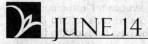

JUNE 14

2 Kings 15:1–16:20

15 In the twenty-seventh year of Jeroboam
king of Israel, Azariah the son of
Amaziah, king of Judah, became king. 2 He was
sixteen years old when he became king, and
he reigned fifty-two years in Jerusalem. His
mother's name *was* Jecholiah of Jerusalem.
3 And he did *what was* right in the sight of the
LORD, according to all that his father Amaziah
had done, 4 except that the high places were not
removed; the people still sacrificed and burned
incense on the high places. 5 Then the LORD
struck the king, so that he was a leper until the
day of his death; so he dwelt in an isolated
house. And Jotham the king's son *was* over the
royal house, judging the people of the land.
6 Now the rest of the acts of Azariah, and all
that he did, *are* they not written in the book of
the chronicles of the kings of Judah? 7 So
Azariah rested with his fathers, and they
buried him with his fathers in the City of David. Then Jotham his son reigned in his place.
8 In the thirty-eighth year of Azariah king of
Judah, Zechariah the son of Jeroboam reigned
over Israel in Samaria six months. 9 And he did
evil in the sight of the LORD, as his fathers had
done; he did not depart from the sins of
Jeroboam the son of Nebat, who had made Israel sin. 10 Then Shallum the son of Jabesh conspired against him, and struck and killed him
in front of the people; and he reigned in his
place.
11 Now the rest of the acts of Zechariah,
indeed they *are* written in the book of the
chronicles of the kings of Israel.
12 This *was* the word of the LORD which He
spoke to Jehu, saying, "Your sons shall sit on
the throne of Israel to the fourth *generation.*"
And so it was.
13 Shallum the son of Jabesh became king in
the thirty-ninth year of Uzziah king of Judah;
and he reigned a full month in Samaria. 14 For
Menahem the son of Gadi went up from
Tirzah, came to Samaria, and struck Shallum
the son of Jabesh in Samaria and killed him;
and he reigned in his place.
15 Now the rest of the acts of Shallum, and
the conspiracy which he led, indeed they *are*
written in the book of the chronicles of the
kings of Israel. 16 Then from Tirzah, Menahem
attacked Tiphsah, all who *were* there, and its
territory. Because they did not surrender,
therefore he attacked *it.* All the women there
who were with child he ripped open.
17 In the thirty-ninth year of Azariah king of
Judah, Menahem the son of Gadi became king
over Israel, *and reigned* ten years in Samaria.
18 And he did evil in the sight of the LORD; he
did not depart all his days from the sins of
Jeroboam the son of Nebat, who had made Israel sin. 19 Pul king of Assyria came against the
land; and Menahem gave Pul a thousand talents of silver, that his hand might be with him
to strengthen the kingdom under his control.
20 And Menahem exacted the money from Israel, from all the very wealthy, from each man
fifty shekels of silver, to give to the king of Assyria. So the king of Assyria turned back, and
did not stay there in the land.
21 Now the rest of the acts of Menahem, and
all that he did, *are* they not written in the book
of the chronicles of the kings of Israel? 22 So
Menahem rested with his fathers. Then Pekahiah his son reigned in his place.
23 In the fiftieth year of Azariah king of Judah,
Pekahiah the son of Menahem became king
over Israel in Samaria, *and reigned* two years.
24 And he did evil in the sight of the LORD; he
did not depart from the sins of Jeroboam the
son of Nebat, who had made Israel sin. 25 Then
Pekah the son of Remaliah, an officer of his,
conspired against him and killed him in Samaria, in the citadel of the king's house, along
with Argob and Arieh; and with him were fifty
men of Gilead. He killed him and reigned in
his place.
26 Now the rest of the acts of Pekahiah, and
all that he did, indeed they *are* written in the
book of the chronicles of the kings of Israel.
27 In the fifty-second year of Azariah king of
Judah, Pekah the son of Remaliah became

king over Israel in Samaria, *and reigned* twenty years. 28And he did evil in the sight of the
LORD; he did not depart from the sins of
Jeroboam the son of Nebat, who had made Israel sin. 29In the days of Pekah king of Israel,
Tiglath-Pileser king of Assyria came and took
Ijon, Abel Beth Maachah, Janoah, Kedesh,
Hazor, Gilead, and Galilee, all the land of
Naphtali; and he carried them captive to Assyria. 30Then Hoshea the son of Elah led a conspiracy against Pekah the son of Remaliah,
and struck and killed him; so he reigned in his
place in the twentieth year of Jotham the son
of Uzziah.
31Now the rest of the acts of Pekah, and all
that he did, indeed they *are* written in the
book of the chronicles of the kings of Israel.
32In the second year of Pekah the son of
Remaliah, king of Israel, Jotham the son of
Uzziah, king of Judah, began to reign. 33He
was twenty-five years old when he became
king, and he reigned sixteen years in Jerusalem. His mother's name *was* Jerusha the
daughter of Zadok. 34And he did *what was*
right in the sight of the LORD; he did according
to all that his father Uzziah had done. 35How-
ever the high places were not removed; the
people still sacrificed and burned incense on
the high places. He built the Upper Gate of the
house of the LORD.
36Now the rest of the acts of Jotham, and all
that he did, *are* they not written in the book of
the chronicles of the kings of Judah? 37In those
days the LORD began to send Rezin king of
Syria and Pekah the son of Remaliah against
Judah. 38So Jotham rested with his fathers, and
was buried with his fathers in the City of David his father. Then Ahaz his son reigned in
his place.
16 In the seventeenth year of Pekah the son
of Remaliah, Ahaz the son of Jotham,
king of Judah, began to reign. 2Ahaz *was* twenty years old when he became king, and he
reigned sixteen years in Jerusalem; and he did
not do *what was* right in the sight of the LORD
his God, as his father David *had done.* 3But he
walked in the way of the kings of Israel; indeed
he made his son pass through the fire, according to the abominations of the nations whom
the LORD had cast out from before the children
of Israel. 4And he sacrificed and burned incense
on the high places, on the hills, and under
every green tree.
5Then Rezin king of Syria and Pekah the son
of Remaliah, king of Israel, came up to Jerusalem to *make* war; and they besieged Ahaz but
could not overcome *him.* 6At that time Rezin
king of Syria captured Elath for Syria, and

16:3 walked in the way of the kings of Israel. This does not necessarily mean that Ahaz participated in the calf worship introduced by Jeroboam I at Bethel and Dan, but that he increasingly brought pagan, idolatrous practices into the worship of the Lord in Jerusalem. These are specified in vv. 10–16 and parallel those of Jeroboam I in the northern kingdom. This included idols to Baal (2 Chr. 28:2). **made his son pass through the fire.** As a part of the ritual worship of Molech, the god of the Moabites, children were sacrificed by fire (3:27). This horrific practice was continually condemned in the Old Testament (Lev. 18:21; 20:2–5; Deut. 18:10; Jer. 7:31; 19:5; 32:35).

drove the men of Judah from Elath. Then the
Edomites went to Elath, and dwell there to
this day.
7So Ahaz sent messengers to Tiglath-Pileser
king of Assyria, saying, "I *am* your servant
and your son. Come up and save me from the
hand of the king of Syria and from the hand of
the king of Israel, who rise up against me."
8And Ahaz took the silver and gold that was
found in the house of the LORD, and in the
treasuries of the king's house, and sent *it as* a
present to the king of Assyria. 9So the king of
Assyria heeded him; for the king of Assyria
went up against Damascus and took it, carried
its people captive to Kir, and killed Rezin.
10Now King Ahaz went to Damascus to meet
Tiglath-Pileser king of Assyria, and saw an
altar that *was* at Damascus; and King Ahaz
sent to Urijah the priest the design of the altar
and its pattern, according to all its workmanship. 11Then Urijah the priest built an altar

16:10 the altar. When Ahaz traveled to Damascus to meet Tiglath-Pileser III, he saw a large altar (v. 15) which was most likely Assyrian. Ahaz sent a sketch of this altar to Urijah the high priest in Jerusalem, and Urijah built an altar just like it. The serious iniquity in this was meddling with and changing, according to personal taste, the furnishings of the temple, the design for which had been given by God (Ex. 25:40; 26:30; 27:1–8; 1 Chr. 28:19). This was like building an idol in the temple, done to please the pagan Assyrian king, whom Ahaz served instead of God.

according to all that King Ahaz had sent from
Damascus. So Urijah the priest made *it* before
King Ahaz came back from Damascus. 12And
when the king came back from Damascus, the
king saw the altar; and the king approached
the altar and made offerings on it. 13So he
burned his burnt offering and his grain offering; and he poured his drink offering and sprinkled the blood of his peace offerings on the
altar. 14He also brought the bronze altar which
was before the LORD, from the front of the temple—from between the *new* altar and the
house of the LORD—and put it on the north
side of the *new* altar. 15Then King Ahaz commanded Urijah the priest, saying, "On the
great *new* altar burn the morning burnt offering, the evening grain offering, the king's
burnt sacrifice, and his grain offering, with the
burnt offering of all the people of the land,
their grain offering, and their drink offerings;
and sprinkle on it all the blood of the burnt
offering and all the blood of the sacrifice. And
the bronze altar shall be for me to inquire *by*."
16Thus did Urijah the priest, according to all
that King Ahaz commanded.
17And King Ahaz cut off the panels of the
carts, and removed the lavers from them; and
he took down the Sea from the bronze oxen
that *were* under it, and put it on a pavement of
stones. 18Also he removed the Sabbath pavilion which they had built in the temple, and he
removed the king's outer entrance from the
house of the LORD, on account of the king of
Assyria.
19Now the rest of the acts of Ahaz which he
did, *are* they not written in the book of the
chronicles of the kings of Judah? 20So Ahaz
rested with his fathers, and was buried with
his fathers in the City of David. Then
Hezekiah his son reigned in his place.

Psalm 73:21–28

21 Thus my heart was grieved,
And I was vexed in my mind.
22 I *was* so foolish and ignorant;
I was *like* a beast before You.
23 Nevertheless I *am* continually with
You;
You hold *me* by my right hand.
24 You will guide me with Your counsel,
And afterward receive me *to* glory.

25 Whom have I in heaven *but You?*
And *there is* none upon earth *that* I
desire besides You.
26 My flesh and my heart fail;
But God *is* the strength of my heart
and my portion forever.

27 For indeed, those who are far from You
shall perish;
You have destroyed all those who
desert You for harlotry.
28 But *it is* good for me to draw near to
God;
I have put my trust in the Lord GOD,
That I may declare all Your works.

Proverbs 18:20–21

20 A man's stomach shall be satisfied
from the fruit of his mouth;
From the produce of his lips he shall
be filled.

21 Death and life *are* in the power of the
tongue,
And those who love it will eat its fruit.

18:21 Death and life. The greatest good and the greatest harm are in the power of the tongue (James 3:6–10).

John 21:1–25

21 After these things Jesus showed Himself
again to the disciples at the Sea of
Tiberias, and in this way He showed *Himself*: 2Si-
mon Peter, Thomas called the Twin, Nathanael
of Cana in Galilee, the *sons* of Zebedee, and two
others of His disciples were together. 3Simon
Peter said to them, "I am going fishing."
They said to him, "We are going with you
also." They went out and immediately got into
the boat, and that night they caught nothing.
4But when the morning had now come, Jesus
stood on the shore; yet the disciples did not
know that it was Jesus. 5Then Jesus said to
them, "Children, have you any food?"
They answered Him, "No."
6And He said to them, "Cast the net on the
right side of the boat, and you will find *some*."
So they cast, and now they were not able to
draw it in because of the multitude of fish.
7Therefore that disciple whom Jesus loved
said to Peter, "It is the Lord!" Now when Simon Peter heard that it was the Lord, he put
on *his* outer garment (for he had removed it),
and plunged into the sea. 8But the other disciples came in the little boat (for they were not
far from land, but about two hundred cubits),
dragging the net with fish. 9Then, as soon as
they had come to land, they saw a fire of coals
there, and fish laid on it, and bread. 10Jesus
said to them, "Bring some of the fish which
you have just caught."

[11]Simon Peter went up and dragged the net to land, full of large fish, one hundred and fifty-three; and although there were so many, the net was not broken. [12]Jesus said to them, "Come *and* eat breakfast." Yet none of the disciples dared ask Him, "Who are You?"—knowing that it was the Lord. [13]Jesus then came and took the bread and gave it to them, and likewise the fish.

[14]This *is* now the third time Jesus showed Himself to His disciples after He was raised from the dead.

[15]So when they had eaten breakfast, Jesus said to Simon Peter, "Simon, *son* of Jonah, do you love Me more than these?"

He said to Him, "Yes, Lord; You know that I love You."

He said to him, "Feed My lambs."

[16]He said to him again a second time, "Simon, *son* of Jonah, do you love Me?"

He said to Him, "Yes, Lord; You know that I love You."

He said to him, "Tend My sheep."

[17]He said to him the third time, "Simon, *son* of Jonah, do you love Me?" Peter was grieved because He said to him the third time, "Do you love Me?"

And he said to Him, "Lord, You know all things; You know that I love You."

Jesus said to him, "Feed My sheep. [18]Most assuredly, I say to you, when you were younger, you girded yourself and walked where you wished; but when you are old, you will stretch out your hands, and another will gird you and carry *you* where you do not wish." [19]This He spoke, signifying by what death he would glorify God. And when He had spoken this, He said to him, "Follow Me."

[20]Then Peter, turning around, saw the disciple whom Jesus loved following, who also had leaned on His breast at the supper, and said, "Lord, who is the one who betrays You?" [21]Peter, seeing him, said to Jesus, "But Lord, what *about* this man?"

[22]Jesus said to him, "If I will that he remain till I come, what *is that* to you? You follow Me."

[23]Then this saying went out among the brethren that this disciple would not die. Yet Jesus did not say to him that he would not die, but, "If I will that he remain till I come, what *is that* to you?"

[24]This is the disciple who testifies of these things, and wrote these things; and we know that his testimony is true.

[25]And there are also many other things that Jesus did, which if they were written one by one, I suppose that even the world itself could not contain the books that would be written. Amen.

21:18,19 A prophecy of Peter's martyrdom. Jesus' call of devotion to Him would also mean that Peter's devotion would entail his own death (Matt. 10:37–39). Whenever any Christian follows Christ, he must be prepared to suffer and die (Matt. 16:24–26). Peter lived 3 decades serving the Lord and anticipating the death that was before him (2 Pet. 1:12–15), but he wrote that such suffering and death for the Lord brings praise to God (1 Pet. 4:14–16). Church tradition records that Peter suffered martyrdom under Nero (ca. A.D. 67–68), being crucified upside down, because he refused to be crucified like his Lord.

DAY 14: How does Jesus deal with Peter's denial of Him during the trial?

In John 21:15–17, the meaning of this section hinges upon the usage of two synonyms for love. In terms of interpretation, when two synonyms are placed in close proximity in context, a difference in meaning, however slight, is emphasized. When Jesus asked Peter if he loved Him, He used a word for love that signified total commitment. Peter responded with a word for love that signified his love for Jesus, but not necessarily his total commitment. This was not because he was reluctant to express that greater love, but because he had been disobedient and denied the Lord in the past. He was, perhaps, now reluctant to make a claim of supreme devotion when, in the past, his life did not support such a claim. Jesus pressed home to Peter the need for unswerving devotion by repeatedly asking Peter if he loved Him supremely. The essential message here is that Jesus demands total commitment from His followers. Their love for Him must place Him above their love for all else. Jesus confronted Peter with love because He wanted Peter to lead the apostles (Matt. 16:18), but in order for Peter to be an effective shepherd, his overwhelming drive must exemplify supreme love for his Lord.

In v. 15, when Jesus asked him if he loved Him "more than these," He probably refers to the fish (v. 11) representing Peter's profession as a fisherman, for he had gone back to it while waiting for Jesus (v. 3). Jesus wanted Peter to love Him so supremely as to forsake all that he was familiar with and be exclusively devoted to being a fisher of men (Matt. 4:19). The phrase may refer to the other disciples, since Peter had claimed he would be more devoted than all the others (Matt. 26:33). "Feed My lambs." The word "feed" conveys the idea of being devoted to the Lord's service as an under-shepherd who cares for His flock (1 Pet. 5:1–4). The word has the idea of constantly feeding and nourishing the sheep. This served as a reminder that the primary duty of the messenger of Jesus Christ is to teach the word of God (2 Tim. 4:2). Acts 1–13 records Peter's obedience to this commission.

In v. 17, "Peter was grieved." The third time Jesus asked Peter, He used Peter's word for love that signified something less than total devotion, questioning even that level of love Peter thought he was safe in claiming. The lessons driven home to Peter grieved his heart, so that he sought for a proper understanding of his heart, not by what he said or had done, but based on the Lord's omniscience (2:24,25).

JUNE 15

2 Kings 17:1–18:37

17 In the twelfth year of Ahaz king of Judah,
Hoshea the son of Elah became king of
Israel in Samaria, *and he reigned* nine years.
2And he did evil in the sight of the LORD, but
not as the kings of Israel who were before
him. 3Shalmaneser king of Assyria came up
against him; and Hoshea became his vassal,
and paid him tribute money. 4And the king of
Assyria uncovered a conspiracy by Hoshea; for
he had sent messengers to So, king of Egypt,
and brought no tribute to the king of Assyria,
as *he had done* year by year. Therefore the king
of Assyria shut him up, and bound him in
prison.

5Now the king of Assyria went throughout
all the land, and went up to Samaria and
besieged it for three years. 6In the ninth year
of Hoshea, the king of Assyria took Samaria
and carried Israel away to Assyria, and placed
them in Halah and by the Habor, the River of
Gozan, and in the cities of the Medes.

7For so it was that the children of Israel had
sinned against the LORD their God, who had
brought them up out of the land of Egypt,
from under the hand of Pharaoh king of
Egypt; and they had feared other gods, 8and
had walked in the statutes of the nations
whom the LORD had cast out from before the
children of Israel, and of the kings of Israel,
which they had made. 9Also the children of Israel secretly did against the LORD their God
things that *were* not right, and they built for
themselves high places in all their cities, from
watchtower to fortified city. 10They set up for
themselves *sacred* pillars and wooden images
on every high hill and under every green tree.
11There they burned incense on all the high
places, like the nations whom the LORD had
carried away before them; and they did
wicked things to provoke the LORD to anger,
12for they served idols, of which the LORD had
said to them, "You shall not do this thing."
13Yet the LORD testified against Israel and
against Judah, by all of His prophets, every
seer, saying, "Turn from your evil ways, and
keep My commandments *and* My statutes,
according to all the law which I commanded
your fathers, and which I sent to you by My
servants the prophets." 14Nevertheless they
would not hear, but stiffened their necks, like
the necks of their fathers, who did not believe
in the LORD their God. 15And they rejected His
statutes and His covenant that He had made
with their fathers, and His testimonies which
He had testified against them; they followed
idols, became idolaters, and *went* after the
nations who *were* all around them, *concerning*
whom the LORD had charged them that they
should not do like them. 16So they left all the
commandments of the LORD their God, made
for themselves a molded image *and* two calves,
made a wooden image and worshiped all the
host of heaven, and served Baal. 17And they
caused their sons and daughters to pass
through the fire, practiced witchcraft and
soothsaying, and sold themselves to do evil in
the sight of the LORD, to provoke Him to anger.
18Therefore the LORD was very angry with Israel, and removed them from His sight; there
was none left but the tribe of Judah alone.

19Also Judah did not keep the commandments of the LORD their God, but walked in the
statutes of Israel which they made. 20And the
LORD rejected all the descendants of Israel,
afflicted them, and delivered them into the
hand of plunderers, until He had cast them
from His sight. 21For He tore Israel from the
house of David, and they made Jeroboam the
son of Nebat king. Then Jeroboam drove Israel from following the LORD, and made them
commit a great sin. 22For the children of Israel
walked in all the sins of Jeroboam which he
did; they did not depart from them, 23until the
LORD removed Israel out of His sight, as He
had said by all His servants the prophets. So

Israel was carried away from their own land to
Assyria, *as it is* to this day.
24Then the king of Assyria brought *people*
from Babylon, Cuthah, Ava, Hamath, and from
Sepharvaim, and placed *them* in the cities of
Samaria instead of the children of Israel; and
they took possession of Samaria and dwelt in
its cities. 25And it was so, at the beginning of
their dwelling there, *that* they did not fear the
LORD; therefore the LORD sent lions among
them, which killed *some* of them. 26So they
spoke to the king of Assyria, saying, "The
nations whom you have removed and placed in
the cities of Samaria do not know the rituals of
the God of the land; therefore He has sent
lions among them, and indeed, they are killing
them because they do not know the rituals of
the God of the land." 27Then the king of Assyria
commanded, saying, "Send there one of the
priests whom you brought from there; let him
go and dwell there, and let him teach them the
rituals of the God of the land." 28Then one of
the priests whom they had carried away from
Samaria came and dwelt in Bethel, and taught
them how they should fear the LORD.
29However every nation continued to make
gods of its own, and put *them* in the shrines on
the high places which the Samaritans had
made, *every* nation in the cities where they
dwelt. 30The men of Babylon made Succoth
Benoth, the men of Cuth made Nergal, the
men of Hamath made Ashima, 31and the Avites
made Nibhaz and Tartak; and the Sepharvites
burned their children in fire to Adrammelech
and Anammelech, the gods of Sepharvaim.
32So they feared the LORD, and from every
class they appointed for themselves priests of
the high places, who sacrificed for them in the
shrines of the high places. 33They feared the
LORD, yet served their own gods—according
to the rituals of the nations from among whom
they were carried away.
34To this day they continue practicing the
former rituals; they do not fear the LORD, nor
do they follow their statutes or their ordinances, or the law and commandment which
the LORD had commanded the children of Jacob, whom He named Israel, 35with whom the
LORD had made a covenant and charged them,
saying: "You shall not fear other gods, nor bow
down to them nor serve them nor sacrifice to
them; 36but the LORD, who brought you up
from the land of Egypt with great power and
an outstretched arm, Him you shall fear, Him
you shall worship, and to Him you shall offer
sacrifice. 37And the statutes, the ordinances,
the law, and the commandment which He
wrote for you, you shall be careful to observe
forever; you shall not fear other gods. 38And
the covenant that I have made with you, you
shall not forget, nor shall you fear other gods.
39But the LORD your God you shall fear; and He
will deliver you from the hand of all your enemies." 40However they did not obey, but they
followed their former rituals. 41So these
nations feared the LORD, yet served their
carved images; also their children and their
children's children have continued doing as
their fathers did, even to this day.

18 Now it came to pass in the third year of
Hoshea the son of Elah, king of Israel,
that Hezekiah the son of Ahaz, king of Judah,
began to reign. 2He was twenty-five years old
when he became king, and he reigned twenty-
nine years in Jerusalem. His mother's name
was Abi the daughter of Zechariah. 3And he did
what was right in the sight of the LORD, according to all that his father David had done.
4He removed the high places and broke the
sacred pillars, cut down the wooden image and
broke in pieces the bronze serpent that Moses
had made; for until those days the children of
Israel burned incense to it, and called it
Nehushtan. 5He trusted in the LORD God of Israel, so that after him was none like him
among all the kings of Judah, nor who were
before him. 6For he held fast to the LORD; he

18:5 He trusted in the LORD God of Israel. The most noble quality of Hezekiah (in dramatic contrast to his father, Ahaz) was that he relied on the Lord as his exclusive hope in every situation. What distinguished him from all other kings of Judah (after the division of the kingdom) was his firm trust in the Lord during a severe national crisis (18:17–19:34). Despite troublesome events, Hezekiah clung tightly to the Lord, faithfully following Him and obeying His commands (v. 6). As a result, the Lord was with him and gave him success (v. 7).

did not depart from following Him, but kept
His commandments, which the LORD had
commanded Moses. 7The LORD was with him;
he prospered wherever he went. And he rebelled against the king of Assyria and did not
serve him. 8He subdued the Philistines, as far
as Gaza and its territory, from watchtower to
fortified city.
9Now it came to pass in the fourth year of
King Hezekiah, which *was* the seventh year of
Hoshea the son of Elah, king of Israel, *that*
Shalmaneser king of Assyria came up against
Samaria and besieged it. 10And at the end of

three years they took it. In the sixth year of
Hezekiah, that *is,* the ninth year of Hoshea
king of Israel, Samaria was taken. [11]Then the
king of Assyria carried Israel away captive to
Assyria, and put them in Halah and by the
Habor, the River of Gozan, and in the cities of
the Medes, [12]because they did not obey the
voice of the LORD their God, but transgressed
His covenant *and* all that Moses the servant of
the LORD had commanded; and they would
neither hear nor do *them.*

[13]And in the fourteenth year of King
Hezekiah, Sennacherib king of Assyria came
up against all the fortified cities of Judah and
took them. [14]Then Hezekiah king of Judah
sent to the king of Assyria at Lachish, saying,
"I have done wrong; turn away from me; whatever you impose on me I will pay." And the
king of Assyria assessed Hezekiah king of Judah three hundred talents of silver and thirty
talents of gold. [15]So Hezekiah gave *him* all the
silver that was found in the house of the LORD
and in the treasuries of the king's house. [16]At
that time Hezekiah stripped *the gold from* the
doors of the temple of the LORD, and *from* the
pillars which Hezekiah king of Judah had
overlaid, and gave it to the king of Assyria.

[17]Then the king of Assyria sent *the* Tartan,
the Rabsaris, *and the* Rabshakeh from Lachish,
with a great army against Jerusalem, to King
Hezekiah. And they went up and came to Jerusalem. When they had come up, they went and
stood by the aqueduct from the upper pool,
which *was* on the highway to the Fuller's Field.
[18]And when they had called to the king, Eliakim
the son of Hilkiah, who *was* over the household,
Shebna the scribe, and Joah the son of Asaph,
the recorder, came out to them. [19]Then *the*
Rabshakeh said to them, "Say now to Hezekiah,
'Thus says the great king, the king of Assyria:
"What confidence *is* this in which you trust?
[20]You speak of *having* plans and power for war;
but *they are* mere words. And in whom do you
trust, that you rebel against me? [21]Now look!
You are trusting in the staff of this broken
reed, Egypt, on which if a man leans, it will go
into his hand and pierce it. So *is* Pharaoh king
of Egypt to all who trust in him. [22]But if you say
to me, 'We trust in the LORD our God,' *is* it not
He whose high places and whose altars
Hezekiah has taken away, and said to Judah
and Jerusalem, 'You shall worship before this
altar in Jerusalem'?" ' [23]Now therefore, I urge
you, give a pledge to my master the king of Assyria, and I will give you two thousand horses—if you are able on your part to put riders
on them! [24]How then will you repel one captain
of the least of my master's servants, and put
your trust in Egypt for chariots and horsemen?
[25]Have I now come up without the LORD against
this place to destroy it? The LORD said to me,
'Go up against this land, and destroy it.' "

[26]Then Eliakim the son of Hilkiah, Shebna,
and Joah said to *the* Rabshakeh, "Please speak
to your servants in Aramaic, for we understand *it;* and do not speak to us in Hebrew in
the hearing of the people who *are* on the wall."

[27]But *the* Rabshakeh said to them, "Has my
master sent me to your master and to you to
speak these words, and not to the men who sit
on the wall, who will eat and drink their own
waste with you?"

[28]Then *the* Rabshakeh stood and called out
with a loud voice in Hebrew, and spoke, saying, "Hear the word of the great king, the king
of Assyria! [29]Thus says the king: 'Do not let
Hezekiah deceive you, for he shall not be able
to deliver you from his hand; [30]nor let
Hezekiah make you trust in the LORD, saying,
"The LORD will surely deliver us; this city shall
not be given into the hand of the king of Assyria." ' [31]Do not listen to Hezekiah; for thus
says the king of Assyria: 'Make *peace* with me
by a present and come out to me; and every
one of you eat from his own vine and every
one from his own fig tree, and every one of
you drink the waters of his own cistern; [32]until
I come and take you away to a land like your
own land, a land of grain and new wine, a land
of bread and vineyards, a land of olive groves
and honey, that you may live and not die. But
do not listen to Hezekiah, lest he persuade you,
saying, "The LORD will deliver us." [33]Has any of
the gods of the nations at all delivered its land
from the hand of the king of Assyria? [34]Where
are the gods of Hamath and Arpad? Where *are*
the gods of Sepharvaim and Hena and Ivah?
Indeed, have they delivered Samaria from my
hand? [35]Who among all the gods of the lands
have delivered their countries from my hand,
that the LORD should deliver Jerusalem from
my hand?' "

[36]But the people held their peace and
answered him not a word; for the king's commandment was, "Do not answer him." [37]Then
Eliakim the son of Hilkiah, who *was* over the
household, Shebna the scribe, and Joah the
son of Asaph, the recorder, came to Hezekiah
with *their* clothes torn, and told him the words
of *the* Rabshakeh.

Psalm 74:1–8

A Contemplation of Asaph.

O God, why have You cast
us off forever?

Why does Your anger smoke against
the sheep of Your pasture?
2 Remember Your congregation, *which*
You have purchased of old,
The tribe of Your inheritance, *which* You
have redeemed—
This Mount Zion where You have
dwelt.
3 Lift up Your feet to the perpetual
desolations.
The enemy has damaged everything in
the sanctuary.
4 Your enemies roar in the midst of Your
meeting place;
They set up their banners *for* signs.
5 They seem like men who lift up
Axes among the thick trees.
6 And now they break down its carved
work, all at once,
With axes and hammers.
7 They have set fire to Your sanctuary;
They have defiled the dwelling place of
Your name to the ground.
8 They said in their hearts,
"Let us destroy them altogether."
They have burned up all the meeting
places of God in the land.

Proverbs 18:22–24

22 *He who* finds a wife finds a good *thing,*
And obtains favor from the LORD.

23 The poor *man* uses entreaties,
But the rich answers roughly.

24 A man *who has* friends must himself be
friendly,
But there is a friend *who* sticks closer
than a brother.

18:24 must himself be friendly. The best text says "may come to ruin" and warns that the person who makes friends too easily and indiscriminately does so to his own destruction. On the other hand, a friend chosen wisely is more loyal than a brother. **friend.** This is a strong word meaning one who loves and was used of Abraham, God's friend (2 Chr. 20:7; Is. 41:8; 1 Sam. 18:1; 2 Sam. 1:26).

Acts 1:1–26

1 The former account I made, O Theophilus, of
all that Jesus began both to do and teach, 2un-
til the day in which He was taken up, after He
through the Holy Spirit had given commandments to the apostles whom He had chosen, 3to
whom He also presented Himself alive after His
suffering by many infallible proofs, being seen
by them during forty days and speaking of the
things pertaining to the kingdom of God.

1:3 presented Himself…by many infallible proofs. John 20:30; 1 Corinthians 15:5–8. To give the apostles confidence to present His message, Jesus entered a locked room (John 20:19), showed His crucifixion wounds (Luke 24:39), and ate and drank with the disciples (Luke 24:41–43). **forty days.** The time period between Jesus' resurrection and ascension during which He appeared at intervals to the apostles and others (1 Cor. 15:5–8) and provided convincing evidence of His resurrection. **kingdom of God.** Here this expression refers to the sphere of salvation, the gracious domain of divine rule over believers' hearts (1 Cor. 6:9; Eph. 5:5; Col. 1:13,14; Rev. 11:15; 12:10). This was the dominant theme during Christ's earthly ministry (Matt. 4:23; 9:35; Mark 1:15; Luke 4:43; 9:2; John 3:3–21).

4And being assembled together with *them,*
He commanded them not to depart from Jerusalem, but to wait for the Promise of the
Father, "which," *He said,* "you have heard
from Me; 5for John truly baptized with water,
but you shall be baptized with the Holy Spirit
not many days from now." 6Therefore, when
they had come together, they asked Him, saying, "Lord, will You at this time restore the
kingdom to Israel?" 7And He said to them, "It
is not for you to know times or seasons which
the Father has put in His own authority. 8But
you shall receive power when the Holy Spirit
has come upon you; and you shall be witnesses to Me in Jerusalem, and in all Judea
and Samaria, and to the end of the earth."
9Now when He had spoken these things,
while they watched, He was taken up, and a
cloud received Him out of their sight. 10And
while they looked steadfastly toward heaven
as He went up, behold, two men stood by
them in white apparel, 11who also said, "Men of
Galilee, why do you stand gazing up into heav-
en? This *same* Jesus, who was taken up from
you into heaven, will so come in like manner
as you saw Him go into heaven."
12Then they returned to Jerusalem from the
mount called Olivet, which is near Jerusalem, a
Sabbath day's journey. 13And when they had
entered, they went up into the upper room
where they were staying: Peter, James, John,
and Andrew; Philip and Thomas; Bartholomew

1:8 The apostles' mission of spreading the gospel was the major reason the Holy Spirit empowered them. This event dramatically altered world history, and the gospel message eventually reached all parts of the earth (Matt. 28:19,20). **receive power.** The apostles had already experienced the Holy Spirit's saving, guiding, teaching, and miracle-working power. Soon they would receive His indwelling presence and a new dimension of power for witness (2:4; 1 Cor. 6:19,20; Eph. 3:16,20). **witnesses.** People who tell the truth about Jesus Christ (John 14:26; 1 Pet. 3:15). The Greek word means "one who dies for his faith" because that was commonly the price of witnessing. **Judea.** The region in which Jerusalem was located. **Samaria.** The region immediately to the north of Judea.

and Matthew; James *the son* of Alphaeus and Simon the Zealot; and Judas *the son* of James.
14These all continued with one accord in prayer
and supplication, with the women and Mary
the mother of Jesus, and with His brothers.
15And in those days Peter stood up in the
midst of the disciples (altogether the number of
names was about a hundred and twenty), and
said, 16"Men *and* brethren, this Scripture had to
be fulfilled, which the Holy Spirit spoke before
by the mouth of David concerning Judas, who
became a guide to those who arrested Jesus;
17for he was numbered with us and obtained a
part in this ministry."
18(Now this man purchased a field with the
wages of iniquity; and falling headlong, he
burst open in the middle and all his entrails
gushed out. 19And it became known to all
those dwelling in Jerusalem; so that field is
called in their own language, Akel Dama, that
is, Field of Blood.)
20"For it is written in the Book of Psalms:

'Let his dwelling place be desolate,
And let no one live in it';

and,

'Let another take his office.'

21"Therefore, of these men who have
accompanied us all the time that the Lord Jesus went in and out among us, 22beginning
from the baptism of John to that day when He
was taken up from us, one of these must become a witness with us of His resurrection."
23And they proposed two: Joseph called
Barsabas, who was surnamed Justus, and
Matthias. 24And they prayed and said, "You, O
Lord, who know the hearts of all, show which
of these two You have chosen 25to take part in
this ministry and apostleship from which Judas by transgression fell, that he might go to
his own place." 26And they cast their lots, and
the lot fell on Matthias. And he was numbered
with the eleven apostles.

DAY 15: When and why did the northern kingdom of Israel come to an end?

In 2 Kings 17:6, it says that the "king of Assyria took Samaria and carried Israel away to Assyria." The capture of Samaria by Sargon II marked the end of the northern kingdom in 722 B.C. According to Assyrian records, the Assyrians deported 27,290 inhabitants of Israel to distant locations. The relocation of populations was characteristic of Assyrian policy during that era. The Israelites were resettled in the upper Tigris-Euphrates Valley and never returned to the Promised Land. "Halah" was a city northeast of Nineveh. The "Habor" River was a northern tributary of the Euphrates. The "cities of the Medes" were northeast of Nineveh. Samaria was resettled with foreigners (v. 24). God did what He said He would do in Deuteronomy 28. The Jews were carried as far east as Susa, where the Book of Esther later took place.

In vv. 7–23, the writer departs from quoting his written sources and gives his own explanation for the captivity of Israel. Judah is included, though her captivity did not occur until 605/604–586 B.C. at the hands of the Babylonians. Her sins were the same. Here is a very full and impressive vindication of God's action in punishing His privileged but rebellious and apostate people. In v. 7, he begins by stating that the Israelites had sinned against the Lord who had redeemed them from Egypt. Gross perversion of the worship of God and national propensity to idolatry finally exhausted divine patience. The idolatry of Israel is described in vv. 7–12. In response to Israel's actions, the Lord sent His prophets to Israel and Judah with a message of repentance (v. 13). However, the people failed to respond to the prophets' messages, because, like their fathers, they did not have faith in the Lord (v. 14). Their lack of faith resulted in disobedience to the Lord's commands and the further pursuit of idolatry (vv. 15–17). The idolatry of Israel (and Judah) brought forth the anger of the Lord, which resulted in exile (v. 18). The "great sin" of both Israel and Judah was their continual following of the sinful pattern of Jeroboam I, departing from the Lord and practicing idolatry, thus bringing down the judgment of captivity predicted by the prophets (vv. 19–23).

JUNE 16

2 Kings 19:1–21:26

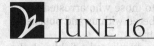

19 And so it was, when King Hezekiah heard *it,* that he tore his clothes, covered himself with sackcloth, and went into the house of the LORD. 2Then he sent Eliakim, who *was* over the household, Shebna the scribe, and the elders of the priests, covered with sackcloth, to Isaiah the prophet, the son of Amoz. 3And they said to him, "Thus says Hezekiah: 'This day *is* a day of trouble, and rebuke, and blasphemy; for the children have come to birth, but *there is* no strength to bring them forth. 4It may be that the LORD your God will hear all the words of *the* Rabshakeh, whom his master the king of Assyria has sent to reproach the living God, and will rebuke the words which the LORD your God has heard. Therefore lift up *your* prayer for the remnant that is left.' "

5So the servants of King Hezekiah came to Isaiah. 6And Isaiah said to them, "Thus you shall say to your master, 'Thus says the LORD: "Do not be afraid of the words which you have heard, with which the servants of the king of Assyria have blasphemed Me. 7Surely I will send a spirit upon him, and he shall hear a rumor and return to his own land; and I will cause him to fall by the sword in his own land." ' "

8Then *the* Rabshakeh returned and found the king of Assyria warring against Libnah, for he heard that he had departed from Lachish. 9And the king heard concerning Tirhakah king of Ethiopia, "Look, he has come out to make war with you." So he again sent messengers to Hezekiah, saying, 10"Thus you shall speak to Hezekiah king of Judah, saying: 'Do not let your God in whom you trust deceive you, saying, "Jerusalem shall not be given into the hand of the king of Assyria." 11Look! You have heard what the kings of Assyria have done to all lands by utterly destroying them; and shall you be delivered? 12Have the gods of the nations delivered those whom my fathers have destroyed, Gozan and Haran and Rezeph, and the people of Eden who *were* in Telassar? 13Where *is* the king of Hamath, the king of Arpad, and the king of the city of Sepharvaim, Hena, and Ivah?' "

14And Hezekiah received the letter from the hand of the messengers, and read it; and Hezekiah went up to the house of the LORD, and spread it before the LORD. 15Then Hezekiah prayed before the LORD, and said: "O LORD God of Israel, *the One* who dwells *between* the cherubim, You are God, You alone, of all the kingdoms of the earth. You have made heaven and earth. 16Incline Your ear, O LORD, and hear; open Your eyes, O LORD, and see; and hear the words of Sennacherib, which he has sent to reproach the living God. 17Truly, LORD, the kings of Assyria have laid waste the nations and their lands, 18and have cast their gods into the fire; for they *were* not gods, but the work of men's hands—wood and stone. Therefore they destroyed them. 19Now therefore, O LORD our God, I pray, save us from his hand, that all the kingdoms of the earth may know that You *are* the LORD God, You alone."

20Then Isaiah the son of Amoz sent to Hezekiah, saying, "Thus says the LORD God of Israel: 'Because you have prayed to Me against Sennacherib king of Assyria, I have heard.' 21This *is* the word which the LORD has spoken concerning him:

'The virgin, the daughter of Zion,
Has despised you, laughed you to scorn;
The daughter of Jerusalem
Has shaken *her* head behind your back!

22 'Whom have you reproached and blasphemed?
Against whom have you raised *your* voice,
And lifted up your eyes on high?
Against the Holy *One* of Israel.
23 By your messengers you have reproached the Lord,
And said: "By the multitude of my chariots
I have come up to the height of the mountains,
To the limits of Lebanon;
I will cut down its tall cedars
And its choice cypress trees;
I will enter the extremity of its borders,
To its fruitful forest.
24 I have dug and drunk strange water,
And with the soles of my feet I have dried up
All the brooks of defense."

25 'Did you not hear long ago
How I made it,
From ancient times that I formed it?
Now I have brought it to pass,
That you should be
For crushing fortified cities *into* heaps of ruins.
26 Therefore their inhabitants had little power;

They were dismayed and confounded;
They were *as* the grass of the field
And the green herb,
As the grass on the housetops
And *grain* blighted before it is grown.
27 'But I know your dwelling place,
Your going out and your coming in,
And your rage against Me.
28 Because your rage against Me and
your tumult
Have come up to My ears,
Therefore I will put My hook in your
nose
And My bridle in your lips,
And I will turn you back
By the way which you came.
29'This *shall be* a sign to you:
You shall eat this year such as grows of
itself,
And in the second year what springs
from the same;
Also in the third year sow and reap,
Plant vineyards and eat the fruit of
them.
30 And the remnant who have escaped of
the house of Judah
Shall again take root downward,
And bear fruit upward.
31 For out of Jerusalem shall go a
remnant,
And those who escape from Mount Zion.
The zeal of the LORD of hosts will do
this.'

32"Therefore thus says the LORD concerning
the king of Assyria:

'He shall not come into this city,
Nor shoot an arrow there,
Nor come before it with shield,
Nor build a siege mound against it.
33 By the way that he came,
By the same shall he return;
And he shall not come into this city,'
Says the LORD.
34 'For I will defend this city, to save it
For My own sake and for My servant
David's sake.' "

35And it came to pass on a certain night that
the angel of the LORD went out, and killed in
the camp of the Assyrians one hundred and
eighty-five thousand; and when *people* arose
early in the morning, there were the
corpses—all dead. 36So Sennacherib king of
Assyria departed and went away, returned
home, and remained at Nineveh. 37Now it came
to pass, as he was worshiping in the temple of
Nisroch his god, that his sons Adrammelech
and Sharezer struck him down with the sword;
and they escaped into the land of Ararat. Then
Esarhaddon his son reigned in his place.

20 In those days Hezekiah was sick and
near death. And Isaiah the prophet, the
son of Amoz, went to him and said to him,
"Thus says the LORD: 'Set your house in order,
for you shall die, and not live.' "
2Then he turned his face toward the wall,
and prayed to the LORD, saying, 3"Remember
now, O LORD, I pray, how I have walked before
You in truth and with a loyal heart, and have
done *what was* good in Your sight." And Hezekiah wept bitterly.
4And it happened, before Isaiah had gone
out into the middle court, that the word of the
LORD came to him, saying, 5"Return and tell
Hezekiah the leader of My people, 'Thus says
the LORD, the God of David your father: "I have
heard your prayer, I have seen your tears;
surely I will heal you. On the third day you
shall go up to the house of the LORD. 6And I will
add to your days fifteen years. I will deliver you
and this city from the hand of the king of Assyria; and I will defend this city for My own
sake, and for the sake of My servant David." ' "
7Then Isaiah said, "Take a lump of figs." So
they took and laid *it* on the boil, and he recovered.
8And Hezekiah said to Isaiah, "What *is* the
sign that the LORD will heal me, and that I shall
go up to the house of the LORD the third day?"
9Then Isaiah said, "This is the sign to you
from the LORD, that the LORD will do the thing
which He has spoken: *shall* the shadow go forward ten degrees or go backward ten degrees?"
10And Hezekiah answered, "It is an easy thing
for the shadow to go down ten degrees; no, but
let the shadow go backward ten degrees."
11So Isaiah the prophet cried out to the LORD,
and He brought the shadow ten degrees backward, by which it had gone down on the sundial of Ahaz.
12At that time Berodach-Baladan the son of
Baladan, king of Babylon, sent letters and a
present to Hezekiah, for he heard that
Hezekiah had been sick. 13And Hezekiah was
attentive to them, and showed them all the
house of his treasures—the silver and gold, the
spices and precious ointment, and all his
armory—all that was found among his treasures. There was nothing in his house or in all
his dominion that Hezekiah did not show them.
14Then Isaiah the prophet went to King
Hezekiah, and said to him, "What did these
men say, and from where did they come to
you?"

So Hezekiah said, "They came from a far
country, from Babylon."
15And he said, "What have they seen in your
house?"
So Hezekiah answered, "They have seen all
that *is* in my house; there is nothing among
my treasures that I have not shown them."
16Then Isaiah said to Hezekiah, "Hear the
word of the LORD: 17'Behold, the days are coming when all that *is* in your house, and what
your fathers have accumulated until this day,
shall be carried to Babylon; nothing shall be
left,' says the LORD. 18'And they shall take away

20:16,17 word of the LORD...carried to Babylon. Isaiah predicted the Babylonian captivity that would come over a century later (586 B.C.), another prophecy historically fulfilled in all of its expected detail.

20:17 nothing shall be left. Hezekiah's sin of parading his wealth before the visitors backfired, though this sin was only symptomatic of the ultimate reason for the captivity. The major cause was the corrupt leadership of Manasseh, Hezekiah's son (21:11–15).

some of your sons who will descend from you,
whom you will beget; and they shall be eunuchs in the palace of the king of Babylon.'"
19So Hezekiah said to Isaiah, "The word of
the LORD which you have spoken *is* good!" For
he said, "Will there not be peace and truth at
least in my days?"
20Now the rest of the acts of Hezekiah—all
his might, and how he made a pool and a tunnel and brought water into the city—*are* they
not written in the book of the chronicles of the
kings of Judah? 21So Hezekiah rested with his
fathers. Then Manasseh his son reigned in his
place.

21 Manasseh *was* twelve years old when he
became king, and he reigned fifty-five
years in Jerusalem. His mother's name *was*
Hephzibah. 2And he did evil in the sight of the
LORD, according to the abominations of the
nations whom the LORD had cast out before
the children of Israel. 3For he rebuilt the high
places which Hezekiah his father had
destroyed; he raised up altars for Baal, and
made a wooden image, as Ahab king of Israel
had done; and he worshiped all the host of
heaven and served them. 4He also built altars
in the house of the LORD, of which the LORD
had said, "In Jerusalem I will put My name."
5And he built altars for all the host of heaven in
the two courts of the house of the LORD. 6Also
he made his son pass through the fire, practiced
soothsaying, used witchcraft, and consulted
spiritists and mediums. He did much evil in
the sight of the LORD, to provoke *Him* to
anger. 7He even set a carved image of Asherah
that he had made, in the house of which the
LORD had said to David and to Solomon his
son, "In this house and in Jerusalem, which I
have chosen out of all the tribes of Israel, I will
put My name forever; 8and I will not make the
feet of Israel wander anymore from the land
which I gave their fathers—only if they are
careful to do according to all that I have commanded them, and according to all the law
that My servant Moses commanded them."
9But they paid no attention, and Manasseh seduced them to do more evil than the nations
whom the LORD had destroyed before the children of Israel.
10And the LORD spoke by His servants the
prophets, saying, 11"Because Manasseh king
of Judah has done these abominations (he has
acted more wickedly than all the Amorites who
were before him, and has also made Judah sin
with his idols), 12therefore thus says the LORD
God of Israel: 'Behold, *I* am bringing *such*
calamity upon Jerusalem and Judah, that whoever hears of it, both his ears will tingle. 13And
I will stretch over Jerusalem the measuring
line of Samaria and the plummet of the house
of Ahab; I will wipe Jerusalem as *one* wipes a
dish, wiping *it* and turning *it* upside down. 14So

21:13 the plummet. These were weighted lines dropped from walls to see whether they were structurally straight (Is. 28:17; Amos 7:7,8). Walls out of line were torn down. The Lord had measured Jerusalem by the standard of His word and had determined that the fate of Samaria (Israel) was also to befall Jerusalem. **wipe Jerusalem.** As one would wipe food off a dish, the Lord would wipe Jerusalem clean off the earth, i.e., obliterate her, and leave her turned upside down, empty, and useless.

I will forsake the remnant of My inheritance
and deliver them into the hand of their enemies; and they shall become victims of plunder to all their enemies, 15because they have
done evil in My sight, and have provoked Me
to anger since the day their fathers came out
of Egypt, even to this day.'"
16Moreover Manasseh shed very much innocent blood, till he had filled Jerusalem from

one end to another, besides his sin by which
he made Judah sin, in doing evil in the sight of
the LORD.
17 Now the rest of the acts of Manasseh—all
that he did, and the sin that he committed—*are*
they not written in the book of the chronicles
of the kings of Judah? 18 So Manasseh rested
with his fathers, and was buried in the garden
of his own house, in the garden of Uzza. Then
his son Amon reigned in his place.
19 Amon *was* twenty-two years old when he
became king, and he reigned two years in Jerusalem. His mother's name *was* Meshul-
lemeth the daughter of Haruz of Jotbah. 20 And
he did evil in the sight of the LORD, as his
father Manasseh had done. 21 So he walked in
all the ways that his father had walked; and he
served the idols that his father had served,
and worshiped them. 22 He forsook the LORD
God of his fathers, and did not walk in the way
of the LORD.
23 Then the servants of Amon conspired
against him, and killed the king in his own
house. 24 But the people of the land executed
all those who had conspired against King
Amon. Then the people of the land made his
son Josiah king in his place.
25 Now the rest of the acts of Amon which he
did, *are* they not written in the book of the
chronicles of the kings of Judah? 26 And he was
buried in his tomb in the garden of Uzza. Then
Josiah his son reigned in his place.

Psalm 74:9–17

9 We do not see our signs;
There is no longer any prophet;
Nor *is there* any among us who knows
how long.
10 O God, how long will the adversary
reproach?
Will the enemy blaspheme Your name
forever?
11 Why do You withdraw Your hand, even
Your right hand?
Take it out of Your bosom and destroy
them.
12 For God *is* my King from of old,
Working salvation in the midst of the
earth.
13 You divided the sea by Your strength;
You broke the heads of the sea
serpents in the waters.
14 You broke the heads of Leviathan in
pieces,
And gave him *as* food to the people
inhabiting the wilderness.
15 You broke open the fountain and the
flood;
You dried up mighty rivers.
16 The day *is* Yours, the night also *is* Yours;
You have prepared the light and the sun.
17 You have set all the borders of the
earth;
You have made summer and winter.

Proverbs 19:1–2

19 Better *is* the poor who walks
in his integrity
Than *one who is* perverse in his lips,
and is a fool.

2 Also it is not good *for* a soul *to be*
without knowledge,
And he sins who hastens with *his* feet.

Acts 2:1–21

2 When the Day of Pentecost had fully come,
they were all with one accord in one place.
2 And suddenly there came a sound from heav-
en, as of a rushing mighty wind, and it filled the
whole house where they were sitting. 3 Then
there appeared to them divided tongues, as of
fire, and *one* sat upon each of them. 4 And they

2:3 The disciples could not comprehend the significance of the Spirit's arrival without the Lord sovereignly illustrating what was occurring with a visible phenomenon. **tongues, as of fire.** Just as the sound, like wind, was symbolic, these were not literal flames of fire but supernatural indicators, like fire, that God had sent the Holy Spirit upon each believer. In Scripture, fire often denoted the divine presence (Ex. 3:2–6). God's use of a firelike appearance here parallels what He did with the dove when Jesus was baptized (Matt. 3:11; Luke 3:16).

were all filled with the Holy Spirit and began to
speak with other tongues, as the Spirit gave
them utterance.
5 And there were dwelling in Jerusalem Jews,
devout men, from every nation under heaven.
6 And when this sound occurred, the multitude
came together, and were confused, because
everyone heard them speak in his own language. 7 Then they were all amazed and marveled, saying to one another, "Look, are not all
these who speak Galileans? 8 And how *is it that*
we hear, each in our own language in which we
were born? 9 Parthians and Medes and Elamites,
those dwelling in Mesopotamia, Judea and
Cappadocia, Pontus and Asia, 10 Phrygia and
Pamphylia, Egypt and the parts of Libya

2:7 Galileans. Inhabitants of the mostly rural area of northern Israel around the Sea of Galilee. Galilean Jews spoke with a distinct regional accent and were considered to be unsophisticated and uneducated by the southern Judean Jews. When Galileans were seen to be speaking so many different languages, the Judean Jews were astonished.

adjoining Cyrene, visitors from Rome, both
Jews and proselytes, [11]Cretans and Arabs—we
hear them speaking in our own tongues the
wonderful works of God." [12]So they were all
amazed and perplexed, saying to one another,
"Whatever could this mean?"
[13]Others mocking said, "They are full of new
wine."
[14]But Peter, standing up with the eleven,
raised his voice and said to them, "Men of
Judea and all who dwell in Jerusalem, let this
be known to you, and heed my words. [15]For
these are not drunk, as you suppose, since it is
only the third hour of the day. [16]But this is
what was spoken by the prophet Joel:

[17] *'And it shall come to pass in the last*
days, says God,
That I will pour out of My Spirit on
all flesh;
Your sons and your daughters shall
prophesy,
Your young men shall see visions,
Your old men shall dream dreams.
[18] *And on My menservants and on My*
maidservants
I will pour out My Spirit in those days;
And they shall prophesy.
[19] *I will show wonders in heaven above*
And signs in the earth beneath:
Blood and fire and vapor of smoke.
[20] *The sun shall be turned into darkness,*
And the moon into blood,
Before the coming of the great and
awesome day of the LORD.
[21] *And it shall come to pass*
That whoever calls on the name of
the LORD
Shall be saved.'

DAY 16: What can we learn about the Holy Spirit's special role from the Book of Acts?

One of the cautions we must exercise in studying and teaching from the Book of Acts has to do with the difference between description and prescription. The difference plays an important role in interpreting the historical biblical books. The Bible's description of an event does not imply that the event or action can, should, or will be repeated.

The role of the Holy Spirit in His arrival as the promised Helper (John 14:17), which Acts describes as a startling audiovisual event (2:1–13), had some partial and selected repetitions (8:14–19; 10:44–48; 19:1–7). These were special cases in which believers are reported to have received or been filled with the Holy Spirit. In each of these cases, the sound of a rushing mighty wind and the tongues as of fire that were present in the original event (2:1–13) were absent, but the people spoke in tongues they did not know (but others recognized). These events should not be taken as the basis for teaching that believers today should expect the same tongue-evidence to accompany the filling of the Holy Spirit. Even in Acts itself, genuine conversions did not necessarily lead to extraordinary filling by the Holy Spirit. For example, a crowd of three thousand people believed and were baptized on the same Day of Pentecost (2:41) that started so dramatically, yet there is no mention of tongues. So, why in some cases did tongues accompany the confirmation of faith? That this actually occurred likely demonstrated that believers were being drawn from very different groups into the church. Each new group received a special welcome from the Holy Spirit. Thus, Samaritans (8:14–19), Gentiles (10:44–48), and believers from the old covenant (19:1–7) were added to the church, and the unity of the church was established. To demonstrate that unity, it was imperative to have some replication in each instance of what had occurred at Pentecost with the believing Jews, such as the presence of the apostles and the coming of the Spirit, manifestly indicated through speaking in the languages of Pentecost.

JUNE 17

2 Kings 22:1–24:20

22 Josiah *was* eight years old when he
became king, and he reigned thirty-one
years in Jerusalem. His mother's name *was*
Jedidah the daughter of Adaiah of Bozkath.
[2]And he did *what was* right in the sight of the
LORD, and walked in all the ways of his father
David; he did not turn aside to the right hand
or to the left.
[3]Now it came to pass, in the eighteenth year

of King Josiah, *that* the king sent Shaphan the scribe, the son of Azaliah, the son of Meshullam, to the house of the LORD, saying: 4"Go up to Hilkiah the high priest, that he may count the money which has been brought into the house of the LORD, which the doorkeepers have gathered from the people. 5And let them deliver it into the hand of those doing the work, who are the overseers in the house of the LORD; let them give it to those who *are* in the house of the LORD doing the work, to repair the damages of the house— 6to carpenters and builders and masons—and to buy timber and hewn stone to repair the house. 7However there need be no accounting made with them of the money delivered into their hand, because they deal faithfully."

8Then Hilkiah the high priest said to Shaphan the scribe, "I have found the Book of the Law in the house of the LORD." And Hilkiah gave the book to Shaphan, and he

22:8 the Book of the Law. A scroll containing the Torah (the Pentateuch), the revelation of God through Moses to Israel (23:2; Deut. 28:61). Manasseh may have destroyed all the copies of God's Law that were not hidden. This could have been the official copy laid beside the ark of the covenant in the Most Holy Place (Deut. 31:25,26). It may have been removed from its place under Ahaz, Manasseh, or Amon (2 Chr. 35:3), but was found during repair work.

read it. 9So Shaphan the scribe went to the king, bringing the king word, saying, "Your servants have gathered the money that was found in the house, and have delivered it into the hand of those who do the work, who oversee the house of the LORD." 10Then Shaphan the scribe showed the king, saying, "Hilkiah the priest has given me a book." And Shaphan read it before the king.

11Now it happened, when the king heard the words of the Book of the Law, that he tore his clothes. 12Then the king commanded Hilkiah the priest, Ahikam the son of Shaphan, Achbor the son of Michaiah, Shaphan the scribe, and Asaiah a servant of the king, saying, 13"Go, inquire of the LORD for me, for the people and for all Judah, concerning the words of this book that has been found; for great *is* the wrath of the LORD that is aroused against us, because our fathers have not obeyed the words of this book, to do according to all that is written concerning us."

14So Hilkiah the priest, Ahikam, Achbor, Shaphan, and Asaiah went to Huldah the prophetess, the wife of Shallum the son of Tikvah, the son of Harhas, keeper of the wardrobe. (She dwelt in Jerusalem in the Second Quarter.) And they spoke with her. 15Then she said to them, "Thus says the LORD God of Israel, 'Tell the man who sent you to Me, 16"Thus says the LORD: 'Behold, I will bring calamity on this place and on its inhabitants—all the words of the book which the king of Judah has read— 17because they have forsaken Me and burned incense to other gods, that they might provoke Me to anger with all the works of their hands. Therefore My wrath shall be aroused against this place and shall not be quenched.' " ' 18But as for the king of Judah, who sent you to inquire of the LORD, in this manner you shall speak to him, 'Thus says the LORD God of Israel: "*Concerning* the words which you have heard— 19because your heart was tender, and you humbled yourself before the LORD when you heard what I spoke against this place and against its inhabitants, that they would become a desolation and a curse, and you tore your clothes and wept before Me, I also have heard *you*," says the LORD. 20"Surely, therefore, I will gather you to your fathers, and you shall be gathered to your grave in peace; and your eyes shall not see all the calamity which I will bring on this place." ' " So they brought back word to the king.

23 Now the king sent them to gather all the elders of Judah and Jerusalem to him. 2The king went up to the house of the LORD with all the men of Judah, and with him all the inhabitants of Jerusalem—the priests and the prophets and all the people, both small and great. And he read in their hearing all the words of the Book of the Covenant which had been found in the house of the LORD.

3Then the king stood by a pillar and made a covenant before the LORD, to follow the LORD and to keep His commandments and His testimonies and His statutes, with all *his* heart and all *his* soul, to perform the words of this covenant that were written in this book. And all the people took a stand for the covenant. 4And the king commanded Hilkiah the high priest, the priests of the second order, and the doorkeepers, to bring out of the temple of the LORD all the articles that were made for Baal, for Asherah, and for all the host of heaven; and he burned them outside Jerusalem in the fields of Kidron, and carried their ashes to Bethel. 5Then he removed the idolatrous priests whom the kings of Judah had ordained to burn incense on the high places in the cities

of Judah and in the places all around Jerusalem, and those who burned incense to Baal, to
the sun, to the moon, to the constellations, and
to all the host of heaven. 6And he brought out
the wooden image from the house of the
LORD, to the Brook Kidron outside Jerusalem,
burned it at the Brook Kidron and ground *it* to
ashes, and threw its ashes on the graves of the
common people. 7Then he tore down the *rit-*
ual booths of the perverted persons that *were*
in the house of the LORD, where the women
wove hangings for the wooden image. 8And he
brought all the priests from the cities of Judah, and defiled the high places where the
priests had burned incense, from Geba to
Beersheba; also he broke down the high
places at the gates which *were* at the entrance
of the Gate of Joshua the governor of the city,
which *were* to the left of the city gate. 9Never-
theless the priests of the high places did not
come up to the altar of the LORD in Jerusalem,
but they ate unleavened bread among their
brethren.

10And he defiled Topheth, which *is* in the
Valley of the Son of Hinnom, that no man might
make his son or his daughter pass through the
fire to Molech. 11Then he removed the horses
that the kings of Judah had dedicated to the
sun, at the entrance to the house of the LORD,
by the chamber of Nathan-Melech, the officer
who *was* in the court; and he burned the chariots of the sun with fire. 12The altars that *were*
on the roof, the upper chamber of Ahaz, which
the kings of Judah had made, and the altars
which Manasseh had made in the two courts
of the house of the LORD, the king broke down
and pulverized there, and threw their dust into
the Brook Kidron. 13Then the king defiled the
high places that *were* east of Jerusalem, which
were on the south of the Mount of Corruption,
which Solomon king of Israel had built for
Ashtoreth the abomination of the Sidonians,
for Chemosh the abomination of the Moabites,
and for Milcom the abomination of the people
of Ammon. 14And he broke in pieces the *sacred*
pillars and cut down the wooden images, and
filled their places with the bones of men.

15Moreover the altar that *was* at Bethel, *and*
the high place which Jeroboam the son of
Nebat, who made Israel sin, had made, both
that altar and the high place he broke down;
and he burned the high place *and* crushed *it*
to powder, and burned the wooden image. 16As
Josiah turned, he saw the tombs that *were*
there on the mountain. And he sent and took
the bones out of the tombs and burned *them*
on the altar, and defiled it according to the
word of the LORD which the man of God proclaimed, who proclaimed these words. 17Then
he said, "What gravestone *is* this that I see?"

So the men of the city told him, "*It is* the
tomb of the man of God who came from Judah
and proclaimed these things which you have
done against the altar of Bethel."

18And he said, "Let him alone; let no one
move his bones." So they let his bones alone,
with the bones of the prophet who came from
Samaria.

19Now Josiah also took away all the shrines
of the high places that *were* in the cities of Samaria, which the kings of Israel had made to
provoke the LORD to anger; and he did to them
according to all the deeds he had done in
Bethel. 20He executed all the priests of the high
places who *were* there, on the altars, and
burned men's bones on them; and he returned
to Jerusalem.

21Then the king commanded all the people,
saying, "Keep the Passover to the LORD your
God, as *it is* written in this Book of the
Covenant." 22Such a Passover surely had never
been held since the days of the judges who
judged Israel, nor in all the days of the kings of
Israel and the kings of Judah. 23But in the eighteenth year of King Josiah this Passover was
held before the LORD in Jerusalem. 24Moreover
Josiah put away those who consulted mediums
and spiritists, the household gods and idols,
all the abominations that were seen in the land
of Judah and in Jerusalem, that he might perform the words of the law which were written
in the book that Hilkiah the priest found in the
house of the LORD. 25Now before him there was
no king like him, who turned to the LORD with
all his heart, with all his soul, and with all his
might, according to all the Law of Moses; nor
after him did *any* arise like him.

23:25 no king like him. Of all the kings in David's line, including David himself, no king more closely approximated the royal ideal of Deuteronomy 17:14–20 than Josiah (Matt. 22:37). Yet, even Josiah fell short of complete obedience because he had multiple wives (vv. 31,36). However, even this righteous king could not turn away the Lord's wrath because of Manasseh's sin (vv. 26,27).

26Nevertheless the LORD did not turn from
the fierceness of His great wrath, with which
His anger was aroused against Judah, because
of all the provocations with which Manasseh
had provoked Him. 27And the LORD said, "I will
also remove Judah from My sight, as I have

removed Israel, and will cast off this city Jerusalem which I have chosen, and the house of which
I said, 'My name shall be there.' "
[28]Now the rest of the acts of Josiah, and all
that he did, *are* they not written in the book of
the chronicles of the kings of Judah? [29]In his
days Pharaoh Necho king of Egypt went to the
aid of the king of Assyria, to the River
Euphrates; and King Josiah went against him.
And *Pharaoh Necho* killed him at Megiddo
when he confronted him. [30]Then his servants
moved his body in a chariot from Megiddo,
brought him to Jerusalem, and buried him in
his own tomb. And the people of the land took
Jehoahaz the son of Josiah, anointed him, and
made him king in his father's place.
[31]Jehoahaz *was* twenty-three years old when
he became king, and he reigned three months
in Jerusalem. His mother's name *was* Hamutal
the daughter of Jeremiah of Libnah. [32]And he
did evil in the sight of the LORD, according to
all that his fathers had done. [33]Now Pharaoh
Necho put him in prison at Riblah in the land
of Hamath, that he might not reign in Jerusalem; and he imposed on the land a tribute of
one hundred talents of silver and a talent of
gold. [34]Then Pharaoh Necho made Eliakim the
son of Josiah king in place of his father Josiah,
and changed his name to Jehoiakim. And
Pharaoh took Jehoahaz and went to Egypt, and
he died there.
[35]So Jehoiakim gave the silver and gold to
Pharaoh; but he taxed the land to give money
according to the command of Pharaoh; he
exacted the silver and gold from the people of
the land, from every one according to his assessment, to give *it* to Pharaoh Necho. [36]Jehoiakim
was twenty-five years old when he became
king, and he reigned eleven years in Jerusalem.
His mother's name *was* Zebudah the daughter
of Pedaiah of Rumah. [37]And he did evil in the
sight of the LORD, according to all that his
fathers had done.

24 In his days Nebuchadnezzar king of
Babylon came up, and Jehoiakim
became his vassal *for* three years. Then he
turned and rebelled against him. [2]And the LORD
sent against him *raiding* bands of Chaldeans,
bands of Syrians, bands of Moabites, and
bands of the people of Ammon; He sent them
against Judah to destroy it, according to the
word of the LORD which He had spoken by His
servants the prophets. [3]Surely at the commandment of the LORD *this* came upon Judah,
to remove *them* from His sight because of the
sins of Manasseh, according to all that he had
done, [4]and also because of the innocent blood
that he had shed; for he had filled Jerusalem

24:1 Nebuchadnezzar. Nebuchadnezzar II was the son of Nabopolassar, king of Babylon from 626 to 605 B.C. As crown prince, Nebuchadnezzar had led his father's army against Pharaoh Necho and the Egyptians at Carchemish on the Euphrates River in northern Syria (605 B.C.). By defeating the Egyptians, Babylon was established as the strongest nation in the ancient Near East. Egypt and its vassals, including Judah, became vassals of Babylon with this victory. Nebuchadnezzar followed up his victory at Carchemish by invading the land of Judah. Later, in 605 B.C., Nebuchadnezzar took some captives to Babylon, including Daniel and his friends (Dan. 1:1–3). Toward the end of 605 B.C., Nabopolassar died and Nebuchadnezzar succeeded him as king of Babylon, 3 years after Jehoiakim had taken the throne in Judah (Jer. 25:1). Nebuchadnezzar reigned from 605 to 562 B.C. **three years.** Nebuchadnezzar returned to the west in 604 B.C. and took tribute from all of the kings of the west, including Jehoiakim of Judah. Jehoiakim submitted to Babylonian rule from 604 to 602 B.C. In 602 B.C., Jehoiakim rebelled against Babylon, disregarding the advice of the prophet Jeremiah (Jer. 27:9–11).

with innocent blood, which the LORD would not
pardon.
[5]Now the rest of the acts of Jehoiakim, and
all that he did, *are* they not written in the book
of the chronicles of the kings of Judah? [6]So
Jehoiakim rested with his fathers. Then Jehoiachin his son reigned in his place.
[7]And the king of Egypt did not come out of
his land anymore, for the king of Babylon had
taken all that belonged to the king of Egypt
from the Brook of Egypt to the River
Euphrates.
[8]Jehoiachin *was* eighteen years old when he
became king, and he reigned in Jerusalem
three months. His mother's name *was*
Nehushta the daughter of Elnathan of Jerusalem. [9]And he did evil in the sight of the LORD,
according to all that his father had done.
[10]At that time the servants of Nebuchadnezzar king of Babylon came up against Jerusalem,
and the city was besieged. [11]And Nebuchadnezzar king of Babylon came against the city, as his
servants were besieging it. [12]Then Jehoiachin
king of Judah, his mother, his servants, his
princes, and his officers went out to the king of
Babylon; and the king of Babylon, in the eighth
year of his reign, took him prisoner.
[13]And he carried out from there all the

treasures of the house of the LORD and the
treasures of the king's house, and he cut in
pieces all the articles of gold which Solomon
king of Israel had made in the temple of the
LORD, as the LORD had said. [14]Also he carried
into captivity all Jerusalem: all the captains
and all the mighty men of valor, ten thousand
captives, and all the craftsmen and smiths.
None remained except the poorest people of
the land. [15]And he carried Jehoiachin captive to
Babylon. The king's mother, the king's wives,
his officers, and the mighty of the land he carried into captivity from Jerusalem to Babylon.
[16]All the valiant men, seven thousand, and
craftsmen and smiths, one thousand, all *who
were* strong *and* fit for war, these the king of
Babylon brought captive to Babylon.

24:14–16 In 597 B.C., Nebuchadnezzar took an additional 10,000 Judeans as captives to Babylon, in particular the leaders of the nation. This included the leaders of the military and those whose skills would support the military. Included in this deportation was the prophet Ezekiel (Ezek. 1:1–3). Only the lower classes remained behind in Jerusalem. The Babylonian policy of captivity was different from that of the Assyrians, who took most of the people into exile and resettled the land of Israel with foreigners (17:24). The Babylonians took only the leaders and the strong, while leaving the weak and poor, elevating those left to leadership and thereby earning their loyalty. Those taken to Babylon were allowed to work and live in the mainstream of society. This kept the captive Jews together, so it would be possible for them to return, as recorded in Ezra.

[17]Then the king of Babylon made Mattaniah,
Jehoiachin's uncle, king in his place, and
changed his name to Zedekiah.
[18]Zedekiah *was* twenty-one years old when
he became king, and he reigned eleven years
in Jerusalem. His mother's name *was* Hamutal
the daughter of Jeremiah of Libnah. [19]He also
did evil in the sight of the LORD, according to
all that Jehoiakim had done. [20]For because of
the anger of the LORD *this* happened in Jerusalem and Judah, that He finally cast them out
from His presence. Then Zedekiah rebelled
against the king of Babylon.

Psalm 74:18–23

18 Remember this, *that* the enemy has
reproached, O LORD,
And *that* a foolish people has
blasphemed Your name.
19 Oh, do not deliver the life of Your
turtledove to the wild beast!
Do not forget the life of Your poor
forever.
20 Have respect to the covenant;
For the dark places of the earth are full
of the haunts of cruelty.
21 Oh, do not let the oppressed return
ashamed!
Let the poor and needy praise Your
name.

22 Arise, O God, plead Your own cause;
Remember how the foolish man
reproaches You daily.
23 Do not forget the voice of Your
enemies;
The tumult of those who rise up
against You increases continually.

Proverbs 19:3

3 The foolishness of a man twists his
way,
And his heart frets against the LORD.

Acts 2:22–47

[22]"Men of Israel, hear these words: Jesus of
Nazareth, a Man attested by God to you by
miracles, wonders, and signs which God did
through Him in your midst, as you yourselves
also know— [23]Him, being delivered by the
determined purpose and foreknowledge of
God, you have taken by lawless hands, have
crucified, and put to death; [24]whom God raised
up, having loosed the pains of death, because
it was not possible that He should be held by
it. [25]For David says concerning Him:

*'I foresaw the LORD always before my
face,
For He is at my right hand, that I may
not be shaken.*
26 *Therefore my heart rejoiced, and my
tongue was glad;
Moreover my flesh also will rest in
hope.*
27 *For You will not leave my soul in
Hades,
Nor will You allow Your Holy One to
see corruption.*
28 *You have made known to me the ways
of life;
You will make me full of joy in Your
presence.'*

[29]"Men *and* brethren, let *me* speak freely to
you of the patriarch David, that he is both dead

and buried, and his tomb is with us to this day.
30Therefore, being a prophet, and knowing
that God had sworn with an oath to him that of
the fruit of his body, according to the flesh, He
would raise up the Christ to sit on his throne,
31he, foreseeing this, spoke concerning the
resurrection of the Christ, that His soul was
not left in Hades, nor did His flesh see corruption. 32This Jesus God has raised up, of
which we are all witnesses. 33Therefore being
exalted to the right hand of God, and having
received from the Father the promise of the
Holy Spirit, He poured out this which you now
see and hear.
34"For David did not ascend into the heavens, but he says himself:

'The LORD said to my Lord,
"Sit at My right hand,
35 *Till I make Your enemies Your*
footstool."'

36"Therefore let all the house of Israel know
assuredly that God has made this Jesus,
whom you crucified, both Lord and Christ."
37Now when they heard *this,* they were cut
to the heart, and said to Peter and the rest of
the apostles, "Men *and* brethren, what shall
we do?"
38Then Peter said to them, "Repent, and let
every one of you be baptized in the name of Jesus Christ for the remission of sins; and you
shall receive the gift of the Holy Spirit. 39For
the promise is to you and to your children, and
to all who are afar off, as many as the Lord our
God will call."
40And with many other words he testified
and exhorted them, saying, "Be saved from this
perverse generation." 41Then those who gladly
received his word were baptized; and that day
about three thousand souls were added *to*
them. 42And they continued steadfastly in the
apostles' doctrine and fellowship, in the breaking of bread, and in prayers. 43Then fear came
upon every soul, and many wonders and signs
were done through the apostles. 44Now all who
believed were together, and had all things in
common, 45and sold their possessions and
goods, and divided them among all, as anyone
had need.
46So continuing daily with one accord in the
temple, and breaking bread from house to
house, they ate their food with gladness and
simplicity of heart, 47praising God and having
favor with all the people. And the Lord added
to the church daily those who were being
saved.

2:42 apostles' doctrine. The foundational content for the believer's spiritual growth and maturity was the Scripture, God's revealed truth, which the apostles received and taught faithfully. **fellowship.** Literally, "partnership" or "sharing." Because Christians become partners with Jesus Christ and all other believers (1 John 1:3), it is their spiritual duty to stimulate one another to righteousness and obedience (Rom. 12:10; 13:8; 15:5; Gal. 5:13; Eph. 4:2,25; 5:21; Col. 3:9; 1 Thess. 4:9; Heb. 3:13; 10:24,25;1 Pet. 4:9,10). **breaking of bread.** A reference to the Lord's Table, or Communion, which is mandatory for all Christians to observe (1 Cor. 11:24–29). **prayers.** Of individual believers and the church corporately (see 1:14,24; 4:24–31; John 14:13,14).

DAY 17: In response to Peter's sermon, what instructions were given on how to become a Christian?

Those who listened to that powerful sermon were "cut to the heart" (v. 37). The Greek word for cut means "pierce" or "stab," and thus denotes something sudden and unexpected. In grief, remorse, and intense spiritual conviction, Peter's listeners were stunned by his indictment that they had killed their Messiah.

"Repent" (v. 38). This refers to a change of mind and purpose that turns an individual from sin to God (1 Thess. 1:9). Such change involves more than fearing the consequences of God's judgment. Genuine repentance knows that the evil of sin must be forsaken and the Person and work of Christ totally and singularly embraced. Peter exhorted his hearers to repent; otherwise, they would not experience true conversion.

"Be baptized." This Greek word means "be dipped" or "immersed" in water. Peter was obeying Christ's command from Matthew 28:19 and urging the people who repented and turned to the Lord Christ for salvation to identify, through the waters of baptism, with His death, burial, and resurrection (19:5; Rom. 6:3,4; 1 Cor. 12:13; Gal. 3:27). This is the first time the apostles publicly enjoined people to obey that ceremony. Prior to this, many Jews had experienced the baptism of

John the Baptist and were also familiar with the baptism of Gentile converts to Judaism (proselytes).

"In the name of Jesus Christ." For the new believer, it was a crucial but costly identification to accept. "For the remission of sins." This might better be translated "because of the remission of sins." Baptism does not produce forgiveness and cleansing from sin. The reality of forgiveness precedes the rite of baptism (v. 41). Genuine repentance brings from God the forgiveness (remission) of sins (Eph. 1:7); and because of that, the new believer was to be baptized.

"Receive the gift of the Holy Spirit." The one-time act by which God places His Spirit into the believer's life.

JUNE 18

2 Kings 25:1–30

25 Now it came to pass in the ninth year of his reign, in the tenth month, on the tenth *day* of the month, *that* Nebuchadnezzar king of Babylon and all his army came against Jerusalem and encamped against it; and they built a siege wall against it all around. [2]So the city was besieged until the eleventh year of King Zedekiah. [3]By the ninth *day* of the *fourth* month the famine had become so severe in the city that there was no food for the people of the land.

[4]Then the city wall was broken through, and all the men of war *fled* at night by way of the gate between two walls, which was by the king's garden, even though the Chaldeans *were* still encamped all around against the city. And *the king* went by way of the plain. [5]But the army of the Chaldeans pursued the king, and they overtook him in the plains of Jericho. All his army was scattered from him. [6]So they took the king and brought him up to the king of Babylon at Riblah, and they pronounced judgment on him. [7]Then they killed the sons of Zedekiah before his eyes, put out the eyes of Zedekiah, bound him with bronze fetters, and took him to Babylon.

[8]And in the fifth month, on the seventh *day* of the month (which *was* the nineteenth year of King Nebuchadnezzar king of Babylon), Nebuzaradan the captain of the guard, a servant of the king of Babylon, came to Jerusalem. [9]He burned the house of the LORD and the king's house; all the houses of Jerusalem, that is, all the houses of the great, he burned with fire. [10]And all the army of the Chaldeans who *were with* the captain of the guard broke down the walls of Jerusalem all around.

[11]Then Nebuzaradan the captain of the guard carried away captive the rest of the people *who* remained in the city and the defectors who had deserted to the king of Babylon, with the rest of the multitude. [12]But the captain of the guard left *some* of the poor of the land as vinedressers and farmers. [13]The bronze pillars that *were* in the house of the LORD, and the carts and the bronze Sea that *were* in the house of the LORD, the Chaldeans broke in pieces, and carried their bronze to Babylon. [14]They also took away the pots, the shovels, the trimmers, the spoons, and all the bronze utensils with which the priests ministered. [15]The firepans and the basins, the things of solid gold and solid silver, the captain of the guard took away. [16]The two pillars, one Sea, and the carts, which Solomon had made for the house of the LORD, the bronze of all these articles was beyond measure. [17]The height of one pillar *was* eighteen cubits, and the capital on it *was* of bronze. The height of the capital was three cubits, and the network and pomegranates all around the capital were all of bronze. The second pillar was the same, with a network.

[18]And the captain of the guard took Seraiah the chief priest, Zephaniah the second priest, and the three doorkeepers. [19]He also took out of the city an officer who had charge of the men of war, five men of the king's close associates who were found in the city, the chief recruiting officer of the army, who mustered the people of the land, and sixty men of the people of the land *who were* found in the city. [20]So Nebuzaradan, captain of the guard, took these and brought them to the king of Babylon at Riblah. [21]Then the king of Babylon struck them and put them to death at Riblah in the land of Hamath. Thus Judah was carried away captive from its own land.

[22]Then he made Gedaliah the son of Ahikam, the son of Shaphan, governor over the people who remained in the land of Judah, whom Nebuchadnezzar king of Babylon had left. [23]Now when all the captains of the armies, they and *their* men, heard that the king of Babylon had made Gedaliah governor, they came to Gedaliah at Mizpah—Ishmael the son of Nethaniah, Johanan the son of Careah, Seraiah the son of Tanhumeth the Netophathite, and Jaazaniah the son of a Maachathite,

they and their men. 24And Gedaliah took an
oath before them and their men, and said to
them, "Do not be afraid of the servants of the
Chaldeans. Dwell in the land and serve the
king of Babylon, and it shall be well with you."
25But it happened in the seventh month that
Ishmael the son of Nethaniah, the son of
Elishama, of the royal family, came with ten
men and struck and killed Gedaliah, the Jews,
as well as the Chaldeans who were with him at
Mizpah. 26And all the people, small and great,
and the captains of the armies, arose and went
to Egypt; for they were afraid of the Chaldeans.
27Now it came to pass in the thirty-seventh
year of the captivity of Jehoiachin king of Judah, in the twelfth month, on the twenty-seventh *day* of the month, *that* Evil-Merodach
king of Babylon, in the year that he began to
reign, released Jehoiachin king of Judah from
prison. 28He spoke kindly to him, and gave him
a more prominent seat than those of the kings
who *were* with him in Babylon. 29So Jehoiachin
changed from his prison garments, and he ate
bread regularly before the king all the days of
his life. 30And as for his provisions, *there was* a
regular ration given him by the king, a portion
for each day, all the days of his life.

Psalm 75:1–10

To the Chief Musician. Set to "Do Not Destroy."
A Psalm of Asaph. A Song.

We give thanks to You,
O God, we give thanks!
For Your wondrous works declare *that*
Your name is near.

75:1 Your name is near. God's name represents His presence. The history of God's supernatural interventions on behalf of His people demonstrated that God was personally immanent. But Old Testament saints did not have the fullness from the permanent, personal indwelling of the Holy Spirit (John 14:1,16,17; 1 Cor. 3:16; 6:19).

2 "When I choose the proper time,
I will judge uprightly.
3 The earth and all its inhabitants are
dissolved;
I set up its pillars firmly. Selah
4 "I said to the boastful, 'Do not deal
boastfully,'
And to the wicked, 'Do not lift up the
horn.
5 Do not lift up your horn on high;
Do *not* speak with a stiff neck.' "
6 For exaltation *comes* neither from the
east
Nor from the west nor from the south.
7 But God *is* the Judge:
He puts down one,
And exalts another.
8 For in the hand of the LORD *there is*
a cup,
And the wine is red;
It is fully mixed, and He pours it out;
Surely its dregs shall all the wicked of
the earth
Drain *and* drink down.
9 But I will declare forever,
I will sing praises to the God of Jacob.
10 "All the horns of the wicked I will also
cut off,
But the horns of the righteous shall
be exalted."

Proverbs 19:4–5

4 Wealth makes many friends,
But the poor is separated from his
friend.
5 A false witness will not go unpunished,
And *he who* speaks lies will not escape.

Acts 3:1–26

3 Now Peter and John went up together to
the temple at the hour of prayer, the ninth
hour. 2And a certain man lame from his mother's womb was carried, whom they laid daily at
the gate of the temple which is called Beautiful,
to ask alms from those who entered the temple;
3who, seeing Peter and John about to go into
the temple, asked for alms. 4And fixing his eyes
on him, with John, Peter said, "Look at us." 5So
he gave them his attention, expecting to receive
something from them. 6Then Peter said, "Silver
and gold I do not have, but what I do have I give
you: In the name of Jesus Christ of Nazareth,
rise up and walk." 7And he took him by the
right hand and lifted *him* up, and immediately
his feet and ankle bones received strength. 8So
he, leaping up, stood and walked and entered
the temple with them—walking, leaping, and
praising God. 9And all the people saw him walking and praising God. 10Then they knew that it
was he who sat begging alms at the Beautiful
Gate of the temple; and they were filled with
wonder and amazement at what had happened
to him.
11Now as the lame man who was healed held
on to Peter and John, all the people ran together

to them in the porch which is called Solomon's, greatly amazed. [12]So when Peter saw *it,* he responded to the people: "Men of Israel, why do you marvel at this? Or why look so intently at us, as though by our own power or godliness we had made this man walk? [13]The God of Abraham, Isaac, and Jacob, the God of our fathers, glorified His Servant Jesus, whom you delivered up and denied in the presence of Pilate, when he was determined to let *Him* go. [14]But you denied the

3:13 The God of Abraham, Isaac, and Jacob. A description of God familiar to Peter's Jewish audience (Ex. 3:6,15; 1 Kin. 18:36; 1 Chr. 29:18; 2 Chr. 30:6; Matt. 22:32). He used this formula, which stressed God's covenant faithfulness, to demonstrate that he declared the same God and Messiah whom the prophets had proclaimed. **His Servant Jesus.** Peter depicted Jesus as God's personal representative. This is an unusual New Testament title for Jesus, used only 4 other places (v. 26; 4:27,30; Matt. 12:18), but a more familiar Old Testament name for Messiah (Is. 42:1–4,19; 49:5–7; 52:13–53:12; Matt. 20:28; John 6:38; 8:28; 13:1–7). **Pilate...determined to let *Him* go.** Pontius Pilate, the Roman governor at Jesus' trial, came from a national tradition that strongly supported justice. He knew Jesus' crucifixion would be unjust and therefore declared Him innocent 6 times (Luke 23:4,14,15,22; John 18:38; 19:4,6) and repeatedly sought to release Him (Luke 23:13–22; John 19:12,13).

Holy One and the Just, and asked for a murderer to be granted to you, [15]and killed the Prince of life, whom God raised from the dead, of which we are witnesses. [16]And His name, through faith in His name, has made this man strong, whom you see and know. Yes, the faith which *comes* through Him has given him this perfect soundness in the presence of you all.

[17]"Yet now, brethren, I know that you did *it* in ignorance, as *did* also your rulers. [18]But those things which God foretold by the mouth of all His prophets, that the Christ would suffer, He has thus fulfilled. [19]Repent therefore and be converted, that your sins may be blotted out, so that times of refreshing may come

3:15 killed...God raised...we are witnesses. Peter's confident and forceful declaration (1 Cor. 15:3–7) was a clear defense of and provided further evidence for Christ's resurrection. Peter's claim was undeniable; the Jews never showed any evidence, such as Jesus' corpse, to disprove it. **Prince of life.** The Greek word for "prince" means originator, pioneer, or beginner of something. Both Hebrews 2:10 and 12:2 translate it "author." It describes Jesus as the Divine Originator of life (Ps. 36:9; Heb. 2:10; 12:2; 1 John 5:11,20).

from the presence of the Lord, [20]and that He may send Jesus Christ, who was preached to you before, [21]whom heaven must receive until the times of restoration of all things, which God has spoken by the mouth of all His holy prophets since the world began. [22]For Moses truly said to the fathers, *'The LORD your God will raise up for you a Prophet like me from your brethren. Him you shall hear in all*

3:19 Repent...be converted. "Converted" is a frequent New Testament word that relates to sinners turning to God (9:35; 14:15; 26:18,20; Luke 1:16,17; 2 Cor. 3:16; 1 Pet. 2:25). **your sins...blotted out.** Ps. 51:9; Is. 43:25; 44:22. Blotted out compares forgiveness to the complete wiping away of ink from the surface of a document (Col. 2:14).

things, whatever He says to you. [23]*And it shall be that every soul who will not hear that Prophet shall be utterly destroyed from among the people.'* [24]Yes, and all the prophets, from Samuel and those who follow, as many as have spoken, have also foretold these days. [25]You are sons of the prophets, and of the covenant which God made with our fathers, saying to Abraham, *'And in your seed all the families of the earth shall be blessed.'* [26]To you first, God, having raised up His Servant Jesus, sent Him to bless you, in turning away every one *of you* from your iniquities."

DAY 18: How did Judah and Jerusalem finally fall?

Responding to King Zedekiah's rebellion in 2 Kings 24:20, Nebuchadnezzar sent his whole army to lay siege against the city of Jerusalem (2 Kin. 25:1). The siege began in January 588 B.C. and lasted until July 586 B.C. In August 586 B.C., one month after the Babylonian breakthrough of Jerusalem's walls (vv. 2–4), Nebuzaradan, the commander of Nebuchadnezzar's own imperial guard, was sent by the king to oversee the destruction of Jerusalem. The dismantling and destruction of Jerusalem was accomplished by the Babylonians in an orderly progression (v. 8).

First, Jerusalem's most important buildings were burned (v. 9). Second, the Babylonian army tore down Jerusalem's outer walls, the city's main defense (v. 10). Third, Nebuzaradan organized and led a forced march of remaining Judeans into exile in Babylon (vv. 11,12). The exiles included survivors from Jerusalem and those who had surrendered to the Babylonians before the capture of the city. Only poor, unskilled laborers were left behind to tend the vineyards and farm the fields. Fourth, the items made with precious metals in the temple were carried away to Babylon (vv. 13–17). Fifth, Nebuzaradan took Jerusalem's remaining leaders to Riblah, where Nebuchadnezzar had them executed. This insured that they would never lead another rebellion against Babylon (vv. 18–21).

"Thus Judah was carried away captive from its own land" (v. 21). Exile was the ultimate curse brought upon Judah because of her disobedience to the Mosaic Covenant (Lev. 26:33; Deut. 28:36,64). The Book of Lamentations records the sorrow of Jeremiah over this destruction of Jerusalem.

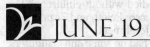

JUNE 19

1 Chronicles 1:1–2:55

1 Adam, Seth, Enosh, [2]Cainan, Mahalalel, Jared, [3]Enoch, Methuselah, Lamech, [4]Noah, Shem, Ham, and Japheth.

[5]The sons of Japheth *were* Gomer, Magog, Madai, Javan, Tubal, Meshech, and Tiras. [6]The sons of Gomer *were* Ashkenaz, Diphath, and Togarmah. [7]The sons of Javan *were* Elishah, Tarshishah, Kittim, and Rodanim.

[8]The sons of Ham *were* Cush, Mizraim, Put, and Canaan. [9]The sons of Cush *were* Seba, Havilah, Sabta, Raama, and Sabtecha. The sons of Raama *were* Sheba and Dedan. [10]Cush begot Nimrod; he began to be a mighty one on the earth. [11]Mizraim begot Ludim, Anamim, Lehabim, Naphtuhim, [12]Pathrusim, Casluhim (from whom came the Philistines and the Caphtorim). [13]Canaan begot Sidon, his firstborn, and Heth; [14]the Jebusite, the Amorite, and the Girgashite; [15]the Hivite, the Arkite, and the Sinite; [16]the Arvadite, the Zemarite, and the Hamathite.

[17]The sons of Shem *were* Elam, Asshur, Arphaxad, Lud, Aram, Uz, Hul, Gether, and Meshech. [18]Arphaxad begot Shelah, and Shelah begot Eber. [19]To Eber were born two sons: the name of one *was* Peleg, for in his days the earth was divided; and his brother's name *was* Joktan. [20]Joktan begot Almodad, Sheleph, Hazarmaveth, Jerah, [21]Hadoram, Uzal, Diklah, [22]Ebal, Abimael, Sheba, [23]Ophir, Havilah, and Jobab. All these *were* the sons of Joktan.

[24]Shem, Arphaxad, Shelah, [25]Eber, Peleg, Reu, [26]Serug, Nahor, Terah, [27]and Abram, who *is* Abraham. [28]The sons of Abraham *were* Isaac and Ishmael.

[29]These *are* their genealogies: The firstborn of Ishmael *was* Nebajoth; then Kedar, Adbeel, Mibsam, [30]Mishma, Dumah, Massa, Hadad, Tema, [31]Jetur, Naphish, and Kedemah. These *were* the sons of Ishmael.

[32]Now the sons born to Keturah, Abraham's concubine, *were* Zimran, Jokshan, Medan, Midian, Ishbak, and Shuah. The sons of Jokshan *were* Sheba and Dedan. [33]The sons of Midian *were* Ephah, Epher, Hanoch, Abida, and Eldaah. All these were the children of Keturah.

[34]And Abraham begot Isaac. The sons of Isaac *were* Esau and Israel. [35]The sons of Esau *were* Eliphaz, Reuel, Jeush, Jaalam, and Korah. [36]And the sons of Eliphaz *were* Teman, Omar, Zephi, Gatam, *and* Kenaz; and *by* Timna, Amalek. [37]The sons of Reuel *were* Nahath, Zerah, Shammah, and Mizzah.

[38]The sons of Seir *were* Lotan, Shobal, Zibeon, Anah, Dishon, Ezer, and Dishan. [39]And the sons of Lotan *were* Hori and Homam; Lotan's sister *was* Timna. [40]The sons of Shobal *were* Alian, Manahath, Ebal, Shephi, and Onam. The sons of Zibeon *were* Ajah and Anah. [41]The son of Anah *was* Dishon. The sons of Dishon *were* Hamran, Eshban, Ithran, and Cheran. [42]The sons of Ezer *were* Bilhan, Zaavan, *and* Jaakan. The sons of Dishan *were* Uz and Aran.

[43]Now these *were* the kings who reigned in the land of Edom before a king reigned over the children of Israel: Bela the son of Beor, and the name of his city was Dinhabah. [44]And when Bela died, Jobab the son of Zerah of Bozrah reigned in his place. [45]When Jobab died, Husham of the land of the Temanites reigned in his place. [46]And when Husham died, Hadad the son of Bedad, who attacked Midian in the field of Moab, reigned in his place. The name of his city *was* Avith. [47]When Hadad died, Samlah of Masrekah reigned in his place. [48]And when Samlah died, Saul of Rehoboth-by-the-River reigned in his place. [49]When Saul died, Baal-Hanan the son of Achbor reigned in his place.

50 And when Baal-Hanan died, Hadad reigned in
his place; and the name of his city was Pai. His
wife's name was Mehetabel the daughter of
Matred, the daughter of Mezahab. 51 Hadad died
also. And the chiefs of Edom were Chief Timnah,
Chief Aliah, Chief Jetheth, 52 Chief Aholibamah,
Chief Elah, Chief Pinon, 53 Chief Kenaz, Chief
Teman, Chief Mibzar, 54 Chief Magdiel, and Chief
Iram. These *were* the chiefs of Edom.

2 These *were* the sons of Israel: Reuben,
Simeon, Levi, Judah, Issachar, Zebulun,
2 Dan, Joseph, Benjamin, Naphtali, Gad, and
Asher.

3 The sons of Judah *were* Er, Onan, and
Shelah. *These* three were born to him by the
daughter of Shua, the Canaanitess. Er, the firstborn of Judah, was wicked in the sight of the
LORD; so He killed him. 4 And Tamar, his
daughter-in-law, bore him Perez and Zerah.
All the sons of Judah *were* five.

5 The sons of Perez *were* Hezron and Hamul.
6 The sons of Zerah *were* Zimri, Ethan, Heman,
Calcol, and Dara—five of them in all.

7 The son of Carmi *was* Achar, the troubler of
Israel, who transgressed in the accursed
thing.

8 The son of Ethan *was* Azariah.

9 Also the sons of Hezron who were born to
him *were* Jerahmeel, Ram, and Chelubai.
10 Ram begot Amminadab, and Amminadab
begot Nahshon, leader of the children of Judah; 11 Nahshon begot Salma, and Salma begot
Boaz; 12 Boaz begot Obed, and Obed begot
Jesse; 13 Jesse begot Eliab his firstborn,
Abinadab the second, Shimea the third,
14 Nethanel the fourth, Raddai the fifth, 15 Ozem
the sixth, *and* David the seventh.

16 Now their sisters *were* Zeruiah and Abigail.
And the sons of Zeruiah *were* Abishai, Joab,
and Asahel—three. 17 Abigail bore Amasa; and
the father of Amasa *was* Jether the Ishmaelite.

18 Caleb the son of Hezron had children by
Azubah, *his* wife, and by Jerioth. Now these
were her sons: Jesher, Shobab, and Ardon.
19 When Azubah died, Caleb took Ephrath as
his wife, who bore him Hur. 20 And Hur begot
Uri, and Uri begot Bezalel.

21 Now afterward Hezron went in to the
daughter of Machir the father of Gilead,
whom he married when he *was* sixty years
old; and she bore him Segub. 22 Segub begot
Jair, who had twenty-three cities in the land of
Gilead. 23 (Geshur and Syria took from them
the towns of Jair, with Kenath and its towns—
sixty towns.) All these *belonged to* the sons of
Machir the father of Gilead. 24 After Hezron
died in Caleb Ephrathah, Hezron's wife Abijah
bore him Ashhur the father of Tekoa.

25 The sons of Jerahmeel, the firstborn of
Hezron, *were* Ram, the firstborn, and Bunah,
Oren, Ozem, *and* Ahijah. 26 Jerahmeel had another wife, whose name was Atarah; she was the
mother of Onam. 27 The sons of Ram, the firstborn of Jerahmeel, were Maaz, Jamin, and Eker.
28 The sons of Onam were Shammai and Jada.
The sons of Shammai *were* Nadab and Abishur.

29 And the name of the wife of Abishur *was*
Abihail, and she bore him Ahban and Molid.
30 The sons of Nadab *were* Seled and Appaim;
Seled died without children. 31 The son of
Appaim *was* Ishi, the son of Ishi *was* Sheshan,
and Sheshan's son *was* Ahlai. 32 The sons of
Jada, the brother of Shammai, *were* Jether and
Jonathan; Jether died without children. 33 The
sons of Jonathan *were* Peleth and Zaza. These
were the sons of Jerahmeel.

34 Now Sheshan had no sons, only daughters.
And Sheshan had an Egyptian servant whose
name *was* Jarha. 35 Sheshan gave his daughter to
Jarha his servant as wife, and she bore him Attai.
36 Attai begot Nathan, and Nathan begot Zabad;
37 Zabad begot Ephlal, and Ephlal begot Obed;
38 Obed begot Jehu, and Jehu begot Azariah;
39 Azariah begot Helez, and Helez begot Eleasah;
40 Eleasah begot Sismai, and Sismai begot
Shallum; 41 Shallum begot Jekamiah, and Jekamiah begot Elishama.

42 The descendants of Caleb the brother of
Jerahmeel *were* Mesha, his firstborn, who was
the father of Ziph, and the sons of Mareshah
the father of Hebron. 43 The sons of Hebron
were Korah, Tappuah, Rekem, and Shema.
44 Shema begot Raham the father of Jorkoam,
and Rekem begot Shammai. 45 And the son of
Shammai *was* Maon, and Maon *was* the father
of Beth Zur.

46 Ephah, Caleb's concubine, bore Haran,
Moza, and Gazez; and Haran begot Gazez.
47 And the sons of Jahdai *were* Regem, Jotham,
Geshan, Pelet, Ephah, and Shaaph.

48 Maachah, Caleb's concubine, bore Sheber
and Tirhanah. 49 She also bore Shaaph the
father of Madmannah, Sheva the father of
Machbenah and the father of Gibea. And the
daughter of Caleb *was* Achsah.

50 These were the descendants of Caleb: The
sons of Hur, the firstborn of Ephrathah, *were*
Shobal the father of Kirjath Jearim, 51 Salma the
father of Bethlehem, *and* Hareph the father of
Beth Gader.

52 And Shobal the father of Kirjath Jearim had
descendants: Haroeh, *and* half of the *families of*
Manuhoth. 53 The families of Kirjath Jearim *were*
the Ithrites, the Puthites, the Shumathites, and
the Mishraites. From these came the
Zorathites and the Eshtaolites.

54 The sons of Salma *were* Bethlehem, the

Netophathites, Atroth Beth Joab, half of the Manahethites, and the Zorites.

55And the families of the scribes who dwelt at Jabez *were* the Tirathites, the Shimeathites, *and* the Suchathites. These *were* the Kenites who came from Hammath, the father of the house of Rechab.

Psalm 76:1–6

To the Chief Musician. On stringed instruments.
A Psalm of Asaph. A Song.

In Judah God *is* known;
His name *is* great in Israel.
2 In Salem also is His tabernacle,
And His dwelling place in Zion.
3 There He broke the arrows of the bow,
The shield and sword of battle. Selah

4 You *are* more glorious and excellent
Than the mountains of prey.
5 The stouthearted were plundered;
They have sunk into their sleep;
And none of the mighty men have
found the use of their hands.
6 At Your rebuke, O God of Jacob,
Both the chariot and horse were cast
into a dead sleep.

Proverbs 19:6–7

6 Many entreat the favor of the nobility,
And every man *is* a friend to one who
gives gifts.
7 All the brothers of the poor hate him;
How much more do his friends go far
from him!
He may pursue *them with* words, *yet* they
abandon *him.*

Acts 4:1–22

4 Now as they spoke to the people, the priests, the captain of the temple, and the Sadducees came upon them, 2being greatly disturbed that they taught the people and preached in Jesus the resurrection from the dead. 3And they laid hands on them, and put *them* in custody until the next day, for it was already evening. 4However, many of those who heard the word believed; and the number of the men came to be about five thousand.

5And it came to pass, on the next day, that their rulers, elders, and scribes, 6as well as Annas the high priest, Caiaphas, John, and Alexander, and as many as were of the family of the high priest, were gathered together at Jerusalem. 7And when they had set them in the midst, they asked, "By what power or by what name have you done this?"

8Then Peter, filled with the Holy Spirit, said to them, "Rulers of the people and elders of Israel: 9If we this day are judged for a good deed *done* to a helpless man, by what means he has been made well, 10let it be known to you all, and to all the people of Israel, that by the name of Jesus Christ of Nazareth, whom you crucified, whom God raised from the dead, by Him this man stands here before you whole. 11This is the *'stone which was rejected by you builders, which has become the chief cornerstone.'* 12Nor is there salvation in any other, for there is no other name under heaven given among men by which we must be saved."

13Now when they saw the boldness of Peter and John, and perceived that they were uneducated and untrained men, they marveled. And they realized that they had been with Jesus. 14And seeing the man who had been healed standing with them, they could say nothing against it. 15But when they had commanded them to go aside out of the council, they conferred among themselves, 16saying, "What shall we do to these men? For, indeed,

4:1 priests. The office of priest in the Old Testament began with Aaron and his sons (Lev. 8). They became the human intermediaries between holy God and sinful humanity. They were characterized by 3 qualities: 1) they were chosen and set apart for priestly service by God; 2) they were to be holy in character; and 3) they were the only ones allowed to come near to God on behalf of the people with the high priest being the chief go-between on the Day of Atonement (Lev. 16). **the captain of the temple.** Chief of the temple police force (composed of Levites) and second-ranking official to the high priest. The Romans had delegated the temple-policing responsibility to the Jews.

4:2 preached in Jesus the resurrection. This part of the apostles' message was the most objectionable to the Jewish leaders. They had executed Christ as a blasphemer and now Peter and John were proclaiming His resurrection.

4:8 filled with the Holy Spirit. Because Peter was under the control of the Spirit, he was able to face persecution and preach the gospel with power (Luke 12:11,12).

4:12 no other name. This refers to the exclusivism of salvation by faith in Jesus Christ. There are only two religious paths: the broad way of works salvation leading to eternal death, and the narrow way of faith in Jesus, leading to eternal life (Matt. 7:13,14; John 10:7,8; 14:6). Sadly, the Sanhedrin and its followers were on the first path.

4:13 uneducated and untrained men. Peter and John were not educated in the rabbinical schools and had no formal training in Old Testament theology.

that a notable miracle has been done through
them *is* evident to all who dwell in Jerusalem,
and we cannot deny *it.* [17]But so that it spreads
no further among the people, let us severely
threaten them, that from now on they speak to
no man in this name."

[18]So they called them and commanded them
not to speak at all nor teach in the name of Jesus.
[19]But Peter and John answered and said to them,
"Whether it is right in the sight of God to listen
to you more than to God, you judge. [20]For we
cannot but speak the things which we have seen
and heard." [21]So when they had further threatened them, they let them go, finding no way of
punishing them, because of the people, since
they all glorified God for what had been done.
[22]For the man was over forty years old on whom
this miracle of healing had been performed.

DAY 19: List the ministries of the Holy Spirit.

Baptismal Medium	1 Corinthians 12:13
Calls to Ministry	Acts 13:2–4
Channel of Divine Revelation	2 Samuel 23:2; Nehemiah 9:30; Zechariah 7:12; John 14:17
Empowers	Exodus 31:1,2; Judges 13:25; Acts 1:8
Fills	Luke 4:1; Acts 2:4; Ephesians 5:18
Guarantees	2 Corinthians 1:22; 5:5; Ephesians 1:14
Guards	2 Timothy 1:14
Helps	John 14:16,26; 15:26; 16:7
Illuminates	1 Corinthians 2:10–13
Indwells	Romans 8:9–11; 1 Corinthians 3:16; 6:19
Intercedes	Romans 8:26,27
Produces Fruit	Galatians 5:22,23
Provides Spiritual Character	Galatians 5:16,18,25
Regenerates	John 3:5,6,8
Restrains/Convicts of Sin	Genesis 6:3; John 16:8–10; Acts 7:51
Sanctifies	Romans 15:16; 1 Corinthians 6:11; 2 Thessalonians 2:13
Seals	2 Corinthians 1:22; Ephesians 1:14; 4:30
Selects Overseers	Acts 20:28
Source of Fellowship	2 Corinthians 13:14; Philippians 2:1
Source of Liberty	2 Corinthians 3:17,18
Source of Power	Ephesians 3:16
Source of Unity	Ephesians 4:3,4
Source of Spiritual Gifts	1 Corinthians 12:4–11
Teaches	John 14:26; Acts 15:28; 1 John 2:20,27

JUNE 20

1 Chronicles 3:1–4:43

3 Now these were the sons of David who
were born to him in Hebron: The firstborn
was Amnon, by Ahinoam the Jezreelitess; the
second, Daniel, by Abigail the Carmelitess; [2]the
third, Absalom the son of Maacah, the daughter
of Talmai, king of Geshur; the fourth, Adonijah
the son of Haggith; [3]the fifth, Shephatiah, by
Abital; the sixth, Ithream, by his wife Eglah.
[4]*These* six were born to him in Hebron. There
he reigned seven years and six months, and in
Jerusalem he reigned thirty-three years. [5]And
these were born to him in Jerusalem: Shimea,
Shobab, Nathan, and Solomon—four by Bath-
shua the daughter of Ammiel. [6]Also *there* were
Ibhar, Elishama, Eliphelet, [7]Nogah, Nepheg,
Japhia, [8]Elishama, Eliada, and Eliphelet—nine *in
all.* [9]*These were* all the sons of David, besides the

3:1 David. The chief reason for such detailed genealogies is that they affirm the line of Christ from Adam (Luke 3:38) through Abraham and David (Matt. 1:1), thus emphasizing the kingdom intentions of God in Christ.

sons of the concubines, and Tamar their sister.
10Solomon's son *was* Rehoboam; Abijah *was*
his son, Asa his son, Jehoshaphat his son,
11Joram his son, Ahaziah his son, Joash his
son, 12Amaziah his son, Azariah his son,
Jotham his son, 13Ahaz his son, Hezekiah his
son, Manasseh his son, 14Amon his son, *and*
Josiah his son. 15The sons of Josiah *were*
Johanan the firstborn, the second Jehoiakim,
the third Zedekiah, and the fourth Shallum.
16The sons of Jehoiakim *were* Jeconiah his son
and Zedekiah his son.

17And the sons of Jeconiah *were* Assir,
Shealtiel his son, 18*and* Malchiram, Pedaiah,
Shenazzar, Jecamiah, Hoshama, and Nedabiah.
19The sons of Pedaiah *were* Zerubbabel and
Shimei. The sons of Zerubbabel *were* Meshul-
lam, Hananiah, Shelomith their sister, 20and
Hashubah, Ohel, Berechiah, Hasadiah, and
Jushab-Hesed—five *in all.*

21The sons of Hananiah *were* Pelatiah and
Jeshaiah, the sons of Rephaiah, the sons of
Arnan, the sons of Obadiah, and the sons of
Shechaniah. 22The son of Shechaniah was Shem-
aiah. The sons of Shemaiah *were* Hattush, Igal,
Bariah, Neariah, and Shaphat—six *in all.* 23The
sons of Neariah *were* Elioenai, Hezekiah, and
Azrikam—three *in all.* 24The sons of Elioenai
were Hodaviah, Eliashib, Pelaiah, Akkub,
Johanan, Delaiah, and Anani—seven *in all.*

4 The sons of Judah *were* Perez, Hezron,
Carmi, Hur, and Shobal. 2And Reaiah the
son of Shobal begot Jahath, and Jahath begot
Ahumai and Lahad. These *were* the families of
the Zorathites. 3These *were the sons of* the
father of Etam: Jezreel, Ishma, and Idbash;
and the name of their sister *was* Hazelelponi;
4and Penuel *was* the father of Gedor, and Ezer
was the father of Hushah.

These *were* the sons of Hur, the firstborn of
Ephrathah the father of Bethlehem.

5And Ashhur the father of Tekoa had two
wives, Helah and Naarah. 6Naarah bore him
Ahuzzam, Hepher, Temeni, and Haahashtari.
These *were* the sons of Naarah. 7The sons of
Helah *were* Zereth, Zohar, and Ethnan; 8and
Koz begot Anub, Zobebah, and the families of
Aharhel the son of Harum.

9Now Jabez was more honorable than his
brothers, and his mother called his name
Jabez, saying, "Because I bore *him* in pain."
10And Jabez called on the God of Israel saying,
"Oh, that You would bless me indeed, and
enlarge my territory, that Your hand would be
with me, and that You would keep *me* from
evil, that I may not cause pain!" So God granted him what he requested.

11Chelub the brother of Shuhah begot
Mehir, who *was* the father of Eshton. 12And
Eshton begot Beth-Rapha, Paseah, and
Tehinnah the father of Ir-Nahash. These *were*
the men of Rechah.

13The sons of Kenaz *were* Othniel and
Seraiah. The sons of Othniel *were* Hathath,
14and Meonothai *who* begot Ophrah. Seraiah
begot Joab the father of Ge Harashim, for
they were craftsmen. 15The sons of Caleb the
son of Jephunneh *were* Iru, Elah, and Naam.
The son of Elah *was* Kenaz. 16The sons of
Jehallelel *were* Ziph, Ziphah, Tiria, and Asarel.
17The sons of Ezrah *were* Jether, Mered,
Epher, and Jalon. And *Mered's wife* bore Miriam, Shammai, and Ishbah the father of Eshtemoa. 18(His wife Jehudijah bore Jered the
father of Gedor, Heber the father of Sochoh,
and Jekuthiel the father of Zanoah.) And these
were the sons of Bithiah the daughter of
Pharaoh, whom Mered took.

19The sons of Hodiah's wife, the sister of
Naham, *were* the fathers of Keilah the Garmite
and of Eshtemoa the Maachathite. 20And the
sons of Shimon *were* Amnon, Rinnah, Ben-
Hanan, and Tilon. And the sons of Ishi *were*
Zoheth and Ben-Zoheth.

21The sons of Shelah the son of Judah *were*
Er the father of Lecah, Laadah the father of
Mareshah, and the families of the house of the
linen workers of the house of Ashbea; 22also
Jokim, the men of Chozeba, and Joash;
Saraph, who ruled in Moab, and Jashubi-
Lehem. Now the records are ancient. 23These
were the potters and those who dwell at
Netaim and Gederah; there they dwelt with
the king for his work.

24The sons of Simeon *were* Nemuel, Jamin,
Jarib, Zerah, *and* Shaul, 25Shallum his son,
Mibsam his son, and Mishma his son. 26And
the sons of Mishma *were* Hamuel his son,
Zacchur his son, and Shimei his son. 27Shimei
had sixteen sons and six daughters; but his
brothers did not have many children, nor did
any of their families multiply as much as the
children of Judah.

28They dwelt at Beersheba, Moladah, Hazar
Shual, 29Bilhah, Ezem, Tolad, 30Bethuel,
Hormah, Ziklag, 31Beth Marcaboth, Hazar

Susim, Beth Biri, and at Shaaraim. These *were*
their cities until the reign of David. [32]And their
villages *were* Etam, Ain, Rimmon, Tochen, and
Ashan—five cities— [33]and all the villages that
were around these cities as far as Baal. These
were their dwelling places, and they maintained their genealogy: [34]Meshobab, Jamlech,
and Joshah the son of Amaziah; [35]Joel, and Jehu
the son of Joshibiah, the son of Seraiah, the son
of Asiel; [36]Elioenai, Jaakobah, Jeshohaiah,
Asaiah, Adiel, Jesimiel, and Benaiah; [37]Ziza the
son of Shiphi, the son of Allon, the son of
Jedaiah, the son of Shimri, the son of
Shemaiah— [38]these mentioned by name *were*
leaders in their families, and their father's
house increased greatly.

[39]So they went to the entrance of Gedor, as
far as the east side of the valley, to seek pasture for their flocks. [40]And they found rich,
good pasture, and the land *was* broad, quiet,
and peaceful; for some Hamites formerly lived
there.

[41]These recorded by name came in the days
of Hezekiah king of Judah; and they attacked
their tents and the Meunites who were found
there, and utterly destroyed them, as it is to
this day. So they dwelt in their place, because
there was pasture for their flocks there. [42]Now
some of them, five hundred men of the sons of
Simeon, went to Mount Seir, having as their
captains Pelatiah, Neariah, Rephaiah, and
Uzziel, the sons of Ishi. [43]And they defeated
the rest of the Amalekites who had escaped.
They have dwelt there to this day.

Psalm 76:7–12

7 You, Yourself, *are* to be feared;
And who may stand in
Your presence
When once You are angry?
8 You caused judgment to be heard from
heaven;
The earth feared and was still,
9 When God arose to judgment,
To deliver all the oppressed of the
earth. Selah

10 Surely the wrath of man shall praise
You;
With the remainder of wrath You shall
gird Yourself.
11 Make vows to the LORD your God, and
pay *them;*
Let all who are around Him bring
presents to Him who ought to be
feared.
12 He shall cut off the spirit
of princes;
He *is* awesome to the kings of
the earth.

76:10 wrath of man shall praise You. The railings against God and His people are turned into praise to God when God providentially brings the wicked down (Is. 36:4–20; Acts 2:23; Rom. 8:28).

76:12 cut off the spirit of princes. God shatters the attitude of proud governmental leaders who rebel against Him.

Proverbs 19:8–9

8 He who gets wisdom loves his own
soul;
He who keeps understanding will find
good.

9 A false witness will not go unpunished,
And *he who* speaks lies shall perish.

Acts 4:23–37

[23]And being let go, they went to their own
companions and reported all that the chief
priests and elders had said to them. [24]So when
they heard that, they raised their voice to God
with one accord and said: "Lord, You *are* God,
who made heaven and earth and the sea, and
all that is in them, [25]who by the mouth of Your
servant David have said:

'Why did the nations rage,
And the people plot vain things?
26 *The kings of the earth took their stand,*
And the rulers were gathered together
Against the LORD and against His
Christ.'

[27]"For truly against Your holy Servant Jesus,
whom You anointed, both Herod and Pontius
Pilate, with the Gentiles and the people of Israel, were gathered together [28]to do whatever
Your hand and Your purpose determined
before to be done. [29]Now, Lord, look on their
threats, and grant to Your servants that with all
boldness they may speak Your word, [30]by
stretching out Your hand to heal, and that
signs and wonders may be done through the
name of Your holy Servant Jesus."

[31]And when they had prayed, the place
where they were assembled together was
shaken; and they were all filled with the Holy
Spirit, and they spoke the word of God with
boldness.

[32]Now the multitude of those who believed

4:24–30 Peter and John's experience did not frighten or discourage the other disciples, but exhilarated them. They took confidence in God's sovereign control of all events, even their sufferings. Furthermore, they were comforted that the opposition whom they were facing was foreseen in the Old Testament (vv. 25,26).

4:32–35 all things in common. Believers understood that all they had belonged to God; and therefore, when a brother or sister had a need, those who could meet it were obligated to do so (James 2:15,16; 1 John 3:17). The method was to give the money to the apostles who would distribute it (vv. 35,37).

4:33 great grace. This means favor and carries a twofold meaning here: 1) favor from the people outside the church. Because of the believers' love and unity, the common people were impressed (2:47); and 2) favor from God who was granting blessing.

were of one heart and one soul; neither did anyone say that any of the things he possessed was
his own, but they had all things in common.

4:36 Barnabas...a Levite. Luke introduces Barnabas as a role model from among those who donated property proceeds. Barnabas was a member of the priestly tribe of the Levites and a native of the island of Cyprus. He becomes an associate of Paul and a prominent figure later in the book (9:26,27; 11:22–24,30; chaps. 13–15). **Cyprus.** The third largest island in the Mediterranean after Sicily and Sardinia, located some 60 miles west off the Syrian coast.

[33]And with great power the apostles gave witness to the resurrection of the Lord Jesus.
And great grace was upon them all. [34]Nor was
there anyone among them who lacked; for all
who were possessors of lands or houses sold
them, and brought the proceeds of the things
that were sold, [35]and laid *them* at the apostles'
feet; and they distributed to each as anyone had
need.

[36]And Joses, who was also named Barnabas
by the apostles (which is translated Son of Encouragement), a Levite of the country of Cyprus, [37]having land, sold *it,* and brought the
money and laid *it* at the apostles' feet.

DAY 20: List the major sermons in Acts.

Sermon	Theme	Reference
Peter to crowds at Pentecost	Peter's explanation of the meaning of Pentecost	Acts 2:14–40
Peter to crowds at the temple	The Jewish people should repent	Acts 3:12–26
Peter to the Sanhedrin	Testimony that a helpless man was healed	Acts 4:5–12
Stephen to the Sanhedrin	Stephen accuses the Jews of killing the Messiah	Acts 7:2–53
Peter to Gentiles	Gentiles can be saved in the same manner as Jews	Acts 10:28–47
Peter to church at Jerusalem	A defense of Peter's ministry to the Gentiles	Acts 11:4–18
Paul to synagogue at Antioch	Jesus was the Messiah of Old Testament prophecies	Acts 13:16–41
Peter to Jerusalem Council	Salvation by grace available to all	Acts 15:7–11
James to Jerusalem Council	Gentile converts do not require circumcision	Acts 15:13–21
Paul to Ephesian elders	Remain faithful in spite of persecution	Acts 20:17–35
Paul to crowd at Jerusalem	Paul's conversion and mission to the Gentiles	Acts 22:1–21
Paul to Sanhedrin	Paul's defense of the gospel	Acts 23:1–6
Paul to King Agrippa	Paul's conversion and zeal for the gospel	Acts 26:2–23
Paul to Jewish leaders at Rome	Paul's statement about his Jewish heritage	Acts 28:17–20

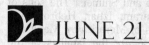

JUNE 21

1 Chronicles 5:1–6:81

5 Now the sons of Reuben the firstborn of Israel—he *was* indeed the firstborn, but
because he defiled his father's bed, his
birthright was given to the sons of Joseph, the
son of Israel, so that the genealogy is not listed
according to the birthright; [2]yet Judah prevailed over his brothers, and from him *came* a
ruler, although the birthright was Joseph's—
[3]the sons of Reuben the firstborn of Israel were
Hanoch, Pallu, Hezron, and Carmi.
[4]The sons of Joel *were* Shemaiah his son, Gog
his son, Shimei his son, [5]Micah his son, Reaiah
his son, Baal his son, [6]and Beerah his son,
whom Tiglath-Pileser king of Assyria carried

into captivity. He *was* leader of the Reubenites.
7And his brethren by their families, when the
genealogy of their generations was registered:
the chief, Jeiel, and Zechariah, 8and Bela the
son of Azaz, the son of Shema, the son of Joel,
who dwelt in Aroer, as far as Nebo and Baal
Meon. 9Eastward they settled as far as the entrance of the wilderness this side of the River
Euphrates, because their cattle had multiplied
in the land of Gilead.

10Now in the days of Saul they made war with
the Hagrites, who fell by their hand; and they
dwelt in their tents throughout the entire *area*
east of Gilead.

11And the children of Gad dwelt next to them
in the land of Bashan as far as Salcah: 12Joel
was the chief, Shapham the next, then Jaanai
and Shaphat in Bashan, 13and their brethren of
their father's house: Michael, Meshullam,
Sheba, Jorai, Jachan, Zia, and Eber—seven *in*
all. 14These *were* the children of Abihail the
son of Huri, the son of Jaroah, the son of
Gilead, the son of Michael, the son of
Jeshishai, the son of Jahdo, the son of Buz;
15Ahi the son of Abdiel, the son of Guni, *was*
chief of their father's house. 16And *the Gadites*
dwelt in Gilead, in Bashan and in its villages,
and in all the common-lands of Sharon within
their borders. 17All these were registered by
genealogies in the days of Jotham king of Judah, and in the days of Jeroboam king of Israel.

18The sons of Reuben, the Gadites, and half
the tribe of Manasseh *had* forty-four thousand
seven hundred and sixty valiant men, men
able to bear shield and sword, to shoot with
the bow, and skillful in war, who went to war.
19They made war with the Hagrites, Jetur,
Naphish, and Nodab. 20And they were helped
against them, and the Hagrites were delivered
into their hand, and all who *were* with them,
for they cried out to God in the battle. He
heeded their prayer, because they put their
trust in Him. 21Then they took away their livestock—fifty thousand of their camels, two
hundred and fifty thousand of their sheep, and
two thousand of their donkeys—also one hundred thousand of their men; 22for many fell
dead, because the war *was* God's. And they
dwelt in their place until the captivity.

23So the children of the half-tribe of Manasseh
dwelt in the land. Their *numbers* increased from
Bashan to Baal Hermon, that is, to Senir, or
Mount Hermon. 24These *were* the heads of
their fathers' houses: Epher, Ishi, Eliel, Azriel,
Jeremiah, Hodaviah, and Jahdiel. They were
mighty men of valor, famous men, *and* heads
of their fathers' houses.

25And they were unfaithful to the God of
their fathers, and played the harlot after the
gods of the peoples of the land, whom God
had destroyed before them. 26So the God of Israel stirred up the spirit of Pul king of Assyria,
that is, Tiglath-Pileser king of Assyria. He carried the Reubenites, the Gadites, and the half-
tribe of Manasseh into captivity. He took them
to Halah, Habor, Hara, and the river of Gozan
to this day.

6 The sons of Levi *were* Gershon, Kohath,
and Merari. 2The sons of Kohath *were*
Amram, Izhar, Hebron, and Uzziel. 3The children of Amram *were* Aaron, Moses, and Miriam. And the sons of Aaron *were* Nadab, Abihu,
Eleazar, and Ithamar. 4Eleazar begot Phinehas,
and Phinehas begot Abishua; 5Abishua begot
Bukki, and Bukki begot Uzzi; 6Uzzi begot Zerahiah, and Zerahiah begot Meraioth; 7Meraioth
begot Amariah, and Amariah begot Ahitub;
8Ahitub begot Zadok, and Zadok begot
Ahimaaz; 9Ahimaaz begot Azariah, and Azariah

6:8 Zadok. By the time of David's reign, the high priestly line had wrongly been shifted to the sons of Ithamar as represented by Abiathar. When Abiathar sided with Adonijah rather than Solomon, Zadok became the ruling high priest (1 Kin. 2:26,27) and restored the high priesthood to the Levitical line through Phinehas (Num. 25:10–13).

begot Johanan; 10Johanan begot Azariah (it was
he who ministered as priest in the temple that
Solomon built in Jerusalem); 11Azariah begot
Amariah, and Amariah begot Ahitub; 12Ahitub
begot Zadok, and Zadok begot Shallum;
13Shallum begot Hilkiah, and Hilkiah begot
Azariah; 14Azariah begot Seraiah, and Seraiah
begot Jehozadak. 15Jehozadak went *into captiv-*
ity when the LORD carried Judah and Jerusalem into captivity by the hand of
Nebuchadnezzar.

16The sons of Levi *were* Gershon, Kohath,
and Merari. 17These are the names of the sons
of Gershon: Libni and Shimei. 18The sons of
Kohath *were* Amram, Izhar, Hebron, and
Uzziel. 19The sons of Merari *were* Mahli and
Mushi. Now these *are* the families of the
Levites according to their fathers: 20Of
Gershon *were* Libni his son, Jahath his son,
Zimmah his son, 21Joah his son, Iddo his son,
Zerah his son, *and* Jeatherai his son. 22The
sons of Kohath *were* Amminadab his son,
Korah his son, Assir his son, 23Elkanah his son,
Ebiasaph his son, Assir his son, 24Tahath his

6:27,28 Samuel's name in this Levitical lineage validates his acceptance into the priesthood (1 Sam. 1:24–28; 2:24–3:1). The fact that Elkanah was from Ephraim (1 Sam. 1:1) indicates where he lived, not his family history (Num. 35:6–8).

son, Uriel his son, Uzziah his son, and Shaul his son. 25The sons of Elkanah *were* Amasai and Ahimoth. 26*As for* Elkanah, the sons of Elkanah *were* Zophai his son, Nahath his son, 27Eliab his son, Jeroham his son, *and* Elkanah his son. 28The sons of Samuel *were Joel* the firstborn, and Abijah the second. 29The sons of Merari *were* Mahli, Libni his son, Shimei his son, Uzzah his son, 30Shimea his son, Haggiah his son, *and* Asaiah his son.

31Now these are the men whom David appointed over the service of song in the house of the LORD, after the ark came to rest. 32They were ministering with music before the dwelling place of the tabernacle of meeting, until Solomon had built the house of the LORD in Jerusalem, and they served in their office according to their order.

33And these *are* the ones who ministered with their sons: Of the sons of the Kohathites *were* Heman the singer, the son of Joel, the son of Samuel, 34the son of Elkanah, the son of Jeroham, the son of Eliel, the son of Toah, 35the son of Zuph, the son of Elkanah, the son of Mahath, the son of Amasai, 36the son of Elkanah, the son of Joel, the son of Azariah, the son of Zephaniah, 37the son of Tahath, the son of Assir, the son of Ebiasaph, the son of Korah, 38the son of Izhar, the son of Kohath, the son of Levi, the son of Israel. 39And his brother Asaph, who stood at his right hand, *was* Asaph the son of Berachiah, the son of Shimea, 40the son of Michael, the son of Baaseiah, the son of Malchijah, 41the son of Ethni, the son of Zerah, the son of Adaiah, 42the son of Ethan, the son of Zimmah, the son of Shimei, 43the son of Jahath, the son of Gershon, the son of Levi.

44Their brethren, the sons of Merari, on the left hand, *were* Ethan the son of Kishi, the son of Abdi, the son of Malluch, 45the son of Hashabiah, the son of Amaziah, the son of Hilkiah, 46the son of Amzi, the son of Bani, the son of Shamer, 47the son of Mahli, the son of Mushi, the son of Merari, the son of Levi.

48And their brethren, the Levites, *were* appointed to every kind of service of the tabernacle of the house of God.

49But Aaron and his sons offered sacrifices on the altar of burnt offering and on the altar of incense, for all the work of the Most Holy *Place,* and to make atonement for Israel, according to all that Moses the servant of God had commanded. 50Now these *are* the sons of Aaron: Eleazar his son, Phinehas his son, Abishua his son, 51Bukki his son, Uzzi his son, Zerahiah his son, 52Meraioth his son, Amariah his son, Ahitub his son, 53Zadok his son, *and* Ahimaaz his son.

54Now these *are* their dwelling places throughout their settlements in their territory, for they were *given* by lot to the sons of Aaron, of the family of the Kohathites: 55They gave them Hebron in the land of Judah, with its surrounding common-lands. 56But the fields of the city and its villages they gave to Caleb the son of Jephunneh. 57And to the sons of Aaron they gave *one of* the cities of refuge, Hebron; also Libnah with its common-lands, Jattir, Eshtemoa with its common-lands, 58Hilen with its common-lands, Debir with its common-lands, 59Ashan with its common-lands, and Beth Shemesh with its common-lands. 60And from the tribe of Benjamin: Geba with its common-lands, Alemeth with its common-lands, and Anathoth with its common-lands. All their cities among their families *were* thirteen.

61To the rest of the family of the tribe of the Kohathites *they gave* by lot ten cities from half the tribe of Manasseh. 62And to the sons of Gershon, throughout their families, *they gave* thirteen cities from the tribe of Issachar, from the tribe of Asher, from the tribe of Naphtali, and from the tribe of Manasseh in Bashan. 63To the sons of Merari, throughout their families, *they gave* twelve cities from the tribe of Reuben, from the tribe of Gad, and from the tribe of Zebulun. 64So the children of Israel gave *these* cities with their common-lands to the Levites. 65And they gave by lot from the tribe of the children of Judah, from the tribe of the children of Simeon, and from the tribe of the children of Benjamin these cities which are called by *their* names.

66Now some of the families of the sons of Kohath *were given* cities as their territory from the tribe of Ephraim. 67And they gave them *one of* the cities of refuge, Shechem with its common-lands, in the mountains of Ephraim, also Gezer with its common-lands, 68Jokmeam with its common-lands, Beth Horon with its common-lands, 69Aijalon with its common-lands, and Gath Rimmon with its common-lands. 70And from the half-tribe of Manasseh: Aner with its common-lands and Bileam with its common-lands, for the rest of the family of the sons of Kohath.

[71]From the family of the half-tribe of
Manasseh the sons of Gershon *were given* Golan
in Bashan with its common-lands and Ashtaroth
with its common-lands. [72]And from the tribe of
Issachar: Kedesh with its common-lands, Daberath with its common-lands, [73]Ramoth with its
common-lands, and Anem with its common-
lands. [74]And from the tribe of Asher: Mashal
with its common-lands, Abdon with its common-lands, [75]Hukok with its common-lands,
and Rehob with its common-lands. [76]And from
the tribe of Naphtali: Kedesh in Galilee with
its common-lands, Hammon with its common-
lands, and Kirjathaim with its common-lands.

[77]From the tribe of Zebulun the rest of the
children of Merari *were given* Rimmon with its
common-lands and Tabor with its common-
lands. [78]And on the other side of the Jordan,
across from Jericho, on the east side of the
Jordan, *they were given* from the tribe of Reuben: Bezer in the wilderness with its common-
lands, Jahzah with its common-lands,
[79]Kedemoth with its common-lands, and
Mephaath with its common-lands. [80]And from
the tribe of Gad: Ramoth in Gilead with its common-lands, Mahanaim with its common-lands,
[81]Heshbon with its common-lands, and Jazer with
its common-lands.

Psalm 77:1–3

To the Chief Musician. To Jeduthun.
A Psalm of Asaph.

I cried out to God with my voice—
To God with my voice;
And He gave ear to me.
2 In the day of my trouble I sought the
Lord;
My hand was stretched out in the night
without ceasing;
My soul refused to be comforted.
3 I remembered God, and was troubled;
I complained, and my spirit was
overwhelmed. Selah

Proverbs 19:10–12

10 Luxury is not fitting for a fool,
Much less for a servant to rule over
princes.
11 The discretion of a man makes him
slow to anger,
And his glory *is* to overlook a
transgression.
12 The king's wrath *is* like the roaring of a
lion,
But his favor *is* like dew on
the grass.

Acts 5:1–21

5 But a certain man named Ananias, with
Sapphira his wife, sold a possession. [2]And
he kept back *part* of the proceeds, his wife also
being aware *of it,* and brought a certain part
and laid *it* at the apostles' feet. [3]But Peter said,
"Ananias, why has Satan filled your heart to lie
to the Holy Spirit and keep back *part* of the
price of the land for yourself? [4]While it
remained, was it not your own? And after it was
sold, was it not in your own control? Why have
you conceived this thing in your heart? You
have not lied to men but to God."

[5]Then Ananias, hearing these words, fell
down and breathed his last. So great fear came
upon all those who heard these things. [6]And
the young men arose and wrapped him up, carried *him* out, and buried *him.*

[7]Now it was about three hours later when his
wife came in, not knowing what had happened.
[8]And Peter answered her, "Tell me whether
you sold the land for so much?"

She said, "Yes, for so much."

[9]Then Peter said to her, "How is it that you
have agreed together to test the Spirit of the
Lord? Look, the feet of those who have buried
your husband *are* at the door, and they will
carry you out." [10]Then immediately she fell
down at his feet and breathed her last. And the
young men came in and found her dead, and
carrying *her* out, buried *her* by her husband.
[11]So great fear came upon all the church and
upon all who heard these things.

5:11 church. This is the first use of "church" in Acts, although it is the most common word used to describe the assembly of those who had believed (cf. 4:32).

[12]And through the hands of the apostles many
signs and wonders were done among the people. And they were all with one accord in Solomon's Porch. [13]Yet none of the rest dared join
them, but the people esteemed them highly.
[14]And believers were increasingly added to the
Lord, multitudes of both men and women, [15]so
that they brought the sick out into the streets
and laid *them* on beds and couches, that at least
the shadow of Peter passing by might fall on
some of them. [16]Also a multitude gathered from
the surrounding cities to Jerusalem, bringing
sick people and those who were tormented by
unclean spirits, and they were all healed.

5:15 shadow of Peter. The people truly believed he had divine healing power and that it might even extend to them through his shadow. But Scripture does not say Peter's shadow ever healed anyone; in fact, the healing power of God through him seemed to go far beyond his shadow (v. 16, "multitude... were all healed"). This outpouring of healing was an answer to the prayer in 4:29,30.

5:16 unclean spirits. They are demons, fallen angels (Rev. 12:3) who are so designated because of their vile wickedness. They frequently live inside unbelievers, particularly those who vent their wicked nature.

[17]Then the high priest rose up, and all those
who *were* with him (which is the sect of the Sadducees), and they were filled with indignation,

5:20 the words of this life. The gospel (Phil. 2:16; 1 John 1:1–4). Jesus Christ came into this world to provide abundant and eternal life to spiritually dead people (John 1:4; 11:25; 1 John 5:20).

[18]and laid their hands on the apostles and put
them in the common prison. [19]But at night an
angel of the Lord opened the prison doors and
brought them out, and said, [20]"Go, stand in the
temple and speak to the people all the words
of this life."
[21]And when they heard *that,* they entered
the temple early in the morning and taught.
But the high priest and those with him came
and called the council together, with all the elders of the children of Israel, and sent to the
prison to have them brought.

DAY 21: Why the severity of judgment upon Ananias and Sapphira?

The account of Ananias and Sapphira as shown in Acts 5 represents the classic example of hypocrisy among Christians who faked their spirituality to impress others (Matt. 6:1–6,16–18; 15:7; 23:13–36). They were in the "multitude of those who believed" (4:32) and were involved with the Holy Spirit (v. 3), but remained hypocrites. They sold a possession and "kept back part of the proceeds" (v. 2). This was not a sin in and of itself. However, they had promised, perhaps publicly, that they were giving the full amount received to the Lord. Their outward sin was lying about how much they were giving to the church, but the deeper, more devastating sin was their spiritual hypocrisy based on selfishness.

Peter addressed Ananias with the words: "Satan filled your heart to lie to the Holy Spirit" (v. 3). Ananias and Sapphira were satanically inspired in contrast to Barnabas's Spirit-filled gesture (4:37). Ananias must have promised the Lord he would give the whole amount. He lied to the ever-present Holy Spirit in him (1 Cor. 6:19,20) and in the church (Eph. 2:21,22). And hearing Peter's words, Ananias fell down and died. The Jews did not embalm, but customarily buried the dead the same day, especially someone who died by divine judgment (see Deut. 21:22,23).

"So great fear came upon all those who heard these things" (v. 5). They were afraid about the seriousness of hypocrisy and sin in the church. The people learned that death can be the consequence of sin (1 Cor. 11:30–32; 1 John 5:16). That fear extended beyond those present to all who heard about the divine judgment (v. 11).

Then the same judgment fell upon Sapphira. Peter said that they had "agreed together to test the Spirit of the Lord" (v. 9). Sapphira had gone too far in presuming upon God's forbearance. The folly of such blatant human presumption had to be shown as a sin, hence the ultimate divine chastening that followed.

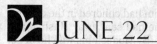

JUNE 22

1 Chronicles 7:1–8:40

7 The sons of Issachar *were* Tola, Puah,
Jashub, and Shimron—four *in all.* [2]The
sons of Tola *were* Uzzi, Rephaiah, Jeriel,
Jahmai, Jibsam, and Shemuel, heads of their
father's house. *The sons* of Tola *were* mighty
men of valor in their generations; their number in the days of David *was* twenty-two thousand six hundred. [3]The son of Uzzi *was*
Izrahiah, and the sons of Izrahiah *were* Michael, Obadiah, Joel, and Ishiah. All five of
them *were* chief men. [4]And with them, by their
generations, according to their fathers' houses, *were* thirty-six thousand troops ready for
war; for they had many wives and sons.

5 Now their brethren among all the families
of Issachar *were* mighty men of valor, listed by
their genealogies, eighty-seven thousand in
all.

6 *The sons* of Benjamin *were* Bela, Becher,
and Jediael—three *in all.* 7 The sons of Bela
were Ezbon, Uzzi, Uzziel, Jerimoth, and Iri—
five *in all.* They *were* heads of *their* fathers'
houses, and they were listed by their genealogies, twenty-two thousand and thirty-four
mighty men of valor.

8 The sons of Becher *were* Zemirah, Joash,
Eliezer, Elioenai, Omri, Jerimoth, Abijah,
Anathoth, and Alemeth. All these *are* the sons
of Becher. 9 And they were recorded by geneal-
ogy according to their generations, heads of
their fathers' houses, twenty thousand two
hundred mighty men of valor. 10 The son of
Jediael *was* Bilhan, and the sons of Bilhan *were*
Jeush, Benjamin, Ehud, Chenaanah, Zethan,
Tharshish, and Ahishahar.

11 All these sons of Jediael *were* heads of
their fathers' houses; *there were* seventeen
thousand two hundred mighty men of valor fit
to go out for war *and* battle. 12 Shuppim and
Huppim *were* the sons of Ir, *and* Hushim *was*
the son of Aher.

13 The sons of Naphtali *were* Jahziel, Guni,
Jezer, and Shallum, the sons of Bilhah.

14 The descendants of Manasseh: his Syrian
concubine bore him Machir the father of
Gilead, the father of Asriel. 15 Machir took as
his wife *the sister* of Huppim and Shuppim,
whose name *was* Maachah. The name of
Gilead's grandson *was* Zelophehad, but
Zelophehad begot only daughters. 16 (Maachah
the wife of Machir bore a son, and she called
his name Peresh. The name of his brother *was*
Sheresh, and his sons *were* Ulam and Rakem.
17 The son of Ulam *was* Bedan.) These *were* the
descendants of Gilead the son of Machir, the
son of Manasseh.

18 His sister Hammoleketh bore Ishhod,
Abiezer, and Mahlah.

19 And the sons of Shemida were Ahian,
Shechem, Likhi, and Aniam.

20 The sons of Ephraim *were* Shuthelah,
Bered his son, Tahath his son, Eladah his son,
Tahath his son, 21 Zabad his son, Shuthelah his
son, and Ezer and Elead. The men of Gath who
were born in *that* land killed *them* because
they came down to take away their cattle.
22 Then Ephraim their father mourned many
days, and his brethren came to comfort him.

23 And when he went in to his wife, she conceived and bore a son; and he called his name
Beriah, because tragedy had come upon his
house. 24 Now his daughter *was* Sheerah, who
built Lower and Upper Beth Horon and Uzzen
Sheerah; 25 and Rephah *was* his son, *as well* as
Resheph, and Telah his son, Tahan his son,
26 Laadan his son, Ammihud his son, Elishama
his son, 27 Nun his son, and Joshua his son.

28 Now their possessions and dwelling places
were Bethel and its towns: to the east Naaran,
to the west Gezer and its towns, and Shechem
and its towns, as far as Ayyah and its towns;
29 and by the borders of the children of Manasseh *were* Beth Shean and its towns, Taanach
and its towns, Megiddo and its towns, Dor and
its towns. In these dwelt the children of Joseph,
the son of Israel.

30 The sons of Asher *were* Imnah, Ishvah,
Ishvi, Beriah, and their sister Serah. 31 The
sons of Beriah *were* Heber and Malchiel, who
was the father of Birzaith. 32 And Heber begot
Japhlet, Shomer, Hotham, and their sister
Shua. 33 The sons of Japhlet *were* Pasach,
Bimhal, and Ashvath. These *were* the children
of Japhlet. 34 The sons of Shemer *were* Ahi,
Rohgah, Jehubbah, and Aram. 35 And the sons
of his brother Helem *were* Zophah, Imna,
Shelesh, and Amal. 36 The sons of Zophah *were*
Suah, Harnepher, Shual, Beri, Imrah, 37 Bezer,
Hod, Shamma, Shilshah, Jithran, and Beera.
38 The sons of Jether *were* Jephunneh, Pispah,
and Ara. 39 The sons of Ulla *were* Arah, Haniel,
and Rizia.

40 All these *were* the children of Asher, heads
of *their* fathers' houses, choice men, mighty
men of valor, chief leaders. And they were
recorded by genealogies among the army fit
for battle; their number *was* twenty-six thousand.

8 Now Benjamin begot Bela his firstborn,
Ashbel the second, Aharah the third,
2 Nohah the fourth, and Rapha the fifth. 3 The
sons of Bela *were* Addar, Gera, Abihud,
4 Abishua, Naaman, Ahoah, 5 Gera, Shephuphan,
and Huram.

6 These *are* the sons of Ehud, who were the
heads of the fathers' *houses* of the inhabitants
of Geba, and who forced them to move to
Manahath: 7 Naaman, Ahijah, and Gera who
forced them to move. He begot Uzza and
Ahihud.

8 Also Shaharaim had children in the country
of Moab, after he had sent away Hushim and
Baara his wives. 9 By Hodesh his wife he begot
Jobab, Zibia, Mesha, Malcam, 10 Jeuz, Sachiah,
and Mirmah. These *were* his sons, heads of
their fathers' *houses.*

11 And by Hushim he begot Abitub and
Elpaal. 12 The sons of Elpaal *were* Eber,
Misham, and Shemed, who built Ono and Lod
with its towns; 13 and Beriah and Shema, who

were heads of their fathers' *houses* of the inhabitants of Aijalon, who drove out the inhabitants
of Gath. [14]Ahio, Shashak, Jeremoth, [15]Zebadiah,
Arad, Eder, [16]Michael, Ispah, and Joha *were* the
sons of Beriah. [17]Zebadiah, Meshullam, Hizki,
Heber, [18]Ishmerai, Jizliah, and Jobab *were* the
sons of Elpaal. [19]Jakim, Zichri, Zabdi, [20]Elienai,
Zillethai, Eliel, [21]Adaiah, Beraiah, and Shimrath
were the sons of Shimei. [22]Ishpan, Eber, Eliel,
[23]Abdon, Zichri, Hanan, [24]Hananiah, Elam,
Antothijah, [25]Iphdeiah, and Penuel *were* the
sons of Shashak. [26]Shamsherai, Shehariah,
Athaliah, [27]Jaareshiah, Elijah, and Zichri *were*
the sons of Jeroham.

[28]These *were* heads of the fathers' *houses* by
their generations, chief men. These dwelt in
Jerusalem.

[29]Now the father of Gibeon, whose wife's
name *was* Maacah, dwelt at Gibeon. [30]And his
firstborn son *was* Abdon, then Zur, Kish, Baal,
Nadab, [31]Gedor, Ahio, Zecher, [32]and Mikloth,
who begot Shimeah. They also dwelt alongside their relatives in Jerusalem, with their
brethren. [33]Ner begot Kish, Kish begot Saul,
and Saul begot Jonathan, Malchishua,
Abinadab, and Esh-Baal. [34]The son of Jonathan
was Merib-Baal, and Merib-Baal begot Micah.
[35]The sons of Micah *were* Pithon, Melech,
Tarea, and Ahaz. [36]And Ahaz begot Jehoaddah;
Jehoaddah begot Alemeth, Azmaveth, and
Zimri; and Zimri begot Moza. [37]Moza begot
Binea, Raphah his son, Eleasah his son, *and*
Azel his son.

[38]Azel had six sons whose names *were* these:
Azrikam, Bocheru, Ishmael, Sheariah, Obadiah,
and Hanan. All these *were* the sons of Azel.
[39]And the sons of Eshek his brother *were* Ulam
his firstborn, Jeush the second, and Eliphelet
the third.

[40]The sons of Ulam were mighty men of
valor—archers. *They* had many sons and
grandsons, one hundred and fifty *in all.* These
were all sons of Benjamin.

Psalm 77:4–9

[4] You hold my eyelids *open;*
I am so troubled that I cannot speak.
[5] I have considered the days of old,
The years of ancient times.
[6] I call to remembrance my song in
the night;
I meditate within my heart,
And my spirit makes diligent search.

[7] Will the Lord cast off forever?
And will He be favorable no more?
[8] Has His mercy ceased forever?
Has *His* promise failed forevermore?

77:4 hold my eyelids *open.* The psalmist was so upset that he could neither sleep nor talk rationally.

77:6 my song in the night. The remembrance of happier times only deepened his depression. **spirit makes diligent search.** His spirit continually meditated on possible solutions to his problems.

[9] Has God forgotten to be gracious?
Has He in anger shut up His tender
mercies? Selah

Proverbs 19:13–14

[13] A foolish son *is* the ruin of his father,
And the contentions of a wife *are* a
continual dripping.

[14] Houses and riches *are* an inheritance
from fathers,
But a prudent wife *is* from the LORD.

19:13 continual dripping. An obstinate, argumentative woman is literally like a leak so unrelenting that one has to run from it or go mad. Here are two ways to devastate a man: an ungodly son and an irritating wife.

19:14 One receives inheritance as a family blessing (a result of human birth), but a wise wife (31:10–31) is a result of divine blessing.

Acts 5:22–42

[22]But when the officers came and did not
find them in the prison, they returned and
reported, [23]saying, "Indeed we found the
prison shut securely, and the guards standing
outside before the doors; but when we opened
them, we found no one inside!" [24]Now when
the high priest, the captain of the temple, and
the chief priests heard these things, they wondered what the outcome would be. [25]So one
came and told them, saying, "Look, the men
whom you put in prison are standing in the
temple and teaching the people!"

[26]Then the captain went with the officers
and brought them without violence, for they
feared the people, lest they should be stoned.
[27]And when they had brought them, they set

them before the council. And the high priest
asked them, 28saying, "Did we not strictly command you not to teach in this name? And look,
you have filled Jerusalem with your doctrine,
and intend to bring this Man's blood on us!"
29But Peter and the *other* apostles answered
and said: "We ought to obey God rather than
men. 30The God of our fathers raised up Jesus
whom you murdered by hanging on a tree. 31Him
God has exalted to His right hand *to be* Prince
and Savior, to give repentance to Israel and forgiveness of sins. 32And we are His witnesses to
these things, and *so* also *is* the Holy Spirit whom
God has given to those who obey Him."
33When they heard *this,* they were furious
and plotted to kill them. 34Then one in the council stood up, a Pharisee named Gamaliel, a
teacher of the law held in respect by all the people, and commanded them to put the apostles
outside for a little while. 35And he said to them:
"Men of Israel, take heed to yourselves what
you intend to do regarding these men. 36For
some time ago Theudas rose up, claiming to be
somebody. A number of men, about four hundred, joined him. He was slain, and all who
obeyed him were scattered and came to nothing. 37After this man, Judas of Galilee rose up in
the days of the census, and drew away many
people after him. He also perished, and all who
obeyed him were dispersed. 38And now I say to
you, keep away from these men and let them
alone; for if this plan or this work is of men, it
will come to nothing; 39but if it is of God, you
cannot overthrow it—lest you even be found to
fight against God."
40And they agreed with him, and when they
had called for the apostles and beaten *them,*
they commanded that they should not speak in
the name of Jesus, and let them go. 41So they
departed from the presence of the council, rejoicing that they were counted worthy to suffer
shame for His name. 42And daily in the temple,
and in every house, they did not cease teaching and preaching Jesus *as* the Christ.

DAY 22: How was the church in Jerusalem spared initially from persecution?

In Acts 5:28, the high priest reminds Peter and the other apostles, "Did we not strictly command you not to teach this name? And look, you have filled Jerusalem with your doctrine." The gospel of Jesus Christ (2:14–40; 4:12,13). "And intend to bring this Man's blood on us." The Sanhedrin had apparently forgotten the brash statement its supporters had made before Pilate that the responsibility for Jesus' death should be on them and their children (Matt. 27:25).

The apostles' response was so fearlessly delivered that the Jews were infuriated and plotted to kill them. Then Gamaliel stood up in the Sanhedrin. Like his grandfather, the prominent rabbi Hillel, Gamaliel was the most noted rabbi of his time and led the liberal faction of the Pharisees. His most famous student was the apostle Paul (22:3). He argued that they needed to take heed as to what they were plotting. He mentioned Theudas (v. 36), an otherwise unknown individual who led a revolt in Judea in the early years of the first century, not to be confused with a later Theudas cited in Josephus as a revolutionary.

And Gamaliel reminded them of how Judas of Galilee rose up (v. 37). He was the founder of the Zealots who led another revolt in Palestine early in the first century. Zealots, a party of Jews who were fanatical nationalists, believed that radical action was required to overthrow the Roman power in Palestine. They even sought to take up arms against Rome.

Gamaliel's counsel was to "let them alone" (v. 38); for if it was the work of men, it would come to nothing. But if it was of God, none could overcome it. Fortunately, the members of the Sanhedrin heeded Gamaliel's words concerning the apostles and restricted their punishment to beating them.

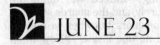

JUNE 23

1 Chronicles 9:1–10:14

9 So all Israel was recorded by genealogies,
and indeed, they *were* inscribed in the book
of the kings of Israel. But Judah was carried
away captive to Babylon because of their
unfaithfulness. 2And the first inhabitants who
dwelt in their possessions in their cities *were* Israelites, priests, Levites, and the Nethinim.
3Now in Jerusalem the children of Judah
dwelt, and some of the children of Benjamin,
and of the children of Ephraim and Manasseh:
4Uthai the son of Ammihud, the son of Omri,
the son of Imri, the son of Bani, of the descendants of Perez, the son of Judah. 5Of the
Shilonites: Asaiah the firstborn and his sons.
6Of the sons of Zerah: Jeuel, and their
brethren—six hundred and ninety. 7Of the
sons of Benjamin: Sallu the son of Meshullam,
the son of Hodaviah, the son of Hassenuah;
8Ibneiah the son of Jeroham; Elah the son of
Uzzi, the son of Michri; Meshullam the son of

Shephatiah, the son of Reuel, the son of
Ibnijah; 9and their brethren, according to their
generations—nine hundred and fifty-six. All
these men *were* heads of a father's *house* in
their fathers' houses.
10Of the priests: Jedaiah, Jehoiarib, and
Jachin; 11Azariah the son of Hilkiah, the son of
Meshullam, the son of Zadok, the son of
Meraioth, the son of Ahitub, the officer over the
house of God; 12Adaiah the son of Jeroham, the
son of Pashur, the son of Malchijah; Maasai the
son of Adiel, the son of Jahzerah, the son of
Meshullam, the son of Meshillemith, the son of
Immer; 13and their brethren, heads of their
fathers' houses—one thousand seven hundred
and sixty. *They were* very able men for the
work of the service of the house of God.
14Of the Levites: Shemaiah the son of Hasshub, the son of Azrikam, the son of
Hashabiah, of the sons of Merari; 15Bakbakkar,
Heresh, Galal, and Mattaniah the son of
Micah, the son of Zichri, the son of Asaph;
16Obadiah the son of Shemaiah, the son of
Galal, the son of Jeduthun; and Berechiah the
son of Asa, the son of Elkanah, who lived in
the villages of the Netophathites.
17And the gatekeepers *were* Shallum, Akkub,
Talmon, Ahiman, and their brethren. Shallum
was the chief. 18Until then *they had been* gatekeepers for the camps of the children of Levi
at the King's Gate on the east.
19Shallum the son of Kore, the son of
Ebiasaph, the son of Korah, and his brethren,
from his father's house, the Korahites, *were* in
charge of the work of the service, gatekeepers
of the tabernacle. Their fathers had been
keepers of the entrance to the camp of the
LORD. 20And Phinehas the son of Eleazar had
been the officer over them in time past; the
LORD *was* with him. 21Zechariah the son of Meshelemiah *was* keeper of the door of the tabernacle of meeting.
22All those chosen as gatekeepers *were* two
hundred and twelve. They were recorded by
their genealogy, in their villages. David and
Samuel the seer had appointed them to their
trusted office. 23So they and their children
were in charge of the gates of the house of the
LORD, the house of the tabernacle, by assignment. 24The gatekeepers were assigned to the
four directions: the east, west, north, and
south. 25And their brethren in their villages
had to come with them from time to time for
seven days. 26For in this trusted office *were*
four chief gatekeepers; they were Levites. And
they had charge over the chambers and treasuries of the house of God. 27And they lodged
all around the house of God because they *had*
the responsibility, and they *were* in charge of
opening *it* every morning.
28Now *some* of them were in charge of the
serving vessels, for they brought them in and
took them out by count. 29*Some* of them *were*
appointed over the furnishings and over all
the implements of the sanctuary, and over the
fine flour and the wine and the oil and the
incense and the spices. 30And *some* of the sons
of the priests made the ointment of the spices.
31Mattithiah of the Levites, the firstborn of
Shallum the Korahite, had the trusted office
over the things that were baked in the pans.
32And some of their brethren of the sons of
the Kohathites *were* in charge of preparing the
showbread for every Sabbath.
33These are the singers, heads of the fathers'
houses of the Levites, *who lodged* in the chambers, *and were* free *from other duties;* for they
were employed in *that* work day and night.
34These heads of the fathers' *houses* of the
Levites *were* heads throughout their generations. They dwelt at Jerusalem.
35Jeiel the father of Gibeon, whose wife's
name *was* Maacah, dwelt at Gibeon. 36His firstborn son *was* Abdon, then Zur, Kish, Baal, Ner,
Nadab, 37Gedor, Ahio, Zechariah, and Mikloth.
38And Mikloth begot Shimeam. They also
dwelt alongside their relatives in Jerusalem,
with their brethren. 39Ner begot Kish, Kish
begot Saul, and Saul begot Jonathan,
Malchishua, Abinadab, and Esh-Baal. 40The
son of Jonathan *was* Merib-Baal, and Merib-
Baal begot Micah. 41The sons of Micah *were*
Pithon, Melech, Tahrea, and Ahaz. 42And Ahaz
begot Jarah; Jarah begot Alemeth, Azmaveth,
and Zimri; and Zimri begot Moza; 43Moza
begot Binea, Rephaiah his son, Eleasah his
son, and Azel his son.
44And Azel had six sons whose names *were*
these: Azrikam, Bocheru, Ishmael, Sheariah,
Obadiah, and Hanan; these *were* the sons of
Azel.

10 Now the Philistines fought against Israel; and the men of Israel fled from
before the Philistines, and fell slain on Mount
Gilboa. 2Then the Philistines followed hard
after Saul and his sons. And the Philistines
killed Jonathan, Abinadab, and Malchishua,
Saul's sons. 3The battle became fierce against
Saul. The archers hit him, and he was wounded by the archers. 4Then Saul said to his
armorbearer, "Draw your sword, and thrust
me through with it, lest these uncircumcised
men come and abuse me." But his armorbearer would not, for he was greatly afraid.
Therefore Saul took a sword and fell on it. 5And
when his armorbearer saw that Saul was dead,

he also fell on his sword and died. 6So Saul and
his three sons died, and all his house died
together. 7And when all the men of Israel who
were in the valley saw that they had fled and
that Saul and his sons were dead, they forsook
their cities and fled; then the Philistines came
and dwelt in them.

8So it happened the next day, when the
Philistines came to strip the slain, that they
found Saul and his sons fallen on Mount
Gilboa. 9And they stripped him and took his
head and his armor, and sent word throughout the land of the Philistines to proclaim the
news *in the temple* of their idols and among
the people. 10Then they put his armor in the
temple of their gods, and fastened his head in
the temple of Dagon.

11And when all Jabesh Gilead heard all that
the Philistines had done to Saul, 12all the valiant
men arose and took the body of Saul and the
bodies of his sons; and they brought them to
Jabesh, and buried their bones under the
tamarisk tree at Jabesh, and fasted seven days.
13So Saul died for his unfaithfulness which
he had committed against the LORD, because
he did not keep the word of the LORD, and also
because he consulted a medium for guidance.
14But *he* did not inquire of the LORD; therefore
He killed him, and turned the kingdom over to
David the son of Jesse.

Psalm 77:10–15

10 And I said, "This *is* my anguish;
But I will remember the years of the
right hand of the Most High."
11 I will remember the works of the LORD;
Surely I will remember Your wonders
of old.
12 I will also meditate on all Your work,
And talk of Your deeds.

77:10 This psalm illustrates one cure for depression. The psalmist does not explain the cause of his despair, but he was definitely locked into gloom. When he thought about God, it only caused him to complain bitterly. But beginning in v. 10, the psalmist's mood starts to change because he commits himself to focusing on God's goodness and past acts of deliverance. His lament then changes into a hymn of praise. **years of the right hand of the Most High.** The psalmist began to remember the times when God used His right hand (power) to strengthen and protect him.

13 Your way, O God, *is* in the sanctuary;
Who *is* so great a God as *our* God?
14 You *are* the God who does wonders;
You have declared Your strength
among the peoples.
15 You have with *Your* arm redeemed
Your people,
The sons of Jacob and Joseph.
Selah

Proverbs 19:15–16

15 Laziness casts *one* into a deep sleep,
And an idle person will suffer hunger.

16 He who keeps the commandment
keeps his soul,
But he who is careless of his ways
will die.

19:16 commandment. Wisdom is equated with God's commandments. In a sense, Proverbs contain the applications and implications of all that is in God's moral law.

Acts 6:1–15

6 Now in those days, when *the number of*
the disciples was multiplying, there arose
a complaint against the Hebrews by the
Hellenists, because their widows were neglected in the daily distribution. 2Then the twelve
summoned the multitude of the disciples and
said, "It is not desirable that we should leave
the word of God and serve tables. 3Therefore,
brethren, seek out from among you seven men
of *good* reputation, full of the Holy Spirit and
wisdom, whom we may appoint over this business; 4but we will give ourselves continually to
prayer and to the ministry of the word."

5And the saying pleased the whole multitude. And they chose Stephen, a man full of
faith and the Holy Spirit, and Philip,
Prochorus, Nicanor, Timon, Parmenas, and
Nicolas, a proselyte from Antioch, 6whom they
set before the apostles; and when they had
prayed, they laid hands on them.

7Then the word of God spread, and the number of the disciples multiplied greatly in Jerusalem, and a great many of the priests were obedient to the faith.

8And Stephen, full of faith and power, did
great wonders and signs among the people.
9Then there arose some from what is called
the Synagogue of the Freedmen (Cyrenians,
Alexandrians, and those from Cilicia and
Asia), disputing with Stephen. 10And they were
not able to resist the wisdom and the Spirit by

6:7 One of Luke's periodic statements summarizing the growth of the church and the spread of the gospel (2:41,47; 4:4; 5:14; 9:31; 12:24; 13:49; 16:5; 19:20). **great many of the priests.** The conversion of large numbers of priests may account for the vicious opposition that arose against Stephen.

6:8 wonders and signs. Acts 4:30; 5:12; 14:3; 15:12. Wonders is the amazement people experience when witnessing supernatural works (miracles). Signs point to the power of God behind miracles—marvels have no value unless they point to God and His truth. Such works were often done by the Holy Spirit through the apostles (5:12–16) and their associates (6:8) to authenticate them as the messengers of God's truth (2 Cor. 12:12; Heb. 2:3,4).

which he spoke. [11]Then they secretly induced
men to say, "We have heard him speak blasphemous words against Moses and God."
[12]And they stirred up the people, the elders,
and the scribes; and they came upon *him*,
seized him, and brought *him* to the council.
[13]They also set up false witnesses who said,
"This man does not cease to speak blasphemous words against this holy place and the
law; [14]for we have heard him say that this Jesus of Nazareth will destroy this place and
change the customs which Moses delivered to
us." [15]And all who sat in the council, looking
steadfastly at him, saw his face as the face of
an angel.

6:15 face of an angel. Pure, calm, unruffled composure, reflecting the presence of God (Ex. 34:29–35).

DAY 23: How did the apostles deal with the first major problem within the church?

By Acts 6:1 the church could have reached over 20,000 men and women. At that time "there arose a complaint against the Hebrews by the Hellenists." Hebrews were the native Jewish population of Palestine; Hellenists were Jews from the Diaspora. The Hellenists' absorption of aspects of Greek culture made them suspect to the Palestinian Jews. The Hellenists believed their widows were not receiving an adequate share of the food the church provided for their care (1 Tim. 5:3–16).

The apostles considered the problem and said they could not "leave the word of God and serve tables" (v. 2). The word translated "tables" can refer to tables used in monetary matters (Matt. 21:12; Mark 11:15; John 2:15), as well as those used for serving meals. To be involved either in financial matters or in serving meals would take the 12 away from their first priority. Prayer and the ministry of the word (v. 2) define the highest priorities of church leaders (v. 4).

Rather, they told the church to pick out "seven men" to take care of it (v. 3). These were not deacons in terms of the later church office (1 Tim. 3:8–13), although they performed some of the same duties. Stephen and Philip (the only ones of the 7 mentioned elsewhere in Scripture) clearly were evangelists, not deacons. Acts later mentions elders (14:23; 20:17), but not deacons.

The 7 men chosen by the church all had Greek names, implying they were all Hellenists. The church, in a display of love and unity, may have chosen them to rectify the apparent imbalance involving the Hellenistic widows. The apostles "prayed…laid hands on them" (v. 6). This expression was used of Jesus when He healed and sometimes indicated being taken prisoner. In the Old Testament, offerers of sacrifices laid their hands on the animal as an expression of identification (Lev. 8:14,18,22; Heb. 6:2). But in the symbolic sense, it signified the affirmation, support, and identification with someone and his ministry (see 1 Tim. 4:14; 5:22; 2 Tim. 1:6; Num. 27:23).

JUNE 24

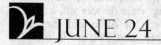

1 Chronicles 11:1–12:40

11 Then all Israel came together to David at
Hebron, saying, "Indeed we *are* your bone
and your flesh. [2]Also, in time past, even when
Saul was king, you *were* the one who led Israel
out and brought them in; and the LORD your
God said to you, 'You shall shepherd My people
Israel, and be ruler over My people Israel.' "
[3]Therefore all the elders of Israel came to the
king at Hebron, and David made a covenant
with them at Hebron before the LORD. And they
anointed David king over Israel, according to
the word of the LORD by Samuel.

[4]And David and all Israel went to Jerusalem,
which is Jebus, where the Jebusites *were*, the
inhabitants of the land. [5]But the inhabitants of
Jebus said to David, "You shall not come in

here!" Nevertheless David took the stronghold of Zion (that is, the City of David). 6 Now
David said, "Whoever attacks the Jebusites
first shall be chief and captain." And Joab the
son of Zeruiah went up first, and became
chief. 7 Then David dwelt in the stronghold;
therefore they called it the City of David. 8 And
he built the city around it, from the Millo to
the surrounding area. Joab repaired the rest
of the city. 9 So David went on and became
great, and the LORD of hosts *was* with him.

10 Now these *were* the heads of the mighty
men whom David had, who strengthened
themselves with him in his kingdom, with all Israel, to make him king, according to the word
of the LORD concerning Israel.

11 And this *is* the number of the mighty men
whom David had: Jashobeam the son of a
Hachmonite, chief of the captains; he had lifted up his spear against three hundred, killed
by him at one time.

12 After him *was* Eleazar the son of Dodo, the
Ahohite, who *was one* of the three mighty men.
13 He was with David at Pasdammim. Now there
the Philistines were gathered for battle, and
there was a piece of ground full of barley. So the
people fled from the Philistines. 14 But they stationed themselves in the middle of *that* field,
defended it, and killed the Philistines. So the
LORD brought about a great victory.

15 Now three of the thirty chief men went
down to the rock to David, into the cave of
Adullam; and the army of the Philistines
encamped in the Valley of Rephaim. 16 David
was then in the stronghold, and the garrison
of the Philistines *was* then in Bethlehem.
17 And David said with longing, "Oh, that someone would give me a drink of water from the
well of Bethlehem, which is by the gate!" 18 So
the three broke through the camp of the
Philistines, drew water from the well of Bethlehem that *was* by the gate, and took *it* and
brought *it* to David. Nevertheless David would
not drink it, but poured it out to the LORD.
19 And he said, "Far be it from me, O my God,
that I should do this! Shall I drink the blood of
these men *who have put* their lives *in jeopardy?*
For at the risk of their lives they brought it."
Therefore he would not drink it. These things
were done by the three mighty men.

20 Abishai the brother of Joab was chief of *another* three. He had lifted up his spear against
three hundred *men,* killed *them,* and won a
name among *these* three. 21 Of the three he was
more honored than the other two men.
Therefore he became their captain. However
he did not attain to the *first* three.

22 Benaiah was the son of Jehoiada, the son
of a valiant man from Kabzeel, who had done
many deeds. He had killed two lion-like
heroes of Moab. He also had gone down and
killed a lion in the midst of a pit on a snowy day.
23 And he killed an Egyptian, a man of *great*
height, five cubits tall. In the Egyptian's hand
there was a spear like a weaver's beam; and he
went down to him with a staff, wrested the
spear out of the Egyptian's hand, and killed
him with his own spear. 24 These *things*
Benaiah the son of Jehoiada did, and won a
name among three mighty men. 25 Indeed he
was more honored than the thirty, but he did
not attain to the *first* three. And David appointed him over his guard.

26 Also the mighty warriors *were* Asahel the
brother of Joab, Elhanan the son of Dodo of
Bethlehem, 27 Shammoth the Harorite, Helez
the Pelonite, 28 Ira the son of Ikkesh the
Tekoite, Abiezer the Anathothite, 29 Sibbechai
the Hushathite, Ilai the Ahohite, 30 Maharai the
Netophathite, Heled the son of Baanah the
Netophathite, 31 Ithai the son of Ribai of Gibeah,
of the sons of Benjamin, Benaiah the Pirathonite,
32 Hurai of the brooks of Gaash, Abiel the
Arbathite, 33 Azmaveth the Baharumite, Eliahba
the Shaalbonite, 34 the sons of Hashem the
Gizonite, Jonathan the son of Shageh the
Hararite, 35 Ahiam the son of Sacar the Hararite,
Eliphal the son of Ur, 36 Hepher the Mecherathite,
Ahijah the Pelonite, 37 Hezro the Carmelite,
Naarai the son of Ezbai, 38 Joel the brother of Na-
than, Mibhar the son of Hagri, 39 Zelek the
Ammonite, Naharai the Berothite (the armor-
bearer of Joab the son of Zeruiah), 40 Ira the
Ithrite, Gareb the Ithrite, 41 Uriah the Hittite,
Zabad the son of Ahlai, 42 Adina the son of Shiza
the Reubenite (a chief of the Reubenites) and
thirty with him, 43 Hanan the son of Maachah,
Joshaphat the Mithnite, 44 Uzzia the Ashterathite,
Shama and Jeiel the sons of Hotham the
Aroerite, 45 Jediael the son of Shimri, and Joha
his brother, the Tizite, 46 Eliel the Mahavite,
Jeribai and Joshaviah the sons of Elnaam,
Ithmah the Moabite, 47 Eliel, Obed, and Jaasiel
the Mezobaite.

12 Now these *were* the men who came to David at Ziklag while he was still a fugitive
from Saul the son of Kish; and they *were*
among the mighty men, helpers in the war,
2 armed with bows, using both the right hand
and the left in *hurling* stones and *shooting*
arrows with the bow. *They were* of Benjamin,
Saul's brethren.

3 The chief *was* Ahiezer, then Joash, the sons
of Shemaah the Gibeathite; Jeziel and Pelet the
sons of Azmaveth; Berachah, and Jehu the
Anathothite; 4 Ishmaiah the Gibeonite, a mighty

man among the thirty, and over the thirty;
Jeremiah, Jahaziel, Johanan, and Jozabad the
Gederathite; 5 Eluzai, Jerimoth, Bealiah,
Shemariah, and Shephatiah the Haruphite;
6 Elkanah, Jisshiah, Azarel, Joezer, and Jasho-
beam, the Korahites; 7 and Joelah and
Zebadiah the sons of Jeroham of Gedor.

8 *Some* Gadites joined David at the stronghold
in the wilderness, mighty men of valor, men
trained for battle, who could handle shield and
spear, whose faces *were like* the faces of lions,
and *were* as swift as gazelles on the mountains:
9 Ezer the first, Obadiah the second, Eliab the
third, 10 Mishmannah the fourth, Jeremiah the
fifth, 11 Attai the sixth, Eliel the seventh,
12 Johanan the eighth, Elzabad the ninth,
13 Jeremiah the tenth, and Machbanai the
eleventh. 14 These *were* from the sons of Gad,
captains of the army; the least was over a hundred, and the greatest was over a thousand.
15 These *are* the ones who crossed the Jordan in
the first month, when it had overflowed all its
banks; and they put to flight all *those* in the valleys, to the east and to the west.

16 Then some of the sons of Benjamin and Judah came to David at the stronghold. 17 And
David went out to meet them, and answered
and said to them, "If you have come peaceably to me to help me, my heart will be united
with you; but if to betray me to my enemies,
since *there is* no wrong in my hands, may the
God of our fathers look and bring judgment."
18 Then the Spirit came upon Amasai, chief of
the captains, *and he said:*

"*We are* yours, O David;
We *are* on your side, O son of Jesse!
Peace, peace to you,
And peace to your helpers!
For your God helps you."

So David received them, and made them captains of the troop.

19 And *some* from Manasseh defected to David when he was going with the Philistines to
battle against Saul; but they did not help them,
for the lords of the Philistines sent him away
by agreement, saying, "He may defect to his
master Saul *and endanger* our heads." 20 When
he went to Ziklag, those of Manasseh who
defected to him were Adnah, Jozabad, Jediael,
Michael, Jozabad, Elihu, and Zillethai, captains of the thousands who *were* from
Manasseh. 21 And they helped David against
the bands *of raiders,* for they *were* all mighty
men of valor, and they were captains in the
army. 22 For at *that* time they came to David day
by day to help him, until *it was* a great army,
like the army of God.

23 Now these *were* the numbers of the divisions *that were* equipped for war, *and* came to
David at Hebron to turn *over* the kingdom of
Saul to him, according to the word of the LORD:
24 of the sons of Judah bearing shield and spear,
six thousand eight hundred armed for war; 25 of
the sons of Simeon, mighty men of valor fit for
war, seven thousand one hundred; 26 of the sons
of Levi four thousand six hundred; 27 Jehoiada,
the leader of the Aaronites, and with him three
thousand seven hundred; 28 Zadok, a young
man, a valiant warrior, and from his father's
house twenty-two captains; 29 of the sons of Benjamin, relatives of Saul, three thousand (until
then the greatest part of them had remained
loyal to the house of Saul); 30 of the sons of
Ephraim twenty thousand eight hundred,
mighty men of valor, famous men throughout
their father's house; 31 of the half-tribe of
Manasseh eighteen thousand, who were designated by name to come and make David king;
32 of the sons of Issachar who had understanding of the times, to know what Israel ought to
do, their chiefs were two hundred; and all their
brethren were at their command; 33 of Zebulun
there were fifty thousand who went out to battle, expert in war with all weapons of war, stouthearted men who could keep ranks; 34 of
Naphtali one thousand captains, and with them
thirty-seven thousand with shield and spear;
35 of the Danites who could keep battle formation, twenty-eight thousand six hundred; 36 of
Asher, those who could go out to war, able to
keep battle formation, forty thousand; 37 of the
Reubenites and the Gadites and the half-tribe of
Manasseh, from the other side of the Jordan,
one hundred and twenty thousand armed for
battle with every *kind* of weapon of war.

38 All these men of war, who could keep
ranks, came to Hebron with a loyal heart, to
make David king over all Israel; and all the
rest of Israel *were* of one mind to make David
king. 39 And they were there with David three
days, eating and drinking, for their brethren
had prepared for them. 40 Moreover those who
were near to them, from as far away as
Issachar and Zebulun and Naphtali, were
bringing food on donkeys and camels, on
mules and oxen—provisions of flour and

12:18 the Spirit. A temporary empowerment by the Holy Spirit to assure David that the Benjamites and Judahites were loyal to him and that the cause was blessed by God.

cakes of figs and cakes of raisins, wine and oil and oxen and sheep abundantly, for *there was* joy in Israel.

Psalm 77:16–20

16 The waters saw You, O God;
The waters saw You, they were afraid;
The depths also trembled.
17 The clouds poured out water;
The skies sent out a sound;
Your arrows also flashed about.
18 The voice of Your thunder *was* in the
whirlwind;
The lightnings lit up the world;
The earth trembled and shook.
19 Your way *was* in the sea,
Your path in the great waters,
And Your footsteps were not known.
20 You led Your people like a flock
By the hand of Moses and Aaron.

Proverbs 19:17–19

17 He who has pity on the poor lends to
the LORD,
And He will pay back what he has
given.

18 Chasten your son while there is hope,
And do not set your heart on his
destruction.

19 *A man of* great wrath will suffer
punishment;
For if you rescue *him,* you will have to
do it again.

Acts 7:1–21

7 Then the high priest said, "Are these
things so?"
2And he said, "Brethren and fathers, listen:
The God of glory appeared to our father Abraham when he was in Mesopotamia, before he
dwelt in Haran, 3and said to him, *'Get out of
your country and from your relatives, and
come to a land that I will show you.'* 4Then he
came out of the land of the Chaldeans and
dwelt in Haran. And from there, when his
father was dead, He moved him to this land in
which you now dwell. 5And *God* gave him no
inheritance in it, not even *enough* to set his
foot on. But even when *Abraham* had no child,
He promised to give it to him for a possession,
and to his descendants after him. 6But God
spoke in this way: that his descendants would
dwell in a foreign land, and that they would
bring them into bondage and oppress *them*
four hundred years. 7*'And the nation to whom
they will be in bondage I will judge,'* said God,
'and after that they shall come out and serve

7:2–53 Stephen's response does not seem to answer the high priest's question. Instead, he gave a masterful, detailed defense of the Christian faith from the Old Testament and concluded by condemning the Jewish leaders for rejecting Jesus.

7:2 The God of glory. A title used only here and in Psalm 29:3. God's glory is the sum of His attributes (Ex. 33:18,19). **Abraham...Mesopotamia, before he dwelt in Haran.** Genesis 12:1–4 refers to the repeat of this call after Abraham had settled in Haran (ca. 500 miles northwest of Ur). Evidently, God had originally called Abraham while he was living in Ur (Gen. 15:7; Neh. 9:7), then repeated that call at Haran (Gen. 11:31–12:3).

Me in this place.' 8Then He gave him the
covenant of circumcision; and so *Abraham*
begot Isaac and circumcised him on the
eighth day; and Isaac *begot* Jacob, and Jacob
begot the twelve patriarchs.
9"And the patriarchs, becoming envious,
sold Joseph into Egypt. But God was with him
10and delivered him out of all his troubles, and
gave him favor and wisdom in the presence of
Pharaoh, king of Egypt; and he made him governor over Egypt and all his house. 11Now a
famine and great trouble came over all the
land of Egypt and Canaan, and our fathers
found no sustenance. 12But when Jacob heard
that there was grain in Egypt, he sent out our
fathers first. 13And the second *time* Joseph was
made known to his brothers, and Joseph's
family became known to the Pharaoh. 14Then
Joseph sent and called his father Jacob and all
his relatives to *him,* seventy-five people. 15So
Jacob went down to Egypt; and he died, he
and our fathers. 16And they were carried back
to Shechem and laid in the tomb that Abraham
bought for a sum of money from the sons of
Hamor, *the father* of Shechem.
17"But when the time of the promise drew
near which God had sworn to Abraham, the
people grew and multiplied in Egypt 18till
another king arose who did not know Joseph.
19This man dealt treacherously with our people, and oppressed our forefathers, making
them expose their babies, so that they might
not live. 20At this time Moses was born, and was
well pleasing to God; and he was brought up in
his father's house for three months. 21But when
he was set out, Pharaoh's daughter took him
away and brought him up as her own son.

DAY 24: What were the sources for the writer of the Chronicles?

The inspiration of Scripture (2 Tim. 3:16) was sometimes accomplished through direct revelation from God without a human writer, e.g., the Mosaic Law. At other times, God used human sources, as mentioned in Luke 1:1–4. Such was the experience of the chronicler as evidenced by the many contributing sources. Whether the material came through direct revelation or by existing resources, God's inspiration through the Holy Spirit prevented the original human authors of Scripture from any error (2 Pet. 1:19–21). Although relatively few scribal errors have been made in copying Scripture, they can be identified and corrected. Thus, the original, inerrant content of the Bible has been preserved.

1. Book of the Kings of Israel/Judah (1 Chr. 9:1; 2 Chr. 16:11; 20:34; 25:26; 27:7; 28:26; 32:32; 35:27; 36:8)
2. The Chronicles of David (1 Chr. 27:24)
3. Book of Samuel (1 Chr. 29:29)
4. Book of Nathan (1 Chr. 29:29; 2 Chr. 9:29)
5. Book of Gad (1 Chr. 29:29)
6. Prophecy of Ahijah the Shilonite (2 Chr. 9:29)
7. Visions of Iddo (2 Chr. 9:29)
8. Records of Shemaiah (2 Chr. 12:15)
9. Records of Iddo (2 Chr. 12:15)
10. Annals of Iddo (2 Chr. 13:22)
11. Annals of Jehu (2 Chr. 20:34)
12. Commentary on the Book of the Kings (2 Chr. 24:27)
13. Acts of Uzziah by Isaiah (2 Chr. 26:22)
14. Letters/Message of Sennacherib (2 Chr. 32:10–17)
15. Vision of Isaiah (2 Chr. 32:32)
16. Words of the Seers (2 Chr 33:18)
17. Sayings of Hozai (2 Chr. 33:19)
18. Written instructions of David and Solomon (2 Chr. 35:4)
19. The Laments (2 Chr. 35:25)

JUNE 25

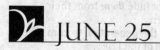

1 Chronicles 13:1–14:17

13 Then David consulted with the captains
of thousands and hundreds, *and* with
every leader. 2And David said to all the assembly of Israel, "If *it seems* good to you, and if it
is of the LORD our God, let us send out to our
brethren everywhere *who are* left in all the
land of Israel, and with them to the priests and
Levites *who are* in their cities *and* their common-lands, that they may gather together to
us; 3and let us bring the ark of our God back to
us, for we have not inquired at it since the
days of Saul." 4Then all the assembly said that
they would do so, for the thing was right in the
eyes of all the people.
5So David gathered all Israel together, from
Shihor in Egypt to as far as the entrance of
Hamath, to bring the ark of God from Kirjath
Jearim. 6And David and all Israel went up to
Baalah, to Kirjath Jearim, which belonged to
Judah, to bring up from there the ark of God
the LORD, who dwells *between* the cherubim,
where *His* name is proclaimed. 7So they carried the ark of God on a new cart from the
house of Abinadab, and Uzza and Ahio drove
the cart. 8Then David and all Israel played *music* before God with all *their* might, with singing, on harps, on stringed instruments, on tambourines, on cymbals, and with trumpets.
9And when they came to Chidon's threshing floor, Uzza put out his hand to hold the
ark, for the oxen stumbled. 10Then the anger
of the LORD was aroused against Uzza, and He
struck him because he put his hand to the ark;
and he died there before God. 11And David
became angry because of the LORD's outbreak
against Uzza; therefore that place is called
Perez Uzza to this day. 12David was afraid of
God that day, saying, "How can I bring the ark
of God to me?"

13:3 the ark of our God. Not only had the ark been stolen and profaned by the Philistines (1 Sam. 5–6), but when it was returned, Saul neglected to seek God's instruction for it. Scripture records only one occasion when Saul sought God's ark after its return (1 Sam. 14:18).

13So David would not move the ark with him
into the City of David, but took it aside into the
house of Obed-Edom the Gittite. 14The ark of
God remained with the family of Obed-Edom
in his house three months. And the LORD
blessed the house of Obed-Edom and all that
he had.

14 Now Hiram king of Tyre sent messengers to David, and cedar trees, with
masons and carpenters, to build him a house.
2So David knew that the LORD had established
him as king over Israel, for his kingdom was
highly exalted for the sake of His people Israel.

3Then David took more wives in Jerusalem,
and David begot more sons and daughters.
4And these are the names of his children
whom he had in Jerusalem: Shammua, Shobab,
Nathan, Solomon, 5Ibhar, Elishua, Elpelet,
6Nogah, Nepheg, Japhia, 7Elishama, Beeliada,
and Eliphelet.

8Now when the Philistines heard that David
had been anointed king over all Israel, all the
Philistines went up to search for David. And
David heard *of it* and went out against them.
9Then the Philistines went and made a raid on
the Valley of Rephaim. 10And David inquired of
God, saying, "Shall I go up against the
Philistines? Will You deliver them into my
hand?"

The LORD said to him, "Go up, for I will
deliver them into your hand."

11So they went up to Baal Perazim, and David defeated them there. Then David said,
"God has broken through my enemies by my
hand like a breakthrough of water." Therefore
they called the name of that place Baal
Perazim. 12And when they left their gods
there, David gave a commandment, and they
were burned with fire.

13Then the Philistines once again made a
raid on the valley. 14Therefore David inquired
again of God, and God said to him, "You shall
not go up after them; circle around them, and
come upon them in front of the mulberry trees.
15And it shall be, when you hear a sound of
marching in the tops of the mulberry trees,
then you shall go out to battle, for God has gone
out before you to strike the camp of the Philistines." 16So David did as God commanded him,
and they drove back the army of the Philistines
from Gibeon as far as Gezer. 17Then the fame of
David went out into all lands, and the LORD
brought the fear of him upon all nations.

14:8–17 The Philistines desired to ruin David before the throne was consolidated. Their plan was to kill David, but God gave him victory over the Philistines (unlike Saul) and thus declared both to the Philistines and Israel His support of Israel's new king.

Psalm 78:1–11

A Contemplation of Asaph.

Give ear, O my people, *to* my law;
Incline your ears to the
words of my mouth.
2 I will open my mouth in a parable;
I will utter dark sayings of old,

78:2 parable. The word is used here in the broader sense of a story with moral and spiritual applications. **dark sayings.** Puzzling, ambiguous information. The lessons of history are not easily discerned correctly. For an infallible interpretation of history, there must be a prophet. The specific puzzle in Israel's history is the nation's rebellious spirit in spite of God's grace.

3 Which we have heard and known,
And our fathers have told us.
4 We will not hide *them* from their
children,
Telling to the generation to come the
praises of the LORD,
And His strength and His wonderful
works that He has done.

5 For He established a testimony in
Jacob,
And appointed a law in Israel,
Which He commanded our fathers,
That they should make them known to
their children;
6 That the generation to come might
know *them*,
The children *who* would be born,
That they may arise and declare *them* to
their children,
7 That they may set their hope in God,
And not forget the works of God,
But keep His commandments;
8 And may not be like their fathers,
A stubborn and rebellious generation,
A generation *that* did not set its heart
aright,
And whose spirit was not faithful to God.

9 The children of Ephraim, *being* armed
and carrying bows,

Turned back in the day of battle.
10 They did not keep the covenant of God;
They refused to walk in His law,
11 And forgot His works
And His wonders that He had
shown them.

Proverbs 19:20–21

20 Listen to counsel and receive
instruction,
That you may be wise in your latter
days.

21 There are many plans in a man's heart,
Nevertheless the LORD's counsel—that
will stand.

Acts 7:22–43

[22]And Moses was learned in all the wisdom of
the Egyptians, and was mighty in words and
deeds.
[23]"Now when he was forty years old, it came
into his heart to visit his brethren, the children
of Israel. [24]And seeing one of *them* suffer
wrong, he defended and avenged him who was

7:23 he was forty years old. Moses' life may be divided into three 40-year periods. The first 40 years encompassed his birth and life in Pharaoh's court; the second, his exile in Midian (vv. 29,30); and the third revolved around the events of the Exodus and the years of Israel's wilderness wandering (v. 36).

oppressed, and struck down the Egyptian.
[25]For he supposed that his brethren would
have understood that God would deliver them
by his hand, but they did not understand.
[26]And the next day he appeared to *two of* them
as they were fighting, and *tried to* reconcile
them, saying, 'Men, you are brethren; why do
you wrong one another?' [27]But he who did his
neighbor wrong pushed him away, saying,
'Who made you a ruler and a judge over us?
[28]*Do you want to kill me as you did the Egyp-*
tian yesterday?' [29]Then, at this saying, Moses
fled and became a dweller in the land of
Midian, where he had two sons.
[30]"And when forty years had passed, an
Angel of the Lord appeared to him in a flame
of fire in a bush, in the wilderness of Mount Sinai. [31]When Moses saw *it,* he marveled at the
sight; and as he drew near to observe, the
voice of the Lord came to him, [32]*saying, 'I am*
the God of your fathers—the God of Abraham,
the God of Isaac, and the God of Jacob.' And
Moses trembled and dared not look. [33]*'Then*
the LORD *said to him, "Take your sandals off*
your feet, for the place where you stand is holy
ground. [34]*I have surely seen the oppression of*
My people who are in Egypt; I have heard their
groaning and have come down to deliver them.
And now come, I will send you to Egypt."'
[35]"This Moses whom they rejected, saying,
'Who made you a ruler and a judge?' is the one
God sent *to be* a ruler and a deliverer by the hand
of the Angel who appeared to him in the bush.
[36]He brought them out, after he had shown wonders and signs in the land of Egypt, and in the
Red Sea, and in the wilderness forty years.
[37]"This is that Moses who said to the children of Israel, *'The* LORD *your God will raise*
up for you a Prophet like me from your
brethren. Him you shall hear.'
[38]"This is he who was in the congregation in
the wilderness with the Angel who spoke to
him on Mount Sinai, and *with* our fathers, the
one who received the living oracles to give to
us, [39]whom our fathers would not obey, but
rejected. And in their hearts they turned back
to Egypt, [40]saying to Aaron, *'Make us gods to*
go before us; as for this Moses who brought
us out of the land of Egypt, we do not know
what has become of him.' [41]And they made a
calf in those days, offered sacrifices to the
idol, and rejoiced in the works of their own
hands. [42]Then God turned and gave them up to
worship the host of heaven, as it is written in
the book of the Prophets:

'Did you offer Me slaughtered animals
and sacrifices during forty years in
the wilderness,
O house of Israel?
43 *You also took up the tabernacle of*
Moloch,
And the star of your god Remphan,
Images which you made to worship;
And I will carry you away beyond
Babylon.'

7:43 *Babylon.* Amos wrote Damascus (Amos 5:27), while Stephen said Babylon. Amos was prophesying the captivity of the northern kingdom in Assyria, a deportation beyond Damascus. Later, the southern kingdom was taken captive to Babylon. Stephen, inspired to do so, extended the prophecy to embrace the judgment on the whole nation summarizing their idolatrous history and its results.

DAY 25: What does it mean that God "gave them up" in Acts 7:42?

"Then God turned and gave them up to worship the host of heaven." Here Stephen quoted from Amos 5:25–27. It means that God judicially abandoned the people to their sin and idolatry (Hos. 4:17). The worship of the sun, moon, and stars began in the wilderness and lasted through the Babylonian captivity (Deut. 4:19; 17:3; 2 Kin. 17:16; 21:3–5; 23:4; 2 Chr. 33:3,5; Jer. 8:2; 19:13; Zeph. 1:5).

Similarly, in Romans 1:24, it states that "God also gave them up to uncleanness, in the lusts of their hearts." The Greek word used is for handing over a prisoner to his sentence. When men consistently abandon God, He will abandon them (Judg. 10:13; 2 Chr. 15:2; 24:20; Ps. 81:11,12; Matt. 15:14). He accomplishes this 1) indirectly and immediately, by removing His restraint and allowing their sin to run its inevitable course and 2) directly and eventually, by specific acts of divine judgment and punishment. "Uncleanness" is a general term often used of decaying matter, like the contents of a grave. It speaks here of sexual immorality (2 Cor. 12:21; Gal. 5:19–23; Eph. 5:3; 1 Thess. 4:7), which begins in the heart and moves to the shame of the body.

And "God gave them up to vile passions" (Rom. 1:26). This is identified in vv. 26, 27 as homosexuality, a sin roundly condemned in Scripture (Gen. 19; Lev. 18:22; 1 Cor. 6:9–11; Gal. 5:19–21; Eph. 5:3–5; 1 Tim. 1:9,10; Jude 7). Rather than the normal Greek term for "women," this is a general word for female. Paul mentions women first to show the extent of debauchery under the wrath of abandonment, because in most cultures women are the last to be affected by moral collapse.

And "God gave them over to a debased mind" (v. 28). This translates a Greek word that means "not passing the test." It was often used to describe useless, worthless metals, discarded because they contained too much impurity. God has tested man's minds and found them worthless and useless (Jer. 6:30).

JUNE 26

1 Chronicles 15:1–16:43

15 *David* built houses for himself in the City
of David; and he prepared a place for the
ark of God, and pitched a tent for it. [2]Then Da-

15:1 *David* built houses for himself. He was able by the alliance and help of Hiram (18:1) to build a palace for himself and separate houses for his wives and their children. While the ark remained near Jerusalem at the home of Obed-Edom for 3 months (13:13,14), David constructed a new tabernacle in Jerusalem to fulfill God's word in Deuteronomy 12:5–7 of a permanent residency.

vid said, "No one may carry the ark of God but
the Levites, for the Lord has chosen them to
carry the ark of God and to minister before Him
forever." [3]And David gathered all Israel together at Jerusalem, to bring up the ark of the Lord
to its place, which he had prepared for it. [4]Then
David assembled the children of Aaron and the
Levites: [5]of the sons of Kohath, Uriel the chief,
and one hundred and twenty of his brethren; [6]of
the sons of Merari, Asaiah the chief, and two
hundred and twenty of his brethren; [7]of the sons
of Gershom, Joel the chief, and one hundred
and thirty of his brethren; [8]of the sons of
Elizaphan, Shemaiah the chief, and two hundred of his brethren; [9]of the sons of Hebron,
Eliel the chief, and eighty of his brethren; [10]of
the sons of Uzziel, Amminadab the chief, and
one hundred and twelve of his brethren.
[11]And David called for Zadok and Abiathar
the priests, and for the Levites: for Uriel,
Asaiah, Joel, Shemaiah, Eliel, and Amminadab.
[12]He said to them, "You *are* the heads of the

15:11 Zadok...Abiathar. These two high priests, heads of the two priestly houses of Eleazar and Ithamar, were colleagues in the high priesthood (2 Sam. 20:25). They served the Lord simultaneously in David's reign. Zadok attended the tabernacle in Gibeon (1 Chr. 16:39), while Abiathar served the temporary place of the ark in Jerusalem. Ultimately, Zadok prevailed (1 Kin. 2:26,27).

fathers' *houses* of the Levites; sanctify yourselves, you and your brethren, that you may
bring up the ark of the LORD God of Israel to *the*
place I have prepared for it. [13]For because you
did not *do it* the first *time,* the LORD our God
broke out against us, because we did not consult
Him about the proper order."

14So the priests and the Levites sanctified
themselves to bring up the ark of the LORD
God of Israel. 15And the children of the Levites
bore the ark of God on their shoulders, by its
poles, as Moses had commanded according to
the word of the LORD.
16Then David spoke to the leaders of the
Levites to appoint their brethren *to be* the
singers accompanied by instruments of music,
stringed instruments, harps, and cymbals, by
raising the voice with resounding joy. 17So the
Levites appointed Heman the son of Joel; and of
his brethren, Asaph the son of Berechiah; and
of their brethren, the sons of Merari, Ethan the
son of Kushaiah; 18and with them their brethren
of the second *rank:* Zechariah, Ben, Jaaziel,
Shemiramoth, Jehiel, Unni, Eliab, Benaiah,
Maaseiah, Mattithiah, Elipheleh, Mikneiah,
Obed-Edom, and Jeiel, the gatekeepers; 19the
singers, Heman, Asaph, and Ethan, *were* to
sound the cymbals of bronze; 20Zechariah,
Aziel, Shemiramoth, Jehiel, Unni, Eliab,
Maaseiah, and Benaiah, with strings according
to Alamoth; 21Mattithiah, Elipheleh, Mikneiah,
Obed-Edom, Jeiel, and Azaziah, to direct with
harps on the Sheminith; 22Chenaniah, leader of
the Levites, was instructor *in charge of* the
music, because he *was* skillful; 23Berechiah
and Elkanah *were* doorkeepers for the ark;
24Shebaniah, Joshaphat, Nethanel, Amasai,
Zechariah, Benaiah, and Eliezer, the priests,
were to blow the trumpets before the ark of
God; and Obed-Edom and Jehiah, doorkeepers for the ark.
25So David, the elders of Israel, and the captains over thousands went to bring up the ark
of the covenant of the LORD from the house of
Obed-Edom with joy. 26And so it was, when
God helped the Levites who bore the ark of
the covenant of the LORD, that they offered
seven bulls and seven rams. 27David was
clothed with a robe of fine linen, as were all
the Levites who bore the ark, the singers, and
Chenaniah the music master *with* the singers.
David also wore a linen ephod. 28Thus all Israel
brought up the ark of the covenant of the LORD
with shouting and with the sound of the horn,
with trumpets and with cymbals, making
music with stringed instruments and harps.
29And it happened, *as* the ark of the covenant
of the LORD came to the City of David, that
Michal, Saul's daughter, looked through a window and saw King David whirling and playing
music; and she despised him in her heart.

16 So they brought the ark of God, and set
it in the midst of the tabernacle that David had erected for it. Then they offered burnt
offerings and peace offerings before God.
2And when David had finished offering the
burnt offerings and the peace offerings, he
blessed the people in the name of the LORD.
3Then he distributed to everyone of Israel,
both man and woman, to everyone a loaf of
bread, a piece *of meat,* and a cake of raisins.
4And he appointed some of the Levites to minister before the ark of the LORD, to commemo-
rate, to thank, and to praise the LORD God of Israel: 5Asaph the chief, and next to him
Zechariah, *then* Jeiel, Shemiramoth, Jehiel,
Mattithiah, Eliab, Benaiah, and Obed-Edom:
Jeiel with stringed instruments and harps, but
Asaph made music with cymbals; 6Benaiah and
Jahaziel the priests regularly *blew* the trumpets before the ark of the covenant of God.
7On that day David first delivered *this psalm*
into the hand of Asaph and his brethren, to
thank the LORD:

8 Oh, give thanks to the LORD!
Call upon His name;
Make known His deeds among the
peoples!
9 Sing to Him, sing psalms to Him;
Talk of all His wondrous works!
10 Glory in His holy name;
Let the hearts of those rejoice who
seek the LORD!
11 Seek the LORD and His strength;
Seek His face evermore!
12 Remember His marvelous works
which He has done,
His wonders, and the judgments of
His mouth,
13 O seed of Israel His servant,
You children of Jacob, His
chosen ones!

14 He *is* the LORD our God;
His judgments *are* in all the earth.
15 Remember His covenant forever,
The word which He commanded, for a
thousand generations,
16 *The covenant which* He made with
Abraham,
And His oath to Isaac,
17 And confirmed it to Jacob for a statute,
To Israel *for* an everlasting covenant,
18 Saying, "To you I will give the land of
Canaan
As the allotment of your inheritance,"
19 When you were few in number,
Indeed very few, and strangers in it.
20 When they went from one nation to
another,
And from *one* kingdom to another
people,

21 He permitted no man to do them
wrong;
Yes, He rebuked kings for their sakes,
22 *Saying,* "Do not touch My anointed
ones,
And do My prophets no harm."

23 Sing to the LORD, all the earth;
Proclaim the good news of His
salvation from day to day.
24 Declare His glory among the nations,
His wonders among all peoples.
25 For the LORD *is* great and greatly to
be praised;
He *is* also to be feared above all gods.
26 For all the gods of the peoples
are idols,
But the LORD made the heavens.
27 Honor and majesty *are* before Him;
Strength and gladness are in His place.

28 Give to the LORD, O families of the
peoples,
Give to the LORD glory and strength.
29 Give to the LORD the glory *due*
His name;
Bring an offering, and come before
Him.
Oh, worship the LORD in the beauty
of holiness!
30 Tremble before Him, all the earth.
The world also is firmly established,
It shall not be moved.

31 Let the heavens rejoice, and let the
earth be glad;
And let them say among the nations,
"The LORD reigns."
32 Let the sea roar, and all its fullness;
Let the field rejoice, and all that *is* in it.
33 Then the trees of the woods shall
rejoice before the LORD,
For He is coming to judge the earth.

34 Oh, give thanks to the LORD, for *He*
is good!
For His mercy *endures* forever.
35 And say, "Save us, O God of our
salvation;
Gather us together, and deliver us
from the Gentiles,
To give thanks to Your holy name,
To triumph in Your praise."

36 Blessed *be* the LORD God of Israel
From everlasting to everlasting!

And all the people said, "Amen!" and praised
the LORD.
37So he left Asaph and his brothers there
before the ark of the covenant of the LORD to
minister before the ark regularly, as every
day's work required; 38and Obed-Edom with
his sixty-eight brethren, including Obed-
Edom the son of Jeduthun, and Hosah, *to be*
gatekeepers; 39and Zadok the priest and his
brethren the priests, before the tabernacle of
the LORD at the high place that *was* at Gibeon,
40to offer burnt offerings to the LORD on the
altar of burnt offering regularly morning and
evening, and *to do* according to all that is written in the Law of the LORD which He commanded Israel; 41and with them Heman and
Jeduthun and the rest who were chosen, who
were designated by name, to give thanks to
the LORD, because His mercy *endures* forever;
42and with them Heman and Jeduthun, to
sound aloud with trumpets and cymbals and
the musical instruments of God. Now the sons
of Jeduthun *were* gatekeepers.
43Then all the people departed, every man to
his house; and David returned to bless his
house.

Psalm 78:12–16

12 Marvelous things He did in the sight of
their fathers,
In the land of Egypt, *in* the field of
Zoan.
13 He divided the sea and caused them to
pass through;
And He made the waters stand up like
a heap.

78:13 waters stand up like a heap. The parting of the Red Sea at the beginning of the Exodus, which allowed Israel to escape from the Egyptian armies, was always considered by the Old Testament saints to be the most spectacular miracle of their history (Ex. 14).

78:15 split the rocks. Twice in the wilderness, when Israel desperately needed a great water supply, God brought water out of rocks (Ex. 17:6; Num. 20:11).

14 In the daytime also He led them with
the cloud,
And all the night with a light of fire.
15 He split the rocks in the wilderness,
And gave *them* drink in abundance like
the depths.
16 He also brought streams out of the
rock,

And caused waters to run down like
rivers.

Proverbs 19:22–24

22 What is desired in a man is kindness,
And a poor man is better than a liar.

23 The fear of the LORD *leads* to life,
And *he who has it* will abide in
satisfaction;
He will not be visited with evil.

24 A lazy *man* buries his hand in the bowl,
And will not so much as bring it to his
mouth again.

Acts 7:44–60

44"Our fathers had the tabernacle of witness
in the wilderness, as He appointed, instructing
Moses to make it according to the pattern that
he had seen, 45which our fathers, having
received it in turn, also brought with Joshua
into the land possessed by the Gentiles, whom
God drove out before the face of our fathers
until the days of David, 46who found favor
before God and asked to find a dwelling for the
God of Jacob. 47But Solomon built Him a house.
48"However, the Most High does not dwell in
temples made with hands, as the prophet says:

49 *'Heaven is My throne,*
And earth is My footstool.
What house will you build for Me? says
the LORD*,*
Or what is the place of My rest?
50 *Has My hand not made all these*
things?'

51"*You* stiff-necked and uncircumcised in
heart and ears! You always resist the Holy Spirit;
as your fathers *did,* so *do* you. 52Which of the
prophets did your fathers not persecute? And
they killed those who foretold the coming of
the Just One, of whom you now have become
the betrayers and murderers, 53who have
received the law by the direction of angels and
have not kept *it.*"
54When they heard these things they were
cut to the heart, and they gnashed at him with
their teeth. 55But he, being full of the Holy
Spirit, gazed into heaven and saw the glory of
God, and Jesus standing at the right hand of
God, 56and said, "Look! I see the heavens
opened and the Son of Man standing at the
right hand of God!"
57Then they cried out with a loud voice,
stopped their ears, and ran at him with one
accord; 58and they cast *him* out of the city and
stoned *him.* And the witnesses laid down their
clothes at the feet of a young man named Saul.
59And they stoned Stephen as he was calling
on *God* and saying, "Lord Jesus, receive my
spirit." 60Then he knelt down and cried out
with a loud voice, "Lord, do not charge them
with this sin." And when he had said this, he
fell asleep.

7:44–50 To counter the false charge that he blasphemed the temple (6:13,14), Stephen recounted its history to show his respect for it.

7:49,50 Quoted from Isaiah 66:1,2. Stephen's point is that God is greater than the temple, and thus the Jewish leaders were guilty of blaspheming by confining God to it.

DAY 26: Why was Stephen martyred?

In the climax of Stephen's sermon (Acts 7:51–53), he indicted the Jewish leaders for rejecting God in the same way that their ancestors had rejected Him in the Old Testament. He told the members of the esteemed Sanhedrin that they were "stiff-necked" like their fathers (Ex. 32:9; 33:5) and "uncircumcised in heart and ears!" Thus they were as unclean before God as the uncircumcised Gentiles (Deut. 10:16; Jer. 4:4; Rom. 2:28,29). "You always resist the Holy Spirit" by rejecting the Spirit's messengers and their message. And when he spoke of the "Just One," Stephen reminds them that they betrayed and murdered Him (v. 52). His words were reminiscent of those from Jesus' sermon in Matthew 23:13–39.

The reaction of the Sanhedrin was that they "gnashed at him with their teeth" (v. 54). That is the fullness of anger and frustration and was in contrast to Stephen, who "being full of the Holy Spirit, gazed into heaven and saw the glory of God, and Jesus standing at the right hand of God" (v. 55). Isaiah (Is. 6:1–3), Ezekiel (Ezek. 1:26–28), Paul (2 Cor. 12:2–4), and John (Rev. 1:10) also received visions of God's glory in heaven.

Stephen's words were so appalling that they took him out of the city and "stoned him." This was the punishment prescribed in the law for blasphemy (Lev. 24:16); however, this was not a formal execution but an act of mob violence. And those who participated "laid down their clothes…Saul" (v. 58). Paul's first appearance in Scripture. That he was near enough to the action to be holding the clothes of Stephen's killers reflects his deep involvement in the sordid affair. And Paul heard those marvelous words of Stephen, "do not charge them with this sin" (v. 60). As had Jesus before him (Luke 23:34), Stephen prayed for God to forgive his killers.

JUNE 27

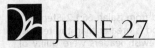

1 Chronicles 17:1–18:17

17 Now it came to pass, when David was
dwelling in his house, that David said to
Nathan the prophet, "See now, I dwell in a
house of cedar, but the ark of the covenant of
the LORD *is* under tent curtains."
[2]Then Nathan said to David, "Do all that *is* in
your heart, for God *is* with you."
[3]But it happened that night that the word of
God came to Nathan, saying, [4]"Go and tell My
servant David, 'Thus says the LORD: "You shall
not build Me a house to dwell in. [5]For I have
not dwelt in a house since the time that I
brought up Israel, even to this day, but have
gone from tent to tent, and from *one* tabernacle
to another. [6]Wherever I have moved about with
all Israel, have I ever spoken a word to any of
the judges of Israel, whom I commanded to
shepherd My people, saying, 'Why have you
not built Me a house of cedar?' " ' [7]Now therefore, thus shall you say to My servant David,
'Thus says the LORD of hosts: "I took you from
the sheepfold, from following the sheep, to be
ruler over My people Israel. [8]And I have been
with you wherever you have gone, and have cut
off all your enemies from before you, and have
made you a name like the name of the great
men who *are* on the earth. [9]Moreover I will
appoint a place for My people Israel, and will
plant them, that they may dwell in a place of
their own and move no more; nor shall the
sons of wickedness oppress them anymore, as
previously, [10]since the time that I commanded
judges *to be* over My people Israel. Also I will
subdue all your enemies. Furthermore I tell
you that the LORD will build you a house. [11]And
it shall be, when your days are fulfilled, when
you must go *to be* with your fathers, that I will
set up your seed after you, who will be of your
sons; and I will establish his kingdom. [12]He
shall build Me a house, and I will establish his
throne forever. [13]I will be his Father, and he
shall be My son; and I will not take My mercy
away from him, as I took *it* from *him* who was
before you. [14]And I will establish him in My
house and in My kingdom forever; and his
throne shall be established forever." ' "
[15]According to all these words and according to all this vision, so Nathan spoke to David.
[16]Then King David went in and sat before
the LORD; and he said: "Who *am* I, O LORD
God? And what is my house, that You have
brought me this far? [17]And *yet* this was a small
thing in Your sight, O God; and You have *also*
spoken of Your servant's house for a great
while to come, and have regarded me according to the rank of a man of high degree, O
LORD God. [18]What more can David *say* to You
for the honor of Your servant? For You know
Your servant. [19]O LORD, for Your servant's
sake, and according to Your own heart, You
have done all this greatness, in making known
all these great things. [20]O LORD, *there is* none
like You, nor *is there any* God besides You,
according to all that we have heard with our
ears. [21]And who *is* like Your people Israel, the
one nation on the earth whom God went to
redeem for Himself *as* a people—to make for
Yourself a name by great and awesome deeds,
by driving out nations from before Your people whom You redeemed from Egypt? [22]For
You have made Your people Israel Your very
own people forever; and You, LORD, have
become their God.
[23]"And now, O LORD, the word which You have
spoken concerning Your servant and concerning his house, *let it* be established forever, and
do as You have said. [24]So let it be established,
that Your name may be magnified forever, saying, 'The LORD of hosts, the God of Israel, *is* Israel's God.' And let the house of Your servant
David be established before You. [25]For You, O
my God, have revealed to Your servant that

17:27 The Davidic Covenant in Chronicles

1. 1 Chr. 17:7–27	God to Nathan to David
2. 1 Chr. 22:6–16	David to Solomon
3. 1 Chr. 28:6,7	David to Solomon
4. 2 Chr. 6:8,9,16,17	Solomon to the nation
5. 2 Chr. 7:17,18	God to Solomon
6. 2 Chr. 13:4,5	Abijah to Jeroboam
7. 2 Chr. 21:7	Chronicler's commentary

You will build him a house. Therefore Your
servant has found it *in his heart* to pray before
You. [26]And now, LORD, You are God, and have
promised this goodness to Your servant.
[27]Now You have been pleased to bless the
house of Your servant, that it may continue
before You forever; for You have blessed it, O
LORD, and *it shall be* blessed forever."

18 After this it came to pass that David attacked the Philistines, subdued them,
and took Gath and its towns from the hand of
the Philistines. [2]Then he defeated Moab, and
the Moabites became David's servants, *and*
brought tribute.

[3]And David defeated Hadadezer king of
Zobah *as far as* Hamath, as he went to establish his power by the River Euphrates. [4]David
took from him one thousand chariots, seven
thousand horsemen, and twenty thousand foot
soldiers. Also David hamstrung all the chariot
horses, except that he spared enough of them
for one hundred chariots.

[5]When the Syrians of Damascus came to help
Hadadezer king of Zobah, David killed twenty-
two thousand of the Syrians. [6]Then David put
garrisons in Syria of Damascus; and the Syrians
became David's servants, *and* brought tribute.
So the LORD preserved David wherever he went.
[7]And David took the shields of gold that were on
the servants of Hadadezer, and brought them to
Jerusalem. [8]Also from Tibhath and from Chun,
cities of Hadadezer, David brought a large
amount of bronze, with which Solomon made
the bronze Sea, the pillars, and the articles of
bronze.

[9]Now when Tou king of Hamath heard that
David had defeated all the army of Hadadezer
king of Zobah, [10]he sent Hadoram his son to
King David, to greet him and bless him,
because he had fought against Hadadezer and
defeated him (for Hadadezer had been at war
with Tou); and *Hadoram brought with him* all
kinds of articles of gold, silver, and bronze.
[11]King David also dedicated these to the LORD,
along with the silver and gold that he had
brought from all *these* nations—from Edom,
from Moab, from the people of Ammon, from
the Philistines, and from Amalek.

[12]Moreover Abishai the son of Zeruiah
killed eighteen thousand Edomites in the
Valley of Salt. [13]He also put garrisons in Edom,
and all the Edomites became David's servants. And the LORD preserved David wherever he went.

[14]So David reigned over all Israel, and
administered judgment and justice to all his
people. [15]Joab the son of Zeruiah *was* over the
army; Jehoshaphat the son of Ahilud *was*
recorder; [16]Zadok the son of Ahitub and Abimelech the son of Abiathar *were* the priests;
Shavsha *was* the scribe; [17]Benaiah the son of
Jehoiada *was* over the Cherethites and the
Pelethites; and David's sons *were* chief ministers at the king's side.

Psalm 78:17–25

17 But they sinned even more against
Him
By rebelling against the Most High in
the wilderness.
18 And they tested God in their heart
By asking for the food of their fancy.

78:18 the food of their fancy. Instead of being grateful for God's marvelous provisions of manna, the Israelites complained against God and Moses. God sent them meat, but also judged them (Num. 11).

19 Yes, they spoke against God:
They said, "Can God prepare a table in
the wilderness?
20 Behold, He struck the rock,
So that the waters gushed out,
And the streams overflowed.
Can He give bread also?
Can He provide meat for His people?"
21 Therefore the LORD heard *this* and was
furious;
So a fire was kindled against Jacob,
And anger also came up against Israel,
22 Because they did not believe in God,
And did not trust in His salvation.
23 Yet He had commanded the clouds
above,
And opened the doors of heaven,
24 Had rained down manna on them
to eat,
And given them of the bread of heaven.
25 Men ate angels' food;
He sent them food to the full.

Proverbs 19:25–26

25 Strike a scoffer, and the simple will
become wary;
Rebuke one who has understanding,
and he will discern knowledge.
26 He who mistreats *his* father *and* chases
away *his* mother
Is a son who causes shame and brings
reproach.

19:25 scoffer...simple...understanding. Three classes of people are noted: 1) scoffers are rebuked for learning nothing; 2) simpletons are warned by observing the rebuke of the scoffer; and 3) the understanding deepen their wisdom from any reproof.

Acts 8:1–25

8 Now Saul was consenting to his death.
At that time a great persecution arose
against the church which was at Jerusalem;
and they were all scattered throughout the
regions of Judea and Samaria, except the apostles. 2And devout men carried Stephen *to his*
burial, and made great lamentation over him.

8:1 consenting. Paul's murderous hatred of all believers was manifested here in his attitude toward Stephen (1 Tim. 1:13–15). **scattered.** Led by a Jew named Saul of Tarsus, the persecution scattered the Jerusalem fellowship and led to the first missionary outreach of the church. Not all members of the Jerusalem church were forced to flee; the Hellenists, because Stephen was likely one, bore the brunt of the persecution (11:19,20). **except the apostles.** They remained because of their devotion to Christ, to care for those at Jerusalem, and to continue evangelizing the region (9:26,27).

8:3 he made havoc of the church. "Made havoc" was used in extrabiblical writings to refer to the destruction of a city or mangling by a wild animal.

3As for Saul, he made havoc of the church,
entering every house, and dragging off men
and women, committing *them* to prison.
4Therefore those who were scattered went
everywhere preaching the word. 5Then Philip
went down to the city of Samaria and preached
Christ to them. 6And the multitudes with one
accord heeded the things spoken by Philip,
hearing and seeing the miracles which he did.
7For unclean spirits, crying with a loud voice,
came out of many who were possessed; and
many who were paralyzed and lame were
healed. 8And there was great joy in that city.
9But there was a certain man called Simon,
who previously practiced sorcery in the city

8:10,11 the great power of God. Simon claimed to be united to God. The early church fathers claimed he was one of the founders of Gnosticism, which asserted there were a series of divine emanations reaching up to God. They were called Powers, and the people believed he was at the top of the ladder.

and astonished the people of Samaria, claiming that he was someone great, 10to whom they
all gave heed, from the least to the greatest,
saying, "This man is the great power of God."
11And they heeded him because he had astonished them with his sorceries for a long time.
12But when they believed Philip as he preached
the things concerning the kingdom of God and
the name of Jesus Christ, both men and
women were baptized. 13Then Simon himself
also believed; and when he was baptized he
continued with Philip, and was amazed, seeing
the miracles and signs which were done.
14Now when the apostles who were at Jerusalem heard that Samaria had received the
word of God, they sent Peter and John to
them, 15who, when they had come down,
prayed for them that they might receive the
Holy Spirit. 16For as yet He had fallen upon
none of them. They had only been baptized in
the name of the Lord Jesus. 17Then they laid
hands on them, and they received the Holy
Spirit.
18And when Simon saw that through the laying on of the apostles' hands the Holy Spirit
was given, he offered them money, 19saying,
"Give me this power also, that anyone on
whom I lay hands may receive the Holy
Spirit."
20But Peter said to him, "Your money perish
with you, because you thought that the gift of
God could be purchased with money! 21You
have neither part nor portion in this matter, for
your heart is not right in the sight of God. 22Re-
pent therefore of this your wickedness, and
pray God if perhaps the thought of your heart
may be forgiven you. 23For I see that you are poisoned by bitterness and bound by iniquity."
24Then Simon answered and said, "Pray to
the Lord for me, that none of the things which
you have spoken may come upon me."
25So when they had testified and preached
the word of the Lord, they returned to Jerusalem, preaching the gospel in many villages of
the Samaritans.

DAY 27: Is the Holy Spirit received subsequent to salvation?

In Acts 8:15, Peter and John were sent to Samaria to pray for those who had responded to the preaching of Philip (Acts 8:4–13) that they might receive the Holy Spirit. "For as yet He had fallen upon none of them" (v. 16). This verse does not support the false notion that Christians receive the Holy Spirit subsequent to salvation. This was a transitional period in which confirmation by the apostles was necessary to verify the inclusion of a new group of people into the church. Because of the animosity that existed between Jews and Samaritans, it was essential for the Samaritans to receive the Spirit in the presence of the leaders of the Jerusalem church, for the purpose of maintaining a unified church. The delay also revealed the Samaritans' need to come under apostolic authority. The same transitional event occurred when the Gentiles were added to the church (11:44–46; 15:6–12; 19:6).

So "they laid hands on them, and they received the Holy Spirit" (v. 17). This signified apostolic affirmation and solidarity. That this actually occurred likely demonstrated that believers also spoke in tongues here, just as those who received the Spirit did on the Day of Pentecost, as the Gentiles did when they received the Spirit (10:46), and as those followers of John did (19:6). As Samaritans, Gentiles, and believers from the Old Covenant were added to the church, the unity of the church was established. No longer could one nation (Israel) be God's witness people, but the church made up of Jews, Gentiles, half-breed Samaritans, and Old Testament saints who became New Testament believers (19:1–7). To demonstrate the unity, it was imperative that there be some replication in each instance of what had occurred at Pentecost with the believing Jews, such as the presence of the apostles and the coming of the Spirit manifestly indicated through speaking in the languages of Pentecost (2:5–12).

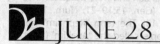

JUNE 28

1 Chronicles 19:1–20:8

19 It happened after this that Nahash the
king of the people of Ammon died, and
his son reigned in his place. 2Then David said, "I
will show kindness to Hanun the son of Nahash,
because his father showed kindness to me." So
David sent messengers to comfort him concerning his father. And David's servants came
to Hanun in the land of the people of Ammon
to comfort him.
3And the princes of the people of Ammon
said to Hanun, "Do you think that David really honors your father because he has sent
comforters to you? Did his servants not come
to you to search and to overthrow and to spy
out the land?"
4Therefore Hanun took David's servants,
shaved them, and cut off their garments in the
middle, at their buttocks, and sent them away.
5Then *some* went and told David about the
men; and he sent to meet them, because the
men were greatly ashamed. And the king said,
"Wait at Jericho until your beards have grown,
and *then* return."
6When the people of Ammon saw that they
had made themselves repulsive to David,
Hanun and the people of Ammon sent a thousand talents of silver to hire for themselves
chariots and horsemen from Mesopotamia,
from Syrian Maacah, and from Zobah. 7So
they hired for themselves thirty-two thousand
chariots, with the king of Maacah and his people, who came and encamped before Medeba.
Also the people of Ammon gathered together
from their cities, and came to battle.
8Now when David heard *of it*, he sent Joab
and all the army of the mighty men. 9Then the
people of Ammon came out and put themselves in battle array before the gate of the
city, and the kings who had come *were* by
themselves in the field.
10When Joab saw that the battle line was
against him before and behind, he chose some
of Israel's best, and put *them* in battle array
against the Syrians. 11And the rest of the people he put under the command of Abishai his
brother, and they set *themselves* in battle array
against the people of Ammon. 12Then he said,
"If the Syrians are too strong for me, then you
shall help me; but if the people of Ammon are
too strong for you, then I will help you. 13Be of
good courage, and let us be strong for our
people and for the cities of our God. And may
the LORD do *what is* good in His sight."
14So Joab and the people who *were* with him
drew near for the battle against the Syrians,
and they fled before him. 15When the people of
Ammon saw that the Syrians were fleeing,
they also fled before Abishai his brother, and
entered the city. So Joab went to Jerusalem.
16Now when the Syrians saw that they had
been defeated by Israel, they sent messengers
and brought the Syrians who were beyond the

River, and Shophach the commander of Hadadezer's army *went* before them. [17]When it was told David, he gathered all Israel, crossed over the Jordan and came upon them, and set up in *battle* array against them. So when David had set up in battle array against the Syrians, they fought with him. [18]Then the Syrians fled before Israel; and David killed seven thousand charioteers and forty thousand foot soldiers of the Syrians, and killed Shophach the commander of the army. [19]And when the servants of Hadadezer saw that they were defeated by Israel, they made peace with David and became his servants. So the Syrians were not willing to help the people of Ammon anymore.

20 It happened in the spring of the year, at the time kings go out *to battle,* that Joab led out the armed forces and ravaged the country of the people of Ammon, and came and besieged Rabbah. But David stayed at Jerusalem. And Joab defeated Rabbah and overthrew it. [2]Then David took their king's crown from his head, and found it to weigh a talent of gold, and *there were* precious stones in it. And it was set on David's head. Also he brought out the spoil of the city in great abundance. [3]And he brought out the people who *were* in it, and put *them* to work with saws, with iron picks, and with axes. So David did to all the cities of the people of Ammon. Then David and all the people returned *to* Jerusalem.

20:1–3 The chronicler was not inspired by God to mention David's sin with Bathsheba and subsequent sins recorded in 2 Samuel 11:2–12:23. The adultery and murder occurred at this time, while David stayed in Jerusalem instead of going to battle. The story was likely omitted because the book was written to focus on God's permanent interest in His people, Israel, and the perpetuity of David's kingdom.

[4]Now it happened afterward that war broke out at Gezer with the Philistines, at which time Sibbechai the Hushathite killed Sippai, *who was one* of the sons of the giant. And they were subdued.

[5]Again there was war with the Philistines, and Elhanan the son of Jair killed Lahmi the brother of Goliath the Gittite, the shaft of whose spear *was* like a weaver's beam.

[6]Yet again there was war at Gath, where there was a man of *great* stature, with twenty-four fingers and toes, six *on each hand* and six *on each foot;* and he also was born to the giant. [7]So when he defied Israel, Jonathan the son of Shimea, David's brother, killed him.

[8]These were born to the giant in Gath, and they fell by the hand of David and by the hand of his servants.

20:4–8 See 2 Samuel 21:15–22. The chronicler chose not to write of some of the darker days in David's reign, especially the revolt of David's son Absalom, for the same reason the iniquity of the king with Bathsheba was left out. This section describes the defeat of 4 Philistine giants at the hands of David and his men. Though these events cannot be located chronologically with any certainty, the narratives of victory provide a fitting preface to David's song of praise, which magnifies God's deliverance (2 Sam. 22:1–51).

20:4 the giant. The Hebrew term is *rapha.* This was not the name of an individual, but a term used collectively for the Rephaim who inhabited the land of Canaan and were noted for their inordinate size (Gen. 15:19–21; Num. 13:33; Deut. 2:11; 3:11,13). The term "Rephaim" was used of the people called the "Anakim" (Deut. 2:10,11,20,21), distinguished for their size and strength. According to Joshua 11:21,22, the "Anakim" were driven from the hill country of Israel and Judah, but remained in the Philistine cities of Gaza, Gath, and Ashdod. Though the Philistines had succumbed to the power of Israel's army, the appearance of some great champion revived their courage and invited their hope for victory against the Israelite invaders.

Psalm 78:26–33

26 He caused an east wind to blow in the heavens;
And by His power He brought in the south wind.
27 He also rained meat on them like the dust,
Feathered fowl like the sand of the seas;
28 And He let *them* fall in the midst of their camp,
All around their dwellings.
29 So they ate and were well filled,
For He gave them their own desire.
30 They were not deprived of their craving;
But while their food *was* still in their mouths,
31 The wrath of God came against them,
And slew the stoutest of them,
And struck down the choice *men* of Israel.

32 In spite of this they still sinned,
And did not believe in His wondrous works.
33 Therefore their days He consumed in futility,
And their years in fear.

Proverbs 19:27–29

27 Cease listening to instruction, my son,
And you will stray from the words of knowledge.
28 A disreputable witness scorns justice,
And the mouth of the wicked devours iniquity.
29 Judgments are prepared for scoffers,
And beatings for the backs of fools.

Acts 8:26–40

26Now an angel of the Lord spoke to Philip,
saying, "Arise and go toward the south along the
road which goes down from Jerusalem to Gaza."
This is desert. 27So he arose and went. And
behold, a man of Ethiopia, a eunuch of great
authority under Candace the queen of the Ethiopians, who had charge of all her treasury, and
had come to Jerusalem to worship, 28was returning. And sitting in his chariot, he was reading
Isaiah the prophet. 29Then the Spirit said to
Philip, "Go near and overtake this chariot."
30So Philip ran to him, and heard him reading
the prophet Isaiah, and said, "Do you understand what you are reading?"
31And he said, "How can I, unless someone
guides me?" And he asked Philip to come up
and sit with him. 32The place in the Scripture
which he read was this:

"He was led as a sheep to the slaughter;
And as a lamb before its shearer is silent,
So He opened not His mouth.
33 *In His humiliation His justice was taken away,*
And who will declare His generation?
For His life is taken from the earth."

34So the eunuch answered Philip and said, "I
ask you, of whom does the prophet say this, of
himself or of some other man?" 35Then Philip
opened his mouth, and beginning at this Scripture, preached Jesus to him. 36Now as they
went down the road, they came to some water.
And the eunuch said, "See, *here is* water. What
hinders me from being baptized?"
37Then Philip said, "If you believe with all
your heart, you may."
And he answered and said, "I believe that Jesus Christ is the Son of God."
38So he commanded the chariot to stand
still. And both Philip and the eunuch went
down into the water, and he baptized him.
39Now when they came up out of the water, the
Spirit of the Lord caught Philip away, so that
the eunuch saw him no more; and he went on
his way rejoicing. 40But Philip was found at
Azotus. And passing through, he preached in
all the cities till he came to Caesarea.

DAY 28: How did Philip bring the gospel to the Ethiopian eunuch?

Philip, who had been involved with the evangelization of the Samaritans, was told by an angel of the Lord to go to an undisclosed location along the road that went down from Jerusalem to Gaza (Acts 8:26). Gaza was one of 5 chief cities of the Philistines. The original city was destroyed in the first century B.C. and a new city was built near the coast.

There Philip met an Ethiopian eunuch. Ethiopia in those days was a large kingdom located south of Egypt. A eunuch can refer to one who had been emasculated or generally, to a government official. It is likely he was both since Luke refers to him as a eunuch and as one who held a position of authority in the queen's court—that of treasurer, much like a Minister of Finance or Secretary of the Treasury. As a physical eunuch, he would have been denied access to the temple (Deut. 23:1) and the opportunity to become a full proselyte to Judaism.

The eunuch was reading Isaiah (Acts 8:28). He knew the importance of seeking God through the Scripture. And the verses he was reading were found in Isaiah 53:7,8. The eunuch's question to Philip was "of whom does the prophet say this, of himself or of some other man?" (v. 34). His confusion was understandable. Even the Jewish religious experts were divided on the meaning of this passage. Some believed the slaughtered sheep represented Israel, others thought Isaiah was referring to himself, and others thought the Messiah was Isaiah's subject.

Philip preached Jesus to the eunuch, who immediately responded with the wish to be baptized. After the baptism, it says that "the Spirit of the Lord caught Philip away" (v. 39). Elijah (1 Kin. 18:12; 2 Kin. 2:16) and Ezekiel (Ezek. 3:12,14; 8:3) were also snatched away in a miraculous fashion. This was a powerful confirmation to the caravan that Philip was God's representative.

JUNE 29

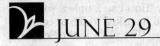

1 Chronicles 21:1–22:19

21 Now Satan stood up against Israel, and
moved David to number Israel. 2So David said to Joab and to the leaders of the people, "Go, number Israel from Beersheba to
Dan, and bring the number of them to me that
I may know *it.*"

21:1 Satan...moved. Second Samuel 24:1 reports that it was God who moved David. This apparent discrepancy is resolved by understanding that God sovereignly and permissively uses Satan to achieve His purposes. God uses Satan to judge sinners (Mark 4:15; 2 Cor. 4:4), to refine saints (Job 1:8–2:10; Luke 22:31,32), to discipline those in the church (1 Cor. 5:1–5; 1 Tim. 1:20), and to further purify obedient believers (2 Cor. 12:7–10). Neither God nor Satan forced David to sin (James 1:13–15), but God allowed Satan to tempt David and he chose to sin. The sin surfaced his proud heart and God dealt with him for it. **number Israel.** David's census brought tragedy because, unlike the census in Moses' time (Num. 1; 2) which God had commanded, this census by David was to gratify his pride in the great strength of his army and consequent military power. He was also putting more trust in his forces than in his God. He was taking credit for his victories by the building of his great army. This angered God, who moved Satan to bring the sin to a head.

3And Joab answered, "May the LORD make
His people a hundred times more than they
are. But, my lord the king, *are* they not all my
lord's servants? Why then does my lord
require this thing? Why should he be a cause
of guilt in Israel?"
4Nevertheless the king's word prevailed
against Joab. Therefore Joab departed and
went throughout all Israel and came to Jerusalem. 5Then Joab gave the sum of the number
of the people to David. All Israel *had* one million one hundred thousand men who drew the
sword, and Judah *had* four hundred and seventy thousand men who drew the sword. 6But
he did not count Levi and Benjamin among
them, for the king's word was abominable to
Joab.
7And God was displeased with this thing;
therefore He struck Israel. 8So David said to
God, "I have sinned greatly, because I have
done this thing; but now, I pray, take away the
iniquity of Your servant, for I have done very
foolishly."
9Then the LORD spoke to Gad, David's seer,
saying, 10"Go and tell David, saying, 'Thus says
the LORD: "I offer you three *things;* choose one
of them for yourself, that I may do *it* to
you." ' "
11So Gad came to David and said to him,
"Thus says the LORD: 'Choose for yourself, 12ei-
ther three years of famine, or three months to
be defeated by your foes with the sword of
your enemies overtaking *you,* or else for three
days the sword of the LORD—the plague in the
land, with the angel of the LORD destroying
throughout all the territory of Israel.' Now
consider what answer I should take back to
Him who sent me."
13And David said to Gad, "I am in great distress. Please let me fall into the hand of the
LORD, for His mercies *are* very great; but do
not let me fall into the hand of man."
14So the LORD sent a plague upon Israel, and
seventy thousand men of Israel fell. 15And God
sent an angel to Jerusalem to destroy it. As he
was destroying, the LORD looked and relented
of the disaster, and said to the angel who was
destroying, "It is enough; now restrain your
hand." And the angel of the LORD stood by the
threshing floor of Ornan the Jebusite.
16Then David lifted his eyes and saw the
angel of the LORD standing between earth and
heaven, having in his hand a drawn sword
stretched out over Jerusalem. So David and
the elders, clothed in sackcloth, fell on their
faces. 17And David said to God, "Was it not I
who commanded the people to be numbered?
I am the one who has sinned and done evil
indeed; but these sheep, what have they done?
Let Your hand, I pray, O LORD my God, be
against me and my father's house, but not
against Your people that they should be
plagued."
18Therefore, the angel of the LORD commanded Gad to say to David that David should
go and erect an altar to the LORD on the
threshing floor of Ornan the Jebusite. 19So David went up at the word of Gad, which he had
spoken in the name of the LORD. 20Now Ornan
turned and saw the angel; and his four sons
who were with him hid themselves, but Ornan
continued threshing wheat. 21So David came
to Ornan, and Ornan looked and saw David.
And he went out from the threshing floor, and
bowed before David with *his* face to the

ground. 22Then David said to Ornan, "Grant
me the place of *this* threshing floor, that I may
build an altar on it to the LORD. You shall grant
it to me at the full price, that the plague may
be withdrawn from the people."
23But Ornan said to David, "Take *it* to yourself, and let my lord the king do *what is* good
in his eyes. Look, I *also* give *you* the oxen for
burnt offerings, the threshing implements for
wood, and the wheat for the grain offering; I
give *it* all."
24Then King David said to Ornan, "No, but I
will surely buy *it* for the full price, for I will not
take what is yours for the LORD, nor offer
burnt offerings with *that which* costs *me* nothing." 25So David gave Ornan six hundred
shekels of gold by weight for the place. 26And
David built there an altar to the LORD, and
offered burnt offerings and peace offerings,
and called on the LORD; and He answered him
from heaven by fire on the altar of burnt offering.
27So the LORD commanded the angel, and he
returned his sword to its sheath.
28At that time, when David saw that the LORD
had answered him on the threshing floor of
Ornan the Jebusite, he sacrificed there. 29For
the tabernacle of the LORD and the altar of the
burnt offering, which Moses had made in the
wilderness, *were* at that time at the high place
in Gibeon. 30But David could not go before it to
inquire of God, for he was afraid of the sword
of the angel of the LORD.
22 Then David said, "This *is* the house of
the LORD God, and this *is* the altar of
burnt offering for Israel." 2So David commanded to gather the aliens who *were* in the
land of Israel; and he appointed masons to cut
hewn stones to build the house of God. 3And
David prepared iron in abundance for the nails
of the doors of the gates and for the joints, and
bronze in abundance beyond measure, 4and
cedar trees in abundance; for the Sidonians
and those from Tyre brought much cedar
wood to David.
5Now David said, "Solomon my son *is* young
and inexperienced, and the house to be built
for the LORD *must be* exceedingly magnificent,
famous and glorious throughout all countries.
I will now make preparation for it." So David
made abundant preparations before his death.
6Then he called for his son Solomon, and
charged him to build a house for the LORD
God of Israel. 7And David said to Solomon:
"My son, as for me, it was in my mind to build
a house to the name of the LORD my God; 8but
the word of the LORD came to me, saying, 'You
have shed much blood and have made great
wars; you shall not build a house for My name,
because you have shed much blood on the
earth in My sight. 9Behold, a son shall be born
to you, who shall be a man of rest; and I will
give him rest from all his enemies all around.
His name shall be Solomon, for I will give
peace and quietness to Israel in his days. 10He
shall build a house for My name, and he shall
be My son, and I *will be* his Father; and I will
establish the throne of his kingdom over Israel forever.' 11Now, my son, may the LORD be
with you; and may you prosper, and build the
house of the LORD your God, as He has said to
you. 12Only may the LORD give you wisdom
and understanding, and give you charge concerning Israel, that you may keep the law of
the LORD your God. 13Then you will prosper, if
you take care to fulfill the statutes and judgments with which the LORD charged Moses
concerning Israel. Be strong and of good
courage; do not fear nor be dismayed. 14Indeed
I have taken much trouble to prepare for the
house of the LORD one hundred thousand talents of gold and one million talents of silver,
and bronze and iron beyond measure, for it is
so abundant. I have prepared timber and stone
also, and you may add to them. 15Moreover
there are workmen with you in abundance:
woodsmen and stonecutters, and all types of
skillful men for every kind of work. 16Of gold
and silver and bronze and iron *there is* no limit.
Arise and begin working, and the LORD be
with you."
17David also commanded all the leaders of
Israel to help Solomon his son, *saying,* 18"*Is* not
the LORD your God with you? And has He *not*
given you rest on every side? For He has
given the inhabitants of the land into my hand,
and the land is subdued before the LORD and
before His people. 19Now set your heart and

22:5 young. Solomon was born early in David's reign (ca. 1000–990 B.C.) and was at this time 20 to 30 years of age. The magnificent and complex challenge of building such a monumental edifice with all its elements required an experienced leader for preparation. **magnificent.** David understood that the temple needed to reflect on earth something of God's heavenly majesty, so he devoted himself to the collection of the plans and materials, tapping the vast amount of spoils from people he had conquered and cities he had sacked (vv. 14–16).

22:11–13 David's spiritual charge to Solomon resembles the Lord's exhortation to Joshua (Josh. 1:6–9). Solomon asked God for and received the very wisdom and understanding his father, David, desired for him (2 Chr. 1:7–12; 1 Kin. 3:3–14). He learned the value of such spiritual counsel and passed it on in Ecclesiastes 12:1,13.

22:14 one hundred thousand...gold. Assuming a talent weighed about 75 pounds, this would be approximately 3,750 tons, a staggering amount of gold. **one million.** This would be approximately 37,500 tons of silver.

20:1 Wine...strong drink. This begins a new theme of temperance (23:20,21,29–35; 31:4,5). Wine was grape juice mixed with water to dilute it, but strong drink was unmixed. While the use of these beverages is not specifically condemned (Deut. 14:26), being intoxicated always is (Is. 28:7). Rulers were not to drink, so their judgment would not be clouded nor their behavior less than exemplary (31:4,5). **mocker...brawler.** "Mocker" is the same word as "scoffer" in 19:25,29; a brawler is violent, loud, and uncontrolled. Both words describe the personality of the drunkard.

your soul to seek the LORD your God. Therefore arise and build the sanctuary of the LORD God, to bring the ark of the covenant of the LORD and the holy articles of God into the house that is to be built for the name of the LORD."

Psalm 78:34–39

34 When He slew them, then they
sought Him;
And they returned and sought
earnestly for God.
35 Then they remembered that God *was*
their rock,
And the Most High God their
Redeemer.
36 Nevertheless they flattered Him with
their mouth,
And they lied to Him with their tongue;
37 For their heart was not steadfast
with Him,
Nor were they faithful in His covenant.
38 But He, *being* full of compassion, forgave
their iniquity,
And did not destroy *them.*
Yes, many a time He turned His
anger away,
And did not stir up all His wrath;
39 For He remembered that they *were*
but flesh,
A breath that passes away and does not
come again.

Proverbs 20:1–2

20 Wine *is* a mocker,
Strong drink *is* a brawler,
And whoever is led astray by it is not
wise.
2 The wrath of a king *is* like the roaring
of a lion;
Whoever provokes him to anger sins
against his own life.

Acts 9:1–21

9 Then Saul, still breathing threats and murder against the disciples of the Lord, went
to the high priest 2and asked letters from him to the synagogues of Damascus, so that if he found any who were of the Way, whether men or women, he might bring them bound to Jerusalem.
3As he journeyed he came near Damascus, and suddenly a light shone around him from
heaven. 4Then he fell to the ground, and heard a voice saying to him, "Saul, Saul, why are you persecuting Me?"
5And he said, "Who are You, Lord?"
Then the Lord said, "I am Jesus, whom you are persecuting. It *is* hard for you to kick against the goads."
6So he, trembling and astonished, said, "Lord, what do You want me to do?"
Then the Lord *said* to him, "Arise and go into the city, and you will be told what you must do."
7And the men who journeyed with him stood speechless, hearing a voice but seeing
no one. 8Then Saul arose from the ground, and when his eyes were opened he saw no one. But they led him by the hand and brought *him*
into Damascus. 9And he was three days without sight, and neither ate nor drank.
10Now there was a certain disciple at Damascus named Ananias; and to him the Lord said in a vision, "Ananias."
And he said, "Here I am, Lord."
11So the Lord *said* to him, "Arise and go to the street called Straight, and inquire at the house of Judas for *one* called Saul of Tarsus,
for behold, he is praying. 12And in a vision he

has seen a man named Ananias coming in and
putting *his* hand on him, so that he might
receive his sight."
[13]Then Ananias answered, "Lord, I have
heard from many about this man, how much
harm he has done to Your saints in Jerusalem.
[14]And here he has authority from the chief
priests to bind all who call on Your name."
[15]But the Lord said to him, "Go, for he is a
chosen vessel of Mine to bear My name
before Gentiles, kings, and the children of Israel. [16]For I will show him how many things he
must suffer for My name's sake."
[17]And Ananias went his way and entered the
house; and laying his hands on him he said,
"Brother Saul, the Lord Jesus, who appeared
to you on the road as you came, has sent me
that you may receive your sight and be filled
with the Holy Spirit." [18]Immediately there fell
from his eyes *something* like scales, and he
received his sight at once; and he arose and
was baptized.
[19]So when he had received food, he was
strengthened. Then Saul spent some days
with the disciples at Damascus.
[20]Immediately he preached the Christ in the
synagogues, that He is the Son of God.
[21]Then all who heard were amazed, and said,
"Is this not he who destroyed those who called
on this name in Jerusalem, and has come here
for that purpose, so that he might bring them
bound to the chief priests?"

DAY 29: How did the apostle Paul come to faith in Jesus Christ?

The apostle Paul was originally named Saul, after the first king of Israel. He was born a Jew, studied in Jerusalem under Gamaliel (Acts 22:3), and became a Pharisee (23:6). He was also a Roman citizen, a right he inherited from his father (22:8). Acts 9:1–19 records the external facts of his conversion (see also 22:1–22; 26:9–20). Philippians 3:1–14 records the internal spiritual conversion.

At the time of his conversion Saul was "still breathing threats and murder" against Christians (Acts 9:1; 1 Tim. 1:12,13; 1 Cor. 15:9). He was in Damascus, the capital of Syria, which apparently had a large population of Jews, including Hellenist believers who fled Jerusalem to avoid persecution (Acts 9:2). He had letters authorizing him to seek out those "who were of the Way." This description of Christianity, derived from Jesus' description of Himself (John 14:6), appears several times in Acts (19:9,23; 22:4; 24:14,22).

The "light…from heaven" (v. 3) that struck him was the appearance of Jesus Christ in glory (22:6; 26:13) and was visible only to Saul (26:9). The voice that asked him, "Why are you persecuting Me?" was that of Jesus (v. 5). An inseparable union exists between Christ and His followers. Saul's persecution represented a direct attack on Christ. Saul arose from that encounter, blinded by the light, and went in obedience to await the next step (v. 6).

Meanwhile, Ananias was being given divine instructions concerning Paul and Paul's ministry. He is told that Saul is a "chosen vessel," literally "a vessel of election" (v. 15). There was perfect continuity between Paul's salvation and his service; God chose him to convey His grace to all men (Gal. 1:1; 1 Tim. 2:7; 2 Tim. 1:11). Paul used this same word 4 times (Rom. 9:21,23; 2 Cor. 4:7; 2 Tim. 2:21). "Before Gentiles, kings, and the children of Israel." Paul began his ministry preaching to Jews (13:14; 14:1; 17:1,10; 18:4; 19:8), but his primary calling was to Gentiles (Rom. 11:13; 15:16). God also called him to minister to kings such as Agrippa (25:23–26:32) and likely Caesar (25:10–12; 2 Tim. 4:16,17).

Ananias went to Paul and "laying his hands on him," he prayed for Paul's healing and that he would "be filled with the Holy Spirit" (v. 17). He was then filled with the Spirit and empowered for service (2:4,14; 4:8,31; 6:5,8).

JUNE 30

1 Chronicles 23:1–25:31

23 So when David was old and full of
days, he made his son Solomon king
over Israel.
[2]And he gathered together all the leaders of
Israel, with the priests and the Levites. [3]Now the
Levites were numbered from the age of thirty
years and above; and the number of individual
males was thirty-eight thousand. [4]Of these,
twenty-four thousand *were* to look after the
work of the house of the LORD, six thousand
were officers and judges, [5]four thousand *were*
gatekeepers, and four thousand praised the
LORD with *musical* instruments, "which I
made," *said David,* "for giving praise."
[6]Also David separated them into divisions
among the sons of Levi: Gershon, Kohath, and
Merari.
[7]Of the Gershonites: Laadan and Shimei.
[8]The sons of Laadan: the first Jehiel, then
Zetham and Joel—three *in all.* [9]The sons of
Shimei: Shelomith, Haziel, and Haran—three

in all. These were the heads of the fathers'
houses of Laadan. [10]And the sons of Shimei:
Jahath, Zina, Jeush, and Beriah. These *were*
the four sons of Shimei. [11]Jahath was the first
and Zizah the second. But Jeush and Beriah
did not have many sons; therefore they were
assigned as one father's house.

[12]The sons of Kohath: Amram, Izhar,
Hebron, and Uzziel—four *in all.* [13]The sons of
Amram: Aaron and Moses; and Aaron was set
apart, he and his sons forever, that he should
sanctify the most holy things, to burn incense
before the LORD, to minister to Him, and to give
the blessing in His name forever. [14]Now the
sons of Moses the man of God were reckoned
to the tribe of Levi. [15]The sons of Moses *were*
Gershon and Eliezer. [16]Of the sons of Gershon,
Shebuel *was* the first. [17]Of the descendants of
Eliezer, Rehabiah was the first. And Eliezer
had no other sons, but the sons of Rehabiah
were very many. [18]Of the sons of Izhar, Shelomith *was* the first. [19]Of the sons of Hebron,
Jeriah *was* the first, Amariah the second,
Jahaziel the third, and Jekameam the fourth.
[20]Of the sons of Uzziel, Michah *was* the first
and Jesshiah the second.

[21]The sons of Merari *were* Mahli and Mushi.
The sons of Mahli *were* Eleazar and Kish.
[22]And Eleazar died, and had no sons, but only
daughters; and their brethren, the sons of
Kish, took them *as wives.* [23]The sons of Mushi
were Mahli, Eder, and Jeremoth—three *in all.*

[24]These *were* the sons of Levi by their fathers'
houses—the heads of the fathers' *houses* as
they were counted individually by the number
of their names, who did the work for the service of the house of the LORD, from the age of
twenty years and above.

[25]For David said, "The LORD God of Israel has
given rest to His people, that they may dwell in
Jerusalem forever"; [26]and also to the Levites,
"They shall no longer carry the tabernacle, or
any of the articles for its service." [27]For by the
last words of David the Levites *were* numbered
from twenty years old and above; [28]because
their duty *was* to help the sons of Aaron in the
service of the house of the LORD, in the courts
and in the chambers, in the purifying of all
holy things and the work of the service of the
house of God, [29]both with the showbread and
the fine flour for the grain offering, with the
unleavened cakes and *what is baked in* the
pan, with what is mixed and with all kinds of
measures and sizes; [30]to stand every morning
to thank and praise the LORD, and likewise at
evening; [31]and at every presentation of a burnt
offering to the LORD on the Sabbaths and on the
New Moons and on the set feasts, by number
according to the ordinance governing them,
regularly before the LORD; [32]and that they
should attend to the needs of the tabernacle of
meeting, the needs of the holy *place,* and the
needs of the sons of Aaron their brethren in
the work of the house of the LORD.

24 Now *these are* the divisions of the sons
of Aaron. The sons of Aaron *were*
Nadab, Abihu, Eleazar, and Ithamar. [2]And
Nadab and Abihu died before their father, and
had no children; therefore Eleazar and Ithamar ministered as priests. [3]Then David with
Zadok of the sons of Eleazar, and Ahimelech
of the sons of Ithamar, divided them according
to the schedule of their service.

[4]There were more leaders found of the sons
of Eleazar than of the sons of Ithamar, and *thus*
they were divided. Among the sons of Eleazar
were sixteen heads of *their* fathers' houses, and
eight heads of their fathers' houses among the
sons of Ithamar. [5]Thus they were divided by lot,
one group as another, for there were officials of
the sanctuary and officials *of the house* of God,
from the sons of Eleazar and from the sons of
Ithamar. [6]And the scribe, Shemaiah the son of
Nethanel, *one of* the Levites, wrote them down
before the king, the leaders, Zadok the priest,
Ahimelech the son of Abiathar, and the heads
of the fathers' *houses* of the priests and Levites,
one father's house taken for Eleazar and *one* for
Ithamar.

[7]Now the first lot fell to Jehoiarib, the second
to Jedaiah, [8]the third to Harim, the fourth to Seo-
rim, [9]the fifth to Malchijah, the sixth to
Mijamin, [10]the seventh to Hakkoz, the eighth to
Abijah, [11]the ninth to Jeshua, the tenth to
Shecaniah, [12]the eleventh to Eliashib, the
twelfth to Jakim, [13]the thirteenth to Huppah, the
fourteenth to Jeshebeab, [14]the fifteenth to
Bilgah, the sixteenth to Immer, [15]the seventeenth to Hezir, the eighteenth to Happizzez,
[16]the nineteenth to Pethahiah, the twentieth to
Jehezekel, [17]the twenty-first to Jachin, the twen-
ty-second to Gamul, [18]the twenty-third to
Delaiah, the twenty-fourth to Maaziah.

[19]This *was* the schedule of their service for
coming into the house of the LORD according
to their ordinance by the hand of Aaron their
father, as the LORD God of Israel had commanded him.

[20]And the rest of the sons of Levi: of the sons
of Amram, Shubael; of the sons of Shubael,
Jehdeiah. [21]Concerning Rehabiah, of the sons
of Rehabiah, the first *was* Isshiah. [22]Of the
Izharites, Shelomoth; of the sons of Shelomoth, Jahath. [23]Of the sons *of Hebron,* Jeriah
was the first, Amariah the second, Jahaziel the
third, *and* Jekameam the fourth. [24]*Of* the sons

of Uzziel, Michah; of the sons of Michah,
Shamir. 25The brother of Michah, Isshiah; of the
sons of Isshiah, Zechariah. 26The sons of Merari
were Mahli and Mushi; the son of Jaaziah,
Beno. 27The sons of Merari by Jaaziah *were*
Beno, Shoham, Zaccur, and Ibri. 28Of Mahli:
Eleazar, who had no sons. 29Of Kish: the son of
Kish, Jerahmeel.

30Also the sons of Mushi *were* Mahli, Eder,
and Jerimoth. These *were* the sons of the
Levites according to their fathers' houses.

31These also cast lots just as their brothers
the sons of Aaron did, in the presence of King
David, Zadok, Ahimelech, and the heads of the
fathers' *houses* of the priests and Levites. The
chief fathers *did* just as their younger brethren.

25 Moreover David and the captains of the
army separated for the service *some* of
the sons of Asaph, of Heman, and of Jeduthun,
who *should* prophesy with harps, stringed
instruments, and cymbals. And the number of
the skilled men performing their service was:
2Of the sons of Asaph: Zaccur, Joseph,
Nethaniah, and Asharelah; the sons of Asaph
were under the direction of Asaph, who prophesied according to the order of the king. 3Of
Jeduthun, the sons of Jeduthun: Gedaliah,
Zeri, Jeshaiah, *Shimei,* Hashabiah, and
Mattithiah, six, under the direction of their
father Jeduthun, who prophesied with a harp
to give thanks and to praise the LORD. 4Of
Heman, the sons of Heman: Bukkiah,
Mattaniah, Uzziel, Shebuel, Jerimoth, Hananiah, Hanani, Eliathah, Giddalti, Romamti-
Ezer, Joshbekashah, Mallothi, Hothir, *and*
Mahazioth. 5All these *were* the sons of Heman
the king's seer in the words of God, to exalt
his horn. For God gave Heman fourteen sons
and three daughters.

25:1 the captains of the army. David relied on his mighty men for help (11:10). **Asaph... Heman...Jeduthun.** David's 3 chief ministers of music (6:31–48). **prophesy.** This is not necessarily to be taken in a revelatory sense, but rather in the sense of proclamation and exhortation through the lyrics of their music (25:2,3). Prophesying is not necessarily predicting the future or even speaking direct revelation. It is proclaiming truth (v. 5) to people (1 Cor. 14:3), and music is a vehicle for such proclamation in praise (v. 3). David and the leaders selected those most capable (v. 7) of leading the people to worship God through their music.

6All these *were* under the direction of their
father for the music *in* the house of the LORD,
with cymbals, stringed instruments, and
harps, for the service of the house of God.
Asaph, Jeduthun, and Heman *were* under the
authority of the king. 7So the number of them,
with their brethren who were instructed in the
songs of the LORD, all who were skillful, *was*
two hundred and eighty-eight.

8And they cast lots for their duty, the small
as well as the great, the teacher with the student.

9Now the first lot for Asaph came out for Joseph; the second for Gedaliah, him with his
brethren and sons, twelve; 10the third for
Zaccur, his sons and his brethren, twelve; 11the
fourth for Jizri, his sons and his brethren,
twelve; 12the fifth for Nethaniah, his sons and
his brethren, twelve; 13the sixth for Bukkiah,
his sons and his brethren, twelve; 14the seventh for Jesharelah, his sons and his brethren,
twelve; 15the eighth for Jeshaiah, his sons and
his brethren, twelve; 16the ninth for Mattaniah,
his sons and his brethren, twelve; 17the tenth
for Shimei, his sons and his brethren, twelve;
18the eleventh for Azarel, his sons and his
brethren, twelve; 19the twelfth for Hashabiah,
his sons and his brethren, twelve; 20the thirteenth for Shubael, his sons and his brethren,
twelve; 21the fourteenth for Mattithiah, his
sons and his brethren, twelve; 22the fifteenth
for Jeremoth, his sons and his brethren,
twelve; 23the sixteenth for Hananiah, his sons
and his brethren, twelve; 24the seventeenth for
Joshbekashah, his sons and his brethren,
twelve; 25the eighteenth for Hanani, his sons
and his brethren, twelve; 26the nineteenth for
Mallothi, his sons and his brethren, twelve;
27the twentieth for Eliathah, his sons and his
brethren, twelve; 28the twenty-first for Hothir,
his sons and his brethren, twelve; 29the twenty-
second for Giddalti, his sons and his brethren,
twelve; 30the twenty-third for Mahazioth, his
sons and his brethren, twelve; 31the twenty-
fourth for Romamti-Ezer, his sons and his
brethren, twelve.

Psalm 78:40–55

40 How often they provoked Him in
 the wilderness,
And grieved Him in the desert!
41 Yes, again and again they tempted
 God,
And limited the Holy One of Israel.
42 They did not remember His power:
The day when He redeemed them
 from the enemy,
43 When He worked His signs in Egypt,

78:41 limited the Holy One. The Israelites did this by doubting God's power.

78:42 did not remember His power. The generations of Israelites which left Egypt and eventually died in the wilderness were characterized by ignoring God's previous acts of power and faithfulness. The following verses (vv. 42–55) rehearse the plagues and miracles of the Exodus from Egypt, which marvelously demonstrated God's omnipotence and covenant love.

And His wonders in the field of Zoan;
44 Turned their rivers into blood,
And their streams, that they could
not drink.
45 He sent swarms of flies among them,
which devoured them,
And frogs, which destroyed them.
46 He also gave their crops to the
caterpillar,
And their labor to the locust.
47 He destroyed their vines with hail,
And their sycamore trees with frost.
48 He also gave up their cattle to the hail,
And their flocks to fiery lightning.
49 He cast on them the fierceness of
His anger,
Wrath, indignation, and trouble,
By sending angels of destruction
among them.
50 He made a path for His anger;
He did not spare their soul from death,
But gave their life over to the plague,
51 And destroyed all the firstborn in
Egypt,
The first of *their* strength in the tents
of Ham.
52 But He made His own people go forth
like sheep,
And guided them in the wilderness like
a flock;
53 And He led them on safely, so that they
did not fear;
But the sea overwhelmed their
enemies.
54 And He brought them to His holy
border,
This mountain *which* His right hand
had acquired.
55 He also drove out the nations before
them,
Allotted them an inheritance by survey,
And made the tribes of Israel dwell in
their tents.

Proverbs 20:3

3 *It is* honorable for a man to stop
striving,
Since any fool can start a quarrel.

Acts 9:22–43

22But Saul increased all the more in strength,
and confounded the Jews who dwelt in Damascus, proving that this *Jesus* is the Christ.
23Now after many days were past, the Jews
plotted to kill him. 24But their plot became
known to Saul. And they watched the gates
day and night, to kill him. 25Then the disciples
took him by night and let *him* down through
the wall in a large basket.
26And when Saul had come to Jerusalem, he
tried to join the disciples; but they were all
afraid of him, and did not believe that he was
a disciple. 27But Barnabas took him and
brought *him* to the apostles. And he declared
to them how he had seen the Lord on the
road, and that He had spoken to him, and how
he had preached boldly at Damascus in the
name of Jesus. 28So he was with them at Jerusalem, coming in and going out. 29And he
spoke boldly in the name of the Lord Jesus
and disputed against the Hellenists, but they
attempted to kill him. 30When the brethren
found out, they brought him down to
Caesarea and sent him out to Tarsus.
31Then the churches throughout all Judea,
Galilee, and Samaria had peace and were edified. And walking in the fear of the Lord and in
the comfort of the Holy Spirit, they were multiplied.
32Now it came to pass, as Peter went
through all *parts of the country,* that he also
came down to the saints who dwelt in Lydda.
33There he found a certain man named Aeneas,
who had been bedridden eight years and was
paralyzed. 34And Peter said to him, "Aeneas, Jesus the Christ heals you. Arise and make your
bed." Then he arose immediately. 35So all who
dwelt at Lydda and Sharon saw him and
turned to the Lord.
36At Joppa there was a certain disciple
named Tabitha, which is translated Dorcas.
This woman was full of good works and
charitable deeds which she did. 37But it happened in those days that she became sick and
died. When they had washed her, they laid *her*
in an upper room. 38And since Lydda was near
Joppa, and the disciples had heard that Peter
was there, they sent two men to him, imploring *him* not to delay in coming to them. 39Then
Peter arose and went with them. When he had
come, they brought *him* to the upper room.

9:30 Caesarea. An important port city on the Mediterranean located 30 miles north of Joppa. As the capital of the Roman province of Judea and the home of the Roman procurator, it served as the headquarters of a large Roman garrison. **sent him out to Tarsus.** Paul disappeared from prominent ministry for several years, although he possibly founded some churches around Syria and Cilicia (15:23; Gal. 1:21).

And all the widows stood by him weeping, showing the tunics and garments which Dorcas had made while she was with them.
40 But Peter put them all out, and knelt down and prayed. And turning to the body he said, "Tabitha, arise." And she opened her eyes, and when she saw Peter she sat up.
41 Then he gave her *his* hand and lifted her up; and when he had called the saints and widows, he presented her alive.
42 And it became known throughout all Joppa, and many believed on the Lord.
43 So it was that he stayed many days in Joppa with Simon, a tanner.

DAY 30: How were the duties of the temple divided up?

Administrative Duties	Supervisors	1 Chronicles 23:4,5
	Bailiffs	1 Chronicles 23:4,5
	Judges	1 Chronicles 23:4,5
	Public administrators	1 Chronicles 26:29,30
Ministerial Duties	Priests	1 Chronicles 24:1,2
	Prophets	1 Chronicles 25:1
	Assistants for sacrifices	1 Chronicles 23:29–31
	Assistants for purification ceremonies	1 Chronicles 23:27,28
Service Duties	Bakers of the Bread of the Presence	1 Chronicles 23:29
	Those who checked the weights and measures	1 Chronicles 23:29
	Custodians	1 Chronicles 23:28
Financial Duties	Those who cared for the treasury	1 Chronicles 26:20
	Those who cared for dedicated items	1 Chronicles 26:26–28
Artistic Duties	Musicians	1 Chronicles 25:6
	Singers	1 Chronicles 25:7
Protective Duties	Temple guards	1 Chronicles 23:5
	Guards for the gates and storehouses	1 Chronicles 26:12–18
Individual Assignments	Recording secretary	1 Chronicles 24:6
	Chaplain to the king	1 Chronicles 25:4
	Private prophet to the king	1 Chronicles 25:2
	Captain of the guard	1 Chronicles 26:1
	Chief officer of the treasury	1 Chronicles 26:23,24

JULY 1

1 Chronicles 26:1–27:34

26 Concerning the divisions of the gatekeepers: of the Korahites, Meshelemiah
the son of Kore, of the sons of Asaph. 2And the
sons of Meshelemiah *were* Zechariah the firstborn, Jediael the second, Zebadiah the third,
Jathniel the fourth, 3Elam the fifth, Jehohanan
the sixth, Eliehoenai the seventh.
4Moreover the sons of Obed-Edom *were*
Shemaiah the firstborn, Jehozabad the second,
Joah the third, Sacar the fourth, Nethanel the
fifth, 5Ammiel the sixth, Issachar the seventh,
Peulthai the eighth; for God blessed him.
6Also to Shemaiah his son were sons born
who governed their fathers' houses, because
they *were* men of great ability. 7The sons of
Shemaiah *were* Othni, Rephael, Obed, and Elzabad, whose brothers Elihu and Semachiah *were*
able men.
8All these *were* of the sons of Obed-Edom,
they and their sons and their brethren, able
men with strength for the work: sixty-two of
Obed-Edom.
9And Meshelemiah had sons and brethren,
eighteen able men.
10Also Hosah, of the children of Merari, had
sons: Shimri the first (for *though* he was not
the firstborn, his father made him the first),
11Hilkiah the second, Tebaliah the third,
Zechariah the fourth; all the sons and brethren
of Hosah *were* thirteen.
12Among these *were* the divisions of the
gatekeepers, among the chief men, *having*
duties just like their brethren, to serve in the
house of the LORD. 13And they cast lots for
each gate, the small as well as the great,
according to their father's house. 14The lot for
the East *Gate* fell to Shelemiah. Then they cast
lots *for* his son Zechariah, a wise counselor,
and his lot came out for the North Gate; 15to
Obed-Edom the South Gate, and to his sons
the storehouse. 16To Shuppim and Hosah *the
lot came out* for the West Gate, with the Shal-
lecheth Gate on the ascending highway—
watchman opposite watchman. 17On the east
were six Levites, on the north four each day,
on the south four each day, and for the storehouse two by two. 18As for the Parbar on the
west, *there were* four on the highway *and* two
at the Parbar. 19These were the divisions of the
gatekeepers among the sons of Korah and
among the sons of Merari.
20Of the Levites, Ahijah *was* over the treasuries
of the house of God and over the treasuries of
the dedicated things. 21The sons of Laadan, the
descendants of the Gershonites of Laadan,
heads of their fathers' *houses,* of Laadan the
Gershonite: Jehieli. 22The sons of Jehieli,
Zetham and Joel his brother, *were* over the
treasuries of the house of the LORD. 23Of the
Amramites, the Izharites, the Hebronites, and
the Uzzielites: 24Shebuel the son of Gershom,
the son of Moses, *was* overseer of the treasuries. 25And his brethren by Eliezer *were*
Rehabiah his son, Jeshaiah his son, Joram his
son, Zichri his son, and Shelomith his son.
26This Shelomith and his brethren *were* over
all the treasuries of the dedicated things
which King David and the heads of fathers'
houses, the captains over thousands and hundreds, and the captains of the army, had dedicated. 27Some of the spoils won in battles they
dedicated to maintain the house of the LORD.
28And all that Samuel the seer, Saul the son of
Kish, Abner the son of Ner, and Joab the son
of Zeruiah had dedicated, every dedicated
thing, was under the hand of Shelomith and
his brethren.
29Of the Izharites, Chenaniah and his sons
performed duties as officials and judges over Israel outside Jerusalem.
30Of the Hebronites, Hashabiah and his
brethren, one thousand seven hundred able
men, had the oversight of Israel on the west

26:1–19 The temple gatekeepers or guards had other duties, such as checking out equipment and utensils; storing, ordering, and maintaining food for the priests and sacrifices; caring for the temple furniture; mixing the incense daily burned; and accounting for gifts brought. Their "duties" (v. 12) are given in 1 Chronicles 9:17–27.

26:20 treasuries. The Levites watched over the store of valuables given to the Lord. This is a general reference to all the precious things committed to their trust, including contributions from David and the people, as well as war spoils given by triumphant soldiers (vv. 26,27).

26:29–32 officials and judges. There were 6,000 magistrates exercising judicial functions throughout the land.

side of the Jordan for all the business of the
LORD, and in the service of the king. [31]Among
the Hebronites, Jerijah *was* head of the
Hebronites according to his genealogy of the
fathers. In the fortieth year of the reign of David they were sought, and there were found
among them capable men at Jazer of Gilead.
[32]And his brethren *were* two thousand seven
hundred able men, heads of fathers' *houses,*
whom King David made officials over the
Reubenites, the Gadites, and the half-tribe of
Manasseh, for every matter pertaining to God
and the affairs of the king.

27 And the children of Israel, according to
their number, the heads of fathers'
houses, the captains of thousands and hundreds and their officers, served the king in
every matter of the *military* divisions. *These
divisions* came in and went out month by
month throughout all the months of the year,
each division *having* twenty-four thousand.

[2]Over the first division for the first month
was Jashobeam the son of Zabdiel, and in his
division *were* twenty-four thousand; [3]*he was* of
the children of Perez, and the chief of all the
captains of the army for the first month. [4]Over
the division of the second month *was* Dodai an
Ahohite, and of his division Mikloth also *was*
the leader; in his division *were* twenty-four
thousand. [5]The third captain of the army for
the third month *was* Benaiah, the son of
Jehoiada the priest, who was chief; in his division *were* twenty-four thousand. [6]This was the
Benaiah *who was* mighty *among* the thirty, and
was over the thirty; in his division *was*
Ammizabad his son. [7]The fourth *captain* for
the fourth month *was* Asahel the brother of
Joab, and Zebadiah his son after him; in his
division *were* twenty-four thousand. [8]The fifth
captain for the fifth month *was* Shamhuth the
Izrahite; in his division were twenty-four thousand. [9]The sixth *captain* for the sixth month
was Ira the son of Ikkesh the Tekoite; in his
division *were* twenty-four thousand. [10]The seventh *captain* for the seventh month *was* Helez
the Pelonite, of the children of Ephraim; in his
division *were* twenty-four thousand. [11]The
eighth *captain* for the eighth month *was*
Sibbechai the Hushathite, of the Zarhites; in his
division *were* twenty-four thousand. [12]The ninth
captain for the ninth month *was* Abiezer the
Anathothite, of the Benjamites; in his division
were twenty-four thousand. [13]The tenth *captain*
for the tenth month *was* Maharai the
Netophathite, of the Zarhites; in his division
were twenty-four thousand. [14]The eleventh *captain* for the eleventh month *was* Benaiah the
Pirathonite, of the children of Ephraim; in his
division *were* twenty-four thousand. [15]The
twelfth *captain* for the twelfth month *was*
Heldai the Netophathite, of Othniel; in his division *were* twenty-four thousand.

[16]Furthermore, over the tribes of Israel: the
officer over the Reubenites *was* Eliezer the
son of Zichri; over the Simeonites, Shephatiah
the son of Maachah; [17]*over* the Levites, Hashabiah the son of Kemuel; over the Aaronites,
Zadok; [18]*over* Judah, Elihu, *one* of David's
brothers; *over* Issachar, Omri the son of Michael; [19]*over* Zebulun, Ishmaiah the son of
Obadiah; *over* Naphtali, Jerimoth the son of
Azriel; [20]*over* the children of Ephraim, Hoshea
the son of Azaziah; *over* the half-tribe of
Manasseh, Joel the son of Pedaiah; [21]*over* the
half-*tribe* of Manasseh in Gilead, Iddo the son
of Zechariah; *over* Benjamin, Jaasiel the son of
Abner; [22]*over* Dan, Azarel the son of Jeroham.
These *were* the leaders of the tribes of Israel.

[23]But David did not take the number of
those twenty years old and under, because the
LORD had said He would multiply Israel like
the stars of the heavens. [24]Joab the son of
Zeruiah began a census, but he did not finish,
for wrath came upon Israel because of this
census; nor was the number recorded in the
account of the chronicles of King David.

[25]And Azmaveth the son of Adiel *was* over
the king's treasuries; and Jehonathan the son
of Uzziah was over the storehouses in the
field, in the cities, in the villages, and in the
fortresses. [26]Ezri the son of Chelub was over
those who did the work of the field for tilling
the ground. [27]And Shimei the Ramathite *was*
over the vineyards, and Zabdi the Shiphmite
was over the produce of the vineyards for the
supply of wine. [28]Baal-Hanan the Gederite was
over the olive trees and the sycamore trees
that *were* in the lowlands, and Joash *was* over
the store of oil. [29]And Shitrai the Sharonite *was*
over the herds that fed in Sharon, and Shaphat
the son of Adlai was over the herds *that were*
in the valleys. [30]Obil the Ishmaelite *was* over
the camels, Jehdeiah the Meronothite *was*
over the donkeys, [31]and Jaziz the Hagrite *was*

27:1–15 This section enumerates the standing army of Israel (288,000 men), which had responsibility to guard the nation and temple. They were divided into 12 divisions, each of which served for one month during the year. When full war occurred, a larger force could be called into action.

over the flocks. All these *were* the officials over King David's property.

32Also Jehonathan, David's uncle, *was* a counselor, a wise man, and a scribe; and Jehiel the son of Hachmoni *was* with the king's sons.
33Ahithophel *was* the king's counselor, and Hushai the Archite *was* the king's companion.
34After Ahithophel *was* Jehoiada the son of Benaiah, then Abiathar. And the general of the king's army *was* Joab.

Psalm 78:56–66

56 Yet they tested and provoked the Most
High God,
And did not keep His testimonies,
57 But turned back and acted unfaithfully
like their fathers;
They were turned aside like a deceitful
bow.
58 For they provoked Him to anger with
their high places,
And moved Him to jealousy with their
carved images.
59 When God heard *this,* He was furious,
And greatly abhorred Israel,
60 So that He forsook the tabernacle of
Shiloh,
The tent He had placed among men,

78:60 tabernacle of Shiloh. Shiloh was an early location of Yahweh worship in the Promised Land. The capture and removal of the ark from Shiloh by the Philistines symbolized God's judgment.

61 And delivered His strength into captivity,
And His glory into the enemy's hand.
62 He also gave His people over to the
sword,
And was furious with His inheritance.
63 The fire consumed their young men,
And their maidens were not given in
marriage.
64 Their priests fell by the sword,
And their widows made no lamentation.
65 Then the Lord awoke as *from* sleep,
Like a mighty man who shouts
because of wine.
66 And He beat back His enemies;
He put them to a perpetual reproach.

Proverbs 20:4–5

4 The lazy *man* will not plow because of
winter;
He will beg during harvest and *have*
nothing.
5 Counsel in the heart of man *is like*
deep water,
But a man of understanding will draw
it out.

20:5 deep water. The wise man has keen discernment reaching to the deepest intentions of the heart to grasp wise counsel (18:4; Heb. 4:12).

Acts 10:1–23

10 There was a certain man in Caesarea called Cornelius, a centurion of what was called the Italian Regiment, 2a devout *man* and one who feared God with all his household, who gave alms generously to the people, and prayed to God always. 3About the ninth hour of the day he saw clearly in a vision an angel of God coming in and saying to him, "Cornelius!"
4And when he observed him, he was afraid, and said, "What is it, lord?"

So he said to him, "Your prayers and your alms have come up for a memorial before God. 5Now send men to Joppa, and send for Simon whose surname is Peter. 6He is lodging with Simon, a tanner, whose house is by the sea. He will tell you what you must do." 7And when the angel who spoke to him had departed, Cornelius called two of his household servants and a devout soldier from among those who waited on him continually. 8So when he had explained all *these* things to them, he sent them to Joppa.

9The next day, as they went on their journey and drew near the city, Peter went up on the housetop to pray, about the sixth hour. 10Then he became very hungry and wanted to eat; but while they made ready, he fell into a trance
11and saw heaven opened and an object like a great sheet bound at the four corners, descending to him and let down to the earth.
12In it were all kinds of four-footed animals of the earth, wild beasts, creeping things, and birds of the air. 13And a voice came to him, "Rise, Peter; kill and eat."

14But Peter said, "Not so, Lord! For I have never eaten anything common or unclean."

15And a voice *spoke* to him again the second time, "What God has cleansed you must not call common." 16This was done three times. And the object was taken up into heaven again.

17Now while Peter wondered within himself what this vision which he had seen meant,

behold, the men who had been sent from
Cornelius had made inquiry for Simon's
house, and stood before the gate. [18]And they
called and asked whether Simon, whose surname was Peter, was lodging there.
[19]While Peter thought about the vision, the
Spirit said to him, "Behold, three men are
seeking you. [20]Arise therefore, go down and
go with them, doubting nothing; for I have sent
them."
[21]Then Peter went down to the men who had
been sent to him from Cornelius, and said,
"Yes, I am he whom you seek. For what reason have you come?"
[22]And they said, "Cornelius *the* centurion, a
just man, one who fears God and has a good
reputation among all the nation of the Jews,
was divinely instructed by a holy angel to summon you to his house, and to hear words from
you." [23]Then he invited them in and lodged
them.
On the next day Peter went away with them,
and some brethren from Joppa accompanied
him.

DAY 1: Who was Cornelius, and why was he so important?

In Acts 10:1, it states that Cornelius was a centurion—one of 60 officers in a Roman legion, each of whom commanded 100 men. He was of the "Italian Regiment" or "Italian Cohort." Ten cohorts of 600 men each made up a legion.

Cornelius was a "devout *man* and one who feared God" (v. 2). This is a technical term used by Jews to refer to Gentiles who had abandoned their pagan religion in favor of worshiping the Lord God. Such a person, while following the ethics of the Old Testament, had not become a full proselyte to Judaism through circumcision. Cornelius was a Gentile who was about to receive the saving knowledge of God in Christ. Cornelius was told in a vision that his prayers, devotion, faith, and goodness were like a fragrant offering rising up to God, "a memorial" (v. 4). He was even given specific directions on how to reach Peter.

The next day "Peter went up on the housetop to pray" (v. 9). All kinds of worship occurred on the flat roofs of Jewish homes (2 Kin. 23:12; Jer. 19:13; 32:29). In a trance Peter sees a great sheet descending from heaven, and "in it were all kinds of four-footed animals," both clean and unclean animals (v. 12). To keep the Israelites separate from their idolatrous neighbors, God set specific dietary restrictions regarding the consumption of such animals (Lev. 11:25,26). But a voice speaks to him and says, "Rise, Peter; kill and eat" (v. 13). With the coming of the New Covenant and the calling of the church, God ended the dietary restrictions (Mark 7:19). "What God has cleansed you must not call common" (v. 15). More than just abolishing the Old Testament dietary restrictions, God made unity possible in the church of both Jews, symbolized by the clean animals, and Gentiles, symbolized by the unclean animals, through the comprehensive sacrificial death of Christ (Eph. 2:14).

The vision and the confirmation by the Holy Spirit (v. 19) made it crystal clear to Peter that the gospel was for all people. The proof is that when the men from Cornelius arrived, he "invited them in" (v. 23). Self-respecting Jews did not invite any Gentiles into their home, especially soldiers of the hated Roman army.

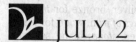

JULY 2

1 Chronicles 28:1–29:30

28 Now David assembled at Jerusalem all
the leaders of Israel: the officers of the
tribes and the captains of the divisions who
served the king, the captains over thousands
and captains over hundreds, and the stewards
over all the substance and possessions of the
king and of his sons, with the officials, the
valiant men, and all the mighty men of valor.
[2]Then King David rose to his feet and said,
"Hear me, my brethren and my people: I *had* it
in my heart to build a house of rest for the ark
of the covenant of the LORD, and for the footstool of our God, and had made preparations to
build it. [3]But God said to me, 'You shall not
build a house for My name, because you *have
been* a man of war and have shed blood.' [4]How-
ever the LORD God of Israel chose me above
all the house of my father to be king over Israel forever, for He has chosen Judah *to be* the
ruler. And of the house of Judah, the house of
my father, and among the sons of my father,
He was pleased with me to make *me* king over
all Israel. [5]And of all my sons (for the LORD has
given me many sons) He has chosen my son
Solomon to sit on the throne of the kingdom of
the LORD over Israel. [6]Now He said to me, 'It is
your son Solomon *who* shall build My house
and My courts; for I have chosen him *to be* My
son, and I will be his Father. [7]Moreover I will
establish his kingdom forever, if he is steadfast to observe My commandments and My
judgments, as it is this day.' [8]Now therefore, in

28:2–8 For the assembly's sake, David testified to the Davidic Covenant originally given by God to him in 2 Samuel 7 (17:7–27; 22:6–16). David makes it clear that Solomon was God's choice (v. 5) as had been frequently intimated (2 Sam. 12:24,25; 1 Kin. 1:13), just as the coming Christ will be God's chosen Son to ultimately fulfill the kingdom promise.

the sight of all Israel, the assembly of the
LORD, and in the hearing of our God, be careful to seek out all the commandments of the
LORD your God, that you may possess this
good land, and leave *it* as an inheritance for
your children after you forever.
9"As for you, my son Solomon, know the
God of your father, and serve Him with a loyal
heart and with a willing mind; for the LORD
searches all hearts and understands all the
intent of the thoughts. If you seek Him, He
will be found by you; but if you forsake Him,
He will cast you off forever. 10Consider now,
for the LORD has chosen you to build a house
for the sanctuary; be strong, and do it."
11Then David gave his son Solomon the
plans for the vestibule, its houses, its treasuries, its upper chambers, its inner chambers,
and the place of the mercy seat; 12and the plans
for all that he had by the Spirit, of the courts
of the house of the LORD, of all the chambers
all around, of the treasuries of the house of
God, and of the treasuries for the dedicated
things; 13also for the division of the priests and
the Levites, for all the work of the service of
the house of the LORD, and for all the articles
of service in the house of the LORD. 14*He gave*
gold by weight for *things* of gold, for all articles used in every kind of service; also *silver*
for all articles of silver by weight, for all articles used in every kind of service; 15the weight
for the lampstands of gold, and their lamps of
gold, by weight for each lampstand and its
lamps; for the lampstands of silver by weight,
for the lampstand and its lamps, according to
the use of each lampstand. 16And by weight *he*
gave gold for the tables of the showbread, for
each table, and silver for the tables of silver;
17also pure gold for the forks, the basins, the
pitchers of pure gold, and the golden bowls—
he gave gold by weight for every bowl; and for
the silver bowls, *silver* by weight for every
bowl; 18and refined gold by weight for the altar
of incense, and for the construction of the
chariot, that is, the gold cherubim that spread
their wings and overshadowed the ark of the
covenant of the LORD. 19"All *this*," *said David*,
"the LORD made me understand in writing, by
His hand upon me, all the works of these plans."
20And David said to his son Solomon, "Be
strong and of good courage, and do *it*; do not
fear nor be dismayed, for the LORD God—my
God—*will be* with you. He will not leave you
nor forsake you, until you have finished all the
work for the service of the house of the LORD.
21*Here are* the divisions of the priests and the
Levites for all the service of the house of God;
and every willing craftsman *will be* with you
for all manner of workmanship, for every kind
of service; also the leaders and all the people
will be completely at your command."

28:19 in writing. David wrote down the plans under the Holy Spirit's divine inspiration (non-canonical, written revelation). This divine privilege was much like that of Moses for the tabernacle (Ex. 25:9,40; 27:8; Heb. 8:5).

28:20,21 Solomon's associates in the building project were God, the owner and general contractor (28:20), plus the human workforce (28:21).

29 Furthermore King David said to all the
assembly: "My son Solomon, whom
alone God has chosen, *is* young and inexperienced; and the work *is* great, because the temple *is* not for man but for the LORD God. 2Now
for the house of my God I have prepared with
all my might: gold for *things to be made of* gold,
silver for *things of* silver, bronze for *things of*
bronze, iron for *things of* iron, wood for *things*
of wood, onyx stones, *stones* to be set, glistening stones of various colors, all kinds of
precious stones, and marble slabs in abundance. 3Moreover, because I have set my
affection on the house of my God, I have given
to the house of my God, over and above all
that I have prepared for the holy house, my
own special treasure of gold and silver: 4three
thousand talents of gold, of the gold of Ophir,
and seven thousand talents of refined silver, to
overlay the walls of the houses; 5the gold for
things of gold and the silver for *things of* silver,
and for all kinds of work *to be done* by the
hands of craftsmen. Who *then* is willing to consecrate himself this day to the LORD?"
6Then the leaders of the fathers' *houses*, leaders
of the tribes of Israel, the captains of thousands

and of hundreds, with the officers over the
king's work, offered willingly. 7They gave for the
work of the house of God five thousand talents
and ten thousand darics of gold, ten thousand
talents of silver, eighteen thousand talents of
bronze, and one hundred thousand talents of
iron. 8And whoever had *precious* stones gave
them to the treasury of the house of the LORD,
into the hand of Jehiel the Gershonite. 9Then
the people rejoiced, for they had offered willingly, because with a loyal heart they had offered willingly to the LORD; and King David
also rejoiced greatly.

10Therefore David blessed the LORD before all
the assembly; and David said:

"Blessed are You, LORD God of Israel,
our Father, forever and ever.
11 Yours, O LORD, *is* the greatness,
The power and the glory,
The victory and the majesty;
For all *that is* in heaven and in earth
is Yours;
Yours *is* the kingdom, O LORD,
And You are exalted as head over all.
12 Both riches and honor *come* from You,
And You reign over all.
In Your hand *is* power and might;
In Your hand *it is* to make great
And to give strength to all.

13 "Now therefore, our God,
We thank You
And praise Your glorious name.
14 But who *am* I, and who *are* my people,
That we should be able to offer so
willingly as this?
For all things *come* from You,
And of Your own we have given You.
15 For we *are* aliens and pilgrims before
You,
As *were* all our fathers;
Our days on earth *are* as a shadow,
And without hope.

16"O LORD our God, all this abundance that
we have prepared to build You a house for
Your holy name is from Your hand, and *is* all
Your own. 17I know also, my God, that You test
the heart and have pleasure in uprightness. As
for me, in the uprightness of my heart I have
willingly offered all these *things;* and now with
joy I have seen Your people, who are present
here to offer willingly to You. 18O LORD God of
Abraham, Isaac, and Israel, our fathers, keep
this forever in the intent of the thoughts of the
heart of Your people, and fix their heart
toward You. 19And give my son Solomon a
loyal heart to keep Your commandments and
Your testimonies and Your statutes, to do all
these things, and to build the temple for which
I have made provision."

20Then David said to all the assembly, "Now
bless the LORD your God." So all the assembly
blessed the LORD God of their fathers, and
bowed their heads and prostrated themselves
before the LORD and the king.

21And they made sacrifices to the LORD and
offered burnt offerings to the LORD on the next
day: a thousand bulls, a thousand rams, a thousand lambs, with their drink offerings, and
sacrifices in abundance for all Israel. 22So they
ate and drank before the LORD with great
gladness on that day. And they made Solomon
the son of David king the second time, and
anointed *him* before the LORD *to be* the leader,
and Zadok *to be* priest. 23Then Solomon sat on
the throne of the LORD as king instead of David his father, and prospered; and all Israel
obeyed him. 24All the leaders and the mighty
men, and also all the sons of King David, submitted themselves to King Solomon. 25So the
LORD exalted Solomon exceedingly in the sight
of all Israel, and bestowed on him *such* royal
majesty as had not been on any king before
him in Israel.

26Thus David the son of Jesse reigned over all
Israel. 27And the period that he reigned over Israel *was* forty years; seven years he reigned in
Hebron, and thirty-three *years* he reigned in Jerusalem. 28So he died in a good old age, full of
days and riches and honor; and Solomon his
son reigned in his place. 29Now the acts of King
David, first and last, indeed they *are* written in
the book of Samuel the seer, in the book of Nathan the prophet, and in the book of Gad the
seer, 30with all his reign and his might, and the
events that happened to him, to Israel, and to
all the kingdoms of the lands.

Psalm 78:67–72

67 Moreover He rejected the tent of Joseph,
And did not choose the tribe of
Ephraim,
68 But chose the tribe of Judah,
Mount Zion which He loved.
69 And He built His sanctuary like the
heights,
Like the earth which He has
established forever.
70 He also chose David His servant,
And took him from the sheepfolds;
71 From following the ewes that had
young He brought him,
To shepherd Jacob His people,
And Israel His inheritance.
72 So he shepherded them according to
the integrity of his heart,

And guided them by the skillfulness
of his hands.

Proverbs 20:6–7

6 Most men will proclaim each his own
goodness,
But who can find a faithful man?

7 The righteous *man* walks in his
integrity;
His children *are* blessed after him.

Acts 10:24–48

24And the following day they entered
Caesarea. Now Cornelius was waiting for
them, and had called together his relatives
and close friends. 25As Peter was coming in,
Cornelius met him and fell down at his feet
and worshiped *him*. 26But Peter lifted him up,
saying, "Stand up; I myself am also a man."
27And as he talked with him, he went in and
found many who had come together. 28Then
he said to them, "You know how unlawful it is
for a Jewish man to keep company with or go
to one of another nation. But God has shown
me that I should not call any man common or
unclean. 29Therefore I came without objection
as soon as I was sent for. I ask, then, for what
reason have you sent for me?"

10:28 unlawful. Literally, "breaking a taboo." Peter followed the Jewish standards and traditions his whole life. His comments reveal his acceptance of a new standard in which Jews no longer were to consider Gentiles profane.

30So Cornelius said, "Four days ago I was
fasting until this hour; and at the ninth hour I
prayed in my house, and behold, a man stood
before me in bright clothing, 31and said,
'Cornelius, your prayer has been heard, and
your alms are remembered in the sight of
God. 32Send therefore to Joppa and call Simon
here, whose surname is Peter. He is lodging in
the house of Simon, a tanner, by the sea.
When he comes, he will speak to you.' 33So I
sent to you immediately, and you have done
well to come. Now therefore, we are all present before God, to hear all the things commanded you by God."

34Then Peter opened *his* mouth and said: "In
truth I perceive that God shows no partiality.
35But in every nation whoever fears Him and
works righteousness is accepted by Him.

10:34 God shows no partiality. Taught in both the Old Testament (Deut. 10:17; 2 Chr. 19:7; Job 34:19) and the New Testament (Rom. 2:11; 3:29,30; James 2:1). The reality of this truth was taking on new dimensions for Peter.

36The word which *God* sent to the children of
Israel, preaching peace through Jesus
Christ—He is Lord of all— 37that word you
know, which was proclaimed throughout all
Judea, and began from Galilee after the baptism which John preached: 38how God anointed Jesus of Nazareth with the Holy Spirit and
with power, who went about doing good and
healing all who were oppressed by the devil,
for God was with Him. 39And we are witnesses
of all things which He did both in the land of
the Jews and in Jerusalem, whom they killed
by hanging on a tree. 40Him God raised up on
the third day, and showed Him openly, 41not to
all the people, but to witnesses chosen before
by God, *even* to us who ate and drank with
Him after He arose from the dead. 42And He
commanded us to preach to the people, and to
testify that it is He who was ordained by God
to be Judge of the living and the dead. 43To Him
all the prophets witness that, through His
name, whoever believes in Him will receive remission of sins."

10:36 preaching peace. Christ, by paying the price of sin through His sacrificial death, established peace between man and God (Rom. 5:1–11).

44While Peter was still speaking these
words, the Holy Spirit fell upon all those who
heard the word. 45And those of the circumcision who believed were astonished, as many as
came with Peter, because the gift of the Holy
Spirit had been poured out on the Gentiles
also. 46For they heard them speak with
tongues and magnify God.

Then Peter answered, 47"Can anyone forbid
water, that these should not be baptized who
have received the Holy Spirit just as we *have?*"
48And he commanded them to be baptized in
the name of the Lord. Then they asked him to
stay a few days.

DAY 2: What does God desire in our giving?

King David called for consecrated giving to the building of the temple, based on his personal example of generosity (1 Chr. 29:3,4). David gave his personal fortune to the temple building, a fortune almost immeasurable. He says that "over and above all that I have prepared for the holy house, my own special treasure of gold and silver: three thousand talents of gold, of the gold of Ophir." Assuming a talent weighed about 75 pounds, this amounts to almost 112 tons of gold. This was held to be the purest and finest in the world (Job 22:24; 28:16; Is. 13:12). Plus the 7,000 talents of silver, which would be 260 tons, the total worth of such precious metals has been estimated in the billions of dollars.

As he addresses the people, David notes the phrase "with a willing mind" (vv. 6–9). Here is the key to all freewill giving, i.e., giving what one desires to give. Tithes were required for taxation, to fund the theocracy, similar to taxation today. The law required that to be paid. This, however, is the voluntary giving from the heart to the Lord. The New Testament speaks of this (Luke 6:38; 2 Cor. 9:1–8) and never demands that a tithe be given to God, but that taxes be paid to one's government (Rom. 13:6,7). Paying taxes and giving God whatever one is willing to give, based on devotion to Him and His glory, is biblical giving.

The people rejoiced in their offering to the temple which was "five thousand talents…of gold" (1 Chr. 29:7). This amounts to 187 tons of gold. Add to that 375 tons of silver, 675 tons of bronze, and 3,750 tons of iron. The sum of all this is staggering and has been estimated into the billions of dollars. David responds to the phenomenal offering expressing amazing sacrifices of wealth with praise in which he acknowledges that all things belong to and come from God (vv. 10–15). David says that opportunities for giving to God are tests of the character, "test the heart," of a believer's devotion to the Lord (v. 17). The king acknowledges that the attitude of one's heart is significantly more important than the amount of offering in one's hand.

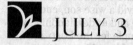

JULY 3

2 Chronicles 1:1–2:18

1 Now Solomon the son of David was strengthened in his kingdom, and the LORD his God
was with him and exalted him exceedingly.
2And Solomon spoke to all Israel, to the captains of thousands and of hundreds, to the
judges, and to every leader in all Israel, the
heads of the fathers' *houses.* 3Then Solomon,
and all the assembly with him, went to the
high place that *was* at Gibeon; for the tabernacle of meeting with God was there, which Moses the servant of the LORD had made in the
wilderness. 4But David had brought up the ark
of God from Kirjath Jearim to *the place* David
had prepared for it, for he had pitched a tent
for it at Jerusalem. 5Now the bronze altar that
Bezalel the son of Uri, the son of Hur, had
made, he put before the tabernacle of the
LORD; Solomon and the assembly sought Him
there. 6And Solomon went up there to the
bronze altar before the LORD, which *was* at the
tabernacle of meeting, and offered a thousand
burnt offerings on it.
7On that night God appeared to Solomon,
and said to him, "Ask! What shall I give you?"
8And Solomon said to God: "You have
shown great mercy to David my father, and
have made me king in his place. 9Now, O LORD
God, let Your promise to David my father be
established, for You have made me king over a
people like the dust of the earth in multitude.
10Now give me wisdom and knowledge, that I
may go out and come in before this people; for
who can judge this great people of Yours?"
11Then God said to Solomon: "Because this
was in your heart, and you have not asked
riches or wealth or honor or the life of your
enemies, nor have you asked long life—but
have asked wisdom and knowledge for yourself, that you may judge My people over whom
I have made you king— 12wisdom and knowledge *are* granted to you; and I will give you
riches and wealth and honor, such as none of
the kings have had who *were* before you, nor
shall any after you have the like."
13So Solomon came to Jerusalem from the
high place that *was* at Gibeon, from before the
tabernacle of meeting, and reigned over Israel.
14And Solomon gathered chariots and horsemen; he had one thousand four hundred chariots and twelve thousand horsemen, whom he
stationed in the chariot cities and with the
king in Jerusalem. 15Also the king made silver
and gold as common in Jerusalem as stones,
and he made cedars as abundant as the
sycamores which *are* in the lowland. 16And Solomon had horses imported from Egypt and
Keveh; the king's merchants bought them in
Keveh at the *current* price. 17They also

1:17 six hundred *shekels.* Assuming a shekel weighs .4 ounces, this represents 15 pounds of silver for one chariot. **one hundred and fifty.** Assuming the weight is in shekels, this would be about 3.75 pounds of silver. Deuteronomy 17:16 warned against the king's amassing horses.

acquired and imported from Egypt a chariot
for six hundred *shekels* of silver, and a horse
for one hundred and fifty; thus, through their
agents, they exported them to all the kings of
the Hittites and the kings of Syria.

2 Then Solomon determined to build a temple for the name of the LORD, and a royal
house for himself. [2]Solomon selected seventy
thousand men to bear burdens, eighty thousand to quarry *stone* in the mountains, and
three thousand six hundred to oversee them.

2:1 temple for the name of the LORD. God's covenant name, Yahweh or Jehovah (Ex. 3:14), is in mind. David wanted to do this, but was not allowed to do any more than plan and prepare (1 Chr. 23–26; 28:11–13), purchase the land (2 Sam. 24:18–25; 1 Chr. 22), and gather the materials (1 Chr. 22:14–16).

[3]Then Solomon sent to Hiram king of Tyre,
saying:

As you have dealt with David my father,
and sent him cedars to build himself a
house to dwell in, *so deal with me.*
[4]Behold, I am building a temple for the
name of the LORD my God, to dedicate *it*
to Him, to burn before Him sweet
incense, for the continual showbread, for
the burnt offerings morning and evening,
on the Sabbaths, on the New Moons, and
on the set feasts of the LORD our God.
This *is an ordinance* forever to Israel.

5 And the temple which I build *will be*
great, for our God is greater than all
gods. [6]But who is able to build Him a
temple, since heaven and the heaven of
heavens cannot contain Him? Who *am* I
then, that I should build Him a temple,
except to burn sacrifice before Him?

7 Therefore send me at once a man
skillful to work in gold and silver, in
bronze and iron, in purple and crimson
and blue, who has skill to engrave with
the skillful men who are with me in
Judah and Jerusalem, whom David my
father provided. [8]Also send me cedar and
cypress and algum logs from Lebanon,
for I know that your servants have skill
to cut timber in Lebanon; and indeed my
servants *will be* with your servants, [9]to
prepare timber for me in abundance, for
the temple which I am about to build
shall be great and wonderful.

10 And indeed I will give to your servants,
the woodsmen who cut timber, twenty
thousand kors of ground wheat, twenty
thousand kors of barley, twenty thousand
baths of wine, and twenty thousand
baths of oil.

[11]Then Hiram king of Tyre answered in writing, which he sent to Solomon:

Because the LORD loves His people, He
has made you king over them.

[12]Hiram also said:

Blessed *be* the LORD God of Israel, who
made heaven and earth, for He has
given King David a wise son, endowed
with prudence and understanding, who
will build a temple for the LORD and a
royal house for himself!

13 And now I have sent a skillful man,
endowed with understanding, Huram my
master *craftsman* [14](the son of a woman of
the daughters of Dan, and his father was a
man of Tyre), skilled to work in gold and
silver, bronze and iron, stone and wood,
purple and blue, fine linen and crimson,
and to make any engraving and to
accomplish any plan which may be given
to him, with your skillful men and with the
skillful men of my lord David your father.

15 Now therefore, the wheat, the barley,
the oil, and the wine which my lord has
spoken of, let him send to his servants.
[16]And we will cut wood from Lebanon,
as much as you need; we will bring it to
you in rafts by sea to Joppa, and you
will carry it up to Jerusalem.

[17]Then Solomon numbered all the aliens
who *were* in the land of Israel, after the census
in which David his father had numbered them;
and there were found to be one hundred and
fifty-three thousand six hundred. [18]And he
made seventy thousand of them bearers of
burdens, eighty thousand stonecutters in the
mountain, and three thousand six hundred
overseers to make the people work.

Psalm 79:1–4

A Psalm of Asaph.

O God, the nations have come into
Your inheritance;
Your holy temple they have defiled;
They have laid Jerusalem in heaps.
2 The dead bodies of Your servants
They have given *as* food for the birds
of the heavens,
The flesh of Your saints to the beasts
of the earth.
3 Their blood they have shed like water
all around Jerusalem,
And *there was* no one to bury *them.*
4 We have become a reproach to our
neighbors,
A scorn and derision to those who are
around us.

79:1–13 The historical basis for this lament psalm was probably Nebuchadnezzar's destruction of the temple in 586 B.C. (Ps. 74; 2 Kin. 25:8–21; Lam. 1–5). The psalm contains prayer for the nation's spiritual needs, curses against the enemies of God's people, and praises in anticipation of God's actions. The psalm helps the believer express his anguish in a disaster when it seems as though God is aloof.

79:1 nations. In this context, the word refers to heathen, pagan people. **inheritance.** The inheritance of God was national Israel, and specifically its capital city, Jerusalem, where the temple was located.

Proverbs 20:8–9

8 A king who sits on the throne of
judgment
Scatters all evil with his eyes.
9 Who can say, "I have made my heart
clean,
I am pure from my sin"?

Acts 11:1–30

11 Now the apostles and brethren who were
in Judea heard that the Gentiles had also
received the word of God. 2And when Peter
came up to Jerusalem, those of the circumcision contended with him, 3saying, "You went
in to uncircumcised men and ate with them!"
4But Peter explained *it* to them in order
from the beginning, saying: 5"I was in the city
of Joppa praying; and in a trance I saw a vision,

11:3 ate with them! The Jewish believers were outraged over such a blatant breach of Jewish custom. It was difficult for them to conceive that Jesus could be equally Lord of Gentile believers.

an object descending like a great sheet, let
down from heaven by four corners; and it
came to me. 6When I observed it intently and
considered, I saw four-footed animals of the
earth, wild beasts, creeping things, and birds
of the air. 7And I heard a voice saying to me,
'Rise, Peter; kill and eat.' 8But I said, 'Not so,
Lord! For nothing common or unclean has at
any time entered my mouth.' 9But the voice
answered me again from heaven, 'What God
has cleansed you must not call common.'
10Now this was done three times, and all were
drawn up again into heaven. 11At that very
moment, three men stood before the house
where I was, having been sent to me from
Caesarea. 12Then the Spirit told me to go with
them, doubting nothing. Moreover these six
brethren accompanied me, and we entered
the man's house. 13And he told us how he had
seen an angel standing in his house, who said
to him, 'Send men to Joppa, and call for Simon
whose surname is Peter, 14who will tell you
words by which you and all your household
will be saved.' 15And as I began to speak, the
Holy Spirit fell upon them, as upon us at the
beginning. 16Then I remembered the word of
the Lord, how He said, 'John indeed baptized
with water, but you shall be baptized with the
Holy Spirit.' 17If therefore God gave them the
same gift as *He gave* us when we believed on
the Lord Jesus Christ, who was I that I could
withstand God?"
18When they heard these things they became
silent; and they glorified God, saying, "Then
God has also granted to the Gentiles repentance to life."
19Now those who were scattered after the
persecution that arose over Stephen traveled
as far as Phoenicia, Cyprus, and Antioch,

11:18 God has also granted to the Gentiles repentance to life. One of the most shocking admissions in Jewish history, but an event that the Old Testament had prophesied (Is. 42:1,6; 49:6; Acts 2:38).

preaching the word to no one but the Jews only. [20]But some of them were men from Cyprus and Cyrene, who, when they had come to Antioch, spoke to the Hellenists, preaching the Lord Jesus. [21]And the hand of the Lord was with them, and a great number believed and turned to the Lord.

[22]Then news of these things came to the ears of the church in Jerusalem, and they sent out Barnabas to go as far as Antioch. [23]When he came and had seen the grace of God, he was glad, and encouraged them all that with purpose of heart they should continue with the Lord. [24]For he was a good man, full of the Holy Spirit and of faith. And a great many people were added to the Lord.

[25]Then Barnabas departed for Tarsus to seek Saul. [26]And when he had found him, he brought him to Antioch. So it was that for a whole year they assembled with the church and taught a great many people. And the disciples were first called Christians in Antioch.

[27]And in these days prophets came from Jerusalem to Antioch. [28]Then one of them, named Agabus, stood up and showed by the Spirit that there was going to be a great famine throughout all the world, which also happened in the days of Claudius Caesar. [29]Then the disciples, each according to his ability, determined to send relief to the brethren dwelling in Judea. [30]This they also did, and sent it to the elders by the hands of Barnabas and Saul.

11:27 prophets. Preachers of the New Testament (1 Cor. 14:32; Eph. 2:20).

11:28 Agabus. One of the Jerusalem prophets who years later played an important part in Paul's ministry (21:10, 11). **a great famine.** Several ancient writers (Tacitus [*Annals* XI.43], Josephus [*Antiquities* XX.ii.5], and Suetonius [*Claudius* 18]) affirm the occurrence of great famines in Israel ca. A.D. 45–46. **all the world.** The famine reached beyond the region of Palestine. **Claudius Caesar.** Emperor of Rome (A.D. 41–54).

DAY 3: How does the baptism with the Holy Spirit (1 Cor. 12:13) relate to the Spirit's activities in the Book of Acts?

Acts describes a number of occasions in which the Holy Spirit "fell on" or "filled" or "came upon" people (2:4; 10:44; 19:6). Here in Acts 11:16,17, Peter recounts how the Holy Spirit fell upon the Gentiles just as it had the early Jewish disciples. Peter identifies these actions by God as a fulfillment of Joel's prophecy (Joel 2:28–32).

Viewed from the perspective of the entire New Testament, these experiences were neither the same nor replacements for what John the Baptist (Mark 1:8) and Paul described as the baptism with the Holy Spirit (1 Cor. 12:13). The *baptism* with the Spirit is the one-time act by which God places believers into His body. The *filling* is a repeated reality of Spirit-controlled behavior that God commands believers to maintain (Eph. 5:18). Peter and others who experienced the special filling on Pentecost Day (2:4) were filled with the Spirit again and again (4:8,31; 6:5; 7:55) and so boldly spoke the word of God. That was just the beginning. The fullness of the Spirit affects all areas of life, not just speaking boldly (Eph. 5:18–33).

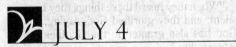

JULY 4

2 Chronicles 3:1–4:22

3 Now Solomon began to build the house of
the LORD at Jerusalem on Mount Moriah, where *the LORD* had appeared to his father David, at the place that David had prepared on the threshing floor of Ornan the Jebusite. [2]And he began to build on the second *day* of the second month in the fourth year of his reign.

[3]This is the foundation which Solomon laid for building the house of God: The length *was* sixty cubits (by cubits according to the former measure) and the width twenty cubits. [4]And the vestibule that *was* in front *of the sanctuary* was twenty cubits long across the width of the house, and the height *was* one hundred and twenty. He overlaid the inside with pure gold. [5]The larger room he paneled with cypress which he overlaid with fine gold, and he carved palm trees and chainwork on it. [6]And he decorated the house with precious stones for beauty, and the gold *was* gold from Parvaim. [7]He also overlaid the house—the beams and doorposts, its walls and doors—with gold; and he carved cherubim on the walls.

[8]And he made the Most Holy Place. Its length was according to the width of the house, twenty cubits, and its width twenty

cubits. He overlaid it with six hundred talents
of fine gold. 9The weight of the nails *was* fifty
shekels of gold; and he overlaid the upper
area with gold. 10In the Most Holy Place he
made two cherubim, fashioned by carving,
and overlaid them with gold. 11The wings of
the cherubim *were* twenty cubits in *overall*
length: one wing *of the one cherub was* five
cubits, touching the wall of the room, and the
other wing *was* five cubits, touching the wing
of the other cherub; 12*one* wing of the other
cherub *was* five cubits, touching the wall of
the room, and the other wing *also was* five
cubits, touching the wing of the other cherub.
13The wings of these cherubim spanned twenty cubits overall. They stood on their feet, and
they faced inward. 14And he made the veil of
blue, purple, crimson, and fine linen, and wove
cherubim into it.

3:10–13 two cherubim. This free-standing set of cherubim was in addition to the more diminutive set on the ark itself.

3:14 veil. The veil separated the Holy Place from the Most Holy Place (the Holy of Holies), which was entered once annually by the high priest on the Day of Atonement (Lev. 16). This highly limited access to the presence of God was eliminated by the death of Christ, when the veil in Herod's temple was torn in two from top to bottom (Matt. 27:51). It signified that believers had immediate, full access to God's presence through their Mediator and High Priest Jesus Christ, who was the perfect, once-for-all sacrifice (Heb. 3:14–16; 9:19–22).

15Also he made in front of the temple two pillars thirty-five cubits high, and the capital that
was on the top of each of *them* was five cubits.
16He made wreaths of chainwork, as in the
inner sanctuary, and put *them* on top of the pillars; and he made one hundred pomegranates,
and put *them* on the wreaths of chainwork.
17Then he set up the pillars before the temple,
one on the right hand and the other on the
left; he called the name of the one on the right
hand Jachin, and the name of the one on the
left Boaz.

4 Moreover he made a bronze altar: twenty
cubits was its length, twenty cubits its
width, and ten cubits its height.
2Then he made the Sea of cast *bronze,* ten
cubits from one brim to the other; *it was* completely round. Its height *was* five cubits, and a

4:1 bronze altar. This is the main altar on which sacrifices were offered (the millennial temple altar, Ezek. 43:13–17). For comparison to the tabernacle's altar, see Exodus 27:1–8; 38:1–7. If the cubit of 18 inches was used rather than the royal cubit of 21 inches, it would make the altar 30 feet by 30 feet by 15 feet high.

4:2 the Sea. This large laver was used for ritual cleansing. In Ezekiel's millennial temple, the laver will apparently be replaced by the waters that flow through the temple (Ezek. 47:1–12).

line of thirty cubits measured its circumference. 3And under it *was* the likeness of oxen
encircling it all around, ten to a cubit, all the
way around the Sea. The oxen *were* cast in two
rows, when it was cast. 4It stood on twelve
oxen: three looking toward the north, three
looking toward the west, three looking toward
the south, and three looking toward the east;
the Sea *was set* upon them, and all their back
parts *pointed* inward. 5It *was* a handbreadth
thick; and its brim was shaped like the brim of
a cup, *like* a lily blossom. It contained three
thousand baths.
6He also made ten lavers, and put five on the
right side and five on the left, to wash in them;
such things as they offered for the burnt offering they would wash in them, but the Sea *was*
for the priests to wash in. 7And he made ten
lampstands of gold according to their design,
and set *them* in the temple, five on the right
side and five on the left. 8He also made ten
tables, and placed *them* in the temple, five on
the right side and five on the left. And he made
one hundred bowls of gold.
9Furthermore he made the court of the
priests, and the great court and doors for the
court; and he overlaid these doors with
bronze. 10He set the Sea on the right side,
toward the southeast.
11Then Huram made the pots and the shovels
and the bowls. So Huram finished doing the
work that he was to do for King Solomon for
the house of God: 12the two pillars and the
bowl-shaped capitals *that were* on top of the
two pillars; the two networks covering the two
bowl-shaped capitals which *were* on top of the
pillars; 13four hundred pomegranates for the
two networks (two rows of pomegranates for
each network, to cover the two bowl-shaped
capitals that *were* on the pillars); 14he also made
carts and the lavers on the carts; 15one Sea and

twelve oxen under it; 16also the pots, the shovels, the forks—and all their articles Huram his
master *craftsman* made of burnished bronze
for King Solomon for the house of the LORD.
17In the plain of Jordan the king had them
cast in clay molds, between Succoth and
Zeredah. 18And Solomon had all these articles
made in such great abundance that the weight
of the bronze was not determined.
19Thus Solomon had all the furnishings
made for the house of God: the altar of gold
and the tables on which *was* the showbread;
20the lampstands with their lamps of pure gold,
to burn in the prescribed manner in front of
the inner sanctuary, 21with the flowers and the
lamps and the wick-trimmers of gold, of purest
gold; 22the trimmers, the bowls, the ladles, and
the censers of pure gold. As for the entry of
the sanctuary, its inner doors to the Most Holy
Place, and the doors of the main hall of the
temple, *were* gold.

Psalm 79:5–10

5 How long, LORD?
Will You be angry forever?
Will Your jealousy burn like fire?
6 Pour out Your wrath on the nations
that do not know You,
And on the kingdoms that do not call
on Your name.
7 For they have devoured Jacob,
And laid waste his dwelling place.

8 Oh, do not remember former iniquities
against us!
Let Your tender mercies come speedily
to meet us,
For we have been brought very low.
9 Help us, O God of our salvation,
For the glory of Your name;
And deliver us, and provide atonement
for our sins,
For Your name's sake!
10 Why should the nations say,
"Where *is* their God?"
Let there be known among the nations
in our sight
The avenging of the blood of Your
servants *which has been* shed.

79:9 atonement. The word, found 3 times in the Psalms (65:3; 78:38), means to cover away sin and its effects. In the Old Testament, atonement was symbolized in sacrificial ritual, though actual forgiveness of sin was ultimately based on the death of Christ applied to the penitent sinner (Heb. 9). **For Your name's sake.** A defeat of a nation was believed to be a defeat of its god. A mark of spiritual maturity is one's concern for the reputation of God.

Proverbs 20:10–12

10 Diverse weights *and* diverse
measures,
They *are* both alike, an abomination
to the LORD.

11 Even a child is known by his deeds,
Whether what he does *is* pure and
right.

12 The hearing ear and the seeing eye,
The LORD has made them both.

Acts 12:1–25

12 Now about that time Herod the king
stretched out *his* hand to harass some
from the church. 2Then he killed James the
brother of John with the sword. 3And because
he saw that it pleased the Jews, he proceeded
further to seize Peter also. Now it was *during*
the Days of Unleavened Bread. 4So when he
had arrested him, he put *him* in prison, and
delivered *him* to four squads of soldiers to
keep him, intending to bring him before the
people after Passover.
5Peter was therefore kept in prison, but constant prayer was offered to God for him by the
church. 6And when Herod was about to bring
him out, that night Peter was sleeping, bound
with two chains between two soldiers; and the
guards before the door were keeping the prison.
7Now behold, an angel of the Lord stood by *him,*
and a light shone in the prison; and he struck
Peter on the side and raised him up, saying,
"Arise quickly!" And his chains fell off *his* hands.
8Then the angel said to him, "Gird yourself and
tie on your sandals"; and so he did. And he said
to him, "Put on your garment and follow me."
9So he went out and followed him, and did not
know that what was done by the angel was real,
but thought he was seeing a vision. 10When they
were past the first and the second guard posts,
they came to the iron gate that leads to the city,
which opened to them of its own accord; and
they went out and went down one street, and
immediately the angel departed from him.
11And when Peter had come to himself, he
said, "Now I know for certain that the Lord
has sent His angel, and has delivered me from
the hand of Herod and *from* all the expectation
of the Jewish people."
12So, when he had considered *this,* he came
to the house of Mary, the mother of John

whose surname was Mark, where many were gathered together praying. [13]And as Peter knocked at the door of the gate, a girl named Rhoda came to answer. [14]When she recognized Peter's voice, because of *her* gladness she did not open the gate, but ran in and announced that Peter stood before the gate. [15]But they said to her, "You are beside yourself!" Yet she kept insisting that it was so. So they said, "It is his angel."

[16]Now Peter continued knocking; and when they opened *the door* and saw him, they were astonished. [17]But motioning to them with his hand to keep silent, he declared to them how the Lord had brought him out of the prison. And he said, "Go, tell these things to James and to the brethren." And he departed and went to another place.

[18]Then, as soon as it was day, there was no small stir among the soldiers about what had become of Peter. [19]But when Herod had searched for him and not found him, he examined the guards and commanded that *they* should be put to death.

And he went down from Judea to Caesarea, and stayed *there.*

[20]Now Herod had been very angry with the people of Tyre and Sidon; but they came to him with one accord, and having made Blastus the king's personal aide their friend, they asked for peace, because their country was supplied with food by the king's *country.*

[21]So on a set day Herod, arrayed in royal apparel, sat on his throne and gave an oration to them. [22]And the people kept shouting, "The voice of a god and not of a man!" [23]Then immediately an angel of the Lord struck him, because he did not give glory to God. And he was eaten by worms and died.

[24]But the word of God grew and multiplied.

[25]And Barnabas and Saul returned from Jerusalem when they had fulfilled *their* ministry, and they also took with them John whose surname was Mark.

12:12 Mary. Mark is called the cousin of Barnabas in Colossians 4:10, so Mary was his aunt. **John...Mark.** Cousin of Barnabas (Col. 4:10), acquaintance of Peter in his youth (1 Pet. 5:13), he accompanied Barnabas and Paul to Antioch (v. 25) and later to Cyprus (13:4,5). He deserted them at Perga (13:13), and Paul refused to take him on his second missionary journey because of that desertion (15:36–41). He accompanied Barnabas to Cyprus (15:39). He disappeared until he was seen with Paul at Rome as an accepted companion and co-worker (Col. 4:10; Philem. 24). During Paul's second imprisonment at Rome, Paul sought John Mark's presence as useful to him (2 Tim. 4:11). He wrote the second Gospel that bears his name, being enriched in his task by the aid of Peter (1 Pet. 5:13).

12:17 James. The Lord's brother, now head of the Jerusalem church. **he departed.** Except for a brief appearance in chapter 15, Peter fades from the scene as the rest of Acts revolves around Paul and his ministry.

DAY 4: Who was the Herod of Acts 12 who violently persecuted the church?

"Herod the king" of v. 1 was Herod Agrippa I, who reigned from A.D. 37 to 44 and was the grandson of Herod the Great. He ran up numerous debts in Rome and fled to Palestine. Imprisoned by Emperor Tiberius after some careless comments, he eventually was released following Tiberius's death, and was made ruler of northern Palestine, to which Judea and Samaria were added in A.D. 41. As a hedge against his shaky relationship with Rome, he curried favor with the Jews by persecuting Christians.

He killed James the brother of John with the sword (v. 2). James was the first of the apostles to be martyred. The manner of his execution indicates James was accused of leading people to follow false gods (Deut. 13:12–15). He also imprisoned Peter and put him in the custody of "four squads" (v. 4). Each squad contained 4 soldiers and rotated the watch on Peter. At all times 2 guards were chained to him in his cell, while the other 2 stood guard outside the cell door (v. 6).

After Peter's rescue by an angel, Herod "put to death" the guards who were in charge (v. 19). According to Justinian's *Code* (ix. 4:4), a guard who allowed a prisoner to escape would suffer the same fatal penalty that awaited the prisoner.

Later, Herod came under the judgment of God. "On a set day" (v. 21), at a feast in honor of Herod's patron, the Roman emperor Claudius, Herod came out "arrayed in royal apparel." According to Josephus, he wore a garment made of silver. When the people began shouting, "The voice of a god and not of a man!" we are told that Herod "did not give glory to God" (v. 22), the crime for which Herod was struck down by an angel (A.D. 44). "And he was eaten by worms" (v. 23). According to Josephus, Herod endured terrible pain for 5 days before he died.

JULY 5

2 Chronicles 5:1–6:42

5 So all the work that Solomon had done for the house of the LORD was finished; and Solomon brought in the things which his father David had dedicated: the silver and the gold and all the furnishings. And he put *them* in the treasuries of the house of God.

5:1 The temple took 7 years, 6 months to build and was completed in Solomon's 11th year (959 B.C.) in the eighth month (1 Kin. 6:38). Since it was dedicated in the seventh month (5:3), its dedication occurred 11 months later to coincide with the Feast of Tabernacles. Why is there so much emphasis in the Old Testament on the temple? 1) It was the center of worship that called people to correct belief through the generations. 2) It was the symbol of God's presence with His people. 3) It was the symbol of forgiveness and grace, reminding the people of the seriousness of sin and the availability of mercy. 4) It prepared the people for the true Lamb of God, Jesus Christ, who would take away sin. 5) It was a place of prayer.

2 Now Solomon assembled the elders of Israel and all the heads of the tribes, the chief fathers of the children of Israel, in Jerusalem, that they might bring the ark of the covenant of the LORD up from the City of David, which *is* Zion. 3 Therefore all the men of Israel assembled with the king at the feast, which *was* in the seventh month. 4 So all the elders of Israel came, and the Levites took up the ark. 5 Then they brought up the ark, the tabernacle of meeting, and all the holy furnishings that *were* in the tabernacle. The priests and the Levites brought them up. 6 Also King Solomon, and all the congregation of Israel who were assembled with him before the ark, were sacrificing sheep and oxen that could not be counted or numbered for multitude. 7 Then the priests brought in the ark of the covenant of the LORD to its place, into the inner sanctuary of the temple, to the Most Holy *Place,* under the wings of the cherubim. 8 For the cherubim spread *their* wings over the place of the ark, and the cherubim overshadowed the ark and its poles. 9 The poles extended so that the ends of the poles of the ark could be seen from *the holy place,* in front of the inner sanctuary; but they could not be seen from outside. And they are there to this day. 10 Nothing was in the ark except the two tablets which Moses put *there* at Horeb, when the LORD made *a covenant* with the children of Israel, when they had come out of Egypt.

11 And it came to pass when the priests came out of the *Most* Holy *Place* (for all the priests who *were* present had sanctified themselves, without keeping to their divisions), 12 and the Levites *who were* the singers, all those of Asaph and Heman and Jeduthun, with their sons and their brethren, stood at the east end of the altar, clothed in white linen, having cymbals, stringed instruments and harps, and with them one hundred and twenty priests sounding with trumpets— 13 indeed it came to pass, when the trumpeters and singers *were* as one, to make one sound to be heard in praising and thanking the LORD, and when they lifted up their voice with the trumpets and cymbals and instruments of music, and praised the LORD, *saying:*

"*For He is* good,
For His mercy *endures* forever,"

5:13,14 the glory of the LORD. The Lord's presence indwelt the temple and the first service of worship was held. In the same manner He descended on the tabernacle (Ex. 40:34–38). He will do likewise on the millennial temple (Ezek. 43:1–5). His glory is representative of His Person (Ex. 33), and entering the temple signified His presence.

that the house, the house of the LORD, was filled with a cloud, 14 so that the priests could not continue ministering because of the cloud; for the glory of the LORD filled the house of God.

6 Then Solomon spoke:

"The LORD said He would dwell in the dark cloud.
2 I have surely built You an exalted house,
And a place for You to dwell in forever."

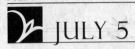

3 Then the king turned around and blessed the whole assembly of Israel, while all the assembly of Israel was standing. 4 And he said: "Blessed *be* the LORD God of Israel, who has fulfilled with His hands *what* He spoke with His mouth to my father David, saying, 5 'Since

the day that I brought My people out of the
land of Egypt, I have chosen no city from any
tribe of Israel *in which* to build a house, that
My name might be there, nor did I choose any
man to be a ruler over My people Israel. [6]Yet I
have chosen Jerusalem, that My name may be
there, and I have chosen David to be over My
people Israel.' [7]Now it was in the heart of my
father David to build a temple for the name of
the LORD God of Israel. [8]But the LORD said to
my father David, 'Whereas it was in your heart
to build a temple for My name, you did well in
that it was in your heart. [9]Nevertheless you
shall not build the temple, but your son who
will come from your body, he shall build the
temple for My name.' [10]So the LORD has fulfilled His word which He spoke, and I have
filled the position of my father David, and sit
on the throne of Israel, as the LORD promised;
and I have built the temple for the name of the
LORD God of Israel. [11]And there I have put the
ark, in which *is* the covenant of the LORD
which He made with the children of Israel."

[12]Then *Solomon* stood before the altar of the
LORD in the presence of all the assembly of Israel, and spread out his hands [13](for Solomon
had made a bronze platform five cubits long,
five cubits wide, and three cubits high, and
had set it in the midst of the court; and he
stood on it, knelt down on his knees before all
the assembly of Israel, and spread out his
hands toward heaven); [14]and he said: "LORD
God of Israel, *there is* no God in heaven or on
earth like You, who keep *Your* covenant and
mercy with Your servants who walk before You
with all their hearts. [15]You have kept what
You promised Your servant David my father;
You have both spoken with Your mouth and fulfilled *it* with Your hand, as *it is* this day. [16]There-
fore, LORD God of Israel, now keep what You
promised Your servant David my father, saying, 'You shall not fail to have a man sit before
Me on the throne of Israel, only if your sons
take heed to their way, that they walk in My
law as you have walked before Me.' [17]And now,
O LORD God of Israel, let Your word come true,
which You have spoken to Your servant David.

[18]"But will God indeed dwell with men on
the earth? Behold, heaven and the heaven of
heavens cannot contain You. How much less
this temple which I have built! [19]Yet regard the
prayer of Your servant and his supplication, O
LORD my God, and listen to the cry and the
prayer which Your servant is praying before
You: [20]that Your eyes may be open toward this
temple day and night, toward the place where
You said *You would* put Your name, that You
may hear the prayer which Your servant
makes toward this place. [21]And may You hear
the supplications of Your servant and of Your
people Israel, when they pray toward this
place. Hear from heaven Your dwelling place,
and when You hear, forgive.

[22]"If anyone sins against his neighbor, and
is forced to take an oath, and comes *and* takes
an oath before Your altar in this temple, [23]then
hear from heaven, and act, and judge Your
servants, bringing retribution on the wicked
by bringing his way on his own head, and justifying the righteous by giving him according
to his righteousness.

[24]"Or if Your people Israel are defeated
before an enemy because they have sinned
against You, and return and confess Your
name, and pray and make supplication before
You in this temple, [25]then hear from heaven
and forgive the sin of Your people Israel, and
bring them back to the land which You gave to
them and their fathers.

[26]"When the heavens are shut up and there
is no rain because they have sinned against
You, when they pray toward this place and
confess Your name, and turn from their sin
because You afflict them, [27]then hear *in* heav-
en, and forgive the sin of Your servants, Your
people Israel, that You may teach them the
good way in which they should walk; and send
rain on Your land which You have given to
Your people as an inheritance.

[28]"When there is famine in the land, pestilence or blight or mildew, locusts or grasshoppers; when their enemies besiege them in the
land of their cities; whatever plague or whatever sickness *there is;* [29]whatever prayer, whatever supplication is *made* by anyone, or by all
Your people Israel, when each one knows his
own burden and his own grief, and spreads
out his hands to this temple: [30]then hear from
heaven Your dwelling place, and forgive, and
give to everyone according to all his ways,
whose heart You know (for You alone know
the hearts of the sons of men), [31]that they may
fear You, to walk in Your ways as long as they
live in the land which You gave to our fathers.

[32]"Moreover, concerning a foreigner, who is
not of Your people Israel, but has come from a
far country for the sake of Your great name
and Your mighty hand and Your outstretched
arm, when they come and pray in this temple;
[33]then hear from heaven Your dwelling place,
and do according to all for which the foreigner
calls to You, that all peoples of the earth may
know Your name and fear You, as *do* Your people
Israel, and that they may know that this temple
which I have built is called by Your name.

[34]"When Your people go out to battle against

their enemies, wherever You send them, and
when they pray to You toward this city which
You have chosen and the temple which I have
built for Your name, [35]then hear from heaven
their prayer and their supplication, and maintain
their cause.

[36]"When they sin against You (for *there is* no
one who does not sin), and You become angry
with them and deliver them to the enemy, and
they take them captive to a land far or near;
[37]*yet* when they come to themselves in the land
where they were carried captive, and repent,
and make supplication to You in the land of
their captivity, saying, 'We have sinned, we
have done wrong, and have committed
wickedness'; [38]and *when* they return to You
with all their heart and with all their soul in
the land of their captivity, where they have
been carried captive, and pray toward their
land which You gave to their fathers, the city
which You have chosen, and toward the temple which I have built for Your name: [39]then
hear from heaven Your dwelling place their
prayer and their supplications, and maintain
their cause, and forgive Your people who have
sinned against You. [40]Now, my God, I pray, let
Your eyes be open and *let* Your ears *be* attentive to the prayer *made* in this place.

41 "Now therefore,
Arise, O LORD God, to Your resting place,
You and the ark of Your strength.
Let Your priests, O LORD God, be
clothed with salvation,
And let Your saints rejoice in
goodness.

42 "O LORD God, do not turn away the face
of Your Anointed;
Remember the mercies of Your
servant David."

Psalm 79:11–13

11 Let the groaning of the prisoner come
before You;
According to the greatness of Your
power
Preserve those who are appointed to
die;
12 And return to our neighbors sevenfold
into their bosom
Their reproach with which they have
reproached You, O Lord.
13 So we, Your people and sheep of Your
pasture,
Will give You thanks forever;
We will show forth Your praise to all
generations.

Proverbs 20:13–14

13 Do not love sleep, lest you come to
poverty;
Open your eyes, *and* you will be
satisfied with bread.

14 "*It is* good for nothing," cries the buyer;
But when he has gone his way, then he
boasts.

Acts 13:1–25

13 Now in the church that was at Antioch
there were certain prophets and teachers: Barnabas, Simeon who was called Niger,
Lucius of Cyrene, Manaen who had been
brought up with Herod the tetrarch, and Saul.
[2]As they ministered to the Lord and fasted, the
Holy Spirit said, "Now separate to Me
Barnabas and Saul for the work to which I
have called them." [3]Then, having fasted and
prayed, and laid hands on them, they sent
them away.

[4]So, being sent out by the Holy Spirit, they
went down to Seleucia, and from there they
sailed to Cyprus. [5]And when they arrived in
Salamis, they preached the word of God in the
synagogues of the Jews. They also had John
as *their* assistant.

[6]Now when they had gone through the
island to Paphos, they found a certain sorcerer, a false prophet, a Jew whose name *was* Bar-
Jesus, [7]who was with the proconsul, Sergius
Paulus, an intelligent man. This man called for
Barnabas and Saul and sought to hear the
word of God. [8]But Elymas the sorcerer (for so
his name is translated) withstood them, seeking to turn the proconsul away from the faith.
[9]Then Saul, who also *is called* Paul, filled with
the Holy Spirit, looked intently at him [10]and
said, "O full of all deceit and all fraud, *you* son
of the devil, *you* enemy of all righteousness,
will you not cease perverting the straight
ways of the Lord? [11]And now, indeed, the hand

13:6 Paphos. The capital of Cyprus and thus the seat of the Roman government. It also was a great center for the worship of Aphrodite (Venus), and thus a hotbed for all kinds of immorality. **a certain sorcerer...a Jew.** "Sorcerer" is better translated "magician." Originally it carried no evil connotation, but later was used to describe all kinds of practitioners and dabblers in the occult. This particular magician put his knowledge to evil use.

of the Lord *is* upon you, and you shall be blind,
not seeing the sun for a time."
And immediately a dark mist fell on him, and
he went around seeking someone to lead him
by the hand. 12Then the proconsul believed,
when he saw what had been done, being
astonished at the teaching of the Lord.
13Now when Paul and his party set sail from
Paphos, they came to Perga in Pamphylia; and
John, departing from them, returned to Jerusalem. 14But when they departed from Perga, they
came to Antioch in Pisidia, and went into the
synagogue on the Sabbath day and sat down.
15And after the reading of the Law and the
Prophets, the rulers of the synagogue sent to
them, saying, "Men *and* brethren, if you have
any word of exhortation for the people, say on."
16Then Paul stood up, and motioning with *his*
hand said, "Men of Israel, and you who fear
God, listen: 17The God of this people Israel
chose our fathers, and exalted the people
when they dwelt as strangers in the land of
Egypt, and with an uplifted arm He brought
them out of it. 18Now for a time of about forty
years He put up with their ways in the wilderness. 19And when He had destroyed seven
nations in the land of Canaan, He distributed
their land to them by allotment.
20"After that He gave *them* judges for about
four hundred and fifty years, until Samuel the
prophet. 21And afterward they asked for a
king; so God gave them Saul the son of Kish,
a man of the tribe of Benjamin, for forty years.
22And when He had removed him, He raised
up for them David as king, to whom also He
gave testimony and said, *'I have found David*
the *son* of Jesse, *a man after My own heart,*
who will do all My will.' 23From this man's
seed, according to *the* promise, God raised up
for Israel a Savior— Jesus— 24after John had
first preached, before His coming, the baptism
of repentance to all the people of Israel. 25And
as John was finishing his course, he said, 'Who
do you think I am? I am not *He.* But behold,
there comes One after me, the sandals of
whose feet I am not worthy to loose.'

13:15 reading of the Law and the Prophets. The reading of the Scriptures. This occupied the third part in the liturgy of the synagogue, after the recitation of the *shema* (Deut. 6:4) and further prayers, but before the teaching, which was usually based on what had been read from the Scriptures. **rulers of the synagogue.** Those who had general oversight of the synagogue, including designating who would read from the Scriptures.

13:22 ***a man after My own heart.*** Some would question the reality of this designation for David since he proved to be such a sinner at times (1 Sam. 11:1–4; 12:9; 21:10–22:1). No man after God's own heart is perfect; yet he will recognize sin and repent of it, as did David (Pss. 32; 38; 51).

DAY 5: How does Acts 13 mark a change in the Book of Acts?

Chapter 13 marks a turning point in Acts in that the first 12 chapters focus on Peter while the remaining chapters revolve around Paul. With Peter, the emphasis is the Jewish church in Jerusalem and Judea; with Paul, the focus is the spread of the Gentile church throughout the Roman world, which began at the church in Antioch. In this church were certain "prophets" (v. 1). These men had a significant role in the apostolic church (1 Cor. 12:28; Eph. 2:20). They were preachers of God's Word and were responsible in the early years of the church to instruct local congregations. On some occasions, they received new revelation that was of a practical nature (11:28; 21:10), a function that ended with the cessation of the temporary sign gifts. Their office was also replaced by pastor-teachers and evangelists (Eph. 4:11).

The leaders in the church in Antioch "ministered to the Lord" (v. 2). This is from a Greek word which in Scripture describes priestly service. Serving in leadership in the church is an act of worship to God and consists of offering spiritual sacrifices to Him, including prayer, oversight of the flock, plus preaching and teaching the Word. And they "fasted." This is often connected with vigilant, passionate prayer (Neh. 1:4; Ps. 35:13; Dan. 9:3; Matt. 17:21; Luke 2:37) and includes either a loss of desire for food or the purposeful setting aside of eating to concentrate on spiritual issues (Matt. 6:16,17).

While they worshiped, the Holy Spirit issued the first missionary outreach: "Separate to Me Barnabas and Saul for the work to which I have called them" (v. 2). Saul and Barnabas chose to begin their missionary outreach in Cyprus because it was Barnabas's home, which was only a two-day journey from Antioch and had a large Jewish population. Here Paul established the custom of preaching to the Jews first whenever he entered a new city because he had an open door, as a Jew, to speak and introduce the gospel. Also, if he preached to Gentiles first, the Jews would never have listened to him.

JULY 6

2 Chronicles 7:1–8:18

7 When Solomon had finished praying, fire
came down from heaven and consumed
the burnt offering and the sacrifices; and the
glory of the LORD filled the temple. [2]And the
priests could not enter the house of the LORD,
because the glory of the LORD had filled the
LORD's house. [3]When all the children of Israel
saw how the fire came down, and the glory of
the LORD on the temple, they bowed their faces
to the ground on the pavement, and worshiped
and praised the LORD, *saying:*

"For *He is* good,
For His mercy *endures* forever."

[4]Then the king and all the people offered
sacrifices before the LORD. [5]King Solomon
offered a sacrifice of twenty-two thousand
bulls and one hundred and twenty thousand
sheep. So the king and all the people dedicated
the house of God. [6]And the priests attended to
their services; the Levites also with instruments of the music of the LORD, which King
David had made to praise the LORD, saying,
"For His mercy *endures* forever," whenever
David offered praise by their ministry. The
priests sounded trumpets opposite them,
while all Israel stood.

[7]Furthermore Solomon consecrated the
middle of the court that *was* in front of the
house of the LORD; for there he offered burnt
offerings and the fat of the peace offerings,
because the bronze altar which Solomon had
made was not able to receive the burnt offerings, the grain offerings, and the fat.

[8]At that time Solomon kept the feast seven
days, and all Israel with him, a very great
assembly from the entrance of Hamath to the
Brook of Egypt. [9]And on the eighth day they
held a sacred assembly, for they observed the
dedication of the altar seven days, and the
feast seven days. [10]On the twenty-third day of
the seventh month he sent the people away to
their tents, joyful and glad of heart for the
good that the LORD had done for David, for Solomon, and for His people Israel. [11]Thus Solomon finished the house of the LORD and the
king's house; and Solomon successfully accomplished all that came into his heart to make in
the house of the LORD and in his own house.

[12]Then the LORD appeared to Solomon by
night, and said to him: "I have heard your
prayer, and have chosen this place for Myself
as a house of sacrifice. [13]When I shut up heav-
en and there is no rain, or command the
locusts to devour the land, or send pestilence
among My people, [14]if My people who are
called by My name will humble themselves,
and pray and seek My face, and turn from
their wicked ways, then I will hear from heav-
en, and will forgive their sin and heal their
land. [15]Now My eyes will be open and My ears
attentive to prayer *made* in this place. [16]For
now I have chosen and sanctified this house,
that My name may be there forever; and My
eyes and My heart will be there perpetually.
[17]As for you, if you walk before Me as your
father David walked, and do according to all
that I have commanded you, and if you keep
My statutes and My judgments, [18]then I will
establish the throne of your kingdom, as I
covenanted with David your father, saying, 'You
shall not fail *to have* a man as ruler in Israel.'

7:17,18 if...then. If there was obedience on the part of the nation, the kingdom would be established and they would have "a man as ruler." Their disobedience was legendary and so was the destruction of their kingdom and their dispersion. When Israel is saved (Rom. 11:25–27; Zech. 12:14), then their King Messiah will set up this glorious kingdom (Rev. 20:1ff.).

[19]"But if you turn away and forsake My
statutes and My commandments which I have
set before you, and go and serve other gods,
and worship them, [20]then I will uproot them
from My land which I have given them; and
this house which I have sanctified for My
name I will cast out of My sight, and will make
it a proverb and a byword among all peoples.
[21]"And *as for* this house, which is exalted,
everyone who passes by it will be astonished
and say, 'Why has the LORD done thus to this
land and this house?' [22]Then they will answer,
'Because they forsook the LORD God of their
fathers, who brought them out of the land of
Egypt, and embraced other gods, and worshiped them and served them; therefore He
has brought all this calamity on them.' "

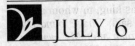

8 It came to pass at the end of twenty years,
when Solomon had built the house of the
LORD and his own house, [2]that the cities which
Hiram had given to Solomon, Solomon built
them; and he settled the children of Israel
there. [3]And Solomon went to Hamath Zobah
and seized it. [4]He also built Tadmor in the
wilderness, and all the storage cities which he

built in Hamath. [5]He built Upper Beth Horon
and Lower Beth Horon, fortified cities *with*
walls, gates, and bars, [6]also Baalath and all the
storage cities that Solomon had, and all the
chariot cities and the cities of the cavalry, and
all that Solomon desired to build in Jerusalem,
in Lebanon, and in all the land of his dominion.
[7]All the people *who were* left of the Hittites,
Amorites, Perizzites, Hivites, and Jebusites, who
were not of Israel— [8]that is, their descendants
who were left in the land after them, whom the
children of Israel did not destroy—from these
Solomon raised forced labor, as it is to this
day. [9]But Solomon did not make the children
of Israel servants for his work. Some *were*
men of war, captains of his officers, captains of
his chariots, and his cavalry. [10]And others *were*
chiefs of the officials of King Solomon: two
hundred and fifty, who ruled over the people.
[11]Now Solomon brought the daughter of
Pharaoh up from the City of David to the
house he had built for her, for he said, "My
wife shall not dwell in the house of David king
of Israel, because *the places* to which the ark of
the LORD has come are holy."

8:11 the daughter of Pharaoh. First Kings 3:1 mentions the marriage and the fact that Solomon brought her to Jerusalem until he could build a house for her. Until that palace was built, Solomon lived in David's palace, but did not allow her to do so, because she was a heathen and because the ark of God had once been in David's house. He surely knew his marriage to this pagan did not please God (Deut. 7:3,4). Eventually his pagan wives caused tragic consequences (1 Kin. 11:1–11).

[12]Then Solomon offered burnt offerings to
the LORD on the altar of the LORD which he
had built before the vestibule, [13]according to
the daily rate, offering according to the commandment of Moses, for the Sabbaths, the
New Moons, and the three appointed yearly
feasts—the Feast of Unleavened Bread, the
Feast of Weeks, and the Feast of Tabernacles.
[14]And, according to the order of David his
father, he appointed the divisions of the
priests for their service, the Levites for their
duties (to praise and serve before the priests)
as the duty of each day required, and the gatekeepers by their divisions at each gate; for so
David the man of God had commanded.
[15]They did not depart from the command of
the king to the priests and Levites concerning
any matter or concerning the treasuries.
[16]Now all the work of Solomon was well-
ordered from the day of the foundation of the
house of the LORD until it was finished. So the
house of the LORD was completed.
[17]Then Solomon went to Ezion Geber and
Elath on the seacoast, in the land of Edom.
[18]And Hiram sent him ships by the hand of his
servants, and servants who knew the sea.
They went with the servants of Solomon to
Ophir, and acquired four hundred and fifty talents of gold from there, and brought it to King
Solomon.

Psalm 80:1–6

To the Chief Musician. Set to "The Lilies."
A Testimony of Asaph. A Psalm.

Give ear, O Shepherd of Israel,
You who lead Joseph like a flock;
You who dwell *between* the cherubim,
shine forth!
2 Before Ephraim, Benjamin, and
Manasseh,
Stir up Your strength,
And come *and* save us!

3 Restore us, O God;
Cause Your face to shine,
And we shall be saved!

4 O LORD God of hosts,
How long will You be angry
Against the prayer of Your people?
5 You have fed them with the bread
of tears,
And given them tears to drink in
great measure.
6 You have made us a strife to our
neighbors,
And our enemies laugh among
themselves.

Proverbs 20:15

15 There is gold and a multitude of rubies,
But the lips of knowledge *are* a
precious jewel.

Acts 13:26–52

[26]"Men *and* brethren, sons of the family of
Abraham, and those among you who fear God,
to you the word of this salvation has been sent.
[27]For those who dwell in Jerusalem, and their
rulers, because they did not know Him, nor
even the voices of the Prophets which are read
every Sabbath, have fulfilled *them* in condemning *Him.* [28]And though they found no cause for
death *in Him,* they asked Pilate that He should
be put to death. [29]Now when they had fulfilled all
that was written concerning Him, they took

Him down from the tree and laid *Him* in a tomb.
30But God raised Him from the dead. 31He was
seen for many days by those who came up with
Him from Galilee to Jerusalem, who are His witnesses to the people. 32And we declare to you
glad tidings—that promise which was made to
the fathers. 33God has fulfilled this for us their
children, in that He has raised up Jesus. As it is
also written in the second Psalm:

13:29,30 tree...tomb...God raised. The Old Testament predicted the crucifixion of Christ on a cross (Ps. 22; Deut. 21), at the time when this particular form of execution was not used. His burial in a "tomb" was also prophesied (Is. 53:9), yet victims of crucifixions were commonly tossed into mass graves. The climax of Paul's message was the resurrection of Christ, the ultimate proof that Jesus is the Messiah and the fulfillment of 3 specific prophecies (vv. 33–35).

'You are My Son,
Today I have begotten You.'

34And that He raised Him from the dead, no
more to return to corruption, He has spoken
thus:

'I will give you the sure mercies of David.'

35Therefore He also says in another *Psalm:*

'You will not allow Your Holy One to
see corruption.'

36"For David, after he had served his own
generation by the will of God, fell asleep, was
buried with his fathers, and saw corruption; 37but
He whom God raised up saw no corruption.
38Therefore let it be known to you, brethren, that
through this Man is preached to you the forgiveness of sins; 39and by Him everyone who
believes is justified from all things from which
you could not be justified by the law of Moses.
40Beware therefore, lest what has been spoken
in the prophets come upon you:

41 *'Behold, you despisers,*
Marvel and perish!
For I work a work in your days,
A work which you will by no means
believe,
Though one were to declare it to you.' "

42So when the Jews went out of the synagogue,
the Gentiles begged that these words might be
preached to them the next Sabbath. 43Now when
the congregation had broken up, many of the
Jews and devout proselytes followed Paul and
Barnabas, who, speaking to them, persuaded
them to continue in the grace of God.

13:39 justified from. This is better translated "freed from." **you could not be justified by the law of Moses.** Keeping the Law of Moses did not free anyone from their sins (Rom. 3:28; 1 Cor. 1:30; Gal. 2:16; 3:11; Phil. 3:9). But the atoning death of Jesus completely satisfied the demands of God's law, making forgiveness of all sins available to all who believe (Gal. 3:16; Col. 2:13,14). Only the forgiveness Christ offers can free people from their sins (Rom. 3:20,22).

13:43 devout proselytes. Full converts to Judaism who had been circumcised. **continue in the grace of God.** Those who are truly saved persevere and validate the reality of their salvation by continuing in the grace of God (John 8:31; 15:1–6; Col. 1:21–23; 1 John 2:19). With such encouragement, Paul and Barnabas hoped to prevent those who were intellectually convinced of the truths of the gospel, yet had stopped short of saving faith, from reverting to legalism rather than embracing Christ completely.

44On the next Sabbath almost the whole city
came together to hear the word of God. 45But
when the Jews saw the multitudes, they were
filled with envy; and contradicting and blaspheming, they opposed the things spoken by
Paul. 46Then Paul and Barnabas grew bold and
said, "It was necessary that the word of God
should be spoken to you first; but since you
reject it, and judge yourselves unworthy of everlasting life, behold, we turn to the Gentiles. 47For
so the Lord has commanded us:

'I have set you as a light to the Gentiles,
That you should be for salvation to the
ends of the earth.' "

13:51 shook off the dust from their feet. The Jews' antagonism toward Gentiles extended to their unwillingness to even bring Gentile dust into Israel. The symbolism of Paul and Barnabas's act is clear that they considered the Jews at Antioch no better than heathen. There could have been no stronger condemnation.

48Now when the Gentiles heard this, they were glad and glorified the word of the Lord. And as many as had been appointed to eternal life believed.

49And the word of the Lord was being spread throughout all the region. 50But the Jews stirred up the devout and prominent women and the chief men of the city, raised up persecution against Paul and Barnabas, and expelled them from their region. 51But they shook off the dust from their feet against them, and came to Iconium. 52And the disciples were filled with joy and with the Holy Spirit.

DAY 6: How does a verse such as 2 Chronicles 7:14 relate to country such as America?

"If My people who are called by My name will humble themselves, and pray and seek My face, and turn from their wicked ways, then I will hear from heaven, and will forgive their sin and heal their land."

Unlike ancient Israel, America is not a covenant nation. God has made no promise to our physical ancestors that guarantees our national status. If Israel had to fulfill the conditions for divine blessing, even though God had covenanted with them as His chosen people, America certainly has no inviolable claim on the blessing of God. As long as unbelief and disobedience to the Word of God color the soul of our nation, we simply cannot expect the blessing of God. Israel didn't get it in her unbelief.

But for those of us who are Christians, the covenant blessings do apply. "If you are Christ's, then you are Abraham's seed, and heirs according to the promise" (Gal. 3:29). All the promises of salvation, mercy, forgiveness of sins, and spiritual prosperity are ours to claim as long as we remain faithful to God.

That is why the spiritual state of the church in our nation is the key to the blessing of the nation as a whole. If God is going to bless America, it will not be for the sake of the nation itself. He blesses the nation, and has always done so, for the sake of His people. If we who are called by His name are not fulfilling the conditions for divine blessing, there is no hope whatsoever for the rest of the nation.

On the other hand, if the church is fit to receive God's blessing, the whole nation will be the beneficiary of that, because the Word of God will be proclaimed with power, God will add to His church, and spiritual blessings of all kinds will result. And those are the truest blessings of all.

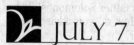

JULY 7

2 Chronicles 9:1–10:19

9 Now when the queen of Sheba heard of the fame of Solomon, she came to Jerusalem to test Solomon with hard questions, *having* a very great retinue, camels that bore spices, gold in abundance, and precious stones; and when she came to Solomon, she spoke with him about all that was in her heart. 2So Solomon answered all her questions; there was nothing so difficult for Solomon that he could not explain it to her. 3And when the queen of Sheba had seen the wisdom of Solomon, the house that he had built, 4the food on his table, the seating of his servants, the service of his waiters and their apparel, his cupbearers and their apparel, and his entryway by which he went up to the house of the LORD, there was no more spirit in her.

5Then she said to the king: "*It was* a true report which I heard in my own land about your words and your wisdom. 6However I did not believe their words until I came and saw with my own eyes; and indeed the half of the greatness of your wisdom was not told me. You exceed the fame of which I heard. 7Happy *are* your men and happy *are* these your servants, who stand continually before you and hear your wisdom! 8Blessed be the LORD your God, who delighted in you, setting you on His throne *to be* king for the LORD your God! Because your God has loved Israel, to establish them forever, therefore He made you king over them, to do justice and righteousness."

9And she gave the king one hundred and twenty talents of gold, spices in great abundance, and precious stones; there never were any spices such as those the queen of Sheba gave to King Solomon.

10Also, the servants of Hiram and the servants of Solomon, who brought gold from Ophir, brought algum wood and precious stones. 11And the king made walkways *of* the algum wood for the house of the LORD and for the king's house, also harps and stringed instruments for singers; and there were none such *as these* seen before in the land of Judah.

12Now King Solomon gave to the queen of Sheba all she desired, whatever she asked, *much more* than she had brought to the king.

So she turned and went to her own country,
she and her servants.
[13]The weight of gold that came to Solomon
yearly was six hundred and sixty-six talents of
gold, [14]besides *what* the traveling merchants
and traders brought. And all the kings of
Arabia and governors of the country brought
gold and silver to Solomon. [15]And King Solomon made two hundred large shields of hammered gold; six hundred *shekels* of hammered
gold went into each shield. [16]*He* also *made*
three hundred shields of hammered gold;
three hundred *shekels* of gold went into each
shield. The king put them in the House of the
Forest of Lebanon.
[17]Moreover the king made a great throne of
ivory, and overlaid it with pure gold. [18]The
throne *had* six steps, with a footstool of gold,
which were fastened to the throne; there were
armrests on either side of the place of the seat,
and two lions stood beside the armrests.
[19]Twelve lions stood there, one on each side of
the six steps; nothing like *this* had been made
for any *other* kingdom.
[20]All King Solomon's drinking vessels *were*
gold, and all the vessels of the House of the
Forest of Lebanon *were* pure gold. Not *one was*
silver, for this was accounted as nothing in the
days of Solomon. [21]For the king's ships went to
Tarshish with the servants of Hiram. Once
every three years the merchant ships came,
bringing gold, silver, ivory, apes, and monkeys.
[22]So King Solomon surpassed all the kings
of the earth in riches and wisdom. [23]And all the
kings of the earth sought the presence of Solomon to hear his wisdom, which God had put
in his heart. [24]Each man brought his present:
articles of silver and gold, garments, armor,
spices, horses, and mules, at a set rate year by
year.
[25]Solomon had four thousand stalls for horses and chariots, and twelve thousand horsemen whom he stationed in the chariot cities
and with the king at Jerusalem.
[26]So he reigned over all the kings from the
River to the land of the Philistines, as far as the
border of Egypt. [27]The king made silver *as common* in Jerusalem as stones, and he made cedar
trees as abundant as the sycamores which *are*
in the lowland. [28]And they brought horses to
Solomon from Egypt and from all lands.
[29]Now the rest of the acts of Solomon, first
and last, *are* they not written in the book of
Nathan the prophet, in the prophecy of Ahijah
the Shilonite, and in the visions of Iddo the
seer concerning Jeroboam the son of Nebat?
[30]Solomon reigned in Jerusalem over all Israel
forty years. [31]Then Solomon rested with his
fathers, and was buried in the City of David
his father. And Rehoboam his son reigned in
his place.

9:29 In later years, Solomon turned away from God; and, due to the influence of his wives, he led the nation into idolatry. This split the kingdom and sowed the seeds that led to its defeat and dispersion. The Chronicles do not record this sad end to Solomon's life because the focus is on encouraging the returning Jews from Babylon with God's pledge to them for a glorious future in the Davidic Covenant.

10 And Rehoboam went to Shechem, for all
Israel had gone to Shechem to make him
king. [2]So it happened, when Jeroboam the son
of Nebat heard *it* (he was in Egypt, where he
had fled from the presence of King Solomon),
that Jeroboam returned from Egypt. [3]Then
they sent for him and called him. And Jeroboam and all Israel came and spoke to Rehoboam, saying, [4]"Your father made our yoke heavy;
now therefore, lighten the burdensome service
of your father and his heavy yoke which he put
on us, and we will serve you."
[5]So he said to them, "Come back to me after
three days." And the people departed.
[6]Then King Rehoboam consulted the elders
who stood before his father Solomon while he
still lived, saying, "How do you advise *me* to
answer these people?"
[7]And they spoke to him, saying, "If you are
kind to these people, and please them, and
speak good words to them, they will be your
servants forever."
[8]But he rejected the advice which the elders
had given him, and consulted the young men
who had grown up with him, who stood before
him. [9]And he said to them, "What advice do
you give? How should we answer this people
who have spoken to me, saying, 'Lighten the
yoke which your father put on us'?"
[10]Then the young men who had grown up
with him spoke to him, saying, "Thus you
should speak to the people who have spoken to
you, saying, 'Your father made our yoke
heavy, but you make *it* lighter on us'—thus
you shall say to them: 'My little *finger* shall be
thicker than my father's waist! [11]And now, whereas my father put a heavy yoke on you, I will add
to your yoke; my father chastised you with
whips, but I *will chastise you* with scourges!' "
[12]So Jeroboam and all the people came to
Rehoboam on the third day, as the king had
directed, saying, "Come back to me the third

day." 13Then the king answered them roughly.
King Rehoboam rejected the advice of the elders, 14and he spoke to them according to the
advice of the young men, saying, "My father
made your yoke heavy, but I will add to it; my
father chastised you with whips, but I *will chastise you* with scourges!" 15So the king did not listen to the people; for the turn *of events* was from
God, that the LORD might fulfill His word, which
He had spoken by the hand of Ahijah the
Shilonite to Jeroboam the son of Nebat.
16Now when all Israel *saw* that the king did
not listen to them, the people answered the
king, saying:

"What share have we in David?
We have no inheritance in the son of
Jesse.
Every man to your tents, O Israel!
Now see to your own house, O David!"

So all Israel departed to their tents. 17But
Rehoboam reigned over the children of Israel
who dwelt in the cities of Judah.
18Then King Rehoboam sent Hadoram, who
was in charge of revenue; but the children of
Israel stoned him with stones, and he died.
Therefore King Rehoboam mounted *his* chariot in haste to flee to Jerusalem. 19So Israel has
been in rebellion against the house of David to
this day.

Psalm 80:7–13

7 Restore us, O God of hosts;
Cause Your face to shine,
And we shall be saved!

8 You have brought a vine out of Egypt;
You have cast out the nations, and
planted it.

80:8 vine out of Egypt. The vine is a metaphor for Israel, whom God delivered out of Egypt and nurtured into a powerful nation (Is. 5:1–7; 27:2–6; Matt. 21:33–40).

9 You prepared *room* for it,
And caused it to take deep root,
And it filled the land.
10 The hills were covered with its shadow,
And the mighty cedars with its boughs.
11 She sent out her boughs to the Sea,
And her branches to the River.
12 Why have You broken down her hedges,
So that all who pass by the way pluck
her *fruit?*
13 The boar out of the woods uproots it,
And the wild beast of the field
devours it.

Proverbs 20:16–18

16 Take the garment of one who is surety
for a stranger,
And hold it as a pledge *when it* is for
a seductress.

20:16 Garments were common security for a loan but they always had to be returned by sundown (Ex. 22:26,27; Deut. 24:10–13). "Seductress" is more likely "foreigner." Anyone who foolishly has taken on the responsibility for the debt of a stranger or an immoral woman will likely never be paid back, so he will never pay his creditor unless his own garment is taken as security.

17 Bread gained by deceit *is* sweet
to a man,
But afterward his mouth will be filled
with gravel.
18 Plans are established by counsel;
By wise counsel wage war.

Acts 14:1–28

14 Now it happened in Iconium that they
went together to the synagogue of the
Jews, and so spoke that a great multitude both
of the Jews and of the Greeks believed. 2But
the unbelieving Jews stirred up the Gentiles
and poisoned their minds against the brethren.
3Therefore they stayed there a long time,
speaking boldly in the Lord, who was bearing
witness to the word of His grace, granting
signs and wonders to be done by their hands.
4But the multitude of the city was divided:
part sided with the Jews, and part with the
apostles. 5And when a violent attempt was

14:4 apostles. Barnabas was not an apostle in the same sense as Paul and the 12 since he was not an eyewitness of the resurrected Christ nor had he been called by Him. It is best to translate "apostles" here as "messengers" (2 Cor. 8:23; Phil. 2:25). The verb means "to send." The 12 and Paul were "apostles of Christ" (2 Cor. 11:13; 1 Thess. 2:6), while Barnabas and others were "apostles of the churches" (2 Cor. 8:23).

made by both the Gentiles and Jews, with
their rulers, to abuse and stone them, [6]they
became aware of it and fled to Lystra and
Derbe, cities of Lycaonia, and to the surrounding region. [7]And they were preaching
the gospel there.
[8]And in Lystra a certain man without strength
in his feet was sitting, a cripple from his mother's womb, who had never walked. [9]*This* man
heard Paul speaking. Paul, observing him
intently and seeing that he had faith to be
healed, [10]said with a loud voice, "Stand up
straight on your feet!" And he leaped and
walked. [11]Now when the people saw what Paul
had done, they raised their voices, saying in
the Lycaonian *language,* "The gods have
come down to us in the likeness of men!"
[12]And Barnabas they called Zeus, and Paul,
Hermes, because he was the chief speaker.
[13]Then the priest of Zeus, whose temple was in
front of their city, brought oxen and garlands
to the gates, intending to sacrifice with the
multitudes.
[14]But when the apostles Barnabas and Paul
heard this, they tore their clothes and ran in
among the multitude, crying out [15]and saying,
"Men, why are you doing these things? We also
are men with the same nature as you, and
preach to you that you should turn from these
useless things to the living God, who made the
heaven, the earth, the sea, and all things that are
in them, [16]who in bygone generations allowed all
nations to walk in their own ways. [17]Neverthe-
less He did not leave Himself without witness, in
that He did good, gave us rain from heaven and
fruitful seasons, filling our hearts with food and
gladness." [18]And with these sayings they could
scarcely restrain the multitudes from sacrificing
to them.
[19]Then Jews from Antioch and Iconium
came there; and having persuaded the multitudes, they stoned Paul *and* dragged *him* out
of the city, supposing him to be dead. [20]How-
ever, when the disciples gathered around him,
he rose up and went into the city. And the next
day he departed with Barnabas to Derbe.
[21]And when they had preached the gospel to
that city and made many disciples, they
returned to Lystra, Iconium, and Antioch,
[22]strengthening the souls of the disciples, exhorting *them* to continue in the faith, and *say-*
ing, "We must through many tribulations enter
the kingdom of God." [23]So when they had appointed elders in every church, and prayed
with fasting, they commended them to the
Lord in whom they had believed. [24]And after
they had passed through Pisidia, they came to
Pamphylia. [25]Now when they had preached the
word in Perga, they went down to Attalia.
[26]From there they sailed to Antioch, where
they had been commended to the grace of
God for the work which they had completed.
[27]Now when they had come and gathered the
church together, they reported all that God had
done with them, and that He had opened the
door of faith to the Gentiles. [28]So they stayed
there a long time with the disciples.

14:15–17 Because the crowd at Lystra was pagan and had no knowledge of the Old Testament, Paul adjusted his message to fit the audience. Instead of proclaiming the God of Abraham, Isaac, and Jacob, he appealed to the universal and rational knowledge of the One who created the world (17:22–26; Jon. 1:9).

14:17 did not leave Himself without witness. God's providence and His creative power testify to man's reason of His existence (Rom. 1:18–20), as does man's own conscience, which contains His moral law (Rom. 2:13–15).

DAY 7: How does Acts 14 demonstrate the varied reactions for preaching the gospel of Christ?

The city of Iconium was a cultural melting pot of native Phrygians, Greeks, Jews, and Roman colonists. A great multitude came to faith as Paul and Barnabas spoke "boldly in the Lord, who was bearing witness to the word of His grace, granting signs and wonders to be done by their hands" (v. 3). Acts of such divine power confirmed that Paul and Barnabas spoke for God. Nevertheless, the gospel message divided the city and a violent attempt was made by both the Gentiles and Jews, with their rulers, to abuse and stone them (v. 5). This proves that their Jewish opponents were the instigators, since stoning was a Jewish form of execution, usually for blasphemy.

Fleeing Iconium, they went to Lystra and Derbe, cities of Lycaonia (v. 6). Lycaonia was a district in the Roman province of Galatia. Lystra was about 18 miles from Iconium and was the home of Lois, Eunice, and Timothy (16:1; 2 Tim. 1:5). The strange reaction by the people of Lystra to the healing of the cripple, who had never walked (v. 8), had its roots in local folklore. According to tradition, the gods Zeus and Hermes visited Lystra incognito, asking for food and lodging. All turned them away except for a peasant named Philemon and his wife, Baucis. The gods took vengeance by drowning everyone in a flood. But they turned the lowly cottage of Philemon and Baucis into a temple, where they were to serve as priest and priestess. Not wanting to repeat their ancestors' mistake, the people of Lystra believed Barnabas to be Zeus and Paul to be Hermes.

"Then Jews from Antioch and Iconium came there…they stoned Paul…supposing him to be dead" (v. 19). Paul did not die from the stoning as some claim, who link it to his third-heaven experience in 2 Corinthians 12. "Supposing" usually means "to suppose something that is not true." The main New Testament use of this word argues that the crowd's supposition was incorrect and that Paul was not dead. Another argument in favor of this position is that if Paul was resurrected, why didn't Luke mention it? Also, the dates of Paul's third-heaven experience and the time of the stoning do not reconcile.

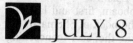

JULY 8

2 Chronicles 11:1–12:16

11 Now when Rehoboam came to Jerusalem, he assembled from the house of Judah and Benjamin one hundred and eighty
thousand chosen *men* who were warriors, to
fight against Israel, that he might restore the
kingdom to Rehoboam.
2But the word of the LORD came to Shemaiah
the man of God, saying, 3"Speak to Rehoboam
the son of Solomon, king of Judah, and to all Israel in Judah and Benjamin, saying, 4'Thus
says the LORD: "You shall not go up or fight
against your brethren! Let every man return to
his house, for this thing is from Me." ' "
Therefore they obeyed the words of the LORD,
and turned back from attacking Jeroboam.
5So Rehoboam dwelt in Jerusalem, and built
cities for defense in Judah. 6And he built Bethlehem, Etam, Tekoa, 7Beth Zur, Sochoh, Adullam,
8Gath, Mareshah, Ziph, 9Adoraim, Lachish,
Azekah, 10Zorah, Aijalon, and Hebron, which
are in Judah and Benjamin, fortified cities.
11And he fortified the strongholds, and put captains in them, and stores of food, oil, and wine.
12Also in every city *he put* shields and spears,
and made them very strong, having Judah and
Benjamin on his side.
13And from all their territories the priests
and the Levites who *were* in all Israel took
their stand with him. 14For the Levites left their
common-lands and their possessions and
came to Judah and Jerusalem, for Jeroboam
and his sons had rejected them from serving
as priests to the LORD. 15Then he appointed for
himself priests for the high places, for the
demons, and the calf idols which he had
made. 16And after *the Levites left,* those from all
the tribes of Israel, such as set their heart to
seek the LORD God of Israel, came to Jerusalem to sacrifice to the LORD God of their
fathers. 17So they strengthened the kingdom of
Judah, and made Rehoboam the son of Solomon strong for three years, because they
walked in the way of David and Solomon for
three years.
18Then Rehoboam took for himself as wife
Mahalath the daughter of Jerimoth the son of
David, *and of* Abihail the daughter of Eliah the
son of Jesse. 19And she bore him children:
Jeush, Shamariah, and Zaham. 20After her he
took Maachah the granddaughter of Absalom;
and she bore him Abijah, Attai, Ziza, and
Shelomith. 21Now Rehoboam loved Maachah
the granddaughter of Absalom more than all
his wives and his concubines; for he took eighteen wives and sixty concubines, and begot twenty-
eight sons and sixty daughters. 22And Rehoboam
appointed Abijah the son of Maachah as chief, *to
be* leader among his brothers; for he *intended* to
make him king. 23He dealt wisely, and dispersed
some of his sons throughout all the territories
of Judah and Benjamin, to every fortified city;
and he gave them provisions in abundance. He
also sought many wives *for them.*

12 Now it came to pass, when Rehoboam
had established the kingdom and had
strengthened himself, that he forsook the law
of the LORD, and all Israel along with him. 2And
it happened in the fifth year of King Rehoboam
that Shishak king of Egypt came up against Jerusalem, because they had transgressed
against the LORD, 3with twelve hundred chariots,
sixty thousand horsemen, and people without

12:2–5 Shishak. He ruled over Egypt ca. 945–924 B.C. An Egyptian record of this invasion written on stone has been found, recording that Shishak's army penetrated all the way north to the Sea of Galilee. He wanted to restore Egypt's once-great power, but was unable to conquer both Israel and Judah. However, he was able to destroy cities in Judah and gain some control of trade routes. Judah came under Egyptian control.

number who came with him out of Egypt—the
Lubim and the Sukkiim and the Ethiopians.
4And he took the fortified cities of Judah and
came to Jerusalem.

5Then Shemaiah the prophet came to
Rehoboam and the leaders of Judah, who were
gathered together in Jerusalem because of
Shishak, and said to them, "Thus says the
LORD: 'You have forsaken Me, and therefore I
also have left you in the hand of Shishak.' "

6So the leaders of Israel and the king humbled themselves; and they said, "The LORD *is*
righteous."

7Now when the LORD saw that they humbled
themselves, the word of the LORD came to
Shemaiah, saying, "They have humbled themselves; *therefore* I will not destroy them, but I will
grant them some deliverance. My wrath shall
not be poured out on Jerusalem by the hand of
Shishak. 8Nevertheless they will be his servants,
that they may distinguish My service from the
service of the kingdoms of the nations."

12:6,7 humbled themselves. In the face of the Egyptian conqueror, the leaders responded to the word of God through the prophet (v. 5) and repented, so that God would end His wrath worked through Shishak.

12:8 Nevertheless. A fitting punishment arose to remind the Jews of their heritage in relationship to Egypt. This was the first major military encounter with Egypt since the Exodus had ended hundreds of years of slavery there. A taste of being enslaved again to a people from whom God had given liberation was bitter. The message was crystal clear—if the Jews would forsake the true worship of God, they would also lose His protective hand of blessing. It was much better to serve God than to have to serve "kingdoms of the nations."

9So Shishak king of Egypt came up against
Jerusalem, and took away the treasures of the
house of the LORD and the treasures of the
king's house; he took everything. He also carried away the gold shields which Solomon had
made. 10Then King Rehoboam made bronze
shields in their place, and committed *them* to
the hands of the captains of the guard, who
guarded the doorway of the king's house.
11And whenever the king entered the house of
the LORD, the guard would go and bring them
out; then they would take them back into the
guardroom. 12When he humbled himself, the
wrath of the LORD turned from him, so as not
to destroy *him* completely; and things also
went well in Judah.

13Thus King Rehoboam strengthened himself in Jerusalem and reigned. Now Rehoboam
was forty-one years old when he became king;
and he reigned seventeen years in Jerusalem,
the city which the LORD had chosen out of all
the tribes of Israel, to put His name there. His
mother's name *was* Naamah, an Ammonitess.
14And he did evil, because he did not prepare
his heart to seek the LORD.

15The acts of Rehoboam, first and last, *are*
they not written in the book of Shemaiah the
prophet, and of Iddo the seer concerning
genealogies? And *there were* wars between
Rehoboam and Jeroboam all their days. 16So
Rehoboam rested with his fathers, and was
buried in the City of David. Then Abijah his
son reigned in his place.

Psalm 80:14–19

14 Return, we beseech You, O God of hosts;
Look down from heaven and see,
And visit this vine
15 And the vineyard which Your right
hand has planted,
And the branch *that* You made strong
for Yourself.
16 *It is* burned with fire, *it is* cut down;
They perish at the rebuke of Your
countenance.
17 Let Your hand be upon the man of Your
right hand,
Upon the son of man *whom* You made
strong for Yourself.

80:17 son of man. In this context, this phrase is primarily a reference to Israel. In a secondary sense, the "son of man" may allude to the Davidic dynasty and even extend to the Messiah, since He is so frequently called by that title in the New Testament.

18 Then we will not turn back from You;
Revive us, and we will call upon Your
name.

19 Restore us, O LORD God of hosts;
Cause Your face to shine,
And we shall be saved!

Proverbs 20:19–21

19 He who goes about *as* a talebearer
reveals secrets;

Therefore do not associate with one who
flatters with his lips.

20 Whoever curses his father or his
mother,
His lamp will be put out in deep
darkness.

21 An inheritance gained hastily at the
beginning
Will not be blessed at the end.

20:21 gained hastily. This implies an unjust method in gaining the inheritance, so that it will be lost by the same unjust ways or by punishment.

Acts 15:1–21

15 And certain *men* came down from Judea and taught the brethren, "Unless you are circumcised according to the custom of Moses, you cannot be saved."
[2]Therefore,
when Paul and Barnabas had no small dissension and dispute with them, they determined that Paul and Barnabas and certain others of them should go up to Jerusalem, to the apostles and elders, about this question.
[3]So, being sent on their way by the church, they passed through Phoenicia and Samaria, describing the conversion of the Gentiles; and they caused great joy to all the brethren.
[4]And
when they had come to Jerusalem, they were received by the church and the apostles and the elders; and they reported all things that God had done with them.
[5]But some of the sect
of the Pharisees who believed rose up, saying, "It is necessary to circumcise them, and to command *them* to keep the law of Moses."
[6]Now the apostles and elders came together
to consider this matter.
[7]And when there had
been much dispute, Peter rose up *and* said to them: "Men *and* brethren, you know that a good while ago God chose among us, that by my mouth the Gentiles should hear the word of the gospel and believe.
[8]So God, who knows
the heart, acknowledged them by giving them the Holy Spirit, just as *He did* to us,
[9]and made
no distinction between us and them, purifying their hearts by faith.
[10]Now therefore, why do
you test God by putting a yoke on the neck of the disciples which neither our fathers nor we were able to bear?
[11]But we believe that
through the grace of the Lord Jesus Christ we shall be saved in the same manner as they."
[12]Then all the multitude kept silent and lis-
tened to Barnabas and Paul declaring how many miracles and wonders God had worked through them among the Gentiles.
[13]And after
they had become silent, James answered, saying, "Men *and* brethren, listen to me:
[14]Simon
has declared how God at the first visited the Gentiles to take out of them a people for His name.
[15]And with this the words of the
prophets agree, just as it is written:

16 *'After this I will return*
And will rebuild the tabernacle of
David, which has fallen down;
I will rebuild its ruins,
And I will set it up;
17 *So that the rest of mankind may seek*
the LORD,
Even all the Gentiles who are called by
My name,
Says the LORD who does all these
things.'

15:19 we should not trouble. The Greek word for "trouble" means "to throw something in the path of someone to annoy them." The decision of the Jerusalem Council, after considering all the evidence, was that keeping the law and observing rituals were not requirements for salvation. The Judaizers were to cease troubling and annoying the Gentiles.

[18]"Known to God from eternity are all His
works.
[19]Therefore I judge that we should not
trouble those from among the Gentiles who are turning to God,
[20]but that we write to them
to abstain from things polluted by idols, *from* sexual immorality, *from* things strangled, and *from* blood.
[21]For Moses has had throughout
many generations those who preach him in every city, being read in the synagogues every Sabbath."

DAY 8: Why is the first church council in Acts 15 the most important ever held?

Throughout its history, the church's leaders have met to settle doctrinal issues. Historians point to 7 ecumenical councils in the church's early history, especially the Councils of Nicea (A.D. 325) and Chalcedon (A.D. 451). Yet the most important council was the first one—the Jerusalem Council—because it established the answer to the most vital doctrinal question of all: "What must a person do to be saved?" The apostles and elders defied efforts to impose legalism and ritualism as necessary prerequisites for salvation. They forever affirmed that salvation is totally by grace through faith in Christ alone.

The Judaizers were false teachers who were self-appointed guardians of legalism. They taught a doctrine of salvation by works through the act of circumcision (v. 1). In answer to this, Peter rose up and gave the first of 3 speeches at the Council that amount to one of the strongest defenses of salvation by grace through faith alone contained in Scripture. Peter began his defense by reviewing how God saved Gentiles in the early days of the church without a requirement of circumcision, law keeping, or ritual—referring to the salvation of Cornelius and his household (10:44–48; 11:17,18). If God did not require any additional qualifications for salvation, neither should the legalists.

The Judaizers could have argued that Cornelius and the others could not have been saved because they did not meet the legalistic requirements. To thwart that potential argument, Peter reiterates that God gave them the Holy Spirit, thus proving the genuineness of their salvation (v. 8). Peter warns the Judaizers that they are putting a yoke on the neck of the disciples—a description of the law and the legalism of the scribes and Pharisees (Matt. 23:4; Luke 11:46). The legalists expected the Gentiles to carry a load they themselves were unwilling to bear. "But we believe that through the grace of the Lord Jesus Christ we shall be saved" (v. 11). His declaration is a resounding affirmation of salvation by grace through faith alone.

JULY 9

2 Chronicles 13:1–14:15

13 In the eighteenth year of King Jeroboam,
Abijah became king over Judah. 2He
reigned three years in Jerusalem. His mother's name *was* Michaiah the daughter of Uriel
of Gibeah.

And there was war between Abijah and
Jeroboam. 3Abijah set the battle in order with an
army of valiant warriors, four hundred thousand choice men. Jeroboam also drew up in battle formation against him with eight hundred
thousand choice men, mighty men of valor.

4Then Abijah stood on Mount Zemaraim,
which *is* in the mountains of Ephraim, and
said, "Hear me, Jeroboam and all Israel:
5Should you not know that the LORD God of Israel gave the dominion over Israel to David
forever, to him and his sons, by a covenant of
salt? 6Yet Jeroboam the son of Nebat, the servant of Solomon the son of David, rose up and
rebelled against his lord. 7Then worthless
rogues gathered to him, and strengthened
themselves against Rehoboam the son of Solomon, when Rehoboam was young and inexperienced and could not withstand them. 8And
now you think to withstand the kingdom of
the LORD, which is in the hand of the sons of
David; and you *are* a great multitude, and with
you are the gold calves which Jeroboam made
for you as gods. 9Have you not cast out the
priests of the LORD, the sons of Aaron, and the
Levites, and made for yourselves priests, like
the peoples of *other* lands, so that whoever
comes to consecrate himself with a young bull
and seven rams may be a priest of *things that
are* not gods? 10But as for us, the LORD *is* our
God, and we have not forsaken Him; and the
priests who minister to the LORD *are* the sons
of Aaron, and the Levites *attend* to *their* duties.
11And they burn to the LORD every morning
and every evening burnt sacrifices and sweet
incense; *they* also *set* the showbread *in order on*
the pure *gold* table, and the lampstand of gold
with its lamps to burn every evening; for we
keep the command of the LORD our God, but
you have forsaken Him. 12Now look, God
Himself is with us as *our* head, and His priests
with sounding trumpets to sound the alarm
against you. O children of Israel, do not fight
against the LORD God of your fathers, for you
shall not prosper!"

13But Jeroboam caused an ambush to go
around behind them; so they were in front of
Judah, and the ambush *was* behind them.

13:15 God struck Jeroboam and all Israel. At the time of certain defeat, with 400,000 troops behind and the same number in front, Judah was saved by divine intervention. What God did is unknown, but the army of Israel began to flee (v. 16), and the soldiers of Judah massacred 500,000 of them in an unimaginable blood bath (v. 17).

13:17 Before the battle, Jeroboam outnumbered Abijah two to one (13:3). After the fray, in which the Lord intervened on behalf of Judah, Abijah outnumbered Jeroboam 4 to 3.

14 And when Judah looked around, to their surprise the battle line *was* at both front and rear;
and they cried out to the LORD, and the priests
sounded the trumpets. 15 Then the men of Judah gave a shout; and as the men of Judah
shouted, it happened that God struck
Jeroboam and all Israel before Abijah and Judah. 16 And the children of Israel fled before Judah, and God delivered them into their hand.
17 Then Abijah and his people struck them with
a great slaughter; so five hundred thousand
choice men of Israel fell slain. 18 Thus the children of Israel were subdued at that time; and
the children of Judah prevailed, because they
relied on the LORD God of their fathers.

19 And Abijah pursued Jeroboam and took
cities from him: Bethel with its villages,
Jeshanah with its villages, and Ephrain with its
villages. 20 So Jeroboam did not recover
strength again in the days of Abijah; and the
LORD struck him, and he died.

21 But Abijah grew mighty, married fourteen
wives, and begot twenty-two sons and sixteen
daughters. 22 Now the rest of the acts of Abijah,
his ways, and his sayings *are* written in the annals of the prophet Iddo.

14 So Abijah rested with his fathers, and they
buried him in the City of David. Then
Asa his son reigned in his place. In his days
the land was quiet for ten years.

2 Asa did *what was* good and right in the eyes
of the LORD his God, 3 for he removed the altars
of the foreign *gods* and the high places, and
broke down the *sacred* pillars and cut down
the wooden images. 4 He commanded Judah to
seek the LORD God of their fathers, and to
observe the law and the commandment. 5 He
also removed the high places and the incense
altars from all the cities of Judah, and the kingdom was quiet under him. 6 And he built fortified cities in Judah, for the land had rest; he
had no war in those years, because the LORD
had given him rest. 7 Therefore he said to Judah, "Let us build these cities and make walls
around *them,* and towers, gates, and bars,
while the land *is* yet before us, because we
have sought the LORD our God; we have
sought *Him,* and He has given us rest on every
side." So they built and prospered. 8 And Asa
had an army of three hundred thousand from
Judah who carried shields and spears, and
from Benjamin two hundred and eighty thousand men who carried shields and drew bows;
all these *were* mighty men of valor.

9 Then Zerah the Ethiopian came out against
them with an army of a million men and three
hundred chariots, and he came to Mareshah.
10 So Asa went out against him, and they set the
troops in battle array in the Valley of
Zephathah at Mareshah. 11 And Asa cried out to
the LORD his God, and said, "LORD, *it is* nothing
for You to help, whether with many or with
those who have no power; help us, O LORD our
God, for we rest on You, and in Your name we
go against this multitude. O LORD, You *are* our
God; do not let man prevail against You!"

12 So the LORD struck the Ethiopians before
Asa and Judah, and the Ethiopians fled. 13 And
Asa and the people who *were* with him pursued them to Gerar. So the Ethiopians were
overthrown, and they could not recover, for
they were broken before the LORD and His
army. And they carried away very much spoil.
14 Then they defeated all the cities around
Gerar, for the fear of the LORD came upon
them; and they plundered all the cities, for
there was exceedingly much spoil in them.
15 They also attacked the livestock enclosures,
and carried off sheep and camels in abundance, and returned to Jerusalem.

Psalm 81:1–5

To the Chief Musician. On an instrument of Gath.
A Psalm of Asaph.

Sing aloud to God our strength;
Make a joyful shout to the God
of Jacob.
2 Raise a song and strike the timbrel,
The pleasant harp with the lute.
3 Blow the trumpet at the time of the
New Moon,
At the full moon, on our solemn feast day.
4 For this *is* a statute for Israel,
A law of the God of Jacob.
5 This He established in Joseph *as* a
testimony,
When He went throughout the land
of Egypt,
Where I heard a language I did not
understand.

81:3 New Moon...full moon. The seventh month of Israel's year (Tishri; Sept./Oct.) culminated the festival year with a succession of celebrations. The month began with the blowing of the trumpets, continued with the Day of Atonement on the tenth day, and celebrated the Feast of Tabernacles on the fifteenth day when the moon was full. The Feast of Tabernacles praised God for His care in the wilderness wanderings and also pointed to the coming kingdom (Matt. 17:1–4).

Proverbs 20:22–23

22 Do not say, "I will recompense evil";
Wait for the LORD, and He will save you.
23 Diverse weights *are* an abomination to
the LORD,
And dishonest scales *are* not good.

Acts 15:22–41

22 Then it pleased the apostles and elders, with
the whole church, to send chosen men of their
own company to Antioch with Paul and Barnabas,
namely, Judas who was also named Barsabas, and
Silas, leading men among the brethren.
23 They wrote this *letter* by them:

The apostles, the elders, and the
brethren,
To the brethren who are of the
Gentiles in Antioch, Syria, and Cilicia:

Greetings.

24 Since we have heard that some who
went out from us have troubled you
with words, unsettling your souls,
saying, "*You must* be circumcised and
keep the law"—to whom we gave no
such commandment— 25 it seemed good
to us, being assembled with one
accord, to send chosen men to you
with our beloved Barnabas and Paul,
26 men who have risked their lives for
the name of our Lord Jesus Christ.
27 We have therefore sent Judas and
Silas, who will also report the same
things by word of mouth. 28 For it
seemed good to the Holy Spirit, and to
us, to lay upon you no greater burden
than these necessary things: 29 that you
abstain from things offered to idols,
from blood, from things strangled, and
from sexual immorality. If you keep
yourselves from these, you will do well.

Farewell.

30 So when they were sent off, they came to
Antioch; and when they had gathered the multitude together, they delivered the letter.
31 When they had read it, they rejoiced over its
encouragement. 32 Now Judas and Silas, themselves being prophets also, exhorted and
strengthened the brethren with many words.
33 And after they had stayed *there* for a time,
they were sent back with greetings from the
brethren to the apostles.
34 However, it seemed good to Silas to remain
there. 35 Paul and Barnabas also remained in
Antioch, teaching and preaching the word of
the Lord, with many others also.
36 Then after some days Paul said to
Barnabas, "Let us now go back and visit our
brethren in every city where we have preached
the word of the Lord, *and see* how they are
doing." 37 Now Barnabas was determined to
take with them John called Mark. 38 But Paul
insisted that they should not take with them
the one who had departed from them in
Pamphylia, and had not gone with them to the
work. 39 Then the contention became so sharp
that they parted from one another. And so
Barnabas took Mark and sailed to Cyprus;
40 but Paul chose Silas and departed, being
commended by the brethren to the grace of
God. 41 And he went through Syria and Cilicia,
strengthening the churches.

15:24 troubled...unsettling. "Troubled" is a different Greek word from the one in v. 19, meaning "to deeply upset," "to deeply disturb," "to perplex," or "to create fear." The Greek word for "unsettling" was used in extrabiblical writings to speak of someone going bankrupt. Together these words aptly describe the chaos caused by the Judaizers.

15:36 *see* how they are doing. In addition to proclaiming the gospel, Paul also recognized his responsibility to mature the new believers in their faith (Matt. 28:19,20; Eph. 4:12,13; Phil. 1:8; Col. 1:28; 1 Thess. 2:17). So he planned his second missionary journey to retrace his first one.

15:39 contention...parted. This was not an amicable parting—they were in sharp disagreement regarding John Mark. The weight of the evidence favors Paul's decision, especially since he was an apostle of Jesus Christ. That alone should have caused Barnabas to submit to his authority. But they eventually did reconcile (1 Cor. 9:6).

15:40 Silas. He was perfectly suited to be Paul's companion, since he was a prophet and could proclaim and teach the Word. Being a Jew gave him access to the synagogues. Because he was a Roman citizen (16:37), he enjoyed the same benefits and protection as Paul. His status as a respected leader in the Jerusalem fellowship helped to reinforce Paul's teaching that Gentile salvation was by grace alone through faith alone.

DAY 9: How did a godly king respond to crises?

Second Chronicles 14:1–16:14 records the reign of Asa in Judah (ca. 911–870 B.C.). First Kings 15:11 says that Asa did as his forefather David had done—honoring God while building the kingdom (vv. 6–8). Times of peace were used for strengthening. "Asa did what was good and right in the eyes of LORD his God" (v. 2). He removed elements of false worship that had accumulated over the years of Solomon, Rehoboam, and Abijah (1 Kin. 15:12,13). Apparently, he did not remove all the high places or, once removed, they reappeared (1 Kin. 15:14; 1 Chr. 15:6). His son Jehoshaphat later had to remove them (2 Chr. 17:6), although not completely (1 Chr. 20:33). This was done in an effort to comply with Deuteronomy 12:2,3.

Asa had an army of 580,000 men "who carried shields and drew bows; all these were mighty men of valor" (v. 8). Yet a major threat developed from Zerah, the Ethiopian, probably on behalf of the Egyptian Pharaoh, who was attempting to regain control as Shishak had during the days of Rehoboam (2 Chr. 12:7,8), ca. 901–900 B.C. The Ethiopians came against them with "an army of a million men and three hundred chariots" (v. 9).

Asa's appeal to God centered on God's omnipotence and reputation and is well worth memorizing. "LORD, it is nothing for You to help, whether with many or with those who have no power; help us,…O LORD, You are our God; do not let man prevail against You!" (v. 11). God's response was to strike the Ethiopian army and overthrow them. "And they carried away very much spoil" (v. 13). It appears that this great horde was a nomadic people who moved with all their possessions and had set up their camp near Gerar. The spoils of Judah's victory were immense.

JULY 10

2 Chronicles 15:1–16:14

15 Now the Spirit of God came upon Azariah
the son of Oded. 2And he went out to
meet Asa, and said to him: "Hear me, Asa, and
all Judah and Benjamin. The LORD *is* with you
while you are with Him. If you seek Him, He
will be found by you; but if you forsake Him,
He will forsake you. 3For a long time Israel *has
been* without the true God, without a teaching
priest, and without law; 4but when in their
trouble they turned to the LORD God of Israel,
and sought Him, He was found by them. 5And
in those times *there was* no peace to the one
who went out, nor to the one who came in, but
great turmoil *was* on all the inhabitants of the
lands. 6So nation was destroyed by nation, and
city by city, for God troubled them with every
adversity. 7But you, be strong and do not let
your hands be weak, for your work shall be
rewarded!"
8And when Asa heard these words and the
prophecy of Oded the prophet, he took
courage, and removed the abominable idols
from all the land of Judah and Benjamin and
from the cities which he had taken in the
mountains of Ephraim; and he restored the
altar of the LORD that *was* before the vestibule
of the LORD. 9Then he gathered all Judah and
Benjamin, and those who dwelt with them
from Ephraim, Manasseh, and Simeon, for
they came over to him in great numbers from
Israel when they saw that the LORD his God
was with him.
10So they gathered together at Jerusalem in
the third month, in the fifteenth year of the
reign of Asa. 11And they offered to the LORD at
that time seven hundred bulls and seven thousand sheep from the spoil they had brought.
12Then they entered into a covenant to seek
the LORD God of their fathers with all their
heart and with all their soul; 13and whoever
would not seek the LORD God of Israel was to
be put to death, whether small or great,
whether man or woman. 14Then they took an
oath before the LORD with a loud voice, with
shouting and trumpets and rams' horns. 15And
all Judah rejoiced at the oath, for they had
sworn with all their heart and sought Him
with all their soul; and He was found by them,
and the LORD gave them rest all around.

15:1 Spirit of God. An act of the Holy Spirit, common in the Old Testament, enabling servants of God to speak or act uniquely for Him. **Azariah.** This man was a prophet mentioned only here, who met Asa as he returned from the victory and spoke to him before all his army.

15:2 The spiritual truth here is basic, namely that God is present and powerful in defense of His obedient people. While good Asa ruled for 41 years, 8 wicked kings ruled in Israel, including Jeroboam, who, along with the others, was a negative illustration of this truth.

[16]Also he removed Maachah, the mother of Asa the king, from *being* queen mother, because she had made an obscene image of Asherah; and Asa cut down her obscene image, then crushed and burned *it* by the Brook Kidron. [17]But the high places were not removed from Israel. Nevertheless the heart of Asa was loyal all his days.

[18]He also brought into the house of God the things that his father had dedicated and that he himself had dedicated: silver and gold and utensils. [19]And there was no war until the thirty-fifth year of the reign of Asa.

16 In the thirty-sixth year of the reign of Asa, Baasha king of Israel came up against Judah and built Ramah, that he might let none go out or come in to Asa king of Judah. [2]Then Asa brought silver and gold from the treasuries of the house of the LORD and of the king's house, and sent to Ben-Hadad king of Syria, who dwelt in Damascus, saying, [3]"*Let there be* a treaty between you and me, as there was between my father and your father. See, I have sent you silver and gold; come, break your treaty with Baasha king of Israel, so that he will withdraw from me."

[4]So Ben-Hadad heeded King Asa, and sent the captains of his armies against the cities of Israel. They attacked Ijon, Dan, Abel Maim, and all the storage cities of Naphtali. [5]Now it happened, when Baasha heard *it,* that he stopped building Ramah and ceased his work. [6]Then King Asa took all Judah, and they carried away the stones and timber of Ramah, which Baasha had used for building; and with them he built Geba and Mizpah.

[7]And at that time Hanani the seer came to Asa king of Judah, and said to him: "Because you have relied on the king of Syria, and have not relied on the LORD your God, therefore the army of the king of Syria has escaped from your hand. [8]Were the Ethiopians and the Lubim not a huge army with very many chariots and horsemen? Yet, because you relied on the LORD, He delivered them into your hand. [9]For the eyes of the LORD run to and fro throughout the whole earth, to show Himself strong on behalf of *those* whose heart *is* loyal to Him. In this you have done foolishly; therefore from now on you shall have wars." [10]Then Asa was angry with the seer, and put him in prison, for *he was* enraged at him because of this. And Asa oppressed *some* of the people at that time.

[11]Note that the acts of Asa, first and last, are indeed written in the book of the kings of Judah and Israel. [12]And in the thirty-ninth year of his reign, Asa became diseased in his feet, and his malady was severe; yet in his disease he did not seek the LORD, but the physicians.

[13]So Asa rested with his fathers; he died in the forty-first year of his reign. [14]They buried him in his own tomb, which he had made for himself in the City of David; and they laid him in the bed which was filled with spices and various ingredients prepared in a mixture of ointments. They made a very great burning for him.

16:7 Hanani. God used this prophet to rebuke Asa 1) for his wicked appropriation of temple treasures devoted to God to purchase power, and 2) for his faithless dependence on a pagan king instead of the Lord, in contrast to before when opposed by Egypt (2 Chr. 14:9–15). **army of the king of Syria has escaped.** Asa forfeited by this sin the opportunity of gaining victory not only over Israel, but also Syria. This could have been a greater victory than over the Ethiopians, which would have deprived Syria of any future successful attacks on Judah. Though God had delivered them when they were outnumbered (13:3ff.; 14:9ff.), the king showed his own spiritual decline both in lack of trust and in his treatment of the prophet of God who spoke truth (v. 10).

Psalm 81:6–10

6 "I removed his shoulder from the burden;
His hands were freed from the baskets.
7 You called in trouble, and I delivered you;
I answered you in the secret place of thunder;
I tested you at the waters of Meribah. Selah

8 "Hear, O My people, and I will admonish you!
O Israel, if you will listen to Me!
9 There shall be no foreign god among you;
Nor shall you worship any foreign god.
10 I *am* the LORD your God,
Who brought you out of the land of Egypt;
Open your mouth wide, and I will fill it.

Proverbs 20:24–25

24 A man's steps *are* of the LORD;
How then can a man understand his own way?
25 *It is* a snare for a man to devote rashly *something as* holy,
And afterward to reconsider *his* vows.

Acts 16:1–21

16 Then he came to Derbe and Lystra. And
behold, a certain disciple was there, named
Timothy, *the* son of a certain Jewish woman who
believed, but his father *was* Greek. 2He was well
spoken of by the brethren who were at Lystra

16:1 a certain disciple...Timothy. A young man (late teens or early 20s) of high regard, a "true son in the faith" (1 Tim. 1:2; 2 Tim. 1:2), who eventually became Paul's right-hand man (1 Cor. 4:17; 1 Thess. 3:2; Phil. 2:19). In essence, he became John Mark's replacement. After being commissioned by the elders of the local church (1 Tim. 4:14; 2 Tim. 1:6), he joined Paul and Silas. **his father *was* Greek.** The grammar likely suggests his father was dead. By being both Jew and Gentile, Timothy had access to both cultures—an indispensable asset for missionary service.

and Iconium. 3Paul wanted to have him go on
with him. And he took *him* and circumcised him
because of the Jews who were in that region, for
they all knew that his father was Greek. 4And as
they went through the cities, they delivered to
them the decrees to keep, which were determined by the apostles and elders at Jerusalem.
5So the churches were strengthened in the faith,
and increased in number daily.

16:3 circumcised him. This was done to aid his acceptance by the Jews and provide full access to the synagogues he would be visiting with Paul and Silas. If Timothy had not been circumcised, the Jews could have assumed he had renounced his Jewish heritage and had chosen to live as a Gentile.

6Now when they had gone through Phrygia
and the region of Galatia, they were forbidden
by the Holy Spirit to preach the word in Asia.

16:6 Holy Spirit...Asia. Paul was not allowed to fulfill his intention to minister in Asia Minor (modern Turkey) and to such cities as Ephesus, Smyrna, Philadelphia, Laodicea, Colosse, Sardis, Pergamos, and Thyatira.

7After they had come to Mysia, they tried to go
into Bithynia, but the Spirit did not permit
them. 8So passing by Mysia, they came down
to Troas. 9And a vision appeared to Paul in the
night. A man of Macedonia stood and pleaded
with him, saying, "Come over to Macedonia
and help us." 10Now after he had seen the
vision, immediately we sought to go to
Macedonia, concluding that the Lord had
called us to preach the gospel to them.

16:9 Macedonia. The region located across the Aegean Sea on the mainland of Greece. The cities of Philippi and Thessalonica were located there. Most significantly, going there was to take the gospel from Asia into Europe.

11Therefore, sailing from Troas, we ran a
straight course to Samothrace, and the next
day came to Neapolis, 12and from there to
Philippi, which is the foremost city of that part
of Macedonia, a colony. And we were staying
in that city for some days. 13And on the
Sabbath day we went out of the city to the
riverside, where prayer was customarily
made; and we sat down and spoke to the
women who met *there.* 14Now a certain woman
named Lydia heard *us.* She was a seller of purple from the city of Thyatira, who worshiped
God. The Lord opened her heart to heed the
things spoken by Paul. 15And when she and
her household were baptized, she begged *us,*
saying, "If you have judged me to be faithful to
the Lord, come to my house and stay." So she
persuaded us.

16Now it happened, as we went to prayer,
that a certain slave girl possessed with a spirit of divination met us, who brought her masters much profit by fortune-telling. 17This girl
followed Paul and us, and cried out, saying,
"These men are the servants of the Most High
God, who proclaim to us the way of salvation."
18And this she did for many days.
But Paul, greatly annoyed, turned and said
to the spirit, "I command you in the name of
Jesus Christ to come out of her." And he came
out that very hour. 19But when her masters
saw that their hope of profit was gone, they
seized Paul and Silas and dragged *them* into
the marketplace to the authorities.
20And they brought them to the magistrates,
and said, "These men, being Jews, exceedingly trouble our city; 21and they teach customs which are not lawful for us, being Romans, to receive or observe."

DAY 10: How did Lydia and the demon-possessed girl in Philippi respond differently to the gospel?

When Paul arrived in Philippi (Acts 16:12), evidently the Jewish community did not have the minimum of 10 Jewish men who were heads of households required to form a synagogue. In such cases, a place of prayer under the open sky and near a river or sea was adopted as a meeting place. Most likely this spot was located where the road leading out of the city crossed the Gangites River. Paul spoke "to the women who met there" (v. 13). In further evidence of the small number of Jewish men, it was women who met to pray, read from the Old Testament law, and discuss what they read.

Lydia was from the city of Thyatira, which was located in the Roman province of Lydia, thus the name "Lydia" was probably associated with her place of origin. She was a "seller of purple" (v. 14). Because purple dye was extremely expensive, purple garments were usually worn by royalty and the wealthy. As a result, Lydia's business turned a nice profit, which enabled her to have a house large enough to accommodate the missionary team (v. 15) and the new church at Philippi (v. 40). "Who worshiped God." Like Cornelius, she believed in the God of Israel but had not become a full proselyte (10:2). The Lord opened her heart, and she and her household were baptized.

Also in Philippi was a slave girl "possessed with a spirit of divination" (v. 16), literally, "a python spirit." That expression comes from Greek mythology. Python was a snake that guarded the oracle at Delphi. Essentially, this girl was a medium in contact with demons who could supposedly predict the future. For several days she followed Paul and rightly cried out in the streets, "These men are the servants of the Most High God" (v. 17). El Elyon, the Absolutely Sovereign God, is an Old Testament title (used about 50 times) for the God of Israel (Gen. 14:18–22; Ps. 78:35; Dan. 5:18). But the spirit was wrong, and Paul finally turned and said to the spirit, "I command you in the name of Jesus Christ to come out of her" (v. 18). The demon left the girl in obedience to Paul's command and his apostolic authority. The ability to cast out demons was a special ability of Christ's apostles (Mark 3:15; 2 Cor. 12:12).

JULY 11

2 Chronicles 17:1–18:34

17 Then Jehoshaphat his son reigned in his
place, and strengthened himself against
Israel. 2And he placed troops in all the fortified
cities of Judah, and set garrisons in the land of
Judah and in the cities of Ephraim which Asa
his father had taken. 3Now the LORD was with
Jehoshaphat, because he walked in the former
ways of his father David; he did not seek the
Baals, 4but sought the God of his father, and
walked in His commandments and not according to the acts of Israel. 5Therefore the LORD
established the kingdom in his hand; and all
Judah gave presents to Jehoshaphat, and he
had riches and honor in abundance. 6And his
heart took delight in the ways of the LORD;
moreover he removed the high places and
wooden images from Judah.
7Also in the third year of his reign he sent
his leaders, Ben-Hail, Obadiah, Zechariah,
Nethanel, and Michaiah, to teach in the cities
of Judah. 8And with them *he sent* Levites:
Shemaiah, Nethaniah, Zebadiah, Asahel,
Shemiramoth, Jehonathan, Adonijah, Tobijah,
and Tobadonijah—the Levites; and with them
Elishama and Jehoram, the priests. 9So they
taught in Judah, and *had* the Book of the Law of
the LORD with them; they went throughout all
the cities of Judah and taught the people.
10And the fear of the LORD fell on all the kingdoms of the lands that *were* around Judah, so
that they did not make war against Jehoshaphat.
11Also *some* of the Philistines brought Jehoshaphat presents and silver as tribute; and the
Arabians brought him flocks, seven thousand
seven hundred rams and seven thousand
seven hundred male goats.
12So Jehoshaphat became increasingly powerful, and he built fortresses and storage cities
in Judah. 13He had much property in the cities
of Judah; and the men of war, mighty men of
valor, *were* in Jerusalem.
14These *are* their numbers, according to their

17:3–9 Jehoshaphat made three strategic moves, spiritually speaking: 1) he obeyed the Lord (17:3–6); 2) he removed false worship from the land (17:6); and 3) he sent out teachers who taught the people the Law of the Lord (17:7–9).

17:12,13 These verses indicate the massive wealth that developed under divine blessing (18:1), as well as formidable military power (vv. 14–19).

fathers' houses. Of Judah, the captains of thousands: Adnah the captain, and with him three hundred thousand mighty men of valor; 15and next to him *was* Jehohanan the captain, and with him two hundred and eighty thousand; 16and next to him *was* Amasiah the son of Zichri, who willingly offered himself to the LORD, and with him two hundred thousand mighty men of valor. 17Of Benjamin: Eliada a mighty man of valor, and with him two hundred thousand men armed with bow and shield; 18and next to him *was* Jehozabad, and with him one hundred and eighty thousand prepared for war. 19These served the king, besides those the king put in the fortified cities throughout all Judah.

18 Jehoshaphat had riches and honor in abundance; and by marriage he allied himself with Ahab. 2After some years he went down to *visit* Ahab in Samaria; and Ahab killed sheep and oxen in abundance for him and the people who were with him, and persuaded him to go up *with him* to Ramoth Gilead. 3So Ahab king of Israel said to Jehoshaphat king of Judah, "Will you go with me *against* Ramoth Gilead?"

And he answered him, "I *am* as you *are,* and my people as your people; *we will be* with you in the war."

4Also Jehoshaphat said to the king of Israel, "Please inquire for the word of the LORD today."

5Then the king of Israel gathered the prophets together, four hundred men, and said to them, "Shall we go to war against Ramoth Gilead, or shall I refrain?"

So they said, "Go up, for God will deliver it into the king's hand."

6But Jehoshaphat said, "*Is there* not still a prophet of the LORD here, that we may inquire of Him?"

7So the king of Israel said to Jehoshaphat, "*There is* still one man by whom we may inquire of the LORD; but I hate him, because he never prophesies good concerning me, but always evil. He *is* Micaiah the son of Imla."

And Jehoshaphat said, "Let not the king say such things!"

8Then the king of Israel called one *of his* officers and said, "Bring Micaiah the son of Imla quickly!"

9The king of Israel and Jehoshaphat king of Judah, clothed in *their* robes, sat each on his throne; and they sat at a threshing floor at the entrance of the gate of Samaria; and all the prophets prophesied before them. 10Now Zedekiah the son of Chenaanah had made horns of iron for himself; and he said, "Thus says the LORD: 'With these you shall gore the Syrians until they are destroyed.' "

11And all the prophets prophesied so, saying, "Go up to Ramoth Gilead and prosper, for the LORD will deliver *it* into the king's hand."

12Then the messenger who had gone to call Micaiah spoke to him, saying, "Now listen, the words of the prophets with one accord encourage the king. Therefore please let your word be like *the word of* one of them, and speak encouragement."

13And Micaiah said, "*As* the LORD lives, whatever my God says, that I will speak."

14Then he came to the king; and the king said to him, "Micaiah, shall we go to war against Ramoth Gilead, or shall I refrain?"

And he said, "Go and prosper, and they shall be delivered into your hand!"

15So the king said to him, "How many times shall I make you swear that you tell me nothing but the truth in the name of the LORD?"

16Then he said, "I saw all Israel scattered on the mountains, as sheep that have no shepherd. And the LORD said, 'These have no master. Let each return to his house in peace.' "

17And the king of Israel said to Jehoshaphat, "Did I not tell you he would not prophesy good concerning me, but evil?"

18Then *Micaiah* said, "Therefore hear the word of the LORD: I saw the LORD sitting on His throne, and all the host of heaven standing on His right hand and His left. 19And the LORD said, 'Who will persuade Ahab king of Israel to go up, that he may fall at Ramoth Gilead?' So one spoke in this manner, and another spoke in that manner. 20Then a spirit came forward and stood before the LORD, and said, 'I will persuade him.' The LORD said to him, 'In what way?' 21So he said, 'I will go out and be a lying spirit in the mouth of all his prophets.' And *the LORD* said, 'You shall persuade *him* and also prevail; go out and do so.' 22Therefore look! The LORD has put a lying spirit in the mouth of these prophets of yours, and the LORD has declared disaster against you."

23Then Zedekiah the son of Chenaanah went near and struck Micaiah on the cheek, and said, "Which way did the spirit from the LORD go from me to speak to you?"

24And Micaiah said, "Indeed you shall see on that day when you go into an inner chamber to hide!"

25Then the king of Israel said, "Take Micaiah, and return him to Amon the governor of the city and to Joash the king's son; 26and say, 'Thus says the king: "Put this *fellow* in prison, and feed him with bread of affliction and water of affliction, until I return in peace." ' "

27But Micaiah said, "If you ever return in peace, the LORD has not spoken by me." And he said, "Take heed, all you people!"

28So the king of Israel and Jehoshaphat the
king of Judah went up to Ramoth Gilead. 29And
the king of Israel said to Jehoshaphat, "I will
disguise myself and go into battle; but you put
on your robes." So the king of Israel disguised
himself, and they went into battle.
30Now the king of Syria had commanded the
captains of the chariots who *were* with him,
saying, "Fight with no one small or great, but
only with the king of Israel."
31So it was, when the captains of the chariots
saw Jehoshaphat, that they said, "It *is* the king
of Israel!" Therefore they surrounded him to
attack; but Jehoshaphat cried out, and the
LORD helped him, and God diverted them from
him. 32For so it was, when the captains of the
chariots saw that it was not the king of Israel,
that they turned back from pursuing him.
33Now a certain man drew a bow at random, and
struck the king of Israel between the joints of
his armor. So he said to the driver of his chariot, "Turn around and take me out of the battle,
for I am wounded." 34The battle increased that
day, and the king of Israel propped *himself* up
in *his* chariot facing the Syrians until evening;
and about the time of sunset he died.

Psalm 81:11–16

11 "But My people would not heed My
voice,
And Israel would *have* none of Me.
12 So I gave them over to their own
stubborn heart,
To walk in their own counsels.

13 "Oh, that My people would listen to Me,
That Israel would walk in My ways!
14 I would soon subdue their enemies,
And turn My hand against their
adversaries.
15 The haters of the LORD would pretend
submission to Him,
But their fate would endure forever.
16 He would have fed them also with the
finest of wheat;
And with honey from the rock I would
have satisfied you."

81:16 honey from the rock. This phrase was first used by Moses in his song of praise (Deut. 32:13). Though honey is sometimes found in the clefts of rocks, the intent of the figure here is more likely to valuable food provided from unlikely places.

Proverbs 20:26–28

26 A wise king sifts out the wicked,
And brings the threshing wheel over
them.
27 The spirit of a man *is* the lamp of the
LORD,
Searching all the inner depths of his
heart.

28 Mercy and truth preserve the king,
And by lovingkindness he upholds his
throne.

20:27 the lamp of the LORD. The "spirit" represents the conscience of man which searches every secret place.

Acts 16:22–40

22Then the multitude rose up together against
them; and the magistrates tore off their clothes
and commanded *them* to be beaten with rods.
23And when they had laid many stripes on them,
they threw *them* into prison, commanding the
jailer to keep them securely. 24Having received
such a charge, he put them into the inner prison
and fastened their feet in the stocks.

16:24 inner prison...in the stocks. The most secure part of the prison. The jailer took further precautions by putting their feet "in the stocks." This particular security measure was designed to produce painful cramping so the prisoner's legs were spread as far apart as possible.

25But at midnight Paul and Silas were praying
and singing hymns to God, and the prisoners
were listening to them. 26Suddenly there was a
great earthquake, so that the foundations of the
prison were shaken; and immediately all the
doors were opened and everyone's chains
were loosed. 27And the keeper of the prison,
awaking from sleep and seeing the prison
doors open, supposing the prisoners had fled,
drew his sword and was about to kill himself.
28But Paul called with a loud voice, saying, "Do
yourself no harm, for we are all here."
29Then he called for a light, ran in, and fell
down trembling before Paul and Silas. 30And he
brought them out and said, "Sirs, what must I
do to be saved?"

[31]So they said, "Believe on the Lord Jesus Christ, and you will be saved, you and your household." [32]Then they spoke the word of the Lord to him and to all who were in his house. [33]And he took them the same hour of the night and washed *their* stripes. And immediately he and all his *family* were baptized. [34]Now when he had brought them into his house, he set food before them; and he rejoiced, having believed in God with all his household.

[35]And when it was day, the magistrates sent the officers, saying, "Let those men go."

[36]So the keeper of the prison reported these words to Paul, saying, "The magistrates have sent to let you go. Now therefore depart, and go in peace."

[37]But Paul said to them, "They have beaten us openly, uncondemned Romans, *and* have thrown *us* into prison. And now do they put us out secretly? No indeed! Let them come themselves and get us out."

[38]And the officers told these words to the magistrates, and they were afraid when they heard that they were Romans. [39]Then they came and pleaded with them and brought *them* out, and asked *them* to depart from the city. [40]So they went out of the prison and entered *the house of* Lydia; and when they had seen the brethren, they encouraged them and departed.

16:27 prison doors open...about to kill himself. Instead of waiting to face humiliation and a painful execution. A Roman soldier, who let a prisoner escape, paid for his negligence with his life (12:19; 27:42).

16:31 Believe on the Lord Jesus Christ. One must believe He is who He claimed to be (John 20:31) and believe in what He did (1 Cor. 15:3, 4; Rom. 1:16). **you and your household.** All of his family, servants, and guests who could comprehend the gospel and believe heard the gospel and believed.

DAY 11: How did Roman law affect Paul and the preaching of the gospel?

The city of Philippi, which was located 10 miles inland from Neapolis, was named for Philip II of Macedon (the father of Alexander the Great). It was a Roman colony (Acts 16:2). Philippi became a Roman colony in 31 B.C., so it carried the right of freedom (it was self-governing and independent of the provincial government), the right of exemption from tax, and the right of holding land in full ownership.

In Acts 16:21, Paul and those with him are accused before the city magistrates as troublemakers who "teach customs…not lawful for us…Romans." It was technically true that Roman citizens were not to engage in any foreign religion that had not been sanctioned by the state. But it was a false charge that they were creating chaos. Every Roman colony had two magistrates serving as judges. In this case, they did not uphold Roman justice: They did not investigate the charges, conduct a proper hearing, or give Paul and Silas the chance to defend themselves. Instead, the magistrates had them beaten with rods. This was an illegal punishment since they had not been convicted of any crime. The officers (v. 35) under the command of the magistrates administered the beating with rods tied together in a bundle. Paul received the same punishment on two other occasions (2 Cor. 11:25).

Later, when Paul told them they were "Romans" (v. 37), it was a real problem. To inflict corporal punishment on a Roman citizen was a serious crime and made more so since Paul and Barnabas did not receive a trial. As a result, the magistrates faced the possibility of being removed from office and having Philippi's privileges as a Roman colony revoked.

JULY 12

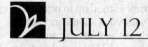

2 Chronicles 19:1–20:37

19 Then Jehoshaphat the king of Judah returned safely to his house in Jerusalem. [2]And Jehu the son of Hanani the seer went out to meet him, and said to King Jehoshaphat, "Should you help the wicked and love those who hate the LORD? Therefore the wrath of the LORD *is* upon you. [3]Nevertheless

19:1–3 Having faced possible death that was diverted by God (18:31), Jehoshaphat was rebuked because of his alliances. The prophet condemned the king's alliance with God's enemy, Ahab (1 Kin. 22:2), yet there was mercy mingled with wrath because of the king's concern personally and nationally for the true worship of God.

good things are found in you, in that you have
removed the wooden images from the land,
and have prepared your heart to seek God."

4So Jehoshaphat dwelt at Jerusalem; and he
went out again among the people from
Beersheba to the mountains of Ephraim, and
brought them back to the LORD God of their fathers. 5Then he set judges in the land throughout all the fortified cities of Judah, city by city,
6and said to the judges, "Take heed to what
you are doing, for you do not judge for man
but for the LORD, who *is* with you in the judgment. 7Now therefore, let the fear of the LORD
be upon you; take care and do *it,* for *there is* no
iniquity with the LORD our God, no partiality,
nor taking of bribes."

8Moreover in Jerusalem, for the judgment of
the LORD and for controversies, Jehoshaphat
appointed some of the Levites and priests,
and some of the chief fathers of Israel, when
they returned to Jerusalem. 9And he commanded them, saying, "Thus you shall act in
the fear of the LORD, faithfully and with a loyal
heart: 10Whatever case comes to you from your
brethren who dwell in their cities, whether of
bloodshed or offenses against law or commandment, against statutes or ordinances,
you shall warn them, lest they trespass
against the LORD and wrath come upon you
and your brethren. Do this, and you will not
be guilty. 11And take notice: Amariah the chief
priest *is* over you in all matters of the LORD;
and Zebadiah the son of Ishmael, the ruler of
the house of Judah, for all the king's matters;
also the Levites *will be* officials before you.
Behave courageously, and the LORD will be
with the good."

20 It happened after this *that* the people
of Moab with the people of Ammon,
and *others* with them besides the Ammonites,
came to battle against Jehoshaphat. 2Then
some came and told Jehoshaphat, saying, "A
great multitude is coming against you from
beyond the sea, from Syria; and they are in
Hazazon Tamar" (which *is* En Gedi). 3And
Jehoshaphat feared, and set himself to seek
the LORD, and proclaimed a fast throughout all
Judah. 4So Judah gathered together to ask *help*
from the LORD; and from all the cities of Judah
they came to seek the LORD.

5Then Jehoshaphat stood in the assembly of
Judah and Jerusalem, in the house of the
LORD, before the new court, 6and said: "O
LORD God of our fathers, *are* You not God in
heaven, and do You *not* rule over all the kingdoms of the nations, and in Your hand *is there*
not power and might, so that no one is able to
withstand You? 7*Are* You not our God, *who*
drove out the inhabitants of this land before
Your people Israel, and gave it to the descendants of Abraham Your friend forever? 8And they
dwell in it, and have built You a sanctuary in it
for Your name, saying, 9'If disaster comes upon
us—sword, judgment, pestilence, or famine—
we will stand before this temple and in Your
presence (for Your name *is* in this temple), and
cry out to You in our affliction, and You will
hear and save.' 10And now, here are the people
of Ammon, Moab, and Mount Seir—whom You
would not let Israel invade when they came out
of the land of Egypt, but they turned from them
and did not destroy them— 11here they are,
rewarding us by coming to throw us out of
Your possession which You have given us to
inherit. 12O our God, will You not judge them?
For we have no power against this great multitude that is coming against us; nor do we
know what to do, but our eyes *are* upon You."

13Now all Judah, with their little ones, their
wives, and their children, stood before the LORD.

14Then the Spirit of the LORD came upon
Jahaziel the son of Zechariah, the son of
Benaiah, the son of Jeiel, the son of Mattaniah,
a Levite of the sons of Asaph, in the midst of
the assembly. 15And he said, "Listen, all you of
Judah and you inhabitants of Jerusalem, and
you, King Jehoshaphat! Thus says the LORD to
you: 'Do not be afraid nor dismayed because
of this great multitude, for the battle *is* not
yours, but God's. 16Tomorrow go down against
them. They will surely come up by the Ascent
of Ziz, and you will find them at the end of the
brook before the Wilderness of Jeruel. 17You
will not *need* to fight in this *battle.* Position
yourselves, stand still and see the salvation of
the LORD, who is with you, O Judah and Jerusalem!' Do not fear or be dismayed; tomorrow
go out against them, for the LORD *is* with you."

18And Jehoshaphat bowed his head with *his*
face to the ground, and all Judah and the
inhabitants of Jerusalem bowed before the
LORD, worshiping the LORD. 19Then the Levites
of the children of the Kohathites and of the
children of the Korahites stood up to praise the
LORD God of Israel with voices loud and high.

20So they rose early in the morning and went
out into the Wilderness of Tekoa; and as they
went out, Jehoshaphat stood and said, "Hear
me, O Judah and you inhabitants of Jerusalem: Believe in the LORD your God, and you
shall be established; believe His prophets, and
you shall prosper." 21And when he had consulted with the people, he appointed those
who should sing to the LORD, and who should
praise the beauty of holiness, as they went out
before the army and were saying:

"Praise the LORD,
For His mercy *endures* forever."

22 Now when they began to sing and to
praise, the LORD set ambushes against the people of Ammon, Moab, and Mount Seir, who
had come against Judah; and they were defeated. 23 For the people of Ammon and Moab
stood up against the inhabitants of Mount Seir
to utterly kill and destroy *them.* And when
they had made an end of the inhabitants of
Seir, they helped to destroy one another.

24 So when Judah came to a place overlook-
ing the wilderness, they looked toward the
multitude; and there *were* their dead bodies,
fallen on the earth. No one had escaped.

25 When Jehoshaphat and his people came to
take away their spoil, they found among them
an abundance of valuables on the dead bodies,
and precious jewelry, which they stripped off
for themselves, more than they could carry
away; and they were three days gathering the
spoil because there was so much. 26 And on the
fourth day they assembled in the Valley of
Berachah, for there they blessed the LORD;
therefore the name of that place was called
The Valley of Berachah until this day. 27 Then
they returned, every man of Judah and Jerusalem, with Jehoshaphat in front of them, to go
back to Jerusalem with joy, for the LORD had
made them rejoice over their enemies. 28 So
they came to Jerusalem, with stringed instruments and harps and trumpets, to the house of
the LORD. 29 And the fear of God was on all the
kingdoms of *those* countries when they heard
that the LORD had fought against the enemies
of Israel. 30 Then the realm of Jehoshaphat was
quiet, for his God gave him rest all around.

31 So Jehoshaphat was king over Judah. *He*
was thirty-five years old when he became
king, and he reigned twenty-five years in Jerusalem. His mother's name *was* Azubah the
daughter of Shilhi. 32 And he walked in the way
of his father Asa, and did not turn aside from
it, doing *what was* right in the sight of the
LORD. 33 Nevertheless the high places were not
taken away, for as yet the people had not directed their hearts to the God of their fathers.

34 Now the rest of the acts of Jehoshaphat,
first and last, indeed they *are* written in the
book of Jehu the son of Hanani, which *is* mentioned in the book of the kings of Israel.

35 After this Jehoshaphat king of Judah allied
himself with Ahaziah king of Israel, who acted
very wickedly. 36 And he allied himself with
him to make ships to go to Tarshish, and they
made the ships in Ezion Geber. 37 But Eliezer
the son of Dodavah of Mareshah prophesied
against Jehoshaphat, saying, "Because you
have allied yourself with Ahaziah, the LORD
has destroyed your works." Then the ships
were wrecked, so that they were not able to go
to Tarshish.

Psalm 82:1–8

A Psalm of Asaph.

God stands in the congregation
of the mighty;
He judges among the gods.
2 How long will you judge unjustly,
And show partiality to the wicked?
Selah

82:1 congregation of the mighty. The scene opens with God having called the world leaders together. **among the gods.** Some have taken this psalm to be about demons or false pagan gods. The best interpretation is that these "gods" are human leaders, such as judges, kings, legislators, and presidents (Ex. 22:8,9,28; Judg. 5:8,9). God the Great Judge presides over these lesser judges.

3 Defend the poor and fatherless;
Do justice to the afflicted and needy.
4 Deliver the poor and needy;
Free *them* from the hand of the wicked.

5 They do not know, nor do they
understand;
They walk about in darkness;
All the foundations of the earth are
unstable.
6 I said, "You *are* gods,
And all of you *are* children of the Most
High.
7 But you shall die like men,
And fall like one of the princes."

82:6 I said. Kings and judges are set up ultimately by the decree of God (Ps. 2:6). God, in effect, invests His authority in human leaders for the stability of the universe (Rom. 13:1–7). But God may revoke this authority (v. 7). ***"You are gods."*** Jesus, in quoting this phrase in John 10:34, supported the interpretation that the "gods" were human beings. In a play on words, He claims that if human leaders can be called "gods," certainly the Messiah can be called God.

8 Arise, O God, judge the earth;
For You shall inherit all nations.

82:8 You shall inherit all nations. The psalmist prayerfully anticipates the future when God will set up His kingdom and restore order and perfect justice to a sin-cursed world (Pss. 96; 97; Is. 11:1–5).

Proverbs 20:29–30

29 The glory of young men *is* their strength,
And the splendor of old men *is* their gray head.
30 Blows that hurt cleanse away evil,
As *do* stripes the inner depths of the heart.

Acts 17:1–15

17 Now when they had passed through Amphipolis and Apollonia, they came to Thessalonica, where there was a synagogue of
the Jews. 2Then Paul, as his custom was, went in to them, and for three Sabbaths reasoned
with them from the Scriptures, 3explaining and demonstrating that the Christ had to suffer and rise again from the dead, and *saying,* "This Jesus whom I preach to you is the Christ." 4And
some of them were persuaded; and a great multitude of the devout Greeks, and not a few of the leading women, joined Paul and Silas.
5But the Jews who were not persuaded, becoming envious, took some of the evil men from the marketplace, and gathering a mob, set all the city in an uproar and attacked the house of Jason, and sought to bring them out
to the people. 6But when they did not find them, they dragged Jason and some brethren to the rulers of the city, crying out, "These who have turned the world upside down have
come here too. 7Jason has harbored them, and these are all acting contrary to the decrees of

17:7 contrary to the decrees of Caesar. One of the most serious crimes in the Roman Empire was to acknowledge allegiance to any king but Caesar (John 19:15).

Caesar, saying there is another king—Jesus."
8And they troubled the crowd and the rulers of
the city when they heard these things. 9So
when they had taken security from Jason and the rest, they let them go.
10Then the brethren immediately sent Paul and Silas away by night to Berea. When they arrived, they went into the synagogue of the
Jews. 11These were more fair-minded than those in Thessalonica, in that they received the word with all readiness, and searched the Scriptures daily *to find out* whether these
things were so. 12Therefore many of them believed, and also not a few of the Greeks, prominent women as well as men. 13But when
the Jews from Thessalonica learned that the word of God was preached by Paul at Berea, they came there also and stirred up the
crowds. 14Then immediately the brethren sent Paul away, to go to the sea; but both Silas and
Timothy remained there. 15So those who conducted Paul brought him to Athens; and receiving a command for Silas and Timothy to come to him with all speed, they departed.

17:15 Athens. The cultural center of Greece. At its zenith, Athens was home to the most renowned philosophers in history, including Socrates, Plato, and Aristotle, who was arguably the most influential philosopher of all. Two other significant philosophers taught there: Epicurus, founder of Epicureanism, and Zeno, founder of Stoicism—two of the dominant philosophies in that day (v. 18).

DAY 12: How did Jehoshaphat express his faith in the face of adversity?

Second Chronicles 20:1–30 is one of the great stories of faith in the Old Testament. Attacked by a great multitude from Moab and Ammon, Jehoshaphat made the appropriate spiritual response, i.e., the king and the nation appealed to God in prayer and fasting. The fast was national, including even the children (v. 13). Jehoshaphat stood in the redecorated center court praying for the nation, appealing to the promises, the glory, and the reputation of God which were at stake since He was identified with Judah (vv. 5–12). In his prayer he acknowledged God's sovereignty (v. 6), God's covenant (v. 7), God's presence (vv. 8,9), God's goodness (v. 10), God's possession (v. 11), and their utter dependence on Him (v. 12).

The Lord responded immediately, sending a message of confidence through the prophet Jahaziel. "Do not be afraid nor dismayed because of this great multitude, for the battle is not yours, but God's. Tomorrow go down against them.... You will not need to fight in this battle. Position yourselves, stand still and see the salvation of the LORD" (v. 15–17).

Here was the praise of faith (vv. 18–21). They were confident enough in God's promise of victory to begin the praise before the battle was won. So great was their trust that the choir marched in front of the army, singing psalms. People were appointed who should "praise the beauty of holiness" (v. 21). The Lord is beautiful in holiness (Ex. 15:11; Ps. 27:4), but the text here would better be translated "in holy attire," which was referring to the manner in which the Levite singers were clothed in symbolic sacred clothing (1 Chr. 16:29) in honor of the Lord's holiness.

Similar to God's intervention in Gideon's day (Judg. 7:15–23), God caused confusion among the enemy, who mistakenly turned upon themselves and slaughtered each other (vv. 22–24). Some think this may have been done by angels who appeared and set off this uncontrolled and deadly panic. The destruction was complete before Jehoshaphat and his army ever met the enemy (v. 24).

JULY 13

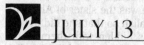

2 Chronicles 21:1–22:12

21 And Jehoshaphat rested with his fathers,
and was buried with his fathers in the
City of David. Then Jehoram his son reigned
in his place. 2He had brothers, the sons of Jehoshaphat: Azariah, Jehiel, Zechariah, Azar-
yahu, Michael, and Shephatiah; all these *were*
the sons of Jehoshaphat king of Israel. 3Their
father gave them great gifts of silver and gold
and precious things, with fortified cities in Judah; but he gave the kingdom to Jehoram,
because he *was* the firstborn.
4Now when Jehoram was established over
the kingdom of his father, he strengthened
himself and killed all his brothers with the
sword, and also *others* of the princes of Israel.
5Jehoram *was* thirty-two years old when he
became king, and he reigned eight years in Jerusalem. 6And he walked in the way of the
kings of Israel, just as the house of Ahab had
done, for he had the daughter of Ahab as a
wife; and he did evil in the sight of the LORD.
7Yet the LORD would not destroy the house of
David, because of the covenant that He had
made with David, and since He had promised
to give a lamp to him and to his sons forever.
8In his days Edom revolted against Judah's
authority, and made a king over themselves.
9So Jehoram went out with his officers, and all
his chariots with him. And he rose by night
and attacked the Edomites who had surrounded him and the captains of the chariots. 10Thus
Edom has been in revolt against Judah's
authority to this day. At that time Libnah revolted against his rule, because he had forsaken
the LORD God of his fathers. 11Moreover he
made high places in the mountains of Judah,
and caused the inhabitants of Jerusalem to commit harlotry, and led Judah astray.
12And a letter came to him from Elijah the
prophet, saying,

Thus says the LORD God of your father
David:
Because you have not walked in the
ways of Jehoshaphat your father, or in
the ways of Asa king of Judah, 13but
have walked in the way of the kings of
Israel, and have made Judah and the
inhabitants of Jerusalem to play the
harlot like the harlotry of the house of
Ahab, and also have killed your brothers,
those of your father's household, *who
were* better than yourself, 14behold, the
LORD will strike your people with a
serious affliction—your children, your
wives, and all your possessions; 15and

21:11 led Judah astray. Undoubtedly he was influenced by his marriage to Ahab's daughter (v. 6) and was influenced in the alliance just like his father (2 Chr. 18:1). They had not learned from Solomon's sinful example (1 Kin. 11:3,4). His wicked wife, Athaliah, later became ruler over Judah and tried to wipe out David's royal line (2 Chr. 22:10).

21:12–15 Elijah, best known for his confrontations with Israel's Ahab and Jezebel (1 Kin. 17–2 Kin. 2:11), confronted prophetically Jehoram's sins of idolatry and murder (21:13). The consequences from God's judgment extended beyond himself to his family and the nation (21:14,15). This event undoubtedly occurred in the early years of Jehoram's coregency with his father Jehoshaphat and shortly before Elijah's departure to heaven, ca. 848 B.C. (2 Kin. 2:11,12).

you *will become* very sick with a disease
of your intestines, until your intestines
come out by reason of the sickness, day
by day.

[16]Moreover the LORD stirred up against
Jehoram the spirit of the Philistines and the
Arabians who *were* near the Ethiopians. [17]And
they came up into Judah and invaded it, and
carried away all the possessions that were
found in the king's house, and also his sons and
his wives, so that there was not a son left to him
except Jehoahaz, the youngest of his sons.
[18]After all this the LORD struck him in his
intestines with an incurable disease. [19]Then it
happened in the course of time, after the end
of two years, that his intestines came out
because of his sickness; so he died in severe
pain. And his people made no burning for him,
like the burning for his fathers.
[20]He was thirty-two years old when he
became king. He reigned in Jerusalem eight
years and, to no one's sorrow, departed.
However they buried him in the City of David,
but not in the tombs of the kings.

22 Then the inhabitants of Jerusalem
made Ahaziah his youngest son king in
his place, for the raiders who came with the
Arabians into the camp had killed all the older
sons. So Ahaziah the son of Jehoram, king of
Judah, reigned. [2]Ahaziah *was* forty-two years
old when he became king, and he reigned one
year in Jerusalem. His mother's name *was*
Athaliah the granddaughter of Omri. [3]He also
walked in the ways of the house of Ahab, for his
mother advised him to do wickedly. [4]Therefore
he did evil in the sight of the LORD, like the
house of Ahab; for they were his counselors
after the death of his father, to his destruction.
[5]He also followed their advice, and went with
Jehoram the son of Ahab king of Israel to war
against Hazael king of Syria at Ramoth Gilead;
and the Syrians wounded Joram. [6]Then he
returned to Jezreel to recover from the
wounds which he had received at Ramah,
when he fought against Hazael king of Syria.
And Azariah the son of Jehoram, king of Judah,
went down to see Jehoram the son of
Ahab in Jezreel, because he was sick.
[7]His going to Joram was God's occasion for
Ahaziah's downfall; for when he arrived, he
went out with Jehoram against Jehu the son of
Nimshi, whom the LORD had anointed to cut
off the house of Ahab. [8]And it happened, when
Jehu was executing judgment on the house of
Ahab, and found the princes of Judah and the
sons of Ahaziah's brothers who served Ahaziah,
that he killed them. [9]Then he searched for
Ahaziah; and they caught him (he was hiding
in Samaria), and brought him to Jehu. When
they had killed him, they buried him, "because,"
they said, "he is the son of Jehoshaphat, who
sought the LORD with all his heart."
So the house of Ahaziah had no one to
assume power over the kingdom.
[10]Now when Athaliah the mother of Ahaziah
saw that her son was dead, she arose and
destroyed all the royal heirs of the house of Judah.
[11]But Jehoshabeath, the daughter of the
king, took Joash the son of Ahaziah, and stole
him away from among the king's sons who
were being murdered, and put him and his
nurse in a bedroom. So Jehoshabeath, the
daughter of King Jehoram, the wife of Jehoiada
the priest (for she was the sister of Ahaziah),
hid him from Athaliah so that she did not kill
him. [12]And he was hidden with them in the
house of God for six years, while Athaliah
reigned over the land.

Psalm 83:1–8

A Song. A Psalm of Asaph.

Do not keep silent, O God!
Do not hold Your peace,
And do not be still, O God!
2 For behold, Your enemies make
a tumult;
And those who hate You have lifted up
their head.
3 They have taken crafty counsel against
Your people,
And consulted together against Your
sheltered ones.
4 They have said, "Come, and let us
cut them off from *being* a nation,
That the name of Israel may be
remembered no more."

83:4 cut them off. The hostile nations, under Satan's influence, repudiated God's promise to preserve forever the nation of Israel (Gen. 17:7,8; Ps. 89:34–37).

5 For they have consulted together with
one consent;
They form a confederacy against
You:
6 The tents of Edom and the
Ishmaelites;
Moab and the Hagrites;
7 Gebal, Ammon, and Amalek;

Philistia with the inhabitants of Tyre;
8 Assyria also has joined with them;
They have helped the children of Lot.
Selah

Proverbs 21:1

21 The king's heart *is* in the hand
of the LORD,
Like the rivers of water;
He turns it wherever He wishes.

Acts 17:16–34

16Now while Paul waited for them at Athens,
his spirit was provoked within him when he
saw that the city was given over to idols.
17Therefore he reasoned in the synagogue
with the Jews and with the *Gentile* worshipers,
and in the marketplace daily with those who
happened to be there. 18Then certain Epicurean and Stoic philosophers encountered
him. And some said, "What does this babbler
want to say?"

17:18 Epicurean and Stoic philosophers. Epicurean philosophy taught that the chief end of man was the avoidance of pain. Epicureans were materialists—they did not deny the existence of God, but they believed He did not become involved with the affairs of men. When a person died, they believed his body and soul disintegrated. Stoic philosophy taught self-mastery—that the goal in life was to reach a place of indifference to pleasure or pain. **babbler.** Literally, "seed picker." Some of the philosophers viewed Paul as an amateur philosopher—one who had no ideas of his own but only picked among prevailing philosophies and constructed one with no depth.

Others said, "He seems to be a proclaimer
of foreign gods," because he preached to
them Jesus and the resurrection.
19And they took him and brought him to the
Areopagus, saying, "May we know what this
new doctrine *is* of which you speak? 20For you
are bringing some strange things to our ears.
Therefore we want to know what these things
mean." 21For all the Athenians and the foreigners who were there spent their time in nothing
else but either to tell or to hear some new
thing.
22Then Paul stood in the midst of the
Areopagus and said, "Men of Athens, I perceive that in all things you are very religious;
23for as I was passing through and considering
the objects of your worship, I even found an
altar with this inscription:

TO THE UNKNOWN GOD.

Therefore, the One whom you worship without knowing, Him I proclaim to you: 24God,
who made the world and everything in it,
since He is Lord of heaven and earth, does not
dwell in temples made with hands. 25Nor is He
worshiped with men's hands, as though He
needed anything, since He gives to all life,
breath, and all things. 26And He has made from
one blood every nation of men to dwell on all
the face of the earth, and has determined their
preappointed times and the boundaries of
their dwellings, 27so that they should seek the
Lord, in the hope that they might grope for
Him and find Him, though He is not far from
each one of us; 28for in Him we live and move
and have our being, as also some of your own
poets have said, 'For we are also His offspring.' 29Therefore, since we are the offspring
of God, we ought not to think that the Divine
Nature is like gold or silver or stone, something shaped by art and man's devising.
30Truly, these times of ignorance God overlooked, but now commands all men everywhere to repent, 31because He has appointed a
day on which He will judge the world in righteousness by the Man whom He has ordained.
He has given assurance of this to all by raising
Him from the dead."
32And when they heard of the resurrection
of the dead, some mocked, while others said,
"We will hear you again on this *matter*." 33So
Paul departed from among them. 34However,
some men joined him and believed, among
them Dionysius the Areopagite, a woman
named Damaris, and others with them.

17:28 in Him we live and move and have our being. A quote from the Cretan poet Epimenides.

17:29 the offspring of God. A quote from Aratus, who came from Paul's home region of Cilicia. **not...like gold or silver.** If man is the offspring of God, as the Greek poet suggested, it is foolish to think that God could be nothing more than a man-made idol. Such reasoning points out the absurdity of idolatry (Is. 44:9–20).

DAY 13: How did Paul address the philosophers of Athens?

In preaching to them Jesus and the resurrection, Paul was brought to the Areopagus (Acts 17:19). This was a court named for the hill on which it once met. Paul was not being formally tried; only being asked to defend his teaching.

Paul immediately mentioned the inscription on one other object of worship: TO THE UNKNOWN GOD. The Athenians were supernaturalists—they believed in supernatural powers that intervened in the course of natural laws. They at least acknowledged the existence of someone beyond their ability to understand who had made all things. Paul thus had the opportunity to introduce them to the Creator-God who could be known. When evangelizing pagans, Paul started from creation, the general revelation of God (14:15–17). When evangelizing Jews, he started from the Old Testament (vv. 10–13).

Declaring to them the "God, who made the world" (v. 24) flatly contradicted both the Epicureans, who believed matter was eternal and therefore had no creator, and the Stoics, who as pantheists believed God was part of everything and could not have created Himself. And adding that "He has made from one blood every nation of men" (v. 26) also confronted them directly. All men are equal in God's sight since all came from one man, Adam. This teaching was a blow to the national pride of the Greeks, who believed all non-Greeks were barbarians. "And has determined their preappointed times and the boundaries of their dwellings." God sovereignly controls the rise and fall of nations and empires (Dan. 2:36–45; Luke 21:24). God is responsible for establishing nations as to their racial identity and their specific geographical locations (Deut. 32:8) and determining the extent of their conquests (Is. 10:12–15).

God's objective for man in revealing Himself as the creator, ruler, and controller of the world was that they "should seek the Lord" (v. 27). Men have no excuse for not knowing about God because He has revealed Himself in man's conscience and in the physical world (Rom. 1:19,20; 2:15).

JULY 14

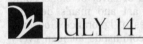

2 Chronicles 23:1–24:27

23 In the seventh year Jehoiada strengthened himself, *and made a* covenant with the captains of hundreds: Azariah the son of Jeroham, Ishmael the son of Jehohanan, Azariah the son of Obed, Maaseiah the son of Adaiah, and Elishaphat the son of Zichri.
2 And they went throughout Judah and gathered the Levites from all the cities of Judah, and the chief fathers of Israel, and they came to Jerusalem.
3 Then all the assembly made a covenant with the king in the house of God. And he said to them, "Behold, the king's son shall reign, as

23:3 as the LORD...said. This is one of the most dramatic moments in messianic history. The human offspring of David have been reduced to one—Joash. If he had died, there would have been no human heir to the Davidic throne, and it would have meant the destruction of the line of the Messiah. However, God remedied the situation by providentially protecting Joash (2 Chr. 22:10–12) and eliminating Athaliah (1 Chr. 23:12–21).

the LORD has said of the sons of David.
4 This *is* what you shall do: One-third of you entering on the Sabbath, of the priests and the Levites, *shall be* keeping watch over the doors;
5 one-third *shall be* at the king's house; and one-third at the Gate of the Foundation. All the people *shall be* in the courts of the house of the LORD.
6 But let no one come into the house of the LORD except the priests and those of the Levites who serve. They may go in, for they *are* holy; but all the people shall keep the watch of the LORD.
7 And the Levites shall surround the king on all sides, every man with his weapons in his hand; and whoever comes into the house, let him be put to death. You are to be with the king when he comes in and when he goes out."
8 So the Levites and all Judah did according to all that Jehoiada the priest commanded. And each man took his men who were to be on duty on the Sabbath, with those who were going *off duty* on the Sabbath; for Jehoiada the priest had not dismissed the divisions.
9 And Jehoiada the priest gave to the captains of hundreds the spears and the large and small shields which *had belonged* to King David, that *were* in the temple of God.
10 Then he set all the people, every man with his weapon in his hand, from the right side of the temple to the left side of the temple, along by the altar and by the temple, all around the king.
11 And they brought out the king's son, put the crown on

him, *gave him* the Testimony, and made him king. Then Jehoiada and his sons anointed him, and said, "*Long* live the king!"

[12]Now when Athaliah heard the noise of the people running and praising the king, she came to the people *in* the temple of the LORD. [13]*When* she looked, there was the king standing by his pillar at the entrance; and the leaders and the trumpeters *were* by the king. All the people of the land were rejoicing and blowing trumpets, also the singers with musical instruments, and those who led in praise. So Athaliah tore her clothes and said, "Treason! Treason!"

[14]And Jehoiada the priest brought out the captains of hundreds who were set over the army, and said to them, "Take her outside under guard, and slay with the sword whoever follows her." For the priest had said, "Do not kill her in the house of the LORD."

[15]So they seized her; and she went by way of the entrance of the Horse Gate *into* the king's house, and they killed her there.

[16]Then Jehoiada made a covenant between himself, the people, and the king, that they should be the LORD's people. [17]And all the people went to the temple of Baal, and tore it down. They broke in pieces its altars and images, and killed Mattan the priest of Baal before the altars. [18]Also Jehoiada appointed the oversight of the house of the LORD to the hand of the priests, the Levites, whom David had assigned in the house of the LORD, to offer the burnt offerings of the LORD, as *it is* written in the Law of Moses, with rejoicing and with singing, *as it was established* by David. [19]And he set the gatekeepers at the gates of the house of the LORD, so that no one *who was* in any way unclean should enter.

[20]Then he took the captains of hundreds, the nobles, the governors of the people, and all the people of the land, and brought the king down from the house of the LORD; and they went through the Upper Gate to the king's house, and set the king on the throne of the kingdom. [21]So all the people of the land rejoiced; and the city was quiet, for they had slain Athaliah with the sword.

24 Joash *was* seven years old when he became king, and he reigned forty years in Jerusalem. His mother's name *was* Zibiah of Beersheba. [2]Joash did *what was* right in the sight of the LORD all the days of Jehoiada the priest. [3]And Jehoiada took two wives for him, and he had sons and daughters.

[4]Now it happened after this *that* Joash set his heart on repairing the house of the LORD. [5]Then he gathered the priests and the Levites, and said to them, "Go out to the cities of Judah, and gather from all Israel money to repair the house of your God from year to year, and see that you do it quickly."

However the Levites did not do it quickly. [6]So the king called Jehoiada the chief *priest,* and said to him, "Why have you not required the Levites to bring in from Judah and from Jerusalem the collection, *according to the commandment* of Moses the servant of the LORD and of the assembly of Israel, for the tabernacle of witness?" [7]For the sons of Athaliah, that wicked woman, had broken into the house of God, and had also presented all the dedicated things of the house of the LORD to the Baals.

[8]Then at the king's command they made a chest, and set it outside at the gate of the house of the LORD. [9]And they made a proclamation throughout Judah and Jerusalem to bring to the LORD the collection *that* Moses the servant of God *had imposed* on Israel in the wilderness. [10]Then all the leaders and all the people rejoiced, brought their contributions, and put *them* into the chest until all had given. [11]So it was, at that time, when the chest was brought to the king's official by the hand of the Levites, and when they saw that *there was* much money, that the king's scribe and the high priest's officer came and emptied the chest, and took it and returned it to its place. Thus they did day by day, and gathered money in abundance.

[12]The king and Jehoiada gave it to those who did the work of the service of the house of the LORD; and they hired masons and carpenters to repair the house of the LORD, and also those who worked in iron and bronze to restore the house of the LORD. [13]So the workmen labored, and the work was completed by them; they restored the house of God to its original condition and reinforced it. [14]When they had finished, they brought the rest of the money before the king and Jehoiada; they made from it articles for the house of the LORD, articles for serving and offering, spoons and vessels of gold and silver. And they offered burnt offerings

24:15,16 Jehoiada. This man was the high priest of Athaliah's and Joash's reigns (2 Chr. 23:1–24:16), who championed God's cause of righteousness during days of evil by: 1) leading the fight against idols; 2) permitting the coup against Athaliah; and 3) granting the throne to Joash to bring about the subsequent revival.

in the house of the LORD continually all the days of Jehoiada.

15But Jehoiada grew old and was full of days, and he died; *he was* one hundred and thirty years old when he died. 16And they buried him in the City of David among the kings, because he had done good in Israel, both toward God and His house.

17Now after the death of Jehoiada the leaders of Judah came and bowed down to the king. And the king listened to them. 18Therefore they left the house of the LORD God of their fathers, and served wooden images and idols; and wrath came upon Judah and Jerusalem because of their trespass. 19Yet He sent prophets to them, to bring them back to the LORD; and they testified against them, but they would not listen.

20Then the Spirit of God came upon Zechariah the son of Jehoiada the priest, who stood above the people, and said to them, "Thus says God: 'Why do you transgress the commandments of the LORD, so that you cannot prosper? Because you have forsaken the LORD, He also has forsaken you.' " 21So they conspired against him, and at the command of the king they stoned him with stones in the court of the house of the LORD. 22Thus Joash the king did not remember the kindness which Jehoiada his father had done to him, but killed his son; and as he died, he said, "The LORD look on *it,* and repay!"

23So it happened in the spring of the year *that* the army of Syria came up against him; and they came to Judah and Jerusalem, and destroyed all the leaders of the people from among the people, and sent all their spoil to the king of Damascus. 24For the army of the Syrians came with a small company of men; but the LORD delivered a very great army into their hand, because they had forsaken the LORD God of their fathers. So they executed judgment against Joash. 25And when they had withdrawn from him (for they left him severely wounded), his own servants conspired against him because of the blood of the sons of Jehoiada the priest, and killed him on his bed. So he died. And they buried him in the City of David, but they did not bury him in the tombs of the kings.

26These are the ones who conspired against him: Zabad the son of Shimeath the Ammonitess, and Jehozabad the son of Shimrith the Moabitess. 27Now *concerning* his sons, and the many oracles about him, and the repairing of the house of God, indeed they *are* written in the annals of the book of the kings. Then Amaziah his son reigned in his place.

Psalm 83:9–18

9 Deal with them as *with* Midian,
As *with* Sisera,
As *with* Jabin at the Brook Kishon,
10 Who perished at En Dor,
Who became *as* refuse on the earth.
11 Make their nobles like Oreb and like Zeeb,
Yes, all their princes like Zebah and Zalmunna,
12 Who said, "Let us take for ourselves
The pastures of God for a possession."
13 O my God, make them like the whirling dust,
Like the chaff before the wind!
14 As the fire burns the woods,
And as the flame sets the mountains on fire,
15 So pursue them with Your tempest,
And frighten them with Your storm.
16 Fill their faces with shame,
That they may seek Your name, O LORD.
17 Let them be confounded and dismayed forever;
Yes, let them be put to shame and perish,
18 That they may know that You, whose name alone *is* the LORD,
Are the Most High over all the earth.

83:18 know...Most High. The purpose of the maledictions against the hostile nations is neither personal nor national, but spiritual: that the nations may know and glorify God. **whose name alone *is* the LORD.** "Alone" should precede "are" in the next phrase. The Gentile nations need to know that the God of the Bible is the only God.

Proverbs 21:2–3

2 Every way of a man *is* right in his own eyes,
But the LORD weighs the hearts.

3 To do righteousness and justice
Is more acceptable to the LORD than sacrifice.

Acts 18:1–28

18 After these things Paul departed from Athens and went to Corinth. 2And he found a certain Jew named Aquila, born in Pontus, who had recently come from Italy

18:1 Corinth. The leading political and commercial center in Greece. It was located at a strategic point on the isthmus of Corinth, which connected the Peloponnesian peninsula with the rest of Greece. Virtually all traffic between northern and southern Greece had to pass through the city. Because Corinth was a trade center and host to all sorts of travelers, it had an unsettled population that was extremely debauched. It also housed the temple of Aphrodite, the goddess of love. One thousand temple priestesses, who were ritual prostitutes, came each evening into the city to practice their trade.

with his wife Priscilla (because Claudius had
commanded all the Jews to depart from
Rome); and he came to them. 3So, because he
was of the same trade, he stayed with them
and worked; for by occupation they were tent-
makers. 4And he reasoned in the synagogue
every Sabbath, and persuaded both Jews and
Greeks.
5When Silas and Timothy had come from
Macedonia, Paul was compelled by the Spirit,
and testified to the Jews *that* Jesus *is* the
Christ. 6But when they opposed him and blasphemed, he shook *his* garments and said to
them, "Your blood *be* upon your *own* heads; I
am clean. From now on I will go to the
Gentiles." 7And he departed from there and
entered the house of a certain *man* named
Justus, *one* who worshiped God, whose house
was next door to the synagogue. 8Then
Crispus, the ruler of the synagogue, believed
on the Lord with all his household. And many
of the Corinthians, hearing, believed and were
baptized.

18:8 Crispus, the ruler of the synagogue. The conversion of this respected leader must have sent shock waves throughout the Jewish community.

9Now the Lord spoke to Paul in the night by
a vision, "Do not be afraid, but speak, and do
not keep silent; 10for I am with you, and no one
will attack you to hurt you; for I have many
people in this city." 11And he continued *there* a
year and six months, teaching the word of
God among them.

18:13 contrary to the law. While Judaism was not an official religion, it was officially tolerated in the Roman world, and Christianity was viewed as a sect of Judaism. The Jews in Corinth claimed that Paul's teaching was external to Judaism and therefore should be banned. Had Gallio ruled in the Jews' favor, Christianity could have been outlawed throughout the empire.

12When Gallio was proconsul of Achaia, the
Jews with one accord rose up against Paul and
brought him to the judgment seat, 13saying,
"This *fellow* persuades men to worship God
contrary to the law."
14And when Paul was about to open *his* mouth,
Gallio said to the Jews, "If it were a matter of
wrongdoing or wicked crimes, O Jews, there
would be reason why I should bear with you.
15But if it is a question of words and names and
your own law, look *to it* yourselves; for I do not
want to be a judge of such *matters*." 16And he
drove them from the judgment seat. 17Then all
the Greeks took Sosthenes, the ruler of the synagogue, and beat *him* before the judgment seat.
But Gallio took no notice of these things.
18So Paul still remained a good while. Then he
took leave of the brethren and sailed for Syria,
and Priscilla and Aquila *were* with him. He had
his hair cut off at Cenchrea, for he had taken a
vow. 19And he came to Ephesus, and left them
there; but he himself entered the synagogue
and reasoned with the Jews. 20When they
asked *him* to stay a longer time with them, he
did not consent, 21but took leave of them, saying, "I must by all means keep this coming feast
in Jerusalem; but I will return again to you, God
willing." And he sailed from Ephesus.
22And when he had landed at Caesarea, and
gone up and greeted the church, he went down to
Antioch. 23After he had spent some time *there*, he
departed and went over the region of Galatia and
Phrygia in order, strengthening all the disciples.
24Now a certain Jew named Apollos, born at
Alexandria, an eloquent man *and* mighty in
the Scriptures, came to Ephesus. 25This man
had been instructed in the way of the Lord;
and being fervent in spirit, he spoke and
taught accurately the things of the Lord,
though he knew only the baptism of John. 26So
he began to speak boldly in the synagogue.
When Aquila and Priscilla heard him, they
took him aside and explained to him the way
of God more accurately. 27And when he

desired to cross to Achaia, the brethren wrote, exhorting the disciples to receive him; and when he arrived, he greatly helped those who had believed through grace; [28]for he vigorously refuted the Jews publicly, showing from the Scriptures that Jesus is the Christ.

DAY 14: How did Aquila and Priscilla help Apollos?

In Acts 18:24, Apollos came to Ephesus and clearly was an Old Testament saint and follower of John the Baptist (v. 25). He came from Alexandria, an important city in Egypt located near the mouth of the Nile. In the first century, it had a large Jewish population. Thus Apollos, though born outside of Israel, was reared in a Jewish cultural setting. It states that he was "mighty in the Scriptures," referring to Apollos's knowledge of the Old Testament Scriptures. That knowledge, combined with his eloquence, allowed him to crush his Jewish opponents in a later debate (v. 28).

He had been instructed in "the way of the Lord" (v. 25). This did not include the Christian faith (v. 26). The Old Testament uses the phrase to describe the spiritual and moral standards God required His people to observe. "He knew only the baptism of John." Despite his knowledge of the Old Testament, Apollos did not fully understand Christian truth. John's baptism was to prepare Israel for the Messiah's arrival. Apollos accepted that message, even acknowledging that Jesus of Nazareth was Israel's Messiah. He did not, however, understand such basic Christian truths as the significance of Christ's death and resurrection, the ministry of the Holy Spirit, and the church as God's new witness people. He was a redeemed Old Testament believer (v. 24).

Fortunately, Aquila and Priscilla completed Apollos's training in divine truth by instructing him in the fullness of the Christian faith (v. 26). After further instruction, he became a powerful Christian preacher. His ministry profoundly influenced the Corinthians (1 Cor. 1:12). Aquila and Priscilla were a husband and wife team who became Paul's close friends and even risked their lives for him (Rom. 16:3,4).

JULY 15

2 Chronicles 25:1–27:9

25 Amaziah *was* twenty-five years old
when he became king, and he reigned
twenty-nine years in Jerusalem. His mother's
name *was* Jehoaddan of Jerusalem. [2]And he
did *what was* right in the sight of the LORD, but
not with a loyal heart.
[3]Now it happened, as soon as the kingdom
was established for him, that he executed his
servants who had murdered his father the
king. [4]However he did not execute their children, but *did* as *it is* written in the Law in the
Book of Moses, where the LORD commanded,
saying, "The fathers shall not be put to death
for their children, nor shall the children be put
to death for their fathers; but a person shall
die for his own sin."
[5]Moreover Amaziah gathered Judah together and set over them captains of thousands and
captains of hundreds, according to *their*
fathers' houses, throughout all Judah and Benjamin; and he numbered them from twenty
years old and above, and found them to be
three hundred thousand choice *men, able* to
go to war, who could handle spear and shield.
[6]He also hired one hundred thousand mighty
men of valor from Israel for one hundred talents of silver. [7]But a man of God came to him,
saying, "O king, do not let the army of Israel
go with you, for the LORD *is* not with Israel—
not with any of the children of Ephraim. [8]But if
you go, be gone! Be strong in battle! *Even so,*
God shall make you fall before the enemy; for
God has power to help and to overthrow."
[9]Then Amaziah said to the man of God, "But
what *shall we* do about the hundred talents
which I have given to the troops of Israel?"
And the man of God answered, "The LORD is
able to give you much more than this." [10]So
Amaziah discharged the troops that had come to
him from Ephraim, to go back home. Therefore
their anger was greatly aroused against Judah,
and they returned home in great anger.
[11]Then Amaziah strengthened himself, and
leading his people, he went to the Valley of Salt
and killed ten thousand of the people of Seir.
[12]Also the children of Judah took captive ten

25:7 man of God. This is a technical term used about 70 times in the Old Testament, always referring to one who spoke for God. He warned Amaziah not to make idolatrous Israel his ally because the Lord was not with Ephraim, i.e., Israel, the capital of idolatry.

25:8 God has power. The man of God reminded the king sarcastically that he would need to be strong, since God wouldn't help.

thousand alive, brought them to the top of the
rock, and cast them down from the top of the
rock, so that they all were dashed in pieces.
[13]But as for the soldiers of the army which
Amaziah had discharged, so that they would
not go with him to battle, they raided the cities
of Judah from Samaria to Beth Horon, killed
three thousand in them, and took much spoil.
[14]Now it was so, after Amaziah came from the
slaughter of the Edomites, that he brought the
gods of the people of Seir, set them up *to be* his
gods, and bowed down before them and burned
incense to them. [15]Therefore the anger of the
LORD was aroused against Amaziah, and He
sent him a prophet who said to him, "Why have
you sought the gods of the people, which could
not rescue their own people from your hand?"
[16]So it was, as he talked with him, that *the
king* said to him, "Have we made you the king's
counselor? Cease! Why should you be killed?"

25:14–16 Amaziah did the unthinkable from both a biblical and political perspective—he embraced the false gods of the people whom he had just defeated. Perhaps he did this because he was seduced by the wicked pleasures of idolatry and because he thought it would help him in assuring no future threat from Edom. However, it only brought destruction to the king, who just wanted to silence the voice of God.

Then the prophet ceased, and said, "I know
that God has determined to destroy you,
because you have done this and have not
heeded my advice."
[17]Now Amaziah king of Judah asked advice
and sent to Joash the son of Jehoahaz, the son
of Jehu, king of Israel, saying, "Come, let us
face one another *in battle.*"
[18]And Joash king of Israel sent to Amaziah
king of Judah, saying, "The thistle that *was* in
Lebanon sent to the cedar that was in Lebanon,
saying, 'Give your daughter to my son as wife';
and a wild beast that *was* in Lebanon passed
by and trampled the thistle. [19]Indeed you say
that you have defeated the Edomites, and your
heart is lifted up to boast. Stay at home now;
why should you meddle with trouble, that you
should fall—you and Judah with you?"
[20]But Amaziah would not heed, for it *came*
from God, that He might give them into the
hand *of their enemies,* because they sought the
gods of Edom. [21]So Joash king of Israel went
out; and he and Amaziah king of Judah faced
one another at Beth Shemesh, which *belongs*
to Judah. [22]And Judah was defeated by Israel,
and every man fled to his tent. [23]Then Joash
the king of Israel captured Amaziah king of Judah, the son of Joash, the son of Jehoahaz, at
Beth Shemesh; and he brought him to Jerusalem, and broke down the wall of Jerusalem
from the Gate of Ephraim to the Corner Gate—
four hundred cubits. [24]And *he took* all the gold
and silver, all the articles that were found in
the house of God with Obed-Edom, the treasures of the king's house, and hostages, and
returned to Samaria.
[25]Amaziah the son of Joash, king of Judah,
lived fifteen years after the death of Joash the
son of Jehoahaz, king of Israel. [26]Now the rest
of the acts of Amaziah, from first to last,
indeed *are* they not written in the book of the
kings of Judah and Israel? [27]After the time that
Amaziah turned away from following the LORD,
they made a conspiracy against him in Jerusalem, and he fled to Lachish; but they sent after
him to Lachish and killed him there. [28]Then
they brought him on horses and buried him
with his fathers in the City of Judah.
26 Now all the people of Judah took Uzziah,
who *was* sixteen years old, and made
him king instead of his father Amaziah. [2]He
built Elath and restored it to Judah, after the
king rested with his fathers.
[3]Uzziah *was* sixteen years old when he
became king, and he reigned fifty-two years in
Jerusalem. His mother's name was Jecholiah
of Jerusalem. [4]And he did *what was* right in
the sight of the LORD, according to all that his
father Amaziah had done. [5]He sought God in
the days of Zechariah, who had understanding
in the visions of God; and as long as he sought
the LORD, God made him prosper.
[6]Now he went out and made war against the
Philistines, and broke down the wall of Gath,
the wall of Jabneh, and the wall of Ashdod; and
he built cities *around* Ashdod and among the
Philistines. [7]God helped him against the
Philistines, against the Arabians who lived in
Gur Baal, and against the Meunites. [8]Also the
Ammonites brought tribute to Uzziah. His
fame spread as far as the entrance of Egypt,
for he became exceedingly strong.
[9]And Uzziah built towers in Jerusalem at the
Corner Gate, at the Valley Gate, and at the corner buttress of the wall; then he fortified
them. [10]Also he built towers in the desert. He
dug many wells, for he had much livestock,
both in the lowlands and in the plains; *he also
had* farmers and vinedressers in the mountains and in Carmel, for he loved the soil.
[11]Moreover Uzziah had an army of fighting

men who went out to war by companies,
according to the number on their roll as prepared by Jeiel the scribe and Maaseiah the officer, under the hand of Hananiah, *one* of the
king's captains. 12 The total number of chief officers of the mighty men of valor *was* two thousand six hundred. 13 And under their authority
was an army of three hundred and seven thousand five hundred, that made war with mighty
power, to help the king against the enemy.
14 Then Uzziah prepared for them, for the entire
army, shields, spears, helmets, body armor,
bows, and slings *to cast* stones. 15 And he made
devices in Jerusalem, invented by skillful men,
to be on the towers and the corners, to shoot
arrows and large stones. So his fame spread
far and wide, for he was marvelously helped
till he became strong.
16 But when he was strong his heart was lifted up, to *his* destruction, for he transgressed
against the LORD his God by entering the temple of the LORD to burn incense on the altar of
incense. 17 So Azariah the priest went in after
him, and with him were eighty priests of the
LORD—valiant men. 18 And they withstood King
Uzziah, and said to him, "*It is* not for you,
Uzziah, to burn incense to the LORD, but for the
priests, the sons of Aaron, who are consecrated
to burn incense. Get out of the sanctuary, for
you have trespassed! You *shall have* no honor
from the LORD God."
19 Then Uzziah became furious; and he *had* a
censer in his hand to burn incense. And while
he was angry with the priests, leprosy broke
out on his forehead, before the priests in the
house of the LORD, beside the incense altar.
20 And Azariah the chief priest and all the priests
looked at him, and there, on his forehead, he
was leprous; so they thrust him out of that
place. Indeed he also hurried to get out,
because the LORD had struck him.
21 King Uzziah was a leper until the day of his
death. He dwelt in an isolated house, because
he was a leper; for he was cut off from the house
of the LORD. Then Jotham his son *was* over the
king's house, judging the people of the land.
22 Now the rest of the acts of Uzziah, from
first to last, the prophet Isaiah the son of Amoz
wrote. 23 So Uzziah rested with his fathers, and
they buried him with his fathers in the field of
burial which *belonged* to the kings, for they
said, "He is a leper." Then Jotham his son
reigned in his place.

27 Jotham *was* twenty-five years old when
he became king, and he reigned sixteen years in Jerusalem. His mother's name
was Jerushah the daughter of Zadok. 2 And he
did *what was* right in the sight of the LORD,
according to all that his father Uzziah had
done (although he did not enter the temple of
the LORD). But still the people acted corruptly.
3 He built the Upper Gate of the house of the
LORD, and he built extensively on the wall of
Ophel. 4 Moreover he built cities in the mountains of Judah, and in the forests he built
fortresses and towers. 5 He also fought with
the king of the Ammonites and defeated them.
And the people of Ammon gave him in that
year one hundred talents of silver, ten thousand kors of wheat, and ten thousand of barley.
The people of Ammon paid this to him in the
second and third years also. 6 So Jotham
became mighty, because he prepared his ways
before the LORD his God.
7 Now the rest of the acts of Jotham, and all
his wars and his ways, indeed they *are* written
in the book of the kings of Israel and Judah.
8 He was twenty-five years old when he became
king, and he reigned sixteen years in Jerusalem. 9 So Jotham rested with his fathers, and
they buried him in the City of David. Then
Ahaz his son reigned in his place.

Psalm 84:1–7

To the Chief Musician. On an instrument of Gath.
A Psalm of the sons of Korah.

How lovely *is* Your tabernacle,
O LORD of hosts!
2 My soul longs, yes, even faints
For the courts of the LORD;
My heart and my flesh cry out for the
living God.

3 Even the sparrow has found a home,
And the swallow a nest for herself,
Where she may lay her young—
Even Your altars, O LORD of hosts,
My King and my God.
4 Blessed *are* those who dwell in Your
house;
They will still be praising You.
Selah

5 Blessed *is* the man whose strength *is*
in You,
Whose heart *is* set on pilgrimage.
6 *As they* pass through the Valley of Baca,
They make it a spring;
The rain also covers it with pools.
7 They go from strength to strength;
Each one appears before God in Zion.

Proverbs 21:4–5

4 A haughty look, a proud heart,
And the plowing of the wicked *are* sin.
5 The plans of the diligent *lead* surely
to plenty,

But *those of* everyone *who is* hasty,
surely to poverty.

Acts 19:1–20

19 And it happened, while Apollos was at
Corinth, that Paul, having passed
through the upper regions, came to Ephesus.
And finding some disciples [2]he said to them,
"Did you receive the Holy Spirit when you
believed?"
So they said to him, "We have not so much
as heard whether there is a Holy Spirit."
[3]And he said to them, "Into what then were
you baptized?"
So they said, "Into John's baptism."
[4]Then Paul said, "John indeed baptized with
a baptism of repentance, saying to the people
that they should believe on Him who would
come after him, that is, on Christ Jesus."
[5]When they heard *this,* they were baptized
in the name of the Lord Jesus. [6]And when Paul
had laid hands on them, the Holy Spirit came
upon them, and they spoke with tongues and
prophesied. [7]Now the men were about twelve
in all.
[8]And he went into the synagogue and spoke
boldly for three months, reasoning and persuading concerning the things of the kingdom
of God. [9]But when some were hardened and
did not believe, but spoke evil of the Way
before the multitude, he departed from them
and withdrew the disciples, reasoning daily in
the school of Tyrannus. [10]And this continued
for two years, so that all who dwelt in Asia
heard the word of the Lord Jesus, both Jews
and Greeks.
[11]Now God worked unusual miracles by the
hands of Paul, [12]so that even handkerchiefs or
aprons were brought from his body to the
sick, and the diseases left them and the evil
spirits went out of them. [13]Then some of the
itinerant Jewish exorcists took it upon themselves to call the name of the Lord Jesus over
those who had evil spirits, saying, "We exor-
cise you by the Jesus whom Paul preaches."
[14]Also there were seven sons of Sceva, a Jewish chief priest, who did so.

19:13 itinerant Jewish exorcists. Simon Magus (8:9–25) and Bar-Jesus (13:6–12) were other possible examples of such charlatans (Matt. 12:27). In contrast to the absolute authority exercised by Jesus and the apostles over demons, those exorcists sought to expel the demons by attempting to call on a more potent spirit being—in this case the Lord Jesus.

19:15 Jesus...Paul I know. Recognizing that the exorcists had no authority over him (unlike Jesus and Paul), the demon rejected their attempt to expel him from his victim. This confirms that the power to cast out demons belonged to Jesus and the apostles and no one else. Even the demons give testimony to that.

19:19 books. Of secret magical spells. Burning them proved the genuineness of the magicians' repentance. Having destroyed these books, they could not easily resume their practices. **fifty thousand *pieces* of silver.** Fifty thousand days' wages for a common laborer—an astonishing sum of money given to indicate how widespread the practice of magic was in Ephesus.

[15]And the evil spirit answered and said, "Jesus I know, and Paul I know; but who are
you?"
[16]Then the man in whom the evil spirit was
leaped on them, overpowered them, and prevailed against them, so that they fled out of
that house naked and wounded. [17]This became
known both to all Jews and Greeks dwelling in
Ephesus; and fear fell on them all, and the
name of the Lord Jesus was magnified. [18]And
many who had believed came confessing and
telling their deeds. [19]Also, many of those who
had practiced magic brought their books
together and burned *them* in the sight of all.
And they counted up the value of them, and *it*
totaled fifty thousand *pieces* of silver. [20]So the
word of the Lord grew mightily and prevailed.

DAY 15: How could the "disciples" of Acts 19:1 not have received the Holy Spirit?

Coming to Ephesus, Paul found "some disciples." They were of John the Baptist (v. 3), hence Old Testament seekers. That they did not yet fully understand the Christian faith is evident from their reply to Paul's question (v. 2). The word "disciple" means "learner," or "follower," and does not always refer to Christians (Matt. 9:14; 11:2; Mark 2:18; Luke 5:33; 7:18,19; 11:1; John 1:35; 6:66). Followers of John the Baptist, like this group, existed into the second century.

"Did you receive the Holy Spirit when you believed?" (v. 2). The question reflects Paul's uncertainty about their spiritual status. Since all Christians receive the Holy Spirit at the moment of salvation, their answer revealed they were not yet fully Christians. They had not yet received Christian baptism (having been baptized only "into John's baptism"), which further evidenced that they were not Christians. These disciples did not realize Jesus of Nazareth was the One to whom John's baptism pointed. Paul gave them instruction not on how to receive the Spirit, but about Jesus Christ. "They were baptized in the name of the Lord Jesus" (v. 5). They believed Paul's presentation of the gospel and came to saving faith in the Lord Jesus Christ (2:41). Although required of all Christians, baptism does not save.

Then "Paul…laid hands on them" (v. 6). This signified their inclusion into the church. Apostles were also present when the church was born (chap. 2), and when the Samaritans (chap. 8) and Gentiles (chap. 10) were included. In each case, God's purpose was to emphasize the unity of the church. And they "spoke with tongues and prophesied." This served as proof that they were part of the church. They also needed tangible evidence that the Holy Spirit now indwelt them, since they had not heard that He had come (v. 2).

JULY 16

2 Chronicles 28:1–29:36

28 Ahaz *was* twenty years old when he became king, and he reigned sixteen years in Jerusalem; and he did not do *what was* right in the sight of the LORD, as his father David *had done.* 2For he walked in the ways of the kings of Israel, and made molded images for the Baals. 3He burned incense in the Valley of the Son of Hinnom, and burned his children in the fire, according to the abominations of the nations whom the LORD had cast out before the children of Israel. 4And he sacrificed and burned incense on the high places, on the hills, and under every green tree.

5Therefore the LORD his God delivered him into the hand of the king of Syria. They defeated him, and carried away a great multitude of them as captives, and brought *them* to Damascus. Then he was also delivered into the hand of the king of Israel, who defeated him with a great slaughter. 6For Pekah the son of Remaliah killed one hundred and twenty thousand in Judah in one day, all valiant men, because they had forsaken the LORD God of their fathers. 7Zichri, a mighty man of Ephraim, killed Maaseiah the king's son, Azrikam the officer over the house, and Elkanah *who was* second to the king. 8And the children of Israel carried away captive of their brethren two hundred thousand women, sons, and daughters; and they also took away much spoil from them, and brought the spoil to Samaria.

9But a prophet of the LORD was there, whose name *was* Oded; and he went out before the army that came to Samaria, and said to them: "Look, because the LORD God of your fathers was angry with Judah, He has delivered them into your hand; but you have killed them in a rage *that* reaches up to heaven. 10And now you propose to force the children of Judah and Jerusalem to be your male and female slaves; *but are* you not also guilty before the LORD your God? 11Now hear me, therefore, and return the captives, whom you have taken captive from your brethren, for the fierce wrath of the LORD *is* upon you."

12Then some of the heads of the children of Ephraim, Azariah the son of Johanan, Berechiah the son of Meshillemoth, Jehizkiah the son of Shallum, and Amasa the son of Hadlai, stood up against those who came from the war, 13and said to them, "You shall not bring the captives here, for we *already* have offended the LORD. You intend to add to our sins and to our guilt; for our guilt is great, and *there is* fierce wrath against Israel." 14So the armed men left the captives and the spoil before the leaders and all the assembly. 15Then the men who were designated by name rose up and took the captives, and from the spoil they clothed all who were naked among them, dressed them and gave them sandals, gave them food and drink, and anointed them; and they let all the feeble ones ride on donkeys. So they brought them to their brethren at Jericho, the city of palm trees. Then they returned to Samaria.

16At the same time King Ahaz sent to the kings of Assyria to help him. 17For again the Edomites had come, attacked Judah, and carried away captives. 18The Philistines also had invaded the cities of the lowland and of the

28:9 Oded. An otherwise unknown prophet, with the same name as an earlier Oded (15:1,8). The prophet said that Israel had won the victory because God was judging Judah. But he protested the viciousness of the killing and the effort to enslave them (v. 10) and warned them of God's wrath for such action (v. 11). Amazingly the apostate and hostile Israelites complied with the prophet's warning (vv. 12–15).

South of Judah, and had taken Beth Shemesh,
Aijalon, Gederoth, Sochoh with its villages,
Timnah with its villages, and Gimzo with its
villages; and they dwelt there. 19For the LORD
brought Judah low because of Ahaz king of Israel, for he had encouraged moral decline in
Judah and had been continually unfaithful to
the LORD. 20Also Tiglath-Pileser king of Assyria
came to him and distressed him, and did not
assist him. 21For Ahaz took part *of the treasures*
from the house of the LORD, from the house of
the king, and from the leaders, and he gave *it*
to the king of Assyria; but he did not help him.
22Now in the time of his distress King Ahaz
became increasingly unfaithful to the LORD.
This *is that* King Ahaz. 23For he sacrificed to
the gods of Damascus which had defeated
him, saying, "Because the gods of the kings of
Syria help them, I will sacrifice to them that
they may help me." But they were the ruin of
him and of all Israel. 24So Ahaz gathered the
articles of the house of God, cut in pieces the
articles of the house of God, shut up the doors
of the house of the LORD, and made for himself
altars in every corner of Jerusalem. 25And in
every single city of Judah he made high places
to burn incense to other gods, and provoked
to anger the LORD God of his fathers.
26Now the rest of his acts and all his ways,
from first to last, indeed they *are* written in the
book of the kings of Judah and Israel. 27So
Ahaz rested with his fathers, and they buried
him in the city, in Jerusalem; but they did not
bring him into the tombs of the kings of Israel.
Then Hezekiah his son reigned in his place.

29 Hezekiah became king *when he was*
twenty-five years old, and he reigned
twenty-nine years in Jerusalem. His mother's
name *was* Abijah the daughter of Zechariah.
2And he did *what was* right in the sight of the
LORD, according to all that his father David
had done.
3In the first year of his reign, in the first
month, he opened the doors of the house of
the LORD and repaired them. 4Then he
brought in the priests and the Levites, and
gathered them in the East Square, 5and said to
them: "Hear me, Levites! Now sanctify yourselves, sanctify the house of the LORD God of
your fathers, and carry out the rubbish from
the holy *place.* 6For our fathers have trespassed and done evil in the eyes of the LORD
our God; they have forsaken Him, have turned
their faces away from the dwelling place of the
LORD, and turned *their* backs *on Him.* 7They
have also shut up the doors of the vestibule,
put out the lamps, and have not burned
incense or offered burnt offerings in the holy
place to the God of Israel. 8Therefore the
wrath of the LORD fell upon Judah and Jerusalem, and He has given them up to trouble, to
desolation, and to jeering, as you see with
your eyes. 9For indeed, because of this our
fathers have fallen by the sword; and our sons,
our daughters, and our wives *are* in captivity.
10"Now *it is* in my heart to make a covenant
with the LORD God of Israel, that His fierce
wrath may turn away from us. 11My sons, do not
be negligent now, for the LORD has chosen you
to stand before Him, to serve Him, and that you
should minister to Him and burn incense."
12Then these Levites arose: Mahath the son
of Amasai and Joel the son of Azariah, of the
sons of the Kohathites; of the sons of Merari,
Kish the son of Abdi and Azariah the son of
Jehallelel; of the Gershonites, Joah the son of
Zimmah and Eden the son of Joah; 13of the
sons of Elizaphan, Shimri and Jeiel; of the
sons of Asaph, Zechariah and Mattaniah; 14of
the sons of Heman, Jehiel and Shimei; and of
the sons of Jeduthun, Shemaiah and Uzziel.
15And they gathered their brethren, sanctified themselves, and went according to the
commandment of the king, at the words of the
LORD, to cleanse the house of the LORD. 16Then
the priests went into the inner part of the
house of the LORD to cleanse *it,* and brought
out all the debris that they found in the temple
of the LORD to the court of the house of the
LORD. And the Levites took *it* out and carried
it to the Brook Kidron.
17Now they began to sanctify on the first *day*
of the first month, and on the eighth day of the
month they came to the vestibule of the LORD.
So they sanctified the house of the LORD in
eight days, and on the sixteenth day of the
first month they finished.
18Then they went in to King Hezekiah and
said, "We have cleansed all the house of the
LORD, the altar of burnt offerings with all its articles, and the table of the showbread with all its

29:3 first year...first month. Hezekiah addressed the spiritual problems first, which reflected his life priorities. Hezekiah correctly diagnosed Judah's ills—she had abandoned the true worship of God. So the king stepped in to reverse the policy of his father (28:22–25) and to repair the temple and return proper temple worship as God had prescribed in His Word (vv. 3–7). He knew such a revival of devotion to God would turn God's wrath away from Judah (v. 10).

articles. 19 Moreover all the articles which King
Ahaz in his reign had cast aside in his transgression we have prepared and sanctified; and
there they *are,* before the altar of the LORD."
20 Then King Hezekiah rose early, gathered
the rulers of the city, and went up to the
house of the LORD. 21 And they brought seven
bulls, seven rams, seven lambs, and seven
male goats for a sin offering for the kingdom,
for the sanctuary, and for Judah. Then he
commanded the priests, the sons of Aaron, to
offer *them* on the altar of the LORD. 22 So they
killed the bulls, and the priests received the
blood and sprinkled *it* on the altar. Likewise
they killed the rams and sprinkled the blood
on the altar. They also killed the lambs and
sprinkled the blood on the altar. 23 Then they
brought out the male goats *for* the sin offering before the king and the assembly, and
they laid their hands on them. 24 And the
priests killed them; and they presented their
blood on the altar as a sin offering to make an
atonement for all Israel, for the king commanded *that* the burnt offering and the sin
offering *be made* for all Israel.
25 And he stationed the Levites in the house
of the LORD with cymbals, with stringed
instruments, and with harps, according to the
commandment of David, of Gad the king's seer,
and of Nathan the prophet; for thus *was* the
commandment of the LORD by His prophets.
26 The Levites stood with the instruments of
David, and the priests with the trumpets.
27 Then Hezekiah commanded *them* to offer the
burnt offering on the altar. And when the burnt
offering began, the song of the LORD *also* began,
with the trumpets and with the instruments of
David king of Israel. 28 So all the assembly worshiped, the singers sang, and the trumpeters
sounded; all *this continued* until the burnt offering was finished. 29 And when they had finished
offering, the king and all who were present
with him bowed and worshiped. 30 Moreover
King Hezekiah and the leaders commanded
the Levites to sing praise to the LORD with the
words of David and of Asaph the seer. So they
sang praises with gladness, and they bowed
their heads and worshiped.
31 Then Hezekiah answered and said, "Now
that you have consecrated yourselves to the
LORD, come near, and bring sacrifices and
thank offerings into the house of the LORD."
So the assembly brought in sacrifices and
thank offerings, and as many as were of a willing heart *brought* burnt offerings. 32 And the
number of the burnt offerings which the
assembly brought was seventy bulls, one hundred rams, *and* two hundred lambs; all these
were for a burnt offering to the LORD. 33 The
consecrated things *were* six hundred bulls and
three thousand sheep. 34 But the priests were
too few, so that they could not skin all the
burnt offerings; therefore their brethren the
Levites helped them until the work was ended
and until the *other* priests had sanctified themselves, for the Levites were more diligent in
sanctifying themselves than the priests. 35 Also
the burnt offerings *were* in abundance, with the
fat of the peace offerings and *with* the drink
offerings for *every* burnt offering.
So the service of the house of the LORD was
set in order. 36 Then Hezekiah and all the people rejoiced that God had prepared the people,
since the events took place so suddenly.

Psalm 84:8–12

8 O LORD God of hosts, hear my prayer;
Give ear, O God of Jacob! Selah
9 O God, behold our shield,
And look upon the face of Your
anointed.

84:9 behold our shield. A metaphor for the king, who also would have participated in a festival at the temple (Ps. 47:9; Hos. 4:18). **the face of Your anointed.** The king is regularly described as God's "anointed" (Pss. 2:2; 18:50; 20:6; 28:8; 89:38,51). The psalmist thus prays that God would look upon the king with favor, blessing his reign with prosperity.

10 For a day in Your courts *is* better than
a thousand.
I would rather be a doorkeeper
in the house of my God
Than dwell in the tents of
wickedness.
11 For the LORD God *is* a sun
and shield;
The LORD will give grace and glory;
No good *thing* will He withhold
From those who walk uprightly.
12 O LORD of hosts,
Blessed *is* the man who trusts
in You!

Proverbs 21:6–8

6 Getting treasures by a lying tongue
Is the fleeting fantasy of those who
seek death.

7 The violence of the wicked will destroy them,
Because they refuse to do justice.
8 The way of a guilty man *is* perverse;
But *as for* the pure, his work *is* right.

Acts 19:21–41

21When these things were accomplished,
Paul purposed in the Spirit, when he had
passed through Macedonia and Achaia, to go
to Jerusalem, saying, "After I have been
there, I must also see Rome." 22So he sent into
Macedonia two of those who ministered to
him, Timothy and Erastus, but he himself
stayed in Asia for a time.

19:21 I must also see Rome. Paul had not visited the Imperial capital; but because of the strategic importance of the church there, he could stay away no longer. In addition, Paul intended to use Rome as a jumping-off point for ministry in the strategic region of Spain (Rom. 15:22–24). This simple declaration marked a turning point in Acts—from this point on, Rome became Paul's goal. He would ultimately arrive there as a Roman prisoner (28:16).

23And about that time there arose a great
commotion about the Way. 24For a certain man
named Demetrius, a silversmith, who made
silver shrines of Diana, brought no small
profit to the craftsmen. 25He called them
together with the workers of similar occupation, and said: "Men, you know that we have
our prosperity by this trade. 26Moreover you
see and hear that not only at Ephesus, but
throughout almost all Asia, this Paul has persuaded and turned away many people, saying
that they are not gods which are made with
hands. 27So not only is this trade of ours in danger of falling into disrepute, but also the temple
of the great goddess Diana may be despised
and her magnificence destroyed, whom all
Asia and the world worship."
28Now when they heard *this,* they were full
of wrath and cried out, saying, "Great *is* Diana
of the Ephesians!" 29So the whole city was
filled with confusion, and rushed into the theater with one accord, having seized Gaius and
Aristarchus, Macedonians, Paul's travel companions. 30And when Paul wanted to go in to
the people, the disciples would not allow him.
31Then some of the officials of Asia, who were
his friends, sent to him pleading that he would
not venture into the theater. 32Some therefore
cried one thing and some another, for the
assembly was confused, and most of them did
not know why they had come together. 33And
they drew Alexander out of the multitude, the
Jews putting him forward. And Alexander motioned with his hand, and wanted to make his
defense to the people. 34But when they found
out that he was a Jew, all with one voice cried
out for about two hours, "Great *is* Diana of the
Ephesians!"

19:31 officials of Asia. Known by the title "Asiarchs," these members of the aristocracy were dedicated to promoting Roman interests. Though only one Asiarch ruled at a time, they bore the title for life. That such powerful, influential men were Paul's friends shows that they did not regard him or his message as criminal. Hence, there was no legitimate cause for the riot.

19:33 Alexander. Probably not the false teacher later active at Ephesus (1 Tim. 1:20) or the individual who opposed Paul at Rome (2 Tim. 4:14), since the name was common. He was either a Christian Jew or a spokesman for Ephesus's Jewish community. Either way, the Jews' motive for putting him forward was the same—to disassociate themselves from the Christians and avoid a massacre of the Jews. **make his defense.** Either of the Christians, or the Jews, depending on which group he represented.

35And when the city clerk had quieted the
crowd, he said: "Men of Ephesus, what man is
there who does not know that the city of the
Ephesians is temple guardian of the great goddess Diana, and of the *image* which fell down
from Zeus? 36Therefore, since these things
cannot be denied, you ought to be quiet and
do nothing rashly. 37For you have brought
these men here who are neither robbers of
temples nor blasphemers of your goddess.
38Therefore, if Demetrius and his fellow craftsmen have a case against anyone, the courts
are open and there are proconsuls. Let them
bring charges against one another. 39But if you
have any other inquiry to make, it shall be
determined in the lawful assembly. 40For we
are in danger of being called in question for
today's uproar, there being no reason which
we may give to account for this disorderly
gathering." 41And when he had said these
things, he dismissed the assembly.

DAY 16: How profound an impact can the gospel have on a society?

Reading Acts 19:1–20, it is clear that the gospel made a tremendous impact on Ephesus. Paul's two years of ministry here along with "unusual miracles," the very public deliverance of a man from an evil spirit, and burning of magic books had left there mark. "So the word of the Lord grew mightily and prevailed" (v. 20).

So much so that Demetrius, a silversmith, took action against them. He was a maker of "silver shrines of Diana" (v. 24), the goddess Diana (also known as Artemis). These shrines were used as household idols and in the worship at the temple of Diana. Worship of her, centered at the great temple of Diana at Ephesus (one of the Seven Wonders of the Ancient World), was widespread throughout the Roman Empire. It is likely that the riot described in this passage took place during the annual spring festival held in her honor at Ephesus. The statement "brought no small profit" suggests Demetrius may have been the head of the silversmiths' guild—which would explain his taking the lead in opposing the Christian preachers.

Demetrius cleverly played upon his hearers' fears of financial ruin, religious zeal, and concern for their city's prestige. The Christian preachers, he argued, threatened the continued prosperity of Ephesus. His audience's violent reaction shows they took the threat seriously (v. 28). That was the impact of the gospel on their daily lives. The frenzied mob gathered in the theater clearly threatened the lives of Gaius and Aristarchus because of their role in the delivery of the Christian message.

JULY 17

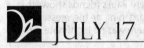

2 Chronicles 30:1–31:21

30 And Hezekiah sent to all Israel and Judah, and also wrote letters to Ephraim and Manasseh, that they should come to the house of the LORD at Jerusalem, to keep the Passover to the LORD God of Israel.
2For the king and his leaders and all the assembly in Jerusalem had agreed to keep the Passover in the second month.
3For they could not keep it at the regular time, because a sufficient number of priests had not consecrated themselves, nor had the people gathered together at Jerusalem.
4And the matter pleased the king and all the assembly.
5So they resolved to make a proclamation throughout all Israel, from Beersheba to Dan, that they should come to keep the Passover to the LORD God of Israel at Jerusalem, since they had not done *it* for a long *time* in the *prescribed* manner.
6Then the runners went throughout all Israel and Judah with the letters from the king and his leaders, and spoke according to the command of the king: "Children of Israel, return to the LORD God of Abraham, Isaac, and Israel; then He will return to the remnant of you who have escaped from the hand of the kings of Assyria.
7And do not be like your fathers and your brethren, who trespassed against the LORD God of their fathers, so that He gave them up to desolation, as you see.
8Now do not be stiff-necked, as your fathers *were, but* yield yourselves to the LORD; and enter His sanctuary, which He has sanctified forever, and serve the LORD your God, that the fierceness of His wrath may turn away from you.
9For if you return to the LORD, your brethren and your children *will be treated* with compassion by those who lead them captive, so that they may come back to this land; for the LORD your God *is* gracious and merciful, and will not turn *His* face from you if you return to Him."
10So the runners passed from city to city through the country of Ephraim and Manasseh, as far as Zebulun; but they laughed at them and mocked them.
11Nevertheless some from Asher, Manasseh, and Zebulun humbled themselves and came to Jerusalem.
12Also the hand of God was on Judah to give them singleness of heart to obey the command of the king and the leaders, at the word of the LORD.
13Now many people, a very great assembly, gathered at Jerusalem to keep the Feast of Unleavened Bread in the second month.
14They arose and took away the altars that *were* in Jerusalem, and they took away all the incense altars and cast *them* into the Brook Kidron.
15Then they slaughtered the Passover *lambs* on the fourteenth *day* of the second month.

30:6 return. The nation was required by law to annually celebrate 3 feasts in Jerusalem: 1) Passover; 2) Pentecost; and 3) Tabernacles (Ex. 23; Lev. 23; Num. 28; 29; Deut. 16). God would have returned to bless the people of the northern apostate and idolatrous kingdom of Israel if they had returned to Him.

The priests and the Levites were ashamed, and
sanctified themselves, and brought the burnt
offerings to the house of the LORD. [16]They
stood in their place according to their custom,
according to the Law of Moses the man of
God; the priests sprinkled the blood *received*
from the hand of the Levites. [17]For *there were*
many in the assembly who had not sanctified
themselves; therefore the Levites had charge
of the slaughter of the Passover *lambs* for
everyone *who was* not clean, to sanctify *them* to
the LORD. [18]For a multitude of the people, many
from Ephraim, Manasseh, Issachar, and
Zebulun, had not cleansed themselves, yet
they ate the Passover contrary to what was
written. But Hezekiah prayed for them, saying, "May the good LORD provide atonement
for everyone [19]*who* prepares his heart to seek
God, the LORD God of his fathers, though *he is*
not *cleansed* according to the purification of
the sanctuary." [20]And the LORD listened to
Hezekiah and healed the people.

[21]So the children of Israel who were present
at Jerusalem kept the Feast of Unleavened
Bread seven days with great gladness; and the
Levites and the priests praised the LORD day
by day, *singing* to the LORD, accompanied by
loud instruments. [22]And Hezekiah gave
encouragement to all the Levites who taught
the good knowledge of the LORD; and they ate
throughout the feast seven days, offering
peace offerings and making confession to the
LORD God of their fathers.

[23]Then the whole assembly agreed to keep
the feast another seven days, and they kept it
another seven days with gladness. [24]For
Hezekiah king of Judah gave to the assembly
a thousand bulls and seven thousand sheep,
and the leaders gave to the assembly a thousand bulls and ten thousand sheep; and a
great number of priests sanctified themselves.
[25]The whole assembly of Judah rejoiced, also
the priests and Levites, all the assembly that
came from Israel, the sojourners who came

30:1–27 Hezekiah reached back to restore the Feast of Unleavened Bread and the Passover (Ex. 12:1–20; Lev. 23:1–8), which apparently had not been properly and regularly observed in some time, perhaps since the division of the kingdom 215 years earlier (v. 5). The Passover would later be revived again by Josiah (2 Chr. 35:1–9) and Zerubbabel (Ezra 6:19–22). It celebrated God's forgiveness and redemption of His believing people.

30:26 nothing like this. A telling statement about the spiritual degeneracy of the divided kingdom since the time of Solomon over 215 years earlier.

from the land of Israel, and those who dwelt in
Judah. [26]So there was great joy in Jerusalem,
for since the time of Solomon the son of David, king of Israel, *there had* been nothing like
this in Jerusalem. [27]Then the priests, the
Levites, arose and blessed the people, and
their voice was heard; and their prayer came
up to His holy dwelling place, to heaven.

31 Now when all this was finished, all Israel
who were present went out to the cities
of Judah and broke the *sacred* pillars in pieces,
cut down the wooden images, and threw down
the high places and the altars—from all Judah,
Benjamin, Ephraim, and Manasseh—until
they had utterly destroyed them all. Then all
the children of Israel returned to their own
cities, every man to his possession.

[2]And Hezekiah appointed the divisions of
the priests and the Levites according to their
divisions, each man according to his service,
the priests and Levites for burnt offerings and
peace offerings, to serve, to give thanks, and to
praise in the gates of the camp of the LORD.
[3]The king also *appointed* a portion of his possessions for the burnt offerings: for the morning and evening burnt offerings, the burnt
offerings for the Sabbaths and the New
Moons and the set feasts, as *it is* written in the
Law of the LORD.

[4]Moreover he commanded the people who
dwelt in Jerusalem to contribute support for
the priests and the Levites, that they might
devote themselves to the Law of the LORD.

[5]As soon as the commandment was circulated, the children of Israel brought in abundance the firstfruits of grain and wine, oil and
honey, and of all the produce of the field; and
they brought in abundantly the tithe of everything. [6]And the children of Israel and Judah,
who dwelt in the cities of Judah, brought the
tithe of oxen and sheep; also the tithe of holy
things which were consecrated to the LORD
their God they laid in heaps.

[7]In the third month they began laying them
in heaps, and they finished in the seventh
month. [8]And when Hezekiah and the leaders
came and saw the heaps, they blessed the LORD
and His people Israel. [9]Then Hezekiah questioned the priests and the Levites concerning

31:6 tithe. Since the priests and Levites served the nation, they were to be supported by the people through the taxation of the tithe. According to Leviticus 27:30–33 and Numbers 18:21,24, the people were to give the tenth (tithe) to supply all the needs of the Levites. Malachi 3:8 says they were robbing God when they did not give the tithe. Deuteronomy 12:6,7 called for a second tithe that was to support the nation's devotion to the temple by being used for the national festivals at the temple in Jerusalem. This was called the festival tithe. Deuteronomy 14:28,29 called for a third tithe every 3 years for the poor. The sum of this tax plan totaled about 23 percent annually.

the heaps. 10And Azariah the chief priest, from
the house of Zadok, answered him and said,
"Since *the people* began to bring the offerings
into the house of the LORD, we have had
enough to eat and have plenty left, for the LORD
has blessed His people; and what is left *is* this
great abundance."
11Now Hezekiah commanded *them* to prepare rooms in the house of the LORD, and they
prepared them. 12Then they faithfully brought
in the offerings, the tithes, and the dedicated
things; Cononiah the Levite had charge of
them, and Shimei his brother *was* the next.
13Jehiel, Azaziah, Nahath, Asahel, Jerimoth,
Jozabad, Eliel, Ismachiah, Mahath, and
Benaiah *were* overseers under the hand of
Cononiah and Shimei his brother, at the commandment of Hezekiah the king and Azariah
the ruler of the house of God. 14Kore the son
of Imnah the Levite, the keeper of the East
Gate, *was* over the freewill offerings to God, to
distribute the offerings of the LORD and the
most holy things. 15And under him *were* Eden,
Miniamin, Jeshua, Shemaiah, Amariah, and
Shecaniah, *his* faithful assistants in the cities
of the priests, to distribute allotments to their
brethren by divisions, to the great as well as
the small.
16Besides those males from three years old
and up who were written in the genealogy,
they distributed to everyone who entered the
house of the LORD his daily portion for the
work of his service, by his division, 17and to
the priests who were written in the genealogy
according to their father's house, and to the
Levites from twenty years old and up according to their work, by their divisions, 18and to all
who were written in the genealogy—their little
ones and their wives, their sons and daughters,
the whole company of them—for in their faithfulness they sanctified themselves in holiness.
19Also for the sons of Aaron the priests, *who*
were in the fields of the common-lands of their
cities, in every single city, *there were* men who
were designated by name to distribute portions to all the males among the priests and to
all who were listed by genealogies among the
Levites.
20Thus Hezekiah did throughout all Judah,
and he did what *was* good and right and true
before the LORD his God. 21And in every work
that he began in the service of the house of
God, in the law and in the commandment, to
seek his God, he did *it* with all his heart. So he
prospered.

Psalm 85:1–7

To the Chief Musician.
A Psalm of the sons of Korah.

LORD, You have been favorable
to Your land;
You have brought back the captivity
of Jacob.
2 You have forgiven the iniquity
of Your people;
You have covered all their sin.
Selah
3 You have taken away all Your wrath;
You have turned from the fierceness
of Your anger.

4 Restore us, O God of our salvation,
And cause Your anger toward us to
cease.
5 Will You be angry with us forever?
Will You prolong Your anger to all
generations?
6 Will You not revive us again,
That Your people may rejoice
in You?
7 Show us Your mercy, LORD,
And grant us Your salvation.

Proverbs 21:9–11

9 Better to dwell in a corner of a
housetop,
Than in a house shared with a
contentious woman.
10 The soul of the wicked desires evil;
His neighbor finds no favor
in his eyes.
11 When the scoffer is punished, the
simple is made wise;
But when the wise is instructed,
he receives knowledge.

Acts 20:1–16

20 After the uproar had ceased, Paul
called the disciples to *himself,*
embraced *them,* and departed to go to
Macedonia. [2]Now when he had gone over that
region and encouraged them with many
words, he came to Greece [3]and stayed three
months. And when the Jews plotted against him
as he was about to sail to Syria, he decided to
return through Macedonia. [4]And Sopater of
Berea accompanied him to Asia—also Aristarchus
and Secundus of the Thessalonians, and Gaius of
Derbe, and Timothy, and Tychicus and Trophimus of Asia. [5]These men, going ahead, waited
for us at Troas. [6]But we sailed away from
Philippi after the Days of Unleavened Bread,
and in five days joined them at Troas, where
we stayed seven days.
[7]Now on the first *day* of the week, when the
disciples came together to break bread, Paul,
ready to depart the next day, spoke to them
and continued his message until midnight.
[8]There were many lamps in the upper room
where they were gathered together. [9]And in a
window sat a certain young man named
Eutychus, who was sinking into a deep sleep.
He was overcome by sleep; and as Paul continued speaking, he fell down from the third
story and was taken up dead. [10]But Paul went
down, fell on him, and embracing *him* said,
"Do not trouble yourselves, for his life is in
him." [11]Now when he had come up, had broken bread and eaten, and talked a long while,
even till daybreak, he departed. [12]And they
brought the young man in alive, and they were
not a little comforted.

20:3 three months. Most or all of it were likely spent in Corinth. **Jews plotted against him.** Tragically, most of the opposition to Paul's ministry stemmed from his fellow countrymen (2 Cor. 11:26). The Jewish community of Corinth hated Paul because of its humiliating debacle before Gallio (18:12–17), and the stunning conversions of two of its most prominent leaders, Crispus (18:8) and Sosthenes (18:17; 1 Cor. 1:1). Luke does not record the details of the Jews' plot, but it undoubtedly involved murdering Paul during the voyage to Palestine. The apostle would have been an easy target on a small ship packed with Jewish pilgrims. Because of that danger, Paul canceled his plans to sail from Greece to Syria. Instead, he decided to go north into Macedonia, cross the Aegean Sea to Asia Minor, and catch another ship from there. That delay cost Paul his opportunity to reach Palestine in time for Passover, but he hurried to be there in time for Pentecost (v. 16).

20:9 young man. The Greek word suggests he was between 7 and 14 years old. His youth, the fumes from the lamps, and the lateness of the hour (v. 7) gradually overcame his resistance. He dozed off, fell out of the open window, and was killed.

20:10 his life is in him. This does not mean that he had not died, but that his life had been restored. As a physician, Luke knew whether someone had died, as he plainly states (v. 9) was the case with Eutychus.

[13]Then we went ahead to the ship and sailed
to Assos, there intending to take Paul on
board; for so he had given orders, intending
himself to go on foot. [14]And when he met us at
Assos, we took him on board and came to
Mitylene. [15]We sailed from there, and the next
day came opposite Chios. The following *day*
we arrived at Samos and stayed at Trogyllium.
The next *day* we came to Miletus. [16]For Paul
had decided to sail past Ephesus, so that he
would not have to spend time in Asia; for he
was hurrying to be at Jerusalem, if possible,
on the Day of Pentecost.

DAY 17: Why did the church gather to worship on Sunday?

"Now on the first day of the week" (Acts 20:7). Sunday was the day the church gathered for worship, because it was the day of Christ's resurrection (Matt. 28:1; Mark 16:2,9; Luke 24:1; John 20:1,19; 1 Cor. 16:2). The writings of the early church fathers confirm that the church continued to meet on Sunday after the close of the New Testament period. Scripture does not require Christians to observe the Saturday Sabbath:

1. The Sabbath was the sign of the Mosaic Covenant (Ex. 31:16,17; Neh. 9:14; Ezek. 20:12), whereas Christians are under the New Covenant (2 Cor. 3; Heb. 8);
2. there is no New Testament command to keep the Sabbath;
3. the first command to keep the Sabbath was not until the time of Moses (Ex. 20:8);

4. the Jerusalem Council (chap. 15) did not order Gentile believers to keep the Sabbath;
5. Paul never cautioned Christians about breaking the Sabbath; and
6. the New Testament explicitly teaches that Sabbath keeping was not a requirement (Rom. 14:5; Gal. 4:10,11; Col. 2:16,17).

JULY 18

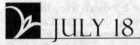

2 Chronicles 32:1–33:25

32 After these deeds of faithfulness,
Sennacherib king of Assyria came and
entered Judah; he encamped against the fortified cities, thinking to win them over to himself. 2And when Hezekiah saw that Sennacherib had come, and that his purpose was
to make war against Jerusalem, 3he consulted
with his leaders and commanders to stop the
water from the springs which *were* outside the
city; and they helped him. 4Thus many people
gathered together who stopped all the springs
and the brook that ran through the land, saying, "Why should the kings of Assyria come
and find much water?" 5And he strengthened
himself, built up all the wall that was broken,
raised *it* up to the towers, and *built* another
wall outside; also he repaired the Millo *in* the
City of David, and made weapons and shields
in abundance. 6Then he set military captains
over the people, gathered them together to
him in the open square of the city gate, and
gave them encouragement, saying, 7"Be
strong and courageous; do not be afraid nor
dismayed before the king of Assyria, nor
before all the multitude that *is* with him; for
there are more with us than with him. 8With
him *is* an arm of flesh; but with us *is* the LORD
our God, to help us and to fight our battles."
And the people were strengthened by the
words of Hezekiah king of Judah.

9After this Sennacherib king of Assyria sent
his servants to Jerusalem (but he and all the
forces with him *laid siege* against Lachish), to
Hezekiah king of Judah, and to all Judah who
were in Jerusalem, saying, 10"Thus says
Sennacherib king of Assyria: 'In what do you
trust, that you remain under siege in Jerusalem? 11Does not Hezekiah persuade you to
give yourselves over to die by famine and by
thirst, saying, "The LORD our God will deliver
us from the hand of the king of Assyria"? 12Has
not the same Hezekiah taken away His high
places and His altars, and commanded Judah
and Jerusalem, saying, "You shall worship
before one altar and burn incense on it"? 13Do
you not know what I and my fathers have done
to all the peoples of *other* lands? Were the
gods of the nations of those lands in any way
able to deliver their lands out of my hand?
14Who *was there* among all the gods of those
nations that my fathers utterly destroyed that
could deliver his people from my hand, that
your God should be able to deliver you from
my hand? 15Now therefore, do not let Hezekiah
deceive you or persuade you like this, and do
not believe him; for no god of any nation or
kingdom was able to deliver his people from
my hand or the hand of my fathers. How much
less will your God deliver you from my hand?' "

16Furthermore, his servants spoke against
the LORD God and against His servant
Hezekiah.

17He also wrote letters to revile the LORD
God of Israel, and to speak against Him, saying,
"As the gods of the nations of *other* lands have
not delivered their people from my hand, so
the God of Hezekiah will not deliver His people from my hand." 18Then they called out with
a loud voice in Hebrew to the people of Jerusalem who *were* on the wall, to frighten them and
trouble them, that they might take the city.
19And they spoke against the God of Jerusalem,
as against the gods of the people of the earth—
the work of men's hands.

20Now because of this King Hezekiah and
the prophet Isaiah, the son of Amoz, prayed
and cried out to heaven. 21Then the LORD sent
an angel who cut down every mighty man of
valor, leader, and captain in the camp of the
king of Assyria. So he returned shamefaced to
his own land. And when he had gone into the
temple of his god, some of his own offspring
struck him down with the sword there.

22Thus the LORD saved Hezekiah and the
inhabitants of Jerusalem from the hand of
Sennacherib the king of Assyria, and from the
hand of all *others,* and guided them on every
side. 23And many brought gifts to the LORD at
Jerusalem, and presents to Hezekiah king of
Judah, so that he was exalted in the sight of all
nations thereafter.

24In those days Hezekiah was sick and near
death, and he prayed to the LORD; and He spoke
to him and gave him a sign. 25But Hezekiah did
not repay according to the favor *shown* him, for
his heart was lifted up; therefore wrath was

looming over him and over Judah and Jerusalem. [26]Then Hezekiah humbled himself for the
pride of his heart, he and the inhabitants of Jerusalem, so that the wrath of the LORD did not
come upon them in the days of Hezekiah.
[27]Hezekiah had very great riches and honor.
And he made himself treasuries for silver, for
gold, for precious stones, for spices, for shields,
and for all kinds of desirable items; [28]store-
houses for the harvest of grain, wine, and oil;
and stalls for all kinds of livestock, and folds for
flocks. [29]Moreover he provided cities for himself, and possessions of flocks and herds in
abundance; for God had given him very much
property. [30]This same Hezekiah also stopped the
water outlet of Upper Gihon, and brought the
water by tunnel to the west side of the City of
David. Hezekiah prospered in all his works.
[31]However, *regarding* the ambassadors of the
princes of Babylon, whom they sent to him to
inquire about the wonder that was *done* in the
land, God withdrew from him, in order to test
him, that He might know all *that was* in his
heart.
[32]Now the rest of the acts of Hezekiah, and
his goodness, indeed they *are* written in the
vision of Isaiah the prophet, the son of Amoz,
and in the book of the kings of Judah and Israel. [33]So Hezekiah rested with his fathers, and
they buried him in the upper tombs of the
sons of David; and all Judah and the inhabitants of Jerusalem honored him at his death.
Then Manasseh his son reigned in his place.
33 Manasseh *was* twelve years old when
he became king, and he reigned fifty-
five years in Jerusalem. [2]But he did evil in the
sight of the LORD, according to the abominations of the nations whom the LORD had cast
out before the children of Israel. [3]For he
rebuilt the high places which Hezekiah his
father had broken down; he raised up altars
for the Baals, and made wooden images; and
he worshiped all the host of heaven and
served them. [4]He also built altars in the house
of the LORD, of which the LORD had said, "In
Jerusalem shall My name be forever." [5]And he
built altars for all the host of heaven in the two
courts of the house of the LORD. [6]Also he
caused his sons to pass through the fire in the
Valley of the Son of Hinnom; he practiced
soothsaying, used witchcraft and sorcery, and
consulted mediums and spiritists. He did
much evil in the sight of the LORD, to provoke
Him to anger. [7]He even set a carved image, the
idol which he had made, in the house of God,
of which God had said to David and to Solomon his son, "In this house and in Jerusalem, which I have chosen out of all the tribes
of Israel, I will put My name forever; [8]and I will
not again remove the foot of Israel from the
land which I have appointed for your fathers—
only if they are careful to do all that I have
commanded them, according to the whole law
and the statutes and the ordinances by the
hand of Moses." [9]So Manasseh seduced Judah
and the inhabitants of Jerusalem to do more
evil than the nations whom the LORD had
destroyed before the children of Israel.
[10]And the LORD spoke to Manasseh and his
people, but they would not listen. [11]Therefore
the LORD brought upon them the captains of
the army of the king of Assyria, who took
Manasseh with hooks, bound him with bronze
fetters, and carried him off to Babylon. [12]Now
when he was in affliction, he implored the
LORD his God, and humbled himself greatly

32:30 A 1,700-foot-long tunnel cut through solid rock (below Jerusalem) redirected water from the spring Gihon outside of Jerusalem (to the east) toward the south of Jerusalem into the pool of Siloam within the city to provide water in time of siege. The tunnel was a remarkable feat of engineering and boring skill, often 60 feet below the ground and large enough to walk through. It was discovered in 1838, but not until 1909 was it cleared of the debris left by the destruction of Jerusalem back in 586 B.C. This may not have been the first water shaft, since David may have entered Jerusalem 300 years earlier through a water shaft (2 Sam. 5:6–8).

33:12,13 Manasseh. This king was very wicked and idolatrous, a murderer of his children, and a desecrater of the temple. God graciously forgave this "chief of sinners" (1 Tim. 1:15) when he repented. He did what he could to reverse the effect of his life (vv. 15–17). Although the people worshiped God and not idols, they were doing it in the wrong place and wrong way. God had commanded them to offer sacrifices only in certain places (Deut. 12:13,14) to keep them from corrupting the prescribed forms and to protect them from pagan religious influence. Disobedience to God's requirements in this matter surely contributed to the decline under the next king, Amon (vv. 21–23), whose corruption his successor, Josiah, had to eliminate (34:3–7).

before the God of his fathers, 13and prayed to
Him; and He received his entreaty, heard his
supplication, and brought him back to Jerusalem into his kingdom. Then Manasseh knew
that the LORD *was* God.

14After this he built a wall outside the City of
David on the west side of Gihon, in the valley,
as far as the entrance of the Fish Gate; and *it*
enclosed Ophel, and he raised it to a very
great height. Then he put military captains in
all the fortified cities of Judah. 15He took away
the foreign gods and the idol from the house
of the LORD, and all the altars that he had built
in the mount of the house of the LORD and in
Jerusalem; and he cast *them* out of the city.
16He also repaired the altar of the LORD, sacrificed peace offerings and thank offerings on it,
and commanded Judah to serve the LORD God
of Israel. 17Nevertheless the people still sacrificed on the high places, *but* only to the LORD
their God.

18Now the rest of the acts of Manasseh, his
prayer to his God, and the words of the seers
who spoke to him in the name of the LORD
God of Israel, indeed they *are written* in the
book of the kings of Israel. 19Also his prayer
and *how God* received his entreaty, and all his
sin and trespass, and the sites where he built
high places and set up wooden images and
carved images, before he was humbled,
indeed they *are* written among the sayings of
Hozai. 20So Manasseh rested with his fathers,
and they buried him in his own house. Then
his son Amon reigned in his place.

21Amon *was* twenty-two years old when he
became king, and he reigned two years in Jerusalem. 22But he did evil in the sight of the
LORD, as his father Manasseh had done; for
Amon sacrificed to all the carved images
which his father Manasseh had made, and
served them. 23And he did not humble himself
before the LORD, as his father Manasseh had
humbled himself; but Amon trespassed more
and more.

24Then his servants conspired against him,
and killed him in his own house. 25But the people of the land executed all those who had conspired against King Amon. Then the people of
the land made his son Josiah king in his place.

Psalm 85:8–13

8 I will hear what God the LORD will
speak,
For He will speak peace
To His people and to His saints;
But let them not turn back to folly.
9 Surely His salvation *is* near to those
who fear Him,

85:9 salvation...who fear Him. Only those who renounce their sinful autonomy and put their complete trust in the living God will participate in the blessings of salvation and the future kingdom (John 3:3–5). **glory may dwell in our land.** The departure of the glory of God, which signified His presence, is described in Ezekiel 10; 11. He withdrew His glory because of the apostasy of the nation immediately preceding the Babylonian exile (Ezek. 8–11). The return of the glory of the Lord in the future millennial temple is foretold in Ezekiel 43:1–4.

85:10 Mercy...truth...righteousness...peace. These 4 spiritual qualities, characterizing the atmosphere of the future kingdom of Christ, will relate to each other in perfect harmony and will saturate kingdom life (vv. 10,13).

That glory may dwell in our land.

10 Mercy and truth have met together;
Righteousness and peace have kissed.
11 Truth shall spring out of the earth,
And righteousness shall look down
from heaven.
12 Yes, the LORD will give *what is* good;
And our land will yield its increase.
13 Righteousness will go before Him,
And shall make His footsteps *our*
pathway.

Proverbs 21:12

12 The righteous *God* wisely considers
the house of the wicked,
Overthrowing the wicked for *their*
wickedness.

Acts 20:17–38

17From Miletus he sent to Ephesus and
called for the elders of the church. 18And when
they had come to him, he said to them: "You
know, from the first day that I came to Asia, in
what manner I always lived among you, 19serv-
ing the Lord with all humility, with many tears
and trials which happened to me by the plotting of the Jews; 20how I kept back nothing that
was helpful, but proclaimed it to you, and
taught you publicly and from house to house,
21testifying to Jews, and also to Greeks, repentance toward God and faith toward our Lord
Jesus Christ. 22And see, now I go bound in the
spirit to Jerusalem, not knowing the things
that will happen to me there, 23except that the
Holy Spirit testifies in every city, saying that

chains and tribulations await me. 24But none of
these things move me; nor do I count my life
dear to myself, so that I may finish my race
with joy, and the ministry which I received
from the Lord Jesus, to testify to the gospel of
the grace of God.
25"And indeed, now I know that you all,
among whom I have gone preaching the kingdom of God, will see my face no more. 26There-
fore I testify to you this day that I *am* innocent
of the blood of all *men*. 27For I have not
shunned to declare to you the whole counsel
of God. 28Therefore take heed to yourselves
and to all the flock, among which the Holy
Spirit has made you overseers, to shepherd
the church of God which He purchased with
His own blood. 29For I know this, that after my
departure savage wolves will come in among
you, not sparing the flock. 30Also from among
yourselves men will rise up, speaking perverse things, to draw away the disciples after
themselves. 31Therefore watch, and remember
that for three years I did not cease to warn
everyone night and day with tears.
32"So now, brethren, I commend you to God
and to the word of His grace, which is able to
build you up and give you an inheritance
among all those who are sanctified. 33I have
coveted no one's silver or gold or apparel.
34Yes, you yourselves know that these hands
have provided for my necessities, and for
those who were with me. 35I have shown you in
every way, by laboring like this, that you must
support the weak. And remember the words
of the Lord Jesus, that He said, 'It is more
blessed to give than to receive.' "
36And when he had said these things, he
knelt down and prayed with them all. 37Then
they all wept freely, and fell on Paul's neck and
kissed him, 38sorrowing most of all for the
words which he spoke, that they would see his
face no more. And they accompanied him to
the ship.

20:19 with many tears. Paul wept because of: 1) those who did not know Christ (Rom. 9:2,3); 2) struggling, immature believers (2 Cor. 2:4); and 3) the threat of false teachers (v. 29,30). **plotting of the Jews.** Ironically, it was the plot of the Jews at Corinth that allowed the Ephesian elders this opportunity to spend time with Paul.

20:22 bound in the spirit. Paul's deep sense of duty toward the Master who had redeemed him and called him to service drove him onward despite the threat of danger and hardship (v. 23).

20:23 Holy Spirit testifies. Paul knew he faced persecution in Jerusalem (Rom.. 15:31), though he would not know the details until he heard Agabus's prophecy (21:10,11).

DAY 18: Why should the church always be on guard?

Paul told the Ephesians that he had declared to them "the whole counsel of God" (Acts 20:27). The entire plan and purpose of God for man's salvation in all its fullness: divine truths of creation, election, redemption, justification, adoption, conversion, sanctification, holy living, and glorification. And now that he was leaving, he gives them a warning.

False teachers were already plaguing the churches of Galatia (Gal. 1:6) and the Corinthian church (2 Cor. 11:4). "Take heed to yourselves" (v. 28), a warning that proved true by later events at Ephesus (1 Tim. 1:3–7,19,20; 6:20,21; Rev. 2:2). Paul repeated this call to self-examination to Timothy when his young son in the faith served as pastor of the Ephesian congregation (1 Tim. 4:16; 2 Tim. 2:20,21). The "overseers" are the same as elders and pastors. The word stresses the leaders' responsibility to watch over and protect their congregations—an appropriate usage in the context of a warning against false teachers. Church rule, which minimizes the biblical authority of elders in favor of a cultural, democratic process, is foreign to the New Testament (1 Thess. 5:12,13; Heb. 13:17).

He warns of "savage wolves" (v. 29)—a term borrowed from Jesus (Matt. 7:15; 10:16). This metaphor stresses the extreme danger false teachers pose to the church. "From among yourselves" (v. 30). Even more deadly than attacks from outside the church are the defections of those (especially leaders) within the church (1 Tim. 1:20; 2 Tim. 1:15; 2:17; Jude 3,4,10–13). These wolves would speak "perverse things." The Greek word means "distorted" or "twisted." False teachers twist God's Word for their own evil ends (13:10; 2 Pet. 3:16).

"So now, brethren, I commend you to God and to the word of His grace, which is able to build you up" (v. 32). The Scriptures, the record of God's gracious dealings with mankind, is the source of spiritual growth for all Christians. And since the church is "the pillar and ground of the truth" (1 Tim. 3:15), its leaders must be familiar with that truth.

JULY 19

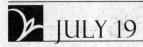

2 Chronicles 34:1–36:23

34 Josiah *was* eight years old when he
became king, and he reigned thirty-one
years in Jerusalem. 2And he did *what was* right
in the sight of the LORD, and walked in the
ways of his father David; *he* did *not* turn aside
to the right hand or to the left.

3For in the eighth year of his reign, while he
was still young, he began to seek the God of
his father David; and in the twelfth year he
began to purge Judah and Jerusalem of the
high places, the wooden images, the carved
images, and the molded images. 4They broke
down the altars of the Baals in his presence,
and the incense altars which *were* above them
he cut down; and the wooden images, the
carved images, and the molded images he
broke in pieces, and made dust of them and
scattered *it* on the graves of those who had
sacrificed to them. 5He also burned the bones
of the priests on their altars, and cleansed Judah and Jerusalem. 6And *so he did* in the cities
of Manasseh, Ephraim, and Simeon, as far as
Naphtali and all around, with axes. 7When he
had broken down the altars and the wooden
images, had beaten the carved images into
powder, and cut down all the incense altars
throughout all the land of Israel, he returned
to Jerusalem.

8In the eighteenth year of his reign, when
he had purged the land and the temple, he
sent Shaphan the son of Azaliah, Maaseiah
the governor of the city, and Joah the son of
Joahaz the recorder, to repair the house of
the LORD his God. 9When they came to Hilkiah
the high priest, they delivered the money that
was brought into the house of God, which the
Levites who kept the doors had gathered from
the hand of Manasseh and Ephraim, from all
the remnant of Israel, from all Judah and Benjamin, and *which* they had brought back to Jerusalem. 10Then they put *it* in the hand of the
foremen who had the oversight of the house of
the LORD; and they gave it to the workmen who
worked in the house of the LORD, to repair and
restore the house. 11They gave *it* to the craftsmen and builders to buy hewn stone and timber for beams, and to floor the houses which
the kings of Judah had destroyed. 12And the
men did the work faithfully. Their overseers
were Jahath and Obadiah the Levites, of the
sons of Merari, and Zechariah and Meshullam,
of the sons of the Kohathites, to supervise.
Others of the Levites, all of whom were skillful
with instruments of music, 13*were* over the burden bearers and *were* overseers of all who did
work in any kind of service. And *some* of the
Levites *were* scribes, officers, and gatekeepers.

14Now when they brought out the money that
was brought into the house of the LORD,
Hilkiah the priest found the Book of the Law of
the LORD *given* by Moses. 15Then Hilkiah
answered and said to Shaphan the scribe, "I
have found the Book of the Law in the house
of the LORD." And Hilkiah gave the book to
Shaphan. 16So Shaphan carried the book to the
king, bringing the king word, saying, "All that
was committed to your servants they are
doing. 17And they have gathered the money
that was found in the house of the LORD, and
have delivered it into the hand of the overseers and the workmen." 18Then Shaphan the
scribe told the king, saying, "Hilkiah the priest
has given me a book." And Shaphan read it
before the king.

19Thus it happened, when the king heard
the words of the Law, that he tore his clothes.
20Then the king commanded Hilkiah, Ahikam
the son of Shaphan, Abdon the son of Micah,
Shaphan the scribe, and Asaiah a servant of
the king, saying, 21"Go, inquire of the LORD for
me, and for those who are left in Israel and Judah, concerning the words of the book that is
found; for great *is* the wrath of the LORD that is
poured out on us, because our fathers have
not kept the word of the LORD, to do according
to all that is written in this book."

22So Hilkiah and those the king *had appoint-
ed* went to Huldah the prophetess, the wife of
Shallum the son of Tokhath, the son of
Hasrah, keeper of the wardrobe. (She dwelt in
Jerusalem in the Second Quarter.) And they
spoke to her to that *effect.*

23Then she answered them, "Thus says the
LORD God of Israel, 'Tell the man who sent you
to Me, 24"Thus says the LORD: 'Behold, I will
bring calamity on this place and on its inhabitants, all the curses that are written in the
book which they have read before the king of
Judah, 25because they have forsaken Me and
burned incense to other gods, that they might
provoke Me to anger with all the works of
their hands. Therefore My wrath will be
poured out on this place, and not be
quenched.' " ' 26But as for the king of Judah,
who sent you to inquire of the LORD, in this
manner you shall speak to him, 'Thus says the
LORD God of Israel: "*Concerning* the words
which you have heard— 27because your heart
was tender, and you humbled yourself before
God when you heard His words against this

place and against its inhabitants, and you
humbled yourself before Me, and you tore
your clothes and wept before Me, I also have
heard *you,*” says the LORD. 28“Surely I will gather you to your fathers, and you shall be gathered to your grave in peace; and your eyes
shall not see all the calamity which I will bring
on this place and its inhabitants.” ’ ” So they
brought back word to the king.

29Then the king sent and gathered all the
elders of Judah and Jerusalem. 30The king
went up to the house of the LORD, with all the
men of Judah and the inhabitants of Jerusalem—the priests and the Levites, and all the
people, great and small. And he read in their
hearing all the words of the Book of the
Covenant which had been found in the house
of the LORD. 31Then the king stood in his place
and made a covenant before the LORD, to follow the LORD, and to keep His commandments
and His testimonies and His statutes with all
his heart and all his soul, to perform the words
of the covenant that were written in this book.
32And he made all who were present in Jerusalem and Benjamin take a stand. So the inhabitants of Jerusalem did according to the
covenant of God, the God of their fathers.
33Thus Josiah removed all the abominations
from all the country that *belonged* to the children of Israel, and made all who were present
in Israel diligently serve the LORD their God.
All his days they did not depart from following
the LORD God of their fathers.

35 Now Josiah kept a Passover to the LORD
in Jerusalem, and they slaughtered the
Passover *lambs* on the fourteenth *day* of the
first month. 2And he set the priests in their
duties and encouraged them for the service of
the house of the LORD. 3Then he said to the
Levites who taught all Israel, who were holy to
the LORD: “Put the holy ark in the house which
Solomon the son of David, king of Israel, built.
It shall no longer *be* a burden on *your* shoulders. Now serve the LORD your God and His
people Israel. 4Prepare *yourselves* according to
your fathers’ houses, according to your divisions, following the written instruction of David
king of Israel and the written instruction of Solomon his son. 5And stand in the holy *place*
according to the divisions of the fathers’ houses of your brethren the *lay* people, and *according to* the division of the father’s house of the
Levites. 6So slaughter the Passover *offerings,*
consecrate yourselves, and prepare *them* for
your brethren, that *they* may do according to
the word of the LORD by the hand of Moses.”

7Then Josiah gave the *lay* people lambs and
young goats from the flock, all for Passover
offerings for all who were present, to the number of thirty thousand, as well as three thousand
cattle; these *were* from the king’s possessions.
8And his leaders gave willingly to the people, to
the priests, and to the Levites. Hilkiah, Zechariah,
and Jehiel, rulers of the house of God, gave to
the priests for the Passover *offerings* two thousand six hundred *from the flock,* and three
hundred cattle. 9Also Conaniah, his brothers
Shemaiah and Nethanel, and Hashabiah and
Jeiel and Jozabad, chief of the Levites, gave to
the Levites for Passover *offerings* five thousand *from the flock* and five hundred cattle.

10So the service was prepared, and the
priests stood in their places, and the Levites in
their divisions, according to the king’s command. 11And they slaughtered the Passover *offerings;* and the priests sprinkled *the blood* with
their hands, while the Levites skinned *the animals.* 12Then they removed the burnt offerings
that *they* might give them to the divisions of
the fathers’ houses of the *lay* people, to offer
to the LORD, as *it is* written in the Book of Moses. And so *they did* with the cattle. 13Also they
roasted the Passover *offerings* with fire
according to the ordinance; but the *other* holy
offerings they boiled in pots, in caldrons, and
in pans, and divided *them* quickly among all
the *lay* people. 14Then afterward they prepared
portions for themselves and for the priests,
because the priests, the sons of Aaron, *were
busy* in offering burnt offerings and fat until
night; therefore the Levites prepared portions
for themselves and for the priests, the sons of
Aaron. 15And the singers, the sons of Asaph,
were in their places, according to the command of David, Asaph, Heman, and Jeduthun
the king’s seer. Also the gatekeepers were at
each gate; they did not have to leave their
position, because their brethren the Levites
prepared portions for them.

35:3 the holy ark. The ark of the covenant which was to remain in the Most Holy Place had been removed, probably by Manasseh who set a carved image in its place (33:7). The law for the carrying of the ark during the tabernacle days, when it was portable, called for poles to be place through rings on the sides and Levites (Kohathites) to carry it by the poles without touching it (Ex. 25:14,15). Now that the temple was built and the ark had a permanent place, it no longer needed to be transported in the old way.

[16]So all the service of the LORD was prepared
the same day, to keep the Passover and to
offer burnt offerings on the altar of the LORD,
according to the command of King Josiah.
[17]And the children of Israel who were present
kept the Passover at that time, and the Feast
of Unleavened Bread for seven days. [18]There
had been no Passover kept in Israel like that
since the days of Samuel the prophet; and
none of the kings of Israel had kept such a
Passover as Josiah kept, with the priests and
the Levites, all Judah and Israel who were
present, and the inhabitants of Jerusalem. [19]In
the eighteenth year of the reign of Josiah this
Passover was kept.

[20]After all this, when Josiah had prepared the
temple, Necho king of Egypt came up to fight
against Carchemish by the Euphrates; and
Josiah went out against him. [21]But he sent messengers to him, saying, "What have I to do with
you, king of Judah? *I have* not *come* against you
this day, but against the house with which I
have war; for God commanded me to make
haste. Refrain *from meddling with* God, who *is*
with me, lest He destroy you." [22]Nevertheless
Josiah would not turn his face from him, but
disguised himself so that he might fight with
him, and did not heed the words of Necho
from the mouth of God. So he came to fight in
the Valley of Megiddo.

35:21 God commanded me. Necho is referring to the true God—whether he had a true revelation or not is unknown. Josiah had no way to know either, and it is apparent he did not believe that Necho spoke the word of God. There is no reason to assume his death was punishment for refusing to believe. He probably thought Necho was lying and, once victorious with Assyria over Babylon, they would together be back to assault Israel.

[23]And the archers shot King Josiah; and the
king said to his servants, "Take me away, for I
am severely wounded." [24]His servants therefore took him out of that chariot and put him in
the second chariot that he had, and they
brought him to Jerusalem. So he died, and was
buried in *one of* the tombs of his fathers. And
all Judah and Jerusalem mourned for Josiah.

[25]Jeremiah also lamented for Josiah. And to
this day all the singing men and the singing
women speak of Josiah in their lamentations.
They made it a custom in Israel; and indeed
they *are* written in the Laments.

[26]Now the rest of the acts of Josiah and his
goodness, according to *what was* written in
the Law of the LORD, [27]and his deeds from first
to last, indeed they *are* written in the book of
the kings of Israel and Judah.

36 Then the people of the land took
Jehoahaz the son of Josiah, and made
him king in his father's place in Jerusalem.
[2]Jehoahaz *was* twenty-three years old when he
became king, and he reigned three months in
Jerusalem. [3]Now the king of Egypt deposed
him at Jerusalem; and he imposed on the land
a tribute of one hundred talents of silver and a
talent of gold. [4]Then the king of Egypt made
Jehoahaz's brother Eliakim king over Judah
and Jerusalem, and changed his name to
Jehoiakim. And Necho took Jehoahaz his
brother and carried him off to Egypt.

[5]Jehoiakim *was* twenty-five years old when
he became king, and he reigned eleven years
in Jerusalem. And he did evil in the sight of
the LORD his God. [6]Nebuchadnezzar king of
Babylon came up against him, and bound him
in bronze *fetters* to carry him off to Babylon.
[7]Nebuchadnezzar also carried off *some* of the
articles from the house of the LORD to Babylon,
and put them in his temple at Babylon. [8]Now
the rest of the acts of Jehoiakim, the abominations which he did, and what was found
against him, indeed they *are* written in the
book of the kings of Israel and Judah. Then
Jehoiachin his son reigned in his place.

[9]Jehoiachin *was* eight years old when he
became king, and he reigned in Jerusalem
three months and ten days. And he did evil in
the sight of the LORD. [10]At the turn of the year
King Nebuchadnezzar summoned *him* and
took him to Babylon, with the costly articles
from the house of the LORD, and made
Zedekiah, *Jehoiakim's* brother, king over Judah
and Jerusalem.

[11]Zedekiah *was* twenty-one years old when
he became king, and he reigned eleven years
in Jerusalem. [12]He did evil in the sight of the
LORD his God, *and* did not humble himself
before Jeremiah the prophet, *who spoke* from
the mouth of the LORD. [13]And he also rebelled
against King Nebuchadnezzar, who had made
him swear *an oath* by God; but he stiffened his
neck and hardened his heart against turning
to the LORD God of Israel. [14]Moreover all the
leaders of the priests and the people transgressed more and more, *according* to all the
abominations of the nations, and defiled the
house of the LORD which He had consecrated
in Jerusalem.

[15]And the LORD God of their fathers sent
warnings to them by His messengers, rising

up early and sending *them,* because He had
compassion on His people and on His
dwelling place. 16But they mocked the messengers of God, despised His words, and
scoffed at His prophets, until the wrath of the
LORD arose against His people, till *there was*
no remedy.
17Therefore He brought against them the
king of the Chaldeans, who killed their young
men with the sword in the house of their
sanctuary, and had no compassion on young
man or virgin, on the aged or the weak; He
gave *them* all into his hand. 18And all the articles from the house of God, great and small,
the treasures of the house of the LORD, and
the treasures of the king and of his leaders,
all *these* he took to Babylon. 19Then they
burned the house of God, broke down the
wall of Jerusalem, burned all its palaces with
fire, and destroyed all its precious possessions. 20And those who escaped from the
sword he carried away to Babylon, where
they became servants to him and his sons
until the rule of the kingdom of Persia, 21to fulfill the word of the LORD by the mouth of
Jeremiah, until the land had enjoyed her
Sabbaths. As long as she lay desolate she
kept Sabbath, to fulfill seventy years.
22Now in the first year of Cyrus king of
Persia, that the word of the LORD by the
mouth of Jeremiah might be fulfilled, the
LORD stirred up the spirit of Cyrus king of
Persia, so that he made a proclamation
throughout all his kingdom, and also *put it* in
writing, saying,

23 Thus says Cyrus king of Persia:
All the kingdoms of the earth the LORD
God of heaven has given me. And He
has commanded me to build Him a
house at Jerusalem which is in Judah.
Who *is* among you of all His people?
May the LORD his God *be* with him, and
let him go up!

36:11–21 The reign of Zedekiah, a.k.a. Mattaniah (ca. 597–586 B.C.). Jeremiah prophesied during this reign (Jer. 1:3) and wrote Lamentations to mourn the destruction of Jerusalem and the temple in 586 B.C. Ezekiel received his commission during this reign (Ezek. 1:1) and prophesied from 592 B.C. to his death in 560 B.C.

Psalm 86:1–5

A Prayer of David.

Bow down Your ear, O LORD, hear me;
For I *am* poor and needy.
2 Preserve my life, for I *am* holy;
You are my God;
Save Your servant who trusts in You!
3 Be merciful to me, O Lord,
For I cry to You all day long.
4 Rejoice the soul of Your servant,
For to You, O Lord, I lift up my soul.
5 For You, Lord, *are* good, and ready to forgive,
And abundant in mercy to all those who call upon You.

Proverbs 21:13–14

13 Whoever shuts his ears to the cry of the poor
Will also cry himself and not be heard.
14 A gift in secret pacifies anger,
And a bribe behind the back, strong wrath.

Acts 21:1–17

21 Now it came to pass, that when we had
departed from them and set sail, running
a straight course we came to Cos, the following *day* to Rhodes, and from there to Patara.
2And finding a ship sailing over to Phoenicia,
we went aboard and set sail. 3When we had
sighted Cyprus, we passed it on the left, sailed
to Syria, and landed at Tyre; for there the ship
was to unload her cargo. 4And finding disciples, we stayed there seven days. They told
Paul through the Spirit not to go up to Jerusalem. 5When we had come to the end of those
days, we departed and went on our way; and
they all accompanied us, with wives and children, till *we were* out of the city. And we knelt

21:2 finding a ship...Phoenicia. Realizing he would never reach Jerusalem in time for Pentecost if he continued to hug the coast, Paul decided to risk sailing directly across the Mediterranean Sea to Tyre (v. 3). The ship they embarked on would have been considerably larger than the small coastal vessels on which they had been sailing. The ship that later took Paul on his ill-fated voyage to Rome held 276 people (27:37); this one was probably of comparable size.

down on the shore and prayed. 6 When we had
taken our leave of one another, we boarded
the ship, and they returned home.
7 And when we had finished *our* voyage from
Tyre, we came to Ptolemais, greeted the
brethren, and stayed with them one day. 8 On
the next *day* we who were Paul's companions
departed and came to Caesarea, and entered
the house of Philip the evangelist, who was *one*
of the seven, and stayed with him. 9 Now this
man had four virgin daughters who prophesied.
10 And as we stayed many days, a certain prophet
named Agabus came down from Judea. 11 When
he had come to us, he took Paul's belt, bound
his *own* hands and feet, and said, "Thus says
the Holy Spirit, 'So shall the Jews at Jerusalem
bind the man who owns this belt, and deliver
him into the hands of the Gentiles.' "
12 Now when we heard these things, both we
and those from that place pleaded with him
not to go up to Jerusalem. 13 Then Paul
answered, "What do you mean by weeping
and breaking my heart? For I am ready not
only to be bound, but also to die at Jerusalem
for the name of the Lord Jesus."
14 So when he would not be persuaded, we
ceased, saying, "The will of the Lord be done."
15 And after those days we packed and went
up to Jerusalem. 16 Also some of the disciples
from Caesarea went with us and brought with
them a certain Mnason of Cyprus, an early
disciple, with whom we were to lodge.
17 And when we had come to Jerusalem, the
brethren received us gladly.

21:9 virgin daughters. That they were virgins may indicate that they had been called by God for special ministry (1 Cor. 7:34). The early church regarded these women as important sources of information on the early years of the church. **prophesied.** Luke does not reveal the nature of their prophecy. They may have had an ongoing prophetic ministry or prophesied only once. Since women are not to be preachers or teachers in the church (1 Cor. 14:34–36; 1 Tim. 2:11,12), they probably ministered to individuals.

DAY 19: Why did Paul not heed all the warnings about going to Jerusalem?

The church in Tyre had been founded by some of those who fled Jerusalem after Stephen's martyrdom (Acts 11:19)—a persecution Paul himself had spearheaded. When Paul arrived there, the disciples there told Paul "to not to go up to Jerusalem" (21:4). This was not a command from the Spirit for Paul not to go to Jerusalem. Rather, the Spirit had revealed to the believers at Tyre that Paul would face suffering in Jerusalem. Understandably, they tried to dissuade him from going there. Paul's mission to Jerusalem had been given him by the Lord Jesus (20:24); the Spirit would never command him to abandon it.

Later, a prophet named Agabus (11:28) met Paul in Caesarea. Although it was located in Judea, the Jews considered Caesarea, seat of the Roman government, to be a foreign city. Old Testament prophets sometimes acted out their prophecies (1 Kin. 11:29–39; Is. 20:2–6; Jer. 13:1–11; Ezek. 4; 5), and Agabus's action of binding his hands and feet with Paul's belt foreshadowed Paul's arrest and imprisonment by the Romans (Acts 21:11). Though falsely accused by the Jews (vv. 27, 28), Paul was arrested and imprisoned by the Romans (vv. 31–33).

Hearing these warnings, it is not surprising that both Paul's friends (Luke and the others traveling with him) and the Caesarean Christians pleaded with Paul to not go. Paul's response is to say, "I am ready not only to be bound, but also to die at Jerusalem for the name of the Lord Jesus" (v. 13). Jesus' name represents all that He is. That said from Paul, his friends response was, "The will of the Lord be done" (v. 14)—a confident expression of trust that God's will is best (1 Sam. 3:18; Matt. 6:10; Luke 22:42; James 4:13–15).

JULY 20

Ezra 1:1–2:70

1 Now in the first year of Cyrus king of Persia,
that the word of the LORD by the mouth of
Jeremiah might be fulfilled, the LORD stirred
up the spirit of Cyrus king of Persia, so that he
made a proclamation throughout all his kingdom, and also *put it* in writing, saying,

2 Thus says Cyrus king of Persia:
All the kingdoms of the earth the LORD
God of heaven has given me. And He
has commanded me to build Him a
house at Jerusalem which *is* in Judah.
3 Who *is* among you of all His people?
May his God be with him, and let him

go up to Jerusalem which *is* in Judah, and build the house of the LORD God of Israel (He *is* God), which *is* in Jerusalem. [4]And whoever is left in any place where he dwells, let the men of his place help him with silver and gold, with goods and livestock, besides the freewill offerings for the house of God which *is* in Jerusalem.

[5]Then the heads of the fathers' *houses* of Judah and Benjamin, and the priests and the Levites, with all whose spirits God had moved, arose to go up and build the house of the LORD which *is* in Jerusalem. [6]And all those who *were* around them encouraged them with articles of silver and gold, with goods and livestock, and with precious things, besides all *that* was willingly offered.

1:5 whose spirits God had moved. The primary underlying message of Ezra and Nehemiah is that the sovereign hand of God is at work in perfect keeping with His plan at His appointed times. The 70 years of captivity were complete, so God stirred up not only the spirit of Cyrus to make the decree, but His own people to go and build up Jerusalem and the temple (1:1).

[7]King Cyrus also brought out the articles of the house of the LORD, which Nebuchadnezzar had taken from Jerusalem and put in the temple of his gods; [8]and Cyrus king of Persia brought them out by the hand of Mithredath the treasurer, and counted them out to Sheshbazzar the prince of Judah. [9]This *is* the number of them: thirty gold platters, one thousand silver platters, twenty-nine knives, [10]thirty gold basins, four hundred and ten silver basins of a similar *kind, and* one thousand other articles. [11]All the articles of gold and silver *were* five thousand four hundred. All *these* Sheshbazzar took with the captives who were brought from Babylon to Jerusalem.

2 Now these *are* the people of the province who came back from the captivity, of those who had been carried away, whom Nebuchadnezzar the king of Babylon had carried away to Babylon, and who returned to Jerusalem and Judah, everyone to his *own* city.

[2]*Those* who came with Zerubbabel *were* Jeshua, Nehemiah, Seraiah, Reelaiah, Mordecai, Bilshan, Mispar, Bigvai, Rehum, *and* Baanah. The number of the men of the people of Israel: [3]the people of Parosh, two thousand one hundred and

2:2 Zerubbabel. This man was the rightful leader of Judah in that he was of the lineage of David through Jehoiachin (1 Chr. 3:17). He did not serve as king (the curse on Jehoiachin's line, Jer. 22:24–30), but was still in the messianic line because the curse was bypassed (Matt. 1:12; Luke 3:27). The curse of the messianic line for Christ was bypassed in Luke's genealogy by tracing the lineage through David's son Nathan. His name means "offspring of Babylon," indicating his place of birth. He, rather than Cyrus's political appointee Sheshbazzar (1:11), led Judah according to God's will. **Jeshua.** The high priest of the first return whose name means "Yahweh saves." He is called Joshua in Haggai 1:1 and Zechariah 3:1. His father Jozadak (Ezra 3:2) had been exiled (1 Chr. 6:15). He came from the lineage of Levi, Aaron, Eleazar, and Phinehas; thus he was legitimately in the line of the high priest (Num. 25:10–13).

seventy-two; [4]the people of Shephatiah, three hundred and seventy-two; [5]the people of Arah, seven hundred and seventy-five; [6]the people of Pahath-Moab, of the people of Jeshua *and* Joab, two thousand eight hundred and twelve; [7]the people of Elam, one thousand two hundred and fifty-four; [8]the people of Zattu, nine hundred and forty-five; [9]the people of Zaccai, seven hundred and sixty; [10]the people of Bani, six hundred and forty-two; [11]the people of Bebai, six hundred and twenty-three; [12]the people of Azgad, one thousand two hundred and twenty-two; [13]the people of Adonikam, six hundred and sixty-six; [14]the people of Bigvai, two thousand and fifty-six; [15]the people of Adin, four hundred and fifty-four; [16]the people of Ater of Hezekiah, ninety-eight; [17]the people of Bezai, three hundred and twenty-three; [18]the people of Jorah, one hundred and twelve; [19]the people of Hashum, two hundred and twenty-three; [20]the people of Gibbar, ninety-five; [21]the people of Bethlehem, one hundred and twenty-three; [22]the men of Netophah, fifty-six; [23]the men of Anathoth, one hundred and twenty-eight; [24]the people of Azmaveth, forty-two; [25]the people of Kirjath Arim, Chephirah, and Beeroth, seven hundred and forty-three; [26]the people of Ramah and Geba, six hundred and twenty-one; [27]the men of Michmas, one hundred and twenty-two; [28]the men of Bethel and Ai, two hundred and twenty-three; [29]the people of Nebo, fifty-two; [30]the people of Magbish, one

hundred and fifty-six; 31the people of the other
Elam, one thousand two hundred and fifty-four;
32the people of Harim, three hundred and twenty; 33the people of Lod, Hadid, and Ono, seven
hundred and twenty-five; 34the people of Jericho,
three hundred and forty-five; 35the people of
Senaah, three thousand six hundred and thirty.

36The priests: the sons of Jedaiah, of the
house of Jeshua, nine hundred and seventy-
three; 37the sons of Immer, one thousand and
fifty-two; 38the sons of Pashhur, one thousand
two hundred and forty-seven; 39the sons of
Harim, one thousand and seventeen.

40The Levites: the sons of Jeshua and
Kadmiel, of the sons of Hodaviah, seventy-four.

41The singers: the sons of Asaph, one hundred and twenty-eight.

42The sons of the gatekeepers: the sons of
Shallum, the sons of Ater, the sons of Talmon,
the sons of Akkub, the sons of Hatita, and the sons
of Shobai, one hundred and thirty-nine *in* all.

43The Nethinim: the sons of Ziha, the sons of
Hasupha, the sons of Tabbaoth, 44the sons of
Keros, the sons of Siaha, the sons of Padon,
45the sons of Lebanah, the sons of Hagabah, the
sons of Akkub, 46the sons of Hagab, the sons of
Shalmai, the sons of Hanan, 47the sons of
Giddel, the sons of Gahar, the sons of Reaiah,
48the sons of Rezin, the sons of Nekoda, the
sons of Gazzam, 49the sons of Uzza, the sons of
Paseah, the sons of Besai, 50the sons of Asnah,
the sons of Meunim, the sons of Nephusim,
51the sons of Bakbuk, the sons of Hakupha, the
sons of Harhur, 52the sons of Bazluth, the sons
of Mehida, the sons of Harsha, 53the sons of
Barkos, the sons of Sisera, the sons of Tamah,
54the sons of Neziah, and the sons of Hatipha.

55The sons of Solomon's servants: the sons
of Sotai, the sons of Sophereth, the sons of
Peruda, 56the sons of Jaala, the sons of Darkon,
the sons of Giddel, 57the sons of Shephatiah,
the sons of Hattil, the sons of Pochereth of
Zebaim, and the sons of Ami. 58All the
Nethinim and the children of Solomon's servants were three hundred and ninety-two.

59And these *were* the ones who came up
from Tel Melah, Tel Harsha, Cherub, Addan,
and Immer; but they could not identify their
father's house or their genealogy, whether
they *were* of Israel: 60the sons of Delaiah, the
sons of Tobiah, and the sons of Nekoda, six
hundred and fifty-two; 61and of the sons of the
priests: the sons of Habaiah, the sons of Koz,
and the sons of Barzillai, who took a wife of
the daughters of Barzillai the Gileadite, and
was called by their name. 62These sought their
listing *among* those who were registered by
genealogy, but they were not found; therefore
they *were excluded* from the priesthood as
defiled. 63And the governor said to them that they
should not eat of the most holy things till a priest
could consult with the Urim and Thummim.

64The whole assembly together *was* forty-
two thousand three hundred *and* sixty, 65be-
sides their male and female servants, of whom
there were seven thousand three hundred and
thirty-seven; and they had two hundred men
and women singers. 66Their horses *were* seven
hundred and thirty-six, their mules two hundred and forty-five, 67their camels four hundred and thirty-five, and *their* donkeys six
thousand seven hundred and twenty.

68*Some* of the heads of the fathers' *houses,*
when they came to the house of the LORD
which *is* in Jerusalem, offered freely for the
house of God, to erect it in its place: 69Accord-
ing to their ability, they gave to the treasury
for the work sixty-one thousand gold drachmas, five thousand minas of silver, and one
hundred priestly garments.

70So the priests and the Levites, *some* of the
people, the singers, the gatekeepers, and the
Nethinim, dwelt in their cities, and all Israel in
their cities.

Psalm 86:6–10

6 Give ear, O LORD, to my prayer;
And attend to the voice of my
supplications.
7 In the day of my trouble I will call upon
You,
For You will answer me.
8 Among the gods *there is* none like You,
O Lord;
Nor *are there any works* like Your
works.
9 All nations whom You have made
Shall come and worship before You,
O Lord,
And shall glorify Your name.
10 For You *are* great, and do wondrous
things;
You alone *are* God.

Proverbs 21:15–16

15 *It is* a joy for the just to do justice,
But destruction *will come* to the
workers of iniquity.
16 A man who wanders from the way of
understanding
Will rest in the assembly of the dead.

Acts 21:18–40

18On the following *day* Paul went in with us to
James, and all the elders were present. 19When

he had greeted them, he told in detail those
things which God had done among the
Gentiles through his ministry. 20And when
they heard *it,* they glorified the Lord. And
they said to him, "You see, brother, how many
myriads of Jews there are who have believed,
and they are all zealous for the law; 21but they
have been informed about you that you teach
all the Jews who are among the Gentiles to forsake Moses, saying that they ought not to circumcise *their* children nor to walk according to
the customs. 22What then? The assembly must
certainly meet, for they will hear that you have
come. 23Therefore do what we tell you: We
have four men who have taken a vow. 24Take
them and be purified with them, and pay their
expenses so that they may shave *their* heads,
and that all may know that those things of
which they were informed concerning you are
nothing, but *that* you yourself also walk orderly
and keep the law. 25But concerning the Gentiles
who believe, we have written *and* decided that
they should observe no such thing, except that
they should keep themselves from *things*
offered to idols, from blood, from things strangled, and from sexual immorality."

21:24 be purified. Having just returned from an extended stay in Gentile lands, Paul was considered ceremonially unclean. He therefore needed to undergo ritual purification before participating (as their sponsor) in the ceremony marking the end of the 4 men's vows. **pay their expenses.** For the temple ceremony in which the 4 would shave their heads and the sacrifices associated with the Nazirite vow. Paying those expenses for another was considered an act of piety; and by so doing, Paul would give further proof that he had not forsaken his Jewish heritage. **shave *their* heads.** A practice commonly associated with a Nazirite vow (Num. 6:18).

26Then Paul took the men, and the next day,
having been purified with them, entered the
temple to announce the expiration of the days
of purification, at which time an offering
should be made for each one of them.
27Now when the seven days were almost
ended, the Jews from Asia, seeing him in the
temple, stirred up the whole crowd and laid
hands on him, 28crying out, "Men of Israel,
help! This is the man who teaches all *men*
everywhere against the people, the law, and
this place; and furthermore he also brought

21:28 the people, the law, and this place. Paul's enemies leveled 3 false charges against him. They claimed that he taught Jews to forsake their heritage—the same lie told by the Judaizers. The second charge, that Paul opposed the law, was a very dangerous one, albeit false, in this setting. Originally, Pentecost was a celebration of the firstfruits of the harvest. But by this time, it had become a celebration of Moses' receiving the law on Mt. Sinai. Thus, the Jewish people were especially zealous for the law during this feast. The third charge, of blaspheming or defiling the temple, had helped bring about the deaths of Jesus (Mark 14:57,58) and Stephen (Acts 6:13). All 3 charges were, of course, totally false.

21:30 doors were shut. This was done by the temple guards, since Paul's death on the temple grounds would defile the temple (2 Kin. 11:15). They made no effort, however, to rescue the apostle from the crowd, which was intent on beating him to death.

Greeks into the temple and has defiled this
holy place." 29(For they had previously seen
Trophimus the Ephesian with him in the city,
whom they supposed that Paul had brought
into the temple.)
30And all the city was disturbed; and the people ran together, seized Paul, and dragged him
out of the temple; and immediately the doors
were shut. 31Now as they were seeking to kill
him, news came to the commander of the garrison that all Jerusalem was in an uproar. 32He
immediately took soldiers and centurions, and
ran down to them. And when they saw the commander and the soldiers, they stopped beating
Paul. 33Then the commander came near and
took him, and commanded *him* to be bound
with two chains; and he asked who he was and
what he had done. 34And some among the multitude cried one thing and some another.
So when he could not ascertain the truth
because of the tumult, he commanded him to
be taken into the barracks. 35When he reached
the stairs, he had to be carried by the soldiers
because of the violence of the mob. 36For the
multitude of the people followed after, crying
out, "Away with him!"
37Then as Paul was about to be led into the
barracks, he said to the commander, "May I
speak to you?"
He replied, "Can you speak Greek? 38Are
you not the Egyptian who some time ago

stirred up a rebellion and led the four thousand assassins out into the wilderness?"
39But Paul said, "I am a Jew from Tarsus, in
Cilicia, a citizen of no mean city; and I implore
you, permit me to speak to the people."
40So when he had given him permission,
Paul stood on the stairs and motioned with his
hand to the people. And when there was a
great silence, he spoke to *them* in the Hebrew
language, saying,

DAY 20: How did God sovereignly restore the Jews to the land?

It was through a proclamation by Cyrus king of Persia. The Lord had prophesied through Isaiah, who said of Cyrus, "He is My shepherd,…saying to Jerusalem, 'You shall be built,' and to the temple, 'Your foundation shall be laid'" (Is. 44:28). The historian Josephus records an account of the day when Daniel read Isaiah's prophecy to Cyrus, and in response he was moved to declare the proclamation of Ezra 1:2–4 (538 B.C.). "That the word of the LORD by the mouth of Jeremiah might be fulfilled." Jeremiah had prophesied the return of the exiles after a 70-year captivity in Babylon (Jer. 25:11; 29:10–14; Dan. 9:2). This was no isolated event, but rather an outworking of the covenant promises made to Abraham in Genesis 12:1–3.

We are told that "the LORD stirred up the spirit of Cyrus." A strong expression of the fact that God sovereignly works in the lives of kings to effect His purposes (Prov. 21:1; Dan. 2:21; 4:17). Cyrus made a proclamation, which was the most common form of spoken, public communication, usually from the central administration. The king would dispatch a herald, perhaps with a written document, into the city. In order to address the people, he would either go to the city gate, where people often congregated for social discourse, or gather the people together in a square, occasionally by the blowing of a horn. The herald would then make the proclamation to the people. A document called the Cyrus Cylinder, recovered in reasonably good condition by archeologists, commissions people from many lands to return to their cities to rebuild the temples to their gods, apparently as some sort of general policy of Cyrus. Whether or not this document was an extension of the proclamation made to the exiles in this passage must remain a matter of speculation.

It is possible that Daniel played a part in the Jews' receiving such favorable treatment (Dan. 6:25–28). According to the Jewish historian Josephus, he was Cyrus's prime minister who shared Isaiah's prophecies with Cyrus (Is. 44:28; 46:1–4). The existence of such documents, written over a century before Cyrus was born, led him to acknowledge that all his power came from the God of Israel and prompted him to fulfill the prophecy.

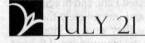

JULY 21

Ezra 3:1–4:24

3 And when the seventh month had come,
and the children of Israel *were* in the cities,
the people gathered together as one man to Jerusalem. 2Then Jeshua the son of Jozadak and
his brethren the priests, and Zerubbabel the
son of Shealtiel and his brethren, arose and
built the altar of the God of Israel, to offer burnt
offerings on it, as *it is* written in the Law of Moses the man of God. 3Though fear *had come* upon
them because of the people of those countries,
they set the altar on its bases; and they offered
burnt offerings on it to the LORD, *both* the morning and evening burnt offerings. 4They also kept
the Feast of Tabernacles, as *it is* written, and *offered* the daily burnt offerings in the number
required by ordinance for each day. 5Afterwards
they offered the regular burnt offering, and *those*
for New Moons and for all the appointed feasts
of the LORD that were consecrated, and *those*
of everyone who willingly offered a freewill
offering to the LORD. 6From the first day of the
seventh month they began to offer burnt
offerings to the LORD, although the foundation
of the temple of the LORD had not been laid.
7They also gave money to the masons and the
carpenters, and food, drink, and oil to the people of Sidon and Tyre to bring cedar logs from
Lebanon to the sea, to Joppa, according to the
permission which they had from Cyrus king
of Persia.
8Now in the second month of the second
year of their coming to the house of God at Jerusalem, Zerubbabel the son of Shealtiel,
Jeshua the son of Jozadak, and the rest of their
brethren the priests and the Levites, and all
those who had come out of the captivity to Jerusalem, began *work* and appointed the
Levites from twenty years old and above to
oversee the work of the house of the LORD.
9Then Jeshua *with* his sons and brothers,
Kadmiel *with* his sons, and the sons of Judah,
arose as one to oversee those working on the
house of God: the sons of Henadad *with* their
sons and their brethren the Levites.

10 When the builders laid the foundation of
the temple of the LORD, the priests stood in
their apparel with trumpets, and the Levites,
the sons of Asaph, with cymbals, to praise the
LORD, according to the ordinance of David
king of Israel. 11 And they sang responsively,
praising and giving thanks to the LORD:

"For *He is* good,
For His mercy *endures* forever toward
Israel."

Then all the people shouted with a great shout,
when they praised the LORD, because the foundation of the house of the LORD was laid.
12 But many of the priests and Levites and
heads of the fathers' *houses,* old men who had
seen the first temple, wept with a loud voice
when the foundation of this temple was laid
before their eyes. Yet many shouted aloud for
joy, 13 so that the people could not discern the
noise of the shout of joy from the noise of the
weeping of the people, for the people shouted
with a loud shout, and the sound was heard
afar off.

3:12 the first temple. The temple built by Solomon (1 Kin. 5–7). **wept with a loud voice.** The first temple had been destroyed 50 years earlier. The old men, who would have been about 60 years or older, knew that this second temple did not begin to match the splendor of Solomon's temple nor did the presence of God reside within it (Hag. 2:1–4; Zech. 4:9,10). The nation was small and weak, the temple smaller and less beautiful by far. There were no riches as in David and Solomon's days. The ark was gone. But most disappointing was the absence of God's Shekinah glory. Thus the weeping. **shouted...for joy.** For those who did not have a point of comparison, this was a great moment. Possibly Psalm 126 was written and sung for this occasion.

4 Now when the adversaries of Judah and
Benjamin heard that the descendants of
the captivity were building the temple of the
LORD God of Israel, 2 they came to Zerubbabel
and the heads of the fathers' *houses,* and said
to them, "Let us build with you, for we seek
your God as you *do;* and we have sacrificed to
Him since the days of Esarhaddon king of Assyria, who brought us here." 3 But Zerubbabel
and Jeshua and the rest of the heads of the
fathers' *houses* of Israel said to them, "You may
do nothing with us to build a house for our
God; but we alone will build to the LORD God
of Israel, as King Cyrus the king of Persia has
commanded us." 4 Then the people of the land
tried to discourage the people of Judah. They
troubled them in building, 5 and hired counselors against them to frustrate their purpose
all the days of Cyrus king of Persia, even until
the reign of Darius king of Persia.
6 In the reign of Ahasuerus, in the beginning
of his reign, they wrote an accusation against
the inhabitants of Judah and Jerusalem.
7 In the days of Artaxerxes also, Bishlam,
Mithredath, Tabel, and the rest of their companions wrote to Artaxerxes king of Persia;
and the letter *was* written in Aramaic script,
and translated into the Aramaic language.
8 Rehum the commander and Shimshai the
scribe wrote a letter against Jerusalem to King
Artaxerxes in this fashion:

9 From Rehum the commander, Shimshai
the scribe, and the rest of their
companions—*representatives* of the
Dinaites, the Apharsathchites, the
Tarpelites, the people of Persia and
Erech and Babylon and Shushan, the
Dehavites, the Elamites, 10 and the rest
of the nations whom the great and noble
Osnapper took captive and settled in the
cities of Samaria and the remainder
beyond the River—and so forth.

11 (This *is* a copy of the letter that they sent him)

To King Artaxerxes from your
servants, the men *of the region* beyond
the River, and so forth:

12 Let it be known to the king that the
Jews who came up from you have
come to us at Jerusalem, and are
building the rebellious and evil city,
and are finishing *its* walls and repairing
the foundations. 13 Let it now be known
to the king that, if this city is built and
the walls completed, they will not pay
tax, tribute, or custom, and the king's
treasury will be diminished. 14 Now
because we receive support from the
palace, it was not proper for us to see
the king's dishonor; therefore we have
sent and informed the king, 15 that
search may be made in the book of the
records of your fathers. And you will
find in the book of the records and
know that this city *is* a rebellious city,
harmful to kings and provinces, and
that they have incited sedition within
the city in former times, for which
cause this city was destroyed.

4:6–23 This section represents later opposition which Ezra chose to put here as a parenthetical continuation of the theme "opposition to resettling and rebuilding Judah." He first referred to the opposition from Israel's enemies under King Ahasuerus (a regal title) or Xerxes (ca. 486–464 B.C.), who ruled at the time of Esther (4:6). Ezra 4:7–23 then recounts opposition in Nehemiah's day under Artaxerxes I (ca. 464–423 B.C.) expressed in a detailed letter of accusation against the Jews (vv. 7–16). It was successful in stopping the work, as the king's reply indicates (vv. 17–23). Most likely, this opposition is that also spoken of in Nehemiah 1:3. All this was the ongoing occurrence of severe animosity between the Israelites and Samaritans, which was later aggravated when the Samaritans built a rival temple on Mt. Gerizim (John 4:9). The opposition to Zerubbabel picks up again at 4:24–5:2 during the reign of Darius I, who actually reigned before either Ahasuerus or Artaxerxes.

16 We inform the king that if this city is
rebuilt and its walls are completed, the
result will be that you will have no
dominion beyond the River.

17The king sent an answer:

To Rehum the commander, *to*
Shimshai the scribe, *to* the rest of their
companions who dwell in Samaria, and
to the remainder beyond the River:

Peace, and so forth.

18 The letter which you sent to us has
been clearly read before me. 19And I
gave the command, and a search has
been made, and it was found that this
city in former times has revolted
against kings, and rebellion and
sedition have been fostered in it.
20There have also been mighty kings
over Jerusalem, who have ruled over all
the region beyond the River; and tax,
tribute, and custom were paid to them.
21Now give the command to make these
men cease, that this city may not be
built until the command is given by me.

22 Take heed now that you do not fail to
do this. Why should damage increase
to the hurt of the kings?

23Now when the copy of King Artaxerxes' letter *was* read before Rehum, Shimshai the
scribe, and their companions, they went up in
haste to Jerusalem against the Jews, and by
force of arms made them cease. 24Thus the
work of the house of God which *is* at Jerusalem
ceased, and it was discontinued until the second year of the reign of Darius king of Persia.

4:21 Now give the command. No small order for one or two workers, but rather the efforts of 50,000 were called to a halt. The king was commissioning a decree of great significance. The original language calls for the difference. This decree would not lose its authority until the king established a new decree.

Psalm 86:11–17

11 Teach me Your way, O LORD;
I will walk in Your truth;
Unite my heart to fear Your name.
12 I will praise You, O Lord my God, with all my heart,
And I will glorify Your name forevermore.
13 For great *is* Your mercy toward me,
And You have delivered my soul from the depths of Sheol.
14 O God, the proud have risen against me,
And a mob of violent *men* have sought my life,
And have not set You before them.
15 But You, O Lord, *are* a God full of compassion, and gracious,
Longsuffering and abundant in mercy and truth.
16 Oh, turn to me, and have mercy on me!
Give Your strength to Your servant,
And save the son of Your maidservant.
17 Show me a sign for good,
That those who hate me may see *it* and be ashamed,
Because You, LORD, have helped me and comforted me.

Proverbs 21:17–18

17 He who loves pleasure *will be* a poor man;
He who loves wine and oil will not be rich.
18 The wicked *shall be* a ransom for the righteous,
And the unfaithful for the upright.

Acts 22:1–30

22 "Brethren and fathers, hear my
defense before you now." 2And when
they heard that he spoke to them in the Hebrew language, they kept all the more silent.

Then he said: 3"I am indeed a Jew, born in
Tarsus of Cilicia, but brought up in this city at
the feet of Gamaliel, taught according to the
strictness of our fathers' law, and was zealous
toward God as you all are today. 4I persecuted
this Way to the death, binding and delivering
into prisons both men and women, 5as also the
high priest bears me witness, and all the council of the elders, from whom I also received

22:3 I am indeed a Jew. A response to the false charges raised by the Asian Jews. **born in Tarsus.** Tarsus was the chief city of Cilicia. **brought up in this city.** Paul was born among the Hellenistic Jews of the Diaspora, but had been brought up in Jerusalem. **Gamaliel.** That Paul had studied under the most celebrated rabbi of that day was further evidence that the charges against him were absurd. **fathers' law.** As a student of Gamaliel, Paul received extensive training both in the Old Testament law and in the rabbinic traditions. Also, though he did not mention it to the crowd, he had been a Pharisee. In light of all that, the charge that Paul opposed the law was ridiculous.

letters to the brethren, and went to Damascus
to bring in chains even those who were there
to Jerusalem to be punished.

6"Now it happened, as I journeyed and came
near Damascus at about noon, suddenly a
great light from heaven shone around me.
7And I fell to the ground and heard a voice saying to me, 'Saul, Saul, why are you persecuting
Me?' 8So I answered, 'Who are You, Lord?'
And He said to me, 'I am Jesus of Nazareth,
whom you are persecuting.'

9"And those who were with me indeed saw
the light and were afraid, but they did not hear
the voice of Him who spoke to me. 10So I said,
'What shall I do, Lord?' And the Lord said to me,
'Arise and go into Damascus, and there you will
be told all things which are appointed for you to
do.' 11And since I could not see for the glory of
that light, being led by the hand of those who
were with me, I came into Damascus.

12"Then a certain Ananias, a devout man
according to the law, having a good testimony
with all the Jews who dwelt *there,* 13came to
me; and he stood and said to me, 'Brother
Saul, receive your sight.' And at that same
hour I looked up at him. 14Then he said, 'The
God of our fathers has chosen you that you
should know His will, and see the Just One,
and hear the voice of His mouth. 15For you will
be His witness to all men of what you have
seen and heard. 16And now why are you waiting? Arise and be baptized, and wash away
your sins, calling on the name of the Lord.'

17"Now it happened, when I returned to Jerusalem and was praying in the temple, that I was
in a trance 18and saw Him saying to me, 'Make
haste and get out of Jerusalem quickly, for
they will not receive your testimony concerning Me.' 19So I said, 'Lord, they know that in
every synagogue I imprisoned and beat those
who believe on You. 20And when the blood of
Your martyr Stephen was shed, I also was
standing by consenting to his death, and
guarding the clothes of those who were killing
him.' 21Then He said to me, 'Depart, for I will
send you far from here to the Gentiles.' "

22And they listened to him until this word,
and *then* they raised their voices and said,
"Away with such a *fellow* from the earth, for he
is not fit to live!" 23Then, as they cried out and
tore off *their* clothes and threw dust into the
air, 24the commander ordered him to be
brought into the barracks, and said that he

22:21–23 Paul's insistence that the Lord had sent him to minister to the despised Gentiles was too much for the crowd. They viewed the teaching that Gentiles could be saved without first becoming Jewish proselytes (thus granting them equal status with the Jewish people before God) as intolerable blasphemy.

should be examined under scourging, so that
he might know why they shouted so against
him. 25And as they bound him with thongs,
Paul said to the centurion who stood by, "Is it
lawful for you to scourge a man who is a
Roman, and uncondemned?"

26When the centurion heard *that,* he went
and told the commander, saying, "Take care
what you do, for this man is a Roman."

27Then the commander came and said to
him, "Tell me, are you a Roman?"

He said, "Yes."

28The commander answered, "With a large
sum I obtained this citizenship."

And Paul said, "But I was born *a citizen.*"

29Then immediately those who were about

to examine him withdrew from him; and the commander was also afraid after he found out that he was a Roman, and because he had bound him.

30 The next day, because he wanted to know for certain why he was accused by the Jews, he released him from *his* bonds, and commanded the chief priests and all their council to appear, and brought Paul down and set him before them.

DAY 21: Who were the people who made so much trouble for those Jews who returned from captivity?

In Ezra 3:3, it mentions "the people of those countries." These were the settlers who had come to occupy the land during the 70 years of Israel's absence. They were deportees brought in from other countries by the Assyrians and the Babylonians. These inhabitants saw the Jews as a threat and quickly wanted to undermine their allegiance to God (4:1,2). These are called "the adversaries"—Israel's enemies in the region, who resisted their reestablishment of the temple.

These enemies came to the Jews offering their assistance, saying, "We have sacrificed to Him" (v. 2). This false claim represented the syncretistic worship of the Samaritans, whose ancestry came from intermarriage with foreign immigrants in Samaria after 722 B.C. (4:10). In the British Museum is a large cylinder; and inscribed on it are the annals of Esarhaddon, an Assyrian king (ca. 681–669 B.C.), who deported a large population of Israelites from Palestine. A consequent settlement of Babylonian colonists took their place and intermarried with remaining Jewish women and their descendants. The result was the mongrel race called Samaritans. They had developed a superstitious form of worshiping God (2 Kin. 17:26–34).

Idolatry had been the chief cause for Judah's deportation to Babylon, and they wanted to avoid it altogether. While they still had their spiritual problems (Ezra 9; 10), they rejected any form of mixed religion, particularly this offer of cooperation which had sabotage as its goal (vv. 4,5). "King Cyrus…commanded us." This note gave authority to their refusal.

Nevertheless, the enemies hired counselors who managed to "frustrate" the work on the temple. This caused a 16-year delay (ca. 536–520 B.C.). As a result, the people took more interest in their personal affairs than in spiritual matters (Hag. 1:2–6).

JULY 22

Ezra 5:1–6:22

5 Then the prophet Haggai and Zechariah the son of Iddo, prophets, prophesied to the
Jews who *were* in Judah and Jerusalem, in the name of the God of Israel, *who was* over them.
2 So Zerubbabel the son of Shealtiel and Jeshua the son of Jozadak rose up and began to build the house of God which *is* in Jerusalem; and the prophets of God *were* with them, helping them.
3 At the same time Tattenai the governor of *the region* beyond the River and Shethar-Boznai and their companions came to them and spoke thus to them: "Who has commanded you to build this temple and finish this wall?"
4 Then, accordingly, we told them the names of the men who were constructing this building.
5 But the eye of their God was upon the elders of the Jews, so that they could not make them cease till a report could go to Darius. Then a written answer was returned

5:1 Haggai and Zechariah. The Book of Haggai is styled as a "royal administrative correspondence" (Hag. 1:13) sent from the Sovereign King of the Universe through the "LORD's messenger," Haggai (Hag. 1:13). Part of its message is addressed specifically to Zerubbabel, the political leader, and Joshua, the religious leader, telling them to take courage and work on the temple because God was with them (Hag. 2:4). These two prophets gave severe reproaches and threats if the people did not return to the building and promised national prosperity if they did. Not long after the exiles heard this message, the temple work began afresh after a 16-year hiatus.

5:5 But the eye of their God was upon the elders. God's hand of protection which led this endeavor allowed the work to continue while official communication was going on with Darius, the Persian king.

concerning this *matter.* [6]This is a copy of the
letter that Tattenai sent:

The governor of *the region* beyond the
River, and Shethar-Boznai, and his
companions, the Persians who *were in
the region* beyond the River, to Darius
the king.

[7](They sent a letter to him, in which was written thus)

To Darius the king:

All peace.

8 Let it be known to the king that we went
into the province of Judea, to the temple
of the great God, which is being built
with heavy stones, and timber is being
laid in the walls; and this work goes on
diligently and prospers in their hands.

9 Then we asked those elders, *and* spoke
thus to them: "Who commanded you to
build this temple and to finish these
walls?" [10]We also asked them their
names to inform you, that we might
write the names of the men who *were*
chief among them.

11 And thus they returned us an answer,
saying: "We are the servants of the
God of heaven and earth, and we are
rebuilding the temple that was built
many years ago, which a great king
of Israel built and completed. [12]But
because our fathers provoked the God
of heaven to wrath, He gave them into
the hand of Nebuchadnezzar king of
Babylon, the Chaldean, *who* destroyed
this temple and carried the people away
to Babylon. [13]However, in the first year of
Cyrus king of Babylon, King Cyrus
issued a decree to build this house of
God. [14]Also, the gold and silver articles of
the house of God, which
Nebuchadnezzar had taken from the
temple that *was* in Jerusalem and carried
into the temple of Babylon—those King
Cyrus took from the temple of Babylon,
and they were given to one named
Sheshbazzar, whom he had made
governor. [15]And he said to him, 'Take
these articles; go, carry them to the
temple *site* that *is* in Jerusalem, and let
the house of God be rebuilt on its former
site.' [16]Then the same Sheshbazzar came
and laid the foundation of the house of
God which *is* in Jerusalem; but from that
time even until now it has been under
construction, and it is not finished."

17 Now therefore, if *it seems* good to the
king, let a search be made in the king's
treasure house, which *is* there in
Babylon, whether it is *so* that a decree
was issued by King Cyrus to build this
house of God at Jerusalem, and let the
king send us his pleasure concerning
this *matter.*

6 Then King Darius issued a decree, and a
search was made in the archives, where
the treasures were stored in Babylon. [2]And at
Achmetha, in the palace that *is* in the province
of Media, a scroll was found, and in it a record
was written thus:

3 In the first year of King Cyrus, King
Cyrus issued a decree *concerning* the
house of God at Jerusalem: "Let the
house be rebuilt, the place where they
offered sacrifices; and let the
foundations of it be firmly laid, its
height sixty cubits *and* its width sixty
cubits, [4]*with* three rows of heavy stones
and one row of new timber. Let the
expenses be paid from the king's
treasury. [5]Also let the gold and silver
articles of the house of God, which
Nebuchadnezzar took from the temple
which *is* in Jerusalem and brought to
Babylon, be restored and taken back to
the temple which *is* in Jerusalem, *each*
to its place; and deposit *them* in the
house of God"—

6 Now *therefore,* Tattenai, governor of
the region beyond the River, and
Shethar-Boznai, and your companions
the Persians who *are* beyond the River,
keep yourselves far from there. [7]Let
the work of this house of God alone; let
the governor of the Jews and the
elders of the Jews build this house of
God on its site.

8 Moreover I issue a decree *as to* what
you shall do for the elders of these
Jews, for the building of this house of
God: Let the cost be paid at the king's
expense from taxes *on the region* beyond
the River; this is to be given immediately
to these men, so that they are not
hindered. [9]And whatever they need—
young bulls, rams, and lambs for the
burnt offerings of the God of heaven,
wheat, salt, wine, and oil, according to
the request of the priests who *are* in
Jerusalem—let it be given them day by
day without fail, [10]that they may offer
sacrifices of sweet aroma to the God of

heaven, and pray for the life of the king
and his sons.

11 Also I issue a decree that whoever
alters this edict, let a timber be pulled
from his house and erected, and let
him be hanged on it; and let his house
be made a refuse heap because of this.
12And may the God who causes His
name to dwell there destroy any king
or people who put their hand to alter it,
or to destroy this house of God which
is in Jerusalem. I Darius issue a
decree; let it be done diligently.

13Then Tattenai, governor of *the region*
beyond the River, Shethar-Boznai, and their
companions diligently did according to what
King Darius had sent. 14So the elders of the Jews
built, and they prospered through the prophesying of Haggai the prophet and Zechariah
the son of Iddo. And they built and finished *it*,
according to the commandment of the God of
Israel, and according to the command of
Cyrus, Darius, and Artaxerxes king of Persia.

6:14 the commandment of the God of Israel...the command of Cyrus. This is not the normal term for commandment, but it is the same word translated "decree" or "administrative order" throughout the book. The message here is powerful. It was the decree from God, the Sovereign of the universe, which gave administrative authority to rebuild the temple. The decrees (same word) of 3 of the greatest monarchs in the history of the ancient Near East were only a secondary issue. God rules the universe and He raises up kings, then pulls them from their thrones when they have served His administration.

15Now the temple was finished on the third day
of the month of Adar, which was in the sixth
year of the reign of King Darius. 16Then the
children of Israel, the priests and the Levites
and the rest of the descendants of the captivity,
celebrated the dedication of this house of God
with joy. 17And they offered sacrifices at the
dedication of this house of God, one hundred
bulls, two hundred rams, four hundred lambs,
and as a sin offering for all Israel twelve male
goats, according to the number of the tribes of
Israel. 18They assigned the priests to their divisions and the Levites to their divisions, over the
service of God in Jerusalem, as it is written in
the Book of Moses.

19And the descendants of the captivity kept
the Passover on the fourteenth *day* of the first
month. 20For the priests and the Levites had
purified themselves; all of them *were ritually*
clean. And they slaughtered the Passover
lambs for all the descendants of the captivity,
for their brethren the priests, and for themselves. 21Then the children of Israel who had
returned from the captivity ate together with
all who had separated themselves from the
filth of the nations of the land in order to seek
the LORD God of Israel. 22And they kept the
Feast of Unleavened Bread seven days with joy;
for the LORD made them joyful, and turned the
heart of the king of Assyria toward them, to
strengthen their hands in the work of the
house of God, the God of Israel.

6:22 turned the heart of the king of Assyria toward them. By turning the heart of the king in their favor in allowing them to complete the rebuilding, God encouraged His people. They understood the verse, "The king's heart is in the hand of the LORD" (Prov. 21:1) better through this ordeal. The title "King of Assyria" was held by every king who succeeded the great Neo-Assyrian Empire regardless of what country they may have come from.

Psalm 87:1–7

A Psalm of the sons of Korah. A Song.

His foundation *is* in the holy
mountains.
2 The LORD loves the gates of Zion
More than all the dwellings of Jacob.
3 Glorious things are spoken of you,
O city of God! Selah

4 "I will make mention of Rahab and
Babylon to those who know Me;
Behold, O Philistia and Tyre,
with Ethiopia:
'This *one* was born there.'"

5 And of Zion it will be said,
"This *one* and that *one* were born
in her;
And the Most High Himself shall
establish her."
6 The LORD will record,
When He registers the peoples:
"This *one* was born there."
Selah

7 Both the singers and the players on
instruments *say,*
"All my springs *are* in you."

Proverbs 21:19–20

19 Better to dwell in the wilderness,
Than with a contentious and angry
woman.

20 *There is* desirable treasure,
And oil in the dwelling of the wise,
But a foolish man squanders it.

Acts 23:1–15

23 Then Paul, looking earnestly at the
council, said, "Men *and* brethren, I
have lived in all good conscience before God
until this day." 2And the high priest Ananias commanded those who stood by him to strike him
on the mouth. 3Then Paul said to him, "God will
strike you, *you* whitewashed wall! For you sit to
judge me according to the law, and do you command me to be struck contrary to the law?"

23:2 high priest Ananias. Not the Annas of the Gospels, this man was one of Israel's cruelest and most corrupt high priests. His pro-Roman policies alienated him from the Jewish people, who murdered him at the outset of the revolt against Rome (A.D. 66). **commanded...to strike him.** An illegal act in keeping with Ananias's brutal character. The verb translated "strike" is used of the mob's beating of Paul (21:32) and the Roman soldiers' beating of Jesus (Matt. 27:30). It was no mere slap on the face, but a vicious blow.

23:3 whitewashed wall. Ezekiel 13:10–16; Matthew 23:27. **contrary to the law.** Outraged by the high priest's flagrant violation of Jewish law, Paul flared up in anger. When Jesus was similarly struck in violation of the law, He reacted by calmly asking the reason for the blow (John 18:23). Paul's reaction was wrong, as he would shortly admit (v. 5). Although an evil man, Ananias still held a God-ordained office and was to be granted the respect that position demanded.

4And those who stood by said, "Do you
revile God's high priest?"
5Then Paul said, "I did not know, brethren,
that he was the high priest; for it is written,
'*You shall not speak evil of a ruler of your
people.*' "
6But when Paul perceived that one part
were Sadducees and the other Pharisees, he
cried out in the council, "Men *and* brethren, I
am a Pharisee, the son of a Pharisee; concerning the hope and resurrection of the dead I am
being judged!"
7And when he had said this, a dissension
arose between the Pharisees and the
Sadducees; and the assembly was divided.
8For Sadducees say that there is no resurrection—and no angel or spirit; but the Pharisees
confess both. 9Then there arose a loud outcry.
And the scribes of the Pharisees' party arose
and protested, saying, "We find no evil in this
man; but if a spirit or an angel has spoken to
him, let us not fight against God."

23:7 a dissension arose. There were major social, political, and theological differences between the Sadducees and Pharisees. By raising the issue of the resurrection, Paul appealed to the Pharisees for support on perhaps the most important theological difference. Since the resurrection of Jesus Christ is also the central theme of Christianity, this was no cynical ploy on Paul's part to divide the Sanhedrin over a trivial point of theology.

10Now when there arose a great dissension,
the commander, fearing lest Paul might be
pulled to pieces by them, commanded the
soldiers to go down and take him by force
from among them, and bring *him* into the
barracks.
11But the following night the Lord stood by
him and said, "Be of good cheer, Paul; for as
you have testified for Me in Jerusalem, so you
must also bear witness at Rome."
12And when it was day, some of the Jews
banded together and bound themselves
under an oath, saying that they would neither eat nor drink till they had killed Paul.
13Now there were more than forty who had
formed this conspiracy. 14They came to the
chief priests and elders, and said, "We have
bound ourselves under a great oath that we
will eat nothing until we have killed Paul.
15Now you, therefore, together with the
council, suggest to the commander that he
be brought down to you tomorrow, as
though you were going to make further
inquiries concerning him; but we are ready
to kill him before he comes near."

DAY 22: How does Psalm 87 describe God's love for Jerusalem?

This psalm describes the Lord's love for Jerusalem and exalts this city as the religious center of the world in the coming messianic kingdom (Ps. 48). Though the nations of the world (even including some of Israel's former enemies) will worship the Lord then, Israel will still be the favored nation (Is. 2:2–4; 19:23–25; 45:22–25; 56:6–8; Zech. 8:20–23; 14:16–19).

"His foundation is in the holy mountains" (v. 1). "His foundation" means "His founded city," namely Jerusalem, located in the hill country of Judea. "The LORD loves the gates of Zion" (v. 2). Zion is a poetic description of Jerusalem, seemingly used by the Old Testament writers when special spiritual and religious significance was being attached to the city. Though God certainly loved other cities in Israel, He did not choose any of them to be His worship center. The gates represent the access of the potential worshiper into the city where he could come into a special worshiping relationship with God. "More than all the dwellings of Jacob." The other cities in Israel were not chosen by God to be the place of His special dwelling.

"Glorious things are spoken of you, O city of God!" (v. 3). Jerusalem was God's city because there God met His people in praise and offerings. "I will make mention of Rahab and Babylon" (v. 4). Rahab was a monster of ancient pagan mythology and symbolized Egypt in the Old Testament (Ps. 89:10; Is. 30:7; 51:9). Two of the superpowers of the ancient world, fierce enemies of Israel, will one day worship the Lord in Zion (Is. 19:19–25). "Philistia...Tyre...Ethiopia" (Ps. 87:4). Three more Gentile nations, ancient enemies of Israel, whose descendants will worship the Lord in Jerusalem (Is. 14:28–32; 18:1–7). This multinational worship is pictured as a great joy to the Lord Himself. "This one was born there" (Ps. 87:6). To be born in Jerusalem will be noted as a special honor in the messianic kingdom (vv. 5,6; also Zech. 8:20–23).

"All my springs are in you" (v. 7). "Springs" is a metaphor for the source of joyful blessings. Eternal salvation, including the death and resurrection of Christ, is rooted in Jerusalem. The prophets also tell of a literal fountain flowing from the temple in Jerusalem which will water the surrounding land (Joel 3:18; Ezek. 47:1–12).

JULY 23

Ezra 7:1–8:36

7 Now after these things, in the reign of
Artaxerxes king of Persia, Ezra the son of
Seraiah, the son of Azariah, the son of Hilkiah,
2the son of Shallum, the son of Zadok, the son
of Ahitub, 3the son of Amariah, the son of
Azariah, the son of Meraioth, 4the son of
Zerahiah, the son of Uzzi, the son of Bukki,
5the son of Abishua, the son of Phinehas, the
son of Eleazar, the son of Aaron the chief
priest— 6this Ezra came up from Babylon; and
he *was* a skilled scribe in the Law of Moses,
which the LORD God of Israel had given. The
king granted him all his request, according to
the hand of the LORD his God upon him. 7*Some*
of the children of Israel, the priests, the Levites,
the singers, the gatekeepers, and the Nethinim
came up to Jerusalem in the seventh year of
King Artaxerxes. 8And Ezra came to Jerusalem in the fifth month, which *was* in the seventh year of the king. 9On the first *day* of the
first month he began *his* journey from Babylon,
and on the first *day* of the fifth month he came
to Jerusalem, according to the good hand of
his God upon him. 10For Ezra had prepared his
heart to seek the Law of the LORD, and to do *it*,
and to teach statutes and ordinances in Israel.
11This *is* a copy of the letter that King
Artaxerxes gave Ezra the priest, the scribe,
expert in the words of the commandments of
the LORD, and of His statutes to Israel:

12 Artaxerxes, king of kings,

To Ezra the priest, a scribe of the Law of the God of heaven:

7:6 a skilled scribe. Ezra's role as a scribe was critical to reinstate the nation since the leaders had to go back to the law and interpret it. This was no small task because many aspects of life had changed in the intervening 1,000 years since the law was first given. Tradition says Ezra had the law memorized and could write it from recall. **the hand of the LORD his God upon him.** This refrain occurs throughout the books of Ezra and Nehemiah. Its resounding presence assures the reader that it was not by the shrewd leadership skills of a few men that Judah, with its temple and walls, was rebuilt in the midst of a powerful Medo-Persian Empire. Rather it was the sovereign hand of the wise and powerful King of the universe that allowed this to happen.

7:10 seek...do...teach. The pattern of Ezra's preparation is exemplary. He studied before he attempted to live a life of obedience, and he studied and practiced the law in his own life before he opened his mouth to teach that law. But the success of Ezra's leadership did not come from his strength alone, but most significantly because "the good hand of his God [was] upon him" (7:9).

Perfect *peace,* and so forth.

13 I issue a decree that all those of the
people of Israel and the priests and
Levites in my realm, who volunteer to
go up to Jerusalem, may go with you.
[14]And whereas you are being sent by the
king and his seven counselors to inquire
concerning Judah and Jerusalem, with
regard to the Law of your God which *is*
in your hand; [15]and *whereas you are* to
carry the silver and gold which the king
and his counselors have freely offered
to the God of Israel, whose dwelling *is*
in Jerusalem; [16]and *whereas* all the silver
and gold that you may find in all the
province of Babylon, along with the
freewill offering of the people and the
priests, *are to be* freely offered for the
house of their God in Jerusalem— [17]now
therefore, be careful to buy with this
money bulls, rams, and lambs, with
their grain offerings and their drink
offerings, and offer them on the altar of
the house of your God in Jerusalem.

18 And whatever seems good to you and
your brethren to do with the rest of the
silver and the gold, do it according to
the will of your God. [19]Also the articles
that are given to you for the service of
the house of your God, deliver in full
before the God of Jerusalem. [20]And
whatever more may be needed for the
house of your God, which you may
have occasion to provide, pay *for it*
from the king's treasury.

21 And I, *even* I, Artaxerxes the king, issue
a decree to all the treasurers who *are in
the region* beyond the River, that
whatever Ezra the priest, the scribe of
the Law of the God of heaven, may
require of you, let it be done diligently,
[22]up to one hundred talents of silver, one
hundred kors of wheat, one hundred
baths of wine, one hundred baths of
oil, and salt without prescribed limit.
[23]Whatever is commanded by the God of
heaven, let it diligently be done for the
house of the God of heaven. For why
should there be wrath against the realm
of the king and his sons?

24 Also we inform you that it shall not be
lawful to impose tax, tribute, or custom
on any of the priests, Levites, singers,
gatekeepers, Nethinim, or servants of
this house of God. [25]And you, Ezra,
according to your God-given wisdom,
set magistrates and judges who may
judge all the people who *are in the
region* beyond the River, all such as
know the laws of your God; and teach
those who do not know *them.* [26]Whoever
will not observe the law of your God
and the law of the king, let judgment be
executed speedily on him, whether *it be*
death, or banishment, or confiscation of
goods, or imprisonment.

[27]Blessed *be* the LORD God of our fathers, who
has put *such a thing* as this in the king's heart,
to beautify the house of the LORD which *is* in Jerusalem, [28]and has extended mercy to me
before the king and his counselors, and before
all the king's mighty princes.

So I was encouraged, as the hand of the
LORD my God *was* upon me; and I gathered
leading men of Israel to go up with me.

8 These *are* the heads of their fathers' *houses,*
and *this is* the genealogy of those who went
up with me from Babylon, in the reign of King
Artaxerxes: [2]of the sons of Phinehas, Gershom;
of the sons of Ithamar, Daniel; of the sons of David, Hattush; [3]of the sons of Shecaniah, of the
sons of Parosh, Zechariah; and registered with
him *were* one hundred and fifty males; [4]of the
sons of Pahath-Moab, Eliehoenai the son of
Zerahiah, and with him two hundred males; [5]of
the sons of Shechaniah, Ben-Jahaziel, and with
him three hundred males; [6]of the sons of Adin,
Ebed the son of Jonathan, and with him fifty
males; [7]of the sons of Elam, Jeshaiah the son of
Athaliah, and with him seventy males; [8]of the
sons of Shephatiah, Zebadiah the son of Michael, and with him eighty males; [9]of the sons
of Joab, Obadiah the son of Jehiel, and with him
two hundred and eighteen males; [10]of the sons
of Shelomith, Ben-Josiphiah, and with him one
hundred and sixty males; [11]of the sons of Bebai,
Zechariah the son of Bebai, and with him twenty-
eight males; [12]of the sons of Azgad, Johanan the
son of Hakkatan, and with him one hundred
and ten males; [13]of the last sons of Adonikam,

whose names *are* these—Eliphelet, Jeiel, and
Shemaiah—and with them sixty males; [14]also of
the sons of Bigvai, Uthai and Zabbud, and with
them seventy males.

[15]Now I gathered them by the river that
flows to Ahava, and we camped there three
days. And I looked among the people and the
priests, and found none of the sons of Levi
there. [16]Then I sent for Eliezer, Ariel,
Shemaiah, Elnathan, Jarib, Elnathan, Nathan,
Zechariah, and Meshullam, leaders; also for
Joiarib and Elnathan, men of understanding.
[17]And I gave them a command for Iddo the
chief man at the place Casiphia, and I told
them what they should say to Iddo *and* his
brethren the Nethinim at the place Casiphia—
that they should bring us servants for the house
of our God. [18]Then, by the good hand of our God
upon us, they brought us a man of understanding, of the sons of Mahli the son of Levi, the son
of Israel, namely Sherebiah, with his sons and
brothers, eighteen men; [19]and Hashabiah, and
with him Jeshaiah of the sons of Merari, his
brothers and their sons, twenty men; [20]also of
the Nethinim, whom David and the leaders had
appointed for the service of the Levites, two
hundred and twenty Nethinim. All of them
were designated by name.

[21]Then I proclaimed a fast there at the river
of Ahava, that we might humble ourselves
before our God, to seek from Him the right
way for us and our little ones and all our possessions. [22]For I was ashamed to request of the
king an escort of soldiers and horsemen to
help us against the enemy on the road,
because we had spoken to the king, saying,
"The hand of our God *is* upon all those for
good who seek Him, but His power and His
wrath *are* against all those who forsake Him."
[23]So we fasted and entreated our God for this,
and He answered our prayer.

[24]And I separated twelve of the leaders of
the priests—Sherebiah, Hashabiah, and ten of
their brethren with them— [25]and weighed out
to them the silver, the gold, and the articles,
the offering for the house of our God which the
king and his counselors and his princes, and
all Israel *who were* present, had offered. [26]I
weighed into their hand six hundred and fifty
talents of silver, silver articles *weighing* one
hundred talents, one hundred talents of gold,
[27]twenty gold basins *worth* a thousand drachmas, and two vessels of fine polished bronze,
precious as gold. [28]And I said to them, "You *are*
holy to the LORD; the articles *are* holy also; and
the silver and the gold *are* a freewill offering to
the LORD God of your fathers. [29]Watch and keep
them until you weigh *them* before the leaders of
the priests and the Levites and heads of the
fathers' *houses* of Israel in Jerusalem, *in* the chambers of the house of the LORD." [30]So the priests
and the Levites received the silver and the gold
and the articles by weight, to bring *them* to Jerusalem to the house of our God.

[31]Then we departed from the river of Ahava
on the twelfth *day* of the first month, to go to
Jerusalem. And the hand of our God was upon
us, and He delivered us from the hand of the
enemy and from ambush along the road. [32]So
we came to Jerusalem, and stayed there three
days.

[33]Now on the fourth day the silver and the
gold and the articles were weighed in the house
of our God by the hand of Meremoth the son of
Uriah the priest, and with him *was* Eleazar the
son of Phinehas; with them *were* the Levites,
Jozabad the son of Jeshua and Noadiah the son
of Binnui, [34]with the number *and* weight of
everything. All the weight was written down at
that time.

[35]The children of those who had been carried away captive, who had come from the captivity, offered burnt offerings to the God of Israel: twelve bulls for all Israel, ninety-six rams,
seventy-seven lambs, and twelve male goats *as*
a sin offering. All *this was* a burnt offering to
the LORD.

[36]And they delivered the king's orders to the
king's satraps and the governors *in the region*
beyond the River. So they gave support to the
people and the house of God.

8:21–23 I proclaimed a fast. The people of Israel would soon begin the long journey. Such travel was dangerous, for the roads were frequented by thieves who robbed for survival. Even messengers traveled with caravans to ensure their safety. Ezra and the people did not want to confuse the king regarding their trust in God's protection so they entreated Him for safety with a prayerful fast. God honored their prayer of faith with His protection.

Psalm 88:1–5

A Song. A Psalm of the sons of Korah.
To the Chief Musician. Set to "Mahalath
Leannoth." A Contemplation of Heman
the Ezrahite.

O LORD, God of my salvation,
I have cried out day
and night before You.
2 Let my prayer come before You;
Incline Your ear to my cry.

3 For my soul is full of troubles,
And my life draws near to the grave.
4 I am counted with those who go down
to the pit;
I am like a man *who has* no strength,
5 Adrift among the dead,
Like the slain who lie in the grave,
Whom You remember no more,
And who are cut off from Your hand.

88:4 go down to the pit. "Pit" is one of several references to the grave in this psalm (the dead, vv. 5, 10; the grave, vv. 3, 5, 11; place of destruction, v. 11).

Proverbs 21:21–22

21 He who follows righteousness, and
mercy
Finds life, righteousness, and honor.
22 A wise *man* scales the city of the
mighty,
And brings down the trusted
stronghold.

Acts 23:16–35

16So when Paul's sister's son heard of their
ambush, he went and entered the barracks and
told Paul. 17Then Paul called one of the centurions to *him* and said, "Take this young man to
the commander, for he has something to tell
him." 18So he took him and brought *him* to the
commander and said, "Paul the prisoner called
me to *him* and asked *me* to bring this young
man to you. He has something to say to you."
19Then the commander took him by the
hand, went aside, and asked privately, "What
is it that you have to tell me?"
20And he said, "The Jews have agreed to ask
that you bring Paul down to the council tomorrow,
as though they were going to inquire more
fully about him. 21But do not yield to them, for
more than forty of them lie in wait for him,
men who have bound themselves by an oath
that they will neither eat nor drink till they
have killed him; and now they are ready, waiting for the promise from you."
22So the commander let the young man
depart, and commanded *him,* "Tell no one
that you have revealed these things to me."
23And he called for two centurions, saying,
"Prepare two hundred soldiers, seventy horsemen, and two hundred spearmen to go to
Caesarea at the third hour of the night; 24and
provide mounts to set Paul on, and bring *him*
safely to Felix the governor." 25He wrote a letter in the following manner:

26 Claudius Lysias,

To the most excellent governor Felix:

Greetings.

27 This man was seized by the Jews and
was about to be killed by them.
Coming with the troops I rescued him,
having learned that he was a Roman.
28And when I wanted to know the
reason they accused him, I brought
him before their council. 29I found out
that he was accused concerning
questions of their law, but had nothing
charged against him deserving of death
or chains. 30And when it was told me
that the Jews lay in wait for the man, I
sent him immediately to you, and also
commanded his accusers to state before
you the charges against him.

Farewell.

31Then the soldiers, as they were commanded, took Paul and brought *him* by night
to Antipatris. 32The next day they left the
horsemen to go on with him, and returned to
the barracks. 33When they came to Caesarea
and had delivered the letter to the governor,
they also presented Paul to him. 34And when

23:16 Paul's sister's son. The only clear reference in Scripture to Paul's family. Why he was in Jerusalem, away from the family home in Tarsus, is not known. Nor is it evident why he would want to warn his uncle, since Paul's family possibly disinherited him when he became a Christian (Phil. 3:8). **entered the barracks and told Paul.** Since Paul was not under arrest, but merely in protective custody, he was able to receive visitors.

23:27 having learned that he was a Roman. Actually, Lysias did not find this out until after he arrested Paul (22:25,26). Lysias sought to portray himself in the best possible light before the governor. For that reason, he also neglected to mention his order to have Paul scourged (22:24) and his mistaken assumption that he was the notorious Egyptian assassin (21:38).

the governor had read *it,* he asked what province he was from. And when he understood that *he was* from Cilicia, [35]he said, "I will hear you when your accusers also have come." And he commanded him to be kept in Herod's Praetorium.

DAY 23: How can Luke's authorship of Acts be defended when his name is not mentioned in the book?

Lack of the author's name is not an unusual challenge in establishing the authorship of a Bible book. Many books of the Bible come to us without obvious human authorship. In most cases, however, internal and external clues lead us to reasonable confidence in identifying the author. One benefit created by initial anonymity involves recognizing that the Bible books originated by the inspiration of the Holy Spirit. It may take some effort to discover whom God used in writing one of those books, but the original Author is not in question.

The Gospel of Luke and Acts of the Apostles share numerous marks of common human authorship. They are addressed to the same person—Theophilus (Luke 1:3; Acts 1:1). They are parallel in style. The second book claims to be an extension of the first.

Luke was in a unique position to record Acts of the Apostles. He was Paul's close friend, traveling companion, and personal physician (Col. 4:14). His work indicates that he was a careful researcher (Luke 1:1–4) and an accurate historian, displaying an intimate knowledge of Roman laws and customs. His records of the geography of Palestine, Asia Minor, and Italy offer flawless details.

In writing Acts, Luke drew on written sources (15:23–29; 23:26–30). He, also, no doubt, interviewed key figures, such as Peter, John, and others in the Jerusalem church. Paul's 2-year imprisonment at Caesarea (24:27) gave Luke ample opportunity to interview Philip and his daughters (important sources of information on the early days of the church). Finally, Luke's frequent use of the first person plural pronouns "we" and "us" (16:10–17; 20:5–21:18; 27:1–28:16) reveals that he was an eyewitness to many of the events recorded in Acts.

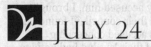

JULY 24

Ezra 9:1–10:44

9 When these things were done, the leaders came to me, saying, "The people of Israel and the priests and the Levites have not separated themselves from the peoples of the lands, with respect to the abominations of the Canaanites, the Hittites, the Perizzites, the Jebusites, the Ammonites, the Moabites, the Egyptians, and the Amorites. [2]For they have taken some of their daughters *as wives* for themselves and their sons, so that the holy seed is mixed with the peoples of *those* lands. Indeed, the hand of the leaders and rulers has been foremost in this trespass." [3]So when I heard this thing, I tore my garment and my robe, and plucked out some of the hair of my head and beard, and sat down astonished. [4]Then everyone who trembled at the words of the God of Israel assembled to me, because of the transgression of those who had been carried away captive, and I sat astonished until the evening sacrifice.

[5]At the evening sacrifice I arose from my fasting; and having torn my garment and my robe, I fell on my knees and spread out my hands to the LORD my God. [6]And I said: "O my God, I am

9:1 When these things were done. This refers to the implementation of the different trusts and duties committed to him. **priests...Levites.** As was the case before the Assyrian and Babylonian deportations, the spiritual leadership defaulted along with the people (Is. 24:2; Jer. 5:30,31; 6:13–15; Hos. 3:9; Mal. 2:1–9; 2 Tim. 4:2–4). **abominations.** The reason for this exclusiveness was to keep the people pure. In the first settlement, Israel was warned not to make covenants with the nations, which would result in intermarriages and inevitably the worship of foreign gods (Ex. 34:10–17; Deut. 7:1–5). To a great extent, the continual violation of this precipitated the 70-year exile from which they had just returned. Ezra found out it had happened again and called for immediate repentance. Nehemiah (Neh. 13:23–27) and Malachi (Mal. 2:14–16) later encountered the same sin. It is unthinkable that the Jews would so quickly go down the same disastrous path of idolatry. Neither wrath from God in the exile to Babylon nor grace from God in the return was enough to keep them from defecting again.

too ashamed and humiliated to lift up my face
to You, my God; for our iniquities have risen
higher than *our* heads, and our guilt has grown
up to the heavens. 7Since the days of our fathers
to this day we *have been* very guilty, and for our
iniquities we, our kings, *and* our priests have
been delivered into the hand of the kings of the
lands, to the sword, to captivity, to plunder, and
to humiliation, as *it is* this day. 8And now for a
little while grace has been *shown* from the LORD
our God, to leave us a remnant to escape, and
to give us a peg in His holy place, that our God
may enlighten our eyes and give us a measure
of revival in our bondage. 9For we *were* slaves.
Yet our God did not forsake us in our bondage;
but He extended mercy to us in the sight of the
kings of Persia, to revive us, to repair the house
of our God, to rebuild its ruins, and to give us a
wall in Judah and Jerusalem. 10And now, O our
God, what shall we say after this? For we have
forsaken Your commandments, 11which You
commanded by Your servants the prophets,
saying, 'The land which you are entering to possess is an unclean land, with the uncleanness of
the peoples of the lands, with their abominations which have filled it from one end to another with their impurity. 12Now therefore, do not
give your daughters as wives for their sons, nor
take their daughters to your sons; and never
seek their peace or prosperity, that you may be
strong and eat the good of the land, and leave *it*
as an inheritance to your children forever.' 13And
after all that has come upon us for our evil deeds
and for our great guilt, since You our God have
punished us less than our iniquities *deserve,* and
have given us *such* deliverance as this, 14should
we again break Your commandments, and join
in marriage with the people *committing* these
abominations? Would You not be angry with us
until You had consumed *us,* so that *there would
be* no remnant or survivor? 15O LORD God of Israel, You *are* righteous, for we are left as a remnant, as *it is* this day. Here we *are* before You, in
our guilt, though no one can stand before You
because of this!"

9:5–15 Ezra's priestly prayer of intercession and confession is like Daniel's (Dan. 9:1–20) and Nehemiah's (Neh. 1:4–11), in that he used plural pronouns that identified himself with the people's sin, even though he did not participate in it. The use of "we," "our," and "us" demonstrates Ezra's understanding that the sin of the few is sufficient to contaminate the many.

10 Now while Ezra was praying, and while
he was confessing, weeping, and bowing
down before the house of God, a very large
assembly of men, women, and children gathered to him from Israel; for the people wept
very bitterly. 2And Shechaniah the son of Jehiel,

10:1 praying...confessing, weeping, and bowing down. Ezra's contrite spirit before the people was evident and they joined him. These extreme expressions of contrition demonstrated the seriousness of the sin and the genuineness of their repentance.

one of the sons of Elam, spoke up and said to
Ezra, "We have trespassed against our God,
and have taken pagan wives from the peoples
of the land; yet now there is hope in Israel in
spite of this. 3Now therefore, let us make a
covenant with our God to put away all these
wives and those who have been born to them,
according to the advice of my master and of
those who tremble at the commandment of our
God; and let it be done according to the law.
4Arise, for *this* matter *is* your *responsibility.* We
also *are* with you. Be of good courage, and do *it.*"
5Then Ezra arose, and made the leaders of
the priests, the Levites, and all Israel swear an
oath that they would do according to this word.
So they swore an oath. 6Then Ezra rose up
from before the house of God, and went into
the chamber of Jehohanan the son of Eliashib;
and *when* he came there, he ate no bread and
drank no water, for he mourned because of the
guilt of those from the captivity.
7And they issued a proclamation throughout
Judah and Jerusalem to all the descendants of
the captivity, that they must gather at Jerusalem, 8and that whoever would not come within
three days, according to the instructions of the
leaders and elders, all his property would be
confiscated, and he himself would be separated
from the assembly of those from the captivity.
9So all the men of Judah and Benjamin gathered at Jerusalem within three days. It *was* the
ninth month, on the twentieth of the month; and
all the people sat in the open square of the house
of God, trembling because of *this* matter and
because of heavy rain. 10Then Ezra the priest
stood up and said to them, "You have transgressed and have taken pagan wives, adding to
the guilt of Israel. 11Now therefore, make confession to the LORD God of your fathers, and do His
will; separate yourselves from the peoples of the
land, and from the pagan wives."

12Then all the assembly answered and said
with a loud voice, "Yes! As you have said, so
we must do. 13But *there are* many people; *it is*
the season for heavy rain, and we are not able
to stand outside. Nor *is this* the work of one or
two days, for *there are* many of us who have
transgressed in this matter. 14Please, let the
leaders of our entire assembly stand; and let
all those in our cities who have taken pagan
wives come at appointed times, together with
the elders and judges of their cities, until the
fierce wrath of our God is turned away from us
in this matter." 15Only Jonathan the son of
Asahel and Jahaziah the son of Tikvah
opposed this, and Meshullam and Shabbethai
the Levite gave them support.
16Then the descendants of the captivity did
so. And Ezra the priest, *with* certain heads of
the fathers' *households,* were set apart by the
fathers' households, each of them by name;
and they sat down on the first day of the tenth
month to examine the matter. 17By the first day
of the first month they finished *questioning* all
the men who had taken pagan wives.
18And among the sons of the priests who
had taken pagan wives *the following* were
found of the sons of Jeshua the son of Jozadak,
and his brothers: Maaseiah, Eliezer, Jarib, and
Gedaliah. 19And they gave their promise that
they would put away their wives; and *being*
guilty, *they presented* a ram of the flock as their
trespass offering.
20Also of the sons of Immer: Hanani and
Zebadiah; 21of the sons of Harim: Maaseiah,
Elijah, Shemaiah, Jehiel, and Uzziah; 22of the
sons of Pashhur: Elioenai, Maaseiah, Ishmael,
Nethanel, Jozabad, and Elasah.
23Also of the Levites: Jozabad, Shimei,
Kelaiah (the same *is* Kelita), Pethahiah, Judah, and Eliezer.
24Also of the singers: Eliashib; and of the
gatekeepers: Shallum, Telem, and Uri.
25And others of Israel: of the sons of Parosh:
Ramiah, Jeziah, Malchiah, Mijamin, Eleazar,
Malchijah, and Benaiah; 26of the sons of Elam:
Mattaniah, Zechariah, Jehiel, Abdi, Jeremoth,
and Eliah; 27of the sons of Zattu: Elioenai, Eli-
ashib, Mattaniah, Jeremoth, Zabad, and Aziza;
28of the sons of Bebai: Jehohanan, Hananiah,
Zabbai, *and* Athlai; 29of the sons of Bani:
Meshullam, Malluch, Adaiah, Jashub, Sheal,
and Ramoth; 30of the sons of Pahath-Moab:
Adna, Chelal, Benaiah, Maaseiah, Mattaniah,
Bezalel, Binnui, and Manasseh; 31*of* the sons of
Harim: Eliezer, Ishijah, Malchijah, Shemaiah,
Shimeon, 32Benjamin, Malluch, *and* Shemariah;
33of the sons of Hashum: Mattenai, Mattattah,
Zabad, Eliphelet, Jeremai, Manasseh, *and*
Shimei; 34of the sons of Bani: Maadai, Amram,
Uel, 35Benaiah, Bedeiah, Cheluh, 36Vaniah,
Meremoth, Eliashib, 37Mattaniah, Mattenai,
Jaasai, 38Bani, Binnui, Shimei, 39Shelemiah, Na-
than, Adaiah, 40Machnadebai, Shashai, Sharai,
41Azarel, Shelemiah, Shemariah, 42Shallum,
Amariah, *and* Joseph; 43of the sons of Nebo:
Jeiel, Mattithiah, Zabad, Zebina, Jaddai, Joel,
and Benaiah.
44All these had taken pagan wives, and *some*
of them had wives *by whom* they had children.

Psalm 88:6–10

6 You have laid me in the lowest pit,
In darkness, in the depths.
7 Your wrath lies heavy upon me,
And You have afflicted *me* with all
Your waves. Selah

88:7 all Your waves. Like the waves rolling onto the seashore, so God has directed trouble after trouble on the psalmist (v. 17).

8 You have put away my acquaintances
far from me;
You have made me an abomination
to them;
I am shut up, and I cannot get out;
9 My eye wastes away because of
affliction.
LORD, I have called daily upon You;
I have stretched out my hands
to You.
10 Will You work wonders for the dead?
Shall the dead arise *and* praise You?
Selah

Proverbs 21:23–24

23 Whoever guards his mouth
and tongue
Keeps his soul from troubles.

24 A proud *and* haughty *man*—
"Scoffer" *is* his name;
He acts with arrogant pride.

Acts 24:1–27

24 Now after five days Ananias the high
priest came down with the elders and a
certain orator *named* Tertullus. These gave
evidence to the governor against Paul.
2And when he was called upon, Tertullus

24:3 Felix. Governor of Judea from A.D. 52 to 59. Felix was a former slave whose brother (a favorite of Emperor Claudius) had obtained for him the position as governor. He was not highly regarded by the influential Romans of his day and accomplished little during his term as governor. He defeated the Egyptian and his followers (21:38), but his brutality angered the Jews and led to his ouster as governor by Emperor Nero two years after Paul's hearing (v. 27).

began his accusation, saying: "Seeing that
through you we enjoy great peace, and prosperity is being brought to this nation by your
foresight, 3we accept *it* always and in all
places, most noble Felix, with all thankfulness.
4Nevertheless, not to be tedious to you any
further, I beg you to hear, by your courtesy, a
few words from us. 5For we have found this
man a plague, a creator of dissension among
all the Jews throughout the world, and a ring-
leader of the sect of the Nazarenes. 6He even
tried to profane the temple, and we seized
him, and wanted to judge him according to
our law. 7But the commander Lysias came by
and with great violence took *him* out of our
hands, 8commanding his accusers to come to
you. By examining him yourself you may
ascertain all these things of which we accuse
him." 9And the Jews also assented, maintaining that these things were so.
10Then Paul, after the governor had nodded
to him to speak, answered: "Inasmuch as I
know that you have been for many years a
judge of this nation, I do the more cheerfully
answer for myself, 11because you may ascertain that it is no more than twelve days since I
went up to Jerusalem to worship. 12And they
neither found me in the temple disputing with
anyone nor inciting the crowd, either in the
synagogues or in the city. 13Nor can they prove
the things of which they now accuse me. 14But
this I confess to you, that according to the
Way which they call a sect, so I worship the
God of my fathers, believing all things which
are written in the Law and in the Prophets. 15I
have hope in God, which they themselves also
accept, that there will be a resurrection of *the*
dead, both of *the* just and *the* unjust. 16This *being* so, I myself always strive to have a conscience without offense toward God and men.
17"Now after many years I came to bring
alms and offerings to my nation, 18in the midst
of which some Jews from Asia found me purified in the temple, neither with a mob nor with
tumult. 19They ought to have been here before
you to object if they had anything against me.
20Or else let those who are *here* themselves say
if they found any wrongdoing in me while I
stood before the council, 21unless *it is* for this
one statement which I cried out, standing
among them, 'Concerning the resurrection of
the dead I am being judged by you this day.' "
22But when Felix heard these things, having
more accurate knowledge of *the* Way, he
adjourned the proceedings and said, "When
Lysias the commander comes down, I will
make a decision on your case." 23So he commanded the centurion to keep Paul and to let
him have liberty, and told him not to forbid
any of his friends to provide for or visit him.
24And after some days, when Felix came
with his wife Drusilla, who was Jewish, he
sent for Paul and heard him concerning the
faith in Christ. 25Now as he reasoned about

24:24 Drusilla. The youngest daughter of Agrippa I (12:1) and Felix's third wife. Felix, struck by her beauty, had lured her away from her husband. At the time of Paul's hearing, she was not yet 20 years old.

24:25 righteousness, self-control, and the judgment. God demands "righteousness" of all men, because of His holy nature (Matt. 5:48; 1 Pet. 1:15,16). For men and women to conform to that absolute standard requires "self-control." The result of failing to exhibit self-control and to conform oneself to God's righteous standard is (apart from salvation) "judgment." **Felix was afraid.** Living with a woman he had lured away from her husband, Felix obviously lacked "righteousness" and "self-control." The realization that he faced "judgment" alarmed him, and he hastily dismissed Paul. **when I have a convenient time.** The moment of conviction passed, and Felix foolishly passed up his opportunity to repent (2 Cor. 6:2).

righteousness, self-control, and the judgment
to come, Felix was afraid and answered, "Go
away for now; when I have a convenient time I
will call for you." 26Meanwhile he also hoped
that money would be given him by Paul, that
he might release him. Therefore he sent for
him more often and conversed with him.
27But after two years Porcius Festus succeeded Felix; and Felix, wanting to do the
Jews a favor, left Paul bound.

DAY 24: How does Ezra's handling of the intermarriage situation fit into the overall pattern of biblical teaching?

Ezra 9 and 10 record a critical time in the reestablishment of the Jewish people in their homeland. In the years before Ezra arrived from Persia, many of the returned Jewish men intermarried with pagan women from the area. This practice reflects no circumstances like we find in the marriages of Rahab or Ruth, Gentiles who became believers in God. The pagan background of these women was not taken into account by their husbands. Ezra received this news as part of the report when he reached Jerusalem.

For Ezra, this was almost the worst possible news. Intermarriage with pagans had historically been a key in the repeated downfalls of the nation. These marriages were an act of disobedience. Ezra was overwhelmed with shame and distress over the situation (Ezra 9:3,4). His grief was open and convicting.

Eventually, the people themselves confessed their error and decided that those who had married pagan women would have to "put away" (divorce) these wives.

God had not changed His mind about divorce. Malachi, who lived in this time period, declared that God hates divorce (Mal. 2:16).

Several important notes can be made about this passage in Ezra. It does not establish a norm about divorce. It is also easy to overlook the fact that while the solution of divorce was a group decision, each of these marriages was examined individually. Presumably, cases in which the women had become believers were treated differently than cases in which the women involved saw questions of faith as violation of the marriage agreement.

In the humility of the guilty and the care in confronting these issues, a great deal of God's mercy comes through. A strict interpretation of the law could have led to the stoning death of all involved. The eagerness to set things right opened the doorway for a solution, even though in some of the cases it involved the grief and sadness of divorce.

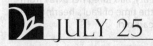

JULY 25

Nehemiah 1:1–2:20

1 The words of Nehemiah the son of
Hachaliah.
It came to pass in the month of Chislev, *in*
the twentieth year, as I was in Shushan the citadel, 2that Hanani one of my brethren came
with men from Judah; and I asked them concerning the Jews who had escaped, who had
survived the captivity, and concerning Jerusalem. 3And they said to me, "The survivors who
are left from the captivity in the province *are*
there in great distress and reproach. The wall
of Jerusalem *is* also broken down, and its
gates are burned with fire."
4So it was, when I heard these words, that I
sat down and wept, and mourned *for many*
days; I was fasting and praying before the God
of heaven.
5And I said: "I pray, LORD God of heaven, O
great and awesome God, *You* who keep *Your*
covenant and mercy with those who love You
and observe Your commandments, 6please let
Your ear be attentive and Your eyes open, that
You may hear the prayer of Your servant
which I pray before You now, day and night,
for the children of Israel Your servants, and
confess the sins of the children of Israel which
we have sinned against You. Both my father's
house and I have sinned. 7We have acted very
corruptly against You, and have not kept the
commandments, the statutes, nor the ordinances which You commanded Your servant
Moses. 8Remember, I pray, the word that You
commanded Your servant Moses, saying, '*If*
you are unfaithful, I will scatter you among the
nations; 9but *if* you return to Me, and keep My
commandments and do them, though some of
you were cast out to the farthest part of the
heavens, *yet* I will gather them from there, and
bring them to the place which I have chosen as
a dwelling for My name.' 10Now these *are* Your
servants and Your people, whom You have redeemed by Your great power, and by Your
strong hand. 11O Lord, I pray, please let Your
ear be attentive to the prayer of Your servant,

1:4 sat down and wept, and mourned *for many* days. Although Nehemiah was neither a prophet nor a priest, he had a deep sense of Jerusalem's significance to God and was greatly distressed that affairs there had not advanced the cause and glory of God.

and to the prayer of Your servants who desire to fear Your name; and let Your servant prosper this day, I pray, and grant him mercy in the sight of this man."

For I was the king's cupbearer.

1:11 the king's cupbearer. As an escort of the monarch at meals, the cupbearer had a unique advantage to petition the king. Not only did the king owe him his life since the cupbearer tested all the king's beverages for possible poison, thus putting his own life at risk, but he also became a close confidant. God sovereignly used this relationship between a Gentile and Jew to deliver His people, such as He did with Joseph, Daniel, Esther, and Mordecai.

2 And it came to pass in the month of Nisan, in the twentieth year of King Artaxerxes, *when* wine *was* before him, that I took the wine and gave it to the king. Now I had never been sad in his presence before. 2Therefore the king said to me, "Why *is* your face sad, since you *are* not sick? This *is* nothing but sorrow of heart."

2:2 dreadfully afraid. Nehemiah feared that either his countenance, his explanation, or his request would anger the king and thus lead to his death (Esth. 4:11 with 5:1–3).

So I became dreadfully afraid, 3and said to the king, "May the king live forever! Why should my face not be sad, when the city, the place of my fathers' tombs, *lies* waste, and its gates are burned with fire?"

4Then the king said to me, "What do you request?"

So I prayed to the God of heaven. 5And I said to the king, "If it pleases the king, and if your servant has found favor in your sight, I ask that you send me to Judah, to the city of my fathers' tombs, that I may rebuild it."

6Then the king said to me (the queen also sitting beside him), "How long will your journey be? And when will you return?" So it pleased the king to send me; and I set him a time.

7Furthermore I said to the king, "If it pleases the king, let letters be given to me for the governors *of the region* beyond the River, that they must permit me to pass through till I come to Judah, 8and a letter to Asaph the keeper of the king's forest, that he must give me timber to make beams for the gates of the citadel which *pertains* to the temple, for the city wall, and for the house that I will occupy." And the king granted *them* to me according to the good hand of my God upon me.

9Then I went to the governors *in the region* beyond the River, and gave them the king's letters. Now the king had sent captains of the army and horsemen with me. 10When Sanballat the Horonite and Tobiah the Ammonite official heard *of it,* they were deeply disturbed that a man had come to seek the well-being of the children of Israel.

2:10 Sanballat...Tobiah. These men were probably also behind the opposition described in Ezra 4:7–23 which stopped the work in Jerusalem. Sanballat served as governor of Samaria and Tobiah, of the region east of the Jordan. These district magistrates were leaders of Samaritan factions (see chap. 6) to the north and east. They had lost any recourse to prevent Judah from rebuilding since God's people were authorized to fortify their settlement against attack from enemies such as these two officials. To overtly attack or oppose the Jews would be to oppose the Persian king.

11So I came to Jerusalem and was there three days. 12Then I arose in the night, I and a few men with me; I told no one what my God had put in my heart to do at Jerusalem; nor was there any animal with me, except the one on which I rode. 13And I went out by night through the Valley Gate to the Serpent Well and the Refuse Gate, and viewed the walls of Jerusalem which were broken down and its gates which were burned with fire. 14Then I went on to the Fountain Gate and to the King's Pool, but *there was* no room for the animal under me to pass. 15So I went up in the night by the valley, and viewed the wall; then I turned back and entered by the Valley Gate, and so returned. 16And the officials did not know where I had gone or what I had done; I had not yet told the Jews, the priests, the nobles, the officials, or the others who did the work.

17Then I said to them, "You see the distress that we *are* in, how Jerusalem *lies* waste, and its gates are burned with fire. Come and let us build the wall of Jerusalem, that we may no longer be a reproach." 18And I told them of the hand of my God which had been good upon me, and also of the king's words that he had spoken to me.

So they said, "Let us rise up and build." Then they set their hands to *this* good *work*.

19 But when Sanballat the Horonite, Tobiah the Ammonite official, and Geshem the Arab heard *of it,* they laughed at us and despised us, and said, "What *is* this thing that you are doing? Will you rebel against the king?"

20 So I answered them, and said to them, "The God of heaven Himself will prosper us; therefore we His servants will arise and build, but you have no heritage or right or memorial in Jerusalem."

Psalm 88:11–18

11 Shall Your lovingkindness be declared
in the grave?
Or Your faithfulness in the place of
destruction?
12 Shall Your wonders be known in the
dark?
And Your righteousness in the land
of forgetfulness?

13 But to You I have cried out, O LORD,
And in the morning my prayer comes
before You.
14 LORD, why do You cast off my soul?
Why do You hide Your face
from me?
15 I *have been* afflicted and ready to die
from *my* youth;
I suffer Your terrors;
I am distraught.
16 Your fierce wrath has gone over me;
Your terrors have cut me off.
17 They came around me all day long
like water;
They engulfed me altogether.
18 Loved one and friend You have put
far from me,
And my acquaintances into
darkness.

Proverbs 21:25–26

25 The desire of the lazy *man* kills him,
For his hands refuse to labor.
26 He covets greedily all day long,
But the righteous gives and does
not spare.

Acts 25:1–27

25 Now when Festus had come to the province, after three days he went up from Caesarea to Jerusalem. 2 Then the high priest and the chief men of the Jews informed him against Paul; and they petitioned him, 3 asking a favor against him, that he would summon him to Jerusalem—while *they* lay in ambush along the road to kill him. 4 But Festus answered that Paul should be kept at Caesarea, and that he himself was going *there* shortly. 5 "Therefore," he said, "let those who have authority among you go down with *me* and accuse this man, to see if there is any fault in him."

6 And when he had remained among them more than ten days, he went down to Caesarea. And the next day, sitting on the judgment seat, he commanded Paul to be brought. 7 When he had come, the Jews who had come down from Jerusalem stood about and laid many serious complaints against Paul, which they could not prove, 8 while he answered for himself, "Neither against the law of the Jews, nor against the temple, nor against Caesar have I offended in anything at all."

9 But Festus, wanting to do the Jews a favor, answered Paul and said, "Are you willing to go up to Jerusalem and there be judged before me concerning these things?"

10 So Paul said, "I stand at Caesar's judgment seat, where I ought to be judged. To the Jews I have done no wrong, as you very well know. 11 For if I am an offender, or have committed anything deserving of death, I do not object to dying; but if there is nothing in these things of which these men accuse me, no one can deliver me to them. I appeal to Caesar."

12 Then Festus, when he had conferred with the council, answered, "You have appealed to Caesar? To Caesar you shall go!"

25:13 King Agrippa. Herod Agrippa II, son of the Herod who killed James and imprisoned Peter (12:1). He was the last of the Herods, who play a prominent role in New Testament history. His great-uncle, Herod Antipas, was the Herod of the Gospels (Mark 6:14–29; Luke 3:1; 13:31–33; 23:7–12), while his great-grandfather, Herod the Great, ruled at the time Jesus was born (Matt. 2:1–19; Luke 1:5). Though not the ruler of Judea, Agrippa was well versed in Jewish affairs (26:3). **Bernice.** Not Agrippa's wife, but his consort and sister. (Their sister, Drusilla, was married to the former governor, Felix). Their incestuous relationship was the talk of Rome, where Agrippa grew up. Bernice for a while became the mistress of Emperor Vespasian, then of his son, Titus, but always returned to her brother.

13And after some days King Agrippa and
Bernice came to Caesarea to greet Festus.
14When they had been there many days,
Festus laid Paul's case before the king, saying: "There is a certain man left a prisoner by
Felix, 15about whom the chief priests and the
elders of the Jews informed *me,* when I was
in Jerusalem, asking for a judgment against
him. 16To them I answered, 'It is not the custom of the Romans to deliver any man to
destruction before the accused meets the
accusers face to face, and has opportunity to
answer for himself concerning the charge
against him.' 17Therefore when they had
come together, without any delay, the next
day I sat on the judgment seat and commanded the man to be brought in. 18When the
accusers stood up, they brought no accusation against him of such things as I supposed,
19but had some questions against him about
their own religion and about a certain Jesus,
who had died, whom Paul affirmed to be
alive. 20And because I was uncertain of such
questions, I asked whether he was willing to
go to Jerusalem and there be judged concerning these matters. 21But when Paul appealed to be reserved for the decision of
Augustus, I commanded him to be kept till I
could send him to Caesar."

22Then Agrippa said to Festus, "I also would
like to hear the man myself."

"Tomorrow," he said, "you shall hear him."

23So the next day, when Agrippa and
Bernice had come with great pomp, and had
entered the auditorium with the commanders
and the prominent men of the city, at Festus'
command Paul was brought in. 24And Festus
said: "King Agrippa and all the men who are
here present with us, you see this man about
whom the whole assembly of the Jews petitioned me, both at Jerusalem and here, crying
out that he was not fit to live any longer. 25But
when I found that he had committed nothing
deserving of death, and that he himself had
appealed to Augustus, I decided to send him.
26I have nothing certain to write to my lord
concerning him. Therefore I have brought
him out before you, and especially before you,
King Agrippa, so that after the examination
has taken place I may have something to
write. 27For it seems to me unreasonable to
send a prisoner and not to specify the charges
against him."

25:26 I have nothing certain. Since Festus did not understand the nature of the charges against Paul, he did not know what to write in his official report to Nero. For a provincial governor to send a prisoner to the emperor with no clear charges against him was foolish, if not dangerous. **especially before you, King Agrippa.** Festus hoped Herod's expertise in Jewish affairs (26:3) would enable him to make sense of the charges against Paul.

DAY 25: What leadership qualities does Nehemiah illustrate in his life?

Like many biblical leaders, Nehemiah demonstrated an understanding of God's call over his life. Whether as cupbearer to a king or as the rebuilder of Jerusalem, Nehemiah pursued his goals with commitment, careful planning, strategic delegation, creative problem solving, focus on the task at hand, and a continual reliance on God, particularly regarding areas beyond his control. Each of the leadership qualities above can be illustrated from Nehemiah's successful completion of the effort to rebuild the walls of Jerusalem.

First, Nehemiah demonstrated his commitment by his interest and his deep concern over the condition of his fellow Jews in Judah. Next, Nehemiah prayed and planned. He claimed God's promise to bring His people back to the Promised Land, but he didn't assume that he would be part of God's action. He declared himself available (1:11; 2:5).

Even when he arrived in Jerusalem, Nehemiah personally inspected the need before he revealed his plans. Then he enlisted the help of the local leadership. He challenged them to take responsibility for the common good. He placed before them a very specific goal—to rebuild the wall. Workers were assigned to work on the wall where it ran closest to their own homes. That way they could see the benefit in having the protective barrier near where they lived.

As the work sped forward, Nehemiah did not allow himself to be distracted by attacks of various kings or tricks from enemies. He took threats seriously enough to arm the people but not so seriously that the work came to a halt. At every turn, we find Nehemiah conferring in prayer with God, placing every decision before the ultimate Decider. Nehemiah succeeded because he never lost sight of the true reasons for the work and the source of power with which to do the work.

JULY 26

Nehemiah 3:1–5:19

3 Then Eliashib the high priest rose up with his brethren the priests and built the Sheep Gate; they consecrated it and hung its doors. They built as far as the Tower of the Hundred, *and* consecrated it, then as far as the Tower of Hananel. [2]Next to *Eliashib* the men of Jericho built. And next to them Zaccur the son of Imri built.

[3]Also the sons of Hassenaah built the Fish Gate; they laid its beams and hung its doors with its bolts and bars. [4]And next to them Meremoth the son of Urijah, the son of Koz, made repairs. Next to them Meshullam the son of Berechiah, the son of Meshezabel, made repairs. Next to them Zadok the son of Baana made repairs. [5]Next to them the Tekoites made repairs; but their nobles did not put their shoulders to the work of their Lord.

[6]Moreover Jehoiada the son of Paseah and Meshullam the son of Besodeiah repaired the Old Gate; they laid its beams and hung its doors, with its bolts and bars. [7]And next to them Melatiah the Gibeonite, Jadon the Meronothite, the men of Gibeon and Mizpah, repaired the residence of the governor *of the region* beyond the River. [8]Next to him Uzziel the son of Harhaiah, one of the goldsmiths, made repairs. Also next to him Hananiah, one of the perfumers, made repairs; and they fortified Jerusalem as far as the Broad Wall. [9]And next to them Rephaiah the son of Hur, leader of half the district of Jerusalem, made repairs. [10]Next to them Jedaiah the son of Harumaph made repairs in front of his house. And next to him Hattush the son of Hashabniah made repairs.

[11]Malchijah the son of Harim and Hashub the son of Pahath-Moab repaired another section, as well as the Tower of the Ovens. [12]And next to him was Shallum the son of Hallohesh, leader of half the district of Jerusalem; he and his daughters made repairs.

[13]Hanun and the inhabitants of Zanoah repaired the Valley Gate. They built it, hung its doors with its bolts and bars, and *repaired* a thousand cubits of the wall as far as the Refuse Gate.

[14]Malchijah the son of Rechab, leader of the district of Beth Haccerem, repaired the Refuse Gate; he built it and hung its doors with its bolts and bars.

[15]Shallun the son of Col-Hozeh, leader of the district of Mizpah, repaired the Fountain Gate; he built it, covered it, hung its doors with its bolts and bars, and repaired the wall of the Pool of Shelah by the King's Garden, as far as the stairs that go down from the City of David. [16]After him Nehemiah the son of Azbuk, leader of half the district of Beth Zur, made repairs as far as *the place* in front of the tombs of David, to the man-made pool, and as far as the House of the Mighty.

[17]After him the Levites, *under* Rehum the son of Bani, made repairs. Next to him Hashabiah, leader of half the district of Keilah, made repairs for his district. [18]After him their brethren, *under* Bavai the son of Henadad, leader of the *other* half of the district of Keilah, made repairs. [19]And next to him Ezer the son of Jeshua, the leader of Mizpah, repaired another section in front of the Ascent to the Armory at the buttress. [20]After him Baruch the son of Zabbai carefully repaired the other section, from the buttress to the door of the house of Eliashib the high priest. [21]After him Meremoth the son of Urijah, the son of Koz, repaired another section, from the door of the house of Eliashib to the end of the house of Eliashib.

[22]And after him the priests, the men of the plain, made repairs. [23]After him Benjamin and Hasshub made repairs opposite their house. After them Azariah the son of Maaseiah, the son of Ananiah, made repairs by his house. [24]After him Binnui the son of Henadad repaired another section, from the house of Azariah to the buttress, even as far as the corner. [25]Palal the son of Uzai *made repairs* opposite the buttress, and on the tower which projects from the king's upper house that *was* by the court of the prison. After him Pedaiah the son of Parosh *made repairs.*

[26]Moreover the Nethinim who dwelt in Ophel *made repairs* as far as *the place* in front of the Water Gate toward the east, and on the projecting tower. [27]After them the Tekoites repaired another section, next to the great projecting tower, and as far as the wall of Ophel.

[28]Beyond the Horse Gate the priests made repairs, each in front of his *own* house. [29]After them Zadok the son of Immer made repairs in front of his *own* house. After him Shemaiah the son of Shechaniah, the keeper of the East Gate, made repairs. [30]After him Hananiah the son of Shelemiah, and Hanun, the sixth son of Zalaph, repaired another section. After him Meshullam the son of Berechiah made repairs in front of his dwelling. [31]After him Malchijah, one of the goldsmiths, made repairs as far as the house of the Nethinim and of the merchants, in front of the Miphkad Gate, and as far as the upper room at the corner. [32]And between the upper room at the corner, as far

as the Sheep Gate, the goldsmiths and the
merchants made repairs.

4 But it so happened, when Sanballat heard
that we were rebuilding the wall, that he
was furious and very indignant, and mocked
the Jews. 2And he spoke before his brethren
and the army of Samaria, and said, "What are
these feeble Jews doing? Will they fortify
themselves? Will they offer sacrifices? Will
they complete it in a day? Will they revive the
stones from the heaps of rubbish—*stones* that
are burned?"

3Now Tobiah the Ammonite *was* beside him,
and he said, "Whatever they build, if even a
fox goes up *on it,* he will break down their
stone wall."

4Hear, O our God, for we are despised; turn
their reproach on their own heads, and give
them as plunder to a land of captivity! 5Do not
cover their iniquity, and do not let their sin be
blotted out from before You; for they have provoked *You* to anger before the builders.

6So we built the wall, and the entire wall was
joined together up to half its *height,* for the
people had a mind to work.

7Now it happened, when Sanballat, Tobiah,
the Arabs, the Ammonites, and the Ashdodites
heard that the walls of Jerusalem were being
restored and the gaps were beginning to be
closed, that they became very angry, 8and all
of them conspired together to come *and*
attack Jerusalem and create confusion. 9Never-
theless we made our prayer to our God, and
because of them we set a watch against them
day and night.

10Then Judah said, "The strength of the
laborers is failing, and *there is* so much rubbish that we are not able to build the wall."

11And our adversaries said, "They will neither know nor see anything, till we come into
their midst and kill them and cause the work
to cease."

12So it was, when the Jews who dwelt near
them came, that they told us ten times, "From
whatever place you turn, *they will be* upon us."
13Therefore I positioned *men* behind the
lower parts of the wall, at the openings; and I
set the people according to their families, with
their swords, their spears, and their bows.
14And I looked, and arose and said to the
nobles, to the leaders, and to the rest of the
people, "Do not be afraid of them. Remember
the Lord, great and awesome, and fight for
your brethren, your sons, your daughters,
your wives, and your houses."

15And it happened, when our enemies heard
that it was known to us, and *that* God had
brought their plot to nothing, that all of us
returned to the wall, everyone to his work.
16So it was, from that time on, *that* half of my
servants worked at construction, while the
other half held the spears, the shields, the
bows, and *wore* armor; and the leaders *were*
behind all the house of Judah. 17Those who
built on the wall, and those who carried burdens, loaded themselves so that with one hand
they worked at construction, and with the
other held a weapon. 18Every one of the
builders had his sword girded at his side as he
built. And the one who sounded the trumpet
was beside me.

19Then I said to the nobles, the rulers, and
the rest of the people, "The work *is* great and
extensive, and we are separated far from one
another on the wall. 20Wherever you hear the
sound of the trumpet, rally to us there. Our
God will fight for us."

21So we labored in the work, and half of *the*
men held the spears from daybreak until the
stars appeared. 22At the same time I also said
to the people, "Let each man and his servant
stay at night in Jerusalem, that they may be
our guard by night and a working party by
day." 23So neither I, my brethren, my servants,
nor the men of the guard who followed me
took off our clothes, *except* that everyone took
them off for washing.

5 And there was a great outcry of the people
and their wives against their Jewish
brethren. 2For there were those who said,
"We, our sons, and our daughters *are* many;
therefore let us get grain, that we may eat and
live."

3There were also *some* who said, "We have
mortgaged our lands and vineyards and
houses, that we might buy grain because of
the famine."

4There were also those who said, "We have
borrowed money for the king's tax *on* our
lands and vineyards. 5Yet now our flesh *is* as
the flesh of our brethren, our children as their
children; and indeed we are forcing our sons
and our daughters to be slaves, and *some* of
our daughters have been brought into slavery.
It is not in our power *to redeem them,* for other
men have our lands and vineyards."

6And I became very angry when I heard
their outcry and these words. 7After serious
thought, I rebuked the nobles and rulers, and
said to them, "Each of you is exacting usury
from his brother." So I called a great assembly
against them. 8And I said to them, "According
to our ability we have redeemed our Jewish
brethren who were sold to the nations. Now
indeed, will you even sell your brethren? Or
should they be sold to us?"

Then they were silenced and found nothing
to say. 9Then I said, "What you are doing *is* not
good. Should you not walk in the fear of our
God because of the reproach of the nations,
our enemies? 10I also, *with* my brethren and my
servants, am lending them money and grain.
Please, let us stop this usury! 11Restore now to
them, even this day, their lands, their vineyards, their olive groves, and their houses, also
a hundredth of the money and the grain, the
new wine and the oil, that you have charged
them."
12So they said, "We will restore *it,* and will
require nothing from them; we will do as you
say."
Then I called the priests, and required an
oath from them that they would do according to this promise. 13Then I shook out the
fold of my garment and said, "So may God
shake out each man from his house, and from
his property, who does not perform this
promise. Even thus may he be shaken out
and emptied."
And all the assembly said, "Amen!" and
praised the LORD. Then the people did according to this promise.
14Moreover, from the time that I was
appointed to be their governor in the land of
Judah, from the twentieth year until the thirty-
second year of King Artaxerxes, twelve years,
neither I nor my brothers ate the governor's
provisions. 15But the former governors who
were before me laid burdens on the people,
and took from them bread and wine, besides
forty shekels of silver. Yes, even their servants
bore rule over the people, but I did not do so,
because of the fear of God. 16Indeed, I also
continued the work on this wall, and we did
not buy any land. All my servants *were* gathered there for the work.
17And at my table *were* one hundred and fifty
Jews and rulers, besides those who came to us
from the nations around us. 18Now *that* which
was prepared daily *was* one ox *and* six choice
sheep. Also fowl were prepared for me, and
once every ten days an abundance of all kinds
of wine. Yet in spite of this I did not demand
the governor's provisions, because the
bondage was heavy on this people.
19Remember me, my God, for good, *according to* all that I have done for this people.

Psalm 89:1–4

A Contemplation of Ethan the Ezrahite.

1 I will sing of the mercies of the
LORD forever;
With my mouth will I make known
Your faithfulness to all generations.
2 For I have said, "Mercy shall be built
up forever;
Your faithfulness You shall establish in the
very heavens."

3 "I have made a covenant with My chosen,
I have sworn to My servant David:
4 'Your seed I will establish forever,
And build up your throne to all
generations.' " Selah

89:3 covenant with My chosen. The Davidic Covenant, culminating in Messiah's reign, was established in 2 Samuel 7 (1 Kin. 8:23; 1 Chr. 17; 2 Chr. 21:7; Pss. 110;132). The covenant was in the form of a royal grant covenant as God, the Great King, chose David as His servant king. In this type of covenant, the person with whom the Lord established the covenant could violate the terms of the covenant and the Lord would still be obligated to maintain the covenant.

89:4 seed...forever...throne. The covenant with David was extended to his descendants. The throne promise guaranteed that the rightful heir to the throne would always be a descendant of David (vv. 29,36; see also 2 Sam. 7:13,16,18; Luke 1:31–33). The genealogies of Jesus qualify Him for the throne (Matt. 1:1–17; Luke 3:23–38).

Proverbs 21:27

27 The sacrifice of the wicked *is* an
abomination;
How much more *when* he brings it
with wicked intent!

Acts 26:1–32

26 Then Agrippa said to Paul, "You are
permitted to speak for yourself."
So Paul stretched out his hand and
answered for himself: 2"I think myself happy,
King Agrippa, because today I shall answer for
myself before you concerning all the things of
which I am accused by the Jews, 3especially
because you are expert in all customs and
questions which have to do with the Jews.
Therefore I beg you to hear me patiently.
4"My manner of life from my youth, which
was spent from the beginning among my own
nation at Jerusalem, all the Jews know. 5They
knew me from the first, if they were willing to testify, that according to the strictest sect of our religion I lived a Pharisee. 6And now I stand and am
judged for the hope of the promise made by God
to our fathers. 7To this *promise* our twelve tribes,

earnestly serving *God* night and day, hope to
attain. For this hope's sake, King Agrippa, I am
accused by the Jews. 8 Why should it be thought
incredible by you that God raises the dead?
9 "Indeed, I myself thought I must do many
things contrary to the name of Jesus of Nazareth. 10 This I also did in Jerusalem, and many of
the saints I shut up in prison, having received
authority from the chief priests; and when they
were put to death, I cast my vote against *them.*
11 And I punished them often in every synagogue and compelled *them* to blaspheme; and
being exceedingly enraged against them, I persecuted *them* even to foreign cities.
12 "While thus occupied, as I journeyed to
Damascus with authority and commission
from the chief priests, 13 at midday, O king,
along the road I saw a light from heaven,
brighter than the sun, shining around me and
those who journeyed with me. 14 And when we
all had fallen to the ground, I heard a voice
speaking to me and saying in the Hebrew language, 'Saul, Saul, why are you persecuting
Me? *It is* hard for you to kick against the
goads.' 15 So I said, 'Who are You, Lord?' And
He said, 'I am Jesus, whom you are persecuting. 16 But rise and stand on your feet; for I
have appeared to you for this purpose, to
make you a minister and a witness both of the
things which you have seen and of the things
which I will yet reveal to you. 17 I will deliver
you from the *Jewish* people, as well as *from* the
Gentiles, to whom I now send you, 18 to open
their eyes, *in order* to turn *them* from darkness
to light, and *from* the power of Satan to God,
that they may receive forgiveness of sins and
an inheritance among those who are sanctified by faith in Me.'
19 "Therefore, King Agrippa, I was not
disobedient to the heavenly vision, 20 but declared first to those in Damascus and in Jerusalem, and throughout all the region of Judea,
and *then* to the Gentiles, that they should
repent, turn to God, and do works befitting
repentance. 21 For these reasons the Jews
seized me in the temple and tried to kill *me.*
22 Therefore, having obtained help from God,
to this day I stand, witnessing both to small
and great, saying no other things than those
which the prophets and Moses said would
come— 23 that the Christ would suffer, that He
would be the first to rise from the dead, and
would proclaim light to the *Jewish* people and
to the Gentiles."
24 Now as he thus made his defense, Festus
said with a loud voice, "Paul, you are beside
yourself! Much learning is driving you mad!"
25 But he said, "I am not mad, most noble
Festus, but speak the words of truth and reason. 26 For the king, before whom I also speak
freely, knows these things; for I am convinced
that none of these things escapes his attention,
since this thing was not done in a corner.
27 King Agrippa, do you believe the prophets? I
know that you do believe."
28 Then Agrippa said to Paul, "You almost
persuade me to become a Christian."

26:24 you are beside yourself! Festus was astonished that a learned scholar like Paul could actually believe that the dead would live again—something no intelligent Roman would accept. Unable to contain himself, he interrupted the proceedings, shouting that Paul's tremendous learning had driven him insane (Mark 3:21; John 8:48,52; 10:20).

26:26 not done in a corner. The death of Jesus and the Christians' claim that He rose from the dead were common knowledge in Palestine.

26:27 do you believe the prophets? Paul's shrewd question put Herod in a dilemma. If he affirmed his belief in the prophets, he would also have to admit that what they taught about Jesus' death and resurrection was true—an admission that would make him appear foolish before his Roman friends. Yet to deny the prophets would outrage his Jewish subjects.

26:28 You almost persuade me. A better translation is "Do you think you can convince me to become a Christian in such a short time?" Recognizing his dilemma, Agrippa parried Paul's question with one of his own.

29 And Paul said, "I would to God that not
only you, but also all who hear me today,
might become both almost and altogether
such as I am, except for these chains."
30 When he had said these things, the king
stood up, as well as the governor and Bernice
and those who sat with them; 31 and when they
had gone aside, they talked among themselves, saying, "This man is doing nothing
deserving of death or chains."
32 Then Agrippa said to Festus, "This man
might have been set free if he had not
appealed to Caesar."

DAY 26: Why did Nehemiah denounce the nobles and rulers?

In Nehemiah 5:1–5, the people were fatigued with hard labor, drained by the relentless harassment of enemies, poor and lacking the necessities of life, lacking tax money and borrowing for it, and working on the wall in the city rather than getting food from the country. On top of this came complaints against the terrible exploitation and extortion by the rich Jews who would not help, but forced people to sell their homes and children, while having no ability to redeem them back. Under normal conditions, the law offered the hope of releasing these young people through the remission of debts which occurred every 7 years or in the 50th year of Jubilee (Lev. 25). The custom of redemption made it possible to "buy back" the enslaved individual at almost any time, but the desperate financial situation of those times made that appear impossible.

So Nehemiah "rebuked the nobles and rulers" (v. 7). They had become the enemy from within. "Exacting usury." Usury can refer to normal interest or it can signify excessive interest. According to Mosaic Law, the Jews were forbidden to take interest from their brothers on the loan of money, food, or anything else. If the person was destitute, they should consider it a gift. If they could pay it back later, it was to be without interest (Lev. 25:36,37; Deut. 23:19,20). Such generosity marked the godly (Ps. 15:5; Jer. 15:10; Prov. 28:8). Interest could be taken from foreigners (v. 20). Interest loans were known to exceed 50 percent at times in ancient nations. Such usury took advantage of people's desperation and was virtually impossible to repay, consuming their entire family assets and reducing the debtors to permanent slavery.

Nehemiah denounced with just severity the evil conduct of selling a brother by means of usury. He contrasted it with his own action of redeeming with his own money some of the Jewish exiles, who through debt had lost their freedom in Babylon (v. 8). Nehemiah set the example again by making loans, but not in exacting usury (v. 10). To remedy the evil that they had brought, those guilty of usury were to return the property they had confiscated from those who couldn't pay the loans back, as well as returning the interest they had charged (v. 11).

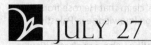

JULY 27

Nehemiah 6:1–7:73

6 Now it happened when Sanballat, Tobiah,
Geshem the Arab, and the rest of our enemies heard that I had rebuilt the wall, and *that* there were no breaks left in it (though at that time I had not hung the doors in the gates),
2that Sanballat and Geshem sent to me, saying, "Come, let us meet together among the villages in the plain of Ono." But they thought to do me harm.
3So I sent messengers to them, saying, "I *am* doing a great work, so that I cannot come down. Why should the work cease while I leave it and go down to you?"
4But they sent me this message four times, and I answered them in the same manner.
5Then Sanballat sent his servant to me as before, the fifth time, with an open letter in his hand.
6In it *was* written:

> It is reported among the nations, and Geshem says, *that* you and the Jews plan to rebel; therefore, according to these rumors, you are rebuilding the wall, that you may be their king.
> 7And you have also appointed prophets to proclaim concerning you at Jerusalem, saying, "*There is* a king in Judah!" Now these matters will be reported to the king. So come, therefore, and let us consult together.

8Then I sent to him, saying, "No such things as you say are being done, but you invent them in your own heart."
9For they all *were trying to* make us afraid, saying, "Their hands will be weakened in the work, and it will not be done."

Now therefore, *O God,* strengthen my hands.

10Afterward I came to the house of Shemaiah the son of Delaiah, the son of Mehetabel, who *was* a secret informer; and he said, "Let us meet together in the house of God, within the temple, and let us close the doors of the temple, for they are coming to kill you; indeed, at night they will come to kill you."

6:5 open letter. Official letters were typically rolled up and sealed with an official signet by the letter's sender or one of his assisting officials. An open or unsealed letter was not only a sign of disrespect and open criticism, but also suggested the information therein was public knowledge. The goal of this document was to intimidate Nehemiah into stopping the work.

6:10 secret informer. When the open letter failed to intimidate Nehemiah into stopping the work and coming to a meeting, his enemies decided to try intimidation from within. They hired a false prophet (v. 12), Shemaiah, to lure Nehemiah into the Holy Place in the temple for refuge from a murder plot. To enter and shut himself in the Holy Place would have been a desecration of the house of God and would have caused people to question his reverence for God. Shemaiah was the son of a priest who was an intimate friend of Nehemiah. This plan would give them grounds to raise an evil report against Nehemiah, who was not a priest and had no right to go into the Holy Place (6:13). It could also make the people question his courage (v. 11).

11 And I said, "Should such a man as I flee? And who *is there* such as I who would go into the temple to save his life? I will not go in!"
12 Then I perceived that God had not sent him at all, but that he pronounced *this* prophecy against me because Tobiah and Sanballat had hired him. 13 For this reason he *was* hired, that I should be afraid and act that way and sin, so *that* they might have *cause* for an evil report, that they might reproach me.

14 My God, remember Tobiah and Sanballat, according to these their works, and the prophetess Noadiah and the rest of the prophets who would have made me afraid.

15 So the wall was finished on the twenty-fifth *day* of Elul, in fifty-two days. 16 And it happened, when all our enemies heard *of it,* and all the nations around us saw *these things,* that they were very disheartened in their own eyes; for they perceived that this work was done by our God.

6:16 this work was done by our God. While modern readers might be tempted to exalt the leadership qualities which brought the work to completion, Nehemiah's conclusion was seen through the eyes of his enemies, i.e., God works through faithful people, but it is God who works.

17 Also in those days the nobles of Judah sent many letters to Tobiah, and *the letters of* Tobiah came to them. 18 For many in Judah were pledged to him, because he was the son-in-law of Shechaniah the son of Arah, and his son Jehohanan had married the daughter of Meshullam the son of Berechiah. 19 Also they reported his good deeds before me, and reported my words to him. Tobiah sent letters to frighten me.

7 Then it was, when the wall was built and I had hung the doors, when the gatekeepers, the singers, and the Levites had been appointed, 2 that I gave the charge of Jerusalem to my brother Hanani, and Hananiah the leader of the citadel, for he *was* a faithful man and feared God more than many.

3 And I said to them, "Do not let the gates of Jerusalem be opened until the sun is hot; and while they stand *guard,* let them shut and bar the doors; and appoint guards from among the inhabitants of Jerusalem, one at his watch station and another in front of his own house."

4 Now the city *was* large and spacious, but the people in it *were* few, and the houses *were* not rebuilt. 5 Then my God put it into my heart to gather the nobles, the rulers, and the people, that they might be registered by genealogy. And I found a register of the genealogy of those who had come up in the first *return,* and found written in it:

6 These *are* the people of the province who came back from the captivity, of those who had been carried away, whom Nebuchadnezzar the king of Babylon had carried away, and who returned to Jerusalem and Judah, everyone to his city.

7 Those who came with Zerubbabel *were* Jeshua, Nehemiah, Azariah, Raamiah, Nahamani, Mordecai, Bilshan, Mispereth, Bigvai, Nehum, and Baanah.

The number of the men of the people of Israel: 8 the sons of Parosh, two thousand one hundred and seventy-two;
9 the sons of Shephatiah, three hundred and seventy-two;
10 the sons of Arah, six hundred and fifty-two;
11 the sons of Pahath-Moab, of the sons of Jeshua and Joab, two thousand eight hundred and eighteen;
12 the sons of Elam, one thousand two hundred and fifty-four;
13 the sons of Zattu, eight hundred and forty-five;
14 the sons of Zaccai, seven hundred and sixty;
15 the sons of Binnui, six hundred and forty-eight;

16 the sons of Bebai, six hundred and
twenty-eight;
17 the sons of Azgad, two thousand three
hundred and twenty-two;
18 the sons of Adonikam, six hundred
and sixty-seven;
19 the sons of Bigvai, two thousand and
sixty-seven;
20 the sons of Adin, six hundred and
fifty-five;
21 the sons of Ater of Hezekiah,
ninety-eight;
22 the sons of Hashum, three hundred
and twenty-eight;
23 the sons of Bezai, three hundred and
twenty-four;
24 the sons of Hariph, one hundred and
twelve;
25 the sons of Gibeon, ninety-five;
26 the men of Bethlehem and Netophah,
one hundred and eighty-eight;
27 the men of Anathoth, one hundred
and twenty-eight;
28 the men of Beth Azmaveth, forty-two;
29 the men of Kirjath Jearim, Chephirah,
and Beeroth, seven hundred and
forty-three;
30 the men of Ramah and Geba, six
hundred and twenty-one;
31 the men of Michmas, one hundred
and twenty-two;
32 the men of Bethel and Ai, one hundred
and twenty-three;
33 the men of the other Nebo, fifty-two;
34 the sons of the other Elam, one
thousand two hundred and fifty-four;
35 the sons of Harim, three hundred
and twenty;
36 the sons of Jericho, three hundred
and forty-five;
37 the sons of Lod, Hadid, and Ono,
seven hundred and twenty-one;
38 the sons of Senaah, three thousand
nine hundred and thirty.

39 The priests: the sons of Jedaiah, of the
house of Jeshua, nine hundred and
seventy-three;
40 the sons of Immer, one thousand and
fifty-two;
41 the sons of Pashhur, one thousand
two hundred and forty-seven;
42 the sons of Harim, one thousand and
seventeen.

43 The Levites: the sons of Jeshua, of
Kadmiel,
and of the sons of Hodevah,
seventy-four.

44 The singers: the sons of Asaph, one
hundred and forty-eight.

45 The gatekeepers: the sons of Shallum,
the sons of Ater,
the sons of Talmon,
the sons of Akkub,
the sons of Hatita,
the sons of Shobai, one hundred and
thirty-eight.

46 The Nethinim: the sons of Ziha,
the sons of Hasupha,
the sons of Tabbaoth,
47 the sons of Keros,
the sons of Sia,
the sons of Padon,
48 the sons of Lebana,
the sons of Hagaba,
the sons of Salmai,
49 the sons of Hanan,
the sons of Giddel,
the sons of Gahar,
50 the sons of Reaiah,
the sons of Rezin,
the sons of Nekoda,
51 the sons of Gazzam,
the sons of Uzza,
the sons of Paseah,
52 the sons of Besai,
the sons of Meunim,
the sons of Nephishesim,
53 the sons of Bakbuk,
the sons of Hakupha,
the sons of Harhur,
54 the sons of Bazlith,
the sons of Mehida,
the sons of Harsha,
55 the sons of Barkos,
the sons of Sisera,
the sons of Tamah,
56 the sons of Neziah,
and the sons of Hatipha.

57 The sons of Solomon's servants: the
sons of Sotai,
the sons of Sophereth,
the sons of Perida,
58 the sons of Jaala,
the sons of Darkon,
the sons of Giddel,
59 the sons of Shephatiah,
the sons of Hattil,
the sons of Pochereth of Zebaim,
and the sons of Amon.
60 All the Nethinim, and the sons of
Solomon's servants, *were* three
hundred and ninety-two.

61 And these *were* the ones who came up

from Tel Melah, Tel Harsha, Cherub,
Addon, and Immer, but they could not
identify their father's house nor their
lineage, whether they *were* of Israel:
62the sons of Delaiah,
the sons of Tobiah,
the sons of Nekoda, six hundred and
forty-two;
63and of the priests: the sons of
Habaiah,
the sons of Koz,
the sons of Barzillai, who took a wife of
the daughters of Barzillai the Gileadite,
and was called by their name.
64These sought their listing *among*
those who were registered by
genealogy, but it was not found;
therefore they were excluded from
the priesthood as defiled. 65And the
governor said to them that they should
not eat of the most holy things till a
priest could consult with the Urim and
Thummim.

66 Altogether the whole assembly *was*
forty-two thousand three hundred
and sixty, 67besides their male and
female servants, of whom *there were*
seven thousand three hundred and
thirty-seven; and they had two hundred
and forty-five men and women singers.
68Their horses were seven hundred and
thirty-six, their mules two hundred and
forty-five, 69*their* camels four hundred
and thirty-five, *and* donkeys six
thousand seven hundred and twenty.

70 And some of the heads of the fathers'
houses gave to the work. The governor
gave to the treasury one thousand gold
drachmas, fifty basins, and five
hundred and thirty priestly garments.
71Some of the heads of the fathers'
houses gave to the treasury of the
work twenty thousand gold drachmas,
and two thousand two hundred silver
minas. 72And that which the rest of the
people gave *was* twenty thousand gold
drachmas, two thousand silver minas,
and sixty-seven priestly garments.

73So the priests, the Levites, the gatekeepers,
the singers, *some* of the people, the Nethinim,
and all Israel dwelt in their cities.

Psalm 89:5–10

5 And the heavens will praise Your
wonders, O LORD;
Your faithfulness also in the assembly
of the saints.
6 For who in the heavens can be
compared to the LORD?
Who among the sons of the mighty can
be likened to the LORD?
7 God is greatly to be feared in the
assembly of the saints,
And to be held in reverence by all *those*
around Him.
8 O LORD God of hosts,
Who *is* mighty like You, O LORD?
Your faithfulness also surrounds You.
9 You rule the raging of the sea;
When its waves rise, You still them.
10 You have broken Rahab in pieces, as
one who is slain;
You have scattered Your enemies with
Your mighty arm.

Proverbs 21:28

28 A false witness shall perish,
But the man who hears *him* will speak
endlessly.

Acts 27:1–26

27 And when it was decided that we
should sail to Italy, they delivered Paul
and some other prisoners to *one* named Julius,
a centurion of the Augustan Regiment. 2So,
entering a ship of Adramyttium, we put to sea,
meaning to sail along the coasts of Asia.
Aristarchus, a Macedonian of Thessalonica,
was with us. 3And the next *day* we landed at
Sidon. And Julius treated Paul kindly and gave
him liberty to go to his friends and receive
care. 4When we had put to sea from there, we
sailed under *the shelter of* Cyprus, because the
winds were contrary. 5And when we had sailed
over the sea which is off Cilicia and
Pamphylia, we came to Myra, *a city* of Lycia.
6There the centurion found an Alexandrian
ship sailing to Italy, and he put us on board.
7When we had sailed slowly many days, and
arrived with difficulty off Cnidus, the wind not

27:1 we. The use of the pronoun "we" marks the return of Paul's close friend Luke, who has been absent since 21:18. He had likely been living near Caesarea so he could care for Paul during his imprisonment. Now he rejoined the apostle for the journey to Rome. **centurion of the Augustan Regiment.** A cohort (regiment) of that name was stationed in Palestine during the reign of Agrippa II. Julius may have been on detached duty, performing such tasks as escorting important prisoners.

permitting us to proceed, we sailed under *the*
shelter of Crete off Salmone. 8Passing it with
difficulty, we came to a place called Fair
Havens, near the city *of* Lasea.
9Now when much time had been spent, and
sailing was now dangerous because the Fast
was already over, Paul advised them, 10saying,
"Men, I perceive that this voyage will end with
disaster and much loss, not only of the cargo
and ship, but also our lives." 11Nevertheless
the centurion was more persuaded by the
helmsman and the owner of the ship than by
the things spoken by Paul. 12And because the
harbor was not suitable to winter in, the majority advised to set sail from there also, if by any
means they could reach Phoenix, a harbor of
Crete opening toward the southwest and
northwest, *and* winter *there.*

27:10 end with disaster. Because of the lateness of the season and the difficulties they had already experienced, Paul wisely counseled them to spend the winter at Fair Havens.

13When the south wind blew softly, supposing that they had obtained *their* desire, putting
out to sea, they sailed close by Crete. 14But not
long after, a tempestuous head wind arose,
called Euroclydon. 15So when the ship was
caught, and could not head into the wind, we
let *her* drive. 16And running under *the shelter of*
an island called Clauda, we secured the skiff
with difficulty. 17When they had taken it on
board, they used cables to undergird the ship;
and fearing lest they should run aground on

27:17 used cables to undergird the ship. A procedure known as frapping. The cables, wrapped around the hull and winched tight, helped the ship endure the battering of the wind and waves. **Syrtis.** A region of sandbars and shoals off the coast of Africa, much feared as a graveyard of ships. **struck sail.** This phrase could best be translated "let down the sea anchor." The sailors undoubtedly did both, since putting out an anchor with the sails up would be self-defeating.

the Syrtis *Sands,* they struck sail and so were
driven. 18And because we were exceedingly
tempest-tossed, the next *day* they lightened
the ship. 19On the third *day* we threw the ship's
tackle overboard with our own hands. 20Now
when neither sun nor stars appeared for many
days, and no small tempest beat on *us,* all hope
that we would be saved was finally given up.
21But after long abstinence from food, then
Paul stood in the midst of them and said,
"Men, you should have listened to me, and not
have sailed from Crete and incurred this disaster and loss. 22And now I urge you to take
heart, for there will be no loss of life among
you, but only of the ship. 23For there stood by
me this night an angel of the God to whom I
belong and whom I serve, 24saying, 'Do not be
afraid, Paul; you must be brought before Caesar; and indeed God has granted you all those
who sail with you.' 25Therefore take heart,
men, for I believe God that it will be just as it
was told me. 26However, we must run aground
on a certain island."

DAY 27: What parts of the Old Testament and what people were active in the events surrounding the return of the Jews from exile?

Five historical books (1 and 2 Chr., Ezra, Neh., and Esth.) come from or cover events after the exile. Three prophetic books (Hag., Zech., and Mal.) come from the same period. The term "post-exilic" is often used to describe these books and people.

First and Second Chronicles provide a summary of history viewed from the final days of the exile. Ezra and Nehemiah journal the thrilling and trying days of the return to Judah and the rebuilding of the nation. Haggai and Zechariah were prophets active during the time recorded in Ezra 4–6 when the temple was under reconstruction. Malachi wrote and prophesied during Nehemiah's revisit to Persia (Neh. 13:6).

Although part of the purpose of these books confirms God's continued covenant with the house of David and the unbroken kingly line, the emphasis shifts from royalty to other servants of God. A scribe, a cupbearer, and prophets become God's central agents. Even Esther, although a queen, had to rely on God rather than her position and power to accomplish God's role for her in preserving the Jews in Persia.

All of this sets the stage for the mixed expectations that surrounded the birth of Jesus, the fulfillment of God's covenant with David, God's personal involvement in the history of salvation.

JULY 28

Nehemiah 8:1–9:38

When the seventh month came, the children of Israel *were* in their cities.
8 Now all the people gathered together as
one man in the open square that *was* in
front of the Water Gate; and they told Ezra the
scribe to bring the Book of the Law of Moses,
which the LORD had commanded Israel. 2So
Ezra the priest brought the Law before the
assembly of men and women and all who *could*
hear with understanding on the first day of the
seventh month. 3Then he read from it in the
open square that *was* in front of the Water
Gate from morning until midday, before the
men and women and those who could understand; and the ears of all the people *were atten-*
tive to the Book of the Law.

4So Ezra the scribe stood on a platform of
wood which they had made for the purpose;
and beside him, at his right hand, stood
Mattithiah, Shema, Anaiah, Urijah, Hilkiah,
and Maaseiah; and at his left hand Pedaiah,
Mishael, Malchijah, Hashum, Hashbadana,
Zechariah, *and* Meshullam. 5And Ezra opened
the book in the sight of all the people, for he
was *standing* above all the people; and when
he opened it, all the people stood up. 6And
Ezra blessed the LORD, the great God.

Then all the people answered, "Amen,
Amen!" while lifting up their hands. And they
bowed their heads and worshiped the LORD
with *their* faces to the ground.

7Also Jeshua, Bani, Sherebiah, Jamin,
Akkub, Shabbethai, Hodijah, Maaseiah, Kelita,
Azariah, Jozabad, Hanan, Pelaiah, and the
Levites, helped the people to understand the
Law; and the people *stood* in their place. 8So
they read distinctly from the book, in the Law
of God; and they gave the sense, and helped
them to understand the reading.

9And Nehemiah, who *was* the governor,
Ezra the priest *and* scribe, and the Levites
who taught the people said to all the people,
"This day *is* holy to the LORD your God; do not
mourn nor weep." For all the people wept,
when they heard the words of the Law.

10Then he said to them, "Go your way, eat
the fat, drink the sweet, and send portions to
those for whom nothing is prepared; for *this*
day *is* holy to our Lord. Do not sorrow, for the
joy of the LORD is your strength."

11So the Levites quieted all the people, saying, "Be still, for the day *is* holy; do not be
grieved." 12And all the people went their way to
eat and drink, to send portions and rejoice
greatly, because they understood the words
that were declared to them.

13Now on the second day the heads of the
fathers' *houses* of all the people, with the priests
and Levites, were gathered to Ezra the scribe,
in order to understand the words of the Law.
14And they found written in the Law, which the
LORD had commanded by Moses, that the children of Israel should dwell in booths during
the feast of the seventh month, 15and that they
should announce and proclaim in all their
cities and in Jerusalem, saying, "Go out to the
mountain, and bring olive branches, branches
of oil trees, myrtle branches, palm branches,
and branches of leafy trees, to make booths,
as *it is* written."

16Then the people went out and brought
them and made themselves booths, each one
on the roof of his house, or in their courtyards
or the courts of the house of God, and in the
open square of the Water Gate and in the open
square of the Gate of Ephraim. 17So the whole
assembly of those who had returned from the
captivity made booths and sat under the
booths; for since the days of Joshua the son of
Nun until that day the children of Israel had
not done so. And there was very great gladness. 18Also day by day, from the first day until
the last day, he read from the Book of the Law
of God. And they kept the feast seven days;
and on the eighth day *there was* a sacred
assembly, according to the *prescribed* manner.
9 Now on the twenty-fourth day of this
month the children of Israel were assembled with fasting, in sackcloth, and with dust
on their heads. 2Then those of Israelite lineage
separated themselves from all foreigners; and
they stood and confessed their sins and the
iniquities of their fathers. 3And they stood up
in their place and read from the Book of the
Law of the LORD their God *for one*-fourth of the
day; and *for another* fourth they confessed and
worshiped the LORD their God.

4Then Jeshua, Bani, Kadmiel, Shebaniah,

9:1 this month. Tishri (Sept./Oct.), 445 B.C. (7:73b; 8:2). **with fasting, in sackcloth, and with dust.** The outward demonstration of deep mourning and heaviness of heart for their iniquity seems to have been done in the spirit of the Day of Atonement which was normally observed on the tenth day of the seventh month (Lev. 16:1–34; 23:26–32).

9:2 separated themselves from all foreigners. This call for divorcing all lawful wives taken from among the heathen was needed, since the last time, prompted 13 years before by Ezra, had only been partially successful. Many had escaped the required action of divorce and kept their pagan wives. Perhaps new defaulters had appeared, also, and were confronted for the first time with this necessary action of divorce. Nehemiah's efforts were successful in removing this evil mixture.

9:3 they stood...read...confessed and worshiped. The succession of events helped to reestablish the essential commitment of Israel to God and His law. They read for 3 hours about the sins of their fathers and for 3 more hours confessed that they had been partakers of similar evil deeds. In response to all of this, they worshiped.

Bunni, Sherebiah, Bani, *and* Chenani stood on the stairs of the Levites and cried out with a loud voice to the LORD their God. 5And the Levites, Jeshua, Kadmiel, Bani, Hashabniah, Sherebiah, Hodijah, Shebaniah, *and* Pethahiah, said:

"Stand up *and* bless the LORD your God
Forever and ever!

"Blessed be Your glorious name,
Which is exalted above all blessing and praise!
6 You alone *are* the LORD;
You have made heaven,
The heaven of heavens, with all their host,
The earth and everything on it,
The seas and all that is in them,
And You preserve them all.
The host of heaven worships You.
7 "You *are* the LORD God,
Who chose Abram,
And brought him out of Ur of the Chaldeans,
And gave him the name Abraham;
8 You found his heart faithful before You,
And made a covenant with him
To give the land of the Canaanites,
The Hittites, the Amorites,
The Perizzites, the Jebusites,
And the Girgashites—
To give *it* to his descendants.
You have performed Your words,
For You *are* righteous.

9 "You saw the affliction of our fathers in Egypt,
And heard their cry by the Red Sea.
10 You showed signs and wonders against Pharaoh,
Against all his servants,
And against all the people of his land.
For You knew that they acted proudly against them.
So You made a name for Yourself, as *it is* this day.
11 And You divided the sea before them,
So that they went through the midst of the sea on the dry land;
And their persecutors You threw into the deep,
As a stone into the mighty waters.
12 Moreover You led them by day with a cloudy pillar,
And by night with a pillar of fire,
To give them light on the road
Which they should travel.

13 "You came down also on Mount Sinai,
And spoke with them from heaven,
And gave them just ordinances and true laws,
Good statutes and commandments.
14 You made known to them Your holy Sabbath,
And commanded them precepts, statutes and laws,
By the hand of Moses Your servant.
15 You gave them bread from heaven for their hunger,
And brought them water out of the rock for their thirst,
And told them to go in to possess the land
Which You had sworn to give them.

16 "But they and our fathers acted proudly,
Hardened their necks,
And did not heed Your commandments.
17 They refused to obey,
And they were not mindful of Your wonders
That You did among them.
But they hardened their necks,
And in their rebellion
They appointed a leader
To return to their bondage.
But You *are* God,
Ready to pardon,
Gracious and merciful,
Slow to anger,
Abundant in kindness,
And did not forsake them.

18 "Even when they made a molded calf
for themselves,
And said, 'This *is* your god
That brought you up out of Egypt,'
And worked great provocations,
19 Yet in Your manifold mercies
You did not forsake them in the
wilderness.
The pillar of the cloud did not depart
from them by day,
To lead them on the road;
Nor the pillar of fire by night,
To show them light,
And the way they should go.
20 You also gave Your good Spirit to
instruct them,
And did not withhold Your manna from
their mouth,
And gave them water for their thirst.
21 Forty years You sustained them in the
wilderness;
They lacked nothing;
Their clothes did not wear out
And their feet did not swell.

22 "Moreover You gave them kingdoms
and nations,
And divided them into districts.
So they took possession of the land of
Sihon,
The land of the king of Heshbon,
And the land of Og king of Bashan.
23 You also multiplied their children as
the stars of heaven,
And brought them into the land
Which You had told their fathers
To go in and possess.
24 So the people went in
And possessed the land;
You subdued before them the
inhabitants of the land,
The Canaanites,
And gave them into their hands,
With their kings
And the people of the land,
That they might do with them as they
wished.
25 And they took strong cities and a rich
land,
And possessed houses full of all goods,
Cisterns *already* dug, vineyards, olive
groves,
And fruit trees in abundance.
So they ate and were filled and grew
fat,
And delighted themselves in Your
great goodness.

26 "Nevertheless they were disobedient
And rebelled against You,
Cast Your law behind their backs
And killed Your prophets, who testified
against them
To turn them to Yourself;
And they worked great provocations.
27 Therefore You delivered them into the
hand of their enemies,
Who oppressed them;
And in the time of their trouble,
When they cried to You,
You heard from heaven;
And according to Your abundant
mercies
You gave them deliverers who saved
them
From the hand of their enemies.

28 "But after they had rest,
They again did evil before You.
Therefore You left them in the hand of
their enemies,
So that they had dominion over them;
Yet when they returned and cried out
to You,
You heard from heaven;
And many times You delivered them
according to Your mercies,
29 And testified against them,
That You might bring them back to
Your law.
Yet they acted proudly,
And did not heed Your
commandments,
But sinned against Your judgments,
'Which if a man does, he shall live by
them.'
And they shrugged their shoulders,
Stiffened their necks,
And would not hear.
30 Yet for many years You had patience
with them,
And testified against them by Your Spirit
in Your prophets.
Yet they would not listen;
Therefore You gave them into the
hand of the peoples of the lands.
31 Nevertheless in Your great mercy
You did not utterly consume them nor
forsake them;
For You *are* God, gracious and
merciful.

32 "Now therefore, our God,
The great, the mighty, and awesome
God,
Who keeps covenant and mercy:
Do not let all the trouble seem small
before You

That has come upon us,
Our kings and our princes,
Our priests and our prophets,
Our fathers and on all Your people,
From the days of the kings of Assyria
until this day.
33 However You *are* just in all that has
befallen us;
For You have dealt faithfully,
But we have done wickedly.
34 Neither our kings nor our princes,
Our priests nor our fathers,
Have kept Your law,
Nor heeded Your commandments and
Your testimonies,
With which You testified against them.
35 For they have not served You in their
kingdom,
Or in the many good *things* that You
gave them,
Or in the large and rich land which
You set before them;
Nor did they turn from their wicked
works.

36 "Here we *are,* servants today!
And the land that You gave to our
fathers,
To eat its fruit and its bounty,
Here we *are,* servants in it!
37 And it yields much increase to the kings
You have set over us,
Because of our sins;
Also they have dominion over our
bodies and our cattle
At their pleasure;
And we *are* in great distress.

38 "And because of all this,
We make a sure *covenant* and write *it;*
Our leaders, our Levites, *and* our
priests seal *it.*"

Psalm 89:11–18

11 The heavens *are* Yours, the earth also
is Yours;
The world and all its fullness, You have
founded them.
12 The north and the south, You have
created them;
Tabor and Hermon rejoice in Your
name.
13 You have a mighty arm;
Strong is Your hand, *and* high is Your
right hand.
14 Righteousness and justice *are* the
foundation of Your throne;
Mercy and truth go before Your face.
15 Blessed *are* the people who know the
joyful sound!
They walk, O LORD, in the light of Your
countenance.
16 In Your name they rejoice all day long,
And in Your righteousness they are
exalted.
17 For You *are* the glory of their strength,
And in Your favor our horn is exalted.
18 For our shield *belongs* to the LORD,
And our king to the Holy One of Israel.

Proverbs 21:29–31

29 A wicked man hardens his face,
But *as for* the upright, he establishes
his way.

21:29 The wicked become obstinate, maintaining what suits them without regard for others or the truth, while good people proceed with integrity.

30 *There is* no wisdom or understanding
Or counsel against the LORD.

31 The horse *is* prepared for the day of
battle,
But deliverance *is* of the LORD.

Acts 27:27–44

27 Now when the fourteenth night had come,
as we were driven up and down in the Adriatic
Sea, about midnight the sailors sensed that
they were drawing near some land. 28 And they
took soundings and found *it* to be twenty fathoms; and when they had gone a little farther,
they took soundings again and found *it* to be
fifteen fathoms. 29 Then, fearing lest we should
run aground on the rocks, they dropped four

27:27 fourteenth night. Since they sailed from Fair Havens (v. 13). ***Adriatic Sea.*** The central Mediterranean Sea, not the present Adriatic Sea located between Italy and Croatia. The modern Adriatic was known in Paul's day as the Gulf of Adria. **sensed.** The sailors probably heard the sound of waves breaking on a shore.

27:28 took soundings. With a weight attached to a length of rope they measured the depth of the sea. **twenty fathoms...fifteen fathoms.** 120 feet...90 feet. The decreasing depth of the water confirmed the ship was approaching land.

anchors from the stern, and prayed for day to
come. [30]And as the sailors were seeking to
escape from the ship, when they had let down
the skiff into the sea, under pretense of putting out anchors from the prow, [31]Paul said to
the centurion and the soldiers, "Unless these
men stay in the ship, you cannot be saved."
[32]Then the soldiers cut away the ropes of the
skiff and let it fall off.

[33]And as day was about to dawn, Paul
implored *them* all to take food, saying, "Today
is the fourteenth day you have waited and continued without food, and eaten nothing.
[34]Therefore I urge you to take nourishment, for
this is for your survival, since not a hair will fall
from the head of any of you." [35]And when he
had said these things, he took bread and gave
thanks to God in the presence of them all; and
when he had broken *it* he began to eat. [36]Then
they were all encouraged, and also took food
themselves. [37]And in all we were two hundred
and seventy-six persons on the ship. [38]So when
they had eaten enough, they lightened the ship
and threw out the wheat into the sea.

[39]When it was day, they did not recognize the
land; but they observed a bay with a beach,
onto which they planned to run the ship if possible. [40]And they let go the anchors and left
them in the sea, meanwhile loosing the rudder
ropes; and they hoisted the mainsail to the
wind and made for shore. [41]But striking a place
where two seas met, they ran the ship aground;
and the prow stuck fast and remained immovable, but the stern was being broken up by the
violence of the waves.

[42]And the soldiers' plan was to kill the prisoners, lest any of them should swim away and
escape. [43]But the centurion, wanting to save
Paul, kept them from *their* purpose, and commanded that those who could swim should
jump *overboard* first and get to land, [44]and the
rest, some on boards and some on *parts* of the
ship. And so it was that they all escaped safely
to land.

27:42 the soldiers' plan was to kill the prisoners. Knowing they could face punishment or death if their prisoners escaped (12:19; 16:27).

DAY 28: How do repentance from sin and rejoicing go together?

In response to the people's request, Ezra brought the Law of the Lord to the people (Nehemiah 8:1). At this time, the Law was a scroll, as opposed to a text consisting of bound pages. Such a reading was required every 7 years at the Feast of Tabernacles (Deut. 31:10–13), even though it had been neglected since the Babylonian captivity until this occasion.

From daybreak to noon, a period of at least 6 hours, the Law was read and explained. Other men, probably priests, stood with Ezra to show agreement, and all of the people stood, as well (Neh. 8:5). This was in respect for God's Word, as though they were in the presence of God Himself. Some of the Levites assisted Ezra with the people's understanding of the Scripture by reading and explaining it (vv. 7,8). This may have involved translation for people who were only Aramaic speakers in exile, but more likely it means "to break down" the text into its parts so that the people could understand it. This was an exposition or explanation of the meaning and not just translation.

When the people heard and understood God's law, they wept (v. 9). Not tears of joy, but penitent sorrow (v. 10) came forth as they were grieved by conviction (v. 11) over the distressing manifestations of sin in transgressing the Lord's commands and the consequent punishments they had suffered in their captivity.

The event called for a holy day of worship to prepare them for the hard days ahead (12:43), so they were encouraged to rejoice. The words they had heard did remind them that God punishes sin, but also that God blesses obedience. That was reason to celebrate. "Do not sorrow, for the joy of the LORD is your strength" (8:10). They had not been utterly destroyed as a nation, in spite of their sin, and were, by God's grace, on the brink of a new beginning. That called for celebration.

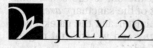

JULY 29

Nehemiah 10:1–11:36

10 Now those who placed *their* seal on *the*
document were:
Nehemiah the governor, the son of
Hacaliah, and Zedekiah,
[2]Seraiah, Azariah, Jeremiah, [3]Pashhur,
Amariah, Malchijah, [4]Hattush, Shebaniah,
Malluch, [5]Harim, Meremoth, Obadiah,
[6]Daniel, Ginnethon, Baruch, [7]Meshullam,
Abijah, Mijamin, [8]Maaziah, Bilgai, and
Shemaiah. These were the priests.

9 The Levites: Jeshua the son of
Azaniah, Binnui of the sons of
Henadad, *and* Kadmiel.
10 Their brethren: Shebaniah, Hodijah,
Kelita, Pelaiah, Hanan, 11 Micha, Rehob,
Hashabiah, 12 Zaccur, Sherebiah, Shebaniah, 13 Hodijah, Bani, *and* Beninu.
14 The leaders of the people: Parosh,
Pahath-Moab, Elam, Zattu, Bani,
15 Bunni, Azgad, Bebai, 16 Adonijah,
Bigvai, Adin, 17 Ater, Hezekiah, Azzur,
18 Hodijah, Hashum, Bezai, 19 Hariph,
Anathoth, Nebai, 20 Magpiash, Meshullam, Hezir, 21 Meshezabel, Zadok,
Jaddua, 22 Pelatiah, Hanan, Anaiah,
23 Hoshea, Hananiah, Hasshub, 24 Hallohesh, Pilha, Shobek, 25 Rehum, Hash-
abnah, Maaseiah, 26 Ahijah, Hanan,
Anan, 27 Malluch, Harim, *and* Baanah.

28 Now the rest of the people—the priests,
the Levites, the gatekeepers, the singers, the
Nethinim, and all those who had separated
themselves from the peoples of the lands to
the Law of God, their wives, their sons, and
their daughters, everyone who had knowl-

10:28 who had separated themselves. These are those who 1) had followed the demand of Ezra and Nehemiah to divorce pagan spouses or 2) had been left in the land but never joined themselves to any heathen, thus remaining separate. Intermarriage with the nations had previously precipitated an influence in Israel which had culminated in Babylonian slavery, thus playing a major role in Israel's unfaithfulness to the covenant.

edge and understanding— 29 these joined with
their brethren, their nobles, and entered into
a curse and an oath to walk in God's Law,
which was given by Moses the servant of God,
and to observe and do all the commandments
of the LORD our Lord, and His ordinances and
His statutes: 30 We would not give our daughters as wives to the peoples of the land, nor
take their daughters for our sons; 31 *if* the peoples of the land brought wares or any grain to
sell on the Sabbath day, we would not buy it
from them on the Sabbath, or on a holy day; and
we would forego the seventh year's *produce* and
the exacting of every debt.

32 Also we made ordinances for ourselves, to
exact from ourselves yearly one-third of a shekel
for the service of the house of our God: 33 for the
showbread, for the regular grain offering, for
the regular burnt offering of the Sabbaths, the
New Moons, and the set feasts; for the holy
things, for the sin offerings to make atonement
for Israel, and all the work of the house of our
God. 34 We cast lots among the priests, the
Levites, and the people, for bringing the wood
offering into the house of our God, according
to our fathers' houses, at the appointed times
year by year, to burn on the altar of the LORD
our God as *it is* written in the Law.

35 And *we made ordinances* to bring the firstfruits of our ground and the firstfruits of all
fruit of all trees, year by year, to the house of

10:35–37 firstfruits...firstborn...firstborn. These laws required the firstfruits of the ground (Ex. 23:19; 34:26; Deut. 26:2), the firstfruits of the trees (Lev. 19:24; Num. 18:13), the firstborn sons redeemed by the estimated price of the priest (Num. 18:15), and the firstborn of the herds and flocks (Ex. 13:12; Num. 18:15,17). All of this was kept at the storehouses near the temple and distributed for the support of the priests and Levites. The Levites then gave a tenth of what they received to the priests (Num. 18:26).

the LORD; 36 to bring the firstborn of our sons
and our cattle, as *it is* written in the Law, and
the firstborn of our herds and our flocks, to
the house of our God, to the priests who minister in the house of our God; 37 to bring the
firstfruits of our dough, our offerings, the fruit
from all kinds of trees, *the* new wine and oil, to
the priests, to the storerooms of the house of
our God; and to bring the tithes of our land to
the Levites, for the Levites should receive the
tithes in all our farming communities. 38 And
the priest, the descendant of Aaron, shall be
with the Levites when the Levites receive
tithes; and the Levites shall bring up a tenth of
the tithes to the house of our God, to the
rooms of the storehouse.

39 For the children of Israel and the children
of Levi shall bring the offering of the grain, of
the new wine and the oil, to the storerooms
where the articles of the sanctuary *are, where*
the priests who minister and the gatekeepers
and the singers *are;* and we will not neglect
the house of our God.

11 Now the leaders of the people dwelt at Jerusalem; the rest of the people cast lots to
bring one out of ten to dwell in Jerusalem, the
holy city, and nine-tenths *were to dwell* in *other*

cities. 2And the people blessed all the men
who willingly offered themselves to dwell at
Jerusalem.

3These *are* the heads of the province who
dwelt in Jerusalem. (But in the cities of Judah
everyone dwelt in his own possession in their
cities—Israelites, priests, Levites, Nethinim,
and descendants of Solomon's servants.) 4Also
in Jerusalem dwelt *some* of the children of Judah and of the children of Benjamin.

The children of Judah: Athaiah the son of
Uzziah, the son of Zechariah, the son of Amariah, the son of Shephatiah, the son of Mahalalel, of the children of Perez; 5and Maaseiah
the son of Baruch, the son of Col-Hozeh, the
son of Hazaiah, the son of Adaiah, the son of
Joiarib, the son of Zechariah, the son of Shiloni.
6All the sons of Perez who dwelt at Jerusalem
were four hundred and sixty-eight valiant men.

7And these are the sons of Benjamin: Sallu
the son of Meshullam, the son of Joed, the son
of Pedaiah, the son of Kolaiah, the son of
Maaseiah, the son of Ithiel, the son of
Jeshaiah; 8and after him Gabbai *and* Sallai,
nine hundred and twenty-eight. 9Joel the son
of Zichri *was* their overseer, and Judah the son
of Senuah *was* second over the city.

10Of the priests: Jedaiah the son of Joiarib,
and Jachin; 11Seraiah the son of Hilkiah, the son
of Meshullam, the son of Zadok, the son of
Meraioth, the son of Ahitub, *was* the leader of
the house of God. 12Their brethren who did the
work of the house *were* eight hundred and
twenty-two; and Adaiah the son of Jeroham,
the son of Pelaliah, the son of Amzi, the son of
Zechariah, the son of Pashhur, the son of
Malchijah, 13and his brethren, heads of the
fathers' *houses, were* two hundred and forty-
two; and Amashai the son of Azarel, the son of
Ahzai, the son of Meshillemoth, the son of
Immer, 14and their brethren, mighty men of valor,
were one hundred and twenty-eight. Their overseer *was* Zabdiel the son of *one of* the great men.

15Also of the Levites: Shemaiah the son of
Hasshub, the son of Azrikam, the son of
Hashabiah, the son of Bunni; 16Shabbethai and
Jozabad, of the heads of the Levites, *had* the
oversight of the business outside of the house
of God; 17Mattaniah the son of Micha, the son
of Zabdi, the son of Asaph, the leader *who*
began the thanksgiving with prayer; Bakbukiah, the second among his brethren; and
Abda the son of Shammua, the son of Galal,
the son of Jeduthun. 18All the Levites in the
holy city *were* two hundred and eighty-four.

19Moreover the gatekeepers, Akkub, Talmon, and their brethren who kept the gates,
were one hundred and seventy-two.

20And the rest of Israel, of the priests *and*
Levites, *were* in all the cities of Judah, everyone in his inheritance. 21But the Nethinim
dwelt in Ophel. And Ziha and Gishpa *were*
over the Nethinim.

22Also the overseer of the Levites at Jerusalem *was* Uzzi the son of Bani, the son of
Hashabiah, the son of Mattaniah, the son of
Micha, of the sons of Asaph, the singers in
charge of the service of the house of God.
23For *it was* the king's command concerning
them that a certain portion should be for the
singers, a quota day by day. 24Pethahiah the
son of Meshezabel, of the children of Zerah
the son of Judah, *was* the king's deputy in all
matters concerning the people.

25And as for the villages with their fields,
some of the children of Judah dwelt in Kirjath
Arba and its villages, Dibon and its villages,
Jekabzeel and its villages; 26in Jeshua, Moladah,
Beth Pelet, 27Hazar Shual, and Beersheba and
its villages; 28in Ziklag and Meconah and its villages; 29in En Rimmon, Zorah, Jarmuth,
30Zanoah, Adullam, and their villages; in Lachish
and its fields; in Azekah and its villages. They
dwelt from Beersheba to the Valley of Hinnom.

31Also the children of Benjamin from Geba
dwelt in Michmash, Aija, and Bethel, and their
villages; 32in Anathoth, Nob, Ananiah; 33in
Hazor, Ramah, Gittaim; 34in Hadid, Zeboim,
Neballat; 35in Lod, Ono, *and* the Valley of
Craftsmen. 36Some of the Judean divisions of
Levites *were* in Benjamin.

Psalm 89:19–29

19 Then You spoke in a vision to Your
holy one,
And said: "I have given help to *one who*
is mighty;
I have exalted one chosen from the
people.
20 I have found My servant David;
With My holy oil I have anointed him,
21 With whom My hand shall be
established;
Also My arm shall strengthen him.
22 The enemy shall not outwit him,
Nor the son of wickedness afflict him.
23 I will beat down his foes before his
face,
And plague those who hate him.
24 "But My faithfulness and My mercy
shall be with him,
And in My name his horn shall be
exalted.
25 Also I will set his hand over the sea,
And his right hand over the rivers.
26 He shall cry to Me, 'You *are* my Father,

My God, and the rock of my salvation.'
27 Also I will make him *My* firstborn,
The highest of the kings of the earth.
28 My mercy I will keep for him forever,
And My covenant shall stand firm with
him.
29 His seed also I will make *to endure*
forever,
And his throne as the days of heaven.

89:27 *My* firstborn. The firstborn child was given a place of special honor and a double portion of the inheritance (Gen. 27; 2 Kin. 2:9). However, in a royal grant covenant, a chosen person could be elevated to the level of firstborn sonship and thus have title to a perpetual gift involving dynastic succession (Ps. 2:7). Though not actually the first, Israel was considered the firstborn among nations (Ex. 4:22); Ephraim the younger was treated as the firstborn (Gen. 48:13–20); and David was the firstborn among kings. In this latter sense of prominent favor, Christ can be called the firstborn over all creation (Col. 1:15), in that He is given the preeminence over all created beings.

Proverbs 22:1–2

22 A *good* name is to be chosen
rather than great riches,
Loving favor rather than silver and gold.

2 The rich and the poor have this in
common,
The LORD *is* the maker of them all.

Acts 28:1–31

28 Now when they had escaped, they then
found out that the island was called
Malta. [2]And the natives showed us unusual
kindness; for they kindled a fire and made us
all welcome, because of the rain that was
falling and because of the cold. [3]But when Paul
had gathered a bundle of sticks and laid *them*
on the fire, a viper came out because of the
heat, and fastened on his hand. [4]So when the
natives saw the creature hanging from his
hand, they said to one another, "No doubt this
man is a murderer, whom, though he has
escaped the sea, yet justice does not allow to
live." [5]But he shook off the creature into the
fire and suffered no harm. [6]However, they
were expecting that he would swell up or suddenly fall down dead. But after they had
looked for a long time and saw no harm come
to him, they changed their minds and said that
he was a god.
[7]In that region there was an estate of the
leading citizen of the island, whose name was
Publius, who received us and entertained us
courteously for three days. [8]And it happened
that the father of Publius lay sick of a fever
and dysentery. Paul went in to him and
prayed, and he laid his hands on him and
healed him. [9]So when this was done, the rest
of those on the island who had diseases also
came and were healed. [10]They also honored us
in many ways; and when we departed, they provided such things as were necessary.

28:8 sick of a fever and dysentery. The gastric fever (caused by a microbe found in goat's milk) that was common on Malta. Dysentery, often the result of poor sanitation, was widespread in the ancient world.

[11]After three months we sailed in an
Alexandrian ship whose figurehead was the
Twin Brothers, which had wintered at the
island. [12]And landing at Syracuse, we stayed
three days. [13]From there we circled round and
reached Rhegium. And after one day the
south wind blew; and the next day we came to
Puteoli, [14]where we found brethren, and were
invited to stay with them seven days. And so
we went toward Rome. [15]And from there, when
the brethren heard about us, they came to
meet us as far as Appii Forum and Three Inns.
When Paul saw them, he thanked God and
took courage.
[16]Now when we came to Rome, the centurion delivered the prisoners to the captain of the
guard; but Paul was permitted to dwell by himself with the soldier who guarded him.
[17]And it came to pass after three days that Paul
called the leaders of the Jews together. So when
they had come together, he said to them: "Men
and brethren, though I have done nothing

28:16 centurion delivered the prisoners to the captain of the guard. Many Greek manuscripts omit this phrase. If part of the original text, it indicates either that Julius delivered the prisoners to his commanding officer or to the commander of the Praetorian Guard. **dwell by himself...guarded.** Possibly through Julius's intervention, Paul was allowed to live under guard in his own rented quarters (v. 30).

against our people or the customs of our
fathers, yet I was delivered as a prisoner from
Jerusalem into the hands of the Romans, [18]who,
when they had examined me, wanted to let *me*
go, because there was no cause for putting me
to death. [19]But when the Jews spoke against *it,*
I was compelled to appeal to Caesar, not that I
had anything of which to accuse my nation.
[20]For this reason therefore I have called for you,
to see *you* and speak with *you,* because for the
hope of Israel I am bound with this chain."
[21]Then they said to him, "We neither received letters from Judea concerning you, nor
have any of the brethren who came reported
or spoken any evil of you. [22]But we desire to
hear from you what you think; for concerning
this sect, we know that it is spoken against
everywhere."
[23]So when they had appointed him a day,
many came to him at *his* lodging, to whom he
explained and solemnly testified of the kingdom of God, persuading them concerning Jesus from both the Law of Moses and the
Prophets, from morning till evening. [24]And
some were persuaded by the things which
were spoken, and some disbelieved. [25]So when
they did not agree among themselves, they
departed after Paul had said one word: "The
Holy Spirit spoke rightly through Isaiah the
prophet to our fathers, [26]saying,

'Go to this people and say:
"Hearing you will hear, and shall not
understand;
And seeing you will see, and not
perceive;
27 *For the hearts of this people have*
grown dull.
Their ears are hard of hearing,
And their eyes they have closed,
Lest they should see with their eyes
and hear with their ears,
Lest they should understand with their
hearts and turn,
So that I should heal them."'

[28]"Therefore let it be known to you that the
salvation of God has been sent to the
Gentiles, and they will hear it!" [29]And when he
had said these words, the Jews departed and
had a great dispute among themselves.
[30]Then Paul dwelt two whole years in his
own rented house, and received all who came
to him, [31]preaching the kingdom of God and
teaching the things which concern the Lord
Jesus Christ with all confidence, no one forbidding him.

DAY 29: How does Nehemiah fit into the time line of world history?

It is unclear how Nehemiah became King Artaxerxes' cupbearer, but the fact that Esther was the king's stepmother may have inclined the king to consider a Jew for such a trusted position. When Nehemiah carried out his mission to rebuild the walls of Jerusalem, the Persian Empire had been dominant for almost 100 years. King Cyrus's decree of repatriation given back in 539 B.C. had instigated a group of Jews to return to Israel under Zerubbabel. Their desperate state almost a century later spurred Nehemiah into action.

Ancient Egyptian documents (Elephantine papyri) dated around the 5th century B.C. independently confirm part of Nehemiah's account. Sanballat the governor of Samaria (2:19), Jehohanan (6:18; 12:23) and Nehemiah himself receive mention.

The events recorded in Nehemiah, along with Malachi's prophecies, make up the final inspired writings of the Old Testament. God chose to then remain silent for 400 years. That silence ended with the announcements of John the Baptist's and Jesus' births.

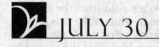

JULY 30

Nehemiah 12:1–13:31

12 Now these *are* the priests and the Levites
who came up with Zerubbabel the son of
Shealtiel, and Jeshua: Seraiah, Jeremiah, Ezra,
[2]Amariah, Malluch, Hattush, [3]Shechaniah,
Rehum, Meremoth, [4]Iddo, Ginnethoi, Abijah,
[5]Mijamin, Maadiah, Bilgah, [6]Shemaiah, Joiarib,
Jedaiah, [7]Sallu, Amok, Hilkiah, *and* Jedaiah.
These *were* the heads of the priests and their
brethren in the days of Jeshua.
[8]Moreover the Levites *were* Jeshua, Binnui,
Kadmiel, Sherebiah, Judah, *and* Mattaniah *who*
led the thanksgiving *psalms,* he and his
brethren. [9]Also Bakbukiah and Unni, their
brethren, *stood* across from them in *their* duties.
[10]Jeshua begot Joiakim, Joiakim begot
Eliashib, Eliashib begot Joiada, [11]Joiada begot
Jonathan, and Jonathan begot Jaddua.
[12]Now in the days of Joiakim, the priests, the
heads of the fathers' *houses were:* of Seraiah,
Meraiah; of Jeremiah, Hananiah; [13]of Ezra,

Meshullam; of Amariah, Jehohanan; 14of
Melichu, Jonathan; of Shebaniah, Joseph; 15of
Harim, Adna; of Meraioth, Helkai; 16of Iddo,
Zechariah; of Ginnethon, Meshullam; 17of
Abijah, Zichri; *the son* of Minjamin; of Moadiah,
Piltai; 18of Bilgah, Shammua; of Shemaiah,
Jehonathan; 19of Joiarib, Mattenai; of Jedaiah,
Uzzi; 20of Sallai, Kallai; of Amok, Eber; 21of
Hilkiah, Hashabiah; *and* of Jedaiah, Nethanel.

22During the reign of Darius the Persian, a
record *was also kept* of the Levites and priests
who had been heads of their fathers' *houses* in
the days of Eliashib, Joiada, Johanan, and
Jaddua. 23The sons of Levi, the heads of the
fathers' *houses* until the days of Johanan the son
of Eliashib, *were* written in the book of the
chronicles.

24And the heads of the Levites *were*
Hashabiah, Sherebiah, and Jeshua the son of
Kadmiel, with their brothers across from
them, to praise *and* give thanks, group alter-
nating with group, according to the command
of David the man of God. 25Mattaniah, Bakbukiah, Obadiah, Meshullam, Talmon, and
Akkub *were* gatekeepers keeping the watch at
the storerooms of the gates. 26These *lived* in
the days of Joiakim the son of Jeshua, the son
of Jozadak, and in the days of Nehemiah the
governor, and of Ezra the priest, the scribe.

27Now at the dedication of the wall of Jerusalem they sought out the Levites in all their
places, to bring them to Jerusalem to celebrate
the dedication with gladness, both with
thanksgivings and singing, *with* cymbals and
stringed instruments and harps. 28And the
sons of the singers gathered together from
the countryside around Jerusalem, from the
villages of the Netophathites, 29from the house
of Gilgal, and from the fields of Geba and
Azmaveth; for the singers had built themselves
villages all around Jerusalem. 30Then the
priests and Levites purified themselves, and
purified the people, the gates, and the wall.

31So I brought the leaders of Judah up on the
wall, and appointed two large thanksgiving
choirs. *One* went to the right hand on the wall
toward the Refuse Gate. 32After them went
Hoshaiah and half of the leaders of Judah,
33and Azariah, Ezra, Meshullam, 34Judah, Benjamin, Shemaiah, Jeremiah, 35and some of the
priests' sons with trumpets—Zechariah the
son of Jonathan, the son of Shemaiah, the son
of Mattaniah, the son of Michaiah, the son of
Zaccur, the son of Asaph, 36and his brethren,
Shemaiah, Azarel, Milalai, Gilalai, Maai,
Nethanel, Judah, *and* Hanani, with the musical
instruments of David the man of God. And
Ezra the scribe *went* before them. 37By the
Fountain Gate, in front of them, they went up
the stairs of the City of David, on the stairway
of the wall, beyond the house of David, as far
as the Water Gate eastward.

38The other thanksgiving choir went the
opposite *way*, and I *was* behind them with half of
the people on the wall, going past the Tower of
the Ovens as far as the Broad Wall, 39and above
the Gate of Ephraim, above the Old Gate,
above the Fish Gate, the Tower of Hananel,
the Tower of the Hundred, as far as the Sheep
Gate; and they stopped by the Gate of the
Prison.

40So the two thanksgiving choirs stood in
the house of God, likewise I and the half of the
rulers with me; 41and the priests, Eliakim,
Maaseiah, Minjamin, Michaiah, Elioenai, Zechariah, *and* Hananiah, with trumpets; 42also
Maaseiah, Shemaiah, Eleazar, Uzzi, Jehohanan,
Malchijah, Elam, and Ezer. The singers sang
loudly with Jezrahiah the director.

43Also that day they offered great sacrifices,
and rejoiced, for God had made them rejoice
with great joy; the women and the children also
rejoiced, so that the joy of Jerusalem was heard
afar off.

44And at the same time some were appointed over the rooms of the storehouse for the
offerings, the firstfruits, and the tithes, to
gather into them from the fields of the cities
the portions specified by the Law for the
priests and Levites; for Judah rejoiced over
the priests and Levites who ministered. 45Both
the singers and the gatekeepers kept the
charge of their God and the charge of the
purification, according to the command of
David *and* Solomon his son. 46For in the days of
David and Asaph of old *there were* chiefs of the
singers, and songs of praise and thanksgiving
to God. 47In the days of Zerubbabel and in the
days of Nehemiah all Israel gave the portions
for the singers and the gatekeepers, a portion for each day. They also consecrated *holy*
things for the Levites, and the Levites consecrated *them* for the children of Aaron.

13 On that day they read from the Book of
Moses in the hearing of the people, and
in it was found written that no Ammonite or
Moabite should ever come into the assembly
of God, 2because they had not met the children of Israel with bread and water, but hired
Balaam against them to curse them. However,
our God turned the curse into a blessing. 3So
it was, when they had heard the Law, that they
separated all the mixed multitude from Israel.

4Now before this, Eliashib the priest, having
authority over the storerooms of the house of
our God, *was* allied with Tobiah. 5And he had

prepared for him a large room, where previously they had stored the grain offerings, the
frankincense, the articles, the tithes of grain,
the new wine and oil, which were commanded
to be given to the Levites and singers and gatekeepers, and the offerings for the priests. 6But
during all this I was not in Jerusalem, for in the
thirty-second year of Artaxerxes king of Babylon I had returned to the king. Then after certain days I obtained leave from the king, 7and I
came to Jerusalem and discovered the evil that
Eliashib had done for Tobiah, in preparing a
room for him in the courts of the house of God.
8And it grieved me bitterly; therefore I threw
all the household goods of Tobiah out of the
room. 9Then I commanded them to cleanse the
rooms; and I brought back into them the articles of the house of God, with the grain offering and the frankincense.

10I also realized that the portions for the
Levites had not been given *them;* for each of
the Levites and the singers who did the work
had gone back to his field. 11So I contended
with the rulers, and said, "Why is the house of
God forsaken?" And I gathered them together
and set them in their place. 12Then all Judah
brought the tithe of the grain and the new wine
and the oil to the storehouse. 13And I appointed
as treasurers over the storehouse Shelemiah
the priest and Zadok the scribe, and of the
Levites, Pedaiah; and next to them *was* Hanan
the son of Zaccur, the son of Mattaniah; for
they were considered faithful, and their task
was to distribute to their brethren.

14Remember me, O my God, concerning
this, and do not wipe out my good deeds that
I have done for the house of my God, and for
its services!

15In those days I saw *people* in Judah treading wine presses on the Sabbath, and bringing
in sheaves, and loading donkeys with wine,
grapes, figs, and all *kinds of* burdens, which
they brought into Jerusalem on the Sabbath
day. And I warned *them* about the day on which
they were selling provisions. 16Men of Tyre
dwelt there also, who brought in fish and all
kinds of goods, and sold *them* on the Sabbath
to the children of Judah, and in Jerusalem.

17Then I contended with the nobles of Judah, and said to them, "What evil thing *is* this
that you do, by which you profane the Sabbath
day? 18Did not your fathers do thus, and did
not our God bring all this disaster on us and
on this city? Yet you bring added wrath on Israel by profaning the Sabbath."

19So it was, at the gates of Jerusalem, as it
began to be dark before the Sabbath, that I
commanded the gates to be shut, and charged
that they must not be opened till after the
Sabbath. Then I posted *some* of my servants at
the gates, *so that* no burdens would be
brought in on the Sabbath day. 20Now the merchants and sellers of all kinds of wares lodged
outside Jerusalem once or twice.

21Then I warned them, and said to them,
"Why do you spend the night around the wall?
If you do *so* again, I will lay hands on you!"
From that time on they came no *more* on the
Sabbath. 22And I commanded the Levites that
they should cleanse themselves, and that they
should go and guard the gates, to sanctify the
Sabbath day.

Remember me, O my God, *concerning* this
also, and spare me according to the greatness
of Your mercy!

23In those days I also saw Jews *who* had married women of Ashdod, Ammon, *and* Moab.
24And half of their children spoke the language
of Ashdod, and could not speak the language of
Judah, but spoke according to the language of
one or the other people.

25So I contended with them and cursed them,
struck some of them and pulled out their hair,
and made them swear by God, *saying,* "You
shall not give your daughters as wives to their
sons, nor take their daughters for your sons or
yourselves. 26Did not Solomon king of Israel
sin by these things? Yet among many nations
there was no king like him, who was beloved of
his God; and God made him king over all Israel. Nevertheless pagan women caused even
him to sin. 27Should we then hear of your doing
all this great evil, transgressing against our
God by marrying pagan women?"

28And *one* of the sons of Joiada, the son of
Eliashib the high priest, *was* a son-in-law of
Sanballat the Horonite; therefore I drove him
from me.

29Remember them, O my God, because they
have defiled the priesthood and the covenant
of the priesthood and the Levites.

30Thus I cleansed them of everything pagan. I
also assigned duties to the priests and the Levites,
each to his service, 31and *to bringing* the wood
offering and the firstfruits at appointed times.

Remember me, O my God, for good!

Psalm 89:30–37

30 "If his sons forsake My law
And do not walk in My judgments,
31 If they break My statutes
And do not keep My
commandments,
32 Then I will punish their transgression
with the rod,
And their iniquity with stripes.

33 Nevertheless My lovingkindness I will
not utterly take from him,
Nor allow My faithfulness to fail.
34 My covenant I will not break,
Nor alter the word that has gone out of
My lips.
35 Once I have sworn by My holiness;
I will not lie to David:
36 His seed shall endure forever,
And his throne as the sun before Me;
37 It shall be established forever like the
moon,
Even *like* the faithful witness
in the sky." Selah

Proverbs 22:3–4

3 A prudent *man* foresees evil and hides
himself,
But the simple pass on and are punished.

4 By humility *and* the fear of the LORD
Are riches and honor and life.

Romans 1:1–32

1 Paul, a bondservant of Jesus Christ, called *to be*
an apostle, separated to the gospel of God
2which He promised before through His
prophets in the Holy Scriptures, 3concerning His
Son Jesus Christ our Lord, who was born of the
seed of David according to the flesh, 4*and* declared *to be* the Son of God with power according to the Spirit of holiness, by the resurrection
from the dead. 5Through Him we have received
grace and apostleship for obedience to the faith
among all nations for His name, 6among whom
you also are the called of Jesus Christ;

7To all who are in Rome, beloved of God,
called *to be* saints:

Grace to you and peace from God our
Father and the Lord Jesus Christ.

8First, I thank my God through Jesus Christ
for you all, that your faith is spoken of throughout the whole world. 9For God is my witness,
whom I serve with my spirit in the gospel of
His Son, that without ceasing I make mention
of you always in my prayers, 10making request
if, by some means, now at last I may find a way
in the will of God to come to you. 11For I long to
see you, that I may impart to you some spiritual gift, so that you may be established— 12that
is, that I may be encouraged together with you
by the mutual faith both of you and me.

13Now I do not want you to be unaware,
brethren, that I often planned to come to you
(but was hindered until now), that I might have
some fruit among you also, just as among the
other Gentiles. 14I am a debtor both to Greeks
and to barbarians, both to wise and to unwise.
15So, as much as is in me, *I am* ready to preach
the gospel to you who are in Rome also.

16For I am not ashamed of the gospel of
Christ, for it is the power of God to salvation
for everyone who believes, for the Jew first
and also for the Greek. 17For in it the righteousness of God is revealed from faith to faith;
as it is written, *"The just shall live by faith."*

18For the wath of God is revealed from heav-
en against all ungodliness and unrighteousness of men, who suppress the truth in

1:17 The just shall live by faith. Paul intends to prove that it has always been God's way to justify sinners by grace on the basis of faith alone. God established Abraham as a pattern of faith (4:22–25; Gal. 3:6,7) and thus calls him the father of all who believe (4:11,16). Elsewhere, Paul uses this same phrase to argue that no one has ever been declared righteous before God except by faith alone (Gal. 3:11) and that true faith will demonstrate itself in action (Phil. 2:12,13). This expression emphasizes that true faith is not a single event, but a way of life—it endures. That endurance is called the perseverance of the saints (Col. 1:22,23; Heb. 3:12–14). One central theme of the story of Job is that no matter what Satan does, saving faith cannot be destroyed.

1:18 wrath of God. This is not an impulsive outburst of anger aimed capriciously at people whom God does not like. It is the settled, determined response of a righteous God against sin.

unrighteousness, 19because what may be
known of God is manifest in them, for God has
shown *it* to them. 20For since the creation of the
world His invisible *attributes* are clearly seen,
being understood by the things that are made,
even His eternal power and Godhead, so that
they are without excuse, 21because, although
they knew God, they did not glorify *Him* as
God, nor were thankful, but became futile in
their thoughts, and their foolish hearts were
darkened. 22Professing to be wise, they
became fools, 23and changed the glory of the
incorruptible God into an image made like
corruptible man—and birds and four-footed
animals and creeping things.

24Therefore God also gave them up to
uncleanness, in the lusts of their hearts, to dis-

1:20 they are without excuse. God holds all men responsible for their refusal to acknowledge what He has shown them of Himself in His creation. Even those who have never had an opportunity to hear the gospel have received a clear witness about the existence and character of God—and have suppressed it. If a person will respond to the revelation he has, even if it is solely natural revelation, God will provide some means for that person to hear the gospel (Acts 8:26–39; 10:1–48; 17:27).

honor their bodies among themselves,
[25]who exchanged the truth of God for the lie, and worshiped and served the creature rather than the Creator, who is blessed forever. Amen.
[26]For this reason God gave them up to vile passions. For even their women exchanged the natural use for what is against nature.
[27]Likewise also the men, leaving the natural use of the woman, burned in their lust for one another, men with men committing what is shameful, and receiving in themselves the penalty of their error which was due.
[28]And even as they did not like to retain God in *their* knowledge, God gave them over to a debased mind, to do those things which are

1:21 knew God. Man is conscious of God's existence, power, and divine nature through general revelation (vv. 19,20). **they did not glorify *Him*.** Man's chief end is to glorify God (Lev. 10:3; 1 Chr. 16:24–29; Ps. 148; Rom. 15:5,6), and Scripture constantly demands it (Ps. 29:1,2; 1 Cor. 10:31; Rev. 4:11). To glorify Him is to honor Him, to acknowledge His attributes, and to praise Him for His perfections (Ex. 34:5–7). It is to recognize His glory and extol Him for it. Failing to give Him glory is man's greatest affront to his Creator (Acts 12:22,23). **nor were thankful.** They refused to acknowledge that every good thing they enjoyed came from God.

not fitting;
[29]being filled with all unrighteousness, sexual immorality, wickedness, covetousness, maliciousness; full of envy, murder, strife, deceit, evil-mindedness; *they are* whisperers,
[30]backbiters, haters of God, violent, proud, boasters, inventors of evil things, disobedient to parents,
[31]undiscerning, untrustworthy, unloving, unforgiving, unmerciful;
[32]who, knowing the righteous judgment of God, that those who practice such things are deserving of death, not only do the same but also approve of those who practice them.

DAY 30: How did Paul maintain his commitment to the gospel?

Paul tells us in Romans 1:16: "I am not ashamed of the gospel of Christ." He had been imprisoned in Philippi (Acts 16:23,24), chased out of Thessalonica (Acts 17:10), smuggled out of Berea (Acts 17:14), laughed at in Athens (Acts 17:32), regarded as a fool in Corinth (1 Cor. 1:18,23), and stoned in Galatia (Acts 14:19), but Paul remained eager to preach the gospel in Rome—the seat of contemporary political power and pagan religion. Neither ridicule, criticism, nor physical persecution could curb his boldness.

"For it is the power of God." The English word "dynamite" comes from this Greek word. Although the message may sound foolish to some (1 Cor. 1:18), the gospel is effective because it carries with it the omnipotence of God. Only God's power is able to overcome man's sinful nature and give him new life (5:6; 8:3; John 1:12; 1 Cor. 1:18,23–25; 2:1–4; 4:20; 1 Pet. 1:23).

"The power of God to salvation." Used 5 times in Romans (the verb form occurs 8 times), this key word basically means "deliverance" or "rescue." The power of the gospel delivers people from lostness (Matt. 18:11), from the wrath of God (Rom. 5:9), from willful spiritual ignorance (Hos. 4:6; 2 Thess. 1:8), from evil self-indulgence (Luke 14:26), and from the darkness of false religion (Col. 1:13; 1 Pet. 2:9). It rescues them from the ultimate penalty of their sin, i.e., eternal separation from God and eternal punishment (Rev. 20:6).

"For everyone who believes." To trust, rely on, or have faith in. When used of salvation, this word usually occurs in the present tense ("is believing") which stresses that faith is not simply a one-time event, but an ongoing condition. True saving faith is supernatural, a gracious gift of God that He produces in the heart (Eph. 2:8) and is the only means by which a person can appropriate true righteousness. Saving faith consists of 3 elements: 1) mental: the mind understands the gospel and the truth about Christ (10:14–17); 2) emotional: one embraces the truthfulness of those facts with sorrow over sin and joy over God's mercy and grace (6:17; 15:13); and 3) volitional: the sinner submits his will to Christ and trusts in Him alone as the only hope of salvation.

JULY 31

Esther 1:1–2:23

1 Now it came to pass in the days of
Ahasuerus (this *was* the Ahasuerus who
reigned over one hundred and twenty-seven
provinces, from India to Ethiopia), [2]in those
days when King Ahasuerus sat on the throne
of his kingdom, which *was* in Shushan the citadel, [3]*that* in the third year of his reign he
made a feast for all his officials and servants—
the powers of Persia and Media, the nobles,
and the princes of the provinces *being* before
him— [4]when he showed the riches of his glorious kingdom and the splendor of his excellent majesty for many days, one hundred and
eighty days *in all.*

[5]And when these days were completed, the
king made a feast lasting seven days for all the
people who were present in Shushan the citadel, from great to small, in the court of the garden of the king's palace. [6]*There were* white and
blue linen *curtains* fastened with cords of fine
linen and purple on silver rods and marble pillars; *and the* couches *were* of gold and silver
on a *mosaic* pavement of alabaster, turquoise,
and white and black marble. [7]And they served
drinks in golden vessels, each vessel being different from the other, with royal wine in abundance, according to the generosity of the king.
[8]In accordance with the law, the drinking was
not compulsory; for so the king had ordered
all the officers of his household, that they
should do according to each man's pleasure.

[9]Queen Vashti also made a feast for the
women *in* the royal palace which *belonged* to
King Ahasuerus.

1:9 Queen Vashti. Greek literature records her name as Amestris. She gave birth (ca. 483 B.C.) to Ahasuerus's third son, Artaxerxes, who later succeeded his father Ahasuerus on the throne (Ezra 7:1).

[10]On the seventh day, when the heart of the
king was merry with wine, he commanded
Mehuman, Biztha, Harbona, Bigtha, Abagtha,
Zethar, and Carcas, seven eunuchs who served in
the presence of King Ahasuerus, [11]to bring Queen
Vashti before the king, *wearing* her royal crown,
in order to show her beauty to the people and
the officials, for she *was* beautiful to behold.
[12]But Queen Vashti refused to come at the king's
command *brought* by *his* eunuchs; therefore the
king was furious, and his anger burned within
him.

[13]Then the king said to the wise men who
understood the times (for this *was* the king's
manner toward all who knew law and justice,
[14]those closest to him *being* Carshena, Shethar,
Admatha, Tarshish, Meres, Marsena, and
Memucan, the seven princes of Persia and
Media, who had access to the king's presence,
and who ranked highest in the kingdom):
[15]"What *shall we* do to Queen Vashti, according
to law, because she did not obey the command
of King Ahasuerus *brought to her* by the
eunuchs?"

[16]And Memucan answered before the king
and the princes: "Queen Vashti has not only
wronged the king, but also all the princes, and
all the people who *are* in all the provinces of
King Ahasuerus. [17]For the queen's behavior
will become known to all women, so that they
will despise their husbands in their eyes,
when they report, 'King Ahasuerus commanded Queen Vashti to be brought in before
him, but she did not come.' [18]This very day the
noble ladies of Persia and Media will say to all
the king's officials that they have heard of the
behavior of the queen. Thus *there will be*
excessive contempt and wrath. [19]If it pleases
the king, let a royal decree go out from him,
and let it be recorded in the laws of the Persians and the Medes, so that it will not be
altered, that Vashti shall come no more before
King Ahasuerus; and let the king give her
royal position to another who is better than
she. [20]When the king's decree which he will
make is proclaimed throughout all his empire
(for it is great), all wives will honor their husbands, both great and small."

[21]And the reply pleased the king and the
princes, and the king did according to the
word of Memucan. [22]Then he sent letters to all
the king's provinces, to each province in its
own script, and to every people in their own
language, that each man should be master in
his own house, and speak in the language of
his own people.

2 After these things, when the wrath of King
Ahasuerus subsided, he remembered
Vashti, what she had done, and what had been
decreed against her. [2]Then the king's servants
who attended him said: "Let beautiful young
virgins be sought for the king; [3]and let the
king appoint officers in all the provinces of his
kingdom, that they may gather all the beautiful
young virgins to Shushan the citadel, into the

women's quarters, under the custody of Hegai
the king's eunuch, custodian of the women.
And let beauty preparations be given *them.*
[4]Then let the young woman who pleases the
king be queen instead of Vashti."
This thing pleased the king, and he did so.
[5]In Shushan the citadel there was a certain
Jew whose name *was* Mordecai the son of Jair,
the son of Shimei, the son of Kish, a Benjamite.

2:5 Mordecai. He was among the fourth generation of deported Jews. **Kish.** Mordecai's great-grandfather who actually experienced the Babylonian deportation. After Babylon fell to Medo-Persia (ca. 539 B.C.), Jews were moved to other parts of the new kingdom. Kish represents a Benjamite family name that could be traced back (ca. 1100 B.C.) to Saul's father (1 Sam. 9:1).

[6]*Kish* had been carried away from Jerusalem
with the captives who had been captured with
Jeconiah king of Judah, whom Nebuchadnezzar
the king of Babylon had carried away. [7]And
Mordecai had brought up Hadassah, that *is,*
Esther, his uncle's daughter, for she had neither father nor mother. The young woman *was*
lovely and beautiful. When her father and
mother died, Mordecai took her as his own
daughter.
[8]So it was, when the king's command and
decree were heard, and when many young
women were gathered at Shushan the citadel,
under the custody of Hegai, that Esther also
was taken to the king's palace, into the care of
Hegai the custodian of the women. [9]Now the
young woman pleased him, and she obtained
his favor; so he readily gave beauty preparations to her, besides her allowance. Then
seven choice maidservants were provided for
her from the king's palace, and he moved her
and her maidservants to the best *place* in the
house of the women.
[10]Esther had not revealed her people or family, for Mordecai had charged her not to reveal *it.*
[11]And every day Mordecai paced in front of the
court of the women's quarters, to learn of Esther's welfare and what was happening to her.
[12]Each young woman's turn came to go in to
King Ahasuerus after she had completed
twelve months' preparation, according to the
regulations for the women, for thus were the
days of their preparation apportioned: six
months with oil of myrrh, and six months with
perfumes and preparations for beautifying
women. [13]Thus *prepared, each* young woman
went to the king, and she was given whatever
she desired to take with her from the women's
quarters to the king's palace. [14]In the evening
she went, and in the morning she returned to
the second house of the women, to the custody
of Shaashgaz, the king's eunuch who kept the
concubines. She would not go in to the king
again unless the king delighted in her and
called for her by name.
[15]Now when the turn came for Esther the
daughter of Abihail the uncle of Mordecai,
who had taken her as his daughter, to go in to
the king, she requested nothing but what
Hegai the king's eunuch, the custodian of the
women, advised. And Esther obtained favor in
the sight of all who saw her. [16]So Esther was
taken to King Ahasuerus, into his royal palace,
in the tenth month, which *is* the month of
Tebeth, in the seventh year of his reign. [17]The
king loved Esther more than all the *other*
women, and she obtained grace and favor in
his sight more than all the virgins; so he set
the royal crown upon her head and made her
queen instead of Vashti. [18]Then the king made
a great feast, the Feast of Esther, for all his
officials and servants; and he proclaimed a
holiday in the provinces and gave gifts according to the generosity of a king.
[19]When virgins were gathered together a
second time, Mordecai sat within the king's
gate. [20]*Now* Esther had not revealed her family
and her people, just as Mordecai had charged
her, for Esther obeyed the command of
Mordecai as when she was brought up by him.
[21]In those days, while Mordecai sat within
the king's gate, two of the king's eunuchs,
Bigthan and Teresh, doorkeepers, became furious and sought to lay hands on King
Ahasuerus. [22]So the matter became known to
Mordecai, who told Queen Esther, and Esther
informed the king in Mordecai's name. [23]And
when an inquiry was made into the matter, it
was confirmed, and both were hanged on a gallows; and it was written in the book of the
chronicles in the presence of the king.

Psalm 89:38–45

[38] But You have cast off and abhorred,
You have been furious with Your
anointed.
[39] You have renounced the covenant of
Your servant;
You have profaned his crown *by casting*
it to the ground.
[40] You have broken down all his hedges;
You have brought his strongholds to
ruin.

41 All who pass by the way plunder him;
He is a reproach to his neighbors.
42 You have exalted the right hand of his
adversaries;
You have made all his enemies rejoice.
43 You have also turned back the edge of
his sword,
And have not sustained him in the
battle.
44 You have made his glory cease,
And cast his throne down to the
ground.
45 The days of his youth You have
shortened;
You have covered him with shame.
Selah

Proverbs 22:5–6

5 Thorns *and* snares *are* in the way of
the perverse;
He who guards his soul will be far from
them.

6 Train up a child in the way he should
go,
And when he is old he will not depart
from it.

22:6 way he should go. There is only one right way, God's way, the way of life. That way is specified in great detail in Proverbs. Since it is axiomatic that early training secures lifelong habits, parents must insist upon this way, teaching God's Word and enforcing it with loving discipline consistently throughout the child's upbringing.

Romans 2:1–29

2 Therefore you are inexcusable, O man,
whoever you are who judge, for in whatever you judge another you condemn yourself;
for you who judge practice the same things.
[2]But we know that the judgment of God is
according to truth against those who practice
such things. [3]And do you think this, O man,
you who judge those practicing such things,
and doing the same, that you will escape the
judgment of God? [4]Or do you despise the riches of His goodness, forbearance, and longsuffering, not knowing that the goodness of God
leads you to repentance? [5]But in accordance
with your hardness and your impenitent heart
you are treasuring up for yourself wrath in the
day of wrath and revelation of the righteous
judgment of God, [6]who *"will render to each one
according to his deeds"*: [7]eternal life to those
who by patient continuance in doing good seek
for glory, honor, and immortality; [8]but to those
who are self-seeking and do not obey the truth,
but obey unrighteousness—indignation and
wrath, [9]tribulation and anguish, on every soul
of man who does evil, of the Jew first and also
of the Greek; [10]but glory, honor, and peace to
everyone who works what is good, to the Jew
first and also to the Greek. [11]For there is no partiality with God.

[12]For as many as have sinned without law
will also perish without law, and as many as
have sinned in the law will be judged by the
law [13](for not the hearers of the law *are* just in
the sight of God, but the doers of the law will
be justified; [14]for when Gentiles, who do not
have the law, by nature do the things in the law,
these, although not having the law, are a law to
themselves, [15]who show the work of the law
written in their hearts, their conscience also
bearing witness, and between themselves *their*
thoughts accusing or else excusing *them*) [16]in
the day when God will judge the secrets of
men by Jesus Christ, according to my gospel.

[17]Indeed you are called a Jew, and rest on the
law, and make your boast in God, [18]and know
His will, and approve the things that are excellent, being instructed out of the law, [19]and are
confident that you yourself are a guide to the
blind, a light to those who are in darkness, [20]an
instructor of the foolish, a teacher of babes,
having the form of knowledge and truth in the

2:6–10 Although Scripture everywhere teaches that salvation is not on the basis of works (4:1–4; Eph. 2:8,9), it consistently teaches that God's judgment is always on the basis of a man's deeds (Is. 3:10,11; Jer. 17:10; John 5:28,29; 1 Cor. 3:8; 2 Cor. 5:10; Gal. 6:7–9; Rom. 14:12). Paul describes the deeds of two distinct groups: the redeemed (vv. 7,10) and the unredeemed (vv. 8,9). The deeds of the redeemed are not the basis of their salvation but the evidence of it. They are not perfect and are prone to sin, but there is undeniable evidence of righteousness in their lives (James 2:14–20,26).

2:11 partiality. Literally, "to receive a face," that is, to give consideration to someone simply because of his position, wealth, influence, popularity, or appearance. Because it is God's nature to be just, it is impossible for Him to be anything but impartial (Acts 10:34; Gal. 2:6; Eph. 6:7,8; Col. 3:25; 1 Pet. 1:17).

law. [21]You, therefore, who teach another, do
you not teach yourself? You who preach that a
man should not steal, do you steal? [22]You who
say, "Do not commit adultery," do you commit
adultery? You who abhor idols, do you rob temples? [23]You who make your boast in the law, do
you dishonor God through breaking the law?
[24]For *"the name of God is blasphemed among
the Gentiles because of you,"* as it is written.
[25]For circumcision is indeed profitable if you
keep the law; but if you are a breaker of the law,
your circumcision has become uncircumcision.
[26]Therefore, if an uncircumcised man keeps
the righteous requirements of the law, will not
his uncircumcision be counted as circumcision? [27]And will not the physically uncircumcised, if he fulfills the law, judge you who, *even*
with *your* written *code* and circumcision, *are* a
transgressor of the law? [28]For he is not a Jew
who *is one* outwardly, nor *is* circumcision that
which *is* outward in the flesh; [29]but *he is* a Jew
who *is one* inwardly; and circumcision *is that* of
the heart, in the Spirit, not in the letter; whose
praise *is* not from men but from God.

DAY 31: Why isn't God directly mentioned in Esther?

The question naturally arises when reading the book. Even the usual clues about God's presence seem absent. No one refers to the Law of God, sacrifices, worship, or prayer. God does not appear to receive public or private recognition for the preservation of the Jews. When it comes to God, Esther seems strangely silent.

In fact, the silence is so obvious that it becomes an argument. Esther challenges the tendency to demand that God prove His power and presence. Must God be apparent? All too quickly we expect God to demonstrate in unmistakable ways His identity. Yet God has repeatedly resisted human ultimatums. God reveals Himself for His own purposes, not human requirements.

Throughout history, God has more readily operated behind the scenes than in plain sight. The Scriptures are filled with unusual circumstances in which God worked obviously. But Esther comes close to revealing God's standard procedure. God's fingerprints are all over Esther's story. His superficial absence points to a deeper presence. God chose to be subtle, but He was there. The events in Esther give us a model for hope when God works in less than obvious ways in our lives.

AUGUST 1

Esther 3:1–4:17

3 After these things King Ahasuerus promoted Haman, the son of Hammedatha the
Agagite, and advanced him and set his seat
above all the princes who *were* with him. 2And
all the king's servants who *were* within the
king's gate bowed and paid homage to Haman,
for so the king had commanded concerning
him. But Mordecai would not bow or pay homage. 3Then the king's servants who *were* within the king's gate said to Mordecai, "Why do
you transgress the king's command?" 4Now it
happened, when they spoke to him daily and he
would not listen to them, that they told *it* to
Haman, to see whether Mordecai's words
would stand; for *Mordecai* had told them that he
was a Jew. 5When Haman saw that Mordecai did
not bow or pay him homage, Haman was filled
with wrath. 6But he disdained to lay hands on
Mordecai alone, for they had told him of the
people of Mordecai. Instead, Haman sought to
destroy all the Jews who *were* throughout the
whole kingdom of Ahasuerus—the people of
Mordecai.

7In the first month, which is the month of
Nisan, in the twelfth year of King Ahasuerus,
they cast Pur (that *is,* the lot), before Haman to
determine the day and the month, until *it fell on*
the twelfth *month,* which *is* the month of Adar.

8Then Haman said to King Ahasuerus,
"There is a certain people scattered and dispersed among the people in all the provinces of
your kingdom; their laws *are* different from all
other people's, and they do not keep the king's
laws. Therefore it *is* not fitting for the king to let
them remain. 9If it pleases the king, let *a decree*
be written that they be destroyed, and I will pay
ten thousand talents of silver into the hands of
those who do the work, to bring *it* into the
king's treasuries."

10So the king took his signet ring from his
hand and gave it to Haman, the son of
Hammedatha the Agagite, the enemy of the
Jews. 11And the king said to Haman, "The
money and the people *are* given to you, to do
with them as seems good to you."

12Then the king's scribes were called on the
thirteenth day of the first month, and *a decree*
was written according to all that Haman commanded—to the king's satraps, to the governors
who *were* over each province, to the officials of
all people, to every province according to its
script, and to every people in their language. In
the name of King Ahasuerus it was written, and
sealed with the king's signet ring. 13And the letters were sent by couriers into all the king's
provinces, to destroy, to kill, and to annihilate all
the Jews, both young and old, little children
and women, in one day, on the thirteenth *day* of
the twelfth month, which *is* the month of Adar,
and to plunder their possessions. 14A copy of
the document was to be issued as law in every
province, being published for all people, that
they should be ready for that day. 15The couriers went out, hastened by the king's command;
and the decree was proclaimed in Shushan the
citadel. So the king and Haman sat down to
drink, but the city of Shushan was perplexed.

4 When Mordecai learned all that had happened, he tore his clothes and put on sackcloth and ashes, and went out into the midst of
the city. He cried out with a loud and bitter
cry. 2He went as far as the front of the king's
gate, for no one *might* enter the king's gate
clothed with sackcloth. 3And in every province
where the king's command and decree
arrived, *there was* great mourning among the
Jews, with fasting, weeping, and wailing; and
many lay in sackcloth and ashes.

4So Esther's maids and eunuchs came and
told her, and the queen was deeply distressed.
Then she sent garments to clothe Mordecai and
take his sackcloth away from him, but he would
not accept *them.* 5Then Esther called Hathach,
one of the king's eunuchs whom he had appointed to attend her, and she gave him a command
concerning Mordecai, to learn what and why
this *was.* 6So Hathach went out to Mordecai in
the city square that *was* in front of the king's
gate. 7And Mordecai told him all that had happened to him, and the sum of money that
Haman had promised to pay into the king's
treasuries to destroy the Jews. 8He also gave him
a copy of the written decree for their destruction, which was given at Shushan, that he might
show it to Esther and explain it to her, and that
he might command her to go in to the king to
make supplication to him and plead before him
for her people. 9So Hathach returned and told
Esther the words of Mordecai.

3:4 he *was* a Jew. It seems evident from Haman's fury and attempted genocide that there were strong anti-Semitic attitudes in Shushan, which seems to explain Mordecai's reluctance to reveal his true ethnic background.

[10]Then Esther spoke to Hathach, and gave him a command for Mordecai: [11]"All the king's servants and the people of the king's provinces know that any man or woman who goes into the inner court to the king, who has not been called, *he has* but one law: put *all* to death, except the one to whom the king holds out the golden scepter, that he may live. Yet I myself have not been called to go in to the king these thirty days." [12]So they told Mordecai Esther's words.

[13]And Mordecai told *them* to answer Esther: "Do not think in your heart that you will escape in the king's palace any more than all the other Jews. [14]For if you remain completely silent at this time, relief and deliverance will arise for the Jews from another place, but you and your father's house will perish. Yet who knows whether you have come to the kingdom for *such* a time as this?"

4:14 relief and deliverance. Mordecai exhibited a healthy faith in God's sovereign power to preserve His people. He may have remembered the Lord's promise to Abraham (Gen. 12:3; 17:1–8). **you...will perish.** Mordecai indicated that Esther would not escape the sentence or be overlooked because of her prominence (4:13). ***such* a time as this.** Mordecai indirectly appealed to God's providential timing.

[15]Then Esther told *them* to reply to Mordecai: [16]"Go, gather all the Jews who are present in Shushan, and fast for me; neither eat nor drink for three days, night or day. My maids and I will fast likewise. And so I will go to the king, which *is* against the law; and if I perish, I perish!"

[17]So Mordecai went his way and did according to all that Esther commanded him.

Psalm 89:46–52

46 How long, LORD?
Will You hide Yourself forever?
Will Your wrath burn like fire?
47 Remember how short my time is;
For what futility have You created all
the children of men?
48 What man can live and not see death?
Can he deliver his life from the power
of the grave? Selah
49 Lord, where *are* Your former
lovingkindnesses,
Which You swore to David in Your truth?

89:46 hide Yourself forever. By God's seeming refusal to answer prayer and restore the Davidic kingship, it seemed as though God was hiding Himself. Of course, the discipline of disobedient kings had been foretold (v. 32). According to the prophets, God would eventually restore Israel and the Davidic throne in an earthly kingdom (Hos. 3:4,5). Never in the Old Testament is there a sense that this Davidic promise would be fulfilled by Christ with a spiritual and heavenly reign.

50 Remember, Lord, the reproach of Your
servants—
How I bear in my bosom *the reproach of*
all the many peoples,
51 With which Your enemies have
reproached, O LORD,
With which they have reproached the
footsteps of Your anointed.

52 Blessed *be* the LORD forevermore!
Amen and Amen.

Proverbs 22:7–8

7 The rich rules over the poor,
And the borrower *is* servant to the
lender.

8 He who sows iniquity will reap sorrow,
And the rod of his anger will fail.

Romans 3:1–31

3 What advantage then has the Jew, or what
is the profit of circumcision? [2]Much in
every way! Chiefly because to them were committed the oracles of God. [3]For what if some
did not believe? Will their unbelief make the
faithfulness of God without effect? [4]Certainly
not! Indeed, let God be true but every man a
liar. As it is written:

"That You may be justified in Your words,
And may overcome when You are
judged."

[5]But if our unrighteousness demonstrates
the righteousness of God, what shall we say?
Is God unjust who inflicts wrath? (I speak as a
man.) [6]Certainly not! For then how will God
judge the world?

[7]For if the truth of God has increased
through my lie to His glory, why am I also still
judged as a sinner? [8]And *why* not *say,* "Let us
do evil that good may come"?—as we are slan-
derously reported and as some affirm that we
say. Their condemnation is just.

3:2 oracles. This Greek word is *logoin,* a diminutive form of the common New Testament word *logos,* which is normally translated "word." These are important sayings or messages, especially supernatural ones. Here Paul uses the word to encompass the entire Old Testament—the Jews received the very words of the true God (Deut. 4:1,2; 6:1,2; Mark 12:24; Luke 16:29; John 5:39). The Jews had a great advantage in having the Old Testament, because it contained the truth about salvation (2 Tim. 3:15) and about the gospel in its basic form (Gal. 3:8). When Paul said "preach the Word" (2 Tim. 4:2), he meant the "oracles of God" (1 Pet. 4:11) recorded in Scripture.

3:11 none...understands. Man is unable to comprehend the truth of God or grasp His standard of righteousness (Pss. 14:2; 53:3; 1 Cor. 2:14). Sadly, his spiritual ignorance does not result from a lack of opportunity, but is an expression of his depravity and rebellion (Eph. 4:18). **none...seeks.** This verse clearly implies that the world's false religions are fallen man's attempts to escape the true God—not to seek Him. Man's natural tendency is to seek his own interests (Phil. 2:21), but his only hope is for God to seek him (John 6:37,44). It is only as a result of God's work in the heart that anyone seeks Him (Ps. 16:8; Matt. 6:33).

9 What then? Are we better *than they?* Not at
all. For we have previously charged both Jews
and Greeks that they are all under sin.
10 As it is written:

"There is none righteous, no, not one;
11 *There is none who understands;*
There is none who seeks after God.
12 *They have all turned aside;*
They have together become
unprofitable;
There is none who does good, no,
not one."
13 *"Their throat is an open tomb;*
With their tongues they have practiced
deceit";
"The poison of asps is under their lips";
14 *"Whose mouth is full of cursing and*
bitterness."
15 *"Their feet are swift to shed blood;*
16 *Destruction and misery are in*
their ways;
17 *And the way of peace they have*
not known."
18 *"There is no fear of God before*
their eyes."

19 Now we know that whatever the law says, it
says to those who are under the law, that every
mouth may be stopped, and all the world may
become guilty before God. 20 Therefore by the
deeds of the law no flesh will be justified in His
sight, for by the law *is* the knowledge of sin.
21 But now the righteousness of God apart
from the law is revealed, being witnessed by
the Law and the Prophets, 22 even the righteousness of God, through faith in Jesus Christ,
to all and on all who believe. For there is no difference; 23 for all have sinned and fall short of
the glory of God, 24 being justified freely by His
grace through the redemption that is in Christ
Jesus, 25 whom God set forth *as* a propitiation by
His blood, through faith, to demonstrate His
righteousness, because in His forbearance God
had passed over the sins that were previously
committed, 26 to demonstrate at the present time
His righteousness, that He might be just and
the justifier of the one who has faith in Jesus.
27 Where *is* boasting then? It is excluded. By
what law? Of works? No, but by the law of
faith. 28 Therefore we conclude that a man is
justified by faith apart from the deeds of the
law. 29 Or *is He* the God of the Jews only? *Is He*
not also the God of the Gentiles? Yes, of the
Gentiles also, 30 since *there is* one God who will
justify the circumcised by faith and the uncircumcised through faith. 31 Do we then make
void the law through faith? Certainly not! On
the contrary, we establish the law.

DAY 1: As sinners, how are we justified before God?

In Romans 3:24, the verb "justified" is a legal or forensic term that comes from the Greek word for "righteous" and means "to declare righteous." This verdict includes pardon from the guilt and penalty of sin and the imputation of Christ's righteousness to the believer's account, which provides for the positive righteousness man needs to be accepted by God. God declares a sinner righteous solely on the basis of the merits of Christ's righteousness. God imputed a believer's sin to Christ's account in His sacrificial death (Is. 53:4,5; 1 Pet. 2:24), and He imputes Christ's perfect obedience to God's law to Christians (5:19; 1 Cor. 1:30; 2 Cor. 5:21; Phil. 3:9). The sinner receives this gift of

God's grace by faith alone (3:22, 25; 4:1–25). Sanctification, the work of God by which He makes righteous those whom He has already justified, is distinct from justification but without exception always follows it (8:30).

"Justified freely by His grace through the redemption that is in Christ Jesus." Justification is a gracious gift God extends to the repentant, believing sinner, wholly apart from human merit or work. The imagery behind the Greek word for "redemption" comes from the ancient slave market. It meant paying the necessary ransom to obtain the prisoner's or slave's release. The only adequate payment to redeem sinners from sin's slavery and its deserved punishment was "in Christ Jesus" (1 Tim. 2:6; 1 Pet. 1:18,19) and was paid to God to satisfy His justice.

"Whom God set forth as a propitiation by His blood" (v. 25). This great sacrifice was not accomplished in secret, but God publicly displayed His Son on Calvary for all to see. Crucial to the significance of Christ's sacrifice, a propitiation carries the idea of appeasement or satisfaction—in this case Christ's violent death satisfied the offended holiness and wrath of God against those for whom Christ died (Is. 53:11; Col. 2:11–14). The Hebrew equivalent of this word was used to describe the mercy seat—the cover to the ark of the covenant—where the high priest sprinkled the blood of the slaughtered animal on the Day of Atonement to make atonement for the sins of the people. In pagan religions, it is the worshiper—not the god—who is responsible to appease the wrath of the offended deity. But in reality, man is incapable of satisfying God's justice apart from Christ, except by spending eternity in hell.

AUGUST 2

Esther 5:1–6:14

5 Now it happened on the third day that Esther put on *her* royal *robes* and stood in the
inner court of the king's palace, across from
the king's house, while the king sat on his
royal throne in the royal house, facing the
entrance of the house. 2So it was, when the
king saw Queen Esther standing in the court,
that she found favor in his sight, and the king
held out to Esther the golden scepter that *was*
in his hand. Then Esther went near and
touched the top of the scepter.
3And the king said to her, "What do you
wish, Queen Esther? What *is* your request? It
shall be given to you—up to half the kingdom!"
4So Esther answered, "If it pleases the king,
let the king and Haman come today to the banquet that I have prepared for him."
5Then the king said, "Bring Haman quickly,
that he may do as Esther has said." So the
king and Haman went to the banquet that Esther had prepared.
6At the banquet of wine the king said to Esther, "What *is* your petition? It shall be granted you. What *is* your request, up to half the
kingdom? It shall be done!"
7Then Esther answered and said, "My petition and request *is this:* 8If I have found favor
in the sight of the king, and if it pleases the
king to grant my petition and fulfill my
request, then let the king and Haman come to
the banquet which I will prepare for them, and
tomorrow I will do as the king has said."
9So Haman went out that day joyful and with
a glad heart; but when Haman saw Mordecai in
the king's gate, and that he did not stand or
tremble before him, he was filled with indignation against Mordecai. 10Nevertheless Haman
restrained himself and went home, and he
sent and called for his friends and his wife
Zeresh. 11Then Haman told them of his great
riches, the multitude of his children, everything in which the king had promoted him,
and how he had advanced him above the officials and servants of the king.
12Moreover Haman said, "Besides, Queen
Esther invited no one but me to come in with
the king to the banquet that she prepared; and
tomorrow I am again invited by her, along
with the king. 13Yet all this avails me nothing,
so long as I see Mordecai the Jew sitting at the
king's gate."
14Then his wife Zeresh and all his friends said
to him, "Let a gallows be made, fifty cubits high,
and in the morning suggest to the king that
Mordecai be hanged on it; then go merrily with
the king to the banquet."
And the thing pleased Haman; so he had the
gallows made.

6 That night the king could not sleep. So one
was commanded to bring the book of the
records of the chronicles; and they were read
before the king. 2And it was found written that
Mordecai had told of Bigthana and Teresh, two
of the king's eunuchs, the doorkeepers who
had sought to lay hands on King Ahasuerus.
3Then the king said, "What honor or dignity has
been bestowed on Mordecai for this?"
And the king's servants who attended him
said, "Nothing has been done for him."

6:1 the book. Five years had intervened since Mordecai's loyal but as yet unrewarded act (2:23). At exactly the proper moment, God providentially intervened so that the king suffered insomnia, called for the book of records, read of Mordecai's unrewarded deeds 5 years past, and then desired to reward him (Dan. 6:18).

4So the king said, "Who *is* in the court?"
Now Haman had *just* entered the outer court
of the king's palace to suggest that the king
hang Mordecai on the gallows that he had prepared for him.
5The king's servants said to him, "Haman is
there, standing in the court."
And the king said, "Let him come in."
6So Haman came in, and the king asked
him, "What shall be done for the man whom
the king delights to honor?"
Now Haman thought in his heart, "Whom
would the king delight to honor more than
me?" 7And Haman answered the king, "*For* the
man whom the king delights to honor, 8let a
royal robe be brought which the king has
worn, and a horse on which the king has ridden, which has a royal crest placed on its
head. 9Then let this robe and horse be delivered to the hand of one of the king's most
noble princes, that he may array the man
whom the king delights to honor. Then parade
him on horseback through the city square,
and proclaim before him: 'Thus shall it be
done to the man whom the king delights to
honor!' "
10Then the king said to Haman, "Hurry, take
the robe and the horse, as you have suggested,
and do so for Mordecai the Jew who sits within the king's gate! Leave nothing undone of all
that you have spoken."
11So Haman took the robe and the horse,
arrayed Mordecai and led him on horseback
through the city square, and proclaimed
before him, "Thus shall it be done to the man
whom the king delights to honor!"
12Afterward Mordecai went back to the
king's gate. But Haman hurried to his house,
mourning and with his head covered. 13When
Haman told his wife Zeresh and all his friends
everything that had happened to him, his wise
men and his wife Zeresh said to him, "If
Mordecai, before whom you have begun to
fall, is of Jewish descent, you will not prevail
against him but will surely fall before him."
14While they *were* still talking with him, the
king's eunuchs came, and hastened to bring
Haman to the banquet which Esther had prepared.

6:13 you have begun to fall. Neither divine prophecy (Ex. 17:14) nor biblical history (1 Sam. 15:8,9) stood in Haman's favor. Haman's entourage seemed to have some knowledge of this biblical history.

Psalm 90:1–6

A Prayer of Moses the man of God.

Lord, You have been our dwelling
place in all generations.
2 Before the mountains were brought
forth,
Or ever You had formed the earth and
the world,
Even from everlasting to everlasting,
You *are* God.

3 You turn man to destruction,
And say, "Return, O children
of men."

90:Title. Moses the man of God. Moses the prophet (Deut. 18:15–22) was unique in that the Lord knew him "face to face" (Deut. 34:10–12). "Man of God" (Deut. 33:1) is a technical term used over 70 times in the Old Testament, always referring to one who spoke for God. It is used of Timothy in the New Testament (1 Tim. 6:11; 2 Tim. 3:17).

90:3 You turn man to destruction. The unusual word for destruction has the idea of crushed matter. Though different from the "dust" of Genesis 3:19, this phrase is no doubt a reference to that passage. Humanity lives under a sovereign decree of death and cannot escape it.

4 For a thousand years in
Your sight
Are like yesterday when it is past,
And *like* a watch in the night.
5 You carry them away *like* a flood;
They are like a sleep.
In the morning they are like grass
which grows up:
6 In the morning it flourishes and
grows up;

In the evening it is cut down and
withers.

Proverbs 22:9

9 He who has a generous eye will be
blessed,
For he gives of his bread to
the poor.

Romans 4:1–25

4 What then shall we say that Abraham our
father has found according to the flesh?
[2]For if Abraham was justified by works, he has
something to boast about, but not before God.
[3]For what does the Scripture say? *"Abraham
believed God, and it was accounted to him for
righteousness."* [4]Now to him who works, the
wages are not counted as grace but as debt.

4:3 A quotation of Genesis 15:6, one of the clearest statements in all Scripture about justification. **believed.** Abraham was a man of faith (1:16; 4:18–21; Gal. 3:6,7,9; Heb. 11:8–10). But faith is not a meritorious work. It is never the ground of justification—it is simply the channel through which it is received and it, too, is a gift. **accounted.** vv. 5,9,10,22. Also translated "imputed" (vv. 6,8,11,23,24). Used in both financial and legal settings, this Greek word means to take something that belongs to someone and credit to another's account. It is a one-sided transaction—Abraham did nothing to accumulate it; God simply credited it to him. God took His own righteousness and credited it to Abraham as if it were actually his. This God did because Abraham believed in Him.

[5]But to him who does not work but believes
on Him who justifies the ungodly, his faith is
accounted for righteousness, [6]just as David
also describes the blessedness of the man to
whom God imputes righteousness apart from
works:

7 *"Blessed are those whose lawless deeds
are forgiven,
And whose sins are covered;*
8 *Blessed is the man to whom the* L*ORD*
shall not impute sin."

[9]*Does* this blessedness then *come* upon the circumcised *only,* or upon the uncircumcised also?
For we say that faith was accounted to Abraham
for righteousness. [10]How then was it accounted?
While he was circumcised, or uncircumcised?
Not while circumcised, but while uncircumcised. [11]And he received the sign of circumcision, a seal of the righteousness of the faith
which *he had while still* uncircumcised, that he
might be the father of all those who believe,
though they are uncircumcised, that righteousness might be imputed to them also,
[12]and the father of circumcision to those who not
only *are* of the circumcision, but who also walk
in the steps of the faith which our father Abraham *had while still* uncircumcised.

4:11,12 the father of all those who believe. Racially, Abraham is the father of all Jews (circumcised); spiritually, he is the father of both believing Jews (v. 12) and believing Gentiles (uncircumcised; v. 11).

[13]For the promise that he would be the heir
of the world *was* not to Abraham or to his seed
through the law, but through the righteousness of faith. [14]For if those who are of the law
are heirs, faith is made void and the promise
made of no effect, [15]because the law brings
about wrath; for where there is no law *there is*
no transgression.
[16]Therefore *it is* of faith that *it might be* according to grace, so that the promise might be sure
to all the seed, not only to those who are of the
law, but also to those who are of the faith of
Abraham, who is the father of us all [17](as it is
written, *"I have made you a father of many
nations"*) in the presence of Him whom he
believed—God, who gives life to the dead and
calls those things which do not exist as though
they did; [18]who, contrary to hope, in hope
believed, so that he became the father of many
nations, according to what was spoken, *"So
shall your descendants be."* [19]And not being
weak in faith, he did not consider his own body,
already dead (since he was about a hundred
years old), and the deadness of Sarah's womb.
[20]He did not waver at the promise of God
through unbelief, but was strengthened in faith,
giving glory to God, [21]and being fully convinced
that what He had promised He was also able to
perform. [22]And therefore *"it was accounted to
him for righteousness."*
[23]Now it was not written for his sake alone
that it was imputed to him, [24]but also for us. It
shall be imputed to us who believe in Him who
raised up Jesus our Lord from the dead, [25]who
was delivered up because of our offenses, and
was raised because of our justification.

DAY 2: Why do Esther and Mordecai appear so secular in their lifestyles?

In contrast to their near contemporaries Ezra, Nehemiah, and Daniel, the central people in Esther seem worldly. The lack of references to God is most obvious in Esther and Mordecai's conversations. Are these all subtle indications that Esther and Mordecai were people whose faith had little or no effect on their daily lives?

The Book of Esther does not settle this question. There are several important factors, however, that might hold us back from jumping to conclusions about Esther and Mordecai. Primary among these is the fact that the book has a limited scope. Only a few key events are recorded. Few if any details of the inner life of either main character are revealed. Yet the integrity of their actions ought to incline us toward giving them the benefit of the doubt when it comes to faith (4:13–16).

Here are a few other considerations regarding this question: 1) While Mordecai's caution about announcing his and Esther's heritage publicly might be questioned, it must also be pointed out that others were also cautious about this same matter (Neh. 2:1–8 makes no mention of God in Nehemiah's conversation with Artaxerxes); 2) Public events such as Passover had fallen out of practice during the captivity, meaning that there were fewer occasions in which faith was practiced in the open (this doesn't mean however that the Jews were not a marked people, since they could be identified for the purpose of Haman's law); 3) When it was appropriate, Esther did openly identify her Jewish heritage (7:3,4). These considerations do not remove the charge that Esther and Mordecai seem less devoted to God than, for example, Daniel. But the fact that God did work out His purposes in their lives comes through clearly in the book.

AUGUST 3

Esther 7:1–8:17

7 So the king and Haman went to dine with
Queen Esther. 2And on the second day, at
the banquet of wine, the king again said to Esther, "What *is* your petition, Queen Esther? It shall be granted you. And what *is* your request, up to half the kingdom? It shall be done!"
3Then Queen Esther answered and said, "If I have found favor in your sight, O king, and if it pleases the king, let my life be given me at my petition, and my people at my request. 4For we have been sold, my people and I, to be destroyed, to be killed, and to be annihilated. Had we been sold as male and female slaves, I would have held my tongue, although the enemy could never compensate for the king's loss."
5So King Ahasuerus answered and said to Queen Esther, "Who is he, and where is he, who would dare presume in his heart to do such a thing?"
6And Esther said, "The adversary and enemy *is* this wicked Haman!"
So Haman was terrified before the king and queen.
7Then the king arose in his wrath from the banquet of wine *and went* into the palace garden; but Haman stood before Queen Esther, pleading for his life, for he saw that evil was determined against him by the king. 8When the king returned from the palace garden to the place of the banquet of wine, Haman had fallen across the couch where Esther *was.* Then the king said, "Will he also assault the queen while I *am* in the house?"
As the word left the king's mouth, they covered Haman's face. 9Now Harbonah, one of the eunuchs, said to the king, "Look! The gallows, fifty cubits high, which Haman made for Mordecai, who spoke good on the king's behalf, is standing at the house of Haman."
Then the king said, "Hang him on it!"
10So they hanged Haman on the gallows that he had prepared for Mordecai. Then the king's wrath subsided.

8 On that day King Ahasuerus gave Queen
Esther the house of Haman, the enemy of the Jews. And Mordecai came before the king, for Esther had told how he *was related* to her.
2So the king took off his signet ring, which he had taken from Haman, and gave it to Mordecai; and Esther appointed Mordecai over the house of Haman.

8:1 the house of Haman. Property of a traitor by Persian custom returned to the king. In this case, he gave it to his queen, Esther, who put Mordecai over it (8:2). The outcome for Haman's wife, Zeresh, and his wise men is unknown (5:14; 6:12,13). Haman's 10 sons later died (9:7–10).

[3]Now Esther spoke again to the king, fell down at his feet, and implored him with tears to counteract the evil of Haman the Agagite, and the scheme which he had devised against the Jews. [4]And the king held out the golden scepter toward Esther. So Esther arose and stood before the king, [5]and said, "If it pleases the king, and if I have found favor in his sight and the thing *seems* right to the king and I am pleasing in his eyes, let it be written to revoke the letters devised by Haman, the son of Hammedatha the Agagite, which he wrote to annihilate the Jews who *are* in all the king's provinces. [6]For how can I endure to see the evil that will come to my people? Or how can I endure to see the destruction of my countrymen?"

[7]Then King Ahasuerus said to Queen Esther and Mordecai the Jew, "Indeed, I have given Esther the house of Haman, and they have hanged him on the gallows because he *tried to* lay his hand on the Jews. [8]You yourselves write *a decree* concerning the Jews, as you please, in the king's name, and seal *it* with the king's signet ring; for whatever is written in the king's name and sealed with the king's signet ring no one can revoke."

[9]So the king's scribes were called at that time, in the third month, which *is* the month of Sivan, on the twenty-third *day;* and it was written, according to all that Mordecai commanded, to the Jews, the satraps, the governors, and the princes of the provinces from India to Ethiopia, one hundred and twenty-seven provinces *in all,* to every province in its own script, to every people in their own language, and to the Jews in their own script and language. [10]And he wrote in the name of King Ahasuerus, sealed *it* with the king's signet ring, and sent letters by couriers on horseback, riding on royal horses bred from swift steeds.

[11]By these letters the king permitted the Jews who *were* in every city to gather together and protect their lives—to destroy, kill, and annihilate all the forces of any people or province that would assault them, *both* little children and women, and to plunder their possessions, [12]on one day in all the provinces of King Ahasuerus, on the thirteenth *day* of the twelfth month, which *is* the month of Adar. [13]A copy of the document was to be issued as a decree in every province and published for all people, so that the Jews would be ready on that day to avenge themselves on their enemies. [14]The couriers who rode on royal horses went out, hastened and pressed on by the king's command. And the decree was issued in Shushan the citadel.

[15]So Mordecai went out from the presence of the king in royal apparel of blue and white, with a great crown of gold and a garment of fine linen and purple; and the city of Shushan rejoiced and was glad. [16]The Jews had light and gladness, joy and honor. [17]And in every province and city, wherever the king's command and decree came, the Jews had joy and gladness, a feast and a holiday. Then many of the people of the land became Jews, because fear of the Jews fell upon them.

8:17 many...people...Jews. The population realized that the God of the Jews greatly exceeded anything that the pantheon of Persian deities could offer (Ex. 15:14–16; Ps. 105:38; Acts 5:11), especially in contrast to their recent defeat by the Greeks.

Psalm 90:7–17

7 For we have been consumed by Your anger,
And by Your wrath we are terrified.
8 You have set our iniquities before You,
Our secret *sins* in the light of Your countenance.
9 For all our days have passed away in Your wrath;
We finish our years like a sigh.
10 The days of our lives *are* seventy years;
And if by reason of strength *they are* eighty years,
Yet their boast *is* only labor and sorrow;
For it is soon cut off, and we fly away.
11 Who knows the power of Your anger?
For as the fear of You, *so is* Your wrath.
12 So teach *us* to number our days,
That we may gain a heart of wisdom.

13 Return, O LORD!
How long?
And have compassion on Your servants.
14 Oh, satisfy us early with Your mercy,
That we may rejoice and be glad all our days!
15 Make us glad according to the days *in which* You have afflicted us,
The years *in which* we have seen evil.
16 Let Your work appear to Your servants,
And Your glory to their children.
17 And let the beauty of the LORD our God be upon us,

90:12 number our days. Evaluate the use of time in light of the brevity of life. **heart of wisdom.** Wisdom repudiates autonomy and focuses on the Lord's sovereignty and revelation.

90:17 the beauty of the LORD. The Lord's beauty implies His delight, approval, and favor. **establish the work of our hands.** By God's mercy and grace, one's life can have value, significance, and meaning (1 Cor. 15:58).

And establish the work of our hands
for us;
Yes, establish the work of our hands.

Proverbs 22:10–11

10 Cast out the scoffer, and contention
will leave;
Yes, strife and reproach will cease.

11 He who loves purity of heart
And has grace on his lips,
The king *will be* his friend.

Romans 5:1–21

5 Therefore, having been justified by faith,
we have peace with God through our Lord
Jesus Christ, 2through whom also we have
access by faith into this grace in which we
stand, and rejoice in hope of the glory of God.
3And not only *that,* but we also glory in tribulations, knowing that tribulation produces perseverance; 4and perseverance, character; and
character, hope. 5Now hope does not disap-
point, because the love of God has been
poured out in our hearts by the Holy Spirit
who was given to us.
6For when we were still without strength, in
due time Christ died for the ungodly. 7For
scarcely for a righteous man will one die; yet
perhaps for a good man someone would even
dare to die. 8But God demonstrates His own
love toward us, in that while we were still sinners, Christ died for us. 9Much more then,
having now been justified by His blood, we
shall be saved from wrath through Him. 10For
if when we were enemies we were reconciled
to God through the death of His Son, much
more, having been reconciled, we shall be
saved by His life. 11And not only *that,* but we
also rejoice in God through our Lord Jesus
Christ, through whom we have now received
the reconciliation.
12Therefore, just as through one man sin
entered the world, and death through sin, and

5:3 tribulations. A word used for pressure, like that of a press squeezing the fluid from olives or grapes. Here they are not the normal pressures of living (8:35), but the inevitable troubles that come to followers of Christ because of their relationship with Him (Matt. 5:10–12; John 15:20; 2 Cor. 4:17; 1 Thess. 3:3; 2 Tim. 3:12; 1 Pet. 4:19). Such difficulties produce rich spiritual benefits (vv. 3,4). **perseverance.** Sometimes translated "patience," this word refers to endurance, the ability to remain under tremendous weight and pressure without succumbing (15:5; Col. 1:22,23; 2 Thess. 1:4; Rev. 14:12).

5:4 character. A better translation is "proven character." The Greek word simply means "proof." It was used of testing metals to determine their purity. Here the proof is Christian character (James 1:12). Christians can glory in tribulations because of what those troubles produce.

5:5 love of God…poured out. God's love for us (v. 8) has been lavishly poured out to the point of overflowing within our hearts. Paul moves from the objective aspects of our security in Christ to the internal, more subjective. God has implanted within our hearts evidence that we belong to Him in that we love the One who first loved us. **Spirit who was given.** A marvelous testimony to God's love for us.

thus death spread to all men, because all
sinned— 13(For until the law sin was in the
world, but sin is not imputed when there is no
law. 14Nevertheless death reigned from Adam to
Moses, even over those who had not sinned
according to the likeness of the transgression of
Adam, who is a type of Him who was to come.
15But the free gift *is* not like the offense. For if by
the one man's offense many died, much more
the grace of God and the gift by the grace of the
one Man, Jesus Christ, abounded to many.
16And the gift *is* not like *that which came* through
the one who sinned. For the judgment *which
came* from one *offense resulted* in condemnation,
but the free gift *which came* from many offenses
resulted in justification. 17For if by the one man's
offense death reigned through the one, much
more those who receive abundance of grace
and of the gift of righteousness will reign in life
through the One, Jesus Christ.)
18Therefore, as through one man's offense
judgment came to all men, resulting in

condemnation, even so through one Man's
righteous act *the free gift came* to all men, resulting in justification of life. [19]For as by one man's
disobedience many were made sinners, so also
by one Man's obedience many will be made
righteous.
[20]Moreover the law entered that the offense
might abound. But where sin abounded, grace
abounded much more, [21]so that as sin reigned
in death, even so grace might reign through
righteousness to eternal life through Jesus
Christ our Lord.

DAY 3: What are the results of being justified by faith?

Having proven that God justifies sinners on the basis of faith alone, Paul now counters the notion that, although believers receive salvation by faith, they will preserve it by good works (Rom. 5:1–11). He argues that they are bound eternally to Jesus Christ, preserved by His power and not by human effort (Is. 11:5; Ps. 36:5; Lam. 3:23; Eph. 1:18–20; 2 Tim. 2:13; Heb. 10:23). "Having been justified by faith" (v. 1). The Greek construction—and its English translation—underscores that justification is a one-time legal declaration with continuing results, not an ongoing process. "We have peace with God." Not a subjective, internal sense of calm and serenity, but an external, objective reality. God has declared Himself to be at war with every human being because of man's sinful rebellion against Him and His laws (v. 10; 1:18; 8:7; Ex. 22:24; Deut. 32:21, 22; Ps. 7:11; John 3:36; Eph. 5:6). But the first great result of justification is that the sinner's war with God is ended forever (Col. 1:21,22). Scripture refers to the end of this conflict as a person's being reconciled to God (vv. 10,11; 2 Cor. 5:18–20).

"Through whom also we have access by faith" (v. 2). Used only twice elsewhere in the New Testament (Eph. 2:18; 3:12), this word always refers to the believer's access to God through Jesus Christ. What was unthinkable to the Old Testament Jew is now available to all who come (Jer. 32:38,40; Heb. 4:16; 10:19–22; Matt. 27:51). "Grace in which we stand." This refers to the permanent, secure position believers enjoy in God's grace (v. 10; 8:31–34; John 6:37; Phil. 1:6; 2 Tim. 1:12; Jude 24). "And rejoice in hope of the glory of God." Unlike the English word "hope," the New Testament word contains no uncertainty. It speaks of something that is certain, but not yet realized. The believer's ultimate destiny is to share in the very glory of God (8:29,30; John 17:22; 2 Cor. 3:18; Phil. 3:20,21; 1 John 3:1,2), and that hope will be realized because Christ Himself secures it (1 Tim. 1:1). Without the clear and certain promises of the Word of God, the believer would have no basis for hope (15:4; Ps. 119:81,114; Eph. 2:12; Jer. 14:8).

AUGUST 4

Esther 9:1–10:3

9 Now in the twelfth month, that *is,* the
month of Adar, on the thirteenth day, *the
time* came for the king's command and his
decree to be executed. On the day that the

9:1 twelfth month. During the period February-March. Here is a powerful statement with regard to God's providential preservation of the Jewish race in harmony with God's unconditional promise to Abraham (Gen. 17:1–8). This providential deliverance stands in contrast to God's miraculous deliverance of the Jews from Egypt; yet in both cases the same end had been accomplished by the supernatural power of God.

enemies of the Jews had hoped to overpower
them, the opposite occurred, in that the Jews
themselves overpowered those who hated
them. [2]The Jews gathered together in their
cities throughout all the provinces of King
Ahasuerus to lay hands on those who sought
their harm. And no one could withstand them,
because fear of them fell upon all people. [3]And
all the officials of the provinces, the satraps,
the governors, and all those doing the king's
work, helped the Jews, because the fear of
Mordecai fell upon them. [4]For Mordecai *was*
great in the king's palace, and his fame spread
throughout all the provinces; for this man
Mordecai became increasingly prominent.
[5]Thus the Jews defeated all their enemies with
the stroke of the sword, with slaughter and
destruction, and did what they pleased with
those who hated them.
[6]And in Shushan the citadel the Jews killed
and destroyed five hundred men. [7]Also
Parshandatha, Dalphon, Aspatha, [8]Poratha,
Adalia, Aridatha, [9]Parmashta, Arisai, Aridai,
and Vajezatha— [10]the ten sons of Haman the
son of Hammedatha, the enemy of the Jews—

they killed; but they did not lay a hand on the plunder.

11On that day the number of those who were killed in Shushan the citadel was brought to the king. 12And the king said to Queen Esther, "The Jews have killed and destroyed five hundred men in Shushan the citadel, and the ten sons of Haman. What have they done in the rest of the king's provinces? Now what *is* your petition? It shall be granted to you. Or what *is* your further request? It shall be done."

13Then Esther said, "If it pleases the king, let it be granted to the Jews who *are* in Shushan to do again tomorrow according to today's decree, and let Haman's ten sons be hanged on the gallows."

14So the king commanded this to be done; the decree was issued in Shushan, and they hanged Haman's ten sons.

15And the Jews who *were* in Shushan gathered together again on the fourteenth day of the month of Adar and killed three hundred men at Shushan; but they did not lay a hand on the plunder.

16The remainder of the Jews in the king's provinces gathered together and protected their lives, had rest from their enemies, and killed seventy-five thousand of their enemies; but they did not lay a hand on the plunder. 17*This was* on the thirteenth day of the month of Adar. And on the fourteenth of *the month* they rested and made it a day of feasting and gladness.

18But the Jews who *were* at Shushan assembled together on the thirteenth *day,* as well as on the fourteenth; and on the fifteenth of *the month* they rested, and made it a day of feasting and gladness. 19Therefore the Jews of the villages who dwelt in the unwalled towns celebrated the fourteenth day of the month of Adar *with* gladness and feasting, as a holiday, and for sending presents to one another.

20And Mordecai wrote these things and sent letters to all the Jews, near and far, who *were* in all the provinces of King Ahasuerus, 21to establish among them that they should celebrate yearly the fourteenth and fifteenth days of the month of Adar, 22as the days on which the Jews had rest from their enemies, as the month which was turned from sorrow to joy for them, and from mourning to a holiday; that they should make them days of feasting and joy, of sending presents to one another and gifts to the poor. 23So the Jews accepted the custom which they had begun, as Mordecai had written to them, 24because Haman, the son of Hammedatha the Agagite, the enemy of all the Jews, had plotted against the Jews to annihilate them, and had cast Pur (that *is,* the lot), to consume them and destroy them; 25but when *Esther* came before the king, he commanded by letter that this wicked plot which *Haman* had devised against the Jews should return on his own head, and that he and his sons should be hanged on the gallows.

26So they called these days Purim, after the name Pur. Therefore, because of all the words of this letter, what they had seen concerning this matter, and what had happened to them, 27the Jews established and imposed it upon themselves and their descendants and all who would join them, that without fail they should celebrate these two days every year, according to the written *instructions* and according to the *prescribed* time, 28*that* these days *should be* remembered and kept throughout every generation, every family, every province, and every city, that these days of Purim should not fail *to be observed* among the Jews, and *that* the memory of them should not perish among their descendants.

29Then Queen Esther, the daughter of Abihail, with Mordecai the Jew, wrote with full authority to confirm this second letter about Purim. 30And *Mordecai* sent letters to all the Jews, to the one hundred and twenty-seven provinces of the kingdom of Ahasuerus, *with* words of peace and truth, 31to confirm these days of Purim at their *appointed* time, as Mordecai the Jew and Queen Esther had prescribed for them, and as they had decreed for themselves and their descendants concerning matters of their fasting and lamenting. 32So the decree of Esther confirmed these matters of Purim, and it was written in the book.

10 And King Ahasuerus imposed tribute on the land and *on* the islands of the sea. 2Now all the acts of his power and his might, and the account of the greatness of Mordecai,

10:3 Mordecai...*was* second. Mordecai joined the top echelon of Jewish international statesmen like Joseph, who ranked second in the Egyptian dynasty (Gen. 41:37–45), and Daniel, who succeeded in both the Babylonian (Dan. 2:46–49; 5:29) and Medo-Persian Empires (Dan. 6:28). **speaking peace.** Less than 10 years later (ca. 465 B.C.), Ahasuerus was assassinated. There are no further details concerning Esther and Mordecai. What Mordecai did for less than a decade on behalf of Israel, Jesus Christ will do for all eternity as the Prince of Peace (Is. 9:6,7; Zech. 9:9,10).

to which the king advanced him, *are* they not
written in the book of the chronicles of the
kings of Media and Persia? 3For Mordecai the
Jew *was* second to King Ahasuerus, and was
great among the Jews and well received by the
multitude of his brethren, seeking the good of
his people and speaking peace to all his countrymen.

Psalm 91:1–6

He who dwells in the secret place
of the Most High
Shall abide under the shadow of the
Almighty.

91:1 secret place of the Most High. An intimate place of divine protection. The use of "Most High" for God emphasizes that no threat can ever overpower Him. **shadow of the Almighty.** In a land where the sun can be oppressive and dangerous, a "shadow" was understood as a metaphor for care and protection.

2 I will say of the LORD, "*He is* my refuge
and my fortress;
My God, in Him I will trust."
3 Surely He shall deliver you from the
snare of the fowler
And from the perilous pestilence.
4 He shall cover you with His feathers,
And under His wings you shall take
refuge;
His truth *shall be your* shield and
buckler.
5 You shall not be afraid of the terror by
night,
Nor of the arrow *that* flies by day,
6 *Nor* of the pestilence *that* walks in
darkness,
Nor of the destruction *that* lays waste
at noonday.

Proverbs 22:12

12 The eyes of the LORD preserve
knowledge,
But He overthrows the words of the
faithless.

Romans 6:1–23

6 What shall we say then? Shall we continue
in sin that grace may abound? 2Certainly
not! How shall we who died to sin live any
longer in it? 3Or do you not know that as many
of us as were baptized into Christ Jesus were
baptized into His death? 4Therefore we were
buried with Him through baptism into death,
that just as Christ was raised from the dead by
the glory of the Father, even so we also should
walk in newness of life.

5For if we have been united together in the
likeness of His death, certainly we also shall
be *in the likeness* of *His* resurrection, 6knowing
this, that our old man was crucified with *Him,*
that the body of sin might be done away with,
that we should no longer be slaves of sin. 7For
he who has died has been freed from sin.
8Now if we died with Christ, we believe that we
shall also live with Him, 9knowing that Christ,
having been raised from the dead, dies no
more. Death no longer has dominion over
Him. 10For *the death* that He died, He died to
sin once for all; but *the life* that He lives, He
lives to God. 11Likewise you also, reckon yourselves to be dead indeed to sin, but alive to
God in Christ Jesus our Lord.

12Therefore do not let sin reign in your mortal body, that you should obey it in its lusts.
13And do not present your members *as* instruments of unrighteousness to sin, but present
yourselves to God as being alive from the
dead, and your members as instruments of
righteousness to God. 14For sin shall not have
dominion over you, for you are not under law
but under grace.

15What then? Shall we sin because we are
not under law but under grace? Certainly not!
16Do you not know that to whom you present
yourselves slaves to obey, you are that one's
slaves whom you obey, whether of sin *leading*
to death, or of obedience *leading* to righteousness? 17But God be thanked that *though* you

6:3 baptized into Christ Jesus. This does not refer to water baptism. Paul is actually using the word "baptized" in a metaphorical sense, as we might in saying someone was immersed in his work or underwent his baptism of fire when experiencing some trouble. All Christians have, by placing saving faith in Him, been spiritually immersed into the Person Christ, that is, united and identified with Him (1 Cor. 6:17; 10:2; Gal. 3:27; 1 Pet. 3:21; 1 John 1:3; Acts 2:38). Certainly water baptism pictures this reality, which is the purpose—to show the transformation of the justified. **into His death.** This means that immersion or identification is specifically with Christ's death and resurrection.

were slaves of sin, yet you obeyed from the
heart that form of doctrine to which you were
delivered. 18And having been set free from sin,
you became slaves of righteousness. 19I speak
in human *terms* because of the weakness of
your flesh. For just as you presented your
members *as* slaves of uncleanness, and of lawlessness *leading* to *more* lawlessness, so now
present your members *as* slaves *of* righteousness for holiness.
20For when you were slaves of sin, you were
free in regard to righteousness. 21What fruit
did you have then in the things of which you
are now ashamed? For the end of those things
is death. 22But now having been set free from
sin, and having become slaves of God, you
have your fruit to holiness, and the end, everlasting life. 23For the wages of sin *is* death, but
the gift of God *is* eternal life in Christ Jesus our
Lord.

DAY 4: In verses such as Romans 5:12 and 6:23, to what kind of death is Paul referring?

The word "death" has three distinct manifestations in biblical terminology: 1) spiritual death or separation from God (Eph. 1:1,2,4,18); 2) physical death (Heb. 9:27); and 3) eternal death (also called the second death), which includes not only eternal separation from God, but eternal torment in the lake of fire (Rev. 20:11–15).

When sin entered the human race through Adam, all these aspects of death came with it. Adam was not originally subject to death; but through his sin, death became a grim certainty for him and his posterity. The "death" referred to in Romans 6:23 includes the first and third descriptions above. That verse establishes two inexorable absolutes: 1) spiritual death and eternal separation from God make up the paycheck for every person's slavery to sin; and 2) eternal life is a free gift God gives undeserving sinners who believe in His Son (Eph. 2:8,9).

AUGUST 5

Job 1:1–2:13

1 There was a man in the land of Uz, whose
name *was* Job; and that man was blameless
and upright, and one who feared God and
shunned evil. 2And seven sons and three
daughters were born to him. 3Also, his possessions were seven thousand sheep, three
thousand camels, five hundred yoke of oxen,
five hundred female donkeys, and a very large
household, so that this man was the greatest
of all the people of the East.
4And his sons would go and feast *in their*
houses, each on his *appointed* day, and would
send and invite their three sisters to eat and
drink with them. 5So it was, when the days of
feasting had run their course, that Job would
send and sanctify them, and he would rise
early in the morning and offer burnt offerings
according to the number of them all. For Job
said, "It may be that my sons have sinned and
cursed God in their hearts." Thus Job did regularly.
6Now there was a day when the sons of God
came to present themselves before the LORD,
and Satan also came among them. 7And the
LORD said to Satan, "From where do you
come?"
So Satan answered the LORD and said, "From
going to and fro on the earth, and from walking back and forth on it."
8Then the LORD said to Satan, "Have you
considered My servant Job, that *there is* none
like him on the earth, a blameless and upright
man, one who fears God and shuns evil?"
9So Satan answered the LORD and said, "Does
Job fear God for nothing? 10Have You not made
a hedge around him, around his household, and
around all that he has on every side? You have
blessed the work of his hands, and his possessions have increased in the land. 11But now,
stretch out Your hand and touch all that he has,
and he will surely curse You to Your face!"
12And the LORD said to Satan, "Behold, all
that he has *is* in your power; only do not lay a
hand on his *person*."
So Satan went out from the presence of the
LORD.
13Now there was a day when his sons and
daughters *were* eating and drinking wine in
their oldest brother's house; 14and a messenger came to Job and said, "The oxen were
plowing and the donkeys feeding beside
them, 15when the Sabeans raided *them* and
took them away—indeed they have killed the
servants with the edge of the sword; and I
alone have escaped to tell you!"
16While he *was* still speaking, another also
came and said, "The fire of God fell from heav-
en and burned up the sheep and the servants,
and consumed them; and I alone have escaped
to tell you!"

1:1–2:13 This section identifies the main persons and sets the stage for the drama to follow. **Uz.** Job's home was a walled city with gates (29:7,8), where he held a position of great respect. The city was in the land of Uz in northern Arabia, adjacent to Midian, where Moses lived for 40 years (Ex. 2:15). **Job.** The story begins on earth with Job as the central figure. He was a rich man with 7 sons and 3 daughters, in his middle years with a grown family. He was good, a family man, rich, and widely known. **blameless...upright,...feared God... shunned evil.** 1:8. Job was not perfect or without sin (6:24; 7:21; 9:20). However, it appears from the language that he had put his trust in God for redemption and faithfully lived a God-honoring, sincere life of integrity and consistency personally, maritally (2:10), and parentally (1:4,5).

1:6 sons of God. Job's life is about to be caught up in heavenly strategies as the scene moves from earth to heaven where God is holding council with His heavenly court. Neither Job nor his friends ever knew about this. The angelic host (38:7; Pss. 29:1; 89:7; Dan. 3:25) came to God's throne to render account of their ministry throughout the earth and heaven (1 Kin. 22:19–22). Like a Judas among the apostles, Satan was with the angels. **Satan.** Emboldened by the success he had with the unfallen Adam in paradise (Gen. 3:6–12,17–19), he was confident that the fear of God in Job, one of a fallen race, would not stand his tests. And he had fallen himself (see Is. 14:12). As opposed to a personal name, Satan as a title means "adversary," in either a personal or judicial sense. This demon is the ultimate spiritual adversary of all time and has been accusing the righteous throughout the ages (Rev. 12:10).

17 While he *was* still speaking, another also came and said, "The Chaldeans formed three bands, raided the camels and took them away, yes, and killed the servants with the edge of the sword; and I alone have escaped to tell you!"

18 While he *was* still speaking, another also came and said, "Your sons and daughters *were* eating and drinking wine in their oldest brother's house, 19 and suddenly a great wind came from across the wilderness and struck the four corners of the house, and it fell on the young people, and they are dead; and I alone have escaped to tell you!"

20 Then Job arose, tore his robe, and shaved his head; and he fell to the ground and worshiped. 21 And he said:

"Naked I came from my mother's
womb,
And naked shall I return there.
The LORD gave, and the LORD has
taken away;
Blessed be the name of the LORD."

22 In all this Job did not sin nor charge God with wrong.

2 Again there was a day when the sons of God came to present themselves before the LORD, and Satan came also among them to present himself before the LORD. 2 And the LORD said to Satan, "From where do you come?"

Satan answered the LORD and said, "From going to and fro on the earth, and from walking back and forth on it."

3 Then the LORD said to Satan, "Have you considered My servant Job, that *there is* none like him on the earth, a blameless and upright man, one who fears God and shuns evil? And still he holds fast to his integrity, although you incited Me against him, to destroy him without cause."

2:3 he holds fast to his integrity. God affirmed that Job had won round one. **without cause.** God uses the same expression the adversary used in Job 1 "for nothing (1:9)...without cause (2:3)." The message behind God's turn of words is that the adversary is the guilty party in this case, not Job who had suffered all the disaster without any personal cause. He had done nothing to incur the pain and loss, though it was massive. The issue was purely a matter of conflict between God and Satan. This is a crucial statement, because when Job's friends tried to explain why all the disasters had befallen him, they always put the blame on Job. Grasping this assessment from God—that Job had not been punished for something, but suffered for nothing related to him personally—is a crucial key to the story. Sometimes suffering is caused by divine purposes unknowable to us.

4 So Satan answered the LORD and said, "Skin for skin! Yes, all that a man has he will give for his life. 5 But stretch out Your hand now, and touch his bone and his flesh, and he will surely curse You to Your face!"

6 And the LORD said to Satan, "Behold, he *is* in your hand, but spare his life."

7So Satan went out from the presence of the
LORD, and struck Job with painful boils from
the sole of his foot to the crown of his head.
8And he took for himself a potsherd with
which to scrape himself while he sat in the
midst of the ashes.
9Then his wife said to him, "Do you still hold
fast to your integrity? Curse God and die!"
10But he said to her, "You speak as one of the
foolish women speaks. Shall we indeed accept
good from God, and shall we not accept adversity?" In all this Job did not sin with his lips.
11Now when Job's three friends heard of all
this adversity that had come upon him, each
one came from his own place—Eliphaz the
Temanite, Bildad the Shuhite, and Zophar the
Naamathite. For they had made an appointment together to come and mourn with him,
and to comfort him. 12And when they raised
their eyes from afar, and did not recognize
him, they lifted their voices and wept; and
each one tore his robe and sprinkled dust on
his head toward heaven. 13So they sat down
with him on the ground seven days and seven
nights, and no one spoke a word to him, for
they saw that *his* grief was very great.

Psalm 91:7–13

7 A thousand may fall at your side,
And ten thousand at your right hand;
But it shall not come near you.
8 Only with your eyes shall you look,
And see the reward of the wicked.

9 Because you have made the LORD,
who is my refuge,
Even the Most High, your dwelling
place,
10 No evil shall befall you,
Nor shall any plague come near your
dwelling;
11 For He shall give His angels charge
over you,
To keep you in all your ways.
12 In *their* hands they shall bear
you up,
Lest you dash your foot against
a stone.
13 You shall tread upon the lion and
the cobra,
The young lion and the serpent you
shall trample underfoot.

Proverbs 22:13–14

13 The lazy *man* says, "*There is* a lion
outside!
I shall be slain in the streets!"

14 The mouth of an immoral woman *is* a
deep pit;
He who is abhorred by the LORD will
fall there.

Romans 7:1–25

7 Or do you not know, brethren (for I speak
to those who know the law), that the law
has dominion over a man as long as he lives?
2For the woman who has a husband is bound
by the law to *her* husband as long as he lives.
But if the husband dies, she is released from
the law of *her* husband. 3So then if, while *her*
husband lives, she marries another man, she
will be called an adulteress; but if her husband
dies, she is free from that law, so that she is no
adulteress, though she has married another
man. 4Therefore, my brethren, you also have
become dead to the law through the body of
Christ, that you may be married to another—
to Him who was raised from the dead, that we
should bear fruit to God. 5For when we were
in the flesh, the sinful passions which were
aroused by the law were at work in our members to bear fruit to death. 6But now we have
been delivered from the law, having died to
what we were held by, so that we should serve
in the newness of the Spirit and not *in* the oldness of the letter.

7:6 delivered from the law. Not freedom to do what God's law forbids (6:1,15; 8:4; 3:31), but freedom from the spiritual liabilities and penalties of God's law. Because we died in Christ when He died, the law with its condemnation and penalties no longer has jurisdiction over us (vv. 1–3). **serve.** This is the verb form of the word for "bondservant," but here it is parallel to being slaves of righteousness (6:22), emphasizing that this service is not voluntary. Not only is the believer able to do what is right, he will do what is right. **the newness of the Spirit.** A new state of mind which the Spirit produces, characterized by a new desire and ability to keep the law of God. **oldness of the letter.** The external, written law code that produced only hostility and condemnation.

7What shall we say then? *Is* the law sin?
Certainly not! On the contrary, I would not
have known sin except through the law. For I
would not have known covetousness unless
the law had said, "*You shall not covet.*" 8But
sin, taking opportunity by the commandment,
produced in me all *manner of evil* desire. For

apart from the law sin *was* dead. [9]I was alive
once without the law, but when the commandment came, sin revived and I died. [10]And the
commandment, which *was* to *bring* life, I
found to *bring* death. [11]For sin, taking occasion
by the commandment, deceived me, and by it
killed *me*. [12]Therefore the law is holy, and the
commandment holy and just and good.
[13]Has then what is good become death to
me? Certainly not! But sin, that it might
appear sin, was producing death in me
through what is good, so that sin through the
commandment might become exceedingly
sinful. [14]For we know that the law is spiritual,
but I am carnal, sold under sin. [15]For what I am
doing, I do not understand. For what I will to
do, that I do not practice; but what I hate, that
I do. [16]If, then, I do what I will not to do, I agree
with the law that *it is* good. [17]But now, *it is* no
longer I who do it, but sin that dwells in me.
[18]For I know that in me (that is, in my flesh)
nothing good dwells; for to will is present with
me, but *how* to perform what is good I do not
find. [19]For the good that I will *to do*, I do not do;
but the evil I will not *to do*, that I practice.
[20]Now if I do what I will not *to do*, it is no longer
I who do it, but sin that dwells in me.
[21]I find then a law, that evil is present with
me, the one who wills to do good. [22]For I delight in the law of God according to the inward
man. [23]But I see another law in my members,
warring against the law of my mind, and bringing me into captivity to the law of sin which is
in my members. [24]O wretched man that I am!
Who will deliver me from this body of death?
[25]I thank God—through Jesus Christ our Lord!
So then, with the mind I myself serve the
law of God, but with the flesh the law of sin.

DAY 5: In Romans 7:7–25, is Paul describing his own experience as a believer or unbeliever?

Paul uses the personal pronoun "I" throughout this passage, using his own experience as an example of what is true of unredeemed humanity (7:7–12) and of true Christians (7:13–25). Some interpret this chronicle of Paul's inner conflict as describing his life before Christ. They point out that Paul describes the person as "sold under sin" (7:14), as having "nothing good" in him (7:18), and as a "wretched man" trapped in a "body of death" (7:24). Those descriptions seem to contradict Paul's earlier description of the believer (6:2,6,7,11,17,18,22).

It is correct, however, to understand Paul here to be speaking about a believer. This person desires to obey God's law and hates sin (7:15,19,21). He is humble, recognizing that nothing good dwells in his humanness (7:18). He sees sin in himself, but not as all that is there (7:17,20–22). And he serves Jesus Christ with his mind (7:25). Paul has already established that none of those attitudes ever describe the unsaved (1:18–21,32; 3:10–20). Paul's use of the present tense verbs in 7:14–25 strongly supports the idea that he was describing his current experience as a Christian.

Even those who agree that Paul was speaking as a genuine believer, however, still find room for disagreement. Some see a carnal, fleshly Christian under the influence of old habits. Others see a legalistic Christian, frustrated by his feeble attempts in his own power to please God by keeping the Mosaic Law. But the personal pronoun "I" refers to the apostle Paul, a standard of spiritual health and maturity. This leads to the conclusion that Paul, in 7:7–25, must be describing all Christians—even the most spiritual and mature—who, when they honestly evaluate themselves against the righteous standard of God's law, realize how far short they fall. Notice, particularly, Paul's honesty and transparency in the four laments (7:14–17,18–20,21–23,24–25).

AUGUST 6

Job 3:1–4:21

3 After this Job opened his mouth and
cursed the day of his *birth*. [2]And Job
spoke, and said:

3 "May the day perish on which I was born,
And the night *in which* it was said,
'A male child is conceived.'
4 May that day be darkness;
May God above not seek it,
Nor the light shine upon it.
5 May darkness and the shadow of death claim it;
May a cloud settle on it;
May the blackness of the day terrify it.
6 *As for* that night, may darkness seize it;
May it not rejoice among the days of the year,
May it not come into the number of the months.
7 Oh, may that night be barren!
May no joyful shout come into it!

8 May those curse it who curse the day,
Those who are ready to arouse
Leviathan.
9 May the stars of its morning be dark;
May it look for light, but *have* none,
And not see the dawning of the day;
10 Because it did not shut up the doors of
my *mother's* womb,
Nor hide sorrow from my eyes.

11 "Why did I not die at birth?
Why did I *not* perish when I came from
the womb?
12 Why did the knees receive me?
Or why the breasts, that I should
nurse?
13 For now I would have lain still and
been quiet,
I would have been asleep;
Then I would have been at rest
14 With kings and counselors of the
earth,
Who built ruins for themselves,
15 Or with princes who had gold,
Who filled their houses *with* silver;
16 Or *why* was I not hidden like a stillborn
child,
Like infants who never saw light?
17 There the wicked cease
from troubling,
And there the weary are at rest.
18 *There* the prisoners rest together;
They do not hear the voice of the
oppressor.
19 The small and great are there,
And the servant *is* free from
his master.

20 "Why is light given to him who is
in misery,
And life to the bitter of soul,
21 Who long for death, but it does not
come,
And search for it more than hidden
treasures;
22 Who rejoice exceedingly,
And are glad when they can find the
grave?
23 *Why is light given* to a man whose way
is hidden,
And whom God has hedged in?
24 For my sighing comes before I eat,
And my groanings pour out like water.
25 For the thing I greatly feared has come
upon me,
And what I dreaded has happened
to me.
26 I am not at ease, nor am I quiet;
I have no rest, for trouble comes."

3:25,26 the thing I greatly feared. Not a particular thing but a generic classification of suffering. The very worst fear that anyone could have was coming to pass in Job's life, and he is experiencing severe anxiety, fearing more.

4 Then Eliphaz the Temanite answered and
said:
2 "*If* one attempts a word with you, will
you become weary?
But who can withhold himself from
speaking?
3 Surely you have instructed many,
And you have strengthened weak
hands.
4 Your words have upheld him who was
stumbling,
And you have strengthened the feeble
knees;
5 But now it comes upon you, and you
are weary;
It touches you, and you are troubled.
6 *Is* not your reverence your confidence?
And the integrity of your ways your
hope?
7 "Remember now, who *ever* perished
being innocent?
Or where were the upright *ever* cut off?
8 Even as I have seen,
Those who plow iniquity

4:7 who *ever* perished being innocent? Eliphaz, recognizing Job's "reverence" and "integrity" (v. 6), was likely encouraging Job at the outset by saying he wouldn't die because he was innocent of any deadly iniquity, but must be guilty of some serious sin because he was reaping such anger from God. This was a moral universe and moral order was at work, he thought. He had oversimplified God's pattern of retribution. This simple axiom, "the righteous will prosper and the wicked will suffer," does not always hold up in human experience. It is true that plowing and sowing iniquity reaps judgment, so Eliphaz was partially right (Gal. 6:7–9; 1 Pet. 3:12), but not everything we reap in life is the result of something we have sown (2 Cor. 12:7–10). Eliphaz was replacing theology with simplistic logic. To say that wherever there is suffering, it is the result of sowing sin is wrong (Ex. 4:11; John 9:1–3).

And sow trouble reap the same.
9 By the blast of God they perish,
And by the breath of His anger they
are consumed.
10 The roaring of the lion,
The voice of the fierce lion,
And the teeth of the young lions are
broken.
11 The old lion perishes for lack of prey,
And the cubs of the lioness are
scattered.
12 "Now a word was secretly brought to
me,
And my ear received a whisper of it.
13 In disquieting thoughts from the
visions of the night,
When deep sleep falls on men,
14 Fear came upon me, and trembling,
Which made all my bones shake.
15 Then a spirit passed before my face;
The hair on my body stood up.
16 It stood still,
But I could not discern its appearance.
A form *was* before my eyes;
There was silence;
Then I heard a voice *saying:*
17 'Can a mortal be more righteous
than God?
Can a man be more pure than his
Maker?
18 If He puts no trust in His servants,
If He charges His angels
with error,
19 How much more those who dwell in
houses of clay,
Whose foundation is in the dust,
Who are crushed before a moth?
20 They are broken in pieces from
morning till evening;
They perish forever, with no one
regarding.
21 Does not their own excellence
go away?
They die, even without wisdom.'

Psalm 91:14–16

14 "Because he has set his love upon Me,
therefore I will deliver him;
I will set him on high, because he has
known My name.
15 He shall call upon Me, and I will
answer him;
I *will be* with him in trouble;
I will deliver him and honor him.
16 With long life I will satisfy him,
And show him My salvation."

91:14 set his love upon Me. God Himself is the speaker in this section (vv. 14–16), and He describes the blessing He gives to those who know and love Him. The word for "love" means a "deep longing" for God or a "clinging" to God.

Proverbs 22:15

15 Foolishness *is* bound up in the heart of
a child;
The rod of correction will drive it far
from him.

Romans 8:1–21

8 *There is* therefore now no condemnation
to those who are in Christ Jesus, who do
not walk according to the flesh, but according
to the Spirit. 2For the law of the Spirit of life in
Christ Jesus has made me free from the law of
sin and death. 3For what the law could not do
in that it was weak through the flesh, God *did*
by sending His own Son in the likeness of sinful flesh, on account of sin: He condemned sin
in the flesh, 4that the righteous requirement of
the law might be fulfilled in us who do not
walk according to the flesh but according to
the Spirit. 5For those who live according to the
flesh set their minds on the things of the flesh,
but those *who live* according to the Spirit, the
things of the Spirit. 6For to be carnally minded
is death, but to be spiritually minded *is* life and

8:1 therefore. The result or consequence of the truth just taught. Normally it marks the conclusion of the verses immediately preceding it. But here it introduces the staggering results of Paul's teaching in the first 7 chapters: that justification is by faith alone on the basis of God's overwhelming grace. **no condemnation.** Occurring only 3 times in the New Testament, all in Romans (5:16,18), "condemnation" is used exclusively in judicial settings as the opposite of justification. It refers to a verdict of guilty and the penalty that verdict demands. No sin a believer can commit—past, present, or future—can be held against him, since the penalty was paid by Christ and righteousness was imputed to the believer. And no sin will ever reverse this divine legal decision. **those...in Christ Jesus.** I.e., every true Christian; to be in Christ means to be united with Him.

peace. [7]Because the carnal mind *is* enmity against God; for it is not subject to the law of God, nor indeed can be. [8]So then, those who are in the flesh cannot please God.

[9]But you are not in the flesh but in the Spirit, if indeed the Spirit of God dwells in you. Now if anyone does not have the Spirit of Christ, he is not His. [10]And if Christ *is* in you, the body *is* dead because of sin, but the Spirit *is* life because of righteousness. [11]But if the Spirit of Him who raised Jesus from the dead dwells in you, He who raised Christ from the dead will also give life to your mortal bodies through His Spirit who dwells in you.

[12]Therefore, brethren, we are debtors—not to the flesh, to live according to the flesh. [13]For if you live according to the flesh you will die; but if by the Spirit you put to death the deeds of the body, you will live. [14]For as many as are led by the Spirit of God, these are sons of God. [15]For you did not receive the spirit of bondage again to fear, but you received the Spirit of adoption by whom we cry out, "Abba, Father." [16]The Spirit Himself bears witness with our spirit that we are children of God, [17]and if children, then heirs—heirs of God and joint heirs with Christ, if indeed we suffer with *Him,* that we may also be glorified together.

[18]For I consider that the sufferings of this present time are not worthy *to be compared* with the glory which shall be revealed in us. [19]For the earnest expectation of the creation eagerly waits for the revealing of the sons of God. [20]For the creation was subjected to futility, not willingly, but because of Him who subjected *it* in hope; [21]because the creation itself also will be delivered from the bondage of corruption into the glorious liberty of the children of God.

8:15 spirit of bondage…to fear. Because of their life of sin, unregenerate people are slaves to their fear of death (Heb. 2:14,15) and to their fear of final punishment (1 John 4:18). **Spirit of adoption.** Not primarily a reference to the transaction by which God adopts us (Eph. 1:5; Gal. 4:5–7), but to a Spirit-produced awareness of the rich reality that God has made us His children, and, therefore, that we can come before Him without fear or hesitation as our beloved Father. It includes the confidence that we are truly sons of God. **Abba.** An informal, Aramaic term for Father that conveys a sense of intimacy. Like the English terms "Daddy" or "Papa," it connotes tenderness, dependence, and a relationship free of fear or anxiety (Mark 14:36).

DAY 6: What kind of relationship does Satan have with God in the Book of Job?

Satan may be God's sworn enemy, but they are not equals. Satan is a creature; God is the Creator. Satan was an angel unwilling to serve in his exalted role, and he rebelled against God.

The continual conflict between Satan and God is illustrated when Satan states that righteous people remain faithful to God only because of what they get. They trust in God only as long as God is nice to them. Satan challenged God's claims of Job's righteousness by calling it untested, if not questionable. Apparently Satan was convinced that he could destroy Job's faith in God by inflicting suffering on him.

Satan suffered another defeat as God demonstrated through Job's life that saving faith can't be destroyed no matter how much trouble the believer suffers or how incomprehensible and undeserved the suffering seems.

After failing to destroy Job, Satan disappears from the story. He remains God's defeated enemy, still raging against God's inevitable triumph.

AUGUST 7

Job 5:1–6:30

5 "Call out now; Is there anyone who will
answer you?
And to which of the holy ones will you
turn?
2 For wrath kills a foolish man,
And envy slays a simple one.
3 I have seen the foolish taking root,
But suddenly I cursed his dwelling
place.
4 His sons are far from safety,
They are crushed in the gate,
And *there is* no deliverer.
5 Because the hungry eat up his harvest,
Taking it even from the thorns,
And a snare snatches their substance.

6 For affliction does not come from the dust,
Nor does trouble spring from the ground;
7 Yet man is born to trouble,
As the sparks fly upward.

8 "But as for me, I would seek God,
And to God I would commit my cause—
9 Who does great things, and unsearchable,
Marvelous things without number.
10 He gives rain on the earth,
And sends waters on the fields.
11 He sets on high those who are lowly,
And those who mourn are lifted to safety.
12 He frustrates the devices of the crafty,
So that their hands cannot carry out their plans.
13 He catches the wise in their own craftiness,
And the counsel of the cunning comes quickly upon them.
14 They meet with darkness in the daytime,
And grope at noontime as in the night.
15 But He saves the needy from the sword,
From the mouth of the mighty,
And from their hand.
16 So the poor have hope,
And injustice shuts her mouth.

17 "Behold, happy *is* the man whom God corrects;
Therefore do not despise the chastening of the Almighty.
18 For He bruises, but He binds up;
He wounds, but His hands make whole.
19 He shall deliver you in six troubles,
Yes, in seven no evil shall touch you.
20 In famine He shall redeem you from death,
And in war from the power of the sword.

5:17 happy *is* the man whom God corrects. Eliphaz put a positive spin on his advice by telling Job that enviable or desirable is the situation of the one God cares enough to chasten. "If only Job admitted his sin, he could be happy again" was the advice.

21 You shall be hidden from the scourge of the tongue,
And you shall not be afraid of destruction when it comes.
22 You shall laugh at destruction and famine,
And you shall not be afraid of the beasts of the earth.
23 For you shall have a covenant with the stones of the field,
And the beasts of the field shall be at peace with you.
24 You shall know that your tent *is* in peace;
You shall visit your dwelling and find nothing amiss.
25 You shall also know that your descendants *shall be* many,
And your offspring like the grass of the earth.
26 You shall come to the grave at a full age,
As a sheaf of grain ripens in its season.
27 Behold, this we have searched out;
It *is* true.
Hear it, and know for yourself."

6 Then Job answered and said:

2 "Oh, that my grief were fully weighed,
And my calamity laid with it on the scales!
3 For then it would be heavier than the sand of the sea—
Therefore my words have been rash.
4 For the arrows of the Almighty *are* within me;
My spirit drinks in their poison;
The terrors of God are arrayed against me.
5 Does the wild donkey bray when it has grass,
Or does the ox low over its fodder?
6 Can flavorless food be eaten without salt?
Or is there *any* taste in the white of an egg?
7 My soul refuses to touch them;
They *are* as loathsome food to me.

8 "Oh, that I might have my request,
That God would grant *me* the thing that I long for!
9 That it would please God to crush me,
That He would loose His hand and cut me off!
10 Then I would still have comfort;
Though in anguish I would exult,
He will not spare;

6:10 the words of the Holy One. Job had not been avoiding the revelation of God that he had received. The commands of the Holy One were precious to him and he had lived by them. This was confusing to him, as he couldn't find any sinful source for his suffering. He would rejoice in his pain if he knew it would soon lead to death, but he couldn't see any hope for death or deliverance in himself (vv. 11–13).

For I have not concealed the words of
the Holy One.
11 "What strength do I have, that I should
hope?
And what *is* my end, that I should
prolong my life?
12 *Is* my strength the strength of stones?
Or is my flesh bronze?
13 *Is* my help not within me?
And is success driven from me?

14 "To him who is afflicted, kindness
should be shown by his friend,
Even though he forsakes the fear of
the Almighty.
15 My brothers have dealt deceitfully like
a brook,
Like the streams of the brooks that
pass away,
16 Which are dark because of the ice,
And into which the snow vanishes.
17 When it is warm, they cease to flow;
When it is hot, they vanish from their
place.
18 The paths of their way turn aside,
They go nowhere and perish.
19 The caravans of Tema look,
The travelers of Sheba hope for them.
20 They are disappointed because they
were confident;
They come there and are confused.
21 For now you are nothing,
You see terror and are afraid.
22 Did I ever say, 'Bring *something* to me'?
Or, 'Offer a bribe for me from your
wealth'?
23 Or, 'Deliver me from the enemy's
hand'?
Or, 'Redeem me from the hand of
oppressors'?

24 "Teach me, and I will hold my tongue;
Cause me to understand wherein I
have erred.
25 How forceful are right words!
But what does your arguing prove?
26 Do you intend to rebuke *my* words,
And the speeches of a desperate one,
which are as wind?
27 Yes, you overwhelm the fatherless,
And you undermine your friend.
28 Now therefore, be pleased to look at
me;
For I would never lie to your face.
29 Yield now, let there be no injustice!
Yes, concede, my righteousness still
stands!
30 Is there injustice on my tongue?
Cannot my taste discern the unsavory?

Psalm 92:1–7

A Psalm. A Song for the Sabbath day.

It is good to give thanks to
the LORD,
And to sing praises to Your name,
O Most High;
2 To declare Your lovingkindness in the
morning,
And Your faithfulness every night,
3 On an instrument of ten strings,
On the lute,
And on the harp,
With harmonious sound.
4 For You, LORD, have made me glad
through Your work;
I will triumph in the works of Your
hands.

5 O LORD, how great are Your works!
Your thoughts are very deep.
6 A senseless man does not know,
Nor does a fool understand this.
7 When the wicked spring up like grass,
And when all the workers of iniquity
flourish,
It is that they may be destroyed
forever.

Proverbs 22:16

16 He who oppresses the poor to increase
his *riches,*
And he who gives to the rich, *will*
surely *come* to poverty.

22:16 These two vices reflect the same selfish attitude: withholding from the poor to keep what one has and giving to the rich to induce them to give one more. Both are unacceptable to God and incur punishment.

Romans 8:22–39

22 For we know that the whole creation groans
and labors with birth pangs together until
now. 23 Not only *that,* but we also who have the
firstfruits of the Spirit, even we ourselves
groan within ourselves, eagerly waiting for
the adoption, the redemption of our body.
24 For we were saved in this hope, but hope
that is seen is not hope; for why does one still
hope for what he sees? 25 But if we hope for
what we do not see, we eagerly wait for *it* with
perseverance.

26 Likewise the Spirit also helps in our weaknesses. For we do not know what we should
pray for as we ought, but the Spirit Himself
makes intercession for us with groanings which
cannot be uttered. 27 Now He who searches the
hearts knows what the mind of the Spirit *is,*
because He makes intercession for the saints
according to *the will of* God.

28 And we know that all things work together
for good to those who love God, to those who
are the called according to *His* purpose. 29 For
whom He foreknew, He also predestined *to be*
conformed to the image of His Son, that He
might be the firstborn among many brethren.
30 Moreover whom He predestined, these He
also called; whom He called, these He also justified; and whom He justified, these He also
glorified.

31 What then shall we say to these things? If
God *is* for us, who *can be* against us? 32 He who
did not spare His own Son, but delivered Him
up for us all, how shall He not with Him also
freely give us all things? 33 Who shall bring a
charge against God's elect? *It is* God who justifies. 34 Who *is* he who condemns? *It is* Christ
who died, and furthermore is also risen, who
is even at the right hand of God, who also
makes intercession for us. 35 Who shall separate us from the love of Christ? *Shall* tribulation, or distress, or persecution, or famine, or
nakedness, or peril, or sword? 36 As it is written:

> *"For Your sake we are killed all day long;*
> *We are accounted as sheep for the slaughter."*

37 Yet in all these things we are more than con-
querors through Him who loved us. 38 For I am
persuaded that neither death nor life, nor angels
nor principalities nor powers, nor things present
nor things to come, 39 nor height nor depth, nor
any other created thing, shall be able to separate
us from the love of God which is in Christ Jesus
our Lord.

8:35–39 This list of experiences and persons that can't separate the believer from God's love in Christ was not just theory to Paul. It was rather a personal testimony from one who had personally survived assaults from these entities and emerged triumphant.

8:35 the love of Christ. Not our love for Christ, but His love for us (John 13:1), specifically here as He demonstrated it in salvation (1 John 4:9,10). **tribulation.** Here the word probably refers to the kind of adversity common to all men. **distress.** This refers to being strictly confined in a narrow, difficult place or being helplessly hemmed in by one's circumstances. **persecution.** Suffering inflicted on us by men because of our relationship with Christ (Matt. 5:10–12).

DAY 7: Explain the process Paul refers to in Romans 8:28–30 and 9:6–29.

With these words, God reveals in human terms His divine role in the process of salvation. Paul's description offends the human spirit because it minimizes our role. Yet only those who see their own helplessness in the face of sin can come to see how gracious God has been in acting and choosing ahead of time. We never surprise God; He always anticipates us! "But God demonstrates His own love toward us, in that while we were still sinners, Christ died for us" (Rom. 5:8).

The term "foreknew" (8:29) does not simply refer to God's omniscience—that in eternity past He knew who would come to Christ. Rather, it speaks of a predetermined choice by God to set His love on us and establish an intimate relationship. The term "election" (9:11) refers to the same action on God's part (1 Pet. 1:1,2,20). Salvation is not initiated by human choice. Even faith is a gift of God (Rom. 1:16; John 6:37; Eph. 2:8,9).

The term "predestined" (8:29) literally means "to mark out, appoint, or determine beforehand." Those God chooses, He destines for His chosen end—that is, likeness to His Son (Eph. 1:4,5,11). The goal of God's predestined purpose for His own is that they would be made like Jesus Christ.

The reality and security of our standing with God rests ultimately in His character and decision, not ours. Paul summarized his teaching about the believer's security in Christ with a thundering litany of questions and answers that haunt believers. They reach their peak with "Who shall separate us from the love of Christ?" (8:35). Paul's answer is an almost poetic expression of praise for God's grace in bringing salvation to completion for all who are chosen and believe—it is a hymn of security.

AUGUST 8

Job 7:1–8:22

7 "*Is there* not a time of hard
service for man on earth?
Are not his days also like the days of a
hired man?
2 Like a servant who earnestly desires
the shade,
And like a hired man who eagerly
looks for his wages,
3 So I have been allotted months of futility,
And wearisome nights have been
appointed to me.
4 When I lie down, I say, 'When shall I
arise,
And the night be ended?'
For I have had my fill of tossing till dawn.
5 My flesh is caked with worms and dust,
My skin is cracked and breaks out
afresh.

6 "My days are swifter than a weaver's
shuttle,
And are spent without hope.
7 Oh, remember that my life *is* a breath!
My eye will never again see good.
8 The eye of him who sees me will see
me no *more;*
While your eyes *are* upon me, I shall no
longer *be.*
9 *As* the cloud disappears and vanishes
away,
So he who goes down to the grave
does not come up.
10 He shall never return to his house,
Nor shall his place know him anymore.

11 "Therefore I will not restrain my mouth;
I will speak in the anguish of my spirit;
I will complain in the bitterness of my
soul.
12 *Am* I a sea, or a sea serpent,
That You set a guard over me?
13 When I say, 'My bed will comfort me,
My couch will ease my complaint,'
14 Then You scare me with dreams
And terrify me with visions,
15 So that my soul chooses strangling
And death rather than my body.
16 I loathe *my life;*
I would not live forever.
Let me alone,
For my days *are but* a breath.

17 "What *is* man, that You should exalt him,
That You should set Your heart on him,
18 That You should visit him every
morning,
And test him every moment?
19 How long?
Will You not look away from me,
And let me alone till I swallow my
saliva?

7:19 till I swallow my saliva. This strange statement was an Arabic proverb, indicating a brief moment. Job was asking for a moment "to catch his breath," or in the case of the proverb, "swallow his saliva."

20 Have I sinned?
What have I done to You, O watcher of
men?
Why have You set me as Your target,
So that I am a burden to myself?
21 Why then do You not pardon my
transgression,
And take away my iniquity?
For now I will lie down in the dust,
And You will seek me diligently,
But I *will* no longer *be.*"

8 Then Bildad the Shuhite answered and
said:

2 "How long will you speak these *things,*
And the words of your mouth *be like* a
strong wind?
3 Does God subvert judgment?
Or does the Almighty pervert justice?
4 If your sons have sinned against Him,
He has cast them away for their
transgression.
5 If you would earnestly seek God
And make your supplication to the
Almighty,
6 If you *were* pure and upright,

8:3 Almighty pervert justice. Bildad took Job's claims for innocence and applied them to his simplistic notion of retribution. He concluded that Job was accusing God of injustice when God must be meting out justice to Job. Job tried to avoid outright accusations of this sort, but the evidence led Bildad to this conclusion because he had no knowledge of the heavenly facts.

Surely now He would awake for you,
And prosper your rightful dwelling place.
7 Though your beginning was small,
Yet your latter end would increase abundantly.
8 "For inquire, please, of the former age,
And consider the things discovered by their fathers;
9 For we *were born* yesterday, and know nothing,
Because our days on earth *are* a shadow.
10 Will they not teach you and tell you,
And utter words from their heart?
11 "Can the papyrus grow up without a marsh?
Can the reeds flourish without water?
12 While it *is* yet green *and* not cut down,
It withers before any *other* plant.
13 So *are* the paths of all who forget God;
And the hope of the hypocrite shall perish,
14 Whose confidence shall be cut off,
And whose trust *is* a spider's web.
15 He leans on his house, but it does not stand.
He holds it fast, but it does not endure.
16 He grows green in the sun,
And his branches spread out in his garden.
17 His roots wrap around the rock heap,
And look for a place in the stones.
18 If he is destroyed from his place,
Then *it* will deny him, *saying,* 'I have not seen you.'
19 "Behold, this is the joy of His way,
And out of the earth others will grow.
20 Behold, God will not cast away the blameless,
Nor will He uphold the evildoers.
21 He will yet fill your mouth with laughing,
And your lips with rejoicing.
22 Those who hate you will be clothed with shame,
And the dwelling place of the wicked will come to nothing."

Psalm 92:8–15

8 But You, LORD, *are* on high forevermore.
9 For behold, Your enemies, O LORD,
For behold, Your enemies shall perish;
All the workers of iniquity shall be scattered.
10 But my horn You have exalted like a wild ox;
I have been anointed with fresh oil.
11 My eye also has seen *my desire* on my enemies;
My ears hear *my desire* on the wicked
Who rise up against me.

92:10 my horn…anointed with fresh oil. This figure is based on a practice of making an animal's horns gleam by rubbing oil on them. Thus God, in effect, had invigorated the psalmist (Pss. 23:5; 133:2).

12 The righteous shall flourish like a palm tree,
He shall grow like a cedar in Lebanon.
13 Those who are planted in the house of the LORD
Shall flourish in the courts of our God.
14 They shall still bear fruit in old age;
They shall be fresh and flourishing,
15 To declare that the LORD is upright;
He is my rock, and *there is* no unrighteousness in Him.

Proverbs 22:17–21

17 Incline your ear and hear the words of the wise,
And apply your heart to my knowledge;
18 For *it is* a pleasant thing if you keep them within you;
Let them all be fixed upon your lips,
19 So that your trust may be in the LORD;
I have instructed you today, even you.
20 Have I not written to you excellent things
Of counsels and knowledge,
21 That I may make you know the certainty of the words of truth,
That you may answer words of truth
To those who send to you?

Romans 9:1–15

9 I tell the truth in Christ, I am not lying, my
conscience also bearing me witness in the
Holy Spirit, [2]that I have great sorrow and continual grief in my heart. [3]For I could wish that
I myself were accursed from Christ for my
brethren, my countrymen according to the
flesh, [4]who are Israelites, to whom *pertain* the
adoption, the glory, the covenants, the giving
of the law, the service *of God,* and the promises; [5]of whom *are* the fathers and from whom,
according to the flesh, Christ *came,* who is
over all, *the* eternally blessed God. Amen.
[6]But it is not that the word of God has taken
no effect. For they *are* not all Israel who *are* of
Israel, [7]nor *are they* all children because they
are the seed of Abraham; but, *"In Isaac your
seed shall be called."* [8]That is, those who *are*
the children of the flesh, these *are* not the
children of God; but the children of the promise are counted as the seed. [9]For this *is* the
word of promise: *"At this time I will come and
Sarah shall have a son."*
[10]And not only *this,* but when Rebecca also had
conceived by one man, *even* by our father Isaac
[11](for *the children* not yet being born, nor having done any good or evil, that the purpose of
God according to election might stand, not of
works but of Him who calls), [12]it was said to
her, *"The older shall serve the younger."* [13]As
it is written, *"Jacob I have loved, but Esau I
have hated."*
[14]What shall we say then? *Is there* unrighteousness with God? Certainly not! [15]For He
says to Moses, *"I will have mercy on whomever I will have mercy, and I will have compassion on whomever I will have compassion."*

9:4 Israelites. The descendants of Abraham through Jacob, whose name God changed to Israel (Gen. 32:28). **adoption.** Not in the sense of providing salvation to every person born a Jew (8:15–23; 9:6), but sovereignly selecting an entire nation to receive His special calling, covenant, and blessing and to serve as His witness nation (Ex. 4:22;19:6; Hos. 11:1; Is. 46:3,4). **glory.** The glory cloud (Shekinah) that pictured God's presence in the Old Testament (Ex. 16:10; 24:16,17; 29:42,43; Lev. 9:23). His glory was supremely present in the Holy of Holies in both the tabernacle and the temple, which served as the throne room of Yahweh, Israel's King (Ex. 25:22; 40:34; 1 Kin. 8:11). **covenants.** A covenant is a legally binding promise, agreement, or contract. Three times in the New Testament the word "covenants" is used in the plural (Gal. 4:24; Eph. 2:12). All but one of God's covenants with man are eternal and unilateral—that is, God promised to accomplish something based on His own character and not on the response or actions of the promised beneficiary. The 6 biblical covenants include: 1) the covenant with Noah (Gen. 9:8–17); 2) the covenant with Abraham (Gen. 12:1–3); 3) the covenant of law given through Moses at Sinai (Ex. 19–31; Deut. 29;30); 4) the priestly covenant (Num. 25:10–13); 5) the covenant of an eternal kingdom through David's greatest Son (2 Sam. 7:8–16); and 6) the New Covenant (Jer. 31:31–34; Ezek. 37:26; Heb. 8:6–13). All but the Mosaic Covenant are eternal and unilateral. It is neither, since Israel's sin abrogated it and it has been replaced by the New Covenant (Heb. 8:7–13).

DAY 8: Describe what Job was going through?

In Job 7:1, he said, "Is there not a time of hard service for man on earth?" He felt like a slave under tyranny of his master, longing for relief and reward (vv. 1,2); he was sleepless (v. 3,4); he was loathsome because of worms and scabs, dried filth and new running sores (v. 5); he was like a weaver's shuttle, tossed back and forth (v. 6); he was like a breath or cloud that comes and goes on its way to death (vv. 7–10). In this discourse, Job attempted to reconcile in his own mind what God was doing.

Job's Living Death

1. Painful boils from head to toe (2:7,13; 30:17)
2. Severe itching/irritation (2:7,8)
3. Great grief (2:13)
4. Lost appetite (3:24; 6:6,7)
5. Agonizing discomfort (3:24)
6. Insomnia (7:4)
7. Worm- and dust-infested flesh (7:5)
8. Continual oozing of boils (7:5)
9. Hallucinations (7:14)
10. Decaying skin (13:28)
11. Shriveled up (16:8; 17:7; 19:20)
12. Severe halitosis (19:17)
13. Teeth fell out (19:20)
14. Relentless pain (30:17)
15. Skin turned black (30:30)
16. Raging fever (30:30)
17. Dramatic weight loss (33:21)

AUGUST 9

Job 9:1–10:22

9 Then Job answered and said:

2 "Truly I know *it is* so,
But how can a man be righteous before God?
3 If one wished to contend with Him,
He could not answer Him one time out of a thousand.
4 *God is* wise in heart and mighty in strength.
Who has hardened *himself* against Him and prospered?
5 He removes the mountains, and they do not know
When He overturns them in His anger;
6 He shakes the earth out of its place,
And its pillars tremble;
7 He commands the sun, and it does not rise;
He seals off the stars;
8 He alone spreads out the heavens,
And treads on the waves of the sea;
9 He made the Bear, Orion, and the Pleiades,
And the chambers of the south;
10 He does great things past finding out,
Yes, wonders without number.
11 If He goes by me, I do not see *Him;*
If He moves past, I do not perceive Him;
12 If He takes away, who can hinder Him?
Who can say to Him, 'What are You doing?'
13 God will not withdraw His anger,
The allies of the proud lie prostrate beneath Him.

14 "How then can I answer Him,
And choose my words *to reason* with Him?
15 For though I were righteous, I could not answer Him;
I would beg mercy of my Judge.
16 If I called and He answered me,
I would not believe that He was listening to my voice.
17 For He crushes me with a tempest,
And multiplies my wounds without cause.
18 He will not allow me to catch my breath,
But fills me with bitterness.
19 If *it is a matter* of strength, indeed *He is* strong;

9:15,20 though I were righteous. He means here, not sinless, but having spiritual integrity, i.e., a pure heart to love, serve, and obey God. He was affirming again that his suffering was not due to sins he was not willing to confess. Even at that, God found something to condemn him for, he felt, making it hopeless, then, to contend with God.

And if of justice, who will appoint my day *in court?*
20 Though I were righteous, my own mouth would condemn me;
Though I *were* blameless, it would prove me perverse.

21 "I am blameless, yet I do not know myself;
I despise my life.
22 It *is* all one *thing;*
Therefore I say, 'He destroys the blameless and the wicked.'
23 If the scourge slays suddenly,
He laughs at the plight of the innocent.
24 The earth is given into the hand of the wicked.
He covers the faces of its judges.
If it is not *He,* who else could it be?

25 "Now my days are swifter than a runner;
They flee away, they see no good.
26 They pass by like swift ships,
Like an eagle swooping on its prey.
27 If I say, 'I will forget my complaint,
I will put off my sad face and wear a smile,'
28 I am afraid of all my sufferings;
I know that You will not hold me innocent.
29 *If* I am condemned,
Why then do I labor in vain?
30 If I wash myself with snow water,
And cleanse my hands with soap,
31 Yet You will plunge me into the pit,
And my own clothes will abhor me.

32 "For *He is* not a man, as I *am,*
That I may answer Him,
And that we should go to court together.
33 Nor is there any mediator between us,
Who may lay his hand on us both.
34 Let Him take His rod away from me,
And do not let dread of Him terrify me.
35 *Then* I would speak and not fear Him,
But it is not so with me.

9:32 *that* we should go to court together. Job acknowledged that, as a mere man, he had no right to call on God to declare his innocence or to contend with God over his innocence. Job was not arguing that he was sinless, but he didn't believe he had sinned to the extent that he deserved his severe suffering. Job held on to the same simplistic system of retribution as that of his accusers, which said that suffering was always caused by sin. And he knew he was not sinless, but he couldn't identify any unconfessed or unrepented sins. "Where is mercy?" he wondered.

9:33–35 any mediator between us. A court official who sees both sides clearly, as well as the source of disagreement, so as to bring resolution was not found. Where was an advocate, an arbitrator, an umpire, or a referee? Was there no one to remove God's rod and call for justice?

10 "My soul loathes my life;
I will give free course to my complaint,
I will speak in the bitterness of my soul.
2 I will say to God, 'Do not condemn me;
Show me why You contend with me.
3 *Does it* seem good to You that You should oppress,
That You should despise the work of Your hands,
And smile on the counsel of the wicked?
4 Do You have eyes of flesh?
Or do You see as man sees?
5 *Are* Your days like the days of a mortal man?
Are Your years like the days of a mighty man,
6 That You should seek for my iniquity
And search out my sin,
7 Although You know that I am not wicked,
And *there is* no one who can deliver from Your hand?

8 'Your hands have made me and fashioned me,
An intricate unity;
Yet You would destroy me.
9 Remember, I pray, that You have made me like clay.
And will You turn me into dust again?
10 Did You not pour me out like milk,
And curdle me like cheese,
11 Clothe me with skin and flesh,
And knit me together with bones and sinews?
12 You have granted me life and favor,
And Your care has preserved my spirit.

13 'And these *things* You have hidden in Your heart;
I know that this *was* with You:
14 If I sin, then You mark me,
And will not acquit me of my iniquity.
15 If I am wicked, woe to me;
Even *if* I am righteous, I cannot lift up my head.
I am full of disgrace;
See my misery!
16 If *my head* is exalted,
You hunt me like a fierce lion,
And again You show Yourself awesome against me.
17 You renew Your witnesses against me,
And increase Your indignation toward me;
Changes and war are *ever* with me.

18 'Why then have You brought me out of the womb?
Oh, that I had perished and no eye had seen me!
19 I would have been as though I had not been.
I would have been carried from the womb to the grave.
20 Are not my days few?
Cease! Leave me alone, that I may take a little comfort,
21 Before I go *to the place from which* I shall not return,
To the land of darkness and the shadow of death,
22 A land as dark as darkness *itself*,
As the shadow of death, without any order,
Where even the light *is* like darkness.' "

Psalm 93:1–5

The LORD reigns, He is clothed with majesty;
The LORD is clothed,
He has girded Himself with strength.
Surely the world is established, so that it cannot be moved.
2 Your throne *is* established from of old;
You *are* from everlasting.

3 The floods have lifted up, O LORD,
The floods have lifted up their voice;
The floods lift up their waves.
4 The LORD on high *is* mightier
Than the noise of many waters,
Than the mighty waves of the sea.
5 Your testimonies are very sure;

Holiness adorns Your house,
O LORD, forever.

Proverbs 22:22–23

22 Do not rob the poor because he *is* poor,
Nor oppress the afflicted at the gate;
23 For the LORD will plead their cause,
And plunder the soul of those who
plunder them.

Romans 9:16–33

16So then *it is* not of him who wills, nor of him
who runs, but of God who shows mercy. 17For
the Scripture says to the Pharaoh, *"For this
very purpose I have raised you up, that I may
show My power in you, and that My name may
be declared in all the earth."* 18Therefore He
has mercy on whom He wills, and whom He
wills He hardens.

19You will say to me then, "Why does He still
find fault? For who has resisted His will?" 20But
indeed, O man, who are you to reply against
God? Will the thing formed say to him who
formed *it*, "Why have you made me like this?"
21Does not the potter have power over the clay,
from the same lump to make one vessel for
honor and another for dishonor?

22*What* if God, wanting to show *His* wrath
and to make His power known, endured with
much longsuffering the vessels of wrath prepared for destruction, 23and that He might
make known the riches of His glory on the vessels of mercy, which He had prepared beforehand for glory, 24even us whom He called, not
of the Jews only, but also of the Gentiles?

25As He says also in Hosea:

*"I will call them My people, who were
not My people,
And her beloved, who was not beloved."*
26 *"And it shall come to pass in the place
where it was said to them,
'You are not My people,'
There they shall be called sons of the
living God."*

27Isaiah also cries out concerning Israel:

*"Though the number of the children of
Israel be as the sand of the sea,
The remnant will be saved.*
28 *For He will finish the work and cut it
short in righteousness,
Because the LORD will make a short
work upon the earth."*

29And as Isaiah said before:

*"Unless the LORD of Sabaoth had left us
a seed,
We would have become like Sodom,
And we would have been made like
Gomorrah."*

30What shall we say then? That Gentiles, who
did not pursue righteousness, have attained to
righteousness, even the righteousness of
faith; 31but Israel, pursuing the law of righteousness, has not attained to the law of righteousness. 32Why? Because *they did* not *seek it*
by faith, but as it were, by the works of the law.
For they stumbled at that stumbling stone.
33As it is written:

*"Behold, I lay in Zion a stumbling stone
and rock of offense,
And whoever believes on Him will not
be put to shame."*

9:20,21 Using the familiar Old Testament analogy of the potter (Is. 64:6–8; Jer. 18:3–16), Paul argues that it is as irrational, and far more arrogant, for men to question God's choice of certain sinners for salvation as for a piece of pottery to question the purposes of the potter.

9:22,23 These verses are not intended to identify the origin of evil or explain fully why God has allowed it, but they do provide 3 reasons He has permitted its presence and contamination: 1) to demonstrate His wrath; 2) to make His power known; and 3) to put the riches of His glorious mercy on display. No one is treated unfairly: Some receive the justice they earn and deserve (6:23); others graciously receive mercy.

DAY 9: Why do righteous and innocent people suffer?

Of course, no human being is truly righteous or innocent. The Bible clearly states that all have sinned (Rom. 3:23). And all sinners deserve to be punished, eternally. That's what makes God's grace so amazing!

In understanding that truth, however, it must be admitted that on a relative human scale, righteous and innocent people exist. That is, some people are more moral and virtuous than others and some are more innocent. Consider, for example, a person who strives to live out the Golden Rule, or another who gives generously to the poor. And certainly most consider small children to have a naive innocence. So this question could be rephrased: "Why do little children and people who live exemplary lives suffer?"

This question reveals the assumption that there is a direct connection between righteousness and innocence on the one hand and pain-free living on the other. There may be a connection, but it is not direct. Indeed, sin eventually does lead to suffering, but suffering is not an infallible indicator of sin. Job's friends could not see beyond this point. For them, a person's suffering was always an effect whose only cause could be that person's sin.

The righteous and the innocent do indeed suffer for a variety of reasons: 1) Sometimes righteous actions in a sinful world involve suffering—as when a righteous person sacrifices his or her life for another; 2) Sometimes the sins of others involve the righteous in suffering—a child may be deeply hurt as a result of his or her parent's actions; 3) The righteous and innocent are not exempt from the painful situations which arise in life in an imperfect and sinful world—like toothaches and smashed fingers; and 4) People sometimes suffer for no specific reason that can be clarified. Job is a perfect illustration of this last experience.

AUGUST 10

Job 11:1–12:25

11 Then Zophar the Naamathite answered and said:

2 "Should not the multitude of words be answered?
And should a man full of talk be vindicated?
3 Should your empty talk make men hold their peace?
And when you mock, should no one rebuke you?
4 For you have said,
'My doctrine *is* pure,
And I am clean in your eyes.'
5 But oh, that God would speak,
And open His lips against you,
6 That He would show you the secrets of wisdom!
For *they would* double *your* prudence.
Know therefore that God exacts from you
Less than your iniquity *deserves.*

7 "Can you search out the deep things of God?
Can you find out the limits of the Almighty?
8 *They are* higher than heaven— what can you do?
Deeper than Sheol—what can you know?
9 Their measure *is* longer than the earth
And broader than the sea.

10 "If He passes by, imprisons, and gathers *to judgment,*
Then who can hinder Him?
11 For He knows deceitful men;
He sees wickedness also.
Will He not then consider *it?*
12 For an empty-headed man will be wise,
When a wild donkey's colt is born a man.

13 "If you would prepare your heart,
And stretch out your hands toward Him;
14 If iniquity *were* in your hand, *and you* put it far away,
And would not let wickedness dwell in your tents;
15 Then surely you could lift up your face without spot;
Yes, you could be steadfast, and not fear;
16 Because you would forget *your* misery,
And remember *it* as waters *that have* passed away,
17 And *your* life would be brighter than noonday.
Though you were dark, you would be like the morning.
18 And you would be secure, because there is hope;
Yes, you would dig *around you, and* take your rest in safety.
19 You would also lie down, and no one would make *you* afraid;
Yes, many would court your favor.
20 But the eyes of the wicked will fail,
And they shall not escape,
And their hope—loss of life!"

12 Then Job answered and said:

2 "No doubt you *are* the people,
And wisdom will die with you!
3 But I have understanding as well as you;
I *am* not inferior to you.

12:2–4 you *are* the people, and wisdom will die with you! Job responded with cutting sarcasm directed at his know-it-all friends (v. 2) and then reminded them that he understood the principles of which they had spoken (v. 3), but they were irrelevant to his situation. On top of that, he despaired at the pain of becoming a derision to his friends, though he was innocent (v. 4).

Indeed, who does not *know* such
things as these?
4 "I am one mocked by his friends,
Who called on God, and He answered
him,
The just and blameless *who is*
ridiculed.
5 A lamp is despised in the thought of
one who is at ease;
It is made ready for those whose feet
slip.
6 The tents of robbers prosper,
And those who provoke God are
secure—
In what God provides by His hand.
7 "But now ask the beasts, and they will
teach you;
And the birds of the air, and they will
tell you;
8 Or speak to the earth, and it will teach
you;
And the fish of the sea will explain to
you.
9 Who among all these does not know
That the hand of the LORD has done this,
10 In whose hand *is* the life of every living
thing,
And the breath of all mankind?
11 Does not the ear test words
And the mouth taste its food?
12 Wisdom *is* with aged men,
And with length of days,
understanding.
13 "With Him *are* wisdom and strength,
He has counsel and understanding.
14 If He breaks *a thing* down, it cannot be
rebuilt;
If He imprisons a man, there can be no
release.
15 If He withholds the waters, they dry
up;
If He sends them out, they overwhelm
the earth.
16 With Him *are* strength and prudence.
The deceived and the deceiver *are* His.
17 He leads counselors away plundered,
And makes fools of the judges.
18 He loosens the bonds of kings,
And binds their waist with a belt.
19 He leads princes away plundered,
And overthrows the mighty.
20 He deprives the trusted ones of
speech,
And takes away the discernment of the
elders.
21 He pours contempt on princes,
And disarms the mighty.
22 He uncovers deep things out of
darkness,
And brings the shadow of death to
light.
23 He makes nations great, and destroys
them;
He enlarges nations, and guides them.
24 He takes away the understanding of
the chiefs of the people of the earth,
And makes them wander in a pathless
wilderness.
25 They grope in the dark without light,
And He makes them stagger like a
drunken *man*.

Psalm 94:1–11

O LORD God, to whom vengeance
belongs—
O God, to whom vengeance belongs,
shine forth!

94:1 to whom vengeance belongs. Vengeance from God is not in the sense of uncontrolled vindictiveness, but in the sense of just retribution by the eternal Judge for trespasses against His law. **shine forth.** Make an appearance. He may even be asking for a theophany (Pss. 50:2; 80:1).

2 Rise up, O Judge of the earth;
Render punishment to the proud.
3 LORD, how long will the wicked,
How long will the wicked triumph?
4 They utter speech, *and* speak insolent
things;
All the workers of iniquity boast in
themselves.
5 They break in pieces Your people,
O LORD,
And afflict Your heritage.

6 They slay the widow and
the stranger,
And murder the fatherless.
7 Yet they say, "The LORD does not see,
Nor does the God of Jacob understand."

8 Understand, you senseless among
the people;
And *you* fools, when will you
be wise?
9 He who planted the ear, shall He not
hear?
He who formed the eye, shall He not
see?
10 He who instructs the nations, shall He
not correct,
He who teaches man knowledge?
11 The LORD knows the thoughts
of man,
That they *are* futile.

Proverbs 22:24–25

24 Make no friendship with an angry
man,
And with a furious man do not go,
25 Lest you learn his ways
And set a snare for your soul.

Romans 10:1–21

10 Brethren, my heart's desire and prayer to
God for Israel is that they may be saved.
[2]For I bear them witness that they have a zeal
for God, but not according to knowledge. [3]For
they being ignorant of God's righteousness,
and seeking to establish their own righteousness, have not submitted to the righteousness
of God. [4]For Christ *is* the end of the law for
righteousness to everyone who believes.
[5]For Moses writes about the righteousness
which is of the law, *"The man who does those
things shall live by them."* [6]But the righteousness of faith speaks in this way, *"Do not say in
your heart, 'Who will ascend into heaven?'"*
(that is, to bring Christ down *from above*) [7]or,
"'Who will descend into the abyss?'" (that is, to
bring Christ up from the dead). [8]But what does
it say? *"The word is near you, in your mouth
and in your heart"* (that is, the word of faith
which we preach): [9]that if you confess with your
mouth the Lord Jesus and believe in your heart
that God has raised Him from the dead, you will
be saved. [10]For with the heart one believes unto
righteousness, and with the mouth confession is
made unto salvation. [11]For the Scripture says,
*"Whoever believes on Him will not be put to
shame."* [12]For there is no distinction between
Jew and Greek, for the same Lord over all is

10:4 Christ *is* the end of the law. Although the Greek word translated "end" can mean either "fulfillment" or "termination," this is not a reference to Christ's having perfectly fulfilled the law through His teaching (Matt. 5:17,18) or through His sinless life (2 Cor. 5:21). Instead, as the second half of the verse shows, Paul means that belief in Christ as Lord and Savior ends the sinner's futile quest for righteousness through his imperfect attempts to save himself by efforts to obey the law (3:20–22; Is. 64:6; Col. 2:13,14).

10:9 confess...the Lord Jesus. Not a simple acknowledgment that He is God and the Lord of the universe, since even demons acknowledge that to be true (James 2:19). This is the deep personal conviction, without reservation, that Jesus is that person's own master or sovereign. This phrase includes repenting from sin, trusting in Jesus for salvation, and submitting to Him as Lord. This is the volitional element of faith. **God has raised Him from the dead.** Christ's resurrection was the supreme validation of His ministry (John 2:18–21). Belief in it is necessary for salvation because it proved that Christ is who He claimed to be and that the Father had accepted His sacrifice in the place of sinners (4:24; Acts 13:32,33; 1 Pet. 1:3,4). Without the resurrection, there is no salvation (1 Cor. 15:14–17).

rich to all who call upon Him. [13]For *"whoever
calls on the name of the LORD shall be saved."*
[14]How then shall they call on Him in whom
they have not believed? And how shall they
believe in Him of whom they have not heard?
And how shall they hear without a preacher?
[15]And how shall they preach unless they are
sent? As it is written:

*"How beautiful are the feet of those
who preach the gospel of peace,
Who bring glad tidings of good things!"*

[16]But they have not all obeyed the gospel. For
Isaiah says, *"LORD, who has believed our
report?"* [17]So then faith *comes* by hearing, and
hearing by the word of God.
[18]But I say, have they not heard? Yes indeed:

*"Their sound has gone out to all the
earth,
And their words to the ends of the
world."*

[19]But I say, did Israel not know? First Moses
says:

"I will provoke you to jealousy by those
who are not a nation,
I will move you to anger by a foolish
nation."

20 But Isaiah is very bold and says:

"I was found by those who did not
seek Me;
I was made manifest to those who
did not ask for Me."

21 But to Israel he says:

"All day long I have stretched out
My hands
To a disobedient and contrary
people."

DAY 10: How was Zophar's argument right and wrong regarding Job's situation?

In Job 11:1–20, Zophar the Naamathite stepped in to interrogate Job. He chose to pound Job with the same law of retaliation. Job must repent, he said, not understanding the reality. He was indignant at Job's protests of innocence. And he moved the allegations against Job to a new level. Not only was Job guilty and unrepentant, he was also an empty talker (vv. 2,3). In fact, Job's long-winded defense of his innocence and God's apparent injustice was sin worthy of rebuke, in Zophar's mind.

In v. 4, Zophar claimed that Job had said, "I am clean in your eyes." Job never claimed sinlessness; in fact, he acknowledged that he had sinned (7:21; 13:26). But he still maintained his innocence of any great transgression or attitude of unrepentance, affirming his sincerity and integrity as a man of faith and obedience to God. This claim infuriated Zophar (v. 5).

Zophar was correct that Job would have been much wiser if he had only known the unknowable secrets of God (v. 6). In this case, the scene in heaven between God and Satan would have clarified everything. But Job couldn't know the secret wisdom of God (vv. 7–9). Zophar should have applied his point to himself. If God's wisdom was so deep, high, long, and broad, how was it that he could understand it and have all the answers? Like his friends, Zophar thought he understood God and reverted to the same law of retaliation, the sowing and reaping principle, to again indict Job. He implied that Job was wicked (vv. 10,11) and thought he was wise, though actually he was out of control as if he were a "wild donkey man" (v. 12).

Zophar set out 4 steps of Job's repentance in vv. 13,14: 1) devote your heart to God; 2) stretch your hands to Him in prayer for forgiveness; 3) put your sin far away; and 4) don't allow any sin in your tent. If Job did these things, he would be blessed (vv. 15–19). If Job didn't repent, he would die (v. 20). Zophar was right that the life of faith in God is based on penitence and obedience. He was right that God blesses His people with hope, security, and peace. But, like his friends, he was wrong in not understanding that God allows unpredictable and seemingly unfair suffering for reasons not known to us. He was wrong in presuming that the answer for Job was repentance.

AUGUST 11

Job 13:1–14:22

13 "Behold, my eye has seen all *this,*
My ear has heard and understood it.
2 What you know, I also know;
I *am* not inferior to you.
3 But I would speak to the Almighty,
And I desire to reason with God.
4 But you forgers of lies,
You *are* all worthless physicians.
5 Oh, that you would be silent,
And it would be your wisdom!
6 Now hear my reasoning,
And heed the pleadings of my lips.
7 Will you speak wickedly for God,
And talk deceitfully for Him?
8 Will you show partiality for Him?
Will you contend for God?
9 Will it be well when He searches you
out?
Or can you mock Him as one mocks a
man?
10 He will surely rebuke you
If you secretly show partiality.
11 Will not His excellence make you
afraid,
And the dread of Him fall upon you?
12 Your platitudes *are* proverbs of ashes,
Your defenses are defenses of clay.
13 "Hold your peace with me, and let me
speak,
Then let come on me what *may!*
14 Why do I take my flesh in my teeth,
And put my life in my hands?
15 Though He slay me, yet will I trust
Him.

13:15 Though He slay me, yet will I trust Him. Job assured his accusers that his convictions were not self-serving, because he was ready to die trusting God. But still he would defend his innocence before God and was confident that he was truly saved and not a hypocrite (v. 16).

13:23 How many *are* my iniquities and sins? Job wanted to know how many so that he could determine if his measure of suffering matched the severity of his sin, and he could then repent for sins he was unaware of.

Even so, I will defend my own ways
before Him.
16 He also *shall* be my salvation,
For a hypocrite could not come before
Him.
17 Listen carefully to my speech,
And to my declaration with your ears.
18 See now, I have prepared *my* case,
I know that I shall be vindicated.
19 Who *is* he *who* will contend with me?
If now I hold my tongue, I perish.

20 "Only two *things* do not do to me,
Then I will not hide myself from You:
21 Withdraw Your hand far from me,
And let not the dread of You make me
afraid.
22 Then call, and I will answer;
Or let me speak, then You respond to me.
23 How many *are* my iniquities and sins?
Make me know my transgression and
my sin.
24 Why do You hide Your face,
And regard me as Your enemy?
25 Will You frighten a leaf driven to and
fro?
And will You pursue dry stubble?
26 For You write bitter things against me,
And make me inherit the iniquities of
my youth.
27 You put my feet in the stocks,
And watch closely all my paths.
You set a limit for the soles of my feet.

28 "*Man* decays like a rotten thing,
Like a garment that is moth-eaten.

14 "Man *who is* born of woman
Is of few days and full of trouble.
2 He comes forth like a flower and fades
away;
He flees like a shadow and does not
continue.
3 And do You open Your eyes on such a
one,
And bring me to judgment with
Yourself?
4 Who can bring a clean *thing* out of an
unclean?
No one!
5 Since his days *are* determined,
The number of his months *is* with You;
You have appointed his limits, so that
he cannot pass.
6 Look away from him that he may rest,
Till like a hired man he finishes his
day.

7 "For there is hope for a tree,
If it is cut down, that it will sprout
again,
And that its tender shoots will not
cease.
8 Though its root may grow old in the
earth,
And its stump may die in the ground,
9 *Yet* at the scent of water it will bud
And bring forth branches like a plant.
10 But man dies and is laid away;
Indeed he breathes his last
And where *is* he?
11 *As* water disappears from the sea,
And a river becomes parched and dries
up,
12 So man lies down and does not rise.
Till the heavens *are* no more,
They will not awake
Nor be roused from their sleep.

13 "Oh, that You would hide me in the
grave,
That You would conceal me until Your
wrath is past,
That You would appoint me a set time,
and remember me!
14 If a man dies, shall he live *again?*
All the days of my hard service I will
wait,
Till my change comes.
15 You shall call, and I will answer You;
You shall desire the work of Your hands.
16 For now You number my steps,
But do not watch over my sin.
17 My transgression *is* sealed up in a bag,
And You cover my iniquity.

18 "But *as* a mountain falls *and* crumbles
away,
And *as* a rock is moved from its place;
19 *As* water wears away stones,
And as torrents wash away the soil of
the earth;
So You destroy the hope of man.

20 You prevail forever against him, and he
passes on;
You change his countenance and send
him away.
21 His sons come to honor, and he does
not know *it;*
They are brought low, and he does not
perceive *it.*
22 But his flesh will be in pain over it,
And his soul will mourn over it."

Psalm 94:12–19

12 Blessed *is* the man whom You instruct,
O LORD,
And teach out of Your law,
13 That You may give him rest from the
days of adversity,
Until the pit is dug for the wicked.
14 For the LORD will not cast off His
people,
Nor will He forsake His inheritance.

94:14 will not cast off His people. God has a permanent commitment to His people, Israel, established through a covenant based on His abiding love (Gen. 15; Jer. 12:15; Mic. 7:18). This important truth serves as a doctrinal basis for Pss. 93–100 and was intended to encourage the nation during difficult times. Paul refers to this in Romans 11:1 as he assures the future salvation of Israel.

15 But judgment will return to
righteousness,
And all the upright in heart will follow
it.
16 Who will rise up for me against the
evildoers?
Who will stand up for me against the
workers of iniquity?
17 Unless the LORD *had been* my help,
My soul would soon have settled in
silence.
18 If I say, "My foot slips,"
Your mercy, O LORD, will hold me up.
19 In the multitude of my anxieties within
me,
Your comforts delight my soul.

Proverbs 22:26–27

26 Do not be one of those who shakes
hands in a pledge,
One of those who is surety for debts;
27 If you have nothing *with which* to pay,
Why should he take away your bed
from under you?

Romans 11:1–18

11 I say then, has God cast away His people?
Certainly not! For I also am an Israelite, of
the seed of Abraham, *of* the tribe of Benjamin.
[2]God has not cast away His people whom He
foreknew. Or do you not know what the
Scripture says of Elijah, how he pleads with
God against Israel, saying, [3]"*LORD, they have
killed Your prophets and torn down Your
altars, and I alone am left, and they seek my
life*"? [4]But what does the divine response say
to him? *"I have reserved for Myself seven thousand men who have not bowed the knee to
Baal."* [5]Even so then, at this present time there is
a remnant according to the election of grace.
[6]And if by grace, then *it is* no longer of works;
otherwise grace is no longer grace. But if *it is* of
works, it is no longer grace; otherwise work is
no longer work.
[7]What then? Israel has not obtained what it
seeks; but the elect have obtained it, and the
rest were blinded. [8]Just as it is written:

11:1 cast away. To thrust away from oneself. The form of the question in the Greek text expects a negative answer. Despite Israel's disobedience (9:1–13; 10:14–21), God has not rejected His people (1 Sam. 12:22; 1 Kin. 6:13; Pss. 89:31–37; 94:14; Is. 49:15; 54:1–10; Jer. 33:19–26). **Certainly not!** The strongest form of negation in Greek.

11:17 branches were broken off. Some, but not all, of the branches of Israel were removed. God always preserved a believing remnant (vv. 3,4). **a wild olive tree,...grafted in.** Olives were an important crop in the ancient world. Although trees often lived for hundreds of years, individual branches eventually stopped producing olives. When that happened, branches from younger trees were grafted in to restore productivity. Paul's point is that the old, unproductive branches (Israel) were broken off and branches from a wild olive tree (Gentiles) were grafted in. **the root and fatness.** Once grafted in, Gentiles partake of the richness of God's covenant blessings as the spiritual heirs of Abraham (4:11; Gal. 3:29). **the olive tree.** The place of divine blessing—God's covenant of salvation made with Abraham (Gen. 12:1–3; 15:1–21; 17:1–27).

"God has given them a spirit of stupor,
Eyes that they should not see
And ears that they should not hear,
To this very day."

9And David says:

"Let their table become a snare and a trap,
A stumbling block and a recompense to them.
10 *Let their eyes be darkened, so that they do not see,*
And bow down their back always."

11I say then, have they stumbled that they
should fall? Certainly not! But through their
fall, to provoke them to jealousy, salvation *has*
come to the Gentiles. 12Now if their fall *is* riches
for the world, and their failure riches for the
Gentiles, how much more their fullness!
13For I speak to you Gentiles; inasmuch as I
am an apostle to the Gentiles, I magnify my ministry, 14if by any means I may provoke to jealousy *those who are* my flesh and save some of
them. 15For if their being cast away *is* the reconciling of the world, what *will* their acceptance *be* but life from the dead?
16For if the firstfruit *is* holy, the lump *is* also
holy; and if the root *is* holy, so *are* the branches.
17And if some of the branches were broken off,
and you, being a wild olive tree, were grafted in
among them, and with them became a partaker of the root and fatness of the olive tree, 18do
not boast against the branches. But if you do
boast, *remember that* you do not support the
root, but the root *supports* you.

DAY 11: What kind of relationship did Job have with God?

Job's biography begins with a 4-part description of his character: "blameless and upright, and one who feared God and shunned evil" (1:1). He prayed for his children and was concerned about their relationship with God (v. 5). He was successful and wealthy—the stereotype of a blessed man. In fact, God adds His own glowing approval of Job, using the same traits that open the book (v. 8).

Faced with the sudden, crushing loss of everything—children, servants, herds—Job's initial response was to grieve and recognize God's sovereignty. "'The LORD gave, and the LORD has taken away; blessed be the name of the LORD.' In all this Job did not sin nor charge God with wrong" (vv. 21b,22).

Under the harsh judgments of his friends, Job eventually struggled to understand why God seemed unwilling to settle matters. Once God did speak, at least part of Job's problem becomes clear—he confused a relationship with God with familiarity with God. The Lord did not rebuke Job's faith or sincerity; instead, God questioned Job's insistence on an answer for his difficulties. By allowing Job to hear just a little of the extent of his ignorance, God showed Job that there was a great deal of knowledge he would never understand. As a creature, Job simply had no right to demand an answer from his Creator. Job's final words are filled with humility and repentance: "I have heard of You by the hearing of the ear, but now my eye sees You. Therefore I abhor myself, and repent in dust and ashes" (42:5,6).

Job spent his last days enjoying the same kind of relationship he had earlier with God. He prayed for his friends and raised another family of godly children. He lived a full life.

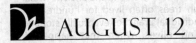

AUGUST 12

Job 15:1–16:22

15 Then Eliphaz the Temanite answered and said:

2 "Should a wise man answer with empty knowledge,
And fill himself with the east wind?
3 Should he reason with unprofitable talk,
Or by speeches with which he can do no good?
4 Yes, you cast off fear,
And restrain prayer before God.
5 For your iniquity teaches your mouth,
And you choose the tongue of the crafty.
6 Your own mouth condemns you, and not I;
Yes, your own lips testify against you.

7 "*Are* you the first man *who* was born?
Or were you made before the hills?
8 Have you heard the counsel of God?
Do you limit wisdom to yourself?
9 What do you know that we do not know?
What do you understand that *is* not in us?

10 Both the gray-haired and the aged *are*
among us,
Much older than your father.
11 *Are* the consolations of God too small
for you,
And the word *spoken* gently with you?
12 Why does your heart carry you away,
And what do your eyes wink at,
13 That you turn your spirit against God,
And let *such* words go out of your
mouth?

14 "What *is* man, that he could be pure?
And *he who is* born of a woman, that he
could be righteous?
15 If *God* puts no trust in His saints,
And the heavens are not pure in His
sight,
16 How much less man, *who is*
abominable and filthy,
Who drinks iniquity like water!

15:14–16 A strong statement with regard to the sinfulness of man (Rom. 3:23) that attacked Job's claim to righteousness. Verse 15 refers to holy angels who fell and brought impurity into the heavens (Rev. 12:1–4). The truth is accurate, that all men are sinners—but irrelevant in Job's case, because his suffering was not due to any sin.

17 "I will tell you, hear me;
What I have seen I will declare,
18 What wise men have told,
Not hiding *anything received* from their
fathers,
19 To whom alone the land was given,
And no alien passed among them:
20 The wicked man writhes with pain all
his days,
And the number of years is hidden
from the oppressor.
21 Dreadful sounds *are* in his ears;
In prosperity the destroyer comes
upon him.
22 He does not believe that he will return
from darkness,
For a sword is waiting for him.
23 He wanders about for bread, *saying,*
'Where *is it?*'
He knows that a day of darkness is
ready at his hand.
24 Trouble and anguish make him afraid;
They overpower him, like a king ready
for battle.
25 For he stretches out his hand against
God,
And acts defiantly against the
Almighty,
26 Running stubbornly against Him
With his strong, embossed shield.

27 "Though he has covered his face with
his fatness,
And made *his* waist heavy with fat,
28 He dwells in desolate cities,
In houses which no one inhabits,
Which are destined to become ruins.
29 He will not be rich,
Nor will his wealth continue,
Nor will his possessions overspread
the earth.
30 He will not depart from darkness;
The flame will dry out his branches,
And by the breath of His mouth he will
go away.
31 Let him not trust in futile *things,*
deceiving himself,
For futility will be his reward.
32 It will be accomplished before his time,
And his branch will not be green.
33 He will shake off his unripe grape like
a vine,
And cast off his blossom like an olive
tree.
34 For the company of hypocrites *will be*
barren,
And fire will consume the tents of
bribery.
35 They conceive trouble and bring forth
futility;
Their womb prepares deceit."

16 Then Job answered and said:

2 "I have heard many such things;
Miserable comforters *are* you all!
3 Shall words of wind have an end?
Or what provokes you that you answer?
4 I also could speak as you *do,*
If your soul were in my soul's place.
I could heap up words against you,
And shake my head at you;
5 *But* I would strengthen you with my
mouth,
And the comfort of my lips would
relieve *your grief.*

6 "Though I speak, my grief is not
relieved;
And *if* I remain silent, how am I eased?
7 But now He has worn me out;
You have made desolate all my
company.

8 You have shriveled me up,
And it is a witness *against me;*
My leanness rises up against me
And bears witness to my face.
9 He tears *me* in His wrath, and hates
me;
He gnashes at me with His teeth;
My adversary sharpens His gaze on
me.
10 They gape at me with their mouth,
They strike me reproachfully on the
cheek,
They gather together against me.
11 God has delivered me to the ungodly,
And turned me over to the hands of
the wicked.
12 I was at ease, but He has shattered me;
He also has taken *me* by my neck, and
shaken me to pieces;
He has set me up for His target,
13 His archers surround me.
He pierces my heart and does not pity;
He pours out my gall on the ground.
14 He breaks me with wound upon
wound;
He runs at me like a warrior.

15 "I have sewn sackcloth over my skin,
And laid my head in the dust.
16 My face is flushed from weeping,
And on my eyelids *is* the shadow of
death;
17 Although no violence *is* in my hands,
And my prayer *is* pure.

18 "O earth, do not cover my blood,
And let my cry have no *resting* place!
19 Surely even now my witness *is* in
heaven,
And my evidence *is* on high.
20 My friends scorn me;
My eyes pour out *tears* to God.
21 Oh, that one might plead for a man
with God,
As a man *pleads* for his neighbor!
22 For when a few years are finished,
I shall go the way of no return.

Psalm 94:20–23

20 Shall the throne of iniquity, which
devises evil by law,
Have fellowship with You?
21 They gather together against the life of
the righteous,
And condemn innocent blood.
22 But the LORD has been my defense,
And my God the rock of my refuge.
23 He has brought on them their own
iniquity,
And shall cut them off in their own
wickedness;
The LORD our God shall cut them off.

Proverbs 22:28–29

28 Do not remove the ancient landmark
Which your fathers have set.

29 Do you see a man *who* excels in his
work?
He will stand before kings;
He will not stand before unknown *men.*

Romans 11:19–36

[19]You will say then, "Branches were broken
off that I might be grafted in." [20]Well *said.*
Because of unbelief they were broken off, and
you stand by faith. Do not be haughty, but fear.
[21]For if God did not spare the natural branches, He may not spare you either. [22]Therefore
consider the goodness and severity of God: on
those who fell, severity; but toward you, goodness, if you continue in *His* goodness. Otherwise you also will be cut off. [23]And they also, if
they do not continue in unbelief, will be grafted in, for God is able to graft them in again.

11:20 unbelief...faith. Branches were broken off and others grafted in based solely on the issue of faith, not race, ethnicity, social or intellectual background, or external morality. Salvation is ever and always by faith alone (1:16,17; Eph. 2:8,9). **fear.** (See 1 Cor. 10:12; 2 Cor. 13:5.) God will judge the apostate church (Rev. 2:15,16; 3:16) just as surely as He judged apostate Israel.

11:22 consider the goodness and severity. All of God's attributes work in harmony. There is no conflict between His goodness and love, and His justice and wrath. Those who accept His gracious offer of salvation experience His goodness (2:4); those who reject it experience His severity (2:5). **those who fell.** The unbelieving Jews described in vv. 12–21. "Fell" translates a Greek word meaning "to fall so as to be completely ruined." Those who reject God's offer of salvation bring upon themselves utter spiritual ruin. **if you continue.** Genuine saving faith always perseveres (John 8:31; 15:5,6; Col. 1:22,23; Heb. 3:12–14; 4:11; 1 John 2:19). **cut off.** From the same Greek root word translated "severity" earlier in the verse. God will deal swiftly and severely with those who reject Him.

[24]For if you were cut out of the olive tree which is wild by nature, and were grafted contrary to nature into a cultivated olive tree, how much more will these, who *are* natural *branches*, be grafted into their own olive tree?

[25]For I do not desire, brethren, that you should be ignorant of this mystery, lest you should be wise in your own opinion, that blindness in part has happened to Israel until the fullness of the Gentiles has come in. [26]And so all Israel will be saved, as it is written:

"The Deliverer will come out of Zion,
And He will turn away ungodliness
from Jacob;
27 *For this is My covenant with them,*
When I take away their sins."

[28]Concerning the gospel *they are* enemies
for your sake, but concerning the election *they*
are beloved for the sake of the fathers. [29]For
the gifts and the calling of God *are* irrevocable. [30]For as you were once disobedient to
God, yet have now obtained mercy through
their disobedience, [31]even so these also have
now been disobedient, that through the mercy
shown you they also may obtain mercy. [32]For
God has committed them all to disobedience, that He might have mercy on all.

[33]Oh, the depth of the riches both of the wisdom and knowledge of God! How unsearchable *are* His judgments and His ways past finding out!

34 *"For who has known the mind of the*
LORD?
Or who has become His counselor?"
35 *"Or who has first given to Him*
And it shall be repaid to him?"

[36]For of Him and through Him and to Him *are* all things, to whom *be* glory forever. Amen.

11:33 wisdom. (See Ps. 104:24; Dan. 2:20; Eph. 3:10; Rev. 7:12.) **knowledge.** God's omniscience (1 Sam. 2:3; 1 Kin. 8:39; Ps. 44:21; 147:5). **judgments.** God's purposes or decrees, which are beyond human understanding (Ps. 36:6). **ways.** The methods God chooses to accomplish His purposes (Job 5:9; 9:10; 26:14).

DAY 12: How did Job's friends fail him?

"I have heard many such things; miserable comforters are you all!" (Job 16:1). Job's friends had come to comfort him. In spite of 7 blissful days of silence at the outset, their mission had failed miserably, and their comfort had turned into more torment for Job. What started out as Eliphaz's sincere efforts to help Job understand his dilemma had turned into rancor and sarcasm. In the end, their haranguing had heightened the frustrations of all parties involved. If the matter were reversed and Job was comforter to his friends, he would never treat them as they have treated him. He would have strengthened and comforted them.

"He tears me in His wrath, and hates me; He gnashes at me with His teeth" (v. 9). "I was at ease, but He has shattered me" (v. 12). These poignant thoughts from Job lamented his suffering as severe judgment from God, who had worn him out, withered his strength, and chewed him up by severe scrutiny ("sharpens His gaze," v. 9). Job refers to God as "my Adversary," who had shattered, shaken, shot at, and sliced him (vv. 12–14).

He had no one to turn to in his sorrow, except God (v. 19), who was silent and had not vindicated him. "My friends scorn me" (v. 20), when they should have comforted him. "Oh, that one might plead for a man with God" (v. 21). The pleading would be for a verdict of innocence on behalf of a friend or neighbor in a court setting before the judge/king. God anticipated the need of an advocate, and He has provided One in the Person of the Lord Jesus Christ (1 Tim. 2:5; 1 John 2:1,2).

AUGUST 13

Job 17:1–18:21

17 "My spirit is broken,
My days are extinguished,
The grave *is ready* for me.
2 *Are* not mockers with me?
And does not my eye dwell on their
provocation?
3 "Now put down a pledge for me with
Yourself.
Who *is* he *who* will shake hands with
me?
4 For You have hidden their heart from
understanding;
Therefore You will not exalt *them*.
5 He who speaks flattery to *his* friends,
Even the eyes of his children will fail.
6 "But He has made me a byword of the
people,

And I have become one in whose face
men spit.
7 My eye has also grown dim because of
sorrow,
And all my members *are* like shadows.
8 Upright *men* are astonished at this,
And the innocent stirs himself up
against the hypocrite.
9 Yet the righteous will hold to his way,
And he who has clean hands will be
stronger and stronger.

10 "But please, come back again,
all of you,
For I shall not find *one* wise *man*
among you.
11 My days are past,
My purposes are broken off,
Even the thoughts of my heart.
12 They change the night into day;
'The light *is* near,' *they say,* in the face
of darkness.
13 If I wait *for* the grave *as* my house,
If I make my bed in the darkness,
14 If I say to corruption, 'You *are* my
father,'
And to the worm, 'You *are* my mother
and my sister,'
15 Where then *is* my hope?
As for my hope, who can see it?
16 *Will* they go down to the gates of
Sheol?
Shall *we have* rest together in the
dust?"

18 Then Bildad the Shuhite answered and
said:

2 "How long *till* you put an end to words?
Gain understanding, and afterward we
will speak.
3 Why are we counted as beasts,
And regarded as stupid in your sight?
4 You who tear yourself in anger,
Shall the earth be forsaken for you?
Or shall the rock be removed from its
place?

5 "The light of the wicked indeed goes
out,
And the flame of his fire does not
shine.
6 The light is dark in his tent,
And his lamp beside him is put out.
7 The steps of his strength are
shortened,
And his own counsel casts him down.
8 For he is cast into a net by his own feet,
And he walks into a snare.
9 The net takes *him* by the heel,
And a snare lays hold of him.
10 A noose *is* hidden for him on the
ground,
And a trap for him in the road.
11 Terrors frighten him on every side,
And drive him to his feet.
12 His strength is starved,
And destruction *is* ready at his side.
13 It devours patches of his skin;
The firstborn of death devours his
limbs.
14 He is uprooted from the shelter of his
tent,
And they parade him before the king
of terrors.
15 They dwell in his tent *who are* none of
his;
Brimstone is scattered on his dwelling.
16 His roots are dried out below,
And his branch withers above.
17 The memory of him perishes from the
earth,
And he has no name among the
renowned.
18 He is driven from light into darkness,
And chased out of the world.
19 He has neither son nor posterity among
his people,
Nor any remaining in his dwellings.
20 Those in the west are astonished at his
day,
As those in the east are frightened.
21 Surely such *are* the dwellings of the
wicked,
And this *is* the place *of him who* does
not know God."

Psalm 95:1–5

Oh come, let us sing to the LORD!
Let us shout joyfully to
the Rock of our salvation.
2 Let us come before His presence with
thanksgiving;
Let us shout joyfully to Him with
psalms.
3 For the LORD *is* the great God,
And the great King above all gods.
4 In His hand *are* the deep places of the
earth;
The heights of the hills *are* His also.
5 The sea *is* His, for He made it;
And His hands formed the dry *land*.

Proverbs 23:1–3

23 When you sit down to eat
with a ruler,
Consider carefully what *is* before you;

95:1 Rock of our salvation. This metaphor for God was especially appropriate in this psalm, which refers (vv. 8,9) to the water that came from the rock in the wilderness (Ex. 17:1–7; Num. 20:1–13; 1 Cor. 10:4).

95:3 the great King above all gods. This is a poetic way of denying the existence of other gods (96:5), which existed only as statues, not persons (Jer. 10:1–10).

95:4 deep places of the earth. This refers to the depths of the seas, valleys, and caverns, and contrasts with the hills. The point (v. 5) is that God was not a local god like the imaginary gods of the heathens, usually put up in high places, but the universal Creator and Ruler of the whole earth.

12:1 present your bodies a living sacrifice. Under the Old Covenant, God accepted the sacrifices of dead animals. But because of Christ's ultimate sacrifice, the Old Testament sacrifices are no longer of any effect (Heb. 9:11,12). For those in Christ, the only acceptable worship is to offer themselves completely to the Lord. Under God's control, the believer's yet unredeemed body can and must be yielded to Him as an instrument of righteousness. **reasonable service.** "Reasonable" is from the Greek for "logic." In light of all the spiritual riches believers enjoy solely as the fruit of God's mercies (Rom. 11:33,36), it logically follows that they owe God their highest form of service. Understood here is the idea of priestly, spiritual service, which was such an integral part of Old Testament worship.

12:2 do not be conformed. "Conformed" refers to assuming an outward expression that does not reflect what is really inside, a kind of masquerade or act. The word's form implies that Paul's readers were already allowing this to happen and must stop. **this world.** Better translated, "age," which refers to the system of beliefs, values—or the spirit of the age—at any time current in the world. This sum of contemporary thinking and values forms the moral atmosphere of our world and is always dominated by Satan (2 Cor. 4:4). **transformed.** The Greek word, from which the English word "metamorphosis" comes, connotes a change in outward appearance. Matthew uses the same word to describe the Transfiguration (Matt. 17:2). Just as Christ briefly and in a limited way displayed outwardly His inner, divine nature and glory at the Transfiguration, Christians should outwardly manifest their inner, redeemed natures, not once, however, but daily (2 Cor. 3:18; Eph. 5:18). **renewing of your mind.** That kind of transformation can occur only as the Holy Spirit changes our thinking through consistent study and meditation of Scripture (Ps. 119:11; Col. 1:28; 3:10, 16; Phil. 4:8). The renewed mind is one saturated with and controlled by the Word of God.

2 And put a knife to your throat
If you *are* a man given to appetite.
3 Do not desire his delicacies,
For they *are* deceptive food.

Romans 12:1–21

12 I beseech you therefore, brethren, by the
mercies of God, that you present your bodies a living sacrifice, holy, acceptable to God,
which is your reasonable service. 2 And do not be
conformed to this world, but be transformed by
the renewing of your mind, that you may prove
what *is* that good and acceptable and perfect
will of God.
3 For I say, through the grace given to me, to
everyone who is among you, not to think *of*
himself more highly than he ought to think, but
to think soberly, as God has dealt to each one a
measure of faith. 4 For as we have many members in one body, but all the members do not
have the same function, 5 so we, *being* many, are
one body in Christ, and individually members
of one another. 6 Having then gifts differing
according to the grace that is given to us, *let us*
use them: if prophecy, *let us prophesy* in proportion to our faith; 7 or ministry, *let us use it* in *our*
ministering; he who teaches, in teaching; 8 he
who exhorts, in exhortation; he who gives,
with liberality; he who leads, with diligence; he
who shows mercy, with cheerfulness.
9 *Let* love *be* without hypocrisy. Abhor what is
evil. Cling to what is good. 10 *Be* kindly affection-
ate to one another with brotherly love, in honor
giving preference to one another; 11 not lagging in
diligence, fervent in spirit, serving the Lord; 12 rejoicing in hope, patient in tribulation, continuing
steadfastly in prayer; 13 distributing to the needs
of the saints, given to hospitality.
14 Bless those who persecute you; bless and
do not curse. 15 Rejoice with those who rejoice,
and weep with those who weep. 16 Be of the
same mind toward one another. Do not set your
mind on high things, but associate with the
humble. Do not be wise in your own opinion.

[17]Repay no one evil for evil. Have regard for good things in the sight of all men. [18]If it is possible, as much as depends on you, live peaceably with all men. [19]Beloved, do not avenge yourselves, but *rather* give place to wrath; for it is written, *"Vengeance is Mine, I will repay,"* says the Lord. [20]Therefore

"If your enemy is hungry, feed him;
If he is thirsty, give him a drink;
For in so doing you will heap coals of fire on his head."

[21]Do not be overcome by evil, but overcome evil with good.

DAY 13: How has God gifted believers to fulfill His purposes?

Romans 12:6–8 describes the general categories of spiritual gifts. These come to us "according to the grace…given"—undeserved and unmerited. The gift itself (1 Cor. 12:4), the specific way in which it is used (1 Cor. 12:5), and the spiritual results (1 Cor. 12:6) are all sovereignly chosen by the Spirit completely apart from personal merit (1 Cor. 12:11).

"Prophecy." This Greek word means "speaking forth" and does not necessarily include prediction of the future or any other mystical or supernatural aspects. Although some prophets in Acts did make predictions of future events (11:27,28; 21:10,11), others made no predictions but spoke the truth of God to encourage and strengthen their hearers (15:32; vv. 22–31). The evidence does suggest, however, that in the first century, before the New Testament was complete and the sign gifts had ceased (1 Cor. 13:8; 2 Cor. 12:12; Heb. 2:3,4), this word may have had both nonrevelatory and revelatory facets. In its nonrevelatory sense, the word "prophecy" simply identifies the skill of public proclamation of the word of God (1 Cor. 14:3,24,25; 1 Pet. 4:11). "In proportion to our faith." Literally, "the faith," or the fully revealed message or body of Christian faith (Jude 3; 2 Tim. 4:2). The preacher must be careful to preach the same message the apostles delivered.

"Ministry" (v. 7). From the same Greek word as "deacon" comes from, it refers to those who serve. This gift, similar to the gift of helps (1 Cor. 12:28), has broad application to include every kind of practical help (Acts 20:35; 1 Cor. 12:28). "Teaching." The ability to interpret, clarify, systematize, and explain God's truth clearly (Acts 18:24,25; 2 Tim. 2:2). Pastors must have the gift of teaching (1 Tim. 3:2; Titus 1:9; 1 Tim. 4:16); but many mature, qualified laymen also have this gift. This differs from preaching (prophecy), not in content, but in the unique skill for public proclamation.

"Exhortation" (v. 8). The gift which enables a believer to effectively call others to obey and follow God's truth. It may be used negatively to admonish and correct regarding sin (2 Tim. 4:2) or positively to encourage, comfort, and strengthen struggling believers (2 Cor. 1:3–5; Heb. 10:24,25). "Gives, with liberality." This denotes the sacrificial sharing and giving of one's resources and self to meet the needs of others (2 Cor. 8:3–5,9; 11; Eph. 4:28). The believer who gives with a proper attitude does not do so for thanks and personal recognition, but to glorify God (Matt. 6:2; Acts 2:44,45; 4:37–5:11; 2 Cor. 8:2–5). "Leads." Literally, "standing before." Paul calls this gift "administrations" (1 Cor. 12:28), a word that means "to guide" and is used of the person who steers a ship (Acts 27:11; Rev. 18:17). Again, the church's leaders must exercise this gift, but it is certainly not limited to them. "Shows mercy, with cheerfulness." One who actively shows sympathy and sensitivity to those in suffering and sorrow and who has both the willingness and the resources to help lessen their afflictions. Frequently, this gift accompanies the gift of exhortation. This attitude is crucial to ensure that the gift of mercy becomes a genuine help, not a discouraging commiseration with those who are suffering (Prov. 14:21,31; Luke 4:18,19).

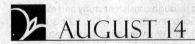

AUGUST 14

Job 19:1–20:29

19 Then Job answered and said:

2 "How long will you torment my soul,
And break me in pieces with words?
3 These ten times you have reproached me;
You are not ashamed *that* you have wronged me.
4 And if indeed I have erred,
My error remains with me.
5 If indeed you exalt *yourselves* against me,
And plead my disgrace against me,
6 Know then that God has wronged me,
And has surrounded me with His net.

7 "If I cry out concerning wrong, I am not heard.
If I cry aloud, *there is* no justice.
8 He has fenced up my way, so that I cannot pass;
And He has set darkness in my paths.

9 He has stripped me of my glory,
And taken the crown *from* my head.
10 He breaks me down on every side,
And I am gone;
My hope He has uprooted like a tree.
11 He has also kindled His wrath against me,
And He counts me as *one of* His enemies.
12 His troops come together
And build up their road against me;
They encamp all around my tent.

13 "He has removed my brothers far from me,
And my acquaintances are completely estranged from me.
14 My relatives have failed,
And my close friends have forgotten me.
15 Those who dwell in my house, and my maidservants,
Count me as a stranger;
I am an alien in their sight.
16 I call my servant, but he gives no answer;
I beg him with my mouth.
17 My breath is offensive to my wife,
And I am repulsive to the children of my own body.
18 Even young children despise me;
I arise, and they speak against me.
19 All my close friends abhor me,
And those whom I love have turned against me.
20 My bone clings to my skin and to my flesh,
And I have escaped by the skin of my teeth.
21 "Have pity on me, have pity on me,
O you my friends,
For the hand of God has struck me!
22 Why do you persecute me as God *does,*
And are not satisfied with my flesh?

23 "Oh, that my words were written!
Oh, that they were inscribed in a book!
24 That they were engraved on a rock
With an iron pen and lead, forever!
25 For I know *that* my Redeemer lives,
And He shall stand at last on the earth;
26 And after my skin is destroyed, this *I know,*
That in my flesh I shall see God,
27 Whom I shall see for myself,
And my eyes shall behold, and not another.
How my heart yearns within me!

19:20 skin of my teeth. This was the origin of a common slang phrase, referring to skin that is thin and fragile. The idea is that he had escaped death by a very slim margin. The loss of all his family, as well as the abuse of his friends was added to the terror of God-forsakeness which had gripped him.

19:23–29 At the point of Job's greatest despair, his faith appeared at its highest as he confidently affirmed that God was his Redeemer. He wanted that confidence in the record for all to know (vv. 23,24). Job wished that the activities of his life were put into words and "inscribed in granite," so all would know that he had not sinned to the magnitude of his suffering. God granted his prayer. God was his Redeemer (Ex. 6:6; Ps. 19:14; 72:14; Is. 43:14; 47:4; 49:26; Jer. 50:34), who would vindicate him in that last day of judgment on the earth when justice was finally done (Jer. 12:1–3; John 5:25,29; Rev. 20:11–15).

28 If you should say, 'How shall we persecute him?'—
Since the root of the matter is found in me,
29 Be afraid of the sword for yourselves;
For wrath *brings* the punishment of the sword,
That you may know *there is* a judgment."

20 Then Zophar the Naamathite answered and said:
2 "Therefore my anxious thoughts make me answer,
Because of the turmoil within me.
3 I have heard the rebuke that reproaches me,
And the spirit of my understanding causes me to answer.

4 "Do you *not* know this of old,
Since man was placed on earth,
5 That the triumphing of the wicked is short,
And the joy of the hypocrite is *but* for a moment?
6 Though his haughtiness mounts up to the heavens,
And his head reaches to the clouds,
7 *Yet* he will perish forever like his own refuse;
Those who have seen him will say,
'Where is he?'

8 He will fly away like a dream, and not
be found;
Yes, he will be chased away like a
vision of the night.
9 The eye *that* saw him will *see him* no
more,
Nor will his place behold him anymore.
10 His children will seek the favor of the
poor,
And his hands will restore his wealth.
11 His bones are full of his youthful vigor,
But it will lie down with him in the
dust.

12 "Though evil is sweet in his mouth,
And he hides it under his tongue,
13 *Though* he spares it and does not
forsake it,
But still keeps it in his mouth,
14 *Yet* his food in his stomach turns sour;
It becomes cobra venom within him.
15 He swallows down riches
And vomits them up again;
God casts them out of his belly.
16 He will suck the poison of cobras;
The viper's tongue will slay him.
17 He will not see the streams,
The rivers flowing with honey and
cream.
18 He will restore that for which he
labored,
And will not swallow *it* down;
From the proceeds of business
He will get no enjoyment.
19 For he has oppressed *and* forsaken the
poor,
He has violently seized a house which
he did not build.

20 "Because he knows no quietness in his
heart,
He will not save anything he desires.
21 Nothing is left for him to eat;
Therefore his well-being will not last.
22 In his self-sufficiency he will be in
distress;
Every hand of misery will come
against him.
23 *When* he is about to fill his stomach,
God will cast on him the fury of His
wrath,
And will rain *it* on him while he is
eating.
24 He will flee from the iron weapon;
A bronze bow will pierce him through.
25 It is drawn, and comes out of the body;
Yes, the glittering *point comes* out of
his gall.
Terrors *come* upon him;
26 Total darkness *is* reserved for his
treasures.
An unfanned fire will consume him;
It shall go ill with him who is left in his
tent.
27 The heavens will reveal his iniquity,
And the earth will rise up against him.
28 The increase of his house will depart,
And his goods will flow away in the day
of His wrath.
29 This *is* the portion from God for a
wicked man,
The heritage appointed to him by
God."

Psalm 95:6–11

6 Oh come, let us worship and bow
down;
Let us kneel before the LORD our
Maker.
7 For He *is* our God,
And we *are* the people of His pasture,
And the sheep of His hand.

Today, if you will hear His voice:
8 "Do not harden your hearts, as in
the rebellion,
As *in* the day of trial in the wilderness,
9 When your fathers tested Me;
They tried Me, though they saw My
work.

95:9 tested Me. This is a reference to the same event (v. 8), also called "Massah" (translated "testing"), when God brought water out of the rock (Ex. 17:7; Deut. 6:16; 9:22; 33:8). The writer to the Hebrews applies the principle of this event to his readers, suggesting that their inclination to doubt the Lord and return to Judaism was parallel with their fathers' inclination to doubt the Lord and go back to Egypt.

10 For forty years I was grieved with *that*
generation,
And said, 'It *is* a people who go astray
in their hearts,
And they do not know My ways.'
11 So I swore in My wrath,
'They shall not enter My rest.' "

Proverbs 23:4–5

4 Do not overwork to be rich;
Because of your own understanding,
cease!
5 Will you set your eyes on that which
is not?

23:4,5 Rather than wearing oneself out pursuing wealth, pursue the wisdom of God and what glorifies Him, and He will bless with prosperity as He chooses.

For *riches* certainly make themselves
wings;
They fly away like an eagle *toward*
heaven.

Romans 13:1–14

13 Let every soul be subject to the governing authorities. For there is no authority
except from God, and the authorities that exist
are appointed by God. 2 Therefore whoever
resists the authority resists the ordinance of
God, and those who resist will bring judgment
on themselves. 3 For rulers are not a terror to
good works, but to evil. Do you want to be
unafraid of the authority? Do what is good,
and you will have praise from the same. 4 For
he is God's minister to you for good. But if you
do evil, be afraid; for he does not bear the
sword in vain; for he is God's minister, an
avenger to *execute* wrath on him who practices
evil. 5 Therefore *you* must be subject, not only
because of wrath but also for conscience'
sake. 6 For because of this you also pay taxes,
for they are God's ministers attending continually to this very thing. 7 Render therefore to
all their due: taxes to whom taxes *are due,* customs to whom customs, fear to whom fear,
honor to whom honor.
8 Owe no one anything except to love one

13:14 But put on the Lord Jesus Christ. This phrase summarizes sanctification, the continuing spiritual process in which those who have been saved by faith are transformed into His image and likeness (2 Cor. 3:18; Gal. 4:19; Phil. 3:13,14; Col. 2:7; 1 John 3:2,3). The image Paul uses to describe that process is taking off and putting on clothing, which is symbolic of thoughts and behavior. **no provision.** This word has the basic meaning of planning ahead or forethought. Most sinful behavior results from wrong ideas and lustful desires we allow to linger in our minds (James 1:14,15).

another, for he who loves another has fulfilled
the law. 9 For the commandments, *"You shall*
not commit adultery," "You shall not murder,"
"You shall not steal," "You shall not bear false
witness," "You shall not covet," and if *there is*
any other commandment, are *all* summed up
in this saying, namely, *"You shall love your*
neighbor as yourself." 10 Love does no harm to
a neighbor; therefore love *is* the fulfillment of
the law.
11 And *do* this, knowing the time, that now *it*
is high time to awake out of sleep; for now our
salvation *is* nearer than when we *first* believed.
12 The night is far spent, the day is at hand.
Therefore let us cast off the works of darkness, and let us put on the armor of light. 13 Let
us walk properly, as in the day, not in revelry
and drunkenness, not in lewdness and lust,
not in strife and envy. 14 But put on the Lord Jesus Christ, and make no provision for the
flesh, to *fulfill its* lusts.

DAY 14: How should a Christian respond to the government?

In Romans 13:1, Paul says, "Let every soul be subject to the governing authorities." This Greek word was used of a soldier's absolute obedience to his superior officer. Scripture makes one exception to this command: when obedience to civil authority would require disobedience to God's word (Ex. 1:17; Dan. 3:16–18; 6:7,10; Acts 4:19,20; 5:28,29). Every position of civil authority without regard to competency, morality, reasonableness, or any other caveat (1 Thess. 4:11,12; 1 Tim. 2:1,2; Titus 3:1,2). "For there is no authority except from God." Since He alone is the sovereign ruler of the universe (Pss. 62:11; 103:19; 1 Tim. 6:15), He has instituted 4 authorities on earth: 1) the government over all citizens; 2) the church over all believers; 3) the parents over all children; and 4) the masters over all employees. Human government's authority is "appointed" and is defined by God. He instituted human government to reward good and to restrain sin in an evil, fallen world.

Since all government is God-ordained, disobedience is rebellion against God (v. 2) and will be met with judgment. Not God's judgment, but punishment from the government for breaking the law. Even the most wicked, godless governments act as a deterrent to crime. Peaceful, law-abiding citizens need not fear the authorities. Few governments will harm those who obey their laws. In fact, governments usually commend such people.

"For because of this you also pay taxes" (v. 6). The Greek word referred specifically to taxes paid by individuals, particularly those living in a conquered nation to their foreign rulers—which makes the tax even more onerous. That tax was usually a combined income and property tax. In this context, however, Paul uses the term in the broadest possible sense to speak of all kinds of taxes. Jesus explicitly taught that taxes are to be paid—even to the pagan Roman government (Matt. 22:17–21). He also set an example by willingly paying the temple tax (Matt. 17:24–27). "Render…to all their due" (v. 7). "Render" translates a Greek word signifying the payment of something owed—not a voluntary contribution—and is reinforced by the word "due." The apostle reiterates that paying taxes is mandatory.

AUGUST 15

Job 21:1–22:30

21 Then Job answered and said:

2 "Listen carefully to my speech,
And let this be your consolation.
3 Bear with me that I may speak,
And after I have spoken, keep mocking.
4 "As for me, *is* my complaint against man?
And if *it were,* why should I not be impatient?
5 Look at me and be astonished;
Put *your* hand over *your* mouth.
6 Even when I remember I am terrified,
And trembling takes hold of my flesh.
7 Why do the wicked live *and* become old,
Yes, become mighty in power?
8 Their descendants are established with them in their sight,
And their offspring before their eyes.
9 Their houses *are* safe from fear,
Neither *is* the rod of God upon them.
10 Their bull breeds without failure;
Their cow calves without miscarriage.
11 They send forth their little ones like a flock,
And their children dance.
12 They sing to the tambourine and harp,
And rejoice to the sound of the flute.
13 They spend their days in wealth,
And in a moment go down to the grave.
14 Yet they say to God, 'Depart from us,
For we do not desire the knowledge of Your ways.
15 Who *is* the Almighty, that we should serve Him?
And what profit do we have if we pray to Him?'
16 Indeed their prosperity *is* not in their hand;
The counsel of the wicked is far from me.

17 "How often is the lamp of the wicked put out?
How often does their destruction come upon them,
The sorrows *God* distributes in His anger?
18 They are like straw before the wind,
And like chaff that a storm carries away.
19 *They say,* 'God lays up one's iniquity for his children';
Let Him recompense him, that he may know *it.*
20 Let his eyes see his destruction,
And let him drink of the wrath of the Almighty.
21 For what does he care about his household after him,
When the number of his months is cut in half?

22 "Can *anyone* teach God knowledge,
Since He judges those on high?
23 One dies in his full strength,
Being wholly at ease and secure;
24 His pails are full of milk,
And the marrow of his bones is moist.
25 Another man dies in the bitterness of his soul,
Never having eaten with pleasure.
26 They lie down alike in the dust,
And worms cover them.

27 "Look, I know your thoughts,
And the schemes *with which* you would wrong me.
28 For you say,
'Where *is* the house of the prince?
And where *is* the tent,
The dwelling place of the wicked?'
29 Have you not asked those who travel the road?
And do you not know their signs?
30 For the wicked are reserved for the day of doom;
They shall be brought out on the day of wrath.
31 Who condemns his way to his face?
And who repays him *for what* he has done?

32 Yet he shall be brought to the grave,
And a vigil kept over the tomb.
33 The clods of the valley shall be sweet
to him;
Everyone shall follow him,
As countless *have gone* before him.
34 How then can you comfort me with
empty words,
Since falsehood remains in your
answers?"

22 Then Eliphaz the Temanite answered
and said:

2 "Can a man be profitable to God,
Though he who is wise may be
profitable to himself?
3 *Is it* any pleasure to the Almighty that
you are righteous?
Or *is it* gain *to Him* that you make your
ways blameless?

4 "Is it because of your fear of Him that
He corrects you,
And enters into judgment with you?
5 *Is* not your wickedness great,
And your iniquity without end?
6 For you have taken pledges from your
brother for no reason,
And stripped the naked of their
clothing.
7 You have not given the weary water to
drink,
And you have withheld bread from the
hungry.
8 But the mighty man possessed the land,
And the honorable man dwelt in it.
9 You have sent widows away empty,
And the strength of the fatherless was
crushed.
10 Therefore snares *are* all around you,
And sudden fear troubles you,
11 Or darkness *so that* you cannot see;
And an abundance of water covers you.

12 "Is not God in the height of heaven?
And see the highest stars, how lofty
they are!
13 And you say, 'What does God know?
Can He judge through the deep
darkness?
14 Thick clouds cover Him, so that He
cannot see,
And He walks above the circle of
heaven.'
15 Will you keep to the old way
Which wicked men have trod,
16 Who were cut down before
their time,
Whose foundations were swept away
by a flood?
17 They said to God, 'Depart from us!
What can the Almighty do to them?'
18 Yet He filled their houses with good
things;
But the counsel of the wicked is far
from me.

19 "The righteous see *it* and are glad,
And the innocent laugh at them:
20 'Surely our adversaries are cut down,
And the fire consumes
their remnant.'

21 "Now acquaint yourself with Him, and
be at peace;
Thereby good will come to you.
22 Receive, please, instruction from His
mouth,
And lay up His words in your heart.
23 If you return to the Almighty, you will
be built up;
You will remove iniquity far from your
tents.
24 Then you will lay your gold in the dust,
And the *gold* of Ophir among the
stones of the brooks.
25 Yes, the Almighty will be your gold
And your precious silver;
26 For then you will have your delight in
the Almighty,
And lift up your face to God.
27 You will make your prayer to Him,
He will hear you,
And you will pay your vows.
28 You will also declare a thing,
And it will be established for you;
So light will shine on your ways.
29 When they cast *you* down, and you say,
'Exaltation *will come!*'
Then He will save the humble *person*.
30 He will *even* deliver one who is not
innocent;
Yes, he will be delivered by the purity
of your hands."

Psalm 96:1–6

Oh, sing to the LORD a new song!
Sing to the LORD, all the earth.
2 Sing to the LORD, bless His name;
Proclaim the good news of His
salvation from day to day.
3 Declare His glory among the nations,
His wonders among all peoples.
4 For the LORD *is* great and greatly to
be praised;
He *is* to be feared above all gods.

96:1 a new song. This new song was intended for the future inauguration of the millennial rule of the Lord over the earth (Pss. 144:9; 149:1; Rev. 5:9; 14:3).

96:3 His glory...nations. The glory of the Lord is more than just His majestic splendor. It includes all of the reasons for admiring and praising Him, such as His acts of creation (Ps. 19:2) and redemption (v. 2).

5 For all the gods of the peoples *are* idols,
But the LORD made the heavens.
6 Honor and majesty *are* before Him;
Strength and beauty *are* in His sanctuary.

Proverbs 23:6–8

6 Do not eat the bread of a miser,
Nor desire his delicacies;
7 For as he thinks in his heart, so *is* he.
"Eat and drink!" he says to you,
But his heart is not with you.
8 The morsel you have eaten, you will vomit up,
And waste your pleasant words.

Romans 14:1–23

14 Receive one who is weak in the faith, *but*
not to disputes over doubtful things. [2]For
one believes he may eat all things, but he who
is weak eats *only* vegetables. [3]Let not him who
eats despise him who does not eat, and let not
him who does not eat judge him who eats; for
God has received him. [4]Who are you to judge
another's servant? To his own master he
stands or falls. Indeed, he will be made to
stand, for God is able to make him stand.
[5]One person esteems *one* day above another; another esteems every day *alike.* Let each
be fully convinced in his own mind. [6]He who
observes the day, observes *it* to the Lord; and
he who does not observe the day, to the Lord
he does not observe *it.* He who eats, eats to
the Lord, for he gives God thanks; and he who
does not eat, to the Lord he does not eat, and
gives God thanks. [7]For none of us lives to himself, and no one dies to himself. [8]For if we live,
we live to the Lord; and if we die, we die to the
Lord. Therefore, whether we live or die, we are
the Lord's. [9]For to this end Christ died and rose
and lived again, that He might be Lord of both
the dead and the living. [10]But why do you judge
your brother? Or why do you show contempt
for your brother? For we shall all stand before
the judgment seat of Christ. [11]For it is written:

"As I live, says the LORD,
Every knee shall bow to Me,
And every tongue shall confess to God."

[12]So then each of us shall give account of
himself to God. [13]Therefore let us not judge
one another anymore, but rather resolve this,
not to put a stumbling block or a cause to fall
in *our* brother's way.
[14]I know and am convinced by the Lord Jesus
that *there is* nothing unclean of itself; but to him
who considers anything to be unclean, to him *it is*
unclean. [15]Yet if your brother is grieved because
of *your* food, you are no longer walking in love.
Do not destroy with your food the one for whom
Christ died. [16]Therefore do not let your good be
spoken of as evil; [17]for the kingdom of God is not
eating and drinking, but righteousness and
peace and joy in the Holy Spirit. [18]For he who
serves Christ in these things *is* acceptable to
God and approved by men.

14:15 grieved. The Greek word refers to causing pain or distress. A weak believer may be hurt when he sees a brother do something he believes is sinful. But still worse, the strong believer may cause his weaker brother to violate his own conscience (1 Cor. 8:8–13). **love.** Love will ensure that the strong Christian is sensitive and understanding of his brother's weaknesses (1 Cor. 8:8–13). **destroy.** This refers to complete devastation. In the New Testament, it is often used to indicate eternal damnation (Matt. 10:28; Luke 13:3; John 3:16; Rom. 2:12). In this context, however, it refers to a serious devastation of one's spiritual growth (Matt. 18:3,6,14).

14:17 kingdom of God. The sphere of salvation where God rules in the hearts of those He has saved. **eating and drinking.** Nonessentials and external observances. **righteousness.** Holy, obedient living (Eph. 6:14; Phil. 1:11). **peace.** The loving tranquillity, produced by the Spirit, that should characterize believers' relationships with God and each other (Gal. 5:22). **joy in the Holy Spirit.** Another part of the Spirit's fruit, this describes an abiding attitude of praise and thanksgiving regardless of circumstances, which flows from one's confidence in God's sovereignty (Gal. 5:22; 1 Thess. 1:6).

[19]Therefore let us pursue the things *which make* for peace and the things by which one may edify another. [20]Do not destroy the work of God for the sake of food. All things indeed *are* pure, but *it is* evil for the man who eats with offense. [21]*It is* good neither to eat meat nor drink wine nor *do anything* by which your brother stumbles or is offended or is made weak. [22]Do you have faith? Have *it* to yourself before God. Happy *is* he who does not condemn himself in what he approves. [23]But he who doubts is condemned if he eats, because *he does* not *eat* from faith; for whatever *is* not from faith is sin.

DAY 15: How is unity maintained within the church when there is so much diversity?

Reading through Romans 14:1–12, it is clear that the diversity of the church displays Christ's power to bring together dissimilar people in genuine unity. Yet Satan often works on man's unredeemed flesh to create division and threaten that unity. The threat to unity Paul addresses in this passage arises when mature (strong) believers—both Jews and Gentiles—conflict with immature (weak) believers. The strong Jewish believers understood their freedom in Christ and realized the ceremonial requirements of the Mosaic Law were no longer binding. The mature Gentiles understood that idols are not gods and, therefore, that they could eat meat that had been offered to them. But in both cases the weaker brothers' consciences were troubled, and they were even tempted to violate their consciences, become more legalistic under the feelings of guilt, or even to sin. Knowing that the mature Jews and Gentiles would be able to understand these struggles, Paul addresses most of his comments to them.

The secret to unity begins with the willingness to "receive one who is weak in the faith" (v. 1). The Greek word refers to personal and willing acceptance of another. This characterizes those believers who are unable to let go of the religious ceremonies and rituals of their past. The weak Jewish believer had difficulty abandoning the rites and prohibitions of the Old Covenant; he felt compelled to adhere to dietary laws, observe the Sabbath, and offer sacrifices in the temple. The weak Gentile believer had been steeped in pagan idolatry and its rituals; he felt that any contact with anything remotely related to his past, including eating meat that had been offered to a pagan deity and then sold in the marketplace, tainted him with sin. Both had very sensitive consciences in these areas and were not yet mature enough to be free of those convictions.

Neither one should "despise…judge" the other (v. 3). "Despise" indicates a contempt for someone as worthless, who deserves only disdain and abhorrence. "Judge" is equally strong and means "to condemn." Paul uses them synonymously: The strong hold the weak in contempt as legalistic and self-righteous; the weak judge the strong to be irresponsible at best and perhaps depraved. "To his own master he stands or falls" (v. 4). How Christ evaluates each believer is what matters, and His judgment does not take into account religious tradition or personal preference.

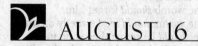

AUGUST 16

Job 23:1–25:6

23 Then Job answered and said:
2 "Even today my complaint is bitter;
My hand is listless because of my groaning.
3 Oh, that I knew where I might find Him,
That I might come to His seat!
4 I would present *my* case before Him,
And fill my mouth with arguments.
5 I would know the words *which* He would answer me,
And understand what He would say to me.
6 Would He contend with me in His great power?
No! But He would take *note* of me.
7 There the upright could reason with Him,
And I would be delivered forever from my Judge.

8 "Look, I go forward, but He is not *there,*
And backward, but I cannot perceive Him;
9 When He works on the left hand, I cannot behold *Him;*
When He turns to the right hand, I cannot see *Him.*
10 But He knows the way that I take;
When He has tested me, I shall come forth as gold.
11 My foot has held fast to His steps;
I have kept His way and not turned aside.
12 I have not departed from the commandment of His lips;

I have treasured the words of His mouth
More than my necessary *food.*

13 "But He *is* unique, and who can make Him change?
And *whatever* His soul desires, *that* He does.
14 For He performs *what is* appointed for me,
And many such *things are* with Him.
15 Therefore I am terrified at His presence;
When I consider *this,* I am afraid of Him.
16 For God made my heart weak,
And the Almighty terrifies me;
17 Because I was not cut off from the presence of darkness,
And He did *not* hide deep darkness from my face.

24 "*Since* times are not hidden from the Almighty,
Why do those who know Him see not His days?
2 "*Some* remove landmarks;
They seize flocks violently and feed *on them;*
3 They drive away the donkey of the fatherless;
They take the widow's ox as a pledge.
4 They push the needy off the road;
All the poor of the land are forced to hide.
5 Indeed, *like* wild donkeys in the desert,
They go out to their work, searching for food.
The wilderness *yields* food for them
and for *their* children.
6 They gather their fodder in the field
And glean in the vineyard of the wicked.
7 They spend the night naked, without clothing,
And have no covering in the cold.
8 They are wet with the showers of the mountains,
And huddle around the rock for want of shelter.
9 "*Some* snatch the fatherless from the breast,
And take a pledge from the poor.
10 They cause *the poor* to go naked, without clothing;
And they take away the sheaves from the hungry.
11 They press out oil within their walls,
And tread winepresses, yet suffer thirst.
12 The dying groan in the city,
And the souls of the wounded cry out;
Yet God does not charge *them* with wrong.
13 "There are those who rebel against the light;
They do not know its ways
Nor abide in its paths.
14 The murderer rises with the light;
He kills the poor and needy;
And in the night he is like a thief.
15 The eye of the adulterer waits for the twilight,
Saying, 'No eye will see me';
And he disguises *his* face.
16 In the dark they break into houses
Which they marked for themselves in the daytime;
They do not know the light.
17 For the morning is the same to them as the shadow of death;
If *someone* recognizes *them,*
They are in the terrors of the shadow of death.
18 "They *should be* swift on the face of the waters,
Their portion *should be* cursed in the earth,
So that no *one would* turn into the way of their vineyards.
19 As drought and heat consume the snow waters,
So the grave *consumes those who* have sinned.
20 The womb *should* forget him,
The worm *should* feed sweetly on him;
He *should* be remembered no more,
And wickedness *should* be broken like a tree.
21 For he preys on the barren *who* do not bear,
And does no good for the widow.
22 "But *God* draws the mighty away with His power;

24:18–21 Again Job referred to the opinions of his counselors, saying that, if their views were correct, all the wicked should be experiencing punishment. But it is obvious they were not.

He rises up, but no *man* is sure of life.
23 He gives them security, and they rely *on it;*
Yet His eyes *are* on their ways.
24 They are exalted for a little while,
Then they are gone.
They are brought low;
They are taken out of the way like all *others;*
They dry out like the heads of grain.

25 "Now if *it is* not *so,* who will prove me a liar,
And make my speech worth nothing?"

25 Then Bildad the Shuhite answered and said:

2 "Dominion and fear *belong* to Him;
He makes peace in His high places.
3 Is there any number to His armies?
Upon whom does His light not rise?
4 How then can man be righteous before God?
Or how can he be pure *who is* born of a woman?
5 If even the moon does not shine,
And the stars are not pure in His sight,
6 How much less man, *who is* a maggot,
And a son of man, *who is* a worm?"

Psalm 96:7–10

7 Give to the LORD, O families of the peoples,
Give to the LORD glory and strength.
8 Give to the LORD the glory *due* His name;
Bring an offering, and come into His courts.
9 Oh, worship the LORD in the beauty of holiness!
Tremble before Him, all the earth.
10 Say among the nations, "The LORD reigns;
The world also is firmly established,
It shall not be moved;
He shall judge the peoples righteously."

96:10 firmly established. Instead of the continuance of international chaos in human history, the world will be settled and efficiently managed by the Messiah in the millennial kingdom (Ps. 2; Mic. 4:1–5). **judge the peoples righteously.** Not only will the Lord establish international peace and stability in the future messianic kingdom, but He will also rule the world with impeccable justice (v. 13; Is. 11:1–5).

Proverbs 23:9

9 Do not speak in the hearing of a fool,
For he will despise the wisdom of your words.

Romans 15:1–24

15 We then who are strong ought to bear
with the scruples of the weak, and not to
please ourselves. 2Let each of us please *his*

15:1 to bear. The word means "to pick up and carry a weight." It is used of carrying a pitcher of water (Mark 14:13), of carrying a man (Acts 21:35), and figuratively of bearing an obligation (Acts 15:10). The strong are not to simply tolerate the weaknesses of their weaker brothers; they are to help the weak shoulder their burdens by showing loving and practical consideration for them (Gal. 6:2; 1 Cor. 9:19–22; Phil. 2:2–4).

neighbor for *his* good, leading to edification.
3For even Christ did not please Himself; but as
it is written, *"The reproaches of those who re-*
proached You fell on Me." 4For whatever
things were written before were written for our
learning, that we through the patience and
comfort of the Scriptures might have hope.
5Now may the God of patience and comfort
grant you to be like-minded toward one another, according to Christ Jesus, 6that you may
with one mind *and* one mouth glorify the God
and Father of our Lord Jesus Christ.
7Therefore receive one another, just as
Christ also received us, to the glory of God.
8Now I say that Jesus Christ has become a servant to the circumcision for the truth of God,
to confirm the promises *made* to the fathers,
9and that the Gentiles might glorify God for
His mercy, as it is written:

"For this reason I will confess to You
among the Gentiles,
And sing to Your name."

10And again he says:

"Rejoice, O Gentiles, with His people!"

11And again:

"Praise the LORD, all you Gentiles!
Laud Him, all you peoples!"

[12]And again, Isaiah says:

"There shall be a root of Jesse;
And He who shall rise to reign over
the Gentiles,
In Him the Gentiles shall hope."

[13]Now may the God of hope fill you with all
joy and peace in believing, that you may
abound in hope by the power of the Holy
Spirit.

[14]Now I myself am confident concerning
you, my brethren, that you also are full of
goodness, filled with all knowledge, able also
to admonish one another. [15]Nevertheless,
brethren, I have written more boldly to you on
some points, as reminding you, because of the
grace given to me by God, [16]that I might be a
minister of Jesus Christ to the Gentiles, ministering the gospel of God, that the offering of
the Gentiles might be acceptable, sanctified
by the Holy Spirit. [17]Therefore I have reason to
glory in Christ Jesus in the things *which pertain* to God. [18]For I will not dare to speak of
any of those things which Christ has not
accomplished through me, in word and deed,
to make the Gentiles obedient—[19]in mighty
signs and wonders, by the power of the Spirit of
God, so that from Jerusalem and round about
to Illyricum I have fully preached the gospel of
Christ. [20]And so I have made it my aim to
preach the gospel, not where Christ was
named, lest I should build on another man's
foundation, [21]but as it is written:

"To whom He was not announced, they
shall see;
And those who have not heard shall
understand."

[22]For this reason I also have been much hindered from coming to you. [23]But now no longer
having a place in these parts, and having a great
desire these many years to come to you, [24]when-
ever I journey to Spain, I shall come to you. For
I hope to see you on my journey, and to be
helped on my way there by you, if first I may enjoy your *company* for a while.

DAY 16: How does Paul exemplify a "minister of Jesus Christ"?

Paul calls himself a "minister of Jesus Christ to the Gentiles" in Romans 15:16. "Minister" was a general Greek term used of public officials. But in the New Testament it is used most often of those who serve God in some form of public worship (e.g., Phil. 2:17; Heb. 1:7,14; 8:1,2,6), including that of a priest (Luke 1:23). Although Paul's practice was always to present the gospel to the Jews first in every city he visited, his primary apostolic calling was to the Gentiles (11:13; Acts 9:15). Having referred to himself as a minister, a word with priestly overtones, Paul explains that his priestly ministry is to present to God an offering of a multitude of Gentile converts.

"Therefore I have reason to glory in Christ Jesus" (v. 17). Literally, "to boast." Paul never boasted in his accomplishments as an apostle, but only in what Christ had accomplished through him (1 Cor. 1:27–29,31; 2 Cor. 10:13–17; 12:5,9; Gal. 6:14; 1 Tim. 1:12–16). In Paul's case, his preaching was accompanied with "signs and wonders" (v. 19). God used them to authenticate true preaching and teaching. "From Jerusalem and round about to Illyricum I have fully preached the gospel of Christ." The region that roughly corresponds to the former European country of Yugoslavia, spanning some 1,400 miles.

Paul's goal was to reach those who had never heard the gospel (v. 20)—the primary function of a New Testament evangelist (Eph. 4:11). But for pastor-teachers, building on the foundation laid by such an evangelist is the crucial part of their ministry (1 Cor. 3:6).

AUGUST 17

Job 26:1–14

26 But Job answered and said:

2 "How have you helped *him who is*
without power?
How have you saved the arm *that has*
no strength?
3 How have you counseled *one who has*
no wisdom?
And *how* have you declared sound
advice to many?
4 To whom have you uttered words?
And whose spirit came from you?

5 "The dead tremble,
Those under the waters and those
inhabiting them.
6 Sheol *is* naked before Him,
And Destruction has no covering.
7 He stretches out the north over empty
space;
He hangs the earth on nothing.
8 He binds up the water in His thick
clouds,

26:7 hangs the earth on nothing. A statement that is accurate, given in ancient time, before scientific verification. This indicates the divine authorship of Scripture.

26:10 a circular horizon. This describes the earth as a circular globe, another scientifically accurate statement at a time when many thought the world was flat.

26:13 His Spirit. Job 33:4. The Holy Spirit worked mightily in creation (Gen. 1:2). **the fleeing serpent.** This is figurative language for the idea that God brought all constellations into subjection under His authority (26:12). "Serpent" could be translated "crooked" and refer to any wayward stars or planets being brought under control by His mighty power.

Yet the clouds are not broken under it.
9 He covers the face of *His* throne,
And spreads His cloud over it.
10 He drew a circular horizon on the face of the waters,
At the boundary of light and darkness.
11 The pillars of heaven tremble,
And are astonished at His rebuke.
12 He stirs up the sea with His power,
And by His understanding He breaks up the storm.
13 By His Spirit He adorned the heavens;
His hand pierced the fleeing serpent.
14 Indeed these *are* the mere edges of His ways,
And how small a whisper we hear of Him!
But the thunder of His power who can understand?"

Psalm 96:11–13

11 Let the heavens rejoice, and let the earth be glad;
Let the sea roar, and all its fullness;
12 Let the field be joyful, and all that *is* in it.
Then all the trees of the woods will rejoice
13 before the LORD.
For He is coming, for He is coming to judge the earth.
He shall judge the world with righteousness,
And the peoples with His truth.

96:13 He is coming. The rule of the Lord described in this psalm is not the present universal kingdom (Ps. 93), but one which will be established when Christ returns to earth.

Proverbs 23:10–12

10 Do not remove the ancient landmark,
Nor enter the fields of the fatherless;
11 For their Redeemer *is* mighty;
He will plead their cause against you.
12 Apply your heart to instruction,
And your ears to words of knowledge.

23:11 Redeemer. In a normal situation the near kinsman would rescue the one who had fallen upon hard times (Lev. 25:25; Ruth 2:20; 3:12,13; 4:1–12) or avenge in the case of a murder (Num. 35:19). "Redeemer" is applied to God as the Savior of His people (e.g., Gen. 48:16; Ex. 6:6; Job 19:25; Ps. 19:14; Is. 41:14; 43:14; 44:24) since the helpless had no voice.

Romans 15:25–33

25 But now I am going to Jerusalem to minister to
the saints. 26 For it pleased those from
Macedonia and Achaia to make a certain contribution for the poor among the saints who are in
Jerusalem. 27 It pleased them indeed, and they
are their debtors. For if the Gentiles have been partakers of their spiritual things, their duty is also to minister to them in material things.
28 Therefore, when I have performed this and
have sealed to them this fruit, I shall go by way
of you to Spain. 29 But I know that when I come
to you, I shall come in the fullness of the blessing of the gospel of Christ.
30 Now I beg you, brethren, through the Lord Jesus Christ, and through the love of the Spirit, that you strive together with me in
prayers to God for me, 31 that I may be deliv-
ered from those in Judea who do not believe, and that my service for Jerusalem may be
acceptable to the saints, 32 that I may come to
you with joy by the will of God, and may be
refreshed together with you. 33 Now the God of
peace *be* with you all. Amen.

DAY 17: Who was Paul the apostle, and why does he seem to have two names?

Paul (Greek name) the apostle was also known as Saul, which was his Hebrew name. Along with his double name, Paul was also able to exercise dual citizenship as a Jewish descendant from the tribe of Benjamin (Phil. 3:5) and as a Roman (Acts 16:37; 22:25). Paul was born about the time of Christ's birth, in Tarsus, located in modern Turkey (Acts 9:11).

Young Saul spent much of his early life in Jerusalem as a student of the celebrated rabbi (teacher) Gamaliel (Acts 22:3). Like his father before him, Paul was a Pharisee (Acts 23:6), a member of the strictest Jewish sect (Phil. 3:5). He actively resisted those who followed Jesus. His first appearance in Scripture occurs in Acts 7:58 as he observed the martyrdom of Stephen.

Miraculously converted while on his way to Damascus (about A.D. 33–34) to persecute Christians, Paul immediately began proclaiming the gospel (Acts 9:20). After narrowly escaping Damascus (Acts 9:23–25; 2 Cor. 11:32,33), Paul spent three years in the wilderness (Gal. 1:17,18). During those years, he received much of his doctrine as direct revelation from the Lord (Gal. 1:11,12).

More than any other individual, Paul was responsible for the spread of Christianity throughout the Roman Empire. He made three missionary journeys along the north side of the Mediterranean Sea, tirelessly preaching the gospel he had once tried to destroy (Acts 26:9). Eventually he was arrested in Jerusalem (Acts 21:27–31), appealed for a hearing before Caesar, and finally reached Rome (chaps. 27; 28). Later, he was released for a short time of ministry then arrested again and martyred at Rome in about A.D. 65–67.

Though physically unimpressive (2 Cor. 10:10; Gal. 4:14), Paul possessed an inner strength granted him through the Holy Spirit's power (Phil. 4:13). The grace of God proved sufficient to provide for his every need (2 Cor. 12:9,10), enabling this noble servant of Christ to successfully finish his spiritual race (2 Tim. 4:7).

AUGUST 18

Job 27:1–28:28

27 Moreover Job continued his discourse, and said:

2 "*As* God lives, *who* has taken away my
justice,
And the Almighty, *who* has made my
soul bitter,
3 As long as my breath *is* in me,
And the breath of God in my nostrils,
4 My lips will not speak wickedness,
Nor my tongue utter deceit.
5 Far be it from me
That I should say you are right;
Till I die I will not put away my
integrity from me.
6 My righteousness I hold fast, and will
not let it go;
My heart shall not reproach *me* as
long as I live.

7 "May my enemy be like the wicked,
And he who rises up against me like
the unrighteous.
8 For what is the hope of the hypocrite,
Though he may gain *much*,
If God takes away his life?
9 Will God hear his cry
When trouble comes upon him?
10 Will he delight himself in the
Almighty?
Will he always call on God?

11 "I will teach you about the hand of God;
What *is* with the Almighty I will not
conceal.
12 Surely all of you have seen *it;*
Why then do you behave with
complete nonsense?

13 "This is the portion of a wicked man
with God,
And the heritage of oppressors,
received from the Almighty:
14 If his children are multiplied, *it is* for
the sword;
And his offspring shall not be satisfied
with bread.
15 Those who survive him shall be buried
in death,
And their widows shall not weep,
16 Though he heaps up silver like dust,
And piles up clothing like clay—
17 He may pile *it* up, but the just will wear
it,
And the innocent will divide the silver.
18 He builds his house like a moth,
Like a booth *which* a watchman makes.
19 The rich man will lie down,
But not be gathered *up;*

He opens his eyes,
And he *is* no more.
20 Terrors overtake him like a flood;
A tempest steals him away in the night.
21 The east wind carries him away, and he is gone;
It sweeps him out of his place.
22 It hurls against him and does not spare;
He flees desperately from its power.
23 *Men* shall clap their hands at him,
And shall hiss him out of his place.

28 "Surely there is a mine for silver,
And a place *where* gold is refined.
2 Iron is taken from the earth,
And copper *is* smelted *from* ore.
3 *Man* puts an end to darkness,
And searches every recess
For ore in the darkness and the shadow of death.
4 He breaks open a shaft away from people;
In places forgotten by feet
They hang far away from men;
They swing to and fro.
5 *As for* the earth, from it comes bread,
But underneath it is turned up as by fire;
6 Its stones *are* the source of sapphires,
And it contains gold dust.
7 *That* path no bird knows,
Nor has the falcon's eye seen it.
8 The proud lions have not trodden it,
Nor has the fierce lion passed over it.
9 He puts his hand on the flint;
He overturns the mountains at the roots.
10 He cuts out channels in the rocks,
And his eye sees every precious thing.
11 He dams up the streams from trickling;
What is hidden he brings forth to light.
12 "But where can wisdom be found?
And where *is* the place of understanding?
13 Man does not know its value,
Nor is it found in the land of the living.
14 The deep says, '*It is* not in me';
And the sea says, '*It is* not with me.'
15 It cannot be purchased for gold,
Nor can silver be weighed *for* its price.
16 It cannot be valued in the gold of Ophir,
In precious onyx or sapphire.
17 Neither gold nor crystal can equal it,
Nor can it be exchanged for jewelry of fine gold.
18 No mention shall be made of coral or quartz,
For the price of wisdom *is* above rubies.
19 The topaz of Ethiopia cannot equal it,
Nor can it be valued in pure gold.
20 "From where then does wisdom come?
And where *is* the place of understanding?
21 It is hidden from the eyes of all living,
And concealed from the birds of the air.
22 Destruction and Death say,
'We have heard a report about it with our ears.'
23 God understands its way,
And He knows its place.
24 For He looks to the ends of the earth,
And sees under the whole heavens,
25 To establish a weight for the wind,
And apportion the waters by measure.
26 When He made a law for the rain,
And a path for the thunderbolt,
27 Then He saw *wisdom* and declared it;
He prepared it, indeed, He searched it out.
28 And to man He said,
'Behold, the fear of the Lord, that *is* wisdom,
And to depart from evil *is* understanding.' "

Psalm 97:1–6

The LORD reigns;
Let the earth rejoice;
Let the multitude of isles be glad!
2 Clouds and darkness surround Him;
Righteousness and justice *are* the foundation of His throne.
3 A fire goes before Him,

97:1 multitude of isles. Refers to all the continents as well as islands of the world (Is. 42:10; Dan. 2:34,35,44; Zech. 14:9).

97:2 Clouds and darkness. Such a description emphasizes the terrifying effect of the Lord's presence, both in the past (Ex. 19:16–18) and in the future Day of the Lord (Joel 2:2; Zeph. 1:15; Matt. 24:29,30).

97:3 burns up His enemies. The Lord will utterly destroy His enemies in the future Day of the Lord (Zech. 14:12).

And burns up His enemies round about.
4 His lightnings light the world;
The earth sees and trembles.
5 The mountains melt like wax at the
presence of the LORD,
At the presence of the Lord of the
whole earth.
6 The heavens declare His
righteousness,
And all the peoples see His glory.

Proverbs 23:13–14

13 Do not withhold correction from a
child,
For *if* you beat him with a rod,
he will not die.
14 You shall beat him with a rod,
And deliver his soul from hell.

Romans 16:1–27

16 I commend to you Phoebe our sister,
who is a servant of the church in

16:1 Phoebe. Means "bright and radiant," which aptly fits Paul's brief description of her personality and Christian character. **servant.** The term from which we get "deacon" and "deaconess" (1 Tim. 3:10,11,13). In the early church, women servants cared for sick believers, the poor, strangers, and those in prison. They instructed the women and children (Titus 2:3–5). Whether Phoebe had an official title or not, she had the great responsibility of delivering this letter to the Roman church. When they had served faithfully and become widowed and destitute, such women were to be cared for by the church (1 Tim. 5:3–16).

Cenchrea, 2 that you may receive her in the
Lord in a manner worthy of the saints, and
assist her in whatever business she has need
of you; for indeed she has been a helper of
many and of myself also.
3 Greet Priscilla and Aquila, my fellow workers in Christ Jesus, 4 who risked their own
necks for my life, to whom not only I give
thanks, but also all the churches of the
Gentiles. 5 Likewise *greet* the church that is in
their house.
Greet my beloved Epaenetus, who is the firstfruits of Achaia to Christ. 6 Greet Mary, who
labored much for us. 7 Greet Andronicus and
Junia, my countrymen and my fellow prisoners,
who are of note among the apostles, who also
were in Christ before me.
8 Greet Amplias, my beloved in the Lord.
9 Greet Urbanus, our fellow worker in Christ,
and Stachys, my beloved. 10 Greet Apelles,
approved in Christ. Greet those who are of the
household of Aristobulus. 11 Greet Herodion,
my countryman. Greet those who are of the
household of Narcissus who are in the Lord.
12 Greet Tryphena and Tryphosa, who have
labored in the Lord. Greet the beloved Persis,
who labored much in the Lord. 13 Greet Rufus,
chosen in the Lord, and his mother and mine.
14 Greet Asyncritus, Phlegon, Hermas,
Patrobas, Hermes, and the brethren who are
with them. 15 Greet Philologus and Julia,
Nereus and his sister, and Olympas, and all
the saints who are with them.
16 Greet one another with a holy kiss. The
churches of Christ greet you.

16:16 holy kiss. Kissing of friends on the forehead, cheek, or beard was common in the Old Testament. The Jews in the New Testament church carried on the practice, and it became especially precious to new believers, who were often outcasts from their own families because of their faith, because of the spiritual kinship it signified.

17 Now I urge you, brethren, note those who
cause divisions and offenses, contrary to the
doctrine which you learned, and avoid them.
18 For those who are such do not serve our
Lord Jesus Christ, but their own belly, and by
smooth words and flattering speech deceive
the hearts of the simple. 19 For your obedience
has become known to all. Therefore I am glad
on your behalf; but I want you to be wise in
what is good, and simple concerning evil.
20 And the God of peace will crush Satan under
your feet shortly.
The grace of our Lord Jesus Christ *be* with
you. Amen.
21 Timothy, my fellow worker, and Lucius, Jason, and Sosipater, my countrymen, greet you.
22 I, Tertius, who wrote *this* epistle, greet you
in the Lord.
23 Gaius, my host and *the host* of the whole
church, greets you. Erastus, the treasurer of
the city, greets you, and Quartus, a brother.
24 The grace of our Lord Jesus Christ *be* with
you all. Amen.

[25]Now to Him who is able to establish you
according to my gospel and the preaching of
Jesus Christ, according to the revelation of the
mystery kept secret since the world began
[26]but now made manifest, and by the prophetic Scriptures made known to all nations, according to the commandment of the everlasting God, for obedience to the faith— [27]to
God, alone wise, *be* glory through Jesus Christ
forever. Amen.

16:26 prophetic Scriptures made known. God had told Israel that He would not only call her to righteousness, but appoint her as a light (of the gospel) to the nations (Is. 42:6; 49:6; 1 Pet. 1:10,11; Gen. 12:3; Ex. 19:6; Is. 49:22; 53:11; 60:3–5; Jer. 31:31,33).

DAY 18: What wise conclusion did Job come to regarding his debate with his friends?

Job said to his friends, "I will teach you about the hand of God" (27:11). Job had pinpointed the issue between him and his friends. They disagreed on the outworking of God's retribution. They agreed that God was powerful, wise, and sovereign. But because Job knew there was no cherished sin in his life that would bring upon him such intense suffering, Job was forced to conclude that the simplistic notion that all suffering comes from sin and all righteousness is rewarded, was wrong. At the outset, Job himself probably believed as the comforters still did, but he had seen that his friends' limitation of God's action was drastically in need of revision; in fact, it was nonsense.

"God understands its way, and He knows its place" (28:23). These are perhaps the most important thoughts in the chapter for the debates. Job and his friends have probed God's wisdom for 3 court rounds and basically have arrived nowhere near the truth. Finally, Job made the point clearly that the divine wisdom necessary to explain his suffering was inaccessible to man. Only God knew all about it, because He knows everything (v. 24). True wisdom belongs to the One who is the Almighty Creator (vv. 25,26). One can only know it if He declares it to him (Deut. 29:29).

"Behold, the fear of the Lord, that is wisdom" (28:28). Job had made the connection that the others would not. While the specific features of God's wisdom may not be revealed to us, the alpha and omega of wisdom is to revere God and avoid sin (Ps. 111:10; Prov. 1:7; 9:10; Eccl. 12:13,14), leaving the unanswered questions to Him in trusting submission. All we can do is trust and obey (Eccl. 12:13), and that is enough wisdom. One may never know the reasons for life's sufferings.

AUGUST 19

Job 29:1–30:31

29 Job further continued his discourse, and said:

2 "Oh, that I were as *in* months past,
As *in* the days *when* God watched over me;
3 When His lamp shone upon my head,
And when by His light I walked *through* darkness;
4 Just as I was in the days of my prime,
When the friendly counsel of God *was* over my tent;
5 When the Almighty *was* yet with me,
When my children *were* around me;
6 When my steps were bathed with cream,
And the rock poured out rivers of oil for me!

7 "When I went out to the gate by the city,
When I took my seat in the open square,
8 The young men saw me and hid,
And the aged arose *and* stood;
9 The princes refrained from talking,
And put *their* hand on their mouth;
10 The voice of nobles was hushed,
And their tongue stuck to the roof of their mouth.
11 When the ear heard, then it blessed me,
And when the eye saw, then it approved me;
12 Because I delivered the poor who cried out,
The fatherless and *the one who* had no helper.

29:5 When the Almighty *was* yet with me. Job felt abandoned by God. But God would demonstrate to Job, by addressing his criticisms, that God was with him all throughout this ordeal.

29:12,13 poor…fatherless…perishing *man*…widow's. All over the ancient Near Eastern world, a man's virtue was measured by his treatment of the weakest and most vulnerable members of society. If he protected and provided for this group, he was respected as being a noble man. These things, which Job had done, his accusers said he must not have done or he wouldn't be suffering (see 22:1–11).

13 The blessing of a perishing *man* came upon me,
And I caused the widow's heart to sing for joy.
14 I put on righteousness, and it clothed me;
My justice *was* like a robe and a turban.
15 I *was* eyes to the blind,
And I *was* feet to the lame.
16 I *was* a father to the poor,
And I searched out the case *that* I did not know.
17 I broke the fangs of the wicked,
And plucked the victim from his teeth.

18 "Then I said, 'I shall die in my nest,
And multiply *my* days as the sand.
19 My root *is* spread out to the waters,
And the dew lies all night on my branch.
20 My glory *is* fresh within me,
And my bow is renewed in my hand.'

21 "*Men* listened to me and waited,
And kept silence for my counsel.
22 After my words they did not speak again,
And my speech settled on them *as dew.*
23 They waited for me *as* for the rain,
And they opened their mouth wide *as* for the spring rain.
24 *If* I mocked at them, they did not believe *it,*
And the light of my countenance they did not cast down.
25 I chose the way for them, and sat as chief;
So I dwelt as a king in the army,
As one *who* comforts mourners.

30 "But now they mock at me,
men younger than I,
Whose fathers I disdained to put with the dogs of my flock.
2 Indeed, what *profit* is the strength of their hands to me?
Their vigor has perished.
3 *They are* gaunt from want and famine,
Fleeing late to the wilderness, desolate and waste,
4 Who pluck mallow by the bushes,
And broom tree roots *for* their food.
5 They were driven out from among *men,*
They shouted at them as *at* a thief.
6 *They had* to live in the clefts of the valleys,
In caves of the earth and the rocks.
7 Among the bushes they brayed,
Under the nettles they nestled.
8 *They were* sons of fools,
Yes, sons of vile men;
They were scourged from the land.

9 "And now I am their taunting song;
Yes, I am their byword.
10 They abhor me, they keep far from me;
They do not hesitate to spit in my face.
11 Because He has loosed my bowstring and afflicted me,
They have cast off restraint before me.
12 At *my* right *hand* the rabble arises;
They push away my feet,
And they raise against me their ways of destruction.
13 They break up my path,
They promote my calamity;
They have no helper.
14 They come as broad breakers;
Under the ruinous storm they roll along.
15 Terrors are turned upon me;
They pursue my honor as the wind,
And my prosperity has passed like a cloud.

16 "And now my soul is poured out because of my *plight;*
The days of affliction take hold of me.
17 My bones are pierced in me at night,
And my gnawing pains take no rest.
18 By great force my garment is disfigured;
It binds me about as the collar of my coat.
19 He has cast me into the mire,
And I have become like dust and ashes.

20 "I cry out to You, but You do not answer me;
I stand up, and You regard me.
21 *But* You have become cruel to me;
With the strength of Your hand You oppose me.
22 You lift me up to the wind and cause me to ride *on it;*

You spoil my success.
23 For I know *that* You will bring me
to death,
And *to* the house appointed for all
living.
24 "Surely He would not stretch out *His*
hand against a heap of ruins,
If they cry out when He destroys *it*.
25 Have I not wept for him who was in
trouble?
Has *not* my soul grieved for the poor?
26 But when I looked for good, evil came
to me;
And when I waited for light, then came
darkness.
27 My heart is in turmoil and cannot rest;
Days of affliction confront me.
28 I go about mourning, but not in the
sun;
I stand up in the assembly *and* cry out
for help.
29 I am a brother of jackals,
And a companion of ostriches.
30 My skin grows black and falls from me;
My bones burn with fever.
31 My harp is *turned* to mourning,
And my flute to the voice of those who
weep.

Psalm 97:7–12

7 Let all be put to shame who serve
carved images,
Who boast of idols.
Worship Him, all *you* gods.
8 Zion hears and is glad,
And the daughters of Judah rejoice
Because of Your judgments, O LORD.
9 For You, LORD, *are* most high above all
the earth;
You are exalted far above all gods.
10 You who love the LORD, hate evil!
He preserves the souls of His saints;
He delivers them out of the hand of the
wicked.
11 Light is sown for the righteous,
And gladness for the upright in heart.
12 Rejoice in the LORD, you righteous,
And give thanks at the remembrance
of His holy name.

Proverbs 23:15–16

15 My son, if your heart is wise,
My heart will rejoice—indeed, I
myself;
16 Yes, my inmost being will rejoice
When your lips speak right things.

1 Corinthians 1:1–31

1 Paul, called *to be* an apostle of Jesus Christ
through the will of God, and Sosthenes *our*
brother,

2 To the church of God which is at Corinth, to
those who are sanctified in Christ Jesus, called
to be saints, with all who in every place call on
the name of Jesus Christ our Lord, both theirs
and ours:

3 Grace to you and peace from God our Father
and the Lord Jesus Christ.

4 I thank my God always concerning you for
the grace of God which was given to you by
Christ Jesus, 5 that you were enriched in everything by Him in all utterance and all knowledge, 6 even as the testimony of Christ was
confirmed in you, 7 so that you come short in
no gift, eagerly waiting for the revelation of
our Lord Jesus Christ, 8 who will also confirm
you to the end, *that you may be* blameless in
the day of our Lord Jesus Christ. 9 God *is* faithful, by whom you were called into the fellowship
of His Son, Jesus Christ our Lord.

10 Now I plead with you, brethren, by the
name of our Lord Jesus Christ, that you all
speak the same thing, and *that* there be no divisions among you, but *that* you be perfectly
joined together in the same mind and in the
same judgment. 11 For it has been declared to
me concerning you, my brethren, by those of
Chloe's *household*, that there are contentions
among you. 12 Now I say this, that each of you
says, "I am of Paul," or "I am of Apollos," or "I
am of Cephas," or "I am of Christ." 13 Is Christ
divided? Was Paul crucified for you? Or were
you baptized in the name of Paul?

14 I thank God that I baptized none of you
except Crispus and Gaius, 15 lest anyone
should say that I had baptized in my own
name. 16 Yes, I also baptized the household of
Stephanas. Besides, I do not know whether I
baptized any other. 17 For Christ did not send
me to baptize, but to preach the gospel, not
with wisdom of words, lest the cross of Christ
should be made of no effect.

18 For the message of the cross is foolishness
to those who are perishing, but to us who are
being saved it is the power of God. 19 For it is
written:

"I will destroy the wisdom of the wise,
And bring to nothing the
understanding of the prudent."

20 Where *is* the wise? Where *is* the scribe?
Where *is* the disputer of this age? Has not God
made foolish the wisdom of this world? 21 For

1:10 speak the same thing. Paul is emphasizing the unity of doctrine in the local assembly of believers, not the spiritual unity of His universal church. Doctrinal unity, clearly and completely based on Scripture, must be the foundation of all church life (John 17:11,21–23; Acts 2:46,47). Both weak commitment to doctrine and commitment to disunity of doctrine will severely weaken a church and destroy the true unity. In its place, there can be only shallow sentimentalism or superficial harmony. **joined together.** The basic idea is that of putting back together something that was broken or separated so it is no longer divided. The term is used in both the New Testament and in classical Greek to speak of mending such things as nets, broken bones or utensils, torn garments, and dislocated joints. **same mind...same judgment.** Philippians 3:15,16. The demand is for unity internally in their individual minds and externally in decisions made among themselves—unified in truth by beliefs, convictions, standards, and in behavior by applied principles of living (Acts 4:32; Eph. 4:3). The only source of such unity is God's Word which establishes the standard of truth on which true unity rests.

1:13 Is Christ divided? No human leader, not even an apostle, should be given the loyalty that belongs only to the Lord. Such elevation of leaders leads only to contention, disputes, and a divided church. Christ is not divided and neither is His body, the church. Paul depreciates his worth in comparison to the Lord Jesus.

1:18 message of the cross. God's total revelation, i.e., the gospel in all its fullness, which centers in the Incarnation and Crucifixion of Christ (2:2); the entire divine plan and provision for the redemption of sinners, which is the theme of all Scripture, is in view. **foolishness.** Translates the word from which "moron" is derived. **perishing...being saved.** Every person is either in the process of salvation (though not completed until the redemption of the body; see Rom. 8:23; 13:11) or the process of destruction. One's response to the cross of Christ determines which. To the Christ-rejectors who are in the process of being destroyed (Eph. 2:1,2) the gospel is nonsense. To those who are believers it is powerful wisdom.

since, in the wisdom of God, the world
through wisdom did not know God, it pleased
God through the foolishness of the message
preached to save those who believe. 22For
Jews request a sign, and Greeks seek after
wisdom; 23but we preach Christ crucified, to
the Jews a stumbling block and to the Greeks
foolishness, 24but to those who are called, both
Jews and Greeks, Christ the power of God and
the wisdom of God. 25Because the foolishness
of God is wiser than men, and the weakness of
God is stronger than men.
26For you see your calling, brethren, that not
many wise according to the flesh, not many
mighty, not many noble, *are called.* 27But God
has chosen the foolish things of the world to
put to shame the wise, and God has chosen
the weak things of the world to put to shame
the things which are mighty; 28and the base
things of the world and the things which are
despised God has chosen, and the things
which are not, to bring to nothing the things
that are, 29that no flesh should glory in His
presence. 30But of Him you are in Christ Jesus,
who became for us wisdom from God—and
righteousness and sanctification and redemption—
31that, as it is written, *"He who glories, let him glory in the LORD."*

DAY 19: Describe the church in Corinth.

The church in Corinth was founded by Paul on his second missionary journey (Acts 18:1ff.). As usual, his ministry began in the synagogue, where he was assisted by two Jewish believers, Priscilla and Aquila, with whom he lived for a while and who were fellow tradesmen. Soon after, Silas and Timothy joined them and Paul began preaching even more intensely in the synagogue. When most of the Jews resisted the gospel, he left the synagogue, but not before Crispus, the leader of the synagogue, his family, and many other Corinthians were converted (Acts 18:5–8).

After ministering in Corinth for over a year and a half (Acts 18:11), Paul was brought before a Roman tribunal by some of the Jewish leaders. Because the charges were strictly religious and not civil, the proconsul, Gallio, dismissed the case. Shortly thereafter, Paul took Priscilla and Aquila with him to Ephesus. From there he returned to Israel (vv. 18–22).

Unable to fully break with the culture from which it came, the church at Corinth was exceptionally factional, showing its carnality and immaturity. After the gifted Apollos had ministered in the church for some time, a group of his admirers established a clique and had little to do with the rest of the church. Another group developed that was loyal to Paul, another claimed special allegiance to Peter (Cephas), and still another to Christ alone (see 1:10–13; 3:1–9).

The most serious problem of the Corinthian church was worldliness, an unwillingness to divorce the culture around them. Most of the believers could not consistently separate themselves from their old, selfish, immoral, and pagan ways. It became necessary for Paul to write to correct this, as well as to command the faithful Christians not only to break fellowship with the disobedient and unrepentant members, but to put those members out of the church (5:9–13).

AUGUST 20

Job 31:1–32:22

31 "I have made a covenant with my eyes;
Why then should I look upon a young woman?
2 For what *is* the allotment of God from above,
And the inheritance of the Almighty from on high?
3 *Is* it not destruction for the wicked,
And disaster for the workers of iniquity?
4 Does He not see my ways,
And count all my steps?

5 "If I have walked with falsehood,
Or if my foot has hastened to deceit,
6 Let me be weighed on honest scales,
That God may know my integrity.
7 If my step has turned from the way,
Or my heart walked after my eyes,
Or if any spot adheres to my hands,
8 *Then* let me sow, and another eat;
Yes, let my harvest be rooted out.

9 "If my heart has been enticed by a woman,
Or *if* I have lurked at my neighbor's door,
10 *Then* let my wife grind for another,
And let others bow down over her.
11 For that *would be* wickedness;
Yes, it *would be* iniquity *deserving of* judgment.
12 For that *would be* a fire *that* consumes to destruction,
And would root out all my increase.

13 "If I have despised the cause of my male or female servant
When they complained against me,
14 What then shall I do when God rises up?
When He punishes, how shall I answer Him?
15 Did not He who made me in the womb make them?
Did not the same One fashion us in the womb?

16 "If I have kept the poor from *their* desire,
Or caused the eyes of the widow to fail,
17 Or eaten my morsel by myself,
So that the fatherless could not eat of it
18 (But from my youth I reared him as a father,
And from my mother's womb I guided *the widow*);
19 If I have seen anyone perish for lack of clothing,
Or any poor *man* without covering;
20 If his heart has not blessed me,
And *if* he was *not* warmed with the fleece of my sheep;
21 If I have raised my hand against the fatherless,
When I saw I had help in the gate;
22 *Then* let my arm fall from my shoulder,
Let my arm be torn from the socket.
23 For destruction *from* God *is* a terror to me,
And because of His magnificence I cannot endure.

24 "If I have made gold my hope,
Or said to fine gold, '*You are* my confidence';
25 If I have rejoiced because my wealth *was* great,
And because my hand had gained much;
26 If I have observed the sun when it shines,
Or the moon moving *in* brightness,
27 So that my heart has been secretly enticed,
And my mouth has kissed my hand;
28 This also *would be* an iniquity *deserving of* judgment,

For I would have denied God *who is*
above.
29 "If I have rejoiced at the destruction of
him who hated me,
Or lifted myself up when evil found him
30 (Indeed I have not allowed my mouth
to sin
By asking for a curse on his soul);
31 If the men of my tent have not said,
'Who is there that has not been
satisfied with his meat?'
32 (*But* no sojourner had to lodge in the
street,
For I have opened my doors to
the traveler);
33 If I have covered my transgressions as
Adam,
By hiding my iniquity in my bosom,
34 Because I feared the great multitude,
And dreaded the contempt of families,
So that I kept silence
And did not go out of the door—
35 Oh, that I had one to hear me!
Here is my mark.
Oh, that the Almighty would answer me,
That my Prosecutor had written a book!

31:35 my Prosecutor had written a book. Job wished that God, the perfect Prosecutor who knows the allegations perfectly, had written a book that would have revealed God's will and wisdom and the reasons for Job's pain. This would have cleared him of all charges by his friends.

36 Surely I would carry it on my shoulder,
And bind it on me *like* a crown;
37 I would declare to Him the number of
my steps;
Like a prince I would approach Him.

38 "If my land cries out against me,
And its furrows weep together;
39 If I have eaten its fruit without money,
Or caused its owners to lose their lives;
40 *Then* let thistles grow instead of wheat,
And weeds instead of barley."

The words of Job are ended.

32 So these three men ceased answering
Job, because he *was* righteous in his
own eyes. 2Then the wrath of Elihu, the son of
Barachel the Buzite, of the family of Ram, was
aroused against Job; his wrath was aroused
because he justified himself rather than God.
3Also against his three friends his wrath was
aroused, because they had found no answer,
and *yet* had condemned Job.
4Now because they *were* years older than he,
Elihu had waited to speak to Job. 5When Elihu
saw that *there was* no answer in the mouth of
these three men, his wrath was aroused.
6So Elihu, the son of Barachel the Buzite,
answered and said:

"I *am* young in years, and you *are* very
old;
Therefore I was afraid,
And dared not declare my opinion to
you.
7 I said, 'Age should speak,
And multitude of years should teach
wisdom.'
8 But *there is* a spirit in man,
And the breath of the Almighty gives
him understanding.
9 Great men are not *always* wise,
Nor do the aged *always* understand
justice.

10 "Therefore I say, 'Listen to me,
I also will declare my opinion.'
11 Indeed I waited for your words,
I listened to your reasonings, while you
searched out what to say.
12 I paid close attention to you;
And surely not one of you convinced Job,
Or answered his words—
13 Lest you say,
'We have found wisdom';
God will vanquish him, not man.
14 Now he has not directed *his* words
against me;
So I will not answer him with your
words.

15 "They are dismayed and answer no
more;
Words escape them.
16 And I have waited, because they did
not speak,
Because they stood still *and* answered
no more.
17 I also will answer my part,
I too will declare my opinion.
18 For I am full of words;
The spirit within me compels me.
19 Indeed my belly *is* like wine *that* has no
vent;
It is ready to burst like new wineskins.
20 I will speak, that I may find relief;
I must open my lips and answer.
21 Let me not, I pray, show partiality to
anyone;

Nor let me flatter any man.
22 For I do not know how to flatter,
Else my Maker would soon take me
away.

Psalm 98:1–3

A Psalm.

Oh, sing to the LORD a new song!
For He has done marvelous things;
His right hand and His holy arm have
gained Him the victory.

98:1 right hand…holy arm. These are symbols of power. **the victory.** The Lord is often pictured in the Old Testament as a divine warrior (Ex. 15:2,3; Pss. 18; 68:1–8; Is. 59:15ff.). According to the prophets, Christ will begin His millennial reign following His victory over the nations of the world which will gather against Israel in the end times (Zech. 14:1–15; Rev. 19:11–21).

2 The LORD has made known His
salvation;
His righteousness He has revealed in
the sight of the nations.
3 He has remembered His mercy and
His faithfulness to the house
of Israel;
All the ends of the earth have seen the
salvation of our God.

Proverbs 23:17–18

17 Do not let your heart envy sinners,
But *be zealous* for the fear of the LORD
all the day;
18 For surely there is a hereafter,
And your hope will not be cut off.

23:18 there is a hereafter. Anyone who might envy sinners needs to know that their prosperity is brief. They will die ("be cut off"); then there will be a time when all iniquities will be dealt with and divine justice will prevail (Ps. 37:28–38). The righteous will live forever.

1 Corinthians 2:1–16

2 And I, brethren, when I came to you, did
not come with excellence of speech or of
wisdom declaring to you the testimony of
God. [2]For I determined not to know anything
among you except Jesus Christ and Him crucified. [3]I was with you in weakness, in fear, and
in much trembling. [4]And my speech and my
preaching *were* not with persuasive words of
human wisdom, but in demonstration of the
Spirit and of power, [5]that your faith should not
be in the wisdom of men but in the power of
God.

[6]However, we speak wisdom among those
who are mature, yet not the wisdom of this
age, nor of the rulers of this age, who are coming to nothing. [7]But we speak the wisdom of
God in a mystery, the hidden *wisdom* which
God ordained before the ages for our glory,

2:7 mystery. This term does not refer to something puzzling, but to truth known to God before time, that He has kept secret until the appropriate time for Him to reveal it. **for our glory.** The truth God established before time and revealed in the New Testament wisdom of the gospel is the truth that God will save and glorify sinners.

[8]which none of the rulers of this age knew; for
had they known, they would not have crucified the Lord of glory.
[9]But as it is written:

"Eye has not seen, nor ear heard,
Nor have entered into the heart of man
The things which God has prepared for
those who love Him."

[10]But God has revealed *them* to us through His
Spirit. For the Spirit searches all things, yes,
the deep things of God. [11]For what man knows
the things of a man except the spirit of the
man which is in him? Even so no one knows
the things of God except the Spirit of God.
[12]Now we have received, not the spirit of the
world, but the Spirit who is from God, that we
might know the things that have been freely
given to us by God.
[13]These things we also speak, not in words
which man's wisdom teaches but which the
Holy Spirit teaches, comparing spiritual things
with spiritual. [14]But the natural man does not
receive the things of the Spirit of God, for they
are foolishness to him; nor can he know *them,*
because they are spiritually discerned. [15]But
he who is spiritual judges all things, yet he
himself is *rightly* judged by no one. [16]For *"who*
has known the mind of the LORD that he may
instruct Him?" But we have the mind of
Christ.

DAY 20: How do we receive spiritual truth?

From 1 Corinthians 2:10–16, it is clear that the wisdom that saves, which man's wisdom can't know, is revealed to us by God. He makes it known by revelation, inspiration, and illumination. Revelation (vv. 10,11) and inspiration (vv. 12,13) were given to those who wrote the Bible. Illumination (vv. 14–16) is given to all believers who seek to know and understand that divinely written truth. In each case, the Holy Spirit is the divine agent doing the work (2 Pet. 1:21).

"God has revealed them" (v. 10). By the Holy Spirit, God disclosed His saving truth (Matt. 11:25; 13:10–13). The Spirit alone was qualified because He knows all that God knows, Himself being God. "To us." As with the "we's" in vv. 6,7 and vv. 12,13, Paul is, first of all, speaking of himself, and, in a sense, of believers who have been given the Word as recorded by the apostles and their associates who wrote the New Testament.

"We have received" (v. 12). The "we" and "us" refer to the apostles and other writers of the Word of God. The means was inspiration (2 Tim. 3:16; 2 Pet. 1:20,21), by which God freely gave the gift of His Word. It was this process of inspiration that turned the spiritual thoughts into spiritual words (v. 13) to give life (Matt. 4:4).

"But the natural man does not receive the things of the Spirit of God" (v. 14). This refers to the unconverted, who lack supernatural life and wisdom. "Because they are spiritually discerned." Through illumination of the Word, the Holy Spirit provides His saints the capacity to discern divine truth, which the spiritually dead are unable to comprehend (John 5:37–39; 1 John 2:20,27). The doctrine of illumination does not mean we know everything (Deut. 29:29), that we do not need teachers (Eph. 4:11,12), or that understanding does not require hard work (2 Tim. 2:15).

AUGUST 21

Job 33:1–34:37

33 "But please, Job, hear my speech,
And listen to all my words.
2 Now, I open my mouth;
My tongue speaks in my mouth.
3 My words *come* from my upright heart;
My lips utter pure knowledge.
4 The Spirit of God has made me,
And the breath of the Almighty gives
me life.
5 If you can answer me,
Set *your words* in order before me;
Take your stand.
6 Truly I *am* as your spokesman before
God;
I also have been formed out of clay.
7 Surely no fear of me will terrify you,
Nor will my hand be heavy on you.

8 "Surely you have spoken in my hearing,
And I have heard the sound of *your*
words, *saying,*
9 'I *am* pure, without transgression;
I *am* innocent, and *there is* no iniquity
in me.
10 Yet He finds occasions against me,
He counts me as His enemy;
11 He puts my feet in the stocks,
He watches all my paths.'

12 "Look, *in* this you are not righteous.
I will answer you,
For God is greater than man.
13 Why do you contend with Him?
For He does not give an accounting of
any of His words.
14 For God may speak in one way, or in
another,
Yet man does not perceive it.
15 In a dream, in a vision of the night,
When deep sleep falls upon men,
While slumbering on their beds,
16 Then He opens the ears of men,
And seals their instruction.
17 In order to turn man *from his* deed,
And conceal pride from man,
18 He keeps back his soul from the Pit,
And his life from perishing by the
sword.

19 "*Man* is also chastened with pain on
his bed,
And with strong *pain* in many of his
bones,
20 So that his life abhors bread,
And his soul succulent food.
21 His flesh wastes away from sight,
And his bones stick out *which once*
were not seen.
22 Yes, his soul draws near the Pit,
And his life to the executioners.

23 "If there is a messenger for him,
A mediator, one among a thousand,
To show man His uprightness,
24 Then He is gracious to him, and says,
'Deliver him from going down to the Pit;

I have found a ransom';
25 His flesh shall be young like a child's,
He shall return to the days of his youth.
26 He shall pray to God, and He will delight in him,
He shall see His face with joy,
For He restores to man His righteousness.
27 Then he looks at men and says,
'I have sinned, and perverted *what was* right,
And it did not profit me.'
28 He will redeem his soul from going down to the Pit,
And his life shall see the light.

29 "Behold, God works all these *things,*
Twice, *in fact,* three *times* with a man,
30 To bring back his soul from the Pit,
That he may be enlightened with the light of life.

31 "Give ear, Job, listen to me;
Hold your peace, and I will speak.
32 If you have anything to say, answer me;
Speak, for I desire to justify you.
33 If not, listen to me;
Hold your peace, and I will teach you wisdom."

34 Elihu further answered and said:

2 "Hear my words, you wise *men;*
Give ear to me, you who have knowledge.
3 For the ear tests words
As the palate tastes food.
4 Let us choose justice for ourselves;
Let us know among ourselves what *is* good.

5 "For Job has said, 'I am righteous,
But God has taken away my justice;
6 Should I lie concerning my right?
My wound *is* incurable, *though I am* without transgression.'
7 What man *is* like Job,
Who drinks scorn like water,
8 Who goes in company with the workers of iniquity,
And walks with wicked men?
9 For he has said, 'It profits a man nothing
That he should delight in God.'

10 "Therefore listen to me, you men of understanding:
Far be it from God *to do* wickedness,
And *from* the Almighty to *commit* iniquity.
11 For He repays man *according to* his work,
And makes man to find a reward according to *his* way.
12 Surely God will never do wickedly,
Nor will the Almighty pervert justice.
13 Who gave Him charge over the earth?
Or who appointed *Him over* the whole world?
14 If He should set His heart on it,
If He should gather to Himself His Spirit and His breath,
15 All flesh would perish together,
And man would return to dust.

16 "If *you have* understanding, hear this;
Listen to the sound of my words:
17 Should one who hates justice govern?
Will you condemn *Him who is* most just?
18 *Is it fitting* to say to a king, '*You are* worthless,'
And to nobles, '*You are* wicked'?
19 Yet He is not partial to princes,
Nor does He regard the rich more than the poor;
For they *are* all the work of His hands.
20 In a moment they die, in the middle of the night;
The people are shaken and pass away;
The mighty are taken away without a hand.

21 "For His eyes *are* on the ways of man,
And He sees all his steps.
22 There is no darkness nor shadow of death

34:1–37 Elihu addressed Job and his accusers. His approach was to quote Job directly (vv. 5–9), then respond to his complaints, but at times he misinterpreted Job's remarks, and at other times he put the words of the accusers in Job's mouth. The most obvious example of the latter wrongdoing was in saying that Job claimed to be sinlessly perfect (v. 6). Job never claimed that; in fact, Job acknowledged his sin (7:21; 13:26). Elihu didn't know it, but God had pronounced Job innocent (1:8; 2:3). In answer to Job's complaints that God seemed unjust, Elihu reminded Job that God was too holy to do anything wrong (v. 10), fair in dealing with people (vv. 11,12), powerful (vv. 13,14), just (vv. 17,18), impartial (vv. 19,20), omniscient (vv. 21,22), the Judge of all (v. 23), and the Sovereign who does what He wills to prevent evil (vv. 24–30).

Where the workers of iniquity may
hide themselves.
23 For He need not further consider a
man,
That he should go before God in
judgment.
24 He breaks in pieces mighty men
without inquiry,
And sets others in their place.
25 Therefore He knows their works;
He overthrows *them* in the night,
And they are crushed.
26 He strikes them as wicked *men*
In the open sight of others,
27 Because they turned back from Him,
And would not consider any of His
ways,
28 So that they caused the cry of the poor
to come to Him;
For He hears the cry of the afflicted.
29 When He gives quietness, who then
can make trouble?
And when He hides *His* face, who then
can see Him,
Whether *it is* against a nation or a man
alone?—
30 That the hypocrite should not reign,
Lest the people be ensnared.
31 "For has *anyone* said to God,
'I have borne *chastening;*
I will offend no more;
32 Teach me *what* I do not see;
If I have done iniquity, I will do no
more'?
33 Should He repay *it* according to your
terms,
Just because you disavow it?
You must choose, and not I;
Therefore speak what you know.
34 "Men of understanding say to me,
Wise men who listen to me:
35 'Job speaks without knowledge,
His words *are* without wisdom.'
36 Oh, that Job were tried to the utmost,
Because *his* answers *are like* those of
wicked men!
37 For he adds rebellion to his sin;
He claps *his hands* among us,
And multiplies his words against God."

Psalm 98:4–9

4 Shout joyfully to the LORD, all the earth;
Break forth in song, rejoice, and sing
praises.
5 Sing to the LORD with the harp,
With the harp and the sound of a
psalm,

98:4 Shout joyfully. A great cheer, greeting and welcoming a king (Zech. 9:9; Matt. 21:4–9). **break forth.** The idea is that of an eruption of praise which could not be contained (Is. 14:7; 44:23; 55:12).

98:8 rivers clap *their* hands. Different parts of nature are pictured as rejoicing in this universal scene of joy (Is. 35:1,2; Rom. 8:19–21).

6 With trumpets and the sound of a horn;
Shout joyfully before the LORD, the King.
7 Let the sea roar, and all its fullness,
The world and those who dwell in it;
8 Let the rivers clap *their* hands;
Let the hills be joyful together
9 before the LORD,
For He is coming to judge the earth.
With righteousness He shall judge the
world,
And the peoples with equity.

Proverbs 23:19–21

19 Hear, my son, and be wise;
And guide your heart in the way.
20 Do not mix with winebibbers,
Or with gluttonous eaters of meat;
21 For the drunkard and the glutton will
come to poverty,
And drowsiness will clothe *a man*
with rags.

1 Corinthians 3:1–23

3 And I, brethren, could not speak to you as
to spiritual *people* but as to carnal, as to
babes in Christ. 2I fed you with milk and not
with solid food; for until now you were not able
to receive it, and even now you are still not able;
3for you are still carnal. For where *there are*
envy, strife, and divisions among you, are you
not carnal and behaving like *mere* men? 4For
when one says, "I am of Paul," and another, "I
am of Apollos," are you not carnal?
5Who then is Paul, and who *is* Apollos, but
ministers through whom you believed, as the
Lord gave to each one? 6I planted, Apollos
watered, but God gave the increase. 7So then
neither he who plants is anything, nor he who
waters, but God who gives the increase. 8Now
he who plants and he who waters are one, and
each one will receive his own reward according
to his own labor.
9For we are God's fellow workers; you are
God's field, *you are* God's building. 10According

3:12 if anyone builds. This is, first of all, in reference to the evangelists and pastors (v. 9), and then to all believers who are called to build the church through faithful ministry. **gold, silver, precious stones.** His quality materials represent dedicated, spiritual service to build the church. **wood, hay, straw.** Inferior materials implying shallow activity with no eternal value. They do not refer to activities that are evil.

3:13 the Day. Refers to the time of the judgment seat of Christ (2 Cor. 5:10). **revealed by fire.** The fire of God's discerning judgment (Job 23:10; Zech. 13:9; 1 Pet. 1:17,18; Rev. 3:18). Second Corinthians 5:10 indicates that the wood, hay, and straw are "worthless" things that don't stand the test of judgment fire.

to the grace of God which was given to me, as
a wise master builder I have laid the foundation, and another builds on it. But let each one
take heed how he builds on it. [11]For no other
foundation can anyone lay than that which is
laid, which is Jesus Christ. [12]Now if anyone
builds on this foundation *with* gold, silver, precious stones, wood, hay, straw, [13]each one's
work will become clear; for the Day will
declare it, because it will be revealed by fire;
and the fire will test each one's work, of what
sort it is. [14]If anyone's work which he has built
on *it* endures, he will receive a reward. [15]If anyone's work is burned, he will suffer loss; but
he himself will be saved, yet so as through
fire.

[16]Do you not know that you are the temple
of God and *that* the Spirit of God dwells in
you? [17]If anyone defiles the temple of God, God
will destroy him. For the temple of God is
holy, which *temple* you are.

[18]Let no one deceive himself. If anyone
among you seems to be wise in this age, let
him become a fool that he may become wise.
[19]For the wisdom of this world is foolishness
with God. For it is written, *"He catches the
wise in their own craftiness"*; [20]and again, *"The
LORD knows the thoughts of the wise, that
they are futile."* [21]Therefore let no one boast in
men. For all things are yours: [22]whether Paul
or Apollos or Cephas, or the world or life or
death, or things present or things to come—
all are yours. [23]And you *are* Christ's, and
Christ *is* God's.

DAY 21: What does it mean to be "carnal"?

The cause of problems in the Corinthian church was more than external, worldly influence. It was also internal carnality (1 Cor. 3:1). The pressures of the world were combined with the weakness of the flesh. Although Corinthian believers were no longer "natural," they were not "spiritual" (fully controlled by the Holy Spirit). In fact, they were "carnal" (controlled by the fallen flesh). Though all believers have the Holy Spirit (Rom. 8:9), they still battle the fallen flesh (Rom. 7:14–25; 8:23).

Paul calls them "babes in Christ." The carnality of those believers was indicative of their immaturity. They had no excuse for not being mature, since Paul implied that he should have been able to write to them as mature, in light of all he had taught them (v. 2). He could only feed them with "milk" (v. 2). Not a reference to certain doctrines, but to the more easily digestible truths of doctrine that were given to new believers. "Solid food" is the deeper features of the doctrines of Scripture. The difference is not in the kind of truth, but degree of depth. Spiritual immaturity makes one unable to receive the richest truths.

Carnality produces the attitude of envy, a severe form of selfishness, which produces the action of strife and the subsequent divisions (v. 3). They end up acting as "mere men." Apart from the will of Spirit, hence carnal, not spiritual. Factionalism was the divisive product of carnality, aligning themselves with "Paul…Apollos" (v. 4). Paul reminds them that all the human instruments God uses to produce salvation life are equally considered and rewarded for their willingness to be used by God. But all the glory goes to Him, who alone saves. Because of that, the silly favoritism is condemned (vv. 5–8).

AUGUST 22

Job 35:1–36:33

35 Moreover Elihu answered and said:

2 "Do you think this is right?
Do you say,
'My righteousness is more than God's'?
3 For you say,
'What advantage will it be to You?
What profit shall I have, more than *if* I
had sinned?'

4 "I will answer you,

And your companions with you.
5 Look to the heavens and see;
And behold the clouds—
They are higher than you.
6 If you sin, what do you accomplish
against Him?
Or, *if* your transgressions are
multiplied, what do you do to Him?
7 If you are righteous, what do you give
Him?
Or what does He receive from your
hand?
8 Your wickedness affects a man such as
you,
And your righteousness a son of man.

9 "Because of the multitude of oppressions
they cry out;
They cry out for help because of the
arm of the mighty.
10 But no one says, 'Where *is* God my
Maker,
Who gives songs in the night,
11 Who teaches us more than the beasts
of the earth,
And makes us wiser than the birds of
heaven?'
12 There they cry out, but He does not
answer,
Because of the pride of evil men.
13 Surely God will not listen to empty *talk,*
Nor will the Almighty regard it.
14 Although you say you do not see Him,
Yet justice *is* before Him, and you must
wait for Him.

35:1–16 Elihu again referred to Job's complaints, first of all his thinking that there appeared to be no advantage to being righteous (v. 3), which Job had said, as recorded in 21:15 and 34:9. The first part of his answer is that Job gained nothing by sinning or not sinning because God was so high that nothing men do affects Him (vv. 5–7). It only affects other men (v. 8). Job had also complained that God did not answer his prayers when he cried under this oppression (see 24:12; 30:20). Elihu coldly gave 3 reasons why Job's prayers had not been heard: pride (vv. 10,12), wrong motives (v. 13), and lack of patient trust (v. 14). Again, all this theoretical talk missed Job's predicament completely because he was righteous. Elihu was no more help than the other counselors.

15 And now, because He has not punished
in His anger,
Nor taken much notice of folly,
16 Therefore Job opens his mouth in vain;
He multiplies words without
knowledge."

36 Elihu also proceeded and said:

2 "Bear with me a little, and I will show you
That *there are* yet words to speak on
God's behalf.
3 I will fetch my knowledge from afar;
I will ascribe righteousness to my
Maker.
4 For truly my words *are* not false;
One who is perfect in knowledge *is*
with you.

5 "Behold, God *is* mighty, but despises *no
one;*
He is mighty in strength of
understanding.
6 He does not preserve the life of the
wicked,
But gives justice to the oppressed.
7 He does not withdraw His eyes from
the righteous;
But *they are* on the throne with kings,
For He has seated them forever,
And they are exalted.
8 And if *they are* bound in fetters,
Held in the cords of affliction,
9 Then He tells them their work and
their transgressions—
That they have acted defiantly.
10 He also opens their ear to instruction,
And commands that they turn from
iniquity.
11 If they obey and serve *Him,*
They shall spend their days in
prosperity,
And their years in pleasures.
12 But if they do not obey,
They shall perish by the sword,
And they shall die without knowledge.

13 "But the hypocrites in heart store up
wrath;
They do not cry for help when He
binds them.
14 They die in youth,
And their life *ends* among the
perverted persons.
15 He delivers the poor in their affliction,
And opens their ears in oppression.

16 "Indeed He would have brought you out
of dire distress,

36:15 opens their ears in oppression. This was a new insight and perhaps the most helpful thing Elihu said. He went beyond all that had been said about God's using suffering to chasten and bring repentance. He was saying that God used suffering to open men's ears, to draw them to Himself. But as long as Job kept complaining, he was turning to iniquity rather than drawing near to God in his suffering (vv. 16–21).

Into a broad place where *there is* no
restraint;
And what is set on your table *would be*
full of richness.
17 But you are filled with the judgment
due the wicked;
Judgment and justice take hold *of you.*
18 Because *there is* wrath, *beware* lest He
take you away with *one* blow;
For a large ransom would not help you
avoid *it.*
19 Will your riches,
Or all the mighty forces,
Keep you from distress?
20 Do not desire the night,
When people are cut off in their place.
21 Take heed, do not turn to iniquity,
For you have chosen this rather than
affliction.

22 "Behold, God is exalted by His power;
Who teaches like Him?
23 Who has assigned Him His way,
Or who has said, 'You have done
wrong'?

24 "Remember to magnify His work,
Of which men have sung.
25 Everyone has seen it;
Man looks on *it* from afar.

26 "Behold, God *is* great, and we do not
know *Him;*
Nor can the number of His years *be*
discovered.
27 For He draws up drops of water,
Which distill as rain from the mist,
28 Which the clouds drop down
And pour abundantly on man.
29 Indeed, can *anyone* understand the
spreading of clouds,
The thunder from His canopy?
30 Look, He scatters His light upon it,
And covers the depths of the sea.
31 For by these He judges the peoples;
He gives food in abundance.
32 He covers *His* hands with lightning,
And commands it to strike.
33 His thunder declares it,
The cattle also, concerning the rising
storm.

Psalm 99:1–9

The LORD reigns;
Let the peoples tremble!
He dwells *between* the cherubim;
Let the earth be moved!
2 The LORD *is* great in Zion,
And He *is* high above all the peoples.
3 Let them praise Your great and
awesome name—
He *is* holy.

4 The King's strength also loves justice;
You have established equity;
You have executed justice and
righteousness in Jacob.
5 Exalt the LORD our God,
And worship at His footstool—
He *is* holy.

6 Moses and Aaron were among His
priests,
And Samuel was among those who
called upon His name;
They called upon the LORD, and He
answered them.
7 He spoke to them in the cloudy pillar;
They kept His testimonies and
the ordinance He gave them.

8 You answered them, O LORD our God;
You were to them God-Who-Forgives,
Though You took vengeance on their
deeds.
9 Exalt the LORD our God,
And worship at His holy hill;
For the LORD our God *is* holy.

99:5 His footstool. In general, this is a metaphor for the temple in Jerusalem (Is. 60:13; Lam. 2:1); but more specifically, for the ark of the covenant (1 Chr. 28:2). Footstools were included with the thrones of the kings of Israel (2 Chr. 9:18).

99:9 His holy hill. This is the hill in Jerusalem where the temple was (Pss. 15:1; 24:3), and where it will be located in the future messianic kingdom (Is. 24:23).

Proverbs 23:22–25

22 Listen to your father who begot you,
And do not despise your mother when
she is old.

23:23 Buy the truth. Obtain the truth at all costs. Then never relinquish it at any price.

23 Buy the truth, and do not sell *it,*
Also wisdom and instruction and
understanding.
24 The father of the righteous will greatly
rejoice,
And he who begets a wise *child* will
delight in him.
25 Let your father and your mother be
glad,
And let her who bore you rejoice.

1 Corinthians 4:1–21

4 Let a man so consider us, as servants of
Christ and stewards of the mysteries of
God. [2]Moreover it is required in stewards that
one be found faithful. [3]But with me it is a very
small thing that I should be judged by you or
by a human court. In fact, I do not even judge
myself. [4]For I know of nothing against myself,
yet I am not justified by this; but He who
judges me is the Lord. [5]Therefore judge nothing before the time, until the Lord comes, who
will both bring to light the hidden things of
darkness and reveal the counsels of the
hearts. Then each one's praise will come from
God.

[6]Now these things, brethren, I have figuratively transferred to myself and Apollos for
your sakes, that you may learn in us not to
think beyond what is written, that none of you
may be puffed up on behalf of one against the
other. [7]For who makes you differ *from another?* And what do you have that you did not
receive? Now if you did indeed receive *it,* why
do you boast as if you had not received *it?*

[8]You are already full! You are already rich!
You have reigned as kings without us—and
indeed I could wish you did reign, that we also
might reign with you! [9]For I think that God
has displayed us, the apostles, last, as men
condemned to death; for we have been made a
spectacle to the world, both to angels and to
men. [10]We *are* fools for Christ's sake, but you
are wise in Christ! We *are* weak, but you *are*
strong! You *are* distinguished, but we *are*
dishonored! [11]To the present hour we both
hunger and thirst, and we are poorly clothed,
and beaten, and homeless. [12]And we labor,
working with our own hands. Being reviled,
we bless; being persecuted, we endure; [13]be-
ing defamed, we entreat. We have been made
as the filth of the world, the offscouring of all
things until now.

[14]I do not write these things to shame you,
but as my beloved children I warn *you.* [15]For
though you might have ten thousand instruc-
tors in Christ, yet *you do* not *have* many
fathers; for in Christ Jesus I have begotten you
through the gospel. [16]Therefore I urge you,
imitate me. [17]For this reason I have sent Timothy to you, who is my beloved and faithful son
in the Lord, who will remind you of my ways
in Christ, as I teach everywhere in every
church.

[18]Now some are puffed up, as though I were
not coming to you. [19]But I will come to you
shortly, if the Lord wills, and I will know, not
the word of those who are puffed up, but the
power. [20]For the kingdom of God *is* not in word
but in power. [21]What do you want? Shall I
come to you with a rod, or in love and a spirit
of gentleness?

4:8 full!...rich!...reigned. In a severe rebuke, Paul heaps on false praise, sarcastically suggesting that those Corinthians who were self-satisfied had already achieved spiritual greatness. They were similar to the Laodiceans (Rev. 3:17). **reign.** Yet, Paul genuinely wished it really were the coronation time of the Millennium, so that they all might share in the glory of the Lord.

DAY 22: How did Paul want to be regarded by the Corinthians?

"Let a man so consider us, as servants of Christ and stewards of the mysteries of God" (1 Cor. 4:1). Paul wanted everyone to view him and his fellow ministers only as the humble messengers God ordained them to be (3:9,22). "Servants." Paul expresses his humility by using a word literally meaning "under rowers," referring to the lowest, most menial, and most despised galley slaves, who rowed on the bottom tier of a ship. "Stewards." Paul defines his responsibilities as an apostle by using a word originally referring to a person entrusted with and responsible for his master's entire household: e.g., buildings, fields, finances, food, other servants, and sometimes even children of the owner. "Mysteries of God." "Mystery" is used in the New Testament to refer to divine revelation previously hidden. Here the word is used in its broadest sense as God's fully revealed truth in the New Testament. It was all that truth which Paul had to oversee and dispense as God's servant and steward.

The most essential quality of a servant or steward is obedient loyalty to his master (vv. 2,17; 7:25; Matt. 24:45–51; Col. 1:7; 4:7). Because of that, Paul said that "it is a very small thing that I should be judged by you or by a human court" (v. 3). Paul is not being arrogant or saying that he is above fellow ministers, other Christians, or even certain unbelievers. He is saying that a human verdict on his life is not the one that matters, even if it was his own.

"For I know of nothing against myself, yet I am not justified by this" (v. 4). Paul was not aware of any unconfessed or habitual sin in his own life, but his limited understanding assumed that his was not the final verdict. Paul's own sincere evaluation of his life did not acquit him of all failures to be faithful. The Lord is the ultimate and only qualified Judge of any man's obedience and faithfulness (2 Tim. 2:15). Since final rewards will be based not just on outward service but on inward devotion (10:31), only God can give the praise each deserves. He will "bring to light the hidden things of darkness…counsels of the hearts" (v. 5).

AUGUST 23

Job 37:1–38:41

37 "At this also my heart trembles,
And leaps from its place.
2 Hear attentively the thunder of His voice,
And the rumbling *that* comes from His mouth.
3 He sends it forth under the whole heaven,
His lightning to the ends of the earth.
4 After it a voice roars;
He thunders with His majestic voice,
And He does not restrain them when His voice is heard.
5 God thunders marvelously with His voice;
He does great things which we cannot comprehend.
6 For He says to the snow, 'Fall *on* the earth';
Likewise to the gentle rain and the heavy rain of His strength.
7 He seals the hand of every man,
That all men may know His work.
8 The beasts go into dens,
And remain in their lairs.
9 From the chamber *of the south* comes the whirlwind,
And cold from the scattering winds *of the north.*
10 By the breath of God ice is given,
And the broad waters are frozen.
11 Also with moisture He saturates the thick clouds;
He scatters His bright clouds.
12 And they swirl about, being turned by His guidance,
That they may do whatever He commands them
On the face of the whole earth.
13 He causes it to come,
Whether for correction,
Or for His land,
Or for mercy.

14 "Listen to this, O Job;
Stand still and consider the wondrous works of God.
15 Do you know when God dispatches them,
And causes the light of His cloud to shine?
16 Do you know how the clouds are balanced,
Those wondrous works of Him who is perfect in knowledge?
17 Why *are* your garments hot,
When He quiets the earth by the south *wind?*
18 With Him, have you spread out the skies,
Strong as a cast metal mirror?

19 "Teach us what we should say to Him,
For we can prepare nothing because of the darkness.
20 Should He be told that I *wish to* speak?
If a man were to speak, surely he would be swallowed up.
21 Even now *men* cannot look at the light *when it is* bright in the skies,
When the wind has passed and cleared them.
22 He comes from the north *as* golden *splendor;*
With God *is* awesome majesty.
23 *As for* the Almighty, we cannot find Him;
He is excellent in power,
In judgment and abundant justice;

He does not oppress.
24 Therefore men fear Him;
He shows no partiality to any *who are* wise of heart."

38 Then the LORD answered Job out of the whirlwind, and said:

2 "Who *is* this who darkens counsel
By words without knowledge?
3 Now prepare yourself like a man;
I will question you, and you shall answer Me.

4 "Where were you when I laid the foundations of the earth?
Tell *Me,* if you have understanding.
5 Who determined its measurements?
Surely you know!
Or who stretched the line upon it?
6 To what were its foundations fastened?
Or who laid its cornerstone,
7 When the morning stars sang together,
And all the sons of God shouted for joy?

8 "Or *who* shut in the sea with doors,
When it burst forth *and* issued from the womb;
9 When I made the clouds its garment,
And thick darkness its swaddling band;
10 When I fixed My limit for it,
And set bars and doors;
11 When I said,
'This far you may come, but no farther,
And here your proud waves must stop!'

12 "Have you commanded the morning since your days *began,*
And caused the dawn to know its place,
13 That it might take hold of the ends of the earth,
And the wicked be shaken out of it?
14 It takes on form like clay *under* a seal,
And stands out like a garment.
15 From the wicked their light is withheld,
And the upraised arm is broken.

16 "Have you entered the springs of the sea?
Or have you walked in search of the depths?
17 Have the gates of death been revealed to you?
Or have you seen the doors of the shadow of death?
18 Have you comprehended the breadth of the earth?
Tell *Me,* if you know all this.

19 "Where *is* the way *to* the dwelling of light?
And darkness, where *is* its place,
20 That you may take it to its territory,
That you may know the paths *to* its home?
21 Do you know *it,* because you were born then,
Or *because* the number of your days *is* great?

22 "Have you entered the treasury of snow,
Or have you seen the treasury of hail,
23 Which I have reserved for the time of trouble,
For the day of battle and war?
24 By what way is light diffused,
Or the east wind scattered over the earth?

25 "Who has divided a channel for the overflowing *water,*
Or a path for the thunderbolt,
26 To cause it to rain on a land *where there is* no one,

38:1 the LORD. Yahweh, the covenant "LORD," was the name used for God in the book's prologue, where the reader was introduced to Job and his relationship with God. However, in chapters 3–37, the name "Yahweh" is not used. God is called "El Shaddai," God the Almighty. In this book that change becomes a way of illustrating that God has been detached and distant. The relationship is restored in rich terms as God reveals Himself to Job using His covenant name. **out of the whirlwind.** Job had repeatedly called God to court in order to verify his innocence. God finally came to interrogate Job on some of the comments he had made to his own accusers. God was about to be Job's vindicator, but He first brought Job to a right understanding of Himself.

38:3 I will question you. God silenced Job's presumption in constantly wanting to ask the questions of God by becoming Job's questioner. It must be noted that God never told Job about the reason for his pain, about the conflict between Himself and Satan, which was the reason for Job's suffering. He never gave Job any explanation at all about the circumstances of his trouble. He did one thing in all He said. He asked Job if he was as eternal, great, powerful, wise, and perfect as God. If not, Job would have been better off to be quiet and trust Him.

A wilderness in which *there is* no man;
27 To satisfy the desolate waste,
And cause to spring forth the growth
of tender grass?
28 Has the rain a father?
Or who has begotten the drops of dew?
29 From whose womb comes the ice?
And the frost of heaven, who gives it
birth?
30 The waters harden like stone,
And the surface of the deep is frozen.

31 "Can you bind the cluster of the
Pleiades,
Or loose the belt of Orion?
32 Can you bring out Mazzaroth in its
season?
Or can you guide the Great Bear with
its cubs?
33 Do you know the ordinances of the
heavens?
Can you set their dominion over the
earth?

34 "Can you lift up your voice to the
clouds,
That an abundance of water may cover
you?
35 Can you send out lightnings, that they
may go,
And say to you, 'Here we *are!*'?
36 Who has put wisdom in the mind?
Or who has given understanding to the
heart?
37 Who can number the clouds by
wisdom?
Or who can pour out the bottles of
heaven,
38 When the dust hardens in clumps,
And the clods cling together?

39 "Can you hunt the prey for the lion,
Or satisfy the appetite of the young
lions,
40 When they crouch in *their* dens,
Or lurk in their lairs to lie in wait?
41 Who provides food for the raven,
When its young ones cry to God,
And wander about for lack of food?

Psalm 100:1–5

A Psalm of Thanksgiving.

Make a joyful shout to the LORD,
all you lands!
2 Serve the LORD with gladness;
Come before His presence with singing.
3 Know that the LORD, He *is* God;
It is He *who* has made us, and not we
ourselves;

100:3 Know. In the sense of experiencing and being completely assured of the truth. **the LORD, He *is* God.** A confession that Israel's covenant God, Yahweh, is the only true God. **made us.** Though God's actual creation of every human being is understood here, this phrase seems to refer to God's making and blessing Israel as a nation (Deut. 32:6,15; Ps. 95:6; Is. 29:22,23; 44:2). **His people...His pasture.** The shepherd image is often ascribed to the king of Israel, as well as to the Lord (Ps. 78:70–72; Is. 44:28; Jer. 10:21; Zech. 10:3; 11:4–17). The figure suggests intimate care (Luke 15:3–6). According to the New Testament, the Lord is also the Shepherd of saints in the church age (John 10:16).

We are His people and the sheep of His
pasture.

4 Enter into His gates with thanksgiving,
And into His courts with praise.
Be thankful to Him, *and* bless His
name.
5 For the LORD *is* good;
His mercy *is* everlasting,
And His truth *endures* to all
generations.

Proverbs 23:26–28

26 My son, give me your heart,
And let your eyes observe my ways.
27 For a harlot *is* a deep pit,
And a seductress *is* a narrow well.
28 She also lies in wait as *for* a victim,
And increases the unfaithful among
men.

1 Corinthians 5:1–13

5 It is actually reported *that there is* sexual
immorality among you, and such sexual
immorality as is not even named among the
Gentiles—that a man has his father's wife!
2And you are puffed up, and have not rather
mourned, that he who has done this deed
might be taken away from among you. 3For I
indeed, as absent in body but present in spirit,
have already judged (as though I were present) him who has so done this deed. 4In the
name of our Lord Jesus Christ, when you are
gathered together, along with my spirit, with
the power of our Lord Jesus Christ, 5deliver
such a one to Satan for the destruction of the
flesh, that his spirit may be saved in the day of
the Lord Jesus.

5:1 sexual immorality. This sin was so vile that even the church's pagan neighbors were doubtless scandalized by it. The Corinthians had rationalized or minimized this sin which was common knowledge, even though Paul had written them before about it (v. 9). The Greek for "immorality" is the root of the English word "pornography." **his father's wife.** The man's stepmother, with whom having sexual relations bore the same sinful stigma as if between him and his natural mother. Incest was punishable by death in the Old Testament (Lev. 18:7,8,29; Deut. 22:30) and was both uncommon ("not even named") and illegal under Roman law.

6 Your glorying *is* not good. Do you not know
that a little leaven leavens the whole lump?
7 Therefore purge out the old leaven, that you
may be a new lump, since you truly are
unleavened. For indeed Christ, our Passover,
was sacrificed for us. 8 Therefore let us keep
the feast, not with old leaven, nor with the
leaven of malice and wickedness, but with the
unleavened *bread* of sincerity and truth.

9 I wrote to you in my epistle not to keep
company with sexually immoral people. 10 Yet *I*
certainly *did* not *mean* with the sexually
immoral people of this world, or with the covetous, or extortioners, or idolaters, since then
you would need to go out of the world. 11 But
now I have written to you not to keep company with anyone named a brother, who is sexually immoral, or covetous, or an idolater, or a
reviler, or a drunkard, or an extortioner—not
even to eat with such a person.

12 For what *have* I *to do* with judging those
also who are outside? Do you not judge those
who are inside? 13 But those who are outside
God judges. Therefore *"put away from yourselves the evil person."*

DAY 23: Why doesn't God answer all of Job's (and our) questions?

This question assumes that if God answered all our questions, it would be easier to believe. This is not true. Trust goes beyond answers. Sometimes, questions become a way to avoid trust.

Take, for example, a little girl invited to jump off the stairs into her father's waiting hands. She asks, "Will you catch me, Daddy?" He answers, "Yes, I will!" She may jump or she may proceed to ask endless versions of her first question. If she does jump, it will be more because of whom she knows her father to be than because of his answer to one of her questions. The fact that she jumps does not mean that she has run out of fears or questions; it means that her trust is greater than her fears or questions.

In the end, we must trust God more than our capacity to understand God's ways. The lesson from Job's experience does not forbid us from asking questions. Often these questions will lead us to the reasons for our suffering. But Job's experience also warns us that we may not be able to understand all our suffering all the time, or even any of it some of the time.

God doesn't answer all of our questions because we are simply unable to understand many of His answers.

AUGUST 24

Job 39:1–40:24

39 "Do you know the time when the
wild mountain goats bear young?
Or can you mark when the deer gives
birth?
2 Can you number the months *that* they
fulfill?
Or do you know the time when they
bear young?
3 They bow down,
They bring forth their young,
They deliver their offspring.
4 Their young ones are healthy,
They grow strong with grain;
They depart and do not return to them.

5 "Who set the wild donkey free?
Who loosed the bonds of the onager,
6 Whose home I have made the
wilderness,
And the barren land his dwelling?
7 He scorns the tumult of the city;
He does not heed the shouts of the
driver.
8 The range of the mountains *is* his
pasture,
And he searches after every green
thing.

9 "Will the wild ox be willing to serve you?
Will he bed by your manger?
10 Can you bind the wild ox in the furrow with ropes?
Or will he plow the valleys behind you?
11 Will you trust him because his strength *is* great?
Or will you leave your labor to him?
12 Will you trust him to bring home your grain,
And gather it to your threshing floor?

13 "The wings of the ostrich wave proudly,
But are her wings and pinions *like the* kindly stork's?
14 For she leaves her eggs on the ground,
And warms them in the dust;
15 She forgets that a foot may crush them,
Or that a wild beast may break them.
16 She treats her young harshly, as though *they were* not hers;
Her labor is in vain, without concern,
17 Because God deprived her of wisdom,
And did not endow her with understanding.
18 When she lifts herself on high,
She scorns the horse and its rider.

19 "Have you given the horse strength?
Have you clothed his neck with thunder?
20 Can you frighten him like a locust?
His majestic snorting strikes terror.
21 He paws in the valley, and rejoices in *his* strength;
He gallops into the clash of arms.
22 He mocks at fear, and is not frightened;
Nor does he turn back from the sword.
23 The quiver rattles against him,
The glittering spear and javelin.
24 He devours the distance with fierceness and rage;
Nor does he come to a halt because the trumpet *has* sounded.
25 At *the blast of* the trumpet he says, 'Aha!'
He smells the battle from afar,
The thunder of captains and shouting.

26 "Does the hawk fly by your wisdom,
And spread its wings toward the south?
27 Does the eagle mount up at your command,
And make its nest on high?
28 On the rock it dwells and resides,
On the crag of the rock and the stronghold.
29 From there it spies out the prey;
Its eyes observe from afar.
30 Its young ones suck up blood;
And where the slain *are,* there it *is.*"

40 Moreover the LORD answered Job, and said:

2 "Shall the one who contends with the Almighty correct *Him?*
He who rebukes God, let him answer it."

3 Then Job answered the LORD and said:

4 "Behold, I am vile;
What shall I answer You?
I lay my hand over my mouth.
5 Once I have spoken, but I will not answer;
Yes, twice, but I will proceed no further."

6 Then the LORD answered Job out of the whirlwind, and said:

7 "Now prepare yourself like a man;
I will question you, and you shall answer Me:

8 "Would you indeed annul My judgment?
Would you condemn Me that you may be justified?
9 Have you an arm like God?
Or can you thunder with a voice like His?
10 Then adorn yourself *with* majesty and splendor,
And array yourself with glory and beauty.
11 Disperse the rage of your wrath;
Look on everyone *who is* proud, and humble him.
12 Look on everyone *who is* proud, *and* bring him low;
Tread down the wicked in their place.
13 Hide them in the dust together,
Bind their faces in hidden *darkness.*
14 Then I will also confess to you
That your own right hand can save you.

15 "Look now at the behemoth, which I made *along* with you;
He eats grass like an ox.
16 See now, his strength *is* in his hips,
And his power *is* in his stomach muscles.
17 He moves his tail like a cedar;
The sinews of his thighs are tightly knit.
18 His bones *are like* beams of bronze,
His ribs like bars of iron.

40:15–24 behemoth. While this is a generic term used commonly in the Old Testament for large cattle or land animals, the description in this passage suggests an extraordinary creature. The hippopotamus has been suggested by the details in the passage (vv. 19–24). However, the short tail of a hippo is hardly consistent with v. 17, where tail could be translated "trunk." It could refer to an elephant, who could be considered "first" or chief of God's creatures whom only He can control (v. 19). Some believe God is describing His most impressive creation of land animals, the dinosaur species, which fit all the characteristics.

19 He *is* the first of the ways of God;
Only He who made him can bring near
His sword.
20 Surely the mountains yield food for him,
And all the beasts of the field play
there.
21 He lies under the lotus trees,
In a covert of reeds and marsh.
22 The lotus trees cover him *with* their
shade;
The willows by the brook surround him.
23 Indeed the river may rage,
Yet he is not disturbed;
He is confident, though the Jordan
gushes into his mouth,
24 *Though* he takes it in his eyes,
Or one pierces *his* nose with a snare.

Psalm 101:1–4

A Psalm of David.

I will sing of mercy and justice;
To You, O LORD, I will sing praises.
2 I will behave wisely in a perfect way.
Oh, when will You come to me?
I will walk within my house with a
perfect heart.

101:2 perfect way. As the king goes, so go his followers (v. 6). **when will You come to me?** This is not an eschatological expectation, but rather a personal expression of David's need for God's immanent involvement in his earthly kingship. **my house.** The king first starts with his own personal life (v. 7) and then looks beyond to his kingdom (vv. 5,8).

3 I will set nothing wicked before my
eyes;
I hate the work of those who fall away;
It shall not cling to me.
4 A perverse heart shall depart from me;
I will not know wickedness.

Proverbs 23:29–30

29 Who has woe?
Who has sorrow?
Who has contentions?
Who has complaints?
Who has wounds without cause?
Who has redness of eyes?
30 Those who linger long at the wine,
Those who go in search of mixed wine.

23:30 mixed wine. Lingering long at the wine is indicative of constant drinking so as to induce drunkenness (1 Tim. 3:3; Titus 1:7). Searching for more to drink indicates the same pursuit.

1 Corinthians 6:1–20

6 Dare any of you, having a matter against
another, go to law before the unrighteous,
and not before the saints? 2Do you not know
that the saints will judge the world? And if the
world will be judged by you, are you unworthy
to judge the smallest matters? 3Do you not
know that we shall judge angels? How much
more, things that pertain to this life? 4If then
you have judgments concerning things pertaining to this life, do you appoint those who
are least esteemed by the church to judge? 5I
say this to your shame. Is it so, that there is not
a wise man among you, not even one, who will
be able to judge between his brethren? 6But
brother goes to law against brother, and that
before unbelievers!

7Now therefore, it is already an utter failure for
you that you go to law against one another. Why

6:2 judge the world. Because Christians will assist Christ to judge the world in the millennial kingdom (Rev. 2:26,27; 3:21; Dan. 7:22), they are more than qualified with the truth, the Spirit, the gifts, and the resources they presently have in Him to settle small matters that come up among themselves in this present life.

do you not rather accept wrong? Why do you not
rather *let yourselves* be cheated? [8]No, you yourselves do wrong and cheat, and *you do* these
things *to your* brethren! [9]Do you not know that
the unrighteous will not inherit the kingdom of
God? Do not be deceived. Neither fornicators,
nor idolaters, nor adulterers, nor homosexuals,
nor sodomites, [10]nor thieves, nor covetous, nor
drunkards, nor revilers, nor extortioners will
inherit the kingdom of God. [11]And such were
some of you. But you were washed, but you were
sanctified, but you were justified in the name of
the Lord Jesus and by the Spirit of our God.

[12]All things are lawful for me, but all things
are not helpful. All things are lawful for me,
but I will not be brought under the power of
any. [13]Foods for the stomach and the stomach
for foods, but God will destroy both it and
them. Now the body *is* not for sexual immorality but for the Lord, and the Lord for the body.
[14]And God both raised up the Lord and will
also raise us up by His power.

[15]Do you not know that your bodies are
members of Christ? Shall I then take the members of Christ and make *them* members of a
harlot? Certainly not! [16]Or do you not know
that he who is joined to a harlot is one body
with her? For *"the two,"* He says, *"shall
become one flesh."* [17]But he who is joined to
the Lord is one spirit *with Him.*

[18]Flee sexual immorality. Every sin that a
man does is outside the body, but he who commits sexual immorality sins against his own
body. [19]Or do you not know that your body is
the temple of the Holy Spirit *who is* in you,
whom you have from God, and you are not
your own? [20]For you were bought at a price;
therefore glorify God in your body and in your
spirit, which are God's.

6:15 members. The believer's body is not only for the Lord here and now (v. 14) but is of the Lord, a part of His body, the church (Eph. 1:22,23). The Christian's body is a spiritual temple in which the Spirit of Christ lives (12:3; John 7:38,39; 20:22; Acts 1:8; Rom. 8:9; 2 Cor. 6:16); therefore, when a believer commits a sexual sin, it involves Christ with a harlot. All sexual sin is harlotry. **Certainly not!** These words translate the strongest Greek negative—"may it never be so."

DAY 24: Who does Paul list among those who will not inherit God's kingdom?

First Corinthians 6:9,10 provides a list of people who will "not inherit the kingdom." The kingdom is the spiritual sphere of salvation where God rules as king over all who belong to Him by faith. All believers are in that spiritual kingdom, yet are waiting to enter into the full inheritance of it in the age to come. While believers can and do commit these sins, they do not characterize them as an unbroken life pattern. When they do, it demonstrates that the person is not in God's kingdom. True believers who do sin, repent of that sin and seek to gain the victory over it (Rom. 7:14–25).

"Fornicators." All who indulge in sexual immorality, but particularly unmarried persons. "Idolaters." Those who worship any false god or follow any false religious system. "Adulterers." Married persons who indulge in sexual acts outside their marriage. "Homosexuals...sodomites." These terms refer to those who exchange and corrupt normal male-female sexual roles and relations. Transvestism, sex changes, and other gender perversions are included (Gen. 1:27; Deut. 22:5). Sodomites are so-called because the sin of male-male sex dominated the city of Sodom (Gen. 18:20; 19:4,5). This sinful perversion is condemned always, in any form, by Scripture (Lev. 18:22; 20:13; Rom. 1:26,27; 1 Tim. 1:10).

"Thieves...covetous." Both are guilty of the same basic sin of greed. Those who are covetous desire what belongs to others; thieves actually take it. "Revilers." People who try to destroy others with words. "Extortioners." Swindlers and embezzlers who steal indirectly, taking unfair advantage of others for their own financial gain.

Paul reminds the Corinthians that "such were some of you" (v. 11). Though not all Christians have been guilty of all those particular sins, every Christian is equally an ex-sinner, since Christ came to save sinners (Matt. 9:13; Rom. 5:20).

AUGUST 25

Job 41:1–42:17

41 "Can you draw out Leviathan with
a hook,
Or *snare* his tongue with a line *which*
you lower?
2 Can you put a reed through his nose,
Or pierce his jaw with a hook?
3 Will he make many supplications to
you?
Will he speak softly to you?

41:1 Leviathan. This term appears in 4 other Old Testament texts (Job 3:8; Pss. 74:14; 104:26; Is. 27:1). In each case Leviathan refers to some mighty creature who can overwhelm man but who is no match for God. Since this creature lives in the sea among ships (Ps. 104:26), some form of sea monster, possibly an ancient dinosaur, is in view. Some feel it was a crocodile, which had scaly hide (v. 15), terrible teeth (v. 14), and speed in the water (v. 32). But crocodiles are not sea creatures, and clearly this one was (v. 31). Some have thought it was a killer whale or a great white shark, because he is the ultimate killer beast over all other proud beasts (v. 34).

4 Will he make a covenant with you?
Will you take him as a servant forever?
5 Will you play with him as *with* a bird,
Or will you leash him for your maidens?
6 Will *your* companions make a banquet of him?
Will they apportion him among the merchants?
7 Can you fill his skin with harpoons,
Or his head with fishing spears?
8 Lay your hand on him;
Remember the battle—
Never do it again!
9 Indeed, *any* hope of *overcoming* him is false;
Shall *one not* be overwhelmed at the sight of him?
10 No one *is so* fierce that he would dare stir him up.
Who then is able to stand against Me?
11 Who has preceded Me, that I should pay *him?*
Everything under heaven is Mine.

12 "I will not conceal his limbs,
His mighty power, or his graceful proportions.
13 Who can remove his outer coat?
Who can approach *him* with a double bridle?
14 Who can open the doors of his face,
With his terrible teeth all around?
15 *His* rows of scales are *his* pride,
Shut up tightly *as with* a seal;
16 One is so near another
That no air can come between them;
17 They are joined one to another,
They stick together and cannot be parted.
18 His sneezings flash forth light,
And his eyes *are* like the eyelids of the morning.
19 Out of his mouth go burning lights;
Sparks of fire shoot out.
20 Smoke goes out of his nostrils,
As *from* a boiling pot and burning rushes.
21 His breath kindles coals,
And a flame goes out of his mouth.
22 Strength dwells in his neck,
And sorrow dances before him.
23 The folds of his flesh are joined together;
They are firm on him and cannot be moved.
24 His heart is as hard as stone,
Even as hard as the lower *millstone.*
25 When he raises himself up, the mighty are afraid;
Because of his crashings they are beside themselves.
26 *Though* the sword reaches him, it cannot avail;
Nor does spear, dart, or javelin.
27 He regards iron as straw,
And bronze as rotten wood.
28 The arrow cannot make him flee;
Slingstones become like stubble to him.
29 Darts are regarded as straw;
He laughs at the threat of javelins.
30 His undersides *are* like sharp potsherds;
He spreads pointed *marks* in the mire.
31 He makes the deep boil like a pot;
He makes the sea like a pot of ointment.
32 He leaves a shining wake behind him;
One would think the deep had white hair.
33 On earth there is nothing like him,
Which is made without fear.
34 He beholds every high *thing;*
He *is* king over all the children of pride."

42 Then Job answered the LORD and said:

2 "I know that You can do everything,
And that no purpose *of Yours* can be withheld from You.
3 *You asked,* 'Who *is* this who hides counsel without knowledge?'
Therefore I have uttered what I did not understand,

Things too wonderful for me, which I
did not know.
4 Listen, please, and let me speak;
You said, 'I will question you, and you
shall answer Me.'
5 "I have heard of You by the hearing of
the ear,
But now my eye sees You.
6 Therefore I abhor *myself,*
And repent in dust and ashes."

7And so it was, after the LORD had spoken
these words to Job, that the LORD said to
Eliphaz the Temanite, "My wrath is aroused
against you and your two friends, for you have
not spoken of Me *what is* right, as My servant
Job *has.* 8Now therefore, take for yourselves
seven bulls and seven rams, go to My servant
Job, and offer up for yourselves a burnt offering; and My servant Job shall pray for you. For
I will accept him, lest I deal with you *according*
to your folly; because you have not spoken of
Me *what is* right, as My servant Job *has.*"
9So Eliphaz the Temanite and Bildad the
Shuhite *and* Zophar the Naamathite went and
did as the LORD commanded them; for the
LORD had accepted Job. 10And the LORD restored Job's losses when he prayed for his
friends. Indeed the LORD gave Job twice as
much as he had before. 11Then all his brothers, all his sisters, and all those who had been
his acquaintances before, came to him and ate
food with him in his house; and they consoled
him and comforted him for all the adversity
that the LORD had brought upon him. Each
one gave him a piece of silver and each a ring
of gold.
12Now the LORD blessed the latter *days* of Job
more than his beginning; for he had fourteen
thousand sheep, six thousand camels, one
thousand yoke of oxen, and one thousand
female donkeys. 13He also had seven sons and
three daughters. 14And he called the name of
the first Jemimah, the name of the second
Keziah, and the name of the third Keren-
Happuch. 15In all the land were found no
women *so* beautiful as the daughters of Job;
and their father gave them an inheritance
among their brothers.
16After this Job lived one hundred and forty
years, and saw his children and grandchildren
for four generations. 17So Job died, old and full
of days.

42:1–6 Job's confession and repentance took place finally. He still did not know why he suffered so profoundly, but he was done complaining, questioning, and challenging God's wisdom and justice. He was reduced to such utter humility, crushed beneath the weight of God's greatness, that all he could do was repent for his insolence. Without answers to all of his questions, Job quietly bowed in humble submission before his Creator and admitted that God was sovereign (Is. 14:24; 46:8–11). Most importantly for the message of the book, Job was still diseased and without his children and possessions, and God had not changed anything (except for the humbling of the heart of His servant). Satan had been proven completely wrong in the charges he brought against Job and in thinking he could destroy true saving faith; Job's companions were completely wrong in the charges they brought against him; but most critically, Job himself was completely wrong in the charges he had raised against God. He expressed his own sorrowful regret that he had not just accepted God's will without such ignorant complaints and questions.

42:5 have heard...now my eye sees You. At last, Job said he understood God whom he had seen with the eyes of faith. He had never so well grasped the greatness, majesty, sovereignty, and independence of God as he did at that moment.

Psalm 101:5–8

5 Whoever secretly slanders his
neighbor,
Him I will destroy;
The one who has a haughty look and a
proud heart,
Him I will not endure.
6 My eyes *shall be* on the faithful of the
land,
That they may dwell with me;
He who walks in a perfect way,
He shall serve me.
7 He who works deceit shall not dwell
within my house;
He who tells lies shall not continue in
my presence.
8 Early I will destroy all the wicked of
the land,
That I may cut off all the evildoers
from the city of the LORD.

Proverbs 23:31–35

31 Do not look on the wine when it is red,
When it sparkles in the cup,

When it swirls around smoothly;
32 At the last it bites like a serpent,
And stings like a viper.
33 Your eyes will see strange things,
And your heart will utter perverse
things.
34 Yes, you will be like one who lies down
in the midst of the sea,
Or like one who lies at the top of the
mast, *saying:*
35 "They have struck me, *but* I was not
hurt;
They have beaten me, but I did not feel
it.
When shall I awake, that I may seek
another *drink?*"

1 Corinthians 7:1–19

7 Now concerning the things of which you
wrote to me:
It is good for a man not to touch a woman.
2 Nevertheless, because of sexual immorality,
let each man have his own wife, and let each
woman have her own husband. 3 Let the husband render to his wife the affection due her,
and likewise also the wife to her husband. 4 The
wife does not have authority over her own
body, but the husband *does.* And likewise the
husband does not have authority over his own
body, but the wife *does.* 5 Do not deprive one
another except with consent for a time, that
you may give yourselves to fasting and
prayer; and come together again so that Satan
does not tempt you because of your lack of
self-control. 6 But I say this as a concession, not
as a commandment. 7 For I wish that all men
were even as I myself. But each one has his
own gift from God, one in this manner and
another in that.
8 But I say to the unmarried and to the widows: It is good for them if they remain even as
I am; 9 but if they cannot exercise self-control,
let them marry. For it is better to marry than
to burn *with passion.*
10 Now to the married I command, *yet* not I
but the Lord: A wife is not to depart from *her*
husband. 11 But even if she does depart, let her
remain unmarried or be reconciled to *her* husband. And a husband is not to divorce *his* wife.
12 But to the rest I, not the Lord, say: If any
brother has a wife who does not believe, and
she is willing to live with him, let him not
divorce her. 13 And a woman who has a husband
who does not believe, if he is willing to live with
her, let her not divorce him. 14 For the unbelieving husband is sanctified by the wife, and the
unbelieving wife is sanctified by the husband;
otherwise your children would be unclean, but
now they are holy. 15 But if the unbeliever
departs, let him depart; a brother or a sister is
not under bondage in such *cases.* But God has
called us to peace. 16 For how do you know, O
wife, whether you will save *your* husband? Or
how do you know, O husband, whether you will
save *your* wife?
17 But as God has distributed to each one, as
the Lord has called each one, so let him walk.
And so I ordain in all the churches. 18 Was anyone called while circumcised? Let him not
become uncircumcised. Was anyone called
while uncircumcised? Let him not be circumcised. 19 Circumcision is nothing and uncircumcision is nothing, but keeping the commandments of God *is what matters.*

7:2 sexual immorality. There is a great danger of sexual sin when single (Matt. 19:12). Marriage is God's only provision for sexual fulfillment. Marriage should not be reduced simply to that, however. Paul has a much higher view and articulates it in Ephesians 5:22,23. He is, here, stressing the issue of sexual sin for people who are single.

7:5 deprive. Literally, "stop depriving each other!" This command may indicate that this kind of deprivation was going on among believers, perhaps reacting to the gross sexual sins of their past and wanting to leave all that behind. Husbands and wives may abstain temporarily from sexual activity, but only when they mutually agree to do so for intercession, as a part of their fasting. **come together again.** Sexual intercourse is to be soon renewed after the spiritual interruption. **so that Satan does not tempt.** After the agreed-upon "time" of abstinence, sexual desires intensify and a spouse becomes more vulnerable to sinful desire.

DAY 25: How does Paul address the issue of divorce for the Corinthian church?

Paul taught about divorce in the context of answering a number of questions that the church had sent to him. The first of those questions had to do with marriage, an area of trouble due to the moral corruption of the surrounding culture that tolerated fornication, adultery, homosexuality, polygamy, and concubinage.

The apostle reminded the believers that his teaching was based on what Jesus had already made clear during His earthly ministry (Matt. 5:31,32; 19:5–8). Jesus Himself based His teaching on the previously revealed word of God (Gen. 2:24; Mal. 2:16).

Paul's departure point for teaching affirmed God's prohibition of divorce. He wrote that in cases where a Christian has already divorced another Christian except for adultery (1 Cor. 7:10,11), neither partner is free to marry another person. They should reconcile or at least remain unmarried.

Paul then added some helpful direction on the issue of marital conflicts created in cases where one spouse becomes a believer (vv. 12–16). First, the believing spouse lives under orders to make the best of the marriage, seeking to win his or her spouse to Christ. If the unbelieving spouse decides to end the marriage, Paul's response is "let him depart" (v. 15). This term refers to divorce (vv. 10,11). When an unbelieving spouse cannot tolerate the partner's faith and wants a divorce, it is best to let that happen in order to preserve peace in the family (12:18). Therefore, the bond of marriage is broken only by death (7:2), adultery (Matt. 19:9), or an unbeliever's departure.

When the bond of marriage is broken in any of those ways, a Christian is free to marry another believer (Rom. 7:15). Throughout Scripture, whenever legitimate divorce occurs, remarriage is an assumed option. When divorce is permitted, so is remarriage.

In general, conversion and obedience to Christ should lead us to greater faithfulness and commitment in every relationship. This extended passage (vv. 1–24) plainly repeats the basic principle that Christians should willingly accept the marital condition and social situations into which God has placed them and be content to serve Him there until He leads them elsewhere.

AUGUST 26

Ecclesiastes 1:1–2:26

1 The words of the Preacher, the son of David, king in Jerusalem.

2 "Vanity of vanities," says the Preacher;
"Vanity of vanities, all *is* vanity."

3 What profit has a man from all his labor
In which he toils under the sun?
4 *One* generation passes away,
and *another* generation comes;
But the earth abides forever.
5 The sun also rises, and the sun goes
down,
And hastens to the place where it
arose.
6 The wind goes toward the south,
And turns around to the north;
The wind whirls about continually,
And comes again on its circuit.
7 All the rivers run into the sea,
Yet the sea *is* not full;
To the place from which the rivers
come,
There they return again.
8 All things *are* full of labor;
Man cannot express *it*.
The eye is not satisfied with seeing,
Nor the ear filled with hearing.
9 That which has been *is* what will be,
That which *is* done is what will be
done,
And *there is* nothing new under the
sun.
10 Is there anything of which it may be
said,
"See, this *is* new"?
It has already been in ancient times
before us.
11 *There is* no remembrance of former
things,
Nor will there be any remembrance of
things that are to come
By *those* who will come after.

12 I, the Preacher, was king over Israel in Jerusalem. 13 And I set my heart to seek and
search out by wisdom concerning all that is
done under heaven; this burdensome task God
has given to the sons of man, by which they
may be exercised. 14 I have seen all the works

1:13 wisdom. Solomon's use of the term, in typical Hebrew fashion, is more practical than philosophical and implies more than knowledge. It carries notions of ability for proper behavior, success, common sense, and wit. **burdensome task.** Man's search to understand is at times difficult, yet God-given (2:26; 3:10; 5:16–19; 6:2; 8:11,15; 9:9; 12:11). **God.** The covenant name, "LORD," is never used in Ecclesiastes. However, "God" is found almost 40 times. The emphasis is more on God's sovereignty in creation and providence than on His covenant relationship through redemption.

that are done under the sun; and indeed, all *is*
vanity and grasping for the wind.

15 *What is* crooked cannot be made
straight,
And what is lacking cannot be
numbered.

16 I communed with my heart, saying, "Look, I
have attained greatness, and have gained more
wisdom than all who were before me in Jerusalem. My heart has understood great wisdom
and knowledge." 17 And I set my heart to know
wisdom and to know madness and folly. I perceived that this also is grasping for the wind.

18 For in much wisdom *is* much grief,
And he who increases knowledge
increases sorrow.

2 I said in my heart, "Come now, I will test
you with mirth; therefore enjoy pleasure";
but surely, this also *was* vanity. 2 I said of laughter—"Madness!"; and of mirth, "What does it
accomplish?" 3 I searched in my heart *how* to
gratify my flesh with wine, while guiding my
heart with wisdom, and how to lay hold on
folly, till I might see what *was* good for the
sons of men to do under heaven all the days of
their lives.

4 I made my works great, I built myself houses, and planted myself vineyards. 5 I made
myself gardens and orchards, and I planted all
kinds of fruit trees in them. 6 I made myself
water pools from which to water the growing
trees of the grove. 7 I acquired male and female
servants, and had servants born in my house.
Yes, I had greater possessions of herds and
flocks than all who were in Jerusalem before
me. 8 I also gathered for myself silver and gold
and the special treasures of kings and of the
provinces. I acquired male and female singers,
the delights of the sons of men, *and* musical
instruments of all kinds.

9 So I became great and excelled more than
all who were before me in Jerusalem. Also my
wisdom remained with me.

10 Whatever my eyes desired I did not
keep from them.
I did not withhold my heart from any
pleasure,
For my heart rejoiced in all my labor;
And this was my reward from all my
labor.
11 Then I looked on all the works that my
hands had done
And on the labor in which I had toiled;
And indeed all *was* vanity and grasping
for the wind.
There was no profit under the sun.

12 Then I turned myself to consider
wisdom and madness and folly;
For what *can* the man *do* who succeeds
the king?—
Only what he has already done.
13 Then I saw that wisdom excels folly
As light excels darkness.
14 The wise man's eyes *are* in his head,
But the fool walks in darkness.
Yet I myself perceived
That the same event happens to them
all.

15 So I said in my heart,
"As it happens to the fool,
It also happens to me,
And why was I then more wise?"
Then I said in my heart,
"This also *is* vanity."
16 For *there is* no more remembrance of
the wise than of the fool forever,
Since all that now *is* will be forgotten in
the days to come.
And how does a wise *man* die?
As the fool!

17 Therefore I hated life because the work that
was done under the sun *was* distressing to me,
for all *is* vanity and grasping for the wind.

18 Then I hated all my labor in which I had
toiled under the sun, because I must leave it to
the man who will come after me. 19 And who
knows whether he will be wise or a fool? Yet
he will rule over all my labor in which I toiled
and in which I have shown myself wise under
the sun. This also *is* vanity. 20 Therefore I
turned my heart and despaired of all the labor
in which I had toiled under the sun. 21 For there
is a man whose labor *is* with wisdom, knowledge, and skill; yet he must leave his heritage
to a man who has not labored for it. This also
is vanity and a great evil. 22 For what has man
for all his labor, and for the striving of his
heart with which he has toiled under the sun?
23 For all his days *are* sorrowful, and his work
burdensome; even in the night his heart takes
no rest. This also is vanity.

24 Nothing *is* better for a man *than* that he
should eat and drink, and *that* his soul should
enjoy good in his labor. This also, I saw, was
from the hand of God. 25 For who can eat, or who
can have enjoyment, more than I? 26 For *God*
gives wisdom and knowledge and joy to a man
who *is* good in His sight; but to the sinner He
gives the work of gathering and collecting, that
he may give to *him who is* good before God.
This also *is* vanity and grasping for the wind.

Psalm 102:1–11

A Prayer of the afflicted, when he is overwhelmed and pours out his complaint before the LORD.

Hear my prayer, O LORD,
And let my cry come to You.
2 Do not hide Your face from me in the day of my trouble;
Incline Your ear to me;
In the day that I call, answer me speedily.

3 For my days are consumed like smoke,
And my bones are burned like a hearth.
4 My heart is stricken and withered like grass,
So that I forget to eat my bread.
5 Because of the sound of my groaning
My bones cling to my skin.
6 I am like a pelican of the wilderness;
I am like an owl of the desert.
7 I lie awake,
And am like a sparrow alone on the housetop.

8 My enemies reproach me all day long;
Those who deride me swear an oath against me.
9 For I have eaten ashes like bread,
And mingled my drink with weeping,
10 Because of Your indignation and Your wrath;
For You have lifted me up and cast me away.
11 My days *are* like a shadow that lengthens,
And I wither away like grass.

102:10,11 a shadow that lengthens. The time of sunset is used to describe the psalmist's desperate sense that his life will end shortly because God has punished him by withdrawing His presence and strength.

Proverbs 24:1–2

24 Do not be envious of evil men,
Nor desire to be with them;
2 For their heart devises violence,
And their lips talk of troublemaking.

1 Corinthians 7:20–40

[20]Let each one remain in the same calling in which he was called. [21]Were you called *while* a slave? Do not be concerned about it; but if you can be made free, rather use *it.* [22]For he who is called in the Lord *while* a slave is the Lord's freedman. Likewise he who is called *while* free is Christ's slave. [23]You were bought at a price; do not become slaves of men. [24]Brethren, let each one remain with God in that *state* in which he was called.

[25]Now concerning virgins: I have no commandment from the Lord; yet I give judgment as one whom the Lord in His mercy has made trustworthy. [26]I suppose therefore that this is good because of the present distress—that *it is* good for a man to remain as he is: [27]Are you bound to a wife? Do not seek to be loosed. Are you loosed from a wife? Do not seek a wife. [28]But even if you do marry, you have not sinned; and if a virgin marries, she has not sinned. Nevertheless such will have trouble in the flesh, but I would spare you.

[29]But this I say, brethren, the time *is* short, so that from now on even those who have wives should be as though they had none, [30]those who weep as though they did not weep, those who rejoice as though they did not rejoice, those who buy as though they did not possess, [31]and those who use this world as not misusing *it.* For the form of this world is passing away.

[32]But I want you to be without care. He who is unmarried cares for the things of the Lord—how he may please the Lord. [33]But he

7:25–40 Having already established that both marriage and singleness are good and right before the Lord (vv. 1–9), and for the person who has the gift of singleness (v. 7), that state has many practical advantages, Paul continued to answer the questions about which the Corinthians had written him. Paul gives 6 reasons for never marrying, in relationship to the downside of marriage, but remaining single (virgins): 1) pressure from the system (vv. 25–27); 2) problems of the flesh (v. 28); 3) passing of the world (vv. 29–31); 4) preoccupations of marriage (vv. 32–35); 5) promises from fathers (vv. 36–38); and 6) permanency of marriage (vv. 39,40).

7:26 present distress. An unspecified, current calamity. Perhaps Paul anticipated the imminent Roman persecutions which began within 10 years after this epistle was written. **remain as he is.** Persecution is difficult enough for a single person to endure, but problems and pain are multiplied for those who are married, especially if they have children.

who is married cares about the things of the
world—how he may please *his* wife. 34There is
a difference between a wife and a virgin. The
unmarried woman cares about the things of
the Lord, that she may be holy both in body
and in spirit. But she who is married cares
about the things of the world—how she may
please *her* husband. 35And this I say for your
own profit, not that I may put a leash on you,
but for what is proper, and that you may serve
the Lord without distraction.
36But if any man thinks he is behaving improp-
erly toward his virgin, if she is past the flower of
youth, and thus it must be, let him do what he
wishes. He does not sin; let them marry. 37Nev-
ertheless he who stands steadfast in his heart,
having no necessity, but has power over his own
will, and has so determined in his heart that he
will keep his virgin, does well. 38So then he who
gives *her* in marriage does well, but he who
does not give *her* in marriage does better.
39A wife is bound by law as long as her husband lives; but if her husband dies, she is at
liberty to be married to whom she wishes, only
in the Lord. 40But she is happier if she remains
as she is, according to my judgment—and I
think I also have the Spirit of God.

7:33,34 how he may please *his* wife...husband. Here is a basic and expected principle for a good marriage—each seeking to please the other.

DAY 26: How does the author's declaration that "all is vanity" relate to the message of Ecclesiastes?

By stating one of his conclusions in the opening lines, the author of Ecclesiastes challenges readers to pay attention. The word translated "vanity" is used in at least three ways throughout the book. In each case, the term refers to the nature and value of human activity "under the sun":

1. "Vanity" refers to the "fleeting" nature of human accomplishments that James later described as like a vapor (James 4:14).
2. "Vanity" can mean "futile" or "meaningless," which points to the cursed condition of the universe and the debilitating effects it has on human earthly experience.
3. "Vanity" can represent "incomprehensible" or "enigmatic," which gives consideration to life's unanswerable questions. Solomon found that the word applied to his entire experiment.

While the context in each of the 37 appearances of "vanity" helps determine the particular meaning Solomon had in mind, his most frequent usage conveyed the idea of "incomprehensible" or "unknowable." He was expressing the human limits when faced with the mysteries of God's purposes. Solomon's final conclusion to "fear God and keep His commandments" (12:13,14) represents more than the book's summary; it states the only hope of the good life and the only reasonable response of faith and obedience to the sovereign God. God precisely superintends all activities under the sun, each in its time according to His perfect plan, while He discloses only as much as His perfect wisdom dictates. All people remain accountable. Those who refuse to take God and His Word seriously are doomed to lives of the severest vanity.

AUGUST 27

Ecclesiastes 3:1–22

3 To everything *there is* a season,
A time for every purpose
under heaven:
2 A time to be born,
And a time to die;
A time to plant,
And a time to pluck *what is* planted;
3 A time to kill,
And a time to heal;
A time to break down,
And a time to build up;
4 A time to weep,
And a time to laugh;
A time to mourn,
And a time to dance;
5 A time to cast away stones,
And a time to gather stones;
A time to embrace,
And a time to refrain from
embracing;
6 A time to gain,
And a time to lose;
A time to keep,
And a time to throw away;
7 A time to tear,
And a time to sew;

A time to keep silence,
And a time to speak;
8 A time to love,
And a time to hate;
A time of war,
And a time of peace.

[9]What profit has the worker from that in which he labors? [10]I have seen the God-given task with which the sons of men are to be occupied. [11]He has made everything beautiful in its time. Also He has put eternity in their hearts, except that no one can find out the work that God does from beginning to end.

[12]I know that nothing *is* better for them than to rejoice, and to do good in their lives, [13]and also that every man should eat and drink and enjoy the good of all his labor—it *is* the gift of God.

3:1–8 a season, a time. Not only does God fix the standard and withhold or dispense satisfaction (2:26), but He also appoints "seasons" and "times." Earthly pursuits are good in their proper place and time, but unprofitable when pursued as the chief goal (vv. 9,10).

3:11 everything. Every activity or event for which a culmination point may be fixed. **beautiful.** Fitting or appropriate. The phrase echoes "God saw…it was very good" (Gen. 1:31). Even in a cursed universe, activity should not be meaningless. Its futility lies in the fickle satisfaction of man and his failure to trust the wisdom of sovereign God. **put eternity in their hearts.** God made men for His eternal purpose, and nothing in post-Fall time can bring them complete satisfaction.

14 I know that whatever God does,
It shall be forever.
Nothing can be added to it,
And nothing taken from it.
God does *it,* that men should fear
before Him.
15 That which is has already been,
And what is to be has already been;
And God requires an account of what
is past.

[16]Moreover I saw under the sun:

In the place of judgment,
Wickedness *was* there;
And *in* the place of righteousness,
Iniquity *was* there.

[17]I said in my heart,

"God shall judge the righteous and the
wicked,
For *there is* a time there for every
purpose and for every work."

[18]I said in my heart, "Concerning the condition
of the sons of men, God tests them, that they
may see that they themselves are *like* animals."
[19]For what happens to the sons of men also
happens to animals; one thing befalls them: as
one dies, so dies the other. Surely, they all
have one breath; man has no advantage over
animals, for all *is* vanity. [20]All go to one place: all
are from the dust, and all return to dust. [21]Who
knows the spirit of the sons of men, which goes
upward, and the spirit of the animal, which
goes down to the earth? [22]So I perceived that
nothing *is* better than that a man should
rejoice in his own works, for that *is* his heritage. For who can bring him to see what will
happen after him?

Psalm 102:12–17

12 But You, O LORD, shall endure forever,
And the remembrance of Your name to
all generations.
13 You will arise *and* have mercy on Zion;
For the time to favor her,
Yes, the set time, has come.
14 For Your servants take pleasure in her
stones,
And show favor to her dust.
15 So the nations shall fear the name of
the LORD,
And all the kings of the earth Your
glory.
16 For the LORD shall build up Zion;
He shall appear in His glory.
17 He shall regard the prayer of the
destitute,
And shall not despise their prayer.

Proverbs 24:3–4

3 Through wisdom a house is built,
And by understanding it is established;
4 By knowledge the rooms are filled
With all precious and pleasant riches.

1 Corinthians 8:1–13

8 Now concerning things offered to idols:
We know that we all have knowledge.
Knowledge puffs up, but love edifies. [2]And if
anyone thinks that he knows anything, he
knows nothing yet as he ought to know. [3]But if
anyone loves God, this one is known by Him.
[4]Therefore concerning the eating of things
offered to idols, we know that an idol *is* nothing in the world, and that *there is* no other God

8:1 things offered to idols. The Greeks and Romans were polytheistic (worshiping many gods) and polydemonistic (believing in many evil spirits). They believed that evil spirits would try to invade human beings by attaching themselves to food before it was eaten, and that the spirits could be removed only by the food's being sacrificed to a god. The sacrifice was meant not only to gain favor with the god but also to cleanse the meat from demonic contamination. Such decontaminated meat was offered to the gods as a sacrifice. That which was not burned on the altar was served at wicked pagan feasts. What was left was sold in the market. After conversion, believers resented eating such food bought out of idol markets, because it reminded sensitive Gentile believers of their previous pagan lives and the demonic worship. **we all have knowledge.** Paul and mature believers knew better than to be bothered by such food offered once to idols and then sold in the marketplace. They knew the deities didn't exist and that evil spirits did not contaminate the food. **love edifies.** Knowledge mingled with love prevents a believer from exercising freedoms that offend weaker believers and, rather, builds the others up in truth and wisdom (13:1–4).

8:7 conscience...is defiled. The consciences of some newer converts were still accusing them strongly with regard to allowing them to eat idol food without feeling spiritually corrupted and guilty. They still imagined that idols were real and evil. A defiled conscience is one that has been violated, bringing fear, shame, and guilt.

8:12 you sin against Christ. A strong warning that causing a brother or sister in Christ to stumble is more than simply an offense against that person. It is a serious offense against the Lord Himself.

but one. 5For even if there are so-called gods,
whether in heaven or on earth (as there are
many gods and many lords), 6yet for us *there is*
one God, the Father, of whom *are* all things,
and we for Him; and one Lord Jesus Christ,
through whom *are* all things, and through
whom we *live.*

7However, *there is* not in everyone that knowledge; for some, with consciousness of the idol,
until now eat *it* as a thing offered to an idol; and
their conscience, being weak, is defiled. 8But
food does not commend us to God; for neither if
we eat are we the better, nor if we do not eat are
we the worse.
9But beware lest somehow this liberty of
yours become a stumbling block to those who
are weak. 10For if anyone sees you who have
knowledge eating in an idol's temple, will not
the conscience of him who is weak be emboldened to eat those things offered to idols? 11And
because of your knowledge shall the weak
brother perish, for whom Christ died? 12But
when you thus sin against the brethren, and
wound their weak conscience, you sin against
Christ. 13Therefore, if food makes my brother
stumble, I will never again eat meat, lest I
make my brother stumble.

DAY 27: In Ecclesiates, what reflections does Solomon give on Genesis?

Toward the end of his life, the penitent King Solomon pondered life in the wake of the Fall and the outworking of man's sin. Solomon drew the following conclusions, possibly from his own study of Genesis:

1. God created the heavens and earth with laws of design and regularity (Eccl. 1:2–7; 3:1–8; Gen. 1:1–31; 8:22).
2. Man is created from dust and returns to dust (Eccl. 3:20; 12:7; Gen. 2:7; 3:19).
3. God placed in man His life-giving breath (Eccl. 12:7; Gen. 2:7).
4. As God ordained it, marriage is one of life's most enjoyable blessings (Eccl. 9:9; Gen. 2:18–25).
5. Divine judgment results from the Fall (Eccl. 3:14–22; 11:9; 12:14; Gen. 2:17; 3:1–19).
6. The effect of the curse on creation is "vanity," i.e., futility (Eccl. 1:5–8; Gen. 3:17–19).
7. Labor after the Fall is difficult and yields little profit (Eccl. 1:3,13; 2:3; 3:9–11; Gen. 3:17–19).
8. Death overcomes all creatures after the Fall (Eccl. 8:8; 9:4,5; Gen. 2:17; 3:19).
9. After the Fall, man's heart is desperately wicked (Eccl. 7:20,29; 8:11; 9:3; Gen. 3:22; 6:5; 8:21).
10. God withholds certain knowledge and wisdom from man for His wise, but unspoken, reasons (Eccl. 6:12; 8:17; Gen. 3:22).

AUGUST 28

Ecclesiastes 4:1–6:12

4 Then I returned and considered all the oppression that is done under the sun:

And look! The tears of the oppressed,
But they have no comforter—
On the side of their oppressors *there is* power,
But they have no comforter.
2 Therefore I praised the dead who were already dead,
More than the living who are still alive.
3 Yet, better than both *is he* who has never existed,
Who has not seen the evil work that is done under the sun.

4 Again, I saw that for all toil and every skillful work a man is envied by his neighbor. This also *is* vanity and grasping for the wind.

5 The fool folds his hands
And consumes his own flesh.
6 Better a handful *with* quietness
Than both hands full, *together with* toil and grasping for the wind.

7 Then I returned, and I saw vanity under the sun:

8 There is one alone, without companion:
He has neither son nor brother.
Yet *there is* no end to all his labors,
Nor is his eye satisfied with riches.
But he never asks,
"For whom do I toil and deprive myself of good?"
This also *is* vanity and a grave misfortune.

9 Two *are* better than one,
Because they have a good reward for their labor.
10 For if they fall, one will lift up his companion.
But woe to him *who is* alone when he falls,
For *he has* no one to help him up.
11 Again, if two lie down together, they will keep warm;
But how can one be warm *alone?*
12 Though one may be overpowered by another, two can withstand him.
And a threefold cord is not quickly broken.

13 Better a poor and wise youth
Than an old and foolish king who will be admonished no more.
14 For he comes out of prison to be king,
Although he was born poor in his kingdom.
15 I saw all the living who walk under the sun;
They were with the second youth who stands in his place.
16 *There was* no end of all the people over whom he was made king;
Yet those who come afterward will not rejoice in him.
Surely this also *is* vanity and grasping for the wind.

5 Walk prudently when you go to the house
of God; and draw near to hear rather than
to give the sacrifice of fools, for they do not
know that they do evil.

2 Do not be rash with your mouth,
And let not your heart utter anything hastily before God.
For God *is* in heaven, and you on earth;
Therefore let your words be few.
3 For a dream comes through much activity,
And a fool's voice *is known* by *his* many words.

4 When you make a vow to God, do not delay to pay it;
For *He has* no pleasure in fools.
Pay what you have vowed—
5 Better not to vow than to vow and not pay.

6 Do not let your mouth cause your flesh to sin,
nor say before the messenger *of God* that it
was an error. Why should God be angry at
your excuse and destroy the work of your
hands? 7 For in the multitude of dreams and
many words *there is* also vanity. But fear God.
8 If you see the oppression of the poor, and
the violent perversion of justice and righteousness in a province, do not marvel at the
matter; for high official watches over high official, and higher officials are over them.
9 Moreover the profit of the land is for all;
even the king is served from the field.

10 He who loves silver will not be satisfied with silver;
Nor he who loves abundance, with increase.
This also *is* vanity.

11 When goods increase,
They increase who eat them;

So what profit have the owners
Except to see *them* with their eyes?

12 The sleep of a laboring man *is* sweet,
Whether he eats little or much;
But the abundance of the rich will not
permit him to sleep.

13 There is a severe evil *which* I have
seen under the sun:
Riches kept for their owner to his hurt.

14 But those riches perish through
misfortune;
When he begets a son, *there is* nothing
in his hand.

15 As he came from his mother's womb,
naked shall he return,
To go as he came;
And he shall take nothing from his
labor
Which he may carry away in his hand.

16 And this also *is* a severe evil—
Just exactly as he came, so shall he go.
And what profit has he who has
labored for the wind?

17 All his days he also eats in darkness,
And *he has* much sorrow and sickness
and anger.

18 Here is what I have seen: *It is* good and fitting *for one* to eat and drink, and to enjoy the
good of all his labor in which he toils under the
sun all the days of his life which God gives
him; for it *is* his heritage. 19 As for every man to
whom God has given riches and wealth, and
given him power to eat of it, to receive his heritage and rejoice in his labor—this *is* the gift of
God. 20 For he will not dwell unduly on the days
of his life, because God keeps *him* busy with
the joy of his heart.

6 There is an evil which I have seen under
the sun, and it *is* common among men: 2 A
man to whom God has given riches and wealth
and honor, so that he lacks nothing for himself
of all he desires; yet God does not give him
power to eat of it, but a foreigner consumes it.
This *is* vanity, and it *is* an evil affliction.
3 If a man begets a hundred *children* and lives
many years, so that the days of his years are
many, but his soul is not satisfied with goodness, or indeed he has no burial, I say *that* a
stillborn child *is* better than he— 4 for it comes
in vanity and departs in darkness, and its name
is covered with darkness. 5 Though it has not
seen the sun or known *anything,* this has more
rest than that man, 6 even if he lives a thousand
years twice—but has not seen goodness. Do
not all go to one place?

7 All the labor of man *is* for his mouth,
And yet the soul is not satisfied.

8 For what more has the wise *man* than
the fool?
What does the poor man have,
Who knows *how* to walk before the
living?

9 Better *is* the sight of the eyes than the
wandering of desire.
This also *is* vanity and grasping for the
wind.

10 Whatever one is, he has been named
already,
For it is known that he *is* man;
And he cannot contend with Him who
is mightier than he.

11 Since there are many things that
increase vanity,
How *is* man the better?

12 For who knows what *is* good for man in
life, all the days of his vain life which he passes like a shadow? Who can tell a man what will
happen after him under the sun?

6:2 God does not give him power to eat. The Lord gives and takes away for His own purposes. So, the blessings of God cannot be assumed or taken for granted. But they should be enjoyed with thankfulness while they are available.

Psalm 102:18–28

18 This will be written for the generation
to come,
That a people yet to be created may
praise the LORD.

19 For He looked down from the height of
His sanctuary;
From heaven the LORD viewed the
earth,

20 To hear the groaning of the prisoner,
To release those appointed to death,

21 To declare the name of the LORD in Zion,
And His praise in Jerusalem,

22 When the peoples are gathered together,
And the kingdoms, to serve the LORD.

23 He weakened my strength in the way;
He shortened my days.

24 I said, "O my God,
Do not take me away in the midst of
my days;
Your years *are* throughout all
generations.

102:25–27 Eternal God created the heavens and earth, which will one day perish (v. 26). Hebrews 1:10–12 applies this passage to the Lord Jesus Christ, who is superior to the angels because: 1) He is eternal, while they had a beginning; and 2) He created, but they were created. This passage clearly affirms the eternality and deity of Christ. The unchangeable God will outlast His creation, even into the new creation (Mal. 3:6; James 1:17; 2 Pet. 3; Rev. 21; 22).

25 Of old You laid the foundation of the
earth,
And the heavens *are* the work of Your
hands.
26 They will perish, but You will endure;
Yes, they will all grow old like a
garment;
Like a cloak You will change them,
And they will be changed.
27 But You *are* the same,
And Your years will have no end.
28 The children of Your servants will
continue,
And their descendants will be
established before You."

Proverbs 24:5–6

5 A wise man *is* strong,
Yes, a man of knowledge increases
strength;
6 For by wise counsel you will wage your
own war,
And in a multitude of counselors *there*
is safety.

1 Corinthians 9:1–27

9 Am I not an apostle? Am I not free? Have I
not seen Jesus Christ our Lord? Are you
not my work in the Lord? [2]If I am not an apostle to others, yet doubtless I am to you. For
you are the seal of my apostleship in the Lord.
[3]My defense to those who examine me is
this: [4]Do we have no right to eat and drink?
[5]Do we have no right to take along a believing
wife, as *do* also the other apostles, the brothers of the Lord, and Cephas? [6]Or *is it* only
Barnabas and I *who* have no right to refrain
from working? [7]Who ever goes to war at his
own expense? Who plants a vineyard and does
not eat of its fruit? Or who tends a flock and
does not drink of the milk of the flock?
[8]Do I say these things as a *mere* man? Or
does not the law say the same also? [9]For it is
written in the law of Moses, *"You shall not*
muzzle an ox while it treads out the grain." Is
it oxen God is concerned about? [10]Or does He
say *it* altogether for our sakes? For our sakes,
no doubt, *this* is written, that he who plows
should plow in hope, and he who threshes in
hope should be partaker of his hope. [11]If we
have sown spiritual things for you, *is it* a great
thing if we reap your material things? [12]If others are partakers of *this* right over you, *are* we
not even more?
Nevertheless we have not used this right,
but endure all things lest we hinder the gospel
of Christ. [13]Do you not know that those who
minister the holy things eat *of the things* of the
temple, and those who serve at the altar partake of *the offerings of* the altar? [14]Even so the
Lord has commanded that those who preach
the gospel should live from the gospel.
[15]But I have used none of these things, nor
have I written these things that it should be
done so to me; for it *would be* better for me to
die than that anyone should make my boasting
void. [16]For if I preach the gospel, I have nothing to boast of, for necessity is laid upon me;
yes, woe is me if I do not preach the gospel!
[17]For if I do this willingly, I have a reward; but
if against my will, I have been entrusted with a
stewardship. [18]What is my reward then? That
when I preach the gospel, I may present the
gospel of Christ without charge, that I may not
abuse my authority in the gospel.
[19]For though I am free from all *men,* I have
made myself a servant to all, that I might win
the more; [20]and to the Jews I became as a Jew,
that I might win Jews; to those *who are* under
the law, as under the law, that I might win
those *who are* under the law; [21]to those *who are*
without law, as without law (not being without
law toward God, but under law toward Christ),
that I might win those *who are* without law; [22]to
the weak I became as weak, that I might win
the weak. I have become all things to all *men,*
that I might by all means save some. [23]Now
this I do for the gospel's sake, that I may be
partaker of it with *you.*
[24]Do you not know that those who run in a
race all run, but one receives the prize? Run in
such a way that you may obtain *it.* [25]And everyone who competes *for the prize* is temperate in
all things. Now they *do it* to obtain a perish-
able crown, but we *for* an imperishable *crown.*
[26]Therefore I run thus: not with uncertainty.
Thus I fight: not as *one who* beats the air. [27]But
I discipline my body and bring *it* into subjection, lest, when I have preached to others, I
myself should become disqualified.

9:24 race. The Greeks enjoyed two great athletic events, the Olympic games and the Isthmian games, and because the Isthmian events were held in Corinth, believers there were quite familiar with this analogy of running to win.

9:26 not with uncertainty. Four times Paul has mentioned his goal of winning people to salvation (vv. 19,22). **beats the air.** Paul changes the metaphor to boxing to illustrate the point that he was no shadow boxer, just waving his arms without effect (1 Tim. 1:18).

DAY 28: How is Jesus Christ seen in the Psalms?

Psalms	New Testament Quote	Significance
2:1–12	Acts 4:25,26; 13:33; Heb. 1:5; 5:5	Incarnation, Crucifixion, Resurrection
8:3–8	1 Cor. 15:27,28; Eph. 1:22; Heb. 2:5–10	Creation
16:8–11	Acts 2:24–31; 13:35–37	Death, Resurrection
22:1–31	Matt. 27:35–46; John 19:23,24; Heb. 2:12; 5:5	Incarnation, Crucifixion, Resurrection
40:6–8	Heb. 10:5–9	Incarnation
41:9	John 13:18,21	Betrayal
45:6,7	Heb. 1:8,9	Deity
68:18	Eph. 4:8	Ascension, Enthronement
69:20,21,25	Matt. 27:34,48; Acts 1:15–20	Betrayal, Crucifixion
72:6–17		Millennial Kingship
78:1,2,15	Matt. 13:35; 1 Cor. 10:4	Theophany, Earthly Teaching Ministry
89:3–37	Acts 2:30	Millennial Kingship
102:25–27	Heb. 1:10–12	Creation, Eternality
109:6–19	Acts 1:15–20	Betrayal
110:1–7	Matt. 22:43–45; Acts. 2:33–35; Heb. 1:13; 5:6–10; 6:20; 7:24	Deity, Ascension, Heavenly Priesthood, Millennial Kingship
118:22,23	Matt. 21:42; Mark 12:10,11; Luke 20:17; Acts 4:8–12; 1 Pet. 2:7	Rejection as Savior
132:12–18	Acts 2:30	Millennial Kingship

AUGUST 29

Ecclesiastes 7:1–29

7 A good name *is* better than precious
ointment,
And the day of death than the day of
one's birth;
2 Better to go to the house of mourning
Than to go to the house of feasting,
For that *is* the end of all men;
And the living will take *it* to heart.
3 Sorrow *is* better than laughter,
For by a sad countenance the heart is
made better.
4 The heart of the wise *is* in the house of
mourning,
But the heart of fools *is* in the house of
mirth.
5 *It is* better to hear the rebuke of the
wise
Than for a man to hear the song of
fools.
6 For like the crackling of thorns under
a pot,
So *is* the laughter of the fool.
This also is vanity.

7 Surely oppression destroys a wise
man's reason,
And a bribe debases the heart.

8 The end of a thing *is* better than its
beginning;
The patient in spirit *is* better than the
proud in spirit.
9 Do not hasten in your spirit to be
angry,
For anger rests in the bosom of fools.
10 Do not say,
"Why were the former days better than
these?"
For you do not inquire wisely
concerning this.

11 Wisdom *is* good with an inheritance,
And profitable to those who see the
sun.
12 For wisdom *is* a defense *as* money *is* a
defense,
But the excellence of knowledge *is that*
wisdom gives life to those who
have it.

13 Consider the work of God;
For who can make straight what
He has made crooked?
14 In the day of prosperity be joyful,
But in the day of adversity
consider:
Surely God has appointed the one
as well as the other,
So that man can find out nothing *that*
will come after him.

15 I have seen everything in my days of vanity:

There is a just *man* who perishes in
his righteousness,
And there is a wicked *man* who
prolongs *life* in his wickedness.

16 Do not be overly righteous,
Nor be overly wise:
Why should you destroy yourself?
17 Do not be overly wicked,
Nor be foolish:
Why should you die before
your time?
18 *It is* good that you grasp this,
And also not remove your hand from
the other;
For he who fears God will escape
them all.

19 Wisdom strengthens the wise
More than ten rulers of the city.
20 For *there is* not a just man on earth
who does good
And does not sin.

21 Also do not take to heart everything
people say,
Lest you hear your servant cursing
you.
22 For many times, also, your own heart
has known
That even you have cursed others.

23 All this I have proved by wisdom.
I said, "I will be wise";
But it *was* far from me.
24 As for that which is far off and
exceedingly deep,
Who can find it out?
25 I applied my heart to know,
To search and seek out wisdom and the
reason *of things,*
To know the wickedness of folly,
Even of foolishness *and* madness.
26 And I find more bitter than death
The woman whose heart *is* snares and
nets,
Whose hands *are* fetters.
He who pleases God shall escape
from her,
But the sinner shall be trapped
by her.

27 "Here is what I have found," says the
Preacher,
"*Adding* one thing to the other to find
out the reason,
28 Which my soul still seeks but I cannot
find:
One man among a thousand I have
found,
But a woman among all these I have
not found.
29 Truly, this only I have found:
That God made man upright,
But they have sought out many
schemes."

Psalm 103:1–5

A Psalm of David.

Bless the LORD, O my soul;
And all that is within me,
bless His holy name!
2 Bless the LORD, O my soul,
And forget not all His benefits:
3 Who forgives all your iniquities,
Who heals all your diseases,
4 Who redeems your life from
destruction,
Who crowns you with lovingkindness
and tender mercies,

103:2 forget not all His benefits. These earthly gifts from God included: 1) forgiveness of sin (v. 3); 2) recovery from sickness (v. 3); 3) deliverance from death (v. 4); 4) abundant lovingkindness and mercy (v. 4); and 5) food to sustain life (v. 5).

103:5 youth is renewed like the eagle's. The mysterious way of the long-lived eagle symbolized strength and speed (Ex. 19:4; Jer. 48:40), which also characterizes human youth. As a general rule, a person blessed of God will grow weak and slow down less rapidly than otherwise (Is. 40:29–31, which uses the same language).

5 Who satisfies your mouth with good
things,
So that your youth is renewed like the
eagle's.

Proverbs 24:7–9

7 Wisdom *is* too lofty for a fool;
He does not open his mouth in the
gate.

8 He who plots to do evil
Will be called a schemer.
9 The devising of foolishness *is* sin,
And the scoffer *is* an abomination to
men.

1 Corinthians 10:1–18

10 Moreover, brethren, I do not want you to
be unaware that all our fathers were
under the cloud, all passed through the sea,
2all were baptized into Moses in the cloud and
in the sea, 3all ate the same spiritual food, 4and
all drank the same spiritual drink. For they
drank of that spiritual Rock that followed them,
and that Rock was Christ. 5But with most of
them God was not well pleased, for *their bodies*
were scattered in the wilderness.
6Now these things became our examples, to
the intent that we should not lust after evil
things as they also lusted. 7And do not become
idolaters as *were* some of them. As it is written,
"The people sat down to eat and drink, and rose
up to play." 8Nor let us commit sexual immorality, as some of them did, and in one day twenty-
three thousand fell; 9nor let us tempt Christ, as
some of them also tempted, and were destroyed
by serpents; 10nor complain, as some of them
also complained, and were destroyed by the
destroyer. 11Now all these things happened to
them as examples, and they were written for
our admonition, upon whom the ends of the
ages have come.
12Therefore let him who thinks he stands take
heed lest he fall. 13No temptation has overtaken
you except such as is common to man; but God
is faithful, who will not allow you to be tempted
beyond what you are able, but with the temptation will also make the way of escape, that you
may be able to bear *it.*

10:4 that spiritual Rock. The Jews had a legend that the actual rock Moses struck followed them throughout their wilderness wanderings, providing water for them. Paul says they have a Rock providing all they need, but it is Christ. Rock (*petra*) refers to a massive cliff, not simply a large stone or boulder, signifying the preincarnate Messiah (Christ), who protected and sustained His people.

10:6 our examples. They died in the wilderness because of their failure of self-discipline and consequent indulgence of every desire (9:27). Four major sins characterized them: idolatry (v. 7); sexual immorality (v. 8); testing God (v. 9); and complaining (v. 10).

10:16 cup of blessing. The proper name given to the third cup during the Passover Feast. At the last Passover with the disciples, Jesus used the third cup as the symbol of His blood shed for sin. That cup became the one used to institute the Lord's Supper. He set the cup apart as a token of salvation blessing before passing it to the 12. **communion.** Means "to have in common, to participate and have partnership with." The same Greek word is used in 1:9; 2 Corinthians 8:4; Philippians 2:1; 3:10. Commemorating the Lord's Supper was a regular and cherished practice in the early church, by which believers remembered their Savior's death and celebrated their common salvation and eternal life which reflected their perfect spiritual oneness. **the blood of Christ.** A vivid phrase used to represent Christ's sacrificial death and full atoning work. **the bread.** This symbolized our Lord's body as the cup symbolized His blood. Both point to His death as a sacrifice for the salvation of men.

[14]Therefore, my beloved, flee from idolatry. [15]I
speak as to wise men; judge for yourselves
what I say. [16]The cup of blessing which we
bless, is it not the communion of the blood of
Christ? The bread which we break, is it not
the communion of the body of Christ? [17]For
we, *though* many, are one bread *and* one body;
for we all partake of that one bread.
[18]Observe Israel after the flesh: Are not those
who eat of the sacrifices partakers of the altar?

DAY 29: When Ecclesiastes encourages readers to "enjoy life," is that unconditional?

Solomon balanced his enjoyment theme with repeated reminders of divine judgment. Even the best moments in life ought not to cut a person off from awareness of God as Provider to whom all will give an account. Solomon declared that the possibility of enjoyment was based on faith (Eccl. 2:24–26).

Part of Ecclesiastes reports the king's experiment in trying to enjoy life without regard for the fear of God's judgment. Solomon discovered that such an effort was in vain. In the end, he came to grasp the importance of obedience.

The tragic results of Solomon's personal experience, coupled with the insight of extraordinary wisdom, make Ecclesiastes a book from which all believers can receive warnings and lessons in their faith (2:1–26). This book demonstrates that a person who sees each day of existence, labor, and basic provision as a gift from God, and accepts whatever God gives, will actually live an abundant life. However, anyone who seeks to be satisfied apart from God will live with futility regardless of personal successes.

AUGUST 30

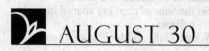

Ecclesiastes 8:1–10:20

8 Who *is* like a wise *man?*
And who knows the interpretation of
a thing?
A man's wisdom makes his face shine,
And the sternness of his face is
changed.

[2]I *say,* "Keep the king's commandment for
the sake of your oath to God. [3]Do not be hasty
to go from his presence. Do not take your
stand for an evil thing, for he does whatever
pleases him."

4 Where the word of a king *is, there is*
power;
And who may say to him, "What are
you doing?"
5 He who keeps his command will
experience nothing harmful;
And a wise man's heart discerns both
time and judgment,
6 Because for every matter there is a
time and judgment,
Though the misery of man increases
greatly.
7 For he does not know what will happen;
So who can tell him when it will occur?
8 No one has power over the spirit to
retain the spirit,
And no one has power in the day of
death.
There is no release from that war,
And wickedness will not deliver those
who are given to it.

[9]All this I have seen, and applied my heart to
every work that is done under the sun: *There is*
a time in which one man rules over another to
his own hurt.
[10]Then I saw the wicked buried, who had
come and gone from the place of holiness, and
they were forgotten in the city where they had
so done. This also *is* vanity. [11]Because the sentence against an evil work is not executed
speedily, therefore the heart of the sons of
men is fully set in them to do evil. [12]Though a
sinner does evil a hundred *times,* and his *days*
are prolonged, yet I surely know that it will be
well with those who fear God, who fear before
Him. [13]But it will not be well with the wicked;
nor will he prolong *his* days, *which are* as a
shadow, because he does not fear before God.
[14]There is a vanity which occurs on earth,
that there are just *men* to whom it happens
according to the work of the wicked; again,
there are wicked *men* to whom it happens
according to the work of the righteous. I said
that this also *is* vanity.
[15]So I commended enjoyment, because a
man has nothing better under the sun than to
eat, drink, and be merry; for this will remain
with him in his labor *all* the days of his life
which God gives him under the sun.
[16]When I applied my heart to know wisdom

8:15 enjoyment. In no way does Solomon commend unbridled, rampant indulgence in sin, which is implied in Christ's account of the man whose barns were full. That man may have justified his sin by quoting this passage (Luke 12:19). His focus here is on the resolve to enjoy life in the face of the injustice which surrounded him.

and to see the business that is done on earth,
even though one sees no sleep day or night,
17then I saw all the work of God, that a man
cannot find out the work that is done under the
sun. For though a man labors to discover *it*, yet
he will not find *it;* moreover, though a wise
man attempts to know *it*, he will not be able to
find *it*.

9 For I considered all this in my heart, so
that I could declare it all: that the righteous and the wise and their works *are* in the
hand of God. People know neither love nor
hatred *by* anything *they see* before them. 2All
things *come* alike to all:

One event *happens* to the righteous
and the wicked;
To the good, the clean, and the
unclean;
To him who sacrifices and him who
does not sacrifice.
As is the good, so *is* the sinner;
He who takes an oath as *he* who fears
an oath.

3This *is* an evil in all that is done under the sun:
that one thing *happens* to all. Truly the hearts
of the sons of men are full of evil; madness *is*
in their hearts while they live, and after that
they go to the dead. 4But for him who is joined
to all the living there is hope, for a living dog is
better than a dead lion.

5 For the living know that they will die;
But the dead know nothing,
And they have no more reward,
For the memory of them is forgotten.
6 Also their love, their hatred, and their
envy have now perished;
Nevermore will they have a share
In anything done under the sun.

7 Go, eat your bread with joy,
And drink your wine with a merry
heart;
For God has already accepted your
works.
8 Let your garments always be white,
And let your head lack no oil.

9Live joyfully with the wife whom you love
all the days of your vain life which He has
given you under the sun, all your days of vanity; for that *is* your portion in life, and in the
labor which you perform under the sun.
10Whatever your hand finds to do, do *it* with
your might; for *there is* no work or device or
knowledge or wisdom in the grave where you
are going.
11I returned and saw under the sun that—

The race *is* not to the swift,
Nor the battle to the strong,
Nor bread to the wise,
Nor riches to men of understanding,
Nor favor to men of skill;
But time and chance happen to them
all.
12 For man also does not know his time:
Like fish taken in a cruel net,
Like birds caught in a snare,
So the sons of men *are* snared in an
evil time,
When it falls suddenly upon them.

13This wisdom I have also seen under the
sun, and it *seemed* great to me: 14*There was* a little city with few men in it; and a great king
came against it, besieged it, and built great
snares around it. 15Now there was found in it a
poor wise man, and he by his wisdom delivered the city. Yet no one remembered that
same poor man.
16Then I said:

"Wisdom *is* better than strength.
Nevertheless the poor man's wisdom *is*
despised,
And his words are not heard.
17 Words of the wise, *spoken* quietly,
should be heard
Rather than the shout of a ruler of
fools.
18 Wisdom *is* better than weapons of war;
But one sinner destroys much good."

10 Dead flies putrefy the perfumer's
ointment,
And cause it to give off a foul odor;
So does a little folly to one respected for
wisdom *and* honor.
2 A wise man's heart *is* at his right hand,
But a fool's heart at his left.
3 Even when a fool walks along the way,
He lacks wisdom,
And he shows everyone *that* he *is* a
fool.

4 If the spirit of the ruler rises against
you,
Do not leave your post;
For conciliation pacifies great offenses.
5 There is an evil I have seen under the
sun,
As an error proceeding from the ruler:
6 Folly is set in great dignity,
While the rich sit in a lowly place.
7 I have seen servants on horses,
While princes walk on the ground like
servants.
8 He who digs a pit will fall into it,
And whoever breaks through a wall
will be bitten by a serpent.
9 He who quarries stones may be hurt
by them,
And he who splits wood may be
endangered by it.
10 If the ax is dull,
And one does not sharpen the edge,
Then he must use more strength;
But wisdom brings success.

10:10 wisdom brings success. A little wisdom will ease the efforts of life. Even though life's experiences often don't turn out the way one would have hoped, wise living usually produces a good outcome. This is a very important conclusion for Solomon's testing of wisdom.

11 A serpent may bite when *it is* not
charmed;
The babbler is no different.
12 The words of a wise man's mouth *are*
gracious,
But the lips of a fool shall swallow him
up;
13 The words of his mouth begin with
foolishness,
And the end of his talk *is* raving
madness.
14 A fool also multiplies words.
No man knows what is to be;
Who can tell him what will be after
him?
15 The labor of fools wearies them,
For they do not even know how to go
to the city!

16 Woe to you, O land, when your king *is*
a child,
And your princes feast in the morning!
17 Blessed *are* you, O land, when your
king *is* the son of nobles,
And your princes feast at the proper
time—
For strength and not for drunkenness!
18 Because of laziness the building decays,
And through idleness of hands the
house leaks.
19 A feast is made for laughter,
And wine makes merry;
But money answers everything.

20 Do not curse the king, even in your
thought;
Do not curse the rich, even in your
bedroom;
For a bird of the air may carry your
voice,
And a bird in flight may tell the matter.

Psalm 103:6–14

6 The LORD executes righteousness
And justice for all who are oppressed.
7 He made known His ways to Moses,
His acts to the children of Israel.
8 The LORD *is* merciful and gracious,
Slow to anger, and abounding in mercy.
9 He will not always strive *with us,*
Nor will He keep *His anger* forever.
10 He has not dealt with us according to
our sins,
Nor punished us according to our
iniquities.

11 For as the heavens are high above the
earth,
So great is His mercy toward those
who fear Him;
12 As far as the east is from the west,
So far has He removed our
transgressions from us.
13 As a father pities *his* children,
So the LORD pities those who fear Him.
14 For He knows our frame;
He remembers that we *are* dust.

Proverbs 24:10–12

10 *If* you faint in the day of adversity,
Your strength *is* small.

11 Deliver *those who* are drawn toward
death,
And hold back *those* stumbling to the
slaughter.
12 If you say, "Surely we did not know
this,"
Does not He who weighs the hearts
consider *it?*
He who keeps your soul, does He *not*
know *it?*
And will He *not* render to *each* man
according to his deeds?

24:12 He who weighs the hearts. God is the One who knows the truth about the motives of the heart and the excuses for failing to do what is right (James 4:17). **render to *each* man according to his deeds.** v. 29; Job 34:11; Jer. 25:14; 50:29.

1 Corinthians 10:19–33

[19]What am I saying then? That an idol is anything, or what is offered to idols is anything?
[20]Rather, that the things which the Gentiles
sacrifice they sacrifice to demons and not to
God, and I do not want you to have fellowship
with demons. [21]You cannot drink the cup of the
Lord and the cup of demons; you cannot partake of the Lord's table and of the table of
demons. [22]Or do we provoke the Lord to jealousy? Are we stronger than He?
[23]All things are lawful for me, but not all
things are helpful; all things are lawful for me,
but not all things edify. [24]Let no one seek his
own, but each one the other's *well-being.*
[25]Eat whatever is sold in the meat market,
asking no questions for conscience' sake; [26]for
"the earth is the LORD's, and all its fullness."
[27]If any of those who do not believe invites
you *to dinner,* and you desire to go, eat whatever is set before you, asking no question for
conscience' sake. [28]But if anyone says to you,

10:19,20 Idols and the things sacrificed to them have no spiritual nature or power in themselves (8:4,8), but they do represent the demonic. If pagan worshipers believe an idol is a god, demons act out the part of the imagined god (2 Thess. 2:9–11). There is not a true god in the idol, but there is a satanic spiritual force (Deut. 32:17; Ps. 106:37).

10:23–30 Paul gives 4 principles for Christian liberty: 1) edification over gratification (v. 23); 2) others over self (v. 24); 3) liberty over legalism (vv. 25–27); and 4) condescension over condemnation (vv. 28–30).

"This was offered to idols," do not eat it for the
sake of the one who told you, and for conscience' sake; for *"the earth is the LORD's, and
all its fullness."* [29]"Conscience," I say, not your
own, but that of the other. For why is my liberty judged by another *man's* conscience? [30]But if
I partake with thanks, why am I evil spoken of
for *the food* over which I give thanks?
[31]Therefore, whether you eat or drink, or
whatever you do, do all to the glory of God.
[32]Give no offense, either to the Jews or to the
Greeks or to the church of God, [33]just as I also
please all *men* in all *things,* not seeking my
own profit, but the *profit* of many, that they
may be saved.

DAY 30: What are the different kinds of Psalms?

The Psalms cover the full breadth of human experience. Some express in general terms while others express in very specific terms the shifting events of life. There's a psalm for almost any kind of day.

One way to categorize the Psalms groups them by five general types:

1. Wisdom Psalms—instructions for wise living (1; 37; 119)
2. Lamentation Psalms—meditations on the pangs of life (3; 17; 120)
3. Penitential Psalms—meditations on the pangs of sin (51)
4. Kingship Psalms—meditations on God's sovereign rule (2; 21; 144)
5. Thanksgiving Psalms—praise and worship offered to God (19; 32; 111)

AUGUST 31

Ecclesiastes 11:1–12:14

11 Cast your bread upon the waters,
For you will find it after many days.
2 Give a serving to seven, and also to
eight,
For you do not know what evil will be
on the earth.
3 If the clouds are full of rain,
They empty *themselves* upon the earth;
And if a tree falls to the south or the
north,
In the place where the tree falls, there
it shall lie.
4 He who observes the wind will not sow,
And he who regards the clouds will not
reap.
5 As you do not know what *is* the way of
the wind,

Or how the bones *grow* in the womb of
her who is with child,
So you do not know the works of God
who makes everything.
6 In the morning sow your seed,
And in the evening do not withhold
your hand;
For you do not know which will
prosper,
Either this or that,
Or whether both alike *will be* good.

7 Truly the light is sweet,
And *it is* pleasant for the eyes to
behold the sun;
8 But if a man lives many years
And rejoices in them all,
Yet let him remember the days of
darkness,
For they will be many.
All that is coming *is* vanity.

9 Rejoice, O young man, in your youth,
And let your heart cheer you in the
days of your youth;
Walk in the ways of your heart,
And in the sight of your eyes;
But know that for all these
God will bring you into judgment.
10 Therefore remove sorrow from your
heart,
And put away evil from your flesh,
For childhood and youth *are* vanity.

12 Remember now your Creator in the
days of your youth,
Before the difficult days come,
And the years draw near when you say,
"I have no pleasure in them":
2 While the sun and the light,
The moon and the stars,
Are not darkened,
And the clouds do not return after the
rain;
3 In the day when the keepers of the
house tremble,
And the strong men bow down;
When the grinders cease because they
are few,
And those that look through the
windows grow dim;
4 When the doors are shut in the streets,
And the sound of grinding is low;
When one rises up at the sound of a
bird,
And all the daughters of music are
brought low.
5 Also they are afraid of height,
And of terrors in the way;
When the almond tree blossoms,
The grasshopper is a burden,
And desire fails.
For man goes to his eternal home,
And the mourners go about the
streets.

6 *Remember your Creator* before the
silver cord is loosed,
Or the golden bowl is broken,
Or the pitcher shattered at the
fountain,
Or the wheel broken at the well.
7 Then the dust will return to the earth
as it was,
And the spirit will return to God who
gave it.

8 "Vanity of vanities," says the Preacher,
"All *is* vanity."

9 And moreover, because the Preacher was
wise, he still taught the people knowledge; yes,
he pondered and sought out *and* set in order
many proverbs. 10 The Preacher sought to find
acceptable words; and *what was* written *was*
upright—words of truth. 11 The words of the wise
are like goads, and the words of scholars are like
well-driven nails, given by one Shepherd. 12 And
further, my son, be admonished by these. Of
making many books *there is* no end, and much
study *is* wearisome to the flesh.
13 Let us hear the conclusion of the whole
matter:

Fear God and keep His
commandments,
For this is man's all.
14 For God will bring every work into
judgment,
Including every secret thing,
Whether good or evil.

Psalm 103:15–22

15 *As for* man, his days *are* like grass;
As a flower of the field, so he
flourishes.
16 For the wind passes over it, and it is
gone,
And its place remembers it no more.
17 But the mercy of the LORD *is* from
everlasting to everlasting
On those who fear Him,
And His righteousness to children's
children,
18 To such as keep His covenant,
And to those who remember His
commandments to do them.
19 The LORD has established His throne
in heaven,

103:17,18 the mercy of the LORD. Those who appeal to God's mercy by proper fear (v. 17) and obedience (v. 18) will overcome the shortness of physical life with eternal life. Luke 1:50 quotes Psalm 103:17.

103:19 His throne in heaven. From everlasting to everlasting God has always ruled over all things (Pss. 11:4; 47:1–9; 148:8–13). This universal kingdom is to be distinguished from God's mediatorial kingdom on earth.

And His kingdom rules over all.
20 Bless the LORD, you His angels,
Who excel in strength, who do His
word,
Heeding the voice of His word.
21 Bless the LORD, all *you* His hosts,
You ministers of His, who do His
pleasure.
22 Bless the LORD, all His works,
In all places of His dominion.

Bless the LORD, O my soul!

Proverbs 24:13–14

13 My son, eat honey because *it is* good,
And the honeycomb *which is* sweet to
your taste;
14 So *shall* the knowledge of wisdom *be* to
your soul;
If you have found *it,* there is
a prospect,
And your hope will not be cut off.

1 Corinthians 11:1–16

11 Imitate me, just as I also *imitate* Christ.
2 Now I praise you, brethren, that you
remember me in all things and keep the traditions just as I delivered *them* to you.
3 But I want
you to know that the head of every man is
Christ, the head of woman *is* man, and the head
of Christ *is* God.
4 Every man praying or prophesying, having *his* head covered, dishonors his
head.
5 But every woman who prays or prophesies with *her* head uncovered dishonors her
head, for that is one and the same as if her head
were shaved.
6 For if a woman is not covered, let
her also be shorn. But if it is shameful for a
woman to be shorn or shaved, let her be covered.
7 For a man indeed ought not to cover *his*
head, since he is the image and glory of God;
but woman is the glory of man.
8 For man is not
from woman, but woman from man.
9 Nor was
man created for the woman, but woman for the
man.
10 For this reason the woman ought to
have *a symbol of* authority on *her* head, because
of the angels.
11 Nevertheless, neither *is* man
independent of woman, nor woman independent of man, in the Lord.
12 For as woman *came*
from man, even so man also *comes* through
woman; but all things are from God.
13 Judge among yourselves. Is it proper for a
woman to pray to God with her head uncovered?
14 Does not even nature itself teach you

11:4 covered, dishonors. Literally, "having down from head," is probably a reference to men wearing a head covering, which seems to have been a local custom. Jews began wearing head coverings during the fourth century A.D., although some may already have been wearing them in New Testament times. Apparently, Corinthian men were doing the same, and Paul informs them that it is a disgrace. Paul is not stating a universal law from God, but acknowledging a local custom, which did reflect divine principle. In that society, a man's uncovered head was a sign of his authority over women, who were to have their heads covered. For a man to cover his head was to suggest a reversal of proper roles.

11:5 woman who prays or prophesies. Paul makes clear directives that women are not to lead or speak in the services of the church (14:34; 1 Tim. 2:12), but they may pray and proclaim the truth to unbelievers, as well as teaching children and other women (1 Tim. 5:16; Titus 2:3,4). Wherever and whenever women do pray and proclaim the Word appropriately, they must do so maintaining a proper distinction from men. **uncovered.** In the culture of Corinth, a woman's covered head while ministering or worshiping was a symbol to signify a subordinate relationship to her husband. The apostle is not laying down an absolute law for women to wear veils or coverings in all churches for all time, but is declaring that the symbols of the divinely established male and female roles are to be genuinely honored in every culture. As in the case of meat offered to idols (chaps. 8; 9), there is nothing spiritual about wearing or not wearing a covering. But manifesting rebellion against God's order was wrong. **dishonors her head.** "Head" may refer to her own self being disgraced by refusing to conform to recognized symbols of submission, or to her husband, who is disgraced by her behavior.

that if a man has long hair, it is a dishonor to
him? 15But if a woman has long hair, it is a
glory to her; for *her* hair is given to her for a
covering. 16But if anyone seems to be contentious, we have no such custom, nor *do* the churches of God.

DAY 31: How does Solomon balance enjoyment in life with the coming judgment?

In Ecclesiastes 11:9–12:8, Solomon crystallizes the book's message. Death is imminent and with it comes retribution. Enjoyment and judgment, though strange partners, come together in this section because both clamor for man's deepest commitment. Surprisingly, one does not win out over the other. In a world created for enjoyment but damaged by sin, judgment and enjoyment/pleasure are held in tension. With too much pleasure, judgment stands as a threatening force; with too much judgment, enjoyment suffers. In the final analysis, both are prominent themes of life that are resolved in our relationship to God, the primary issue of life and this book.

"Rejoice…judgment" (11:9). The two terms seem to cancel out the other. How can this be explained? Enjoy life but do not commit iniquity. The balance that is called for insures that enjoyment is not reckless, sinful abandonment. Pleasure is experienced in faith and obedience, for as Solomon has said repeatedly, one can only receive true satisfaction as a gift from God.

"Fear God" (12:13,14). Solomon's final word on the issues raised in this book, as well as life itself, focuses on one's relationship to God. All of the concern for a life under the sun, with its pleasures and uncertainties, was behind Solomon. Such things seemed comparatively irrelevant to him as he faced the end of his life. But death, in spite of the focused attention he had given to it in Ecclesiastes, was not the greatest equalizer. Judgment/retribution is the real equalizer as Solomon saw it, for God will bring every person's every act to judgment. Unbelievers will stand at the Great White Throne judgment (Rev. 20:11–15) and believers before Christ at the Bema judgment (1 Cor. 3:10–15; 2 Cor. 5:9,10). When all is said and done, the certainty and finality of retribution give life the meaning for which David's ofttimes foolish son had been searching. Whatever may be one's portion in life, accountability to the God, whose ways are often mysterious, is both eternal and irrevocable.

SEPTEMBER 1

Song of Solomon 1:1–2:17

1 The song of songs, which *is* Solomon's.

THE SHULAMITE

2 Let him kiss me with the kisses of his
mouth—
For your love *is* better than wine.
3 Because of the fragrance of your good
ointments,
Your name *is* ointment poured forth;
Therefore the virgins love you.
4 Draw me away!

THE DAUGHTERS OF JERUSALEM

We will run after you.

THE SHULAMITE

The king has brought me into his
chambers.

THE DAUGHTERS OF JERUSALEM

We will be glad and rejoice in you.

We will remember your love more
than wine.

THE SHULAMITE

Rightly do they love you.

5 I *am* dark, but lovely,
O daughters of Jerusalem,
Like the tents of Kedar,
Like the curtains of Solomon.
6 Do not look upon me, because
I *am* dark,
Because the sun has tanned me.
My mother's sons were angry with me;
They made me the keeper of the
vineyards,
But my own vineyard I have not kept.

(TO HER BELOVED)

7 Tell me, O you whom I love,
Where you feed *your flock,*
Where you make *it* rest at noon.
For why should I be as one who veils
herself
By the flocks of your companions?

THE BELOVED

8 If you do not know, O fairest among
women,
Follow in the footsteps of the flock,
And feed your little goats
Beside the shepherds' tents.
9 I have compared you, my love,
To my filly among Pharaoh's chariots.
10 Your cheeks are lovely with
ornaments,
Your neck with chains *of gold.*

THE DAUGHTERS OF JERUSALEM

11 We will make you ornaments of gold
With studs of silver.

THE SHULAMITE

12 While the king *is* at his table,
My spikenard sends forth its
fragrance.
13 A bundle of myrrh *is* my beloved
to me,
That lies all night between my breasts.
14 My beloved *is* to me a cluster of henna
blooms
In the vineyards of En Gedi.

THE BELOVED

15 Behold, you *are* fair, my love!
Behold, you *are* fair!
You *have* dove's eyes.

THE SHULAMITE

16 Behold, you *are* handsome, my
beloved!
Yes, pleasant!
Also our bed *is* green.
17 The beams of our houses *are* cedar,
And our rafters of fir.

2 I *am* the rose of Sharon,
And the lily of the valleys.

THE BELOVED

2 Like a lily among thorns,
So is my love among the daughters.

THE SHULAMITE

3 Like an apple tree among the trees of
the woods,
So *is* my beloved among the sons.
I sat down in his shade with great
delight,
And his fruit *was* sweet to my taste.

THE SHULAMITE TO THE DAUGHTERS
OF JERUSALEM

4 He brought me to the banqueting
house,
And his banner over me *was* love.
5 Sustain me with cakes of raisins,
Refresh me with apples,
For I *am* lovesick.

6 His left hand *is* under my head,
And his right hand embraces me.
7 I charge you, O daughters of Jerusalem,
By the gazelles or by the does
of the field,
Do not stir up nor awaken love
Until it pleases.

THE SHULAMITE

8 The voice of my beloved!
Behold, he comes
Leaping upon the mountains,
Skipping upon the hills.
9 My beloved is like a gazelle or a young
stag.
Behold, he stands behind our wall;
He is looking through the windows,
Gazing through the lattice.
10 My beloved spoke, and said to me:
"Rise up, my love, my fair one,
And come away.
11 For lo, the winter is past,
The rain is over *and* gone.
12 The flowers appear on the earth;
The time of singing has come,
And the voice of the turtledove
Is heard in our land.
13 The fig tree puts forth her green figs,
And the vines *with* the tender grapes
Give a *good* smell.
Rise up, my love, my fair one,
And come away!

14 "O my dove, in the clefts of the rock,
In the secret *places* of the cliff,
Let me see your face,
Let me hear your voice;
For your voice *is* sweet,
And your face *is* lovely."

HER BROTHERS

15 Catch us the foxes,
The little foxes that spoil the vines,
For our vines *have* tender grapes.

THE SHULAMITE

16 My beloved *is* mine, and I *am* his.
He feeds *his flock* among the lilies.

2:7 I charge you. This refrain, which is repeated before the wedding (3:5) and also afterward (8:4), explicitly expresses the Shulamite's commitment to a chaste life before and during marriage. She invites accountability to the daughters of Jerusalem.

(TO HER BELOVED)

17 Until the day breaks
And the shadows flee away,
Turn, my beloved,
And be like a gazelle
Or a young stag
Upon the mountains of Bether.

Psalm 104:1–9

Bless the LORD, O my soul!

O LORD my God, You are very great:
You are clothed with honor and
majesty,
2 Who cover *Yourself* with light as *with* a
garment,
Who stretch out the heavens like
a curtain.
3 He lays the beams of His upper
chambers in the waters,
Who makes the clouds His chariot,
Who walks on the wings of the wind,
4 Who makes His angels spirits,
His ministers a flame of fire.

104:4 spirits...flame of fire. Hebrews 1:7 attributes these characteristics to angels describing their swiftness and destructiveness, as God's instruments of judgment.

5 *You who* laid the foundations
of the earth,
So *that* it should not be moved forever,
6 You covered it with the deep as *with* a
garment;
The waters stood above the mountains.
7 At Your rebuke they fled;
At the voice of Your thunder they
hastened away.
8 They went up over the mountains;
They went down into the valleys,
To the place which You founded for
them.
9 You have set a boundary that they may
not pass over,
That they may not return to cover the
earth.

Proverbs 24:15–16

15 Do not lie in wait, O wicked *man*,
against the dwelling of the
righteous;
Do not plunder his resting place;

16 For a righteous *man* may fall seven
times
And rise again,
But the wicked shall fall by calamity.

1 Corinthians 11:17–34

[17]Now in giving these instructions I do not
praise *you,* since you come together not for the
better but for the worse. [18]For first of all, when
you come together as a church, I hear that
there are divisions among you, and in part I
believe it. [19]For there must also be factions
among you, that those who are approved may
be recognized among you. [20]Therefore when
you come together in one place, it is not to eat
the Lord's Supper. [21]For in eating, each one
takes his own supper ahead of *others;* and one
is hungry and another is drunk. [22]What! Do you
not have houses to eat and drink in? Or do you
despise the church of God and shame those
who have nothing? What shall I say to you?
Shall I praise you in this? I do not praise *you.*

11:17–34 The early church love feasts (Jude 12) usually closed with observance of the Lord's Supper. The worldly, carnal church at Corinth had turned those sacred meals into gluttonous, drunken revelries. Beyond that, wealthy believers brought ample food and drink for themselves but refused to share, letting their poorer brethren go away hungry (v. 21).

[23]For I received from the Lord that which I
also delivered to you: that the Lord Jesus on
the *same* night in which He was betrayed took
bread; [24]and when He had given thanks, He broke
it and said, "Take, eat; this is My body which is
broken for you; do this in remembrance of
Me." [25]In the same manner *He* also *took* the
cup after supper, saying, "This cup is the new
covenant in My blood. This do, as often as you
drink *it,* in remembrance of Me."

[26]For as often as you eat this bread and
drink this cup, you proclaim the Lord's death
till He comes.

[27]Therefore whoever eats this bread or
drinks *this* cup of the Lord in an unworthy
manner will be guilty of the body and blood of
the Lord. [28]But let a man examine himself, and
so let him eat of the bread and drink of the
cup. [29]For he who eats and drinks in an unworthy manner eats and drinks judgment to himself, not discerning the Lord's body. [30]For this
reason many *are* weak and sick among you,
and many sleep. [31]For if we would judge ourselves, we would not be judged. [32]But when we
are judged, we are chastened by the Lord, that
we may not be condemned with the world.

[33]Therefore, my brethren, when you come
together to eat, wait for one another. [34]But if
anyone is hungry, let him eat at home, lest you
come together for judgment. And the rest I
will set in order when I come.

11:27,29 in an unworthy manner. I.e., ritualistically, indifferently, with an unrepentant heart, a spirit of bitterness, or any other ungodly attitude.

11:30 sleep. I.e., are dead. The offense was so serious that God put the worst offenders to death, an extreme but effective form of church purification (Luke 13:1–5; Acts 5:1–11; 1 John 5:16).

DAY 1: What is the central theme of the Song of Solomon?

Solomon, who reigned over the united kingdom 40 years (971–931 B.C.), appears 7 times by name in this book (1:1,5; 3:7,9,11; 8:11,12). In view of his writing skills, musical giftedness (1 Kin. 4:32), and the authorial, not dedicatory, sense of 1:1, this piece of Scripture could have been penned at any time during Solomon's reign. Knowing that this portion of Scripture comprises one song by one author, it is best taken as a unified piece of poetic, Wisdom literature rather than a series of love poems without a common theme or author.

Two people dominate this true-life, dramatic love song. Solomon, whose kingship is mentioned 5 times (1:4,12; 3:9,11; 7:5), appears as "the beloved." The Shulamite maiden (6:13) remains obscure; most likely she was a resident of Shunem, 3 miles north of Jezreel in lower Galilee. Some suggest she is Pharaoh's daughter (1 Kin. 3:1), although the Song provides no evidence for this conclusion. Others favor Abishag, the Shunammite who cared for King David (1 Kin. 1:1–4,15). An unknown maiden from Shunem, whose family had possibly been employed by Solomon (8:11), seems most reasonable. She would have been Solomon's first wife (Eccl. 9:9), before he sinned by adding 699 other wives and 300 concubines (1 Kin. 11:3).

In contrast to the two distorted extremes of ascetic abstinence and lustful perversion outside of marriage, Solomon's ancient love song exalts the purity of marital affection and romance. It parallels and enhances other portions of Scripture which portray God's plan for marriage, including the beauty and sanctity of sexual intimacy between husband and wife. The Song rightfully stands alongside other classic Scripture passages which expand on this theme (Gen. 2:24; Ps. 45; Prov. 5:15–23; 1 Cor. 7:1–5; 13:1–8; Eph. 5:18–33; Col. 3:18,19; 1 Pet. 3:1–7). Hebrews 13:4 captures the heart of this song: "Marriage is honorable among all, and the bed undefiled; but fornicators and adulterers God will judge."

SEPTEMBER 2

Song of Solomon 3:1–4:16

The Shulamite

3 By night on my bed I sought the one
I love;
I sought him, but I did not find him.
2 "I will rise now," *I said,*
"And go about the city;
In the streets and in the squares
I will seek the one I love."
I sought him, but I did not find him.
3 The watchmen who go about the city
found me;
I said,
"Have you seen the one I love?"

4 Scarcely had I passed by them,
When I found the one I love.
I held him and would not let him go,
Until I had brought him to the house
of my mother,
And into the chamber of her who
conceived me.

5 I charge you, O daughters of Jerusalem,
By the gazelles or by the does of the
field,
Do not stir up nor awaken love
Until it pleases.

3:5 As in 2:7, the beloved knows that the intensity of her love for Solomon cannot yet be experienced until the wedding, so she invites the daughters of Jerusalem to keep her accountable regarding sexual purity. Up to this point, the escalating desire of the Shulamite for Solomon has been expressed in veiled and delicate ways as compared to the explicit and open expressions which follow, as would be totally appropriate for a married couple (4:1ff.).

The Shulamite

6 Who *is* this coming out of the
wilderness
Like pillars of smoke,
Perfumed with myrrh and
frankincense,
With all the merchant's fragrant
powders?
7 Behold, it *is* Solomon's couch,
With sixty valiant men around it,
Of the valiant of Israel.
8 They all hold swords,
Being expert in war.
Every man *has* his sword on his thigh
Because of fear in the night.

9 Of the wood of Lebanon
Solomon the King
Made himself a palanquin:
10 He made its pillars *of* silver,
Its support *of* gold,
Its seat *of* purple,
Its interior paved *with* love
By the daughters of Jerusalem.
11 Go forth, O daughters of Zion,
And see King Solomon with the crown
With which his mother crowned him
On the day of his wedding,
The day of the gladness of his heart.

The Beloved

4 Behold, you *are* fair, my love!
Behold, you *are* fair!
You *have* dove's eyes behind your veil.
Your hair *is* like a flock of goats,
Going down from Mount Gilead.
2 Your teeth *are* like a flock of shorn
sheep
Which have come up from the
washing,
Every one of which bears twins,
And none *is* barren among them.
3 Your lips *are* like a strand of scarlet,
And your mouth is lovely.
Your temples behind your veil
Are like a piece of pomegranate.
4 Your neck *is* like the tower of David,
Built for an armory,

On which hang a thousand bucklers,
All shields of mighty men.
5 Your two breasts *are* like two fawns,
Twins of a gazelle,
Which feed among the lilies.

6 Until the day breaks
And the shadows flee away,
I will go my way to the mountain of myrrh
And to the hill of frankincense.

7 You *are* all fair, my love,
And *there is* no spot in you.
8 Come with me from Lebanon, *my* spouse,
With me from Lebanon.
Look from the top of Amana,
From the top of Senir and Hermon,
From the lions' dens,
From the mountains of the leopards.
9 You have ravished my heart,
My sister, *my* spouse;
You have ravished my heart
With one *look* of your eyes,
With one link of your necklace.
10 How fair is your love,
My sister, *my* spouse!
How much better than wine is your love,
And the scent of your perfumes
Than all spices!
11 Your lips, O *my* spouse,
Drip as the honeycomb;
Honey and milk *are* under your tongue;
And the fragrance of your garments
Is like the fragrance of Lebanon.

12 A garden enclosed
Is my sister, *my* spouse,
A spring shut up,
A fountain sealed.
13 Your plants *are* an orchard of pomegranates
With pleasant fruits,
Fragrant henna with spikenard,
14 Spikenard and saffron,
Calamus and cinnamon,
With all trees of frankincense,
Myrrh and aloes,
With all the chief spices—
15 A fountain of gardens,
A well of living waters,
And streams from Lebanon.

THE SHULAMITE

16 Awake, O north *wind*,
And come, O south!
Blow upon my garden,
That its spices may flow out.
Let my beloved come to his garden
And eat its pleasant fruits.

Psalm 104:10–23

10 He sends the springs into the valleys;
They flow among the hills.
11 They give drink to every beast of the field;
The wild donkeys quench their thirst.
12 By them the birds of the heavens have their home;
They sing among the branches.
13 He waters the hills from His upper chambers;
The earth is satisfied with the fruit of Your works.

14 He causes the grass to grow for the cattle,
And vegetation for the service of man,
That he may bring forth food from the earth,
15 And wine *that* makes glad the heart of man,
Oil to make *his* face shine,
And bread *which* strengthens man's heart.
16 The trees of the LORD are full *of sap*,
The cedars of Lebanon which He planted,
17 Where the birds make their nests;
The stork has her home in the fir trees.
18 The high hills *are* for the wild goats;
The cliffs are a refuge for the rock badgers.

19 He appointed the moon for seasons;
The sun knows its going down.
20 You make darkness, and it is night,
In which all the beasts of the forest creep about.
21 The young lions roar after their prey,
And seek their food from God.
22 *When* the sun rises, they gather together
And lie down in their dens.
23 Man goes out to his work
And to his labor until the evening.

Proverbs 24:17–18

17 Do not rejoice when your enemy falls,
And do not let your heart be glad when he stumbles;
18 Lest the LORD see *it*, and it displease Him,
And He turn away His wrath from him.

1 Corinthians 12:1–31

12 Now concerning spiritual *gifts,* brethren,
I do not want you to be ignorant: [2]You
know that you were Gentiles, carried away to
these dumb idols, however you were led.
[3]Therefore I make known to you that no one
speaking by the Spirit of God calls Jesus accursed, and no one can say that Jesus is Lord
except by the Holy Spirit.

12:1 spiritual *gifts*. The NKJV translators italicized "gifts" to indicate that the word is not in the original but is implied by the context (vv. 4,9,28,30,31; 14:1). The Greek literally means "pertaining to the Spirit," referring to that which has spiritual qualities or characteristics or is under some form of spiritual control. Spiritual gifts are divine enablements for ministry that the Holy Spirit gives in some measure to all believers and that are to be completely under His control and used for the building of the church to Christ's glory (Rom. 12:4–8). These had to be distinguished from the mystical experiences called "ecstasy" (supernatural, sensuous communion with a deity) and "enthusiasm" (divination, dreams, revelations, visions) that were found in the pagan religions of Corinth.

12:2 Gentiles. That is, non-Christian pagans (1 Thess. 4:5; 1 Pet. 2:12). **carried away.** Incredibly, some church members were mimicking certain dramatic and bizarre practices of the mystery religions in which they had been formerly involved. The practice of ecstasy, considered to be the highest expression of religious experience, involved supposed supernatural interaction with a deity, induced through frenzied hypnotic chants and ceremonies. The practice frequently included drunkenness (Eph. 5:18) and sexual orgies, to which the devotees willfully yielded themselves to be led into gross sin.

12:3 accursed. This is the most severe kind of condemnation. Some of the Corinthians were fleshly and given over to ecstasies that were controlled by demons. In that condition, they actually claimed to be prophesying or teaching in the Spirit while demonically blaspheming the name of the Lord whom they were supposed to be worshiping. They had been judging the use of gifts on the basis of experience and not content. Satan always assaults the Person of Christ. It is possible that the curser of Christ was a Gentile claiming to be a Christian, but holding to a philosophy that all matter was evil, including the human Jesus (i.e., pregnosticism). They might have said that the Christ spirit left the human Jesus before His death, and therefore Jesus died a cursed death as a mere man. **Jesus is Lord.** The validity of any speaking exercise is determined by the truthfulness of it. If the speaker affirms the lordship of Jesus, it is the truth from the Holy Spirit. What a person believes and says about Jesus Christ is the test of whether he speaks from the Holy Spirit. He always leads people to Christ's lordship (2:8–14; John 15:26; 1 John 5:6–8).

[4]There are diversities of gifts, but the same
Spirit. [5]There are differences of ministries, but
the same Lord. [6]And there are diversities of
activities, but it is the same God who works all
in all. [7]But the manifestation of the Spirit is
given to each one for the profit *of all:* [8]for to
one is given the word of wisdom through the
Spirit, to another the word of knowledge
through the same Spirit, [9]to another faith by
the same Spirit, to another gifts of healings by
the same Spirit, [10]to another the working of
miracles, to another prophecy, to another discerning of spirits, to another *different* kinds of
tongues, to another the interpretation of
tongues. [11]But one and the same Spirit works
all these things, distributing to each one individually as He wills.
[12]For as the body is one and has many members, but all the members of that one body,
being many, are one body, so also *is* Christ. [13]For
by one Spirit we were all baptized into one
body—whether Jews or Greeks, whether
slaves or free—and have all been made to
drink into one Spirit. [14]For in fact the body is
not one member but many.
[15]If the foot should say, "Because I am not a
hand, I am not of the body," is it therefore not
of the body? [16]And if the ear should say, "Because I am not an eye, I am not of the body," is
it therefore not of the body? [17]If the whole
body *were* an eye, where *would be* the hearing?
If the whole *were* hearing, where *would be* the
smelling? [18]But now God has set the members,
each one of them, in the body just as He
pleased. [19]And if they were all one member,
where *would* the body *be?*
[20]But now indeed *there are* many members,
yet one body. [21]And the eye cannot say to the
hand, "I have no need of you"; nor again the

head to the feet, "I have no need of you." [22]No,
much rather, those members of the body
which seem to be weaker are necessary. [23]And
those *members* of the body which we think to
be less honorable, on these we bestow greater
honor; and our unpresentable *parts* have
greater modesty, [24]but our presentable *parts*
have no need. But God composed the body,
having given greater honor to that *part* which
lacks it, [25]that there should be no schism in the
body, but *that* the members should have the
same care for one another. [26]And if one member suffers, all the members suffer with *it;* or if
one member is honored, all the members
rejoice with *it.*

[27]Now you are the body of Christ, and members individually. [28]And God has appointed
these in the church: first apostles, second
prophets, third teachers, after that miracles,
then gifts of healings, helps, administrations,
varieties of tongues. [29]*Are* all apostles? *Are* all
prophets? *Are* all teachers? *Are* all workers of
miracles? [30]Do all have gifts of healings? Do all
speak with tongues? Do all interpret? [31]But earnestly desire the best gifts. And yet I show you
a more excellent way.

DAY 2: How does Paul's teaching in 1 Corinthians help resolve the controversy over the sign gifts discussed in chapters 12–14?

Three chapters in this letter are devoted to the subject of spiritual gifts in the church. Paul knew that the subject was controversial but vital to a healthy church. The atmosphere of false religions that abounded in Corinth caused counterfeit spiritual manifestations that had to be confronted. Paul informed the church and challenged the believers in Corinth to regulate their behavior by the truth and the Spirit.

The categories of giftedness in these verses do not refer to natural talents, skills, or abilities. Believers and unbelievers alike possess such resources. No, these gifts are sovereignly and supernaturally bestowed by the Holy Spirit on all believers (12:7,11), enabling them to spiritually edify each other effectively and thus honor the Lord.

The varieties of spiritual gifts fall roughly into two general types: 1) speaking gifts, and 2) serving gifts (12:8–10; Rom. 12:6–8; 1 Pet. 4:10,11). The speaking or verbal gifts (prophecy, knowledge, wisdom, teaching, and exhortation) and the serving, nonverbal gifts (leadership, helps, giving, mercy, faith, and discernment) are all permanent and will operate throughout the church age. Their purpose is to build up the church and glorify God. The list here and in Romans 12:3–8 is best seen as representative of categories of giftedness from which the Holy Spirit draws to give each believer whatever kind or combination of kinds He chooses (12:11). Some believers may be gifted in similar ways to others but are personally unique because the Spirit suits each grace gift to the individual.

A special category made up of miracles, healing, languages, and the interpretation of languages, served as a set of temporary sign gifts limited to the apostolic age and have, therefore, ceased. Their purpose was to authenticate the apostles and their message as the true word of God. Once God's Word was complete and became self-authenticating, they were no longer required.

SEPTEMBER 3

Song of Solomon 5:1–6:13

THE BELOVED

5 I have come to my garden,
my sister, *my* spouse;
I have gathered my myrrh with my
spice;
I have eaten my honeycomb with
my honey;
I have drunk my wine with
my milk.

(TO HIS FRIENDS)

Eat, O friends!
Drink, yes, drink deeply,
O beloved ones!

5:1 I have. While the guests feasted, the couple consummated their marriage (Gen. 29:23; Deut. 22:13–21) and Solomon announced the blessing (Gen. 2:25). **Eat, O friends!** Given the intimate and private nature of sexual union, it seems difficult to understand anyone but God speaking these words (Prov. 5:21). This is the divine affirmation of sexual love between husband and wife as holy and beautiful.

THE SHULAMITE

2 I sleep, but my heart is awake;
It is the voice of my beloved!
He knocks, *saying,*
"Open for me, my sister, my love,
My dove, my perfect one;
For my head is covered with dew,
My locks with the drops of the night."
3 I have taken off my robe;
How can I put it on *again?*
I have washed my feet;
How can I defile them?
4 My beloved put his hand
By the latch *of the door,*
And my heart yearned for him.
5 I arose to open for my beloved,
And my hands dripped *with* myrrh,
My fingers with liquid myrrh,
On the handles of the lock.

6 I opened for my beloved,
But my beloved had turned away
and was gone.
My heart leaped up when he spoke.
I sought him, but I could not find him;
I called him, but he gave me no
answer.
7 The watchmen who went about the city
found me.
They struck me, they wounded me;
The keepers of the walls
Took my veil away from me.
8 I charge you, O daughters of Jerusalem,
If you find my beloved,
That you tell him I *am* lovesick!

THE DAUGHTERS OF JERUSALEM

9 What *is* your beloved
More than *another* beloved,
O fairest among women?
What *is* your beloved
More than *another* beloved,
That you so charge us?

THE SHULAMITE

10 My beloved *is* white and ruddy,
Chief among ten thousand.
11 His head *is like* the finest gold;
His locks *are* wavy,
And black as a raven.
12 His eyes *are* like doves
By the rivers of waters,
Washed with milk,
And fitly set.
13 His cheeks *are* like a bed of spices,
Banks of scented herbs.
His lips *are* lilies,
Dripping liquid myrrh.
14 His hands *are* rods of gold
Set with beryl.
His body *is* carved ivory
Inlaid *with* sapphires.
15 His legs *are* pillars of marble
Set on bases of fine gold.
His countenance *is* like Lebanon,
Excellent as the cedars.
16 His mouth *is* most sweet,
Yes, he *is* altogether lovely.
This *is* my beloved,
And this *is* my friend,
O daughters of Jerusalem!

THE DAUGHTERS OF JERUSALEM

6 Where has your beloved gone,
O fairest among women?
Where has your beloved
turned aside,
That we may seek him with you?

THE SHULAMITE

2 My beloved has gone to his garden,
To the beds of spices,
To feed *his flock* in the gardens,
And to gather lilies.
3 I *am* my beloved's,
And my beloved *is* mine.
He feeds *his flock* among the lilies.

THE BELOVED

4 O my love, you *are as* beautiful as
Tirzah,
Lovely as Jerusalem,
Awesome as *an army* with banners!
5 Turn your eyes away from me,
For they have overcome me.
Your hair *is* like a flock of goats
Going down from Gilead.
6 Your teeth *are* like a flock of sheep
Which have come up from the
washing;
Every one bears twins,
And none *is* barren among them.
7 Like a piece of pomegranate
Are your temples behind your veil.

8 There are sixty queens
And eighty concubines,
And virgins without number.
9 My dove, my perfect one,
Is the only one,
The only one of her mother,
The favorite of the one who bore her.
The daughters saw her
And called her blessed,
The queens and the concubines,
And they praised her.

10 Who is she who looks forth as the
morning,
Fair as the moon,
Clear as the sun,
Awesome as *an army* with banners?

The Shulamite

11 I went down to the garden of nuts
To see the verdure of the valley,
To see whether the vine had budded
And the pomegranates had bloomed.
12 Before I was even aware,
My soul had made me
As the chariots of my noble people.

The Beloved and His Friends

13 Return, return, O Shulamite;
Return, return, that we may look upon
you!

The Shulamite

What would you see in the Shulamite—
As it were, the dance of the two camps?

Psalm 104:24–30

24 O Lord, how manifold are Your works!
In wisdom You have made them all.
The earth is full of Your possessions—
25 This great and wide sea,
In which *are* innumerable teeming
things,
Living things both small and great.
26 There the ships sail about;
There is that Leviathan
Which You have made to play there.

27 These all wait for You,
That You may give *them* their food in
due season.
28 *What* You give them they gather in;
You open Your hand, they are filled
with good.
29 You hide Your face, they are troubled;
You take away their breath, they die
and return to their dust.
30 You send forth Your Spirit, they are
created;
And You renew the face of the earth.

Proverbs 24:19–20

19 Do not fret because of evildoers,
Nor be envious of the wicked;
20 For there will be no prospect for the
evil *man;*
The lamp of the wicked will be put out.

1 Corinthians 13:1–13

13 Though I speak with the tongues of men
and of angels, but have not love, I have
become sounding brass or a clanging cymbal.
2And though I have *the gift of* prophecy, and
understand all mysteries and all knowledge,
and though I have all faith, so that I could
remove mountains, but have not love, I am
nothing. 3And though I bestow all my goods to
feed *the poor,* and though I give my body to be
burned, but have not love, it profits me nothing.
4Love suffers long *and* is kind; love does not
envy; love does not parade itself, is not puffed

13:1–13 Spiritual gifts were present in Corinth (1:7); right doctrine was even in place (11:2); but love was absent. This led to the quarrels and exhibitions of selfishness and pride that plagued the church—notably in the area of spiritual gifts. Instead of selfishly and jealously desiring showy gifts which they don't have, believers should pursue the greatest thing of all—love for one another. This chapter is considered by many the greatest literary passage ever penned by Paul. It is central to his earnestly dealing with spiritual gifts (chaps. 12–14), because after discussing the endowment of gifts (chap. 12) and before presenting the function of gifts (chap. 14), he addresses the attitude necessary in all ministry in the church (chap. 13).

13:1 tongues of men. That this gift was actual languages is established in Acts 2:4–12, affirmed in this text by Paul's calling it "of men"—clearly a reference to human language. This was the gift which the Corinthians prized so highly, abused so greatly, and counterfeited so disastrously. God gave the ability to speak in a language not known to the speaker, as a sign with limited function (14:1–33). **tongues...of angels.** The apostle was writing in general hypothetical terms. There is no biblical teaching of any special angelic language that people could learn to speak. **love.** Self-giving love that is more concerned with giving than receiving (John 3:16; 14:1; Matt. 5:44,45; John 13:1,34,35; 15:9; Rom. 5:10; Eph. 2:4–7; Phil. 2:2; Col. 3:14; Heb. 10:24). Without love, no matter how linguistically gifted one is to speak his own language, other languages, or even (hypothetically) the speech of angels, his speech is noise only. In New Testament times, rites honoring the pagan deities Cybele, Bacchus, and Dionysius included ecstatic noises accompanied by gongs, cymbals, and trumpets. Unless the speech of the Corinthians was done in love, it was no better than the gibberish of pagan ritual.

13:4–7 In the previous comments (vv. 1–3), the focus is on the emptiness produced when love is absent from ministry. In these verses, the fullness of love is described, in each case by what love does. Love is action, not abstraction. Positively, love is patient with people and gracious to them with generosity. Negatively, love never envies, or brags, or is arrogant, since that is the opposite of selfless service to others. Never rude or overbearing, love never wants its own way, is not irritated or angered in personal offense, and finds no pleasure in someone else's sin, even the sin of an enemy. On the positive side again, love is devoted to truth in everything. With regard to "all things" within God's righteous and gracious will, love protects, believes, hopes, and endures what others reject.

up; 5does not behave rudely, does not seek its
own, is not provoked, thinks no evil; 6does not
rejoice in iniquity, but rejoices in the truth;
7bears all things, believes all things, hopes all
things, endures all things.

8Love never fails. But whether *there are*
prophecies, they will fail; whether *there are*
tongues, they will cease; whether *there is*
knowledge, it will vanish away. 9For we know
in part and we prophesy in part. 10But when
that which is perfect has come, then that
which is in part will be done away.

11When I was a child, I spoke as a child, I
understood as a child, I thought as a child; but
when I became a man, I put away childish
things. 12For now we see in a mirror, dimly, but
then face to face. Now I know in part, but then
I shall know just as I also am known.

13And now abide faith, hope, love, these
three; but the greatest of these *is* love.

DAY 3: What about interpretations of Song of Solomon that allergorize it to mean God's love for Israel or Christ's love for the church?

The Song has suffered strained interpretations over the centuries by those who use the "allegorical" method of interpretation, claiming that this song has no actual historical basis, but rather that it depicts God's love for Israel and/or Christ's love for the church. The misleading idea from hymnology that Christ is the rose of Sharon and the lily of the valleys results from this method (2:1). The "typological" variation admits the historical reality, but concludes that it ultimately pictures Christ's bridegroom love for His bride the church.

A more satisfying way to approach Solomon's Song is to take it at face value and interpret it in the normal historical sense, understanding the frequent use of poetic imagery to depict reality. To do so understands that Solomon recounts phases of his relationship with the Shulamite: 1) his own days of courtship, 2) the early days of his first marriage, followed by 3) the maturing of this royal couple through the good and bad days of life. The Song of Solomon expands on the ancient marriage instructions of Genesis 2:24, thus providing spiritual music for a lifetime of marital harmony. It is given by God to demonstrate His intention for the romance and loveliness of marriage, the most precious of human relations and "the grace of life" (1 Pet. 3:7).

SEPTEMBER 4

Song of Solomon 7:1–8:14

THE BELOVED

7 How beautiful are your feet in sandals,
O prince's daughter!
The curves of your thighs *are* like
jewels,
The work of the hands of a skillful
workman.
2 Your navel *is* a rounded goblet;
It lacks no blended beverage.
Your waist *is* a heap of wheat
Set about with lilies.
3 Your two breasts *are* like two fawns,
Twins of a gazelle.
4 Your neck *is* like an ivory tower,
Your eyes *like* the pools in Heshbon
By the gate of Bath Rabbim.
Your nose *is* like the tower of Lebanon
Which looks toward Damascus.
5 Your head *crowns* you like *Mount*
Carmel,
And the hair of your head
is like purple;
A king *is* held captive by *your* tresses.
6 How fair and how pleasant you are,
O love, with your delights!
7 This stature of yours is like a palm tree,

And your breasts *like* its clusters.
8 I said, "I will go up to the palm tree,
I will take hold of its branches."
Let now your breasts be like clusters of the vine,
The fragrance of your breath like apples,
9 And the roof of your mouth like the best wine.

The Shulamite

The wine goes *down* smoothly for my beloved,
Moving gently the lips of sleepers.
10 I *am* my beloved's,
And his desire *is* toward me.
11 Come, my beloved,
Let us go forth to the field;
Let us lodge in the villages.
12 Let us get up early to the vineyards;
Let us see if the vine has budded,
Whether the grape blossoms are open,
And the pomegranates are in bloom.
There I will give you my love.
13 The mandrakes give off a fragrance,
And at our gates *are* pleasant *fruits*,
All manner, new and old,
Which I have laid up for you, my beloved.

8 Oh, that you were like my brother,
Who nursed at my mother's breasts!
If I should find you outside,
I would kiss you;
I would not be despised.
2 I would lead you *and* bring you
Into the house of my mother,
She *who* used to instruct me.
I would cause you to drink of spiced wine,
Of the juice of my pomegranate.

(To the Daughters of Jerusalem)

3 His left hand *is* under my head,
And his right hand embraces me.
4 I charge you, O daughters of Jerusalem,
Do not stir up nor awaken love
Until it pleases.

A Relative

5 Who *is* this coming up from the wilderness,
Leaning upon her beloved?

I awakened you under the apple tree.
There your mother brought you forth;
There she *who* bore you brought *you* forth.

The Shulamite to Her Beloved

6 Set me as a seal upon your heart,
As a seal upon your arm;
For love *is as* strong as death,
Jealousy *as* cruel as the grave;
Its flames *are* flames of fire,
A most vehement flame.
7 Many waters cannot quench love,
Nor can the floods drown it.
If a man would give for love
All the wealth of his house,
It would be utterly despised.

8:6,7 For love. This represents the 1 Corinthians 13:1–8 of the Old Testament. Four qualities of love appear: 1) love is unyielding in marriage, as death is to life; 2) love is intense like the brightest flame, perhaps as bright as the glory of the Lord; 3) love is invincible or unquenchable, even when flooded by difficulty; and 4) love is so priceless that it cannot be bought, only given away.

The Shulamite's Brothers

8 We have a little sister,
And she has no breasts.
What shall we do for our sister
In the day when she is spoken for?
9 If she *is* a wall,
We will build upon her
A battlement of silver;
And if she *is* a door,
We will enclose her
With boards of cedar.

The Shulamite

10 I *am* a wall,
And my breasts like towers;
Then I became in his eyes
As one who found peace.
11 Solomon had a vineyard at Baal Hamon;
He leased the vineyard to keepers;
Everyone was to bring for its fruit
A thousand silver *coins*.

(To Solomon)

12 My own vineyard *is* before me.
You, O Solomon, *may have* a thousand,
And those who tend its fruit two hundred.

The Beloved

13 You who dwell in the gardens,

The companions listen for your voice—
Let me hear it!

THE SHULAMITE

14 Make haste, my beloved,
And be like a gazelle
Or a young stag
On the mountains of spices.

Psalm 104:31–35

31 May the glory of the LORD endure
forever;
May the LORD rejoice in His works.
32 He looks on the earth, and it
trembles;
He touches the hills, and they smoke.
33 I will sing to the LORD as long
as I live;
I will sing praise to my God while I
have my being.
34 May my meditation be sweet to Him;
I will be glad in the LORD.
35 May sinners be consumed from the
earth,
And the wicked be no more.

Bless the LORD, O my soul!
Praise the LORD!

Proverbs 24:21–22

21 My son, fear the LORD and the king;
Do not associate with those given to
change;

24:21 the king. Loyalty to the king is proper because he is the agent of the Lord's wisdom (Deut. 17:14–20; Rom. 13:1–7). That loyalty includes having no part with rebels who seek to subvert or overthrow him ("change"). Peter draws on this verse in his call to good citizenship in 1 Peter 1:17; 2:17.

22 For their calamity will rise suddenly,
And who knows the ruin those two can
bring?

1 Corinthians 14:1–20

14 Pursue love, and desire spiritual *gifts,* but
especially that you may prophesy. 2For he
who speaks in a tongue does not speak to men
but to God, for no one understands *him;* however, in the spirit he speaks mysteries. 3But he
who prophesies speaks edification and exhortation and comfort to men. 4He who speaks in a

14:1 Pursue love. A command for every believer. Because lovelessness was a root spiritual problem in the Corinthian church, the godly love just described should have been sought after by them with particular determination and diligence. **desire spiritual *gifts*.** Love does not preclude the use of these enablements. Since Paul has addressed not desiring showy gifts (12:31) and not elevating one over the other (12:14–25), some might think it best to set them all aside for unity's sake. Spiritual gifts, on the other hand, are sovereignly bestowed by God on each believer and necessary for the building of the church (12:1–10). Desire for them, in this context, is in reference to their use collectively and faithfully in His service—not a personal yearning to have an admired gift that one did not possess. As a congregation, the Corinthians should be wanting the full expression of all the gifts to be exercised. "You" is plural, emphasizing the corporate desire of the church. **especially...prophesy.** This spiritual gift was desirable in the life of the church to serve in a way that tongues cannot, namely, by edifying the entire church (v. 5).

tongue edifies himself, but he who prophesies
edifies the church. 5I wish you all spoke with
tongues, but even more that you prophesied;
for he who prophesies *is* greater than he who
speaks with tongues, unless indeed he interprets, that the church may receive edification.
6But now, brethren, if I come to you speaking
with tongues, what shall I profit you unless I
speak to you either by revelation, by knowledge, by prophesying, or by teaching? 7Even
things without life, whether flute or harp, when
they make a sound, unless they make a distinction in the sounds, how will it be known what is
piped or played? 8For if the trumpet makes an
uncertain sound, who will prepare for battle? 9So
likewise you, unless you utter by the tongue
words easy to understand, how will it be known
what is spoken? For you will be speaking into
the air. 10There are, it may be, so many kinds of
languages in the world, and none of them *is* without significance. 11Therefore, if I do not know the
meaning of the language, I shall be a foreigner
to him who speaks, and he who speaks *will be* a
foreigner to me. 12Even so you, since you are
zealous for spiritual *gifts, let it be* for the edification of the church *that* you seek to excel.
13Therefore let him who speaks in a tongue
pray that he may interpret. 14For if I pray in a
tongue, my spirit prays, but my understanding

14:18 I speak with tongues more than you all. Paul emphasized that by writing all of this, he was not condemning genuine tongues (plural). Nor, as some may have thought to accuse him, was he envious of a gift he did not possess. At that point, he stopped speaking hypothetically about counterfeit tongue-speaking. He actually had more occasions to use the true gift than all of them (though we have no record of a specific instance). He knew the true gift and had used it properly. It is interesting, however, that the New Testament makes no mention of Paul's actually exercising that gift. Nor does Paul in his own writings make mention of a specific use of it by any Christian.

is unfruitful. [15]What is *the conclusion* then? I
will pray with the spirit, and I will also pray
with the understanding. I will sing with the
spirit, and I will also sing with the understanding. [16]Otherwise, if you bless with the spirit,
how will he who occupies the place of the
uninformed say "Amen" at your giving of
thanks, since he does not understand what
you say? [17]For you indeed give thanks well, but
the other is not edified.

[18]I thank my God I speak with tongues more
than you all; [19]yet in the church I would rather
speak five words with my understanding, that
I may teach others also, than ten thousand
words in a tongue.

[20]Brethren, do not be children in understanding; however, in malice be babes, but in understanding be mature.

DAY 4: What was at the heart of Paul's concern for the use of the gift of tongues in the church in Corinth?

In the section of 1 Corinthians 14:2–39, although it is not indicated consistently in some translations, the distinction between the singular tongue and the plural tongues is foundational to the proper interpretation of this chapter. Paul seems to use the singular to distinguish the counterfeit gift of pagan gibberish and the plural to indicate the genuine gift of a foreign language (v. 2). It was perhaps in recognition of that, that the King James Version (KJV) translators added consistently the word "unknown" before every singular form (see vv. 2,4,13,14,19,27). The implications of that distinction will be noted as appropriate. Against the backdrop of carnality and counterfeit ecstatic speech learned from the experience of the pagans, Paul covers 3 basic issues with regard to speaking in languages by the gift of the Holy Spirit: 1) its position, inferior to prophecy (vv. 1–19); 2) its purpose, a sign to unbelievers not believers (vv. 20–25); and 3) its procedure, systematic, limited, and orderly (vv. 26–40).

"He who speaks in a tongue" (v. 2). This is singular, indicating that it refers to the false gibberish of the counterfeit pagan ecstatic speech. The singular is used because gibberish can't be plural; there are not various kinds of nonlanguage. There are, however, various languages; hence, when speaking of the true gift of language, Paul uses the plural to make the distinction (vv. 6,18,22,23,29). The only exception is in vv. 27,28, where it refers to a single person speaking a single genuine language. "No one understands him;…in the spirit he speaks mysteries." The carnal Corinthians using the counterfeit ecstatic speech of paganism were not interested in being understood, but in making a dramatic display. The spirit by which they spoke was not the Holy Spirit, but their own human spirit or some demon. And the mysteries they declared were the type associated with the pagan mystery religions, which was espoused to be the depths that only the initiated few were privileged to know and understand. Those mysteries were totally unlike the ones mentioned in Scripture (e.g., Matt. 13:11; Eph. 3:9), which are divine revelations of truths previously hidden (12:7; Eph. 3:3–6). "Does not speak to men but to God." This is better translated, "to a god." The Greek text has no definite article. Their gibberish was worship of pagan deities. The Bible records no incident of any believer ever speaking to God in any other than normal human language.

SEPTEMBER 5

Isaiah 1:1–2:22

1 The vision of Isaiah the son of Amoz, which
he saw concerning Judah and Jerusalem in
the days of Uzziah, Jotham, Ahaz, *and*
Hezekiah, kings of Judah.

2 Hear, O heavens, and give ear, O earth!
For the LORD has spoken:
"I have nourished and brought up
children,
And they have rebelled against Me;
3 The ox knows its owner

And the donkey its master's crib;
But Israel does not know,
My people do not consider."

4 Alas, sinful nation,
A people laden with iniquity,
A brood of evildoers,
Children who are corrupters!
They have forsaken the LORD,
They have provoked to anger
The Holy One of Israel,
They have turned away backward.

5 Why should you be stricken again?
You will revolt more and more.
The whole head is sick,
And the whole heart faints.
6 From the sole of the foot even to the head,
There is no soundness in it,
But wounds and bruises and putrefying sores;
They have not been closed or bound up,
Or soothed with ointment.

7 Your country *is* desolate,
Your cities *are* burned with fire;
Strangers devour your land in your presence;
And *it is* desolate, as overthrown by strangers.
8 So the daughter of Zion is left as a booth in a vineyard,
As a hut in a garden of cucumbers,
As a besieged city.
9 Unless the LORD of hosts
Had left to us a very small remnant,
We would have become like Sodom,
We would have been made like Gomorrah.

10 Hear the word of the LORD,
You rulers of Sodom;
Give ear to the law of our God,
You people of Gomorrah:
11 "To what purpose *is* the multitude of your sacrifices to Me?"
Says the LORD.

1:11 I have had enough...I do not delight. God found all sacrifices meaningless and even abhorrent if the offerer failed in obedience to His laws. Rebellion is equated to the sin of witchcraft and stubbornness to iniquity and idolatry.

"I have had enough of burnt offerings of rams
And the fat of fed cattle.
I do not delight in the blood of bulls,
Or of lambs or goats.

12 "When you come to appear before Me,
Who has required this from your hand,
To trample My courts?
13 Bring no more futile sacrifices;
Incense is an abomination to Me.
The New Moons, the Sabbaths, and the calling of assemblies—
I cannot endure iniquity and the sacred meeting.
14 Your New Moons and your appointed feasts
My soul hates;
They are a trouble to Me,
I am weary of bearing *them*.

1:14 My soul hates. It is impossible to doubt the Lord's total aversion toward hypocritical religion. Other practices God hates include robbery for burnt offering (61:8), serving other gods (Jer. 44:4), harboring evil against a neighbor and love for a false oath (Zech. 8:16), divorce (Mal. 2:16), and the one who loves violence (Ps. 11:5).

15 When you spread out your hands,
I will hide My eyes from you;
Even though you make many prayers,
I will not hear.
Your hands are full of blood.
16 "Wash yourselves, make yourselves clean;
Put away the evil of your doings from before My eyes.
Cease to do evil,
17 Learn to do good;
Seek justice,
Rebuke the oppressor;
Defend the fatherless,
Plead for the widow.

18 "Come now, and let us reason together,"
Says the LORD,
"Though your sins are like scarlet,
They shall be as white as snow;
Though they are red like crimson,
They shall be as wool.
19 If you are willing and obedient,
You shall eat the good of the land;
20 But if you refuse and rebel,
You shall be devoured by the sword";

1:18 scarlet,...crimson. The two colors speak of the guilt of those whose hands were "full of blood" (v. 15). Fullness of blood speaks of extreme iniquity and perversity (59:3; Ezek. 9:9,10; 23:37,45). **white as snow;...as wool.** Snow and wool are substances that are naturally white, and therefore portray what is clean, the blood-guilt (v. 15) having been removed (Ps. 51:7). Isaiah was a prophet of grace, but forgiveness is not unconditional. It comes through repentance as v. 19 indicates.

For the mouth of the LORD has spoken.

21 How the faithful city has become
a harlot!
It was full of justice;
Righteousness lodged in it,
But now murderers.
22 Your silver has become dross,
Your wine mixed with water.
23 Your princes *are* rebellious,
And companions of thieves;
Everyone loves bribes,
And follows after rewards.
They do not defend the fatherless,
Nor does the cause of the widow come
before them.

24 Therefore the Lord says,
The LORD of hosts, the Mighty One of
Israel,
"Ah, I will rid Myself of My adversaries,
And take vengeance on My enemies.
25 I will turn My hand against you,
And thoroughly purge away your dross,
And take away all your alloy.
26 I will restore your judges as at the first,
And your counselors as at the
beginning.
Afterward you shall be called the city
of righteousness, the faithful city."

27 Zion shall be redeemed with justice,
And her penitents with righteousness.
28 The destruction of transgressors and of
sinners *shall be* together,
And those who forsake the LORD shall
be consumed.
29 For they shall be ashamed of the
terebinth trees
Which you have desired;
And you shall be embarrassed because
of the gardens
Which you have chosen.
30 For you shall be as a terebinth whose
leaf fades,
And as a garden that has no water.
31 The strong shall be as tinder,
And the work of it as a spark;
Both will burn together,
And no one shall quench *them*.

2 The word that Isaiah the son of Amoz saw
concerning Judah and Jerusalem.

2 Now it shall come to pass in the latter
days
That the mountain of the LORD's house
Shall be established on the top of the
mountains,
And shall be exalted above the hills;
And all nations shall flow to it.
3 Many people shall come and say,
"Come, and let us go up to the mountain
of the LORD,
To the house of the God of Jacob;
He will teach us His ways,
And we shall walk in His paths."
For out of Zion shall go forth the law,
And the word of the LORD from
Jerusalem.
4 He shall judge between the nations,
And rebuke many people;
They shall beat their swords into
plowshares,
And their spears into pruning hooks;
Nation shall not lift up sword against
nation,
Neither shall they learn war anymore.

5 O house of Jacob, come and let us walk
In the light of the LORD.

6 For You have forsaken Your people, the
house of Jacob,
Because they are filled with eastern
ways;
They *are* soothsayers like the Philistines,
And they are pleased with the children
of foreigners.
7 Their land is also full of silver and gold,
And there is no end to their treasures;
Their land is also full of horses,
And there is no end to their chariots.
8 Their land is also full of idols;
They worship the work of their own
hands,
That which their own fingers have made.
9 People bow down,
And each man humbles himself;
Therefore do not forgive them.

10 Enter into the rock, and hide in the dust,
From the terror of the LORD
And the glory of His majesty.
11 The lofty looks of man shall be humbled,

The haughtiness of men shall be
bowed down,
And the LORD alone shall be exalted in
that day.

12 For the day of the LORD of hosts
Shall come upon everything proud and
lofty,
Upon everything lifted up—
And it shall be brought low—
13 Upon all the cedars of Lebanon *that are*
high and lifted up,
And upon all the oaks of Bashan;
14 Upon all the high mountains,
And upon all the hills *that are* lifted up;
15 Upon every high tower,
And upon every fortified wall;
16 Upon all the ships of Tarshish,
And upon all the beautiful sloops.
17 The loftiness of man shall be bowed
down,
And the haughtiness of men shall be
brought low;
The LORD alone will be exalted in that
day,
18 But the idols He shall utterly abolish.
19 They shall go into the holes of the
rocks,
And into the caves of the earth,
From the terror of the LORD
And the glory of His majesty,
When He arises to shake the earth
mightily.

2:19 holes of the rocks,...caves of the earth. Revelation 6:12,15,16 uses this passage and 2:21 to describe man's flight from the terrors of tribulation during the period before Christ's personal return to earth. This shows that the final fulfillment of this prophecy will be during Daniel's 70th week.

20 In that day a man will cast away his
idols of silver
And his idols of gold,
Which they made, *each* for himself to
worship,
To the moles and bats,
21 To go into the clefts of the rocks,
And into the crags of the rugged rocks,
From the terror of the LORD
And the glory of His majesty,
When He arises to shake the earth
mightily.

22 Sever yourselves from such a man,
Whose breath *is* in his nostrils;
For of what account is he?

Psalm 105:1–6

Oh, give thanks to the LORD!
Call upon His name;
Make known His deeds among the
peoples!
2 Sing to Him, sing psalms to Him;
Talk of all His wondrous works!
3 Glory in His holy name;
Let the hearts of those rejoice who
seek the LORD!
4 Seek the LORD and His strength;
Seek His face evermore!
5 Remember His marvelous works
which He has done,
His wonders, and the judgments
of His mouth,
6 O seed of Abraham His servant,
You children of Jacob, His chosen
ones!

Proverbs 24:23–25

23 These *things* also *belong* to the wise:
It is not good to show partiality in
judgment.
24 He who says to the wicked, "You *are*
righteous,"
Him the people will curse;
Nations will abhor him.
25 But those who rebuke *the wicked* will
have delight,
And a good blessing will come upon
them.

1 Corinthians 14:21–40

21 In the law it is written:
*"With men of other tongues and other
lips
I will speak to this people;
And yet, for all that, they will not hear
Me,"*

says the Lord.
22 Therefore tongues are for a sign, not to
those who believe but to unbelievers; but prophesying is not for unbelievers but for those who
believe. 23 Therefore if the whole church
comes together in one place, and all speak
with tongues, and there come in *those who are*
uninformed or unbelievers, will they not say
that you are out of your mind? 24 But if all
prophesy, and an unbeliever or an uninformed
person comes in, he is convinced by all, he is
convicted by all. 25 And thus the secrets of his

heart are revealed; and so, falling down on *his* face, he will worship God and report that God is truly among you.

[26]How is it then, brethren? Whenever you come together, each of you has a psalm, has a teaching, has a tongue, has a revelation, has an interpretation. Let all things be done for edification. [27]If anyone speaks in a tongue, *let there be* two or at the most three, *each* in turn, and let one interpret. [28]But if there is no interpreter, let him keep silent in church, and let him speak to himself and to God. [29]Let two or three prophets speak, and let the others judge. [30]But if *anything* is revealed to another who sits by, let the first keep silent. [31]For you can all prophesy one by one, that all may learn and all may be encouraged. [32]And the spirits of the prophets are subject to the prophets. [33]For God is not *the author* of confusion but of peace, as in all the churches of the saints.

[34]Let your women keep silent in the churches, for they are not permitted to speak; but *they are* to be submissive, as the law also says. [35]And if they want to learn something, let them ask their own husbands at home; for it is shameful for women to speak in church.

[36]Or did the word of God come *originally* from you? Or *was it* you only that it reached? [37]If anyone thinks himself to be a prophet or spiritual, let him acknowledge that the things which I write to you are the commandments of the Lord. [38]But if anyone is ignorant, let him be ignorant.

[39]Therefore, brethren, desire earnestly to prophesy, and do not forbid to speak with tongues. [40]Let all things be done decently and in order.

14:33 confusion. Here is the key to the whole chapter. The church at worship before God should reflect His character and nature because He is a God of peace and harmony, order and clarity, not strife and confusion (Rom. 15:33; 2 Thess. 3:16; Heb. 13:20). **as in all the churches.** This phrase does not belong in v. 33, but at the beginning of v. 34, as a logical introduction to a universal principle for churches.

DAY 5: Who was Isaiah the prophet?

Isaiah, the son of Amoz, ministered in and around Jerusalem as a prophet to Judah during the reigns of 4 kings of Judah: Uzziah (called "Azariah" in 2 Kings), Jotham, Ahaz, and Hezekiah (1:1), from ca. 739 to 686 B.C. He evidently came from a family of some rank, because he had easy access to the king (7:3) and intimacy with a priest (8:2). He was married and had two sons who bore symbolic names: "Shear-Jashub" ("a remnant shall return," 7:3) and "Maher-Shalal-Hash-Baz" ("hasting to the spoil, hurrying to the prey," 8:3). When called by God to prophesy, in the year of King Uzziah's death (ca. 739 B.C.), he responded with a cheerful readiness, though he knew from the beginning that his ministry would be one of fruitless warning and exhortation (6:9–13). Having been reared in Jerusalem, he was an appropriate choice as a political and religious counselor to the nation.

Isaiah was a contemporary of Hosea and Micah. His writing style has no rival in its versatility of expression, brilliance of imagery, and richness of vocabulary. The early church father Jerome likened him to Demosthenes, the legendary Greek orator. His writing features a range of 2,186 different words, compared to 1,535 in Ezekiel, 1,653 in Jeremiah, and 2,170 in the Psalms. Second Chronicles 32:32 records that he wrote a biography of King Hezekiah, also. The prophet lived until at least 681 B.C. when he penned the account of Sennacherib's death (37:38). Tradition has it that he met his death under King Manasseh (ca. 695–642 B.C.) by being cut in two with a wooden saw (Heb. 11:37).

SEPTEMBER 6

Isaiah 3:1–4:6

3 For behold, the Lord,
the LORD of hosts,
Takes away from Jerusalem and from
Judah
The stock and the store,
The whole supply of bread and the
whole supply of water;
2 The mighty man and the man of war,
The judge and the prophet,
And the diviner and the elder;
3 The captain of fifty and the honorable
man,
The counselor and the skillful artisan,
And the expert enchanter.
4 "I will give children *to be* their princes,
And babes shall rule over them.
5 The people will be oppressed,
Every one by another and every one
by his neighbor;

The child will be insolent toward
the elder,
And the base toward the honorable."
6 When a man takes hold of his brother
In the house of his father, *saying,*
"You have clothing;
You be our ruler,
And *let* these ruins *be* under your
power,"
7 In that day he will protest, saying,
"I cannot cure *your* ills,
For in my house *is* neither food nor
clothing;
Do not make me a ruler of the people."
8 For Jerusalem stumbled,
And Judah is fallen,
Because their tongue and their doings
Are against the LORD,
To provoke the eyes of His glory.
9 The look on their countenance
witnesses against them,
And they declare their sin as Sodom;
They do not hide *it*.
Woe to their soul!
For they have brought evil upon
themselves.

3:8 Jerusalem...Judah. The fall of Jerusalem in 586 B.C. was only a partial fulfillment of this prophecy. The final fulfillment awaits the times just prior to Christ's Second Coming. **against the LORD.** The root of Zion's problem surfaces: overt rebellion against the Lord. The people sinned shamelessly; they made no effort to conceal it (3:9).

10 "Say to the righteous that *it shall be* well
with them,
For they shall eat the fruit of their
doings.
11 Woe to the wicked! *It shall be* ill *with
him,*
For the reward of his hands shall be
given him.
12 *As for* My people, children *are* their
oppressors,
And women rule over them.
O My people! Those who lead you
cause *you* to err,
And destroy the way of your paths."

13 The LORD stands up to plead,
And stands to judge the people.
14 The LORD will enter into judgment
With the elders of His people
And His princes:
"For you have eaten up the vineyard;
The plunder of the poor *is* in your
houses.
15 What do you mean by crushing My
people
And grinding the faces of the poor?"
Says the Lord GOD of hosts.

16 Moreover the LORD says:

"Because the daughters of Zion are
haughty,
And walk with outstretched necks
And wanton eyes,
Walking and mincing *as* they go,
Making a jingling with their feet,
17 Therefore the Lord will strike with a
scab
The crown of the head of the
daughters of Zion,
And the LORD will uncover their secret
parts."
18 In that day the Lord will take away the
finery:
The jingling anklets, the scarves, and
the crescents;
19 The pendants, the bracelets, and the
veils;
20 The headdresses, the leg ornaments,
and the headbands;
The perfume boxes, the charms,
21 and the rings;
The nose jewels,
22 the festal apparel, and the mantles;
The outer garments, the purses,
23 and the mirrors;
The fine linen, the turbans, and the
robes.

24 And so it shall be:

Instead of a sweet smell there will be a
stench;
Instead of a sash, a rope;
Instead of well-set hair, baldness;
Instead of a rich robe, a girding of
sackcloth;
And branding instead of beauty.
25 Your men shall fall by the sword,
And your mighty in the war.
26 Her gates shall lament and mourn,
And she *being* desolate shall sit on the
ground.

4 And in that day seven women shall
take hold of one man, saying,
"We will eat our own food and wear our
own apparel;

4:2 Branch. This messianic title occurs also in Jeremiah 23:5; 33:15; Zechariah 3:8; 6:12. The thought behind the title relates to 2 Samuel 23:5, that of growth. The life of the Branch will bear spiritual fruit (John 15:4,5).

Only let us be called by your name,
To take away our reproach."

2 In that day the Branch of the LORD
shall be beautiful and glorious;
And the fruit of the earth *shall be*
excellent and appealing
For those of Israel who have escaped.

3And it shall come to pass that *he who is* left
in Zion and remains in Jerusalem will be
called holy—everyone who is recorded among
the living in Jerusalem. 4When the Lord has
washed away the filth of the daughters of Zion,
and purged the blood of Jerusalem from her
midst, by the spirit of judgment and by the spirit of burning, 5then the LORD will create above
every dwelling place of Mount Zion, and
above her assemblies, a cloud and smoke by
day and the shining of a flaming fire by night.
For over all the glory there *will be* a covering.
6And there will be a tabernacle for shade in the
daytime from the heat, for a place of refuge,
and for a shelter from storm and rain.

Psalm 105:7–22

7 He *is* the LORD our God;
His judgments *are* in all the earth.
8 He remembers His covenant forever,
The word *which* He commanded, for a
thousand generations,

105:8 a thousand generations. A reference to an exceedingly long time (a generation is normally 40 years) which would encompass the remainder of human history; i.e., forever (Deut. 7:9; 1 Chr. 16:15).

9 *The covenant* which He made with
Abraham,
And His oath to Isaac,
10 And confirmed it to Jacob for a statute,
To Israel *as* an everlasting covenant,
11 Saying, "To you I will give the land of
Canaan
As the allotment of your inheritance,"
12 When they were few in number,
Indeed very few, and strangers in it.
13 When they went from one nation to
another,
From *one* kingdom to another people,
14 He permitted no one to do them
wrong;
Yes, He rebuked kings for their sakes,
15 *Saying,* "Do not touch My anointed
ones,
And do My prophets no harm."
16 Moreover He called for a famine
in the land;
He destroyed all the provision of
bread.
17 He sent a man before them—
Joseph—*who* was sold as a slave.
18 They hurt his feet with fetters,
He was laid in irons.
19 Until the time that his word came to pass,
The word of the LORD tested him.
20 The king sent and released him,
The ruler of the people let him go free.
21 He made him lord of his house,
And ruler of all his possessions,
22 To bind his princes at his pleasure,
And teach his elders wisdom.

Proverbs 24:26–27

26 He who gives a right answer kisses
the lips.
27 Prepare your outside work,
Make it fit for yourself in the field;
And afterward build your house.

1 Corinthians 15:1–28

15 Moreover, brethren, I declare to you the
gospel which I preached to you, which
also you received and in which you stand, 2by
which also you are saved, if you hold fast that
word which I preached to you—unless you
believed in vain.
3For I delivered to you first of all that which I
also received: that Christ died for our sins according to the Scriptures, 4and that He was
buried, and that He rose again the third day according to the Scriptures, 5and that He was seen
by Cephas, then by the twelve. 6After that He
was seen by over five hundred brethren at once,
of whom the greater part remain to the present,
but some have fallen asleep. 7After that He was
seen by James, then by all the apostles. 8Then
last of all He was seen by me also, as by one
born out of due time.
9For I am the least of the apostles, who am not
worthy to be called an apostle, because I persecuted the church of God. 10But by the grace of

15:5–7 The testimony of eyewitnesses, recorded in the New Testament, was added to support the reality of the resurrection. These included: 1) John and Peter together (John 20:19,20), but probably also separately before (Luke 24:34); 2) the 12 (John 20:19,20; Luke 24:36; Acts 1:22); 3) the 500, only referred to here, had all seen the risen Christ (Matt. 28:9; Mark 16:9,12,14; Luke 24:31–39; John 21:1–23); 4) James, either one of the two so-named apostles (son of Zebedee or son of Alphaeus; Mark 3:17,18) or even James the half brother of the Lord, the author of the epistle by that name and the key leader in the Jerusalem church (Acts 15:13–21); and 5) the apostles (John 20:19–29). Such unspecified appearances occurred over a 40-day period (Acts 1:3) to all the apostles.

15:25 all enemies under His feet. This figure comes from the common practice of kings always sitting enthroned above their subjects, so that when the subjects bowed or kneeled, they were lower than the sovereign's feet. With enemies, the monarch might put his foot on the neck of a conquered ruler, symbolizing that enemy's total subjugation. In the millennial kingdom, Christ's foes will be in subjection to Him.

15:26, 27 last enemy…death. Christ has broken the power of Satan, who held the power of death (Heb. 2:14), at the Cross. But Satan will not be permanently divested of his weapon of death until the end of the Millennium (Rev. 20:1–10). At that point, having fulfilled completely the prophecy of Psalm 8:6 (v. 27a), Christ then will deliver the kingdom to His Father, and the eternal glory of Revelation 21 and 22 will begin.

God I am what I am, and His grace toward me
was not in vain; but I labored more abundantly
than they all, yet not I, but the grace of God
which was with me. 11Therefore, whether *it was*
I or they, so we preach and so you believed.
12Now if Christ is preached that He has been
raised from the dead, how do some among you
say that there is no resurrection of the dead?
13But if there is no resurrection of the dead,
then Christ is not risen. 14And if Christ is not
risen, then our preaching *is* empty and your
faith *is* also empty. 15Yes, and we are found
false witnesses of God, because we have testified of God that He raised up Christ, whom He
did not raise up—if in fact the dead do not rise.
16For if *the* dead do not rise, then Christ is not
risen. 17And if Christ is not risen, your faith *is*
futile; you are still in your sins! 18Then also
those who have fallen asleep in Christ have perished. 19If in this life only we have hope in
Christ, we are of all men the most pitiable.
20But now Christ is risen from the dead, *and*
has become the firstfruits of those who have
fallen asleep. 21For since by man *came* death,
by Man also *came* the resurrection of the dead.
22For as in Adam all die, even so in Christ all
shall be made alive. 23But each one in his own
order: Christ the firstfruits, afterward those
who are Christ's at His coming. 24Then *comes*
the end, when He delivers the kingdom to God
the Father, when He puts an end to all rule and
all authority and power. 25For He must reign till
He has put all enemies under His feet. 26The
last enemy *that* will be destroyed *is* death. 27For
"He has put all things under His feet." But
when He says "all things are put under *Him*,"
it is evident that He who put all things under
Him is excepted. 28Now when all things are
made subject to Him, then the Son Himself will
also be subject to Him who put all things under
Him, that God may be all in all.

DAY 6: What difference would it make if the Resurrection of Christ never really happened?

"How do some among you say that there is no resurrection of the dead?" (1 Cor. 15:12). The Corinthian Christians believed in Christ's resurrection, or else they could not have been Christians (John 6:44; 11:25; Acts 4:12; 2 Cor. 4:14; 1 Thess. 4:16). But some had particular difficulty accepting and understanding the resurrection of believers. Some of this confusion was a result of their experiences with pagan philosophies and religions. A basic tenet of much of ancient Greek philosophy was dualism, which taught that everything physical was intrinsically evil; so the idea of a resurrected body was repulsive and disgusting (Acts 17:32). In addition, perhaps some Jews in the Corinthian church formerly may have been influenced by the Sadducees, who did not believe in the resurrection even though it is taught in the Old Testament (Job 19:26; Pss. 16:8–11; 17:15; Dan. 12:2). On the other hand, New Testament teaching in the words of our Lord Himself was extensive on the resurrection (John 5:28,29; 6:44; 11:25; 14:19), and it was the theme of the apostolic preaching (Acts 4:1,2). In spite of that clarity, the church at Corinth was in doubt about the resurrection.

In vv. 13–19, Paul gives 6 disastrous consequences if there were no resurrection: 1) preaching Christ would be senseless (v. 14); 2) faith in Christ would be useless (v. 14); 3) all the witnesses and preachers of the resurrection would be liars (v. 15); 4) no one would be redeemed from sin (v. 17); 5) all former believers would have perished (v. 18); and 6) Christians would be the most pitiable people on earth (v. 19).

SEPTEMBER 7

Isaiah 5:1–6:13

5 Now let me sing to my Well-beloved
A song of my Beloved regarding His vineyard:
My Well-beloved has a vineyard
On a very fruitful hill.
2 He dug it up and cleared out its stones,
And planted it with the choicest vine.
He built a tower in its midst,
And also made a winepress in it;
So He expected *it* to bring forth *good* grapes,
But it brought forth wild grapes.

5:2 *good* grapes,...wild grapes. The owner made every conceivable provision for the vine's productivity and protection, illustrating the Lord's purely gracious choice of Israel. Justifiably, He expected a good yield from His investment, but the vine's produce was "sour berries," inedible and fit only for dumping.

3 "And now, O inhabitants of Jerusalem and men of Judah,
Judge, please, between Me and My vineyard.
4 What more could have been done to My vineyard
That I have not done in it?
Why then, when I expected *it* to bring forth *good* grapes,
Did it bring forth wild grapes?
5 And now, please let Me tell you what I will do to My vineyard:
I will take away its hedge, and it shall be burned;
And break down its wall, and it shall be trampled down.
6 I will lay it waste;
It shall not be pruned or dug,
But there shall come up briers and thorns.
I will also command the clouds
That they rain no rain on it."
7 For the vineyard of the LORD of hosts *is* the house of Israel,
And the men of Judah are His pleasant plant.
He looked for justice, but behold, oppression;
For righteousness, but behold, a cry *for help*.

8 Woe to those who join house to house;
They add field to field,
Till *there is* no place
Where they may dwell alone in the midst of the land!
9 In my hearing the LORD of hosts *said,*
"Truly, many houses shall be desolate,
Great and beautiful ones, without inhabitant.
10 For ten acres of vineyard shall yield one bath,
And a homer of seed shall yield one ephah."
11 Woe to those who rise early in the morning,
That they may follow intoxicating drink;
Who continue until night, *till* wine inflames them!
12 The harp and the strings,
The tambourine and flute,
And wine are in their feasts;
But they do not regard the work of the LORD,
Nor consider the operation of His hands.
13 Therefore my people have gone into captivity,
Because *they have* no knowledge;
Their honorable men *are* famished,
And their multitude dried up with thirst.
14 Therefore Sheol has enlarged itself
And opened its mouth beyond measure;
Their glory and their multitude and their pomp,

And he who is jubilant, shall descend
into it.
15 People shall be brought down,
Each man shall be humbled,
And the eyes of the lofty shall be
humbled.
16 But the LORD of hosts shall be exalted
in judgment,
And God who is holy shall be hallowed
in righteousness.
17 Then the lambs shall feed in their
pasture,
And in the waste places of the fat ones
strangers shall eat.

18 Woe to those who draw iniquity with
cords of vanity,
And sin as if with a cart rope;
19 That say, "Let Him make speed *and*
hasten His work,
That we may see *it;*
And let the counsel of the Holy One of
Israel draw near and come,
That we may know *it.*"

20 Woe to those who call evil good, and
good evil;
Who put darkness for light, and light
for darkness;
Who put bitter for sweet, and sweet for
bitter!

21 Woe to *those who are* wise in their own
eyes,
And prudent in their own sight!

22 Woe to men mighty at drinking wine,
Woe to men valiant for mixing
intoxicating drink,
23 Who justify the wicked for a bribe,
And take away justice from the
righteous man!

24 Therefore, as the fire devours the
stubble,
And the flame consumes the chaff,
So their root will be as rottenness,
And their blossom will ascend like
dust;
Because they have rejected the law of
the LORD of hosts,
And despised the word of the Holy
One of Israel.
25 Therefore the anger of the LORD is
aroused against His people;
He has stretched out His hand against
them
And stricken them,
And the hills trembled.
Their carcasses *were* as refuse in the
midst of the streets.

For all this His anger is not turned away,
But His hand *is* stretched out still.

26 He will lift up a banner to the nations
from afar,
And will whistle to them from the end
of the earth;
Surely they shall come with speed,
swiftly.
27 No one will be weary or stumble
among them,
No one will slumber or sleep;
Nor will the belt on their loins be loosed,
Nor the strap of their sandals be broken;
28 Whose arrows *are* sharp,
And all their bows bent;
Their horses' hooves will seem like flint,
And their wheels like a whirlwind.
29 Their roaring *will be* like a lion,
They will roar like young lions;
Yes, they will roar
And lay hold of the prey;
They will carry *it* away safely,
And no one will deliver.
30 In that day they will roar against them
Like the roaring of the sea.
And if *one* looks to the land,
Behold, darkness *and* sorrow;
And the light is darkened by the clouds.

6 In the year that King Uzziah died, I saw
the Lord sitting on a throne, high and lifted up, and the train of His *robe* filled the temple. 2 Above it stood seraphim; each one had six
wings: with two he covered his face, with two
he covered his feet, and with two he flew. 3 And
one cried to another and said:

"Holy, holy, holy *is* the LORD of hosts;
The whole earth *is* full of His glory!"

4 And the posts of the door were shaken by the
voice of him who cried out, and the house was
filled with smoke.
5 So I said:

"Woe *is* me, for I am undone!
Because I *am* a man of unclean lips,
And I dwell in the midst of a people of
unclean lips;
For my eyes have seen the King,
The LORD of hosts."

6 Then one of the seraphim flew to me, having in his hand a live coal *which* he had taken
with the tongs from the altar. 7 And he touched
my mouth *with it,* and said:

"Behold, this has touched your lips;
Your iniquity is taken away,
And your sin purged."

8 Also I heard the voice of the Lord, saying:

"Whom shall I send,
And who will go for Us?"

Then I said, "Here *am* I! Send me."
9 And He said, "Go, and tell this people:

'Keep on hearing, but do not
understand;
Keep on seeing, but do not perceive.'

10 "Make the heart of this people dull,
And their ears heavy,
And shut their eyes;
Lest they see with their eyes,
And hear with their ears,
And understand with their heart,
And return and be healed."

11 Then I said, "Lord, how long?"
And He answered:

"Until the cities are laid waste
and without inhabitant,
The houses are without a man,
The land is utterly desolate,
12 The LORD has removed men far away,
And the forsaken places *are* many in
the midst of the land.
13 But yet a tenth *will be* in it,
And will return and be for consuming,
As a terebinth tree or as an oak,
Whose stump *remains* when it is cut
down.
So the holy seed *shall be* its stump."

Psalm 105:23–36

23 Israel also came into Egypt,
And Jacob dwelt in the land of Ham.
24 He increased His people greatly,
And made them stronger than their
enemies.
25 He turned their heart to hate His
people,
To deal craftily with His servants.

26 He sent Moses His servant,
And Aaron whom He had chosen.
27 They performed His signs among them,
And wonders in the land of Ham.
28 He sent darkness, and made *it* dark;
And they did not rebel against His
word.
29 He turned their waters into blood,
And killed their fish.
30 Their land abounded with frogs,
Even in the chambers of their kings.
31 He spoke, and there came swarms of
flies,
And lice in all their territory.
32 He gave them hail for rain,
And flaming fire in their land.
33 He struck their vines also, and their fig
trees,
And splintered the trees of their
territory.
34 He spoke, and locusts came,
Young locusts without number,
35 And ate up all the vegetation in their
land,
And devoured the fruit of their ground.
36 He also destroyed all the firstborn in
their land,
The first of all their strength.

Proverbs 24:28–29

28 Do not be a witness against your
neighbor without cause,
For would you deceive with your lips?
29 Do not say, "I will do to him just as he
has done to me;
I will render to the man according to
his work."

1 Corinthians 15:29–58

29 Otherwise, what will they do who are baptized for the dead, if the dead do not rise at all?
Why then are they baptized for the dead?
30 And why do we stand in jeopardy every
hour? 31 I affirm, by the boasting in you which
I have in Christ Jesus our Lord, I die daily. 32 If,
in the manner of men, I have fought with
beasts at Ephesus, what advantage *is it* to me?
If *the* dead do not rise, *"Let us eat and drink,
for tomorrow we die!"*
33 Do not be deceived: "Evil company corrupts good habits." 34 Awake to righteousness,

15:29 This difficult verse has numerous possible interpretations. Other Scripture passages, however, clarify certain things which it does *not* mean. It does not teach, for example, that a dead person can be saved by another person's being baptized on his behalf, because baptism never has a part in a person's salvation (Eph. 2:8; Rom. 3:28; 4:3; 6:3,4). A reasonable view seems to be that "they…who are baptized" refers to living believers who give outward testimony to their faith in baptism by water because they were first drawn to Christ by the exemplary lives, faithful influence, and witness of believers who had subsequently died. Paul's point is that, if there is no resurrection and no life after death, then why are people coming to Christ to follow the hope of those who have died?

and do not sin; for some do not have the
knowledge of God. I speak *this* to your shame.
35 But someone will say, "How are the dead
raised up? And with what body do they come?"
36 Foolish one, what you sow is not made alive
unless it dies. 37 And what you sow, you do not
sow that body that shall be, but mere grain—
perhaps wheat or some other *grain*. 38 But God
gives it a body as He pleases, and to each seed
its own body.
39 All flesh *is* not the same flesh, but *there is*
one *kind of* flesh of men, another flesh of animals, another of fish, *and* another of birds.
40 *There are* also celestial bodies and terrestrial bodies; but the glory of the celestial *is*
one, and the *glory* of the terrestrial *is* another.
41 *There is* one glory of the sun, another glory
of the moon, and another glory of the stars;
for *one* star differs from *another* star in glory.
42 So also *is* the resurrection of the dead. *The*
body is sown in corruption, it is raised in incorruption. 43 It is sown in dishonor, it is raised in
glory. It is sown in weakness, it is raised in
power. 44 It is sown a natural body, it is raised a
spiritual body. There is a natural body, and
there is a spiritual body. 45 And so it is written,
"The first man Adam became a living being."
The last Adam *became* a life-giving spirit.

15:42b–44 Focusing directly on the resurrection body, Paul gives 4 sets of contrasts to show how the new body will differ from the present one (v. 54; Phil. 3:20,21): 1) no more sickness and death ("corruption"); 2) no more shame because of sin ("dishonor"); 3) no more frailty in temptation ("weakness"); and 4) no more limits to the time/space sphere ("natural").

46 However, the spiritual is not first, but the
natural, and afterward the spiritual. 47 The first
man *was* of the earth, *made* of dust; the second Man *is* the Lord from heaven. 48 As *was* the
man of dust, so also *are* those *who are made* of
dust; and as *is* the heavenly *Man*, so also *are*
those *who are* heavenly. 49 And as we have
borne the image of the *man* of dust, we shall
also bear the image of the heavenly *Man*.
50 Now this I say, brethren, that flesh and
blood cannot inherit the kingdom of God; nor
does corruption inherit incorruption. 51 Behold,
I tell you a mystery: We shall not all sleep, but
we shall all be changed— 52 in a moment, in the
twinkling of an eye, at the last trumpet. For the
trumpet will sound, and the dead will be raised
incorruptible, and we shall be changed. 53 For this
corruptible must put on incorruption, and this
mortal *must* put on immortality. 54 So when this corruptible has put on incorruption, and this mortal
has put on immortality, then shall be brought to
pass the saying that is written: *"Death is swal-*
lowed up in victory."

15:52 twinkling of an eye. This was Paul's way of showing how brief the "moment" will be. The Greek word for "twinkling" refers to any rapid movement. Since the eye can move more rapidly than any other part of our visible bodies, it seems to well illustrate the sudden transformation of raptured believers. **trumpet will sound.** To herald the end of the church era, when all believers will be removed from the earth at the rapture (1 Thess. 4:16). **dead...raised.** According to 1 Thessalonians 4:16, they are first and the living saints follow.

55 *"O Death, where is your sting?*
O Hades, where is your victory?"

56 The sting of death *is* sin, and the strength of
sin *is* the law. 57 But thanks *be* to God, who
gives us the victory through our Lord Jesus
Christ.
58 Therefore, my beloved brethren, be steadfast, immovable, always abounding in the work
of the Lord, knowing that your labor is not in
vain in the Lord.

DAY 7: Describe Isaiah's vision of heaven.

In Isaiah 6:1, Isaiah says that he "saw the Lord sitting on a throne, high and lifted up." The prophet became unconscious of the outside world and with his inner eye saw what God revealed to him. This experience recalls the experience of John's prophetic vision in Revelation 4:1–11. The throne was greatly elevated, emphasizing the Most High God. His "train" refers to the hem or fringe of the Lord's glorious robe that filled the temple. Though Isaiah may have been at the earthly temple, this describes a vision which transcends the earthly. The throne of God is in the heavenly temple (Rev. 4:1–6; 5:1–7; 11:19; 15:5–8).

The seraphim above the throne (v. 2) are an order of angelic creatures who bear a similarity to the 4 living creatures of Revelation 4:6, which in turn resemble the cherubim of Ezekiel 10:1ff. "Six wings." Two wings covered the faces of the seraphim because they dared not gaze directly at God's glory. Two covered their feet, acknowledging their lowliness even though engaged in divine service. With two they flew in serving the One on the throne. Thus, 4 wings related to worship, emphasizing the priority of praise.

"One cried to another and said: 'Holy, holy, holy' " (v. 3). The seraphs were speaking to each other in antiphonal praise. The primary thrust of the 3-fold repetition of God's holiness is to emphasize God's separateness from and independence of His fallen creation, though it implies secondarily that God is 3 Persons. The earth is the worldwide display of His immeasurable glory, perfections, and attributes as seen in creation (Rom. 1:20). Fallen man has nevertheless refused to glorify Him as God (Rom. 1:23). "And the posts of the door were shaken…smoke" (v. 4). The shaking and smoke symbolize God's holiness as it relates to His wrath and judgment (Ex. 19:16–20; Rev. 15:8).

Isaiah's vision made him painfully aware of his sin and broke him; in this way God has prepared him for his cleansing and his commission. "Woe is me…I am a man of unclean lips" (v. 5). If the lips are unclean, so is the heart. This vision of God's holiness vividly reminded the prophet of his own unworthiness which deserved judgment. Job (Job 42:6) and Peter (Luke 5:8) came to the same realization about themselves when confronted with the presence of the Lord (Ezek. 1:28–2:7; Rev. 1:17). The hot coal taken from the altar of incense in heaven (Rev. 8:3–5) is emblematic of God's purifying work (v. 6). Repentance is painful. Spiritual cleansing for special service to the Lord, not salvation, is in view (v. 8).

SEPTEMBER 8

Isaiah 7:1–8:22

7 Now it came to pass in the days of Ahaz
the son of Jotham, the son of Uzziah, king
of Judah, *that* Rezin king of Syria and Pekah the
son of Remaliah, king of Israel, went up to Jerusalem to *make* war against it, but could not
prevail against it. 2And it was told to the house
of David, saying, "Syria's forces are deployed
in Ephraim." So his heart and the heart of his
people were moved as the trees of the woods
are moved with the wind.

3Then the LORD said to Isaiah, "Go out now
to meet Ahaz, you and Shear-Jashub your son,
at the end of the aqueduct from the upper
pool, on the highway to the Fuller's Field, 4and
say to him: 'Take heed, and be quiet; do not
fear or be fainthearted for these two stubs of
smoking firebrands, for the fierce anger of
Rezin and Syria, and the son of Remaliah. 5Be-
cause Syria, Ephraim, and the son of Remaliah
have plotted evil against you, saying, 6"Let us
go up against Judah and trouble it, and let us
make a gap in its wall for ourselves, and set a
king over them, the son of Tabel"— 7thus says
the Lord GOD:

"It shall not stand,
Nor shall it come to pass.
8 For the head of Syria *is* Damascus,
And the head of Damascus *is* Rezin.
Within sixty-five years Ephraim will be
broken,
So that it will not *be* a people.
9 The head of Ephraim *is* Samaria,
And the head of Samaria *is* Remaliah's
son.
If you will not believe,
Surely you shall not be established." ' "

10Moreover the LORD spoke again to Ahaz,
saying, 11"Ask a sign for yourself from the LORD
your God; ask it either in the depth or in the
height above."

12But Ahaz said, "I will not ask, nor will I test
the LORD!"

13Then he said, "Hear now, O house of David!
Is it a small thing for you to weary men, but will
you weary my God also? 14Therefore the Lord
Himself will give you a sign: Behold, the virgin
shall conceive and bear a Son, and shall call His
name Immanuel. 15Curds and honey He shall
eat, that He may know to refuse the evil and
choose the good. 16For before the Child shall
know to refuse the evil and choose the good,
the land that you dread will be forsaken by
both her kings. 17The LORD will bring the king
of Assyria upon you and your people and your
father's house—days that have not come since
the day that Ephraim departed from Judah."

7:18 fly…bee. Egypt was full of flies, and Assyria was a country noted for beekeeping. These insects represented the armies from the powerful countries which the Lord would summon to overrun Judah and take the people into exile.

18 And it shall come to pass in that day
That the LORD will whistle for the fly
That *is* in the farthest part of the rivers
of Egypt,
And for the bee that *is* in the land of
Assyria.
19 They will come, and all of them will rest
In the desolate valleys and in the clefts
of the rocks,
And on all thorns and in all pastures.

20 In the same day the Lord will shave
with a hired razor,
With those from beyond the River,
with the king of Assyria,
The head and the hair of the legs,
And will also remove the beard.

21 It shall be in that day
That a man will keep alive a young cow
and two sheep;
22 So it shall be, from the abundance of
milk they give,
That he will eat curds;
For curds and honey everyone will eat
who is left in the land.

23 It shall happen in that day,
That wherever there could be a
thousand vines
Worth a thousand *shekels* of silver,
It will be for briers and thorns.
24 With arrows and bows *men* will come
there,
Because all the land will become briers
and thorns.
25 And to any hill which could be dug
with the hoe,
You will not go there for fear of briers
and thorns;
But it will become a range for oxen
And a place for sheep to roam.

8 Moreover the LORD said to me, "Take a
large scroll, and write on it with a man's
pen concerning Maher-Shalal-Hash-Baz. 2And
I will take for Myself faithful witnesses to
record, Uriah the priest and Zechariah the son
of Jeberechiah."

3Then I went to the prophetess, and she conceived and bore a son. Then the LORD said to
me, "Call his name Maher-Shalal-Hash-Baz; 4for
before the child shall have knowledge to cry
'My father' and 'My mother,' the riches of Damascus and the spoil of Samaria will be taken
away before the king of Assyria."

5The LORD also spoke to me again, saying:

6 "Inasmuch as these people refused
The waters of Shiloah that flow softly,
And rejoice in Rezin and in Remaliah's
son;
7 Now therefore, behold, the Lord
brings up over them
The waters of the River, strong and
mighty—
The king of Assyria and all his glory;
He will go up over all his channels
And go over all his banks.
8 He will pass through Judah,
He will overflow and pass over,
He will reach up to the neck;
And the stretching out of his wings
Will fill the breadth of Your land,
O Immanuel.

9 "Be shattered, O you peoples, and be
broken in pieces!
Give ear, all you from far countries.
Gird yourselves, but be broken in
pieces;
Gird yourselves, but be broken in
pieces.
10 Take counsel together, but it will come
to nothing;
Speak the word, but it will not stand,
For God *is* with us."

8:10 God *is* with us. The Hebrew is *Immanuel.* The name of the virgin's child (7:14) guaranteed the eventual triumph of the faithful remnant of Israel.

11For the LORD spoke thus to me with a
strong hand, and instructed me that I should
not walk in the way of this people, saying:

12 "Do not say, 'A conspiracy,'
Concerning all that this people call a
conspiracy,
Nor be afraid of their threats, nor be
troubled.
13 The LORD of hosts, Him you shall
hallow;
Let Him *be* your fear,
And *let* Him *be* your dread.
14 He will be as a sanctuary,
But a stone of stumbling and a rock of
offense
To both the houses of Israel,
As a trap and a snare to the inhabitants
of Jerusalem.
15 And many among them shall
stumble;
They shall fall and be broken,
Be snared and taken."

16 Bind up the testimony,
Seal the law among my disciples.
17 And I will wait on the LORD,
Who hides His face from the house of Jacob;
And I will hope in Him.
18 Here am I and the children whom the LORD has given me!
We are for signs and wonders in Israel
From the LORD of hosts,
Who dwells in Mount Zion.

19And when they say to you, "Seek those
who are mediums and wizards, who whisper
and mutter," should not a people seek their
God? *Should they seek* the dead on behalf of the
living? 20To the law and to the testimony! If
they do not speak according to this word, *it is*
because *there is* no light in them.

21They will pass through it hard-pressed and
hungry; and it shall happen, when they are
hungry, that they will be enraged and curse
their king and their God, and look upward.
22Then they will look to the earth, and see trouble and darkness, gloom of anguish; and *they will be* driven into darkness.

8:19 *seek* the dead. People of Isaiah's day were using spiritualists to communicate with the dead as King Saul did through the medium at En Dor (1 Sam. 28:8–19). The law strictly forbade such consultations (Lev. 19:26; Deut. 18:10,11).

Psalm 105:37–45

37 He also brought them out with silver and gold,
And *there was* none feeble among His tribes.
38 Egypt was glad when they departed,
For the fear of them had fallen upon them.
39 He spread a cloud for a covering,
And fire to give light in the night.
40 *The people* asked, and He brought quail,
And satisfied them with the bread of heaven.
41 He opened the rock, and water gushed out;
It ran in the dry places *like* a river.

42 For He remembered His holy promise,
And Abraham His servant.
43 He brought out His people with joy,
His chosen ones with gladness.
44 He gave them the lands of the Gentiles,
And they inherited the labor of the nations,
45 That they might observe His statutes
And keep His laws.

Praise the LORD!

Proverbs 24:30–34

30 I went by the field of the lazy *man*,
And by the vineyard of the man devoid of understanding;
31 And there it was, all overgrown with thorns;
Its surface was covered with nettles;
Its stone wall was broken down.
32 When I saw *it*, I considered *it* well;
I looked on *it and* received instruction:
33 A little sleep, a little slumber,
A little folding of the hands to rest;
34 So shall your poverty come *like* a prowler,
And your need like an armed man.

1 Corinthians 16:1–24

16 Now concerning the collection for the
saints, as I have given orders to the churches of Galatia, so you must do also: 2On the first
day of the week let each one of you lay something aside, storing up as he may prosper, that
there be no collections when I come. 3And when
I come, whomever you approve by *your* letters I
will send to bear your gift to Jerusalem. 4But if it
is fitting that I go also, they will go with me.
5Now I will come to you when I pass
through Macedonia (for I am passing through Macedonia). 6And it may be that I will remain, or even spend the winter with you, that you may send me on my journey, wherever I go.
7For I do not wish to see you now on the way; but I hope to stay a while with you, if the Lord permits.
8But I will tarry in Ephesus until Pentecost.

16:1 collection. An offering for destitute believers in the overpopulated, famine stricken city of Jerusalem (see Acts 11:28). Paul had previously solicited funds from the churches of Galatia, Macedonia, and Achaia (Rom. 15:26; Luke 10:25–37; 2 Cor. 8:1–5; 9:12–15; Gal. 6:10; 1 John 3:17).

16:2 as he may prosper. No required amount or percentage for giving to the Lord's work is specified in the New Testament. All giving to the Lord is to be freewill giving and completely discretionary (Luke 6:38; 2 Cor. 9:6–8). This is not to be confused with the Old Testament required giving of 3 tithes (Lev. 27:30; Num. 18:21–26; Deut. 14:28,29; Mal. 3:8–10), which totaled about 23 percent annually to fund the national government of Israel, take care of public festivals, and provide welfare. Modern parallels to the Old Testament tithe are found in the taxation system of countries (Rom. 13:6). Old Testament giving to God was not regulated as to amount (see Ex. 25:1,2; 35:21; 36:6; Prov. 3:9,10; 11:24).

9For a great and effective door has opened to
me, and *there are* many adversaries.
10And if Timothy comes, see that he may be
with you without fear; for he does the work of
the Lord, as I also *do.* 11Therefore let no one
despise him. But send him on his journey in
peace, that he may come to me; for I am waiting for him with the brethren.
12Now concerning *our* brother Apollos, I
strongly urged him to come to you with the brethren, but he was quite unwilling to come at this time; however, he will come when he has a convenient time.
13Watch, stand fast in the faith, be brave, be
strong. 14Let all *that* you *do* be done with love.

16:9 many adversaries. Perhaps no New Testament church had such fierce opposition as the one in Ephesus. In spite of that opposition, the door for the gospel was open wide (2 Cor. 2:12,13 where Paul also had an open door, but no heart to remain and preach) and Paul stayed. At the end of the experience of opposition described in 2 Corinthians 1:8–10, he wrote 1 Corinthians.

15I urge you, brethren—you know the household of Stephanas, that it is the firstfruits of Achaia, and *that* they have devoted themselves to the ministry of the saints—
16that you also submit to such, and to everyone who works and labors with *us.*
17I am glad about the coming of Stephanas, Fortunatus, and Achaicus, for what was lacking on your part they supplied. 18For they
refreshed my spirit and yours. Therefore acknowledge such men.
19The churches of Asia greet you. Aquila and Priscilla greet you heartily in the Lord, with the church that is in their house. 20All the
brethren greet you.
Greet one another with a holy kiss.
21The salutation with my own hand—Paul's.
22If anyone does not love the Lord Jesus Christ, let him be accursed. O Lord, come!
23The grace of our Lord Jesus Christ *be* with
you. 24My love *be* with you all in Christ Jesus. Amen.

DAY 8: From Isaiah 7 and 8, list a few of the many prophecies from Isaiah that were fulfilled in the New Testament.

In Isaiah 7:14, since Ahaz refused to choose a sign, the Lord chose His own sign, whose implementation would occur far beyond Ahaz's lifetime. "The virgin." This prophecy reached forward to the virgin birth of the Messiah, as the New Testament notes (Matt. 1:23). The Hebrew word refers to an unmarried woman and means "virgin" (Gen. 24:43; Prov. 30:19; Song 1:3; 6:8), so the birth of Isaiah's own son (8:3) could not have fully satisified the prophecy. "Shall call His name Immanuel." The title, applied to Jesus in Matthew 1:23, means "God with us."

Isaiah 8:14. "Sanctuary…stone of stumbling." Isaiah found encouragement in the Lord as his holy place of protection from his accusers. The New Testament applies this verse to corporate Israel in her ongoing rejection of Jesus as Messiah (Luke 2:34; Rom. 9:32,33; 1 Pet. 2:8). "Both the houses of Israel." They will be collapsed until the return of the Messiah to the earth restores them.

Isaiah 8:15. "Many…shall stumble." Another prediction anticipated the stumbling of Israel, which included her rejection of her Messiah at His first advent (Luke 20:18; Rom. 9:32; 28:16).

Isaiah 8:17. "Wait on…hope." The speaker is Isaiah whose disposition was to await the Lord's deliverance, the national salvation promised the faithful remnant (40:31; 49:23).

Isaiah 8:18. "I and the children." In their historical setting, the words refer to Isaiah and his two sons, whose names had prophetic significance (i.e., as "signs and wonders"). In Hebrews 2:13, these verses emphasize the point that Christ had fully identified Himself with mankind by taking a human nature. And He demonstrated the reality of His human nature by His reliance upon God during His earthly sojourn.

SEPTEMBER 9

Isaiah 9:1–10:34

9 Nevertheless the gloom *will* not *be* upon her who *is* distressed,
As when at first He lightly esteemed
The land of Zebulun and the land of Naphtali,
And afterward more heavily oppressed *her*,
By the way of the sea, beyond the Jordan,
In Galilee of the Gentiles.
2 The people who walked in darkness
Have seen a great light;
Those who dwelt in the land of the shadow of death,
Upon them a light has shined.

3 You have multiplied the nation
And increased its joy;
They rejoice before You
According to the joy of harvest,
As *men* rejoice when they divide the spoil.
4 For You have broken the yoke of his burden
And the staff of his shoulder,
The rod of his oppressor,
As in the day of Midian.
5 For every warrior's sandal from the noisy battle,
And garments rolled in blood,
Will be used for burning *and* fuel of fire.

6 For unto us a Child is born,
Unto us a Son is given;
And the government will be upon His shoulder.
And His name will be called
Wonderful, Counselor, Mighty God,
Everlasting Father, Prince of Peace.
7 Of the increase of *His* government and peace
There will be no end,
Upon the throne of David and over His kingdom,
To order it and establish it with judgment and justice
From that time forward, even forever.
The zeal of the LORD of hosts will perform this.

8 The Lord sent a word against Jacob,
And it has fallen on Israel.
9 All the people will know—
Ephraim and the inhabitant of Samaria—

9:6 Child…Son. These terms elaborate further on Immanuel, the child to be born to the virgin (7:14). The virgin's child will also be the royal Son of David, with rights to the Davidic throne (9:7; Matt. 1:21; Luke 1:31–33; 2:7,11). **government.** In fulfillment of this verse and Psalm 2:9, the Son will rule the nations of the world (Rev. 2:27; 19:15). **Wonderful, Counselor.** The remaining 3 titles consist of two words each, so the intention was probably that each pair of words indicate one title: "Wonderful Counselor." In contrast to Ahaz, this King will implement supernatural wisdom in discharging His office (2 Sam. 16:23; 1 Kin. 3:28). **Mighty God.** As a powerful warrior, the Messiah will accomplish the military exploits mentioned in 9:3–5. **Everlasting Father.** The Messiah will be a Father to His people eternally. As Davidic King, He will compassionately care for and discipline them (40:11; 63:16; 64:8; Pss. 68:5,6; 103:13; Prov. 3:12). **Prince of Peace.** The government of Immanuel will procure and perpetuate peace among the nations of the world (2:4; 11:6–9; Mic. 4:3).

9:7 throne of David. The virgin's Son will be the rightful heir to David's throne and will inherit the promises of the Davidic Covenant (2 Sam. 7:12–16; Ps. 89:1–37; Matt. 1:1).

Who say in pride and arrogance of heart:
10 "The bricks have fallen down,
But we will rebuild with hewn stones;
The sycamores are cut down,
But we will replace *them* with cedars."
11 Therefore the LORD shall set up
The adversaries of Rezin against him,
And spur his enemies on,
12 The Syrians before and the Philistines behind;
And they shall devour Israel with an open mouth.

For all this His anger is not turned away,
But His hand *is* stretched out still.

13 For the people do not turn to Him who strikes them,
Nor do they seek the LORD of hosts.
14 Therefore the LORD will cut off head and tail from Israel,
Palm branch and bulrush in one day.
15 The elder and honorable, he *is* the head;
The prophet who teaches lies, he *is* the tail.

16 For the leaders of this people cause *them* to err,
And *those who are* led by them are destroyed.
17 Therefore the Lord will have no joy in their young men,
Nor have mercy on their fatherless and widows;
For everyone *is* a hypocrite and an evildoer,
And every mouth speaks folly.

For all this His anger is not turned away,
But His hand *is* stretched out still.

18 For wickedness burns as the fire;
It shall devour the briers and thorns,
And kindle in the thickets of the forest;
They shall mount up *like* rising smoke.
19 Through the wrath of the LORD of hosts
The land is burned up,
And the people shall be as fuel for the fire;
No man shall spare his brother.
20 And he shall snatch on the right hand
And be hungry;
He shall devour on the left hand
And not be satisfied;
Every man shall eat the flesh of his own arm.
21 Manasseh *shall devour* Ephraim, and Ephraim Manasseh;
Together they *shall be* against Judah.

For all this His anger is not turned away,
But His hand *is* stretched out still.

10 "Woe to those who decree unrighteous decrees,
Who write misfortune,
Which they have prescribed
2 To rob the needy of justice,
And to take what is right from the poor of My people,
That widows may be their prey,
And *that* they may rob the fatherless.
3 What will you do in the day of punishment,
And in the desolation *which* will come from afar?
To whom will you flee for help?
And where will you leave your glory?
4 Without Me they shall bow down among the prisoners,
And they shall fall among the slain."

For all this His anger is not turned away,
But His hand *is* stretched out still.

5 "Woe to Assyria, the rod of My anger
And the staff in whose hand is My indignation.
6 I will send him against an ungodly nation,
And against the people of My wrath
I will give him charge,
To seize the spoil, to take the prey,
And to tread them down like the mire of the streets.
7 Yet he does not mean so,
Nor does his heart think so;
But *it is* in his heart to destroy,
And cut off not a few nations.
8 For he says,
'*Are* not my princes altogether kings?
9 *Is* not Calno like Carchemish?
Is not Hamath like Arpad?
Is not Samaria like Damascus?
10 As my hand has found the kingdoms of the idols,
Whose carved images excelled those of Jerusalem and Samaria,
11 As I have done to Samaria and her idols,
Shall I not do also to Jerusalem and her idols?' "

12 Therefore it shall come to pass, when the
Lord has performed all His work on Mount
Zion and on Jerusalem, *that He will say,* "I will
punish the fruit of the arrogant heart of the king
of Assyria, and the glory of his haughty looks."
13 For he says:

"By the strength of my hand I have done *it,*
And by my wisdom, for I am prudent;
Also I have removed the boundaries of the people,
And have robbed their treasuries;
So I have put down the inhabitants like a valiant *man.*
14 My hand has found like a nest the riches of the people,
And as one gathers eggs *that are* left,
I have gathered all the earth;
And there was no one who moved *his* wing,
Nor opened *his* mouth with even a peep."

15 Shall the ax boast itself against him who chops with it?
Or shall the saw exalt itself against him who saws with it?
As if a rod could wield *itself* against those who lift it up,
Or as if a staff could lift up, *as if it were* not wood!

16 Therefore the Lord, the Lord of hosts,
Will send leanness among his fat ones;
And under his glory
He will kindle a burning
Like the burning of a fire.
17 So the Light of Israel will be for a fire,
And his Holy One for a flame;
It will burn and devour
His thorns and his briers in one day.
18 And it will consume the glory of his forest and of his fruitful field,
Both soul and body;
And they will be as when a sick man wastes away.
19 Then the rest of the trees of his forest
Will be so few in number
That a child may write them.

20 And it shall come to pass in that day
That the remnant of Israel,
And such as have escaped of the house of Jacob,
Will never again depend on him who defeated them,
But will depend on the LORD, the Holy One of Israel, in truth.
21 The remnant will return, the remnant of Jacob,
To the Mighty God.
22 For though your people, O Israel, be as the sand of the sea,
A remnant of them will return;
The destruction decreed shall overflow with righteousness.
23 For the Lord GOD of hosts
Will make a determined end
In the midst of all the land.

24 Therefore thus says the Lord GOD of hosts: "O My people, who dwell in Zion, do not be afraid of the Assyrian. He shall strike you with a rod and lift up his staff against you, in the manner of Egypt. 25 For yet a very little while and the indignation will cease, as will My anger in their destruction." 26 And the LORD of hosts will stir up a scourge for him like the slaughter of Midian at the rock of Oreb; *as* His rod was on the sea, so will He lift it up in the manner of Egypt.

27 It shall come to pass in that day
That his burden will be taken away from your shoulder,
And his yoke from your neck,
And the yoke will be destroyed because of the anointing oil.

28 He has come to Aiath,
He has passed Migron;
At Michmash he has attended to his equipment.
29 They have gone along the ridge,
They have taken up lodging at Geba.
Ramah is afraid,
Gibeah of Saul has fled.
30 Lift up your voice,
O daughter of Gallim!
Cause it to be heard as far as Laish—
O poor Anathoth!
31 Madmenah has fled,
The inhabitants of Gebim seek refuge.
32 As yet he will remain at Nob that day;
He will shake his fist at the mount of the daughter of Zion,
The hill of Jerusalem.

33 Behold, the Lord,
The LORD of hosts,
Will lop off the bough with terror;
Those of high stature *will be* hewn down,
And the haughty will be humbled.
34 He will cut down the thickets of the forest with iron,
And Lebanon will fall by the Mighty One.

Psalm 106:1–5

Praise the LORD!

Oh, give thanks to the LORD, for *He is* good!
For His mercy *endures* forever.
2 Who can utter the mighty acts of the LORD?
Who can declare all His praise?
3 Blessed *are* those who keep justice,
And he who does righteousness at all times!

4 Remember me, O LORD, with the favor *You have toward* Your people.
Oh, visit me with Your salvation,
5 That I may see the benefit of Your chosen ones,
That I may rejoice in the gladness of Your nation,
That I may glory with Your inheritance.

Proverbs 25:1–2

25 These also *are* proverbs of Solomon which the men of Hezekiah king of Judah copied:

2 *It is* the glory of God to conceal a matter,
But the glory of kings *is* to search out a matter.

2 Corinthians 1:1–24

1 Paul, an apostle of Jesus Christ by the will of
God, and Timothy *our* brother,

To the church of God which is at Corinth,
with all the saints who are in all Achaia:

[2]Grace to you and peace from God our
Father and the Lord Jesus Christ.

[3]Blessed *be* the God and Father of our Lord
Jesus Christ, the Father of mercies and God of
all comfort, [4]who comforts us in all our tribulation, that we may be able to comfort those
who are in any trouble, with the comfort with
which we ourselves are comforted by God.

1:4 tribulation. This term refers to crushing pressure, because in Paul's life and ministry there was always something attempting to weaken him, restrict or confine his ministry, or even crush out his life. But no matter what confronted him, Paul knew God would sustain and strengthen him (12:9,10; Rom. 8:31–38; Phil. 1:6). **that we may be able to comfort.** Comfort from God is not an end in itself. Its purpose is that believers also might be comforters. Having humiliated and convicted the Corinthians, God used Paul to return to them with a strengthening message after he himself had received divine strengthening (6:1–13; 12:6–11; Luke 22:31,32).

[5]For as the sufferings of Christ abound in us,
so our consolation also abounds through
Christ. [6]Now if we are afflicted, *it is* for your
consolation and salvation, which is effective
for enduring the same sufferings which we
also suffer. Or if we are comforted, *it is* for
your consolation and salvation. [7]And our hope
for you *is* steadfast, because we know that as
you are partakers of the sufferings, so also *you
will partake* of the consolation.

[8]For we do not want you to be ignorant,
brethren, of our trouble which came to us in
Asia: that we were burdened beyond measure,
above strength, so that we despaired even of
life. [9]Yes, we had the sentence of death in ourselves, that we should not trust in ourselves but
in God who raises the dead, [10]who delivered us
from so great a death, and does deliver us; in
whom we trust that He will still deliver *us,* [11]you
also helping together in prayer for us, that
thanks may be given by many persons on our
behalf for the gift *granted* to us through many.

[12]For our boasting is this: the testimony of our
conscience that we conducted ourselves in the

1:8 trouble which came to us in Asia. This was a recent occurrence (following the writing of 1 Corinthians) that happened in or around the city of Ephesus. The details of this situation are not known. **despaired even of life.** Paul faced something that was beyond human survival and was extremely discouraging because he believed it threatened to end his ministry prematurely. The Greek word for "despaired" literally means "no passage," the total absence of an exit (2 Tim. 4:6). The Corinthians were aware of what had happened to Paul, but did not realize the utter severity of it, or what God was doing through those circumstances.

1:9 the sentence of death. The word for "sentence" is a technical term that indicated the passing of an official resolution, in this case the death sentence. Paul was so absolutely sure he was going to die for the gospel that he had pronounced the sentence upon himself. **not trust in ourselves but in God.** God's ultimate purpose for Paul's horrible extremity. The Lord took him to the point at which he could not fall back on any intellectual, physical, or emotional human resource (12:9,10). **who raises the dead.** A Jewish descriptive term for God used in synagogue worship language. Paul understood that trust in God's power to raise the dead was the only hope of rescue from his extreme circumstances.

world in simplicity and godly sincerity, not with
fleshly wisdom but by the grace of God, and
more abundantly toward you. [13]For we are not
writing any other things to you than what you
read or understand. Now I trust you will understand, even to the end [14](as also you have understood us in part), that we are your boast as you
also *are* ours, in the day of the Lord Jesus.

[15]And in this confidence I intended to come
to you before, that you might have a second
benefit— [16]to pass by way of you to Macedonia,
to come again from Macedonia to you, and be
helped by you on my way to Judea. [17]There-
fore, when I was planning this, did I do it lightly? Or the things I plan, do I plan according to
the flesh, that with me there should be Yes,
Yes, and No, No? [18]But *as* God *is* faithful, our
word to you was not Yes and No. [19]For the Son
of God, Jesus Christ, who was preached
among you by us—by me, Silvanus, and Timothy—was not Yes and No, but in Him was
Yes. [20]For all the promises of God in Him *are*

Yes, and in Him Amen, to the glory of God through us. [21]Now He who establishes us with you in Christ and has anointed us *is* God, [22]who also has sealed us and given us the Spirit in our hearts as a guarantee.

[23]Moreover I call God as witness against my soul, that to spare you I came no more to Corinth. [24]Not that we have dominion over your faith, but are fellow workers for your joy; for by faith you stand.

DAY 9: Why did Paul write a second book to the Corinthians?

Paul's association with the church of Corinth began on his second missionary journey (Acts 18:1–18), when he spent 18 months (Acts 18:11) ministering there. After leaving Corinth, Paul heard of immorality in the Corinthian church and wrote a letter (since lost) to confront that sin, referred to in 1 Corinthians 5:9. During his ministry in Ephesus, he received further reports of trouble in the Corinthian church in the form of divisions among them (1 Cor. 1:11). In addition, the Corinthians wrote Paul a letter (1 Cor. 7:1), asking for clarification of some issues. Paul responded by writing the letter known as 1 Corinthians. Planning to remain at Ephesus a little longer (1 Cor. 16:8,9), Paul sent Timothy to Corinth (1 Cor. 4:17; 16:10,11). Disturbing news reached the apostle (possibly from Timothy) of further difficulties at Corinth, including the arrival of self-styled false apostles.

To create the platform to teach their false gospel, the false apostles began by assaulting the character of Paul. They had to convince the people to turn from Paul to them if they were to succeed in preaching demon doctrine. Temporarily abandoning the work at Ephesus, Paul went immediately to Corinth. The visit (known as the "painful visit," 2 Cor. 2:1) was not a successful one from Paul's perspective—someone in the Corinthian church even openly insulted him (2:5–8,10; 7:12). Saddened by the Corinthians' lack of loyalty to defend him, seeking to spare them further reproof (1:23), and perhaps hoping time would bring them to their senses, Paul returned to Ephesus. From Ephesus, Paul wrote what is known as the "severe letter" (2:4) and sent it with Titus to Corinth (7:5–16). Leaving Ephesus after the riot sparked by Demetrius (Acts 19:23–20:1), Paul went to Troas to meet Titus (2:12,13). But Paul was so anxious for news of how the Corinthians had responded to the "severe letter" that he could not minister there though the Lord had opened the door (2:12; 7:5). So he left for Macedonia to look for Titus (2:13). To Paul's immense relief and joy, Titus met him with the news that the majority of the Corinthians had repented of their rebellion against Paul (7:7). Wise enough to know that some rebellious attitudes still smoldered under the surface and could erupt again, Paul wrote the Corinthians the letter called 2 Corinthians. In this letter, though the apostle expressed his relief and joy at their repentance (7:8–16), his main concern was to defend his apostleship (chaps. 1–7), exhort the Corinthians to resume preparations for the collection for the poor at Jerusalem (chaps. 8, 9), and confront the false apostles head on (chaps. 10–13). He then went to Corinth, as he had written (12:14; 13:1,2). The Corinthians' participation in the Jerusalem offering (Rom. 15:26) implies that Paul's third visit to that church was successful.

SEPTEMBER 10

Isaiah 11:1–12:6

11 There shall come forth a Rod from
the stem of Jesse,
And a Branch shall grow out of his roots.
2 The Spirit of the LORD shall rest upon
Him,
The Spirit of wisdom and
understanding,
The Spirit of counsel and might,
The Spirit of knowledge and of the fear
of the LORD.
3 His delight *is* in the fear of the LORD,
And He shall not judge by the sight of
His eyes,
Nor decide by the hearing of His ears;
4 But with righteousness He shall judge
the poor,
And decide with equity for the meek of
the earth;
He shall strike the earth with the rod
of His mouth,

11:1 stem...roots. With the Babylonian captivity of 586 B.C., the Davidic dynasty appeared as decimated as the Assyrian army. A major difference between the two was the life remaining in the stump and roots of the Davidic line. That life was to manifest itself in new growth in the form of the Rod and Branch. **Jesse.** Jesse was David's father through whose line the messianic king was to come (Ruth 4:22; 1 Sam. 16:1,12,13). **Branch.** This is a title for the Messiah (see 4:2).

11:2 The Spirit of the Lord. As the Spirit of the Lord came upon David when he was anointed king (1 Sam 16:13; Ps. 51:11), so He will rest upon David's descendant, Christ, who will rule the world. **Spirit...the Lord...Him.** This verse refers to the 3 persons of the Holy Trinity (see 6:3). **wisdom and understanding...counsel and might...knowledge and...fear of the Lord.** These are Spirit-imparted qualifications that will enable the Messiah to rule justly and effectively.

And with the breath of His lips He shall
slay the wicked.
5 Righteousness shall be the belt of His
loins,
And faithfulness the belt of His waist.
6 "The wolf also shall dwell with the lamb,
The leopard shall lie down with the
young goat,
The calf and the young lion and the
fatling together;
And a little child shall lead them.
7 The cow and the bear shall graze;
Their young ones shall lie down
together;
And the lion shall eat straw like the ox.
8 The nursing child shall play by the
cobra's hole,
And the weaned child shall put his
hand in the viper's den.
9 They shall not hurt nor destroy in all
My holy mountain,
For the earth shall be full of the
knowledge of the Lord
As the waters cover the sea.
10 "And in that day there shall be a Root
of Jesse,
Who shall stand as a banner to the
people;
For the Gentiles shall seek Him,
And His resting place shall be
glorious."

11:10 in that day. The time of universal peace will come in the future reign of the Lord. **Gentiles shall seek Him.** The Root of Jesse will also attract non-Jews who inhabit the future kingdom (49:6; 52:10; 60:3; 66:18). Paul saw God's ministry to Gentiles during the church age as an additional implication of this verse (Rom. 15:12).

11 It shall come to pass in that day
That the Lord shall set His hand again
the second time
To recover the remnant of His people
who are left,
From Assyria and Egypt,
From Pathros and Cush,
From Elam and Shinar,
From Hamath and the islands of the sea.

12 He will set up a banner for the nations,
And will assemble the outcasts
of Israel,
And gather together the dispersed
of Judah
From the four corners of the earth.
13 Also the envy of Ephraim shall depart,
And the adversaries of Judah shall be
cut off;
Ephraim shall not envy Judah,
And Judah shall not harass Ephraim.
14 But they shall fly down upon the
shoulder of the Philistines toward
the west;
Together they shall plunder the people
of the East;
They shall lay their hand on Edom
and Moab;
And the people of Ammon shall obey
them.
15 The Lord will utterly destroy the
tongue of the Sea of Egypt;
With His mighty wind He will shake
His fist over the River,
And strike it in the seven streams,
And make *men* cross over dryshod.
16 There will be a highway for the
remnant of His people
Who will be left from Assyria,
As it was for Israel
In the day that he came up from the
land of Egypt.

12 And in that day you will say:

"O Lord, I will praise You;
Though You were angry with me,
Your anger is turned away, and You
comfort me.
2 Behold, God *is* my salvation,
I will trust and not be afraid;
'For Yah, the Lord, *is* my strength and
song;
He also has become my salvation.' "

3 Therefore with joy you will draw water
From the wells of salvation.

4 And in that day you will say:

"Praise the Lord, call upon His name;

Declare His deeds among the peoples,
Make mention that His name
is exalted.
5 Sing to the LORD,
For He has done excellent things;
This *is* known in all the earth.
6 Cry out and shout, O inhabitant
of Zion,
For great *is* the Holy One of Israel in
your midst!"

Psalm 106:6–18

6 We have sinned with our fathers,
We have committed iniquity,
We have done wickedly.
7 Our fathers in Egypt did not
understand Your wonders;
They did not remember the multitude
of Your mercies,
But rebelled by the sea—the Red Sea.
8 Nevertheless He saved them for His
name's sake,
That He might make His mighty power
known.
9 He rebuked the Red Sea also, and it
dried up;
So He led them through the depths,
As through the wilderness.
10 He saved them from the hand of him
who hated *them,*
And redeemed them from the hand of
the enemy.
11 The waters covered their enemies;
There was not one of them left.
12 Then they believed His words;
They sang His praise.

13 They soon forgot His works;
They did not wait for His counsel,
14 But lusted exceedingly in the
wilderness,
And tested God in the desert.
15 And He gave them their request,
But sent leanness into their soul.

16 When they envied Moses in the camp,
And Aaron the saint of the LORD,
17 The earth opened up and swallowed
Dathan,
And covered the faction of Abiram.
18 A fire was kindled in their company;
The flame burned up the wicked.

Proverbs 25:3–5

3 *As* the heavens for height and the
earth for depth,
So the heart of kings *is* unsearchable.

4 Take away the dross from silver,
And it will go to the silversmith *for*
jewelry.
5 Take away the wicked from before the
king,
And his throne will be established in
righteousness.

2 Corinthians 2:1–17

2 But I determined this within myself, that I
would not come again to you in sorrow.
2For if I make you sorrowful, then who is he
who makes me glad but the one who is made
sorrowful by me?

2:2 Although Paul was sensitive to the Corinthians' pain and sadness from the past confrontation, because of his commitment to purity he would confront them again if necessary. "The one who is made sorrowful" refers to one convicted by his sin. In particular, there was apparently on Paul's last visit, a man in the church who confronted him with the accusations taken from the false teachers. The church had not dealt with that man in Paul's defense, and Paul was deeply grieved over that lack of loyalty. The only thing that would bring Paul joy would be repentance from such a one and any who agreed with him, and Paul had been waiting for it.

3And I wrote this very thing to you, lest,
when I came, I should have sorrow over those
from whom I ought to have joy, having confidence in you all that my joy is *the joy* of you all.
4For out of much affliction and anguish of heart
I wrote to you, with many tears, not that you
should be grieved, but that you might know
the love which I have so abundantly for you.
5But if anyone has caused grief, he has not
grieved me, but all of you to some extent—not
to be too severe. 6This punishment which *was*
inflicted by the majority *is* sufficient for such a
man, 7so that, on the contrary, you *ought* rather
to forgive and comfort *him,* lest perhaps such
a one be swallowed up with too much sorrow.
8Therefore I urge you to reaffirm *your* love to
him. 9For to this end I also wrote, that I might
put you to the test, whether you are obedient
in all things. 10Now whom you forgive anything, I also *forgive.* For if indeed I have forgiven anything, I have forgiven that one for
your sakes in the presence of Christ, 11lest Satan should take advantage of us; for we are not
ignorant of his devices.

[12]Furthermore, when I came to Troas to *preach* Christ's gospel, and a door was opened to me by the Lord, [13]I had no rest in my spirit, because I did not find Titus my brother; but taking my leave of them, I departed for Macedonia.

[14]Now thanks *be* to God who always leads us in triumph in Christ, and through us diffuses the fragrance of His knowledge in every place. [15]For we are to God the fragrance of Christ among those who are being saved and among those who are perishing. [16]To the one *we are* the aroma of death *leading* to death, and to the other the aroma of life *leading* to life. And who *is* sufficient for these things? [17]For we are not, as so many, peddling the word of God; but as of sincerity, but as from God, we speak in the sight of God in Christ.

2:17 not, as so many. Or, "not as the majority." This specifically refers to the false teachers in Corinth and to the many other teachers and philosophers of that day who operated by human wisdom (1 Cor. 1:19,20). **peddling.** From a Greek verb that means "to corrupt," this word came to refer to corrupt hucksters or con men who by their cleverness and deception were able to sell as genuine an inferior product that was only a cheap imitation. The false teachers in the church were coming with clever, deceptive rhetoric to offer a degraded, adulterated message that mixed paganism and Jewish tradition. They were dishonest men seeking personal profit and prestige at the expense of gospel truth and people's souls.

DAY 10: What was Paul's rationale for forgiveness?

Second Corinthians 2:5–11 is one of the best texts in all of Scripture on the godly motivation for forgiveness. Paul said, "If anyone has caused grief" (v. 5). The Greek construction of this clause assumes the condition to be true—Paul is acknowledging the reality of the offense and its ongoing effect, not on him, but on the church. With this deflection of any personal vengeance, he sought to soften the charge against the penitent offender and allow the church to deal with the man and those who were with him objectively, apart from Paul's personal anguish or offense.

"This punishment…inflicted by the majority" (v. 6). This indicates that the church in Corinth had followed the biblical process in disciplining the sinning man (Matt. 18:15–20; 2 Thess. 3:6,14). The Greek word for "punishment," used frequently in secular writings but only here in the New Testament, denoted an official legal penalty or commercial sanction that was enacted against an individual or group (city, nation). "Is sufficient." The process of discipline and punishment was enough. Now it was time to show mercy because the man had repented (Matt. 18:18,23–35; Gal. 6:1,2; Eph. 4:32; Col. 3:13; Heb. 12:11).

"You ought rather to forgive and comfort him" (v. 7). It was time to grant forgiveness so the man's joy would be restored (Ps. 51:12,14; Is. 42:2,3). Paul knew there was—and is—no place in the church for man-made limits on God's grace, mercy, and forgiveness toward repentant sinners. Such restrictions could only rob the fellowship of the joy of unity (Matt. 18:34,35; Mark 11:25,26). "Therefore I urge you to reaffirm your love to him."

SEPTEMBER 11

Isaiah 13:1–14:32

13 The burden against Babylon which Isaiah the son of Amoz saw.

2 "Lift up a banner on the high mountain,
Raise your voice to them;
Wave your hand, that they may enter
the gates of the nobles.
3 I have commanded My sanctified ones;
I have also called My mighty ones for
My anger—
Those who rejoice in My exaltation."
4 The noise of a multitude in the
mountains,
Like that of many people!
A tumultuous noise of the kingdoms of
nations gathered together!
The LORD of hosts musters
The army for battle.
5 They come from a far country,
From the end of heaven—
The LORD and His weapons
of indignation,
To destroy the whole land.
6 Wail, for the day of the LORD *is* at hand!
It will come as destruction from the
Almighty.
7 Therefore all hands will be limp,

Every man's heart will melt,
8 And they will be afraid.
Pangs and sorrows will take hold of *them;*
They will be in pain as a woman in childbirth;
They will be amazed at one another;
Their faces *will be like* flames.
9 Behold, the day of the LORD comes,
Cruel, with both wrath and fierce anger,
To lay the land desolate;
And He will destroy its sinners from it.
10 For the stars of heaven and their constellations
Will not give their light;
The sun will be darkened in its going forth,
And the moon will not cause its light to shine.

11 "I will punish the world for *its* evil,
And the wicked for their iniquity;
I will halt the arrogance of the proud,
And will lay low the haughtiness of the terrible.
12 I will make a mortal more rare than fine gold,
A man more than the golden wedge of Ophir.
13 Therefore I will shake the heavens,
And the earth will move out of her place,
In the wrath of the LORD of hosts
And in the day of His fierce anger.
14 It shall be as the hunted gazelle,
And as a sheep that no man takes up;
Every man will turn to his own people,
And everyone will flee to his own land.
15 Everyone who is found will be thrust through,
And everyone who is captured will fall by the sword.
16 Their children also will be dashed to pieces before their eyes;
Their houses will be plundered
And their wives ravished.

17 "Behold, I will stir up the Medes against them,
Who will not regard silver;
And *as for* gold, they will not delight in it.
18 Also *their* bows will dash the young men to pieces,
And they will have no pity on the fruit of the womb;
Their eye will not spare children.
19 And Babylon, the glory of kingdoms,
The beauty of the Chaldeans' pride,
Will be as when God overthrew Sodom and Gomorrah.
20 It will never be inhabited,
Nor will it be settled from generation to generation;
Nor will the Arabian pitch tents there,
Nor will the shepherds make their sheepfolds there.
21 But wild beasts of the desert will lie there,
And their houses will be full of owls;
Ostriches will dwell there,
And wild goats will caper there.
22 The hyenas will howl in their citadels,
And jackals in their pleasant palaces.
Her time *is* near to come,
And her days will not be prolonged."

14 For the LORD will have mercy on Jacob,
and will still choose Israel, and settle them
in their own land. The strangers will be joined
with them, and they will cling to the house of
Jacob. 2Then people will take them and bring
them to their place, and the house of Israel
will possess them for servants and maids in
the land of the LORD; they will take them captive whose captives they were, and rule over
their oppressors.
3It shall come to pass in the day the LORD
gives you rest from your sorrow, and from
your fear and the hard bondage in which you
were made to serve, 4that you will take up this
proverb against the king of Babylon, and say:

"How the oppressor has ceased,
The golden city ceased!
5 The LORD has broken the staff of the wicked,
The scepter of the rulers;
6 He who struck the people in wrath with a continual stroke,
He who ruled the nations in anger,
Is persecuted *and* no one hinders.
7 The whole earth is at rest *and* quiet;
They break forth into singing.
8 Indeed the cypress trees rejoice over you,
And the cedars of Lebanon,
Saying, 'Since you were cut down,
No woodsman has come up against us.'

9 "Hell from beneath is excited about you,
To meet *you* at your coming;
It stirs up the dead for you,
All the chief ones of the earth;
It has raised up from their thrones

All the kings of the nations.
10 They all shall speak and say to you:
'Have you also become as weak as we?
Have you become like us?
11 Your pomp is brought down to Sheol,
And the sound of your stringed
instruments;
The maggot is spread under you,
And worms cover you.'

12 "How you are fallen from heaven,
O Lucifer, son of the morning!
How you are cut down to the ground,
You who weakened the nations!
13 For you have said in your heart:
'I will ascend into heaven,
I will exalt my throne above the stars
of God;
I will also sit on the mount of the
congregation
On the farthest sides of the north;
14 I will ascend above the heights of the
clouds,
I will be like the Most High.'

14:12–14 fallen from heaven,...be like the Most High. Jesus' use of v. 12 to describe Satan's fall (Luke 10:18; Rev. 12:8–10) has led many to see more than a reference to the king of Babylon. Just as the Lord addressed Satan in His words to the serpent (Gen. 3:14,15), this inspired dirge speaks to the king of Babylon and to the devil who energized him. See Ezekiel 28:12–17 for similar language to the king of Tyre and Satan behind him.

14:12 heaven. The scene suddenly shifts from the underworld to heaven to emphasize the unbridled pride of the king and Satan energizing him. **Lucifer, son of the morning.** Literally, "Lucifer" means "shining one," but translators have often rendered it "morning star." Tradition of the time saw the stars as representing gods battling among themselves for places of preeminence.

14:13,14 I will. Five "I wills" emphasize the arrogance of the king of Babylon and of Satan from whom he takes his cue.

15 Yet you shall be brought down to
Sheol,
To the lowest depths of the Pit.
16 "Those who see you will gaze at you,
And consider you, *saying:*
'*Is* this the man who made the earth
tremble,
Who shook kingdoms,
17 Who made the world as a wilderness
And destroyed its cities,
Who did not open the house of his
prisoners?'

18 "All the kings of the nations,
All of them, sleep in glory,
Everyone in his own house;
19 But you are cast out of your grave
Like an abominable branch,
Like the garment of those who are slain,
Thrust through with a sword,
Who go down to the stones of the pit,
Like a corpse trodden underfoot.
20 You will not be joined with them in
burial,
Because you have destroyed your land
And slain your people.
The brood of evildoers shall never be
named.
21 Prepare slaughter for his children
Because of the iniquity of their fathers,
Lest they rise up and possess the land,
And fill the face of the world with cities."

22 "For I will rise up against them," says
the LORD of hosts,
"And cut off from Babylon the name
and remnant,
And offspring and posterity," says the
LORD.
23 "I will also make it a possession for the
porcupine,
And marshes of muddy water;
I will sweep it with the broom of
destruction," says the LORD of
hosts.

24 The LORD of hosts has sworn, saying,
"Surely, as I have thought, so it shall
come to pass,
And as I have purposed, *so* it shall
stand:
25 That I will break the Assyrian in My
land,
And on My mountains tread him
underfoot.
Then his yoke shall be removed from
them,
And his burden removed from their
shoulders.
26 This *is* the purpose that is purposed
against the whole earth,
And this *is* the hand that is stretched
out over all the nations.
27 For the LORD of hosts has purposed,
And who will annul *it?*
His hand *is* stretched out,
And who will turn it back?"

28This is the burden which came in the year that King Ahaz died.

29 "Do not rejoice, all you of Philistia,
Because the rod that struck you
is broken;
For out of the serpent's roots will come
forth a viper,
And its offspring *will be* a fiery flying
serpent.
30 The firstborn of the poor will feed,
And the needy will lie down in safety;
I will kill your roots with famine,
And it will slay your remnant.
31 Wail, O gate! Cry, O city!
All you of Philistia *are* dissolved;
For smoke will come from the north,
And no one *will be* alone in his appointed times."

32 What will they answer the messengers
of the nation?
That the LORD has founded Zion,
And the poor of His people shall take
refuge in it.

Psalm 106:19–23

19 They made a calf in Horeb,
And worshiped the molded image.
20 Thus they changed their glory
Into the image of an ox that eats grass.
21 They forgot God their Savior,
Who had done great things in Egypt,
22 Wondrous works in the land of Ham,
Awesome things by the Red Sea.
23 Therefore He said that He would
destroy them,
Had not Moses His chosen one stood
before Him in the breach,
To turn away His wrath, lest He
destroy *them.*

Proverbs 25:6–7

6 Do not exalt yourself in the presence of
the king,
And do not stand in the place of the
great;
7 For *it is* better that he say to you,
"Come up here,"

25:6,7 In the royal court, as in all of life, self-seeking and pride bring one down. Do not intrude into such a place, for the elevating of the humble is honorable, but the humbling of the proud is disgraceful (Luke 14:8–10; James 4:7–10).

Than that you should be put lower in
the presence of the prince,
Whom your eyes have seen.

2 Corinthians 3:1–18

3 Do we begin again to commend ourselves?
Or do we need, as some others, epistles of
commendation to you or *letters* of commendation from you? 2You are our epistle written in
our hearts, known and read by all men; 3clear-
ly you are an epistle of Christ, ministered by
us, written not with ink but by the Spirit of the
living God, not on tablets of stone but on
tablets of flesh, *that is,* of the heart.
4And we have such trust through Christ
toward God. 5Not that we are sufficient of ourselves to think of anything as *being* from ourselves, but our sufficiency *is* from God, 6who
also made us sufficient as ministers of the new
covenant, not of the letter but of the Spirit; for
the letter kills, but the Spirit gives life.
7But if the ministry of death, written *and*
engraved on stones, was glorious, so that the
children of Israel could not look steadily at the
face of Moses because of the glory of his

3:18 we all. Not just Moses, or prophets, apostles, and preachers, but all believers. **with unveiled face.** Believers in the New Covenant have nothing obstructing their vision of Christ and His glory as revealed in the Scripture. **beholding as in a mirror.** Paul's emphasis here is not so much on the reflective capabilities of the mirror as it is on the intimacy of it. A person can bring a mirror right up to his face and get an unobstructed view. Mirrors in Paul's day were polished metal, and thus offered a far from perfect reflection. Though the vision is unobstructed and intimate, believers do not see a perfect representation of God's glory now, but will one day (1 Cor. 13:12). **being transformed.** A continual, progressive transformation. **into the same image.** As they gaze at the glory of the Lord, believers are continually being transformed into Christlikeness. The ultimate goal of the believer is to be like Christ (Rom. 8:29; Phil. 3:12–14; 1 John 3:2), and by continually focusing on Him the Spirit transforms the believer more and more into His image. **from glory to glory.** From one level of glory to another level of glory—from one level of manifesting Christ to another. This verse describes progressive sanctification. The more believers grow in their knowledge of Christ, the more He is revealed in their lives (Phil. 3:12–14).

countenance, which *glory* was passing away,
[8]how will the ministry of the Spirit not be more
glorious? [9]For if the ministry of condemnation
had glory, the ministry of righteousness
exceeds much more in glory. [10]For even what
was made glorious had no glory in this
respect, because of the glory that excels. [11]For
if what is passing away *was* glorious, what
remains *is* much more glorious.
[12]Therefore, since we have such hope, we
use great boldness of speech— [13]unlike Moses, *who* put a veil over his face so that the
children of Israel could not look steadily at the
end of what was passing away. [14]But their
minds were blinded. For until this day the
same veil remains unlifted in the reading of
the Old Testament, because the *veil* is taken
away in Christ. [15]But even to this day, when
Moses is read, a veil lies on their heart. [16]Nev-
ertheless when one turns to the Lord, the veil
is taken away. [17]Now the Lord is the Spirit; and
where the Spirit of the Lord *is,* there *is* liberty.
[18]But we all, with unveiled face, beholding as in
a mirror the glory of the Lord, are being transformed into the same image from glory to
glory, just as by the Spirit of the Lord.

DAY 11: What credentials of his apostleship did Paul give to the Corinthians?

Because Paul did not want to allow the false teachers to accuse him of being proud, he began his defense in 2 Corinthians 3:1 by posing two questions rather than making any overt claims. "Do we begin again to commend ourselves?" The Greek word for "commend" means "to introduce." Thus Paul was asking the Corinthians if he needed to reintroduce himself, as if they had never met, and prove himself once more. The form of the question demanded a negative answer. "Or do we need, as some others,…letters of commendation from you?" The false teachers also accused Paul of not possessing the appropriate documents to prove his legitimacy. Such letters were often used to introduce and authenticate someone to the first-century churches (1 Cor. 16:3,10,11). The false teachers undoubtedly arrived in Corinth with such letters, which they may have forged (Acts 15:1,5) or obtained under false pretenses from prominent members of the Jerusalem church. Paul's point was that he did not need secondhand testimony when the Corinthians had firsthand proof of his sincere and godly character, as well as the truth of his message that regenerated them.

"You are our epistle written in our hearts" (v. 2). An affirmation of Paul's affection for the believers in Corinth—he held them close to his heart. "Known and read by all men." The transformed lives of the Corinthians were Paul's most eloquent testimonial, better than any secondhand letter. Their changed lives were like an open letter that could be seen and read by all men as a testimony to Paul's faithfulness and the truth of his message.

"You are an epistle of Christ" (v. 3). The false teachers did not have a letter of commendation signed by Christ, but Paul had the Corinthian believers' changed lives as proof that Christ had transformed them. "Written not with ink." Paul's letter was no human document written with ink that can fade. It was a living one. "Spirit of the living God." Paul's letter was alive, written by Christ's divine, supernatural power through the transforming work of the Holy Spirit (1 Cor. 2:4,5; 1 Thess. 1:5). "Tablets of stone." A reference to the Ten Commandments. "Tablets of flesh…of the heart." More than just writing His Law on stone, God was writing His Law on the hearts of those people He transformed. The false teachers claimed external adherence to the Mosaic Law as the basis of salvation, but the transformed lives of the Corinthians proved that salvation was an internal change wrought by God in the heart.

SEPTEMBER 12

Isaiah 15:1–16:14

15 The burden against Moab.

Because in the night Ar of Moab is laid
    waste
And destroyed,
Because in the night Kir of Moab is
    laid waste
And destroyed,
2 He has gone up to the temple and Dibon,
To the high places to weep.
Moab will wail over Nebo and over
    Medeba;
On all their heads *will be* baldness,
And every beard cut off.
3 In their streets they will clothe
    themselves with sackcloth;
On the tops of their houses
And in their streets
Everyone will wail, weeping bitterly.
4 Heshbon and Elealeh will cry out,
Their voice shall be heard as far as
    Jahaz;

Therefore the armed soldiers of Moab
will cry out;
His life will be burdensome to him.

5 "My heart will cry out for Moab;
His fugitives *shall flee* to Zoar,
Like a three-year-old heifer.
For by the Ascent of Luhith
They will go up with weeping;
For in the way of Horonaim
They will raise up a cry of destruction,
6 For the waters of Nimrim will be
desolate,
For the green grass has withered
away;
The grass fails, there is nothing green.
7 Therefore the abundance they have
gained,
And what they have laid up,
They will carry away to the Brook of
the Willows.
8 For the cry has gone all around the
borders of Moab,
Its wailing to Eglaim
And its wailing to Beer Elim.
9 For the waters of Dimon will be full of
blood;
Because I will bring more upon Dimon,
Lions upon him who escapes from
Moab,
And on the remnant of the land."

16 Send the lamb to the ruler
of the land,
From Sela to the wilderness,
To the mount of the daughter
of Zion.
2 For it shall be as a wandering bird
thrown out of the nest;
So shall be the daughters of Moab at
the fords of the Arnon.
3 "Take counsel, execute judgment;
Make your shadow like the night
in the middle of the day;
Hide the outcasts,
Do not betray him who escapes.
4 Let My outcasts dwell with you,
O Moab;
Be a shelter to them from the face of
the spoiler.
For the extortioner is at an end,
Devastation ceases,
The oppressors are consumed out of
the land.
5 In mercy the throne will be
established;
And One will sit on it in truth, in the
tabernacle of David,
Judging and seeking justice and
hastening righteousness."

6 We have heard of the pride of Moab—
He is very proud—
Of his haughtiness and his pride and
his wrath;
But his lies *shall* not *be* so.
7 Therefore Moab shall wail for Moab;
Everyone shall wail.
For the foundations of Kir Hareseth
you shall mourn;
Surely *they are* stricken.

8 For the fields of Heshbon languish,
And the vine of Sibmah;
The lords of the nations have broken
down its choice plants,
Which have reached to Jazer
And wandered through the wilderness.
Her branches are stretched out,
They are gone over the sea.
9 Therefore I will bewail the vine of
Sibmah,
With the weeping of Jazer;
I will drench you with my tears,
O Heshbon and Elealeh;
For battle cries have fallen
Over your summer fruits and your
harvest.

16:9 I will bewail. Isaiah displayed genuine emotion over the destruction of so rich an agricultural resource. This reflected the Lord's response, too.

10 Gladness is taken away,
And joy from the plentiful field;
In the vineyards there will be no
singing,
Nor will there be shouting;
No treaders will tread out wine in the
presses;
I have made their shouting cease.
11 Therefore my heart shall resound like
a harp for Moab,
And my inner being for Kir Heres.

12 And it shall come to pass,
When it is seen that Moab is weary on
the high place,
That he will come to his sanctuary
to pray;
But he will not prevail.

13 This *is* the word which the LORD has spoken concerning Moab since that time. 14 But
now the LORD has spoken, saying, "Within
three years, as the years of a hired man, the

glory of Moab will be despised with all that great multitude, and the remnant *will be* very small *and* feeble."

Psalm 106:24–31

24 Then they despised the pleasant land;
They did not believe His word,
25 But complained in their tents,
And did not heed the voice of the LORD.
26 Therefore He raised His hand *in an oath* against them,
To overthrow them in the wilderness,
27 To overthrow their descendants among the nations,
And to scatter them in the lands.

28 They joined themselves also to Baal of Peor,
And ate sacrifices made to the dead.
29 Thus they provoked *Him* to anger with their deeds,
And the plague broke out among them.
30 Then Phinehas stood up and intervened,
And the plague was stopped.
31 And that was accounted to him for righteousness
To all generations forevermore.

Proverbs 25:8–10

8 Do not go hastily to court;
For what will you do in the end,
When your neighbor has put you to shame?

106:28 Baal of Peor. Refers to Baal, a god of the Moabites, whose worship occurred at the location of the mountain called Peor (Num. 23:28). **sacrifices made to the dead.** This most likely refers to sacrifices made to lifeless idols (1 Thess. 1:9). Israel should have been worshiping "the living God" (Deut. 5:26; 1 Sam. 17:26,36; Pss. 42:2; 84:2; Jer. 10:3–10; Dan. 6:20,26).

106:31 accounted to him for righteousness. This was a just and rewardable action, evidencing faith in God. As with Abraham (Gen. 15:6 and Rom. 4:3; Gal. 3:6; James 2:23), so it was also with Phinehas. The everlasting covenant of perpetual priesthood through Aaron, from the house of Levi, was first made by God in Leviticus 24:8,9. This covenant was reaffirmed in Numbers 18:8,19. In this text, the covenant is further specified to be through the line of faithful Phinehas.

9 Debate your case with your neighbor,
And do not disclose the secret to another;
10 Lest he who hears *it* expose your shame,
And your reputation be ruined.

2 Corinthians 4:1–18

4 Therefore, since we have this ministry, as
we have received mercy, we do not lose
heart. 2But we have renounced the hidden
things of shame, not walking in craftiness nor
handling the word of God deceitfully, but by
manifestation of the truth commending ourselves to every man's conscience in the sight
of God. 3But even if our gospel is veiled, it is
veiled to those who are perishing, 4whose
minds the god of this age has blinded, who do
not believe, lest the light of the gospel of the
glory of Christ, who is the image of God,
should shine on them. 5For we do not preach
ourselves, but Christ Jesus the Lord, and ourselves your bondservants for Jesus' sake. 6For
it is the God who commanded light to shine
out of darkness, who has shone in our hearts
to *give* the light of the knowledge of the glory
of God in the face of Jesus Christ.
7But we have this treasure in earthen vessels, that the excellence of the power may be
of God and not of us. 8*We are* hard-pressed on
every side, yet not crushed; *we are* perplexed,
but not in despair; 9persecuted, but not forsaken; struck down, but not destroyed— 10al-
ways carrying about in the body the dying of
the Lord Jesus, that the life of Jesus also may
be manifested in our body. 11For we who live
are always delivered to death for Jesus' sake,
that the life of Jesus also may be manifested in
our mortal flesh. 12So then death is working in
us, but life in you.
13And since we have the same spirit of faith,
according to what is written, *"I believed and
therefore I spoke,"* we also believe and therefore speak, 14knowing that He who raised up
the Lord Jesus will also raise us up with Jesus,
and will present *us* with you. 15For all things
are for your sakes, that grace, having spread
through the many, may cause thanksgiving to
abound to the glory of God.
16Therefore we do not lose heart. Even though
our outward man is perishing, yet the inward
man is being renewed day by day. 17For our light
affliction, which is but for a moment, is working
for us a far more exceeding *and* eternal weight of
glory, 18while we do not look at the things which
are seen, but at the things which are not seen.
For the things which are seen *are* temporary,
but the things which are not seen *are* eternal.

4:16 our outward man is perishing. The physical body is in the process of decay and will eventually die. On the surface Paul was referring to the normal aging process, but with the added emphasis that his lifestyle sped up that process. While not an old man, Paul wore himself out in ministry, both in the effort and pace he maintained, plus the number of beatings and attacks he absorbed from his enemies (6:4–10; 11:23–27). **inward *man*.** The soul of every believer i.e., the new creation—the eternal part of the believer (Eph. 4:24; Col. 3:10). **being renewed.** The growth and maturing process of the believer is constantly occurring. While the physical body is decaying, the inner self of the believer continues to grow and mature into Christlikeness (Eph. 3:16–20).

4:17 our light affliction...for a moment. The Greek word for "light" means "a weightless trifle" and "affliction" refers to intense pressure. From a human perspective, Paul's own testimony lists a seemingly unbearable litany of sufferings and persecutions he endured throughout his life (11:23–33), yet he viewed them as weightless and lasting for only a brief moment. **eternal weight of glory.** The Greek word for "weight" refers to a heavy mass. For Paul, the future glory he would experience with the Lord far outweighed any suffering he experienced in this world (Rom. 8:17,18; 1 Pet. 1:6,7).

DAY 12: Why do people not respond to the gospel?

Paul said "if our gospel is veiled, it is veiled to those who are perishing" (2 Cor. 4:3). The false teachers accused Paul of preaching an antiquated message. So Paul showed that the problem was not with the message or the messenger, but with the hearers headed for hell (1 Cor. 2:14). The preacher cannot persuade people to believe; only God can do that.

"Whose minds the god of this age has blinded" (v. 4). Satan (Matt. 4:8; John 12:31; 14:30; 16:11; Eph. 2:2; 2 Tim. 2:26; 1 John 5:19) is the god of this age—the current world mind-set expressed by the ideals, opinions, goals, hopes, and views of the majority of people. It encompasses the world's philosophies, education, and commerce. Satan blinds men to God's truth through the world system he has created. Without a godly influence, man left to himself will follow that system, which panders to the depravity of unbelievers and deepens their moral darkness (Matt. 13:19). Ultimately, it is God who allows such blindness (John 12:40).

"For we do not preach ourselves, but Christ Jesus" (v. 5). The false teachers accused Paul of preaching for his own benefit, yet they were the ones guilty of doing so. In contrast, Paul was always humble (12:5,9; 1 Cor. 2:3); he never promoted himself, but always preached Christ Jesus as Lord (1 Cor. 2:2). "For it is the God who commanded light to shine out of darkness, who has shone in our hearts to give the light of the knowledge of the glory of God" (v. 6). A direct reference to God as Creator, who commanded physical light into existence (Gen. 1:3). The same God who created physical light in the universe is the same God who must create supernatural light in the soul and usher believers from the kingdom of darkness to His kingdom of light (Col. 1:13). That means to know that Christ is God incarnate. To be saved, one must understand that the glory of God shone in Jesus Christ.

SEPTEMBER 13

Isaiah 17:1–18:7

17 The burden against Damascus.

"Behold, Damascus will cease from
being a city,
And it will be a ruinous heap.
2 The cities of Aroer *are* forsaken;
They will be for flocks
Which lie down, and no one will make
them afraid.
3 The fortress also will cease from
Ephraim,
The kingdom from Damascus,
And the remnant of Syria;
They will be as the glory of the
children of Israel,"
Says the LORD of hosts.
4 "In that day it shall come to pass
That the glory of Jacob will wane,
And the fatness of his flesh
grow lean.
5 It shall be as when the harvester gathers
the grain,
And reaps the heads with his arm;

It shall be as he who gathers heads
of grain
In the Valley of Rephaim.
6 Yet gleaning grapes will be left in it,
Like the shaking of an olive tree,
Two *or* three olives at the top of the
uppermost bough,
Four *or* five in its most fruitful
branches,"
Says the LORD God of Israel.

7 In that day a man will look to his
Maker,
And his eyes will have respect for the
Holy One of Israel.
8 He will not look to the altars,
The work of his hands;
He will not respect what his fingers
have made,
Nor the wooden images nor the
incense altars.

9 In that day his strong cities will be as a
forsaken bough
And an uppermost branch,
Which they left because of the children
of Israel;
And there will be desolation.

10 Because you have forgotten the God of
your salvation,
And have not been mindful of the Rock
of your stronghold,
Therefore you will plant pleasant plants
And set out foreign seedlings;
11 In the day you will make your plant to
grow,
And in the morning you will make your
seed to flourish;
But the harvest *will be* a heap of ruins
In the day of grief and desperate
sorrow.

12 Woe to the multitude of many people
Who make a noise like the roar of the
seas,
And to the rushing of nations
That make a rushing like the rushing
of mighty waters!
13 The nations will rush like the rushing
of many waters;
But *God* will rebuke them and they will
flee far away,
And be chased like the chaff of the
mountains before the wind,
Like a rolling thing before the
whirlwind.
14 Then behold, at eventide, trouble!
And before the morning, he *is* no
more.
This *is* the portion of those who
plunder us,
And the lot of those who rob us.

18 Woe to the land shadowed
with buzzing wings,
Which *is* beyond the rivers of Ethiopia,
2 Which sends ambassadors by sea,
Even in vessels of reed on the waters,
saying,
"Go, swift messengers, to a nation tall
and smooth *of skin,*
To a people terrible from their
beginning onward,
A nation powerful and treading down,
Whose land the rivers divide."

3 All inhabitants of the world and
dwellers on the earth:
When he lifts up a banner on the
mountains, you see *it;*
And when he blows a trumpet, you
hear *it.*
4 For so the LORD said to me,
"I will take My rest,
And I will look from My dwelling place
Like clear heat in sunshine,
Like a cloud of dew in the heat of
harvest."

18:4 I will take My rest. The Lord will wait patiently until the appropriate time to intervene in human affairs, until sunshine and dew have built to an opportune climactic moment.

5 For before the harvest, when the bud
is perfect
And the sour grape is ripening in the
flower,
He will both cut off the sprigs with
pruning hooks
And take away *and* cut down the
branches.
6 They will be left together for the
mountain birds of prey
And for the beasts of the earth;
The birds of prey will summer on them,
And all the beasts of the earth will
winter on them.
7 In that time a present will be brought to
the LORD of hosts
From a people tall and smooth *of skin,*
And from a people terrible from their
beginning onward,

A nation powerful and treading down,
Whose land the rivers divide—
To the place of the name of the LORD of
hosts,
To Mount Zion.

Psalm 106:32–39

32 They angered *Him* also at the waters of
strife,
So that it went ill with Moses on
account of them;
33 Because they rebelled against His
Spirit,
So that he spoke rashly with his lips.
34 They did not destroy the peoples,
Concerning whom the LORD had
commanded them,
35 But they mingled with the Gentiles
And learned their works;
36 They served their idols,
Which became a snare to them.
37 They even sacrificed their sons
And their daughters to demons,
38 And shed innocent blood,
The blood of their sons and daughters,
Whom they sacrificed to the idols of
Canaan;
And the land was polluted with blood.
39 Thus they were defiled by their own
works,
And played the harlot by their own
deeds.

Proverbs 25:11–12

11 A word fitly spoken *is like* apples of gold
In settings of silver.
12 *Like* an earring of gold and an
ornament of fine gold
Is a wise rebuker to an obedient ear.

2 Corinthians 5:1–21

5 For we know that if our earthly house, *this*
tent, is destroyed, we have a building from
God, a house not made with hands, eternal in
the heavens. 2 For in this we groan, earnestly
desiring to be clothed with our habitation
which is from heaven, 3 if indeed, having been
clothed, we shall not be found naked. 4 For we
who are in *this* tent groan, being burdened,
not because we want to be unclothed, but further clothed, that mortality may be swallowed
up by life. 5 Now He who has prepared us for
this very thing *is* God, who also has given us
the Spirit as a guarantee.
6 So *we are* always confident, knowing that
while we are at home in the body we are
absent from the Lord. 7 For we walk by faith,
not by sight. 8 We are confident, yes, well
pleased rather to be absent from the body and
to be present with the Lord.
9 Therefore we make it our aim, whether
present or absent, to be well pleasing to Him.
10 For we must all appear before the judgment
seat of Christ, that each one may receive the
things *done* in the body, according to what he
has done, whether good or bad. 11 Knowing,
therefore, the terror of the Lord, we persuade
men; but we are well known to God, and I also
trust are well known in your consciences.
12 For we do not commend ourselves again to
you, but give you opportunity to boast on our
behalf, that you may have *an answer* for those
who boast in appearance and not in heart.
13 For if we are beside ourselves, *it is* for God;
or if we are of sound mind, *it is* for you. 14 For
the love of Christ compels us, because we
judge thus: that if One died for all, then all
died; 15 and He died for all, that those who live
should live no longer for themselves, but for
Him who died for them and rose again.

5:10 This describes the believer's deepest motivation and highest aim in pleasing God—the realization that every Christian is inevitably and ultimately accountable to Him. **the judgment seat of Christ.** "Judgment seat" metaphorically refers to the place where the Lord will sit to evaluate believers' lives for the purpose of giving them eternal rewards. It was an elevated platform where victorious athletes (e.g., during the Olympics) went to receive their crowns. The term is also used in the New Testament to refer to the place of judging, as when Jesus stood before Pontius Pilate (Matt. 27:19; John 19:13), but here the reference is definitely from the athletic analogy. Corinth had such a platform where both athletic rewards and legal justice were dispensed (Acts 18:12–16), so the Corinthians understood Paul's reference. **the things *done* in the body.** Actions which happened during the believer's time of earthly ministry. This does not include sins, since their judgment took place at the Cross (Eph 1:7). Paul was referring to all those activities believers do during their lifetimes, which relate to their eternal reward and praise from God. What Christians do in their temporal bodies will, in His eyes, have an impact for eternity (1 Cor. 4:3–5; Rom. 12:1,2: Rev. 22:12). **whether good or bad.** These Greek terms do not refer to moral good and moral evil. Matters of sin have been completely dealt with by the death of the Savior. Rather, Paul was comparing worthwhile, eternally valuable activities with useless ones.

[16]Therefore, from now on, we regard no one according to the flesh. Even though we have known Christ according to the flesh, yet now we know *Him thus* no longer. [17]Therefore, if anyone *is* in Christ, *he is* a new creation; old things have passed away; behold, all things have become new. [18]Now all things *are* of God, who has reconciled us to Himself through Jesus Christ, and has given us the ministry of reconciliation, [19]that is, that God was in Christ reconciling the world to Himself, not imputing their trespasses to them, and has committed to us the word of reconciliation.

5:19 God was in Christ. God by His own will and design used His Son, the only acceptable and perfect sacrifice, as the means to reconcile sinners to Himself. **reconciling the world.** God initiates the change in the sinner's status in that He brings him from a position of alienation to a state of forgiveness and right relationship with Himself. This again is the essence of the gospel. The word "world" should not be interpreted in any universalistic sense, which would say that everyone will be saved or even potentially reconciled. "World" refers rather to the entire sphere of mankind or humanity (Titus 2:11; 3:4), the category of beings to whom God offers reconciliation—people from every ethnic group, without distinction. The intrinsic merit of Christ's reconciling death is infinite and the offer is unlimited. However, actual atonement was made only for those who believe (John 10:11,15; 17:9; Acts 13:48; 20:28; Rom. 8:32,33; Eph. 5:25).

[20]Now then, we are ambassadors for Christ, as though God were pleading through us: we implore *you* on Christ's behalf, be reconciled to God. [21]For He made Him who knew no sin *to be* sin for us, that we might become the righteousness of God in Him.

5:21 Here Paul summarized the heart of the gospel, explaining how sinners can be reconciled to God through Jesus Christ. These 15 Greek words express the doctrines of imputation and substitution like no other single verse. **who knew no sin.** Jesus Christ, the sinless Son of God (Gal. 4:4,5; Luke 23:4,14,22,47; John 8:46; Heb. 4:15; 7:26; 1 Pet. 1:19; 2:22–24; 3:18; Rev. 5:2–10). **sin for us.** God the Father, using the principle of imputation, treated Christ as if He were a sinner though He was not, and had Him die as a substitute to pay the penalty for the sins of those who believe in Him (Is. 53:4–6; Gal. 3:10–13; 1 Pet. 2:24). On the cross, He did not become a sinner (as some suggest), but remained as holy as ever. He was treated as if He were guilty of all the sins ever committed by all who would ever believe, though He committed none. The wrath of God was exhausted on Him and the just requirement of God's law met for those for whom He died. **the righteousness of God.** Another reference to justification and imputation. The righteousness that is credited to the believer's account is the righteousness of Jesus Christ, God's Son. As Christ was not a sinner, but was treated as if He were, so believers who have not yet been made righteous (until glorification) are treated as if they were righteous.

DAY 13: What does Paul mean when he writes about being "in Christ" and someone being a "new creation" (2 Cor. 5:17)?

Paul uses the term "in Christ" when he writes about various aspects of our relationship with Jesus Christ as Lord and Savior. These two words comprise a brief but profound statement of the inexhaustible significance of the believer's redemption (salvation), which includes the following:

1. The believer's security in Christ, who bore in His body God's judgment against sin.
2. The believer's acceptance in (through) Christ with whom God alone is well pleased.
3. The believer's future assurance in Him who is the resurrection to eternal life and the sole guarantor of the believer's inheritance in heaven.
4. The believer's participation in the divine nature of Christ, the everlasting Word (2 Pet. 1:4).

All of the changes that Christ brings to the believer's life result in a state that can be rightly called "a new creation." The terms describe something created at a qualitatively new level of excellence. They parallel other biblical concepts like regeneration and new birth (John 3:3; Eph. 2:1–3; Titus 3:5; 1 Pet. 1:23; 1 John 2:29; 3:9; 5:4). The expression includes the Christian's forgiveness of sins paid for in Christ's substitutionary death (Gal. 6:15; Eph. 4:24).

SEPTEMBER 14

Isaiah 19:1–20:6

19 The burden against Egypt.

Behold, the LORD rides on a swift cloud,
And will come into Egypt;
The idols of Egypt will totter at His presence,
And the heart of Egypt will melt in its midst.

2 "I will set Egyptians against Egyptians;
Everyone will fight against his brother,
And everyone against his neighbor,
City against city, kingdom against kingdom.
3 The spirit of Egypt will fail in its midst;
I will destroy their counsel,
And they will consult the idols and the charmers,
The mediums and the sorcerers.
4 And the Egyptians I will give
Into the hand of a cruel master,
And a fierce king will rule over them,"
Says the Lord, the LORD of hosts.

5 The waters will fail from the sea,
And the river will be wasted and dried up.
6 The rivers will turn foul;
The brooks of defense will be emptied and dried up;
The reeds and rushes will wither.
7 The papyrus reeds by the River, by the mouth of the River,
And everything sown by the River,
Will wither, be driven away, and be no more.
8 The fishermen also will mourn;
All those will lament who cast hooks into the River,
And they will languish who spread nets on the waters.
9 Moreover those who work in fine flax
And those who weave fine fabric will be ashamed;
10 And its foundations will be broken.
All who make wages *will be* troubled of soul.

11 Surely the princes of Zoan *are* fools;
Pharaoh's wise counselors give foolish counsel.
How do you say to Pharaoh, "I *am* the son of the wise,
The son of ancient kings?"
12 Where *are* they?
Where are your wise men?
Let them tell you now,
And let them know what the LORD of hosts has purposed against Egypt.
13 The princes of Zoan have become fools;
The princes of Noph are deceived;
They have also deluded Egypt,
Those who are the mainstay of its tribes.
14 The LORD has mingled a perverse spirit in her midst;
And they have caused Egypt to err in all her work,
As a drunken man staggers in his vomit.
15 Neither will there be *any* work for Egypt,
Which the head or tail,
Palm branch or bulrush, may do.

16 In that day Egypt will be like women, and will be afraid and fear because of the waving of the hand of the LORD of hosts, which He waves over it. 17 And the land of Judah will be a terror to Egypt; everyone who makes mention of it will be afraid in himself, because of the counsel of the LORD of hosts which He has determined against it.

18 In that day five cities in the land of Egypt will speak the language of Canaan and swear by the LORD of hosts; one will be called the City of Destruction.

19 In that day there will be an altar to the LORD in the midst of the land of Egypt, and a pillar to the LORD at its border. 20 And it will be for a sign and for a witness to the LORD of hosts in the land of Egypt; for they will cry to the LORD because of the oppressors, and He will send them a Savior and a Mighty One, and He will deliver them. 21 Then the LORD will be known to Egypt, and the Egyptians will know the LORD in that day, and will make sacrifice

19:18 five cities. Humanly speaking, the chances of even one Egyptian city turning to the Lord were remote, but divinely speaking, there will be 5 times that many. **language of Canaan.** Egypt is to speak the language of Judah. Not only are they to fear Judah (v. 17), they are also to convert to Judah's form of worship. **swear by the LORD of hosts.** Egypt will "in that day" turn to God in a dramatic way. This prophecy anticipates the personal reign of the Davidic King on earth.

and offering; yes, they will make a vow to the
LORD and perform *it.* 22And the LORD will strike
Egypt, He will strike and heal *it;* they will
return to the LORD, and He will be entreated
by them and heal them.
23In that day there will be a highway from
Egypt to Assyria, and the Assyrian will come
into Egypt and the Egyptian into Assyria, and
the Egyptians will serve with the Assyrians.
24In that day Israel will be one of three with
Egypt and Assyria—a blessing in the midst of the
land, 25whom the LORD of hosts shall bless, saying, "Blessed *is* Egypt My people, and Assyria the
work of My hands, and Israel My inheritance."

19:25 My people,...the work of My hands. Elsewhere Scripture uses these epithets to speak only of Israel (10:24; 29:23; 43:6,7; 45:11; 60:21; 64:8; Pss. 100:3; 110:3; 138:8; Jer. 11:4; Hos 1:10; 2:23). In the future kingdom, Israel is to be God's instrument for drawing other nations into His fold.

20 In the year that Tartan came to
Ashdod, when Sargon the king of Assyria sent him, and he fought against Ashdod
and took it, 2at the same time the LORD spoke
by Isaiah the son of Amoz, saying, "Go, and
remove the sackcloth from your body, and
take your sandals off your feet." And he did so,
walking naked and barefoot.
3Then the LORD said, "Just as My servant
Isaiah has walked naked and barefoot three
years *for* a sign and a wonder against Egypt and
Ethiopia, 4so shall the king of Assyria lead away
the Egyptians as prisoners and the Ethiopians
as captives, young and old, naked and barefoot,
with their buttocks uncovered, to the shame of
Egypt. 5Then they shall be afraid and ashamed
of Ethiopia their expectation and Egypt their
glory. 6And the inhabitant of this territory will
say in that day, 'Surely such *is* our expectation,
wherever we flee for help to be delivered from
the king of Assyria; and how shall we escape?'"

Psalm 106:40–48

40 Therefore the wrath of the LORD was
kindled against His people,
So that He abhorred His own
inheritance.
41 And He gave them into the hand
of the Gentiles,
And those who hated them ruled over
them.
42 Their enemies also oppressed them,
And they were brought into subjection
under their hand.
43 Many times He delivered them;
But they rebelled in their counsel,
And were brought low for their
iniquity.
44 Nevertheless He regarded their
affliction,
When He heard their cry;
45 And for their sake He remembered His
covenant,
And relented according to the
multitude of His mercies.
46 He also made them to be pitied
By all those who carried them away
captive.

47 Save us, O LORD our God,
And gather us from among the Gentiles,
To give thanks to Your holy name,
To triumph in Your praise.

48 Blessed *be* the LORD God of Israel
From everlasting to everlasting!
And let all the people say, "Amen!"
Praise the LORD!

Proverbs 25:13

13 Like the cold of snow in time of harvest
Is a faithful messenger to those who
send him,
For he refreshes the soul of his masters.

2 Corinthians 6:1–18

6 We then, *as* workers together *with Him*
also plead with *you* not to receive the
grace of God in vain. 2For He says:

"In an acceptable time I have heard you,
And in the day of salvation I have
helped you."

Behold, now *is* the accepted time; behold, now
is the day of salvation.
3We give no offense in anything, that our
ministry may not be blamed. 4But in all *things*
we commend ourselves as ministers of God: in
much patience, in tribulations, in needs, in distresses, 5in stripes, in imprisonments, in
tumults, in labors, in sleeplessness, in fastings;
6by purity, by knowledge, by longsuffering, by
kindness, by the Holy Spirit, by sincere love,
7by the word of truth, by the power of God, by
the armor of righteousness on the right hand
and on the left, 8by honor and dishonor, by evil
report and good report; as deceivers, and *yet*
true; 9as unknown, and *yet* well known; as
dying, and behold we live; as chastened, and

6:2 Paul emphasized his point by quoting Isaiah 49:8. He was passionately concerned that the Corinthians adhere to the truth because it was God's time to save and they were messengers for helping to spread that message. **now *is* the day of salvation.** Paul applied Isaiah's words to the present situation. There is a time in God's economy when He listens to sinners and responds to those who are repentant—and it was and is that time (Prov. 1:20–23; Is. 55:6; Heb. 3:7,8; 4:7). However, there will also be an end to that time (Gen. 6:3; Prov. 1:24–33; John 9:4), which is why Paul's exhortation was so passionate.

6:7 by the word of truth. The Scriptures, the revealed Word of God (Col. 1:5; James 1:18). During his entire ministry, Paul never operated beyond the boundaries of the direction and guidance of divine revelation. **by the power of God.** Paul did not rely on his own strength when he ministered (1 Cor. 1:18; 2:1–5; Rom. 1:16). **by the armor of righteousness.** Paul did not fight Satan's kingdom with human resources, but with spiritual virtue (10:3–5; Eph. 6:10–18). **the right hand...the left.** Paul had both offensive tools, such as the sword of the Spirit, and defensive tools, such as the shield of faith and the helmet of salvation, at his disposal.

yet not killed; 10 as sorrowful, yet always rejoicing; as poor, yet making many rich; as having
nothing, and *yet* possessing all things.
11 O Corinthians! We have spoken openly to
you, our heart is wide open. 12 You are not
restricted by us, but you are restricted by your
own affections. 13 Now in return for the same (I
speak as to children), you also be open.
14 Do not be unequally yoked together with
unbelievers. For what fellowship has righteousness with lawlessness? And what communion
has light with darkness? 15 And what accord has
Christ with Belial? Or what part has a believer
with an unbeliever? 16 And what agreement has
the temple of God with idols? For you are the
temple of the living God. As God has said:

"I will dwell in them
And walk among them.
I will be their God,
And they shall be My people."

17 Therefore

"Come out from among them
And be separate, says the Lord.
Do not touch what is unclean,
And I will receive you."
18 *"I will be a Father to you,*
And you shall be My sons and
daughters,
Says the LORD Almighty."

DAY 14: What did Paul mean by warning believers to not become "unequally yoked together with unbelievers"?

Paul's use of this phrase in 2 Corinthians 6:14 is an illustration taken from Old Testament prohibitions to Israel regarding the work-related joining together of two different kinds of livestock (Deut. 22:10). By this analogy, Paul taught that it is not right to join together in common spiritual enterprise with unbelievers—a relationship that would be detrimental to the Christian's testimony within the body of Christ. It is impossible under such an arrangement for things to be done to God's glory (1 Cor. 5:9–13; 6:15–18; 10:7–21; James 4:4; 1 John 2:15). This was especially important for the Corinthians because of the threats from the false teachers and the surrounding pagan idolatry. But this command does not mean believers should end all associations with unbelievers. That would defy the purpose for which God saved believers and left them on earth (Matt. 28:19,20; 1 Cor. 9:19–23).

"And what accord has Christ with Belial?" (v. 15). An ancient name for Satan, the utterly worthless one (Deut. 13:13). This contrasts sharply with Jesus Christ, the worthy One with whom believers are to be in fellowship. "And what agreement has the temple of God with idols?" (v. 16). The temple of God (true Christianity) and idols (idolatrous, demonic false religions) are utterly incompatible. "You are the temple of the living God." Believers individually are spiritual houses (5:1) in which the Spirit of Christ dwells. "As God has said." Paul supported his statement by referring to a blend of Old Testament texts (Lev. 26:11,12; Jer. 24:7; 31:33; Ezek. 37:26,27; Hos. 2:2,3).

Paul drew from Isaiah 52:11 and elaborated on the command to be spiritually separated. It is not only irrational and sacrilegious but disobedient to be bound together with unbelievers. When believers are saved, they are to disengage themselves from all forms of false religion and make a clean break from all sinful habits and old idolatrous patterns. "Be separate." This is a command for believers to be as Christ was (Heb. 7:26).

SEPTEMBER 15

Isaiah 21:1–22:25

21 The burden against the Wilderness of
the Sea.

As whirlwinds in the South pass
through,
So it comes from the desert, from a
terrible land.
2 A distressing vision is declared to me;
The treacherous dealer deals
treacherously,
And the plunderer plunders.
Go up, O Elam!
Besiege, O Media!
All its sighing I have made to cease.
3 Therefore my loins are filled with pain;
Pangs have taken hold of me, like the
pangs of a woman in labor.
I was distressed when *I* heard *it;*
I was dismayed when *I* saw *it.*
4 My heart wavered, fearfulness
frightened me;
The night for which I longed He
turned into fear for me.
5 Prepare the table,
Set a watchman in the tower,
Eat and drink.
Arise, you princes,
Anoint the shield!

6 For thus has the Lord said to me:
"Go, set a watchman,
Let him declare what he sees."
7 And he saw a chariot *with* a pair of
horsemen,
A chariot of donkeys, *and* a chariot of
camels,
And he listened earnestly with great
care.
8 Then he cried, "A lion, my Lord!
I stand continually on the watchtower
in the daytime;
I have sat at my post every night.
9 And look, here comes a chariot of men
with a pair of horsemen!"
Then he answered and said,
"Babylon is fallen, is fallen!
And all the carved images of her gods
He has broken to the ground."
10 Oh, my threshing and the grain of my
floor!
That which I have heard from the LORD
of hosts,

21:9 Babylon is fallen, is fallen! The watchman proclaimed the tragic end of mighty Babylon, which initially fell to the Assyrians in 689 B.C. and again to the Persians in 539 B.C. Yet Isaiah's prediction looked forward to the ultimate fall of the great enemy of God, as verified by John's citation of this verse in Revelation 14:8; 18:2 (Jer. 50:2; 51:8,49).

The God of Israel,
I have declared to you.

11 The burden against Dumah.

He calls to me out of Seir,
"Watchman, what of the night?
Watchman, what of the night?"
12 The watchman said,
"The morning comes, and also the night.
If you will inquire, inquire;
Return! Come back!"

13 The burden against Arabia.

In the forest in Arabia you will lodge,
O you traveling companies of
Dedanites.
14 O inhabitants of the land of Tema,
Bring water to him who is thirsty;
With their bread they met him who fled.
15 For they fled from the swords, from
the drawn sword,
From the bent bow, and from the
distress of war.

16 For thus the LORD has said to me: "Within
a year, according to the year of a hired man, all
the glory of Kedar will fail; 17 and the remainder of the number of archers, the mighty men
of the people of Kedar, will be diminished; for
the LORD God of Israel has spoken *it.*"

22 The burden against the Valley of
Vision.

What ails you now, that you have all
gone up to the housetops,
2 You who are full of noise,
A tumultuous city, a joyous city?
Your slain *men are* not slain with the
sword,
Nor dead in battle.
3 All your rulers have fled together;
They are captured by the archers.
All who are found in you are bound
together;
They have fled from afar.
4 Therefore I said, "Look away from me,

22:1 Valley of Vision. This referred to Israel, since God often revealed Himself to Jerusalem in visions. However, the unrepentant inhabitants displayed a marked lack of vision in their oblivion to the destruction that awaited them. **What ails you...?** The prophet reproached the people for celebrating with wild parties when they should have been in deep repentance because of their sins. Apparently he anticipated a condition that arose in conjunction with Jerusalem's fall to the Babylonians in 586 B.C. But similar incursions by the Assyrians in either 711 or 701 B.C., from which the Lord delivered the city, had prompted the revelry among the people.

I will weep bitterly;
Do not labor to comfort me
Because of the plundering of the
daughter of my people."

5 For *it is* a day of trouble and treading
down and perplexity
By the Lord GOD of hosts
In the Valley of Vision—
Breaking down the walls
And of crying to the mountain.
6 Elam bore the quiver
With chariots of men *and* horsemen,
And Kir uncovered the shield.
7 It shall come to pass *that* your choicest
valleys
Shall be full of chariots,
And the horsemen shall set themselves
in array at the gate.

8 He removed the protection of Judah.
You looked in that day to the armor of
the House of the Forest;
9 You also saw the damage to the city
of David,
That it was great;
And you gathered together the waters
of the lower pool.
10 You numbered the houses of Jerusalem,
And the houses you broke down
To fortify the wall.
11 You also made a reservoir between the
two walls
For the water of the old pool.
But you did not look to its Maker,
Nor did you have respect for Him who
fashioned it long ago.

12 And in that day the Lord GOD of hosts
Called for weeping and for mourning,
For baldness and for girding with
sackcloth.
13 But instead, joy and gladness,
Slaying oxen and killing sheep,
Eating meat and drinking wine:
"Let us eat and drink, for tomorrow we
die!"

22:13 Let us eat and drink, for tomorrow we die! Paul cites the same philosophy (1 Cor. 15:32): If there is no resurrection, enjoyment in this life is all that matters. It utterly disregards God's eternal values.

14 Then it was revealed in my hearing by
the LORD of hosts,
"Surely for this iniquity there will be no
atonement for you,
Even to your death," says the Lord
GOD of hosts.

15 Thus says the Lord GOD of hosts:

"Go, proceed to this steward,
To Shebna, who *is* over the house,
and say:
16 'What have you here, and whom have
you here,
That you have hewn a sepulcher here,
As he who hews himself a sepulcher
on high,
Who carves a tomb for himself in a
rock?
17 Indeed, the LORD will throw you away
violently,
O mighty man,
And will surely seize you.
18 He will surely turn violently and toss
you like a ball
Into a large country;
There you shall die, and there your
glorious chariots
Shall be the shame of your master's
house.
19 So I will drive you out of your office,
And from your position he will pull you
down.

20 'Then it shall be in that day,
That I will call My servant Eliakim the
son of Hilkiah;
21 I will clothe him with your robe
And strengthen him with your belt;
I will commit your responsibility into
his hand.
He shall be a father to the inhabitants
of Jerusalem
And to the house of Judah.

[22] The key of the house of David
I will lay on his shoulder;
So he shall open, and no one shall shut;
And he shall shut, and no one shall open.

22:22 key of the house of David. This authority to admit or refuse admittance into the king's presence evidenced the king's great confidence in Eliakim. Jesus applied this terminology to Himself as one who could determine who would enter His future Davidic kingdom (Rev. 3:7).

[23] I will fasten him *as* a peg in a secure
place,
And he will become a glorious throne
to his father's house.

[24]"They will hang on him all the glory of his
father's house, the offspring and the posterity,
all vessels of small quantity, from the cups to
all the pitchers. [25]In that day,' says the LORD of
hosts, 'the peg that is fastened in the secure
place will be removed and be cut down and
fall, and the burden that *was* on it will be cut
off; for the LORD has spoken.' "

Psalm 107:1–9

Oh, give thanks to the LORD,
for *He is* good!
For His mercy *endures* forever.
[2] Let the redeemed of the LORD say *so,*
Whom He has redeemed from the
hand of the enemy,
[3] And gathered out of the lands,
From the east and from the west,
From the north and from the south.
[4] They wandered in the wilderness in a
desolate way;
They found no city to dwell in.
[5] Hungry and thirsty,
Their soul fainted in them.
[6] Then they cried out to the LORD in
their trouble,
And He delivered them out of their
distresses.
[7] And He led them forth by the right way,
That they might go to a city for a
dwelling place.
[8] Oh, that *men* would give thanks to the
LORD *for* His goodness,
And *for* His wonderful works to the
children of men!
[9] For He satisfies the longing soul,
And fills the hungry soul with
goodness.

Proverbs 25:14–16

[14] Whoever falsely boasts of giving
Is like clouds and wind without rain.
[15] By long forbearance a ruler is
persuaded,
And a gentle tongue breaks a bone.
[16] Have you found honey?
Eat only as much as you need,
Lest you be filled with it and vomit.

2 Corinthians 7:1–16

7 Therefore, having these promises, beloved,
let us cleanse ourselves from all filthiness
of the flesh and spirit, perfecting holiness in the
fear of God.
[2]Open *your hearts* to us. We have wronged
no one, we have corrupted no one, we have
cheated no one. [3]I do not say *this* to condemn;
for I have said before that you are in our
hearts, to die together and to live together.
[4]Great *is* my boldness of speech toward you,
great *is* my boasting on your behalf. I am filled
with comfort. I am exceedingly joyful in all our
tribulation.

7:1 these promises. The Old Testament promises Paul quoted in 6:16–18. Scripture often encourages believers to action based on God's promises (Rom. 12:1; 2 Pet. 1:3). **let us cleanse ourselves.** The form of this Greek verb indicates that this is something each Christian must do in his own life. **filthiness.** This Greek word, which appears only here in the New Testament, was used 3 times in the Greek Old Testament to refer to religious defilement or unholy alliances with idols, idol feasts, temple prostitutes, sacrifices, and festivals of worship. **flesh and spirit.** False religion panders to the human appetites represented by both "flesh and spirit." While some believers for a time might avoid succumbing to fleshly sins associated with false religion, the Christian who exposes his mind to false teaching cannot avoid contamination by the devilish ideologies and blasphemies that assault the purity of divine truth and blaspheme God's name. **perfecting holiness.** The Greek word for "perfecting" means "to finish" or "to complete" (8:6). "Holiness" refers to separation from all that would defile both the body and the mind. Complete or perfect holiness was embodied only in Christ; thus, believers are to pursue Him (3:18; Lev. 20:26; Matt. 5:48; Rom. 8:29; Phil. 3:12–14; 1 John 3:2,3).

5For indeed, when we came to Macedonia,
our bodies had no rest, but we were troubled
on every side. Outside *were* conflicts, inside
were fears. 6Nevertheless God, who comforts
the downcast, comforted us by the coming of
Titus, 7and not only by his coming, but also by
the consolation with which he was comforted
in you, when he told us of your earnest desire,
your mourning, your zeal for me, so that I
rejoiced even more.
8For even if I made you sorry with my letter,
I do not regret it; though I did regret it. For I
perceive that the same epistle made you
sorry, though only for a while. 9Now I rejoice,
not that you were made sorry, but that your
sorrow led to repentance. For you were made
sorry in a godly manner, that you might suffer
loss from us in nothing. 10For godly sorrow
produces repentance *leading* to salvation, not
to be regretted; but the sorrow of the world
produces death. 11For observe this very thing,
that you sorrowed in a godly manner: What
diligence it produced in you, *what* clearing *of
yourselves, what* indignation, *what* fear, *what*
vehement desire, *what* zeal, *what* vindication!
In all *things* you proved yourselves to be clear
in this matter. 12Therefore, although I wrote to
you, *I did* not *do it* for the sake of him who had
done the wrong, nor for the sake of him who
suffered wrong, but that our care for you in
the sight of God might appear to you.
13Therefore we have been comforted in your
comfort. And we rejoiced exceedingly more
for the joy of Titus, because his spirit has been
refreshed by you all. 14For if in anything I have
boasted to him about you, I am not ashamed. But
as we spoke all things to you in truth, even so
our boasting to Titus was found true. 15And his
affections are greater for you as he remembers
the obedience of you all, how with fear and
trembling you received him. 16Therefore I rejoice
that I have confidence in you in everything.

DAY 15: What are the characteristics of true repentance?

Paul's first letter to the Corinthians produced a sorrow in the believers that led them to repent of their sins (2 Cor. 7:9). "Repentance" refers to the desire to turn from sin and restore one's relationship to God. "Godly sorrow produces repentance leading to salvation" (v. 10). "Godly sorrow" refers to sorrow that is according to the will of God and produced by the Holy Spirit. True repentance cannot occur apart from such a genuine sorrow over one's sin. Repentance is at the very heart of and proves one's salvation: unbelievers repent of their sin initially when they are saved, and then as believers, repent of their sins continually to keep the joy and blessing of their relationship to God.

Verse 11 provides a look at how genuine repentance will manifest itself in one's attitudes. "Diligence." Better translated, "earnestness" or "eagerness." It is the initial reaction of true repentance to eagerly and aggressively pursue righteousness. This is an attitude that ends indifference to sin and complacency about evil and deception. "What clearing of yourselves." A desire to clear one's name of the stigma that accompanies sin. The repentant sinner restores the trust and confidence of others by making his genuine repentance known. "Indignation." Often associated with righteous indignation and holy anger. Repentance leads to anger over one's sin and displeasure at the shame it has brought on the Lord's name and His people. "Fear." This is reverence toward God, who is the One most offended by sin. Repentance leads to a healthy fear of the One who chastens and judges sin. "Vehement desire." This could be translated "yearning," or "a longing for," and refers to the desire of the repentant sinner to restore the relationship with the one who was sinned against. "Zeal." This refers to loving someone or something so much that one hates anyone or anything that harms the object of this love. "Vindication." This could be translated "avenging of wrong," and refers to the desire to see justice done. The repentant sinner no longer tries to protect himself; he wants to see the sin avenged no matter what it might cost him. "To be clear in this matter." The essence of repentance is an aggressive pursuit of holiness, which was characteristic of the Corinthians. The Greek word for "clear" means "pure" or "holy." They demonstrated the integrity of their repentance by their purity.

SEPTEMBER 16

Isaiah 23:1–24:23

23 The burden against Tyre.

Wail, you ships of Tarshish!
For it is laid waste,
So that there is no house, no harbor;
From the land of Cyprus it is revealed
to them.
2 Be still, you inhabitants of the
coastland,
You merchants of Sidon,
Whom those who cross the sea have
filled.
3 And on great waters the grain of Shihor,

23:1 Tyre. A Phoenician seaport on the Mediterranean Sea, located about 35 miles north of Mt. Carmel and 28 miles west of Mt. Hermon, Tyre supplied lumber for King Solomon's temple (1 Kin. 5:1,7–12) and sailors for his navy (1 Kin. 9:26,27). **laid waste.** Tyre was under siege 5 times between this prophecy and 332 B.C. Only the last of these attacks (in 332 B.C., by Alexander the Great) completely leveled and subdued the city. Ezekiel prophesied this destruction in Ezekiel 26:3–27:36.

The harvest of the River, *is* her revenue;
And she is a marketplace for the nations.

4 Be ashamed, O Sidon;
For the sea has spoken,
The strength of the sea, saying,
"I do not labor, nor bring forth children;
Neither do I rear young men,
Nor bring up virgins."
5 When the report *reaches* Egypt,
They also will be in agony at the report of Tyre.
6 Cross over to Tarshish;
Wail, you inhabitants of the coastland!
7 *Is* this your joyous *city,*
Whose antiquity *is* from ancient days,
Whose feet carried her far off to dwell?
8 Who has taken this counsel against Tyre, the crowning *city,*
Whose merchants *are* princes,
Whose traders *are* the honorable of the earth?
9 The LORD of hosts has purposed it,
To bring to dishonor the pride of all glory,
To bring into contempt all the honorable of the earth.

10 Overflow through your land like the River,
O daughter of Tarshish;
There is no more strength.
11 He stretched out His hand over the sea,
He shook the kingdoms;
The LORD has given a commandment against Canaan
To destroy its strongholds.
12 And He said, "You will rejoice no more,
O you oppressed virgin daughter of Sidon.
Arise, cross over to Cyprus;
There also you will have no rest."

13 Behold, the land of the Chaldeans,
This people *which* was not;
Assyria founded it for wild beasts of the desert.
They set up its towers,
They raised up its palaces,
And brought it to ruin.
14 Wail, you ships of Tarshish!
For your strength is laid waste.

15 Now it shall come to pass in that day that
Tyre will be forgotten seventy years, according to the days of one king. At the end of seventy years it will happen to Tyre as *in* the song
of the harlot:

16 "Take a harp, go about the city,
You forgotten harlot;
Make sweet melody, sing many songs,
That you may be remembered."

17 And it shall be, at the end of seventy years,
that the LORD will deal with Tyre. She will
return to her hire, and commit fornication
with all the kingdoms of the world on the face
of the earth. 18 Her gain and her pay will be set
apart for the LORD; it will not be treasured nor
laid up, for her gain will be for those who dwell
before the LORD, to eat sufficiently, and for fine
clothing.

24 Behold, the LORD makes the earth empty and makes it waste,
Distorts its surface
And scatters abroad its inhabitants.
2 And it shall be:
As with the people, so with the priest;
As with the servant, so with his master;
As with the maid, so with her mistress;
As with the buyer, so with the seller;
As with the lender, so with the borrower;
As with the creditor, so with the debtor.
3 The land shall be entirely emptied and utterly plundered,
For the LORD has spoken this word.
4 The earth mourns *and* fades away,
The world languishes *and* fades away;
The haughty people of the earth languish.
5 The earth is also defiled under its inhabitants,
Because they have transgressed the laws,
Changed the ordinance,
Broken the everlasting covenant.
6 Therefore the curse has devoured the earth,

And those who dwell in it are desolate.
Therefore the inhabitants of the earth
are burned,
And few men *are* left.

7 The new wine fails, the vine languishes,
All the merry-hearted sigh.
8 The mirth of the tambourine ceases,
The noise of the jubilant ends,
The joy of the harp ceases.
9 They shall not drink wine with a song;
Strong drink is bitter to those who
drink it.
10 The city of confusion is broken down;
Every house is shut up, so that none
may go in.
11 *There is* a cry for wine in the streets,
All joy is darkened,
The mirth of the land is gone.
12 In the city desolation is left,
And the gate is stricken with
destruction.
13 When it shall be thus in the midst of
the land among the people,
It shall be like the shaking of an olive
tree,
Like the gleaning of grapes when the
vintage is done.

14 They shall lift up their voice, they shall
sing;
For the majesty of the LORD
They shall cry aloud from the sea.
15 Therefore glorify the LORD in the
dawning light,
The name of the LORD God of Israel in
the coastlands of the sea.
16 From the ends of the earth we have
heard songs:
"Glory to the righteous!"
But I said, "I am ruined, ruined!
Woe to me!
The treacherous dealers have dealt
treacherously,
Indeed, the treacherous dealers have
dealt very treacherously."

17 Fear and the pit and the snare
Are upon you, O inhabitant of the
earth.
18 And it shall be
That he who flees from the noise
of the fear
Shall fall into the pit,
And he who comes up from the midst
of the pit
Shall be caught in the snare;
For the windows from on high are open,
And the foundations of the earth are
shaken.

19 The earth is violently broken,
The earth is split open,
The earth is shaken exceedingly.
20 The earth shall reel to and fro like a
drunkard,
And shall totter like a hut;
Its transgression shall be heavy upon it,
And it will fall, and not rise again.

21 It shall come to pass in that day
That the LORD will punish on high the
host of exalted ones,
And on the earth the kings of the
earth.
22 They will be gathered together,
As prisoners are gathered in the pit,
And will be shut up in the prison;
After many days they will be punished.
23 Then the moon will be disgraced
And the sun ashamed;
For the LORD of hosts will reign
On Mount Zion and in Jerusalem
And before His elders, gloriously.

24:18 windows from on high. In Noah's day, God judged with a flood (Gen. 7:11). He will judge again from heaven, but not with a flood. Revelation 6:13,14; 8:3–13; 16:1–21. **foundations of the earth.** Unparalleled earthquakes will mark the future visitation during and after the fulfillment of Daniel's 70-week prophecy (13:13; Matt. 24:7; Rev. 6:12,14; 8:5; 11:19; 16:18).

24:23 moon...disgraced...sun ashamed. In the eternal state after Christ's millennial reign, the glory of God and of the Lamb will replace the sun and moon as sources of light (Rev. 21:23). **reign...in Jerusalem.** In Revelation 11:15–17; 19:6,16 (Luke 1:31–33), John confirmed this clear prophecy of Messiah's future earthly reign in Jerusalem.

Psalm 107:10–22

10 Those who sat in darkness and in the
shadow of death,
Bound in affliction and irons—
11 Because they rebelled against the
words of God,
And despised the counsel of the Most
High,
12 Therefore He brought down their
heart with labor;
They fell down, and *there was* none
to help.
13 Then they cried out to the LORD in their
trouble,

And He saved them out of their
distresses.
14 He brought them out of darkness and
the shadow of death,
And broke their chains in pieces.
15 Oh, that *men* would give thanks to the
LORD *for* His goodness,
And *for* His wonderful works to the
children of men!
16 For He has broken the gates of bronze,
And cut the bars of iron in two.

17 Fools, because of their transgression,
And because of their iniquities, were
afflicted.
18 Their soul abhorred all manner of food,
And they drew near to the gates of
death.
19 Then they cried out to the LORD in
their trouble,
And He saved them out of their
distresses.
20 He sent His word and healed them,
And delivered *them* from their
destructions.
21 Oh, that *men* would give thanks to the
LORD *for* His goodness,
And *for* His wonderful works to the
children of men!
22 Let them sacrifice the sacrifices of
thanksgiving,
And declare His works with rejoicing.

Proverbs 25:17

17 Seldom set foot in your neighbor's
house,
Lest he become weary of you
and hate you.

2 Corinthians 8:1–24

8 Moreover, brethren, we make known to
you the grace of God bestowed on the
churches of Macedonia: [2]that in a great trial of
affliction the abundance of their joy and their
deep poverty abounded in the riches of their
liberality. [3]For I bear witness that according to
their ability, yes, and beyond *their* ability, *they*
were freely willing, [4]imploring us with much
urgency that we would receive the gift and the
fellowship of the ministering to the saints.
[5]And not *only* as we had hoped, but they first
gave themselves to the Lord, and *then* to us by
the will of God. [6]So we urged Titus, that as he
had begun, so he would also complete this
grace in you as well. [7]But as you abound in
everything—in faith, in speech, in knowledge,
in all diligence, and in your love for us—*see*
that you abound in this grace also.
[8]I speak not by commandment, but I am testing the sincerity of your love by the diligence of
others. [9]For you know the grace of our Lord Jesus Christ, that though He was rich, yet for
your sakes He became poor, that you through
His poverty might become rich.
[10]And in this I give advice: It is to your
advantage not only to be doing what you
began and were desiring to do a year ago; [11]but
now you also must complete the doing *of it;*
that as *there was* a readiness to desire *it,* so
there also *may be* a completion out of what *you*
have. [12]For if there is first a willing mind, *it is*
accepted according to what one has, *and* not
according to what he does not have.
[13]For *I do* not *mean* that others should be
eased and you burdened; [14]but by an equality,

8:9 though He was rich. A reference to the eternality and preexistence of Christ. As the Second Person of the Trinity, Christ is as rich as God is rich. He owns everything, and possesses all power, authority, sovereignty, glory, honor, and majesty (Is. 9:6; Mic. 5:2; John 1:1; 8:58; 10:30; 17:5; Col. 1:15–18; 2:9; Heb. 1:3). **He became poor.** A reference to Christ's Incarnation (John 1:14; Rom. 1:3; 8:3; Gal. 4:4; Col. 1:20; 1 Tim. 3:16; Heb. 2:7). He laid aside the independent exercise of all His divine prerogatives, left His place with God, took on human form, and died on a cross like a common criminal (Phil. 2:5–8). **that you...might become rich.** Believers become spiritually rich through the sacrifice and impoverishment of Christ (Phil. 2:5–8). They become rich in salvation, forgiveness, joy, peace, glory, honor, and majesty (1 Cor. 1:4,5; 3:22; Eph. 1:3; 1 Pet. 1:3,4). They become joint heirs with Christ (Rom. 8:17).

8:12 willing mind. Paul spoke of a readiness and eagerness to give. God is most concerned with the heart attitude of the giver, not the amount he gives (9:7; Mark 12:41–44). **according to what one has.** Whatever one has is the resource out of which he should give. That is why there are no set amounts or percentages for giving anywhere stated in the New Testament. The implication is that if one has much, he can give much; if he has little, he can give only little (9:6). **not according to what he does not have.** Believers do not need to go into debt to give nor lower themselves to a poverty level. God never asks believers to impoverish themselves. The Macedonians received a special blessing of grace from God to give the way they did.

that now at this time your abundance *may sup-*
ply their lack, that their abundance also may *sup-*
ply your lack—that there may be equality. 15As it
is written, *"He who gathered much had nothing*
left over, and he who gathered little had no lack."
16But thanks *be* to God who puts the same
earnest care for you into the heart of Titus. 17For
he not only accepted the exhortation, but being
more diligent, he went to you of his own accord.
18And we have sent with him the brother whose
praise *is* in the gospel throughout all the churches, 19and not only *that,* but who was also chosen
by the churches to travel with us with this gift,
which is administered by us to the glory of the
Lord Himself and *to show* your ready mind,
20avoiding this: that anyone should blame us in
this lavish gift which is administered by us—
21providing honorable things, not only in the
sight of the Lord, but also in the sight of men.
22And we have sent with them our brother
whom we have often proved diligent in many
things, but now much more diligent, because
of the great confidence which *we have* in you.
23If *anyone inquires* about Titus, *he is* my partner and fellow worker concerning you. Or if
our brethren *are inquired about, they are* messengers of the churches, the glory of Christ.
24Therefore show to them, and before the
churches, the proof of your love and of our
boasting on your behalf.

DAY 16: How did the Macedonians exemplify freewill giving?

The generosity of the churches of Macedonia that Paul addresses in 2 Corinthians 8:1 was motivated by God's grace. Paul did not merely commend those churches for a noble human work, but instead gave the credit to God for what He did through them. Paul's reference was to the churches at Philippi, Thessalonica, and Berea (Acts 17:11). This was basically an impoverished province that had been ravaged by many wars and even then was being plundered by Roman authority and commerce.

In spite of their difficult circumstances, the churches' joy rose above their pain because of their devotion to the Lord and the causes of His kingdom. It was through the "abundance of their joy" (v. 2) that it was given despite their "deep poverty." "Poverty" refers to the most severe type of economic deprivation, the kind that caused a person to become a beggar. "Riches of their liberality." The Greek word for "liberality" can be translated "generosity" or "sincerity." It is the opposite of duplicity or being double-minded. The Macedonian believers were rich in their single-minded, selfless generosity to God and to others.

In v. 3, Paul highlighted 3 elements of the Macedonians' giving which summed up the concept of freewill giving: 1) "according to their ability." Giving is proportionate—God sets no fixed amount or percentage and expects His people to give based on what they have (Luke 6:38; 1 Cor. 16:2); 2) "beyond their ability." Giving is sacrificial. God's people are to give according to what they have, yet it must be in proportions that are sacrificial (Matt. 6:25–34; Mark 12:41–44; Phil. 4:19); and 3) "freely willing"—literally "one who chooses his own course of action." Giving is voluntary—God's people are not to give out of compulsion, manipulation, or intimidation. Freewill giving has always been God's plan (9:6; Gen. 4:2–4; 8:20; Ex. 25:1,2; 35:4,5,21,22; 36:5–7; Num. 18:12; Deut. 16:10,17; 1 Chr. 29:9; Prov. 3:9,10; 11:24; Luke 19:1–8). Freewill giving is not to be confused with tithing, which related to the national taxation system of Israel (Lev. 27:30) and is paralleled in the New Testament and the present by paying taxes (Matt. 22:21; Rom. 13:6,7).

SEPTEMBER 17

Isaiah 25:1–26:21

25 O LORD, You *are* my God.
I will exalt You,
I will praise Your name,
For You have done wonderful *things;*
Your counsels of old *are* faithfulness
and truth.
2 For You have made a city a ruin,
A fortified city a ruin,
A palace of foreigners to be a city no
more;
It will never be rebuilt.
3 Therefore the strong people will glorify
You;
The city of the terrible nations will fear
You.
4 For You have been a strength to the poor,
A strength to the needy in his distress,
A refuge from the storm,
A shade from the heat;
For the blast of the terrible ones *is* as a
storm *against* the wall.
5 You will reduce the noise of aliens,
As heat in a dry place;
As heat in the shadow of a cloud,
The song of the terrible ones will be
diminished.

6 And in this mountain
The LORD of hosts will make for all
people
A feast of choice pieces,
A feast of wines on the lees,
Of fat things full of marrow,
Of well-refined wines on the lees.
7 And He will destroy on this mountain
The surface of the covering cast over
all people,
And the veil that is spread over all
nations.
8 He will swallow up death forever,
And the Lord GOD will wipe away tears
from all faces;
The rebuke of His people
He will take away from all the earth;
For the LORD has spoken.

25:8 swallow up death. God will swallow up death, which itself functions as a swallower of human beings (5:14; Prov. 1:12). Paul notes the fulfillment of this promise in the resurrection of believers (1 Cor. 15:54). **wipe away tears.** The Lord God will remove the sorrow associated with death (65:19). Revelation alludes to the tender action of this verse twice—once in 7:17 to describe the bliss of the redeemed in heaven, and once in 21:4 to describe ideal conditions in the New Jerusalem. **rebuke...He will take away.** Israel will be the head of the nations and no longer the tail (Deut. 28:13).

9 And it will be said in that day:
"Behold, this *is* our God;
We have waited for Him, and He will
save us.
This *is* the LORD;
We have waited for Him;
We will be glad and rejoice in His
salvation."
10 For on this mountain the hand of the
LORD will rest,
And Moab shall be trampled down
under Him,
As straw is trampled down for the
refuse heap.
11 And He will spread out His hands in
their midst
As a swimmer reaches out to swim,
And He will bring down their pride
Together with the trickery of their
hands.
12 The fortress of the high fort of your walls
He will bring down, lay low,
And bring to the ground, down to the
dust.

26 In that day this song will be sung in the land of Judah:

"We have a strong city;
God will appoint salvation *for* walls and
bulwarks.
2 Open the gates,
That the righteous nation which keeps
the truth may enter in.
3 You will keep *him* in perfect peace,
Whose mind *is* stayed *on You,*
Because he trusts in You.

26:3 perfect peace,...trusts in You. A fixed disposition of trust in the Lord brings a peace that the wicked can never know (48:22; 57:21). Such reliance precludes double-mindedness (James 1:6–8) and serving two masters (Matt. 6:24).

4 Trust in the LORD forever,
For in YAH, the LORD, *is* everlasting
strength.
5 For He brings down those who dwell
on high,
The lofty city;
He lays it low,
He lays it low to the ground,
He brings it down to the dust.
6 The foot shall tread it down—
The feet of the poor
And the steps of the needy."
7 The way of the just *is* uprightness;
O Most Upright,
You weigh the path of the just.
8 Yes, in the way of Your judgments,
O LORD, we have waited for You;
The desire of *our* soul *is* for
Your name
And for the remembrance of You.
9 With my soul I have desired You
in the night,
Yes, by my spirit within me I will seek
You early;
For when Your judgments *are* in the
earth,
The inhabitants of the world will learn
righteousness.
10 Let grace be shown to the wicked,
Yet he will not learn righteousness;
In the land of uprightness he will deal
unjustly,

And will not behold the majesty
of the LORD.
11 LORD, *when* Your hand is lifted up,
they will not see.
But they will see and be ashamed
For *their* envy of people;
Yes, the fire of Your enemies shall
devour them.

12 LORD, You will establish peace for us,
For You have also done all our works
in us.
13 O LORD our God, masters besides You
Have had dominion over us;
But by You only we make mention of
Your name.
14 *They are* dead, they will not live;
They are deceased, they will not rise.
Therefore You have punished and
destroyed them,
And made all their memory to perish.
15 You have increased the nation, O LORD,
You have increased the nation;
You are glorified;
You have expanded all the borders of
the land.

26:15 have increased the nation. With prophetic certainty from the perspective of Israel's future restoration, Isaiah saw the expansion of Israel's borders as an accomplished fact.

16 LORD, in trouble they have visited You,
They poured out a prayer *when* Your
chastening *was* upon them.
17 As a woman with child
Is in pain and cries out in her pangs,
When she draws near the time of her
delivery,
So have we been in Your sight, O LORD.
18 We have been with child, we have been
in pain;
We have, as it were, brought forth
wind;
We have not accomplished any
deliverance in the earth,
Nor have the inhabitants of the world
fallen.

19 Your dead shall live;
Together with my dead body they shall
arise.
Awake and sing, you who dwell in dust;
For your dew *is like* the dew of herbs,
And the earth shall cast out the dead.

20 Come, my people, enter your chambers,
And shut your doors behind you;
Hide yourself, as it were, for a little
moment,
Until the indignation is past.
21 For behold, the LORD comes out of His
place
To punish the inhabitants of the earth
for their iniquity;
The earth will also disclose her blood,
And will no more cover her slain.

Psalm 107:23–32

23 Those who go down to the sea in ships,
Who do business on great waters,
24 They see the works of the LORD,
And His wonders in the deep.
25 For He commands and raises the
stormy wind,
Which lifts up the waves of the sea.
26 They mount up to the heavens,
They go down again to the depths;
Their soul melts because of trouble.
27 They reel to and fro, and stagger like a
drunken man,
And are at their wits' end.
28 Then they cry out to the LORD in their
trouble,
And He brings them out of their
distresses.
29 He calms the storm,
So that its waves are still.
30 Then they are glad because they are
quiet;
So He guides them to their desired
haven.
31 Oh, that *men* would give thanks to the
LORD *for* His goodness,
And *for* His wonderful works to the
children of men!
32 Let them exalt Him also in the
assembly of the people,
And praise Him in the company of the
elders.

Proverbs 25:18–19

18 A man who bears false witness against
his neighbor
Is like a club, a sword, and a sharp
arrow.

19 Confidence in an unfaithful *man* in
time of trouble
Is like a bad tooth and a foot out of
joint.

2 Corinthians 9:1–15

9 Now concerning the ministering to the
saints, it is superfluous for me to write to
you; 2for I know your willingness, about which
I boast of you to the Macedonians, that Achaia

was ready a year ago; and your zeal has stirred
up the majority. [3]Yet I have sent the brethren, lest
our boasting of you should be in vain in this
respect, that, as I said, you may be ready; [4]lest
if *some* Macedonians come with me and find
you unprepared, we (not to mention you!)
should be ashamed of this confident boasting.
[5]Therefore I thought it necessary to exhort
the brethren to go to you ahead of time, and
prepare your generous gift beforehand, which
you had previously promised, that it may be
ready as *a matter of* generosity and not as a
grudging obligation.
[6]But this *I say:* He who sows sparingly will
also reap sparingly, and he who sows bountifully will also reap bountifully. [7]*So let* each one
give as he purposes in his heart, not grudgingly
or of necessity; for God loves a cheerful giver.
[8]And God *is* able to make all grace abound
toward you, that you, always having all sufficiency in all *things,* may have an abundance for
every good work. [9]As it is written:

"He has dispersed abroad,
He has given to the poor;
His righteousness endures forever."

[10]Now may He who supplies seed to the
sower, and bread for food, supply and multiply
the seed you have *sown* and increase the fruits
of your righteousness, [11]while *you are* enriched
in everything for all liberality, which causes
thanksgiving through us to God. [12]For the
administration of this service not only supplies
the needs of the saints, but also is abounding
through many thanksgivings to God, [13]while,
through the proof of this ministry, they glorify
God for the obedience of your confession to
the gospel of Christ, and for *your* liberal sharing with them and all *men,* [14]and by their prayer
for you, who long for you because of the
exceeding grace of God in you. [15]Thanks *be* to
God for His indescribable gift!

9:12 administration of this service. "Administration," which may also be translated "service," is a priestly word from which we get "liturgy." Paul viewed the entire collection project as a spiritual, worshipful enterprise that was primarily being offered to God to glorify Him. **supplies the needs of the saints.** The Greek word for "supplies" is a doubly intense term that could be rendered "really, fully supplying." This indicates the Jerusalem church had an extremely great need. Many residents of Jerusalem had undoubtedly lost their jobs in the waves of persecution that came after the martyrdom of Stephen (Acts 8:1). However, the Corinthians were wealthy enough (they had not yet suffered persecution and deprivation like the Macedonians) to help meet the huge need with a generous monetary gift.

9:15 Paul summarized his discourse by comparing the believer's act of giving with what God did in giving Jesus Christ (Rom. 8:32), "His indescribable gift." God buried His Son and reaped a vast harvest of those who put their faith in the resurrected Christ (John 12:24). That makes it possible for believers to joyfully, sacrificially, and abundantly sow and reap. As they give in this manner, they show forth Christ's likeness (John 12:25,26; Eph. 5:1,2).

DAY 17: What does God look for in our financial giving?

"He who sows sparingly will also reap sparingly, and he who sows bountifully will also reap bountifully" (2 Cor. 9:6). The simple, self-evident agrarian principle—which Paul applied to Christian giving—that the harvest is directly proportionate to the amount of seed sown (Prov. 11:24,25; 19:17; Luke 6:38; Gal. 6:7). When a generous believer gives by faith and trust in God, with a desire to produce the greatest possible blessing, that person will receive that kind of a harvest of blessing (Prov. 3:9,10; 28:27; Mal. 3:10). God gives a return on the amount one invests with Him (Luke 6:38).

"So let each one give as he purposes in his heart" (v. 7). The term translated "purposes" indicates a premeditated, predetermined plan of action that is done from the heart voluntarily, but not impulsively. "Grudgingly." Literally, "with grief," "sorrow," or "sadness," which indicates an attitude of depression, regret, and reluctance that accompanies something done strictly out of a sense of duty and obligation, but not joy. "Of necessity" or "compulsion." This refers to external pressure and coercion, quite possibly accompanied by legalism. Believers are not to give based on the demands of others or according to any arbitrary standards or set amounts. "God loves a cheerful giver." God has a unique, special love for those who are happily committed to generous giving. The Greek word for "cheerful" is the word from which we get "hilarious," which suggests that God loves a heart that is enthusiastically thrilled with the pleasure of giving.

God possesses an infinite amount of grace, and He gives it lavishly, without holding back (v. 9). Here "grace" does not refer to spiritual graces but to money and material needs. When the believer generously—and wisely—gives of his material resources, God graciously replenishes them so he always has plenty and will not be in need (2 Chr. 31:10). "Always having all sufficiency." In secular Greek philosophy, this was the proud contentment of self-sufficiency that supposedly led to true happiness. Paul sanctifies the secular term and says that God, not man, will supply everything needed for real happiness and contentment (Phil. 4:19). "May have an abundance for every good work." God gives back lavishly to generous, cheerful givers, not so they may satisfy selfish, nonessential desires, but so they may meet the variety of needs others have (Deut. 15:10,11).

SEPTEMBER 18

Isaiah 27:1–28:29

27 In that day the LORD with His severe
sword, great and strong,
Will punish Leviathan the fleeing
serpent,
Leviathan that twisted serpent;
And He will slay the reptile that *is* in
the sea.

2 In that day sing to her,
"A vineyard of red wine!
3 I, the LORD, keep it,
I water it every moment;
Lest any hurt it,
I keep it night and day.
4 Fury *is* not in Me.
Who would set briers *and* thorns
Against Me in battle?
I would go through them,
I would burn them together.
5 Or let him take hold of My strength,
That he may make peace with Me;
And he shall make peace with Me."

6 Those who come He shall cause to
take root in Jacob;
Israel shall blossom and bud,
And fill the face of the world with fruit.

7 Has He struck Israel as He struck
those who struck him?
Or has He been slain according to the
slaughter of those who were slain
by Him?
8 In measure, by sending it away,
You contended with it.
He removes *it* by His rough wind
In the day of the east wind.
9 Therefore by this the iniquity of Jacob
will be covered;
And this *is* all the fruit of taking away
his sin:
When he makes all the stones of the
altar
Like chalkstones that are beaten to dust,
Wooden images and incense altars
shall not stand.

10 Yet the fortified city *will be* desolate,
The habitation forsaken and left like a
wilderness;
There the calf will feed, and there it
will lie down
And consume its branches.
11 When its boughs are withered, they
will be broken off;
The women come *and* set them on fire.
For it *is* a people of no understanding;
Therefore He who made them will not
have mercy on them,
And He who formed them will show
them no favor.

12 And it shall come to pass in that day
That the LORD will thresh,
From the channel of the River to the
Brook of Egypt;
And you will be gathered one by one,
O you children of Israel.

13 So it shall be in that day:
The great trumpet will be blown;
They will come, who are about to
perish in the land of Assyria,
And they who are outcasts in the land
of Egypt,
And shall worship the LORD in the holy
mount at Jerusalem.

28 Woe to the crown of pride,
to the drunkards of Ephraim,
Whose glorious beauty *is* a fading
flower
Which *is* at the head of the verdant
valleys,
To those who are overcome with wine!
2 Behold, the Lord has a mighty and
strong one,
Like a tempest of hail and a destroying
storm,

Like a flood of mighty waters
overflowing,
Who will bring *them* down to the earth
with *His* hand.
3 The crown of pride, the drunkards of
Ephraim,
Will be trampled underfoot;
4 And the glorious beauty is a fading
flower
Which *is* at the head of the verdant
valley,
Like the first fruit before the summer,
Which an observer sees;
He eats it up while it is still in his hand.

5 In that day the LORD of hosts will be
For a crown of glory and a diadem of
beauty
To the remnant of His people,
6 For a spirit of justice to him who sits in
judgment,
And for strength to those who turn
back the battle at the gate.

7 But they also have erred through wine,
And through intoxicating drink are out
of the way;
The priest and the prophet have erred
through intoxicating drink,
They are swallowed up by wine,
They are out of the way through
intoxicating drink;
They err in vision, they stumble *in*
judgment.
8 For all tables are full of vomit *and* filth;
No place *is clean.*

9 "Whom will he teach knowledge?
And whom will he make to understand
the message?
Those *just* weaned from milk?
Those *just* drawn from the breasts?
10 For precept *must be* upon precept,
precept upon precept,
Line upon line, line upon line,
Here a little, there a little."

11 For with stammering lips and another
tongue
He will speak to this people,
12 To whom He said, "This *is* the rest *with
which*
You may cause the weary to rest,"
And, "This *is* the refreshing";
Yet they would not hear.
13 But the word of the LORD was to them,
"Precept upon precept, precept upon
precept,
Line upon line, line upon line,
Here a little, there a little,"
That they might go and fall backward,
and be broken
And snared and caught.

14 Therefore hear the word of the LORD,
you scornful men,
Who rule this people who *are*
in Jerusalem,
15 Because you have said, "We have made
a covenant with death,
And with Sheol we are in agreement.
When the overflowing scourge passes
through,
It will not come to us,
For we have made lies our refuge,
And under falsehood we have hidden
ourselves."

16 Therefore thus says the Lord GOD:

"Behold, I lay in Zion a stone for
a foundation,
A tried stone, a precious cornerstone,
a sure foundation;

28:16 stone for a foundation,...a sure foundation. The Lord God contrasted the only sure refuge with the false refuge of relying on foreigners (v. 15). This directly prophesied the coming of the Messiah (Matt. 21:42; Mark 12:10; Luke 20:17; Acts 4:11; Rom. 9:33; Eph. 2:20; 1 Pet. 2:6–8; 8:14,15; Ps. 118:22). **will not act hastily.** The Greek Old Testament interprets this Hebrew verb for "hurry" in the sense of "put to shame," furnishing the basis of the New Testament citations of this verse (Rom. 9:33; 10:11; 1 Pet. 2:6).

Whoever believes will not act hastily.
17 Also I will make justice the measuring
line,
And righteousness the plummet;
The hail will sweep away the refuge
of lies,
And the waters will overflow the hiding
place.
18 Your covenant with death will be
annulled,
And your agreement with Sheol will not
stand;
When the overflowing scourge passes
through,
Then you will be trampled down by it.
19 As often as it goes out it will take you;
For morning by morning it will pass
over,
And by day and by night;
It will be a terror just to understand
the report."

20 For the bed is too short to stretch out *on,*
And the covering so narrow that one cannot wrap himself *in it.*
21 For the LORD will rise up as *at* Mount Perazim,
He will be angry as in the Valley of Gibeon—
That He may do His work, His awesome work,
And bring to pass His act, His unusual act.
22 Now therefore, do not be mockers,
Lest your bonds be made strong;
For I have heard from the Lord GOD of hosts,
A destruction determined even upon the whole earth.

28:23 Give ear. The parable of a farmer underlined the lessons of judgment threats in vv. 18–22. As the farmer does his different tasks, each in the right season and proportion, so God adopts His measures to His purposes: now mercy, then judgment; punishing sooner, then later. His purpose was not to destroy His people, any more than the farmer's object in his threshing or plowing is to destroy his crop.

23 Give ear and hear my voice,
Listen and hear my speech.
24 Does the plowman keep plowing all day to sow?
Does he keep turning his soil and breaking the clods?
25 When he has leveled its surface,
Does he not sow the black cummin
And scatter the cummin,
Plant the wheat in rows,
The barley in the appointed place,
And the spelt in its place?
26 For He instructs him in right judgment,
His God teaches him.
27 For the black cummin is not threshed with a threshing sledge,
Nor is a cartwheel rolled over the cummin;
But the black cummin is beaten out with a stick,
And the cummin with a rod.
28 Bread *flour* must be ground;
Therefore he does not thresh it forever,
Break *it with* his cartwheel,
Or crush it *with* his horsemen.
29 This also comes from the LORD of hosts,
Who is wonderful in counsel *and* excellent in guidance.

Psalm 107:33–43

33 He turns rivers into a wilderness,
And the watersprings into dry ground;
34 A fruitful land into barrenness,
For the wickedness of those who dwell in it.
35 He turns a wilderness into pools of water,
And dry land into watersprings.
36 There He makes the hungry dwell,
That they may establish a city for a dwelling place,
37 And sow fields and plant vineyards,
That they may yield a fruitful harvest.
38 He also blesses them, and they multiply greatly;
And He does not let their cattle decrease.

39 When they are diminished and brought low
Through oppression, affliction, and sorrow,
40 He pours contempt on princes,
And causes them to wander in the wilderness *where there is* no way;
41 Yet He sets the poor on high, far from affliction,
And makes *their* families like a flock.
42 The righteous see *it* and rejoice,
And all iniquity stops its mouth.

43 Whoever *is* wise will observe these *things,*
And they will understand the lovingkindness of the LORD.

Proverbs 25:20

20 *Like* one who takes away a garment in cold weather,
And like vinegar on soda,
Is one who sings songs to a heavy heart.

25:20 vinegar on soda. Pouring vinegar on an alkali (e.g., baking soda) produces a reaction like boiling or turning tranquility into agitation. So is the effect of singing joyful songs without sympathy to the sorrowful.

2 Corinthians 10:1–18

10 Now I, Paul, myself am pleading with you
by the meekness and gentleness of
Christ—who in presence *am* lowly among you,
but being absent am bold toward you. 2But I beg
you that when I am present I may not be bold
with that confidence by which I intend to be bold
against some, who think of us as if we walked
according to the flesh. 3For though we walk in
the flesh, we do not war according to the flesh.
4For the weapons of our warfare *are* not carnal
but mighty in God for pulling down strongholds,
5casting down arguments and every high thing
that exalts itself against the knowledge of God,
bringing every thought into captivity to the obedience of Christ, 6and being ready to punish all
disobedience when your obedience is fulfilled.
7Do you look at things according to the outward appearance? If anyone is convinced in
himself that he is Christ's, let him again consider this in himself, that just as he *is* Christ's,
even so we *are* Christ's. 8For even if I should
boast somewhat more about our authority,
which the Lord gave us for edification and not
for your destruction, I shall not be ashamed—
9lest I seem to terrify you by letters. 10"For *his*
letters," they say, "*are* weighty and powerful,
but *his* bodily presence *is* weak, and *his* speech
contemptible." 11Let such a person consider
this, that what we are in word by letters when
we are absent, such *we will* also *be* in deed
when we are present.
12For we dare not class ourselves or compare ourselves with those who commend
themselves. But they, measuring themselves
by themselves, and comparing themselves
among themselves, are not wise. 13We, however,
will not boast beyond measure, but within the
limits of the sphere which God appointed us—
a sphere which especially includes you. 14For
we are not overextending ourselves (as
though *our authority* did not extend to you),
for it was to you that we came with the gospel
of Christ; 15not boasting of things beyond measure, *that is,* in other men's labors, but having
hope, *that* as your faith is increased, we shall
be greatly enlarged by you in our sphere, 16to
preach the gospel in the *regions* beyond you,
and not to boast in another man's sphere of
accomplishment.
17But *"he who glories, let him glory in the
Lord."* 18For not he who commends himself is
approved, but whom the Lord commends.

10:4 our warfare. The motif of the Christian life as warfare is a common one in the New Testament (6:7; Eph. 6:10–18; 1 Tim. 1:18; 2 Tim. 2:3,4; 4:7). **carnal.** Human. **strongholds.** The metaphor would have been readily understandable to the Corinthians since Corinth, like most ancient cities, had a fortress in which its residents could take refuge. The formidable spiritual strongholds manned by the forces of hell can be demolished only by spiritual weapons wielded by godly believers—singularly the "sword of the Spirit" (Eph. 6:17), since only the truth of God's Word can defeat satanic falsehoods. This is the true spiritual warfare. Believers are not instructed in the New Testament to assault demons or Satan, but to assault error with the truth. That is our battle (John 17:17; Heb. 4:12).

10:5 arguments. Thoughts, ideas, speculations, reasonings, philosophies, and false religions are the ideological forts in which men barricade themselves against God and the gospel (1 Cor. 3:20). **every thought into captivity.** Emphasizes the total destruction of the fortresses of human and satanic wisdom and the rescuing of those inside from the damning lies that had enslaved them.

DAY 18: Why does the tone of 2 Corinthians change so abruptly between 9:15 and 10:1?

Even a casual reader usually notices the abrupt change in tone that occurs between the ninth and tenth chapters. This apparent difference has prompted various explanations of the relationship between chapters 1–9 and 10–13.

Some argue that chapters 10–13 were originally part of the "severe letter" (2:4), and hence belong chronologically before chapters 1–9. Chapters 10–13 cannot, however, have been written before chapters 1–9, since they refer to Titus's visit as a past event (12:18; 8:6). Further, the offender whose defiance of Paul prompted the "severe letter" (2:5–8) is nowhere mentioned in chapters 10–13.

Others agree that chapters 10–13 belong after chapters 1–9, but believe they form a separate letter. They assume that Paul, after sending chapters 1–9 to the Corinthians, received reports of new trouble at Corinth and wrote chapters 10–13 in response. A variation of this view is that Paul paused in his writing of 2 Corinthians after chapters 1–9, then heard bad news from Corinth before he resumed writing chapters 10–13. This view preserves the unity of 2 Corinthians; however, Paul does not mention anywhere in chapters 10–13 that he received any fresh news from Corinth.

The best interpretation views 2 Corinthians as a unified letter, with chapters 1–9 addressed to the repentant majority (2:6) and chapters 10–13 to the minority still influenced by the false teachers. The support for this view is that: 1) there is no historical evidence (from Greek manuscripts, the writings of the church fathers, or early translations) that chapters 10–13 ever circulated as a separate letter—all Greek manuscripts have them following chapters 1–9; 2) the differences in tone between chapters 10–13 and 1–9 have been exaggerated (11:11; 12:14 with 6:11; 7:2); and 3) chapters 10–13 form the logical conclusion to chapters 1–9, as Paul prepared the Corinthians for his promised visit (1:15,16; 2:1–3).

SEPTEMBER 19

Isaiah 29:1–24

29 "Woe to Ariel, to Ariel, the city
where David dwelt!
Add year to year;
Let feasts come around.
2 Yet I will distress Ariel;
There shall be heaviness and sorrow,
And it shall be to Me as Ariel.
3 I will encamp against you all around,
I will lay siege against you with a mound,
And I will raise siegeworks against you.
4 You shall be brought down,
You shall speak out of the ground;
Your speech shall be low, out of the dust;
Your voice shall be like a medium's, out of the ground;
And your speech shall whisper out of the dust.

5 "Moreover the multitude of your foes
Shall be like fine dust,
And the multitude of the terrible ones
Like chaff that passes away;
Yes, it shall be in an instant, suddenly.
6 You will be punished by the LORD of hosts
With thunder and earthquake and great noise,
With storm and tempest
And the flame of devouring fire.
7 The multitude of all the nations who fight against Ariel,
Even all who fight against her and her fortress,
And distress her,
Shall be as a dream of a night vision.
8 It shall even be as when a hungry man dreams,
And look—he eats;
But he awakes, and his soul is still empty;
Or as when a thirsty man dreams,
And look—he drinks;
But he awakes, and indeed *he is* faint,
And his soul still craves:
So the multitude of all the nations shall be,
Who fight against Mount Zion."

9 Pause and wonder!
Blind yourselves and be blind!
They are drunk, but not with wine;
They stagger, but not with intoxicating drink.
10 For the LORD has poured out on you
The spirit of deep sleep,
And has closed your eyes, namely, the prophets;
And He has covered your heads,
namely, the seers.

29:10 spirit of deep sleep. Because Israel refused to hear her true prophets initially, their ability to hear has been impaired. God gave them up judicially to their own hardness of heart. Paul applied this verse specifically to the general condition of Israel's blindness during the age of the church (Rom. 11:8). **prophets... seers.** False prophets and seers have blinded their listeners with their false prophecies.

29:13 hearts far from Me. Empty ritualism does not bring closeness to God. Jesus used this verse to describe the Judaism of His day (Matt. 15:7–9; Mark 7:6,7).

11 The whole vision has become to you like the words of a book that is sealed, which *men* deliver to one who is literate, saying, "Read this, please."
And he says, "I cannot, for it *is* sealed."
12 Then the book is delivered to one who is illiterate, saying, "Read this, please."
And he says, "I am not literate."
13 Therefore the Lord said:

"Inasmuch as these people draw near
with their mouths

And honor Me with their lips,
But have removed their hearts far from Me,
And their fear toward Me is taught by the commandment of men,
14 Therefore, behold, I will again do a marvelous work
Among this people,
A marvelous work and a wonder;
For the wisdom of their wise *men* shall perish,
And the understanding of their prudent *men* shall be hidden."
15 Woe to those who seek deep to hide their counsel far from the LORD,
And their works are in the dark;
They say, "Who sees us?" and, "Who knows us?"
16 Surely you have things turned around!
Shall the potter be esteemed as the clay;
For shall the thing made say of him who made it,
"He did not make me"?
Or shall the thing formed say of him who formed it,
"He has no understanding"?

17 *Is* it not yet a very little while
Till Lebanon shall be turned into a fruitful field,
And the fruitful field be esteemed as a forest?
18 In that day the deaf shall hear the words of the book,
And the eyes of the blind shall see out of obscurity and out of darkness.
19 The humble also shall increase *their* joy in the LORD,
And the poor among men shall rejoice
In the Holy One of Israel.
20 For the terrible one is brought to nothing,
The scornful one is consumed,
And all who watch for iniquity are cut off—
21 Who make a man an offender by a word,
And lay a snare for him who reproves in the gate,
And turn aside the just by empty words.

22 Therefore thus says the LORD, who redeemed Abraham, concerning the house of Jacob:

"Jacob shall not now be ashamed,
Nor shall his face now grow pale;
23 But when he sees his children,
The work of My hands, in his midst,
They will hallow My name,
And hallow the Holy One of Jacob,
And fear the God of Israel.
24 These also who erred in spirit will come to understanding,
And those who complained will learn doctrine."

29:22 redeemed Abraham. God delivered Abraham from his pagan background when He brought him from beyond the Euphrates River into the land of Canaan (Josh. 24:2,3). Paul elaborates on this theme in Romans 4:1–22. **not now be ashamed.** Israel in her history had frequently suffered disgrace, but the personal presence of the Messiah is to change that (45:17; 49:23; 50:7; 54:4). After the salvation of Israel in the end time, the children of Jacob will no longer cause their forefathers to blush over their wickedness.

Psalm 108:1–6

A Song. A Psalm of David.

O God, my heart is steadfast;
I will sing and give praise, even with my glory.
2 Awake, lute and harp!
I will awaken the dawn.
3 I will praise You, O LORD, among the peoples,
And I will sing praises to You among the nations.
4 For Your mercy *is* great above the heavens,
And Your truth *reaches* to the clouds.

5 Be exalted, O God, above the heavens,
And Your glory above all the earth;
6 That Your beloved may be delivered,
Save *with* Your right hand, and hear me.

Proverbs 25:21–22

21 If your enemy is hungry, give him bread to eat;
And if he is thirsty, give him water to drink;

25:21,22 As metals are melted by placing fiery coals on them, so is the heart of an enemy softened by such kindness. Contrast the coals of judgment in Psalm 140:10. Paul quotes this proverb in Romans 12:20.

22 For *so* you will heap coals of fire on his
head,
And the LORD will reward you.

2 Corinthians 11:1–15

11 Oh, that you would bear with me in a little
folly—and indeed you do bear with me.
2For I am jealous for you with godly jealousy.
For I have betrothed you to one husband, that
I may present *you as* a chaste virgin to Christ.
3But I fear, lest somehow, as the serpent
deceived Eve by his craftiness, so your minds
may be corrupted from the simplicity that is in
Christ. 4For if he who comes preaches another
Jesus whom we have not preached, or *if* you
receive a different spirit which you have not
received, or a different gospel which you have
not accepted—you may well put up with it!
5For I consider that I am not at all inferior to
the most eminent apostles. 6Even though *I am*
untrained in speech, yet *I am* not in knowledge. But we have been thoroughly manifested among you in all things.
7Did I commit sin in humbling myself that you
might be exalted, because I preached the
gospel of God to you free of charge? 8I robbed
other churches, taking wages *from them* to
minister to you. 9And when I was present with
you, and in need, I was a burden to no one, for
what I lacked the brethren who came from
Macedonia supplied. And in everything I kept
myself from being burdensome to you, and so
I will keep *myself.* 10As the truth of Christ is in
me, no one shall stop me from this boasting in
the regions of Achaia. 11Why? Because I do not
love you? God knows!
12But what I do, I will also continue to do, that
I may cut off the opportunity from those who
desire an opportunity to be regarded just as we
are in the things of which they boast. 13For such
are false apostles, deceitful workers, transforming themselves into apostles of Christ. 14And no
wonder! For Satan himself transforms himself
into an angel of light. 15Therefore *it is* no great
thing if his ministers also transform themselves
into ministers of righteousness, whose end will
be according to their works.

11:7 free of charge. Greek culture measured the importance of a teacher by the fee he could command. The false apostles therefore accused Paul of being a counterfeit, since he refused to charge for his services (1 Cor. 9:1–15). They convinced the Corinthians to be offended by Paul's refusal to accept support from them, offering that as evidence that he did not love them (v. 11). Paul's resort to manual labor to support himself (Acts 18:1–3) also embarrassed the Corinthians, who felt such work to be beneath the dignity of an apostle. With biting irony Paul asked his accusers how foregoing his right to support could possibly be a sin. In fact, by refusing support he had humbled himself so they could be exalted, i.e., lifted out of their sin and idolatry.

11:13–15 No longer speaking with veiled irony or defending himself, Paul bluntly and directly exposed the false apostles for what they were—emissaries of Satan. Not only was their claim to apostleship false, so also was their doctrine. As satanic purveyors of false teaching, they were under the curse of Galatians 1:8,9. Paul's forceful language may seem harsh, but it expressed the godly jealousy he felt for the Corinthians. Paul was unwilling to sacrifice truth for the sake of unity.

DAY 19: Why was Paul so emotional about the Corinthians' spiritual welfare?

In 2 Corinthians 11:2, Paul said, "I am jealous for you with godly jealousy." Paul was concerned to the point of jealousy, a zeal for their spiritual purity. Jealousy inspired by zeal for God's causes, and thus similar to God's own jealousy for His holy name and His people's loyalty (Ex. 20:5; 34:14; Deut. 4:24; 5:9; 6:15; 32:16,21; Josh. 24:19; Ps. 78:58; Ezek. 39:25; Nah. 1:2). "I have betrothed you to one husband." As their spiritual father (12:14; 1 Cor. 4:15; 9:1,2), Paul portrayed the Corinthians like a daughter, whom he betrothed to Jesus Christ (at their conversion). "A chaste virgin to Christ." Having betrothed or pledged the Corinthians to Christ, Paul wanted them to be pure until the marriage day finally arrived (Rev. 19:7).

Paul compared the danger facing the Corinthian church to Eve's deception by Satan (v. 3). He feared the Corinthians, like Eve, would fall prey to satanic lies and have their minds corrupted. The tragic result would be the abandonment of their simple devotion to Christ in favor of the sophisticated error of the false apostles. Paul's allusion to Genesis 3 implies that the false apostles were Satan's emissaries—a truth that he later made explicit (vv. 13–15).

The false apostles came into the Corinthian church from the outside—just as Satan did into the Garden (v. 4). It is likely that they were Palestinian Jews (v. 22; Acts 6:1) who allegedly sought to bring the Corinthians under the sway of the Jerusalem church. They were in a sense Judaizers, seeking to impose Jewish customs on the Corinthians. Unlike the Judaizers who plagued the Galatian churches (Gal. 5:2), however, the false apostles at Corinth apparently did not insist that the Corinthians be circumcised. Nor did they practice a rigid legalism; in fact, they apparently encouraged licentiousness (12:21). Their fascination with rhetoric and oratory (10:10) suggests they had been influenced by Greek culture and philosophy.

Though their teaching may have differed from the Galatian Judaizers, it was just as deadly. "Another Jesus...a different spirit...a different gospel" (v. 4). Paul's quarrel with the false apostles was not personal, but doctrinal. Those who adulterated the true gospel received Paul's strongest condemnation (Gal. 1:6–9). Paul's fear that the Corinthians would embrace the damning lies of the false apostles prompted his jealous concern for them.

SEPTEMBER 20

Isaiah 30:1–32:20

30 "Woe to the rebellious children,"
says the LORD,
"Who take counsel, but not of Me,
And who devise plans, but not of My
Spirit,
That they may add sin to sin;

30:1 not of Me...not of My Spirit. Hezekiah's advisers urged him to turn to the Egyptians, not to God, for help against the invading Assyrians. Isaiah denounced this reliance on Egypt rather than God, who had forbidden such alliances.

2 Who walk to go down to Egypt,
And have not asked My advice,
To strengthen themselves in the
strength of Pharaoh,
And to trust in the shadow of Egypt!
3 Therefore the strength of Pharaoh
Shall be your shame,
And trust in the shadow of Egypt
Shall be *your* humiliation.
4 For his princes were at Zoan,
And his ambassadors came to Hanes.
5 They were all ashamed of a people *who*
could not benefit them,
Or be help or benefit,
But a shame and also a reproach."

6 The burden against the beasts of the South.

Through a land of trouble and anguish,
From which *came* the lioness and lion,
The viper and fiery flying serpent,
They will carry their riches on the
backs of young donkeys,
And their treasures on the humps of
camels,
To a people *who* shall not profit;
7 For the Egyptians shall help in vain
and to no purpose.
Therefore I have called her
Rahab-Hem-Shebeth.
8 Now go, write it before them on a tablet,
And note it on a scroll,
That it may be for time to come,
Forever and ever:
9 That this *is* a rebellious people,
Lying children,
Children *who* will not hear the law of
the LORD;
10 Who say to the seers, "Do not see,"
And to the prophets, "Do not prophesy
to us right things;
Speak to us smooth things, prophesy
deceits.
11 Get out of the way,
Turn aside from the path,
Cause the Holy One of Israel
To cease from before us."

12 Therefore thus says the Holy One of Israel:

"Because you despise this word,
And trust in oppression and perversity,
And rely on them,
13 Therefore this iniquity shall be to you
Like a breach ready to fall,
A bulge in a high wall,
Whose breaking comes suddenly,
in an instant.
14 And He shall break it like the breaking
of the potter's vessel,
Which is broken in pieces;
He shall not spare.
So there shall not be found among its
fragments

A shard to take fire from the hearth,
Or to take water from the cistern."

15For thus says the Lord GOD, the Holy One
of Israel:

"In returning and rest you shall be saved;
In quietness and confidence shall be your strength."
But you would not,
16 And you said, "No, for we will flee on horses"—
Therefore you shall flee!
And, "We will ride on swift *horses*"—
Therefore those who pursue you shall be swift!
17 One thousand *shall flee* at the threat of one,
At the threat of five you shall flee,
Till you are left as a pole on top of a mountain
And as a banner on a hill.

18 Therefore the LORD will wait, that He may be gracious to you;
And therefore He will be exalted, that He may have mercy on you.
For the LORD *is* a God of justice;
Blessed *are* all those who wait for Him.

19 For the people shall dwell in Zion at Jerusalem;
You shall weep no more.
He will be very gracious to you at the sound of your cry;
When He hears it, He will answer you.
20 And *though* the Lord gives you
The bread of adversity and the water of affliction,
Yet your teachers will not be moved into a corner anymore,
But your eyes shall see your teachers.
21 Your ears shall hear a word behind you, saying,
"This *is* the way, walk in it,"
Whenever you turn to the right hand
Or whenever you turn to the left.
22 You will also defile the covering of your images of silver,
And the ornament of your molded images of gold.
You will throw them away as an unclean thing;
You will say to them, "Get away!"

23 Then He will give the rain for your seed
With which you sow the ground,
And bread of the increase of the earth;
It will be fat and plentiful.
In that day your cattle will feed
In large pastures.
24 Likewise the oxen and the young donkeys that work the ground
Will eat cured fodder,
Which has been winnowed with the shovel and fan.
25 There will be on every high mountain
And on every high hill
Rivers *and* streams of waters,
In the day of the great slaughter,
When the towers fall.
26 Moreover the light of the moon will be as the light of the sun,
And the light of the sun will be sevenfold,
As the light of seven days,
In the day that the LORD binds up the bruise of His people
And heals the stroke of their wound.

27 Behold, the name of the LORD comes from afar,
Burning *with* His anger,
And *His* burden *is* heavy;
His lips are full of indignation,
And His tongue like a devouring fire.
28 His breath is like an overflowing stream,
Which reaches up to the neck,
To sift the nations with the sieve of futility;
And *there shall be* a bridle in the jaws of the people,
Causing *them* to err.

29 You shall have a song
As in the night *when* a holy festival is kept,
And gladness of heart as when one goes with a flute,
To come into the mountain of the LORD,
To the Mighty One of Israel.
30 The LORD will cause His glorious voice to be heard,
And show the descent of His arm,
With the indignation of *His* anger
And the flame of a devouring fire,
With scattering, tempest, and hailstones.
31 For through the voice of the LORD
Assyria will be beaten down,
As He strikes with the rod.
32 And *in* every place where the staff of punishment passes,
Which the LORD lays on him,
It will be with tambourines and harps;
And in battles of brandishing He will fight with it.
33 For Tophet *was* established of old,

Yes, for the king it is prepared.
He has made *it* deep and large;
Its pyre *is* fire with much wood;
The breath of the LORD, like a stream
of brimstone,
Kindles it.

30:33 Tophet. Literally, a place of abomination. Idolatrous Israel had burned to death human victims in this valley just south of Jerusalem, an area sometimes called the Valley of Hinnom (2 Kin. 23:10; Jer. 19:6). Later it became known as Gehenna, the place of refuse for the city, with constantly burning fires, symbolizing hell. The defeat was to be so complete that the fire burns continually.

31 Woe to those who go down to
Egypt for help,
And rely on horses,
Who trust in chariots because *they are*
many,
And in horsemen because they are
very strong,
But who do not look to the Holy One
of Israel,
Nor seek the LORD!
2 Yet He also *is* wise and will bring
disaster,
And will not call back His words,
But will arise against the house of
evildoers,
And against the help of those who
work iniquity.
3 Now the Egyptians *are* men, and not God;
And their horses are flesh, and not
spirit.
When the LORD stretches out His hand,
Both he who helps will fall,
And he who is helped will fall down;
They all will perish together.

4 For thus the LORD has spoken to me:

"As a lion roars,
And a young lion over his prey
(When a multitude of shepherds is
summoned against him,
He will not be afraid of their voice
Nor be disturbed by their noise),
So the LORD of hosts will come down
To fight for Mount Zion and for its hill.
5 Like birds flying about,
So will the LORD of hosts defend
Jerusalem.
Defending, He will also deliver *it;*
Passing over, He will preserve *it.*"

6 Return *to Him* against whom the children of
Israel have deeply revolted. 7 For in that day
every man shall throw away his idols of silver
and his idols of gold—sin, which your own
hands have made for yourselves.

8 "Then Assyria shall fall by a sword not
of man,
And a sword not of mankind
shall devour him.
But he shall flee from the sword,
And his young men shall become
forced labor.
9 He shall cross over to his stronghold
for fear,
And his princes shall be afraid of the
banner,"
Says the LORD,
Whose fire *is* in Zion
And whose furnace *is* in Jerusalem.

32 Behold, a king will reign
in righteousness,
And princes will rule with justice.
2 A man will be as a hiding place from
the wind,
And a cover from the tempest,
As rivers of water in a dry place,
As the shadow of a great rock in a
weary land.
3 The eyes of those who see will not be
dim,
And the ears of those who hear will
listen.
4 Also the heart of the rash will
understand knowledge,
And the tongue of the stammerers will
be ready to speak plainly.
5 The foolish person will no longer be
called generous,
Nor the miser said *to be* bountiful;
6 For the foolish person will speak
foolishness,
And his heart will work iniquity:
To practice ungodliness,
To utter error against the LORD,
To keep the hungry unsatisfied,
And he will cause the drink of the
thirsty to fail.
7 Also the schemes of the schemer *are*
evil;
He devises wicked plans
To destroy the poor with lying words,
Even when the needy speaks justice.
8 But a generous man devises generous
things,

And by generosity he shall stand.

9 Rise up, you women who are at ease,
Hear my voice;
You complacent daughters,
Give ear to my speech.
10 In a year and *some* days
You will be troubled, you complacent
women;
For the vintage will fail,
The gathering will not come.
11 Tremble, you *women* who are at ease;
Be troubled, you complacent ones;
Strip yourselves, make yourselves bare,
And gird *sackcloth* on *your* waists.

12 People shall mourn upon their breasts
For the pleasant fields, for the fruitful
vine.
13 On the land of my people will come up
thorns *and* briers,
Yes, on all the happy homes *in* the
joyous city;
14 Because the palaces will be forsaken,
The bustling city will be deserted.
The forts and towers will become lairs
forever,
A joy of wild donkeys, a pasture of
flocks—
15 Until the Spirit is poured upon us from
on high,
And the wilderness becomes a fruitful
field,
And the fruitful field is counted as a
forest.
16 Then justice will dwell in the
wilderness,
And righteousness remain in the
fruitful field.
17 The work of righteousness will be
peace,
And the effect of righteousness,
quietness and assurance forever.
18 My people will dwell in a peaceful
habitation,
In secure dwellings, and in quiet
resting places,
19 Though hail comes down on the forest,
And the city is brought low in
humiliation.
20 Blessed *are* you who sow beside
all waters,
Who send out freely the feet of the ox
and the donkey.

Psalm 108:7–13

7 God has spoken in His holiness:
"I will rejoice;
I will divide Shechem
And measure out the Valley
of Succoth.
8 Gilead *is* Mine; Manasseh *is* Mine;
Ephraim also *is* the helmet for My
head;
Judah *is* My lawgiver.
9 Moab *is* My washpot;
Over Edom I will cast My shoe;
Over Philistia I will triumph."
10 Who will bring me *into* the strong city?
Who will lead me to Edom?
11 *Is it* not *You,* O God, *who* cast us off?
And *You,* O God, *who* did not go out
with our armies?
12 Give us help from trouble,
For the help of man is useless.
13 Through God we will do valiantly,
For *it is* He *who* shall tread down
our enemies.

Proverbs 25:23–24

23 The north wind brings forth rain,
And a backbiting tongue an angry
countenance.

24 *It is* better to dwell in a corner of a
housetop,
Than in a house shared with a
contentious woman.

2 Corinthians 11:16–33

16I say again, let no one think me a fool. If
otherwise, at least receive me as a fool, that I
also may boast a little. 17What I speak, I speak
not according to the Lord, but as it were, foolishly, in this confidence of boasting. 18Seeing
that many boast according to the flesh, I also
will boast. 19For you put up with fools gladly,
since you *yourselves* are wise! 20For you put up
with it if one brings you into bondage, if one
devours *you,* if one takes *from you,* if one
exalts himself, if one strikes you on the face.
21To *our* shame I say that we were too weak for
that! But in whatever anyone is bold—I speak
foolishly—I am bold also.

11:19–21 These verses contain some of the most scathing sarcasm Paul ever penned, demonstrating the seriousness of the situation at Corinth and revealing the jealous concern of a godly pastor. Paul did not view his disagreement with the false apostles as a mere academic debate; the souls of the Corinthians and the purity of the gospel were at stake.

[22]Are they Hebrews? So *am* I. Are they Israelites? So *am* I. Are they the seed of Abraham?
So *am* I. [23]Are they ministers of Christ?—I
speak as a fool—I *am* more: in labors more
abundant, in stripes above measure, in prisons
more frequently, in deaths often. [24]From the
Jews five times I received forty *stripes* minus
one. [25]Three times I was beaten with rods; once
I was stoned; three times I was shipwrecked; a
night and a day I have been in the deep; [26]*in* journeys often, *in* perils of waters, *in* perils of robbers, *in* perils of *my own* countrymen, *in* perils
of the Gentiles, *in* perils in the city, *in* perils in
the wilderness, *in* perils in the sea, *in* perils
among false brethren; [27]in weariness and toil, in
sleeplessness often, in hunger and thirst, in fastings often, in cold and nakedness— [28]besides
the other things, what comes upon me daily:
my deep concern for all the churches. [29]Who is
weak, and I am not weak? Who is made to
stumble, and I do not burn *with indignation?*
[30]If I must boast, I will boast in the things
which concern my infirmity. [31]The God and
Father of our Lord Jesus Christ, who is blessed
forever, knows that I am not lying. [32]In Damascus the governor, under Aretas the king, was
guarding the city of the Damascenes with a
garrison, desiring to arrest me; [33]but I was let
down in a basket through a window in the
wall, and escaped from his hands.

11:20 brings you into bondage. The Greek verb translated by this phrase appears elsewhere in the New Testament only in Galatians 2:4, where it speaks of the Galatians' enslavement by the Judaizers. The false apostles had robbed the Corinthians of their freedom in Christ (Gal. 5:1). **devours *you*.** Or "preys upon you." This probably refers to the false teachers' demands for financial support (the same verb appears in Luke 20:47 where Jesus denounces the Pharisees for devouring widows' houses). **takes *from you*.** Better translated "takes advantage of you." The false apostles were attempting to catch the Corinthians like fish in a net (Luke 5:5,6). **exalts himself.** This refers to one who is presumptuous, puts on airs, acts arrogantly, or lords it over people (1 Pet. 5:3). **strikes you on the face.** The false apostles may have physically abused the Corinthians, but the phrase is more likely used in a metaphorical sense (1 Cor. 9:27) to speak of the false teachers' humiliation of the Corinthians. To strike someone on the face was a sign of disrespect and contempt (1 Kin. 22:24; Luke 22:64; Acts 23:2).

DAY 20: What had being a minister of Christ cost the apostle Paul?

Contrasting his ministry to the false apostles in 2 Corinthians 11:23, Paul spoke of "in labors more abundant, in stripes above measure, in prisons more frequently, in deaths often." This is a general summation of Paul's sufferings for the gospel. The next few verses give specific examples, many of which are not found in Acts.

"Forty stripes minus one" (v. 24). Deuteronomy 25:1–3 set 40 as the maximum number that could legally be administered. In Paul's day the Jews reduced that number by one to avoid accidentally going over the maximum. Jesus warned that His followers would receive such beatings (Matt. 10:17).

"Beaten with rods" (v. 25). Refers to Roman beatings with flexible sticks tied together (Acts 16:22,23). "Once I was stoned"—at Lystra (Acts 14:19,20). "Three times I was shipwrecked." Not including the shipwreck on his journey as a prisoner to Rome (Acts 27), which had not yet taken place. Paul had been on several sea voyages up to this time, giving ample opportunity for the 3 shipwrecks to have occurred. "A night and a day I have been in the deep." At least one of the shipwrecks was so severe that Paul spent an entire day floating on the wreckage, waiting to be rescued.

"In perils" (v. 26). Those connected with his frequent travels. "Waters" (rivers) and "robbers" posed a serious danger to travelers in the ancient world. Paul's journey from Perga to Pisidian Antioch (Acts 13:14), for example, required him to travel through the robber-infested Taurus Mountains and to cross two dangerous, flood-prone rivers. Paul was frequently in danger from his "own countrymen" (Acts 9:23,29; 13:45; 14:2,19; 17:5; 18:6,12–16; 20:3,19; 21:27–32) and, less often, from "Gentiles" (Acts 16:16–40; 19:23–20:1). "False brethren." Those who appeared to be Christians, but were not, such as the false apostles (v. 13) and the Judaizers (Gal. 2:4).

And far worse than the occasional physical suffering Paul endured —weariness and toil, sleeplessness, hunger, thirst, fastings, and cold—was the constant, daily burden of concern for the churches that he felt (v. 28). Those who were "weak" (Rom. 14; 1 Cor. 8) in faith or were "made to stumble" into sin caused him intense emotional pain.

SEPTEMBER 21

Isaiah 33:1–34:17

33 Woe to you who plunder, though
you *have* not *been* plundered;
And you who deal treacherously,
though they have not dealt
treacherously with you!
When you cease plundering,
You will be plundered;
When you make an end of dealing
treacherously,
They will deal treacherously with you.

2 O LORD, be gracious to us;
We have waited for You.
Be their arm every morning,
Our salvation also in the time of trouble.
3 At the noise of the tumult the people
shall flee;
When You lift Yourself up, the nations
shall be scattered;
4 And Your plunder shall be gathered
Like the gathering of the caterpillar;
As the running to and fro of locusts,
He shall run upon them.

5 The LORD is exalted, for He dwells on
high;
He has filled Zion with justice and
righteousness.
6 Wisdom and knowledge will be the
stability of your times,
And the strength of salvation;
The fear of the LORD *is* His treasure.

7 Surely their valiant ones shall cry
outside,
The ambassadors of peace shall weep
bitterly.
8 The highways lie waste,
The traveling man ceases.
He has broken the covenant,
He has despised the cities,
He regards no man.
9 The earth mourns *and* languishes,
Lebanon is shamed *and* shriveled;
Sharon is like a wilderness,
And Bashan and Carmel shake off
their fruits.

10 "Now I will rise," says the LORD;
"Now I will be exalted,
Now I will lift Myself up.
11 You shall conceive chaff,
You shall bring forth stubble;
Your breath, *as* fire, shall devour you.
12 And the people shall be *like* the
burnings of lime;
Like thorns cut up they shall be
burned in the fire.
13 Hear, you *who are* afar off, what I have
done;
And you *who are* near, acknowledge
My might."

14 The sinners in Zion are afraid;
Fearfulness has seized the hypocrites:
"Who among us shall dwell with the
devouring fire?
Who among us shall dwell with
everlasting burnings?"

33:17 King in His beauty. The prophecy moves beyond Hezekiah in his sackcloth, oppressed by his enemy, to the Messiah in His beauty. Seeing Him in glory is another reward of the righteous. The near-future deliverance from Sennacherib anticipates a more distant wonder when the Messiah will sit on His throne.

15 He who walks righteously and speaks
uprightly,
He who despises the gain of oppressions,
Who gestures with his hands, refusing
bribes,
Who stops his ears from hearing of
bloodshed,
And shuts his eyes from seeing evil:
16 He will dwell on high;
His place of defense *will be* the fortress
of rocks;
Bread will be given him,
His water *will be* sure.

17 Your eyes will see the King in His beauty;
They will see the land that is very far off.
18 Your heart will meditate on terror:
"Where *is* the scribe?
Where *is* he who weighs?
Where *is* he who counts the towers?"
19 You will not see a fierce people,
A people of obscure speech, beyond
perception,
Of a stammering tongue *that you*
cannot understand.

20 Look upon Zion, the city of our
appointed feasts;
Your eyes will see Jerusalem, a quiet
home,
A tabernacle *that* will not be
taken down;

Not one of its stakes will ever be
removed,
Nor will any of its cords be broken.
21 But there the majestic LORD *will be* for us
A place of broad rivers *and* streams,
In which no galley with oars will sail,
Nor majestic ships pass by
22 (For the LORD *is* our Judge,
The LORD *is* our Lawgiver,
The LORD *is* our King;
He will save us);
23 Your tackle is loosed,
They could not strengthen their mast,
They could not spread the sail.

Then the prey of great plunder is divided;
The lame take the prey.
24 And the inhabitant will not say, "I am
sick";
The people who dwell in it *will be*
forgiven *their* iniquity.

34 Come near, you nations,
to hear;
And heed, you people!
Let the earth hear, and all that is in it,
The world and all things that come
forth from it.
2 For the indignation of the LORD *is*
against all nations,
And *His* fury against all their armies;
He has utterly destroyed them,
He has given them over to the slaughter.
3 Also their slain shall be thrown out;
Their stench shall rise from their
corpses,
And the mountains shall be melted
with their blood.
4 All the host of heaven shall be dissolved,
And the heavens shall be rolled up like
a scroll;
All their host shall fall down
As the leaf falls from the vine,
And as *fruit* falling from a fig tree.
5 "For My sword shall be bathed in heaven;
Indeed it shall come down on Edom,
And on the people of My curse, for
judgment.
6 The sword of the LORD is filled with
blood,
It is made overflowing with fatness,
With the blood of lambs and goats,
With the fat of the kidneys of rams.
For the LORD has a sacrifice in Bozrah,
And a great slaughter in the land of
Edom.
7 The wild oxen shall come down with
them,
And the young bulls with the mighty bulls;
Their land shall be soaked with blood,
And their dust saturated with fatness."
8 For *it is* the day of the LORD's vengeance,
The year of recompense for the cause
of Zion.
9 Its streams shall be turned into pitch,
And its dust into brimstone;
Its land shall become burning pitch.
10 It shall not be quenched night or day;
Its smoke shall ascend forever.
From generation to generation it shall
lie waste;
No one shall pass through it forever
and ever.
11 But the pelican and the porcupine shall
possess it,
Also the owl and the raven shall dwell
in it.
And He shall stretch out over it
The line of confusion and the stones
of emptiness.
12 They shall call its nobles to the kingdom,
But none *shall be* there, and all its
princes shall be nothing.

13 And thorns shall come up in its palaces,
Nettles and brambles in its fortresses;
It shall be a habitation of jackals,
A courtyard for ostriches.
14 The wild beasts of the desert shall also
meet with the jackals,
And the wild goat shall bleat to its
companion;
Also the night creature shall rest there,
And find for herself a place of rest.
15 There the arrow snake shall make her
nest and lay *eggs*
And hatch, and gather *them* under her
shadow;
There also shall the hawks be gathered,
Every one with her mate.

16 "Search from the book of the LORD,
and read:
Not one of these shall fail;
Not one shall lack her mate.
For My mouth has commanded it, and
His Spirit has gathered them.
17 He has cast the lot for them,
And His hand has divided it among
them with a measuring line.
They shall possess it forever;
From generation to generation they
shall dwell in it."

Psalm 109:1–5

To the Chief Musician. A Psalm of David.

Do not keep silent,
O God of my praise!

2 For the mouth of the wicked and the mouth of the deceitful
Have opened against me;
They have spoken against me with a lying tongue.
3 They have also surrounded me with words of hatred,
And fought against me without a cause.
4 In return for my love they are my accusers,
But I *give myself to* prayer.
5 Thus they have rewarded me evil for good,
And hatred for my love.

Proverbs 25:25–26

25 *As* cold water to a weary soul,
So *is* good news from a far country.

26 A righteous *man* who falters before the wicked
Is like a murky spring and a polluted well.

25:26 murky spring. The righteous one who sins muddies the water for the wicked who see him and for whom he should serve as an example of righteousness (Ps. 17:5).

2 Corinthians 12:1–21

12 It is doubtless not profitable for me to boast. I will come to visions and revelations of the Lord: [2]I know a man in Christ who fourteen years ago—whether in the body I do not know, or whether out of the body I do not know, God knows—such a one was caught up to the third heaven. [3]And I know such a man—whether in the body or out of the body I do not know, God knows— [4]how he was caught up into Paradise and heard inexpressible words, which it is not lawful for a man to utter. [5]Of such a one I will boast; yet of myself I will not boast, except in my infirmities. [6]For though I might desire to boast, I will not be a fool; for I will speak the truth. But I refrain, lest anyone should think of me above what he sees me *to be* or hears from me.

[7]And lest I should be exalted above measure by the abundance of the revelations, a thorn in the flesh was given to me, a messenger of Satan to buffet me, lest I be exalted above measure. [8]Concerning this thing I pleaded with the Lord three times that it might depart from me. [9]And He said to me, "My grace is sufficient for you, for My strength is made perfect in weakness." Therefore most gladly I will rather boast in my infirmities, that the power of Christ may rest upon me. [10]Therefore I take pleasure in infirmities, in reproaches, in needs, in persecutions, in distresses, for Christ's sake. For when I am weak, then I am strong.

[11]I have become a fool in boasting; you have compelled me. For I ought to have been commended by you; for in nothing was I behind the most eminent apostles, though I am nothing. [12]Truly the signs of an apostle were accomplished among you with all perseverance, in

12:2–4 Since it took place 14 years before the writing of 2 Corinthians, the specific vision Paul relates cannot be identified with any incident recorded in Acts. It probably took place between his return to Tarsus from Jerusalem (Acts 9:30) and the start of his missionary journeys (Acts 13:1–3). **caught up to the third heaven...caught up into Paradise.** Paul was not describing two separate visions—"the third heaven" and "Paradise" are the same place (Rev. 2:7, which says the tree of life is in Paradise, with Rev. 22:14, which says it is in heaven). The first heaven is the earth's atmosphere (Gen. 8:2; Deut. 11:11; 1 Kin. 8:35); the second is interplanetary and interstellar space (Gen. 15:5; Ps. 8:3; Is. 13:10); and the third the abode of God (1 Kin. 8:30; 2 Chr. 30:27; Ps. 123:1).

12:8 I pleaded...three times. Paul, longing for relief from this painful hindrance to his ministry, went to his Lord, begging Him (the use of the definite article with "Lord" shows Paul's prayer was directed to Jesus) to remove it. The demons are only subject to His authority. The 3-fold repetition of Paul's request parallels that of Jesus in Gethsemane (Mark 14:32–41). Both Paul and Jesus had their requests denied, but were granted grace to endure their ordeals.

12:9 My grace is sufficient for you. The present tense of the verb translated "is sufficient" reveals the constant availability of divine grace. God would not remove the thorn, as Paul had requested, but would continually supply him with grace to endure it (1 Cor. 15:10; Phil. 4:13; Col. 1:29). **My strength is made perfect in weakness.** The weaker the human instrument, the more clearly God's grace shines forth.

signs and wonders and mighty deeds. [13]For what is it in which you were inferior to other churches, except that I myself was not burdensome to you? Forgive me this wrong!

[14]Now *for* the third time I am ready to come to you. And I will not be burdensome to you; for I do not seek yours, but you. For the children ought not to lay up for the parents, but the parents for the children. [15]And I will very gladly spend and be spent for your souls; though the more abundantly I love you, the less I am loved.

[16]But be that *as it may,* I did not burden you. Nevertheless, being crafty, I caught you by cunning! [17]Did I take advantage of you by any of those whom I sent to you? [18]I urged Titus, and sent our brother with *him.* Did Titus take advantage of you? Did we not walk in the same spirit? Did *we* not *walk* in the same steps?

[19]Again, do you think that we excuse ourselves to you? We speak before God in Christ. But *we do* all things, beloved, for your edification. [20]For I fear lest, when I come, I shall not find you such as I wish, and *that* I shall be found by you such as you do not wish; lest *there be* contentions, jealousies, outbursts of wrath, selfish ambitions, backbitings, whisperings, conceits, tumults; [21]lest, when I come again, my God will humble me among you, and I shall mourn for many who have sinned before and have not repented of the uncleanness, fornication, and lewdness which they have practiced.

DAY 21: To what was Paul referring by the term "thorn in the flesh"?

Paul began his account about the "thorn in the flesh" by indicating the reason it was given to him—"lest I should be exalted above measure." The assault was painful, but purposeful. As with Job, Satan was the immediate cause, but God was the ultimate cause. God was allowing Satan to bring this severe trouble in the church for the purpose of humbling Paul who, having had so many revelations, including a trip to heaven and back, would have been proud.

Paul's use of the word "messenger" (Greek, *angellos,* or angel) from Satan suggests the "thorn in the flesh" (literally, "a stake for the flesh") was a demon, not a physical illness. Of the 188 uses of the Greek word *angellos* in the New Testament, at least 180 are in reference to angels. This angel was from Satan, a demon afflicting Paul.

Possibly, the best explanation for this demon was that he was indwelling the ring leader of the Corinthian conspiracy, the leader of the false apostles. Through them he was tearing up Paul's beloved church and thus driving a painful stake through Paul. Further support for this view comes from the context of chapters 10–13, which is one of fighting adversaries (the false prophets). The verb translated "buffet" always refers to ill treatment from other people (Matt. 26:67; Mark 14:65; 1 Cor. 4:11; 1 Pet. 2:20). Finally, the Old Testament describes Israel's personal opponents as thorns (Num. 33:55; Josh. 23:13; Judg. 2:3; Ezek. 28:24).

SEPTEMBER 22

Isaiah 35:1–36:22

35 The wilderness and the wasteland
shall be glad for them,
And the desert shall rejoice and
blossom as the rose;
2 It shall blossom abundantly and rejoice,
Even with joy and singing.
The glory of Lebanon shall be given to it,
The excellence of Carmel and Sharon.
They shall see the glory of the LORD,
The excellency of our God.

3 Strengthen the weak hands,
And make firm the feeble knees.
4 Say to those *who are* fearful-hearted,
"Be strong, do not fear!
Behold, your God will come *with*
vengeance,
With the recompense of God;
He will come and save you."

5 Then the eyes of the blind shall be
opened,
And the ears of the deaf shall be
unstopped.
6 Then the lame shall leap like a deer,
And the tongue of the dumb sing.
For waters shall burst forth in the
wilderness,
And streams in the desert.
7 The parched ground shall become a pool,
And the thirsty land springs of water;

35:6 lame...sing. God's restoration in the millennial age is to include physical restoration to the afflicted. Jesus' First Coming gave a foretaste of that future day (Matt. 11:5; 12:22; Mark 7:37; Luke 7:21; Acts 3:8).

In the habitation of jackals, where
each lay,
There shall be grass with reeds and
rushes.
8 A highway shall be there, and a road,
And it shall be called the Highway of
Holiness.

35:8 Highway of Holiness. This refers to the way leading the redeemed back to Jerusalem, the throne of the Messiah, literally and spiritually. Christ Himself is to be the leader on that way, called in 40:3, the "way of the LORD."

The unclean shall not pass over it,
But it *shall be* for others.
Whoever walks the road, although
a fool,
Shall not go astray.
9 No lion shall be there,
Nor shall *any* ravenous beast go up on it;
It shall not be found there.
But the redeemed shall walk *there,*
10 And the ransomed of the LORD shall
return,
And come to Zion with singing,
With everlasting joy on their heads.
They shall obtain joy and gladness,
And sorrow and sighing shall flee away.

36 Now it came to pass in the fourteenth
year of King Hezekiah *that* Sennacherib
king of Assyria came up against all the fortified cities of Judah and took them. [2]Then the
king of Assyria sent *the* Rabshakeh with a
great army from Lachish to King Hezekiah at
Jerusalem. And he stood by the aqueduct
from the upper pool, on the highway to the
Fuller's Field. [3]And Eliakim the son of Hilkiah,
who was over the household, Shebna the
scribe, and Joah the son of Asaph, the
recorder, came out to him.

[4]Then *the* Rabshakeh said to them, "Say
now to Hezekiah, 'Thus says the great king,
the king of Assyria: "What confidence is this in
which you trust? [5]I say you speak of having
plans and power for war; but *they are* mere
words. Now in whom do you trust, that you
rebel against me? [6]Look! You are trusting in
the staff of this broken reed, Egypt, on which
if a man leans, it will go into his hand and
pierce it. So *is* Pharaoh king of Egypt to all
who trust in him.

[7]"But if you say to me, 'We trust in the LORD
our God,' *is it* not He whose high places and
whose altars Hezekiah has taken away, and said
to Judah and Jerusalem, 'You shall worship
before this altar'?" ' [8]Now therefore, I urge you,
give a pledge to my master the king of Assyria,
and I will give you two thousand horses—if
you are able on your part to put riders on
them! [9]How then will you repel one captain of
the least of my master's servants, and put your

36:10 The LORD said. Rabshakeh's boastful claim of the authority from Judah's God for his mission may have been a ploy on his part to get a surrender, but it aligned with Isaiah's prophecy that the Assyrians would be His instrument to punish His people (8:7,8; 10:5,6). The Assyrians may have heard this from partisans or may not have known this, but Judah did.

trust in Egypt for chariots and horsemen?
[10]Have I now come up without the LORD against
this land to destroy it? The LORD said to me,
'Go up against this land, and destroy it.' "

[11]Then Eliakim, Shebna, and Joah said to *the*
Rabshakeh, "Please speak to your servants in
Aramaic, for we understand *it;* and do not
speak to us in Hebrew in the hearing of the
people who *are* on the wall."

[12]But *the* Rabshakeh said, "Has my master
sent me to your master and to you to speak these
words, and not to the men who sit on the wall, who
will eat and drink their own waste with you?"

[13]Then *the* Rabshakeh stood and called out
with a loud voice in Hebrew, and said, "Hear
the words of the great king, the king of Assyria! [14]Thus says the king: 'Do not let
Hezekiah deceive you, for he will not be able
to deliver you; [15]nor let Hezekiah make you
trust in the LORD, saying, "The LORD will surely deliver us; this city will not be given into the
hand of the king of Assyria." ' [16]Do not listen to
Hezekiah; for thus says the king of Assyria:
'Make *peace* with me *by a* present and come
out to me; and every one of you eat from his
own vine and every one from his own fig tree,
and every one of you drink the waters of his
own cistern; [17]until I come and take you away
to a land like your own land, a land of grain
and new wine, a land of bread and vineyards.
[18]*Beware* lest Hezekiah persuade you, saying,
"The LORD will deliver us." Has any one of the
gods of the nations delivered its land from the
hand of the king of Assyria? [19]Where *are* the gods
of Hamath and Arpad? Where *are* the gods of
Sepharvaim? Indeed, have they delivered Samaria from my hand? [20]Who among all the

gods of these lands have delivered their countries from my hand, that the LORD should
deliver Jerusalem from my hand?' "
[21]But they held their peace and answered
him not a word; for the king's commandment
was, "Do not answer him." [22]Then Eliakim the
son of Hilkiah, who *was* over the household,
Shebna the scribe, and Joah the son of Asaph,
the recorder, came to Hezekiah with *their*
clothes torn, and told him the words of *the*
Rabshakeh.

Psalm 109:6–13

6 Set a wicked man over him,
And let an accuser stand at his right
hand.
7 When he is judged, let him be found
guilty,
And let his prayer become sin.
8 Let his days be few,
And let another take his office.
9 Let his children be fatherless,
And his wife a widow.
10 Let his children continually be
vagabonds, and beg;
Let them seek *their bread* also from
their desolate places.
11 Let the creditor seize all that he has,
And let strangers plunder his labor.
12 Let there be none to extend mercy to
him,
Nor let there be any to favor his
fatherless children.
13 Let his posterity be cut off,
And in the generation following let
their name be blotted out.

Proverbs 25:27–28

27 *It is* not good to eat much honey;
So to seek one's own glory *is not* glory.
28 Whoever *has* no rule over his own spirit
Is like a city broken down, without walls.

25:28 city broken down. Such are exposed and vulnerable to the incursion of evil thoughts and successful temptations.

2 Corinthians 13:1–14

13 This *will be* the third *time* I am coming to
you. *"By the mouth of two or three wit-*
nesses every word shall be established." [2]I
have told you before, and foretell as if I were
present the second time, and now being
absent I write to those who have sinned before,
and to all the rest, that if I come again I will not
spare— [3]since you seek a proof of Christ
speaking in me, who is not weak toward you,
but mighty in you. [4]For though He was crucified in weakness, yet He lives by the power of
God. For we also are weak in Him, but we
shall live with Him by the power of God
toward you.
[5]Examine yourselves *as to* whether you are
in the faith. Test yourselves. Do you not know
yourselves, that Jesus Christ is in you?—unless indeed you are disqualified. [6]But I trust
that you will know that we are not disqualified.
[7]Now I pray to God that you do no evil, not
that we should appear approved, but that you
should do what is honorable, though we may
seem disqualified. [8]For we can do nothing
against the truth, but for the truth. [9]For we are
glad when we are weak and you are strong.
And this also we pray, that you may be made
complete. [10]Therefore I write these things
being absent, lest being present I should use
sharpness, according to the authority which
the Lord has given me for edification and not
for destruction.
[11]Finally, brethren, farewell. Become complete. Be of good comfort, be of one mind, live
in peace; and the God of love and peace will be
with you.
[12]Greet one another with a holy kiss.
[13]All the saints greet you.
[14]The grace of the Lord Jesus Christ, and
the love of God, and the communion of the
Holy Spirit *be* with you all. Amen.

13:12 a holy kiss. A sign of greeting in biblical times (Matt. 26:49; Luke 7:45), much like the modern handshake. For Christians, it further expressed brotherly love and unity (Rom. 16:16; 1 Cor. 16:20; 1 Thess. 5:26; 1 Pet. 5:14).

DAY 22: What was Paul's final warning to the Corinthians?

In 2 Corinthians 12:20,21, it is clear that when he visited them, Paul did not want to find the Corinthians in the same sorry spiritual condition as on his last visit (the "painful visit," 2:1). If he found that they were not what he wished (i.e., still practicing the sins he listed), they would find him not as they wished—he would have had to discipline them (13:2). To find the Corinthians still living in unrepentant sin would both humiliate and sadden Paul. This warning (and the one in 13:2) was designed to prevent that from happening.

"I will not spare" (v. 2). Paul informed the Corinthians that he would deal biblically with any sin he found in Corinth. Those Corinthians still seeking proof that Paul was a genuine apostle would have it when he arrived (v. 3). They may have gotten more than they bargained for, however, for Paul was going to use his apostolic authority and power to deal with any sin and rebellion he found there. Christ's power was to be revealed through Paul against the sinning Corinthians (1 Cor. 11:30–32). Paul was to come to Corinth armed with the irresistible power of the risen, glorified Christ (v. 4).

In vv. 5,6, the Greek grammar places great emphasis on the pronouns "yourselves" and "you." Paul turned the tables on his accusers. Instead of presuming to evaluate his apostleship, they needed to test the genuineness of their faith (James 2:14–26). He pointed out the incongruity of the Corinthians' believing (as they did) that their faith was genuine and his apostleship false. Paul was their spiritual father (1 Cor. 4:15). If his apostleship was counterfeit, so was their faith. The genuineness of their salvation was proof of the genuineness of his apostleship.

SEPTEMBER 23

Isaiah 37:1–38:22

37 And so it was, when King Hezekiah
heard *it,* that he tore his clothes, covered himself with sackcloth, and went into the
house of the LORD. [2]Then he sent Eliakim, who
was over the household, Shebna the scribe, and
the elders of the priests, covered with sackcloth, to Isaiah the prophet, the son of Amoz.
[3]And they said to him, "Thus says Hezekiah:
'This day *is* a day of trouble and rebuke and
blasphemy; for the children have come to
birth, but *there is* no strength to bring them
forth. [4]It may be that the LORD your God will
hear the words of *the* Rabshakeh, whom his
master the king of Assyria has sent to reproach the living God, and will rebuke the
words which the LORD your God has heard.
Therefore lift up *your* prayer for the remnant
that is left.' "

[5]So the servants of King Hezekiah came to
Isaiah. [6]And Isaiah said to them, "Thus you
shall say to your master, 'Thus says the LORD:
"Do not be afraid of the words which you have
heard, with which the servants of the king of
Assyria have blasphemed Me. [7]Surely I will
send a spirit upon him, and he shall hear a
rumor and return to his own land; and I will
cause him to fall by the sword in his own
land." ' "

[8]Then *the* Rabshakeh returned, and found
the king of Assyria warring against Libnah, for
he heard that he had departed from Lachish.
[9]And the king heard concerning Tirhakah
king of Ethiopia, "He has come out to make
war with you." So when he heard *it,* he sent
messengers to Hezekiah, saying, [10]"Thus you
shall speak to Hezekiah king of Judah, saying:
'Do not let your God in whom you trust
deceive you, saying, "Jerusalem shall not be
given into the hand of the king of Assyria."
[11]Look! You have heard what the kings of Assyria have done to all lands by utterly destroying them; and shall you be delivered? [12]Have
the gods of the nations delivered those whom
my fathers have destroyed, Gozan and Haran
and Rezeph, and the people of Eden who *were*
in Telassar? [13]Where *is* the king of Hamath,
the king of Arpad, and the king of the city of
Sepharvaim, Hena, and Ivah?' "

[14]And Hezekiah received the letter from the
hand of the messengers, and read it; and
Hezekiah went up to the house of the LORD,
and spread it before the LORD. [15]Then
Hezekiah prayed to the LORD, saying: [16]"O
LORD of hosts, God of Israel, *the One* who
dwells *between* the cherubim, You *are* God,
You alone, of all the kingdoms of the earth.
You have made heaven and earth. [17]Incline
Your ear, O LORD, and hear; open Your eyes, O
LORD, and see; and hear all the words of
Sennacherib, which he has sent to reproach
the living God. [18]Truly, LORD, the kings of As-
syria have laid waste all the nations and their
lands, [19]and have cast their gods into the fire;
for they *were* not gods, but the work of men's
hands—wood and stone. Therefore they
destroyed them. [20]Now therefore, O LORD our
God, save us from his hand, that all the kingdoms of the earth may know that You *are* the
LORD, You alone."

[21]Then Isaiah the son of Amoz sent to
Hezekiah, saying, "Thus says the LORD God of
Israel, 'Because you have prayed to Me against
Sennacherib king of Assyria, [22]this *is* the word
which the LORD has spoken concerning him:

"The virgin, the daughter of Zion,
Has despised you, laughed you to
scorn;
The daughter of Jerusalem

Has shaken *her* head behind your back!

23 "Whom have you reproached and blasphemed?
Against whom have you raised *your* voice,
And lifted up your eyes on high?
Against the Holy One of Israel.
24 By your servants you have reproached the Lord,
And said, 'By the multitude of my chariots
I have come up to the height of the mountains,
To the limits of Lebanon;
I will cut down its tall cedars
And its choice cypress trees;
I will enter its farthest height,
To its fruitful forest.
25 I have dug and drunk water,
And with the soles of my feet I have dried up
All the brooks of defense.'

26 "Did you not hear long ago
How I made it,
From ancient times that I formed it?
Now I have brought it to pass,
That you should be
For crushing fortified cities *into* heaps of ruins.
27 Therefore their inhabitants *had* little power;
They were dismayed and confounded;
They were *as* the grass of the field
And the green herb,
As the grass on the housetops
And grain blighted before it is grown.

28 "But I know your dwelling place,
Your going out and your coming in,
And your rage against Me.
29 Because your rage against Me and your tumult
Have come up to My ears,
Therefore I will put My hook in your nose
And My bridle in your lips,
And I will turn you back
By the way which you came." '

30 "This *shall be* a sign to you:
You shall eat this year such as grows of itself,
And the second year what springs from the same;
Also in the third year sow and reap,
Plant vineyards and eat the fruit of them.
31 And the remnant who have escaped of the house of Judah
Shall again take root downward,
And bear fruit upward.
32 For out of Jerusalem shall go a remnant,
And those who escape from Mount Zion.
The zeal of the LORD of hosts will do this.

33 "Therefore thus says the LORD concerning
the king of Assyria:

'He shall not come into this city,
Nor shoot an arrow there,
Nor come before it with shield,
Nor build a siege mound against it.
34 By the way that he came,
By the same shall he return;
And he shall not come into this city,'
Says the LORD.
35 'For I will defend this city, to save it
For My own sake and for My servant David's sake.' "

36 Then the angel of the LORD went out, and
killed in the camp of the Assyrians one hundred and eighty-five thousand; and when *peo-*
ple arose early in the morning, there were the
corpses—all dead. 37 So Sennacherib king of
Assyria departed and went away, returned
home, and remained at Nineveh. 38 Now it came
to pass, as he was worshiping in the house of
Nisroch his god, that his sons Adrammelech
and Sharezer struck him down with the sword;
and they escaped into the land of Ararat. Then
Esarhaddon his son reigned in his place.

37:29 hook in your nose...bridle in your lips. In judging Sennacherib, the Lord treated him as an obstinate animal with a ring in his nose and/or a bridle in his mouth. Some ancient sources indicate that captives were led before a king by a cord attached to a hook or ring through the upper lip and nose. Thus, he was to be brought back to his own country.

37:36 the angel of the LORD. This was Isaiah's only use of a title that is frequent in the Old Testament, one referring to the Lord Himself. **killed.** Secular records also mention this massive slaughter of Assyrian troops, without noting its supernatural nature, of course.

38 In those days Hezekiah was sick and
near death. And Isaiah the prophet, the
son of Amoz, went to him and said to him,
"Thus says the LORD: 'Set your house in order,
for you shall die and not live.' "
2Then Hezekiah turned his face toward the
wall, and prayed to the LORD, 3and said, "Remember now, O LORD, I pray, how I have
walked before You in truth and with a loyal
heart, and have done *what is* good in Your
sight." And Hezekiah wept bitterly.
4And the word of the LORD came to Isaiah,
saying, 5"Go and tell Hezekiah, 'Thus says the
LORD, the God of David your father: "I have
heard your prayer, I have seen your tears;
surely I will add to your days fifteen years. 6I
will deliver you and this city from the hand of
the king of Assyria, and I will defend this
city." ' 7And this *is* the sign to you from the
LORD, that the LORD will do this thing which
He has spoken: 8Behold, I will bring the shadow on the sundial, which has gone down with
the sun on the sundial of Ahaz, ten degrees
backward." So the sun returned ten degrees on
the dial by which it had gone down.
9This is the writing of Hezekiah king of Judah, when he had been sick and had recovered from his sickness:

10 I said,
"In the prime of my life
I shall go to the gates of Sheol;
I am deprived of the remainder of my
years."
11 I said,
"I shall not see YAH,
The LORD in the land of the living;
I shall observe man no more among
the inhabitants of the world.
12 My life span is gone,
Taken from me like a shepherd's tent;
I have cut off my life like a weaver.
He cuts me off from the loom;
From day until night You make an end
of me.
13 I have considered until morning—
Like a lion,
So He breaks all my bones;
From day until night You make an end
of me.
14 Like a crane *or* a swallow, so I
chattered;
I mourned like a dove;
My eyes fail *from looking* upward.
O LORD, I am oppressed;
Undertake for me!
15 "What shall I say?
He has both spoken to me,
And He Himself has done *it*.
I shall walk carefully all my years
In the bitterness of my soul.
16 O Lord, by these *things men* live;
And in all these *things is* the life of my
spirit;
So You will restore me and make me
live.
17 Indeed *it was* for *my own* peace
That I had great bitterness;
But You have lovingly *delivered* my
soul from the pit of corruption,
For You have cast all my sins behind
Your back.
18 For Sheol cannot thank You,
Death cannot praise You;
Those who go down to the pit cannot
hope for Your truth.
19 The living, the living man, he shall
praise You,
As I *do* this day;
The father shall make known Your
truth to the children.

20 "The LORD *was ready* to save me;
Therefore we will sing my songs with
stringed instruments
All the days of our life, in the house of
the LORD."

21Now Isaiah had said, "Let them take a
lump of figs, and apply *it* as a poultice on the
boil, and he shall recover."
22And Hezekiah had said, "What *is* the sign
that I shall go up to the house of the LORD?"

Psalm 109:14–20

14 Let the iniquity of his fathers be
remembered before the LORD,
And let not the sin of his mother be
blotted out.
15 Let them be continually before the LORD,
That He may cut off the memory of
them from the earth;
16 Because he did not remember to show
mercy,
But persecuted the poor and needy man,
That he might even slay the broken in
heart.
17 As he loved cursing, so let it come to
him;
As he did not delight in blessing, so let it
be far from him.
18 As he clothed himself with cursing as
with his garment,
So let it enter his body like water,
And like oil into his bones.
19 Let it be to him like the garment which
covers him,

And for a belt with which he girds
himself continually.
20 *Let* this *be* the LORD's reward to my
accusers,
And to those who speak evil against my
person.

Proverbs 26:1

26 As snow in summer and rain
in harvest,
So honor is not fitting for a fool.

Galatians 1:1–24

1 Paul, an apostle (not from men nor through
man, but through Jesus Christ and God the
Father who raised Him from the dead), [2]and
all the brethren who are with me,

To the churches of Galatia:

[3]Grace to you and peace from God the
Father and our Lord Jesus Christ, [4]who gave
Himself for our sins, that He might deliver us
from this present evil age, according to the
will of our God and Father, [5]to whom *be* glory
forever and ever. Amen.

[6]I marvel that you are turning away so soon
from Him who called you in the grace of Christ,
to a different gospel, [7]which is not another; but
there are some who trouble you and want to
pervert the gospel of Christ. [8]But even if we,
or an angel from heaven, preach any other
gospel to you than what we have preached to
you, let him be accursed. [9]As we have said
before, so now I say again, if anyone preaches
any other gospel to you than what you have
received, let him be accursed.

[10]For do I now persuade men, or God? Or do
I seek to please men? For if I still pleased men,
I would not be a bondservant of Christ.

[11]But I make known to you, brethren, that the
gospel which was preached by me is not
according to man. [12]For I neither received it
from man, nor was I taught *it,* but *it came*
through the revelation of Jesus Christ.

[13]For you have heard of my former conduct
in Judaism, how I persecuted the church of
God beyond measure and *tried to* destroy it.
[14]And I advanced in Judaism beyond many of
my contemporaries in my own nation, being
more exceedingly zealous for the traditions of
my fathers.

[15]But when it pleased God, who separated
me from my mother's womb and called *me*
through His grace, [16]to reveal His Son in me,
that I might preach Him among the Gentiles, I
did not immediately confer with flesh and
blood, [17]nor did I go up to Jerusalem to those
who were apostles before me; but I went to
Arabia, and returned again to Damascus.

[18]Then after three years I went up to Jerusalem to see Peter, and remained with him fifteen days. [19]But I saw none of the other apostles except James, the Lord's brother. [20](Now
concerning the things which I write to you,
indeed, before God, I do not lie.)

[21]Afterward I went into the regions of Syria
and Cilicia. [22]And I was unknown by face to the
churches of Judea which *were* in Christ. [23]But
they were hearing only, "He who formerly persecuted us now preaches the faith which he once
tried to destroy." [24]And they glorified God in me.

1:12 neither received it from man, nor was I taught *it*. In contrast to the Judaizers, who received their religious instruction from rabbinic tradition. Most Jews did not study the actual Scriptures; instead they used human interpretations of Scripture as their religious authority and guide. Many of their traditions not only were not taught in Scripture but also contradicted it (Mark 7:13). **through the revelation.** This refers to the unveiling of something previously kept secret—in this case, Jesus Christ. While he knew about Christ, Paul subsequently met Him personally on the road to Damascus and received the truth of the gospel from Him (Acts 9:1–16).

1:17 Jerusalem...Arabia,...Damascus. Rather than immediately travel to Jerusalem to be instructed by the apostles, Paul instead went to Nabatean Arabia, a wilderness desert that stretched east of Damascus down to the Sinai peninsula. After being prepared for ministry by the Lord, he returned to minister in nearby Damascus.

1:18 three years. The approximate time from Paul's conversion to his first journey to Jerusalem. During those years he made a visit to Damascus and resided in Arabia, under the instruction of the Lord. This visit is discussed in Acts 9:26–30. **up to Jerusalem.** Travelers in Israel always speak of going up to Jerusalem because of its higher elevation. **see.** Better translated, "to become acquainted with." **Peter.** The apostle who was the personal companion of the Lord and the most powerful spokesman in the early years of the Jerusalem church (Acts 1–12).

DAY 23: What was so shocking to Paul about the Galatians?

That the Galatians were "turning away" (1:6). This is better translated "deserting." The Greek word was used of military desertion, which was punishable by death. The form of this Greek verb indicates that the Galatian believers were voluntarily deserting grace to pursue the legalism taught by the false teachers. "So soon." This Greek word can mean either "easily" or "quickly" and sometimes both. No doubt both senses characterized the Galatians' response to the false teachers' heretical doctrines. "Called you." This could be translated, "Who called you once and for all" (2 Thess. 2:13,14; 2 Tim. 1:8,9; 1 Pet. 1:15), and refers to God's effectual call to salvation. "Grace of Christ." God's free and sovereign act of mercy in granting salvation through the death and resurrection of Christ, totally apart from any human work or merit. "Different gospel." The Judaizers' perversion of the true gospel. They added the requirements, ceremonies, and standards of the Old Covenant as necessary prerequisites to salvation.

"Some who trouble you" (v. 7). The Greek word could be translated "disturb" and means "to shake back and forth," meaning to agitate or stir up. Here, it refers to the deep emotional disturbance the Galatian believers experienced. "Pervert." To turn something into its opposite. By adding law to the gospel of Christ, the false teachers were effectively destroying grace, turning the message of God's undeserved favor toward sinners into a message of earned and merited favor. "The gospel of Christ." The good news of salvation by grace alone through faith alone in Christ alone.

Throughout history God has devoted certain objects, individuals, and groups of people to destruction or to be "accursed" (Josh. 6:17,18; 7:1,25,26). Here the Judaizers are identified as members of this infamous company. "But even if we, or an angel from heaven" (v. 8). Paul's point is hypothetical, calling on the most unlikely examples for false teaching—himself and holy angels. The Galatians should receive no messenger, regardless of how impeccable his credentials, if his doctrine of salvation differs in the slightest degree from God's truth revealed through Christ and the apostles. "Accursed." The translation of the familiar Greek word *anathama,* which refers to devoting someone to destruction in eternal hell (Rom. 9:3; 1 Cor. 12:3; 16:22).

SEPTEMBER 24

Isaiah 39:1–40:31

39 At that time Merodach-Baladan the son
of Baladan, king of Babylon, sent letters and a present to Hezekiah, for he heard
that he had been sick and had recovered. 2And
Hezekiah was pleased with them, and showed them the house of his treasures—the silver and gold, the spices and precious ointment, and all his armory—all that was found among his treasures. There was nothing in his house or in all his dominion that Hezekiah did not show them.

3Then Isaiah the prophet went to King Hezekiah, and said to him, "What did these men say, and from where did they come to you?"

So Hezekiah said, "They came to me from a far country, from Babylon."

4And he said, "What have they seen in your house?"

So Hezekiah answered, "They have seen all that *is* in my house; there is nothing among my treasures that I have not shown them."

5Then Isaiah said to Hezekiah, "Hear the
word of the LORD of hosts: 6'Behold, the days
are coming when all that *is* in your house, and what your fathers have accumulated until this day, shall be carried to Babylon; nothing shall
be left,' says the LORD. 7'And they shall take
away *some* of your sons who will descend from you, whom you will beget; and they shall be eunuchs in the palace of the king of Babylon.' "
8So Hezekiah said to Isaiah, "The word of
the LORD which you have spoken *is* good!" For he said, "At least there will be peace and truth in my days."

40 "Comfort, yes, comfort
My people!"
Says your God.
2 "Speak comfort to Jerusalem, and cry
out to her,
That her warfare is ended,

40:1,2 Comfort,...comfort. The prophecy addressed God's prophets, instructing them to emphasize the theme of comfort to a captive people in a foreign land many miles from their home city of Jerusalem. God has good plans for great blessing to Israel in the future because they are His covenant people, who are never to be permanently cast away (Rom. 11:2).

That her iniquity is pardoned;
For she has received from the LORD's hand
Double for all her sins."

3 The voice of one crying in the wilderness:
"Prepare the way of the LORD;
Make straight in the desert
A highway for our God.
4 Every valley shall be exalted
And every mountain and hill brought low;
The crooked places shall be made straight
And the rough places smooth;

40:3,4 Prepare the way. The remnant of Israel could remove obstacles from the coming Messiah's path through repentance from their sins. John the Baptist reminded his listeners of this necessity (Matt. 3:2), as did Jesus (Matt. 4:17; Mark 1:15). These verses reflect the custom of some eastern monarchs to send heralds before them to clear away obstacles, make causeways, straighten crooked roads and valleys, and level hills (45:1,2). John had the task of getting people ready for the Messiah's arrival.

5 The glory of the LORD shall be revealed,
And all flesh shall see *it* together;
For the mouth of the LORD has spoken."

6 The voice said, "Cry out!"
And he said, "What shall I cry?"

"All flesh *is* grass,
And all its loveliness *is* like the flower of the field.
7 The grass withers, the flower fades,
Because the breath of the LORD blows upon it;
Surely the people *are* grass.
8 The grass withers, the flower fades,
But the word of our God stands forever."

9 O Zion,
You who bring good tidings,
Get up into the high mountain;
O Jerusalem,
You who bring good tidings,
Lift up your voice with strength,
Lift *it* up, be not afraid;
Say to the cities of Judah,
"Behold your God!"

10 Behold, the Lord GOD shall come with a strong *hand,*
And His arm shall rule for Him;
Behold, His reward *is* with Him,
And His work before Him.
11 He will feed His flock like a shepherd;
He will gather the lambs with His arm,
And carry *them* in His bosom,
And gently lead those who are with young.

12 Who has measured the waters in the hollow of His hand,
Measured heaven with a span
And calculated the dust of the earth in a measure?
Weighed the mountains in scales
And the hills in a balance?
13 Who has directed the Spirit of the LORD,
Or *as* His counselor has taught Him?
14 With whom did He take counsel, and *who* instructed Him,
And taught Him in the path of justice?
Who taught Him knowledge,
And showed Him the way of understanding?

40:13,14 directed the Spirit of the LORD. Isaiah pointed to the incomparable wisdom of God. Paul alluded to this verse in connection with God's wisdom in dealing with Jews and Gentiles (Rom. 11:34) and with God's impartation of wisdom to the spiritual believer (1 Cor. 2:16).

15 Behold, the nations *are* as a drop in a bucket,
And are counted as the small dust on the scales;
Look, He lifts up the isles as a very little thing.
16 And Lebanon *is* not sufficient to burn,
Nor its beasts sufficient for a burnt offering.
17 All nations before Him *are* as nothing,
And they are counted by Him less than nothing and worthless.

18 To whom then will you liken God?
Or what likeness will you compare to Him?
19 The workman molds an image,
The goldsmith overspreads it with gold,
And the silversmith casts silver chains.
20 Whoever *is* too impoverished for *such* a contribution

Chooses a tree *that* will not rot;
He seeks for himself a skillful workman
To prepare a carved image *that* will not totter.

21 Have you not known?
Have you not heard?
Has it not been told you from the beginning?
Have you not understood from the foundations of the earth?
22 *It is* He who sits above the circle of the earth,
And its inhabitants *are* like grasshoppers,
Who stretches out the heavens like a curtain,
And spreads them out like a tent to dwell in.
23 He brings the princes to nothing;
He makes the judges of the earth useless.

24 Scarcely shall they be planted,
Scarcely shall they be sown,
Scarcely shall their stock take root in the earth,
When He will also blow on them,
And they will wither,
And the whirlwind will take them away like stubble.

25 "To whom then will you liken Me,
Or *to whom* shall I be equal?" says the Holy One.
26 Lift up your eyes on high,
And see who has created these *things*,
Who brings out their host by number;
He calls them all by name,
By the greatness of His might
And the strength of *His* power;
Not one is missing.

27 Why do you say, O Jacob,
And speak, O Israel:
"My way is hidden from the LORD,
And my just claim is passed over by my God"?
28 Have you not known?
Have you not heard?
The everlasting God, the LORD,
The Creator of the ends of the earth,
Neither faints nor is weary.
His understanding is unsearchable.
29 He gives power to the weak,
And to *those who have* no might He increases strength.
30 Even the youths shall faint and be weary,
And the young men shall utterly fall,
31 But those who wait on the LORD
Shall renew *their* strength;
They shall mount up with wings like eagles,
They shall run and not be weary,
They shall walk and not faint.

40:28 Neither faints nor is weary. God was not too weak to act on their behalf, nor was fatigue an obstacle for the Creator in caring for His people (vv. 29,30). Though even the young and strong become tired and fall, the Ancient of Days never does. **unsearchable.** To the human mind, God's wisdom is not fully comprehensible in how He chooses to fulfill His promises to deliver Israel. Paul saw a further illustration of this truth in God's plan for the final restoration of Israel (Rom. 11:33; see Is. 40:13).

40:31 wait on the LORD. There is a general principle here that patient, praying believers are blessed by God with strength in their trials (2 Cor. 12:8–10). The Lord also expected His people to be patient and await His coming in glory at the end to fulfill the promises of national deliverance, when believing Israel would become stronger than they had ever been.

Psalm 109:21–25

21 But You, O GOD the Lord,
Deal with me for Your name's sake;
Because Your mercy *is* good, deliver me.
22 For I *am* poor and needy,
And my heart is wounded within me.
23 I am gone like a shadow when it lengthens;
I am shaken off like a locust.
24 My knees are weak through fasting,
And my flesh is feeble from lack of fatness.
25 I also have become a reproach to them;
When they look at me, they shake their heads.

Proverbs 26:2

2 Like a flitting sparrow, like a flying swallow,
So a curse without cause shall not alight.

Galatians 2:1–21

2 Then after fourteen years I went up again
to Jerusalem with Barnabas, and also took
Titus with *me*. 2And I went up by revelation,
and communicated to them that gospel which
I preach among the Gentiles, but privately to
those who were of reputation, lest by any
means I might run, or had run, in vain. 3Yet not
even Titus who *was* with me, being a Greek,
was compelled to be circumcised. 4And *this
occurred* because of false brethren secretly
brought in (who came in by stealth to spy out
our liberty which we have in Christ Jesus, that
they might bring us into bondage), 5to whom
we did not yield submission even for an hour,
that the truth of the gospel might continue
with you.
6But from those who seemed to be something—whatever they were, it makes no difference to me; God shows personal favoritism to
no man—for those who seemed *to be something* added nothing to me. 7But on the contrary, when they saw that the gospel for the
uncircumcised had been committed to me, as
the gospel for the circumcised *was* to Peter
8(for He who worked effectively in Peter for
the apostleship to the circumcised also
worked effectively in me toward the Gentiles),
9and when James, Cephas, and John, who
seemed to be pillars, perceived the grace that
had been given to me, they gave me and
Barnabas the right hand of fellowship, that we
should go to the Gentiles and they to the circumcised. 10*They desired* only that we should
remember the poor, the very thing which I
also was eager to do.
11Now when Peter had come to Antioch, I
withstood him to his face, because he was to
be blamed; 12for before certain men came from
James, he would eat with the Gentiles; but
when they came, he withdrew and separated
himself, fearing those who were of the circumcision. 13And the rest of the Jews also played
the hypocrite with him, so that even Barnabas
was carried away with their hypocrisy.
14But when I saw that they were not
straightforward about the truth of the gospel, I
said to Peter before *them* all, "If you, being a
Jew, live in the manner of Gentiles and not as
the Jews, why do you compel Gentiles to live as
Jews? 15We *who are* Jews by nature, and not sinners of the Gentiles, 16knowing that a man is not
justified by the works of the law but by faith in
Jesus Christ, even we have believed in Christ
Jesus, that we might be justified by faith in
Christ and not by the works of the law; for by
the works of the law no flesh shall be justified.
17"But if, while we seek to be justified by
Christ, we ourselves also are found sinners, *is*
Christ therefore a minister of sin? Certainly
not! 18For if I build again those things which I
destroyed, I make myself a transgressor. 19For
I through the law died to the law that I might
live to God. 20I have been crucified with Christ;
it is no longer I who live, but Christ lives in
me; and the *life* which I now live in the flesh I
live by faith in the Son of God, who loved me
and gave Himself for me. 21I do not set aside
the grace of God; for if righteousness *comes*
through the law, then Christ died in vain."

2:20 I have been crucified with Christ. When a person trusts in Christ for salvation, he spiritually participates with the Lord in His crucifixion and His victory over sin and death. **no longer I who live, but Christ lives in me.** The believer's old self is dead, having been crucified with Christ (Rom. 6:3,5). The believer's new man has the privilege of the indwelling Christ empowering him and living through him (Rom. 8:9,10). **gave Himself for me.** The manifestation of Christ's love for the believer through His sacrificial death on the cross (John 10:17,18; Rom. 5:6–8; Eph. 5:25–30).

DAY 24: What led Paul to confront Peter with his hypocrisy?

It took place in the first Gentile church, which was at Antioch, where we are told that Peter "stood condemned" (Gal. 2:11). Peter had been in Antioch for some time, eating with Gentiles. When Judaizers came, pretending to be sent by James (v. 12), they lied, giving false claims of support from the apostles. Peter had already given up all Mosaic ceremony (Acts 10:9–22); nevertheless, he "withdrew." The Greek term refers to strategic military withdrawal. The verb's form may imply that Peter's withdrawal was gradual and deceptive. To eat with the Judaizers and decline invitations to eat with the Gentiles, which he had previously done, meant that Peter was affirming the very dietary restrictions he knew God had abolished (Acts 10:15) and thus striking a blow at the gospel of grace. "Fearing those...of the circumcision"—the true motivation behind Peter's defection. He was afraid of losing popularity with the legalistic, Judaizing segment of people in the church, even though they were self-righteous hypocrites promoting a heretical doctrine.

The Jewish believers in Antioch followed Peter's example and "played the hypocrite" (v. 13). This Greek word refers to an actor who wore a mask to depict a mood or certain character. In the spiritual sense, it refers to someone who masks his true character by pretending to be something he is not (Matt. 6:1–6). They were committed to the gospel of grace, but pretended to accept Jewish legalism. By withdrawing from the Gentile Christians, Peter and the other Jewish believers were not walking in line, "straightforward," with God's Word (v. 14). Before his gradual withdrawal, Peter regularly had fellowship and ate with the Gentiles, thus modeling the ideal of Christian love and liberty between Jew and Gentile. By his Judaizing mandate, he was declaring theirs was the right way.

Paul's rebuke of Peter in vv. 15,16 serves as one of the most dynamic statements in the New Testament on the absolute and unwavering necessity of the doctrine of justification by grace through faith. Peter's apparent repentance acknowledged Paul's apostolic authority and his own submission to the truth (2 Pet. 3:15,16).

SEPTEMBER 25

Isaiah 41:1–42:25

41 "Keep silence before Me,
O coastlands,
And let the people renew *their* strength!
Let them come near, then let them speak;
Let us come near together for judgment.

2 "Who raised up one from the east?
Who in righteousness called him to His feet?
Who gave the nations before him,
And made *him* rule over kings?
Who gave *them* as the dust *to* his sword,
As driven stubble to his bow?
3 Who pursued them, *and* passed safely
By the way *that* he had not gone with his feet?
4 Who has performed and done *it,*
Calling the generations from the beginning?
'I, the LORD, am the first;
And with the last I *am* He.' "

41:4 first...last. He existed before history and will exist after it (44:6; 48:12; Rev. 1:17; 2:8; 22:13). ***I am* He.** It is legitimate to translate the two Hebrew words thus represented by "I am" (see also 42:8; 43:10,13; 46:4), a messianic title appropriated by Jesus frequently as explicit testimony to His deity (e.g., Mark 13:6; 14:62; Luke 21:8; John 8:28,58; 13:19). The title comes originally from the Lord's self-revelation to Moses in Exodus 3:14.

5 The coastlands saw *it* and feared,
The ends of the earth were afraid;
They drew near and came.
6 Everyone helped his neighbor,
And said to his brother,
"Be of good courage!"
7 So the craftsman encouraged the goldsmith;
He who smooths *with* the hammer
inspired him who strikes the anvil,
Saying, "It *is* ready for the soldering";
Then he fastened it with pegs,
That it might not totter.

8 "But you, Israel, *are* My servant,
Jacob whom I have chosen,
The descendants of Abraham My friend.
9 *You* whom I have taken from the ends of the earth,
And called from its farthest regions,
And said to you,
'You *are* My servant,
I have chosen you and have not cast you away:
10 Fear not, for I *am* with you;
Be not dismayed, for I *am* your God.
I will strengthen you,
Yes, I will help you,
I will uphold you with My righteous right hand.'

11 "Behold, all those who were incensed against you
Shall be ashamed and disgraced;
They shall be as nothing,
And those who strive with you shall perish.
12 You shall seek them and not find them—
Those who contended with you.
Those who war against you
Shall be as nothing,
As a nonexistent thing.
13 For I, the LORD your God, will hold your right hand,

Saying to you, 'Fear not, I will help you.'

14 "Fear not, you worm Jacob,
You men of Israel!
I will help you," says the LORD
And your Redeemer, the Holy One
of Israel.
15 "Behold, I will make you into a new
threshing sledge with sharp teeth;
You shall thresh the mountains and
beat *them* small,
And make the hills like chaff.
16 You shall winnow them, the wind shall
carry them away,
And the whirlwind shall scatter them;
You shall rejoice in the LORD,
And glory in the Holy One of Israel.

17 "The poor and needy seek water, but
there is none,
Their tongues fail for thirst.
I, the LORD, will hear them;
I, the God of Israel, will not forsake them.
18 I will open rivers in desolate heights,
And fountains in the midst of the valleys;
I will make the wilderness a pool of
water,
And the dry land springs of water.
19 I will plant in the wilderness the cedar
and the acacia tree,
The myrtle and the oil tree;
I will set in the desert the cypress tree
and the pine
And the box tree together,
20 That they may see and know,
And consider and understand together,
That the hand of the LORD has done
this,
And the Holy One of Israel has
created it.

21 "Present your case," says the LORD.
"Bring forth your strong *reasons,*" says
the King of Jacob.
22 "Let them bring forth and show us what
will happen;
Let them show the former things, what
they *were,*
That we may consider them,
And know the latter end of them;
Or declare to us things to come.
23 Show the things that are to come
hereafter,
That we may know that you *are* gods;
Yes, do good or do evil,
That we may be dismayed and see *it*
together.
24 Indeed you *are* nothing,
And your work *is* nothing;
He who chooses you *is* an abomination.

25 "I have raised up one from the north,
And he shall come;
From the rising of the sun he shall call
on My name;
And he shall come against princes as
though mortar,
As the potter treads clay.
26 Who has declared from the beginning,
that we may know?
And former times, that we may say,
'*He is* righteous'?
Surely *there is* no one who shows,
Surely *there is* no one who declares,
Surely *there is* no one who hears
your words.
27 The first time *I said* to Zion,
'Look, there they are!'
And I will give to Jerusalem one who
brings good tidings.
28 For I looked, and *there was* no man;
I looked among them, but *there was* no
counselor,
Who, when I asked of them, could
answer a word.
29 Indeed they *are* all worthless;
Their works *are* nothing;
Their molded images *are* wind and
confusion.

42 "Behold! My Servant whom
I uphold,
My Elect One *in whom* My soul delights!
I have put My Spirit upon Him;
He will bring forth justice to the
Gentiles.
2 He will not cry out, nor raise *His voice,*
Nor cause His voice to be heard in the
street.
3 A bruised reed He will not break,
And smoking flax He will not quench;
He will bring forth justice for truth.
4 He will not fail nor be discouraged,
Till He has established justice
in the earth;
And the coastlands shall wait for
His law."

5 Thus says God the LORD,
Who created the heavens and
stretched them out,
Who spread forth the earth and that
which comes from it,
Who gives breath to the people on it,
And spirit to those who walk on it:
6 "I, the LORD, have called You
in righteousness,
And will hold Your hand;
I will keep You and give You as a
covenant to the people,

As a light to the Gentiles,
7 To open blind eyes,
To bring out prisoners from the prison,
Those who sit in darkness from the prison house.
8 I *am* the LORD, that *is* My name;
And My glory I will not give to another,
Nor My praise to carved images.
9 Behold, the former things have come to pass,
And new things I declare;
Before they spring forth I tell you of them."

10 Sing to the LORD a new song,
And His praise from the ends of the earth,
You who go down to the sea, and all that is in it,
You coastlands and you inhabitants of them!
11 Let the wilderness and its cities lift up *their voice,*
The villages *that* Kedar inhabits.
Let the inhabitants of Sela sing,
Let them shout from the top of the mountains.
12 Let them give glory to the LORD,
And declare His praise in the coastlands.
13 The LORD shall go forth like a mighty man;
He shall stir up *His* zeal like a man of war.
He shall cry out, yes, shout aloud;
He shall prevail against His enemies.

14 "I have held My peace a long time,
I have been still and restrained Myself.
Now I will cry like a woman in labor,
I will pant and gasp at once.
15 I will lay waste the mountains and hills,
And dry up all their vegetation;
I will make the rivers coastlands,
And I will dry up the pools.
16 I will bring the blind by a way they did not know;
I will lead them in paths they have not known.
I will make darkness light before them,
And crooked places straight.
These things I will do for them,
And not forsake them.
17 They shall be turned back,
They shall be greatly ashamed,
Who trust in carved images,
Who say to the molded images,
'You *are* our gods.'

18 "Hear, you deaf;
And look, you blind, that you may see.
19 Who *is* blind but My servant,
Or deaf as My messenger *whom* I send?
Who *is* blind as *he who is* perfect,
And blind as the LORD's servant?
20 Seeing many things, but you do not observe;
Opening the ears, but he does not hear."
21 The LORD is well pleased for His righteousness' sake;
He will exalt the law and make *it* honorable.
22 But this *is* a people robbed and plundered;
All of them are snared in holes,
And they are hidden in prison houses;
They are for prey, and no one delivers;
For plunder, and no one says, "Restore!"
23 Who among you will give ear to this?
Who will listen and hear for the time to come?
24 Who gave Jacob for plunder, and Israel to the robbers?
Was it not the LORD,
He against whom we have sinned?
For they would not walk in His ways,
Nor were they obedient to His law.
25 Therefore He has poured on him the fury of His anger
And the strength of battle;
It has set him on fire all around,
Yet he did not know;
And it burned him,
Yet he did not take *it* to heart.

Psalm 109:26–31

26 Help me, O LORD my God!
Oh, save me according to Your mercy,
27 That they may know that this *is* Your hand—
That You, LORD, have done it!
28 Let them curse, but You bless;
When they arise, let them be ashamed,
But let Your servant rejoice.
29 Let my accusers be clothed with shame,
And let them cover themselves with their own disgrace as with a mantle.
30 I will greatly praise the LORD with my mouth;
Yes, I will praise Him among the multitude.
31 For He shall stand at the right hand of the poor,
To save *him* from those who condemn him.

Proverbs 26:3–4

3 A whip for the horse,
A bridle for the donkey,
And a rod for the fool's back.
4 Do not answer a fool according to his folly,
Lest you also be like him.

Galatians 3:1–29

3 O foolish Galatians! Who has bewitched
you that you should not obey the truth,
before whose eyes Jesus Christ was clearly
portrayed among you as crucified? [2]This only

3:1 foolish. This refers not to lack of intelligence, but to lack of obedience (Luke 24:25; 1 Tim. 6:9; Titus 3:3). Paul expressed his shock, surprise, and outrage at the Galatians' defection. **Who...?** The Judaizers, the Jewish false teachers were plaguing the Galatian churches. **bewitched.** Charmed or misled by flattery and false promises. The term suggests an appeal to the emotions by the Judaizers. **clearly portrayed.** The Greek word describes the posting of official notices in public places. Paul's preaching had publicly displayed the true gospel of Jesus Christ before the Galatians. **crucified.** The crucifixion of Christ was a one-time historical fact with continuing results into eternity. Christ's sacrificial death provides eternal payment for believers' sins (Heb. 7:25) and does not need to be supplemented by any human works.

I want to learn from you: Did you receive the
Spirit by the works of the law, or by the hearing of faith? [3]Are you so foolish? Having begun
in the Spirit, are you now being made perfect
by the flesh? [4]Have you suffered so many
things in vain—if indeed *it was* in vain?
[5]Therefore He who supplies the Spirit to you
and works miracles among you, *does He do it*
by the works of the law, or by the hearing of
faith?—[6]just as Abraham *"believed God, and it
was accounted to him for righteousness."*
[7]Therefore know that *only* those who are of
faith are sons of Abraham. [8]And the Scripture,
foreseeing that God would justify the Gentiles
by faith, preached the gospel to Abraham
beforehand, *saying, "In you all the nations
shall be blessed."* [9]So then those who *are* of
faith are blessed with believing Abraham.
[10]For as many as are of the works of the law
are under the curse; for it is written, *"Cursed
is everyone who does not continue in all things*

3:2 Did you receive the Spirit...? The answer to Paul's rhetorical question is obvious. The Galatians had received the Spirit when they were saved (Rom. 8:9; 1 Cor. 12:13; 1 John 3:24; 4:13), not through keeping the law, but through saving faith granted when hearing the gospel (Rom. 10:17). The hearing *of* faith is actually hearing *with* faith. Paul appealed to the Galatians' own salvation to refute the Judaizers' false teaching that keeping the law is necessary for salvation.

3:3 Are you so foolish? Incredulous at how easily the Galatians had been duped, Paul asked a second rhetorical question, again rebuking them for their foolishness. **begun in the Spirit,...by the flesh.** The notion that sinful, weak, fallen human nature could improve on the saving work of the Holy Spirit was ludicrous to Paul.

*which are written in the book of the law, to do
them."* [11]But that no one is justified by the law
in the sight of God *is* evident, for *"the just shall
live by faith."* [12]Yet the law is not of faith, but
"the man who does them shall live by them."
[13]Christ has redeemed us from the curse of
the law, having become a curse for us (for it is
written, *"Cursed is everyone who hangs on a
tree"*), [14]that the blessing of Abraham might
come upon the Gentiles in Christ Jesus, that we
might receive the promise of the Spirit
through faith.
[15]Brethren, I speak in the manner of men:
Though *it is* only a man's covenant, yet *if it is*
confirmed, no one annuls or adds to it. [16]Now
to Abraham and his Seed were the promises
made. He does not say, "And to seeds," as of
many, but as of one, *"And to your Seed,"* who
is Christ. [17]And this I say, *that* the law, which
was four hundred and thirty years later, cannot
annul the covenant that was confirmed before
by God in Christ, that it should make the
promise of no effect. [18]For if the inheritance *is*
of the law, *it is* no longer of promise; but God
gave *it* to Abraham by promise.
[19]What purpose then *does* the law *serve?* It was
added because of transgressions, till the Seed
should come to whom the promise was made;
and it was appointed through angels by the hand
of a mediator. [20]Now a mediator does not *mediate*
for one *only,* but God is one.
[21]*Is* the law then against the promises of God?
Certainly not! For if there had been a law given
which could have given life, truly righteousness

would have been by the law. [22]But the Scripture has confined all under sin, that the promise by faith in Jesus Christ might be given to those who believe. [23]But before faith came, we were kept under guard by the law, kept for the faith which would afterward be revealed. [24]Therefore the law was our tutor *to bring us* to Christ, that we might be justified by faith. [25]But after faith has come, we are no longer under a tutor.

[26]For you are all sons of God through faith in Christ Jesus. [27]For as many of you as were baptized into Christ have put on Christ. [28]There is neither Jew nor Greek, there is neither slave nor free, there is neither male nor female; for you are all one in Christ Jesus. [29]And if you *are* Christ's, then you are Abraham's seed, and heirs according to the promise.

3:28 you are all one in Christ Jesus. All those who are one with Jesus Christ are one with one another. This verse does not deny that God has designed for racial, social, and sexual distinctions among Christians, but it affirms that those do not imply spiritual inequality before God. Nor is this spiritual equality incompatible with the God-ordained roles of headship and submission in the church, society, and at home. Jesus Christ, though fully equal with the Father, assumed a submissive role during His incarnation (Phil. 2:5–8).

DAY 25: Who is the "Servant" of Isaiah 42?

Others deserve the title "my servant" (v. 1), but this personal Servant of the Lord is the Messiah, who was chosen (Luke 9:35; 1 Pet. 1:20; Rev. 13:8) because the Lord delights in Him (Matt. 3:17; 17:5) and puts His Spirit upon Him (11:2; 59:21; Matt. 3:16; Luke 4:18). "He will bring forth justice to the Gentiles." At His Second Coming, Christ will rule over a kingdom in which justice prevails throughout the world. The millennial kingdom is not for Israel alone, though the Messiah will reign on the throne of David in Jerusalem, and Israel will be the glorious people. In fact, all the nations of the world will experience the righteousness and justice of the Messiah King.

"He will not cry out…in the street" (v. 2). The quiet and submissive demeanor of Christ at His first advent fulfilled this prophecy (Matt. 11:28–30; 1 Pet. 2:23). "A bruised reed…smoking flax" (v. 3). The Servant will bring comfort and encouragement to the weak and oppressed (Matt. 12:18–20). "Till He has established justice in the earth" (v. 4). Isaiah looked beyond the First Coming of Christ to His Second Coming. Jesus fulfilled vv. 1a,2,3 at His First Coming and will fulfill vv. 1b,4 at His Second Coming, when He rules the earth in perfect justice with "a rod of iron" (Ps. 2:8,9; Rev. 2:27).

"I, the LORD,…will…give you as a covenant to the people" (v. 6). The Servant is a covenant in that He personifies and provides the blessings of salvation to God's people Israel. He is the Mediator of a better covenant than the one with Moses, i.e., the New Covenant (Jer. 31:31–34; Heb. 8:6,10–12). "As a light to the Gentiles." Simeon saw the beginning of this fulfillment at Christ's First Coming (Luke 2:32). He came as the Messiah of Israel, yet the Savior of the world, who revealed Himself to a non-Jewish immoral woman by the well in Samaria (John 4:25,26) and commanded His followers to preach the gospel of salvation to everyone in the world (Matt. 28:19,20). Certainly the church, made up mostly of Gentiles grafted into the trunk of blessing (Rom. 9:24–30; 11:11–24), fulfills this promise, as does the future kingdom on earth when the Servant will use Israel to shine and enlighten all the nations of the earth (49:6; 19:24).

SEPTEMBER 26

Isaiah 43:1–44:28

43 But now, thus says the LORD,
who created you, O Jacob,
And He who formed you, O Israel:
"Fear not, for I have redeemed you;
I have called *you* by your name;
You *are* Mine.
2 When you pass through the waters,
I *will be* with you;
And through the rivers,
they shall not overflow you.
When you walk through the fire, you
shall not be burned,
Nor shall the flame scorch you.
3 For I *am* the LORD your God,
The Holy One of Israel, your Savior;
I gave Egypt for your ransom,
Ethiopia and Seba in your place.
4 Since you were precious in
My sight,
You have been honored,
And I have loved you;
Therefore I will give men for you,
And people for your life.
5 Fear not, for I *am* with you;

I will bring your descendants from the
east,
And gather you from the west;
6 I will say to the north, 'Give them up!'
And to the south, 'Do not keep them
back!'
Bring My sons from afar,
And My daughters from the ends of
the earth—
7 Everyone who is called by My name,
Whom I have created for My glory;
I have formed him, yes, I have made
him."

8 Bring out the blind people who have
eyes,
And the deaf who have ears.
9 Let all the nations be gathered together,
And let the people be assembled.
Who among them can declare this,
And show us former things?
Let them bring out their witnesses,
that they may be justified;
Or let them hear and say, "*It is* truth."
10 "You *are* My witnesses," says the LORD,
"And My servant whom I have chosen,
That you may know and believe Me,
And understand that I *am* He.
Before Me there was no God formed,
Nor shall there be after Me.
11 I, *even* I, *am* the LORD,
And besides Me *there is* no savior.
12 I have declared and saved,
I have proclaimed,
And *there was* no foreign *god* among you;
Therefore you *are* My witnesses,"
Says the LORD, "that I *am* God.
13 Indeed before the day *was,* I *am* He;
And *there is* no one who can deliver out
of My hand;
I work, and who will reverse it?"

14 Thus says the LORD, your Redeemer,
The Holy One of Israel:
"For your sake I will send to Babylon,
And bring them all down as fugitives—
The Chaldeans, who rejoice in their
ships.
15 I *am* the LORD, your Holy One,
The Creator of Israel, your King."

16 Thus says the LORD, who makes a way
in the sea
And a path through the mighty waters,
17 Who brings forth the chariot and
horse,
The army and the power
(They shall lie down together, they
shall not rise;
They are extinguished, they are
quenched like a wick):
18 "Do not remember the former things,
Nor consider the things of old.
19 Behold, I will do a new thing,
Now it shall spring forth;
Shall you not know it?
I will even make a road in the
wilderness
And rivers in the desert.
20 The beast of the field will honor Me,
The jackals and the ostriches,
Because I give waters in the wilderness
And rivers in the desert,
To give drink to My people, My chosen.
21 This people I have formed for Myself;
They shall declare My praise.

22 "But you have not called upon Me,
O Jacob;
And you have been weary of Me,
O Israel.
23 You have not brought Me the sheep
for your burnt offerings,
Nor have you honored Me with your
sacrifices.
I have not caused you to serve with
grain offerings,
Nor wearied you with incense.
24 You have bought Me no sweet cane
with money,
Nor have you satisfied Me with the fat
of your sacrifices;
But you have burdened Me with
your sins,
You have wearied Me with your
iniquities.

25 "I, *even* I, *am* He who blots out your
transgressions for My own sake;
And I will not remember your sins.
26 Put Me in remembrance;
Let us contend together;
State your *case,* that you may
be acquitted.
27 Your first father sinned,

43:25 I, *even* I...not remember your sins. This verse is probably the high point of grace in the Old Testament. In spite of Israel's utter unworthiness, the Lord in His grace has devised a way that He can forgive their sins and grant righteousness, without compromising His holiness. This He would accomplish through the work of His Servant (53:6). In spite of her failures, Israel will always be God's chosen people.

And your mediators have transgressed
against Me.
28 Therefore I will profane the princes of
the sanctuary;
I will give Jacob to the curse,
And Israel to reproaches.

44 "Yet hear me now, O Jacob
My servant,
And Israel whom I have chosen.
2 Thus says the LORD who made you
And formed you from the womb, *who*
will help you:
'Fear not, O Jacob My servant;
And you, Jeshurun, whom I have
chosen.
3 For I will pour water on him who is
thirsty,
And floods on the dry ground;
I will pour My Spirit on your
descendants,
And My blessing on your offspring;
4 They will spring up among the grass
Like willows by the watercourses.'
5 One will say, 'I *am* the LORD's';
Another will call *himself* by the name
of Jacob;
Another will write *with* his hand,
'The LORD's,'
And name *himself* by the name of Israel.

6 "Thus says the LORD, the King of Israel,
And his Redeemer, the LORD of hosts:
'I *am* the First and I *am* the Last;
Besides Me *there is* no God.
7 And who can proclaim as I do?
Then let him declare it and set it in
order for Me,
Since I appointed the ancient people.
And the things that are coming and
shall come,
Let them show these to them.
8 Do not fear, nor be afraid;
Have I not told you from that time,
and declared *it?*
You *are* My witnesses.
Is there a God besides Me?
Indeed *there is* no other Rock;
I know not *one.*' "

9 Those who make an image, all of them
are useless,
And their precious things shall not
profit;
They *are* their own witnesses;
They neither see nor know, that they
may be ashamed.
10 Who would form a god or mold an image
That profits him nothing?
11 Surely all his companions would be
ashamed;
And the workmen, they *are* mere men.
Let them all be gathered together,
Let them stand up;
Yet they shall fear,
They shall be ashamed together.

12 The blacksmith with the tongs works
one in the coals,
Fashions it with hammers,
And works it with the strength of his
arms.
Even so, he is hungry, and his strength
fails;
He drinks no water and is faint.

13 The craftsman stretches out *his* rule,
He marks one out with chalk;
He fashions it with a plane,
He marks it out with the compass,
And makes it like the figure of a man,
According to the beauty of a man, that
it may remain in the house.
14 He cuts down cedars for himself,
And takes the cypress and the oak;
He secures *it* for himself among the
trees of the forest.
He plants a pine, and the rain
nourishes *it.*

15 Then it shall be for a man to burn,
For he will take some of it and warm
himself;
Yes, he kindles *it* and bakes bread;
Indeed he makes a god and worships *it;*
He makes it a carved image, and falls
down to it.
16 He burns half of it in the fire;
With this half he eats meat;
He roasts a roast, and is satisfied.
He even warms *himself* and says,
"Ah! I am warm,
I have seen the fire."
17 And the rest of it he makes into a god,
His carved image.
He falls down before it and worships *it,*
Prays to it and says,
"Deliver me, for you *are* my god!"

18 They do not know nor understand;
For He has shut their eyes, so that
they cannot see,
And their hearts, so that they cannot
understand.
19 And no one considers in his heart,
Nor *is there* knowledge nor
understanding to say,
"I have burned half of it in the fire,
Yes, I have also baked bread on its coals;

I have roasted meat and eaten *it;*
And shall I make the rest of it an
abomination?
Shall I fall down before a block of
wood?"
20 He feeds on ashes;
A deceived heart has turned him
aside;
And he cannot deliver his soul,
Nor say, "*Is there* not a lie in my right
hand?"

21 "Remember these, O Jacob,
And Israel, for you *are* My servant;
I have formed you, you *are* My
servant;
O Israel, you will not be forgotten by Me!
22 I have blotted out, like a thick cloud,
your transgressions,
And like a cloud, your sins.
Return to Me, for I have redeemed you."

23 Sing, O heavens, for the LORD
has done *it!*
Shout, you lower parts of the earth;
Break forth into singing, you
mountains,
O forest, and every tree in it!
For the LORD has redeemed Jacob,
And glorified Himself in Israel.

24 Thus says the LORD, your Redeemer,
And He who formed you from the
womb:
"I *am* the LORD, who makes all *things,*
Who stretches out the heavens all
alone,
Who spreads abroad the earth by Myself;
25 Who frustrates the signs of the
babblers,
And drives diviners mad;
Who turns wise men backward,
And makes their knowledge
foolishness;
26 Who confirms the word of His servant,
And performs the counsel of His
messengers;
Who says to Jerusalem, 'You shall be
inhabited,'
To the cities of Judah, 'You shall be built,'
And I will raise up her waste places;
27 Who says to the deep, 'Be dry!
And I will dry up your rivers';
28 Who says of Cyrus, '*He is* My
shepherd,
And he shall perform all My pleasure,
Saying to Jerusalem, "You shall be
built,"
And to the temple, "Your foundation
shall be laid." '

44:28 Cyrus,...My shepherd. The prophecy—given a century and a half before Cyrus lived and became king of Persia—predicted God's use of the Persian king to gather the faithful remnant of Israel back to the land. In this role, Cyrus prefigured the Lord's Servant, who will shepherd the sheep of Israel in their final regathering (Mic. 5:4). The title "shepherd" applied to kings as leaders of God's people (2 Sam. 5:2; Jer. 3:15). In Acts 13:22, Paul compares David to the standard of Cyrus's obedience. **Jerusalem...the temple.** In 538 B.C., Cyrus decreed the rebuilding of the temple (Ezra 1:1,2; 6:3), thus fulfilling Isaiah's prophecy. The returning Jews completed the work in 516 B.C. (Ezra 6:15).

Psalm 110:1–7

A Psalm of David.

The LORD said to my Lord,
"Sit at My right hand,
Till I make Your enemies
Your footstool."
2 The LORD shall send the rod of Your
strength out of Zion.
Rule in the midst of Your enemies!

3 Your people *shall be* volunteers
In the day of Your power;
In the beauties of holiness, from the
womb of the morning,
You have the dew of Your youth.
4 The LORD has sworn
And will not relent,
"You *are* a priest forever
According to the order of
Melchizedek."
5 The Lord *is* at Your right hand;
He shall execute kings in the day of
His wrath.
6 He shall judge among the nations,
He shall fill *the places* with dead bodies,
He shall execute the heads of many
countries.
7 He shall drink of the brook by the
wayside;
Therefore He shall lift up the head.

Proverbs 26:5–9

5 Answer a fool according to his folly,
Lest he be wise in his own eyes.
6 He who sends a message by the hand
of a fool
Cuts off *his own* feet *and* drinks
violence.

7 *Like* the legs of the lame that hang limp
Is a proverb in the mouth of fools.
8 Like one who binds a stone in a sling
Is he who gives honor to a fool.
9 *Like* a thorn *that* goes into the hand of
a drunkard
Is a proverb in the mouth of fools.

Galatians 4:1–31

4 Now I say *that* the heir, as long as he is a child, does not differ at all from a slave, though he is master of all, [2]but is under guardians and stewards until the time appointed by the father. [3]Even so we, when we were children, were in bondage under the elements of the world. [4]But when the fullness of the time had come, God sent forth His Son, born of a woman, born under the law, [5]to redeem those who were under the law, that we might receive the adoption as sons.

[6]And because you are sons, God has sent forth the Spirit of His Son into your hearts, crying out, "Abba, Father!" [7]Therefore you are no longer a slave but a son, and if a son, then an heir of God through Christ.

[8]But then, indeed, when you did not know God, you served those which by nature are not gods. [9]But now after you have known God, or rather are known by God, how *is it that* you turn again to the weak and beggarly elements, to which you desire again to be in bondage? [10]You observe days and months and seasons and years. [11]I am afraid for you, lest I have labored for you in vain.

[12]Brethren, I urge you to become like me, for I *became* like you. You have not injured me at all. [13]You know that because of physical infirmity I preached the gospel to you at the first. [14]And my trial which was in my flesh you did not despise or reject, but you received me as an angel of God, *even* as Christ Jesus. [15]What then was the blessing you *enjoyed?* For I bear you witness that, if possible, you would have plucked out your own eyes and given them to me. [16]Have I therefore become your enemy because I tell you the truth?

[17]They zealously court you, *but* for no good; yes, they want to exclude you, that you may be zealous for them. [18]But it is good to be zealous in a good thing always, and not only when I am present with you. [19]My little children, for whom I labor in birth again until Christ is formed in you, [20]I would like to be present with you now and to change my tone; for I have doubts about you.

[21]Tell me, you who desire to be under the law, do you not hear the law? [22]For it is written that Abraham had two sons: the one by a bondwoman, the other by a freewoman. [23]But he *who was* of the bondwoman was born according to the flesh, and he of the freewoman through promise, [24]which things are symbolic. For these are the two covenants: the one from Mount Sinai which gives birth to bondage, which is Hagar— [25]for this Hagar is Mount Sinai in Arabia, and corresponds to Jerusalem which now is, and is in bondage with her children— [26]but the Jerusalem above is free, which is the mother of us all. [27]For it is written:

4:4 the fullness of the time. In God's timetable, when the exact religious, cultural, and political conditions demanded by His perfect plan were in place, Jesus came into the world. **God sent forth His Son.** As a father set the time for the ceremony of his son becoming of age and being released from the guardians, stewards, and tutors, so God sent His Son at the precise moment to bring all who believe out from under bondage to the law—a truth Jesus repeatedly affirmed (John 5:30,36,37; 6:39,44,57; 8:16,18,42; 12:49; 17:21,25;20:21). That the Father sent Jesus into the world teaches His preexistence as the eternal second member of the Trinity. **born of a woman.** This emphasizes Jesus' full humanity, not merely His virgin birth (Is. 7:14; Matt. 1:20–25). Jesus had to be fully God for His sacrifice to be of the infinite worth needed to atone for sin. But He also had to be fully man so He could take upon Himself the penalty of sin as the substitute for man. **under the law.** Like all men, Jesus was obligated to obey God's law. Unlike anyone else, however, He perfectly obeyed that law (John 8:46; 2 Cor. 5:21; Heb. 4:15; 7:26; 1 Pet. 2:22; 1 John 3:5). His sinlessness made Him the unblemished sacrifice for sins, who "fulfilled all righteousness," i.e., perfectly obeyed God in everything. That perfect righteousness is what is imputed to those who believe in Him.

4:5 those...under the law. Guilty sinners who are under the law's demands and its curses and in need of a Savior. **the adoption as sons.** "Adoption" is the act of bringing someone who is the offspring of another into one's own family. Since unregenerate people are by nature children of the devil, the only way they can become God's children is by spiritual adoption.

"Rejoice, O barren,
You who do not bear!
Break forth and shout,
You who are not in labor!
For the desolate has many more children
Than she who has a husband."

[28]Now we, brethren, as Isaac *was,* are children of promise. [29]But, as he who was born according to the flesh then persecuted him *who was born* according to the Spirit, even so *it is* now. [30]Nevertheless what does the Scripture say? *"Cast out the bondwoman and her son, for the son of the bondwoman shall not be heir with the son of the freewoman."* [31]So then, brethren, we are not children of the bondwoman but of the free.

DAY 26: How does Psalm 110 exalt Jesus Christ?

This psalm contains one of the most exalted prophetic portions of Scripture presenting Jesus Christ as both a holy king and a royal high priest—something that no human monarch of Israel ever experienced. It, along with Psalm 118, is by far the most quoted psalm in the New Testament (Matt. 22:44; 26:64; Mark 12:36; 14:62; Luke 20:42,43; 22:69; Acts 2:34,35; Heb. 1:13; 5:6; 7:17,21; 10:13). While portraying the perfect king, the perfect high priest, and the perfect government, Psalm 110 declares Christ's current role in heaven as the resurrected Savior (110:1) and His future role on earth as the reigning Monarch (110:2–7). This psalm is decidedly messianic and millennial in content. Jesus Christ (Matt. 22:43,44) verifies the Davidic authorship.

"The LORD said to my Lord" (v. 1). Refers to the divine/human King of Israel—the Lord Jesus Christ. Christ's humanity descended from David, which is demanded by the Davidic promise of 2 Samuel 7:12. Using this passage, Christ also declared His deity in the Gospels (Matt. 22:44; Mark 12:36; Luke 20:42–43) by arguing that only God could have been lord to King David. "My right hand." God the Father invited God the Son in His ascension to sit at the place of honor in the heavenly throne room (Acts. 2:22–36; Heb. 10:10–12). "Your enemies Your footstool." Footstool was an ancient Near Eastern picture of absolute victory portraying the idea that one's enemy was now underfoot (Pss. 8:6,7; 47:3; Is. 66:1; 1 Cor. 15:27).

"You are a priest" (v. 4). The first time in the history of Israel when a king simultaneously served as high priest. Christ (a.k.a. "Branch," Is. 4:2; Jer. 23:5,6; Zech. 3:8; 6:12,13) will build the temple at which the world will worship God (2 Sam. 7:13; Is. 2:2–4; Ezek. 40–48). "Forever." Christ represents the final and foremost high priest in the history of Israel. "The order of Melchizedek." This high priest could not be of Aaron's lineage in that he would not be eternal, not be of Judah, not be a king, and not be of the New Covenant (Jer. 31:31–33; Heb. 8,9). Melchizedek, which means "king of righteousness," served as the human priest/king of Salem in Genesis 14:17–20 and provides a picture of the order of Christ's priesthood (Heb. 5:6; 7:17,21).

SEPTEMBER 27

Isaiah 45:1–46:13

45 "Thus says the LORD to His anointed,
To Cyrus, whose right hand
I have held—
To subdue nations before him
And loose the armor of kings,
To open before him the double doors,
So that the gates will not be shut:
2 'I will go before you
And make the crooked places straight;
I will break in pieces the gates of
bronze
And cut the bars of iron.
3 I will give you the treasures of
darkness
And hidden riches of secret places,
That you may know that I, the LORD,
Who call *you* by your name,
Am the God of Israel.
4 For Jacob My servant's sake,
And Israel My elect,
I have even called you by your name;
I have named you, though you have
not known Me.

45:1 His anointed. This word is the one translated from the Hebrew by the transliteration—"Messiah." It is the word used for the messianic Redeemer King in Psalm 2:2 and Daniel 9:25,26, but here refers to Cyrus, as the king set apart by God's providence for divine purposes. Though not a worshiper of the Lord, the Persian monarch played an unusual role as Israel's shepherd (44:28) and God's anointed judge on nations.

5 I *am* the LORD, and *there is* no other;
There is no God besides Me.
I will gird you, though you have not
known Me,
6 That they may know from the rising of
the sun to its setting
That *there is* none besides Me.
I *am* the LORD, and *there is* no other;
7 I form the light and create darkness,
I make peace and create calamity;
I, the LORD, do all these *things*.'

8 "Rain down, you heavens, from above,
And let the skies pour down
righteousness;
Let the earth open, let them bring
forth salvation,
And let righteousness spring up
together.
I, the LORD, have created it.

9 "Woe to him who strives with his
Maker!
Let the potsherd *strive* with the
potsherds of the earth!
Shall the clay say to him who forms it,
'What are you making?'
Or shall your handiwork *say*, 'He has
no hands'?
10 Woe to him who says to *his* father,
'What are you begetting?'
Or to the woman, 'What have you
brought forth?' "

11 Thus says the LORD,
The Holy One of Israel, and his Maker:
"Ask Me of things to come concerning
My sons;
And concerning the work of My hands,
you command Me.
12 I have made the earth,
And created man on it.
I—My hands—stretched out the
heavens,
And all their host I have commanded.
13 I have raised him up in righteousness,
And I will direct all his ways;
He shall build My city
And let My exiles go free,
Not for price nor reward,"
Says the LORD of hosts.

14 Thus says the LORD:
"The labor of Egypt and merchandise of
Cush
And of the Sabeans, men of stature,
Shall come over to you, and they shall
be yours;
They shall walk behind you,
They shall come over in chains;
And they shall bow down to you.
They will make supplication to you,
saying, 'Surely God *is* in you,
And *there is* no other;
There is no other God.' "

15 Truly You *are* God, who hide Yourself,
O God of Israel, the Savior!
16 They shall be ashamed
And also disgraced, all of them;
They shall go in confusion together,
Who are makers of idols.
17 *But* Israel shall be saved by the LORD
With an everlasting salvation;
You shall not be ashamed or disgraced
Forever and ever.

18 For thus says the LORD,
Who created the heavens,
Who is God,
Who formed the earth and made it,
Who has established it,
Who did not create it in vain,
Who formed it to be inhabited:
"I *am* the LORD, and *there is* no other.
19 I have not spoken in secret,
In a dark place of the earth;
I did not say to the seed of Jacob,
'Seek Me in vain';
I, the LORD, speak righteousness,
I declare things that are right.

20 "Assemble yourselves and come;
Draw near together,
You *who have* escaped from the
nations.
They have no knowledge,
Who carry the wood of their carved
image,
And pray to a god *that* cannot save.
21 Tell and bring forth *your case*;
Yes, let them take counsel together.
Who has declared this from ancient
time?
Who has told it from that time?
Have not I, the LORD?
And *there is* no other God besides Me,
A just God and a Savior;
There is none besides Me.

45:21 *there is* no other...*There is* none. The Lord restated the truth expressed by Moses in Deuteronomy 4:35. The scribe who asked Jesus about the greatest commandment cited this same principle in agreeing with Jesus' answer to his question (Mark 12:32).

22 "Look to Me, and be saved,
All you ends of the earth!
For I *am* God, and *there is* no other.
23 I have sworn by Myself;
The word has gone out of My mouth *in* righteousness,
And shall not return,
That to Me every knee shall bow,
Every tongue shall take an oath.

45:23 every knee shall bow. In the kingdom age, all nations will worship the one true God of Israel. A further meaning, justified by the New Testament, applies this verse to believers' accountability to God when He evaluates their works (Rom. 14:11). In assigning the words another meaning, Paul relates the words to the coming universal acknowledgment that "Jesus Christ is Lord, to the glory of God the Father" (Phil. 2:10,11).

24 He shall say,
'Surely in the LORD I have righteousness and strength.
To Him *men* shall come,
And all shall be ashamed
Who are incensed against Him.
25 In the LORD all the descendants of Israel
Shall be justified, and shall glory.' "

46 Bel bows down, Nebo stoops;
Their idols were on the beasts and on the cattle.
Your carriages *were* heavily loaded,
A burden to the weary *beast.*
2 They stoop, they bow down together;
They could not deliver the burden,
But have themselves gone into captivity.

3 "Listen to Me, O house of Jacob,
And all the remnant of the house of Israel,
Who have been upheld *by Me* from birth,
Who have been carried from the womb:
4 Even to *your* old age, I *am* He,
And *even* to gray hairs I will carry *you!*
I have made, and I will bear;
Even I will carry, and will deliver *you.*
5 "To whom will you liken Me, and make *Me* equal
And compare Me, that we should be alike?
6 They lavish gold out of the bag,
And weigh silver on the scales;
They hire a goldsmith, and he makes it a god;
They prostrate themselves, yes, they worship.
7 They bear it on the shoulder, they carry it
And set it in its place, and it stands;
From its place it shall not move.
Though *one* cries out to it, yet it cannot answer
Nor save him out of his trouble.

8 "Remember this, and show yourselves men;
Recall to mind, O you transgressors.
9 Remember the former things of old,
For I *am* God, and *there is* no other;
I am God, and *there is* none like Me,
10 Declaring the end from the beginning,
And from ancient times *things* that are not *yet* done,
Saying, 'My counsel shall stand,
And I will do all My pleasure,'
11 Calling a bird of prey from the east,
The man who executes My counsel, from a far country.
Indeed I have spoken *it;*
I will also bring it to pass.
I have purposed *it;*
I will also do it.

12 "Listen to Me, you stubborn-hearted,
Who *are* far from righteousness:
13 I bring My righteousness near, it shall not be far off;
My salvation shall not linger.
And I will place salvation in Zion,
For Israel My glory.

Psalm 111:1–6

Praise the LORD!
I will praise the LORD with *my* whole heart,
In the assembly of the upright and *in* the congregation.
2 The works of the LORD *are* great,
Studied by all who have pleasure in them.
3 His work *is* honorable and glorious,
And His righteousness endures forever.
4 He has made His wonderful works to be remembered;
The LORD *is* gracious and full of compassion.

5 He has given food to those who fear
Him;
He will ever be mindful of His
covenant.
6 He has declared to His people the
power of His works,
In giving them the heritage of the
nations.

Proverbs 26:10

10 The great *God* who formed everything
Gives the fool *his* hire and the
transgressor *his* wages.

Galatians 5:1–26

5 Stand fast therefore in the liberty by which
Christ has made us free, and do not be
entangled again with a yoke of bondage. [2]In-
deed I, Paul, say to you that if you become

5:1 Stand fast. Stay where you are, Paul asserts, because of the benefit of being free from the law and the flesh as a way of salvation and the fullness of blessing by grace. **free.** Deliverance from the curse that the law pronounces on the sinner who has been striving unsuccessfully to achieve his own righteousness (3:13,22–26; 4:1–7), but who has now embraced Christ and the salvation granted to him by grace. **entangled again.** Better translated "to be burdened by," "to be oppressed by," or "to be subject to," because of its connection with a yoke. **yoke of bondage.** "Yoke" refers to the apparatus used to control a domesticated animal. The Jews referred to the "yoke of the law" as a good thing, the essence of true religion. Paul argued that for those who pursued it as a way of salvation, the law was a yoke of slavery.

circumcised, Christ will profit you nothing.
[3]And I testify again to every man who becomes
circumcised that he is a debtor to keep the
whole law. [4]You have become estranged from
Christ, you who *attempt to* be justified by law;
you have fallen from grace. [5]For we through
the Spirit eagerly wait for the hope of righteousness by faith. [6]For in Christ Jesus neither
circumcision nor uncircumcision avails anything, but faith working through love.
[7]You ran well. Who hindered you from obeying the truth? [8]This persuasion does not *come*
from Him who calls you. [9]A little leaven leavens
the whole lump. [10]I have confidence in you, in
the Lord, that you will have no other mind; but

5:6 neither circumcision nor uncircumcision avails anything. Nothing done or not done in the flesh, even religious ceremony, makes any difference in one's relationship to God. What is external is immaterial and worthless, unless it reflects genuine internal righteousness (Rom. 2:25–29). **faith working through love.** Saving faith proves its genuine character by works of love. The one who lives by faith is internally motivated by love for God and Christ (Matt. 22:37–40), which supernaturally issues forth in reverent worship, genuine obedience, and self-sacrificing love for others.

he who troubles you shall bear his judgment,
whoever he is.
[11]And I, brethren, if I still preach circumcision, why do I still suffer persecution? Then
the offense of the cross has ceased. [12]I could
wish that those who trouble you would even
cut themselves off!
[13]For you, brethren, have been called to liberty; only do not *use* liberty as an opportunity
for the flesh, but through love serve one
another. [14]For all the law is fulfilled in one
word, *even* in this: *"You shall love your neighbor as yourself."* [15]But if you bite and devour
one another, beware lest you be consumed by
one another!
[16]I say then: Walk in the Spirit, and you shall
not fulfill the lust of the flesh. [17]For the flesh
lusts against the Spirit, and the Spirit against the
flesh; and these are contrary to one another, so
that you do not do the things that you wish.
[18]But if you are led by the Spirit, you are not
under the law.
[19]Now the works of the flesh are evident,
which are: adultery, fornication, uncleanness,
lewdness, [20]idolatry, sorcery, hatred, contentions, jealousies, outbursts of wrath, selfish
ambitions, dissensions, heresies, [21]envy, murders, drunkenness, revelries, and the like; of
which I tell you beforehand, just as I also told
you in time past, that those who practice such
things will not inherit the kingdom of God.
[22]But the fruit of the Spirit is love, joy,
peace, longsuffering, kindness, goodness,
faithfulness, [23]gentleness, self-control. Against
such there is no law. [24]And those *who are*
Christ's have crucified the flesh with its passions and desires. [25]If we live in the Spirit, let
us also walk in the Spirit. [26]Let us not become
conceited, provoking one another, envying
one another.

DAY 27: Describe the fruit of the Spirit.

The fruit of the Spirit are the godly attitudes that characterize the lives of only those who belong to God by faith in Christ and possess the Spirit of God. The Spirit produces fruit which consists of 9 characteristics or attitudes that are inextricably linked with each other and are commanded of believers throughout the New Testament.

"Love." One of several Greek words for love, *agape,* is the love of choice, referring not to an emotional affection, physical attraction, or a familial bond, but to respect, devotion, and affection that leads to willing, self-sacrificial service (John 15:13; Rom. 5:8; 1 John 3:16,17). "Joy." A happiness based on unchanging divine promises and eternal spiritual realities. It is the sense of well-being experienced by one who knows all is well between himself and the Lord (1 Pet. 1:8). Joy is not the result of favorable circumstances, and even occurs when those circumstances are the most painful and severe (John 16:20–22). Joy is a gift from God, and as such, believers are not to manufacture it but to delight in the blessing they already possess (Rom. 14:17; Phil. 4:4). "Peace." The inner calm that results from confidence in one's saving relationship with Christ. The verb form denotes binding together and is reflected in the expression "having it all together." Like joy, peace is not related to one's circumstances (John 14:27; Rom. 8:28; Phil. 4:6,7,9).

"Longsuffering." Patience which refers to the ability to endure injuries inflicted by others and the willingness to accept irritating or painful situations (Eph. 4:2; Col. 3:12; 1 Tim. 1:15,16). "Kindness." Tender concern for others, reflected in a desire to treat others gently, just as the Lord treats all believers (Matt. 11:28,29; 19:13,14; 2 Tim. 2:24). "Goodness." Moral and spiritual excellence manifested in active kindness (Rom. 5:7). Believers are commanded to exemplify goodness (6:10; 2 Thess. 1:11). "Faithfulness." Loyalty and trustworthiness (Lam. 3:22; Phil. 2:7–9; 1 Thess. 5:24; Rev. 2:10).

"Gentleness." Better translated "meekness." It is a humble and gentle attitude that is patiently submissive in every offense, while having no desire for revenge or retribution. In the New Testament, it is used to describe 3 attitudes: submission to the will of God (Col. 3:12), teachability (James 1:21), and consideration of others (Eph. 4:2). "Self-control." This refers to restraining passions and appetites (1 Cor. 9:25; 2 Pet. 1:5,6). "No law." When a Christian walks by the Spirit and manifests His fruit, he needs no external law to produce the attitudes and behavior that please God (Rom. 8:4).

SEPTEMBER 28

Isaiah 47:1–48:22

47 "Come down and sit in the dust,
O virgin daughter of Babylon;
Sit on the ground without a throne,
O daughter of the Chaldeans!
For you shall no more be called
Tender and delicate.
2 Take the millstones and grind meal.
Remove your veil,
Take off the skirt,
Uncover the thigh,
Pass through the rivers.
3 Your nakedness shall be uncovered,
Yes, your shame will be seen;
I will take vengeance,
And I will not arbitrate with a man."

4 *As for* our Redeemer, the LORD of hosts
is His name,
The Holy One of Israel.

5 "Sit in silence, and go into darkness,
O daughter of the Chaldeans;
For you shall no longer be called
The Lady of Kingdoms.
6 I was angry with My people;
I have profaned My inheritance,
And given them into your hand.
You showed them no mercy;
On the elderly you laid your yoke
very heavily.
7 And you said, 'I shall be a lady forever,'
So that you did not take these *things*
to heart,
Nor remember the latter end of them.

8 "Therefore hear this now, *you who are*
given to pleasures,
Who dwell securely,
Who say in your heart, 'I *am*, and *there*
is no one else besides me;
I shall not sit *as* a widow,
Nor shall I know the loss of children';
9 But these two *things* shall come to you
In a moment, in one day:
The loss of children, and widowhood.
They shall come upon you in their
fullness
Because of the multitude of your
sorceries,
For the great abundance of your
enchantments.

10 "For you have trusted in your wickedness;
You have said, 'No one sees me';

Your wisdom and your knowledge have
warped you;
And you have said in your heart,
'I *am,* and *there is* no one else besides
me.'
11 Therefore evil shall come upon you;
You shall not know from where it
arises.
And trouble shall fall upon you;
You will not be able to put it off.
And desolation shall come upon you
suddenly,
Which you shall not know.

12 "Stand now with your enchantments
And the multitude of your sorceries,
In which you have labored from your
youth—
Perhaps you will be able to profit,
Perhaps you will prevail.
13 You are wearied in the multitude of
your counsels;
Let now the astrologers, the stargazers,
And the monthly prognosticators
Stand up and save you
From what shall come upon you.
14 Behold, they shall be as stubble,
The fire shall burn them;
They shall not deliver themselves
From the power of the flame;
It shall not *be* a coal to be warmed by,
Nor a fire to sit before!
15 Thus shall they be to you
With whom you have labored,
Your merchants from your youth;
They shall wander each one to his
quarter.
No one shall save you.

48 "Hear this, O house of Jacob,
Who are called by the name
of Israel,
And have come forth from the
wellsprings of Judah;
Who swear by the name of the LORD,
And make mention of the God of Israel,
But not in truth or in righteousness;
2 For they call themselves after
the holy city,
And lean on the God of Israel;
The LORD of hosts *is* His name:

3 "I have declared the former things from
the beginning;
They went forth from My mouth,
and I caused them to hear it.
Suddenly I did *them,* and they came
to pass.
4 Because I knew that you *were* obstinate,
And your neck *was* an iron sinew,
And your brow bronze,
5 Even from the beginning I have
declared *it* to you;
Before it came to pass I proclaimed *it*
to you,
Lest you should say, 'My idol has done
them,
And my carved image and my molded
image
Have commanded them.'

6 "You have heard;
See all this.
And will you not declare *it?*
I have made you hear new things from
this time,
Even hidden things, and you did not
know them.

48:6 new things. From this point onward, the prophecies of the Messiah's First and Second Coming and the restoration of Israel have a new distinctiveness. Babylon becomes the Babylon of Revelation (v. 20), and God uses Isaiah to communicate truths about the messianic kingdom on earth and the new heavens and new earth that follow it (e.g., 11:1–5; 65:17). Verse 7 indicates that God had never before revealed these features about the future.

7 They are created now and not from the
beginning;
And before this day you have not heard
them,
Lest you should say, 'Of course I knew
them.'
8 Surely you did not hear,
Surely you did not know;
Surely from long ago your ear was not
opened.
For I knew that you would deal very
treacherously,
And were called a transgressor from
the womb.

9 "For My name's sake I will defer
My anger,
And *for* My praise I will restrain it
from you,
So that I do not cut you off.
10 Behold, I have refined you, but not as
silver;
I have tested you in the furnace of
affliction.
11 For My own sake, for My own sake,
I will do *it;*

48:10,11 refined...tested. Since Isaiah's time, Israel's testings have included the Babylonian captivity and present worldwide dispersion from her land; unlike silver purged in the furnace, the purging of Israel is not complete, and they are not refined. But God keeps up the afflictions until they are, so His name is not defamed through the destruction of Israel. The nation will be purged (Zech. 13:1). God's plan is such that He alone, not man or man-made idols, will receive credit for Israel's salvation (42:8; Rom. 11:25–27,33–36). The adversaries of God are never to be given legitimate reasons for scoffing at God and His work.

For how should *My name* be profaned?
And I will not give My glory to another.

12 "Listen to Me, O Jacob,
And Israel, My called:
I *am* He, I *am* the First,
I *am* also the Last.
13 Indeed My hand has laid the
foundation of the earth,
And My right hand has stretched out
the heavens;
When I call to them,
They stand up together.

14 "All of you, assemble yourselves,
and hear!
Who among them has declared these
things?
The LORD loves him;
He shall do His pleasure on Babylon,
And His arm *shall be against* the
Chaldeans.
15 I, *even* I, have spoken;
Yes, I have called him,
I have brought him, and his way will
prosper.

16 "Come near to Me, hear this:
I have not spoken in secret from the
beginning;
From the time that it was, I *was* there.
And now the Lord GOD and His Spirit
Have sent Me."

17 Thus says the LORD, your Redeemer,
The Holy One of Israel:
"I *am* the LORD your God,
Who teaches you to profit,
Who leads you by the way you should
go.
18 Oh, that you had heeded My
commandments!
Then your peace would have been like
a river,
And your righteousness like the waves
of the sea.
19 Your descendants also would have
been like the sand,
And the offspring of your body like the
grains of sand;
His name would not have been cut off
Nor destroyed from before Me."

20 Go forth from Babylon!
Flee from the Chaldeans!
With a voice of singing,
Declare, proclaim this,
Utter it to the end of the earth;
Say, "The LORD has redeemed
His servant Jacob!"
21 And they did not thirst
When He led them through the
deserts;
He caused the waters to flow from the
rock for them;
He also split the rock, and the waters
gushed out.
22 "*There is* no peace," says the LORD, "for
the wicked."

Psalm 111:7–10

7 The works of His hands *are* verity and
justice;
All His precepts *are* sure.
8 They stand fast forever and ever,
And are done in truth and uprightness.
9 He has sent redemption to His people;
He has commanded His covenant
forever:
Holy and awesome *is* His name.
10 The fear of the LORD *is* the beginning
of wisdom;
A good understanding have all those
who do *His commandments.*
His praise endures forever.

Proverbs 26:11–12

11 As a dog returns to his own vomit,
So a fool repeats his folly.
12 Do you see a man wise in his own
eyes?
There is more hope for a fool than for
him.

Galatians 6:1–18

6 Brethren, if a man is overtaken in any trespass, you who *are* spiritual restore such a one in a spirit of gentleness, considering yourself lest you also be tempted. 2 Bear one another's burdens, and so fulfill the law of Christ.

[3]For if anyone thinks himself to be something,
when he is nothing, he deceives himself. [4]But
let each one examine his own work, and then
he will have rejoicing in himself alone, and not in
another. [5]For each one shall bear his own load.
[6]Let him who is taught the word share in all
good things with him who teaches.
[7]Do not be deceived, God is not mocked; for
whatever a man sows, that he will also reap.
[8]For he who sows to his flesh will of the flesh
reap corruption, but he who sows to the Spirit
will of the Spirit reap everlasting life. [9]And let
us not grow weary while doing good, for in
due season we shall reap if we do not lose

6:8 sows to his flesh. Here it means pandering to the flesh's evil desires. **corruption.** From the Greek word for degeneration, as in decaying food. Sin always corrupts and, when left unchecked, always makes a person progressively worse in character (Rom. 6:23). **sows to the Spirit.** To walk by the Holy Spirit. **everlasting life.** This expression describes not only a life that endures forever but, primarily, the highest quality of living that one can experience (Ps. 51:12; John 10:10; Eph. 1:3,18).

heart. [10]Therefore, as we have opportunity, let
us do good to all, especially to those who are
of the household of faith.

6:10 opportunity. This Greek word refers to a distinct, fixed time period rather than occasional moments. Paul's point is that the believer's entire life provides the unique privilege by which he can serve others in Christ's name. **especially...the household of faith.** Our love for fellow Christians is the primary test of our love for God.

[11]See with what large letters I have written
to you with my own hand! [12]As many as desire
to make a good showing in the flesh, these
would compel you to be circumcised, only that
they may not suffer persecution for the cross
of Christ. [13]For not even those who are circumcised keep the law, but they desire to have
you circumcised that they may boast in your
flesh. [14]But God forbid that I should boast
except in the cross of our Lord Jesus Christ,
by whom the world has been crucified to me,
and I to the world. [15]For in Christ Jesus neither
circumcision nor uncircumcision avails anything, but a new creation.
[16]And as many as walk according to this
rule, peace and mercy *be* upon them, and upon
the Israel of God.
[17]From now on let no one trouble me, for I
bear in my body the marks of the Lord Jesus.
[18]Brethren, the grace of our Lord Jesus
Christ *be* with your spirit. Amen.

DAY 28: How do we restore a believer overtaken in sin?

In Galatians 6:1, Paul addresses the situation where someone is overtaken in a sin, which may imply the person was actually seen committing the sin or that he was caught or snared by the sin itself. Those believers who are walking in the Spirit, filled with the Spirit, and evidencing the fruit of the Spirit are to "restore" such a one. This is sometimes used metaphorically of settling disputes or arguments. It means "to mend" or "repair" and was used of setting a broken bone or repairing a dislocated limb (Heb. 12:12,13; Rom. 15:1; 1 Thess. 5:14). The basic process of restoration is outlined in Matthew 18:15–20. "In a spirit of gentleness, considering yourself lest you also be tempted." The Greek form strongly emphasizes a continual, diligent attentiveness.

"Bear one another's burdens, and so fulfill the law of Christ" (v. 2). "Burdens" are extra heavy loads, which here represent difficulties or problems people have trouble dealing with. "Bear" connotes carrying something with endurance. The law of love which fulfills the entire law (John 13:34; Rom. 13:8,10).

"But let each one examine his own work" (v. 4). Literally, "to approve something after testing it." Believers first must be sure their lives are right with God before giving spiritual help to others (Matt. 7:3–5). "Have rejoicing in himself." If a believer rejoices or boasts, it should be only boasting in the Lord for what God has done in him (2 Cor. 10:12–18), not for what he supposedly has accomplished compared to other believers.

"For each one shall bear his own load" (v. 5). This is not a contradiction to v. 2. "Load" has no connotation of difficulty; it refers to life's routine obligations and each believer's ministry calling (Matt. 11:30; 1 Cor. 3:12–15; 2 Cor. 5:10). God requires faithfulness in meeting those responsibilities.

SEPTEMBER 29

Isaiah 49:1–50:11

49 "Listen, O coastlands, to Me,
And take heed, you peoples
from afar!
The LORD has called Me from the womb;
From the matrix of My mother He has
made mention of My name.
2 And He has made My mouth like a
sharp sword;
In the shadow of His hand He has
hidden Me,
And made Me a polished shaft;
In His quiver He has hidden Me."

3 "And He said to me,
'You *are* My servant, O Israel,
In whom I will be glorified.'
4 Then I said, 'I have labored in vain,
I have spent my strength for nothing
and in vain;
Yet surely my just reward *is* with
the LORD,
And my work with my God.' "

5 "And now the LORD says,
Who formed Me from the womb *to be*
His Servant,
To bring Jacob back to Him,
So that Israel is gathered to Him
(For I shall be glorious in the eyes of
the LORD,
And My God shall be My strength),
6 Indeed He says,
'It is too small a thing that You should
be My Servant
To raise up the tribes of Jacob,
And to restore the preserved ones
of Israel;
I will also give You as a light to the
Gentiles,
That You should be My salvation to the
ends of the earth.' "
7 Thus says the LORD,
The Redeemer of Israel, their Holy
One,
To Him whom man despises,
To Him whom the nation abhors,
To the Servant of rulers:
"Kings shall see and arise,
Princes also shall worship,
Because of the LORD who is faithful,
The Holy One of Israel;
And He has chosen You."
8 Thus says the LORD:

49:8 acceptable time…day of salvation. The Messiah is represented as asking for the grace of God to be given to sinners. God gives His favorable answer in a time of grace (61:1) when salvation's day comes to the world (Gal. 4:4,5; Heb. 4:7). At His appointed time in the future, the Lord will, by His Servant, accomplish the final deliverance of Israel. Paul applied these words to his ministry of proclaiming the gospel of God's grace to all people (2 Cor. 6:2). **a covenant to the people.** When the Lord saves and regathers Israel, they will return to the land, to which Joshua brought their ancestors after their exit from Egypt, now restored and glorious (44:26; Josh. 13:1–8).

"In an acceptable time I have heard You,
And in the day of salvation I have
helped You;
I will preserve You and give You
As a covenant to the people,
To restore the earth,
To cause them to inherit the desolate
heritages;
9 That You may say to the prisoners,
'Go forth,'
To those who *are* in darkness, 'Show
yourselves.'
"They shall feed along the roads,
And their pastures *shall be* on all
desolate heights.
10 They shall neither hunger nor thirst,
Neither heat nor sun shall strike them;
For He who has mercy on them will
lead them,
Even by the springs of water He will
guide them.
11 I will make each of My mountains
a road,
And My highways shall be elevated.
12 Surely these shall come from afar;
Look! Those from the north and the
west,
And these from the land of Sinim."

13 Sing, O heavens!
Be joyful, O earth!
And break out in singing,
O mountains!
For the LORD has comforted His
people,
And will have mercy on His afflicted.
14 But Zion said, "The LORD has forsaken
me,
And my Lord has forgotten me."

15 "Can a woman forget her nursing child,
And not have compassion on the son
of her womb?
Surely they may forget,
Yet I will not forget you.
16 See, I have inscribed you on the palms
of My hands;
Your walls *are* continually before Me.
17 Your sons shall make haste;
Your destroyers and those who laid
you waste
Shall go away from you.
18 Lift up your eyes, look around and see;
All these gather together *and* come
to you.
As I live," says the LORD,
"You shall surely clothe yourselves with
them all as an ornament,
And bind them *on you* as a bride *does.*

19 "For your waste and desolate places,
And the land of your destruction,
Will even now be too small for the
inhabitants;
And those who swallowed you up will
be far away.
20 The children you will have,
After you have lost the others,
Will say again in your ears,
'The place *is* too small for me;
Give me a place where I may dwell.'
21 Then you will say in your heart,
'Who has begotten these for me,
Since I have lost my children
and am desolate,
A captive, and wandering to and fro?
And who has brought these up?
There I was, left alone;
But these, where *were* they?' "
22 Thus says the Lord GOD:

"Behold, I will lift My hand in an oath
to the nations,
And set up My standard for the peoples;
They shall bring your sons in *their*
arms,
And your daughters shall be carried on
their shoulders;
23 Kings shall be your foster fathers,
And their queens your nursing
mothers;
They shall bow down to you with *their*
faces to the earth,
And lick up the dust of your feet.
Then you will know that I *am* the LORD,
For they shall not be ashamed who
wait for Me."

24 Shall the prey be taken from the mighty,
Or the captives of the righteous be
delivered?
25 But thus says the LORD:

"Even the captives of the mighty shall
be taken away,
And the prey of the terrible be
delivered;
For I will contend with him who
contends with you,
And I will save your children.
26 I will feed those who oppress you with
their own flesh,
And they shall be drunk with their own
blood as with sweet wine.
All flesh shall know
That I, the LORD, *am* your Savior,
And your Redeemer, the Mighty One
of Jacob."

50 Thus says the LORD:

"Where *is* the certificate of your mother's
divorce,
Whom I have put away?
Or which of My creditors *is it* to whom
I have sold you?
For your iniquities you have sold
yourselves,
And for your transgressions your
mother has been put away.
2 Why, when I came, *was there* no man?
Why, when I called, *was there* none to
answer?
Is My hand shortened at all that it
cannot redeem?
Or have I no power to deliver?
Indeed with My rebuke I dry up the sea,
I make the rivers a wilderness;
Their fish stink because *there is* no
water,
And die of thirst.
3 I clothe the heavens with blackness,
And I make sackcloth their covering."

4 "The Lord GOD has given Me
The tongue of the learned,
That I should know how to speak
A word in season to *him who is* weary.
He awakens Me morning by morning,
He awakens My ear
To hear as the learned.
5 The Lord GOD has opened My ear;
And I was not rebellious,
Nor did I turn away.
6 I gave My back to those who struck
Me,
And My cheeks to those who plucked
out the beard;

I did not hide My face from shame and
spitting.

7 "For the Lord GOD will help Me;
Therefore I will not be disgraced;
Therefore I have set My face like a flint,
And I know that I will not be ashamed.

50:6 My back...My cheeks...My face. The Servant remained obedient though provoked to rebel by excessively vile treatment. Jesus fulfilled this prophecy by remaining submissive to the Father's will (Matt. 26:67; 27:26,30; Mark 14:65; 15:19; Luke 22:63; John 18:22).

50:7 set My face like a flint. So sure was He of the Lord God's help that He resolutely determined to remain unswayed by whatever hardship might await Him (Ezek. 3:8,9). Jesus demonstrated this determination in setting His face to go to Jerusalem to be crucified (Luke 9:51).

8 *He is* near who justifies Me;
Who will contend with Me?
Let us stand together.
Who *is* My adversary?
Let him come near Me.
9 Surely the Lord GOD will help Me;
Who *is* he *who* will condemn Me?
Indeed they will all grow old like
a garment;
The moth will eat them up.

10 "Who among you fears the LORD?
Who obeys the voice of His Servant?
Who walks in darkness
And has no light?
Let him trust in the name of the LORD
And rely upon his God.
11 Look, all you who kindle a fire,
Who encircle *yourselves* with sparks:
Walk in the light of your fire and in the
sparks you have kindled—
This you shall have from My hand:
You shall lie down in torment.

Psalm 112:1–4

Praise the LORD!

Blessed *is* the man *who* fears the LORD,
Who delights greatly in His
commandments.
2 His descendants will be mighty on earth;
The generation of the upright will be
blessed.
3 Wealth and riches *will be* in his house,
And his righteousness endures forever.
4 Unto the upright there arises light in
the darkness;
He is gracious, and full of compassion,
and righteous.

Proverbs 26:13–15

13 The lazy *man* says, "*There is* a lion
in the road!
A fierce lion *is* in the streets!"
14 *As* a door turns on its hinges,
So *does* the lazy *man* on his bed.
15 The lazy *man* buries his hand
in the bowl;
It wearies him to bring it back
to his mouth.

Ephesians 1:1–23

1 Paul, an apostle of Jesus Christ by the will of
God,

To the saints who are in Ephesus, and faithful in Christ Jesus:

2 Grace to you and peace from God our Father
and the Lord Jesus Christ.
3 Blessed *be* the God and Father of our Lord
Jesus Christ, who has blessed us with every
spiritual blessing in the heavenly *places* in
Christ, 4 just as He chose us in Him before the
foundation of the world, that we should be
holy and without blame before Him in love,
5 having predestined us to adoption as sons by
Jesus Christ to Himself, according to the good
pleasure of His will, 6 to the praise of the glory
of His grace, by which He made us accepted in
the Beloved.
7 In Him we have redemption through His
blood, the forgiveness of sins, according to
the riches of His grace 8 which He made to
abound toward us in all wisdom and prudence, 9 having made known to us the mystery
of His will, according to His good pleasure
which He purposed in Himself, 10 that in the
dispensation of the fullness of the times He
might gather together in one all things in
Christ, both which are in heaven and which
are on earth—in Him. 11 In Him also we have
obtained an inheritance, being predestined
according to the purpose of Him who works
all things according to the counsel of His will,
12 that we who first trusted in Christ should be
to the praise of His glory.
13 In Him you also *trusted,* after you heard
the word of truth, the gospel of your salvation;
in whom also, having believed, you were sealed

with the Holy Spirit of promise, [14]who is the guarantee of our inheritance until the redemption of the purchased possession, to the praise of His glory.

1:13,14 sealed with the Holy Spirit. God's own Spirit comes to indwell the believer and secures and preserves his eternal salvation. The sealing of which Paul speaks refers to an official mark of identification placed on a letter, contract, or other document. That document was thereby officially under the authority of the person whose stamp was on the seal. Four primary truths are signified by the seal: 1) security (Dan. 6:17; Matt. 27:62–66); 2) authenticity (1 Kin. 21:6–16); 3) ownership (Jer. 32:10); and 4) authority (Esth. 8:8–12). The Holy Spirit is given by God as His pledge of the believer's future inheritance in glory (2 Cor. 1:21).

[15]Therefore I also, after I heard of your faith in
the Lord Jesus and your love for all the saints, [16]do
not cease to give thanks for you, making mention
of you in my prayers: [17]that the God of our Lord
Jesus Christ, the Father of glory, may give to you
the spirit of wisdom and revelation in the knowledge of Him, [18]the eyes of your understanding
being enlightened; that you may know what is the hope of His calling, what are the riches of the glory of His inheritance in the saints, [19]and
what *is* the exceeding greatness of His power toward us who believe, according to the working of His mighty power [20]which He worked in
Christ when He raised Him from the dead and seated *Him* at His right hand in the heavenly
places, [21]far above all principality and power and might and dominion, and every name that is named, not only in this age but also in that which is to come.

[22]And He put all *things* under His feet, and gave Him *to be* head over all *things* to the church,
[23]which is His body, the fullness of Him who fills all in all.

1:19,20 exceeding greatness of His power. God's great power, that very power which raised Jesus from the dead and lifted Him by ascension back to glory to take His seat at God's right hand, is given to every believer at the time of salvation and is always available (Acts 1:8; Col. 1:29). Paul therefore did not pray that God's power be given to believers but that they be aware of the power they already possessed in Christ and use it (3:20).

DAY 29: Why does Paul use the word "mystery" so often in his letter to the Ephesians?

Paul actually uses the word "mystery" six times in this letter (1:9; 3:3,4,9; 5:32; 6:19). By comparison, the word appears twice in Romans, once in 1 Corinthians, four times in Colossians, once in 1 Timothy, and nowhere else. Contrary to our use of "mystery" as a series of clues to be figured out, Paul's use of the word points to mystery as a heretofore unrevealed truth that has been made clear. The word "mystery" preserves the sense that the revealed truth has such awesome implications that it continues to amaze and humble those who accept it.

Ephesians introduces various aspects of the "mystery." Paul explained his use of the word in 3:4–6 by saying, "that the Gentiles should be fellow heirs, of the same body, and partakers of His promise in Christ through the gospel." When the unsearchable riches of Christ are preached among the Gentiles, one result is an understanding of the "fellowship of the mystery" (3:9). And when God's plan for human marriage is used to explain the unique relationship between Christ and His bride, the church, Paul reminded his readers that the real subject is a great mystery (5:32). And finally, Paul asked the Ephesians to pray for him that he would be able "boldly to make known the mystery of the gospel" (6:19). The gospel is not mysterious because it is hard to understand. It is mysterious because it is unexpected, unmerited, and free. Though Paul didn't use the word in this passage, his summary of the mystery for the Ephesians can be found in 2:8,9: "For by grace you have been saved through faith, and that not of yourselves; it is the gift of God, not of works, lest anyone should boast."

SEPTEMBER 30

Isaiah 51:1–52:15

51 "Listen to Me, you who follow
after righteousness,
You who seek the LORD:
Look to the rock *from which* you were
hewn,
And to the hole of the pit *from which*
you were dug.
2 Look to Abraham your father,
And to Sarah *who* bore you;

For I called him alone,
And blessed him and increased him."

3 For the LORD will comfort Zion,
He will comfort all her waste places;
He will make her wilderness like Eden,
And her desert like the garden
of the LORD;
Joy and gladness will be found in it,
Thanksgiving and the voice of melody.

4 "Listen to Me, My people;
And give ear to Me, O My nation:
For law will proceed from Me,
And I will make My justice rest
As a light of the peoples.
5 My righteousness *is* near,
My salvation has gone forth,
And My arms will judge the peoples;
The coastlands will wait upon Me,
And on My arm they will trust.
6 Lift up your eyes to the heavens,
And look on the earth beneath.
For the heavens will vanish away
like smoke,
The earth will grow old like a garment,
And those who dwell in it will die in
like manner;
But My salvation will be forever,
And My righteousness will not
be abolished.

51:6 heavens will vanish...earth will grow old. This begins to take place in the time of tribulation (Rev. 6:12–14; 8:12,13; 16:8–10,21), setting the stage, along with the earthly judgments on land, sea, and fresh water (Rev. 6:14; 8:6–11; 16:3–5), for a renewed earth during the Millennium. The actual "uncreation" or destruction of the present universe, of which Peter wrote (2 Pet. 3:10–13), occurs at the end of Christ's millennial reign on the earth, when a new heaven and a new earth will replace the present creation (2 Pet. 3:10; Rev. 21:1).

7 "Listen to Me, you who know
righteousness,
You people in whose heart *is* My law:
Do not fear the reproach of men,
Nor be afraid of their insults.
8 For the moth will eat them up like
a garment,
And the worm will eat them like wool;
But My righteousness will be forever,
And My salvation from generation to
generation."

9 Awake, awake, put on strength,
O arm of the LORD!
Awake as in the ancient days,
In the generations of old.
Are You not *the arm* that cut Rahab
apart,
And wounded the serpent?
10 *Are* You not *the One* who dried up
the sea,
The waters of the great deep;
That made the depths of the sea a road
For the redeemed to cross over?
11 So the ransomed of the LORD shall
return,
And come to Zion with singing,
With everlasting joy on their heads.
They shall obtain joy and gladness;
Sorrow and sighing shall flee away.

12 "I, *even* I, *am* He who comforts you.
Who *are* you that you should be afraid
Of a man *who* will die,
And of the son of a man *who* will be
made like grass?
13 And you forget the LORD your Maker,
Who stretched out the heavens
And laid the foundations of the earth;
You have feared continually every day
Because of the fury of the oppressor,
When *he has* prepared to destroy.
And where *is* the fury of the oppressor?
14 The captive exile hastens, that he may
be loosed,
That he should not die in the pit,
And that his bread should not fail.
15 But I *am* the LORD your God,
Who divided the sea whose waves
roared—
The LORD of hosts *is* His name.
16 And I have put My words in your mouth;
I have covered you with the shadow
of My hand,
That I may plant the heavens,
Lay the foundations of the earth,
And say to Zion, 'You *are* My people.' "

17 Awake, awake!
Stand up, O Jerusalem,
You who have drunk at the hand
of the LORD
The cup of His fury;
You have drunk the dregs of the cup
of trembling,
And drained *it* out.
18 *There is* no one to guide her
Among all the sons she has brought
forth;
Nor *is there any* who takes her by the
hand

Among all the sons she has brought up.
19 These two *things* have come to you;
Who will be sorry for you?—
Desolation and destruction, famine and
sword—
By whom will I comfort you?
20 Your sons have fainted,
They lie at the head of all the streets,
Like an antelope in a net;
They are full of the fury of the LORD,
The rebuke of your God.

21 Therefore please hear this, you
afflicted,
And drunk but not with wine.
22 Thus says your Lord,
The LORD and your God,
Who pleads the cause of His people:
"See, I have taken out of your hand
The cup of trembling,
The dregs of the cup of My fury;
You shall no longer drink it.
23 But I will put it into the hand of those
who afflict you,
Who have said to you,
'Lie down, that we may walk over you.'
And you have laid your body like the
ground,
And as the street, for those who walk
over."

52 Awake, awake!
Put on your strength, O Zion;
Put on your beautiful garments,
O Jerusalem, the holy city!
For the uncircumcised and the unclean
Shall no longer come to you.
2 Shake yourself from the dust, arise;
Sit down, O Jerusalem!
Loose yourself from the bonds
of your neck,
O captive daughter of Zion!

3 For thus says the LORD:

"You have sold yourselves for nothing,
And you shall be redeemed without
money."

4 For thus says the Lord GOD:

"My people went down at first
Into Egypt to dwell there;
Then the Assyrian oppressed them
without cause.
5 Now therefore, what have I here,"
says the LORD,
"That My people are taken away for
nothing?
Those who rule over them
Make them wail," says the LORD,
"And My name *is* blasphemed
continually every day.
6 Therefore My people shall know My
name;
Therefore *they shall know* in that day
That I *am* He who speaks:
'Behold, *it is* I.' "

7 How beautiful upon the mountains
Are the feet of him who brings
good news,
Who proclaims peace,
Who brings glad tidings of good *things*,
Who proclaims salvation,
Who says to Zion,
"Your God reigns!"
8 Your watchmen shall lift up *their* voices,
With their voices they shall sing
together;
For they shall see eye to eye
When the LORD brings back Zion.
9 Break forth into joy, sing together,
You waste places of Jerusalem!
For the LORD has comforted His
people,
He has redeemed Jerusalem.
10 The LORD has made bare His holy arm
In the eyes of all the nations;
And all the ends of the earth shall see
The salvation of our God.

11 Depart! Depart! Go out from there,
Touch no unclean *thing*;
Go out from the midst of her,
Be clean,
You who bear the vessels of the LORD.
12 For you shall not go out with haste,
Nor go by flight;
For the LORD will go before you,
And the God of Israel *will be* your rear
guard.
13 Behold, My Servant shall deal
prudently;
He shall be exalted and extolled and
be very high.
14 Just as many were astonished at you,
So His visage was marred more than
any man,

52:14 His visage was marred. The Servant must undergo inhuman cruelty to the point that He no longer looks like a human being. His appearance is so awful that people look at Him in astonishment (53:2,3; Ps. 22:6; Matt. 26:67; 27:30; John 19:3).

And His form more than the sons of
men;
15 So shall He sprinkle many nations.
Kings shall shut their mouths at Him;
For what had not been told them they
shall see,
And what they had not heard they shall
consider.

52:15 sprinkle many nations. In His disfigured state, the Servant will perform a priestly work of cleansing not just Israel but many outside the nation (Ex. 29:21; Lev. 4:6; 8:11; 14:7; Num. 8:7; 19:18,19; Heb. 9:13). **shut their mouths.** At His exaltation, human leaders in the highest places will be speechless and in awe before the once-despised Servant (Ps. 2). When He takes His throne, they will see the unfolding of power and glory such as they have never heard. Paul applied the principle in this verse to his apostolic mission of preaching the gospel of Christ where Christ was yet unknown (Rom. 15:21).

Psalm 112:5–10

5 A good man deals graciously and lends;
He will guide his affairs with discretion.
6 Surely he will never be shaken;
The righteous will be in everlasting
remembrance.
7 He will not be afraid of evil tidings;
His heart is steadfast, trusting in the
LORD.
8 His heart *is* established;
He will not be afraid,
Until he sees *his desire* upon his
enemies.

9 He has dispersed abroad,
He has given to the poor;
His righteousness endures forever;
His horn will be exalted with honor.
10 The wicked will see *it* and be grieved;
He will gnash his teeth and melt away;
The desire of the wicked shall perish.

Proverbs 26:16

16 The lazy *man is* wiser in his own eyes
Than seven men who can answer
sensibly.

Ephesians 2:1–22

2 And you *He made alive,* who were dead in
trespasses and sins, [2]in which you once
walked according to the course of this world,
according to the prince of the power of the air,
the spirit who now works in the sons of
disobedience, [3]among whom also we all once
conducted ourselves in the lusts of our flesh,
fulfilling the desires of the flesh and of the
mind, and were by nature children of wrath,
just as the others.

2:1 dead in trespasses and sins. A sobering reminder of the total sinfulness and lostness from which believers have been redeemed. "In" indicates the realm or sphere in which unregenerate sinners exist. They are not dead because of sinful acts that have been committed but because of their sinful nature (Matt. 12:35; 15:18,19).

[4]But God, who is rich in mercy, because of
His great love with which He loved us, [5]even
when we were dead in trespasses, made us
alive together with Christ (by grace you have
been saved), [6]and raised *us* up together, and
made *us* sit together in the heavenly *places* in
Christ Jesus, [7]that in the ages to come He
might show the exceeding riches of His grace
in *His* kindness toward us in Christ Jesus. [8]For
by grace you have been saved through faith,
and that not of yourselves; *it is* the gift of God,
[9]not of works, lest anyone should boast. [10]For
we are His workmanship, created in Christ Jesus for good works, which God prepared
beforehand that we should walk in them.
[11]Therefore remember that you, once Gentiles
in the flesh—who are called Uncircumcision
by what is called the Circumcision made in the
flesh by hands— [12]that at that time you were
without Christ, being aliens from the commonwealth of Israel and strangers from the
covenants of promise, having no hope and
without God in the world. [13]But now in Christ
Jesus you who once were far off have been
brought near by the blood of Christ.
[14]For He Himself is our peace, who has made
both one, and has broken down the middle wall
of separation, [15]having abolished in His flesh the
enmity, *that is,* the law of commandments *contained* in ordinances, so as to create in Himself
one new man *from* the two, *thus* making peace,
[16]and that He might reconcile them both to God
in one body through the cross, thereby putting to
death the enmity. [17]And He came and preached
peace to you who were afar off and to those who
were near. [18]For through Him we both have
access by one Spirit to the Father.

[19]Now, therefore, you are no longer strangers and foreigners, but fellow citizens with the saints and members of the household of God, [20]having been built on the foundation of the apostles and prophets, Jesus Christ Himself being the chief corner*stone,* [21]in whom the whole building, being fitted together, grows into a holy temple in the Lord, [22]in whom you also are being built together for a dwelling place of God in the Spirit.

2:21 a holy temple in the Lord. Every new believer is a new stone in Christ's temple, the church, Christ's body of believers (1 Pet. 2:5). Christ's building of His church will not be complete until every person who will believe in Him has done so (2 Pet. 3:9).

DAY 30: How were Gentiles brought into the family of God?

Historically, the Gentiles (the "uncircumcision") experienced two types of alienation. The first was social, resulting from the animosity that had existed between Jews and Gentiles for thousands of years. Jews considered Gentiles to be outcasts, objects of derision and reproach. The second and more significant type of alienation was spiritual, because Gentiles as a people were cut off from God in 5 different ways (Eph. 2:11,12): 1) they were "without Christ," the Messiah, having no Savior and Deliverer and without divine purpose or destiny. 2) They were "aliens from the commonwealth of Israel." God's chosen people, the Jews, were a nation whose supreme King and Lord was God Himself, and from whose unique blessing and protection they benefitted. 3) Gentiles were "strangers from the covenants of promise," not able to partake of God's divine covenants in which He promised to give His people a land, a priesthood, a people, a nation, a kingdom, and a King—and to those who believe in Him, eternal life and heaven. 4) They had "no hope" because they had been given no divine promise. 5) They were "without God in the world." While Gentiles had many gods, they did not recognize the true God because they did not want Him.

"But now in Christ Jesus you who once were far off have been brought near by the blood of Christ" (v. 13). "Far off" was a common term in rabbinical writings used to describe Gentiles, those who were apart from the true God (Is. 57:19; Acts 2:39). Every person who trusts in Christ alone for salvation, Jew or Gentile, is brought into spiritual union and intimacy with God. This is the reconciliation of 2 Corinthians 5:18–21. The atoning work accomplished by Christ's death on the cross washes away the penalty of sin and ultimately even its presence. "He Himself" (v. 14). Through His death, Christ abolished Old Testament ceremonial laws, feasts, and sacrifices which uniquely separated Jews from Gentiles. God's moral law (as summarized in the Ten Commandments and written on the hearts of all men, Rom. 2:15) was not abolished but subsumed in the New Covenant, however, because it reflects His own holy nature (Matt. 5:17–19.)

OCTOBER 1

Isaiah 53:1–54:17

53 Who has believed our report?
And to whom has the arm of
the LORD been revealed?
2 For He shall grow up before Him as a
tender plant,
And as a root out of dry ground.
He has no form or comeliness;
And when we see Him,
There is no beauty that we should
desire Him.
3 He is despised and rejected by men,
A Man of sorrows and acquainted with
grief.
And we hid, as it were, *our* faces from
Him;
He was despised, and we did not
esteem Him.

4 Surely He has borne our griefs
And carried our sorrows;
Yet we esteemed Him stricken,
Smitten by God, and afflicted.
5 But He *was* wounded for our
transgressions,
He was bruised for our iniquities;
The chastisement for our peace *was*
upon Him,
And by His stripes we are healed.
6 All we like sheep have gone astray;
We have turned, every one, to his own
way;
And the LORD has laid on Him the
iniquity of us all.

53:6 All we…every one,…us all. Every person has sinned (Rom. 3:9,23), but the Servant has sufficiently shouldered the consequences of sin and the righteous wrath deserved by sinners (1 Tim. 2:5,6; 4:10; 1 John 2:2). The manner in which God laid our iniquity on Him was that God treated Him as if He had committed every sin ever committed by every person who would ever believe, though He was perfectly innocent of any sin. God did so to Him, so that wrath being spent and justice satisfied, God could then give to the account of sinners who believe, the righteousness of Christ, treating them as if they had done only the righteous acts of Christ. In both cases, this is substitution.

7 He was oppressed and He was afflicted,
Yet He opened not His mouth;
He was led as a lamb to the slaughter,
And as a sheep before its shearers is
silent,
So He opened not His mouth.
8 He was taken from prison and from
judgment,
And who will declare His generation?
For He was cut off from the land of the
living;
For the transgressions of My people
He was stricken.
9 And they made His grave with the
wicked—
But with the rich at His death,
Because He had done no violence,
Nor *was any* deceit in His mouth.

10 Yet it pleased the LORD to bruise Him;
He has put *Him* to grief.
When You make His soul an offering
for sin,
He shall see *His* seed, He shall prolong
His days,
And the pleasure of the LORD shall
prosper in His hand.

53:10 it pleased the LORD. Though the Servant did not deserve to die, it was the Lord's will for Him to do so (Matt. 26:39; Luke 22:42; John 12:27; Acts 2:23). **an offering for sin.** Fulfilled by the Servant as the Lamb of God (v. 7; John 1:29). Christ is the Christian's Passover (1 Cor. 5:7). This conclusively eliminates the error that Christ's atonement provides present-day healing for those who pray in faith. His death was an atonement for sin, not sickness. **see *His* seed,…prolong *His* days.** To see His seed, the Servant must rise from the dead. He will do this and live to reign forever.

11 He shall see the labor of His soul,
and be satisfied.
By His knowledge My righteous
Servant shall justify many,
For He shall bear their iniquities.
12 Therefore I will divide Him a portion
with the great,
And He shall divide the spoil with the
strong,
Because He poured out His soul unto
death,
And He was numbered with the
transgressors,
And He bore the sin of many,

And made intercession for the
transgressors.

54 "Sing, O barren,
You *who* have not borne!
Break forth into singing, and cry
aloud,
You *who* have not labored with child!
For more *are* the children of the
desolate
Than the children of the married
woman," says the LORD.
2 "Enlarge the place of your tent,
And let them stretch out the curtains
of your dwellings;
Do not spare;
Lengthen your cords,
And strengthen your stakes.
3 For you shall expand to the right and
to the left,
And your descendants will inherit the
nations,
And make the desolate cities inhabited.
4 "Do not fear, for you will not be ashamed;
Neither be disgraced, for you will not
be put to shame;
For you will forget the shame of your
youth,
And will not remember the reproach of
your widowhood anymore.
5 For your Maker *is* your husband,
The LORD of hosts *is* His name;
And your Redeemer *is* the Holy One of
Israel;
He is called the God of the whole
earth.
6 For the LORD has called you
Like a woman forsaken and grieved in
spirit,
Like a youthful wife when you were
refused,"
Says your God.
7 "For a mere moment I have forsaken
you,
But with great mercies I will gather
you.
8 With a little wrath I hid My face from
you for a moment;
But with everlasting kindness I will
have mercy on you,"
Says the LORD, your Redeemer.
9 "For this *is* like the waters of Noah to
Me;
For as I have sworn
That the waters of Noah would no
longer cover the earth,
So have I sworn
That I would not be angry with you,
nor rebuke you.
10 For the mountains shall depart
And the hills be removed,
But My kindness shall not depart from
you,
Nor shall My covenant of peace be
removed,"
Says the LORD, who has mercy on you.

11 "O you afflicted one,
Tossed with tempest, *and* not comforted,
Behold, I will lay your stones with
colorful gems,
And lay your foundations with
sapphires.
12 I will make your pinnacles of rubies,
Your gates of crystal,
And all your walls of precious stones.
13 All your children *shall be* taught by the
LORD,
And great *shall be* the peace of your
children.
14 In righteousness you shall be
established;
You shall be far from oppression, for
you shall not fear;
And from terror, for it shall not come
near you.
15 Indeed they shall surely assemble, *but*
not because of Me.
Whoever assembles against you shall
fall for your sake.

16 "Behold, I have created the blacksmith
Who blows the coals in the fire,
Who brings forth an instrument for his
work;
And I have created the spoiler to
destroy.
17 No weapon formed against you shall
prosper,
And every tongue *which* rises against
you in judgment
You shall condemn.
This *is* the heritage of the servants of
the LORD,
And their righteousness *is* from Me,"
Says the LORD.

Psalm 113:1–4

Praise the LORD!

Praise, O servants of the LORD,
Praise the name of the LORD!
2 Blessed be the name of the LORD
From this time forth and forevermore!
3 From the rising of the sun to its going
down

The LORD's name *is* to be praised.
4 The LORD *is* high above all nations,
His glory above the heavens.

Proverbs 26:17–19

17 He who passes by *and* meddles in a quarrel not his own
Is like one who takes a dog by the ears.
18 Like a madman who throws firebrands, arrows, and death,
19 *Is* the man *who* deceives his neighbor,
And says, "I was only joking!"

Ephesians 3:1–21

3 For this reason I, Paul, the prisoner of
Christ Jesus for you Gentiles— [2]if indeed
you have heard of the dispensation of the
grace of God which was given to me for you,
[3]how that by revelation He made known to me
the mystery (as I have briefly written already,
[4]by which, when you read, you may understand my knowledge in the mystery of
Christ), [5]which in other ages was not made
known to the sons of men, as it has now been
revealed by the Spirit to His holy apostles and
prophets: [6]that the Gentiles should be fellow
heirs, of the same body, and partakers of His
promise in Christ through the gospel, [7]of
which I became a minister according to the
gift of the grace of God given to me by the
effective working of His power.
[8]To me, who am less than the least of all the
saints, this grace was given, that I should
preach among the Gentiles the unsearchable
riches of Christ, [9]and to make all see what *is*
the fellowship of the mystery, which from the
beginning of the ages has been hidden in God
who created all things through Jesus Christ;
[10]to the intent that now the manifold wisdom
of God might be made known by the church
to the principalities and powers in the heavenly *places,* [11]according to the eternal purpose
which He accomplished in Christ Jesus our
Lord, [12]in whom we have boldness and access
with confidence through faith in Him. [13]Therefore I ask that you do not lose heart at
my tribulations for you, which is your glory.
[14]For this reason I bow my knees to the Father of our Lord Jesus Christ, [15]from whom the
whole family in heaven and earth is named,
[16]that He would grant you, according to the
riches of His glory, to be strengthened with
might through His Spirit in the inner man,
[17]that Christ may dwell in your hearts through
faith; that you, being rooted and grounded in
love, [18]may be able to comprehend with all the
saints what *is* the width and length and depth
and height— [19]to know the love of Christ
which passes knowledge; that you may be
filled with all the fullness of God.
[20]Now to Him who is able to do exceedingly
abundantly above all that we ask or think, according to the power that works in us, [21]to Him
be glory in the church by Christ Jesus to all
generations, forever and ever. Amen.

3:19 to know the love of Christ. Not the love believers have for Christ, but the love of and from Christ that He places in their hearts before they can truly and fully love Him or anyone else (Rom. 5:5). **which passes knowledge.** Knowledge of Christ's love is far beyond the capability of human reason and experience. It is only known by those who are God's children (Phil. 4:7). **filled with all the fullness of God.** To be so strong spiritually, so compelled by divine love, that one is totally dominated by the Lord with nothing left of self. Human comprehension of the fullness of God is impossible, because even the most spiritual and wise believer cannot completely grasp the full extent of God's attributes and characteristics—His power, majesty, wisdom, love, mercy, patience, kindness, and everything He is and does. But believers can experience the greatness of God in their lives as a result of total devotion to Him. Note the fullness of God, here; the fullness of Christ in 4:13; and the fullness of the Spirit in 5:18.

DAY 1: How explicit does Isaiah 53 get regarding the Messiah?

Isaiah begins in v. 1 by saying, "Who has believed our report?" The question implied that, in spite of these and other prophecies, only a few would recognize the Servant when He appeared. This anticipation found literal fulfillment at Christ's First Advent. Israel did not welcome Him at His First Advent (John 1:9–11; 12:38). Paul applied the same prophecy to the world at large (Rom. 10:16). At His First Coming, the nation did not recognize the mighty, incarnate power of God in the Person of Jesus, their Deliverer.

Yet Messiah Jesus was observed carefully by God ("before Him", v. 2), who ordered every minute circumstance of His life. "Dry ground…no beauty that we should desire Him." The Servant will arise in lowly conditions and wear none of the usual emblems of royalty, making His true identity visible only to the discerning eye of faith.

"Despised…rejected…despised" (v. 3). The prophet foresees the hatred and rejection by mankind toward the Messiah/Servant, who suffered not only external abuse, but also internal grief over those He came to save. "We hid…we did not esteem." By using the first person, the prophet spoke for his unbelieving nation's aversion to a crucified Messiah and their lack of respect for the incarnate Son of God.

"Surely He has borne our griefs and carried our sorrows" (v. 4). Isaiah was saying that the Messiah would bear the consequences of the sins of men, namely the griefs and sorrows of life, though incredibly the Jews who watched Him die thought He was being punished by God for His own sins. Matthew found an analogical fulfillment of these words in Jesus' healing ministry (Matt. 8:16,17), because sickness results from sin for which the Servant paid with His life. In eternity, all sickness will be removed, so ultimately it is included in the benefits of the atonement.

"He was wounded for our transgressions…bruised for our iniquities" (v. 5). The Servant suffered not for His own sin, since He was sinless (Heb. 4:15; 7:26), but as the substitute for sinners. The emphasis here is on Christ being the substitute recipient of God's wrath on sinners (2 Cor. 5:21; Gal. 1:3,4; Heb. 10:9,10). "Chastisement for our peace." He suffered the chastisement of God in order to procure our peace with God. "By His stripes we are healed." The stripe that caused His death has brought salvation to those for whose sins He died. Peter confirms this in 1 Peter 2:24.

OCTOBER 2

Isaiah 55:1–56:12

55 "Ho! Everyone who thirsts,
Come to the waters;
And you who have no money,
Come, buy and eat.
Yes, come, buy wine and milk
Without money and without price.

55:1 Everyone. The Servant's redemptive work and glorious kingdom is for the benefit of all who are willing to come (53:6). The prophet invites his readers to participate in the benefits obtained by the suffering of the Servant in chapter 53 and described in chapter 54. **no money,…without money and without price.** Benefits in the Servant's kingdom will be free because of His redemptive work (53:6,8,11; Eph. 2:8,9). **wine and milk.** Symbols for abundance, satisfaction, and prosperity (Song 5:1; Joel 3:18).

2 Why do you spend money for *what is* not bread,
And your wages for *what* does not satisfy?
Listen carefully to Me, and eat *what is* good,
And let your soul delight itself in abundance.
3 Incline your ear, and come to Me.
Hear, and your soul shall live;
And I will make an everlasting covenant with you—
The sure mercies of David.
4 Indeed I have given him *as* a witness to the people,
A leader and commander for the people.
5 Surely you shall call a nation you do not know,
And nations *who* do not know you shall run to you,
Because of the LORD your God,
And the Holy One of Israel;
For He has glorified you."
6 Seek the LORD while He may be found,
Call upon Him while He is near.
7 Let the wicked forsake his way,
And the unrighteous man his thoughts;
Let him return to the LORD,
And He will have mercy on him;
And to our God,
For He will abundantly pardon.

8 "For My thoughts *are* not your thoughts,
Nor *are* your ways My ways," says the LORD.
9 "For *as* the heavens are higher than the earth,
So are My ways higher than your ways,
And My thoughts than your thoughts.
10 "For as the rain comes down, and the snow from heaven,
And do not return there,
But water the earth,

55:6,7 Here is one of the clearest Old Testament invitations to salvation now and kingdom blessing later. It gives an excellent example of how people were saved during the Old Testament period. Salvation grace and mercy were available to the soul that was willing to 1) seek the Lord (Deut. 4:29; 2 Chr. 15:4) and 2) call on Him while He is still available (65:1; Ps. 32:6; Prov. 8:17; Matt. 25:1–13). Such true seeking in faith is accompanied by repentance, which is described as forsaking ways and thoughts and turning from sinful living to the Lord. A sinner must come, believing in God, recognizing his sin, and desiring forgiveness and deliverance from that sin. At the same time he must recognize his own inability to be righteous or to satisfy God and cast himself on God's mercy. It is then that he receives a complete pardon. His sin has been covered by the substitution of the Messiah in his place (chap. 53).

And make it bring forth and bud,
That it may give seed to the sower
And bread to the eater,
11 So shall My word be that goes forth
from My mouth;
It shall not return to Me void,
But it shall accomplish what I please,
And it shall prosper *in the thing* for
which I sent it.

12 "For you shall go out with joy,
And be led out with peace;
The mountains and the hills
Shall break forth into singing before you,
And all the trees of the field shall clap
their hands.
13 Instead of the thorn shall come up the
cypress tree,
And instead of the brier shall come up
the myrtle tree;
And it shall be to the LORD for a name,
For an everlasting sign *that* shall not
be cut off."

56 Thus says the LORD:
"Keep justice, and do righteousness,
For My salvation *is* about to come,
And My righteousness to be revealed.
2 Blessed *is* the man *who* does this,
And the son of man *who* lays hold on it;
Who keeps from defiling the Sabbath,
And keeps his hand from doing any
evil."

3 Do not let the son of the foreigner
Who has joined himself to the LORD
Speak, saying,
"The LORD has utterly separated me
from His people";
Nor let the eunuch say,
"Here I am, a dry tree."
4 For thus says the LORD:
"To the eunuchs who keep My
Sabbaths,
And choose what pleases Me,
And hold fast My covenant,
5 Even to them I will give in My house
And within My walls a place and a name
Better than that of sons and daughters;
I will give them an everlasting name
That shall not be cut off.

6 "Also the sons of the foreigner
Who join themselves to the LORD, to
serve Him,
And to love the name of the LORD, to be
His servants—
Everyone who keeps from defiling the
Sabbath,
And holds fast My covenant—
7 Even them I will bring to My holy
mountain,
And make them joyful in My house of
prayer.
Their burnt offerings and their
sacrifices
Will be accepted on My altar;
For My house shall be called a house
of prayer for all nations."
8 The Lord GOD, who gathers the
outcasts of Israel, says,
"Yet I will gather to him
Others besides those who are gathered
to him."

9 All you beasts of the field, come to
devour,
All you beasts in the forest.
10 His watchmen *are* blind,
They are all ignorant;
They *are* all dumb dogs,
They cannot bark;
Sleeping, lying down, loving to
slumber.
11 Yes, *they are* greedy dogs
Which never have enough.
And they *are* shepherds
Who cannot understand;
They all look to their own way,
Every one for his own gain,
From his *own* territory.
12 "Come," *one says,* "I will bring wine,

And we will fill ourselves with
intoxicating drink;
Tomorrow will be as today,
And much more abundant."

Psalm 113:5–9

5 Who *is* like the LORD our God,
Who dwells on high,
6 Who humbles Himself to behold
The things that are in the heavens and
in the earth?

7 He raises the poor out of the dust,
And lifts the needy out of the ash heap,
8 That He may seat *him* with princes—
With the princes of His people.
9 He grants the barren woman a home,
Like a joyful mother of children.

Praise the LORD!

113:9 the barren woman. Sarah (Gen. 21:2), Rebekah (Gen. 25:21), and Rachel (Gen. 30:23) would be the most significant since the outcome of the Abrahamic Covenant depended on these childless women being blessed by God to be mothers.

Proverbs 26:20–21

20 Where *there is* no wood, the fire
goes out;
And where *there is* no talebearer,
strife ceases.
21 *As* charcoal *is* to burning coals, and
wood to fire,
So *is* a contentious man to
kindle strife.

Ephesians 4:1–32

4 I, therefore, the prisoner of the Lord, beseech you to walk worthy of the calling with
which you were called, 2with all lowliness and
gentleness, with longsuffering, bearing with
one another in love, 3endeavoring to keep the
unity of the Spirit in the bond of peace. 4*There*
is one body and one Spirit, just as you were
called in one hope of your calling; 5one Lord,
one faith, one baptism; 6one God and Father of
all, who *is* above all, and through all, and in
you all.
7But to each one of us grace was given
according to the measure of Christ's gift.
8Therefore He says:

"When He ascended on high,
He led captivity captive,
And gave gifts to men."

9(Now this, *"He ascended"*—what does it mean
but that He also first descended into the lower
parts of the earth? 10He who descended is also
the One who ascended far above all the heavens, that He might fill all things.)
11And He Himself gave some *to be* apostles,
some prophets, some evangelists, and some
pastors and teachers, 12for the equipping of the
saints for the work of ministry, for the edifying
of the body of Christ, 13till we all come to the
unity of the faith and of the knowledge of the
Son of God, to a perfect man, to the measure
of the stature of the fullness of Christ; 14that we
should no longer be children, tossed to and fro
and carried about with every wind of doctrine,
by the trickery of men, in the cunning craftiness of deceitful plotting, 15but, speaking the

4:12 equipping. This refers to restoring something to its original condition, or its being made fit or complete. In this context, it refers to leading Christians from sin to obedience. Scripture is the key to this process (2 Tim. 3:16,17; John 15:3). **saints.** All who believe in Jesus Christ. **the work of ministry.** The spiritual service required of every Christian, not just of church leaders (1 Cor. 15:58). **the edifying of the body of Christ.** The spiritual edification, nurturing, and development of the church (Acts 20:32).

4:14 carried about with every wind of doctrine. Spiritually immature believers who are not grounded in the knowledge of Christ through God's Word are inclined to uncritically accept every sort of beguiling doctrinal error and fallacious interpretation of Scripture promulgated by deceitful, false teachers in the church. They must learn discernment (1 Thess. 5:21,22). The New Testament is replete with warnings of such danger (Acts 20:30,31; Rom. 16:17,18; Gal. 1:6,7; 1 Tim. 4:1–7; 2 Tim. 2:15–18; 2 Pet. 2:1–3).

truth in love, may grow up in all things into
Him who is the head—Christ— 16from whom
the whole body, joined and knit together by
what every joint supplies, according to the
effective working by which every part does its
share, causes growth of the body for the edifying of itself in love.
17This I say, therefore, and testify in the
Lord, that you should no longer walk as the

rest of the Gentiles walk, in the futility of their
mind, [18]having their understanding darkened,
being alienated from the life of God, because
of the ignorance that is in them, because of
the blindness of their heart; [19]who, being past
feeling, have given themselves over to lewdness, to work all uncleanness with greediness.
[20]But you have not so learned Christ, [21]if
indeed you have heard Him and have been
taught by Him, as the truth is in Jesus: [22]that
you put off, concerning your former conduct,
the old man which grows corrupt according to
the deceitful lusts, [23]and be renewed in the
spirit of your mind, [24]and that you put on the
new man which was created according to God,
in true righteousness and holiness.
[25]Therefore, putting away lying, *"Let each
one of you speak truth with his neighbor,"* for
we are members of one another. [26]*"Be angry,
and do not sin"*: do not let the sun go down on
your wrath, [27]nor give place to the devil. [28]Let
him who stole steal no longer, but rather let
him labor, working with *his* hands what is
good, that he may have something to give him
who has need. [29]Let no corrupt word proceed
out of your mouth, but what is good for necessary edification, that it may impart grace to
the hearers. [30]And do not grieve the Holy
Spirit of God, by whom you were sealed for
the day of redemption. [31]Let all bitterness,
wrath, anger, clamor, and evil speaking be put
away from you, with all malice. [32]And be kind to
one another, tenderhearted, forgiving one
another, even as God in Christ forgave you.

DAY 2: Define the spiritually gifted men Christ calls to serve His church in Ephesians 4:11.

"Apostles." A term used particularly of the 12 disciples who had seen the risen Christ (Acts 1:22), including Matthias, who replaced Judas. Later, Paul was uniquely set apart as the apostle to the Gentiles (Gal. 1:15–17) and was numbered with the other apostles. Those apostles were chosen directly by Christ, so as to be called "apostles of Christ" (Gal. 1:1; 1 Pet. 1:1). They were given 3 basic responsibilities: 1) to lay the foundation of the church (2:20); 2) to receive, declare, and write God's Word (3:5; Acts 11:28; 21:10,11); and 3) to give confirmation of that Word through signs, wonders, and miracles (2 Cor. 12:12; Acts 8:6,7). The term "apostle" is used in more general ways of other men in the early church, such as Barnabas (Acts 14:4), Silas, Timothy, and others (Rom. 16:7; Phil. 2:25). They are called "apostles of the churches" (2 Cor. 8:23) rather than "apostles of Jesus Christ" like the 13. They were not self-perpetuating nor was any apostle who died replaced.

"Prophets." Not ordinary believers who had the gift of prophecy but specially commissioned men in the early church. The office of prophet seems to have been exclusively for work within a local congregation. They were not "sent ones" as were the apostles (Acts 13:1), but, as with the apostles, their office ceased with the completion of the New Testament. They sometimes spoke practical direct revelation for the church from God (Acts 11:21–28) or expounded revelation already given (implied in Acts 13:1). Their messages were to be judged by other prophets for validity (1 Cor. 14:32) and had to conform to the teaching of the apostles (v. 37). Those two offices were replaced by the evangelists and teaching pastors.

"Evangelists." Men who proclaim the good news of salvation in Jesus Christ to unbelievers. The related verb translated "to preach the gospel" is used 54 times and the related noun translated "gospel" is used 76 times in the New Testament.

"Pastors and teachers." This phrase is best understood in context as a single office of leadership in the church. The Greek word translated "and" can mean "in particular" (1 Tim. 5:17). The normal meaning of pastor is "shepherd," so the two functions together define the teaching shepherd. He is identified as one who is under the "great Pastor" Jesus (Heb. 13:20,21; 1 Pet. 2:25). One who holds this office is also called an "elder" (Titus 1:5–9) and "bishop" (1 Tim. 3:1–7).

OCTOBER 3

Isaiah 57:1–58:14

57 The righteous perishes,
And no man takes *it* to heart;
Merciful men *are* taken away,
While no one considers
That the righteous is taken away from
evil.

2 He shall enter into peace;
They shall rest in their beds,
Each one walking *in* his uprightness.

3 "But come here,
You sons of the sorceress,
You offspring of the adulterer and the
harlot!
4 Whom do you ridicule?
Against whom do you make a wide
mouth

And stick out the tongue?
Are you not children of transgression,
Offspring of falsehood,
5 Inflaming yourselves with gods under
every green tree,
Slaying the children in the valleys,
Under the clefts of the rocks?
6 Among the smooth *stones* of the stream
Is your portion;
They, they, *are* your lot!
Even to them you have poured a drink
offering,
You have offered a grain offering.
Should I receive comfort in these?

7 "On a lofty and high mountain
You have set your bed;
Even there you went up
To offer sacrifice.
8 Also behind the doors and their posts
You have set up your remembrance;
For you have uncovered yourself *to*
those other than Me,
And have gone up to them;
You have enlarged your bed
And made *a covenant* with them;
You have loved their bed,
Where you saw *their* nudity.
9 You went to the king with ointment,
And increased your perfumes;
You sent your messengers far off,
And *even* descended to Sheol.
10 You are wearied in the length of
your way;
Yet you did not say, 'There is no hope.'
You have found the life of your hand;
Therefore you were not grieved.

11 "And of whom have you been afraid,
or feared,
That you have lied
And not remembered Me,
Nor taken *it* to your heart?
Is it not because I have held My peace
from of old
That you do not fear Me?
12 I will declare your righteousness
And your works,
For they will not profit you.
13 When you cry out,
Let your collection *of idols* deliver you.
But the wind will carry them all away,
A breath will take *them.*
But he who puts his trust in Me shall
possess the land,
And shall inherit My holy mountain."

14 And one shall say,
"Heap it up! Heap it up!
Prepare the way,
Take the stumbling block out of the
way of My people."
15 For thus says the High and Lofty One
Who inhabits eternity, whose name *is*
Holy:
"I dwell in the high and holy *place,*
With him *who* has a contrite and
humble spirit,
To revive the spirit of the humble,
And to revive the heart of the contrite
ones.
16 For I will not contend forever,
Nor will I always be angry;
For the spirit would fail before Me,
And the souls *which* I have made.
17 For the iniquity of his covetousness
I was angry and struck him;
I hid and was angry,
And he went on backsliding in the way
of his heart.
18 I have seen his ways, and will heal him;
I will also lead him,
And restore comforts to him
And to his mourners.

19 "I create the fruit of the lips:
Peace, peace to *him who is* far off and
to *him who is* near,"
Says the LORD,
"And I will heal him."
20 But the wicked *are* like the troubled sea,
When it cannot rest,
Whose waters cast up mire and dirt.
21 "*There is* no peace,"
Says my God, "for the wicked."

58 "Cry aloud, spare not;
Lift up your voice like a trumpet;
Tell My people their transgression,
And the house of Jacob their sins.
2 Yet they seek Me daily,
And delight to know My ways,
As a nation that did righteousness,
And did not forsake the ordinance of
their God.
They ask of Me the ordinances of
justice;
They take delight in approaching God.
3 'Why have we fasted,' *they say,* 'and You
have not seen?
Why have we afflicted our souls, and
You take no notice?'

"In fact, in the day of your fast you find
pleasure,
And exploit all your laborers.
4 Indeed you fast for strife and debate,

And to strike with the fist of wickedness.
You will not fast as *you do* this day,
To make your voice heard on high.
5 Is it a fast that I have chosen,
A day for a man to afflict his soul?
Is it to bow down his head like a bulrush,
And to spread out sackcloth and ashes?
Would you call this a fast,
And an acceptable day to the LORD?

6 "*Is* this not the fast that I have chosen:
To loose the bonds of wickedness,
To undo the heavy burdens,
To let the oppressed go free,
And that you break every yoke?
7 *Is it* not to share your bread with the hungry,
And that you bring to your house the poor who are cast out;
When you see the naked, that you cover him,
And not hide yourself from your own flesh?

58:3–7 Why…? The people complained when God did not recognize their religious actions, but God responded that their fastings had been only halfhearted. Hypocritical fasting resulted in contention, quarreling, and pretense, excluding the possibility of genuine prayer to God. Fasting consisted of more than just an outward ritual and a mock repentance. It involved penitence over sin and consequent humility, disconnecting from sin and oppression of others, feeding the hungry, and acting humanely toward those in need.

8 Then your light shall break forth like the morning,
Your healing shall spring forth speedily,
And your righteousness shall go before you;
The glory of the LORD shall be your rear guard.
9 Then you shall call, and the LORD will answer;
You shall cry, and He will say, 'Here I *am*.'

"If you take away the yoke from your midst,
The pointing of the finger, and speaking wickedness,
10 *If* you extend your soul to the hungry
And satisfy the afflicted soul,
Then your light shall dawn in the darkness,
And your darkness shall *be* as the noonday.
11 The LORD will guide you continually,
And satisfy your soul in drought,
And strengthen your bones;
You shall be like a watered garden,
And like a spring of water, whose waters do not fail.
12 Those from among you
Shall build the old waste places;
You shall raise up the foundations of many generations;
And you shall be called the Repairer of the Breach,
The Restorer of Streets to Dwell In.

13 "If you turn away your foot from the Sabbath,
From doing your pleasure on My holy day,
And call the Sabbath a delight,
The holy *day* of the LORD honorable,
And shall honor Him, not doing your own ways,
Nor finding your own pleasure,
Nor speaking *your own* words,
14 Then you shall delight yourself in the LORD;
And I will cause you to ride on the high hills of the earth,
And feed you with the heritage of Jacob your father.
The mouth of the LORD has spoken."

58:14 delight yourself in the LORD. Repentant ones walking in fellowship with the Lord experience satisfaction of soul (Ps. 37:4). Their satisfaction will not come from material goods.

Psalm 114:1–8

When Israel went out of Egypt,
The house of Jacob from a people of strange language,
2 Judah became His sanctuary,
And Israel His dominion.

3 The sea saw *it* and fled;
Jordan turned back.
4 The mountains skipped like rams,
The little hills like lambs.
5 What ails you, O sea, that you fled?
O Jordan, *that* you turned back?

6 O mountains, *that* you skipped like
rams?
O little hills, like lambs?

7 Tremble, O earth, at the presence
of the Lord,
At the presence of the God of Jacob,
8 Who turned the rock *into* a pool of
water,
The flint into a fountain of waters.

Proverbs 26:22

22 The words of a talebearer *are* like tasty
trifles,
And they go down into the inmost body.

Ephesians 5:1–16

5 Therefore be imitators of God as dear children. 2And walk in love, as Christ also has
loved us and given Himself for us, an offering
and a sacrifice to God for a sweet-smelling
aroma.
3But fornication and all uncleanness or covetousness, let it not even be named among
you, as is fitting for saints; 4neither filthiness,
nor foolish talking, nor coarse jesting, which
are not fitting, but rather giving of thanks. 5For
this you know, that no fornicator, unclean person, nor covetous man, who is an idolater, has
any inheritance in the kingdom of Christ and
God. 6Let no one deceive you with empty
words, for because of these things the wrath
of God comes upon the sons of disobedience.
7Therefore do not be partakers with them.
8For you were once darkness, but now *you*
are light in the Lord. Walk as children of light
9(for the fruit of the Spirit *is* in all goodness,
righteousness, and truth), 10finding out what is
acceptable to the Lord. 11And have no fellowship with the unfruitful works of darkness, but
rather expose *them.* 12For it is shameful even to
speak of those things which are done by them
in secret. 13But all things that are exposed are
made manifest by the light, for whatever
makes manifest is light. 14Therefore He says:

"Awake, you who sleep,
Arise from the dead,
And Christ will give you light."

15See then that you walk circumspectly, not
as fools but as wise, 16redeeming the time, because the days are evil.

DAY 3: What should the standard be for a Christian's life?

"Be imitators of God," says Paul in Ephesians 5:1. The Christian has no greater calling or purpose than that of imitating his Lord. That is the very purpose of sanctification, growing in likeness to the Lord while serving Him on earth (Matt. 5:48). The Christian life is designed to reproduce godliness as modeled by the Savior and Lord, Jesus Christ, in whose image believers have been recreated through the new birth (Rom. 8:29; 2 Cor. 3:18; 1 Pet. 1:14–16). As God's dear children, believers are to become more and more like their heavenly Father (Matt. 5:48; 1 Pet. 1:15,16).

"And walk in love, as Christ also has loved us and given Himself for us" (v. 2). The Lord is the supreme example in His self-sacrificing love for lost sinners (4:32; Rom. 5:8–10). He took human sin upon Himself and gave up His very life that men might be redeemed from their sin. They are henceforth to be imitators of His great love in the newness and power of the Holy Spirit, who enables them to demonstrate divine love. "A sweet-smelling aroma." Christ's offering of Himself for fallen man pleased and glorified His heavenly Father, because it demonstrated in the most complete and perfect way God's sovereign, perfect, unconditional, and divine kind of love.

In absolute contrast to God's holiness and love, such sins as "fornication…covetousness" (v. 3), by which Satan seeks to drive God's children as far away as possible from His image and will, are so godless that the world should never have reason even to suspect their presence in Christians. The 3 inappropriate sins of the tongue (v. 4) include any speech that is obscene and degrading or foolish and dirty, as well as suggestive and immoral wit. All such are destructive of holy living and godly testimony and should be confessed, forsaken, and replaced by open expressions of thankfulness to God (Col. 3:8).

OCTOBER 4

Isaiah 59:1–60:22

59 Behold, the LORD's hand is
not shortened,
That it cannot save;
Nor His ear heavy,
That it cannot hear.
2 But your iniquities have separated you
from your God;
And your sins have hidden *His* face
from you,
So that He will not hear.
3 For your hands are defiled with blood,
And your fingers with iniquity;

Your lips have spoken lies,
Your tongue has muttered perversity.
4 No one calls for justice,
Nor does *any* plead for truth.
They trust in empty words and speak lies;
They conceive evil and bring forth iniquity.
5 They hatch vipers' eggs and weave the spider's web;
He who eats of their eggs dies,
And *from* that which is crushed a viper breaks out.
6 Their webs will not become garments,
Nor will they cover themselves with their works;
Their works *are* works of iniquity,
And the act of violence *is* in their hands.
7 Their feet run to evil,
And they make haste to shed innocent blood;
Their thoughts *are* thoughts of iniquity;
Wasting and destruction *are* in their paths.
8 The way of peace they have not known,
And *there is* no justice in their ways;
They have made themselves crooked paths;
Whoever takes that way shall not know peace.
9 Therefore justice is far from us,
Nor does righteousness overtake us;
We look for light, but there is darkness!
For brightness, *but* we walk in blackness!
10 We grope for the wall like the blind,
And we grope as if *we had* no eyes;
We stumble at noonday as at twilight;
We are as dead *men* in desolate places.
11 We all growl like bears,
And moan sadly like doves;
We look for justice, but *there is* none;
For salvation, *but* it is far from us.
12 For our transgressions are multiplied before You,
And our sins testify against us;
For our transgressions *are* with us,
And *as for* our iniquities, we know them:
13 In transgressing and lying against the LORD,
And departing from our God,
Speaking oppression and revolt,
Conceiving and uttering from the heart words of falsehood.
14 Justice is turned back,
And righteousness stands afar off;
For truth is fallen in the street,
And equity cannot enter.
15 So truth fails,
And he *who* departs from evil makes himself a prey.

Then the LORD saw *it,* and it displeased Him
That *there was* no justice.
16 He saw that *there was* no man,
And wondered that *there was* no intercessor;
Therefore His own arm brought salvation for Him;
And His own righteousness, it sustained Him.
17 For He put on righteousness as a breastplate,
And a helmet of salvation on His head;
He put on the garments of vengeance for clothing,
And was clad with zeal as a cloak.

59:15,16 the LORD saw...no intercessor. The Lord was aware of Israel's tragic condition and of the absence of anyone to intervene on His behalf. The Lord took it on Himself to change Israel's condition through the intervention of His Suffering Servant (53:12).

59:17 righteousness as a breastplate...helmet of salvation. Figuratively speaking, the Lord armed Himself for the deliverance of His people and for taking vengeance on enemies who would seek His destruction. Paul drew on this terminology in describing a believer's spiritual preparation for warding off the attacks of Satan (Eph. 6:14,17; 1 Thess. 5:8).

18 According to *their* deeds, accordingly He will repay,
Fury to His adversaries,
Recompense to His enemies;
The coastlands He will fully repay.
19 So shall they fear
The name of the LORD from the west,
And His glory from the rising of the sun;
When the enemy comes in like a flood,
The Spirit of the LORD will lift up a standard against him.

20 "The Redeemer will come to Zion,
And to those who turn from transgression in Jacob,"
Says the LORD.

21"As for Me," says the LORD, "this *is* My
covenant with them: My Spirit who *is* upon you,
and My words which I have put in your mouth,
shall not depart from your mouth, nor from the
mouth of your descendants, nor from the
mouth of your descendants' descendants," says
the LORD, "from this time and forevermore."

60 Arise, shine;
For your light has come!
And the glory of the LORD is risen
upon you.
2 For behold, the darkness shall cover
the earth,
And deep darkness the people;
But the LORD will arise over you,
And His glory will be seen upon you.
3 The Gentiles shall come to your light,
And kings to the brightness of your
rising.

4 "Lift up your eyes all around, and see:
They all gather together, they come to
you;
Your sons shall come from afar,
And your daughters shall be nursed at
your side.
5 Then you shall see and become radiant,
And your heart shall swell with joy;
Because the abundance of the sea shall
be turned to you,
The wealth of the Gentiles shall come
to you.
6 The multitude of camels shall cover
your *land,*
The dromedaries of Midian and Ephah;
All those from Sheba shall come;
They shall bring gold and incense,
And they shall proclaim the praises of
the LORD.
7 All the flocks of Kedar shall be
gathered together to you,
The rams of Nebaioth shall minister to
you;
They shall ascend with acceptance on
My altar,
And I will glorify the house of My
glory.

8 "Who *are* these *who* fly like a cloud,
And like doves to their roosts?
9 Surely the coastlands shall wait for Me;
And the ships of Tarshish *will come*
first,
To bring your sons from afar,
Their silver and their gold with them,
To the name of the LORD your God,
And to the Holy One of Israel,
Because He has glorified you.

10 "The sons of foreigners shall build up
your walls,
And their kings shall minister to you;
For in My wrath I struck you,
But in My favor I have had mercy
on you.
11 Therefore your gates shall be open
continually;
They shall not be shut day or night,
That *men* may bring to you the wealth
of the Gentiles,
And their kings in procession.
12 For the nation and kingdom which will
not serve you shall perish,
And *those* nations shall be utterly
ruined.

13 "The glory of Lebanon shall come to you,
The cypress, the pine, and the box tree
together,
To beautify the place of My sanctuary;
And I will make the place of My feet
glorious.
14 Also the sons of those who afflicted you
Shall come bowing to you,
And all those who despised you shall
fall prostrate at the soles of your
feet;
And they shall call you The City of the
LORD,
Zion of the Holy One of Israel.

15 "Whereas you have been forsaken and
hated,
So that no one went through *you,*
I will make you an eternal excellence,
A joy of many generations.
16 You shall drink the milk of the
Gentiles,
And milk the breast of kings;
You shall know that I, the LORD, *am*
your Savior
And your Redeemer, the Mighty One
of Jacob.

17 "Instead of bronze I will bring gold,
Instead of iron I will bring silver,
Instead of wood, bronze,
And instead of stones, iron.
I will also make your officers peace,
And your magistrates righteousness.
18 Violence shall no longer be heard in
your land,
Neither wasting nor destruction within
your borders;
But you shall call your walls Salvation,
And your gates Praise.

19 "The sun shall no longer be your light
by day,

Nor for brightness shall the moon give
light to you;
But the LORD will be to you an
everlasting light,
And your God your glory.

60:19 sun shall no longer...everlasting light. Isaiah, looking beyond the millennial kingdom, sees a view of the New Jerusalem following the Millennium (Rev. 21:23; 22:5). His prophetic perspective did not allow him to distinguish the eternal phase of the future kingdom from the temporal one, just as the Old Testament prophets could not distinguish between the First and Second Advent of Christ (1 Pet. 1:10,11).

20 Your sun shall no longer go down,
Nor shall your moon withdraw itself;
For the LORD will be your everlasting
light,
And the days of your mourning shall be
ended.
21 Also your people *shall* all *be* righteous;
They shall inherit the land forever,
The branch of My planting,
The work of My hands,
That I may be glorified.
22 A little one shall become a thousand,
And a small one a strong nation.
I, the LORD, will hasten it in its time."

Psalm 115:1–8

Not unto us, O LORD, not unto us,
But to Your name give glory,
Because of Your mercy,
Because of Your truth.
2 Why should the Gentiles say,
"So where *is* their God?"

3 But our God *is* in heaven;
He does whatever He pleases.
4 Their idols *are* silver and gold,
The work of men's hands.
5 They have mouths, but they do not
speak;
Eyes they have, but they do not see;
6 They have ears, but they do not hear;
Noses they have, but they do not smell;
7 They have hands, but they do not
handle;
Feet they have, but they do not walk;
Nor do they mutter through their
throat.
8 Those who make them are like them;
So is everyone who trusts in them.

Proverbs 26:23

23 Fervent lips with a wicked heart
Are like earthenware covered with
silver dross.

26:23 earthenware covered. A cheap veneer of silver over a common clay pot hiding its commonness and fragility is like the deception spoken by evil people. This thought is expanded in vv. 24–28.

Ephesians 5:17–33

17 Therefore do not be unwise, but understand what the will of the Lord *is.* 18 And do not
be drunk with wine, in which is dissipation;
but be filled with the Spirit, 19 speaking to one

5:18 but be filled with the Spirit. True communion with God is not induced by drunkenness but by the Holy Spirit. Paul is not speaking of the Holy Spirit's indwelling (Rom. 8:9) or the baptism by Christ with the Holy Spirit (1 Cor. 12:13), because every Christian is indwelt and baptized by the Spirit at the time of salvation. He is rather giving a command for believers to live continually under the influence of the Spirit by letting the Word control them, pursuing pure lives, confessing all known sin, dying to self, surrendering to God's will, and depending on His power in all things. Being filled with the Spirit is living in the conscious presence of the Lord Jesus Christ, letting His mind, through the Word, dominate everything that is thought and done. Being filled with the Spirit is the same as walking in the Spirit.

another in psalms and hymns and spiritual
songs, singing and making melody in your
heart to the Lord, 20 giving thanks always for all
things to God the Father in the name of our
Lord Jesus Christ, 21 submitting to one another
in the fear of God.

22 Wives, submit to your own husbands, as to
the Lord. 23 For the husband is head of the
wife, as also Christ is head of the church; and
He is the Savior of the body. 24 Therefore, just
as the church is subject to Christ, so *let* the
wives *be* to their own husbands in everything.

25 Husbands, love your wives, just as Christ
also loved the church and gave Himself for
her, 26 that He might sanctify and cleanse her

with the washing of water by the word, 27 that
He might present her to Himself a glorious
church, not having spot or wrinkle or any such
thing, but that she should be holy and without
blemish. 28 So husbands ought to love their
own wives as their own bodies; he who loves
his wife loves himself. 29 For no one ever hated
his own flesh, but nourishes and cherishes it,
just as the Lord *does* the church. 30 For we are
members of His body, of His flesh and of His
bones. 31 *"For this reason a man shall leave his*
father and mother and be joined to his wife,
and the two shall become one flesh." 32 This is
a great mystery, but I speak concerning
Christ and the church. 33 Nevertheless let each
one of you in particular so love his own wife as
himself, and let the wife *see* that she respects
her husband.

DAY 4: How do the principles of submission and love in Ephesians 5:21–33 work in a marriage?

The section that begins with a call to wise living (5:15) leads up to Paul's general counsel about submission (5:21). This last verse serves to introduce the next section (5:22–6:9), which spells out the godly expectations for various relationships. Here Paul stated unequivocally that every Spirit-filled Christian is to be a humble, submissive Christian. This is foundational to all the relationships in this section. No believer is inherently superior to any other believer. In their standing before God, all believers are equal in every way (3:28).

Having established the foundational principle of submission (5:21), Paul applied it first to the wife. The command is unqualified and applicable to every Christian wife, no matter what her own abilities, education, knowledge of Scripture, spiritual maturity, or any other qualities might be in relation to those of her husband. The submission is not the husband's to command but for the wife to willingly and lovingly offer. The phrase "your own husband" limits the wife's submission to the one man whom God has placed over her.

The Spirit-filled wife recognizes that her husband's role in giving leadership is not only God-ordained but also a reflection of Christ's own loving, authoritative headship of the church. As the Lord delivered His church from the dangers of sin, death, and hell, so the husband provides for, protects, preserves, and loves his wife, leading her to blessing as she submits (Titus 1:4; 2:13; 3:6).

Paul has much more to say to the man who has been placed in the role of authority within marriage. That authority comes with supreme responsibilities for husbands in regard to their wives. Husbands are to love their wives with the same sacrificial love that Christ has for His church. Christ gave everything He had, including His own life, for the sake of His church, and that is the standard of sacrifice for a husband's love of his wife.

The clarity of God's guidelines makes it certain that problems in marriage must always be traced in both directions so that each partner clearly understands his or her roles and responsibilities. Failure to love is just as often the source of marital trouble as failure to submit.

OCTOBER 5

Isaiah 61:1–62:12

61 "The Spirit of the Lord GOD *is*
upon Me,
Because the LORD has anointed Me
To preach good tidings to the poor;
He has sent Me to heal the
brokenhearted,
To proclaim liberty to the captives,
And the opening of the prison to *those*
who are bound;
2 To proclaim the acceptable year of the
LORD,
And the day of vengeance of our God;
To comfort all who mourn,

61:1,2 The Spirit...acceptable year of the LORD. The Servant of the Lord (42:1) will be the ultimate Preacher and the Redeemer of Israel who rescues them. Jesus speaks of the initial fulfillment of this promise, referring it to His ministry of providing salvation's comfort to the spiritually oppressed (Luke 4:18,19). He says specifically, "Today this Scripture is fulfilled in your hearing" (Luke 4:21). The Jews who were saved during Christ's ministry, and those being saved during this church age still do not fulfill the promise of the salvation of the nation to come in the end time (Zech. 12:10–13:1; Rom. 11:25–27).

3 To console those who mourn in Zion,
To give them beauty for ashes,
The oil of joy for mourning,
The garment of praise for the spirit
of heaviness;
That they may be called trees of
righteousness,
The planting of the LORD, that He may
be glorified."

4 And they shall rebuild the old ruins,
They shall raise up the former
desolations,
And they shall repair the ruined cities,
The desolations of many generations.
5 Strangers shall stand and feed your
flocks,
And the sons of the foreigner
Shall be your plowmen and your
vinedressers.
6 But you shall be named the priests of
the LORD,
They shall call you the servants of
our God.
You shall eat the riches of the Gentiles,
And in their glory you shall boast.
7 Instead of your shame *you shall have*
double *honor,*
And *instead of* confusion they shall
rejoice in their portion.
Therefore in their land they shall
possess double;
Everlasting joy shall be theirs.

8 "For I, the LORD, love justice;
I hate robbery for burnt offering;
I will direct their work in truth,
And will make with them an
everlasting covenant.
9 Their descendants shall be known
among the Gentiles,
And their offspring among
the people.
All who see them shall acknowledge
them,
That they *are* the posterity *whom* the
LORD has blessed."

10 I will greatly rejoice in the LORD,
My soul shall be joyful in my God;
For He has clothed me with the
garments of salvation,
He has covered me with the robe of
righteousness,
As a bridegroom decks *himself* with
ornaments,
And as a bride adorns *herself* with her
jewels.
11 For as the earth brings forth its bud,
As the garden causes the things that
are sown in it to spring forth,
So the Lord GOD will cause
righteousness and praise to spring
forth before all the nations.

61:10 clothed me...covered me. Here is the Old Testament picture of imputed righteousness, the essential heart of the New Covenant. When a penitent sinner recognizes he can't achieve his own righteousness by works (Rom. 3:19–22; 2 Cor. 5:21; Phil. 3:8,9) and repents and calls on the mercy of God, the Lord covers him with His own divine righteousness by grace through his faith.

62 For Zion's sake I will not hold
My peace,
And for Jerusalem's sake I will not rest,
Until her righteousness goes forth as
brightness,
And her salvation as a lamp *that* burns.
2 The Gentiles shall see your
righteousness,
And all kings your glory.
You shall be called by a new name,
Which the mouth of the LORD will
name.
3 You shall also be a crown of glory
In the hand of the LORD,
And a royal diadem
In the hand of your God.
4 You shall no longer be termed Forsaken,
Nor shall your land any more be
termed Desolate;
But you shall be called Hephzibah, and
your land Beulah;
For the LORD delights in you,
And your land shall be married.
5 For *as* a young man marries a virgin,
So shall your sons marry you;
And *as* the bridegroom rejoices over
the bride,
So shall your God rejoice over you.

6 I have set watchmen on your walls,
O Jerusalem;
They shall never hold their peace day
or night.
You who make mention of the LORD,
do not keep silent,
7 And give Him no rest till He
establishes
And till He makes Jerusalem a praise
in the earth.

8 The LORD has sworn by His right hand
And by the arm of His strength:
"Surely I will no longer give your grain
As food for your enemies;
And the sons of the foreigner shall not
drink your new wine,
For which you have labored.
9 But those who have gathered it shall
eat it,
And praise the LORD;
Those who have brought it together
shall drink it in My holy courts."

10 Go through,
Go through the gates!
Prepare the way for the people;
Build up,
Build up the highway!
Take out the stones,
Lift up a banner for the peoples!

11 Indeed the LORD has proclaimed
To the end of the world:
"Say to the daughter of Zion,
'Surely your salvation is coming;
Behold, His reward *is* with Him,
And His work before Him.' "
12 And they shall call them The Holy
People,
The Redeemed of the LORD;
And you shall be called Sought Out,
A City Not Forsaken.

Psalm 115:9–13

9 O Israel, trust in the LORD;
He *is* their help and their shield.
10 O house of Aaron, trust in the LORD;
He *is* their help and their shield.
11 You who fear the LORD, trust in the
LORD;
He *is* their help and their shield.

12 The LORD has been mindful of *us;*
He will bless us;
He will bless the house of Israel;
He will bless the house of Aaron.
13 He will bless those who fear the LORD,
Both small and great.

Proverbs 26:24–26

24 He who hates, disguises *it* with his lips,
And lays up deceit within himself;
25 When he speaks kindly, do not believe
him,
For *there are* seven abominations in his
heart;
26 *Though his* hatred is covered by deceit,
His wickedness will be revealed before
the assembly.

Ephesians 6:1–24

6 Children, obey your parents in the Lord,
for this is right. 2"*Honor your father and*
mother," which is the first commandment
with promise: 3"*that it may be well with you*
and you may live long on the earth."
4And you, fathers, do not provoke your children to wrath, but bring them up in the training and admonition of the Lord.
5Bondservants, be obedient to those who are
your masters according to the flesh, with fear
and trembling, in sincerity of heart, as to Christ;
6not with eyeservice, as men-pleasers, but as
bondservants of Christ, doing the will of God
from the heart, 7with goodwill doing service, as
to the Lord, and not to men, 8knowing that whatever good anyone does, he will receive the same
from the Lord, whether *he is* a slave or free.
9And you, masters, do the same things to
them, giving up threatening, knowing that
your own Master also is in heaven, and there
is no partiality with Him.
10Finally, my brethren, be strong in the Lord
and in the power of His might. 11Put on the
whole armor of God, that you may be able to
stand against the wiles of the devil. 12For we do
not wrestle against flesh and blood, but
against principalities, against powers, against

6:10 be strong in the Lord and in the power of His might. Ultimately, Satan's power over Christians is already broken and the great war is won through Christ's crucifixion and resurrection, which forever conquered the power of sin and death (Rom. 5:18–21; 1 Cor. 15:56,57; Heb. 2:14). However, in life on earth, battles of temptation go on regularly. The Lord's power, the strength of His Spirit, and the force of biblical truth are required for victory.

6:13 Therefore take up the whole armor of God. Paul again emphasized the necessity of the Christian's appropriating God's full spiritual armor by obedience in taking it up or putting it on (v. 11). The first 3 pieces of armor (girdle, breastplate, and shoes/boots, vv. 14,15) were worn continually on the battlefield; the last 3 (shield, helmet, and sword, vv. 16,17) were kept ready for use when actual fighting began. **the evil day.** Since the Fall of man, every day has been evil, a condition that will persist until the Lord returns and establishes His own righteous kingdom on earth. **having done all, to stand.** Standing firm against the enemy without wavering or falling is the goal.

the rulers of the darkness of this age, against
spiritual *hosts* of wickedness in the heavenly
places. [13]Therefore take up the whole armor of
God, that you may be able to withstand in the
evil day, and having done all, to stand.
[14]Stand therefore, having girded your waist
with truth, having put on the breastplate of
righteousness, [15]and having shod your feet with
the preparation of the gospel of peace; [16]above
all, taking the shield of faith with which you will
be able to quench all the fiery darts of the
wicked one. [17]And take the helmet of salvation,
and the sword of the Spirit, which is the word
of God; [18]praying always with all prayer and supplication in the Spirit, being watchful to this end
with all perseverance and supplication for all
the saints— [19]and for me, that utterance may be
given to me, that I may open my mouth boldly
to make known the mystery of the gospel, [20]for
which I am an ambassador in chains; that in it I
may speak boldly, as I ought to speak.
[21]But that you also may know my affairs *and*
how I am doing, Tychicus, a beloved brother
and faithful minister in the Lord, will make all
things known to you; [22]whom I have sent to
you for this very purpose, that you may know
our affairs, and *that* he may comfort your
hearts.
[23]Peace to the brethren, and love with faith,
from God the Father and the Lord Jesus
Christ. [24]Grace *be* with all those who love our
Lord Jesus Christ in sincerity. Amen.

DAY 5: Why does Paul insist in Ephesians 6:10–17 that Christians must be prepared for spiritual battle?

The true believer described in chapters 1–3, who lives the Spirit-controlled life described in 4:1–6:9, can be sure to encounter spiritual warfare. So Paul closed his letter with warnings about upcoming battles and instructions about victorious living. The Lord provides His saints with sufficient armor to combat and defeat the adversary. Ephesians 6:10–13 briefly sets forth the basic truths regarding the believer's necessary spiritual preparation as well as truths about the enemy, the battle, and the victory. Verses 14–17 specify the six most necessary pieces of spiritual armor with which God equips His children to resist and overcome Satan's assaults. The spiritual equipment parallels the standard military equipment worn by soldiers in Paul's day:

1. Belt of truth—The soldier wore a tunic of loose-fitting clothing. Since ancient combat was largely hand-to-hand, the tunic was a potential hindrance and danger. The belt cinched up the loose material. The belt that pulls together all the spiritual loose ends is "truth" or, better, "truthfulness."
2. Breastplate of righteousness—A tough, sleeveless piece of leather or heavy material covered the soldier's full torso, protecting his heart and other vital organs. Because righteousness, or holiness, is such a distinctive characteristic of God Himself, it is easy to understand why it is the Christian's chief protection against Satan and his schemes.
3. Boots of the gospel—Roman soldiers wore boots with nails in them to grip the ground in combat. The gospel of peace pertains to the good news that through Christ believers are at peace with God, and He is on their side (Rom. 5:6–10).
4. Shield of faith—This Greek word usually refers to the large shield that protected the soldier's entire body. The believer's continual trust in God's Word and promise is "above all" absolutely necessary to protect him or her from temptations to every sort of sin.
5. Helmet of salvation—The helmet protected the head, always a major target in battle. This passage is speaking to those who are already saved; therefore, it does not refer to attaining salvation. Rather, since Satan seeks to destroy a believer's assurance of salvation with his weapons of doubt and discouragement, the believer must be as conscious of his or her confident status in Christ as he or she would be aware of a helmet on the head.
6. Sword of the Spirit—A sword was the soldier's only weapon. In the same way, God's Word is the only weapon that a believer needs, infinitely more powerful than any of Satan's devices.

OCTOBER 6

Isaiah 63:1–64:12

63 Who *is* this who comes from Edom,
With dyed garments from Bozrah,
This *One who is* glorious in His
apparel,
Traveling in the greatness of His
strength?—
"I who speak in righteousness, mighty
to save."
2 Why *is* Your apparel red,

And Your garments like one who treads
in the winepress?
3 "I have trodden the winepress alone,
And from the peoples no one *was* with
Me.
For I have trodden them in My anger,
And trampled them in My fury;
Their blood is sprinkled upon My
garments,
And I have stained all My robes.
4 For the day of vengeance *is* in My
heart,
And the year of My redeemed has
come.
5 I looked, but *there was* no one to help,
And I wondered
That *there was* no one to uphold;
Therefore My own arm brought
salvation for Me;
And My own fury, it sustained Me.
6 I have trodden down the peoples in My
anger,
Made them drunk in My fury,
And brought down their strength to
the earth."

7 I will mention the lovingkindnesses of
the LORD
And the praises of the LORD,
According to all that the LORD has
bestowed on us,
And the great goodness toward the
house of Israel,
Which He has bestowed on them
according to His mercies,
According to the multitude of His
lovingkindnesses.
8 For He said, "Surely they *are* My people,
Children *who* will not lie."
So He became their Savior.
9 In all their affliction He was afflicted,
And the Angel of His Presence saved
them;

63:7 lovingkindnesses...lovingkindnesses. All the plurals in this verse imply that language is inadequate to recite all the goodness and undeserved mercies God has showered on the nation time after time because of His everlasting covenant with them. By His elective choice, they became His people and He their Savior (43:1,3). This guarantees that they will not always be false ("lie"), but someday true and faithful to God because of His sovereign election of them.

In His love and in His pity He
redeemed them;
And He bore them and carried them
All the days of old.
10 But they rebelled and grieved His Holy
Spirit;
So He turned Himself against them as
an enemy,
And He fought against them.

11 Then he remembered the days of old,
Moses *and* his people, *saying:*
"Where *is* He who brought them up out
of the sea
With the shepherd of His flock?
Where *is* He who put His Holy Spirit
within them,
12 Who led *them* by the right hand of
Moses,
With His glorious arm,
Dividing the water before them
To make for Himself an everlasting
name,
13 Who led them through the deep,
As a horse in the wilderness,
That they might not stumble?"
14 As a beast goes down into the valley,
And the Spirit of the LORD causes him
to rest,
So You lead Your people,
To make Yourself a glorious name.

15 Look down from heaven,
And see from Your habitation, holy and
glorious.
Where *are* Your zeal and Your strength,
The yearning of Your heart and Your
mercies toward me?
Are they restrained?
16 Doubtless You *are* our Father,
Though Abraham was ignorant of us,
And Israel does not acknowledge us.
You, O LORD, *are* our Father;
Our Redeemer from Everlasting *is*
Your name.
17 O LORD, why have You made us stray
from Your ways,
And hardened our heart from Your fear?
Return for Your servants' sake,
The tribes of Your inheritance.
18 Your holy people have possessed *it* but
a little while;
Our adversaries have trodden down
Your sanctuary.
19 We have become *like* those of old, over
whom You never ruled,
Those who were never called by Your
name.

64 Oh, that You would rend the heavens!
That You would come down!
That the mountains might shake at
Your presence—
2 As fire burns brushwood,
As fire causes water to boil—
To make Your name known to Your
adversaries,
That the nations may tremble at Your
presence!
3 When You did awesome things *for
which* we did not look,
You came down,
The mountains shook at Your
presence.
4 For since the beginning of the world
Men have not heard nor perceived by
the ear,
Nor has the eye seen any God besides
You,
Who acts for the one who waits for
Him.
5 You meet him who rejoices and does
righteousness,
Who remembers You in Your ways.
You are indeed angry, for we have
sinned—
In these ways we continue;
And we need to be saved.
6 But we are all like an unclean *thing,*
And all our righteousnesses *are* like
filthy rags;
We all fade as a leaf,
And our iniquities, like the wind,
Have taken us away.
7 And *there is* no one who calls on Your
name,
Who stirs himself up to take hold
of You;
For You have hidden Your face
from us,
And have consumed us because of
our iniquities.

8 But now, O LORD,
You *are* our Father;
We *are* the clay, and You our potter;
And all we *are* the work of Your hand.
9 Do not be furious, O LORD,
Nor remember iniquity forever;
Indeed, please look—we all *are* Your
people!
10 Your holy cities are a wilderness,
Zion is a wilderness,
Jerusalem a desolation.
11 Our holy and beautiful temple,
Where our fathers praised You,
Is burned up with fire;
And all our pleasant things are laid
waste.
12 Will You restrain Yourself because of
these *things,* O LORD?
Will You hold Your peace, and afflict
us very severely?

64:11 burned up with fire;...laid waste. Through prophetic revelation Isaiah uttered these words many years before the fall of Jerusalem and the destruction of the temple in 586 B.C. Yet he lamented over the fallen state as though it had already occurred. God's people were in desperate straits and their prayers urgent and persistent: "How can You stand by when Your people and Your land are so barren?"

Psalm 115:14–18

14 May the LORD give you increase more
and more,
You and your children.
15 *May* you *be* blessed by the LORD,
Who made heaven and earth.

16 The heaven, *even* the heavens, *are* the
LORD's;
But the earth He has given to the
children of men.
17 The dead do not praise the LORD,
Nor any who go down into silence.
18 But we will bless the LORD
From this time forth and forevermore.

Praise the LORD!

Proverbs 26:27

27 Whoever digs a pit will fall into it,
And he who rolls a stone will have it
roll back on him.

Philippians 1:1–30

1 Paul and Timothy, bondservants of Jesus
Christ,

To all the saints in Christ Jesus who are in Philippi, with the bishops and deacons:

2 Grace to you and peace from God our
Father and the Lord Jesus Christ.
3 I thank my God upon every remembrance
of you, 4 always in every prayer of mine making
request for you all with joy, 5 for your fellowship
in the gospel from the first day until now, 6 being confident of this very thing, that He who
has begun a good work in you will complete *it*
until the day of Jesus Christ; 7 just as it is right

for me to think this of you all, because I have you in my heart, inasmuch as both in my chains and in the defense and confirmation of the gospel, you all are partakers with me of grace. [8]For God is my witness, how greatly I long for you all with the affection of Jesus Christ.

[9]And this I pray, that your love may abound still more and more in knowledge and all discernment, [10]that you may approve the things that are excellent, that you may be sincere and without offense till the day of Christ, [11]being filled with the fruits of righteousness which *are* by Jesus Christ, to the glory and praise of God.

[12]But I want you to know, brethren, that the things *which happened* to me have actually turned out for the furtherance of the gospel, [13]so that it has become evident to the whole palace guard, and to all the rest, that my chains are in Christ; [14]and most of the brethren in the Lord, having become confident by my chains, are much more bold to speak the word without fear.

[15]Some indeed preach Christ even from envy and strife, and some also from goodwill: [16]The former preach Christ from selfish ambition, not sincerely, supposing to add affliction to my chains; [17]but the latter out of love, knowing that I am appointed for the defense of the gospel. [18]What then? Only *that* in every way, whether in pretense or in truth, Christ is preached; and in this I rejoice, yes, and will rejoice.

[19]For I know that this will turn out for my deliverance through your prayer and the supply of the Spirit of Jesus Christ, [20]according to my earnest expectation and hope that in nothing I shall be ashamed, but with all boldness, as always, so now also Christ will be magnified in my body, whether by life or by death. [21]For to me, to live *is* Christ, and to die *is* gain. [22]But if *I* live on in the flesh, this *will mean* fruit from *my* labor; yet what I shall choose I cannot tell. [23]For I am hard-pressed between the two, having a desire to depart and be with Christ, *which is* far better. [24]Nevertheless to remain in the flesh *is* more needful for you. [25]And being confident of this, I know that I shall remain and continue with you all for your progress and joy of faith, [26]that your rejoicing for me may be more abundant in Jesus Christ by my coming to you again.

[27]Only let your conduct be worthy of the gospel of Christ, so that whether I come and see you or am absent, I may hear of your affairs, that you stand fast in one spirit, with one mind striving together for the faith of the gospel, [28]and not in any way terrified by your adversaries, which is to them a proof of perdition, but to you of salvation, and that from God. [29]For to you it has been granted on behalf of Christ, not only to believe in Him, but also to suffer for His sake, [30]having the same conflict which you saw in me and now hear *is* in me.

1:18 I rejoice,…will rejoice. Paul's joy was not tied to his circumstances or his critics (Ps. 4:7,8; Rom. 12:12; 2 Cor. 6:10). He was glad when the gospel was proclaimed with authority, no matter who received credit. He endured the unjust accusations without bitterness at his accusers. Rather, he rejoiced that they preached Christ, even in a pretense of godliness.

DAY 6: What was Paul's prayer for the Philippians?

"That your love may abound still more and more in knowledge" (1:9). This is from the Greek word that describes genuine, full, or advanced knowledge. Biblical love is not an empty sentimentalism but is anchored deeply in the truth of Scripture and regulated by it. "Discernment." The English word "aesthetic" comes from this Greek word, which speaks of moral perception, insight, and the practical application of knowledge. Love is not blind, but perceptive, and it carefully scrutinizes to distinguish between right and wrong.

"That you may approve the…excellent" (v. 10). "Approve" in classical Greek described the assaying of metals or the testing of money for authenticity. "Excellent" means "to differ." Believers need the ability to distinguish those things that are truly important so they can establish the right priorities. "Sincere and without offense." "Sincere" means "genuine" and may have originally meant "tested by sunlight." In the ancient world, dishonest pottery dealers filled cracks in their inferior products with wax before glazing and painting them, making worthless pots difficult to distinguish from expensive ones. The only way to avoid being defrauded was to hold the pot to the sun, making the wax-filled cracks obvious. Dealers marked their fine pottery that could withstand "sun testing" as *sine cera*—"without wax." "Without offense" can be translated "blameless," referring to relational integrity. Christians are to live lives of true integrity that do not cause others to sin.

"Being filled with the fruits of righteousness" (v. 11). This is better translated, "the fruit righteousness produces." "Which are by Jesus Christ." This speaks of the salvation transformation provided by our Lord and His ongoing work of power through His Spirit in us. "To the glory and praise of God." The ultimate end of all Paul's prayers was that God be glorified.

OCTOBER 7

Isaiah 65:1–66:24

65 "I was sought by *those who* did not ask
for Me;
I was found by *those who* did not seek
Me.
I said, 'Here I am, here I am,'
To a nation *that* was not called by My
name.

65:1 not ask…not seek…not called. Though Israel sought the Lord, they did so only superficially. They did not genuinely seek Him. The New Testament assigns an additional sense to the words in Romans 10:20, applying them to Gentiles who find Him through the work of His sovereign grace.

2 I have stretched out My hands all day
long to a rebellious people,
Who walk in a way *that is* not good,
According to their own thoughts;
3 A people who provoke Me to anger
continually to My face;
Who sacrifice in gardens,
And burn incense on altars of brick;
4 Who sit among the graves,
And spend the night in the tombs;
Who eat swine's flesh,
And the broth of abominable things is
in their vessels;
5 Who say, 'Keep to yourself,
Do not come near me,
For I am holier than you!'
These *are* smoke in My nostrils,
A fire that burns all the day.

6 "Behold, *it is* written before Me:
I will not keep silence, but will repay—
Even repay into their bosom—
7 Your iniquities and the iniquities of
your fathers together,"
Says the LORD,
"Who have burned incense on the
mountains
And blasphemed Me on the hills;
Therefore I will measure their former
work into their bosom."

8 Thus says the LORD:

"As the new wine is found in the cluster,
And *one* says, 'Do not destroy it,
For a blessing *is* in it,'
So will I do for My servants' sake,
That I may not destroy them all.
9 I will bring forth descendants from
Jacob,
And from Judah an heir of My
mountains;
My elect shall inherit it,
And My servants shall dwell there.
10 Sharon shall be a fold of flocks,
And the Valley of Achor a place for
herds to lie down,
For My people who have sought Me.

11 "But you *are* those who forsake the LORD,
Who forget My holy mountain,
Who prepare a table for Gad,
And who furnish a drink offering for
Meni.
12 Therefore I will number you for the
sword,
And you shall all bow down to the
slaughter;
Because, when I called, you did not
answer;
When I spoke, you did not hear,
But did evil before My eyes,
And chose *that* in which I do not
delight."

13 Therefore thus says the Lord GOD:

"Behold, My servants shall eat,
But you shall be hungry;
Behold, My servants shall drink,
But you shall be thirsty;
Behold, My servants shall rejoice,
But you shall be ashamed;
14 Behold, My servants shall sing for joy
of heart,
But you shall cry for sorrow of heart,
And wail for grief of spirit.
15 You shall leave your name as a curse to
My chosen;

For the Lord GOD will slay you,
And call His servants by another name;
16 So that he who blesses himself in the earth
Shall bless himself in the God of truth;
And he who swears in the earth
Shall swear by the God of truth;
Because the former troubles are forgotten,
And because they are hidden from My eyes.

17 "For behold, I create new heavens and a new earth;
And the former shall not be remembered or come to mind.
18 But be glad and rejoice forever in what I create;
For behold, I create Jerusalem *as* a rejoicing,
And her people a joy.
19 I will rejoice in Jerusalem,
And joy in My people;
The voice of weeping shall no longer be heard in her,
Nor the voice of crying.

20 "No more shall an infant from there *live but a few* days,
Nor an old man who has not fulfilled his days;
For the child shall die one hundred years old,
But the sinner *being* one hundred years old shall be accursed.
21 They shall build houses and inhabit *them;*
They shall plant vineyards and eat their fruit.
22 They shall not build and another inhabit;
They shall not plant and another eat;
For as the days of a tree, *so shall be* the days of My people,
And My elect shall long enjoy the work of their hands.
23 They shall not labor in vain,
Nor bring forth children for trouble;
For they *shall be* the descendants of the blessed of the LORD,
And their offspring with them.

24 "It shall come to pass
That before they call, I will answer;
And while they are still speaking, I will hear.
25 The wolf and the lamb shall feed together,
The lion shall eat straw like the ox,
And dust *shall be* the serpent's food.
They shall not hurt nor destroy in all My holy mountain,"
Says the LORD.

66 Thus says the LORD:

"Heaven *is* My throne,
And earth *is* My footstool.
Where *is* the house that you will build Me?
And where *is* the place of My rest?
2 For all those *things* My hand has made,
And all those *things* exist,"
Says the LORD.
"But on this *one* will I look:
On *him who is* poor and of a contrite spirit,
And who trembles at My word.

66:1,2 Isaiah began the final summary of his prophecy with a reminder that God is not looking for a temple of stone, since as Creator of all things, the whole universe is His dwelling place. Stephen cited this passage before the Sanhedrin to point out their error in limiting God to a temple made with hands (Acts 7:49,50). On the contrary, God is looking for a heart to dwell in, a heart that is tender and broken, not one concerned with the externalities of religion. God is looking to dwell in the heart of a person who takes His Word seriously.

3 "He who kills a bull *is as if* he slays a man;
He who sacrifices a lamb, *as if* he breaks a dog's neck;
He who offers a grain offering, *as if he offers* swine's blood;
He who burns incense, *as if* he blesses an idol.
Just as they have chosen their own ways,
And their soul delights in their abominations,
4 So will I choose their delusions,
And bring their fears on them;
Because, when I called, no one answered,
When I spoke they did not hear;
But they did evil before My eyes,
And chose *that* in which I do not delight."

5 Hear the word of the LORD,
You who tremble at His word:
"Your brethren who hated you,

Who cast you out for My name's sake,
said,
'Let the LORD be glorified,
That we may see your joy.'
But they shall be ashamed."

6 The sound of noise from the city!
A voice from the temple!
The voice of the LORD,
Who fully repays His enemies!

7 "Before she was in labor, she gave birth;
Before her pain came,
She delivered a male child.
8 Who has heard such a thing?
Who has seen such things?
Shall the earth be made to give birth in
one day?
Or shall a nation be born at once?
For as soon as Zion was in labor,
She gave birth to her children.
9 Shall I bring to the time of birth, and not
cause delivery?" says the LORD.
"Shall I who cause delivery shut up *the
womb?*" says your God.
10 "Rejoice with Jerusalem,
And be glad with her, all you who love
her;
Rejoice for joy with her, all you who
mourn for her;
11 That you may feed and be satisfied
With the consolation of her bosom,
That you may drink deeply and be
delighted
With the abundance of her glory."

12 For thus says the LORD:

"Behold, I will extend peace to her like
a river,
And the glory of the Gentiles like a
flowing stream.
Then you shall feed;
On *her* sides shall you be carried,
And be dandled on *her* knees.
13 As one whom his mother comforts,
So I will comfort you;
And you shall be comforted in
Jerusalem."

14 When you see *this,* your heart shall
rejoice,
And your bones shall flourish like grass;
The hand of the LORD shall be known
to His servants,
And *His* indignation to His enemies.
15 For behold, the LORD will come with fire
And with His chariots, like a whirlwind,
To render His anger with fury,
And His rebuke with flames of fire.
16 For by fire and by His sword
The LORD will judge all flesh;
And the slain of the LORD shall be many.

17 "Those who sanctify themselves and
purify themselves,
To go to the gardens
After an *idol* in the midst,
Eating swine's flesh and the
abomination and the mouse,
Shall be consumed together," says the
LORD.

18 "For I *know* their works and their thoughts.
It shall be that I will gather all nations and
tongues; and they shall come and see My glory.
19 I will set a sign among them; and those among
them who escape I will send to the nations: *to*
Tarshish and Pul and Lud, who draw the bow,
and Tubal and Javan, *to* the coastlands afar off
who have not heard My fame nor seen My
glory. And they shall declare My glory among
the Gentiles. 20 Then they shall bring all your
brethren for an offering to the LORD out of all
nations, on horses and in chariots and in litters,
on mules and on camels, to My holy mountain
Jerusalem," says the LORD, "as the children of Israel bring an offering in a clean vessel into the
house of the LORD. 21 And I will also take some of
them for priests *and* Levites," says the LORD.

22 "For as the new heavens and the new
earth
Which I will make shall remain before
Me," says the LORD,
"So shall your descendants and your
name remain.
23 And it shall come to pass
That from one New Moon to another,
And from one Sabbath to another,
All flesh shall come to worship before
Me," says the LORD.

24 "And they shall go forth and look
Upon the corpses of the men
Who have transgressed against Me.
For their worm does not die,
And their fire is not quenched.
They shall be an abhorrence to all
flesh."

Psalm 116:1–4

I love the LORD, because He has heard
My voice *and* my supplications.
2 Because He has inclined His ear to me,
Therefore I will call *upon Him* as long
as I live.

3 The pains of death surrounded me,
And the pangs of Sheol laid hold of me;
I found trouble and sorrow.

4 Then I called upon the name of the LORD:
"O LORD, I implore You, deliver my soul!"

Proverbs 26:28

28 A lying tongue hates *those who are* crushed by it,
And a flattering mouth works ruin.

Philippians 2:1–30

2 Therefore if *there is* any consolation in
Christ, if any comfort of love, if any fellowship of the Spirit, if any affection and mercy,
2fulfill my joy by being like-minded, having the
same love, *being* of one accord, of one mind.
3*Let* nothing *be done* through selfish ambition
or conceit, but in lowliness of mind let each
esteem others better than himself. 4Let each of
you look out not only for his own interests, but
also for the interests of others.
5Let this mind be in you which was also in
Christ Jesus, 6who, being in the form of God,
did not consider it robbery to be equal with
God, 7but made Himself of no reputation, taking the form of a bondservant, *and* coming in
the likeness of men. 8And being found in
appearance as a man, He humbled Himself
and became obedient to *the point of* death,
even the death of the cross. 9Therefore God
also has highly exalted Him and given Him
the name which is above every name, 10that at
the name of Jesus every knee should bow, of
those in heaven, and of those on earth, and of
those under the earth, 11and *that* every tongue
should confess that Jesus Christ *is* Lord, to the
glory of God the Father.
12Therefore, my beloved, as you have always
obeyed, not as in my presence only, but now
much more in my absence, work out your own
salvation with fear and trembling; 13for it is
God who works in you both to will and to do
for *His* good pleasure.
14Do all things without complaining and disputing, 15that you may become blameless and
harmless, children of God without fault in the
midst of a crooked and perverse generation,
among whom you shine as lights in the world,
16holding fast the word of life, so that I may
rejoice in the day of Christ that I have not run
in vain or labored in vain.
17Yes, and if I am being poured out *as a drink
offering* on the sacrifice and service of your
faith, I am glad and rejoice with you all. 18For
the same reason you also be glad and rejoice
with me.
19But I trust in the Lord Jesus to send Timothy to you shortly, that I also may be encouraged when I know your state. 20For I have no
one like-minded, who will sincerely care for
your state. 21For all seek their own, not the
things which are of Christ Jesus. 22But you
know his proven character, that as a son with
his father he served with me in the gospel.
23Therefore I hope to send him at once, as soon
as I see how it goes with me. 24But I trust in the

2:2 fulfill my joy. This can also be translated "make my joy complete." Paul's joy was tied to a concern for the unity of believers (Heb. 13:17). **like-minded.** The Greek word means "think the same way." This exhortation is not optional or obscure, but is repeated throughout the New Testament (Rom. 15:5; 1 Cor. 1:10; 2 Cor. 13:11–13). **same love.** Believers are to love others in the body of Christ equally—not because they are all equally attractive, but by showing the same kind of sacrificial, loving service to all that was shown to them by Christ. **one accord.** This may also be translated "united in spirit" and perhaps is a term specially coined by Paul. It literally means "one-souled" and describes people who are knit together in harmony, having the same desires, passions, and ambitions.

2:6 being in the form of God. Paul affirms that Jesus eternally has been God. The usual Greek word for "being" is not used here. Instead, Paul chose another term that stresses the essence of a person's nature—his continuous state or condition. Paul also could have chosen one of two Greek words for "form," but he chose the one that specifically denotes the essential, unchanging character of something—what it is in and of itself. The fundamental doctrine of Christ's deity has always encompassed these crucial characteristics (John 1:1,3,4,14; 8:58; Col. 1:15–17; Heb. 1:3). **not...robbery.** The Greek word is translated "robbery" here because it originally meant "a thing seized by robbery." It eventually came to mean anything clutched, embraced, or prized, and thus is sometimes translated "grasped" or "held on to." Though Christ had all the rights, privileges, and honors of Deity—which He was worthy of and could never be disqualified from—His attitude was not to cling to those things or His position but to be willing to give them up for a season. **equal with God.** The Greek word for "equal" defines things that are exactly the same in size, quantity, quality, character, and number. In every sense, Jesus is equal to God and constantly claimed to be so during His earthly ministry (John 5:18; 10:33,38; 14:9; 20:28; Heb. 1:1–3).

Lord that I myself shall also come shortly.
[25]Yet I considered it necessary to send to you
Epaphroditus, my brother, fellow worker, and
fellow soldier, but your messenger and the
one who ministered to my need; [26]since he was
longing for you all, and was distressed
because you had heard that he was sick. [27]For
indeed he was sick almost unto death; but God
had mercy on him, and not only on him but on
me also, lest I should have sorrow upon sorrow. [28]Therefore I sent him the more eagerly,
that when you see him again you may rejoice,
and I may be less sorrowful. [29]Receive him
therefore in the Lord with all gladness, and
hold such men in esteem; [30]because for the
work of Christ he came close to death, not
regarding his life, to supply what was lacking
in your service toward me.

DAY 7: How did Christ humble Himself for our salvation?

In Philippians 2:7, Paul writes that Christ "made Himself of no reputation." This is more clearly translated "emptied Himself." This was a self-renunciation, not an emptying Himself of Deity nor an exchange of Deity for humanity. Jesus did, however, renounce or set aside His privileges in several areas: 1) heavenly glory—while on earth He gave up the glory of a face-to-face relationship with God (John 17:5); 2) independent authority—during His Incarnation Christ completely submitted Himself to the will of His Father (Matt. 26:39; John 5:30); 3) divine prerogatives—He set aside the voluntary display of His divine attributes and submitted Himself to the Spirit's direction (Matt. 24:36; John 1:45–49); 4) eternal riches—while on earth Christ was poor and owned very little (2 Cor. 8:9); and 5) a favorable relationship with God—He felt the Father's wrath for human sin while on the cross (Matt. 27:46; 2 Cor. 5:21).

"Taking the form of a bondservant" (v. 7). Again, Paul uses the Greek word "form," which indicates exact essence. As a true servant, Jesus submissively did the will of His Father (Is. 52:13,14). "Coming in the likeness of men." Christ became more than God in a human body, but He took on all the essential attributes of humanity (Luke 2:52; Gal. 4:4; Col. 1:22). He became the God-Man: fully God and fully man.

"And being found in appearance as a man" (v. 8). Christ's humanity is described from the viewpoint of those who saw Him. Paul is implying that, although He outwardly looked like a man, there was much more to Him (His deity) than many people recognized naturally (John 6:42; 8:48). "He humbled Himself." After the humbling of incarnation, Jesus further humbled Himself in that He subjected Himself to persecution and suffering (Is. 53:7; Matt. 26:62–64; Mark 14:60,61; 1 Pet. 2:23). "Obedient…death." Beyond even persecution, Jesus went to the lowest point or furthest extent in His humiliation in dying as a criminal, following God's plan for Him. "The cross." Even further humiliation was His because Jesus' death was not by ordinary means, but was accomplished by crucifixion—the cruelest, most excruciating, most degrading form of death ever devised.

OCTOBER 8

Jeremiah 1:1–2:37

1 The words of Jeremiah the son of Hilkiah, of
the priests who *were* in Anathoth in the land
of Benjamin, [2]to whom the word of the LORD
came in the days of Josiah the son of Amon,
king of Judah, in the thirteenth year of his reign.
[3]It came also in the days of Jehoiakim the son of
Josiah, king of Judah, until the end of the
eleventh year of Zedekiah the son of Josiah,
king of Judah, until the carrying away of Jerusalem captive in the fifth month.

[4]Then the word of the LORD came to me,
saying:

5 "Before I formed you in the womb I
knew you;
Before you were born I sanctified you;
I ordained you a prophet to the
nations."

[6]Then said I:

"Ah, Lord GOD!
Behold, I cannot speak, for I *am* a
youth."

[7]But the LORD said to me:

"Do not say, 'I *am* a youth,'

1:5 Before I formed you… This is not reincarnation; it is God's all-knowing cognizance of Jeremiah and sovereign plan for him before he was conceived (Paul's similar realization, Gal. 1:15).

For you shall go to all to whom I send
you,
And whatever I command you, you
shall speak.
8 Do not be afraid of their faces,
For I *am* with you to deliver you," says
the LORD.

9Then the LORD put forth His hand and
touched my mouth, and the LORD said to me:

"Behold, I have put My words in your
mouth.
10 See, I have this day set you over the
nations and over the kingdoms,
To root out and to pull down,
To destroy and to throw down,
To build and to plant."

11Moreover the word of the LORD came to
me, saying, "Jeremiah, what do you see?"
And I said, "I see a branch of an almond
tree."
12Then the LORD said to me, "You have seen
well, for I am ready to perform My word."
13And the word of the LORD came to me the
second time, saying, "What do you see?"
And I said, "I see a boiling pot, and it is facing away from the north."
14Then the LORD said to me:

"Out of the north calamity shall break
forth
On all the inhabitants of the land.
15 For behold, I am calling
All the families of the kingdoms of the
north," says the LORD;
"They shall come and each one set his
throne
At the entrance of the gates of
Jerusalem,
Against all its walls all around,
And against all the cities of Judah.
16 I will utter My judgments
Against them concerning all their
wickedness,
Because they have forsaken Me,
Burned incense to other gods,
And worshiped the works of their own
hands.

17 "Therefore prepare yourself and arise,
And speak to them all that I command
you.
Do not be dismayed before their faces,
Lest I dismay you before them.
18 For behold, I have made you this day
A fortified city and an iron pillar,
And bronze walls against the whole
land—
Against the kings of Judah,
Against its princes,
Against its priests,
And against the people of the land.
19 They will fight against you,
But they shall not prevail against you.
For I *am* with you," says the LORD, "to
deliver you."

2 Moreover the word of the LORD came to
me, saying, 2"Go and cry in the hearing of
Jerusalem, saying, 'Thus says the LORD:

"I remember you,
The kindness of your youth,
The love of your betrothal,
When you went after Me in the
wilderness,
In a land not sown.
3 Israel *was* holiness to the LORD,
The firstfruits of His increase.
All that devour him will offend;
Disaster will come upon them," says
the LORD.' "

4Hear the word of the LORD, O house of Jacob
and all the families of the house of Israel. 5Thus
says the LORD:

"What injustice have your fathers found
in Me,
That they have gone far from Me,
Have followed idols,
And have become idolaters?
6 Neither did they say, 'Where *is* the
LORD,
Who brought us up out of the land of
Egypt,
Who led us through the wilderness,
Through a land of deserts and pits,
Through a land of drought and the
shadow of death,
Through a land that no one crossed
And where no one dwelt?'
7 I brought you into a bountiful country,
To eat its fruit and its goodness.
But when you entered, you defiled My
land
And made My heritage an
abomination.
8 The priests did not say, 'Where *is* the
LORD?'
And those who handle the law did not
know Me;
The rulers also transgressed against Me;
The prophets prophesied by Baal,
And walked after *things that* do not
profit.
9 "Therefore I will yet bring charges
against you," says the LORD,

"And against your children's children
I will bring charges.
10 For pass beyond the coasts of Cyprus and see,
Send to Kedar and consider diligently,
And see if there has been such *a thing.*
11 Has a nation changed *its* gods,
Which *are* not gods?
But My people have changed their Glory
For *what* does not profit.
12 Be astonished, O heavens, at this,
And be horribly afraid;
Be very desolate," says the LORD.
13 "For My people have committed two evils:
They have forsaken Me, the fountain of living waters,
And hewn themselves cisterns—broken cisterns that can hold no water.

14 "*Is* Israel a servant?
Is he a homeborn *slave?*
Why is he plundered?
15 The young lions roared at him, *and* growled;
They made his land waste;
His cities are burned, without inhabitant.
16 Also the people of Noph and Tahpanhes
Have broken the crown of your head.
17 Have you not brought this on yourself,
In that you have forsaken the LORD your God
When He led you in the way?
18 And now why take the road to Egypt,
To drink the waters of Sihor?
Or why take the road to Assyria,
To drink the waters of the River?
19 Your own wickedness will correct you,
And your backslidings will rebuke you.
Know therefore and see that *it is* an evil and bitter *thing*
That you have forsaken the LORD your God,
And the fear of Me *is* not in you,"
Says the Lord GOD of hosts.

20 "For of old I have broken your yoke *and* burst your bonds;
And you said, 'I will not transgress,'
When on every high hill and under every green tree
You lay down, playing the harlot.
21 Yet I had planted you a noble vine, a seed of highest quality.
How then have you turned before Me
Into the degenerate plant of an alien vine?
22 For though you wash yourself with lye, and use much soap,
Yet your iniquity is marked before Me,"
says the Lord GOD.

23 "How can you say, 'I am not polluted,
I have not gone after the Baals'?
See your way in the valley;
Know what you have done:
You are a swift dromedary breaking loose in her ways,
24 A wild donkey used to the wilderness,
That sniffs at the wind in her desire;
In her time of mating, who can turn her away?
All those who seek her will not weary themselves;
In her month they will find her.
25 Withhold your foot from being unshod, and your throat from thirst.
But you said, 'There is no hope.
No! For I have loved aliens, and after them I will go.'

26 "As the thief is ashamed when he is found out,
So is the house of Israel ashamed;
They and their kings and their princes, and their priests and their prophets,
27 Saying to a tree, 'You *are* my father,'
And to a stone, 'You gave birth to me.'
For they have turned *their* back to Me, and not *their* face.
But in the time of their trouble
They will say, 'Arise and save us.'
28 But where *are* your gods that you have made for yourselves?
Let them arise,
If they can save you in the time of your trouble;
For *according to* the number of your cities
Are your gods, O Judah.

29 "Why will you plead with Me?
You all have transgressed against Me,"
says the LORD.
30 "In vain I have chastened your children;
They received no correction.
Your sword has devoured your prophets
Like a destroying lion.
31 "O generation, see the word of the LORD!
Have I been a wilderness to Israel,
Or a land of darkness?
Why do My people say, 'We are lords;
We will come no more to You'?

32 Can a virgin forget her ornaments,
Or a bride her attire?
Yet My people have forgotten Me days without number.

33 "Why do you beautify your way to seek love?
Therefore you have also taught
The wicked women your ways.
34 Also on your skirts is found
The blood of the lives of the poor innocents.
I have not found it by secret search,
But plainly on all these things.
35 Yet you say, 'Because I am innocent,
Surely His anger shall turn from me.'
Behold, I will plead My case against you,
Because you say, 'I have not sinned.'
36 Why do you gad about so much to change your way?
Also you shall be ashamed of Egypt as you were ashamed of Assyria.
37 Indeed you will go forth from him
With your hands on your head;
For the LORD has rejected your trusted allies,
And you will not prosper by them.

Psalm 116:5–14

5 Gracious *is* the LORD, and righteous;
Yes, our God *is* merciful.
6 The LORD preserves the simple;
I was brought low, and He saved me.
7 Return to your rest, O my soul,
For the LORD has dealt bountifully with you.

8 For You have delivered my soul from death,
My eyes from tears,
And my feet from falling.
9 I will walk before the LORD
In the land of the living.
10 I believed, therefore I spoke,
"I am greatly afflicted."
11 I said in my haste,
"All men *are* liars."

12 What shall I render to the LORD
For all His benefits toward me?
13 I will take up the cup of salvation,
And call upon the name of the LORD.
14 I will pay my vows to the LORD
Now in the presence of all His people.

Proverbs 27:1

27 Do not boast about tomorrow,
For you do not know what a day may bring forth.

Philippians 3:1–21

3 Finally, my brethren, rejoice in the Lord.
For me to write the same things to you *is*
not tedious, but for you *it is* safe.
[2]Beware of dogs, beware of evil workers,
beware of the mutilation! [3]For we are the circumcision, who worship God in the Spirit,

3:2 dogs. During the first century, dogs roamed the streets and were essentially wild scavengers. Because dogs were such filthy animals, the Jews loved to refer to Gentiles as dogs. Yet here Paul refers to Jews, specifically the Judaizers, as dogs to describe their sinful, vicious, and uncontrolled character. **evil workers.** The Judaizers prided themselves on being workers of righteousness. Yet Paul described their works as evil, since any attempt to please God by one's own efforts and draw attention away from Christ's accomplished redemption is the worst kind of wickedness. **mutilation.** In contrast to the Greek word for "circumcision," which means "to cut around," this term means "to cut down (off)." Like the prophets of Baal (1 Kin. 18:28) and pagans who mutilated their bodies in their frenzied rituals, which were forbidden in the Old Testament (Lev. 19:28; 21:5; Deut. 14:1), the Judaizers' circumcision was, ironically, no spiritual symbol; it was merely physical mutilation.

rejoice in Christ Jesus, and have no confidence in the flesh, [4]though I also might have
confidence in the flesh. If anyone else thinks
he may have confidence in the flesh, I more
so: [5]circumcised the eighth day, of the stock
of Israel, *of* the tribe of Benjamin, a Hebrew
of the Hebrews; concerning the law, a
Pharisee; [6]concerning zeal, persecuting the
church; concerning the righteousness which
is in the law, blameless.
[7]But what things were gain to me, these I
have counted loss for Christ. [8]Yet indeed I also
count all things loss for the excellence of the
knowledge of Christ Jesus my Lord, for whom
I have suffered the loss of all things, and count
them as rubbish, that I may gain Christ [9]and
be found in Him, not having my own righteousness, which *is* from the law, but that
which *is* through faith in Christ, the righteousness which is from God by faith; [10]that I may
know Him and the power of His resurrection,
and the fellowship of His sufferings, being
conformed to His death, [11]if, by any means, I
may attain to the resurrection from the dead.

3:7 what things were gain…I have counted loss. The Greek word for "gain" is an accounting term that means "profit." The Greek word for "loss" also is an accounting term used to describe a business loss. Paul used the language of business to describe the spiritual transaction that occurred when Christ redeemed him. All his Jewish religious credentials that he thought were in his profit column were actually worthless and damning (Luke 18:9–14). Thus, he put them in his loss column when he saw the glories of Christ.

3:8 knowledge of Christ Jesus. To "know" Christ is not simply to have intellectual knowledge about Him. Paul used the Greek verb that means to know "experientially" or "personally" (John 10:27; 17:3; 2 Cor. 4:6; 1 John 5:20). It is equivalent to shared life with Christ. It also corresponds to a Hebrew word used of God's knowledge of His people (Amos 3:2) and their knowledge of Him in love and obedience (Jer. 31:34; Hos. 6:3; 8:2). **rubbish.** The Greek word refers to garbage or waste and can even be translated "dung" or "manure."

[12]Not that I have already attained, or am
already perfected; but I press on, that I may
lay hold of that for which Christ Jesus has also
laid hold of me. [13]Brethren, I do not count
myself to have apprehended; but one thing *I*
do, forgetting those things which are behind
and reaching forward to those things which
are ahead, [14]I press toward the goal for the
prize of the upward call of God in Christ Jesus.
[15]Therefore let us, as many as are mature,
have this mind; and if in anything you think
otherwise, God will reveal even this to you.
[16]Nevertheless, to *the degree* that we have
already attained, let us walk by the same rule,
let us be of the same mind.
[17]Brethren, join in following my example,
and note those who so walk, as you have us for
a pattern. [18]For many walk, of whom I have
told you often, and now tell you even weeping,
that they are the enemies of the cross of
Christ: [19]whose end *is* destruction, whose god
is their belly, and *whose* glory *is* in their
shame—who set their mind on earthly things.
[20]For our citizenship is in heaven, from which
we also eagerly wait for the Savior, the Lord Jesus Christ, [21]who will transform our lowly body
that it may be conformed to His glorious body,
according to the working by which He is able
even to subdue all things to Himself.

DAY 8: Who was the prophet Jeremiah?

Jeremiah, who served as both a priest and a prophet, was the son of a priest named Hilkiah. He was from the small village of Anathoth (1:1), today called Anata, about 3 miles northeast of Jerusalem. As an object lesson to Judah, Jeremiah remained unmarried (16:1–4). He was assisted in ministry by a scribe named Baruch, to whom Jeremiah dictated and who copied and had custody over the writings compiled from the prophet's messages (36:4,32; 45:1). Jeremiah has been known as "the weeping prophet" (9:1; 13:17; 14:17), living a life of conflict because of his predictions of judgment by the invading Babylonians. He was threatened, tried for his life, put in stocks, forced to flee from Jehoiakim, publicly humiliated by a false prophet, and thrown into a pit.

Jeremiah carried out a ministry directed mostly to his own people in Judah, but which expanded to other nations at times. He appealed to his countrymen to repent and avoid God's judgment via an invader (chaps. 7; 26). Once invasion was certain after Judah refused to repent, he pled with them not to resist the Babylonian conqueror in order to prevent total destruction (chap. 27). He also called on delegates of other nations to heed his counsel and submit to Babylon (chap. 27), and he predicted judgments from God on various nations (25:12–38; chaps. 46–51).

The dates of his ministry, which spanned 5 decades, are from the Judean king Josiah's thirteenth year, noted in 1:2 (627 B.C.), to beyond the fall of Jerusalem to Babylon in 586 B.C. (chaps. 39; 40; 52). After 586 B.C., Jeremiah was forced to go with a fleeing remnant of Judah to Egypt (chaps. 43; 44).

OCTOBER 9

Jeremiah 3:1–4:31

3 "They say, 'If a man divorces his wife,
And she goes from him
And becomes another man's,
May he return to her again?'
Would not that land be greatly
polluted?
But you have played the harlot with
many lovers;
Yet return to Me," says the LORD.

2 "Lift up your eyes to the desolate
heights and see:
Where have you not lain *with men?*
By the road you have sat for them
Like an Arabian in the wilderness;
And you have polluted the land
With your harlotries and your
wickedness.
3 Therefore the showers have been
withheld,
And there has been no latter rain.
You have had a harlot's forehead;
You refuse to be ashamed.
4 Will you not from this time cry to Me,
'My Father, You *are* the guide of my
youth?
5 Will He remain angry forever?
Will He keep it to the end?'
Behold, you have spoken and done evil
things,
As you were able."

6The LORD said also to me in the days of
Josiah the king: "Have you seen what backsliding Israel has done? She has gone up on every
high mountain and under every green tree,
and there played the harlot. 7And I said, after
she had done all these *things,* 'Return to Me.'
But she did not return. And her treacherous
sister Judah saw it. 8Then I saw that for all the
causes for which backsliding Israel had committed adultery, I had put her away and given
her a certificate of divorce; yet her treacherous sister Judah did not fear, but went and
played the harlot also. 9So it came to pass,
through her casual harlotry, that she defiled
the land and committed adultery with stones
and trees. 10And yet for all this her treacherous
sister Judah has not turned to Me with her
whole heart, but in pretense," says the LORD.
11Then the LORD said to me, "Backsliding Israel has shown herself more righteous than
treacherous Judah. 12Go and proclaim these
words toward the north, and say:

'Return, backsliding Israel,' says the
LORD;
'I will not cause My anger to fall on
you.
For I *am* merciful,' says the LORD;
'I will not remain angry forever.
13 Only acknowledge your iniquity,
That you have transgressed against the
LORD your God,
And have scattered your charms
To alien deities under every green
tree,
And you have not obeyed My voice,'
says the LORD.

14"Return, O backsliding children," says the
LORD; "for I am married to you. I will take you,
one from a city and two from a family, and I
will bring you to Zion. 15And I will give you

3:14 I am married to you. God pictured His covenant relationship with Israel as a marriage and pleaded with mercy for Judah to repent and return. He will take her back. Hosea's restoration of Gomer was a picture of God taking back His wicked, adulterous people.

shepherds according to My heart, who will
feed you with knowledge and understanding.
16"Then it shall come to pass, when you are
multiplied and increased in the land in those
days," says the LORD, "that they will say no
more, 'The ark of the covenant of the LORD.' It
shall not come to mind, nor shall they remember it, nor shall they visit *it,* nor shall it be
made anymore.
17"At that time Jerusalem shall be called The
Throne of the LORD, and all the nations shall
be gathered to it, to the name of the LORD, to
Jerusalem. No more shall they follow the dictates of their evil hearts.
18"In those days the house of Judah shall
walk with the house of Israel, and they shall
come together out of the land of the north to
the land that I have given as an inheritance to
your fathers.
19"But I said:

'How can I put you among the children
And give you a pleasant land,
A beautiful heritage of the hosts of
nations?'

"And I said:

'You shall call Me, "My Father,"
And not turn away from Me.'
20 Surely, *as* a wife treacherously departs
from her husband,
So have you dealt treacherously with
Me,
O house of Israel," says the LORD.

21 A voice was heard on the desolate
heights,
Weeping *and* supplications of the
children of Israel.
For they have perverted their way;
They have forgotten the LORD their God.

22 "Return, you backsliding children,
And I will heal your backslidings."

"Indeed we do come to You,
For You are the LORD our God.
23 Truly, in vain *is salvation hoped for* from the hills,
And from the multitude of mountains;
Truly, in the LORD our God
Is the salvation of Israel.
24 For shame has devoured
The labor of our fathers from our youth—
Their flocks and their herds,
Their sons and their daughters.
25 We lie down in our shame,
And our reproach covers us.
For we have sinned against the LORD our God,
We and our fathers,
From our youth even to this day,
And have not obeyed the voice of the LORD our God."

4 "If you will return, O Israel," says the LORD,
"Return to Me;
And if you will put away your abominations out of My sight,
Then you shall not be moved.
2 And you shall swear, 'The LORD lives,'
In truth, in judgment, and in righteousness;
The nations shall bless themselves in Him,
And in Him they shall glory."

3 For thus says the LORD to the men of Judah and Jerusalem:

"Break up your fallow ground,
And do not sow among thorns.
4 Circumcise yourselves to the LORD,
And take away the foreskins of your hearts,
You men of Judah and inhabitants of Jerusalem,
Lest My fury come forth like fire,
And burn so that no one can quench *it,*
Because of the evil of your doings."

5 Declare in Judah and proclaim in Jerusalem, and say:

"Blow the trumpet in the land;
Cry, 'Gather together,'
And say, 'Assemble yourselves,
And let us go into the fortified cities.'
6 Set up the standard toward Zion.
Take refuge! Do not delay!
For I will bring disaster from the north,
And great destruction."

4:4 Circumcise. This surgery (Gen. 17:10–14) was to cut away flesh that could hold disease in its folds and could pass the disease on to wives. It was important for the preservation of God's people physically. But it was also a symbol of the need for the heart to be cleansed from sin's deadly disease. The essential surgery needed to happen on the inside, where God calls for taking away fleshly things that keep the heart from being spiritually devoted to Him and from true faith in Him and His will. Jeremiah later expanded on this theme (31:31–34).

7 The lion has come up from his thicket,
And the destroyer of nations is on his way.
He has gone forth from his place
To make your land desolate.
Your cities will be laid waste,
Without inhabitant.
8 For this, clothe yourself with sackcloth,
Lament and wail.
For the fierce anger of the LORD
Has not turned back from us.

9 "And it shall come to pass in that day," says the LORD,
"*That* the heart of the king shall perish,
And the heart of the princes;
The priests shall be astonished,
And the prophets shall wonder."

10 Then I said, "Ah, Lord GOD!
Surely You have greatly deceived this people and Jerusalem,
Saying, 'You shall have peace,'
Whereas the sword reaches to the heart."

11 At that time it will be said
To this people and to Jerusalem,
"A dry wind of the desolate heights *blows* in the wilderness
Toward the daughter of My people—
Not to fan or to cleanse—
12 A wind too strong for these will come for Me;
Now I will also speak judgment against them."

13 "Behold, he shall come up like clouds,
And his chariots like a whirlwind.
His horses are swifter than eagles.
Woe to us, for we are plundered!"

14 O Jerusalem, wash your heart from
wickedness,
That you may be saved.
How long shall your evil thoughts
lodge within you?
15 For a voice declares from Dan
And proclaims affliction from Mount
Ephraim:
16 "Make mention to the nations,
Yes, proclaim against Jerusalem,
That watchers come from a far country
And raise their voice against the cities
of Judah.
17 Like keepers of a field they are against
her all around,
Because she has been rebellious
against Me," says the LORD.

18 "Your ways and your doings
Have procured these *things* for you.
This *is* your wickedness,
Because it is bitter,
Because it reaches to your heart."

19 O my soul, my soul!
I am pained in my very heart!
My heart makes a noise in me;
I cannot hold my peace,
Because you have heard, O my soul,
The sound of the trumpet,
The alarm of war.
20 Destruction upon destruction is cried,
For the whole land is plundered.
Suddenly my tents are plundered,
And my curtains in a moment.
21 How long will I see the standard,
And hear the sound of the trumpet?

22 "For My people *are* foolish,
They have not known Me.
They *are* silly children,
And they have no understanding.
They *are* wise to do evil,
But to do good they have no
knowledge."

23 I beheld the earth, and indeed *it was*
without form, and void;
And the heavens, they *had* no light.
24 I beheld the mountains, and indeed
they trembled,
And all the hills moved back and forth.
25 I beheld, and indeed *there was* no man,
And all the birds of the heavens had fled.
26 I beheld, and indeed the fruitful land
was a wilderness,
And all its cities were broken down
At the presence of the LORD,
By His fierce anger.
27 For thus says the LORD:
"The whole land shall be desolate;
Yet I will not make a full end.
28 For this shall the earth mourn,
And the heavens above be black,
Because I have spoken.
I have purposed and will not relent,
Nor will I turn back from it.
29 The whole city shall flee from the noise
of the horsemen and bowmen.
They shall go into thickets and climb
up on the rocks.
Every city *shall be* forsaken,
And not a man shall dwell in it.

30 "And *when* you *are* plundered,
What will you do?
Though you clothe yourself with
crimson,
Though you adorn *yourself* with
ornaments of gold,
Though you enlarge your eyes with
paint,
In vain you will make yourself fair;
Your lovers will despise you;
They will seek your life.

31 "For I have heard a voice as of a woman
in labor,
The anguish as of her who brings forth
her first child,
The voice of the daughter of Zion
bewailing herself;
She spreads her hands, *saying,*
'Woe *is* me now, for my soul is weary
Because of murderers!'

Psalm 116:15–19

15 Precious in the sight of the LORD
Is the death of His saints.
16 O LORD, truly I *am* Your servant;
I *am* Your servant, the son of Your
maidservant;
You have loosed my bonds.
17 I will offer to You the sacrifice of
thanksgiving,
And will call upon the name of the
LORD.
18 I will pay my vows to the LORD
Now in the presence of all His people,
19 In the courts of the LORD's house,
In the midst of you, O Jerusalem.
Praise the LORD!

Proverbs 27:2

2 Let another man praise you, and not
your own mouth;
A stranger, and not your own lips.

Philippians 4:1–23

4 Therefore, my beloved and longed-for
brethren, my joy and crown, so stand fast
in the Lord, beloved.
2 I implore Euodia and I implore Syntyche to
be of the same mind in the Lord. 3 And I urge
you also, true companion, help these women
who labored with me in the gospel, with
Clement also, and the rest of my fellow workers, whose names *are* in the Book of Life.
4 Rejoice in the Lord always. Again I will say,
rejoice!

4:4 Rejoice in the Lord. Paul's familiar theme throughout the epistle, which has already been heard in chapters 1 and 2. "In the Lord" signifies the sphere in which the believers' joy exists—a sphere unrelated to the circumstances of life, but related to an unassailable, unchanging relationship to the sovereign Lord.

4:12 abased…abound. Paul knew how to get along with humble means (food, clothing, daily necessities) and how to live in prosperity ("to overflow"). **to be full and to be hungry.** The Greek word translated "to be full" was used of feeding and fattening animals. Paul knew how to be content when he had plenty to eat and when he was deprived of enough to eat.

4:13 I can do all things. Paul uses a Greek verb that means "to be strong" or "to have strength" (Acts 19:16,20; James 5:16). He had strength to withstand "all things" (vv. 11,12), including both difficulty and prosperity in the material world. **through Christ who strengthens me.** The Greek word for strengthen means "to put power in." Because believers are in Christ (Gal. 2:20), He infuses them with His strength to sustain them until they receive some provision (Eph. 3:16–20; 2 Cor. 12:10).

5 Let your gentleness be known to all men.
The Lord *is* at hand.
6 Be anxious for nothing, but in everything
by prayer and supplication, with thanksgiving,
let your requests be made known to God; 7 and
the peace of God, which surpasses all understanding, will guard your hearts and minds
through Christ Jesus.
8 Finally, brethren, whatever things are true,
whatever things *are* noble, whatever things
are just, whatever things *are* pure, whatever
things *are* lovely, whatever things *are* of good
report, if *there is* any virtue and if *there is* anything praiseworthy—meditate on these
things. 9 The things which you learned and
received and heard and saw in me, these do,
and the God of peace will be with you.
10 But I rejoiced in the Lord greatly that now
at last your care for me has flourished again;
though you surely did care, but you lacked
opportunity. 11 Not that I speak in regard to
need, for I have learned in whatever state I
am, to be content: 12 I know how to be abased,
and I know how to abound. Everywhere and
in all things I have learned both to be full and
to be hungry, both to abound and to suffer
need. 13 I can do all things through Christ who
strengthens me.
14 Nevertheless you have done well that you
shared in my distress. 15 Now you Philippians
know also that in the beginning of the gospel,
when I departed from Macedonia, no church
shared with me concerning giving and receiving but you only. 16 For even in Thessalonica
you sent *aid* once and again for my necessities. 17 Not that I seek the gift, but I seek the
fruit that abounds to your account. 18 Indeed I
have all and abound. I am full, having received
from Epaphroditus the things *sent* from you, a
sweet-smelling aroma, an acceptable sacrifice,
well pleasing to God. 19 And my God shall supply all your need according to His riches in
glory by Christ Jesus. 20 Now to our God and
Father *be* glory forever and ever. Amen.
21 Greet every saint in Christ Jesus. The
brethren who are with me greet you. 22 All the
saints greet you, but especially those who are
of Caesar's household.
23 The grace of our Lord Jesus Christ be with
you all. Amen.

DAY 9: How do we keep the peace of God in our lives?

Paul tells us to "be anxious for nothing" (Phil. 4:6). Fret and worry indicate a lack of trust in God's wisdom, sovereignty, or power. Delighting in the Lord and meditating on His Word are a great antidote to anxiety (Ps. 1:2). "In everything by prayer and supplication, with thanksgiving,…requests." All difficulties are within God's purposes. Gratitude to God accompanies all true prayer.

"And the peace of God" (v. 7). Inner calm or tranquillity is promised to the believer who has a thankful attitude based on an unwavering confidence that God is able and willing to do what is best for His children (Rom. 8:28). "Which surpasses all understanding." This refers to the divine origin of peace. It transcends human intellect, analysis, and insight. "Will guard." A military term meaning "to keep watch over." God's peace guards believers from anxiety, doubt, fear, and distress. "Your hearts and minds." Paul was not making a distinction between the two—he was giving a comprehensive statement referring to the whole inner person. Because of the believer's union with Christ, He guards his inner being with His peace.

And believers are to think on what is true (v. 8), what is found in God (2 Tim. 2:25), in Christ (Eph. 4:20,21), in the Holy Spirit (John 16:13), and in God's Word (John 17:17). They are to think on what is "worthy of respect," whatever is worthy of awe and adoration, i.e., the sacred as opposed to the profane. The believer is to think in harmony with God's divine standard of holiness and on what is morally clean and undefiled. Believers are to focus on whatever is lovely, "pleasing" or "amiable," and that which is highly regarded or thought well of. If they follow the truth of God proclaimed, along with the example of that truth lived by Paul before them, "the God of peace will be with [them]" (v. 9). God is peace (Rom. 16:20; Eph. 2:14), makes peace with sinners through Christ (2 Cor. 5:18–20), and gives perfect peace in trouble (v. 7).

OCTOBER 10

Jeremiah 5:1–6:30

5 "Run to and fro through the streets
of Jerusalem;
See now and know;
And seek in her open places
If you can find a man,
If there is *anyone* who executes
judgment,
Who seeks the truth,
And I will pardon her.
2 Though they say, '*As* the LORD lives,'
Surely they swear falsely."

3 O LORD, *are* not Your eyes on the
truth?
You have stricken them,
But they have not grieved;
You have consumed them,
But they have refused to receive
correction.
They have made their faces harder
than rock;
They have refused to return.

4 Therefore I said, "Surely these *are*
poor.
They are foolish;
For they do not know the way of the
LORD,
The judgment of their God.
5 I will go to the great men and speak to
them,
For they have known the way of the
LORD,
The judgment of their God."
But these have altogether broken the
yoke
And burst the bonds.
6 Therefore a lion from the forest shall
slay them,
A wolf of the deserts shall destroy
them;
A leopard will watch over their cities.
Everyone who goes out from there
shall be torn in pieces,
Because their transgressions are many;
Their backslidings have increased.

7 "How shall I pardon you for this?
Your children have forsaken Me
And sworn by *those that are* not gods.
When I had fed them to the full,
Then they committed adultery
And assembled themselves by troops
in the harlots' houses.
8 They were *like* well-fed lusty stallions;
Every one neighed after his neighbor's
wife.
9 Shall I not punish *them* for these *things?*"
says the LORD.
"And shall I not avenge Myself on such
a nation as this?

10 "Go up on her walls and destroy,
But do not make a complete end.
Take away her branches,
For they *are* not the LORD's.
11 For the house of Israel and the house
of Judah
Have dealt very treacherously with
Me," says the LORD.

12 They have lied about the LORD,
And said, "*It is* not He.
Neither will evil come upon us,
Nor shall we see sword or famine.
13 And the prophets become wind,
For the word *is* not in them.
Thus shall it be done to them."

5:10 not the LORD's. The people, depicted as vine branches to be destroyed (11:16,17), did not genuinely know the Lord in a saving relationship, but had forsaken Him and given allegiance to other gods. The description of having eyes but not seeing and ears but not hearing (v. 21) is used by Isaiah (6:9) and Jesus Christ (Matt. 13:13) for such false professors as these branches. Jesus also referred to false branches which were burned (John 15:2,6).

14 Therefore thus says the LORD God of hosts:

"Because you speak this word,
Behold, I will make My words in your mouth fire,
And this people wood,
And it shall devour them.
15 Behold, I will bring a nation against you from afar,
O house of Israel," says the LORD.
"It *is* a mighty nation,
It *is* an ancient nation,
A nation whose language you do not know,
Nor can you understand what they say.
16 Their quiver *is* like an open tomb;
They *are* all mighty men.
17 And they shall eat up your harvest and your bread,
Which your sons and daughters should eat.
They shall eat up your flocks and your herds;
They shall eat up your vines and your fig trees;
They shall destroy your fortified cities,
In which you trust, with the sword.

18 "Nevertheless in those days," says the LORD, "I will not make a complete end of you.
19 And it will be when you say, 'Why does the LORD our God do all these *things* to us?' then you shall answer them, 'Just as you have forsaken Me and served foreign gods in your land, so you shall serve aliens in a land *that is* not yours.'

20 "Declare this in the house of Jacob
And proclaim it in Judah, saying,
21 'Hear this now, O foolish people,
Without understanding,
Who have eyes and see not,
And who have ears and hear not:
22 Do you not fear Me?' says the LORD.
'Will you not tremble at My presence,
Who have placed the sand as the bound of the sea,
By a perpetual decree, that it cannot pass beyond it?
And though its waves toss to and fro,
Yet they cannot prevail;
Though they roar, yet they cannot pass over it.
23 But this people has a defiant and rebellious heart;
They have revolted and departed.
24 They do not say in their heart,
"Let us now fear the LORD our God,
Who gives rain, both the former and the latter, in its season.
He reserves for us the appointed weeks of the harvest."
25 Your iniquities have turned these *things* away,
And your sins have withheld good from you.

26 'For among My people are found wicked *men;*
They lie in wait as one who sets snares;
They set a trap;
They catch men.
27 As a cage is full of birds,
So their houses *are* full of deceit.
Therefore they have become great and grown rich.
28 They have grown fat, they are sleek;
Yes, they surpass the deeds of the wicked;
They do not plead the cause,
The cause of the fatherless;
Yet they prosper,
And the right of the needy they do not defend.
29 Shall I not punish *them* for these *things?*' says the LORD.
'Shall I not avenge Myself on such a nation as this?'

30 "An astonishing and horrible thing
Has been committed in the land:
31 The prophets prophesy falsely,
And the priests rule by their *own* power;
And My people love *to have it* so.
But what will you do in the end?

6 "O you children of Benjamin,
Gather yourselves to flee from the midst of Jerusalem!
Blow the trumpet in Tekoa,
And set up a signal-fire in Beth Haccerem;
For disaster appears out of the north,

And great destruction.
2 I have likened the daughter of Zion
To a lovely and delicate woman.
3 The shepherds with their flocks shall
come to her.
They shall pitch *their* tents against her
all around.
Each one shall pasture in his own place."

4 "Prepare war against her;
Arise, and let us go up at noon.
Woe to us, for the day goes away,
For the shadows of the evening are
lengthening.
5 Arise, and let us go by night,
And let us destroy her palaces."

6 For thus has the LORD of hosts said:

"Cut down trees,
And build a mound against Jerusalem.
This *is* the city to be punished.
She *is* full of oppression in her midst.
7 As a fountain wells up with water,
So she wells up with her wickedness.
Violence and plundering are heard in
her.
Before Me continually *are* grief and
wounds.
8 Be instructed, O Jerusalem,
Lest My soul depart from you;
Lest I make you desolate,
A land not inhabited."

9 Thus says the LORD of hosts:

"They shall thoroughly glean as a vine
the remnant of Israel;
As a grape-gatherer, put your hand
back into the branches."

10 To whom shall I speak and give warning,
That they may hear?
Indeed their ear *is* uncircumcised,
And they cannot give heed.
Behold, the word of the LORD is a
reproach to them;
They have no delight in it.
11 Therefore I am full of the fury of the
LORD.
I am weary of holding *it* in.
"I will pour it out on the children
outside,
And on the assembly of young men
together;
For even the husband shall be taken
with the wife,
The aged with *him who is* full of days.
12 And their houses shall be turned over
to others,
Fields and wives together;
For I will stretch out My hand
Against the inhabitants of the land,"
says the LORD.
13 "Because from the least of them even to
the greatest of them,
Everyone *is* given to covetousness;
And from the prophet even to the
priest,
Everyone deals falsely.
14 They have also healed the hurt of My
people slightly,
Saying, 'Peace, peace!'
When *there is* no peace.

6:14 'Peace, peace!' Wicked leaders among the prophets and priests (v. 13) proclaimed peace falsely and gave weak and brief comfort. They provided no true healing from the spiritual wound, not having discernment to deal with the sin and its effects (v. 15). The need was to return to obedience (v. 16).

15 Were they ashamed when they had
committed abomination?
No! They were not at all ashamed;
Nor did they know how to blush.
Therefore they shall fall among those
who fall;
At the time I punish them,
They shall be cast down," says the
LORD.

16 Thus says the LORD:

"Stand in the ways and see,
And ask for the old paths, where the
good way *is,*
And walk in it;
Then you will find rest for your souls.
But they said, 'We will not walk *in it.*'
17 Also, I set watchmen over you, *saying,*
'Listen to the sound of the trumpet!'
But they said, 'We will not listen.'
18 Therefore hear, you nations,
And know, O congregation, what *is*
among them.
19 Hear, O earth!
Behold, I will certainly bring calamity
on this people—
The fruit of their thoughts,
Because they have not heeded My
words
Nor My law, but rejected it.
20 For what purpose to Me

Comes frankincense from Sheba,
And sweet cane from a far country?
Your burnt offerings *are* not
acceptable,
Nor your sacrifices sweet to Me."

21 Therefore thus says the LORD:

"Behold, I will lay stumbling blocks
before this people,
And the fathers and the sons together
shall fall on them.
The neighbor and his friend shall
perish."

22 Thus says the LORD:

"Behold, a people comes from the north
country,
And a great nation will be raised from
the farthest parts of the earth.
23 They will lay hold on bow and spear;
They *are* cruel and have no mercy;
Their voice roars like the sea;
And they ride on horses,
As men of war set in array against you,
O daughter of Zion."

24 We have heard the report of it;
Our hands grow feeble.
Anguish has taken hold of us,
Pain as of a woman in labor.
25 Do not go out into the field,
Nor walk by the way.
Because of the sword of the enemy,
Fear *is* on every side.
26 O daughter of my people,
Dress in sackcloth
And roll about in ashes!
Make mourning *as for* an only son,
most bitter lamentation;
For the plunderer will suddenly come
upon us.

27 "I have set you *as* an assayer *and* a
fortress among My people,
That you may know and test their way.
28 They *are* all stubborn rebels, walking
as slanderers.
They are bronze and iron,
They *are* all corrupters;
29 The bellows blow fiercely,
The lead is consumed by the fire;
The smelter refines in vain,
For the wicked are not drawn off.
30 *People* will call them rejected silver,
Because the LORD has rejected them."

Psalm 117:1–2

Praise the LORD, all you Gentiles!
Laud Him, all you peoples!

2 For His merciful kindness is great
toward us,
And the truth of the LORD *endures*
forever.

Praise the LORD!

Proverbs 27:3–4

3 A stone *is* heavy and sand *is* weighty,
But a fool's wrath *is* heavier than both
of them.

4 Wrath *is* cruel and anger a torrent,
But who *is* able to stand before
jealousy?

Colossians 1:1–29

1 Paul, an apostle of Jesus Christ by the will of
God, and Timothy our brother,

2 To the saints and faithful brethren in Christ
who are in Colosse:

Grace to you and peace from God our
Father and the Lord Jesus Christ.

3 We give thanks to the God and Father of
our Lord Jesus Christ, praying always for you,
4 since we heard of your faith in Christ Jesus
and of your love for all the saints; 5 because of
the hope which is laid up for you in heaven, of
which you heard before in the word of the
truth of the gospel, 6 which has come to you, as
it has also in all the world, and is bringing
forth fruit, as *it is* also among you since the
day you heard and knew the grace of God in
truth; 7 as you also learned from Epaphras, our
dear fellow servant, who is a faithful minister
of Christ on your behalf, 8 who also declared to
us your love in the Spirit.

9 For this reason we also, since the day we
heard it, do not cease to pray for you, and to ask
that you may be filled with the knowledge of
His will in all wisdom and spiritual understanding; 10 that you may walk worthy of the
Lord, fully pleasing *Him*, being fruitful in
every good work and increasing in the knowledge of God; 11 strengthened with all might,
according to His glorious power, for all
patience and longsuffering with joy; 12 giving
thanks to the Father who has qualified us to
be partakers of the inheritance of the saints in
the light. 13 He has delivered us from the power
of darkness and conveyed *us* into the kingdom
of the Son of His love, 14 in whom we have
redemption through His blood, the forgiveness of sins.

15 He is the image of the invisible God, the
firstborn over all creation. 16 For by Him all things
were created that are in heaven and that are on
earth, visible and invisible, whether thrones or

1:12 qualified us. The Greek word means "to make sufficient," "to empower," or "to authorize." God qualifies us only through the finished work of the Savior. Apart from God's grace through Jesus Christ, all people would be qualified only to receive His wrath. **inheritance.** Literally, "for the portion of the lot." Each believer will receive his own individual portion of the total divine inheritance, an allusion to the partitioning of Israel's inheritance in Canaan (Num. 26:52–56; 33:51–54; Josh. 14:1,2). **in the light.** Scripture represents "light" intellectually as divine truth (Ps. 119:130) and morally as divine purity (Eph. 5:8–14; 1 John 1:5). The saints' inheritance exists in the spiritual realm of truth and purity where God Himself dwells (1 Tim. 6:16). Light, then, is a synonym for God's kingdom.

1:19 all the fullness. A term likely used by those in the Colossian heresy to refer to divine powers and attributes they believed were divided among various emanations. Paul countered that by asserting that the fullness of Deity—all the divine powers and attributes—was not spread out among created beings but completely dwelt in Christ alone.

1:27 Gentiles:...Christ in you. The Old Testament predicted the coming of the Messiah and that the Gentiles would partake of salvation (Is. 42:6; 45:21,22; 49:6; 52:10; 60:1–3; Pss. 22:27; 65:5; 98:2,3), but it did not reveal that the Messiah would actually live in each member of His redeemed church, made up mostly of Gentiles. That believers, both Jew and Gentile, now possess the surpassing riches of the indwelling Christ is the glorious revealed mystery. **the hope of glory.** The indwelling Spirit of Christ is the guarantee to each believer of future glory.

dominions or principalities or powers. All
things were created through Him and for Him.
17And He is before all things, and in Him all
things consist. 18And He is the head of the body,
the church, who is the beginning, the firstborn
from the dead, that in all things He may have
the preeminence.
19For it pleased *the Father that* in Him all the
fullness should dwell, 20and by Him to reconcile all things to Himself, by Him, whether
things on earth or things in heaven, having
made peace through the blood of His cross.
21And you, who once were alienated and
enemies in your mind by wicked works, yet
now He has reconciled 22in the body of His
flesh through death, to present you holy, and
blameless, and above reproach in His sight—
23if indeed you continue in the faith, grounded
and steadfast, and are not moved away from
the hope of the gospel which you heard,
which was preached to every creature under
heaven, of which I, Paul, became a minister.
24I now rejoice in my sufferings for you, and
fill up in my flesh what is lacking in the afflictions of Christ, for the sake of His body, which
is the church, 25of which I became a minister
according to the stewardship from God which
was given to me for you, to fulfill the word of
God, 26the mystery which has been hidden
from ages and from generations, but now has
been revealed to His saints. 27To them God
willed to make known what are the riches of
the glory of this mystery among the Gentiles:
which is Christ in you, the hope of glory. 28Him
we preach, warning every man and teaching
every man in all wisdom, that we may present
every man perfect in Christ Jesus. 29To this
end I also labor, striving according to His
working which works in me mightily.

DAY 10: How does Colossians 1:15,16 define Christ as God?

The Greek word for "image" means "copy" or "likeness." Jesus Christ is the perfect image—the exact likeness—of God and is in the very form of God (Phil. 2:6; John 1:14; 14:9) and has been so from all eternity. By describing Jesus in this manner, Paul emphasizes that He is both the representation and manifestation of God. Thus, He is fully God in every way (2:9; John 8:58; 10:30–33; Heb. 1:8).

"The firstborn over all creation." The Greek word for "firstborn" can refer to one who was born first chronologically, but most often refers to preeminence in position or rank (Heb. 1:6; Rom. 8:29). In both Greek and Jewish culture, the firstborn was the ranking son who had received the right of inheritance from his father, whether he was born first or not. It is used of Israel who, not being the first nation, was however the preeminent nation (Ex. 4:22; Jer. 31:9). Firstborn in this context clearly means highest in rank, not first created (Ps. 89:27; Rev. 1:5) for several reasons:

1. Christ cannot be both "first begotten" and "only begotten" (John 1:14,18; 3:16,18; 1 John 4:9);

2. when the "firstborn" is one of a class, the class is in the plural form (v. 18; Rom. 8:29), but "creation," the class here, is in a singular form;

3. if Paul was teaching that Christ was a created being, he was agreeing with the heresy he was writing to refute; and

4. it is impossible for Christ to be both created and the Creator of everything (v. 16).

Thus Jesus is the firstborn in the sense that He has the preeminence (v. 18) and possesses the right of inheritance "over all creation" (Heb. 1:2; Rev. 5:1–7,13). He existed before the creation and is exalted in rank above it.

The false teachers had incorporated into their heresy the worship of angels, including the lie that Jesus was one of them, merely a spirit created by God and inferior to Him. Paul rejected that and made it clear that angels, whatever their rank, whether holy or fallen, are mere creatures, and their Creator is none other than the preeminent One, the Lord Savior, Jesus Christ (v. 16). The purpose of His catalog of angelic ranks is to show the immeasurable superiority of Christ over any being the false teachers might suggest.

OCTOBER 11

Jeremiah 7:1–8:22

7 The word that came to Jeremiah from the
LORD, saying, 2"Stand in the gate of the
LORD's house, and proclaim there this word,

7:1 The word that came. This was Jeremiah's first temple sermon (v. 2); another is found in chapter 26. God was aroused against the sins He names (vv. 6,19), especially at His temple becoming a den of thieves (v. 11). The point of this message, however, was that if Israel would repent, even at this late hour, God would still keep the conqueror from coming (vv. 3,7). They must reject lies such as the false hope that peace is certain, based on the reasoning that the Lord would never bring calamity on His own temple (v. 4). They must turn from their sins (vv. 3,5,9) and end their hypocrisy (v. 10).

and say, 'Hear the word of the LORD, all *you of*
Judah who enter in at these gates to worship
the LORD!' " 3Thus says the LORD of hosts, the
God of Israel: "Amend your ways and your
doings, and I will cause you to dwell in this
place. 4Do not trust in these lying words, saying,
'The temple of the LORD, the temple of the
LORD, the temple of the LORD *are* these.'
5"For if you thoroughly amend your ways
and your doings, if you thoroughly execute
judgment between a man and his neighbor, 6*if*
you do not oppress the stranger, the fatherless,
and the widow, and do not shed innocent
blood in this place, or walk after other gods to
your hurt, 7then I will cause you to dwell in
this place, in the land that I gave to your
fathers forever and ever.
8"Behold, you trust in lying words that cannot
profit. 9Will you steal, murder, commit
adultery, swear falsely, burn incense to Baal,
and walk after other gods whom you do not
know, 10and *then* come and stand before Me in
this house which is called by My name, and
say, 'We are delivered to do all these abominations'?
11Has this house, which is called by My
name, become a den of thieves in your eyes?
Behold, I, even I, have seen *it*," says the LORD.
12"But go now to My place which *was* in
Shiloh, where I set My name at the first, and
see what I did to it because of the wickedness
of My people Israel. 13And now, because you
have done all these works," says the LORD,
"and I spoke to you, rising up early and speaking,
but you did not hear, and I called you, but
you did not answer, 14therefore I will do to the
house which is called by My name, in which
you trust, and to this place which I gave to you
and your fathers, as I have done to Shiloh.
15And I will cast you out of My sight, as I have
cast out all your brethren—the whole posterity
of Ephraim.
16"Therefore do not pray for this people, nor
lift up a cry or prayer for them, nor make intercession
to Me; for I will not hear you. 17Do you
not see what they do in the cities of Judah and
in the streets of Jerusalem? 18The children
gather wood, the fathers kindle the fire, and
the women knead dough, to make cakes for
the queen of heaven; and *they* pour out drink
offerings to other gods, that they may provoke
Me to anger. 19Do they provoke Me to anger?"
says the LORD. "*Do they* not *provoke* themselves,
to the shame of their own faces?"
20Therefore thus says the Lord GOD: "Behold,
My anger and My fury will be poured
out on this place—on man and on beast, on

7:18 the queen of heaven. The Jews were worshiping Ishtar, an Assyrian and Babylonian goddess also called Ashtoreth and Astarte, the wife of Baal or Molech. Because these deities symbolized generative power, their worship involved prostitution.

7:22 I did not...command. Bible writers sometimes use apparent negation to make a comparative emphasis. What God commanded His people at the Exodus was not so much the offerings as it was the heart obedience which prompted the offerings.

the trees of the field and on the fruit of the
ground. And it will burn and not be quenched."
[21]Thus says the LORD of hosts, the God of Israel: "Add your burnt offerings to your sacrifices and eat meat. [22]For I did not speak to your
fathers, or command them in the day that I
brought them out of the land of Egypt, concerning burnt offerings or sacrifices. [23]But this
is what I commanded them, saying, 'Obey My
voice, and I will be your God, and you shall be
My people. And walk in all the ways that I
have commanded you, that it may be well with
you.' [24]Yet they did not obey or incline their
ear, but followed the counsels *and* the dictates
of their evil hearts, and went backward and
not forward. [25]Since the day that your fathers
came out of the land of Egypt until this day, I
have even sent to you all My servants the
prophets, daily rising up early and sending
them. [26]Yet they did not obey Me or incline
their ear, but stiffened their neck. They did
worse than their fathers.
[27]"Therefore you shall speak all these words
to them, but they will not obey you. You shall
also call to them, but they will not answer you.
[28]"So you shall say to them, 'This *is* a nation
that does not obey the voice of the LORD their
God nor receive correction. Truth has perished and has been cut off from their mouth.
[29]Cut off your hair and cast *it* away, and take up
a lamentation on the desolate heights; for the
LORD has rejected and forsaken the generation of His wrath.' [30]For the children of Judah
have done evil in My sight," says the LORD.
"They have set their abominations in the
house which is called by My name, to pollute
it. [31]And they have built the high places of
Tophet, which *is* in the Valley of the Son of
Hinnom, to burn their sons and their daughters in the fire, which I did not command, nor
did it come into My heart.
[32]"Therefore behold, the days are coming,"
says the LORD, "when it will no more be called
Tophet, or the Valley of the Son of Hinnom, but
the Valley of Slaughter; for they will bury in
Tophet until there is no room. [33]The corpses of
this people will be food for the birds of the
heaven and for the beasts of the earth. And no
one will frighten *them away.* [34]Then I will cause
to cease from the cities of Judah and from the
streets of Jerusalem the voice of mirth and the
voice of gladness, the voice of the bridegroom
and the voice of the bride. For the land shall
be desolate.

8 "At that time," says the LORD, "they shall
bring out the bones of the kings of Judah,
and the bones of its princes, and the bones of
the priests, and the bones of the prophets, and
the bones of the inhabitants of Jerusalem, out
of their graves. [2]They shall spread them
before the sun and the moon and all the host
of heaven, which they have loved and which
they have served and after which they have
walked, which they have sought and which
they have worshiped. They shall not be gathered nor buried; they shall be like refuse on
the face of the earth. [3]Then death shall be chosen rather than life by all the residue of those
who remain of this evil family, who remain in
all the places where I have driven them," says
the LORD of hosts.
[4]"Moreover you shall say to them, 'Thus says
the LORD:

"Will they fall and not rise?
Will one turn away and not return?
5 Why has this people slidden back,
Jerusalem, in a perpetual backsliding?
They hold fast to deceit,
They refuse to return.
6 I listened and heard,
But they do not speak aright.
No man repented of his wickedness,
Saying, 'What have I done?'
Everyone turned to his own course,
As the horse rushes into the battle.

7 "Even the stork in the heavens
Knows her appointed times;
And the turtledove, the swift, and the
swallow
Observe the time of their coming.
But My people do not know the
judgment of the LORD.

8 "How can you say, 'We *are* wise,
And the law of the LORD *is* with us'?
Look, the false pen of the scribe
certainly works falsehood.
9 The wise men are ashamed,

They are dismayed and taken.
Behold, they have rejected the word of the LORD;
So what wisdom do they have?
10 Therefore I will give their wives to others,
And their fields to those who will inherit *them;*
Because from the least even to the greatest
Everyone is given to covetousness;
From the prophet even to the priest
Everyone deals falsely.
11 For they have healed the hurt of the daughter of My people slightly,
Saying, 'Peace, peace!'
When *there is* no peace.
12 Were they ashamed when they had committed abomination?
No! They were not at all ashamed,
Nor did they know how to blush.
Therefore they shall fall among those who fall;
In the time of their punishment
They shall be cast down," says the LORD.

13 "I will surely consume them," says the LORD.
"No grapes *shall be* on the vine,
Nor figs on the fig tree,
And the leaf shall fade;
And *the things* I have given them shall pass away from them." ' "

14 "Why do we sit still?
Assemble yourselves,
And let us enter the fortified cities,
And let us be silent there.
For the LORD our God has put us to silence
And given us water of gall to drink,
Because we have sinned against the LORD.
15 "*We* looked for peace, but no good *came;*
And for a time of health, and there was trouble!
16 The snorting of His horses was heard from Dan.
The whole land trembled at the sound of the neighing of His strong ones;
For they have come and devoured the land and all that is in it,
The city and those who dwell in it."

17 "For behold, I will send serpents among you,
Vipers which cannot be charmed,
And they shall bite you," says the LORD.

18 I would comfort myself in sorrow;
My heart *is* faint in me.
19 Listen! The voice,
The cry of the daughter of my people
From a far country:
"*Is* not the LORD in Zion?
Is not her King in her?"

"Why have they provoked Me to anger
With their carved images—
With foreign idols?"

20 "The harvest is past,
The summer is ended,
And we are not saved!"

21 For the hurt of the daughter of my people I am hurt.
I am mourning;
Astonishment has taken hold of me.
22 *Is there* no balm in Gilead,
Is there no physician there?
Why then is there no recovery
For the health of the daughter of my people?

Psalm 118:1–4

Oh, give thanks to the LORD, for *He is* good!
For His mercy *endures* forever.
2 Let Israel now say,
"His mercy *endures* forever."
3 Let the house of Aaron now say,
"His mercy *endures* forever."
4 Let those who fear the LORD now say,
"His mercy *endures* forever."

Proverbs 27:5–6

5 Open rebuke *is* better
Than love carefully concealed.
6 Faithful *are* the wounds of a friend,
But the kisses of an enemy *are* deceitful.

Colossians 2:1–23

2 For I want you to know what a great conflict I have for you and those in Laodicea, and *for* as many as have not seen my face in the flesh, 2that their hearts may be encouraged, being knit together in love, and *attaining* to all riches of the full assurance of understanding, to the knowledge of the mystery of God, both of the Father and of Christ, 3in whom are hidden all the treasures of wisdom and knowledge.

4Now this I say lest anyone should deceive you with persuasive words. 5For though I am absent in the flesh, yet I am with you in spirit, rejoicing to see your *good* order and the steadfastness of your faith in Christ.

6As you therefore have received Christ Jesus the Lord, so walk in Him, 7rooted and built up

in Him and established in the faith, as you have
been taught, abounding in it with thanksgiving.
[8]Beware lest anyone cheat you through philosophy and empty deceit, according to the tradition of men, according to the basic principles
of the world, and not according to Christ. [9]For
in Him dwells all the fullness of the Godhead
bodily; [10]and you are complete in Him, who is
the head of all principality and power.
[11]In Him you were also circumcised with the
circumcision made without hands, by putting
off the body of the sins of the flesh, by the circumcision of Christ, [12]buried with Him in baptism, in which you also were raised with *Him*
through faith in the working of God, who
raised Him from the dead. [13]And you, being
dead in your trespasses and the uncircumcision of your flesh, He has made alive together
with Him, having forgiven you all trespasses,
[14]having wiped out the handwriting of requirements that was against us, which was contrary
to us. And He has taken it out of the way, having nailed it to the cross. [15]Having disarmed
principalities and powers, He made a public
spectacle of them, triumphing over them in it.
[16]So let no one judge you in food or in drink,
or regarding a festival or a new moon or sabbaths, [17]which are a shadow of things to come,
but the substance is of Christ. [18]Let no one
cheat you of your reward, taking delight in *false*
humility and worship of angels, intruding into
those things which he has not seen, vainly
puffed up by his fleshly mind, [19]and not holding
fast to the Head, from whom all the body, nourished and knit together by joints and ligaments,
grows with the increase *that is* from God.

2:14 wiped out the handwriting. The Greek word translated "handwriting" referred to the handwritten certificate of debt by which a debtor acknowledged his indebtedness. All people (Rom. 3:23) owe God an unpayable debt for violating His law (Gal. 3:10; James 2:10; Matt. 18:23–27) and are thus under sentence of death (Rom. 6:23). Paul graphically compares God's forgiveness of believers' sins to wiping ink off a parchment. Through Christ's sacrificial death on the cross, God has totally erased our certificate of indebtedness and made our forgiveness complete. **nailed it to the cross.** This is another metaphor for forgiveness. The list of the crimes of a crucified criminal was nailed to the cross with that criminal to declare the violations he was being punished for. Believers' sins were all put to Christ's account, nailed to His cross as He paid the penalty in their place for them all, thus satisfying the just wrath of God against crimes requiring punishment in full.

[20]Therefore, if you died with Christ from the
basic principles of the world, why, as *though*
living in the world, do you subject yourselves
to regulations— [21]"Do not touch, do not taste,
do not handle," [22]which all concern things
which perish with the using—according to the
commandments and doctrines of men?
[23]These things indeed have an appearance of
wisdom in self-imposed religion, *false* humility,
and neglect of the body, *but are* of no value
against the indulgence of the flesh.

DAY 11: What were the false teachers trying to do to the Colossians?

"Beware lest anyone cheat you," Paul warns in Colossians 2:8. Here is the term for robbery. False teachers who are successful in getting people to believe lies rob them of truth, salvation, and blessing. "Through philosophy and empty deceit." "Philosophy" ("love of wisdom") appears only here in the New Testament. The word referred to more than merely the academic discipline, but described any theory about God, the world, or the meaning of life. Those embracing the Colossian heresy used it to describe the supposed higher knowledge they claimed to have attained. Paul, however, equates the false teachers' philosophy with "empty deceit"; that is, with worthless deception. "According to the basic principles of the world." Far from being advanced, profound knowledge, the false teachers' beliefs were simplistic and immature like all the rest of the speculations, ideologies, philosophies, and psychologies the fallen satanic and human system invents.

"For in Him dwells all the fullness of the Godhead bodily" (v. 9). Christ possesses the fullness of the divine nature and attributes. In Greek philosophical thought, matter was evil; spirit was good. Thus, it was unthinkable that God would ever take on a human body. Paul refutes that false teaching by stressing the reality of Christ's Incarnation. Jesus was not only fully God, but fully human as well. "And you are complete in Him" (v. 10). Believers are complete in Christ, both positionally by the imputed perfect righteousness of Christ and the complete sufficiency of all heavenly resources for spiritual maturity. "Who is the head of all principality and power." Jesus Christ is the creator and ruler of the universe and all its spiritual beings, not a lesser being emanating from God as the Colossian errorists maintained.

OCTOBER 12

Jeremiah 9:1–10:25

9 Oh, that my head were waters,
And my eyes a fountain of tears,
That I might weep day and night
For the slain of the daughter of my people!

9:1 waters,...tears. Jeremiah cared so greatly that he longed for the relief of flooding tears or a place of retreat to be free of the burden of Judah's sins for a while.

2 Oh, that I had in the wilderness
A lodging place for travelers;
That I might leave my people,
And go from them!
For they *are* all adulterers,
An assembly of treacherous men.

3 "And *like* their bow they have bent their tongues *for* lies.
They are not valiant for the truth on the earth.
For they proceed from evil to evil,
And they do not know Me," says the LORD.

4 "Everyone take heed to his neighbor,
And do not trust any brother;
For every brother will utterly supplant,
And every neighbor will walk with slanderers.

5 Everyone will deceive his neighbor,
And will not speak the truth;
They have taught their tongue to speak lies;
They weary themselves to commit iniquity.

6 Your dwelling place *is* in the midst of deceit;
Through deceit they refuse to know Me," says the LORD.

7 Therefore thus says the LORD of hosts:

"Behold, I will refine them and try them;
For how shall I deal with the daughter of My people?

8 Their tongue *is* an arrow shot out;
It speaks deceit;
One speaks peaceably to his neighbor with his mouth,
But in his heart he lies in wait.

9 Shall I not punish them for these *things?*" says the LORD.
"Shall I not avenge Myself on such a nation as this?"

10 I will take up a weeping and wailing for the mountains,
And for the dwelling places of the wilderness a lamentation,
Because they are burned up,
So that no one can pass through;
Nor can *men* hear the voice of the cattle.
Both the birds of the heavens and the beasts have fled;
They are gone.

11 "I will make Jerusalem a heap of ruins, a den of jackals.
I will make the cities of Judah desolate, without an inhabitant."

12 Who *is* the wise man who may understand
this? And *who is he* to whom the mouth of the
LORD has spoken, that he may declare it? Why
does the land perish *and* burn up like a wilderness, so that no one can pass through?
13 And the LORD said, "Because they have forsaken My law which I set before them, and
have not obeyed My voice, nor walked according to it, 14 but they have walked according to
the dictates of their own hearts and after the
Baals, which their fathers taught them,"
15 therefore thus says the LORD of hosts, the
God of Israel: "Behold, I will feed them, this
people, with wormwood, and give them water
of gall to drink. 16 I will scatter them also among
the Gentiles, whom neither they nor their
fathers have known. And I will send a sword
after them until I have consumed them."

17 Thus says the LORD of hosts:

"Consider and call for the mourning women,
That they may come;
And send for skillful *wailing* women,
That they may come.

18 Let them make haste
And take up a wailing for us,
That our eyes may run with tears,
And our eyelids gush with water.

19 For a voice of wailing is heard from Zion:
'How we are plundered!
We are greatly ashamed,
Because we have forsaken the land,
Because we have been cast out of our dwellings.' "

20 Yet hear the word of the LORD,
O women,
And let your ear receive the word of
His mouth;
Teach your daughters wailing,
And everyone her neighbor a
lamentation.
21 For death has come through our
windows,
Has entered our palaces,
To kill off the children—*no longer to be*
outside!
And the young men—*no longer* on the
streets!

22Speak, "Thus says the LORD:

'Even the carcasses of men shall fall as
refuse on the open field,
Like cuttings after the harvester,
And no one shall gather *them.*'"

23Thus says the LORD:

"Let not the wise *man* glory in his
wisdom,
Let not the mighty *man* glory in his
might,
Nor let the rich *man* glory in his riches;
24 But let him who glories glory in this,
That he understands and knows Me,
That I *am* the LORD, exercising
lovingkindness, judgment, and
righteousness in the earth.
For in these I delight," says the LORD.

25"Behold, the days are coming," says the
LORD, "that I will punish all *who are* circumcised with the uncircumcised— 26Egypt, Judah, Edom, the people of Ammon, Moab, and
all *who are* in the farthest corners, who dwell
in the wilderness. For all *these* nations *are*
uncircumcised, and all the house of Israel *are*
uncircumcised in the heart."

10 Hear the word which the LORD speaks to
you, O house of Israel.
2Thus says the LORD:

"Do not learn the way of the Gentiles;
Do not be dismayed at the signs of
heaven,
For the Gentiles are dismayed at them.
3 For the customs of the peoples *are*
futile;
For *one* cuts a tree from the forest,
The work of the hands of the
workman, with the ax.
4 They decorate it with silver and gold;
They fasten it with nails and hammers
So that it will not topple.
5 They *are* upright, like a palm tree,
And they cannot speak;
They must be carried,
Because they cannot go *by themselves.*
Do not be afraid of them,
For they cannot do evil,
Nor can they do any good."

6 Inasmuch as *there is* none like You,
O LORD
(You *are* great, and Your name *is* great
in might),
7 Who would not fear You, O King of the
nations?
For this is Your rightful due.
For among all the wise *men* of the
nations,
And in all their kingdoms,
There is none like You.

10:7 King. God, who sovereignly created and controls all things (vv. 12,16; Deut. 4:35), is alone the eternal, living God (Pss. 47; 145) worthy of trust. By contrast, earthly idols have to be fashioned by men (v. 9) and will perish (v. 15).

8 But they are altogether dull-hearted
and foolish;
A wooden idol *is* a worthless doctrine.
9 Silver is beaten into plates;
It is brought from Tarshish,
And gold from Uphaz,
The work of the craftsman
And of the hands of the metalsmith;
Blue and purple *are* their clothing;
They *are* all the work of skillful *men.*
10 But the LORD *is* the true God;
He *is* the living God and the
everlasting King.
At His wrath the earth will tremble,
And the nations will not be able to
endure His indignation.

11Thus you shall say to them: "The gods that
have not made the heavens and the earth shall
perish from the earth and from under these
heavens."

12 He has made the earth by His power,
He has established the world by His
wisdom,
And has stretched out the heavens at
His discretion.
13 When He utters His voice,
There is a multitude of waters in the
heavens:

"And He causes the vapors to ascend
from the ends of the earth.
He makes lightning for the rain,
He brings the wind out of His
treasuries."

14 Everyone is dull-hearted, without
knowledge;
Every metalsmith is put to shame by
an image;
For his molded image *is* falsehood,
And *there is* no breath in them.
15 They *are* futile, a work of errors;
In the time of their punishment they
shall perish.
16 The Portion of Jacob *is* not like them,
For He *is* the Maker of all *things,*
And Israel *is* the tribe of His
inheritance;
The LORD of hosts *is* His name.

17 Gather up your wares from the land,
O inhabitant of the fortress!

18 For thus says the LORD:
"Behold, I will throw out at this time
The inhabitants of the land,
And will distress them,
That they may find *it so.*"

19 Woe is me for my hurt!
My wound is severe.
But I say, "Truly this *is* an infirmity,
And I must bear it."
20 My tent is plundered,
And all my cords are broken;
My children have gone from me,
And they *are* no more.
There is no one to pitch my tent
anymore,
Or set up my curtains.

21 For the shepherds have become
dull-hearted,
And have not sought the LORD;
Therefore they shall not prosper,
And all their flocks shall be scattered.
22 Behold, the noise of the report has
come,
And a great commotion out of the
north country,
To make the cities of Judah desolate,
a den of jackals.

23 O LORD, I know the way of man *is* not
in himself;
It is not in man who walks to direct his
own steps.
24 O LORD, correct me, but with justice;
Not in Your anger, lest You bring me to
nothing.
25 Pour out Your fury on the Gentiles,
who do not know You,
And on the families who do not call on
Your name;
For they have eaten up Jacob,
Devoured him and consumed him,
And made his dwelling place desolate.

Psalm 118:5–9

5 I called on the LORD in distress;
The LORD answered me *and set me* in a
broad place.
6 The LORD *is* on my side;
I will not fear.
What can man do to me?
7 The LORD is for me among those who
help me;
Therefore I shall see *my desire* on
those who hate me.
8 *It is* better to trust in the LORD
Than to put confidence in man.
9 *It is* better to trust in the LORD
Than to put confidence in princes.

Proverbs 27:7

7 A satisfied soul loathes the
honeycomb,
But to a hungry soul every bitter thing
is sweet.

Colossians 3:1–25

3 If then you were raised with Christ, seek
those things which are above, where
Christ is, sitting at the right hand of God. 2 Set
your mind on things above, not on things on

3:2 Set your mind. This can also be translated "think" or "have this inner disposition." As a compass points north, the believer's entire disposition should point itself toward the things of heaven. Heavenly thoughts can only come by understanding heavenly realities from Scripture (Rom. 8:5; 12:2; Phil. 1:23; 4:8; 1 John 2:15–17).

the earth. 3 For you died, and your life is hidden with Christ in God. 4 When Christ *who is*
our life appears, then you also will appear with
Him in glory.

5 Therefore put to death your members which
are on the earth: fornication, uncleanness, passion, evil desire, and covetousness, which is
idolatry. 6 Because of these things the wrath of
God is coming upon the sons of disobedience,

[7]in which you yourselves once walked when you
lived in them.
[8]But now you yourselves are to put off all
these: anger, wrath, malice, blasphemy, filthy
language out of your mouth. [9]Do not lie to one
another, since you have put off the old man
with his deeds, [10]and have put on the new *man*
who is renewed in knowledge according to the
image of Him who created him, [11]where there
is neither Greek nor Jew, circumcised nor
uncircumcised, barbarian, Scythian, slave *nor*
free, but Christ *is* all and in all.
[12]Therefore, as *the* elect of God, holy and
beloved, put on tender mercies, kindness, humility, meekness, longsuffering; [13]bearing with one
another, and forgiving one another, if anyone has
a complaint against another; even as Christ forgave you, so you also *must do.* [14]But above all
these things put on love, which is the bond of
perfection. [15]And let the peace of God rule in
your hearts, to which also you were called in one
body; and be thankful. [16]Let the word of Christ
dwell in you richly in all wisdom, teaching and
admonishing one another in psalms and hymns
and spiritual songs, singing with grace in your
hearts to the Lord. [17]And whatever you do in word
or deed, *do* all in the name of the Lord Jesus, giving thanks to God the Father through Him.
[18]Wives, submit to your own husbands, as is
fitting in the Lord.
[19]Husbands, love your wives and do not be
bitter toward them.
[20]Children, obey your parents in all things,
for this is well pleasing to the Lord.

3:20 in all things. The only limit on a child's obedience is when parents demand something contrary to God's Word. For example, some children will act contrary to their parents' wishes even in coming to Christ (Luke 12:51–53; 14:26).

[21]Fathers, do not provoke your children, lest
they become discouraged.
[22]Bondservants, obey in all things your masters according to the flesh, not with eyeservice,
as men-pleasers, but in sincerity of heart, fearing God. [23]And whatever you do, do it heartily,
as to the Lord and not to men, [24]knowing that
from the Lord you will receive the reward of
the inheritance; for you serve the Lord Christ.
[25]But he who does wrong will be repaid for what
he has done, and there is no partiality.

DAY 12: What should a believer's relationship be to the Word of God?

In Colossians 3:16, Pauls says to "let the word of Christ dwell in you richly." This is Scripture, the Holy Spirit inspired Scripture, the word of revelation He brought into the world. "Dwell" means "to live in" or "to be at home," and "richly" may be more fully rendered "abundantly or extravagantly rich." Scripture should permeate every aspect of the believer's life and control every thought, word, and deed (Ps. 119:11; Matt. 13:9; Phil. 2:16; 2 Tim. 2:15). This concept is parallel to being filled with the Spirit in Ephesians 5:18 since the results of each are the same. In Ephesians 5:18, the power and motivation for all the effects is the filling of the Holy Spirit; here it is the word richly dwelling. Those two realities are really one. The Holy Spirit fills the life controlled by His Word. This emphasizes that the filling of the Spirit is not some ecstatic or emotional experience, but a steady controlling of the life by obedience to the truth of God's Word.

"Teaching and admonishing one another in psalms and hymns and spiritual songs" (v. 17). The early church sang the Psalms. Old Testament psalms put to music, primarily, but the term was used also of vocal music in general. "Hymns"—perhaps songs of praise distinguished from the Psalms which exalted God, in that they focused on the Lord Jesus Christ. "Spiritual songs"—probably songs of personal testimony expressing truths of the grace of salvation in Christ. "With grace in your hearts to the Lord"—not just public, but private. The Lord Himself is both the source and the object of the believer's song-filled heart. That such music pleases God can be seen in the account of the temple dedication, when the singing so honored the Lord that His glory came down (2 Chr. 5:12,14).

OCTOBER 13

Jeremiah 11:1–12:17

11 The word that came to Jeremiah from the
LORD, saying, [2]"Hear the words of this
covenant, and speak to the men of Judah and to
the inhabitants of Jerusalem; [3]and say to them,
'Thus says the LORD God of Israel: "Cursed *is*
the man who does not obey the words of this
covenant [4]which I commanded your fathers in
the day I brought them out of the land of Egypt,
from the iron furnace, saying, 'Obey My voice,

and do according to all that I command you; so
shall you be My people, and I will be your God,'
5that I may establish the oath which I have
sworn to your fathers, to give them 'a land flowing with milk and honey,' as *it is* this day." ' "
And I answered and said, "So be it, LORD."
6Then the LORD said to me, "Proclaim all
these words in the cities of Judah and in the
streets of Jerusalem, saying: 'Hear the words
of this covenant and do them. 7For I earnestly
exhorted your fathers in the day I brought
them up out of the land of Egypt, until this day,
rising early and exhorting, saying, "Obey My
voice." 8Yet they did not obey or incline their
ear, but everyone followed the dictates of his
evil heart; therefore I will bring upon them all
the words of this covenant, which I commanded *them* to do, but *which* they have not done.' "
9And the LORD said to me, "A conspiracy has
been found among the men of Judah and among
the inhabitants of Jerusalem. 10They have
turned back to the iniquities of their forefathers
who refused to hear My words, and they have
gone after other gods to serve them; the house
of Israel and the house of Judah have broken
My covenant which I made with their fathers."
11Therefore thus says the LORD: "Behold, I
will surely bring calamity on them which they
will not be able to escape; and though they cry
out to Me, I will not listen to them. 12Then the
cities of Judah and the inhabitants of Jerusalem
will go and cry out to the gods to whom they
offer incense, but they will not save them at all
in the time of their trouble. 13For *according to*
the number of your cities were your gods, O Judah; and *according to* the number of the streets
of Jerusalem you have set up altars to *that*
shameful thing, altars to burn incense to Baal.
14"So do not pray for this people, or lift up a
cry or prayer for them; for I will not hear *them*
in the time that they cry out to Me because of
their trouble.

15 "What has My beloved to do in My
house,
Having done lewd deeds with many?
And the holy flesh has passed from
you.
When you do evil, then you rejoice.
16 The LORD called your name,
Green Olive Tree, Lovely *and* of Good
Fruit.
With the noise of a great tumult
He has kindled fire on it,
And its branches are broken.

17"For the LORD of hosts, who planted you, has
pronounced doom against you for the evil of the
house of Israel and of the house of Judah, which

11:15 My beloved. A phrase showing God's sensitive regard for His relationship to Israel as a nation (2:2; 12:7). It does not carry the assumption, however, that every individual is spiritually saved (5:10a). **lewd deeds.** Shameful idolatry that defiled all that befits true temple worship, such as the examples in Ezekiel 8:6–13. These were gross violations of the first 3 commandments (Ex. 20:2–7). **holy flesh.** In some way, they corrupted the animal sacrifices by committing sin which they enjoyed.

they have done against themselves to provoke
Me to anger in offering incense to Baal."
18Now the LORD gave me knowledge *of it,*
and I know *it;* for You showed me their doings.
19But I *was* like a docile lamb brought to the
slaughter; and I did not know that they had
devised schemes against me, *saying,* "Let us
destroy the tree with its fruit, and let us cut
him off from the land of the living, that his
name may be remembered no more."

20 But, O LORD of hosts,
You who judge righteously,
Testing the mind and the heart,
Let me see Your vengeance on them,
For to You I have revealed my cause.

21"Therefore thus says the LORD concerning
the men of Anathoth who seek your life, saying,
'Do not prophesy in the name of the LORD, lest
you die by our hand'— 22therefore thus says the
LORD of hosts: 'Behold, I will punish them. The
young men shall die by the sword, their sons
and their daughters shall die by famine; 23and
there shall be no remnant of them, for I will
bring catastrophe on the men of Anathoth, *even*
the year of their punishment.' "

12 Righteous *are* You, O LORD,
when I plead with You;
Yet let me talk with You about *Your*
judgments.
Why does the way of the wicked
prosper?
Why are those happy who deal so
treacherously?
2 You have planted them, yes, they have
taken root;
They grow, yes, they bear fruit.
You *are* near in their mouth
But far from their mind.
3 But You, O LORD, know me;
You have seen me,

And You have tested my heart toward
You.
Pull them out like sheep for the
slaughter,
And prepare them for the day of
slaughter.
4 How long will the land mourn,
And the herbs of every field wither?
The beasts and birds are consumed,
For the wickedness of those who dwell
there,
Because they said, "He will not see our
final end."

5 "If you have run with the footmen, and
they have wearied you,
Then how can you contend with horses?
And *if* in the land of peace,
In which you trusted, *they wearied you*,
Then how will you do in the floodplain
of the Jordan?

12:5 If you have run. The Lord replied to Jeremiah telling him that if he grew faint with lesser trials and felt like quitting, what would he do when the battle got even harder? **floodplain of the Jordan.** The river in flood stage overflowed its banks into a plain that grew up as a thicket. The point is that Jeremiah needed to be ready to deal with tougher testings, pictured by the invader's overwhelming the land like a flood, or posing high danger as in the Jordan thicket where concealed wild animals could terrify a person.

6 For even your brothers, the house of
your father,
Even they have dealt treacherously
with you;
Yes, they have called a multitude after
you.
Do not believe them,
Even though they speak smooth words
to you.

7 "I have forsaken My house, I have left
My heritage;
I have given the dearly beloved of My
soul into the hand of her enemies.
8 My heritage is to Me like a lion in the
forest;
It cries out against Me;
Therefore I have hated it.
9 My heritage *is* to Me *like* a speckled
vulture;
The vultures all around *are* against her.
Come, assemble all the beasts of the
field,
Bring them to devour!

10 "Many rulers have destroyed My
vineyard,
They have trodden My portion
underfoot;
They have made My pleasant portion a
desolate wilderness.
11 They have made it desolate;
Desolate, it mourns to Me;
The whole land is made desolate,
Because no one takes *it* to heart.
12 The plunderers have come
On all the desolate heights in the
wilderness,
For the sword of the LORD shall devour
From *one* end of the land to the *other*
end of the land;
No flesh shall have peace.
13 They have sown wheat but reaped
thorns;
They have put themselves to pain *but*
do not profit.
But be ashamed of your harvest
Because of the fierce anger of the
LORD."

14 Thus says the LORD: "Against all My evil
neighbors who touch the inheritance which I
have caused My people Israel to inherit—behold, I will pluck them out of their land and
pluck out the house of Judah from among them.
15 Then it shall be, after I have plucked them out,
that I will return and have compassion on them
and bring them back, everyone to his heritage
and everyone to his land. 16 And it shall be, if
they will learn carefully the ways of My people,
to swear by My name, 'As the LORD lives,' as
they taught My people to swear by Baal, then
they shall be established in the midst of My people. 17 But if they do not obey, I will utterly pluck
up and destroy that nation," says the LORD.

Psalm 118:10–14

10 All nations surrounded me,
But in the name of the LORD I will
destroy them.
11 They surrounded me,
Yes, they surrounded me;
But in the name of the LORD I will
destroy them.
12 They surrounded me like bees;
They were quenched like a fire of
thorns;
For in the name of the LORD I will
destroy them.

13 You pushed me violently, that I might
fall,
But the LORD helped me.
14 The LORD *is* my strength and song,
And He has become my salvation.

Proverbs 27:8

8 Like a bird that wanders from its nest
Is a man who wanders from his place.

Colossians 4:1–18

4 Masters, give your bondservants what is
just and fair, knowing that you also have
a Master in heaven.
2Continue earnestly in prayer, being vigilant
in it with thanksgiving; 3meanwhile praying
also for us, that God would open to us a door
for the word, to speak the mystery of Christ,
for which I am also in chains, 4that I may make
it manifest, as I ought to speak.
5Walk in wisdom toward those *who are* outside, redeeming the time. 6*Let* your speech
always *be* with grace, seasoned with salt, that
you may know how you ought to answer each
one.
7Tychicus, a beloved brother, faithful minister, and fellow servant in the Lord, will tell you
all the news about me. 8I am sending him to
you for this very purpose, that he may know
your circumstances and comfort your hearts,
9with Onesimus, a faithful and beloved brother, who is *one* of you. They will make known to
you all things which *are happening* here.
10Aristarchus my fellow prisoner greets you,
with Mark the cousin of Barnabas (about
whom you received instructions: if he comes
to you, welcome him), 11and Jesus who is called
Justus. These *are my* only fellow workers for
the kingdom of God who are of the circumcision; they have proved to be a comfort to me.
12Epaphras, who is *one* of you, a bondservant
of Christ, greets you, always laboring fervently
for you in prayers, that you may stand perfect
and complete in all the will of God. 13For I bear
him witness that he has a great zeal for you,
and those who are in Laodicea, and those in
Hierapolis. 14Luke the beloved physician and
Demas greet you. 15Greet the brethren who are
in Laodicea, and Nymphas and the church that
is in his house.
16Now when this epistle is read among you,
see that it is read also in the church of the
Laodiceans, and that you likewise read the *epistle* from Laodicea. 17And say to Archippus,
"Take heed to the ministry which you have
received in the Lord, that you may fulfill it."
18This salutation by my own hand—Paul. Remember my chains. Grace *be* with you. Amen.

4:2 Continue earnestly. The Greek word means "to be courageously persistent" or "to hold fast and not let go" and refers here to persistent prayer (Acts 1:14; Rom. 12:12; Eph. 6:18; 1 Thess. 5:17; Luke 11:5–10; 18:1–8). **being vigilant.** In its most general sense this means to stay awake while praying. But Paul has in mind the broader implication of staying alert for specific needs about which to pray rather than being vague and unfocused.

4:6 with grace. To speak what is spiritual, wholesome, fitting, kind, sensitive, purposeful, complimentary, gentle, truthful, loving, and thoughtful. **seasoned with salt.** Just as salt not only flavors but prevents corruption, the Christian's speech should act not only as a blessing to others but as a purifying influence within the decaying society of the world.

4:18 by my own hand. Paul usually dictated his letters to an amanuensis (recording secretary), but would often add his own greeting in his own writing at the end of his letters (1 Cor. 16:21; Gal. 6:11; 2 Thess. 3:17; Philem. 19).

DAY 13: What were the Prison Epistles, and what prison was Paul in when he wrote them?

Four of Paul's letters are grouped as the Prison Epistles: Ephesians, Philippians, Colossians, and Philemon. Each of them includes clear internal references to the writer's prison surroundings (Eph. 3:1; 4:1; 6:20; Phil. 1:7,13,14,17; Col. 4:3,10,18; Philem. 1,9,10,13,23). The similarities between the details of Paul's imprisonment given in Acts and in the Prison Epistles support the traditional position that the letters were written from Rome. Among these details are: 1) Paul was guarded by soldiers (Acts 28:16; Phil. 1:13,14); 2) Paul was permitted to receive visitors (Acts 28:30; Phil. 4:18); and 3) Paul had the opportunity to preach the gospel (Acts 28:31; Eph. 6:18–20; Phil. 1:12–14; Col.4:2-4).

Caesarea and Ephesus have also been suggested as Paul's possible location when he wrote at least some of these letters. Paul was imprisoned in Caesarea for two years (Acts 24:27), but his opportunities to receive visitors and proclaim the gospel were severely limited during that time (Acts 23:35). The Prison Epistles express Paul's hope for a favorable verdict (Phil. 1:25; 2:24; Philem. 23). In Caesarea, however, Paul's only hope for release was either to bribe Felix (Acts 24:26) or agree to stand trial at Jerusalem under Festus (Acts 25:9). In the Prison Epistles, Paul expected the decision in his case to be final (Phil. 1:20–23; 2:17,23). That could not have been true at Caesarea, since Paul could and did appeal his case to the emperor.

Ephesus has been the other suggested location. Most of the same difficulties faced by the Caesarea suggestion face those who support Ephesus. The most telling argument against Ephesus as the point of origin for the Prison Epistles, however, is that there is no evidence that Paul was ever imprisoned at Ephesus.

In light of the serious difficulties faced by both the Caesarean and Ephesian views, no reason remains for rejecting the traditional view that Paul wrote the Prison Epistles from Rome while awaiting a hearing before the emperor on his appeal for justice as a Roman citizen.

OCTOBER 14

Jeremiah 13:1–14:22

13 Thus the LORD said to me: "Go and get yourself a linen sash, and put it around your waist, but do not put it in water." 2 So I got a sash according to the word of the LORD, and put *it* around my waist.

13:1 a linen sash. One of several signs Jeremiah enacted to illustrate God's message involved putting a linen sash (generally the inner garment against the skin) around his waist. This depicted Israel's close intimacy with God in the covenant, so that they could glorify Him (v. 11). **do not put it in water.** Signified the moral filth of the nation. Buried and allowed time to rot (v. 7), the sash pictured Israel as useless to God due to sin (v. 10). Hiding it by the Euphrates (v. 6) pointed to the land of Babylon, where God would exile Israel to deal with her pride (v. 9).

3 And the word of the LORD came to me the second time, saying, 4 "Take the sash that you acquired, which *is* around your waist, and arise, go to the Euphrates, and hide it there in a hole in the rock." 5 So I went and hid it by the Euphrates, as the LORD commanded me.

6 Now it came to pass after many days that the LORD said to me, "Arise, go to the Euphrates, and take from there the sash which I commanded you to hide there." 7 Then I went to the Euphrates and dug, and I took the sash from the place where I had hidden it; and there was the sash, ruined. It was profitable for nothing.

8 Then the word of the LORD came to me, saying, 9 "Thus says the LORD: 'In this manner I will ruin the pride of Judah and the great pride of Jerusalem. 10 This evil people, who refuse to hear My words, who follow the dictates of their hearts, and walk after other gods to serve them and worship them, shall be just like this sash which is profitable for nothing. 11 For as the sash clings to the waist of a man, so I have caused the whole house of Israel and the whole house of Judah to cling to Me,' says the LORD, 'that they may become My people, for renown, for praise, and for glory; but they would not hear.'

12 "Therefore you shall speak to them this word: 'Thus says the LORD God of Israel: "Every bottle shall be filled with wine." '

"And they will say to you, 'Do we not certainly know that every bottle will be filled with wine?'

13 "Then you shall say to them, 'Thus says the LORD: "Behold, I will fill all the inhabitants of this land—even the kings who sit on David's throne, the priests, the prophets, and all the inhabitants of Jerusalem—with drunkenness! 14 And I will dash them one against another, even the fathers and the sons together," says the LORD. "I will not pity nor spare nor have mercy, but will destroy them." ' "

15 Hear and give ear:
Do not be proud,
For the LORD has spoken.
16 Give glory to the LORD your God
Before He causes darkness,
And before your feet stumble
On the dark mountains,
And while you are looking for light,
He turns it into the shadow of death
And makes *it* dense darkness.
17 But if you will not hear it,
My soul will weep in secret for *your* pride;

My eyes will weep bitterly
And run down with tears,
Because the LORD's flock has been taken captive.

18 Say to the king and to the queen mother,
"Humble yourselves;
Sit down,
For your rule shall collapse, the crown of your glory."
19 The cities of the South shall be shut up,
And no one shall open *them;*
Judah shall be carried away captive, all of it;
It shall be wholly carried away captive.

20 Lift up your eyes and see
Those who come from the north.
Where *is* the flock *that* was given to you,
Your beautiful sheep?
21 What will you say when He punishes you?
For you have taught them
To be chieftains, to be head over you.
Will not pangs seize you,
Like a woman in labor?
22 And if you say in your heart,
"Why have these things come upon me?"
For the greatness of your iniquity
Your skirts have been uncovered,
Your heels made bare.
23 Can the Ethiopian change his skin or the leopard its spots?
Then may you also do good who are accustomed to do evil.

24 "Therefore I will scatter them like stubble
That passes away by the wind of the wilderness.
25 This is your lot,
The portion of your measures from Me," says the LORD,
"Because you have forgotten Me
And trusted in falsehood.
26 Therefore I will uncover your skirts over your face,
That your shame may appear.
27 I have seen your adulteries
And your *lustful* neighings,
The lewdness of your harlotry,
Your abominations on the hills in the fields.
Woe to you, O Jerusalem!
Will you still not be made clean?"

14 The word of the LORD that came to Jeremiah concerning the droughts.

2 "Judah mourns,
And her gates languish;
They mourn for the land,
And the cry of Jerusalem has gone up.
3 Their nobles have sent their lads for water;
They went to the cisterns *and* found no water.
They returned with their vessels empty;
They were ashamed and confounded
And covered their heads.
4 Because the ground is parched,
For there was no rain in the land,
The plowmen were ashamed;
They covered their heads.
5 Yes, the deer also gave birth in the field,
But left because there was no grass.
6 And the wild donkeys stood in the desolate heights;
They sniffed at the wind like jackals;
Their eyes failed because *there was* no grass."

7 O LORD, though our iniquities testify against us,
Do it for Your name's sake;
For our backslidings are many,
We have sinned against You.
8 O the Hope of Israel, his Savior in time of trouble,
Why should You be like a stranger in the land,
And like a traveler *who* turns aside to tarry for a night?
9 Why should You be like a man astonished,
Like a mighty one *who* cannot save?
Yet You, O LORD, *are* in our midst,
And we are called by Your name;
Do not leave us!

10 Thus says the LORD to this people:

"Thus they have loved to wander;
They have not restrained their feet.
Therefore the LORD does not accept them;
He will remember their iniquity now,
And punish their sins."

11 Then the LORD said to me, "Do not pray
for this people, for *their* good. 12 When they
fast, I will not hear their cry; and when they
offer burnt offering and grain offering, I will
not accept them. But I will consume them by
the sword, by the famine, and by the pestilence."
13 Then I said, "Ah, Lord GOD! Behold, the

prophets say to them, 'You shall not see the
sword, nor shall you have famine, but I will
give you assured peace in this place.' "
[14]And the LORD said to me, "The prophets
prophesy lies in My name. I have not sent
them, commanded them, nor spoken to them;
they prophesy to you a false vision, divination,
a worthless thing, and the deceit of their heart.
[15]Therefore thus says the LORD concerning the
prophets who prophesy in My name, whom I
did not send, and who say, 'Sword and famine
shall not be in this land'—'By sword and
famine those prophets shall be consumed!
[16]And the people to whom they prophesy shall
be cast out in the streets of Jerusalem because
of the famine and the sword; they will have no
one to bury them—them nor their wives, their
sons nor their daughters—for I will pour their
wickedness on them.'
[17]"Therefore you shall say this word to
them:

'Let my eyes flow with tears night and
day,
And let them not cease;
For the virgin daughter of my people
Has been broken with a mighty stroke,
with a very severe blow.
18 If I go out to the field,
Then behold, those slain with the sword!
And if I enter the city,
Then behold, those sick from famine!
Yes, both prophet and priest go about
in a land they do not know.' "

19 Have You utterly rejected Judah?
Has Your soul loathed Zion?
Why have You stricken us so that *there is* no healing for us?
We looked for peace, but *there was* no
good;
And for the time of healing, and there
was trouble.
20 We acknowledge, O LORD, our
wickedness
And the iniquity of our fathers,
For we have sinned against You.
21 Do not abhor *us*, for Your name's sake;
Do not disgrace the throne of Your
glory.
Remember, do not break Your
covenant with us.
22 Are there any among the idols of the
nations that can cause rain?
Or can the heavens give showers?
Are You not He, O LORD our God?
Therefore we will wait for You,
Since You have made all these.

Psalm 118:15–20

15 The voice of rejoicing and salvation
Is in the tents of the righteous;
The right hand of the LORD does
valiantly.
16 The right hand of the LORD is exalted;
The right hand of the LORD does
valiantly.
17 I shall not die, but live,
And declare the works of the LORD.
18 The LORD has chastened me severely,
But He has not given me over to death.

19 Open to me the gates of righteousness;
I will go through them,
And I will praise the LORD.
20 This is the gate of the LORD,
Through which the righteous shall
enter.

118:19 gates of righteousness. Most likely a figurative reference, i.e., spiritual gates through which the righteous pass (Ps. 100:4) rather than to the gates of the temple.

118:20 the gate. This points to the entryway which leads to the presence of the Lord. Jesus may have had this psalm in mind when He taught about "the narrow gate" in Matthew 7:13,14.

Proverbs 27:9

9 Ointment and perfume delight the heart,
And the sweetness of a man's friend
gives delight by hearty counsel.

1 Thessalonians 1:1–10

1 Paul, Silvanus, and Timothy,

To the church of the Thessalonians in God
the Father and the Lord Jesus Christ:

Grace to you and peace from God our
Father and the Lord Jesus Christ.
[2]We give thanks to God always for you all,
making mention of you in our prayers, [3]re-
membering without ceasing your work of
faith, labor of love, and patience of hope in our
Lord Jesus Christ in the sight of our God and
Father, [4]knowing, beloved brethren, your election by God. [5]For our gospel did not come to
you in word only, but also in power, and in the
Holy Spirit and in much assurance, as you
know what kind of men we were among you
for your sake.

6And you became followers of us and of the
Lord, having received the word in much affliction, with joy of the Holy Spirit, 7so that you
became examples to all in Macedonia and
Achaia who believe. 8For from you the word of
the Lord has sounded forth, not only in
Macedonia and Achaia, but also in every
place. Your faith toward God has gone out, so
that we do not need to say anything. 9For they
themselves declare concerning us what manner of entry we had to you, and how you
turned to God from idols to serve the living
and true God, 10and to wait for His Son from
heaven, whom He raised from the dead, *even*
Jesus who delivers us from the wrath to come.

1:6 followers. The Thessalonians had become third-generation mimics of Christ. Christ is the first; Paul is the second; and the Thessalonians are the third (1 Cor. 4:16; 11:1). **joy of the Holy Spirit.** Joy in the midst of suffering evidenced the reality of their salvation, which included the indwelling Holy Spirit (1 Cor. 3:16; 6:19).

DAY 14: Why was Paul writing to the Thessalonians?

Paul had originally traveled 100 miles from Philippi via Amphipolis and Apollonia to Thessalonica on his second missionary journey (A.D. 50; Acts 16:1–18:22). As his custom was upon arrival, he sought out the synagogue in which to teach the local Jews the gospel (Acts 17:1,2). On that occasion, he dialogued with them from the Old Testament concerning Christ's death and resurrection in order to prove that Jesus of Nazareth was truly the promised Messiah (Acts 17:2,3). Some Jews believed and soon after, Hellenistic proselytes and some wealthy women of the community also were converted (Acts 17:4).

Because of their effective ministry, the Jews had Paul's team evicted from the city (Acts 17:5–9), so they went south to evangelize Berea (Acts 17:10). There Paul had a similar experience to Thessalonica with conversions followed by hostility, so the believers sent Paul away. He headed for Athens, while Silvanus and Timothy remained in Berea (Acts 17:11–14). They rejoined Paul in Athens (Acts 17:15,16 with 1 Thess. 3:1), from which Timothy was later dispatched back to Thessalonica (3:2). Apparently, Silas afterwards traveled from Athens to Philippi while Paul journeyed on alone to Corinth (Acts 18:1). It was after Timothy and Silvanus rejoined Paul in Corinth (Acts 18:5) that he wrote 1 Thessalonians in response to Timothy's good report of the church.

Paul undoubtedly had multiple reasons for writing, all coming out of his supreme concern for the flock from which he had been separated. Some of Paul's purposes clearly included: 1) encouraging the church (1:2–10); 2) answering false allegations (2:1–12); 3) comforting the persecuted flock (2:13–16); 4) expressing his joy in their faith (2:17–3:13); 5) reminding them of the importance of moral purity (4:1–8); 6) condemning the sluggard lifestyle (4:9–12); 7) correcting a wrong understanding of prophetic events (4:13–5:11); 8) defusing tensions within the flock (5:12–15); and 9) exhorting the flock in the basics of Christian living (5:16–22).

OCTOBER 15

Jeremiah 15:1–16:21

15 Then the LORD said to me, "*Even* if Moses and Samuel stood before Me, My
mind *would* not *be* favorable toward this people. Cast *them* out of My sight, and let them go
forth. 2And it shall be, if they say to you,
'Where should we go?' then you shall tell
them, 'Thus says the LORD:

"Such as *are* for death, to death;
And such as *are* for the sword, to the
sword;
And such as *are* for the famine, to the
famine;
And such as *are* for the captivity, to the
captivity." '

3"And I will appoint over them four forms *of
destruction*," says the LORD: "the sword to slay,
the dogs to drag, the birds of the heavens and
the beasts of the earth to devour and destroy.
4I will hand them over to trouble, to all kingdoms of the earth, because of Manasseh the
son of Hezekiah, king of Judah, for what he
did in Jerusalem.

5 "For who will have pity on you,
O Jerusalem?
Or who will bemoan you?
Or who will turn aside to ask how you
are doing?
6 You have forsaken Me," says the LORD,
"You have gone backward.

Therefore I will stretch out My hand
against you and destroy you;
I am weary of relenting!
7 And I will winnow them with a
winnowing fan in the gates of the
land;
I will bereave *them* of children;
I will destroy My people,
Since they do not return from their
ways.
8 Their widows will be increased to Me
more than the sand of the seas;
I will bring against them,
Against the mother of the young men,
A plunderer at noonday;
I will cause anguish and terror to fall
on them suddenly.
9 "She languishes who has borne seven;
She has breathed her last;
Her sun has gone down
While *it was* yet day;
She has been ashamed and
confounded.
And the remnant of them I will deliver
to the sword
Before their enemies," says the LORD.

15:1–9 It was ineffective at this point to intercede for the nation. Even prayers by Moses (Num. 14:11–25) and Samuel (1 Sam. 12:19–25), eminent in intercession, would not defer judgment, where unrepentance persists. Chief among things provoking judgment was the intense sin of King Manasseh. Noted in v. 4, this provocation is recounted in 2 Kings 21:1–18, 2 Kings 23:26, which says the Lord did not relent from His anger because of this.

10 Woe is me, my mother,
That you have borne me,
A man of strife and a man of contention
to the whole earth!
I have neither lent for interest,
Nor have men lent to me for interest.
Every one of them curses me.
11 The LORD said:
"Surely it will be well with your
remnant;
Surely I will cause the enemy to
intercede with you
In the time of adversity and in the time
of affliction.
12 Can anyone break iron,
The northern iron and the bronze?
13 Your wealth and your treasures
I will give as plunder without price,
Because of all your sins,
Throughout your territories.
14 And I will make *you* cross over with
your enemies
Into a land *which* you do not know;
For a fire is kindled in My anger,
Which shall burn upon you."
15 O LORD, You know;
Remember me and visit me,
And take vengeance for me on my
persecutors.
In Your enduring patience, do not take
me away.
Know that for Your sake I have
suffered rebuke.
16 Your words were found, and I ate
them,
And Your word was to me the joy and
rejoicing of my heart;
For I am called by Your name,
O LORD God of hosts.
17 I did not sit in the assembly of the
mockers,
Nor did I rejoice;
I sat alone because of Your hand,
For You have filled me with indignation.
18 Why is my pain perpetual
And my wound incurable,
Which refuses to be healed?
Will You surely be to me like an
unreliable stream,
As waters *that* fail?
19 Therefore thus says the LORD:
"If you return,
Then I will bring you back;
You shall stand before Me;
If you take out the precious from the vile,
You shall be as My mouth.
Let them return to you,
But you must not return to them.
20 And I will make you to this people a
fortified bronze wall;
And they will fight against you,
But they shall not prevail against you;
For I *am* with you to save you
And deliver you," says the LORD.
21 "I will deliver you from the hand of the
wicked,
And I will redeem you from the grip of
the terrible."

16 The word of the LORD also came to me,
saying, 2 "You shall not take a wife, nor
shall you have sons or daughters in this place."
3 For thus says the LORD concerning the sons

16:2 You shall not take a wife. Since destruction and exile are soon to fall on Judah, the prophet must not have a wife and family. God's kindness will keep him from anxiety over them in the awful situation of suffering and death (v. 4).

and daughters who are born in this place, and
concerning their mothers who bore them and
their fathers who begot them in this land:
4“They shall die gruesome deaths; they shall
not be lamented nor shall they be buried, *but*
they shall be like refuse on the face of the earth.
They shall be consumed by the sword and by
famine, and their corpses shall be meat for the
birds of heaven and for the beasts of the earth.”
5For thus says the LORD: “Do not enter the
house of mourning, nor go to lament or
bemoan them; for I have taken away My peace
from this people,” says the LORD, “lovingkindness and mercies. 6Both the great and the
small shall die in this land. They shall not be
buried; neither shall men lament for them, cut
themselves, nor make themselves bald for
them. 7Nor shall *men* break *bread* in mourning
for them, to comfort them for the dead; nor
shall *men* give them the cup of consolation to
drink for their father or their mother. 8Also
you shall not go into the house of feasting to
sit with them, to eat and drink.”
9For thus says the LORD of hosts, the God
of Israel: “Behold, I will cause to cease from
this place, before your eyes and in your days,
the voice of mirth and the voice of gladness, the
voice of the bridegroom and the voice of the
bride.
10“And it shall be, when you show this people all these words, and they say to you, ‘Why
has the LORD pronounced all this great disaster against us? Or what *is* our iniquity? Or
what *is* our sin that we have committed
against the LORD our God?’ 11then you shall say
to them, ‘Because your fathers have forsaken
Me,’ says the LORD; ‘they have walked after
other gods and have served them and worshiped them, and have forsaken Me and not
kept My law. 12And you have done worse than
your fathers, for behold, each one follows the
dictates of his own evil heart, so that no one
listens to Me. 13Therefore I will cast you out of
this land into a land that you do not know, neither you nor your fathers; and there you shall
serve other gods day and night, where I will
not show you favor.’
14“Therefore behold, the days are coming,”
says the LORD, “that it shall no more be said,
‘The LORD lives who brought up the children of
Israel from the land of Egypt,’ 15but, ‘The LORD
lives who brought up the children of Israel
from the land of the north and from all the
lands where He had driven them.’ For I will
bring them back into their land which I gave to
their fathers.
16“Behold, I will send for many fishermen,”
says the LORD, “and they shall fish them; and
afterward I will send for many hunters, and
they shall hunt them from every mountain
and every hill, and out of the holes of the
rocks. 17For My eyes *are* on all their ways; they
are not hidden from My face, nor is their iniquity hidden from My eyes. 18And first I will
repay double for their iniquity and their sin,
because they have defiled My land; they have
filled My inheritance with the carcasses of their
detestable and abominable idols.”

19 O LORD, my strength and
my fortress,
My refuge in the day of affliction,
The Gentiles shall come to You
From the ends of the earth and say,
“Surely our fathers have inherited lies,
Worthlessness and unprofitable *things*.”
20 Will a man make gods for himself,
Which *are* not gods?

21 “Therefore behold, I will this once
cause them to know,
I will cause them to know
My hand and My might;
And they shall know that My name *is*
the LORD.

Psalm 118:21–24

21 I will praise You,
For You have answered me,
And have become my salvation.

22 The stone *which* the builders
rejected
Has become the chief cornerstone.
23 This was the LORD's doing;
It *is* marvelous in our eyes.
24 This *is* the day the LORD has made;
We will rejoice and be glad in it.

Proverbs 27:10

10 Do not forsake your own friend or your
father's friend,
Nor go to your brother's house in the
day of your calamity;
Better *is* a neighbor nearby than a
brother far away.

118:22 stone...builders rejected...chief cornerstone. Peter identified the chief cornerstone in the New Testament as Christ (Acts 4:11; 1 Pet. 2:7). In the parable of the vineyard (Matt. 21:42; Mark 12:10–11; Luke 20:17), the rejected son of the vineyard owner is likened to the rejected stone which became the chief cornerstone. Christ was that rejected stone. Jewish leaders were pictured as builders of the nation. Now, this passage in v. 22 has a historical basis which is paralleled in its major features by analogy with the rejection of Christ who came to deliver/save the nation. Moses' experience, as a type of Christ, pictured Christ's rejection. On at least 3 occasions, Moses (stone) was rejected by the Jews (builders) as their God sent the deliverer (chief cornerstone). For examples see Exodus 2:11–15; 14:10–14; 16:1–20.

1 Thessalonians 2:1–20

2 For you yourselves know, brethren, that
our coming to you was not in vain. [2]But
even after we had suffered before and were
spitefully treated at Philippi, as you know, we
were bold in our God to speak to you the
gospel of God in much conflict. [3]For our
exhortation *did* not *come* from error or
uncleanness, nor *was it* in deceit.

[4]But as we have been approved by God to be
entrusted with the gospel, even so we speak,
not as pleasing men, but God who tests our
hearts. [5]For neither at any time did we use flattering words, as you know, nor a cloak for covetousness—God *is* witness. [6]Nor did we seek
glory from men, either from you or from others,
when we might have made demands as apostles
of Christ. [7]But we were gentle among you, just
as a nursing *mother* cherishes her own children.
[8]So, affectionately longing for you, we were well
pleased to impart to you not only the gospel of
God, but also our own lives, because you had
become dear to us. [9]For you remember,
brethren, our labor and toil; for laboring night
and day, that we might not be a burden to any of
you, we preached to you the gospel of God.

2:7,8 gentle...as a nursing *mother*. Paul may have had in mind Moses' portrayal of himself as a nursing mother to Israel (Num. 11:12). He used the same tender picture with the Corinthians (2 Cor. 12:14,15) and the Galatians (Gal. 4:19). Paul's affection for the Thessalonians was like that felt by a mother willing to sacrifice her life for her child as was Christ who was willing to give up His own life for those who would be born again into the family of God (Matt. 20:28)

[10]You *are* witnesses, and God *also*, how
devoutly and justly and blamelessly we
behaved ourselves among you who believe;
[11]as you know how we exhorted, and comforted, and charged every one of you, as a father
does his own children, [12]that you would walk
worthy of God who calls you into His own
kingdom and glory.

[13]For this reason we also thank God without
ceasing, because when you received the word
of God which you heard from us, you welcomed *it* not *as* the word of men, but as it is in
truth, the word of God, which also effectively
works in you who believe. [14]For you, brethren,
became imitators of the churches of God
which are in Judea in Christ Jesus. For you
also suffered the same things from your own
countrymen, just as they *did* from the
Judeans, [15]who killed both the Lord Jesus and
their own prophets, and have persecuted us;
and they do not please God and are contrary
to all men, [16]forbidding us to speak to the
Gentiles that they may be saved, so as always
to fill up *the measure of* their sins; but wrath
has come upon them to the uttermost.

[17]But we, brethren, having been taken away
from you for a short time in presence, not in
heart, endeavored more eagerly to see your
face with great desire. [18]Therefore we wanted
to come to you—even I, Paul, time and
again—but Satan hindered us. [19]For what *is*
our hope, or joy, or crown of rejoicing? *Is it* not
even you in the presence of our Lord Jesus
Christ at His coming? [20]For you are our glory
and joy.

DAY 15: What is the effect of the Word of God working in a person's life?

"We also thank God without ceasing," Paul said, "because when you received the word of God which you heard from us, you welcomed it not as the word of men, but as it is in truth, the word of God" (1 Thess. 2:13). Paul's message from God is equated with the Old Testament (Mark 7:13). It was the message taught by the apostles (Acts 4:31; 6:2). Peter preached it to the Gentiles (Acts 11:1). It was the word Paul preached on his first missionary journey (Acts 13:5,7,44,48,49), his second (Acts 16:32; 17:13; 18:11), and his third (Acts 19:10).

"Which also effectively works in you who believe." The work of God's Word includes:

- saving (Rom. 10:17; 1 Pet. 1:23);
- teaching and training (2 Tim. 3:16,17);
- guiding (Ps. 119:105);
- counseling (Ps. 119:24);
- reviving (Ps. 119:154);
- restoring (Ps. 19:7);
- warning and rewarding (Ps. 19:11);
- nourishing (1 Pet. 2:2);
- judging (Heb. 4:12);
- sanctifying (John 17:17);
- freeing (John 8:31,32);
- enriching (Col. 3:16);
- protecting (Ps. 119:11);
- strengthening (Ps. 119:28);
- making wise (Ps. 119:17–100);
- rejoicing the heart (Ps. 19:8);
- and prospering (Josh. 1:8,9).

OCTOBER 16

Jeremiah 17:1–18:23

17 "The sin of Judah *is* written
with a pen of iron;
With the point of a diamond *it is*
engraved
On the tablet of their heart,
And on the horns of your altars,

17:1 The sin of Judah. Reasons for the judgment continue here: 1) idolatry (vv. 1–4), 2) relying on the flesh (v. 5), and 3) dishonesty in amassing wealth (v. 11). **pen of iron.** The names of idols were engraved on the horns of their altars with such a tool. The idea is that Judah's sin was permanent, etched in them as if into stone. How much different to have God's word written on the heart.

2 While their children remember
Their altars and their wooden images
By the green trees on the high hills.
3 O My mountain in the field,
I will give as plunder your wealth, all
your treasures,
And your high places of sin within all
your borders.
4 And you, even yourself,
Shall let go of your heritage which I
gave you;
And I will cause you to serve your
enemies
In the land which you do not know;
For you have kindled a fire in My
anger *which* shall burn forever."

5 Thus says the LORD:

"Cursed *is* the man who trusts in man
And makes flesh his strength,
Whose heart departs from the LORD.
6 For he shall be like a shrub in the
desert,
And shall not see when good comes,
But shall inhabit the parched places in
the wilderness,
In a salt land *which is* not inhabited.

7 "Blessed *is* the man who trusts in the
LORD,
And whose hope is the LORD.
8 For he shall be like a tree planted by
the waters,
Which spreads out its roots by the
river,
And will not fear when heat comes;
But its leaf will be green,
And will not be anxious in the year of
drought,
Nor will cease from yielding fruit.

9 "The heart *is* deceitful above all *things*,
And desperately wicked;
Who can know it?
10 I, the LORD, search the heart,
I test the mind,
Even to give every man according to
his ways,
According to the fruit of his doings.

11 "*As* a partridge that broods but does not
hatch,
So is he who gets riches, but not by
right;
It will leave him in the midst of his
days,
And at his end he will be a fool."

12 A glorious high throne from the
beginning
Is the place of our sanctuary.
13 O LORD, the hope of Israel,
All who forsake You shall be ashamed.
"Those who depart from Me

Shall be written in the earth,
Because they have forsaken the LORD,
The fountain of living waters."

14 Heal me, O LORD, and I shall be healed;
Save me, and I shall be saved,
For You *are* my praise.
15 Indeed they say to me,
"Where *is* the word of the LORD?
Let it come now!"
16 As for me, I have not hurried away
from *being* a shepherd *who* follows
You,
Nor have I desired the woeful day;
You know what came out of my lips;
It was right there before You.
17 Do not be a terror to me;
You *are* my hope in the day of doom.
18 Let them be ashamed who persecute
me,
But do not let me be put to shame;
Let them be dismayed,
But do not let me be dismayed.
Bring on them the day of doom,
And destroy them with double
destruction!

19 Thus the LORD said to me: "Go and stand in
the gate of the children of the people, by
which the kings of Judah come in and by
which they go out, and in all the gates of Jerusalem; 20 and say to them, 'Hear the word of the
LORD, you kings of Judah, and all Judah, and
all the inhabitants of Jerusalem, who enter by
these gates. 21 Thus says the LORD: "Take heed
to yourselves, and bear no burden on the
Sabbath day, nor bring *it* in by the gates of Jerusalem; 22 nor carry a burden out of your houses on the Sabbath day, nor do any work, but
hallow the Sabbath day, as I commanded your
fathers. 23 But they did not obey nor incline
their ear, but made their neck stiff, that they
might not hear nor receive instruction.
24 "And it shall be, if you heed Me carefully,"
says the LORD, "to bring no burden through
the gates of this city on the Sabbath day, but
hallow the Sabbath day, to do no work in it,
25 then shall enter the gates of this city kings
and princes sitting on the throne of David, riding in chariots and on horses, they and their
princes, accompanied by the men of Judah and
the inhabitants of Jerusalem; and this city shall
remain forever. 26 And they shall come from the
cities of Judah and from the places around Jerusalem, from the land of Benjamin and from
the lowland, from the mountains and from the
South, bringing burnt offerings and sacrifices,
grain offerings and incense, bringing sacrifices of praise to the house of the LORD.
27 "But if you will not heed Me to hallow the
Sabbath day, such as not carrying a burden
when entering the gates of Jerusalem on the
Sabbath day, then I will kindle a fire in its
gates, and it shall devour the palaces of Jerusalem, and it shall not be quenched." ' "

18 The word which came to Jeremiah from
the LORD, saying: 2 "Arise and go down to
the potter's house, and there I will cause you to
hear My words." 3 Then I went down to the potter's house, and there he was, making something at the wheel. 4 And the vessel that he
made of clay was marred in the hand of the
potter; so he made it again into another vessel,
as it seemed good to the potter to make.
5 Then the word of the LORD came to me, saying: 6 "O house of Israel, can I not do with you
as this potter?" says the LORD. "Look, as the
clay *is* in the potter's hand, so *are* you in My
hand, O house of Israel! 7 The instant I speak

18:2–6 potter's house. God sent Jeremiah to a potter, who gave him an illustration by shaping a vessel. The prophet secured a vessel and used it for his own illustration (19:1ff.). Jeremiah watched the potter at his wheel. The soft clay became misshapen, but the potter shaped it back into a good vessel. God will so do with Judah if she repents.

concerning a nation and concerning a kingdom, to pluck up, to pull down, and to destroy
it, 8 if that nation against whom I have spoken
turns from its evil, I will relent of the disaster
that I thought to bring upon it. 9 And the instant
I speak concerning a nation and concerning a
kingdom, to build and to plant *it,* 10 if it does evil
in My sight so that it does not obey My voice,
then I will relent concerning the good with
which I said I would benefit it.
11 "Now therefore, speak to the men of Judah
and to the inhabitants of Jerusalem, saying,
'Thus says the LORD: "Behold, I am fashioning
a disaster and devising a plan against you. Return now every one from his evil way, and
make your ways and your doings good." ' "
12 And they said, "That is hopeless! So we will
walk according to our own plans, and we will
every one obey the dictates of his evil heart."
13 Therefore thus says the LORD:

"Ask now among the Gentiles,
Who has heard such things?
The virgin of Israel has done a very
horrible thing.

18:12 That is hopeless! Jeremiah brought the inhabitants of Jerusalem to the point where they actually stated their condition honestly. The prophet's threats were useless because they were so far gone—abandoned to their sins and the penalty. All hypocrisy was abandoned in favor of honesty, without repentance. Repentance was not in Israel (v. 18; 19:15). This explains a seeming paradox, that Israel can repent and avert judgment, yet Jeremiah is not to pray for Israel (7:16; 11:14). It would do no good to pray for their change since they steeled themselves against any change.

14 Will *a man* leave the snow water of
Lebanon,
Which comes from the rock of the field?
Will the cold flowing waters be
forsaken for strange waters?
15 "Because My people have forgotten Me,
They have burned incense to
worthless idols.
And they have caused themselves to
stumble in their ways,
From the ancient paths,
To walk in pathways and not on a
highway,
16 To make their land desolate *and* a
perpetual hissing;
Everyone who passes by it will be
astonished
And shake his head.
17 I will scatter them as with an east wind
before the enemy;
I will show them the back and not the
face
In the day of their calamity."

18 Then they said, "Come and let us devise
plans against Jeremiah; for the law shall not
perish from the priest, nor counsel from the
wise, nor the word from the prophet. Come
and let us attack him with the tongue, and let
us not give heed to any of his words."

19 Give heed to me, O LORD,
And listen to the voice of those who
contend with me!
20 Shall evil be repaid for good?
For they have dug a pit for my life.
Remember that I stood before You
To speak good for them,
To turn away Your wrath
from them.
21 Therefore deliver up their children to
the famine,
And pour out their *blood*
By the force of the sword;
Let their wives *become* widows
And bereaved of their children.
Let their men be put to death,
Their young men *be* slain
By the sword in battle.
22 Let a cry be heard from their houses,
When You bring a troop suddenly upon
them;
For they have dug a pit to take me,
And hidden snares for my feet.
23 Yet, LORD, You know all their counsel
Which is against me, to slay *me*.
Provide no atonement for their iniquity,
Nor blot out their sin from Your sight;
But let them be overthrown before You.
Deal *thus* with them
In the time of Your anger.

Psalm 118:25–29

25 Save now, I pray, O LORD;
O LORD, I pray, send now prosperity.
26 Blessed *is* he who comes in the name
of the LORD!
We have blessed you from the house of
the LORD.
27 God *is* the LORD,
And He has given us light;
Bind the sacrifice with cords to the
horns of the altar.
28 You *are* my God, and I will praise You;
You are my God, I will exalt You.
29 Oh, give thanks to the LORD, for *He is*
good!
For His mercy *endures* forever.

Proverbs 27:11–12

11 My son, be wise, and make my heart
glad,
That I may answer him who
reproaches me.
12 A prudent *man* foresees evil *and* hides
himself;
The simple pass on *and* are punished.

1 Thessalonians 3:1–13

3 Therefore, when we could no longer endure
it, we thought it good to be left in Athens
alone, 2 and sent Timothy, our brother and minister of God, and our fellow laborer in the gospel
of Christ, to establish you and encourage you
concerning your faith, 3 that no one should be
shaken by these afflictions; for you yourselves
know that we are appointed to this. 4 For, in fact,

3:2 establish...encourage...your faith. This was a common ministry concern and practice of Paul (Acts 14:22; 15:32; 18:23). Paul's concern did not focus on health, wealth, self-esteem, or ease of life, but rather the spiritual quality of life. Their faith was of supreme importance in Paul's mind as evidenced by 5 mentions in vv. 1–10. Faith includes the foundation of the body of doctrine (Jude 3) and their believing response to God in living out that truth (Heb. 11:6).

3:5 the tempter. Satan had already been characterized as a hinderer (2:18) and now as a tempter in the sense of trying/testing for the purpose of causing failure (Matt. 4:3; 1 Cor. 7:5; James 1:12–18). Paul was not ignorant of Satan's schemes (2 Cor. 2:11; 11:23) nor vulnerable to his methods (Eph. 6:11), so Paul took action to counterattack Satan's expected maneuver and to assure that all his efforts were not useless.

we told you before when we were with you that
we would suffer tribulation, just as it happened,
and you know. 5 For this reason, when I could no
longer endure it, I sent to know your faith, lest
by some means the tempter had tempted you,
and our labor might be in vain.

6 But now that Timothy has come to us from
you, and brought us good news of your faith and
love, and that you always have good remembrance of us, greatly desiring to see us, as we
also *to see* you— 7 therefore, brethren, in all our
affliction and distress we were comforted concerning you by your faith. 8 For now we live, if
you stand fast in the Lord.

9 For what thanks can we render to God for
you, for all the joy with which we rejoice for
your sake before our God, 10 night and day praying exceedingly that we may see your face and
perfect what is lacking in your faith?

11 Now may our God and Father Himself, and
our Lord Jesus Christ, direct our way to you.
12 And may the Lord make you increase and
abound in love to one another and to all, just as
we *do* to you, 13 so that He may establish your
hearts blameless in holiness before our God
and Father at the coming of our Lord Jesus
Christ with all His saints.

DAY 16: What was Paul's prayer for the Thessalonians?

"Now may our God...direct our way to you" (1 Thess. 3:11). Paul knew that Satan had hindered his return (2:18). Even though Timothy had visited and returned with a good report, Paul still felt the urgency to see his spiritual children again. Paul followed the biblical admonition of the Psalms (Ps. 37:1–5) and Proverbs (Prov. 3:5,6) to entrust difficult situations to God.

"May the Lord make you increase and abound in love to one another" (v. 12). With over 30 positive and negative "one anothers" in the New Testament, love appears by far most frequently (4:9; Rom. 12:10; 13:8; 2 Thess. 1:3; 1 Pet. 1:22; 1 John 3:11,23; 4:7,11; 2 John 5). It is the overarching term that includes all of the other "one anothers." Its focus is on believers in the church. "And to all." In light of the fact that God loved the world and sent His Son to die for human sin, believers who were loved when they were unlovely (Rom. 5:8) are to love unbelievers (Matt. 5:43,44). Other New Testament commands concerning all men include pursuing peace (Rom. 12:18), doing good (Gal. 6:10), being patient (Phil. 4:5), praying (1 Tim. 2:1), showing consideration (Titus 3:2), and honoring (1 Pet. 2:17).

"So that He may establish your hears blameless in holiness before our God." Paul prayed that there would be no grounds of accusation because of unholiness. "At the coming of our Lord Jesus Christ with all His saints." Since this exact term is not used elsewhere in the New Testament of angels but is commonly used for believers, it is best to understand the coming of the Lord to rapture all His church and take them to heaven to enjoy His presence.

OCTOBER 17

Jeremiah 19:1–20:18

19 Thus says the LORD: "Go and get a potter's earthen flask, and *take* some of the
elders of the people and some of the elders of
the priests. 2 And go out to the Valley of the
Son of Hinnom, which *is* by the entry of the
Potsherd Gate; and proclaim there the words
that I will tell you, 3 and say, 'Hear the word of
the LORD, O kings of Judah and inhabitants of
Jerusalem. Thus says the LORD of hosts, the
God of Israel: "Behold, I will bring such a
catastrophe on this place, that whoever hears
of it, his ears will tingle.

4“Because they have forsaken Me and made this an alien place, because they have burned incense in it to other gods whom neither they, their fathers, nor the kings of Judah have known, and have filled this place with the blood of the innocents 5(they have also built the high places of Baal, to burn their sons with fire *for* burnt offerings to Baal, which I did not command or speak, nor did it come into My mind), 6therefore behold, the days are coming,” says the LORD, “that this place shall no more be called Tophet or the Valley of the Son of Hinnom, but the Valley of Slaughter. 7And I will make void the counsel of Judah and Jerusalem in this place, and I will cause them to fall by the sword before their enemies and by the hands of those who seek their lives; their corpses I will give as meat for the birds of the heaven and for the beasts of the earth. 8I will make this city desolate and a hissing; everyone who passes by it will be astonished and hiss because of all its plagues. 9And I will cause them to eat the flesh of their sons and the flesh of their daughters, and everyone shall eat the flesh of his friend in the siege and in the desperation with which their enemies and those who seek their lives shall drive them to despair.” ’

10“Then you shall break the flask in the sight of the men who go with you, 11and say to them, ‘Thus says the LORD of hosts: “Even so I will break this people and this city, as *one* breaks a potter’s vessel, which cannot be made whole again; and they shall bury *them* in Tophet till *there is* no place to bury. 12Thus I will do to this place,” says the LORD, “and to its inhabitants, and make this city like Tophet. 13And the houses of Jerusalem and the houses of the kings of Judah shall be defiled like the place of Tophet, because of all the houses on whose roofs they have burned incense to all the host of heaven, and poured out drink offerings to other gods.” ’ ”

14Then Jeremiah came from Tophet, where the LORD had sent him to prophesy; and he stood in the court of the Lord’s house and said to all the people, 15“Thus says the LORD of hosts, the God of Israel: ‘Behold, I will bring on this city and on all her towns all the doom that I have pronounced against it, because they have stiffened their necks that they might not hear My words.’ ”

20 Now Pashhur the son of Immer, the priest who *was* also chief governor in the house of the LORD, heard that Jeremiah prophesied these things. 2Then Pashhur struck Jeremiah the prophet, and put him in the stocks that *were* in the high gate of Benjamin, which *was* by the house of the LORD.

20:2 struck Jeremiah. Pashur or others acting on his authority delivered 40 lashes (see Deut. 25:3) to the prophet. **put him in the stocks.** Hands, feet, and neck were fastened in holes, bending the body to a distorted posture, causing excruciating pain. **high gate.** The northern gate of the upper temple court.

3And it happened on the next day that Pashhur brought Jeremiah out of the stocks. Then Jeremiah said to him, “The LORD has not called your name Pashhur, but Magor-Missabib. 4For thus says the LORD: ‘Behold, I will make you a terror to yourself and to all your friends; and they shall fall by the sword of their enemies, and your eyes shall see *it*. I will give all Judah into the hand of the king of Babylon, and he shall carry them captive to Babylon and slay them with the sword. 5Moreover I will deliver all the wealth of this city, all its produce, and all its precious things; all the treasures of the kings of Judah I will give into the hand of their enemies, who will plunder them, seize them, and carry them to Babylon. 6And you, Pashhur, and all who dwell in your house, shall go into captivity. You shall go to Babylon, and there you shall die, and be buried there, you and all your friends, to whom you have prophesied lies.’ ”

7 O LORD, You induced me, and I was persuaded;
You are stronger than I, and have prevailed.
I am in derision daily;
Everyone mocks me.
8 For when I spoke, I cried out;
I shouted, “Violence and plunder!”
Because the word of the LORD was made to me
A reproach and a derision daily.
9 Then I said, “I will not make mention of Him,
Nor speak anymore in His name.”
But *His word* was in my heart like a burning fire
Shut up in my bones;
I was weary of holding *it* back,
And I could not.
10 For I heard many mocking:
“Fear on every side!”
“Report,” *they say,* “and we will report it!”
All my acquaintances watched for my stumbling, *saying,*

"Perhaps he can be induced;
Then we will prevail against him,
And we will take our revenge on him."

11 But the LORD *is* with me as a mighty, awesome One.
Therefore my persecutors will stumble, and will not prevail.
They will be greatly ashamed, for they will not prosper.
Their everlasting confusion will never be forgotten.
12 But, O LORD of hosts,
You who test the righteous,
And see the mind and heart,
Let me see Your vengeance on them;
For I have pleaded my cause before You.
13 Sing to the LORD! Praise the LORD!
For He has delivered the life of the poor
From the hand of evildoers.
14 Cursed *be* the day in which I was born!
Let the day not be blessed in which my mother bore me!
15 Let the man *be* cursed
Who brought news to my father, saying,
"A male child has been born to you!"
Making him very glad.
16 And let that man be like the cities
Which the LORD overthrew, and did not relent;
Let him hear the cry in the morning
And the shouting at noon,
17 Because he did not kill me from the womb,
That my mother might have been my grave,
And her womb always enlarged *with me.*
18 Why did I come forth from the womb to see labor and sorrow,
That my days should be consumed with shame?

Psalm 119:1–8

א ALEPH

Blessed *are* the undefiled in the way,
Who walk in the law of the LORD!
2 Blessed *are* those who keep His testimonies,
Who seek Him with the whole heart!
3 They also do no iniquity;
They walk in His ways.
4 You have commanded *us*
To keep Your precepts diligently.
5 Oh, that my ways were directed
To keep Your statutes!
6 Then I would not be ashamed,
When I look into all Your commandments.
7 I will praise You with uprightness of heart,
When I learn Your righteous judgments.
8 I will keep Your statutes;
Oh, do not forsake me utterly!

119:1–176 This longest of psalms and chapters in the Bible stands as the "Mt. Everest" of the Psalter. It joins Psalms 1 and 19 in exalting God's Word. The author is unknown for certain, although David, Daniel, or Ezra have reasonably been suggested. The psalmist apparently wrote while under some sort of serious duress as comes through in many verses. This is an acrostic psalm (Pss. 9; 10; 25; 34; 37; 111; 112; 145) composed of 22 sections, each containing 8 lines. All 8 lines of the first section start with the first letter of the Hebrew alphabet; thus the psalm continues until all 22 letters have been used in order. The 8 different terms referring to Scripture occurring throughout the psalm are: 1) law, 2) testimonies, 3) precepts, 4) statutes, 5) commandments, 6) judgments, 7) word, and 8) ordinances. From before sunrise to beyond sunset the Word of God dominated the psalmist's life: 1) before dawn (v. 147), 2) daily (v. 97), 3) 7 times daily (v. 164), 4) nightly (vv. 55,148), and 5) at midnight (v. 62).

Proverbs 27:13

13 Take the garment of him who is surety for a stranger,
And hold it in pledge *when* he is surety for a seductress.

1 Thessalonians 4:1–18

4 Finally then, brethren, we urge and exhort
in the Lord Jesus that you should abound
more and more, just as you received from us
how you ought to walk and to please God; [2]for
you know what commandments we gave you
through the Lord Jesus.
[3]For this is the will of God, your sanctification:
that you should abstain from sexual immorality;
[4]that each of you should know how to possess
his own vessel in sanctification and honor, [5]not
in passion of lust, like the Gentiles who do not
know God; [6]that no one should take advantage
of and defraud his brother in this matter,
because the Lord *is* the avenger of all such, as

we also forewarned you and testified. 7For
God did not call us to uncleanness, but in holiness. 8Therefore he who rejects *this* does not
reject man, but God, who has also given us
His Holy Spirit.
9But concerning brotherly love you have no
need that I should write to you, for you yourselves are taught by God to love one another;
10and indeed you do so toward all the brethren
who are in all Macedonia. But we urge you,
brethren, that you increase more and more;
11that you also aspire to lead a quiet life, to mind
your own business, and to work with your own
hands, as we commanded you, 12that you may
walk properly toward those who are outside,
and *that* you may lack nothing.
13But I do not want you to be ignorant,
brethren, concerning those who have fallen
asleep, lest you sorrow as others who have no
hope. 14For if we believe that Jesus died and
rose again, even so God will bring with Him
those who sleep in Jesus.
15For this we say to you by the word of the
Lord, that we who are alive *and* remain until
the coming of the Lord will by no means precede those who are asleep. 16For the Lord
Himself will descend from heaven with a
shout, with the voice of an archangel, and with
the trumpet of God. And the dead in Christ
will rise first. 17Then we who are alive *and*
remain shall be caught up together with them
in the clouds to meet the Lord in the air. And
thus we shall always be with the Lord. 18There-
fore comfort one another with these words.

4:13 those who have fallen asleep. Sleep is the familiar New Testament euphemism for death which describes the appearance of the deceased. It describes the dead body not the soul (2 Cor. 5:1–9; Phil. 1:23). Sleep is used of Jairus's daughter (Matt. 9:24), whom Jesus raised from the dead, and Stephen, who was stoned to death (Acts 7:60; John 11:11; 1 Cor. 7:39; 15:6,18,51; 2 Pet. 3:4). Those who sleep are identified in v. 16 as "the dead in Christ." The people, in ignorance, had come to the conclusion that those who die miss the Lord's return, and they were grieved over their absence at such a glorious event. Thus the departure of a loved one brought great anguish to the soul.

4:18 comfort one another. The primary purpose of this passage is not to teach a scheme of prophecy, but rather to provide encouragement to those Christians whose loved ones have died. The comfort here is based on the following: 1) the dead will be resurrected and will participate in the Lord's coming for His own; 2) when Christ comes, the living will be reunited forever with their loved ones; and 3) they all will be with the Lord eternally (v. 17).

DAY 17: How does Paul describe the return of Jesus Christ in 1 Thessalonians 4:15,16?

It is clear the Thessalonians had come to believe in and hope for the reality of their Savior's return (1:3,9,10; 2:19; 5:1,2). They were living in expectation of that coming, eagerly awaiting Christ. First Thessalonians 4:13 indicates they were even agitated about some things that might affect their participation in it. They knew Christ's return was the climactic event in redemptive history and didn't want to miss it. The major question they had was: "What happens to the Christians who die before He comes? Do they miss His return?" Clearly, they had an imminent view of Christ's return, and Paul had left the impression it could happen in their lifetime. Their confusion came as they were being persecuted, an experience they thought they were to be delivered from by the Lord's return (3:3,4).

Paul answers by saying "the Lord Himself will descend with a shout" (v. 16). This fulfills the pledge of John 14:1–3 (Acts 1:11). Until then He remains in heaven (1:10; Heb. 1:1–3). "With the voice of an archangel." Perhaps it is Michael, the archangel, whose voice is heard as he is identified with Israel's resurrection in Daniel 12:1–3. At that moment, the dead rise first. They will not miss the Rapture but will be the first participants. "And with the trumpet of God." This trumpet is illustrated by the trumpet of Exodus 19:16–19, which called the people out of the camp to meet God. It will be a trumpet of deliverance (Zeph. 1:16; Zech. 9:14).

After the dead come forth, their spirits, already with the Lord (2 Cor. 5:8; Phil. 1:23), now being joined to resurrected new bodies, the living Christians will be raptured, "caught up" (v. 17). This passage along with John 14:1–3 and 1 Corinthians 15:51,52 form the biblical basis for "the Rapture" of the church.

OCTOBER 18

Jeremiah 21:1–22:30

21 The word which came to Jeremiah from
the LORD when King Zedekiah sent to
him Pashhur the son of Melchiah, and
Zephaniah the son of Maaseiah, the priest, saying, 2"Please inquire of the LORD for us, for
Nebuchadnezzar king of Babylon makes war
against us. Perhaps the LORD will deal with us
according to all His wonderful works, that *the
king* may go away from us."
3Then Jeremiah said to them, "Thus you
shall say to Zedekiah, 4'Thus says the LORD God
of Israel: "Behold, I will turn back the weapons
of war that *are* in your hands, with which you
fight against the king of Babylon and the
Chaldeans who besiege you outside the walls;
and I will assemble them in the midst of this
city. 5I Myself will fight against you with an outstretched hand and with a strong arm, even in
anger and fury and great wrath. 6I will strike
the inhabitants of this city, both man and beast;
they shall die of a great pestilence. 7And afterward," says the LORD, "I will deliver Zedekiah
king of Judah, his servants and the people, and
such as are left in this city from the pestilence
and the sword and the famine, into the hand of
Nebuchadnezzar king of Babylon, into the
hand of their enemies, and into the hand of
those who seek their life; and he shall strike
them with the edge of the sword. He shall not
spare them, or have pity or mercy." '
8"Now you shall say to this people, 'Thus
says the LORD: "Behold, I set before you the
way of life and the way of death. 9He who remains in this city shall die by the sword, by
famine, and by pestilence; but he who goes
out and defects to the Chaldeans who besiege
you, he shall live, and his life shall be as a
prize to him. 10For I have set My face against
this city for adversity and not for good," says
the LORD. "It shall be given into the hand of
the king of Babylon, and he shall burn it with
fire." '
11"And concerning the house of the king of
Judah, *say,* 'Hear the word of the LORD, 12O
house of David! Thus says the LORD:

"Execute judgment in the morning;
And deliver *him who is* plundered
Out of the hand of the oppressor,
Lest My fury go forth like fire
And burn so that no one can quench *it,*
Because of the evil of your doings.

13 "Behold, I *am* against you, O inhabitant
of the valley,
And rock of the plain," says the LORD,
"Who say, 'Who shall come down
against us?
Or who shall enter our dwellings?'
14 But I will punish you according to the
fruit of your doings," says the LORD;
"I will kindle a fire in its forest,
And it shall devour all things around
it." ' "

22 Thus says the LORD: "Go down to the
house of the king of Judah, and there
speak this word, 2and say, 'Hear the word of
the LORD, O king of Judah, you who sit on the
throne of David, you and your servants and
your people who enter these gates! 3Thus says
the LORD: "Execute judgment and righteousness, and deliver the plundered out of the
hand of the oppressor. Do no wrong and do no
violence to the stranger, the fatherless, or the
widow, nor shed innocent blood in this place.
4For if you indeed do this thing, then shall
enter the gates of this house, riding on horses
and in chariots, accompanied by servants and
people, kings who sit on the throne of David.
5But if you will not hear these words, I swear
by Myself," says the LORD, "that this house
shall become a desolation." ' "
6For thus says the LORD to the house of the
king of Judah:

"You *are* Gilead to Me,
The head of Lebanon;
Yet I surely will make you
a wilderness,
Cities *which* are not inhabited.
7 I will prepare destroyers
against you,
Everyone with his weapons;
They shall cut down your choice
cedars
And cast *them* into the fire.

8And many nations will pass by this city; and
everyone will say to his neighbor, 'Why has
the LORD done so to this great city?' 9Then
they will answer, 'Because they have forsaken
the covenant of the LORD their God, and worshiped other gods and served them.' "

10 Weep not for the dead, nor bemoan
him;
Weep bitterly for him who
goes away,
For he shall return no more,
Nor see his native country.

11For thus says the LORD concerning Shallum

the son of Josiah, king of Judah, who reigned instead of Josiah his father, who went from this place: "He shall not return here anymore, [12]but he shall die in the place where they have led him captive, and shall see this land no more.

13 "Woe to him who builds his house by unrighteousness
And his chambers by injustice,
Who uses his neighbor's service without wages
And gives him nothing for his work,
14 Who says, 'I will build myself a wide house with spacious chambers,
And cut out windows for it,
Paneling *it* with cedar
And painting *it* with vermilion.'

15 "Shall you reign because you enclose *yourself* in cedar?
Did not your father eat and drink,
And do justice and righteousness?
Then *it was* well with him.
16 He judged the cause of the poor and needy;
Then *it was* well.
Was not this knowing Me?" says the LORD.
17 "Yet your eyes and your heart *are* for nothing but your covetousness,
For shedding innocent blood,
And practicing oppression and violence."

[18]Therefore thus says the LORD concerning Jehoiakim the son of Josiah, king of Judah:

"They shall not lament for him,
Saying, 'Alas, my brother!' or 'Alas, my sister!'
They shall not lament for him,
Saying, 'Alas, master!' or 'Alas, his glory!'
19 He shall be buried with the burial of a donkey,

22:18,19 Jehoiakim. Ruling from 609 to 598 B.C., he was also wicked in taxing the people (2 Kin. 23:35) and making them build his splendid palace without pay, violating God's law in Leviticus 19:13 and Deuteronomy 24:14,15. He was slain in Babylon's second siege and his corpse dishonored, being left like a dead donkey on the ground for scavengers to feed on.

Dragged and cast out beyond the gates of Jerusalem.

20 "Go up to Lebanon, and cry out,
And lift up your voice in Bashan;
Cry from Abarim,
For all your lovers are destroyed.
21 I spoke to you in your prosperity,
But you said, 'I will not hear.'
This *has been* your manner from your youth,
That you did not obey My voice.
22 The wind shall eat up all your rulers,
And your lovers shall go into captivity;
Surely then you will be ashamed and humiliated
For all your wickedness.
23 O inhabitant of Lebanon,
Making your nest in the cedars,
How gracious will you be when pangs come upon you,
Like the pain of a woman in labor?

[24]"*As* I live," says the LORD, "though Coniah
the son of Jehoiakim, king of Judah, were the
signet on My right hand, yet I would pluck you
off; [25]and I will give you into the hand of those
who seek your life, and into the hand *of those*
whose face you fear—the hand of Nebuchadnezzar king of Babylon and the hand of the
Chaldeans. [26]So I will cast you out, and your
mother who bore you, into another country
where you were not born; and there you shall
die. [27]But to the land to which they desire to
return, there they shall not return.

28 "Is this man Coniah a despised, broken idol—
A vessel in which *is* no pleasure?
Why are they cast out, he and his descendants,
And cast into a land which they do not know?
29 O earth, earth, earth,
Hear the word of the LORD!
30 Thus says the LORD:
'Write this man down as childless,
A man *who* shall not prosper in his days;
For none of his descendants shall prosper,
Sitting on the throne of David,
And ruling anymore in Judah.' "

Psalm 119:9–16

ב BETH
9 How can a young man cleanse his way?
By taking heed according to Your word.

10 With my whole heart I have sought
You;
Oh, let me not wander from Your
commandments!
11 Your word I have hidden in
my heart,
That I might not sin against You.
12 Blessed *are* You, O LORD!
Teach me Your statutes.
13 With my lips I have declared
All the judgments of Your mouth.
14 I have rejoiced in the way of Your
testimonies,
As *much as* in all riches.
15 I will meditate on Your precepts,
And contemplate Your ways.
16 I will delight myself in Your statutes;
I will not forget Your word.

Proverbs 27:14

14 He who blesses his friend with a loud
voice, rising early in the morning,
It will be counted a curse to him.

1 Thessalonians 5:1–28

5 But concerning the times and the seasons,
brethren, you have no need that I should
write to you. [2]For you yourselves know perfectly that the day of the Lord so comes as a
thief in the night. [3]For when they say, "Peace
and safety!" then sudden destruction comes
upon them, as labor pains upon a pregnant
woman. And they shall not escape. [4]But you,
brethren, are not in darkness, so that this Day
should overtake you as a thief. [5]You are all
sons of light and sons of the day. We are not of
the night nor of darkness. [6]Therefore let us
not sleep, as others *do,* but let us watch and be
sober. [7]For those who sleep, sleep at night,
and those who get drunk are drunk at night.
[8]But let us who are of the day be sober, putting
on the breastplate of faith and love, and *as* a
helmet the hope of salvation. [9]For God did not
appoint us to wrath, but to obtain salvation
through our Lord Jesus Christ, [10]who died for
us, that whether we wake or sleep, we should
live together with Him.
[11]Therefore comfort each other and edify
one another, just as you also are doing.
[12]And we urge you, brethren, to recognize
those who labor among you, and are over you
in the Lord and admonish you, [13]and to esteem
them very highly in love for their work's sake.
Be at peace among yourselves.
[14]Now we exhort you, brethren, warn those
who are unruly, comfort the fainthearted, uphold the weak, be patient with all. [15]See that no
one renders evil for evil to anyone, but always
pursue what is good both for yourselves and
for all.
[16]Rejoice always, [17]pray without ceasing, [18]in
everything give thanks; for this is the will of
God in Christ Jesus for you.
[19]Do not quench the Spirit. [20]Do not despise
prophecies. [21]Test all things; hold fast what is
good. [22]Abstain from every form of evil.
[23]Now may the God of peace Himself sanctify you completely; and may your whole spirit, soul, and body be preserved blameless at
the coming of our Lord Jesus Christ. [24]He who
calls you *is* faithful, who also will do *it.*
[25]Brethren, pray for us.
[26]Greet all the brethren with a holy kiss.
[27]I charge you by the Lord that this epistle be
read to all the holy brethren.
[28]The grace of our Lord Jesus Christ *be* with
you. Amen.

5:12 recognize. This does not mean simple face recognition, but that the people are to know their pastors well enough to have an intimate appreciation for them and to respect them because of their value. The work of pastors is summarized in a 3-fold description which includes: 1) laboring, working to the point of exhaustion; 2) overseeing, literally standing before the flock to lead them in the way of righteousness; and 3) admonishing, instructing in the truths of God's Word.

5:19 quench. The fire of God's Spirit is not to be doused with sin. Believers are also instructed to not grieve the Holy Spirit (Eph. 4:30) but to be controlled by the Holy Spirit (Eph. 5:18) and to walk by the Holy Spirit (Gal. 5:16).

5:23 God...sanctify you. Only God (Rom. 15:33; 16:20; Phil. 4:9; Heb. 13:20) "Himself" can separate us from sin to holiness "completely." **whole spirit, soul, and body.** This comprehensive reference makes the term "completely" more emphatic. By using spirit and soul, Paul was not indicating that the immaterial part of man could be divided into two substances (Heb. 4:12). The two words are used interchangeably throughout Scripture (Heb. 6:19; 10:39; 1 Pet. 2:11; 2 Pet. 2:8).

DAY 18: When Paul refers to the "Day of the Lord" in 1 Thessalonians 5:2, what does he mean?

There are 19 indisputable uses of "the Day of the Lord" in the Old Testament and 4 in the New Testament (Acts 2:20; 2 Thess. 2:2; 2 Pet. 3:10). The Old Testament prophets used "Day of the Lord" to describe near historical judgments (Is. 13:6–22; Ezek. 30:2–19; Joel 1:15; 3:14; Amos 5:18–20; Zeph. 1:14–18) or far eschatological divine judgments (Joel 2:30–32; Zech. 14:1; Mal. 4:1,5). Six times it is referred to as the "day of doom" and 4 times as the "day of vengeance." The New Testament calls it a day of "wrath," a day of "visitation," and the "Great Day of God Almighty" (Rev. 16:14). These are terrifying judgments from God (Joel 2:30,31; 2 Thess. 1:7–10) for the overwhelming sinfulness of the world.

The future "Day of the Lord" which unleashes God's wrath falls into two parts: 1) the end of the 7-year tribulation period (Rev. 19:11–21), and 2) the end of the Millennium. These two are actually 1,000 years apart, and Peter refers to the end of the 1,000-year period in connection with the final "Day of the Lord" (2 Pet. 3:10; Rev. 20:7–15). Here, Paul refers to that aspect of the "Day of the Lord," which concludes the Tribulation period. When Paul uses the phrase "a thief in the night," it is never used to refer to the Rapture of the church. It is used of Christ's coming in judgment on the Day of the Lord at the end of the 7-year Tribulation which is distinct from the Rapture of the church, and it is used of the judgment which concludes the Millennium (2 Pet. 3:10). As a thief comes unexpectedly and without warning, so will the Day of the Lord come in both its final phases.

OCTOBER 19

Jeremiah 23:1–24:10

23 "Woe to the shepherds who destroy and
scatter the sheep of My pasture!" says
the LORD. 2Therefore thus says the LORD God of
Israel against the shepherds who feed My people: "You have scattered My flock, driven them away, and not attended to them. Behold, I will attend to you for the evil of your doings," says
the LORD. 3"But I will gather the remnant of My
flock out of all countries where I have driven them, and bring them back to their folds; and
they shall be fruitful and increase. 4I will set up
shepherds over them who will feed them; and they shall fear no more, nor be dismayed, nor shall they be lacking," says the LORD.

5 "Behold, *the* days are coming," says the
LORD,
"That I will raise to David a Branch of
righteousness;
A King shall reign and prosper,
And execute judgment and
righteousness in the earth.
6 In His days Judah will be saved,
And Israel will dwell safely;
Now this *is* His name by which He will
be called:

THE LORD OUR RIGHTEOUSNESS.

7"Therefore, behold, *the* days are coming,"
says the LORD, "that they shall no longer say,
'As the LORD lives who brought up the children of Israel from the land of Egypt,'
8but, 'As
the LORD lives who brought up and led the descendants of the house of Israel from the north country and from all the countries where I had driven them.' And they shall dwell in their own land."

9 My heart within me is broken
Because of the prophets;

23:3,4 I will gather. God pledged to restore exiled Israelites to their ancient soil. The land in view was Palestine, being contrasted with all the other countries (v. 3), thus assuring that the regathering would be as literal as the scattering. The restoration of Judah from Babylon is referred to in language which in its fullness can only refer to the final restoration of God's people ("out of all countries" and v. 8), under the Messiah. "Nor shall they be lacking" indicates that no one will be missing or detached. These are prophecies not yet fulfilled.

23:4 shepherds...will feed them. Zerubbabel, Ezra, Nehemiah, and others were small fulfillments compared to the consummate shepherding of the Messiah Jesus.

23:5 Branch. The Messiah is pictured as a branch (literally, "shoot") out of David's family tree (23:5; 33:15,16; Is. 4:2; 11:1–5; Zech. 3:8; 6:12,13), who will rule over God's people in the future.

All my bones shake.
I am like a drunken man,
And like a man whom wine has overcome,
Because of the LORD,
And because of His holy words.
10 For the land is full of adulterers;
For because of a curse the land mourns.
The pleasant places of the wilderness are dried up.
Their course of life is evil,
And their might *is* not right.

11 "For both prophet and priest are profane;
Yes, in My house I have found their wickedness," says the LORD.
12 "Therefore their way shall be to them
Like slippery *ways;*
In the darkness they shall be driven on
And fall in them;
For I will bring disaster on them,
The year of their punishment," says the LORD.

13 "And I have seen folly in the prophets of Samaria:
They prophesied by Baal
And caused My people Israel to err.
14 Also I have seen a horrible thing in the prophets of Jerusalem:
They commit adultery and walk in lies;
They also strengthen the hands of evildoers,
So that no one turns back from his wickedness.
All of them are like Sodom to Me,
And her inhabitants like Gomorrah.

15 "Therefore thus says the LORD of hosts concerning the prophets:

'Behold, I will feed them with wormwood,
And make them drink the water of gall;
For from the prophets of Jerusalem
Profaneness has gone out into all the land.' "

16 Thus says the LORD of hosts:

"Do not listen to the words of the prophets who prophesy to you.
They make you worthless;
They speak a vision of their own heart,
Not from the mouth of the LORD.
17 They continually say to those who despise Me,
'The LORD has said, "You shall have peace" ';
And *to* everyone who walks according to the dictates of his own heart, they say,
'No evil shall come upon you.' "

18 For who has stood in the counsel of the LORD,
And has perceived and heard His word?
Who has marked His word and heard *it?*
19 Behold, a whirlwind of the LORD has gone forth in fury—
A violent whirlwind!
It will fall violently on the head of the wicked.
20 The anger of the LORD will not turn back
Until He has executed and performed the thoughts of His heart.
In the latter days you will understand it perfectly.

21 "I have not sent these prophets, yet they ran.
I have not spoken to them, yet they prophesied.
22 But if they had stood in My counsel,
And had caused My people to hear My words,
Then they would have turned them from their evil way
And from the evil of their doings.

23 "*Am* I a God near at hand," says the LORD,
"And not a God afar off?
24 Can anyone hide himself in secret places,
So I shall not see him?" says the LORD;
"Do I not fill heaven and earth?" says the LORD.

25 "I have heard what the prophets have said
who prophesy lies in My name, saying, 'I have
dreamed, I have dreamed!' 26 How long will *this*
be in the heart of the prophets who prophesy
lies? Indeed *they are* prophets of the deceit of
their own heart, 27 who try to make My people
forget My name by their dreams which everyone tells his neighbor, as their fathers forgot
My name for Baal.

28 "The prophet who has a dream, let him tell a dream;
And he who has My word, let him speak My word faithfully.
What *is* the chaff to the wheat?" says the LORD.
29 "*Is* not My word like a fire?" says the LORD,

23:29 like a fire...hammer. God's word has irresistible qualities to prevail over the deception in the shepherds' false messages.

"And like a hammer *that* breaks the
rock in pieces?

30"Therefore behold, I *am* against the
prophets," says the LORD, "who steal My words
every one from his neighbor. 31Behold, I *am*
against the prophets," says the LORD, "who use
their tongues and say, 'He says.' 32Behold, I *am*
against those who prophesy false dreams," says
the LORD, "and tell them, and cause My people to
err by their lies and by their recklessness. Yet I did
not send them or command them; therefore they
shall not profit this people at all," says the LORD.
33"So when these people or the prophet or the
priest ask you, saying, 'What is the oracle of the
LORD?' you shall then say to them, 'What oracle?'
I will even forsake you," says the LORD.
34"And *as for* the prophet and the priest and the
people who say, 'The oracle of the LORD!' I will
even punish that man and his house. 35Thus
every one of you shall say to his neighbor, and
every one to his brother, 'What has the LORD
answered?' and, 'What has the LORD spoken?'
36And the oracle of the LORD you shall mention
no more. For every man's word will be his oracle,
for you have perverted the words of the living
God, the LORD of hosts, our God. 37Thus you
shall say to the prophet, 'What has the LORD
answered you?' and, 'What has the LORD spoken?'
38But since you say, 'The oracle of the
LORD!' therefore thus says the LORD: 'Because
you say this word, "The oracle of the LORD!" and
I have sent to you, saying, "Do not say, 'The oracle
of the LORD!' " 39therefore behold, I, even I,
will utterly forget you and forsake you, and the
city that I gave you and your fathers, and *will
cast you* out of My presence. 40And I will bring an
everlasting reproach upon you, and a perpetual
shame, which shall not be forgotten.' "

24 The LORD showed me, and there were
two baskets of figs set before the temple
of the LORD, after Nebuchadnezzar king of
Babylon had carried away captive Jeconiah
the son of Jehoiakim, king of Judah, and the
princes of Judah with the craftsmen and
smiths, from Jerusalem, and had brought
them to Babylon. 2One basket *had* very good
figs, like the figs *that are* first ripe; and the
other basket *had* very bad figs which could not
be eaten, they were so bad. 3Then the LORD
said to me, "What do you see, Jeremiah?"

And I said, "Figs, the good figs, very good;
and the bad, very bad, which cannot be eaten,
they are so bad."

4Again the word of the LORD came to me, saying,
5"Thus says the LORD, the God of Israel:
'Like these good figs, so will I acknowledge
those who are carried away captive from Judah,
whom I have sent out of this place for *their own*
good, into the land of the Chaldeans. 6For I will
set My eyes on them for good, and I will bring
them back to this land; I will build them and not
pull *them* down, and I will plant them and not
pluck *them* up. 7Then I will give them a heart to
know Me, that I *am* the LORD; and they shall be
My people, and I will be their God, for they
shall return to Me with their whole heart.

8"And as the bad figs which cannot be eaten,
they are so bad'—surely thus says the LORD—
'so will I give up Zedekiah the king of Judah,
his princes, the residue of Jerusalem who
remain in this land, and those who dwell in the
land of Egypt. 9I will deliver them to trouble
into all the kingdoms of the earth, for *their*
harm, *to be* a reproach and a byword, a taunt
and a curse, in all places where I shall drive
them. 10And I will send the sword, the famine,
and the pestilence among them, till they are
consumed from the land that I gave to them
and their fathers.' "

Psalm 119:17–24

ג GIMEL

17 Deal bountifully with Your servant,
That I may live and keep Your word.
18 Open my eyes, that I may see
Wondrous things from Your law.
19 I *am* a stranger in the earth;
Do not hide Your commandments
from me.
20 My soul breaks with longing
For Your judgments at all times.
21 You rebuke the proud— the cursed,
Who stray from Your commandments.
22 Remove from me reproach and
contempt,

119:18 Open my eyes. Perhaps this is the supreme prayer that a student of Scripture could speak since it confesses the student's inadequacy and the divine Author's sufficiency (vv. 98,99,105,130).

For I have kept Your testimonies.
23 Princes also sit *and* speak against me,
But Your servant meditates on Your statutes.
24 Your testimonies also *are* my delight
And my counselors.

Proverbs 27:15–16

15 A continual dripping on a very rainy day
And a contentious woman are alike;
16 Whoever restrains her restrains the wind,
And grasps oil with his right hand.

2 Thessalonians 1:1–12

Greeting

1 Paul, Silvanus, and Timothy,

To the church of the Thessalonians in God our Father and the Lord Jesus Christ:

2 Grace to you and peace from God our Father and the Lord Jesus Christ.

3 We are bound to thank God always for you,
brethren, as it is fitting, because your faith grows
exceedingly, and the love of every one of you all
abounds toward each other, 4 so that we ourselves boast of you among the churches of God
for your patience and faith in all your persecutions and tribulations that you endure, 5 *which is*
manifest evidence of the righteous judgment of
God, that you may be counted worthy of the
kingdom of God, for which you also suffer;
6 since *it is* a righteous thing with God to repay
with tribulation those who trouble you, 7 and to
give you who are troubled rest with us when the
Lord Jesus is revealed from heaven with His
mighty angels, 8 in flaming fire taking vengeance
on those who do not know God, and on those
who do not obey the gospel of our Lord Jesus
Christ. 9 These shall be punished with everlasting destruction from the presence of the Lord
and from the glory of His power, 10 when He
comes, in that Day, to be glorified in His saints
and to be admired among all those who believe,
because our testimony among you was believed.

11 Therefore we also pray always for you that
our God would count you worthy of *this* calling,
and fulfill all the good pleasure of *His* goodness
and the work of faith with power, 12 that the
name of our Lord Jesus Christ may be glorified
in you, and you in Him, according to the grace
of our God and the Lord Jesus Christ.

DAY 19: What should a believer's attitude be toward suffering?

In 2 Thessalonians 1:4, Paul speaks of the "patience and faith" of the Thessalonians. Nowhere was their growth in faith and love more evident than in the way they patiently and faithfully endured hostilities and suffering from the enemies of Christ. Although there was no need to speak, since the Thessalonians' lives spoke clearly enough (1 Thess. 1:8), Paul's joy before the Lord over their perseverance bubbled up.

Having a right attitude toward suffering (v. 5) is essential, and that required attitude is concern for the kingdom of God. They were not self-centered but concentrated on God's kingdom. Their focus was not on personal comfort, fulfillment, and happiness, but on the glory of God and the fulfillment of His purposes. They were not moaning about the injustice of their persecutions. Rather, they were patiently enduring the sufferings they did not deserve (v. 4). This very attitude was "manifest evidence" or positive proof that God's wise process of purging, purifying, and perfecting through suffering was working to make His beloved people worthy of the kingdom (2:12) by being perfected (James 1:2–4; 1 Pet. 5:10).

For believers, afflictions are to be expected (1 Thess. 3:3) as they live and develop Christian character in a satanic world. Suffering is not to be thought of as evidence that God has forsaken them, but as evidence that He is with them, perfecting them (Matt. 5:10; Rom. 8:18; 2 Cor. 12:10). So the Thessalonians demonstrated that their salvation, determined by faith alone in the Lord Jesus Christ, was genuine because they, like Christ, were willing to suffer on account of God and His kingdom. They suffered unjustly as objects of man's wrath against Christ and His kingdom (Acts 5:41; Phil. 3:10; Col. 1:24).

OCTOBER 20

Jeremiah 25:1–26:24

25 The word that came to Jeremiah concerning all the people of Judah, in the
fourth year of Jehoiakim the son of Josiah, king
of Judah (which *was* the first year of
Nebuchadnezzar king of Babylon), 2 which
Jeremiah the prophet spoke to all the people
of Judah and to all the inhabitants of Jerusalem, saying: 3 "From the thirteenth year of
Josiah the son of Amon, king of Judah, even to
this day, this *is* the twenty-third year in which

the word of the LORD has come to me; and I
have spoken to you, rising early and speaking,
but you have not listened. 4And the LORD has
sent to you all His servants the prophets, rising early and sending *them,* but you have not
listened nor inclined your ear to hear. 5They
said, 'Repent now everyone of his evil way and
his evil doings, and dwell in the land that the
LORD has given to you and your fathers forever and ever. 6Do not go after other gods to
serve them and worship them, and do not
provoke Me to anger with the works of your
hands; and I will not harm you.' 7Yet you have
not listened to Me," says the LORD, "that you
might provoke Me to anger with the works of
your hands to your own hurt.

8"Therefore thus says the LORD of hosts:
'Because you have not heard My words, 9be-
hold, I will send and take all the families of the
north,' says the LORD, 'and Nebuchadnezzar
the king of Babylon, My servant, and will
bring them against this land, against its inhabitants, and against these nations all around,
and will utterly destroy them, and make them
an astonishment, a hissing, and perpetual desolations. 10Moreover I will take from them the
voice of mirth and the voice of gladness, the
voice of the bridegroom and the voice of the
bride, the sound of the millstones and the light
of the lamp. 11And this whole land shall be a
desolation *and* an astonishment, and these
nations shall serve the king of Babylon seventy
years.

25:11 seventy years. Here is the first specific statement on the length of the exile . This period probably began in the fourth year of Jehoiakim, when Jerusalem was first captured and the temple treasures were taken. It ends with the decree of Cyrus to let the Jews return, spanning from ca. 605/04 B.C. to 536/35 B.C. The exact number of Sabbath years is 490 years, the period from Saul to the Babylonian captivity. This was retribution for their violation of the Sabbath law (Lev. 26:34,35; 2 Chr. 36:21).

12"Then it will come to pass, when seventy
years are completed, *that* I will punish the king
of Babylon and that nation, the land of the
Chaldeans, for their iniquity,' says the LORD;
'and I will make it a perpetual desolation. 13So I
will bring on that land all My words which I
have pronounced against it, all that is written
in this book, which Jeremiah has prophesied
concerning all the nations. 14(For many nations
and great kings shall be served by them also;
and I will repay them according to their deeds
and according to the works of their own
hands.)' "

15For thus says the LORD God of Israel to me:
"Take this wine cup of fury from My hand, and
cause all the nations, to whom I send you, to
drink it. 16And they will drink and stagger and
go mad because of the sword that I will send
among them."

17Then I took the cup from the LORD's hand,
and made all the nations drink, to whom the
LORD had sent me: 18Jerusalem and the cities
of Judah, its kings and its princes, to make
them a desolation, an astonishment, a hissing,
and a curse, as *it is* this day; 19Pharaoh king of
Egypt, his servants, his princes, and all his
people; 20all the mixed multitude, all the kings
of the land of Uz, all the kings of the land of
the Philistines (namely, Ashkelon, Gaza,
Ekron, and the remnant of Ashdod); 21Edom,
Moab, and the people of Ammon; 22all the kings
of Tyre, all the kings of Sidon, and the kings of
the coastlands which *are* across the sea;
23Dedan, Tema, Buz, and all *who are* in the farthest corners; 24all the kings of Arabia and all
the kings of the mixed multitude who dwell in
the desert; 25all the kings of Zimri, all the
kings of Elam, and all the kings of the Medes;
26all the kings of the north, far and near, one
with another; and all the kingdoms of the world
which *are* on the face of the earth. Also the
king of Sheshach shall drink after them.

27"Therefore you shall say to them, 'Thus
says the LORD of hosts, the God of Israel:
"Drink, be drunk, and vomit! Fall and rise no
more, because of the sword which I will send
among you." ' 28And it shall be, if they refuse to
take the cup from your hand to drink, then
you shall say to them, 'Thus says the LORD of
hosts: "You shall certainly drink! 29For behold,
I begin to bring calamity on the city which is
called by My name, and should you be utterly
unpunished? You shall not be unpunished, for
I will call for a sword on all the inhabitants of
the earth," says the LORD of hosts.'

30"Therefore prophesy against them all these
words, and say to them:

'The LORD will roar from on high,
And utter His voice from His holy
habitation;
He will roar mightily against His fold.
He will give a shout, as those who
tread *the grapes,*
Against all the inhabitants of the earth.
31 A noise will come to the ends of the
earth—

For the LORD has a controversy with
the nations;
He will plead His case with all flesh.
He will give those *who are* wicked to
the sword,' says the LORD."

32 Thus says the LORD of hosts:

"Behold, disaster shall go forth
From nation to nation,
And a great whirlwind shall be
raised up
From the farthest parts of the earth.

33 "And at that day the slain of the LORD shall be
from *one* end of the earth even to the *other* end
of the earth. They shall not be lamented, or
gathered, or buried; they shall become refuse
on the ground.

34 "Wail, shepherds, and cry!
Roll about *in the ashes,*
You leaders of the flock!
For the days of your slaughter and
your dispersions are fulfilled;
You shall fall like a precious vessel.
35 And the shepherds will have no way
to flee,
Nor the leaders of the flock to escape.
36 A voice of the cry of the shepherds,
And a wailing of the leaders to the
flock *will be heard.*
For the LORD has plundered their
pasture,
37 And the peaceful dwellings are cut down
Because of the fierce anger of the
LORD.
38 He has left His lair like the lion;
For their land is desolate
Because of the fierceness of the
Oppressor,
And because of His fierce anger."

26 In the beginning of the reign of
Jehoiakim the son of Josiah, king of Judah, this word came from the LORD, saying,
2 "Thus says the LORD: 'Stand in the court of the
LORD's house, and speak to all the cities of Judah, which come to worship *in* the LORD's
house, all the words that I command you to
speak to them. Do not diminish a word. 3 Perhaps everyone will listen and turn from his
evil way, that I may relent concerning the
calamity which I purpose to bring on them
because of the evil of their doings.' 4 And you
shall say to them, 'Thus says the LORD: "If you
will not listen to Me, to walk in My law which
I have set before you, 5 to heed the words of
My servants the prophets whom I sent to you,
both rising up early and sending *them* (but
you have not heeded), 6 then I will make this
house like Shiloh, and will make this city a
curse to all the nations of the earth." ' "
7 So the priests and the prophets and all the
people heard Jeremiah speaking these words
in the house of the LORD. 8 Now it happened,
when Jeremiah had made an end of speaking
all that the LORD had commanded *him* to
speak to all the people, that the priests and the
prophets and all the people seized him, saying,
"You will surely die! 9 Why have you prophesied in the name of the LORD, saying, 'This
house shall be like Shiloh, and this city shall be
desolate, without an inhabitant'?" And all the
people were gathered against Jeremiah in the
house of the LORD.
10 When the princes of Judah heard these
things, they came up from the king's house to
the house of the LORD and sat down in the
entry of the New Gate of the LORD's *house.*
11 And the priests and the prophets spoke to
the princes and all the people, saying, "This
man deserves to die! For he has prophesied
against this city, as you have heard with your
ears."
12 Then Jeremiah spoke to all the princes and
all the people, saying: "The LORD sent me to
prophesy against this house and against this
city with all the words that you have heard.

26:12 Jeremiah spoke. Leaders and people threatened to kill him (v. 8). The prophet defended himself while in extreme danger. He did not compromise but displayed tremendous spiritual courage. He was ready to die (v. 14), yet warned the crowd that God would hold the guilty accountable (v. 15).

13 Now therefore, amend your ways and your
doings, and obey the voice of the LORD your
God; then the LORD will relent concerning the
doom that He has pronounced against you.
14 As for me, here I am, in your hand; do with
me as seems good and proper to you. 15 But
know for certain that if you put me to death,
you will surely bring innocent blood on yourselves, on this city, and on its inhabitants; for
truly the LORD has sent me to you to speak all
these words in your hearing."
16 So the princes and all the people said to
the priests and the prophets, "This man does
not deserve to die. For he has spoken to us in
the name of the LORD our God."
17 Then certain of the elders of the land rose
up and spoke to all the assembly of the people,

saying: [18]"Micah of Moresheth prophesied in
the days of Hezekiah king of Judah, and spoke
to all the people of Judah, saying, 'Thus says
the LORD of hosts:

"Zion shall be plowed *like* a field,
Jerusalem shall become heaps of
ruins,
And the mountain of the temple
Like the bare hills of the forest." '

[19]Did Hezekiah king of Judah and all Judah
ever put him to death? Did he not fear the
LORD and seek the LORD's favor? And the LORD
relented concerning the doom which He had
pronounced against them. But we are doing
great evil against ourselves."

[20]Now there was also a man who prophesied
in the name of the LORD, Urijah the son of
Shemaiah of Kirjath Jearim, who prophesied
against this city and against this land according to all the words of Jeremiah. [21]And when
Jehoiakim the king, with all his mighty men
and all the princes, heard his words, the king
sought to put him to death; but when Urijah
heard *it,* he was afraid and fled, and went to
Egypt. [22]Then Jehoiakim the king sent men to
Egypt: Elnathan the son of Achbor, and *other*
men *who went* with him to Egypt. [23]And they
brought Urijah from Egypt and brought him
to Jehoiakim the king, who killed him with the
sword and cast his dead body into the graves
of the common people.

[24]Nevertheless the hand of Ahikam the son
of Shaphan was with Jeremiah, so that they
should not give him into the hand of the people
to put him to death.

Psalm 119:25–32

ד DALETH

25 My soul clings to the dust;
Revive me according to Your word.
26 I have declared my ways, and You
answered me;
Teach me Your statutes.
27 Make me understand the way of Your
precepts;
So shall I meditate on Your wonderful
works.
28 My soul melts from heaviness;
Strengthen me according to Your
word.
29 Remove from me the way of lying,
And grant me Your law graciously.
30 I have chosen the way of truth;
Your judgments I have laid *before me.*
31 I cling to Your testimonies;
O LORD, do not put me to shame!
32 I will run the course of Your
commandments,
For You shall enlarge my heart.

Proverbs 27:17

17 *As* iron sharpens iron,
So a man sharpens the countenance of
his friend.

27:17 iron sharpens iron. The benefits of intellectual and theological discussion encourage joy through a keener mind and the improvement of good character which the face will reveal.

2 Thessalonians 2:1–17

2 Now, brethren, concerning the coming of
our Lord Jesus Christ and our gathering
together to Him, we ask you, [2]not to be soon
shaken in mind or troubled, either by spirit or
by word or by letter, as if from us, as though
the day of Christ had come. [3]Let no one
deceive you by any means; for *that Day will*
not come unless the falling away comes first,
and the man of sin is revealed, the son of
perdition, [4]who opposes and exalts himself

2:7 the mystery of lawlessness. This is the spirit of lawlessness already prevalent in society (1 John 3:4; 5:17), but still a mystery in that it is not fully revealed as it will be in the one who so blatantly opposes God that he blasphemously assumes the place of God on earth which God has reserved for Jesus Christ. The spirit of such a man is already in operation (1 John 2:18; 4:3), but the man who fully embodies that spirit has not come. **taken out of the way.** This refers not to spatial removal (therefore it could not be the Rapture of the church) but rather "a stepping aside." The idea is "out of the way," not gone. This restraint will be in place until the Antichrist is revealed, at the midpoint of the Tribulation, leaving him 42 months to reign (Dan. 7:25; Rev. 13:5).

2:9,10 the *lawless one.* He will do mighty acts pointing to himself as supernaturally empowered. His whole operation will be deceptive, luring the world to worship him and be damned. The career of the coming lawless one is more fully described in Revelation 13:1–18.

above all that is called God or that is worshiped, so that he sits as God in the temple of
God, showing himself that he is God.
5Do you not remember that when I was still
with you I told you these things? 6And now you
know what is restraining, that he may be
revealed in his own time. 7For the mystery of
lawlessness is already at work; only He who
now restrains *will do so* until He is taken out of
the way. 8And then the lawless one will be
revealed, whom the Lord will consume with
the breath of His mouth and destroy with the
brightness of His coming. 9The coming of the
lawless one is according to the working of Satan, with all power, signs, and lying wonders,
10and with all unrighteous deception among
those who perish, because they did not receive
the love of the truth, that they might be saved.
11And for this reason God will send them strong
delusion, that they should believe the lie, 12that
they all may be condemned who did not believe
the truth but had pleasure in unrighteousness.
13But we are bound to give thanks to God
always for you, brethren beloved by the Lord,
because God from the beginning chose you for
salvation through sanctification by the Spirit
and belief in the truth, 14to which He called you
by our gospel, for the obtaining of the glory of
our Lord Jesus Christ. 15Therefore, brethren,
stand fast and hold the traditions which you
were taught, whether by word or our epistle.
16Now may our Lord Jesus Christ Himself,
and our God and Father, who has loved us and
given *us* everlasting consolation and good
hope by grace, 17comfort your hearts and establish you in every good word and work.

DAY 20: What is the "falling away" that Paul speaks of in 2 Thessalonians 2:3,4?

The Day of the Lord cannot occur until a deliberate abandonment of a formerly professed position, allegiance, or commitment occurs (the term was used to refer to military, political, or religious rebellion). Some have suggested, on questionable linguistic evidence, that this refers to a "departure" in the sense of the Rapture. Context, however, points to a religious defection, which is further described in v. 4. The language indicates a specific event, not general apostasy which exists now and always will. Rather, Paul has in mind *the* apostasy. This is an event which is clearly and specifically identifiable and unique, the consummate act of rebellion, an event of final magnitude. The key to identifying the event is to identify the main person, which Paul does, calling him the "man of sin." Some texts have "man of lawlessness," but there is no real difference in meaning since sin equals lawlessness (1 John 3:4). This is the one who is called "the prince who is to come" (Dan. 9:26) and "the little horn" (Dan. 7:8), whom John calls "the beast" (Rev. 13:2–10,18) and most know as the Antichrist. The context and language clearly identify a real person in future times who actually does the things prophesied of him in Scripture. He is also called "the son of perdition" or destruction, a term used of Judas Iscariot (John 17:12).

"The falling away" is the abomination of desolation that takes place at the midpoint of the Tribulation spoken of in Daniel 9:27; 11:31 and Matthew 24:15. This man is not Satan, although Satan is the force behind him (v. 9) and he has motives like the desires of the devil (Is. 14:13,14). Paul is referring to the very act of ultimate apostasy which reveals the final Antichrist and sets the course for the events that usher in the Day of the Lord. Apparently, he will be seen as supportive of religion so that God and Christ will not appear as his enemies until the apostasy. He exalts himself and opposes God by moving into the temple, the place for worship of God, declaring himself to be God and demanding the worship of the world. In this act of satanic self-deification, he commits the great apostasy in defiance of God.

OCTOBER 21

Jeremiah 27:1–28:17

27 In the beginning of the reign of
Jehoiakim the son of Josiah, king of Judah, this word came to Jeremiah from the
LORD, saying, 2"Thus says the LORD to me:
'Make for yourselves bonds and yokes, and put
them on your neck, 3and send them to the king
of Edom, the king of Moab, the king of the
Ammonites, the king of Tyre, and the king of
Sidon, by the hand of the messengers who
come to Jerusalem to Zedekiah king of Judah.
4And command them to say to their masters,
"Thus says the LORD of hosts, the God of Israel—thus you shall say to your masters: 5'I
have made the earth, the man and the beast that
are on the ground, by My great power and by
My outstretched arm, and have given it to
whom it seemed proper to Me. 6And now I have
given all these lands into the hand of Nebuchadnezzar the king of Babylon, My servant; and the

beasts of the field I have also given him to
serve him. [7]So all nations shall serve him and
his son and his son's son, until the time of his
land comes; and then many nations and great
kings shall make him serve them. [8]And it shall
be, *that* the nation and kingdom which will not
serve Nebuchadnezzar the king of Babylon,
and which will not put its neck under the yoke
of the king of Babylon, that nation I will punish,'
says the LORD, 'with the sword, the famine, and
the pestilence, until I have consumed them by
his hand. [9]Therefore do not listen to your

27:8 yoke of...Babylon. The point of the object lesson is simple. Any nation that will serve Babylon willingly may stay in their own land, but nations that will not submit voluntarily to Babylon will suffer destruction. Consequently, Judah should submit and not be removed from the land (vv. 9–18).

prophets, your diviners, your dreamers, your
soothsayers, or your sorcerers, who speak to
you, saying, "You shall not serve the king of
Babylon." [10]For they prophesy a lie to you, to
remove you far from your land; and I will drive
you out, and you will perish. [11]But the nations
that bring their necks under the yoke of the
king of Babylon and serve him, I will let them
remain in their own land,' says the LORD, 'and
they shall till it and dwell in it.' " ' "

[12]I also spoke to Zedekiah king of Judah
according to all these words, saying, "Bring
your necks under the yoke of the king of
Babylon, and serve him and his people, and
live! [13]Why will you die, you and your people, by
the sword, by the famine, and by the pestilence,
as the LORD has spoken against the nation that
will not serve the king of Babylon? [14]Therefore
do not listen to the words of the prophets who
speak to you, saying, 'You shall not serve the
king of Babylon,' for they prophesy a lie to you;
[15]for I have not sent them," says the LORD, "yet
they prophesy a lie in My name, that I may
drive you out, and that you may perish, you and
the prophets who prophesy to you."

[16]Also I spoke to the priests and to all this
people, saying, "Thus says the LORD: 'Do not
listen to the words of your prophets who
prophesy to you, saying, "Behold, the vessels
of the LORD's house will now shortly be
brought back from Babylon"; for they prophesy a lie to you. [17]Do not listen to them; serve
the king of Babylon, and live! Why should this
city be laid waste? [18]But if they *are* prophets,
and if the word of the LORD is with them, let
them now make intercession to the LORD of
hosts, that the vessels which are left in the
house of the LORD, *in* the house of the king of
Judah, and at Jerusalem, do not go to Babylon.'

[19]"For thus says the LORD of hosts concerning the pillars, concerning the Sea, concerning the carts, and concerning the remainder
of the vessels that remain in this city, [20]which
Nebuchadnezzar king of Babylon did not take,
when he carried away captive Jeconiah the
son of Jehoiakim, king of Judah, from Jerusalem to Babylon, and all the nobles of Judah
and Jerusalem— [21]yes, thus says the LORD of
hosts, the God of Israel, concerning the vessels that remain in the house of the LORD, and
in the house of the king of Judah and of Jerusalem: [22]'They shall be carried to Babylon, and
there they shall be until the day that I visit
them,' says the LORD. 'Then I will bring them
up and restore them to this place.' "

28

And it happened in the same year, at
the beginning of the reign of Zedekiah
king of Judah, in the fourth year *and* in the
fifth month, *that* Hananiah the son of Azur the
prophet, who *was* from Gibeon, spoke to me in
the house of the LORD in the presence of the
priests and of all the people, saying, [2]"Thus
speaks the LORD of hosts, the God of Israel,
saying: 'I have broken the yoke of the king of
Babylon. [3]Within two full years I will bring
back to this place all the vessels of the LORD's
house, that Nebuchadnezzar king of Babylon
took away from this place and carried to
Babylon. [4]And I will bring back to this place

28:2,3 I have broken the yoke. The false prophet, of the kind Jeremiah warned of in 27:14–16, boldly predicted victory over Babylon and the return of the temple vessels within two years. In actuality, Babylon achieved its third and final step in conquering Judah 11 years later (586 B.C.) as in chapters 39, 40, and 52.

Jeconiah the son of Jehoiakim, king of Judah,
with all the captives of Judah who went to
Babylon,' says the LORD, 'for I will break the
yoke of the king of Babylon.' "

[5]Then the prophet Jeremiah spoke to the
prophet Hananiah in the presence of the
priests and in the presence of all the people
who stood in the house of the LORD, [6]and the
prophet Jeremiah said, "Amen! The LORD do
so; the LORD perform your words which you
have prophesied, to bring back the vessels of

the LORD's house and all who were carried away captive, from Babylon to this place. [7]Nevertheless hear now this word that I speak in your hearing and in the hearing of all the people: [8]The prophets who have been before me and before you of old prophesied against many countries and great kingdoms—of war and disaster and pestilence. [9]As for the prophet who prophesies of peace, when the word of the prophet comes to pass, the prophet will be known *as* one whom the LORD has truly sent."

[10]Then Hananiah the prophet took the yoke off the prophet Jeremiah's neck and broke it. [11]And Hananiah spoke in the presence of all the people, saying, "Thus says the LORD: 'Even so I will break the yoke of Nebuchadnezzar king of Babylon from the neck of all nations within the space of two full years.' " And the prophet Jeremiah went his way.

[12]Now the word of the LORD came to Jeremiah, after Hananiah the prophet had broken the yoke from the neck of the prophet Jeremiah, saying, [13]"Go and tell Hananiah, saying, 'Thus says the LORD: "You have broken the yokes of wood, but you have made in their place yokes of iron." [14]For thus says the LORD of hosts, the God of Israel: "I have put a yoke of iron on the neck of all these nations, that they may serve Nebuchadnezzar king of Babylon; and they shall serve him. I have given him the beasts of the field also." ' "

[15]Then the prophet Jeremiah said to Hananiah the prophet, "Hear now, Hananiah, the LORD has not sent you, but you make this people trust in a lie. [16]Therefore thus says the LORD: 'Behold, I will cast you from the face of the earth. This year you shall die, because you have taught rebellion against the LORD.' "

[17]So Hananiah the prophet died the same year in the seventh month.

Psalm 119:33–40

ה HE
33 Teach me, O LORD, the way of Your
statutes,
And I shall keep it *to* the end.
34 Give me understanding, and I shall
keep Your law;
Indeed, I shall observe it with *my*
whole heart.
35 Make me walk in the path of Your
commandments,
For I delight in it.
36 Incline my heart to Your testimonies,
And not to covetousness.
37 Turn away my eyes from looking at
worthless things,
And revive me in Your way.
38 Establish Your word to Your servant,
Who *is devoted* to fearing You.
39 Turn away my reproach which I dread,
For Your judgments *are* good.
40 Behold, I long for Your precepts;
Revive me in Your righteousness.

119:39 good. The very attributes of God (v. 68) become the characteristics of Scripture: 1) trustworthy (v. 42); 2) true (vv. 43,142,151,160); 3) faithful (v. 86); 4) unchangeable (v. 89); 5) eternal (vv. 90,152); 6) light (v. 105); and 7) pure (v. 140).

Proverbs 27:18

18 Whoever keeps the fig tree will eat its
fruit;
So he who waits on his master will be
honored.

2 Thessalonians 3:1–18

3 Finally, brethren, pray for us, that the word of the Lord may run *swiftly* and be glorified, just as *it is* with you, [2]and that we

3:1 pray for us. Paul frequently enlisted prayer support from the churches for his ministry (Rom. 15:30–32; Eph. 6:18,19; Col. 4:2,3; 1 Thess. 5:25; Philem. 22). In particular, he asked them to pray that the word of God would continue to spread rapidly as it had been already (Acts 6:7; 12:24; 13:44–49) and be received with the honor it deserved.

may be delivered from unreasonable and wicked men; for not all have faith.

[3]But the Lord is faithful, who will establish you and guard *you* from the evil one. [4]And we have confidence in the Lord concerning you, both that you do and will do the things we command you. [5]Now may the Lord direct your hearts into the love of God and into the patience of Christ.

[6]But we command you, brethren, in the name of our Lord Jesus Christ, that you withdraw from every brother who walks disorderly and not according to the tradition which he received from us. [7]For you yourselves know how you ought to follow us, for we were not disorderly among you; [8]nor did we eat anyone's bread free of charge, but worked with labor and toil night and day, that we might not be a burden to any of

you, [9]not because we do not have authority, but
to make ourselves an example of how you
should follow us.
[10]For even when we were with you, we commanded you this: If anyone will not work, neither shall he eat. [11]For we hear that there are
some who walk among you in a disorderly
manner, not working at all, but are busybodies.
[12]Now those who are such we command and exhort through our Lord Jesus Christ that they
work in quietness and eat their own bread.
[13]But *as for* you, brethren, do not grow weary
in doing good. [14]And if anyone does not obey
our word in this epistle, note that person and do
not keep company with him, that he may be
ashamed. [15]Yet do not count *him* as an enemy,
but admonish *him* as a brother.
[16]Now may the Lord of peace Himself give
you peace always in every way. The Lord *be*
with you all.
[17]The salutation of Paul with my own hand,
which is a sign in every epistle; so I write.
[18]The grace of our Lord Jesus Christ *be* with
you all. Amen.

DAY 21: How does Paul's teaching on church discipline in 2 Thessalonians 3:6–15 fit with other major biblical passages on this subject?

Paul addressed a particular issue of church discipline with the Thessalonians in 3:6–15. Helpful parallel passages that should be consulted in studying this one include Matthew 18:15–20, 1 Corinthians 5:1–13, Galatians 6:1–5, and 1 Timothy 5:19,20.

This passage (3:6–15) gives specific direction on the nature of the church's response to someone who deliberately refuses to follow God's Word, expecting to benefit from fellowship with God's people while being unwilling to participate in a meaningful way. Paul's directions were not mere suggestions, but rather they carried the weight and authority of a judge's court order which the apostle delivered and enforced (vv. 4,6,10,12). In Paul's words, "If anyone will not work, neither shall he eat" (3:10). These were fellow believers acting in a parasitic way, sapping the generosity of other believers. Paul had already addressed this pattern in his first letter (1 Thess. 4:11). If there were any questions, Paul called them to imitate him (v. 7; 1 Thess. 1:6) because he imitated Christ (1 Cor. 4:16; 11:1; Eph. 5:1).

This passage offers an emphatic command, a personal confrontation, and a compassionate caution. First, vv. 6 and 14 instruct the rest of the church to "withdraw" and "not keep company" with such a person. In other words, Paul was commanding the church to disfellowship blatantly disobedient Christians in order to produce shame (v. 14) and, hopefully, repentance. Second, Paul was giving the sluggards a direct command to "work in quietness and eat their own bread" (v. 12), removing any excuse that they had not been warned about discipline. Third, Paul added two crucial words of caution. He reminded the believers that genuinely needy people deserved help. He urged them, "Do not grow weary in doing good" (v. 13). He also cautioned them to limit their disciplinary withdrawal. "Yet do not count him as an enemy, but admonish him as a brother" (v. 15). While an unrepentant pattern of sin should be handled decisively, they should continually remember that the person being disciplined is a brother or sister in the Lord. All further warnings to this person about his or her sin should be done with love and concern, praying for this fellow believer's restoration.

The goal for any prescription for church discipline must be the restoration of the sinning person. If successful, Jesus said that "you have gained your brother" (Matt. 18:15). The idea is not merely to punish the offender or to shun him completely, but to remove him as a detrimental influence from the fellowship of the church, and henceforth to regard him as an evangelistic prospect rather than a brother. Ultimately, the sin for which he is excommunicated is a hardhearted impenitence.

OCTOBER 22

Jeremiah 29:1–30:24

29 Now these *are* the words of the letter
that Jeremiah the prophet sent from Jerusalem to the remainder of the elders who
were carried away captive—to the priests, the
prophets, and all the people whom Nebuchadnezzar had carried away captive from Jerusalem to Babylon. [2](This happened after Jeconiah
the king, the queen mother, the eunuchs, the
princes of Judah and Jerusalem, the craftsmen, and the smiths had departed from Jerusalem.) [3]*The letter was sent* by the hand of
Elasah the son of Shaphan, and Gemariah the
son of Hilkiah, whom Zedekiah king of Judah
sent to Babylon, to Nebuchadnezzar king of
Babylon, saying,

4 Thus says the LORD of hosts, the God
of Israel, to all who were carried away
captive, whom I have caused to be

carried away from Jerusalem to
Babylon:
5 Build houses and dwell *in them;* plant
gardens and eat their fruit. [6]Take wives
and beget sons and daughters; and
take wives for your sons and give your
daughters to husbands, so that they
may bear sons and daughters—that
you may be increased there, and not
diminished. [7]And seek the peace of the
city where I have caused you to be
carried away captive, and pray to the
LORD for it; for in its peace you will
have peace. [8]For thus says the LORD of
hosts, the God of Israel: Do not let your
prophets and your diviners who are in
your midst deceive you, nor listen to
your dreams which you cause to be
dreamed. [9]For they prophesy falsely to
you in My name; I have not sent them,
says the LORD.
10 For thus says the LORD: After seventy
years are completed at Babylon, I will
visit you and perform My good word
toward you, and cause you to return to
this place. [11]For I know the thoughts
that I think toward you, says the LORD,
thoughts of peace and not of evil, to
give you a future and a hope. [12]Then
you will call upon Me and go and pray
to Me, and I will listen to you. [13]And you
will seek Me and find *Me,* when you
search for Me with all your heart. [14]I
will be found by you, says the LORD,
and I will bring you back from your
captivity; I will gather you from all the
nations and from all the places where I
have driven you, says the LORD, and I
will bring you to the place from which I
cause you to be carried away captive.
15 Because you have said, "The LORD has
raised up prophets for us in Babylon"—
[16]therefore thus says the LORD
concerning the king who sits on the
throne of David, concerning all the
people who dwell in this city, and
concerning your brethren who have not
gone out with you into captivity— [17]thus
says the LORD of hosts: Behold, I will
send on them the sword, the famine,
and the pestilence, and will make them
like rotten figs that cannot be eaten,
they are so bad. [18]And I will pursue
them with the sword, with famine, and
with pestilence; and I will deliver them
to trouble among all the kingdoms of

29:14 I will be found by you. The Lord would answer their prayer by returning the Jews to their land, Daniel's example and God's response (Dan. 9:4–27). Fulfillment would occur in the era of Ezra and Nehemiah, and beyond this in even fuller measure after the Second Advent of their Messiah (Dan. 2:35,45; 7:13,14,27; 12:1–3,13).

the earth—to be a curse, an
astonishment, a hissing, and a reproach
among all the nations where I have
driven them, [19]because they have not
heeded My words, says the LORD,
which I sent to them by My servants
the prophets, rising up early and
sending *them;* neither would you heed,
says the LORD. [20]Therefore hear the
word of the LORD, all you of the
captivity, whom I have sent from
Jerusalem to Babylon.
21 Thus says the LORD of hosts, the God of
Israel, concerning Ahab the son of
Kolaiah, and Zedekiah the son of
Maaseiah, who prophesy a lie to you in
My name: Behold, I will deliver them
into the hand of Nebuchadnezzar king
of Babylon, and he shall slay them
before your eyes. [22]And because of
them a curse shall be taken up by all
the captivity of Judah who *are* in
Babylon, saying, "The LORD make you
like Zedekiah and Ahab, whom the king
of Babylon roasted in the fire";
[23]because they have done disgraceful
things in Israel, have committed
adultery with their neighbors' wives,
and have spoken lying words in My
name, which I have not commanded
them. Indeed I know, and *am* a witness,
says the LORD.
24 You shall also speak to Shemaiah the
Nehelamite, saying, [25]Thus speaks the
LORD of hosts, the God of Israel, saying:
You have sent letters in your name to
all the people who *are* at Jerusalem, to
Zephaniah the son of Maaseiah the
priest, and to all the priests, saying,
[26]"The LORD has made you priest
instead of Jehoiada the priest, so that
there should be officers *in* the house
of the LORD over every man *who* is
demented and considers himself a

prophet, that you should put him in
prison and in the stocks. 27Now
therefore, why have you not rebuked
Jeremiah of Anathoth who makes
himself a prophet to you? 28For he has
sent to us *in* Babylon, saying, 'This
captivity is long; build houses and
dwell *in them,* and plant gardens and
eat their fruit.' "

29 Now Zephaniah the priest read this
letter in the hearing of Jeremiah the
prophet. 30Then the word of the LORD
came to Jeremiah, saying: 31Send to all
those in captivity, saying, Thus says the
LORD concerning Shemaiah the
Nehelamite: Because Shemaiah has
prophesied to you, and I have not sent
him, and he has caused you to trust in
a lie— 32therefore thus says the LORD:
Behold, I will punish Shemaiah the
Nehelamite and his family: he shall not
have anyone to dwell among this
people, nor shall he see the good that I
will do for My people, says the LORD,
because he has taught rebellion
against the LORD.

30 The word that came to Jeremiah from
the LORD, saying, 2"Thus speaks the
LORD God of Israel, saying: 'Write in a book for
yourself all the words that I have spoken to you.
3For behold, the days are coming,' says the
LORD, 'that I will bring back from captivity My
people Israel and Judah,' says the LORD. 'And I
will cause them to return to the land that I gave
to their fathers, and they shall possess it.' "
4Now these *are* the words that the LORD
spoke concerning Israel and Judah.
5"For thus says the LORD:

'We have heard a voice of trembling,
Of fear, and not of peace.
6 Ask now, and see,
Whether a man is ever in labor with
child?
So why do I see every man *with* his
hands on his loins
Like a woman in labor,
And all faces turned pale?
7 Alas! For that day *is* great,
So that none *is* like it;
And it *is* the time of Jacob's trouble,
But he shall be saved out of it.

8 'For it shall come to pass in that day,'
Says the LORD of hosts,
'*That* I will break his yoke from your
neck,
And will burst your bonds;
Foreigners shall no more enslave them.
9 But they shall serve the LORD
their God,
And David their king,
Whom I will raise up for them.

10 'Therefore do not fear, O My servant
Jacob,' says the LORD,
'Nor be dismayed, O Israel;
For behold, I will save you from afar,
And your seed from the land of their
captivity.
Jacob shall return, have rest and be
quiet,
And no one shall make *him* afraid.
11 For I *am* with you,' says the LORD,
'to save you;
Though I make a full end of all nations
where I have scattered you,
Yet I will not make a complete end
of you.
But I will correct you in justice,
And will not let you go altogether
unpunished.'

12"For thus says the LORD:

'Your affliction *is* incurable,
Your wound *is* severe.
13 *There is* no one to plead
your cause,
That you may be bound up;
You have no healing medicines.
14 All your lovers have forgotten you;
They do not seek you;
For I have wounded you with the
wound of an enemy,
With the chastisement of a
cruel one,
For the multitude of your iniquities,
Because your sins have increased.
15 Why do you cry about your affliction?
Your sorrow *is* incurable.
Because of the multitude of your
iniquities,
Because your sins have increased,

30:7 time of Jacob's trouble. This period of unprecedented difficulty for Israel, as the verse defines, is set in a context of Israel's final restoration. It is best equated with the time of tribulation (vv. 8,9) just before Christ's Second Advent mentioned elsewhere (Dan. 12:1; Matt. 24:21,22) and described in detail by Revelation 6–19.

I have done these things to you.

16 'Therefore all those who devour you
shall be devoured;
And all your adversaries, every one of
them, shall go into captivity;
Those who plunder you shall become
plunder,
And all who prey upon you I will make
a prey.
17 For I will restore health to you
And heal you of your wounds,' says the
LORD,
'Because they called you an outcast
saying:
"This *is* Zion;
No one seeks her." '

18 "Thus says the LORD:

'Behold, I will bring back the captivity
of Jacob's tents,
And have mercy on his dwelling
places;
The city shall be built upon its own
mound,
And the palace shall remain according
to its own plan.
19 Then out of them shall proceed
thanksgiving
And the voice of those who make
merry;
I will multiply them, and they shall not
diminish;
I will also glorify them, and they shall
not be small.
20 Their children also shall be as before,
And their congregation shall be
established before Me;
And I will punish all who oppress them.
21 Their nobles shall be from among them,
And their governor shall come from
their midst;
Then I will cause him to draw near,
And he shall approach Me;
For who *is* this who pledged his heart
to approach Me?' says the LORD.
22 'You shall be My people,
And I will be your God.' "

23 Behold, the whirlwind of the LORD
Goes forth with fury,
A continuing whirlwind;
It will fall violently on the head of the
wicked.
24 The fierce anger of the LORD will not
return until He has done it,
And until He has performed the intents
of His heart.

In the latter days you will consider it.

Psalm 119:41–48

ו WAW

41 Let Your mercies come also to me,
O LORD—
Your salvation according to Your word.
42 So shall I have an answer for him who
reproaches me,
For I trust in Your word.
43 And take not the word of truth utterly
out of my mouth,
For I have hoped in Your ordinances.
44 So shall I keep Your law continually,
Forever and ever.
45 And I will walk at liberty,
For I seek Your precepts.
46 I will speak of Your testimonies also
before kings,
And will not be ashamed.
47 And I will delight myself in Your
commandments,
Which I love.
48 My hands also I will lift up to Your
commandments,
Which I love,
And I will meditate on Your statutes.

Proverbs 27:19

19 As in water face *reflects* face,
So a man's heart *reveals* the man.

1 Timothy 1:1–20

1 Paul, an apostle of Jesus Christ, by the commandment of God our Savior and the Lord
Jesus Christ, our hope,

2 To Timothy, a true son in the faith:

Grace, mercy, *and* peace from God our
Father and Jesus Christ our Lord.

3 As I urged you when I went into
Macedonia—remain in Ephesus that you may
charge some that they teach no other doctrine, 4 nor give heed to fables and endless
genealogies, which cause disputes rather than
godly edification which is in faith. 5 Now the
purpose of the commandment is love from a
pure heart, *from* a good conscience, and *from*
sincere faith, 6 from which some, having
strayed, have turned aside to idle talk, 7 desiring to be teachers of the law, understanding
neither what they say nor the things which
they affirm.

8 But we know that the law *is* good if one uses
it lawfully, 9 knowing this: that the law is not
made for a righteous person, but for *the* lawless
and insubordinate, for *the* ungodly and for sinners, for *the* unholy and profane, for murderers
of fathers and murderers of mothers, for

1:4 fables and endless genealogies. Legends and fanciful stories manufactured from elements of Judaism (v. 7; Titus 1:14), which probably dealt with allegorical or fictitious interpretations of Old Testament genealogical lists. In reality, they were "doctrines of demons" (4:1), posing as God's truth (4:7).

1:8 the law *is* good. The Greek word for "good" can be translated "useful." The law is good or useful because it reflects God's holy will and righteous standard (Ps. 19:7; Rom. 7:12) which accomplishes its purpose in showing sinners their sin (Rom. 3:19) and their need for a Savior (Gal. 3:24). The law forces people to recognize that they are guilty of disobeying God's commands, and it thereby condemns every person and sentences them to hell.

1:13 because I did *it* ignorantly in unbelief. Paul was neither a Jewish apostate nor a Pharisee who clearly understood Jesus' teaching and still rejected Him. He was a zealous, fastidious Jew trying to earn his salvation, thus lost and damned. His plea of ignorance was not a claim to innocence nor an excuse denying his guilt. It was simply a statement indicating that he did not understand the truth of Christ's gospel and was honestly trying to protect his religion. His willing repentance when confronted by Christ is evidence that he had not understood the ramifications of his actions—he truly thought he was doing God a service (Acts 26:9).

manslayers, 10for fornicators, for sodomites, for
kidnappers, for liars, for perjurers, and if there
is any other thing that is contrary to sound
doctrine, 11according to the glorious gospel of
the blessed God which was committed to my
trust.
12And I thank Christ Jesus our Lord who has
enabled me, because He counted me faithful,
putting *me* into the ministry, 13although I was
formerly a blasphemer, a persecutor, and an
insolent man; but I obtained mercy because I
did *it* ignorantly in unbelief. 14And the grace of
our Lord was exceedingly abundant, with faith
and love which are in Christ Jesus. 15This *is* a
faithful saying and worthy of all acceptance,
that Christ Jesus came into the world to save
sinners, of whom I am chief. 16However, for
this reason I obtained mercy, that in me first
Jesus Christ might show all longsuffering, as
a pattern to those who are going to believe on
Him for everlasting life. 17Now to the King
eternal, immortal, invisible, to God who alone
is wise, *be* honor and glory forever and ever.
Amen.
18This charge I commit to you, son Timothy,
according to the prophecies previously made
concerning you, that by them you may wage the
good warfare, 19having faith and a good conscience, which some having rejected, concerning the faith have suffered shipwreck, 20of
whom are Hymenaeus and Alexander, whom I
delivered to Satan that they may learn not to
blaspheme.

DAY 22: Who is Timothy?

Timothy received his name, which means "one who honors God," from his mother (Eunice) and grandmother (Lois), devout Jews who became believers in the Lord Jesus Christ (2 Tim. 1:5) and taught Timothy the Old Testament Scriptures from his childhood (2 Tim. 3:15). His father was a Greek (Acts 16:1) who may have died before Timothy met Paul.

Timothy was from Lystra (Acts 16:1–3), a city in the Roman province of Galatia (part of modern Turkey). Paul led Timothy to Christ (1:2,18; 1 Cor. 4:17; 2 Tim. 1:2), undoubtedly during his ministry in Lystra on his first missionary journey (Acts 14:6–23). When he revisited Lystra on his second missionary journey, Paul chose Timothy to accompany him (Acts 16:1–3). Although Timothy was very young (probably in his late teens or early twenties, since about 15 years later Paul referred to him as a young man; 4:12), he had a reputation for godliness (Acts 16:2). Timothy was to be Paul's disciple, friend, and colaborer for the rest of the apostle's life, ministering with him in Berea (Acts 17:14), Athens (Acts 17:15), Corinth (Acts 18:5; 2 Cor. 1:19), and accompanying him on his trip to Jerusalem (Acts 20:4). He was with Paul in his first Roman imprisonment and went to Philippi (2:19–23) after Paul's release. In addition, Paul frequently mentions Timothy in his epistles. Paul often sent Timothy to churches as his representative (1 Cor. 4:17; 16:10; Phil. 2:19; 1 Thess. 3:2), and 1 Timothy finds him on another assignment, serving as pastor of the church at Ephesus (1:3).

OCTOBER 23

Jeremiah 31:1–32:44

31 "At the same time," says the LORD, "I will be the God of all the families of Israel, and they shall be My people."

2 Thus says the LORD:

"The people who survived the sword
Found grace in the wilderness—
Israel, when I went to give him rest."

3 The LORD has appeared of old to me, *saying:*
"Yes, I have loved you with an everlasting love;
Therefore with lovingkindness I have drawn you.
4 Again I will build you, and you shall be rebuilt,
O virgin of Israel!
You shall again be adorned with your tambourines,
And shall go forth in the dances of those who rejoice.
5 You shall yet plant vines on the mountains of Samaria;
The planters shall plant and eat *them* as ordinary food.
6 For there shall be a day
When the watchmen will cry on Mount Ephraim,
'Arise, and let us go up *to* Zion,
To the LORD our God.' "

7 For thus says the LORD:

"Sing with gladness for Jacob,
And shout among the chief of the nations;
Proclaim, give praise, and say,
'O LORD, save Your people,
The remnant of Israel!'
8 Behold, I will bring them from the north country,
And gather them from the ends of the earth,
Among them the blind and the lame,
The woman with child
And the one who labors with child, together;
A great throng shall return there.
9 They shall come with weeping,
And with supplications I will lead them.
I will cause them to walk by the rivers of waters,
In a straight way in which they shall not stumble;
For I am a Father to Israel,
And Ephraim *is* My firstborn.

10 "Hear the word of the LORD, O nations,
And declare *it* in the isles afar off, and say,
'He who scattered Israel will gather him,
And keep him as a shepherd *does* his flock.'
11 For the LORD has redeemed Jacob,
And ransomed him from the hand of one stronger than he.
12 Therefore they shall come and sing in the height of Zion,
Streaming to the goodness of the LORD—
For wheat and new wine and oil,
For the young of the flock and the herd;
Their souls shall be like a well-watered garden,
And they shall sorrow no more at all.

13 "Then shall the virgin rejoice in the dance,
And the young men and the old, together;
For I will turn their mourning to joy,
Will comfort them,
And make them rejoice rather than sorrow.
14 I will satiate the soul of the priests with abundance,
And My people shall be satisfied with My goodness, says the LORD."

15 Thus says the LORD:

"A voice was heard in Ramah,
Lamentation *and* bitter weeping,
Rachel weeping for her children,
Refusing to be comforted for her children,
Because they *are* no more."

16 Thus says the LORD:

"Refrain your voice from weeping,
And your eyes from tears;
For your work shall be rewarded, says the LORD,
And they shall come back from the land of the enemy.
17 There is hope in your future, says the LORD,
That *your* children shall come back to their own border.
18 "I have surely heard Ephraim bemoaning himself:

'You have chastised me, and I was
chastised,
Like an untrained bull;
Restore me, and I will return,
For You *are* the LORD my God.
19 Surely, after my turning, I repented;
And after I was instructed, I struck
myself on the thigh;
I was ashamed, yes, even humiliated,
Because I bore the reproach of my
youth.'
20 *Is* Ephraim My dear son?
Is he a pleasant child?
For though I spoke against him,
I earnestly remember him still;
Therefore My heart yearns for him;
I will surely have mercy on him, says
the LORD.

21 "Set up signposts,
Make landmarks;
Set your heart toward the highway,
The way in *which* you went.
Turn back, O virgin of Israel,
Turn back to these your cities.
22 How long will you gad about,
O you backsliding daughter?
For the LORD has created a new thing
in the earth—
A woman shall encompass a man."

23 Thus says the LORD of hosts, the God of Israel: "They shall again use this speech in the
land of Judah and in its cities, when I bring
back their captivity: 'The LORD bless you, O
home of justice, *and* mountain of holiness!'
24 And there shall dwell in Judah itself, and in all
its cities together, farmers and those going out
with flocks. 25 For I have satiated the weary soul,
and I have replenished every sorrowful soul."
26 After this I awoke and looked around, and
my sleep was sweet to me.
27 "Behold, the days are coming, says the
LORD, that I will sow the house of Israel and the
house of Judah with the seed of man and the
seed of beast. 28 And it shall come to pass, *that* as
I have watched over them to pluck up, to break
down, to throw down, to destroy, and to afflict,
so I will watch over them to build and to plant,
says the LORD. 29 In those days they shall say no
more:

'The fathers have eaten sour grapes,
And the children's teeth are set on
edge.'

30 But every one shall die for his own iniquity;
every man who eats the sour grapes, his teeth
shall be set on edge.
31 "Behold, the days are coming, says the
LORD, when I will make a new covenant with
the house of Israel and with the house of Judah— 32 not according to the covenant that I
made with their fathers in the day *that* I took
them by the hand to lead them out of the land
of Egypt, My covenant which they broke,
though I was a husband to them, says the
LORD. 33 But this *is* the covenant that I will
make with the house of Israel after those days,
says the LORD: I will put My law in their minds,
and write it on their hearts; and I will be their
God, and they shall be My people. 34 No more
shall every man teach his neighbor, and every
man his brother, saying, 'Know the LORD,' for
they all shall know Me, from the least of them
to the greatest of them, says the LORD. For I
will forgive their iniquity, and their sin I will
remember no more."

35 Thus says the LORD,
Who gives the sun for a light by day,
The ordinances of the moon and the
stars for a light by night,
Who disturbs the sea,
And its waves roar
(The LORD of hosts *is* His name):

36 "If those ordinances depart
From before Me, says the LORD,
Then the seed of Israel shall also cease
From being a nation before Me
forever."

37 Thus says the LORD:

"If heaven above can be measured,
And the foundations of the earth
searched out beneath,
I will also cast off all the seed of Israel
For all that they have done, says the
LORD.

38 "Behold, the days are coming, says the
LORD, that the city shall be built for the LORD
from the Tower of Hananel to the Corner
Gate. 39 The surveyor's line shall again extend
straight forward over the hill Gareb; then it
shall turn toward Goath. 40 And the whole valley of the dead bodies and of the ashes, and all
the fields as far as the Brook Kidron, to the
corner of the Horse Gate toward the east, *shall
be* holy to the LORD. It shall not be plucked up
or thrown down anymore forever."

32 The word that came to Jeremiah from
the LORD in the tenth year of Zedekiah
king of Judah, which was the eighteenth year
of Nebuchadnezzar. 2 For then the king of
Babylon's army besieged Jerusalem, and Jeremiah the prophet was shut up in the court of
the prison, which *was in* the king of Judah's

house. [3]For Zedekiah king of Judah had shut him up, saying, "Why do you prophesy and say, 'Thus says the LORD: "Behold, I will give this city into the hand of the king of Babylon, and he shall take it; [4]and Zedekiah king of Judah shall not escape from the hand of the Chaldeans, but shall surely be delivered into the hand of the king of Babylon, and shall speak with him face to face, and see him eye to eye; [5]then he shall lead Zedekiah to Babylon, and there he shall be until I visit him," says the LORD; "though you fight with the Chaldeans, you shall not succeed" '?"

[6]And Jeremiah said, "The word of the LORD came to me, saying, [7]'Behold, Hanamel the son of Shallum your uncle will come to you, saying, "Buy my field which *is* in Anathoth, for the right of redemption *is* yours to buy *it*." ' [8]Then Hanamel my uncle's son came to me in the court of the prison according to the word of the LORD, and said to me, 'Please buy my field that *is* in Anathoth, which *is* in the country of Benjamin; for the right of inheritance *is* yours, and the redemption yours; buy *it* for yourself.' Then I knew that this was the word of the LORD. [9]So I bought the field from Hanamel, the son of my uncle who *was* in Anathoth, and weighed *out to* him the money—seventeen shekels of silver. [10]And I signed the deed and sealed *it*, took witnesses, and weighed the money on the scales. [11]So I took the purchase deed, *both* that which was sealed *according* to the law and custom, and that which was open; [12]and I gave the purchase deed to Baruch the son of Neriah, son of Mahseiah, in the presence of Hanamel my uncle's *son*, and in the presence of the witnesses who signed the purchase deed, before all the Jews who sat in the court of the prison.

[13]"Then I charged Baruch before them, saying, [14]'Thus says the LORD of hosts, the God of Israel: "Take these deeds, both this purchase deed which is sealed and this deed which is open, and put them in an earthen vessel, that they may last many days." [15]For thus says the LORD of hosts, the God of Israel: "Houses and fields and vineyards shall be possessed again in this land." '

[16]"Now when I had delivered the purchase deed to Baruch the son of Neriah, I prayed to the LORD, saying: [17]'Ah, Lord GOD! Behold, You have made the heavens and the earth by Your great power and outstretched arm. There is nothing too hard for You. [18]*You* show lovingkindness to thousands, and repay the iniquity of the fathers into the bosom of their children after them—the Great, the Mighty God, whose name *is* the LORD of hosts. [19]*You* *are* great in counsel and mighty in work, for Your eyes *are* open to all the ways of the sons of men, to give everyone according to his ways and according to the fruit of his doings. [20]You have set signs and wonders in the land of Egypt, to this day, and in Israel and among *other* men; and You have made Yourself a name, as it is this day. [21]You have brought Your people Israel out of the land of Egypt with signs and wonders, with a strong hand and an outstretched arm, and with great terror; [22]You have given them this land, of which You swore to their fathers to give them—"a land flowing with milk and honey." [23]And they came in and took possession of it, but they have not obeyed Your voice or walked in Your law. They have done nothing of all that You commanded them to do; therefore You have caused all this calamity to come upon them.

[24]'Look, the siege mounds! They have come to the city to take it; and the city has been given into the hand of the Chaldeans who fight against it, because of the sword and famine and pestilence. What You have spoken has happened; there You see *it!* [25]And You have said to me, O Lord GOD, "Buy the field for money, and take witnesses"!—yet the city has been given into the hand of the Chaldeans.' "

[26]Then the word of the LORD came to Jeremiah, saying, [27]"Behold, I *am* the LORD, the God of all flesh. Is there anything too hard for Me? [28]Therefore thus says the LORD: 'Behold, I will give this city into the hand of the Chaldeans, into the hand of Nebuchadnezzar king of Babylon, and he shall take it. [29]And the Chaldeans who fight against this city shall come and set fire to this city and burn it, with the houses on whose roofs they have offered incense to Baal and poured out drink offerings to other gods, to provoke Me to anger; [30]because the children of Israel and the children of

32:14 Take these deeds. Title deeds to the land, kept for security reasons in a pottery jar, would attest in a future day to one's claim of possession. Men of Anathoth did return to Jerusalem from Babylon (Ezra 2:23). Also, some of the poor of the land, left by the Babylonians (chap. 39), could have included certain inhabitants of Anathoth. In a still future day, God will be able (vv. 17,27) to make this land good to a resurrected Jeremiah and confirm to the right people that they are the prophet/priest's descendants.

Judah have done only evil before Me from their youth. For the children of Israel have provoked Me only to anger with the work of their hands,' says the LORD. 31'For this city has been to Me *a provocation of* My anger and My fury from the day that they built it, even to this day; so I will remove it from before My face 32because of all the evil of the children of Israel and the children of Judah, which they have done to provoke Me to anger—they, their kings, their princes, their priests, their prophets, the men of Judah, and the inhabitants of Jerusalem. 33And they have turned to Me the back, and not the face; though I taught them, rising up early and teaching *them,* yet they have not listened to receive instruction. 34But they set their abominations in the house which is called by My name, to defile it. 35And they built the high places of Baal which *are* in the Valley of the Son of Hinnom, to cause their sons and their daughters to pass through *the fire* to Molech, which I did not command them, nor did it come into My mind that they should do this abomination, to cause Judah to sin.'

36"Now therefore, thus says the LORD, the God of Israel, concerning this city of which you say, 'It shall be delivered into the hand of the king of Babylon by the sword, by the famine, and by the pestilence: 37Behold, I will gather them out of all countries where I have driven them in My anger, in My fury, and in great wrath; I will bring them back to this place, and I will cause them to dwell safely. 38They shall be My people, and I will be their God; 39then I will give them one heart and one way, that they may fear Me forever, for the good of them and their children after them. 40And I will make an everlasting covenant with them, that I will not turn away from doing them good; but I will put My fear in their hearts so that they will not depart from Me. 41Yes, I will rejoice over them to do them good, and I will assuredly plant them in this land, with all My heart and with all My soul.'

42"For thus says the LORD: 'Just as I have brought all this great calamity on this people, so I will bring on them all the good that I have promised them. 43And fields will be bought in this land of which you say, "*It is* desolate, without man or beast; it has been given into the hand of the Chaldeans." 44Men will buy fields for money, sign deeds and seal *them,* and take witnesses, in the land of Benjamin, in the places around Jerusalem, in the cities of Judah, in the cities of the mountains, in the cities of the lowland, and in the cities of the South; for I will cause their captives to return,' says the LORD."

Psalm 119:49–56

ז ZAYIN

49 Remember the word to Your servant,
Upon which You have caused me to hope.
50 This *is* my comfort in my affliction,
For Your word has given me life.
51 The proud have me in great derision,
Yet I do not turn aside from Your law.
52 I remembered Your judgments of old, O LORD,
And have comforted myself.
53 Indignation has taken hold of me
Because of the wicked, who forsake Your law.
54 Your statutes have been my songs
In the house of my pilgrimage.
55 I remember Your name in the night, O LORD,
And I keep Your law.
56 This has become mine,
Because I kept Your precepts.

Proverbs 27:20

20 Hell and Destruction are never full;
So the eyes of man are never satisfied.

27:20 Hell and Destruction. Man's desires are never filled up. They are as insatiable as the place of eternal punishment which never overfills.

1 Timothy 2:1–15

2 Therefore I exhort first of all that supplications, prayers, intercessions, *and* giving of thanks be made for all men, 2for kings and all who are in authority, that we may lead a quiet and peaceable life in all godliness and reverence. 3For this *is* good and acceptable in the sight of God our Savior, 4who desires all men to be saved and to come to the knowledge of the truth. 5For *there is* one God and one Mediator between God and men, *the* Man Christ Jesus, 6who gave Himself a ransom for all, to be testified in due time, 7for which I was appointed a preacher and an apostle—I am speaking the truth in Christ *and* not lying—a teacher of the Gentiles in faith and truth.

8I desire therefore that the men pray everywhere, lifting up holy hands, without wrath and doubting; 9in like manner also, that the women adorn themselves in modest apparel, with propriety and moderation, not with braided hair or gold or pearls or costly clothing, 10but, which is

proper for women professing godliness, with
good works. 11Let a woman learn in silence with
all submission. 12And I do not permit a woman to
teach or to have authority over a man, but to be
in silence. 13For Adam was formed first, then
Eve. 14And Adam was not deceived, but the
woman being deceived, fell into transgression.
15Nevertheless she will be saved in childbearing
if they continue in faith, love, and holiness, with
self-control.

2:1 supplications. The Greek word is from a root that means "to lack," "to be deprived," or "to be without." Thus this kind of prayer occurs because of a need. The lost have a great need for salvation, and believers should always be asking God to meet that need. **intercessions.** This word comes from a root meaning "to fall in with someone" or "to draw near so as to speak intimately." The verb from which this word derives is used of Christ's and the Spirit's intercession for believers (Rom. 8:26; Heb. 7:25). Paul's desire is for the Ephesian Christians to have compassion for the lost, to understand the depths of their pain and misery, and to come intimately to God pleading for their salvation.

2:9 adorn...modest apparel. The Greek word for "adorn" means "to arrange," "to put in order," or "to make ready." A woman is to arrange herself appropriately for the worship service, which includes wearing decent clothing which reflects a properly adorned chaste heart. **propriety and moderation.** The Greek word for "propriety" refers to modesty mixed with humility, which carries the underlying idea of shame. It can also refer to a rejection of anything dishonorable to God or to grief over sin. "Moderation" basically refers to self-control over sexual passions. Godly women hate sin and control their passions so as not to lead another into sin.

DAY 23: What is the "New Covenant" in Jeremiah 31:31–34?

God announced here the coming establishment of a New Covenant with His people. This covenant will be different from the one "I made with their fathers in the day that I took them by the hand to lead them out of the land of Egypt, My covenant which they broke." The New Covenant is given in these terms: "I will put My law in their minds, and write it on their hearts; and I will be their God, and they shall be My people."

The fulfillment of this New Covenant was to individuals, as well as to Israel as a nation (v. 36; Rom. 11:16–27). It is set 1) in the framework of a reestablishment in their land (vv. 38–40 and chaps. 30–33) and 2) in the time after the ultimate difficulty (30:7).

In principle, this covenant, also announced by Jesus Christ (Luke 22:20), began to be exercised with spiritual aspects realized for Jewish and Gentile believers in the church era (1 Cor. 11:25; Heb. 8:7–13; 9:15; 10:14–17; 12:24; 13:20). It has already begun to take effect with "a remnant according to the election of grace" (Rom. 11:5). The New Covenant will be also realized by the people of Israel in the last days, including the regathering to their ancient land, Palestine (chaps. 30–33). The streams of the Abrahamic, Davidic, and New Covenants find their confluence in the millennial kingdom ruled over by the Messiah.

OCTOBER 24

Jeremiah 33:1–34:22

33 Moreover the word of the LORD came to
Jeremiah a second time, while he was
still shut up in the court of the prison, saying,
2"Thus says the LORD who made it, the LORD
who formed it to establish it (the LORD *is* His
name): 3'Call to Me, and I will answer you, and
show you great and mighty things, which you
do not know.'
4"For thus says the LORD, the God of Israel,
concerning the houses of this city and the houses of the kings of Judah, which have been pulled
down *to fortify* against the siege mounds and
the sword: 5'They come to fight with the
Chaldeans, but *only* to fill their places with the
dead bodies of men whom I will slay in My
anger and My fury, all for whose wickedness I
have hidden My face from this city. 6Behold, I
will bring it health and healing; I will heal them
and reveal to them the abundance of peace and
truth. 7And I will cause the captives of Judah and
the captives of Israel to return, and will rebuild
those places as at the first. 8I will cleanse them
from all their iniquity by which they have

sinned against Me, and I will pardon all their
iniquities by which they have sinned and by
which they have transgressed against Me.
9 Then it shall be to Me a name of joy, a praise,
and an honor before all nations of the earth,
who shall hear all the good that I do to them;
they shall fear and tremble for all the goodness
and all the prosperity that I provide for it.'

10 "Thus says the LORD: 'Again there shall be
heard in this place—of which you say, "It *is*
desolate, without man and without beast"—in
the cities of Judah, in the streets of Jerusalem
that are desolate, without man and without
inhabitant and without beast, 11 the voice of joy
and the voice of gladness, the voice of the
bridegroom and the voice of the bride, the
voice of those who will say:

"Praise the LORD of hosts,
For the LORD *is* good,
For His mercy *endures* forever"—

and of those *who will* bring the sacrifice of
praise into the house of the LORD. For I will
cause the captives of the land to return as at
the first,' says the LORD.

12 "Thus says the LORD of hosts: 'In this place
which is desolate, without man and without
beast, and in all its cities, there shall again be a
dwelling place of shepherds causing *their*
flocks to lie down. 13 In the cities of the mountains, in the cities of the lowland, in the cities of
the South, in the land of Benjamin, in the
places around Jerusalem, and in the cities of
Judah, the flocks shall again pass under the
hands of him who counts *them,*' says the LORD.

14 'Behold, the days are coming,' says the
LORD, 'that I will perform that good thing
which I have promised to the house of Israel
and to the house of Judah:

15 'In those days and at that time
I will cause to grow up to David
A Branch of righteousness;
He shall execute judgment and
righteousness in the earth.
16 In those days Judah will be saved,
And Jerusalem will dwell safely.
And this *is the name* by which she will
be called:

THE LORD OUR RIGHTEOUSNESS.'

17 "For thus says the LORD: 'David shall never
lack a man to sit on the throne of the house of
Israel; 18 nor shall the priests, the Levites, lack
a man to offer burnt offerings before Me, to
kindle grain offerings, and to sacrifice continually.' "

33:15 A Branch. This is the Messiah King in David's lineage. He is the King whose reign immediately follows the Second Coming when He appears in power (Dan. 2:35,45; 7:13,14,27; Matt. 16:27–28; 24:30; 26:64).

19 And the word of the LORD came to
Jeremiah, saying, 20 "Thus says the LORD: 'If
you can break My covenant with the day and
My covenant with the night, so that there will
not be day and night in their season, 21 then My
covenant may also be broken with David My
servant, so that he shall not have a son to
reign on his throne, and with the Levites, the
priests, My ministers. 22 As the host of heaven
cannot be numbered, nor the sand of the sea
measured, so will I multiply the descendants
of David My servant and the Levites who minister to Me.' "

23 Moreover the word of the LORD came to
Jeremiah, saying, 24 "Have you not considered
what these people have spoken, saying, 'The
two families which the LORD has chosen, He
has also cast them off'? Thus they have despised My people, as if they should no more
be a nation before them.

25 "Thus says the LORD: 'If My covenant *is* not
with day and night, *and if* I have not appointed
the ordinances of heaven and earth, 26 then I
will cast away the descendants of Jacob and
David My servant, *so* that I will not take *any* of
his descendants *to be* rulers over the descendants of Abraham, Isaac, and Jacob. For I will
cause their captives to return, and will have
mercy on them.' "

34 The word which came to Jeremiah
from the LORD, when Nebuchadnezzar
king of Babylon and all his army, all the kingdoms of the earth under his dominion, and all
the people, fought against Jerusalem and all
its cities, saying, 2 "Thus says the LORD, the
God of Israel: 'Go and speak to Zedekiah king
of Judah and tell him, "Thus says the LORD: 'Behold, I will give this city into the hand of the
king of Babylon, and he shall burn it with fire.
3 And you shall not escape from his hand, but
shall surely be taken and delivered into his
hand; your eyes shall see the eyes of the king
of Babylon, he shall speak with you face to face,
and you shall go to Babylon.' " ' 4 Yet hear the
word of the LORD, O Zedekiah king of Judah!
Thus says the LORD concerning you: 'You
shall not die by the sword. 5 You shall die in
peace; as in the ceremonies of your fathers,

the former kings who were before you, so
they shall burn *incense* for you and lament for
you, *saying,* "Alas, lord!" For I have pronounced the word, says the LORD.' "
6Then Jeremiah the prophet spoke all these
words to Zedekiah king of Judah in Jerusalem,
7when the king of Babylon's army fought
against Jerusalem and all the cities of Judah
that were left, against Lachish and Azekah; for
only these fortified cities remained of the
cities of Judah.
8*This is* the word that came to Jeremiah from
the LORD, after King Zedekiah had made a
covenant with all the people who *were* at Jerusalem to proclaim liberty to them: 9that every
man should set free his male and female
slave—a Hebrew man or woman—that no one
should keep a Jewish brother in bondage.
10Now when all the princes and all the people,
who had entered into the covenant, heard that
everyone should set free his male and female
slaves, that no one should keep them in
bondage anymore, they obeyed and let *them*
go. 11But afterward they changed their minds
and made the male and female slaves return,
whom they had set free, and brought them
into subjection as male and female slaves.
12Therefore the word of the LORD came to
Jeremiah from the LORD, saying, 13"Thus says
the LORD, the God of Israel: 'I made a covenant
with your fathers in the day that I brought
them out of the land of Egypt, out of the house
of bondage, saying, 14"At the end of seven years
let every man set free his Hebrew brother, who
has been sold to him; and when he has served
you six years, you shall let him go free from
you." But your fathers did not obey Me nor
incline their ear. 15Then you recently turned
and did what was right in My sight—every
man proclaiming liberty to his neighbor; and
you made a covenant before Me in the house
which is called by My name. 16Then you
turned around and profaned My name, and
every one of you brought back his male and
female slaves, whom you had set at liberty, at
their pleasure, and brought them back into
subjection, to be your male and female slaves.'
17"Therefore thus says the LORD: 'You have
not obeyed Me in proclaiming liberty, every
one to his brother and every one to his neighbor. Behold, I proclaim liberty to you,' says
the LORD—'to the sword, to pestilence, and to
famine! And I will deliver you to trouble
among all the kingdoms of the earth. 18And I
will give the men who have transgressed My
covenant, who have not performed the words of
the covenant which they made before Me, when
they cut the calf in two and passed between the

34:18,21 cut the calf in two. God will give the guilty over to death before the conqueror, for they denied the covenant ratified by blood (v. 21). In this custom, as in Genesis 15:8–17, two parties laid out parts of a sacrifice on two sides, then walked between the parts. By that symbolic action, each pledged to fulfill his promise, agreeing in effect, "May my life (represented by the blood) be poured out if I fail to honor my part."

parts of it— 19the princes of Judah, the princes
of Jerusalem, the eunuchs, the priests, and all
the people of the land who passed between the
parts of the calf— 20I will give them into the
hand of their enemies and into the hand of
those who seek their life. Their dead bodies
shall be for meat for the birds of the heaven
and the beasts of the earth. 21And I will give
Zedekiah king of Judah and his princes into
the hand of their enemies, into the hand of
those who seek their life, and into the hand of
the king of Babylon's army which has gone
back from you. 22Behold, I will command,' says
the LORD, 'and cause them to return to this
city. They will fight against it and take it and
burn it with fire; and I will make the cities of
Judah a desolation without inhabitant.' "

Psalm 119:57–64

ח HETH
57 *You are* my portion, O LORD;
I have said that I would keep Your words.
58 I entreated Your favor with *my* whole heart;
Be merciful to me according to Your word.
59 I thought about my ways,
And turned my feet to Your testimonies.
60 I made haste, and did not delay
To keep Your commandments.
61 The cords of the wicked have bound me,
But I have not forgotten Your law.
62 At midnight I will rise to give thanks to You,
Because of Your righteous judgments.
63 I *am* a companion of all who fear You,
And of those who keep Your precepts.
64 The earth, O LORD, is full of Your mercy;
Teach me Your statutes.

Proverbs 27:21

21 The refining pot *is* for silver and the
furnace for gold,
And a man *is valued* by what others say
of him.

1 Timothy 3:1–16

3 This *is* a faithful saying: If a man desires
the position of a bishop, he desires a good
work. 2A bishop then must be blameless, the
husband of one wife, temperate, sober-minded,

3:1 desires...desires. Two different Greek words are used. The first means "to reach out after." It describes external action not internal motive. The second means "a strong passion" and refers to an inward desire. Taken together, these two words aptly describe the type of man who belongs in the ministry—one who outwardly pursues it because he is driven by a strong internal desire. **bishop.** The word means "overseer" and identifies the men who are responsible to lead the church (5:17; 1 Thess. 5:12; Heb. 13:7). In the New Testament the words "bishop," "elder," "overseer," and "pastor" are used interchangeably to describe the same men (Acts 20:17,28; Titus 1:5–9; 1 Pet. 5:1,2). Bishops (pastors, overseers, elders) are responsible to lead (5:17), preach and teach (5:17), help the spiritually weak (1 Thess. 5:12–14), care for the church (1 Pet. 5:1,2), and ordain other leaders (4:14).

of good behavior, hospitable, able to teach; 3not
given to wine, not violent, not greedy for
money, but gentle, not quarrelsome, not covetous; 4one who rules his own house well, having
his children in submission with all reverence
5(for if a man does not know how to rule his
own house, how will he take care of the church
of God?); 6not a novice, lest being puffed up
with pride he fall into the *same* condemnation
as the devil. 7Moreover he must have a good
testimony among those who are outside, lest
he fall into reproach and the snare of the devil.
8Likewise deacons *must be* reverent, not
double-tongued, not given to much wine, not
greedy for money, 9holding the mystery of the

3:6 not a novice, lest...puffed up with pride. Putting a new convert into a leadership role would tempt him to pride. Elders, therefore, are to be drawn from the spiritually mature men of the congregation. **fall into the *same* condemnation as the devil.** Satan's condemnation was due to pride over his position. It resulted in his fall from honor and authority. The same kind of fall and judgment could easily happen to a new and weak believer put in a position of spiritual leadership.

3:8 deacons. From a word group meaning "to serve." Originally referring to menial tasks such as waiting on tables (Acts 6:1–4), "deacon" came to denote any service in the church. Deacons serve under the leadership of elders, helping them exercise oversight in the practical matters of church life. Scripture defines no official or specific responsibilities for deacons. They are to do whatever the elders assign them or whatever spiritual ministry is necessary.

faith with a pure conscience. 10But let these
also first be tested; then let them serve as deacons, being *found* blameless. 11Likewise, *their*
wives *must be* reverent, not slanderers, temperate, faithful in all things. 12Let deacons be
the husbands of one wife, ruling *their* children
and their own houses well. 13For those who
have served well as deacons obtain for themselves a good standing and great boldness in
the faith which is in Christ Jesus.
14These things I write to you, though I hope
to come to you shortly; 15but if I am delayed, *I*
write so that you may know how you ought to
conduct yourself in the house of God, which is
the church of the living God, the pillar and
ground of the truth. 16And without controversy
great is the mystery of godliness:

God was manifested in the flesh,
Justified in the Spirit,
Seen by angels,
Preached among the Gentiles,
Believed on in the world,
Received up in glory.

DAY 24: What does it mean for an elder to be "the husband of one wife"?

In 1 Timothy 3:2, the Greek is literally a "one-woman man." This says nothing about marriage or divorce (v. 4). The issue is not the elder's marital status but his moral and sexual purity. This qualification heads the list, because it is in this area that leaders are most prone to fail. Various interpretations of this qualification have been offered. Some see it as a prohibition against polygamy—an unnecessary injunction since polygamy was not common in Roman society and clearly forbidden by Scripture (Gen. 2:24), the teaching of Jesus (Matt. 19:5,6; Mark 10:6–9), and Paul (Eph. 5:31). A polygamist could not even have been a church member, let alone a church leader. Others see this requirement as barring those who remarried after the death of their wives. But, as already noted, the issue is sexual purity, not marital status. Further, the Bible encourages remarriage after widowhood (5:14; 1 Cor. 7:39). Some believe that Paul here excludes divorced men from church leadership. That again ignores the fact that this qualification does not deal with marital status. Nor does the Bible prohibit all remarriage after divorce (Matt. 5:31,32; 19:9; 1 Cor. 7:15). Finally, some think that this requirement excludes single men from church leadership. But if that were Paul's intent, he would have disqualified himself (1 Cor. 7:8).

A "one-woman man" is one totally devoted to his wife, maintaining singular devotion, affection, and sexual purity in both thought and deed. To violate this is to forfeit blamelessness and no longer be "above reproach" (Titus 1:6,7).

OCTOBER 25

Jeremiah 35:1–36:32

35 The word which came to Jeremiah from
the LORD in the days of Jehoiakim the
son of Josiah, king of Judah, saying, 2"Go to the
house of the Rechabites, speak to them, and
bring them into the house of the LORD, into one
of the chambers, and give them wine to drink."
3Then I took Jaazaniah the son of Jeremiah,
the son of Habazziniah, his brothers and all his
sons, and the whole house of the Rechabites,
4and I brought them into the house of the
LORD, into the chamber of the sons of Hanan
the son of Igdaliah, a man of God, which *was* by
the chamber of the princes, above the chamber of Maaseiah the son of Shallum, the keeper of the door. 5Then I set before the sons of
the house of the Rechabites bowls full of wine,
and cups; and I said to them, "Drink wine."
6But they said, "We will drink no wine, for
Jonadab the son of Rechab, our father, commanded us, saying, 'You shall drink no wine,
you nor your sons, forever. 7You shall not build
a house, sow seed, plant a vineyard, nor have
any of these; but all your days you shall dwell
in tents, that you may live many days in the
land where you are sojourners.' 8Thus we have
obeyed the voice of Jonadab the son of Rechab,
our father, in all that he charged us, to drink no
wine all our days, we, our wives, our sons, or
our daughters, 9nor to build ourselves houses
to dwell in; nor do we have vineyard, field, or
seed. 10But we have dwelt in tents, and have
obeyed and done according to all that Jonadab
our father commanded us. 11But it came to pass,
when Nebuchadnezzar king of Babylon came
up into the land, that we said, 'Come, let us go
to Jerusalem for fear of the army of the
Chaldeans and for fear of the army of the Syrians.' So we dwell at Jerusalem."
12Then came the word of the LORD to
Jeremiah, saying, 13"Thus says the LORD of
hosts, the God of Israel: 'Go and tell the men
of Judah and the inhabitants of Jerusalem,
"Will you not receive instruction to obey My
words?" says the LORD. 14"The words of
Jonadab the son of Rechab, which he commanded his sons, not to drink wine, are performed; for to this day they drink none, and
obey their father's commandment. But
although I have spoken to you, rising early and
speaking, you did not obey Me. 15I have also
sent to you all My servants the prophets, rising
up early and sending *them,* saying, 'Turn now
everyone from his evil way, amend your
doings, and do not go after other gods to serve
them; then you will dwell in the land which I
have given you and your fathers.' But you have
not inclined your ear, nor obeyed Me. 16Surely
the sons of Jonadab the son of Rechab have
performed the commandment of their father,
which he commanded them, but this people
has not obeyed Me." '
17"Therefore thus says the LORD God of
hosts, the God of Israel: 'Behold, I will bring on
Judah and on all the inhabitants of Jerusalem
all the doom that I have pronounced against
them; because I have spoken to them but they
have not heard, and I have called to them but
they have not answered.' "
18And Jeremiah said to the house of the
Rechabites, "Thus says the LORD of hosts,
the God of Israel: 'Because you have obeyed
the commandment of Jonadab your father, and
kept all his precepts and done according to all
that he commanded you, 19therefore thus says
the LORD of hosts, the God of Israel: "Jonadab
the son of Rechab shall not lack a man to stand
before Me forever." ' "

36 Now it came to pass in the fourth year
of Jehoiakim the son of Josiah, king of

Judah, *that* this word came to Jeremiah from the LORD, saying: 2"Take a scroll of a book and write on it all the words that I have spoken to you against Israel, against Judah, and against all the nations, from the day I spoke to you, from the days of Josiah even to this day. 3It may be that the house of Judah will hear all the adversities which I purpose to bring upon them, that everyone may turn from his evil way, that I may forgive their iniquity and their sin."

4Then Jeremiah called Baruch the son of Neriah; and Baruch wrote on a scroll of a book, at the instruction of Jeremiah, all the words of the LORD which He had spoken to him. 5And Jeremiah commanded Baruch, saying, "I *am*

36:4 Baruch wrote. Jeremiah's recording secretary wrote the prophet's messages and penned them a second time after the first scroll was burned (36:32). He also read the messages in the temple (v. 10) and in the palace (v. 15). Later, Jehudi read a small part of the first scroll before King Jehoiakim (vv. 21–23).

confined, I cannot go into the house of the LORD. 6You go, therefore, and read from the scroll which you have written at my instruction, the words of the LORD, in the hearing of the people in the LORD's house on the day of fasting. And you shall also read them in the hearing of all Judah who come from their cities. 7It may be that they will present their supplication before the LORD, and everyone will turn from his evil way. For great *is* the anger and the fury that the LORD has pronounced against this people." 8And Baruch the son of Neriah did according to all that Jeremiah the prophet commanded him, reading from the book the words of the LORD in the LORD's house.

9Now it came to pass in the fifth year of Jehoiakim the son of Josiah, king of Judah, in the ninth month, *that* they proclaimed a fast before the LORD to all the people in Jerusalem, and to all the people who came from the cities of Judah to Jerusalem. 10Then Baruch read from the book the words of Jeremiah in the house of the LORD, in the chamber of Gemariah the son of Shaphan the scribe, in the upper court at the entry of the New Gate of the LORD's house, in the hearing of all the people.

11When Michaiah the son of Gemariah, the son of Shaphan, heard all the words of the LORD from the book, 12he then went down to the king's house, into the scribe's chamber; and there all the princes were sitting—Elishama the scribe, Delaiah the son of Shemaiah, Elnathan the son of Achbor, Gemariah the son of Shaphan, Zedekiah the son of Hananiah, and all the princes. 13Then Michaiah declared to them all the words that he had heard when Baruch read the book in the hearing of the people. 14Therefore all the princes sent Jehudi the son of Nethaniah, the son of Shelemiah, the son of Cushi, to Baruch, saying, "Take in your hand the scroll from which you have read in the hearing of the people, and come." So Baruch the son of Neriah took the scroll in his hand and came to them. 15And they said to him, "Sit down now, and read it in our hearing." So Baruch read *it* in their hearing.

16Now it happened, when they had heard all the words, that they looked in fear from one to another, and said to Baruch, "We will surely tell the king of all these words." 17And they asked Baruch, saying, "Tell us now, how did you write all these words—at his instruction?"

18So Baruch answered them, "He proclaimed with his mouth all these words to me, and I wrote *them* with ink in the book."

19Then the princes said to Baruch, "Go and hide, you and Jeremiah; and let no one know where you are."

20And they went to the king, into the court; but they stored the scroll in the chamber of Elishama the scribe, and told all the words in the hearing of the king. 21So the king sent Jehudi to bring the scroll, and he took it from Elishama the scribe's chamber. And Jehudi read it in the hearing of the king and in the hearing of all the princes who stood beside the king. 22Now the king was sitting in the winter house in the ninth month, with *a fire* burning on the hearth before him. 23And it happened, when Jehudi had read three or four columns, *that the king* cut it with the scribe's knife and cast *it* into the fire that *was* on the hearth, until all the scroll was consumed in the fire that *was* on the hearth. 24Yet they were not afraid, nor did they tear their garments, the king nor any

36:23 cut it. As often as Jehudi read "three or four columns," the king cut it up, doing so all the way through the whole scroll because he rejected the message (v. 29). Jehoiakim is the king who sent men to Egypt (chap. 26) to bring back God's faithful prophet, Urijah, so that he could execute him.

of his servants who heard all these words.
25 Nevertheless Elnathan, Delaiah, and Gemariah
implored the king not to burn the scroll; but he
would not listen to them. 26 And the king commanded Jerahmeel the king's son, Seraiah the
son of Azriel, and Shelemiah the son of Abdeel,
to seize Baruch the scribe and Jeremiah the
prophet, but the LORD hid them.
27 Now after the king had burned the scroll
with the words which Baruch had written at
the instruction of Jeremiah, the word of the
LORD came to Jeremiah, saying: 28 "Take yet
another scroll, and write on it all the former
words that were in the first scroll which
Jehoiakim the king of Judah has burned. 29 And
you shall say to Jehoiakim king of Judah,
'Thus says the LORD: "You have burned this
scroll, saying, 'Why have you written in it that
the king of Babylon will certainly come and
destroy this land, and cause man and beast to
cease from here?' " 30 Therefore thus says the
LORD concerning Jehoiakim king of Judah: "He
shall have no one to sit on the throne of David,
and his dead body shall be cast out to the heat
of the day and the frost of the night. 31 I will punish him, his family, and his servants for their
iniquity; and I will bring on them, on the inhabitants of Jerusalem, and on the men of Judah
all the doom that I have pronounced against
them; but they did not heed." ' "
32 Then Jeremiah took another scroll and
gave it to Baruch the scribe, the son of Neriah,
who wrote on it at the instruction of Jeremiah
all the words of the book which Jehoiakim
king of Judah had burned in the fire. And
besides, there were added to them many similar words.

Psalm 119:65–72

ט TETH

65 You have dealt well with Your servant,
O LORD, according to Your word.
66 Teach me good judgment and
knowledge,
For I believe Your commandments.
67 Before I was afflicted I went astray,
But now I keep Your word.
68 You *are* good, and do good;
Teach me Your statutes.
69 The proud have forged a lie against
me,
But I will keep Your precepts with *my*
whole heart.
70 Their heart is as fat as grease,
But I delight in Your law.
71 *It is* good for me that I have been
afflicted,
That I may learn Your statutes.
72 The law of Your mouth *is* better to me
Than thousands of *coins of* gold and
silver.

Proverbs 27:22

22 Though you grind a fool in a mortar
with a pestle along with crushed
grain,
Yet his foolishness will not depart from
him.

1 Timothy 4:1–16

4 Now the Spirit expressly says that in latter
times some will depart from the faith, giving heed to deceiving spirits and doctrines of
demons, 2 speaking lies in hypocrisy, having
their own conscience seared with a hot iron,
3 forbidding to marry, *and commanding* to
abstain from foods which God created to be
received with thanksgiving by those who

4:1 the Spirit expressly says. Paul repeats to Timothy the warning he had given many years earlier to the Ephesian elders (Acts 20:29,30). The Holy Spirit through the Scriptures has repeatedly warned of the danger of apostasy (Matt. 24:4–12; Acts 20:29,30; 2 Thess. 2:3–12; Heb. 3:12; 5:11–6:8; 10:26–31; 2 Pet. 3:3; 1 John 2:18; Jude 18). **in latter times.** The period from the First Coming of Christ until His return (Acts 2:16,17; Heb. 1:1,2; 9:26; 1 Pet. 1:20; 1 John 2:18). Apostasy will exist throughout that period, reaching a climax shortly before Christ returns (Matt. 24:12). **depart from the faith.** Those who fall prey to the false teachers will abandon the Christian faith. The Greek word for "depart" is the source of the English word "apostatize" and refers to someone moving away from an original position. These are professing or nominal Christians who associate with those who truly believe the gospel but defect after believing lies and deception, thus revealing their true nature as unconverted. **deceiving spirits.** Those demonic spirits, either directly or through false teachers, who have wandered away from the truth and lead others to do the same. **doctrines of demons.** Not teaching about demons, but false teaching that originates from them. To sit under such teaching is to hear lies from the demonic realm (Eph. 6:12; James 3:15; 2 John 7–11). The influence of demons will reach its peak during the Tribulation (2 Thess. 2:9; Rev. 9:2–11; 16:14; 20:2,3,8,10). Satan and demons constantly work the deceptions that corrupt and pervert God's Word.

4:6 nourished...words of faith...good doctrine. Continual feeding on the truths of Scripture is essential to the spiritual health of all Christians (2 Tim. 3:16,17), but especially of spiritual leaders like Timothy. Only by reading the Word, studying it, meditating on it, and mastering its contents can a pastor fulfill his mandate (2 Tim. 2:15). Timothy had been doing so since childhood (2 Tim. 3:15), and Paul urged him to continue (v. 16; 2 Tim. 3:14). "Words of faith" is a general reference to Scripture, God's revealed truth. "Good doctrine" indicates the theology Scripture teaches.

believe and know the truth. [4]For every creature of God *is* good, and nothing is to be
refused if it is received with thanksgiving; [5]for
it is sanctified by the word of God and prayer.
[6]If you instruct the brethren in these things,
you will be a good minister of Jesus Christ,
nourished in the words of faith and of the good
doctrine which you have carefully followed. [7]But
reject profane and old wives' fables, and exercise yourself toward godliness. [8]For bodily exercise profits a little, but godliness is profitable for
all things, having promise of the life that now is
and of that which is to come. [9]This *is* a faithful
saying and worthy of all acceptance. [10]For to this
end we both labor and suffer reproach, because
we trust in the living God, who is *the* Savior of
all men, especially of those who believe. [11]These
things command and teach.
[12]Let no one despise your youth, but be an
example to the believers in word, in conduct,
in love, in spirit, in faith, in purity. [13]Till I come,
give attention to reading, to exhortation, to
doctrine. [14]Do not neglect the gift that is in
you, which was given to you by prophecy with
the laying on of the hands of the eldership.
[15]Meditate on these things; give yourself
entirely to them, that your progress may be
evident to all. [16]Take heed to yourself and to
the doctrine. Continue in them, for in doing
this you will save both yourself and those who
hear you.

DAY 25: What specific instructions did Paul give Timothy that would apply to a young person?

A young person seeking to live as a disciple of Jesus Christ can find essential guidelines in 4:12–16, where Paul listed five areas (verse 12) in which Timothy was to be an example to the church:

1. In "word" or speech—see also Matthew 12:34–37; Ephesians 4:25,29,31.
2. In "conduct" or righteous living—see also Titus 2:10; 1 Peter 1:15; 2:12; 3:16.
3. In "love" or self-sacrificial service for others—see also John 15:13.
4. In "faith" or faithfulness or commitment, not belief—see also 1 Corinthians 4:2.
5. In "purity" and particularly sexual purity—see also 4:2.

The verses that follow hold several other building blocks to a life of discipleship:

1. Timothy was to be involved in the public reading, study, and application of Scripture (v. 13).
2. Timothy was to diligently use his spiritual gift that others had confirmed and affirmed in a public way (v. 14).
3. Timothy was to be committed to a process of progress in his walk with Christ (v. 15).
4. Timothy was to "take heed" to pay careful attention to "yourself and to the doctrine" (v. 16).

The priorities of a godly leader should be summed up in Timothy's personal holiness and public teaching. All of Paul's exhortations in vv. 6–16 fit into one or the other of those two categories. By careful attention to his own godly life and faithful preaching of the Word, Timothy would continue to be the human instrument God would use to bring the gospel and to save some who heard him. Though salvation is God's work, it is His pleasure to do it through human instruments.

OCTOBER 26

Jeremiah 37:1–38:28

37 Now King Zedekiah the son of Josiah
reigned instead of Coniah the son of
Jehoiakim, whom Nebuchadnezzar king of
Babylon made king in the land of Judah. [2]But
neither he nor his servants nor the people of
the land gave heed to the words of the LORD
which He spoke by the prophet Jeremiah.
[3]And Zedekiah the king sent Jehucal the son
of Shelemiah, and Zephaniah the son of
Maaseiah, the priest, to the prophet Jeremiah,
saying, "Pray now to the LORD our God for us."
[4]Now Jeremiah was coming and going among
the people, for they had not *yet* put him in

prison. 5Then Pharaoh's army came up from
Egypt; and when the Chaldeans who were
besieging Jerusalem heard news of them, they
departed from Jerusalem.
6Then the word of the LORD came to the
prophet Jeremiah, saying, 7"Thus says the
LORD, the God of Israel, 'Thus you shall say to
the king of Judah, who sent you to Me to
inquire of Me: "Behold, Pharaoh's army which
has come up to help you will return to Egypt,
to their own land. 8And the Chaldeans shall
come back and fight against this city, and take
it and burn it with fire." ' 9Thus says the LORD:
'Do not deceive yourselves, saying, "The
Chaldeans will surely depart from us," for they
will not depart. 10For though you had defeated
the whole army of the Chaldeans who fight
against you, and there remained *only* wounded
men among them, they would rise up, every
man in his tent, and burn the city with fire.' "
11And it happened, when the army of the
Chaldeans left *the siege* of Jerusalem for fear of
Pharaoh's army, 12that Jeremiah went out of Jerusalem to go into the land of Benjamin to claim
his property there among the people. 13And
when he was in the Gate of Benjamin, a captain
of the guard *was* there whose name *was* Irijah
the son of Shelemiah, the son of Hananiah; and
he seized Jeremiah the prophet, saying, "You
are defecting to the Chaldeans!"
14Then Jeremiah said, "False! I am not
defecting to the Chaldeans." But he did not listen to him.
So Irijah seized Jeremiah and brought him
to the princes. 15Therefore the princes were
angry with Jeremiah, and they struck him and
put him in prison in the house of Jonathan the
scribe. For they had made that the prison.
16When Jeremiah entered the dungeon and
the cells, and Jeremiah had remained there
many days, 17then Zedekiah the king sent and
took him *out*. The king asked him secretly in
his house, and said, "Is there *any* word from
the LORD?"
And Jeremiah said, "There is." Then he
said, "You shall be delivered into the hand of
the king of Babylon!"
18Moreover Jeremiah said to King Zedekiah,
"What offense have I committed against you,
against your servants, or against this people,
that you have put me in prison? 19Where now
are your prophets who prophesied to you, saying, 'The king of Babylon will not come
against you or against this land'? 20Therefore
please hear now, O my lord the king. Please,
let my petition be accepted before you, and do
not make me return to the house of Jonathan
the scribe, lest I die there."
21Then Zedekiah the king commanded that
they should commit Jeremiah to the court of
the prison, and that they should give him daily
a piece of bread from the bakers' street, until
all the bread in the city was gone. Thus
Jeremiah remained in the court of the prison.

38 Now Shephatiah the son of Mattan,
Gedaliah the son of Pashhur, Jucal the
son of Shelemiah, and Pashhur the son of
Malchiah heard the words that Jeremiah had
spoken to all the people, saying, 2"Thus says
the LORD: 'He who remains in this city shall die
by the sword, by famine, and by pestilence; but
he who goes over to the Chaldeans shall live;
his life shall be as a prize to him, and he shall
live.' 3Thus says the LORD: 'This city shall surely be given into the hand of the king of
Babylon's army, which shall take it.' "
4Therefore the princes said to the king,
"Please, let this man be put to death, for thus
he weakens the hands of the men of war who
remain in this city, and the hands of all the
people, by speaking such words to them. For
this man does not seek the welfare of this
people, but their harm."
5Then Zedekiah the king said, "Look, he *is* in
your hand. For the king can *do* nothing against
you." 6So they took Jeremiah and cast him into
the dungeon of Malchiah the king's son, which
was in the court of the prison, and they let
Jeremiah down with ropes. And in the dungeon
there was no water, but mire. So Jeremiah sank
in the mire.

38:6 no water, but mire. The murderous princes (v. 4) would let God's spokesman die of thirst, hunger, hypothermia, or suffocation if he sank too deeply into the bottom of the cistern.

7Now Ebed-Melech the Ethiopian, one of
the eunuchs, who was in the king's house,
heard that they had put Jeremiah in the dungeon. When the king was sitting at the Gate of
Benjamin, 8Ebed-Melech went out of the
king's house and spoke to the king, saying:
9"My lord the king, these men have done evil
in all that they have done to Jeremiah the
prophet, whom they have cast into the dungeon, and he is likely to die from hunger in the
place where he is. For *there is* no more bread
in the city." 10Then the king commanded Ebed-
Melech the Ethiopian, saying, "Take from
here thirty men with you, and lift Jeremiah the
prophet out of the dungeon before he dies."
11So Ebed-Melech took the men with him and

went into the house of the king under the treasury, and took from there old clothes and old
rags, and let them down by ropes into the dungeon to Jeremiah. 12 Then Ebed-Melech the
Ethiopian said to Jeremiah, "Please put these
old clothes and rags under your armpits, under
the ropes." And Jeremiah did so. 13 So they pulled
Jeremiah up with ropes and lifted him out of the
dungeon. And Jeremiah remained in the court
of the prison.

14 Then Zedekiah the king sent and had
Jeremiah the prophet brought to him at the
third entrance of the house of the LORD. And
the king said to Jeremiah, "I will ask you
something. Hide nothing from me."

15 Jeremiah said to Zedekiah, "If I declare *it* to
you, will you not surely put me to death? And if
I give you advice, you will not listen to me."

16 So Zedekiah the king swore secretly to
Jeremiah, saying, "*As* the LORD lives, who
made our very souls, I will not put you to
death, nor will I give you into the hand of
these men who seek your life."

17 Then Jeremiah said to Zedekiah, "Thus
says the LORD, the God of hosts, the God of Israel: 'If you surely surrender to the king of
Babylon's princes, then your soul shall live;
this city shall not be burned with fire, and you
and your house shall live. 18 But if you do not
surrender to the king of Babylon's princes,
then this city shall be given into the hand of
the Chaldeans; they shall burn it with fire, and
you shall not escape from their hand.' "

19 And Zedekiah the king said to Jeremiah, "I
am afraid of the Jews who have defected to the
Chaldeans, lest they deliver me into their
hand, and they abuse me."

20 But Jeremiah said, "They shall not deliver
you. Please, obey the voice of the LORD which
I speak to you. So it shall be well with you, and
your soul shall live. 21 But if you refuse to surrender, this *is* the word that the LORD has
shown me: 22 'Now behold, all the women who
are left in the king of Judah's house *shall be*
surrendered to the king of Babylon's princes,
and those *women* shall say:

"Your close friends have set upon you
And prevailed against you;
Your feet have sunk in the mire,
And they have turned away again."

23 'So they shall surrender all your wives and
children to the Chaldeans. You shall not
escape from their hand, but shall be taken by
the hand of the king of Babylon. And you shall
cause this city to be burned with fire.' "

24 Then Zedekiah said to Jeremiah, "Let no
one know of these words, and you shall not die.
25 But if the princes hear that I have talked with
you, and they come to you and say to you, 'Declare to us now what you have said to the king,
and also what the king said to you; do not hide
it from us, and we will not put you to death,'
26 then you shall say to them, 'I presented my
request before the king, that he would not make
me return to Jonathan's house to die there.' "

27 Then all the princes came to Jeremiah and
asked him. And he told them according to all
these words that the king had commanded. So
they stopped speaking with him, for the conversation had not been heard. 28 Now Jeremiah
remained in the court of the prison until the
day that Jerusalem was taken. And he was
there when Jerusalem was taken.

Psalm 119:73–80

י YOD

73 Your hands have made me and
fashioned me;
Give me understanding, that I may
learn Your commandments.
74 Those who fear You will be glad when
they see me,
Because I have hoped in Your word.
75 I know, O LORD, that Your judgments
are right,
And *that* in faithfulness You have
afflicted me.
76 Let, I pray, Your merciful kindness be
for my comfort,
According to Your word to Your servant.
77 Let Your tender mercies come to me,
that I may live;
For Your law *is* my delight.
78 Let the proud be ashamed,
For they treated me wrongfully with
falsehood;
But I will meditate on Your precepts.
79 Let those who fear You turn to me,
Those who know Your testimonies.
80 Let my heart be blameless regarding
Your statutes,
That I may not be ashamed.

Proverbs 27:23–27

23 Be diligent to know the state of your
flocks,
And attend to your herds;
24 For riches *are* not forever,
Nor does a crown *endure* to all
generations.
25 *When* the hay is removed, and the
tender grass shows itself,
And the herbs of the mountains are
gathered in,

[26] The lambs *will provide* your clothing,
And the goats the price of a field;
[27] *You shall have* enough goats' milk for
your food,
For the food of your household,
And the nourishment of your
maidservants.

1 Timothy 5:1–25

5 Do not rebuke an older man, but exhort
him as a father, younger men as brothers,
[2]older women as mothers, younger women as
sisters, with all purity.
[3]Honor widows who are really widows. [4]But

5:3 Honor. "To show respect or care," "to support," or "to treat graciously." Although it includes meeting all kinds of needs, Paul had in mind here not only this broad definition but primarily financial support (Ex. 20:12; Matt. 15:1–6; 27:9). **really widows.** Not all widows are truly alone and without resources. Financial support from the church is mandatory only for widows who have no means to provide for their daily needs.

if any widow has children or grandchildren,
let them first learn to show piety at home and
to repay their parents; for this is good and
acceptable before God. [5]Now she who is really
a widow, and left alone, trusts in God and continues in supplications and prayers night and
day. [6]But she who lives in pleasure is dead
while she lives. [7]And these things command,
that they may be blameless. [8]But if anyone
does not provide for his own, and especially
for those of his household, he has denied the
faith and is worse than an unbeliever.
[9]Do not let a widow under sixty years old be
taken into the number, *and not unless* she has
been the wife of one man, [10]well reported for
good works: if she has brought up children, if
she has lodged strangers, if she has washed
the saints' feet, if she has relieved the afflicted,
if she has diligently followed every good work.
[11]But refuse *the* younger widows; for when
they have begun to grow wanton against
Christ, they desire to marry, [12]having
condemnation because they have cast off their
first faith. [13]And besides they learn *to be* idle,
wandering about from house to house, and
not only idle but also gossips and busybodies,
saying things which they ought not. [14]There-
fore I desire that *the* younger *widows* marry,
bear children, manage the house, give no
opportunity to the adversary to speak
reproachfully. [15]For some have already turned
aside after Satan. [16]If any believing man or
woman has widows, let them relieve them, and
do not let the church be burdened, that it may
relieve those who are really widows.
[17]Let the elders who rule well be counted
worthy of double honor, especially those who
labor in the word and doctrine. [18]For the

5:17 elders. This identifies the "bishop" (3:1) or overseer, who is also called pastor (Eph. 4:11). **rule well.** Elders are spiritual rulers in the church. **double honor.** Elders who serve with greater commitment, excellence, and effort should have greater acknowledgment from their congregations. This expression does not mean such men should receive exactly twice as much remuneration as others, but because they have earned such respect they should be paid more generously. **especially.** Means "chiefly" or "particularly." Implicit is the idea that some elders will work harder than others and be more prominent in ministry. **labor.** Literally, "work to the point of fatigue or exhaustion." The Greek word stresses the effort behind the work more than the amount of work. **word and doctrine.** Or better, "preaching and teaching." The first emphasizes proclamation along with exhortation and admonition and calls for a heart response to the Lord. The second is an essential fortification against heresy and puts more stress on instruction.

Scripture says, *"You shall not muzzle an ox
while it treads out the grain,"* and, "The laborer *is* worthy of his wages." [19]Do not receive an
accusation against an elder except from two or
three witnesses. [20]Those who are sinning

5:23 No longer drink only water. "Water" in the ancient world was often polluted and carried many diseases. Therefore Paul urged Timothy not to risk illness, not even for the sake of a commitment to abstinence from wine. Apparently Timothy avoided wine so as not to place himself in harm's way. **use a little wine...infirmities.** Paul wanted Timothy to use wine which, because of fermentation, acted as a disinfectant to protect his health problems due to the harmful effects of impure water.

rebuke in the presence of all, that the rest also
may fear.
21 I charge *you* before God and the Lord Jesus Christ and the elect angels that you
observe these things without prejudice, doing
nothing with partiality. 22 Do not lay hands on
anyone hastily, nor share in other people's
sins; keep yourself pure.
23 No longer drink only water, but use a little
wine for your stomach's sake and your frequent infirmities.
24 Some men's sins are clearly evident, preceding *them* to judgment, but those of some
men follow later. 25 Likewise, the good works *of*
some are clearly evident, and those that are
otherwise cannot be hidden.

DAY 26: Why should elders be chosen very carefully?

Paul cautions Timothy: "Do not lay hands on anyone hastily" (1 Tim. 5:22). This regards the ceremony that affirmed a man's suitability for and acceptance into public ministry as an elder/pastor/overseer. This came from the Old Testament practice of laying hands on a sacrificial animal to identify with it (Ex. 29:10,15,19). "Hastily" refers to proceeding with this ceremony without a thorough investigation and preparation period to be certain of the man's qualifications (as in 3:1–7). "Nor share in other people's sins." This refers to the sin of hasty ordination, which makes those responsible culpable for the man's sin of serving as an unqualified elder and, thus, misleading people. "Keep yourself pure." Some versions translate "pure" as "free from sin." Paul wanted Timothy, by not participating in the recognition of unqualified elders, to remain untainted by others' sins. The church desperately needed qualified spiritual leaders, but the selection had to be carefully executed.

In v. 24, Paul adds that "some men's sins are clearly evident." The sins of some men are manifest for all to see, thus disqualifying them out of hand for service as elders. "Preceding them to judgment." The known sins of the unqualified announce those men's guilt and unfitness before all. "Judgment" refers to the church's process for determining men's suitability to serve as elders. "But those of some men follow later." The sins of other candidates for elder will come to light in time, perhaps even during the scrutiny of the evaluation process.

The same is true of good works (v. 25). Some are evident; others come to light later. Time and truth go hand in hand. The whole emphasis in this instruction regarding choosing elders, according to the qualifications of 3:1–7, is to be patient, fair, impartial, and pure (vv. 21–25). Such an approach will yield the right choices.

OCTOBER 27

Jeremiah 39:1–40:16

39 In the ninth year of Zedekiah king of
Judah, in the tenth month, Nebuchadnezzar king of Babylon and all his army came
against Jerusalem, and besieged it. 2 In the eleventh year of Zedekiah, in the fourth month, on
the ninth *day* of the month, the city was penetrated.
3 Then all the princes of the king of Babylon
came in and sat in the Middle Gate: Nergal-
Sharezer, Samgar-Nebo, Sarsechim, Rabsaris,
Nergal-Sarezer, Rabmag, with the rest of the
princes of the king of Babylon.
4 So it was, when Zedekiah the king of Judah
and all the men of war saw them, that they fled
and went out of the city by night, by way of the
king's garden, by the gate between the two
walls. And he went out by way of the plain.
5 But the Chaldean army pursued them and
overtook Zedekiah in the plains of Jericho.
And when they had captured him, they
brought him up to Nebuchadnezzar king of
Babylon, to Riblah in the land of Hamath,
where he pronounced judgment on him.
6 Then the king of Babylon killed the sons of
Zedekiah before his eyes in Riblah; the king of
Babylon also killed all the nobles of Judah.
7 Moreover he put out Zedekiah's eyes, and
bound him with bronze fetters to carry him
off to Babylon. 8 And the Chaldeans burned the
king's house and the houses of the people with
fire, and broke down the walls of Jerusalem.
9 Then Nebuzaradan the captain of the guard
carried away captive to Babylon the remnant
of the people who remained in the city and
those who defected to him, with the rest of the
people who remained. 10 But Nebuzaradan the
captain of the guard left in the land of Judah
the poor people, who had nothing, and gave
them vineyards and fields at the same time.
11 Now Nebuchadnezzar king of Babylon gave
charge concerning Jeremiah to Nebuzaradan
the captain of the guard, saying, 12 "Take him
and look after him, and do him no harm; but

do to him just as he says to you." [13]So
Nebuzaradan the captain of the guard sent
Nebushasban, Rabsaris, Nergal-Sharezer,
Rabmag, and all the king of Babylon's chief
officers; [14]then they sent *someone* to take
Jeremiah from the court of the prison, and
committed him to Gedaliah the son of Ahikam,
the son of Shaphan, that he should take him
home. So he dwelt among the people.

[15]Meanwhile the word of the LORD had come
to Jeremiah while he was shut up in the court
of the prison, saying, [16]"Go and speak to Ebed-
Melech the Ethiopian, saying, 'Thus says the
LORD of hosts, the God of Israel: "Behold, I will
bring My words upon this city for adversity
and not for good, and they shall be *performed*
in that day before you. [17]But I will deliver you in
that day," says the LORD, "and you shall not be
given into the hand of the men of whom you
are afraid. [18]For I will surely deliver you, and
you shall not fall by the sword; but your life
shall be as a prize to you, because you have
put your trust in Me," says the LORD.' "

40 The word that came to Jeremiah from
the LORD after Nebuzaradan the captain of the guard had let him go from Ramah,
when he had taken him bound in chains
among all who were carried away captive from
Jerusalem and Judah, who were carried away
captive to Babylon.

[2]And the captain of the guard took Jeremiah
and said to him: "The LORD your God has pronounced this doom on this place. [3]Now the
LORD has brought *it,* and has done just as He
said. Because you *people* have sinned against
the LORD, and not obeyed His voice, therefore
this thing has come upon you. [4]And now look,
I free you this day from the chains that *were*
on your hand. If it seems good to you to come
with me to Babylon, come, and I will look after
you. But if it seems wrong for you to come
with me to Babylon, remain here. See, all the
land *is* before you; wherever it seems good
and convenient for you to go, go there."

[5]Now while Jeremiah had not yet gone
back, *Nebuzaradan said,* "Go back to Gedaliah
the son of Ahikam, the son of Shaphan, whom
the king of Babylon has made governor over
the cities of Judah, and dwell with him
among the people. Or go wherever it seems
convenient for you to go." So the captain of the
guard gave him rations and a gift and let him
go. [6]Then Jeremiah went to Gedaliah the son
of Ahikam, to Mizpah, and dwelt with him
among the people who were left in the land.

[7]And when all the captains of the armies who
were in the fields, they and their men, heard
that the king of Babylon had made Gedaliah
the son of Ahikam governor in the land, and
had committed to him men, women, children,
and the poorest of the land who had not been
carried away captive to Babylon, [8]then they
came to Gedaliah at Mizpah—Ishmael the son
of Nethaniah, Johanan and Jonathan the sons
of Kareah, Seraiah the son of Tanhumeth, the
sons of Ephai the Netophathite, and Jezaniah
the son of a Maachathite, they and their men.
[9]And Gedaliah the son of Ahikam, the son of
Shaphan, took an oath before them and their
men, saying, "Do not be afraid to serve the
Chaldeans. Dwell in the land and serve the
king of Babylon, and it shall be well with you.
[10]As for me, I will indeed dwell at Mizpah and
serve the Chaldeans who come to us. But you,
gather wine and summer fruit and oil, put *them*
in your vessels, and dwell in your cities that
you have taken." [11]Likewise, when all the Jews
who *were* in Moab, among the Ammonites, in
Edom, and who *were* in all the countries, heard
that the king of Babylon had left a remnant of
Judah, and that he had set over them Gedaliah
the son of Ahikam, the son of Shaphan, [12]then
all the Jews returned out of all places where
they had been driven, and came to the land of
Judah, to Gedaliah at Mizpah, and gathered
wine and summer fruit in abundance.

[13]Moreover Johanan the son of Kareah and
all the captains of the forces that *were* in the
fields came to Gedaliah at Mizpah, [14]and said to
him, "Do you certainly know that Baalis the
king of the Ammonites has sent Ishmael the
son of Nethaniah to murder you?" But Gedaliah
the son of Ahikam did not believe them.

[15]Then Johanan the son of Kareah spoke
secretly to Gedaliah in Mizpah, saying, "Let
me go, please, and I will kill Ishmael the son of
Nethaniah, and no one will know *it.* Why
should he murder you, so that all the Jews
who are gathered to you would be scattered,
and the remnant in Judah perish?"

[16]But Gedaliah the son of Ahikam said to
Johanan the son of Kareah, "You shall not do
this thing, for you speak falsely concerning
Ishmael."

Psalm 119:81–88

כ KAPH

81 My soul faints for Your salvation,
But I hope in Your word.
82 My eyes fail *from searching*
Your word,
Saying, "When will You comfort me?"
83 For I have become like a wineskin in
smoke,

119:83 a wineskin in smoke. Just as smoke will dry out, stiffen, and crack a wineskin thus making it useless, so the psalmist's affliction has debilitated him.

Yet I do not forget Your statutes.
84 How many *are* the days of Your servant?
When will You execute judgment on those who persecute me?
85 The proud have dug pits for me,
Which *is* not according to Your law.
86 All Your commandments *are* faithful;
They persecute me wrongfully;
Help me!
87 They almost made an end of me on earth,
But I did not forsake Your precepts.
88 Revive me according to Your lovingkindness,
So that I may keep the testimony of Your mouth.

Proverbs 28:1

28 The wicked flee when no one pursues,
But the righteous are bold as a lion.

28:1 A guilty conscience imagines accusers everywhere (Num. 32:23; Ps. 53:5), while a clear conscience has boldness to face everyone.

1 Timothy 6:1–21

6 Let as many bondservants as are under the yoke count their own masters worthy of all honor, so that the name of God and *His* doctrine may not be blasphemed. 2And those who have believing masters, let them not despise *them* because they are brethren, but rather serve *them* because those who are benefited are believers and beloved. Teach and exhort these things.

3If anyone teaches otherwise and does not consent to wholesome words, *even* the words of our Lord Jesus Christ, and to the doctrine which accords with godliness, 4he is proud, knowing nothing, but is obsessed with disputes and arguments over words, from which come envy, strife, reviling, evil suspicions, 5useless wranglings of men of corrupt minds and destitute of the truth, who suppose that

6:3 Paul identifies 3 characteristics of false teachers: 1) they "teach otherwise"—a different doctrine, or any teaching that contradicts God's revelation in Scripture; 2) they do "not consent to wholesome words"—they do not agree with sound, healthy teaching, specifically the teaching contained in Scripture; and 3) they reject "doctrine which accords with godliness"—teaching not based on Scripture will always result in an unholy life. Instead of godliness, false teachers will be marked by sin.

godliness is a *means of* gain. From such withdraw yourself.

6Now godliness with contentment is great gain. 7For we brought nothing into *this* world, *and it is* certain we can carry nothing out. 8And having food and clothing, with these we shall be content. 9But those who desire to be rich fall into temptation and a snare, and *into* many foolish and harmful lusts which drown men in destruction and perdition. 10For the love of money is a root of all *kinds of* evil, for which some have strayed from the faith in their greediness, and pierced themselves through with many sorrows.

11But you, O man of God, flee these things and pursue righteousness, godliness, faith, love, patience, gentleness. 12Fight the good fight of faith, lay hold on eternal life, to which you were also called and have confessed the good confession in the presence of many witnesses. 13I urge

6:12 Fight the good fight of faith. The Greek word for "fight" gives us the English word "agonize" and was used in both military and athletic endeavors to describe the concentration, discipline, and extreme effort needed to win. The "good fight of faith" is the spiritual conflict with Satan's kingdom of darkness in which all men of God are necessarily involved. **lay hold on eternal life.** Paul is here admonishing Timothy to "get a grip" on the reality of the matters associated with eternal life, so that he would live and minister with a heavenly and eternal perspective (Phil. 3:20; Col. 3:2). **to which you were also called.** Refers to God's effectual, sovereign call of Timothy to salvation. **good confession.** Timothy's public confession of faith in the Lord Jesus Christ, which likely occurred at his baptism and again when he was ordained to the ministry (4:14; 2 Tim. 1:6).

you in the sight of God who gives life to all
things, and *before* Christ Jesus who witnessed
the good confession before Pontius Pilate, [14]that
you keep *this* commandment without spot,
blameless until our Lord Jesus Christ's appearing, [15]which He will manifest in His own time, *He
who is* the blessed and only Potentate, the King
of kings and Lord of lords, [16]who alone has
immortality, dwelling in unapproachable light,
whom no man has seen or can see, to whom *be*
honor and everlasting power. Amen.
[17]Command those who are rich in this present age not to be haughty, nor to trust in
uncertain riches but in the living God, who
gives us richly all things to enjoy. [18]*Let them* do
good, that they be rich in good works, ready to
give, willing to share, [19]storing up for themselves a good foundation for the time to come,
that they may lay hold on eternal life.

6:17–19 Paul counsels Timothy what to teach those who are rich in material possessions, those who have more than the mere essentials of food, clothing, and shelter. Paul does not condemn such people nor command them to get rid of their wealth. He does call them to be good stewards of their God-given resources (Deut. 8:18; 1 Sam. 2:7; 1 Chr. 29:12).

[20]O Timothy! Guard what was committed to
your trust, avoiding the profane *and* idle babblings and contradictions of what is falsely
called knowledge— [21]by professing it some
have strayed concerning the faith.
Grace *be* with you. Amen.

DAY 27: How can a believer find genuine contentment?

In 1 Timonty 6:6, the Greek word for "contentment" means "self-sufficiency" and was used by Stoic philosophers to describe a person who was unflappable and unmoved by external circumstances. Christians are to be satisfied and sufficient and not to seek for more than what God has already given them. He is the source of true contentment (2 Cor. 3:5; 9:8; Phil. 4:11–13,19).

"Having food and clothing,...be content" (v. 8). The basic necessities of life are what ought to make Christians content. Paul does not condemn having possessions as long as God graciously provides them (v. 17). He does, however, condemn a self-indulgent desire for money, which results from discontentment.

"But those who desire to be rich fall into temptation" (v. 9). "Desire" refers to a settled wish born of reason and clearly describes those guilty of greed. The form of the Greek verb for "fall" indicates that those who have such a desire are continually falling into temptation. Greedy people are compulsive—they are continually trapped in sins by their consuming desire to acquire more. "In destruction and perdition." Such greed may lead these people to suffer the tragic end of destruction and hell. These terms refer to the eternal punishment of the wicked.

"For the love of money" (v. 10). Literally, "affection for silver." In the context, this sin applies to false teachers specifically, but the principle is true universally. Money itself is not evil since it is a gift from God (Deut. 8:18). Paul condemns only the love of it (Matt. 6:24), which is so characteristic of false teachers (1 Pet. 5:2; 2 Pet. 2:1–3,15). "Some have strayed from the faith." From the body of Christian truth. Gold has replaced God for these apostates, who have turned away from pursuing the things of God in favor of money.

OCTOBER 28

Jeremiah 41:1–42:22

41 Now it came to pass in the seventh month
that Ishmael the son of Nethaniah, the
son of Elishama, of the royal family and of the
officers of the king, came with ten men to
Gedaliah the son of Ahikam, at Mizpah. And
there they ate bread together in Mizpah. [2]Then
Ishmael the son of Nethaniah, and the ten men
who were with him, arose and struck Gedaliah
the son of Ahikam, the son of Shaphan, with
the sword, and killed him whom the king of
Babylon had made governor over the land.
[3]Ishmael also struck down all the Jews who
were with him, *that is,* with Gedaliah at
Mizpah, and the Chaldeans who were found
there, the men of war.
[4]And it happened, on the second day after
he had killed Gedaliah, when as yet no one
knew *it,* [5]that certain men came from
Shechem, from Shiloh, and from Samaria,
eighty men with their beards shaved and their
clothes torn, having cut themselves, with
offerings and incense in their hand, to bring
them to the house of the LORD. [6]Now Ishmael
the son of Nethaniah went out from Mizpah to

meet them, weeping as he went along; and it
happened as he met them that he said to them,
"Come to Gedaliah the son of Ahikam!" [7]So it
was, when they came into the midst of the city,
that Ishmael the son of Nethaniah killed them
and cast them into the midst of a pit, he and the
men who were with him. [8]But ten men were
found among them who said to Ishmael, "Do
not kill us, for we have treasures of wheat, barley, oil, and honey in the field." So he desisted
and did not kill them among their brethren.
[9]Now the pit into which Ishmael had cast all the
dead bodies of the men whom he had slain,
because of Gedaliah, *was* the same one Asa the
king had made for fear of Baasha king of Israel. Ishmael the son of Nethaniah filled it with
the slain. [10]Then Ishmael carried away captive
all the rest of the people who *were* in Mizpah,
the king's daughters and all the people who
remained in Mizpah, whom Nebuzaradan the
captain of the guard had committed to
Gedaliah the son of Ahikam. And Ishmael the
son of Nethaniah carried them away captive
and departed to go over to the Ammonites.

[11]But when Johanan the son of Kareah and
all the captains of the forces that *were* with
him heard of all the evil that Ishmael the son
of Nethaniah had done, [12]they took all the men
and went to fight with Ishmael the son of
Nethaniah; and they found him by the great
pool that *is* in Gibeon. [13]So it was, when all the
people who *were* with Ishmael saw Johanan the
son of Kareah, and all the captains of the forces
who *were* with him, that they were glad. [14]Then
all the people whom Ishmael had carried away
captive from Mizpah turned around and came
back, and went to Johanan the son of Kareah.
[15]But Ishmael the son of Nethaniah escaped
from Johanan with eight men and went to the
Ammonites.

[16]Then Johanan the son of Kareah, and all
the captains of the forces that were with him,
took from Mizpah all the rest of the people
whom he had recovered from Ishmael the son
of Nethaniah after he had murdered Gedaliah
the son of Ahikam—the mighty men of war
and the women and the children and the
eunuchs, whom he had brought back from
Gibeon. [17]And they departed and dwelt in the
habitation of Chimham, which is near Bethlehem, as they went on their way to Egypt, [18]be-
cause of the Chaldeans; for they were afraid of
them, because Ishmael the son of Nethaniah
had murdered Gedaliah the son of Ahikam,
whom the king of Babylon had made governor
in the land.

42 Now all the captains of the forces,
Johanan the son of Kareah, Jezaniah
the son of Hoshaiah, and all the people, from
the least to the greatest, came near [2]and said
to Jeremiah the prophet, "Please, let our petition be acceptable to you, and pray for us to
the LORD your God, for all this remnant (since
we are left *but* a few of many, as you can see),
[3]that the LORD your God may show us the way
in which we should walk and the thing we
should do."

[4]Then Jeremiah the prophet said to them, "I
have heard. Indeed, I will pray to the LORD
your God according to your words, and it shall
be, *that* whatever the LORD answers you, I will
declare *it* to you. I will keep nothing back from
you."

[5]So they said to Jeremiah, "Let the LORD be
a true and faithful witness between us, if we do
not do according to everything which the
LORD your God sends us by you. [6]Whether *it is*
pleasing or displeasing, we will obey the voice
of the LORD our God to whom we send you,
that it may be well with us when we obey the
voice of the LORD our God."

[7]And it happened after ten days that the
word of the LORD came to Jeremiah. [8]Then he
called Johanan the son of Kareah, all the captains of the forces which *were* with him, and all
the people from the least even to the greatest,
[9]and said to them, "Thus says the LORD, the
God of Israel, to whom you sent me to present
your petition before Him: [10]'If you will still
remain in this land, then I will build you and
not pull *you* down, and I will plant you and not
pluck *you* up. For I relent concerning the disaster that I have brought upon you. [11]Do not
be afraid of the king of Babylon, of whom you
are afraid; do not be afraid of him,' says the
LORD, 'for I *am* with you, to save you and deliver you from his hand. [12]And I will show you
mercy, that he may have mercy on you and
cause you to return to your own land.'

[13]"But if you say, 'We will not dwell in this
land,' disobeying the voice of the LORD your
God, [14]saying, 'No, but we will go to the land of
Egypt where we shall see no war, nor hear the
sound of the trumpet, nor be hungry for
bread, and there we will dwell'— [15]Then hear
now the word of the LORD, O remnant of Judah! Thus says the LORD of hosts, the God of
Israel: 'If you wholly set your faces to enter
Egypt, and go to dwell there, [16]then it shall be
that the sword which you feared shall overtake you there in the land of Egypt; the famine
of which you were afraid shall follow close
after you there *in* Egypt; and there you shall

die. 17So shall it be with all the men who set their faces to go to Egypt to dwell there. They shall die by the sword, by famine, and by pestilence. And none of them shall remain or escape from the disaster that I will bring upon them.'

18"For thus says the LORD of hosts, the God of Israel: 'As My anger and My fury have been poured out on the inhabitants of Jerusalem, so will My fury be poured out on you when you enter Egypt. And you shall be an oath, an astonishment, a curse, and a reproach; and you shall see this place no more.'

19"The LORD has said concerning you, O remnant of Judah, 'Do not go to Egypt!' Know certainly that I have admonished you this day. 20For you were hypocrites in your hearts when you sent me to the LORD your God, saying, 'Pray for us to the LORD our God, and according to all that the LORD your God says, so declare to us and we will do *it.*' 21And I have this day declared *it* to you, but you have not obeyed the voice of the LORD your God, or anything which He has sent you by me. 22Now therefore, know certainly that you shall die by the sword, by famine, and by pestilence in the place where you desire to go to dwell."

Psalm 119:89–96

ל LAMED

89 Forever, O LORD,
Your word is settled in heaven.
90 Your faithfulness *endures* to all
generations;
You established the earth, and it
abides.
91 They continue this day according to
Your ordinances,
For all *are* Your servants.
92 Unless Your law *had been* my delight,
I would then have perished in my
affliction.
93 I will never forget Your precepts,
For by them You have given me life.
94 I *am* Yours, save me;
For I have sought Your precepts.
95 The wicked wait for me to destroy me,
But I will consider Your testimonies.
96 I have seen the consummation of all
perfection,
But Your commandment *is* exceedingly
broad.

Proverbs 28:2

2 Because of the transgression of a land,
many *are* its princes;
But by a man of understanding *and*
knowledge
Right will be prolonged.

28:2 many *are* its princes. Unrighteousness in a nation produces political instability with many vying for power, thus the tenure of each leader is shortened. Wisdom promotes social order and long rule.

2 Timothy 1:1–18

1 Paul, an apostle of Jesus Christ by the will of God, according to the promise of life which is in Christ Jesus,

2To Timothy, a beloved son:

Grace, mercy, *and* peace from God the Father and Christ Jesus our Lord.

3I thank God, whom I serve with a pure conscience, as *my* forefathers *did,* as without ceasing I remember you in my prayers night and day, 4greatly desiring to see you, being mindful of your tears, that I may be filled with joy,

1:4 mindful of your tears. Paul perhaps remembered this occurring at their latest parting, which occurred after a short visit to Ephesus, following the writing of 1 Timothy and prior to Paul's arrest at Troas and his second imprisonment in Rome. Years before, Paul had a similar parting with the elders at Ephesus (Acts 20:36–38).

5when I call to remembrance the genuine faith that is in you, which dwelt first in your grandmother Lois and your mother Eunice, and I am persuaded is in you also. 6Therefore I remind you to stir up the gift of God which is in you through the laying on of my hands. 7For God has not given us a spirit of fear, but of power and of love and of a sound mind.

8Therefore do not be ashamed of the testimony of our Lord, nor of me His prisoner, but share with me in the sufferings for the gospel according to the power of God, 9who has saved us and called *us* with a holy calling, not according to our works, but according to His own purpose and grace which was given to us in Christ Jesus before time began, 10but has now been revealed by the appearing of our Savior Jesus Christ, *who* has abolished death and brought life and immortality to light through the gospel, 11to which I was appointed a preacher, an apostle, and a teacher of the Gentiles. 12For this reason I also suffer these things; nevertheless I am not ashamed,

1:7 a spirit of fear. The Greek word, which can also be translated "timidity," denotes a cowardly, shameful fear caused by a weak, selfish character. The threat of Roman persecution, which was escalating under Nero, the hostility of those in the Ephesian church who resented Timothy's leadership, and the assaults of false teachers with their sophisticated systems of deceptions may have been overwhelming Timothy. But if he was fearful, it didn't come from God. **power.** Positively, God has already given believers all the spiritual resources they need for every trial and threat (Matt. 10:19,20). Divine power—effective, productive spiritual energy belongs to believers (Eph. 1:18–20; 3:20; Zech. 4:6). **love.** This kind of love centers on pleasing God and seeking others' welfare before one's own (Rom. 14:8; Gal. 5:22,25; Eph. 3:19; 1 Pet. 1:22; 1 John 4:18). **sound mind.** Refers to a disciplined, self-controlled, and properly prioritized mind. This is the opposite of fear and cowardice that causes disorder and confusion. Focusing on the sovereign nature and perfect purposes of our eternal God allows believers to control their lives with godly wisdom and confidence in every situation.

1:12 I also suffer. Paul had no fear of persecution and death from preaching the gospel in a hostile setting because he was so confident God had sealed his future glory and blessing. **know whom I have believed.** "Know" describes the certainty of Paul's intimate, saving knowledge—the object of which was God Himself. The form of the Greek verb translated "I have believed" refers to something that began in the past and has continuing results. This knowing is equal to "the knowledge of the truth" (3:7; 1 Tim. 2:4). **He is able to keep what I have committed.** Paul's life in time and eternity had been given to his Lord. He lived with unwavering confidence and boldness because of the revealed truth about God's power and faithfulness and his own experience of an unbreakable relationship to the Lord (Rom. 8:31–39). **that Day.** Also called "Day of Christ" (Phil. 1:10), when believers will stand before the judgment seat and be rewarded.

for I know whom I have believed and am persuaded that He is able to keep what I have committed to Him until that Day.
13Hold fast the pattern of sound words which you have heard from me, in faith and love which are in Christ Jesus. 14That good thing which was committed to you, keep by the Holy Spirit who dwells in us.

15This you know, that all those in Asia have turned away from me, among whom are Phygellus and Hermogenes. 16The Lord grant mercy to the household of Onesiphorus, for he often refreshed me, and was not ashamed of my chain; 17but when he arrived in Rome, he sought me out very zealously and found *me.* 18The Lord grant to him that he may find mercy from the Lord in that Day—and you know very well how many ways he ministered *to me* at Ephesus.

DAY 28: Why did Paul write 2 Timothy?

Paul was released from his first Roman imprisonment for a short period of ministry during which he wrote 1 Timothy and Titus. Second Timothy, however, finds Paul once again in a Roman prison (1:16; 2:9), apparently rearrested as part of Nero's persecution of Christians. Unlike Paul's confident hope of release during his first imprisonment (Phil. 1:19,25,26; 2:24; Philem. 22), this time he had no such hopes (4:6–8). In his first imprisonment in Rome (ca. A.D. 60–62), before Nero had begun the persecution of Christians (A.D. 64), he was only under house arrest and had opportunity for much interaction with people and ministry (Acts 28:16–31). At this time, 5 or 6 years later (ca. A.D. 66–67), however, he was in a cold cell (4:13), in chains (2:9), and with no hope of deliverance (4:6).

Abandoned by virtually all of those close to him for fear of persecution (1:15; 4:9–12,16) and facing imminent execution, Paul wrote to Timothy, urging him to hasten to Rome for one last visit with the apostle (4:9,21). Whether Timothy made it to Rome before Paul's execution is not known. According to tradition, Paul was not released from this second Roman imprisonment but suffered the martyrdom he had foreseen (4:6).

In this letter, Paul, aware the end was near, passed the nonapostolic mantle of ministry to Timothy (2:2) and exhorted him to continue faithful in his duties (1:6), hold on to sound doctrine (1:13,14), avoid error (2:15–18), accept persecution for the gospel (2:3,4; 3:10–12), put his confidence in the Scripture, and preach it relentlessly (3:15–4:5).

OCTOBER 29

Jeremiah 43:1–44:30

43 Now it happened, when Jeremiah had stopped speaking to all the people all the words of the LORD their God, for which the LORD their God had sent him to them, all these words, 2that Azariah the son of Hoshaiah, Johanan the son of Kareah, and all the proud men spoke, saying to Jeremiah, "You speak falsely! The LORD our God has not sent you to say, 'Do not go to Egypt to dwell there.' 3But Baruch the son of Neriah has set you against us, to deliver us into the hand of the Chaldeans, that they may put us to death or carry us away captive to Babylon." 4So Johanan the son of Kareah, all the captains of the forces, and all the people would not obey the voice of the LORD, to remain in the land of Judah. 5But Johanan the son of Kareah and all the captains of the forces took all the remnant of Judah who had returned to dwell in the land of Judah, from all nations where they had been driven— 6men, women, children, the king's daughters, and every person whom Nebuzaradan the captain of the guard had left with Gedaliah the son of Ahikam, the son of Shaphan, and Jeremiah the prophet and Baruch the son of Neriah. 7So they went to the land of Egypt, for they did not obey the voice of the LORD. And they went as far as Tahpanhes.

43:1–7 when Jeremiah...stopped speaking. The incorrigible, disobedient leaders accused him of deceit and forced Jeremiah and the remnant to go to Egypt, despite the fact that all his prophecies regarding Babylon had come to pass. In so doing, they went out of God's protection into His judgment, as all who are disobedient to His Word do.

8Then the word of the LORD came to Jeremiah in Tahpanhes, saying, 9"Take large stones in your hand, and hide them in the sight of the men of Judah, in the clay in the brick courtyard which *is* at the entrance to Pharaoh's house in Tahpanhes; 10and say to them, 'Thus says the LORD of hosts, the God of Israel: "Behold, I will send and bring Nebuchadnezzar the king of Babylon, My servant, and will set his throne above these stones that I have hidden. And he will spread his royal pavilion over them. 11When he comes, he shall strike the land of Egypt *and deliver* to death *those appointed* for death, and to captivity *those appointed* for captivity, and to the sword *those appointed* for the sword. 12I will kindle a fire in the houses of the gods of Egypt, and he shall burn them and carry them away captive. And he shall array himself with the land of Egypt, as a shepherd puts on his garment, and he shall go out from there in peace. 13He shall also break the *sacred* pillars of Beth Shemesh that *are* in the land of Egypt; and the houses of the gods of the Egyptians he shall burn with fire." ' "

44 The word that came to Jeremiah concerning all the Jews who dwell in the land of Egypt, who dwell at Migdol, at Tahpanhes, at Noph, and in the country of Pathros, saying, 2"Thus says the LORD of hosts, the God of Israel: 'You have seen all the calamity that I have brought on Jerusalem and on all the cities of Judah; and behold, this day they *are* a desolation, and no one dwells in them, 3because of their wickedness which they have committed to provoke Me to anger, in that they went to burn incense *and* to serve other gods whom they did not know, they nor you nor your fathers. 4However I have sent to you all My servants the prophets, rising early and sending *them,* saying, "Oh, do not do this abominable thing that I hate!" 5But they did not listen or incline their ear to turn from their wickedness, to burn no incense to other gods. 6So My fury and My anger were poured out and kindled in the cities of Judah and in the streets of Jerusalem; and they are wasted *and* desolate, as it is this day.'

7"Now therefore, thus says the LORD, the God of hosts, the God of Israel: 'Why do you commit *this* great evil against yourselves, to cut off from you man and woman, child and infant, out of Judah, leaving none to remain, 8in that you provoke Me to wrath with the works of your hands, burning incense to other gods in the land of Egypt where you have gone to dwell, that you may cut yourselves off and be a curse and a reproach among all the nations of the earth? 9Have you forgotten the wickedness of your fathers, the wickedness of the kings of Judah, the wickedness of their wives, your own wickedness, and the wickedness of your wives, which they committed in the land of Judah and in the streets of Jerusalem? 10They have not been humbled, to this day, nor have they feared; they have not walked in My law or in My statutes that I set before you and your fathers.'

11"Therefore thus says the LORD of hosts, the

God of Israel: 'Behold, I will set My face against
you for catastrophe and for cutting off all Judah.
[12]And I will take the remnant of Judah who have
set their faces to go into the land of Egypt to
dwell there, and they shall all be consumed *and*
fall in the land of Egypt. They shall be consumed by the sword *and* by famine. They shall
die, from the least to the greatest, by the sword
and by famine; and they shall be an oath, an
astonishment, a curse and a reproach! [13]For I
will punish those who dwell in the land of Egypt,
as I have punished Jerusalem, by the sword, by
famine, and by pestilence, [14]so that none of the
remnant of Judah who have gone into the land
of Egypt to dwell there shall escape or survive,
lest they return to the land of Judah, to which
they desire to return and dwell. For none shall
return except those who escape.' "

[15]Then all the men who knew that their wives
had burned incense to other gods, with all the
women who stood by, a great multitude, and all
the people who dwelt in the land of Egypt, in
Pathros, answered Jeremiah, saying: [16]"*As for*
the word that you have spoken to us in the
name of the LORD, we will not listen to you! [17]But
we will certainly do whatever has gone out of
our own mouth, to burn incense to the queen of
heaven and pour out drink offerings to her, as
we have done, we and our fathers, our kings and
our princes, in the cities of Judah and in the
streets of Jerusalem. For *then* we had plenty of
food, were well-off, and saw no trouble. [18]But
since we stopped burning incense to the queen
of heaven and pouring out drink offerings to
her, we have lacked everything and have been
consumed by the sword and by famine."

[19]*The women also said,* "And when we
burned incense to the queen of heaven and
poured out drink offerings to her, did we
make cakes for her, to worship her, and pour
out drink offerings to her without our husbands' *permission?*"

[20]Then Jeremiah spoke to all the people—
the men, the women, and all the people who
had given him *that* answer—saying: [21]"The
incense that you burned in the cities of Judah
and in the streets of Jerusalem, you and your
fathers, your kings and your princes, and the
people of the land, did not the LORD remember
them, and did it *not* come into His mind? [22]So
the LORD could no longer bear *it,* because of
the evil of your doings *and* because of the
abominations which you committed.
Therefore your land is a desolation, an astonishment, a curse, and without an inhabitant, as
it is this day. [23]Because you have burned
incense and because you have sinned against
the LORD, and have not obeyed the voice of the
LORD or walked in His law, in His statutes or in
His testimonies, therefore this calamity has
happened to you, as *at* this day."

[24]Moreover Jeremiah said to all the people
and to all the women, "Hear the word of the
LORD, all Judah who *are* in the land of Egypt!
[25]Thus says the LORD of hosts, the God of Israel,
saying: 'You and your wives have spoken with
your mouths and fulfilled with your hands, saying, "We will surely keep our vows that we have
made, to burn incense to the queen of heaven
and pour out drink offerings to her." You will
surely keep your vows and perform your
vows!' [26]Therefore hear the word of the LORD,
all Judah who dwell in the land of Egypt: 'Behold, I have sworn by My great name,' says the
LORD, 'that My name shall no more be named
in the mouth of any man of Judah in all the land
of Egypt, saying, "The Lord GOD lives." [27]Be-
hold, I will watch over them for adversity and
not for good. And all the men of Judah who *are*
in the land of Egypt shall be consumed by the
sword and by famine, until there is an end to
them. [28]Yet a small number who escape the
sword shall return from the land of Egypt to
the land of Judah; and all the remnant of Judah,
who have gone to the land of Egypt to dwell
there, shall know whose words will stand,
Mine or theirs. [29]And this *shall be* a sign to you,'
says the LORD, 'that I will punish you in this
place, that you may know that My words will
surely stand against you for adversity.'

[30]"Thus says the LORD: 'Behold, I will give
Pharaoh Hophra king of Egypt into the hand
of his enemies and into the hand of those who
seek his life, as I gave Zedekiah king of Judah
into the hand of Nebuchadnezzar king of
Babylon, his enemy who sought his life.' "

Psalm 119:97–104

מ MEM

97 Oh, how I love Your law!
It *is* my meditation all the day.
98 You, through Your commandments,
make me wiser than my enemies;
For they *are* ever with me.
99 I have more understanding than all my
teachers,
For Your testimonies *are* my
meditation.
100 I understand more than the
ancients,
Because I keep Your precepts.
101 I have restrained my feet from every
evil way,
That I may keep Your word.
102 I have not departed from Your
judgments,

For You Yourself have taught me.
103 How sweet are Your words to my taste,
Sweeter than honey to my mouth!
104 Through Your precepts I get understanding;
Therefore I hate every false way.

Proverbs 28:3

3 A poor man who oppresses the poor
Is like a driving rain which leaves no food.

28:3 oppresses the poor. When the poor come to power and oppress their own, it is as bad as a destructive storm washing the fields clean instead of watering the crop.

2 Timothy 2:1–26

2 You therefore, my son, be strong in the
grace that is in Christ Jesus. 2And the
things that you have heard from me among
many witnesses, commit these to faithful men
who will be able to teach others also. 3You

2:2 faithful men who will be able to teach others. Timothy was to take the divine revelation he had learned from Paul and teach it to other faithful men—men with proven spiritual character and giftedness, who would in turn pass on those truths to another generation. From Paul to Timothy to faithful men to others encompasses 4 generations of godly leaders. That process of spiritual reproduction, which began in the early church, is to continue until the Lord returns.

therefore must endure hardship as a good
soldier of Jesus Christ. 4No one engaged in
warfare entangles himself with the affairs of
this life, that he may please him who enlisted
him as a soldier. 5And also if anyone competes
in athletics, he is not crowned unless he competes according to the rules. 6The hardworking farmer must be first to partake of the
crops. 7Consider what I say, and may the Lord
give you understanding in all things.

8Remember that Jesus Christ, of the seed of
David, was raised from the dead according to
my gospel, 9for which I suffer trouble as an
evildoer, *even* to the point of chains; but the
word of God is not chained. 10Therefore I

2:8 Remember…Jesus Christ. The supreme model of a faithful teacher (v. 2), soldier (vv. 3,4), athlete (v. 5), and farmer (v. 6). Timothy was to follow His example in teaching, suffering, pursuing the prize, and planting the seeds of truth for a spiritual harvest. **of the seed of David.** As David's descendant, Jesus is the rightful heir to his throne (Luke 1:32,33). The Lord's humanity is stressed. **raised from the dead.** The resurrection of Christ is the central truth of the Christian faith (1 Cor. 15:3,4,17,19). By it, God affirmed the perfect redemptive work of Jesus Christ (Rom. 1:4).

endure all things for the sake of the elect, that
they also may obtain the salvation which is in
Christ Jesus with eternal glory.
11*This is* a faithful saying:

For if we died with *Him*,
We shall also live with *Him*.
12 If we endure,
We shall also reign with *Him*.
If we deny *Him*,
He also will deny us.
13 If we are faithless,
He remains faithful;
He cannot deny Himself.

14Remind *them* of these things, charging *them*
before the Lord not to strive about words to no
profit, to the ruin of the hearers. 15Be diligent to
present yourself approved to God, a worker
who does not need to be ashamed, rightly dividing the word of truth. 16But shun profane *and*
idle babblings, for they will increase to more
ungodliness. 17And their message will spread
like cancer. Hymenaeus and Philetus are of this
sort, 18who have strayed concerning the truth,
saying that the resurrection is already past; and
they overthrow the faith of some. 19Neverthe-
less the solid foundation of God stands, having
this seal: "The Lord knows those who are His,"
and, "Let everyone who names the name of
Christ depart from iniquity."
20But in a great house there are not only vessels of gold and silver, but also of wood and
clay, some for honor and some for dishonor.
21Therefore if anyone cleanses himself from
the latter, he will be a vessel for honor, sanctified and useful for the Master, prepared for
every good work. 22Flee also youthful lusts;
but pursue righteousness, faith, love, peace
with those who call on the Lord out of a pure
heart. 23But avoid foolish and ignorant disputes, knowing that they generate strife. 24And

a servant of the Lord must not quarrel but be
gentle to all, able to teach, patient, [25]in humility correcting those who are in opposition, if
God perhaps will grant them repentance, so
that they may know the truth, [26]and *that* they
may come to their senses *and escape* the snare
of the devil, having been taken captive by him
to *do* his will.

DAY 29: How is the Christian life compared to being a soldier, an athlete, and a farmer?

"Endure hardship as a good soldier" (2 Tim. 2:3). The metaphor of the Christian life as warfare (against the evil world system, the believer's sinful human nature, and Satan) is a familiar one in the New Testament (2 Cor. 10:3–5; Eph. 6:10–20; 1 Thess. 4:8; 1 Tim. 1:18; 4:7; 6:12). Here Paul is dealing with the conflict against the hostile world and the persecution. "No one engaged in warfare entangles himself" (v. 4). Just as a soldier called to duty is completely severed from the normal affairs of civilian life, so also must the good soldier of Jesus Christ refuse to allow the things of the world to distract him (James 4:4; 1 John 2:15–17).

"If anyone competes in athletics" (v. 5). The Greek verb expresses the effort and determination needed to compete successfully in an athletic event (1 Cor. 9:24). This is a useful picture of spiritual effort and untiring pursuit of the victory to those familiar with events such as the Olympic Games and the Isthmian Games (held in Corinth). "Crowned…rules." All an athlete's hard work and discipline will be wasted if he or she fails to compete according to the rules. This is a call to obey the Word of God in the pursuit of spiritual victory.

"The hardworking farmer" (v. 6). "Hardworking" is from a Greek verb meaning "to labor to the point of exhaustion." Ancient farmers worked long hours of backbreaking labor under all kinds of conditions with the hope that their physical effort would be rewarded by a good harvest. Paul is urging Timothy not to be lazy or indolent but to labor intensely (Col. 1:28,29) with a view to the harvest.

OCTOBER 30

Jeremiah 45:1–46:28

45 The word that Jeremiah the prophet
spoke to Baruch the son of Neriah,
when he had written these words in a book at
the instruction of Jeremiah, in the fourth year
of Jehoiakim the son of Josiah, king of Judah,
saying, [2]"Thus says the LORD, the God of Israel,
to you, O Baruch: [3]'You said, "Woe is me now!
For the LORD has added grief to my sorrow.
I fainted in my sighing, and I find no rest." '
[4]"Thus you shall say to him, 'Thus says the
LORD: "Behold, what I have built I will break
down, and what I have planted I will pluck up,
that is, this whole land. [5]And do you seek great
things for yourself? Do not seek *them;* for
behold, I will bring adversity on all flesh," says
the LORD. "But I will give your life to you as a
prize in all places, wherever you go." ' "

45:3 Woe is me now! Baruch felt anxiety as his own cherished plans of a bright future were apparently dashed; even death became a darkening peril (v. 5). Also, he was possibly pressed by human questionings about God carrying through with such calamity (v. 4). Jeremiah spoke to encourage him (v. 2).

45:5 you seek great things. Baruch had his expectations far too high and that made the disasters harder to bear. It is enough that he be content just to live. Jeremiah, who once also complained, learned by his own suffering to encourage complainers.

46 The word of the LORD which came to
Jeremiah the prophet against the
nations. [2]Against Egypt.
Concerning the army of Pharaoh Necho,
king of Egypt, which was by the River
Euphrates in Carchemish, and which
Nebuchadnezzar king of Babylon defeated in
the fourth year of Jehoiakim the son of Josiah,
king of Judah:

3 "Order the buckler and shield,
And draw near to battle!
4 Harness the horses,
And mount up, you horsemen!
Stand forth with *your* helmets,
Polish the spears,
Put on the armor!
5 Why have I seen them dismayed *and*
turned back?
Their mighty ones are beaten down;
They have speedily fled,
And did not look back,
For fear *was* all around," says the LORD.

6 "Do not let the swift flee away,
Nor the mighty man escape;
They will stumble and fall
Toward the north, by the River
Euphrates.
7 "Who *is* this coming up like a flood,
Whose waters move like the rivers?
8 Egypt rises up like a flood,
And *its* waters move like the rivers;
And he says, 'I will go up *and* cover the
earth,
I will destroy the city and its
inhabitants.'
9 Come up, O horses, and rage,
O chariots!
And let the mighty men come forth:
The Ethiopians and the Libyans who
handle the shield,
And the Lydians who handle *and* bend
the bow.
10 For this *is* the day of the Lord GOD of
hosts,
A day of vengeance,
That He may avenge Himself on His
adversaries.
The sword shall devour;
It shall be satiated and made drunk
with their blood;
For the Lord GOD of hosts has a
sacrifice
In the north country by the River
Euphrates.
11 "Go up to Gilead and take balm,
O virgin, the daughter of Egypt;
In vain you will use many medicines;
You shall not be cured.
12 The nations have heard of your shame,
And your cry has filled the land;
For the mighty man has stumbled
against the mighty;
They both have fallen together."

13 The word that the LORD spoke to Jeremiah the prophet, how Nebuchadnezzar king of Babylon would come *and* strike the land of Egypt.

14 "Declare in Egypt, and proclaim in
Migdol;
Proclaim in Noph and in Tahpanhes;
Say, 'Stand fast and prepare yourselves,
For the sword devours all around you.'
15 Why are your valiant *men* swept away?
They did not stand
Because the LORD drove them away.
16 He made many fall;
Yes, one fell upon another.
And they said, 'Arise!
Let us go back to our own people
And to the land of our nativity
From the oppressing sword.'
17 They cried there,
'Pharaoh, king of Egypt, *is but* a noise.
He has passed by the appointed time!'

18 "*As* I live," says the King,
Whose name *is* the LORD of hosts,
"Surely as Tabor *is* among the
mountains
And as Carmel by the sea, *so* he shall
come.
19 O you daughter dwelling in Egypt,
Prepare yourself to go into captivity!
For Noph shall be waste and desolate,
without inhabitant.
20 "Egypt *is* a very pretty heifer,
But destruction comes, it comes from
the north.
21 Also her mercenaries are in her midst
like fat bulls,
For they also are turned back,
They have fled away together.
They did not stand,
For the day of their calamity had come
upon them,
The time of their punishment.
22 Her noise shall go like a serpent,
For they shall march with an army
And come against her with axes,
Like those who chop wood.
23 "They shall cut down her forest," says
the LORD,
"Though it cannot be searched,
Because they *are* innumerable,
And more numerous than
grasshoppers.
24 The daughter of Egypt shall be
ashamed;
She shall be delivered into
the hand
Of the people of the north."

25 The LORD of hosts, the God of Israel, says: "Behold, I will bring punishment on Amon of No, and Pharaoh and Egypt, with their gods and their kings—Pharaoh and those who trust
in him. 26 And I will deliver them into the hand of those who seek their lives, into the hand of Nebuchadnezzar king of Babylon and the hand of his servants. Afterward it shall be inhabited as in the days of old," says the LORD.

27 "But do not fear, O My servant Jacob,
And do not be dismayed, O Israel!
For behold, I will save you from afar,

And your offspring from the land of
their captivity;
Jacob shall return, have rest and be at
ease;
No one shall make *him* afraid.
28 Do not fear, O Jacob My servant," says
the LORD,
"For I *am* with you;
For I will make a complete end of all
the nations
To which I have driven you,
But I will not make a complete end of
you.
I will rightly correct you,
For I will not leave you wholly
unpunished."

Psalm 119:105–112

נ NUN
105 Your word *is* a lamp to my feet
And a light to my path.
106 I have sworn and confirmed
That I will keep Your righteous
judgments.
107 I am afflicted very much;
Revive me, O LORD, according to Your
word.
108 Accept, I pray, the freewill offerings of
my mouth, O LORD,
And teach me Your judgments.
109 My life *is* continually in my hand,
Yet I do not forget Your law.
110 The wicked have laid a snare for me,
Yet I have not strayed from Your
precepts.
111 Your testimonies I have taken as a
heritage forever,
For they *are* the rejoicing of my heart.
112 I have inclined my heart to perform
Your statutes
Forever, to the very end.

Proverbs 28:4

4 Those who forsake the law praise the
wicked,
But such as keep the law contend with
them.

2 Timothy 3:1–17

3 But know this, that in the last days perilous times will come: [2]For men will be lovers
of themselves, lovers of money, boasters,
proud, blasphemers, disobedient to parents,
unthankful, unholy, [3]unloving, unforgiving,
slanderers, without self-control, brutal, despisers of good, [4]traitors, headstrong, haughty,
lovers of pleasure rather than lovers of God,
[5]having a form of godliness but denying its

3:1 the last days. This phrase refers to this age, the time since the First Coming of the Lord Jesus. **perilous times.** "Perilous" is used to describe the savage nature of two demon-possessed men (Matt. 8:28). The word for "times" had to do with epochs rather than clock or calendar time. Such savage, dangerous eras or epochs will increase in frequency and severity as the return of Christ approaches (v. 13). The church age is fraught with these dangerous movements accumulating strength as the end nears.

power. And from such people turn away! [6]For
of this sort are those who creep into households and make captives of gullible women
loaded down with sins, led away by various
lusts, [7]always learning and never able to come
to the knowledge of the truth. [8]Now as Jannes
and Jambres resisted Moses, so do these also
resist the truth: men of corrupt minds, disap-

3:8 Jannes and Jambres. Although their names are not mentioned in the Old Testament, they were likely two of the Egyptian magicians that opposed Moses (Ex. 7:11,22; 8:7,18,19; 9:11). According to Jewish tradition, they pretended to become Jewish proselytes, instigated the worship of the golden calf, and were killed with the rest of the idolaters (Ex. 32). Paul's choice of them as examples may indicate the false teachers at Ephesus were practicing deceiving signs and wonders.

proved concerning the faith; [9]but they will
progress no further, for their folly will be manifest to all, as theirs also was.
[10]But you have carefully followed my doctrine, manner of life, purpose, faith, longsuffering, love, perseverance, [11]persecutions,
afflictions, which happened to me at Antioch,
at Iconium, at Lystra—what persecutions I
endured. And out of *them* all the Lord delivered me. [12]Yes, and all who desire to live godly
in Christ Jesus will suffer persecution. [13]But
evil men and impostors will grow worse and
worse, deceiving and being deceived. [14]But
you must continue in the things which you
have learned and been assured of, knowing
from whom you have learned *them*, [15]and that
from childhood you have known the Holy

Scriptures, which are able to make you wise for salvation through faith which is in Christ Jesus.
16All Scripture *is* given by inspiration of God, and *is* profitable for doctrine, for reproof, for correction, for instruction in righteousness,
17that the man of God may be complete, thoroughly equipped for every good work.

DAY 30: How does 2 Timothy 3:16 describe Scripture?

"All Scripture"—both Old Testament and New Testament Scripture are included (2 Pet. 3:15,16, which identify New Testament writings as Scripture). "Is given by inspiration of God." Literally, "breathed out by God" or "God-breathed." Sometimes God told the Bible writers the exact words to say (Jer. 1:9), but more often He used their minds, vocabularies, and experiences to produce His own infallible, inerrant Word (1 Thess. 2:13; Heb. 1:1; 2 Pet. 1:20,21). It is important to note that inspiration applies only to the original autographs of Scripture, not the Bible writers; there are no inspired Scripture writers, only inspired Scripture. So identified is God with His Word that when Scripture speaks, God speaks (Rom. 9:17; Gal. 3:8). Scripture is called "the oracles of God" (Rom. 3:2; 1 Pet. 4:11) and cannot be altered (John 10:35; Matt. 5:17,18; Luke 16:17; Rev. 22:18,19).

"And is profitable for doctrine." The divine instruction or doctrinal content of both the Old Testament and the New Testament (2:15; Acts 20:18,20,21,27; 1 Cor. 2:14–16; Col. 3:16; 1 John 2:20,24,27). The Scripture provides the comprehensive and complete body of divine truth necessary for life and godliness. "For reproof." Rebuke for wrong behavior or wrong belief. The Scripture exposes sin (Heb. 4:12,13) that can then be dealt with through confession and repentance. "For correction." The restoration of something to its proper condition. The word appears only here in the New Testament, but was used in extrabiblical Greek of righting a fallen object or helping back to their feet those who had stumbled. Scripture not only rebukes wrong behavior but also points the way back to godly living. "For instruction in righteousness." Scripture provides positive training ("instruction" originally referred to training a child) in godly behavior, not merely rebuke and correction of wrong behavior (Acts 20:32; 1 Tim. 4:6; 1 Pet. 2:1,2).

OCTOBER 31

Jeremiah 47:1–48:47

47 The word of the LORD that came to Jeremiah the prophet against the Philistines, before Pharaoh attacked Gaza.
2Thus says the LORD:

"Behold, waters rise out of the north,
And shall be an overflowing flood;
They shall overflow the land and all that is in it,
The city and those who dwell within;
Then the men shall cry,
And all the inhabitants of the land shall wail.
3 At the noise of the stamping hooves of his strong horses,
At the rushing of his chariots,
At the rumbling of his wheels,
The fathers will not look back for *their* children,
Lacking courage,
4 Because of the day that comes to plunder all the Philistines,
To cut off from Tyre and Sidon every helper who remains;
For the LORD shall plunder the Philistines,
The remnant of the country of Caphtor.
5 Baldness has come upon Gaza,
Ashkelon is cut off
With the remnant of their valley.
How long will you cut yourself?

6 "O you sword of the LORD,
How long until you are quiet?
Put yourself up into your scabbard,
Rest and be still!
7 How can it be quiet,
Seeing the LORD has given it a charge
Against Ashkelon and against the seashore?
There He has appointed it."

48 Against Moab.
Thus says the LORD of hosts,
the God of Israel:

"Woe to Nebo!
For it is plundered,
Kirjathaim is shamed *and* taken;
The high stronghold is shamed and dismayed—
2 No more praise of Moab.
In Heshbon they have devised evil against her:

'Come, and let us cut her off as a
nation.'
You also shall be cut down,
O Madmen!
The sword shall pursue you;
3 A voice of crying *shall be* from
Horonaim:
'Plundering and great destruction!'
4 "Moab is destroyed;
Her little ones have caused a cry to be
heard;
5 For in the Ascent of Luhith they
ascend with continual weeping;
For in the descent of Horonaim the
enemies have heard a cry of
destruction.

6 "Flee, save your lives!
And be like the juniper in the
wilderness.
7 For because you have trusted in your
works and your treasures,
You also shall be taken.
And Chemosh shall go forth into
captivity,
His priests and his princes together.
8 And the plunderer shall come against
every city;
No one shall escape.
The valley also shall perish,
And the plain shall be destroyed,
As the LORD has spoken.

9 "Give wings to Moab,
That she may flee and get away;
For her cities shall be desolate,
Without any to dwell in them.
10 Cursed *is* he who does the work of the
LORD deceitfully,
And cursed *is* he who keeps back his
sword from blood.
11 "Moab has been at ease from his youth;
He has settled on his dregs,
And has not been emptied from vessel
to vessel,
Nor has he gone into captivity.
Therefore his taste remained in him,
And his scent has not changed.
12 "Therefore behold, the days are
coming," says the LORD,
"That I shall send him wine-workers
Who will tip him over
And empty his vessels
And break the bottles.
13 Moab shall be ashamed of Chemosh,
As the house of Israel was ashamed of
Bethel, their confidence.

48:11,12 This wine-making imagery is vivid. In the production of sweet wine, the juice was left in a wineskin until the sediment or dregs settled onto the bottom. Then it was poured into another skin until more dregs were separated. This process continued until the dregs were all removed and a pure, sweet wine obtained. Moab was not taken from suffering to suffering so that her bitter dregs would be removed through the purging of pain. Thus the nation was settled into the thickness and bitterness of its own sin. Judgment from God was coming to smash them.

14 "How can you say, 'We *are* mighty
And strong men for the war'?
15 Moab is plundered and gone up *from*
her cities;
Her chosen young men have gone
down to the slaughter," says the
King,
Whose name *is* the LORD of hosts.

16 "The calamity of Moab *is* near at hand,
And his affliction comes quickly.
17 Bemoan him, all you who are around
him;
And all you who know his name,
Say, 'How the strong staff is broken,
The beautiful rod!'

18 "O daughter inhabiting Dibon,
Come down from *your* glory,
And sit in thirst;
For the plunderer of Moab has come
against you,
He has destroyed your strongholds.
19 O inhabitant of Aroer,
Stand by the way and watch;
Ask him who flees
And her who escapes;
Say, 'What has happened?'
20 Moab is shamed, for he is broken
down.
Wail and cry!
Tell it in Arnon, that Moab is
plundered.

21 "And judgment has come on the plain
country:
On Holon and Jahzah and Mephaath,
22 On Dibon and Nebo and Beth
Diblathaim,
23 On Kirjathaim and Beth Gamul and
Beth Meon,

24 On Kerioth and Bozrah,
On all the cities of the land of Moab,
Far or near.
25 The horn of Moab is cut off,
And his arm is broken," says the LORD.
26 "Make him drunk,
Because he exalted *himself* against the LORD.
Moab shall wallow in his vomit,
And he shall also be in derision.
27 For was not Israel a derision to you?
Was he found among thieves?
For whenever you speak of him,
You shake *your head in scorn.*
28 You who dwell in Moab,
Leave the cities and dwell in the rock,
And be like the dove *which* makes her nest
In the sides of the cave's mouth.

29 "We have heard the pride of Moab
(He *is* exceedingly proud),
Of his loftiness and arrogance and pride,
And of the haughtiness of his heart."

30 "I know his wrath," says the LORD,
"But it *is* not right;
His lies have made nothing right.
31 Therefore I will wail for Moab,
And I will cry out for all Moab;
I will mourn for the men of Kir Heres.
32 O vine of Sibmah! I will weep for you with the weeping of Jazer.
Your plants have gone over the sea,
They reach to the sea of Jazer.
The plunderer has fallen on your summer fruit and your vintage.
33 Joy and gladness are taken
From the plentiful field
And from the land of Moab;
I have caused wine to fail from the winepresses;
No one will tread with joyous shouting—
Not joyous shouting!

34 "From the cry of Heshbon to Elealeh and to Jahaz
They have uttered their voice,
From Zoar to Horonaim,
Like a three-year-old heifer;
For the waters of Nimrim also shall be desolate.

35 "Moreover," says the LORD,
"I will cause to cease in Moab
The one who offers *sacrifices* in the high places
And burns incense to his gods.
36 Therefore My heart shall wail like flutes for Moab,
And like flutes My heart shall wail
For the men of Kir Heres.
Therefore the riches they have acquired have perished.

37 "For every head *shall be* bald, and every beard clipped;
On all the hands *shall be* cuts, and on the loins sackcloth—
38 A general lamentation
On all the housetops of Moab,
And in its streets;
For I have broken Moab like a vessel in which *is* no pleasure," says the LORD.
39 "They shall wail:
'How she is broken down!
How Moab has turned her back with shame!'
So Moab shall be a derision
And a dismay to all those about her."

40 For thus says the LORD:

"Behold, one shall fly like an eagle,
And spread his wings over Moab.
41 Kerioth is taken,
And the strongholds are surprised;
The mighty men's hearts in Moab on that day shall be
Like the heart of a woman in birth pangs.
42 And Moab shall be destroyed as a people,
Because he exalted *himself* against the LORD.
43 Fear and the pit and the snare *shall be* upon you,
O inhabitant of Moab," says the LORD.
44 "He who flees from the fear shall fall into the pit,
And he who gets out of the pit shall be caught in the snare.
For upon Moab, upon it I will bring
The year of their punishment," says the LORD.

45 "Those who fled stood under the shadow of Heshbon
Because of exhaustion.
But a fire shall come out of Heshbon,
A flame from the midst of Sihon,
And shall devour the brow of Moab,
The crown of the head of the sons of tumult.
46 Woe to you, O Moab!
The people of Chemosh perish;

For your sons have been taken captive,
And your daughters captive.

47 “Yet I will bring back the captives of
Moab
In the latter days,” says the LORD.

Thus far *is* the judgment of Moab.

Psalm 119:113–120

ס SAMEK
113 I hate the double-minded,
But I love Your law.
114 You *are* my hiding place and my shield;
I hope in Your word.
115 Depart from me, you evildoers,
For I will keep the commandments of
my God!
116 Uphold me according to Your word,
that I may live;
And do not let me be ashamed of my
hope.
117 Hold me up, and I shall be safe,
And I shall observe Your statutes
continually.
118 You reject all those who stray from
Your statutes,
For their deceit *is* falsehood.
119 You put away all the wicked of the
earth *like* dross;
Therefore I love Your testimonies.
120 My flesh trembles for fear of You,
And I am afraid of Your judgments.

Proverbs 28:5

5 Evil men do not understand justice,
But those who seek the LORD
understand all.

2 Timothy 4:1–22

4 I charge *you* therefore before God and the
Lord Jesus Christ, who will judge the living and the dead at His appearing and His
kingdom: 2Preach the word! Be ready in season *and* out of season. Convince, rebuke, exhort, with all longsuffering and teaching. 3For
the time will come when they will not endure
sound doctrine, but according to their own
desires, *because* they have itching ears, they
will heap up for themselves teachers; 4and they
will turn *their* ears away from the truth, and be
turned aside to fables. 5But you be watchful in
all things, endure afflictions, do the work of an
evangelist, fulfill your ministry.
6For I am already being poured out as a
drink offering, and the time of my departure is
at hand. 7I have fought the good fight, I have
finished the race, I have kept the faith. 8Finally,

4:2 the word. The entire written Word of God, His complete revealed truth as contained in the Bible (3:15,16; Acts 20:27). **Be ready.** The Greek word has a broad range of meanings, including suddenness or forcefulness. Here the form of the verb suggests the complementary ideas of urgency, preparedness, and readiness. It was used of a soldier prepared to go into battle or a guard who was continually alert for any surprise attack—attitudes which are imperative for a faithful preacher. **in season *and* out of season.** The faithful preacher must proclaim the Word when it is popular and/or convenient and when it is not; when it seems suitable to do so and when it seems not. The dictates of popular culture, tradition, reputation, acceptance, or esteem in the community (or in the church) must never alter the true preacher's commitment to proclaim God's Word. **Convince, rebuke.** The negative side of preaching the Word (the "reproof" and "correction"; 3:16). The Greek word for "convince" refers to correcting behavior or false doctrine by using careful biblical argument to help a person understand the error of his actions. The Greek word for "rebuke" deals more with correcting the person's motives by convicting him of his sin and leading him to repentance.

there is laid up for me the crown of righteousness, which the Lord, the righteous Judge, will
give to me on that Day, and not to me only but
also to all who have loved His appearing.
9Be diligent to come to me quickly; 10for
Demas has forsaken me, having loved this
present world, and has departed for
Thessalonica—Crescens for Galatia, Titus for
Dalmatia. 11Only Luke is with me. Get Mark
and bring him with you, for he is useful to me
for ministry. 12And Tychicus I have sent to
Ephesus. 13Bring the cloak that I left with
Carpus at Troas when you come—and the
books, especially the parchments.
14Alexander the coppersmith did me much
harm. May the Lord repay him according to
his works. 15You also must beware of him, for
he has greatly resisted our words.
16At my first defense no one stood with me,
but all forsook me. May it not be charged
against them.
17But the Lord stood with me and strengthened me, so that the message might be
preached fully through me, and *that* all the
Gentiles might hear. Also I was delivered out

of the mouth of the lion. [18]And the Lord will
deliver me from every evil work and preserve
me for His heavenly kingdom. To Him *be* glory
forever and ever. Amen!
[19]Greet Prisca and Aquila, and the household
of Onesiphorus. [20]Erastus stayed in Corinth,
but Trophimus I have left in Miletus sick.
[21]Do your utmost to come before winter.
Eubulus greets you, as well as Pudens,
Linus, Claudia, and all the brethren.
[22]The Lord Jesus Christ be with your spirit.
Grace be with you. Amen.

DAY 31: Describe how Paul recaps his life in 2 Timothy 4:6–8.

"For I am already being poured out as a drink offering" (v. 6). Meaning his death was imminent. In the Old Testament sacrificial system, a drink offering was the final offering that followed the burnt and grain offerings prescribed for the people of Israel (Num. 15:1–16). Paul saw his coming death as his final offering to God in a life that had already been full of sacrifices to Him. "My departure" speaks of Paul's death. The Greek word essentially refers to the loosening of something, such as the mooring ropes of a ship or the ropes of a tent; thus it eventually acquired the secondary meaning of "departure."

"I have fought…have finished…have kept" (v. 7). The form of the 3 Greek verbs indicates completed action with continuing results. Paul saw his life as complete—he had been able to accomplish through the Lord's power all that God called him to do. He was a soldier, an athlete, and a guardian. "The faith." The truths and standards of the revealed Word of God.

"Finally, there is laid up for me the crown of righteousness" (v. 8). The Greek word for "crown" literally means "surrounding," and it was used of the plaited wreaths or garlands placed on the heads of dignitaries and victorious military officers or athletes. Linguistically, "of righteousness" can mean either that righteousness is the source of the crown or that righteousness is the nature of the crown. The crown represents eternal righteousness received through the imputed righteousness of Christ at salvation (Rom. 4:6,11). The Holy Spirit works practical righteousness (sanctification) in the believer throughout his lifetime of struggle with sin (Rom. 6:13,19; 8:4). But only when the struggle is complete will the Christian receive Christ's righteousness perfected in him (glorification) when he enters heaven (Gal. 5:5).

NOVEMBER 1

Jeremiah 49:1–50:46

49 Against the Ammonites.
Thus says the LORD:

"Has Israel no sons?
Has he no heir?
Why *then* does Milcom inherit Gad,
And his people dwell in its cities?
2 Therefore behold, the days are coming," says the LORD,
"That I will cause to be heard an alarm of war
In Rabbah of the Ammonites;
It shall be a desolate mound,
And her villages shall be burned with fire.
Then Israel shall take possession of his inheritance," says the LORD.
3 "Wail, O Heshbon, for Ai is plundered!
Cry, you daughters of Rabbah,
Gird yourselves with sackcloth!
Lament and run to and fro by the walls;
For Milcom shall go into captivity
With his priests and his princes together.
4 Why do you boast in the valleys,
Your flowing valley, O backsliding daughter?
Who trusted in her treasures, *saying,*
'Who will come against me?'
5 Behold, I will bring fear upon you,"
Says the Lord GOD of hosts,
"From all those who are around you;
You shall be driven out, everyone headlong,
And no one will gather those who wander off.
6 But afterward I will bring back
The captives of the people of Ammon,"
says the LORD.

7 Against Edom.
Thus says the LORD of hosts:

"*Is* wisdom no more in Teman?
Has counsel perished from the prudent?
Has their wisdom vanished?
8 Flee, turn back, dwell in the depths,
O inhabitants of Dedan!
For I will bring the calamity of Esau upon him,
The time *that* I will punish him.
9 If grape-gatherers came to you,
Would they not leave *some* gleaning grapes?
If thieves by night,
Would they not destroy until they have enough?
10 But I have made Esau bare;
I have uncovered his secret places,
And he shall not be able to hide himself.
His descendants are plundered,
His brethren and his neighbors,
And he *is* no more.
11 Leave your fatherless children,
I will preserve *them* alive;
And let your widows trust in Me."

12 For thus says the LORD: "Behold, those whose
judgment *was* not to drink of the cup have
assuredly drunk. And *are* you the one who will
altogether go unpunished? You shall not go
unpunished, but you shall surely drink *of it.*
13 For I have sworn by Myself," says the LORD,
"that Bozrah shall become a desolation, a
reproach, a waste, and a curse. And all its cities
shall be perpetual wastes."

14 I have heard a message from the LORD,
And an ambassador has been sent to the nations:
"Gather together, come against her,
And rise up to battle!

15 "For indeed, I will make you small among nations,
Despised among men.
16 Your fierceness has deceived you,
The pride of your heart,
O you who dwell in the clefts of the rock,
Who hold the height of the hill!
Though you make your nest as high as the eagle,
I will bring you down from there,"
says the LORD.
17 "Edom also shall be an astonishment;
Everyone who goes by it will be astonished
And will hiss at all its plagues.
18 As in the overthrow of Sodom and Gomorrah
And their neighbors," says the LORD,
"No one shall remain there,
Nor shall a son of man dwell in it.

19 "Behold, he shall come up like a lion from the floodplain of the Jordan
Against the dwelling place of the strong;
But I will suddenly make him run away from her.
And who *is* a chosen *man that* I may appoint over her?
For who *is* like Me?
Who will arraign Me?

And who *is* that shepherd
Who will withstand Me?"

20 Therefore hear the counsel of the LORD
that He has taken against Edom,
And His purposes that He has
proposed against the inhabitants
of Teman:
Surely the least of the flock shall draw
them out;
Surely He shall make their dwelling
places desolate with them.
21 The earth shakes at the noise
of their fall;
At the cry its noise is heard
at the Red Sea.
22 Behold, He shall come up and fly
like the eagle,
And spread His wings over Bozrah;
The heart of the mighty men of Edom
in that day shall be
Like the heart of a woman in birth pangs.

23 Against Damascus.

"Hamath and Arpad are shamed,
For they have heard bad news.
They are fainthearted;
There is trouble on the sea;
It cannot be quiet.
24 Damascus has grown feeble;
She turns to flee,
And fear has seized *her.*
Anguish and sorrows have taken her
like a woman in labor.
25 Why is the city of praise not deserted,
the city of My joy?
26 Therefore her young men shall fall in
her streets,
And all the men of war shall be cut off
in that day," says the LORD of hosts.
27 "I will kindle a fire in the wall
of Damascus,
And it shall consume the palaces of
Ben-Hadad."

28 Against Kedar and against the kingdoms of
Hazor, which Nebuchadnezzar king of Babylon
shall strike.

Thus says the LORD:

"Arise, go up to Kedar,
And devastate the men of the East!
29 Their tents and their flocks they shall
take away.
They shall take for themselves their
curtains,
All their vessels and their camels;
And they shall cry out to them,
'Fear *is* on every side!'

30 "Flee, get far away! Dwell in the depths,
O inhabitants of Hazor!" says the LORD.
"For Nebuchadnezzar king of Babylon
has taken counsel against you,
And has conceived a plan against you.

31 "Arise, go up to the wealthy nation that
dwells securely," says the LORD,
"Which has neither gates nor bars,
Dwelling alone.
32 Their camels shall be for booty,
And the multitude of their cattle for
plunder.
I will scatter to all winds those in the
farthest corners,
And I will bring their calamity from all
its sides," says the LORD.
33 "Hazor shall be a dwelling for jackals,
a desolation forever;
No one shall reside there,
Nor son of man dwell in it."

34 The word of the LORD that came to Jeremiah the prophet against Elam, in the beginning of the reign of Zedekiah king of Judah,
saying, 35 "Thus says the LORD of hosts:

'Behold, I will break the bow of Elam,
The foremost of their might.
36 Against Elam I will bring the four
winds
From the four quarters of heaven,
And scatter them toward all those winds;
There shall be no nations where the
outcasts of Elam will not go.
37 For I will cause Elam to be dismayed
before their enemies
And before those who seek their life.
I will bring disaster upon them,
My fierce anger,' says the LORD;
'And I will send the sword after them
Until I have consumed them.
38 I will set My throne in Elam,
And will destroy from there the king
and the princes,' says the LORD.

39 'But it shall come to pass in the latter
days:
I will bring back the captives of Elam,'
says the LORD."

50 The word that the LORD spoke against Babylon *and* against the land of the Chaldeans by Jeremiah the prophet.

2 "Declare among the nations,
Proclaim, and set up a standard;
Proclaim—do not conceal *it*—
Say, 'Babylon is taken, Bel is shamed.
Merodach is broken in pieces;
Her idols are humiliated,
Her images are broken in pieces.'

3 For out of the north a nation comes up
against her,
Which shall make her land desolate,
And no one shall dwell therein.
They shall move, they shall depart,
Both man and beast.

4 "In those days and in that time,"
says the LORD,
"The children of Israel shall come,
They and the children of Judah together;
With continual weeping they shall come,
And seek the LORD their God.
5 They shall ask the way to Zion,
With their faces toward it, *saying*,
'Come and let us join ourselves
to the LORD
In a perpetual covenant
That will not be forgotten.'

6 "My people have been lost sheep.
Their shepherds have led them astray;
They have turned them away *on* the
mountains.
They have gone from mountain to hill;
They have forgotten their resting place.
7 All who found them have devoured them;
And their adversaries said, 'We have
not offended,
Because they have sinned against the
LORD, the habitation of justice,
The LORD, the hope of their fathers.'

8 "Move from the midst of Babylon,
Go out of the land of the Chaldeans;
And be like the rams before the flocks.
9 For behold, I will raise and cause to
come up against Babylon
An assembly of great nations
from the north country,
And they shall array themselves
against her;
From there she shall be captured.
Their arrows *shall be* like *those* of an
expert warrior;
None shall return in vain.
10 And Chaldea shall become plunder;
All who plunder her shall be satisfied,"
says the LORD.

11 "Because you were glad, because you
rejoiced,
You destroyers of My heritage,
Because you have grown fat like a
heifer threshing grain,
And you bellow like bulls,
12 Your mother shall be deeply ashamed;
She who bore you shall be ashamed.
Behold, the least of the nations *shall be*
a wilderness,
A dry land and a desert.
13 Because of the wrath of the LORD
She shall not be inhabited,
But she shall be wholly desolate.
Everyone who goes by Babylon shall
be horrified
And hiss at all her plagues.

14 "Put yourselves in array against
Babylon all around,
All you who bend the bow;
Shoot at her, spare no arrows,
For she has sinned against the LORD.
15 Shout against her all around;
She has given her hand,
Her foundations have fallen,
Her walls are thrown down;
For it *is* the vengeance of the LORD.
Take vengeance on her.
As she has done, so do to her.
16 Cut off the sower from Babylon,
And him who handles the sickle at
harvest time.
For fear of the oppressing sword
Everyone shall turn to his own people,
And everyone shall flee to his own land.

17 "Israel *is* like scattered sheep;
The lions have driven *him* away.
First the king of Assyria devoured him;
Now at last this Nebuchadnezzar king
of Babylon has broken his bones."

18 Therefore thus says the LORD of hosts, the God of Israel:

"Behold, I will punish the king of
Babylon and his land,
As I have punished the king of Assyria.
19 But I will bring back Israel to his home,
And he shall feed on Carmel and
Bashan;
His soul shall be satisfied on Mount
Ephraim and Gilead.
20 In those days and in that time," says
the LORD,
"The iniquity of Israel shall be sought,
but *there shall be* none;
And the sins of Judah, but they shall
not be found;
For I will pardon those whom I preserve.

21 "Go up against the land of Merathaim,
against it,
And against the inhabitants of Pekod.
Waste and utterly destroy them," says
the LORD,
"And do according to all that I have
commanded you.
22 A sound of battle *is* in the land,
And of great destruction.

23 How the hammer of the whole earth
has been cut apart and broken!
How Babylon has become a desolation
among the nations!

50:23 hammer of the whole earth. The description was of Babylon's former conquering force, and God's breaking the "hammer" He had once used. The fact that God used Babylon as His executioner was no commendation of that nation (Hab. 1:6,7).

I have laid a snare for you;
24 You have indeed been trapped,
O Babylon,
And you were not aware;
You have been found and also caught,
Because you have contended against
the LORD.
25 The LORD has opened His armory,
And has brought out the weapons of
His indignation;
For this *is* the work of the Lord GOD
of hosts
In the land of the Chaldeans.
26 Come against her from the farthest
border;
Open her storehouses;
Cast her up as heaps of ruins,
And destroy her utterly;
Let nothing of her be left.
27 Slay all her bulls,
Let them go down to the slaughter.
Woe to them!
For their day has come, the time of
their punishment.
28 The voice of those who flee and escape
from the land of Babylon
Declares in Zion the vengeance of the
LORD our God,
The vengeance of His temple.

29 "Call together the archers against
Babylon.
All you who bend the bow, encamp
against it all around;
Let none of them escape.
Repay her according to her work;
According to all she has done, do to her;
For she has been proud against the
LORD,
Against the Holy One of Israel.
30 Therefore her young men shall fall in
the streets,
And all her men of war shall be cut off
in that day," says the LORD.

31 "Behold, I *am* against you,
O most haughty one!" says the Lord
GOD of hosts;
"For your day has come,
The time *that* I will punish you.
32 The most proud shall stumble and fall,
And no one will raise him up;
I will kindle a fire in his cities,
And it will devour all around him."

33 Thus says the LORD of hosts:

"The children of Israel *were* oppressed,
Along with the children of Judah;
All who took them captive have held
them fast;
They have refused to let them go.
34 Their Redeemer *is* strong;
The LORD of hosts *is* His name.
He will thoroughly plead their case,
That He may give rest to the land,
And disquiet the inhabitants of Babylon.

35 "A sword *is* against the Chaldeans,"
says the LORD,
"Against the inhabitants of Babylon,
And against her princes and her wise
men.
36 A sword *is* against the soothsayers,
and they will be fools.
A sword *is* against her mighty men,
and they will be dismayed.
37 A sword *is* against their horses,
Against their chariots,
And against all the mixed peoples who
are in her midst;
And they will become like women.
A sword *is* against her treasures, and
they will be robbed.
38 A drought *is* against her waters, and they
will be dried up.
For it *is* the land of carved images,
And they are insane with *their* idols.

39 "Therefore the wild desert beasts shall
dwell *there* with the jackals,
And the ostriches shall dwell in it.
It shall be inhabited no more forever,
Nor shall it be dwelt in from generation
to generation.
40 As God overthrew Sodom and Gomorrah
And their neighbors," says the LORD,
"*So* no one shall reside there,
Nor son of man dwell in it.

41 "Behold, a people shall come from the
north,
And a great nation and many kings
Shall be raised up from the ends of the
earth.
42 They shall hold the bow and the lance;
They *are* cruel and shall not show mercy.

Their voice shall roar like the sea;
They shall ride on horses,
Set in array, like a man for the battle,
Against you, O daughter of Babylon.

43 "The king of Babylon has heard the
report about them,
And his hands grow feeble;
Anguish has taken hold of him,
Pangs as of a woman in childbirth.

44 "Behold, he shall come up like a lion
from the floodplain of the Jordan
Against the dwelling place of the strong;
But I will make them suddenly run
away from her.
And who *is* a chosen *man that* I may
appoint over her?
For who *is* like Me?
Who will arraign Me?
And who *is* that shepherd
Who will withstand Me?"

45 Therefore hear the counsel of the LORD
that He has taken against Babylon,
And His purposes that He has
proposed against the land of the
Chaldeans:
Surely the least of the flock shall draw
them out;
Surely He will make their dwelling
place desolate with them.
46 At the noise of the taking of Babylon
The earth trembles,
And the cry is heard among the nations.

Psalm 119:121–128

ע AYIN
121 I have done justice and righteousness;
Do not leave me to my oppressors.
122 Be surety for Your servant for good;
Do not let the proud oppress me.
123 My eyes fail *from seeking* Your
salvation
And Your righteous word.
124 Deal with Your servant according to
Your mercy,
And teach me Your statutes.
125 I *am* Your servant;
Give me understanding,
That I may know Your testimonies.
126 *It is* time for *You* to act, O LORD,
For they have regarded Your law as
void.
127 Therefore I love Your commandments
More than gold, yes, than fine gold!
128 Therefore all *Your* precepts *concerning*
all *things*
I consider *to be* right;
I hate every false way.

Proverbs 28:6

6 Better *is* the poor who walks in his
integrity
Than one perverse *in his* ways, though
he *be* rich.

Titus 1:1–16

1 Paul, a bondservant of God and an apostle of
Jesus Christ, according to the faith of God's
elect and the acknowledgment of the truth
which accords with godliness, [2]in hope of eternal life which God, who cannot lie, promised
before time began, [3]but has in due time manifested His word through preaching, which
was committed to me according to the commandment of God our Savior;

1:1 bondservant. Paul pictures himself as the most menial slave of New Testament times, indicating his complete and willing servitude to the Lord, by whom all believers have been "bought at a price" (1 Cor. 6:20; 1 Pet. 1:18,19). This is the only time Paul referred to himself as a "bondservant of God" (Rom. 1:1; Gal. 1:10; Phil. 1:1). He was placing himself alongside Old Testament men of God (Rev. 15:3).

[4]To Titus, a true son in *our* common faith:

Grace, mercy, *and* peace from God the
Father and the Lord Jesus Christ our Savior.
[5]For this reason I left you in Crete, that you
should set in order the things that are lacking,
and appoint elders in every city as I commanded you— [6]if a man is blameless, the husband of one wife, having faithful children not
accused of dissipation or insubordination. [7]For a
bishop must be blameless, as a steward of God,
not self-willed, not quick-tempered, not given to
wine, not violent, not greedy for money, [8]but
hospitable, a lover of what is good, sober-
minded, just, holy, self-controlled, [9]holding
fast the faithful word as he has been taught,
that he may be able, by sound doctrine, both
to exhort and convict those who contradict.
[10]For there are many insubordinate, both
idle talkers and deceivers, especially those of
the circumcision, [11]whose mouths must be
stopped, who subvert whole households,
teaching things which they ought not, for the
sake of dishonest gain. [12]One of them, a prophet
of their own, said, "Cretans *are* always liars, evil
beasts, lazy gluttons." [13]This testimony is true.
Therefore rebuke them sharply, that they may

1:12 a prophet. Epimenides, the highly esteemed sixth century B.C. Greek poet and native of Crete, had characterized his own people as the dregs of Greek culture. Elsewhere, Paul also quoted pagan sayings (Acts 17:28; 1 Cor. 15:33). This quote is directed at the false teachers' character.

be sound in the faith, [14]not giving heed to Jewish fables and commandments of men who turn from the truth. [15]To the pure all things are pure, but to those who are defiled and unbelieving nothing is pure; but even their mind and conscience are defiled. [16]They profess to know God, but in works they deny *Him,* being abominable, disobedient, and disqualified for every good work.

1:14 fables and commandments of men. Paul reemphasized (v. 10, "those of the circumcision") that most of the false teachers were Jewish. They taught the same kind of externalism and unscriptural laws and traditions that both Isaiah and Jesus railed against (Is. 29:13; Matt. 15:1–9; Mark 7:5–13).

1:15 defiled. The outwardly despicable things that those men practiced (vv. 10–12) were simply reflections of their inner corruption. **mind and conscience.** If the mind is defiled, it cannot accurately inform the conscience, so conscience cannot warn the person. When conscience is accurately and fully infused with God's truth, it functions as the warning system God designed.

DAY 1: Who was Titus, and what was his role in the church?

Although Luke did not mention Titus by name in the Book of Acts, it seems probable that Titus, a Gentile (Gal. 2:3), met and may have been led to faith in Christ by Paul (Titus 1:4) before or during the apostle's first missionary journey. Later, Titus ministered for a period of time with Paul on the Island of Crete and was left behind to continue and strengthen the work (1:5). After Artemas or Tychicus (3:12) arrived to direct the ministry there, Paul wanted Titus to join him in the city of Nicopolis, in the province of Achaia in Greece, and stay through the winter (3:12).

Because of his involvement with the church at Corinth during Paul's third missionary journey, Titus is mentioned 9 times in 2 Corinthians, where Paul refers to him as "my brother" (2:13) and "my partner and fellow worker" (8:23). The young elder was already familiar with Judaizers, false teachers in the church, who among other things insisted that all Christians, Gentile as well as Jew, were bound by the Mosaic Law. Titus had accompanied Paul and Barnabas years earlier to the Council of Jerusalem where that heresy was the subject (Acts 15; Gal. 2:1–5).

Crete, one of the largest islands in the Mediterranean Sea, measuring 160 miles long by 35 miles at its widest, lying south of the Aegean Sea, had been briefly visited by Paul on his voyage to Rome (Acts 27). He returned there for ministry and later left Titus to continue the work, much as he left Timothy at Ephesus (1 Tim. 1:3), while he went on to Macedonia. He most likely wrote to Titus in response to a letter from Titus or a report from Crete.

NOVEMBER 2

Jeremiah 51:1–52:34

51 Thus says the LORD:
"Behold, I will raise up against Babylon,
Against those who dwell in Leb Kamai,
A destroying wind.
2 And I will send winnowers to Babylon,
Who shall winnow her and empty
her land.
For in the day of doom
They shall be against her all around.
3 Against *her* let the archer bend his bow,
And lift himself up against *her*
in his armor.
Do not spare her young men;
Utterly destroy all her army.
4 Thus the slain shall fall in the land of
the Chaldeans,
And *those* thrust through in her
streets.
5 For Israel is not forsaken, nor Judah,
By his God, the LORD of hosts,
Though their land was filled with sin
against the Holy One of Israel."
6 Flee from the midst of Babylon,
And every one save his life!

Do not be cut off in her iniquity,
For this *is* the time of the LORD's
vengeance;
He shall recompense her.
7 Babylon *was* a golden cup in the LORD's
hand,
That made all the earth drunk.
The nations drank her wine;
Therefore the nations are deranged.
8 Babylon has suddenly fallen
and been destroyed.
Wail for her!
Take balm for her pain;
Perhaps she may be healed.

51:8 suddenly fallen. The focus was first on Babylon's sudden fall on one night in 539 B.C. (Dan. 5:30). The far view looks at the destruction of the final Babylon near the Second Advent when it will be absolutely sudden (Rev. 18).

9 We would have healed Babylon,
But she is not healed.
Forsake her, and let us go everyone to
his own country;
For her judgment reaches to heaven
and is lifted up to the skies.
10 The LORD has revealed our
righteousness.
Come and let us declare in Zion the
work of the LORD our God.

11 Make the arrows bright!
Gather the shields!
The LORD has raised up the spirit
of the kings of the Medes.
For His plan *is* against Babylon to
destroy it,
Because it *is* the vengeance of the
LORD,
The vengeance for His temple.
12 Set up the standard on the walls
of Babylon;
Make the guard strong,
Set up the watchmen,
Prepare the ambushes.
For the LORD has both devised
and done
What He spoke against the inhabitants
of Babylon.
13 O you who dwell by many waters,
Abundant in treasures,
Your end has come,
The measure of your covetousness.
14 The LORD of hosts has sworn by
Himself:
"Surely I will fill you with men, as with
locusts,
And they shall lift up a shout against you."

15 He has made the earth by His power;
He has established the world by His
wisdom,
And stretched out the heaven by His
understanding.
16 When He utters *His* voice—
There is a multitude of waters in the
heavens:
"He causes the vapors to ascend from
the ends of the earth;
He makes lightnings for the rain;
He brings the wind out of His
treasuries."

17 Everyone is dull-hearted, without
knowledge;
Every metalsmith is put to shame by
the carved image;
For his molded image *is* falsehood,
And *there is* no breath in them.
18 They *are* futile, a work of errors;
In the time of their punishment they
shall perish.
19 The Portion of Jacob *is* not like them,
For He *is* the Maker of all things;
And *Israel is* the tribe of His
inheritance.
The LORD of hosts *is* His name.

51:15–19 He has made the earth. God's almighty power and wisdom in creation are evidences of His superiority to all idols (vv. 17,18), who along with their worshipers will all be destroyed by His mighty power (vv. 15,16,19), as in Babylon's case.

20 "You *are* My battle-ax *and* weapons
of war:
For with you I will break the nation in
pieces;
With you I will destroy kingdoms;
21 With you I will break in pieces the
horse and its rider;
With you I will break in pieces the
chariot and its rider;
22 With you also I will break in pieces
man and woman;
With you I will break in pieces old and
young;

With you I will break in pieces the
young man and the maiden;
23 With you also I will break in pieces the
shepherd and his flock;
With you I will break in pieces the
farmer and his yoke of oxen;
And with you I will break in pieces
governors and rulers.

24 "And I will repay Babylon
And all the inhabitants of Chaldea
For all the evil they have done
In Zion in your sight," says the LORD.

25 "Behold, I *am* against you, O destroying
mountain,
Who destroys all the earth,"
says the LORD.
"And I will stretch out My hand
against you,
Roll you down from the rocks,
And make you a burnt mountain.
26 They shall not take from you a stone
for a corner
Nor a stone for a foundation,
But you shall be desolate forever,"
says the LORD.

27 Set up a banner in the land,
Blow the trumpet among the nations!
Prepare the nations against her,
Call the kingdoms together against her:
Ararat, Minni, and Ashkenaz.
Appoint a general against her;
Cause the horses to come up like the
bristling locusts.
28 Prepare against her the nations,
With the kings of the Medes,
Its governors and all its rulers,
All the land of his dominion.
29 And the land will tremble and sorrow;
For every purpose of the LORD shall be
performed against Babylon,
To make the land of Babylon
a desolation without inhabitant.
30 The mighty men of Babylon have
ceased fighting,
They have remained in their
strongholds;
Their might has failed,
They became *like* women;
They have burned her dwelling places,
The bars of her *gate* are broken.
31 One runner will run to meet another,
And one messenger to meet another,
To show the king of Babylon that his
city is taken on *all* sides;
32 The passages are blocked,
The reeds they have burned with fire,
And the men of war are terrified.

33 For thus says the LORD of hosts, the God of
Israel:

"The daughter of Babylon *is* like a
threshing floor
When it is time to thresh her;
Yet a little while
And the time of her harvest will come."

34 "Nebuchadnezzar the king of Babylon
Has devoured me, he has crushed me;
He has made me an empty vessel,
He has swallowed me up like a monster;
He has filled his stomach with my
delicacies,
He has spit me out.
35 Let the violence *done* to me and my
flesh *be* upon Babylon,"
The inhabitant of Zion will say;
"And my blood be upon the inhabitants
of Chaldea!"
Jerusalem will say.

36 Therefore thus says the LORD:

"Behold, I will plead your case and take
vengeance for you.
I will dry up her sea and make her
springs dry.
37 Babylon shall become a heap,
A dwelling place for jackals,
An astonishment and a hissing,
Without an inhabitant.
38 They shall roar together like lions,
They shall growl like lions' whelps.
39 In their excitement I will prepare
their feasts;
I will make them drunk,
That they may rejoice,
And sleep a perpetual sleep
And not awake," says the LORD.
40 "I will bring them down
Like lambs to the slaughter,
Like rams with male goats.

41 "Oh, how Sheshach is taken!
Oh, how the praise of the whole earth
is seized!
How Babylon has become desolate
among the nations!
42 The sea has come up over Babylon;
She is covered with the multitude
of its waves.
43 Her cities are a desolation,
A dry land and a wilderness,
A land where no one dwells,
Through which no son of man passes.
44 I will punish Bel in Babylon,
And I will bring out of his mouth what
he has swallowed;

And the nations shall not stream to
him anymore.
Yes, the wall of Babylon shall fall.

45 "My people, go out of the midst of her!
And let everyone deliver himself from
the fierce anger of the LORD.
46 And lest your heart faint,
And you fear for the rumor that *will be*
heard in the land
(A rumor will come *one* year,
And after that, in *another* year
A rumor *will come,*
And violence in the land,
Ruler against ruler),
47 Therefore behold, the days are coming
That I will bring judgment on the
carved images of Babylon;
Her whole land shall be ashamed,
And all her slain shall fall in her midst.
48 Then the heavens and the earth and all
that *is* in them
Shall sing joyously over Babylon;
For the plunderers shall come to her
from the north," says the LORD.

49 As Babylon *has caused* the slain
of Israel to fall,
So at Babylon the slain of all the earth
shall fall.
50 You who have escaped the sword,
Get away! Do not stand still!
Remember the LORD afar off,
And let Jerusalem come to your mind.

51 We are ashamed because we have
heard reproach.
Shame has covered our faces,
For strangers have come into
the sanctuaries of the LORD's house.
52 "Therefore behold, the days are
coming," says the LORD,
"That I will bring judgment on her
carved images,
And throughout all her land the
wounded shall groan.
53 Though Babylon were to mount up to
heaven,
And though she were to fortify the
height of her strength,
Yet from Me plunderers would come to
her," says the LORD.

54 The sound of a cry *comes* from
Babylon,
And great destruction from the land of
the Chaldeans,
55 Because the LORD is plundering
Babylon
And silencing her loud voice,
Though her waves roar like great
waters,
And the noise of their voice is uttered,
56 Because the plunderer comes against
her, against Babylon,
And her mighty men are taken.
Every one of their bows is broken;
For the LORD *is* the God of recompense,
He will surely repay.

57 "And I will make drunk
Her princes and wise men,
Her governors, her deputies, and her
mighty men.
And they shall sleep a perpetual sleep
And not awake," says the King,
Whose name *is* the LORD of hosts.

58 Thus says the LORD of hosts:

"The broad walls of Babylon shall be
utterly broken,
And her high gates shall be burned
with fire;
The people will labor in vain,
And the nations, because of the fire;
And they shall be weary."

59 The word which Jeremiah the prophet commanded Seraiah the son of Neriah, the son of
Mahseiah, when he went with Zedekiah the
king of Judah to Babylon in the fourth year of
his reign. And Seraiah *was* the quartermaster.
60 So Jeremiah wrote in a book all the evil that
would come upon Babylon, all these words that
are written against Babylon.
61 And Jeremiah
said to Seraiah, "When you arrive in Babylon
and see it, and read all these words,
62 then you
shall say, 'O LORD, You have spoken against
this place to cut it off, so that none shall remain
in it, neither man nor beast, but it shall be desolate forever.'
63 Now it shall be, when you have
finished reading this book, *that* you shall tie a
stone to it and throw it out into the Euphrates.
64 Then you shall say, 'Thus Babylon shall sink
and not rise from the catastrophe that I will
bring upon her. And they shall be weary.' "

Thus far *are* the words of Jeremiah.

52 Zedekiah *was* twenty-one years old
when he became king, and he reigned
eleven years in Jerusalem. His mother's name
was Hamutal the daughter of Jeremiah of
Libnah.
2 He also did evil in the sight of the
LORD, according to all that Jehoiakim had
done.
3 For because of the anger of the LORD
this happened in Jerusalem and Judah, till He
finally cast them out from His presence. Then
Zedekiah rebelled against the king of Babylon.
4 Now it came to pass in the ninth year of his
reign, in the tenth month, on the tenth *day* of

the month, *that* Nebuchadnezzar king of Babylon and all his army came against Jerusalem and encamped against it; and *they* built a siege wall against it all around. [5]So the city was besieged until the eleventh year of King Zedekiah. [6]By the fourth month, on the ninth day of the month, the famine had become so severe in the city that there was no food for the people of the land. [7]Then the city *wall* was broken through, and all the men of war fled and went out of the city at night by way of the gate between the two walls, which *was* by the king's garden, even though the Chaldeans *were* near the city all around. And they went by way of the plain.

[8]But the army of the Chaldeans pursued the king, and they overtook Zedekiah in the plains of Jericho. All his army was scattered from him. [9]So they took the king and brought him up to the king of Babylon at Riblah in the land of Hamath, and he pronounced judgment on him. [10]Then the king of Babylon killed the sons of Zedekiah before his eyes. And he killed all the princes of Judah in Riblah. [11]He also put out the eyes of Zedekiah; and the king of Babylon bound him in bronze fetters, took him to Babylon, and put him in prison till the day of his death.

[12]Now in the fifth month, on the tenth *day* of the month (which *was* the nineteenth year of King Nebuchadnezzar king of Babylon), Nebuzaradan, the captain of the guard, *who* served the king of Babylon, came to Jerusalem. [13]He burned the house of the LORD and the king's house; all the houses of Jerusalem, that is, all the houses of the great, he burned with fire. [14]And all the army of the Chaldeans who *were* with the captain of the guard broke down all the walls of Jerusalem all around. [15]Then Nebuzaradan the captain of the guard carried away captive *some* of the poor people, the rest of the people who remained in the city, the defectors who had deserted to the king of Babylon, and the rest of the craftsmen. [16]But Nebuzaradan the captain of the guard left *some* of the poor of the land as vinedressers and farmers.

[17]The bronze pillars that *were* in the house of the LORD, and the carts and the bronze Sea that *were* in the house of the LORD, the Chaldeans broke in pieces, and carried all their bronze to Babylon. [18]They also took away the pots, the shovels, the trimmers, the bowls, the spoons, and all the bronze utensils with which the *priests* ministered. [19]The basins, the firepans, the bowls, the pots, the lampstands, the spoons, and the cups, whatever *was* solid gold and whatever *was* solid silver, the captain of the guard took away. [20]The two pillars, one Sea, the twelve bronze bulls which *were* under *it, and* the carts, which King Solomon had made for the house of the LORD—the bronze of all these articles was beyond measure. [21]Now *concerning* the pillars: the height of one pillar *was* eighteen cubits, a measuring line of twelve cubits could measure its circumference, and its thickness *was* four fingers; *it was* hollow. [22]A capital of bronze *was* on it; and the height of one capital *was* five cubits, with a network and pomegranates all around the capital, all of bronze. The second pillar, with pomegranates was the same. [23]There were ninety-six pomegranates on the sides; all the pomegranates, all around on the network, *were* one hundred.

[24]The captain of the guard took Seraiah the chief priest, Zephaniah the second priest, and the three doorkeepers. [25]He also took out of the city an officer who had charge of the men of war, seven men of the king's close associates who were found in the city, the principal scribe of the army who mustered the people of the land, and sixty men of the people of the land who were found in the midst of the city. [26]And Nebuzaradan the captain of the guard took these and brought them to the king of Babylon at Riblah. [27]Then the king of Babylon struck them and put them to death at Riblah in the land of Hamath. Thus Judah was carried away captive from its own land.

[28]These *are* the people whom Nebuchadnezzar carried away captive: in the seventh year, three thousand and twenty-three Jews; [29]in the eighteenth year of Nebuchadnezzar he carried away captive from Jerusalem eight hundred and thirty-two persons; [30]in the twenty-third year of Nebuchadnezzar, Nebuzaradan the captain of the guard carried away captive of the Jews seven hundred and forty-five persons. All the persons *were* four thousand six hundred.

[31]Now it came to pass in the thirty-seventh year of the captivity of Jehoiachin king of Judah, in the twelfth month, on the twenty-fifth *day* of the month, *that* Evil-Merodach king of Babylon, in the *first* year of his reign, lifted up the head of Jehoiachin king of Judah and brought him out of prison. [32]And he spoke kindly to him and gave him a more prominent seat than those of the kings who *were* with him in Babylon. [33]So Jehoiachin changed from his prison garments, and he ate bread regularly before the *king* all the days of his life. [34]And as for his provisions, there was a regular ration given him by the king of Babylon, a portion for each day until the day of his death, all the days of his life.

Psalm 119:129–136

פ PE

129 Your testimonies are wonderful;
Therefore my soul keeps them.
130 The entrance of Your words
gives light;
It gives understanding to the simple.
131 I opened my mouth and panted,
For I longed for Your commandments.
132 Look upon me and be merciful to me,
As Your custom *is* toward those who
love Your name.
133 Direct my steps by Your word,
And let no iniquity have dominion over
me.
134 Redeem me from the oppression of
man,
That I may keep Your precepts.
135 Make Your face shine upon Your
servant,
And teach me Your statutes.
136 Rivers of water run down from my
eyes,
Because *men* do not keep Your law.

Proverbs 28:7–8

7 Whoever keeps the law *is* a discerning
son,
But a companion of gluttons shames
his father.
8 One who increases his possessions
by usury and extortion
Gathers it for him who will pity the
poor.

Titus 2:1–15

2 But as for you, speak the things which are
proper for sound doctrine: [2]that the older
men be sober, reverent, temperate, sound in
faith, in love, in patience; [3]the older women
likewise, that they be reverent in behavior, not
slanderers, not given to much wine, teachers
of good things— [4]that they admonish the
young women to love their husbands, to love
their children, [5]*to be* discreet, chaste, home-
makers, good, obedient to their own husbands,
that the word of God may not be blasphemed.
[6]Likewise, exhort the young men to be
sober-minded, [7]in all things showing yourself *to*
be a pattern of good works; in doctrine *showing*
integrity, reverence, incorruptibility, [8]sound
speech that cannot be condemned, that one
who is an opponent may be ashamed, having
nothing evil to say of you.
[9]*Exhort* bondservants to be obedient to their
own masters, to be well pleasing in all *things*,
not answering back, [10]not pilfering, but showing all good fidelity, that they may adorn the
doctrine of God our Savior in all things.
[11]For the grace of God that brings salvation
has appeared to all men, [12]teaching us that,

2:4 admonish the young women. Their own examples of godliness (v. 3) give older women the right and the credibility to instruct younger women in the church. The obvious implication is that older women must exemplify the virtues (vv. 4,5) that they "admonish." **love their husbands.** Like the other virtues mentioned here, this one is unconditional. It is based on God's will, not on a husband's worthiness. The Greek word *phileo* emphasizes affection.

2:9 bondservants. The term applies generally to all employees, but direct reference is to slaves—men, women, and children who, in the Roman Empire and in much of the ancient world, were owned by their masters. They had few, if any, civil rights and often were accorded little more dignity or care than domestic animals. The New Testament nowhere condones or condemns the practice of slavery, but it everywhere teaches that freedom from the bondage of sin is infinitely more important than freedom from any human bondage a person may have to endure (see Rom. 6:22). **obedient…well pleasing.** Paul clearly teaches that, even in the most servile of circumstances, believers are "to be obedient" and seek to please those for whom they work, whether their "masters" are believers or unbelievers, fair or unfair, kind or cruel. How much more obligated are believers to respect and obey employers for whom they work voluntarily! As with wives' obedience to their husbands (v. 5), the only exception would involve a believer's being required to disobey God's Word.

2:14 redeem…purify. Another expression (v. 12) summarizes the dual effect of salvation (regeneration and sanctification). To "redeem" is to release someone held captive on the payment of a ransom. The price was Christ's blood paid to satisfy God's justice. **special people.** People who are special by virtue of God's decree and confirmed by the grace of salvation which they have embraced (1 Cor. 6:19,20; 1 Pet. 2:9). **zealous.** Good works are the product, not the means, of salvation (Eph. 2:10).

denying ungodliness and worldly lusts, we should live soberly, righteously, and godly in the present age, [13]looking for the blessed hope and glorious appearing of our great God and Savior Jesus Christ, [14]who gave Himself for us, that He might redeem us from every lawless deed and purify for Himself *His* own special people, zealous for good works.

[15]Speak these things, exhort, and rebuke with all authority. Let no one despise you.

DAY 2: How does the Book of Titus indicate that the message was intended for more than just Titus and the Christians on Crete?

Titus 2:11–13 presents the heart of Paul's letter to Titus. The apostle had already emphasized that God's sovereign purpose in calling out elders (1:5) and in commanding His people to live righteously (vv. 1–10) is to provide the witness that brings God's plan and purpose of salvation to fulfillment. Paul condensed the saving plan of God into 3 realities: 1) salvation from the penalty (v. 11); 2) salvation from the power (v. 12); and 3) salvation from the presence of sin (v. 13).

As Paul described the "grace of God that brings salvation" (v. 11), he was not simply referring to the divine attribute of grace, but Jesus Christ Himself, grace incarnate, God's supremely gracious gift to fallen mankind (John 1:14). The term "all men" does not teach universal salvation. "All men" is used as "man" in 3:4 to refer to humanity in general, as a category, not to every individual. Jesus Christ made a sufficient sacrifice to cover every sin of every one who believes (John 3:16–18; 1 Tim. 2:5,6; 4:10; 1 John 2:2). Paul makes clear in the opening words of this letter to Titus that salvation becomes effective only through "the faith of God's elect" (1:1). Paul was well aware that the gospel had universal implications. Out of all humanity, only those who believe will be saved (John 1:12; 3:16; 5:24,38,40; 6:40; 10:9; Rom. 10:9–17).

NOVEMBER 3

Lamentations 1:1–2:22

1 How lonely sits the city
That was full of people!
How like a widow is she,
Who *was* great among the nations!
The princess among the provinces
Has become a slave!

2 She weeps bitterly in the night,
Her tears *are* on her cheeks;
Among all her lovers
She has none to comfort *her.*
All her friends have dealt
treacherously with her;
They have become her enemies.

3 Judah has gone into captivity,
Under affliction and hard servitude;
She dwells among the nations,
She finds no rest;
All her persecutors overtake her in
dire straits.

4 The roads to Zion mourn
Because no one comes to the set feasts.
All her gates are desolate;
Her priests sigh,
Her virgins are afflicted,
And she *is* in bitterness.

5 Her adversaries have become the
master,
Her enemies prosper;
For the LORD has afflicted her
Because of the multitude of her transgressions.
Her children have gone into captivity
before the enemy.

6 And from the daughter of Zion
All her splendor has departed.
Her princes have become like deer
That find no pasture,
That flee without strength
Before the pursuer.

7 In the days of her affliction and
roaming,
Jerusalem remembers all her pleasant
things
That she had in the days of old.
When her people fell into the hand of
the enemy,
With no one to help her,
The adversaries saw her
And mocked at her downfall.

8 Jerusalem has sinned gravely,
Therefore she has become vile.
All who honored her despise her
Because they have seen her
nakedness;
Yes, she sighs and turns away.

9 Her uncleanness *is* in her skirts;
She did not consider her destiny;
Therefore her collapse was awesome;
She had no comforter.
"O LORD, behold my affliction,
For *the* enemy is exalted!"

10 The adversary has spread his hand
Over all her pleasant things;
For she has seen the nations enter
her sanctuary,
Those whom You commanded
Not to enter Your assembly.

11 All her people sigh,
They seek bread;
They have given their valuables for food
to restore life.
"See, O LORD, and consider,
For I am scorned."

12 "*Is it* nothing to you, all you who pass by?
Behold and see
If there is any sorrow like my sorrow,
Which has been brought on me,
Which the LORD has inflicted
In the day of His fierce anger.

13 "From above He has sent fire into my
bones,
And it overpowered them;
He has spread a net for my feet
And turned me back;
He has made me desolate
And faint all the day.

14 "The yoke of my transgressions was
bound;
They were woven together by His hands,
And thrust upon my neck.
He made my strength fail;
The Lord delivered me into the hands
of *those whom* I am not able to
withstand.

15 "The Lord has trampled underfoot all
my mighty *men* in my midst;
He has called an assembly against me
To crush my young men;
The Lord trampled *as* in a winepress
The virgin daughter of Judah.

16 "For these *things* I weep;
My eye, my eye overflows with water;
Because the comforter, who should
restore my life,
Is far from me.
My children are desolate
Because the enemy prevailed."

17 Zion spreads out her hands,
But no one comforts her;
The LORD has commanded concerning
Jacob
That those around him *become*
his adversaries;
Jerusalem has become an unclean
thing among them.

18 "The LORD is righteous,
For I rebelled against His
commandment.
Hear now, all peoples,
And behold my sorrow;
My virgins and my young men
Have gone into captivity.

19 "I called for my lovers,
But they deceived me;
My priests and my elders
Breathed their last in the city,
While they sought food
To restore their life.

20 "See, O LORD, that I *am* in distress;
My soul is troubled;
My heart is overturned within me,
For I have been very rebellious.
Outside the sword bereaves,
At home *it is* like death.

21 "They have heard that I sigh,
But no one comforts me.
All my enemies have heard of my
trouble;
They are glad that You have done *it*.
Bring on the day You have announced,
That they may become like me.

22 "Let all their wickedness come
before You,
And do to them as You have done
to me
For all my transgressions;
For my sighs *are* many,
And my heart *is* faint."

2 How the Lord has covered
the daughter of Zion
With a cloud in His anger!
He cast down from heaven to the earth
The beauty of Israel,
And did not remember His footstool
In the day of His anger.

1:21,22 Bring on the day. A prayer that God will likewise bring other ungodly people into judgment, especially Babylon (2:20–22; 3:64–66; 4:21,22). Such prayers are acceptable against the enemies of God (Ps. 109:14,15).

2 The Lord has swallowed up and has
not pitied
All the dwelling places of Jacob.
He has thrown down in His wrath
The strongholds of the daughter
of Judah;
He has brought *them* down to the
ground;
He has profaned the kingdom
and its princes.

3 He has cut off in fierce anger
Every horn of Israel;
He has drawn back His right hand
From before the enemy.
He has blazed against Jacob like a
flaming fire
Devouring all around.

4 Standing like an enemy, He has bent
His bow;
With His right hand, like an adversary,
He has slain all *who were* pleasing to
His eye;
On the tent of the daughter of Zion,
He has poured out His fury like fire.

5 The Lord was like an enemy.
He has swallowed up Israel,
He has swallowed up all her palaces;
He has destroyed her strongholds,
And has increased mourning and
lamentation
In the daughter of Judah.

6 He has done violence to His tabernacle,
As if it were a garden;
He has destroyed His place of
assembly;
The LORD has caused
The appointed feasts and Sabbaths to
be forgotten in Zion.
In His burning indignation He has
spurned the king and the priest.

7 The Lord has spurned His altar,
He has abandoned His sanctuary;
He has given up the walls of her
palaces
Into the hand of the enemy.
They have made a noise in the house
of the LORD
As on the day of a set feast.

8 The LORD has purposed to destroy
The wall of the daughter of Zion.
He has stretched out a line;
He has not withdrawn His hand from
destroying;
Therefore He has caused the rampart
and wall to lament;
They languished together.

9 Her gates have sunk into the ground;
He has destroyed and broken her bars.
Her king and her princes *are* among
the nations;
The Law *is* no *more,*
And her prophets find no vision from
the LORD.

10 The elders of the daughter of Zion
Sit on the ground *and* keep silence;
They throw dust on their heads
And gird themselves with sackcloth.
The virgins of Jerusalem
Bow their heads to the ground.

11 My eyes fail with tears,
My heart is troubled;
My bile is poured on the ground
Because of the destruction of the
daughter of my people,
Because the children and the infants
Faint in the streets of the city.

12 They say to their mothers,
"Where *is* grain and wine?"
As they swoon like the wounded
In the streets of the city,
As their life is poured out
In their mothers' bosom.

13 How shall I console you?
To what shall I liken you,
O daughter of Jerusalem?
What shall I compare with you,
that I may comfort you,
O virgin daughter of Zion?
For your ruin *is* spread wide as the sea;
Who can heal you?

14 Your prophets have seen for you
False and deceptive visions;
They have not uncovered your iniquity,
To bring back your captives,
But have envisioned for you false
prophecies and delusions.

15 All who pass by clap *their* hands at you;
They hiss and shake their heads
At the daughter of Jerusalem:
"*Is* this the city that is called
'The perfection of beauty,
The joy of the whole earth'?"

16 All your enemies have opened their
mouth against you;
They hiss and gnash *their* teeth.
They say, "We have swallowed *her* up!
Surely this *is* the day we have waited
for;
We have found *it,* we have seen *it!*"

17 The LORD has done what He purposed;
He has fulfilled His word
Which He commanded in days of old.
He has thrown down and has not
pitied,
And He has caused an enemy
to rejoice over you;
He has exalted the horn of your
adversaries.
18 Their heart cried out to the Lord,
"O wall of the daughter of Zion,
Let tears run down like a river day
and night;
Give yourself no relief;
Give your eyes no rest.
19 "Arise, cry out in the night,
At the beginning of the watches;
Pour out your heart like water before
the face of the Lord.
Lift your hands toward Him
For the life of your young children,
Who faint from hunger at the head
of every street."
20 "See, O LORD, and consider!
To whom have You done this?
Should the women eat their offspring,
The children they have cuddled?
Should the priest and prophet be slain
In the sanctuary of the Lord?

2:20 See, O LORD, and consider! The chapter closes by placing the issue before God. **women eat their offspring.** Hunger became so desperate in the 18-month siege that women resorted to the unbelievable—even eating their children (4:10; Lev. 26:29; Deut. 28:53,56,57; Jer. 19:9).

21 "Young and old lie
On the ground in the streets;
My virgins and my young men
Have fallen by the sword;
You have slain *them* in the day of Your
anger,
You have slaughtered *and* not pitied.
22 "You have invited as to a feast day
The terrors that surround me.
In the day of the LORD's anger
There was no refugee or survivor.
Those whom I have borne and
brought up
My enemies have destroyed."

Psalm 119:137–144

צ TSADDE
137 Righteous *are* You, O LORD,
And upright *are* Your judgments.
138 Your testimonies, *which* You have
commanded,
Are righteous and very faithful.
139 My zeal has consumed me,
Because my enemies have forgotten
Your words.
140 Your word *is* very pure;
Therefore Your servant loves it.
141 I *am* small and despised,
Yet I do not forget Your precepts.
142 Your righteousness *is* an everlasting
righteousness,
And Your law *is* truth.
143 Trouble and anguish have overtaken
me,
Yet Your commandments *are* my
delights.
144 The righteousness of Your testimonies
is everlasting;
Give me understanding, and I shall live.

Proverbs 28:9–10

9 One who turns away his ear from
hearing the law,
Even his prayer *is* an abomination.
10 Whoever causes the upright to go
astray in an evil way,
He himself will fall into his own pit;
But the blameless will inherit good.

Titus 3:1–15

3 Remind them to be subject to rulers and
authorities, to obey, to be ready for every
good work, 2to speak evil of no one, to be
peaceable, gentle, showing all humility to all
men. 3For we ourselves were also once foolish,
disobedient, deceived, serving various lusts
and pleasures, living in malice and envy, hate-

3:1–11 In his closing remarks, Paul admonished Titus to remind believers under his care of their attitudes toward: 1) the unsaved rulers (v. 1) and people in general (v. 2); 2) their previous state as unbelievers lost in sin (v. 3); 3) of their gracious salvation through Jesus Christ (vv. 4–7); 4) of their righteous testimony to the unsaved world (v. 8); 5) and of their responsibility to oppose false teachers and factious members within the church (vv. 9–11). All of these matters are essential to effective evangelism.

ful and hating one another. [4]But when the kindness and the love of God our Savior toward man appeared, [5]not by works of righteousness which we have done, but according to His mercy He saved us, through the washing of regeneration and renewing of the Holy Spirit, [6]whom He poured out on us abundantly through Jesus Christ our Savior, [7]that having been justified by His grace we should become heirs according to the hope of eternal life.

[8]This is a faithful saying, and these things I want you to affirm constantly, that those who have believed in God should be careful to maintain good works. These things are good and profitable to men.

[9]But avoid foolish disputes, genealogies, contentions, and strivings about the law; for they are unprofitable and useless. [10]Reject a divisive man after the first and second admonition, [11]knowing that such a person is warped and sinning, being self-condemned.

[12]When I send Artemas to you, or Tychicus, be diligent to come to me at Nicopolis, for I have decided to spend the winter there. [13]Send Zenas the lawyer and Apollos on their journey with haste, that they may lack nothing. [14]And let our *people* also learn to maintain good works, to *meet* urgent needs, that they may not be unfruitful.

[15]All who *are* with me greet you. Greet those who love us in the faith.

Grace *be* with you all. Amen.

3:3 ourselves. It is not that every believer has committed every sin listed here, but rather that before salvation every life is characterized by such sins. That sobering truth should make believers humble in dealing with the unsaved, even those who are grossly immoral and ungodly. If it weren't for God's grace to His own, they would all be wicked.

DAY 3: What is the Book of Lamentations about?

The prophetic seeds of Jerusalem's destruction were sown through Joshua 800 years in advance (Josh. 23:15,16). Now, for over 40 years, Jeremiah had prophesied of coming judgment and been scorned by the people for preaching doom (ca. 645–605 B.C.). When that judgment came on the disbelieving people from Nebuchadnezzar and the Babylonian army, Jeremiah still responded with great sorrow and compassion toward his suffering and obstinate people. Lamentations relates closely to the Book of Jeremiah, describing the anguish over Jerusalem's receiving God's judgment for unrepentant sins. In the book that bears his name, Jeremiah had predicted the calamity in chapters 1–29. In Lamentations, he concentrates in more detail on the bitter suffering and heartbreak that was felt over Jerusalem's devastation (Ps. 46:4,5). So critical was Jerusalem's destruction that the facts are recorded in 4 separate Old Testament chapters: 2 Kings 25; Jeremiah 39:1–11; 52; and 2 Chronicles 36:11–21.

All 154 verses have been recognized by the Jews as a part of their sacred canon. Along with Ruth, Esther, Song of Solomon, and Ecclesiastes, Lamentations is included among the Old Testament books of the Megilloth, or "five scrolls," which were read in the synagogue on special occasions. Lamentations is read on the ninth of Ab (July/Aug.) to remember the date of Jerusalem's destruction by Nebuchadnezzar. Interestingly, this same date later marked the destruction of Herod's temple by the Romans in A.D. 70.

NOVEMBER 4

Lamentations 3:1–5:22

3 I *am* the man *who* has seen affliction
by the rod of His wrath.
2 He has led me and made *me* walk
In darkness and not *in* light.
3 Surely He has turned His hand
against me
Time and time again throughout the day.
4 He has aged my flesh and my skin,
And broken my bones.
5 He has besieged me
And surrounded *me* with bitterness
and woe.
6 He has set me in dark places
Like the dead of long ago.
7 He has hedged me in so that I cannot
get out;
He has made my chain heavy.
8 Even when I cry and shout,
He shuts out my prayer.
9 He has blocked my ways with hewn
stone;
He has made my paths crooked.
10 He *has been* to me a bear lying in wait,

3:8 He shuts out my prayer. God's nonresponse to Jeremiah's prayers was not because Jeremiah was guilty of personal sin (Ps. 66:18); rather, it was due to Israel's perpetual sin without repentance (Jer. 19:15). God's righteousness to judge that sin must pursue its course (Jer. 7:16; 11:14). Jeremiah knew that, yet prayed, wept (vv. 48–51), and longed to see repentance.

Like a lion in ambush.
11 He has turned aside my ways and torn
me in pieces;
He has made me desolate.
12 He has bent His bow
And set me up as a target for the arrow.

13 He has caused the arrows of His quiver
To pierce my loins.
14 I have become the ridicule of all my
people—
Their taunting song all the day.
15 He has filled me with bitterness,
He has made me drink wormwood.

16 He has also broken my teeth with
gravel,
And covered me with ashes.
17 You have moved my soul far from
peace;
I have forgotten prosperity.
18 And I said, "My strength and my hope
Have perished from the LORD."

19 Remember my affliction and roaming,
The wormwood and the gall.
20 My soul still remembers
And sinks within me.
21 This I recall to my mind,
Therefore I have hope.

22 *Through* the LORD's mercies we are not
consumed,
Because His compassions fail not.
23 *They are* new every morning;
Great *is* Your faithfulness.
24 "The LORD *is* my portion," says my soul,

3:22–24 His compassions fail not. As bleak as the situation of judgment had become, God's covenant lovingkindness was always present (vv. 31,32), and His incredible faithfulness always endured so that Judah would not be destroyed forever (Mal. 3:6).

"Therefore I hope in Him!"

25 The LORD *is* good to those who wait
for Him,
To the soul *who* seeks Him.
26 *It is* good that *one* should hope
and wait quietly
For the salvation of the LORD.
27 *It is* good for a man to bear
The yoke in his youth.

28 Let him sit alone and keep silent,
Because *God* has laid *it* on him;
29 Let him put his mouth in the dust—
There may yet be hope.
30 Let him give *his* cheek to the one who
strikes him,
And be full of reproach.

31 For the Lord will not cast off forever.
32 Though He causes grief,
Yet He will show compassion
According to the multitude of His
mercies.
33 For He does not afflict willingly,
Nor grieve the children of men.

34 To crush under one's feet
All the prisoners of the earth,
35 To turn aside the justice *due* a man
Before the face of the Most High,
36 Or subvert a man in his cause—
The Lord does not approve.

37 Who *is* he *who* speaks and it comes
to pass,
When the Lord has not commanded *it?*
38 *Is it* not from the mouth of the Most
High
That woe and well-being proceed?
39 Why should a living man complain,
A man for the punishment of his sins?

40 Let us search out and examine our ways,
And turn back to the LORD;
41 Let us lift our hearts and hands
To God in heaven.
42 We have transgressed and rebelled;
You have not pardoned.

43 You have covered *Yourself* with anger
And pursued us;
You have slain *and* not pitied.
44 You have covered Yourself with a
cloud,
That prayer should not pass through.
45 You have made us an offscouring and
refuse
In the midst of the peoples.

46 All our enemies
Have opened their mouths against us.

47 Fear and a snare have come upon us,
Desolation and destruction.
48 My eyes overflow with rivers of water
For the destruction of the daughter
of my people.

49 My eyes flow and do not cease,
Without interruption,
50 Till the LORD from heaven
Looks down and sees.
51 My eyes bring suffering to my soul
Because of all the daughters of my city.

52 My enemies without cause
Hunted me down like a bird.
53 They silenced my life in the pit
And threw stones at me.
54 The waters flowed over my head;
I said, "I am cut off!"

55 I called on Your name, O LORD,
From the lowest pit.
56 You have heard my voice:
"Do not hide Your ear
From my sighing, from my cry
for help."
57 You drew near on the day I called
on You,
And said, "Do not fear!"

58 O Lord, You have pleaded the case
for my soul;
You have redeemed my life.
59 O LORD, You have seen *how* I am
wronged;
Judge my case.
60 You have seen all their vengeance,
All their schemes against me.

61 You have heard their reproach,
O LORD,
All their schemes against me,
62 The lips of my enemies
And their whispering against me
all the day.
63 Look at their sitting down and their
rising up;
I *am* their taunting song.

64 Repay them, O LORD,
According to the work of their hands.
65 Give them a veiled heart;
Your curse *be* upon them!
66 In Your anger,
Pursue and destroy them
From under the heavens of the LORD.

4 How the gold has become dim!
How changed the fine gold!
The stones of the sanctuary
are scattered
At the head of every street.

2 The precious sons of Zion,
Valuable as fine gold,
How they are regarded as clay pots,
The work of the hands of the potter!

3 Even the jackals present their breasts
To nurse their young;
But the daughter of my people *is* cruel,
Like ostriches in the wilderness.

4 The tongue of the infant clings
To the roof of its mouth for thirst;
The young children ask for bread,
But no one breaks *it* for them.

5 Those who ate delicacies
Are desolate in the streets;
Those who were brought up in scarlet
Embrace ash heaps.

6 The punishment of the iniquity of the
daughter of my people
Is greater than the punishment of the
sin of Sodom,
Which was overthrown in a moment,
With no hand to help her!

7 Her Nazirites were brighter than snow
And whiter than milk;
They were more ruddy in body
than rubies,
Like sapphire in their appearance.

8 *Now* their appearance is blacker
than soot;
They go unrecognized in the streets;
Their skin clings to their bones,
It has become as dry as wood.

9 *Those* slain by the sword are better off
Than *those* who die of hunger;
For these pine away,
Stricken *for lack* of the fruits
of the field.

10 The hands of the compassionate women
Have cooked their own children;
They became food for them
In the destruction of the daughter of
my people.

11 The LORD has fulfilled His fury,
He has poured out His fierce anger.
He kindled a fire in Zion,
And it has devoured its foundations.

12 The kings of the earth,
And all inhabitants of the world,
Would not have believed
That the adversary and the enemy
Could enter the gates of Jerusalem—
13 Because of the sins of her prophets
And the iniquities of her priests,

Who shed in her midst
The blood of the just.

14 They wandered blind in the streets;
They have defiled themselves with blood,
So that no one would touch their garments.

15 They cried out to them,
"Go away, unclean!
Go away, go away,
Do not touch us!"
When they fled and wandered,
Those among the nations said,
"They shall no longer dwell *here.*"

16 The face of the LORD scattered them;
He no longer regards them.
The people do not respect the priests
Nor show favor to the elders.

17 Still our eyes failed us,
Watching vainly for our help;
In our watching we watched
For a nation *that* could not save *us.*

18 They tracked our steps
So that we could not walk in our streets.
Our end was near;
Our days were over,
For our end had come.

19 Our pursuers were swifter
Than the eagles of the heavens.
They pursued us on the mountains
And lay in wait for us in the wilderness.

20 The breath of our nostrils, the anointed of the LORD,
Was caught in their pits,
Of whom we said, "Under his shadow
We shall live among the nations."

21 Rejoice and be glad, O daughter of Edom,
You who dwell in the land of Uz!
The cup shall also pass over to you
And you shall become drunk and make yourself naked.

22 *The punishment of* your iniquity is accomplished,
O daughter of Zion;
He will no longer send you into captivity.
He will punish your iniquity,
O daughter of Edom;
He will uncover your sins!

5 Remember, O LORD, what has come upon us;
Look, and behold our reproach!

2 Our inheritance has been turned over to aliens,
And our houses to foreigners.

3 We have become orphans and waifs,
Our mothers *are* like widows.

4 We pay for the water we drink,
And our wood comes at a price.

5 *They* pursue at our heels;
We labor *and* have no rest.

6 We have given our hand *to* the Egyptians
And the Assyrians, to be satisfied with bread.

7 Our fathers sinned *and are* no more,
But we bear their iniquities.

8 Servants rule over us;
There is none to deliver *us* from their hand.

9 We get our bread *at the risk* of our lives,
Because of the sword in the wilderness.

10 Our skin is hot as an oven,
Because of the fever of famine.

11 They ravished the women in Zion,
The maidens in the cities of Judah.

12 Princes were hung up by their hands,
And elders were not respected.

13 Young men ground at the millstones;
Boys staggered under *loads of* wood.

14 The elders have ceased *gathering at* the gate,
And the young men from their music.

15 The joy of our heart has ceased;
Our dance has turned into mourning.

16 The crown has fallen *from* our head.
Woe to us, for we have sinned!

17 Because of this our heart is faint;
Because of these *things* our eyes grow dim;

18 Because of Mount Zion which is desolate,
With foxes walking about on it.

19 You, O LORD, remain forever;
Your throne from generation to generation.

20 Why do You forget us forever,
And forsake us for so long a time?

21 Turn us back to You, O LORD, and we will be restored;
Renew our days as of old,

22 Unless You have utterly rejected us,
And are very angry with us!

Psalm 119:145–152

ק QOPH

145 I cry out with *my* whole heart;
Hear me, O LORD!

I will keep Your statutes.
146 I cry out to You;
Save me, and I will keep Your
testimonies.
147 I rise before the dawning of the
morning,
And cry for help;
I hope in Your word.
148 My eyes are awake through the *night*
watches,
That I may meditate on Your word.
149 Hear my voice according to Your
lovingkindness;
O LORD, revive me according to Your
justice.
150 They draw near who follow after
wickedness;
They are far from Your law.
151 You *are* near, O LORD,
And all Your commandments *are* truth.
152 Concerning Your testimonies,
I have known of old that You have
founded them forever.

Proverbs 28:11

11 The rich man *is* wise in his own eyes,
But the poor who has understanding
searches him out.

Philemon 1–25

Paul, a prisoner of Christ Jesus, and Timothy *our* brother,

To Philemon our beloved *friend* and fellow
laborer, [2]to the beloved Apphia, Archippus our
fellow soldier, and to the church in your house:

[3]Grace to you and peace from God our Father
and the Lord Jesus Christ.

[4]I thank my God, making mention of you
always in my prayers, [5]hearing of your love and
faith which you have toward the Lord Jesus and
toward all the saints, [6]that the sharing of your faith
may become effective by the acknowledgment of

1 prisoner of Christ Jesus. At the time of writing, Paul was a prisoner in Rome. Paul was imprisoned for the sake of and by the sovereign will of Christ (Eph. 3:1; 4:1; 6:19,20; Phil. 1:13; Col. 4:3). By beginning with his imprisonment and not his apostolic authority, Paul made this letter a gentle and singular appeal to a friend. A reminder of Paul's severe hardships was bound to influence Philemon's willingness to do the comparatively easy task Paul was about to request.

every good thing which is in you in Christ Jesus. [7]For we have great joy and consolation in
your love, because the hearts of the saints have
been refreshed by you, brother.

[8]Therefore, though I might be very bold in
Christ to command you what is fitting, [9]*yet* for
love's sake I rather appeal *to you*—being such
a one as Paul, the aged, and now also a prisoner of Jesus Christ— [10]I appeal to you for my
son Onesimus, whom I have begotten *while* in
my chains, [11]who once was unprofitable to you,
but now is profitable to you and to me.

[12]I am sending him back. You therefore
receive him, that is, my own heart, [13]whom I
wished to keep with me, that on your behalf he
might minister to me in my chains for the
gospel. [14]But without your consent I wanted to
do nothing, that your good deed might not be by
compulsion, as it were, but voluntary.

[15]For perhaps he departed for a while for this
purpose, that you might receive him forever, [16]no
longer as a slave but more than a slave—a
beloved brother, especially to me but how much
more to you, both in the flesh and in the Lord.

16 more than a slave—a beloved brother. Paul did not call for Onesimus's freedom (1 Cor. 7:20–22), but that Philemon would receive his slave now as a fellow believer in Christ (Eph. 6:9; Col. 4:1; 1 Tim. 6:2). Christianity never sought to abolish slavery, but rather to make the relationships within it just and kind. **in the flesh.** In this physical life (Phil. 1:22), as they worked together. **in the Lord.** The master and slave were to enjoy spiritual oneness and fellowship as they worshiped and ministered together.

[17]If then you count me as a partner, receive
him as *you would* me. [18]But if he has wronged
you or owes anything, put that on my account.
[19]I, Paul, am writing with my own hand. I will
repay—not to mention to you that you owe me
even your own self besides. [20]Yes, brother, let
me have joy from you in the Lord; refresh my
heart in the Lord.

[21]Having confidence in your obedience, I
write to you, knowing that you will do even
more than I say. [22]But, meanwhile, also prepare
a guest room for me, for I trust that through
your prayers I shall be granted to you.

[23]Epaphras, my fellow prisoner in Christ Jesus, greets you, [24]*as do* Mark, Aristarchus,
Demas, Luke, my fellow laborers.

[25]The grace of our Lord Jesus Christ *be* with
your spirit. Amen.

DAY 4: What is the background for the Book of Philemon?

Philemon had been saved under Paul's ministry, probably at Ephesus (v. 19), several years earlier. Wealthy enough to have a large house (v. 2), Philemon also owned at least one slave, a man named Onesimus (literally, "useful"; a common name for slaves). Onesimus was not a believer at the time he stole some money (v. 18) from Philemon and ran away. Like countless thousands of other runaway slaves, Onesimus fled to Rome, seeking to lose himself in the imperial capital's teeming and nondescript slave population. Through circumstances not recorded in Scripture, Onesimus met Paul in Rome and became a Christian.

The apostle quickly grew to love the runaway slave (vv. 12,16) and longed to keep Onesimus in Rome (v. 13), where he was providing valuable service to Paul in his imprisonment (v. 11). But by stealing and running away from Philemon, Onesimus had both broken Roman law and defrauded his master. Paul knew those issues had to be dealt with and decided to send Onesimus back to Colosse. It was too hazardous for him to make the trip alone (because of the danger of slave-catchers), so Paul sent him back with Tychicus, who was returning to Colosse with the Epistle to the Colossians (Col. 4:7–9). Along with Onesimus, Paul sent Philemon this beautiful personal letter, urging him to forgive Onesimus and welcome him back to service as a brother in Christ (vv. 15–17).

NOVEMBER 5

Ezekiel 1:1–2:10

1 Now it came to pass in the thirtieth year, in
the fourth *month*, on the fifth *day* of the
month, as I *was* among the captives by the
River Chebar, *that* the heavens were opened
and I saw visions of God. 2On the fifth *day* of
the month, which *was* in the fifth year of King
Jehoiachin's captivity, 3the word of the LORD
came expressly to Ezekiel the priest, the son
of Buzi, in the land of the Chaldeans by the
River Chebar; and the hand of the LORD was
upon him there.
4Then I looked, and behold, a whirlwind was
coming out of the north, a great cloud with
raging fire engulfing itself; and brightness *was*
all around it and radiating out of its midst like
the color of amber, out of the midst of the fire.
5Also from within it *came* the likeness of four
living creatures. And this *was* their appearance: they had the likeness of a man. 6Each
one had four faces, and each one had four
wings. 7Their legs *were* straight, and the soles
of their feet *were* like the soles of calves' feet.
They sparkled like the color of burnished
bronze. 8The hands of a man *were* under their
wings on their four sides; and each of the four
had faces and wings. 9Their wings touched one
another. *The creatures* did not turn when they
went, but each one went straight forward.
10As for the likeness of their faces, *each* had
the face of a man; each of the four had the face
of a lion on the right side, each of the four had
the face of an ox on the left side, and each of the
four had the face of an eagle. 11Thus *were* their
faces. Their wings stretched upward; two *wings*
of each one touched one another, and two covered their bodies. 12And each one went straight
forward; they went wherever the spirit wanted
to go, and they did not turn when they went.
13As for the likeness of the living creatures,
their appearance *was* like burning coals of fire,
like the appearance of torches going back and
forth among the living creatures. The fire was
bright, and out of the fire went lightning. 14And
the living creatures ran back and forth, in
appearance like a flash of lightning.
15Now as I looked at the living creatures,
behold, a wheel *was* on the earth beside each
living creature with its four faces. 16The
appearance of the wheels and their workings

1:4 whirlwind...fire. Judgment on Judah in a further and totally devastating phase (beyond the 597 B.C. deportation) is to come out of the north, and did come from Babylon in 588–586 (as Jer. 39; 40). Its terror is depicted by a fiery whirlwind emblematic of God's judgments and the golden brightness signifying dazzling glory.

1:16 wheel in the middle of a wheel. This depicted the gigantic (v. 15, "on the earth" and "so high," v. 18) energy of the complicated revolutions of God's massive judgment machinery bringing about His purposes with unerring certainty.

was like the color of beryl, and all four had the
same likeness. The appearance of their workings *was,* as it were, a wheel in the middle of a
wheel. 17When they moved, they went toward
any one of four directions; they did not turn
aside when they went. 18As for their rims, they
were so high they were awesome; and their
rims *were* full of eyes, all around the four of
them. 19When the living creatures went, the
wheels went beside them; and when the living
creatures were lifted up from the earth, the
wheels were lifted up. 20Wherever the spirit
wanted to go, they went, *because* there the
spirit went; and the wheels were lifted together
with them, for the spirit of the living creatures
was in the wheels. 21When those went, *these*
went; when those stood, *these* stood; and when
those were lifted up from the earth, the wheels
were lifted up together with them, for the spirit
of the living creatures *was* in the wheels.

22The likeness of the firmament above the
heads of the living creatures *was* like the color
of an awesome crystal, stretched out over their
heads. 23And under the firmament their wings
spread out straight, one toward another. Each
one had two which covered one side, and each
one had two which covered the other side of the
body. 24When they went, I heard the noise of
their wings, like the noise of many waters, like
the voice of the Almighty, a tumult like the noise
of an army; and when they stood still, they let
down their wings. 25A voice came from above
the firmament that *was* over their heads; whenever they stood, they let down their wings.

26And above the firmament over their heads
was the likeness of a throne, in appearance
like a sapphire stone; on the likeness of the
throne *was* a likeness with the appearance of a
man high above it. 27Also from the appearance
of His waist and upward I saw, as it were, the
color of amber with the appearance of fire all
around within it; and from the appearance of
His waist and downward I saw, as it were, the
appearance of fire with brightness all around.
28Like the appearance of a rainbow in a cloud
on a rainy day, so *was* the appearance of the
brightness all around it. This *was* the appearance of the likeness of the glory of the LORD.

So when I saw *it,* I fell on my face, and I
heard a voice of One speaking.

2 And He said to me, "Son of man, stand on
your feet, and I will speak to you." 2Then
the Spirit entered me when He spoke to me,
and set me on my feet; and I heard Him who
spoke to me. 3And He said to me: "Son of man,
I am sending you to the children of Israel, to a
rebellious nation that has rebelled against Me;
they and their fathers have transgressed
against Me to this very day. 4For *they are* impudent and stubborn children. I am sending you
to them, and you shall say to them, 'Thus says
the Lord GOD.' 5As for them, whether they hear
or whether they refuse—for they *are* a rebellious house—yet they will know that a prophet
has been among them.

6"And you, son of man, do not be afraid of
them nor be afraid of their words, though
briers and thorns *are* with you and you dwell
among scorpions; do not be afraid of their
words or dismayed by their looks, though
they *are* a rebellious house. 7You shall speak
My words to them, whether they hear or
whether they refuse, for they *are* rebellious.
8But you, son of man, hear what I say to you. Do
not be rebellious like that rebellious house;
open your mouth and eat what I give you."

9Now when I looked, there was a hand
stretched out to me; and behold, a scroll of a
book *was* in it. 10Then He spread it before me;
and *there was* writing on the inside and on the
outside, and written on it *were* lamentations
and mourning and woe.

Psalm 119:153–160

ר RESH

153 Consider my affliction and deliver me,
For I do not forget Your law.
154 Plead my cause and redeem me;
Revive me according to Your word.
155 Salvation *is* far from the wicked,
For they do not seek Your statutes.
156 Great *are* Your tender mercies,
O LORD;
Revive me according to Your
judgments.
157 Many *are* my persecutors and my
enemies,
Yet I do not turn from Your
testimonies.
158 I see the treacherous, and am
disgusted,
Because they do not keep Your word.

2:2 the Spirit entered me. What God commands a servant to do (v. 1), He gives power to fulfill by His Spirit (3:14; Zech. 4:6). This pictures the selective empowering by the Holy Spirit to enable an individual for special service to the Lord, which occurred frequently in the Old Testament. (For examples see 11:5; 37:1; Num. 24:2; Judg. 3:10; 6:34; 11:29; 13:25; 1 Sam. 10:10; 16:13,14; 19:20; 2 Chr. 15:1; Luke 4:18.)

159 Consider how I love Your precepts;
Revive me, O LORD, according to Your lovingkindness.
160 The entirety of Your word *is* truth,
And every one of Your righteous judgments *endures* forever.

Proverbs 28:12

12 When the righteous rejoice, *there is* great glory;
But when the wicked arise, men hide themselves.

Hebrews 1:1–14

1 God, who at various times and in various
ways spoke in time past to the fathers by the
prophets, [2]has in these last days spoken to us
by *His* Son, whom He has appointed heir of all
things, through whom also He made the
worlds; [3]who being the brightness of *His* glory
and the express image of His person, and up-
holding all things by the word of His power,
when He had by Himself purged our sins, sat
down at the right hand of the Majesty on high,
[4]having become so much better than the
angels, as He has by inheritance obtained a
more excellent name than they.

1:2 last days. Jews understood the "last days" to mean the time when the Messiah (Christ) would come (Num. 24:14; Jer. 33:14–16; Mic. 5:1,2; Zech. 9:9,16). The fulfillment of the messianic prophecies commenced with the advent of the Messiah. Since He came, it has been the "last days" (1 Cor. 10:11; James 5:3; 1 Pet. 1:20; 4:7; 1 John 2:18). In the past, God gave revelation through His prophets; but in these times, beginning with the Messiah's Advent, God spoke the message of redemption through the Son. **heir.** Everything that exists will ultimately come under the control of the Son of God, the Messiah. This "inheritance" is the full extension of the authority which the Father has given to the Son (Dan. 7:13,14; Matt. 28:18), as the "firstborn." **worlds.** The word can also be translated "ages." It refers to time, space, energy, and matter—the entire universe and everything that makes it function (John 1:3).

---

[5]For to which of the angels did He ever say:

"You are My Son,
Today I have begotten You"?

And again:

"I will be to Him a Father,
And He shall be to Me a Son"?

[6]But when He again brings the firstborn into the world, He says:

"Let all the angels of God worship Him."

[7]And of the angels He says:

"Who makes His angels spirits
And His ministers a flame of fire."

[8]But to the Son *He says:*

"Your throne, O God, is forever and ever;
A scepter of righteousness is the scepter of Your kingdom.
9 *You have loved righteousness and hated lawlessness;*
Therefore God, Your God, has anointed You
With the oil of gladness more than Your companions."

1:8,9 *He says.* Quoting from Psalm 45:6,7, the writer argues for the Deity and the lordship of the Son over creation (v. 3). The text is all the more significant since the declaration of the Son's Deity is presented as the words of the Father Himself (Is. 9:6; Jer. 23:5,6; John 5:18; Titus 2:13; 1 John 5:20). It is clear that the writer of Hebrews had the 3 messianic offices in mind: Prophet (v. 1), Priest (v. 3), and King (vv. 3,8). Induction into those 3 offices required anointing (v. 9). The title "Messiah" ("Christ") means "anointed one" (Is. 61:1–3; Luke 4:16–21).

---

[10]And:

"You, LORD, in the beginning laid the foundation of the earth,
And the heavens are the work of Your hands.
11 *They will perish, but You remain;*
And they will all grow old like a garment;
12 *Like a cloak You will fold them up,*
And they will be changed.
But You are the same,
And Your years will not fail."

[13]But to which of the angels has He ever said:

"Sit at My right hand,
Till I make Your enemies Your footstool"?

[14]Are they not all ministering spirits sent forth to minister for those who will inherit salvation?

DAY 5: To which Hebrews was this book written?

Although the author and the original recipients of this letter are unknown, the title, dating as early as the second century A.D., had been "To the Hebrews." The title certainly fits the content. The epistle exudes a Jewish mind-set. References to Hebrew history and religion abound. And since no particular Gentile or pagan practice gains any attention in the book, the church has kept the traditional title.

A proper interpretation of this epistle requires the recognition that it addresses 3 distinct groups of Hebrews:

1. Hebrew Christians who suffered rejection and persecution by fellow Jews (10:32–34), although none as yet had been martyred (12:4). The letter was written to give them encouragement and confidence in Christ, their Messiah and High Priest. They were an immature group of believers who were tempted to hold on to the symbolic and spiritually powerless rituals and traditions of Judaism.

2. Jewish unbelievers who were intellectually convinced of the basic truths of the gospel but who had not placed their faith in Jesus Christ as their own Savior and Lord. They were intellectually persuaded but spiritually uncommitted. These unbelievers are addressed in such passages as 2:1–3; 6:4–6; 10:26–29; and 12:15–17.

3. Jewish unbelievers who were attracted by the gospel and the Person of Christ but who had reached no final conviction about Him. Chapter 9 is largely devoted to them.

NOVEMBER 6

Ezekiel 3:1–4:17

3 Moreover He said to me, "Son of man,
eat what you find; eat this scroll, and go,
speak to the house of Israel." 2So I opened my
mouth, and He caused me to eat that scroll.
3And He said to me, "Son of man, feed your
belly, and fill your stomach with this scroll that
I give you." So I ate, and it was in my mouth
like honey in sweetness.
4Then He said to me: "Son of man, go to the
house of Israel and speak with My words to
them. 5For you *are* not sent to a people of unfamiliar speech and of hard language, *but* to the
house of Israel, 6not to many people of unfamiliar speech and of hard language, whose
words you cannot understand. Surely, had I
sent you to them, they would have listened to
you. 7But the house of Israel will not listen to
you, because they will not listen to Me; for all the
house of Israel *are* impudent and hard-hearted.
8Behold, I have made your face strong against
their faces, and your forehead strong against
their foreheads. 9Like adamant stone, harder
than flint, I have made your forehead; do not
be afraid of them, nor be dismayed at their
looks, though they *are* a rebellious house."
10Moreover He said to me: "Son of man, receive
into your heart all My words that I speak to you,
and hear with your ears. 11And go, get to the captives, to the children of your people, and speak
to them and tell them, 'Thus says the Lord GOD,'
whether they hear, or whether they refuse."

3:8,9 I have made your face strong. What God commands ("do not be afraid") He gives sufficiency to do ("I have made"), so God will enable the prophet to live up to his name (which means "strengthened by God"). 2:2; 3:14,24; Is. 41:10; Jer. 1:8,17.

3:9 rebellious. It is sad to observe that the exile and affliction did not make the Jews more responsive to God; rather, they were hardened by their sufferings. God gave Ezekiel a "hardness" to surpass the people and sustain his ministry as prophet to the exiles.

12Then the Spirit lifted me up, and I heard
behind me a great thunderous voice: "Blessed
is the glory of the LORD from His place!" 13*I* also
heard the noise of the wings of the living creatures that touched one another, and the noise
of the wheels beside them, and a great thunderous noise. 14So the Spirit lifted me up and
took me away, and I went in bitterness, in the
heat of my spirit; but the hand of the LORD was
strong upon me. 15Then I came to the captives
at Tel Abib, who dwelt by the River Chebar;
and I sat where they sat, and remained there
astonished among them seven days.
16Now it came to pass at the end of seven
days that the word of the LORD came to me,
saying, 17"Son of man, I have made you a
watchman for the house of Israel; therefore
hear a word from My mouth, and give them
warning from Me: 18When I say to the wicked,
'You shall surely die,' and you give him no

3:17 a watchman. This role was spiritually analogous to the role of watchmen on a city wall, vigilant to spot the approach of an enemy and warn the residents to muster a defense. The prophet gave timely warnings of approaching judgment. The work of a watchman is vividly set forth in 2 Samuel 18:24–27 and 2 Kings 9:17–20.

warning, nor speak to warn the wicked from
his wicked way, to save his life, that same
wicked *man* shall die in his iniquity; but his
blood I will require at your hand. [19]Yet, if you
warn the wicked, and he does not turn from
his wickedness, nor from his wicked way, he
shall die in his iniquity; but you have delivered
your soul.

[20]"Again, when a righteous *man* turns from
his righteousness and commits iniquity, and I
lay a stumbling block before him, he shall die;
because you did not give him warning, he
shall die in his sin, and his righteousness
which he has done shall not be remembered;
but his blood I will require at your hand. [21]Nev-
ertheless if you warn the righteous *man* that
the righteous should not sin, and he does not
sin, he shall surely live because he took warning; also you will have delivered your soul."

[22]Then the hand of the LORD was upon me
there, and He said to me, "Arise, go out into
the plain, and there I shall talk with you."

[23]So I arose and went out into the plain, and
behold, the glory of the LORD stood there, like
the glory which I saw by the River Chebar; and
I fell on my face. [24]Then the Spirit entered me
and set me on my feet, and spoke with me and
said to me: "Go, shut yourself inside your
house. [25]And you, O son of man, surely they
will put ropes on you and bind you with them,
so that you cannot go out among them. [26]I will
make your tongue cling to the roof of your
mouth, so that you shall be mute and not be
one to rebuke them, for they *are* a rebellious
house. [27]But when I speak with you, I will open
your mouth, and you shall say to them, 'Thus
says the Lord GOD.' He who hears, let him hear;
and he who refuses, let him refuse; for they *are*
a rebellious house.

4 "You also, son of man, take a clay tablet
and lay it before you, and portray on it a
city, Jerusalem. [2]Lay siege against it, build a
siege wall against it, and heap up a mound
against it; set camps against it also, and place
battering rams against it all around. [3]Moreover
take for yourself an iron plate, and set it *as* an
iron wall between you and the city. Set your
face against it, and it shall be besieged, and
you shall lay siege against it. This *will be* a
sign to the house of Israel.

[4]"Lie also on your left side, and lay the iniquity of the house of Israel upon it. *According* to
the number of the days that you lie on it, you
shall bear their iniquity. [5]For I have laid on you
the years of their iniquity, according to the number of the days, three hundred and ninety days;
so you shall bear the iniquity of the house of Israel. [6]And when you have completed them, lie
again on your right side; then you shall bear the
iniquity of the house of Judah forty days. I have
laid on you a day for each year.

[7]"Therefore you shall set your face toward
the siege of Jerusalem; your arm *shall be*
uncovered, and you shall prophesy against it.
[8]And surely I will restrain you so that you cannot turn from one side to another till you have
ended the days of your siege.

[9]"Also take for yourself wheat, barley,
beans, lentils, millet, and spelt; put them into
one vessel, and make bread of them for yourself. *During* the number of days that you lie on
your side, three hundred and ninety days, you
shall eat it. [10]And your food which you eat *shall*
be by weight, twenty shekels a day; from time
to time you shall eat it. [11]You shall also drink
water by measure, one-sixth of a hin; from
time to time you shall drink. [12]And you shall
eat it *as* barley cakes; and bake it using fuel of
human waste in their sight."

[13]Then the LORD said, "So shall the children
of Israel eat their defiled bread among the
Gentiles, where I will drive them."

[14]So I said, "Ah, Lord GOD! Indeed I have
never defiled myself from my youth till now; I
have never eaten what died of itself or was
torn by beasts, nor has abominable flesh ever
come into my mouth."

[15]Then He said to me, "See, I am giving you
cow dung instead of human waste, and you
shall prepare your bread over it."

[16]Moreover He said to me, "Son of man,
surely I will cut off the supply of bread in Jerusalem; they shall eat bread by weight and with
anxiety, and shall drink water by measure and
with dread, [17]that they may lack bread and water,
and be dismayed with one another, and waste
away because of their iniquity.

Psalm 119:161–168

ש SHIN

161 Princes persecute me without a cause,
But my heart stands in awe of Your
word.

162 I rejoice at Your word
As one who finds great treasure.
163 I hate and abhor lying,
But I love Your law.
164 Seven times a day I praise You,
Because of Your righteous judgments.
165 Great peace have those who love Your law,
And nothing causes them to stumble.
166 LORD, I hope for Your salvation,
And I do Your commandments.
167 My soul keeps Your testimonies,
And I love them exceedingly.
168 I keep Your precepts and Your testimonies,
For all my ways *are* before You.

Proverbs 28:13

13 He who covers his sins will not prosper,
But whoever confesses and forsakes *them* will have mercy.

Hebrews 2:1–18

2 Therefore we must give the more earnest
heed to the things we have heard, lest we
drift away. 2For if the word spoken through
angels proved steadfast, and every transgression and disobedience received a just reward,
3how shall we escape if we neglect so great a
salvation, which at the first began to be spoken by the Lord, and was confirmed to us by
those who heard *Him,* 4God also bearing witness both with signs and wonders, with various
miracles, and gifts of the Holy Spirit, according
to His own will?

5For He has not put the world to come, of
which we speak, in subjection to angels. 6But
one testified in a certain place, saying:

"What is man that You are mindful of him,
Or the son of man that You take care of him?
7 *You have made him a little lower than the angels;*
You have crowned him with glory and honor,
And set him over the works of Your hands.
8 *You have put all things in subjection under his feet."*

For in that He put all in subjection under him,
He left nothing *that is* not put under him. But
now we do not yet see all things put under
him. 9But we see Jesus, who was made a little
lower than the angels, for the suffering of
death crowned with glory and honor, that He,
by the grace of God, might taste death for
everyone.

10For it was fitting for Him, for whom *are* all
things and by whom *are* all things, in bringing
many sons to glory, to make the captain of
their salvation perfect through sufferings.
11For both He who sanctifies and those who
are being sanctified *are* all of one, for which
reason He is not ashamed to call them
brethren, 12saying:

"I will declare Your name to My brethren;
In the midst of the assembly I will sing praise to You."

13And again:

"I will put My trust in Him."

And again:

2:4 signs…wonders,…miracles…gifts. The supernatural powers demonstrated by Jesus and by His apostles were the Father's divine confirmation of the gospel of Jesus Christ, His Son (John 10:38; Acts 2:22; Rom. 15:19; 1 Cor. 14:22; 2 Cor. 12:12). This authentication of the message was the purpose of such miraculous deeds. **the Holy Spirit.** The epistle's first reference to the Holy Spirit refers in passing to His ministry of confirming the message of salvation by means of miraculous gifts. Mentioned elsewhere in the epistle are the Holy Spirit's involvement in the revelation of Scripture (3:7; 10:15), in teaching (9:8), in presalvation operations (6:4, perhaps His convicting work; 10:29, common grace), and in ministry to Christ (9:14).

2:14 partaken…shared. The Greek word for "partaken" means fellowship, communion, or partnership. "Shared" means to take hold of something that is not related to one's own kind. The Son of God was not by nature "flesh and blood," but took upon Himself that nature for the sake of providing redemption for mankind. **death…power of death.** This is the ultimate purpose of the Incarnation: Jesus came to earth to die. By dying, He was able to conquer death in His resurrection (John 14:19). By conquering death, He rendered Satan powerless against all who are saved. Satan's using the power of death is subject to God's will (Job 2:6).

"Here am I and the children whom God
has given Me."

[14]Inasmuch then as the children have partaken of flesh and blood, He Himself likewise shared in the same, that through death
He might destroy him who had the power of
death, that is, the devil, [15]and release those
who through fear of death were all their lifetime subject to bondage. [16]For indeed He
does not give aid to angels, but He does give
aid to the seed of Abraham. [17]Therefore, in
all things He had to be made like *His*
brethren, that He might be a merciful and
faithful High Priest in things *pertaining* to
God, to make propitiation for the sins of the
people. [18]For in that He Himself has suffered,
being tempted, He is able to aid those who
are tempted.

2:17 propitiation. The word means "to conciliate" or "satisfy." Christ's work of propitiation is related to His High Priestly ministry. By His partaking of a human nature, Christ demonstrated His mercy to mankind and His faithfulness to God by satisfying God's requirement for sin and thus obtaining for His people full forgiveness.

DAY 6: How can we know whether Ezekiel's language is descriptive of a literal event or symbolic of an idea or principle?

Ezekiel's life offered his audience a sequence of experiences and actions that became teachable moments. Some of these were scenes in visions that held special significance. For example, the first three chapters of the book report extended visions in which the prophet saw a whirlwind, heavenly creatures, and an edible scroll. He also received his call to the prophetic ministry.

In addition, Ezekiel carried out certain unusual or highly symbolic actions that were intended to picture a message or convey a warning. In 4:1–3, the prophet was directed to carve on a clay tablet and then use an iron plate as a sign about the danger facing Jerusalem. Other acted-out sermons followed: symbolic sleeping postures (4:4–8), siege bread making and baking (4:9–17), and haircutting and burning (5:1–4). God instructed Ezekiel to respond even to the tragedies in his life in such a way that a message was communicated to the people. The prophet learned of his wife's impending death but was told by God that his loss would provide an important lesson the people needed to hear. Just as Ezekiel was not allowed to mourn, the people would not be allowed to mourn when they finally faced the "death" of Jerusalem. "'Thus Ezekiel is a sign to you; according to all that he has done you shall do; and when this comes, you shall know that I am the Lord God'" (Ezek. 24:24).

The unique nature of Ezekiel's approach creates a striking contrast between the clarity of his message and the willful rejection of that message by the people. His ministry removed every excuse.

NOVEMBER 7

Ezekiel 5:1–6:14

5 "And you, son of man, take a sharp sword,
take it as a barber's razor, and pass *it* over
your head and your beard; then take scales to
weigh and divide the *hair*. [2]You shall burn with
fire one-third in the midst of the city, when the
days of the siege are finished; then you shall
take one-third and strike around *it* with the
sword, and one-third you shall scatter in the
wind: I will draw out a sword after them. [3]You
shall also take a small number of them and bind
them in the edge of your *garment*. [4]Then take
some of them again and throw them into the
midst of the fire, and burn them in the fire.
From there a fire will go out into all the house
of Israel.
[5]"Thus says the Lord God: 'This *is* Jerusalem; I have set her in the midst of the nations
and the countries all around her. [6]She has
rebelled against My judgments by doing
wickedness more than the nations, and
against My statutes more than the countries
that *are* all around her; for they have refused
My judgments, and they have not walked in
My statutes.' [7]Therefore thus says the Lord
God: 'Because you have multiplied *disobedi-*
ence more than the nations that *are* all around
you, have not walked in My statutes nor kept
My judgments, nor even done according to
the judgments of the nations that *are* all
around you'— [8]therefore thus says the Lord

5:1–4 a barber's razor. The sign in Ezekiel's shaving his hair illustrated the severe humiliation to come at the hand of enemies, emphasizing calamities to three segments of Jerusalem due to the Babylonian conquest. Some were punished by fire, i.e., pestilence and famine (v. 12), others died by the enemy's sword, and some were dispersed and pursued by death (v. 12). A small part of his hair clinging to his garment (v. 3) depicted a remaining remnant, some of whom were subject to further calamity (v. 4; 6:8; Jer. 41–44).

GOD: 'Indeed I, even I, *am* against you and will
execute judgments in your midst in the sight
of the nations. 9And I will do among you what
I have never done, and the like of which I will
never do again, because of all your abominations. 10Therefore fathers shall eat *their* sons
in your midst, and sons shall eat their
fathers; and I will execute judgments among
you, and all of you who remain I will scatter
to all the winds.

11'Therefore, *as* I live,' says the Lord GOD,
'surely, because you have defiled My sanctuary with all your detestable things and with all
your abominations, therefore I will also diminish *you;* My eye will not spare, nor will I have
any pity. 12One-third of you shall die of the
pestilence, and be consumed with famine in
your midst; and one-third shall fall by the
sword all around you; and I will scatter another third to all the winds, and I will draw out a
sword after them.

13'Thus shall My anger be spent, and I will
cause My fury to rest upon them, and I will be
avenged; and they shall know that I, the LORD,
have spoken *it* in My zeal, when I have spent
My fury upon them. 14Moreover I will make
you a waste and a reproach among the nations
that *are* all around you, in the sight of all who
pass by.

15'So it shall be a reproach, a taunt, a lesson,
and an astonishment to the nations that *are* all
around you, when I execute judgments among
you in anger and in fury and in furious rebukes.
I, the LORD, have spoken. 16When I send
against them the terrible arrows of famine
which shall be for destruction, which I will
send to destroy you, I will increase the famine
upon you and cut off your supply of bread. 17So
I will send against you famine and wild beasts,
and they will bereave you. Pestilence and blood
shall pass through you, and I will bring the
sword against you. I, the LORD, have spoken.' "

6 Now the word of the LORD came to me,
saying: 2"Son of man, set your face toward
the mountains of Israel, and prophesy against
them, 3and say, 'O mountains of Israel, hear
the word of the Lord GOD! Thus says the Lord
GOD to the mountains, to the hills, to the
ravines, and to the valleys: "Indeed I, *even* I,
will bring a sword against you, and I will
destroy your high places. 4Then your altars
shall be desolate, your incense altars shall be
broken, and I will cast down your slain *men*
before your idols. 5And I will lay the corpses of
the children of Israel before their idols, and I
will scatter your bones all around your altars.
6In all your dwelling places the cities shall be
laid waste, and the high places shall be desolate, so that your altars may be laid waste and
made desolate, your idols may be broken and
made to cease, your incense altars may be cut
down, and your works may be abolished. 7The
slain shall fall in your midst, and you shall know
that I *am* the LORD.

6:7 you shall know that I *am* the LORD. This clause recurs in vv. 10,13,14, and 60 times elsewhere in the book. It shows that the essential reason for judgment is the violation of the character of God. This is repeatedly acknowledged in Leviticus 18–26, where the motive for all obedience to God's law is the fact that He is the Lord God.

8"Yet I will leave a remnant, so that you may
have *some* who escape the sword among the
nations, when you are scattered through the
countries. 9Then those of you who escape will
remember Me among the nations where they
are carried captive, because I was crushed by
their adulterous heart which has departed
from Me, and by their eyes which play the harlot after their idols; they will loathe themselves for the evils which they committed in
all their abominations. 10And they shall know
that I *am* the LORD; I have not said in vain that
I would bring this calamity upon them."

11"Thus says the Lord GOD: "Pound your
fists and stamp your feet, and say, 'Alas, for all
the evil abominations of the house of Israel!
For they shall fall by the sword, by famine,
and by pestilence. 12He who is far off shall die
by the pestilence, he who is near shall fall by
the sword, and he who remains and is
besieged shall die by the famine. Thus will I
spend My fury upon them. 13Then you shall
know that I *am* the LORD, when their slain are

among their idols all around their altars, on every high hill, on all the mountaintops, under every green tree, and under every thick oak, wherever they offered sweet incense to all their idols. [14]So I will stretch out My hand against them and make the land desolate, yes, more desolate than the wilderness toward Diblah, in all their dwelling places. Then they shall know that I *am* the LORD.' " ' "

Psalm 119:169–176

ת TAU

169 Let my cry come before You, O LORD;
Give me understanding according to
Your word.
170 Let my supplication come before You;
Deliver me according to Your word.
171 My lips shall utter praise,
For You teach me Your statutes.
172 My tongue shall speak of Your word,
For all Your commandments *are*
righteousness.
173 Let Your hand become my help,
For I have chosen Your precepts.
174 I long for Your salvation, O LORD,
And Your law *is* my delight.
175 Let my soul live, and it shall praise You;
And let Your judgments help me.
176 I have gone astray like a lost sheep;
Seek Your servant,
For I do not forget Your
commandments.

Proverbs 28:14

14 Happy *is* the man who is always reverent,
But he who hardens his heart will fall
into calamity.

Hebrews 3:1–19

3 Therefore, holy brethren, partakers of the heavenly calling, consider the Apostle and High Priest of our confession, Christ Jesus,
[2]who was faithful to Him who appointed Him,
as Moses also *was faithful* in all His house. [3]For
this One has been counted worthy of more glory than Moses, inasmuch as He who built the house has more honor than the house. [4]For
every house is built by someone, but He who built all things *is* God. [5]And Moses indeed *was*
faithful in all His house as a servant, for a testimony of those things which would be spoken *afterward,* [6]but Christ as a Son over His own house, whose house we are if we hold fast the confidence and the rejoicing of the hope firm to the end.
[7]Therefore, as the Holy Spirit says:

"Today, if you will hear His voice,
8 *Do not harden your hearts as in the*
rebellion,
In the day of trial in the wilderness,
9 *Where your fathers tested Me,*
tried Me,
And saw My works forty years.
10 *Therefore I was angry with that*
generation,
And said, 'They always go astray in
their heart,
And they have not known My ways.'
11 *So I swore in My wrath,*
'They shall not enter My rest.' "

[12]Beware, brethren, lest there be in any of you an evil heart of unbelief in departing from the living God; [13]but exhort one another daily,
while it is called *"Today,"* lest any of you be hardened through the deceitfulness of sin.
[14]For we have become partakers of Christ if we hold the beginning of our confidence steadfast to the end, [15]while it is said:

"Today, if you will hear His voice,

3:1 consider. The writer asks for the readers' complete attention and diligent observation of the superiority of Jesus Christ. **Apostle and High Priest.** An apostle is a "sent one" who has the rights, power, and authority of the one who sends him. Jesus was sent to earth by the Father (John 3:17,34; 5:36–38; 8:42). The topic of the High Priesthood of Christ, which was begun in 2:17,18 and is mentioned again here, will be taken up again in greater detail in 4:14–10:18. Meanwhile, the writer presents the supremacy of Christ to Moses (vv. 1–6), to Joshua (4:8), and to all other national heroes and Old Testament preachers whom Jews held in high esteem. Jesus Himself spoke of His superiority to Moses in the same context in which He spoke of His being sent by the Father (John 5:36–38,45–47; Luke 16:29–31). Moses had been sent by God to deliver His people from historical Egypt and its bondage (Ex. 3:10). Jesus was sent by God to deliver His people from spiritual Egypt and its bondage (2:15). **of our confession.** Christ is the center of our confession of faith in the gospel, both in creed and public testimony. The term is used again in 4:14 and 10:23. In all 3 uses in Hebrews, there is a sense of urgency. Surely, the readers would not give up Christ, whom they had professed, and reject what He had done for them, if they could understand the superiority of His Person and work.

Do not harden your hearts as in the
rebellion."

[16]For who, having heard, rebelled? Indeed, *was it* not all who came out of Egypt, *led* by Moses? [17]Now with whom was He angry forty years? *Was it* not with those who sinned, whose corpses fell in the wilderness? [18]And to whom did He swear that they would not enter His rest, but to those who did not obey? [19]So we see that they could not enter in because of unbelief.

DAY 7: What are the central warnings for believers in the Book of Hebrews?

Beyond its value as a doctrinal treatise, this book is intensely practical in its application to everyday living. The writer himself even refers to his letter as a "word of exhortation" (13:22). Exhortations designed to stir the readers into action are found throughout the text. Those exhortations are given in the form of 6 warnings:

1. Warning against drifting from "the things we have heard" (2:1–4)
2. Warning against disbelieving the "voice" of God (3:7–14)
3. Warning against degenerating from "the elementary principles of Christ" (5:11–6:20)
4. Warning against despising "the knowledge of the truth" (10:26–39)
5. Warning against devaluing "the grace of God" (12:15–17)
6. Warning against departing from Him "who speaks" (12:25–29)

For example, when the writer warns of the danger of drifting (2:1), he uses some vivid nautical terms. The phrase "earnest heed" refers to mooring a ship by securing it to a dock. The second phrase "drift away" was often used of a ship that had been allowed to drift past the harbor. The warning is to secure oneself to the truth of the gospel in such a way as to not pass by the only harbor of salvation. The alternate tendency toward apathy points to those who make a shipwreck of their lives.

NOVEMBER 8

Ezekiel 7:1–8:18

7 Moreover the word of the LORD came to me, saying, [2]"And you, son of man, thus says the Lord GOD to the land of Israel:

'An end! The end has come upon the
four corners of the land.
3 Now the end *has come* upon you,
And I will send My anger against you;
I will judge you according to your
ways,
And I will repay you for all your
abominations.
4 My eye will not spare you,
Nor will I have pity;
But I will repay your ways,
And your abominations will be in your
midst;
Then you shall know that I *am* the
LORD!'

[5]"Thus says the Lord GOD:

'A disaster, a singular disaster;
Behold, it has come!
6 An end has come,
The end has come;
It has dawned for you;
Behold, it has come!
7 Doom has come to you, you who dwell
in the land;
The time has come,
A day of trouble *is* near,
And not of rejoicing in the mountains.
8 Now upon you I will soon pour out
My fury,
And spend My anger upon you;
I will judge you according to your
ways,
And I will repay you for all your
abominations.

9 'My eye will not spare,
Nor will I have pity;
I will repay you according to your
ways,
And your abominations will be
in your midst.
Then you shall know that I *am* the
LORD who strikes.
10 'Behold, the day!
Behold, it has come!
Doom has gone out;
The rod has blossomed,
Pride has budded.
11 Violence has risen up into a rod of
wickedness;
None of them *shall remain,*
None of their multitude,
None of them;
Nor *shall there be* wailing for them.
12 The time has come,

The day draws near.

'Let not the buyer rejoice,
Nor the seller mourn,
For wrath *is* on their whole multitude.
13 For the seller shall not return to what
has been sold,
Though he may still be alive;
For the vision concerns the whole
multitude,
And it shall not turn back;
No one will strengthen himself
Who lives in iniquity.

14 'They have blown the trumpet and
made everyone ready,
But no one goes to battle;
For My wrath *is* on all their multitude.
15 The sword *is* outside,
And the pestilence and famine within.
Whoever *is* in the field
Will die by the sword;
And whoever *is* in the city,
Famine and pestilence will devour him.

16 'Those who survive will escape and be
on the mountains
Like doves of the valleys,
All of them mourning,
Each for his iniquity.
17 Every hand will be feeble,
And every knee will be *as* weak *as* water.
18 They will also be girded with
sackcloth;
Horror will cover them;
Shame *will be* on every face,
Baldness on all their heads.

19 'They will throw their silver into the
streets,
And their gold will be like refuse;
Their silver and their gold will not be
able to deliver them
In the day of the wrath of the LORD;
They will not satisfy their souls,
Nor fill their stomachs,
Because it became their stumbling
block of iniquity.

20 'As for the beauty of his ornaments,
He set it in majesty;
But they made from it
The images of their abominations—
Their detestable things;
Therefore I have made it
Like refuse to them.
21 I will give it as plunder
Into the hands of strangers,
And to the wicked of the earth as spoil;
And they shall defile it.
22 I will turn My face from them,
And they will defile My secret place;
For robbers shall enter it and defile it.

23 'Make a chain,
For the land is filled with crimes
of blood,
And the city is full of violence.
24 Therefore I will bring the worst
of the Gentiles,
And they will possess their houses;
I will cause the pomp of the strong to
cease,
And their holy places shall be defiled.
25 Destruction comes;
They will seek peace, but *there shall be*
none.
26 Disaster will come upon disaster,
And rumor will be upon rumor.
Then they will seek a vision from a
prophet;
But the law will perish from the priest,
And counsel from the elders.

27 'The king will mourn,
The prince will be clothed with
desolation,
And the hands of the common people
will tremble.
I will do to them according to their
way,
And according to what they deserve
I will judge them;
Then they shall know that I *am* the
LORD!' "

8 And it came to pass in the sixth year, in the
sixth *month,* on the fifth *day* of the month,
as I sat in my house with the elders of Judah
sitting before me, that the hand of the Lord
GOD fell upon me there. 2Then I looked, and
there was a likeness, like the appearance of
fire—from the appearance of His waist and
downward, fire; and from His waist and
upward, like the appearance of brightness, like
the color of amber. 3He stretched out the form
of a hand, and took me by a lock of my hair; and
the Spirit lifted me up between earth and heav-
en, and brought me in visions of God to Jerusalem, to the door of the north gate of the inner
court, where the seat of the image of jealousy
was, which provokes to jealousy. 4And behold,
the glory of the God of Israel *was* there, like
the vision that I saw in the plain.
5Then He said to me, "Son of man, lift your
eyes now toward the north." So I lifted my eyes
toward the north, and there, north of the altar
gate, was this image of jealousy in the entrance.
6Furthermore He said to me, "Son of man,
do you see what they are doing, the great

8:3 in visions of God. Ezekiel 8–11 deals with details conveyed only to Ezekiel in visions. Ezekiel's trip to Jerusalem was in spirit only, while his body physically remained in his house. In visions he went to Jerusalem and in visions he returned to Babylon (11:24). After God finished the visions, Ezekiel told his home audience what he had seen. The visions are not a description of deeds done in the past in Israel, but a survey of Israel's current condition, as they existed at that very time. **the seat...image of jealousy.** God represents to Ezekiel the image of an idol (Deut. 4:16) in the entrance to the inner court of the temple. It is called "the image of jealousy" because it provoked the Lord to jealousy (5:13; 16:38; 36:6; 38:19; Ex. 20:5).

abominations that the house of Israel commits
here, to make Me go far away from My sanctuary? Now turn again, you will see greater
abominations." [7]So He brought me to the door
of the court; and when I looked, there was a
hole in the wall. [8]Then He said to me, "Son of
man, dig into the wall"; and when I dug into
the wall, there was a door.
[9]And He said to me, "Go in, and see the
wicked abominations which they are doing
there." [10]So I went in and saw, and there—
every sort of creeping thing, abominable
beasts, and all the idols of the house of Israel,
portrayed all around on the walls. [11]And there
stood before them seventy men of the elders of
the house of Israel, and in their midst stood
Jaazaniah the son of Shaphan. Each man had a
censer in his hand, and a thick cloud of incense
went up. [12]Then He said to me, "Son of man,
have you seen what the elders of the house of
Israel do in the dark, every man in the room of
his idols? For they say, 'The LORD does not see
us, the LORD has forsaken the land.' "
[13]And He said to me, "Turn again, *and* you
will see greater abominations that they are
doing." [14]So He brought me to the door of the
north gate of the LORD's house; and to my dismay, women were sitting there weeping for
Tammuz.
[15]Then He said to me, "Have you seen *this,* O
son of man? Turn again, you will see greater
abominations than these." [16]So He brought me
into the inner court of the LORD's house; and
there, at the door of the temple of the LORD,
between the porch and the altar, *were* about
twenty-five men with their backs toward the
temple of the LORD and their faces toward the

8:14 weeping for Tammuz. Yet a greater abomination than the secret cult was Israel's engaging in the Babylonian worship of Tammuz or Dumuzi (Duzu), beloved of Ishtar, the god of spring vegetation. Vegetation burned in the summer, died in the winter, and came to life in the spring. The women mourned over the god's demise in July and longed for his revival. The fourth month of the Hebrew calendar still bears the name Tammuz. With the worship of this idol were connected the basest immoralities.

east, and they were worshiping the sun
toward the east.
[17]And He said to me, "Have you seen *this,* O
son of man? Is it a trivial thing to the house of
Judah to commit the abominations which they
commit here? For they have filled the land
with violence; then they have returned to provoke Me to anger. Indeed they put the branch
to their nose. [18]Therefore I also will act in fury.
My eye will not spare nor will I have pity; and
though they cry in My ears with a loud voice,
I will not hear them."

Psalm 120:1–7

A Song of Ascents.

In my distress I cried to the LORD,
And He heard me.
2 Deliver my soul, O LORD, from lying lips
And from a deceitful tongue.

3 What shall be given to you,
Or what shall be done to you,
You false tongue?
4 Sharp arrows of the warrior,
With coals of the broom tree!

5 Woe is me, that I dwell in Meshech,
That I dwell among the tents of Kedar!
6 My soul has dwelt too long
With one who hates peace.

120:4 Sharp arrows...coals. Lies and false accusations are likened to 1) the pain/injury inflicted in battle by arrows and 2) the pain of being burned with charcoal made from the wood of a broom tree (a desert bush that grows 10 to 15 feet high).

7 I *am for* peace;
But when I speak, they *are* for war.

Proverbs 28:15

15 *Like* a roaring lion and a charging bear
Is a wicked ruler over poor people.

Hebrews 4:1–16

4 Therefore, since a promise remains of entering His rest, let us fear lest any of you seem
to have come short of it. 2 For indeed the gospel
was preached to us as well as to them; but the
word which they heard did not profit them, not
being mixed with faith in those who heard *it.*
3 For we who have believed do enter that rest, as
He has said:

"So I swore in My wrath,
'They shall not enter My rest,'"

although the works were finished from the
foundation of the world. 4 For He has spoken in
a certain place of the seventh *day* in this way:
"And God rested on the seventh day from all
His works"; 5 and again in this *place: "They*
shall not enter My rest."
6 Since therefore it remains that some *must*
enter it, and those to whom it was first preached
did not enter because of disobedience, 7 again
He designates a certain day, saying in David, *"Today,"* after such a long time, as it has been said:

"Today, if you will hear His voice,
Do not harden your hearts."

8 For if Joshua had given them rest, then He
would not afterward have spoken of another
day. 9 There remains therefore a rest for the
people of God. 10 For he who has entered His
rest has himself also ceased from his works as
God *did* from His.
11 Let us therefore be diligent to enter that
rest, lest anyone fall according to the same
example of disobedience. 12 For the word of
God *is* living and powerful, and sharper than
any two-edged sword, piercing even to the
division of soul and spirit, and of joints and
marrow, and is a discerner of the thoughts
and intents of the heart. 13 And there is no creature hidden from His sight, but all things *are*
naked and open to the eyes of Him to whom
we *must give* account.
14 Seeing then that we have a great High
Priest who has passed through the heavens,
Jesus the Son of God, let us hold fast *our* confession. 15 For we do not have a High Priest
who cannot sympathize with our weaknesses,
but was in all *points* tempted as *we are, yet*
without sin. 16 Let us therefore come boldly to
the throne of grace, that we may obtain mercy
and find grace to help in time of need.

4:12 two-edged sword. While the Word of God is comforting and nourishing to those who believe, it is a tool of judgment and execution for those who have not committed themselves to Jesus Christ. Some of the Hebrews were merely going through the motions of belonging to Christ. Intellectually, they were at least partly persuaded, but inside they were not committed to Him. God's Word would expose their shallow beliefs and even their false intentions (1 Sam. 16:7; 1 Pet. 4:5). **division of soul and spirit.** These terms do not describe two separate entities (any more than "thoughts and intents" do) but are used as one might say "heart and soul" to express fullness (Luke 10:27; Acts 4:32; 1 Thess. 5:23). Elsewhere these two terms are used interchangeably to describe man's immaterial self, his eternal inner person.

DAY 8: What does Hebrews 4:14–16 teach about prayer?

Just as the high priest under the Old Covenant passed through 3 areas (the outer court, the Holy Place, and the Holy of Holies) to make the atoning sacrifice, Jesus passed through 3 heavens (the atmospheric heaven, the stellar heaven, and God's abode; 2 Cor. 12:2–4) after making the perfect, final sacrifice (v. 14). Once a year on the Day of Atonement the high priest of Israel would enter the Holy of Holies to make atonement for the sins of the people (Lev. 16). That tabernacle was but a limited copy of the heavenly reality (8:1–5). When Jesus entered into the heavenly Holy of Holies, having accomplished redemption, the earthly facsimile was replaced by the reality of heaven itself. Freed from that which is earthly, the Christian faith is characterized by the heavenly (3:1; Eph. 1:3; 2:6; Phil. 3:20; Col. 1:5; 1 Pet. 1:4).

And Jesus as our High Priest was "in all points tempted as we are, yet without sin" (v. 15). Jesus became fully capable of understanding and sympathizing with His human brethren.

"Let us therefore come boldly to the throne of grace" (v. 16). Most ancient rulers were unapproachable by anyone but their highest advisers (Esth. 4:11). In contrast, the Holy Spirit calls for all to come confidently before God's throne to receive mercy and grace through Jesus Christ. The ark of the covenant was viewed as the place on earth where God sat enthroned between the cherubim (2 Kin. 19:15; Jer. 3:16,17). Oriental thrones included a footstool—yet another metaphor for the ark (Ps. 132:7). It was at the throne of God that Christ made atonement for sins, and it is there that grace is dispensed to believers for all the issues of life (2 Cor. 4:15; 9:8; 12:9; Eph. 1:7; 2:7).

NOVEMBER 9

Ezekiel 9:1–10:22

9 Then He called out in my hearing with a
loud voice, saying, "Let those who have
charge over the city draw near, each *with* a
deadly weapon in his hand." 2And suddenly six
men came from the direction of the upper
gate, which faces north, each with his battle-ax
in his hand. One man among them *was*
clothed with linen and had a writer's inkhorn
at his side. They went in and stood beside the
bronze altar.
3Now the glory of the God of Israel had
gone up from the cherub, where it had been,
to the threshold of the temple. And He called
to the man clothed with linen, who *had* the
writer's inkhorn at his side; 4and the LORD said
to him, "Go through the midst of the city,
through the midst of Jerusalem, and put a
mark on the foreheads of the men who sigh
and cry over all the abominations that are
done within it."

9:3 the glory...had gone up. The glory of God departs before the destruction of the city and temple. The gradual departure of God from His temple is depicted in stages: the glory resides in the temple's Most Holy Place, between the wings of the cherubs on each side of the ark of the covenant over the mercy seat, then leaves to the front door (9:3; 10:4), later to the east gate by the outer wall (10:18,19), and finally to the Mount of Olives to the east, having fully departed (11:22,23). The glory will return in the future kingdom of Messiah (43:2–7).

5To the others He said in my hearing, "Go
after him through the city and kill; do not let
your eye spare, nor have any pity. 6Utterly slay
old *and* young men, maidens and little children and women; but do not come near anyone on whom *is* the mark; and begin at My
sanctuary." So they began with the elders who
were before the temple. 7Then He said to
them, "Defile the temple, and fill the courts
with the slain. Go out!" And they went out and
killed in the city.
8So it was, that while they were killing them,
I was left *alone;* and I fell on my face and cried
out, and said, "Ah, Lord GOD! Will You destroy
all the remnant of Israel in pouring out Your
fury on Jerusalem?"
9Then He said to me, "The iniquity of the
house of Israel and Judah *is* exceedingly
great, and the land is full of bloodshed, and
the city full of perversity; for they say, 'The
LORD has forsaken the land, and the LORD
does not see!' 10And as for Me also, My eye will
neither spare, nor will I have pity, *but* I will recompense their deeds on their own head."
11Just then, the man clothed with linen, who
had the inkhorn at his side, reported back and
said, "I have done as You commanded me."
10 And I looked, and there in the firmament
that was above the head of the cherubim,
there appeared something like a sapphire
stone, having the appearance of the likeness
of a throne. 2Then He spoke to the man
clothed with linen, and said, "Go in among the
wheels, under the cherub, fill your hands with
coals of fire from among the cherubim, and
scatter *them* over the city." And he went in as I
watched.
3Now the cherubim were standing on the
south side of the temple when the man went
in, and the cloud filled the inner court. 4Then
the glory of the LORD went up from the

10:2 fill...with coals. God specifies that the marking angel (9:2,11) reach into the war machine and fill his hands with fiery coals in the presence of the angels of chapter 1. These coals picture the fires of judgment which God's angels are to "scatter" on Jerusalem. In Isaiah 6, "coals" were used for the purification of the prophet; here they were for the destruction of the wicked (Heb. 12:29). Fire did destroy Jerusalem in 586 B.C.

cherub, *and paused* over the threshold of the
temple; and the house was filled with the
cloud, and the court was full of the brightness
of the LORD's glory. 5And the sound of the
wings of the cherubim was heard *even* in the
outer court, like the voice of Almighty God
when He speaks.

6Then it happened, when He commanded
the man clothed in linen, saying, "Take fire
from among the wheels, from among the
cherubim," that he went in and stood beside
the wheels. 7And the cherub stretched out his
hand from among the cherubim to the fire
that *was* among the cherubim, and took *some*
of it and put *it* into the hands of the *man*
clothed with linen, who took *it* and went out.
8The cherubim appeared to have the form of a
man's hand under their wings.

9And when I looked, there were four wheels
by the cherubim, one wheel by one cherub
and another wheel by each other cherub; the
wheels appeared *to have* the color of a beryl
stone. 10*As for* their appearance, all four looked
alike—as it were, a wheel in the middle of a
wheel. 11When they went, they went toward
any of their four directions; they did not turn
aside when they went, but followed in the
direction the head was facing. They did not
turn aside when they went. 12And their whole
body, with their back, their hands, their wings,
and the wheels that the four had, *were* full of
eyes all around. 13As for the wheels, they were
called in my hearing, "Wheel."

14Each one had four faces: the first face *was*
the face of a cherub, the second face the face
of a man, the third the face of a lion, and the
fourth the face of an eagle. 15And the cherubim were lifted up. This *was* the living creature I saw by the River Chebar. 16When the
cherubim went, the wheels went beside them;
and when the cherubim lifted their wings to
mount up from the earth, the same wheels also
did not turn from beside them. 17When *the*
cherubim stood still, *the wheels* stood still, and
when *one* was lifted up, *the other* lifted itself up,
for the spirit of the living creature *was* in them.

18Then the glory of the LORD departed from
the threshold of the temple and stood over the
cherubim. 19And the cherubim lifted their
wings and mounted up from the earth in my
sight. When they went out, the wheels *were*
beside them; and they stood at the door of the
east gate of the LORD's house, and the glory of
the God of Israel *was* above them.

20This *is* the living creature I saw under the
God of Israel by the River Chebar, and I knew
they *were* cherubim. 21Each one had four faces
and each one four wings, and the likeness of
the hands of a man *was* under their wings.
22And the likeness of their faces *was* the same
as the faces which I had seen by the River
Chebar, their appearance and their persons.
They each went straight forward.

10:9–17 wheels by the cherubim. This whole section is similar to 1:4–21. Four wheels on God's chariot mingled with the 4 angels (1:15–21) coordinated with each other in precision, and each with a different one of the cherubim. All looked so much alike that it was as if one wheel blended entirely with another (v. 10). As their appearance was so unified, their action was in unison and instant (v. 11). The cherubim had bodies like men and their chariot wheels were full of eyes denoting full perception both to see the sinners and their fitting judgment. The color beryl is a sparkling yellow or gold.

Psalm 121:1–8

A Song of Ascents.

I will lift up my eyes to the hills—
From whence comes my help?
2 My help *comes* from the LORD,
Who made heaven and earth.

3 He will not allow your foot to be moved;
He who keeps you will not slumber.
4 Behold, He who keeps Israel
Shall neither slumber nor sleep.

5 The LORD *is* your keeper;
The LORD *is* your shade at your right hand.
6 The sun shall not strike you by day,
Nor the moon by night.

7 The LORD shall preserve you from all evil;
He shall preserve your soul.
8 The LORD shall preserve your going out and your coming in
From this time forth, and even forevermore.

Proverbs 28:16

16 A ruler who lacks understanding *is* a great oppressor,
But he who hates covetousness will prolong *his* days.

Hebrews 5:1–14

5 For every high priest taken from among
men is appointed for men in things *pertaining* to God, that he may offer both gifts and
sacrifices for sins. [2]He can have compassion on
those who are ignorant and going astray, since
he himself is also subject to weakness. [3]Be-
cause of this he is required as for the people,
so also for himself, to offer *sacrifices* for sins.
[4]And no man takes this honor to himself, but
he who is called by God, just as Aaron *was.*
[5]So also Christ did not glorify Himself to become High Priest, but *it was* He who said to
Him:

"You are My Son,
Today I have begotten You."

[6]As *He* also says in another *place:*

"You are a priest forever
According to the order of
Melchizedek";

[7]who, in the days of His flesh, when He had offered up prayers and supplications, with vehement cries and tears to Him who was able to
save Him from death, and was heard because
of His godly fear, [8]though He was a Son, *yet* He
learned obedience by the things which He suffered. [9]And having been perfected, He became
the author of eternal salvation to all who obey
Him, [10]called by God as High Priest *"according
to the order of Melchizedek,"* [11]of whom we
have much to say, and hard to explain, since
you have become dull of hearing.

5:11 dull. The Hebrews' spiritual lethargy and slow response to gospel teaching prevented additional teaching at this time. This is a reminder that failure to appropriate the truth of the gospel produces stagnation in spiritual advancement and the inability to understand or assimilate additional teaching (John 16:12). Such a situation exists also among the Gentiles who have received revelatory truth (natural or general revelation) from God in the creation (Rom. 1:18–20). Rejection of that revelation results in a process of hardening (Rom. 1:21–32). The Hebrews had not only received the same general revelation, they had also received special revelation consisting of the Old Testament scriptures (Rom. 9:4), the Messiah Himself (Rom. 9:5), and the teaching of the apostles (2:3,4). Until the Hebrews obeyed the revelation they had received and obtained eternal salvation (v. 8), additional teaching about the Messiah's Melchizedekan priesthood would be of no profit to them.

[12]For though by this time you ought to be
teachers, you need *someone* to teach you again
the first principles of the oracles of God; and you
have come to need milk and not solid food. [13]For
everyone who partakes *only* of milk *is* unskilled
in the word of righteousness, for he is a babe.
[14]But solid food belongs to those who are of full
age, *that is,* those who by reason of use have their
senses exercised to discern both good and evil.

DAY 9: Why does it say that Jesus "learned obedience"?

The context of Hebrews 5:7 makes it clear that "who, in the days of His flesh" refers back to Christ, the main subject in v. 5. In Gethsemane, Jesus agonized and wept, but committed Himself to do the Father's will in accepting the cup of suffering which would bring His death (Matt. 26:38–46; Luke 22:44,45). Anticipating bearing the burden of judgment for sin, Jesus felt its fullest pain and grief (Is. 52:14; 53:3–5,10). Though He bore the penalty in silence and did not seek to deliver Himself from it (Is. 53:7), He did cry out from the agony of the fury of God's wrath poured on His perfectly holy and obedient Person (Matt. 27:46; 2 Cor. 5:21). Jesus asked to be saved from remaining in death, i.e., to be resurrected (Ps. 16:9,10).

"Though He was a Son, yet He learned obedience by the things which He suffered" (v. 8). Christ did not need to suffer in order to conquer or correct any disobedience. In His deity (as the Son of God), He understood obedience completely. As the incarnate Lord, He humbled Himself to learn (Luke 2:52). He learned obedience for the same reasons He bore temptation: to confirm His humanity and experience its sufferings to the fullest (2:10; Luke 2:52; Phil. 2:8). Christ's obedience was also necessary so that He could fulfill all righteousness (Matt. 5:13) and thus prove to be the perfect sacrifice to take the place of sinners (1 Pet. 3:18). He was the perfectly righteous One, whose righteousness would be imputed to sinners (Rom. 3:24–26).

"And having been perfected, He became the author of eternal salvation" (v. 9). Because of the perfect righteousness of Jesus Christ and His perfect sacrifice for sin, He became the cause of salvation. True salvation evidences itself in obedience to Christ, from the initial obedience to the gospel command to repent and believe (Acts 5:32; Rom. 1:5; 2 Thess. 1:8; 1 Pet. 1:2,22; 4:17) to a life pattern of obedience to the Word (Rom. 6:16).

NOVEMBER 10

Ezekiel 11:1–12:28

11 Then the Spirit lifted me up and brought me to the East Gate of the LORD's house, which faces eastward; and there at the door of the gate were twenty-five men, among whom I saw Jaazaniah the son of Azzur, and Pelatiah the son of Benaiah, princes of the people. 2And He said to me: "Son of man, these *are* the men who devise iniquity and give wicked counsel in this city, 3who say, '*The time is* not near to build houses; this *city is* the caldron, and we *are* the meat.' 4Therefore prophesy against them, prophesy, O son of man!"

5Then the Spirit of the LORD fell upon me, and said to me, "Speak! 'Thus says the LORD: "Thus you have said, O house of Israel; for I know the things that come into your mind. 6You have multiplied your slain in this city, and you have filled its streets with the slain." 7Therefore thus says the Lord GOD: "Your slain whom you have laid in its midst, they *are* the meat, and this *city is* the caldron; but I shall bring you out of the midst of it. 8You have feared the sword; and I will bring a sword upon you," says the Lord GOD. 9"And I will bring you out of its midst, and deliver you into the hands of strangers, and execute judgments on you. 10You shall fall by the sword. I will judge you at the border of Israel. Then you shall know that I *am* the LORD. 11This *city* shall not be your caldron, nor shall you be the meat in its midst. I will judge you at the border of Israel. 12And you shall know that I *am* the LORD; for you have not walked in My statutes nor executed My judgments, but have done according to the customs of the Gentiles which *are* all around you." ' "

13Now it happened, while I was prophesying, that Pelatiah the son of Benaiah died. Then I fell on my face and cried with a loud voice, and said, "Ah, Lord GOD! Will You make a complete end of the remnant of Israel?"

14Again the word of the LORD came to me, saying, 15"Son of man, your brethren, your relatives, your countrymen, and all the house of Israel in its entirety, *are* those about whom the inhabitants of Jerusalem have said, 'Get far away from the LORD; this land has been given to us as a possession.' 16Therefore say, 'Thus says the Lord GOD: "Although I have cast them far off among the Gentiles, and although I have scattered them among the countries, yet I shall be a little sanctuary for them in the countries where they have gone." ' 17Therefore say, 'Thus says the Lord GOD: "I will gather you from the peoples, assemble you from the countries where you have been scattered, and I will give you the land of Israel." ' 18And they will go there, and they will take away all its detestable things and all its abominations from there. 19Then I will give them one heart, and I will put a new spirit within them, and take the stony heart out of their flesh, and give them a heart of flesh, 20that they may walk in My statutes and keep My judgments and do them; and they shall be My people, and I will be their God. 21But *as for those* whose hearts follow the desire for their detestable things and their abominations, I will recompense their deeds on their own heads," says the Lord GOD.

22So the cherubim lifted up their wings, with the wheels beside them, and the glory of the God of Israel *was* high above them. 23And the glory of the LORD went up from the midst of the city and stood on the mountain, which *is* on the east side of the city.

24Then the Spirit took me up and brought me in a vision by the Spirit of God into Chaldea, to those in captivity. And the vision that I had seen went up from me. 25So I spoke to those in captivity of all the things the LORD had shown me.

12 Now the word of the LORD came to me, saying: 2"Son of man, you dwell in the midst of a rebellious house, which has eyes to see but does not see, and ears to hear but does not hear; for they *are* a rebellious house.

3"Therefore, son of man, prepare your belongings for captivity, and go into captivity by day in their sight. You shall go from your place into captivity to another place in their sight. It may be that they will consider, though they *are* a rebellious house. 4By day you shall bring out your belongings in their sight, as

12:3 prepare…for captivity. This dramatic object lesson by the prophet called for carrying belongings out in a stealthy way as an act that depicted baggage for exile, just the bare necessities. His countrymen carried out such baggage when they went into captivity or sought to escape during Babylon's takeover of Jerusalem (vv. 7,11). Some attempting to escape were caught as in a net, like King Zedekiah who was overtaken, blinded, and forced into exile. Verse 9 indicates that Ezekiel actually did what he was told.

though going into captivity; and at evening
you shall go in their sight, like those who go
into captivity. [5]Dig through the wall in their
sight, and carry *your belongings* out through it.
[6]In their sight you shall bear *them* on *your*
shoulders *and* carry *them* out at twilight; you
shall cover your face, so that you cannot see
the ground, for I have made you a sign to the
house of Israel."

[7]So I did as I was commanded. I brought out
my belongings by day, as though going into
captivity, and at evening I dug through the
wall with my hand. I brought *them* out at twilight, *and* I bore *them* on *my* shoulder in their
sight.

[8]And in the morning the word of the LORD
came to me, saying, [9]"Son of man, has not the
house of Israel, the rebellious house, said to
you, 'What are you doing?' [10]Say to them,
'Thus says the Lord GOD: "This burden *con-*
cerns the prince in Jerusalem and all the
house of Israel who are among them." ' [11]Say,
'I *am* a sign to you. As I have done, so shall it
be done to them; they shall be carried away
into captivity.' [12]And the prince who *is* among
them shall bear *his belongings* on *his* shoulder
at twilight and go out. They shall dig through
the wall to carry *them* out through it. He shall
cover his face, so that he cannot see the
ground with *his* eyes. [13]I will also spread My
net over him, and he shall be caught in My
snare. I will bring him to Babylon, *to* the land
of the Chaldeans; yet he shall not see it,
though he shall die there. [14]I will scatter to
every wind all who *are* around him to help
him, and all his troops; and I will draw out the
sword after them.

[15]"Then they shall know that I *am* the LORD,
when I scatter them among the nations and
disperse them throughout the countries. [16]But
I will spare a few of their men from the sword,
from famine, and from pestilence, that they
may declare all their abominations among the
Gentiles wherever they go. Then they shall
know that I *am* the LORD."

[17]Moreover the word of the LORD came to
me, saying, [18]"Son of man, eat your bread
with quaking, and drink your water with
trembling and anxiety. [19]And say to the people of the land, 'Thus says the Lord GOD to
the inhabitants of Jerusalem *and* to the land
of Israel: "They shall eat their bread with
anxiety, and drink their water with dread, so
that her land may be emptied of all who are
in it, because of the violence of all those who
dwell in it. [20]Then the cities that are inhabited
shall be laid waste, and the land shall become
desolate; and you shall know that I *am* the
LORD." ' "

[21]And the word of the LORD came to me, saying, [22]"Son of man, what *is* this proverb *that*
you *people* have about the land of Israel, which
says, 'The days are prolonged, and every
vision fails'? [23]Tell them therefore, 'Thus says
the Lord GOD: "I will lay this proverb to rest,
and they shall no more use it as a proverb in
Israel." But say to them, "The days are at
hand, and the fulfillment of every vision. [24]For
no more shall there be any false vision or flattering divination within the house of Israel.
[25]For I *am* the LORD. I speak, and the word
which I speak will come to pass; it will no
more be postponed; for in your days, O rebellious house, I will say the word and perform
it," says the Lord GOD.' "

[26]Again the word of the LORD came to me,
saying, [27]"Son of man, look, the house of Israel
is saying, 'The vision that he sees *is* for many
days *from now,* and he prophesies of times far
off.' [28]Therefore say to them, 'Thus says the
Lord GOD: "None of My words will be postponed any more, but the word which I speak
will be done," says the Lord GOD.' "

12:22 this proverb. Delay had given the people the false impression that the stroke of judgment would never come. In fact, a saying had become popular, no doubt developed by false prophets who caused the people to reject Ezekiel's visions and prophecies (v. 27) and who gave "flattering divinations" (vv. 23,24).

Psalm 122:1–5

A Song of Ascents. Of David.

I was glad when they said to me,
"Let us go into the house
of the LORD."
2 Our feet have been standing
Within your gates, O Jerusalem!

3 Jerusalem is built
As a city that is compact together,
4 Where the tribes go up,
The tribes of the LORD,
To the Testimony of Israel,
To give thanks to the name
of the LORD.
5 For thrones are set there
for judgment,
The thrones of the house of David.

Proverbs 28:17–18

17 A man burdened with bloodshed
will flee into a pit;
Let no one help him.
18 Whoever walks blamelessly will be
saved,
But *he who is* perverse *in his* ways
will suddenly fall.

Hebrews 6:1–20

6 Therefore, leaving the discussion of the elementary *principles* of Christ, let us go on to
perfection, not laying again the foundation of
repentance from dead works and of faith
toward God, 2of the doctrine of baptisms, of
laying on of hands, of resurrection of the
dead, and of eternal judgment. 3And this we
will do if God permits.

6:1 leaving. This "leaving" does not mean to despise or abandon the basic doctrines. They are the place to start, not stop. They are the gate of entrance on the road to salvation in Christ. **elementary *principles* of Christ.** As "the oracles of God" in 5:12 refers to the Old Testament, so does this phrase. The writer is referring to basic Old Testament teaching that prepared the way for Messiah—the beginning teaching about Christ. These Old Testament "principles" include the 6 features listed in vv. 1,2. **go on to perfection.** Salvation by faith in Messiah Jesus. The verb is passive, so as to indicate "let us be carried to salvation." That is not a matter of learners being carried by teachers, but both being carried forward by God. The writer warns his Jewish readers that there is no value in stopping with the Old Testament basics and repeating ("laying again") what was only intended to be foundational.

4For *it is* impossible for those who were
once enlightened, and have tasted the heavenly gift, and have become partakers of the Holy
Spirit, 5and have tasted the good word of God
and the powers of the age to come, 6if they fall
away, to renew them again to repentance, since
they crucify again for themselves the Son of
God, and put *Him* to an open shame.
7For the earth which drinks in the rain that
often comes upon it, and bears herbs useful
for those by whom it is cultivated, receives
blessing from God; 8but if it bears thorns and
briers, *it is* rejected and near to being cursed,
whose end *is* to be burned.

6:4 enlightened. They had received instruction in biblical truth which was accompanied by intellectual perception. Understanding the gospel is not the equivalent of regeneration (10:26,32). In John 1:9, it is clear that enlightening is not the equivalent of salvation. **tasted the heavenly gift.** Tasting in the figurative sense in the New Testament refers to consciously experiencing something (2:9). The experience might be momentary or continuing. Christ's "tasting" of death (2:9) was obviously momentary and not continuing or permanent. All men experience the goodness of God, but that does not mean they are all saved (Matt. 5:45; Acts 17:25). Many Jews, during the Lord's earthly ministry experienced the blessings from heaven He brought—in healings and deliverance from demons, as well as eating the food He created miraculously (John 6). Whether the gift refers to Christ (John 6:51; 2 Cor. 9:15) or to the Holy Spirit (Acts 2:38; 1 Pet. 1:12), experiencing either one was not the equivalent of salvation (John 16:8; Acts 7:51).

9But, beloved, we are confident of better
things concerning you, yes, things that
accompany salvation, though we speak in this
manner. 10For God *is* not unjust to forget your
work and labor of love which you have shown
toward His name, *in that* you have ministered
to the saints, and do minister. 11And we desire
that each one of you show the same diligence
to the full assurance of hope until the end,
12that you do not become sluggish, but imitate
those who through faith and patience inherit
the promises.
13For when God made a promise to Abraham,
because He could swear by no one greater, He
swore by Himself, 14saying, *"Surely blessing I
will bless you, and multiplying I will multiply
you."* 15And so, after he had patiently endured, he
obtained the promise. 16For men indeed swear
by the greater, and an oath for confirmation *is* for
them an end of all dispute. 17Thus God, determining to show more abundantly to the heirs of
promise the immutability of His counsel, confirmed *it* by an oath, 18that by two immutable
things, in which it *is* impossible for God to lie, we
might have strong consolation, who have fled for
refuge to lay hold of the hope set before *us.*
19This *hope* we have as an anchor of the soul,
both sure and steadfast, and which enters the
Presence behind the veil, 20where the forerunner has entered for us, *even* Jesus, having
become High Priest forever according to the
order of Melchizedek.

DAY 10: To whom is Hebrews 6:4–6, and particularly the phrase "once enlightened," directed?

The phrase "once enlightened" is often taken to refer to Christians. The accompanying warning, then, is taken to indicate the danger of losing their salvation if they "fall away" and "crucify again for themselves the Son of God." But the immediate context has no mention of their being saved. They are not described with any terms that apply only to believers (such as holy, born again, righteous, or saints).

The interpretive problem arises from inaccurately identifying the spiritual condition of the ones being addressed. In this case, they were unbelievers who had been exposed to God's redemptive truth and, perhaps, had made a profession of faith but had not exercised genuine saving faith. Another passage (10:26) addresses the same issue. The subject here is people who come in contact with the gospel but are spiritually unchanged by it. Apostate Christians are Christians in name only, not genuine believers who are often incorrectly thought to lose their salvation because of their sins.

There is no possibility of these verses referring to someone losing their salvation. Many Scripture passages make unmistakably clear that salvation is eternal (see, e.g., John 10:27–29; Rom. 8:35,38,39; Phil. 1:6; 1 Pet. 1:4,5). Those who want to make this passage mean that believers can lose salvation will have to admit that it would then also make the point that one could never get it back again.

NOVEMBER 11

Ezekiel 13:1–14:23

13 And the word of the LORD came to me,
saying, 2"Son of man, prophesy against
the prophets of Israel who prophesy, and say
to those who prophesy out of their own heart,
'Hear the word of the LORD!' "
3Thus says the Lord GOD: "Woe to the foolish prophets, who follow their own spirit and
have seen nothing! 4O Israel, your prophets
are like foxes in the deserts. 5You have not
gone up into the gaps to build a wall for the
house of Israel to stand in battle on the day of
the LORD. 6They have envisioned futility and
false divination, saying, 'Thus says the LORD!'
But the LORD has not sent them; yet they hope
that the word may be confirmed. 7Have you
not seen a futile vision, and have you not spoken false divination? You say, 'The LORD says,'
but I have not spoken."
8Therefore thus says the Lord GOD: "Because you have spoken nonsense and envisioned lies, therefore I *am* indeed against
you," says the Lord GOD. 9"My hand will be
against the prophets who envision futility and
who divine lies; they shall not be in the assembly of My people, nor be written in the record
of the house of Israel, nor shall they enter into
the land of Israel. Then you shall know that I
am the Lord GOD.
10"Because, indeed, because they have
seduced My people, saying, 'Peace!' when *there*
is no peace—and one builds a wall, and they
plaster it with untempered *mortar*— 11say to
those who plaster *it* with untempered *mortar,*
that it will fall. There will be flooding rain, and
you, O great hailstones, shall fall; and a stormy
wind shall tear *it* down. 12Surely, when the wall
has fallen, will it not be said to you, 'Where *is*
the mortar with which you plastered *it?*' "

13:10,11 builds a wall. False prophets had lulled the people into false security. Phony "peace" promises, while sin continued on the brink of God's judgment, was a way, so to speak, of erecting a defective "wall" and whitewashing it to make it look good. Such an unsafe "wall" was doomed to collapse (v. 11) when God would bring His storm, picturing the invaders' assault (v. 11).

13Therefore thus says the Lord GOD: "I will
cause a stormy wind to break forth in My
fury; and there shall be a flooding rain in My
anger, and great hailstones in fury to consume
it. 14So I will break down the wall you have
plastered with untempered *mortar,* and bring
it down to the ground, so that its foundation
will be uncovered; it will fall, and you shall be
consumed in the midst of it. Then you shall
know that I *am* the LORD.
15"Thus will I accomplish My wrath on the
wall and on those who have plastered it with
untempered *mortar;* and I will say to you, 'The
wall *is* no *more,* nor those who plastered it,
16*that is,* the prophets of Israel who prophesy
concerning Jerusalem, and who see visions of

peace for her when *there is* no peace,' " says
the Lord GOD.
17"Likewise, son of man, set your face against
the daughters of your people, who prophesy
out of their own heart; prophesy against them,
18and say, 'Thus says the Lord GOD: "Woe to
the *women* who sew *magic* charms on their
sleeves and make veils for the heads of people
of every height to hunt souls! Will you hunt
the souls of My people, and keep yourselves
alive? 19And will you profane Me among My
people for handfuls of barley and for pieces of
bread, killing people who should not die, and
keeping people alive who should not live, by
your lying to My people who listen to lies?"
20"Therefore thus says the Lord GOD: "Behold, I *am* against your *magic* charms by which
you hunt souls there like birds. I will tear them
from your arms, and let the souls go, the souls
you hunt like birds. 21I will also tear off your
veils and deliver My people out of your hand,
and they shall no longer be as prey in your
hand. Then you shall know that I *am* the LORD.
22"Because with lies you have made the
heart of the righteous sad, whom I have not
made sad; and you have strengthened the
hands of the wicked, so that he does not turn
from his wicked way to save his life. 23There-
fore you shall no longer envision futility nor
practice divination; for I will deliver My people
out of your hand, and you shall know that I *am*
the LORD." ' "
14 Now some of the elders of Israel came to
me and sat before me. 2And the word of
the LORD came to me, saying, 3"Son of man,
these men have set up their idols in their
hearts, and put before them that which causes
them to stumble into iniquity. Should I let
Myself be inquired of at all by them?
4"Therefore speak to them, and say to them,
'Thus says the Lord GOD: "Everyone of the
house of Israel who sets up his idols in his
heart, and puts before him what causes him to
stumble into iniquity, and then comes to the
prophet, I the LORD will answer him who comes,
according to the multitude of his idols, 5that I
may seize the house of Israel by their heart,
because they are all estranged from Me by
their idols." '
6"Therefore say to the house of Israel, 'Thus
says the Lord GOD: "Repent, turn away from
your idols, and turn your faces away from all
your abominations. 7For anyone of the house of
Israel, or of the strangers who dwell in Israel,
who separates himself from Me and sets up his
idols in his heart and puts before him what
causes him to stumble into iniquity, then comes
to a prophet to inquire of him concerning Me,
I the LORD will answer him by Myself. 8I will
set My face against that man and make him a
sign and a proverb, and I will cut him off from
the midst of My people. Then you shall know
that I *am* the LORD.
9"And if the prophet is induced to speak anything, I the LORD have induced that prophet,
and I will stretch out My hand against him and
destroy him from among My people Israel.
10And they shall bear their iniquity; the punishment of the prophet shall be the same as the
punishment of the one who inquired, 11that the
house of Israel may no longer stray from Me,
nor be profaned anymore with all their transgressions, but that they may be My people and
I may be their God," says the Lord GOD.' "
12The word of the LORD came again to me,
saying: 13"Son of man, when a land sins against
Me by persistent unfaithfulness, I will stretch
out My hand against it; I will cut off its supply
of bread, send famine on it, and cut off man
and beast from it. 14Even *if* these three men,
Noah, Daniel, and Job, were in it, they would
deliver *only* themselves by their righteousness," says the Lord GOD.
15"If I cause wild beasts to pass through the
land, and they empty it, and make it so desolate that no man may pass through because of
the beasts, 16*even though* these three men *were*
in it, *as* I live," says the Lord GOD, "they would
deliver neither sons nor daughters; only they
would be delivered, and the land would be
desolate.
17"Or *if* I bring a sword on that land, and say,
'Sword, go through the land,' and I cut off man
and beast from it, 18even *though* these three men
were in it, *as* I live," says the Lord GOD, "they

14:14–20 Noah, Daniel, and Job. Jeremiah 7:16 and 15:1–4 provide a close parallel to this passage. According to Jeremiah, even Moses and Samuel, well known for their power in intercessory prayer, would not prevail to deliver Jerusalem and the people. The 3 Old Testament heroes mentioned in this section exhibited power in intercession on behalf of others (Gen. 6:18; Job 42:7–10; Dan. 1; 2) at strategic points in redemptive history, and even they could not deliver anyone but themselves if they were there praying earnestly. Even the presence and prayers of the godly could not stop the coming judgment. Genesis 18:22–32 and Jeremiah 5:1–4 provide rare exceptions to the principle that one man's righteousness is no protection for others.

would deliver neither sons nor daughters, but
only they themselves would be delivered.
19 “Or *if* I send a pestilence into that land and
pour out My fury on it in blood, and cut off
from it man and beast, 20 even *though* Noah,
Daniel, and Job *were* in it, *as* I live,” says the
Lord GOD, “they would deliver neither son nor
daughter; they would deliver *only* themselves
by their righteousness.”
21 For thus says the Lord GOD: “How much
more it shall be when I send My four severe
judgments on Jerusalem—the sword and
famine and wild beasts and pestilence—to cut
off man and beast from it? 22 Yet behold, there
shall be left in it a remnant who will be
brought out, *both* sons and daughters; surely
they will come out to you, and you will see
their ways and their doings. Then you will be
comforted concerning the disaster that I have
brought upon Jerusalem, all that I have
brought upon it. 23 And they will comfort you,
when you see their ways and their doings; and
you shall know that I have done nothing without
cause that I have done in it,” says the Lord GOD.

Psalm 122:6–9

6 Pray for the peace of Jerusalem:
“May they prosper who love you.
7 Peace be within your walls,
Prosperity within your palaces.”
8 For the sake of my brethren and
companions,
I will now say, “Peace *be* within you.”
9 Because of the house of the LORD
our God
I will seek your good.

Proverbs 28:19

19 He who tills his land will have plenty
of bread,
But he who follows frivolity will have
poverty enough!

Hebrews 7:1–28

7 For this Melchizedek, king of Salem,
priest of the Most High God, who met
Abraham returning from the slaughter of the
kings and blessed him, 2 to whom also Abraham gave a tenth part of all, first being translated “king of righteousness,” and then also
king of Salem, meaning “king of peace,” 3 without father, without mother, without genealogy,
having neither beginning of days nor end of
life, but made like the Son of God, remains a
priest continually.
4 Now consider how great this man *was,* to
whom even the patriarch Abraham gave a
tenth of the spoils. 5 And indeed those who are
of the sons of Levi, who receive the priesthood,
have a commandment to receive tithes from
the people according to the law, that is, from
their brethren, though they have come from
the loins of Abraham; 6 but he whose genealogy
is not derived from them received tithes from
Abraham and blessed him who had the promises. 7 Now beyond all contradiction the lesser is
blessed by the better. 8 Here mortal men receive
tithes, but there he *receives them,* of whom it is
witnessed that he lives. 9 Even Levi, who
receives tithes, paid tithes through Abraham,
so to speak, 10 for he was still in the loins of his
father when Melchizedek met him.
11 Therefore, if perfection were through the
Levitical priesthood (for under it the people
received the law), what further need *was there*
that another priest should rise according to the
order of Melchizedek, and not be called according to the order of Aaron? 12 For the priesthood
being changed, of necessity there is also a
change of the law. 13 For He of whom these
things are spoken belongs to another tribe,
from which no man has officiated at the altar.
14 For *it is* evident that our Lord arose from
Judah, of which tribe Moses spoke nothing
concerning priesthood. 15 And it is yet far more
evident if, in the likeness of Melchizedek, there
arises another priest 16 who has come, not
according to the law of a fleshly commandment, but according to the power of an endless life. 17 For He testifies:

“You are a priest forever
According to the order of
Melchizedek.”

18 For on the one hand there is an annulling
of the former commandment because of its
weakness and unprofitableness, 19 for the law
made nothing perfect; on the other hand, *there*
is the bringing in of a better hope, through
which we draw near to God.
20 And inasmuch as *He was* not *made priest*
without an oath 21 (for they have become priests

7:19 the law made nothing perfect. The law saved no one (Rom. 3:19,20); rather it cursed everyone (Gal. 3:10–13). **draw near to God.** This is the key phrase in this passage. Drawing near to God is the essence of Christianity as compared with the Levitical system, which kept people outside His presence. As believer priests, we are all to draw near to God—that is a characteristic of the priesthood (Ex. 19:22; Matt. 27:51).

without an oath, but He with an oath by Him who said to Him:

"The LORD has sworn
And will not relent,
'You are a priest forever
According to the order of
Melchizedek'"),

[22]by so much more Jesus has become a surety of a better covenant.

[23]Also there were many priests, because they were prevented by death from continuing. [24]But He, because He continues forever, has an unchangeable priesthood. [25]Therefore He is also able to save to the uttermost those who come to God through Him, since He always lives to make intercession for them.

[26]For such a High Priest was fitting for us, *who is* holy, harmless, undefiled, separate from sinners, and has become higher than the heavens; [27]who does not need daily, as those high priests, to offer up sacrifices, first for His own sins and then for the people's, for this He did once for all when He offered up Himself. [28]For the law appoints as high priests men who have weakness, but the word of the oath, which came after the law, *appoints* the Son who has been perfected forever.

7:25 uttermost. Virtually the same concept as was expressed in "perfection" (v. 11) and "make perfect" (v. 19). The Greek term is used only here and in Luke 13:11 (the woman's body could not be straightened completely). **intercession.** The word means "to intercede on behalf of another." It was used to refer the bringing of a petition to a king on behalf of someone. The High Priestly intercessory prayer of Christ in John 17 is an example. Since rabbis assigned intercessory powers to angels, perhaps the people were treating angels as intercessors. The writer makes it clear that only Christ is the intercessor (1 Tim. 2:5).

DAY 11: Who was Melchizedek, and why was he so important?

Melchizedek shows up abruptly and briefly in the Old Testament, but his special role in Abraham's life makes him a significant figure. He is mentioned again in Psalm 110:4, the passage under consideration in Hebrews 4:14–7:28. As the king of Salem and priest of the Most High God in the time of Abraham, Melchizedek offered a historical precedent for the role of king-priest (Gen. 14:18–20), filled perfectly by Jesus Christ.

By using the two Old Testament references to Melchizedek, the writer (7:1–28) explains the superiority of Christ's priesthood by reviewing Melchizedek's unique role as a type of Christ and his superiority to the Levitical high priesthood. The Levitical priesthood was hereditary, but Melchizedek's was not. Through Abraham's honor, Melchizedek's rightful role was established. The major ways in which the Melchizedekan priesthood was superior to the Levitical priesthood are these:

1. The receiving of tithes (7:2–10), as when Abraham the ancestor of the Levites gave Melchizedek a tithe of the spoils.
2. The giving of the blessing (7:1,6,7), as when Abraham accepted Melchizedek's blessing.
3. The continual replacement of the Levitical priesthood (7:11–19), which passed down from father to son.
4. The perpetuity of the Melchizedekan priesthood (7:3,8,16,17,20–28), since the record about his priesthood does not record his death.

NOVEMBER 12

Ezekiel 15:1–16:63

15 Then the word of the LORD came to me, saying: [2]"Son of man, how is the wood of the vine *better* than any other wood, the vine branch which is among the trees of the forest? [3]Is wood taken from it to make any object? Or can *men* make a peg from it to hang any vessel

15:1–3 Then the word...came. Israel, often symbolized by a vine (17:6–10; Gen. 49:22; Jer. 2:21), had become useful for nothing. Failing to do the very thing God set her apart to do—bear fruit—she no longer served any purpose and was useless (v. 2). Other trees can be used for construction of certain things, but a fruitless vine is useless (v. 3). It has no value. In every age, the people of God have their value in their fruitfulness.

on? 4Instead, it is thrown into the fire for fuel;
the fire devours both ends of it, and its middle
is burned. Is it useful for *any* work? 5Indeed,
when it was whole, no object could be made
from it. How much less will it be useful for *any*
work when the fire has devoured it, and it is
burned?

6"Therefore thus says the Lord GOD: 'Like
the wood of the vine among the trees of the
forest, which I have given to the fire for fuel,
so I will give up the inhabitants of Jerusalem;
7and I will set My face against them. They will
go out from *one* fire, but *another* fire shall
devour them. Then you shall know that I *am*
the LORD, when I set My face against them.
8Thus I will make the land desolate, because
they have persisted in unfaithfulness,' says the
Lord GOD."

16 Again the word of the LORD came to me,
saying, 2"Son of man, cause Jerusalem to
know her abominations, 3and say, 'Thus says
the Lord GOD to Jerusalem: "Your birth and
your nativity *are* from the land of Canaan; your
father *was* an Amorite and your mother a
Hittite. 4*As for* your nativity, on the day you
were born your navel cord was not cut, nor
were you washed in water to cleanse *you;* you
were not rubbed with salt nor wrapped in
swaddling cloths. 5No eye pitied you, to do any
of these things for you, to have compassion on
you; but you were thrown out into the open
field, when you yourself were loathed on the
day you were born.

6"And when I passed by you and saw you
struggling in your own blood, I said to you in
your blood, 'Live!' Yes, I said to you in your
blood, 'Live!' 7I made you thrive like a plant in
the field; and you grew, matured, and became
very beautiful. *Your* breasts were formed,
your hair grew, but you *were* naked and bare.

8"When I passed by you again and looked
upon you, indeed your time *was* the time of
love; so I spread My wing over you and covered your nakedness. Yes, I swore an oath to
you and entered into a covenant with you, and
you became Mine," says the Lord GOD.

16:8 the time of love. This refers to the marriageable state. Spreading his "wing" was a custom of espousal (Ruth 3:9) and indicates that God entered into a covenant with the young nation at Mt. Sinai (Ex. 19:5–8). Making a covenant signifies marriage, the figure of God's relation to Israel (Jer. 2:2; 3:1ff.; Hos. 2:2–23).

9"Then I washed you in water; yes, I thoroughly washed off your blood, and I anointed
you with oil. 10I clothed you in embroidered
cloth and gave you sandals of badger skin; I
clothed you with fine linen and covered you
with silk. 11I adorned you with ornaments, put
bracelets on your wrists, and a chain on your
neck. 12And I put a jewel in your nose, earrings
in your ears, and a beautiful crown on your
head. 13Thus you were adorned with gold and silver, and your clothing *was of* fine linen, silk, and
embroidered cloth. You ate *pastry of* fine flour,
honey, and oil. You were exceedingly beautiful,
and succeeded to royalty. 14Your fame went out
among the nations because of your beauty, for it
was perfect through My splendor which I had
bestowed on you," says the Lord GOD.

15"But you trusted in your own beauty,
played the harlot because of your fame, and
poured out your harlotry on everyone passing
by who *would have* it. 16You took some of your
garments and adorned multicolored high
places for yourself, and played the harlot on
them. *Such* things should not happen, nor be.
17You have also taken your beautiful jewelry
from My gold and My silver, which I had given
you, and made for yourself male images and
played the harlot with them. 18You took your
embroidered garments and covered them,
and you set My oil and My incense before
them. 19Also My food which I gave you—the
pastry of fine flour, oil, and honey *which* I fed
you—you set it before them as sweet incense;
and *so* it was," says the Lord GOD.

20"Moreover you took your sons and your
daughters, whom you bore to Me, and these
you sacrificed to them to be devoured. *Were*
your *acts* of harlotry a small matter, 21that you
have slain My children and offered them up to
them by causing them to pass through *the*
fire? 22And in all your abominations and acts of
harlotry you did not remember the days of
your youth, when you were naked and bare,
struggling in your blood.

23"Then it was so, after all your wickedness—
'Woe, woe to you!' says the Lord GOD— 24*that*
you also built for yourself a shrine, and made
a high place for yourself in every street. 25You
built your high places at the head of every
road, and made your beauty to be abhorred.
You offered yourself to everyone who passed
by, and multiplied your acts of harlotry. 26You
also committed harlotry with the Egyptians,
your very fleshly neighbors, and increased
your acts of harlotry to provoke Me to anger.

27"Behold, therefore, I stretched out My
hand against you, diminished your allotment,
and gave you up to the will of those who hate

you, the daughters of the Philistines, who
were ashamed of your lewd behavior. [28]You
also played the harlot with the Assyrians,
because you were insatiable; indeed you
played the harlot with them and still were not
satisfied. [29]Moreover you multiplied your acts
of harlotry as far as the land of the trader,
Chaldea; and even then you were not satisfied.

[30]"How degenerate is your heart!" says the
Lord GOD, "seeing you do all these *things,* the
deeds of a brazen harlot.

[31]"You erected your shrine at the head of
every road, and built your high place in every
street. Yet you were not like a harlot, because
you scorned payment. [32]*You are* an adulterous
wife, *who* takes strangers instead of her husband. [33]Men make payment to all harlots, but
you made your payments to all your lovers,
and hired them to come to you from all around
for your harlotry. [34]You are the opposite of
other women in your harlotry, because no one
solicited you to be a harlot. In that you gave
payment but no payment was given you, therefore you are the opposite."

[35]'Now then, O harlot, hear the word of the
LORD! [36]Thus says the Lord GOD: "Because
your filthiness was poured out and your
nakedness uncovered in your harlotry with
your lovers, and with all your abominable
idols, and because of the blood of your children which you gave to them, [37]surely, therefore, I will gather all your lovers with whom
you took pleasure, all those you loved, *and* all
those you hated; I will gather them from all
around against you and will uncover your
nakedness to them, that they may see all your
nakedness. [38]And I will judge you as women
who break wedlock or shed blood are judged;
I will bring blood upon you in fury and jealousy. [39]I will also give you into their hand, and
they shall throw down your shrines and break
down your high places. They shall also strip
you of your clothes, take your beautiful jewelry, and leave you naked and bare.

[40]"They shall also bring up an assembly
against you, and they shall stone you with
stones and thrust you through with their
swords. [41]They shall burn your houses with
fire, and execute judgments on you in the
sight of many women; and I will make you
cease playing the harlot, and you shall no
longer hire lovers. [42]So I will lay to rest My
fury toward you, and My jealousy shall depart
from you. I will be quiet, and be angry no
more. [43]Because you did not remember the
days of your youth, but agitated Me with all
these *things,* surely I will also recompense
your deeds on *your own* head," says the Lord
GOD. "And you shall not commit lewdness in
addition to all your abominations.

[44]"Indeed everyone who quotes proverbs
will use *this* proverb against you: 'Like mother,
like daughter!' [45]You *are* your mother's daughter, loathing husband and children; and you
are the sister of your sisters, who loathed their
husbands and children; your mother *was* a
Hittite and your father an Amorite.

[46]"Your elder sister *is* Samaria, who dwells
with her daughters to the north of you; and
your younger sister, who dwells to the south of
you, *is* Sodom and her daughters. [47]You did not
walk in their ways nor act according to their
abominations; but, as *if that were* too little, you
became more corrupt than they in all your ways.

[48]"*As* I live," says the Lord GOD, "neither
your sister Sodom nor her daughters have
done as you and your daughters have done.
[49]Look, this was the iniquity of your sister
Sodom: She and her daughter had pride, fullness of food, and abundance of idleness; neither did she strengthen the hand of the poor
and needy. [50]And they were haughty and committed abomination before Me; therefore I
took them away as I saw *fit.*

[51]"Samaria did not commit half of your sins;
but you have multiplied your abominations
more than they, and have justified your sisters
by all the abominations which you have done.
[52]You who judged your sisters, bear your own
shame also, because the sins which you committed were more abominable than theirs;
they are more righteous than you. Yes, be disgraced also, and bear your own shame,
because you justified your sisters.

[53]"When I bring back their captives, the captives of Sodom and her daughters, and the
captives of Samaria and her daughters, then *I
will also bring back* the captives of your captivity among them, [54]that you may bear your own
shame and be disgraced by all that you did
when you comforted them. [55]When your sisters, Sodom and her daughters, return to their
former state, and Samaria and her daughters
return to their former state, then you and your
daughters will return to your former state.
[56]For your sister Sodom was not a byword in
your mouth in the days of your pride, [57]before
your wickedness was uncovered. It was like
the time of the reproach of the daughters of
Syria and all *those* around her, and of the
daughters of the Philistines, who despise you
everywhere. [58]You have paid for your lewdness and your abominations," says the LORD.
[59]For thus says the Lord GOD: "I will deal with
you as you have done, who despised the oath
by breaking the covenant.

[60]"Nevertheless I will remember My covenant with you in the days of your youth, and I will establish an everlasting covenant with you. [61]Then you will remember your ways and be ashamed, when you receive your older and your younger sisters; for I will give them to you for daughters, but not because of My covenant with you. [62]And I will establish My covenant with you. Then you shall know that I *am* the LORD, [63]that you may remember and be ashamed, and never open your mouth anymore because of your shame, when I provide you an atonement for all you have done," says the Lord GOD.' "

16:60 I will remember My covenant. God is gracious and He always finds a covenant basis on which He can exercise His grace. The Lord will remember the Abrahamic Covenant (Gen. 12:1ff.) made with Israel in her youth. Restoration will be by grace, not merit. **an everlasting covenant.** This is the New Covenant, which is unconditional, saving, and everlasting (37:26; Is. 59:21; 61:8; Jer. 31:31–34; Heb. 8:6–13). The basis of God's grace will not be the Mosaic Covenant, which the Jews could never fulfill, even with the best intentions (Ex. 24:1ff.). When God establishes His eternal covenant, Israel will know that God is the Lord because of His grace.

Psalm 123:1–4

A Song of Ascents.

Unto You I lift up my eyes,
O You who dwell in the heavens.
2 Behold, as the eyes of servants
look to the hand of their masters,
As the eyes of a maid to the hand
of her mistress,
So our eyes *look* to the LORD our God,
Until He has mercy on us.

3 Have mercy on us, O LORD, have
mercy on us!
For we are exceedingly filled with
contempt.
4 Our soul is exceedingly filled
With the scorn of those who are at ease,
With the contempt of the proud.

Proverbs 28:20

20 A faithful man will abound with
blessings,
But he who hastens to be rich
will not go unpunished.

Hebrews 8:1–13

8 Now *this is* the main point of the things we are saying: We have such a High Priest, who is seated at the right hand of the throne of the Majesty in the heavens, [2]a Minister of the sanctuary and of the true tabernacle which the Lord erected, and not man.

[3]For every high priest is appointed to offer both gifts and sacrifices. Therefore *it is* necessary that this One also have something to offer. [4]For if He were on earth, He would not be a priest, since there are priests who offer the gifts according to the law; [5]who serve the copy and shadow of the heavenly things, as Moses was divinely instructed when he was about to make the tabernacle. For He said, *"See that you make all things according to the pattern shown you on the mountain."* [6]But now He has obtained a more excellent ministry, inasmuch as He is also Mediator of a better covenant, which was established on better promises.

8:5 The quote is from Exodus 25:40. **copy and shadow.** This does not mean that there are actual buildings in heaven which were copied in the tabernacle, but rather that the heavenly realities were adequately symbolized and represented in the earthly tabernacle model.

[7]For if that first *covenant* had been faultless, then no place would have been sought for a second. [8]Because finding fault with them, He says: *"Behold, the days are coming, says the LORD, when I will make a new covenant with the house of Israel and with the house of Judah— [9]not according to the covenant that I made with their fathers in the day when I took them by the hand to lead them out of the land of Egypt; because they did not continue in My covenant, and I disregarded them, says the LORD. [10]For this is the covenant that I will make with the house of Israel after those days, says the LORD: I will put My laws in their mind and write them on their hearts; and I will be their God, and they shall be My people. [11]None of them shall teach his neighbor, and none his brother, saying, 'Know the LORD,' for all shall know Me, from the least of them to the greatest of them. [12]For I will be merciful to their unrighteousness, and their sins and their lawless deeds I will remember no more."*

[13]In that He says, *"A new covenant,"* He has made the first obsolete. Now what is becoming obsolete and growing old is ready to vanish away.

DAY 12: Who was the prophet Ezekiel?

If the "thirtieth year" of Ezekiel 1:1 refers to Ezekiel's age, he was 25 when taken captive and 30 when called into ministry. Thirty was the age when priests commenced their office, so it was a notable year for Ezekiel. His ministry began in 593/92 B.C. and extended at least 22 years until 571/70 B.C. (25:17). He was a contemporary of both Jeremiah (who was about 20 years older) and Daniel (who was the same age), whom he names in 14:14,20; 28:3 as an already well-known prophet. Like Jeremiah (Jer. 1:1) and Zechariah (Zech. 1:1 with Neh. 12:16), Ezekiel was both a prophet and a priest (1:3). Because of his priestly background, he was particularly interested in and familiar with the temple details. So God used him to write much about them (8:1–11:25; 40:1–47:12).

Ezekiel and his wife (who is mentioned in 24:15–27) were among 10,000 Jews taken captive to Babylon in 597 B.C. (2 Kin. 24:11–18). They lived in Tel Abib (3:15) on the bank of the Chebar River, probably southeast of Babylon. Domestically, Ezekiel and the 10,000 lived more as colonists than captives, being permitted to farm tracts of land under somewhat favorable conditions (Jer. 29). Ezekiel even had his own house (3:24; 20:1). Ezekiel writes of his wife's death in exile (Ezek. 24:18), but the book does not mention Ezekiel's death, which rabbinical tradition suggests occurred at the hands of an Israelite prince whose idolatry he rebuked around 560 B.C.

Prophetically, false prophets deceived the exiles with assurances of a speedy return to Judah (13:3,16; Jer. 29:1). From 593 to 585 B.C., Ezekiel warned that their beloved Jerusalem would be destroyed and their exile prolonged, so there was no hope of immediate return. In 585 B.C., an escapee from Jerusalem, who had evaded the Babylonians, reached Ezekiel with the first news that the city had fallen in 586 B.C., about 6 months earlier (33:21). That dashed the false hopes of any immediate deliverance for the exiles, so the remainder of Ezekiel's prophecies related to Israel's future restoration to its homeland and the final blessings of the messianic kingdom.

NOVEMBER 13

Ezekiel 17:1–18:32

17 And the word of the LORD came to me,
saying, 2"Son of man, pose a riddle, and
speak a parable to the house of Israel, 3and
say, 'Thus says the Lord GOD:

"A great eagle with large wings and
long pinions,
Full of feathers of various colors,
Came to Lebanon
And took from the cedar the highest
branch.
4 He cropped off its topmost young twig
And carried it to a land of trade;
He set it in a city of merchants.
5 Then he took some of the seed
of the land
And planted it in a fertile field;
He placed *it* by abundant waters
And set it like a willow tree.
6 And it grew and became a spreading
vine of low stature;
Its branches turned toward him,
But its roots were under it.
So it became a vine,
Brought forth branches,
And put forth shoots.

7 "But there was another great eagle with
large wings and many feathers;
And behold, this vine bent its roots
toward him,
And stretched its branches toward
him,
From the garden terrace where it had
been planted,
That he might water it.
8 It was planted in good soil by many
waters,
To bring forth branches, bear fruit,
And become a majestic vine." '

9"Say, 'Thus says the Lord GOD:

"Will it thrive?
Will he not pull up its roots,
Cut off its fruit,
And leave it to wither?
All of its spring leaves will wither,
And no great power or many people
Will be needed to pluck it up
by its roots.
10 Behold, *it is* planted,
Will it thrive?
Will it not utterly wither when the east
wind touches it?
It will wither in the garden terrace
where it grew." ' "

11Moreover the word of the LORD came to
me, saying, 12"Say now to the rebellious house:
'Do you not know what these *things mean?*'
Tell *them,* 'Indeed the king of Babylon went to
Jerusalem and took its king and princes, and
led them with him to Babylon. 13And he took

the king's offspring, made a covenant with him, and put him under oath. He also took away the mighty of the land, [14]that the kingdom might be brought low and not lift itself up, *but* that by keeping his covenant it might stand. [15]But he rebelled against him by sending his ambassadors to Egypt, that they might give him horses and many people. Will he prosper? Will he who does such *things* escape? Can he break a covenant and still be delivered?

[16]'*As* I live,' says the Lord GOD, 'surely in the place *where* the king *dwells* who made him king, whose oath he despised and whose covenant he broke—with him in the midst of Babylon he shall die. [17]Nor will Pharaoh with *his* mighty army and great company do anything in the war, when they heap up a siege mound and build a wall to cut off many persons. [18]Since he despised the oath by breaking the covenant, and in fact gave his hand and still did all these *things,* he shall not escape.' "

[19]Therefore thus says the Lord GOD: "*As* I live, surely My oath which he despised, and My covenant which he broke, I will recompense on his own head. [20]I will spread My net over him, and he shall be taken in My snare. I will bring him to Babylon and try him there for the treason which he committed against Me. [21]All his fugitives with all his troops shall fall by the sword, and those who remain shall be scattered to every wind; and you shall know that I, the LORD, have spoken."

[22]Thus says the Lord GOD: "I will take also *one* of the highest branches of the high cedar and set *it* out. I will crop off from the topmost of its young twigs a tender one, and will plant *it* on a high and prominent mountain. [23]On the mountain height of Israel I will plant it; and it will bring forth boughs, and bear fruit, and be a majestic cedar. Under it will dwell birds of every sort; in the shadow of its branches they will dwell. [24]And all the trees of the field shall know that I, the LORD, have brought down the high tree and exalted the low tree, dried up the green tree and made the dry tree flourish; I, the LORD, have spoken and have done *it.*"

17:22,23 ***one* of the highest branches.** This is messianic prophecy stating that God will provide the Messiah from the royal line of David ("the high cedar") and establish Him in His kingdom (like a mountain, Dan. 2:35,44,45). He will be "a high branch" reigning in the height of success. "Branch" is a name for the Messiah (34:23,24; 37:24,25; Is. 4:2; Jer. 23:5; 33:15; Zech. 3:8; 6:12). The Messiah will be "a tender one" (v. 22) who grows into a "majestic cedar" (v. 23). Under His kingdom rule, all nations will be blessed and Israel restored.

18 The word of the LORD came to me again, saying, [2]"What do you mean when you use this proverb concerning the land of Israel, saying:

'The fathers have eaten sour grapes,
And the children's teeth are set on
edge'?

[3]"*As* I live," says the Lord GOD, "You shall no longer use this proverb in Israel.

4 "Behold, all souls are Mine;
The soul of the father
As well as the soul of the son is Mine;
The soul who sins shall die.

18:4 The soul who sins shall die. God played no favorites, but was fair in holding each individual accountable for his own sin. The death is physical death which, for many, results in eternal death.

5 But if a man is just
And does what is lawful and right;
6 If he has not eaten on the mountains,
Nor lifted up his eyes to the idols of the
house of Israel,
Nor defiled his neighbor's wife,
Nor approached a woman during her
impurity;
7 If he has not oppressed anyone,
But has restored to the debtor his
pledge;
Has robbed no one by violence,
But has given his bread to the hungry
And covered the naked with clothing;
8 If he has not exacted usury
Nor taken any increase,
But has withdrawn his hand from
iniquity
And executed true judgment between
man and man;
9 *If* he has walked in My statutes
And kept My judgments faithfully—
He *is* just;
He shall surely live!"
Says the Lord GOD.

10 "If he begets a son *who is* a robber
Or a shedder of blood,
Who does any of these *things*

11 And does none of those *duties,*
But has eaten on the mountains
Or defiled his neighbor's wife;
12 If he has oppressed the poor and needy,
Robbed by violence,
Not restored the pledge,
Lifted his eyes to the idols,
Or committed abomination;
13 If he has exacted usury
Or taken increase—
Shall he then live?
He shall not live!
If he has done any of these abominations,
He shall surely die;
His blood shall be upon him.

14 "*If,* however, he begets a son
Who sees all the sins which his father
has done,
And considers but does not do likewise;
15 *Who* has not eaten on the mountains,
Nor lifted his eyes to the idols of the
house of Israel,
Nor defiled his neighbor's wife;
16 Has not oppressed anyone,
Nor withheld a pledge,
Nor robbed by violence,
But has given his bread to the hungry
And covered the naked with clothing;
17 *Who* has withdrawn his hand from
the poor
And not received usury or increase,
But has executed My judgments
And walked in My statutes—
He shall not die for the iniquity of his
father;
He shall surely live!
18 "*As for* his father,
Because he cruelly oppressed,
Robbed his brother by violence,
And did what *is* not good among his
people,
Behold, he shall die for his iniquity.

19"Yet you say, 'Why should the son not bear
the guilt of the father?' Because the son has done
what is lawful and right, and has kept all My
statutes and observed them, he shall surely
live. 20The soul who sins shall die. The son shall
not bear the guilt of the father, nor the father bear
the guilt of the son. The righteousness of the
righteous shall be upon himself, and the wickedness of the wicked shall be upon himself.

21"But if a wicked man turns from all his sins
which he has committed, keeps all My
statutes, and does what is lawful and right, he
shall surely live; he shall not die. 22None of the
transgressions which he has committed shall
be remembered against him; because of the
righteousness which he has done, he shall live.
23Do I have any pleasure at all that the wicked
should die?" says the Lord GOD, "*and* not that
he should turn from his ways and live?

24"But when a righteous man turns away
from his righteousness and commits iniquity,
and does according to all the abominations
that the wicked *man* does, shall he live? All
the righteousness which he has done shall not
be remembered; because of the unfaithfulness
of which he is guilty and the sin which he has
committed, because of them he shall die.

25"Yet you say, 'The way of the Lord is not
fair.' Hear now, O house of Israel, is it not My
way which is fair, and your ways which are not
fair? 26When a righteous *man* turns away from
his righteousness, commits iniquity, and dies
in it, it is because of the iniquity which he has
done that he dies. 27Again, when a wicked *man*
turns away from the wickedness which he
committed, and does what is lawful and right,
he preserves himself alive. 28Because he considers and turns away from all the transgressions which he committed, he shall surely
live; he shall not die. 29Yet the house of Israel
says, 'The way of the Lord is not fair.' O house
of Israel, is it not My ways which are fair, and
your ways which are not fair?

30"Therefore I will judge you, O house of Israel, every one according to his ways," says the
Lord GOD. "Repent, and turn from all your
transgressions, so that iniquity will not be your
ruin. 31Cast away from you all the transgressions which you have committed, and get yourselves a new heart and a new spirit. For why
should you die, O house of Israel? 32For I have
no pleasure in the death of one who dies," says
the Lord GOD. "Therefore turn and live!"

Psalm 124:1–8

A Song of Ascents. Of David.

"If it had not been the LORD who was
on our side,"
Let Israel now say—
2 "If it had not been the LORD who was
on our side,
When men rose up against us,
3 Then they would have swallowed us
alive,
When their wrath was kindled
against us;
4 Then the waters would have
overwhelmed us,
The stream would have gone over
our soul;
5 Then the swollen waters
Would have gone over our soul."

6 Blessed *be* the LORD,

Who has not given us *as* prey to their
teeth.
7 Our soul has escaped as a bird from
the snare of the fowlers;
The snare is broken, and we have
escaped.
8 Our help *is* in the name of the LORD,
Who made heaven and earth.

Proverbs 28:21

21 To show partiality *is* not good,
Because for a piece of bread a man will
transgress.

Hebrews 9:1–28

9 Then indeed, even the first *covenant* had
ordinances of divine service and the earthly sanctuary. 2For a tabernacle was prepared:
the first *part,* in which *was* the lampstand, the
table, and the showbread, which is called the
sanctuary; 3and behind the second veil, the part
of the tabernacle which is called the Holiest of
All, 4which had the golden censer and the ark
of the covenant overlaid on all sides with gold,
in which *were* the golden pot that had the
manna, Aaron's rod that budded, and the tablets of the covenant; 5and above it were the
cherubim of glory overshadowing the mercy
seat. Of these things we cannot now speak in
detail.
6Now when these things had been thus prepared, the priests always went into the first
part of the tabernacle, performing the services. 7But into the second part the high priest
went alone once a year, not without blood,
which he offered for himself and *for* the people's sins *committed* in ignorance; 8the Holy
Spirit indicating this, that the way into the
Holiest of All was not yet made manifest while
the first tabernacle was still standing. 9It *was*
symbolic for the present time in which both
gifts and sacrifices are offered which cannot
make him who performed the service perfect
in regard to the conscience— 10*concerned* only
with foods and drinks, various washings, and
fleshly ordinances imposed until the time of
reformation.
11But Christ came *as* High Priest of the good
things to come, with the greater and more perfect tabernacle not made with hands, that is,
not of this creation. 12Not with the blood of
goats and calves, but with His own blood He
entered the Most Holy Place once for all, having obtained eternal redemption. 13For if the
blood of bulls and goats and the ashes of a
heifer, sprinkling the unclean, sanctifies for the
purifying of the flesh, 14how much more shall
the blood of Christ, who through the eternal
Spirit offered Himself without spot to God,
cleanse your conscience from dead works to
serve the living God? 15And for this reason He
is the Mediator of the new covenant, by means of
death, for the redemption of the transgressions
under the first covenant, that those who are
called may receive the promise of the eternal
inheritance.
16For where there *is* a testament, there must
also of necessity be the death of the testator.
17For a testament *is* in force after men are dead,
since it has no power at all while the testator
lives. 18Therefore not even the first *covenant*
was dedicated without blood. 19For when Moses had spoken every precept to all the people
according to the law, he took the blood of
calves and goats, with water, scarlet wool, and
hyssop, and sprinkled both the book itself and
all the people, 20saying, *"This is the blood of the
covenant which God has commanded you."*
21Then likewise he sprinkled with blood both the
tabernacle and all the vessels of the ministry.
22And according to the law almost all things are

9:8 The Levitical system did not provide any direct access into God's presence for His people. Rather, it kept them away. Nearness had to be provided by another way (v. 12). This is the primary lesson which the Holy Spirit taught concerning the tabernacle. It teaches how inaccessible God is apart from the death of Jesus Christ. **Holy Spirit.** By the Spirit-inspired instruction given for the Holiest of All, He was indicating that there was no way to God in the ceremonial system. Only Christ could open the way (John 14:6).

9:27 to die once. This is a general rule for all mankind. There have been very rare exceptions (e.g., Lazarus died twice, John 11:43,44). Those, like Lazarus, who were raised from the dead by a miraculous act of our Lord were not resurrected to a glorified body and unending life. They only experienced resuscitation. Another exception will be those who don't die even once, but who will be "caught up…to meet the Lord in the air" (1 Thess. 4:17; Enoch, Gen. 5:24; Elijah, 2 Kin. 2:11). **the judgment.** A general term encompassing the judgment of all people, believers (2 Cor. 5:10) and unbelievers (Rev. 20:11–15).

purified with blood, and without shedding of
blood there is no remission.
[23]Therefore *it was* necessary that the
copies of the things in the heavens should be
purified with these, but the heavenly things
themselves with better sacrifices than these.
[24]For Christ has not entered the holy places
made with hands, *which are* copies of the
true, but into heaven itself, now to appear in
the presence of God for us; [25]not that He
should offer Himself often, as the high priest
enters the Most Holy Place every year with
blood of another— [26]He then would have had
to suffer often since the foundation of the
world; but now, once at the end of the ages,
He has appeared to put away sin by the sacrifice of Himself. [27]And as it is appointed for
men to die once, but after this the judgment,
[28]so Christ was offered once to bear the sins
of many. To those who eagerly wait for Him
He will appear a second time, apart from sin,
for salvation.

DAY 13: Why does Hebrews have so much about blood, including a statement such as "without shedding of blood there is no remission" (9:22)?

Beginning with 9:7, the writer examined the significance of the blood of sacrifice. This term is especially central to 9:1–10:18 where the passage identifies the deaths of Old Testament sacrifices with the death of Christ (9:12–14). Note, however, that this shedding of blood in and of itself was an insufficient sacrifice. Christ had not only to shed His blood, but He also had to die—10:10 indicates that He gave His body as a sacrificial offering. Without His death, His blood had no saving value.

The expression, then, "blood of Christ" (9:14) refers not simply to the fluid but to the whole atoning sacrificial work of Christ in His death. Blood is used as a substitute word for death (see, e.g., Matt. 23:30,35; 27:6,8,24,25; John 6:54–56; Acts 18:6; 20:26). By reviewing the significance of the blood sacrifices in the Old Testament, the writer was pointing to a pattern of lessons that prepared the world to understand the necessity of Christ's death. The emphatic phrase "without shedding of blood there is no remission" (9:22) simply repeats the lesson that sin creates a debt that must be paid by someone. "It is the blood that makes atonement for the soul" (Lev. 17:11). The phraseology is reminiscent of Christ's words, "For this is My blood of the new covenant, which is shed for many for the remission of sins" (Matt. 26:28). Remission means forgiveness in these verses—forgiveness for the sinner and payment of the debt. Christ's death (blood) provides the remission.

NOVEMBER 14

Ezekiel 19:1–20:49

19 "Moreover take up a lamentation for the
princes of Israel, [2]and say:

'What *is* your mother? A lioness:
She lay down among the lions;
Among the young lions she nourished
her cubs.
3 She brought up one of her cubs,
And he became a young lion;
He learned to catch prey,
And he devoured men.
4 The nations also heard of him;
He was trapped in their pit,
And they brought him with chains to
the land of Egypt.
5 'When she saw that she waited, *that*
her hope was lost,
She took another of her cubs *and* made
him a young lion.
6 He roved among the lions,
And became a young lion;
He learned to catch prey;
He devoured men.
7 He knew their desolate places,
And laid waste their cities;
The land with its fullness was
desolated
By the noise of his roaring.
8 Then the nations set against him
from the provinces on every side,
And spread their net over him;
He was trapped in their pit.
9 They put him in a cage with chains,
And brought him to the king of Babylon;
They brought him in nets,
That his voice should no longer be
heard on the mountains of Israel.

10 'Your mother *was* like a vine in your
bloodline,
Planted by the waters,
Fruitful and full of branches
Because of many waters.
11 She had strong branches for scepters
of rulers.

She towered in stature above the thick
branches,
And was seen in her height amid the
dense foliage.
12 But she was plucked up in fury,
She was cast down to the ground,
And the east wind dried her fruit.
Her strong branches were broken and
withered;
The fire consumed them.
13 And now she *is* planted in the wilderness,
In a dry and thirsty land.
14 Fire has come out from a rod of her
branches
And devoured her fruit,
So that she has no strong branch—
a scepter for ruling.' "

This *is* a lamentation, and has become a
lamentation.

20 It came to pass in the seventh year, in
the fifth *month,* on the tenth *day* of the
month, *that* certain of the elders of Israel came
to inquire of the LORD, and sat before me.
[2]Then the word of the LORD came to me, saying, [3]"Son of man, speak to the elders of Israel,
and say to them, 'Thus says the Lord GOD:
"Have you come to inquire of Me? *As* I live,"
says the Lord GOD, "I will not be inquired of by
you." ' [4]Will you judge them, son of man, will
you judge *them?* Then make known to them
the abominations of their fathers.

[5]"Say to them, 'Thus says the Lord GOD:
"On the day when I chose Israel and raised
My hand in an oath to the descendants of the
house of Jacob, and made Myself known to
them in the land of Egypt, I raised My hand in
an oath to them, saying, 'I *am* the LORD your
God.' [6]On that day I raised My hand in an oath
to them, to bring them out of the land of Egypt
into a land that I had searched out for them,
'flowing with milk and honey,' the glory of all
lands. [7]Then I said to them, 'Each of you,
throw away the abominations which are
before his eyes, and do not defile yourselves
with the idols of Egypt. I *am* the LORD your
God.' [8]But they rebelled against Me and would
not obey Me. They did not all cast away the
abominations which were before their eyes,
nor did they forsake the idols of Egypt. Then I
said, 'I will pour out My fury on them and fulfill My anger against them in the midst of the
land of Egypt.' [9]But I acted for My name's
sake, that it should not be profaned before the
Gentiles among whom they *were,* in whose
sight I had made Myself known to them, to
bring them out of the land of Egypt.

[10]"Therefore I made them go out of the land
of Egypt and brought them into the wilderness.
[11]And I gave them My statutes and showed
them My judgments, 'which, *if* a man does, he
shall live by them.' [12]Moreover I also gave
them My Sabbaths, to be a sign between them
and Me, that they might know that I *am* the
LORD who sanctifies them. [13]Yet the house of
Israel rebelled against Me in the wilderness;
they did not walk in My statutes; they despised My judgments, 'which, *if* a man does,
he shall live by them'; and they greatly defiled
My Sabbaths. Then I said I would pour out My
fury on them in the wilderness, to consume
them. [14]But I acted for My name's sake, that it
should not be profaned before the Gentiles, in
whose sight I had brought them out. [15]So I
also raised My hand in an oath to them in the
wilderness, that I would not bring them into
the land which I had given *them,* 'flowing with
milk and honey,' the glory of all lands, [16]be-
cause they despised My judgments and did
not walk in My statutes, but profaned My
Sabbaths; for their heart went after their
idols. [17]Nevertheless My eye spared them
from destruction. I did not make an end of
them in the wilderness.

[18]"But I said to their children in the wilderness, 'Do not walk in the statutes of your
fathers, nor observe their judgments, nor defile
yourselves with their idols. [19]I *am* the LORD
your God: Walk in My statutes, keep My judgments, and do them; [20]hallow My Sabbaths, and
they will be a sign between Me and you, that
you may know that I *am* the LORD your God.'

[21]"Notwithstanding, the children rebelled
against Me; they did not walk in My statutes,
and were not careful to observe My judgments, 'which, *if* a man does, he shall live by
them'; but they profaned My Sabbaths. Then I
said I would pour out My fury on them and fulfill My anger against them in the wilderness.
[22]Nevertheless I withdrew My hand and acted
for My name's sake, that it should not be profaned in the sight of the Gentiles, in whose
sight I had brought them out. [23]Also I raised
My hand in an oath to those in the wilderness,
that I would scatter them among the Gentiles
and disperse them throughout the countries,
[24]because they had not executed My judgments, but had despised My statutes, profaned
My Sabbaths, and their eyes were fixed on
their fathers' idols.

[25]"Therefore I also gave them up to statutes
that were not good, and judgments by which
they could not live; [26]and I pronounced them
unclean because of their ritual gifts, in that
they caused all their firstborn to pass through
the fire, that I might make them desolate and
that they might know that I am the LORD." '

[27]"Therefore, son of man, speak to the house
of Israel, and say to them, 'Thus says the Lord
GOD: "In this too your fathers have blasphemed Me, by being unfaithful to Me. [28]When
I brought them into the land *concerning* which
I had raised My hand in an oath to give them,
and they saw all the high hills and all the thick
trees, there they offered their sacrifices and
provoked Me with their offerings. There they
also sent up their sweet aroma and poured out
their drink offerings. [29]Then I said to them,
'What *is* this high place to which you go?' So
its name is called Bamah to this day." ' [30]There-
fore say to the house of Israel, 'Thus says the
Lord GOD: "Are you defiling yourselves in the
manner of your fathers, and committing harlotry according to their abominations? [31]For
when you offer your gifts and make your sons
pass through the fire, you defile yourselves
with all your idols, even to this day. So shall I
be inquired of by you, O house of Israel? *As* I
live," says the Lord GOD, "I will not be
inquired of by you. [32]What you have in your
mind shall never be, when you say, 'We will be
like the Gentiles, like the families in other
countries, serving wood and stone.'

[33]"*As* I live," says the Lord GOD, "surely with
a mighty hand, with an outstretched arm, and
with fury poured out, I will rule over you. [34]I
will bring you out from the peoples and gather
you out of the countries where you are scattered, with a mighty hand, with an outstretched
arm, and with fury poured out. [35]And I will bring
you into the wilderness of the peoples, and
there I will plead My case with you face to face.
[36]Just as I pleaded My case with your fathers in
the wilderness of the land of Egypt, so I will
plead My case with you," says the Lord GOD.

[37]"I will make you pass under the rod, and I
will bring you into the bond of the covenant; [38]I
will purge the rebels from among you, and
those who transgress against Me; I will bring
them out of the country where they dwell, but
they shall not enter the land of Israel. Then
you will know that I *am* the LORD.

[39]"As for you, O house of Israel," thus says
the Lord GOD: "Go, serve every one of you his
idols—and hereafter—if you will not obey Me;
but profane My holy name no more with your
gifts and your idols. [40]For on My holy mountain, on the mountain height of Israel," says
the Lord GOD, "There all the house of Israel,
all of them in the land, shall serve Me; there I
will accept them, and there I will require your
offerings and the firstfruits of your sacrifices,
together with all your holy things. [41]I will
accept you as a sweet aroma when I bring you
out from the peoples and gather you out of the
countries where you have been scattered; and
I will be hallowed in you before the Gentiles.
[42]Then you shall know that I *am* the LORD,
when I bring you into the land of Israel, into
the country *for* which I raised My hand in an
oath to give to your fathers. [43]And there you
shall remember your ways and all your doings
with which you were defiled; and you shall
loathe yourselves in your own sight because
of all the evils that you have committed. [44]Then
you shall know that I *am* the LORD, when I
have dealt with you for My name's sake, not
according to your wicked ways nor according
to your corrupt doings, O house of Israel,"
says the Lord GOD.' "

[45]Furthermore the word of the LORD came to
me, saying, [46]"Son of man, set your face toward
the south; preach against the south and prophesy against the forest land, the South, [47]and say
to the forest of the South, 'Hear the word of the
LORD! Thus says the Lord GOD: "Behold, I will
kindle a fire in you, and it shall devour every
green tree and every dry tree in you; the blazing flame shall not be quenched, and all faces
from the south to the north shall be scorched
by it. [48]All flesh shall see that I, the LORD, have
kindled it; it shall not be quenched." ' "

[49]Then I said, "Ah, Lord GOD! They say of
me, 'Does he not speak parables?' "

20:37 pass under the rod. God used a shepherd figure here, apt since He was their Great Shepherd (34:11–13; Jer. 23:5–8). As a shepherd, God brings His sheep home to their fold (Jer. 33:13), has them file in, separating sheep from goats (Matt. 25), passing under His shepherd's rod to be noted and checked for injury. He will bring them into the bond of the New Covenant by giving them His Spirit with life (36:24–27; 37:14; 39:29). This is Israel's final salvation (Rom. 11:26–33).

20:39 If they persist in their stubborn idolatry, God will allow them to follow it to their doom. He would also rather have them as out-and-out idolaters rather than hypocritical patronizers of His worship like they had been (Amos 5:21–26).

Psalm 125:1–5

A Song of Ascents.

Those who trust in the LORD
Are like Mount Zion,
Which cannot be moved, *but* abides
forever.

2 As the mountains surround Jerusalem,
So the LORD surrounds His people
From this time forth and forever.

3 For the scepter of wickedness
shall not rest
On the land allotted to the righteous,
Lest the righteous reach out their
hands to iniquity.

4 Do good, O LORD, to *those who are* good,
And to *those who are* upright in their
hearts.

5 As for such as turn aside to their
crooked ways,
The LORD shall lead them away
With the workers of iniquity.

Peace *be* upon Israel!

Proverbs 28:22

22 A man with an evil eye hastens after
riches,
And does not consider that poverty will
come upon him.

Hebrews 10:1–18

10 For the law, having a shadow of the good
things to come, *and* not the very image of
the things, can never with these same sacrifices, which they offer continually year by year,
make those who approach perfect. 2For then
would they not have ceased to be offered? For
the worshipers, once purified, would have had
no more consciousness of sins. 3But in those
sacrifices there is a reminder of sins every
year. 4For *it is* not possible that the blood of
bulls and goats could take away sins.
5Therefore, when He came into the world,
He said:

"Sacrifice and offering You did not desire,
But a body You have prepared for Me.
6 *In burnt offerings and sacrifices for sin*
You had no pleasure.
7 *Then I said, 'Behold, I have come—*
In the volume of the book it is written
of Me—
To do Your will, O God.' "

8Previously saying, *"Sacrifice and offering,*
burnt offerings, and offerings for sin You did
not desire, nor had pleasure in them" (which
are offered according to the law), 9then He
said, *"Behold, I have come to do Your will, O*
God." He takes away the first that He may
establish the second. 10By that will we have

10:5,6 You did not desire. God was not pleased with sacrifices given by a person who did not give them out of a sincere heart (Ps. 51:17; Is. 1:11; Jer. 6:20; Hos. 6:6; Amos 5:21–25). To sacrifice only as a ritual, without obedience, was a mockery and worse than no sacrifice at all (Is. 1:11–18).

been sanctified through the offering of the
body of Jesus Christ once *for all.*
11And every priest stands ministering daily
and offering repeatedly the same sacrifices,
which can never take away sins. 12But this Man,
after He had offered one sacrifice for sins forever, sat down at the right hand of God, 13from
that time waiting till His enemies are made His
footstool. 14For by one offering He has perfected forever those who are being sanctified.
15But the Holy Spirit also witnesses to us; for
after He had said before,
16*"This is the covenant that I will make with*
them after those days, says the LORD: I will put
My laws into their hearts, and in their minds I
will write them," 17*then He adds, "Their sins*
and their lawless deeds I will remember no
more." 18Now where there is remission of
these, *there is* no longer an offering for sin.

10:10 sanctified. "Sanctify" means to "make holy," to be set apart from sin for God (1 Thess. 4:3). When Christ fulfilled the will of God, He provided for the believer a continuing, permanent condition of holiness (Eph. 4:24; 1 Thess. 3:13). This is the believer's positional sanctification as opposed to the progressive sanctification that results from daily walking by the will of God (Rom. 6:19; 12:1,2; 2 Cor. 7:1). **body.** Refers to His atoning death, as the term "blood" has been used to do (9:7,12,14,18,22). Mention of the body of Christ in such a statement is unusual in the New Testament, but it is logically derived from the quotation from Psalm 40:6.

DAY 14: What was the problem with the Old Testament sacrificial system?

"For the law, having a shadow of the good things to come, and not the very image" (Heb. 10:1). The Greek term translated "shadow" refers to a pale reflection, as contrasted with a sharp, distinct one. The term behind "very image," on the other hand, indicates an exact and distinct replica (Col. 2:17). "Can never…make those who approach perfect." This term is used repeatedly in Hebrews to refer to salvation. As much as those living under the law desired to approach God, the Levitical system provided no way to enter His holy presence (Pss. 15:1; 16:11; 24:3,4).

If sin had really been overpowered by that system of sacrifices, the Old Testament believers' consciences would have been cleansed from condemning guilt (v. 2). There was not freedom of conscience under the Old Covenant. The Old Testament sacrifices not only could not remove sin, but their constant repetition was a constant reminder of that deficiency (v. 3). The promise of the New Covenant was that the sin would be removed and even God would "remember" their sins "no more" (8:12, quoting Jer. 31:34).

"For it is not possible that the blood of bulls and goats could take away sins" (v. 4). The Levitical system was not designed by God to remove or forgive sins. It was preparatory for the coming of the Messiah (Gal. 3:24) in that it made the people expectant (1 Pet. 1:10). It revealed the seriousness of their sinful condition, in that even temporary covering required the death of an animal. It revealed the reality of God's holiness and righteousness by indicating that sin had to be covered. Finally, it revealed the necessity of full and complete forgiveness so that God could have desired fellowship with His people.

NOVEMBER 15

Ezekiel 21:1–22:31

21 And the word of the LORD came to me,
saying, [2]"Son of man, set your face toward
Jerusalem, preach against the holy places, and
prophesy against the land of Israel; [3]and say to
the land of Israel, 'Thus says the LORD: "Behold, I *am* against you, and I will draw My
sword out of its sheath and cut off both righteous and wicked from you. [4]Because I will cut
off both righteous and wicked from you, therefore My sword shall go out of its sheath
against all flesh from south *to* north, [5]that all
flesh may know that I, the LORD, have drawn
My sword out of its sheath; it shall not return
anymore." ' [6]Sigh therefore, son of man, with a
breaking heart, and sigh with bitterness
before their eyes. [7]And it shall be when they
say to you, 'Why are you sighing?' that you
shall answer, 'Because of the news; when it
comes, every heart will melt, all hands will be
feeble, every spirit will faint, and all knees will
be weak *as* water. Behold, it is coming and
shall be brought to pass,' says the Lord GOD."
[8]Again the word of the LORD came to me,
saying, [9]"Son of man, prophesy and say, 'Thus
says the LORD!' Say:

'A sword, a sword is sharpened
And also polished!
10 Sharpened to make a dreadful
slaughter,
Polished to flash like lightning!
Should we then make mirth?
It despises the scepter of My son,
As it does all wood.
11 And He has given it to be polished,
That it may be handled;
This sword is sharpened, and it is
polished
To be given into the hand of the slayer.'

12 "Cry and wail, son of man;
For it will be against My people,
Against all the princes of Israel.
Terrors including the sword will be
against My people;
Therefore strike *your* thigh.

13 "Because *it is* a testing,
And what if *the sword* despises even
the scepter?
The scepter shall be no *more,*"

says the Lord GOD.

14 "You therefore, son of man, prophesy,
And strike *your* hands together.
The third time let the sword do double
damage.
It *is* the sword *that* slays,
The sword that slays the great *men,*
That enters their private chambers.
15 I have set the point of the sword against
all their gates,
That the heart may melt and many
may stumble.
Ah! *It is* made bright;
It is grasped for slaughter:

16 "Swords at the ready!
Thrust right!
Set your blade!
Thrust left—
Wherever your edge is ordered!

17 "I also will beat My fists together,
And I will cause My fury to rest;
I, the LORD, have spoken."

[18]The word of the LORD came to me again,
saying: [19]"And son of man, appoint for yourself

two ways for the sword of the king of Babylon
to go; both of them shall go from the same
land. Make a sign; put *it* at the head of the
road to the city. 20 Appoint a road for the sword
to go to Rabbah of the Ammonites, and to Judah, into fortified Jerusalem. 21 For the king of
Babylon stands at the parting of the road, at
the fork of the two roads, to use divination: he
shakes the arrows, he consults the images, he
looks at the liver. 22 In his right hand is the
divination for Jerusalem: to set up battering
rams, to call for a slaughter, to lift the voice with
shouting, to set battering rams against the
gates, to heap up a *siege* mound, and to build a
wall. 23 And it will be to them like a false divination in the eyes of those who have sworn oaths
with them; but he will bring their iniquity to
remembrance, that they may be taken.
24 "Therefore thus says the Lord GOD: 'Because you have made your iniquity to be
remembered, in that your transgressions are
uncovered, so that in all your doings your sins
appear—because you have come to remembrance, you shall be taken in hand.
25 'Now to you, O profane, wicked prince of
Israel, whose day has come, whose iniquity
shall end, 26 thus says the Lord GOD:

"Remove the turban, and take off
the crown;
Nothing *shall remain* the same.
Exalt the humble, and humble the
exalted.
27 Overthrown, overthrown,
I will make it overthrown!
It shall be no *longer,*
Until He comes whose right it is,
And I will give it *to Him.*" '

28 "And you, son of man, prophesy and say,
'Thus says the Lord GOD concerning the
Ammonites and concerning their reproach,'
and say:

'A sword, a sword *is* drawn,
Polished for slaughter,
For consuming, for flashing—
29 While they see false visions for you,
While they divine a lie to you,
To bring you on the necks of the
wicked, the slain
Whose day has come,
Whose iniquity *shall* end.

30 'Return *it* to its sheath.
I will judge you
In the place where you were created,
In the land of your nativity.
31 I will pour out My indignation on you;
I will blow against you with the fire
of My wrath,
And deliver you into the hands of brutal
men *who are* skillful to destroy.
32 You shall be fuel for the fire;
Your blood shall be in the midst
of the land.
You shall not be remembered,
For I the LORD have spoken.' "

22 Moreover the word of the LORD came
to me, saying, 2 "Now, son of man, will
you judge, will you judge the bloody city? Yes,
show her all her abominations! 3 Then say,
'Thus says the Lord GOD: "The city sheds
blood in her own midst, that her time may
come; and she makes idols within herself to
defile herself. 4 You have become guilty by the
blood which you have shed, and have defiled
yourself with the idols which you have made.
You have caused your days to draw near, and
have come to *the end of* your years; therefore I
have made you a reproach to the nations, and
a mockery to all countries. 5 *Those* near and
those far from you will mock you as infamous
and full of tumult.
6 "Look, the princes of Israel: each one has
used his power to shed blood in you. 7 In you
they have made light of father and mother; in
your midst they have oppressed the stranger;
in you they have mistreated the fatherless and
the widow. 8 You have despised My holy things
and profaned My Sabbaths. 9 In you are men
who slander to cause bloodshed; in you are
those who eat on the mountains; in your midst
they commit lewdness. 10 In you men uncover
their fathers' nakedness; in you they violate
women who are set apart during their impurity.
11 One commits abomination with his neighbor's
wife; another lewdly defiles his daughter-in-law;
and another in you violates his sister, his
father's daughter. 12 In you they take bribes to
shed blood; you take usury and increase; you

21:27 Until He comes. The 3-fold mention of "overthrown" expresses the severest degree of unsettled and chaotic conditions. Israel was to experience severe instability and even the kingly privilege will not be Israel's again until the Messiah comes, "to whom it rightly belongs," or "whose right it is" (Gen. 49:10). God will give the kingship to Him (Jer. 23:5–8), the greater "David" (Ezek. 37:24). His "right" is that perfect combination of priestly and royal offices (Heb. 5–7).

---

have made profit from your neighbors by
extortion, and have forgotten Me," says the
Lord GOD.
13"Behold, therefore, I beat My fists at the
dishonest profit which you have made, and at
the bloodshed which has been in your midst.
14Can your heart endure, or can your hands
remain strong, in the days when I shall deal
with you? I, the LORD, have spoken, and will do
it. 15I will scatter you among the nations, disperse you throughout the countries, and remove your filthiness completely from you. 16You
shall defile yourself in the sight of the nations;
then you shall know that I *am* the LORD." ' "
17The word of the LORD came to me, saying,
18"Son of man, the house of Israel has become
dross to Me; they *are* all bronze, tin, iron, and
lead, in the midst of a furnace; they have
become dross from silver. 19Therefore thus
says the Lord GOD: 'Because you have all
become dross, therefore behold, I will gather
you into the midst of Jerusalem. 20*As men*
gather silver, bronze, iron, lead, and tin into
the midst of a furnace, to blow fire on it, to
melt *it;* so I will gather *you* in My anger and
in My fury, and I will leave *you there* and melt
you. 21Yes, I will gather you and blow on you
with the fire of My wrath, and you shall be
melted in its midst. 22As silver is melted in the
midst of a furnace, so shall you be melted in
its midst; then you shall know that I, the
LORD, have poured out My fury on you.' "
23And the word of the LORD came to me, saying, 24"Son of man, say to her: 'You *are* a land
that is not cleansed or rained on in the day of
indignation.' 25The conspiracy of her prophets
in her midst is like a roaring lion tearing the
prey; they have devoured people; they have
taken treasure and precious things; they have
made many widows in her midst. 26Her priests
have violated My law and profaned My holy
things; they have not distinguished between
the holy and unholy, nor have they made
known *the difference* between the unclean and
the clean; and they have hidden their eyes
from My Sabbaths, so that I am profaned
among them. 27Her princes in her midst *are*
like wolves tearing the prey, to shed blood, to
destroy people, and to get dishonest gain.
28Her prophets plastered them with untempered *mortar,* seeing false visions, and divin-
ing lies for them, saying, 'Thus says the Lord
GOD,' when the LORD had not spoken. 29The
people of the land have used oppressions, committed robbery, and mistreated the poor and
needy; and they wrongfully oppress the stranger. 30So I sought for a man among them who
would make a wall, and stand in the gap before
Me on behalf of the land, that I should not
destroy it; but I found no one. 31Therefore I
have poured out My indignation on them; I
have consumed them with the fire of My
wrath; and I have recompensed their deeds on
their own heads," says the Lord GOD.

22:30 So I sought for a man. Ezekiel and Jeremiah were faithful, but apart from them God sought a man capable of advocacy for Israel when its sin had gone so far. But no one could lead the people to repentance and draw the nation back from the brink of the judgment that came in 586 B.C. (Jer. 7:26,36; 19:15). Only God's Messiah, God Himself, will have the character and the credentials sufficient to do what no man can do, intercede for Israel (Is. 59:16–19; 63:5; Rev. 5). He was rejected by them in His earthly ministry, so the effects of this judgment continue today, until they turn to Him in faith (Zech. 12:10; 13:1).

Psalm 126:1–6

A Song of Ascents.

When the LORD brought back
the captivity of Zion,
We were like those who dream.
2 Then our mouth was filled with
laughter,
And our tongue with singing.
Then they said among the nations,
"The LORD has done great things
for them."
3 The LORD has done great things
for us,
And we are glad.

4 Bring back our captivity, O LORD,
As the streams in the South.

5 Those who sow in tears
Shall reap in joy.
6 He who continually goes forth
weeping,
Bearing seed for sowing,
Shall doubtless come again
with rejoicing,
Bringing his sheaves *with him.*

Proverbs 28:23

23 He who rebukes a man will find more
favor afterward
Than he who flatters with the tongue.

Hebrews 10:19–39

19 Therefore, brethren, having boldness to enter the Holiest by the blood of Jesus, 20 by a new and living way which He consecrated for us, through the veil, that is, His flesh, 21 and *having* a High Priest over the house of God, 22 let us draw near with a true heart in full assurance of faith, having our hearts sprinkled from an evil conscience and our bodies washed with pure water. 23 Let us hold fast the confession of *our* hope without wavering, for He who promised *is* faithful. 24 And let us consider one another in order to stir up love and good works, 25 not forsaking the assembling of ourselves together, as *is* the manner of some, but exhorting *one another,* and so much the more as you see the Day approaching.

10:20 new. In Greek, this word originally meant "newly slain," but was understood as "recent" when the epistle was written. The way is new because the covenant is new. It is not a way provided by the Levitical system. **living way.** Though it is the path of eternal life, it was not opened by Christ's sinless life—it required His death. The Hebrews were invited to embark on this way which is characterized by the eternal life of the Son of God who loved them and gave Himself for them (John 14:6; Gal. 2:20). The Christian faith was known as "the Way" among the Jews of Jerusalem (Acts 9:2), as well as among the Gentiles (Acts 19:23). Those receiving this epistle understood quite clearly that the writer was inviting them to become Christians—to join those who had been persecuted for their faith. True believers in their midst were even then suffering persecution, and those who had not committed themselves to the Way were asked to become targets of the same persecution.

26 For if we sin willfully after we have received the knowledge of the truth, there no longer remains a sacrifice for sins, 27 but a certain fearful expectation of judgment, and fiery indignation which will devour the adversaries. 28 Anyone who has rejected Moses' law dies without mercy on *the testimony of* two or three witnesses. 29 Of how much worse punishment, do you suppose, will he be thought worthy who has trampled the Son of God underfoot, counted the blood of the covenant by which he was sanctified a common thing, and insulted the Spirit of grace? 30 For we know Him who said, *"Vengeance is Mine, I will repay,"* says the Lord. And again, *"The* LORD *will judge His people."* 31 It is a fearful thing to fall into the hands of the living God.

32 But recall the former days in which, after you were illuminated, you endured a great struggle with sufferings: 33 partly while you were made a spectacle both by reproaches and tribulations, and partly while you became companions of those who were so treated; 34 for you had compassion on me in my chains, and joyfully accepted the plundering of your goods, knowing that you have a better and an enduring possession for yourselves in heaven. 35 Therefore do not cast away your confidence, which has great reward. 36 For you have need of endurance, so that after you have done the will of God, you may receive the promise:

37 *"For yet a little while,*
And He who is coming will come
and will not tarry.
38 *Now the just shall live by faith;*
But if anyone draws back,
My soul has no pleasure in him."

39 But we are not of those who draw back to perdition, but of those who believe to the saving of the soul.

DAY 15: How do we draw near to God?

"Let us draw near with a true heart" (Heb. 10:22). Based on what had been written, this was the heart of the invitation to those in the assembly who had not come to Christ. The same invitation is found in the first New Testament book to be written (James 4:8), where James reveals the corollary of drawing near to God: God will draw near to you. Asaph taught that it is a good thing to draw near to God (Ps. 73:28). The full restoration of Israel to God's blessing is dependent upon their drawing near to Him (Jer. 30:18–22). In other words, it is an eschatological invitation coming to them in "these last days" (Heb. 1:2). This verse describes the prerequisites for entering the presence of God (Ps. 15): sincerity, security, salvation, and sanctification. The Greek term behind "true" carries the ideas of being sincere, genuine, and without ulterior motive (Jer. 24:7; Matt. 15:8). This one thing these particular Hebrews lacked: genuine commitment to Christ.

"In full assurance of faith." Utter confidence in the promises of God is intended by the phrase. Such confidence will result in heartfelt assurance or security which will allow them to persevere through the coming trials. This is the first of a familiar triad: faith, hope (v. 23), and love (v. 24).

"Having our hearts sprinkled…with pure water." The imagery in this verse is taken from the sacrificial ceremonies of the Old Covenant, where blood was sprinkled as a sign of cleansing, and the priests were continually washing themselves and the sacred vessels in basins of clear water. The "washing with pure water" does not refer to Christian baptism, but to the Holy Spirit's purifying one's life by means of the Word of God (Eph. 5:25,26; Titus 3:5). This is purely a New Covenant picture (Jer. 31:33; Ezek. 36:25,26).

NOVEMBER 16

Ezekiel 23:1–24:27

23 The word of the LORD came again to me, saying:

2 "Son of man, there were two women,
The daughters of one mother.
3 They committed harlotry in Egypt,
They committed harlotry in their youth;
Their breasts were there embraced,
Their virgin bosom was there pressed.
4 Their names: Oholah the elder and Oholibah her sister;
They were Mine,
And they bore sons and daughters.
As for their names,
Samaria *is* Oholah, and Jerusalem *is* Oholibah.

5 "Oholah played the harlot even though she was Mine;
And she lusted for her lovers, the neighboring Assyrians,
6 *Who were* clothed in purple,
Captains and rulers,
All of them desirable young men,
Horsemen riding on horses.
7 Thus she committed her harlotry with them,
All of them choice men of Assyria;
And with all for whom she lusted,
With all their idols, she defiled herself.
8 She has never given up her harlotry *brought* from Egypt,
For in her youth they had lain with her,
Pressed her virgin bosom,
And poured out their immorality upon her.

9 "Therefore I have delivered her
Into the hand of her lovers,
Into the hand of the Assyrians,
For whom she lusted.
10 They uncovered her nakedness,
Took away her sons and daughters,
And slew her with the sword;
She became a byword among women,
For they had executed judgment on her.

11 "Now although her sister Oholibah saw
this, she became more corrupt in her lust than
she, and in her harlotry more corrupt than her
sister's harlotry.

12 "She lusted for the neighboring Assyrians,
Captains and rulers,
Clothed most gorgeously,
Horsemen riding on horses,
All of them desirable young men.
13 Then I saw that she was defiled;
Both *took* the same way.
14 But she increased her harlotry;
She looked at men portrayed on the wall,
Images of Chaldeans portrayed in vermilion,
15 Girded with belts around their waists,
Flowing turbans on their heads,
All of them looking like captains,
In the manner of the Babylonians of Chaldea,
The land of their nativity.
16 As soon as her eyes saw them,
She lusted for them
And sent messengers to them in Chaldea.

17 "Then the Babylonians came to her, into the bed of love,
And they defiled her with their immorality;
So she was defiled by them, and alienated herself from them.
18 She revealed her harlotry and uncovered her nakedness.
Then I alienated Myself from her,
As I had alienated Myself from her sister.

19 "Yet she multiplied her harlotry
In calling to remembrance the days of her youth,
When she had played the harlot in the land of Egypt.
20 For she lusted for her paramours,
Whose flesh *is like* the flesh of donkeys,
And whose issue *is like* the issue of horses.

21 Thus you called to remembrance the
lewdness of your youth,
When the Egyptians pressed your
bosom
Because of your youthful breasts.

22"Therefore, Oholibah, thus says the Lord
GOD:

'Behold, I will stir up your lovers
against you,
From whom you have alienated yourself,
And I will bring them against you from
every side:
23 The Babylonians,
All the Chaldeans,
Pekod, Shoa, Koa,
All the Assyrians with them,
All of them desirable young men,
Governors and rulers,
Captains and men of renown,
All of them riding on horses.
24 And they shall come against you
With chariots, wagons, and war-horses,
With a horde of people.
They shall array against you
Buckler, shield, and helmet all around.

'I will delegate judgment to them,
And they shall judge you according to
their judgments.
25 I will set My jealousy against you,
And they shall deal furiously with you;
They shall remove your nose
and your ears,
And your remnant shall fall by the
sword;
They shall take your sons and your
daughters,
And your remnant shall be devoured
by fire.
26 They shall also strip you of your clothes
And take away your beautiful jewelry.

27 'Thus I will make you cease your
lewdness and your harlotry
Brought from the land of Egypt,
So that you will not lift your eyes to
them,
Nor remember Egypt anymore.'

28"For thus says the Lord GOD: 'Surely I will
deliver you into the hand of those you hate,
into the hand *of those* from whom you alienated yourself. 29They will deal hatefully with you,
take away all you have worked for, and leave
you naked and bare. The nakedness of your
harlotry shall be uncovered, both your lewdness and your harlotry. 30I will do these *things*
to you because you have gone as a harlot after
the Gentiles, because you have become
defiled by their idols. 31You have walked in the
way of your sister; therefore I will put her cup
in your hand.'

32"Thus says the Lord GOD:

'You shall drink of your sister's cup,
The deep and wide one;
You shall be laughed to scorn
And held in derision;
It contains much.
33 You will be filled with drunkenness and
sorrow,
The cup of horror and desolation,
The cup of your sister Samaria.
34 You shall drink and drain it,
You shall break its shards,
And tear at your own breasts;
For I have spoken,'
Says the Lord GOD.

35"Therefore thus says the Lord GOD:

'Because you have forgotten Me and
cast Me behind your back,
Therefore you shall bear the *penalty*
Of your lewdness and your harlotry.' "

36The LORD also said to me: "Son of man, will
you judge Oholah and Oholibah? Then declare to them their abominations. 37For they
have committed adultery, and blood *is* on their
hands. They have committed adultery with
their idols, and even *sacrificed* their sons whom
they bore to Me, passing them through *the fire,*
to devour *them.* 38Moreover they have done this
to Me: They have defiled My sanctuary on the
same day and profaned My Sabbaths. 39For
after they had slain their children for their
idols, on the same day they came into My sanctuary to profane it; and indeed thus they have
done in the midst of My house.

40"Furthermore you sent for men to come
from afar, to whom a messenger *was* sent; and
there they came. And you washed yourself for
them, painted your eyes, and adorned yourself
with ornaments. 41You sat on a stately couch,
with a table prepared before it, on which you
had set My incense and My oil. 42The sound of
a carefree multitude *was* with her, and
Sabeans *were* brought from the wilderness
with men of the common sort, who put
bracelets on their wrists and beautiful crowns
on their heads. 43Then I said concerning *her*
who had grown old in adulteries, 'Will they
commit harlotry with her now, and she *with*
them?' 44Yet they went in to her, as men go in to
a woman who plays the harlot; thus they went
in to Oholah and Oholibah, the lewd women.
45But righteous men will judge them after the
manner of adulteresses, and after the manner

of women who shed blood, because they *are*
adulteresses, and blood *is* on their hands.
46“For thus says the Lord GOD: ‘Bring up an
assembly against them, give them up to trouble and plunder. 47The assembly shall stone
them with stones and execute them with their
swords; they shall slay their sons and their
daughters, and burn their houses with fire.
48Thus I will cause lewdness to cease from the
land, that all women may be taught not to
practice your lewdness. 49They shall repay you
for your lewdness, and you shall pay for your
idolatrous sins. Then you shall know that I *am*
the Lord GOD.’ ”

24 Again, in the ninth year, in the tenth
month, on the tenth *day* of the month,
the word of the LORD came to me, saying,
2“Son of man, write down the name of the day,
this very day—the king of Babylon started his
siege against Jerusalem this very day. 3And
utter a parable to the rebellious house, and
say to them, ‘Thus says the Lord GOD:

“Put on a pot, set *it* on,
And also pour water into it.
4 Gather pieces *of meat* in it,
Every good piece,
The thigh and the shoulder.
Fill *it* with choice cuts;
5 Take the choice of the flock.
Also pile *fuel* bones under it,
Make it boil well,
And let the cuts simmer in it.”

6“Therefore thus says the Lord GOD:

“Woe to the bloody city,
To the pot whose scum *is* in it,
And whose scum is not gone from it!
Bring it out piece by piece,
On which no lot has fallen.
7 For her blood is in her midst;
She set it on top of a rock;
She did not pour it on the ground,
To cover it with dust.
8 That it may raise up fury and take
vengeance,
I have set her blood on top of a rock,
That it may not be covered.”

9“Therefore thus says the Lord GOD:

“Woe to the bloody city!
I too will make the pyre great.
10 Heap on the wood,
Kindle the fire;
Cook the meat well,
Mix in the spices,
And let the cuts be burned up.
11 “Then set the pot empty on the coals,
That it may become hot and its bronze
may burn,
That its filthiness may be melted in it,
That its scum may be consumed.
12 She has grown weary with lies,
And her great scum has not gone
from her.
Let her scum *be* in the fire!
13 In your filthiness *is* lewdness.
Because I have cleansed you,
and you were not cleansed,
You will not be cleansed of your
filthiness anymore,
Till I have caused My fury to rest
upon you.
14 I, the LORD, have spoken *it;*
It shall come to pass, and I will do *it;*
I will not hold back,
Nor will I spare,
Nor will I relent;
According to your ways
And according to your deeds
They will judge you,”
Says the Lord GOD.’ ”

15Also the word of the LORD came to me, saying, 16“Son of man, behold, I take away from
you the desire of your eyes with one stroke;
yet you shall neither mourn nor weep, nor
shall your tears run down. 17Sigh in silence,
make no mourning for the dead; bind your turban on your head, and put your sandals on your
feet; do not cover *your* lips, and do not eat man’s
bread *of sorrow.*”
18So I spoke to the people in the morning,
and at evening my wife died; and the next
morning I did as I was commanded.
19And the people said to me, “Will you not
tell us what these *things signify* to us, that you
behave so?”
20Then I answered them, “The word of the
LORD came to me, saying, 21‘Speak to the
house of Israel, “Thus says the Lord GOD: ‘Behold, I will profane My sanctuary, your arrogant boast, the desire of your eyes, the delight

24:16–27 Ezekiel’s wife died as a sign to Israel. All personal sorrow was eclipsed in the universal calamity. Just as Ezekiel was not to mourn the death of his wife (v. 17), so Israel was not to mourn the death of her families (vv. 19–24). Though the text emphasizes how precious his wife was, the “desire of [his] eyes” (vv. 16,21), his “boast” and “delight” (v. 21), he was obedient and submitted to God’s will. He became a heartbreaking sign to his people.

of your soul; and your sons and daughters
whom you left behind shall fall by the sword.
[22]And you shall do as I have done; you shall not
cover *your* lips nor eat man's bread *of sorrow.*
[23]Your turbans shall be on your heads and your
sandals on your feet; you shall neither mourn
nor weep, but you shall pine away in your iniquities and mourn with one another. [24]Thus
Ezekiel is a sign to you; according to all that he
has done you shall do; and when this comes,
you shall know that I *am* the Lord GOD.' "
[25]'And you, son of man—*will it* not *be* in the
day when I take from them their stronghold,
their joy and their glory, the desire of their
eyes, and that on which they set their minds,
their sons and their daughters: [26]*that* on that day
one who escapes will come to you to let *you* hear
it with *your* ears? [27]On that day your mouth will
be opened to him who has escaped; you shall
speak and no longer be mute. Thus you will be
a sign to them, and they shall know that I *am*
the LORD.' "

Psalm 127:1–5

A Song of Ascents. Of Solomon.

Unless the LORD builds the house,
They labor in vain who build it;
Unless the LORD guards the city,
The watchman stays awake in vain.
2 *It is* vain for you to rise up early,
To sit up late,
To eat the bread of sorrows;
For so He gives His beloved sleep.

3 Behold, children *are* a heritage from
the LORD,
The fruit of the womb *is* a reward.

127:3 heritage...reward. Children are a blessing from the Lord. There are overtones of God's promise to Abraham to make his offspring like the dust of the earth and the stars of heaven (Gen. 13:16; 15:5).

4 Like arrows in the hand of a warrior,
So *are* the children of one's youth.
5 Happy *is* the man who has his quiver
full of them;
They shall not be ashamed,
But shall speak with their enemies in
the gate.

Proverbs 28:24

24 Whoever robs his father or his mother,
And says, "*It is* no transgression,"
The same *is* companion to a destroyer.

Hebrews 11:1–16

11 Now faith is the substance of things hoped
for, the evidence of things not seen. [2]For
by it the elders obtained a *good* testimony.
[3]By faith we understand that the worlds were
framed by the word of God, so that the things
which are seen were not made of things which
are visible.
[4]By faith Abel offered to God a more excellent sacrifice than Cain, through which he
obtained witness that he was righteous, God
testifying of his gifts; and through it he being
dead still speaks.
[5]By faith Enoch was taken away so that he
did not see death, *"and was not found, because*
God had taken him"; for before he was taken
he had this testimony, that he pleased God.
[6]But without faith *it is* impossible to please
Him, for he who comes to God must believe
that He is, and *that* He is a rewarder of those
who diligently seek Him.

11:6 impossible to please. Enoch pleased God because he had faith. Without such faith it is not possible for anyone to "walk with God" or "please Him" (10:38). **He is.** The emphasis here is on "He," the true God. Genuine faith does not simply believe that *a* divine being exists, but that the God of Scripture is the *only* real and true God who exists. Not believing that God exists is equivalent to calling Him a liar (1 John 5:10). **rewarder.** A person must believe not only that the true God exists, but also that He will reward men's faith in Him with forgiveness and righteousness, because He has promised to do so (10:35; Gen. 15:1; Deut. 4:29; 1 Chr. 28:9; Ps. 58:11; Is. 40:10).

[7]By faith Noah, being divinely warned of
things not yet seen, moved with godly fear,
prepared an ark for the saving of his household, by which he condemned the world and
became heir of the righteousness which is
according to faith.
[8]By faith Abraham obeyed when he was
called to go out to the place which he would
receive as an inheritance. And he went out,
not knowing where he was going. [9]By faith he
dwelt in the land of promise as *in* a foreign
country, dwelling in tents with Isaac and Jacob, the heirs with him of the same promise;
[10]for he waited for the city which has foundations, whose builder and maker *is* God.
[11]By faith Sarah herself also received
strength to conceive seed, and she bore a

11:13–16 strangers and pilgrims. See Genesis 23:4. Their faith was patient and endured great hardships because they believed God had something better. They had no desire to go back to Ur, but did long for heaven (Job 19:25,26; Ps. 27:4).

child when she was past the age, because she judged Him faithful who had promised. 12 Therefore from one man, and him as good as dead, were born *as many* as the stars of the sky in multitude—innumerable as the sand which is by the seashore.

13 These all died in faith, not having received the promises, but having seen them afar off were assured of them, embraced *them* and confessed that they were strangers and pilgrims on the earth. 14 For those who say such things declare plainly that they seek a homeland. 15 And truly if they had called to mind that *country* from which they had come out, they would have had opportunity to return. 16 But now they desire a better, that is, a heavenly *country*. Therefore God is not ashamed to be called their God, for He has prepared a city for them.

DAY 16: Why are so many Old Testament people listed in chapter 11?

The eleventh chapter of Hebrews offers a moving account of faithful Old Testament saints who remain models of faith. The chapter has received such titles as "The Saint's Hall of Fame," "The Honor Roll of Old Testament Saints," and "Heroes of the Faith." Their lives attest to the value of living by faith. They compose the "cloud of witnesses" (12:1) who give powerful testimony to the Hebrews that they should come to faith in Christ.

This passage begins with an emphatic statement about the nature of faith. Faith involves the most solid possible conviction—the God-given present assurance of a future reality. True faith is not based on empirical evidence but on divine assurance and is a gift of God (Eph. 2:8).

The names, accomplishments, and sufferings described in this chapter illustrate the range of faithfulness in the lives of saints. Some experienced great success in this world; whereas others suffered great affliction. The point is that they all courageously and uncompromisingly followed God, regardless of the earthly outcome. They placed their trust in Him and in His promises (see 6:12; 2 Tim. 3:12).

NOVEMBER 17

Ezekiel 25:1–26:21

25 The word of the LORD came to me, saying, 2 "Son of man, set your face against the Ammonites, and prophesy against them. 3 Say to the Ammonites, 'Hear the word of the Lord GOD! Thus says the Lord GOD: "Because you said, 'Aha!' against My sanctuary when it was profaned, and against the land of Israel when it was desolate, and against the house of Judah when they went into captivity, 4 indeed, therefore, I will deliver you as a possession to the men of the East, and they shall set their encampments among you and make their dwellings among you; they shall eat your fruit, and they shall drink your milk. 5 And I will make Rabbah a stable for camels and Ammon a resting place for flocks. Then you shall know that I *am* the LORD."

6 "For thus says the Lord GOD: "Because you clapped *your* hands, stamped your feet, and rejoiced in heart with all your disdain for the land of Israel, 7 indeed, therefore, I will stretch out My hand against you, and give you as plunder to the nations; I will cut you off from the peoples, and I will cause you to perish from the countries; I will destroy you, and you shall know that I *am* the LORD."

8 "Thus says the Lord GOD: "Because Moab and Seir say, 'Look! The house of Judah *is* like all the nations,' 9 therefore, behold, I will clear the territory of Moab of cities, of the cities on its frontier, the glory of the country, Beth Jeshimoth, Baal Meon, and Kirjathaim. 10 To the men of the East I will give it as a possession, together with the Ammonites, that the Ammonites may not be remembered among the nations. 11 And I will execute judgments upon Moab, and they shall know that I *am* the LORD."

12 "Thus says the Lord GOD: "Because of what Edom did against the house of Judah by taking vengeance, and has greatly offended by avenging itself on them," 13 therefore thus says the Lord GOD: "I will also stretch out My hand against Edom, cut off man and beast from it, and make it desolate from Teman; Dedan shall fall by the sword. 14 I will lay My

vengeance on Edom by the hand of My people
Israel, that they may do in Edom according to
My anger and according to My fury; and they
shall know My vengeance," says the Lord GOD.
15"Thus says the Lord GOD: "Because the
Philistines dealt vengefully and took vengeance
with a spiteful heart, to destroy because of the
old hatred," 16therefore thus says the Lord
GOD: "I will stretch out My hand against the
Philistines, and I will cut off the Cherethites
and destroy the remnant of the seacoast. 17I
will execute great vengeance on them with
furious rebukes; and they shall know that I *am*
the LORD, when I lay My vengeance upon
them." ' "

26 And it came to pass in the eleventh
year, on the first *day* of the month, *that*
the word of the LORD came to me, saying,
2"Son of man, because Tyre has said against
Jerusalem, 'Aha! She is broken who *was* the
gateway of the peoples; now she is turned
over to me; I shall be filled; she is laid waste.'
3"Therefore thus says the Lord GOD: 'Behold, I *am* against you, O Tyre, and will cause
many nations to come up against you, as the
sea causes its waves to come up. 4And they
shall destroy the walls of Tyre and break
down her towers; I will also scrape her dust
from her, and make her like the top of a rock. 5It
shall be *a place for* spreading nets in the midst
of the sea, for I have spoken,' says the Lord
GOD; 'it shall become plunder for the nations.
6Also her daughter *villages* which *are* in the
fields shall be slain by the sword. Then they
shall know that I *am* the LORD.'
7"For thus says the Lord GOD: 'Behold, I will
bring against Tyre from the north Nebuchadnezzar king of Babylon, king of kings, with
horses, with chariots, and with horsemen, and
an army with many people. 8He will slay with
the sword your daughter *villages* in the fields;
he will heap up a siege mound against you,
build a wall against you, and raise a defense
against you. 9He will direct his battering rams
against your walls, and with his axes he will
break down your towers. 10Because of the
abundance of his horses, their dust will cover
you; your walls will shake at the noise of the
horsemen, the wagons, and the chariots,
when he enters your gates, as men enter a city
that has been breached. 11With the hooves of
his horses he will trample all your streets; he
will slay your people by the sword, and your
strong pillars will fall to the ground. 12They will
plunder your riches and pillage your merchandise; they will break down your walls and
destroy your pleasant houses; they will lay
your stones, your timber, and your soil in the
midst of the water. 13I will put an end to the
sound of your songs, and the sound of your
harps shall be heard no more. 14I will make
you like the top of a rock; you shall be *a place*
for spreading nets, and you shall never be
rebuilt, for I the LORD have spoken,' says the
Lord GOD.
15"Thus says the Lord GOD to Tyre: 'Will
the coastlands not shake at the sound of your
fall, when the wounded cry, when slaughter is
made in the midst of you? 16Then all the
princes of the sea will come down from their
thrones, lay aside their robes, and take off
their embroidered garments; they will clothe
themselves with trembling; they will sit on
the ground, tremble *every* moment, and be
astonished at you. 17And they will take up a
lamentation for you, and say to you:

"How you have perished,
O one inhabited by seafaring men,
O renowned city,
Who was strong at sea,
She and her inhabitants,
Who caused their terror *to be*
on all her inhabitants!
18 Now the coastlands tremble on the day
of your fall;
Yes, the coastlands by the sea are
troubled at your departure." '

19"For thus says the Lord GOD: 'When I
make you a desolate city, like cities that are
not inhabited, when I bring the deep upon
you, and great waters cover you, 20then I will
bring you down with those who descend into
the Pit, to the people of old, and I will make
you dwell in the lowest part of the earth, in
places desolate from antiquity, with those who
go down to the Pit, so that you may never be
inhabited; and I shall establish glory in the
land of the living. 21I will make you a terror,
and you *shall be* no *more;* though you are
sought for, you will never be found again,' says
the Lord GOD."

Psalm 128:1–6

A Song of Ascents.

Blessed *is* every one who fears
the LORD,
Who walks in His ways.
2 When you eat the labor of your hands,
You *shall be* happy, and *it shall be* well
with you.
3 Your wife *shall be* like a fruitful vine
In the very heart of your house,

128:1 who fears the LORD. A good working definition is provided by the parallel line, "who walks in His ways." Fathers (Ps. 128:1, 4), mothers (Prov. 31:30), and children (Ps. 34:11) are to fear the Lord. This psalm may have been the basis for Jesus' illustration of the two builders (Matt. 7:24–27).

Your children like olive plants
All around your table.
4 Behold, thus shall the man be blessed
Who fears the LORD.

5 The LORD bless you out of Zion,
And may you see the good
of Jerusalem
All the days of your life.
6 Yes, may you see your children's
children.

Peace *be* upon Israel!

Proverbs 28:25

25 He who is of a proud heart stirs up
strife,
But he who trusts in the LORD will be
prospered.

Hebrews 11:17–40

[17]By faith Abraham, when he was tested, offered up Isaac, and he who had received the promises offered up his only begotten *son,* [18]of whom it was said, *"In Isaac your seed shall be called,"* [19]concluding that God *was* able to raise *him* up, even from the dead, from which he also received him in a figurative sense.

[20]By faith Isaac blessed Jacob and Esau concerning things to come.

[21]By faith Jacob, when he was dying, blessed each of the sons of Joseph, and worshiped, *leaning* on the top of his staff.

[22]By faith Joseph, when he was dying, made mention of the departure of the children of Israel, and gave instructions concerning his bones.

[23]By faith Moses, when he was born, was hidden three months by his parents, because they saw *he was* a beautiful child; and they were not afraid of the king's command.

[24]By faith Moses, when he became of age, refused to be called the son of Pharaoh's daughter, [25]choosing rather to suffer affliction with the people of God than to enjoy the passing pleasures of sin, [26]esteeming the reproach of Christ greater riches than the treasures in Egypt; for he looked to the reward.

[27]By faith he forsook Egypt, not fearing the wrath of the king; for he endured as seeing Him who is invisible. [28]By faith he kept the Passover and the sprinkling of blood, lest he who destroyed the firstborn should touch them.

[29]By faith they passed through the Red Sea as by dry *land, whereas* the Egyptians, attempting to do so, were drowned.

[30]By faith the walls of Jericho fell down after they were encircled for seven days. [31]By faith the harlot Rahab did not perish with those who did not believe, when she had received the spies with peace.

[32]And what more shall I say? For the time would fail me to tell of Gideon and Barak and Samson and Jephthah, also *of* David and Samuel and the prophets: [33]who through faith subdued kingdoms, worked righteousness, obtained promises, stopped the mouths of lions, [34]quenched the violence of fire, escaped the edge of the sword, out of weakness were made strong, became valiant in battle, turned to flight the armies of the aliens. [35]Women received their dead raised to life again.

Others were tortured, not accepting deliverance, that they might obtain a better resurrection. [36]Still others had trial of mockings and scourgings, yes, and of chains and imprisonment. [37]They were stoned, they were sawn in two, were tempted, were slain with the sword. They wandered about in sheepskins and goatskins, being destitute, afflicted, tormented— [38]of whom the world was not worthy. They wandered in deserts and mountains, *in* dens and caves of the earth.

[39]And all these, having obtained a good testimony through faith, did not receive the promise, [40]God having provided something better for us, that they should not be made perfect apart from us.

11:19 even from the dead. Believing that God's promise regarding Isaac was unconditional, Abraham came to the conclusion that God would fulfill that promise even if it required raising Isaac from the dead (Gen. 22:5). **figurative sense.** The word is the same as in 9:9, which is the basis for the English word "parable." Abraham received Isaac back from the dead, as it were, even though Isaac had not been slain.

DAY 17: How did faith shape the life of Moses?

In Hebrews 11:24, we are told that "By faith Moses, when he became of age," refused the fame he could have in Egypt if he would have capitalized on his position as the adopted son of Pharaoh's daughter (Ex. 2:10). "Choosing rather to suffer affliction with the people of God" (v. 25). Moses would have sinned had he refused to take on the responsibility God gave him regarding Israel, and he had a clear and certain conviction that "God would deliver them by his hand" (Acts 7:25). Moses repudiated the pleasures of Egypt.

"Esteeming the reproach of Christ greater riches than the treasures of Egypt" (v. 26). Moses suffered reproach for the sake of Christ in the sense that he identified with the Messiah's people in their suffering (v. 25). In addition, Moses identified himself with the Messiah because of his own role as leader and prophet (12:2; Deut. 18:15; Pss. 69:9; 89:51). Moses knew of the sufferings and glory of the Messiah (John 5:46; Acts 26:22,23; 1 Pet. 1:10–12).

"By faith he forsook Egypt" (v. 27). Moses left Egypt for the first time when he fled for his life after killing the Egyptian slave master (Ex. 2:14,15). That time he did fear Pharaoh's wrath. On the second occasion, he turned his back on Egypt and all that it represented. This leaving was not for fear of Pharaoh, so it is the one in view here. "Seeing Him who is invisible." Moses' faith was such that he responded to God's commands as though God were standing visibly before him. This was the basis for his loyalty to God, and it should be a believer's example for loyalty (2 Cor. 4:16–18).

NOVEMBER 18

Ezekiel 27:1–28:26

27 The word of the LORD came again to
me, saying, [2]"Now, son of man, take up
a lamentation for Tyre, [3]and say to Tyre, 'You
who are situated at the entrance of the sea,
merchant of the peoples on many coastlands,
thus says the Lord GOD:

"O Tyre, you have said,
'I *am* perfect in beauty.'
4 Your borders *are* in the midst of the seas.
Your builders have perfected your beauty.
5 They made all *your* planks of fir trees from Senir;
They took a cedar from Lebanon to make you a mast.
6 *Of* oaks from Bashan they made your oars;
The company of Ashurites have inlaid your planks
With ivory from the coasts of Cyprus.
7 Fine embroidered linen from Egypt was what you spread for your sail;
Blue and purple from the coasts of Elishah was what covered you.

8 "Inhabitants of Sidon and Arvad were your oarsmen;
Your wise men, O Tyre, were in you;
They became your pilots.
9 Elders of Gebal and its wise men
Were in you to caulk your seams;
All the ships of the sea
And their oarsmen were in you
To market your merchandise.

10 "Those from Persia, Lydia, and Libya
Were in your army as men of war;
They hung shield and helmet in you;
They gave splendor to you.
11 Men of Arvad with your army *were* on your walls *all* around,
And the men of Gammad were in your towers;
They hung their shields on your walls *all* around;
They made your beauty perfect.

[12]"Tarshish *was* your merchant because of
your many luxury goods. They gave you silver,
iron, tin, and lead for your goods. [13]Javan,
Tubal, and Meshech *were* your traders. They
bartered human lives and vessels of bronze for
your merchandise. [14]Those from the house of
Togarmah traded for your wares with horses,
steeds, and mules. [15]The men of Dedan *were*
your traders; many isles *were* the market of your
hand. They brought you ivory tusks and
ebony as payment. [16]Syria *was* your merchant
because of the abundance of goods you made.
They gave you for your wares emeralds, purple, embroidery, fine linen, corals, and rubies.
[17]Judah and the land of Israel *were* your
traders. They traded for your merchandise
wheat of Minnith, millet, honey, oil, and balm.
[18]Damascus *was* your merchant because of the
abundance of goods you made, because of
your many luxury items, with the wine of
Helbon and with white wool. [19]Dan and Javan
paid for your wares, traversing back and forth.
Wrought iron, cassia, and cane were among
your merchandise. [20]Dedan *was* your merchant
in saddlecloths for riding. [21]Arabia and all the

princes of Kedar *were* your regular merchants. They traded with you in lambs, rams, and goats. [22]The merchants of Sheba and Raamah *were* your merchants. They traded for your wares the choicest spices, all kinds of precious stones, and gold. [23]Haran, Canneh, Eden, the merchants of Sheba, Assyria, *and* Chilmad *were* your merchants. [24]These *were* your merchants in choice items—in purple clothes, in embroidered garments, in chests of multicolored apparel, in sturdy woven cords, which were in your marketplace.

25 "The ships of Tarshish were carriers of your merchandise.
You were filled and very glorious in the midst of the seas.
26 Your oarsmen brought you into many waters,
But the east wind broke you in the midst of the seas.

27 "Your riches, wares, and merchandise,
Your mariners and pilots,
Your caulkers and merchandisers,
All your men of war who *are* in you,
And the entire company which *is* in your midst,
Will fall into the midst of the seas on the day of your ruin.
28 The common-land will shake at the sound of the cry of your pilots.

29 "All who handle the oar,
The mariners,
All the pilots of the sea
Will come down from their ships
and stand on the shore.
30 They will make their voice heard because of you;
They will cry bitterly and cast dust on their heads;
They will roll about in ashes;
31 They will shave themselves completely bald because of you,
Gird themselves with sackcloth,
And weep for you
With bitterness of heart *and* bitter wailing.
32 In their wailing for you
They will take up a lamentation,
And lament for you:
'What *city is* like Tyre,
Destroyed in the midst of the sea?

33 'When your wares went out by sea,
You satisfied many people;
You enriched the kings of the earth
With your many luxury goods and your merchandise.
34 But you are broken by the seas in the depths of the waters;
Your merchandise and the entire company will fall in your midst.
35 All the inhabitants of the isles will be astonished at you;
Their kings will be greatly afraid,
And *their* countenance will be troubled.
36 The merchants among the peoples will hiss at you;
You will become a horror, and *be* no more forever.' " ' "

28 The word of the LORD came to me again, saying, [2]"Son of man, say to the prince of Tyre, 'Thus says the Lord GOD:

"Because your heart *is* lifted up,
And you say, 'I *am* a god,
I sit *in* the seat of gods,
In the midst of the seas,'
Yet you *are* a man, and not a god,
Though you set your heart as the heart of a god
3 (Behold, you *are* wiser than Daniel!
There is no secret that can be hidden from you!
4 With your wisdom and your understanding
You have gained riches for yourself,
And gathered gold and silver into your treasuries;
5 By your great wisdom in trade you have increased your riches,
And your heart is lifted up because of your riches),"

[6]"Therefore thus says the Lord GOD:

"Because you have set your heart as the heart of a god,
7 Behold, therefore, I will bring strangers against you,
The most terrible of the nations;
And they shall draw their swords against the beauty of your wisdom,
And defile your splendor.
8 They shall throw you down into the Pit,
And you shall die the death of the slain
In the midst of the seas.
9 "Will you still say before him who slays you,
'I *am* a god?'
But you *shall be* a man, and not a god,
In the hand of him who slays you.
10 You shall die the death of the uncircumcised
By the hand of aliens;
For I have spoken," says the Lord GOD.' "

[11]Moreover the word of the LORD came to me, saying, [12]"Son of man, take up a lamentation for the king of Tyre, and say to him, 'Thus says the Lord GOD:

"You *were* the seal of perfection,
Full of wisdom and perfect in beauty.
13 You were in Eden, the garden of God;
Every precious stone *was* your covering:
The sardius, topaz, and diamond,
Beryl, onyx, and jasper,
Sapphire, turquoise, and emerald with gold.
The workmanship of your timbrels and pipes
Was prepared for you on the day you were created.

28:12 the seal of perfection. The Lord led Ezekiel to address the king as the one to be judged, but clearly the power behind him was Satan. This phrase must be associated with Satan as one perfect in angelic beauty before he rebelled against God. But it can also relate to "perfection" in the same context of Tyre's enterprise, topmost in its trade to the ancient world (27:3,4,11), glorious in her seafaring efforts (27:24), and the crowning city (Is. 23:8), i.e., "perfect" as Jerusalem also is said to be (16:14; Lam. 2:15). **Full of wisdom.** This referred to Satan's wisdom as an angel and to Tyre's wisdom (skill) in trade (27:8,9; 28:4).

14 "You *were* the anointed cherub who covers;
I established you;
You were on the holy mountain of God;
You walked back and forth in the midst of fiery stones.
15 You *were* perfect in your ways from the day you were created,
Till iniquity was found in you.
16 "By the abundance of your trading
You became filled with violence within,
And you sinned;
Therefore I cast you as a profane thing
Out of the mountain of God;
And I destroyed you, O covering cherub,
From the midst of the fiery stones.
17 "Your heart was lifted up because of your beauty;
You corrupted your wisdom for the sake of your splendor;
I cast you to the ground,
I laid you before kings,
That they might gaze at you.
18 "You defiled your sanctuaries
By the multitude of your iniquities,
By the iniquity of your trading;
Therefore I brought fire from your midst;
It devoured you,
And I turned you to ashes upon the earth
In the sight of all who saw you.
19 All who knew you among the peoples are astonished at you;
You have become a horror,
And *shall be* no more forever." ' "

28:1–19 This section concerning the king of Tyre is similar to Isaiah 14:3–23 referring to the king of Babylon. In both passages, some of the language best fits Satan. Most likely, both texts primarily describe the human king who is being used by Satan, much like Peter when Jesus said to him, "Get behind Me, Satan!" (Matt. 16:23). The judgment can certainly apply to Satan, also.

20 Then the word of the LORD came to me, saying,
21 "Son of man, set your face toward Sidon,
and prophesy against her, 22 and say, 'Thus says
the Lord GOD:

"Behold, I *am* against you, O Sidon;
I will be glorified in your midst;
And they shall know that I *am* the LORD,
When I execute judgments in her and am hallowed in her.
23 For I will send pestilence upon her,
And blood in her streets;
The wounded shall be judged in her midst
By the sword against her on every side;
Then they shall know that I *am* the LORD.

24 "And there shall no longer be a pricking
brier or a painful thorn for the house of Israel
from among all *who are* around them, who despise them. Then they shall know that I *am* the
Lord GOD."
25 Thus says the Lord GOD: "When I have
gathered the house of Israel from the peoples
among whom they are scattered, and am hallowed in them in the sight of the Gentiles, then
they will dwell in their own land which I gave
to My servant Jacob. 26 And they will dwell
safely there, build houses, and plant vineyards; yes, they will dwell securely, when I
execute judgments on all those around them
who despise them. Then they shall know that
I *am* the LORD their God." ' "

Psalm 129:1–4

A Song of Ascents.

"Many a time they have afflicted me
from my youth,"
Let Israel now say—
2 "Many a time they have afflicted me
from my youth;
Yet they have not prevailed against me.
3 The plowers plowed on my back;
They made their furrows long."
4 The LORD *is* righteous;
He has cut in pieces the cords
of the wicked.

Proverbs 28:26

26 He who trusts in his own heart
is a fool,
But whoever walks wisely will be
delivered.

Hebrews 12:1–29

12 Therefore we also, since we are surrounded by so great a cloud of witnesses, let us
lay aside every weight, and the sin which so easily ensnares *us,* and let us run with endurance
the race that is set before us, 2looking unto Jesus, the author and finisher of *our* faith, who for
the joy that was set before Him endured the
cross, despising the shame, and has sat down
at the right hand of the throne of God.
3For consider Him who endured such hostility from sinners against Himself, lest you
become weary and discouraged in your souls.
4You have not yet resisted to bloodshed, striving against sin. 5And you have forgotten the
exhortation which speaks to you as to sons:

*"My son, do not despise the chastening
of the LORD,
Nor be discouraged when you are
rebuked by Him;*
6 *For whom the LORD loves He chastens,
And scourges every son whom He
receives."*

12:4 bloodshed. None of the Hebrews had experienced such intense exhaustion or persecution that it brought them to death or martyrdom. Since Stephen (Acts 7:60), James (Acts 12:1), and others (Acts 9:1; 22:4; 26:10) had faced martyrdom in Jerusalem, it would appear to rule out that city as the residence of this epistle's recipients.

7If you endure chastening, God deals with
you as with sons; for what son is there whom
a father does not chasten? 8But if you are without chastening, of which all have become partakers, then you are illegitimate and not sons.
9Furthermore, we have had human fathers
who corrected *us,* and we paid *them* respect.
Shall we not much more readily be in subjection to the Father of spirits and live? 10For they
indeed for a few days chastened *us* as seemed
best to them, but He for *our* profit, that *we* may
be partakers of His holiness. 11Now no chastening seems to be joyful for the present, but
painful; nevertheless, afterward it yields the
peaceable fruit of righteousness to those who
have been trained by it.
12Therefore strengthen the hands which
hang down, and the feeble knees, 13and make
straight paths for your feet, so that what is lame
may not be dislocated, but rather be healed.
14Pursue peace with all *people,* and holiness,
without which no one will see the Lord: 15look-
ing carefully lest anyone fall short of the grace
of God; lest any root of bitterness springing up
cause trouble, and by this many become
defiled; 16lest there *be* any fornicator or profane person like Esau, who for one morsel of
food sold his birthright. 17For you know that
afterward, when he wanted to inherit the
blessing, he was rejected, for he found no
place for repentance, though he sought it diligently with tears.

12:14 Pursue...holiness. In this epistle, it is explained as 1) a drawing near to God with full faith and a cleansed conscience (10:14,22), and 2) a genuine acceptance of Christ as the Savior and sacrifice for sin, bringing the sinner into fellowship with God. Unbelievers will not be drawn to accept Christ if believers' lives do not demonstrate the qualities God desires, including peace and holiness (John 13:35; 1 Tim. 4:3; 5:23; 1 Pet. 1:16).

18For you have not come to the mountain
that may be touched and that burned with fire,
and to blackness and darkness and tempest,
19and the sound of a trumpet and the voice of
words, so that those who heard *it* begged that
the word should not be spoken to them anymore. 20(For they could not endure what was
commanded: *"And if so much as a beast touches the mountain, it shall be stoned or shot with
an arrow."* 21And so terrifying was the sight

that Moses said, *"I am exceedingly afraid and trembling."*)

22 But you have come to Mount Zion and to the city of the living God, the heavenly Jerusalem, to an innumerable company of angels, 23 to the general assembly and church of the firstborn *who are* registered in heaven, to God the Judge of all, to the spirits of just men made perfect, 24 to Jesus the Mediator of the new covenant, and to the blood of sprinkling that speaks better things than *that of* Abel.

25 See that you do not refuse Him who speaks. For if they did not escape who refused Him who spoke on earth, much more *shall we not escape* if we turn away from Him who *speaks* from heaven, 26 whose voice then shook the earth; but now He has promised, saying, *"Yet once more I shake not only the earth, but also heaven."* 27 Now this, *"Yet once more,"* indicates the removal of those things that are being shaken, as of things that are made, that the things which cannot be shaken may remain.

28 Therefore, since we are receiving a kingdom which cannot be shaken, let us have grace, by which we may serve God acceptably with reverence and godly fear. 29 For our God *is* a consuming fire.

12:29 consuming fire. See Deuteronomy 4:24. God's law given at Sinai prescribed many severe punishments, but the punishment is far worse for those who reject His offer of salvation through His own Son, Jesus Christ (Luke 3:16,17).

DAY 18: How does Hebrews 12:1 represent a crucial transition for its readers?

"Therefore we also, since we are surrounded by so great a cloud of witnesses." This is a very crucial transition word offering an emphatic conclusion to the section which began in 10:19. The deceased people of chapter 11 give witness to the value and blessing of living by faith. Motivation for running "the race" is not in the possibility of receiving praise from "observing" heavenly saints. Rather, the runner is inspired by the godly examples those saints set during their lives. The great crowd are not comprised of spectators but rather are ones whose past life of faith encourages others to live that way (11:2,4,5,33,39).

"Let us run with endurance the race that is set before us." The reference is to those Hebrews who had made a profession of Christ, but had not gone all the way to full faith. They had not yet begun the race, which starts with salvation. The writer has invited them to accept salvation in Christ and join the race. "Let us lay aside every weight." Different from the "sin" mentioned next, this refers to the main encumbrance weighing down the Hebrews which was the Levitical system with its stifling legalism. The athlete would strip away every piece of unnecessary clothing before competing in the race. The outward things emphasized by the Levitical system not only impede, they "ensnare." "And sin." In this context, this focuses first on the particular sin of unbelief—refusing to turn away from the Levitical sacrifices to the perfect sacrifice, Jesus Christ (John 16:8–11), as well as other sins cherished by the unbeliever. The athletic metaphor presents the faith-filled life as a demanding, grueling effort. The English word "agony" is derived from the Greek word used here for "endurance."

"Looking unto Jesus" (v. 2). They were to fix their eyes on Jesus as the object of faith and salvation (11:26,27; Acts 7:55,56; Phil. 3:8). "The author…of our faith." The term means originator or preeminent example. "The finisher…of our faith." The term is "perfecter," having the idea of carrying through to perfect completion (John 19:30). Jesus persevered so that He might receive the joy of accomplishment of the Father's will and exaltation (1:9; Ps. 16:9–11; Luke 10:21–24).

NOVEMBER 19

Ezekiel 29:1–30:26

29 In the tenth year, in the tenth *month,* on the twelfth *day* of the month, the word of the LORD came to me, saying, 2 "Son of man, set your face against Pharaoh king of Egypt, and prophesy against him, and against all Egypt. 3 Speak, and say, 'Thus says the Lord GOD:

"Behold, I *am* against you,
O Pharaoh king of Egypt,
O great monster who lies in the midst
of his rivers,
Who has said, 'My River *is* my own;
I have made *it* for myself.'
4 But I will put hooks in your jaws,
And cause the fish of your rivers
to stick to your scales;
I will bring you up out of the midst of
your rivers,
And all the fish in your rivers will stick
to your scales.

5 I will leave you in the wilderness,
You and all the fish of your rivers;
You shall fall on the open field;
You shall not be picked up or gathered.
I have given you as food
To the beasts of the field
And to the birds of the heavens.

6 “Then all the inhabitants of Egypt
Shall know that I *am* the LORD,
Because they have been a staff of reed
to the house of Israel.
7 When they took hold of you with
the hand,
You broke and tore all their shoulders;
When they leaned on you,
You broke and made all their backs
quiver.”

8 “Therefore thus says the Lord GOD: “Surely
I will bring a sword upon you and cut off from
you man and beast. 9 And the land of Egypt
shall become desolate and waste; then they will
know that I *am* the LORD, because he said, ‘The
River *is* mine, and I have made *it.*’ 10 Indeed,
therefore, I *am* against you and against your
rivers, and I will make the land of Egypt utterly waste and desolate, from Migdol *to* Syene,
as far as the border of Ethiopia. 11 Neither foot
of man shall pass through it nor foot of beast
pass through it, and it shall be uninhabited
forty years. 12 I will make the land of Egypt desolate in the midst of the countries *that are* desolate; and among the cities *that are* laid waste,
her cities shall be desolate forty years; and I
will scatter the Egyptians among the nations
and disperse them throughout the countries.”

13 “Yet, thus says the Lord GOD: “At the end of
forty years I will gather the Egyptians from the
peoples among whom they were scattered. 14 I
will bring back the captives of Egypt and cause
them to return to the land of Pathros, to the
land of their origin, and there they shall be a
lowly kingdom. 15 It shall be the lowliest of kingdoms; it shall never again exalt itself above the
nations, for I will diminish them so that they
will not rule over the nations anymore. 16 No
longer shall it be the confidence of the house
of Israel, but will remind them of *their* iniquity
when they turned to follow them. Then they
shall know that I *am* the Lord GOD.” ’ ”

17 And it came to pass in the twenty-seventh
year, in the first *month,* on the first *day* of the
month, *that* the word of the LORD came to me,
saying, 18 “Son of man, Nebuchadnezzar king of
Babylon caused his army to labor strenuously
against Tyre; every head *was* made bald, and
every shoulder rubbed raw; yet neither he nor
his army received wages from Tyre, for the
labor which they expended on it. 19 Therefore
thus says the Lord GOD: ‘Surely I will give the
land of Egypt to Nebuchadnezzar king of
Babylon; he shall take away her wealth, carry
off her spoil, and remove her pillage; and that
will be the wages for his army. 20 I have given
him the land of Egypt *for* his labor, because
they worked for Me,’ says the Lord GOD.

21 ‘In that day I will cause the horn of the
house of Israel to spring forth, and I will open
your mouth to speak in their midst. Then they
shall know that I *am* the LORD.’ ”

29:21 I will cause the horn…to spring forth. God caused Israel’s power to return and restored her authority as the power in an animal’s horn (1 Sam. 2:1). Though other nations subdued her, her latter end in messianic times will be blessed. **I will open your mouth.** Most likely this refers to the day when Ezekiel’s writings would be understood by looking back at their fulfillment. His muteness had already ceased in 586/585 B.C. when Jerusalem fell (33:21,22).

30 The word of the LORD came to me
again, saying, 2 “Son of man, prophesy
and say, ‘Thus says the Lord GOD:

“Wail, ‘Woe to the day!’
3 For the day *is* near,
Even the day of the LORD *is* near;
It will be a day of clouds, the time
of the Gentiles.
4 The sword shall come upon Egypt,
And great anguish shall be
in Ethiopia,
When the slain fall in Egypt,
And they take away her wealth,
And her foundations are broken down.

5 “Ethiopia, Libya, Lydia, all the mingled people,
Chub, and the men of the lands who are allied,
shall fall with them by the sword.”
6 “Thus says the LORD:

“Those who uphold Egypt shall fall,
And the pride of her power shall come
down.
From Migdol *to* Syene
Those within her shall fall by the
sword,”
Says the Lord GOD.

7 “They shall be desolate in the midst
of the desolate countries,

And her cities shall be in the midst
of the cities *that are* laid waste.
8 Then they will know that I *am* the
LORD,
When I have set a fire in Egypt
And all her helpers are destroyed.
9 On that day messengers shall go forth
from Me in ships
To make the careless Ethiopians
afraid,
And great anguish shall come upon
them,
As on the day of Egypt;
For indeed it is coming!"

10 "Thus says the Lord GOD:

"I will also make a multitude of Egypt to
cease
By the hand of Nebuchadnezzar king of
Babylon.
11 He and his people with him, the most
terrible of the nations,
Shall be brought to destroy the land;
They shall draw their swords against
Egypt,
And fill the land with the slain.
12 I will make the rivers dry,
And sell the land into the hand of the
wicked;
I will make the land waste, and all that
is in it,
By the hand of aliens.
I, the LORD, have spoken."

13 "Thus says the Lord GOD:

"I will also destroy the idols,
And cause the images to cease from
Noph;
There shall no longer be princes from
the land of Egypt;
I will put fear in the land of Egypt.
14 I will make Pathros desolate,
Set fire to Zoan,
And execute judgments in No.
15 I will pour My fury on Sin,
the strength of Egypt;
I will cut off the multitude of No,
16 And set a fire in Egypt;
Sin shall have great pain,
No shall be split open,
And Noph *shall be in* distress daily.
17 The young men of Aven and Pi Beseth
shall fall by the sword,
And these *cities* shall go into
captivity.
18 At Tehaphnehes the day shall
also be darkened,
When I break the yokes
of Egypt there.
And her arrogant strength shall cease
in her;
As for her, a cloud shall cover her,
And her daughters shall go into
captivity.
19 Thus I will execute judgments on
Egypt,
Then they shall know that I *am* the
LORD." ' "

20 And it came to pass in the eleventh year, in
the first *month,* on the seventh *day* of the
month, *that* the word of the LORD came to me,
saying, 21 "Son of man, I have broken the arm
of Pharaoh king of Egypt; and see, it has not
been bandaged for healing, nor a splint put on
to bind it, to make it strong enough to hold a
sword. 22 Therefore thus says the Lord GOD:
'Surely I *am* against Pharaoh king of Egypt,
and will break his arms, both the strong one
and the one that was broken; and I will make
the sword fall out of his hand. 23 I will scatter
the Egyptians among the nations, and disperse them throughout the countries. 24 I will
strengthen the arms of the king of Babylon
and put My sword in his hand; but I will break
Pharaoh's arms, and he will groan before him
with the groanings of a mortally wounded
man. 25 Thus I will strengthen the arms of the
king of Babylon, but the arms of Pharaoh shall
fall down; they shall know that I *am* the LORD,
when I put My sword into the hand of the king
of Babylon and he stretches it out against the
land of Egypt. 26 I will scatter the Egyptians
among the nations and disperse them throughout the countries. Then they shall know that I
am the LORD.' "

Psalm 129:5–8

5 Let all those who hate Zion
Be put to shame and turned back.
6 Let them be as the grass *on* the
housetops,
Which withers before it grows up,
7 With which the reaper does not fill
his hand,
Nor he who binds sheaves, his arms.
8 Neither let those who pass by
them say,
"The blessing of the LORD *be*
upon you;
We bless you in the name
of the LORD!"

Proverbs 28:27

27 He who gives to the poor will not lack,
But he who hides his eyes will have
many curses.

Hebrews 13:1–25

13 Let brotherly love continue. 2Do not forget to entertain strangers, for by so *doing*
some have unwittingly entertained angels.
3Remember the prisoners as if chained with
them—those who are mistreated—since you
yourselves are in the body also.
4Marriage *is* honorable among all, and the
bed undefiled; but fornicators and adulterers
God will judge.

13:4 honorable. God highly honors marriage, which He instituted at creation (Gen. 2:24); but some people in the early church considered celibacy to be holier than marriage, an idea Paul strongly denounces in 1 Timothy 4:3. Sexual activity in a marriage is pure, but any sexual activity outside marriage brings one under divine judgment. **God will judge.** God prescribes serious consequences for sexual immorality.

5*Let your* conduct *be* without covetousness;
be content with such things as you have. For
He Himself has said, *"I will never leave you*
nor forsake you." 6So we may boldly say:

"The LORD is my helper;
I will not fear.
What can man do to me?"

7Remember those who rule over you, who
have spoken the word of God to you, whose
faith follow, considering the outcome of *their*
conduct. 8Jesus Christ *is* the same yesterday,
today, and forever. 9Do not be carried about
with various and strange doctrines. For *it is*
good that the heart be established by grace,
not with foods which have not profited those
who have been occupied with them.
10We have an altar from which those who
serve the tabernacle have no right to eat. 11For
the bodies of those animals, whose blood is
brought into the sanctuary by the high priest
for sin, are burned outside the camp. 12There-
fore Jesus also, that He might sanctify the people with His own blood, suffered outside the
gate. 13Therefore let us go forth to Him, outside
the camp, bearing His reproach. 14For here we
have no continuing city, but we seek the one to
come. 15Therefore by Him let us continually
offer the sacrifice of praise to God, that is, the
fruit of *our* lips, giving thanks to His name.
16But do not forget to do good and to share, for
with such sacrifices God is well pleased.
17Obey those who rule over you, and be submissive, for they watch out for your souls, as
those who must give account. Let them do so
with joy and not with grief, for that would be
unprofitable for you.
18Pray for us; for we are confident that we
have a good conscience, in all things desiring
to live honorably. 19But I especially urge *you* to
do this, that I may be restored to you the
sooner.
20Now may the God of peace who brought up
our Lord Jesus from the dead, that great
Shepherd of the sheep, through the blood of
the everlasting covenant, 21make you complete
in every good work to do His will, working in
you what is well pleasing in His sight, through
Jesus Christ, to whom *be* glory forever and
ever. Amen.
22And I appeal to you, brethren, bear with
the word of exhortation, for I have written to
you in few words. 23Know that *our* brother
Timothy has been set free, with whom I shall
see you if he comes shortly.
24Greet all those who rule over you, and all
the saints. Those from Italy greet you.
25Grace *be* with you all. Amen.

13:17 rule over you. The pastors/elders of the church exercise the very authority of Christ when they preach, teach, and apply Scripture (Acts 20:28; 1 Thess. 5:12,13). They serve the church on behalf of Christ and must give Him an account of their faithfulness. These may include both secular and spiritual rulers. Even those who do not acknowledge God are nevertheless ordained and used by Him (Rom. 13:1,4). **joy.** The church is responsible to help its leaders do their work with satisfaction and delight.

13:21 make you complete. This is not the Greek word for "perfect" or "perfection" used throughout Hebrews to indicate salvation but is a word which is translated "prepared" in 10:5 and "framed" in 11:3. It refers to believers being edified. The verb has the idea of equipping by means of adjusting, shaping, mending, restoring, or preparing (11:3; 1 Cor. 1:10; 2 Cor. 13:11; 2 Tim. 3:17).

DAY 19: Did the writer of Hebrews actually think Christians might entertain angels (13:2)?

The last chapter of the epistle focuses on some of the essential practical ethics of Christian living. These ethics help portray the true gospel to the world, encourage others to believe in Christ, and bring glory to God. The first of these is love for fellow believers (John 13:35). Although the primary reference would be to Christians, the writer must have had emotions similar to those of the apostle Paul when it came to considering his fellow Hebrews (see Rom. 9:3,4).

"Do not forget to entertain strangers, for by so doing some have unwittingly entertained angels" (v. 2). The second grace needing development was the extension of love to those who were strangers (Rom. 12:3; 1 Tim. 3:2). Hospitality in the ancient world often included putting up a guest overnight or longer. This is hardest to do when experiencing a time of persecution. The Hebrews would not know whether a guest would prove to be a spy or a fellow believer being pursued. To bring up "angels" was not given as the ultimate motivation for hospitality but to reveal that one never knows how far-reaching an act of kindness might be (Matt. 25:40,45). This is exactly what happened to Abraham and Sarah (Gen. 18:1–3), Lot (Gen. 19:1,2), Gideon (Judg. 6:11–24), and Manoah (Judg. 13:6–20).

NOVEMBER 20

Ezekiel 31:1–32:32

31 Now it came to pass in the eleventh year, in the third *month*, on the first *day* of the month, *that* the word of the LORD came to me, saying, 2"Son of man, say to Pharaoh king of Egypt and to his multitude:

'Whom are you like in your greatness?
3 Indeed Assyria *was* a cedar
in Lebanon,
With fine branches that shaded the
forest,
And of high stature;
And its top was among the thick boughs.
4 The waters made it grow;
Underground waters gave it height,
With their rivers running around the
place where it was planted,
And sent out rivulets to all the trees
of the field.
5 'Therefore its height was exalted above
all the trees of the field;
Its boughs were multiplied,
And its branches became long because
of the abundance of water,
As it sent them out.
6 All the birds of the heavens made their
nests in its boughs;
Under its branches all the beasts of the
field brought forth their young;
And in its shadow all great nations
made their home.
7 'Thus it was beautiful in greatness and
in the length of its branches,
Because its roots reached to abundant
waters.
8 The cedars in the garden of God could
not hide it;
The fir trees were not like its boughs,
And the chestnut trees were not like its
branches;
No tree in the garden of God was like it
in beauty.
9 I made it beautiful with a multitude of
branches,
So that all the trees of Eden envied it,
That *were* in the garden of God.'

10"Therefore thus says the Lord GOD: 'Because you have increased in height, and it set its top among the thick boughs, and its heart was lifted up in its height, 11therefore I will deliver it into the hand of the mighty one of the nations, and he shall surely deal with it; I have driven it out for its wickedness. 12And aliens, the most terrible of the nations, have cut it down and left it; its branches have fallen on the mountains and in all the valleys; its boughs lie broken by all the rivers of the land; and all the peoples of the earth have gone from under its shadow and left it.

13 'On its ruin will remain all the birds of
the heavens,

31:2–18 Whom are you like...? Ezekiel filled this chapter with a metaphor/analogy comparing Egypt to a huge tree that dominates a forest to a king/nation that dominates the world (17:22–24; Dan. 4:1–12,19–27). He reasoned that just as a strong tree like Assyria (v. 3) fell (ca. 609 B.C.), so will Egypt (ca. 568 B.C.). If the Egyptians tend to be proud and feel invincible, let them remember how powerful Assyria had fallen already.

And all the beasts of the field will come
to its branches—

14"So that no trees by the waters may ever
again exalt themselves for their height, nor set
their tops among the thick boughs, that no tree
which drinks water may ever be high enough
to reach up to them.

'For they have all been delivered to
death,
To the depths of the earth,
Among the children of men who go
down to the Pit.'

15"Thus says the Lord GOD: 'In the day when
it went down to hell, I caused mourning. I covered the deep because of it. I restrained its
rivers, and the great waters were held back. I
caused Lebanon to mourn for it, and all the
trees of the field wilted because of it. 16I made
the nations shake at the sound of its fall, when
I cast it down to hell together with those who
descend into the Pit; and all the trees of Eden,
the choice and best of Lebanon, all that drink
water, were comforted in the depths of the
earth. 17They also went down to hell with it,
with those slain by the sword; and *those who
were* its *strong* arm dwelt in its shadows
among the nations.

18"To which of the trees in Eden will you
then be likened in glory and greatness? Yet
you shall be brought down with the trees of
Eden to the depths of the earth; you shall lie
in the midst of the uncircumcised, with *those*
slain by the sword. This *is* Pharaoh and all his
multitude,' says the Lord GOD."

32 And it came to pass in the twelfth year,
in the twelfth *month,* on the first *day* of
the month, *that* the word of the LORD came to
me, saying, 2"Son of man, take up a lamentation for Pharaoh king of Egypt, and say to him:

'You are like a young lion among
the nations,
And you *are* like a monster in the seas,
Bursting forth in your rivers,
Troubling the waters with your feet,
And fouling their rivers.'

3"Thus says the Lord GOD:

'I will therefore spread My net over you
with a company of many people,
And they will draw you up in My net.
4 Then I will leave you on the land;
I will cast you out on the open fields,
And cause to settle on you all the birds
of the heavens.
And with you I will fill the beasts of the
whole earth.
5 I will lay your flesh on the mountains,
And fill the valleys with your carcass.
6 'I will also water the land with the flow
of your blood,
Even to the mountains;
And the riverbeds will be full of you.
7 When *I* put out your light,
I will cover the heavens, and make its
stars dark;
I will cover the sun with a cloud,
And the moon shall not give her light.
8 All the bright lights of the heavens
I will make dark over you,
And bring darkness upon your land,'
Says the Lord GOD.

9"I will also trouble the hearts of many peoples, when I bring your destruction among the
nations, into the countries which you have not
known. 10Yes, I will make many peoples astonished at you, and their kings shall be horribly
afraid of you when I brandish My sword before
them; and they shall tremble *every* moment,
every man for his own life, in the day of your fall.'

11"For thus says the Lord GOD: 'The sword
of the king of Babylon shall come upon you.
12By the swords of the mighty warriors, all of
them the most terrible of the nations, I will
cause your multitude to fall.

'They shall plunder the pomp of Egypt,
And all its multitude shall be
destroyed.
13 Also I will destroy all its animals
From beside its great waters;
The foot of man shall muddy them
no more,
Nor shall the hooves of animals muddy
them.
14 Then I will make their waters clear,
And make their rivers run like oil,'
Says the Lord GOD.

15 'When I make the land of Egypt desolate,
And the country is destitute of all that
once filled it,
When I strike all who dwell in it,
Then they shall know that I *am*
the LORD.

16 'This *is* the lamentation
With which they shall lament her;
The daughters of the nations shall
lament her;
They shall lament for her, for Egypt,
And for all her multitude,'
Says the Lord GOD."

17It came to pass also in the twelfth year, on
the fifteenth *day* of the month, *that* the word of
the LORD came to me, saying:

18 "Son of man, wail over the multitude
of Egypt,
And cast them down to the depths of
the earth,
Her and the daughters of the famous
nations,
With those who go down to the Pit:
19 'Whom do you surpass in beauty?
Go down, be placed with the
uncircumcised.'

20 "They shall fall in the midst of *those*
slain by the sword;
She is delivered to the sword,
Drawing her and all her multitudes.
21 The strong among the mighty
Shall speak to him out of the midst
of hell
With those who help him:
'They have gone down,
They lie with the uncircumcised,
slain by the sword.'

22 "Assyria *is* there, and all her company,
With their graves all around her,
All of them slain, fallen by the sword.
23 Her graves are set in the recesses of
the Pit,
And her company is all around her
grave,
All of them slain, fallen by the sword,
Who caused terror in the land
of the living.

24 "There *is* Elam and all her multitude,
All around her grave,
All of them slain, fallen by the sword,
Who have gone down uncircumcised
to the lower parts of the earth,
Who caused their terror in the land
of the living;
Now they bear their shame with those
who go down to the Pit.
25 They have set her bed in the midst of
the slain,
With all her multitude,
With her graves all around it,
All of them uncircumcised, slain
by the sword;
Though their terror was caused
In the land of the living,
Yet they bear their shame
With those who go down to the Pit;
It was put in the midst of the slain.

26 "There *are* Meshech and Tubal and all
their multitudes,
With all their graves around it,
All of them uncircumcised, slain
by the sword,
Though they caused their terror in the
land of the living.
27 They do not lie with the mighty
Who are fallen of the uncircumcised,
Who have gone down to hell with their
weapons of war;
They have laid their swords under
their heads,
But their iniquities will be on their
bones,
Because of the terror of the mighty in
the land of the living.
28 Yes, you shall be broken in the midst
of the uncircumcised,
And lie with *those* slain by the sword.

29 "There *is* Edom,
Her kings and all her princes,
Who despite their might
Are laid beside *those* slain by the
sword;
They shall lie with the uncircumcised,
And with those who go down to the Pit.
30 There *are* the princes of the north,
All of them, and all the Sidonians,
Who have gone down with the slain
In shame at the terror which they
caused by their might;
They lie uncircumcised with *those* slain
by the sword,
And bear their shame with those who
go down to the Pit.

31 "Pharaoh will see them
And be comforted over all his
multitude,
Pharaoh and all his army,
Slain by the sword,"
Says the Lord GOD.

32 "For I have caused My terror in the
land of the living;
And he shall be placed in the midst of
the uncircumcised
With *those* slain by the sword,
Pharaoh and all his multitude,"
Says the Lord GOD.

Psalm 130:1–4

A Song of Ascents.

Out of the depths I have cried to
You, O LORD;
2 Lord, hear my voice!
Let Your ears be attentive
To the voice of my supplications.

3 If You, LORD, should mark iniquities,
O Lord, who could stand?
4 But *there is* forgiveness with You,
That You may be feared.

Proverbs 28:28

28 When the wicked arise, men hide
themselves;
But when they perish, the righteous
increase.

James 1:1–27

1 James, a bondservant of God and of the Lord
Jesus Christ,

To the twelve tribes which are scattered
abroad:

Greetings.

[2]My brethren, count it all joy when you fall
into various trials, [3]knowing that the testing of
your faith produces patience. [4]But let patience
have *its* perfect work, that you may be perfect
and complete, lacking nothing. [5]If any of you
lacks wisdom, let him ask of God, who gives to
all liberally and without reproach, and it will
be given to him. [6]But let him ask in faith, with
no doubting, for he who doubts is like a wave
of the sea driven and tossed by the wind. [7]For
let not that man suppose that he will receive
anything from the Lord; [8]*he is* a double-minded
man, unstable in all his ways.

1:6 ask in faith. Prayer must be offered with confident trust in a sovereign God (Heb. 11:1). **with no doubting.** This refers to having one's thinking divided within himself, not merely because of mental indecision but an inner moral conflict or distrust in God. **wave of the sea.** The person who doubts God's ability or willingness to provide this wisdom is like the billowing, restless sea, moving back and forth with its endless tides, never able to settle (Josh. 24:15; 1 Kin. 18:21; Rev. 3:16).

[9]Let the lowly brother glory in his exaltation, [10]but the rich in his humiliation, because
as a flower of the field he will pass away. [11]For
no sooner has the sun risen with a burning
heat than it withers the grass; its flower falls,
and its beautiful appearance perishes. So the
rich man also will fade away in his pursuits.
[12]Blessed *is* the man who endures temptation; for when he has been approved, he will
receive the crown of life which the Lord has
promised to those who love Him. [13]Let no one
say when he is tempted, "I am tempted by
God"; for God cannot be tempted by evil, nor
does He Himself tempt anyone. [14]But each one
is tempted when he is drawn away by his own

1:14 drawn away. This Greek word was used to describe wild game being lured into traps. Just as animals can be drawn to their deaths by attractive baits, temptation promises people something good, which is actually harmful. **his own desires.** This refers to lust, the strong desire of the human soul to enjoy or acquire something to fulfill the flesh. Man's fallen nature has the propensity to strongly desire whatever sin will satisfy it (Rom. 7:8–25). "His own" describes the individual nature of lust—it is different for each person as a result of inherited tendencies, environment, upbringing, and personal choices. The Greek grammar also indicates that these "desires" are the direct agent or cause of one's sinning. **enticed.** A fishing term that means "to capture" or "to catch with bait" (2 Pet. 2:14,18). It is a parallel to "drawn away."

desires and enticed. [15]Then, when desire has
conceived, it gives birth to sin; and sin, when
it is full-grown, brings forth death.
[16]Do not be deceived, my beloved brethren.
[17]Every good gift and every perfect gift is from
above, and comes down from the Father of
lights, with whom there is no variation or
shadow of turning. [18]Of His own will He
brought us forth by the word of truth, that we
might be a kind of firstfruits of His creatures.
[19]So then, my beloved brethren, let every
man be swift to hear, slow to speak, slow to
wrath; [20]for the wrath of man does not produce
the righteousness of God.
[21]Therefore lay aside all filthiness and overflow of wickedness, and receive with meekness the implanted word, which is able to save
your souls.
[22]But be doers of the word, and not hearers
only, deceiving yourselves. [23]For if anyone is a
hearer of the word and not a doer, he is like a
man observing his natural face in a mirror;
[24]for he observes himself, goes away, and
immediately forgets what kind of man he was.
[25]But he who looks into the perfect law of liberty and continues *in it*, and is not a forgetful
hearer but a doer of the work, this one will be
blessed in what he does.
[26]If anyone among you thinks he is religious,
and does not bridle his tongue but deceives
his own heart, this one's religion *is* useless.
[27]Pure and undefiled religion before God and
the Father is this: to visit orphans and widows
in their trouble, *and* to keep oneself unspotted
from the world.

DAY 20: How can James expect Christians to "count it all joy" when they face difficulties and trials (1:2)?

The Greek word for "count" may also be translated "consider" or "evaluate." The natural human response to trials is not to rejoice; therefore the believer must make a conscious commitment to face them with joy. "Trials" connote troubles or things that break the pattern of peace, comfort, joy, and happiness in someone's life. The verb form of this word means "to put someone or something to the test," with the purpose of discovering that person's nature or that thing's quality. God brings such tests to prove—and increase—the strength and quality of one's faith and to demonstrate its validity (vv. 2–12). Every trial becomes a test of faith designed to strengthen. If the believer fails the test by wrongly responding, that test then becomes a temptation or a solicitation to evil.

"Knowing that the testing of your faith produces patience" (v. 3). This means "proof" or "proving." This testing produces "endurance" or "perseverance." Through tests, a Christian will learn to withstand and even cherish the benefit of the pressure of a trial until God removes it at His appointed time.

"But let patience have its perfect work" (v. 4). This is not a reference to sinless perfection (3:2), but to spiritual maturity (1 John 2:14). The testing of faith drives believers to deeper communion and greater trust in Christ—qualities that in turn produce a stable, godly, and righteous character. "That you may be…complete." From a compound Greek word that means "all the portions whole."

NOVEMBER 21

Ezekiel 33:1–34:31

33 Again the word of the LORD came to me,
saying, 2"Son of man, speak to the children of your people, and say to them: 'When I
bring the sword upon a land, and the people of
the land take a man from their territory and
make him their watchman, 3when he sees the
sword coming upon the land, if he blows the
trumpet and warns the people, 4then whoever
hears the sound of the trumpet and does not
take warning, if the sword comes and takes
him away, his blood shall be on his *own* head.
5He heard the sound of the trumpet, but did
not take warning; his blood shall be upon himself. But he who takes warning will save his
life. 6But if the watchman sees the sword coming and does not blow the trumpet, and the
people are not warned, and the sword comes
and takes *any* person from among them, he is
taken away in his iniquity; but his blood I will
require at the watchman's hand.'

7"So you, son of man: I have made you a
watchman for the house of Israel; therefore
you shall hear a word from My mouth and
warn them for Me. 8When I say to the wicked,
'O wicked *man*, you shall surely die!' and you
do not speak to warn the wicked from his way,
that wicked *man* shall die in his iniquity; but
his blood I will require at your hand. 9Never-
theless if you warn the wicked to turn from his
way, and he does not turn from his way, he
shall die in his iniquity; but you have delivered
your soul.

10"Therefore you, O son of man, say to the
house of Israel: 'Thus you say, "If our transgressions and our sins *lie* upon us, and we
pine away in them, how can we then live?" '
11Say to them: '*As* I live,' says the Lord GOD, 'I
have no pleasure in the death of the wicked, but
that the wicked turn from his way and live.
Turn, turn from your evil ways! For why should
you die, O house of Israel?'

12"Therefore you, O son of man, say to the
children of your people: 'The righteousness of
the righteous man shall not deliver him in the
day of his transgression; as for the wickedness
of the wicked, he shall not fall because of it in
the day that he turns from his wickedness; nor
shall the righteous be able to live because of *his*
righteousness in the day that he sins.' 13When I
say to the righteous *that* he shall surely live,

33:2–9 watchman. Such men as Jeremiah and Ezekiel (3:16–21) were spiritual watchmen (33:7–9), warning that God would bring a sword on His people so that they had opportunity to prepare and be safe. This analogy came from the custom of putting guards on the city wall watching for the approach of danger, then trumpeting the warning.

33:4 his blood…on his *own* head. Once the watchman did his duty, the responsibility passed to each person. Each person is accountable for his own response to God's warnings, whether to die in judgment or to live as one who heeded and repented. Ezekiel had been a very faithful and obedient "watchman."

but he trusts in his own righteousness and commits iniquity, none of his righteous works shall
be remembered; but because of the iniquity
that he has committed, he shall die. [14]Again,
when I say to the wicked, 'You shall surely
die,' if he turns from his sin and does what is
lawful and right, [15]*if* the wicked restores the
pledge, gives back what he has stolen, and
walks in the statutes of life without committing
iniquity, he shall surely live; he shall not die.
[16]None of his sins which he has committed
shall be remembered against him; he has done
what is lawful and right; he shall surely live.

[17]"Yet the children of your people say, 'The
way of the Lord is not fair.' But it is their way
which is not fair! [18]When the righteous turns
from his righteousness and commits iniquity,
he shall die because of it. [19]But when the wicked
turns from his wickedness and does what is
lawful and right, he shall live because of it.
[20]Yet you say, 'The way of the Lord is not fair.'
O house of Israel, I will judge every one of you
according to his own ways."

[21]And it came to pass in the twelfth year of
our captivity, in the tenth *month,* on the fifth
day of the month, *that* one who had escaped
from Jerusalem came to me and said, "The
city has been captured!"

[22]Now the hand of the LORD had been upon
me the evening before the man came who had
escaped. And He had opened my mouth; so
when he came to me in the morning, my
mouth was opened, and I was no longer mute.

[23]Then the word of the LORD came to me,
saying: [24]"Son of man, they who inhabit those
ruins in the land of Israel are saying, 'Abraham was only one, and he inherited the land.
But we *are* many; the land has been given to
us as a possession.'

[25]"Therefore say to them, 'Thus says the
Lord GOD: "You eat *meat* with blood, you lift up
your eyes toward your idols, and shed blood.
Should you then possess the land? [26]You rely
on your sword, you commit abominations, and
you defile one another's wives. Should you
then possess the land?"'

[27]"Say thus to them, 'Thus says the Lord
GOD: "*As* I live, surely those who *are* in the
ruins shall fall by the sword, and the one who
is in the open field I will give to the beasts to
be devoured, and those who *are* in the strongholds and caves shall die of the pestilence.
[28]For I will make the land most desolate, her
arrogant strength shall cease, and the mountains of Israel shall be so desolate that no one
will pass through. [29]Then they shall know that
I *am* the LORD, when I have made the land
most desolate because of all their abominations which they have committed."'

[30]"As for you, son of man, the children of
your people are talking about you beside the
walls and in the doors of the houses; and they
speak to one another, everyone saying to his
brother, 'Please come and hear what the word
is that comes from the LORD.' [31]So they come
to you as people do, they sit before you *as* My
people, and they hear your words, but they do
not do them; for with their mouth they show
much love, *but* their hearts pursue their *own*
gain. [32]Indeed you *are* to them as a very lovely song of one who has a pleasant voice and
can play well on an instrument; for they hear
your words, but they do not do them. [33]And
when this comes to pass—surely it will
come—then they will know that a prophet has
been among them."

34 And the word of the LORD came to me,
saying, [2]"Son of man, prophesy against
the shepherds of Israel, prophesy and say to
them, 'Thus says the Lord GOD to the shepherds: "Woe to the shepherds of Israel who
feed themselves! Should not the shepherds
feed the flocks? [3]You eat the fat and clothe yourselves with the wool; you slaughter the fatlings,
but you do not feed the flock. [4]The weak you
have not strengthened, nor have you healed
those who were sick, nor bound up the broken, nor brought back what was driven away,
nor sought what was lost; but with force and
cruelty you have ruled them. [5]So they were
scattered because *there was* no shepherd; and
they became food for all the beasts of the field
when they were scattered. [6]My sheep wandered through all the mountains, and on every
high hill; yes, My flock was scattered over the
whole face of the earth, and no one was seeking or searching *for them."*

[7]"Therefore, you shepherds, hear the word
of the LORD: [8]"*As* I live," says the Lord GOD,
"surely because My flock became a prey, and
My flock became food for every beast of the
field, because *there was* no shepherd, nor did
My shepherds search for My flock, but the
shepherds fed themselves and did not feed My
flock"— [9]therefore, O shepherds, hear the
word of the LORD! [10]Thus says the Lord GOD:
"Behold, I *am* against the shepherds, and I
will require My flock at their hand; I will cause
them to cease feeding the sheep, and the
shepherds shall feed themselves no more; for
I will deliver My flock from their mouths, that
they may no longer be food for them."

[11]"For thus says the Lord GOD: "Indeed I
Myself will search for My sheep and seek
them out. [12]As a shepherd seeks out his flock

on the day he is among his scattered sheep, so
will I seek out My sheep and deliver them
from all the places where they were scattered
on a cloudy and dark day. 13And I will bring
them out from the peoples and gather them
from the countries, and will bring them to
their own land; I will feed them on the mountains of Israel, in the valleys and in all the
inhabited places of the country. 14I will feed
them in good pasture, and their fold shall be
on the high mountains of Israel. There they
shall lie down in a good fold and feed in rich
pasture on the mountains of Israel. 15I will feed
My flock, and I will make them lie down," says
the Lord GOD. 16"I will seek what was lost and
bring back what was driven away, bind up the
broken and strengthen what was sick; but I
will destroy the fat and the strong, and feed
them in judgment."

17"And *as for* you, O My flock, thus says the
Lord GOD: "Behold, I shall judge between
sheep and sheep, between rams and goats. 18*Is
it* too little for you to have eaten up the good
pasture, that you must tread down with your
feet the residue of your pasture—and to have
drunk of the clear waters, that you must foul
the residue with your feet? 19And *as for* My
flock, they eat what you have trampled with
your feet, and they drink what you have fouled
with your feet."

20"Therefore thus says the Lord GOD to
them: "Behold, I Myself will judge between
the fat and the lean sheep. 21Because you have
pushed with side and shoulder, butted all the
weak ones with your horns, and scattered
them abroad, 22therefore I will save My flock,
and they shall no longer be a prey; and I will
judge between sheep and sheep. 23I will establish one shepherd over them, and he shall
feed them—My servant David. He shall feed
them and be their shepherd. 24And I, the LORD,
will be their God, and My servant David a
prince among them; I, the LORD, have spoken.

25"I will make a covenant of peace with them,
and cause wild beasts to cease from the land;
and they will dwell safely in the wilderness
and sleep in the woods. 26I will make them and
the places all around My hill a blessing; and I
will cause showers to come down in their season; there shall be showers of blessing. 27Then
the trees of the field shall yield their fruit, and
the earth shall yield her increase. They shall
be safe in their land; and they shall know that
I *am* the LORD, when I have broken the bands
of their yoke and delivered them from the
hand of those who enslaved them. 28And they
shall no longer be a prey for the nations, nor
shall beasts of the land devour them; but they
shall dwell safely, and no one shall make *them*
afraid. 29I will raise up for them a garden of
renown, and they shall no longer be consumed
with hunger in the land, nor bear the shame of
the Gentiles anymore. 30Thus they shall know
that I, the LORD their God, *am* with them, and
they, the house of Israel, *are* My people," says
the Lord GOD.' "

31"You are My flock, the flock of My pasture;
you *are* men, *and* I *am* your God," says the
Lord GOD.

Psalm 130:5–8

5 I wait for the LORD, my soul waits,
And in His word I do hope.
6 My soul *waits* for the Lord
More than those who watch for the morning—
Yes, more than those who watch for the morning.
7 O Israel, hope in the LORD;
For with the LORD *there is* mercy,
And with Him *is* abundant redemption.
8 And He shall redeem Israel
From all his iniquities.

Proverbs 29:1

29 He who is often rebuked,
and hardens *his* neck,
Will suddenly be destroyed, and that without remedy.

James 2:1–26

2 My brethren, do not hold the faith of our
Lord Jesus Christ, *the Lord* of glory, with
partiality. 2For if there should come into your
assembly a man with gold rings, in fine apparel,

2:1 the faith. This refers not to the act of believing, but to the entire Christian faith (Jude 3), which has as its central focus Jesus Christ. ***the Lord* of glory.** Christ is the One who reveals the glory of God. In His Incarnation, He showed only impartiality (Matt. 22:16)—for example, consider the nonelite people included in His genealogy, His choice of the humble village of Nazareth as His residence for 30 years, and His willingness to minister in Galilee and Samaria, both regions held in contempt by Israel's leaders. **partiality.** Originally, this word referred to raising someone's face or elevating the person, but it came to refer to exalting someone strictly on a superficial, external basis, such as appearance, race, wealth, rank, or social status.

and there should also come in a poor man in
filthy clothes, 3and you pay attention to the one
wearing the fine clothes and say to him, "You sit
here in a good place," and say to the poor man,
"You stand there," or, "Sit here at my footstool,"
4have you not shown partiality among yourselves, and become judges with evil thoughts?
5Listen, my beloved brethren: Has God not
chosen the poor of this world *to be* rich in faith
and heirs of the kingdom which He promised to
those who love Him? 6But you have dishonored
the poor man. Do not the rich oppress you and
drag you into the courts? 7Do they not blaspheme that noble name by which you are called?
8If you really fulfill *the* royal law according to
the Scripture, *"You shall love your neighbor as
yourself,"* you do well; 9but if you show partiality, you commit sin, and are convicted by the
law as transgressors. 10For whoever shall keep
the whole law, and yet stumble in one *point,* he
is guilty of all. 11For He who said, *"Do not commit adultery,"* also said, *"Do not murder."* Now
if you do not commit adultery, but you do murder, you have become a transgressor of the
law. 12So speak and so do as those who will be
judged by the law of liberty. 13For judgment is
without mercy to the one who has shown no
mercy. Mercy triumphs over judgment.
14What *does it* profit, my brethren, if someone says he has faith but does not have works?
Can faith save him? 15If a brother or sister is
naked and destitute of daily food, 16and one of
you says to them, "Depart in peace, be warmed
and filled," but you do not give them the
things which are needed for the body, what
does it profit? 17Thus also faith by itself, if it
does not have works, is dead.
18But someone will say, "You have faith, and I
have works." Show me your faith without your
works, and I will show you my faith by my
works. 19You believe that there is one God. You
do well. Even the demons believe—and tremble! 20But do you want to know, O foolish man,
that faith without works is dead? 21Was not
Abraham our father justified by works when
he offered Isaac his son on the altar? 22Do you
see that faith was working together with his
works, and by works faith was made perfect?
23And the Scripture was fulfilled which says,
*"Abraham believed God, and it was accounted
to him for righteousness."* And he was called
the friend of God. 24You see then that a man is
justified by works, and not by faith only.
25Likewise, was not Rahab the harlot also
justified by works when she received the messengers and sent *them* out another way?
26For as the body without the spirit is dead,
so faith without works is dead also.

2:8 royal law. This is better translated "sovereign law." The idea is that this law is supreme or binding. **love your neighbor as yourself.** This sovereign law (quoted from Lev. 19:18), when combined with the command to love God (Deut. 6:4,5), summarizes all the Law and the Prophets (Matt. 22:36–40; Rom. 13:8–10). James is not advocating some kind of emotional affection for oneself—self-love is clearly a sin (2 Tim. 3:2). Rather, the command is to pursue meeting the physical health and spiritual well-being of one's neighbors (all within the sphere of our influence; Luke 10:30–37) with the same intensity and concern as one does naturally for oneself (Phil. 2:3,4).

2:19 You believe that there is one God. A clear reference to the passage most familiar to his Jewish readers: the *Shema* (Deut. 6:4,5), the most basic doctrine of the Old Testament. **demons believe.** Even fallen angels affirm the oneness of God and tremble at its implications. Demons are essentially orthodox in their doctrine (Matt. 8:29,30; Mark 5:7; Luke 4:41; Acts 19:15). But orthodox doctrine by itself is no proof of saving faith. They know the truth about God, Christ, and the Spirit, but hate it and them.

DAY 21: If salvation is by faith in Christ alone, how can James write "faith without works is dead" (2:20)?

"Do you want to know, O foolish man, that faith without works is dead?" Literally, "empty, defective." The objector's claim of belief is fraudulent, and his faith is a sham. James is not contrasting two methods of salvation (faith versus works). Instead, he contrasts two kinds of faith: living faith that saves and dead faith that does not (1 John 3:7–10).

"Was not Abraham our father justified by works…?" (v. 21). This does not contradict Paul's clear teaching that Abraham was justified before God by grace alone through faith alone (Rom. 3:20; 4:1–25; Gal. 3:6,11). For several reasons, James cannot mean that Abraham was constituted righteous before God because of his own good works: 1) James already stressed that salvation is a gracious gift (1:17,18); 2) in the middle of this disputed passage (v. 23), James quoted Genesis 15:6, which forcefully claims that God credited righteousness to Abraham solely on the basis of his faith (Rom. 1:17; 3:24; 4:1–25); and 3) the work that James said justified Abraham was his offering up of Isaac (Gen. 22:9,12), an event that occurred many years after he first exercised faith and was declared righteous before God (Gen. 12:1–7; 15:6). Instead, Abraham's offering of Isaac demonstrated the genuineness of his faith and the reality of his justification before God. James is emphasizing the vindication before others of a man's claim to salvation. James's teaching perfectly complements Paul's writings; salvation is determined by faith alone (Eph. 2:8,9) and demonstrated by faithfulness to obey God's will alone (Eph. 2:10).

"And by works faith was made perfect" (v. 22). This refers to bringing something to its end or to its fullness. Just as a fruit tree has not arrived at its goal until it bears fruit, faith has not reached its end until it demonstrates itself in a righteous life.

NOVEMBER 22

Ezekiel 35:1–36:38

35 Moreover the word of the LORD came
to me, saying, 2"Son of man, set your
face against Mount Seir and prophesy against
it, 3and say to it, 'Thus says the Lord GOD:

"Behold, O Mount Seir, I *am* against
you;
I will stretch out My hand against you,
And make you most desolate;
4 I shall lay your cities waste,
And you shall be desolate.
Then you shall know that I *am* the
LORD.

5"Because you have had an ancient hatred,
and have shed *the blood of* the children of Israel by the power of the sword at the time of
their calamity, when their iniquity *came to an*
end, 6therefore, *as* I live," says the Lord GOD,
"I will prepare you for blood, and blood shall
pursue you; since you have not hated blood,
therefore blood shall pursue you. 7Thus I will
make Mount Seir most desolate, and cut off
from it the one who leaves and the one who
returns. 8And I will fill its mountains with the
slain; on your hills and in your valleys and in all
your ravines those who are slain by the sword
shall fall. 9I will make you perpetually desolate,
and your cities shall be uninhabited; then you
shall know that I *am* the LORD.

10"Because you have said, 'These two
nations and these two countries shall be mine,
and we will possess them,' although the LORD
was there, 11therefore, *as* I live," says the Lord
GOD, "I will do according to your anger and
according to the envy which you showed in
your hatred against them; and I will make
Myself known among them when I judge you.
12Then you shall know that I *am* the LORD. I
have heard all your blasphemies which you
have spoken against the mountains of Israel,
saying, 'They are desolate; they are given to
us to consume.' 13Thus with your mouth you
have boasted against Me and multiplied your
words against Me; I have heard *them.*"

14"Thus says the Lord GOD: "The whole earth
will rejoice when I make you desolate. 15As you
rejoiced because the inheritance of the house
of Israel was desolate, so I will do to you; you
shall be desolate, O Mount Seir, as well as all of
Edom—all of it! Then they shall know that I
am the LORD."'

36 "And you, son of man, prophesy to the
mountains of Israel, and say, 'O mountains of Israel, hear the word of the LORD!
2Thus says the Lord GOD: "Because the enemy
has said of you, 'Aha! The ancient heights have
become our possession,'"' 3therefore prophesy, and say, 'Thus says the Lord GOD: "Because they made *you* desolate and swallowed

36:1 This chapter presents the prerequisite regeneration which Israel must experience before they can nationally enter into the promised blessings. This chapter must be understood to speak of a literal Israel, a literal land, and a literal regeneration, leading to a literal kingdom under Messiah. **prophesy to the mountains.** vv. 1,4,6,8. Ezekiel addresses Israel's mountains as symbolic of the whole nation. He promises: 1) to give these mountains again to dispersed Israel (v. 12); 2) to cause fruit to grow on them (v. 8); 3) to rebuild cities and to multiply people there (v. 10); and 4) to bless in a greater way than in the past (v. 11). This promise can only be fulfilled in future millennial blessing to Israel that she has not yet experienced, because it includes the salvation of the New Covenant (vv. 25–27,29,31,33).

you up on every side, so that you became the
possession of the rest of the nations, and you
are taken up by the lips of talkers and slandered by the people"— [4]therefore, O mountains of Israel, hear the word of the Lord GOD!
Thus says the Lord GOD to the mountains, the
hills, the rivers, the valleys, the desolate
wastes, and the cities that have been forsaken,
which became plunder and mockery to the
rest of the nations all around— [5]therefore thus
says the Lord GOD: "Surely I have spoken in
My burning jealousy against the rest of the
nations and against all Edom, who gave My
land to themselves as a possession, with
wholehearted joy *and* spiteful minds, in order
to plunder its open country." '
[6]"Therefore prophesy concerning the land
of Israel, and say to the mountains, the hills,
the rivers, and the valleys, 'Thus says the Lord
GOD: "Behold, I have spoken in My jealousy
and My fury, because you have borne the
shame of the nations." [7]Therefore thus says
the Lord GOD: "I have raised My hand in an
oath that surely the nations that *are* around
you shall bear their own shame. [8]But you, O
mountains of Israel, you shall shoot forth your
branches and yield your fruit to My people Israel, for they are about to come. [9]For indeed I
am for you, and I will turn to you, and you
shall be tilled and sown. [10]I will multiply men
upon you, all the house of Israel, all of it; and
the cities shall be inhabited and the ruins
rebuilt. [11]I will multiply upon you man and
beast; and they shall increase and bear young;
I will make you inhabited as in former times,
and do better *for you* than at your beginnings.
Then you shall know that I *am* the LORD. [12]Yes,
I will cause men to walk on you, My people Israel; they shall take possession of you, and
you shall be their inheritance; no more shall
you bereave them *of children."*
[13]"Thus says the Lord GOD: "Because they
say to you, 'You devour men and bereave your
nation *of children,'* [14]therefore you shall devour
men no more, nor bereave your nation anymore," says the Lord GOD. [15]"Nor will I let you
hear the taunts of the nations anymore, nor
bear the reproach of the peoples anymore, nor
shall you cause your nation to stumble anymore," says the Lord GOD.' "
[16]Moreover the word of the LORD came to
me, saying: [17]"Son of man, when the house of
Israel dwelt in their own land, they defiled it
by their own ways and deeds; to Me their way
was like the uncleanness of a woman in her
customary impurity. [18]Therefore I poured out
My fury on them for the blood they had shed
on the land, and for their idols *with which* they
had defiled it. [19]So I scattered them among the
nations, and they were dispersed throughout
the countries; I judged them according to
their ways and their deeds. [20]When they came
to the nations, wherever they went, they profaned My holy name—when they said of
them, 'These *are* the people of the LORD, *and*
yet they have gone out of His land.' [21]But I had
concern for My holy name, which the house
of Israel had profaned among the nations
wherever they went.
[22]"Therefore say to the house of Israel,
'Thus says the Lord GOD: "I do not do *this* for
your sake, O house of Israel, but for My holy
name's sake, which you have profaned among
the nations wherever you went. [23]And I will
sanctify My great name, which has been profaned among the nations, which you have profaned in their midst; and the nations shall
know that I *am* the LORD," says the Lord GOD,
"when I am hallowed in you before their eyes.
[24]For I will take you from among the nations,
gather you out of all countries, and bring you
into your own land. [25]Then I will sprinkle clean
water on you, and you shall be clean; I will
cleanse you from all your filthiness and from
all your idols. [26]I will give you a new heart and
put a new spirit within you; I will take the
heart of stone out of your flesh and give you a
heart of flesh. [27]I will put My Spirit within you
and cause you to walk in My statutes, and you
will keep My judgments and do *them.* [28]Then
you shall dwell in the land that I gave to your
fathers; you shall be My people, and I will be
your God. [29]I will deliver you from all your
uncleannesses. I will call for the grain and
multiply it, and bring no famine upon you.
[30]And I will multiply the fruit of your trees and
the increase of your fields, so that you need
never again bear the reproach of famine
among the nations. [31]Then you will remember
your evil ways and your deeds that *were* not

36:25–27 I will cleanse you. Along with the physical reality of a return to the land, God pledged spiritual renewal: 1) cleansing from sin; 2) a new heart of the New Covenant (Jer. 31:31–34); 3) a new spirit or disposition inclined to worship Him; and 4) His Spirit dwelling in them, enabling them to walk in obedience to His word. This has not happened, because Israel has not trusted Jesus Christ as Messiah and Savior, but it will before the kingdom of Messiah (Zech. 12–14; Rom. 11:25–27; Rev. 11:13).

36:26,27 What was figuratively described in v. 25 is explained as literal in vv. 26,27. The gift of the "new heart" signifies the new birth, which is regeneration by the Holy Spirit (11:18–20). The "heart" stands for the whole nature. The "spirit" indicates the governing power of the mind which directs thought and conduct. A "stony heart" is stubborn and self-willed. A "heart of flesh" is pliable and responsive. The evil inclination is removed and a new nature replaces it. This is New Covenant character as in Jeremiah 31:31–34.

good; and you will loathe yourselves in your own sight, for your iniquities and your abominations. [32]Not for your sake do I do *this*," says the Lord GOD, "let it be known to you. Be ashamed and confounded for your own ways, O house of Israel!"

[33]"Thus says the Lord GOD: "On the day that I cleanse you from all your iniquities, I will also enable *you* to dwell in the cities, and the ruins shall be rebuilt. [34]The desolate land shall be tilled instead of lying desolate in the sight of all who pass by. [35]So they will say, 'This land that was desolate has become like the garden of Eden; and the wasted, desolate, and ruined cities *are now* fortified *and* inhabited.' [36]Then the nations which are left all around you shall know that I, the LORD, have rebuilt the ruined places *and* planted what was desolate. I, the LORD, have spoken *it*, and I will do *it*."

[37]"Thus says the Lord GOD: "I will also let the house of Israel inquire of Me to do this for them: I will increase their men like a flock. [38]Like a flock *offered as* holy *sacrifices*, like the flock at Jerusalem on its feast days, so shall the ruined cities be filled with flocks of men. Then they shall know that I *am* the LORD."'"

Psalm 131:1–3

A Song of Ascents. Of David.

LORD, my heart is not haughty,
Nor my eyes lofty.
Neither do I concern myself with great matters,
Nor with things too profound for me.

2 Surely I have calmed and quieted my soul,
Like a weaned child with his mother;
Like a weaned child *is* my soul within me.

3 O Israel, hope in the LORD
From this time forth and forever.

Proverbs 29:2–3

2 When the righteous are in authority,
the people rejoice;
But when a wicked *man* rules, the
people groan.

3 Whoever loves wisdom makes his
father rejoice,
But a companion of harlots wastes *his*
wealth.

James 3:1–18

3 My brethren, let not many of you become teachers, knowing that we shall receive a stricter judgment. [2]For we all stumble in many things. If anyone does not stumble in word, he *is* a perfect man, able also to bridle the whole body. [3]Indeed, we put bits in horses' mouths that they may obey us, and we turn their whole body. [4]Look also at ships: although they are so large and are driven by fierce winds, they are turned by a very small rudder wherever the pilot desires. [5]Even so the tongue is a little member and boasts great things.

See how great a forest a little fire kindles! [6]And the tongue *is* a fire, a world of iniquity. The tongue is so set among our members that it defiles the whole body, and sets on fire the course of nature; and it is set on fire by hell. [7]For every kind of beast and bird, of reptile and creature of the sea, is tamed and has been tamed by mankind. [8]But no man can tame the tongue. *It is* an unruly evil, full of deadly poison. [9]With it we bless our God and Father, and

3:6 tongue *is* a fire. Like fire, the tongue's sinful words can spread destruction rapidly; or as its accompanying smoke, those words can permeate and ruin everything around it. **defiles.** This means "to pollute or contaminate" (Mark 7:20; Jude 23). **the course of nature.** Better translated "the circle of life," this underscores that the tongue's evil can extend beyond the individual to affect everything in his sphere of influence. **hell.** A translation of the Greek word *gehenna* (or valley of Hinnom). In Christ's time, this valley that lay southwest of Jerusalem's walls served as the city dump and was known for its constantly burning fire. Jesus used that place to symbolize the eternal place of punishment and torment (Mark 9:43,45). To James "hell" conjures up not just the place but the satanic host that will some day inherit it—they use the tongue as a tool for evil.

with it we curse men, who have been made in the similitude of God. 10Out of the same mouth proceed blessing and cursing. My brethren, these things ought not to be so. 11Does a spring send forth fresh *water* and bitter from the same opening? 12Can a fig tree, my brethren, bear olives, or a grapevine bear figs? Thus no spring yields both salt water and fresh.

13Who *is* wise and understanding among you? Let him show by good conduct *that* his works *are done* in the meekness of wisdom. 14But if you have bitter envy and self-seeking in your hearts, do not boast and lie against the truth. 15This wisdom does not descend from above, but *is* earthly, sensual, demonic. 16For where envy and self-seeking *exist,* confusion and every evil thing *are* there. 17But the wisdom that is from above is first pure, then peaceable, gentle, willing to yield, full of mercy and good fruits, without partiality and without hypocrisy. 18Now the fruit of righteousness is sown in peace by those who make peace.

DAY 22: How does James explain the difference between the two kinds of wisdom in the world (3:13–18)?

The term "wise" in v. 13 is the common Greek word for speculative knowledge and philosophy, but the Hebrews infused it with the much richer meaning of skillfully applying knowledge to the matter of practical living. This passage points out that two groups of people can be called wise; but in each case, the source of wisdom and the character of the "wise" are entirely opposite.

Wisdom from above (v. 17) includes the following characteristics: 1) pure. This refers to spiritual integrity and moral sincerity. Every genuine Christian has this kind of heart motivation (Pss. 24:3,4; 51:7; Matt. 5:8; Rom. 7:22,23; Heb. 12:14); 2) peaceable. Means "peace loving" or "peace promoting" (Matt. 5:9); 3) gentle. This word is difficult to translate, but most nearly means a character trait of sweet reasonableness. Such a person will submit to all kinds of mistreatment and difficulty with an attitude of kind, courteous, patient humility, without any thought of hatred or revenge (Matt. 5:10,11); 4) willing to yield. The original term described someone who was teachable, compliant, easily persuaded, and who willingly submitted to military discipline or moral and legal standards. For believers, it defines obedience to God's standards (Matt. 5:3–5); 5) full of mercy. The gift of showing concern for those who suffer pain and hardship, and the ability to forgive quickly (Matt. 5:7; Rom. 12:8); 6) without partiality. The Greek word occurs only here in the New Testament and denotes a consistent, unwavering person who is undivided in his commitment and conviction and does not make unfair distinctions.

NOVEMBER 23

Ezekiel 37:1–38:23

37 The hand of the LORD came upon me and brought me out in the Spirit of the LORD, and set me down in the midst of the valley; and it *was* full of bones. 2Then He caused me to pass by them all around, and behold, *there were* very many in the open valley; and indeed *they were* very dry. 3And He said to me, "Son of man, can these bones live?"

So I answered, "O Lord GOD, You know."

4Again He said to me, "Prophesy to these bones, and say to them, 'O dry bones, hear the word of the LORD! 5Thus says the Lord GOD to these bones: "Surely I will cause breath to enter into you, and you shall live. 6I will put sinews on you and bring flesh upon you, cover you with skin and put breath in you; and you shall live. Then you shall know that I *am* the LORD." ' "

37:3 can these bones live? The many dry bones (v. 2) picture the nation Israel (v. 11) as apparently dead in their dispersion and waiting for national resurrection. The people knew about the doctrine of individual resurrection; otherwise, this prophecy would have had no meaning (1 Kin. 17; 2 Kin. 4; 13:21; Is. 25:8; 26:19; Dan. 12:2; Hos. 13:14).

37:4–6 Prophesy to these bones. Ezekiel is to proclaim God's pledge to reassemble Israelites from the world and restore the nation of Israel to life (v. 5) and give them His Spirit (v. 14) in true salvation and spiritual life. Clearly, God is promising the resurrection of the nation of Israel and its spiritual regeneration (36:25–27).

7So I prophesied as I was commanded; and as I prophesied, there was a noise, and suddenly a rattling; and the bones came together, bone to bone. 8Indeed, as I looked, the sinews and the flesh came upon them, and the skin covered them over; but *there was* no breath in them.

9 Also He said to me, "Prophesy to the breath, prophesy, son of man, and say to the breath, 'Thus says the Lord GOD: "Come from the four winds, O breath, and breathe on these slain, that they may live." ' " 10 So I prophesied as He commanded me, and breath came into them, and they lived, and stood upon their feet, an exceedingly great army.

11 Then He said to me, "Son of man, these bones are the whole house of Israel. They indeed say, 'Our bones are dry, our hope is lost, and we ourselves are cut off!' 12 Therefore prophesy and say to them, 'Thus says the Lord GOD: "Behold, O My people, I will open your graves and cause you to come up from your graves, and bring you into the land of Israel. 13 Then you shall know that I *am* the LORD, when I have opened your graves, O My people, and brought you up from your graves. 14 I will put My Spirit in you, and you shall live, and I will place you in your own land. Then you shall know that I, the LORD, have spoken *it* and performed *it*," says the LORD.' "

15 Again the word of the LORD came to me, saying, 16 "As for you, son of man, take a stick for yourself and write on it: 'For Judah and for the children of Israel, his companions.' Then take another stick and write on it, 'For Joseph, the stick of Ephraim, and *for* all the house of Israel, his companions.' 17 Then join them one to another for yourself into one stick, and they will become one in your hand.

18 "And when the children of your people speak to you, saying, 'Will you not show us what you *mean* by these?'— 19 say to them, 'Thus says the Lord GOD: "Surely I will take the stick of Joseph, which *is* in the hand of Ephraim, and the tribes of Israel, his companions; and I will join them with it, with the stick of Judah, and make them one stick, and they will be one in My hand." ' 20 And the sticks on which you write will be in your hand before their eyes.

21 "Then say to them, 'Thus says the Lord GOD: "Surely I will take the children of Israel from among the nations, wherever they have gone, and will gather them from every side and bring them into their own land; 22 and I will make them one nation in the land, on the mountains of Israel; and one king shall be king over them all; they shall no longer be two nations, nor shall they ever be divided into two kingdoms again. 23 They shall not defile themselves anymore with their idols, nor with their detestable things, nor with any of their transgressions; but I will deliver them from all their dwelling places in which they have sinned, and will cleanse them. Then they shall be My people, and I will be their God.

24 "David My servant *shall be* king over them, and they shall all have one shepherd; they shall also walk in My judgments and observe My statutes, and do them. 25 Then they shall dwell in the land that I have given to Jacob My servant, where your fathers dwelt; and they shall dwell there, they, their children, and their children's children, forever; and My servant David *shall be* their prince forever. 26 Moreover I will make a covenant of peace with them, and it shall be an everlasting covenant with them; I will establish them and multiply them, and I will set My sanctuary in their midst forevermore. 27 My tabernacle also shall be with them; indeed I will be their God, and they shall be My people. 28 The nations also will know that I, the LORD, sanctify Israel, when My sanctuary is in their midst forevermore." ' "

38 Now the word of the LORD came to me, saying, 2 "Son of man, set your face against Gog, of the land of Magog, the prince of Rosh, Meshech, and Tubal, and prophesy against him, 3 and say, 'Thus says the Lord GOD: "Behold, I *am* against you, O Gog, the prince of Rosh, Meshech, and Tubal. 4 I will turn you around, put hooks into your jaws, and lead you out, with all your army, horses, and horsemen, all splendidly clothed, a great company *with* bucklers and shields, all of them handling swords. 5 Persia, Ethiopia, and Libya are with them, all of them *with* shield and helmet; 6 Gomer and all its troops; the house of Togarmah *from* the far north and all its troops—many people *are* with you.

7 "Prepare yourself and be ready, you and all your companies that are gathered about you; and be a guard for them. 8 After many days you will be visited. In the latter years you will come into the land of those brought back from the sword *and* gathered from many people on the mountains of Israel, which had long been desolate; they were brought out of the nations, and now all of them dwell safely. 9 You will ascend, coming like a storm, covering the land like a cloud, you and all your troops and many peoples with you."

10 'Thus says the Lord GOD: "On that day it shall come to pass *that* thoughts will arise in your mind, and you will make an evil plan: 11 You will say, 'I will go up against a land of unwalled villages; I will go to a peaceful people, who dwell safely, all of them dwelling without walls, and having neither bars nor gates'— 12 to take plunder and to take booty, to stretch out your hand against the waste places *that are again* inhabited, and against a people gathered

from the nations, who have acquired livestock
and goods, who dwell in the midst of the land.
[13]Sheba, Dedan, the merchants of Tarshish,
and all their young lions will say to you, 'Have
you come to take plunder? Have you gathered
your army to take booty, to carry away silver
and gold, to take away livestock and goods, to
take great plunder?' " '
[14]"Therefore, son of man, prophesy and say
to Gog, 'Thus says the Lord GOD: "On that day
when My people Israel dwell safely, will you
not know *it?* [15]Then you will come from your
place out of the far north, you and many peoples with you, all of them riding on horses, a
great company and a mighty army. [16]You will
come up against My people Israel like a cloud,
to cover the land. It will be in the latter days
that I will bring you against My land, so that
the nations may know Me, when I am hallowed
in you, O Gog, before their eyes." [17]Thus says
the Lord GOD: "Are *you* he of whom I have
spoken in former days by My servants the
prophets of Israel, who prophesied for years in
those days that I would bring you against them?
[18]"And it will come to pass at the same time,
when Gog comes against the land of Israel,"
says the Lord GOD, "*that* My fury will show in
My face. [19]For in My jealousy *and* in the fire of
My wrath I have spoken: 'Surely in that day
there shall be a great earthquake in the land of
Israel, [20]so that the fish of the sea, the birds of
the heavens, the beasts of the field, all creeping
things that creep on the earth, and all men who
are on the face of the earth shall shake at My
presence. The mountains shall be thrown
down, the steep places shall fall, and every
wall shall fall to the ground.' [21]I will call for a
sword against Gog throughout all My mountains," says the Lord GOD. "Every man's
sword will be against his brother. [22]And I will
bring him to judgment with pestilence and
bloodshed; I will rain down on him, on his
troops, and on the many peoples who *are* with
him, flooding rain, great hailstones, fire, and
brimstone. [23]Thus I will magnify Myself and
sanctify Myself, and I will be known in the
eyes of many nations. Then they shall know
that I *am* the LORD." '

Psalm 132:1–9

A Song of Ascents.

LORD, remember David
And all his afflictions;
[2] How he swore to the LORD,
And vowed to the Mighty One of Jacob:
[3] "Surely I will not go into the chamber of
my house,
Or go up to the comfort of my bed;
[4] I will not give sleep to my eyes
Or slumber to my eyelids,
[5] Until I find a place for the LORD,
A dwelling place for the Mighty One
of Jacob."

[6] Behold, we heard of it in Ephrathah;
We found it in the fields of the woods.
[7] Let us go into His tabernacle;
Let us worship at His footstool.
[8] Arise, O LORD, to Your resting place,
You and the ark of Your strength.
[9] Let Your priests be clothed with
righteousness,
And let Your saints shout for joy.

Proverbs 29:4

[4] The king establishes the land by
justice,
But he who receives bribes
overthrows it.

James 4:1–17

4 Where do wars and fights *come* from
among you? Do *they* not *come* from your
desires for pleasure that war in your members?
[2]You lust and do not have. You murder and
covet and cannot obtain. You fight and war. Yet
you do not have because you do not ask. [3]You
ask and do not receive, because you ask amiss,
that you may spend *it* on your pleasures. [4]Adul-
terers and adulteresses! Do you not know that
friendship with the world is enmity with God?
Whoever therefore wants to be a friend of the
world makes himself an enemy of God. [5]Or do
you think that the Scripture says in vain, "The
Spirit who dwells in us yearns jealously"?
[6]But He gives more grace. Therefore He
says:

"God resists the proud,
But gives grace to the humble."

4:4 friendship. Appearing only here in the New Testament, the Greek word describes love in the sense of a strong emotional attachment. Those with a deep and intimate longing for the things of the world give evidence that they are not redeemed (1 John 2:15–17). **enmity with God.** The necessary corollary to friendship with the world. The sobering truth that unbelievers are God's enemies is taught throughout Scripture (Deut. 32:41–43; Pss. 21:8; 68:21; 72:9; 110:1,2; Is. 42:13; Nah. 1:2,8; Luke 19:27; Rom. 5:10; 8:5–7; 1 Cor. 15:25).

4:6 more grace. The only ray of hope in man's spiritual darkness is the sovereign grace of God, which alone can rescue man from his propensity to lust for evil things. That God gives "more grace" shows that His grace is greater than the power of sin, the flesh, the world, and Satan (Rom. 5:20). The Old Testament quote (from Prov. 3:34; 1 Pet. 5:5) reveals who obtains God's grace—the humble, not the proud enemies of God. The word "humble" does not define a special class of Christians, but encompasses all believers (Is. 57:15; 66:2; Matt. 18:3,4).

7Therefore submit to God. Resist the devil
and he will flee from you. 8Draw near to God
and He will draw near to you. Cleanse *your*
hands, *you* sinners; and purify *your* hearts, *you*
double-minded. 9Lament and mourn and weep!
Let your laughter be turned to mourning and
your joy to gloom. 10Humble yourselves in the
sight of the Lord, and He will lift you up.
11Do not speak evil of one another, brethren.
He who speaks evil of a brother and judges his
brother, speaks evil of the law and judges the
law. But if you judge the law, you are not a
doer of the law but a judge. 12There is one Lawgiver, who is able to save and to destroy. Who
are you to judge another?
13Come now, you who say, "Today or tomorrow we will go to such and such a city, spend
a year there, buy and sell, and make a profit";
14whereas you do not know what *will happen*
tomorrow. For what *is* your life? It is even a
vapor that appears for a little time and then
vanishes away. 15Instead you *ought* to say, "If
the Lord wills, we shall live and do this or
that." 16But now you boast in your arrogance.
All such boasting is evil.
17Therefore, to him who knows to do good
and does not do *it*, to him it is sin.

DAY 23: What do the 10 commands that fill James 4:7–10 have to do with grace?

These verses contain a series of 10 commands that prepare a person to receive saving grace. These commands delineate a person's response to God's gracious offer of salvation and reveal what it means to be humble. Each command uses a Greek imperative to define the expected action:

1. Submit to God (v. 7)—James used the word to describe a willing, conscious submission to God's authority as sovereign ruler of the universe.
2. Resist the devil (v. 7)—those who consciously "take [their] stand against" Satan and transfer their allegiance to God will find that Satan "will flee from" them; he is a defeated foe.
3. Draw near to God (v. 8)—pursue an intimate love relationship with God (Phil. 3:10).
4. Cleanse your hands (v. 8)—the added term "sinners" addresses the unbelievers' need to recognize and confess their sin (5:20).
5. Purify your hearts (v. 8)—cleansing the hands symbolizes external behavior; this phrase refers to the inner thoughts, motives, and desires of the heart (Ps. 24:3,4).
6. Lament (v. 9)—to be afflicted, wretched, and miserable. This is the state of those truly broken over their sin (Matt. 5:4).
7. Mourn (v. 9)—the internal experience of brokenness over sin (Ps. 51:17; Matt. 5:4).
8. Weep (v. 9)—the outward manifestation of inner sorrow over sin (Mark 14:72).
9. Grieve without laughter or joy (v. 9)—the signs of denial; the flippant laughter of those foolishly indulging in worldly pleasures without regard to God, life, death, sin, judgment, or holiness.
10. Humble yourself (v. 10)—this final command sums up the preceding 9. The word "humble" comes from a word meaning "to make oneself low." Those conscious of being in the presence of the majestic, infinitely holy God are humble (Is. 6:5).

NOVEMBER 24

Ezekiel 39:1–40:49

39 "And you, son of man, prophesy against
Gog, and say, 'Thus says the Lord GOD:
"Behold, I *am* against you, O Gog, the prince of
Rosh, Meshech, and Tubal; 2and I will turn
you around and lead you on, bringing you up
from the far north, and bring you against the
mountains of Israel. 3Then I will knock the bow
out of your left hand, and cause the arrows to
fall out of your right hand. 4You shall fall upon
the mountains of Israel, you and all your troops
and the peoples who *are* with you; I will give
you to birds of prey of every sort and *to* the
beasts of the field to be devoured. 5You shall
fall on the open field; for I have spoken," says
the Lord GOD. 6"And I will send fire on Magog
and on those who live in security in the coast-

lands. Then they shall know that I *am* the
LORD. 7So I will make My holy name known in
the midst of My people Israel, and I will not *let*
them profane My holy name anymore. Then
the nations shall know that *I am* the LORD, the
Holy One in Israel. 8Surely it is coming, and it
shall be done," says the Lord GOD. "This *is* the
day of which I have spoken.
9"Then those who dwell in the cities of Israel
will go out and set on fire and burn the weapons,
both the shields and bucklers, the bows and
arrows, the javelins and spears; and they will
make fires with them for seven years. 10They
will not take wood from the field nor cut down
any from the forests, because they will make
fires with the weapons; and they will plunder
those who plundered them, and pillage those
who pillaged them," says the Lord GOD.
11"It will come to pass in that day *that* I will
give Gog a burial place there in Israel, the valley of those who pass by east of the sea; and it
will obstruct travelers, because there they will
bury Gog and all his multitude. Therefore
they will call *it* the Valley of Hamon Gog. 12For
seven months the house of Israel will be burying them, in order to cleanse the land. 13In-
deed all the people of the land will be burying,
and they will gain renown for it on the day that
I am glorified," says the Lord GOD. 14"They will
set apart men regularly employed, with the
help of a search party, to pass through the land
and bury those bodies remaining on the
ground, in order to cleanse it. At the end of
seven months they will make a search. 15The
search party will pass through the land; and
when anyone sees a man's bone, he shall set up
a marker by it, till the buriers have buried it in
the Valley of Hamon Gog. 16*The* name of *the*
city *will* also *be* Hamonah. Thus they shall
cleanse the land." '
17"And as for you, son of man, thus says the
Lord GOD, 'Speak to every sort of bird and to
every beast of the field:

"Assemble yourselves and come;
Gather together from all sides to My
    sacrificial meal
Which I am sacrificing for you,
A great sacrificial meal on the
    mountains of Israel,
That you may eat flesh and drink
    blood.
18 You shall eat the flesh of the mighty,
Drink the blood of the princes of the
    earth,
Of rams and lambs,
Of goats and bulls,
All of them fatlings of Bashan.
19 You shall eat fat till you are full,
And drink blood till you are drunk,
At My sacrificial meal
Which I am sacrificing for you.
20 You shall be filled at My table
With horses and riders,
With mighty men
And with all the men of war,"
    says the Lord GOD.

21"I will set My glory among the nations; all
the nations shall see My judgment which I
have executed, and My hand which I have laid
on them. 22So the house of Israel shall know
that I *am* the LORD their God from that day forward. 23The Gentiles shall know that the house
of Israel went into captivity for their iniquity;
because they were unfaithful to Me, therefore
I hid My face from them. I gave them into the
hand of their enemies, and they all fell by the
sword. 24According to their uncleanness and
according to their transgressions I have dealt
with them, and hidden My face from them." '
25"Therefore thus says the Lord GOD: 'Now I
will bring back the captives of Jacob, and have
mercy on the whole house of Israel; and I will
be jealous for My holy name— 26after they
have borne their shame, and all their unfaithfulness in which they were unfaithful to Me,
when they dwelt safely in their *own* land and no
one made *them* afraid. 27When I have brought
them back from the peoples and gathered
them out of their enemies' lands, and I am hallowed in them in the sight of many nations,
28then they shall know that I *am* the LORD their
God, who sent them into captivity among the
nations, but also brought them back to their
land, and left none of them captive any longer.
29And I will not hide My face from them anymore; for I shall have poured out My Spirit on
the house of Israel,' says the Lord GOD."

40 In the twenty-fifth year of our captivity,
at the beginning of the year, on the
tenth *day* of the month, in the fourteenth year
after the city was captured, on the very same
day the hand of the LORD was upon me; and
He took me there. 2In the visions of God He
took me into the land of Israel and set me on a
very high mountain; on it toward the south
was something like the structure of a city. 3He
took me there, and behold, *there was* a man
whose appearance *was* like the appearance of
bronze. He had a line of flax and a measuring
rod in his hand, and he stood in the gateway.
4And the man said to me, "Son of man, look
with your eyes and hear with your ears, and
fix your mind on everything I show you; for
you *were* brought here so that I might show
them to you. Declare to the house of Israel
everything you see." 5Now there was a wall all

around the outside of the temple. In the man's
hand was a measuring rod six cubits *long,*
each being a cubit and a handbreadth; and he
measured the width of the wall structure, one
rod; and the height, one rod.

[6]Then he went to the gateway which faced
east; and he went up its stairs and measured
the threshold of the gateway, *which was* one
rod wide, and the other threshold *was* one rod
wide. [7]Each gate chamber *was* one rod long
and one rod wide; between the gate chambers
was a space of five cubits; and the threshold of
the gateway by the vestibule of the inside gate
was one rod. [8]He also measured the vestibule
of the inside gate, one rod. [9]Then he measured
the vestibule of the gateway, eight cubits; and
the gateposts, two cubits. The vestibule of the
gate *was* on the inside. [10]In the eastern gateway *were* three gate chambers on one side and
three on the other; the three *were* all the same
size; also the gateposts were of the same size
on this side and that side.

1.5 ft = 1 cubit

[11]He measured the width of the entrance to
the gateway, ten cubits; *and* the length of the
gate, thirteen cubits. [12]*There was* a space in front
of the gate chambers, one cubit *on this side* and
one cubit on that side; the gate chambers *were*
six cubits on this side and six cubits on that
side. [13]Then he measured the gateway from
the roof of *one* gate chamber to the roof of the
other; the width *was* twenty-five cubits, as door
faces door. [14]He measured the gateposts, sixty
cubits high, and the court all around the gateway *extended* to the gatepost. [15]*From* the front
of the entrance gate to the front of the
vestibule of the inner gate *was* fifty cubits.
[16]*There were* beveled window *frames* in the gate
chambers and in their intervening archways
on the inside of the gateway all around, and
likewise in the vestibules. *There were* windows
all around on the inside. And on each gatepost
were palm trees.

[17]Then he brought me into the outer court;
and *there were* chambers and a pavement
made all around the court; thirty chambers
faced the pavement. [18]The pavement was by
the side of the gateways, corresponding to the
length of the gateways; *this was* the lower
pavement. [19]Then he measured the width from
the front of the lower gateway to the front of
the inner court exterior, one hundred cubits
toward the east and the north.

[20]On the outer court was also a gateway facing north, and he measured its length and its
width. [21]Its gate chambers, three on this side
and three on that side, its gateposts and its
archways, had the same measurements as the
first gate; its length *was* fifty cubits and its
width twenty-five cubits. [22]Its windows and
those of its archways, and also its palm trees,
had the same measurements as the gateway
facing east; it was ascended by seven steps,
and its archway *was* in front of it. [23]A gate of the
inner court was opposite the northern gateway,
just as the eastern *gateway;* and he measured
from gateway to gateway, one hundred cubits.

[24]After that he brought me toward the south,
and there a gateway was facing south; and he
measured its gateposts and archways according to these same measurements. [25]*There were*
windows in it and in its archways all around
like those windows; its length *was* fifty cubits
and its width twenty-five cubits. [26]Seven steps
led up to it, and its archway *was* in front of
them; and it had palm trees on its gateposts,
one on this side and one on that side. [27]*There*
was also a gateway on the inner court, facing
south; and he measured from gateway to gateway toward the south, one hundred cubits.

[28]Then he brought me to the inner court
through the southern gateway; he measured the
southern gateway according to these same
measurements. [29]Also its gate chambers, its
gateposts, and its archways *were* according to
these same measurements; *there were* windows
in it and in its archways all around; *it was* fifty
cubits long and twenty-five cubits wide. [30]*There*
were archways all around, twenty-five cubits
long and five cubits wide. [31]Its archways faced
the outer court, palm trees *were* on its gateposts,
and going up to it *were* eight steps.

[32]And he brought me into the inner court
facing east; he measured the gateway according to these same measurements. [33]Also its
gate chambers, its gateposts, and its archways
were according to these same measurements;
and *there were* windows in it and in its archways all around; *it was* fifty cubits long and
twenty-five cubits wide. [34]Its archways faced
the outer court, and palm trees *were* on its
gateposts on this side and on that side; and
going up to it *were* eight steps.

[35]Then he brought me to the north gateway
and measured *it* according to these same
measurements— [36]also its gate chambers, its
gateposts, and its archways. It had windows all
around; its length *was* fifty cubits and its width
twenty-five cubits. [37]Its gateposts faced the
outer court, palm trees *were* on its gateposts
on this side and on that side, and going up to it
were eight steps.

[38]*There was* a chamber and its entrance by
the gateposts of the gateway, where they
washed the burnt offering. [39]In the vestibule of
the gateway *were* two tables on this side and
two tables on that side, on which to slay the

burnt offering, the sin offering, and the trespass offering. 40 At the outer side of the *ves-*
tibule, as one goes up to the entrance of the
northern gateway, *were* two tables; and on the
other side of the vestibule of the gateway *were*
two tables. 41 Four tables *were* on this side and
four tables on that side, by the side of the
gateway, eight tables on which they slaughtered *the sacrifices.* 42 *There were* also four
tables of hewn stone for the burnt offering,
one cubit and a half long, one cubit and a half
wide, and one cubit high; on these they laid
the instruments with which they slaughtered
the burnt offering and the sacrifice. 43 Inside
were hooks, a handbreadth wide, fastened all
around; and the flesh of the sacrifices *was* on
the tables.

44 Outside the inner gate *were* the chambers
for the singers in the inner court, one facing
south at the side of the northern gateway, and
the other facing north at the side of the southern gateway. 45 Then he said to me, "This chamber which faces south *is* for the priests who
have charge of the temple. 46 The chamber
which faces north *is* for the priests who have
charge of the altar; these *are* the sons of Zadok,
from the sons of Levi, who come near the LORD
to minister to Him."

47 And he measured the court, one hundred
cubits long and one hundred cubits wide,
foursquare. The altar *was* in front of the temple. 48 Then he brought me to the vestibule of
the temple and measured the doorposts of the
vestibule, five cubits on this side and five
cubits on that side; and the width of the gateway was three cubits on this side and three
cubits on that side. 49 The length of the vestibule
was twenty cubits, and the width eleven cubits;
and by the steps which led up to it *there were*
pillars by the doorposts, one on this side and
another on that side.

Psalm 132:10–18

10 For Your servant David's sake,
Do not turn away the face of Your
Anointed.

11 The LORD has sworn *in* truth to David;
He will not turn from it:
"I will set upon your throne the fruit of
your body.
12 If your sons will keep My covenant
And My testimony which I shall teach
them,
Their sons also shall sit upon your
throne forevermore."

13 For the LORD has chosen Zion;
He has desired *it* for His dwelling place:
14 "This *is* My resting place forever;
Here I will dwell, for I have desired it.
15 I will abundantly bless her provision;
I will satisfy her poor with bread.
16 I will also clothe her priests with
salvation,
And her saints shall shout aloud for joy.
17 There I will make the horn of David
grow;
I will prepare a lamp for My Anointed.
18 His enemies I will clothe with shame,
But upon Himself His crown shall
flourish."

Proverbs 29:5

5 A man who flatters his neighbor
Spreads a net for his feet.

James 5:1–20

5 Come now, *you* rich, weep and howl for
your miseries that are coming upon *you!*
2 Your riches are corrupted, and your garments
are moth-eaten. 3 Your gold and silver are cor-
roded, and their corrosion will be a witness
against you and will eat your flesh like fire.
You have heaped up treasure in the last days.
4 Indeed the wages of the laborers who mowed
your fields, which you kept back by fraud, cry
out; and the cries of the reapers have reached
the ears of the Lord of Sabaoth. 5 You have lived
on the earth in pleasure and luxury; you have
fattened your hearts as in a day of slaughter.
6 You have condemned, you have murdered
the just; he does not resist you.

7 Therefore be patient, brethren, until the
coming of the Lord. See *how* the farmer waits
for the precious fruit of the earth, waiting
patiently for it until it receives the early and latter rain. 8 You also be patient. Establish your
hearts, for the coming of the Lord is at hand.

9 Do not grumble against one another,
brethren, lest you be condemned. Behold, the
Judge is standing at the door! 10 My brethren,
take the prophets, who spoke in the name of
the Lord, as an example of suffering and patience. 11 Indeed we count them blessed who

132:10 A prayer that God's promise and favor would not be withheld from David's descendants on the throne of Judah. **Your Anointed.** As David had been anointed king (1 Sam. 16:13), so a greater King had been anointed, namely Christ, but not yet seated on the throne (Is. 61:1; Luke 4:18,19).

5:7 patient. The word emphasizes patience with people (1 Thess. 5:14), not trials or circumstances (as in 1:3). Specifically, James has in mind patience with the oppressive rich. **the coming.** The Second Coming of Christ. Realizing the glory that awaits them at Christ's return should motivate believers to patiently endure mistreatment (Rom. 8:18). **the early and latter rain.** The "early" rain falls in Israel during October and November and softens the ground for planting. The "latter" rain falls in March and April, immediately before the spring harvest. Just as the farmer waits patiently from the early rain to the latter for his crop to ripen, so must Christians patiently wait for the Lord's return (Gal. 6:9; 2 Tim. 4:8; Titus 2:13).

endure. You have heard of the perseverance
of Job and seen the end *intended by* the
Lord—that the Lord is very compassionate
and merciful.
[12]But above all, my brethren, do not swear,
either by heaven or by earth or with any other
oath. But let your "Yes" be "Yes," and *your*
"No," "No," lest you fall into judgment.
[13]Is anyone among you suffering? Let him
pray. Is anyone cheerful? Let him sing psalms.
[14]Is anyone among you sick? Let him call for
the elders of the church, and let them pray
over him, anointing him with oil in the name of
the Lord. [15]And the prayer of faith will save the
sick, and the Lord will raise him up. And if he
has committed sins, he will be forgiven. [16]Con-
fess *your* trespasses to one another, and pray
for one another, that you may be healed. The
effective, fervent prayer of a righteous man
avails much. [17]Elijah was a man with a nature
like ours, and he prayed earnestly that it
would not rain; and it did not rain on the land
for three years and six months. [18]And he

5:14 anointing him with oil. Literally, "rubbing him with oil": 1) possibly this is a reference to ceremonial anointing (Lev. 14:18; Mark 6:13); 2) on the other hand, James may have had in mind medical treatment of believers physically bruised and battered by persecution. Perhaps it is better to understand the anointing in a metaphorical sense of the elders' encouraging, comforting, and strengthening the believer.

prayed again, and the heaven gave rain, and
the earth produced its fruit.
[19]Brethren, if anyone among you wanders
from the truth, and someone turns him back,
[20]let him know that he who turns a sinner from
the error of his way will save a soul from death
and cover a multitude of sins.

5:14,15 sick. James directs those who are "sick," meaning weakened by their suffering, to call for the elders of the church for strength, support, and prayer.

5:15 prayer of faith. The prayer offered on their behalf by the elders. **save the sick.** Deliver them from their suffering because they have been weakened by their infirmity, not from their sin, which was confessed. **committed sins...be forgiven.** Not by the elders, since God alone can forgive sins (Is. 43:25; Dan. 9:9; Mark 2:7). That those who are suffering called for the elders implies they had a contrite, repentant heart, and that part of their time with the overseers would involve confessing their sins to God.

DAY 24: What warning does James give to the rich?

In James 5:1, he begins: "Come now, you rich, weep and howl for your miseries that are coming upon you!" James condemns them not for being wealthy, but for misusing their resources. Unlike the believing rich in Timothy's congregation (1 Tim. 6:17–19), these are the wicked wealthy who profess Christian faith and have associated themselves with the church, but whose real god is money.

"Indeed the wages...you kept back" (v. 4). The rich had gained some of their wealth by oppressing and defrauding their day laborers—a practice strictly forbidden in the Old Testament (Lev. 19:13; Deut. 24:14,15). The One who hears the cries of the defrauded laborers, James warns, is the Lord of hosts, the commander of the armies of heaven (angels). The Bible teaches that angels will be involved in the judgment of unbelievers (Matt. 13:39–41,49; 16:27; 25:31; 2 Thess. 1:7,8).

"You have lived on the earth in pleasure and luxury" (v. 5). After robbing their workers to accumulate their wealth, the rich indulged themselves in an extravagant lifestyle. "Pleasure" has the connotation of wanton pleasure. "Luxury" leads to vice when a person becomes consumed with the pursuit of pleasure, since a life without self-denial soon becomes out of control in every area. Like fattened cattle ready to be slaughtered, the rich that James condemns had indulged themselves to the limit.

"You have condemned... murdered the just" (v. 6). This describes the next step in the sinful progression of the rich. Hoarding led to fraud, which led to self-indulgence. Finally, that overindulgence has consumed the rich to the point that they will do anything to sustain their lifestyle. "Condemned" comes from a word meaning "to sentence." The implication is that the rich were using the courts to commit judicial murder (2:6).

NOVEMBER 25

Ezekiel 41:1–42:20

41 Then he brought me into the sanctuary
and measured the doorposts, six cubits
wide on one side and six cubits wide on the
other side—the width of the tabernacle. [2]The
width of the entryway *was* ten cubits, and the
side walls of the entrance *were* five cubits on
this side and five cubits on the other side; and
he measured its length, forty cubits, and its
width, twenty cubits.
[3]Also he went inside and measured the
doorposts, two cubits; and the entrance, six
cubits *high;* and the width of the entrance,
seven cubits. [4]He measured the length, twenty
cubits; and the width, twenty cubits, beyond
the sanctuary; and he said to me, "This *is* the
Most Holy *Place.*"
[5]Next, he measured the wall of the temple,
six cubits. The width of each side chamber all
around the temple *was* four cubits on every
side. [6]The side chambers *were* in three stories,
one above the other, thirty chambers in each
story; they rested on ledges which *were* for
the side chambers all around, that they might
be supported, but not fastened to the wall of
the temple. [7]As one went up from story to
story, the side chambers became wider all
around, because their supporting ledges in
the wall of the temple ascended like steps;
therefore the width of the structure increased
as one went up *from* the lowest *story* to the
highest by way of the middle one. [8]I also saw
an elevation all around the temple; it was the
foundation of the side chambers, a full rod,
that is, six cubits *high.* [9]The thickness of the
outer wall of the side chambers *was* five
cubits, and so also the remaining terrace by
the place of the side chambers of the temple.
[10]And between *it and* the *wall* chambers was a
width of twenty cubits all around the temple on
every side. [11]The doors of the side chambers
opened on the terrace, one door toward the
north and another toward the south; and the
width of the terrace *was* five cubits all around.
[12]The building that faced the separating
courtyard at its western end *was* seventy cubits
wide; the wall of the building *was* five cubits
thick all around, and its length ninety cubits.
[13]So he measured the temple, one hundred
cubits long; and the separating courtyard with
the building and its walls *was* one hundred
cubits long; [14]also the width of the eastern face
of the temple, including the separating courtyard, *was* one hundred cubits. [15]He measured
the length of the building behind it, facing the
separating courtyard, with its galleries on the
one side and on the other side, one hundred
cubits, as well as the inner temple and the
porches of the court, [16]their doorposts and the
beveled window frames. And the galleries all
around their three stories opposite the threshold were paneled with wood from the ground to
the windows—the windows were covered—
[17]from the space above the door, even to the
inner room, as well as outside, and on every
wall all around, inside and outside, by measure.
[18]And *it was* made with cherubim and palm
trees, a palm tree between cherub and
cherub. *Each* cherub had two faces, [19]so that
the face of a man *was* toward a palm tree on
one side, and the face of a young lion toward a
palm tree on the other side; thus *it was* made
throughout the temple all around. [20]From the
floor to the space above the door, and on the
wall of the sanctuary, cherubim and palm
trees *were* carved.
[21]The doorposts of the temple *were* square,
as was the front of the sanctuary; their appearance was similar. [22]The altar *was* of wood,
three cubits high, and its length two cubits. Its
corners, its length, and its sides *were* of wood;
and he said to me, "This *is* the table that *is* before the LORD."
[23]The temple and the sanctuary had two
doors. [24]The doors had two panels *apiece,* two
folding panels: two *panels* for one door and
two panels for the other *door.* [25]Cherubim and
palm trees *were* carved on the doors of the
temple just as they *were* carved on the walls. A
wooden canopy *was* on the front of the
vestibule outside. [26]*There were* beveled window

frames and palm trees on one side and on the
other, on the sides of the vestibule—also on the
side chambers of the temple and on the canopies.

42 Then he brought me out into the outer
court, by the way toward the north;
and he brought me into the chamber which
was opposite the separating courtyard, and
which *was* opposite the building toward the
north. 2Facing the length, *which was* one hundred cubits (the width was fifty cubits), was
the north door. 3Opposite the inner court of
twenty *cubits,* and opposite the pavement of
the outer court, *was* gallery against gallery in
three *stories.* 4In front of the chambers, toward
the inside, *was* a walk ten cubits wide, at a distance of one cubit; and their doors faced
north. 5Now the upper chambers *were* shorter,
because the galleries took away *space* from
them more than from the lower and middle
stories of the building. 6For they *were* in three
stories and did not have pillars like the pillars
of the courts; therefore *the upper level* was
shortened more than the lower and middle
levels from the ground up. 7And a wall which
was outside ran parallel to the chambers, at
the front of the chambers, toward the outer
court; its length *was* fifty cubits. 8The length of
the chambers toward the outer court *was* fifty
cubits, whereas that facing the temple *was* one
hundred cubits. 9At the lower chambers *was*
the entrance on the east side, as one goes into
them from the outer court.

10Also *there were* chambers in the thickness
of the wall of the court toward the east, opposite the separating courtyard and opposite the
building. 11*There was* a walk in front of them
also, and their appearance *was* like the chambers which *were* toward the north; they *were* as
long and as wide as the others, and all their
exits and entrances *were* according to plan.
12And corresponding to the doors of the chambers that *were* facing south, as one enters them,
there was a door in front of the walk, the way
directly in front of the wall toward the east.

13Then he said to me, "The north chambers
and the south chambers, which *are* opposite
the separating courtyard, *are* the holy chambers where the priests who approach the LORD
shall eat the most holy offerings. There they
shall lay the most holy offerings—the grain
offering, the sin offering, and the trespass
offering—for the place *is* holy. 14When the
priests enter them, they shall not go out of the
holy *chamber* into the outer court; but there
they shall leave their garments in which they
minister, for they *are* holy. They shall put on
other garments; then they may approach *that*
which *is* for the people."

15Now when he had finished measuring the
inner temple, he brought me out through the
gateway that faces toward the east, and measured it all around. 16He measured the east
side with the measuring rod, five hundred
rods by the measuring rod all around. 17He
measured the north side, five hundred rods
by the measuring rod all around. 18He measured the south side, five hundred rods by the
measuring rod. 19He came around to the west
side *and* measured five hundred rods by the
measuring rod. 20He measured it on the four
sides; it had a wall all around, five hundred *cubits* long and five hundred wide, to separate
the holy areas from the common.

Psalm 133:1–3

A Song of Ascents. Of David.

Behold, how good and how
pleasant *it is*
For brethren to dwell together
in unity!

2 *It is* like the precious oil upon the head,
Running down on the beard,
The beard of Aaron,
Running down on the edge of his
garments.

3 *It is* like the dew of Hermon,
Descending upon the mountains of Zion;
For there the LORD commanded the
blessing—
Life forevermore.

133:2 oil upon. Most likely refers to the anointing of Aaron as high priest of the nation (Ex. 29:7; 30:30), which would picture a rich spiritual blessing as a first priority.

Proverbs 29:6

6 By transgression an evil man is snared,
But the righteous sings and rejoices.

1 Peter 1:1–25

1 Peter, an apostle of Jesus Christ,

To the pilgrims of the Dispersion in Pontus,
Galatia, Cappadocia, Asia, and Bithynia, 2elect
according to the foreknowledge of God the
Father, in sanctification of the Spirit, for obedience and sprinkling of the blood of Jesus Christ:

Grace to you and peace be multiplied.

3Blessed *be* the God and Father of our Lord

1:4 inheritance. Peter showed those persecuted Christians how to look past their troubles to their eternal inheritance. Life, righteousness, joy, peace, perfection, God's presence, Christ's glorious companionship, rewards, and all else God has planned is the Christian's heavenly inheritance (v. 5; Matt. 25:34; Acts 26:18; Eph. 1:11; Col. 1:12; Heb. 9:15; also Pss. 16:5; 23; 26; 72; Lam. 3:24). According to Ephesians 1:14, the indwelling Holy Spirit is the resident guarantee of that inheritance. **incorruptible.** The inheritance is not subject to passing away nor liable to decay. The word was used in secular Greek of something that was unravaged by an invading army (Matt. 6:19–21). **undefiled.** This word means unpolluted, unstained with evil. The undefiled inheritance of the Christian is in marked contrast to an earthly inheritance, all of which is corrupted and defiled. **does not fade away.** "Fading" was often used of flowers that wither and decay. Though earthly inheritances eventually fade away, the eternal inheritance of a Christian has no decaying elements.

Jesus Christ, who according to His abundant
mercy has begotten us again to a living hope
through the resurrection of Jesus Christ from
the dead, 4to an inheritance incorruptible and
undefiled and that does not fade away, reserved in heaven for you, 5who are kept by the
power of God through faith for salvation ready
to be revealed in the last time.
6In this you greatly rejoice, though now for
a little while, if need be, you have been grieved
by various trials, 7that the genuineness of your
faith, *being* much more precious than gold that
perishes, though it is tested by fire, may be
found to praise, honor, and glory at the revelation of Jesus Christ, 8whom having not seen
you love. Though now you do not see *Him,* yet
believing, you rejoice with joy inexpressible
and full of glory, 9receiving the end of your
faith—the salvation of *your* souls.
10Of this salvation the prophets have
inquired and searched carefully, who prophesied of the grace *that would come* to you,
11searching what, or what manner of time,
the Spirit of Christ who was in them was
indicating when He testified beforehand the
sufferings of Christ and the glories that
would follow. 12To them it was revealed that,
not to themselves, but to us they were ministering the things which now have been
reported to you through those who have
preached the gospel to you by the Holy Spirit
sent from heaven—things which angels
desire to look into.
13Therefore gird up the loins of your mind,
be sober, and rest *your* hope fully upon the
grace that is to be brought to you at the revelation of Jesus Christ; 14as obedient children,
not conforming yourselves to the former
lusts, *as* in your ignorance; 15but as He who
called you *is* holy, you also be holy in all *your*
conduct, 16because it is written, *"Be holy, for I
am holy."*
17And if you call on the Father, who without
partiality judges according to each one's
work, conduct yourselves throughout the time
of your stay *here* in fear; 18knowing that you
were not redeemed with corruptible things,
like silver or gold, from your aimless conduct
received by tradition from your fathers, 19but
with the precious blood of Christ, as of a lamb
without blemish and without spot. 20He indeed
was foreordained before the foundation of the
world, but was manifest in these last times for
you 21who through Him believe in God, who
raised Him from the dead and gave Him glory,
so that your faith and hope are in God.
22Since you have purified your souls in obeying the truth through the Spirit in sincere love
of the brethren, love one another fervently
with a pure heart, 23having been born again,
not of corruptible seed but incorruptible,
through the word of God which lives and
abides forever, 24because

"All flesh is as grass,
And all the glory of man as the flower
of the grass.
The grass withers,
And its flower falls away,
25 *But the word of the LORD endures*
forever."

Now this is the word which by the gospel was
preached to you.

1:7 genuineness of your faith. God's purpose in allowing trouble is to test the reality of one's faith. But the benefit of such a testing, or "fire," is immediately for the Christian, not God. When a believer comes through a trial still trusting the Lord, he is assured that his faith is genuine (Gen. 22:1–12; Job 1:20–22). **revelation of Jesus Christ.** The revelation or unveiling of Christ refers to His Second Coming, particularly focusing on the time when He comes to call and reward His redeemed people (v. 13; 4:13; 1 Cor. 1:7), i.e., the Rapture (1 Thess. 4:13–18).

DAY 25: Why did Peter write his first epistle?

When the city of Rome burned, the Romans believed that their emperor, Nero, had set the city on fire, probably because of his incredible lust to build. In order to build more, he had to destroy what already existed.

The Romans were totally devastated. Their culture, in a sense, went down with the city. All the religious elements of their life were destroyed—their great temples, shrines, and even their household idols were burned up. This had great religious implications because it made them believe that their deities had been unable to deal with this conflagration and were also victims of it. The people were homeless and hopeless. Many had been killed. Their bitter resentment was severe, so Nero realized that he had to redirect the hostility.

The emperor's chosen scapegoat was the Christians, who were already hated because they were associated with Jews, and because they were seen as being hostile to the Roman culture. Nero spread the word quickly that the Christians had set the fires. As a result, a vicious persecution against Christians began, and soon spread throughout the Roman Empire, touching places north of the Taurus mountains, like Pontus, Galatia, Cappadocia, Asia, and Bithynia (1:1), and impacting the Christians, whom Peter calls "pilgrims." These "pilgrims" were probably Gentiles, for the most part (1:14,18; 2:9,10; 4:3), possibly led to Christ by Paul and his associates and established on Paul's teachings. But they needed spiritual strengthening because of their sufferings. Thus the apostle Peter, under the inspiration of the Holy Spirit, wrote this epistle to strengthen them.

NOVEMBER 26

Ezekiel 43:1–44:31

43 Afterward he brought me to the gate,
the gate that faces toward the east. [2]And
behold, the glory of the God of Israel came from
the way of the east. His voice *was* like the sound
of many waters; and the earth shone with His
glory. [3]*It was* like the appearance of the vision
which I saw—like the vision which I saw when I
came to destroy the city. The visions *were* like
the vision which I saw by the River Chebar; and
I fell on my face. [4]And the glory of the LORD
came into the temple by way of the gate which
faces toward the east. [5]The Spirit lifted me up
and brought me into the inner court; and
behold, the glory of the LORD filled the temple.
[6]Then I heard *Him* speaking to me from the
temple, while a man stood beside me. [7]And He
said to me, "Son of man, *this is* the place of My
throne and the place of the soles of My feet,
where I will dwell in the midst of the children
of Israel forever. No more shall the house of
Israel defile My holy name, they nor their
kings, by their harlotry or with the carcasses
of their kings on their high places. [8]When they
set their threshold by My threshold, and their
doorpost by My doorpost, with a wall between
them and Me, they defiled My holy name by
the abominations which they committed;
therefore I have consumed them in My anger.
[9]Now let them put their harlotry and the carcasses of their kings far away from Me, and I
will dwell in their midst forever.
[10]"Son of man, describe the temple to the
house of Israel, that they may be ashamed of
their iniquities; and let them measure the pattern. [11]And if they are ashamed of all that they
have done, make known to them the design of
the temple and its arrangement, its exits and
its entrances, its entire design and all its ordinances, all its forms and all its laws. Write *it*
down in their sight, so that they may keep its
whole design and all its ordinances, and perform them. [12]This *is* the law of the temple: The
whole area surrounding the mountaintop *is*
most holy. Behold, this *is* the law of the temple.
[13]"These are the measurements of the altar
in cubits (the cubit *is* one cubit and a handbreadth): the base one cubit high and one
cubit wide, with a rim all around its edge of
one span. This *is* the height of the altar: [14]from
the base on the ground to the lower ledge, two
cubits; the width of the ledge, one cubit; from
the smaller ledge to the larger ledge, four
cubits; and the width of the ledge, *one* cubit.
[15]The altar hearth *is* four cubits high, with four
horns extending upward from the hearth.
[16]The altar hearth *is* twelve *cubits* long, twelve
wide, square at its four corners; [17]the ledge,
fourteen *cubits* long and fourteen wide on its
four sides, with a rim of half a cubit around it;
its base, one cubit all around; and its steps face
toward the east."
[18]And He said to me, "Son of man, thus says
the Lord GOD: 'These *are* the ordinances for
the altar on the day when it is made, for sacrificing burnt offerings on it, and for sprinkling
blood on it. [19]You shall give a young bull for a
sin offering to the priests, the Levites, who are
of the seed of Zadok, who approach Me to

minister to Me,’ says the Lord GOD. 20“You
shall take some of its blood and put *it* on the
four horns of the altar, on the four corners of
the ledge, and on the rim around it; thus you
shall cleanse it and make atonement for it.
21Then you shall also take the bull of the sin
offering, and burn it in the appointed place of
the temple, outside the sanctuary. 22On the
second day you shall offer a kid of the goats
without blemish for a sin offering; and they
shall cleanse the altar, as they cleansed *it* with
the bull. 23When you have finished cleansing
it, you shall offer a young bull without blemish, and a ram from the flock without blemish.
24When you offer them before the LORD, the
priests shall throw salt on them, and they will
offer them up *as* a burnt offering to the LORD.
25Every day for seven days you shall prepare a
goat *for* a sin offering; they shall also prepare
a young bull and a ram from the flock, both
without blemish. 26Seven days they shall make
atonement for the altar and purify it, and so
consecrate *it.* 27When these days are over it
shall be, on the eighth day and thereafter, that
the priests shall offer your burnt offerings and
your peace offerings on the altar; and I will accept you,’ says the Lord GOD.”

44 Then He brought me back to the outer
gate of the sanctuary which faces toward
the east, but it *was* shut. 2And the LORD said to
me, “This gate shall be shut; it shall not be
opened, and no man shall enter by it, because
the LORD God of Israel has entered by it; therefore it shall be shut. 3*As for* the prince, *because* he
is the prince, he may sit in it to eat bread before
the LORD; he shall enter by way of the vestibule
of the gateway, and go out the same way.”

4Also He brought me by way of the north
gate to the front of the temple; so I looked, and
behold, the glory of the LORD filled the house
of the LORD; and I fell on my face. 5And the
LORD said to me, “Son of man, mark well, see
with your eyes and hear with your ears, all
that I say to you concerning all the ordinances
of the house of the LORD and all its laws. Mark
well who may enter the house and all who go
out from the sanctuary.

6“Now say to the rebellious, to the house of
Israel, ‘Thus says the Lord GOD: “O house of
Israel, let Us have no more of all your
abominations. 7When you brought in foreigners, uncircumcised in heart and uncircumcised in flesh, to be in My sanctuary to
defile it—My house—and when you offered
My food, the fat and the blood, then they
broke My covenant because of all your
abominations. 8And you have not kept charge
of My holy things, but you have set *others* to

44:5–9 Mark well who may enter. Since the Lord’s glory fills the temple, it is sanctified (v. 4), and God is particular about what kind of people worship there. Sins of the past, as in chapters 8–11, must not be repeated, and if they are, those sins will exclude their perpetrators from the temple. Only the circumcised in heart may enter (Deut. 30:6; Jer. 4:4; Rom. 2:25–29), whether of Israel or another nation (vv. 7,9). Many peoples other than Jews will go into the kingdom in unresurrected bodies, because they have believed in Jesus Christ and are ready for His coming. They will escape His deadly judgment and populate and reproduce in the 1,000-year kingdom. Such circumcision pertains to a heart which is sincere about removing sin and being devoted to the Lord (Jer. 29:13). In the Millennium, a Jew with an uncircumcised heart will be considered a foreigner (v. 9). “Uncircumcised in flesh” refers to sinners, and “foreigner” identifies rejecters of the true God.

keep charge of My sanctuary for you.” 9Thus
says the Lord GOD: “No foreigner, uncircumcised in heart or uncircumcised in flesh, shall
enter My sanctuary, including any foreigner
who *is* among the children of Israel.

10“And the Levites who went far from Me,
when Israel went astray, who strayed away
from Me after their idols, they shall bear their
iniquity. 11Yet they shall be ministers in My
sanctuary, *as* gatekeepers of the house and
ministers of the house; they shall slay the burnt
offering and the sacrifice for the people, and
they shall stand before them to minister to
them. 12Because they ministered to them before
their idols and caused the house of Israel to
fall into iniquity, therefore I have raised My
hand in an oath against them,” says the Lord
GOD, “that they shall bear their iniquity. 13And
they shall not come near Me to minister to Me
as priest, nor come near any of My holy things,
nor into the Most Holy *Place;* but they shall
bear their shame and their abominations
which they have committed. 14Nevertheless I
will make them keep charge of the temple, for
all its work, and for all that has to be done in it.

15“But the priests, the Levites, the sons of
Zadok, who kept charge of My sanctuary when
the children of Israel went astray from Me,
they shall come near Me to minister to Me; and
they shall stand before Me to offer to Me the fat
and the blood,” says the Lord GOD. 16“They
shall enter My sanctuary, and they shall come

near My table to minister to Me, and they shall
keep My charge. 17 And it shall be, whenever
they enter the gates of the inner court, that
they shall put on linen garments; no wool shall
come upon them while they minister within
the gates of the inner court or within the
house. 18 They shall have linen turbans on their
heads and linen trousers on their bodies; they
shall not clothe themselves with *anything that
causes* sweat. 19 When they go out to the outer
court, to the outer court to the people, they
shall take off their garments in which they have
ministered, leave them in the holy chambers,
and put on other garments; and in their holy
garments they shall not sanctify the people.

20 "They shall neither shave their heads, nor
let their hair grow long, but they shall keep
their hair well trimmed. 21 No priest shall drink
wine when he enters the inner court. 22 They
shall not take as wife a widow or a divorced
woman, but take virgins of the descendants of
the house of Israel, or widows of priests.

23 "And they shall teach My people *the difference* between the holy and the unholy, and
cause them to discern between the unclean
and the clean. 24 In controversy they shall stand
as judges, *and* judge it according to My judgments. They shall keep My laws and My
statutes in all My appointed meetings, and
they shall hallow My Sabbaths.

25 "They shall not defile *themselves* by coming
near a dead person. Only for father or mother,
for son or daughter, for brother or unmarried
sister may they defile themselves. 26 After he is
cleansed, they shall count seven days for him.
27 And on the day that he goes to the sanctuary to
minister in the sanctuary, he must offer his sin
offering in the inner court," says the Lord GOD.

28 "It shall be, in regard to their inheritance,
that I *am* their inheritance. You shall give them
no possession in Israel, for I *am* their possession. 29 They shall eat the grain offering, the sin
offering, and the trespass offering; every dedicated thing in Israel shall be theirs. 30 The best
of all firstfruits of any kind, and every sacrifice
of any kind from all your sacrifices, shall be
the priest's; also you shall give to the priest
the first of your ground meal, to cause a blessing to rest on your house. 31 The priests shall
not eat anything, bird or beast, that died naturally or was torn *by wild beasts*.

Psalm 134:1–3

A Song of Ascents.

Behold, bless the LORD,
All *you* servants of the LORD,
Who by night stand in the house
of the LORD!

2 Lift up your hands *in* the sanctuary,
And bless the LORD.

3 The LORD who made heaven and earth
Bless you from Zion!

Proverbs 29:7

7 The righteous considers the cause of
the poor,
But the wicked does not understand
such knowledge.

1 Peter 2:1–25

2 Therefore, laying aside all malice, all
deceit, hypocrisy, envy, and all evil speaking, 2 as newborn babes, desire the pure milk of
the word, that you may grow thereby, 3 if indeed
you have tasted that the Lord *is* gracious.

2:2 desire the pure milk of the word. Spiritual growth is always marked by a craving for and a delight in God's Word with the intensity with which a baby craves milk (Job 23:12; Pss. 1:1,2; 19:7–11; 119:16,24,35,47,48,72,92,97,103,111, 113,127,159,167,174; Jer. 15:16). A Christian develops a desire for the truth of God's Word by: 1) remembering his life's source (1:25; Is. 55:10,11; John 15:3; Heb. 4:12); 2) eliminating sin from his life (v. 1); 3) admitting his need for God's truth (v. 2,"as newborn babes"; Matt. 4:4); 4) pursuing spiritual growth (v. 2, "that you may grow thereby"); and 5) surveying his blessings (v. 3,"Lord is gracious").

4 Coming to Him *as to* a living stone, rejected
indeed by men, but chosen by God *and* precious, 5 you also, as living stones, are being
built up a spiritual house, a holy priesthood, to
offer up spiritual sacrifices acceptable to God
through Jesus Christ. 6 Therefore it is also contained in the Scripture,

"Behold, I lay in Zion
A chief cornerstone, elect, precious,
And he who believes on Him will by no
means be put to shame."

7 Therefore, to you who believe, *He is* precious; but to those who are disobedient,

"The stone which the builders rejected
Has become the chief cornerstone,"

8 and

"A stone of stumbling
And a rock of offense."

They stumble, being disobedient to the word,
to which they also were appointed.
9But you *are* a chosen generation, a royal
priesthood, a holy nation, His own special people, that you may proclaim the praises of Him
who called you out of darkness into His marvelous light; 10who once *were* not a people but
are now the people of God, who had not
obtained mercy but now have obtained mercy.
11Beloved, I beg *you* as sojourners and pilgrims, abstain from fleshly lusts which war
against the soul, 12having your conduct honorable among the Gentiles, that when they speak
against you as evildoers, they may, by *your*
good works which they observe, glorify God in
the day of visitation.

2:11 abstain from fleshly lusts. Perhaps more literally, "hold yourself away from fleshly lusts." In order to have an impact on the world for God, Christians must be disciplined in an inward and private way by avoiding the desires of the fallen nature (Gal. 5:19–21, where "fleshly lusts" include much more than sexual temptations). **which war against the soul.** "War," i.e., to carry on a military campaign. Fleshly lusts are personified as if they were an army of rebels or guerrillas who incessantly search out and try to destroy the Christian's joy, peace, and usefulness (4:2,3).

13Therefore submit yourselves to every ordinance of man for the Lord's sake, whether to
the king as supreme, 14or to governors, as to
those who are sent by him for the punishment
of evildoers and *for the* praise of those who do
good. 15For this is the will of God, that by doing
good you may put to silence the ignorance of
foolish men— 16as free, yet not using liberty as
a cloak for vice, but as bondservants of God.
17Honor all *people.* Love the brotherhood. Fear
God. Honor the king.
18Servants, *be* submissive to *your* masters
with all fear, not only to the good and gentle,
but also to the harsh. 19For this *is* commendable, if because of conscience toward God one
endures grief, suffering wrongfully. 20For what
credit *is it* if, when you are beaten for your
faults, you take it patiently? But when you do
good and suffer, if you take it patiently, this *is*
commendable before God. 21For to this you
were called, because Christ also suffered for
us, leaving us an example, that you should follow His steps:

2:13 submit yourselves. "Submit" is a military term meaning "to arrange in military fashion under the commander," "to put oneself in an attitude of submission." As citizens in the world and under civil law and authority, God's people are to live in a humble, submissive way in the midst of any hostile, godless, slandering society (vv. 21–23; Prov. 24:21; Jer. 29:4–14; Matt. 22:21; Rom. 13:1ff., 1 Tim. 2:1; Heb. 10:32–34). **for the Lord's sake.** Though the Christian's true citizenship is in heaven, he still must live as an obedient citizen in this world so that God will be honored and glorified. Rebellious conduct by a Christian brings dishonor on Christ.

22 *"Who committed no sin,*
Nor was deceit found in His mouth";

23who, when He was reviled, did not revile in
return; when He suffered, He did not threat-
en, but committed *Himself* to Him who judges
righteously; 24who Himself bore our sins in His
own body on the tree, that we, having died to
sins, might live for righteousness—by whose
stripes you were healed. 25For you were like
sheep going astray, but have now returned to
the Shepherd and Overseer of your souls.

DAY 26: How are Christians described in 1 Peter 2:9?

Believers there are described as "a chosen generation." Peter uses Old Testament concepts to emphasize the privileges of New Testament Christians (Deut. 7:6–8). In strong contrast to the disobedient who are appointed by God to wrath (v. 8), Christians are chosen by God to salvation (1:2).

They are also called "a royal priesthood." The concept of a kingly priesthood is drawn from Exodus 19:6. Israel temporarily forfeited this privilege because of its apostasy and because its wicked leaders executed the Messiah. At the present time, the church is a royal priesthood united with the royal priest, Jesus Christ. A royal priesthood is not only a priesthood that belongs to and serves the king, but is also a priesthood which exercises rule. This will ultimately be fulfilled in Christ's future kingdom (1 Cor. 6:1–4; Rev. 5:10; 20:6).

And they are described as "a holy nation." Another allusion to Exodus 19:6 (Lev. 19:2; 20:26;

Deut. 7:6; Is. 62:12). Tragically, Israel temporarily forfeited the great privilege of being the unique people of God through unbelief. Until Israel's future acceptance of its Messiah, God has replaced the nation with the church. "His own special people." This combines phraseology found in Exodus 19:5; Isaiah 43:21; Malachi 3:17. "That you may proclaim the praises of Him who called you." To "proclaim" means to tell forth, to tell something not otherwise known. "Praises" are excellencies, virtues, eminent qualities.

NOVEMBER 27

Ezekiel 45:1–46:24

45 "Moreover, when you divide the land
by lot into inheritance, you shall set
apart a district for the LORD, a holy section of
the land; its length *shall be* twenty-five thousand *cubits,* and the width ten thousand. It *shall*
be holy throughout its territory all around. 2Of
this there shall be a square plot for the sanctuary, five hundred by five hundred *rods,* with
fifty cubits around it for an open space. 3So this
is the district you shall measure: twenty-five
thousand *cubits* long and ten thousand wide; in
it shall be the sanctuary, the Most Holy *Place.*
4It shall be a holy *section* of the land, belonging
to the priests, the ministers of the sanctuary,
who come near to minister to the LORD; it shall
be a place for their houses and a holy place for
the sanctuary. 5*An area* twenty-five thousand
cubits long and ten thousand wide shall belong
to the Levites, the ministers of the temple;
they shall have twenty chambers as a possession.
6"You shall appoint as the property of the
city *an area* five thousand *cubits* wide and
twenty-five thousand long, adjacent to the district of the holy *section;* it shall belong to the
whole house of Israel.
7"The prince shall have *a section* on one side
and the other of the holy district and the city's
property; and bordering on the holy district
and the city's property, extending westward
on the west side and eastward on the east
side, the length *shall be* side by side with one
of the *tribal* portions, from the west border to
the east border. 8The land shall be his possession in Israel; and My princes shall no more
oppress My people, but they shall give *the rest*
of the land to the house of Israel, according to
their tribes."
9"Thus says the Lord GOD: "Enough, O princes
of Israel! Remove violence and plundering, execute justice and righteousness, and stop dispos-
sessing My people," says the Lord GOD. 10"You
shall have honest scales, an honest ephah, and
an honest bath. 11The ephah and the bath shall
be of the same measure, so that the bath contains one-tenth of a homer, and the ephah one-
tenth of a homer; their measure shall be according to the homer. 12The shekel *shall be* twenty
gerahs; twenty shekels, twenty-five shekels,
and fifteen shekels shall be your mina.
13"This *is* the offering which you shall offer:
you shall give one-sixth of an ephah from a
homer of wheat, and one-sixth of an ephah
from a homer of barley. 14The ordinance concerning oil, the bath of oil, *is* one-tenth of a
bath from a kor. *A kor is* a homer or ten baths,
for ten baths *are* a homer. 15And one lamb shall
be given from a flock of two hundred, from the
rich pastures of Israel. These shall be for grain
offerings, burnt offerings, and peace offerings, to make atonement for them," says the
Lord GOD. 16"All the people of the land shall
give this offering for the prince in Israel.
17Then it shall be the prince's part *to give* burnt
offerings, grain offerings, and drink offerings,
at the feasts, the New Moons, the Sabbaths,
and at all the appointed seasons of the house of
Israel. He shall prepare the sin offering, the
grain offering, the burnt offering, and the peace
offerings to make atonement for the house of
Israel."

45:9–12 The leaders of the land are urged to be thoroughly honest in their commercial dealings. This warning shows that there will be sin in the Millennium. The believing Jews who entered the 1,000-year reign of Christ on earth and inherited the promised kingdom will be fully human and capable of such sins. There also will be children who do not necessarily believe, as the final rebellion against King Messiah and His temple proves (Rev. 20:7–9).

18"Thus says the Lord GOD: "In the first *month,*
on the first *day* of the month, you shall take a
young bull without blemish and cleanse the
sanctuary. 19The priest shall take some of the
blood of the sin offering and put *it* on the doorposts of the temple, on the four corners of the
ledge of the altar, and on the gateposts of the
gate of the inner court. 20And so you shall do on

the seventh *day* of the month for everyone who has sinned unintentionally or in ignorance. Thus you shall make atonement for the temple.

21“In the first *month,* on the fourteenth day of the month, you shall observe the Passover, a feast of seven days; unleavened bread shall be eaten. 22And on that day the prince shall prepare for himself and for all the people of the land a bull *for* a sin offering. 23On the seven days of the feast he shall prepare a burnt offering to the LORD, seven bulls and seven rams without blemish, daily for seven days, and a kid of the goats daily *for* a sin offering. 24And he shall prepare a grain offering of one ephah for each bull and one ephah for each ram, together with a hin of oil for each ephah.

25“In the seventh *month,* on the fifteenth day of the month, at the feast, he shall do likewise for seven days, according to the sin offering, the burnt offering, the grain offering, and the oil.”

46 Thus says the Lord GOD: “The gateway of the inner court that faces toward the east shall be shut the six working days; but on the Sabbath it shall be opened, and on the day of the New Moon it shall be opened. 2The prince shall enter by way of the vestibule of the gateway from the outside, and stand by the gatepost. The priests shall prepare his burnt offering and his peace offerings. He shall worship at the threshold of the gate. Then he shall go out, but the gate shall not be shut until evening. 3Likewise the people of the land shall worship at the entrance to this gateway before the LORD on the Sabbaths and the New Moons. 4The burnt offering that the prince offers to the LORD on the Sabbath day *shall be* six lambs without blemish, and a ram without blemish; 5and the grain offering *shall be one* ephah for a ram, and the grain offering for the lambs, as much as he wants to give, as well as a hin of oil with every ephah. 6On the day of the New Moon *it shall be* a young bull without blemish, six lambs, and a ram; they shall be without blemish. 7He shall prepare a grain offering of an ephah for a bull, an ephah for a ram, as much as he wants to give for the lambs, and a hin of oil with every ephah. 8When the prince enters, he shall go in by way of the vestibule of the gateway, and go out the same way.

9“But when the people of the land come before the LORD on the appointed feast days, whoever enters by way of the north gate to worship shall go out by way of the south gate; and whoever enters by way of the south gate shall go out by way of the north gate. He shall not return by way of the gate through which he came, but shall go out through the opposite gate. 10The prince shall then be in their midst. When they go in, he shall go in; and when they go out, he shall go out. 11At the festivals and the appointed feast days the grain offering shall be an ephah for a bull, an ephah for a ram, as much as he wants to give for the lambs, and a hin of oil with every ephah.

12“Now when the prince makes a voluntary burnt offering or voluntary peace offering to the LORD, the gate that faces toward the east shall then be opened for him; and he shall prepare his burnt offering and his peace offerings as he did on the Sabbath day. Then he shall go out, and after he goes out the gate shall be shut.

13“You shall daily make a burnt offering to the LORD *of* a lamb of the first year without blemish; you shall prepare it every morning. 14And you shall prepare a grain offering with it every morning, a sixth of an ephah, and a third of a hin of oil to moisten the fine flour. This grain offering is a perpetual ordinance, to be made regularly to the LORD. 15Thus they shall prepare the lamb, the grain offering, and the oil, *as* a regular burnt offering every morning.”

16‘Thus says the Lord GOD: “If the prince gives a gift *of some* of his inheritance to any of his sons, it shall belong to his sons; it is their possession by inheritance. 17But if he gives a gift of some of his inheritance to one of his servants, it shall be his until the year of liberty, after which it shall return to the prince. But his inheritance shall belong to his sons; it shall become theirs. 18Moreover the prince shall not take any of the people’s inheritance by evicting them from their property; he shall provide an inheritance for his sons from his own property, so that none of My people may be scattered from his property.” ’ ”

19Now he brought me through the entrance, which *was* at the side of the gate, into the holy chambers of the priests which face toward the north; and there a place *was* situated at their extreme western end. 20And he said to me, “This *is* the place where the priests shall boil the trespass offering and the sin offering, *and* where they shall bake the grain offering, so that they do not bring *them* out into the outer court to sanctify the people.”

21Then he brought me out into the outer court and caused me to pass by the four corners of the court; and in fact, in every corner of the court *there was another* court. 22In the four corners of the court *were* enclosed courts, forty *cubits* long and thirty wide; all four corners *were* the same size. 23*There was* a row *of building stones* all around in them, all around

the four of them; and cooking hearths were made under the rows of stones all around.
24And he said to me, "These *are* the kitchens where the ministers of the temple shall boil the sacrifices of the people."

Psalm 135:1–7

Praise the LORD!

Praise the name of the LORD;
Praise *Him,* O you servants of the LORD!
2 You who stand in the house of the LORD,
In the courts of the house of our God,
3 Praise the LORD, for the LORD *is* good;
Sing praises to His name, for *it is* pleasant.
4 For the LORD has chosen Jacob for Himself,
Israel for His special treasure.

5 For I know that the LORD *is* great,
And our Lord *is* above all gods.
6 Whatever the LORD pleases He does,
In heaven and in earth,
In the seas and in all deep places.
7 He causes the vapors to ascend from the ends of the earth;
He makes lightning for the rain;
He brings the wind out of His treasuries.

Proverbs 29:8

8 Scoffers set a city aflame,
But wise *men* turn away wrath.

1 Peter 3:1–22

3 Wives, likewise, *be* submissive to your own
husbands, that even if some do not obey
the word, they, without a word, may be won by
the conduct of their wives, 2when they
observe your chaste conduct *accompanied* by
fear. 3Do not let your adornment be *merely* outward—arranging the hair, wearing gold, or
putting on *fine* apparel— 4rather *let it be* the
hidden person of the heart, with the incorruptible *beauty* of a gentle and quiet spirit,
which is very precious in the sight of God.
5For in this manner, in former times, the holy
women who trusted in God also adorned
themselves, being submissive to their own
husbands, 6as Sarah obeyed Abraham, calling
him lord, whose daughters you are if you do
good and are not afraid with any terror.
7Husbands, likewise, dwell with *them* with
understanding, giving honor to the wife, as to
the weaker vessel, and as *being* heirs together
of the grace of life, that your prayers may not
be hindered.

3:1 likewise. In chapter 2, Peter taught that living successfully as a Christian in a hostile world would require relating properly in two places: the civil society (2:13–17) and the workplace (2:18–25). At the start of this chapter, he added two more places: the family (vv. 1–7) and the local church (vv. 8,9). ***be submissive.*** Peter insisted that if Christians are to be a witness for their Lord, they must submit not only to the civil, but also to the social order which God has designed. **own husbands.** Women are not inferior to men in any way, any more than submissive Christians are inferior to pagan rulers or non-Christian bosses (Gal. 3:28). But wives have been given a role which puts them in submission to the headship which resides in their own husbands (1 Cor. 11:1–9; Eph. 5:22; Col. 3:18; Titus 2:4,5).

3:7 Husbands, likewise. Submission is the responsibility of a Christian husband, as well (Eph. 5:21). Though not submitting to his wife as a leader, a believing husband must submit to the loving duty of being sensitive to the needs, fears, and feelings of his wife. In other words, a Christian husband needs to subordinate his needs to hers, whether she is a Christian or not. Peter specifically notes consideration, chivalry, and companionship. **weaker vessel.** While she is fully equal in Christ and not inferior spiritually because she is a woman (Gal. 3:28), she is physically weaker and in need of protection, provision, and strength from her husband. **heirs together of the grace of life.** Here the "grace of life" is not salvation, but marriage—the best relationship earthly life has to offer. The husband must cultivate companionship and fellowship with his wife, Christian or not (Eccl. 9:9).

8Finally, all *of you be* of one mind, having compassion for one another; love as brothers, *be* tenderhearted, *be* courteous; 9not returning evil for
evil or reviling for reviling, but on the contrary
blessing, knowing that you were called to this,
that you may inherit a blessing. 10For

"He who would love life
And see good days,
Let him refrain his tongue from evil,
And his lips from speaking deceit.
11 *Let him turn away from evil and do good;*
Let him seek peace and pursue it.
12 *For the eyes of the LORD are on the righteous,*

3:15 sanctify the Lord God in your hearts. "Christ" is to be preferred here, so the reading is "set apart in your hearts Christ as Lord." The heart is the sanctuary in which He prefers to be worshiped. Live in submissive communion with the Lord Jesus, loving and obeying Him—and you have nothing to fear. **always *be* ready to *give* a defense.** The English word "apologetics" comes from the Greek word here translated "defense." Peter is using the word in an informal sense (Phil. 1:16,17) and is insisting that the believer must understand what he believes and why one is a Christian, and then be able to articulate one's beliefs humbly, thoughtfully, reasonably, and biblically. **the hope that is in you.** Salvation with its anticipation of eternal glory.

And His ears are open to their prayers;
But the face of the L*ORD is against*
those who do evil."

13And who *is* he who will harm you if you
become followers of what is good? 14But even if
you should suffer for righteousness' sake, *you*
are blessed. *"And do not be afraid of their*
threats, nor be troubled." 15But sanctify the
Lord God in your hearts, and always *be* ready to
give a defense to everyone who asks you a reason for the hope that is in you, with meekness
and fear; 16having a good conscience, that when
they defame you as evildoers, those who revile
your good conduct in Christ may be ashamed.
17For *it is* better, if it is the will of God, to suffer
for doing good than for doing evil.

18For Christ also suffered once for sins, the
just for the unjust, that He might bring us to
God, being put to death in the flesh but made
alive by the Spirit, 19by whom also He went and
preached to the spirits in prison, 20who formerly were disobedient, when once the Divine
longsuffering waited in the days of Noah, while
the ark was being prepared, in which a few,
that is, eight souls, were saved through water.
21There is also an antitype which now saves
us—baptism (not the removal of the filth of the
flesh, but the answer of a good conscience
toward God), through the resurrection of Jesus Christ, 22who has gone into heaven and is
at the right hand of God, angels and authorities
and powers having been made subject to Him.

DAY 27: How does Peter use familiar terms such as "spirit," "abyss," "flood," and "baptism" in 1 Peter 3:18–22?

This passage proves to be one of the most difficult texts in the New Testament to translate and interpret. The line between Old Testament allusions and New Testament applications gets blurred. Peter's overall purpose of this passage, which was to encourage his readers in their suffering, must be kept in mind during interpretation. The apostle repeatedly reminded them that even Christ suffered unjustly because it was God's will (vv. 17,18) and accomplished God's purposes.

Therefore, although Jesus experienced a violent physical execution that terminated His earthly life when He was "put to death in the flesh" (v. 18; Heb. 5:7), nevertheless He was "made alive by the Spirit" (v. 18). This is not a reference to the Holy Spirit, but to Jesus' true inner life, His own spirit. Contrasted with His flesh (humanness) which was dead for three days, His spirit (Deity) remained alive, literally "in spirit" (Luke 23:46).

Part of God's purpose in Christ's death involved His activities between His death and resurrection. His living spirit went to the demon spirits bound in the Abyss and proclaimed victory in spite of death. Peter further explained that the Abyss is inhabited by bound demons that have been there since the time of Noah. They were sent there because they overstepped the limits of God's tolerance with their wickedness. Not even 120 years of Noah's example and preaching had stemmed the tide of wickedness in his time (Gen. 6:1–8). Thus God bound these demons permanently in the Abyss until their final sentencing.

Peter's analogy spotlights the ministry of Jesus Christ in saving us as surely as the ark saved Noah's family. He is not referring to water baptism here but to a figurative immersion in Christ that keeps us safe from the flood of God's sure judgment. The resurrection of Christ demonstrates God's acceptance of Christ's substitutionary death for the sins of those who believe (Acts 2:30,31; Rom. 1:4). God's judgment fell on Christ just as the judgment of the floodwaters fell on the ark. The believer who is in Christ is thus in the ark of safety that will sail over the waters of judgment into eternal glory (Rom. 6:1–4).

NOVEMBER 28

Ezekiel 47:1–48:35

47 Then he brought me back to the door
of the temple; and there was water,
flowing from under the threshold of the temple toward the east, for the front of the temple
faced east; the water was flowing from under
the right side of the temple, south of the altar.
[2]He brought me out by way of the north gate,
and led me around on the outside to the outer
gateway that faces east; and there was water,
running out on the right side.

[3]And when the man went out to the east
with the line in his hand, he measured one
thousand cubits, and he brought me through
the waters; the water *came up to my* ankles.
[4]Again he measured one thousand and
brought me through the waters; the water
came up to my knees. Again he measured one
thousand and brought me through; the water
came up to my waist. [5]Again he measured one
thousand, *and it was* a river that I could not
cross; for the water was too deep, water in
which one must swim, a river that could not be
crossed. [6]He said to me, "Son of man, have you
seen *this?*" Then he brought me and returned
me to the bank of the river.

[7]When I returned, there, along the bank of
the river, *were* very many trees on one side and
the other. [8]Then he said to me: "This water
flows toward the eastern region, goes down
into the valley, and enters the sea. *When it*
reaches the sea, *its* waters are healed. [9]And it
shall be *that* every living thing that moves,
wherever the rivers go, will live. There will be
a very great multitude of fish, because these
waters go there; for they will be healed, and
everything will live wherever the river goes.
[10]It shall be *that* fishermen will stand by it from
En Gedi to En Eglaim; they will be *places* for
spreading their nets. Their fish will be of the
same kinds as the fish of the Great Sea,
exceedingly many. [11]But its swamps and
marshes will not be healed; they will be given
over to salt. [12]Along the bank of the river, on
this side and that, will grow all *kinds of* trees
used for food; their leaves will not wither, and
their fruit will not fail. They will bear fruit
every month, because their water flows from
the sanctuary. Their fruit will be for food, and
their leaves for medicine."

[13]Thus says the Lord GOD: "These *are* the
borders by which you shall divide the land as an
inheritance among the twelve tribes of Israel.
Joseph *shall have two* portions. [14]You shall inherit it equally with one another; for I raised My
hand in an oath to give it to your fathers, and
this land shall fall to you as your inheritance.

[15]"This *shall be* the border of the land on the
north: from the Great Sea, *by* the road to
Hethlon, as one goes to Zedad, [16]Hamath,
Berothah, Sibraim (which *is* between the border of Damascus and the border of Hamath),
to Hazar Hatticon (which *is* on the border of
Hauran). [17]Thus the boundary shall be from
the Sea to Hazar Enan, the border of Damascus; and as for the north, northward, it is the
border of Hamath. *This is* the north side.

[18]"On the east side you shall mark out the
border from between Hauran and Damascus,
and between Gilead and the land of Israel, along
the Jordan, and along the eastern side of the
sea. *This is* the east side.

[19]"The south side, toward the South, *shall be*
from Tamar to the waters of Meribah by
Kadesh, along the brook to the Great Sea.
This is the south side, toward the South.

[20]"The west side *shall be* the Great Sea, from
the *southern* boundary until one comes to a
point opposite Hamath. This *is* the west side.

[21]"Thus you shall divide this land among
yourselves according to the tribes of Israel. [22]It
shall be that you will divide it by lot as an
inheritance for yourselves, and for the strangers who dwell among you and who bear children among you. They shall be to you as
native-born among the children of Israel; they
shall have an inheritance with you among the
tribes of Israel. [23]And it shall be *that* in whatever tribe the stranger dwells, there you shall
give *him* his inheritance," says the Lord GOD.

48 "Now these *are* the names of the
tribes: From the northern border
along the road to Hethlon at the entrance of
Hamath, to Hazar Enan, the border of Damascus northward, in the direction of Hamath,
there shall be one *section for* Dan from its east
to its west side; [2]by the border of Dan, from
the east side to the west, one *section for* Asher;
[3]by the border of Asher, from the east side to
the west, one *section for* Naphtali; [4]by the border of Naphtali, from the east side to the west,
one *section for* Manasseh; [5]by the border of
Manasseh, from the east side to the west, one
section for Ephraim; [6]by the border of
Ephraim, from the east side to the west, one
section for Reuben; [7]by the border of Reuben,
from the east side to the west, one *section for*
Judah; [8]by the border of Judah, from the east
side to the west, shall be the district which
you shall set apart, twenty-five thousand *cubits*
in width, and *in* length the same as one of the

other portions, from the east side to the west,
with the sanctuary in the center.
9"The district that you shall set apart for the
LORD *shall be* twenty-five thousand *cubits* in
length and ten thousand in width. 10To
these—to the priests—the holy district shall
belong: on the north twenty-five thousand *cu-*
bits in length, on the west ten thousand in
width, on the east ten thousand in width, and
on the south twenty-five thousand in length.
The sanctuary of the LORD shall be in the center. 11*It shall be* for the priests of the sons of
Zadok, who are sanctified, who have kept My
charge, who did not go astray when the children of Israel went astray, as the Levites went
astray. 12And *this* district of land that is set
apart shall be to them a thing most holy by the
border of the Levites.
13"Opposite the border of the priests, the
Levites *shall have an area* twenty-five thousand *cubits* in length and ten thousand in
width; its entire length *shall be* twenty-five
thousand and its width ten thousand. 14And
they shall not sell or exchange any of it; they
may not alienate this best *part* of the land, for
it is holy to the LORD.
15"The five thousand *cubits* in width that
remain, along the edge of the twenty-five
thousand, shall be for general use by the city,
for dwellings and common-land; and the city
shall be in the center. 16These *shall be* its measurements: the north side four thousand five
hundred *cubits,* the south side four thousand
five hundred, the east side four thousand five
hundred, and the west side four thousand five
hundred. 17The common-land of the city shall
be: to the north two hundred and fifty *cubits,*
to the south two hundred and fifty, to the east
two hundred and fifty, and to the west two
hundred and fifty. 18The rest of the length,
alongside the district of the holy *section, shall*
be ten thousand *cubits* to the east and ten thousand to the west. It shall be adjacent to the district of the holy *section,* and its produce shall
be food for the workers of the city. 19The workers of the city, from all the tribes of Israel, shall
cultivate it. 20The entire district *shall be* twenty-
five thousand *cubits* by twenty-five thousand *cu-*
bits, foursquare. You shall set apart the holy district with the property of the city.
21"The rest *shall belong* to the prince, on one
side and on the other of the holy district and of
the city's property, next to the twenty-five thousand *cubits* of the *holy* district as far as the eastern border, and westward next to the twenty-
five thousand as far as the western border,
adjacent to the *tribal* portions; *it shall belong* to
the prince. It shall be the holy district, and the
sanctuary of the temple *shall be* in the center.
22Moreover, apart from the possession of the
Levites and the possession of the city *which*
are in the midst of what *belongs* to the prince,
the area between the border of Judah and the
border of Benjamin shall belong to the prince.
23"As for the rest of the tribes, from the east
side to the west, Benjamin *shall have* one *sec-*
tion; 24by the border of Benjamin, from the
east side to the west, Simeon *shall have* one
section; 25by the border of Simeon, from the
east side to the west, Issachar *shall have* one
section; 26by the border of Issachar, from the
east side to the west, Zebulun *shall have* one
section; 27by the border of Zebulun, from the
east side to the west, Gad *shall have* one *sec-*
tion; 28by the border of Gad, on the south side,
toward the South, the border shall be from
Tamar *to* the waters of Meribah *by* Kadesh,
along the brook to the Great Sea. 29This *is* the
land which you shall divide by lot as an inheritance among the tribes of Israel, and these
are their portions," says the Lord GOD.
30"These *are* the exits of the city. On the
north side, measuring four thousand five hundred *cubits* 31(the gates of the city *shall be*
named after the tribes of Israel), the three
gates northward: one gate for Reuben, one
gate for Judah, and one gate for Levi; 32on the
east side, four thousand five hundred *cubits,*
three gates: one gate for Joseph, one gate for
Benjamin, and one gate for Dan; 33on the south
side, measuring four thousand five hundred
cubits, three gates: one gate for Simeon, one
gate for Issachar, and one gate for Zebulun;
34on the west side, four thousand five hundred
cubits with their three gates: one gate for Gad,
one gate for Asher, and one gate for Naphtali.
35All the way around *shall be* eighteen thousand *cubits;* and the name of the city from *that*
day *shall be:* THE LORD *IS* THERE."

48:35 the name. The city is called YHWH Shammah, "The LORD Is There." The departed glory of God (chaps. 8–11) has returned (44:1,2), and His dwelling, the temple, is in the very center of the district given over to the Lord. With this final note, all of the unconditional promises which God had made to Israel in the Abrahamic Covenant (Gen. 12), the Levitic Covenant (Num. 25), the Davidic Covenant (2 Sam. 7), and the New Covenant (Jer. 31) have been fulfilled. So this final verse provides the consummation of Israel's history—the returned presence of God!

Psalm 135:8–14

8 He destroyed the firstborn of Egypt,
Both of man and beast.
9 He sent signs and wonders into the
midst of you, O Egypt,
Upon Pharaoh and all his servants.
10 He defeated many nations
And slew mighty kings—
11 Sihon king of the Amorites,
Og king of Bashan,
And all the kingdoms of Canaan—
12 And gave their land *as* a heritage,
A heritage to Israel His people.

13 Your name, O LORD, *endures* forever,
Your fame, O LORD, throughout all
generations.
14 For the LORD will judge His people,
And He will have compassion
on His servants.

Proverbs 29:9

9 *If* a wise man contends with
a foolish man,
Whether *the fool* rages or laughs, *there*
is no peace.

29:9 contends. A fool may respond to wisdom with anger or laughter; but in either case, no agreement can be reached.

1 Peter 4:1–19

4 Therefore, since Christ suffered for us in
the flesh, arm yourselves also with the
same mind, for he who has suffered in the
flesh has ceased from sin, [2]that he no longer
should live the rest of *his* time in the flesh for
the lusts of men, but for the will of God. [3]For
we *have spent* enough of our past lifetime in
doing the will of the Gentiles—when we
walked in lewdness, lusts, drunkenness, revelries, drinking parties, and abominable idola-
tries. [4]In regard to these, they think it strange
that you do not run with *them* in the same flood
of dissipation, speaking evil of *you.* [5]They will
give an account to Him who is ready to judge the
living and the dead. [6]For this reason the gospel
was preached also to those who are dead, that
they might be judged according to men in the
flesh, but live according to God in the spirit.
[7]But the end of all things is at hand; therefore be serious and watchful in your prayers.
[8]And above all things have fervent love for one

4:9 *Be* hospitable to one another. The Greek word means "love of strangers." Love is intensely practical, not just emotional. In Peter's day, love included opening one's home and caring for other needy Christians, such as traveling preachers. It also included opening one's home for church services. Scripture also teaches that Christians should be hospitable to strangers (Ex. 22:21; Deut. 14:28,29; Heb. 13:1,2).

another, for *"love will cover a multitude of*
sins." [9]*Be* hospitable to one another without
grumbling. [10]As each one has received a gift,
minister it to one another, as good stewards of
the manifold grace of God. [11]If anyone speaks,
let him speak as the oracles of God. If anyone
ministers, *let him do it* as with the ability
which God supplies, that in all things God may
be glorified through Jesus Christ, to whom
belong the glory and the dominion forever
and ever. Amen.
[12]Beloved, do not think it strange concerning the fiery trial which is to try you, as
though some strange thing happened to you;
[13]but rejoice to the extent that you partake of
Christ's sufferings, that when His glory is
revealed, you may also be glad with exceeding
joy. [14]If you are reproached for the name of
Christ, blessed *are you,* for the Spirit of glory
and of God rests upon you. On their part He is
blasphemed, but on your part He is glorified.
[15]But let none of you suffer as a murderer, a
thief, an evildoer, or as a busybody in other
people's matters. [16]Yet if *anyone suffers* as a
Christian, let him not be ashamed, but let him
glorify God in this matter.

4:12 the fiery trial. Peter probably wrote this letter shortly before or after the burning of Rome and at the beginning of the horrors of a 200-year period of Christian persecution. Peter explains that 4 attitudes are necessary in order to be triumphant in persecution: 1) expect it (v. 12); 2) rejoice in it (vv. 13,14); 3) evaluate its cause (vv. 15–18); and 4) entrust it to God (v. 19). **some strange thing happened.** "Happened" means "to fall by chance." A Christian must not think that his persecution is something that happened accidentally. God allowed it and designed it for the believer's testing, purging, and cleansing.

17For the time *has come* for judgment to
begin at the house of God; and if *it begins* with
us first, what will *be* the end of those who do
not obey the gospel of God? 18Now

"If the righteous one is scarcely saved,
Where will the ungodly and the sinner
appear?"

19Therefore let those who suffer according to
the will of God commit their souls *to Him* in
doing good, as to a faithful Creator.

DAY 28: What did Peter mean when he said "the end of all things is at hand" (1 Pet. 4:7)?

The Greek word for "end" is never used in the New Testament as a chronological end, as if something simply stops. Instead, the word means a consummation, a goal achieved, a result attained, or a realization. Having emphasized triumphant suffering through death, Peter here begins to emphasize triumphant suffering through the Second Coming of Christ (1:3; 2:12), which is the goal of all things. He is calling believers to live obediently and expectantly in the light of Christ's return. "Is at hand." The idea is that of a process consummated with a resulting nearness, i.e., "imminent." Peter is reminding the readers of this letter that the return of Jesus Christ could be at any moment (Rom. 13:12; 1 Thess. 1:10; James 5:7,8; Rev. 22:20).

"Be serious and watchful." To be "serious" implies here not to be swept away by emotions or passions, thus maintaining a proper eternal perspective on life. The doctrine of the imminent return of Christ should not turn the Christian into a zealous fanatic who does nothing but wait for it to occur. Instead, it should lead the believer into a watchful pursuit of holiness. Moreover, a watchful attitude creates a pilgrim mentality (2:11). It reminds the Christian that he is a citizen of heaven only sojourning on earth. It should also remind him that he will face the record of his service to God and be rewarded for what stands the test at the judgment seat of Christ, which follows the return of Christ to rapture His church. "And watchful in your prayers." A mind victimized by emotion and passion, out of control, or knocked out of balance by worldly lusts and pursuits, is a mind that cannot know the fullness of holy communion in prayer with God (3:7). A mind fixed on His return is purified (1 John 3:3) and enjoys the fullness of fellowship with the Lord.

NOVEMBER 29

Daniel 1:1–2:49

1 In the third year of the reign of Jehoiakim
king of Judah, Nebuchadnezzar king of
Babylon came to Jerusalem and besieged it.
2And the Lord gave Jehoiakim king of Judah
into his hand, with some of the articles of the
house of God, which he carried into the land
of Shinar to the house of his god; and he
brought the articles into the treasure house of
his god.
3Then the king instructed Ashpenaz, the
master of his eunuchs, to bring some of the
children of Israel and some of the king's descendants and some of the nobles, 4young men in
whom *there was* no blemish, but good-looking,
gifted in all wisdom, possessing knowledge
and quick to understand, who *had* ability to
serve in the king's palace, and whom they
might teach the language and literature of the
Chaldeans. 5And the king appointed for them a
daily provision of the king's delicacies and of
the wine which he drank, and three years of
training for them, so that at the end of *that*
time they might serve before the king. 6Now
from among those of the sons of Judah were
Daniel, Hananiah, Mishael, and Azariah. 7To
them the chief of the eunuchs gave names: he
gave Daniel *the name* Belteshazzar; to
Hananiah, Shadrach; to Mishael, Meshach;
and to Azariah, Abed-Nego.
8But Daniel purposed in his heart that he
would not defile himself with the portion of
the king's delicacies, nor with the wine which
he drank; therefore he requested of the chief
of the eunuchs that he might not defile himself. 9Now God had brought Daniel into the
favor and goodwill of the chief of the eunuchs.
10And the chief of the eunuchs said to Daniel,
"I fear my lord the king, who has appointed

1:8 Daniel purposed. The pagan food and drink was devoted to idols. To indulge was to be understood as honoring these deities. Daniel "purposed in his heart" (Prov. 4:23) not to engage in compromise by being untrue to God's call of commitment (Ex. 34:14,15). Also, foods that God's law prohibited (Lev. 1:1) were items that pagans consumed; to partake entailed direct compromise (Dan. 1:12). Moses took this stand (Heb. 11:24–26), as did the psalmist (Ps. 119:115) and Jesus (Heb. 7:26).

your food and drink. For why should he see
your faces looking worse than the young men
who *are* your age? Then you would endanger
my head before the king."

[11]So Daniel said to the steward whom the
chief of the eunuchs had set over Daniel,
Hananiah, Mishael, and Azariah, [12]"Please test
your servants for ten days, and let them give
us vegetables to eat and water to drink. [13]Then
let our appearance be examined before you,
and the appearance of the young men who eat
the portion of the king's delicacies; and as you
see fit, *so* deal with your servants." [14]So he consented with them in this matter, and tested
them ten days.

[15]And at the end of ten days their features
appeared better and fatter in flesh than all the
young men who ate the portion of the king's
delicacies. [16]Thus the steward took away their
portion of delicacies and the wine that they
were to drink, and gave them vegetables.

[17]As for these four young men, God gave
them knowledge and skill in all literature and
wisdom; and Daniel had understanding in all
visions and dreams.

[18]Now at the end of the days, when the king
had said that they should be brought in, the
chief of the eunuchs brought them in before
Nebuchadnezzar. [19]Then the king interviewed
them, and among them all none was found like
Daniel, Hananiah, Mishael, and Azariah; therefore they served before the king. [20]And in all matters of wisdom *and* understanding about which
the king examined them, he found them ten times
better than all the magicians *and* astrologers who
were in all his realm. [21]Thus Daniel continued
until the first year of King Cyrus.

2 Now in the second year of Nebuchadnezzar's
reign, Nebuchadnezzar had dreams; and his
spirit was *so* troubled that his sleep left him.
[2]Then the king gave the command to call the
magicians, the astrologers, the sorcerers, and
the Chaldeans to tell the king his dreams. So
they came and stood before the king. [3]And the
king said to them, "I have had a dream, and my
spirit is anxious to know the dream."

[4]Then the Chaldeans spoke to the king in
Aramaic, "O king, live forever! Tell your servants
the dream, and we will give the interpretation."

[5]The king answered and said to the
Chaldeans, "My decision is firm: if you do not
make known the dream to me, and its interpretation, you shall be cut in pieces, and your
houses shall be made an ash heap. [6]However,
if you tell the dream and its interpretation, you
shall receive from me gifts, rewards, and great
honor. Therefore tell me the dream and its
interpretation."

[7]They answered again and said, "Let the
king tell his servants the dream, and we will
give its interpretation."

[8]The king answered and said, "I know for
certain that you would gain time, because you
see that my decision is firm: [9]if you do not
make known the dream to me, *there is only*
one decree for you! For you have agreed to
speak lying and corrupt words before me till
the time has changed. Therefore tell me the
dream, and I shall know that you can give me
its interpretation."

[10]The Chaldeans answered the king, and
said, "There is not a man on earth who can tell
the king's matter; therefore no king, lord, or
ruler has *ever* asked such things of any magician, astrologer, or Chaldean. [11]*It is* a difficult
thing that the king requests, and there is no
other who can tell it to the king except the
gods, whose dwelling is not with flesh."

[12]For this reason the king was angry and
very furious, and gave the command to
destroy all the wise *men* of Babylon. [13]So the
decree went out, and they began killing the
wise *men;* and they sought Daniel and his
companions, to kill *them.*

[14]Then with counsel and wisdom Daniel
answered Arioch, the captain of the king's
guard, who had gone out to kill the wise *men*
of Babylon; [15]he answered and said to Arioch
the king's captain, "Why is the decree from the
king so urgent?" Then Arioch made the decision known to Daniel.

[16]So Daniel went in and asked the king to
give him time, that he might tell the king the
interpretation. [17]Then Daniel went to his house,
and made the decision known to Hananiah,
Mishael, and Azariah, his companions, [18]that
they might seek mercies from the God of heav-
en concerning this secret, so that Daniel and
his companions might not perish with the rest
of the wise *men* of Babylon. [19]Then the secret
was revealed to Daniel in a night vision. So
Daniel blessed the God of heaven.

[20]Daniel answered and said:

"Blessed be the name of God forever
    and ever,
For wisdom and might are His.
21 And He changes the times and the
    seasons;
He removes kings and raises up kings;
He gives wisdom to the wise
And knowledge to those who have
    understanding.
22 He reveals deep and secret things;
He knows what *is* in the darkness,
And light dwells with Him.

23 "I thank You and praise You,
O God of my fathers;
You have given me wisdom and might,
And have now made known to me what
we asked of You,
For You have made known to us the
king's demand."

24 Therefore Daniel went to Arioch, whom
the king had appointed to destroy the wise
men of Babylon. He went and said thus to him:
"Do not destroy the wise *men* of Babylon; take
me before the king, and I will tell the king the
interpretation."
25 Then Arioch quickly brought Daniel
before the king, and said thus to him, "I have
found a man of the captives of Judah, who will
make known to the king the interpretation."
26 The king answered and said to Daniel,
whose name *was* Belteshazzar, "Are you able
to make known to me the dream which I have
seen, and its interpretation?"
27 Daniel answered in the presence of the
king, and said, "The secret which the king has
demanded, the wise *men,* the astrologers, the
magicians, and the soothsayers cannot declare
to the king. 28 But there is a God in heaven who
reveals secrets, and He has made known to
King Nebuchadnezzar what will be in the latter
days. Your dream, and the visions of your head
upon your bed, were these: 29 As for you, O
king, thoughts came *to* your *mind while* on your
bed, *about* what would come to pass after this;
and He who reveals secrets has made known
to you what will be. 30 But as for me, this secret
has not been revealed to me because I have
more wisdom than anyone living, but for *our*
sakes who make known the interpretation to
the king, and that you may know the thoughts
of your heart.
31 "You, O king, were watching; and behold,
a great image! This great image, whose splendor *was* excellent, stood before you; and its
form *was* awesome. 32 This image's head *was* of
fine gold, its chest and arms of silver, its belly
and thighs of bronze, 33 its legs of iron, its feet
partly of iron and partly of clay. 34 You watched
while a stone was cut out without hands,
which struck the image on its feet of iron and
clay, and broke them in pieces. 35 Then the iron,
the clay, the bronze, the silver, and the gold
were crushed together, and became like chaff
from the summer threshing floors; the wind
carried them away so that no trace of them
was found. And the stone that struck the
image became a great mountain and filled the
whole earth.
36 "This *is* the dream. Now we will tell the
interpretation of it before the king. 37 You, O
king, *are* a king of kings. For the God of heav-
en has given you a kingdom, power, strength,
and glory; 38 and wherever the children of men
dwell, or the beasts of the field and the birds
of the heaven, He has given *them* into your
hand, and has made you ruler over them all—
you *are* this head of gold. 39 But after you shall
arise another kingdom inferior to yours; then
another, a third kingdom of bronze, which
shall rule over all the earth. 40 And the fourth
kingdom shall be as strong as iron, inasmuch
as iron breaks in pieces and shatters everything; and like iron that crushes, *that kingdom*
will break in pieces and crush all the others.
41 Whereas you saw the feet and toes, partly of
potter's clay and partly of iron, the kingdom
shall be divided; yet the strength of the iron
shall be in it, just as you saw the iron mixed
with ceramic clay. 42 And *as* the toes of the feet
were partly of iron and partly of clay, *so* the
kingdom shall be partly strong and partly
fragile. 43 As you saw iron mixed with ceramic
clay, they will mingle with the seed of men;
but they will not adhere to one another, just as
iron does not mix with clay. 44 And in the days
of these kings the God of heaven will set up a
kingdom which shall never be destroyed; and
the kingdom shall not be left to other people;
it shall break in pieces and consume all these
kingdoms, and it shall stand forever. 45 Inasmuch as you saw that the stone was cut out of
the mountain without hands, and that it broke
in pieces the iron, the bronze, the clay, the silver, and the gold—the great God has made
known to the king what will come to pass
after this. The dream is certain, and its interpretation is sure."

2:36–45 we will tell the interpretation. Five empires in succession would rule over Israel, here pictured by parts of a statue (body). In Daniel 7, the same empires are represented by 4 great beasts. These empires are Babylon, Medo-Persia, Greece, Rome, and the later revived Rome, each one differentiated from the previous as indicated by the declining quality of the metal. A stone picturing Christ (Luke 20:18) at His Second Coming (as the Son of Man also does in Dan. 7:13,14) will destroy the fourth empire in its final phase with catastrophic suddenness (2:34,35,44,45). Christ's total shattering of Gentile power will result in the establishment of His millennial kingdom, the ultimate empire, and then continuing on eternally (2:44; 7:27).

[46]Then King Nebuchadnezzar fell on his face, prostrate before Daniel, and commanded that they should present an offering and incense to him. [47]The king answered Daniel, and said, "Truly your God *is* the God of gods, the Lord of kings, and a revealer of secrets, since you could reveal this secret." [48]Then the king promoted Daniel and gave him many great gifts; and he made him ruler over the whole province of Babylon, and chief administrator over all the wise *men* of Babylon. [49]Also Daniel petitioned the king, and he set Shadrach, Meshach, and Abed-Nego over the affairs of the province of Babylon; but Daniel *sat* in the gate of the king.

Psalm 135:15–21

15 The idols of the nations *are* silver and
gold,
The work of men's hands.
16 They have mouths, but they do not
speak;
Eyes they have, but they do not see;
17 They have ears, but they do not hear;
Nor is there *any* breath in their
mouths.
18 Those who make them are like them;
So is everyone who trusts in them.

19 Bless the LORD, O house of Israel!
Bless the LORD, O house of Aaron!
20 Bless the LORD, O house of Levi!
You who fear the LORD, bless the LORD!
21 Blessed be the LORD out of Zion,
Who dwells in Jerusalem!
Praise the LORD!

Proverbs 29:10

10 The bloodthirsty hate the blameless,
But the upright seek his well-being.

1 Peter 5:1–14

5 The elders who are among you I exhort, I who am a fellow elder and a witness of the sufferings of Christ, and also a partaker of the glory that will be revealed: [2]Shepherd the flock of God which is among you, serving as overseers, not by compulsion but willingly, not for dishonest gain but eagerly; [3]nor as being lords over those entrusted to you, but being examples to the flock; [4]and when the Chief Shepherd appears, you will receive the crown of glory that does not fade away.

[5]Likewise you younger people, submit yourselves to *your* elders. Yes, all of *you* be submissive to one another, and be clothed with humility, for

"God resists the proud,
But gives grace to the humble."

[6]Therefore humble yourselves under the mighty hand of God, that He may exalt you in due time, [7]casting all your care upon Him, for He cares for you.

5:6 under the mighty hand of God. This is an Old Testament symbol of the power of God working in the experience of men, always accomplishing His sovereign purpose (Ex. 3:19,20; Job 30:20,21; Ezek. 20:33,37; Mic. 6:8). The readers of Peter's letter were not to fight the sovereign hand of God, even when it brought them through testings. One of the evidences of lack of submission and humility is impatience with God in His work of humbling believers. **exalt you in due time.** God will lift up the suffering, submissive believers in His wisely appointed time. See Job 42.

[8]Be sober, be vigilant; because your adversary the devil walks about like a roaring lion, seeking whom he may devour. [9]Resist him, steadfast in the faith, knowing that the same sufferings are experienced by your brotherhood in the world. [10]But may the God of all grace, who called us to His eternal glory by Christ Jesus, after you have suffered a while, perfect, establish, strengthen, and settle *you.* [11]To Him *be* the glory and the dominion forever and ever. Amen.

[12]By Silvanus, our faithful brother as I consider him, I have written to you briefly, exhorting and testifying that this is the true grace of God in which you stand.

[13]She who is in Babylon, elect together with *you,* greets you; and *so does* Mark my son. [14]Greet one another with a kiss of love.

Peace to you all who are in Christ Jesus. Amen.

DAY 29: How are pastors to care for their congregations?

First Peter 5:2 gives this exhortation to the elders: "Shepherd the flock of God." After the motivation (v. 1) comes the exhortation (vv. 2–4). Since the primary objective of shepherding is feeding, or teaching, every elder must be able to teach (John 21:15–17; 1 Tim. 3:2; Titus 1:9). Involved with the feeding of the flock is also protecting the flock (Acts 20:28–30). In both duties, it must be remembered that the flock belongs to God, not to the pastor. God entrusts some of His flock to the pastor of a church to lead, care for, and feed (v. 3).

"Not by compulsion but willingly." Specifically, Peter may be warning the elders against a first danger—laziness. The divine calling (1 Cor. 9:16), along with the urgency of the task (Rom. 1:15), should prevent laziness and indifference. "Not for dishonest gain." False teachers are always motivated by a second danger, money, and use their power and position to rob people of their own wealth (2 Pet. 2:1–3). Scripture is clear that churches should pay their shepherds well (1 Cor. 9:7–14; 1 Tim. 5:17,18); but a desire for undeserved money must never be a motive for ministers to serve (1 Tim. 3:3; 6:9–11; 2 Tim. 2:4; Titus 1:7; 2 Pet. 2:3; see also Jer. 6:13; 8:10; Mic. 3:11; Mal. 1:10).

"Nor as being lords" (v. 3). This is the third major temptation for a pastor: demagoguery. In this context, "lords" means to dominate someone or some situation. It implies leadership by manipulation and intimidation. Rather, true spiritual leadership is by example (1 Tim. 4:12).

NOVEMBER 30

Daniel 3:1–4:37

3 Nebuchadnezzar the king made an image of gold, whose height *was* sixty cubits *and* its width six cubits. He set it up in the plain of Dura, in the province of Babylon.
2And King Nebuchadnezzar sent *word* to gather together the satraps, the administrators, the governors, the counselors, the treasurers, the judges, the magistrates, and all the officials of the provinces, to come to the dedication of the image which King Nebuchadnezzar had set up.
3So the satraps, the administrators, the governors, the counselors, the treasurers, the judges, the magistrates, and all the officials of the provinces gathered together for the dedication of the image that King Nebuchadnezzar had set up; and they stood before the image that Nebuchadnezzar had set up.
4Then a herald cried aloud: "To you it is commanded, O peoples, nations, and languages,
5*that* at the time you hear the sound of the horn, flute, harp, lyre, *and* psaltery, in symphony with all kinds of music, you shall fall down and worship the gold image that King Nebuchadnezzar has set up;
6and whoever does not fall down and worship shall be cast immediately into the midst of a burning fiery furnace."
7So at that time, when all the people heard the sound of the horn, flute, harp, *and* lyre, in symphony with all kinds of music, all the people, nations, and languages fell down *and* worshiped the gold image which King Nebuchadnezzar had set up.
8Therefore at that time certain Chaldeans came forward and accused the Jews.
9They spoke and said to King Nebuchadnezzar, "O king, live forever!
10You, O king, have made a decree that everyone who hears the sound of the horn, flute, harp, lyre, *and* psaltery, in symphony with all kinds of music, shall fall down and worship the gold image;
11and whoever does not fall down and worship shall be cast into the midst of a burning fiery furnace.
12There are certain Jews whom you have set over the affairs of the province of Babylon: Shadrach, Meshach, and Abed-Nego; these men, O king, have not paid due regard to you. They do not serve your gods or worship the gold image which you have set up."
13Then Nebuchadnezzar, in rage and fury, gave the command to bring Shadrach, Meshach, and Abed-Nego. So they brought these men before the king.
14Nebuchadnezzar spoke, saying to them, "*Is it* true, Shadrach, Meshach, and Abed-Nego, *that* you do not serve my gods or worship the gold image which I have set up?
15Now if you are ready at the time you hear the sound of the horn, flute, harp, lyre, *and* psaltery, in symphony with all kinds of music, and you fall down and worship the image which I have made, *good!* But if you do

3:1 image of gold. The statue, which the king arrogantly made, represented himself as an expression of his greatness and glory and reflected the dream where he was the head of gold (2:38). It was not necessarily made of solid gold, but more likely would have been overlaid with gold, like many objects found in the ruins of Babylon. The word for "image" usually means a human form. The height of the figure was about 90 feet and the width 9 feet; it would have been comparable in height to date palms found in that area. The self-deifying statue of the king need not have been grotesquely thin in proportion to the height since a massive base could have contributed to the height. This established the worship of Nebuchadnezzar and the nation under his power, in addition to the other gods.

3:15 who *is* the god...? The king's challenge would return to embarrass him. The true God was able to deliver, just as He was able to reveal a dream and its meaning. Nebuchadnezzar had earlier called him "the God of gods" (2:47); but having let that fade from his attention, he soon would be shocked and humiliated when God took up his challenge (3:28,29).

not worship, you shall be cast immediately into
the midst of a burning fiery furnace. And who *is*
the god who will deliver you from my hands?"
16 Shadrach, Meshach, and Abed-Nego
answered and said to the king, "O Nebuchadnezzar, we have no need to answer you in this
matter. 17 If that *is the case,* our God whom we
serve is able to deliver us from the burning
fiery furnace, and He will deliver *us* from your
hand, O king. 18 But if not, let it be known to
you, O king, that we do not serve your gods,
nor will we worship the gold image which you
have set up."
19 Then Nebuchadnezzar was full of fury, and
the expression on his face changed toward
Shadrach, Meshach, and Abed-Nego. He spoke
and commanded that they heat the furnace
seven times more than it was usually heated.
20 And he commanded certain mighty men of
valor who *were* in his army to bind Shadrach,
Meshach, and Abed-Nego, *and* cast *them* into
the burning fiery furnace. 21 Then these men
were bound in their coats, their trousers, their
turbans, and their *other* garments, and were
cast into the midst of the burning fiery furnace. 22 Therefore, because the king's command was urgent, and the furnace exceedingly hot, the flame of the fire killed those men
who took up Shadrach, Meshach, and Abed-
Nego. 23 And these three men, Shadrach,
Meshach, and Abed-Nego, fell down bound
into the midst of the burning fiery furnace.
24 Then King Nebuchadnezzar was astonished; and he rose in haste *and* spoke, saying
to his counselors, "Did we not cast three men
bound into the midst of the fire?"

They answered and said to the king, "True,
O king."
25 "Look!" he answered, "I see four men
loose, walking in the midst of the fire; and they
are not hurt, and the form of the fourth is like
the Son of God."
26 Then Nebuchadnezzar went near the
mouth of the burning fiery furnace *and* spoke,
saying, "Shadrach, Meshach, and Abed-Nego,
servants of the Most High God, come out, and
come *here.*" Then Shadrach, Meshach, and
Abed-Nego came from the midst of the fire.
27 And the satraps, administrators, governors,
and the king's counselors gathered together,
and they saw these men on whose bodies the
fire had no power; the hair of their head was
not singed nor were their garments affected,
and the smell of fire was not on them.
28 Nebuchadnezzar spoke, saying, "Blessed
be the God of Shadrach, Meshach, and Abed-
Nego, who sent His Angel and delivered His
servants who trusted in Him, and they have
frustrated the king's word, and yielded their
bodies, that they should not serve nor worship
any god except their own God! 29 Therefore I
make a decree that any people, nation, or language which speaks anything amiss against
the God of Shadrach, Meshach, and Abed-
Nego shall be cut in pieces, and their houses
shall be made an ash heap; because there is
no other God who can deliver like this."
30 Then the king promoted Shadrach, Meshach,
and Abed-Nego in the province of Babylon.

4 Nebuchadnezzar the king,

To all peoples, nations, and languages
that dwell in all the earth:

Peace be multiplied to you.

2 I thought it good to declare the signs
and wonders that the Most High God
has worked for me.

3 How great *are* His signs,
And how mighty His wonders!
His kingdom *is* an everlasting
kingdom,
And His dominion *is* from generation
to generation.

4 I, Nebuchadnezzar, was at rest in my
house, and flourishing in my palace.
5 I saw a dream which made me afraid,
and the thoughts on my bed and the
visions of my head troubled me.
6 Therefore I issued a decree to bring in
all the wise *men* of Babylon before me,
that they might make known to me the
interpretation of the dream. 7 Then the
magicians, the astrologers, the
Chaldeans, and the soothsayers came
in, and I told them the dream; but they
did not make known to me its
interpretation. 8 But at last Daniel came
before me (his name *is* Belteshazzar,
according to the name of my god; in
him *is* the Spirit of the Holy God), and
I told the dream before him, *saying:*
9 "Belteshazzar, chief of the magicians,

because I know that the Spirit of the Holy God *is* in you, and no secret troubles you, explain to me the visions of my dream that I have seen, and its interpretation.

10 "These *were* the visions of my head
while on my bed:

I was looking, and behold,
A tree in the midst of the earth,
And its height was great.
11 The tree grew and became strong;
Its height reached to the heavens,
And it could be seen to the ends
of all the earth.
12 Its leaves *were* lovely,
Its fruit abundant,
And in it *was* food for all.
The beasts of the field found shade
under it,
The birds of the heavens dwelt in its
branches,
And all flesh was fed from it.

13 "I saw in the visions of my head *while* on
my bed, and there was a watcher, a holy
one, coming down from heaven. 14He
cried aloud and said thus:

'Chop down the tree and cut off its
branches,
Strip off its leaves and scatter its fruit.
Let the beasts get out from under it,
And the birds from its branches.
15 Nevertheless leave the stump and
roots in the earth,
Bound with a band of iron and bronze,
In the tender grass of the field.
Let it be wet with the dew of heaven,
And *let* him graze with the beasts
On the grass of the earth.
16 Let his heart be changed from *that*
of a man,
Let him be given the heart of a beast,
And let seven times pass over him.

17 'This decision *is* by the decree of the
watchers,
And the sentence by the word of the
holy ones,
In order that the living may know
That the Most High rules in the
kingdom of men,
Gives it to whomever He will,
And sets over it the lowest of men.'

18 "This dream I, King Nebuchadnezzar,
have seen. Now you, Belteshazzar,
declare its interpretation, since all the
wise *men* of my kingdom are not able to
make known to me the interpretation;
but you *are* able, for the Spirit of the
Holy God *is* in you."

19 Then Daniel, whose name *was*
Belteshazzar, was astonished for a
time, and his thoughts troubled him.
So the king spoke, and said,
"Belteshazzar, do not let the dream or
its interpretation trouble you."
Belteshazzar answered and said,
"My lord, *may* the dream concern
those who hate you, and its
interpretation concern your enemies!

20 "The tree that you saw, which grew
and became strong, whose height
reached to the heavens and which
could be seen by all the earth, 21whose
leaves *were* lovely and its fruit
abundant, in which *was* food for all,
under which the beasts of the field
dwelt, and in whose branches the birds
of the heaven had their home— 22it *is*
you, O king, who have grown and
become strong; for your greatness has
grown and reaches to the heavens, and
your dominion to the end of the earth.

23 "And inasmuch as the king saw a
watcher, a holy one, coming down from
heaven and saying, 'Chop down the
tree and destroy it, but leave its stump
and roots in the earth, *bound* with a
band of iron and bronze in the tender
grass of the field; let it be wet with the
dew of heaven, and let him graze with
the beasts of the field, till seven times
pass over him'; 24this is the interpretation,
O king, and this is the decree of the
Most High, which has come upon my
lord the king: 25They shall drive you
from men, your dwelling shall be with
the beasts of the field, and they shall
make you eat grass like oxen. They
shall wet you with the dew of heaven,
and seven times shall pass over you, till
you know that the Most High rules in
the kingdom of men, and gives it to
whomever He chooses.

26 "And inasmuch as they gave the
command to leave the stump *and* roots
of the tree, your kingdom shall be
assured to you, after you come to know
that Heaven rules. 27Therefore, O king,
let my advice be acceptable to you;
break off your sins by *being* righteous,
and your iniquities by showing mercy
to *the* poor. Perhaps there may be a
lengthening of your prosperity."

28 All *this* came upon King
Nebuchadnezzar. 29At the end of the
twelve months he was walking about
the royal palace of Babylon. 30The king
spoke, saying, "Is not this great
Babylon, that I have built for a royal
dwelling by my mighty power and for
the honor of my majesty?"

31 While the word *was still* in the king's
mouth, a voice fell from heaven: "King
Nebuchadnezzar, to you it is spoken:
the kingdom has departed from you!
32And they shall drive you from men,
and your dwelling *shall be* with the
beasts of the field. They shall make
you eat grass like oxen; and seven
times shall pass over you, until you
know that the Most High rules in the
kingdom of men, and gives it to
whomever He chooses."

33 That very hour the word was fulfilled
concerning Nebuchadnezzar; he was
driven from men and ate grass like oxen;
his body was wet with the dew of heaven
till his hair had grown like eagles'
feathers and his nails like birds' *claws.*

34 And at the end of the time I,
Nebuchadnezzar, lifted my eyes to
heaven, and my understanding
returned to me; and I blessed the Most
High and praised and honored Him
who lives forever:

For His dominion *is* an everlasting
dominion,
And His kingdom *is* from generation to
generation.
35 All the inhabitants of the earth *are*
reputed as nothing;
He does according to His will in the
army of heaven
And *among* the inhabitants of the
earth.
No one can restrain His hand
Or say to Him, "What have You done?"

36 At the same time my reason returned
to me, and for the glory of my
kingdom, my honor and splendor
returned to me. My counselors and
nobles resorted to me, I was restored
to my kingdom, and excellent majesty
was added to me. 37Now I,
Nebuchadnezzar, praise and extol and
honor the King of heaven, all of whose
works *are* truth, and His ways justice.
And those who walk in pride He is able
to put down.

Psalm 136:1–9

Oh, give thanks to the LORD,
for *He is* good!
For His mercy *endures* forever.
2 Oh, give thanks to the God of gods!
For His mercy *endures* forever.
3 Oh, give thanks to the Lord of lords!
For His mercy *endures* forever:

4 To Him who alone does great wonders,
For His mercy *endures* forever;
5 To Him who by wisdom made the
heavens,
For His mercy *endures* forever;
6 To Him who laid out the earth above
the waters,
For His mercy *endures* forever;
7 To Him who made great lights,
For His mercy *endures* forever—
8 The sun to rule by day,
For His mercy *endures* forever;
9 The moon and stars to rule by night,
For His mercy *endures* forever.

Proverbs 29:11

11 A fool vents all his feelings,
But a wise *man* holds them back.

2 Peter 1:1–21

1 Simon Peter, a bondservant and apostle of Jesus Christ,

To those who have obtained like precious faith with us by the righteousness of our God and Savior Jesus Christ:

2Grace and peace be multiplied to you in the
knowledge of God and of Jesus our Lord, 3as
His divine power has given to us all things that *pertain* to life and godliness, through the knowledge of Him who called us by glory and
virtue, 4by which have been given to us exceedingly great and precious promises, that through these you may be partakers of the divine nature, having escaped the corruption *that is* in the world through lust.

1:4 partakers of the divine nature. This expression is not different from the concepts of being born again, born from above (John 3:3; James 1:18; 1 Pet. 1:23), being in Christ (Rom. 8:1), or being the home of the Trinity (John 14:17–23). The precious promises of salvation result in becoming God's children in the present age (John 1:12; Rom. 8:9; Gal. 2:20; Col. 1:27), and thereby sharing in God's nature by the possession of His eternal life.

5But also for this very reason, giving all diligence, add to your faith virtue, to virtue knowledge, 6to knowledge self-control, to self-control
perseverance, to perseverance godliness, 7to
godliness brotherly kindness, and to brotherly
kindness love. 8For if these things are yours
and abound, *you* will be neither barren nor
unfruitful in the knowledge of our Lord Jesus
Christ. 9For he who lacks these things is short-
sighted, even to blindness, and has forgotten
that he was cleansed from his old sins.
10Therefore, brethren, be even more diligent
to make your call and election sure, for if you
do these things you will never stumble; 11for so
an entrance will be supplied to you abundantly
into the everlasting kingdom of our Lord and
Savior Jesus Christ.
12For this reason I will not be negligent to
remind you always of these things, though
you know and are established in the present
truth. 13Yes, I think it is right, as long as I am
in this tent, to stir you up by reminding *you*,
14knowing that shortly I *must* put off my tent,
just as our Lord Jesus Christ showed me.
15Moreover I will be careful to ensure that you
always have a reminder of these things after
my decease.
16For we did not follow cunningly devised
fables when we made known to you the power
and coming of our Lord Jesus Christ, but
were eyewitnesses of His majesty. 17For He
received from God the Father honor and glory
when such a voice came to Him from the
Excellent Glory: "This is My beloved Son, in
whom I am well pleased." 18And we heard this
voice which came from heaven when we were
with Him on the holy mountain.
19And so we have the prophetic word confirmed, which you do well to heed as a light
that shines in a dark place, until the day dawns
and the morning star rises in your hearts;
20knowing this first, that no prophecy of
Scripture is of any private interpretation, 21for
prophecy never came by the will of man, but
holy men of God spoke *as they were* moved by
the Holy Spirit.

1:21 by the will of man. As Scripture is not of human origin, neither is it the result of human will. The emphasis in the phrase is that no part of Scripture was ever at any time produced because men wanted it so. The Bible is not the product of human effort. The prophets, in fact, sometimes wrote what they could not fully understand (1 Pet. 1:10,11), but were nonetheless faithful to write what God revealed to them. **moved by the Holy Spirit.** Grammatically, this means that they were continually carried or borne along by the Spirit of God. The Holy Spirit thus is the divine author and originator, the producer of the Scriptures. In the Old Testament alone, the human writers refer to their writings as the words of God over 3,800 times (e.g., Jer. 1:4; 3:2; Rom. 3:2; 1 Cor. 2:10). Though the human writers of Scripture were active rather than passive in the process of writing Scripture, God the Holy Spirit superintended them so that, using their own individual personalities, thought processes, and vocabulary, they composed and recorded without error the exact words God wanted written. The original copies of Scripture are therefore inspired, i.e., God-breathed (2 Tim. 3:16) and inerrant, i.e., without error (John 10:34,35; 17:17; Titus 1:2). Peter defined the process of inspiration which created an inerrant original text (Prov. 30:5; 1 Cor. 14:36; 1 Thess. 2:13).

DAY 30: Who was the fourth person in the fiery furnace of Daniel 3:19–25?

The delivery of Shadrach, Meshach, and Abed-Nego from the flames was an astonishing, miraculous event. The furnace was real, and the flames were hot. The guards who carried the young men close enough to cast them in the furnace were killed. Why complicate this miracle with a fourth person in the furnace? Because the king himself noticed the discrepancy between the number he had thrown into the flames and the number he saw strolling about. The truth usually includes unexpected complications.

The king concluded the fourth person was a heavenly being. He identified the visitor in two different ways: 1) "like the Son of God" (3:25); 2) "Angel" (3:28). When he commanded the three friends to exit the furnace, the king did not extend an invitation to God's special servant.

Viewed from the context of all of Scripture, the fourth person could possibly have been the Second Person of the Godhead (Jesus Christ) in a preincarnate appearance. For other similar Old Testament instances, see Exodus 3:2, Joshua 5:13–15, and Judges 6:11ff. While the term "Angel" is used in these reports, the person had a special connection with the Lord. He wasn't an angel, but the Angel of the Lord. His presence may be startling but He does not have the stunning and awe-inspiring appearance of an angel. The king saw four men in the furnace. The one who appeared miraculously he identified as the Son of God. It may well have been an inspired exclamation.

DECEMBER 1

Daniel 5:1–6:28

5 Belshazzar the king made a great feast for
a thousand of his lords, and drank wine in
the presence of the thousand. 2While he tasted
the wine, Belshazzar gave the command to
bring the gold and silver vessels which his father Nebuchadnezzar had taken from the temple which *had been* in Jerusalem, that the king
and his lords, his wives, and his concubines
might drink from them. 3Then they brought
the gold vessels that had been taken from the
temple of the house of God which *had been* in
Jerusalem; and the king and his lords, his
wives, and his concubines drank from them.
4They drank wine, and praised the gods of gold
and silver, bronze and iron, wood and stone.

5In the same hour the fingers of a man's
hand appeared and wrote opposite the lampstand on the plaster of the wall of the king's
palace; and the king saw the part of the hand
that wrote. 6Then the king's countenance
changed, and his thoughts troubled him, so
that the joints of his hips were loosened and
his knees knocked against each other. 7The
king cried aloud to bring in the astrologers,
the Chaldeans, and the soothsayers. The king
spoke, saying to the wise *men* of Babylon,
"Whoever reads this writing, and tells me its
interpretation, shall be clothed with purple and
have a chain of gold around his neck; and he
shall be the third ruler in the kingdom." 8Now
all the king's wise *men* came, but they could
not read the writing, or make known to the
king its interpretation. 9Then King Belshazzar
was greatly troubled, his countenance was
changed, and his lords were astonished.

10The queen, because of the words of the
king and his lords, came to the banquet hall.
The queen spoke, saying, "O king, live forever! Do not let your thoughts trouble you, nor
let your countenance change. 11There is a man
in your kingdom in whom *is* the Spirit of the
Holy God. And in the days of your father, light
and understanding and wisdom, like the wisdom of the gods, were found in him; and King
Nebuchadnezzar your father—your father the
king—made him chief of the magicians,
astrologers, Chaldeans, *and* soothsayers. 12In-
asmuch as an excellent spirit, knowledge,
understanding, interpreting dreams, solving
riddles, and explaining enigmas were found in
this Daniel, whom the king named Belteshazzar, now let Daniel be called, and he will
give the interpretation."

13Then Daniel was brought in before the king.
The king spoke, and said to Daniel, "*Are* you
that Daniel who is one of the captives from
Judah, whom my father the king brought from
Judah? 14I have heard of you, that the Spirit of
God *is* in you, and *that* light and understanding
and excellent wisdom are found in you. 15Now
the wise *men,* the astrologers, have been
brought in before me, that they should read this
writing and make known to me its interpretation, but they could not give the interpretation of
the thing. 16And I have heard of you, that you can
give interpretations and explain enigmas. Now if
you can read the writing and make known to me
its interpretation, you shall be clothed with purple and *have* a chain of gold around your neck,
and shall be the third ruler in the kingdom."

17Then Daniel answered, and said before the
king, "Let your gifts be for yourself, and give
your rewards to another; yet I will read the
writing to the king, and make known to him the
interpretation. 18O king, the Most High God
gave Nebuchadnezzar your father a kingdom
and majesty, glory and honor. 19And because of
the majesty that He gave him, all peoples,
nations, and languages trembled and feared
before him. Whomever he wished, he executed; whomever he wished, he kept alive;
whomever he wished, he set up; and whomever he wished, he put down. 20But when his
heart was lifted up, and his spirit was hardened in pride, he was deposed from his kingly
throne, and they took his glory from him.
21Then he was driven from the sons of men, his
heart was made like the beasts, and his
dwelling *was* with the wild donkeys. They fed
him with grass like oxen, and his body was wet
with the dew of heaven, till he knew that the
Most High God rules in the kingdom of men,
and appoints over it whomever He chooses.

22"But you his son, Belshazzar, have not
humbled your heart, although you knew all
this. 23And you have lifted yourself up against
the Lord of heaven. They have brought the
vessels of His house before you, and you and
your lords, your wives and your concubines,
have drunk wine from them. And you have
praised the gods of silver and gold, bronze and
iron, wood and stone, which do not see or hear
or know; and the God who *holds* your breath in
His hand and owns all your ways, you have not
glorified. 24Then the fingers of the hand were
sent from Him, and this writing was written.
25"And this is the inscription that was written:

MENE, MENE, TEKEL, UPHARSIN.

26This *is* the interpretation of *each* word. MENE:
God has numbered your kingdom, and finished

it; [27]TEKEL: You have been weighed in the balances, and found wanting; [28]PERES: Your kingdom has been divided, and given to the Medes
and Persians." [29]Then Belshazzar gave the
command, and they clothed Daniel with purple and *put* a chain of gold around his neck,
and made a proclamation concerning him that
he should be the third ruler in the kingdom.

5:25–29 MENE, MENE. This means "counted" or "appointed" and is doubled for stronger emphasis. *Tekel* means "weighed" or "assessed" by the God who weighs actions (1 Sam. 2:3; Ps. 62:9). *Peres* denotes "divided," i.e., to the Medes and Persians. *Pharsin* in v. 25 is the plural of *peres,* possibly emphasizing the parts in the division. The "U" prefix on *pharsin* has the idea of the English "and."

[30]That very night Belshazzar, king of the
Chaldeans, was slain. [31]And Darius the Mede
received the kingdom, *being* about sixty-two
years old.

6 It pleased Darius to set over the kingdom
one hundred and twenty satraps, to be
over the whole kingdom; [2]and over these,
three governors, of whom Daniel *was* one,
that the satraps might give account to them,
so that the king would suffer no loss. [3]Then
this Daniel distinguished himself above the
governors and satraps, because an excellent
spirit *was* in him; and the king gave thought to
setting him over the whole realm. [4]So the governors and satraps sought to find *some* charge
against Daniel concerning the kingdom; but
they could find no charge or fault, because he
was faithful; nor was there any error or fault
found in him. [5]Then these men said, "We shall
not find any charge against this Daniel unless
we find *it* against him concerning the law of
his God."

[6]So these governors and satraps thronged
before the king, and said thus to him: "King
Darius, live forever! [7]All the governors of the
kingdom, the administrators and satraps, the
counselors and advisors, have consulted
together to establish a royal statute and to
make a firm decree, that whoever petitions
any god or man for thirty days, except you, O
king, shall be cast into the den of lions. [8]Now,
O king, establish the decree and sign the writing, so that it cannot be changed, according to
the law of the Medes and Persians, which does
not alter." [9]Therefore King Darius signed the
written decree.

6:3 an excellent spirit. Daniel, over 80, had enjoyed God's blessing throughout his life (1:20,21; 2:49; 4:8; 5:12). **over the whole realm.** Daniel was the favorite of the king. He had experience, wisdom, a sense of history, leadership, a good reputation, ability, attitude, and revelation from the God of heaven. Apparently, God wanted him in the place of influence to encourage and assist in the Jews' return to Judah, since the return was made in Cyrus's first year (539–537 B.C.), right before the lions' den incident. From the record of Ezra 1 and 6, all the basic elements of the return appear: 1) the temple was to be rebuilt with the cost paid from Cyrus's treasury; 2) all Jews who visited could return, and those who stayed were urged to assist financially; and 3) the gold and silver vessels stolen from the temple by Nebuchadnezzar were to be taken back. To account for such favor toward the Jews, it is easy to think of Daniel not only influencing Cyrus to write such a decree, but even formulating it for him.

[10]Now when Daniel knew that the writing
was signed, he went home. And in his upper
room, with his windows open toward Jerusalem, he knelt down on his knees three times
that day, and prayed and gave thanks before
his God, as was his custom since early days.
[11]Then these men assembled and found
Daniel praying and making supplication
before his God. [12]And they went before the
king, and spoke concerning the king's decree:
"Have you not signed a decree that every man
who petitions any god or man within thirty
days, except you, O king, shall be cast into the
den of lions?"

The king answered and said, "The thing *is*
true, according to the law of the Medes and
Persians, which does not alter."
[13]So they answered and said before the king,
"That Daniel, who is one of the captives from
Judah, does not show due regard for you, O
king, or for the decree that you have signed,
but makes his petition three times a day."
[14]And the king, when he heard *these* words,
was greatly displeased with himself, and set
his heart on Daniel to deliver him; and he labored till the going down of the sun to deliver
him. [15]Then these men approached the king,
and said to the king, "Know, O king, that *it is*
the law of the Medes and Persians that no
decree or statute which the king establishes
may be changed."

16 So the king gave the command, and they
brought Daniel and cast *him* into the den of
lions. *But* the king spoke, saying to Daniel,
"Your God, whom you serve continually, He
will deliver you." 17 Then a stone was brought and
laid on the mouth of the den, and the king sealed
it with his own signet ring and with the signets
of his lords, that the purpose concerning Daniel
might not be changed.

18 Now the king went to his palace and spent
the night fasting; and no musicians were
brought before him. Also his sleep went from
him. 19 Then the king arose very early in the
morning and went in haste to the den of lions.
20 And when he came to the den, he cried out
with a lamenting voice to Daniel. The king
spoke, saying to Daniel, "Daniel, servant of
the living God, has your God, whom you serve
continually, been able to deliver you from the
lions?"

21 Then Daniel said to the king, "O king, live
forever! 22 My God sent His angel and shut the
lions' mouths, so that they have not hurt me,
because I was found innocent before Him; and
also, O king, I have done no wrong before you."

23 Now the king was exceedingly glad for him,
and commanded that they should take Daniel
up out of the den. So Daniel was taken up out
of the den, and no injury whatever was found
on him, because he believed in his God.

24 And the king gave the command, and they
brought those men who had accused Daniel,
and they cast *them* into the den of lions—
them, their children, and their wives; and the
lions overpowered them, and broke all their
bones in pieces before they ever came to the
bottom of the den.

25 Then King Darius wrote:

To all peoples, nations, and languages
that dwell in all the earth:

Peace be multiplied to you.

26 I make a decree that in every dominion
of my kingdom *men must* tremble and
fear before the God of Daniel.

For He *is* the living God,
And steadfast forever;
His kingdom *is the one* which shall not
be destroyed,
And His dominion *shall endure*
to the end.

27 He delivers and rescues,
And He works signs and wonders
In heaven and on earth,
Who has delivered Daniel from the
power of the lions.

28 So this Daniel prospered in the reign of
Darius and in the reign of Cyrus the Persian.

Psalm 136:10–26

10 To Him who struck Egypt in their
firstborn,
For His mercy *endures* forever;
11 And brought out Israel from among
them,
For His mercy *endures* forever;
12 With a strong hand, and with an
outstretched arm,
For His mercy *endures* forever;
13 To Him who divided the Red Sea
in two,
For His mercy *endures* forever;
14 And made Israel pass through the
midst of it,
For His mercy *endures* forever;
15 But overthrew Pharaoh and his
army in the Red Sea,
For His mercy *endures* forever;
16 To Him who led His people through
the wilderness,
For His mercy *endures* forever;
17 To Him who struck down
great kings,
For His mercy *endures* forever;
18 And slew famous kings,
For His mercy *endures* forever—
19 Sihon king of the Amorites,
For His mercy *endures* forever;
20 And Og king of Bashan,
For His mercy *endures* forever—
21 And gave their land as a heritage,
For His mercy *endures* forever;
22 A heritage to Israel His servant,
For His mercy *endures* forever.

23 Who remembered us in our
lowly state,
For His mercy *endures* forever;
24 And rescued us from our enemies,
For His mercy *endures* forever;
25 Who gives food to all flesh,
For His mercy *endures* forever.

26 Oh, give thanks to the God
of heaven!
For His mercy *endures* forever.

Proverbs 29:12–13

12 If a ruler pays attention to lies,
All his servants *become* wicked.

13 The poor *man* and the oppressor
have this in common:
The LORD gives light to the eyes
of both.

2 Peter 2:1–22

2 But there were also false prophets among the people, even as there will be false teachers among you, who will secretly bring in destructive heresies, even denying the Lord who bought them, *and* bring on themselves swift destruction. [2]And many will follow their destructive ways, because of whom the way of truth will be blasphemed. [3]By covetousness they will exploit you with deceptive words; for a long time their judgment has not been idle, and their destruction does not slumber.

[4]For if God did not spare the angels who sinned, but cast *them* down to hell and delivered *them* into chains of darkness, to be reserved for judgment; [5]and did not spare the ancient world, but saved Noah, *one of* eight *people,* a preacher of righteousness, bringing in the flood on the world of the ungodly; [6]and turning the cities of Sodom and Gomorrah into ashes, condemned *them* to destruction, making *them* an example to those who afterward would live ungodly; [7]and delivered righteous Lot, *who was* oppressed by the filthy conduct of the wicked [8](for that righteous man, dwelling among them, tormented *his* righteous soul from day to day by seeing and hearing *their* lawless deeds)— [9]*then* the Lord knows how to deliver the godly out of temptations and to reserve the unjust under punishment for the day of judgment, [10]and especially those who walk according to the flesh in the lust of uncleanness and despise authority. *They are* presumptuous, self-willed. They are not afraid to speak evil of dignitaries, [11]whereas angels, who are greater in power and might, do not bring a reviling accusation against them before the Lord.

[12]But these, like natural brute beasts made to be caught and destroyed, speak evil of the things they do not understand, and will utterly perish in their own corruption, [13]*and* will receive the wages of unrighteousness, *as* those who count it pleasure to carouse in the daytime. *They are* spots and blemishes, carousing in their own deceptions while they feast with you, [14]having eyes full of adultery and that cannot cease from sin, enticing unstable souls. They have a heart trained in covetous practices, *and are* accursed children. [15]They have forsaken the right way and gone astray, following the way of Balaam the *son* of Beor, who loved the wages of unrighteousness; [16]but he was rebuked for his iniquity: a dumb donkey speaking with a man's voice restrained the madness of the prophet.

[17]These are wells without water, clouds carried by a tempest, for whom is reserved the blackness of darkness forever.

[18]For when they speak great swelling *words* of emptiness, they allure through the lusts of the flesh, through lewdness, the ones who have actually escaped from those who live in error. [19]While they promise them liberty, they themselves are slaves of corruption; for by whom a person is overcome, by him also he is brought into bondage. [20]For if, after they have escaped the pollutions of the world through the knowledge of the Lord and Savior Jesus Christ, they are again entangled in them and overcome, the latter end is worse for them than the beginning. [21]For it would have been better for them not to have known the way of righteousness, than having known *it,* to turn from the holy commandment delivered to them. [22]But it has happened to them according to the true proverb: *"A dog returns to his own vomit,"* and, "a sow, having washed, to her wallowing in the mire."

2:11 angels, who are greater in power. A reference to the holy angels, who are greater in power than human beings. **do not bring a reviling accusation.** Unlike false teachers who are defiant toward higher powers, the holy angels so revere their Lord that they will not speak insults against any authority. Even the archangel Michael, recognizing the great presence and power of Satan, refused to speak evil of him (Jude 8,9), but called on the Lord to do so. No believer should be so boldly foolish as to mock or command the power of supernatural demons, especially Satan.

2:19 promise them liberty. False teachers promise those "trying to escape" the struggles of life the very freedom they seek. **slaves of corruption.** The false teachers can't deliver the freedom they promise, because they themselves are enslaved to the very corruption which people are trying to escape. **overcome,...bondage.** Whoever puts himself, in the name of freedom, into the hands of a false teacher, who is a prisoner himself, also becomes a prisoner. Bondage to corruption awaits all followers of false teachers.

DAY 1: Who were the false teachers that Peter describes in 2 Peter 2:1?

Peter described false teachers in detail in this chapter so that Christians would always recognize their characteristics and methods. The greatest sin of Christ-rejecters and the most damning work of Satan is misrepresentation of the truth and its consequent deception. Nothing is more wicked than for someone to claim to speak for God to the salvation of souls when in reality he speaks for Satan to the damnation of souls.

Peter says they will be from "among the people." "The people" is used in the New Testament of Israel (Acts 26:17,23). Peter's point, though, is that Satan has always endeavored to infiltrate groups of believers with the deceptions of false teachers (John 8:44). Since Eve, he has been in the deceit business (2 Cor. 11:3,4). The false teachers parade themselves as Christian pastors, teachers, and evangelists and "secretly bring in destructive heresies." "Heresies" means self-designed religious lies which lead to division and faction (1 Cor. 11:19; Gal. 5:20). The Greek word for "destructive" basically means damnation. This word is used 6 times in this letter and always speaks of final damnation (vv. 1–3; 3:7,16). This is why it is so tragic when a church makes a virtue out of the toleration of unscriptural teachings and ideas in the name of love and unity (2 Thess. 3:14; 1 Tim. 4:1–5; Titus 3:9–11).

"Denying the Lord." This phrase exposes the depth of the crime and guilt of the false teachers. This unusual Greek word for "Lord" appears 10 times in the New Testament and means one who has supreme authority, whether human authority or divine authority. Peter here warns that false prophets deny the sovereign lordship of Jesus Christ. Though their heresies may include the denial of the virgin birth, deity, bodily resurrection, and Second Coming of Christ, the false teachers' basic error is that they will not submit their lives to the rule of Christ. All false religions have an erroneous Christology.

DECEMBER 2

Daniel 7:1–8:27

7 In the first year of Belshazzar king of
Babylon, Daniel had a dream and visions
of his head *while* on his bed. Then he wrote
down the dream, telling the main facts.
2 Daniel spoke, saying, "I saw in my vision by
night, and behold, the four winds of heaven
were stirring up the Great Sea. 3 And four great
beasts came up from the sea, each different
from the other. 4 The first *was* like a lion, and
had eagle's wings. I watched till its wings were
plucked off; and it was lifted up from the earth
and made to stand on two feet like a man, and
a man's heart was given to it.
5 "And suddenly another beast, a second, like
a bear. It was raised up on one side, and *had*
three ribs in its mouth between its teeth. And
they said thus to it: 'Arise, devour much flesh!'
6 "After this I looked, and there was another,
like a leopard, which had on its back four
wings of a bird. The beast also had four heads,
and dominion was given to it.
7 "After this I saw in the night visions, and
behold, a fourth beast, dreadful and terrible,
exceedingly strong. It had huge iron teeth; it
was devouring, breaking in pieces, and trampling the residue with its feet. It *was* different
from all the beasts that *were* before it, and it had
ten horns. 8 I was considering the horns, and
there was another horn, a little one, coming
up among them, before whom three of the
first horns were plucked out by the roots. And
there, in this horn, *were* eyes like the eyes of a
man, and a mouth speaking pompous words.

9 "I watched till thrones were put in place,
And the Ancient of Days was seated;
His garment *was* white as snow,
And the hair of His head *was* like
pure wool.
His throne *was* a fiery flame,
Its wheels a burning fire;
10 A fiery stream issued
And came forth from before Him.
A thousand thousands ministered
to Him;
Ten thousand times ten thousand
stood before Him.
The court was seated,
And the books were opened.

11 "I watched then because of the sound of
the pompous words which the horn was
speaking; I watched till the beast was slain,
and its body destroyed and given to the burning flame. 12 As for the rest of the beasts, they
had their dominion taken away, yet their lives
were prolonged for a season and a time.

13 "I was watching in the night visions,
And behold, *One* like the Son of Man,
Coming with the clouds of heaven!
He came to the Ancient of Days,
And they brought Him near before Him.
14 Then to Him was given dominion and
glory and a kingdom,

That all peoples, nations, and
languages should serve Him.
His dominion *is* an everlasting
dominion,
Which shall not pass away,
And His kingdom *the one*
Which shall not be destroyed.

15“I, Daniel, was grieved in my spirit within
my body, and the visions of my head troubled
me. 16I came near to one of those who stood
by, and asked him the truth of all this. So he
told me and made known to me the interpretation of these things: 17‘Those great beasts,
which are four, *are* four kings *which* arise out
of the earth. 18But the saints of the Most High
shall receive the kingdom, and possess the
kingdom forever, even forever and ever.’

19“Then I wished to know the truth about the
fourth beast, which was different from all the
others, exceedingly dreadful, *with* its teeth of
iron and its nails of bronze, *which* devoured,
broke in pieces, and trampled the residue with
its feet; 20and the ten horns that *were* on its
head, and the other *horn* which came up, before
which three fell, namely, that horn which had
eyes and a mouth which spoke pompous words,
whose appearance *was* greater than his fellows.
21“I was watching; and the same horn was
making war against the saints, and prevailing
against them, 22until the Ancient of Days came,
and a judgment was made *in favor* of the
saints of the Most High, and the time came for
the saints to possess the kingdom.
23“Thus he said:

‘The fourth beast shall be
A fourth kingdom on earth,
Which shall be different from all *other*
kingdoms,
And shall devour the whole earth,
Trample it and break it in pieces.
24 The ten horns *are* ten kings
Who shall arise from this kingdom.
And another shall rise after them;
He shall be different from the first *ones,*
And shall subdue three kings.
25 He shall speak *pompous* words against
the Most High,
Shall persecute the saints of the Most
High,
And shall intend to change times
and law.
Then *the saints* shall be given into
his hand
For a time and times and half a time.
26 ‘But the court shall be seated,
And they shall take away his dominion,
To consume and destroy *it* forever.
27 Then the kingdom and dominion,
And the greatness of the kingdoms
under the whole heaven,
Shall be given to the people, the saints
of the Most High.
His kingdom *is* an everlasting kingdom,
And all dominions shall serve and
obey Him.’

28“This *is* the end of the account. As for me,
Daniel, my thoughts greatly troubled me, and
my countenance changed; but I kept the matter in my heart.”

8 In the third year of the reign of King
Belshazzar a vision appeared *to* me—to
me, Daniel—after the one that appeared to me
the first time. 2I saw in the vision, and it so happened while I was looking, that I *was* in
Shushan, the citadel, which *is* in the province
of Elam; and I saw in the vision that I was by
the River Ulai. 3Then I lifted my eyes and saw,
and there, standing beside the river, was a ram
which had two horns, and the two horns *were*
high; but one *was* higher than the other, and
the higher *one* came up last. 4I saw the ram
pushing westward, northward, and southward,
so that no animal could withstand him; nor *was*
there any that could deliver from his hand, but
he did according to his will and became great.
5And as I was considering, suddenly a male
goat came from the west, across the surface of

8:3–9 This imagery unfolded historically. The ram pictures the Medo-Persian Empire as a whole, its two horns standing for the two entities (the Medes and the Persians) that merged into one. The history of this empire is briefly noted in v. 4, as it is seen conquering from the east to the west, south and north, under Cyrus, as predicted also by Isaiah 150 years earlier (Is. 45:1–7). The higher horn, which appeared last, represents Persia. The goat (v. 5) represents Greece with its great horn Alexander, who with his army of 35,000 moved with such speed that he is pictured as not even touching the ground. The broken horn is Alexander in his death; the 4 horns are generals who became kings over 4 sectors of the Grecian Empire after Alexander (7:6). The small horn is Antiochus Epiphanes, who rose from the third empire to rule the Syrian division in 175–164 B.C. and is the same king dominant in 11:21–35. In 7:8,24–26, a similar “little horn” clearly represents the final Antichrist. The reason both are described as “little horns” is because one prefigures the other.

the whole earth, without touching the ground;
and the goat *had* a notable horn between his
eyes. [6]Then he came to the ram that had two
horns, which I had seen standing beside the
river, and ran at him with furious power. [7]And I
saw him confronting the ram; he was moved
with rage against him, attacked the ram, and
broke his two horns. There was no power in
the ram to withstand him, but he cast him
down to the ground and trampled him; and
there was no one that could deliver the ram
from his hand.
[8]Therefore the male goat grew very great;
but when he became strong, the large horn
was broken, and in place of it four notable
ones came up toward the four winds of heav-
en. [9]And out of one of them came a little horn
which grew exceedingly great toward the
south, toward the east, and toward the Glorious *Land.* [10]And it grew up to the host of heav-
en; and it cast down *some* of the host and *some*
of the stars to the ground, and trampled them.
[11]He even exalted *himself* as high as the Prince
of the host; and by him the daily *sacrifices*
were taken away, and the place of His sanctuary was cast down. [12]Because of transgression,
an army was given over *to the horn* to oppose
the daily *sacrifices;* and he cast truth down to
the ground. He did *all this* and prospered.
[13]Then I heard a holy one speaking; and *another* holy one said to that certain *one* who was
speaking, "How long *will* the vision *be, concerning* the daily *sacrifices* and the transgression of
desolation, the giving of both the sanctuary and
the host to be trampled underfoot?"
[14]And he said to me, "For two thousand
three hundred days; then the sanctuary shall
be cleansed."
[15]Then it happened, when I, Daniel, had
seen the vision and was seeking the meaning,
that suddenly there stood before me one having the appearance of a man. [16]And I heard a
man's voice between *the banks of* the Ulai, who
called, and said, "Gabriel, make this *man*
understand the vision." [17]So he came near
where I stood, and when he came I was afraid
and fell on my face; but he said to me, "Understand, son of man, that the vision *refers* to the
time of the end."
[18]Now, as he was speaking with me, I was in
a deep sleep with my face to the ground; but
he touched me, and stood me upright. [19]And
he said, "Look, I am making known to you what
shall happen in the latter time of the indignation; for at the appointed time the end *shall be.*
[20]The ram which you saw, having the two
horns—*they are* the kings of Media and Persia.
[21]And the male goat *is* the kingdom of Greece.
The large horn that *is* between its eyes *is* the
first king. [22]As for the broken *horn* and the
four that stood up in its place, four kingdoms
shall arise out of that nation, but not with its
power.

23 "And in the latter time of their kingdom,
When the transgressors have reached
their fullness,
A king shall arise,
Having fierce features,
Who understands sinister schemes.
24 His power shall be mighty, but not by
his own power;
He shall destroy fearfully,
And shall prosper and thrive;
He shall destroy the mighty, and *also*
the holy people.

25 "Through his cunning
He shall cause deceit to prosper
under his rule;
And he shall exalt *himself* in his heart.
He shall destroy many in *their*
prosperity.
He shall even rise against the Prince
of princes;
But he shall be broken without *human*
means.

26 "And the vision of the evenings
and mornings
Which was told is true;
Therefore seal up the vision,
For *it refers* to many days
in the future."

[27]And I, Daniel, fainted and was sick for days;
afterward I arose and went about the king's
business. I was astonished by the vision, but no
one understood it.

Psalm 137:1–6

By the rivers of Babylon,
There we sat down, yea, we wept
When we remembered Zion.
2 We hung our harps
Upon the willows in the midst of it.

137:1 the rivers of Babylon. The Tigris and Euphrates Rivers. **we wept.** They even wept when the exile was over and the second temple was being built (Ezra 3:12), so deep was their sorrow. **Zion.** The dwelling place of God on earth (Pss. 9:11; 76:2) which was destroyed by the Babylonians (2 Chr. 36:19; Pss. 74:6–8; 79:1; Is. 64:10,11; Jer. 52:12–16; Lam. 2:4).

3 For there those who carried us away
captive asked of us a song,
And those who plundered us *requested*
mirth,
Saying, "Sing us *one* of the songs
of Zion!"

4 How shall we sing the LORD's song
In a foreign land?
5 If I forget you, O Jerusalem,
Let my right hand forget *its skill!*
6 If I do not remember you,
Let my tongue cling to the roof of my
mouth—
If I do not exalt Jerusalem
Above my chief joy.

Proverbs 29:14

14 The king who judges the poor with
truth,
His throne will be established
forever.

2 Peter 3:1–18

3 Beloved, I now write to you this second epistle (in *both of* which I stir up your pure minds by way of reminder), [2]that you may be mindful of the words which were spoken before by the holy prophets, and of the commandment of us, the apostles of the Lord and Savior, [3]knowing this first: that scoffers will come in the last days, walking according to their own lusts, [4]and saying, "Where is the promise of His coming? For since the fathers fell asleep, all things continue as *they were* from the beginning of creation." [5]For this they willfully forget: that by the word of God the heavens were of old, and the earth standing out of water and in the water, [6]by which the world *that* then existed perished, being flooded with water. [7]But the heavens and the earth *which* are now preserved by the same word, are reserved for fire until the day of judgment and perdition of ungodly men.

[8]But, beloved, do not forget this one thing, that with the Lord one day *is* as a thousand years, and a thousand years as one day. [9]The Lord is not slack concerning *His* promise, as some count slackness, but is longsuffering toward us, not willing that any should perish but that all should come to repentance.

[10]But the day of the Lord will come as a thief in the night, in which the heavens will pass away with a great noise, and the elements will melt with fervent heat; both the earth and the works that are in it will be burned up. [11]Therefore, since all these things will be dissolved, what manner *of persons* ought you to be in holy conduct and godliness, [12]looking for and hastening the coming of the day of God, because of which the heavens will be dissolved, being on fire, and the elements will melt with fervent heat? [13]Nevertheless we, according to His promise, look for new heavens and a new earth in which righteousness dwells.

[14]Therefore, beloved, looking forward to these things, be diligent to be found by Him in peace, without spot and blameless; [15]and consider *that* the longsuffering of our Lord *is* salvation—as also our beloved brother Paul, according to the wisdom given to him, has written to you, [16]as also in all his epistles, speaking in them of these things, in which are some things hard to understand, which untaught and unstable *people* twist to their own destruction, as *they do* also the rest of the Scriptures.

3:3 knowing this first. "First" here means the preeminent matter, not the first in a list. Peter's priority in this section of his letter is to warn Christians about how the false teachers would try to deny this judgment and steal the hope of believers. **scoffers will come.** False teachers argue against the Second Coming of Christ or any teaching of Scripture through ridicule (Is. 5:19; Jude 18). **in the last days.** This phrase refers to that entire period of time from the arrival of the Messiah to His return (Acts 2:17; Gal. 4:4; 2 Tim. 3:1; Heb. 1:2; 1 Pet. 1:20; 1 John 2:18,19; James 5:3; Jude 18). The entire age will be marked by saboteurs of the Christian truth and especially the hope of Christ's return.

3:16 hard to understand. Since Paul had (by the time Peter wrote) written all his letters and died, the readers of 2 Peter would have already received letters about future events from Paul. Some of Paul's explanations were difficult (not impossible) to interpret. Nevertheless, Peter uses Paul as a support for his teaching.

[17]You therefore, beloved, since you know *this* beforehand, beware lest you also fall from your own steadfastness, being led away with the error of the wicked; [18]but grow in the grace and knowledge of our Lord and Savior Jesus Christ.

To Him *be* the glory both now and forever. Amen.

DAY 2: How can we answer those who doubt Daniel's authorship because his prophecies are so astonishingly accurate?

Confidence in the divine origin of Scripture does not rely on blind faith. There are reasonable explanations and acceptable corroborating evidence that point to the trustworthiness of the Bible. Daniel's use of what is now called Imperial Aramaic in writing the book points to an early date. The Dead Sea Scrolls offer evidence that also pushes back the date for Daniel.

When accurate prophecy and possible miracles are discounted by definition as unacceptable, proving Daniel's value becomes challenging. But the problem has little to do with lack of evidence and much to do with willful unbelief. Skeptical interpreters, unwilling to acknowledge supernatural prophecies in Daniel that came to pass (over 100 in chapter 11 alone that were fulfilled), attempt to replace miraculous foresight with simple observation. They assume that the writer of Daniel was actually living in the time of Antiochus and reported current events in prophetic form. That is, the writer wrote as though he was predicting certain events, when, in reality, he was writing after the events had occurred. For scholars like these, no amount of fulfilled prophecy will be enough to convince them. They actually become a reminder to believers that people are not argued into the kingdom of God. The most compelling evidence as well as the most resistant people both need the assistance of God's Spirit in arriving at genuine faith.

DECEMBER 3

Daniel 9:1–10:21

9 In the first year of Darius the son of
Ahasuerus, of the lineage of the Medes,
who was made king over the realm of the
Chaldeans— 2in the first year of his reign I,
Daniel, understood by the books the number
of the years *specified* by the word of the LORD
through Jeremiah the prophet, that He would
accomplish seventy years in the desolations of
Jerusalem.
3Then I set my face toward the Lord God to
make request by prayer and supplications,
with fasting, sackcloth, and ashes. 4And I
prayed to the LORD my God, and made confession, and said, "O Lord, great and awesome
God, who keeps His covenant and mercy with
those who love Him, and with those who keep
His commandments, 5we have sinned and
committed iniquity, we have done wickedly
and rebelled, even by departing from Your
precepts and Your judgments. 6Neither have we
heeded Your servants the prophets, who spoke
in Your name to our kings and our princes, to
our fathers and all the people of the land. 7O
Lord, righteousness *belongs* to You, but to us
shame of face, as *it is* this day—to the men of
Judah, to the inhabitants of Jerusalem and all
Israel, those near and those far off in all the
countries to which You have driven them,
because of the unfaithfulness which they have
committed against You.
8"O Lord, to us *belongs* shame of face, to our
kings, our princes, and our fathers, because we
have sinned against You. 9To the Lord our God
belong mercy and forgiveness, though we have
rebelled against Him. 10We have not obeyed the
voice of the LORD our God, to walk in His laws,
which He set before us by His servants the
prophets. 11Yes, all Israel has transgressed Your
law, and has departed so as not to obey Your
voice; therefore the curse and the oath written
in the Law of Moses the servant of God have
been poured out on us, because we have sinned
against Him. 12And He has confirmed His
words, which He spoke against us and against
our judges who judged us, by bringing upon us
a great disaster; for under the whole heaven
such has never been done as what has been
done to Jerusalem.
13"As *it is* written in the Law of Moses, all
this disaster has come upon us; yet we have
not made our prayer before the LORD our God,
that we might turn from our iniquities and
understand Your truth. 14Therefore the LORD
has kept the disaster in mind, and brought it
upon us; for the LORD our God *is* righteous in
all the works which He does, though we have
not obeyed His voice. 15And now, O Lord our
God, who brought Your people out of the land
of Egypt with a mighty hand, and made
Yourself a name, as *it is* this day—we have
sinned, we have done wickedly!
16"O Lord, according to all Your righteousness, I pray, let Your anger and Your fury be
turned away from Your city Jerusalem, Your
holy mountain; because for our sins, and for the
iniquities of our fathers, Jerusalem and Your
people *are* a reproach to all *those* around us.
17Now therefore, our God, hear the prayer of
Your servant, and his supplications, and for the
Lord's sake cause Your face to shine on Your
sanctuary, which is desolate. 18O my God, incline
Your ear and hear; open Your eyes and see our

desolations, and the city which is called by Your
name; for we do not present our supplications
before You because of our righteous deeds, but
because of Your great mercies. [19]O Lord, hear! O
Lord, forgive! O Lord, listen and act! Do not
delay for Your own sake, my God, for Your city
and Your people are called by Your name."
[20]Now while I *was* speaking, praying, and
confessing my sin and the sin of my people Israel, and presenting my supplication before
the LORD my God for the holy mountain of my
God, [21]yes, while I *was* speaking in prayer, the
man Gabriel, whom I had seen in the vision at
the beginning, being caused to fly swiftly,
reached me about the time of the evening
offering. [22]And he informed *me,* and talked
with me, and said, "O Daniel, I have now come
forth to give you skill to understand. [23]At the
beginning of your supplications the command
went out, and I have come to tell *you,* for you
are greatly beloved; therefore consider the
matter, and understand the vision:

24 "Seventy weeks are determined
For your people and for your holy city,
To finish the transgression,
To make an end of sins,
To make reconciliation for iniquity,
To bring in everlasting righteousness,
To seal up vision and prophecy,
And to anoint the Most Holy.

25 "Know therefore and understand,
That from the going forth of the
command
To restore and build Jerusalem
Until Messiah the Prince,
There shall be seven weeks and
sixty-two weeks;
The street shall be built again,
and the wall,
Even in troublesome times.

26 "And after the sixty-two weeks
Messiah shall be cut off, but not
for Himself;
And the people of the prince who is
to come
Shall destroy the city and the
sanctuary.
The end of it *shall be* with a flood,
And till the end of the war desolations
are determined.

27 Then he shall confirm a covenant
with many for one week;
But in the middle of the week
He shall bring an end to sacrifice
and offering.
And on the wing of abominations shall
be one who makes desolate,
Even until the consummation,
which is determined,
Is poured out on the desolate."

10 In the third year of Cyrus king of Persia
a message was revealed to Daniel, whose
name was called Belteshazzar. The message
was true, but the appointed time *was* long; and
he understood the message, and had understanding of the vision. [2]In those days I, Daniel,
was mourning three full weeks. [3]I ate no pleasant food, no meat or wine came into my mouth,
nor did I anoint myself at all, till three whole
weeks were fulfilled.
[4]Now on the twenty-fourth day of the first
month, as I was by the side of the great river,
that *is,* the Tigris, [5]I lifted my eyes and looked,
and behold, a certain man clothed in linen,
whose waist *was* girded with gold of Uphaz!
[6]His body *was* like beryl, his face like the
appearance of lightning, his eyes like torches
of fire, his arms and feet like burnished
bronze in color, and the sound of his words
like the voice of a multitude.
[7]And I, Daniel, alone saw the vision, for the
men who were with me did not see the vision;
but a great terror fell upon them, so that they fled
to hide themselves. [8]Therefore I was left alone
when I saw this great vision, and no strength
remained in me; for my vigor was turned to
frailty in me, and I retained no strength. [9]Yet I
heard the sound of his words; and while I
heard the sound of his words I was in a deep
sleep on my face, with my face to the ground.

9:24–26 Seventy weeks...until. These are weeks of years, whereas weeks of days are described in a different way (10:2,3). The time spans from the Persian Artaxerxes' decree to rebuild Jerusalem, ca. 445 B.C. (Neh. 2:1–8), to the Messiah's kingdom. This panorama includes: 1) 7 weeks or 49 years, possibly closing Nehemiah's career in the rebuilding of the "street and wall," as well as the end of the ministry of Malachi and the close of the Old Testament; 2) 62 weeks or 434 more years for a total of 483 years to the First Advent of Messiah. This was fulfilled at the Triumphal Entry on 9 Nisan, A.D. 30 (Matt. 21:1–11). The Messiah will be "cut off" (a common reference to death); and 3) the final 7 years or 70th week of the time of Antichrist (v. 27). Roman people, from whom the Antichrist will come, will "destroy the city" of Jerusalem and its temple in A.D. 70.

10 Suddenly, a hand touched me, which made me tremble on my knees and *on* the palms of my hands. 11 And he said to me, "O Daniel, man greatly beloved, understand the words that I speak to you, and stand upright, for I have now been sent to you." While he was speaking this word to me, I stood trembling.

12 Then he said to me, "Do not fear, Daniel, for from the first day that you set your heart to understand, and to humble yourself before your God, your words were heard; and I have come because of your words. 13 But the prince of the kingdom of Persia withstood me twenty-one days; and behold, Michael, one of the chief princes, came to help me, for I had been left alone there with the kings of Persia. 14 Now I have come to make you understand what will happen to your people in the latter days, for the vision *refers* to *many* days yet *to come.*"

10:13 prince of...Persia. The 3-week delay was due to an evil angel opposing Gabriel in heavenly warfare (Rev. 16:12–14). This angel was specially anointed with Persian power in an effort to thwart the work of God. This tells us that Satan engages in heavenly warfare to influence generations and nations against God and His people (Eph. 6:10ff.). **Michael.** This is the chief angel of heaven (10:21; 12:1; Jude 9; Rev. 12:7). Michael remained to assure that the Jews would be free to return to their land.

15 When he had spoken such words to me, I turned my face toward the ground and became speechless. 16 And suddenly, *one* having the likeness of the sons of men touched my lips; then I opened my mouth and spoke, saying to him who stood before me, "My lord, because of the vision my sorrows have overwhelmed me, and I have retained no strength. 17 For how can this servant of my lord talk with you, my lord? As for me, no strength remains in me now, nor is any breath left in me."

18 Then again, *the one* having the likeness of a man touched me and strengthened me. 19 And he said, "O man greatly beloved, fear not! Peace *be* to you; be strong, yes, be strong!"

So when he spoke to me I was strengthened, and said, "Let my lord speak, for you have strengthened me."

20 Then he said, "Do you know why I have come to you? And now I must return to fight with the prince of Persia; and when I have gone forth, indeed the prince of Greece will come. 21 But I will tell you what is noted in the Scripture of Truth. (No one upholds me against these, except Michael your prince.

10:21 Scripture of Truth. God's plan of certain and true designs for men and nations, which He can reveal according to His discretion (11:2; Is. 46:9–11). **except Michael.** The angel with Michael intended to handle the demons of Persia and Greece. This actually forms the heavenly basis for the earthly unfolding of history in 11:2–35.

Psalm 137:7–9

7 Remember, O LORD, against the sons
of Edom
The day of Jerusalem,
Who said, "Raze *it,* raze *it,*
To its very foundation!"

8 O daughter of Babylon, who are
to be destroyed,
Happy the one who repays you
as you have served us!
9 Happy the one who takes and dashes
Your little ones against the rock!

Proverbs 29:15

15 The rod and rebuke give wisdom,
But a child left *to himself* brings shame
to his mother.

1 John 1:1–10

1 That which was from the beginning, which we have heard, which we have seen with our eyes, which we have looked upon, and our hands have handled, concerning the Word of life— 2 the life was manifested, and we have seen, and bear witness, and declare to you that eternal life which was with the Father and was manifested to us— 3 that which we have seen and heard we declare to you, that you also may have fellowship with us; and truly our fellowship *is*

1:2,3 manifested,...seen,...bear witness,...declare. John dramatically reemphasizes through repetition of these terms in vv. 2,3 (v. 1) the authority of his own personal experience as an eyewitness of Jesus' life. Such repetition pointedly reminds his readers that John's personal testimony refutes the false teachers who boasted arrogantly and wrongly about the Christ they had never seen or known.

with the Father and with His Son Jesus Christ. 4 And these things we write to you that your joy may be full.

5 This is the message which we have heard from Him and declare to you, that God is light and in Him is no darkness at all. 6 If we say that we have fellowship with Him, and walk in darkness, we lie and do not practice the truth. 7 But if we walk in the light as He is in the light, we have fellowship with one another, and the blood of Jesus Christ His Son cleanses us from all sin.

8 If we say that we have no sin, we deceive ourselves, and the truth is not in us. 9 If we confess our sins, He is faithful and just to forgive us *our* sins and to cleanse us from all unrighteousness. 10 If we say that we have not sinned, we make Him a liar, and His word is not in us.

DAY 3: Contrast how the lives of true believers and false teachers differ.

In 1 John 1:7, a genuine Christian walks habitually in the light (truth and holiness), not in darkness (falsehood and sin). Their walk also results in cleansing from sin as the Lord continually forgives His own. Since those walking in the light share in the character of God, they will be habitually characterized by His holiness (3 John 11), indicating their true fellowship with Him (James 1:27). A genuine Christian does not walk in darkness but only in the light (2 Cor. 6:14; Eph. 5:8; Col. 1:12,13).

Not only did the false teachers walk in darkness (v. 8), but they went so far as to deny totally the existence of a sin nature in their lives. If someone never admits to being a sinner, salvation cannot result. Not only did the false teachers make false claims to fellowship and disregard sin (v. 6), they are also characterized by deceit regarding sinlessness (Eccl. 7:20; Rom. 3:23).

In the lives of genuine believers, a continual confession of sin is an indication of genuine salvation (v. 9). While the false teachers would not admit their sin, the genuine Christian admitted and forsook it (Ps. 32:3–5; Prov. 28:13). The term "confess" means to say the same thing about sin as God does—to acknowledge His perspective about sin. While v. 7 is from God's perspective, v. 9 is from the Christian's perspective. Confession of sin characterizes genuine Christians, and God continually cleanses those who are confessing (v. 7). Rather than focusing on confession for every single sin as necessary, John has especially in mind here a settled recognition and acknowledgment that one is a sinner in need of cleansing and forgiveness (Eph. 4:32; Col. 2:13).

DECEMBER 4

Daniel 11:1–12:13

11 "Also in the first year of Darius the Mede, I, *even* I, stood up to confirm and strengthen him.) 2 And now I will tell you the truth: Behold, three more kings will arise in Persia, and the fourth shall be far richer than *them* all; by his strength, through his riches, he shall stir up all against the realm of Greece. 3 Then a mighty king shall arise, who shall rule with great dominion, and do according to his will. 4 And when he has arisen, his kingdom shall be broken up and divided toward the four winds of heaven, but not among his posterity nor according to his dominion with which he ruled; for his kingdom shall be uprooted, even for others besides these.

5 "Also the king of the South shall become strong, as well as *one* of his princes; and he shall gain power over him and have dominion. His dominion *shall be* a great dominion. 6 And at the end of *some* years they shall join forces, for the daughter of the king of the South shall go to the king of the North to make an agreement; but she shall not retain the power of her authority, and neither he nor his authority shall stand; but she shall be given up, with those who brought her, and with him who begot her, and with him who strengthened her in *those* times. 7 But from a branch of her roots *one* shall arise in his place, who shall come with an army, enter the fortress of the king of the North, and deal with them and prevail. 8 And he shall also carry their gods captive to Egypt, with their princes *and* their precious articles of

11:2–45 As in 8:3–26, this prophecy sweeps all the way from the history of spiritual conflict in Israel (11:2–35) to the Tribulation (vv. 36–42) when Michael aids in fully delivering Israel (12:1). The detail of this history is so minute and accurate, so confirmed by history, that unbelieving critics have, without evidence, insisted that it was actually written 400 years later than Daniel, after it had happened, which would make the prophet a deceiver. The prophecy actually looks ahead from Daniel to the final Antichrist.

silver and gold; and he shall continue *more* years than the king of the North.

9“Also *the king of the North* shall come to the kingdom of the king of the South, but shall return to his own land. 10However his sons shall stir up strife, and assemble a multitude of great forces; and *one* shall certainly come and overwhelm and pass through; then he shall return to his fortress and stir up strife.

11“And the king of the South shall be moved with rage, and go out and fight with him, with the king of the North, who shall muster a great multitude; but the multitude shall be given into the hand of his *enemy.* 12When he has taken away the multitude, his heart will be lifted up; and he will cast down tens of thousands, but he will not prevail. 13For the king of the North will return and muster a multitude greater than the former, and shall certainly come at the end of some years with a great army and much equipment.

14“Now in those times many shall rise up against the king of the South. Also, violent men of your people shall exalt themselves in fulfillment of the vision, but they shall fall. 15So the king of the North shall come and build a siege mound, and take a fortified city; and the forces of the South shall not withstand *him.* Even his choice troops *shall have* no strength to resist. 16But he who comes against him shall do according to his own will, and no one shall stand against him. He shall stand in the Glorious Land with destruction in his power.

17“He shall also set his face to enter with the strength of his whole kingdom, and upright ones with him; thus shall he do. And he shall give him the daughter of women to destroy it; but she shall not stand *with him,* or be for him. 18After this he shall turn his face to the coastlands, and shall take many. But a ruler shall bring the reproach against them to an end; and with the reproach removed, he shall turn back on him. 19Then he shall turn his face toward the fortress of his own land; but he shall stumble and fall, and not be found.

20“There shall arise in his place one who imposes taxes *on* the glorious kingdom; but within a few days he shall be destroyed, but not in anger or in battle. 21And in his place shall arise a vile person, to whom they will not give the honor of royalty; but he shall come in peaceably, and seize the kingdom by intrigue. 22With the force of a flood they shall be swept away from before him and be broken, and also the prince of the covenant. 23And after the league *is made* with him he shall act deceitfully, for he shall come up and become strong with a small *number of* people. 24He shall enter peaceably, even into the richest places of the province; and he shall do *what* his fathers have not done, nor his forefathers: he shall disperse among them the plunder, spoil, and riches; and he shall devise his plans against the strongholds, but *only* for a time.

25“He shall stir up his power and his courage against the king of the South with a great army. And the king of the South shall be stirred up to battle with a very great and mighty army; but he shall not stand, for they shall devise plans against him. 26Yes, those who eat of the portion of his delicacies shall destroy him; his army shall be swept away, and many shall fall down slain. 27Both these kings' hearts *shall be* bent on evil, and they shall speak lies at the same table; but it shall not prosper, for the end *will* still *be* at the appointed time. 28While returning to his land with great riches, his heart shall be *moved* against the holy covenant; so he shall do *damage* and return to his own land.

29“At the appointed time he shall return and go toward the south; but it shall not be like the former or the latter. 30For ships from Cyprus shall come against him; therefore he shall be grieved, and return in rage against the holy covenant, and do *damage.*

“So he shall return and show regard for those who forsake the holy covenant. 31And forces shall be mustered by him, and they shall defile the sanctuary fortress; then they shall take away the daily *sacrifices,* and place *there* the abomination of desolation. 32Those who do wickedly against the covenant he shall

11:31 defile the sanctuary. Antiochus's soldiers, no doubt working with apostate Jews, guarded the temple, halting all worship, while others attacked the city on the Sabbath, slaughtering men, women, and children. Soldiers desecrated Israel's temple, banned circumcision and daily sacrifices (1 Macc. 1:44–54), and sacrificed a pig on the altar. The Syrians on Chislev (Dec. 15, 167 B.C.) even imposed an idol statue in honor of the Olympian god Zeus into the temple. Jews called it "the abomination that causes desolation," i.e., emptying or ruining for Jewish worship. **abomination of desolation.** Antiochus's soldiers profaned God's temple by spreading sow's broth on the altar and banning daily sacrifices (8:14) as described in 1 Maccabees 1:44–54. Both Daniel and Jesus said this atrocity was only a preview of the abomination that would happen later under the final Antichrist (9:27; Matt. 24:15).

corrupt with flattery; but the people who
know their God shall be strong, and carry out
great exploits. 33And those of the people who
understand shall instruct many; yet *for many*
days they shall fall by sword and flame, by captivity and plundering. 34Now when they fall,
they shall be aided with a little help; but many
shall join with them by intrigue. 35And *some* of
those of understanding shall fall, to refine
them, purify *them,* and make *them* white, *until*
the time of the end; because *it is* still for the
appointed time.

36"Then the king shall do according to his
own will: he shall exalt and magnify himself
above every god, shall speak blasphemies
against the God of gods, and shall prosper till
the wrath has been accomplished; for what
has been determined shall be done. 37He shall
regard neither the God of his fathers nor the
desire of women, nor regard any god; for he
shall exalt himself above *them* all. 38But in their
place he shall honor a god of fortresses; and a
god which his fathers did not know he shall
honor with gold and silver, with precious
stones and pleasant things. 39Thus he shall act
against the strongest fortresses with a foreign
god, which he shall acknowledge, *and*
advance *its* glory; and he shall cause them to
rule over many, and divide the land for gain.

40"At the time of the end the king of the
South shall attack him; and the king of the
North shall come against him like a whirlwind, with chariots, horsemen, and with many
ships; and he shall enter the countries, overwhelm *them,* and pass through. 41He shall also
enter the Glorious Land, and many *countries*
shall be overthrown; but these shall escape
from his hand: Edom, Moab, and the prominent people of Ammon. 42He shall stretch out
his hand against the countries, and the land of
Egypt shall not escape. 43He shall have power
over the treasures of gold and silver, and over
all the precious things of Egypt; also the
Libyans and Ethiopians *shall follow* at his
heels. 44But news from the east and the north
shall trouble him; therefore he shall go out
with great fury to destroy and annihilate many.
45And he shall plant the tents of his palace
between the seas and the glorious holy mountain; yet he shall come to his end, and no one
will help him.

12 "At that time Michael shall stand up,
The great prince who stands *watch*
over the sons of your people;
And there shall be a time of trouble,
Such as never was since there was a
nation,
Even to that time.
And at that time your people shall be
delivered,
Every one who is found written
in the book.
2 And many of those who sleep in the
dust of the earth shall awake,
Some to everlasting life,
Some to shame *and* everlasting
contempt.
3 Those who are wise shall shine
Like the brightness of the firmament,
And those who turn many
to righteousness
Like the stars forever and ever.

4"But you, Daniel, shut up the words, and seal
the book until the time of the end; many shall
run to and fro, and knowledge shall increase."

5Then I, Daniel, looked; and there stood two
others, one on this riverbank and the other on
that riverbank. 6And *one* said to the man
clothed in linen, who *was* above the waters of
the river, "How long shall the fulfillment of
these wonders *be?*"

7Then I heard the man clothed in linen, who
was above the waters of the river, when he held
up his right hand and his left hand to heaven,
and swore by Him who lives forever, that *it
shall be* for a time, times, and half *a time;* and
when the power of the holy people has been
completely shattered, all these *things* shall be
finished.

8Although I heard, I did not understand.
Then I said, "My lord, what *shall be* the end of
these *things?*"

9And he said, "Go *your way,* Daniel, for the
words *are* closed up and sealed till the time of
the end. 10Many shall be purified, made white,
and refined, but the wicked shall do wickedly;
and none of the wicked shall understand, but
the wise shall understand.

11"And from the time *that* the daily *sacrifice*
is taken away, and the abomination of desolation is set up, *there shall be* one thousand two
hundred and ninety days. 12Blessed *is* he who
waits, and comes to the one thousand three
hundred and thirty-five days.

13"But you, go *your way* till the end; for you
shall rest, and will arise to your inheritance at
the end of the days."

Psalm 138:1–3

A Psalm of David.

I will praise You with my whole heart;
Before the gods I will sing praises
to You.
2 I will worship toward Your holy temple,

And praise Your name
For Your lovingkindness and Your
truth;
For You have magnified Your word
above all Your name.
3 In the day when I cried out, You
answered me,
And made me bold *with* strength
in my soul.

Proverbs 29:16

16 When the wicked are multiplied,
transgression increases;
But the righteous will see
their fall.

1 John 2:1–29

2 My little children, these things I write to
you, so that you may not sin. And if anyone
sins, we have an Advocate with the Father, Jesus Christ the righteous. [2]And He Himself is
the propitiation for our sins, and not for ours
only but also for the whole world.
[3]Now by this we know that we know Him, if
we keep His commandments. [4]He who says, "I
know Him," and does not keep His commandments, is a liar, and the truth is not in him.
[5]But whoever keeps His word, truly the love of
God is perfected in him. By this we know that
we are in Him. [6]He who says he abides in Him
ought himself also to walk just as He walked.
[7]Brethren, I write no new commandment to
you, but an old commandment which you
have had from the beginning. The old commandment is the word which you heard from
the beginning. [8]Again, a new commandment I
write to you, which thing is true in Him and in
you, because the darkness is passing away,
and the true light is already shining.
[9]He who says he is in the light, and hates
his brother, is in darkness until now. [10]He who
loves his brother abides in the light, and
there is no cause for stumbling in him. [11]But
he who hates his brother is in darkness and
walks in darkness, and does not know where
he is going, because the darkness has blinded
his eyes.

12 I write to you, little children,
Because your sins are
forgiven you for His
name's sake.
13 I write to you, fathers,
Because you have known Him *who*
is from the beginning.
I write to you, young men,
Because you have overcome the
wicked one.
I write to you, little children,
Because you have known the
Father.
14 I have written to you, fathers,
Because you have known Him *who*
is from the beginning.
I have written to you, young men,
Because you are strong, and the
word of God abides in you,
And you have overcome
the wicked one.

[15]Do not love the world or the things in the
world. If anyone loves the world, the love of
the Father is not in him. [16]For all that *is* in the
world—the lust of the flesh, the lust of the
eyes, and the pride of life—is not of the Father
but is of the world. [17]And the world is passing
away, and the lust of it; but he who does the
will of God abides forever.
[18]Little children, it is the last hour; and as
you have heard that the Antichrist is coming,
even now many antichrists have come, by
which we know that it is the last hour. [19]They
went out from us, but they were not of us; for
if they had been of us, they would have continued with us; but *they went out* that they
might be made manifest, that none of them
were of us.
[20]But you have an anointing from the Holy
One, and you know all things. [21]I have not

2:16 all that *is* in the world. While the world's philosophies and ideologies and much that it offers may appear attractive and appealing, that is deception. Its true and pervasive nature is evil, harmful, ruinous, and satanic. Its deadly theories are raised up against the knowledge of God and hold the souls of men captive (2 Cor. 10:3–5). **lust.** John uses the term negatively here for a strong desire for evil things. **flesh.** The term refers to the sin nature of man; the rebellious self dominated by sin and in opposition to God (Rom. 7:15–25; 8:2–8; Gal. 5:19–21). Satan uses the evil world system to incite the flesh. **eyes.** Satan uses the eyes as a strategic avenue to incite wrong desires (Josh. 7:20,21; 2 Sam. 11:2; Matt. 5:27–29). Satan's temptation of Eve involved being attracted to something beautiful in appearance, but the result was spiritual death (Gen. 3:6, "pleasant to the eyes"). **the pride of life.** The phrase has the idea of arrogance over one's circumstances, which produced haughtiness or exaggeration, parading what one possessed to impress other people (James 4:16).

2:19 They went out from us,...none of them were of us. The first characteristic mentioned of antichrists, i.e., false teachers and deceivers (vv. 22–26), is that they depart from the faithful. They arise from within the church and depart from true fellowship and lead people out with them. The verse also places emphasis on the doctrine of the perseverance of the saints. Those genuinely born again endure in faith and fellowship and the truth (1 Cor. 11:19; 2 Tim. 2:12). The ultimate test of true Christianity is endurance (Mark 13:13; Heb. 3:14). The departure of people from the truth and the church is their unmasking.

written to you because you do not know the
truth, but because you know it, and that no lie
is of the truth.
[22]Who is a liar but he who denies that Jesus
is the Christ? He is antichrist who denies the
Father and the Son. [23]Whoever denies the Son
does not have the Father either; he who
acknowledges the Son has the Father also.
[24]Therefore let that abide in you which you
heard from the beginning. If what you heard
from the beginning abides in you, you also will
abide in the Son and in the Father. [25]And this
is the promise that He has promised us—eternal life.
[26]These things I have written to you concerning those who *try to* deceive you. [27]But the
anointing which you have received from Him
abides in you, and you do not need that anyone
teach you; but as the same anointing teaches
you concerning all things, and is true, and is
not a lie, and just as it has taught you, you will
abide in Him.
[28]And now, little children, abide in Him, that
when He appears, we may have confidence
and not be ashamed before Him at His coming.
[29]If you know that He is righteous, you know
that everyone who practices righteousness is
born of Him.

DAY 4: How does 1 John help us understand some of the destructive teaching that attacked Christianity in the first century?

Paul, Peter, and John all faced early forms of a system of false teaching that later became known as Gnosticism. That term (derived from the Greek word "knowledge") refers to the habit that gnostics had of claiming an elevated knowledge, a higher truth known only to those in on the deep things. Those initiated into this mystical knowledge of truth had a higher internal authority than Scripture. This resulted in a chaotic situation in which the gnostics tried to judge divine revelation by human ideas rather than judging human ideas by divine revelation (1 John 2:15–17).

Philosophically, the heresy relied on a distortion of Platonism. It advocated a dualism in which matter was inherently evil and spirit was good. One of the direct errors of this heresy involved attributing some form of deity to Christ but denying His true humanity, supposedly to preserve Him from evil (which they concluded He would be if He actually came in the flesh). Such a view destroys not only the true humanity of Jesus, but also the atonement work of Christ. Jesus must not only have been truly God, but also the truly human (physically real) man who actually suffered and died upon the cross in order to be the acceptable substitutionary sacrifice for sin (Heb. 2:14–17). The biblical view of Jesus affirms His complete humanity, as well as His full deity.

The gnostic heresy, even in John's day, featured two basic forms: 1) Docetism; and 2) the error of Cerinthus. Docetism (from a Greek word that means, "to appear") asserted that Jesus' physical body was not real but only "seemed" to be physical. John forcefully and repeatedly affirmed the physical reality of Jesus. He reminded his readers that he was an eyewitness to Him ("heard," "seen," "handled," "Jesus Christ has come in the flesh"; 1 John 1:1–4; 4:2,3). The other form of early Gnosticism was traced back to Cerinthus by the early church apologist Irenaeus. Cerinthus taught that Christ's "spirit" descended on the human Jesus at His baptism but left Him shortly before His crucifixion. John asserted that the Jesus who was baptized at the beginning of His ministry was the same Person who was crucified on the cross (1 John 5:6).

John does not directly specify the early gnostic beliefs, but his arguments offer clear clues about his targets. Further, John's wisdom was to avoid direct attacks on rapidly shifting heresies, but to provide a timely, positive restatement of the fundamentals of the faith that would provide timeless truth and answers for later generations of Christians.

DECEMBER 5

Hosea 1:1–2:23

1 The word of the LORD that came to Hosea the
son of Beeri, in the days of Uzziah, Jotham,
Ahaz, *and* Hezekiah, kings of Judah, and in the
days of Jeroboam the son of Joash, king of Israel.

2 When the LORD began to speak by Hosea, the
LORD said to Hosea:

"Go, take yourself a wife of harlotry
And children of harlotry,
For the land has committed
great harlotry
By departing from the LORD."

1:2 children of harlotry. This points to the future unfaithfulness of their mother. The children were possibly not fathered by Hosea. That Hosea's marriage to Gomer was to depict God's marriage to Israel is clearly set forth and becomes the key to the theme of the book.

3 So he went and took Gomer the daughter of
Diblaim, and she conceived and bore him a
son. 4 Then the LORD said to him:

"Call his name Jezreel,
For in a little *while*
I will avenge the bloodshed of Jezreel
on the house of Jehu,
And bring an end to the kingdom of
the house of Israel.
5 It shall come to pass in that day
That I will break the bow of Israel in
the Valley of Jezreel."

6 And she conceived again and bore a daughter. Then *God* said to him:

"Call her name Lo-Ruhamah,
For I will no longer have mercy
on the house of Israel,
But I will utterly take them away.
7 Yet I will have mercy on the house
of Judah,
Will save them by the LORD their God,
And will not save them by bow,
Nor by sword or battle,
By horses or horsemen."

8 Now when she had weaned Lo-Ruhamah,
she conceived and bore a son. 9 Then *God* said:

"Call his name Lo-Ammi,
For you *are* not My people,
And I will not be your *God*.

10 "Yet the number of the children of Israel
Shall be as the sand of the sea,
Which cannot be measured or
numbered.
And it shall come to pass
In the place where it was said to them,
'You *are* not My people,'
There it shall be said to them,
'*You are* sons of the living God.'
11 Then the children of Judah and the
children of Israel
Shall be gathered together,
And appoint for themselves one head;
And they shall come up out of the land,
For great *will be* the day of Jezreel!

2 Say to your brethren,
'My people,'
And to your sisters, 'Mercy *is shown.*'

2 "Bring charges against your mother,
bring charges;
For she *is* not My wife, nor *am* I her
Husband!
Let her put away her harlotries from
her sight,
And her adulteries from between
her breasts;
3 Lest I strip her naked
And expose her, as in the day she was
born,
And make her like a wilderness,
And set her like a dry land,
And slay her with thirst.

4 "I will not have mercy on her children,
For they *are* the children of harlotry.
5 For their mother has played the harlot;
She who conceived them has behaved
shamefully.
For she said, 'I will go after my lovers,
Who give *me* my bread and my water,
My wool and my linen,
My oil and my drink.'

6 "Therefore, behold,
I will hedge up your way with thorns,
And wall her in,
So that she cannot find her paths.
7 She will chase her lovers,
But not overtake them;
Yes, she will seek them, but not find
them.
Then she will say,
'I will go and return to my first husband,
For then *it was* better for me than now.'
8 For she did not know

That I gave her grain, new wine, and oil,
And multiplied her silver and gold—
Which they prepared for Baal.

9 "Therefore I will return and take away
My grain in its time
And My new wine in its season,
And will take back My wool and My linen,
Given to cover her nakedness.
10 Now I will uncover her lewdness
in the sight of her lovers,
And no one shall deliver her from
My hand.
11 I will also cause all her mirth to cease,
Her feast days,
Her New Moons,
Her Sabbaths—
All her appointed feasts.
12 "And I will destroy her vines and
her fig trees,
Of which she has said,
'These *are* my wages that my lovers
have given me.'
So I will make them a forest,
And the beasts of the field shall eat them.
13 I will punish her
For the days of the Baals to which she
burned incense.
She decked herself with her earrings
and jewelry,
And went after her lovers;
But Me she forgot," says the LORD.

14 "Therefore, behold, I will allure her,
Will bring her into the wilderness,
And speak comfort to her.
15 I will give her her vineyards from there,
And the Valley of Achor as a door
of hope;
She shall sing there,
As in the days of her youth,
As in the day when she came up from
the land of Egypt.

16 "And it shall be, in that day,"
Says the LORD,
"*That* you will call Me 'My Husband,'
And no longer call Me 'My Master,'
17 For I will take from her mouth the
names of the Baals,
And they shall be remembered by their
name no more.
18 In that day I will make a covenant for
them
With the beasts of the field,
With the birds of the air,
And *with* the creeping things of the
ground.
Bow and sword of battle I will shatter
from the earth,
To make them lie down safely.

19 "I will betroth you to Me forever;
Yes, I will betroth you to Me
In righteousness and justice,
In lovingkindness and mercy;
20 I will betroth you to Me in faithfulness,
And you shall know the LORD.

2:19,20 I will betroth you. Repeated 3 times, the term emphasizes the intensity of God's restoring love for the nation. In that day, Israel will no longer be thought of as a prostitute. Israel brings nothing to the marriage; God makes all the promises and provides all the dowry. These verses are recited by every orthodox Jew as he places the phylacteries on his hand and forehead (Deut. 11:18). The regeneration/conversion of the nation is much like that of an individual (2 Cor. 5:16–19).

21 "It shall come to pass in that day
That I will answer," says the LORD;
"I will answer the heavens,
And they shall answer the earth.
22 The earth shall answer
With grain,
With new wine,
And with oil;
They shall answer Jezreel.
23 Then I will sow her for Myself in the
earth,
And I will have mercy on *her who had*
not obtained mercy;
Then I will say to *those who were* not
My people,
'You *are* My people!'
And they shall say, '*You are* my God!' "

Psalm 138:4–6

4 All the kings of the earth shall praise
You, O LORD,
When they hear the words of Your
mouth.
5 Yes, they shall sing of the ways of the
LORD,
For great *is* the glory of the LORD.
6 Though the LORD *is* on high,
Yet He regards the lowly;
But the proud He knows from afar.

Proverbs 29:17

17 Correct your son, and he will give
you rest;
Yes, he will give delight to your soul.

1 John 3:1–24

3 Behold what manner of love the Father
has bestowed on us, that we should be
called children of God! Therefore the world
does not know us, because it did not know
Him. 2Beloved, now we are children of God;
and it has not yet been revealed what we shall
be, but we know that when He is revealed, we
shall be like Him, for we shall see Him as He
is. 3And everyone who has this hope in Him
purifies himself, just as He is pure.

3:3 purifies himself, just as He is pure. This is the key verse to 2:28–3:3. Living in the reality of Christ's return makes a difference in a Christian's behavior. Since Christians someday will be like Him, a desire should grow within the Christian to become like Him now. That was Paul's passion, expressed in Philippians 3:12–14. That calls for a purifying of sin, in which we play a part (2 Cor. 7:1; 1 Tim. 5:22; 1 Pet. 1:22).

4Whoever commits sin also commits lawlessness, and sin is lawlessness. 5And you
know that He was manifested to take away our
sins, and in Him there is no sin. 6Whoever
abides in Him does not sin. Whoever sins has
neither seen Him nor known Him.
7Little children, let no one deceive you. He
who practices righteousness is righteous, just
as He is righteous. 8He who sins is of the devil,
for the devil has sinned from the beginning.
For this purpose the Son of God was manifested, that He might destroy the works of the
devil. 9Whoever has been born of God does
not sin, for His seed remains in him; and he
cannot sin, because he has been born of God.
10In this the children of God and the children of the devil are manifest: Whoever does
not practice righteousness is not of God, nor *is*
he who does not love his brother. 11For this is
the message that you heard from the beginning, that we should love one another, 12not as
Cain *who* was of the wicked one and murdered
his brother. And why did he murder him?
Because his works were evil and his brother's
righteous.
13Do not marvel, my brethren, if the world
hates you. 14We know that we have passed

3:16 By this we know love. With this phrase, John introduces the standard of love that is reflected in genuine Christianity. It becomes the measuring stick for every expression of love (see v. 18). John presents this characteristic of Satan's children in terms of their lack of love. Satan's children are marked by indifference toward others' needs. **He laid down His life for us.** This expression is unique to John (John 10:11,15,17,18; 13:37,38; 15:13) and speaks of divesting oneself of something. Christian love is self-sacrificing and giving. Christ's giving up His life for believers epitomized the true nature of Christian love (John 15:12,13; Phil. 2:5–8; 1 Pet. 2:19–23). **we also ought to lay down *our* lives for the brethren.** God calls Christians to that same standard of love for one another as He had for us.

from death to life, because we love the
brethren. He who does not love *his* brother
abides in death. 15Whoever hates his brother is
a murderer, and you know that no murderer
has eternal life abiding in him.
16By this we know love, because He laid
down His life for us. And we also ought to lay
down *our* lives for the brethren. 17But whoever
has this world's goods, and sees his brother in
need, and shuts up his heart from him, how
does the love of God abide in him?
18My little children, let us not love in word or
in tongue, but in deed and in truth. 19And by
this we know that we are of the truth, and shall
assure our hearts before Him. 20For if our heart
condemns us, God is greater than our heart, and
knows all things. 21Beloved, if our heart does
not condemn us, we have confidence toward
God. 22And whatever we ask we receive from
Him, because we keep His commandments
and do those things that are pleasing in His
sight. 23And this is His commandment: that we
should believe on the name of His Son Jesus
Christ and love one another, as He gave us
commandment.
24Now he who keeps His commandments
abides in Him, and He in him. And by this we
know that He abides in us, by the Spirit whom
He has given us.

DAY 5: What 4 reasons does John give for why believers cannot habitually practice sin (1 John 3:4–10)?

This passage begins with the phrase "Whoever commits sin" (v. 4). "Commits" translates a Greek verb that conveys the idea of habitual practice. Although genuine Christians have a sin nature (1:8) and do behave sinfully, their confession of sin (1:9; 2:1) and acceptance of forgiveness prevent sin from becoming the unbroken pattern of their lives (John 8:31,34–36; Rom. 6:11; 2 John 9). God builds a certain growing awareness about sin that provides 4 effective reasons why true Christians cannot habitually practice sin:

1. Genuine Christians cannot practice sin because sin is incompatible with the law of God, which they love (3:4; Ps. 119:34,77,97; Rom. 7:12,22); whereas habitual sin betrays the ultimate sense of rebellion—living as if there were no law or ignoring what laws exist (James 4:17)—in short, lawlessness.

2. Genuine Christians cannot practice sin because sin is incompatible with the work of Christ (3:5). Christ died to sanctify (make holy) the believer (2 Cor. 5:21; Eph. 5:25–27). Habitual sin contradicts Christ's work of breaking the dominion of sin in the believer's life (Rom. 6:1–15).

3. Genuine Christians cannot practice sin because Christ came to destroy the works of the arch-sinner, Satan (3:8). The devil is still operating, but he has been defeated, and in Christ we escape his tyranny. The day will come when all of Satan's activity will cease in the universe, and he will be sent to hell forever (Rev. 20:10).

4. Genuine Christians cannot practice sin because sin is incompatible with the ministry of the Holy Spirit, who has imparted a new nature to the believer (3:9; John 3:5–8). This new nature shuns sin and exhibits the habitual character of righteousness produced by the Holy Spirit (Gal. 5:22–24).

DECEMBER 6

Hosea 3:1–4:19

3 Then the LORD said to me, "Go again, love a
woman *who is* loved by a lover and is committing adultery, just like the love of the LORD
for the children of Israel, who look to other
gods and love *the* raisin cakes *of the pagans.*"
2So I bought her for myself for fifteen *shekels*
of silver, and one and one-half homers of barley. 3And I said to her, "You shall stay with me
many days; you shall not play the harlot, nor
shall you have a man—so, too, *will* I *be* toward
you."
4For the children of Israel shall abide many
days without king or prince, without sacrifice
or *sacred* pillar, without ephod or teraphim.
5Afterward the children of Israel shall return
and seek the LORD their God and David their
king. They shall fear the LORD and His goodness in the latter days.

4 Hear the word of the LORD,
You children of Israel,
For the LORD *brings* a charge against
the inhabitants of the land:

"There is no truth or mercy
Or knowledge of God in the land.
2 *By* swearing and lying,
Killing and stealing and committing
adultery,
They break all restraint,
With bloodshed upon bloodshed.
3 Therefore the land will mourn;
And everyone who dwells there will
waste away
With the beasts of the field
And the birds of the air;
Even the fish of the sea will be taken
away.

4 "Now let no man contend, or rebuke
another;
For your people *are* like those who
contend with the priest.
5 Therefore you shall stumble in the day;
The prophet also shall stumble with
you in the night;
And I will destroy your mother.
6 My people are destroyed for lack of
knowledge.

3:1 Go again, love. Having been previously separated, Hosea was commanded to pursue his estranged wife, Gomer, thereby illustrating God's unquenchable love for faithless Israel. **raisin cakes.** Eaten as a part of special occasions (2 Sam. 6:19), they may have been used in idolatrous ceremonies, possibly as an aphrodisiac (Song 2:5).

3:2 bought her. Probably from a slave auction, Hosea purchased Gomer for 15 shekels of silver and 1 1/2 homers of barley. Together, the total may have equaled 30 pieces of silver, the price paid for a common slave (Ex. 21:32). Barley was the offering of one accused of adultery (Num. 5:15).

Because you have rejected knowledge,
I also will reject you from being priest
for Me;
Because you have forgotten the law
of your God,
I also will forget your children.

7 "The more they increased,
The more they sinned against Me;
I will change their glory into shame.
8 They eat up the sin of My people;
They set their heart on their iniquity.
9 And it shall be: like people, like priest.
So I will punish them for their ways,
And reward them for their deeds.
10 For they shall eat, but not have enough;
They shall commit harlotry,
but not increase;
Because they have ceased obeying
the LORD.

11 "Harlotry, wine, and new wine enslave
the heart.
12 My people ask counsel from their
wooden *idols,*
And their staff informs them.
For the spirit of harlotry has caused
them to stray,
And they have played the harlot
against their God.
13 They offer sacrifices on the
mountaintops,
And burn incense on the hills,
Under oaks, poplars, and terebinths,
Because their shade *is* good.
Therefore your daughters commit
harlotry,
And your brides commit adultery.
14 "I will not punish your daughters when
they commit harlotry,
Nor your brides when they commit
adultery;
For *the men* themselves go apart with
harlots,
And offer sacrifices with a ritual harlot.
Therefore people *who* do not
understand will be trampled.

15 "Though you, Israel, play the harlot,
Let not Judah offend.
Do not come up to Gilgal,
Nor go up to Beth Aven,
Nor swear an oath, *saying,* 'As the
LORD lives'—

16 "For Israel is stubborn
Like a stubborn calf;
Now the LORD will let them forage
Like a lamb in open country.

17 "Ephraim *is* joined to idols,
Let him alone.
18 Their drink is rebellion,
They commit harlotry continually.
Her rulers dearly love dishonor.
19 The wind has wrapped her up
in its wings,
And they shall be ashamed because
of their sacrifices.

Psalm 138:7–8

7 Though I walk in the midst of trouble,
You will revive me;
You will stretch out Your hand
Against the wrath of my enemies,
And Your right hand will save me.
8 The LORD will perfect *that which*
concerns me;
Your mercy, O LORD, *endures* forever;
Do not forsake the works of Your hands.

Proverbs 29:18

18 Where *there is* no revelation, the
people cast off restraint;
But happy *is* he who keeps the law.

29:18 no revelation. This proverb looks both to the lack of the Word (1 Sam. 3:1) and the lack of hearing the Word (Amos 8:11,12), which leads to lawless rebellion (Ex. 32:25; Lev. 13:45; Num. 5:18). The proverb then contrasts the joy and glory of a lawful society (28:14; Mal. 4:4).

1 John 4:1–21

4 Beloved, do not believe every spirit, but
test the spirits, whether they are of God;
because many false prophets have gone out
into the world. 2By this you know the Spirit of
God: Every spirit that confesses that Jesus
Christ has come in the flesh is of God, 3and
every spirit that does not confess that Jesus
Christ has come in the flesh is not of God. And
this is the *spirit* of the Antichrist, which you
have heard was coming, and is now already in
the world.

4You are of God, little children, and have
overcome them, because He who is in you is
greater than he who is in the world. 5They are
of the world. Therefore they speak *as* of the
world, and the world hears them. 6We are of
God. He who knows God hears us; he who is
not of God does not hear us. By this we know
the spirit of truth and the spirit of error.

7Beloved, let us love one another, for love is
of God; and everyone who loves is born of
God and knows God. 8He who does not love

4:1 do not believe every spirit. The mention of the Holy Spirit in 3:24 prompts John to inform his readers that those other spirits exist, i.e., demonic spirits, who produce false prophets and false teachers to propagate their false doctrine (1 Tim. 4:1,2). Christians are to have a healthy skepticism regarding any teaching, unlike some among John's congregations who were too open-minded to anyone claiming a new teaching regarding the faith. **test.** The word "test" is a metallurgist's term used for assaying metals to determine their purity and value. Christians must test any teaching with a view to approving or disapproving it, rigorously comparing any teaching to the Scripture. **the spirits,...many false prophets.** By juxtaposing "spirits" with "false prophets," John reminds his readers that behind human teachers who propagate false doctrine and error are demons inspired by Satan. Human false prophets and teachers are the physical expressions of demonic, spiritual sources (Matt. 7:15; Mark 13:22).

4:17 Love...perfected among us. John is not suggesting sinless perfection, but rather mature love marked by confidence in the face of judgment. Confidence is a sign that love is mature. **as He is, so are we.** Jesus was God's Son in whom He was well pleased on earth. We also are God's children (3:11) and the objects of His gracious goodness. If Jesus called God Father, so may we, since we are accepted in the Beloved (Eph. 1:6). In v. 18, the same truth is stated negatively. The love that builds confidence also banishes fears. We love God and reverence Him, but we do not love God and come to Him in love and at the same time hide from Him in terror (Rom. 8:14,15; 2 Tim. 1:7). Fear involves torment or punishment, a reality the sons of God will never experience, because they are forgiven.

does not know God, for God is love. 9In this
the love of God was manifested toward us, that
God has sent His only begotten Son into the
world, that we might live through Him. 10In
this is love, not that we loved God, but that He
loved us and sent His Son *to be* the propitiation
for our sins. 11Beloved, if God so loved us, we
also ought to love one another.
12No one has seen God at any time. If we
love one another, God abides in us, and His
love has been perfected in us. 13By this we
know that we abide in Him, and He in us,
because He has given us of His Spirit. 14And
we have seen and testify that the Father has
sent the Son *as* Savior of the world. 15Whoever
confesses that Jesus is the Son of God, God
abides in him, and he in God. 16And we have
known and believed the love that God has for
us. God is love, and he who abides in love
abides in God, and God in him.
17Love has been perfected among us in this:
that we may have boldness in the day of judgment; because as He is, so are we in this world.
18There is no fear in love; but perfect love casts
out fear, because fear involves torment. But he
who fears has not been made perfect in love.
19We love Him because He first loved us.
20If someone says, "I love God," and hates
his brother, he is a liar; for he who does not
love his brother whom he has seen, how can
he love God whom he has not seen? 21And this
commandment we have from Him: that he
who loves God *must* love his brother also.

DAY 6: What are the 5 reasons that John gives us for why believers love?

In stark contrast to the self-centered and destructive philosophies and practices of the false teachers, John unfolds the powerful reasons why Christians practice love. In 1 John 4:7–21, the apostle includes 5 such reasons:

1. Christians habitually practice love because God, who indwells them, is the essence of love. The Gnostics believed that God was immaterial spirit and light, but never defined the source of love as coming from His inmost being. As God is Spirit (John 4:24), light (1:5), and a consuming fire (Heb. 12:9), so He is love (4:7,8). Love is inherent in all He is and does. Even His judgment and wrath are perfectly harmonized with His love.

2. Christians habitually practice love because they desire to imitate the supreme example of God's sacrificial love in sending His Son for us (4:9).

3. Christians habitually practice love because love is the heart of Christian witness (4:12). Nobody can see God loving since He is invisible. Jesus no longer is in the world to manifest the love of God. The only demonstration of God's love in this age is the church. That testimony is critical (John 13:35; 2 Cor. 5:18–20).

4. Christians habitually practice love because love is the Christian's assurance (4:13–16; 3:21). Love banishes self-condemnation. When a Christian recognizes in his life the manifestation of love in actions, it results in confidence about his relationship with God.

5. Christians habitually practice love because love is the Christian's confidence in judgment (4:17–20; 3:16–23). Confidence is a sign that love is mature. This is not to suggest sinless perfection in a Christian's life, but rather a habitual practice of love marked by confidence in the face of judgment. Christians love, not in order to escape judgment, but because they have escaped judgment.

DECEMBER 7

Hosea 5:1–6:11

5 "Hear this, O priests!
Take heed, O house of Israel!
Give ear, O house of the king!
For yours *is* the judgment,
Because you have been a snare
to Mizpah
And a net spread on Tabor.
2 The revolters are deeply involved
in slaughter,
Though I rebuke them all.
3 I know Ephraim,
And Israel is not hidden from Me;
For now, O Ephraim, you commit
harlotry;
Israel is defiled.

4 "They do not direct their deeds
Toward turning to their God,
For the spirit of harlotry is in their midst,
And they do not know the LORD.
5 The pride of Israel testifies to his face;
Therefore Israel and Ephraim stumble
in their iniquity;
Judah also stumbles with them.
6 "With their flocks and herds
They shall go to seek the LORD,
But they will not find *Him;*
He has withdrawn Himself from them.
7 They have dealt treacherously
with the LORD,
For they have begotten pagan children.
Now a New Moon shall devour them
and their heritage.

8 "Blow the ram's horn in Gibeah,
The trumpet in Ramah!
Cry aloud *at* Beth Aven,
'*Look* behind you, O Benjamin!'
9 Ephraim shall be desolate in the day
of rebuke;
Among the tribes of Israel I make
known what is sure.

10 "The princes of Judah are like those
who remove a landmark;
I will pour out My wrath on them
like water.
11 Ephraim is oppressed *and* broken in
judgment,
Because he willingly walked by *human*
precept.
12 Therefore I *will be* to Ephraim like a
moth,
And to the house of Judah like
rottenness.

13 "When Ephraim saw his sickness,
And Judah *saw* his wound,
Then Ephraim went to Assyria
And sent to King Jareb;
Yet he cannot cure you,
Nor heal you of your wound.
14 For I *will be* like a lion to Ephraim,
And like a young lion to the house of
Judah.
I, *even* I, will tear *them* and go away;
I will take *them* away, and no one shall
rescue.
15 I will return again to My place
Till they acknowledge their offense.
Then they will seek My face;
In their affliction they will earnestly
seek Me."

6 Come, and let us return to the LORD;
For He has torn, but He will heal us;
He has stricken, but He will bind us up.
2 After two days He will revive us;
On the third day He will raise us up,
That we may live in His sight.
3 Let us know,
Let us pursue the knowledge of the LORD.
His going forth is established as the
morning;
He will come to us like the rain,
Like the latter *and* former rain to the
earth.

4 "O Ephraim, what shall I do to you?
O Judah, what shall I do to you?
For your faithfulness is like a morning
cloud,
And like the early dew it goes away.
5 Therefore I have hewn *them* by the
prophets,

I have slain them by the words
of My mouth;
And your judgments *are like* light
that goes forth.
6 For I desire mercy and not sacrifice,
And the knowledge of God more
than burnt offerings.

7 "But like men they transgressed the
covenant;
There they dealt treacherously with Me.
8 Gilead *is* a city of evildoers
And defiled with blood.
9 As bands of robbers lie in wait for a man,
So the company of priests murder on
the way to Shechem;
Surely they commit lewdness.
10 I have seen a horrible thing in the
house of Israel:
There *is* the harlotry of Ephraim;
Israel is defiled.
11 Also, O Judah, a harvest is appointed
for you,
When I return the captives of My people.

Psalm 139:1–6

For the Chief Musician. A Psalm of David.

O LORD, You have searched me
and known *me.*

139:1 searched me. As it has been in David's life, he prays later that it will continue to be (vv. 23,24). David understands that nothing inside of him can be hidden from God.

2 You know my sitting down and my
rising up;
You understand my thought afar off.
3 You comprehend my path and my lying
down,
And are acquainted with all my ways.
4 For *there is* not a word on my tongue,
But behold, O LORD, You know it
altogether.
5 You have hedged me behind and before,
And laid Your hand upon me.
6 *Such* knowledge *is* too wonderful
for me;
It is high, I cannot *attain* it.

Proverbs 29:19

19 A servant will not be corrected by
mere words;
For though he understands,
he will not respond.

1 John 5:1–21

5 Whoever believes that Jesus is the Christ
is born of God, and everyone who loves
Him who begot also loves him who is begotten
of Him. 2By this we know that we love the
children of God, when we love God and keep
His commandments. 3For this is the love of
God, that we keep His commandments. And
His commandments are not burdensome. 4For
whatever is born of God overcomes the world.
And this is the victory that has overcome the
world—our faith. 5Who is he who overcomes
the world, but he who believes that Jesus is the
Son of God?

5:4 overcomes. John clearly defines who these overcomers are: they are all who believe that Jesus is God's Son, and all that means. The overcomers are believers—all of them (2:13). The word for "overcomer" comes from a Greek word meaning "to conquer," "to have victory," "to have superiority," or "conquering power." The word reflects a genuine superiority that leads to overwhelming success. The victory is demonstrable; it involves overthrowing an enemy so that the victory is seen by all. Jesus also used this word to describe Himself (John 16:33). Because of believers' union with Christ, they too partake in His victory (Rom. 8:37; 2 Cor. 2:14). The word "overcomes" in the original language conveys the idea that the believer has continual victory over the world.

6This is He who came by water and blood—
Jesus Christ; not only by water, but by water
and blood. And it is the Spirit who bears witness, because the Spirit is truth. 7For there are
three that bear witness in heaven: the Father,
the Word, and the Holy Spirit; and these three
are one. 8And there are three that bear witness
on earth: the Spirit, the water, and the blood;
and these three agree as one.
9If we receive the witness of men, the witness
of God is greater; for this is the witness of God
which He has testified of His Son. 10He who
believes in the Son of God has the witness in
himself; he who does not believe God has made
Him a liar, because he has not believed the testimony that God has given of His Son. 11And this
is the testimony: that God has given us eternal
life, and this life is in His Son. 12He who has the
Son has life; he who does not have the Son of
God does not have life. 13These things I have
written to you who believe in the name of the
Son of God, that you may know that you have

5:13 These things. This has reference to all that John has written in his letter. **that you may know that you have eternal life.** Assurance of eternal life constitutes the first Christian certainty. While John wrote his Gospel to bring unbelievers to faith (John 20:31), he wrote the epistle to give believers confidence that they possessed eternal life. The false brethren's departure left John's congregations shaken (2:19). He assured those who remained that since they adhered to the fundamentals of the faith (a proper view of Christ, obedience, love), their salvation was sure. **eternal life.** This does not refer primarily to a period of time but a person (v. 20; John 17:3). Eternal life is a relationship with the Person of Jesus Christ and possessing His nature (vv. 11,12).

5:21 keep yourselves from idols. John contrasts the term "idols" with "the true God" of v. 20. He has reference here to the false teachers that withdrew from the brotherhood with which they had been formerly associated (2:19). Their false beliefs and practices are the idols from which the readers are commanded to protect themselves. The false teachers upheld the world's philosophy as superior to God's revelation as demonstrated in their perversion of basic Christian teaching. In closing, John once again highlights the importance of adherence to the fundamentals of the faith.

eternal life, and that you may *continue to* believe in the name of the Son of God.

14 Now this is the confidence that we have in Him, that if we ask anything according to His will, He hears us.
15 And if we know that He hears us, whatever we ask, we know that we have the petitions that we have asked of Him.

16 If anyone sees his brother sinning a sin *which does* not *lead* to death, he will ask, and He will give him life for those who commit sin not *leading* to death. There is sin *leading* to death. I do not say that he should pray about that.
17 All unrighteousness is sin, and there is sin not *leading* to death.

18 We know that whoever is born of God does not sin; but he who has been born of God keeps himself, and the wicked one does not touch him.

19 We know that we are of God, and the whole world lies *under the sway of* the wicked one.

20 And we know that the Son of God has come and has given us an understanding, that we may know Him who is true; and we are in Him who is true, in His Son Jesus Christ. This is the true God and eternal life.

21 Little children, keep yourselves from idols. Amen.

DAY 7: What are the 3 characteristics of an "overcomer"?

"Whoever believes that Jesus is the Christ is born of God" (1 John 5:1). Saving faith is the first characteristic of an overcomer. The term "believes" conveys the idea of continuing faith, making the point that the mark of genuine believers is that they continue in faith throughout their life. Saving belief is not simply intellectual acceptance, but wholehearted dedication to Jesus Christ that is permanent. The object of the believer's faith is Jesus, particularly that He is the promised Messiah or "Anointed One" whom God sent to be the Savior from sin. Whoever places faith in Jesus Christ as the only Savior has been born again and, as a result, is an overcomer (v. 5). To be "born of God" is a reference to the new birth and is the same word that Jesus used in John 3:7. The tense of the Greek verb indicates that ongoing faith is the result of the new birth and, therefore, the evidence of the new birth. The sons of God will manifest the reality that they have been born again by continuing to believe in God's Son, the Savior. The new birth brings us into a permanent faith relationship with God and Christ.

"And everyone who loves Him who begot also loves him who is begotten of Him" (v. 1). Love is the second characteristic of the overcomer. The overcomer not only believes in God, but loves both God and fellow believers. The moral test is again in view.

"By this we know that we love the children of God, when we love God and keep His commandments" (v. 2). John repeats this phrase twice in these 2 verses. Obedience is the third characteristic of an overcomer. In these verses, John weaves faith, love, and obedience all together inextricably. They exist mutually in a dynamic relationship—as the genuine proof of love is obedience, so the genuine proof of faith is love. The word "keep" conveys the idea of constant obedience (John 8:31,32; 14:15,21; 15:10).

DECEMBER 8

Hosea 7:1–8:14

7 "When I would have healed
Israel,
Then the iniquity of Ephraim was
uncovered,
And the wickedness of Samaria.
For they have committed fraud;
A thief comes in;
A band of robbers takes spoil outside.
2 They do not consider in their hearts
That I remember all their wickedness;
Now their own deeds have surrounded
them;
They are before My face.
3 They make a king glad with their
wickedness,
And princes with their lies.

4 "They *are* all adulterers.
Like an oven heated by a baker—
He ceases stirring *the fire* after
kneading the dough,
Until it is leavened.
5 In the day of our king
Princes have made *him* sick, inflamed
with wine;
He stretched out his hand with scoffers.
6 They prepare their heart like an oven,
While they lie in wait;
Their baker sleeps all night;
In the morning it burns like a flaming
fire.
7 They are all hot, like an oven,
And have devoured their judges;
All their kings have fallen.
None among them calls upon Me.

8 "Ephraim has mixed himself among
the peoples;
Ephraim is a cake unturned.
9 Aliens have devoured his strength,
But he does not know *it;*
Yes, gray hairs are here and there
on him,
Yet he does not know *it.*

7:4–7 The civil leaders' evil lust burned so passionately all night, that the prophet repeatedly described it like a consuming oven (vv. 4,6,7), so hot that the baker could forego stirring the fire during the entire night and still have adequate heat for baking the next morning.

10 And the pride of Israel testifies to his
face,
But they do not return to the LORD
their God,
Nor seek Him for all this.

11 "Ephraim also is like a silly dove,
without sense—
They call to Egypt,
They go to Assyria.
12 Wherever they go, I will spread My net
on them;
I will bring them down like birds
of the air;
I will chastise them
According to what their congregation
has heard.

13 "Woe to them, for they have fled from Me!
Destruction to them,
Because they have transgressed
against Me!
Though I redeemed them,
Yet they have spoken lies against Me.
14 They did not cry out to Me with
their heart
When they wailed upon their beds.

"They assemble together for grain
and new wine,
They rebel against Me;
15 Though I disciplined *and* strengthened
their arms,
Yet they devise evil against Me;
16 They return, *but* not to the Most High;
They are like a treacherous bow.
Their princes shall fall by the sword
For the cursings of their tongue.
This *shall be* their derision in the land
of Egypt.

8 "*Set* the trumpet to your mouth!
He shall come like an eagle against
the house of the LORD,
Because they have transgressed
My covenant
And rebelled against My law.
2 Israel will cry to Me,
'My God, we know You!'
3 Israel has rejected the good;
The enemy will pursue him.

4 "They set up kings, but not by Me;
They made princes, but I did not
acknowledge *them.*
From their silver and gold
They made idols for themselves—
That they might be cut off.
5 Your calf is rejected, O Samaria!
My anger is aroused against them—

How long until they attain to innocence?
6 For from Israel *is* even this:
A workman made it, and it *is* not God;
But the calf of Samaria shall be broken to pieces.

7 "They sow the wind,
And reap the whirlwind.
The stalk has no bud;
It shall never produce meal.
If it should produce,
Aliens would swallow it up.
8 Israel is swallowed up;
Now they are among the Gentiles
Like a vessel in which *is* no pleasure.
9 For they have gone up to Assyria,
Like a wild donkey alone by itself;
Ephraim has hired lovers.
10 Yes, though they have hired among the nations,
Now I will gather them;
And they shall sorrow a little,
Because of the burden of the king of princes.

11 "Because Ephraim has made many altars for sin,
They have become for him altars for sinning.
12 I have written for him the great things of My law,
But they were considered a strange thing.
13 *For* the sacrifices of My offerings they sacrifice flesh and eat *it,*
But the LORD does not accept them.
Now He will remember their iniquity and punish their sins.
They shall return to Egypt.

14 "For Israel has forgotten his Maker,
And has built temples;
Judah also has multiplied fortified cities;
But I will send fire upon his cities,
And it shall devour his palaces."

Psalm 139:7–12

7 Where can I go from Your Spirit?
Or where can I flee from Your presence?
8 If I ascend into heaven, You *are* there;
If I make my bed in hell, behold, You *are there.*
9 *If* I take the wings of the morning,
And dwell in the uttermost parts of the sea,
10 Even there Your hand shall lead me,
And Your right hand shall hold me.
11 If I say, "Surely the darkness shall fall on me,"

139:9 the wings of the morning. In conjunction with "the uttermost parts of the sea," David uses this literary figure to express distance.

Even the night shall be light about me;
12 Indeed, the darkness shall not hide from You,
But the night shines as the day;
The darkness and the light *are* both alike *to You.*

Proverbs 29:20

20 Do you see a man hasty in his words?
There is more hope for a fool than for him.

2 John 1–13

The Elder,

To the elect lady and her children, whom I love in truth, and not only I, but also all those who have known the truth,
2 because of the truth which abides in us and will be with us forever:

3 Grace, mercy, *and* peace will be with you from God the Father and from the Lord Jesus Christ, the Son of the Father, in truth and love.

4 I rejoiced greatly that I have found *some* of your children walking in truth, as we received commandment from the Father.
5 And now I plead with you, lady, not as though I wrote a new

1 The Elder. John uses this title to emphasize his advanced age, his spiritual authority over the congregations in Asia Minor, and the strength of his own personal eyewitness testimony to the life of Jesus and all that He taught (vv. 4–6). **the elect lady and her children.** Some think that this phrase refers metaphorically to a particular local church, while "her children" would refer to members of the congregation. The more natural understanding in context, however, is that it refers to a particular woman and her children (i.e., offspring) who were well known to John. **whom I love in truth.** The basis of Christian hospitality is the truth (vv. 1–3). John accentuates the need for truth by repeating the term "truth" 5 times in the opening 4 verses. Truth refers to the basics or fundamentals of the faith that John has discussed in 1 John, as well as the truths expressed in 2 John 4–6. Truth is the necessary condition of unity and, as a result, the basis of hospitality.

commandment to you, but that which we have
had from the beginning: that we love one
another. [6]This is love, that we walk according
to His commandments. This is the commandment, that as you have heard from the beginning, you should walk in it.

[7]For many deceivers have gone out into the
world who do not confess Jesus Christ *as* coming in the flesh. This is a deceiver and an
antichrist. [8]Look to yourselves, that we do not
lose those things we worked for, but *that* we
may receive a full reward.

[9]Whoever transgresses and does not abide in
the doctrine of Christ does not have God. He
who abides in the doctrine of Christ has both
the Father and the Son. [10]If anyone comes to
you and does not bring this doctrine, do not
receive him into your house nor greet him; [11]for
he who greets him shares in his evil deeds.

[12]Having many things to write to you, I did
not wish *to do so* with paper and ink; but I hope to come to you and speak face to face, that our joy may be full.

[13]The children of your elect sister greet you.
Amen.

10 do not receive him into your house nor greet him. John's prohibition is not a case of entertaining people who disagree on minor matters. These false teachers were carrying on a regular campaign to destroy the basic, fundamental truths of Christianity. Complete disassociation from such heretics is the only appropriate course of action for genuine believers. No benefit or aid of any type (not even a greeting) is permissible. Believers should aid only those who proclaim the truth (vv. 5–8).

DAY 8: Why is it so important to John to "confess Jesus Christ as coming in the flesh" (2 John 7)?

John's purpose was to strengthen Christians to resist the tide of heresy that was rising against the church. Much of this false teaching was an early form of Gnosticism.

The gnostic idea that matter was evil and only spirit was good led to the idea that either the body should be treated harshly, a form of asceticism (Col. 2:21–23), or that sin committed in the body had no connection or effect on one's spirit. In other words, the false teaching sought to drive a wedge between body and soul. This is why it often maintained that Jesus could not have been God and man at the same time.

The result of this error in teaching was compounded when some, including John's opponents, concluded that sins committed in the physical body did not matter. Absolute indulgence in immorality was permissible. One could deny sin even existed (1 John 1:8–10) and disregard God's law (1 John 3:4).

As a bulwark against this heresy, John lifted the confession that "Jesus Christ [came] in the flesh" (v. 7). What Christians do in their physical life is directly connected with what they do in their spiritual life. John emphasized the need for obedience to God's laws, for he defined the true love for God as obedience to His commandments (1 John 5:3). Jesus, in His human living, offered the perfect example of that kind of love.

DECEMBER 9

Hosea 9:1–10:15

9 Do not rejoice, O Israel, with joy
like *other* peoples,
For you have played the harlot against
your God.
You have made love *for* hire on every
threshing floor.
2 The threshing floor and the winepress
Shall not feed them,
And the new wine shall fail in her.
3 They shall not dwell in the LORD's land,
But Ephraim shall return to Egypt,
And shall eat unclean *things* in Assyria.
4 They shall not offer wine *offerings*
to the LORD,
Nor shall their sacrifices be pleasing
to Him.
It shall be like bread of mourners to them;
All who eat it shall be defiled.
For their bread *shall be* for their *own*
life;
It shall not come into the house
of the LORD.

5 What will you do in the appointed day,
And in the day of the feast of the LORD?
6 For indeed they are gone because
of destruction.
Egypt shall gather them up;
Memphis shall bury them.
Nettles shall possess their valuables
of silver;
Thorns *shall be* in their tents.

7 The days of punishment have come;
The days of recompense have come.
Israel knows!
The prophet *is* a fool,
The spiritual man *is* insane,
Because of the greatness of your
iniquity and great enmity.
8 The watchman of Ephraim *is* with
my God;
But the prophet *is* a fowler's snare
in all his ways—
Enmity in the house of his God.

9:7,8 The prophets were God's inspired messengers and watchmen (Ezek. 3:17; 33:1–7), yet Israel considered them fools and madmen.

9 They are deeply corrupted,
As in the days of Gibeah.
He will remember their iniquity;
He will punish their sins.
10 "I found Israel
Like grapes in the wilderness;
I saw your fathers
As the firstfruits on the fig tree in its
first season.
But they went to Baal Peor,
And separated themselves *to that* shame;
They became an abomination like the
thing they loved.
11 *As for* Ephraim, their glory shall fly away
like a bird—
No birth, no pregnancy, and no
conception!
12 Though they bring up their children,
Yet I will bereave them to the last man.
Yes, woe to them when I depart from
them!
13 Just as I saw Ephraim like Tyre, planted
in a pleasant place,
So Ephraim will bring out his children
to the murderer."

14 Give them, O LORD—
What will You give?
Give them a miscarrying womb
And dry breasts!

15 "All their wickedness *is* in Gilgal,
For there I hated them.
Because of the evil of their deeds
I will drive them from My house;
I will love them no more.
All their princes *are* rebellious.
16 Ephraim is stricken,
Their root is dried up;
They shall bear no fruit.
Yes, were they to bear children,
I would kill the darlings of their womb."

17 My God will cast them away,
Because they did not obey Him;
And they shall be wanderers among
the nations.

10 Israel empties *his* vine;
He brings forth fruit for himself.
According to the multitude of his fruit
He has increased the altars;
According to the bounty of his land
They have embellished *his sacred* pillars.
2 Their heart is divided;
Now they are held guilty.
He will break down their altars;
He will ruin their *sacred* pillars.

3 For now they say,
"We have no king,
Because we did not fear the LORD.
And as for a king, what would he do
for us?"
4 They have spoken words,
Swearing falsely in making
a covenant.
Thus judgment springs up like
hemlock in the furrows of the field.
5 The inhabitants of Samaria fear
Because of the calf of Beth Aven.
For its people mourn for it,
And its priests shriek for it—
Because its glory has departed
from it.
6 *The idol* also shall be carried to Assyria
As a present for King Jareb.
Ephraim shall receive shame,
And Israel shall be ashamed
of his own counsel.

7 *As for* Samaria, her king is cut off
Like a twig on the water.
8 Also the high places of Aven, the sin
of Israel,
Shall be destroyed.
The thorn and thistle shall grow on
their altars;

10:8 Cover us!...Fall on us! The captivity would be so severe that the people would pray for the mountains and hills to fall on them, similar to the last days (Luke 23:30; Rev. 6:16).

They shall say to the mountains,
"Cover us!"
And to the hills, "Fall on us!"

9 "O Israel, you have sinned from the days of Gibeah;
There they stood.
The battle in Gibeah against the children of iniquity
Did not overtake them.
10 When *it is* My desire, I will chasten them.
Peoples shall be gathered against them
When I bind them for their two transgressions.
11 Ephraim *is* a trained heifer
That loves to thresh *grain;*
But I harnessed her fair neck,
I will make Ephraim pull *a plow.*
Judah shall plow;
Jacob shall break his clods."
12 Sow for yourselves righteousness;
Reap in mercy;
Break up your fallow ground,
For *it is* time to seek the LORD,
Till He comes and rains righteousness on you.
13 You have plowed wickedness;
You have reaped iniquity.
You have eaten the fruit of lies,
Because you trusted in your own way,
In the multitude of your mighty men.
14 Therefore tumult shall arise among your people,
And all your fortresses shall be plundered
As Shalman plundered Beth Arbel in the day of battle—
A mother dashed in pieces upon *her* children.
15 Thus it shall be done to you, O Bethel,
Because of your great wickedness.
At dawn the king of Israel
Shall be cut off utterly.

Psalm 139:13–16

13 For You formed my inward parts;
You covered me in my mother's womb.
14 I will praise You, for I am fearfully *and* wonderfully made;
Marvelous are Your works,
And *that* my soul knows very well.
15 My frame was not hidden from You,
When I was made in secret,
And skillfully wrought in the lowest parts of the earth.
16 Your eyes saw my substance, being yet unformed.
And in Your book they all were written,
The days fashioned for me,
When *as yet there were* none of them.

139:13 formed...covered. By virtue of the divinely designed period of pregnancy, God providentially watches over the development of the child while yet in the mother's womb.

139:16 Your book. This figure of speech likens God's mind to a book of remembrance. **none of them.** God sovereignly ordained David's life before he was conceived.

Proverbs 29:21

21 He who pampers his servant from childhood
Will have him as a son in the end.

3 John 1–14

The Elder,

To the beloved Gaius, whom I love in truth:

2Beloved, I pray that you may prosper in all
things and be in health, just as your soul prospers. 3For I rejoiced greatly when brethren
came and testified of the truth *that is* in you,
just as you walk in the truth. 4I have no greater
joy than to hear that my children walk in truth.
5Beloved, you do faithfully whatever you do

4 I have no greater joy. John's personal affection for Gaius radiated especially from his personal conduct (Luke 6:46). **my children.** The word "my" is emphatic in the original. John's heart delighted in the proper conduct of his spiritual children in the faith. Those who walk (conduct) in the truth (belief) have integrity—there is no dichotomy between professing and living. He had strong fatherly affection for them (1 Cor. 4:14–16; 1 Thess. 2:11; 3:1–10).

for the brethren and for strangers, [6]who have
borne witness of your love before the church.
If you send them forward on their journey in a
manner worthy of God, you will do well, [7]be-
cause they went forth for His name's sake,
taking nothing from the Gentiles. [8]We therefore ought to receive such, that we may
become fellow workers for the truth.
[9]I wrote to the church, but Diotrephes, who
loves to have the preeminence among them,
does not receive us. [10]Therefore, if I come, I
will call to mind his deeds which he does, prating against us with malicious words. And not
content with that, he himself does not receive
the brethren, and forbids those who wish to,
putting *them* out of the church.
[11]Beloved, do not imitate what is evil, but
what is good. He who does good is of God, but
he who does evil has not seen God.
[12]Demetrius has a *good* testimony from all,
and from the truth itself. And we also bear witness, and you know that our testimony is true.
[13]I had many things to write, but I do not
wish to write to you with pen and ink; [14]but I
hope to see you shortly, and we shall speak
face to face.

Peace to you. Our friends greet you. Greet the friends by name.

DAY 9: What was the problem with Diotrephes in 3 John 9,10?

John apparently had written a previous letter to the church (v. 9), perhaps on the subject of hospitality, but it was lost. Perhaps Diotrephes never read it to the church because he rejected John's authority (vv. 9,10). "Diotrephes, who loves to have the preeminence." The word "preeminence" has the idea of "desiring to be first." It conveys the idea of someone who is selfish, self-centered, and self-seeking. The language suggests a self-promoting demagogue, who served no one, but wanted all to serve only him. Diotrephes' actions directly contradict Jesus' and the New Testament's teaching on servant leadership in the church (Matt. 20:20–28; Phil. 2:5–11; 1 Tim. 3:3; 1 Pet. 5:3). "Diotrephes,…does not receive us." Diotrephes modeled the opposite of kindness and hospitality to God's servants, even denying John's apostolic authority over the local congregation, and as a result, denying the revelation of God that came through that authority. His pride endeavored to supplant the rule of Christ through John in the church. Diotrephes' character was the very opposite of the gentle and loving Gaius who readily showed hospitality.

"If I come, I will call to mind his deeds" (v. 10). John's apostolic authority meant that Diotrephes had to answer for his behavior. The apostle did not overlook this usurping of Christ's place in the church. Verse 10 indicates that Diotrephes was guilty of 4 things: 1) "prating against us." The word "prating" comes from a word meaning "to bubble up" and has the idea of useless, empty jabber, i.e., talking nonsense. The charges against John were completely unjustified; 2) "with malicious words." Not only were Diotrephes' charges false, they were evil; 3) "does not receive the brethren." He not only slandered John but also deliberately defied other believers; and 4) "putting them out of the church." The original language indicates that Diotrephes' habit was to excommunicate those who resisted his authority. To accept John's authority (v. 9), as well as being hospitable to the traveling ministers, directly threatened the authority that Diotrephes coveted.

DECEMBER 10

Hosea 11:1–12:14

11 "When Israel *was* a child,
I loved him,
And out of Egypt I called My son.
2 *As* they called them,
So they went from them;
They sacrificed to the Baals,
And burned incense to carved images.

3 "I taught Ephraim to walk,
Taking them by their arms;
But they did not know that I healed them.
4 I drew them with gentle cords,
With bands of love,
And I was to them as those who take
the yoke from their neck.
I stooped *and* fed them.
5 "He shall not return to the land of Egypt;
But the Assyrian shall be his king,

11:1 In tender words reminiscent of the Exodus from Egypt (Ex. 4:22,23), the Lord reassured Israel of His intense love for her. His compassion for her was aroused (Is. 12:1; 40:1,2; 49:13; Jer. 31:10–14; Zech. 1:12–17). See Matthew 2:15 for Matthew's analogical use of this verse in relationship to Jesus Christ.

Because they refused to repent.
6 And the sword shall slash in his cities,
Devour his districts,
And consume *them,*
Because of their own counsels.
7 My people are bent on backsliding
from Me.
Though they call to the Most High,
None at all exalt *Him.*

8 "How can I give you up, Ephraim?
How can I hand you over, Israel?
How can I make you like Admah?
How can I set you like Zeboiim?
My heart churns within Me;
My sympathy is stirred.
9 I will not execute the fierceness
of My anger;
I will not again destroy Ephraim.
For I *am* God, and not man,
The Holy One in your midst;
And I will not come with terror.

10 "They shall walk after the LORD.
He will roar like a lion.
When He roars,
Then *His* sons shall come trembling
from the west;
11 They shall come trembling like a bird
from Egypt,
Like a dove from the land of Assyria.
And I will let them dwell in their
houses,"
Says the LORD.

12 "Ephraim has encircled Me with lies,
And the house of Israel with deceit;
But Judah still walks with God,
Even with the Holy One *who is* faithful.

12 "Ephraim feeds on the wind,
And pursues the east wind;
He daily increases lies and desolation.
Also they make a covenant with the
Assyrians,
And oil is carried to Egypt.

2 "The LORD also *brings* a charge against
Judah,
And will punish Jacob according to his
ways;
According to his deeds He will
recompense him.
3 He took his brother by the heel in the
womb,
And in his strength he struggled with
God.
4 Yes, he struggled with the Angel and
prevailed;
He wept, and sought favor from Him.
He found Him *in* Bethel,
And there He spoke to us—
5 That is, the LORD God of hosts.
The LORD *is* His memorable name.
6 So you, by *the help of* your God, return;
Observe mercy and justice,
And wait on your God continually.

7 "A cunning Canaanite!
Deceitful scales *are* in his hand;
He loves to oppress.
8 And Ephraim said,
'Surely I have become rich,
I have found wealth for myself;
In all my labors
They shall find in me no iniquity
that *is* sin.'

9 "But I *am* the LORD your God,
Ever since the land of Egypt;
I will again make you dwell in tents,
As in the days of the appointed feast.
10 I have also spoken by the prophets,
And have multiplied visions;
I have given symbols through the
witness of the prophets."

11 Though Gilead *has* idols—
Surely they are vanity—
Though they sacrifice bulls in Gilgal,
Indeed their altars *shall be* heaps in the
furrows of the field.

12 Jacob fled to the country of Syria;
Israel served for a spouse,
And for a wife he tended *sheep.*
13 By a prophet the LORD brought Israel
out of Egypt,
And by a prophet he was preserved.
14 Ephraim provoked *Him* to anger most
bitterly;
Therefore his Lord will leave the guilt
of his bloodshed upon him,
And return his reproach upon him.

Psalm 139:17–24

17 How precious also are Your thoughts
to me, O God!
How great is the sum of them!
18 *If* I should count them, they would be
more in number than the sand;
When I awake, I am still with You.

19 Oh, that You would slay the wicked,
O God!
Depart from me, therefore, you
bloodthirsty men.
20 For they speak against You wickedly;
Your enemies take *Your name* in vain.
21 Do I not hate them, O LORD, who hate
You?

And do I not loathe those who rise up
against You?
22 I hate them with perfect hatred;
I count them my enemies.

23 Search me, O God, and know my heart;
Try me, and know my anxieties;
24 And see if *there is any* wicked way in me,
And lead me in the way everlasting.

Proverbs 29:22

22 An angry man stirs up strife,
And a furious man abounds in
transgression.

Jude 1–25

Jude, a bondservant of Jesus Christ, and
brother of James,

To those who are called, sanctified by God
the Father, and preserved in Jesus Christ:

2 Mercy, peace, and love be multiplied to you.

3 Beloved, while I was very diligent to write to
you concerning our common salvation, I found it
necessary to write to you exhorting you to contend earnestly for the faith which was once for all
delivered to the saints. 4 For certain men have
crept in unnoticed, who long ago were marked
out for this condemnation, ungodly men, who
turn the grace of our God into lewdness and deny
the only Lord God and our Lord Jesus Christ.
5 But I want to remind you, though you once
knew this, that the Lord, having saved the people out of the land of Egypt, afterward
destroyed those who did not believe. 6 And the
angels who did not keep their proper domain,
but left their own abode, He has reserved in
everlasting chains under darkness for the judgment of the great day; 7 as Sodom and Gomorrah,
and the cities around them in a similar manner
to these, having given themselves over to sexual immorality and gone after strange flesh, are
set forth as an example, suffering the vengeance of eternal fire.

8 Likewise also these dreamers defile the
flesh, reject authority, and speak evil of dignitaries. 9 Yet Michael the archangel, in contend-
ing with the devil, when he disputed about the
body of Moses, dared not bring against him a
reviling accusation, but said, "The Lord
rebuke you!" 10 But these speak evil of whatever they do not know; and whatever they know
naturally, like brute beasts, in these things
they corrupt themselves. 11 Woe to them! For
they have gone in the way of Cain, have run
greedily in the error of Balaam for profit, and
perished in the rebellion of Korah.

12 These are spots in your love feasts, while
they feast with you without fear, serving *only*
themselves. *They are* clouds without water,
carried about by the winds; late autumn trees
without fruit, twice dead, pulled up by the
roots; 13 raging waves of the sea, foaming up
their own shame; wandering stars for whom is
reserved the blackness of darkness forever.

14 Now Enoch, the seventh from Adam, prophesied about these men also, saying, "Behold,
the Lord comes with ten thousands of His
saints, 15 to execute judgment on all, to convict all
who are ungodly among them of all their ungodly deeds which they have committed in an
ungodly way, and of all the harsh things which
ungodly sinners have spoken against Him."

16 These are grumblers, complainers, walking
according to their own lusts; and they mouth
great swelling *words,* flattering people to gain

3 contend earnestly. While the salvation of those to whom he wrote was not in jeopardy, false teachers preaching and living out a counterfeit gospel were misleading those who needed to hear the true gospel. Jude wrote this urgent imperative for Christians to wage war against error in all forms and fight strenuously for the truth, like a soldier who has been entrusted with a sacred task of guarding a holy treasure (1 Tim. 6:12; 2 Tim. 4:7). **the faith.** This is the whole body of revealed salvation truth contained in the Scriptures. Here is a call to know sound doctrine (Eph. 4:14; Col. 3:16: 1 Pet. 2:2; 1 John 2:12–14), to be discerning in sorting out truth from error (1 Thess. 5:20–22), and to be willing to confront and attack error (2 Cor. 10:3–5; Phil. 1:17,27; 1 Tim. 1:18; 6:12; 2 Tim. 1:13; 4:7,8; Titus 1:13). **once for all delivered...saints.** God's revelation was delivered once as a unit, at the completion of the Scripture, and is not to be edited by either deletion or addition (Deut. 4:2; 12:32; Prov. 30:6; Rev. 22:18,19). Scripture is complete, sufficient, and finished; therefore it is fixed for all time. Nothing is to be added to the body of the inspired Word because nothing else is needed.

13 raging waves. Apostates promise powerful ministry, but are quickly exposed as wreakers of havoc and workers of worthless shame (Is. 57:20). **wandering stars.** This most likely refers to a meteor or shooting star which has an uncontrolled moment of brilliance and then fades away forever into nothing. Apostates promise enduring spiritual direction but deliver a brief, aimless, and worthless flash.

advantage. [17]But you, beloved, remember the
words which were spoken before by the apostles of our Lord Jesus Christ: [18]how they told
you that there would be mockers in the last
time who would walk according to their own
ungodly lusts. [19]These are sensual persons, who
cause divisions, not having the Spirit.
[20]But you, beloved, building yourselves up on
your most holy faith, praying in the Holy Spirit,
[21]keep yourselves in the love of God, looking
for the mercy of our Lord Jesus Christ unto
eternal life.
[22]And on some have compassion, making a
distinction; [23]but others save with fear, pulling
them out of the fire, hating even the garment
defiled by the flesh.

24 Now to Him who is able to keep you
from stumbling,
And to present *you* faultless
Before the presence of His glory with
exceeding joy,
25 To God our Savior,
Who alone is wise,
Be glory and majesty,
Dominion and power,
Both now and forever.
Amen.

DAY 10: Who was Jude, and why did he write his letter?

Although Jude (Judas) was a common name in Palestine (at least 8 are named in the New Testament), the author of Jude generally has been accepted as Jude, Christ's half brother. He is to be differentiated from the apostle Judas, the son of James (Luke 6:16; Acts 1:13). Several lines of thought lead to this conclusion: 1) Jude's appeal to being the "brother of James," the leader of the Jerusalem Council (Acts 15) and another half brother of Jesus (v. 1; Gal. 1:19); 2) Jude's salutation being similar to James's (James 1:1); and 3) Jude's not identifying himself as an apostle (v. 1), but rather distinguishing between himself and the apostles (v. 17).

Jude lived at a time when Christianity was under severe political attack from Rome and aggressive spiritual infiltration from gnosticlike apostates and libertines who sowed abundant seed for a gigantic harvest of doctrinal error. It could be that this was the forerunner to full-blown Gnosticism which the apostle John would confront over 25 years later in his epistles. Except for John, who lived at the close of the century, all of the other apostles had been martyred; and Christianity was thought to be extremely vulnerable. Thus, Jude called the church to fight, in the midst of intense spiritual warfare, for the truth.

Jude is the only New Testament book devoted exclusively to confronting "apostasy," meaning defection from the true, biblical faith (vv. 3,17). Apostates are described elsewhere in 2 Thessalonians 2:10; Hebrews 10:29; 2 Peter 2:1–22; 1 John 2:18–23. He wrote to condemn the apostates and to urge believers to contend for the faith. He called for discernment on the part of the church and a rigorous defense of biblical truth. He followed the earlier examples of: 1) Christ (Matt. 7:15ff.; 16:6–12; 24:11ff; Rev. 2; 3); 2) Paul (Acts 20:29,30; 1 Tim. 4:1; 2 Tim. 3:1–5; 4:3,4); 3) Peter (2 Pet. 2:1,2; 3:3,4); and 4) John (1 John 4:1–6; 2 John 6–11).

DECEMBER 11

Hosea 13:1–14:9

13 When Ephraim spoke,
trembling,
He exalted *himself* in Israel;
But when he offended through Baal
worship, he died.
2 Now they sin more and more,
And have made for themselves molded
images,
Idols of their silver, according to their
skill;
All of it *is* the work of craftsmen.
They say of them,
"Let the men who sacrifice kiss the calves!"
3 Therefore they shall be like the
morning cloud
And like the early dew that passes away,
Like chaff blown off from a threshing
floor
And like smoke from a chimney.
4 "Yet I *am* the LORD your God
Ever since the land of Egypt,
And you shall know no God but Me;
For *there is* no savior besides Me.
5 I knew you in the wilderness,
In the land of great drought.
6 When they had pasture, they were
filled;
They were filled and their heart was
exalted;
Therefore they forgot Me.
7 "So I will be to them like a lion;

Like a leopard by the road I will lurk;
8 I will meet them like a bear deprived *of her cubs;*
I will tear open their rib cage,
And there I will devour them like a lion.
The wild beast shall tear them.

9 "O Israel, you are destroyed,
But your help *is* from Me.
10 I will be your King;
Where *is any other,*
That he may save you in all your cities?
And your judges to whom you said,
'Give me a king and princes'?
11 I gave you a king in My anger,
And took *him* away in My wrath.

12 "The iniquity of Ephraim *is* bound up;
His sin *is* stored up.
13 The sorrows of a woman in childbirth shall come upon him.
He *is* an unwise son,
For he should not stay long where children are born.

14 "I will ransom them from the power of the grave;
I will redeem them from death.
O Death, I will be your plagues!
O Grave, I will be your destruction!
Pity is hidden from My eyes."

13:14 Placing the strong affirmation of deliverance so abruptly after a denunciation intensified the wonder of His unrequited love (11:8,9; Lev. 26:44). This can apply to God's restoration of Israel from Assyria, and in future times from all the lands of the Dispersion, preserving them and bringing them back to their land for the kingdom of Messiah (Ezek. 37). It also speaks of the time of personal resurrection as in Daniel 12:2,3. Repentant Israelites will be restored to the land and even raised from death to glory. Paul uses this text in 1 Corinthians 15:55 to celebrate the future resurrection of the church. The Messiah's great victory over death and the grave is the firstfruits of the full harvest to come, when all believers will likewise experience the power of His resurrection.

15 Though he is fruitful among *his* brethren,
An east wind shall come;
The wind of the LORD shall come up from the wilderness.
Then his spring shall become dry,
And his fountain shall be dried up.
He shall plunder the treasury of every desirable prize.
16 Samaria is held guilty,
For she has rebelled against her God.
They shall fall by the sword,
Their infants shall be dashed in pieces,
And their women with child ripped open.

14 O Israel, return to the LORD your God,
For you have stumbled because of your iniquity;
2 Take words with you,
And return to the LORD.
Say to Him,
"Take away all iniquity;
Receive *us* graciously,
For we will offer the sacrifices of our lips.
3 Assyria shall not save us,
We will not ride on horses,
Nor will we say anymore to the work of our hands, *'You are* our gods.'
For in You the fatherless finds mercy."

4 "I will heal their backsliding,
I will love them freely,
For My anger has turned away from him.
5 I will be like the dew to Israel;
He shall grow like the lily,
And lengthen his roots like Lebanon.
6 His branches shall spread;
His beauty shall be like an olive tree,
And his fragrance like Lebanon.
7 Those who dwell under his shadow shall return;
They shall be revived *like* grain,
And grow like a vine.
Their scent *shall be* like the wine of Lebanon.

8 "Ephraim *shall say,* 'What have I to do anymore with idols?'
I have heard and observed him.
I *am* like a green cypress tree;
Your fruit is found in Me."

9 Who *is* wise?
Let him understand these things.
Who is prudent?
Let him know them.
For the ways of the LORD *are* right;
The righteous walk in them,
But transgressors stumble in them.

Psalm 140:1–5

To the Chief Musician. A Psalm of David.

Deliver me, O LORD, from evil men;
Preserve me from violent men,

2 Who plan evil things in *their* hearts;
They continually gather together *for* war.
3 They sharpen their tongues like a serpent;
The poison of asps *is* under their lips. Selah
4 Keep me, O LORD, from the hands of the wicked;
Preserve me from violent men,
Who have purposed to make my steps stumble.
5 The proud have hidden a snare for me, and cords;
They have spread a net by the wayside;
They have set traps for me. Selah

Proverbs 29:23

23 A man's pride will bring him low,
But the humble in spirit will retain honor.

Revelation 1:1–20

1 The Revelation of Jesus Christ, which God
gave Him to show His servants things which
must shortly take place. And He sent and signified *it* by His angel to His servant John, 2who
bore witness to the word of God, and to the
testimony of Jesus Christ, to all things that he
saw. 3Blessed *is* he who reads and those who
hear the words of this prophecy, and keep
those things which are written in it; for the
time *is* near.
4John, to the seven churches which are in
Asia:

1:4 seven churches which are in Asia. Asia Minor, equivalent to modern Turkey, was composed of 7 postal districts. At the center of those districts were 7 key cities which served as central points for the dissemination of information. It is to the churches in those cities that John writes. **who is and who was and who is to come.** God's eternal presence is not limited by time. He has always been present and will come in the future. **the seven Spirits.** There are 2 possible meanings: 1) a reference to Isaiah's prophecy concerning the 7-fold ministry of the Holy Spirit (Is. 11:2); or 2) more likely, it is a reference to the lampstand with 7 lamps (a menorah) in Zechariah—also a description of the Holy Spirit (4:5; 5:6; Zech. 4:1–10). In either case, 7 is the number of completeness, so John is identifying the fullness of the Holy Spirit.

Grace to you and peace from Him who is
and who was and who is to come, and from the
seven Spirits who are before His throne, 5and
from Jesus Christ, the faithful witness, the
firstborn from the dead, and the ruler over the
kings of the earth.
To Him who loved us and washed us from
our sins in His own blood, 6and has made us
kings and priests to His God and Father, to
Him *be* glory and dominion forever and ever.
Amen.
7Behold, He is coming with clouds, and
every eye will see Him, even they who pierced
Him. And all the tribes of the earth will mourn
because of Him. Even so, Amen.
8"I am the Alpha and the Omega, *the*
Beginning and *the* End," says the Lord, "who
is and who was and who is to come, the Almighty."
9I, John, both your brother and companion
in the tribulation and kingdom and patience of
Jesus Christ, was on the island that is called
Patmos for the word of God and for the testimony of Jesus Christ. 10I was in the Spirit on
the Lord's Day, and I heard behind me a loud
voice, as of a trumpet, 11saying, "I am the

1:10 in the Spirit. This was not a dream. John was supernaturally transported out of the material world awake—not sleeping—to an experience beyond the normal senses. The Holy Spirit empowered his senses to perceive revelation from God (Acts 10:11). **Lord's Day.** This phrase appears in many early Christian writings and refers to Sunday, the day of the Lord's resurrection. Some have suggested this phrase refers to "the Day of the Lord," but the context doesn't support that interpretation, and the grammatical form of the word "Lord" is adjectival, thus "the Lord's day." **loud voice.** Throughout Revelation, a loud sound or voice indicates the solemnity of what God is about to reveal.

Alpha and the Omega, the First and the Last,"
and, "What you see, write in a book and send
it to the seven churches which are in Asia: to
Ephesus, to Smyrna, to Pergamos, to Thyatira,
to Sardis, to Philadelphia, and to Laodicea."
12Then I turned to see the voice that spoke
with me. And having turned I saw seven gold-
en lampstands, 13and in the midst of the seven
lampstands *One* like the Son of Man, clothed
with a garment down to the feet and girded
about the chest with a golden band. 14His head

and hair *were* white like wool, as white as snow,
and His eyes like a flame of fire; [15]His feet *were*
like fine brass, as if refined in a furnace, and
His voice as the sound of many waters; [16]He had
in His right hand seven stars, out of His mouth
went a sharp two-edged sword, and His countenance *was* like the sun shining in its strength.
[17]And when I saw Him, I fell at His feet as dead.
But He laid His right hand on me, saying to me,
"Do not be afraid; I am the First and the Last. [18]I
am He who lives, and was dead, and behold, I
am alive forevermore. Amen. And I have the
keys of Hades and of Death. [19]Write the things
which you have seen, and the things which are,
and the things which will take place after this.
[20]The mystery of the seven stars which you saw
in My right hand, and the seven golden lampstands: The seven stars are the angels of the
seven churches, and the seven lampstands
which you saw are the seven churches.

1:17 fell at His feet. A common response to seeing the awesome glory of the Lord (Gen. 17:3; Num. 16:22; Ezek. 1:28; Is. 6:1–8; Acts 9:4). **First and the Last.** Jesus Christ applies this Old Testament name for Yahweh (22:13; Is. 41:4; 44:6; 48:12) to Himself, clearly claiming to be God. Idols will come and go. He was before them, and He will remain after them.

DAY 11: What is the background for the Book of Revelation?

Revelation begins with John, the last surviving apostle and an old man, in exile on the small barren island of Patmos, located in the Aegean Sea southwest of Ephesus. The Roman authorities had banished him there because of his faithful preaching of the gospel (1:9). While on Patmos, John received a series of visions that laid out the future history of the world.

When he was arrested, John was in Ephesus, ministering to the church there and in the surrounding cities. Seeking to strengthen those congregations, he could no longer minister to them in person and, following the divine command (1:11), John addressed Revelation to them (1:4). The churches had begun to feel the effects of persecution; at least one man—probably a pastor—had already been martyred (2:13), and John himself had been exiled. But the storm of persecution was about to break in full fury upon the 7 churches so dear to the apostle's heart (2:10). To those churches, Revelation provided a message of hope: God is in sovereign control of all the events of human history; and though evil often seems pervasive and wicked men all-powerful, their ultimate doom is certain. Christ will come in glory to judge and rule.

Unlike most books of the Bible, Revelation contains its own title: "The Revelation of Jesus Christ" (1:1). "Revelation" (Greek, *apokalupsis*) means "an uncovering," "an unveiling," or "a disclosure." In all its uses, "revelation" refers to something or someone, once hidden, becoming visible. What this book reveals or unveils is Jesus Christ in glory. Truths about Him and His final victory, that the rest of Scripture merely allude to, become clearly visible through revelation about Jesus Christ.

DECEMBER 12

Joel 1:1–3:21

1 The word of the LORD that came to Joel the
son of Pethuel.

2 Hear this, you elders,
And give ear, all you inhabitants of the land!
Has *anything like* this happened in your days,
Or even in the days of your fathers?
3 Tell your children about it,
Let your children *tell* their children,
And their children another generation.
4 What the chewing locust left, the swarming locust has eaten;
What the swarming locust left, the crawling locust has eaten;
And what the crawling locust left, the consuming locust has eaten.
5 Awake, you drunkards, and weep;
And wail, all you drinkers of wine,
Because of the new wine,
For it has been cut off from your mouth.
6 For a nation has come up against My land,
Strong, and without number;
His teeth *are* the teeth of a lion,
And he has the fangs of a fierce lion.

1:2 Hear...give ear. The gravity of the situation demanded the undivided focus of their senses, emphasizing the need to make a conscious, purposeful decision in the matter. The terminology was commonly used in "lawsuit" passages (Is. 1:2; Hos. 4:1), intimating that Israel was found guilty and that the present judgment was her "sentence." **elders...all you inhabitants.** The former term refers to the civil and religious leaders, who, in light of their position, were exhorted to lead by example the entire population toward repentance.

7 He has laid waste My vine,
And ruined My fig tree;
He has stripped it bare and thrown *it* away;
Its branches are made white.

8 Lament like a virgin girded with sackcloth
For the husband of her youth.
9 The grain offering and the drink offering
Have been cut off from the house of the LORD;
The priests mourn, who minister to the LORD.
10 The field is wasted,
The land mourns;
For the grain is ruined,
The new wine is dried up,
The oil fails.
11 Be ashamed, you farmers,
Wail, you vinedressers,
For the wheat and the barley;
Because the harvest of the field has perished.
12 The vine has dried up,
And the fig tree has withered;
The pomegranate tree,
The palm tree also,
And the apple tree—
All the trees of the field are withered;
Surely joy has withered away from the sons of men.

13 Gird yourselves and lament, you priests;
Wail, you who minister before the altar;
Come, lie all night in sackcloth,
You who minister to my God;
For the grain offering and the drink offering
Are withheld from the house of your God.
14 Consecrate a fast,
Call a sacred assembly;
Gather the elders
And all the inhabitants of the land
Into the house of the LORD your God,
And cry out to the LORD.

15 Alas for the day!
For the day of the LORD *is* at hand;
It shall come as destruction from the Almighty.
16 Is not the food cut off before our eyes,
Joy and gladness from the house of our God?
17 The seed shrivels under the clods,
Storehouses are in shambles;
Barns are broken down,
For the grain has withered.
18 How the animals groan!
The herds of cattle are restless,
Because they have no pasture;
Even the flocks of sheep suffer punishment.

19 O LORD, to You I cry out;
For fire has devoured the open pastures,
And a flame has burned all the trees of the field.
20 The beasts of the field also cry out to You,
For the water brooks are dried up,
And fire has devoured the open pastures.

2 Blow the trumpet in Zion,
And sound an alarm in My holy mountain!
Let all the inhabitants of the land tremble;
For the day of the LORD is coming,
For it is at hand:
2 A day of darkness and gloominess,
A day of clouds and thick darkness,
Like the morning *clouds* spread over the mountains.
A people *come,* great and strong,
The like of whom has never been;
Nor will there ever be any *such* after them,
Even for many successive generations.

3 A fire devours before them,
And behind them a flame burns;
The land *is* like the Garden of Eden before them,
And behind them a desolate wilderness;
Surely nothing shall escape them.
4 Their appearance is like the appearance of horses;
And like swift steeds, so they run.

5 With a noise like chariots
Over mountaintops they leap,
Like the noise of a flaming fire that
devours the stubble,
Like a strong people set in battle array.

6 Before them the people writhe in pain;
All faces are drained of color.
7 They run like mighty men,
They climb the wall like men of war;
Every one marches in formation,
And they do not break ranks.
8 They do not push one another;
Every one marches in his own column.
Though they lunge between the
weapons,
They are not cut down.
9 They run to and fro in the city,
They run on the wall;
They climb into the houses,
They enter at the windows like a thief.

10 The earth quakes before them,
The heavens tremble;
The sun and moon grow dark,
And the stars diminish their brightness.
11 The LORD gives voice before His army,
For His camp is very great;
For strong *is the One* who executes
His word.
For the day of the LORD *is* great and
very terrible;
Who can endure it?

12 "Now, therefore," says the LORD,
"Turn to Me with all your heart,
With fasting, with weeping, and with
mourning."
13 So rend your heart, and not your
garments;
Return to the LORD your God,
For He *is* gracious and merciful,
Slow to anger, and of great kindness;
And He relents from doing harm.
14 Who knows *if* He will turn and relent,
And leave a blessing behind Him—
A grain offering and a drink offering
For the LORD your God?

15 Blow the trumpet in Zion,
Consecrate a fast,
Call a sacred assembly;
16 Gather the people,
Sanctify the congregation,
Assemble the elders,
Gather the children and nursing babes;
Let the bridegroom go out from his
chamber,
And the bride from her dressing room.

17 Let the priests, who minister to the LORD,
Weep between the porch and the altar;
Let them say, "Spare Your people,
O LORD,
And do not give Your heritage
to reproach,
That the nations should rule over them.
Why should they say among the peoples,
'Where *is* their God?' "

18 Then the LORD will be zealous for
His land,
And pity His people.
19 The LORD will answer and say
to His people,
"Behold, I will send you grain and new
wine and oil,
And you will be satisfied by them;
I will no longer make you a reproach
among the nations.

20 "But I will remove far from you the
northern *army,*
And will drive him away into a barren
and desolate land,
With his face toward the eastern sea
And his back toward the western sea;
His stench will come up,
And his foul odor will rise,
Because he has done monstrous things."

21 Fear not, O land;
Be glad and rejoice,
For the LORD has done marvelous
things!
22 Do not be afraid, you beasts of the
field;
For the open pastures are springing up,
And the tree bears its fruit;
The fig tree and the vine yield their
strength.
23 Be glad then, you children of Zion,
And rejoice in the LORD your God;
For He has given you the former rain
faithfully,
And He will cause the rain to come
down for you—
The former rain,
And the latter rain in the first *month.*
24 The threshing floors shall be full of
wheat,
And the vats shall overflow with new
wine and oil.

25 "So I will restore to you the years that
the swarming locust has eaten,
The crawling locust,
The consuming locust,
And the chewing locust,
My great army which I sent among you.

26 You shall eat in plenty and be satisfied,
And praise the name of the LORD your God,
Who has dealt wondrously with you;
And My people shall never be put to shame.
27 Then you shall know that I *am* in the midst of Israel:
I *am* the LORD your God
And there is no other.
My people shall never be put to shame.

28 "And it shall come to pass afterward
That I will pour out My Spirit on all flesh;
Your sons and your daughters shall prophesy,
Your old men shall dream dreams,
Your young men shall see visions.

2:28 afterward. The abundance of material blessings would be followed by the outpouring of spiritual blessings. When coupled with the other temporal phrases within the passage ("in those days" [v. 29] and "before the coming of the great and awesome day of the LORD" [v. 31]), the term points to a Second Advent fulfillment time frame. **all flesh.** Since the context is "your sons and your daughters," "all flesh" best refers to the house of Israel only. The nations are the recipients of God's wrath, not the effusion of His Spirit (3:2,9ff.).

29 And also on *My* menservants and on *My* maidservants
I will pour out My Spirit in those days.

30 "And I will show wonders in the heavens and in the earth:
Blood and fire and pillars of smoke.
31 The sun shall be turned into darkness,
And the moon into blood,
Before the coming of the great and awesome day of the LORD.
32 And it shall come to pass
That whoever calls on the name of the LORD
Shall be saved.
For in Mount Zion and in Jerusalem there shall be deliverance,
As the LORD has said,
Among the remnant whom the LORD calls.

3 "For behold, in those days and at that time,
When I bring back the captives of Judah and Jerusalem,
2 I will also gather all nations,
And bring them down to the Valley of Jehoshaphat;
And I will enter into judgment with them there
On account of My people, My heritage Israel,
Whom they have scattered among the nations;
They have also divided up My land.
3 They have cast lots for My people,
Have given a boy *as payment* for a harlot,
And sold a girl for wine, that they may drink.

4 "Indeed, what have you to do with Me,
O Tyre and Sidon, and all the coasts of Philistia?
Will you retaliate against Me?
But if you retaliate against Me,
Swiftly and speedily I will return your retaliation upon your own head;
5 Because you have taken My silver and My gold,
And have carried into your temples My prized possessions.
6 Also the people of Judah and the people of Jerusalem
You have sold to the Greeks,
That you may remove them far from their borders.

7 "Behold, I will raise them
Out of the place to which you have sold them,
And will return your retaliation upon your own head.
8 I will sell your sons and your daughters
Into the hand of the people of Judah,
And they will sell them to the Sabeans,
To a people far off;
For the LORD has spoken."

9 Proclaim this among the nations:
"Prepare for war!
Wake up the mighty men,
Let all the men of war draw near,
Let them come up.
10 Beat your plowshares into swords
And your pruning hooks into spears;
Let the weak say, 'I *am* strong.' "
11 Assemble and come, all you nations,
And gather together all around.
Cause Your mighty ones to go down there, O LORD.

12 "Let the nations be wakened, and come up to the Valley of Jehoshaphat;
For there I will sit to judge all the surrounding nations.

13 Put in the sickle, for the harvest is ripe.
Come, go down;
For the winepress is full,
The vats overflow—
For their wickedness *is* great."

14 Multitudes, multitudes in the valley
of decision!
For the day of the LORD *is* near in the
valley of decision.
15 The sun and moon will grow dark,
And the stars will diminish their
brightness.
16 The LORD also will roar from Zion,
And utter His voice from Jerusalem;
The heavens and earth will shake;
But the LORD will be a shelter for His
people,
And the strength of the children
of Israel.

17 "So you shall know that I *am* the LORD
your God,
Dwelling in Zion My holy mountain.
Then Jerusalem shall be holy,
And no aliens shall ever pass through
her again."
18 And it will come to pass in that day
That the mountains shall drip
with new wine,
The hills shall flow with milk,
And all the brooks of Judah shall be
flooded with water;
A fountain shall flow from the house of
the LORD
And water the Valley of Acacias.

19 "Egypt shall be a desolation,
And Edom a desolate wilderness,
Because of violence *against* the people
of Judah,
For they have shed innocent blood in
their land.
20 But Judah shall abide forever,
And Jerusalem from generation to
generation.
21 For I will acquit them of the guilt of
bloodshed, whom I had not
acquitted;
For the LORD dwells in Zion."

Psalm 140:6–13

6 I said to the LORD: "You *are* my God;
Hear the voice of my supplications,
O LORD.
7 O GOD the Lord, the strength of my
salvation,
You have covered my head in the day
of battle.
8 Do not grant, O LORD, the desires of
the wicked;
Do not further his *wicked* scheme,
Lest they be exalted. Selah

9 "*As for* the head of those who
surround me,
Let the evil of their lips cover them;
10 Let burning coals fall upon them;
Let them be cast into the fire,
Into deep pits, that they rise not up
again.
11 Let not a slanderer be established in
the earth;
Let evil hunt the violent man to
overthrow *him*."

12 I know that the LORD will
maintain
The cause of the afflicted,
And justice for the poor.
13 Surely the righteous shall give thanks
to Your name;
The upright shall dwell in Your presence.

Proverbs 29:24

24 Whoever is a partner with a thief hates
his own life;
He swears to tell the truth, but reveals
nothing.

Revelation 2:1–29

2 "To the angel of the church of Ephesus
write,
'These things says He who holds the seven
stars in His right hand, who walks in the midst
of the seven golden lampstands: 2"I know your
works, your labor, your patience, and that you
cannot bear those who are evil. And you have
tested those who say they are apostles and are
not, and have found them liars; 3and you have
persevered and have patience, and have labored
for My name's sake and have not become weary.
4Nevertheless I have *this* against you, that you
have left your first love. 5Remember therefore

2:4 left your first love. To be a Christian is to love the Lord Jesus Christ (John 14:21,23; 1 Cor. 16:22). But the Ephesians' passion and fervor for Christ had become cold, mechanical orthodoxy. Their doctrinal and moral purity, their undiminished zeal for the truth, and their disciplined service were no substitute for the love for Christ they had forsaken.

2:8 Smyrna. Smyrna means "myrrh," the substance used for perfume and often for anointing a dead body for aromatic purposes. Called the crown of Asia, this ancient city (modern Izmir, Turkey) was the most beautiful in Asia Minor and a center of science and medicine. Always on the winner's side in the Roman wars, Smyrna's intense loyalty to Rome resulted in a strong emperor-worship cult. Fifty years after John's death, Polycarp, the pastor of the church in Smyrna, was burned alive at the age of 86 for refusing to worship Caesar. A large Jewish community in the city also proved hostile to the early church.

2:13 where Satan's throne *is*. The headquarters of satanic opposition and a Gentile base for false religions. On the acropolis in Pergamos was a huge, throne-shaped altar to Zeus. In addition, Asklepios, the god of healing, was the god most associated with Pergamos. His snakelike form is still the medical symbol today. The famous medical school connected to his temple mingled medicine with superstition. One prescription called for the worshiper to sleep on the temple floor, allowing snakes to crawl over his body and infuse him with their healing power.

from where you have fallen; repent and do the
first works, or else I will come to you quickly
and remove your lampstand from its place—
unless you repent. [6]But this you have, that you
hate the deeds of the Nicolaitans, which I also
hate.
[7]"He who has an ear, let him hear what the
Spirit says to the churches. To him who overcomes I will give to eat from the tree of life,
which is in the midst of the Paradise of God." '
[8]"And to the angel of the church in Smyrna
write,
'These things says the First and the Last,
who was dead, and came to life: [9]"I know your
works, tribulation, and poverty (but you are
rich); and *I know* the blasphemy of those who
say they are Jews and are not, but *are* a synagogue of Satan. [10]Do not fear any of those
things which you are about to suffer. Indeed,
the devil is about to throw *some* of you into
prison, that you may be tested, and you will
have tribulation ten days. Be faithful until
death, and I will give you the crown of life.
[11]"He who has an ear, let him hear what the
Spirit says to the churches. He who overcomes
shall not be hurt by the second death." '
[12]"And to the angel of the church in
Pergamos write,
'These things says He who has the sharp
two-edged sword: [13]"I know your works, and
where you dwell, where Satan's throne *is*. And
you hold fast to My name, and did not deny
My faith even in the days in which Antipas *was*
My faithful martyr, who was killed among you,
where Satan dwells. [14]But I have a few things
against you, because you have there those
who hold the doctrine of Balaam, who taught
Balak to put a stumbling block before the children of Israel, to eat things sacrificed to idols,
and to commit sexual immorality. [15]Thus you
also have those who hold the doctrine of the
Nicolaitans, which thing I hate. [16]Repent, or
else I will come to you quickly and will fight
against them with the sword of My mouth.
[17]"He who has an ear, let him hear what the
Spirit says to the churches. To him who overcomes I will give some of the hidden manna to
eat. And I will give him a white stone, and on the
stone a new name written which no one knows
except him who receives *it*." '
[18]"And to the angel of the church in Thyatira
write,
'These things says the Son of God, who has
eyes like a flame of fire, and His feet like fine
brass: [19]"I know your works, love, service,
faith, and your patience; and *as* for your
works, the last *are* more than the first. [20]Nevertheless I have a few things against you,
because you allow that woman Jezebel, who
calls herself a prophetess, to teach and seduce
My servants to commit sexual immorality and
eat things sacrificed to idols. [21]And I gave her
time to repent of her sexual immorality, and
she did not repent. [22]Indeed I will cast her into
a sickbed, and those who commit adultery
with her into great tribulation, unless they
repent of their deeds. [23]I will kill her children
with death, and all the churches shall know

2:24 the depths of Satan. This unbelievable libertinism and license was the fruit of pregnostic teaching that one was free to engage and explore the sphere of Satan and participate in evil with the body without harming the spirit.

that I am He who searches the minds and
hearts. And I will give to each one of you
according to your works.
24 "Now to you I say, and to the rest in Thyatira,
as many as do not have this doctrine, who have
not known the depths of Satan, as they say, I
will put on you no other burden. 25 But hold fast
what you have till I come. 26 And he who overcomes, and keeps My works until the end, to
him I will give power over the nations—

27 *'He shall rule them with a rod of iron;*
They shall be dashed to pieces like the potter's vessels'—

as I also have received from My Father; 28 and
I will give him the morning star.
29 "He who has an ear, let him hear what the
Spirit says to the churches." '

DAY 12: Who was the prophet Joel, and what was he writing about?

The author identified himself only as "Joel the son of Pethuel" (1:1). The prophecy provides little else about the man. Even the name of his father is not mentioned elsewhere in the Old Testament. Although he displayed a profound zeal for the temple sacrifices (1:9; 2:13–16), his familiarity with pastoral and agricultural life and his separation from the priests (1:13,14; 2:17) suggest he was not a Levite. Extrabiblical tradition records that he was from the tribe of Reuben, from the town of Bethom or Bethharam, located northeast of the Dead Sea on the border of Reuben and Gad. The context of the prophecy, however, hints that he was a Judean from the Jerusalem vicinity, since the tone of a stranger is absent.

The theme of Joel is the Day of the Lord. It permeates all parts of Joel's message, making it the most sustained treatment in the entire Old Testament (1:15; 3:14). The phrase is employed 19 times by 8 different Old Testament authors (Is. 2:12; 13:6,9; Ezek. 13:5; 30:3; Joel 1:15; 2:1,11,31; 3:14; Amos 5:18 [2x],20; Obad. 15; Zeph. 1:7,14 [2x]; Zech. 14:1; Mal. 4:5). The phrase does not have reference to a chronological time period, but to a general period of wrath and judgment uniquely belonging to the Lord. It is exclusively the day which unveils His character—mighty, powerful, and holy, thus terrifying His enemies. The Day of the Lord does not always refer to an eschatological event; on occasion it has a near historical fulfillment, as seen in Ezekiel 13:5, where it speaks of the Babylonian conquest and destruction of Jerusalem. As is common in prophecy, the near fulfillment is a historic event upon which to comprehend the more distant, eschatological fulfillment.

DECEMBER 13

Amos 1:1–3:15

1 The words of Amos, who was among the sheep-
breeders of Tekoa, which he saw concerning
Israel in the days of Uzziah king of Judah, and in
the days of Jeroboam the son of Joash, king of
Israel, two years before the earthquake.
2 And he said:

"The LORD roars from Zion,
And utters His voice from Jerusalem;
The pastures of the shepherds mourn,
And the top of Carmel withers."

3 Thus says the LORD:

"For three transgressions of Damascus, and for four,
I will not turn away its *punishment,*
Because they have threshed Gilead with implements of iron.
4 But I will send a fire into the house of Hazael,
Which shall devour the palaces of Ben-Hadad.
5 I will also break the *gate* bar of Damascus,
And cut off the inhabitant from the Valley of Aven,
And the one who holds the scepter from Beth Eden.
The people of Syria shall go captive to Kir,"
Says the LORD.

6 Thus says the LORD:

"For three transgressions of Gaza, and for four,
I will not turn away its *punishment,*
Because they took captive the whole captivity
To deliver *them* up to Edom.
7 But I will send a fire upon the wall of Gaza,
Which shall devour its palaces.
8 I will cut off the inhabitant from Ashdod,
And the one who holds the scepter from Ashkelon;

I will turn My hand against Ekron,
And the remnant of the Philistines
shall perish,"
Says the Lord GOD.

9 Thus says the LORD:

"For three transgressions of Tyre,
and for four,
I will not turn away its *punishment,*
Because they delivered up the whole
captivity to Edom,
And did not remember the covenant
of brotherhood.
10 But I will send a fire upon the wall of
Tyre,
Which shall devour its palaces."

11 Thus says the LORD:

"For three transgressions of Edom,
and for four,
I will not turn away its *punishment,*
Because he pursued his brother with
the sword,
And cast off all pity;
His anger tore perpetually,
And he kept his wrath forever.
12 But I will send a fire upon Teman,
Which shall devour the palaces of
Bozrah."

13 Thus says the LORD:

"For three transgressions of the people
of Ammon, and for four,
I will not turn away its *punishment,*
Because they ripped open the women
with child in Gilead,
That they might enlarge their territory.
14 But I will kindle a fire in the wall of
Rabbah,
And it shall devour its palaces,
Amid shouting in the day of battle,
And a tempest in the day of the
whirlwind.
15 Their king shall go into captivity,
He and his princes together,"
Says the LORD.

2 Thus says the LORD:

"For three transgressions of Moab,
and for four,
I will not turn away its *punishment,*
Because he burned the bones of the
king of Edom to lime.
2 But I will send a fire upon Moab,
And it shall devour the palaces of
Kerioth;
Moab shall die with tumult,
With shouting *and* trumpet sound.
3 And I will cut off the judge from its
midst,
And slay all its princes with him,"
Says the LORD.

4 Thus says the LORD:

"For three transgressions of Judah,
and for four,
I will not turn away its *punishment,*
Because they have despised the law of
the LORD,
And have not kept His
commandments.
Their lies lead them astray,
Lies which their fathers followed.
5 But I will send a fire upon Judah,
And it shall devour the palaces
of Jerusalem."

6 Thus says the LORD:

"For three transgressions of Israel,
and for four,
I will not turn away its *punishment,*
Because they sell the righteous for
silver,
And the poor for a pair of sandals.
7 They pant after the dust of the earth
which is on the head of the poor,
And pervert the way of the humble.
A man and his father go in to the *same*
girl,
To defile My holy name.
8 They lie down by every altar on clothes
taken in pledge,
And drink the wine of the condemned
in the house of their god.

9 "Yet *it was* I *who* destroyed the Amorite
before them,
Whose height *was* like the height of
the cedars,
And he *was as* strong as the oaks;
Yet I destroyed his fruit above
And his roots beneath.
10 Also *it was* I *who* brought you up from
the land of Egypt,
And led you forty years through the
wilderness,
To possess the land of the Amorite.
11 I raised up some of your sons as
prophets,
And some of your young men as
Nazirites.
Is it not so, O you children of Israel?"
Says the LORD.
12 "But you gave the Nazirites wine to
drink,

And commanded the prophets saying,
'Do not prophesy!'

13 "Behold, I am weighed down by you,
As a cart full of sheaves is weighed down.
14 Therefore flight shall perish from the swift,
The strong shall not strengthen his power,
Nor shall the mighty deliver himself;
15 He shall not stand who handles the bow,
The swift of foot shall not escape,
Nor shall he who rides a horse deliver himself.
16 The most courageous men of might
Shall flee naked in that day,"
Says the LORD.

3 Hear this word that the LORD has spoken
against you, O children of Israel, against
the whole family which I brought up from the
land of Egypt, saying:

2 "You only have I known of all the families of the earth;
Therefore I will punish you for all your iniquities."
3 Can two walk together, unless they are agreed?
4 Will a lion roar in the forest, when he has no prey?
Will a young lion cry out of his den, if he has caught nothing?
5 Will a bird fall into a snare on the earth, where there is no trap for it?
Will a snare spring up from the earth, if it has caught nothing at all?
6 If a trumpet is blown in a city, will not the people be afraid?
If there is calamity in a city, will not the LORD have done *it?*

7 Surely the Lord GOD does nothing,
Unless He reveals His secret to His servants the prophets.
8 A lion has roared!
Who will not fear?
The Lord GOD has spoken!
Who can but prophesy?

9 "Proclaim in the palaces at Ashdod,
And in the palaces in the land of Egypt, and say:
'Assemble on the mountains of Samaria;
See great tumults in her midst,
And the oppressed within her.
10 For they do not know to do right,'
Says the LORD,
'Who store up violence and robbery in their palaces.' "

11 Therefore thus says the Lord GOD:

"An adversary *shall be* all around the land;
He shall sap your strength from you,
And your palaces shall be plundered."

12 Thus says the LORD:

"As a shepherd takes from the mouth of a lion
Two legs or a piece of an ear,
So shall the children of Israel be taken out
Who dwell in Samaria—
In the corner of a bed and on the edge of a couch!
13 Hear and testify against the house of Jacob,"
Says the Lord GOD, the God of hosts,
14 "That in the day I punish Israel for their transgressions,
I will also visit *destruction* on the altars of Bethel;
And the horns of the altar shall be cut off
And fall to the ground.
15 I will destroy the winter house along with the summer house;
The houses of ivory shall perish,
And the great houses shall have an end,"
Says the LORD.

Psalm 141:1–4

A Psalm of David.

LORD, I cry out to You;
Make haste to me!
Give ear to my voice when I cry out to You.
2 Let my prayer be set before You *as* incense,
The lifting up of my hands *as* the evening sacrifice.

3 Set a guard, O LORD, over my mouth;
Keep watch over the door of my lips.
4 Do not incline my heart to any evil thing,
To practice wicked works
With men who work iniquity;
And do not let me eat of their delicacies.

Proverbs 29:25

25 The fear of man brings a snare,
But whoever trusts in the LORD shall be safe.

Revelation 3:1–22

3 "And to the angel of the church in Sardis
write,
'These things says He who has the seven
Spirits of God and the seven stars: "I know your
works, that you have a name that you are alive,
but you are dead. 2Be watchful, and strengthen
the things which remain, that are ready to die,
for I have not found your works perfect before
God. 3Remember therefore how you have
received and heard; hold fast and repent. Therefore if you will not watch, I will come upon you
as a thief, and you will not know what hour I will
come upon you. 4You have a few names even in
Sardis who have not defiled their garments; and
they shall walk with Me in white, for they are
worthy. 5He who overcomes shall be clothed in
white garments, and I will not blot out his name
from the Book of Life; but I will confess his
name before My Father and before His angels.
6"He who has an ear, let him hear what the
Spirit says to the churches." '
7"And to the angel of the church in
Philadelphia write,
'These things says He who is holy, He who
is true, *"He who has the key of David, He who
opens and no one shuts, and shuts and no one
opens"*: 8"I know your works. See, I have set
before you an open door, and no one can shut
it; for you have a little strength, have kept My
word, and have not denied My name. 9Indeed
I will make *those* of the synagogue of Satan,
who say they are Jews and are not, but lie—
indeed I will make them come and worship
before your feet, and to know that I have loved
you. 10Because you have kept My command to
persevere, I also will keep you from the hour
of trial which shall come upon the whole
world, to test those who dwell on the earth.
11Behold, I am coming quickly! Hold fast what
you have, that no one may take your crown.
12He who overcomes, I will make him a pillar
in the temple of My God, and he shall go out
no more. I will write on him the name of My
God and the name of the city of My God, the
New Jerusalem, which comes down out of
heaven from My God. And *I will write on him*
My new name.
13"He who has an ear, let him hear what the
Spirit says to the churches." '
14"And to the angel of the church of the
Laodiceans write,
'These things says the Amen, the Faithful
and True Witness, the Beginning of the creation of God: 15"I know your works, that you
are neither cold nor hot. I could wish you were
cold or hot. 16So then, because you are lukewarm, and neither cold nor hot, I will vomit
you out of My mouth. 17Because you say, 'I am
rich, have become wealthy, and have need of
nothing'—and do not know that you are
wretched, miserable, poor, blind, and naked—
18I counsel you to buy from Me gold refined in
the fire, that you may be rich; and white garments, that you may be clothed, *that* the
shame of your nakedness may not be
revealed; and anoint your eyes with eye salve,
that you may see. 19As many as I love, I rebuke
and chasten. Therefore be zealous and repent.
20Behold, I stand at the door and knock. If anyone hears My voice and opens the door, I will
come in to him and dine with him, and he with
Me. 21To him who overcomes I will grant to sit
with Me on My throne, as I also overcame and
sat down with My Father on His throne.
22"He who has an ear, let him hear what the
Spirit says to the churches." ' "

3:10 keep you from the hour of trial. Christ's description must refer to the time of tribulation, the 7-year period before Christ's earthly kingdom is consummated, featuring the unleashing of divine wrath in judgments expressed as seals, trumpets, and bowls. This period is described in detail throughout chapters 6–19. The latter half is called "the Great Tribulation" (7:14; Matt. 24:21) and is identified as to time in 11:2,3; 12:6,14; 13:5. The verb "to keep" is followed by a preposition whose normal meaning is "from" or "out of"—this phrase, "keep…from" supports the pretribulational Rapture of the church. This period is the same as Daniel's 70th week (Dan. 9:24–27) and "the time of Jacob's trouble" (Jer. 30:7).

3:16 lukewarm. I.e., tepid. Nearby Hierapolis was famous for its hot springs, and Colosse for its cold, refreshing mountain stream. But Laodicea had dirty, tepid water that flowed for miles through an underground aqueduct. Visitors, unaccustomed to it, immediately spat it out. The church at Laodicea was neither cold, openly rejecting Christ, nor hot, filled with spiritual zeal. Instead, its members were lukewarm, hypocrites professing to know Christ, but not truly belonging to Him (Matt. 7:21ff.). **I will vomit you out of My mouth.** Just like the tepid water of Laodicea, these self-deceived hypocrites sickened Christ.

DAY 13: Who was the prophet Amos, and what is the background behind his messages?

Amos was from Tekoa, a small village 10 miles south of Jerusalem. He was the only prophet to give his occupation before declaring his divine commission. He was not of priestly or noble descent, but worked as a "sheepbreeder" (1:1; 2 Kin. 3:4) and a "tender of sycamore fruit" (7:14) and was a contemporary of Jonah (2 Kin. 14:25), Hosea (Hos. 1:1), and Isaiah (Is. 1:1).

Amos was a Judean prophet called to deliver a message primarily to the northern tribes of Israel (7:15). Politically, it was a time of prosperity under the long and secure reign of Jeroboam II who, following the example of his father Joash (2 Kin. 13:25), significantly "restored the territory of Israel" (2 Kin. 14:25). It was also a time of peace with both Judah (5:5) and her more distant neighbors. The ever-present menace of Assyria was subdued earlier that century because of Nineveh's repentance at the preaching of Jonah (Jon. 3:10). Spiritually, however, it was a time of rampant corruption and moral decay (4:1; 5:10–13; 2 Kin. 14:24).

Amos addresses Israel's two primary sins: 1) an absence of true worship and 2) a lack of justice. In the midst of their ritualistic performance of worship, they were not pursuing the Lord with their hearts (4:4,5; 5:4–6) nor following His standard of justice with their neighbors (5:10–13; 6:12). This apostasy, evidenced by continual, willful rejection of the prophetic message of Amos, is promised divine judgment. Because of His covenant, however, the Lord will not abandon Israel altogether, but will bring future restoration to the righteous remnant (9:7–15).

DECEMBER 14

Amos 4:1–5:27

4 Hear this word, you cows of Bashan,
who *are* on the mountain
of Samaria,
Who oppress the poor,
Who crush the needy,
Who say to your husbands, "Bring
wine, let us drink!"
2 The Lord GOD has sworn by His
holiness:
"Behold, the days shall come upon you
When He will take you away with
fishhooks,
And your posterity with fishhooks.
3 You will go out *through* broken *walls*,
Each one straight ahead of her,
And you will be cast into Harmon,"
Says the LORD.

4 "Come to Bethel and transgress,
At Gilgal multiply transgression;
Bring your sacrifices every morning,
Your tithes every three days.
5 Offer a sacrifice of thanksgiving with
leaven,
Proclaim *and* announce the freewill
offerings;
For this you love,
You children of Israel!"
Says the Lord GOD.

6 "Also I gave you cleanness of teeth
in all your cities.
And lack of bread in all your places;
Yet you have not returned to Me,"
Says the LORD.

7 "I also withheld rain from you,
When *there were* still three months to
the harvest.
I made it rain on one city,
I withheld rain from another city.
One part was rained upon,
And where it did not rain the part
withered.
8 So two *or* three cities wandered to
another city to drink water,
But they were not satisfied;
Yet you have not returned to Me,"
Says the LORD.

9 "I blasted you with blight and mildew.
When your gardens increased,
Your vineyards,
Your fig trees,
And your olive trees,
The locust devoured *them;*
Yet you have not returned to Me,"
Says the LORD.

10 "I sent among you a plague after the
manner of Egypt;
Your young men I killed with a sword,
Along with your captive horses;
I made the stench of your camps come
up into your nostrils;
Yet you have not returned to Me,"
Says the LORD.

11 "I overthrew *some* of you,
As God overthrew Sodom and
Gomorrah,
And you were like a firebrand plucked
from the burning;

Yet you have not returned to Me,"
Says the LORD.

12 "Therefore thus will I do to you, O Israel;
Because I will do this to you,
Prepare to meet your God, O Israel!"

13 For behold,
He who forms mountains,
And creates the wind,
Who declares to man what his
thought *is,*
And makes the morning darkness,
Who treads the high places of the
earth—
The LORD God of hosts *is* His name.

5 Hear this word which I take up against you, a lamentation, O house of Israel:

2 The virgin of Israel has fallen;
She will rise no more.
She lies forsaken on her land;
There is no one to raise her up.

3 For thus says the Lord GOD:
"The city that goes out by a thousand
Shall have a hundred left,
And that which goes out by a hundred
Shall have ten left to the house of Israel."

4 For thus says the LORD to the house of Israel:
"Seek Me and live;
5 But do not seek Bethel,
Nor enter Gilgal,
Nor pass over to Beersheba;
For Gilgal shall surely go into captivity,
And Bethel shall come to nothing.
6 Seek the LORD and live,
Lest He break out like fire *in* the house
of Joseph,
And devour *it,*
With no one to quench *it* in Bethel—
7 You who turn justice to wormwood,
And lay righteousness to rest in the
earth!"
8 He made the Pleiades and Orion;
He turns the shadow of death into
morning
And makes the day dark as night;
He calls for the waters of the sea
And pours them out on the face of the
earth;
The LORD *is* His name.
9 He rains ruin upon the strong,
So that fury comes upon the fortress.
10 They hate the one who rebukes in the
gate,
And they abhor the one who speaks
uprightly.
11 Therefore, because you tread down
the poor
And take grain taxes from him,
Though you have built houses of hewn
stone,
Yet you shall not dwell in them;
You have planted pleasant vineyards,
But you shall not drink wine from them.
12 For I know your manifold transgressions
And your mighty sins:
Afflicting the just *and* taking bribes;
Diverting the poor *from justice* at the
gate.
13 Therefore the prudent keep silent
at that time,
For it *is* an evil time.

14 Seek good and not evil,
That you may live;
So the LORD God of hosts will be
with you,
As you have spoken.
15 Hate evil, love good;
Establish justice in the gate.
It may be that the LORD God of hosts
Will be gracious to the remnant
of Joseph.

16 Therefore the LORD God of hosts, the Lord,
says this:
"*There shall be* wailing in all streets,
And they shall say in all the highways,
'Alas! Alas!'
They shall call the farmer to mourning,
And skillful lamenters to wailing.
17 In all vineyards *there shall be* wailing,
For I will pass through you,"
Says the LORD.

18 Woe to you who desire the day
of the LORD!
For what good *is* the day of the LORD
to you?
It *will be* darkness, and not light.
19 It *will be* as though a man fled from a
lion,
And a bear met him!
Or *as though* he went into the house,
Leaned his hand on the wall,
And a serpent bit him!
20 *Is* not the day of the LORD darkness,
and not light?
Is it not very dark, with no brightness
in it?

21 "I hate, I despise your feast days,
And I do not savor your sacred
assemblies.
22 Though you offer Me burnt offerings
and your grain offerings,

I will not accept *them*,
Nor will I regard your fattened peace
offerings.
23 Take away from Me the noise
of your songs,
For I will not hear the melody of your
stringed instruments.
24 But let justice run down like water,
And righteousness like a mighty stream.

25 "Did you offer Me sacrifices
and offerings
In the wilderness forty years,
O house of Israel?
26 You also carried Sikkuth your king
And Chiun, your idols,
The star of your gods,
Which you made for yourselves.
27 Therefore I will send you into captivity
beyond Damascus,"
Says the LORD, whose name *is* the God
of hosts.

5:25,26 In addition to worshiping the Lord in the wilderness, Israel also worshiped other gods, carrying along "Sikkuth [or "tabernacle"] your king [or "Molech"] and Chiun, your idols." Molech worship included the astrological worship of Saturn and the host of heaven and the actual sacrificing of children (2 Kin. 17:16,17). Warned against Molech worship (Deut. 18:9–13), Israel nevertheless pursued all facets of it, continuing with Solomon (1 Kin. 11:7) and his descendants (1 Kin. 12:28; 2 Kin. 17:16,17; Jer. 32:35) until Josiah (2 Kin. 23:10). Stephen recited Amos 5:25–27 when he recounted the sins of Israel in Acts 7:42,43.

Psalm 141:5–10

5 Let the righteous strike me;
It shall be a kindness.
And let him rebuke me;
It shall be as excellent oil;
Let my head not refuse it.

For still my prayer *is* against the deeds
of the wicked.
6 Their judges are overthrown by the
sides of the cliff,
And they hear my words, for they are
sweet.
7 Our bones are scattered at the mouth
of the grave,
As when one plows and breaks up the
earth.

8 But my eyes *are* upon You,
O GOD the Lord;
In You I take refuge;
Do not leave my soul destitute.
9 Keep me from the snares they have
laid for me,
And from the traps of the workers of
iniquity.
10 Let the wicked fall into their own nets,
While I escape safely.

Proverbs 29:26

26 Many seek the ruler's favor,
But justice for man *comes* from the LORD.

Revelation 4:1–11

4 After these things I looked, and behold, a
door *standing* open in heaven. And the first
voice which I heard *was* like a trumpet speaking
with me, saying, "Come up here, and I will show
you things which must take place after this."
2 Immediately I was in the Spirit; and behold,
a throne set in heaven, and *One* sat on the
throne. 3 And He who sat there was like a
jasper and a sardius stone in appearance; and
there was a rainbow around the throne, in
appearance like an emerald. 4 Around the
throne *were* twenty-four thrones, and on the
thrones I saw twenty-four elders sitting,
clothed in white robes; and they had crowns of
gold on their heads. 5 And from the throne proceeded lightnings, thunderings, and voices.
Seven lamps of fire *were* burning before the
throne, which are the seven Spirits of God.
6 Before the throne *there was* a sea of glass,
like crystal. And in the midst of the throne,

4:4 twenty-four elders. Their joint rule with Christ, their white garments (19:7,8), and their golden crowns (2:10) all seem to indicate that these 24 represent the redeemed (vv. 9–11; 5:5–14; 7:11–17; 11:16–18; 14:3; 19:4). The question is, Which redeemed? Not Israel, since the nation is not yet saved, glorified, and coronated. That is still to come at this point in the events of the end. Their resurrection and glory will come at the end of the 7-year tribulation time (Dan. 12:1–3). Tribulation saints aren't yet saved (7:9,10). Only one group will be complete and glorified at that point—the church. Here elders represent the church, which sings the song of redemption (5:8–10). They are the overcomers who have their crowns and live in the place prepared for them, where they have gone with Jesus (John 14:1–4).

and around the throne, *were* four living creatures full of eyes in front and in back. [7]The first living creature *was* like a lion, the second living creature like a calf, the third living creature had a face like a man, and the fourth living creature *was* like a flying eagle. [8]*The* four living creatures, each having six wings, were full of eyes around and within. And they do not rest day or night, saying:

"Holy, holy, holy,
Lord God Almighty,
Who was and is and is to come!"

[9]Whenever the living creatures give glory and honor and thanks to Him who sits on the throne, who lives forever and ever, [10]the twenty-four elders fall down before Him who sits on the throne and worship Him who lives forever and ever, and cast their crowns before the throne, saying:

11 "You are worthy, O Lord,
To receive glory and honor and power;
For You created all things,
And by Your will they exist and were
created."

DAY 14: Are there different approaches to interpreting the Book of Revelation?

No other New Testament book poses more serious and difficult interpretive challenges than Revelation. The book's vivid imagery and striking symbolism have produced 4 main interpretive approaches:

The *preterist* approach interprets Revelation as a description of first-century events in the Roman Empire. This view conflicts with the book's own often repeated claim to be prophecy (1:3; 22:7,10,18,19). It is impossible to see all the events in Revelation as already fulfilled. The Second Coming of Christ, for example, obviously did not take place in the first century.

The *historicist* approach views Revelation as a panoramic view of church history from apostolic times to the present—seeing in the symbolism such events as the barbarian invasions of Rome, the rise of the Roman Catholic Church, the emergence of Islam, and the French Revolution. This interpretive method robs Revelation of any meaning for those to whom it was written. It also ignores the time limitations the book itself places on the unfolding events (11:2; 12:6,14; 13:5). Historicism has produced many different—and often conflicting—interpretations of the actual historical events contained in Revelation.

The *idealist* approach interprets Revelation as a timeless depiction of the cosmic struggle between the forces of good and evil. In this view, the book contains neither historical allusions nor predictive prophecy. This view also ignores Revelation's prophetic character and, if carried to its logical conclusion, severs the book from any connection with actual historical events. Revelation then becomes merely a collection of stories designed to teach spiritual truth.

The *futurist* approach insists that the events of chapters 6–22 are yet future and that those chapters literally and symbolically depict actual people and events yet to appear on the world scene. It describes the events surrounding the Second Coming of Jesus Christ (chaps. 6–19), the Millennium and final judgment (chap. 20), and the eternal state (chaps. 21; 22). Only this view does justice to Revelation's claim to be prophecy and interprets the book by the same grammatical-historical method as chapters 1–3 and the rest of Scripture.

DECEMBER 15

Amos 6:1–7:17

6 Woe to you *who are* at ease
in Zion,
And trust in Mount Samaria,
Notable persons in the chief nation,
To whom the house of Israel comes!
2 Go over to Calneh and see;
And from there go to Hamath the
great;
Then go down to Gath of the
Philistines.
Are you better than these kingdoms?
Or is their territory greater than your
territory?
3 *Woe to* you who put far off the day
of doom,
Who cause the seat of violence
to come near;
4 Who lie on beds of ivory,
Stretch out on your couches,
Eat lambs from the flock
And calves from the midst of the stall;
5 Who sing idly to the sound of stringed
instruments,
And invent for yourselves musical
instruments like David;
6 Who drink wine from bowls,
And anoint yourselves with the best
ointments,

But are not grieved for the affliction of
Joseph.
7 Therefore they shall now go captive as
the first of the captives,
And those who recline at banquets
shall be removed.

8 The Lord GOD has sworn by Himself,
The LORD God of hosts says:
"I abhor the pride of Jacob,
And hate his palaces;
Therefore I will deliver up *the* city
And all that is in it."

9 Then it shall come to pass, that if ten men
remain in one house, they shall die. 10 And
when a relative *of the dead,* with one who will
burn *the bodies,* picks up the bodies to take
them out of the house, he will say to one inside
the house, "*Are there* any more with you?"
Then someone will say, "None."
And he will say, "Hold your tongue! For we
dare not mention the name of the LORD."

6:10 one who will burn. This could refer to cremation, demanded by the excessive number killed and because of fear of epidemics. With rare exceptions (1 Sam. 31:12), corpses were buried in ancient Israel. **dare not mention...the LORD.** Previously welcomed as a friend, the Lord came in judgment as a foe. Survivors would not want to invoke His name out of fear.

11 For behold, the LORD gives a
command:
He will break the great house
into bits,
And the little house into pieces.
12 Do horses run on rocks?
Does *one* plow *there* with oxen?
Yet you have turned justice into gall,
And the fruit of righteousness into
wormwood,
13 You who rejoice over Lo Debar,
Who say, "Have we not taken Karnaim
for ourselves
By our own strength?"
14 "But, behold, I will raise up a nation
against you,
O house of Israel,"
Says the LORD God of hosts;
"And they will afflict you from the
entrance of Hamath
To the Valley of the Arabah."

7 Thus the Lord GOD showed me: Behold,
He formed locust swarms at the beginning
of the late crop; indeed *it was* the late crop
after the king's mowings. 2 And so it was, when
they had finished eating the grass of the land,
that I said:

"O Lord GOD, forgive, I pray!
Oh, that Jacob may stand,
For he *is* small!"
3 *So* the LORD relented concerning this.
"It shall not be," said the LORD.

4 Thus the Lord GOD showed me: Behold,
the Lord GOD called for conflict by fire, and it
consumed the great deep and devoured the
territory. 5 Then I said:

"O Lord GOD, cease, I pray!
Oh, that Jacob may stand,
For he *is* small!"
6 *So* the LORD relented concerning this.
"This also shall not be," said the Lord
GOD.

7 Thus He showed me: Behold, the Lord
stood on a wall *made* with a plumb line, with a
plumb line in His hand. 8 And the LORD said to
me, "Amos, what do you see?"
And I said, "A plumb line."
Then the Lord said:

"Behold, I am setting a plumb line
In the midst of My people Israel;
I will not pass by them anymore.
9 The high places of Isaac shall be
desolate,
And the sanctuaries of Israel shall
be laid waste.
I will rise with the sword against the
house of Jeroboam."

10 Then Amaziah the priest of Bethel sent to
Jeroboam king of Israel, saying, "Amos has
conspired against you in the midst of the
house of Israel. The land is not able to bear all
his words. 11 For thus Amos has said:

'Jeroboam shall die by the sword,
And Israel shall surely be led
away captive
From their own land.' "

12 Then Amaziah said to Amos:
"Go, you seer!
Flee to the land of Judah.
There eat bread,
And there prophesy.
13 But never again prophesy at Bethel,
For it *is* the king's sanctuary,
And it *is* the royal residence."

14 Then Amos answered, and said to Amaziah:

"I *was* no prophet,
Nor *was* I a son of a prophet,
But I *was* a sheepbreeder
And a tender of sycamore fruit.
15 Then the LORD took me as I followed
the flock,
And the LORD said to me,
'Go, prophesy to My people Israel.'
16 Now therefore, hear the word
of the LORD:
You say, 'Do not prophesy against Israel,
And do not spout against the house
of Isaac.'

17 "Therefore thus says the LORD:

'Your wife shall be a harlot in the city;
Your sons and daughters shall fall by
the sword;
Your land shall be divided by *survey*
line;
You shall die in a defiled land;
And Israel shall surely be led away
captive
From his own land.' "

Psalm 142:1–7

A Contemplation of David. A Prayer when he was in the cave.

I cry out to the LORD with my voice;
With my voice to the LORD
I make my supplication.
2 I pour out my complaint before Him;
I declare before Him my trouble.
3 When my spirit was overwhelmed
within me,
Then You knew my path.
In the way in which I walk
They have secretly set a snare
for me.
4 Look on *my* right hand and see,
For *there is* no one who acknowledges
me;
Refuge has failed me;

142:1–7 Under the same circumstances as Psalm 57 (according to the superscription), David recounted his desperate days hiding in the cave of Adullam (1 Sam. 22:1) while Saul sought him to take his life (1 Sam. 18–24). It appears that David's situation, for the moment at least, seems hopeless without God's intervention. Psalm 91 provides the truths that bring the solution.

No one cares for my soul.
5 I cried out to You, O LORD:
I said, "You *are* my refuge,
My portion in the land of the living.
6 Attend to my cry,
For I am brought very low;
Deliver me from my persecutors,
For they are stronger than I.
7 Bring my soul out of prison,
That I may praise Your name;
The righteous shall surround me,
For You shall deal bountifully with me."

Proverbs 29:27

27 An unjust man *is* an abomination
to the righteous,
And *he who is* upright in the way *is* an
abomination to the wicked.

Revelation 5:1–14

5 And I saw in the right *hand* of Him who sat on the throne a scroll written inside and on the back, sealed with seven seals. 2 Then I saw a strong angel proclaiming with a loud voice, "Who is worthy to open the scroll and to loose its seals?" 3 And no one in heaven or on the earth or under the earth was able to open the scroll, or to look at it.

5:1 a scroll written inside and on the back. This is typical of various kinds of contracts in the ancient world, including deeds, marriage contracts, rental and lease agreements, and wills. The inside of the scroll contained all the details of the contract, and the outside—or back—contained a summary of the document. In this case it almost certainly is a deed—the title deed to the earth (Jer. 32:7ff.). **sealed with seven seals.** Romans sealed their wills 7 times—on the edge at each roll—to prevent unauthorized entry. Hebrew title deeds required a minimum of 3 witnesses and 3 separate seals, with more important transactions requiring more witnesses and seals.

4 So I wept much, because no one was found worthy to open and read the scroll, or to look at it. 5 But one of the elders said to me, "Do not weep. Behold, the Lion of the tribe of Judah, the Root of David, has prevailed to open the scroll and to loose its seven seals."

6 And I looked, and behold, in the midst of the throne and of the four living creatures, and in the midst of the elders, stood a Lamb as

though it had been slain, having seven horns
and seven eyes, which are the seven Spirits of
God sent out into all the earth. 7Then He came
and took the scroll out of the right hand of
Him who sat on the throne.

8Now when He had taken the scroll, the four
living creatures and the twenty-four elders fell
down before the Lamb, each having a harp,
and golden bowls full of incense, which are the
prayers of the saints. 9And they sang a new
song, saying:

> "You are worthy to take the scroll,
> And to open its seals;
> For You were slain,
> And have redeemed us to God
> by Your blood
> Out of every tribe and tongue and
> people and nation,
> 10 And have made us kings and priests
> to our God;
> And we shall reign on the earth."

11Then I looked, and I heard the voice of many
angels around the throne, the living creatures,
and the elders; and the number of them was
ten thousand times ten thousand, and thousands of thousands, 12saying with a loud voice:

> "Worthy is the Lamb who was slain
> To receive power and riches and
> wisdom,
> And strength and honor and glory and
> blessing!"

13And every creature which is in heaven and
on the earth and under the earth and such as are
in the sea, and all that are in them, I heard saying:

> "Blessing and honor and glory and power
> *Be* to Him who sits on the throne,
> And to the Lamb, forever and ever!"

14Then the four living creatures said, "Amen!"
And the twenty-four elders fell down and worshiped Him who lives forever and ever.

DAY 15: Describe the worship in Revelation 5.

"The four living creatures and the twenty-four elders fell down before the Lamb, each having a harp" (v. 8). These ancient stringed instruments not only accompanied the songs of God's people (1 Chr. 25:6; Ps. 33:2), but also accompanied prophecy (1 Sam. 10:5). The 24 elders, representative of the redeemed church, played their harps in praise and in a symbolic indication that all the prophets had said was about to be fulfilled. "Each having...bowls full of incense, which are the prayers of the saints." These golden, wide-mouth saucers were common in the tabernacle and temple. Incense was a normal part of the Old Testament ritual. Priests stood twice daily before the inner veil of the temple and burned incense so that the smoke would carry into the Holy of Holies and be swept into the nostrils of God. That symbolized the people's prayers rising to Him. Specifically, these prayers represent all that the redeemed have ever prayed concerning ultimate and final redemption. This becomes a major theme throughout the book (11:17,18; 13:7,9,10; 14:12; 16:6; 17:6; 18:20,24; 19:8; 20:9).

"And they sang a new song" (v. 9). The Old Testament is filled with references to a new song that flows from a heart that has experienced God's redemption or deliverance (14:3; Pss. 33:3; 96:1; 144:9). This new song anticipates the final, glorious redemption that God is about to begin. "For You were slain, and have redeemed us to God by Your blood." The sacrificial death of Christ on behalf of sinners made Him worthy to take the scroll.

DECEMBER 16

Amos 8:1–9:15

8 Thus the Lord GOD showed me: Behold, a
basket of summer fruit. 2And He said,
"Amos, what do you see?"
So I said, "A basket of summer fruit."
Then the LORD said to me:

> "The end has come upon My people
> Israel;
> I will not pass by them anymore.
> 3 And the songs of the temple
> Shall be wailing in that day,"
> Says the Lord GOD—
> "Many dead bodies everywhere,
> They shall be thrown out in silence."

> 4 Hear this, you who swallow up the
> needy,
> And make the poor of the land fail,

5Saying:

> "When will the New Moon be past,
> That we may sell grain?
> And the Sabbath,
> That we may trade wheat?
> Making the ephah small and the
> shekel large,
> Falsifying the scales by deceit,
> 6 That we may buy the poor for silver,
> And the needy for a pair of sandals—
> Even sell the bad wheat?"

7 The LORD has sworn by the pride
of Jacob:
"Surely I will never forget any of their
works.
8 Shall the land not tremble for this,
And everyone mourn who dwells in it?
All of it shall swell like the River,
Heave and subside
Like the River of Egypt.

9 "And it shall come to pass in that day,"
says the Lord GOD,
"That I will make the sun go down at
noon,
And I will darken the earth in broad
daylight;
10 I will turn your feasts into mourning,
And all your songs into lamentation;
I will bring sackcloth on every waist,
And baldness on every head;
I will make it like mourning for an only
son,
And its end like a bitter day.

11 "Behold, the days are coming," says the
Lord GOD,
"That I will send a famine on the land,
Not a famine of bread,
Nor a thirst for water,
But of hearing the words of the LORD.
12 They shall wander from sea to sea,
And from north to east;
They shall run to and fro, seeking the
word of the LORD,
But shall not find *it.*

13 "In that day the fair virgins
And strong young men
Shall faint from thirst.
14 Those who swear by the sin of Samaria,
Who say,
'As your god lives, O Dan!'
And, 'As the way of Beersheba lives!'
They shall fall and never rise again."

9 I saw the Lord standing by the altar, and He
said:

"Strike the doorposts, that the
thresholds may shake,
And break them on the heads of them
all.
I will slay the last of them with the
sword.
He who flees from them shall not get
away,
And he who escapes from them shall
not be delivered.
2 "Though they dig into hell,
From there My hand shall take them;
Though they climb up to heaven,
From there I will bring them down;
3 And though they hide themselves on
top of Carmel,
From there I will search and take them;
Though they hide from My sight at the
bottom of the sea,
From there I will command the
serpent, and it shall bite them;
4 Though they go into captivity before
their enemies,
From there I will command the sword,
And it shall slay them.
I will set My eyes on them for harm
and not for good."

5 The Lord GOD of hosts,
He who touches the earth and it melts,
And all who dwell there mourn;
All of it shall swell like the River,
And subside like the River of Egypt.
6 He who builds His layers in the sky,
And has founded His strata in the earth;
Who calls for the waters of the sea,
And pours them out on the face of the
earth—
The LORD *is* His name.

7 "*Are* you not like the people of Ethiopia
to Me,
O children of Israel?" says the LORD.
"Did I not bring up Israel from the land
of Egypt,
The Philistines from Caphtor,
And the Syrians from Kir?
8 "Behold, the eyes of the Lord GOD *are*
on the sinful kingdom,
And I will destroy it from the face of
the earth;
Yet I will not utterly destroy the house
of Jacob,"
Says the LORD.

9 "For surely I will command,
And will sift the house of Israel among
all nations,
As *grain* is sifted in a sieve;
Yet not the smallest grain shall fall to
the ground.
10 All the sinners of My people shall die
by the sword,
Who say, 'The calamity shall not
overtake nor confront us.'

11 "On that day I will raise up
The tabernacle of David, which has
fallen down,
And repair its damages;
I will raise up its ruins,
And rebuild it as in the days of old;
12 That they may possess the remnant of
Edom,

And all the Gentiles who are called by
My name,"
Says the LORD who does this thing.

13 "Behold, the days are coming," says the
LORD,
"When the plowman shall overtake the
reaper,
And the treader of grapes him who
sows seed;
The mountains shall drip with sweet
wine,
And all the hills shall flow *with it.*
14 I will bring back the captives of My
people Israel;
They shall build the waste cities and
inhabit *them;*
They shall plant vineyards and drink
wine from them;
They shall also make gardens and eat
fruit from them.
15 I will plant them in their land,
And no longer shall they be pulled up
From the land I have given them,"
Says the LORD your God.

9:15 no longer shall they be pulled up from the land. The ultimate fulfillment of God's land promise to Abraham (Gen. 12:7; 15:7; 17:8) will occur during Christ's millennial reign on earth (Joel 2:26,27).

Psalm 143:1–6

A Psalm of David.

Hear my prayer, O LORD,
Give ear to my supplications!
In Your faithfulness answer me,
And in Your righteousness.
2 Do not enter into judgment with Your
servant,
For in Your sight no one living is
righteous.

3 For the enemy has persecuted my soul;
He has crushed my life to the ground;
He has made me dwell in darkness,
Like those who have long been dead.
4 Therefore my spirit is overwhelmed
within me;
My heart within me is distressed.

5 I remember the days of old;
I meditate on all Your works;
I muse on the work of Your hands.
6 I spread out my hands to You;
My soul *longs* for You like a thirsty
land. Selah

Proverbs 30:1–4

30 The words of Agur the son of Jakeh, *his* utterance. This man declared to Ithiel—to Ithiel and Ucal:

30:1–33 The words of Agur. This is a collection of proverbs written by an unknown sage who was likely a student of wisdom at the time of Solomon (1 Kin. 4:30,31). Agur reflects humility (vv. 1–4), a deep hatred for arrogance (vv. 7–9), and a keen theological mind (vv. 5,6).

2 Surely I *am* more stupid than *any* man,
And do not have the understanding of
a man.
3 I neither learned wisdom
Nor have knowledge of the Holy One.
4 Who has ascended into heaven,
or descended?
Who has gathered the wind in His fists?
Who has bound the waters in a garment?
Who has established all the ends of the
earth?
What *is* His name, and what *is* His
Son's name,
If you know?

30:4 Who...What...? These questions can be answered only by revelation from God. A man can know the "what" about creative wisdom through observation of the physical world and its inner workings, but cannot know the "who." The "who" can be known only when God reveals Himself, which He has in Scripture. This is the testimony and conclusion of Job (Job 42:1–6), Solomon (Eccl. 12:1–14), Isaiah (Is. 40:12–17; 46:8–11; 66:18,19), and Paul (Rom. 8:18–39). **His Son's name.** Jesus Christ. John 1:1–18.

Revelation 6:1–17

6 Now I saw when the Lamb opened one of
the seals; and I heard one of the four living creatures saying with a voice like thunder,
"Come and see." 2And I looked, and behold, a
white horse. He who sat on it had a bow; and
a crown was given to him, and he went out
conquering and to conquer.

6:1 the seals. In chapter 5, Christ was the only One found worthy to open the little scroll—the title deed to the universe. As He breaks the 7 seals that secure the scroll, each seal unleashes a new demonstration of God's judgment on the earth in the future tribulation period. These seal judgments include all the judgments to the end. The seventh seal contains the 7 trumpets; the seventh trumpet contains the 7 bowls.

3When He opened the second seal, I heard
the second living creature saying, "Come and
see." 4Another horse, fiery red, went out. And
it was granted to the one who sat on it to take
peace from the earth, and that *people* should
kill one another; and there was given to him a
great sword.
5When He opened the third seal, I heard the
third living creature say, "Come and see." So I
looked, and behold, a black horse, and he who
sat on it had a pair of scales in his hand. 6And
I heard a voice in the midst of the four living
creatures saying, "A quart of wheat for a denarius, and three quarts of barley for a denarius; and do not harm the oil and the wine."
7When He opened the fourth seal, I heard
the voice of the fourth living creature saying,
"Come and see." 8So I looked, and behold, a
pale horse. And the name of him who sat on it
was Death, and Hades followed with him. And
power was given to them over a fourth of the
earth, to kill with sword, with hunger, with
death, and by the beasts of the earth.
9When He opened the fifth seal, I saw under
the altar the souls of those who had been slain
for the word of God and for the testimony
which they held. 10And they cried with a loud
voice, saying, "How long, O Lord, holy and
true, until You judge and avenge our blood on
those who dwell on the earth?" 11Then a white
robe was given to each of them; and it was said
to them that they should rest a little while
longer, until both *the number of* their fellow servants and their brethren, who would be killed as
they *were,* was completed.
12I looked when He opened the sixth seal,
and behold, there was a great earthquake; and
the sun became black as sackcloth of hair, and
the moon became like blood. 13And the stars of
heaven fell to the earth, as a fig tree drops its
late figs when it is shaken by a mighty wind.
14Then the sky receded as a scroll when it is
rolled up, and every mountain and island was
moved out of its place. 15And the kings of the
earth, the great men, the rich men, the commanders, the mighty men, every slave and
every free man, hid themselves in the caves
and in the rocks of the mountains, 16and said to
the mountains and rocks, "Fall on us and hide
us from the face of Him who sits on the throne
and from the wrath of the Lamb! 17For the
great day of His wrath has come, and who is
able to stand?"

DAY 16: How does Amos 9:11 relate to the Jerusalem Council of Acts 15?

In Amos 9:11, the Lord promised that He "will raise up the tabernacle of David, which has fallen down." At the Jerusalem Council, convened to discuss whether Gentiles should be allowed into the church without requiring circumcision, James quotes this passage (Acts 15:15,16) to support Peter's report of how God had "visited the Gentiles to take out of them a people for His name" (Acts 15:14). Some have thus concluded that the passage was fulfilled in Jesus, the greater Son of David, through whom the dynasty of David was reestablished. The Acts reference, however, is best seen as an illustration of Amos's words and not the fulfillment. The temporal allusions to a future time ("On that day," 9:11), when Israel will "possess the remnant of Edom, and all the Gentiles" (9:12), when the Lord "will plant them in their land, and no longer shall they be pulled up from the land I have given them" (9:15), all make it clear that the prophet is speaking of Messiah's return at the Second Advent to sit upon the throne of David (Is. 9:7), not the establishment of the church by the apostles.

DECEMBER 17

Obadiah 1–21

The vision of Obadiah.

Thus says the Lord GOD concerning
Edom
(We have heard a report from the
LORD,
And a messenger has been sent among
the nations, *saying,*
"Arise, and let us rise up against her
for battle"):
2 "Behold, I will make you small among
the nations;
You shall be greatly despised.

1 The vision. The prophetic word often came from God in the form of a vision (Hab. 1:1). **Thus says the Lord God.** Although the background of the prophet is obscure, the source of his message is not. It was supernaturally given by God and was not motivated by unholy vengeance. **Edom.** Descendants of Esau (Gen. 25:30; 36:1ff.), the Edomites settled in the region south of the Dead Sea. **Arise,...rise up against her.** The prophet heard of an international plot to overthrow Edom. The selfish motives of Edom's enemies were divinely controlled by the Lord's "messengers" to serve His sovereign purposes (Ps. 104:4).

3 The pride of your heart has deceived you,
You who dwell in the clefts of the rock,
Whose habitation is high;
You who say in your heart, 'Who will bring me down to the ground?'
4 Though you ascend *as* high as the eagle,
And though you set your nest among the stars,
From there I will bring you down,"
says the LORD.
5 "If thieves had come to you,
If robbers by night—
Oh, how you will be cut off!—
Would they not have stolen till they had enough?
If grape-gatherers had come to you,
Would they not have left *some* gleanings?
6 "Oh, how Esau shall be searched out!
How his hidden treasures shall be sought after!
7 All the men in your confederacy
Shall force you to the border;
The men at peace with you
Shall deceive you *and* prevail against you.
Those who eat your bread shall lay a trap for you.
No one is aware of it.
8 "Will I not in that day," says the LORD,
"Even destroy the wise *men* from Edom,
And understanding from the mountains of Esau?
9 Then your mighty men, O Teman, shall be dismayed,
To the end that everyone from the mountains of Esau
May be cut off by slaughter.
10 "For violence against your brother Jacob,
Shame shall cover you,
And you shall be cut off forever.
11 In the day that you stood on the other side—
In the day that strangers carried captive his forces,
When foreigners entered his gates
And cast lots for Jerusalem—
Even you *were* as one of them.
12 "But you should not have gazed on the day of your brother
In the day of his captivity;
Nor should you have rejoiced over the children of Judah
In the day of their destruction;
Nor should you have spoken proudly
In the day of distress.
13 You should not have entered the gate of My people
In the day of their calamity.
Indeed, you should not have gazed on their affliction
In the day of their calamity,
Nor laid *hands* on their substance
In the day of their calamity.
14 You should not have stood at the crossroads
To cut off those among them who escaped;
Nor should you have delivered up those among them who remained
In the day of distress.
15 "For the day of the LORD upon all the nations *is* near;
As you have done, it shall be done to you;
Your reprisal shall return upon your own head.
16 For as you drank on My holy mountain,
So shall all the nations drink continually;
Yes, they shall drink, and swallow,
And they shall be as though they had never been.
17 "But on Mount Zion there shall be deliverance,
And there shall be holiness;
The house of Jacob shall possess their possessions.
18 The house of Jacob shall be a fire,
And the house of Joseph a flame;
But the house of Esau *shall be* stubble;
They shall kindle them and devour them,
And no survivor shall *remain* of the house of Esau,"
For the LORD has spoken.

19 The South shall possess the mountains of Esau,
And the Lowland shall possess Philistia.
They shall possess the fields of Ephraim
And the fields of Samaria.
Benjamin *shall possess* Gilead.
20 And the captives of this host of the children of Israel
Shall possess the land of the Canaanites
As far as Zarephath.
The captives of Jerusalem who are in Sepharad
Shall possess the cities of the South.
21 Then saviors shall come to Mount Zion
To judge the mountains of Esau,
And the kingdom shall be the LORD's.

Psalm 143:7–12

7 Answer me speedily, O LORD;
My spirit fails!
Do not hide Your face from me,
Lest I be like those who go down into the pit.
8 Cause me to hear Your lovingkindness in the morning,
For in You do I trust;
Cause me to know the way in which I should walk,
For I lift up my soul to You.
9 Deliver me, O LORD, from my enemies;
In You I take shelter.
10 Teach me to do Your will,
For You *are* my God;
Your Spirit *is* good.
Lead me in the land of uprightness.
11 Revive me, O LORD, for Your name's sake!
For Your righteousness' sake bring my soul out of trouble.
12 In Your mercy cut off my enemies,
And destroy all those who afflict my soul;
For I *am* Your servant.

Proverbs 30:5

5 Every word of God *is* pure;
He *is* a shield to those who put their trust in Him.

Revelation 7:1–17

7 After these things I saw four angels standing
at the four corners of the earth, holding the
four winds of the earth, that the wind should not
blow on the earth, on the sea, or on any tree.
2 Then I saw another angel ascending from the
east, having the seal of the living God. And he
cried with a loud voice to the four angels to
whom it was granted to harm the earth and the
sea, 3 saying, "Do not harm the earth, the sea, or
the trees till we have sealed the servants of our
God on their foreheads." 4 And I heard the number of those who were sealed. One hundred *and*
forty-four thousand of all the tribes of the children of Israel *were* sealed:

7:4 One hundred *and* forty-four thousand. A missionary corps of redeemed Jews who are instrumental in the salvation of many Jews and Gentiles during the Tribulation (vv. 9–17). They will be the firstfruits of a new redeemed Israel (v. 4; Zech. 12:10). Finally, Israel will be the witness nation she refused to be in the Old Testament (Rom. 11:25–27). **all the tribes of the children of Israel.** By sovereign election, God will seal 12,000 from each of the 12 tribes, promising His protection while they accomplish their mission.

5 of the tribe of Judah twelve thousand *were* sealed;
of the tribe of Reuben twelve thousand *were* sealed;
of the tribe of Gad twelve thousand *were* sealed;
6 of the tribe of Asher twelve thousand *were* sealed;
of the tribe of Naphtali twelve thousand *were* sealed;
of the tribe of Manasseh twelve thousand *were* sealed;
7 of the tribe of Simeon twelve thousand *were* sealed;
of the tribe of Levi twelve thousand *were* sealed;
of the tribe of Issachar twelve thousand *were* sealed;
8 of the tribe of Zebulun twelve thousand *were* sealed;
of the tribe of Joseph twelve thousand *were* sealed;

7:1–17 Chapter 7 forms a parenthesis between the sixth seal (6:12–17) and the seventh seal (8:1) and answers the question posed at the end of chapter 6. Two distinct groups will survive the divine fury: 1) 144,000 Jewish evangelists on earth (vv. 1–8) and 2) their converts in heaven (vv. 9–17).

of the tribe of Benjamin twelve
thousand *were* sealed.

9After these things I looked, and behold, a
great multitude which no one could number,
of all nations, tribes, peoples, and tongues,
standing before the throne and before the
Lamb, clothed with white robes, with palm
branches in their hands, 10and crying out with
a loud voice, saying, "Salvation *belongs* to our
God who sits on the throne, and to the Lamb!"
11All the angels stood around the throne and
the elders and the four living creatures, and
fell on their faces before the throne and worshiped God, 12saying:

"Amen! Blessing and glory and wisdom,
Thanksgiving and honor and power
and might,
Be to our God forever and ever.
Amen."

13Then one of the elders answered, saying to
me, "Who are these arrayed in white robes,
and where did they come from?"
14And I said to him, "Sir, you know."
So he said to me, "These are the ones who
come out of the great tribulation, and washed
their robes and made them white in the blood of
the Lamb. 15Therefore they are before the
throne of God, and serve Him day and night in
His temple. And He who sits on the throne will
dwell among them. 16They shall neither hunger
anymore nor thirst anymore; the sun shall not
strike them, nor any heat; 17for the Lamb who is
in the midst of the throne will shepherd them
and lead them to living fountains of waters. And
God will wipe away every tear from their eyes."

DAY 17: Who make up the "great multitude" of Revelation 7:9?

While the tribulation period will be a time of judgment, it will also be a time of unprecedented redemption (v. 14; 6:9–11; 20:4; Is. 11:10; Matt. 24:14). This is noted in v. 9 with the "great multitude which no one could number, of all nations, tribes, peoples, and tongues, standing before the throne and before the Lamb."

John is told that "These are the ones who come out of the great tribulation" (v. 14). These people didn't go with the raptured church, since they were not yet saved. During the 7-year period, they will be saved, martyred, and enter heaven. Though it is a time of unparalleled judgment, it is also a time of unparalleled grace in salvation (Matt. 24:12–14). "And washed their robes and made them white in the blood of the Lamb" (Rev. 7:14). Salvation's cleansing is in relationship to the atoning sacrifice of Christ (1:5; 5:9; Rom. 3:24,25; 5:9).

"Therefore they are before the throne of God, and serve Him day and night in His temple" (v. 15). This refers to the heavenly throne of God. During the Millennium, there will also be a temple on earth—a special holy place where God dwells in a partially restored, but still fallen universe (see Ezek. 40–48). In the final, eternal state with its new heavens and earth, there is no temple; God Himself, who will fill all, will be its temple (21:22). "And He who sits on the throne will dwell among them." The preferred reading is that He "will spread His tent over them." God's presence will become their canopy of shelter to protect them from all the terrors of a fallen world and the indescribable horrors they have experienced on the earth during the time of tribulation.

DECEMBER 18

Jonah 1:1–4:11

1 Now the word of the LORD came to Jonah the
son of Amittai, saying, 2"Arise, go to Nineveh,
that great city, and cry out against it; for their
wickedness has come up before Me." 3But
Jonah arose to flee to Tarshish from the presence of the LORD. He went down to Joppa, and
found a ship going to Tarshish; so he paid the
fare, and went down into it, to go with them to
Tarshish from the presence of the LORD.
4But the LORD sent out a great wind on the
sea, and there was a mighty tempest on the sea,
so that the ship was about to be broken up.

1:3 But Jonah arose to flee to Tarshish. This is the only recorded instance of a prophet refusing God's commission (Jer. 20:7–9). The location of Tarshish, known for its wealth (Ps. 72:10; Jer. 10:9; Ezek. 27:12,25), is uncertain. The Greek historian Herodotus identified it with Tartessus, a merchant city in southern Spain. The prophet went as far west in the opposite direction as possible, showing his reluctance to bring salvation blessing to Gentiles. **from the presence of the LORD.** While no one can escape from the Lord's omnipresence (Ps. 139:7–12), it is thought that the prophet was attempting to flee His manifest presence in the temple at Jerusalem (Gen. 4:16; Jon. 2:4).

5Then the mariners were afraid; and every
man cried out to his god, and threw the cargo
that *was* in the ship into the sea, to lighten the
load. But Jonah had gone down into the lowest
parts of the ship, had lain down, and was fast
asleep.
6So the captain came to him, and said to
him, "What do you mean, sleeper? Arise, call
on your God; perhaps your God will consider
us, so that we may not perish."
7And they said to one another, "Come, let us
cast lots, that we may know for whose cause
this trouble *has come* upon us." So they cast
lots, and the lot fell on Jonah. 8Then they said
to him, "Please tell us! For whose cause *is* this
trouble upon us? What is your occupation?
And where do you come from? What is your
country? And of what people are you?"
9So he said to them, "I *am* a Hebrew; and I
fear the LORD, the God of heaven, who made
the sea and the dry *land.*"
10Then the men were exceedingly afraid,
and said to him, "Why have you done this?"
For the men knew that he fled from the presence of the LORD, because he had told them.
11Then they said to him, "What shall we do to
you that the sea may be calm for us?"—for the
sea was growing more tempestuous.
12And he said to them, "Pick me up and throw
me into the sea; then the sea will become calm
for you. For I know that this great tempest *is*
because of me."
13Nevertheless the men rowed hard to
return to land, but they could not, for the sea
continued to grow more tempestuous against
them. 14Therefore they cried out to the LORD
and said, "We pray, O LORD, please do not let
us perish for this man's life, and do not charge
us with innocent blood; for You, O LORD, have
done as it pleased You." 15So they picked up Jonah and threw him into the sea, and the sea
ceased from its raging. 16Then the men feared
the LORD exceedingly, and offered a sacrifice
to the LORD and took vows.
17Now the LORD had prepared a great fish to
swallow Jonah. And Jonah was in the belly of
the fish three days and three nights.

1:17 a great fish. The species of fish is uncertain; the Hebrew word for whale is not here employed. God sovereignly prepared (literally, "appointed") a great fish to rescue Jonah. Apparently Jonah sank into the depth of the sea before the fish swallowed him (2:3,5,6).

2 Then Jonah prayed to the LORD his God
from the fish's belly. 2And he said:

"I cried out to the LORD because
of my affliction,
And He answered me.

"Out of the belly of Sheol I cried,
And You heard my voice.
3 For You cast me into the deep,
Into the heart of the seas,
And the floods surrounded me;
All Your billows and Your waves
passed over me.
4 Then I said, 'I have been cast out of
Your sight;
Yet I will look again toward Your holy
temple.'
5 The waters surrounded me, *even*
to my soul;
The deep closed around me;
Weeds were wrapped around my head.
6 I went down to the moorings of the
mountains;
The earth with its bars *closed* behind
me forever;
Yet You have brought up my life from
the pit,
O LORD, my God.

7 "When my soul fainted within me,
I remembered the LORD;
And my prayer went *up* to You,
Into Your holy temple.
8 "Those who regard worthless idols
Forsake their own Mercy.
9 But I will sacrifice to You
With the voice of thanksgiving;
I will pay what I have vowed.
Salvation *is* of the LORD."
10So the LORD spoke to the fish, and it vom-
ited Jonah onto dry *land.*

3 Now the word of the LORD came to Jonah
the second time, saying, 2"Arise, go to
Nineveh, that great city, and preach to it the
message that I tell you." 3So Jonah arose and
went to Nineveh, according to the word of the
LORD. Now Nineveh was an exceedingly great
city, a three-day journey *in extent.* 4And Jonah
began to enter the city on the first day's walk.
Then he cried out and said, "Yet forty days,
and Nineveh shall be overthrown!"
5So the people of Nineveh believed God,
proclaimed a fast, and put on sackcloth, from
the greatest to the least of them. 6Then word
came to the king of Nineveh; and he arose from
his throne and laid aside his robe, covered *himself* with sackcloth and sat in ashes. 7And he
caused *it* to be proclaimed and published

throughout Nineveh by the decree of the king
and his nobles, saying,

> Let neither man nor beast, herd nor
> flock, taste anything; do not let them
> eat, or drink water. 8But let man and
> beast be covered with sackcloth, and
> cry mightily to God; yes, let every one
> turn from his evil way and from the
> violence that is in his hands. 9Who can
> tell *if* God will turn and relent, and turn
> away from His fierce anger, so that we
> may not perish?

10Then God saw their works, that they
turned from their evil way; and God relented
from the disaster that He had said He would
bring upon them, and He did not do it.

4 But it displeased Jonah exceedingly, and
he became angry. 2So he prayed to the
LORD, and said, "Ah, LORD, was not this what I
said when I was still in my country? Therefore
I fled previously to Tarshish; for I know that
You *are* a gracious and merciful God, slow to
anger and abundant in lovingkindness, One
who relents from doing harm. 3Therefore now,
O LORD, please take my life from me, for *it is*
better for me to die than to live!"

4:1,2 Jonah, because of his rejection of Gentiles and distaste for their participation in salvation, was displeased at God's demonstration of mercy toward the Ninevites, thereby displaying the real reason for his original flight to Tarshish. From the very beginning, Jonah had clearly understood the gracious character of God (1 Tim. 2:4; 2 Pet. 3:9). He had received pardon, but didn't want Nineveh to know God's mercy (a similar attitude in Luke 15:25ff.).

4Then the LORD said, "*Is it* right for you to be
angry?"
5So Jonah went out of the city and sat on the
east side of the city. There he made himself a
shelter and sat under it in the shade, till he
might see what would become of the city.
6And the LORD God prepared a plant and made
it come up over Jonah, that it might be shade
for his head to deliver him from his misery.
So Jonah was very grateful for the plant. 7But
as morning dawned the next day God prepared a worm, and it *so* damaged the plant
that it withered. 8And it happened, when the
sun arose, that God prepared a vehement east
wind; and the sun beat on Jonah's head, so
that he grew faint. Then he wished death for
himself, and said, "*It is* better for me to die
than to live."
9Then God said to Jonah, "*Is it* right for you
to be angry about the plant?"
And he said, "*It is* right for me to be angry,
even to death!"
10But the LORD said, "You have had pity on
the plant for which you have not labored, nor
made it grow, which came up in a night and
perished in a night. 11And should I not pity
Nineveh, that great city, in which are more
than one hundred and twenty thousand persons who cannot discern between their right
hand and their left—and much livestock?"

Psalm 144:1–8

A Psalm of David.

Blessed *be* the LORD my Rock,
Who trains my hands for war,
And my fingers for battle—
2 My lovingkindness and my fortress,
My high tower and my deliverer,
My shield and *the One* in whom I take
refuge,
Who subdues my people under me.

3 LORD, what *is* man, that You take
knowledge of him?
Or the son of man, that You are
mindful of him?
4 Man is like a breath;
His days *are* like a passing shadow.

5 Bow down Your heavens, O LORD,
and come down;
Touch the mountains, and they shall
smoke.
6 Flash forth lightning and scatter them;
Shoot out Your arrows and destroy
them.
7 Stretch out Your hand from above;
Rescue me and deliver me out of great
waters,
From the hand of foreigners,
8 Whose mouth speaks lying words,
And whose right hand *is* a right hand
of falsehood.

Proverbs 30:6–9

6 Do not add to His words,
Lest He rebuke you, and you be found
a liar.

7 Two *things* I request of You
(Deprive me not before I die):
8 Remove falsehood and lies far from
me;
Give me neither poverty nor riches—
Feed me with the food allotted to me;

9 Lest I be full and deny *You,*
And say, "Who *is* the LORD?"
Or lest I be poor and steal,
And profane the name of my God.

Revelation 8:1–13

8 When He opened the seventh seal, there
was silence in heaven for about half an
hour. 2And I saw the seven angels who stand
before God, and to them were given seven
trumpets. 3Then another angel, having a gold-
en censer, came and stood at the altar. He was
given much incense, that he should offer *it*
with the prayers of all the saints upon the
golden altar which was before the throne.
4And the smoke of the incense, with the
prayers of the saints, ascended before God
from the angel's hand. 5Then the angel took
the censer, filled it with fire from the altar, and
threw *it* to the earth. And there were noises,
thunderings, lightnings, and an earthquake.
6So the seven angels who had the seven
trumpets prepared themselves to sound.
7The first angel sounded: And hail and fire
followed, mingled with blood, and they were
thrown to the earth. And a third of the trees
were burned up, and all green grass was
burned up.
8Then the second angel sounded: And *some-*
thing like a great mountain burning with fire
was thrown into the sea, and a third of the sea
became blood. 9And a third of the living creatures in the sea died, and a third of the ships
were destroyed.
10Then the third angel sounded: And a great
star fell from heaven, burning like a torch, and
it fell on a third of the rivers and on the springs
of water. 11The name of the star is Wormwood.
A third of the waters became wormwood, and
many men died from the water, because it was
made bitter.
12Then the fourth angel sounded: And a
third of the sun was struck, a third of the
moon, and a third of the stars, so that a third
of them were darkened. A third of the day did
not shine, and likewise the night.
13And I looked, and I heard an angel flying
through the midst of heaven, saying with a
loud voice, "Woe, woe, woe to the inhabitants
of the earth, because of the remaining blasts
of the trumpet of the three angels who are
about to sound!"

DAY 18: Why did Jonah run from his mission to Nineveh?

Jonah, though a prophet of Israel, is not remembered for his ministry in Israel, which could explain why the Pharisees erringly claimed in Jesus' day that no prophet had come from Galilee (John 7:52). Rather, the book relates the account of his call to preach repentance to Nineveh and his refusal to go. Nineveh, the capital of Assyria and infamous for its cruelty, was a historical nemesis of Israel and Judah. The focus of this book is on that Gentile city, which was founded by Nimrod, great-grandson of Noah (Gen. 10:6–12). Perhaps the largest city in the ancient world (1:2; 3:2,3; 4:11), it was nevertheless destroyed about 150 years after the repentance of the generation in the time of Jonah's visit (612 B.C.), as Nahum prophesied (Nah. 1:1ff.).

Israel's political distaste for Assyria, coupled with a sense of spiritual superiority as the recipient of God's covenant blessing, produced a recalcitrant attitude in Jonah toward God's request for missionary service. Jonah was sent to Nineveh in part to shame Israel by the fact that a pagan city repented at the preaching of a stranger, whereas Israel would not repent though preached to by many prophets. He was soon to learn that God's love and mercy extends to all of His creatures (4:2,10,11), not just His covenant people (Gen. 9:27; 12:3; Lev. 19:33,34; 1 Sam. 2:10; Is. 2:2; Joel 2:28–32).

DECEMBER 19

Micah 1:1–3:12

1 The word of the LORD that came to Micah of Moresheth in the days of Jotham, Ahaz, *and* Hezekiah, kings of Judah, which he saw concerning Samaria and Jerusalem.

2 Hear, all you peoples!
Listen, O earth, and all that is in it!
Let the Lord GOD be a witness
against you,
The Lord from His holy temple.
3 For behold, the LORD is coming out of
His place;
He will come down
And tread on the high places of the
earth.
4 The mountains will melt under Him,
And the valleys will split
Like wax before the fire,
Like waters poured down a steep place.
5 All this is for the transgression of Jacob
And for the sins of the house of Israel.
What *is* the transgression of Jacob?
Is it not Samaria?

And what *are* the high places of Judah?
Are they not Jerusalem?

6 "Therefore I will make Samaria a heap
of ruins in the field,
Places for planting a vineyard;
I will pour down her stones into the
valley,
And I will uncover her foundations.
7 All her carved images shall be beaten
to pieces,
And all her pay as a harlot shall be
burned with the fire;
All her idols I will lay desolate,
For she gathered *it* from the pay of a
harlot,
And they shall return to the pay of a
harlot."

8 Therefore I will wail and howl,
I will go stripped and naked;
I will make a wailing like the jackals
And a mourning like the ostriches,
9 For her wounds *are* incurable.
For it has come to Judah;
It has come to the gate of My people—
To Jerusalem.

10 Tell *it* not in Gath,
Weep not at all;
In Beth Aphrah
Roll yourself in the dust.
11 Pass by in naked shame, you
inhabitant of Shaphir;
The inhabitant of Zaanan does not
go out.
Beth Ezel mourns;
Its place to stand is taken away from you.

12 For the inhabitant of Maroth pined
for good,
But disaster came down from the LORD
To the gate of Jerusalem.
13 O inhabitant of Lachish,
Harness the chariot to the swift steeds
(She *was* the beginning of sin to the
daughter of Zion),
For the transgressions of Israel were
found in you.
14 Therefore you shall give presents to
Moresheth Gath;
The houses of Achzib *shall be* a lie to
the kings of Israel.
15 I will yet bring an heir to you,
O inhabitant of Mareshah;
The glory of Israel shall come to
Adullam.
16 Make yourself bald and cut off your hair,
Because of your precious children;
Enlarge your baldness like an eagle,
For they shall go from you into captivity.

2

Woe to those who devise iniquity,
And work out evil on their beds!
At morning light they practice it,
Because it is in the power of their hand.
2 They covet fields and take *them*
by violence,
Also houses, and seize *them*.
So they oppress a man and his house,
A man and his inheritance.

3 Therefore thus says the LORD:
"Behold, against this family
I am devising disaster,
From which you cannot remove your
necks;
Nor shall you walk haughtily,
For this *is* an evil time.
4 In that day *one* shall take up a proverb
against you,
And lament with a bitter lamentation,
saying:
'We are utterly destroyed!
He has changed the heritage of my
people;
How He has removed *it* from me!
To a turncoat He has divided
our fields.' "

5 Therefore you will have no one to
determine boundaries by lot
In the assembly of the LORD.

6 "Do not prattle," *you say to those*
who prophesy.
So they shall not prophesy to you;
They shall not return insult for insult.
7 *You who are* named the house of Jacob:
"Is the Spirit of the LORD restricted?
Are these His doings?
Do not My words do good
To him who walks uprightly?

2:7 Spirit of the LORD. God responded to the evil prophets that their message affirming sin in the nation was inconsistent with the Holy Spirit and His true message to Micah (3:8). God's words do reward the righteous, but they also rebuke those engaging in evil deeds.

8 "Lately My people have risen up as an
enemy—
You pull off the robe with the garment
From those who trust *you*, as they
pass by,
Like men returned from war.
9 The women of My people you cast out

From their pleasant houses;
From their children
You have taken away My glory forever.

10 "Arise and depart,
For this *is* not *your* rest;
Because it is defiled, it shall destroy,
Yes, with utter destruction.
11 If a man should walk in a false spirit
And speak a lie, *saying,*
'I will prophesy to you of wine and drink,'
Even he would be the prattler of this people.

2:6–11 False prophets, commanding Micah to cease prophesying, would certainly not prophesy against the people's evil doing. They would not confront them with the divine standard of holiness. Rather, their false message (v. 7) had stopped the mouths of the true prophets and had permitted the rulers to engage in social atrocities (vv. 8,9), leading the people to destruction (v. 10). They didn't want true prophecies; therefore, they got what they wanted (Is. 30:10). It is best to understand that Micah speaks in v. 6 and God in vv. 7–11.

12 "I will surely assemble all of you, O Jacob,
I will surely gather the remnant of Israel;
I will put them together like sheep of the fold,
Like a flock in the midst of their pasture;
They shall make a loud noise because of *so many* people.
13 The one who breaks open will come up before them;
They will break out,
Pass through the gate,
And go out by it;
Their king will pass before them,
With the LORD at their head."

3 And I said:
"Hear now, O heads of Jacob,
And you rulers of the house of Israel:
Is it not for you to know justice?
2 You who hate good and love evil;
Who strip the skin from My people,
And the flesh from their bones;
3 Who also eat the flesh of My people,
Flay their skin from them,
Break their bones,
And chop *them* in pieces
Like *meat* for the pot,
Like flesh in the caldron."

4 Then they will cry to the LORD,
But He will not hear them;
He will even hide His face from them at that time,
Because they have been evil in their deeds.

5 Thus says the LORD concerning the prophets
Who make my people stray;
Who chant "Peace"
While they chew with their teeth,
But who prepare war against him
Who puts nothing into their mouths:
6 "Therefore you shall have night without vision,
And you shall have darkness without divination;
The sun shall go down on the prophets,
And the day shall be dark for them.
7 So the seers shall be ashamed,
And the diviners abashed;
Indeed they shall all cover their lips;
For *there is* no answer from God."
8 But truly I am full of power by the Spirit of the LORD,
And of justice and might,
To declare to Jacob his transgression
And to Israel his sin.
9 Now hear this,
You heads of the house of Jacob
And rulers of the house of Israel,
Who abhor justice
And pervert all equity,
10 Who build up Zion with bloodshed
And Jerusalem with iniquity:
11 Her heads judge for a bribe,
Her priests teach for pay,
And her prophets divine for money.
Yet they lean on the LORD, and say,
"Is not the LORD among us?
No harm can come upon us."
12 Therefore because of you
Zion shall be plowed *like* a field,
Jerusalem shall become heaps of ruins,
And the mountain of the temple
Like the bare hills of the forest.

Psalm 144:9–15

9 I will sing a new song to You, O God;
On a harp of ten strings I will sing praises to You,
10 *The One* who gives salvation to kings,
Who delivers David His servant
From the deadly sword.

11 Rescue me and deliver me from the
hand of foreigners,
Whose mouth speaks lying words,
And whose right hand *is* a right hand
of falsehood—
12 That our sons *may be* as plants grown
up in their youth;
That our daughters *may be* as pillars,
Sculptured in palace style;
13 *That* our barns *may be* full,
Supplying all kinds of produce;
That our sheep may bring forth
thousands
And ten thousands in our fields;
14 *That* our oxen *may be* well laden;
That there be no breaking in or going
out;
That there be no outcry in our streets.
15 Happy *are* the people who are in such a
state;
Happy *are* the people whose God *is* the
LORD!

Proverbs 30:10

10 Do not malign a servant to his master,
Lest he curse you, and you be found
guilty.

Revelation 9:1–21

9 Then the fifth angel sounded: And I saw a
star fallen from heaven to the earth. To
him was given the key to the bottomless pit.
[2]And he opened the bottomless pit, and smoke
arose out of the pit like the smoke of a great
furnace. So the sun and the air were darkened

9:3 locusts. A grasshopperlike insect that descends in swarms so thick they can obscure the sun and strip bare all vegetation. In the 1950s a locust swarm devoured every growing thing for several hundred thousand square miles in the Middle East. These are not normal locusts, however, but specially prepared ones that are merely the outward form of demons, who, like locusts, will bring swarming desolation (Joel 2:1–5). "Like" appears 9 times in John's description. He finds it difficult to describe what he sees in a way the reader can understand. **scorpions.** An arachnid that inhabits warm, dry regions and has an erect tail tipped with a venomous stinger. A scorpion's victim often rolls on the ground in agony, foams at the mouth, and grinds his teeth in pain. The demons in locust form are able to inflict the physical—and perhaps, spiritual—pain like the scorpion (v. 5).

because of the smoke of the pit. [3]Then out of
the smoke locusts came upon the earth. And to
them was given power, as the scorpions of the
earth have power. [4]They were commanded not
to harm the grass of the earth, or any green
thing, or any tree, but only those men who do
not have the seal of God on their foreheads.
[5]And they were not given *authority* to kill
them, but to torment them *for* five months.
Their torment *was* like the torment of a scorpion when it strikes a man. [6]In those days men
will seek death and will not find it; they will
desire to die, and death will flee from them.
[7]The shape of the locusts was like horses
prepared for battle. On their heads were
crowns of something like gold, and their faces
were like the faces of men. [8]They had hair like
women's hair, and their teeth were like lions'
teeth. [9]And they had breastplates like breastplates of iron, and the sound of their wings *was*
like the sound of chariots with many horses
running into battle. [10]They had tails like scorpions, and there were stings in their tails. Their
power *was* to hurt men five months. [11]And they
had as king over them the angel of the bottomless pit, whose name in Hebrew *is*
Abaddon, but in Greek he has the name
Apollyon.

9:11 Abaddon,...Apollyon. Although locusts normally have no king (Prov. 30:27), these demonic creatures do. His name in both Hebrew and Greek means "destroyer." There is a hierarchy of power among the demons, just as among the holy angels. Apparently, "the angel of the bottomless pit" is one of Satan's most trusted leaders or possibly Satan himself.

[12]One woe is past. Behold, still two more
woes are coming after these things.
[13]Then the sixth angel sounded: And I heard
a voice from the four horns of the golden altar
which is before God, [14]saying to the sixth
angel who had the trumpet, "Release the four
angels who are bound at the great river
Euphrates." [15]So the four angels, who had
been prepared for the hour and day and
month and year, were released to kill a third of
mankind. [16]Now the number of the army of the
horsemen *was* two hundred million; I heard
the number of them. [17]And thus I saw the horses in the vision: those who sat on them had
breastplates of fiery red, hyacinth blue, and
sulfur yellow; and the heads of the horses *were*

like the heads of lions; and out of their mouths came fire, smoke, and brimstone. [18]By these three *plagues* a third of mankind was killed—by the fire and the smoke and the brimstone which came out of their mouths. [19]For their power is in their mouth and in their tails; for their tails *are* like serpents, having heads; and with them they do harm.

[20]But the rest of mankind, who were not killed by these plagues, did not repent of the works of their hands, that they should not worship demons, and idols of gold, silver, brass, stone, and wood, which can neither see nor hear nor walk. [21]And they did not repent of their murders or their sorceries or their sexual immorality or their thefts.

DAY 19: Who was the prophet Micah, and what was his message?

The first verse establishes Micah as the author. Beyond that, little is known about him. His parentage is not given, but his name suggests a godly heritage. He traces his roots to the town of Moresheth (1:1,14), located in the foothills of Judah, approximately 25 miles southwest of Jerusalem, on the border of Judah and Philistia, near Gath. From a productive agricultural area, he was like Amos, a country resident removed from the national politics and religion, yet chosen by God (3:8) to deliver a message of judgment to the princes and people of Jerusalem.

Primarily, Micah proclaimed a message of judgment to a people persistently pursuing evil. Similar to other prophets (Hos. 4:1; Amos 3:1), Micah presented his message in lawsuit/courtroom terminology (1:2; 6:1,2). The prophecy is arranged in 3 oracles or cycles, each beginning with the admonition to "hear" (1:2; 3:1; 6:1). Within each oracle, he moves from doom to hope—doom because they have broken God's law given at Sinai; hope because of God's unchanging covenant with their forefathers (7:20). One-third of the book targets the sins of his people; another third looks at the punishment of God to come; and another third promises hope for the faithful after the judgment. Thus, the theme of the inevitability of divine judgment for sin is coupled together with God's immutable commitment to His covenant promises. The combination of God's 1) absolute consistency in judging sin and 2) unbending commitment to His covenant through the remnant of His people provides the hearers with a clear disclosure of the character of the Sovereign of the universe. Through divine intervention, He will bring about both judgment on sinners and blessing on those who repent.

DECEMBER 20

Micah 4:1–5:15

4 Now it shall come to pass
in the latter days
That the mountain of the LORD's house
Shall be established on the top of the
mountains,
And shall be exalted above the hills;
And peoples shall flow to it.
2 Many nations shall come and say,
"Come, and let us go up to the mountain
of the LORD,
To the house of the God of Jacob;
He will teach us His ways,
And we shall walk in His paths."
For out of Zion the law shall go forth,
And the word of the LORD from
Jerusalem.
3 He shall judge between many peoples,
And rebuke strong nations afar off;
They shall beat their swords
into plowshares,
And their spears into pruning hooks;
Nation shall not lift up sword against
nation,
Neither shall they learn war anymore.
4 But everyone shall sit under his vine
and under his fig tree,
And no one shall make *them* afraid;
For the mouth of the LORD of hosts
has spoken.
5 For all people walk each in the name of
his god,
But we will walk in the name of the LORD
our God
Forever and ever.
6 "In that day," says the LORD,

4:1 In a reversal of 3:12, Micah shifted from impending judgment to prophecies of the future millennial kingdom ("the latter days") in which Mt. Zion (v. 3), the center of Messiah's coming earthly kingdom, shall be raised both spiritually and physically (Zech. 14:9,10). This discussion continues to 5:15.

"I will assemble the lame,
I will gather the outcast
And those whom I have afflicted;
7 I will make the lame a remnant,
And the outcast a strong nation;
So the LORD will reign over them in
Mount Zion
From now on, even forever.
8 And you, O tower of the flock,
The stronghold of the daughter of Zion,
To you shall it come,
Even the former dominion shall come,
The kingdom of the daughter
of Jerusalem."

9 Now why do you cry aloud?
Is there no king in your midst?
Has your counselor perished?
For pangs have seized you like a
woman in labor.
10 Be in pain, and labor to bring forth,
O daughter of Zion,
Like a woman in birth pangs.
For now you shall go forth from the city,
You shall dwell in the field,
And to Babylon you shall go.
There you shall be delivered;
There the LORD will redeem you
From the hand of your enemies.

11 Now also many nations have gathered
against you,
Who say, "Let her be defiled,
And let our eye look upon Zion."
12 But they do not know the thoughts of
the LORD,
Nor do they understand His counsel;
For He will gather them like sheaves to
the threshing floor.

13 "Arise and thresh, O daughter of Zion;
For I will make your horn iron,
And I will make your hooves bronze;
You shall beat in pieces many peoples;
I will consecrate their gain to the LORD,
And their substance to the Lord of the
whole earth."

5 Now gather yourself in troops,
O daughter of troops;
He has laid siege against us;
They will strike the judge of Israel with
a rod on the cheek.

2 "But you, Bethlehem Ephrathah,
Though you are little among the
thousands of Judah,
Yet out of you shall come forth to Me
The One to be Ruler in Israel,
Whose goings forth *are* from of old,
From everlasting."

3 Therefore He shall give them up,
Until the time *that* she who is in labor
has given birth;
Then the remnant of His brethren
Shall return to the children of Israel.
4 And He shall stand and feed *His flock*
In the strength of the LORD,
In the majesty of the name of the LORD
His God;
And they shall abide,
For now He shall be great
To the ends of the earth;
5 And this *One* shall be peace.

When the Assyrian comes into our land,
And when he treads in our palaces,
Then we will raise against him
Seven shepherds and eight princely
men.
6 They shall waste with the sword the
land of Assyria,
And the land of Nimrod at its entrances;
Thus He shall deliver *us* from
the Assyrian,
When he comes into our land
And when he treads within our borders.

7 Then the remnant of Jacob
Shall be in the midst of many peoples,
Like dew from the LORD,
Like showers on the grass,
That tarry for no man
Nor wait for the sons of men.
8 And the remnant of Jacob
Shall be among the Gentiles,
In the midst of many peoples,
Like a lion among the beasts of the
forest,
Like a young lion among flocks of sheep,
Who, if he passes through,
Both treads down and tears in pieces,
And none can deliver.
9 Your hand shall be lifted against your
adversaries,
And all your enemies shall be cut off.

10 "And it shall be in that day," says the
LORD,
"That I will cut off your horses from
your midst
And destroy your chariots.
11 I will cut off the cities of your land
And throw down all your strongholds.
12 I will cut off sorceries from your hand,
And you shall have no soothsayers.
13 Your carved images I will also cut off,
And your *sacred* pillars from your midst;
You shall no more worship the work of
your hands;

14 I will pluck your wooden images from
your midst;
Thus I will destroy your cities.
15 And I will execute vengeance in anger
and fury
On the nations that have not heard."

And their eyelids are lifted up.
14 *There is* a generation whose teeth *are*
like swords,
And whose fangs *are like* knives,
To devour the poor from off the earth,
And the needy from *among* men.

Psalm 145:1–9

A Praise of David.

I will extol You, my God, O King;
And I will bless Your name forever
and ever.
2 Every day I will bless You,
And I will praise Your name forever
and ever.
3 Great *is* the LORD, and greatly
to be praised;
And His greatness *is* unsearchable.
4 One generation shall praise Your
works to another,
And shall declare Your mighty acts.
5 I will meditate on the glorious splendor
of Your majesty,
And on Your wondrous works.
6 *Men* shall speak of the might of Your
awesome acts,
And I will declare Your greatness.
7 They shall utter the memory of Your
great goodness,
And shall sing of Your righteousness.
8 The LORD *is* gracious and full of
compassion,
Slow to anger and great in mercy.
9 The LORD *is* good to all,
And His tender mercies *are* over all
His works.

Proverbs 30:11–14

11 *There is* a generation *that* curses
its father,
And does not bless its mother.
12 *There is* a generation *that is* pure in its
own eyes,
Yet is not washed from its filthiness.
13 *There is* a generation—oh, how lofty
are their eyes!

30:11–14 *There is* a generation. These proverbs condemn various forms of unwise behavior and are connected with this common phrase which points to the fact that certain sins can uniquely permeate a whole society or time period.

Revelation 10:1–11

10 I saw still another mighty angel coming
down from heaven, clothed with a cloud.
And a rainbow *was* on his head, his face *was*
like the sun, and his feet like pillars of fire. 2He
had a little book open in his hand. And he set
his right foot on the sea and *his* left *foot* on the
land, 3and cried with a loud voice, as *when* a
lion roars. When he cried out, seven thunders
uttered their voices. 4Now when the seven
thunders uttered their voices, I was about to
write; but I heard a voice from heaven saying
to me, "Seal up the things which the seven
thunders uttered, and do not write them."

10:1 another mighty angel. Many commentators understand this to be Jesus Christ. But the Greek word translated "another" means one of the same kind, i.e., a created being. This is not one of the 7 angels responsible for sounding the trumpets (8:2), but one of the highest ranking in heaven, filled with splendor, greatness, and strength (5:2; 8:3; 18:1). **rainbow.** Perhaps God included this to remind John that, even in judgment, He will always remember His Noahic Covenant and protect His own. **feet like pillars of fire.** This angel's feet and legs indicate the firm resolve with which he will execute the Day of the Lord.

5The angel whom I saw standing on the sea
and on the land raised up his hand to heaven
6and swore by Him who lives forever and ever,
who created heaven and the things that are in it,
the earth and the things that are in it, and the
sea and the things that are in it, that there should
be delay no longer, 7but in the days of the sounding of the seventh angel, when he is about to
sound, the mystery of God would be finished,
as He declared to His servants the prophets.
8Then the voice which I heard from heaven
spoke to me again and said, "Go, take the little
book which is open in the hand of the angel
who stands on the sea and on the earth."
9So I went to the angel and said to him,
"Give me the little book."
And he said to me, "Take and eat it; and it

will make your stomach bitter, but it will be as sweet as honey in your mouth."
10Then I took the little book out of the angel's hand and ate it, and it was as sweet as honey in my mouth. But when I had eaten it, my stomach became bitter.
11And he said to me, "You must prophesy again about many peoples, nations, tongues, and kings."

DAY 20: Is the Bethlehem of Micah 5:2–4 the birthplace of Christ?

"But you, Bethlehem Ephrathah, though you are little among the thousands of Judah, yet out of you shall come forth to Me the One to be Ruler in Israel" (v. 2). This town south of Jerusalem was the birthplace of David and later Jesus Christ (1 Sam. 16; Matt. 2:5; Luke 2:4–7). The name "Bethlehem" means "house of bread" because the area was a grain-producing region in Old Testament times. The name "Ephrathah" ("fruitful") differentiates it from the Galilean town by the same name. The town, known for her many vineyards and olive orchards, was small in size but not in honor. "Whose goings forth are from of old, from everlasting." This speaks of eternal God's incarnation in the Person of Jesus Christ. It points to His millennial reign as King of kings (Is. 9:6).

"Therefore He shall give them up, until the time that she who is in labor has given birth" (v. 3). A reference to the interval between Messiah's rejection at His First Advent and His Second Advent, during the times of the Gentiles when Israel rejects Christ and is under the domination of enemies. Regathering of the "remnant of His brethren" did not occur at the First Advent but is slated for the Second Advent (Is. 10:20–22; 11:11–16). Nor can "return" speak of Gentiles, since it cannot be said that they "returned" to the Lord. Rather, the context of 5:3,4 is millennial and cannot be made to fit the First Advent. Thus, "she who is in labor" must denote the nation of Israel (Rev. 12:1–6).

Verse 4 clearly depicts the millennial rule of Christ, sitting upon the throne of David (Is. 6:1–3).

DECEMBER 21

Micah 6:1–7:20

6 Hear now what the LORD says:

"Arise, plead your case before the
mountains,
And let the hills hear your voice.
2 Hear, O you mountains, the LORD's
complaint,
And you strong foundations of the earth;
For the LORD has a complaint against
His people,
And He will contend with Israel.

3 "O My people, what have I done to you?
And how have I wearied you?
Testify against Me.
4 For I brought you up from the land of
Egypt,
I redeemed you from the house of
bondage;
And I sent before you Moses, Aaron,
and Miriam.
5 O My people, remember now
What Balak king of Moab counseled,
And what Balaam the son of Beor
answered him,
From Acacia Grove to Gilgal,
That you may know the righteousness
of the LORD."

6 With what shall I come before the LORD,
And bow myself before the High God?
Shall I come before Him with burnt
offerings,
With calves a year old?
7 Will the LORD be pleased with
thousands of rams,
Ten thousand rivers of oil?
Shall I give my firstborn *for* my
transgression,
The fruit of my body *for* the sin
of my soul?

8 He has shown you, O man, what *is* good;

6:6,7 Micah, as though speaking on behalf of the people, asked rhetorically how, in light of God's faithfulness toward them, they could continue their hypocrisy by being outwardly religious but inwardly sinful.

6:8 Micah's terse response indicated the people should have known the answer to the rhetorical question. Spiritual blindness had led them to offer everything except the one thing He wanted—a spiritual commitment of the heart from which right behavior would ensue (Deut. 10:12–19; Matt. 22:37–39). This theme is often represented in the Old Testament (1 Sam. 15:22; Is. 1:11–20; Jer. 7:21–23; Hos. 6:6; Amos 5:15).

And what does the LORD require of you
But to do justly,
To love mercy,
And to walk humbly with
your God?

9 The LORD's voice cries to the city—
Wisdom shall see Your name:

"Hear the rod!
Who has appointed it?
10 Are there yet the treasures of
wickedness
In the house of the wicked,
And the short measure *that is* an
abomination?
11 Shall I count pure *those* with the
wicked scales,
And with the bag of deceitful weights?
12 For her rich men are full of violence,
Her inhabitants have spoken lies,
And their tongue is deceitful in their
mouth.

13 "Therefore I will also make *you* sick by
striking you,
By making *you* desolate because of
your sins.
14 You shall eat, but not be satisfied;
Hunger *shall be* in your midst.
You may carry *some* away, but shall
not save *them;*
And what you do rescue I will give over
to the sword.

15 "You shall sow, but not reap;
You shall tread the olives, but not anoint
yourselves with oil;
And *make* sweet wine, but not drink
wine.
16 For the statutes of Omri are kept;
All the works of Ahab's house *are done;*
And you walk in their counsels,
That I may make you a desolation,
And your inhabitants a hissing.
Therefore you shall bear the reproach
of My people."

7 Woe is me!
For I am like those who gather
summer fruits,
Like those who glean vintage grapes;
There is no cluster to eat
Of the first-ripe fruit *which* my soul
desires.
2 The faithful *man* has perished from
the earth,
And *there is* no one upright among men.
They all lie in wait for blood;
Every man hunts his brother with a net.
3 That they may successfully do evil with
both hands—
The prince asks *for gifts,*
The judge *seeks* a bribe,
And the great *man* utters his evil desire;
So they scheme together.
4 The best of them *is* like a brier;
The most upright *is sharper* than a
thorn hedge;
The day of your watchman and your
punishment comes;
Now shall be their perplexity.

5 Do not trust in a friend;
Do not put your confidence in a
companion;
Guard the doors of your mouth
From her who lies in your bosom.
6 For son dishonors father,
Daughter rises against her mother,
Daughter-in-law against her
mother-in-law;
A man's enemies *are* the men of his
own household.
7 Therefore I will look to the LORD;
I will wait for the God of my salvation;
My God will hear me.
8 Do not rejoice over me, my enemy;
When I fall, I will arise;
When I sit in darkness,
The LORD *will be* a light to me.
9 I will bear the indignation of the LORD,
Because I have sinned against Him,
Until He pleads my case
And executes justice for me.
He will bring me forth to the light;
I will see His righteousness.
10 Then *she who is* my enemy will see,
And shame will cover her who said
to me,
"Where is the LORD your God?"
My eyes will see her;
Now she will be trampled down
Like mud in the streets.

11 *In* the day when your walls
are to be built,
In that day the decree shall go far
and wide.
12 *In* that day they shall come to you
From Assyria and the fortified cities,
From the fortress to the River,
From sea to sea,
And mountain *to* mountain.
13 Yet the land shall be desolate
Because of those who dwell in it,
And for the fruit of their deeds.

14 Shepherd Your people with Your staff,
The flock of Your heritage,

Who dwell solitarily *in* a woodland,
In the midst of Carmel;
Let them feed *in* Bashan and Gilead,
As in days of old.

15 "As in the days when you came out of
the land of Egypt,
I will show them wonders."

16 The nations shall see and be ashamed
of all their might;
They shall put *their* hand over *their*
mouth;
Their ears shall be deaf.
17 They shall lick the dust like a serpent;
They shall crawl from their holes like
snakes of the earth.
They shall be afraid of the LORD our
God,
And shall fear because of You.
18 Who *is* a God like You,
Pardoning iniquity
And passing over the transgression of
the remnant of His heritage?

He does not retain His anger forever,
Because He delights *in* mercy.
19 He will again have compassion on us,
And will subdue our iniquities.

You will cast all our sins
Into the depths of the sea.
20 You will give truth to Jacob
And mercy to Abraham,
Which You have sworn to our fathers
From days of old.

Psalm 145:10–16

10 All Your works shall praise You,
O LORD,
And Your saints shall bless You.
11 They shall speak of the glory of Your
kingdom,
And talk of Your power,
12 To make known to the sons of men
His mighty acts,
And the glorious majesty of His
kingdom.
13 Your kingdom *is* an everlasting kingdom,
And Your dominion *endures*
throughout all generations.

14 The LORD upholds all who fall,
And raises up all *who are* bowed down.
15 The eyes of all look expectantly to You,
And You give them their food in due
season.
16 You open Your hand
And satisfy the desire of every living
thing.

Proverbs 30:15

15 The leech has two daughters—
Give *and* Give!

There are three *things that* are never
satisfied,
Four never say, "Enough!":

Revelation 11:1–19

11 Then I was given a reed like a measuring
rod. And the angel stood, saying, "Rise
and measure the temple of God, the altar, and
those who worship there. 2 But leave out the
court which is outside the temple, and do not
measure it, for it has been given to the
Gentiles. And they will tread the holy city
underfoot *for* forty-two months. 3 And I will
give *power* to my two witnesses, and they will
prophesy one thousand two hundred and sixty
days, clothed in sackcloth."

4 These are the two olive trees and the two
lampstands standing before the God of the
earth. 5 And if anyone wants to harm them, fire
proceeds from their mouth and devours their
enemies. And if anyone wants to harm them,
he must be killed in this manner. 6 These have
power to shut heaven, so that no rain falls in
the days of their prophecy; and they have
power over waters to turn them to blood, and
to strike the earth with all plagues, as often as
they desire.

7 When they finish their testimony, the beast
that ascends out of the bottomless pit will
make war against them, overcome them, and
kill them. 8 And their dead bodies *will lie* in the
street of the great city which spiritually is
called Sodom and Egypt, where also our Lord
was crucified. 9 Then *those* from the peoples,
tribes, tongues, and nations will see their dead
bodies three-and-a-half days, and not allow
their dead bodies to be put into graves. 10 And
those who dwell on the earth will rejoice over
them, make merry, and send gifts to one
another, because these two prophets tormented those who dwell on the earth.

11:7 the beast. The first of 36 references to this person in Revelation, who is none other than the Antichrist (see chap. 13). That he will ascend out of the bottomless pit indicates that his power is satanic. **kill them.** Their ministry completed, God will withdraw the two witnesses' supernatural protection. The beast will then be able to accomplish what many had died trying to do.

11Now after the three-and-a-half days the
breath of life from God entered them, and they
stood on their feet, and great fear fell on those
who saw them. 12And they heard a loud voice
from heaven saying to them, "Come up here."
And they ascended to heaven in a cloud, and
their enemies saw them. 13In the same hour
there was a great earthquake, and a tenth of
the city fell. In the earthquake seven thousand
people were killed, and the rest were afraid and
gave glory to the God of heaven.
14The second woe is past. Behold, the third
woe is coming quickly.

11:13 earthquake. God punctuates the ascension of His prophets with a shattering earthquake. The destruction and loss of life may be primarily among the leaders of the Antichrist's forces. **the rest.** This refers to the Jews still living, who will not yet have come to faith in Christ. **gave glory to the God of heaven.** A genuine experience of the salvation of Jews (Luke 17:18,19), in contrast to those who blaspheme and refuse to glorify God (16:9). This makes a key fulfillment of Zechariah's prophecy (12:10; 13:1) and Paul's (Rom. 11:25–27).

15Then the seventh angel sounded: And there
were loud voices in heaven, saying, "The kingdoms of this world have become *the kingdoms*
of our Lord and of His Christ, and He shall
reign forever and ever!" 16And the twenty-four
elders who sat before God on their thrones fell
on their faces and worshiped God, 17saying:

"We give You thanks, O Lord God
Almighty,
The One who is and who was and who
is to come,
Because You have taken Your great
power and reigned.
18 The nations were angry, and Your
wrath has come,
And the time of the dead, that they
should be judged,
And that You should reward Your
servants the prophets and the
saints,
And those who fear Your name, small
and great,
And should destroy those who destroy
the earth."

19Then the temple of God was opened in
heaven, and the ark of His covenant was seen in
His temple. And there were lightnings, noises,
thunderings, an earthquake, and great hail.

DAY 21: Who are the "two witnesses" of Revelation 11?

In v. 3, John is told that "I will give power to my two witnesses." These individuals are granted special power and authority by God to preach a message of judgment and salvation during the second half of the Tribulation. The Old Testament required 2 or more witnesses to confirm testimony (Deut. 17:6; 19:15; Matt. 18:16; John 8:17; Heb. 10:28), and these 2 prophets will be the culmination of God's testimony to Israel: a message of judgment from God and of His gracious offer of the gospel to all who will repent and believe. "They will prophesy one thousand two hundred and sixty days," which is 42 months or 3 1/2 years, "clothed in sackcloth." Coarse, rough cloth made from goat or camel hair. Wearing garments made from it expressed penitence, humility, and mourning. The witnesses are mourning because of the wretched wickedness of the world, God's judgment on it, and the desecration of the temple and the holy city by the Antichrist.

The imagery in v. 4 is drawn from Zechariah 3, 4. Zechariah's vision had both a near fulfillment (the rebuilding of the temple by Joshua and Zerubbabel) and a far future fulfillment (the 2 witnesses, whose ministry points toward Israel's final restoration in the Millennium). "Two olive trees and the two lampstands." Olive oil was commonly used in lamps; together the olive trees and lampstands symbolize the light of spiritual revival. The 2 witnesses' preaching will spark a revival, just as Joshua's and Zerubbabel's did in Israel after the Babylonian captivity.

While it is impossible to be dogmatic about the identity of these 2 witnesses, several observations from vv. 5,6 suggest they might be Moses and Elijah: 1) like Moses, they strike the earth with plagues, and like Elijah, they have the power to keep it from raining; 2) Jewish tradition expected both Moses (Deut. 18:15–18) and Elijah (Mal. 4:5,6) to return in the future (John 1:21); 3) both Moses and Elijah were present at the Transfiguration, the preview of Christ's Second Coming; 4) both Moses and Elijah used supernatural means to provoke repentance; 5) Elijah was taken up alive into heaven, and God buried Moses' body where it would never be found; and 6) the length of the drought the 2 witnesses bring (3 1/2 years) is the same as that brought by Elijah (James 5:17).

DECEMBER 22

Nahum 1:1–3:19

1 The burden against Nineveh. The book of the vision of Nahum the Elkoshite.

2 God *is* jealous, and the LORD avenges;
The LORD avenges and *is* furious.
The LORD will take vengeance on His adversaries,
And He reserves *wrath* for His enemies;
3 The LORD *is* slow to anger and great in power,
And will not at all acquit *the wicked.*

The LORD has His way
In the whirlwind and in the storm,
And the clouds *are* the dust of His feet.
4 He rebukes the sea and makes it dry,
And dries up all the rivers.
Bashan and Carmel wither,
And the flower of Lebanon wilts.
5 The mountains quake before Him,
The hills melt,
And the earth heaves at His presence,
Yes, the world and all who dwell in it.

6 Who can stand before His indignation?
And who can endure the fierceness of His anger?
His fury is poured out like fire,
And the rocks are thrown down by Him.

7 The LORD *is* good,
A stronghold in the day of trouble;
And He knows those who trust in Him.
8 But with an overflowing flood
He will make an utter end of its place,
And darkness will pursue His enemies.

9 What do you conspire against the LORD?
He will make an utter end *of it.*
Affliction will not rise up a second time.
10 For while tangled *like* thorns,
And while drunken *like* drunkards,
They shall be devoured like stubble fully dried.
11 From you comes forth *one*
Who plots evil against the LORD,
A wicked counselor.

12 Thus says the LORD:
"Though *they are* safe, and likewise many,
Yet in this manner they will be cut down
When he passes through.
Though I have afflicted you,
I will afflict you no more;

1:11 wicked counselor. The phrase, literally, "counselor of Belial," suggests satanic influence on the leadership, identified as the king of Assyria (3:18). Specific reference could be to Ashurbanipal (669–633 B.C.) or more likely to Sennacherib (705–681 B.C.), who invaded Judah in 701 B.C. and of whom Isaiah speaks in similar language (Is. 10:7).

13 For now I will break off his yoke from you,
And burst your bonds apart."

14 The LORD has given a command concerning you:
"Your name shall be perpetuated no longer.
Out of the house of your gods
I will cut off the carved image and the molded image.
I will dig your grave,
For you are vile."

15 Behold, on the mountains
The feet of him who brings good tidings,
Who proclaims peace!
O Judah, keep your appointed feasts,
Perform your vows.
For the wicked one shall no more pass through you;
He is utterly cut off.

2 He who scatters has come up before your face.
Man the fort!
Watch the road!
Strengthen *your* flanks!
Fortify *your* power mightily.

2 For the LORD will restore the excellence of Jacob
Like the excellence of Israel,
For the emptiers have emptied them out
And ruined their vine branches.

3 The shields of his mighty men *are* made red,
The valiant men *are* in scarlet.
The chariots *come* with flaming torches
In the day of his preparation,
And the spears are brandished.
4 The chariots rage in the streets,
They jostle one another in the broad roads;
They seem like torches,
They run like lightning.

5 He remembers his nobles;
They stumble in their walk;
They make haste to her walls,
And the defense is prepared.
6 The gates of the rivers are opened,
And the palace is dissolved.
7 It is decreed:
She shall be led away captive,
She shall be brought up;
And her maidservants shall lead *her* as with the voice of doves,
Beating their breasts.

8 Though Nineveh of old *was* like a pool of water,
Now they flee away.
"Halt! Halt!" *they cry;*
But no one turns back.
9 Take spoil of silver!
Take spoil of gold!
There is no end of treasure,
Or wealth of every desirable prize.
10 She is empty, desolate, and waste!
The heart melts, and the knees shake;
Much pain *is* in every side,
And all their faces are drained of color.

11 Where *is* the dwelling of the lions,
And the feeding place of the young lions,
Where the lion walked, the lioness *and* lion's cub,
And no one made *them* afraid?
12 The lion tore in pieces enough for his cubs,
Killed for his lionesses,
Filled his caves with prey,
And his dens with flesh.

13 "Behold, I *am* against you," says the LORD of hosts, "I will burn your chariots in smoke, and the sword shall devour your young lions; I will cut off your prey from the earth, and the voice of your messengers shall be heard no more."

3 Woe to the bloody city!
It *is* all full of lies *and* robbery.
Its victim never departs.
2 The noise of a whip
And the noise of rattling wheels,
Of galloping horses,
Of clattering chariots!
3 Horsemen charge with bright sword and glittering spear.
There is a multitude of slain,
A great number of bodies,
Countless corpses—
They stumble over the corpses—
4 Because of the multitude of harlotries of the seductive harlot,
The mistress of sorceries,
Who sells nations through her harlotries,
And families through her sorceries.

5 "Behold, I *am* against you," says the LORD of hosts;
"I will lift your skirts over your face,
I will show the nations your nakedness,
And the kingdoms your shame.
6 I will cast abominable filth upon you,
Make you vile,
And make you a spectacle.
7 It shall come to pass *that* all who look upon you
Will flee from you, and say,
'Nineveh is laid waste!
Who will bemoan her?'
Where shall I seek comforters for you?"

8 Are you better than No Amon
That was situated by the River,
That had the waters around her,
Whose rampart *was* the sea,
Whose wall *was* the sea?
9 Ethiopia and Egypt *were* her strength,
And *it was* boundless;
Put and Lubim were your helpers.
10 Yet she *was* carried away,
She went into captivity;
Her young children also were dashed to pieces
At the head of every street;
They cast lots for her honorable men,
And all her great men were bound in chains.
11 You also will be drunk;
You will be hidden;
You also will seek refuge from the enemy.

12 All your strongholds *are* fig trees with ripened figs:
If they are shaken,
They fall into the mouth of the eater.
13 Surely, your people in your midst *are* women!
The gates of your land are wide open for your enemies;
Fire shall devour the bars of your *gates.*

3:1 bloody city. The first accusation was a charge well documented in history. Assyria proved to be an unusually cruel, bloodthirsty nation. **lies.** Assyria employed falsehood and treachery to subdue her enemies (2 Kin. 18:28–32). **robbery.** Preying upon her victims, she filled her cities with the goods of other nations.

14 Draw your water for the siege!
Fortify your strongholds!
Go into the clay and tread the mortar!
Make strong the brick kiln!
15 There the fire will devour you,
The sword will cut you off;
It will eat you up like a locust.

Make yourself many— like the locust!
Make yourself many— like the
swarming locusts!
16 You have multiplied your merchants
more than the stars of heaven.
The locust plunders and flies away.
17 Your commanders *are* like *swarming*
locusts,
And your generals like great
grasshoppers,
Which camp in the hedges on a cold day;
When the sun rises they flee away,
And the place where they *are* is not
known.

18 Your shepherds slumber, O king
of Assyria;
Your nobles rest *in the dust.*
Your people are scattered on the
mountains,
And no one gathers them.
19 Your injury *has* no healing,
Your wound is severe.
All who hear news of you
Will clap *their* hands over you,
For upon whom has not your
wickedness passed continually?

Psalm 145:17–21

17 The LORD *is* righteous in all His ways,
Gracious in all His works.
18 The LORD *is* near to all who call upon
Him,
To all who call upon Him in truth.
19 He will fulfill the desire of those who
fear Him;
He also will hear their cry and save
them.
20 The LORD preserves all who love Him,
But all the wicked He will destroy.
21 My mouth shall speak the praise of the
LORD,
And all flesh shall bless His holy name
Forever and ever.

Proverbs 30:16

16 The grave,
The barren womb,
The earth *that* is not satisfied with
water—
And the fire never says, "Enough!"

Revelation 12:1–17

12 Now a great sign appeared in heaven: a
woman clothed with the sun, with the
moon under her feet, and on her head a gar-
land of twelve stars. 2Then being with child, she
cried out in labor and in pain to give birth.
3And another sign appeared in heaven:
behold, a great, fiery red dragon having seven
heads and ten horns, and seven diadems on
his heads. 4His tail drew a third of the stars of

12:3 great, fiery red dragon. The woman's mortal enemy is Satan, who appears as a dragon 13 times in this book (v. 9; 20:2). Red speaks of bloodshed (John 8:44). **seven heads and ten horns, and seven diadems.** Figurative language depicting Satan's domination of 7 past worldly kingdoms and 10 future kingdoms (Dan. 7:7,20,24). Satan has and will rule the world until the seventh trumpet blows (11:15). He has inflicted relentless pain on Israel (Dan. 8:24), desiring to kill the woman before she could bring forth the child that would destroy him.

heaven and threw them to the earth. And the
dragon stood before the woman who was
ready to give birth, to devour her Child as
soon as it was born. 5She bore a male Child
who was to rule all nations with a rod of iron.
And her Child was caught up to God and His
throne. 6Then the woman fled into the wilderness, where she has a place prepared by God,
that they should feed her there one thousand
two hundred and sixty days.
7And war broke out in heaven: Michael and
his angels fought with the dragon; and the
dragon and his angels fought, 8but they did
not prevail, nor was a place found for them in
heaven any longer. 9So the great dragon was
cast out, that serpent of old, called the Devil
and Satan, who deceives the whole world; he
was cast to the earth, and his angels were cast
out with him.
10Then I heard a loud voice saying in heav-
en, "Now salvation, and strength, and the
kingdom of our God, and the power of His
Christ have come, for the accuser of our
brethren, who accused them before our God
day and night, has been cast down. 11And they
overcame him by the blood of the Lamb and
by the word of their testimony, and they did
not love their lives to the death. 12Therefore rejoice, O heavens, and you who dwell in them!

12:9 dragon was cast...to the earth. Satan and his demons were cast out of heaven at the time of their original rebellion, but still have access to it (Job 1:6; 2:1). That access will then be denied, and they will be forever barred from heaven. **Devil and Satan.** "Devil" comes from a Greek verb meaning "to slander" or "to falsely accuse." He is a malignant liar (John 8:44; 1 John 3:8). His accusations against believers (v. 10) are unsuccessful because of Christ our Advocate (1 John 2:1). Satan, meaning "adversary" or "enemy," appears especially in Job and the Gospels. **deceives the whole world.** As he has throughout human history, Satan will deceive people during the Tribulation (13:14; 20:3; John 8:44). After his temporary release from the bottomless pit at the end of the Millennium, he will briefly resume his deceitful ways (20:8,10).

Woe to the inhabitants of the earth and the
sea! For the devil has come down to you, having great wrath, because he knows that he has
a short time."
13Now when the dragon saw that he had
been cast to the earth, he persecuted the
woman who gave birth to the male *Child.* 14But
the woman was given two wings of a great
eagle, that she might fly into the wilderness to
her place, where she is nourished for a time
and times and half a time, from the presence
of the serpent. 15So the serpent spewed water
out of his mouth like a flood after the woman,
that he might cause her to be carried away by
the flood. 16But the earth helped the woman,
and the earth opened its mouth and swallowed up the flood which the dragon had
spewed out of his mouth. 17And the dragon
was enraged with the woman, and he went to
make war with the rest of her offspring, who
keep the commandments of God and have the
testimony of Jesus Christ.

DAY 22: Who was the prophet Nahum, and how was his message related to the prophet Jonah?

The significance of the writing prophets was not their personal lives; it was their message. Thus, background information about the prophet from within the prophecy is rare. Occasionally one of the historical books will shed additional light. In the case of Nahum, nothing is provided except that he was an Elkoshite (1:1), referring either to his birthplace or his place of ministry. Attempts to identify the location of Elkosh have been unsuccessful. Suggestions include Al Qosh, situated in northern Iraq (thus Nahum would have been a descendant of the exiles taken to Assyria in 722 B.C.), Capernaum ("town of Nahum"), or a location in southern Judah (1:15). His birthplace or locale is not significant to the interpretation of the book.

Nahum forms a sequel to the Book of Jonah, who prophesied over a century earlier. Jonah recounts the remission of God's promised judgment toward Nineveh, while Nahum depicts the later execution of God's judgment. Nineveh was proud of her invulnerable city, with her walls reaching 100 feet high and with a moat 150 feet wide and 60 feet deep. But Nahum established the fact that the sovereign God (1:2–5) would bring vengeance upon those who violated His law (1:8,14; 3:5–7). The same God had a retributive judgment against evil which is also redemptive, bestowing His loving kindnesses upon the faithful (1:7,12,13,15; 2:2). The prophecy brought comfort to Judah and all who feared the cruel Assyrians. Nahum said Nineveh would end "with an overflowing flood" (1:8); and it happened when the Tigris River overflowed to destroy enough of the walls to let the Babylonians through. Nahum also predicted that the city would be hidden (3:11). After its destruction in 612 B.C., the site was not rediscovered until 1842 A.D.

DECEMBER 23

Habakkuk 1:1–3:19

1 The burden which the prophet Habakkuk saw.

2 O LORD, how long shall I cry,
And You will not hear?
Even cry out to You, "Violence!"
And You will not save.
3 Why do You show me iniquity,
And cause *me* to see trouble?
For plundering and violence *are* before me;
There is strife, and contention arises.
4 Therefore the law is powerless,
And justice never goes forth.
For the wicked surround the righteous;
Therefore perverse judgment proceeds.

5 "Look among the nations and watch—
Be utterly astounded!
For *I will* work a work in your days
Which you would not believe, though it
were told *you*.
6 For indeed I am raising up the
Chaldeans,
A bitter and hasty nation
Which marches through the breadth of
the earth,
To possess dwelling places *that are* not
theirs.
7 They are terrible and dreadful;
Their judgment and their dignity
proceed from themselves.
8 Their horses also are swifter than
leopards,
And more fierce than evening wolves.
Their chargers charge ahead;
Their cavalry comes from afar;
They fly as the eagle *that* hastens to eat.

9 "They all come for violence;
Their faces are set *like* the east wind.
They gather captives like sand.
10 They scoff at kings,
And princes are scorned by them.
They deride every stronghold,
For they heap up earthen *mounds*
and seize it.
11 Then *his* mind changes, and he
transgresses;
He commits offense,
Ascribing this power to his god."

12 Are You not from everlasting,
O LORD my God, my Holy One?
We shall not die.
O LORD, You have appointed them for
judgment;
O Rock, You have marked them for
correction.
13 *You are* of purer eyes than to behold evil,
And cannot look on wickedness.
Why do You look on those who deal
treacherously,
And hold Your tongue when the
wicked devours
A *person* more righteous than he?
14 *Why* do You make men like fish
of the sea,
Like creeping things *that have* no ruler
over them?
15 They take up all of them with a hook,
They catch them in their net,
And gather them in their dragnet.
Therefore they rejoice and are glad.
16 Therefore they sacrifice to their net,
And burn incense to their dragnet;
Because by them their share
is sumptuous
And their food plentiful.
17 Shall they therefore empty their net,
And continue to slay nations without
pity?

2 I will stand my watch
And set myself on the rampart,
And watch to see what He will say to me,
And what I will answer when I am
corrected.

2 Then the LORD answered me and said:

"Write the vision
And make *it* plain on tablets,
That he may run who reads it.
3 For the vision *is* yet for an appointed
time;
But at the end it will speak, and it will
not lie.
Though it tarries, wait for it;
Because it will surely come,
It will not tarry.

4 "Behold the proud,
His soul is not upright in him;
But the just shall live by his faith.

2:4 the just shall live by his faith. In contrast to the proud, the just will be truly preserved through his faithfulness to God. This is the core of God's message to/through Habakkuk. Both the aspect of justification by faith, as noted by Paul's usage in Romans 1:17 and Galatians 3:11, as well as the aspect of sanctification by faith, as employed by the writer of Hebrews (10:38), reflect the essence of Habakkuk; no conflict exists. The emphasis in both Habakkuk and the New Testament references goes beyond the act of faith to include the continuity of faith. Faith is not a one-time act, but a way of life. The true believer, declared righteous by God, will persevere in faith as the pattern of his life (Col. 1:22,23; Heb. 3:12–14).

5 "Indeed, because he transgresses by wine,
He is a proud man,
And he does not stay at home.
Because he enlarges his desire as hell,
And he *is* like death, and cannot be
satisfied,
He gathers to himself all nations
And heaps up for himself all peoples.

6 "Will not all these take up a proverb
against him,

And a taunting riddle against him,
and say,
'Woe to him who increases
What is not his—how long?
And to him who loads himself with
many pledges'?
7 Will not your creditors rise up
suddenly?
Will they not awaken who oppress you?
And you will become their booty.
8 Because you have plundered many
nations,
All the remnant of the people shall
plunder you,
Because of men's blood
And the violence of the land *and* the city,
And of all who dwell in it.

9 "Woe to him who covets evil gain for his
house,
That he may set his nest on high,
That he may be delivered from the
power of disaster!
10 You give shameful counsel to your house,
Cutting off many peoples,
And sin *against* your soul.
11 For the stone will cry out from the wall,
And the beam from the timbers will
answer it.

12 "Woe to him who builds a town with
bloodshed,
Who establishes a city by iniquity!
13 Behold, *is it* not of the LORD of hosts
That the peoples labor to feed the fire,
And nations weary themselves in vain?
14 For the earth will be filled
With the knowledge of the glory
of the LORD,
As the waters cover the sea.

15 "Woe to him who gives drink to his
neighbor,
Pressing *him to* your bottle,
Even to make *him* drunk,
That you may look on his nakedness!
16 You are filled with shame instead of
glory.
You also—drink!
And be exposed as uncircumcised!
The cup of the LORD's right hand *will
be* turned against you,
And utter shame will be on your glory.
17 For the violence *done to* Lebanon will
cover you,
And the plunder of beasts *which* made
them afraid,
Because of men's blood
And the violence of the land *and* the
city,
And of all who dwell in it.

18 "What profit is the image, that its maker
should carve it,
The molded image, a teacher of lies,
That the maker of its mold should trust
in it,
To make mute idols?
19 Woe to him who says to wood, 'Awake!'
To silent stone, 'Arise! It shall teach!'
Behold, it is overlaid with gold and
silver,
Yet in it there is no breath at all.

20 "But the LORD is in His holy temple.
Let all the earth keep silence before
Him."

3 A prayer of Habakkuk the prophet, on
Shigionoth.

2 O LORD, I have heard Your speech
and was afraid;
O LORD, revive Your work in the midst
of the years!
In the midst of the years make *it*
known;
In wrath remember mercy.
3 God came from Teman,
The Holy One from Mount Paran.
Selah

His glory covered the heavens,
And the earth was full of His praise.
4 *His* brightness was like the light;
He had rays *flashing* from His hand,
And there His power *was* hidden.
5 Before Him went pestilence,
And fever followed at His feet.
6 He stood and measured the earth;
He looked and startled the nations.
And the everlasting mountains were
scattered,
The perpetual hills bowed.
His ways *are* everlasting.
7 I saw the tents of Cushan in affliction;
The curtains of the land of Midian
trembled.
8 O LORD, were *You* displeased with the
rivers,
Was Your anger against the rivers,
Was Your wrath against the sea,
That You rode on Your horses,
Your chariots of salvation?
9 Your bow was made quite ready;
Oaths were sworn over *Your* arrows.
Selah

You divided the earth with rivers.
10 The mountains saw You *and* trembled;
The overflowing of the water passed by.
The deep uttered its voice,

And lifted its hands on high.
11 The sun and moon stood still in their habitation;
At the light of Your arrows they went,
At the shining of Your glittering spear.

12 You marched through the land in indignation;
You trampled the nations in anger.
13 You went forth for the salvation of Your people,
For salvation with Your Anointed.
You struck the head from the house of the wicked,
By laying bare from foundation to neck. Selah

14 You thrust through with his own arrows
The head of his villages.
They came out like a whirlwind to scatter me;
Their rejoicing was like feasting on the poor in secret.
15 You walked through the sea with Your horses,
Through the heap of great waters.

16 When I heard, my body trembled;
My lips quivered at *the* voice;
Rottenness entered my bones;
And I trembled in myself,
That I might rest in the day of trouble.
When he comes up to the people,
He will invade them with his troops.

17 Though the fig tree may not blossom,
Nor fruit be on the vines;
Though the labor of the olive may fail,
And the fields yield no food;
Though the flock may be cut off from the fold,
And there be no herd in the stalls—
18 Yet I will rejoice in the LORD,
I will joy in the God of my salvation.
19 The LORD God is my strength;
He will make my feet like deer's *feet,*
And He will make me walk on my high hills.

To the Chief Musician. With my stringed instruments.

Psalm 146:1–10

Praise the LORD!

Praise the LORD, O my soul!
2 While I live I will praise the LORD;
I will sing praises to my God while I have my being.
3 Do not put your trust in princes,
Nor in a son of man, in whom *there is* no help.
4 His spirit departs, he returns to his earth;
In that very day his plans perish.

5 Happy *is he* who *has* the God of Jacob for his help,
Whose hope *is* in the LORD his God,
6 Who made heaven and earth,
The sea, and all that *is* in them;
Who keeps truth forever,
7 Who executes justice for the oppressed,
Who gives food to the hungry.
The LORD gives freedom to the prisoners.

8 The LORD opens *the eyes of* the blind;
The LORD raises those who are bowed down;
The LORD loves the righteous.
9 The LORD watches over the strangers;
He relieves the fatherless and widow;
But the way of the wicked He turns upside down.

10 The LORD shall reign forever—
Your God, O Zion, to all generations.

Praise the LORD!

Proverbs 30:17

17 The eye *that* mocks *his* father,
And scorns obedience to *his* mother,
The ravens of the valley will pick it out,
And the young eagles will eat it.

30:17 eye *that* mocks. This proverb vividly speaks to the tragic results of disregarding parental respect and authority and the destruction it brings. **ravens...young eagles.** These birds scavenge the unburied corpse of a child who dies prematurely because of rebellion (1 Sam. 17:44; 1 Kin. 14:11; Jer. 16:4; Ezek. 29:5; 39:4).

Revelation 13:1–18

13 Then I stood on the sand of the sea. And
I saw a beast rising up out of the sea,
having seven heads and ten horns, and on his
horns ten crowns, and on his heads a blasphemous name. 2Now the beast which I saw was
like a leopard, his feet were like *the feet of* a
bear, and his mouth like the mouth of a lion.
The dragon gave him his power, his throne,

13:3 his deadly wound was healed. This statement could refer to one of the kingdoms that was destroyed and revived (i.e., the Roman Empire). But more likely it refers to a fake death and resurrection enacted by the Antichrist, as part of his lying deception (vv. 12,14; 17:8,11; 2 Thess. 2:9). **world marveled.** People in the world will be astounded and fascinated when Antichrist appears to rise from the dead. His charisma, brilliance, and attractive but deluding powers will cause the world to follow him unquestioningly (v. 14; 2 Thess. 2:8–12).

13:18 His number *is* 666. This is the essential number of a man. The number 6 falls one short of God's perfect number, 7, and thus represents human imperfection. Antichrist, the most powerful human the world will ever know, will still be a man, i.e., a 6. The ultimate in human and demonic power is a 6, not perfect, as God is. The 3-fold repetition of the number is intended to reiterate and underscore man's identity. When Antichrist is finally revealed, there will be some way to identify him with this basic number of a man, or his name may have the numerical equivalent of 666. (In many languages, including Hebrew, Greek, and Latin, letters have numerical equivalents.) Because this text reveals very little about the meaning of 666, it is unwise to speculate beyond what is said.

and great authority. 3And I saw one of his
heads as if it had been mortally wounded, and
his deadly wound was healed. And all the
world marveled and followed the beast. 4So
they worshiped the dragon who gave authority to the beast; and they worshiped the beast,
saying, "Who *is* like the beast? Who is able to
make war with him?"

5And he was given a mouth speaking great
things and blasphemies, and he was given
authority to continue for forty-two months.
6Then he opened his mouth in blasphemy
against God, to blaspheme His name, His tabernacle, and those who dwell in heaven. 7It
was granted to him to make war with the
saints and to overcome them. And authority
was given him over every tribe, tongue, and
nation. 8All who dwell on the earth will worship him, whose names have not been written
in the Book of Life of the Lamb slain from the
foundation of the world.

9If anyone has an ear, let him hear. 10He who
leads into captivity shall go into captivity; he
who kills with the sword must be killed with
the sword. Here is the patience and the faith of
the saints.

11Then I saw another beast coming up out of
the earth, and he had two horns like a lamb
and spoke like a dragon. 12And he exercises all
the authority of the first beast in his presence,
and causes the earth and those who dwell in it
to worship the first beast, whose deadly
wound was healed. 13He performs great signs,
so that he even makes fire come down from
heaven on the earth in the sight of men. 14And
he deceives those who dwell on the earth by
those signs which he was granted to do in the
sight of the beast, telling those who dwell on
the earth to make an image to the beast who
was wounded by the sword and lived. 15He was
granted *power* to give breath to the image of
the beast, that the image of the beast should
both speak and cause as many as would not
worship the image of the beast to be killed.
16He causes all, both small and great, rich and
poor, free and slave, to receive a mark on their
right hand or on their foreheads, 17and that no
one may buy or sell except one who has the
mark or the name of the beast, or the number
of his name.

18Here is wisdom. Let him who has understanding calculate the number of the beast, for
it is the number of a man: His number *is* 666.

DAY 23: Who was Habakkuk, and where did his questions for God take him?

As with many of the Minor Prophets, nothing is known about the prophet except that which can be inferred from the book. In the case of Habakkuk, internal information is virtually nonexistent, making conclusions about his identity and life conjectural. His simple introduction as "the prophet Habakkuk" may imply that he needed no introduction since he was a well-known prophet of his day. It is certain that he was a contemporary of Jeremiah, Ezekiel, Daniel, and Zephaniah.

The opening verses reveal a historical situation similar to the days of Amos and Micah. Justice had essentially disappeared from the land. Violence and wickedness were pervasive, existing unchecked. In the midst of these dark days, the prophet cried out for divine intervention (1:2–4). God's response, that He was sending the Chaldeans to judge Judah (1:5–11), creates an even greater theological dilemma for Habakkuk: Why didn't God purge His people and restore their righteousness? How could God use the Chaldeans to judge a people more righteous than they (1:12–2:1)? God's answer that He would judge the Chaldeans, also (2:2–20), did not fully satisfy the prophet's theological quandary; in fact, it only intensified it. In Habakkuk's mind, the issue crying for resolution is no longer God's righteous response toward evil (or lack thereof), but the vindication of God's character and covenant with His people (1:13). Like Job, the prophet argued with God; and through that experience, he achieved a deeper understanding of God's sovereign character and a firmer faith in Him (Job 42:5,6; Is. 55:8,9). Ultimately, Habakkuk realized that God was not to be worshiped merely because of the temporal blessings He bestowed, but for His own sake (3:17–19).

DECEMBER 24

Zephaniah 1:1–3:20

1 The word of the LORD which came to Zephaniah the son of Cushi, the son of Gedaliah, the son of Amariah, the son of Hezekiah, in the days of Josiah the son of Amon, king of Judah.

2 "I will utterly consume everything
From the face of the land,"
Says the LORD;
3 "I will consume man and beast;
I will consume the birds of the heavens,
The fish of the sea,
And the stumbling blocks along with the wicked.
I will cut off man from the face of the land,"
Says the LORD.
4 "I will stretch out My hand against Judah,
And against all the inhabitants of Jerusalem.
I will cut off every trace of Baal from this place,
The names of the idolatrous priests with the *pagan* priests—
5 Those who worship the host of heaven on the housetops;
Those who worship and swear *oaths* by the LORD,
But who *also* swear by Milcom;
6 Those who have turned back from *following* the LORD,
And have not sought the LORD, nor inquired of Him."

7 Be silent in the presence of the Lord GOD;
For the day of the LORD *is* at hand,
For the LORD has prepared a sacrifice;
He has invited His guests.
8 "And it shall be,
In the day of the LORD's sacrifice,
That I will punish the princes and the king's children,

1:8 the princes...king's children. Judgment began with the royal house. Lacking commitment to God's covenant, they had adopted the customs and idolatrous practices of the heathen. Since Josiah was only 8 years old when he assumed rulership (ca. 640 B.C.), the reference would not be to his children but to the princes of the royal house or to the children of the king who would be ruling when the prophecy was fulfilled (2 Kin. 25:7; Jer. 39:6).

And all such as are clothed with foreign apparel.
9 In the same day I will punish
All those who leap over the threshold,
Who fill their masters' houses with violence and deceit.

10 "And there shall be on that day,"
says the LORD,
"The sound of a mournful cry from the Fish Gate,
A wailing from the Second Quarter,
And a loud crashing from the hills.
11 Wail, you inhabitants of Maktesh!
For all the merchant people are cut down;
All those who handle money are cut off.
12 "And it shall come to pass at that time
That I will search Jerusalem with lamps,
And punish the men
Who are settled in complacency,
Who say in their heart,
'The LORD will not do good,
Nor will He do evil.'
13 Therefore their goods shall become booty,
And their houses a desolation;
They shall build houses, but not inhabit *them;*
They shall plant vineyards, but not drink their wine."
14 The great day of the LORD *is* near;
It is near and hastens quickly.

The noise of the day of the LORD
is bitter;
There the mighty men shall cry out.
15 That day *is* a day of wrath,
A day of trouble and distress,
A day of devastation and desolation,
A day of darkness and gloominess,
A day of clouds and thick darkness,
16 A day of trumpet and alarm
Against the fortified cities
And against the high towers.

17 "I will bring distress upon men,
And they shall walk like blind men,
Because they have sinned against
the LORD;
Their blood shall be poured out like
dust,
And their flesh like refuse."

18 Neither their silver nor their gold
Shall be able to deliver them
In the day of the LORD's wrath;
But the whole land shall be devoured
By the fire of His jealousy,
For He will make speedy riddance
Of all those who dwell in the land.

2 Gather yourselves together,
yes, gather together,
O undesirable nation,
2 Before the decree is issued,
Or the day passes like chaff,
Before the LORD's fierce anger comes
upon you,
Before the day of the LORD's anger
comes upon you!
3 Seek the LORD, all you meek of the earth,
Who have upheld His justice.
Seek righteousness, seek humility.
It may be that you will be hidden
In the day of the LORD's anger.

4 For Gaza shall be forsaken,
And Ashkelon desolate;
They shall drive out Ashdod at
noonday,
And Ekron shall be uprooted.
5 Woe to the inhabitants of the seacoast,
The nation of the Cherethites!
The word of the LORD *is* against you,
O Canaan, land of the Philistines:
"I will destroy you;
So there shall be no inhabitant."

6 The seacoast shall be pastures,
With shelters for shepherds and folds
for flocks.
7 The coast shall be for the remnant of
the house of Judah;
They shall feed *their* flocks there;
In the houses of Ashkelon they shall lie
down at evening.
For the LORD their God will intervene
for them,
And return their captives.

8 "I have heard the reproach of Moab,
And the insults of the people of
Ammon,
With which they have reproached
My people,
And made arrogant threats against
their borders.
9 Therefore, as I live,"
Says the LORD of hosts, the God
of Israel,
"Surely Moab shall be like Sodom,
And the people of Ammon like
Gomorrah—
Overrun with weeds and saltpits,
And a perpetual desolation.
The residue of My people shall
plunder them,
And the remnant of My people shall
possess them."

10 This they shall have for their pride,
Because they have reproached and
made arrogant threats
Against the people of the LORD
of hosts.
11 The LORD *will be* awesome to them,
For He will reduce to nothing all the
gods of the earth;
People shall worship Him,
Each one from his place,
Indeed all the shores of the nations.

12 "You Ethiopians also,
You shall be slain by My sword."

13 And He will stretch out His hand against
the north,
Destroy Assyria,
And make Nineveh a desolation,
As dry as the wilderness.
14 The herds shall lie down in her midst,
Every beast of the nation.
Both the pelican and the bittern
Shall lodge on the capitals *of* her *pillars;*
Their voice shall sing in the windows;
Desolation *shall be* at the threshold;
For He will lay bare the cedar work.
15 This is the rejoicing city
That dwelt securely,
That said in her heart,
"I *am it,* and *there is* none besides me."
How has she become a desolation,
A place for beasts to lie down!
Everyone who passes by her
Shall hiss and shake his fist.

3 Woe to her who is rebellious
and polluted,
To the oppressing city!
2 She has not obeyed *His* voice,
She has not received correction;
She has not trusted in the LORD,
She has not drawn near to her God.

3 Her princes in her midst *are* roaring
lions;
Her judges *are* evening wolves
That leave not a bone till morning.
4 Her prophets are insolent, treacherous
people;
Her priests have polluted the sanctuary,
They have done violence to the law.
5 The LORD *is* righteous in her midst,
He will do no unrighteousness.
Every morning He brings His justice
to light;
He never fails,
But the unjust knows no shame.

6 "I have cut off nations,
Their fortresses are devastated;
I have made their streets desolate,
With none passing by.
Their cities are destroyed;
There is no one, no inhabitant.
7 I said, 'Surely you will fear Me,
You will receive instruction'—
So that her dwelling would not be
cut off,
Despite everything for which I
punished her.
But they rose early and corrupted all
their deeds.

8 "Therefore wait for Me," says the LORD,
"Until the day I rise up for plunder;
My determination *is* to gather the
nations
To My assembly of kingdoms,
To pour on them My indignation,
All My fierce anger;
All the earth shall be devoured
With the fire of My jealousy.

9 "For then I will restore to the peoples a
pure language,
That they all may call on the name of
the LORD,
To serve Him with one accord.
10 From beyond the rivers of Ethiopia
My worshipers,
The daughter of My dispersed ones,
Shall bring My offering.
11 In that day you shall not be shamed for
any of your deeds
In which you transgress against Me;
For then I will take away from your
midst
Those who rejoice in your pride,
And you shall no longer be haughty
In My holy mountain.
12 I will leave in your midst
A meek and humble people,
And they shall trust in the name
of the LORD.
13 The remnant of Israel shall do no
unrighteousness
And speak no lies,
Nor shall a deceitful tongue be found
in their mouth;
For they shall feed *their* flocks
and lie down,
And no one shall make *them* afraid."

14 Sing, O daughter of Zion!
Shout, O Israel!
Be glad and rejoice with all *your* heart,
O daughter of Jerusalem!
15 The LORD has taken away your
judgments,
He has cast out your enemy.
The King of Israel, the LORD, *is* in your
midst;
You shall see disaster no more.

16 In that day it shall be said to Jerusalem:
"Do not fear;
Zion, let not your hands be weak.
17 The LORD your God in your midst,
The Mighty One, will save;
He will rejoice over you with gladness,
He will quiet *you* with His love,
He will rejoice over you with singing."

18 "I will gather those who sorrow over the
appointed assembly,
Who are among you,
To whom its reproach *is* a burden.
19 Behold, at that time
I will deal with all who afflict you;
I will save the lame,
And gather those who were driven out;
I will appoint them for praise and fame

3:8 The prophet transitions from the historical invasion of Judah by Babylon to the future day of the Lord. He speaks of the Great Tribulation, when the Lord will gather all the nations for judgment (Joel 3:1,2,12–17; Zech. 12:2,3; 14:2; Matt. 24:21). The faithful remnant, presumably the meek of 2:1–3, are exhorted to wait in trust for Him to carry out His judgment.

In every land where they were put to
shame.
20 At that time I will bring you back,
Even at the time I gather you;
For I will give you fame and praise
Among all the peoples of the earth,
When I return your captives
before your eyes,"
Says the LORD.

Psalm 147:1–6

Praise the LORD!
For *it is* good to sing praises
to our God;
For *it is* pleasant, *and* praise is beautiful.

2 The LORD builds up Jerusalem;
He gathers together the outcasts
of Israel.
3 He heals the brokenhearted
And binds up their wounds.
4 He counts the number of the stars;
He calls them all by name.
5 Great *is* our Lord, and mighty in power;
His understanding *is* infinite.
6 The LORD lifts up the humble;
He casts the wicked down to the ground.

Proverbs 30:18–19

18 There are three *things which* are too
wonderful for me,
Yes, four *which* I do not understand:
19 The way of an eagle in the air,
The way of a serpent on a rock,
The way of a ship in the midst of the
sea,
And the way of a man with a virgin.

Revelation 14:1–20

14 Then I looked, and behold, a Lamb standing on Mount Zion, and with Him one
hundred *and* forty-four thousand, having His
Father's name written on their foreheads.
2And I heard a voice from heaven, like the
voice of many waters, and like the voice of loud
thunder. And I heard the sound of harpists
playing their harps. 3They sang as it were a
new song before the throne, before the four
living creatures, and the elders; and no one
could learn that song except the hundred *and*
forty-four thousand who were redeemed from
the earth. 4These are the ones who were not
defiled with women, for they are virgins.
These are the ones who follow the Lamb
wherever He goes. These were redeemed
from *among* men, *being* firstfruits to God and
to the Lamb. 5And in their mouth was found no
deceit, for they are without fault before the
throne of God.
6Then I saw another angel flying in the
midst of heaven, having the everlasting gospel
to preach to those who dwell on the earth—to
every nation, tribe, tongue, and people— 7say-
ing with a loud voice, "Fear God and give
glory to Him, for the hour of His judgment has
come; and worship Him who made heaven
and earth, the sea and springs of water."
8And another angel followed, saying,
"Babylon is fallen, is fallen, that great city,
because she has made all nations drink of the
wine of the wrath of her fornication."

14:8 Babylon is fallen. Lack of response to the first angel's message causes a second angel to pronounce this judgment. Babylon refers to the entire worldwide political, economic, and religious kingdom of Antichrist. The original city of Babylon was the birthplace of idolatry where the residents built the Tower of Babel, a monument to rebelliousness and false religion. Such idolatry was subsequently spread when God confounded man's language and scattered them around the world (Gen. 11:1–9). **wine of the wrath of her fornication.** This pictures Babylon causing the world to become intoxicated with her pleasures and enter an orgy of rebellion, hatred, and idolatry toward God. Fornication is spiritual prostitution to Antichrist's false system, which will fall for such iniquity.

9Then a third angel followed them, saying
with a loud voice, "If anyone worships the
beast and his image, and receives *his* mark on
his forehead or on his hand, 10he himself shall
also drink of the wine of the wrath of God,
which is poured out full strength into the cup
of His indignation. He shall be tormented with
fire and brimstone in the presence of the holy
angels and in the presence of the Lamb. 11And
the smoke of their torment ascends forever
and ever; and they have no rest day or night,
who worship the beast and his image, and
whoever receives the mark of his name."
12Here is the patience of the saints; here *are*
those who keep the commandments of God
and the faith of Jesus.
13Then I heard a voice from heaven saying
to me, "Write: 'Blessed *are* the dead who die in
the Lord from now on.' "
"Yes," says the Spirit, "that they may rest
from their labors, and their works follow them."
14Then I looked, and behold, a white cloud,
and on the cloud sat *One* like the Son of Man,

having on His head a golden crown, and in His hand a sharp sickle. [15]And another angel came out of the temple, crying with a loud voice to Him who sat on the cloud, "Thrust in Your sickle and reap, for the time has come for You to reap, for the harvest of the earth is ripe." [16]So He who sat on the cloud thrust in His sickle on the earth, and the earth was reaped.

[17]Then another angel came out of the temple which is in heaven, he also having a sharp sickle.

[18]And another angel came out from the altar, who had power over fire, and he cried with a loud cry to him who had the sharp sickle, saying, "Thrust in your sharp sickle and gather the clusters of the vine of the earth, for her grapes are fully ripe." [19]So the angel thrust his sickle into the earth and gathered the vine of the earth, and threw *it* into the great winepress of the wrath of God. [20]And the winepress was trampled outside the city, and blood came out of the winepress, up to the horses' bridles, for one thousand six hundred furlongs.

14:19 winepress. This vivid imagery signifies a horrendous slaughter or bloodbath (Is. 63:2,3; Lam. 1:15; Joel 3:13). Here it refers to the slaughter of all the enemies of God who are still alive, facing the destruction at Armageddon, the final battle against God's enemies, staged on the Plain of Esdraelon. The bloody imagery comes from the fresh juice of stomped grapes splattering and running down a trough from the upper vat to the lower vat of a stone winepress.

DAY 24: What is known about Zephaniah, and what was his message for Judah?

Little is known about the author, Zephaniah. Three other Old Testament individuals share his name. He traces his genealogy back 4 generations to King Hezekiah (ca. 715–686 B.C.), standing alone among the prophets descended from royal blood (1:1). Royal genealogy would have given him the ear of Judah's king, Josiah, during whose reign he preached.

The prophet himself dates his message during the reign of Josiah (640–609 B.C.). The moral and spiritual conditions detailed in the book (1:4–6; 3:1–7) seem to place the prophecy prior to Josiah's reforms, when Judah was still languishing in idolatry and wickedness. It was in 628 B.C. that Josiah tore down all the altars to Baal, burned the bones of false prophets, and broke the carved idols (2 Chr. 34:3–7); and in 622 B.C., the Book of the Law was found (2 Chr. 34:8–35:19). Consequently, Zephaniah most likely prophesied from 635 to 625 B.C. and was a contemporary of Jeremiah.

Zephaniah's message on the Day of the Lord warned Judah that the final days were near, through divine judgment at the hands of Nebuchadnezzar, ca. 605–586 B.C. (1:4–13). Yet, it also looks beyond to the far fulfillment in the judgments of Daniel's 70th week (1:18; 3:8). The expression "Day of the Lord" is employed by the author more often than by any other Old Testament writer and is described as a day that is near (1:7), and as a day of wrath, trouble, distress, devastation, desolation, darkness, gloominess, clouds, thick darkness, trumpet, and alarm (1:15,16,18). Yet even within these oracles of divine wrath, the prophet exhorted the people to seek the Lord, offering a shelter in the midst of judgment (2:3) and proclaiming the promise of eventual salvation for His believing remnant (2:7; 3:9–20).

DECEMBER 25

Haggai 1:1–2:23

1 In the second year of King Darius, in the sixth month, on the first day of the month, the word of the LORD came by Haggai the prophet to Zerubbabel the son of Shealtiel, governor of Judah, and to Joshua the son of Jehozadak, the high priest, saying, [2]"Thus speaks the LORD of hosts, saying: 'This people says, "The time has not come, the time that the LORD's house should be built." ' "

[3]Then the word of the LORD came by Haggai the prophet, saying, [4]"*Is it* time for you yourselves to dwell in your paneled houses, and this temple *to lie* in ruins?" [5]Now therefore, thus says the LORD of hosts: "Consider your ways!

[6] "You have sown much, and bring in little;
You eat, but do not have enough;
You drink, but you are not filled
with drink;
You clothe yourselves, but no one
is warm;
And he who earns wages,
Earns wages *to put* into a bag with
holes."

[7]Thus says the LORD of hosts: "Consider your ways! [8]Go up to the mountains and bring wood and build the temple, that I may take pleasure in it and be glorified," says the LORD.

9“*You* looked for much, but indeed *it came to*
little; and when you brought it home, I blew it
away. Why?” says the LORD of hosts. “Because
of My house that *is in* ruins, while every one
of you runs to his own house. 10Therefore the
heavens above you withhold the dew, and the
earth withholds its fruit. 11For I called for a
drought on the land and the mountains, on the
grain and the new wine and the oil, on whatever the ground brings forth, on men and livestock, and on all the labor of *your* hands.”

12Then Zerubbabel the son of Shealtiel, and
Joshua the son of Jehozadak, the high priest,
with all the remnant of the people, obeyed the
voice of the LORD their God, and the words of
Haggai the prophet, as the LORD their God had
sent him; and the people feared the presence of
the LORD. 13Then Haggai, the LORD’s messenger,
spoke the LORD’s message to the people, saying, “I *am* with you, says the LORD.” 14So the

1:13 I *am* with you. Oppressed by hostilities from without and famine from within, the Lord responded to their genuine repentance and obedience, assuring them of His presence with them. This should have evoked a memory of God’s word to Joshua and the returning people centuries before (Josh. 1:5).

LORD stirred up the spirit of Zerubbabel the son
of Shealtiel, governor of Judah, and the spirit of
Joshua the son of Jehozadak, the high priest,
and the spirit of all the remnant of the people;
and they came and worked on the house of the
LORD of hosts, their God, 15on the twenty-
fourth day of the sixth month, in the second
year of King Darius.

2 In the seventh *month,* on the twenty-first of
the month, the word of the LORD came by
Haggai the prophet, saying: 2“Speak now to
Zerubbabel the son of Shealtiel, governor of
Judah, and to Joshua the son of Jehozadak, the
high priest, and to the remnant of the people,
saying: 3‘Who is left among you who saw this
temple in its former glory? And how do you see
it now? In comparison with it, *is this* not in your
eyes as nothing? 4Yet now be strong, Zerubbabel,’ says the LORD; ‘and be strong, Joshua,
son of Jehozadak, the high priest; and be strong,
all you people of the land,’ says the LORD, ‘and
work; for I *am* with you,’ says the LORD of hosts.
5‘*According to* the word that I covenanted with
you when you came out of Egypt, so My Spirit
remains among you; do not fear!’

6“For thus says the LORD of hosts: ‘Once
more (it *is* a little while) I will shake heaven
and earth, the sea and dry land; 7and I will
shake all nations, and they shall come to the
Desire of All Nations, and I will fill this temple
with glory,’ says the LORD of hosts. 8‘The silver
is Mine, and the gold *is* Mine,’ says the LORD
of hosts. 9‘The glory of this latter temple shall
be greater than the former,’ says the LORD of
hosts. ‘And in this place I will give peace,’ says
the LORD of hosts.”

2:7 Desire of All Nations. While some view the phrase as referring to Jerusalem (e.g., Ezra 6:3–9), it seems preferable to see a reference here to the Messiah, the Deliverer for whom all the nations ultimately long. **I will fill this temple with glory.** There is no Scripture to indicate that God’s glory ever did come to Zerubbabel’s temple, as the first temple was filled with the Shekinah glory (1 Kin. 8:10,11; 2 Chr. 5:13,14). However, His glory will fill the millennial temple (Ezek. 43:5). This glorification cannot refer to Christ’s physical presence in Herod’s temple, for the events of vv. 6–9 cannot be accounted for historically. The context speaks of the establishment of His earthly, Davidic, millennial kingdom and His presence in the temple during that kingdom.

10On the twenty-fourth *day* of the ninth
month, in the second year of Darius, the word
of the LORD came by Haggai the prophet, saying, 11“Thus says the LORD of hosts: ‘Now, ask
the priests *concerning the* law, saying, 12“If one
carries holy meat in the fold of his garment,
and with the edge he touches bread or stew,
wine or oil, or any food, will it become
holy?” ’ ”

Then the priests answered and said, “No.”

13And Haggai said, “If *one who is* unclean *be-*
cause of a dead body touches any of these, will
it be unclean?”

So the priests answered and said, “It shall
be unclean.”

14Then Haggai answered and said, “ ‘So is
this people, and so is this nation before Me,’
says the LORD, ‘and so is every work of their
hands; and what they offer there is unclean.

15‘And now, carefully consider from this day
forward: from before stone was laid upon
stone in the temple of the LORD— 16since those
days, when *one* came to a heap of twenty
ephahs, there were *but* ten; when *one* came to

the wine vat to draw out fifty baths from the
press, there were *but* twenty. [17]I struck you
with blight and mildew and hail in all the
labors of your hands; yet you did not *turn* to
Me,' says the LORD. [18]'Consider now from this
day forward, from the twenty-fourth day of the
ninth month, from the day that the foundation
of the LORD's temple was laid—consider it: [19]Is
the seed still in the barn? As yet the vine, the
fig tree, the pomegranate, and the olive tree
have not yielded *fruit. But* from this day I will
bless *you.*' "

[20]And again the word of the LORD came to
Haggai on the twenty-fourth day of the month,
saying, [21]"Speak to Zerubbabel, governor of
Judah, saying:

'I will shake heaven and earth.
22 I will overthrow the throne of
kingdoms;
I will destroy the strength of the
Gentile kingdoms.
I will overthrow the chariots
And those who ride in them;
The horses and their riders shall
come down,
Every one by the sword of his brother.

[23]'In that day,' says the LORD of hosts, 'I will
take you, Zerubbabel My servant, the son of
Shealtiel,' says the LORD, 'and will make you
like a signet *ring;* for I have chosen you,' says
the LORD of hosts."

Psalm 147:7–11

7 Sing to the LORD with thanksgiving;
Sing praises on the harp to
our God,
8 Who covers the heavens
with clouds,
Who prepares rain for the earth,
Who makes grass to grow on the
mountains.
9 He gives to the beast its food,
And to the young ravens that cry.

10 He does not delight in the strength
of the horse;
He takes no pleasure in the legs of a
man.
11 The LORD takes pleasure in those who
fear Him,
In those who hope in His mercy.

Proverbs 30:20

20 This *is* the way of an adulterous
woman:
She eats and wipes her mouth,
And says, "I have done no
wickedness."

Revelation 15:1–8

15 Then I saw another sign in heaven, great
and marvelous: seven angels having the
seven last plagues, for in them the wrath of
God is complete.

[2]And I saw *something* like a sea of glass mingled with fire, and those who have the victory
over the beast, over his image and over his
mark *and* over the number of his name, standing on the sea of glass, having harps of God.
[3]They sing the song of Moses, the servant of
God, and the song of the Lamb, saying:

"Great and marvelous *are* Your works,
Lord God Almighty!
Just and true *are* Your ways,
O King of the saints!
4 Who shall not fear You, O Lord, and
glorify Your name?
For *You* alone *are* holy.
For all nations shall come and worship
before You,
For Your judgments have been
manifested."

[5]After these things I looked, and behold, the
temple of the tabernacle of the testimony in heav-
en was opened. [6]And out of the temple came the
seven angels having the seven plagues, clothed in
pure bright linen, and having their chests girded
with golden bands. [7]Then one of the four living
creatures gave to the seven angels seven golden
bowls full of the wrath of God who lives forever
and ever. [8]The temple was filled with smoke from
the glory of God and from His power, and no one
was able to enter the temple till the seven plagues
of the seven angels were completed.

15:3 song of Moses. Sung by the people of Israel immediately after their passage through the Red Sea and their deliverance from the Egyptian armies (Ex. 15:1–21; Deut. 32:1–43), this was a song of victory and deliverance that the redeemed who overcome Antichrist and his system will readily identify with. **song of the Lamb.** See 5:8–14. These two songs celebrate two great redemptive events: 1) deliverance of Israel by God from Egypt through Moses and 2) deliverance of sinners by God from sin through Christ. **Great and marvelous *are* Your works.** This statement from the song of the Lamb extols God's powerful works in creation as He providentially upholds the universe (Ps. 139:14). **Almighty.** God is omnipotent (Amos 4:13). **King of the saints.** God is sovereign over the redeemed of every nation (Jer. 10:7).

DAY 25: What is the primary message of the Book of Haggai?

In 538 B.C., as a result of the proclamation of Cyrus the Persian (Ezra 1:1–4), Israel was allowed to return from Babylon to her homeland under the civil leadership of Zerubbabel and the spiritual guidance of Joshua the high priest (Ezra 3:2). About 50,000 Jews returned. In 536 B.C., they began to rebuild the temple (Ezra 3:1–4:5); but opposition from neighbors and indifference by the Jews caused the work to be abandoned (Ezra 4:1–24). Sixteen years later Haggai and Zechariah were commissioned by the Lord to stir up the people to 1) not only rebuild the temple, but also to 2) reorder their spiritual priorities (Ezra 5:1–6:22). As a result, the temple was completed 4 years later (ca. 516 B.C.; Ezra 6:15).

The primary theme is the rebuilding of God's temple, which had been lying in ruins since its destruction by Nebuchadnezzar in 586 B.C. By means of 5 messages from the Lord, Haggai exhorted the people to renew their efforts to build the house of the Lord. He motivated them by noting that the drought and crop failures were caused by misplaced spiritual priorities (1:9–11).

But to Haggai, the rebuilding of the temple was not an end in itself. The temple represented God's dwelling place, His manifest presence with His chosen people. The destruction of the temple by Nebuchadnezzar followed the departure of God's dwelling glory (Ezek. 8–11). To the prophet, the rebuilding of the temple invited the return of God's presence to their midst. Using the historical situation as a springboard, Haggai reveled in the supreme glory of the ultimate messianic temple yet to come (2:7), encouraging them with the promise of even greater peace (2:9), prosperity (2:19), divine rulership (2:21,22), and national blessing (2:23) during the Millennium.

DECEMBER 26

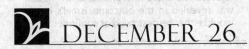

Zechariah 1:1–3:10

1 In the eighth month of the second year of
Darius, the word of the LORD came to
Zechariah the son of Berechiah, the son of
Iddo the prophet, saying, 2"The LORD has been
very angry with your fathers. 3Therefore say
to them, 'Thus says the LORD of hosts: "Return
to Me," says the LORD of hosts, "and I will
return to you," says the LORD of hosts. 4"Do not
be like your fathers, to whom the former
prophets preached, saying, 'Thus says the
LORD of hosts: "Turn now from your evil ways
and your evil deeds."' But they did not hear nor
heed Me," says the LORD.

5 "Your fathers, where *are* they?
And the prophets, do they live forever?
6 Yet surely My words and My statutes,
Which I commanded My servants the
prophets,
Did they not overtake your fathers?

"So they returned and said:

'Just as the LORD of hosts determined
to do to us,
According to our ways and according
to our deeds,
So He has dealt with us.'"'"

7On the twenty-fourth day of the eleventh
month, which is the month Shebat, in the second year of Darius, the word of the LORD came
to Zechariah the son of Berechiah, the son of
Iddo the prophet: 8I saw by night, and behold,
a man riding on a red horse, and it stood
among the myrtle trees in the hollow; and
behind him *were* horses: red, sorrel, and
white. 9Then I said, "My lord, what *are* these?"
So the angel who talked with me said to me, "I
will show you what they *are*."

10And the man who stood among the myrtle
trees answered and said, "These *are the ones*
whom the LORD has sent to walk to and fro
throughout the earth."

11So they answered the Angel of the LORD,
who stood among the myrtle trees, and said, "We
have walked to and fro throughout the earth,
and behold, all the earth is resting quietly."

12Then the Angel of the LORD answered and
said, "O LORD of hosts, how long will You not
have mercy on Jerusalem and on the cities of
Judah, against which You were angry these
seventy years?"

13And the LORD answered the angel who
talked to me, *with* good *and* comforting words.
14So the angel who spoke with me said to me,
"Proclaim, saying, 'Thus says the LORD of hosts:

"I am zealous for Jerusalem
And for Zion with great zeal.
15 I am exceedingly angry with the
nations at ease;
For I was a little angry,
And they helped—*but* with evil *intent*."

16"Therefore thus says the LORD:

"I am returning to Jerusalem with
mercy;
My house shall be built in it," says the
LORD of hosts,

"And a *surveyor's* line shall be stretched
out over Jerusalem." '

17"Again proclaim, saying, 'Thus says the
LORD of hosts:

"My cities shall again spread out
through prosperity;
The LORD will again comfort Zion,
And will again choose Jerusalem." ' "

18Then I raised my eyes and looked, and
there *were* four horns. 19And I said to the angel
who talked with me, "What *are* these?"

So he answered me, "These *are* the horns that
have scattered Judah, Israel, and Jerusalem."

20Then the LORD showed me four craftsmen.
21And I said, "What are these coming to do?"

So he said, "These *are* the horns that scattered Judah, so that no one could lift up his
head; but the craftsmen are coming to terrify
them, to cast out the horns of the nations that
lifted up *their* horn against the land of Judah to
scatter it."

2 Then I raised my eyes and looked, and
behold, a man with a measuring line in his
hand. 2So I said, "Where are you going?"

And he said to me, "To measure Jerusalem,
to see what *is* its width and what *is* its length."

3And there *was* the angel who talked with
me, going out; and another angel was coming
out to meet him, 4who said to him, "Run, speak
to this young man, saying: 'Jerusalem shall be
inhabited *as* towns without walls, because of
the multitude of men and livestock in it. 5For I,'
says the LORD, 'will be a wall of fire all around
her, and I will be the glory in her midst.' "

6"Up, up! Flee from the land of the north,"
says the LORD; "for I have spread you abroad
like the four winds of heaven," says the LORD.
7"Up, Zion! Escape, you who dwell with the
daughter of Babylon."

8For thus says the LORD of hosts: "He sent
Me after glory, to the nations which plunder
you; for he who touches you touches the apple
of His eye. 9For surely I will shake My hand
against them, and they shall become spoil for
their servants. Then you will know that the
LORD of hosts has sent Me.

10"Sing and rejoice, O daughter of Zion! For
behold, I am coming and I will dwell in your
midst," says the LORD. 11"Many nations shall be
joined to the LORD in that day, and they shall
become My people. And I will dwell in your
midst. Then you will know that the LORD of
hosts has sent Me to you. 12And the LORD will
take possession of Judah as His inheritance in
the Holy Land, and will again choose Jerusalem.
13Be silent, all flesh, before the LORD, for He is
aroused from His holy habitation!"

3 Then he showed me Joshua the high
priest standing before the Angel of the
LORD, and Satan standing at his right hand to
oppose him. 2And the LORD said to Satan, "The
LORD rebuke you, Satan! The LORD who has
chosen Jerusalem rebuke you! *Is* this not a
brand plucked from the fire?"

3:1 Satan. This could also be translated "adversary" and thus the person's identity would be unknown. However, because the activity of accusation is so in keeping with Satan (Job 1; 2; Rev. 12:10), his identification is preferable. The malicious adversary stands in the presence of the Lord to proclaim Israel's sins and their unworthiness of God's favor. The situation is crucial: If Joshua is vindicated, Israel is accepted; if Joshua is rejected, Israel is rejected. The entire plan of God for the nation was revealed in the outcome. Israel's hopes would either be destroyed or confirmed.

3Now Joshua was clothed with filthy garments, and was standing before the Angel.
4Then He answered and spoke to those who
stood before Him, saying, "Take away the
filthy garments from him." And to him He said,
"See, I have removed your iniquity from you,
and I will clothe you with rich robes."

5And I said, "Let them put a clean turban on
his head."

So they put a clean turban on his head, and
they put the clothes on him. And the Angel of
the LORD stood by.

6Then the Angel of the LORD admonished
Joshua, saying, 7"Thus says the LORD of hosts:

'If you will walk in My ways,
And if you will keep My command,
Then you shall also judge My house,
And likewise have charge of My
courts;
I will give you places to walk
Among these who stand here.

8 'Hear, O Joshua, the high priest,
You and your companions who sit
before you,
For they are a wondrous sign;
For behold, I am bringing forth My
Servant the BRANCH.
9 For behold, the stone
That I have laid before Joshua:
Upon the stone *are* seven eyes.
Behold, I will engrave its inscription,'
Says the LORD of hosts,

3:9 the stone. Here is another reference to the Messiah. In Psalm 118:22,23; Isaiah 8:13–15; 28:16; Daniel 2:35,45; Matthew 21:42; Ephesians 2:19–22; 1 Peter 2:6–8, He is a rejected stone, a stone of stumbling, a stone of refuge, a destroying stone, and a foundation stone. Here He is the precious foundation stone, with "7 eyes" symbolic of His omniscience and infinite intelligence (4:10; Is. 11:2; Col. 2:3; Rev. 5:6). The engraving may be a reference to the cornerstone of the temple building, on which will be engraved an inscription attesting to the divine Builder and the purpose for which the building was erected. As such, it is closely tied to the removal of "the iniquity of that land in one day," symbolized by the removal of filthy garments in v. 4. The phrase looks to the future day when there will be cleansing and forgiveness for the nation as a whole (12:10–13:1; Rom. 11:25–27), made possible through Christ's redemptive provision at Calvary.

'And I will remove the iniquity of that
land in one day.
10 In that day,' says the LORD of hosts,
'Everyone will invite his neighbor
Under his vine and under his fig tree.' "

Psalm 147:12–20

12 Praise the LORD, O Jerusalem!
Praise your God, O Zion!
13 For He has strengthened the bars of
your gates;
He has blessed your children within
you.
14 He makes peace *in* your borders,
And fills you with the finest wheat.
15 He sends out His command *to the* earth;
His word runs very swiftly.
16 He gives snow like wool;
He scatters the frost like ashes;
17 He casts out His hail like morsels;
Who can stand before His cold?
18 He sends out His word and melts
them;
He causes His wind to blow, *and* the
waters flow.

19 He declares His word to Jacob,
His statutes and His judgments to
Israel.
20 He has not dealt thus with any nation;
And *as for His* judgments, they have
not known them.
Praise the LORD!

Proverbs 30:21–23

21 For three *things* the earth is perturbed,
Yes, for four it cannot bear up:
22 For a servant when he reigns,
A fool when he is filled with food,
23 A hateful *woman* when she is married,
And a maidservant who succeeds her
mistress.

Revelation 16:1–21

16 Then I heard a loud voice from the temple saying to the seven angels, "Go and pour out the bowls of the wrath of God on the earth."

2 So the first went and poured out his bowl
upon the earth, and a foul and loathsome sore
came upon the men who had the mark of the
beast and those who worshiped his image.
3 Then the second angel poured out his bowl
on the sea, and it became blood as of a dead
man; and every living creature in the sea died.
4 Then the third angel poured out his bowl
on the rivers and springs of water, and they
became blood. 5 And I heard the angel of the
waters saying:

"You are righteous, O Lord,
The One who is and who was and who
is to be,
Because You have judged these things.
6 For they have shed the blood of saints
and prophets,
And You have given them blood to
drink.
For it is their just due."

16:5 who is and who was and who is to be. This phrase expresses God's eternality (1:4,8; 4:8; 11:17). Verse 6 says that the eternal God will judge justly because they have killed the believers and preachers of the gospel (6:9–11; 7:9–17; 11:18; 17:6; 18:20). This slaughter will have no parallel in history (Matt. 24:21) and neither will the vengeance of God (Rom. 12:19–21).

7 And I heard another from the altar saying,
"Even so, Lord God Almighty, true and righteous *are* Your judgments."
8 Then the fourth angel poured out his bowl
on the sun, and power was given to him to
scorch men with fire. 9 And men were
scorched with great heat, and they blasphemed the name of God who has power over

these plagues; and they did not repent and
give Him glory.
10 Then the fifth angel poured out his bowl
on the throne of the beast, and his kingdom
became full of darkness; and they gnawed
their tongues because of the pain. 11 They blasphemed the God of heaven because of their
pains and their sores, and did not repent of
their deeds.
12 Then the sixth angel poured out his bowl
on the great river Euphrates, and its water was
dried up, so that the way of the kings from the
east might be prepared. 13 And I saw three
unclean spirits like frogs *coming* out of the
mouth of the dragon, out of the mouth of the
beast, and out of the mouth of the false
prophet. 14 For they are spirits of demons, performing signs, *which* go out to the kings of the
earth and of the whole world, to gather them
to the battle of that great day of God Almighty.
15 "Behold, I am coming as a thief. Blessed *is*
he who watches, and keeps his garments, lest
he walk naked and they see his shame."
16 And they gathered them together to the
place called in Hebrew, Armageddon.
17 Then the seventh angel poured out his
bowl into the air, and a loud voice came out of
the temple of heaven, from the throne, saying,
"It is done!" 18 And there were noises and thunderings and lightnings; and there was a great
earthquake, such a mighty and great earthquake as had not occurred since men were on
the earth. 19 Now the great city was divided
into three parts, and the cities of the nations
fell. And great Babylon was remembered
before God, to give her the cup of the wine of
the fierceness of His wrath. 20 Then every
island fled away, and the mountains were not
found. 21 And great hail from heaven fell upon
men, *each hailstone* about the weight of a talent. Men blasphemed God because of the
plague of the hail, since that plague was
exceedingly great.

16:16 Armageddon. The Hebrew name for Mt. Megiddo, 60 miles north of Jerusalem. The battle will rage on the nearby plains, site of Barak's victory over the Canaanites (Judg. 4) and Gideon's victory over the Midianites (Judg. 7). Napoleon called this valley the greatest battlefield he had ever seen. But the Battle of Armageddon will not be limited to the Megiddo plains—it will encompass the length of Palestine.

DAY 26: What was Zechariah's relationship to Haggai?

Like Jeremiah and Ezekiel, Zechariah was also a priest (Neh. 12:12–16). According to tradition, he was a member of the Great Synagogue, a council of 120 originated by Nehemiah and presided over by Ezra. This council later developed into the ruling elders of the nation, called the Sanhedrin. He was born in Babylon and joined his grandfather, Iddo, in the group of exiles who first returned to Jerusalem under the leadership of Zerubbabel and Joshua the high priest (Neh. 12:4). Because he is occasionally mentioned as the son of his grandfather (Ezra 5:1; 6:14; Neh. 12:16), it is thought that his father, Berechiah, died at an early age before he could succeed his father into the priesthood.

Zechariah joined Haggai in rousing the people from their indifference, challenging them to resume the building of the temple. Haggai's primary purpose was to rebuild the temple. His preaching has a tone of rebuke for the people's indifference, sin, and lack of trust in God. He was used to start the revival, while Zechariah was used to keep it going strong with a more positive emphasis, calling the people to repentance and reassuring them regarding future blessings. Zechariah sought to encourage the people to build the temple in view of the promise that someday the Messiah would come to inhabit it. The people were not just building for the present, but with the future hope of the Messiah in mind. He encouraged the people, still downtrodden by the Gentile powers (1:8–12), with the reality that the Lord remembers His covenant promises to them and that He would restore and bless them. Thus the name of the book (which means "The LORD remembers") contains in seed form the theme of the prophecy.

DECEMBER 27

Zechariah 4:1–6:15

4 Now the angel who talked with me came
back and wakened me, as a man who is
wakened out of his sleep. 2 And he said to me,
"What do you see?"
So I said, "I am looking, and there *is* a lampstand of solid gold with a bowl on top of it, and
on the *stand* seven lamps with seven pipes to
the seven lamps. 3 Two olive trees *are* by it, one
at the right of the bowl and the other at its
left." 4 So I answered and spoke to the angel

who talked with me, saying, "What *are* these,
my lord?"
5 Then the angel who talked with me answered
and said to me, "Do you not know what these
are?"
And I said, "No, my lord."
6 So he answered and said to me:

"This *is* the word of the LORD to
Zerubbabel:
'Not by might nor by power,
but by My Spirit,'
Says the LORD of hosts.
7 'Who *are* you, O great mountain?
Before Zerubbabel *you shall become*
a plain!
And he shall bring forth the capstone
With shouts of "Grace, grace to it!" ' "

8 Moreover the word of the LORD came to me,
saying:

9 "The hands of Zerubbabel
Have laid the foundation of this temple;
His hands shall also finish *it*.
Then you will know
That the LORD of hosts has sent Me to
you.
10 For who has despised the day of small
things?
For these seven rejoice to see
The plumb line in the hand of
Zerubbabel.
They are the eyes of the LORD,
Which scan to and fro throughout the
whole earth."

11 Then I answered and said to him, "What
are these two olive trees—at the right of the
lampstand and at its left?" 12 And I further
answered and said to him, "What *are these* two
olive branches that *drip* into the receptacles of
the two gold pipes from which the golden *oil*
drains?"

4:10 the day of small things. Though the rebuilding of a temple smaller than Solomon's may have been discouraging to some (Ezra 3:12; Hag. 2:3), the Lord announced that His pleasure was upon this work, and that His omniscient care ("7 eyes") was watching over and taking pleasure in its completion. He said in effect, "Don't despise what God is pleased with." This was only a picture of the glorious restoration when the Messiah comes to reign. That temple will make all others pale by comparison (Ezek. 40–48).

13 Then he answered me and said, "Do you
not know what these *are?*"
And I said, "No, my lord."
14 So he said, "These *are* the two anointed
ones, who stand beside the Lord of the whole
earth."

5 Then I turned and raised my eyes, and saw
there a flying scroll.
2 And he said to me, "What do you see?"
So I answered, "I see a flying scroll. Its
length *is* twenty cubits and its width ten cubits."
3 Then he said to me, "This *is* the curse that
goes out over the face of the whole earth:
'Every thief shall be expelled,' according *to*
this side of *the scroll;* and, 'Every perjurer
shall be expelled,' according *to* that side of it."

4 "I will send out *the curse,*" says the LORD
of hosts;
"It shall enter the house of the thief
And the house of the one who swears
falsely by My name.
It shall remain in the midst of his house
And consume it, with its timber and
stones."

5 Then the angel who talked with me came
out and said to me, "Lift your eyes now, and
see what this *is* that goes forth."
6 So I asked, "What *is* it?" And he said, "It *is* a
basket that is going forth."
He also said, "This *is* their resemblance
throughout the earth: 7 Here *is* a lead disc lifted
up, and this *is* a woman sitting inside the basket"; 8 then he said, "This *is* Wickedness!" And
he thrust her down into the basket, and threw
the lead cover over its mouth. 9 Then I raised my
eyes and looked, and there *were* two women,
coming with the wind in their wings; for they
had wings like the wings of a stork, and they lifted up the basket between earth and heaven.
10 So I said to the angel who talked with me,
"Where are they carrying the basket?"
11 And he said to me, "To build a house for it
in the land of Shinar; when it is ready, *the basket* will be set there on its base."

6 Then I turned and raised my eyes and
looked, and behold, four chariots *were*
coming from between two mountains, and the
mountains *were* mountains of bronze. 2 With
the first chariot *were* red horses, with the second chariot black horses, 3 with the third chariot white horses, and with the fourth chariot
dappled horses—strong *steeds.* 4 Then I
answered and said to the angel who talked
with me, "What *are* these, my lord?"
5 And the angel answered and said to me,
"These *are* four spirits of heaven, who go out
from *their* station before the Lord of all the

earth. 6 The one with the black horses is going
to the north country, the white are going after
them, and the dappled are going toward the
south country." 7 Then the strong *steeds* went
out, eager to go, that they might walk to and
fro throughout the earth. And He said, "Go,
walk to and fro throughout the earth." So they
walked to and fro throughout the earth. 8 And
He called to me, and spoke to me, saying, "See,
those who go toward the north country have
given rest to My Spirit in the north country."
9 Then the word of the LORD came to me, saying: 10 "Receive *the gift* from the captives—from
Heldai, Tobijah, and Jedaiah, who have come
from Babylon—and go the same day and enter
the house of Josiah the son of Zephaniah. 11 Take
the silver and gold, make an elaborate crown,
and set *it* on the head of Joshua the son of Jehozadak, the high priest. 12 Then speak to him,
saying, 'Thus says the LORD of hosts, saying:

"Behold, the Man whose name *is* the
BRANCH!
From His place He shall branch out,
And He shall build the temple of the
LORD;
13 Yes, He shall build the temple of the
LORD.
He shall bear the glory,
And shall sit and rule on His throne;
So He shall be a priest on His throne,
And the counsel of peace shall be
between them both." '

14 "Now the elaborate crown shall be for a
memorial in the temple of the LORD for Helem,
Tobijah, Jedaiah, and Hen the son of
Zephaniah. 15 Even those from afar shall come
and build the temple of the LORD. Then you
shall know that the LORD of hosts has sent Me
to you. And *this* shall come to pass if you diligently obey the voice of the LORD your God."

6:12–15 In this brief section, 8 facts are given about the Messiah, the BRANCH: 1) He will come from Israel ("His place," v. 12); 2) He will build the millennial temple (vv. 12b,13a); 3) He will be glorious (v. 13); 4) He will be king and priest (v. 13); 5) He makes peace (v. 13); 6) He opens the kingdom to Gentiles (v. 15a); 7) He will corroborate God's Word (v. 15b); and 8) He demands obedience (v. 15c). This, as always, is the essential matter. After Israel believes, the Messiah will come to set up His kingdom (12:10–13:1; 14:9–21). Faith and cleansing must come first.

Psalm 148:1–6

Praise the LORD!

Praise the LORD from the heavens;
Praise Him in the heights!
2 Praise Him, all His angels;
Praise Him, all His hosts!
3 Praise Him, sun and moon;
Praise Him, all you stars of light!
4 Praise Him, you heavens of heavens,
And you waters above the heavens!

5 Let them praise the name of
the LORD,
For He commanded and they were
created.
6 He also established them forever
and ever;
He made a decree which shall not
pass away.

Proverbs 30:24–28

24 There are four *things which* are little
on the earth,
But they *are* exceedingly wise:
25 The ants *are* a people not strong,
Yet they prepare their food in the
summer;
26 The rock badgers are a feeble folk,
Yet they make their homes in the
crags;
27 The locusts have no king,
Yet they all advance in ranks;
28 The spider skillfully grasps with its
hands,
And it is in kings' palaces.

30:24–28 four *things which* are little. These verses picture 4 creatures which survive due to natural instinct. The wisdom seen in each of these reveals the beauty of the wise Creator and His creation (Ps. 8:3–9) and becomes a model for the principle that labor, diligence, organization, planning, and resourcefulness are better than strength, thus implying the superiority of wisdom over might.

Revelation 17:1–18

17 Then one of the seven angels who had
the seven bowls came and talked with
me, saying to me, "Come, I will show you the
judgment of the great harlot who sits on many
waters, 2 with whom the kings of the earth
committed fornication, and the inhabitants of

the earth were made drunk with the wine of
her fornication."
[3]So he carried me away in the Spirit into the
wilderness. And I saw a woman sitting on a
scarlet beast *which was* full of names of blasphemy, having seven heads and ten horns.
[4]The woman was arrayed in purple and scarlet,
and adorned with gold and precious stones and
pearls, having in her hand a golden cup full of
abominations and the filthiness of her fornication. [5]And on her forehead a name *was* written:

MYSTERY, BABYLON THE GREAT, THE
MOTHER OF HARLOTS AND OF THE
ABOMINATIONS OF THE EARTH.

[6]I saw the woman, drunk with the blood of the
saints and with the blood of the martyrs of Jesus. And when I saw her, I marveled with
great amazement.
[7]But the angel said to me, "Why did you marvel? I will tell you the mystery of the woman and
of the beast that carries her, which has the
seven heads and the ten horns. [8]The beast that
you saw was, and is not, and will ascend out of
the bottomless pit and go to perdition. And those
who dwell on the earth will marvel, whose
names are not written in the Book of Life from
the foundation of the world, when they see the
beast that was, and is not, and yet is.
[9]"Here *is* the mind which has wisdom: The
seven heads are seven mountains on which
the woman sits. [10]There are also seven kings.
Five have fallen, one is, *and* the other has not
yet come. And when he comes, he must continue a short time. [11]The beast that was, and is
not, is himself also the eighth, and is of the
seven, and is going to perdition.
[12]"The ten horns which you saw are ten
kings who have received no kingdom as yet,
but they receive authority for one hour as
kings with the beast. [13]These are of one mind,
and they will give their power and authority to
the beast. [14]These will make war with the
Lamb, and the Lamb will overcome them, for
He is Lord of lords and King of kings; and
those *who are* with Him *are* called, chosen,
and faithful."
[15]Then he said to me, "The waters which
you saw, where the harlot sits, are peoples,
multitudes, nations, and tongues. [16]And the
ten horns which you saw on the beast, these
will hate the harlot, make her desolate and
naked, eat her flesh and burn her with fire.
[17]For God has put it into their hearts to fulfill
His purpose, to be of one mind, and to give
their kingdom to the beast, until the words of
God are fulfilled. [18]And the woman whom you
saw is that great city which reigns over the
kings of the earth."

17:5 forehead. It was customary for Roman prostitutes to wear a headband with their name on it (Jer. 3:3), parading their wretchedness for all to see. The harlot's forehead is emblazoned with a 3-fold title descriptive of the world's final false religious system. **MYSTERY.** A New Testament mystery is truth once hidden, but in the New Testament revealed. Spiritual Babylon's true identity is yet to be revealed. Thus, the precise details of how it will be manifested in the world are not yet known. **BABYLON THE GREAT.** This Babylon is distinct from the historical, geographical city of Babylon (which still existed in John's day). The details of John's vision cannot be applied to any historical city (14:8). **MOTHER OF HARLOTS.** All false religion stems ultimately from Babel or Babylon (Gen. 11).

DAY 27: What is God's word to inspire Zerubbabel to act on His promise?

Zechariah 4:6 states: "This is the word of the LORD to Zerubbabel." The purpose of the vision was to encourage Zerubbabel to complete the temple rebuilding, to assure him of divine enablement for that venture and the endless supply for the future glory of the Messiah's kingdom and temple. The lampstand pictured Israel fully supplied by God to be His light then and in the future. It must be noted that the church has temporarily taken this role presently (Eph. 5:8,9; Rev. 1:12,13,20), until Israel's salvation and restoration to covenant blessing and usefulness.

"'Not by might...power, but by My Spirit.'" Neither human might, wealth, or physical stamina would be sufficient to complete the work. Only an abundant supply of the power of the Holy Spirit, pictured by the "bowl" (v. 2), would enable him to carry out the task and enable Israel in the Messiah's kingdom to be a light again to the world by the operation of the Spirit (Ezek. 36:24).

"'Who are you, O great mountain? Before Zerubbabel you shall become a plain'" (v. 7). Because the outcome is guaranteed (vv. 6,9), any mountainlike opposition will be leveled by God to become like a flat surface. No obstacle will be able to stop the completion of the temple in Zerubbabel's time or in the final kingdom of the Messiah (Ezek. 40–48). "'He shall bring forth the capstone.'" The final stone of the building will be put into place, signifying its completion."'With shouts of "Grace, grace to it!"'" This blessing signifying shouts of joy and thanksgiving came to pass (Ezra 3:11–13) over the completion of the temple. Contrast this attitude with that of the people seeing the unfinished temple (Hag. 2:3).

DECEMBER 28

Zechariah 7:1–9:17

7 Now in the fourth year of King Darius it
came to pass *that* the word of the LORD
came to Zechariah, on the fourth *day* of the
ninth month, Chislev, [2]when *the people* sent
Sherezer, with Regem-Melech and his men, *to*
the house of God, to pray before the LORD, [3]*and*
to ask the priests who *were* in the house of the
LORD of hosts, and the prophets, saying,
"Should I weep in the fifth month and fast as I
have done for so many years?"
[4]Then the word of the LORD of hosts came to
me, saying, [5]"Say to all the people of the land,
and to the priests: 'When you fasted and
mourned in the fifth and seventh *months* during those seventy years, did you really fast for
Me—for Me? [6]When you eat and when you
drink, do you not eat and drink *for yourselves?*
[7]*Should you* not *have obeyed* the words which
the LORD proclaimed through the former
prophets when Jerusalem and the cities
around it were inhabited and prosperous, and
the South and the Lowland were inhabited?' "
[8]Then the word of the LORD came to
Zechariah, saying, [9]"Thus says the LORD of
hosts:

'Execute true justice,
Show mercy and compassion
Everyone to his brother.
10 Do not oppress the widow or the fatherless,
The alien or the poor.
Let none of you plan evil in his heart
Against his brother.'

[11]"But they refused to heed, shrugged their
shoulders, and stopped their ears so that they
could not hear. [12]Yes, they made their hearts
like flint, refusing to hear the law and the words
which the LORD of hosts had sent by His Spirit
through the former prophets. Thus great wrath
came from the LORD of hosts. [13]Therefore it
happened, *that* just as He proclaimed and they
would not hear, so they called out and I would
not listen," says the LORD of hosts. [14]"But I scattered them with a whirlwind among all the
nations which they had not known. Thus the
land became desolate after them, so that no one
passed through or returned; for they made the
pleasant land desolate."

8 Again the word of the LORD of hosts came,
saying, [2]"Thus says the LORD of hosts:

'I am zealous for Zion with great zeal;
With great fervor I am zealous for her.'

[3]"Thus says the LORD:

'I will return to Zion,
And dwell in the midst of Jerusalem.
Jerusalem shall be called the City of Truth,
The Mountain of the LORD of hosts,
The Holy Mountain.'

[4]"Thus says the LORD of hosts:

'Old men and old women shall again sit
In the streets of Jerusalem,
Each one with his staff in his hand
Because of great age.
5 The streets of the city
Shall be full of boys and girls
Playing in its streets.'

[6]"Thus says the LORD of hosts:

'If it is marvelous in the eyes of the remnant of this people in these days,
Will it also be marvelous in My eyes?'
Says the LORD of hosts.

[7]"Thus says the LORD of hosts:

'Behold, I will save My people from the land of the east
And from the land of the west;
8 I will bring them *back,*
And they shall dwell in the midst of Jerusalem.
They shall be My people
And I will be their God,
In truth and righteousness.'

[9]"Thus says the LORD of hosts:

'Let your hands be strong,
You who have been hearing in these days
These words by the mouth of the prophets,
Who *spoke* in the day the foundation was laid

For the house of the LORD of hosts,
That the temple might be built.
10 For before these days
There were no wages for man nor any
hire for beast;
There was no peace from the enemy for
whoever went out or came in;
For I set all men, everyone, against his
neighbor.

11 But now I *will* not *treat* the remnant of this people as in the former days,' says the LORD of hosts.

12 'For the seed *shall be* prosperous,
The vine shall give its fruit,
The ground shall give her increase,
And the heavens shall give their dew—
I will cause the remnant of this people
To possess all these.
13 And it shall come to pass
That just as you were a curse among
the nations,
O house of Judah and house of Israel,
So I will save you, and you shall
be a blessing.
Do not fear,
Let your hands be strong.'

14 "For thus says the LORD of hosts:

'Just as I determined to punish you
When your fathers provoked Me to
wrath,'
Says the LORD of hosts,
'And I would not relent,
15 So again in these days
I am determined to do good
To Jerusalem and to the house
of Judah.
Do not fear.
16 These *are* the things you shall do:
Speak each man the truth to his
neighbor;
Give judgment in your gates for truth,
justice, and peace;
17 Let none of you think evil in your heart
against your neighbor;
And do not love a false oath.
For all these *are things* that I hate,'
Says the LORD."

18 Then the word of the LORD of hosts came to me, saying, 19 "Thus says the LORD of hosts:

'The fast of the fourth *month,*
The fast of the fifth,
The fast of the seventh,
And the fast of the tenth,
Shall be joy and gladness and cheerful
feasts
For the house of Judah.
Therefore love truth and peace.'

20 "Thus says the LORD of hosts:

'Peoples shall yet come,
Inhabitants of many cities;
21 The inhabitants of one *city* shall go to
another, saying,
"Let us continue to go and pray before
the LORD,
And seek the LORD of hosts.
I myself will go also."
22 Yes, many peoples and strong nations
Shall come to seek the LORD of hosts in
Jerusalem,
And to pray before the LORD.'

23 "Thus says the LORD of hosts: 'In those days ten men from every language of the nations shall grasp the sleeve of a Jewish man, saying, "Let us go with you, for we have heard *that* God *is* with you." ' "

9 The burden of the word of the LORD
Against the land of Hadrach,
And Damascus its resting place
(For the eyes of men
And all the tribes of Israel
Are on the LORD);
2 Also *against* Hamath, *which* borders
on it,
And *against* Tyre and Sidon, though
they are very wise.
3 For Tyre built herself a tower,
Heaped up silver like the dust,
And gold like the mire of the streets.
4 Behold, the Lord will cast her out;
He will destroy her power in the sea,
And she will be devoured by fire.
5 Ashkelon shall see *it* and fear;
Gaza also shall be very sorrowful;
And Ekron, for He dried up her
expectation.

9:1–8 This oracle features a series of judgments announced against the nations surrounding Israel (vv. 1–7), with deliverance promised for His people (v. 8). Most understand this to be a prophecy of the victories of the famous Greek conqueror, Alexander the Great, given approximately 200 years before he marched through Palestine. He provides an analogy of Christ returning to judge the nations and save Israel at the end of the Great Tribulation (Matt. 24:21).

The king shall perish from Gaza,
And Ashkelon shall not be inhabited.

6 "A mixed race shall settle in Ashdod,
And I will cut off the pride of the
Philistines.
7 I will take away the blood from his
mouth,
And the abominations from between
his teeth.
But he who remains, even he *shall be*
for our God,
And shall be like a leader in Judah,
And Ekron like a Jebusite.
8 I will camp around My house
Because of the army,
Because of him who passes by and him
who returns.
No more shall an oppressor pass
through them,
For now I have seen with My eyes.

9 "Rejoice greatly, O daughter of Zion!
Shout, O daughter of Jerusalem!
Behold, your King is coming to you;
He *is* just and having salvation,
Lowly and riding on a donkey,
A colt, the foal of a donkey.
10 I will cut off the chariot from Ephraim
And the horse from Jerusalem;
The battle bow shall be cut off.
He shall speak peace to the nations;
His dominion *shall be* 'from sea to sea,
And from the River to the ends
of the earth.'

11 "As for you also,
Because of the blood of your covenant,
I will set your prisoners free from the
waterless pit.
12 Return to the stronghold,
You prisoners of hope.
Even today I declare
That I will restore double to you.
13 For I have bent Judah, My *bow,*
Fitted the bow with Ephraim,
And raised up your sons, O Zion,
Against your sons, O Greece,
And made you like the sword
of a mighty man."

14 Then the LORD will be seen over them,
And His arrow will go forth like
lightning.
The Lord GOD will blow the trumpet,
And go with whirlwinds from the
south.
15 The LORD of hosts will defend them;
They shall devour and subdue with
slingstones.
They shall drink *and* roar as if with
wine;
They shall be filled *with blood* like
basins,
Like the corners of the altar.
16 The LORD their God will save them in
that day,
As the flock of His people.
For they *shall be like* the jewels of a
crown,
Lifted like a banner over His land—
17 For how great is its goodness
And how great its beauty!
Grain shall make the young men thrive,
And new wine the young women.

Psalm 148:7–14

7 Praise the LORD from the earth,
You great sea creatures and all the
depths;
8 Fire and hail, snow and clouds;
Stormy wind, fulfilling His word;
9 Mountains and all hills;
Fruitful trees and all cedars;
10 Beasts and all cattle;
Creeping things and flying fowl;
11 Kings of the earth and all peoples;
Princes and all judges of the earth;
12 Both young men and maidens;
Old men and children.

13 Let them praise the name of the LORD,
For His name alone is exalted;
His glory *is* above the earth and heaven.
14 And He has exalted the horn of His
people,
The praise of all His saints—
Of the children of Israel,
A people near to Him.

Praise the LORD!

148:14 the horn. Refers in general to the strength and prosperity of the nation, which became the cause of praise for Israel. This suggests that Israel enjoyed better times than in the past, e.g., during David's and Solomon's reigns or after returning from the Babylonian captivity. **A people near to Him.** Also "My chosen [people]" (Is. 43:20) and "His special treasure" (Ps. 135:4).

Proverbs 30:29–31

29 There are three *things which* are
majestic in pace,
Yes, four *which* are stately in walk:

30 A lion, *which is* mighty among beasts
And does not turn away from any;
31 A greyhound,
A male goat also,
And a king *whose* troops *are* with him.

30:29–31 three *things*...majestic in pace,... four. The 3 creatures and the king all picture wise, stately, and orderly deportment. Each offers a glimpse of the Creator's power and wisdom (Job 38:1–42:6) and illustrates the dignity and confidence of those who walk wisely.

Revelation 18:1–24

18 After these things I saw another angel
coming down from heaven, having great
authority, and the earth was illuminated with
his glory. 2And he cried mightily with a loud
voice, saying, "Babylon the great is fallen, is
fallen, and has become a dwelling place of
demons, a prison for every foul spirit, and a
cage for every unclean and hated bird! 3For all
the nations have drunk of the wine of the
wrath of her fornication, the kings of the earth
have committed fornication with her, and the
merchants of the earth have become rich
through the abundance of her luxury."
4And I heard another voice from heaven saying, "Come out of her, my people, lest you
share in her sins, and lest you receive of her
plagues. 5For her sins have reached to heaven,
and God has remembered her iniquities. 6Ren-
der to her just as she rendered to you, and
repay her double according to her works; in
the cup which she has mixed, mix double for
her. 7In the measure that she glorified herself
and lived luxuriously, in the same measure
give her torment and sorrow; for she says in
her heart, 'I sit *as* queen, and am no widow,
and will not see sorrow.' 8Therefore her
plagues will come in one day—death and
mourning and famine. And she will be utterly
burned with fire, for strong *is* the Lord God
who judges her.
9"The kings of the earth who committed fornication and lived luxuriously with her will
weep and lament for her, when they see the
smoke of her burning, 10standing at a distance
for fear of her torment, saying, 'Alas, alas, that
great city Babylon, that mighty city! For in one
hour your judgment has come.'
11"And the merchants of the earth will weep
and mourn over her, for no one buys their
merchandise anymore: 12merchandise of gold
and silver, precious stones and pearls, fine
linen and purple, silk and scarlet, every kind of
citron wood, every kind of object of ivory,
every kind of object of most precious wood,
bronze, iron, and marble; 13and cinnamon and
incense, fragrant oil and frankincense, wine
and oil, fine flour and wheat, cattle and sheep,
horses and chariots, and bodies and souls of
men. 14The fruit that your soul longed for has
gone from you, and all the things which are
rich and splendid have gone from you, and you
shall find them no more at all. 15The merchants
of these things, who became rich by her, will
stand at a distance for fear of her torment,
weeping and wailing, 16and saying, 'Alas, alas,
that great city that was clothed in fine linen,
purple, and scarlet, and adorned with gold and
precious stones and pearls! 17For in one hour
such great riches came to nothing.' Every
shipmaster, all who travel by ship, sailors, and
as many as trade on the sea, stood at a distance
18and cried out when they saw the smoke of her
burning, saying, 'What *is* like this great city?'
19"They threw dust on their heads and cried
out, weeping and wailing, and saying, 'Alas,
alas, that great city, in which all who had ships
on the sea became rich by her wealth! For in
one hour she is made desolate.'
20"Rejoice over her, O heaven, and *you* holy
apostles and prophets, for God has avenged
you on her!"
21Then a mighty angel took up a stone like a
great millstone and threw *it* into the sea, saying, "Thus with violence the great city Babylon
shall be thrown down, and shall not be found
anymore. 22The sound of harpists, musicians,
flutists, and trumpeters shall not be heard in
you anymore. No craftsman of any craft shall
be found in you anymore, and the sound of a
millstone shall not be heard in you anymore.
23The light of a lamp shall not shine in you anymore, and the voice of bridegroom and bride
shall not be heard in you anymore. For your
merchants were the great men of the earth,
for by your sorcery all the nations were
deceived. 24And in her was found the blood of
prophets and saints, and of all who were slain
on the earth."

18:24 blood of prophets and saints. The religious and commercial/political systems embodied in Babylon will commit unspeakable atrocities against God's people (6:10; 11:7; 13:7,15; 17:6; 19:2). God will avenge that slaughter of His people (19:2).

DAY 28: If Zechariah 9:9 refers to the First Advent of Christ, how does v. 10 relate to that?

"Behold, your King is coming to you;…riding on a donkey" (v. 9). Unlike Alexander the Great, this King comes riding on a donkey (Jer. 17:25). This was fulfilled at Christ's Triumphal Entry into Jerusalem (Matt. 21:1–5; John 12:12–16). The Jews should have been looking for someone from the line of David (2 Sam. 7; 1 Chr. 17). Four elements in this verse describe the Messiah's character: 1) He is King; 2) He is just; 3) He brings salvation; and 4) He is humble.

Zechariah moves to the Second Advent of Christ and the establishment of His universal kingdom in v. 10. "His dominion shall be 'from sea to sea.'" Not characterized by bloodshed, the Messiah's rule will be a kingdom of peace in which weapons of warfare will be destroyed or converted to peaceful uses (Is. 2:4; 9:5–7; 11:1–10; Mic. 5:2,10–15), and peace spreads from the Euphrates River (the terminus of civilization) to the world.

The two advents of Christ are here compressed as though they were one as in Isaiah 61:1–3 (Luke 4:16,21). Verse 9 refers to His First Coming and v. 10 is His Second. Old Testament prophets didn't see the great time period between the two comings. The church age was a "mystery" hidden from them (Eph. 3:1–9; Col. 1:27).

DECEMBER 29

Zechariah 10:1–12:14

10 Ask the LORD for rain
In the time of the latter rain.
The LORD will make flashing clouds;
He will give them showers of rain,
Grass in the field for everyone.

2 For the idols speak delusion;
The diviners envision lies,
And tell false dreams;
They comfort in vain.
Therefore *the people* wend their way
like sheep;
They are in trouble because
there is no shepherd.

3 "My anger is kindled against
the shepherds,
And I will punish the goatherds.
For the LORD of hosts will visit His flock,
The house of Judah,
And will make them as His royal horse
in the battle.
4 From him comes the cornerstone,
From him the tent peg,
From him the battle bow,
From him every ruler together.
5 They shall be like mighty men,
Who tread down *their enemies*
In the mire of the streets in the battle.
They shall fight because the LORD is
with them,
And the riders on horses shall be put
to shame.

6 "I will strengthen the house of Judah,
And I will save the house of Joseph.
I will bring them back,
Because I have mercy on them.
They shall be as though I had not cast
them aside;
For I *am* the LORD their God,
And I will hear them.
7 *Those of* Ephraim shall be like a mighty
man,
And their heart shall rejoice as if with
wine.
Yes, their children shall see *it* and be
glad;
Their heart shall rejoice in the LORD.
8 I will whistle for them and gather
them,
For I will redeem them;
And they shall increase as they once
increased.

9 "I will sow them among the peoples,
And they shall remember Me in far
countries;
They shall live, together with their
children,
And they shall return.
10 I will also bring them back from the
land of Egypt,
And gather them from Assyria.
I will bring them into the land of Gilead
and Lebanon,
Until no *more room* is found for them.
11 He shall pass through the sea with
affliction,
And strike the waves of the sea:
All the depths of the River shall dry up.
Then the pride of Assyria shall be
brought down,
And the scepter of Egypt shall depart.

12 "So I will strengthen them in the LORD,
And they shall walk up and down in
His name,"
Says the LORD.

11 Open your doors, O Lebanon,
That fire may devour your cedars.
[2] Wail, O cypress, for the cedar has fallen,
Because the mighty *trees* are ruined.
Wail, O oaks of Bashan,
For the thick forest has come down.
[3] *There is* the sound of wailing shepherds!
For their glory is in ruins.
There is the sound of roaring lions!
For the pride of the Jordan is in ruins.

[4]Thus says the LORD my God, "Feed the
flock for slaughter, [5]whose owners slaughter
them and feel no guilt; those who sell them
say, 'Blessed be the LORD, for I am rich'; and
their shepherds do not pity them. [6]For I will no
longer pity the inhabitants of the land," says
the LORD. "But indeed I will give everyone into
his neighbor's hand and into the hand of his
king. They shall attack the land, and I will not
deliver *them* from their hand."

[7]So I fed the flock for slaughter, in particular
the poor of the flock. I took for myself two
staffs: the one I called Beauty, and the other I
called Bonds; and I fed the flock. [8]I dismissed
the three shepherds in one month. My soul
loathed them, and their soul also abhorred me.
[9]Then I said, "I will not feed you. Let what is
dying die, and what is perishing perish. Let
those that are left eat each other's flesh." [10]And
I took my staff, Beauty, and cut it in two, that I
might break the covenant which I had made
with all the peoples. [11]So it was broken on that
day. Thus the poor of the flock, who were watching me, knew that it *was* the word of the LORD.
[12]Then I said to them, "If it is agreeable to you,
give *me* my wages; and if not, refrain." So they
weighed out for my wages thirty *pieces* of silver.

[13]And the LORD said to me, "Throw it to the
potter"—that princely price they set on me. So
I took the thirty *pieces* of silver and threw
them into the house of the LORD for the potter.
[14]Then I cut in two my other staff, Bonds, that
I might break the brotherhood between Judah
and Israel.

[15]And the LORD said to me, "Next, take for
yourself the implements of a foolish shepherd.
[16]For indeed I will raise up a shepherd in the land
who will not care for those who are cut off, nor
seek the young, nor heal those that are broken,
nor feed those that still stand. But he will eat the
flesh of the fat and tear their hooves in pieces.

[17] "Woe to the worthless shepherd,
Who leaves the flock!
A sword *shall be* against his arm
And against his right eye;
His arm shall completely wither,
And his right eye shall be totally blinded."

12 The burden of the word of the LORD
against Israel. Thus says the LORD, who
stretches out the heavens, lays the foundation
of the earth, and forms the spirit of man within him: [2]"Behold, I will make Jerusalem a cup
of drunkenness to all the surrounding peoples,
when they lay siege against Judah and Jerusalem. [3]And it shall happen in that day that I will
make Jerusalem a very heavy stone for all peoples; all who would heave it away will surely be
cut in pieces, though all nations of the earth
are gathered against it. [4]In that day," says the
LORD, "I will strike every horse with confusion,
and its rider with madness; I will open My eyes
on the house of Judah, and will strike every
horse of the peoples with blindness. [5]And the
governors of Judah shall say in their heart,
'The inhabitants of Jerusalem *are* my strength
in the LORD of hosts, their God.' [6]In that day I
will make the governors of Judah like a
firepan in the woodpile, and like a fiery torch
in the sheaves; they shall devour all the surrounding peoples on the right hand and on the
left, but Jerusalem shall be inhabited again in
her own place—Jerusalem.

[7]"The LORD will save the tents of Judah first,
so that the glory of the house of David and the
glory of the inhabitants of Jerusalem shall not
become greater than that of Judah. [8]In that
day the LORD will defend the inhabitants of Jerusalem; the one who is feeble among them in
that day shall be like David, and the house of
David *shall be* like God, like the Angel of the
LORD before them. [9]It shall be in that day *that*
I will seek to destroy all the nations that come
against Jerusalem.

[10]"And I will pour on the house of David and

12:10 I will pour. God, in His own perfect time and by His own power, will sovereignly act to save Israel. This was prophesied by other prophets (Ezek. 39:29; Joel 2:28–32) and by the apostle Paul (Rom. 11:25–27). **Spirit of grace and supplication.** The Holy Spirit is so identified because He brings saving grace and because that grace produces sorrow that will result in repentant prayer to God for forgiveness (Matt. 5:4; Heb. 10:29). **look on Me whom they pierced.** Israel's repentance will come because they look to Jesus, the One whom they rejected and crucified (Is. 53:5; John 19:37), in faith at the Second Advent (Rom. 11:25–27). When God says they pierced "Me," He is certainly affirming the incarnation of Deity—Jesus was God.

on the inhabitants of Jerusalem the Spirit of
grace and supplication; then they will look on
Me whom they pierced. Yes, they will mourn for
Him as one mourns for *his* only *son,* and grieve
for Him as one grieves for a firstborn. [11]In that
day there shall be a great mourning in Jerusalem, like the mourning at Hadad Rimmon in the
plain of Megiddo. [12]And the land shall mourn,
every family by itself: the family of the house of
David by itself, and their wives by themselves;
the family of the house of Nathan by itself, and
their wives by themselves; [13]the family of the
house of Levi by itself, and their wives by themselves; the family of Shimei by itself, and their
wives by themselves; [14]all the families that
remain, every family by itself, and their wives
by themselves.

Psalm 149:1–4

Praise the LORD!

Sing to the LORD a new song,
And His praise in the assembly of saints.

2 Let Israel rejoice in their Maker;
Let the children of Zion be joyful in
their King.
3 Let them praise His name with the
dance;
Let them sing praises to Him with the
timbrel and harp.
4 For the LORD takes pleasure in His
people;
He will beautify the humble with
salvation.

Proverbs 30:32–33

32 If you have been foolish in exalting
yourself,
Or if you have devised evil, *put your*
hand on *your* mouth.
33 For *as* the churning of milk produces
butter,
And wringing the nose produces blood,
So the forcing of wrath produces strife.

Revelation 19:1–21

19 After these things I heard a loud voice of
a great multitude in heaven, saying,
"Alleluia! Salvation and glory and honor and
power *belong* to the Lord our God! [2]For true
and righteous *are* His judgments, because He
has judged the great harlot who corrupted the
earth with her fornication; and He has
avenged on her the blood of His servants *shed*
by her." [3]Again they said, "Alleluia! Her smoke
rises up forever and ever!" [4]And the twenty-
four elders and the four living creatures fell
down and worshiped God who sat on the
throne, saying, "Amen! Alleluia!" [5]Then a voice
came from the throne, saying, "Praise our
God, all you His servants and those who fear
Him, both small and great!"

[6]And I heard, as it were, the voice of a great
multitude, as the sound of many waters and as
the sound of mighty thunderings, saying,
"Alleluia! For the Lord God Omnipotent
reigns! [7]Let us be glad and rejoice and give
Him glory, for the marriage of the Lamb has
come, and His wife has made herself ready."
[8]And to her it was granted to be arrayed in fine
linen, clean and bright, for the fine linen is the
righteous acts of the saints.

[9]Then he said to me, "Write: 'Blessed *are*
those who are called to the marriage supper of
the Lamb!' " And he said to me, "These are the
true sayings of God." [10]And I fell at his feet to
worship him. But he said to me, "See *that you*
do not *do that!* I am your fellow servant, and of
your brethren who have the testimony of Jesus. Worship God! For the testimony of Jesus
is the spirit of prophecy."

19:11 heaven opened. The One who ascended to heaven (Acts 1:9–11) and had been seated at the Father's right hand (Heb. 8:1; 10:12; 1 Pet. 3:22) will return to take back the earth from the usurper and establish His kingdom (5:1–10). The nature of this event shows how it differs from the Rapture. At the Rapture, Christ meets His own in the air—in this event, He comes with them to earth. At the Rapture, there is no judgment—in this event, it is all judgment. This event is preceded by blackness—the darkened sun, moon gone out, stars fallen, smoke—then lightning and blinding glory as Jesus comes. Such details are not included in Rapture passages (John 14:1–3; 1 Thess. 4:13–18). **white horse.** In the Roman triumphal processions, the victorious general rode his white war horse up the Via Sacra to the temple of Jupiter on the Capitoline Hill. Jesus' First Coming was in humiliation on a colt (Zech. 9:9). John's vision portrays Him as the conqueror on His warhorse, coming to destroy the wicked, to overthrow the Antichrist, to defeat Satan, and to take control of the earth (2 Cor. 2:14). **Faithful and True.** True to His word, Jesus will return to earth (Matt. 24:27–31). **makes war.** This startling statement, appearing only here and 2:16, vividly portrays the holy wrath of God against sinners (Ps. 7:11). God's patience will be exhausted with sinful, rebellious mankind.

[11]Now I saw heaven opened, and behold, a white horse. And He who sat on him *was* called Faithful and True, and in righteousness He judges and makes war. [12]His eyes *were* like a flame of fire, and on His head *were* many crowns. He had a name written that no one knew except Himself. [13]He *was* clothed with a robe dipped in blood, and His name is called The Word of God. [14]And the armies in heaven, clothed in fine linen, white and clean, followed Him on white horses. [15]Now out of His mouth goes a sharp sword, that with it He should strike the nations. And He Himself will rule them with a rod of iron. He Himself treads the winepress of the fierceness and wrath of Almighty God. [16]And He has on *His* robe and on His thigh a name written:

KING OF KINGS AND LORD OF LORDS.

[17]Then I saw an angel standing in the sun; and he cried with a loud voice, saying to all the birds that fly in the midst of heaven, "Come and gather together for the supper of the great God, [18]that you may eat the flesh of kings, the flesh of captains, the flesh of mighty men, the flesh of horses and of those who sit on them, and the flesh of all *people,* free and slave, both small and great."

[19]And I saw the beast, the kings of the earth, and their armies, gathered together to make war against Him who sat on the horse and against His army. [20]Then the beast was captured, and with him the false prophet who worked signs in his presence, by which he deceived those who received the mark of the beast and those who worshiped his image. These two were cast alive into the lake of fire burning with brimstone. [21]And the rest were killed with the sword which proceeded from the mouth of Him who sat on the horse. And all the birds were filled with their flesh.

19:20 beast was captured, and...the false prophet. In an instant, the world's armies are without their leaders. The beast is Antichrist (13:1–4); the false prophet is his religious cohort (13:11–17). **cast alive.** The bodies of the beast and the false prophet will be transformed, and they will be banished directly to the lake of fire (Dan. 7:11)—the first of countless millions of unregenerate men (20:15) and fallen angels (Matt. 25:41) to arrive in that dreadful place. That these two still appear there 1,000 years later (20:10) refutes the false doctrine of annihilationism. **lake of fire.** The final hell, the place of eternal punishment for all unrepentant rebels, angelic or human (20:10,15).

DAY 29: What is the "marriage of the Lamb" in Revelation 19:7–9 about?

Hebrew weddings consisted of 3 phases: 1) betrothal (often when the couple were children); 2) presentation (the festivities, often lasting several days, that preceded the ceremony); and 3) the ceremony (the exchanging of vows). The church was betrothed to Christ by His sovereign choice in eternity past (Eph. 1:4; Heb. 13:20) and will be presented to Him at the Rapture (John 14:1–3; 1 Thess. 4:13–18). The final supper will signify the end of the ceremony. This symbolic meal will take place at the establishment of the millennial kingdom and last throughout that 1,000-year period (21:2). While the term "bride" often refers to the church, and does so here (2 Cor. 11:2; Eph. 5:22–24), it ultimately expands to include all the redeemed of all ages.

"And to her it was granted to be arrayed in fine linen,…the righteous acts of the saints" (v. 8). Not Christ's imputed righteousness granted to believers at salvation, but the practical results of that righteousness in believers' lives, i.e., the outward manifestation of inward virtue.

"'Blessed are those who are called to the marriage supper of the Lamb!" (v. 9). This is not the bride (the church) but the guests. The bride doesn't get invited; she invites. These are those saved before Pentecost, all the faithful believers saved by grace through faith up to the birth of the church (Acts 2:1ff.). Though they are not the bride, they still are glorified and reign with Christ in the millennial kingdom. It is really differing imagery rather than differing reality. The guests also will include tribulation saints and believers alive in earthly bodies in the kingdom. The church is the bride, pure and faithful—never a harlot, like Israel was (see Hos. 2). So the church is the bride during the presentation feast in heaven, then comes to earth for the celebration of the final meal (the Millennium). After that event, the new order comes and the marriage is consummated (21:1,2).

DECEMBER 30

Zechariah 13:1–14:21

13 "In that day a fountain shall be opened for the house of David and for the inhabitants of Jerusalem, for sin and for uncleanness.

2"It shall be in that day," says the LORD of hosts, "*that* I will cut off the names of the idols from the land, and they shall no longer be remembered. I will also cause the prophets and the unclean spirit to depart from the land.
3It shall come to pass *that* if anyone still prophesies, then his father and mother who begot him will say to him, 'You shall not live, because you have spoken lies in the name of the LORD.' And his father and mother who begot him shall thrust him through when he prophesies.
4"And it shall be in that day *that* every prophet will be ashamed of his vision when he prophesies; they will not wear a robe of coarse hair to deceive. 5But he will say, 'I *am* no prophet, I *am* a farmer; for a man taught me to keep cattle from my youth.' 6And *one* will say to him, 'What are these wounds between your arms?' Then he will answer, '*Those* with which I was wounded in the house of my friends.'

7 "Awake, O sword, against My Shepherd,
Against the Man who is My Companion,"
Says the LORD of hosts.
"Strike the Shepherd,
And the sheep will be scattered;
Then I will turn My hand against the little ones.
8 And it shall come to pass in all the land,"
Says the LORD,
"*That* two-thirds in it shall be cut off *and* die,
But *one*-third shall be left in it:
9 I will bring the *one*-third through the fire,
Will refine them as silver is refined,
And test them as gold is tested.
They will call on My name,
And I will answer them.
I will say, 'This *is* My people';
And each one will say, 'The LORD *is* my God.' "

14 Behold, the day of the LORD is coming,
And your spoil will be divided in your midst.
2 For I will gather all the nations to battle against Jerusalem;
The city shall be taken,
The houses rifled,
And the women ravished.
Half of the city shall go into captivity,
But the remnant of the people shall not be cut off from the city.

3 Then the LORD will go forth
And fight against those nations,
As He fights in the day of battle.
4 And in that day His feet will stand on the Mount of Olives,
Which faces Jerusalem on the east.
And the Mount of Olives shall be split in two,
From east to west,

13:7 My Shepherd,...the Man who is My Companion. God spoke of the True Shepherd, that mighty Man who is His intimate associate; thus He identified Christ as His coequal, affirming the deity of Christ (John 1:1; 10:30; 14:9). **Strike the Shepherd.** In 11:17, it was the worthless shepherd who was to be struck; now it is the Good Shepherd (12:10) whose death was designed by God from before the foundation of the world (Is. 53:10; Acts 2:23; 1 Pet. 1:18–20). **sheep...scattered.** Jesus applies this prophecy to the disciples who defected from Him after His arrest (Matt. 26:56; Mark 14:50), including Peter's denial (Matt. 26:33–35,69–75). **the little ones.** The same as the "poor of the flock" (11:7). The reference is to the remnant of believers, among the Jews, who were faithful to the Messiah after His crucifixion. Turning God's hand "against" them could mean they would suffer persecution, which they did (John 15:18,20; 16:2; James 1:1), or it could be translated "upon" and refer to God's protection of the faithful.

14:3,4 His feet will stand on the Mount of Olives. To prevent the eradication of His remnant, the Lord will personally intervene to fight against the gathered nations. Just as He fought for His people in the past, so He will do in the future as the ultimate Warrior-King. Jesus will literally return to the Mount of Olives, located east of the Kidron Valley, just as the angels announced at His Ascension (Acts 1:11). When He does, there will be a tremendous topographical upheaval (perhaps an earthquake), a phenomenon not uncommon when God announces His coming in judgment (Mic. 1:2–4; Nah. 1:5; Rev. 16:18–21). The reaction of people is given in Revelation 6:15–17.

Making a very large valley;
Half of the mountain shall move toward
the north
And half of it toward the south.

5 Then you shall flee *through* My
mountain valley,
For the mountain valley shall reach
to Azal.
Yes, you shall flee
As you fled from the earthquake
In the days of Uzziah king of Judah.
Thus the LORD my God will come,
And all the saints with You.

6 It shall come to pass in that day
That there will be no light;
The lights will diminish.
7 It shall be one day
Which is known to the LORD—
Neither day nor night.
But at evening time it shall happen
That it will be light.

8 And in that day it shall be
That living waters shall flow
from Jerusalem,
Half of them toward the eastern sea
And half of them toward the western sea;
In both summer and winter it shall
occur.
9 And the LORD shall be King over
all the earth.
In that day it shall be—
"The LORD *is* one,"
And His name one.

10All the land shall be turned into a plain from
Geba to Rimmon south of Jerusalem. *Jerusalem*
shall be raised up and inhabited in her place
from Benjamin's Gate to the place of the First
Gate and the Corner Gate, and *from* the Tower
of Hananel to the king's winepresses.

11 *The people* shall dwell in it;
And no longer shall there be utter
destruction,
But Jerusalem shall be safely inhabited.

12And this shall be the plague with which the
LORD will strike all the people who fought
against Jerusalem:

Their flesh shall dissolve while they
stand on their feet,
Their eyes shall dissolve in their
sockets,
And their tongues shall dissolve in their
mouths.
13 It shall come to pass in that day
That a great panic from the LORD will
be among them.
Everyone will seize the hand of his
neighbor,
And raise his hand against his
neighbor's hand;
14 Judah also will fight at Jerusalem.
And the wealth of all the surrounding
nations
Shall be gathered together:
Gold, silver, and apparel in great
abundance.

15 Such also shall be the plague
On the horse *and* the mule,
On the camel and the donkey,
And on all the cattle that will be in
those camps.
So *shall* this plague *be.*

16And it shall come to pass *that* everyone
who is left of all the nations which came
against Jerusalem shall go up from year to
year to worship the King, the LORD of hosts,
and to keep the Feast of Tabernacles. 17And it
shall be *that* whichever of the families of the
earth do not come up to Jerusalem to worship
the King, the LORD of hosts, on them there will
be no rain. 18If the family of Egypt will not come
up and enter in, they *shall have* no *rain;* they
shall receive the plague with which the LORD
strikes the nations who do not come up to keep
the Feast of Tabernacles. 19This shall be the
punishment of Egypt and the punishment of all
the nations that do not come up to keep the
Feast of Tabernacles.

20In that day "HOLINESS TO THE LORD"
shall be *engraved* on the bells of the horses.
The pots in the LORD's house shall be like the
bowls before the altar. 21Yes, every pot in Jerusalem and Judah shall be holiness to the LORD
of hosts. Everyone who sacrifices shall come
and take them and cook in them. In that day
there shall no longer be a Canaanite in the
house of the LORD of hosts.

Psalm 149:5–9

5 Let the saints be joyful in glory;
Let them sing aloud on their beds.
6 *Let* the high praises of God *be* in their
mouth,
And a two-edged sword in their hand,
7 To execute vengeance on the nations,
And punishments on the peoples;
8 To bind their kings with chains,
And their nobles with fetters of iron;
9 To execute on them the written
judgment—
This honor have all His saints.

Praise the LORD!

Proverbs 31:1–9

31 The words of King Lemuel, the utterance
which his mother taught him:

2 What, my son?
And what, son of my womb?
And what, son of my vows?
3 Do not give your strength to women,
Nor your ways to that which destroys
kings.

4 *It is* not for kings, O Lemuel,
It is not for kings to drink wine,
Nor for princes intoxicating drink;
5 Lest they drink and forget the law,
And pervert the justice of all the
afflicted.
6 Give strong drink to him who is perishing,
And wine to those who are bitter of heart.
7 Let him drink and forget his poverty,
And remember his misery no more.
8 Open your mouth for the speechless,
In the cause of all *who are* appointed
to die.
9 Open your mouth, judge righteously,
And plead the cause of the poor and
needy.

Revelation 20:1–15

20 Then I saw an angel coming down from
heaven, having the key to the bottomless pit and a great chain in his hand. 2He laid
hold of the dragon, that serpent of old, who is
the Devil and Satan, and bound him for a thousand years; 3and he cast him into the bottomless pit, and shut him up, and set a seal on
him, so that he should deceive the nations no
more till the thousand years were finished.
But after these things he must be released for
a little while.
4And I saw thrones, and they sat on them,
and judgment was committed to them. Then *I*
saw the souls of those who had been beheaded for their witness to Jesus and for the word
of God, who had not worshiped the beast or his
image, and had not received *his* mark on their
foreheads or on their hands. And they lived and
reigned with Christ for a thousand years. 5But
the rest of the dead did not live again until the
thousand years were finished. This *is* the first
resurrection. 6Blessed and holy *is* he who has
part in the first resurrection. Over such the
second death has no power, but they shall be
priests of God and of Christ, and shall reign
with Him a thousand years.
7Now when the thousand years have
expired, Satan will be released from his prison
8and will go out to deceive the nations which
are in the four corners of the earth, Gog and
Magog, to gather them together to battle,
whose number *is* as the sand of the sea. 9They
went up on the breadth of the earth and surrounded the camp of the saints and the
beloved city. And fire came down from God
out of heaven and devoured them. 10The devil,
who deceived them, was cast into the lake of
fire and brimstone where the beast and the
false prophet *are*. And they will be tormented
day and night forever and ever.
11Then I saw a great white throne and Him
who sat on it, from whose face the earth and
the heaven fled away. And there was found no
place for them. 12And I saw the dead, small and

20:5 first resurrection. Scripture teaches 2 kinds of resurrections: the "resurrection of life" and "the resurrection of condemnation" (John 5:29; Dan. 12:2; Acts 24:15). The first kind of resurrection is described as "the resurrection of the just" (Luke 14:14), the resurrection of "those who are Christ's at His coming" (1 Cor. 15:23), and the "better resurrection" (Heb. 11:35). It includes only the redeemed of the church age (1 Thess. 4:13–18), the Old Testament (Dan. 12:2), and the Tribulation (v. 4). They will enter the kingdom in resurrection bodies, along with believers who survived the Tribulation. The second kind of resurrection, then, will be the resurrection of the unconverted who will receive their final bodies suited for torment in hell.

20:12 standing before God. In a judicial sense, as guilty, condemned prisoners before the bar of divine justice. There are no living sinners left in the destroyed universe since all sinners were killed and all believers glorified. **books.** These books record every thought, word, and deed of sinful men—all recorded by divine omniscience. They will provide the evidence for eternal condemnation. ***Book* of Life.** It contains the names of all the redeemed (Dan. 12:1). **judged according to their works.** Their thoughts (Luke 8:17; Rom. 2:16), words (Matt. 12:37), and actions (Matt. 16:27) will be compared to God's perfect, holy standard (Matt. 5:48; 1 Pet. 1:15,16) and will be found wanting (Rom. 3:23). This also implies that there are degrees of punishment in hell (Matt. 10:14,15; 11:22; Mark 12:38–40; Luke 12:47,48; Heb. 10:29).

great, standing before God, and books were
opened. And another book was opened, which
is *the Book* of Life. And the dead were judged
according to their works, by the things which
were written in the books. [13]The sea gave up
the dead who were in it, and Death and Hades
delivered up the dead who were in them. And
they were judged, each one according to his
works. [14]Then Death and Hades were cast into
the lake of fire. This is the second death. [15]And
anyone not found written in the Book of Life
was cast into the lake of fire.

DAY 30: What is the Millennium?

In Revelation 20:2, Satan is bound for "a thousand years." This is the first of 6 references to the length of the millennial kingdom (vv. 3,4,5,6,7). There are 3 main views of the duration and nature of this period:

1) Premillennialism sees this as a literal 1,000-year period during which Jesus Christ, in fulfillment of numerous Old Testament prophecies (e.g., 2 Sam. 7:12–16; Ps. 2; Is. 11:6–12; 24:23; Hos. 3:4,5; Joel 3:9–21; Amos 9:8–15; Mic. 4:1–8; Zeph. 3:14–20; Zech. 14:1–11; Matt. 24:29–31,36–44), reigns on the earth. Using the same general principles of interpretation for both prophetic and nonprophetic passages leads most naturally to Premillennialism. Another strong argument supporting this view is that so many biblical prophecies have already been literally fulfilled, suggesting that future prophecies will likewise be fulfilled literally.

2) Postmillennialism understands the reference to a 1,000-year period as only symbolic of a golden age of righteousness and spiritual prosperity. It will be ushered in by the spread of the gospel during the present church age and brought to completion when Christ returns. According to this view, references to Christ's reign on earth primarily describe His spiritual reign in the hearts of believers in the church.

3) Amillennialism understands the 1,000 years to be merely symbolic of a long period of time. This view interprets Old Testament prophecies of a Millennium as being fulfilled spiritually now in the church (either on earth or in heaven) or as references to the eternal state. Using the same literal, historical, grammatical principles of interpretation so as to determine the normal sense of language, one is left with the inescapable conclusion that Christ will return and reign in a real kingdom on earth for 1,000 years. There is nothing in the text to render the conclusion that "a thousand years" is symbolic.

DECEMBER 31

Malachi 1:1–4:6

1 The burden of the word of the LORD to Israel by Malachi.

2 "I have loved you," says the LORD.
"Yet you say, 'In what way have You loved us?'
Was not Esau Jacob's brother?"
Says the LORD.
"Yet Jacob I have loved;
3 But Esau I have hated,
And laid waste his mountains and his heritage
For the jackals of the wilderness."

4 Even though Edom has said,
"We have been impoverished,
But we will return and build the desolate places,"

Thus says the LORD of hosts:
"They may build, but I will throw down;
They shall be called the Territory of Wickedness,
And the people against whom the LORD will have indignation forever.
5 Your eyes shall see,
And you shall say,
'The LORD is magnified beyond the border of Israel.'

6 "A son honors *his* father,
And a servant *his* master.
If then I am the Father,
Where *is* My honor?
And if I *am* a Master,
Where *is* My reverence?
Says the LORD of hosts
To you priests who despise My name.
Yet you say, 'In what way have we despised Your name?'

7 "You offer defiled food on My altar,
But say,
'In what way have we defiled You?'
By saying,
'The table of the LORD is contemptible.'

8 And when you offer the blind as a
sacrifice,
Is it not evil?
And when you offer the lame and sick,
Is it not evil?
Offer it then to your governor!
Would he be pleased with you?
Would he accept you favorably?"
Says the LORD of hosts.

9 "But now entreat God's favor,
That He may be gracious to us.
While this is being *done* by your hands,
Will He accept you favorably?"
Says the LORD of hosts.
10 "Who *is there* even among you who
would shut the doors,
So that you would not kindle fire *on*
My altar in vain?
I have no pleasure in you,"
Says the LORD of hosts,
"Nor will I accept an offering from your
hands.
11 For from the rising of the sun, even to
its going down,
My name *shall be* great among the
Gentiles;
In every place incense *shall be* offered
to My name,
And a pure offering;
For My name shall be great among the
nations,"
Says the LORD of hosts.

12 "But you profane it,
In that you say,
'The table of the LORD is defiled;
And its fruit, its food, *is* contemptible.'
13 You also say,
'Oh, what a weariness!'
And you sneer at it,"
Says the LORD of hosts.
"And you bring the stolen, the lame,
and the sick;
Thus you bring an offering!
Should I accept this from your hand?"
Says the LORD.
14 "But cursed *be* the deceiver
Who has in his flock a male,
And takes a vow,
But sacrifices to the Lord what is
blemished—
For I *am* a great King,"
Says the LORD of hosts,
"And My name *is to be* feared among
the nations.

2 "And now, O priests, this
commandment is for you.
2 If you will not hear,
And if you will not take *it* to heart,
To give glory to My name,"
Says the LORD of hosts,
"I will send a curse upon you,
And I will curse your blessings.
Yes, I have cursed them already,
Because you do not take *it* to heart.

3 "Behold, I will rebuke your descendants
And spread refuse on your faces,
The refuse of your solemn feasts;
And *one* will take you away with it.
4 Then you shall know that I have sent
this commandment to you,
That My covenant with Levi may
continue,"
Says the LORD of hosts.
5 "My covenant was with him, *one* of life
and peace,
And I gave them to him *that he might*
fear *Me;*
So he feared Me
And was reverent before My name.
6 The law of truth was in his mouth,
And injustice was not found on his lips.
He walked with Me in peace and equity,
And turned many away from iniquity.
7 "For the lips of a priest should keep
knowledge,
And *people* should seek the law from
his mouth;
For he is the messenger of the LORD of
hosts.
8 But you have departed from the way;
You have caused many to stumble at
the law.
You have corrupted the covenant of
Levi,"
Says the LORD of hosts.
9 "Therefore I also have made you
contemptible and base
Before all the people,
Because you have not kept My ways
But have shown partiality in the law."

10 Have we not all one Father?
Has not one God created us?
Why do we deal treacherously with
one another
By profaning the covenant of the
fathers?
11 Judah has dealt treacherously,
And an abomination has been
committed in Israel and
in Jerusalem,
For Judah has profaned
The LORD's holy *institution* which He
loves:

He has married the daughter of a
foreign god.
12 May the LORD cut off from the tents of
Jacob
The man who does this, being awake
and aware,
Yet who brings an offering to the LORD
of hosts!

13 And this is the second thing you do:
You cover the altar of the LORD with
tears,
With weeping and crying;
So He does not regard the offering
anymore,
Nor receive *it* with goodwill from your
hands.
14 Yet you say, "For what reason?"
Because the LORD has been witness
Between you and the wife of your youth,
With whom you have dealt
treacherously;
Yet she is your companion
And your wife by covenant.
15 But did He not make *them* one,
Having a remnant of the Spirit?
And why one?
He seeks godly offspring.
Therefore take heed to your spirit,
And let none deal treacherously with
the wife of his youth.

16 "For the LORD God of Israel says
That He hates divorce,
For it covers one's garment with
violence,"
Says the LORD of hosts.
"Therefore take heed to your spirit,
That you do not deal treacherously."

17 You have wearied the LORD with your
words;
Yet you say,
"In what way have we wearied *Him*?"
In that you say,
"Everyone who does evil
Is good in the sight of the LORD,
And He delights in them,"
Or, "Where *is* the God of justice?"

3 "Behold, I send My messenger,
And he will prepare the way before Me.
And the Lord, whom you seek,
Will suddenly come to His temple,
Even the Messenger of the covenant,
In whom you delight.
Behold, He is coming,"
Says the LORD of hosts.

2 "But who can endure the day of His
coming?

3:1 My messenger. It was a custom of the Near Eastern kings to send messengers before them to remove obstacles to their visit. Employing a wordplay on the name of Malachi, "the LORD's messenger", the Lord Himself announced He was sending one who would "prepare the way before Me." This is "the voice of one crying in the wilderness" (Is. 40:3) and the Elijah of 4:5 who comes before the Lord. The New Testament clearly identifies him as John the Baptist (Matt. 3:3; 11:10,14; 17:12ff.; Mark 1:2; Luke 1:17; 7:26,27; John 1:23).

And who can stand when He appears?
For He *is* like a refiner's fire
And like launderers' soap.
3 He will sit as a refiner and a purifier of
silver;
He will purify the sons of Levi,
And purge them as gold and silver,
That they may offer to the LORD
An offering in righteousness.

4 "Then the offering of Judah
and Jerusalem
Will be pleasant to the LORD,
As in the days of old,
As in former years.
5 And I will come near you for judgment;
I will be a swift witness
Against sorcerers,
Against adulterers,
Against perjurers,
Against those who exploit wage
earners and widows and orphans,
And against those who turn away an
alien—
Because they do not fear Me,"
Says the LORD of hosts.

6 "For I *am* the LORD, I do not change;
Therefore you are not consumed,
O sons of Jacob.
7 Yet from the days of your fathers
You have gone away from My
ordinances
And have not kept *them*.
Return to Me, and I will return to you,"
Says the LORD of hosts.
"But you said,
'In what way shall we return?'

8 "Will a man rob God?
Yet you have robbed Me!
But you say,
'In what way have we robbed You?'
In tithes and offerings.

9 You are cursed with a curse,
For you have robbed Me,
Even this whole nation.
10 Bring all the tithes into the storehouse,
That there may be food in My house,
And try Me now in this,"
Says the LORD of hosts,
"If I will not open for you the windows
of heaven
And pour out for you *such* blessing
That *there will* not *be room* enough *to receive it.*

11 "And I will rebuke the devourer for
your sakes,
So that he will not destroy the fruit of
your ground,
Nor shall the vine fail to bear fruit for
you in the field,"
Says the LORD of hosts;
12 And all nations will call you blessed,
For you will be a delightful land,"
Says the LORD of hosts.

13 "Your words have been harsh
against Me,"
Says the LORD,
"Yet you say,
'What have we spoken
against You?'
14 You have said,
'It is useless to serve God;
What profit *is it* that we have kept His
ordinance,
And that we have walked as mourners
Before the LORD of hosts?
15 So now we call the proud blessed,
For those who do wickedness are
raised up;
They even tempt God and go free.' "

16 Then those who feared the LORD spoke
to one another,
And the LORD listened and heard *them;*
So a book of remembrance was written
before Him
For those who fear the LORD
And who meditate on His name.

17 "They shall be Mine," says the LORD of
hosts,
"On the day that I make them
My jewels.
And I will spare them
As a man spares his own son who
serves him."
18 Then you shall again discern
Between the righteous and the wicked,
Between one who serves God
And one who does not serve Him.

4 "For behold, the day is coming,
Burning like an oven,
And all the proud, yes, all who do
wickedly will be stubble.
And the day which is coming shall
burn them up,"
Says the LORD of hosts,
"That will leave them neither root nor
branch.
2 But to you who fear My name
The Sun of Righteousness shall arise
With healing in His wings;
And you shall go out
And grow fat like stall-fed calves.

4:2 Sun of Righteousness. While the wicked will be devoured by the heat of the Lord's wrath, those who fear Him will feel His warmth with healing in His "rays" or "beams" (Is. 30:26; 60:1,3). The reference is to the Messiah; He is "the Lord our Righteousness" (Ps. 84:11; Jer. 23:5,6; 1 Cor. 1:30). **healing.** The reference should not be limited to the physical recovery from the harm done by the wicked (3:5). This sickness is inextricably linked with sin, with healing coming only through the suffering of the Servant (Ps. 103:3; Is. 53:5; 57:18,19; 1 Pet. 2:24).

3 You shall trample the wicked,
For they shall be ashes under the soles
of your feet
On the day that I do *this,*"
Says the LORD of hosts.
4 "Remember the Law of Moses,
My servant,
Which I commanded him in Horeb for
all Israel,
With the statutes and judgments.
5 Behold, I will send you Elijah the
prophet
Before the coming of the great and
dreadful day of the LORD.
6 And he will turn
The hearts of the fathers to the children,
And the hearts of the children to their
fathers,
Lest I come and strike the earth with a
curse."

Psalm 150:1–6

Praise the LORD!

Praise God in His sanctuary;
Praise Him in His mighty firmament!

2 Praise Him for His mighty acts;
Praise Him according to His excellent
greatness!
3 Praise Him with the sound of
the trumpet;
Praise Him with the lute and harp!
4 Praise Him with the timbrel and dance;
Praise Him with stringed instruments
and flutes!
5 Praise Him with loud cymbals;
Praise Him with clashing cymbals!
6 Let everything that has breath praise
the LORD.

Praise the LORD!

Proverbs 31:10–31

10 Who can find a virtuous wife?
For her worth *is* far above rubies.
11 The heart of her husband safely trusts
her;
So he will have no lack of gain.
12 She does him good and not evil
All the days of her life.
13 She seeks wool and flax,
And willingly works with her hands.
14 She is like the merchant ships,
She brings her food from afar.
15 She also rises while it is yet night,
And provides food for her household,
And a portion for her maidservants.
16 She considers a field and buys it;
From her profits she plants a vineyard.
17 She girds herself with strength,
And strengthens her arms.
18 She perceives that her merchandise
is good,
And her lamp does not go out by night.
19 She stretches out her hands to the
distaff,

31:10–31 This poem offers a beautiful description of the excellent wife as defined by a wife and mother (v. 1). Spiritual and practical wisdom plus moral virtues mark the character of this woman in contrast to the immoral women of v. 3. While the scene here is of a wealthy home and the customs of the ancient Near East, the principles apply to every family. They are set forth as the prayer of every mother for the future wife of her son, and literarily arranged with each of the 22 verses beginning with the 22 letters of the Hebrew alphabet in consecutive order.

And her hand holds the spindle.
20 She extends her hand to the poor,
Yes, she reaches out her hands to the
needy.
21 She is not afraid of snow for her
household,
For all her household *is* clothed with
scarlet.
22 She makes tapestry for herself;
Her clothing *is* fine linen and purple.
23 Her husband is known in the gates,
When he sits among the elders of the
land.
24 She makes linen garments and sells
them,
And supplies sashes for the merchants.
25 Strength and honor *are* her clothing;
She shall rejoice in time to come.
26 She opens her mouth with wisdom,
And on her tongue *is* the law of
kindness.
27 She watches over the ways of her
household,
And does not eat the bread of idleness.
28 Her children rise up and call her
blessed;
Her husband *also,* and he praises her:
29 "Many daughters have done well,
But you excel them all."
30 Charm *is* deceitful and beauty *is*
passing,
But a woman *who* fears the LORD, she
shall be praised.
31 Give her of the fruit of her hands,
And let her own works praise her in
the gates.

Revelation 21:1–22:21

21 Now I saw a new heaven and a new
earth, for the first heaven and the first
earth had passed away. Also there was no
more sea. 2Then I, John, saw the holy city,
New Jerusalem, coming down out of heaven
from God, prepared as a bride adorned for her
husband. 3And I heard a loud voice from heav-
en saying, "Behold, the tabernacle of God *is*
with men, and He will dwell with them, and
they shall be His people. God Himself will be
with them *and be* their God. 4And God will
wipe away every tear from their eyes; there
shall be no more death, nor sorrow, nor crying. There shall be no more pain, for the former things have passed away."
5Then He who sat on the throne said, "Behold, I make all things new." And He said to me,
"Write, for these words are true and faithful."
6And He said to me, "It is done! I am the
Alpha and the Omega, the Beginning and the

21:2 New Jerusalem. This is the capital city of heaven, a place of perfect holiness. It is seen "coming down out of heaven," indicating it already existed; but it descends into the new heavens and new earth from its place on high. This is the city where the saints will live (John 14:1–3). **bride.** An important New Testament metaphor for the church (Matt. 25:1–13; Eph. 5:25–27). John's imagery here extends from the third part of the Jewish wedding, the ceremony. Believers (the bride) in the New Jerusalem come to meet Christ (the bridegroom) in the final ceremony of redemptive history (19:7). The whole city, occupied by all the saints, is called the bride, so that all saints must be finally included in the bride imagery and bridal blessing. God has brought home a bride for His beloved Son. All the saints live with Christ in the Father's house (a promise made before the church began; John 14:2).

End. I will give of the fountain of the water of
life freely to him who thirsts. 7He who overcomes shall inherit all things, and I will be his
God and he shall be My son. 8But the cowardly,
unbelieving, abominable, murderers, sexually
immoral, sorcerers, idolaters, and all liars shall
have their part in the lake which burns with fire
and brimstone, which is the second death."

9Then one of the seven angels who had the
seven bowls filled with the seven last plagues
came to me and talked with me, saying, "Come,
I will show you the bride, the Lamb's wife."
10And he carried me away in the Spirit to a
great and high mountain, and showed me the
great city, the holy Jerusalem, descending out
of heaven from God, 11having the glory of God.
Her light *was* like a most precious stone, like
a jasper stone, clear as crystal. 12Also she had
a great and high wall with twelve gates, and
twelve angels at the gates, and names written
on them, which are *the names* of the twelve
tribes of the children of Israel: 13three gates on
the east, three gates on the north, three gates
on the south, and three gates on the west.

14Now the wall of the city had twelve foundations, and on them were the names of the
twelve apostles of the Lamb. 15And he who
talked with me had a gold reed to measure the
city, its gates, and its wall. 16The city is laid out
as a square; its length is as great as its
breadth. And he measured the city with the
reed: twelve thousand furlongs. Its length,
breadth, and height are equal. 17Then he
measured its wall: one hundred *and* forty-four
cubits, *according* to the measure of a man, that
is, of an angel. 18The construction of its wall was
of jasper; and the city *was* pure gold, like clear
glass. 19The foundations of the wall of the city
were adorned with all kinds of precious stones:
the first foundation *was* jasper, the second sapphire, the third chalcedony, the fourth emerald, 20the fifth sardonyx, the sixth sardius, the
seventh chrysolite, the eighth beryl, the ninth
topaz, the tenth chrysoprase, the eleventh
jacinth, and the twelfth amethyst. 21The twelve
gates *were* twelve pearls: each individual gate
was of one pearl. And the street of the city *was*
pure gold, like transparent glass.

22But I saw no temple in it, for the Lord God
Almighty and the Lamb are its temple. 23The
city had no need of the sun or of the moon to
shine in it, for the glory of God illuminated it.
The Lamb *is* its light. 24And the nations of
those who are saved shall walk in its light, and
the kings of the earth bring their glory and
honor into it. 25Its gates shall not be shut at all by
day (there shall be no night there). 26And they
shall bring the glory and the honor of the
nations into it. 27But there shall by no means
enter it anything that defiles, or causes an
abomination or a lie, but only those who are
written in the Lamb's Book of Life.

22 And he showed me a pure river of
water of life, clear as crystal, proceeding from the throne of God and of the Lamb.
2In the middle of its street, and on either side
of the river, *was* the tree of life, which bore
twelve fruits, each *tree* yielding its fruit every
month. The leaves of the tree *were* for the
healing of the nations. 3And there shall be no
more curse, but the throne of God and of the
Lamb shall be in it, and His servants shall
serve Him. 4They shall see His face, and His
name *shall be* on their foreheads. 5There shall
be no night there: They need no lamp nor
light of the sun, for the Lord God gives them
light. And they shall reign forever and ever.

6Then he said to me, "These words *are* faithful and true." And the Lord God of the holy
prophets sent His angel to show His servants
the things which must shortly take place.

7"Behold, I am coming quickly! Blessed *is*
he who keeps the words of the prophecy of
this book."

8Now I, John, saw and heard these things.
And when I heard and saw, I fell down to worship before the feet of the angel who showed
me these things.

9Then he said to me, "See *that you do* not *do*
that. For I am your fellow servant, and of
your brethren the prophets, and of those who
keep the words of this book. Worship God."

[10]And he said to me, "Do not seal the words of
the prophecy of this book, for the time is at
hand. [11]He who is unjust, let him be unjust
still; he who is filthy, let him be filthy still; he
who is righteous, let him be righteous still;
he who is holy, let him be holy still."

[12]"And behold, I am coming quickly, and My
reward *is* with Me, to give to every one according to his work. [13]I am the Alpha and the
Omega, *the* Beginning and *the* End, the First
and the Last."

[14]Blessed *are* those who do His commandments, that they may have the right to the tree
of life, and may enter through the gates into
the city. [15]But outside *are* dogs and sorcerers
and sexually immoral and murderers and idolaters, and whoever loves and practices a lie.

[16]"I, Jesus, have sent My angel to testify to
you these things in the churches. I am the
Root and the Offspring of David, the Bright
and Morning Star."

[17]And the Spirit and the bride say, "Come!"
And let him who hears say, "Come!" And let
him who thirsts come. Whoever desires, let
him take the water of life freely.

[18]For I testify to everyone who hears the
words of the prophecy of this book: If anyone
adds to these things, God will add to him the
plagues that are written in this book; [19]and if
anyone takes away from the words of the book
of this prophecy, God shall take away his part
from the Book of Life, from the holy city, and
from the things which are written in this book.

[20]He who testifies to these things says,
"Surely I am coming quickly."

Amen. Even so, come, Lord Jesus!

[21]The grace of our Lord Jesus Christ *be* with
you all. Amen.

DAY 31: What is the Book of Malachi about?

Only 50,000 exiles had returned to Judah from Babylon (538–536 B.C.). The temple had been rebuilt under the leadership of Zerubbabel (516 B.C.) and the sacrificial system renewed. Ezra had returned in 458 B.C., followed by Nehemiah in 445 B.C. After being back in the land of Palestine for only a century, the ritual of the Jews' religious routine led to hard-heartedness toward God's great love for them and to widespread departure from His law by both people and priest. Malachi rebuked and condemned these abuses, forcefully indicting the people and calling them to repentance. When Nehemiah returned from Persia the second time (ca. 424 B.C.), he vigorously rebuked them for these abuses in the temple and priesthood, for the violation of the Sabbath rest, and for the unlawful divorce of their Jewish wives so they could marry Gentile women (Neh. 13).

As over two millennia of Old Testament history since Abraham concluded, none of the glorious promises of the Abrahamic, Davidic, and New Covenants had been fulfilled in their ultimate sense. Although there had been a few high points in Israel's history, e.g., Joshua, David, and Josiah, the Jews had seemingly lost all opportunity to receive God's favor. Less than 100 years after returning from captivity, they had already sunk to a depth of sin that exceeded the former iniquities which brought on the Assyrian and Babylonian deportations. Beyond this, the long-anticipated Messiah had not arrived and did not seem to be in sight.

So, Malachi wrote the capstone prophecy of the Old Testament in which he delivered God's message of judgment on Israel for their continuing sin and God's promise that one day in the future, when the Jews would repent, the Messiah would be revealed and God's covenant promises would be fulfilled. There were over 400 years of divine silence, with only Malachi's words ringing condemnation in their ears, before another prophet arrived with a message from God. That was John the Baptist preaching, "Repent, for the kingdom of heaven is at hand!" (Matt. 3:2). Messiah had come.